Downtown Boston

Greater Boston

North Reading

Billerica

Wilmington

Reading

Peabody

Salem

Bedford

Burlington

Woburn

Stoneham

Wakefield

Breakheart Res.

Lynn Woods Res.

Lynn

Lexington

Winchester

Middlesex Fells Res.

Melrose

Saugus

Arlington

Medford

Malden

Everett

Revere

Broad Sound

Waltham

Belmont

Somerville

Chelsea

Tufts University

Brandeis University

Bentley College

Cambridge

Harvard University

Logan International Airport

Winthrop

Watertown

MIT

Boston University

Boston Inner Harbor

Newton

Boston College

Chestnut Hill Res.

BOSTON

Castle Island

Boston Harbor

Brookline

Pine Manor College

Jamaica Pond

Dorchester Bay

Boston Harbor Islands

Wellesley

Babson College

Arnold Arboretum

Franklin Park

Long Island Causeway

Needham

Stony Brook Res.

Quincy Bay

Dedham

Milton

Quincy

Westwood

Norwood

Blue Hills Res.

Braintree

Canton

Randolph

N

LG

0   2 miles

0   2 kilometers

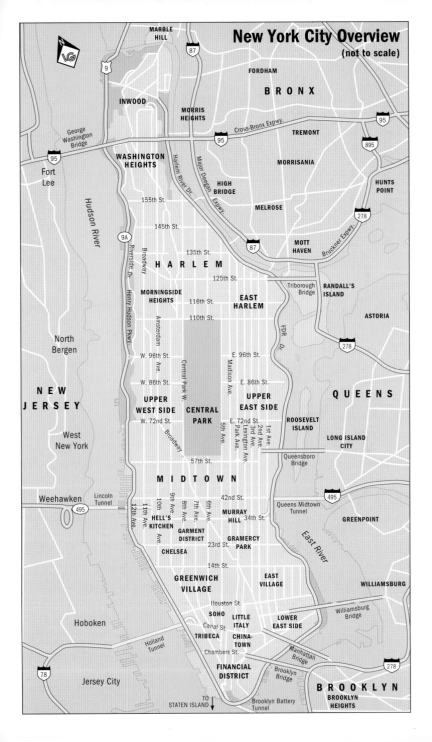

New York City Overview
(not to scale)

MARBLE HILL

FORDHAM

B R O N X

INWOOD

MORRIS HEIGHTS

Cross-Bronx Expwy.

TREMONT

George Washington Bridge

WASHINGTON HEIGHTS

Fort Lee

MORRISANIA

HUNTS POINT

Hudson River

HIGH BRIDGE

MELROSE

155th St.

145th St.

Harlem River Dr.

Major Deegan Expwy.

Bruckner Expwy.

135th St.

MOTT HAVEN

H A R L E M

125th St.

9A

Riverside Dr.

Broadway

Triborough Bridge

RANDALL'S ISLAND

MORNINGSIDE HEIGHTS

116th St.

EAST HARLEM

ASTORIA

Henry Hudson Pkwy.

110th St.

Amsterdam

FDR Dr.

North Bergen

W. 96th St.

E. 96th St.

Central Park W.

Madison Ave.

W. 86th St.

E. 86th St.

N E W

UPPER WEST SIDE

UPPER EAST SIDE

Q U E E N S

J E R S E Y

W. 72nd St.

CENTRAL PARK

E. 72nd St.

5th Ave.

Lexington Ave.

Park Ave.

1st Ave.

2nd Ave.

3rd Ave.

ROOSEVELT ISLAND

West New York

Broadway

LONG ISLAND CITY

57th St.

Queensboro Bridge

Weehawken

Lincoln Tunnel

M I D T O W N

42nd St.

Queens Midtown Tunnel

GREENPOINT

9th Ave.

8th Ave.

7th Ave.

6th Ave.

MURRAY HILL

34th St.

East River

10th Ave.

11th Ave.

12th Ave.

HELL'S KITCHEN

GARMENT DISTRICT

23rd St.

GRAMERCY PARK

CHELSEA

14th St.

GREENWICH VILLAGE

EAST VILLAGE

WILLIAMSBURG

Williamsburg Bridge

Hoboken

Houston St.

SOHO

LITTLE ITALY

LOWER EAST SIDE

Canal St.

TRIBECA

CHINA-TOWN

Manhattan Bridge

Chambers St.

Holland Tunnel

Jersey City

FINANCIAL DISTRICT

Brooklyn Bridge

B R O O K L Y N

TO STATEN ISLAND

Brooklyn Battery Tunnel

BROOKLYN HEIGHTS

MTA New York City Subway

Metropolitan Transportation Authority

with bus, railroad, and ferry connections

Key

MTA New York City Transit
Subway in four boroughs,
buses in five boroughs, and the
MTA Staten Island Railway

The subway operates 24 hours a
day, but not all lines operate at all
times. For more information, call our
Travel Information Center (6AM to
10PM) at 718-330-1234.
Non-English-speaking customers
call 718-330-4847 (6AM to 10PM).

visit www.mta.info

To show service more clearly, geography on
this map has been modified.
© 2007 Metropolitan Transportation Authority
Design: Michael Hertz Associates, NYC.
April 2007

- Local service only
- All trains stop
(local and express service)
- Free subway transfer
- Free out-of-system subway
transfer (excluding single-
ride ticket)
- Normal service
- Additional express
service
- Commuter rail service
- Bus or AIRTRAIN to airport
- Accessible station

Part-time line
extension
Part-time
service
Full time
service

Terminal

Police

See Service Guide
below for details about
specific lines

New York City: Downtown Manhattan

New York City: Midtown Manhattan

Grand Army Plaza
E. 60th St.
5 Av/59 St N,R,W
Lexington Av/59 St N,R,W
Roosevelt Island Tramway
E. 59th St.
59 St 4,5,6
Bloomingdale's
Queensboro Bridge
57 St F
Plaza Hotel
F.A.O. Schwarz
E. 58th St.
Madison-Lexington Venture Building
Marborough Gallery
Trump Tower
IBM Building
E. 57th St.
Second Ave.
First Ave.
E. 56th St.
Museum of Modern Art
St. Thomas
Museum of Television & Radio
Central Synagogue
Citicorp Center
E. 55th St.
E. 54th St.
St. Peter's
Seagram Building
E. 53rd St.
CBS Building
5 Av/53 St E,V
St. Patrick's Cathedral
Lexington Av/53 St E,V
E. 52nd St.
Radio City Music Hall
51 St 6
E. 51st St.
W 50 Sts Rockefeller Center B,D,F,V
Rockefeller Center
St. Batholemew's
E. 50th St.
TURTLE BAY
Sak's Fifth Avenue
Waldorf-Astoria Hotel
E. 49th St.
Fifth Ave.
Madison Ave.
Park Ave.
Lexington Ave.
E. 48th St.
E. 47th St.
United Nations
Algonquin Hotel
E. 46th St.
E. 45th St.
Met Life Building
E. 44th St.
Grand Central Terminal
Grand Central 42 St 5,4,5,6,7
Chrysler Building
E. 43rd St.
Ford Foundation
42 St B,D,F,V
5 Av 7
E. 42nd St.
Daily News Building
Bryant Park
New York Public Library
Whitney Museum Branch
E. 41st St.
Queens Midtown Tunnel
W. 40th St.
E. 40th St.
FDR Dr.
American Standard Building
MURRAY HILL
E. 39th St.
East River
W. 38th St.
E. 38th St.
Park Ave.
HERALD SQUARE W. 37th St.
Pierpont Morgan Library
E. 37th St.
Third Ave.
W. 36th St.
E. 36th St.
W. 35th St.
E. 35th St.
Empire State Building
E. 34th St.
34 St Herald Sq B,D,F,N, Q,R,V,W
W. 33rd St.
33 St 6
E. 33rd St.
W. 32nd St.
E. 32nd St.
Second Ave.
First Ave.
Lexington Ave.
E. 31st St.
E. 30th St.
28 St N,R
E. 29th St.
28 St 6
E. 28th St.
Madison Ave.
Park Ave.
E. 27th St.
Avenue of the Americas (6th Ave.)
W. 26th St.
E. 26th St.
W. 25th St.
Madison Square Park
E. 25th St.
W. 24th St.
Metropolitan Life Insurance Buildings
E. 24th St.
23 St N,R
23 St 6
E. 23rd St.
Peter Cooper Rd.
23rd Street
Flatiron Building
W. 22nd St.
E. 22nd St.
Broadway
W. 21st St.
Gramercy Park
E. 21st St.
W. 20th St.
E. 20th St.
GRAMERCY PARK
W. 19th St.
Theodore Roosevelt Birthplace
E. 19th St.
Irving Pl.
E. 18th St.
W. 18th St.
Fifth Ave.
W. 17th St.
E. 17th St.
First Ave.
W. 16th St.
UNION SQUARE
E. 16th St.
STUYVESANT SQUARE
Third Ave.
6 Av L
W. 15th St.
14 St-Union Sq L,N,Q,R,W,4,5,6
E. 15th St.
3 Av L
1 Av L
Ave. A
Ave. B
Ave. C
Ave. D
4 St F,V
W. 14th St.
E. 14th St.

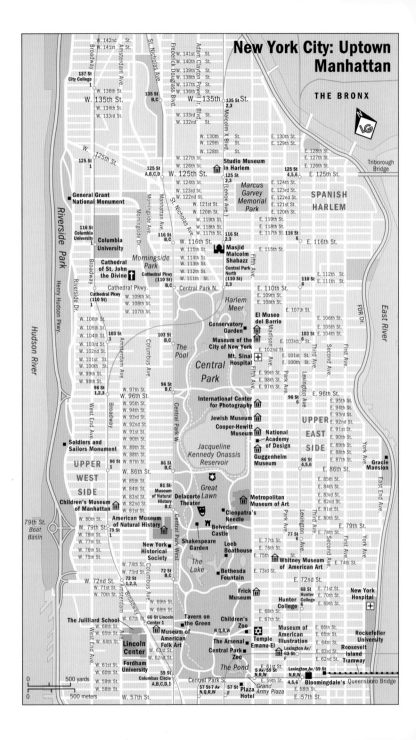

New York City: Uptown Manhattan

THE BRONX

SPANISH HARLEM

Triborough Bridge

Riverside Park

Hudson River

Henry Hudson Pkwy.

Riverside Dr.

Broadway

East River

FDR Dr.

UPPER EAST SIDE

UPPER WEST SIDE

Central Park

Morningside Park

The Pool

The Lake

Jacqueline Kennedy Onassis Reservoir

Great Lawn

The Pond

Harlem Meer

Marcus Garvey Memorial Park

Conservatory Garden

W. 142nd St.
W. 141st St.
Amsterdam Ave.
St. Nicholas Ave.
Frederick Douglass Blvd.
Adam Clayton Powell Jr. Blvd.
W. 141st St.
W. 140th St.
W. 139th St.
W. 138th St.
W. 137th St.
W. 136th St.

Broadway

137 St City College
1

135 St B,C

135 St
B,C

W. 135th St.
W. 134th St.
W. 133rd St.
W. 132nd St.

W. 135th

135 St St.
2,3

Malcolm X Blvd.

W. 130th St.
W. 129th St.
W. 128th St.
W. 127th St.
W. 126th St.

125 St 1

125 St
1

Studio Museum in Harlem

W. 125th St.

125 St
A,B,C,D

125 St
2,3

E. 130th St.
E. 129th St.

125 St
4,5,6

E. 128th St.
E. 127th St.
E. 126th St.
E. 125th St.

General Grant National Monument

W. 124th St.
W. 123rd St.
W. 122nd St.
W. 121st St.

(Lenox Ave.)

E. 124th St.
E. 123rd St.
E. 122nd St.
E. 121st St.
E. 120th St.

Morningside Dr.

Manhattan Ave.

St. Nicholas Ave.

116 St Columbia University
1

Columbia University

116 St
1

W. 119th St.
W. 118th St.
W. 117th St.

116 St
2,3

E. 119th St.
E. 118th St.
E. 117th St. 116 St
6

Cathedral of St. John the Divine

Cathedral Pkwy. (110 St)

Masjid Malcolm Shabazz

W. 116th St.
W. 115th St.
W. 114th St.
W. 113th St.
W. 112th St.
W. 111th St.

Fifth Ave.

E. 115th St.

Central Park North (110 St)
B,C

Central Park N.

Central Park North (110 St)
2,3

110 St
6

E. 112th St.
E. 111th St.

Cathedral Pkwy. (110 St)

W. 109th St.
W. 108th St.
W. 107th St.

E. 110th St.
E. 109th St.
E. 108th St.
E. 107th St.

W. 106th St.
W. 105th St.
W. 104th St.
W. 103rd St.
W. 102nd St.

El Museo del Barrio

E. 106th St.
E. 105th St.
E. 104th St.

Madison Ave.

103 St
1

103 St
B,C

Museum of the City of New York

103 St
6

E. 103rd St.

Amsterdam Ave.

Columbus Ave.

Mt. Sinai Hospital

Third Ave.

Second Ave.

First Ave.

W. 101st St.
W. 100th St.
W. 99th St.
W. 98th St.

E. 102nd St.
E. 101st St.
E. 100th St.
E. 99th St.

Fifth Ave.

Park Ave.

Lexington Ave.

E. 98th St.
E. 97th St.

96 St
1,2,3

W. 97th St.
W. 96th St.

96 St
B,C

W. 95th St.
W. 94th St.
W. 93rd St.
W. 92nd St.
W. 91st St.

96 St
6

E. 96th St.
E. 95th St.
E. 94th St.
E. 93rd St.
E. 92nd St.
E. 91st St.

West End Ave.

Broadway

Central Park W.

International Center for Photography

Jewish Museum

Cooper-Hewitt Museum

National Academy of Design

Guggenheim Museum

E. 90th St.
E. 89th St.
E. 88th St.
E. 87th St.

York Ave.

Soldiers and Sailors Monument

W. 90th St.
W. 89th St.
W. 88th St.
W. 87th St.

86 St
1

W. 86th St.

86 St
B,C

W. 85th St.
W. 84th St.
W. 83rd St.
W. 82nd St.
W. 81st St.

86 St
4,5,6

E. 86th St.
E. 85th St.
E. 84th St.
E. 83rd St.
E. 82nd St.
E. 81st St.

Gracie Mansion

East End Ave.

Children's Museum of Manhattan

81 St-Museum of Natural History
B,C

Delacorte Theater

Metropolitan Museum of Art

E. 80th St.

American Museum of Natural History

W. 80th St.
W. 79th St
79 St
1

Cleopatra's Needle

Belvedere Castle

E. 79th St.

79th St. Boat Basin

W. 78th St.
W. 77th St.
W. 76th St.
W. 75th St.

77 St
6

E. 78th St.
E. 77th St.

Shakespeare Garden

Loeb Boathouse

E. 76th St.
E. 75th St.

New York Historical Society

Whitney Museum of American Art

E. 74th St.

Columbus Ave.

72 St
B,C

Bethesda Fountain

E. 73rd St.

W. 73rd St.
72 St
1,2,3

W. 72nd St.
W. 71st St.
W. 70th St.

E. 72nd St.

Amsterdam Ave.

Frick Museum

68 St Hunter College
6

E. 71st St.
E. 70th St.
E. 69th St.

New York Hospital

W. 69th St.
W. 68th St.

Hunter College

The Juilliard School

66 St Lincoln Center 1

W. 67th St.
W. 66th St.

Tavern on the Green

Children's Zoo

Museum of American Illustration

E. 68th St.

Rockefeller University

Museum of American Folk Art

The Arsenal

Temple Emanu-El

E. 67th St.
E. 66th St.
E. 65th St.
E. 64th St.

Roosevelt Island Tramway

Lincoln Center

W. 65th St.
W. 64th St.
W. 63rd St.
W. 62nd St.

Central Park Zoo

N,Q,R,W

Lexington Av/ 63 St
F

E. 63rd St.

Fordham University

W. 61st St.
W. 60th St.

59 St Columbus Circle A,B,C,D,1

The Pond

5 Av/59 St
N,R,W

E. 61st St.
E. 60th St.

59 St
N,R,W

Lexington Av/59 St

W. 59th St.
W. 58th St.

Central Park S.

57 St-7 Av
N,Q,R,W

57 St
F

Plaza Hotel

Grand Army Plaza

4,5,6

Bloomingdale's

E. 59th St.
E. 58th St.

Queensboro Bridge

W. 57th St.

E. 57th St.

0   500 yards

0   500 meters

Washington D.C.: Downtown

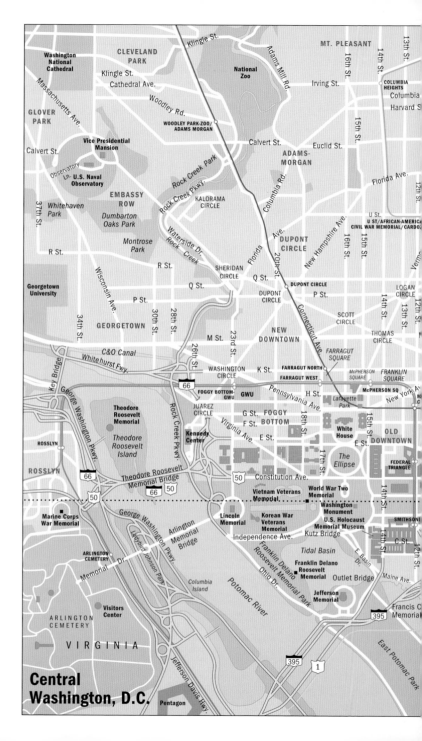

Central
Washington, D.C.

Washington, D.C.: The Mall Area

Massachusetts Ave.

4th St.

G St.

G St.

National Building Museum

2nd St.

395

3rd St.

1st St.

New Jersey Ave.

McCollough Ct.

N. Capitol St.

F St.

E St.

National Postal Museum

UNION STATION

Union Station

Columbus Circle

G St.

3rd St.

2nd St.

D.C. thouse

C St.

Federal Courthouse

Department of Labor

Louisiana Ave.

Delaware Ave.

Russell Senate Office Building

Dirksen Senate Office Building

Maryland Ave.

A St.

Constitution Ave.

tional llery of Art est Wing)

National Gallery of Art (East Wing)

NW

NE

U.S. Supreme Court

Capitol Reflecting Pool

U.S. Capitol

E. Capitol St.

Folger Shakespeare Library

SW

SE

Library of Congress (Jefferson Bldg.)

Library of Congress (Adams Bldg.)

efferson Dr.

ional and Space eum

U.S. Botanic Garden

aryland Ave.

Voice of America Studio

Department of Health and Human Services

1st St.

Washington Ave.

Rayburn House Office Building

Longworth House Office Building

Cannon House Office Building

Library of Congress (Madison Bldg.)

D St.

FEDERAL CENTER SW

2nd St.

Delaware Ave.

Washington Ave.

Ivy St.

CAPITOL SOUTH

North Carolina Ave.

Folger Park

4th St.

Virginia Ave.

chool St.

E St. SW.

Southwest Fwy.

E St.

Garfield Park

Duddington Pl.

South Carolina Ave.

G St. SW.

395

3rd St. SW

Delaware Ave. SW

Randall Recreation Center

S. Capitol St.

Carrolsburg Pl. SW

New Jersey Ave.

K St. SE

L St. SE

Half St. SE

2nd St. SE

Prospect St.

34th St.

33rd St.

N St.

31st St.

Old Stone House

Olive St.

GEORGETOWN

M St.

C&O Creek

Whitehurst Fwy.

South St.

29

Rock Creek

26th St.

L St.

25th St.

24th St.

New Ham

WASHINGTON CIRCLE

GWU Hospi

FOGGY BOTTOM-GWU

George Washington University

Water St. (under freeway)

K St. (under freeway)

66

Francis Scott Key Memorial Bridge

Thompson Boat Center

Watergate Hotel

Watergate Hotel Complex

JUAREZ CIRCLE

24th St.

George Washington Pkwy.

Theodore Roosevelt Memorial

Theodore Roosevelt Island

Georgetown Channel

Rock Creek Pkwy.

Kennedy Center for the Performing Arts

FOGGY BOTTOM

23rd St.

Virgin

Fort Myer Dr.

N. Lynn St.

N. Moore St.

19th St.

N. Kent St.

ROSSLYN

Wilson

Footbridge

Arlington Ridge Rd.

ROSSLYN

Fairfax Dr.

66

Theodore Roosevelt Memorial Bridge

66

50

S
Departm

Nation
Academ
of Scien

50

N. Nash St.

Dark Star Park

50

NW

SW

Henry
Bacon

Mead Dr.

Marine Corps War Memorial (Iwo Jima Statue)

Netherlands Carillon

12th St.

Lincoln Memoria

George Washington Memorial Pkwy.

Arlington Memorial Bridge

Ericsson Memorial

ARLINGTON

Ladybird Johnson Park

ARLINGTON CEMETERY

Grave of President John F. Kennedy

Memorial Dr.

Jefferson Davis Hwy.

Columbia Island

Arlington House

Robert E. Lee Memorial

Visitor Center

ARLINGTON NATIONAL CEMETERY

Tomb of the Unknown Soldier

Footbridge

Lyndon B. Johnson Memorial

N

LG

0   1500 feet

0   500 meters

V I R G I N I A

Jefferson Pl.
Connecticut Ave.
20th St.
19th St.
18th St.
17th St.
DeSales St.
M St.

National Geographic Society

THOMAS CIRCLE

Massachusetts Ave.

11th St.
12th St.
13th St.

M St.
L St.
9th St.

MT. VERNON SQUARE

K St.
15th St.
Vermont Ave.

The Washington Post

16th St.

K St.
I St.

FARRAGUT NORTH

FARRAGUT SQUARE

McPHERSON SQUARE

FRANKLIN SQUARE
McPHERSON SQ

New York Ave.

D.C. Convention Center

Pennsylvania Ave.

FARRAGUT WEST

H St.

U.S. Chamber of Commerce

St. John's Church

15th St.

National Museum of Women in the Arts

H St.

Decatur House

Lafayette Park

New York Ave. Presbyterian Church

Martin Luther King Jr. Library

G Pl.
10th St.

World Bank

Renwick Gallery

Jackson Pl.

Blair House

U.S. Treasury

14th St.

G St.

METRO CENTER

G St.

G St.
F St.

Old Executive Office Building

Madison Pl.

White House

Natl. Theatre

Warner Theatre

Ford's Theatre

F St.

General Services Administration

Octagon

State Pl.

Treasury Pl.

E St.

Federal Bureau of Investigation

E St.

Corcoran Gallery

Interior Department

Red Cross

D St.

Ellipse Rd. NW

17th St.

The Ellipse

Pennsylvania Ave. S.

District Building

Pennsylvania Ave.

11th St.

Old Post Office

9th St.

Department of Justice

National Archives

D.A.R. and Constitution Hall

C St.

Department of Commerce

Ronald Reagan Building

FEDERAL TRIANGLE

Internal Revenue Service

Organization of American States

Constitution Ave.

Constitution Ave.

Constitution Gardens

Vietnam Veterans Memorial

Memorial to the Signers of the Declaration of Independence

World War Two Memorial

Natl. Museum of American History

Natl. Museum of Natural History

Madison Dr.

Reflecting Pool

Washington Monument

THE MALL

West Potomac Park

Sylvan Theatre

14th St.

Freer Gallery of Art

SMITHSONIAN

Smithsonian Castle

Arts & Industries Building

Korean War Veterans Memorial

D.C. War Memorial

Kutz Bridge

Independence Ave.

U.S. Holocaust Memorial Museum

Department of Agriculture

Sackler Gallery

Natl. Museum of African Art

Independence Ave.

Japanese Lantern

E. Basin Dr.

15th St.

Bureau of Engraving and Printing

C St.

Department of Energy

9th St.

Franklin Delano Roosevelt Memorial Park

Franklin Delano Roosevelt Memorial

Tidal Basin

Tidal Basin Boathouse

D St.

L'Enfant Promenade

L'Enfant Plaza

W. Basin Dr.

Cherry Trees

Outlet Bridge

Maine Ave.

12th St. Expwy.

Ohio Dr.

Jefferson Memorial

Francis Case Memorial Bridge

H St.

Maine Ave.
Water St.

Potomac River

George Mason Memorial Bridge

Rochambeau Memorial Bridge

Williams Memorial Bridge

395

Washington Channel

Natl. Park Service Visitors Welcome Center and Park Police Headquarters

East Potomac Park

395

1

Washington, D.C.: White House Area, Foggy Bottom, and Nearby Arlington

Washington D.C. Metro

Vancouver

Seattle

Portland

Bus Route
Streetcar
MAX
Fareless Square

TO PORTLAND INTERNATIONAL AIRPORT (2mi.)

500 yards
500 meters

NE 20th Ave.   SE 20th Ave.
                    SE 19th Ave.
        SE 18th Ave.
        SE 17th Ave.
        SE 16th St.
        SE 15th St.   SE Stark St.
        SE 14th St.
        SE 13th St.
        SE 12th St.

NE 12th Ave.   SE 12th Ave.

Buckman Field

NE Irving St.

                    SE 11th Ave.
        SE Ankeny Blvd   SE 10th Ave.
                    SE 9th Ave.
        SE Washington St.   SE 8th Ave.

NE Glisan St.
NE Flanders St.
NE Everett St.   SE Ankeny St.   SE Taylor St.
NE Davis St.   SE Ash St.   SE Salmon St.
NE Couch St.   SE Pine St.   SE Main St.
        SE Oak St.   SE Madison St.
NE Grand Ave.   SE 7th Ave.
        SE 6th Ave.   SE Hawthorne Blvd.
        SE Alder St.

Lloyd Center

NE Multnomah St.

NE Hassalo St.
NE Holladay St.   SE Grand Ave.
NE Oregon St.   SE Belmont St.
NE Irving St.   SE Morrison St.   TO REED COLLEGE (2mi.)
        SE Martin Luther King Jr. Blvd.   SE Yamhill St.

Convention Center
Oregon Convention Center   Lloyd Blvd.   SE Stark St.
                        SE 3rd Ave.
                SE 2nd Ave.
                SE 1st Ave.

E Burnside St.

Willamette River

Rose Garden Arena
Rose Quarter TC   Burnside Bridge   Water Ave.
                TO OREGON MUSEUM OF SCIENCE AND INDUSTRY (50yd.)

Steel Bridge   Portland Saturday Market
Old Town   Skidmore Fountain   Morrison Bridge

NW Front Ave. (Naito Pkwy.)   NW 1st Ave.   Willamette River
Chinese Classical Garden   NW 2nd Ave.   SW Front Ave. (Naito Pkwy.)
        NW 3rd Ave.   Hawthorne Bridge

Union Station (Amtrak)   NW 4th Ave.   CHINATOWN   SW Ankeny St.
Greyhound Station   NW 5th Ave.   SW Pine St.
        NW 6th Ave.   SW Oak St.   Transit Mall   SW Taylor St.   Morrison
NW Broadway Ave.   U.S. Outdoor Store   Mall   SW Salmon St.   Yamhill Dist.
NW 8th Ave.   Mall   Portland Building
NW Park Ave.   Powell's Book Store   PIONEER COURTHOUSE SQUARE   Portland Building   City Hall   SW 1st Ave.
NW 9th Ave.   SW Stark St.   SW Taylor St.   SW 2nd Ave.
NW 10th Ave.   SW Washington St.   SW Broadway Ave.   SW Salmon St.   SW 3rd Ave.
        SW Alder St.   SW Madison St.   SW 4th Ave.
NW 11th Ave.   SW Washington St.   Galleria   SW 5th Ave.
PEARL DISTRICT   W Burnside St.   Library   SW 6th Ave.
NW 12th St.   SW Morrison St.   SW Jefferson St.
NW 13th St.   SW Yamhill St.   Library   SW 9th Ave.   SW Columbia St.
NW 14th St.   SW Main St.   Portland Art Museum   SW 10th Ave.   SW Clay St.
        SW 13th Ave.   SW 12th Ave.   SW Market St.
NW Lovejoy St.   SW 14th Ave.   Portland State University   SW Mill St.
NW Kearney St.   SW 15th Ave.   SW Montgomery St.
NW Johnson St.   SW 16th Ave.
NW Irving St.   SW 17th Ave.

NW Hoyt St.
NW Glisan St.
NW Everett St.
NW Davis St.
NW Couch St.

NW 16th Ave.
NW 17th Ave.   Civic Stadium   King's Hill
NW 18th Ave.   Civic Stadium   PGE Park
NW 19th Ave.   PGE Park   Goose Hollow
NW 20th Ave.   SW 18th Ave.
NW 21st Ave.   SW 21st Ave.   TO WASHINGTON PARK ZOO (1.5 mi.)
Couch Park   SW 22nd Ave.
NW 22nd Ave.
NW 23rd Ave.   SW 23rd Ave.

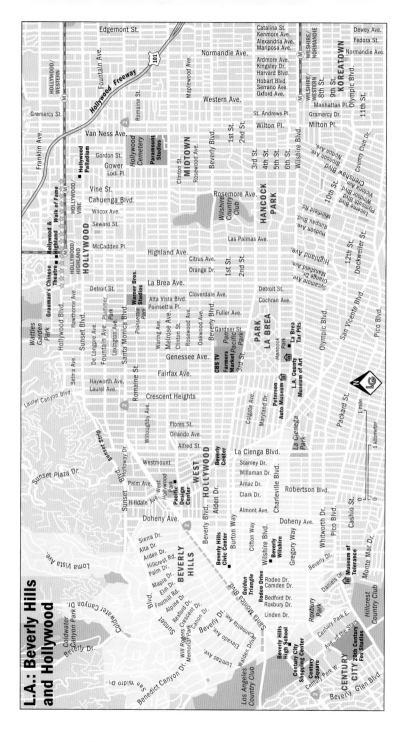

L.A.: Beverly Hills and Hollywood

Metropolitan
Los Angeles

N

0   2 miles
0   2 kilometers

Metro Green Line
Metro Blue Line
Metro Red Line

Pacific Ocean

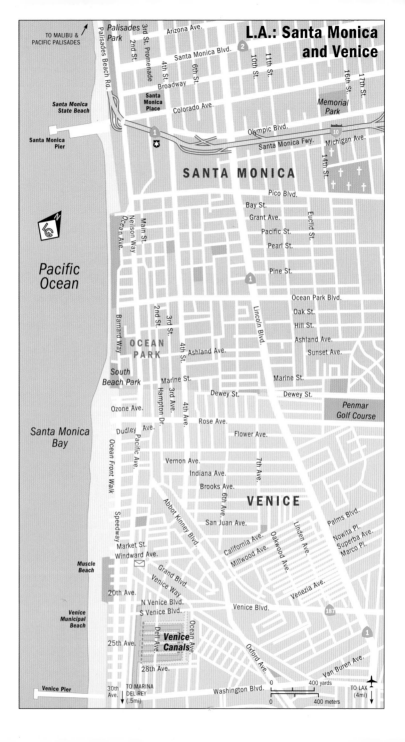

L.A.: Santa Monica and Venice

TO MALIBU & PACIFIC PALISADES

Palisades Park

Palisades Beach Rd.

2nd St.

3rd St.

3rd St. Promenade

4th St.

Broadway

6th St.

5th St.

Arizona Ave.

Santa Monica Blvd.

10th St.

11th St.

16th St.

17th St.

14th St.

Memorial Park

Santa Monica State Beach

Santa Monica Pier

Santa Monica Place

Colorado Ave.

Olympic Blvd.

Santa Monica Fwy.

Michigan Ave.

SANTA MONICA

Pico Blvd.

Bay St.

Grant Ave.

Pacific St.

Pearl St.

Pine St.

Euclid St.

Nelson Way

Ocean Ave.

Main St.

Pacific Ocean

Ocean Park Blvd.

Oak St.

Hill St.

Ashland Ave.

Sunset Ave.

Lincoln Blvd.

2nd St.

3rd St.

4th St.

Barnard Way

OCEAN PARK

Ashland Ave.

South Beach Park

Marine St.

3rd Ave.

Hampton Dr.

4th Ave.

Dewey St.

Marine St.

Dewey St.

Penmar Golf Course

Ozone Ave.

Rose Ave.

Dudley Ave.

Pacific Ave.

Flower Ave.

Santa Monica Bay

Ocean Front Walk

Vernon Ave.

Indiana Ave.

Brooks Ave.

7th Ave.

6th Ave.

VENICE

San Juan Ave.

Abbot Kinney Blvd.

California Ave.

Millwood Ave.

Oakwood Ave.

Linden Ave.

Palms Blvd.

Nowita Pl.

Superba Ave.

Marco Pl.

Speedway

Market St.

Windward Ave.

Muscle Beach

Grand Blvd.

Venice Way

Venezia Ave.

20th Ave.

N Venice Blvd.

S Venice Blvd.

Venice Blvd.

Venice Municipal Beach

25th Ave.

Del Ave.

Ocean Ave.

Venice Canals

Oxford Ave.

28th Ave.

Venice Pier

30th Ave.

TO MARINA DEL REY (.5mi)

Washington Blvd.

Van Buren Ave.

TO LAX (4mi)

0   400 yards

0   400 meters

San Francisco: MUNI Metro System

Embarcadero
Montgomery
Powell
Civic Center
Van Ness
Folsom & Embarcadero
Brannan & Embarcadero
2nd St & King (PacBell Park)
Caltrain Station/ (4th St. & King)
BART
Duboce & Church
Duboce Park/ Duboce & Noe
Carl & Cole
UCSF
Judah & 19th Ave.
Judah & 9th Ave.
Judah & Sunset
Church
Castro
16th St.
Ocean Beach
Church & 18th St.
Church & 24th St.
24th St.
Taraval & Sunset
Taraval & 22nd Ave.
Forest Hill
West Portal
San Francisco Zoo
St. Francis Circle
Church & 30th St.
San Jose & Randall
Junipero Serra & Ocean
Ocean & Jules
City College
Glen Park
Stonestown
SF State
Randolph & Arch
Broad & Plymouth
Balboa Park
San Jose & Geneva
Randolph & 19th Ave.
SAN FRANCISCO
SAN MATEO COUNTY
Daly City

0   1 mile
0   1 kilometer

- N — Judah
- J — Church
- L — Taraval
- M — Oceanview
- K — Ingleside
- ● Subway station
- ●● Surface station
- ⊟ Subway transfer station
- ⊟ Surface transfer station

San Francisco: BART System

North Concord/Martinez
Pittsburg/ Bay Point
Concord
CONTRA COSTA COUNTY
Richmond
El Cerrito del Norte
Pleasant Hill
MARIN COUNTY
El Cerrito Plaza
Walnut Creek
North Berkeley
Berkeley
San Francisco Bay
Ashby
Orinda
Lafayette
Ft. Cronkhite
Rockridge
MacArthur
19th St./Oakland
Oakland City Center/ 12th St.
Embarcadero
Montgomery St.
Powell St.
Civic Center
West Oakland
Lake Merritt
Fruitvale
16th St./Mission
24th St./Mission
Coliseum/ Oakland Airport
Glen Park
Balboa Park
Caltrain
SAN FRANCISCO
Oakland International Airport
San Leandro
Daly City
Colma
Bay Fair
Castro Valley
Dublin/ Pleasanton
South San Francisco
San Bruno
San Francisco Bay
Hayward
ALAMEDA COUNTY
San Francisco International Airport
South Hayward
SAN MATEO COUNTY
Millbrae
Union City
Fremont

- ▬ Richmond-Daly City
- ▬ Pittsburg/Bay Point-Millbrae
- ▬ Fremont-Daly City
- ▬ Fremont-Richmond
- ▬ Dublin/Pleasanton-SFO
- ▬ SFO-Millbrae
- ⊶ CalTrain Shuttle

0   4 miles
0   4 kilometers

San Francisco Transportation

San Francisco Bay

Marina Park

Fo
Ma

Crissy
Field

Marina Blvd.

30

22

28

Palace of
Fine Arts and
Exploratorium

TO GOLDEN GATE
BRIDGE

29

GG

30X

30X

MARINA

Bay

Doyle Dr.

76 ≡ 28 ≡ 76

101

Franc

82X

29

Chestnut St.

30 — 43

Lombard St.

76 — 82

30

82X

101

Greenwich

PRESIDIO

29

29

41 45

PACIFIC
HEIGHTS

Union St.

Octavia

Green

Vallejo

41, 45

22

Broadway

Arguello Blvd.

Walnut St.

Baker

Broderick

Pacific Ave.

Jackson St

West Pacific Ave.

33

Cherry St.

Maple St.

Spruce St.

Locust St.

Laurel St.

Presidio Ave.

3

24

Alta
Park

12

Washingtor

Fillmore

Webster

Buchanan

Lafaye
Par

44

3

California St.

JAPAN-
TOWN

8th Ave.

1   4

33

Arguello

Blvd.

2

Pine St.

Bush St.

1AX

1AX 31AX 31BX

4

2   3   4

Lyon

Divisadero St.

Pierce

Scott

Geary Expressw

4

Geary Blvd.

GG

38 ≡ 38L

38AX, BX

Masonic Ave.

Steiner St.

22

Laguna

44

University of
San Francisco

Turk St.

31

31

31BX

Golden Gate Ave.

24

5

McAllister

Fulton St.

Cabrillo St.

WESTERN
ADDITION

ALAMO
SQUARE

Grove St.

21

21

33

5

Fulton St.

Grove St.

Hayes St.

43

21

Oak St.

Page St.

Haight St.

Fell St.

Panhandle

16AX, BX

16AX, BX

Golden Gate
Park

7

37
37

HAIGHT-
ASHBURY

37

66   71   7

6

Oak St.

Buena
Vista
Park

Waller St.

Duboce Ave.

N

24

3

14t

7

43

Clayton St.

6

33

37

Frederick St.

15th

16AX, BX

71

7th Ave.

8th Ave.

6th Ave.

5th Ave.

4th Av.

3rd Ave.

2nd Av.

9th Ave.

N

66

35

37

Market St.

22

16th
Miss
Dolo
17th

6   66

66

Parnassus Ave.

43

37

F

18th St.

33

Mission
Dolores
Park

19th

66

44

UCSF
Medical
Center

Stanyan St.

37

35

CASTRO

Castro St.

Douglas St.

24

Noe St.

Sanchez St.

Church St.

20t

Liberty St.

Hil

36

Clarendon Ave.

K   M

37

Diamond St.

Alvarado St.

22n

48

48

23

36

43   36

Twin
Peaks

TO ALCATRAZ

0   200 yards
0   200 meters

N
LG

F	Muni Metro/ Historic Streetcar
15	Muni Bus Line
	Cable Car
ba	BART Subway
	CalTran (service to San Jose)
82X	Peak Hours Only
	Route Terminus
SM	SamTrans (service to San Mateo)
GG	Golden Gate Transit (service to Marin)

Hyde St.
Pier

Fisherman's
Wharf

Pier 39

Jefferson St.

19 F

Beach St.

North Point

47 82X

39

15 53

TELEGRAPH
HILL

30

Columbus Ave.

Leavenworth

Stockton

Grant

Powell St.

Mason

NORTH
BEACH

39

Coit
Tower

82X

RUSSIAN
HILL

Taylor St.

Jones

Filbert

41 45

POWELL-HYDE LINE

30

Kearny St.

Montgomery St.

Battery

Sansome

The Embarcadero

F

POWELL-MASON LINE

19

30X 4, 149, 47, 76

Van Ness Ave.

30X

12

15

CHINATOWN

9X

41

JACKSON
SQUARE

Front

Davis

12

Drumm

Ferry
Building

BART TO EAST BAY

Clay St.

Sacramento

1
1

CALIFORNIA ST. LINE

NOB HILL

4

45, 30
9A, BX

9X

30X

15

41

ba

1

Stuart St.

41

30X

80X

30X

Spear St.

Main St.

Beale St.

Fremont St.

1st St.

82X

Bay Bridge

80

1AX,BX 31AX,BX 38AX,BX

Sutter

76

Post

76

UNION
SQUARE

2 3 4

2 3 4

Geary St.

Market St.

9

15

ba

Transbay
Terminal

76

15

2nd St.

76

80X

X18 X08

38

38L

38 38L

27

O'Farrell

Ellis

Eddy

Larkin

Hyde St.

31

31

Turk St.

27

1AX

J K L M N F

5

Mission St.

3rd St.

4th St.

5th St.

6th St.

SOMA

9X

12 31X

30

15

45

42

Pac Bell
Ballpark

China
Basin

CIVIC
CENTER

42 49 47

21

21

16AX, BX

16AX, BX

Market St.

ba

Mission St.

SM

Howard St.

5

12

9X

9AX, BX

9AX, BX

Folsom St.

30 15

45

76

101

7 6

ba

14 14L 47

9th St.

10th St.

12

Harrison St.

80

Bramman St.

41

CalTran
Depot

N

76

Central Freeway

49

14 14L 47

11th St.

12th St.

27

27

9

Townsend

King St.

CHINA
BASIN

7th St.

Owens St.

China Basin St.

12

27

9

9AX 9BX 14X 9X

19

15

Central
Basin

53

22

53

53

33

Potrero St.

San Bruno Ave.

Hampshire St.

Mariposa St.

Texas St.

Missouri St.

22

280

Indiana St.

Minnesota St.

Pennsylvania St.

22

22

48

MISSION

ba

26

14 14L

33

Bryant St.

Florida St.

Alabama St.

Shotwell St.

SM

SM

Harrison St.

Folsom St.

101

12

York St.

Rhode Island St.

De Haro St.

Kansas St.

Carolina St.

Arkansas St.

Wisconsin St.

Connecticut St.

Mississippi St.

53

19

48

3rd St.

Illinois St.

Tennessee St.

48

Valencia St.

Mission St.

Capp St.

S. Van Ness Ave.

SF
General

33

48

Vermont St.

CalTran
Station

N

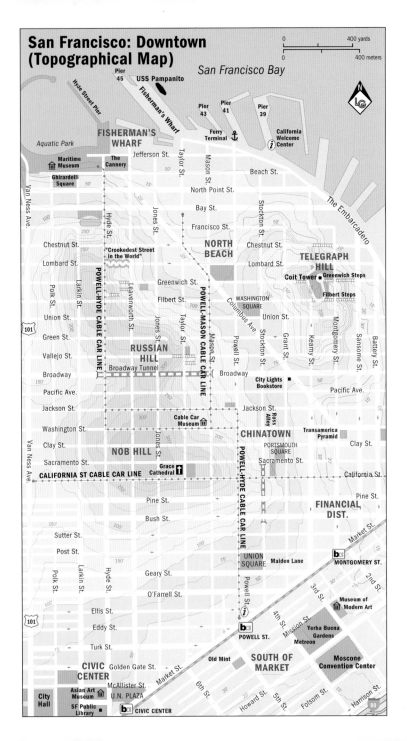

San Francisco: Downtown (Topographical Map)

San Francisco Bay

0   400 yards

0   400 meters

N

Pier 45   USS Pampanito

Hyde Street Pier

Fisherman's Wharf

Pier 43

Pier 41

Pier 39

Ferry Terminal

California Welcome Center

FISHERMAN'S WHARF

Aquatic Park

The Embarcadero

Maritime Museum

The Cannery

Jefferson St.

Beach St.

Ghirardelli Square

Taylor St.

Mason St.

North Point St.

Van Ness Ave.

Jones St.

Bay St.

Francisco St.

Stockton St.

Hyde St.

Chestnut St.

"Crookedest Street in the World"

NORTH BEACH

Chestnut St.

TELEGRAPH HILL

Lombard St.

Lombard St.

Coit Tower

Greenwich Steps

Polk St.

Larkin St.

POWELL-HYDE CABLE CAR LINE

Leavenworth St.

Greenwich St.

Filbert St.

POWELL-MASON CABLE CAR LINE

Columbus Ave.

WASHINGTON SQUARE

Filbert Steps

Union St.

Jones St.

Taylor St.

Union St.

Stockton St.

Grant St.

Kearny St.

Montgomery St.

Sansome St.

Battery St.

Green St.

RUSSIAN HILL

Vallejo St.

Powell St.

Broadway

Broadway Tunnel

Broadway

City Lights Bookstore

Pacific Ave.

Pacific Ave.

Jackson St.

Jackson St.

Ross Alley

Washington St.

Cable Car Museum

Transamerica Pyramid

CHINATOWN

Clay St.

Jones St.

PORTSMOUTH SQUARE

Clay St.

NOB HILL

Sacramento St.

POWELL-HYDE CABLE CAR LINE

Sacramento St.

Van Ness Ave.

CALIFORNIA ST CABLE CAR LINE

Grace Cathedral

California St.

Pine St.

Pine St.

Bush St.

FINANCIAL DIST.

Sutter St.

Market St.

Post St.

Polk St.

Larkin St.

Hyde St.

Geary St.

UNION SQUARE

Maiden Lane

MONTGOMERY ST.

O'Farrell St.

Powell St.

3rd St.

2nd St.

Ellis St.

Museum of Modern Art

Eddy St.

POWELL ST.

4th St.

Mission St.

Yerba Buena Gardens

Turk St.

Metreon

CIVIC CENTER

Golden Gate St.

Market St.

Old Mint

SOUTH OF MARKET

Moscone Convention Center

McAllister St.

6th St.

5th St.

Harrison St.

City Hall

Asian Art Museum

U.N. PLAZA

Howard St.

Folsom St.

SF Public Library

CIVIC CENTER

80

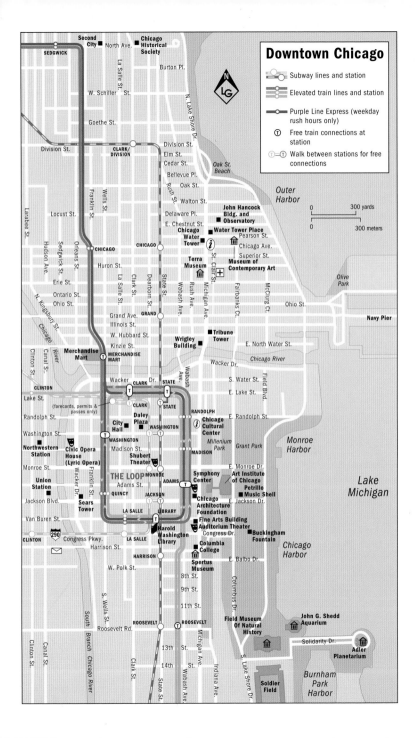

Downtown Chicago

- Subway lines and station
- Elevated train lines and station
- Purple Line Express (weekday rush hours only)
- ⓘ Free train connections at station
- ⓘ–ⓘ Walk between stations for free connections

Second City ■ North Ave. ■ **Chicago Historical Society**

SEDGWICK

Burton Pl.

W. Schiller St.

La Salle Dr.

Goethe St.

N. Lake Shore Dr.

Division St.

Division St.

CLARK/DIVISION

Elm St.

Cedar St.

Bellevue Pl.

Oak St.

Oak St. Beach

Walton St.

Delaware Pl.

E. Chestnut St.

John Hancock Bldg. and Observatory ■

Chicago Water Tower ■

Water Tower Place

ⓘ

Pearson St.

Chicago Ave.

Terra Museum 🏛

St. Clair St.

Museum of Contemporary Art ✚

Superior St.

Locust St.

Franklin St.

Wells St.

CHICAGO

CHICAGO

Huron St.

Clark St.

Dearborn St.

State St.

Rush Ave.

Wabash Ave.

Michigan Ave.

Fairbanks Ct.

McClurg Ct.

Olive Park

Larabee St.

Hudson Ave.

Sedgwick St.

Orleans St.

Erie St.

La Salle St.

Ontario St.

Ohio St.

Ohio St.

Navy Pier

N. Kingsbury St.

Chicago River

Grand Ave.

GRAND

Illinois St.

W. Hubbard St.

Kinzie St.

Wrigley Building ■

■ **Tribune Tower**

E. North Water St.

Merchandise Mart ⓘ

MERCHANDISE MART

Wacker Dr.

Chicago River

Wacker Dr.

Canal St.

Wabash Ave.

S. Water St.

Field Blvd.

Canal St.

CLINTON

Lake St.

Wacker Dr.

CLARK

STATE

E. Lake St.

Randolph St.

(farecards, permits & passes only)

CLARK

STATE

RANDOLPH

Daley Plaza

City Hall

WASHINGTON

Chicago Cultural Center ⓘ

E. Randolph St.

Washington St.

Northwestern Station 🚇

Civic Opera House (Lyric Opera)

WASHINGTON

Madison St.

Shubert Theater

THE LOOP

MADISON

Millenium Park

Grant Park

Monroe Harbor

Monroe St.

Franklin St.

Wacker Dr.

MONROE

Adams St.

ADAMS

Symphony Center

Art Institute of Chicago

E. Monroe Dr.

Union Station 🚇

Jackson Blvd.

QUINCY

JACKSON

ⓘ

Petrillo Music Shell ■

E. Jackson Dr.

Lake Michigan

Van Buren St.

Sears Tower ■

LA SALLE

LIBRARY

Chicago Architecture Foundation ■

Fine Arts Building ■

Auditorium Theater ■

Buckingham Fountain ■

CLINTON

290

Congress Pkwy.

LA SALLE

Harold Washington Library 🏛

Congress Dr.

Chicago Harbor

Harrison St.

HARRISON

Columbia College 🏛

E. Balbo Dr.

W. Polk St.

Spertus Museum 🏛

8th St.

S. Wells St.

Clark St.

9th St.

11th St.

Columbus Dr.

S. Lake Shore Dr.

South Branch Chicago River

ROOSEVELT

ⓘ

ROOSEVELT

Roosevelt Rd.

Field Museum Of Natural History 🏛

John G. Shedd Aquarium 🏛

Clinton St.

13th St.

State St.

Wabash Ave.

Michigan Ave.

Indiana Ave.

Solidarity Dr.

Adler Planetarium 🏛

14th St.

Soldier Field

Burnham Park Harbor

0 ___ 300 yards

0 ___ 300 meters

Outer Harbor

Seattle

LET'S GO

■ PAGES PACKED WITH ESSENTIAL INFORMATION

"Value-packed, unbeatable, accurate, and comprehensive."

—The Los Angeles Times

"The guides are aimed not only at young budget travelers but at the independent traveler; a sort of streetwise cookbook for traveling alone."

—The New York Times

"Unbeatable; good sight-seeing advice; up-to-date info on restaurants, hotels, and inns; a commitment to money-saving travel; and a wry style that brightens nearly every page."

—The Washington Post

■ THE BEST TRAVEL BARGAINS IN YOUR BUDGET

"All the dirt, dirt cheap."

—People

"Let's Go follows the creed that you don't have to toss your life's savings to the wind to travel—unless you want to."

—The Salt Lake Tribune

■ REAL ADVICE FOR REAL EXPERIENCES

"The writers seem to have experienced every rooster-packed bus and lunar-surfaced mattress about which they write."

—The New York Times

"[Let's Go's] devoted updaters really walk the walk (and thumb the ride, and trek the trail). Learn how to fish, haggle, find work—anywhere."

—Food & Wine

"A world-wise traveling companion—always ready with friendly advice and helpful hints, all sprinkled with a bit of wit."

—The Philadelphia Inquirer

■ A GUIDE WITH A SPIRIT AND A SOCIAL CONSCIENCE

"Lighthearted and sophisticated, informative and fun to read. [Let's Go] helps the novice traveler navigate like a knowledgeable old hand."

—Atlanta Journal-Constitution

"The serious mission at the book's core reveals itself in exhortations to respect the culture and the environment—and, if possible, to visit as a volunteer, a student, or a teacher rather than a tourist."

—San Francisco Chronicle

LET'S GO PUBLICATIONS

TRAVEL GUIDES

Australia 9th edition
Austria & Switzerland 12th edition
Brazil 1st edition
Britain 2008
California 10th edition
Central America 9th edition
Chile 2nd edition
China 5th edition
Costa Rica 3rd edition
Eastern Europe 13th edition
Ecuador 1st edition
Egypt 2nd edition
Europe 2008
France 2008
Germany 13th edition
Greece 9th edition
Hawaii 4th edition
India & Nepal 8th edition
Ireland 13th edition
Israel 4th edition
Italy 2008
Japan 1st edition
Mexico 22nd edition
New Zealand 8th edition
Peru 1st edition
Puerto Rico 3rd edition
Southeast Asia 9th edition
Spain & Portugal 2008
Thailand 3rd edition
USA 24th edition
Vietnam 2nd edition
Western Europe 2008

ROADTRIP GUIDE

Roadtripping USA 2nd edition

ADVENTURE GUIDES

Alaska 1st edition
Pacific Northwest 1st edition
Southwest USA 3rd edition

CITY GUIDES

Amsterdam 5th edition
Barcelona 3rd edition
Boston 4th edition
London 16th edition
New York City 16th edition
Paris 14th edition
Rome 12th edition
San Francisco 4th edition
Washington, D.C. 13th edition

POCKET CITY GUIDES

Amsterdam
Berlin
Boston
Chicago
London
New York City
Paris
San Francisco
Venice
Washington, D.C.

LET'S GO

USA

SERGIO IBARRA EDITOR
ALEX BREAUX ASSOCIATE EDITOR
VANESSA DUBE ASSOCIATE EDITOR
JAMES O'KEEFE ASSOCIATE EDITOR

RESEARCHER-WRITERS

ELISE EGGART	**CAROLINE PIERCE**
CARA B. EISENPRESS	**MELISSA POCEK**
JESSICA ESTEP	**P. KIRK REARDON**
RACHEL GARWIN	**LIZ TINGUE**
DAN NALBANDYAN	**STEPHEN TRAVIERSO**
MATT ZIMMERMAN	

MAISIE CLARK MAP EDITOR
ANNE BENSSON MANAGING EDITOR

ST. MARTIN'S PRESS NEW YORK

Maps by David Lindroth copyright © 2008 by St. Martin's Press.

Distributed outside the USA and Canada by Macmillan.

ISBN-13: 978-0-312-37445-7
ISBN-10: 0-312-37445-3
Twenty-fourth Edition
10 9 8 7 6 5 4 3 2 1

Let's Go: USA is written by Let's Go Publications, 67 Mount Auburn St., Cambridge, MA 02138, USA.

Let's Go® and the LG logo are trademarks of Let's Go, Inc.

HOW TO USE THIS BOOK

For each edition, *Let's Go* sends dozens of researchers across the United States in search of the most authentic cuisine, the most bizarre Americana, and the best deals on the continent. This year's edition is revised, revamped, and ready to hit the road, complete with expanded national parks coverage, improved maps, and new daytrips. Here's what you'll find inside:

ORGANIZATION. This book will walk you (and probably ride with you) state by state through the US, starting in New York City and zigzagging from New England down through the South and up to the Pacific Northwest. Each chapter begins with a highlights box to help you pinpoint the best a region has to offer. To find the right region in a hurry, use the black tabs on the side of the book to guide you.

HELPFUL INFORMATION. The **Essentials** chapter (p. 11) is full of useful tips to help you plan a budget, navigate transportation, and pack just the right gear. **Life and Times** (p. 53) will get you up to speed with American history, food, and culture. The opportunities for study, work, and volunteerism in **Beyond Tourism** (p. 75) will inform you of exciting ways to make a difference during your travels.

PHONE CODES AND TELEPHONE NUMBERS. Phone numbers in text are preceded by the ☎ icon. The three-digit area code for each town appears opposite its name and is also denoted by the ☎ icon. Be prepared to dial the area code before the phone number—ten-digit dialing is required to dial between area codes.

PRICE RANGES AND RANKINGS. Our researchers list establishments in order of value from best to worst. Our favorites are denoted by the *Let's Go* thumbs-up (◙), our way of telling you that an establishment is too good to miss. Since the best value is not always the cheapest price, we have also incorporated a system of price ranges (p. xi). GLBT establishments are listed at the end of each section.

FEATURES. "The Local Story" tries to get at regional culture in a way that other coverage can't. You'll hear about an age-old rivalry between cheesesteak stands in Philadelphia, riveting shootouts in the Wild West, and a rumored entrance to Hell. In keeping with our renewed focus on socially conscious travel, "Giving Back" highlights service opportunities like maintaining the Appalachian Trail and participating in great fundraising opportunities for local communities and causes. We know you're traveling on a budget, so we've incorporated "The Big Splurge" to tell you when an extravagance is worth the sticker shock and "The Hidden Deal" to help your pennies go further. New for 2008, "Americana" features describe the unique American experience.

USA: Chapters

New England
pp. 228-301

Mid-Atlantic
pp. 86-227

Great Lakes
pp. 476-571

Florida
pp. 431-475

The South
pp. 302-430

Great Plains
pp. 572-626

Texas
pp. 627-662

Rocky Mountains
pp. 663-748

The Southwest
pp. 749-849

Pacific Northwest
pp. 935-986

California
pp. 850-934

MAINE

VERMONT
NEW HAMPSHIRE
MASSACHUSETTS
Boston
RHODE ISLAND
CONNECTICUT
New York City
NEW JERSEY
Philadelphia
DELAWARE
MARYLAND
Baltimore
Washington, DC
WEST VIRGINIA
VIRGINIA

NEW YORK
PENNSYLVANIA
Pittsburgh
OHIO
Cleveland
Detroit
MICHIGAN
INDIANA
ILLINOIS
Chicago
Milwaukee
WISCONSIN
St Paul
Minneapolis
MINNESOTA

NORTH DAKOTA
SOUTH DAKOTA
NEBRASKA
IOWA
Kansas City
MISSOURI
St. Louis
KANSAS
Tulsa
OKLAHOMA

KENTUCKY
Nashville
TENNESSEE
Memphis
ARKANSAS
MISSISSIPPI
ALABAMA
GEORGIA
Atlanta
SOUTH CAROLINA
NORTH CAROLINA
Charlotte

LOUISIANA
New Orleans
Gulf of Mexico

Orlando
Tampa
Miami

ATLANTIC OCEAN

Dallas
Austin
Houston
TEXAS

MEXICO

Denver
COLORADO
WYOMING
MONTANA
IDAHO
UTAH
Salt Lake City
NEVADA
Las Vegas
ARIZONA
Phoenix
NEW MEXICO
Albuquerque

Vancouver
Seattle
WASHINGTON
OREGON

San Francisco
San Diego
Los Angeles

PACIFIC OCEAN

0   200 miles
0   200 kilometers

N

CONTENTS

PRICE RANGES
USA

①②③④⑤

Our researchers list establishments in order of value from best to worst; our favorites are denoted by the Let's Go thumbs-up (◪). However, because the best value is not always the cheapest price, we have also incorporated a system of price ranges, based on a rough expectation of what you'll spend. For **accommodations,** we base our range on the cheapest price for which a single traveler can stay for one night. For **restaurants** and other dining establishments, we estimate the average amount a traveler will spend. The table tells you what you'll *typically* find in the USA at the corresponding price range; keep in mind that no system can allow for every individual establishment's quirks, and you'll typically get more for your money in larger cities. In other words: expect anything.

ACCOMMODATIONS	RANGE	WHAT YOU'RE *LIKELY* TO FIND
❶	under $30	Camping and most dorm rooms, such as HI or other hostels. Expect bunk beds and a communal bath; you may have to provide or rent linens.
❷	$30-45	Upper-end hostels or a small B&B. You may have a private bathroom or a sink in your room.
❸	$46-70	A small room with a private bath. Should have decent amenities, such as phone and TV. Breakfast may be included in the price of a room.
❹	$71-100	A room of your own with a private bath. May have more amenities or be in a more touristed area.
❺	over $100	Large, posh hotels. If it doesn't have the perks you want, you've paid too much.

FOOD	RANGE	WHAT YOU'RE *LIKELY* TO FIND
❶	under $7	Mostly sandwich shops or greasy spoons. Don't worry about tucking your shirt in.
❷	$7-9	Sandwiches, appetizers at a bar, or low-priced entrees. May be sit-down or takeout.
❸	$10-13	Mid-priced entrees, possibly with soup or salad. Tip will bump you up a couple dollars, since you'll probably have a waiter or waitress.
❹	$14-17	A somewhat fancy restaurant or steakhouse. Either way, you'll have a special knife. Some restaurants may have a dress code; many will look down on T-shirts and jeans.
❺	over $17	Food with foreign names and a decent wine list. Slacks and dress shirts may be expected.

RESEARCHER-WRITERS

Elise Eggart
Idaho, Oregon, and Washington

What happens when you take a Southern Belle and let her have her way with the wet and wild Northwest? If you're Elise, you send back new and updated coverage on some of the most gorgeous National Parks, hippiest small towns, and classiest inexpensive wineries. This recent college grad was the perfect match for the route; no potato, hop, or latte was free from her discerning eye and strong attention to detail.

Cara B. Eisenpress
The Great Plains

Despite some initial anxiety about America's Heartland—and a few priceless camping fiascos—Cara dove (and drove) headfirst into the quintessential American experience, thriving on a largely meat-and-potatoes diet and meticulously reporting on all the establishments fit to list in our latest guide. Brimming with passion and self-described "infinite, undying, unquantifiable" love for the road, Cara drifted across mid-America to the tune of the latest country jams.

Jessica Estep
Texas, Oklahoma, and Kansas

Researching a region as vast as TX, OK, and KS is no small feat. Covering the region in the middle of summer and driving a bumperless car is enough to make the cagiest traveler say "uncle." Rocking out during long car rides and sporadic cell phone reception, Jessica sent copy that had a little extra spunk. Team USA marveled at her fearless trailblazing ways as she sent back new regional coverage cool enough to keep any traveler excited.

Rachel Garwin
The Rockies

Rachel—that notorious goddess of the great outdoors—camps and climbs like it's her job, so reading her coverage of the Rockies was like savoring a scoop of homemade chocolate ice cream against a breath-taking alpine backdrop. When she wasn't making her jam-packed itinerary look easy, Rachel rocked out to world-class bluegrass, sampled the ever-tasty Rocky Mountain oyster, and came up with copy as on-the-mark as it was eloquent.

Dan Nalbandyan
Mid-Atlantic

Dan's coverage of the timeless Mid-Atlantic is larger than life, thanks to his experience navigating impossible Philadelphian traffic, partying like a rockstar in Ocean City, and taking hipper-than-hip New York City by storm. Despite a tight schedule, a tighter budget, and a daunting laundry list of establishments to review, Dan fearlessly rose to the occasion, writing with such wit and snark as to make you laugh, cry, salivate, and keep coming back for more.

Caroline Pierce
The Southwest

Helicopter or mule ride? Are vortexes and UFOs real? How many nights can I go without showering? It's questions like these that kept spunky Caroline on her toes as she deftly researched her way through the Southwest. Treks through National Parks were a piece of cake for this stalwart and creative researcher. Caroline's copy came alive with her enthusiasm, her sense of adventure, and her (mouth-watering) love for pancakes and Mexican food.

Melissa Pocek *The Carolinas, Georgia, and Florida*

From the Research Triangle to the tips of Key West, Melissa endured extreme temperatures, computer crashes, and long nights to bring her enthusiasm to our readers. Her sunny disposition and positive attitude were assets on the road, and came through in her thoughtful postcards. Melissa's commitment to socially responsible travel and honesty made her a great match for *Let's Go*.

P. Kirk Reardon *The Great Lakes*

An LG veteran, free-spirited Kirk dominated the open road and the backcountry areas of his route. Newly armed with his driver's license and his diploma, Kirk cut through copy like a seasoned pro. Whether biking through Chicago or traipsing through Michigan's Northern Peninsula, Kirk always brought his open mind and his boundless appetite for adventure to his work.

Liz Tingue *California and Nevada*

With a dash of eye liner and bangs blowing in the wind, Liz took the West Coast by storm. This MA native hit up all the Vegas and SoCal hot spots, and survived Death Valley only to keep it classy in San Diego. By crashing on couches and forming friendships, Liz never failed to write inspired copy while still finding time to taste Napa's finest wine and soak up some Pacific waves and rays.

Stephen Travierso *The South*

Driving drama in the Deep South was not enough to faze our resident actor. Stephen charmed his way across the South, blending in with locals whenever possible to get the inside scoop. His commitment to the job proved to be pivotal as he updated the Big Easy's coverage with strong details and the utmost sensitivity. The South is still happening, and Stephen made sure to let us know it's still open for business.

Matt Zimmerman *New England*

Matt's love for the open road helped him tear through New England. He took no prisoners, but still asked all the necessary questions. This accomplished musician from the "Volunteer State" (TN) is a true outdoorsman, camping most nights and taking full advantage of hikes and scenery. With untamed hair, detailed copy, and entertaining stories, Matt was a natural who kept an eye out for adventure at all times.

CONTRIBUTING WRITERS

Andrew Stillman *Seattle and Washington State*
Joe Tartakoff *Tijuana, Mexico*
Melinda Biocchi, Sade Jimoh *Boston*

ABOUT LET'S GO

NOT YOUR PARENTS' TRAVEL GUIDE

At Let's Go, we see every trip as the chance of a lifetime. If your dream is to grab a machete and forge through the jungles of Costa Rica, we can take you there. If you'd rather bask in the Riviera sun at a beachside cafe, we'll set you a table. We write for readers who know that there's more to travel than sharing double deckers with tourists and who believe that travel can change both themselves and the world—whether they plan to spend six days in Mexico City or six months in Europe. We'll show you just how far your money can go, and prove that the greatest limitation on your adventures is not your wallet, but your imagination.

BEYOND THE TOURIST EXPERIENCE

To help you gain a deeper connection with the places you travel, our fearless researchers scour the globe to give you the heads-up on both world-renowned and off-the-beaten-track attractions, sights, and destinations. They engage with the local culture only to emerge with the freshest insights on everything from local festivals to regional cuisine. We've also opened our pages to respected writers and scholars to hear their takes on the countries and regions we cover, and asked travelers who have worked, studied, or volunteered abroad to contribute first-person accounts of their experiences. In addition, we increased our coverage of responsible travel and expanded each guide's Beyond Tourism chapter to share more ideas about how to give back while on the road.

FORTY-EIGHT YEARS OF WISDOM

Let's Go got its start in 1960, when a group of creative and well-traveled students compiled their experience and advice into a 20-page mimeographed pamphlet, which they gave to travelers on charter flights to Europe. Four and a half decades later, we've expanded to cover six continents and all kinds of travel—while retaining our founders' adventurous attitude toward the world. Laced with witty prose and total candor, our guides are still researched and written entirely by students on shoestring budgets, experienced travelers who know that train strikes, stolen luggage, food poisoning, and marriage proposals are all part of a day's work.

THE LET'S GO COMMUNITY

More than just a travel guide company, Let's Go is a community. Our small staff comes together because of our shared passion for travel and our desire to help other travelers see the world the way it was meant to be seen. We love it when our readers become part of the Let's Go community as well—when you travel, drop us a postcard (67 Mt. Auburn St., Cambridge, MA 02138, USA), send us an e-mail (feedback@letsgo.com), or post on our forum (http://www.letsgo.com/connect/forum) to tell us about your adventures and discoveries.

For more information, visit us online: www.letsgo.com.

ACKNOWLEDGMENTS

LET'S GO

TEAM USA THANKS: Our fantastic RWs, who through their hard work and awesome adventures helped make this a Wet Hot American Summer; Anne, for sharing, oversharing, and always being a high; Maisie, for being a delicious little map flooze; Trang, for taking it all in good stride; Prod, for helping America stay beautiful; the 4th floor, for putting up with our bitchin' tunes; the office, for being hot.

SERGIO THANKS: The ⬛Plastics (Dube, Breaux, Jimmy), for cakes, capes, and SOMLs; Anne, for trusting me with this giant burn book; Julie, for emo hits; Maisie, for direction; Gordon, for rehab; Ingrid and Conroy, for Last Senior Standing; 6 Exeter, for MTV Hits and family dinners; Sammy, for being around in spirit; Inés, for liking me the way I are; my family, for love and support 3000 mi. away.

VANESSA THANKS: Breaux, Jimmy, & Serge for a hilarious SOMS, and for crowning me La Princesa; my siblings, for going first; M&D, for letting me be the "!"; Nanni & Grampy for being awesome; J.Crew, Dick Wolf, DVR, and my hair-dryer for the daily support.

ALEX THANKS: Maverick, Hollywood, and Sundown for the laughing usually with me and not at me; my eating partner Maisie; Anne and her American lifestyle; Unique Pizza (RIP), abbrevs.; my parents for their love (and cookies) and my brother for educational G-Chats.

JAMES THANKS: Breaux, Dube, and Serge for putting up with my antics; Maisie, for the fascist map dictatorship; ASF, LG, and SO, for not calling the police; Mom, Dad, et al. for support, financial and otherwise; AF, LF, NG, MP, PS for good fun; Provincetown, for the SARS.

MAISIE THANKS: Sergio, Jimmy, Alex, and Vanessa, for keeping it American; Anne, for keeping it clean; Mapland, for keeping it real; Anna Rachlin, for keeping me sane!

Editor
Sergio Ibarra
Associate Editors
Vanessa Dube, Alex Breaux, James O'Keefe
Managing Editor
Anne Bensson
Map Editor
Maisie Clark
Typesetter
Ankur Ghosh

Publishing Director
Jennifer Q. Wong
Editor-in-Chief
Silvia Gonzalez Killingsworth
Production Manager
Victoria Esquivel-Korsiak
Cartography Manager
Thomas MacDonald Barron
Editorial Managers
Anne Bensson, Calina Ciobanu, Rachel Nolan
Financial Manager
Sara Culver
Business and Marketing Manager
Julie Vodhanel
Personnel Manager
Victoria Norelid
Production Associate
Jansen A. S. Thurmer
Director of E-Commerce & IT
Patrick Carroll
Website Manager
Kathryne A. Bevilacqua
Office Coordinators
Juan L. Peña, Bradley J. Jones

Director of Advertising Sales
Hunter McDonald
Senior Advertising Associate
Daniel Lee

President
William Hauser
General Managers
Bob Rombauer, Jim McKellar

The United States

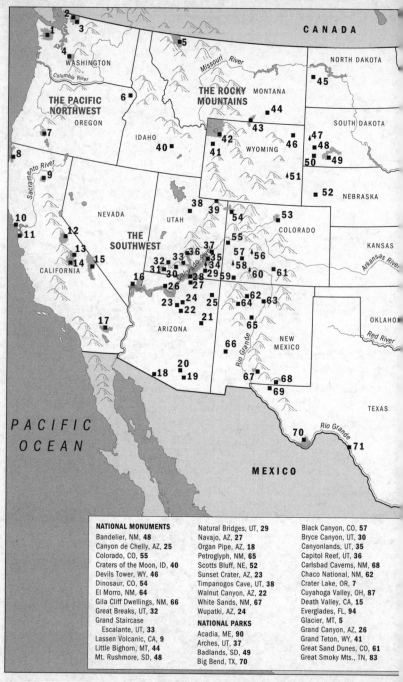

PACIFIC OCEAN

CANADA

MEXICO

NATIONAL MONUMENTS
Bandelier, NM, **48**
Canyon de Chelly, AZ, **25**
Colorado, CO, **55**
Craters of the Moon, ID, **40**
Devils Tower, WY, **46**
Dinosaur, CO, **54**
El Morro, NM, **64**
Gila Cliff Dwellings, NM, **66**
Great Breaks, UT, **32**
Grand Staircase
  Escalante, UT, **33**
Lassen Volcanic, CA, **9**
Little Bighorn, MT, **44**
Mt. Rushmore, SD, **48**

Natural Bridges, UT, **29**
Navajo, AZ, **27**
Organ Pipe, AZ, **18**
Petroglyph, NM, **65**
Scotts Bluff, NE, **52**
Sunset Crater, AZ, **23**
Timpanogos Cave, UT, **38**
Walnut Canyon, AZ, **22**
White Sands, NM, **67**
Wupatki, AZ, **24**

NATIONAL PARKS
Acadia, ME, **90**
Arches, UT, **37**
Badlands, SD, **49**
Big Bend, TX, **70**

Black Canyon, CO, **57**
Bryce Canyon, UT, **30**
Canyonlands, UT, **35**
Capitol Reef, UT, **36**
Carlsbad Caverns, NM, **68**
Chaco National, NM, **62**
Crater Lake, OR, **7**
Cuyahoga Valley, OH, **87**
Death Valley, CA, **15**
Everglades, FL, **94**
Glacier, MT, **5**
Grand Canyon, AZ, **26**
Grand Teton, WY, **41**
Great Sand Dunes, CO, **61**
Great Smoky Mts., TN, **83**

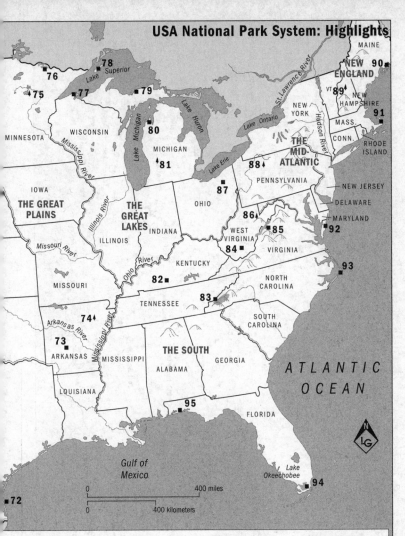

USA National Park System: Highlights

USA Transportation Network

☐ Major bus (Greyhound) hubs
◉ Other major cities
〜〜〜 Amtrak routes

DISCOVER THE UNITED STATES

The United States has its relics, of course: preserved colonial settlements on the Eastern seaboard, Spanish ruins in Florida, vestiges of native dwellings built and abandoned long before Christopher Columbus was even a twinkle in his mother's eye. Yet in the end, visitors to the US often come away struck by the sheer depth of the New World's infatuation with, well, newness. A nation of johnny-come-latelys, America cuts its teeth on stories of people and places reinventing themselves practically overnight. Movie stars become governors, sleepy cow towns become biotech meccas, and no one blinks at these madcap reversals because America is a country where looking forward trumps looking back time and time again.

Too often, it's the big cities of the United States that dominate the tourist imagination: the lights of New York, the monuments of Washington, D.C., the trolley cars of San Francisco. And perhaps these cities do give a glimpse of America in microcosm, whether it's the glamour of a gallery opening or the broken-window dreariness of a housing project. Still, seeing America's true colors means leaving the cities behind for a spell and heading out to review the high-school marching band in an Alabama whistle-stop or to ponder the solemn immensity of Montana's Big Sky country. It's not that these two worlds are always so far apart; it's just that America is big and brash and bewildering enough that you'll need six or seven sides of the story to start wrapping your mind around the place. Relentlessly literal, exasperatingly impetuous, disarmingly provincial, America will sweep you off your feet and leave you yearning for another dose of its star-spangled energy.

USA FACTS AND FIGURES

POPULATION: 295,734,134.

LARGEST CITIES: New York City, Los Angeles, Chicago, Houston, Philadelphia.

MILES OF HIGHWAY: 3,980,688 (of which 2,577,693 mi. are paved).

MILES DRIVEN EACH YEAR: 1½ trillion (to the sun and back 7500 times).

COMMON PET NAMES: Patches, Misty, Buster, Princess, Bear, Sheba.

TVS PER HOUSE: 2.4.

WHEN TO GO

In general, the US tourist season consists of the summer months between Memorial Day and Labor Day (May 23-Sept. 4, 2008). National parks flood with visitors during the high season, but cities are less affected by seasonal variation. For regions where winter sports are popular or the winters are mild, as in the mountains and the southern US, the peak season is generally inverted (Dec.-Apr.).

WHAT TO DO

Even this book's more than one thousand pages can't do justice to the vibrant, diverse offerings of the US. No two trips are the same, and visitors who travel to several regions may feel like they've visited different countries. Nevertheless, there are a few common themes that should be a part of any thorough exploration.

MUST-SEE CITIES

No visitor should pass up the glitz and glamour of Los Angeles, the round-the-clock excitement of New York City, or the multicultural metropolis of Miami. Nonetheless, the curious traveler should also take time to explore the wealth of lesser-known American cities with their own regional flavor. Hidden between the twin giants of New York and Boston, compact and walkable **Providence, RI** (p. 290), beckons with a slower, more inviting pace. Standing guard as the gateway to the West, **St. Louis, MO** (p. 608), combines distinctive neighborhoods and eclectic dining with an energetic nightlife scene fueled by the world's biggest brewery, Anheuser-Busch. Travelers to **Charleston, SC** (p. 355), are rewarded with lush gardens, antebellum plantations, and Southern charm. No party animal should miss Mardi Gras in **New Orleans, LA** (p. 413), where the city's carefree attitude, rich musical tradition, and sumptuous Creole cookin' cast an enchanting spell. Arts and crafts enthusiasts flock to **Santa Fe, NM** (p. 824), where old adobe churches, gorgeous galleries, and authentic Southwestern cuisine share the streets with the ritzy shops and restaurants serving the city's wealthy second-homers. The bohemian metropolis of **Portland, OR** (p. 936), known as the microbrewery capital of North America, is worth seeing for its fantastic open-air market alone.

COLLEGE TOWNS

America's colleges, from sprawling state universities to tiny liberal arts academies, have engendered unique communities with youthful vitality and alternative spirit. **Ann Arbor, MI** (p. 501), is the epitome of an American college town, boasting an unparalleled bar scene and a mishmash of Midwest hipsters while still maintaining a relaxed, friendly atmosphere. Not to be outdone, **Madison, WI** (p. 539) holds its own as both a state capital and a youthful romping ground. The 50,000 students who run amuck in **Austin, TX** (p. 633), spurn stereotypes about the conservative Lone Star State, creating a liberal haven where collegiate energy and Southwestern grit thrive side by side. A bastion of hippie culture, **Boulder, CO** (p. 671), gives a new meaning to the Rocky Mountain high. The mountain hamlet of **Middlebury, VT** (p. 254), combines rural charm with a touch of youthful rowdiness. An increasingly diverse student community gives the Southern establishment a run for its money in **Charlottesville, VA** (p. 215), a gorgeous town known for its rolling hills and splendid architecture. **Missoula, MT** (p. 729), is one of the most fascinatingly cosmopolitan cities in the Prairie States. **Berkeley, CA** (p. 867), perhaps the most famous American college town, has become a city in its own right without sacrificing its collegiate charms.

AMERICANA

America boasts the biggest, smallest, and zaniest of almost everything. Kitschy roadside attractions dot the country's dusty roads, putting on public display a vast and truly baffling material culture. Out west in Polson, MT, the **Miracle of America Museum** (p. 734) enshrines reg'lar ol' American living. Evidence of American architectural ingenuity can be found at the **Corn Palace** in Mitchell, SD (p. 579); this gargantuan structure is rebuilt every year with a fresh crop. America also claims the largest **operational chainsaw** near Marquette, MI (p. 512), and the world's largest **folding pocketknife** in Natchitoches, LA (p. 418), neither of which can quite compete with the magnitude of **Carhenge**—a scale model of Stonehenge built from 36 old cars just north of Alliance, NE (p. 603). Bigger and brighter still are the lights of **Times Square** in New York (p. 103) and **the Strip** in Las Vegas, NV (p. 755). And no tour of American kitsch would be complete without a trip to the heart and soul of all Americana—Elvis's **Graceland** (p. 328).

BASEBALL STADIUMS

The Great American Pastime is enshrined in its ballparks, where baseball zealots cheer on their favorite
teams. Nothing beats catching a game on a balmy
summer evening. The oldest ballpark still in use is
Fenway Park (p. 270) in Boston, MA, where the Red
Sox have played since 1912. The Chicago Cubs
make their home at **Wrigley Field** (p. 526), whose ivy-
clad outfield fences are an enduring symbol of baseball's storied past. Known as the "House that Ruth
Built," **Yankee Stadium** (p. 106) in the Bronx has more
history than any other stadium and is still widely considered the greatest ballpark in America. On the West
Coast, **Dodger Stadium** (p. 903) rivals its East Coast
predecessors with breathtaking views of downtown
Los Angeles and the promise of beautiful weather.
But while many purists cling to these relics of baseball's heyday, a wave of modern stadiums has ushered in a new era, and today the competition among
cities for the best ballpark often overshadows team
rivalries. **Camden Yards** (p. 181) in Baltimore, MD,
perfectly bridges the gap between old and new, combining brick architecture with the most modern
amenities. Perhaps the most impressive new stadium
is the Pittsburgh Pirates' **PNC Park** (p. 169), a classically styled ballpark that offers striking views of the
Pittsburgh skyline and the chance to blast a homer
into the Allegheny River. At **SBC Park** (p. 865), Giants
fans munch on gourmet concessions and cheer as
their sluggers launch dingers into the San Francisco
Bay, while at **Mile High Stadium** (p. 668), Colorado
fans decide which Rockies to gape at: the ones playing ball or the ones towering over the bleachers.

NATIONAL PARKS

From haunting red buttes to endless caves, the
national parks of the United States protect some of
the most phenomenal natural scenery in the world.
While much of the land's beauty can be seen along
the byways, the truly miraculous works of nature are
cared for by the National Park Service. The easternmost park in the US, **Acadia National Park, ME** (p. 235),
features unspoiled rocky beaches and dense pine forests. **Shenandoah National Park, VA** (p. 217), made its
way into history as America's first land reclamation
project, and today lures travelers with its mountain
vistas. **Great Smoky Mountains National Park, TN** (p.
318), the largest national park east of the Mississippi,
also contains the International Biosphere Reserve
and World Heritage Site. Farther west lie America's
larger, better-known parks. Arguably the most
famous (and most crowded) of these is **Yellowstone**

SAVORY SPECIALTIES

1. Chicken 'n' waffles. The ultimate soul food combination: warm
waffles and crispy fried chicken.
Ladle on the syrup in Atlanta, GA,
or Los Angeles, CA.

2. Creole and Cajun. From
chicken gumbo to shrimp
étouffée, Louisiana serves a jambalaya of cultural cuisines.

3. Fish boils. Feast like a lumberjack on whitefish plucked from
Lake Michigan and served straight
out of a bubbling cauldron.

4. Texas barbecue. Clark's in
Tioga, TX (p. 642), 1½ hr. north of
Dallas, has perfected the cowboy's craft of serving slow-cooked
meat smothered in spicy sauce.

5. Philadelphia cheesesteak.
Heavyweights Geno's and Pat's
(p. 153) have been duking it out
for nearly 50 years for the title of
Philly cheesesteak champion.

6. Cuban. Miami, FL, simmers
with *cocina cubana* so delicious,
you'll want to make it your vice.

7. Saltwater taffy. Beloved by
children (and despised by den-
tists), this East Coast shore treat
is sweet, sticky, and delicious.

8. Cincinnati chili. Cincinnati
(OH) chili sets itself apart from its
Texan counterpart by its thinner
consistency and unusual spices.

9. Deep-dish pizza. A Chicago,
IL, classic, the double-thick crust
comes piled high with toppings.

10. New Mexican chiles.
Make like a native Southwest-
erner and add red or green chili
sauce to eggs, enchiladas, and
everything in between.

DISCOVER

National Park, WY (p. 700), home to the geyser called Old Faithful. **Grand Canyon National Park, AZ** (p. 784), wows visitors with...well, the Grand Canyon, while **Yosemite National Park, CA** (p. 926), draws hordes of trekkers, trailers, and tourists with steep mountains and stunning waterfalls. Smaller—but no less breathtaking—are the otherworldly hoodoos (pillar-like rock formations) of **Bryce Canyon National Park, UT** (p. 776), the varied and dramatic terrain of **Waterton-Glacier International Peace Park, MT** (p. 734), and the awe-inspiring mountains of **Grand Teton National Park, WY** (p. 712).

🔖 LET'S GO PICKS

BEST SPOTS TO SHOW OFF YOUR BIRTHDAY SUIT: The dippin' is skinny at **Austin, TX's** Hippie Hollow (p. 637), while the prowl is clothing optional at **Cougar Hot Springs** (p. 947) in Eugene, OR.

MOST UNAPPETIZING BEER NAMES: South Carolina's **Mullet** (p. 362), and Louisiana's **funkybuttjuice** (p. 413) definitely rank among the nation's finest name-impaired beverages.

BEST FAKES: Tour five continents in a day, from a miniature Eiffel Tower to New York City to the Egyptian pyramids, on The Strip in **Las Vegas, NV** (p. 755). Ogle a replica of Jerusalem at the Holy Land Experience in **Orlando, FL** (p. 440). See the Mississippi River in miniature at the Mud Island River Park in **Memphis, TN** (p. 330); only 3½hr. away, a model Parthenon perches in the "Athens of the South," **Nashville, TN** (p. 314). Can't make it to Italy? Head to Presbyterian Memorial Church in **St. Augustine, FL**, the spitting image of St. Mark's Cathedral.

BEST GATORS: Make friends with America's scariest reptiles in places like **Natchitoches, LA** (p. 418); the **Everglades, FL** (p. 460); **St. Augustine, FL** (p. 449); and **Myrtle Beach, SC** (p. 362).

BEST ALTERNATIVE TO A GLASS: Enjoy a "beer boot" at the Essen Haus in Madison, WI (p. 544).

BEST OPPORTUNITIES FOR MULTI-TASKING: At Soapbox, a "laundrolounge" in **Wilmington, NC,** you can party and do your laundry at the same time (p. 354). Lace up your bowling shoes and pray for a strike at the **Boone, NC** Bowling Center's weekly "Christian Cosmic Bowling" night (p. 347).

MOST LIKELY TO HAVE PIRATES: The *José Gasparilla's* crew of buccaneers invades **Tampa, FL** in the first week of February (p. 443). **Alexandria Bay, NY,** hosts an annual Pirate Week (p. 139), while an altogether different kind of pirates play ball at PNC Park in **Pittsburgh, PA** (p. 165).

BEST REENACTMENTS: Listen to Pilgrims narrate the tale of the Mayflower at Plimoth Plantation in **Plymouth, MA** (p. 277). At Saloon #10 in the gambling town of **Deadwood, SD,** the shooting of outlaw Wild Bill Hickok is reenacted several times a day (p. 588). Get your American heritage fix in Colonial **Williamsburg, VA.**

BEST PLACES TO CATCH SOME RAYS: Show off your tan among spring-breakers and NASCAR drivers in sunny **Daytona Beach, FL** (p. 445), or see and be seen on eclectic **Venice Beach, CA** (p. 894). To run with a different crowd, join the wild ponies in **Assateague, MD** (p. 184).

DISCOVER

SCALING THE WEST (3 WEEKS)

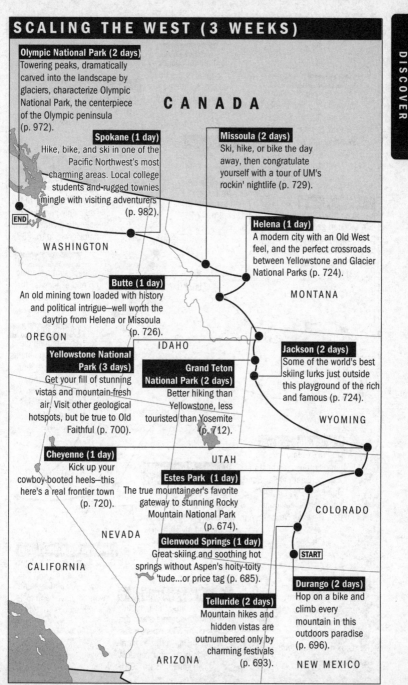

CANADA

Olympic National Park (2 days)
Towering peaks, dramatically carved into the landscape by glaciers, characterize Olympic National Park, the centerpiece of the Olympic peninsula (p. 972).

Spokane (1 day)
Hike, bike, and ski in one of the Pacific Northwest's most charming areas. Local college students and rugged townies mingle with visiting adventurers (p. 982).

Missoula (2 days)
Ski, hike, or bike the day away, then congratulate yourself with a tour of UM's rockin' nightlife (p. 729).

END

WASHINGTON

Helena (1 day)
A modern city with an Old West feel, and the perfect crossroads between Yellowstone and Glacier National Parks (p. 724).

Butte (1 day)
An old mining town loaded with history and political intrigue—well worth the daytrip from Helena or Missoula (p. 726).

MONTANA

OREGON

IDAHO

Yellowstone National Park (3 days)
Get your fill of stunning vistas and mountain-fresh air. Visit other geological hotspots, but be true to Old Faithful (p. 700).

Grand Teton National Park (2 days)
Better hiking than Yellowstone, less touristed than Yosemite (p. 712).

Jackson (2 days)
Some of the world's best skiing lurks just outside this playground of the rich and famous (p. 724).

WYOMING

Cheyenne (1 day)
Kick up your cowboy-booted heels—this here's a real frontier town (p. 720).

UTAH

Estes Park (1 day)
The true mountaineer's favorite gateway to stunning Rocky Mountain National Park (p. 674).

COLORADO

Glenwood Springs (1 day)
Great skiing and soothing hot springs without Aspen's hoity-toity 'tude...or price tag (p. 685).

NEVADA

START

CALIFORNIA

Durango (2 days)
Hop on a bike and climb every mountain in this outdoors paradise (p. 696).

Telluride (2 days)
Mountain hikes and hidden vistas are outnumbered only by charming festivals (p. 693).

ARIZONA

NEW MEXICO

DISCOVER

SOUTHWEST ADVENTURE (2½ WEEKS)

Moab (1 day)
The mountain biking capital of the US attracts enthusiasts from all over to its famed slick-rock trails (p. 768).

Grand Canyon (2 days)
Share the breathtaking view with the hordes of visitors on the South Rim, or head to the North Rim to savor the canyon's beauty by yourself (p. 784).

Arches National Park (1 day)
The richest collection of rock arches in the world, tucked away in one of Utah's more remote areas (p. 771).

Capitol Reef (1 day)
The hundred-mile Waterpocket Fold amazes geologists, backcountry hikers, and everyone in between (p. 774).

Mesa Verde National Park (1 day)
Clamber among ancient cliff dwellings at the US's only park devoted solely to archaeological preservation (p. 698).

Las Vegas (2 days)
Catch a cheap flight to Sin City and gamble away the money you saved in one of the Strip's shimmering casinos (p. 751).

Durango (1 day)
The perfect spot to saddle up and experience the mountains of Colorado (p. 696).

END

START

Santa Fe (2 days)
Hike around the Pendos Mountains, visit the city's art galleries, and wind down your trip with some excellent Mexican food (p. 824).

Death Valley (2 days)
Due to extreme temperatures, it's best to visit the Death Valley Sand Dunes (p. 921) at this aptly-named National Park between Nov. and Apr.

White Sands National Monument (1 day)
Giant, blindingly white dunes roll for miles in all directions—sunset is particularly stunning (p. 844).

Carlsbad Caverns (1 day)
Don't forget your flashlight when you explore this enormous underground world of caves and rock formations (p. 847).

Joshua Tree (1 day)
Survey 794,000 acres from atop Ryan Mountain (p. 919) or from the ground on Geology Tour Rd. Look out for ancient petroglyphs.

Flagstaff and Sedona (1 day)
Free-spirited folk, superb outdoor activities, and the chance to experience a spine-tingling vortex await at two of Arizona's coolest destinations (p. 793).

CURTAIN CALL (3 WEEKS)

Cambridge (1 day)
The American Repertory Theater yields ground-breaking results every season, employing highly-skilled actors and exploring alternative means in telling both new works and classics (p. 273).

Chicago (4 days)
See blockbuster musicals and off-beat parodies at the Steppenwolf Theater and Goodwin Theatre where leading men such as John Malkovich and Gary Sinise sometimes star (p. 514).

Williamstown (3 days)
The Tony-award-winning Williamstown Theater Festival host plays and musicals on two mainstages and several secondary stages around town every summer from mid-June to late Aug. (p. 287).

New Haven (1 day)
Check out the Yale Repertory Theatre. Each year Yale Rep produces exciting new plays and bold interpretations of the classics (p. 298).

New York City (5 days)
Enjoy talented actors, great stories, and million dollar productions on Broadway. For less mainstream shows, don't forget about off-Broadway (p. 88).

Providence (1 day)
Don't miss fresh interpretations of classics and works from emerging playwrights at the regionally acclaimed Trinity Repertory Company (p. 290).

Nashville (1 day)
Enjoy important Broadway shows and special engagements at the Tennessee Performance Arts Center, which houses the The Nashville Ballet, Nashville Opera Association, and the Tennessee Repertory Theatre (p. 310).

Louisville (2 days)
The well-respected Actors Theatre hosts contemporary comedies and dramas. Don't miss the Kentucky Shakespeare Festival from June to July, held in outdoor amphitheaters (p. 304).

Washington, D.C. (3 days)
Venture to the Arena Stage, often called the best regional company in America. Don't miss the famous Woolly Mammoth Theater Company, which offers pay-what-you-can and under-25 performances of contemporary works (p. 188).

DISCOVER

USA NATIONAL PARKS (1 MONTH)

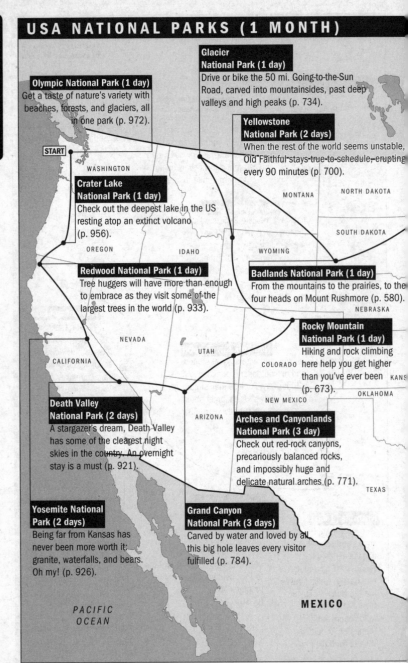

Glacier National Park (1 day)
Drive or bike the 50 mi. Going-to-the-Sun Road, carved into mountainsides, past deep valleys and high peaks (p. 734).

Olympic National Park (1 day)
Get a taste of nature's variety with beaches, forests, and glaciers, all in one park (p. 972).

Yellowstone National Park (2 days)
When the rest of the world seems unstable, Old Faithful stays true to schedule, erupting every 90 minutes (p. 700).

START

WASHINGTON

Crater Lake National Park (1 day)
Check out the deepest lake in the US resting atop an extinct volcano (p. 956).

MONTANA   NORTH DAKOTA

SOUTH DAKOTA

OREGON   IDAHO   WYOMING

Badlands National Park (1 day)
From the mountains to the prairies, to the four heads on Mount Rushmore (p. 580).

Redwood National Park (1 day)
Tree huggers will have more than enough to embrace as they visit some of the largest trees in the world (p. 933).

NEBRASKA

Rocky Mountain National Park (1 day)
Hiking and rock climbing here help you get higher than you've ever been (p. 673).

NEVADA

UTAH

CALIFORNIA

COLORADO   KANS

NEW MEXICO   OKLAHOMA

Death Valley National Park (2 days)
A stargazer's dream, Death Valley has some of the clearest night skies in the country. An overnight stay is a must (p. 921).

ARIZONA

Arches and Canyonlands National Park (3 day)
Check out red-rock canyons, precariously balanced rocks, and impossibly huge and delicate natural arches (p. 771).

TEXAS

Yosemite National Park (2 days)
Being far from Kansas has never been more worth it; granite, waterfalls, and bears. Oh my! (p. 926).

Grand Canyon National Park (3 days)
Carved by water and loved by all, this big hole leaves every visitor fulfilled (p. 784).

PACIFIC OCEAN

MEXICO

CANADA

Voyageurs National Park (1 day)
Cast a line at Voyageurs, home to some great fishing lakes (p. 567).

Acadia National Park (1 day)
Look out for the nesting peregrine falcons, bike the carriage roads, or watch the sunrise from the highest mountain on the coast (p. 235).

END

MINNESOTA

WISCONSIN

Lake Superior

Lake Michigan

Lake Huron

MICHIGAN

Lake Ontario

Lake Erie

MAINE

NEW HAMPSHIRE

VERMONT

NEW YORK

MASS.

RHODE ISLAND

CONNECTICUT

IOWA

ILLINOIS

INDIANA

OHIO

PENNSYLVANIA

NEW JERSEY

DELAWARE

WEST VIRGINIA

MARYLAND

Washington, DC

MISSOURI

KENTUCKY

VIRGINIA

Shenandoah National Park (2 days)
Driving through the length of the park, which includes mineral-encrusted caves and Civil War battlefields, is a treat to many (p. 217).

ARKANSAS

TENNESSEE

NORTH CAROLINA

SOUTH CAROLINA

Mammoth Cave National Park (1 day)
No digging is required to go down deep; Mammoth Cave is already the longest cave system in the world (p. 306).

ALABAMA

GEORGIA

Great Smokey Mountains National Park (2 days)
A stop here will let you get a taste of the eastern hiking gem, the Appalachian Trail (p. 318).

LOUISIANA

MISSISSIPPI

FLORIDA

ATLANTIC OCEAN

Gulf of Mexico

0   400 miles

0   400 kilometers

BBQ NATION (11 DAYS)

Louisville (1 day)
Make your first meaty meal a good one: award-winning barbecue makes Mark's Feed Store the perfect place to eat like an animal (p. 304).

Charleston (1 day)
Just because Sticky Fingers is a Southern chain doesn't mean it ain't finger-lickin' good (p. 355).

Nashville (1 day)
The flashing neon pigs above Jack's Bar-B-Que only hint at the amount of delicious pulled pork waiting inside (p. 310).

Durham (1 day)
Dig into a daily special at Bullock's and join the local debate over whether true barbecue sauce should be ketchup- or vinegar-based (p. 333).

Memphis (1 day)
Eat like the King at Rendezvous, one of Elvis's favorite barbecue spots (p. 325).

START

Austin (1 day)
Still got a craving for slow-cooked meat? Finish up your tour by gorging yourself on Ruby's perfectly crisp brisket (p. 633).

END

Columbia (1 day)
Maurice's Gourmet Barbecue holds the world record for most barbecue sold in one day—maybe with your help they can break their own record! (p. 360).

Houston (1 day)
Texas's royal family is a regular at Otto's Barbecue—they've even re-named W's favorite dish the Bush Plate (p. 645).

Savannah (1 day)
Wall's skimps on the seating, but its scrumptious barbecue is worth the wait for a table (p. 380).

Tuscaloosa (1 day)
If legendary Dreamland Barbecue had a menu, it would only need to have one item: ribs (p. 392).

Birmingham (1 day)
Start the Alabama leg of your trip off right with an enormous rack of the state's best ribs from Jim and Nick's (p. 389).

ESSENTIALS

PLANNING YOUR TRIP

> **ENTRANCE REQUIREMENTS.**
> **Passport** (p. 12). Required of citizens of countries other than the US and Canada.
> **Visa** (p. 13). Generally required of citizens of all countries other than the US and Canada, but requirement can be waived for residents of certain countries.
> **Inoculations** (p. 22). None required.
> **Work Permit** (p. 13). Required of all foreigners planning to work in the US.

EMBASSIES AND CONSULATES

US CONSULAR SERVICES ABROAD

Contact the nearest embassy or consulate to obtain info on the visas necessary to travel to the US. Listings of foreign embassies in the US and US embassies abroad can be found at www.embassyworld.com. The **US State Department** (http://travel.state.gov) provides a complete list of US embassy and consulate websites.

Australia: Moonah Pl., Yarralumla **(Canberra)**, ACT 2600 (☎61 02 6214 5600; http://usembassy-australia.state.gov). **Consulates:** 553 St. Kilda Rd., **Melbourne,** VIC 3004 (☎61 03 9526 5900; fax 9510 4646); 16 St. George's Terr., 13th fl., **Perth,** WA 6000 (☎61 08 9202 1224; fax 9231 9444); MLC Centre, Level 59, 19-29 Martin Pl., **Sydney,** NSW 2000 (☎61 02 9373 9200; fax 9373 9125).

Canada: 490 Sussex Dr., **Ottawa,** ON K1N 1G8 (☎1 613-238-5335; www.usembassycanada.gov). **Consulates:** 615 Macleod Tr. SE, Ste. 1050, **Calgary,** AB T2G 4T8 (☎403-266-8962; fax 264-6630); Ste. 904, Purdy's Wharf Tower II, 1969 Upper Water St., **Halifax,** NS B3J 3R7 (mailing address: P.O. Box 2130, CRO, Halifax, NS B3J 3B7; ☎902-429-2480; fax 423-6861); 1155 St. Alexandre St., **Montréal,** QC H3B 1Z1 (mailing address: P.O. Box 65, Station Desjardins, Montréal, QC H5B 1G1; ☎514-398-9695; fax 398-0973); 2 Place Terrasse Dufferin, B.P. 939, **Québec City,** QC G1R 4T9 (☎418-692-2095; fax 692-4640); 360 University Ave., **Toronto,** ON M5G 1S4 (☎416-595-1700; fax 595-0051); 1095 W. Pender 668-St., **Vancouver,** BC V6E 2M6 (☎604-685-4311; fax 685-5285); 201 Portage Ave., Ste. 860, **Winnipeg,** MB R3B 3K6 (☎204-940-1800; fax 940-1809).

Ireland: 42 Elgin Rd., Ballsbridge, Dublin 4 (☎353 01 668 8777; http://dublin.usembassy.gov).

New Zealand: 29 Fitzherbert Terr., Thorndon, **Wellington** (mailing address: P.O. Box 1190, Wellington, New Zealand; ☎644 462 600; www.usembassy.org.nz). **Consulate:** Citibank Building, 23 Customs St., 3rd fl., **Auckland** (mailing address: Private Bag 92022, Auckland, New Zealand; ☎649 303 2724, ext. 225, 226, or 250; fax 366 0870).

UK: 24 Grosvenor Sq., **London,** W1A 1AE, England (☎44 02074 999 000; www.usembassy.org.uk). **Consulates:** Danesfort House, 223 Stranmillis Rd., **Belfast,** N. Ireland BT9 5GR (☎44 02890 386 100; fax 681 301); 3 Regent Terr., **Edinburgh,** Scotland EH7 5BW (☎44 01315 568 315; fax 576 023).

CONSULAR SERVICES IN THE US

IN WASHINGTON, D.C.

Australia: 1601 Massachusetts Ave. NW, 20036 (☎202-797-3000; www.austemb.org).

Canada: 501 Pennsylvania Ave. NW, 20001 (☎202-682-1740; www.canadianembassy.org).

Ireland: 2234 Mass. Ave. NW, 20008 (☎202-462-3939; www.irelandemb.org).

New Zealand: 37 Observatory Circle NW, 20008 (☎202-328-4800; www.nzemb.org).

UK: 3100 Massachusetts Ave. NW, 20008 (☎202-588-7800; www.britainusa.com/consular/embassy).

TOURIST OFFICES

The US does not have a central tourism office; each state is responsible for its own tourist information. State tourist offices can be particularly helpful in guiding visitors to highlights of the region. *Let's Go* lists the location and phone number of state tourist offices with each state's introduction. Consult www.towd.com for the tourism websites of specific states.

DOCUMENTS AND FORMALITIES

PASSPORTS

REQUIREMENTS

All non-US and non-Canadian citizens need valid passports to enter **the US** and re-enter their home countries. Canadians can enter and leave the US with proof of citizenship and photo ID (a driver's license and birth certificate should suffice), but a Canadian passport is highly recommended. **The US** does not allow entrance if the holder's passport expires in under 6 months after the date of their departure; returning home with an expired passport is illegal and may result in a fine.

NEW PASSPORTS

Citizens of Australia, Canada, Ireland, New Zealand, the UK, and the US can apply for a passport at any passport office or at selected post offices and courts of law. Citizens of these countries may also download passport applications from the official website of their country's government or passport office. Any new passport or renewal applications must be filed well in advance of the departure date, though most passport offices offer rush services for a very steep fee. Note, however, that "rushed" passports still take up to two weeks to arrive. For more information, see the following websites: http://www.passports.gov.au (Australia); http://www.ppt.gc.ca (Canada); http://foreignaffairs.gov.ie (Ireland); http://www.passports.govt.nz (NZ); http://www.ukpa.gov.uk (UK); http://www.state.gov (US).

PASSPORT MAINTENANCE

Photocopy the page of your passport with your photo, as well as your visas, traveler's check serial numbers, and any other important documents. Carry one set of copies in a safe place, apart from the originals, and leave another set at home. Consulates also recommend that you carry an expired passport or an official copy of your birth certificate in a part of your baggage separate from other documents.

If you lose your passport, immediately notify the local police and the nearest embassy or consulate of your home government. To expedite its replacement, you must show ID and proof of citizenship; it also helps to know all information previously recorded in the passport. In some cases, a replacement may take weeks to process, and it may be valid only for a limited time. Any visas stamped in your old passport will be irretrievably lost.

VISAS, INVITATIONS, AND WORK PERMITS

VISAS

As of August 2005, citizens of certain non-English-speaking countries need a visa in addition to a valid passport for entrance into the US. Citizens of Canada do not need visas; citizens of Australia, Ireland, New Zealand, the UK, and most European countries can waive US visas through the **Visa Waiver Program (VWP).** Visitors qualify for VWP if they are traveling only for business or pleasure (*not* work or study), are staying for fewer than **90 days,** have proof of intent to leave (e.g., a return plane ticket), possess an I-94W form (an arrival/departure certificate issued upon arrival), are traveling on an approved air or sea carrier (most major carriers qualify—contact the carrier if you are in doubt), and have no visa ineligiblities (e.g., a criminal record). Visitors in the VWP must possess a **machine-readable passport** to be admitted to the US without a visa. See http://travel.state.gov or contact your local consulate for a list of countries participating in the VWP. For stays of longer than 90 days in the US, all travelers (except Canadians) must have a visa; travelers eligible to waive their visas and who wish to stay for more than 90 days must receive a visa before entering the US.

Each applicant for a visitor visa must pay a non-refundable fee of $100. In some cases, there may be a reciprocal issuance fee, depending on the applicant's nationality. This fee is refundable if your application is denied. How long you can stay in the US on a particular visit will be determined by a US official upon your arrival but is usually six months for tourism and business trips. Visas can be purchased **at any US Consular office or at the Consular office with jurisdiction over an applicant's country. Expect an application to take anywhere from three days to four weeks or longer to process at different consulates.**

Double-check entrance requirements at the nearest embassy or consulate of **the US** (listed under **US Consular Services Abroad,** on p. 11) for up-to-date info before departure. US citizens can also consult http://travel.state.gov.

Entering **the US** to study requires a special visa. For more information, see **Beyond Tourism** (p. 82).

WORK PERMITS

Admission as a visitor does not include the right to work, which is authorized only by a work permit, or Employment Authorization Document. To apply for a work permit, you must file an INS Form I-765 online or by mail to the US Citizenship and Immigration Services. There is a nonrefundable filing fee of $175. For more information on this process, visit the US Citizenship and Immigration Services website at http://uscis.gov.

IDENTIFICATION

When you travel, always carry at least two forms of identification on your person, including a photo ID; a passport and a driver's license or birth certificate is usually an adequate combination. Never carry all your IDs together; split them up in case of theft or loss, and keep photocopies of all of them in your luggage and at home.

STUDENT, TEACHER, AND YOUTH IDENTIFICATION

The **International Student Identity Card (ISIC),** the most widely accepted form of student ID, provides discounts on some sights, accommodations (20% or more off rooms in many chain hotels), food, and transportation (e.g., 5-15% off Alamo Car rentals); access to a 24hr. emergency helpline; and insurance benefits for US cardholders (see **Insurance,** p. 22). Applicants must be full-time secondary or post-secondary school students. Because of the proliferation of fake ISICs, some services (particularly airlines) require additional proof of student identity.

The **International Teacher Identity Card (ITIC)** offers teachers the same insurance coverage as the ISIC and similar but limited discounts. For travelers who are under 26 years old but are not students, the **International Youth Travel Card (IYTC)** also offers many of the same benefits as the ISIC.

Each of these identity cards costs US$22 or equivalent. ISICs and ITICs are valid until the new year unless purchased between September and December, in which case they are valid until the beginning of the following new year. Thus, a card purchased in March 2006 will be valid until December 31, 2006, while a card purchased in November 2006 will be valid until December 31, 2007. IYTCs are valid for one year from the date of issue. To learn more about ISICs, ITICs, and IYTCs, see www.myisic.com. Many student travel agencies (p. 26) issue the cards; for a list of issuing agencies or more information, consult the **International Student Travel Confederation (ISTC)** website (www.istc.org).

The **International Student Exchange Card (ISE Card)** is a similar identification card available to students, faculty, and youths aged 12 to 26. The card provides discounts, medical benefits (covers up to $2,000 in medical expenses), access to a 24hr. emergency helpline, and the ability to purchase student airfares. An ISE Card costs $25; call ☎800-255-8000 for more info, or visit www.isecard.com.

CUSTOMS

Upon entering **the US**, you must declare certain items from abroad and pay a duty on the value of those articles if they exceed the allowance established by **the US** customs service. Note that goods and gifts purchased at **duty-free** shops abroad are not exempt from duty or sales tax; "duty-free" merely means that you need not pay a tax in the country of purchase. Upon returning home, you must likewise declare all articles acquired abroad and pay a duty on the value of articles in excess of your home country's allowance. In order to expedite your return, make a list of any valuables brought from home and register them with customs before traveling abroad, and be sure to keep receipts for all goods acquired abroad.

MONEY

CURRENCY AND EXCHANGE

The currency chart below is based on August 2007 exchange rates between local currency and Australian dollars (AUS$), Canadian dollars (CDN$), European Union euros (EUR€), New Zealand dollars (NZ$), and British pounds (UK£). Check a large newspaper or the currency converter on websites like www.xe.com or www.bloomberg.com for up-to-date figures.

DOLLAR ($)		
AUS$1= US$0.83	US$1= AUS$1.20	
CDN$1= US$0.96	US$1= CDN$1.04	
EUR€1= US$1.38	US$1= EUR€0.72	
NZ$1= US$1	US$1= NZ$1	
UK£1= US$2.03	US$1= UK£0.49	

As a general rule, it's cheaper to convert money in **the US** than at home. While currency exchange will probably be available in your arrival airport, it's wise to bring enough foreign currency to last for the first 24 to 72 hours of your trip. When changing money abroad, try to go to banks that have no more than a 5% margin between buy and sell prices. Since you lose money with each transaction, **convert large sums** (unless the currency is depreciating rapidly), but **no more than you'll need.** If you use traveler's checks or bills, carry some in small denominations ($50 or less) for times when you are forced to exchange money at disadvantageous rates, but bring a range of denominations since charges may be levied per check cashed. Store your money in a variety of forms; ideally, at any given time you will be carrying some cash, some traveler's checks, and an ATM and/or credit card.

TRAVELER'S CHECKS

Traveler's checks are one of the safest and least troublesome means of carrying funds. American Express and Visa are the most-recognized brands. Many banks and agencies sell them for a small commission. Check issuers provide refunds if the checks are lost or stolen, and many provide additional services, such as toll-free refund hotlines abroad, emergency message services, and assistance with lost and stolen credit cards or passports. Traveler's checks are readily accepted in all regions of the US. Ask about toll-free refund hotlines and the location of refund centers when purchasing checks, and always carry emergency cash.

American Express: Checks available with commission at select banks, at all AmEx offices, and online (www.americanexpress.com; US residents only). American Express cardholders can also purchase checks by phone (☎800-721-9768). Checks available in Australian, British, Canadian, European, and Japanese currencies, among others. American Express also offers the Travelers Cheque Card, a prepaid reloadable card. Cheques for Two can be signed by either of two people traveling together. For purchase locations or more information, contact AmEx's service centers: in Australia ☎800 688 022, in New Zealand 423 74 409, in the UK 0800 587 6023, in the US and Canada 800-221-7282; elsewhere, call the US collect at 1-800-964-6665.

Travelex: Thomas Cook MasterCard and Interpayment Visa traveler's checks available. For information about Thomas Cook MasterCard in Canada and the US call ☎800-223-7373, in the UK 0800 622 101; elsewhere call the UK collect at +44 1733 318 950. For information about Interpayment Visa in the US and Canada call ☎800-732-1322, in the UK 0800 515 884; elsewhere call the UK collect at +44 1733 318 949. For more information, visit www.travelex.com.

Visa: Checks available (generally with commission) at banks worldwide. For the location of the nearest office, call the Visa Travelers Cheque Global Refund and Assistance Center: in the UK ☎0800 515 884, in the US 800-227-6811, elsewhere call the UK collect at +44 2079 378 091. Checks available in British, Canadian, European, Japanese, and US currencies, among others. Visa also offers TravelMoney, a prepaid debit card that can be reloaded online or by phone. For more information on Visa travel services, see http://usa.visa.com/personal/using_visa/travel_with_visa.html.

CREDIT, DEBIT, AND ATM CARDS

Where they are accepted, **credit cards** often offer superior exchange rates—up to 5% better than the retail rate used by banks and other currency exchange establishments. Credit cards may also offer services such as insurance or emergency help, and are sometimes required to reserve hotel rooms or rental cars. **MasterCard** and **Visa** are the most frequently accepted; **American Express** cards work at some ATMs and at AmEx offices and major airports.

The use of **ATM cards** is widespread in the US. Depending on the system that your home bank uses, you can most likely access your personal bank account while traveling. ATMs get the same wholesale exchange rate as credit cards, but there is often a limit on the amount of money you can withdraw per day (usually around $500). There is typically also a surcharge of $1-5 per withdrawal.

Debit cards are as convenient as credit cards but have a more immediate impact on your funds. A debit card can be used wherever its associated credit card company (usually MasterCard or Visa) is accepted, yet the money is withdrawn directly from the holder's checking account. Debit cards often also function as ATM cards and can be used to withdraw cash from associated banks and ATMs throughout the US. Ask your local bank about obtaining one.

The two major international money networks are **MasterCard/Maestro/Cirrus** (for ATM locations ☎800-424-7787 or www.mastercard.com) and **Visa/PLUS** (for ATM locations ☎800-843-7587 or www.visa.com). Most ATMs charge a transaction fee that is paid to the bank that owns the ATM.

GETTING MONEY FROM HOME

If you run out of money while traveling, the easiest and cheapest solution is to have someone back home make a deposit to your bank account. If that is impossible, consider one of the following options.

WIRING MONEY

It is possible to arrange a **bank money transfer,** in which a bank at home wires money to a bank in **the US**. This is the cheapest way to transfer cash, but it's also the slowest, usually taking several days or more. Note that some banks may only release your funds in local currency, potentially sticking you with a poor exchange rate; inquire about this in advance. Money transfer services like **Western Union** are faster and more convenient than bank transfers—but also much pricier. Western Union has many locations worldwide. To find one, visit www.westernunion.com, or call in Australia ☎800 173 833, in Canada and the US 800-325-6000, or in the UK 0800 833 833. To wire money within the US using a credit card (Discover, MasterCard, Visa), ☎800-225-5227. Money transfer services are also available to **American Express** cardholders and at selected **Thomas Cook** offices.

COSTS

The cost of your trip will vary considerably, depending on where you go, how you travel, and where you stay. The most significant expenses will probably be your round-trip (return) **airfare** to the US (see **Getting to the US: By Plane,** p. 25) and a **railpass** or **bus pass.** Be sure to factor in gas, which costs about $3 per gallon in the US as of August 2007. Before you go, spend some time calculating a reasonable daily **budget.**

STAYING ON A BUDGET

To give you a general idea, a bare-bones day in the US (camping or sleeping in hostels/guesthouses, buying food at supermarkets) costs about $40; a slightly more comfortable day (sleeping in hostels/guesthouses and occasional budget hotel, eating one meal per day at a restaurant, going out at night) costs around $75; and for a luxurious day, the sky's the limit. Don't forget to factor in emergency reserve funds (at least $200) when planning how much money you'll need.

TIPS FOR SAVING MONEY

Some simpler ways include searching out opportunities for free entertainment, splitting accommodation and food costs with trustworthy fellow travelers, and buying food in supermarkets rather than eating out. Bring a **sleepsack** (see p. 18) to save on sheet charges in hostels, and do your **laundry** in the sink (unless you're explicitly prohibited from doing so). Museums often have certain days once a month or once a week when admission is free; plan accordingly. If you are eligible, consider getting an ISIC or an IYTC; many sights and museums offer reduced admission to students and youths. For getting around quickly, bikes are the most economical option. Renting a bike is cheaper than renting a moped or scooter. Don't forget about walking, though; you can learn a lot about a city by seeing it on foot. Drinking at bars and clubs quickly becomes expensive. It's cheaper to buy alcohol at a supermarket and indulge before going out (known colloquially as "pregaming" among college students). That said, there is no way to get around spending money. Though staying within budget is important, don't do so at the expense of your health or a great travel experience.

TIPPING AND BARGAINING

In the US, it is customary to tip waitstaff and taxi drivers 15-20% (at your discretion). Tips are usually not included in restaurant bills unless you have a large party (generally six or more). At the airport and in hotels, porters expect a $1-2 per bag tip to carry your bags—more if the bags are heavy. Bargaining is generally frowned upon and fruitless, except in open-air flea markets and farmers' markets.

TAXES

State sales tax ranges 4-10% in the US, though some states have no sales tax, and many states do not tax grocery items, clothing, or prescription drugs. Many states and counties, especially in the South, charge a tax on hotel rooms; rates vary 3-18%. Sales tax is not usually included in the listing prices in *Let's Go*.

PACKING

Pack lightly: Lay out only what you absolutely need, then take half the clothes and twice the money. The Travelite FAQ (www.travelite.org) is a good resource for tips on traveling light. The online **Universal Packing List** (http://upl.codeq.info) will generate a customized list of suggested items based on your trip length, the expected climate, your planned activities, and other factors. If you plan to do a lot of hiking, also consult **The Great Outdoors**, p. 43. Some frequent travelers keep a bag packed with all the essentials: passport, money belt, hat, socks, etc. Then, when they decide to leave, they know they haven't forgotten anything.

> **Luggage:** If you plan to cover most of your itinerary by foot, a sturdy **frame backpack** is unbeatable. (For the basics to keep in mind when buying a pack, see p. 45.) Toting a **suitcase** or **trunk** is fine if you plan to live in one or two cities and explore from there, but not a great idea if you plan to move around frequently. In addition to your main piece of luggage, a **daypack** (a small backpack or courier bag) is useful.

> **Clothing:** No matter when you're traveling, it's a good idea to bring a warm jacket or wool sweater, a rain jacket (Gore-Tex® is both waterproof and breathable), sturdy shoes or hiking boots, and thick socks. Flip-flops or waterproof sandals are must-haves for grubby hostel showers, and extra socks are always a good idea. You may also want a few outfits for going out, and maybe a

TOP TEN LIST

TOP TEN WAYS TO SAVE IN THE US

A trip to the United States can be impossibly expensive—but it doesn't have to be. With a few small changes to your traveling routine, you can save lots more of your dollars for souvenirs.

1. Buy food and drinks at grocery stores or farmers' markets instead of restaurants and bars.
2. If you'll be visiting two or more national parks, **invest in a National Parks Pass,** valid at any park in the US for a full year.
3. Take advantage of flyers and coupons in weekly papers that will allow you to bypass cover charges at clubs.
4. Buy a CityPass (www.citypass.com), which lets you skip the line at major tourist attractions in any of 10 cities and areas, and discounts admission.
5. Snap up free Internet access in libraries and in Visitors Centers.
6. Use public transit or walk as much as possible.
7. Don't pay for entertainment. Most US cities have frequent (and fun!) free festivals and concerts.
8. In major cities, make your base on the outskirts of town, where restaurants and accommodations tend to be cheaper.
9. Travel by train. A 30-day Amtrak Pass is helpful when traveling frequently.
10. If you have to fly, check out low-fare carriers. Southwest, jetBlue, and Independence Air all fly to smaller airports, which means cheaper tickets.

nicer pair of shoes. If you plan to visit religious or cultural sites, remember that you will need modest and respectful dress.

Sleepsack: Some hostels require that you either provide your own linen or rent sheets from them. Save cash by making your own sleepsack: fold a full-size sheet in half the long way, then sew it closed along the long side and one of the short sides.

Converters and Adapters: In the US, electricity is 120 volts AC, which is incompatible with the 220/240V appliances found in most other countries. Appliances from anywhere outside North America will need an adapter (which changes the shape of the plug, $5) and a converter (which changes the voltage, $10-30). Australians and New Zealanders (who use 230V at home) won't need a converter, but will need an adapter. For more on all things adaptable, check out http://kropla.com/electric.htm.

Toiletries: Toiletries are readily available in supermarkets and pharmacies, but it may be hard to find your preferred brand; bring extras. Contact lenses are likely to be expensive and difficult to find, so bring enough extra pairs and solution for your entire trip. Bring your glasses and a copy of your prescription in case you need emergency replacements.

First-Aid Kit: For a basic first-aid kit, pack bandages, a pain reliever, antibiotic cream, a thermometer, a multifunction pocketknife, tweezers, moleskin, decongestant, motion-sickness remedy, diarrhea or upset-stomach medication (Pepto Bismol® or Imodium®), an antihistamine, sunscreen, insect repellent, burn ointment, and an epinephrine kit (EpiPen®) in case of severe allergic reactions.

Film: Buying film and developing it in the US can be expensive (about $13 for a roll of 24 color exposures), so consider bringing enough film for your entire trip. Less serious photographers may want to bring a disposable camera or two. Despite disclaimers, air-port security X-rays can fog film, so buy a lead-lined pouch at a camera store or ask security to hand-inspect it. Always pack film in your carry-on luggage, since higher-intensity X-rays are used on checked luggage. If you don't want to bother with film, consider using a digital camera. Although a steep initial investment, a digital camera means you never have to buy film again. Bring along a large enough memory card and extra batteries. For more on digital cameras, visit www.shortcourses.com/choosing/contents.htm.

Other Useful Items: For safety purposes, bring a **money belt** and a small **padlock.** Basic **outdoors equipment** (plastic water bottle, compass, waterproof matches, pocketknife, sunglasses, sunscreen, hat) may also prove useful. **Quick repairs** of torn garments can be done on the road with a needle and thread; also consider bringing electrical tape for patching tears. If you want to do laundry by hand, bring detergent, a small rubber ball to stop up the sink, and string for a makeshift clothes line. Other things you're liable to forget include: an umbrella, sealable **plastic bags** (for damp clothes, soap, food, shampoo, and other spillables), an **alarm clock,** safety pins, rubber bands, a flashlight, earplugs, garbage bags, and a small calculator. A **cell phone** can be a lifesaver (literally) on the road; see p. 35 for information on acquiring one that will work in the US.

Important Documents: Don't forget your passport, traveler's checks, ATM and/or credit cards, adequate ID, and photocopies of all of the aforementioned in case these documents are lost or stolen (see p. 12). Also check that you have any of the following that might apply to you: a hosteling membership card (see p. 37); driver's license (see p. 12); travel insurance forms (see p. 22); ISIC (see p. 13), and/or rail or bus pass (see p. 29).

SAFETY AND HEALTH

GENERAL ADVICE

In any type of crisis situation, the most important thing to do is **stay calm.** Your country's embassy abroad (p. 11) is usually your best resource when things go wrong; registering with that embassy upon arrival in the country is often a good idea. The government offices listed in the **Travel Advisories** box (p. 20) can provide information on the services they offer their citizens in case of emergencies abroad.

LOCAL LAWS AND POLICE

DRIVING

If you are using a **car,** learn local driving signals and wear a seatbelt. You must obey all posted signs, including speed limit signs. If a police car sounds its siren behind you, slow down and pull over as soon as it is safe to do so. If an emergency vehicle approaches from either direction with its sirens on, slow down and pull over to the side of the road until the vehicle has passed and is several hundred feet away. The only exception to this law occurs if an emergency vehicle is approaching from the opposite direction on a divided highway; in this case, motorists on the side opposite the emergency vehicle need not pull over. Most localities require you to stop when school buses are picking up or dropping off passengers except, as above, when they are on the opposite side of a divided highway.

Local police are often a good resource for help. If your car breaks down or you find yourself stranded, call or wait for local or state highway police to arrive.

DRUGS AND ALCOHOL

In the US, the drinking age is 21, and drinking restrictions are particularly strict. Younger travelers should expect to be asked to show government-issued identification when purchasing any alcoholic beverage. Drinking and driving is prohibited everywhere and is widely considered to be extremely dangerous. Open alcoholic beverage containers in your car will incur heavy fines; a failed sobriety test will mean fines, a suspended license, imprisonment, or all three. Most localities restrict where and when alcohol can be sold. Sales usually stop at a certain time at night and are often prohibited entirely on Sundays. Narcotics like marijuana, heroin, and cocaine are highly illegal in the US. If you carry prescription drugs while you travel, keep a copy of the prescription with you, especially at border crossings.

SPECIFIC CONCERNS

NATURAL DISASTERS

EARTHQUAKES. Earthquakes occur frequently in certain parts of the US, particularly California, but most are too small to be felt. If a strong earthquake does occur, it will last at most 1-2 minutes. Open a door to provide an escape route and protect yourself by moving underneath a sturdy doorway, table, or desk. If you are outside, move to an open area free from buildings, trees, and power lines.

TORNADOES AND HURRICANES. Tornadoes have been reported in every US state, though they are most common in the Great Plains during the spring and summer. If you are inside during a tornado, move to a basement or interior location away from windows. If you are outside, lie flat on the ground in a low place away from power lines. Hurricanes are most common on the Atlantic and Gulf of Mexico coasts. Often, these areas are evacuated in anticipation of particularly severe hurricanes. If you are not advised to evacuate, stay inside, away from windows.

LANDSLIDES/MUDSLIDES. Heavy rain, flooding, or snow runoff combined with hilly terrain can lead to landslides or mudslides, particularly on slopes where vegetation has been removed. This will most likely not be a concern in cities; however, if you are hiking after a heavy rainfall, be aware of the possibility of a slide. If you are caught in a mudslide or landslide, try to get out of its path and run to high ground or shelter. If escape is not possible, curl into a ball and protect your head.

FOREST FIRES. Dry spells are common in the western US. In 2003, forest fires ravaged much of the eastern Cascades, as well as parts of California and Oregon. If you are hiking or camping and smell smoke, see flames, or hear fire, leave the area immediately. To prevent forest fires, always make sure campfires are completely extinguished; during high levels of fire danger, campfires will most likely be prohibited. Before you go hiking or camping, be sure to check with local authorities for the level of fire danger in the area.

TERRORISM

In light of the September 11, 2001 terrorist attacks, there is an elevated risk of further terrorist activities in the US. The threat of an attack is generally not specific or great enough to warrant avoiding certain places or modes of transportation. After the September 11 attacks, the Department of Homeland Security (DHS) was created to protect the US from further terrorist threats. Local and national news media often report changes in threat status, and travelers should be alert to these changes. The box on **travel advisories** (see below) lists offices to contact and webpages to visit to get the most updated list of your home country's government's advisories about travel.

PERSONAL SAFETY

EXPLORING AND TRAVELING

To avoid unwanted attention, try to blend in as much as possible. Respecting local customs (in many cases, dressing more conservatively than you would at home) may placate would-be hecklers. Familiarize yourself with your surroundings before setting out, and carry yourself with confidence. Check maps in shops and restaurants rather than on the street. If you are traveling alone, be sure someone at home knows your itinerary, and never admit that you're by yourself. When walking at night, stick to busy, well-lit streets and avoid dark alleyways. If you ever feel uncomfortable, leave the area as quickly and directly as you can.

There is no sure-fire way to avoid all the threatening situations you might encounter while traveling, but a good **self-defense course** will give you concrete ways to react to unwanted advances. **Impact, Prepare, and Model Mugging** can refer you to local self-defense courses in the US. Visit www.impactsafety.org (Impact), www.prepareinc.com (Prepare), or www.modelmugging.org (Model Mugging) for a list of nearby chapters. Impact workshops (2-4hr.) start at $50; full courses (20hr.) run $350-500.

TRAVEL ADVISORIES. The following government offices provide travel information and advisories by telephone, by fax, or via the web:

Australian Department of Foreign Affairs and Trade: ☎1300 555 135; www.dfat.gov.au.

Canadian Department of Foreign Affairs and International Trade (DFAIT): ☎800-267-8376; www.dfait-maeci.gc.ca. Call for their free booklet, *Bon Voyage...But.*

New Zealand Ministry of Foreign Affairs: ☎044 398 000; www.mft.govt.nz/travel/index.html.

UK Foreign and Commonwealth Office: ☎02070 081 500; www.fco.gov.uk.

US Department of State: ☎202-647-5225; http://travel.state.gov. Visit the website for the booklet *A Safe Trip Abroad.*

If you are using a **car,** learn local driving signals and wear a seatbelt. Children under 40 lbs. should ride only in specially-designed carseats, available for a small fee from most car rental agencies ($7-10 per day); infants under 1 year or 20 lb. must ride in rear-facing carseats. All children under 12 must sit in the rear seat of the car. Study route maps before you hit the road, and if you plan on spending a lot of time driving, consider bringing spare parts. If your car breaks down, wait for the police to assist you. For long drives in desolate areas, invest in a cellular phone and a roadside assistance program (see p. 31). Park your vehicle in a garage or well-traveled area, and use a steering wheel locking device in larger cities. **Sleeping in your car** is one of the most dangerous (and often illegal) ways to get your rest. For info on the perils of **hitchhiking,** see p. 33.

POSSESSIONS AND VALUABLES

Never leave your belongings unattended; crime occurs in even the most demure-looking hostel or hotel. Bring your own padlock for hostel lockers, and don't ever store valuables in any locker. Be particularly careful on **buses** and **trains;** horror stories abound about determined thieves who wait for travelers to fall asleep. Carry your backpack in front of you where you can see it. When traveling with others, sleep in alternate shifts. When alone, use good judgment in selecting a train compartment: never stay in an empty one, and use a lock to secure your pack to the luggage rack. Try to sleep on top bunks with your luggage stored above you (if not in bed with you), and keep documents and valuables on your person.

There are a few steps you can take to minimize the financial risk associated with traveling. First, **bring as little with you as possible.** Second, buy a few combination **padlocks** to secure your belongings either in your pack or in a hostel or train station locker. Third, **carry as little cash as possible.** Keep your traveler's checks and ATM/credit cards in a **money belt**—not a "fanny pack"—along with your passport and ID cards. Fourth, **keep a small cash reserve separate from your primary stash.** This should be about $50 sewn into or stored in the depths of your pack, along with your traveler's check numbers and important photocopies.

In large cities **con artists** often work in groups that may include children. Beware of certain classics: sob stories that require money, rolls of bills "found" on the street, mustard spilled (or saliva spit) onto your shoulder to distract you while they snatch your bag. **Never let your passport and your bags out of your sight.** Beware of **pickpockets** in city crowds, especially on public transit. Also, be alert in public telephone booths: If you must say your calling card number, do so very quietly; if you punch it in, make sure no one can look over your shoulder.

If you will be traveling with electronic devices, such as a computer or a PDA, check whether your homeowner's insurance covers loss, theft, or damage when you travel. If not, you might consider purchasing a low-cost travel insurance policy. **Safeware** (☎800-800-1492; www.safeware.com) specializes in covering computers and charges $90 for 90-day comprehensive coverage up to $4000.

PRE-DEPARTURE HEALTH

In your **passport,** write the names of anyone you wish to be contacted in case of a medical emergency, and list any allergies or medical conditions. Matching a prescription to a foreign equivalent is not always safe or possible, so if you take prescription drugs, carry up-to-date, legible prescriptions or a statement from your doctor with the medication's trade name, manufacturer, chemical name, and dosage. While traveling, be sure to keep all medication with you in your carry-on luggage. For tips on packing a basic **first-aid kit** and other health essentials, see p. 18.

ESSENTIALS

IMMUNIZATIONS AND PRECAUTIONS

Although no inoculations are required for US tourists, travelers over two years old should make sure that the following vaccines are up to date: MMR (for measles, mumps, and rubella); DTaP or Td (for diphtheria, tetanus, and pertussis); IPV (for polio); Hib (for *Haemophilus influenza B*); and HepB (for Hepatitis B). For recommendations on immunizations and prophylaxis, consult the CDC (see below) in the US or the equivalent in your home country, and check with a doctor.

INSURANCE

Travel insurance covers four basic areas: medical/health problems, property loss, trip cancellation/interruption, and emergency evacuation. Though regular insurance policies may well extend to travel-related accidents, you may consider purchasing separate travel insurance if the cost of potential trip cancellation, interruption, or emergency medical evacuation is greater than you can absorb. Prices for travel insurance purchased separately generally run about $50 per week for full coverage, while trip cancellation/interruption may be purchased separately at a rate of $3-5 per day depending on length of stay.

Medical insurance (especially university policies) often covers costs incurred abroad; check with your provider. **Homeowners' insurance** (or your family's coverage) often covers theft during travel and loss of travel documents (passport, plane ticket, railpass, etc.) up to $500.

ISIC and **ITIC** (see p. 13) provide basic insurance benefits to US cardholders, including $100 per day of in-hospital sickness for up to 100 days and $10,000 of accident-related medical reimbursement (see www.isicus.com for details). Cardholders have access to a toll-free 24hr. helpline for medical, legal, and financial emergencies. **American Express** (☎800-338-1670) grants most cardholders automatic collision and theft car rental insurance on rentals made with the card.

USEFUL ORGANIZATIONS AND PUBLICATIONS

The US Centers for Disease Control and Prevention (CDC; ☎877-FYI-TRIP; www.cdc.gov/travel) maintains an international travelers' hotline and an informative website. Consult the appropriate government agency of your home country for consular information sheets on health, entry requirements, and other issues for various countries (see the listings in the box on Travel Advisories, p. 20). For quick information on health and other travel warnings, call the Overseas Citizens Services (M-F 8am-8pm ☎888-407-4747, from overseas 202-501-4444), or contact a passport agency, embassy, or consulate abroad. For information on medical evacuation services and travel insurance firms, see the US government's website at http://travel.state.gov/travel/abroad_health.html or the British Foreign and Commonwealth Office (www.fco.gov.uk). For general health info, contact the American Red Cross (☎800-564-1234; www.redcross.org).

STAYING HEALTHY

Common sense is the simplest prescription for good health while you travel. Drink lots of fluids to prevent dehydration and constipation, and wear sturdy, broken-in shoes and clean socks.

ONCE IN THE US

ENVIRONMENTAL HAZARDS

Heat exhaustion and dehydration: Heat exhaustion leads to nausea, heavy sweating, excessive thirst, headaches, and dizziness. Avoid it by drinking plenty of fluids, eating salty foods (e.g., crackers), abstaining from dehydrating beverages (e.g., alcohol and caffeinated beverages), and always wearing sunscreen. Continuous heat stress can eventually lead to heatstroke, characterized by a rising temperature, severe headache, delirium and cessation of sweating. Cool off victims with wet towels and take them to a doctor. The southern US is particularly prone to heat waves, though travelers in all areas should be cautious in summer and bring plenty of water on hiking or camping trips.

High Altitude: The Rocky, Sierra Nevada, and Cascades mountains in the western US are at particularly high altitudes. When visiting these locations, allow your body a couple of days to adjust to less oxygen before exerting yourself. Note that alcohol is more potent and UV rays are stronger at high elevations.

Hypothermia and frostbite: Travelers to the US during the winter months should be aware of the dangers of cold exposure. A rapid drop in body temperature is the clearest sign of overexposure to cold. Victims may shiver, feel exhausted, have poor coordination or slurred speech, hallucinate, or experience mental lethargy. *Do not let hypothermia victims fall asleep.* To avoid hypothermia, keep dry, wear warm, moisture-wicking layers (polyester, wool, silk), limit alcohol and caffeine intake, drink a lot of water, and eat plenty of carbohydrates. When the temperature is below freezing, watch out for frostbite, especially on ears, nose, hands, and feet. If skin turns white or purple, waxy, and cold, come out of the cold immediately and call for medical assistance. Do not rub the area. Drink warm, non-alcoholic, non-caffeinated fluids, and avoid gradually thawing the area until medical help arrives. To prevent frostbite, dress warmly, stay out of the wind, and apply skin moisturizer to any exposed body part.

Sunburn: Always wear sunscreen (SPF 30 or higher) when spending excessive amounts of time outdoors. If you are planning on spending time near water, in the desert, or in the snow, you are at higher risk of getting burned, even through clouds. If you get sunburned, drink more fluids than usual and apply an aloe-based lotion. Severe sunburns can lead to sun poisoning, a condition that affects the entire body, causing fever, fatigue, and a blistering skin rash. Sun poisoning should always be treated by a doctor.

INSECT-BORNE DISEASES

Many diseases are transmitted by insects—mainly mosquitoes, fleas, ticks, and lice. Be aware of insects in wet or forested areas, especially while hiking and camping; wear long pants and long sleeves, tuck your pants into your socks, and use a mosquito net. Use insect repellents such as DEET and soak or spray your gear with permethrin (licensed in the US only for use on clothing). **Mosquitoes,** carriers of diseases including malaria, dengue fever, and yellow fever, can be particularly dangerous in wet, swampy, or wooded areas such as the southeastern US. **Ticks,** carriers of Lyme and other diseases, can be particularly dangerous in rural and forested regions, particularly the northeast, central north, and Pacific coast.

Lyme disease: A bacterial infection carried by ticks and marked by a circular bull's-eye rash of 2 in. or more. Later symptoms include fever, headache, fatigue, and aches and pains. Antibiotics are effective if administered early. Left untreated, Lyme disease can cause chronic joint pain, heart irregularities, and problems with the nervous system. If you find a tick attached to your skin, grasp its body with fine-tipped tweezers and steadily pull away from the skin. Do not try to remove ticks with petroleum jelly, nail polish remover, or a hot match. Cleanse the area with antiseptic. Removing a tick within 24hr. greatly reduces the chance of Lyme disease transmission. Tick bites usually occur in moist, shaded environments and wooded areas of the northeastern, central northern, and Pacific coastal regions and are most common during the late spring and summer months. If you are going to be hiking in these areas, wear long clothes and use DEET.

West Nile Virus: The West Nile Virus has been detected in all 48 continental states and is transmitted through the bite of an infected mosquito. Most victims do not have any symptoms, but some develop mild flu-like symptoms; less than 1% develop more severe symptoms including meningitis or encephalitis. Those at highest risk are the elderly and those with lowered immune systems, but people of all ages can develop a serious illness. To minimize the risk of infection, limit outdoor activity when mosquitoes are most active (dawn, dusk, and early evening), wear long clothes, and use DEET.

FOOD- AND WATER-BORNE DISEASES

In the US, city and suburban tap water is treated to be safe for drinking, though travelers should still exercise caution in remote rural areas or areas with untreated well water. Raw shellfish, unpasteurized milk, or dishes containing raw eggs may still present health risks. Watch out for food from markets or street vendors that may have been cooked in unhygienic conditions.

Backcountry hikers may purify their own water by bringing it to a rolling boil or treating it with **iodine tablets;** note, however, that some parasites such as giardia have exteriors that resist iodine treatment, so boiling is a more reliable treatment. Always wash your hands before eating or bring a quick-drying purifying liquid hand cleaner.

Gastroenteritis/Stomach Flu: Caused by a class of viruses called Noroviruses; spreads via contact with the body fluids of infected people, including exposure to contaminated foods or touching contaminated objects, and direct contact with infected persons. Symptoms appear within 48hr. of infection and include vomiting, nausea, chills, diarrhea, and abdominal cramping. Though the symptoms usually pass within a few days, the disease can be contagious for several weeks and a doctor should be consulted if any of these symptoms develop.

Giardiasis: Transmitted through parasites (microbes, tapeworms, etc. in contaminated water and food) and acquired by drinking untreated water from streams or lakes. Symptoms include diarrhea, abdominal cramps, bloating, fatigue, weight loss, and nausea. If untreated it can lead to severe dehydration. Giardiasis occurs worldwide.

OTHER INFECTIOUS DISEASES

Rabies: Transmitted through the saliva of infected animals; fatal if untreated. By the time symptoms (thirst and muscle spasms) appear, the disease is in its terminal stage. If you are bitten, wash the wound thoroughly, seek immediate medical care, and try to have the animal located. A rabies vaccine, which consists of 3 shots given over a 21-day period, is available and recommended for developing world travel, but is only semi-effective. Rabies is found all over the world, and is often transmitted through dogs, but travelers to backcountry and wooded areas should be wary of all wild animals.

HIV and AIDS: For detailed information on Acquired Immune Deficiency Syndrome (AIDS) in the US, call the US Centers for Disease Control's 24hr. hotline at ☎770-488-7100, or contact the Joint United Nations Programme on HIV/AIDS (UNAIDS), 20 ave. Appia, CH-1211 Geneva 27, Switzerland (☎+41 22 791 3666; fax 22 791 4187).

Sexually Transmitted Infections (STIs): Gonorrhea, chlamydia, genital warts, syphilis, herpes, and other STIs are easier to catch than HIV and can be just as deadly. **Hepatitis** B and C can also be transmitted sexually. Though condoms may protect you from some STIs, oral or even tactile contact can lead to transmission. If you think you may have contracted an STI, see a doctor immediately.

OTHER HEALTH CONCERNS

MEDICAL CARE ON THE ROAD

Medical care in the US is among the best in the world. In case of medical emergency, dial ☎911 from any phone and an operator will send out paramedics, a fire brigade, or the police as needed. Emergency care is available at any emergency room on a walk-in basis. If you do not have insurance, you will have to pay for medical care. Appointments are required for non-emergency medical services. If you are concerned about obtaining medical assistance while traveling, you may wish to employ special support services. The *MedPass* from **GlobalCare, Inc.,** 6875 Shiloh Rd. East, Alpharetta, GA 30005 (☎800-860-1111; www.globalcare.net), provides 24hr. international medical assistance, support, and medical evacuation resources. If your regular **insurance** policy does not cover travel abroad, you may wish to purchase additional coverage (see p. 22).

Those with medical conditions (such as diabetes, allergies to antibiotics, epilepsy, or heart conditions) may want to obtain a **MedicAlert** membership (first year $35, annually thereafter $20), which includes a stainless steel ID tag, among other benefits, like a 24hr. collect-call number. Contact the MedicAlert Foundation, 2323 Colorado Ave., Turlock, CA 95382, USA (☎888-633-4298, outside US ☎209-668-3333; www.medicalert.org).

WOMEN'S HEALTH

Women traveling in the backcountry are vulnerable to **urinary tract (including bladder and kidney) infections.** Over-the-counter medicines can sometimes alleviate symptoms, but if they persist, see a doctor. **Vaginal yeast infections** may flare up in hot and humid climates. Wearing loosely fitting trousers or a skirt and cotton underwear will help, as will over-the-counter remedies like Monostat or Gynelotrimin. **Tampons, pads,** and **contraceptive devices** are widely available in the US, but your favorite brand may not be stocked—bring extras of anything you can't live without. **Abortion** is legal in the US; for more information contact Planned Parenthood (☎800-230-7526; www.plannedparenthood.org).

GETTING TO THE US

BY PLANE

When it comes to airfare, a little effort can save you a bundle. If your plans are flexible enough to deal with the restrictions, courier fares are the cheapest. Tickets bought from consolidators and standby seating are also good deals, but last-minute specials, airfare wars, and charter flights often beat these fares. The key is to hunt around, be flexible, and ask persistently about discounts. Students, seniors, and those under 26 should never pay full price for a ticket.

AIRFARES

Airfares to the US peak during the summer, especially between June and **September;** holidays are also expensive. Generally, the cheapest times to travel are **during the winter** and **during school sessions**, but it depends on the high-season months of your destination. Midweek (M-Th morning) round-trip flights run $40-50 cheaper than weekend flights, but they are generally more crowded and less likely to permit frequent-flier upgrades. Not fixing a return date ("open return") or arriving in and departing from different cities ("open-jaw") can be pricier than round-trip flights. Patching one-way flights together is the most expensive way to travel. Flights between state capitals or regional hubs—New York, Los Angeles, Boston, Chicago, Washington, D.C.—will tend to be cheaper.

If the US is only one stop on a more extensive globe-hop, consider a round-the-world (RTW) ticket. Tickets usually include at least five stops and are valid for about a year; prices range US$1200-5000. Try **Northwest Airlines/KLM** (☎800-225-2525; www.nwa.com) or **Star Alliance,** a consortium of 16 airlines including United Airlines (www.staralliance.com).

ESSENTIALS

Fares for round-trip flights to the US's East Coast from Western Europe cost €440-875, €220-550 in the low season (Sept.-May); round-trip flights from Australia or New Zealand to the US's West Coast usually cost AUS$1020-1800.

BUDGET AND STUDENT TRAVEL AGENCIES

While knowledgeable agents specializing in flights to **the US** can make your life easy and help you save, they may not spend the time to find you the lowest possible fare—they get paid on commission. Travelers holding **ISICs** and **IYTCs** (see p. 13) qualify for big discounts from student travel agencies. Most flights from budget agencies are on major airlines, but in peak season some may sell seats on less reliable chartered aircraft.

STA Travel, 5900 Wilshire Blvd., Ste. 900, Los Angeles, CA 90036, USA (24hr. reservations and info ☎800-781-4040; www.statravel.com). A student and youth travel organization with over 400 offices worldwide (check their website for a listing of all their offices), including US offices in Boston, Chicago, Los Angeles, New York, Seattle, San Francisco, and Washington, D.C. Ticket booking, travel insurance, railpasses, and more. Walk-in offices are located throughout Australia (☎134 STA), New Zealand (☎0508 782 872), and the UK (☎0871 2 300 040).

Travel CUTS (Canadian Universities Travel Services Limited), 187 College St., Toronto, ON M5T 1P7, Canada; 124 MacDougal Street, New York, NY 10012 (☎800-592-2887; 212-674-2887; www.travelcuts.com). Offices across Canada and the US including Los Angeles, New York, Seattle, and San Francisco.

USIT, 19-21 Aston Quay, Dublin 2, Ireland (☎01 602 1904; www.usit.ie), Ireland's leading student/budget travel agency has 20 offices throughout Northern Ireland and the Republic of Ireland. Offers programs to work, study, and volunteer worldwide.

> ✈ **FLIGHT PLANNING ON THE INTERNET.** The Internet may be the budget traveler's dream when it comes to finding and booking bargain fares, but the array of options can be overwhelming. Many airlines offer last-minute deals on the web. Check individual airlines' websites for more information.
>
> **STA** (www.sta-travel.com) and **StudentUniverse** (www.studentuniverse.com) provide quotes on student tickets, while **Orbitz** (www.orbitz.com), **Expedia** (www.expedia.com), and **Travelocity** (www.travelocity.com) offer full travel services. **Priceline** (www.priceline.com) lets you specify a price, and obligates you to buy any ticket that meets or beats it; **Hotwire** (www.hotwire.com) offers bargain fares, but won't reveal the airline or flight times until purchase. Other sites that compile deals include www.bestfares.com, www.flights.com, www.lowestfare.com, www.onetravel.com, and www.travelzoo.com.
>
> Increasingly, there are online tools available to help sift through multiple offers; **SideStep** (www.sidestep.com) and **Booking Buddy** (www.bookingbuddy.com) let you enter your trip information once and search multiple sites.
>
> An indispensable resource is the **Air Traveler's Handbook** (www.faqs.org/faqs/travel/air/handbook), a comprehensive listing of links to everything you need to know before you board a plane.

COMMERCIAL AIRLINES

The commercial airlines' lowest regular offer is the **APEX** (Advance Purchase Excursion) fare, which provides confirmed reservations and allows "open-jaw" tickets. Generally, reservations must be made seven to 21 days ahead of departure, with seven- to 14-day minimum-stay and up to 90-day maximum-stay restrictions. These fares carry hefty cancellation and change penalties (fees rise in summer).

Book peak-season APEX fares early. Use **Expedia** (www.expedia.com) or **Traveloc-ity** (www.travelocity.com) to get an idea of the lowest published fares, then use the resources outlined here to try and beat those fares. Low-season fares should be appreciably cheaper than the **high-season** (mid-June to Aug.) ones listed here.

TRAVELING FROM THE UK AND IRELAND

Round-trip fares from the UK and Ireland to the eastern US range $200-750, with flights from London usually cheapest at $200-600. Standard commercial carriers like **American** (☎800-433-7300; www.aa.com), **United** (☎800-539-2929 or 800-864-8331; www.ual.com), and **Northwest** (☎800-447-4747; www.nwa.com) will proba-bly offer the most convenient flights, but they may not be the cheapest. Check **Lufthansa** (☎800-399-5838 or 800-645-3880; http://www.lufthansa.com), **British Air-ways** (☎800-247-9297; www.britishairways.com), **Air France** (☎800-237-2747; www.airfrance.us), and **Alitalia** (☎800-223-5730; www.alitaliausa.com) for cheap tickets from destinations in Europe to all over the US. Discount airlines such as **Icelandair** (☎800-223-5500 ext. 2; www.icelandair.com) may provide cheaper flights, though cheaper flights often mean fewer departure points.

TRAVELING FROM AUSTRALIA AND NEW ZEALAND

Check **Air New Zealand** (☎0800 737 000; www.airnewzealand.com), **Quantas Airways** (Australia ☎131 313, New Zealand 0800 101 500; www.qantas.com.au), and **Sin-gapore Air** (Australia ☎131 011, New Zealand 0800 808 909; www.sin-gaporeair.com) for cheap tickets from Australia and New Zealand to the US.

STANDBY FLIGHTS

Traveling standby requires considerable flexibility in arrival and departure dates and cities. Companies dealing in standby flights sell vouchers rather than tickets, along with the promise to get you to your destination (or near your destination) within a certain window of time (typically 1-5 days). You call in before your spe-cific window of time to hear your flight options and the probability that you will be able to board each flight. You can then decide which flights you want to try to make, show up at the appropriate airport at the appropriate time, present your voucher, and board if space is available. Vouchers can usually be bought for both one-way and round-trip travel. You may receive a monetary refund only if every available flight within your date range is full; if you opt not to take an available (but perhaps less convenient) flight, you can only get credit toward future travel. Carefully read agreements with any company offering standby flights as tricky fine print can leave you in the lurch. To check on a company's service record in the US, contact the Better Business Bureau (☎703-276-0100; www.bbb.org).

TICKET CONSOLIDATORS

Ticket consolidators, or **"bucket shops,"** buy unsold tickets in bulk from commer-cial airlines and sell them at discounted rates. The best place to look is in the Sun-day travel section of any major newspaper (such as *The New York Times*), where many bucket shops place tiny ads. Call quickly, as availability is typically extremely limited. Not all bucket shops are reliable, so insist on a receipt that gives full details of restrictions, refunds, and tickets, and pay by credit card (in spite of the 2-5% fee) so you can stop payment if you never receive your tickets. For more info, see www.travel-library.com/air-travel/consolidators.html.

CHARTER FLIGHTS

Charters are flights a tour operator contracts with an airline to fly extra loads of passengers during peak season. Charter flights fly less frequently than major air-lines, make refunds particularly difficult, and are almost always fully booked.

Schedules and itineraries may also change or be cancelled at the last moment (as late as 48hr. before the trip, and without a full refund), and check-in, boarding, and baggage claim are often much slower. However, they can also be cheaper.

Discount clubs and fare brokers offer members savings on last-minute charter and tour deals. Study contracts closely; you don't want to end up with an unwanted overnight layover. **Travelers Advantage** (☎800-835-8747; www.travelersadvantage.com; $10 monthly fee includes discounts and cheap flight directories) specializes in tour and travel packages.

BORDER CROSSINGS

ENTERING THE US BY CAR

If you plan to drive to the US from either Canada or Mexico, you must enter the country through a staffed and open port of entry. Any other entry is illegal and can result in deportation or fines. It is always a bad idea to carry illegal drugs and substances over the border.

FROM CANADA. Crossing into the United States from Canada is usually an easy process. However, it can be more difficult depending on who is crossing, what time of day or year it is, and the border guards themselves. There are many crossing points along the US-Canada border, most of which accept both commercial flow and traveler flow. Usually, there is a negligible delay in crossing the border into the US, but some points might be backed up for 10-20min. or more, depending on traffic and weather conditions. For required documents, see **Documents and Formalities,** p. 12. Although it is common to cross the border without incident or delay, it is also possible that border guards will want to check your vehicle or your documents. In an effort to decrease the risk of terrorism, both the US and Canada are tightening security measures and routinely performing more random checks during border crossings.

FROM MEXICO. As with the US-Canada border, there are many crossing points along the US-Mexico border. Mexican citizens entering the US are required to present both a passport and a non-immigrant visa upon entry. US citizens returning to the US from Mexico are technically not required to present a passport, but it is best to do so anyway to avoid delays. Travelers who are not citizens of the US or Mexico need the documentation required to enter the US via air in order to cross the overland border. Delays in crossing the US-Mexico border are generally short, but can be longer depending on traffic conditions. Customs and border patrol officials have the right to conduct random searches upon entry, and tightened security measures make these searches even more common.

GETTING AROUND THE US

BY PLANE

Basic round-trip fares within the US range roughly $80-500. Commercial carriers like American and United will probably offer the most convenient flights, but they may not be the cheapest. You will probably find flying one of the following "no-frills" airlines to be a better deal, if any of their limited departure points is convenient for you. Many of these airlines also offer one-way flights without the high fees imposed by some major airlines, and do not charge extra for travelers who are not staying over a Saturday night.

AirTran (☎800-247-8726; www.airtran.com). Cross-country and regional flights between 40+ US cities, including Atlanta, Boston, Los Angeles, Washington, D.C., and many small local or regional airports.

America West (☎800-428-4322; www.usairways.com). An extensive flight network, now owned by US Air, serving the continental US, Alaska, Hawaii, Canada, and Mexico with destinations concentrated in the western US.

ATA (☎800-435-9282; www.ata.com). Serves over 45 cities in the continental US, Hawaii, Mexico, and the Caribbean.

Frontier (☎800-432-1359; www.frontierairlines.com). Serves an extensive network of cities and smaller airports in the continental US, Alaska, and Mexico.

JetBlue (☎800-538-2583 or internationally 001 801 365 2525; www.jetblue.com). Serves 30+ locations in the US and Puerto Rico.

Southwest Airlines (☎800-435-9792; www.southwest.com). Serves 60+ locations in the US.

BY BUS

Buses generally offer the most frequent and complete service between the cities and towns of the US. Often, a bus is the only way to reach smaller locales without a car. In rural areas, however, bus lines tend to be sparse.

GREYHOUND

Greyhound (☎800-231-2222; www.greyhound.com) operates the most routes in the US. Schedule information is available at any Greyhound terminal or agency and on their web page.

Advance Purchase Fares: Reserving space far ahead of time ensures a lower fare, but expect smaller discounts June 5 to Sept. 15. Fares are often lower for 14-day, 7-day, or 3-day advance purchases. Call for up-to-date pricing or check their website.

Discounted Fares: Student Advantage cardholders (15% off); over 62 (5% off walk-up fares); military personnel and dependent family members (10% off); Veterans Advantage cardholders (15% off); children under 12 traveling with a full-fare adult (40% off).

Domestic Discovery Passes: US travelers can purchase a pass that allows unlimited travel within the continental US. Passes can be purchased on the Greyhound website. (7-60 days, US$249-689). Child, student, and senior discounts apply.

International Discovery Passes: For travelers from outside North America. Ameripass 4-60 days, US$179-639. Passes can be purchased on the Greyhound website. Child, student, and senior discounts apply.

BY TRAIN

Locomotion is still one of the least expensive (and most pleasant) ways to tour the US, but discounted air travel may be cheaper, and much faster, than train travel. As with airlines, you can save money by purchasing your tickets far in advance, so plan ahead and make reservations early. It is essential to travel light on trains, since many stations will not check luggage. **Amtrak** (☎800-872-7245; www.amtrak.com) provides the only nationwide rail service in the US; round-trip fares usually range $20-500, but check their website for special deals.

BY CAR

The US is most easily traversed by car, and once in the car, by highway. "I" (as in "I-90") refers to interstate highways, "U.S." (as in "U.S. 1") to US highways, and "Rte." (as in "Rte. 7") to state and local highways. There are often local alternatives to highways, which are worth investigating if you have extra time en route.

HOW TO NAVIGATE THE INTERSTATES

In the 1950s, President Dwight D. Eisenhower envisioned a well-organized **interstate highway system.** His dream has been realized: there is now a comprehensive, well-maintained, efficient means of traveling between major cities and between states. Luckily for travelers, the highways are named with an intuitive numbering system. Even-numbered interstates run east-west and odd ones run north-south, decreasing in number toward the south and the west. North-south routes begin on the West Coast with I-5 and end with I-95 on the East Coast. The southernmost east-west route is I-4 in Florida. The northernmost east-west route is I-94, stretching from Montana to Wisconsin. Three-digit numbers signify branches of other interstates (e.g., I-285 is a branch of I-85) that often skirt around large cities.

RENTING

Having a car will give you far better access to most places in the US. While some cities have excellent public transit, others have none, and it is often difficult to get from place to place without a car. Overall, driving is certainly your best option for seeing the US. The drawbacks of car rentals, however, include steep prices (a compact car rents for $25-45 per day) and high minimum ages for rentals (usually 25). Most branches rent to drivers ages 21 to 24 with an additional fee. A few establishments will rent to those over 18, but this is rare and will almost certainly be accompanied by a hefty fee. When evaluating rental costs it is important to note that cheaper cars tend to be less reliable and harder to handle on difficult terrain. Less expensive 4WD vehicles in particular tend to be more top-heavy, and are more dangerous when navigating especially bumpy roads.

RENTAL AGENCIES

You can generally make reservations before you leave by calling major international offices in your home country. Occasionally, however, the price and availability of information they give isn't the same as what the local offices in your country will tell you. Try checking with both numbers to make sure you get the best price and accurate information. Local desk numbers are included in town listings; for home-country numbers, call your toll-free directory.

Car rental agencies fall into two categories: national companies with hundreds of branches, and local agencies that serve only one city or region. National chains usually allow you to pick up a car in one city and drop it off in another (for a hefty charge). **Alamo** (☎800-462-5266; www.alamo.com) rents to ages 21 to 24 with a clean driving record and major credit card for an increased rate. **Enterprise** (☎800-261-7331; www.enterprise.com) and **Dollar** (☎800-800-3665; www.dollar.com) rent to customers ages 21 to 24, while most, but not all, **Thrifty** (☎800-847-4389; www.thrifty.com) locations do likewise for varying surcharges. **Rent-A-Wreck** (☎800-944-7501; www.rent-a-wreck.com) specializes in supplying vehicles that are past their prime for lower prices; a bare-bones compact less than eight years old rents for around $30. There may be a charge for a **collision and damage waiver (CDW),** which usually comes to about $12-15 per day. Major credit cards (including MasterCard and American Express) will sometimes cover the CDW if you use their card to rent a car; call your credit card company for specifics. Most agencies have frequent special rates—be sure to check online or ask the agent before renting.

COSTS

Rental car prices start at around $20-50 a day. Expect to pay more for larger cars and for 4WD. Many rental packages offer unlimited miles, although some do have mileage restrictions. Return the car with a full tank of gas to avoid high fuel charges. Be sure to ask whether the price includes **insurance** against theft and collision. If you are driving a conventional vehicle on an **unpaved road** in a rental car, you are almost never covered by insurance. Insurance plans almost always come with a **deductible.** This means you pay for all damages up to that sum, unless they are the fault of another vehicle. The deductible applies to collisions with other vehicles; collisions with non-vehicles, such as trees, will cost you even more.

AUTO TRANSPORT COMPANIES

These services match drivers with car owners who need cars moved from one city to another. Travelers give the company their desired destination and the company finds a car that needs to go there. Expenses include gas and tolls. Some companies insure their cars; with others, your security deposit covers any breakdowns or damage. You must be over 21, have a valid license, and agree to drive about 400 mi. per day on a fairly direct route. One popular company is **Auto Driveaway Co.,** 11 East Adams, Ste. 1402, Chicago, IL 60603 (☎800-346-2277; www.autodriveaway.com). Another option is **Across America Driveaway,** 10811 Washington Blvd. #302, Culver City, CA 90232 (☎800-677-6686 or 310-798-3374; www.schultz-international.com).

DRIVING PERMITS AND CAR INSURANCE

INTERNATIONAL DRIVING PERMIT (IDP)

If you do not have a license issued by a US state or Canadian province or territory, you might want an **International Driving Permit (IDP)**—it is not required, but may help with police if your license is not written in English. Although the IDP does not require a driving test, you must carry your home license with your IDP at all times. Your IDP, valid for one year, must be issued in your own country before you depart. You must be over 18 to be eligible. An application for an IDP usually requires one or two photos, a current local license, an additional form of identification, and a fee. To apply, contact the national or local branch of your home country's automobile association. Be careful when purchasing an IDP online or anywhere other than your home automobile association. Many vendors sell permits of questionable legitimacy for higher prices.

CAR INSURANCE

Most credit cards cover standard insurance. If you rent, lease, or borrow a car, you may need to certify that you have liability insurance. If you do not have car insurance, most rental companies provide their own basic liability coverage for the duration of the rental.

ON THE ROAD

While driving, be sure to buckle up. ◪**Seatbelts** are required by law in most regions. The **speed limit** in the US varies considerably from region to region. Most urban highways have a 55-65 mph (89kph) limit, while rural routes range from 65 mph (104kph) to 75 mph (120kph). Heed the limit; not only does it save gas, but most local and state police forces make frequent use of radar to catch speed demons. Gasoline prices vary significantly. They are generally much cheaper on the East Coast than on the West, and small, independent stations often offer better prices than national chains. Expect to pay at least $3 per gallon (3.8 liters).

DANGERS

Road conditions vary considerably throughout the country. Some cities have excellent roads, while others have roads riddled with potholes. In rural areas, you may find dirt roads which are considerably slower than paved streets. Watch for signs warning about animal crossings; depending on the region, signs could caution drivers to look for ducks, longhorn, moose, or other animals. Another danger on the road is weather. Depending on the region, snow, ice, sleet, or rain can make driving particularly dangerous. Pay attention to road conditions in bad weather, especially at night, and slow down or pull over if it becomes unsafe to drive.

▋ DRIVING PRECAUTIONS. When traveling in the summer or in the desert, bring substantial amounts of **water** (at least 5L per person per day) for drinking and for the radiator. For long drives to unpopulated areas, register with police before beginning the trek, and again upon arrival at the destination. When traveling long distances, make sure tires are in good repair and have enough air, and get good maps. Since gas stations are harder to come by in rural areas, make sure you have enough gas to get to your destination, or that you know of a station on your route. A **compass** and a **car manual** can also be very useful. You should always carry a **spare tire**, a **jack, jumper cables, extra oil, flares, a flashlight,** and **heavy blankets** (in case your car breaks down at night or in the winter). If you don't know how to **change a tire,** learn before heading out, especially if you are planning on traveling in deserted areas. Blowouts on dirt roads are exceedingly common. If you do have a breakdown, **stay with your car;** if you wander off, there's less likelihood trackers will find you.

CAR ASSISTANCE

Most automobile clubs offer free towing, emergency roadside assistance, travel-related discounts, and random goodies. Travelers should strongly consider membership if planning an extended roadtrip.

American Automobile Association (AAA). Provides 24hr. emergency road service (☎800-222-4357) anywhere in the US. Free trip-planning services, maps, and guidebooks. Free towing and fee-free American Express Travelers Cheques from over 1000 offices across the country and online. Discounts on Hertz car rental (5-20%), Amtrak tickets (10%), and various motel chains and theme parks. Basic membership $48, Associate Membership $12. To sign up, call ☎800-564-6222 or go to www.aaa.com.

BY BICYCLE

U-shaped **Kryptonite** or **Citadel** locks ($30-60) carry insurance against theft for one or two years if your bike is registered with the police. **Bike Nashbar** (☎800-627-4227; www.nashbar.com) sells bike locks and accessories, ships throughout the US and Canada, and will beat any competitor's price. Their tech line (☎800-888-2710; open M-F 6am-8pm EST) fields maintenance questions. The **Adventure Cycling Association,** 150 E. Pine St., P.O. Box 8308, Missoula, MT 59802 (☎800-755-2453; www.adv-cycling.org), is a national, nonprofit organization that researches long-distance routes and organizes bike tours. Annual membership ($33) includes maps, member discounts, and a subscription to *Adventure Cyclist* magazine.

BY THUMB

> **!** *Let's Go* never recommends hitchhiking as a safe means of transportation, and none of the information presented here is intended to do so.

Let's Go strongly urges you to consider the risks before you choose to hitchhike. Hitching means entrusting your life to a stranger and risking assault, sexual harassment, theft, and unsafe driving. For women traveling alone (or even in pairs), hitching is just too dangerous. A man and a woman are a less dangerous combination; two men will have a harder time getting a lift, while three men will go nowhere. In the US, hitchhiking is actually illegal in many states. It is also fairly uncommon; not only is it dangerous to be picked up on the road, but it is unlikely that your hitchhiking attempts will be very successful.

KEEPING IN TOUCH

BY EMAIL AND INTERNET

Though in some places it's possible to forge a remote link with your home server, in most cases this is a much slower (and more expensive) way of checking email than taking advantage of free **web-based email accounts** (e.g., www.hotmail.com and www.yahoo.com). **Internet cafes** and free Internet terminals at public libraries or universities are listed in the **Practical Information** sections of major cities. Prices vary by location but are generally around $2-6 per half-hour. For lists of additional cybercafes, check www.netcafeguide.com or www.cybercafes.com.

Increasingly, travelers find that taking their **laptop computers** on the road with them can be a convenient option for staying connected. Laptop users can call an Internet service provider via a modem using long-distance phone cards specifically intended for such calls. They may also find Internet cafes that allow them to connect their laptops to the Internet. And most excitingly, travelers with wireless-enabled computers can take advantage of an increasing number of Internet "hotspots," where they can get online for free or for a small fee. Newer computers can detect these hotspots automatically; websites like www.jiwire.com, www.wifihotspotlist.com, www.locfinder.net, and www.wififreespot.com can help you find them. For information on **insuring your laptop** while traveling, see p. 21.

WARY WI-FI. Wireless hot spots make Internet access possible in public and remote places. Unfortunately, they also pose **security risks.** Hot spots are public, open networks that use unencrypted, unsecured connections. They are susceptible to hacks and "packet sniffing"—ways of stealing passwords and other private information. To prevent problems, disable ad hoc mode, turn off file sharing, turn off network discovery, encrypt your e-mail, turn on your firewall, beware of phony networks, and watch for over-the-shoulder creeps. Ask the establishment whose wireless you're using for the name of the network so you know you're on the right one. If you are in the vicinity and do not plan to access the Internet, turn off your wireless adapter completely.

BY TELEPHONE

CALLING HOME FROM THE US

You can usually make **direct international calls** from pay phones, but if you aren't using a phone card, you may need to feed the machine regularly. **Prepaid phone cards are a common and relatively inexpensive means of calling abroad.** Each one comes with a Personal Identification Number (PIN) and a toll-free access number. You call the access number and then follow the directions for dialing your PIN. To purchase prepaid phone cards, check online for the best rates; www.calling-cards.com is a good place to start. Online providers generally send your access number and PIN via email, with no actual "card" involved. You can also call home with prepaid phone cards purchased in the US (see **Calling Within the US,** below).

Another option is to purchase a **calling card,** linked to a major national telecommunications service in your home country. Calls are billed collect or to your account. To obtain a calling card, contact the appropriate company listed below. Where available, there are often advantages to purchasing calling cards online, including better rates and immediate access to your account. To call home with a calling card, contact the operator for your service provider in the US by dialing the appropriate toll-free access number (listed below in the third column).

Placing a **collect call** through an international operator can be expensive, but may be necessary. You can frequently call collect without even possessing a company's calling card just by calling its access number and following the instructions.

PLACING INTERNATIONAL CALLS. To call the US from home or to call home from the US, dial:

1. The **international dialing prefix.** To call from **Australia,** dial 0011; **Canada** or the **US,** 011; **Ireland, New Zealand,** or the **UK,** 00.
2. The **country code** of the country you want to call. To call **Australia,** dial 61; **Canada** or the **US,** 1; **Ireland,** 353; **New Zealand,** 64; the **UK,** 44.
3. The **city/area code.** Let's Go lists the city/area codes for cities and towns in the US opposite the city or town name, next to a ☎. If the first digit is a zero (e.g., 020 for London), omit the zero when calling from abroad (e.g., dial 20 from Canada to reach London).
4. The **local number.**

CALLING WITHIN THE US

The simplest way to call within the country is to use a coin-operated phone. **Prepaid phone cards** (available at newspaper kiosks and convenience stores), which

ESSENTIALS

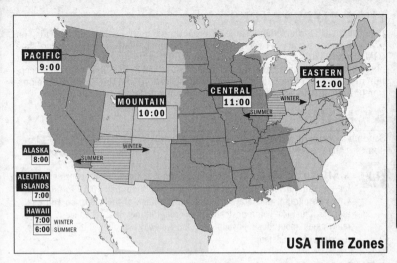

USA Time Zones

carry a certain amount of phone time depending on the card's denomination, usually save time and money in the long run. Most prepaid telephone cards come with a PIN and a toll-free access number. Call the access number and follow the directions on the card to check your minutes. These cards can be used to make international as well as domestic calls. Phone rates typically tend to be highest in the morning, lower in the evening, and lowest on Sunday and late at night.

CELLULAR PHONES

While pay phones can be found in almost every city and town in the US, if you already own a cell phone you can avoid the hassle of scrounging up change or a phone card. Cell phone reception is clear and reliable throughout the country, though in remote areas or in the mountains, reception can be spotty; your provider may also slap on additional roaming fees of up to $1.25 per minute. Travelers who already use US cell phones may want to consider upgrading from local to national service plans to avoid long-distance and roaming charges. Call your service provider to check their coverage policies.

The international standard for cell phones is **Global System for Mobile Communication (GSM).** If you want to use a foreign cell phone in the US, you will be able to make and receive calls if your phone is **GSM-compatible.** The downside is that GSM-compatible phones will only get coverage in relatively populated areas and, even then, only if the phone is from North America or a **tri-band** phone. A tri-band phone allows you to use both European frequencies as well as the North American frequency. You will also need a **SIM (Subscriber Identity Module) card,** a country-specific, thumbnail-sized chip that gives you a local phone number and plugs you into the local network. Many SIM cards are **prepaid:** they come with calling time included and you don't need to sign up for a monthly service plan. Incoming calls are frequently free. When you use up the prepaid time, you can buy additional cards or vouchers (usually available at convenience stores) to add more. For more information on GSM phones, check out www.telestial.com, www.roadpost.com, or www.planetomni.com. If your cell phone is not GSM-compatible, consider purchasing a cell phone with **prepaid minutes.** Verizon (www.verizonwireless.com) and T-mobile (www.tmobile.com) are well-known cellular providers that offer prepaid plans for a variety of budgets.

ESSENTIALS

TIME DIFFERENCES

Because the US is divided into three different time zones (see the time zone map on p. 35), regions can vary between five and eight hours behind Greenwich Mean Time (GMT). New York, NY is five hours behind GMT, while Los Angeles, CA is eight hours behind. The majority of the US observes **Daylight Saving Time,** with the exception of Arizona (not including the Navajo Reservation) and the Eastern Time portion of Indiana. Clocks change for Daylight Saving at 2am local time.

BY MAIL

Sending a postcard within the US costs $0.26, while sending letters (up to 13 oz.) domestically costs $0.41 for the first ounce and $0.17 for each additional ounce.

> ★TIP **MAIL YOURSELF.** To keep in touch with friends and family consider mailing a picture of yourself. Go to the nearest print shop, pay $0.19 to print out your photograph, and draw a line down the back of the photo so you can address it-just like you a postcard. Then drop it in the mail. Let's face it: no on really cares about those museum postcards anyway-especially if they could see a picture of you instead.

SENDING MAIL HOME FROM THE US

Airmail is the best way to send mail home from the US; write "airmail" on the front of the envelope. **Aerogrammes,** printed sheets that fold into envelopes and travel via airmail, are available at most post offices. If regular airmail is too slow, **Federal Express (FedEx)** (☎800-247-4747) can get a letter from New York City to Sydney in two business days for a whopping $50. By **US Express Mail,** a letter will arrive within three to five days and will cost $25. **Surface mail** is by far the cheapest and slowest way to send mail. It takes one to two months to cross the Atlantic and one to three to cross the Pacific—good for heavy items you won't need for a while, such as souvenirs or other articles you've acquired along the way that are weighing down your pack. These are standard rates for mail from the US to:

Australia: Allow 4-7 days for regular airmail home. Postcards/aerogrammes cost $0.90. Letters up to 2oz. cost $1.80; packages up to 1lb. $10, up to 4lb. $28.

Canada: Allow 4-7 days for regular airmail home. Postcards/aerogrammes cost $0.69. Letters up to 2oz. cost $1.00; packages up to 1lb. $5, up to 4lb. $16.

Ireland: Allow 4-7 days for regular airmail home. Postcards/aerogrammes cost $0.90. Letters up to 2oz. cost $1.80; packages up to 1lb. $10, up to 4lb. $30.

New Zealand: Allow 4-7 days for regular airmail home. Postcards/aerogrammes cost $0.90. Letters up to 2oz. cost $1.80; packages up to 1lb. $10, up to 4lb. $28.

UK: Allow 4-7 days for regular airmail home. Postcards/aerogrammes cost $0.90. Letters up to 2oz. cost $1.80; packages up to 1lb. $11, up to 4lb. $30.

SENDING MAIL TO THE US

To ensure timely delivery of your mail, mark envelopes "airmail" or "par avion." In addition to the standard postage system whose rates are listed below, **Federal Express** (www.fedex.com; Australia ☎13 26 10, Canada 800-463-3339, Ireland 1800 535 800, New Zealand 0800 733 339, the UK 0800 123 800) handles express mail services from most countries to the US.

There are several ways to arrange pickup of letters sent to you while you are traveling in the US. Many hostels and hotels will agree to accept mail for guests; after confirming with your hotel or hostel that this is possible, have mail sent directly to your attention at the establishment's street address. Mail can also be sent via **General Delivery** (Poste Restante) to almost any city or town in the US with a post office, **and it is very reliable.** Address letters like so:

> Rip Van Winkle
> c/o General Delivery
> Post Office Street Address
> Phoenicia, NY 12464 USA

The mail will go to a special desk in the central post office, unless you specify a post office by street address or postal code. It's best to use the largest post office, since mail may be sent there regardless. It is usually safer and quicker, though more expensive, to send mail express or registered. Bring your passport (or other photo ID) for pickup. *Let's Go* lists post offices and postal codes in the **Practical Information** section for each city and most towns.

American Express's travel offices throughout the world offer a free **Client Letter Service** (mail held up to 30 days and forwarded upon request) for cardholders who contact them in advance. Some offices provide these services to non-cardholders (especially AmEx Travelers Cheque holders), but call ahead to make sure. *Let's Go* lists AmEx locations for most large cities in **Practical Information** sections; for a complete list, call ☎ 800-528-4800 or visit www.americanexpress.com/travel.

ACCOMMODATIONS

HOSTELS

Many hostels are laid out dorm-style—with large single-sex rooms and bunk beds—although private rooms that sleep two to four are becoming more common. Often, they have kitchens and utensils for your use, bike or moped rentals, storage areas, transportation to airports, breakfast and other meals, laundry facilities, and Internet access. There can be drawbacks: some hostels close during certain daytime "lockout" hours, have a curfew, don't accept reservations, impose a maximum stay, or, less frequently, require that you do chores. In the US, a dorm bed in a hostel will average around $15-25, and a private room will cost from $50-65.

A HOSTELER'S BILL OF RIGHTS. There are certain standard features that we do not include in our hostel listings. Unless we state otherwise, you can expect that every hostel has no lockout, no curfew, a kitchen, free hot showers, some system of secure luggage storage, and no key deposit.

HOSTELLING INTERNATIONAL

Joining the youth hostel association in your own country (listed below) automatically grants you membership privileges in **Hostelling International (HI),** a federation of national hosteling associations. Non-HI members may be allowed to stay in some hostels, but will have to pay extra to do so. HI hostels are scattered throughout the US, and **are typically less expensive than private hostels.** HI's umbrella organization's website (www.hihostels.com), which lists the web addresses and phone numbers of all national associations, can be a great place to begin researching hostels in a specific region. Other comprehensive hostel websites include www.hostelhandbook.com and www.hostels.com.

Most HI hostels also honor **guest memberships**—you'll get a blank card with space for six validation stamps. Each night you'll pay a nonmember supplement (one-sixth the membership fee) and earn one guest stamp; get six stamps and

you're a member. The FreeNites program, a new membership benefit, allows hostelers to gain points toward free rooms. Most student travel agencies (p. 26) sell HI cards, as do all of the national hosteling organizations listed below. All prices listed below are valid for **one-year memberships.**

Australian Youth Hostels Association (AYHA), 422 Kent St., Sydney, NSW 200 (☎02 9261 1111; www.yha.com.au). AUS$52, under 18 AUS$19.

Hostelling International-Canada (HI-C), 205 Catherine St. Ste. 400, Ottawa, ON K2P 1C3 (☎613-237-7884; www.hihostels.ca). CDN$35, under 18 free.

An Óige (Irish Youth Hostel Association), 61 Mountjoy St., Dublin 7 (☎830 4555; www.irelandyha.org). EUR€20, under 18 EUR€10.

Hostelling International Northern Ireland (HINI), 22-32 Donegall Rd., Belfast BT12 5JN (☎02890 32 47 33; www.hini.org.uk). UK£15, under 25 UK£10.

Youth Hostels Association of New Zealand Inc. (YHANZ), Level 1, 166 Moorhouse Ave., P.O. Box 436, Christchurch (☎0800 278 299 (NZ only) or 03 379 9970; www.yha.org.nz). NZ$40, under 18 free.

Scottish Youth Hostels Association (SYHA), 7 Glebe Cres., Stirling FK8 2JA (☎01786 89 14 00; www.syha.org.uk). UK£8, under 18 UK£4.

Youth Hostels Association (England and Wales), Trevelyan House, Dimple Rd., Matlock, Derbyshire DE4 3YH (☎08707 708 868; www.yha.org.uk). UK£16, under 26 UK£10.

Hostelling International-USA, 8401 Colesville Rd., Ste. 600, Silver Spring, MD 20910 (☎301-495-1240; www.hiayh.org). US$28, under 18 free.

BOOKING HOSTELS ONLINE. To ensure that you've got a bed for the night, make a reservation online. Click on the **Hostelworld** booking engine at **www.letsgo.com,** and you'll have access to bargain accommodations from Argentina to Zimbabwe with no added commission.

HOTELS

Budget hotel singles in the US cost about $45-70 per night, doubles $90-110. The cheapest options are usually at the generic chains common in most regions. You'll typically have a private bathroom and shower with hot water, although cheaper places may offer a shared bath. If you make reservations in writing, the hotel will send you a confirmation and may request payment for the first night. It is often easiest to make reservations over the phone with a credit card. Check out www.hotels.com and www.all-hotels.com for **listings of hotels** across the US.

OTHER TYPES OF ACCOMMODATIONS

YMCAS AND YWCAS

Young Men's Christian Association (YMCA) and **Young Women's Christian Association (YWCA)** lodgings are usually cheaper than a hotel but more expensive than a hostel. Not all locations offer lodging; those that do are often located in urban downtowns. Many YMCAs accept women and families; some will not lodge those under 18 without parental permission.

YMCA of the USA, 101 North Wacker Dr., Chicago, IL 60606 (☎800-872-9622; www.ymca.net). Provides a listing of the nearly 1000 Ys across the US and Canada, as well as info on prices and services.

YWCA of the USA, 1015 18th St. NW, Ste. 1100, Washington, DC 20036 (☎202-467-0801; www.ywca.org). Provides a directory of YWCAs across the US.

YMCA Canada, 42 Charles St. E, 6th fl., Toronto, ON M4Y 1T4 (☎416-967-9622; www.ymca.ca). Offers info on Ys in Canada.

European Alliance of YMCAs, Na Porici 12, CZ-115 30 Prague, Czech Republic. (☎+420 22 487 20 20; www.internationalymca.org). Maintains listings of Ys in Europe.

BED & BREAKFASTS (B&BS)

For a cozy alternative to impersonal hotel rooms, B&Bs (private homes with rooms available to travelers) range from acceptable to sublime. Rooms in B&Bs generally cost **$70-90** for a single and **$90-100** for a double in **the US**. Any number of websites provide listings for B&Bs; check out **Bed & Breakfast Inns Online** (www.bbonline.com), **InnFinder** (www.inncrawler.com), **InnSite** (www.innsite.com), **BedandBreakfast.com** (www.bedandbreakfast.com), **Pamela Lanier's Bed & Breakfast Guide Online** (www.lanierbb.com), or **BNBFinder.com** (www.bnbfinder.com).

UNIVERSITY DORMS

Many **colleges** and **universities** open their residence halls to travelers when school is not in session; some even do so during term-time. Getting a room may take a couple of phone calls and require advanced planning, but rates tend to be very low, and many dorms offer free local calls and Internet access. Some universities that host travelers include the University of Texas in Austin, TX (☎512-476-5678) and Ohio State University in Columbus, OH (☎614-292-8266). Most colleges and universities don't advertise dorm vacancies, so it's good to contact individual schools in the regions where you'll be staying.

HOME EXCHANGES AND HOSPITALITY CLUBS

Home exchange offers the traveler various types of homes (houses, apartments, condominiums, villas, even castles in some cases), plus the opportunity to live like a native and to cut down on accommodation fees. For more information, contact **HomeExchange.com**, P.O. Box 787, Hermosa Beach, CA 90254, USA (☎800-877-8723; www.homeexchange.com), or **Intervac International Home Exchange** (☎800-756-4663; www.intervac.com).

Hospitality clubs link their members with individuals or families abroad who are willing to host travelers for free (or for a small fee) to promote cultural exchange and general good karma. In exchange, members usually must be willing to host travelers in their own homes; a small membership fee may also be required. **Global-Freeloaders.com** (www.globalfreeloaders.com) and **The Hospitality Club** (www.hospitalityclub.org) are good places to start. **Servas** (www.servas.org) is an established, more formal, peace-based organization, and requires a fee and an interview to join. An Internet search will find many similar organizations, some of which cater to special interests (e.g., women, GLBT travelers, or members of certain professions). As always, use common sense when planning to stay with (or host) someone whom you do not know well.

LONG-TERM ACCOMMODATIONS

Travelers planning to stay in the US for extended periods of time may find it most cost-effective to rent an **apartment.** Rent prices vary greatly between different regions and cities within the US: a basic one-bedroom (or studio) apartment in Boston, MA, will cost more than a studio in Des Moines, IA, but a studio in San Francisco, CA or New York City, NY will cost more than a studio in Boston. For most major cities in the US you should expect to pay at least $700-1500 per month. Besides the rent itself, prospective tenants usually are also required to front a security deposit (frequently one month's rent, which is returned after the lease is

ESSENTIALS

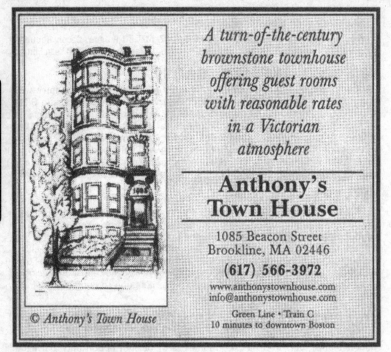
up) and the last month's rent. Aside from studio apartments, travelers can often find unoccupied bedrooms in multi-bedroom apartments. As long as you don't mind sharing a kitchen or bathroom with other tenants, this is often a cheaper and more convenient way of renting. A good online resource for finding apartment and housing rentals in the US is **www.craigslist.org,** which is free and posts daily listings for most major US cities. Other websites and services match potential roommates.

If you decide to rent, make sure you have a written agreement or lease, and that you are clear on all specifics regarding your rental. Never sign an agreement that seems questionable and don't deal with landlords whom you don't trust. A good way to avoid getting ripped off is to check with the housing department in the city or region for laws and regulations for tenants and landlords.

Another option for shorter stays (2-3 months) is **subletting,** which is popular and often easy in the summer months. Subletting involves making an agreement with the current tenants of a house or apartment to occupy their residence for a set amount of time. Sublets often come with furniture and are much more relaxed than formal lease agreements, which usually are set for a year. Before subletting, make sure that it is legal in your city or region, and make sure that the landlord of the property is aware of the sublet agreement.

Aside from renting an apartment or house, there are many other ways to find long-term housing during stays in the United States. Many hostels, motels, hotels, and YMCAs have **long-term options** for visitors who wish to stay for an extended period of time. Also, homestays often provide a long-term option, whether for school, work, or some other arrangement. For accommodations not arranged through a university or organization, it is best to check newspapers or online lists (like www.craigslist.org) for lodging opportunities.

CAMPING

For those with the proper equipment, camping is one of the least expensive and most enjoyable ways to travel in the US. Camping opportunities are boundless and accessible to inexperienced travelers. Generally, private campgrounds have sites for a small fee and offer safety and security. Well-equipped campsites (usually including prepared tent sites, toilets, and water) go for $10-25 per night in the US. **Backcountry camping,** which lacks all of the above amenities, is often free but can cost up to $20 at some national parks. Most campsites are first-come, first-served.

Depending on the region of the country in which you plan to camp, **wild animal safety** may be a concern. For more information on outdoor activities in the US, including camping and wildlife safety, see **The Great Outdoors,** below.

THE GREAT OUTDOORS

The **Great Outdoor Recreation Pages** (www.gorp.com) provide excellent general information for travelers planning on camping or spending time in the outdoors.

USEFUL RESOURCES

A variety of publishing companies offer hiking guidebooks to meet the educational needs of novice or expert. For information about camping, hiking, and biking, write or call the publishers listed below to receive a free catalog.

Family Campers and RVers, 4804 Transit Rd., Bldg. #2, Depew, NY 14043 (☎800-245-9755; www.fcrv.org). Membership (US$25) includes *Camping Today* magazine.

Sierra Club Books, 85 Second St., 2nd fl., San Francisco, CA 94105 (☎415-977-5500; www.sierraclub.org). Publishes general resource books on hiking, camping, and backpacking, as well as specific guides on regions and cities in the US.

The Mountaineers Books, 1001 SW Klickitat Way, Ste. 201, Seattle, WA 98134 (☎206-223-6303; www.mountaineersbooks.org). Over 600 titles on hiking, biking, mountaineering, natural history, and conservation.

Wilderness Press, 1200 5th St., Berkeley, CA 94710 (☎510-558-1666 or toll free 800-443-7227; www.wildernesspress.com). Carries over 100 hiking guides and maps for destinations across North America, focusing mainly on the western US.

Woodall Publications Corporation, 2575 Vista Del Mar Dr., Ventura, CA 93001 (☎877-680-6155; www.woodalls.com). Annually updates campground directories and has extensive national parks coverage.

NATIONAL PARKS

National Parks protect some of North America's most spectacular scenery. Though their primary purpose is preservation, the parks also host recreational activities such as ranger talks, guided hikes, marked trails, skiing, and snowshoe expeditions. For info, contact the **National Park Service,** 1849 C St. NW, Washington, D.C. 20240 (☎202-208-6843; www.nps.gov).

Entrance fees vary. The larger and more popular parks charge a $4-20 entry fee for cars and sometimes a $2-7 fee for pedestrians and cyclists. The **Interagency Annual Pass** ($80), has replaced the old **National Parks Pass** and the **Golden Eagle Passport** hologram, allows the passport-holder's party (up to 3 adults, unlimited children) entry into all public lands across the country, including national parks and sites managed by the US Fish and Wildlife Service, the US Forest Service, and the Bureau of Land Management. National Parks Passes purchased in 2008 will expire 12 months from the date of first use (punched at the first gate entry).

Interagency Annual Passes can be purchased at park entrances and also by writing to National Park Foundation, P.O. Box 34108, Washington, D.C. 20043 (send $80 plus shipping and handling), online at www.nationalparks.org, or by calling ☎888-467-2757. US citizens or residents over 62 qualify for the **Senior Pass** ($10 one-time fee), which entitles the holder's party to free park entry, a 50% discount on camping, and 50% reductions on various recreational fees for the passport holder. Disabled persons can enjoy the same privileges with the **Access Pass** (free).

Most national parks have both backcountry and developed **camping.** Some welcome RVs, and a few offer grand lodges. At the more popular parks in the US, reservations, available through MISTIX (☎800-365-2267; www.recreation.gov) are essential, no more than five months in advance. Indoor accommodations should be reserved months in advance. Campgrounds often observe first come, first served policies; many fill up by late morning.

LEAVE NO TRACE. *Let's Go* encourages travelers to embrace the "Leave No Trace" ethic, minimizing their impact on natural environments and protecting them for future generations. Trekkers and wilderness enthusiasts should set up camp on durable surfaces, use cookstoves instead of campfires, bury human waste away from water supplies, bag trash and carry it out with them, and respect wildlife and natural objects. For more detailed information, contact the **Leave No Trace Center for Outdoor Ethics,** P.O. Box 997, Boulder, CO 80306 (☎800-332-4100 or 303-442-8222; www.lnt.org).

NATIONAL FORESTS

Often less accessible and less crowded, **US National Forests** (www.fs.fed.us) are a purist's alternative to parks. While some have recreational facilities, most are equipped only for primitive camping—pit toilets and sites without water are the norm. When charged, entrance fees are $10-20, but camping is generally free or $3-5. Necessary **wilderness permits** for backpackers can be obtained at the US Forest Service field office in the area. *The Guide to Your National Forests* is available at all Forest Service branches, or you can call or write the main office (USDA Forest Service, Information Center, 1400 Independence Ave. SW, Washington, D.C. 20250; ☎202-205-8333). This booklet includes a list of all National Forest addresses; request maps and other info directly from the forest(s) you plan to visit. Reservations with varying fees are available for most forests, but are usually only needed during high season at popular sites. Call the National Recreation Reservation Center up to one year in advance (☎877-444-6777, international 518-885-3639; www.reserveusa.com).

WILDERNESS SAFETY

Staying **warm, dry,** and **well hydrated** is key to a happy and safe wilderness experience. For any hike, prepare yourself for an emergency by packing a first-aid kit, a reflector, a whistle, high-energy food, extra water, raingear, a hat, mittens, and extra socks. For warmth, wear wool or insulating synthetic materials designed for the outdoors. **Cotton** (known in the hiking world as "death cloth") is a bad choice because it dries painfully slowly.

Check **weather forecasts** often and pay attention to the skies when hiking, as weather patterns can change suddenly. Always let someone—a friend, your hostel, a park ranger, or a local hiking organization—know where you are and when. Know your physical limits and do not attempt to hike beyond your ability. See **Safety and Health,** p. 18, for information on outdoor medical concerns.

WILDLIFE

BEARS. The US is home to two species of bear, the brown bear (also called the grizzly bear) and the black bear. Grizzlies prefer semi-open spaces in mountainous areas, while black bears stick to forested regions. If you see a bear, calmly walk (don't run) in the other direction. The best way to avoid danger is to completely avoid the bear—bears will attack if they are surprised, threatened, or protecting their territory or cubs. Sing or talk loudly on the trail and hike in groups, if possible. If the black bear charges or attacks, the National Forest Service recommends that you stand your ground and fight back. For grizzly bears, the protocol for encounters is different. If you encounter a grizzly bear, the National Forest Service recommends that you play dead. Curl up in a ball facing downward, use your hands and arms to protect the back of your neck and face, and keep your pack on for added protection. Do not move or make noise until you are sure the bear has left the area. See the National Forest Service bear safety page at http://www.fs.fed.us/r1/wildlife/igbc/Safety/cwi/menu.htm for more information.

To avoid attracting bears, don't leave food or other scented items (trash, toiletries, the clothes that you cooked in) near your tent. Putting these objects into canisters is now mandatory in some parks. **Bear-bagging,** hanging edibles and other good-smelling objects from a tree out of reach of hungry paws, is the best way to keep your toothpaste from becoming a condiment. Bears are also attracted to any **perfume,** as are bugs, so leave cologne, scented soap, deodorant, and hairspray at home.

SNAKES. Poisonous snakes are hazards in many wilderness areas in the US and Canada. The two most dangerous are coral snakes and rattlesnakes. Coral snakes make their home in the Southwestern US and can be identified by black, yellow, and red bands. Rattlesnakes live in desert and marsh areas, and will shake the rattle at the end of their tail when threatened. Don't attempt to handle or kill a snake; if you see one, back away slowly. If you are bitten, clean the wound immediately, apply a pressure bandage, keep the wound below the heart (to slow the flow of venom through the blood stream), and immobilize the limb. Do not attempt to suck the venom out with your mouth and do not ice the wound—studies have shown that cooling the wound makes it more difficult to extract the venom. Seek immediate medical attention for any snakebite that breaks the skin.

MOOSE. Mountain regions in the north are moose stomping grounds. These big, antlered animals have been known to charge humans, so never feed or walk toward a moose. If a moose charges, get behind a tree immediately and raise your arms in the air with your fingers spread (but don't wave them) so that you appear larger. If the moose attacks you, curl up in the fetal position on the ground, cover your head with your arms, and stay still.

MOSQUITOES. While mosquitoes are certainly not as dangerous as bears or snakes, they can be a camper's main source of agony. Though these creatures start cropping up in spring, the peak season in the US runs June-August before tapering off at the approach of fall. Be especially careful around damp or swampy areas and at dawn and dusk. Mosquitoes can bite through thin fabric, so cover up as much as possible with thicker materials. 100% DEET is useful, but mosquitoes can be so ravenous that nothing short of a mosquito hood and netting really stops every jab.

CAMPING AND HIKING EQUIPMENT

WHAT TO BUY

Good camping equipment is both sturdy and light. North American suppliers tend to offer the most competitive prices.

Sleeping Bags: Most sleeping bags are rated by season; "summer" means 30-40°F (around 0°C) at night; "four-season" or "winter" often means below 0°F (-17°C). Bags are made of **down** (warm and light, but expensive, and miserable when wet) or of **synthetic** material (heavy, durable, and warm when wet). Prices range $50-250 for a summer synthetic to $200-300 for a good down winter bag. **Sleeping bag pads** include foam pads ($10-30), air mattresses ($15-50), and self-inflating mats ($30-120). Bring a **stuff sack** to store your bag and keep it dry.

Tents: The best tents are free-standing (with their own frames and suspension systems), set up quickly, and only require staking in high winds. Low-profile dome tents are the best all-around. Worthy 2-person tents start at $100, 4-person at $160. Make sure your tent has a rain fly and seal its seams with waterproofer. Other useful accessories include a **battery-operated lantern,** a plastic **groundcloth,** and a nylon **tarp.**

Backpacks: Internal-frame packs mold well to your back, keep a lower center of gravity, and flex adequately to allow for difficult trails, while **external-frame packs** are more comfortable for long hikes over even terrain, as they carry weight higher and distribute it more evenly. Your pack should have a strong, padded hip-belt to transfer weight to your legs. There are models designed specifically for women. Any serious backpacking requires at least 4000 in^3 (16,000cc), plus 500 in^3 for sleeping bags in internal-frame packs. Sturdy backpacks cost anywhere from $125-420—it's worth it to spend a good amount on your pack. When hunting for the perfect pack, fill up models with something heavy, strap it on correctly, and walk around the store to get a sense of how it distributes weight. Buy a **rain cover** ($10-20) or store all belongings in plastic bags.

Boots: Wear hiking boots with good **ankle support** that fit snugly and comfortably over 1-2 pairs of **wool socks** and a pair of thin **liner socks.** To spare yourself blisters, break in your boots over several weeks before you go.

Other Necessities: Synthetic layers, like those made of polypropylene or polyester, and a pile jacket will keep you warm even when wet. A **space blanket** ($5-15) will help you to retain body heat and doubles as a groundcloth. Plastic **water bottles** are vital; look for shatter- and leak-resistant models. Carry **water-purification tablets** for when you can't boil water. Although most campgrounds provide campfire sites, you may want to bring a small **metal grate** or **grill.** For those places that forbid fires or the gathering of firewood, you'll need a **camp stove** (the classic Coleman starts at $50) and a propane-filled **fuel bottle** to operate it. Also bring a **first-aid kit, pocketknife, insect repellent,** and **waterproof matches** or a **lighter.**

WHERE TO BUY IT

The online and mail-order companies listed below offer lower prices than many retail stores. A visit to a local camping or outdoors store will give you a good sense of the look and weight of certain items before you buy.

Campmor, 400 Corporate Dr., PO Box 680, Mahwah, NJ 07430 (☎800-525-4784; www.campmor.com).

Cotswold Outdoor, Unit 11 Kemble Business Park, Crudwell, Malmesbury Wiltshire, SN16 9SH, UK (☎08704 427 755; www.cotswoldoutdoor.com).

Discount Camping, 833 Main North Rd., Pooraka, South Australia 5095, Australia (☎618 8262 3399; www.discountcamping.com.au).

Eastern Mountain Sports (EMS), 1 Vose Farm Rd., Peterborough, 03458 NH (☎888-463-6367; www.ems.com).

Gear-Zone, 8 Burnet Rd., Sweetbriar Rd. Industrial Estate, Norwich, NR3 2BS, UK (☎1603 410 108; www.gear-zone.co.uk).

L.L. Bean, Freeport, ME 04033, USA (US and Canada ☎800-441-5713; UK 0800 891 297; www.llbean.com).

Mountain Designs, 443a Nudgee Rd., Hendra, Queensland 4011, Australia (☎+617 3114 4300; www.mountaindesigns.com).

Recreational Equipment, Inc. (REI), Sumner, WA 98352 (US and Canada ☎800-426-4840, elsewhere 253-891-2500; www.rei.com).

CAMPERS AND RVS

Much to the chagrin of outdoors purists, the US is a haven for the corpulent homes-on-wheels known as **recreational vehicles (RVs).** Renting an RV costs more than tent camping or hosteling but often less than staying in hotels while renting a car (see **Rental Cars,** p. 30). The convenience of bringing along your own bedroom, bathroom, and kitchen makes RVing an attractive option, especially for older travelers and families with children. Rates vary widely by region, season (**July and Aug.** are the most expensive months), and type of RV. Rental prices for a standard RV are about **$900 per week. Cruise America,** 11 West Hampton Ave., Mesa, AZ 85210 (US ☎800-327-7799, elsewhere 480-464-7300; www.cruiseamerica.com), rents and sells RVs at more than 135 locations in the US and Canada.

ORGANIZED ADVENTURE TRIPS

Organized adventure tours offer another way of exploring the wild. Activities include hiking, biking, skiing, canoeing, kayaking, rafting, climbing, photo safaris, and archaeological digs. Tourism bureaus often can suggest parks, trails, and outfitters. Organizations that specialize in camping and outdoor equipment like REI and EMS (see above) also are good sources for information.

Specialty Travel Index, P.O. Box 458, San Anselmo, CA 94979 (US ☎888-624-4030, elsewhere 415-455-1643; www.specialtytravel.com).

TrekAmerica, P.O. Box 189, Rockaway, NJ 07866 (US ☎800-221-0596 or 973-983-1144, elsewhere +44 01295 256 777; www.trekamerica.com). Operates tours in the western US, including the Southwest, the Pacific Northwest, and California.

The National Outdoor Leadership School (NOLS), 284 Lincoln St., Lander, WY 82520 (☎800-710-6657; www.nols.edu). Offers educational wilderness trips all over the world, including many in the US. They also offer courses in wilderness medicine training and leave-no-trace ethics.

Outward Bound, 100 Mystery Point Rd., Garrison, NY 10524 (☎866-467-7651; www.outwardboundwilderness.com). Offers expedition courses in outdoor education throughout the US. Courses range from several days to over 40 days, and include special focuses, such as life and career renewal and trips for couples.

The Sierra Club, 85 2nd St., 2nd fl., San Francisco, CA 94105 (☎415-977-5500; www.sierraclub.org/outings), plans adventure outings at branches throughout the US.

SPECIFIC CONCERNS

SUSTAINABLE TRAVEL

As the number of travelers on the road continues to rise, the detrimental effect they can have on natural environments becomes an increasing concern. With this in mind, Let's Go promotes the philosophy of **sustainable travel.** Through a sensitivity to issues of ecology and sustainability, today's travelers can be a powerful force in preserving as well as restoring the places they visit.

Ecotourism, a rising trend in sustainable travel, focuses on the conservation of natural habitats and using them to build up the economy without exploitation or

ESSENTIALS

ESSENTIALS

> **ECOTOURISM RESOURCES.** For more information on environmentally responsible tourism, contact one of the organizations below:
> **Conservation International,** 2011 Crystal Dr., Ste. 500, Arlington, VA 22202, USA (☎800-406-2306 or 703-341-2400; www.conservation.org).
> **Green Globe 21,** Green Globe vof, Verbenalaan 1, 2111 ZL Aerdenhout, The Netherlands (☎31 23 544 0306; www.greenglobe.com).
> **International Ecotourism Society,** 1333 H St. NW, Ste. 300E, Washington, D.C. 20005, USA (☎202-347-9203; www.ecotourism.org).
> **United Nations Environment Program (UNEP),** 39-43 Quai André Citroën, 75739 Paris Cedex 15, France (☎33 1 44 37 14 50; www.uneptie.org/pc/tourism).

overdevelopment. Travelers can make a difference: by doing advance research, by supporting organizations and by patronizing establishments that pay attention to their impact on their natural surroundings. Consult www.planeta.com and www.earthfoot.org for info about ecotourism and links to related reading. For more information on ecotourism in the United States, see **Beyond Tourism,** p. 75.

RESPONSIBLE TRAVEL

The impact of your tourist dollars on the destinations you visit should not be underestimated. The choices you make during your trip can have potent effects on local communities—for better or for worse. Travelers who care about the destinations and environments they visit should become aware of the social and cultural implications of the choices they make when they travel. Simple decisions such as buying local products instead of globally-available products and paying a fair price for the product or service can have a strong, positive effect on the community.

Community-based tourism aims to channel tourist dollars into the local economy by emphasizing tours and cultural programs that are run by members of the host community and that often benefit disadvantaged groups. This type of tourism also benefits the tourists themselves, as these tours often take them beyond the traditional tours of the region. An excellent resource for general information on community-based travel is *Ethical Travel Guide* (UK£13), a project of **Tourism Concern** (☎+44 020 7133 3330; www.tourismconcern.org.uk).

TRAVELING ALONE

There are many benefits to traveling alone, including independence and greater interaction with locals. On the other hand, any solo traveler is a more vulnerable target of harassment and street theft. As a lone traveler, try not to stand out as a tourist, look confident, and be especially careful in deserted or very crowded areas. Stay away from areas that are not well-lit. If questioned, never admit that you are traveling alone. Maintain regular contact with someone at home who knows your itinerary, and always research your destination before traveling. For more tips, pick up *Traveling Solo* by Eleanor Berman (Globe Pequot Press, US$18), visit www.travelaloneandloveit.com, or subscribe to **Connecting: Solo Travel Network,** 689 Park Rd., Unit 6, Gibsons, BC V0N 1V7, Canada (☎800-557-1757; www.cstn.org; membership US$30-50).

WOMEN TRAVELERS

Women exploring on their own inevitably face some additional safety concerns, but it's easy to be adventurous without taking undue risks. If you are concerned, consider staying in hostels which offer single rooms that lock from the inside or in religious organizations with single-sex rooms. Stick to centrally located accommodations and avoid solitary late-night treks or metro rides.

Always carry extra cash for a phone call, bus, or taxi. **Hitchhiking** is never safe for lone women, or even for two women traveling together. Look as if you know where you're going and approach older women or couples for directions if you're lost or uncomfortable.

Generally, the less you look like a tourist, the better off you'll be. Dress conservatively, especially in rural areas. Wearing a conspicuous **wedding band** sometimes helps to prevent unwanted advances.

Your best answer to verbal harassment is no answer at all; feigning deafness, sitting motionless, and staring straight ahead at nothing in particular will usually do the trick. The extremely persistent can sometimes be dissuaded by a firm, loud, and very public "Go away!" in the appropriate language. Don't hesitate to seek out a police officer or a passerby if you are being harassed. Memorize the emergency numbers in places you visit, and consider carrying a whistle on your keychain. A self-defense course will both prepare you for a potential attack and raise your level of awareness of your surroundings (see **Personal Safety**, p. 20). Also be sure you are aware of the health concerns that women face when traveling (see p. 25).

GLBT TRAVELERS

American cities are generally accepting of all sexualities, and thriving gay, lesbian, bisexual, and transgendered (GLBT) communities can be found in most cosmopolitan areas. Most college towns are GLBT-friendly as well. Still, homophobia is not uncommon, particularly in rural areas. To avoid unwanted attention in rural areas, refrain from public displays of affection. *Let's Go* includes local GLBT info lines and community centers when available.

To avoid hassles at airports and border crossings, transgendered travelers should make sure that all of their travel documents consistently report the same gender. Many countries (including Australia, Canada, Ireland, New Zealand, the UK, and the US) will amend the passports of post-operative transsexuals to reflect their true gender, although governments are generally less willing to amend documents for pre-operative transsexuals and other transgendered individuals.

Listed below are contact organizations, mail-order bookstores, and publishers that offer materials addressing some specific concerns. **Out and About** (www.planetout.com) offers a weekly newsletter and a comprehensive site to address gay travel concerns. The online newspaper **365gay.com** also has a travel section (www.365gay.com/travel/travelchannel.htm).

Gay's the Word, 66 Marchmont St., London WC1N 1AB, UK (☎44 020 7278 7654; http://freespace.virgin.net/gays.theword/). The largest gay and lesbian bookshop in the UK, with both fiction and non-fiction titles. Mail-order service available.

Giovanni's Room, 345 South 12th St., Philadelphia, PA 19107 (☎215-923-2960; www.queerbooks.com). An international lesbian and gay bookstore with mail-order service (carries many of the publications listed below).

International Lesbian and Gay Association (ILGA), 17 Rue de la Charité, 1210 Brussels, Belgium (☎32 2 502 2471; www.ilga.org). Provides political information, such as homosexuality laws of individual countries.

TRAVELERS WITH DISABILITIES

Federal law dictates that all public buildings in the US should be wheelchair-accessible, and building codes make disabled access more the norm than the

▼ **ADDITIONAL RESOURCES: GLBT**
Spartacus 2007: International Gay Guide. Bruno Gmunder Verlag (US$33).
Damron Men's Travel Guide, Damron Road Atlas, Damron Accommodations Guide, Damron City Guide, and *Damron Women's Traveller.* Damron Travel Guides (US$18-24). For info, call ☎800-462-6654 or visit www.damron.com.
The Gay Vacation Guide: The Best Trips and How to Plan Them, Mark Chesnut. Kensington Books (US$15).
Gayellow Pages USA/Canada, Frances Green. Gayellow Pages (US$20). They also publish smaller regional editions. Visit Gayellow pages online at http://gayellowpages.com.

exception. Still, those with disabilities should inform airlines and hotels of their disabilities when making reservations; time may be needed to prepare accommodations. Call ahead to restaurants, museums, and other facilities to find out if they are handicapped- accessible. **Visiting rugged parks may be difficult or impossible if you have severe disabilities, but many parks do have handicapped-accessible trails.**

In the US, both Amtrak and major airlines will accommodate disabled passengers if notified at least 72hr. in advance. Amtrak offers a 15% discount to physically disabled travelers (☎800-872-7245). Greyhound buses will provide a 50% discount for a companion if the ticket is purchased at least 24 hr. in advance. If you are without a fellow traveler, call Greyhound (☎800-752-4841, TDD 800-345-3109) at least two days before you plan to leave and they will make arrangements to assist you. For info on transportation availability in individual US cities, contact the local chapter of the **Easter Seal Society** (☎800-221-6827; www.easter-seals.org).

Certified guide dogs entering the US must have originated from or lived for six months in an area that is free from rabies (including Australia, Canada, Ireland, New Zealand, and the UK), or they must have unexpired vaccination certificates. For a list of rabies-free areas, see www.cdc.gov/ncidod/dvrd/rabies. In all areas in the US, guide dogs are legally allowed, free of charge, on public transit and in all "public establishments," including hotels, restaurants, and stores.

If you are planning to visit a national park or attraction run by the National Park Service, obtain a free **Access Pass,** available at all park entrances and from federal offices whose functions relate to land, forests, or wildlife. The passport entitles disabled travelers and their families to free admission to any public land and provides a lifetime 50% discount on campsite and parking fees.

USEFUL ORGANIZATIONS

Accessible Journeys, 35 West Sellers Ave., Ridley Park, PA 19078, USA (☎800-846-4537; www.disabilitytravel.com). Designs tours for the wheelchair-bound and slow walkers. The site has tips and forums for all travelers.

Flying Wheels Travel, 143 W. Bridge St., Owatonna, MN 55060, USA (☎507-451-5005; www.flyingwheelstravel.com). Specializes in escorted trips to Europe for people with physical disabilities; plans custom trips worldwide.

The Guided Tour, Inc., 7900 Old York Rd., Ste. 114B, Elkins Park, PA 19027, USA (☎800-783-5841; www.guidedtour.com). Organizes travel programs for persons with developmental and physical challenges in the US.

Mobility International USA (MIUSA), P.O. Box 10767, Eugene, OR 97440, USA (☎541-343-1284; www.miusa.org). Provides a variety of books and other publications containing information for travelers with disabilities.

Society for Accessible Travel and Hospitality (SATH), 347 Fifth Ave., Ste. 610, New York, NY 10016, USA (☎212-447-7284; www.sath.org). Advocacy group that publishes free online travel info. Annual membership US$49, students and seniors US$29.

MINORITY TRAVELERS

The US is a multicultural nation, but general attitudes toward race relations in the US differ from region to region. Racial and ethnic minorities sometimes face blatant or subtle discrimination and/or harassment. Remain calm and report individuals to a supervisor and establishments to the **Better Business Bureau** for the region (www.bbb.org, or call the operator for local listings); contact the police in extreme situations. Let's Go always welcomes reader input regarding discriminatory establishments. Be aware that racial tensions do exist, even in large, ostensibly progressive areas, and try to avoid confrontations.

In towns along the US-Mexican border, the **Border Patrol** for the US Immigration and Naturalization Service (INS) remains on a constant lookout for Mexican nationals who have crossed the border illegally. In border towns, they may pull over anyone who looks suspicious, search their vehicles for smuggled goods or people, and ask for identification.

FURTHER RESOURCES

United States Department of Justice (www.usdoj.gov/pclo).

Go Girl! The Black Woman's Book of Travel and Adventure, Elaine Lee. Eighth Mountain Press ($25).

The African-American Travel Guide, Wayne C. Robinson. Hunter Publishing ($16).

DIETARY CONCERNS

Vegetarians should have an array of options in most parts of the country, especially along the veggie-friendly West Coast. Let's Go often indicates vegetarian options in restaurant listings; other places to look for vegetarian and vegan cuisine are local health food stores, as well as large natural food chains such as **Trader Joe's** and **Wild Oats.** Vegan options may be more difficult to find in smaller towns; be prepared to make your own meals. The travel section of the **The Vegetarian Resource Group's** website, at www.vrg.org/travel, has a comprehensive list of organizations and websites that are geared toward helping traveling vegetarians and vegans. For more information, visit your local bookstore or health food store, and consult The Vegetarian Traveler: Where to Stay if You're Vegetarian, Vegan, or Environmentally Sensitive, by Jed and Susan Civic (Larson Publications; $16), or Vegetarian Restaurants & Natural Food Stores in the US: A Comprehensive Guide to Over 2500 Vegetarian Eateries, by John Howley (Torchlight Publications; $16). Vegetarians will also find numerous resources on the web; try www.vegdining.com, www.happycow.net, and www.vegetariansabroad.com.

Travelers who keep kosher should contact synagogues in larger cities for information on kosher restaurants. Your own synagogue or college Hillel should have access to lists of Jewish institutions across the nation. Search for kosher restaurants by state, city, or category at www.shamash.org/kosher. If you are strict in your observance, you may have to prepare your own food on the road. A good resource is the Jewish Travel Guide, edited by Michael Zaidner (Vallentine Mitchell; US$19). Travelers looking for **halal** restaurants may find www.zabihah.com a useful resource.

OTHER RESOURCES

Let's Go tries to cover all aspects of budget travel, but we can't put everything in our guides. Listed below are books and websites that can serve as jumping-off points for your own research.

ESSENTIALS

USEFUL PUBLICATIONS

The Road Atlas United States 2005, Rand McNally ($20). For more info, visit www.Rand-McNally.com.

The Next Exit: The Most Complete Interstate Highway Guide Ever Printed, edited by Mark T. Watson ($15).

Colman National Forest Campground & Recreation Directory. Our Forests ($20).

American Ways: A Guide for Foreigners in the United States, Gary Althen, Amanda R. Doran, and Susan J. Szmania ($27).

Speak American: A Survival Guide to the Language and Culture of the USA, Dileri Dorunda Johnston ($8).

America Bizarro: A Guide to Freaky Festivals, Groovy Gatherings, Kooky Contests, and Other Strange Happenings Across the USA, Nelson Taylor ($15).

Eat Your Way Across the USA, Jane and Michael Stern ($15).

Hip Hotels USA, Herbert Ypma ($30).

WORLD WIDE WEB

Almost every aspect of budget travel is accessible via the web. In 10min. at the keyboard, you can make a hostel reservation, get advice on travel hotspots from other travelers, or find out how much a train from Denver to Detroit costs. Listed here are some regional and travel-related sites to start your search; other relevant websites are listed throughout the book.

 WWW.LETSGO.COM. Our website features extensive content from our guides; a community forum where travelers can connect with each other, ask questions or advice, and share stories and tips; and expanded resources to help you plan your trip. Browse by destination and find info on ordering titles. Check back often to see constant updates, exciting new tips, prize giveaways, and researcher blogs to whet your appetite for travel, *Let's Go* style. See you soon!

THE ART OF TRAVEL

BootsnAll.com: www.bootsnall.com. Numerous resources for independent travelers, from planning your trip to reporting on it when you get back.

How to See the World: www.artoftravel.com. A compendium of great travel tips, from cheap flights to self defense to interacting with local culture.

Travel Intelligence: www.travelintelligence.net. A large collection of travel writing by distinguished travel writers.

Travel Library: www.travel-library.com. Fantastic links for general info and personal travelogues.

World Hum: www.worldhum.com. An independently produced collection of "travel dispatches from a shrinking planet."

INFORMATION ON THE USA

Atevo Travel: www.atevo.com. Detailed travel tips and suggested itineraries.

CIA World Factbook: www.odci.gov/cia/publications/factbook/index.html. Tons of vital statistics on the US's geography, government, economy, and people.

Geographia: www.geographia.com. Highlights, culture, and people of the US.

PlanetRider: www.planetrider.com. A subjective list of links to the "best" websites covering the culture and tourist attractions of the US.

World Travel Guide: www.travel-guides.com. Helpful practical info.

LIFE AND TIMES

HISTORY

10,000 BC
The first Americans arrive in North America via the Bering Strait.

WATER UNDER THE BRIDGE. Archaeologists believe that the first inhabitants of the Americas crossed the Bering Sea from Siberia by a **land bridge** during the last Ice Age—approximately 12,000 years ago. Scientists have raised different theories to explain this migration: the pursuit of bison, a shift in the living conditions in Asia, or just wanderlust. Gradually, the Asiatic migrants came to inhabit all corners of their new continent. The earliest Native American cultures were nomadic, flourishing as they followed ▓**megafauna** (giant mammals similar to today's horses, armadillos, and lions). Around AD 200, the ancestors of today's Pueblos fostered advanced civilizations; ruins are visible in the Anasazi Great Houses of **Chaco Canyon** (p. 839).

A BRAVE NEW WORLD. Though no one is certain, it is likely that the earliest Europeans to arrive in America did so accidentally, when storms blew their ships off course. Textbooks place the discovery of the Americas in 1492, when **Christopher Columbus,** an Italian explorer, found his voyage to the East blocked by Hispaniola in the Caribbean Sea. Columbus thought he had reached the Spice Islands of the East Indies, and dubbed the inhabitants "Indians." Columbus's arrival marked the beginning of European conquest. In addition to establishing what would become a permanent European presence in the New World, conquests brought disease and death to the Native Americans.

AD 1499
The United States of Vespuccia? Amerigo Vespucci explores the continents that will soon bear his (first) name.

In the centuries after Columbus's voyage, Europeans rushed to the New World in search of gold and silver, prestige for themselves, colonies for their motherland, and in some cases, religious freedom. The Spanish expanded into the southern and southwestern regions what is now the US, while the French and Dutch created more modest empires to the north. The English settled the New World's east coast, and after a few failed attempts, established a successful colony at **Jamestown** (p. 212) in 1607. Their prosperity and growth hinged on the indigenous tobacco plant, a product that gained instant popularity in England. In the years after 1620, the **Puritans,** religious separatists who had been persecuted by the Presbyterians in England, fled to present-day Massachusetts, settling at the famous Plymouth Rock (p. 277). The Puritan founding of Plimoth spawned the popular myth of the first American Thanksgiving.

1584-1590
Unsolved Mystery: the colonists at Roanoke, an island off the coast of South Carolina, mysteriously disappear.

1692
Toil and trouble: witch hunters terrorize Salem, MA.

REVOLUTION AND INDEPENDENCE. In order to protect her holdings in the Americas from an impending French influence, Britain entered the **French and Indian War** in 1754, fighting battles against French and Native American joint forces. The British triumphed, but their victory was bittersweet: Britain's power in the Americas seemed irrelevant once the colonists no longer needed protection from the French. Furthermore, the struggle more than doubled Britain's government expenditures. British leaders decided to shift the economic burden onto American colonists: the new taxes angered colonists, who rallied against "taxation without representation." Colonial committees created the **First Continental Congress,** which attempted to convince England of the colonists' rights. Tensions peaked in 1773 when patriots in Boston staged the **Boston Tea Party,** dumping over 10,000 pounds of tea into Boston Harbor to protest unfair tea taxation. This marked the beginning of violence between Great Britain and the colonies and led to the Second Continental Congress. This Congress prepared the colonies for the war, which officially began in April 1775, at the battles of Lexington and Concord. In 1776, **Thomas Jefferson** drafted the **Declaration of Independence,** and it was adopted on **July 4th,** which remains the USA's most important non-religious national holiday. Fighting continued throughout the east coast until October 1781, when, outnumbered by colonial rebels and their French allies, the British surrendered, ending the **Revolutionary War** and finally granting the colonists their independence.

1773
Costume party? Dressed as Mohawk Indians, colonists dump British tea into the harbor during the Boston Tea Party.

July 4, 1776
The Declaration of Independence, written by Thomas Jefferson, is signed by the Continental Congress.

THE CONSTITUTION, PROTECTOR OF FREEDOM. In 1787, the state legislatures of the original 13 states sent 55 delegates to draft what was to become the **Constitution,** which is still the governing code of law in America today. The **Bill of Rights,** a set of 10 constitutional amendments, was passed shortly after the Constitution, and remains a cornerstone of the American political system. This document includes protection of personal rights: freedom of speech, press, and religion, respectively. When the Constitution was ratified, **George Washington,** the former Commander-in-Chief of the Continental Army, was unanimously elected the first President of the United States.

MANIFEST DESTINY. After Jefferson was elected third President of the US, he purchased the **Louisiana Territory** from Napoleon in 1803—for less than $0.03 an acre. The purchase began an era known as "manifest destiny": the belief that it was the will of God for America to stretch from the Atlantic to the Pacific. The sprawling landmass stretched south from Montana to Louisiana and west from the Mississippi River to the Rocky Mountains. The next year, Jefferson sent **Meriwether Lewis** and **William Clark** to explore the territory and find a river route to the Pacific Ocean. Lewis and Clark never found a waterway linking the oceans, but with the help of a Shoshone guide, **Sacagawea,** they charted the land west of the Mississippi. In the decades that followed, droves of people moved west along the grueling **Oregon Trail** in search of a new life. Over 40,000 prospectors traveled to California between 1848 and 1849 in a mass migration now known as the **Gold Rush.**

1803
You bought what?! Thomas Jefferson purchases the Louisiana territory for $0.03 per acre. A year later, Lewis and Clark head west to explore America's new territory.

When the independent Republic of Texas (formerly part of Mexico) became a US state in 1845, President James Polk decided to expand into Mexican territory. The tension that resulted from the Texas War of Independence and Polk's designs on Mexico's territory led to the **Mexican-American War.** American soldiers offered protection for the Texans from Native Americans in exchange for surrender. Mexican troops were forced to capitulate when US troops invaded Mexico City. The treaty that ended the war in February 1848 granted the US nearly two-fifths of Mexico's territory, including modern-day New Mexico, California, Nevada, Utah, most of Arizona and Colorado, and parts of Wyoming, Kansas, and Oklahoma.

The **Homestead Act** of 1862 prompted the cultivation of the Great Plains by distributing government land to those who would farm the land and settle it. This large-scale settlement led to bloody battles with the Sioux, Hunkpapas, and Cheyenne Native American tribes who had long inhabited the Plains and saw the settlement as an invasion of their lands. From 1866 to 1891 conflicts with Native Americans raged on, leading to the **Allotment Act** of 1891, which established Native American land reservations in order to end the fighting.

SLAVERY IN THE NEW WORLD. The first **Africans** were brought to America in 1619 on a Dutch slave ship that landed in Jamestown, VA. The demand for cheap labor in America increased from the late 1500s into the 1600s, and white settlers began to invade Native American communities looking for slaves. Native Americans, however, suffered fatally from European diseases, leading colonial America to rely on African slaves to provide labor. Thousands of Africans were forced across the Atlantic to be auctioned off into US slavery, a harrowing journey known as the **Middle Passage.** This lasted until 1808, when the slave trade was abolished. Slave ownership, however, continued until the mid-19th century.

The existence of slavery exacerbated existing ideological differences between the North and the South. The South's agricultural economy was driven by slave labor, while the industrialized North relied on manufacturing and trade. Because the federal government was designed to prevent the "tyranny" of pre-Revolution days, each state in the Union could decide to allow or prohibit slavery independently. As the Northern states became more insistent that territories and new states should be kept as "free states", the Southern states dug in their heels, citing the Revolutionary ideal of states' rights. Meanwhile, Northern abolitionists joined with free African-Americans to form the **Underground Railroad,** an escape route in which "conductors" secretly transported escaped slaves into the free Northern states. Southern slave-owners often chased slaves down in an attempt to reclaim their "property," further fueling tensions between the North and South. In the end, only a fierce, bloody conflict could decide which region would prevail.

"A HOUSE DIVIDED": THE CIVIL WAR. Tensions between the North and South came to a head when **Abraham Lincoln,** an antislavery Congressman from Illinois, was elected President in 1860. In response, South Carolina, a hotbed of pro-slavery sentiment, seceded from the Union and 10 other Southern states quickly followed suit. These rebellious states became the **Confederate States of America** under the Presidency of Jefferson Davis. Lincoln refused to accept the secession, setting the stage for war. On April 12, 1861, Southern troops fired on Fort Sumter (p. 358) in Charleston, SC, and the **Civil War (**or the War

1838
The US government forces Cherokee Indians to leave their homes and march west on the Trail of Tears.

1848
"What a girl wants": Elizabeth Cady Stanton, Lucretia Mott, and others give new meaning to women's rights at the Seneca Falls Convention.

1849
Golden Slumbers: Gold Rush fever hits California and lures settlers west.

1860
Eleven southern states secede from the Union and form the Confederate States of America.

LIFE AND TIMES

1862
President Abraham Lincoln issues the Emancipation Proclamation, ending slavery in the US.

1865
Gen. Robert E. Lee of the Confederate Army surrenders to the Union, ending the Civil War.

of Northern Aggression as it is known in the South) began. For four years the country endured a bloody conflict. Lincoln led the Union to eventual victory, but the price was high; the war claimed more American lives than any other conflict in US history. Lincoln was assassinated at the Ford Theater on April 14, 1865, by Southern sympathizer John Wilkes Booth.

RECONSTRUCTION, INVENTION, AND INDUSTRIALIZATION.
The period after the war brought with it a period of transition: Reconstruction in the South and the Industrial Revolution in the North. While the North's rapid industrialization made it a contender in the world economy, the South's agricultural economy entered a slow decline. Injured and embittered by the war and dependent on an outdated agricultural tradition, Southerners struggled to readjust to new socio-economic conditions. Meanwhile, newly-freed blacks faced a difficult transition from plantation life to free life. **Jim Crow** laws imposed by white politicians espoused a doctrine of segregation, impeding African-Americans' civil rights—forcing them to be segregated from whites in public areas, such as schools and buses. Even drinking fountains were classified according to race. Freedom from slavery, however, also meant new opportunities for African-Americans. Black colleges were founded, and a few prominent African-Americans were able to gain some political power. For many blacks, though, segregation, Jim Crow laws, and racist sentiment led to share-crop farming for white landowners, which was not much different from slavery.

During the **"Gilded Age"** of the 1870s, captains of industry Cornelius Vanderbilt, Andrew Carnegie, and John D. Rockefeller built commercial empires and enormous personal fortunes amid an atmosphere of widespread corruption. However, massive wealth didn't trickle down to farmers and industrial workers, who faced low wages, violent strike break-ups, and unsafe working conditions. But the Industrial Age wasn't all bad. Major developments in transportation were a cornerstone of industrialization. Between 1850 and 1890, miles of **railroad** track in the nation increased from around 9000 to over 200,000. Aviation became popular after the **Wright Brothers** flew the first

1876
Say what? Alexander Graham Bell invents the first telephone.

airplane at Kitty Hawk, NC (p. 348) in 1903. **Thomas Edison** started the nation's first electricity generating station (in addition to inventing appliances like the **lightbulb**), and Rockefeller began turning oil into the energy powerhouse it is today. In 1876, **Alexander Graham Bell** invented the **telephone,** forever changing communication.

1879
Seeing the light: Thomas Edison invents the ▨ **lightbulb** after many failed attempts.

THE WORLD MOVES: IMPERIALISM, IMMIGRATION, AND WWI. The United States' victory in the **Spanish-American War** of 1898 seemed to validate its internationalist policies. Believing that the US should be a leader in world affairs, and continuing its tradition of Manifest Destiny, the nation acquired colonies in the Philippines, Puerto Rico, and Guam.

While the US displayed its proud face all over the globe, the late 19th and early 20th centuries brought a flood of new foreign faces to the nation. The flood of **European immigration** began in 1880, when nearly four million Italian immigrants fled

Italy's dismal economic climate for American shores. Between 1880 and 1900, the US population grew by 50 percent. New York's **Ellis Island** (p. 98) became the center for processing immigrants. Near Ellis Island, the **Statue of Liberty** (p. 98), a gift to the US from the people of France, greeted the shiploads of "tired, poor, huddled masses" yearning for the freedom promised by the Constitution.

In 1901, **Teddy Roosevelt** took over the presidency following the assassination of William McKinley, and brought a youthful, progressive approach to the government. In response to the corrupt, monopolistic practices of big business, Roosevelt and his progressive **Bull Moose Party** promoted anti-trust reforms to regulate large companies. In foreign affairs, Roosevelt established the US as an international police power; recommending that the nation "speak softly and carry a big stick." Meanwhile, a new breed of journalists, known as the "muckrakers," began writing articles to unveil the Industrial Age's rampant corruption. One of the most famous of these works, Upton Sinclair's *The Jungle*, was a graphic exposé of the meatpacking industry.

After vowing to keep the US out of "Europe's War," President **Woodrow Wilson** entered **World War I.** US troops landed in Europe in 1917 and fought until Germany's defeat the next year. The expansion of the US Armed Forces that was necessary to carry out the war meant that 6% of the labor force aged 15-44 was deployed, and at least a fifth of the nation's resources were devoted to the war. The war, and the US's sudden involvement, called for extensive production of military products. In fact, from an economic point of view, the money spent by the US on the war was completely offset by the increases in production that were necessary to fight it. Though the metal-consuming war jump-started America's industrial economy and established the US as a major international power, the war killed 10 million people, including 130,174 Americans. Ultimately, this human loss left Americans wary of future combat in Europe.

ROARING 20S, GREAT DEPRESSION, AND WWII. After the war, Americans returned their attention to the home front, and the United States entered a new age of affluence. Labor unrest and racial tension were blamed on communist influences, and during 1919 the US experienced a **"Red Scare"** as unease over the spread of communism increased. The same year, the perceived moral decline of America was addressed by the immensely unpopular **Prohibition** laws, which outlawed alcohol. In spite of these restrictions, America's fun-loving spirit thrived as Mafia-run ◼**"speakeasies"** replaced neighborhood saloons and created a huge black market for bootleg liquor. The jazz scene raged, giving this era of music, leisure, and decadence the apt name **"The Jazz Age."**

During this period, women **suffragists** such as **Susan B. Anthony** mobilized for the right to vote, putting intense pressure on politicians at every level of the government. These efforts eventually met with success in 1920 with the passage of the 19th Amendment to the US Constitution, which extended suffrage to women.

1896
First silent movie is shown in New York City. Popcorn sales skyrocket.

1903
Let's go fly a kite...or a plane: Orville and Wilbur Wright make the first successful airplane flight.

1908
"Baby, you can drive my car": Henry Ford's $850 Model T zooms onto the market.

1917
The US enters WWI.

LIFE AND TIMES

1927
Charles Lindbergh
makes the first
solo flight across
the Atlantic Ocean.

Oct. 29, 1929
The New York Stock
Exchange crashes,
sparking a world-
wide depression.

Dec. 7, 1941
The attack on Pearl
Harbor pushes the
US into WWII.

1947
Play ball!
Jackie Robinson
joins the Brooklyn
Dodgers, becoming
the first African-
American to play
Major League
Baseball.

The economic boom of the **"Roaring 20s"** was driven largely by overextended credit. The facade of economic stability crumbled on "Black Thursday," October 24, 1929, when the New York Stock Exchange crashed. This downfall initiated a period of world-wide financial collapse known as the **Great Depression.** In an urban, mechanized age, millions of workers (25-50% of the work force) were left unemployed and struggled to provide for their families. The United States, like the rest of the developed world, rebounded slowly, and poor economic conditions continued for almost a decade despite **New Deal** policies like the Social Security Act initiated by President **Franklin D. Roosevelt.**

In the aftermath of the Depression, Nazi Germany plowed through Europe. American civilians were largely unaware of the extent of the horrors in Europe because of Nazi cover-ups. The US entered **World War II** only after the Japanese attack on Pearl Harbor, Hawaii on December 7, 1941. Joining the Allied Powers, the US waged a war on two fronts, fighting both the Germans in Europe and the Japanese in the Pacific. The European front was resolved with the German surrender on May 8, 1945, less than a year after the immense **D-Day** invasion of continental Europe in June 1944. The war in the Pacific continued until August of 1945, when the US dropped two newly developed **nuclear bombs** on Japan, killing 80,000 civilians and demonstrating to the world the power of nuclear warfare. Defeating Germany and her allies in Europe and Asia established the US military as a permanent global force.

THE COLD WAR. Spared the wartime devastation faced by Europe and East Asia and empowered by nationalistic pride, the US economy boomed after the war and secured the nation's status as the world's dominant economic and military power. The US population increased during this period, as jubilation over victory and a throng of men returning from war created the **Baby Boomer generation.** While the 1950s are often nostalgically recalled as a golden age of prosperity and traditional values, the decade did experience international tumult and angst.

The ideological gulf between the world's two nuclear powers—the democratic, capitalist US and the totalitarian, communist Soviet Union—initiated the half-century **Cold War** between the two nations. Tension with the Soviet Union heightened as **President Harry Truman** installed the foreign policy of communist containment to prevent the spread of communism beyond the Soviet Union's borders. Fear of communism led to American military involvement in Asia, where the Maoist revolution in China had emboldened imitators in surrounding countries. From 1950 to 1953, the United States fought the **Korean War** on behalf of the South Koreans, who had been attacked by the communist North Korean government. The Soviet launch of Sputnik, the first artificial satellite, in 1957 rekindled fears that communist regimes were surpassing America in many ways. The **Cuban Missile Crisis** in 1962, during which **President John F. Kennedy** negotiated the removal of Soviet missiles from a Cuban base, narrowly avoiding nuclear war, reinforced the perception that the United States had to protect the world from Soviet invasion.

Exploiting rising anti-communist feeling at home, the **House Un-American Activities Committee,** led by **Senator Joseph McCarthy,** conducted so-called witch-hunts delving into every aspect of American public life to root out communist sympathizers, with a special focus on Hollywood and the media as a whole. The power of McCarthy and the HUAC waned as the vast majority of accusations were proven to be unfounded.

In 1963, Lee Harvey Oswald assassinated President Kennedy during a parade in Dallas, TX. The assassination of the young, charismatic President mirrored America's larger loss of innocence and optimism. Throughout the rest of the decade, cultural strife, stemming from the long-fought civil rights movement and the bloody, controversial Vietnam War, altered the nation's social fabric.

ALL YOU NEED IS LOVE...AND PROTEST. Driven by the dictates of the containment policy instituted after WWII, the US became embroiled in Vietnamese politics, culminating in a large-scale deployment of combat troops in 1965 to protect the South Vietnamese state from the aggression of Ho Chi Minh's communist government to the north. The **Vietnam War** was seen as a test of America's foreign policy, making retreat difficult even when it became apparent that military officials had underestimated the situation in Vietnam and that a U.S. victory was unlikely. Though most Americans supported the war at first, opposition grew as it dragged on and citizens began to question its moral premises. Vietnam was the first war "fought on television," where graphic images of war never before seen by Americans, contributed to the perception of the war as a hopeless endeavor. Members of the new hippie generation responded with shouts of "Make Love, Not War" at the 1969 **Woodstock** music festival. The youth protests catalyzed wrenching generational clashes that eventually climaxed in riots and violence at the **1968 Democratic National Convention** and the National Guard shooting of anti-war protestors at **Kent State** in 1970.

The Vietnam War was not the only cause that captured the hearts and minds of idealistic young Americans. **Rosa Parks's** refusal to give up a bus seat in Montgomery, AL (p. 384) in 1955 sparked a period of feverish activity culminating in the **civil rights movement,** in which African-Americans strove for recognition of equality. The struggle was characterized by countless demonstrations, marches, and sit-ins in the heart of a defiant and often violent South. Activists were drenched with fire hoses, arrested, and even killed by local mobs and policemen. The movement crested with a march on Washington, D.C. in 1963, where **Dr. Martin Luther King, Jr.** delivered his famous "I Have A Dream" speech, calling for non-violent racial integration. The tone of the civil rights movement changed as some blacks became fed up with peaceful demonstrations and turned to the more militant rhetoric of **Malcolm X,** who espoused separatist "Black Power," and the **Black Panthers**, who used more aggressive tactics to assert African-Americans' rights.

The second wave of the **women's movement** arose at this time as well. Sparked by **Betty Friedan's** book *The Feminine Mys-*

1954
The Supreme Court decision in *Brown v. Board of Education* ends racial segregation in American public schools.

1961
Make Peace, not War:
President John F. Kennedy establishes the Peace Corps to aid impoverished nations.

1969
"If you believe, they put a man on the moon": Neil Armstrong becomes ▩ **the first man on the moon.**

LIFE AND TIMES

tique, American women sought to erase the line between men's and women's roles in society, demanding equal pay and access to male-dominated professions. Outside the **Miss America Pageant** in 1968, women crowned a sheep "Miss America" and exuberantly threw away their bras and high heels. The sexual revolution, fueled by the introduction and commercial use of the birth control pill, focused the debate on abortion and reproductive rights. The 1973 Supreme Court decision in **Roe v. Wade** legalized abortion, but the battle between its opponents and advocates still divides the nation.

Despite civil rights legislation and anti-poverty measures passed under **President Lyndon B. Johnson's** Great Society agenda, the specter of the Vietnam War overshadowed his presidency. By the end of these tumultuous years, the nation had dropped seven million tons of bombs on former Indochina—twice the amount used against America's WWII enemies—and victory was still out of reach. Under **President Richard Nixon,** America extracted the last of its troops from Vietnam.

In 1972, five burglars were caught breaking into the Democratic National Convention Headquarters in the **Watergate** (p. 199) apartments. Their attempt to bug the offices led to a broader scandal involving Nixon himself. Aided by the information of top FBI official Mark Felt (an anonymous source known until 2005 as "Deep Throat"), *Washington Post* reporters Carl Bernstein and Bob Woodward published a series of articles that exposed Nixon's links to the scandal and ultimately led to his resignation.

By the mid-1970s, America was disillusioned with both the government and the idealistic counterculture of the previous decade. Frivolous activities, like dancing in platform shoes and powder blue suits under flashing lights—a phenomenon known as **disco**—became the mark of a generation that just wanted to have fun. Unfortunately, the international situation remained tense. The oil-rich Arab nations boycotted the US, causing an **energy crisis** in 1973 that drove up gas prices, frustrated autophile Americans, and precipitated an economic recession.

1974
The Watergate scandal causes President Richard Nixon to resign.

THE 1980S. In 1980, **Ronald Reagan,** a politically conservative former California governor and actor, was elected to the White House. Reagan knew how to give the people what they needed: money. He cut spending on public programs and lowered taxes. Though the decade's conservatives embraced social goals, the Reagan revolution was economic. **Reaganomics** cut taxes for big corporations, reduced government spending, and attempted to limit inflation, initiating a "trickle-down" effect and spurring consumption. On the foreign policy front, the straight-talking cowboy president negotiated the end of the Cold War.

THE 1990S: BILLS, BILLS, BILLS. The US remained an active force in the world through the early 1990s. **President George H.W. Bush** directed "Operation Desert Storm" in 1990 as a response to Iraq's invasion of neighboring Kuwait. The war freed Kuwait, but its popularity in the US was compromised by the economic recession that followed. In 1992, Americans elected young Democrat **Bill Clinton,** who promised a new era of government activism after years of laissez-faire rule.

1980
Stroke of genius? The Rubik's Cube becomes the hottest toy on the market.

Clinton found himself plagued with his own problems: a suspicious Arkansas real estate development project called Whitewater, an alleged extramarital affair with Gennifer Flowers, and accusations of sexual harassment from Paula Jones. Yet Clinton's public approval remained high, especially after the nation supported him in a struggle against Congressional Republicans whose attempts to balance the budget led to two government shutdowns between 1995 and 1996. Clinton was re-elected in 1996, but new scandal erupted in 1998 as reports of an inappropriate relationship between Clinton and White House intern **Monica Lewinsky** were plastered across the American media. Clinton initially denied the allegations, but later admitted that he lied, resulting in impeachment for perjury and obstruction of justice. The trial in the Senate ended with a vote for informal censure over conviction, and Clinton remained in office. Despite the scandal, 90s America saw its lowest unemployment and inflation rates in modern history, as well as increased homeownership, decreased crime and welfare rolls, and the first balanced budget in years.

The United States also saw the introduction of the **World Wide Web** in 1991, plus a vast increase in the use of **personal computers (PCs).** As the decade progressed, PCs became more prevalent and **email** jumped in popularity; by the turn of the century, 100 million Americans were using the Internet. The sudden demand for the Internet set the stage for the so-called **dot-com boom** of the 1990s. California's **Silicon Valley** played host to many of the startup Internet companies that enjoyed unbelievable success in the stock market. The dot-com bubble, however, was short-lived, and burst early on in the 21st century.

A NEW ENEMY: TERROR. On **September 11th, 2001,** the most severe terrorist attack in the history of the United States occurred when four planes were hijacked by Al-Qaeda terrorists. The site of the most violent crash was the World Trade Center in New York City, where approximately 3000 lives were taken. Since September 11th, **President George W. Bush** has initiated a **War on Terrorism** designed to identify and capture terrorists, particularly those of Al-Qaeda. Immediately following the attacks on the US, patriotism was high, and Bush received sweeping support for the US invasion of Afghanistan and the toppling of the ruling Taliban, who had supported Al-Qaeda terrorists. The War on Terrorism became more controversial at home when Attorney General John Ashcroft proposed (and Congress passed) measures like the **PATRIOT Act,** which were designed to protect the country from terrorists, but which many believe to endanger key civil liberties.

RECENT NEWS. President Bush declared war on Iraq in March 2003 to "disarm Iraq and free its people." Major fighting ended only three weeks after the American army entered Iraq, but US forces remain years later, trying to stabilize the nation in the face of bloody insurgent violence and heated domestic unrest.

It appears that the war in Iraq—which has grown to be an increasingly contentious issue at home and abroad—will be a

1981
The first personal computers hit the market.

1991
The US enters the Gulf War in the Middle East.

1997
"I'm the king of the world!" Tear-jerker *Titanic* becomes the highest grossing film of all time.

1998
Office Space: A White House sex scandal involving President Bill Clinton and intern Monica Lewinsky shocks the public.

2001
Terrorists crash two airplanes into the World Trade Center towers of New York City, killing thousands.

LIFE AND TIMES

LIFE AND TIMES

2003
President Bush calls for the invasion of Iraq.

2003
Space shuttle Columbia explodes, prompting major changes in the US's space program.

2004
A curse is lifted: The Boston Red Sox win baseball's World Series for the first time in 86 years.

focal point for presidential hopefuls in 2008, who in 2007 have begun to clamor for nominations from their respective parties. Democrats are eager to capture the presidency in the wake of the highly controversial Bush administration, with candidates Senators Hillary Clinton and Barack Obama leading an aggressive charge. Early polls show Republican favorites Fred Thompson and former New York City Mayor Rudolph Giuliani as likely candidates for the GOP nomination.

Hurricane Katrina ravaged the Deep South in late August of 2005, tearing through the region and leaving a trail of destruction in its wake. By any standard one of the costliest and deadliest hurricanes in the history of the United States, Katrina left a permanent impact on many beloved American cities, including New Orleans, which suffered as many as 53 levee breaches and causing severe flooding in approximately 80% of the city. New Orleans is currently on its way to recovery.

Global warming has also proven to be a troubling dilemma, jumping to the forefront of political discourse. In 2006, former vice-president Al Gore unveiled his groundbreaking, Oscar-winning documentary *An Inconvenient Truth*, which explores contemporary data and predictions for climate change.

PEOPLE

Considering that Native Americans make up less than 1 percent of the population, the US truly is a "country of immigrants." While the country's population is and always has been mostly white, waves of immigration of various ethnic groups at different points in history have changed US demographics. The US population is currently 76% white, 14% Hispanic and Latino, 12% African-American, and 4% Asian. Non-white populations are often concentrated in urban areas.

The **Establishment Clause** of the US Constitution states that the government and public institutions must remain neutral to religion. This "separation of church and state" ensures that Americans have the freedom to practice any religion they choose (or none at all) and still receive equal treatment from the government. Still, since the Puritans, religion has been a defining characteristic of the American ethic, and some studies have concluded that as many as 90% of Americans do have some religious affiliation. Christianity dominates: 76% of Americans identify themselves as Catholic, Protestant, Mormon, or another sect of Christianity. The so-called **Bible Belt** is composed of a number of Southern and Midwestern states where fervent Protestantism is a defining factor of local culture and politics.

English is the official language of the US, and even those who speak another language often speak English as well. American dialects vary by region, but these differences are limited to individual words and expressions. In some regions of the country—particularly California, Texas, the Southwest, and Miami—an influx of Spanish-speaking immigrants has made Spanish almost as prevalent as English. In fact, the US contains the world's fifth-largest Spanish speaking population.

CULTURE

FOOD

While fast-food chains freckle the country and trends like low-carb diets curb the nation's eating habits, authentic American food tastes best at the regional level.

Local agricultural production, immigration patterns, and cultures have resulted in unique and delicious foods that far outshine the burger-and-fries stereotype of American cuisine.

NORTHEAST. When America's English settlers landed in the Northeast, they combined staple meats and vegetables with uniquely American foodstuffs like turkey, maple syrup, clams, lobster, cranberries, and corn. Such treasures as Boston brown bread, Indian pudding, New England clam chowder, and Maine boiled lobster resulted. The shellfish in the Northeast is second to none.

SOUTH. Be prepared for some home cookin'! Fried chicken, biscuits, mashed potatoes, and collard greens are some highlights of Southeastern cuisine. Cheese grits or cornbread are a savory supplement to lunch and dinner dishes.

LOUISIANA. Chefs in New Orleans (p. 401), where creole and Cajun seasonings tantalize the taste buds, are among the best in the country. Locals and tourists alike regard crawfish, fried catfish, jambalaya (rice cooked with ham, sausage, shrimp, and herbs), and gumbo (a soup with okra, meat, and vegetables) as delicacies. The faint of heart beware: Cajun and creole cooking is notoriously spicy.

TEXAS. From beef to pork to beef again, Texans like to throw it on the grill. Eat at any of their many barbecue joints and they'll tell you that the real secret is in the sauce. For those in the mood for Mexican, *enchiladas*, *burritos*, *nachos*, and *fajitas* are scrumptious Tex-Mex options.

SOUTHWEST. Strongly influenced by Mexican cuisine, Southwestern grub relies on traditional Mexican ingredients like corn, flour, and chilies. Salsa made from tomatoes, chilies (especially New Mexico's famous hatch chilies), and *tomatillos* adds spice to most dishes, including *quesadillas*, *chiles rellenos*, and *tacos*.

CALIFORNIA. California's trend-setting status in the US extends beyond fashion and movies to fresh and natural foods. Home to acres of orange groves and avocado trees, California offers an array of organic produce mixed into everything from smoothies to salads. Grapes also grow plentifully in the numerous vineyards that line the fields of Napa Valley (p. 873) and central California, the US's illustrious wine country.

NORTHWEST. In close proximity to the arctic water frequented by halibut and salmon, many cities in the Pacific Northwest are known for superior seafood, which can be found in everything from chowder to *tacos*. If you're looking for a cold one to wash down your seafood, Portland, OR (p. 936) is the microbrewery capital of North America and has the beer to prove it.

CUSTOMS AND ETIQUETTE

TABLE MANNERS. In the US, having good table manners means quiet eating. Loud chewing, talking with food in your mouth, slurping, or burping are all considered to be offensive dining habits. Tipping etiquette generally requires a 10-15% tip at lunch and a 15-20% tip at dinner for servers at sit-down restaurants.

PUBLIC BEHAVIOR. Dress in the US tends to be more casual than in Europe. Toplessness on beaches, particularly by women, is a grave fashion faux pas. Many establishments require customers to wear a shirt and shoes. The most acceptable forms of public affection are hugging and holding hands; kissing in public will usually attract some uncomfortable stares. Although most cities are tolerant of homosexuality, gay or lesbian couples should be aware that they may receive unwanted attention for public displays of affection, especially in rural areas.

LIFE AND TIMES

GESTURES. One of the most offensive gestures in the US is extending the middle finger at someone. Known as "giving the finger" or even "flipping the bird," this gesture is considered rude and obscene. A "thumbs up" gesture, though, is a sign of approval. It is also a widely recognized signal for hitchhiking, which *Let's Go* does not recommend.

THE ARTS

It did not take long for hearty American individualism to make its mark on the global canon, previously dominated by age-old European traditions. From the 19th-century Transcendentalist literature of New England to the unique musical stylings of bluegrass and jazz, America has established itself time and again as an innovator in the world of creative arts.

LITERATURE

THE FIRST FEW PAGES. The first best-seller printed in America, the *Bay Psalm Book*, was published in Cambridge, MA, in 1640. Very few enduring classics were created until the early 1800s, when artists began to explore the unique American experience in their writing. **James Fenimore Cooper's** *Last of the Mohicans* (1826), **Nathaniel Hawthorne's** *The Scarlet Letter* (1850), and **Herman Melville's** *Moby Dick* (1851)—American classics that have stood the test of time—all feature strong individualists who navigate the rugged American landscape. By the mid-19th century, the work of **New England Transcendentalists** like **Henry David Thoreau** *(Walden,* 1854*)* and **Ralph Waldo Emerson** *(Nature,* 1836*)* embodied a spirit of anti-materialism by focusing on self-reflection and a retreat into nature. **Walt Whitman** promoted an innovative style of poetry with his revolutionary free verse expressing both his distaste for the conditions of the 19th century and his idealistic views about American democracy. Later in the century, **Mark Twain** became one of America's most beloved storytellers with his homespun tales out of Hannibal, MO. His novel *The Adventures of Huckleberry Finn* (1885) uses a young boy's journey to express social criticism and glorify the human spirit.

Literature also provided 19th-century American women the opportunity to express themselves and to comment critically on contemporary society. In 1852, **Harriet Beecher Stowe** published *Uncle Tom's Cabin*, a depiction of slavery that, according to some scholars, contributed to the outbreak of the Civil War and the abolitionist movement. Poet **Emily Dickinson** secretly scribbled away in her native Amherst, MA, home; unfortunately, her untitled and unpunctuated verses weren't discovered until after her death in 1886.

EARLY 20TH-CENTURY EXPLORATIONS. Amidst the economic prosperity of the 1920s, a reflective, self-centered movement fomented in American literature in response to changing cultural values. **F. Scott Fitzgerald's** works *(The Great Gatsby)* portray restless individuals who are financially secure but unfulfilled by their conspicuous consumption. Scarred by the massive destruction caused by WWI mechanization, many American writers of the **Lost Generation**—including Fitzgerald, **Ernest Hemingway** *(The Old Man and the Sea)*, **T.S. Eliot** ("The Love Song of J. Alfred Prufrock"), **Ezra Pound,** and **e.e. cummings**—moved abroad. This group's sophisticated works were enlightened by their expat status, which gave them a platform from which to convey an increasing disillusionment with the contemporary American experience. The **Harlem Renaissance,** a convergence of African-American artistic and political action in New York City, was spurred by the **Great Migration,** a large-scale African-American migration from the rural South to the urban North, and it fed off the excitement of the Jazz Age. **Langston Hughes** *(Montage of a Dream Deferred)*, **Nella Larsen** *(Quicksand)*, and **Zora Neale Hur-**

ston *(Their Eyes Were Watching God)* brought an awareness of black talent and creativity to a broader audience as they struggled to define African-American identity and the black experience in America. The Harlem Renaissance also saw the rise of more radical black intellectualism led by **Marcus Garvey,** champion of the **Pan-African** movement, and **Alain Locke,** who wrote the essay "The New Negro."

In the 1930s and 40s, as America struggled to recover from the Great Depression, the plight of decaying agricultural life and faltering industry of the Deep South and West began to infiltrate literature. **William Faulkner** *(The Sound and the Fury)* juxtaposed avant-garde stream-of-consciousness techniques with stories rooted in the social decay of the rural South. Nobel Prize recipient **John Steinbeck** is best known for his 1939 novel *The Grapes of Wrath*, which depicts the condition of migrant laborers heading from the Great Plains to California in the wake of the Great Depression. The plays of **Tennessee Williams** *(A Streetcar Named Desire)* portray family dynamics within uprooted lower-class Southern families. **Clifford Odets's** play *Waiting for Lefty (1935)*, detailing the plight of frustrated factory workers, was a grassroots hit, and audiences often joined with the actors in chanting the play's final lines, "Strike! Strike!" In his remarkable autobiography, *Black Boy* (1945), **Richard Wright** recounts growing up in the Jim Crow South.

POST-WAR MALAISE. In the conformist 1950s, literature provided an outlet for commentary on America's underlying social problems. **Ralph Ellison's** *Invisible Man*, published in 1952, confronted the division between white and black identities in America. In 1955, **Vladimir Nabokov,** a Russian émigré, redefined literary style for a whole generation of writers with his controversial story about unconventional love between a gnarly old man and his prepubescent young protégé, *Lolita*. **Gwendolyn Brooks,** the first black writer to win a Pulitzer Prize, published intense poetry highlighting social problems like abortion, gangs, and juvenile delinquency. Members of the **Beat Generation,** led by cult heroes **Jack Kerouac** *(On the Road)* and **Allen Ginsberg** *(Howl)*, lived wildly and espoused a free-thinking attitude. Playwright **Arthur Miller** delved into the American psyche with *Death of a Salesman* (1949), in which he explored the frailty of the American dream. He later wrote *The Crucible*, a play detailing the Salem witch-hunts, as a critique of Sen. McCarthy's communist "witch-hunts" (p. 59).

As Americans increasingly questioned social conventions in the 1960s, writers began to explore more unorthodox material. **Anne Sexton** revealed the depths of her own mental breakdown in *Live or Die* (1966), while **Sylvia Plath** paved the way for feminist authors, exposed her psychological deterioration, and foreshadowed her own suicide in *The Bell Jar* (1963). The essays and stories of **James Baldwin** *(The Fire Next Time)* warned both white and black Americans about the self-destructive implications of racial hatred. **Flannery O'Connor** exposed the eerie, grotesque underbelly of the contemporary South in short stories such as "A Good Man is Hard to Find" (1953).

The search for identity and the attempt to reconcile artistic and social agendas continued into the 1970s and 80s. **E.L. Doctorow's** *Ragtime* (1975) evokes vibrant images of turn-of-the-century America, weaving together historical and fictional figures. **Toni Morrison** *(Beloved)* won the Nobel Prize for her visceral interpretations of the tension between gender, ethnic, and cultural identities. **Don DeLillo's** *White Noise* (1985) continues the American absurdist tradition and, using both humor and uncanny insight, delves into America's obsession with mortality. Many stories have also focused on the fast pace and commercialism of modern society. In *American Psycho* (1991), **Bret Easton Ellis** exposes the conspicuous consumption of New York City in the 1980s, while the plays of **David Mamet** *(Glengarry Glen Ross)* are known for confronting the gritty underside of American business. Among more recent authors, the prolific **Philip Roth** *(American Pastoral)* contin-

LIFE AND TIMES

ues to disassemble the American dream. **David Sedaris** *(Me Talk Pretty One Day)* draws raves for his hilarious, self-deprecating columns and essays about his childhood, family life, and his experience as an American living in France. Distressingly young **Jonathan Safran Foer's** newest novel, *Extremely Loud and Incredibly Close*, explores the post-9/11 world and a young person's place in it.

MUSIC

The United States have given birth to a plethora of musical genres, whose styles and songs have intermingled to produce the many distinct styles that can be heard today. **Scott Joplin** meshed African-American harmony and rhythm with classical European style to develop the first American piano form, **ragtime.** From this rich, upbeat, piano-banging dance music of the 19th century to the Deep South's mournful blues, early African-American music defined **soul.** The 1950s saw a new, "edgy" style of music arise from America's youth: **rock 'n' roll.** Soul and gospel music evolved into R&B, jazz, funk, and later, hip-hop, while rock exploded in the 60s and 70s into today's genre of "classic rock." Recent decades have ushered in new styles of rap, metal, grunge alternative, and teeny-bopper "bubblegum" pop.

SINGIN' THE BLUES. As with ragtime, black Southerners were primarily responsible for the blues, which was originally a blend of Northwest African slave calls and Native American song and verse forms. Blues songs were popularized by legendary "father of the blues" **W.C. Handy.** His "St. Louis Blues" remains one of the most recorded songs ever. As Southern blacks migrated to industrial centers during the early 20th century, the blues, augmented by the contributions of women like **Mamie Smith, Billie Holiday,** and **Bessie Smith,** found an audience in the North. The blues heavily influenced the development of other popular American musical styles, most notably jazz and rock 'n' roll.

AND ALL THAT JAZZ. Ragtime, blues, and military brass combined in New Orleans in the early 20th century to create America's classical music, jazz. Its emphasis on improvisation and unique tonal and harmonic rules distinguished it from previous genres. The work of all-time jazz greats like **Louis Armstrong, Dizzy Gillespie,** and **Ella Fitzgerald** influenced the work of later classical composers; **Leonard Bernstein's** classical orchestrations and **George Gershwin's** theatrical style can both trace their roots and distinctly American sound to the jazz tradition. Early jazz also led to the era of big band music, during which the legendary **Duke Ellington** and the swing orchestra of **Glenn Miller** reigned supreme.

COUNTRY ROADS, TAKE ME HOME. Country music has its roots in the Appalachian Mountains, among a poor rural white population that put a new spin on its ancestral European folk traditions. Sentimental, often spiritual lyrics were combined with simple melodies to create a characteristically honest American sound. The genre owes much of its attitude and sound to classic heroes: **Hank Williams** cultivated an air of tragic, honky-tonk mystique, while **Johnny Cash** left his mark with brazen, devil-may-care honesty. Commercially, country didn't catch on until it was given a boost by radio and Nashville's famous 1930s program the **Grand Ole Opry,** which allowed country artists like **Willie Nelson** and **Emmylou Harris** to capture both Southern and Northern audiences. Recently, country artists like **Garth Brooks, Tim McGraw,** and **LeAnn Rimes,** as well as country-pop crossovers like the **Dixie Chicks** and **Faith Hill,** have combined to bring modern country into the mainstream.

Folk music, a related genre, has often embraced political and social activism through its lyrics and spirit. **Woody Guthrie's** music touched upon issues of patriotism amidst the Great Depression ("This Land is Your Land"). Thanks to artists like **Bob Dylan** and **Joan Baez,** folk music became more popular in the 1960s, speaking to social protesters across the nation. During the hippie generation, people used songs like "We Shall Overcome" and "Where Have all the Flowers Gone?" to express their opinions about relevant issues and to unify their protests. Folk survives today in coffee shops, on street corners, and in musicians like **Dar Williams.**

PUT ANOTHER DIME IN THE JUKEBOX, BABY. No one can say exactly how rock 'n' roll was started, but it grew out of an attempt to reconcile African-American rhythm and blues with the traditionally white country western music. **Elvis Presley** was the crowned "King," after he became the first artist to cross the racial barrier in music, uniting country and R&B. His rock kingdom, **Graceland** (p. 328), is a popular attraction for Memphis tourists. During the 1950s and 60s rock 'n' roll's driving, danceable rhythms, rebellious attitude, and fascination with electric instruments dominated the popular music charts. As teenagers looked for something more exciting and daring to express their style, rock 'n' roll reflected the new post-WWII optimism and innocence throughout America. The genre has produced most of America's more famous music icons—before Elvis, there was **Chuck Berry** and then **Jerry Lee Lewis,** who ushered in a new era of poodle skirts and slicked-back hair. In the 60s and 70s, rock used bluegrass melodies, classic beats, and the wailing guitar solos made famous by **Jimi Hendrix** and **Led Zeppelin** to create classic rock, a genre that lives on with artists like **Bruce Springsteen** and **Aerosmith.**

MO' MUSIC. In 1961 **Berry Gordy, Jr.** started a little company in Detroit that revolutionized American music. **Motown** was an all-black record label that produced hit artists like **The Supremes, The Temptations, Marvin Gaye,** and **The Jackson Five,** which provided **Michael Jackson's** first entry into the music world. Descended from gospel and the blues, the unmistakable "Motown sound" combined smooth lyrics with funk backing, sparking a new genre of soul music. Unlike previous African-American musical acts, Motown artists did not strive to integrate their sound into the white music world. Rather, Motown singers were the first African-American musicians to infuse their music with a socio-political message. Listeners changed **Martha and the Vandellas'** song "Dancing in the Street" from a party song into a theme song for civil rights riots in 1967 Detroit. **James Brown's** song "Say it Loud, I'm Black and I'm Proud" (1968) espoused black power and black pride. Today's R&B, however, has drifted far from its roots and is often inseparable from hip-hop. Artists like **R. Kelly** and **Beyoncé** have led R&B's charge toward hip-hop and the mainstream pop music. R&B's links to Motown are now barely visible.

DISCO BALLS, HAIR BANDS, AND GANGSTA RAP. The 1970s will be forever remembered as the era of disco. Disco divas like **Gloria Gaynor** ("I Will Survive") and funk bands like **The Bee-Gees** dominated American nightlife and fostered a culture that celebrated dancing, drugs, and excess. The 1980s witnessed a rap revolution, spawned by East Coast stars **Public Enemy, Run-DMC,** and the **Beastie Boys.** The 80s also ushered in the popularity of "hair bands" like **Poison** and punk rockers like **The Ramones,** not to mention that little entertainer named **Madonna.** In the early 90s, grunge music escaped from the garage and broke into the national spotlight largely because of Seattle's **Nirvana** and **Pearl Jam.** The West Coast birthed the "gangsta rap" movement (Dr. Dre, Snoop Dogg) in the 90s, prompting much debate over the promotion of violence and excessive misogyny in its lyrics. The legendary East Coast-West Coast feud between NYC's **Notorious B.I.G.** and L.A.'s **Tupac Shakur** split the rap community and ended with both rappers' deaths six months apart in 1996-97. **Eminem** rocketed to international stardom with provocative lyrics and outlandish persona, **50 Cent** stormed onto the scene as a tough-talking, big-selling bully, and **Jay-Z** cemented a place in the up-and-coming world of contemporary rap.

DIRTY POP. Pop-Punk broke into the mainstream during the 1990s with **Green Day's** rise to fame. With the help of artists like **Blink-182** and **Good Charlotte,** this toned-down and upbeat version of the 80's heavy punk has continued to have a major presence in young America's iPod. But the late 90s and the new millennium have been primarily dominated by a resurgence of bubblegum pop and dance tunes. Barely 16 years old when their first album was released, the **New Kids on the Block** spearheaded the boy-band phenomenon. The MTV generation of consumer teens has sustained the popularity of young superstars like **Britney Spears** and **Justin Timberlake.** Although some purists criticize the genre for lacking real musical substance, pop's prominence on the Billboard charts indicates that young fans couldn't care less. **Kelly Clarkson,** winner of the first season of the reality TV competition *American Idol*, exemplifies pop's stronghold in American culture.

GREAT AMERICAN COMPOSERS. It may lag behind some European countries in famous orchestral composers per capita, but the US has had its fair share of musical heavy-hitters. One of the earliest American composers was **William Billings,** a Boston-born composer of patriotic hymns such as *Chester* (1778). The 19th century played host to the "March King," **John Philip Sousa,** whose work includes the US's official march, *The Stars and Stripes Forever*, which is a favorite at Fourth of July celebrations. **Charles Ives** moonlighted as a composer, winning the 1947 Pulitzer Prize for Music for his *Third Symphony.* **George Gershwin** *(Rhapsody in Blue)* made his mark in classical composition during the early 20th century before extending his talents to Broadway and Hollywood. He later teamed up with his brother, **Ira Gershwin,** to write and compose classics like the operetta *Porgy and Bess.* Born in 1900, when the music world had not yet fully recognized Americans as great composers, **Aaron Copland** is considered by many to be the pioneer of American classical music. He is best known for his concert *(Appalachian Spring)* and ballet *(Billy the Kid)* works, but he also composed jazz and movie soundtracks. Perhaps the most influential classical composer of the 20th century, **Leonard Bernstein** is best known for his scores for Broadway musicals *West Side Story* and *On the Town*. He also played an important role in the increased popular acceptance of classical music. **Stephen Sondheim** learned his craft from a legend, **Oscar Hammerstein II,** and has since set the standard for Broadway musical composition. Winner of seven Tony Awards for his work on Broadway, Sondheim has also received acclaim for his big-screen compositions, and won the 1990 Academy Award for Best Original Song for *Sooner or Later.*

FILM

SILENT CINEMA AND PRE-CODE TALKIES. Before sound was wedded to image in the first "talkie"—1927's *The Jazz Singer*—silent films ruled the screen. Silent films quickly went out of fashion once sound entered the picture, and aspiring filmmakers were lured to the West Coast by incentives from the Los Angeles Chamber of Commerce, with the lure of sunshine, a potentially cheap labor force, inexpensive land for studio construction, and varied landscapes for all genres of film. By these virtues, **Hollywood, CA** quickly became the center of the movie business. In the 1920s, movie stars such as comedians **Charlie Chaplin** and **Buster Keaton,** the swashbuckling daredevil **Douglas Fairbanks,** and the hopeless romantic **Clara Bow** emerged as bankable celebrities. Films such as *Sunrise* (1927) and *The Crowd* (1928) combined innovative cinematography and compelling narratives that remain popular to this day. Early films did not ignore socially charged topics. D.W. Griffith's first American epic feature, *The Birth of a Nation*, chronicled the Civil War and its aftermath during Reconstruction. The iconoclastic film argued for white supremacy, a racist message that was met with considerable controversy and protest. In conjunction with public's visceral reaction to *The Birth of a Nation*, critics began wondering publicly about the moral value of movies and their power as a medium. In an effort to prevent what seemed like imminent federal regulation, filmmakers created the **Motion Pictures Producers and Distributors of America (MPPDA),** a self-regulating board that would address these pertinent concerns internally.

CLASSICALLY COOL. The film industry's success led to the expansion of the **studio system.** Giant Hollywood production houses like **Paramount, MGM, 20th Century Fox,** and **Warner** exerted their influence over selected films, budgets, scripts, actors, writers, and directors, editing, scoring and publicity. American film's **golden age** took place during the height of the studio era, when Hollywood's four major studios standardized and dominated films. **Victor Fleming's** *Gone with the Wind* (1939), a Civil War epic, was the first large-scale movie extravaganza, redefining the bounds of cinematic scope. **Frank Capra,** who explored American values in films like *It's a Wonderful Life* (1946) and *Mr. Smith Goes to Washington* (1939), brought a conscience to entertainment. Michael Curtiz's *Casablanca* (1942), starring **Humphrey Bogart,** was a classic cinematic romance with a patriotic and politicized background. In 1941, **Orson Welles** unveiled his intricate masterpiece, *Citizen Kane,* a landmark work that revolutionized the potential of narrative structure. Fantasy dominated ticket sales: **Walt Disney's** animated *Snow White* (1937), *Pinocchio* (1940), *Dumbo* (1941), and Fleming's *The Wizard of Oz* (1939) kept producers well-fed, while *Frankenstein* (1931) and *King Kong* (1933) were wildly successful as well.

EPICS, HORROR, AND THE CELEBRITY. Heightened tensions with the Soviet Union led to paranoid witch-hunt investigations conducted by the **House of Representatives' Un-American Activities Committee (HUAC),** which aimed to root out suspected communists in Hollywood but ended up repressing liberal themes in films. The resulting communist anxiety manifested itself in films concerning invading armies of evil aliens such as *Invasion of the Body Snatchers* (1956) and *The War of the Worlds* (1953). Competition from television prompted innovations and gimmicks such as cine-rama, 3-D, Smell-O-Vision, and CinemaScope to bring audiences back to the cinema. The revival of epic films like *The Ten Commandments* (1956), *Ben-Hur* (1959), and *Spartacus* (1960) took advantage of the new big-screen format. Meanwhile, **Alfred Hitchcock** created horror films like *Vertigo* (1958) and *Psycho* (1960) that still evoke jumps and screams from viewers.

The 1950s also saw the emergence of a cult of glamour surrounding the most luminous celebrities and creating the star system. Cloaked in glitz and scandal, sex symbols **Marilyn Monroe, James Dean** *(Rebel Without a Cause),* **Elizabeth Taylor,** and **Rock Hudson** drew audiences to movies by name recognition alone. These stars, along with actors **Marlon Brando** *(A Streetcar Named Desire)* and **Audrey Hepburn** *(Breakfast at Tiffany's),* brought their own mystique to the screen, and cemented cinema's omnipresence in America's consciousness. The phenomenon of the Hollywood celebrity is alive and well today.

THE NEW CLASSICS. The 1960s and early 70s saw widespread social upheaval involving political, sexual, social tensions. Adapting to the demands of younger, more liberal audiences, studios enlisted directors influenced by the French New Wave as well as artists from other media to direct features. With studios more willing to gamble, and a new movie ratings board—the **Motion Picture Association of America (MPAA)**—to replace censorship, the work of a number of innovative filmmakers began to enter the mainstream. **Stanley Kubrick's** *Dr. Strangelove* (1964), *2001: A Space Odyssey* (1968), and *A Clockwork Orange* (1971) brought a literary importance to filmmaking. **Dennis Hopper's** *Easy Rider* (1969) depicted counter-cultural youth rebellion and disillusionment with the American dream, while acclaimed *To Kill A Mockingbird* (1962) and *The Manchurian Candidate* (1962) established film as a means of expressing social and political criticism. **Blax-**

LIFE AND TIMES

ploitation, a new genre that emerged in the early 1970s sensationalized portrayals of urban African-Americans with films like *Shaft*.

Throughout the 1970s, experimentalism largely gave way to less embellished treatment of equally serious issues. Film-schooled directors like **Martin Scorsese** *(Taxi Driver)*, **Francis Ford Coppola** *(The Godfather)*, and **Michael Cimino** *(The Deer Hunter)* brought technical skill to their exploration of the darker side of humanity. An influx of foreign filmmakers, like Milos Forman *(One Flew Over the Cuckoo's Nest)* and Roman Polański *(Chinatown)*, rejuvenated creativity in American film.

PAYING THE BILLS. Driven by the mass global distribution of American cinema and the development of high-tech special effects, the late 1970s and 80s witnessed the birth of the **blockbuster. Steven Spielberg's** *Jaws* kicked off the trend in 1973 by piloting the now standard advertising methods of TV previews, movie merchandise, media stunts, and theme music publicity. Following this breakout success, Spielberg produced *E.T.* (1982) and *Raiders of the Lost Ark* (1981). **George Lucas** followed the special effects trend with his *Star Wars* trilogy in the late 70s and early 80s. Though such films were criticized for a reliance on effects, they almost single-handedly restored Hollywood as America's choice for entertainment.

Despite Hollywood's increasing commercialism, quite a bit of highly imaginative work emerged during this period, including Rob Reiner's *This Is Spinal Tap* (1984), a hilarious mockumentary of popular music, and David Lynch's *Blue Velvet* (1986), a disturbing look at the primal terror beneath the tranquil surface of suburbia. Blockbuster productions swept through the 1990s, with high-budget money makers like the dinosaur thriller *Jurassic Park* (1993), and the decadent love story *Titanic* (1997) drawing the largest crowds. Recently, a revolution in digital film technology has spawned such hits as *Shrek* (2001), *Finding Nemo* (2003), *The Incredibles* (2004), and *Ratatouille* (2007) that cater to children and adult audiences with lush computer animation and layered jokes that combine pop culture with whimsical farce.

INDEPENDENT(LY) AWESOME. The recognition of independent, or **indie,** films—films that are either produced independently of any major studio or at least do not follow standard studio conventions—marks cinema's most interesting turn in the last several years. Brothers **Joel and Ethan Coen** have created some of the most creative and original work of late, including the gruesome comedy *Fargo* (1996) and the hilarious, off-beat *The Big Lebowski* (1998). **Quentin Tarantino's** cool action *(Reservoir Dogs, Pulp Fiction)*, **Paul Thomas Anderson's** emotionally charged and frequently sprawling storytelling style *(Boogie Nights, Magnolia)*, and **Wes Anderson's** dark, quirky humor *(Rushmore, The Royal Tenenbaums, The Life Aquatic with Steve Zissou)* have all infused American cinema with fresh, new life. Recently, however, films have been tackling heavier issues. **Michael Moore's** ultra-liberal documentaries *Bowling for Columbine, Fahrenheit 9/11,* and *Sicko* and Mel Gibson's graphic and highly controversial film *The Passion of the Christ* are only a few examples. Small-budget documentaries including Moore's queries into American culture and politics, **Morgan Spurlock's** fast-food exposé *Supersize Me* (2004), **Jeffrey Blitz's** *Spellbound* (2004), which chronicles the dark side of spelling bees, and **Al Gore's** *An Inconvenient Truth* (2006), which illuminates the graveness of global warming, have also gained popularity recently.

FINE ARTS

American art has often been dismissed as a poor reflection of European trends. Despite this stereotype, it has a rich history grounded in the country's expansion. Its raw and uncontrolled nature is reflected not only in the grandiose 19th-century landscape paintings that capture the beauty of the untamed West, but also in the unwieldy lines and shapes of American 20th-century abstract expressionism.

PAINTING. Portraiture flourished in colonial America. John Singleton Copley, Charles Willson Peale, and Gilbert Stuart rendered intimate likenesses of iconic revolutionary figures from Paul Revere to George Washington. In the first half of the 19th century, Thomas Cole and Asher B. Durand produced ambitious landscapes with didactic overtones. Cole was one of the earliest artists in the **Hudson River School,** a group of painters who combined expressive depictions of nature with ideas about the divine. Later, **Winslow Homer's** vibrant watercolors captured the wild side of nature in sweeping seascapes, while softer American Impressionists like Childe Hassam depicted the effects of light in New England city scenes. The turn of the 20th century saw an emphasis on Realism and the depiction of urban life. The group of painters known as the **Ash Can School,** led by Robert Henri, promoted "art for art's sake." By the 1940s, **Abstract Expressionism** was reborn in the US. Country-wide anxiety over international unrest and the threat of war bore heavily on the American psyche. In drip paintings and color field works, painters like **Jackson Pollock** and **Mark Rothko** reflected the ironic mix of swaggering confidence and frenetic insecurity that characterized Cold War America. Ushering in the age of **Pop Art, Roy Lichtenstein** and **Andy Warhol** used mass-produced, cartoonish images to satirize the icons of American popular culture. Art that enshrined the mundane blurred the boundaries between "high culture" and "mass culture," and became symbolic of the growing **postmodernist** movement. The 1980s art boom, centered around private galleries in New York City and L.A., ushered in a decade of slick, idyllic paintings and the kitschy sculptures of **Jeff Koons.**

PHOTOGRAPHY. Beginning in the early 20th century, photography became the medium of choice for artists with a social conscience. **Jakob Riis** and **Lewis Hine** photographed the urban poor and child laborers, while **Walker Evans** and **Dorothea Lange** captured destitute farmers during the Great Depression. **Ansel Adams** used his photographs of rugged Western landscapes as tools in his quest for natural conservation in the 40s, 50s, and 60s. **Robert Frank's** snapshots caught the social transitions and tensions of 1960s America. In the 1970s, photography came into its own as back-to-basics 35mm photographs pushed the boundaries of defined art.

THE MEDIA

America is wired. Images, sounds, and stories from the television, radio, Internet, newspapers, and magazines infiltrate every aspect of the American lifestyle. Fads have been popularized and fortunes have been made thanks solely to the power of mass media, but because of its pervasive power, constant debate rages over who should be held responsible for the media's content. Despite controversy about policing the industry, American consumption of new media continues to grow.

TELEVISION. TV sets are found in over 98% of US homes. Competition between the five national **networks** (ABC, CBS, CW, Fox, NBC), cable television, and satellite TV has triggered exponential growth in TV culture. Network prime time (8-11 EST) often features America's most popular shows like courtroom drama *Law and Order* (NBC), desert island drama, *Lost* (ABC), and hospital drama *Grey's Anatomy* (ABC). **Cable TV** provides special-interest channels that cover every subject from cooking to sports to science fiction. **Premium stations** air recently released movies along with regular programming; one favorite is HBO, which boasts the fame-oriented *Entourage* and Showtime's *Weeds*. Travelers will find that some hotel rooms come equipped with basic cable, while others offer premium stations and pay-per-view channels.

Although **reality television** began with MTV's *"The Real World"* in 1992, it surged to what seemed to be its peak after *Survivor's* (CBS) popularity in the early 21st century, and it has made a comeback with such ultra-popular shows *American Idol* (Fox) and **Donald Trump's** *The Apprentice* (NBC). On *Idol*, contestants compete for a recording contract and instant fame, while Trump's contestants compete for the chance to work for "The Donald" himself. The father of modern reality television, *Survivor*, has slipped considerably since its early days. Still, the cable station MTV seems to have gotten it right: teenagers still spend hours glued to reality programs *The Real World* and *Road Rules*.

Comedy programs also dominate much of TV-land. The long-running *Saturday Night Live* (NBC) is a perennial favorite and has helped launch the careers of comedians **Will Ferrell** and **Al Franken,** while late-night television is sustained by the comic stylings of talk-show hosts like David Letterman on *The Late Show* (CBS) and Conan O'Brien on *Late Night* (NBC). Recently, fake news correspondents who sensationalize political bloopers and provide social commentary like *The Colbert Report* with **Stephen Colbert** and *The Daily Show* with **Jon Stewart** have generated an avid viewership. Daytime programming is less watched and tends to fill the hours with tawdry **soap operas** and **talk shows.**

Television is the point of entry to **worldwide news** for most Americans. Twenty-four hour news coverage is available on cable stations such as **CNN, MSNBC,** and the **Fox News Channel.** Each major network presents local and national nightly news (usually at 5 and/or 11pm EST), while prime-time "newsmagazines" like *60 Minutes* (CBS), *Dateline* (NBC), and *20/20* (ABC) specialize in investigative reports and special-interest stories. **ESPN,** a cable channel, gives viewers "all sports, all the time" and has capitalized on America's sporting obsession with the ever-popular *SportsCenter*, the definitive sports news show. The **Public Broadcasting System (PBS)** is commercial-free and funded by viewer contributions, the federal government, and corporate grants. Its repertoire includes educational children's shows like *Sesame Street*—America's seminal childhood TV-watching experience—as well as nature programs, mystery shows, and British comedies.

PRINT. Despite the onset of sophisticated technologies like TV and the Internet, Americans still cherish the feel of glossy pages and the smell of newsprint. Newsstands still crowd city corners and transportation terminals throughout the country. Publications cover all areas of society, culture, and politics; whether it's for lounging away a Sunday afternoon at home or passing time in a doctor's waiting room, print media is holding its ground against digital competitors.

Ranging from trashy tabloids like the *National Enquirer* to the most influential and respected news breakers, American print media is notably diverse. Often subject to criticism for being too liberal, or sensational, it remains generally accurate and accountable. Some of the nation's most well-respected newspapers include *The New York Times* and *The Washington Post*, though every major city has at least one major paper. Women's magazines such as *Cosmopolitan* and men's magazines like *GQ* center on sex and fashion. *The New Yorker* amuses subscribers with short stories, essays, and cartoons. Entertainment magazines like *People* and *US Weekly* chronicle celebrity gossip, while *Rolling Stone* focuses on music. Financial wizards swear by *The Wall Street Journal* and *Forbes*. Sports buffs troll the pages of *Sports Illustrated*, the country's preeminent sports magazine.

RADIO. Before television transformed American culture, the radio was the country's primary source of entertainment and news. Classic comedy programs like *The Jack Benny Show* and the crackly news coverage of **Edward R. Murrow** amused and informed Americans for decades. WDIA, an all black radio station in the late 1940s, expounded ideas about religion and politics and was instrumental in uniting the African-American community in the years leading up to the civil rights movement. Even though television's moving images and crisper sounds have reduced radio's earlier, widespread popularity, it remains a treasured medium in America's car-dependent culture. Radio is generally divided into AM and FM; talk radio comprises most of the low-frequency AM slots, while the high-powered FM stations feature most of the music. Each broadcaster owns a four-letter call-name, with "W" as the first letter for those east of the Mississippi River (as in WJMN), and "K" to the west (as in KPFA).

The more intellectually-minded listen to **National Public Radio (NPR).** Full of classical music and social pundits, NPR disseminates information about everything from general news on *Morning Edition* to car repair on the irreverent but useful *Car Talk.* Supplying the country's regional needs, local stations give up-to-the-minute news reports and air a wide range of music.

INTERNET. In the late 90s, the Internet—which got its humble start at the hands of the US government as a small networking device—exploded with the mass production of personal computers and software by **Apple** and **Microsoft** and the subsequent creation of user-friendly services like **amazon.com** and **America Online (AOL).** The rise of the Internet has firmly cemented email in the lives of most Americans, and such simple, free hosts as **hotmail.com** and **gmail.com** seem to be here to stay.

Since then, the Internet has been steadily increasing in importance. News-hungry intellectuals can find to-the-minute updates on all the stories fit to print on **cnn.com** and **nytimes.com,** making radio, television, and print seem less important. The rise of sophisticated search engines like **google.com** made the burgeoning digital world possible, along with the preeminence of flashy and lucrative Internet start-up companies.

The turn of the millennium brought with it the expansion of the Internet, revolutionizing the way Americans watch TV and listen to music. **Napster,** a slick program designed to let users "share" music for free, burst onto the web in the late 90s only to be quashed by music companies, who demanded legislation outlawing file-sharing. The Internet, however, quickly created other options: **iTunes,** for instance, allows users to buy music, movies, and TV shows for immediate download.

SPORTS AND RECREATION

For Americans, professional sports are inseparable from commercialism and regional allegiances. Dressed in colorful jerseys and bloated with cheap beer, Americans fill stadiums or lounge at home to cheer on their local teams. The best athletes come from all over the world to compete in America's biggest sports, providing for intense competition and thrilling entertainment.

BASEBALL. The slow-paced, tension-inducing game of baseball captures the hearts of dreaming Little League children and earns its place as America's national pastime. Baseball in the US centers on the **Major League Baseball (MLB)** season, which lasts from spring training in early March until October. Every fall, the **World Series** garners national attention by matching the league's top two teams.

(AMERICAN) FOOTBALL. Not for the weak, football combines the toughness of boxing with the athleticism of basketball. Nowhere is the commercialism of American sports more spectacularly displayed than at the annual **Super Bowl.** Every January, the **National Football League (NFL)** season ends with a championship featuring the league's two best teams and million-dollar commercial campaigns.

BASKETBALL. The professional basketball teams making up the **National Basketball Association (NBA)** hail from almost every major city. NBA players have come a long way since the first teams, who played with peach baskets and Converse All-

Star sneakers. Today, professional basketball games are fast-paced, aerial shows. Women have gotten into the game with the **WNBA**, a young but exciting league.

ICE HOCKEY. The **National Hockey League (NHL)**, comprised of both American and Canadian teams, features great ice hockey and some of the best fights in professional sports. Recent rule changes encouraging higher scoring and implementing shoot-outs replacing ties have improved the game. As NHL teams vie for the **Stanley Cup,** the tension of competition often results in crowd-pleasing team brawls.

SOCCER. **Major League Soccer (MLS)** is an up-and-coming sport that is beginning to acquire foreign talent (including David Beckham of the Los Angeles Galaxy) in an attempt to gain respect from abroad and to bolster talent. As professional American talent continues to sign with European teams, the U.S.'s status as a sleeping giant in global soccer is indisputable. Following a disappointing 2006 World Cup, the US national team seeks to improve its standing at the 2010 cup.

COLLEGE SPORTS. Sticking with their school allegiances, many Americans live and die by their college's sporting endeavors. College teams compete within regional conferences, creating fierce rivalries fueled by hordes of fanatical student and alumni supporters. Football draws the biggest crowds, and each January the National Champion is decided on a rotating basis at either the **Rose Bowl, Fiesta Bowl, Orange Bowl,** or **Sugar Bowl.** Enthusiasm for college hoops often surpasses that for the pros, and women's college basketball has become increasingly popular in recent years. Every spring, hoops fan-demonium reaches fever pitch during the NCAA tournament, fondly referred to as **March Madness.** While more and more high-school players are skipping college to play professionally, the college courts are still a great place to see the NBA superstars of tomorrow.

OTHER SPORTS. Other sports claim smaller niches of the American spectatorship. Both golf and tennis have internationally publicized tournaments known as the **US Open.** Now America's largest spectator sport, **NASCAR auto racing** draws droves of fans with the Daytona 500 and Indianapolis 500. Gamblers and boozers alike enjoy the coveted **Triple Crown** of horse racing, which is composed of the **Kentucky Derby,** the **Preakness,** and the **Belmont Stakes.**

NATIONAL HOLIDAYS

DATE (2008)	
January 1	New Year's Day
January 16	Martin Luther King, Jr. Day
February 20	Presidents Day
May 29	Memorial Day
July 4	Independence Day
September 4	Labor Day
October 9	Columbus Day
November 11	Veterans Day
November 23	Thanksgiving
December 25	Christmas Day

BEYOND TOURISM

A PHILOSOPHY FOR TRAVELERS

As a tourist, you are always a foreigner. While hostel-hopping and sightseeing can be great fun, you may want to consider going *beyond* tourism. Experiencing a foreign place through studying, volunteering, or working can help reduce that touristy stranger-in-a-strange-land feeling. Furthermore, travelers can make a positive impact on the natural and cultural environments they visit. With this Beyond Tourism chapter, *Let's Go* hopes to promote a better understanding of the US and to provide suggestions for those who want to get more than a photo album out of their travels. The "Giving Back" sidebar features also highlight regional Beyond Tourism opportunities.

Opportunities for **volunteerism** abound, with both local and international organizations. **Studying** in a new environment can be enlightening, whether through direct enrollment in a local university or in an independent research project. **Working** is a way to immerse yourself in local culture while financing your travels.

As a **volunteer** in the US, you can participate in projects either on a short-term basis or as the main component of your trip. Opportunities for volunteerism, activism, and conservation abound and can be found in cities, National Parks, and everywhere in between. Spend a few hours bringing food to the homeless (p. 76), several days building a house for a low-income family in the Mississippi Delta with Habitat for Humanity (p. 77), or months mentoring a child through Big Brothers Big Sisters of America (p. 77). Later in this chapter, we recommend organizations that will help you find the opportunities that best suit your interests, whether you're looking to pitch in for a day or a year.

Studying at a college or language program, either by enrolling in a local university or through a study-abroad program, allows for intellectual exploration while living as a "real" American student.

Travelers may also structure their trips by the **work** that they can do along the way—by taking either odd jobs or full-time stints in cities where they plan an extended visit. Regardless of whether you are looking for temporary work or something more permanent, a good place to start your search is the local newspaper, which is usually the best source of up-to-date job information. Internet search engines like **www.monster.com** are also helpful. Before signing on, be sure you have the correct visa and working papers (see **Visa Information,** p. 13).

BEYOND TOURISM HIGHLIGHTS

DISCOVER the natural beauty of the Southwest while volunteering at Utah's Canyonlands National Park (p. 80).

IMMERSE yourself in architect Paolo Soleri's experimental community while working and learning about ecologically-friendly architecture (p. 81).

STUDY at one of America's private or public universities and experience the life of an American college student (p. 82).

VOLUNTEERING

Volunteering can be a powerful and fulfilling experience, especially when combined with the thrill of traveling in a new place. The sheer size of the US guarantees that no matter where you are and what you're interested in, there will be a way for you to get involved. In urban areas, mentoring and literacy programs and organizations that work to combat hunger and homelessness offer an abundance of volunteer opportunities. Environmental conservation has become a popular activity for visitors to the many national and state parks. Search engines like **www.volunteermatch.org** are a useful resource for finding local opportunities.

Most people who volunteer in the US do so on a short-term basis, at organizations that make use of drop-in or once-a-week volunteers. The best way to find opportunities that match your interests and schedule may be to check with local or national volunteer centers like the ones listed below. Social outreach work is generally the most common short-term volunteer activity—it can take as little as an afternoon to make a difference in a community.

Those looking for longer, more intensive volunteer opportunities usually go through a parent organization that takes care of logistical details and often provides a group environment and support system—for a fee. There are two main types of organizations—religious and non-sectarian—although there are rarely restrictions on participation for either.

> **WHY PAY MONEY TO VOLUNTEER?** Many volunteers are surprised to learn that some organizations require large fees or "donations." While this may seem ridiculous at first glance, such fees often keep the organization afloat, in addition to covering administrative expenses and airfare, room, and board for the volunteers. Other organizations must rely on private donations and government subsidies. If you're concerned about how a program spends its fees, request an annual report or financial account. A reputable organization won't refuse to inform you of how volunteer money is spent. Pay-to-volunteer programs might be a good idea for young travelers who are looking for more support and structure (such as pre-arranged transportation and housing), or anyone who would rather not create a volunteer experience from scratch.

URBAN ISSUES

Urban communities in the US face distinct and varied crises, such as hunger, homelessness, and lack of affordable health care. There are numerous opportunities to get involved in these communities and make a difference. Interested individuals can find short- and long-term volunteer opportunities through volunteer search engines, such as **www.volunteersolutions.org** and **www.networkforgood.org,** that help individuals locate organizations that fit their interests and locations.

America's Second Harvest, 35 E. Wacker Dr., #2000, Chicago, IL 60601 (☎800-771-2303 or 312-263-2303; www.2ndharvest.org). As the US's largest hunger organization, Second Harvest oversees more than 200 food banks throughout the country and feeds more than 23 million people each year. Sort and repackage salvaged food, prepare and serve food at a shelter, or tutor children.

Common Ground, 14 E. 28th Street., New York, NY 10016 (☎212-389-9300; www.commonground.org). Common Ground community seeks to "solve homelessness" through its programs in Manhattan, the Hudson Valley, and Connecticut. Volunteers work to move disadvantaged individuals from the streets to shelters, and finally into homes built and maintained by Common Ground. The organization also shapes policy and creates preventative programs to fight homelessness.

National Coalition for the Homeless, 1012 14th St. NW, #600, Washington, D.C. 20005 (☎202-737-6444; www.nationalhomeless.org). Maintains a website with listings of local homeless assistance programs and shelters, food banks, hospitals, and advocacy groups across the country.

BEYOND TOURISM

SCI International Voluntary Service, 5505 Walnut Level Rd., Crozet, VA 22932 (☎206-350-6585; www.sci-ivs.org). Service Civil International organizes teams for 2- to 4-week work camps or 3- to 12-month volunteer postings on grassroots projects. Most camps also include opportunities to study social justice issues. Volunteers must be over 16. Fees run from $115, and include SCI-IVS membership, housing, and meals; additional fees apply to applicants who register through international affiliates.

RURAL DEVELOPMENT

America's rural communities, once the backbone of an agricultural economy, now struggle against urban sprawl, land-use debates, and adapting to a changing socio-economic landscape.

Foundation for the Mid-South, 134 East Amite St., Jackson, MS 39201 (☎601-355-8167; http://www.fndmidsouth.org). Working in Louisiana, Mississippi, and Alabama, the Foundation for the Mid-South seeks to bring volunteers together to improve the region's schools, communities, and economy. Programs such as "Communities of Opportunity" and "Mid-South Middle Start" work toward area-specific goals of economic empowerment and improving middle-school education.

Habitat for Humanity International, 121 Habitat St., Americus, GA 31709 (☎229-924-6935, ext. 2551 or 2552; www.habitat.org). Volunteers build houses throughout the US (and in 100 other countries) to benefit low-income families. Projects take anywhere from 2 weeks to 3 years. Short-term program costs range $900-4000; check with local branches for free volunteer opportunities.

Northeast Regional Center for Rural Development, Penn State University 7 Armsby Building, University Park, PA 16802 (☎814-863-4656; http://www.nercrd.psu.edu). Guided by principles of economic viability, improving the quality of life for rural communities, and helping these communities adapt to changing socioeconomic conditions, the Northeast Regional Center for Rural Development provides grants for volunteer initiatives attacking poverty, land use, and community development.

YOUTH PROGRAMS

Educational and mentoring programs throughout the US also offer instruction and support to youth in need. These programs are most appropriate for volunteers who are willing to make a long-term commitment to working with their students.

Big Brothers Big Sisters of America, 230 N. 13th St., Philadelphia, PA 19107 (☎215-567-7000; www.bbbsa.org). This century-old organization provides mentorship, friendship, and support to hundreds of thousands of American kids. Paired "Bigs" and "Littles" work on homework together, participate in community service, or just hang out.

Boys and Girls Clubs of America, 1275 Peachtree St., Atlanta, GA 30309 (☎404-487-5700; www.bcga.org). Boys and Girls Clubs of America seek to instill "competence, usefulness, belonging, and influence" in their community youth. Clubs are open daily, and memberships are affordable, creating a unique space for children who have limited recreation opportunities. Programs range from character and leadership initiatives to arts enrichment.

Child Welfare League of America, 2345 Crystal Dr., Ste. 250, Arlington, VA 22202 (☎703-412-2400; www.cwla.org). Almost 800 public and private not-for-profit organizations make up the Child Welfare League of America, which works to help 3.5 million children who have been abused or neglected. Programs include family foster care, child mental health, juvenile justice, and housing issues. Their website maintains current research for youth advocates, as well as a database of publications and program opportunities.

BEYOND TOURISM

Do Something!, Inc. 24-32 Union Square East, 4th fl., New York, NY 10003 (http://www.dosomething.org). Founded by Dress-for-Success CEO Nancy Lublin, Do Something! uses the Internet to inspire and empower young volunteers who want to make a difference. The foundation distributes over $1 million in grant money each year to fund projects developed by young adults, and the website does everything from suggesting project ideas to connecting volunteers with programs in their neighborhoods.

Good Shepherd Services, 305 Seventh Ave., 9th fl., New York, NY 10001 (☎917-318-9993; http://www.goodsheperds.org). Good Shepherd operates one-on-one mentoring, group mentoring, and tutoring services for vulnerable adolescents in Manhattan, Brooklyn, the Bronx, and Queens. Mentors and tutors work with youth placed in residential programs and foster boarding homes, teaching job skills and inspiring career readiness.

The National Mentoring Partnership, 1600 Duke St., Ste. 300, Alexandria, VA 22314 (☎703-224-2200; www.mentoring.org). Advocates the expansion of mentoring programs with the goal of serving the 17.6 million children in the US who could benefit from mentor relationships. Maintains a database of mentoring opportunities, including state and local mentoring partnerships, programs, and volunteer centers.

MEDICAL OUTREACH

You don't need an M.D. to give back through medical outreach programs in the US. Volunteers are needed to staff offices, participate in emergency relief, and connect with those in need.

American Red Cross National Headquarters, 2025 E St. NW, Washington, D.C. 20006 (☎800-733-2767; www.redcross.org/donate/volunteer). The American Red Cross is the gold standard for volunteers, with programs ranging from disaster services to youth volunteering and HIV/AIDS mentoring. The website's volunteer-match service puts volunteers in touch with needy areas that can benefit from their specific skill sets.

Body Health Resources Corporation, 250 W. 57th St., New York, NY 10107 (www.thebody.com). "The Body" is an extensive, informative website about all things HIV/AIDS-related. Check out the "Helping and Getting Help" section of the website for a list of regional service organizations throughout the US that are in need of volunteers.

Meals on Wheels Association of America, 203 S. Union St., Alexandria, VA 22314 (☎703-548-5558; www.mowaa.org). Buy, prepare, and deliver meals to the elderly and the poor. Public awareness and research projects also available. Search the website for the region in which you would like to serve.

National Hospice Foundation, 1700 Diagonal Rd., Ste. 625, Alexandria, VA 22314 (☎703-837-1500; www.hospiceinfo.org). Hospices offer emotional and spiritual support for those close to death, as well as counseling for their families. Search by name, state, or ZIP code to find a US hospice in need of volunteers.

Partners in Health, 614 Huntington Ave, Boston, MA 02115 (☎617-432-5256; www.pih.org). Run by Dr. Paul Farmer, the subject of Tracy Kidder's bestseller *Mountains Beyond Mountains*, Partners in Health focuses on health initiatives worldwide. In Boston, their Prevention and Access to Care and Treatment (PACT) serves the neediest HIV/AIDS patients in the area. Volunteers are needed as translators in the Boston office, and for other staff tasks.

Project Hope, 255 Carter Hall Ln., Millwood, VA 22646 (☎800-544-4673; www.projecthope.org). Project Hope celebrates its 50th anniversary in 2008, continuing to serve those in need of healthcare across the globe. In the US, volunteers for Project Hope can register on their website to work on disaster relief or special missions with the US Navy.

United States Office of Minority Health's Resource Center, P.O. Box 37337, Washington, D.C. 20013 (☎800-444-6472; www.omhrc.gov). Provides one of the most comprehensive lists of US state, federal, and other service organizations.

LITERACY PROGRAMS

A quarter of American adults are not proficient in reading. Many experience diffi-culties because they did not finish high school, while others are immigrants or per-sons suffering from learning or vision disabilities.

America's Literacy Directory (☎800-228-8813; www.literacydirectory.org/volun-teer.asp). A service of the National Institute for Literacy, this online directory allows you to search for volunteer opportunities among more than 5000 literacy programs for adults and young adults.

Proliteracy Worldwide, 1320 Jamesville Ave., Syracuse, NY 13210 (☎888-528-2224 or 315-422-9121; www.proliteracy.org). The world's largest adult volunteer literacy organi-zation, with chapters in the US. Tutors teach basic literacy or English for Speakers of Other Languages (ESOL) to individuals and families.

Reading is Fundamental, Inc., 1825 Connecticut Ave. NW, Ste. 400, Washington, D.C. 20009 (☎877-RIF-READ or 202-536-3400; www.rif.org). Oldest and largest family liter-acy program in the US. Volunteers can get involved nationwide by participating in read-ings at public libraries, fundraising, and organizing book orders for community events.

ECOTOURISM AND CONSERVATION

Ecotourism organizations have blossomed in the US, offering (sometimes) costly activities and tours developed to minimize environmental impact. More innovative programs arrange outings engineered to improve the environment and quality of life at the local level, while providing volunteers with the opportunity to research and experience the wilderness, and to build work skills. Additionally, conserva-tion groups work to protect America's wilderness and wildlife.

American Society for the Prevention of Cruelty to Animals (ASPCA), 424 E. 92nd St., New York, NY 10128 (☎212-876-7700; www.aspca.org). Promotes the humane treat-ment of animals through awareness programs, public policy efforts, shelter support, and animal medical treatment. Look under "Find a Shelter" on their website to find a list of shelters needing volunteers, or apply to volunteer at the ASPCA's headquarters in New York City. The ASPCA is partnered with www.petfinder.com, which also has a data-base of shelters and rescue groups.

Backroads, 801 Cedar St. Berkeley, CA 94710 (☎510-527-1555; www.backroads.com). Week-long walking, biking, and multi-sport trips designed to minimize environmental impact by avoiding mechanized transport. Destinations include San Juan Islands, WA; the Gulf Coast; and northern New England. Most courses $1200-2000.

Earth Share, 7735 Old Georgetown Rd., Ste. 900, Bethesda, MD 20814 (☎800-875-3863 or 240-333-0300; www.earthshare.org). A network of national conservation organi-zations that offers links to short- and long-term volunteer opportunities with community and state organizations in 19 states.

Earthwatch Institute, 3 Clock Tower Pl., Ste. 100, Box 75, Maynard, MA 01754 (☎800-776-0188 or 978-461-0081; www.earthwatch.org). Arranges 1- to 3-week programs to promote the conservation of natural resources and aid in field research. Under the supervi-sion of leading scientists, volunteer teams perform tasks like tracking wildlife in Alaska's temperate rainforests or excavating prehistoric pueblos in the Southwest. Volunteers must be over 16. Expeditions generally cost $700-4000, depending on length and location.

Environmental Careers Organization, 30 Winter St., Boston, MA 02108 (☎617-426-4375; www.eco.org). Develop skills in communications, outreach, or as a field technician for organizations like the Bureau of Land Management, US Geological Survey, and the Envi-ronmental Protection Agency. 3-month to 2-year paid internships in 35 states and 3 US ter-ritories. Internships mostly available in summer but also during the year.

National Outdoor Leadership School (NOLS), 284 Lincoln St., Lander, WY 82520 (☎800-710-6657; www.nols.edu). Designs 2- to 12-week wilderness expeditions that foster leadership abilities and backcountry skills, such as backpacking, wilderness medicine, and caving. Age requirements vary by expedition. Most courses cost at least $100 per day.

Natural Resources Conservation Service, Attn: Conservation Communications Staff, P.O. Box 2890, Washington, D.C. 20013 (☎202-720-3210; www.nrcs.usda.gov). Volunteer on private farms and ranches, in classrooms, or in offices promoting conservation and improving habitats. Give tours and speeches, take photographs, or organize exhibits with specialists.

Orion Grassroots Network, 187 Main St., Great Barrington, MA 01230 (☎888-909-6568; www.oriononline.org). A network of 795 nonprofits and community organizations that matches volunteers with paid and unpaid environmental internships.

Volunteers-in-Parks (National Park Service), 1849 C St. NW, Washington, D.C. 20240 (☎202-354-1800; www.nps.gov/volunteer). From the Great Smoky Mountains to Alaska's Glacier Bay, volunteers learn about park management, wildlife research, and environmental education by giving tours, monitoring wildlife, picking up trash, and planting trees in national parks. Applicants from abroad may receive free, reimbursed, or reduced-cost housing and food from the International Volunteers-in-Parks program.

World-Wide Opportunities on Organic Farms USA, P.O. Box 510, Felton, CA 95018 (☎831-425-3276; www.wwoofusa.org). Learn about organic farming and permaculture on one of over 200 host farms across the United States. Volunteers devote about 6hr. per day to farm work in exchange for accommodations and meals. Volunteers must be over 18 or accompanied by a legal guardian. Requested stay lengths vary from a weekend to 3 months. Membership $20; 2-person membership $30.

PROGRAMS IN THE ARTS

The creatively inclined can pursue numerous forms of artistic expression in the US—the bohemian quarters of New York City and San Francisco, as well as the wide-open spaces of the American interior, offer all types of artistic opportunities.

VISUAL AND PERFORMING ARTS

Chautauqua Institution, P.O. Box 28, Chautauqua, NY 14722 (☎800-836-ARTS/2782; www.chautauqua-inst.org). A National Historic Landmark that offers intensive summer programs in art, dance, music, and theater for talented students. Programs range 2-7 weeks. Need- and talent-based scholarships available.

New York Foundation for the Arts, 155 Ave. of the Americas, 14th fl., New York, NY 10013 (☎212-366-6900; www.nyfa.org). From dance to music to visual arts, NYFA provides a national database of resources in the arts, including listings of current job and internship openings and schedules for art events. The "For Artists" link on the website posts audition notices, calls for entry, and information about workshops.

National Association of Schools of Theatre, 11250 Roger Bacon Dr., Ste. 21, Reston, VA 20190 (☎703-437-0700; http://nast.arts-accredit.org). Supplies a list of accredited degree- and non-degree-granting institutions in the US that offer theater programs.

Santa Fe Art Institute, P.O. Box 24044, Santa Fe, NM 87502 (☎505-424-5050; www.sfai.org). A world-class artistic center, the Santa Fe Art Institute offers 1-week workshops ($900 includes residency and tuition) and allows participants to learn from professional resident artists. Need-based scholarships are available.

Summer Theater, Box 727, Saxtons River, VT 05154 (www.summertheater.com). Each year, small local theaters throughout the country put out a series of dramatic productions, including musicals, comedy, drama, and opera. Tickets are affordable, and many young and talented actors get their first experiences on the stage. For audition and performance information, contact the individual summer theaters listed on the website.

FILM

Indiewire.com, 304 Hudson St., 6th fl., New York, NY 10013 (☎212-675-3908; www.indiewire.com). Explore the student and independent film scene in the US while you get the low-down on upcoming film festivals, lectures, and symposia. Classifieds list paid and unpaid positions for actors, crew, writers, and producers; you can also meet and find collaborators for your own projects.

New York Film Academy (NYFA), 100 E. 17th St., New York, NY 10003 (☎212-674-4300; www.nyfa.com). NYFA allows would-be actors, filmmakers, and screenwriters the chance to hone their skills on studio sets in several cities. Program lengths vary from 1 week to 1 year, and include classes in acting, screenwriting, digital imaging, filmmaking, comedy, and 3D animation. Programs cost $1500-25,000.

University of Southern California School of Cinema-Television, Summer Program Enrollment Office, 850 W. 34th St., Los Angeles, CA 90089 (☎213-740-1742; www.uscsummerfilm.com). Boasting an alumni list that includes *Star Wars* mastermind George Lucas, screenwriter John Milius *(Apocalypse Now)*, and producer Laura Ziskin *(Spiderman)*, the world-renowned film school offers summer workshops with classes in writing, digital imaging, directing, and producing. University housing is available, as are classes for students who have already logged some hours (or years) in the industry. Students also have access to free seminars, workshops, and screenings.

POETRY

Writer's Colonies allow writers to pursue writing projects without distraction. Residencies range from 1 week to several months; some programs include workshops and conferences. Costs generally cover room and board, though fellowships are occasionally available. A directory of several writer's colonies is available at www.poewar.com/articles/colonies.htm; for a more comprehensive listing of artist's retreats, try *Artist's Communities: A Directory of Residencies in the United States that Offer Time and Space for Creativity,* by Tricia Snell (Allworth Press 2000).

Poets and Writers, Inc., 72 Spring St., Ste. 301, New York, NY 10012 (☎212-226-3586; www.pw.org). Provides links to writing programs at universities in the US as well as an extensive list of conferences and residencies for writers.

Poetry Slam Incorporated, 11462 East Ln., Whitmore Lake, MI 48189 (☎810-231-5435; www.poetryslam.com). All across the country, poets perform 3-5min. of their work in cafes and bars, and are judged by audience members on performance and writing ability. Poetry Slam Inc. compiles a massive list of these venues; most have at least 1 night per week devoted to slams or readings. Admission prices range from free to a small cover charge; you may have to sign up in advance to perform.

ARCHITECTURE AND DESIGN

Arcosanti, HC74, P.O. Box 4136, Mayer, AZ 86333 (☎928-632-7135; www.arcosanti.org). Founded by Frank Lloyd Wright's disciple Paolo Soleri (who still lives here), Arcosanti is a community 70 mi. north of Phoenix based on Soleri's theory of "arcology"—the symbiotic relationship between architecture and ecology. It hosts 1-week ($485) and 5-week ($1175) workshops in which participants help expand the settlement while learning about Soleri's project and developing their skills at construction and planning. An all-expenses-paid 3-month internship is available for those with some prior architectural background after they have completed the 5-week workshop.

Ecological Design Institute, P.O. Box 989, Sausalito, CA 94966 (☎415-332-5806; www.ecodesign.org). Integrating technology and nature into their vision of green design, EDI promotes education for sustainability, highlighting design projects along the West Coast that practice these principles. Their website has a list of institutions in the US that offer workshops and classes in ecologically friendly design and construction.

STUDYING

Study-abroad programs range from basic language and culture courses to college-level classes, which can often be taken for credit. In order to choose a program that best fits your needs, research as much as you can before making your decision—determine costs and duration, as well as what kind of students participate in the program and what sort of accommodations are provided.

> **VISA INFORMATION.** All foreign students must have a **visa** to study in the US. Travelers must also provide proof of intent to leave, like a return plane ticket or an I-94 card. Foreign students who want to study in the US must apply for either an M-1 visa (non-academic or vocational studies) or an F-1 visa (for full-time students enrolled in a program to study or conduct research at an accredited US college or university). See www.unitedstatesvisas.gov/studying.html for further information. To get a visa or study permit, apply at a US embassy or consulate in your home country. If English is not your native language, you will probably want to take the Test of English as a Foreign Language (TOEFL), administered in many countries. The international students office at the institution you will be attending can give you specifics. Contact **TOEFL/TSE Publications,** Rosedale Road, Princeton, NJ, 08541, USA (☎877-863-3546, outside the US ☎609-921-9000; www.toefl.org). US **visa extensions** are sometimes attainable with a completed I-539 form; call the Bureau of Citizenship and Immigration Service's (BCIS) forms request line (☎800-375-5283) or get it online at www.ucis.gov/files/form/i-539.pdf. See **http://travel.state.gov/visa** for more info. Security measures have made the visa application process more rigorous and lengthier. **Apply well in advance of your travel date.** The process may seem complex, but you must take the proper steps or risk deportation.

In programs that have large groups of students who speak the same language, there is a trade-off. You may feel more comfortable in the community, but you will not have the same opportunity to practice a foreign language or befriend other international students. For accommodations, dorm life provides a better opportunity to mingle with fellow students, but there is less of a chance to experience the local scene. If you live with a family, there is the potential to build lifelong friendships with natives and to experience day-to-day life in more depth, but conditions may vary greatly from family to family.

UNIVERSITIES

Most university-level study abroad programs in the US are conducted in English, with many offering classes for English learners and beginner- and lower-level language courses. Those relatively fluent in English may find it cheaper to enroll directly in a US university, though getting college credit may be more difficult. You can search **www.studyabroad.com** for various semester-abroad programs that meet your criteria, including your desired location and focus of study. The list below includes organizations that can help place students in university programs abroad, and those that have their own branch in the US.

In order to live the life of a real American college student, consider a visiting-student program lasting either a semester or a full year. (Some institutions have trimesters, but most American universities have a fall semester Sept.-Dec. and a spring semester Jan.-May.) The best method is to contact colleges and universities in your home country to see what kinds of exchanges they have with those in the

US; college students can often receive credit for study abroad. A more complicated option for advanced English speakers is to enroll directly in an American institution. Each state maintains a public university system. The US also hosts a number of reputable private universities, as well as innumerable community, professional, and technical colleges. Tuition costs, however, are high in the US, and a full course of undergraduate study entails a four-year commitment.

LANGUAGE SCHOOLS

Language schools can be independently run international or local organizations or divisions of foreign universities. They rarely offer college credit, but are a good alternative to university study if you desire greater focus on the language or a less rigorous courseload. These programs are also good for younger high school students who might not feel comfortable with older students in a university program.

American Language Programs, 56 Hobbs Brook Rd., Boston, MA 02493 (☎ 781-888-1515; www.alp-online.com). ALP runs programs in Arizona, California, Florida, New York, and Massachusetts that include homestays and intensive English training. $900-1080 per week (15-25hr.) for 1 person, $1600-1960 for 2 people.

Berlitz Languages, Inc., 40 West 51st St., New York, NY 10020 (☎ 212-765-1000; www.berlitz.com). Berlitz has over 60 language centers throughout the US that offer private, group, and immersion classes (with optional homestays) for all ages.

Eurocentres, P.O. Box 16602, Alexandria, VA 22302 (☎ 703-243-7884; www.eurocentres.com) or in Europe, Head Office, Seestr. 247, CH-8038 Zurich, Switzerland (☎ 011 41 44 485 50 40). Language programs for beginning to advanced students with homestays in the US.

WORKING

Like volunteering, work opportunities tend to fall into two categories: long term and short term. Some travelers want long-term jobs that allow them to get to know another part of the world as a member of the community, while others seek out short-term jobs to finance the next leg of their travels. In the US, people who want to work long-term should consider exchange programs. Short-term work is most often found in service industries and agriculture.

For either type of work, local newspapers are the best places to start searching. Internet search engines like **www.monster.com** and **www.hotjobs.yahoo.com** are also helpful. Note that working abroad often requires a special work visa; see the box below for more information.

LONG-TERM WORK

If you're planning on spending a substantial amount of time (more than 3 months) working in the US, search for a job well in advance. International placement agencies and websites are geared toward pairing US employers with international travelers. Although they are often available only to college students, **internships** are a good way to segue into working abroad, despite frequently meager paychecks. Be wary of advertisements for companies claiming to be able get you a job abroad for a fee—often the same listings are available online or in newspapers. Some reputable organizations include:

Alliances Abroad Group, Inc., 1221 S. Mopac Expwy., Ste. 250, Austin, TX 78746 (☎ 866-ABROAD; www.alliancesabroad.com). Organizes summer work in the service industry for university students ages 18-28.

VISA INFORMATION. All foreign visitors are required to have a **visa** if they intend to work in the US. In addition, travelers must provide proof of intent to leave, such as a return plane ticket or an I-94 card. A **work permit** (or "green card") is also required. Your employer must obtain this document, usually by demonstrating that you have skills that locals lack. Friends in the US can sometimes help expedite permits or arrange work-for-accommodations exchanges. To **obtain visas and work permits,** contact a US embassy or consulate (see **Embassies and Consulates,** p. 11). Visa extensions in the US are sometimes attainable with a completed I-539 form; request forms from the Bureau of Citizenship and Immigration Service (☎800-870-3676; http://uscis.gov/graphics/formsfee/forms/index.htm). See **http://travel.state.gov/visa** for more information. Security measures have made the visa application process more rigorous, and therefore lengthier. **Apply well in advance of your travel date.** The process may seem complex, but the alternative could be deportation.

British Universities North American Club (BUNAC), 16 Bowling Green Ln., London, EC1R OQH, UK (☎+44 020 7251 3472, US 203-264-0901; www.bunac.com). Arranges short- and long-term job placements, visas, and work authorization in the US for individuals over 18. Work placement includes summer jobs, work training programs, and camp counselor positions. Some programs are open to non-students.

Camp America, 37a Queen's Gate, London, SW7 5HR, UK (☎+44 020 7581 7373, US 203-399-5000; www.campamerica.co.uk). Summer camp jobs are popular in the US; most last about 9 weeks and can include time afterward for travel. Camp America places counselors in a variety of camps, including religious camps and camps for disadvantaged or special-needs children. Positions in service areas, such as kitchen or maintenance, are also available. **Camp Counselors USA,** 2330 Marinship Way, Ste. 250, Sausalito, CA 94965 (☎415-339-2728; www.ccusa.com), also places counselors and has positions in specialty areas such as outdoor sports and the arts.

Council Exchanges, 3 Copley Pl., 2nd fl., Boston, MA 02116 (☎617-247-0350; www.councilexchanges.org). Charges a $300-475 fee for arranging working authorizations valid for 3-6 months. Extensive information about job opportunities in the US.

International Cooperative Education, 15 Spiros Way, Menlo Park, CA, 94025 (☎650-323-4944; www.icemenlo.com). Finds summer jobs for students in the US. Costs include a $200 application fee and a $600 fee for placement.

JOBS YOU ARRANGE

Looking beyond job placement programs may be the best way to find a job opportunity that fits your needs, skills, and time. However, most job service and search engines do not assist potential employees in acquiring visas or work permits, which you must have before applying for temporary work or internships. Keep in mind that individual employers may have specific policies with regard to non-US citizens, and allow for extra time to process applications.

About Jobs, 180 State Rd., Ste. 2U, Sagamore Beach, MA 02562 (☎508-888-6889; www.aboutjobs.com). Has summer jobs, internships, and resort work in North America.

Cool Works, P.O. Box 272, 511 Hwy. 89, Gardiner, MT 59030 (☎406-848-2380; www.coolworks.com). Options include work at state parks, ski resorts, camps, ranches, and amusement parks.

JobsAbroad.com. Find internships and jobs on this user-friendly site. Committed to providing the most comprehensive employment directories, jobsabroad.com supplies the most up-to-date and accurate information on the web for both international and native travelers.

BEYOND TOURISM

Net-Temps.com. Net-Temps assists staffing companies in sourcing and hiring the most qualified candidates. Search by keyword or location for full-time and temporary jobs. Membership with Net-Temps is free for job-seekers. Users can search thousands of new job postings, create a free Job Search Assistant, and post up to 3 resumes and cover letters. Provides resume-writing and interviewing tips.

AU PAIR WORK

Au pairs are typically women (though sometimes men), aged 18-27, who work as live-in nannies, caring for children and doing light housework in foreign countries in exchange for room, board, and a small stipend. Most former au pairs speak favorably of their experience. One perk of the job is that it allows you to really get to know the country without the high expenses of traveling. Drawbacks, however, often include mediocre pay and long hours. In the US, weekly salaries typically fall below $200, with at least 45hr. of work expected. Au pairs are expected to speak English and have at least 200hr. of childcare experience. Much of the au pair experience depends on the family with whom you are placed. A good starting point for those seeking employment is **Childcare International, Ltd.** (Trafalgar House, Greenville Pl., London NW7 3SA, UK. ☎ +44 020 8906-3116; fax 8906-3461; www.child-int.co.uk.) A similar placement agency in the US is **InterExchange.** (161 Sixth Ave., New York, NY 10013. ☎ 212-924-0446; fax 924-0575; www.interexchange.org.)

SHORT-TERM WORK

Traveling for long periods of time can get expensive; many travelers try their hand at odd jobs for a few weeks at a time to help finance another month or two of travel. A popular option is to work several hours a day at a hostel in exchange for free or discounted room and/or board. Most often, these short-term jobs are found by word of mouth, or simply by talking to the owner of a hostel or restaurant. Due to the high turnover in the tourism industry, many places are eager for help, even if it is only temporary. Good sites to search for hostels in the US along with the availability of short-term jobs are **hostels.com, hiayh.org,** and **usahostels.com.** *Let's Go* lists temporary jobs of this nature whenever possible; look in the practical information sections of larger cities. Help-wanted sections in local newspapers and on websites like **www.craigslist.org** are helpful resources for short-term jobs in popular destinations. It is illegal to take a paid job without a work permit or visa.

FURTHER READING ON BEYOND TOURISM.

Alternatives to the Peace Corps: A Guide of Global Volunteer Opportunities, by Paul Backhurst. Food First Books, 2005 ($12).

The Back Door Guide to Short-Term Job Adventures: Internships, Summer Jobs, Seasonal Work, Volunteer Vacations, and Transitions Abroad, by Michael Landes. Ten Speed Press, 2005 ($22).

Green Volunteers: The World Guide to Voluntary Work in Nature Conservation, ed. Fabio Ausenda. Universe, 2007 ($15).

International Job Finder: Where the Jobs Are Worldwide, by Daniel Lauber and Kraig Rice. Planning Communications, 2002 ($20).

Live and Work Abroad: A Guide for Modern Nomads, by Huw Francis and Michelyne Callan. Vacation-Work Publications, 2001 ($16).

Volunteer Vacations: Short-Term Adventures That Will Benefit You and Others, by Doug Cutchins, Anne Geissinger, and Bill McMillon. Chicago Review Press, 2006 ($18).

Work Your Way Around the World, by Susan Griffith. Vacation-Work Publications, 2007 ($22).

MID-ATLANTIC

From the Eastern seaboard of New York south through Virginia, the mid-Atlantic states claim many of the nation's major historical, political, and economic centers. This region has witnessed the rotation of US capitals: first Philadelphia, PA; then Princeton, NJ; Annapolis, MD; Trenton, NJ; New York, NY; and finally Washington, D.C. During the Civil War, the mid-Atlantic even housed the Confederate capital, Richmond, VA. Urban centers cover much of the land, but the great outdoors have survived. The Appalachian Trail meanders through the region, and New York's Adirondacks compose the largest national park in the lower 48 states.

HIGHLIGHTS OF THE MID-ATLANTIC

GAPE at the obelisk **Washington Monument** (p. 195), the glistening **Empire State Building** (p. 101), and the jagged crack in the **Liberty Bell** (p. 154).

ABSORB the majesty of world-class art at the **Metropolitan Museum of Art** (p. 108), the **Museum of Modern Art** (p. 109), and the **National Gallery of Art** (p. 196).

GIGGLE at the colonial costumes of reenactors in **Philadelphia** (p. 148), **Gettysburg** (p. 163), and **Williamsburg** (p. 210).

CATCH some rays during a break from **Atlantic City's** slot machines (p. 142), or spread your towel next to a starlet in the **Hamptons** (p. 117).

WHISTLE along with the heartstopping showtunes of a **Broadway** musical (p. 110).

NEW YORK

The Empire State offers a little bit of everything: the excitement of New York City, the grandeur of Niagara Falls, and the natural beauty of the Catskills and Adirondacks. While "The City that Never Sleeps" attracts cosmopolitan adventure-seekers, those grooving to a mellower tune head upstate. Here, surrounded by cool waterways and wooded mountainsides, you may find it difficult to remember that lattes and Prada even exist. Still, while the easy rolling cities of upstate New York are natural and sweet, there's nothing like the juicy tang of the Big Apple.

⁊ PRACTICAL INFORMATION

Capital: Albany.

Visitor Info: Division of Tourism, 1 Commerce Plaza, Albany 12245 (☎518-474-4116 or 800-225-5697; www.iloveny.state.ny.us). Operators available M-F 8:30am-4:45pm. **New York State Office of Parks and Recreation and Historic Preservation,** Empire State Plaza, Agency Bldg. 1, Albany 12238 (☎518-474-0456). Open M-F 9am-5pm.

Postal Abbreviation: NY. **Sales Tax:** 7-9%, depending on county.

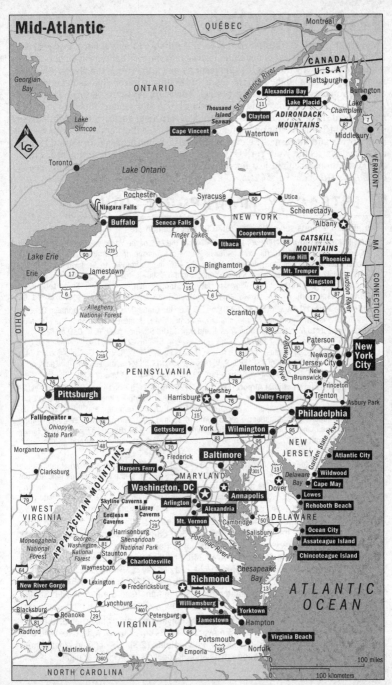

Mid-Atlantic

100 miles

100 kilometers

NEW YORK CITY ☎212

The self-proclaimed "Capital of the World" puts its money where its mouth is. Eight million New Yorkers pack themselves into the city limits, and each one can tell you exactly why theirs is the greatest city on earth. This is the place where the legendary Yankees hold court, the lights of Broadway never dim, and every street corner promises a hot dog and a pretzel. Towering skyscrapers form the hub of American business by day, and the pounding beats of legendary clubs thump from neon-tinged shadows by night. When an act of terrorism destroyed the twin towers of the World Trade Center on September 11, 2001, New Yorkers were awakened to both horror and heroism. The city has moved on, but it hasn't forgotten. Day or night, every street in New York City's five boroughs is ready to spring into action, and every moment might just become a New York Minute. For more info, check out 📖*Let's Go: New York City.*

✈ INTERCITY TRANSPORTATION

Airports: 4 airports serve the New York City metropolitan area.

John F. Kennedy Airport (JFK; ☎718-244-4444), at the end of the Van Wyck Expwy., in southern Queens. The airport is 15 mi. from midtown Manhattan, but the drive can take 1hr. JFK handles most international and many domestic flights. The AirTrain runs from JFK to 2 subway stops leading into the city. From Howard Beach Station, connect to the A subway train. From Jamaica Station, connect to E, J, or Z subway train. (Allow 1hr. for entire trip; AirTrain every 4-8min. 6am-11pm, every 12min. 11pm-6am; $5 plus subway fare on MetroCard.) Taxi to Manhattan $45, plus tolls and tip.

LaGuardia Airport (LGA; ☎718-533-3400), off Exit 7 on the Grand Central Pkwy., in northern Queens. LaGuardia is 9 mi. from midtown Manhattan, a 25min. drive. Domestic flights only. The MTA M60 bus connects to Manhattan subway lines 1 and 9 at 110th St./Broadway; A, B, C, D at 125th St./ St. Nicholas Ave.; 2, 3 at 125th St./Lenox (6th) Ave.; 4, 5, 6 at 125th St./Lexington Ave. The Q33 bus goes to Jackson Heights/Roosevelt Ave. in Queens for 7, E, F, G, R, V; the Q48 bus goes to 74th St./Broadway in Queens for 7, E, F, G, R, V. (Allow at least 1½hr. for all routes. M60 runs daily 5am-1am, Q33 and Q48 24hr.; all buses $2.) Taxi to Manhattan $45, plus tolls and tip.

Newark Liberty International Airport (EWR; ☎973-961-6000), off Exit 14 on I-95, 16 mi. west of Midtown in Newark, NJ. Domestic and international flights. Olympia Airport Express (☎973-964-6233) travels from the airport to Port Authority, Grand Central Terminal, and Penn Station (15-60min.); departs for Port Authority every 5-10min. 4:15am-11:45pm, departs for Penn Station 4am-11pm, departs for Grand Central every 20-30min. 4am-11pm; $14. Bus #107 by the New Jersey Transit Authority (☎973-762-5100) covers Newark, Newark International Airport (North Terminal), and Port Authority (25min., every 30-45min. 5:20am-1am, $4.40).

Islip Long Island MacArthur Airport (ISP; ☎631-467-3210), 50 mi. from midtown Manhattan in Ronkonkoma, NY. Take the shuttle van service or the S57 bus to the Ronkonkoma train station. Shuttle ($5) departs from the baggage claim every 30min. 6am-10:30pm. Bus ($1.50) departs every hr., no service Su. From Ronkonkoma, the Long Island Rail Road (LIRR) runs trains into Penn Station (1½hr.; on-peak departs about every 30min., off-peak every hr.; $9.50-13).

Trains: Grand Central Terminal, 42nd St. and Park Ave. (Subway: 4, 5, 6, 7, S to 42nd St./Grand Central), handles **Metro-North** (☎800-638-7646) commuter lines. **Amtrak** (☎800-872-7245; www.amtrak.com) runs out of **Penn Station,** 33rd St. and 8th Ave. (Subway: 34th St./Penn Station/7th Ave.; 34th St./Penn Station/8th Ave.) To **Boston** (4-5hr., 10 per day, $78), **Philadelphia** (1½hr., 10 per day, $45), and **Washington, D.C.** (3-4hr., 10 per day, $67). The **Long Island Railroad (LIRR;** ☎718-217-5477) and **NJ Transit** (☎973-762-5100) commuter rails also run from Penn Station. At 33rd St. and 6th Ave., **PATH** (☎800-234-7284) trains depart for New Jersey.

Buses: Greyhound (☎800-229-9424; www.greyhound.com) buses leave the **Port Authority Terminal,** 42nd St. and 8th Ave. (☎564-8484. Subway: A, C, E to 42nd St./Port Authority.) To **Boston** (4-6hr., $35), **Philadelphia** (2-3hr., $21), and **Washington, D.C.** (4½hr., $37). Watch for con artists and pickpockets, especially at night.

◪ ORIENTATION

NYC is comprised of five **boroughs:** the Bronx, Brooklyn, Manhattan, Queens, and Staten Island. Flanked on the east by the East River (actually a strait) and on the west by the Hudson River, **Manhattan** is an island, measuring only 13 mi. long and 2½ mi. wide. **Queens** and **Brooklyn** are on the other side of the East River. **Staten Island,** southwest of Manhattan, is the most residential borough. North of Manhattan sits the **Bronx,** the only borough connected by land to the rest of the US.

BOROUGHS

MANHATTAN

Above 14th Street, Manhattan is an organized grid of avenues running north-south and streets east-west. Street numbers increase as you travel north. Avenues are slightly less predictable: some are numbered, while others are named. The numbers of the avenues increase as you go west. **Broadway** defies the pattern, cutting diagonally east across the island at 23rd St. **Central Park** and **Fifth Avenue** (south of 59th St., north of 110th St.) separate the city into the East Side and West Side. **Washington Heights** is located north of 155th St.; **Morningside Heights** (above 110th St. and below 125th St.) is sandwiched between **Harlem** (150s to 110th St.) and the **Upper West Side** (110th St. to 59th St., west of Central Park). The museum-heavy **Upper East Side** is across Central Park, above 59th St. on 5th Ave. **Midtown** (59th St. to 42nd St.) includes Times Square and the Theater District. **Lower Midtown** (41st St. to 14th St.) includes **Herald Square, Chelsea,** and **Union Square.**

   Below 14th St., the city dissolves into a confusing tangle of old, narrow streets that aren't numbered south of Houston St. The bohemian **East Village** and **Alphabet City** are grid-like, with alphabetized avenues from Ave. A to Ave. D, east of First Ave. Intellectual **Greenwich Village,** to the west, is especially complicated west of 6th Ave. Moving south, trendy **SoHo** (South of Houston St.) and **TriBeCa** (Triangle Below Canal St.) are just west of historically ethnic enclaves **Little Italy, Chinatown,** and the **Lower East Side.** The **Financial District/Wall Street area** at the tip of Manhattan, set over the original Dutch layout, is full of narrow, winding, one-way streets.

BROOKLYN

The **Brooklyn-Queens Expressway (BQE)** links to the **Belt Parkway** and circumscribes Brooklyn. Ocean Pkwy., Ocean Ave., Coney Island Ave., and diagonal Flatbush Ave. run from the beaches of southern Brooklyn (**Coney Island** and **Brighton Beach**) to the heart of the borough in **Prospect Park.** The streets of western Brooklyn (including **Park Slope**) are aligned with the western shore and intersect central Brooklyn's main arteries at a 45-degree angle. In northern Brooklyn (including **Greenpoint, Brooklyn Heights,** and **Downtown Brooklyn**), several avenues—Atlantic Ave., Eastern Pkwy., and Flushing Ave.—travel east into Queens.

QUEENS

The streets of Queens resemble neither the orderly grid of Upper Manhattan nor the haphazard angles of Greenwich Village. Streets run north-south and are numbered west to east, from 1st St. in **Astoria** to 271st St. in **Glen Oaks.** Avenues run perpendicular to streets and are numbered north to south, from 2nd Ave. to 165th Ave. The address of an establishment often tells you the closest cross-street (for example, the establishment at 45-07 32nd Ave. is near the intersection with 45th St.). Pick up the useful Queens Bus Map, free and available on most Queens buses.

THE BRONX

Major highways divide the Bronx. The **Major Deegan Expressway (I-87)** runs up the western border of the borough, right next to the Harlem River. The **Cross-Bronx**

Manhattan
SEE MAP, p. 91

◭ ACCOMMODATIONS

Big Apple Hostel,	1	B3
Carlton Arms Hotel,	2	C4
Central Park Hostel,	3	B1
Chelsea International Hostel,	4	B5
Chelsea Star Hotel,	5	B4
Gershwin Hotel,	6	C4
Hotel Stanford,	7	C4
Jazz on the Park,	8	B1
Larchmont Hotel,	9	C5
New York International Hostel (HI),	10	B1

🍎 FOOD

Becco,	11	B3
Big Nick's Burger Joint and Pizza Joint,	12	B2
Cafe Mogador,	13	C5
Chinatown Ice-Cream Factory,	14	C6
Doyers Vietnamese Restaurant,	15	C6
Frank,	16	C5
Fried Dumpling,	17	C6
Gray's Papaya,	18	B2
Il Vagabondo,	19	C3
Island Burgers and Shakes,	20	B3
Joe's Shanghai,	21	C6
Kangsuh Korean Restaurant,	22	C4
Katz's Delicatessen,	23	D6
Kossar's Bialys,	24	D6
La Mela,	25	C6
Lips,	26	B5
Lombardi's Coal Oven Pizza,	27	C6
Mottsu,	28	C6
Moustache,	29	B5
Payard,	30	C2
Pop Burger,	31	B5
Say Cheese!,	32	B4
Shake Shack,	33	C4
Vermicelli,	34	C2
Zabar's,	35	B2

🍷 NIGHTLIFE: BARS

The Big Easy,	36	C1
Circa Tabac,	37	C6
d.b.a.,	38	B5
Dive 75,	39	B2
Dorrian's Red Hand,	40	C2
The Evelyn Lounge,	41	B2
Joe's Pub,	42	C6
Local 138,	43	D6
Lotus Lounge,	44	D8
Milady's,	45	C6
The White Horse Tavern,	46	B5

🍷 NIGHTLIFE: DANCE CLUBS

Cielo,	47	C6
Eugene,	48	C4
Happy Ending,	49	B5
Tribe,	50	D5

🍷 NIGHTLIFE: GLBT

Boiler Room,	51	C5
g,	52	B5
Henrietta Hudson,	53	B5
SBNY,	54	C5

Expressway (I-95) runs across the borough, turning north on its eastern most edge. Up the center of the borough runs the **Bronx River Parkway.** Many avenues run north-south, including **Jerome Avenue** on the western side and **White Plains Road** and **Boston Road** to the east. East-west streets include **Tremont Avenue, Fordham Road,** and the **Pelham Parkway.**

STATEN ISLAND

Unlike the rest of the city, Staten Island is quite spread out. Pick up necessary maps of Staten Island's bus routes as well as other pamphlets at the **Chamber of Commerce,** 130 Bay St. (☎718-727-1900), left from the ferry station.

🖅 LOCAL TRANSPORTATION

Public Transit: The **Metropolitan Transportation Authority (MTA)** runs the city's subways, buses, and trains. The **subway** system is open 24hr.; once inside, a passenger may transfer onto any other subway train without restrictions. Maps are available in any station. **Buses,** often slower than subways, stop roughly every 2 blocks and run throughout the city. Blue signposts announce bus numbers; glass-walled shelters display schedules and route maps. In the outer boroughs, some buses are run by independent contractors. Be sure to grab a borough bus map. **MetroCard** electronic fare cards for subways and buses have a pre-set value (e.g. 12 rides for the price of 10) and allow free bus and subway transfers within 2hr. of your first swipe. The 1-day ($7), 7-day ($24), and 30-day ($76) "Unlimited Rides" MetroCards (as opposed to $2 "Pay-Per-Ride" cards) are good for tourists visiting many sights.

🔢 PRACTICAL INFORMATION

Visitor Info: NYC & Company, 810 7th Ave. (☎212-484-1222; www.nycvisit.com). Open M-F 8:30am-6pm, Sa-Su 9am-5pm. Also in Grand Central and Penn Station.

Manhattan

SEE MAP KEY, p. 90

○ SIGHTS

1 Columbia University
2 Cathedral of St. John the Divine
3 Guggenheim Museum
4 Metropolitan Museum of Art
5 American Museum of Natural History
6 Whitney Museum
7 Frick Collection
8 Lincoln Center for the Performing Arts
9 Columbus Circle
10 Carnegie Hall
11 Museum of Modern Art
12 Rockefeller Center
13 St. Patrick's Cathedral
14 Port Authority Bus Terminal
15 Times Square
16 New York Public Library
17 Grand Central Station
18 United Nations
19 General Post Office
20 Penn Station
21 Empire State Building
22 Union Square
23 Washington Square
24 World Trade Center Site
25 Battery Park

SEE COLOR INSETS FOR MORE
NEW YORK CITY MAPS

GLBT Resources: Callen-Lorde Community Health Center, 356 W. 18th St. (☎212-271-7200), between 8th and 9th Ave. Open M and W 8:30am-8pm, Tu 8:30am-12:30pm and 2:15-8pm, Th-F 9am-4:30pm, and Sa 9:30am-1:30pm; service may be limited on weekends and morning hours. **Gay Men's Health Crisis-Geffen Clinic,** 119 W. 24th St. (☎212-807-6655), between 6th and 7th Ave. Walk-in counseling M-F 10am-6pm. Open M-F 11am-8pm. **Gay and Lesbian Switchboard,** ☎212-989-0999. Operates M-F 4pm-midnight, Sa noon-5pm.

Hotlines: AIDS Hotline, ☎800-825-5448. Operates daily 9am-9pm. **Crime Victims' Hotline,** ☎212-577-7777. **Sex Crimes Report Line,** ☎212-267-7273. Both 24hr.

Medical Services: Doctors Walk-in Clinic, 55 E. 34th St. (☎212-252-6001, ext. 2), between Park and Madison Ave. Open M-Th 8am-8pm, F 8am-7pm, Sa 9am-3pm, Su 9am-2pm. Last walk-in 1hr. before closing.

Post Office: General Post Office, 421 8th Ave. (☎212-330-3002), at W. 32nd St. Open 24hr. General Delivery at 390 9th Ave., at W. 30th St. **Postal Code:** 10001.

Area Codes: 212, 347, or 646 (Manhattan); 718 (other 4 boroughs); 917 (cell phones). All New York City calls made within and between all 5 area codes must be dialed using 10-digit dialing.

◢ ACCOMMODATIONS

Accommodations are very expensive, with a capital "V." Travelers can expect a basic dorm bed in a hostel to run around $35, with private rooms running at rates closer to $50. Hotel singles start around $60, with the upper-limit being determined by the highest number you can think of, times three.

HOSTELS

 Central Park Hostel, 19 W. 103rd St. (☎212-678-0491; www.centralparkhostel.com), between Manhattan Ave. and Central Park W. Subway: 103rd St./Central Park W. 5-story walk-up brownstone with a nice lounge and clean guest rooms, all with A/C. Lobby has murals and funky tiled floor. Internet access $2 per 20min. Lockers available. Linen and towels included. Key deposit $2. 13-night max. stay. Reservations recommended. Dorms $26-35; private doubles and studio apartments $109-149. Cash only. ❶

◪ **New York International Hostel (HI),** 891 Amsterdam Ave. (☎212-932-2300; www.hinewyork.org), at 103rd St. Subway: 103 St./Broadway; 103rd St./Central Park W. Housed in a landmark building, this is the largest youth hostel in the US, with 624 beds available for its steady stream of guests. A/C, spotless bathrooms, dining rooms, garden, kitchens, tight security, and TV lounges. Internet access $2 per 20min. Linen and towels included. 26-night max. stay, extendable upon request. Check-in after 4pm. Check-out 11am. Credit card reservations required. 6-8 and 10-12 bed dorms $35, members $32; 4-bed dorms $38/35; rooms with queen bed and 2 bunks $120, with bath $135. AmEx/MC/V. ❷

Big Apple Hostel, 119 W. 45th St. (☎212-302-2603; www.bigapplehostel.com), between 6th and 7th Ave. Subway: 42nd St./Times Sq. Great location just off Times Square. Clean, carpeted rooms (co-ed and single-sex), kitchen, deck with grill, common rooms, and laundry facilities. No elevator. Internet access $1 per 8min. Safe at reception ($0.25). 21-day max. stay. Reception 24hr. Check-in noon. Check-out 11am. Aug.-Sept. reservations only accepted on website or by fax. 4-bed dorms $37-40, in late Dec. $45-60; private rooms $100-125/125-180. MC/V. ❷

Chelsea International Hostel, 251 W. 20th St. (☎212-647-0010; www.chelseahostel.com), between 7th and 8th Ave. Subway: 23rd St./7th Ave.; 23rd St./8th Ave. Popular with European escape artists. Courtyard, kitchens, laundry, and TV rooms. Internet $2 per 20min. Key deposit $10. Passport required. Check-in 24hr. Check-out noon. Reservations recommended 1-3 months in advance. 4-6 person dorms $30, with bath $34, A/C $2 extra; private rooms $70, with A/C $80. AmEx/D/MC/V. ❷

Jazz on the Park, 36 W. 106th St./Duke Ellington Blvd. (☎212-932-1600), between Manhattan Ave. and Central Park W. Subway: 103rd St./Central Park W. Brightly colored hostel with fun decor and 255 beds. A/C and lockers. Live jazz in the lounge on weekends; weekly organized events. Internet access $1 per 9min. Breakfast, linens, and towels included. Laundry. Check-in and check-out 11am. Call ahead to check room availability; reservations recommended. 10- to 12-bed dorms up to $27; 6- to 8-bed dorms $29; 4-bed dorms $32; private rooms $75-130. Prices vary by season. MC/V. ❶

HOTELS AND GUEST HOUSES

▨ **Carlton Arms Hotel,** 160 E. 25th St. (☎212-679-0680; www.carltonarms.com), between 3rd and Lexington Ave. Subway: 23rd St. The insignia shield for this hip hotel sports the Latin phrase for "There's no mint on your pillow." What it lacks in mints, TV, and phones, it makes up for in wild decor. 54 spacious rooms, all with A/C and sink, some with private bath. Check-in 10am. Check-out 11:30am. Reserve for summer 1 month in advance. Rooms $80, with bath $110. Student discount around $10. MC/V. ❸

▨ **Gershwin Hotel,** 7 E. 27th St. (☎212-545-8000; www.gershwinhotel.com), between Madison and 5th Ave. Subway: 28th St./Broadway; 28th St./Park Ave. S. The hotel's red facade is ornamented with stunning glass protrusions. Warhol in the lobby. Private rooms with A/C, bath, cable TV, and phone. Wi-Fi $10 per day, $35 per week. Reception 24hr. Check-in 3pm. Check-out 11am. 6- to 10-bed dorms $40-45; economy rooms $109; standard $109-199; suites available. AmEx/MC/V. ❸

Hotel Stanford, 43 W. 32nd St. (☎212-563-1500 or 800-365-1114; www.hotelstanford.com), between 5th Ave. and Broadway. Subway: 34th St./Herald Sq. This Herald Sq. hotel's lobby has sparkling lights, a marble floor, and great service. Impeccable rooms with A/C, bath, cable TV, fridge, hair dryer, phone, and safe. Breakfast included. Wi-Fi $20 per 24hr. Check-in 3pm. Check-out noon. Reservations recommended. Doubles $139-239; queens $149-249. AmEx/MC/V. ❺

Larchmont Hotel, 27 W. 11th St. (☎212-989-9333; www.larchmonthotel.com), between Fifth and Sixth Ave. Subway: 14th St./Union Sq. Spacious, clean, quiet rooms in whitewashed Greenwich Village brownstone.

BIG APPLE FOR SMALL POTATOES

New York City is not for the faint of heart, and most assuredly not for the slim of wallet: locals and tourists alike know that the price for living in the center of the world is quite steep. Unbelievably, a quality Friday in New York, complete with breakfast, lunch, dinner, and a day's entertainment, can be had for as little as $12.

Breakfast starts at **Kossar's Bialys,** 367 Grand St., on the Lower East Side, where one onion bialy runs just $0.60. The bialy (Polish for "white") is a soft disc of white bread with a bit of onion powder baked in.

Many of New York's most entertaining sights and activities are free. See the famed **St. Paul's Cathedral** or check out Chelsea's hip **art galleries** without spending a dime.

There's no better lunchtime deal in the city than the "Recession Special" at **Gray's Papaya,** 402 6th Ave.: two hot dogs and a smoothie run just $3.50.

After 4pm on Friday, enjoy free admission to one of New York's most popular (and priciest) museums, the **Museum of Modern Art,** 11 W. 53rd St.

At dinnertime, head to Chinatown, where **Fried Dumpling** will sell you five of its namesakes for $1. Odds are you won't be spending more than $5 here.

Round out your day with ice cream ($3) at the **Chinatown Ice Cream Factory,** 65 Bayard St.

A/C, closet, desk, TV, wash basin, and continental breakfast. Shared bath. Check-in 3pm. Check-out noon. Reserve 4-6 weeks ahead. Singles $80-115; doubles $109-135; queens 129-145. AmEx/MC/V. ❹

Chelsea Star Hotel, 300 W. 30th St. (☎212-244-7827 or 877-827-6969; www.starhotelny.com), at 8th Ave. Subway: 34th St./Penn Station/8th Ave. Madonna reportedly lived here as a struggling artist. Stay in 1 of the 16 themed rooms. All rooms with shared bath (20 rooms, 4 per bath) and A/C. Rooftop terrace. Internet access $2 per 20min; free Wi-Fi. Safe deposit box $5. 14-night max. stay. Reception 24hr. Check-in 1pm. Check-out 11am. Reserve at least 1 month ahead. Dorms $29-40; singles $89-119; doubles $109-139; quads $129-159. AmEx/D/MC/V. ❸

◘ FOOD

There's an eatery of any specialty for any budget anywhere you care to look in New York. If you have a rumble in your belly and a charge card in your wallet, the city can be your succulent oyster of culinary delight, and a good meal will find you.

CHINATOWN

▨ **Doyers Vietnamese Restaurant,** 11-13 Doyers St. (☎212-693-0725), between Bowery and Pell St. Follow the steps downstairs. Doyers (formerly known as Vietnam) has great Vietnamese cuisine, served quickly by the friendly staff. Appetizers are delicious and often unusual—try the shrimp paste grilled on sugar cane ($6.25). Also excellent are the hot pot soups ($19, serves 4-6) stuffed with simmering meat, vegetables, and seafood. Serves beer. Open M-Th and Su 11am-10pm, F-Sa 11am-11pm. AmEx. ❷

▨ **Joe's Shanghai,** 9 Pell St. (☎212-233-8888), between Bowery and Mott St. Also at 13621 37th Ave., in Flushing, Queens. From fried turnip shortcakes ($3.65) to crispy whole yellowfish ($14.35), this branch of the Queens legend serves tasty Shanghai specialties. Be prepared for communal tables, long lines on weekends, and prices slightly above a typical Chinatown restaurant. Open daily 11am-11:15pm. Cash only. ❸

Chinatown Ice Cream Factory, 65 Bayard St. (☎212-608-4170; www.chinatownicecreamfactory.com), at Elizabeth St. Unbeatable homemade ice cream in exotic flavors like lychee, black sesame, ginger, red bean, and green tea. 1 scoop $3, 2 scoops $4.65, 3 scoops $5.75. Crowded, but the line moves quickly. Open daily 11am-10pm; in warm weather until 11pm. ❶

Fried Dumpling, 106 Mosco St. (☎212-693-1060), between Mulberry and Mott St. For half the price of a subway ride ($1), get 5 dumplings or 4 pork buns. The only other items are soy bean juice (small $0.75, large $1.50) and hot-and-sour soup ($1). Open daily 10am-6pm. Cash only. ❶

LITTLE ITALY AND NOLITA

▨ **Lombardi's Coal Oven Pizza,** 32 Spring St. (☎212-941-7994), between Mott and Mulberry St. Lombardi's credits itself with creating the NY-style thin-crust, coal-oven pizza. Their large pie ($17.50) feeds 2. Toppings $3 for 1, $5 for 2, $6 for 3. Reservations accepted for groups of 6 or more. Try to visit on off-peak hours: the line is invariably out the door. Open M-Th and Su 11:30am-11pm, F-Sa 11:30am-midnight. Cash only. ❸

La Mela, 167 Mulberry St. (☎212-431-9493), between Broome and Grand St. Raucous dining, chummy staff, and a couple of Italian banjo players stirring up the amore. Generous portions served family-style. House wine $28 per 1.5L. Huge dessert concoction (ice cream, cake, coconut, glazed bananas) $7 per person. Pasta $7-10. 4-course dinners $28 per person, 3-course $24; min. 2 people. Family-style only after 6pm. Open M-Th and Su noon-2am, F-Sa noon-3am. AmEx/MC/V. ❷

Mottsu, 285 Mott St. (☎212-343-8017), between E. Houston and Spring St. One of Nolita's few sushi spots, popular with a young college crowd. Tuna roll $5.50. Eel-avocado roll $6.25. Open M-Th 12:30-3pm and 5:30-10:30pm, F 12:30-3pm and 5-11:30pm, Sa 5-11:30pm, Su 5-10pm. ❸

LOWER EAST SIDE

Shake Shack, at the southeast corner of Madison Sq. Park (☎212-889-6600; www.shakeshacknyc.com). Subway: 23rd St. A good, old-fashioned burger-and-shake stand beneath the leafy trees of Madison Sq. Park. Burgers are spiced and cooked to perfection; the frozen custards, which come in ever-changing flavors like fig, chocolate spice, and peanut butter chocolate chip, are to-die-for. The Shake Shack draws huge crowds, and they come for a reason. Shack burger with lettuce, tomato, and Shack Sauce $4.50. French fries $2. Open in summer daily 11am-11pm. ❶

Katz's Delicatessen, 205 E. Houston St. (☎212-254-2246), between Orchard and Ludlow St. Subway: Lower East Side/2nd Ave. The setting of a scene in "When Harry Met Sally" (1989), Katz's has been an LES institution since 1888—be prepared to pay extra for its fame. Knishes and franks $3. Reuben, cheesesteak, and corned beef sandwiches from $10. Open M-Tu and Su 8am-10pm, W-Th 8am-11pm, F-Sa 8am-3am. ❸

Kossar's Bialys, 367 Grand St. (☎212-473-4810), between Essex and Norfolk St. Subway: Delancey St. New York City's best bialy emporium. What's a bialy? Find out here. One regular onion bialy $0.60; large $1.50. Bagels also served. Open all night Sa. Open M-Th 6am-8pm, F 6am-5pm, Sa 9pm to Su 8pm. ❶

GREENWICH VILLAGE

Lips, 2 Bank St. (☎212-675-7710; www.lipsnyc.com), at Greenwich Ave. Subway: 14th St./8th Ave.; 14th St./7th Ave. Italian-Continental cuisine and impromptu drag "performances" from a high-heeled staff in a room decked out with lips. Try the RuPaul (grilled chicken with mashed potatoes and spinach; $16). Entrees $15-24. Su brunch 11:30am-4pm. Reservations recommended. Open M-Th 5:30-midnight, F-Sa 5:30pm-1:30am, Su 5:30pm-11pm. ❹

Moustache, 90 Bedford St. (☎212-229-2220), between Barrow and Grove St. Subway: Christopher St. Sumptuous Middle Eastern fare served on copper tabletops. Inhale the enticing smell of fresh pita. Try the succulent leg of lambwich ($9). Lentil soup $4. Salads $5-10.50. Falafel sandwich $6. Open daily noon-11pm. ❷

EAST VILLAGE

Cafe Mogador, 101 St. Mark's Place (☎212-677-2226), at 1st. Ave. This perpetually crowded East Village spot serves up a feast of Moroccan delights. Among appetizers, the *baba ghanoush* ($4.25) is a standout; for something more substantial, look to the grill menu, which offers skewered chicken, lamb, or *merguez* (Moroccan beef sausage) on a bed of basmati rice ($12-14.50). Other entrees $9.50-$19. Open M-Th and Su 9am-12:30am, F-Sa 9am-1:30am. ❸

Frank, 88 2nd Ave. (☎212-420-1232), between E. 5th and 6th St. Subway: Astor Pl. At this Italian bistro, the menu, like the restaurant itself, is happily cramped—daily specials are relegated to the chalkboards. Try the roasted rosemary chicken with mashed potatoes, gravy, olives, and slow cooked tomatoes ($13), or the spinach and gorgonzola *gnocchi* special ($15). Delivery available. Open M-Th 10:30am-1am, F-Sa 10:30am-2am, Su 10:30am-midnight. Cash only. ❸

CHELSEA

🔳 **Kangsuh Korean Restaurant,** 1250 Broadway (☎212-564-6845), on 32nd St. between 5th and 6th Ave; entrance off 32nd St. Subway: Herald Sq. Homestyle Korean cooking served family-style with efficient service in a clean, 2-story restaurant. The delectable *hwe dup bap* lunch special (spicy sashimi salad with rice; $10) and the *kalbi* (barbe-cued short ribs; $12) draw hordes of hungry patrons. Entrees $10-18. Open 24hr. ❹

Pop Burger, 58-60 9th Ave. (☎212-414-8686), between 14th and 15th St. Subway: 14th St./7th Ave; 14th St. The fast-food front counter and wait-service back lounge cater to both those who pop "mini" burgers (2 for $5) and those who nibble filet mignon ($25). The food is acclaimed, and the stainless-steel interior looks a little out of this world. Chocolate, strawberry, and vanilla shakes $5.25. Beer $5. Open daily 11am-1am. Lounge open M-Tu and Su 5pm-2am, W-Sa 5pm-4am. ❸

THEATER DISTRICT

🍴 **Becco,** 355 W. 46th St. (☎212-397-7597; www.becconyc.com), between 8th and 9th Ave. Great Italian food for a moderate splurge. 70 wines priced at $20 per bottle. $17 *prix-fixe* lunch (dinner $22) includes a gourmet antipasto platter or caesar salad, plus unlimited servings of the 3 pastas of the day. Try the mesclun salad with Tuscan beans and ripe tomatoes, tossed with an aged Chianti vinaigrette ($8), or the grilled Atlantic salmon with poached potatoes, green beans, and grain mustard ($24). Lunch $14 food min. per person, dinner $16. Open daily noon-3pm and 5pm-midnight. ❹

Island Burgers and Shakes, 766 9th Ave. (☎212-307-7934; http://island.city-search.com), between 51st and 52nd St. Burgers so good that Island sells more than 150 lb. of meat per day. For $0.50 extra, each of the 50 burger varieties ($6-9) can be ordered with grilled chicken instead of beef; you can also design your own. Sadly, no fries. Open daily noon-10:30pm, F until 11pm. Cash only. ❷

Say Cheese!, 649 9th Ave. (☎212-265-8840), between 45th and 46th St. This tiny soup-and-sandwich joint specializes in any and all permutations of grilled cheese ($4.50-8.50). The Chokes on Tuna (tuna fish plus artichokes, fresh oregano, roasted garlic, and American cheese on pizza bianca; $7.50) is a must; the Big Cheese (grilled cheese with red peppers and sauteed onions on olive bread; $7.50), also deserves some praise. Open daily 11am-11pm. ❷

UPPER EAST SIDE

🍴 **Payard,** 1032 Lexington Ave. (☎212-717-5252; www.payard.com), between 73rd and 74th St. Subway: 77th St. With prices as rich as the pastries (which is saying some-thing), this decadent Parisian-style patisserie-bistro serves some of the most sinful des-serts ($7-11) in town. Gourmet sandwiches and savory tarts $12-14. Try the potato *tourte* ($13), with goat's milk brie, mushrooms, caramelized onions, and walnuts. Open M-Th noon-10:30pm, F-Sa noon-11pm. ❹

Il Vagabondo, 351 E. 62nd St. (☎212-832-9221), between 1st and 2nd Ave. Sub-way: 59th St. An Upper East Side staple since 1971. You won't find many tourists here, but the regulars have been flocking to this Italian spot for decades. Don't miss the series of creative veal entrees ($21.50). Lunch entrees $8-29. Dinner $18-39. Open for lunch M-F 12pm-3pm; dinner M-Sa 5:30-11:30pm, Su 5:30-11pm. ❺

Vermicelli, 1492 2nd Ave. (☎212-288-8868), between 77th and 78th St. Subway: 77th St. The name suggests an Italian cookery, but this smallish uptown restaurant actually specializes in Vietnamese. Barbecued chicken with warm vermicelli, corian-der, and roasted peanuts $9. The $6-7 box lunches, served with vegetables, soup, salad, and steamed rice, are a popular eat-on-the-go option. Try the spicy lemon-grass chicken with peppers. Open daily 11:30am-10:45pm. Free delivery. ❷

UPPER WEST SIDE

🍴 **Big Nick's Burger Joint and Pizza Joint,** 2175 Broadway (☎212-362-9238 or 724-2010), at 77th St. Subway: 79th St. Telephone-book-like menu (27 pages thick!). Burgers and pizza are obvious choices, but you can also get all-day breakfast and vegan and vegetarian options. Wrestle with a plate-sized burger ($6-8), a full homestyle Italian dinner ($8-15), or sweet potato fries ($3.25). Open daily 6am-5am (the next morning). Free delivery. 2nd location: 70 W. 71st St. (☎212-799-4444), at Columbus Ave. ❷

🏙 **Zabar's,** 2245 Broadway (☎212-787-2000), between 80th and 81st St. Subway: 79th St. All the imported delicacies you need for a 4-star meal at home. In a pinch? Arrive with a toothpick and make a meal of the legendary free samples. On weekend mornings, masses of hungry New Yorkers stand in line for bagels and coffee. Open M-F 8am-7:30pm, Sa 8am-8pm, Su 9am-6pm. Cafe open M-Sa 7:30am-7pm, Su 8am-6pm. ❸

Gray's Papaya, 2090 Broadway (☎212-799-0243), at 72nd St. Subway: 72nd St. A local landmark chain featuring 3 lively standing-room-only locations with amazing deals on hot dogs. The "recession special" is 2 franks and 1 fruit drink (banana daiquiri, pineapple, piña colada, papaya) for $3.50. Also at 539 8th Ave. and 402 6th Ave. Open 24hr. ❶

HARLEM AND MORNINGSIDE HEIGHTS

🏙 **Amir's Falafel,** 2911A Broadway (☎212-749-7500), between 113th and 114th St. Subway: 110th St.; 116th St. Small and simple, with Middle Eastern staples like *Shawarma* and *baba ghanoush*. Substantial vegetarian options (platters $6.50). Falafel $4. Open daily 11am-11pm. Free delivery within Morningside Heights. Cash only. ❶

🏙 **Amy Ruth's,** 113 W. 116th St. (☎212-280-8779; www.amyruthsrestaurant.com), between Adam Clayton Powell Blvd. and Lenox (6th) Ave. Subway: 116th St. Named in honor of the owner's grandmother, this intimate restaurant serves cuisine straight from a southern kitchen. Try the "Yasmin Cornelius" (chicken wings and waffles; $9) or the "James Ford" (pan-seared jumbo shrimp; $18). Open M-Th 7:30am-11pm, F 7:30am to Su 11pm. Free delivery. ❸

Hispaniola, 839 W. 181st St. (☎212-740-5222; www.hispaniolarestaurant.com), at Cabrini Blvd. Subway: 181st St./Ft. Washington Ave. Delectable Dominican-Asian fusion cuisine. Innovative sushi includes tempura coconut shrimp pineapple rolls ($10) and tilapia asparagus mesclun rolls ($10). The $14 "conto boxes" come with coconut shrimp and salad, plus grilled salmon, miso butterfish, fried chicken, or steak. Sandwiches $8-10. Entrees $15-26. Happy hour M-F 4-8pm. Open M-Sa 11am-4pm and 5:30pm-2am. Kitchen closes at midnight. ❹

BROOKLYN

🏙 **Planet Thailand,** 115 Berry St. (☎718-599-5758), between N. 7th and 8th St. Subway: Bedford Ave. High-ceilinged space that's too trendy for a sign. Expansive menu includes Thai beef and chicken curries ($9), pad thai ($8-9), hibachi table fare ($10-17), and Japanese items (sushi dinner from $11). If you go on a weekend night, be prepared to wait: Planet Thailand takes no reservations, and people from across the city flock here. DJ daily 9pm. Open M-Th and Su 11:30am-midnight, F-Sa 11:30am-1am. Cash only. ❸

DuMont Restaurant, 432 Union Ave. (☎718-486-7717), at Devoe St. Subway: Lorimer St. Excellent service, a solid wine list, and garden dining in warm weather. Feels like a French speakeasy—if France had ever endured prohibition. A handful of plates remain on the menu day to day, of which the burger ($11) and the DuMac and Cheese ($10) are signature pieces. Brunch Sa-Su. Dinner entrees $12-24. Open M-Th 11am-3pm and 6-11pm, F-Sa 11am-3pm and 6pm-midnight, Su 11am-3:30pm and 6pm-11pm. ❹

Jacques Torres Chocolate, 66 Water St. (☎718-875-9772), between Dock and Main St. Subway: High St.; York St. Watch chefs make chocolate almonds ($5 per ¼ lb.), chocolate croissants ($1.50), and chocolate bars ($4). Truffles ($0.80) take center stage, coming in varieties such as fresh-squeezed lemon, cappuccino, and Love Potion #9. Hot chocolate $2.50. Mocha cappuccino $3. Open M-Sa 9am-7pm, Su 10am-6pm. ❶

QUEENS

▨ Flushing Noodle, 135-42 Roosevelt Ave. (☎718-353-1166). Subway: Flushing/Main St. One of Flushing's finest Chinese noodle shops. Try the spare ribs ($9), or choose from all manner of noodles ($4-12). Lunch specials ($5.50; 11am-3:30pm) give you 37 entree choices. Limited seating, always packed. Takeout available. Open daily 9am-10pm. ❶

Bohemian Hall and Beer Garden, 29-19 24th Ave. (☎718-274-4925; www.bohemian-hall.com). Subway: 30th Ave. Operated by the Bohemian Citizens' Benevolent Society, this Czech restaurant and 900-seat outdoor beer garden is packed every night. Enjoy Bohemian staples like fried cheese with french fries ($8) and crunchy pork schnitzel ($10.50). Open M-F 5pm-3am, Sa-Su noon-3am. ❸

◉ SIGHTS

THE STATUE OF LIBERTY AND ELLIS ISLAND

The Statue of Liberty, long a symbol of hope for immigrants, stands at the entrance to New York Harbor. In 1886, the French government presented Frederic-Auguste Bartholdi's sculpture to the US as a sign of goodwill. The statue's crown and torch were closed in September 2001; views are limited to the 150-ft. concrete pedestal. Ellis Island, accessible by the same ferry, was the processing point for millions of immigrants from 1897 to 1938. The museum chronicles immigrant life in the New World. *(Subway: 4, 5 to Bowling Green; R, W to Whitehall St.; 1, 9 to South Ferry. ☎212-363-3200; www.nps.gov/stli. Ferries leave for Liberty Island from the piers at Battery Park every 30min. M-F 9:15am-3:30pm, Sa-Su 9am-4pm. Ferry information ☎212-269-5755; www.statueoflibertyferry.com. Tickets for ferry with access to Liberty Island and Ellis Island $11.50, seniors $9.50, ages 4-12 $4.50, under 4 free. Audio tour $6.)*

FINANCIAL DISTRICT AND CIVIC CENTER

The southern tip of Manhattan is home to many of the financial powerhouses of the world. The physical proof is in the skyline: the **Wall Street** area, less than half a mile long, has one of the highest concentrations of skyscrapers in the world. Crooked streets reflect the city's original Dutch layout; lower Manhattan was the first part of the island to be settled. *(Subway: 1, 9 to Wall St./William St.; 4, 5 to Bowling Green, Wall St./Broadway; N, R, W to Rector St., Whitehall St.; 1, 2, 4, 5, A, C, J, M, Z to Fulton St./Broadway/Nassau St.; J, M, Z to Broad St.)*

FINANCIAL DISTRICT. Once the northern border of the New Amsterdam settlement, Wall St. was named for the wall built in 1653 to shield the Dutch colony from British invasion. By the early 19th century, the area was the financial capital of the US. On the southwest corner of Wall and Broad St. stands the **New York Stock Exchange.** This 1903 temple to capitalism sees billions of dollars change hands daily. The exchange, founded in 1792 at 68 Wall St., is now off-limits to tourists. Around the corner, at the end of Wall St., stands the seemingly ancient **Trinity Church,** with its delicately crafted steeple. *(74 Trinity Place. ☎212-602-0800.)* Peter Minuit purchased Manhattan for the equivalent of $24 at **Bowling Green,** at the intersection of Battery Pl., Broadway, and Whitehall St. The Beaux Arts **Alexander Hamilton US Custom House** overlooks the park. *(1 Bowling Green St.)*

WORLD TRADE CENTER MEMORIAL SITE (GROUND ZERO). The site where the WTC once stood is a sobering spectacle. The poignancy of the vast empty landscape can only really be understood in person. Plans have finally been solidified for the new **Freedom Tower,** which, when completed in 2010 or 2011, will be the world's tallest building at 1776 ft. On August 2, 2004, construction began on a 945-ft.-tall skyscraper, slated to open before the Freedom Tower is completed. The site will also hold a subway terminal and memorials to the victims of the 9/11 attacks.

CIVIC CENTER. The city's center of government is located north of its financial district. The New York City mayor's office is in **City Hall;** around it are courthouses, civic buildings, and federal buildings. The building's interior is closed indefinitely to the public. *(Broadway at Murray St., off Park Row.)* The **Woolworth Building,** a 1913 Neo-Gothic skyscraper and "Cathedral of Commerce" built for $15.5 million to house F.W. Woolworth's five-and-dime store empire, looms south of City Hall. *(233 Broadway, between Barclay St. and Park Pl. Closed to the public.)* A block and a half south on Broadway lies **St. Paul's Chapel,** Manhattan's oldest public building in continuous use. George Washington prayed here on his inauguration day. *(Between Vesey and Fulton St. ☎ 212-602-0747. Open M-F 9am-3pm, Su 7am-3pm. Free. Su mass 8 and 10am.)*

SOUTH STREET SEAPORT. The shipping industry thrived at the South Street Seaport for most of the 19th century, when New York City was the most important port city in the US. During the 20th century, bars, brothels, and crime flourished. Now a 12-block "museum without walls," the seaport displays old schooners, sailboats, and houses. *(Between FDR Dr. and Water St., and between Beekman and John St. Subway: 2, 3, 4, 5, A, C, J, M, Z to Fulton St./Broadway/Nassau St. Visitors Center: 12 Fulton St. ☎ 212-748-8600; www.southstseaport.org. Open Apr.-Oct. Tu-Su 10am-6pm; Nov.-Mar daily 10am-5pm, M limited gallery availability. Ships, shops, and tours $8, students and seniors $6, ages 5-12 $4, under 5 free. Walking around the museum is free.)*

CHINATOWN AND LITTLE ITALY

Mott and **Pell Street,** which form the unofficial center of Chinatown, brim with restaurants and commercial activity. Baby jackets, bamboo hats, and miniature Buddhas crowd the storefronts. **Canal Street** offers tons of low-priced, creatively labeled merchandise (those are *not* Rolexes). **Mulberry Street** remains the heart of Little Italy, which has been largely taken over by Chinatown in recent decades. *(Subway: A, C, E to Canal St./6th Ave.; J, M, Z to Canal St./Centre St.; N, Q, R, W to Canal St./Broadway; 6 to Canal St./Lafayette St.; F to E Broadway; B, D, F, V to Broadway/Lafayette St.)*

LOWER EAST SIDE

The Lower East Side was once the most densely settled area in New York City. The Irish came in the mid-1800s, Eastern Europeans in the 50 years preceding WWI, African-Americans and Puerto Ricans post-WWII, and Latin Americans and Asians in the 80s and 90s. Main thoroughfares like E. Broadway reflect the area's multicultural roots. Orchard St., a historic shopping area that fills up on Sundays, still has traces of the Jewish ghetto that once occupied the area. *(Subway: F, V to Lower East Side/2nd Ave.; F to E Broadway; F, J, M, Z to Delancey St./Essex St.)* A free weekly tour of the Lower East Side meets in front of Katz's Delicatessen (p. 95) on Houston Street (Su 11am). At the **Lower East Side Tenement Museum,** tours lead through three meticulously restored apartments of immigrant families. *(108 Orchard St. ☎ 212-431-0233. Open M 11am-5:30pm, Tu-F 11am-6pm, Sa-Su 10:45am-6pm. Tours depart every 15min. $17, seniors and students $13.)* The **Eldridge Street Synagogue** (12 Eldridge St. ☎ 212-219-0888) and **Congregation Anshe Chesed** *(172-176 Norfolk St., at Stanton St. ☎ 212-865-0600)* are noteworthy, splendid synagogues worth a peek.

SOHO AND TRIBECA

The architecture in the area **South of Houston**—with Canal St. on the south, Broadway on the west, and Crosby St. on the east—is American Industrial, notable for its cast-iron facades. SoHo is filled with artists and galleries (see **Galleries,** p. 142), chic boutiques, and expensive shopping. *(Subway: C, E to Spring St./Ave. of the Americas (6th Ave.); 6 to Spring St./Lafayette St.; N, R, W to Prince St.; 1, 9 to W Houston St.; B, D, F, V to Broadway/Lafayette St.)* **TriBeCa,** or **Triangle Below Canal Street,** contains trendy lofts, restaurants, bars, and galleries—without the upscale airs. Admire the cast-iron

SOUND BITES

There are few things like being overheard on the streets of New York City. Snippets of thousands of conversations fly through the air like maniacal taxi drivers through rush-hour traffic, pausing only as they collide occasionally with the gridlock of your ears.

Fortunately, there is a website that makes sense of it all: www.overheardinnewyork.com. The site is updated daily by hordes of loyal readers who submit aural findings from one-liners to diatribes. This fascinating collection of conversational odds-and-ends creates a brilliant mosaic of how the city thinks—or, at the very least, how it mocks.

Within the annals of Overheard, nothing is sacred. Religion, politics, sex, gender, economic status—all are held up to the withering light of decontextualized irony. Of particular note are the numerous documented interactions between "yuppies" and "hobos."

And while Overheard may be nothing more than the jaded footnote to a New York minute, it provides an immediate glimpse into the true life of the city, a pulsing, irresistible vitality that will have you systematically forging through the site's archives in no time.

And who knows? You might even find yourself overheard somewhere in the mix (we did); but don't worry, we're sure it sounded smarter at the time...

edifices lining White St., Thomas St., and Broadway, the Federal-style buildings on Harrison St., and the shops, galleries, and bars on Church and Reade St. *(Subway: 1, 9 to Canal St./Varick St.; A, C, E to Canal St./Ave. of the Americas (6th Ave.); 1, 9 to Franklin St.; 1, 2, 3, 9 to Chambers St./W Broadway; A, C to Chambers St./Church St.)*

GREENWICH VILLAGE

The wandering streets of Greenwich Village bristle with activism and artistry. Once a hilly farming area, the neighborhood developed in the mid 19th century into a high-society playground that fostered literary creativity. Henry James captured the Village's spirit in his 1880 novel, *Washington Square.* The last 50 years have brought the Beat movement, the emergence of a thriving gay community around Christopher St., and the punk scene. Gentrification in the 80s and 90s made the Village a fashionable settlement for wealthier New Yorkers with more spunk than their uptown counterparts. *(Subway: W 4th St.; 14th St./8th Ave.; 14th St./7th Ave.; 14th St./Ave. of the Americas (6th Ave.); 8th Ave., Ave. of the Americas (6th Ave.); 14th St./Union Sq.; Houston St., Christopher St.; 8th St./NYU; 6th Ave., 8th Ave.; Bleecker St.)*

WASHINGTON SQUARE. Washington Square Park has a rich history. On the north side of the park is **The Row,** a stretch of 1830s brick residences that were once populated by writers, dandies, and professionals. At the north end of the park stands the **Washington Memorial Arch,** built in 1889 to commemorate the centennial of George Washington's inauguration. **New York University,** the country's largest private university, has some of the Village's least appealing contemporary architecture. On the park's southeast side, where Washington Sq. S. meets LaGuardia Pl., NYU's **Loeb Student Center** sports pieces of scrap metal representing birds in flight.

WEST VILLAGE. The area of Greenwich Village west of 6th Ave. boasts eclectic summer street life and excellent nightlife. A visible gay community thrives around **Sheridan Square,** at 7th Ave., W. 4th St., and Christopher St. The 1969 Stonewall Riot, arguably the beginning of the modern gay rights movement, started here. The neighborhood is a magnet for literary pilgrimages. **Chumley's,** a former speakeasy, was a hangout for such authors as Ernest Hemingway and John Dos Passos. *(86 Bedford St., between Grove and Barrow St. ☎ 212-675-4449. Open M-F 4pm for drinks, 5pm for dinner; Sa-Su noon for brunch, 5pm for dinner.)* Off 10th St. and 6th Ave., you'll see an iron gate and street sign marking **Patchin Place.** Theodore Dreiser, e. e. cummings, and Djuna Barnes lived in the 145-year-old buildings that line this path. The Village's narrowest building, **75½ Bedford Street,** only 9½ ft. in width, housed writer Edna St. Vincent Millay in the 20s, when she founded the nearby **Cherry Lane Theater,** 38 Commerce St. Actors Lionel Barrymore and Cary Grant also once called the cramped quarters home.

EAST VILLAGE

The East Village—north of Houston St., east of Broadway, and south of 14th St.—was carved out of the Bowery and the Lower East Side in the early 60s, when artists and writers moved here to escape high rent in Greenwich Village. Today the East Village's wide-ranging population includes punks, hippies, ravers, rastas, guppies, goths, and beatniks—expect the unexpected. **St. Mark's Place** is full of tiny ethnic eateries, street-level shops, sidewalk vendors, and tattoo shops. Bustling with street life, **Astor Place,** at the intersection of Lafayette, E. 8th St., and 4th Ave., is distinguished by a black cube balanced on its corner. Tensions of gentrification have made the East Village into one of the city's most politicized neighborhoods. *(Subway: 6 to Astor Pl., Bleecker St.; L to 1st Ave., 3rd Ave.; F, V to Lower East Side/2nd Ave.)*

LOWER MIDTOWN

UNION SQUARE. At the intersection of 4th Ave. and Broadway, Union Square and the surrounding area sizzled with high society before the Civil War. Today, the park hosts the **Union Square Greenmarket,** a pleasant farmers' market. Local artists give live performances on the green while jugglers, breakdancers, and magicians take to the nearby streets. *(Between Broadway and Park Ave. S., between 14th and 17th St. Subway: 4, 5, 6, L, N, Q, R, W to 14th St./Union Sq. Greenmarket open M, W, and F-Sa 8am-6pm.)* Originally named the Fuller Building, the photogenic **Flatiron Building** was nicknamed after its dramatic wedge shape, imposed by the intersection of Broadway, 5th Ave., 22nd St., and 23rd St.

CHELSEA. Home to fashionable clubs, bars, and restaurants, Chelsea (west of 5th Ave., between 14th and 30th St.) boasts a large GLBT community, a growing artsy-yuppie population, and **art galleries** (p. 109) fleeing high SoHo rents. *(Subway: 1, 2, 3, 9 to 14th St./7th Ave.; A, C, E, L to 14th St./8th Ave.; C, E to 23rd St./8th Ave.; 1, 9 to 23rd St., 28th St./7th Ave.)* **Hotel Chelsea,** between 7th and 8th Ave., has pampered the likes of Sex Pistols bassist Sid Vicious. Countless writers have sought inspiration here, including Vladimir Nabokov and Dylan Thomas. *(222 W. 23rd St., between 7th and 8th Ave. ☎ 212-243-3700.)*

HERALD SQUARE AREA. Herald Sq. is between 34th and 35th St., between Broadway and 6th Ave. The area is a center for shopping. *(Subway: B, D, F, N, Q, R, V, W to 34th St./Herald Sq.)* The **Empire State Building,** now the city's tallest building, dominates postcards, movies, and the city's skyline. The limestone-and-granite structure stretches 1454 ft. into the sky, and its 73 elevators run through 2 mi. of shafts. The nighttime view from the **observation deck,** located 1050 ft. above street level, is spectacular; on a clear night, hawk-eyed observers can see as far as Connecticut. *(350 5th Ave., at 34th St. Observatory: ☎ 212-736-3100. Open daily 8am-2am. Last entry 1:15am. $12, seniors $11, under 12 $7. Skyride: ☎ 212-279-9777. Open daily 10am-10pm. $17, seniors, military, and ages 12-17 $15, ages 4-11 $11.)* East on 34th St. stands **Macy's.** This Goliath of department stores sponsors the **Macy's Thanksgiving Day Parade,** a NYC tradition buoyed by 10-story Snoopys, marching bands, and floats. *(Between 7th Ave. and Broadway, in Herald Sq.)* The **Garment District,** surrounding Macy's but selling cheaper clothing, purportedly contained the world's highest concentration of apparel workers during the 30s. Today, it's a good bet for bargain shoppers with the patience to rummage. *(Between Broadway and 8th Ave.)*

MIDTOWN

East of 8th Ave., from about 42nd St. to 59th St., lie Midtown's mammoth office buildings, posh hotels, and high-brow stores. *(Subway: 4, 5, 6, 7, S to 42nd St./Grand Central; B, D, F, V to 42nd St./Ave. of the Americas (6th Ave.); 7 to 5th Ave./42nd St.; E, V to 5th Ave./53rd St.; N, R, W to 5th Ave./59th St.; 1, 2, 3, 7, 9, N, Q, R, S, W to 42nd St./Times Square; A, C, E to 42nd St./Port Authority; 7, B, D, F, V to 42nd St./Bryant Park.)*

FIFTH AVENUE. A monumental building in the style of a classical temple, the main branch of the **New York Public Library,** between 40th and 42nd St., contains the world's 7th-largest research library and an immense reading room in a truly imposing structure. *(42nd St. and 5th Ave. ☎ 212-869-8089.)* Behind the library, **Bryant Park** features free summertime cultural events, like classic film screenings and live comedy. *(☎ 212-484-1222 for events schedule. Open daily 7am-9pm.)* Designed by James Renwick, the twin spires of **St. Patrick's Cathedral** stretch 330 ft. into the air, making it the largest Catholic cathedral in the US. *(51st St. ☎ 212-753-2261.)*

ROCKEFELLER CENTER. The main entrance to Rockefeller Center is on 5th Ave. between 49th and 50th St. **The Channel Gardens,** so named because they sit between the **Maison Française** on the left and the **British Empire Building** on the right, usher pedestrians toward **Tower Plaza.** This sunken space, topped by the gold-leafed statue of Prometheus, is surrounded by the flags of over 100 countries. During spring and summer an **ice-skating rink** lies dormant beneath an overpriced cafe. The rink, which is better for people-watching than for skating, reopens in winter in time for the **annual Christmas tree lighting,** one of New York City's greatest traditions. **Tours of Rockefeller Center** are available through NBC. *(Tours depart every 2hr. from the GE Building. M-Sa 10am-5pm, Su 10am-3pm. No children under 6. $12, seniors and ages 6-12 $10; groups of 10 or more $10 per person.)*

Behind Tower Plaza is the **General Electric Building,** a 70-story skyscraper. **NBC,** which makes its home here, offers an hour-long **Studio Tour** that traces the network's history, from its 1st radio broadcast in 1926, through the heyday of TV programming in the 50s and 60s, to today's sitcoms and reality TV shows. The tour leads visitors through six studios, including the infamous 6339 square-foot 8H studio, now the home of the legendary *Saturday Night Live. (Departs every 30min. from the NBC Experience Store in the GE Building (every 15min. F-Su); M-Th 8:30am-4:30pm, F-Sa 9:30pm-5:30pm, Su 9:30am-4:30pm; no children under 6. $18.50, seniors and ages 6-12 $15.50.)* A block north is **Radio City Music Hall.** Having narrowly escaped demolition in 1979, this Art Deco landmark received a complete interior restoration shortly thereafter. Radio City's main attraction is the Rockettes, a high-stepping, long-legged troupe of dancers. Tours of the Music Hall take visitors through The Great Stage and various rehearsal halls. *(50th St. at 6th Ave. ☎ 212-247-4777. Tours depart every 30min. daily 11am-3pm. $17, seniors $14, under 12 $10.)*

PARK AVENUE. A luxurious boulevard with greenery running down its center, **Park Avenue,** between 45th and 59th St., is lined with office buildings and hotels. Completed in 1913, the **Grand Central Terminal** has a richly classical main facade on 42nd St., topped by a beautiful sculpture of Mercury, the Roman god of transportation. An info booth sits in the middle of the commuter-filled Concourse. *(Between 42nd and 45th St.)* Several blocks uptown is the *crème de la crème* of Park Avenue hotels, the **Waldorf-Astoria.** *(Between 49th and 50th St.)* The **Seagram Building,** Ludwig Mies Van der Rohe's dark, graceful modern monument, stands a few blocks uptown. *(375 Park Ave., between 52nd and 53rd St.)*

UNITED NATIONS AREA. The **United Nations,** a "center for harmonizing the actions of nations" founded in 1945 in the aftermath of WWII, is located in international territory along what would be 1st Ave. The UN complex consists of the Secretariat Building (the skyscraper), the General Assembly Building, the Hammarskjöld Library, and the Conference Building. The only way into the General Assembly Building is by guided tour. *(1st Ave., between 42nd and 48th St. ☎212-963-4475. 1hr. tours depart from the UN visitors' entrance at 1st Ave. and 46th St. Held every 15min. in 20 languages. Mar.-Dec. M-F 9:30am-4:45pm, Sa-Su 10am-4:30pm; Jan.-Feb. M-F only. $13, over 62 $9, students $8.50, ages 5-14 $7.)* At the **Chrysler Building,** a spire influenced by a radiator tops the Art Deco palace. *(On 42nd St. and Lexington Ave.)*

TIMES SQUARE AND THE THEATER DISTRICT. Times Square, at the intersection of 42nd St., 7th Ave., and Broadway, once gave New York City its reputation for strip clubs and filth. Today, the smut has been replaced by 30 ft. tall billboards, bopping Disney musicals, MTV's Total Request Live studio, and nearly 40 million tourists per year. The outgoing flock to take a picture with the **Naked Cowboy,** a local phenomenon who has become a fixture in the Square, roaming the area freely at all times of the day. Every New Year's Eve, thousands pack into the Square to count down seconds to the new year as a shimmering crystal ball drops at midnight. For info on rush ticketing or anything else, stop by the **Times Square Visitors Center,** 1560 Broadway, at W. 46th St. *(☎212-869-1890; www.timessquarebid.com. Open daily 8am-8pm.)*

57TH STREET AND CENTRAL PARK SOUTH. Luxury hotels, including the **Essex House** and the **St. Moritz** overlook Central Park from their perch on Central Park S., between 5th and 8th Ave., where 59th St. should be. Amid 57th St.'s galleries and stores, New York City's musical center is **Carnegie Hall** (p. 113). A $60 million restoration has returned the 1891 building to its earlier splendor. *(881 7th Ave., at W. 57th St. ☎212-247-7800; www.carnegiehall.org. 1hr. tours M-F 11:30am, 2, 3pm. Purchase tickets at box office on tour days. $10, seniors and students $7, under 12 $3.)*

CENTRAL PARK

> Central Park is fairly safe during the day, but less so at night. Don't be afraid to go to events in the Park at night, but take well-traveled paths and go with someone. Do not wander darker paths at night, especially if you are a woman. In an **emergency,** use one of the call-boxes throughout the park. The **24hr. Police Line** is ☎570-4820.

Central Park was founded in the mid-19th century when wealthy New Yorkers advocated the creation of a park in the style of the public grounds of Europe. Frederick Law Olmsted and Calvert Vaux designed the park in 1858; their Greensward plan took 15 years and 20,000 workers to implement. Expansive fields like the **Sheep Meadow,** from 66th to 69th St., and the **Great Lawn,** from 80th to 85th St., complement developed spaces such as the **Mall,** between 66th and 71st St., the **Shakespeare Garden,** at 80th St., and the **Imagine Mosaic,** commemorating John Lennon, on the western side of the park at 72nd St. Don't miss free summer shows at **Central Park Summerstage** and **Shakespeare in Central Park.** *(Free park maps at Belvedere Castle, located mid-park at 79th St.; the Charles A. Dana Discovery Center, at 110th St. near 5th Ave.; the North Meadow Recreation Center, mid-park at 97th St.; and the Dairy, mid-park near 65th St.)*

UPPER EAST SIDE

Since the late 19th and early 20th centuries, when some of New York City's wealthiest citizens built elaborate mansions along **Fifth Avenue,** the Upper East Side has been home to the city's fanciest residents. Today, some of these mansions have been turned into museums, such as the Frick Collection and the Cooper-Hewitt Museum. They are just two of the world-famous museums that line **Museum Mile,** from 82nd to 104th St. on 5th Ave. (p. 107). **Park Avenue** from 59th to 96th St. is lined with dignified apartment buildings. Lexington and 3rd Ave. are commercial, but as you go east, the neighborhood becomes more and more residential. *(Subway: N, R, W to Fifth Ave./59th St.; 4, 5, 6, N, R, W to 59th St./Lexington Ave.; F to Lexington Ave./63rd St.; 6 to 68th Sts., 77th St., 96th St.; 4, 5, 6 to 86th St./Lexington Ave.)*

UPPER WEST SIDE

While Central Park W. and Riverside Dr. flank the Upper West Side with residential quietude, Columbus Ave., Amsterdam Ave., and Broadway are abuzz with action. Organic fruit and progressive politics dominate the area between 59th and 110th St., west of Central Park. *(Subway: 1, 9, A, B, C, D to 59th St./Columbus Circle; 1, 9 to 66th St., 79th St., 86th St./Broadway; 1, 2, 3, 9 to 72nd St./Broadway; B, C to 72nd St., 81st St., 86th St., 96th St./Central Park W; 1, 2, 3, 9 to 96th St./Broadway.)*

LINCOLN CENTER. Broadway intersects Columbus Ave. at **Lincoln Center,** the city's cultural hub (p. 112). The airy architecture recalls the public plazas of Rome and Venice, but the center's performance spaces for opera, ballet, and classical music take center stage. *(Between 62nd and 66th St.)*

MORNINGSIDE HEIGHTS. Above 110th St. and below 125th St., between Amsterdam Ave. and the Hudson River, **Morningside Heights** centers around **Columbia University's** urban campus. *(Subway: 1 to Cathedral Pkwy. (110th St.), 116th St./Columbia University, 125th St./Broadway.)* The centerpiece of the campus is the majestic Roman Classical **Low Library,** which looms over College Walk, the school's central promenade. *(Morningside Dr. and Broadway, from 114th to 120th St.)* The still-unfinished cathedral of **St. John the Divine,** under construction since 1892, is the largest in the world. It features altars and bays dedicated both to the sufferings of Christ and to the experiences of immigrants, victims of genocide, and AIDS patients. *(Amsterdam Ave., between 110th and 113th St. Subway: 1 to Cathedral Pkwy. (110th St.)/Broadway. ☎ 212-316-7540, tours 212-932-7347, parish box office 212-662-2133; www.stjohndivine.org. Open daily 7am-6pm. Holy Eucharist M-Sa 8:30am and 12:15pm; Su sermon 9am. Tours Tu-Sa 11am, Su 1pm. $5, seniors and students $4.)* **Riverside Church,** near Columbia, has an observation deck in its tower with a stunning view, as well as the world's largest carillon (74 bells), a gift from John D. Rockefeller, Jr. *(490 Riverside Dr., at 120th St. Subway: 1 to 116th St./Columbia University. ☎ 212-870-6792; www.theriversidechurchny.org. Open M-F 9am-4:30pm. Services Su 10:45am. Tours Su 12:30pm, after services, and upon request. Free.)* **Grant's Tomb,** a huge presidential grave commemorating the Union Civil War general, lies at 122nd St. and Riverside Dr. *(Open daily 9am-5pm. Free.)*

HARLEM

Manhattan's largest neighborhood extends from 110th S. to the 150s, between the Hudson and East Rivers. Harlem began its transformation into a black neighborhood between 1910 and 1920. The 20s brought prosperity and the artistic Harlem Renaissance; Civil Rights and radical Black Power activism came in the 60s. Today, thanks to community activism and the recent economic boom, Harlem is thriving. *(Subway: 6 to 103rd St., Central Park N. (110th St.), 116th St./Lexington Ave.; 4, 5, 6 to 125th St./Lexington Ave.; 2, 3 to Central Park N. (110th St.), 116th St., 125th St., 135th St./ Lenox (6th) Ave.; 3 to 145th St./Lenox (6th) Ave., 148th St.; B, C to Cathedral Pkwy. (110th St.), 116th St., 135th St. at Central Park W; A, B, C, D to 125th St./Central Park W, 145th St./St. Nicholas Ave.; 1, 9 to 125th St., 137th St., 145th St./Broadway.)*

SUGAR HILL. African-Americans with "sugar" (money) moved here in the 20s and 30s. Musical legends Duke Ellington and W.C. Handy lived in the neighborhood, while prominent leaders W.E.B. DuBois and Thurgood Marshall inhabited 409 Edgecombe Ave. Some of the city's most notable gangsters operated here. The area is also the birthplace of Sugarhill Records, the rap label that created the Sugarhill Gang. Their 1979 *Rapper's Delight* became the first hip-hop song to enter the top 40.

Today, skyrocketing real estate prices in Manhattan have once more made Sugar Hill's beautiful brownstones prized possessions. *(143rd to 155th St., between St. Nicholas and Edgecombe Ave. Subway: A, B, C, D to 145th St./St. Nicholas Ave.)*

WASHINGTON HEIGHTS. North of 155th St., **Washington Heights** affords a taste of urban life with an ethnic flavor. Eat a Greek dinner, buy Armenian pastries and vegetables from a South African vendor, and discuss the Talmud with a **Yeshiva University** student. Fort Tryon Park is home to **The Cloisters**, a museum specializing in medieval art. The **George Washington Bridge,** a major artery for travelers, is close by. *(Subway: C to 155th St./St. Nicholas Ave., 163rd St.; 1, A, C to 168th St./Broadway; A to 175th St., 181st St., 190th St.; 1, 9 to 181st St./St. Nicholas Ave., 191st St.)*

BROOKLYN

Part of NYC since 1898, Brooklyn is now the most populous borough. In the coverage below, neighborhoods are arranged from north to south.

WILLIAMSBURG AND GREENPOINT. Home to a growing number of artists, Williamsburg's galleries match its artsy population (see **Galleries,** p. 109). **Greenpoint,** bounded by Java St. to the north, Meserole St. to the south, and Franklin St. to the west, is Brooklyn's northernmost border and home to a large Polish population. The birthplace of Mae West and the Union's Civil War ironclad *USS Monitor*, Greenpoint features charming Italianate and Greek revival houses built during the 1850s shipbuilding boom. *(Subway: L to Bedford Ave.; G to Nassau Ave.)*

FULTON LANDING. Fulton Landing is reminiscent of the days when the ferry—not the subway or the car—was the primary means of transportation between Brooklyn and Manhattan. Completed in 1883, the nearby ▧**Brooklyn Bridge**—spanning the gap between lower Manhattan and Brooklyn—is the product of elegant calculation, careful design, and human exertion. A walk across the bridge at sunrise or sunset is one of the most exhilarating strolls New York City has to offer. *(From Brooklyn: entrance at the end of Adams St., at Tillary St. Subway: A, C to High St./Cadman Plaza E. From Manhattan: entrance at Park Row. Subway: 4, 5, 6, J, M, Z to Brooklyn Bridge/City Hall.)*

DOWNTOWN. Brooklyn Heights, a well-preserved 19th-century residential area, sprang up with the development of steamboat transportation between Brooklyn and Manhattan in 1814. Rows of posh Greek Revival and Italianate houses in this area essentially created New York City's first suburb. **Montague Street,** the main drag, has the stores, cafes, and mid-priced restaurants of a cute college town. **Downtown** is the location of Brooklyn's **Civic Center** and holds several grand municipal buildings. *(Subway: 2, 3, 4, 5, M, R to Court St./Borough Hall.)*

PROSPECT PARK. Park Slope is a residential neighborhood with charming brownstones. Neighboring **Prospect Park,** the borough's answer to Central Park, has a zoo, an ice-skating rink, and a children's museum. Central Park designers Frederick Law Olmsted and Calvert Vaux created the park in the mid-1800s. In the 1890s, the 80 ft. high **Memorial Arch** was built in Grand Army Plaza to commemorate the Union's Civil War victory. *(Bounded by Prospect Park W., Flatbush Ave., Ocean Ave., Parkside Ave., and Prospect Park SW. Subway: 2, 3 to Grand Army Plaza; F to 15 St./Prospect Park; B, Q, S to Prospect Park.)*

BROOKLYN BOTANIC GARDEN. Adjacent to the park, this 52-acre fairyland features the **Fragrance Garden for the Blind** (with mint, lemon, violet, and other appetizing aromas) and the more formal **Cranford Rose Garden.** *(1000 Washington Ave.; entrances also on Eastern Pkwy. and on Flatbush Ave. Subway: S to Botanic Garden; B, Q, S to Prospect Park; 2, 3 to Eastern Pkwy./Brooklyn Museum. ☎718-623-7000, events hotline 623-7333; www.bbg.org. Open mid.-Mar. to Oct. Tu-F 8am-6pm, Sa-Su 10am-6pm; Nov. to mid-Mar.*

Tu-F 8am-4:30pm, Sa-Su 10am-4:30pm. $8, students with ID and seniors $4, under 12 free; school groups free. Free Tu and Sa 10am-noon; seniors also free F.)

CONEY ISLAND. Once an elite resort (until the subway made it accessible to the masses), **Coney Island** is now a rickety slice of Americana. The **Cyclone,** 834 Surf Ave., built in 1927, was once the most terrifying roller coaster in the world. Meet sharks and other beasts at the famed **New York Aquarium.** *(At Surf and W. 8th St. Subway: F, Q to W. 8th St./NY Aquarium.* ☎ *718-265-3474; www.nyaquarium.com. Open June-Sept. M-F 10am-6pm, Sa-Su and holidays 10am-7pm; Sept.-Oct. and Apr.-May. M-F 10am-5pm, Sa-Su and holidays 10am-5:30pm; Nov.-Apr. daily 10am-4:30pm. Wheelchair-accessible. $12, seniors and ages 2-12 $8. No bikes, in-line skates, or pets allowed.)*

QUEENS

ASTORIA AND LONG ISLAND CITY. In the northwest corner of Queens lies Astoria, where Greek-, Italian-, and Spanish-speaking communities mingle amid lively shopping districts and cultural attractions. Long Island City is just south, across the river from the Upper East Side. *(Astoria is in the northwestern corner of Queens, across the river from Manhattan. Long Island City is southwest of Astoria, and can be reached by walking south on 21st or 31st St. Subway: All N, W stops between 36th Ave. and Astoria Ditmars Blvd; G, R, V to 36th St. or Steinway St.)*

SOCRATES SCULPTURE PARK. Led by sculptor Mark di Suvero, artists transformed this former landfill into an artistic exhibition space with 35 stunning dayglo and rusted metal abstractions. *(At the end of Broadway, across the Vernon Blvd. intersection. Subway: N, W to Broadway.* ☎ *718-956-1819; www.socratessculpturepark.org. Park offices located across from Broadway entrance. Open daily 10am-dusk. Free.)*

ISAMU NOGUCHI MUSEUM. Abstract carvings and otherworldly forms are the order of the day at this sparsely decorated museum, dedicated to the art of Japanese sculptor Isamu Noguchi. A **sculpture garden,** featuring Noguchi's work in stone, abuts the main exhibition hall. *(Across Vernon Blvd. from the Socrates Sculpture Garden. Subway: N, W to Broadway. Walk 10 blocks from the subway station toward the Manhattan skyline.* ☎ *718-204-7088; www.noguchi.org. Open W-F 10am-5pm, Sa-Su 11am-6pm. $10, students and seniors $5, under 12 free.)*

FLUSHING AND FLUSHING MEADOWS PARK. Flushing boasts colonial neighborhood landmarks, a bustling downtown, and a huge Asian immigrant population. Nearby **Flushing Meadows-Corona Park** was the site of the 1939 and 1964 World's Fair, and now holds **Shea Stadium** (home of the Mets), the **USTA National Tennis Center** (where the US Open is played), and the engaging, kid-friendly **New York Hall of Science.** *(47-01 111th St., at 48th Ave. Subway: 7 to 111th St.* ☎ *718-699-0005; www.nyhallsci.org. Open July-Aug. M-F 9:30am-5pm, Sa-Su 10am-6pm; Sept.-June Tu-Th 9:30am-2pm, F 9:30am-5pm, Sa-Su 10am-6pm. $11, seniors, students, and ages 5-17 $8, ages 2-4 $3, under 2 free. Free Sept.-June F 2-5pm and Su 10-11am.)* The **Unisphere,** a 380-ton steel globe in front of the New York City Building, is the futuristic structure featured in the 1997 movie *Men In Black. (Subway: 7 to Flushing/Main St., 111th St., or Willets Point.)*

THE BRONX

The relentless stream of immigration, once Italian and Irish but now mostly Hispanic and Russian, has created vibrant ethnic neighborhoods (including a Little Italy that puts its Manhattan counterpart to shame).

YANKEE STADIUM. In 1923, Babe Ruth's success as a hitter inspired the construction of the Yankees' own ballpark. Inside the 11½-acre park (the field itself measures only 3½ acres), monuments honor Yankee greats like Lou Gehrig, Joe

DiMaggio, and the Great Bambino himself. *(E. 161st St., at River Ave. Subway: 4, B, D to 161st St./Yankee Stadium. ☎ 718-293-6000; www.yankees.com. 1hr. tours start at noon. In summer $15, seniors and under 14 $8; in winter $12/6.)*

THE BRONX ZOO. The hugely popular **Bronx Zoo/Wildlife Conservation Park** houses over 4000 animals. Soar on the **Skyfari** aerial tramway ($2) between Wild Asia and the **Children's Zoo,** or ride a camel. *(Subway: 2, 5 to West Farms Sq./E. Tremont Ave. Follow Boston Rd. for 3 blocks until the Bronx Park S. gate. Bus: Bx9, Bx12, Bx19, Bx22, and Q44 pass various entrances to the zoo. ☎ 718-367-1010; www.bronxzoo.com. Open May-Oct. daily M-F 10am-5pm, Sa-Su 10am-5:30pm; Nov.-Apr. M-Tu and Th-Su only. Parts of the zoo closed Nov.-Apr. $14, seniors $12, ages 2-12 $10. W free, donation suggested.)*

NEW YORK BOTANICAL GARDEN. Located adjacent to the zoo, the city's most extensive botanical garden (250 acres) includes a 40-acre **hemlock forest** kept in its natural state. Although it costs an extra few dollars to enter, the different ecosystems in the gorgeous domed greenhouse **Conservatory** are worth a visit. *(Bronx River Pkwy. Exit 7W and Fordham Rd. Subway: 4 to Bedford Park Blvd./Lehman College; B, D to Bedford Park Blvd. Walk 8 blocks east or take the Bx26 bus. Bus: Bx19 or Bx26. Train: Metro-North Harlem line goes from Grand Central Terminal to Botanical Garden station. ☎ 718-817-8700; www.nybg.org. Open Apr.-Oct. Tu-Su 10am-6pm; Nov.-Mar. Tu-Su 10am-5pm. $18, seniors and students $16, children 2-12 $5. Call for tours.)*

BELMONT. Arthur Ave. is the center of this uptown **Little Italy,** which is home to wonderful homestyle southern Italian cooking. To get a concentrated sense of the area, stop into **Arthur Avenue Retail Market,** 2344 Arthur Ave., between 186th and Crescent St. Be sure to save your "Sopranos" jokes. *(Centering on Arthur Ave. and E. 187th St., near the Southern Blvd. entrance to the Bronx Zoo. Subway: B, D to Fordham Rd./ Grand Concourse. Walk 11 blocks east or take Bx12 to Arthur Ave. and head south.)*

STATEN ISLAND

Staten Island has a lot to offer, but tourism is often limited. Its parks are vast and lush, and there are beaches, historical sites, and gardens to explore. The **Staten Island Ferry** is itself a sight; it offers the best and cheapest (free) tour of NY's harbor. *(Leaves from South Ferry in Manhattan. Subway: N, R to Whitehall St.; 1, 9 to South Ferry.)* The 19th-century **Snug Harbor Cultural Center** houses the **Newhouse Center for Contemporary Art,** a small gallery with a summer sculpture show, and the **Staten Island Botanical Garden.** *(1000 Richmond Terr. Bus S40. ☎ 718-448-2500. Garden and Newhouse Center $6, students and seniors $5, under 12 $3. Botanical Garden: ☎ 718-273-8200. Open daily dawn-dusk. Free.)*

▥ MUSEUMS

Whether you're looking to examine medieval armor, T. Rex fossils, or abstract color field paintings, New York City has a museum for you. For listings of current and upcoming exhibits, consult *The New Yorker*, *New York* magazine, and Friday's *The New York Times* "Weekend" section. Beware: most museums are closed on Mondays and packed elbow-tight on weekends. Many request a "donation" in place of an admission fee—don't be embarrassed to give as little as $1.

UPPER WEST SIDE

▨ AMERICAN MUSEUM OF NATURAL HISTORY. A statue of Teddy Roosevelt on a horse graces this ecofact repository, which is one of the world's largest museums devoted to science. The main draw is the 4th-floor dinosaur halls, which display real fossils in 85% of the exhibits (most museums use fossil casts). Perhaps the most impressive part of the museum is the sparkling Hayden Planetarium in the

Rose Center for Earth and Space. *(Central Park W., between 77th and 81st St. Subway: 81st St. ☎212-769-5100. Open daily 10am-5:45pm; Rose Center also open F until 8:45pm. Wheelchair-accessible. Suggested donation $15, students and seniors $11, children $8.50; with Planetarium or IMAX Theatre $22/16.50/13.)*

NEW-YORK HISTORICAL SOCIETY. Founded in 1804, this is New York City's oldest continuously operating museum. The Neoclassical building houses a library and museum with exhibits on subjects ranging from slavery to early New York restaurant menus. On the 2nd floor is a comprehensive collection of landscapes from the Hudson River School of painters and Thomas Cole's grand five-painting series, "The Course of Empire." *(2 W. 77th St., at Central Park W. Subway: 79th St.; 72nd St./Central Park W./81st St. ☎212-873-3400; www.nyhistory.org. Open Tu-Th and Sa-Su 10am-6pm, F 10am-8pm. Wheelchair-accessible. $10, seniors $7, students $6, children free. Free F 6-8pm.)*

UPPER EAST SIDE

■ **METROPOLITAN MUSEUM OF ART.** The largest in the Western Hemisphere, the Met's collection boasts over 2 million works spanning 5000 years. Highlights are the Egyptian holdings (including the reconstructed Temple of Dendur), the European paintings collection, and exhibits of American art. The Costume Institute houses over 75,000 costumes and accessories from the 17th century to the present. *(1000 Fifth Ave., at 82nd St. Subway: 86th St./Lexington Ave. ☎212-535-7710, concerts and lectures 570-3949, wheelchair info 535-7710. Open Tu-Th and Su 9:30am-5:15pm, F-Sa 9:30am-8:45pm. Suggested donation $20, seniors $15, students $10.)*

■ **GUGGENHEIM MUSEUM.** The Guggenheim's most famous exhibit is the building itself, an inverted white multi-ridged shell designed by Frank Lloyd Wright and hailed as a modern masterpiece. Interdependent gallery spaces make up a spiral design. The large collection of modern and postmodern paintings includes significant works in Cubism, Surrealism, American Minimalism, and Abstract Expressionism. *(1071 5th Ave., at 89th St. Subway: 86th St./Lexington Ave. ☎212-423-3500. Open M-W and Sa-Su 10am-5:45pm, F 10am-7:45pm. $18, students and seniors $15, under 12 free.)*

FRICK COLLECTION. Henry Clay Frick left his house and art collection to the city, and the museum retains the elegance of his chateau. The Living Hall displays 17th-century furniture, Persian rugs, Holbein portraits, and paintings by El Greco, Rembrandt, Velázquez, and Titian. The courtyard is inhabited by elegant statues surrounding the garden pool and fountain. *(1 E. 70th St., at 5th Ave. Subway: 68th St. ☎212-288-0700. Open Tu-Sa 10am-6pm, Su 11am-5pm. Wheelchair-accessible. $15, seniors $10, students $5. Children under 10 not allowed, under 16 must be accompanied by an adult.)*

MUSEUM OF THE CITY OF NEW YORK. This fascinating museum details the history of the Big Apple, from the construction of the Empire State Building to the history of Broadway. Cultural history of all varieties is on parade—don't miss the model ships, NYC paintings, Yankees World Series trophies (if you can stomach the sight of them), and hot pants. *(1220 5th Ave., at 103rd St. Subway: 103rd St. ☎212-534-1672. Open Tu-Su 10am-5pm. Suggested donation $9, students and seniors $5, under 12 free.)*

THE JEWISH MUSEUM. The gallery's permanent collection details Jewish art and culture throughout history using ancient Biblical artifacts and ceremonial objects, as well as contemporary works by Marc Chagall, Frank Stella, and George Segal. *(1109 5th Ave., at 92nd St. Subway: 96th St. ☎212-423-3200. Open M-W and Sa-Su 11am-5:45pm, Th 11am-8pm. $10, students and seniors $7.50, members and under 12 free. Sa free.)*

WHITNEY MUSEUM OF AMERICAN ART. The museum with a historical mandate to champion the works of living American artists has assembled the largest collection of 20th- and 21st-century American art in the world, including Jasper Johns's

Three Flags and Frank Stella's *Brooklyn Bridge*. *(945 Madison Ave., at 75th St. Subway: 77th St. ☎212-570-3676. Open W-Th and Sa-Su 11am-6pm, F 1-9pm. $15, students and seniors $10, under 12 free. F 6-9pm pay-what-you-wish.)*

MIDTOWN

▨ **MUSEUM OF MODERN ART.** In 2005, MoMA reopened its doors to the public after an extensive (and expensive) reconstruction; the new space, nearly twice the size of the former, was conceived by Yoshio Taniguchi and cost $858 million. The results are nearly as impressive as the collections of 19th- and 20th-century art, including Matisse's *The Dance*, van Gogh's *Starry Night*, and Warhol's signature *Marilyn Monroe*. *(11 W. 53rd St., between 5th and 6th Ave. Subway: 5th Ave./53rd St.; 5th Ave./59th St. ☎212-708-9400. Open M 10:30am-5:30pm, W-Th 10:30am-5:30pm, F 10:30am-8pm, Sa-Su 10:30am-5:30pm. $20, seniors $16, students $12. F 4-8pm free.)*

PALEY CENTER FOR MEDIA. More archive than museum, this shrine to modern media, formerly the Museum of Television and Radio, contains over 100,000 easily accessible TV and radio programs. Unique screenings focus on social, historical, or artistic topics and can't be seen anywhere else. *(25 W. 52nd St., between 5th and 6th Ave. Subway: 47th-50th St. Rockefeller Center/6th Ave.; 5th Ave./53rd St. ☎212-621-6600. Open Tu-W and F-Su noon-6pm, Th noon-8pm. $10, students and seniors $8, under 13 $5.)*

BROOKLYN

▨ **BROOKLYN MUSEUM OF ART (BMA).** If it weren't for the Met, the BMA would be NYC's most magnificent museum. Oceanic and New World art collections reside on the 1st floor; ancient Greek, Roman, Middle Eastern, and Egyptian galleries are on the 3rd floor. *(200 Eastern Pkwy., at Washington Ave. Subway: Eastern Pkwy./Brooklyn Museum. ☎718-638-5000. Open W-F 10am-5pm, Sa-Su 11am-6pm. 1st Sa of each month free arts and entertainment events 5-11pm. $8, students and seniors $4, under 12 free.)*

▛ GALLERIES

New York City's galleries provide a riveting—and free—introduction to the contemporary art world. To get started, pick up a free copy of *The Gallery Guide* at any major museum or gallery. Most galleries are open from Tuesday to Saturday, from 10 or 11am to 5 or 6pm. Galleries are usually only open on weekend afternoons in the summer, and many are closed from late July to early September.

Artists Space, 38 Greene St. 3rd fl. (☎212-226-3970; www.artistsspace.org), at Grand St. Subway: 1, 9 to Canal St./Varick St.; A, C, E to Canal St./Ave. of the Americas (6th Ave.). This nonprofit gallery, founded in 1972, champions work by emerging and unaffiliated artists, focusing on architecture and design. The space often features multiple small exhibits. The Irving Sandler Artists File, containing slides and digitized images of works by more than 3000 unaffiliated artists, is open to critics, curators, and the public by appointment (F-Sa). Open Tu-Sa (Tu-F in July) 11am-6pm. Closed Aug.

The Drawing Center, 35 Wooster St. (☎212-219-2166; www.drawingcenter.org), between Grand and Broome St. Subway: 1, 9 to Canal St./Varick St.; A, C, E to Canal St./Ave. of the Americas (6th Ave.). Specializing in original works on paper, this nonprofit space sets up high-quality rotating exhibits. Open Tu-F 10am-6pm, Sa 11am-6pm. Closed Aug. Suggested donation $3. More space at the **Drawing Room,** 40 Wooster St.

525 W. 22nd St., between 10th and 11th Ave. Houses a handful of excellent, petite galleries of contemporary art, including the **303 Gallery** (☎212-255-1121; www.303gallery.com), **D'Amelio Terras** (☎212-352-9460; www.damelioterras.com), and the **DCA Gallery** (☎212-255-5511; www.dcagallery.com). Call for hours.

LULLABY OF BROADWAY

Few things make theater-lovers' hearts palpitate like the word "Broadway." More than just a slanty, inscrutable thoroughfare, the "Great White Way" is the home of "legit" (live) theater in the United States. The basic breakdown is between "tuners" (musicals, generally comedies) and "straight plays" (no singing or dancing, alas), though the "one-hander" (solo shows that usually feature a single, well-known performer like Billy Crystal or Whoopi Goldberg) has become increasingly common in recent years.

A show "bows" (plays its first performance) long before "opening night" (the final performance before reviews run in the newspapers, always accompanied by a large party), but "previews" (pre-opening performances where the show is still being finished) generally aren't any cheaper. A show's "scribe" (playwright) is considered to be its primary artistic force, but the "helmer" (stage director) can just as easily lay claim to that title.

The $100 "ducats" (tickets) purchased by "auds" (audiences) go toward recouping the show's "capitalization" (the cost of mounting the show, frequently over $10 million for big musicals). "Tonys" (Antoinette M. Perry Awards) can help fuel successful shows, but the peculiar alchemy of luck, glitz, and talent that makes a hit is all part of the magic of Broadway.

529 W. 20th St., between 10th and 11th Ave. This 11-floor colossus boasts over 20 contemporary art galleries, including the **I-20 Gallery** (☎212-645-1100; www.I-20.com), the **ACA Galleries** (☎212-206-8080; www.acagalleries.com), and the famed **Dorfman Projects** (☎212-352-2272; www.dorfman-projects.com). Call for hours.

Leo Castelli, 59 E. 79th St. (☎212-249-4470; www.castelligallery.com), between Park and Madison Ave. Subway: 6 to 77th St. Founded in 1957 by Leo Castelli, a highly influential art dealer known for showcasing the early efforts of Frank Stella and Andy Warhol. Displays works by both established and up-and-coming artists. Open mid-Aug. to late June Tu-Sa 10am-6pm; late June to mid-Aug. Tu-F 11am-5pm. Occasionally closed; call ahead.

🎭 ENTERTAINMENT

Publications with noteworthy entertainment and nightlife sections are the *Village Voice, New York* magazine, and the Sunday edition of the *New York Times*. *The New Yorker* has the most comprehensive theater survey.

THEATER

Broadway tickets usually start from $50. **TKTS,** Duffy Square, at 47th St. and Broadway, sells tickets for many Broadway and some off-Broadway shows at a 25-50% discount on the day of the performance. The lines begin to form an hour or so before the booths open, but they move fairly quickly. More tickets become available as showtime approaches, so you may find fewer possibilities if you go too early. (☎768-1818. Tickets sold M-Sa 3-8pm for evening performances, W and Sa 10am-2pm for matinees, Su 11am-7pm for matinees and evening performances.) An additional ticket booth is located at the South St. Seaport. (At the corner of Front St. and John St. Open M-Sa 11am-6pm and Su 11am-4pm.) Reserve full-price tickets over the phone and pay by credit card using **Tele-Charge** (☎239-6200 or 800-432-7250) for Broadway shows; **Ticket Central** (☎279-4200) for off-Broadway shows; and **Ticketmaster** (☎307-4100 or 800-755-4000) for all types of shows. All three services have a per-ticket service charge; be sure to inquire before purchasing. You can avoid these fees if you buy your tickets from the theater box office.

Shakespeare in the Park (☎539-8750) is a New York City summer tradition. From June through August, two plays are presented at the **Delacorte Theater** in Central Park, near the 81st St. entrance on the Upper West Side, just north of the main road. Tickets are free, but lines form extremely early.

EXPERIMENTAL/PERFORMANCE SPACES

🏚The Kitchen, 512 W. 19th St., between 10th and 11th Ave., is a world-renowned arts showcase in an unassuming Meatpacking District location. The space features experimental and avant-garde film and video, as well as concerts, dance performances, art exhibits, public lectures, and poetry readings. Every September, The Kitchen holds a neighborhood street fair, featuring the work of local artists. (Subway: 23rd St./8th Ave. ☎212-255-5793; www.thekitchen.org. Box office open Tu-Sa 2-6pm. Gallery open Tu-Sa 12-6pm.) The **Knitting Factory,** 74 Leonard St., between Broadway and Church St., is a multi-level performance space featuring several shows nightly, ranging from avant-garde and indie rock to jazz and hip-hop. (Subway: Franklin St. ☎212-219-3006; www.knittingfactory.com. Tickets are available for purchase on the Internet, phone, or at the box office. Cover $5-25. Box office open M-Sa 10am-2am, Su 2pm-2am. Bar open 6pm-4am.)

JAZZ JOINTS

The **JVC Jazz Festival** puts on all-star performances from June to July. Many events are outdoors and free. Check the newspaper or call ☎212-501-1390. Annual festivals sponsored by major corporations draw local talent and industry giants. The concerts take place throughout the city (some free), but center at TriBeCa's **Knitting Factory** (see above). **Smoke,** 2751 Broadway, between 105th and 106th St., may no longer be a den of fumes, but the fantastic music keeps it smokin'. A sultry cocktail lounge jumps with jazz every night, and, although slightly congested, the intimate space swells with music. Surprise guests have included jazz legends like Dr. Lonnie Smith, George Benson, and Ronnie Cuber; the regular lineup features John Farnsworth, Larry Willis, and Steve Wilson. (Subway: 103rd St./Broadway. ☎212-864-6662; www.smokejazz.com. Sets usually at 9, 11pm, 12:30am. "After Work Special" M-Th 5:30-7pm; beer and burger $10. Tu and Th jam sessions 6-8:30pm. Jazz vocalist series Su 6-8:30pm. 21+. F-Sa cover $16-20; $20 drink min. per person per set. Retro Happy hour daily 5-8pm; mixed drinks $3, other drinks $2 off. Open daily 5pm-4am.) **Detour,** 349 E. 13th St., between 1st and 2nd Ave., is a critically acclaimed club with nightly jazz and no cover—a perfect combo. The nondescript exterior is at odds with the impressively packed calendar. (Subway: First Ave. ☎212-533-6212; www.jazzatdetour.com. Mixed drinks $6. Bottled beer $5-6. Wine $6-8. Happy hour daily 4-7pm; drinks $3. 21+. 2-drink min. Open M-Tu and Su 4pm-2am, W-Sa 4pm-4am.) The **Cotton Club,** 656 W. 125th St., on the corner of Riverside Dr., has been around since 1923 and seen jazz greats like Lena Horne, Ethel Waters, and Calloway. (Subway: 125th St./Broadway. ☎212-663-7980 or 800-640-7980; www.cottonclub-newyork.com. M evening swing/big band. Th-Sa evenings buffet dinner and jazz show. M and Th-Sa evenings 21+; call for age restrictions at other events. Cover Su brunch and gospel shows $25; dinner jazz shows $32. Call 2 weeks in advance for reservations and schedule.)

ROCK, POP, PUNK, FUNK

New York City has a long history of producing bands on the vanguard of popular music and performance. **Music festivals** provide the opportunity to see tons of bands at a (relatively) low price. The **CMJ Music Marathon** (☎877-633-7848) runs for four nights in late October or early November and includes over 400 bands and workshops on the alternative music scene. **The Digital Club Festival** (☎677-3530), a newly reconfigured indie-fest, visits New York City in late July. The **Macintosh New York Music Festival** presents over 350 bands over a week-long period in July.

🏚**SOBs (Sounds of Brazil),** 204 Varick St., at W. Houston St., is a dinner-dance club that has some of NYC's best live music and hip-hop's best talents, including recent acts Talib Kweli, Blackalicious, and the Black Eyed Peas. Brazilian food goes well

MID-ATLANTIC

with the sounds: try the braised chicken with rice and okra ($19) or crab cakes with avocado relish ($23). Monday nights feature a 1hr. Latin dance class ($5) at 7pm; Latin bands play at 9pm. Friday nights showcase emerging artists; the late-night French-Caribbean dance party ($15-30) starts at midnight. (Subway: Houston St. ☎212-243-4940; www.sobs.com. Sa samba 6:30pm-4am $20. Box office, next door at 200 Varick St., open M-F 11am-6pm, Sa noon-6pm. Usually 21+, sometimes 18+. Opens M-Sa at 6:30pm.) ▪Southpaw, 125 5th Ave., between Sterling and St. John's Pl., in Park Slope, Brooklyn, is a former 99-cent store that now hosts DJs, local musicians, and plenty of well-known talent. Past performers include Ben Lee, the late Elliott Smith, and members of the Wu-Tang Clan. (Subway: Union St., 7th Ave., Bergen St. ☎718-230-0236; www.spsounds.com. Most shows 18+. Cover $7-20. Doors usually open around 8pm.) ▪Mercury Lounge, 217 E. Houston St., between Essex and Ludlow St., is a converted gravestone parlor—there's a tombstone in the bar's counter top—that attracts an amazing range of big-name acts to its fairly small-time room in addition to some lesser-known up-and-comers. Alterna-rockers and singer-songwriters are frequent performers: past stand-outs include spoken-word artist Maggie Estep, Morphine, and Mary Lou Lord. (Subway: Delancey St. ☎212-260-4700; www.mercuryloungenyc.com. 21+. Cover varies. Box office open M-Sa noon-7pm.)

OPERA AND DANCE

You can do it all at ▪Lincoln Center, the world's largest cultural complex, where many of the best opera, dance, and performance groups set up shop. (Between 62nd and 66th St. and Columbus and Amsterdam Ave. ☎212-875-5456. Subway: 66th St.) Check *The New York Times* listings. The **Metropolitan Opera Company's** premier outfit performs on a Lincoln Center stage as big as a football field. You can stand in the orchestra for $20 or all the way back in the Family Circle for $15. (☎212-362-6000; www.metopera.org. Season Sept.-May M-Sa. Box office open M-Sa 10am-8pm, Su noon-6pm. Upper balcony around $65.) The **New York City Opera** has also come into its own. "City" has a split season (Sept.-Nov. and Mar.-Apr.) and keeps prices low. (☎212-870-5630, rush tickets 212-870-5630; www.nycopera.com. Box office open M 10am-7:30pm, Tu-Sa 10am-8:30pm, Su 11:30am-7:30pm. Tickets $12-105, $16 student rush tickets the morning of the performance.) **Dicapo Opera Theatre,** 184 E. 76th St., between 3rd and Lexington Ave., is a small company that garners standing ovations after nearly every performance. (☎212-288-9438; www.dicapo.com. Subway: 23rd St./Broadway. Tickets around $50.)

The **New York State Theater** in Lincoln Center is home to the late George Balanchine's ▪New York City Ballet. Tickets for the *Nutcracker* in November and December sell out almost immediately. (☎212-870-5570, rush tickets 212-870-7766; www.nycballet.com. Season Nov.-Mar. Tickets $16-88, student rush tickets $12.) The **American Ballet Theatre** dances at the Metropolitan Opera House. (☎212-477-3030, box office 362-6000; www.abt.org. Tickets $20-90.) **City Center,** 131 W. 55th St. (☎212-581-1212; www.citycenter.org), has the city's best dance, from modern to ballet, including the unbelievable ▪Alvin Ailey American Dance Theater. Other dance venues include **Dance Theater Workshop,** 219 W. 19th St. (☎212-924-0077; www.dtw.org), between 7th and 8th Ave.; **Joyce Theater,** 175 8th Ave. (☎212-242-0800; www.joyce.org), between 18th and 19th St.; and **Thalia Spanish Theater,** 41-17 Greenpoint Ave. (☎718-729-3880), between 41st and 42nd St. in Queens.

CLASSICAL MUSIC

Lincoln Center has the most selection in its halls. The **Great Performers Series** packs the Avery Fisher and Alice Tully Halls and the Walter Reade Theater from October until May (see above for contact info; tickets from $20). **Avery Fisher Hall** presents the annual **Mostly Mozart Festival.** Show up early; there are usually recitals 1hr. before the main concert that are free to ticket holders. (☎212-875-5766. July-Aug. Tickets $25-70.) The **New York Philharmonic** begins its regular season in mid-September. Students and seniors can sometimes get $10 tickets the day of; call ahead. (☎212-875-5656. Tickets approximately $20-100.) For a few weeks in late June, the Philharmonic holds **free concerts** (☎212-875-5709) on the Great Lawn in Central Park, at Prospect Park in Brooklyn, at Van Cortlandt Park in the Bronx, and elsewhere. Free outdoor events at Lincoln Center (☎212-875-5928) occur all summer.

Carnegie Hall, on 7th Ave., at 57th St., sometimes offers rush tickets (☎212-247-7800. Box office open early Sept.-June M-Sa 11am-6pm, Su noon-6pm; July-early Sept. M-F 11am-6pm. Tickets $20-80.) A good, cheap way to absorb New York City musical culture is to visit a music school. Except for opera and ballet productions ($5-12), concerts are usually free and frequent. The best options are the **Juilliard School of Music,** Lincoln Center (☎769-7406), the **Mannes College of Music,** 150 W. 85th St. (☎212-580-0210), and the **Manhattan School of Music,** 120 Claremont Ave. (☎212-749-2802).

SPORTS

Most cities are content to have one major-league team in each big-time sport. New York City has two baseball teams, two hockey teams, NBA and WNBA basketball teams, two football teams...and one lonely soccer squad. The beloved **Mets** bat at **Shea Stadium** in Queens. (Subway: Willets Point-Shea Stadium. ☎718-507-6387. $13-30.) The **Yankees** play at **Yankee Stadium** in the Bronx. (Subway: 161st St. ☎718-293-4300. $12-63.) Both the **Giants** and the **Jets** play football across the river at **Giants Stadium** in East Rutherford, NJ (☎201-507-8900; tickets from $25; long waitlist for single-game tickets), and the **New York/New Jersey Metrostars** play soccer in the same venue. The **Knickerbockers** (that's the **Knicks** to you), as well as the WNBA's **Liberty,** play basketball at **Madison Square Garden** (☎212-465-5800; from $25 and $10, respectively), where the **Rangers** also play hockey (from $25). The **Islanders** hit the ice at the **Nassau Veterans Memorial Coliseum** in Uniondale. (☎516-794-9300. Tickets $27-70.) New York City also hosts a number of other world-class events. Get tickets three months in advance for the prestigious **US Open,** held in late August and early September at the USTA Tennis Center in Flushing Meadows, Queens. (☎888-673-6849. Tickets $33-69.) On the 1st Sunday in November, two million spectators witness the 30,000 runners of the **New York City Marathon.** The race begins on the Verrazano Bridge and ends at Central Park's Tavern on the Green (☎212-860-4455).

🗽 NIGHTLIFE

Whether you prefer a Chelsea nightclub or Harlem jazz, a smoky Brooklyn bar or a Lower East Side be-seen-ery, New York has it all. A number of publications print daily, weekly, and monthly nightlife calenders; try the *Village Voice*, *New York* magazine, and *The New York Times* (particularly the Sunday edition).

BARS

LOWER EAST SIDE

🍸 **Local 138,** 138 Ludlow St. (212-477-0280), between Stanton and Rivington St. Subway: Delancey/Essex St. Neighborhood bar with nary a decoration: just tables, bar, and booths. Lay low and grab a beer ($5), watch a game on TV, or make friends with the locals. Happy hour daily 4-9pm with $3 drafts. Open daily 4pm-4am.

Lotus Lounge, 35 Clinton St. (☎212-253-1144), at Stanton St. Subway: Delancey St./ Essex St. A lovely, low-key cafe by day; an even lovelier, lantern-lit bar by night. Bookshelves line the back wall. Live DJ nightly, starting around 10pm. Happy hour daily 4-8pm; Buds $2, drafts $3, and pitchers $15. Open M-Sa 8am-4am, Su 8am-2am.

SOHO AND TRIBECA

■ **Circa Tabac,** 32 Watts St. (☎212-941-1781), between 6th Ave. and Thompson St. Subway: Spring St./Ave. of the Americas (6th Ave.). Claims to be the world's 1st, and perhaps only, cigarette lounge. The bar has remained a smoker's haven despite Mayor Bloomberg's ban, thanks to the same law that protects cigar lounges. 180 kinds of cigarettes ($9-25), plus beer ($5-6) and mixed drinks ($8-12). $5 cutter fee if you bring your own cigars. Open daily 5pm-4am.

Milady's, 160 Prince St. (☎212-226-9069), at Thompson St. Subway: Spring St./Ave. of the Americas (6th Ave.). Down-to-earth staff matches no-frills atmosphere. Bottled beer ($3.50), drafts ($3.50-5), and SoHo's only pool table ($1 per game). Open daily 11am-4am. Kitchen open M-Th 11am-midnight, F-Sa 11am-1am, Su 11am-11pm.

GREENWICH VILLAGE

■ **Blind Tiger Alehouse,** 281 Bleecker St. (☎212-675-3848; www.blindtigeralehouse.com), at 10th St. Subway: Christopher St. Neighborhood pub that draws a diverse group of regulars for an amazing selection of microbrews and tasty freebies. M 6pm free hot dogs steamed in Brooklyn Beer. W 6pm free gourmet cheese tasting. Sa-Su noon free bagels and cream cheese. Happy hour M-F noon-8pm; $1 off pints and $3.50 mixed drinks. Open daily 11:30am-4am. Kitchen closes 2am.

The White Horse Tavern, 567 Hudson St. (☎212-243-9260), at W. 11th St. Subway: Christopher St. Boisterous students playing drinking games, plus locals who reminisce about the tavern's $0.20 beers. Poet Dylan Thomas drank himself to death here—literally. Expansive interior with jukebox. Outdoor patio. Beer $4-5. Open daily 6pm-4am.

EAST VILLAGE

■ **d.b.a.,** 41 1st Ave. (☎212-475-5097), between E. 2nd and 3rd St. Subway: Lower East Side/2nd Ave. For your inner alcohol connoisseur. With 19 premium beers on tap ($6-7), well over 100 bottled imports and microbrews, 50 bourbons, 130 single-malt whiskeys ($5-8), and 45 different tequilas, this friendly space lives up to its motto, "drink good stuff." Outdoor beer garden open until 10pm; space heaters keep it toasty on cold nights. Happy hour 5-7pm; $4 drinks. Open daily 1pm-4am.

Joe's Pub, 425 Lafayette St. (☎212-539-8777; www.joespub.com), between Astor Pl. and E. 4th St. Subway: Astor Pl. Located at the Joseph Papp Public Theater, in a building that once housed the city's first major public library. Norwegian acid-folk, classical chamber music, and dance contests all happily coexist in Joe's Pub. 2-3 bands perform each night; set times around 7, 9, and/or 11pm. Late-night DJs spin hip-hop, rock, and 80s hits for the large, dancing crowd. Open daily 6pm-4am.

UPPER EAST SIDE

The Big Easy, 1768 2nd Ave. (☎212-348-0879), at 92nd St. Subway: 96th St. Perfect for those who miss college, with 5 beirut tables. Good for cheap, strong drinks before a long night. M beirut. Tu Bud $2. W karaoke. 11pm-midnight. Open daily 5pm-4am.

Dorrian's Red Hand, 1616 2nd Ave. (☎212-772-6600), at 84th St. Subway: 86th St. The preppy hot spot all the others aspire to be. The still-in-college, recently graduated, and young moneyed come to this Irish pub to meet, mingle, and down some drinks ($5-8). Open M-Th and Su 11:30am-1am, F-Sa 11:30am-2am.

UPPER WEST SIDE

Dive 75, 101 W. 75th St. (☎212-501-9283), between Columbus and Amsterdam St. Subway: 72nd St. All the joys of your favorite dive, without the nauseating bathroom. Locals lounge on couches, soaking in pop-rock tunes from the jukebox. A stack of board games sits in the corner. Wi-Fi. M in football season free wings. Th palm readings. Happy hour 5-7pm. Open daily M-Th 5pm-4am, F 2pm-4am, Sa-Su noon-4am.

The Evelyn Lounge, 380 Columbus Ave. (☎212-724-2363), at 78th St. Subway: 81st St. Lively upscale bar complete with brick, vintage sofas, and fireplaces. Popular with the after-work and late-night set. The lounge downstairs has 5 more rooms and 2 additional bars and is open on weekends. DJs spin dance and hip-hop. Cultured locals sip martinis ($9-10) and beer ($5-6). Open M-Th 6pm-4am, F-Su 5pm-4am.

BROOKLYN

🔖 **Galapagos,** 70 N. 6th St. (☎718-782-5188; www.galapagosartspace.com), between Kent and Wythe St., in Williamsburg. Subway: Bedford Ave. In June 2008, Galapagos will relocate to 16 Main St., in the DUMBO (Down Under the Manhattan Bridge Overpass) neighborhood of Brooklyn. Once a mayonnaise factory, now one of the hipper cultural spots in the city. Sleek decor, complete with enormous reflecting pool. M 9:30pm free bawdy burlesque show. Tu-W live rock bands ($6-7). F "floating burlesque" 10pm-1am ($5). Su 7pm *Ocularis,* an avant-garde and experimental film screening ($7). More live bands throughout the week ($5-8). DJs every Tu-Sa, start late (usually after 11pm; no cover). Happy hour M-Sa 6-8pm. Check website for event calendar. Open M-Th and Su 6pm-2am, F-Sa 6pm-4am.

The Gate, 321 5th Ave. (☎718-768-4329), corner of 3rd St. Subway: Union St. A few short years ago, Park Slope was a nightlife wasteland, but The Gate's welcoming atmosphere and 24 beers on tap ($4-5) paved the way for a 5th Ave. renaissance. Outdoor patio fills when the weather is warm. Happy hour M-Th 4-8pm, F 3-7pm; $1 off drafts and well drinks. Open M-Th 4pm-4am, F 3pm-4am, Sa-Su 1pm-4am.

Pete's Candy Store, 709 Lorimer St. (☎718-302-3770; www.petescandystore.com), between Frost and Richardson St. Subway: Lorimer St. This soda-shop-turned-bar includes a "make-out" hallway and a small performance room in the back. Pomegranate margarita $8, other mixed drinks $6-8. A local crowd comes for live local music nightly at 9pm. M night spelling bee or stand-up comedy. Tu bingo and W Quizz-Off (both 7-9pm) are extremely popular. During the summer, stop by the barbecues (Su 5-9pm, $5) in the backyard for burgers, hot dogs, and salads. Open M-Tu and Su 5pm-2am, W-Sa 5pm-4am.

DANCE CLUBS

Club scenes are about carefree crowds, unlimited fun, and huge wallet damage. It pays to call ahead to put your name on the guest list. Come after 11pm; the real party starts around 1 or 2am. For serious partiers, a few after-hours clubs keep at it until 5-6am. All clubs listed are 21+ unless otherwise noted. Be prepared with multiple forms of ID.

🔖 **Happy Ending,** 302 Broome St. (☎212-334-9676; www.happyendinglounge.com), between Eldridge and Forsyth St. Subway: F, J, M, Z to Delancey St./Essex St. This bar and lounge was converted from a massage parlor (yes, *that* kind). Mirrors etched with naked women remain, and the saunas have become semi-private booths, their waist-high shower heads left intact. The canopy outside still reads "Xie He Health Club"; you're in the right place. Beer $3-6. Mixed drinks $6-10. Popular W 8pm reading series; 3rd W of each month is erotica-themed. Th 10pm "Something Tight" gay dance party. There's a DJ every night downstairs. Open Tu-Sa 10pm-4am, Su 7pm-4am.

🔖 **Cielo,** 18 Little W 12th St. (☎917-312-8892), between Washington and Greenwich St. A proudly exclusive and surprisingly intimate dance club centered on a sunken dance floor. High-caliber DJs spin electronica, nu jazz, future soul, and deep house every night.

MID-ATLANTIC

The clientele is stylish and the door is tightly guarded; plan your outfit well. Extremely expensive bottle service only at tables. Cover $10-20. Open W-Sa 10pm-4am.

■ **Tribe,** 132 1st Ave. (☎212-979-8965; www.tribebar.com), at St. Mark's Pl. Subway: 6 to Astor Pl. A glamorous dark-wood-and-leather bar with colorful but subtle backlighting. Comfortable lounge areas offer just enough room for a late-night dance party with DJ. Ladies must remove their shoes before dancing on the leather furniture. Late 20s crowd. DJ nightly from 9pm: lots of hip-hop, rock, 80s, and pop. Beer $4-6. Mixed drinks $7-11. Tu 7-10pm live funk, rock, and indie music. Happy hour daily 5-9pm; $3 domestic beers and $5 well drinks. Open daily 5pm-4am.

Eugene, 27 W. 24th St. (☎212-462-0999), between 5th and 6th Ave. Subway: 23rd St./ 7th Ave.; 6 to 23rd St./Park Ave. S; F, V to 23rd St./Ave. of the Americas (6th Ave.); N, R to 23rd St./Broadway. Vegas-casino atmosphere with an Atlantic City crowd. Doubles as an expensive restaurant by day. Party heats up when the DJ arrives around 11pm. Plenty of nooks for private moments with bridge-and-tunnel crowd. Drinks $9-12. Dress to impress. Cover W $15-20, Th-Sa $20. Bar and dance floor open Th-Sa 5pm-4am.

GLBT NIGHTLIFE

Gay nightlife in New York City is centered in **Chelsea,** especially along 8th Ave. in the 20s and in the **West Village,** on Christopher St.

Boiler Room, 86 E. 4th St. (☎212-254-7536), between 1st and 2nd Ave. Subway: Lower East Side/2nd Ave. Popular locale caters to alternative types, NYU students, and refugees from the Chelsea scene. Predominantly gay men, but a mixed crowd, especially on weekends. Jukebox and pool table. Beer $4. Happy hour daily 4-8pm and 10pm-4am; 2-for-1 draft and domestic beers. Open daily 4pm-4am.

g, 223 W. 19th St. (☎212-929-1085), between 7th and 8th Ave. Subway: 18th St./7th Ave. Glitzy, popular bar shaped like an oval racetrack—perhaps an appropriate choice, given the pumped-up Chelsea men who speed around this circuit to the sound of DJ-ed house. Drinks (all beginning with "G") $6-8. Open daily 4pm-4am.

Henrietta Hudson, 438 Hudson St. (☎212-924-3347; www.henriettahudsons.com), between Morton and Barrow St. Subway: Christopher St. Young, clean-cut lesbian crowd. Transitions from after-work hangout to weekend late-night hot spot. Pool table and 2nd bar in quiet back room. Also gay male- and straight-friendly. Busiest Th-Sa. M old school. Tu requests. W karaoke. Th world. F house. Sa pop. Su Latin. Cover Sa-Su $7-10. Happy hour M-F 5-7pm; beer $3. Open M-F 4pm-4am, Sa 1pm-4am, Su 3pm-4am.

SBNY, 50 W. 17th St. (☎212-691-0073; www.splashbar.com), between 5th and 6th Ave. Subway: 18th St./7th Ave.; 23rd St./Ave. of the Americas (6th Ave.). One of the most popular gay mega-bars, the renovated **S**plash **B**ar **N**ew **Y**ork (formerly known as Splash) is a huge 2-fl. complex. A crowded scene, with industrial decor, a dance fl., and high-energy house music. Mixed drinks $6-7.50. 21+ usually, 18+ occasionally. Cover M-Th $5 after 11pm, F $20. Th before midnight no cover with college ID. Happy hour; M-Sa 4-9pm, Su 4-7pm 2-for-1 drinks. Open M-Th and Su 4pm-4am, F-Sa 4pm-5am.

LONG ISLAND   ☎631

Long Island, a suburban landscape stretching 120 mi. east of Manhattan, is both a home to over 2.7 million New Yorkers (excluding those who live in Queens and Brooklyn) and a sleepy summertime vacation spot for wealthy Manhattanites. Not surprisingly, it is expensive and difficult to navigate without a car.

⎕ PRACTICAL INFORMATION. Long Island Railroad (LIRR) services the island from Penn Station in Manhattan (34th St. at 7th Ave.; Subway: 1, 2, 3 to 34th St./ Penn Station/7th Ave.; A, C, E to 34th St./Penn Station/8th Ave.) and stops in

Jamaica, Queens (Subway: E, J, Z), before proceeding to "points east." (☎ 718-217-5477. Fares vary daily and by zone.) To reach **Fire Island,** take the LIRR to Sayville, Bayshore, or Patchogue. The **Sayville Ferry** serves Cherry Grove, the Pines, and Sailor's Haven. (☎ 589-0810. Round-trip $14, under 12 $6.50.) The **Bay Shore Ferry** sails to Fair Harbor, Ocean Beach, Ocean Bay Park, Saltaire, and Kismet. (☎ 665-3600. Round-trip $15, under 12 $7.) The **Patchogue Ferry** shuttles to Davis Park and Watch Hill. (☎ 475-1665. Round-trip $14, under 12 $9.) The Hamptons are accessible by LIRR or by car. Take the Long Island Expwy. to Exit 70, go south to Rte. 27 (Sunset Hwy. or Montauk Hwy.), and head east to Montauk (approx. 50 mi. on Rte. 27). **Long Island Convention and Visitors Bureau** has four locations throughout the island. Call ☎ 951-2423 or 877-386-6654 for locations and hours. **Area Code:** 631 and 516. In listings, 631 unless otherwise noted.

FIRE ISLAND

Tranquil towns dot Fire Island, and the state protects most Fire Island areas by declaring them either state parks or federal "wilderness areas." This lack of infrastructure ensures both peace and inconvenience; visitors must often take water taxis to travel between towns. Fire Island's 17 summer communities have forged distinct niches—middle-class residential clusters, openly gay communities, and havens for vacationing Hollywood stars. Two prominent Fire Island resort hamlets, **Cherry Grove** and **Fire Island Pines** (called **"the Pines"**), host largely gay communities—and parties that rage late into the night. Crowded "streets," or wooden pathways, border spectacular beaches. Weekdays provide an opportunity to enjoy the island in a low-key setting, Thursdays and Sundays offer an ideal balance of sanity and scene, and Fridays and Saturdays see mounting crowds and prices.

Gay nightlife on Fire Island has an established rhythm that may be confusing to newcomers. Since neither Cherry Grove nor the Pines is very big, it's best just to ask around. More commercial than the Pines, the roadless Grove is lined with narrow, raised boardwalks leading to the small, uniformly shingled houses overflowing with men. Lesbian couples make up the majority of the town's population. A night in Cherry Grove usually begins at the **Ice Palace,** attached to the **Cherry Grove Beach Hotel,** where you can disco until dawn. (☎ 597-6600. Open daily July-Aug. noon-4am; Sept.-June noon-10pm). Most go to the Pines for late-night partying; you can catch a water taxi from the docks at Cherry Grove or walk 10min. up the beach. Houses here are spacious and often stunningly modern. Unfortunately, the Pines' active nighttime scene has a bit of a secret club feel to it—you need to be in the know or look like you are. **Tea Dance** (a.k.a. "Low Tea," 5-8pm) takes place inside and around the **Yacht Club** bar/club beside the **Botel Hotel** (☎ 597-6500). Move on to disco **High Tea** at 8pm in the **Pavilion** (☎ 597-6131), the premier disco in Cherry Grove, but make sure you have somewhere to disappear to during "disco naptime" (after 10pm). You can unabashedly dance until dawn at the **Island Club and Bistro** (☎ 597-6001), better known as the **Sip-and-Twirl.** The Pavilion becomes hot again late-night on weekends, including Sundays during the summer.

THE HAMPTONS AND MONTAUK

West Hampton, Southampton, Bridgehampton, and East Hampton make up the entity known as **the Hamptons,** where high-society roams the sidewalks before heading to the beach for the afternoon. Prices are very high here; try going to **Montauk,** at the eastern tip of Long Island, for slightly cheaper accommodations. While lodging anywhere on the South Fork requires some research and often reservations, clean rooms can be found at **Tipperary Inn ❺,** 432 West Lake Ln., accessible via the S-94 bus to Montauk Dock. The inn provides A/C, TV, phone, and fridge. (☎ 668-2010. Rooms for 2-6 people $160-215, higher rates late Aug. and early Sept.)

Many beaches in the Hamptons require a permit to park, but anyone can walk on for free. Sights include the **Montauk Point Lighthouse and Museum,** off Rte. 27 at the far eastern tip of the island, which was built in 1796 by special order of President George Washington. (☎668-2544. Open June-Sept. M-F and Su 10:30am-5:30pm, Sa 10:30am-7pm; call for low-season info. $7, seniors $6, under 12 $3.) Whaling buffs shouldn't miss the **Sag Harbor Whaling Museum,** at the corner of Main and Garden St. in Sag Harbor. (☎725-0770. Open May-Sept. M-Sa 10am-5pm, Su 1-5pm. $5, students and seniors $3, under 12 free. Tours by appointment only; $3.)

THE CATSKILLS   ☎845

According to legend, the Catskills cradled Rip Van Winkle during his century-long repose. The mountain region is still an ideal spot for solitude, despite the infamous Woodstock rock festival of 1969 that forever changed the small town of Bethel. Today, the region's best attractions are miles of pristine hiking and skiing trails and the crystal-clear fishing streams of the Catskill Forest Preserve. Small mountain villages are home to art galleries and shops permeated with local flavor.

🛈 PRACTICAL INFORMATION. Traveling from I-87, follow Rte. 28 W from Exit 19 to reach the many small villages in the area. Rte. 212 from Exit 20 or the Rte. 23-23A loop—termed the "Rip Van Winkle Trail"—from Exit 21, are also easy ways to explore the region. Pay particular attention to warnings for deer in the road! **Adirondack/Pine Hill Trailways** provides excellent service throughout the Catskills. The main stop is in **Kingston,** 400 Washington Ave., on the corner of N. Front St. (☎331-0744 or 800-776-7548; www.trailwaysny.com. Ticket office open daily 5:45am-11pm.) Buses run to New York City (2hr., 10-15 per day, $21). Other stops in the area include Delhi, Hunter, Pine Hill, and Woodstock; each connects with Albany, Cooperstown, New York City, and Utica. Two stationary tourist cabooses, one at the traffic circle in Kingston and one on Rte. 209 in Ellenville, dispense information, including the extremely useful brochure *Ulster County: Catskills Region Travel Guide.* (Open May-Oct. daily 9am-5pm, but hours vary depending on volunteer availability.) Further information on the region can be obtained from the Catskills regional office of the **NY Department of Environmental Conservation** (☎256-3009; www.dec.state.ny.us). **Area Code:** 845, unless otherwise noted.

CATSKILL FOREST PRESERVE

The nearly 300,000-acre **Catskill Forest Preserve** contains many small towns and outdoor opportunities. Besides immaculately maintained state campgrounds, ranger stations distribute free permits for **backcountry camping ❶,** which are required for stays over three days or groups of 10 or more. Hiking trails are generally well maintained, though less-used paths sometimes fall into disrepair. Lean-tos are also maintained, but can become crowded. For more info, call the **Department of Environmental Conservation** (☎256-3000; open M-F 8:30am-4:45pm) or ask a ranger at one of the campgrounds. Most campgrounds sit at trailheads that mark great day-long jaunts. Reservations are a must in the summer, especially on weekends. **Required permits for fishing** (out-of-state residents $15 per day, $25 per week) are available in sporting goods stores and at many campgrounds. Ski season runs from November to April—ski down one of the many slopes along Rte. 28 and Rte. 23A.

KINGSTON

Kingston, was founded by the Dutch in the mid-1600s as the first capital city of New York state. Although much quieter now that the state government has changed locales, parts of Kingston still retain a colonial flavor. The rough stone **Senate House,** 296 Fair St., was the home of merchant Abraham Van Gaasbeek and was used as a meeting place for the rebel colonists' State Senate. Today, the house is filled with antique artifacts indicating its rich history. A nearby museum chronicles art and life in colonial New York. (☎338-2786. Open mid-Apr. to Oct. M and W-Sa 10am-5pm, Su 11am-5pm. Tours every 30min. $4, seniors $3, under 12 $1.) For bells and whistles, stop by the **Volunteer Fireman's Hall and Museum,** 265 Fair St., an 1857 fire station that is full of firefighting memorabilia and even has a working antique fire alarm system. (☎331-0866. Open Apr.-Oct. W-F 11am-3pm, Sa 10am-4pm. Donations accepted.) The **Stockade District,** an area bound by Washington Ave. to the west and Clinton Ave. to the east, was originally surrounded by 14 ft. high wooden walls for protection from the Esopus Indians, but now is the commercial and historical center of town. Built in 1774, the site of New York's first two-year college is now home to **El Rodeo ❶,** 35 Crown St., where quesadillas and fajitas have replaced exams and books. (☎340-9895. Entrees $5-10. Opens M-F at 11am, Sa at noon, Su at 3pm; closes when crowds filter out.)

WOODSTOCK

Once home to painters of the Hudson River School, Woodstock combines chintzy, neo-hippie flair with an historic setting and a vibrant art scene. Local info abounds at the **Woodstock Chamber of Commerce,** 10 Rock City Rd. (☎679-6234; www.woodstockchamber.org.) Dubbed the "local Louvre" by *Life* magazine, the **Woodstock Artists Association Museum,** 28 Tinker St. presents the work of historically notable regional artists in pleasant galleries. (☎679-2940; www.woodstockart.org. Suggested donation $5. Open M, Th, Su noon-5pm, F-Sa noon-6pm.) The **Center for Photography at Woodstock,** 59 Tinker St., provides numerous lectures and classes as well as rotating exhibits. (679-9957; www.cpw.org. Open W-Su 9am-5pm). For those inclined to cycle the steep winding backroads of the Catskills, **Overlook Mountain Bikes,** 93 Tinker St., provides rentals. (☎679-2122. $30 per day. Open W-Sa 11am-6pm, Su 11am-5pm.) Lodging in Woodstock is expensive, but the nearby **Kenneth L. Wilson Campground ❶** has 76 sites nestled in a tranquil forest. The lake allows for canoeing, kayaking, and paddleboating. From Rte. 28, exit onto Rte. 212, then make a hard right onto Wittenburg Rd./County Rte. 40 and follow it 5 mi. to the campground. (☎679-7020. Reception 8am-9pm. Weekend reservations recommended. Registration fee $2.75. Sites $17. Day use $4 per car, $1 per pedestrian or biker. Canoes and 2-person kayaks $15 per 4hr. Paddleboats $5 per hr.) Well worth the expense, **Oriole 9 ❹,** 17 Tinker St., serves enormous salads ($9) and a small but carefully chosen set of entrees ($15-25) in a chic setting. (☎679-5763; www.oriole9.com, open M-Tu 8:30am-4:30pm, W-Su 8:30am-10pm.)

PHOENICIA

Phoenicia is a small town in the heart of the Catskills. **Esopus Creek,** to the west, has great trout fishing, and **The Town Tinker,** 10 Bridge St., rents inner tubes for river-riding on the ripples and rapids. (☎688-5553; www.towntinker.com. Inner tubes $10 per day, with seat $12. Driver's license or $15-75 deposit required. Life jackets required; $3. Wet suits $15. Package with seated tube, life jacket, and single transport $20; package with wetsuit $30. Wet suits not necessary on hot summer days. "Tube taxi" transportation $5 per trip on either the Mountain Railroad or a bus. Open mid-May to Sept. daily 9am-6pm; last rental 3:30-4pm.) A more relaxing alternative is the 100-year-old, volunteer-run **Catskill Mountain Railroad,** which follows Esopus Creek for three scenic miles from Bridge St. to Mt. Pleasant along antique tracks. (☎688-7400; www.catskillmtrailroad.com. May-early Sept. 11am-5pm, Oct. noon-4pm. Two routes run Sa-Su and holidays, 1 trip per hr. Shuttle $5, round-trip $8; ages 4-11 $5. Round-trip scenic route $12/8.) The **Kaleidostore,** in Emerson Pl. on Rte. 28, brings art to a new level with the world's largest kaleidoscope. The best way to view the 60 ft. mirrors is to lie in the middle of the floor as music and color wash over you. (☎688-5800. Open Th-Su 10am-6pm, but call ahead. $7, seniors $5, under 12 free.) A 12 mi. round-trip hike to the 4180 ft. summit of **Slide Mountain** rewards hikers with 360° views of New Jersey, Pennsylvania, and the Hudson Highlands; begin at Woodland Valley Campground (see-below). Nestled in the woods, the **Zen Mountain Monastery,** off Rte. 40 north of Rte. 28, entered on the National Register of Historic Places, houses 35-40 Buddhists who live and work together while receiving Zen training. (☎688-2228. Phone lines open Tu 2-5pm, W-Sa 8:30am-5pm. Closed to the public except during meditation training sessions W 7pm and Su 8:45am. Free; suggested donation $5, lunch provided.)

With 72 sites, the secluded **Woodland Valley Campground ❶,** on Woodland Valley Rd. off High St., 7 mi. southeast of Phoenicia, has a stream, showers ($0.25 per 6min.), and access to day hikes to Giant Ledge or Wittenberg Mountain. (☎688-7647. Reception daily 8am-9pm. Open late May-early Oct. Registration fee $2.75. Sites $15.) Customers line up outside of award-winning **Sweet Sue's ❶,** on Main St., to take a stab at finishing thick french toast and stacks of 23 varieties of enormous 9 in. pancakes. (☎688-7852. Entrees $7-9. Open M and W-Su 7am-3pm.) With a menu longer than Main St., **Brio's ❷,** 68 Main St., serves everything from omelets ($5-7) to burritos ($7-9) to hungry locals. (☎688-5370. Takeout available. Open M-Th and Su 7am-10pm, F-Sa 7am-11pm.)

PINE HILL

The small town of Pine Hill sits near **Belleayre Mountain,** which offers hiking trails and **"Sky Rides"** on a chairlift to the summit in summer, and downhill and cross-country ski slopes when the snow starts to fall. (☎254-5600 or 800-942-6904. Lift tickets M-F $35, Sa-Su $42; over 62 and ages 13-22 $30/34. Equipment rental $25. Sky Ride $8, seniors and ages 13-17 $5. Open mid-June to mid-Oct. Sa-Su 10am-6pm.) **Belleayre Music Festival,** held at the Belleayre Mt. ski resort, hosts classical, jazz, country, opera, and folk concerts in a pavilion during July and August. Past performers include musical legends Ray Charles and Ritchie Havens. (☎800-942-6904; www.belleayremusic.org. Lawn tickets $15, some concerts free.) The **Belleayre Beach at Pine Hills,** half a mile south of Pine Hills on Rte. 28, provides warm-weather recreation, including swimming, hiking, volleyball, and a playground. (☎800-942-6904. Open late May to mid-June Sa-Su 10am-6pm; mid-June to Sept. M-F 10am-6pm, Sa-Su 10am-7:30pm. Lifeguards while park is open. $6 per car, $1 per pedestrian.) For info on the mountain and beach, visit www.belleayre.com.

ALBANY   ☎518

Albany, the capital of New York State and the oldest continuous European settlement of the original 13 colonies, calls itself "the most livable city in America." Albany has the intensity you'd expect from the capital of one of America's most influential states, but outside the government offices, upstate New York's tranquility endures. On weekdays, downtown shops and restaurants thrive off of political purse-strings, while weekend nightlife erupts outside the government center.

■ 🚄 **TRANSPORTATION AND PRACTICAL INFORMATION.** Amtrak, 525 East St. (☎462-5710; www.amtrak.com; station and ticket booth open daily 4:30am-10pm), across the Hudson from downtown, has **train** service to Buffalo (5hr., 4 per day, $50-60) and New York City (2½hr., 8-9 per day, $43-50). Greyhound, 34 Hamilton St. (☎436-9651 or 800-231-2222; www.greyhound.com; station open 24hr., ticket window open daily noon-11:30pm), runs **buses** to Buffalo (6½hr., 7-8 per day, $56) and New York City (3hr., 15 per day, $34). Be careful here at night. From the same station, Adirondack Trailways (☎800-776-7548; www.trailwaysny.com) sends **trains** to Kingston (1hr., 7 per day, $11) and Lake Placid (4hr., 1 per day, $29).

The **Capital District Transportation Authority** (**CDTA;** ☎482-8822; www.cdta.org) runs buses in Albany, Schenectady, and Troy (all fares $1, day pass $3). Get schedules and shuttle routes at the Amtrak and bus stations and Visitors Center. The **Albany Visitors Center,** 25 Quackenbush Sq., at Clinton Ave. and Broadway, runs trolley and horse-drawn carriage tours of downtown and has self-guided walking tours. (☎434-0405; www.albany.org. Open M-F 9am-4pm, Sa-Su 10am-4pm. Carriage tours Aug.-Sept. Th 10am. Trolley tours W and F-Sa 11am. July-Aug. arrive 20min. early for a film about the city. Tours $10, seniors $5.) **Internet Access: Albany Public Library,** 161 Washington Ave. (☎427-4300. Open June-Sept. M-Th 9am-9pm, F 9am-6pm, Sa 9am-5pm; Sept.-June also open Su 1-5pm.) **Post Office:** Capitol Plz., near State St. (☎462-4635. Open M-F 9am-4:45pm.) **Postal Code:** 12224.

🏠 **ACCOMMODATIONS.** Five gorgeous rooms at the **Pine Haven Bed & Breakfast** ➍, 531 Western Ave., at Madison Ave., make this ornate Victorian house a haven indeed. (☎482-1574; www.pinehavenbedandbreakfast.com. A/C, cable TV, parking, Wi-Fi. Reservations required. Rooms $69-109.) **Thompson's Lake State Park** ➊, 18 mi. southwest of Albany, is the closest campground, with 140 wooded sites within walking distance of the lake's sandy beach. Take Madison Ave./Rte. 20 north to Rte. 85. Follow Rte. 85 out of Albany, turn right on Rte. 157, and look for signs. (☎872-1674. Hot showers. Registration fee $2.75. Sites $13. Row boats $5 per hr., $20 per day. Paddle boats $4 per 30min. Lifeguard on duty June-Sept. M-F 10am-6pm, Sa-Su 10am-7pm.) **Red Carpet Inn** ➌, 500 Northern Blvd., between downtown and the airport, has decent rooms with A/C and cable TV. Take Exit 6 from I-90 and turn onto Northern Blvd. (☎462-5562. Rooms $54-60.)

🍴🍸 **FOOD AND NIGHTLIFE.** Lark Street is full of ethnic haunts and coffee-shops with a young, quirky atmosphere, while N. Pearl St. and S. Pearl Street are dotted with traditional American eateries and a number of bars catering to government employees. The two-floor **Bomber's Burrito Bar** ➊, 258 Lark St., offers food, a lounge, pool tables, and New York's longest happy hour (pints $2.50 11am-8pm). Twelve-inch burritos and mountainous nachos share the menu with barbecue tofu fries and witty catchphrases like "we know how to roll a fatty." (☎463-9639. Burritos $6.75. Open daily 11am-1am. Delivery 11am-2pm.) Local art decorates the walls at **The Muddy Cup** ➋, 1038 Madison Ave., a popular hangout for college kids. (☎458-6120; www.muddycup.com. Free Wi-Fi. Open M-Th and Su 7am-midnight, F-Sa 7am-2am.) Head to the **Bayou Cafe** ➌, 79 N. Pearl St., for tangy Cajun food and a wild southern setting. With no set closing time (establishments can serve until 3am on weekends), live rock and blues play long into the night Thursday through Saturday. (☎462-9033; www.bayoucafe.com. Entrees $8-16. Open M-F at 11:30am, Sa at 4:30pm.) **De Johns Restaurant and Pub** ➍, 288 Lark St., is an award-winning spot for candlelit dinners and excellent service. Smoked chicken carbonara and pecan-encrusted trout topped with sherry are specialties. (☎465-5275; www.dejohns.com. Sandwiches $8-10. Entrees $15-18. Open M-Th 4-11pm, F 4pm-midnight, Sa-Su 11am-midnight.)

👁️🎭 **SIGHTS AND ENTERTAINMENT.** Albany's sights center around the **Rock-efeller Empire State Plaza,** between State and Madison St., a modernist Stonehenge made of 900,000 cubic yards of concrete and 232,000 tons of steel. The plaza includes state offices, a bus terminal, a post office, a food court, several war memorials, and the largest outdoor display of modern art in the country, set in (and around) two large reflecting pools. The **Plaza Information Center,** in the north concourse, is the departure spot for Plaza Tours, which visit the buildings, memorials, and works of art. (Information center ☎474-2418, tours ☎473-7521. Open M-F 8:30am-5pm. Tours M-F 11am and 1pm. Free.) The huge flying saucer at one end of the Plaza is the **Empire Center for the Performing Arts,** also known as **"The Egg,"** a venue for professional theater, dance, and concerts. (☎473-1845. Box office open June-Sept. M-F 10am-4pm; Sept.-May M-F 10am-5pm, Sa 11am-2pm. Tickets $8-40.) Across the street, the ■New York State Museum has exhibits on the state's cities, history, people, and wildlife. Both kids and adults will delight in the museum's working carousel, built in 1895. One wing is dedicated to the memory of the World Trade Center, housing large portions of the buildings, crushed FDNY trucks, and the famous American flag recovered from under the wreckage. This powerful exhibit is not to be missed. (☎474-5877. Open daily 9:30am-5pm. Donations accepted.) Between the museum and The Egg, an elevator ride up the 42 floors of the **Corning Tower Observation Deck** provides a 60 mi. view on clear days. (☎474-2418. Open M-F 10am-2:30pm. Photo ID required. Free.) Since 1899, the magnificent **New York State Capitol,** adjacent to the plaza, has provided New York politicians with luxury quarters amidst a tempest of political activity. Tours leave from the **Plaza Information Center.** (☎474-2418. Tours M-F 10am, noon, 2, 3pm; Sa-Su 11am, 1, 3pm. No backpacks allowed. Free.) An art deco interior, attached coffee shop and real buttered popcorn recommend the **Spectrum 8 Theatre,** 290 Delaware Ave., which shows a broad range of independent, foreign, and Hollywood films. (☎449-1192; www.spectrum8.com. Call ahead for show times. Tickets $8.50 with student discount.) The **Capitol Repertory Theatre,** 111 N. Pearl St., stages some of Albany's best plays in a modern theater. (☎445-7469. Box office open M 10am-5pm, Tu-Th 10am-7:30pm, F 10am-8pm, Sa 10am-8:30pm, Su noon-4pm. Tickets $31-39.) Reminiscent of majestic movie theatres of yore, the **Palace Theatre,** 19 Clinton Ave., presents concerts, plays, musicals, and comedy shows. (☎465-3334. Box office open M-F 10am-6pm; Sept.-June also Sa 10am-2pm. Tickets $15-60.)

Bounded by State St. and Madison Ave. north of downtown, **Washington Park** has tulip gardens, tennis courts, and plenty of room to sprawl. The **Park Playhouse** stages free musical theater in a pastoral setting from July to mid-August. (☎434-2035; www.parkplayhouse.com.) **Alive at Five** hosts free concerts on Thursdays 5-8pm at the **Tricentennial Plaza,** across from Bank of America on Broadway, or in the amphitheater in the Hudson Riverfront Park. (☎434-2032. Open June-July. More info at Visitors Center.) The annual **Tulip Festival** (☎434-2032), held in early May in **Washington Park,** celebrates the town's Dutch heritage and over 100,000 tulips in full bloom with food, song, dance, crafts, and a Tulip Queen crowning. Call the **Albany Alive Line** (☎434-1217) or visit www.albanyevents.org for info. The **Mohawk-Hudson Bikeway** (☎386-2225) passes along old railroad grades and canal towpaths, weaving through the capital area and along the Hudson River. The **Down Tube Cycle Shop,** 466 Madison Ave., has rentals. (☎434-1711. $25 per day, $35 per 2 days. Open Apr.-Sept. M-F 11am-7pm, Sa 10am-5pm; Sept.-Apr. M-F 10am-6pm.)

COOPERSTOWN ☎845

In the early 19th century, four cloth bases were placed in a diamond on the Cooperstown green, and an America's favorite past time, baseball, was born. Set on a hill overlooking Otsego Lake, Cooperstown pays homage to the sport's history and legends. Each year, half a million fans make the pilgrimage to the town's pristine streets, wearing their favorite team uniforms and baseball caps. But small Cooperstown is more than just a baseball town. Wander farther afield and you'll find hiking, farmers' markets, and art galleries in "America's most perfect village."

■ **TAKE ME OUT TO THE BALLGAME.** Cooperstown is accessible from **I-90** and **I-88** via **Route 28.** Only four blocks by five blocks, the town is centered around **Main Street (Route 31),** which is chock full of baseball shops and restaurants. Street parking is rare in Cooperstown; park in the free lots just outside of town on

Maple St. off Glen Ave. (Rte. 28), Rte. 28 south of town, or adjacent to the Fenimore Art Museum—it's an easy walk to Main St. **Trolleys** leave from the lots every 20min., dropping riders off at major stops in town, including the **Hall of Fame,** the **Farmer's** and **Fenimore Museums, Doubleday Field,** the Pine Hill Trailways stop, and the **Chamber of Commerce.** (Trolleys run late June-early Sept. daily 8:30am-9pm; early June to mid-June and mid-Sept. to mid-Oct. Sa-Su 8:30am-6pm. All-day pass $3, children $1.) **Pine Hill Trailways** (☎547-2519 or 800-858-8555; open M-F 8am-5:30pm, Sa 9am-noon), picks up visitors at AAA Tri-County Motor Club at the corner of Elm St. and Chestnut St., and goes to Kingston (3½hr., 2 per day, $23) and New York City (5½hr., 2 per day, $45). The **Cooperstown Area Chamber of Commerce and Visitor Information Center,** 31 Chestnut St., on Rte. 28 near Main St., provides maps and information on lodging and attractions. (☎547-9983; www.cooperstown-chamber.org. Open daily June-Sept. 9am-7pm; Oct.-May 9am-5pm.) **Internet Access: Village Library of Cooperstown,** 22 Main St. (☎547-8344. Open M-Tu and Th-F 9am-5pm, W 9am-8pm, Sa 10am-2pm.) **Post Office:** 40 Main St. (☎547-2311. Open M-F 8:30am-5pm, Sa 8:30am-noon.) **Postal Code:** 13326.

⌐ TAKE ME OUT WITH THE CROWD. Lodgers can really strike out during peak season, between late June and mid-September. It's cheapest to camp, or to travel in the low season, when many motels and guest houses slash rates by $20-50. The **Mohican Motel ❹,** 90 Chestnut St., a 10min. walk from the Hall of Fame, offers well-kept rooms with cable TV and A/C. (☎547-5101. 2- to 6-person rooms late June to early Sept. M-F and Su $96-149, Sa $136-189. Apr. to late June and early Sept. to late Oct. M-F and Su $57-84, Sa $77-104.) The beautiful pines and lakeside view of **Glimmerglass State Park ❶,** 8 mi. north of Cooperstown on Rte. 31, on the north shore of Lake Otsego, make it an ideal camping location, with 43 campsites, including four wheelchair-accessible sites. The park offers hiking and biking; in the summer, visitors can swim, fish, and boat in the lake's cool water. (☎547-8662. Park open 8am-sunset. Free hot showers. Dump station. No hookups. Beach opens at 11am. Lifeguard on duty 11am-7pm. Registration fee $2.75. Sites $13. Day use $7 per vehicle.) The **Cooperstown Beaver Valley Campground ❶** has wooded sites, cabins, a pool, recreation area, small pond, and, naturally, a well-maintained baseball diamond. Drive south of town 5 mi. on Rte. 28 and follow the signs. (☎293-7324 or 800-726-7314. Showers $0.25 per 6min. Sites $28-33, with hookup $37. Cabins without indoor plumbing or linens $70.)

◖ BUY ME SOME PEANUTS AND CRACKER JACKS. The popular **Doubleday Cafe ❶,** 93 Main St., serves meals amidst eye-catching memorabilia while TVs show baseball games taking place around the country. (☎547-5468. Omelets $2-4. Hot sandwiches $3-9. Kitchen open June-Sept. M-Th and Su 7am-10pm, F-Sa 7am-11pm; Oct.-May M-Th and Su 7am-9pm, F-Sa 7am-10pm. Bar open later.) For elegant dishes, **Hoffman Lane Bistro ❸,** 2 Hoffman Ln., off Main St. across from the Hall of Fame, has airy rooms and outdoor seating along a quiet side street. (☎547-7055. Entrees $13-20. Kitchen open daily 5-10pm. Bar open M-Th and Su until 1am, F-Sa until 2am.) Follow your nose to **Schneider's Bakery ❶,** 157 Main St., and your taste buds will thank you. A Cooperstown institution, this bakery has been serving their $0.55 "old-fashioneds"—homemade doughnuts—since 1887. (☎547-9631. Open M-W 6:30am-5:30pm, Th-Sa 6:30am-8pm, Su 7:30am-5:30pm.)

◖ I DON'T CARE IF I EVER GET BACK. With almost 400,000 visitors per year, the ◤**National Baseball Hall of Fame and Museum,** on Main St., is an enormous, glowing monument to America's national pastime. Containing more than 35,000 pieces of memorabilia, the museum is a haven for baseball fans, with baseballs from every "no-hitter" in history and a collection of World Series rings. Exhibits include the multimedia presentation "The Baseball Experience," the history of African-Americans and women in baseball, and of course, the luminous Hall of Fame itself, where plaques commemorate the best players the sport has ever seen. (☎547-7200 or 888-425-5633; www.baseballhalloffame.org. Open daily Apr.-Oct. 9am-9pm; Nov.-Mar. 9am-5pm. $14.50, seniors $9.50, ages 7-12 $5.) The biggest event of the year, drawing over 20,000 visitors, is the annual **Hall of Fame Induction Weekend**, when new members of the Hall of Fame are inducted with an appropriate level of pomp and circumstance. On the last weekend in July, the ceremonies are held at the **Clark Sports Center** on Susquehanna Ave., a 10min. walk from the Hall. The event is free and open to the public. The annual **Hall of Fame Game** between two rotating Major League teams is played every June on the intimate Doubleday Field. Contact the Hall of Fame for tickets and info on these two events and reserve accommodations far in advance.

Overlooking a refined lawn and Lake Otsego, the **Fenimore Art Museum,** on Lake Rd./Rte. 80, 1 mi. from Main St., houses a collection of American folk art, Hudson River School paintings, an impressive array of Native American art, and the personal effects of James Fenimore Cooper. The Browere busts—true-to-life sculptures of American greats like John Adams and the Marquis De Lafayette, are a definite highlight. (☎547-1400 or 888-547-1450; www.fenimoreartmuseum.org. Open June-Oct. daily 10am-5pm; Apr.-May and Nov.-Dec. Tu-Su 10am-4pm. $11, seniors $9.50, students $5, ages 7-12 $5.) Go back in time to an 1845 farming village at the **Farmer's Museum,** complete with blacksmiths, musicians, displays about farming, and the unmistakable aroma of farm animals. (☎888-547-1450; www.farmersmuseum.org. Open June-Oct. daily 10am-5pm; Apr.-May by tour only Tu-F 10:30am and noon. $9, seniors $8, students with ID $5, ages 7-12 $4. Combo ticket for Hall of Fame, Fenimore Museum, and Farmer's Museum $29, children $12.) Eight miles north of Cooperstown on Lake Rd./Rte. 80, the **Glimmerglass Opera** stages summer performances of contemporary works as well as new takes on old favorites. (☎547-5704; www.glimmerglass.org. Box office at 18 Chestnut St. in Cooperstown open June-Aug. M-Sa 9am-6pm; Dec.-May M-F 10am-5pm. Tickets M-Th $35-97, F-Su $63-110.)

ITHACA AND THE FINGER LAKES ☎607

According to Iroquois legend, when the Great Spirit laid his hand upon the earth to bless it, the impression of his fingers resulted in the Finger Lakes: Canandaigua, Cayuga, Seneca, and eight others. From the shores of the lakes rise steep rolling hills and breathtaking gorges; millennia of rainfall and snowmelt have carved more than a thousand waterfalls into the stratified rock. Cornell University and Ithaca College overlook downtown Ithaca, where classic college town bookstores and cafes line the streets. Beyond the city lies a more potent treasure—the region's rich vineyards, where the fruits of the land fill many a visitor's glass.

🖥🔁 TRANSPORTATION AND PRACTICAL INFORMATION. Downtown Ithaca centers around **Ithaca Commons,** a pedestrian area with shops and restaurants. A steep uphill walk leads to Cornell's campus. Adjacent to Cornell and overflowing with students, the **Collegetown** area is packed with hole-in-the-wall bars, cheap ethnic restaurants, and family-run diners. Ithaca Bus Terminal, 710 W. State St., at Rte. 13 (☎272-7930), houses ShortLine (☎277-8800; www.shortlinebus.com), with service to New York City (5hr., 8 per day, $43), and Greyhound (☎800-231-2222; www.greyhound.com; open 6:30am-6pm), with **bus** service to Buffalo (3½hr., 3 per day, $31), New York City (5hr., 3 per day, $44), and Philadelphia (8hr., 3 per day, $57). Although Ithaca sits close to the base of Cayuga Lake, **Tompkins Consolidated Area Transit (T-CAT);** (☎277-7433) is the only way to get there without a car. Buses stop at Ithaca Commons; westbound buses also stop on Seneca St. and eastbound buses stop on Green St. (www.tcatbus.com; buses run daily; times vary by route. Schedules available from the Visitors Center. $1.50, ages 6-17 $1.25, seniors $0.75.) The **Ithaca/Tompkins County Convention and Visitors Bureau,** 904 E. Shore Dr., has maps and the free, invaluable *Ithaca Gorges & Waterfalls* guide to outdoor recreation. (☎272-1313 or 800-284-8422; www.visitithaca.com. Open mid-May to early Sept. M-F 9am-5pm, Sa 10am-5pm, Su 10am-4pm; mid-Sept. to early May M-F 9am-5pm.) Info is also available at the **Clinton House,** 116 N. Cayuga St. (Open M-F 10am-5:30pm, Sa 10am-2pm and 3-5pm.) **Internet Access: Tompkins County Public Library,** 101 E. Green St. (☎272-4557. Open July-Aug. M-Th 10am-8:15pm, F-Sa 10am-5pm; Sept.-June also Su 1-5pm.) **Post Office:** 213 N. Tioga St., at E. Buffalo. (☎800-275-8777. Open M-F 8:30am-5pm, Sa 8:30am-noon.) **Postal Code:** 14850.

◪ ACCOMMODATIONS. Budget accommodations are surprisingly abundant in Ithaca. Camping is beautiful during the summer months, and reasonably priced B&Bs are a great option during the winter. The motels lining the many roads to the city are affordable any time of year. The **Sweet Dreams B&B ❸,** 228 Wood St., rests a few blocks south of downtown and is accessible from Albany St. With only two guest rooms, this cozy B&B ensures friendly interaction with the kind owners. (☎272-7727. Reservations required. Rooms $75-85.) A "way cool family-friendly earthy groovy place," the **Turtle Dreams B&B ❸,** 418 Lafayette Road, lives up to its motto with negotiable group rates, ample organic breakfasts, and a lovely setting in the Finger Lakes countryside. From Ithaca, take Rte. 366 west to Church St. in McLean. The B&B is 2½ mi. down the road on the right. (☎838-3492. www.dreamingturtles.com. Rooms with shared bath M-F $50, Sa-Su $55; with private bath $60/65. Just outside Cornell, the **Embassy Motel ❸,** 1083 Dryden Rd. on Rte. 366, has the cheapest rates in town and clean, simple rooms with A/C and cable TV. (☎272-3721. Rooms $45-85, from $75 during summer.) Featuring a waterfall that plummets 215 ft. (a bigger drop than Niagara Falls), **Taughannock Falls State Park ❶,** 8 mi. north on Rte. 89, offers woodland camping, access to the shores of Cayuga Lake, and Saturday evening concerts in July and August. (☎387-6739. Free hot showers. Sites $13, with electricity M-Th $19, F-Su $22. 4-person cabins $40 per night, $160 per week. Registration fee $2.75. Day use $7.) A huge, foaming waterfall dominates the entrance to the campsite at **Buttermilk Falls ❶,** on Rte. 13 south of Ithaca. The closest park to Ithaca, Buttermilk has 60 small sites in a birch forest, and miles of trails trace Buttermilk Creek through the woods and across idyllic bridges. (☎273-5761. Free showers. Sites $13. Registration fee $2.75. Day use $7.)

◨ FOOD. **◪Wegmans ❶,** 500 S. Meadow St., is food paradise for the budget traveler. Food by the pound is available at a wok bar, wing bar, cheese bar, or pizza bar ($5-7 per lb.); the deli sells mammoth 14 in. subs ($7); the candy section holds over 50 tubes of sweets stretching to the ceiling; and the produce section offers every fruit and vegetable imaginable at near-wholesale prices. (☎277-5800. Open 24hr.) Restaurants in Ithaca are focused around Ithaca Commons and Collegetown. With a menu including everything that can possibly be done to a bagel, creative sandwiches ($6-7), and bar with local brews, **Collegetown Bagels ❷,** 415 College Ave., is a haven for local students. (☎273-0982. Open daily 6:30am-2am.) With a new menu twice a day, jazz and folk music on the weekends, and ethnically-themed Sunday nights, **Moosewood Restaurant ❷,** 215 N. Cayuga, at Seneca St. in the Dewitt Mall, features a completely vegetarian selection of fresh and creative dishes and was named one of the 13 most influential restaurants of the 20th century. (☎273-9610. Dinner $10-16. Open Sept.-May M-Th 11:30am-3pm and 5:30-8:30pm, F-Sa 11:30am-3pm and 5:30-9pm, Su 5:30-8:30pm; June-Oct. M-Th 11:30am-3pm and 5:30-9pm, F-Sa 11:30am-3pm and 6-9:30pm, Su 5:30-8:30pm.) Choose from a daily menu of tapas ($2-8) at **Just a Taste ❸,** 116 N. Aurora St. Wine flights ($6-11) and rich desserts ($2-5) are perfect for the outdoor patio during the summer. (☎277-9463. Open M-Th and Su 5:30-10pm, F-Sa 5:30-11pm.) At **Gino's NY Pizzeria ❶,** 106 N. Aurora St., a 16 oz. soda and the two largest slices of pizza you will ever consume ($3) could keep you going all the way to New York City. (☎277-2777. Open M-Th and Su 10:30am-10pm, F-Sa 10:30am-2am.)

◙ **SIGHTS. Cornell University,** the youngest of the Ivy League schools, sits on a steep hill in Ithaca between two tremendous gorges. Accessed by a steep flight of steps across University Ave. from the Johnson Art Museum, the suspension bridge above Fall Creek provides a heart-pounding walk above one gorge, while the **College Avenue Stone Arch Bridge** above Cascadilla Creek has a brilliant sunset view. The **Information and Referral Center,** in the 2nd floor lobby of Day Hall on East Ave., has info on campus sights and activities and offers **campus tours** that showcase the blend of architectural styles and landscaping that make Cornell one of the most beautiful campuses in the US. (☎254-4636. Open M-Sa 8am-5pm, Su 12pm-1pm; phone also staffed M-F 8am-10pm. Tours Apr.-Nov. M-F 9, 11am, 1, and 3pm; Sa 9, 10:30am, 1pm; Su 1pm. Dec.-Mar. daily 1pm. Free.) The funky, box-like cement edifice at the top of the hill houses Cornell's **Herbert F. Johnson Museum of Art,** at the corner of University Ave. and Central Ave. The museum holds a small but impressive collection of works by Giacometti, Matisse, O'Keeffe, Picasso, and Degas, as well as an equally impressive 5th floor Asian art exhibit and rooftop sculpture garden. (☎255-6464. Open Tu-Su 10am-5pm. Free.) Part museum and part paleontology lab, the **Museum of the Earth,** north along Rte. 96, gives visitors a look back into the Finger Lakes' natural history. (☎273-6623; www.museumoftheearth.org. $8, seniors and students $5, ages 3-17 $3.) The extensive **botanical gardens** and **arboretum** that compose the **Cornell Plantations** lie serenely in the northeast corner of campus. Visitors can ramble through the Slim Jim Woods, drive to Grossman Pond, or take a short hike to a lookout point with a view of campus and the surrounding area. (☎255-3020. www.plantations.cornell.edu. Open daily dawn-dusk. Free.) Parking permits ($1) are required at the art museum and gift shop (Open M-F 9am-4pm) and are available at the booths at each entrance to campus.

Information on hiking in the region can be found in the *Passport to the Trails of Tompkins County* ($1), available at the Ithaca Visitors Center. A community gathering place on weekends, the **Ithaca Farmers' Market,** 3rd St. off Rte. 13, has much more than produce under its eaves: vendors also bring ethnic food, cider tastings, and hand-crafted furniture to the market. (☎273-7109. Open Apr.-Dec. Sa 9am-3pm; May-Oct. also Su 9am-3pm, June-Aug. Tu 3-7pm.) The fertile soil and cool climate of the Finger Lakes region has made it the heart of New York's wine industry. Designated **wine trails** provide opportunities for wine tasting and vineyard touring—the fall harvest is the best time to visit. (For more information, contact the Visitors Bureau, p. 125.) The trail closest to Ithaca, the **Cayuga Trail** (☎800-684-5217; www.cayugawinetrail.com) contains 15 vineyards, 11 of which are located along Rte. 89 between Seneca Falls and Ithaca. Other wineries are on the **Seneca Lake Trail** (☎877-536-2717; www.senecalakewine.com), with 25 wineries encircling the lake on Rte. 414 (east side) and Rte. 14 (west side). The **Keuka Trail** (☎800-440-4898; www.keukawinetrail.com), with nine wineries along Rte. 54 and 76, is near Ithaca. Some wineries offer free picnic facilities and tours. All give free tastings; may require the purchase of a glass for a nominal charge.

🎵 🎭 **ENTERTAINMENT AND NIGHTLIFE.** Befitting its Ivy League roots, Cornell offers excellent theater productions year-round. The **Hangar Theatre,** 2 mi. from downtown at the Rte. 89 N. Treman Marina entrance, stages musicals and plays. **The Wedge,** an experimental theater in the same building, gives free performances before and after the mainstage show. (☎273-8588; www.hangarthe-atre.org. Shows Tu-Th and Su 7:30pm, F-Sa 8pm; matinees Sa 3pm, and some Su 2pm. $12-31. Call ahead for Wedge showtimes.) The intimate 73-seat **Kitchen Theatre,** 116 N. Cayuga, is always cooking up something new, hosting everything from one-man shows to full plays. After the main performance, "Kitchen Sink" shows—experimental and cutting-edge theater—are often performed. (☎272-0403. $16-20, students $12. Kitchen Sink shows $5, with ticket to main show $4.) In the same building, the **Ticket Center at Clinton House** sells tickets to events at the Hangar Theatre, the Kitchen Theatre, and many local college theater events. (☎273-4497 or 800-284-8422. Open M-Sa 10am-5:30pm.) The free and widely available *Ithaca Times* has complete listings of entertainment options.With over 300 screenings a year, **Cornell Cinema,** Willard Straight Hall on Cornell's campus, has a film for every taste. (☎255-3522; http://cinema.cornell.edu. Screenings most nights. $6.50, students $4.) A romantic path along the **Cascadilla Creek** gorge starts near the Stone Arch Bridge on College Ave. Student favorites lining College Ave. make up the Collegetown district. **Stella's,** 403 College Ave., has the dual personality of most college students—there is a cafe on one side where intellectuals linger over offerings like the Velvet Hammer (two shots of espresso, steamed milk, and raspberry; $4) and a funky jazz bar where patrons down hip drinks and forget what they learned in class. (☎277-1490. Free Wi-Fi. No cover. Kitchen closes at midnight; cafe open in summer daily 7am-1:30am. Jazz bar open daily 11am-1am.) Named after a local serial killer, **Rulloff's,** 411 College Ave., has a large bar in a dimly-lit pub overflowing with college students. At 5:30pm, during Happy hour, and at half past midnight, the bartender spins the "wheel of fortune" to pick the night's drink special, while $6 pitchers keep the college crowd happy. (☎272-6067; www.rulloffs.com. 21+. Open M-Sa 11:30am-1am, Su 10am-1am.) With plush curtains and masks on the walls, it's Mardi Gras all year long at **Maxie's Supper Club,** 635 W. State St. Between the Shrimp and Grits ($11), Cajun Bloody Mary ($6), and live music on Sunday nights, you'll swear you're in New Orleans. (☎272-4136; www.maxies.com. Raw bar and "mini-plates" $8-16. Entrees $14-24. Su brunch 11am-3pm. Live music T and Su. Raw bar open daily 4pm-midnight, half-price 4-6pm. Kitchen open M-Th and Su 5pm-midnight, F-Sa 5pm-1am. Bar open daily 4pm-1am.)

SENECA FALLS ☎315

In 1848, Seneca Falls hosted the first Women's Rights Convention, forever emblazoning the town in American history books. An essential first stop is the **Seneca Falls Heritage Area Visitor's Center,** 115 Fall St. (☎568-2703. Open M-F 9am-4pm, Sa 10am-4pm, Su noon-4pm.) ■**Women's Rights National Park,** 136 Fall St., sits next to the frame of the Wesleyan Chapel, where the Women's Rights Convention was held. It's an excellent spot to contemplate the convention's powerful Declaration of Sentiments, immortalized on the outdoor memorial. The **Elizabeth Cady Stanton Home** and the **McClintock House,** both part of the park, are nearby. (☎568-2991; www.nps.gov/wori. Open daily 9am-5pm, but call ahead as hours vary seasonally. $3, under 17 free.) Documenting the lives of more than 100 great American women, the **National Women's Hall of Fame,** 76 Fall St., allows you to nominate your favorite heroine. (☎568-8060; www.greatwomen.org. Open May-Sept. M-Sa 10am-4pm; Oct.-Apr. W-Sa 11am-4pm. $3, seniors and students $1.50, families $7.)

The best deal in town for lodging is the **Starlite Motel ❸,** on Rtes. 5 and 20 west of Seneca Falls, where the rooms have A/C, HBO, and kitchenettes. (☎568-6149. Rooms in summer $55-75; in low season $40-75.) South of Seneca Falls on Rte. 89, **Cayuga Lake State Campgrounds ❶** offers more than 250 campsites and a prime beach location. (☎568-5163. Sites $13, with electricity $19. Registration fee $2.75. Day use $7 per vehicle.) Comfy leather couches line the large interior of **Zuzu's**

Cafe ❶, 107 Fall St, serving coffee, ice cream, and light lunches. (☎568-2929. Free Wi-Fi. M-Th and Su 6:30am-10pm, F-Sa 6:30am-11pm.) With deep red booths and a slick retro decor, **Downtown Deli ❶**, 53 Fall St., serves large sandwiches and wraps. In summer, they grill on the deck overlooking the canal. (☎568-9943; www.downtowndelis.com. Subs $4. Open M-F 7:30am-9pm, Sa 9am-9pm, Su 9am-5pm.)

BUFFALO   ☎716

Combining a vibrant cultural scene with rough-around-the-edges charm, Buffalo is a metropolis of synergy. The city is an architectural delight, filled with everything from Gothic church spires to the angular simplicity of homes designed by Frank Lloyd Wright. Here, classic cafes and budget-friendly diners share the streets with hip clubs and professional theater companies. From the downtown skyline to funky Elmwood Village, Buffalo balances small-town warmth with big-city culture.

E TRANSPORTATION. Buffalo Niagara International Airport (BUF), 4200 Genesee St. (☎630-6000; www.buffaloairport.com) in Cheektowaga, 10 mi. east of downtown off Hwy. 33. Take the MetroLink Airport-Downtown Express (#204) from the **Transportation Center,** 181 Ellicott St., at N. Division St. Airport Taxi Service (☎633-8294 or 800-551-9369; www.buffaloairporttaxi.com) offers shuttles to downtown for $15. Call or reserve online. Amtrak, 75 Exchange St. (☎856-2075; www.amtrak.com; office open M-F 6am-3:30pm), at Washington St., runs **trains** to New York City (8½hr., 3 per day, $85) and Toronto (4½hr., 1 per day, $46). Greyhound, in the Buffalo Metropolitan Transportation Center (☎855-7531 or 800-454-2487; www.greyhound.com; station open 24hr.), sends **buses** to: Boston (11½hr., 12 per day, $65); New York City (8½hr., 13 per day, $78); Niagara Falls, ON (1hr., 7 per day, $4); Toronto, ON (2½hr., 12 per day, $16). The **Niagara Frontier Transit Authority (NFTA)** offers bus and rail service in the city (☎855-300; www.nfta.com; $1.50-2.25; seniors, children, and disabled $0.65-0.95), with additional buses to Niagara Falls, NY, and free rides on the above-ground Main St. Metro Rail. For a taxi call **Cheektowaga Taxi,** ☎822-1738.

◪ PRACTICAL INFORMATION. The Visitor Center, 617 Main St., is in the Theater District. (☎852-2356 or 800-283-3256; www.visitbuffaloniagara.com. Open M-F 9am-5pm.) For **GLBT resources** visit: **Pride Buffalo, Inc.,** 266 Elmwood Ave., Ste. 207 (☎879-0999; www.pridebuffalo.org); or **PFLAG,** P.O. Box 617 (☎883-0384; www.pflag-buffalo-niagara.org). **Police:** (non-emergency) ☎855-2222. **Suicide, Rape, Crisis, and Emergency Mental Health Hotline:** ☎834-3131. Operates 24hr. **Medical Services: Buffalo General Hospital,** 100 High St. (☎859-5600). Take the Metro Rail to the Allen-Hospital stop, go up Main St., and turn right on High St. **Internet Access: Buffalo and Erie County Public Library,** 1 Lafayette Sq. at Washington St. (☎858-8900. Internet access with $1 temporary library membership. Wi-Fi. Open M-Sa 8:30am-6pm, Su 1-5pm.) **Post Office:** 701 Washington St. (☎856-4603. Open M-F 8:30am-5:30pm, Sa 8:30am-1pm.) **Postal Code:** 14203.

◪◪ ACCOMMODATIONS AND FOOD. Budget lodgings are a rarity in Buffalo, but chain motels can be found near the airport and off I-90, 8-10 mi. northeast of downtown. Set in the heart of downtown, **◪Hostel Buffalo (HI) ❶**, 667 Main St., has cheery common rooms, a kitchen, and a genial staff. It also has free linen, laundry facilities, and Internet. (☎852-5222; www.hostelbuffalo.com. Reception 24hr. with reservation, otherwise daily Oct.-May 9-11am; July-Aug. 9-11am and 4-11pm; Sept.-June 9-11am and 5-10pm. Check-out 10:45am. Reservations recommended in summer. Wheelchair-accessible. Dorms $23, members $20; private rooms $50-$65; each additional adult $10, each additional child $5.) The **Lenox Hotel & Suites ❸**,

140 North St., at Delaware Ave., has old-fashioned rooms 5min. from Allentown and the Elmwood Village nightlife. Take bus #11, 20, or 25 to North St. (☎884-1700; www.lenoxhotelandsuites.com. A/C, cable TV, coin-op laundry, free parking, kitchens available. Singles from $59; suites $69-119.)

Elmwood Village, up Elmwood Ave. between Virginia Ave. and Forest Ave., is full of funky boutiques, coffee shops, and ethnic restaurants. Despite its imposing statue, **Gabriel's Gate ❷,** 145 Allen St., is a friendly, rustic saloon. Enjoy the famous "Richmond Ave." burger ($5) or the portobello sandwich ($6) from the comfy shaded patio. (☎886-0602. Open M-W and Su 11:30am-midnight, Th 11:30am-1am, F-Sa 11:30am-2am.) Skip chain coffeeshops in favor of **Spot Coffee ❷,** 227 Delaware Ave., where you can get anything from a plain cup o' joe to specialty espresso drinks and iced blended shakes. A funky side room features mismatched furniture and local musicians on Wednesday and Sunday evenings. (☎856-2739. Coffee drinks $2-4. Open M-Th 6am-11pm, F 6am-midnight, Sa 7am-midnight, Su 7am-11pm. Kitchen closes 2hr. before cafe.) Smells of hot sauce fill the street in front of **Anchor Bar ❸,** 1047 Main St., home to the 1964 birth of the buffalo wing. (☎886-8920. Open Th 11am-11pm, F 11am-1am, Sa-Su noon-1am.) After a late, late night out, locals head to **Jim's Steak Out ❶,** 92 W Chippewa, for enormous steak hoagies ($7). (☎854-6666. Open M-W 10:30am-2am, Th-Su 10:30am-5am.)

◪ 🖪 SIGHTS AND ENTERTAINMENT. The **Albright-Knox Art Gallery,** 1285 Elmwood Ave., houses an internationally recognized collection of over 6000 modern pieces, including Picassos and Rothkos. (Take bus #20. ☎882-8700; www.albrightknox.org. Open W-Su 10am-5pm, F 10am-10pm. $10, seniors and students $8, 12 and under free; F 3-10pm free.) Next to the gallery, **Delaware Park,** the center of Buffalo's park system, was designed by landscape architect Frederick Law Olmsted. Frank Lloyd Wright also designed several important houses in the area. Architecture buffs can take a 2hr. self-guided **walking tour** of historic downtown Buffalo; pick up the free guide *Walk Buffalo* at the tourist office. For a great view of Buffalo, head to **Buffalo City Hall,** 65 Niagara Sq., take the elevator to the 25th floor, and walk up three more flights for a spectacular panoramic view from the outdoor observation deck. (☎851-5891. Open M-F 9am-4pm. Free.) **Shea's Performing Arts Center,** 646 Main St. (☎847-1400; www.sheas.org), features Broadway musicals in an elegant opera house, while the **Irish Classical Theatre Company,** 625 Main St. (☎853-4282), performs the works of Gaelic playwrights in a three-row theater-in-

ON THE MENU

AMERICAN DELICACY: BUFFALO WINGS

Once a city of immigrants, modern Buffalo has inherited a rich culinary tradition. This illustrious tradition that includes the German-influenced specialty "beef in weck" and the Irish-Catholic inspired "fish fry" peaked with the invention of of the Buffalo wing. In 1964, at the Italian-American Anchor Bar, the city gave its most famous contribution to appetizer menus everywhere. Attempting to placate her hungry son, Teressa Bellissimo deep-fried leftover chicken wings and covered them in a sauce consisting of cayenne pepper, vinegar, butter, salt, and garlic—resulting in the Buffalo wing we know and love today. At the time the recipe was created, chicken wings were typically thrown away or reserved for making stock. In Buffalo, the best-known places for authentic wings are the Anchor Bar and at Duff's. The Anchor Bar serves more than 36,000 pounds of wings per month. However, locals do not call them "Buffalo wings," but rather "chicken wings" or just plain "wings." Buffalo wings have not only captured America's appetite, but have become a staple of American culture supported by the now defunct professional roller hockey team in Buffalo named the Buffalo Wings and The National Wing Festival held every Labor Day weekend in downtown Buffalo.

the-round. The **Studio Arena Theatre,** 710 Main St. (☎856-8025), is a nationally-recognized company. The Allentown Village Society organizes the **Allentown Art Festival,** a two-day celebration of local artists, craftsmen, and musicians. (☎881-4269; www.allentownartfestival.com.) The **Buffalo Niagara Guitar Festival** (☎845-7156; www.guitarfestival.org) is America's first and largest all-guitar music festival, featuring luminaries like Bo Diddley. From September to January, **Ralph Wilson Stadium,** in Orchard Park, hosts the NFL's **Buffalo Bills** (☎648-1800; www.buffalobills.com), while the NHL's **Sabres** (☎855-4444, ext. 82; www.sabres.com) play at the **HSBC Arena,** 1 Seymour H. Knox III Plaza, from September to April.

NIGHTLIFE. Downtown, bars and clubs are concentrated on **Chippewa Street** and **Franklin Street,** but live music can be found throughout the city. From Thursday to Saturday bars are open until 4am, and thousands of Western New Yorkers are out all night. Pick up a copy of *Artvoice* (www.artvoice.com) for event listings in Buffalo. Music is burned into the walls at **Nietzsche's,** 248 Allen St., where Ani DiFranco and the 10,000 Maniacs got their big breaks. (☎886-8539; www.nietzsches.com. Beer on tap from $2.50. Live rock, reggae, blues, or jazz every night. M open mic night. 21+; call ahead for special 18+ nights. Open daily noon-4am.) **Buffalo Smokehouse and Sky Bar,** 257 Franklin St., is a BBQ joint on the first floor and Buffalo's only open-air rooftop lounge on top. Patrons ride a glass elevator up to the sky bar to relax above the bustling scene below. (☎853-3600. Entrees $10-14. Sky bar cover $3-4 after 10pm. Open daily 11am-4am, weather permitting.) **Club Marcella,** 622 Main St., is a gay nightclub, but clubbers of all persuasions party on its two dance floors. (☎847-6850; www.marcellashowclub.com. Th drag shows. Sa hip-hop. 18+. Cover usually $3. Open W-Su 9pm-4am.)

NIAGARA FALLS
☎716

Niagara Falls is flat-out spectacular, earning its ranking as one of the seven natural wonders of the world. The giant Falls are best viewed from the Canadian side of the Niagara River, where the natural grandeur is complemented by well-developed tourist attractions, nightlife, and a thriving honeymoon industry. Meanwhile, on the American side, a giant resort-casino built on Seneca tribal land promises to revitalize the area. Although the area around the falls teems with commercialized gimmicks, the real draw is the Falls' magnificence—something not to be missed.

BORDER CROSSING. Traveling between the US and Canada is generally an easy process, but security is still taken very seriously. Crossing can be as simple as a wave of the passport or as time-consuming as a full search of your car. To keep things moving along, make sure to have all necessary documents handy. It is illegal to cross the border anywhere except at an open crossing station. See **Essentials,** p. 11, for more details on documents and procedures.

TRANSPORTATION

Trains: In Canada, **VIA Rail Canada,** 4267 Bridge St. (☎888-842-7245). Take the Niagara Falls Shuttle (see **Public Transit,** below) from downtown. Open M-F 6am-8pm, Sa-Su 7am-8pm. Runs to **New York City** (10hr.; 11:30am; M-Th and Sa CDN$86, F and Su CDN$102) and **Toronto** (2hr.; daily 5:45am, M-F 6:45am, Sa-Su 7:40am; CDN$31, with ISIC CDN$22). In the US, **Amtrak,** at 27th and Lockport St. (☎285-4224; www.amtrak.com), 1 block east of Hyde Park Blvd. Open daily 7:30am-5:30pm. Runs to **New York City** (9hr.; M-Th and Sa $71, F and Su $85) and **Toronto** (3hr.; M-Th and Sa $23, F and Su $30). Taxis meet each incoming train ($7-10 to downtown), or wait for bus #52 (runs daily 7am-4:30pm).

Buses: In Canada, the **bus terminal,** 4267 Bridge St. (☎357-2133; www.greyhound.com), across from the train station, is open daily 7am-10:30pm. **Greyhound** buses go to **Toronto** (2hr., 23 per day, CDN$28). **The Magic Bus** (☎877-856-6610; www.magicbuscompany.com) runs between Hostelling International hostels at Niagara Falls and Toronto (Tu, Th, and Sa-Su 5pm; CDN$20). In the US, **Niagara Falls Bus Terminal,** at 4th and Niagara St. (☎282-1331), is open M-F 9am-4pm, Sa-Su 9am-noon. **Greyhound** buses go directly to **New York City** (8hr., 1 per day, $78). To get a bus in Buffalo, take bus #40 "Grand Island" from the Niagara Falls bus terminal to the **Buffalo Transportation Center,** 181 Ellicott St. (1hr., 19 per day, $2.25).

Public Transit: In Canada, the **Niagara Falls Shuttle** (☎356-1179) runs between the bus and train stations, downtown, and other touristy areas. (June 20-Aug. 31 every 30min. 8:45am-2am. All-day pass CDN$6.) **Niagara Frontier Metro Transit System** (☎285-2002; www.nfta.com) provides local city transit in the US ($1.50). **ITA Buffalo Shuttle** (☎800-551-9369) has service from the Niagara Falls info center and major hotels to Buffalo Niagara International Airport ($30).

Taxi: In Canada, **Niagara Falls Taxi,** ☎905-357-4000. In the US, **Blue United Cab,** ☎285-9331. Travelers should beware of taxi drivers who charge full fare for each rider.

Bike Rental: In Canada, **Leisure Trails,** 4362 Leader Ln. (☎905-371-9888), near the Niagara Whirlpool. $5 per hr., $20 per day, including lock and helmet. Open daily 9am-6pm, but later drop-offs can be arranged. In the US, **Bikes & Hikes,** 526 Niagara St. (☎278-0047). $12 per, including helmet, lock, and map.

ORIENTATION AND PRACTICAL INFORMATION

Niagara Falls spans the US-Canadian border (addresses given here are in New York, unless otherwise noted). Take **U.S. 190** to the Robert Moses Pkwy., which leads directly to the Falls and downtown. On the **Canadian** side, most attractions are scattered along **Niagara Parkway (River Road),** and the main entertainment and shopping district is **Clifton Hill** between Victoria Ave. and River Rd. On the **American** side, **Niagara Street** is the main east-west artery, ending at the **Rainbow Bridge,** which crosses to Canada (US $2.50 per car, US $0.50 per pedestrian; tolls only charged going into US). North-south streets are numbered, increasing toward the east. Budget motels line **Route 62 (Niagara Falls Boulevard)** outside of town. Many businesses in the Niagara area accept both American and Canadian currency.

Visitor Info: In Canada, **Niagara Falls Tourism,** 5515 Stanley Ave. (☎800-563-2557 or 905-356-6061; www.discoverniagara.com), has information about the Canadian side. Open M-F 8am-6pm, Sa 10am-6pm, Su 10am-4pm. In the US, the **Orin Lehman Visitors Center** (☎278-1796) is in front of the Falls' observation deck; the entrance is marked by a garden. Open daily 7am-10:15pm.

Hotlines: Sexual Assault Crisis Line, ☎905-682-4584.

Medical Services: In Canada, **Greater Niagara General Hospital,** 5546 Portage Rd. (☎905-358-0171). In the US, **Niagara Falls Memorial Medical Center,** 621 10th St. (☎278-4000; www.nfmmc.org).

Internet Access: In Canada, **Niagara Falls Public Library,** 4848 Victoria Ave. (☎905-356-8080), offers free Internet access. Open M-Th 9am-9pm, F-Sa 9am-5:30pm. In the US, **Niagara Falls Public Library,** 1425 Main St. (☎286-4894; www.niagarafallspubliclib.org), also has free access. Open M-W 9am-9pm, Th-F 9am-5pm.

Post Office: In Canada, 4500 Queen Ave. (☎800-267-1177). Open M-F 8am-5pm. In the US, 615 Main St. (☎285-7561). Open M-F 8:30am-5pm, Sa 8:30am-2pm. **Postal Code:** L2E 2L0 (ON). 14302 (NY). **Area Code:** 905 (ON). 716 (NY). In text, 716 unless otherwise noted.

ACCOMMODATIONS

Many newlyweds spend their honeymoons by the awesome beauty of the Falls. In Canada, cheap motels (from CDN$35) advertising free wedding certificates line **Lundy's Lane,** while many moderately priced B&Bs overlook the gorge on **River Road** between the Rainbow Bridge and the Whirlpool Bridge.

Hostelling International Niagara Falls (HI), 4549 Cataract Ave., Niagara Falls, ON (☎905-357-0770 or 888-749-0058). Just off Bridge St., about 2 blocks from the bus station and VIA Rail. The inside of this hostel is brightly painted with earth-friendly messages. Daily social activities, Fair Trade coffee, and an organic garden. Internet access CDN$1 per 15min. Lockers CDN$2. Linen CDN$2, free with ISIC. Laundry and kitchen facilities. Key deposit CDN$5. Reception in summer 24hr.; in winter 8am-midnight. Check-out 11am. Quiet hours 11pm-7am. Reservations recommended May-Nov. Dorms CDN$26, members CDN$22; singles $58/48. ❶

Backpacker's International Hostel, 4219 Huron St., Niagara Falls, ON, at Zimmerman Ave. (☎905-357-4266 or 800-891-7022; www.backpackers.ca), a 5min. walk from the bus station. Take Bridge St. to Zimmerman Ave.; the hostel is a few blocks to the right. In a beautiful home with clean dorms, private rooms, and tasty breakfasts. Bike rentals CDN$15 per day. Free Internet access. Breakfast, linens, and parking included. Reception 24hr. with reservation. Dorms CDN$25; singles CDN$55; doubles CDN$65. ❶

Bampfield Hall Bed & Breakfast, 4671 Zimmerman Ave., Niagara Falls, ON (☎905-353-8522 or 877-353-8522; www.niagaraniagara.com). Located right off the Niagara River Pkwy., this beautiful, newly restored B&B offers well-decorated and comfortable rooms at fairly reasonable rates. Includes an antique hat museum on premises. No smoking. Reservations required. Rooms CDN$80-115; low season from CDN$65. 10% cash discount. ❸

FOOD

Niagara Cumpir ❶, 4941 Victoria Ave., ON, serves a young clientele affordable Mediterranean and American fare on two spacious patios. Falafel (CDN$3.75), and a whole pizza with any or all toppings (CDN$12) delight patrons dining al fresco. (☎905-356-9900. Open M-Th 11am-11pm, F-Sa 11am-3am, Su 11am-9pm.) The oldest restaurant in town, **Simon's Restaurant ❷,** 4116 Bridge St., ON, just one block from the HI hostel, is more than a hundred years old. Huge breakfasts (CDN$6) and classic cheeseburgers (CDN$3) at historic prices prove why this diner is still a local favorite. (☎905-356-5310. Open M-Sa 5:30am-7pm, Su 5:30am-2pm.) For a touristy location without the touristy prices, head to **Spicy Olive ❸,** 5026 Center St., ON. The hip atmosphere and live music on weekends set this place a step above the other restaurants in the surrounding area. (☎905-371-2323. Entrees CDN$12-20. Open daily noon-2am.)

SIGHTS

In Canada, walk the ◙**promenade** from Clifton Hill to Table Rock Point for spectacular views of Bridal Veil Falls and Horseshoe Falls. Both sides of the border provide plenty of additional attractions. In Canada, the **casinos** and entertainment industry keep tourists occupied, while the American side enjoys a full calendar of historical and cultural festivals (☎800-338-7890; www.niagara-usa.com).

CANADIAN SIDE. On the Canadian side, **Queen Victoria Park** provides the best view of **Horseshoe Falls.** Starting 1hr. after sunset, the Falls are illuminated for 3hr. every night, and a fireworks display lights up the sky every Friday and Sunday at 10pm (May 16-Sept. 1). Parking close to the park is expensive (CDN$12 per hr.), but farther down Niagara Pkwy., across from the Greenhouse, parking is CDN$3 per hr. **People Movers** buses tourists through the 19 mi. area on the Canadian side of the Falls, stopping at attractions along the way. Fare includes rides on the incline railway to nearby casinos. (☎877-642-7275. Mid-June to early Sept. daily 9am-11pm; low-season hours vary. CDN$7.50, children 6-12 CDN$4.50.) Bikers, in-line skaters, and walkers enjoy the 20mi. **Niagara River Recreation Trail,** which runs from Fort Erie to Fort George and passes historical sights dating back to the War of 1812. Far above the crowds and excitement, **Skylon Tower** has the highest view of the Falls at 520 ft. above ground and 775 ft. above the base of the falls. On a clear day, you can see all the way to Toronto. The tower's **Observation Deck** also offers incredible views. *(5200 Robinson St. ☎ 905-356-2651. Open June-Oct. M-F 8am-11pm, Sa-Su 8am-midnight; Nov.-May daily 9am-11pm. CDN$11, children 6-12 CDN$6.45; families CDN$7.)* The **Adventure Pass** includes entrance to the Maid of the Mist boat tour; Journey Behind the Falls, a tour behind Horseshoe Falls; White Water Walk, a long boardwalk next to the Niagara River Rapids; the Butterfly Conservatory, on the grounds of the world-famous Niagara Parks Botanical Gardens; CDN$2 discounts for the Spanish Aero Car, an aerial cable ride over the rapids' whirlpool waters; and all-day transportation on the People Movers. *(Adventure Pass: CDN$43, children CDN$26. www.niagara-parks.com has details and sells passes online. Maid of the Mist: ☎ 905-357-7393. www.maidofthemist.com. Open in summer daily 9:45am-5:45pm. Trips every 15min. CDN$13, children CDN$8. Journey Behind the Falls: ☎ 905-354-1551. Open in summer daily 9am-7:30pm. CDN$10/6. White Water Walk: ☎ 905-374-1221. Open in summer daily 9am-5pm. CDN$8/5. Guided tours available. Butterfly Conservatory: ☎ 905-358-0025. Open in summer daily 9am-7:30pm, call for updated times. CDN$10/6. Aero Car: ☎ 905-354-8983. Open in summer daily 9am-6:45pm. CDN$11/7.)*

In contrast to the natural wonder of the Falls, attractions of a different sort exist on **Clifton Hill,** in the form of fun-houses, wax museums, arcades, and thrill rides.

AMERICAN SIDE. For over 150 years, the **Maid of the Mist** boat tour has entertained visitors with the awe-inspiring (and wet) views from the feet of both Falls. (☎ 284-8897. Open Apr.-Oct. daily 10am-6pm. Tours in summer every 15min. $11.50, ages 6-12 $6.75, $1 for entrance to observation deck only.) The **Cave of the Winds Tour** hands out souvenir (read: ineffective) yellow raincoats and sandals for a drenching hike to the base of the Bridal Veil Falls, including an optional walk to Hurricane Deck where gale-force waves slam down from above. (☎278-1730. Open May to mid-Oct.; hours vary depending on season and weather conditions. Trips leave every 15min. Must be at least 42 in. tall. $8, ages 6-12 $7.) The **Master Pass,** available at the park's Visitors Center, covers admission to the Maid of the Mist; the Cave of the Winds Tour; the **Discovery Geological Museum,** in Prospect Park, which has gorge trail hikes and an elevator ride that simulates the geological history of the Falls; the **Aquarium of Niagara,** which houses the endangered Peruvian penguin; and the **Niagara Scenic Trolley,** a tram-guided tour of the park and the best transportation between the sights on the American side. *(Master Pass: $27.50, ages 6-12 $19.25. Geological Museum: ☎278-1780. Film every 30min. Open June-Aug. daily 9am-7pm; Sept.-May 9am-5pm. $5, children $3. Aquarium: 701 Whirlpool St., across from the Geological Museum. ☎285-3575; www.aquariumofniagara.org. Open daily 9am-5pm. $7.50, children and seniors $5.50. Trolley: ☎278-1730. Runs every 10-20min. Open May-Aug. M-Th and Su 9am-9pm, F-Sa 9am-10pm. $2, ages 6-12 $1.)* The **Niagara Power Project,** 4 mi. north on Robert Moses Pkwy., features hands-on exhibits and videos on energy, hydropower, and local history. *(5777 Lewiston Rd. ☎286-6661. Open daily 9am-5pm. Call ahead to arrange a guided tour. Free.)* Eight miles north in Lewiston, NY, at the foot of 4th St., the 150-acre state **Artpark** focuses on visual and performing arts, offering opera, musicals, pops concerts, and rock shows. *(☎800-659-7275. Box office open M-F 10am-4pm, later on event days. Shows May-Aug.; call for schedule. Shows at 8pm. Tickets $15-40.)* Nestled between Niagara River and

Lake Ontario, **Old Fort Niagara** was built for French troops in 1726 and was the site of battles during the French and Indian War and the American Revolution. *(Follow Robert Moses Pkwy. north from Niagara Falls. ☎ 745-7611. www.oldfortniagara.org. Open June-Aug. daily 9am-8pm; low-season hours vary. $10, seniors $9, ages 6-12 $6.)*

NORTHERN NEW YORK

THE ADIRONDACKS   ☎ 518

The largest state park in the US, Adirondacks State Park encompasses six million acres of cloud-topped mountains, glittering lakes, and knotted pine trees. Thousands of miles of trails carve through the mountainous terrain, leading to scenic vistas and isolated streams. In the green valleys between the peaks, small towns fit snugly between surrounding lakes and forests. The park's size makes it one of the few places in the Northeast where hikers can still spend days without seeing another soul, providing true solitude for the world-weary traveler. Of the six million acres in the Adirondacks State Park, 40% are open to the public and provide a slew of outdoor activities. Fourteen scenic byways offer passage to even the most remote villages, and waterways carry kayakers, canoers, and whitewater rafters through breathtaking gorges and forests.

◪ PRACTICAL INFORMATION

Adirondacks Trailways (☎ 800-858-8555) services the region. From Albany, buses set out for Lake Placid and Lake George. From the Lake George bus stop at Lake George Hardware, 35 Montcalm St., buses go to Albany (4 per day, $14), Lake Placid (1-2 per day, $20), and New York City (4-5 per day, $49). The **Adirondack Mountain Club (ADK)** is the best source of info on outdoor activities in the region. Two excellent booklets available for free through the ADK are the *Adirondacks Waterways* and the *Adirondack Great Walks and Day Hikes* guides, which detail hundreds of hikes and paddles of all difficulty levels throughout the park. Offices are located at 814 Goggins Rd., in Lake George (☎ 668-4447; www.adk.org; open M-Sa 8:30am-5pm), and at Adirondack Loj Rd., in Lake Placid (☎ 523-3441; phone lines operate M-Th and Sa-Su 8am-8pm, F 8am-10pm.) The Lake Placid ADK, also known as the **High Peaks Information Center,** 3 mi. east of Lake Placid then 5 mi. down Adirondack Loj Rd. in the Loj itself, is the area's best resource for weather conditions, trail closures, and backcountry info. The center has washrooms (showers $0.25 per min.) and sells basic outdoor equipment, trail snacks, and a variety of helpful guides ($11-25), including the ADK guides specific to each region ($20). The center also runs an education program that provides outdoors training via one to three day excursions or lecture sessions. Classes include canoeing, rock climbing, and wilderness medicine. (☎ 523-3441. Classes $35-265; includes all food and equipment. Open May-Oct. M-Th and Su 8am-5pm, F-Sa 8am-8pm; Oct.-May daily 8am-5pm. Hours increase with seasonal traffic. Parking $9.)

TUPPER LAKE/BLUE MOUNTAIN LAKE

The western part of the Adirondacks, where small lakes and hamlets speckle the forests, is perfect for a relaxing mountain getaway. The 21 exhibits at the ◪**Adirondack Museum,** off Rte. 30 in Blue Mountain Lake, showcase the history, culture, and lifestyles of Adirondacks residents through the ages. The collection of 25 boats and the richly decorated railcar are among the more impressive exhibits. (☎ 352-7311; www.adkmuseum.org. Open late May to mid-Oct. daily 10am-5pm. $15; military, seniors, students $13; ages 13-17 $6; under 13 free.) In late June, Tupper hosts the **Tin Man Triathlon,** a 1¼ mi. swim, 56 mi. bike ride, and 13 mi. run through town. (Tupper Lake Chamber of Commerce: 60 Park St. ☎ 359-3328 or 888-887-5253. Open daily 9am-5pm.) There are many lodging options throughout the western Adirondacks, especially along Rtes. 3 and 30. Two miles east of Tupper Lake, **Northwood Cabins ❸,** 92 Tupper-Sara Hwy., rents nine cabins with cable TV and heat; some have kitchenettes and fireplaces. The soft beds and friendly owner offer a welcome alternative to the damp floor of the Adirondack forest. (☎ 359-9606 or 800-727-5756. Open mid-May to mid-Oct. Cabins $42-68.) Locals indulge in the half pound Lumberjack burger ($4.50) at the homely **Lumberjack Inn ❷,** 76 Main St., in Tupper Lake. (☎ 359-2910. Open daily 7am-8pm.) At the intersection of Rtes. 30 and 28 in Long Lake, **Hoss's General Store** provides camping supplies and groceries for visitors looking to hit the trails. (☎ 624-2451. Open daily July-Aug. 9am-10pm; Sept.-June 9am-5pm.) Hoss's also houses a bakery and an **Internet** cafe. (☎ 624-6466. Internet access $5 per 15min., including complimentary beverage. Open daily 10am-6pm.) The **Adirondack Park Visitor Interpretive Center,** just west of Newcomb on Rte. 28 N, is a great place to get park information and catch sight of moose, bears, minks, and otters. (☎ 582-2000. Visitors Center open daily 9am-5pm; trails open dawn-dusk. Free.)

AUSABLE CHASM/TICONDEROGA

At the eastern end of the park, hikers revel in the above-treeline views of the High Peaks region and the beauty of nearby Lake Champlain. The ADK runs two lodges near Lake Placid. The ◨**Adirondack Loj ❷,** at the end of Adirondack Loj Rd., off Rte. 73, lures hikers looking for a place to rest their sore feet. The den—heated by an imposing fieldstone fireplace in the winter—is the perfect place to warm up after exploring the wilderness trails on skis or snowshoes. In summer, guests swim, fish, and canoe on Heart Lake, located 100 ft. from the lodge's doorstep. (☎ 523-3441. Breakfast included. Reservations highly recommended. Lunch $7.50. Dinner $16. Snowshoe rentals $10 per day; cross-country ski rentals $20 per day. Canoe or kayak rental 8am-8pm; $5 per hr., guests $3. Bunks $45-55; lean-tos $26; campsites $23; canvas cabin $32; private rooms $110; 4-person wood cabins $100; 16-person $320.) ADK's second lodge, the **John's Brook Lodge ❷,** offers the outdoor-savvy a more secluded and rustic atmosphere. From Lake Placid, follow Rte. 73 for 15 mi. through Keene to Keene Valley, turn right at the Ausable Inn, and drive 5 mi. to the parking lot at the end of the dirt road (parking $5). Reaching the lodge requires a 3½ mi. hike over the rolling hills and through the damp Adirondack woods. Though the basic comforts of linens and showers are not available, three complimentary meals await the weary hiker. John's Brook is no secret, however, and beds fill completely on weekends. (Call the Adirondack Loj for reservations, ☎ 523-3441. Blankets provided. July to mid-Oct. bunks $42-45.) Twelve miles south of Plattsburgh on Rte. 9 lies one of the state's most beautiful campgrounds, **Ausable Point ❶.** Situated on the sandy banks of Lake Champlain, the park is ideal for camping or as a boating daytrip. (☎ 561-7080. Office open 8am-9pm. Registration fee $3. Sites $17, with electricity $20. Day use $6 per car. Make reservations far in advance for prime waterfront sites during weekends and holidays. Lifeguard on duty June to late Aug. M-F 10am-7pm, Sa-Su 10am-8pm.) **Backcountry camping ❶** rules have recently changed in sections of the eastern half of the High Peaks region, where self-issued permits are required. Be aware of your surroundings: camping is prohibited except at prescribed sites; campfires are banned within the entire section. A recent increase in bear activity has prompted rangers to enforce the mandatory use of bear canisters for food. Areas affected by these changes are identified on the new maps sold by the ADK and can be viewed or purchased at the High Peaks Information Center ($8). Otherwise, camping is free anywhere on public land in the backcountry as long as it is at least 150 ft. away from a trail, road, water source, or campground, and below 3500 ft. in altitude. Inquire about the locations of free trailside shelters before planning a hike in the forest. Contact the **Department of Environmental Conservation** (☎402-9428) for more info on backwoods camping. When you get sick of s'mores, join the locals in Ticonderoga at **Burleigh's Luncheonette ❶,** where you can munch on sandwiches ($3-5) and hearty breakfasts ($2.50-4) amidst 50's decor. (☎585-6262. Open M-Sa 7am-4pm.) A number of the trails that wind their way through the highest peaks begin at the Adirondack Loj at the end of Adirondack Loj Rd. 3 mi. east of town along Rte. 73. **Algonquin Peak,** an 8 mi. round-trip hike, has a total rise in elevation of nearly 3,000 ft., but yields a spectacular, above-treeline view. **Mount Marcy,** a 7½ mi. hike to the state's highest peak (5344 ft.), is a daytrip that promises to test even the most avid hiker, finishing with a 360 degree aerial view of Adirondack Park and a commanding view of Lake Placid to the northwest.

Stroll down **Ausable Chasm,** a gorge cut deep into the earth by the roaring Ausable River, 12 mi. south of Plattsburgh on Rte. 9. Seemingly untouched by civilization, the chasm has many waterfalls and is surrounded by the Adirondack forest. At the conclusion of the walk, the relatively calm water provides the opportunity to raft through a labyrinth of age-old rock formations. (☎800-537-1211; www.ausablechasm.com. Open mid-May to late June daily 9:30am-4pm; late June to Sept. M-Th and Su 9:30am-5pm, F-Sa 9:30am-6:30pm. Entrance to the walkway $16, seniors and ages 12-19 $14, ages 5-11 $9. Entrance and raft trip $24/22/17.) Farther south along the shores of Lake Champlain, 1 mi. east of Ticonderoga, lies ⬛**Fort Ticonderoga.** Bronze cannons stand guard over the ancient waterways that held the "key to the continent" during the wars for control of the colonies. The fully restored fortress houses a museum full of historical weapons and artifacts, provides daily historical talks and musket demonstrations, and stages reenactments of historical battles. (☎585-2821; www.fort-ticonderoga.org. Open May-late Oct. daily 9am-5pm. $12, seniors $11, ages 7-12 $6.) Experienced rock climbers and those who want to break into the sport should consult the knowledgeable staff at **The Mountaineer,** in Keene Valley, between I-87 and Lake Placid on Rte. 73. The Mountaineer reels in all types of alpine enthusiasts with the **Adirondack International Mountainfest,** a weekend of clinics and classes for all manner of mountain sports. (☎576-2281. Open in summer M and F-Su 8am-7pm, Tu-Th 9am-6pm; in low season M-F 9am-5:30pm, Sa 8am-5:30pm, Su 9am-5:30pm. Snowshoes $15 per day, ice-climbing boots and crampons $20 per day, rock shoes $12 per day. Mountainfest is held in Jan. on Martin Luther King Day weekend.)

LAKE PLACID   ☎518

Tucked away among the High Peaks Mountains, Lake Placid lives and breathes winter sports. However, it still maintains a lively summer schedule full of outdoors events. Host to the Olympic Winter Games in both 1932 and 1980, this modest city has managed to maintain a small-town ambience while basking in glory. World-class athletes train year-round in the town's extensive facilities, lending it an international flavor that distinguishes Lake Placid from its Adirondack neighbors.

⬛ ⬛ **ORIENTATION AND PRACTICAL INFORMATION.** Lake Placid sits at the intersection of Rtes. 86 and 73 in the northeastern quarter of Adirondack Park. Rte. 73 runs north and connects with Rte. 86 south of the Olympic Skating Center, becoming Main St. as it runs north through the town. Downtown Lake Placid is located on Main St. along the shores of Lake Placid. **Adirondack Trailways** (☎800-776-7548; open M-Sa 8am-7pm, Su 9am-5pm) stops at Lake Placid IGA, 6137 Sentinel Rd., and has extensive service in the area. Destinations include the Albany airport ($27), Lake George ($15), and New York City ($63). The **Placid Xpress** shuttle

LAKE PLACID ■ 137

travels through town every 15-20min. with stops at the various parking areas, including free municipal lots. (☎523-2585. Route maps, including low-season routes, available at the Visitors Center. Runs July-Sept. 8am-10pm; low-season hours vary. Free.) The Lake Placid that exists today is a product of its rich Olympic past. The **Olympic Regional Development Authority,** 2634 Main St., inside the Olympic Center, operates the sports facilities. (☎523-1655 or 800-462-6236; www.orda.org. Open M-F 8:30am-5pm.) Also in the Olympic Center is the **Lake Placid-Essex County Visitors Bureau,** which provides information about food, lodging, weather, and attractions in the area. (☎523-2445; www.lakeplacid.com. Open M-F 8am-5pm, Sa-Su 9am-4pm; closed Su in the spring and fall.) **Internet Access: Lake Placid Public Library,** 2417 Main St. (☎523-3200. Free. Open M-Th 10am-5:30pm, F 10am-7pm, Sa 10am-4pm.) The Visitors Center has free limited Internet service. (15min. limit when others are waiting). **Post Office:** 2591 Main St. (☎523-3071. Open M-F 8:30am-5pm, Sa 8am-noon.) **Postal Code:** 12946.

▐ ACCOMMODATIONS. If you avoid the resorts on the west end of town, both lodgings and food are reasonable in Lake Placid. Many inexpensive motels line Rtes. 86 and 73 just east of town. Just half a mile south of downtown on Rte. 73, the 25 comfortable bunks at the ▓**High Peaks Hostel ❶** will make any traveler feel at home. The complimentary homemade breakfasts, well-equipped kitchens, free linens and towels, and friendly owners make this an excellent lodging option. (☎523-4951. Lockout 9am-4pm. Bunks $30. Cash only.) Two state park campgrounds, some of the nicest in the area, are within 10 mi. of Lake Placid. **Meadowbrook State Park ❶,** 5 mi. west of town on Rte. 86 in Ray Brook, has relatively secluded, wooded campsites and provides easy access to several trailheads. (☎891-4351. Hot showers. Sites $11. Registration $3. Day use $4 per car, $1 per pedestrian.) **Wilmington Notch State Campground ❶,** about 9 mi. east of Lake Placid on Rte. 86, also has shady, if somewhat more crowded, sites close to all of the trailheads and ski slopes of Whiteface Mountain. (☎946-7172. Hot showers. Open May to mid-Oct. Registration 8am-9pm. Sites $13. Day use $4 per car.)

▐▐ FOOD AND NIGHTLIFE. Lake Placid Village, concentrated primarily along Main St., has a number of reasonably priced dining establishments. The lunch buffet in the Terrace Dining Room at the **Hilton Hotel ❷,** 1 Mirror Lake Dr., serves all-you-can-eat sandwiches, soups, salads, and a hot entree ($8) with a view overlooking the lake. (☎523-4411. Buffet daily noon-2pm.) Bright orange walls, local artwork, and the biggest muffins you'll ever see ($2) greet patrons at **Soulshine Bagels ❶,** 2526 Main St. In addition to a vegetarian-friendly menu, this cafe boasts some genuine local flavor. (☎523-9772. Open daily 6:30am-5pm, summer until 9pm.) On the shore of Mirror Lake, **The Cottage ❷,** 5 Mirror Lake Dr., creates sandwiches and salads (all under $9) that patrons can enjoy on the deck. (☎523-9845. Open daily 11:30am-midnight or 1am, depending on crowd. Kitchen closes at 10pm.) The **Lake Placid Pub and Brewery ❸,** 14 Mirror Lake Dr., off the east end of Main St., which features dishes like bangers and mash (English sausage in local Ubu Ale with red potatoes; $9), and drink specials like Two-for Tuesdays which includes two pints for the price of one after 6pm is a local favorite. (☎523-3813. Entrees $10-17. Open daily 11:30am-3am. Kitchen closes at 11pm.) One of Lake Placid's few late-night hot spots, **Wise Guys,** 3 School St., east of the Olympic Center, has both a sports bar and a dance club. (☎523-4446. Cover Sa-Su up to $3. Bar open M-F 3pm-3am, Sa-Su noon-3am. Club open Th-Sa 9pm-3am.)

◪ SIGHTS. The **Olympic Center,** in downtown Lake Placid, houses the 1932 and 1980 hockey arenas, as well as the petite, memorabilia-stuffed **Winter Olympic Museum.** Packed with ice skates, bobsleds, and medals, the museum is a walk through decades of Olympic glory. (☎523-1655, ext. 226; www.orda.org. Open daily 10am-5pm. $4, seniors $3, ages 7-12 $2. **Public Skating:** ☎523-1655. Open year-round M-F 8-9:30pm; call ahead for weekend hours. $5, children and seniors $4; skate rental $3.) During the summer, purchase tickets to watch ski jumpers and aerial freestylists practice for upcoming competitions by sailing down astroturf-covered ramps onto astroturf-covered hillsides or into a swimming pool in the **Olympic Jumping Complex,** just east of town on Rte. 73. Travelers can take a chairlift and an elevator to the top of the ramp for a look down. (☎523-2202. Open Dec.-Sept. daily 9am-4pm; call ahead for hours in Apr. and May. $9 with chairlift; seniors and children $6.) About 5 mi. east of town on Rte. 73, the **Verizon Sports Complex** at **Mount Van Hoevenberg** offers bobsled rides down the actual 1980 Olympic track. Reaching speeds of 50 mph around gut-wrenching curves, the bobsleds run on ice during the winter ($65) and wheels during the summer ($55). If rocketing down the side of the mountain at high speeds isn't for you, narrated bus tours drive more slowly up and down the mountain for a view of the tracks. (☎523-4436. Open W-Su 10am-12:30pm and 1:30-4pm. Winter bobsled runs Dec.-Mar.; summer June-Nov. Must be at least 48 in. tall; under 18 must have parent present. Bus tours 9am-4pm. $5, seniors and ages 7-12 $4.) Whip yourself into shape Olympian-style at the cross-country skiing venue. Cross-country skiing and biathlon courses are available to the public in the winter, and mountain biking trails are uncovered in the summertime. Cross-country ski and bike rentals are available inside the complex. (☎523-2811. Open for skiing daily 9am-4:30pm; last rental 4pm. Trail fee $14 per day, seniors and students $12, over 70 free. Equipment rental $16 per day, under 18 $12 per day. Open for biking mid-June to early Sept. daily 10am-5pm; early Sept. to early Oct. Sa-Su 10am-5pm. Trail fee $6 per day, $10 per 2 days. Bike rental $10-50 per day; helmet required and included with bike rental, $3 per day.) For those planning to take in all or most of Lake Placid's Olympic attractions, the **Olympic Sites Passport** is the best bargain. For $29 per person, the pass includes entrance to the Olympic Jumping Complex (including chairlift and elevator ride), the bus tour of the bobsledding complex, a $5 coupon toward a bobsled ride on Mt. Van Hoevenberg, admission to the Winter Sports Museum, the **Scenic Gondola Ride** to the top of Little Whiteface, and access to the **Veterans Memorial Highway** that climbs Whiteface Mountain. Purchase the passport at any Olympic venue or at the **Olympic Center Box Office** in Lake Placid (☎523-3330).

With 3430 ft. of vertical drop, the most east of the Rockies, the ski runs of **Whiteface Mountain,** east of Lake Placid on Rte. 86. Offers winter fun for all levels of experience. Considered the best ski area in the east, the mountain hosts international competitions. (☎877-754-3223; www.whiteface.com. Lift tickets $64.)

After touring the Olympic venues, get outfitted for your own sporting adventures at **High Peaks Cyclery,** 2733 Main St. Renting and selling all manner of bicycles, climbing gear, camping equipment, skis, snowshoes, and much more, the experts there can prepare you for any outing. If you aren't ready to head out alone, inquire about guide services. (☎523-3764. Open M-Sa 9am-6pm, Su 10am-5pm. Bikes $25-50 per day. Tents $15-20 per day. Cross-country skis $20-35 per day. Snowshoes $15 per day.) To climb the 4867 ft. summit of Whiteface Mountain without breaking a sweat, drive your car up ◙**Veterans Memorial Highway,** 11 mi. east of Lake Placid on Rte. 86. Waiting at the summit is a castle in the clouds, perched on 250 ft. of solid granite that must be ascended via an elevator or a spectacular ridge trail. (☎946-7175. Open daily July-Sept. 8:30am-5pm; mid-May to July and Sept. to mid-Oct. 9am-4pm, longer if weather permits. $9 per car or motorcycle; $4 per passenger.) Eight miles east of town on Rte. 86, 700 ft. of waterfalls cascade down through the small, picturesque **High Falls Gorge.** Winter admission comes with ice cleats for steady footing and hot chocolate to warm chilled bones. (☎946-2278;

ww.highfallsgorge.com. Open daily July-Aug. 9am-5:30pm, Sept.-June 9am-5pm. Last entry 30min. before close. In summer $10, ages 4-12 $6; call for winter rates.)

Lost in the intensity of the Olympic legacy, visitors to Lake Placid often forget the lake's unparalleled peace. Departing from the Lake Placid Marina on the west end of town, **tour boat cruises** glide around the 16 mi. lake in long, sleek, turn-of-the-century boats, providing glimpses of the stately homes that line the shores and illuminating the area's history. (☎523-9704. Cruises depart mid-May to late June M-F 10:30am and 2:30pm; Sa-Su 10:30am, 2:30, 4pm; late June-Sept. daily 10:30am, 1, 2:30, 4pm; Sept. to mid-Oct. daily 10:30am, 1:30, 3pm. Arrive at least 15min. early. $8, seniors $7, children $5.50.) **Mirror Lake Boat Rentals,** 1 Main St., rents boats. (☎524-7890. Open daily May to mid-Oct. 10am-sunset. Paddleboats, canoes, and hydrobikes $22 per hr. Sailboats and electric cruisers $45 per hr.) For a cool dip in the water, head to the **Mirror Lake Public Beach** on Parkside Dr. (☎523-3109. Lifeguards on duty late June to Sept. 9am-7pm, weather permitting. Free.)

Athletics and natural beauty embody the spirit of Lake Placid, but no trip to upstate New York can be complete without a sampling of its famous vineyards. Selections of the award-winning wine produced by Finger Lakes-based **Swedish Hill Winery** are available 1 mi. east of downtown on Rte. 73. After sampling there, bring your glass with you to complete your tasting tour with another eight tastes at the **Goose Watch Winery,** 2527 Main St., in the Alpine Mall, for an additional $0.01. (☎523-1955. Open M-Th 10am-6pm, F-Sa 10am-9pm, Su noon-6pm. 8 tastes and a wine glass $3.) Nearby Saranac Lake hosts a 10-day, no-holds-barred **carnival** in early February, for which an ice palace is created. (Saranac Lake Chamber of Commerce: 39 Main St. ☎891-1990; www.saranaclake.com.)

THOUSAND ISLAND SEAWAY ☎315

Spanning 100 mi. from the mouth of Lake Ontario to the first of the locks on the St. Lawrence River, the Thousand Island region of the St. Lawrence Seaway forms a natural US-Canadian border. Surveys conducted by the US and Canadian governments determined that there are 1,864 islands—at least one square foot of land above water year-round with at least two trees growing on it—in the seaway. Many islands, however, are developed with private residences, lighthouses, and towering 19th-century castles. The Thousand Island region is a fisherman's paradise and a mecca for vacationers, with an incredible array of festivals during the lazy hazy days of summer.

■⁊ ORIENTATION AND PRACTICAL INFORMATION. The Thousand Island region hugs the St. Lawrence River and is less than 2hr. from Syracuse by way of **I-81 North.** From southwest to northeast, **Cape Vincent, Clayton,** and **Alexandria Bay** ("Alex Bay" to locals) are the main towns in the area. Cape Vincent, the smallest of the three, maintains a rich French heritage along the shores of Lake Ontario. Clayton, the most authentically nautical of the three seaside hamlets, boasts museums and galleries, as well as marinas and boats. Alex Bay is alive with countless riverside bars, clubs, and restaurants, and hosts themed weeks throughout the summer, such as "Pirate Week" in August, when pirate ships and scalawags take control of the town. For Wellesley Island, Alexandria Bay, and the eastern 500 islands, stay on I-81 until you reach Rte. 12 E. For Clayton and points west, take Exit 47 and follow Rte. 12 to Rte. 12 E. **Greyhound,** (☎788-8110 or 800-231-2222; www.greyhound.com. Open M-F 9am-1pm, 3-4pm, and 6:10-6:30pm; Sa-Su only at departure times.) 540 State St., in Watertown, runs to Albany (6hr., 2 per day, $38), New York City (8hr., 2 per day, $68), and Syracuse (1¾hr., 2 per day, $13-15). **Thousand Islands Bus Lines** (☎287-2790) departs from the same station M-F at 1pm for Alexandria Bay ($5.60) and Clayton ($3.55). Return trips leave Clayton from Gray's

Florist, 234 James St. (departs daily 8:45am), and Alexandria Bay from the Dockside Cafe, 17 Market St. (departs daily 8:30am). The **Clayton Chamber of Commerce**, 517 Riverside Dr., hands out the free and helpful *Clayton Vacation Guide* and *Thousand Islands Seaway Region Travel Guide.* (☎686-3771; www.1000islands-clayton.com. Open mid-June to mid-Sept. daily 9am-5pm; mid-Sept. to mid-June M-F 9am-5pm.) The **Alexandria Bay Chamber of Commerce**, 7 Market St., is just off James St. and offers the *Alexandria Bay Vacation Guide* to aid your travel in the area. (☎482-9531; www.alexbay.org. Open May-Sept. M-F 8am-4:30pm, Sa 10am-4:30pm.) The **Cape Vincent Chamber of Commerce**, 175 James St., by the ferry landing, welcomes visitors and distributes the *Cape Vincent Vacation Guide.* (☎654-2481; www.capevincent.org. Open May-Oct. Tu-Sa 9am-5pm; late May-early Sept. also M and Su 10am-4pm.) **Internet Access:** In Clayton, **Hawn Memorial Library**, 220 John St. (☎686-3762. Free. Open M and Th-F 10am-5pm, Tu-W 10am-8pm, Sa 9am-noon.) In Alexandria Bay, **Macsherry Library**, 112 Walton St. (☎482-2241. Free. Open M-Th 9am-noon, 1-5pm, 7-9pm; F-Sa 9am-noon and 1-5pm.) In Cape Vincent, **Cape Vincent Community Library**, 157 N. Real, at Gouvello St. (☎654-2132. Free. Open Tu and Th 9am-8pm, F-Sa 9am-1pm.) **Clayton Post Office:** 236 John St. (☎686-3311. Open M-F 9am-4:30pm, Sa 9am-noon.) **Postal Code:** 13624. **Alexandria Bay Post Office:** 13 Bethune St. (☎482-9521. Open M-F 8:30am-5pm, Sa 9am-noon.) **Postal Code:** 13607. **Cape Vincent Post Office:** 362 Broadway St., across from the village green. (☎654-2424. Open M-F 8am-1pm and 2-4:30pm, Sa 9:30-11:30am.) **Postal Code:** 13618.

⚡TIP **SAIL AWAY.** The boundary between the US and Canada in the Thousand Island Seaway is complex and can be tricky for boaters who wish to explore the islands on both sides of the border. In foreign waters, a vessel doesn't have to pass through customs as long as it's in motion. Back on dry land, customs procedures usually take place at small booths on the dock.

⌐ ACCOMMODATIONS. Near Cape Vincent, where Lake Ontario meets the St. Lawrence, **▩Tibbett's Point Lighthouse Hostel (HI) ❶**, 33439 County Rte. 6, is a friendly beacon for the weary traveler. Take Rte. 12 E into town, turn left on Broadway, and follow the river until the road ends. (☎654-3450. Full kitchen with microwave. Check-in 5-10pm. Check-out 7-9am. Open mid-May to late Oct. Reservations strongly recommended on weekends July-Aug. Dorms $17, members $14. Cash only.) The **Bridgeview Motel ❷**, 42823 Rte. 12 between Alex Bay and Clayton, offers clean, no-frills rooms with A/C and TVs for reasonable rates. (☎482-4906. Open May to mid-Oct. Rooms $39-59.)

There are numerous state and private campgrounds in the area (especially along Rte. 12 E.). However, these sites are usually close together and fill up well in advance on weekends. **▩Wellesley Island ❶**, across the toll bridge ($2) on I-81 N before Canada, boasts 2600 acres of marshes and woodland for hiking and cross-country skiing. The beach in the park hosts swimmers in the summer and ice fishers in the winter. (☎482-2722. 438 sites plus cabins. Waterfront sites B19-23 or B1-8 are incredible, but require reservations far in advance. Hot showers and nature center. Sites $13-19, with electricity $19. Full hookup $25. Registration fee $2.75. Cabins with 4 beds, refrigerator, stove, microwave, and picnic table $40-51. Day use $7 per car. Boat rentals $15 per day for rowboats and canoes, $60 per day plus gas for 16 ft. motor boats. Lifeguard on duty mid-June to early Sept. daily 11am-8pm, weather permitting.) The less crowded **Burnham Point State Park ❶**, on Rte. 12 E, 4½ mi. east of Cape Vincent and 11 mi. west of Clayton, may not have a beach, but it does have a wonderful view of the water and two picnic areas among 50 somewhat-cramped sites. (☎654-2324. Open late May-early Sept. daily 7am-

9:30pm. Wheelchair-accessible. Sites $13-19, with electricity $19-23. Registration $2.75. Day use $6 per car. Boat dockage $6 per day.) Reservations for all state parks cost $9 (☎800-456-2267; www.reserveamerica.com).

🄲🄳 **FOOD AND NIGHTLIFE.** The Thousand Island Seaway hosts diverse food options, and the nightlife at Alex Bay ranges from comfortable seaside decks to wild bars. The most popular destination for cheap eats in Alex Bay is **Poor John's ❶,** off James St. at the main intersection downtown, where locals line up for double-stacked burgers ($2.50) and ice cream cones. (☎408-2502. Open daily 11am-10pm. Kitchen closes 7pm.) **Captain's Table ❸,** a restaurant that floats in Alex Bay, offers the best view in the Thousand Islands. Turn left at Uncle Sam Tours, then follow the road to the parking lot. While the main level serves expensive entrees ($11-32), savvy travelers head upstairs for an ample lounge menu (sandwiches $7-8) and a beautiful view. (☎482-7777. Open daily 7am-9:30pm.) Dispensing both hot coffee and cool decorating advice, **Taste of Design ❶,** 288 E Broadway in Cape Vincent, combines cafe offerings with an interior designer's studio. (☎654-2007. Free Wi-Fi. Opens M-F 6:30am and Sa-Su 8:00am.) **Aubrey's Inn ❷,** 126 S. James St. in Cape Vincent, serves ample homestyle meals at delightfully low prices in a nautically themed dining room. (☎654-3754. Breakfast $1.50-6. Most entrees $7-9. Open daily 7am-9pm.) Nightlife in the Thousand Islands region is located in the heart of Alexandria Bay. Numerous bars and clubs line the docks of the seaway and most offer live music and drink specials, but the liveliest place is **Skiffs,** at the corner of James and Market St. (☎482-7543. Open M-Th 1pm-2am, F-Su noon-2am.)

🄶 **EXPLORING THE SEAWAY.** Clayton and Cape Vincent tend to be quieter and less expensive, while Alex Bay is busier and more touristy. Popular activities include scenic tours of the waterways and ferry rides. With fact-packed live narrations, **Uncle Sam Boat Tours,** 47 James St., in Alexandria Bay, delivers good views of the islands and their plush estates, including the famous **Boldt Castle** on Heart Island. (☎482-2611 or 800-253-9229; www.unclesamboattour.com. Tours leave daily from Alex Bay May-late Oct. $7-35, ages 4-12 $4.50-25; prices vary with type and duration of tour. Boldt Castle: $7, ages 4-12 $3. Reserve in advance for lunch or dinner cruises.) In Alexandria Bay, **Empire Boat Lines,** 4 Church St., sends out smaller boats able to navigate very close to the islands, and provides scenic tours, trips to Boldt Castle, and regular service to **Singer Castle,** which is packed full of secret rooms and passageways. (☎482-8687 or 888-449-2539. Tours $13-30, ages 7-14 $10-24. Singer Castle $10, ages 6-12 $5.) **Ferries** run from Cape Vincent to **Wolfe Island,** in Canada, a quaint stop with a strawberry farm, a golf course, and a free ferry ride from the shops and restaurants of Kingston. (☎783-0638. Ferries depart from the Cape Vincent Ferry Dock along Club St. May to mid-Oct., 10 per day. Tickets may be purchased on the ferry. $2 per person, $12 per car, $2 per bicycle. Picture ID required.)

For many, fishing trips and charters are the preferred way to explore the islands and waterways. **Fishing licenses** are available at the **Town Clerk's Office,** 405 Riverside Dr., in Clayton. (☎686-3512. Open M-F 9am-noon and 1-4pm. Licenses $15 per day, $25 per week, $40 per season.) Many bait shops and sporting goods stores stay open longer hours and sell licenses to fishermen. Tell the tale of the big one that got away with **1000 Islands Fishing Charters,** 335 Riverside Dr., inside the 1000 Islands Inn in Clayton. Offering both drift fishing trips with larger groups of people and private charters, 1000 Islands can accommodate your preferences. (☎686-2381 or 877-544-4241. Trips July-late Aug. Reservations required. 4hr. "Drift Trip" $50 per person; tackle and bait included. 7½hr. private charter $75-160 per person, depending upon the number of people in the group; tackle included.) Check out **Hunt's Dive Shop,** 40782 Rte. 12 between Alex Bay and Clayton, for an underwater peek at the wrecks that line the seaway floor. (☎686-1070. Equipment rental $50 per person. Must have certification. Open May-Sept. daily 9am-5:30pm.)

The **Antique Boat Museum,** 750 Mary St., in Clayton, houses, canoes, yachts, speedboats and skiffs of all types. Admission includes free rentals on a variety of skiffs. On Wednesdays in summer, the museum offers free sailing classes to increase boating awareness. (☎686-4104. Open mid-May to mid-Oct. daily 9am-5pm. Call for info on sailing classes. $12, seniors $8, students and ages 6-17 $10, under 5 free.) **French Creek Marina,** 250 Wahl St. (☎686-3621), off Strawberry Ln. just south of the junction of Rtes. 12 and 12 E, rents 14 ft. fishing boats ($50 per day), launches boats ($5 per boat), and provides overnight docking ($20 per boat).

NEW JERSEY

It's difficult to appreciate the wealth and variety of destinations in the Garden State the way many travelers see it: cruising the New Jersey Turnpike on the way to somewhere else. From antiquing to gambling to reenactments of George Washington crossing the Delaware, New Jersey bursts with history and activity. One of New Jersey's best-kept secrets is its 127 miles of white-sand beaches. Between the dazzle of Atlantic City's casinos and the tranquility of Cape May's "diamond" sand, the Jersey shore is one of the region's prime vacation spots.

◪ PRACTICAL INFORMATION

Capital: Trenton.

Visitor Info: State Division of Tourism, P.O. Box 820, Trenton 08625 (☎609-777-0885; www.visitnj.org). **State Bird:** The mosquito.

Postal Abbreviation: NJ. **Sales Tax:** 6%; no tax on clothing. **Tolls:** Keep a fistful of change handy; New Jersey's tunnels, bridges, and turnpikes are littered with toll booths.

ATLANTIC CITY   ☎609

For 70 years, board game enthusiasts have been wheeling and dealing with Atlantic City geography, famously depicted on the Monopoly game board. Meanwhile, the opulence of the original Boardwalk and Park Place faded into neglect and then into mega-dollar tackiness. During a 70s refurbishment effort, giant casino-resorts were built over the rubble of the old boardwalk, sacrificing the city's old-time charm in hopes of attracting tourist dollars with glitz and glamour. The reincarnation failed to turn Atlantic City into a second Las Vegas, leaving poverty and crime lurking around the fringes of the modern downtown. Yet there is still plenty to enjoy: gambling, tanning, games, and rides make Atlantic City an exhilarating destination.

▐ TRANSPORTATION

Atlantic City sits about 30 mi. north of the southern tip of the New Jersey shoreline. It is accessible by car via the **Garden State Parkway** and the **Atlantic City Expressway,** and easily reached by train or bus from Philadelphia or New York City.

Airport: Atlantic City International (ACY; ☎645-7895 or 800-892-0354; www.acairport.com), 20min. west of Atlantic City in Egg Harbor.

Buses: Greyhound, 1995 Atlantic Ave. (☎345-6617; www.greyhound.com). Buses travel to **New York City Port Authority** (2½hr., every 30min., from $25), **Philadelphia** (1½hr., $12), and most major casinos several times per day. **New Jersey Transit**

(☎800-772-2222; www.nj.com/njtransit), on Atlantic Ave. between Michigan and Ohio St., has service to **New York City** (2½hr., 1 per hr., $29 round-trip).

Taxi: Atlantic City Airport Taxi (☎383-1457). **Egg Harbor Atlantic City Taxi Alliance** (☎457-0624). $27 flat rate from airport to Atlantic City. $8 max. within the city.

Alternative Forms of Transportation: Plentiful **Rolling Chair Rides** (☎347-7148) takes 2-3 passengers to the Boardwalk; fares are charged by number of blocks traveled. The **Atlantic City Jitney** (☎344-8642) minibuses serve the entire city ($1.50).

Free Parking: Meterless parking is available in some residential areas. Try Oriental Ave. at New Jersey Ave. for free 3hr. parking within walking distance of the Boardwalk, but be careful at night: this area is relatively isolated.

◢◀ 🔢 ORIENTATION AND PRACTICAL INFORMATION

Attractions cluster on and around the **Boardwalk,** which runs east-west along the Atlantic Ocean. Running parallel to the Boardwalk, **Pacific** and **Atlantic Avenue** offer cheap restaurants, hotels, and convenience stores. Getting around on foot is easy on the Boardwalk. **Parking lots** abound nearby. Atlantic Ave. can be dangerous after dark, and any street farther out can be dangerous even by day.

Visitor Info: Atlantic Expressway Visitors Center, 1 mi. after the Pleasantville Toll Plaza (☎449-7130). Offers pamphlets, brochures, and help with free parking. Open daily 9am-5pm. **Atlantic City Convention Center and Visitors Bureau,** 2314 Pacific Ave. (☎888-228-4748; www.atlanticcitynj.com), near the Boardwalk. Open daily 9am-5pm. On the Boardwalk, try the **Visitor Info Center** at Mississippi St. (☎888-228-4748). Open late May to early Sept. M-W 9:30am-5:30pm, Th-Su 9:30am-8pm; mid-Sept. to mid-May daily 9:30am-5:30pm.

Medical Services: Atlantic City Medical Center, 1925 Pacific Ave. (☎344-4081).

Hotlines: Rape and Abuse (☎522-6489). **Gambling Abuse** (☎588-5515). Both 24hr.

Post Office: 1701 Pacific Ave. (☎345-4212), at Illinois Ave. Open M-F 8:30am-6pm, Sa 8:30am-12:30pm. **Postal Code:** 08401.

🏠 ACCOMMODATIONS

Lodging prices in Atlantic City have skyrocketed in recent years. Less expensive motels cluster around the Black Horse Pike about 1 mi. from downtown. For accommodations closer to the beach, particularly for summer and holiday weekends, reservations made several months in advance are essential.

Inn of the Irish Pub, 164 St. James Pl. (☎344-9063; www.theirishpub.com), between New York and Tennessee Ave. Just off the boardwalk, the inn specializes in simple, comfortable rooms cooled by ocean breezes. Entertainment nightly in downstairs pub. 21+ only. Key deposit $5. One-time service fee $2. Singles with shared bath M-Th and Su $25, F-Sa $30; doubles with shared bath $40/55, with private shower and twin beds $55/90. AmEx/D/MC/V. ❸

Red Carpet Motel, 1630 Albany Ave. (☎348-3171), off the Black Horse Pike on the way into town. Comfortable, basic rooms for low prices. Because the area is isolated, be careful at night. Cable TV, restaurant. In summer singles M-F $69, Sa-Su $99-159; doubles $75/109-169. Low-season singles $45-60; doubles $55-80. ❸

Shady Pines Campground, 443 S. 6th Ave. (☎652-1516), in Absecon, 6 mi. from Atlantic City. Take Exit 12 from the Expwy. or Exit 40 from the Garden State Pkwy. This leafy, 140-site campground sports firewood service, laundry, a playground, a pool, and new restrooms and showers. Quiet hours 10pm-7am. Open Mar.-Oct. Call ahead for summer weekend reservations. Sites with full hookup $39. MC/V. ❷

⬛ FOOD

Along the Boardwalk, shore favorites like hot dogs, pizza, and funnel cake compete with all-you-can-eat buffets for the business of hungry beachgoers. Bored by Boardwalk fare? More diverse options can be found farther west, in town.

Inn of the Irish Pub, 164 St. James Pl. (☎345-9613; www.theirishpub.com). Serves filling pub grub in the inn. The "Poor Richard" lunch special (11:30am-2pm; $2) includes a sandwich and cup of soup. Sandwiches $5. Platters $6. Dinner specials $6. Domestic drafts $1. Su all-you-can-eat brunch $7. Open 24hr. Cash only. ❶

White House Sub Shop, 2301 Arctic Ave. (☎345-8599), at Mississippi Ave. According to local legend, Frank Sinatra had these immense subs (even the half-size sandwiches are nearly a foot in length) flown to him while he was on tour. Pictures of White House Sub-lovers Joe DiMaggio, Wayne Newton, and Mr. T adorn the walls. Half sandwiches $5-7, whole $9-14. Open M-F 7am-9pm, Sa-Su 7am-9:30pm. Cash only. ❷

Tony's Baltimore Grille, 2800 Atlantic Ave. (☎345-5766), at Iowa Ave. Personal jukeboxes add to the old-time atmosphere, while the $8-9 pizzas are hard to resist. Open 24hr. Kitchen open daily 11am-3am. Cash only. ❷

◉⬛ CAINO, BOARDWALK, AND BEACHES

All casinos on the Boardwalk fall within a dice toss of one another. The farthest south is the elegant **Hilton** (☎347-7111 or 800-257-8677; www.hiltonac.com), on the boardwalk between Providence and Boston Ave., and the farthest north is the gaudy **Showboat,** 801 Boardwalk (☎343-4000 or 800-342-7724; www.harrahs.com/our_casinos/sac), at Delaware Ave. Donald Trump's glittering **Trump Taj Mahal,** 1000 Boardwalk (☎449-1000; www.trumptaj.com), at Virginia Ave., is an Atlantic City landmark too glitzy to miss. In true Monopoly form, Trump owns two other hotel-casinos in the city: the recently remodeled **Trump Plaza,** at Mississippi and Boardwalk (☎441-6000 or 800-677-7378; www.trumpplaza.com), lures in classy types looking for an elegant stay and offers decent views of the boardwalk from the game floor; while the **Trump Marina's** motto—"Play hard, live wild"—appeals to a younger, more scantily dressed crowd on Huron Blvd. (☎441-2000; www.trump-marina.com), at the Marina. In summer, energetic partiers "rock the dock" at Trump Castle's indoor/outdoor bar and restaurant, **The Deck** (☎877-477-4697). The roomy, high-ceilinged **Caesar's Boardwalk Resort and Casino,** 2100 Pacific Ave. (☎348-4411 or 800-433-0104; www.caesarsatlanticcity.com), at Arkansas Ave., is the classic choice for those looking to toss the dice. Under the gold- and glass-decorated ceiling of the **Tropicana** (☎340-4000), at Brighton Ave. and the Boardwalk, bit players rub elbows with high rollers at the roulette tables. A few blocks down at the intersection of the Boardwalk and Park Place, the grandiose **Bally's** (☎340-2000) draws in a similarly diverse crowd. Newer casinos include **The Borgata** (☎317-1000 or 866-692-6742; www.theborgata.com), a scintillating golden beacon in the Marina district, near the Trump Marina Hotel Casino and Harrah's; and **Resorts Atlantic City** (☎344-6000 or 800-336-6378; www.resortsac.com), next to the Taj Mahal. **Resorts Atlantic City** offers scandalous-sounding "rendezvous rooms" in addition to its regular hotel and casino operations. All are open 24hr.

The Boardwalk's many arcades and carnival games test a different kind of luck. The historic **Steel Pier** (☎345-4893 or 866-386-6659; www.steelpier.com), at Virginia Ave., across from the Trump Taj Mahal, juts into the coastal waters with a Ferris wheel that spins riders over the Atlantic. (Open M-F 3pm-midnight, Sa-Su noon-1am. Rides $25 for 35 tickets, W-Th all-day unlimited pass $35.) **Go-karts** and **paintball** are popular among more active thrill-seekers, who crowd around Schiff's **Central Pier Arcade & Speedway,** at the Boardwalk and Tennessee Ave., near St.

James Pl. (☎345-5219). For something a little sandier, step off the boardwalk and onto **Atlantic City Beach.** (Open daily 6am-10pm. Free.)

CAPE MAY   ☎609

At the southern extreme of New Jersey's coastline, Cape May is the oldest seashore resort in the US. The town dates back to the mid-1700s, when wealthy Philadelphians would come to the tranquil shore to rest and relax. Today, Cape May is best known for the Victorian-era houses and hotels that give the resort its nickname, Gingerbread Town. Architecture isn't Cape May's only claim to fame; the town is also known for its fine dining, bird-watching, and sparkling white beaches.

⚎ 🔃 ORIENTATION AND PRACTICAL INFORMATION. At the tip of a peninsula which pokes out into the Delaware Bay, Cape May is easily accessible by car or bus. Start digging for loose change as you follow the tollbooth-laden **Garden State Parkway** as far south as it goes (most tolls are less than a dollar). Watch for signs to Cape May until Lafayette St., which leads directly into town. Alternatively, take the slower, scenic **Ocean Drive** (Rte. 9) 40 mi. south along the shore from Atlantic City. **NJ Transit** (☎ 800-772-2222) makes a stop at the bus depot on the corner of Lafayette and Ocean St. and runs to: Atlantic City (2hr., every hr., $4.75); New York City (5hr., 4 per day, $33); Philadelphia (2½hr., 18 per day, $18). From the D.C. area, the 1¾hr. **Cape May-Lewes Ferry** is a pleasant and more direct alternative to the potentially laborious 3-4hr. drive north to New Jersey. (☎ 800-643-3779; www.capemaylewesferry.com. Office open daily 8:30am-4:30pm. 8 per day. Reservations required; call at least 24hr. in advance. Check-in 30min. prior to departure. Apr.-Oct. passenger cars $29, motorcycles $24, cyclists and pedestrians $9.50; Nov.-Mar. $23/18/7.) **Cape May Seashore Lines** runs three old-fashioned trains per day to attractions along the 26 mi. stretch to Tuckahoe. (☎884-2675; www.capemayseashorelines.org. $5, ages 2-12 $2.50.) Bike the beach with the help of **Shields's Bike Rentals,** 11 Gurney Ave. (☎898-1818. Open daily 7am-7pm. $4 per hr., $9 per day; surreys $15/30.) Other services include: **Welcome Center,** 609 Lafayette St. (☎884-9562; open daily 8:30am-4:30pm); **Chamber of Commerce,** 513 Washington St. Mall (☎884-5508; www.capemaychamber.com; open M-F 9am-5pm, Sa-Su 10am-6pm); **Washington Street Mall Information Booth,** at Ocean St. (☎800-275-4278; www.capemaymac.org; open in summer daily 9:15am-4pm and 6-9pm; call for low-season hours); **Internet** at the **Cape May City Library** (☎884-9568; www.capemay.county.lib.nj.us; free; open M, W, F 9am-5pm; Tu and Th 9am-5pm and 7-9pm; Sa 9am-4pm); **Post Office,** 700 Washington St., at Franklin St. (☎884-3578; open M-F 9am-5pm, Sa 8:30am-12:30pm). **Postal Code:** 08204.

🏠 ACCOMMODATIONS. Sleeping does not come cheaply in Cape May. Luxurious hotels and Victorian B&Bs along the beach run $85-250 per night. Farther from the shore, prices drop. Although the **Hotel Clinton ❷,** 202 Perry St. at S. Lafayette St., may lack stately suites and A/C, the Italian family-owned establishment offers 16 breezy rooms, the most affordable rates in town, and very charismatic proprietors; unwind on the spacious porch and 2nd-story balcony, which overlooks central Cape May. (☎884-3993. Open mid-June to Sept. Reservations recommended. Singles with shared bath M-F $35, Sa-Su $40; doubles with shared bath $45/50. Cash or traveler's checks only.) Antique furniture fills the air-conditioned rooms at **Poor Richard's Inn ❹,** 17 Jackson St., an elegant option less than a block from the beach. (☎884-3536; www.poorrichardsinn.com. Continental breakfast included. Check-in 1-10pm. Check-out 10:30am. Memorial Day-Oct. doubles $110-180; call for low season rates.) Campgrounds line U.S. 9 just north of Cape May. In a prime seashore location, **Cape Island Campground ❷,** 709 Rte. 9, is connected to Cape May by **Seashore Lines** (p. 145). The campground has mini-golf, two pools, a playground, a store, and laundry. (☎884-5777 or 800-437-7443; www.capeisland.com. Sites with water and electricity $27-40; with sewage, cable, and lamppost $32-46. MC/V.)

◧◩ **FOOD AND NIGHTLIFE.** Along **Beach Avenue**, generic burger joints and posh beachside restaurants tempt Cape May's sun-lovers. For those hunting for fudge and saltwater taffy, the **Washington Street Mall** houses several popular food stores and eateries. Start the morning off right with a gourmet breakfast on the porch of the **Mad Batter ❸**, 19 Jackson St. at the Carroll Villa Hotel. Try the blueberry pancakes with warm syrup ($7.75) or the orange and almond french toast for $7. (☎884-5970; www.madbatter.com. Lunch entrees $10-13. Dinner entrees $24-31. Open daily 8am-10pm.) A meal in the smoky interior of **Ugly Mug ❹**, 426 Washington St. Mall, is well worth the risk of suffocation. For some fresh air, devour that New England cup o' chowder ($3) on the patio. (☎884-3459. Dinner entrees $16-25. Open M-Sa 11am-2am, Su noon-2am. Hot food served until 11pm. MC/V.) Check your email beachside at the ◧**Magic Brain Cybercafe ❷**, 31 Perry St., a spotless Internet cafe with an amicable staff and a variety of pastries and espresso drinks. (☎884-8188; www.magicbraincybercafe.com. Internet access $4 per 15min., $7 per 30min., $12 per hr. Open daily 8am-6pm. Cash only.) The rock scene collects around **Carney's**, 429 Beach Ave., with nightly entertainment in the summer beginning at 10pm. (☎884-4424. Tu karaoke. Su jams 4-9pm. 21+ after 10pm. Cover $5. Happy hour daily 3-6pm. Open daily 11:30am-2am. Kitchen closes 10pm.)

◪ **HITTING THE BEACH.** Cape May's sands actually sparkle, studded with the famous Cape May "diamonds" (actually quartz pebbles). A **beach tag** is required for those over age 11 from late May to early September 10am-5pm. Buy tags from roaming vendors on any beach access ramp or from the **Beach Tag Office**, 714 Beach Ave. (☎884-9522. Open daily 10am-5pm. Day pass $4, 3-day pass $9, week pass $13, season pass $25.) For a bit of exercise and a spectacular view, ascend the 199 steps to the beacon of the 1859 **Cape May Lighthouse** in **Cape May Point State Park**, west of town at the end of the point. (Lighthouse ☎884-8656, Visitors Center 884-2159; www.capemaymac.org. Park open daily 8am-dusk. Free. Lighthouse open daily 10am-4pm; extended hours in summer. Call ahead for more info.) The behemoth bunker next to the lighthouse is a WWII gun emplacement, once used to scan the shore for German U-boats. In summer, shuttles run 5 mi. from the depot on Lafayette St. to the lighthouse ($5, ages 3-12 $4). Three **trails** start at the Lighthouse Visitors Center: the red (½ mi., wheelchair-accessible), yellow (1¼ mi., moderate and flat), and blue trails (2 mi., moderate and flat, last leg takes hikers along the oceanfront back to the start) boast excellent bird-watching and clearly marked paths through marsh and oceanside dunes. Bicyclists or serious hikers may want to consider taking the 40 mi. section of the **New Jersey Coastal Heritage Trail** from Cape May to Ocean City. The trail passes the Hereford Inlet Lighthouse, the Wetlands Institute, and Corson's Inlet State Park. Get a glimpse at more than 300 types of feathered vacationers at the **Cape May Bird Observatory**, 701 E. Lake Dr., on Cape May Point. Bird maps, field trips, and workshops are available, along with advice about where to go for the best birdwatching. (☎861-0700; www.njaudubon.org/Centers/CMBO. Open daily 9am-4:30pm.) For a look at some larger creatures, **Cape May Whale Watch and Research Center** offers 2-3hr. tours. (☎898-0055 or 888-531-0055; www.capemaywhalewatch.com. Trips run Apr.-Dec. $25-35, ages 7-12 $15-23. One child under 6 free with each paid adult.) **South End Surf Shop**, 311 Beach Ave., rents boards to budding surfers. (☎898-0988. Open Apr.-Sept. daily 9am-10pm. Surfboard $20 per day, $35 for 2 days.) If you want to venture a little farther, **Miss Chris Marina**, on the corner of 3rd St. and Wilson Dr., rents **kayaks**. (☎884-3351. Open daily 6am-7pm. Single kayak $20 per hr.; double $30 per hr.)

THE WILDWOODS ☎ 609

The Wildwoods—Wildwood, North Wildwood, and Wildwood Crest—occupy a barrier island north of Cape May along Jersey's southern coast. A quieter alternative to Atlantic City's crowds, the Wildwoods are home to many miles of pristine, guarded **beaches** covered with a fine, silky sand. (Department of Recreation ☎ 522-5837. Beach open June-Sept. daily 6am-10pm; lifeguards on duty 10am-5:30pm.) If bobbing in the ocean doesn't suit your tastes, boat rentals from **Lake View Dock,** at Park Blvd. and Sunset Lake, can get you out on the water without getting soaked. (☎ 522-0471. Paddleboat $25 per hr. Single kayak $25 per hr. Jet ski $60 per 30min.) Back on land, **Morey's Piers,** on the boardwalk between 25th Ave. and Spencer Ave., will entertain the entire family with roller coasters, carnival games, and waterslides; booths throughout the park proudly feature the fried oreo, a local delicacy. (☎ 522-3900. Rides and games $50 for a 70-ticket card; most rides use 3-8 tickets.) Throughout Wildwood Crest, rows of restored doo-wop style motels take kitsch to a glorious extreme with bright colors, classic neon signs, and names like "The Astronaut" and "Waikiki." Wildwood's motels recall the best of the rock 'n' roll-happy 50s. In summer, the **Doo-Wop Preservation League** leads tours of the architectural landmarks around town. (☎ 729-4000. Tours meet at the Wildwoods Convention Center, 4501 Boardwalk. June-Aug. Tu and Th 7pm. $10, children $5.)

The recently renovated ▧**Caribbean Motel ❸**, 5600 Ocean Ave. in Wildwood Crest, one of the most distinctive of Wildwood's historic motels, offers accommodations close to the beach at comparatively reasonable rates. (☎ 522-8292; www.caribbeanmotel.com. Doubles June-Aug. M-Th and Su $69-165, F-Sa $100-199. Doubles May and Sept.-Oct. $54-79/69-100. AmEx/D/MC/V.) On the mainland, **Acorn Campgrounds ❷**, 419 Rte. 47 S., in nearby Green Creek, ensures its visitors remain happy campers with its selection of modern bathhouses, swimming pools, weekend movies, and free Wi-Fi. (☎ 886-7119; www.acorncampground.com. Sites with electricity and water hookups $40 per day, $240 per week; with full hookup $45/270. MC/V.)

Shore treats like hot dogs and taffy abound along the 2 mi. stretch of boardwalk, while slightly fancier restaurants line New Jersey Ave. and Atlantic Ave. in Wildwood and around Pacific Ave. in Wildwood Crest. If you're famished from a day on the sands, head across the street to **Boardwalk Bar & Grill ❷**, 3500 Atlantic Ave., and try tackling the 1 lb. Kahuna Burger ($9)—finishing it gets your picture in their Hall of Fame. (☎ 522-2431; www.boardwalkbarandgrill.com. M-F live music. Tu karaoke.) **Russo's Restaurant & Bar ❹**, 4415 Park Blvd., cooks up satisfying Italian specialties and seafood entrees. (☎ 522-7038. Entrees $12-20. M-F and Su early-bird entrees 5-6pm, $11. Open daily 7am-3am. Kitchen closes 10pm.) There's no better relief from Wildwood's summer sun than a sundae enjoyed in one of the Cadillac-shaped booths at 50s-themed **Cool Scoops Ice Cream Parlour ❶**, 1111 New Jersey Ave. (☎ 729-2665; www.coolscoops.com).

Wildwood is best reached via the **Garden State Parkway** or the slower, scenic **Rte. 9.** From the west, take the **Atlantic City Expressway,** then follow the Parkway south. **NJ Transit** (☎ 800-772-2222; www.nj.com/njtransit) runs buses from the Wildwood Bus Terminal, 4510 Washington Ave., daily to Cape May, Atlantic City, and Philadelphia with connections to New York City. Within Wildwood, the **Five Mile Beach Electric Trolleys** (☎ 884-5230; www.gatrolley.com) make a loop through the city with routes to neighboring towns ($1-2). The **Greater Wildwood Chamber of Commerce,** 3306 Pacific Ave., has helpful brochures about local attractions and events. (☎ 729-4000; www.gwcoc.com. Open M-F 9am-5pm.) **Internet Access: Wildwood Crest Public Library,** 6301 Ocean Ave. (☎ 522-0564. Free. Opens daily at 9am. Closing times vary seasonally; call for hours.) **Post Office:** 3311 Atlantic Ave. (☎ 800-275-8777. Open M-F 7am-5:30pm, Sa 9am-2pm.) **Postal Code:** 08260.

MID-ATLANTIC

PENNSYLVANIA

Established as a colony to protect Quakers from persecution, the state of Pennsylvania has always been central to the American fight for religious and political freedoms. In 1776, it was the birthplace of the Declaration of Independence. In 1976, Philadelphia groomed its historic shrines for the nation's bicentennial, and today its many colonial monuments serve as the centerpiece of the city's ambitious renewal. Pittsburgh, the steel city with a raw image, was once dirty enough to fool streetlights into burning during the day, but has lately begun a cultural renaissance of sorts. Removed from the noise of its urban areas, central Pennsylvania's landscape has retained much of the rustic beauty discovered by colonists centuries ago, from the farms of Lancaster County to the gorges of the Allegheny Plateau.

🛈 PRACTICAL INFORMATION

Capital: Harrisburg.

Visitor Info: Pennsylvania Travel and Tourism, 400 North St., Harrisburg 17120, 4th fl. (☎717-787-5453 or 800-237-4363; www.experiencepa.com). Open daily 8am-5pm. **Bureau of State Parks,** Rachel Carson State Office Bldg., 400 Market St., Harrisburg 17108 (☎888-727-2757; www.dcnr.state.pa.us/stateparks). Open M-Sa 7am-5pm.

Postal Abbreviation: PA. **Sales Tax:** 6% (7% in Philadelphia and Pittsburgh).

PHILADELPHIA ☎215

William Penn founded the City of Brotherly Love with his band of Quakers in 1682. But it was Ben, not Penn, who laid the foundations for the metropolis it is today. Benjamin Franklin, the ingenious American ambassador, inventor, and womanizer, almost single-handedly built Philadelphia into an American colonial capital; his likeness is ever-present in the city's museums and landmarks, and his name graces a park, a highway, and a bridge, among many other prominent features. Sightseers will eat up Philly's historic attractions, world-class museums, and architectural accomplishments along with the famous cheesesteaks and endless culinary choices within the city's ethnic neighborhoods.

⛟ INTERCITY TRANSPORTATION

Airport: Philadelphia International (PHL; ☎800-745-4283 or 937-6937; www.phl.org), 8 mi. southwest of Center City on I-76. **SEPTA Regional Rail—Airport Line R1** (☎580-7800; www.septa.org) runs from the airport to the 30th St. station daily every 30min. 5am-12:09am.; $5.50. A taxi to downtown costs $25. Most auto rental companies and hotels offer free shuttles.

Trains: Amtrak, 30th St. Station (☎800-872-7245; www.amtrak.com), at Market St. in University City. Station open 24hr. To: **Baltimore** (1-2hr., M-F 10 per day, $40); **Boston** (5-6hr., 10 per day, $74); **New York City** (1½-2hr., 10 per day, $45); **Pittsburgh** (7½hr., 2 per day, $45); **Washington, D.C.** (1½-2hr., 10 per day, $43). Ticket office open M-F 5:10am-10:30pm, Sa-Su 6:10am-10:30pm.

Buses: Greyhound, 1001 Filbert St. (☎800-231-2222; www.greyhound.com), at 10th St. in downtown. To: **Atlantic City** (1-1½hr., 18 per day, $11.50); **Baltimore** (3hr., 7 per day, $19); **Boston** (7hr., 16 per day, $55); **New York City** (2-3hr., 24 per day, $21); **Pittsburgh** (6-7hr., 7 per day, $41); **Washington, D.C.** (3hr., 10 per day, $25). Station open 24hr. **New Jersey Transit** (☎569-3752 or 800-772-3606; ticket window open daily 5:45am-9:30pm) in the same station, runs to **Atlantic City** (1½hr., every 30min., $13) and to points on the New Jersey shore.

Downtown Philadelphia

▲ ACCOMMODATIONS
Alexander Inn, **14**
Bank St. Hostel (HI), **6**
Chamounix Hostel (HI), **1**
La Reserve, **15**
Timberlane Campground, **22**

● FOOD
Abner's Cheesesteaks, **10**
Alma de Cuba, **11**
Bassett's Ice Cream, **5**
Chinese Restaurant, **4**
DiBruno Brothers, **18**
Famous 4th St. Deli, **20**
Jamaican Jerk Hut, **16**
Jim's Steaks, **17**
Pat's and Geno's, **19**
Pink Rose Pastry Shop, **21**
Sang Kee Peking
Duck House, **2**
Singapore, **3**
Smokey Joe's, **9**
Tandoor India Restaurant, **8**

■ NIGHTLIFE
The Khyber, **7**
Moriarty's, **13**
Woody's, **12**

MID-ATLANTIC

⚡ ORIENTATION

Penn planned his city as a logical, easily accessible grid, though the prevalence of one-way streets can cause a migraine behind the wheel. Whether you are walking or driving, the maps and arrows pointing to major destinations that are posted on every downtown street corner are lifesavers. The north-south streets ascend numerically from the **Delaware River,** flowing from **Penn's Landing** and **Independence Hall** on the east side to the **Schuylkill River** (SKOO-kill) on the west side. The first street is **Front;** others follow consecutively from 2nd to 69th across the Schuylkill. Moving outward from the downtown area known as **Center City** along Rte. 676, poorer areas lie to the south and northeast, and more affluent neighborhoods are in the northwest. The intersection of **Broad (14th)** and **Market Street** is the focal point of Center City, marked by ornate City Hall. Street addresses often refer to alleys not pictured on standard city maps. The **SEPTA transportation map,** available free from the tourist office, is probably the most complete map.

Driving around town is not difficult, but finding a place to park your car (and then paying for it) can be a nightmare. If you are extremely lucky or patient, you may be able to find curbside metered parking. Otherwise, parking in most lots near the historic sites is about $13 per day or $3-4 per 30min. If you are willing to get up early, most lots run an "early bird special," charging only $8-10 per day—as long as you park before 9 or 10am and leave before 6pm. Meterless 2hr. parking spaces are sometimes available in the Washington Sq. district or on the cobblestones of Dock St. There is also parking directly behind the Philadelphia Art Museum for $5-8, though it is far from downtown. A final option is to park outside the city, ride the train into Philly, and then walk, bike, or bus to downtown destinations (see **Local Transportation,** below). Public transit can be unsafe after dark.

The **Historic District** stretches from Front St. to 6th St. and from Race St. to South St. The **Washington Square District** runs from 6th St. to Broad St. and Vine St. to South St. The northern half of the historic district is also referred to as **Old City,** while the southern half is also called **Society Hill.** The affluent **Rittenhouse Square District** lies to the west of **Society Hill,** between Walnut and Pine St. **Chinatown** comprises the blocks around the intersection of 10th and Arch St., while the **Museum District,** in the northwest quadrant of the city, is centered around the Benjamin Franklin Pkwy. Across the Schuylkill River to the west, **University City** includes the sprawling campuses of the University of Pennsylvania and Drexel University.

⬒ LOCAL TRANSPORTATION

Public Transit: Southeastern Pennsylvania Transportation Authority (SEPTA), 1234 Market St. (☎ 580-7800). Extensive bus and rail service to the suburbs. Buses serve the 5-county area. Most operate 5am-2am, some 24hr. There are 2 major subway routes: the blue, east-west **Market Street line** (including 30th St. Station and the historic area); and the orange, north-south **Broad Street line** (including the stadium complex in south Philadelphia). The subway is unsafe after dark; buses are often safer. Pick up a free SEPTA system map at any subway stop. Single ride $2 with cash, transfers $0.60; pre-paid tokens $1.30, 2 token min. All-day pass $5.50, weekly pass $19, monthly pass $70. The subway closes around midnight, when **all-night shuttle** service begins, stopping at major subway stops about every 10-15min. until morning.

Tours: In the tourist area, **Phlash** buses provide non-narrative transport between 19 of the major downtown sights. (☎ 923-8522; www.phillyphlash.com. Mar.-Nov. daily 10am-6pm. $1, day pass $4.) The trolleys of **Philadelphia Sightseeing Tours** have knowledgeable drivers and guides and the longest tours in the city. (☎ 925-8687; www.phillytour.com. Apr.-Nov. M-F 9:30am-5:30pm, Sa-Su 9:30am-6pm. $27, seniors

$25, ages 6-12 $10.) To enjoy first-class narration while feeling the wind in your hair, try the open-air double-decker buses of the **Big Bus Company.** (☎866-324-4287; www.bigbustours.com. Runs daily 9am-6pm. $27, seniors $25, ages 4-12 $10.) Finally, the kazoo-blowing amphibious vehicles of **Ride the Ducks** stop at 10 city locations before cruising the river. (☎227-3825; www.phillyducks.com. Runs daily Mar.-Dec. 10am-7pm. $25, seniors $24, ages 3-12 $15.)

Taxi: Yellow Cab, ☎333-3333. **City Cab,** ☎492-6500.

Car Rental: Alamo, ☎492-3960 or 800-327-9633.

Bike Rental: Frankenstein Bike Worx, 1529 Spruce St. (☎893-0415). The shop is tough to spot, but look for stairs going underground. Open May-Sept. M-Sa 11am-6:30pm, Su noon-4pm. Bikes $8 per hr., $25 per day.

▨ PRACTICAL INFORMATION

Visitor Info: The Independence Visitor Center (☎925-6100 or 800-537-7676; www.independencevisitorcenter.com), at 6th and Market St. Has brochures and event schedules as well as desks for the city and National Park Service. The Center also sells tickets for the Philly Phlash and other tour bus services. Open daily 8:30am-5pm.

GLBT Resources: Gay and Lesbian Peer Counseling Services, ☎732-8255. Operates M-F 6-9pm. **William Way Lesbian, Gay, and Bisexual Community Center,** 1315 Spruce St. (☎732-2220; www.waygay.org). Has info about GLBT events and activities. Open M-F 9am-10pm, Sa 10am-7pm, Su 10:30am-7pm.

Hotlines: Suicide and Crisis Intervention, ☎686-4420. **Youth Crisis Line,** ☎787-0633. **Women Against Abuse,** ☎386-7777. All operate 24hr.

Internet Access: The **Free Library of Philadelphia** (p. 158) offers free Internet access with ID. Open M-W 9am-9pm, Th-Sa 9am-5pm. The **Ben Franklin Parkway, Independence Visitors Center,** and **Reading Terminal Market** all have free Wi-Fi.

Post Office: 1234 Market St. (☎800-275-8767), in downtown. Open daily 8:30am-5:30pm. **Postal Code:** 19104.

▌ ACCOMMODATIONS

Inexpensive lodging in Philadelphia is uncommon, but with advance arrangements, it is possible to get rooms close to Center City for around $70. The motels near the airport at Exit 9A on I-95 sacrifice location for affordable rates. **Bed and Breakfast Connections/Bed and Breakfast of Philadelphia,** in Devon, PA, books rooms in Philadelphia and southeastern Pennsylvania. (☎610-687-3565; www.bnb-philadelphia.com. Open M-F 9am-5pm. Reserve at least a week in advance; one-time registration fee $10. Singles $60-90; doubles $75-250.)

▨ **Chamounix Mansion International Youth Hostel (HI),** 3250 Chamounix Dr. (☎878-3676 or 800-379-0017; www.philahostel.org). Take bus #38 from lower Market St. to Ford and Cranston Rd.; from Ford Rd., turn left on Chamounix Dr. An energetic staff maintains the lavish 80-bed Chamounix hostel. Bikes, free parking, kitchen, and piano. In the summer, call ahead to ensure availability. Linen $2. Laundry $2. Internet access $1 per 5min; Wi-Fi available. Check-in 8-11am and 4:30pm-midnight. Lockout 11am-4:30pm. Curfew midnight. Dorms $23, members $20. MC/V. ❶

Bank Street Hostel (HI), 32 S. Bank St. (☎922-0222 or 800-392-4678; www.bank-streethostel.com). From the bus station, walk down Market St.; from City Center and University City, take SEPTA Market St. line to the 2nd St. Station; hostel is located in an alleyway between 2nd and 3rd St. 70 beds and A/C, kitchen, pool table, and TV. Movies nightly 9pm. Laundry $3. Linen $3. Internet access $1 per 4min; Wi-Fi available. Lockout 10:30am-4:30pm. Curfew 2:30am. Dorms $25, members $22. MC/V ❶

La Reserve (Bed and Breakfast Center City), 1804 Pine St. (☎735-1137; www.lare-servebandb.com). Take I-676 to the 23rd St. Exit and bear right. After 10 blocks, turn left onto Pine St. A stately house with a Steinway in the entryway and 8 guest rooms with 19th-century decor. A/C, full breakfast, and Wi-Fi. Doubles $89-159. Student discount 10-20%. AmEx/D/MC/V. ❹

Alexander Inn (☎923-3535 or 877-253-9466; www.alexanderinn.com), at 12th and Spruce St. Popular with the professional set and close to Center City's arts venues. Spacious rooms with A/C, access to a fitness room, cable TV, hot breakfast, Wi-Fi, and just about everything else you could imagine. Rooms $99-159. MC/V. ❺

Timberlane Campground, 117 Timberlane Rd. (☎856-423-6677; www.timberlane-campground.com), 15 mi. from Center City, across the Delaware River in Clarksboro, NJ. Take U.S. 295 S. to the first turnoff for Exit 18A, then follow the campground signs for ½ mi., and turn right on Friendship Rd. Timberlane is 1 block down on the right. Batting cages, fishing pond, hot showers, pool, and toilets. Reservations recommended. Sites $30, with hookup $37. ❶

◘ FOOD

Street vendors are major players in Philly's cuisine scene, hawking cheesesteaks, hoagies, cashews, soft pretzels and Italian ice ("water ice" in Philly-speak) on every corner. Ethnic eateries gather in several areas: **South Street,** between Front and 7th St.; **18th Street,** around Sansom St.; and **2nd Street,** between Chestnut and Market St. The nation's third-largest **Chinatown** (bounded by 11th, 8th, Arch, and Vine St.) has reasonable restaurants, bakeries, and markets, all worth a lunchtime wander. The immense **Italian Market** spans the storefronts, sidewalks, and stalls around 9th St. below Christian St. Make yourself a gourmet Mediterranean picnic from the thousands of meats, cheeses, and olives available at **DiBruno Brothers,** 930 S. 9th St. (☎888-322-4337; http://dibruno.com. Open M 9am-5pm, Tu-Sa 8am-6pm, Su 8am-2pm. AmEx/MC/V.) Philadelphia's original farmers' market (since 1893), the **Reading Terminal Market,** at 12th and Arch St., across from the Pennsylvania Convention Center, is the largest indoor market in the US. A food court on steroids, the market has everything from traditional Amish meat mongers to trendy Asian-fusion stalls. Most places have seating for the jumbled lunchtime crowd of cops, moms, and suits. (☎922-2317; www.readingterminalmarket.org. Open M-Sa 8am-6pm; Amish merchants W 8am-3pm, Th-Sa 8am-5pm.)

HISTORIC DISTRICT

Famous 4th Street Delicatessen, 700 S. 4th St. (☎922-3274 or 888-922-3535), at Bainbridge St. This deli rivals New York City's finest. A landmark since 1923, it has earned a cult following for its pricey but filling corned beef sandwiches ($11.25), classic reubens ($12), and borscht ($5). The voracious can upgrade their sandwiches to size Zaftig. Open M-Sa 7:30am-6pm, Su 7:30am-4pm. AmEx/MC/V. ❷

Jim's Steaks, 400 South St. (☎928-1911; www.jimsteaks.com), at 4th St. Customers flock to this Philly classic at all hours for authentic hoagies ($6 and up), cheesesteaks ($7), and takeout beer. Right up there with Philadelphia institutions Geno's and Pat's. The crowds that wind around the corner at lunchtime know their stuff. Open M-Th 10am-1am, F-Sa 11am-3am, Su noon-10pm. Cash only. ❶

Pink Rose Pastry Shop, 630 S. 4th St. (☎592-0565; www.pinkrosepastry.com), at Bainbridge St., across from the deli. Friendly students serve homemade delicacies at tables graced with freshly cut flowers and grandmotherly decorations. The sour cream apple pie ($5.25) is unbelievable. Open M-Th 8am-10:30pm, F 8am-11:30pm, Sa 9:30am-11pm, Su 9am-10:30pm. AmEx/MC/V. ❶

CHINATOWN

Chinese Restaurant, 104 N. 10th St. (☎928-0261). It doesn't get more authentic than this cheap little restaurant, crowded with locals. The small menu, only recently translated into English, offers far-out fare like oxtail noodle soup ($5). Open M-Th and Sa-Su 9am-8pm. Cash only. ❶

Singapore, 1006 Race St. (☎922-3288), between 10th and 11th St. The health-conscious flock here for kosher-vegetarian roast "pork" with black bean sauce ($7) or the tofu pot with assorted vegetables ($10). The $7.50 lunch specials come with soup, a spring roll, and rice. Dim Sum sampler $10 per person, 2 person min. Open daily 11am-11pm. AmEx/D/MC/V. ❷

Sang Kee Peking Duck House, 238 N. 9th St. (☎925-7532), near Arch St. The extensive menu reaches far into all aspects of Chinese cuisine, but as the name suggests, roast duck (half duck $19.50, whole $27.50) is what fills the tables in Sang Kee's simple dining room. Entrees $7-11. Open M-Th and Su 11am-11pm, F-Sa 11am-midnight. Cash only. ❸

CENTER CITY

Alma de Cuba, 1623 Walnut St. (☎988-1799; www.almadecubarestaurant.com), near Rittenhouse Sq. A cool spot for hot Latin food, with a hipster lounge downstairs and a stylish dining room on the 2nd fl. Try the *sancocho de pollo* soup ($7), made with coconut-chicken broth. Lunch entrees $10-14. Dinner entrees from $21. W live Cuban jazz 9pm-midnight. Happy hour M-F 5-7pm; free tapas and discounted drinks. Open M-Th 5-11pm, F-Sa 5pm-midnight, Su 5-10pm. MC/V. ❹

Jamaican Jerk Hut, 1436 South St. (☎545-8644), near Broad St. While chefs jerk Negril garlic shrimp ($15) to perfection, Bob Marley tunes blast on the backyard veranda. Bring your own beverages, but beware the $2 corking fee on your wine or 6-pack. Entrees $9-18. F-Sa live music 7pm; cover $2. Open M-Th 11am-11:30pm, F-Sa 11am-2am. Cash only. ❹

Bassett's Ice Cream (☎925-4315), in Reading Terminal Market at 12th and Arch St. Established in 1861, Bassett's is the state's oldest ice-creamery, and some say the best in the nation. Originals like pumpkin ice cream may be throwbacks to the olden days, but modern concoctions—moose tracks and mocha chip, for instance—also await. 2 scoops $2.75, 3 scoops $3.70. Open M-F 9am-6pm, Sa 8am-6pm. Cash only. ❶

UNIVERSITY CITY

Tandoor India Restaurant, 106 S. 40th St. (☎222-7122), between Chestnut and Walnut St. Every campus may have a good, cheap Indian restaurant, but this

ON THE MENU

A BEEFY RIVALRY

In a town known for its cheesesteaks and, not surprisingly, for its staggering obesity rates, every Philadelphian has a favorite corner shop to loudly champion whenever the subject of cheesesteaks arises. Even after Mayor Street created a city-wide "Health and Fitness Czar" (shortly after Philly surpassed Houston in 2000 as "fattest city" in a *Men's Health* survey), cheesesteak consumption remained astronomical. Philadelphia is bursting with shops serving up the caloric concoctions, but none is more famous than **Pat's King of Steaks** (☎468-1546; www.patskingofsteaks.com), unless it's his cross-street rival, the larger, more neon **Geno's Steaks** (☎389-0659; www.genosteaks.com).

Pat Olivieri founded his cheesesteak shop on a corner in 1930, amid rumors that he invented the famous sandwich. Some 36 years later, Joe Vento, foiled by a pre-existing store called "Joe's," was inspired by some alleyway graffiti to name his shop, and later his son, Geno. The flashier Geno's boasts fans like Justin Timberlake and Jessica Simpson, while the more sedate Pat's has hosted Steve Case and Larry King. Tourists can sample either side of the controversy (or both) for $6.25 per steak daily at 9th St. and Passyunk Ave.—just be prepared to order quickly, or get roundly cursed by the hungry crowd in line behind you.

is one of the best. Vegetarians come for the *bhindi* (spicy okra; $8). Lunch buffet daily 11:30am-3:30pm ($8); dinner buffet daily 4-10pm ($11). Student discount on buffets 20%. Open daily 11:30am-10:30pm. AmEx/D/MC/V. ❷

Smokey Joe's, 208 S. 40th St. (☎222-0770), between Locust and Walnut St. Hearty meals at student-friendly prices. Burgers $6.50-$8.25. Open daily 11am-2am. AmEx/D/MC/V. ❷

Abner's Cheesesteaks, 3813 Chestnut St. (☎662-0100), at 38th St. This bright, spacious, and cleaner-than-average joint is a local favorite. Cheesesteak $5.25. Open M-Th 11am-midnight, F-Sa 11am-3am, Su 11am-11pm. AmEx/D/MC/V. ❷

◎ SIGHTS

INDEPENDENCE MALL

REVOLUTIONARY SIGHTS. The **Independence National Historical Park,** bounded by Market, Walnut, 2nd, and 7th St., contains dozens of historical buildings. The National Park Service map, available at the Visitors Center, marks sundry minor historical houses that often provide a more illuminating stop than the major buildings. At night, the patriotic **Lights of Liberty Show** illuminates the park. A 1hr., half-mile guided walking tour with an elaborate audio program narrates the events of the Revolution while the $12 million laser light show projects five-story-tall film sequences onto historic buildings. (*Park:* ☎965-7676 or 800-537-7676; *www.independencevisitorcenter.com. Open daily June-Aug. 8:30am-5:30pm; Sept.-May 9am-5pm. Free. Light Show: PECO Energy Liberty Center, at the corner of 6th and Chestnut St. ☎542-3789 or 877-462-1775; www.lightsofliberty.org. Shows May-Aug. Tu-Sa, Sept.-Oct. Th-Sa; all shows begin at dusk. $19.50, seniors and students $16.50, under 12 $13. Parking available on 6th St. between Arch and Market St., under the Visitors Center.*) Directly across from the Visitors Center is a new security building that visitors must pass through to get to the Liberty Bell, Independence Hall, and Congress Hall. No tickets are required to go through the security building. While freedom still rings at the **Liberty Bell Center,** the Liberty Bell unfortunately does not (it cracked the first time it was rung). The petite bell inside the center is also visible through a glass wall from Chestnut Street. (*On Market St., between 5th and 6th St. ☎597-8974. Open daily 9am–5pm. Free.*) One of the most significant sites in American history, **Independence Hall** is also one of Philadelphia's most popular attractions. After Jefferson drafted the Declaration of Independence, the delegates signed the document here in 1776, then reconvened in 1787 to ink their names onto the US Constitution. Today, knowledgeable park rangers take visitors on a brief but informative tour through the nation's first capitol building. (*Between 5th and 6th St. on Chestnut St. Open daily 9am-5pm. Tickets, distributed at the Visitors Center, are required for admittance to the free guided tours that leave every 15min.*) The US Congress assembled in nearby **Congress Hall** from 1790 to 1800, when Philadelphia was the nation's first capital. While soaking up the history, rest in the plush Senate chairs. (*At Chestnut and 6th St. Open daily 9am-5pm.*)

The First Continental Congress, predecessor of the US Congress, united against the British in 1774 in **Carpenters' Hall.** Now a mini-museum heralding the carpenters responsible for Old City Hall and the Pennsylvania State House, the hall also houses the oldest continuously operating trade guild in America, founded in 1724. The hall is located in a fenced green area that also contains a military museum, the nation's second bank, and several historical homes worth a look. (*320 Chestnut St. ☎925-0167; www.carpentershall.org. Open Mar.-Dec. Tu-Su 10am-4pm; Jan.-Feb. W-Su 10am-4pm. Free.*) Behind the Visitors Center, the **National Constitution Center** provides visitors with a multimedia introduction to the Constitution and a variety of exhibits that give a more in-depth look at its history. (*525 Arch St., in Independence National Historical Park. ☎409-6600 or 866-917-1787; www.constitutioncenter.org. Open M-F and Su*

9:30am-5pm, Sa 9:30am-6pm. 17min. multimedia presentation prior to entrance to exhibits; last show 4:10pm. $12, seniors $11, ages 4-12 $8, military free.)

OTHER SIGHTS. The rest of the park preserves residential and commercial buildings of the Revolutionary era. On the northern edge of the mall, a white molding delineates the size and location of Ben Franklin's home in ■**Franklin Court.** The original abode was razed by the statesman's heirs in 1812 in order to erect an apartment complex. The site contains a museum of Franklin's inventions and personal possessions, a 20min. movie, a replica of Franklin's printing office with a working 18th-century printing press, and a post office. This post office was the first in the nation. *(318 Market St., between 3rd and 4th St. ☎ 597-8974. Open in summer daily 9am-5pm; call for winter hours. Free.)* On a more somber note, a statue of George Washington presides over the **Tomb of the Unknown Soldier,** in Washington Sq., where an eternal flame commemorates fallen Revolutionary War heroes.

Located next to Independence Park is the **Federal Reserve Bank of Philadelphia,** which exhibits money from the 13 original colonies and even a $100,000 bill featuring President Woodrow Wilson. *(100 N. 6th St., between Arch and Race St. ☎ 574-6257; www.phil.frb.org. Open Mar.-May and Sept.-Dec. M-F 9:30am-4:30pm; June-Aug. also Sa 10am-4pm and Su noon-4pm; Jan.-Feb. M-F 10am-2pm only. Free.)* Philadelphia's official history museum, the **Atwater Kent Museum,** has a wide range of rare Pennsylvania artifacts, including the wampum belt given to William Penn by the Lenni Lenape at Shakamaxon in 1682 and a giant floor map of Philadelphia. *(16 S. 7th St. ☎ 685-4830; www.philadelphiahistory.org. Open W-Su 1-5pm. $5, ages 13-17 and seniors $3, under 12 free.)*

OUTSIDE INDEPENDENCE MALL

COLONIAL MADNESS. A penniless Ben Franklin arrived in Philadelphia in 1723 and strolled by the rowhouses that line the narrow **Elfreth's Alley,** near 2nd and Arch St. The oldest continuously inhabited street in America now houses a museum that provides a glimpse into the daily lives of Philadelphians throughout the years. *(Museum: 124 Elfreth's Alley. ☎ 574-0560; www.elfrethsalley.org. Open Mar.-Oct. M-Sa 10am-5pm, Su noon-5pm; Nov.-Feb. Th-Sa 10am-5pm, Su noon-5pm. 20min. tours; last tour 4:40pm. $5, ages 6-18 $1.)* Several blocks away, the **Betsy Ross House** is a child-oriented museum honoring America's most beloved seamstress and her masterpiece, the American flag. *(239 Arch St. ☎ 686-1252; www.betsyrosshouse.org. Open Apr.-Sept. daily 10am-5pm; Oct.-Mar. Tu-Su 10am-5pm. $3, children and students $2. Audio tour $4.)*

OTHER SIGHTS. For those who like to get off on the right foot, the Temple University School of Podiatric Medicine contains the **Shoe Museum.** The collection of 900 pairs features footwear from the famous feet of Julius Erving, Reggie Jackson, Lady Bird Johnson, Nancy Reagan, Joan Rivers, and others. Recent additions to the collection include Ella Fitzgerald's gold boots and a pair of 6 in. tall blue satin platform sandals worn by Sally Struthers on the popular television show *All in the Family.* *(8th and Race Sts., 6th fl. ☎ 625-5243. Tours by appointment only W and F 9am-1pm. Free.)* The powder-blue **Benjamin Franklin Bridge,** the longest suspension bridge in the world when it opened in 1926, off Race and 5th St., connects Philadelphia to New Jersey, and provides an expansive view of the city.

SOCIETY HILL AND THE WATERFRONT

Society Hill proper begins on Walnut St., between Front and 7th St., east of Independence Mall, and is bordered on the east by the Delaware River. The neighborhood is filled with townhouses over 200 years old and cobblestone walks illuminated by electric "gaslights." The restaurants along the commercialized waterfront are great places to watch ships go by during the day or see the back-lit Philadelphia skyline by night.

HISTORICAL SIGHTS. Historic **Head House Square,** at 2nd and Pine St., is America's oldest firehouse and marketplace, and now contains restaurants and boutiques. Bargain hunters can test their haggling skills at an outdoor arts and crafts fair. (☎ 790-0782. Open June-Aug. Sa noon-11pm, Su noon-6pm. Free workshops Su 1-3pm.) Each January, sequin- and feather-clad participants join in a rowdy New Year's Day Mummer's Parade, which began in celebration of the masked festival actors known as "mummers." South of Head House Sq., the **Mummer's Museum** swells with glamorous old costumes. (1100 S. 2nd St., at Washington Ave. ☎ 336-3050; www.riverfrontmummers.com. Open May-Sept. Tu-W and F-Sa 9:30am-4:30pm, Th 9:30am-9:30pm, Su noon-4:30pm; July-Aug. closed Su; Oct.-Apr. Tu-Sa 9:30am-4:30pm, Su noon-4:30pm. Free string band concerts Tu 8pm. $3.50; seniors, students, and under 12 $2.50.)

ON THE WATERFRONT. A looming neon sign at the easternmost end of Market St. welcomes visitors to **Penn's Landing.** There are free concerts throughout the year, and the walk from the Market St. entrance over the footbridge to South St. is a gorgeous night trek. (☎ 629-3257; www.pennslandingcorp.com. Major bands Apr.-Oct. Th 8pm. Children's theater Su 10am-noon.) Philadelphian shipbuilding, cargo, and immigration unfold at the **Independence Seaport Museum,** at Penn's Landing. Kids can get their sea legs at the "Boats Float" exhibit. Near the museum a host of old ships bobs at the dock, including the *U.S.S. Olympia,* the oldest steel warship still afloat, and the *U.S.S. Becuna,* a WWII submarine. (☎ 925-5439; www.phillyseaport.org. Open daily 10am-5pm. Museum and ships $9, seniors and students $8, children $6.)

CENTER CITY

As the financial and commercial hub of Philly, Center City barely has enough room to accommodate the professionals who cram into the area bounded by 12th, 23rd, Vine, and Pine St. Rife with activity during the day, the region retires early at night.

ART AND ARCHITECTURE. The country's first school and art museum, the **Pennsylvania Academy of Fine Art** has permanent displays of works by Winslow Homer and Mary Cassatt, while current students show their theses and accomplished alumni get their own exhibits each May. A new building across the street displays more than 250 paintings in 15 gallery rooms. (118 N. Broad St., at Cherry St. ☎ 972-7600; www.pafa.org. Open Tu-Sa 10am-5pm, Su 11am-5pm. Tours 45min.-1hr.; M-F at 11:30am and 12:30pm, Sa-Su at noon and 1pm. $7, seniors and students $6, ages 5-18 $5.) Presiding over Center City, the granite-and-marble **City Hall** took 30 years to build. Until 1908, it reigned as the tallest building in the US, aided by the 37 ft. statue of William Penn bedecked in a hat and stockings at its summit. A law prohibited building anything higher than Penn's hat in Philadelphia until entrepreneurs overturned it in the mid-80s. (At Broad and Market St. ☎ 686-2840. Open M-F 9:30am-4:30pm. Tower-only tour every 15min. daily 9:15am-4:15pm, 5 people max. per tour; reservations recommended. Free.) The **Masonic Temple** is a commanding building that contains a research library, a cache of period art, and breathtaking architecture. The short tours give a glance at the Masons' secretive history. (1 N. Broad St. ☎ 988-1900; www.pagrandlodge.org. Entry by tour only. Tours Tu-Th 11am, 2, 3pm; Sat 10, 11am. $8, students $6, seniors $5, under 12 $5.)

RITTENHOUSE SQUARE

In the early 20th century, architect Paul Phillipe Cert overhauled the Rittenhouse Sq. District, leaving his mark on the ritzy, brick-laden neighborhood southeast of Center City. This area is the city's musical and dramatic heart, housing several performing arts centers. **Rittenhouse Square Park,** bordered by Walnut and 18th St., is an energetic but relaxing stretch of green in the bustling neighborhood.

RITTENHOUSE MUSEUMS. It's a good idea to completely digest lunch before viewing the bizarre and often gory medical abnormalities displayed at the intriguing █**Mütter Museum,** run by the College of Physicians of Philadelphia. Among the potentially unsettling fascinations are a wall of skulls and a collection of preserved body parts of famous people, including John Marshall's bladder stones and a cancerous section of John Wilkes Booth's neck. The museum also contains a Level 4 biohazard suit, a medicinal herb garden, and a bizarre gift shop. *(19 S. 22nd St. ☎563-3737, ext. 211. Open daily 10am-5pm. $12; ages 6-18, seniors, and students $8.)* Just south of the square, the nondescript exterior of the █**Rosenbach Museum and Library** hides an enormous, must-see collection of rare books and manuscripts, from a handwritten copy of James Joyce's *Ulysses* to Lewis Carroll's copy of *Alice in Wonderland* with original sketches. *(2010 Delancey St. ☎732-1600; www.rosenbach.org. Open Tu and Th-F 10am-5pm. Exhibition and tour $8, seniors and students $5.)*

PARKWAY/MUSEUM DISTRICT

Nicknamed "America's Champs-Elysées," the **Benjamin Franklin Parkway** sports a colorful international flag row in downtown Philly. **Logan Circle,** one of the city's five original town squares, was the site of public executions until 1823 but now delights the children who frolic in the **Swann Memorial Fountain.** Designed by Alexander Calder, the fountain represents the Wissahickon Creek, the Schuylkill River, and the Delaware River, the three bodies of water that surround the city.

SCIENCE. A modern assemblage of everything scientific, the highly interactive █**Franklin Institute** would make the old inventor proud. The complex includes three floors of exhibits dedicated to the laws of science, an IMAX theater, a flight simulator used by the Navy, and free shows on everything from dissecting a cow's eye to putting on a spacesuit. The "skybike" allows kids and adults to pedal across a tightrope suspended in a cage nearly four stories high. *(At 20th St. and Ben Franklin Pkwy. ☎448-1200; www.fi.edu. Open daily 9:30am-5pm; IMAX W and F-Sa until 9pm. $13.75, ages 4-11 and seniors $11. Skybike $2. IMAX Theater ☎448-1111; $9, with museum entry $5.)* Part of the Institute, the **Fels Planetarium** takes visitors on daily tours of the stars and stages MTV2's SonicVision hourly from 9pm-midnight on weekends. *(222 N. 20th St. One show included in Franklin Institute ticket. $8, ages 4-11 and seniors $5.)* Just down the parkway, the **Academy of Natural Sciences,** graced by a whimsical statue of two velociraptors in chase, allows budding archaeologists to try their hand at digging up dinosaur fossils. *(1900 Ben Franklin Pkwy., at 19th St. ☎299-1000; www.acnatsci.org. Open M-F 10am-4:30pm, Sa-Su 10am-5pm. Wheelchair-accessible. $10; ages 3-12, military, and seniors $8. AAA discount $1.)*

ART. Sylvester Stallone may have etched the sight of the █**Philadelphia Museum of Art** into the minds of movie buffs everywhere when he bolted up its stately front stairs in *Rocky* (1976), but it is the artwork within that has earned the museum its fine reputation. The world-class collection includes famous works such as Van Gogh's *Sunflowers*, Cezanne's *Large Bathers*, and Toulouse-Lautrec's *At the Moulin Rouge*. The museum also contains a Japanese tea house and extensive Asian, Egyptian, and American art collections. *(Ben Franklin Pkwy. and 26th St. ☎763-8100; www.philamuseum.org. Open Tu-Su 10am-5pm, F 10am-8:45pm. Tours daily 10am-3pm. Live jazz, appetizers, and wine F 5:45pm-8:15pm. $14, seniors $12, ages 13-18 $10, under 13 free; Su free.)* A casting of *The Gates of Hell* outside the **Rodin Museum** guards the most extensive collection of the prolific sculptor's works this side of the Seine. One of the five original castings of *The Thinker* (1880) marks the museum entrance from afar. *(Ben Franklin Pkwy. and 22nd St. ☎763-8100; www.rodinmuseum.org. Open Tu-Su 10am-5pm. Suggested donation $3. 1hr. audio tour $5.)* For lesser-known talents, check out the **Galleries at Moore College of Art and Design,** a series of exhibition halls featuring works by Moore College's students and alumni. *(Ben Franklin Pkwy. at 20th St. ☎965-4045; www.thegalleriesatmoore.org. Open Tu-F 11am-7pm, Sa 11am-5pm. Free.)*

BOOKS AND INMATES. The **Free Library of Philadelphia** has earned a stellar reputation for its orchestral music and rare book collection, one of the nation's largest. Philadelphia art students frequently seek inspiration within the classical architecture of the building. *(At 20th and Vine St. ☎ 686-5322; www.library.phila.gov. Open M-W 9am-9pm, Th-Sa 9am-5pm. Tour of rare books M-F 11am. Free.)* In a reversal of convention, guests line up to get into prison at the castle-like **Eastern State Penitentiary,** once a ground-breaking institution for criminal rehabilitation. Tours twist through the smoldering dimness Al Capone once called home, and guides recount fascinating stories of daring inmates and their attempted escapes. The Halloween Haunted House (late Sept.-Nov.) is not for the faint of heart. *(2124 Fairmount Ave. at 22nd St. ☎ 236-3300; www.easternstate.org. Open W-Su 10am-5pm. Last entry 4pm. Entry includes guided tours every hr. $9, seniors and students $7, ages 7-12 $4; under 7 not permitted.)*

UNIVERSITY CITY

In West Philly, across the Schuylkill from Center City, the **University of Pennsylvania** and **Drexel University** make up University City (U-City), a neighborhood comprised almost entirely of students. The Penn campus, a thriving assemblage of green lawns and red brick quadrangles, contrasts sharply with the dilapidated buildings surrounding it. Ritzy shops and cafes spice up 36th St., while a statue of the omnipresent Benjamin Franklin greets visitors at the campus entrance on 34th and Walnut St. Much of the area surrounding University City is unsafe at night.

U-CITY SIGHTS. The **University Museum of Archaeology and Anthropology** journeys through three floors of the world's major cultures under a beautiful stone and glass rotunda. *(At 33rd and Spruce St. ☎ 898-4001; www.upenn.edu/museum. Open Tu-Sa 10am-4:30pm, Su 1-5pm. $8, ages 6-17, seniors, and students $5.)* In 1965, Andy Warhol had his first one-man show at the cutting-edge **Institute of Contemporary Art.** Today, the ICA features works by some of the newest big names on the art scene. *(118 S. 36th, at Sansom St. ☎ 898-7108; www.icaphila.org. Open W-F noon-8pm, Sa-Su 11am-5pm. $6; artists, seniors, and students $3; Su 11am-1pm free.)* North of the university area, the **Philadelphia Zoo,** the country's oldest zoo, houses more than 2000 animals, including lowland gorillas, bearded pigs, and giant anteaters. The endangered animals exhibit provides a glimpse of some extremely rare species. If you'd rather get a bird's-eye view, take a ride on the Zooballoon and rise 400 ft. above the giraffes and zebras below. *(3260 South St., at 34th and Girard St. ☎ 243-1100; www.philadelphiazoo.org. Open daily Feb.-Nov. 9:30am-5pm; Dec.-Jan. 9:30am-4pm. Mar.-Nov. $17, ages 2-11 and seniors $14; Dec.-Feb. $13. Zooballoon M-F $8, Sa-Su $10. Parking $10.)*

🎵 ENTERTAINMENT

The non-profit **Kimmel Center for the Performing Arts,** 260 S. Broad St., the home of eight resident performing companies and the manager of multiple theaters in the city, dominates Philadelphia's performing arts scene. The **Philadelphia Orchestra** performs in the Center's **Verizon Hall** from September to May, while **Philadance,** a contemporary dance company, and the **Philadelphia Chamber Music Society** reside in the smaller **Perelman Hall.** The Center's **Academy of Music,** at Broad and Locust St., was modeled after Milan's La Scala and is the nation's oldest continuously-running opera house. The Academy hosts the **Opera Company of Philadelphia** (☎ 732-8400) and the six annual productions of the **Pennsylvania Ballet** (☎ 893-1955). The outdoor **Mann Music Center,** at 52nd St. and Parkside Ave., in Fairmount Park, hosts big name entertainers like Tony Bennett, Willie Nelson, and the Gipsy Kings, as well as a variety of jazz and rock concerts. (For all performances, contact Kimmel Center: ☎ 790-5800 or 893-1999; www.kimmelcenter.org. Box office open daily 10am-6pm or until performances begin. Schedule and ticket prices vary.)

The 120-year-old, still independent **Trocadero,** 1003 Arch St., at 10th St., is the nation's oldest operating Victorian theater. It hosts both local and big-name rock bands. (☎922-5483; www.thetroc.com. Box office open M-F 11:30am-6pm, Sa 11:30am-5pm.) The **Robin Hood Dell East,** on Ridge Ave., near 33rd St., in Fairmount Park, brings in top names in pop, jazz, and gospel in July and August. In September, theatrical entertainment graces its stage. (☎685-9560; www.delleast.com. Box office open M-F 10am-5pm, Sa-Su 10am-showtime.) The students of the world-renowned **Curtis Institute of Music,** 1726 Locust St., give free concerts. (☎893-5252; www.curtis.edu. Mid-Oct. to Apr. M, W, and F 8pm.) The **University of the Arts Merriam Theater,** 250 S. Broad St., in Center City, stages performances ranging from student works to Broadway hits. Katharine Hepburn, Laurence Olivier, and Sammy Davis, Jr. have all graced this stage. (☎732-5446; www.merriamtheater.org. Box office open M-Sa 10am-5:30pm.) The Old City, from Chestnut to Vine St. and Front to 4th St., comes alive for the **First Friday** celebration, when streets fill with live music and 40 art galleries, museums, and restaurants open their doors to entice visitors with free food and sparkling wine. (☎800-555-5191; www.old-city.org. Oct.-June first F of each month 5-9pm.)

Philly gets physical with plenty of sports venues—four professional teams play just a short ride away on the Broad St. subway line. Baseball's **Phillies** (☎463-1000; www.phillies.com) step up to the plate at **Citizens Bank Park,** 1 Citizens Bank Way, just off Pattison Ave. between 11th and Darien St. Football's **Eagles** (☎463-5500; www.philadelphiaeagles.com) bask in the cheers of their famously rowdy fans at **Lincoln Financial Field,** at Broad St. and Pattison Ave. Across the street, basketball aficionados fill the **Wachovia Center** (☎336-3600; box office open M-F 9am-6pm, Sa 10am-4pm) for the NBA's **76ers** (☎339-7676; www.sixers.com) and the NHL's **Flyers** (☎755-9700; www.philadelphiaflyers.com). Baseball and hockey tickets start at $10; football and basketball tickets run $15-50. Since the venues are in close proximity, expect parking difficulty on game nights.

⚡ NIGHTLIFE

Check the Friday *Philadelphia Inquirer* for entertainment listings. The free Thursday *City Paper* and the Wednesday *Philadelphia Weekly* have listings of city events. Gay and lesbian weeklies *Au Courant* (free) and *Philadelphia Gay News* ($0.75) list events throughout the Delaware Valley. Many pubs line **2nd Street** near Chestnut St., close to the Bank St. Hostel, catering to a young, bar-hopping crowd. Continuing south to Society Hill, an older crowd fills dozens of more expensive bars and cafes. **Delaware Avenue,** or **Columbus Boulevard,** running along Penn's Landing, has recently become a trendy spot full of nightclubs and dance clubs that attract droves of yuppies and students. Most bars and clubs that cater to a gay clientele congregate along **Camac, South 12th,** and **South 13th Street.**

The Khyber, 56 S. 2nd St. (☎238-5888; www.thekhyber.com). A speakeasy during the days of Prohibition, the Khyber now legally gathers a young crowd to listen to a range of punk, metal, and hip-hop music. The ornate wooden bar was shipped over from England in 1876. Vegetarian sandwiches $3. Live music daily 10pm. 21+. Cover $8. Happy hour M-F 5-8pm; domestic beer $1. Open M-F noon-2am, Sa-Su 1pm-2am. Cash only.

Moriarty's, 1116 Walnut St. (☎627-7676; www.moriartysrestaurant.com), near 11th St. and the Forest Theater. This Irish pub draws a sizeable crowd late into the night with a quiet, comfortable bar scene and good Mexican food. Over 28 beers on tap. Daily drink specials. Happy hour 5-7pm; drafts $3. Open daily 11am-2am. Kitchen closes 1am.

Woody's, 202 S. 13th St. (☎545-1893; www.woodysbar.com), at Walnut St. An outgoing gay crowd frequents this lively club. Most nights, patrons are a happy mix of ages, genders, and sexual orientations. M karaoke. Happy hour daily 5-7pm. Bar open daily 11am-2am. Kitchen open daily noon-3:30pm and 4-11pm.

⚠ OUTDOOR ACTIVITIES

Philly's finest outdoor opportunities can be found in the resplendent **Fairmount Park** (www.phila.gov/fairpark; open dawn-dusk). Ten times the size of New York City's Central Park, Fairmount is covered with bike trails and picnic areas, offering city-weary vacationers outdoor adventures and views of the Schuylkill River. The **Andorra Natural Area** inside the park is a 210-acre preserve of native plants and includes an environmental education center on the banks of Wissahickon Creek. **Mountain biking** is very popular in the Wissahickon and Pennypacker Valleys north of Philadelphia, where both flat and more challenging trails are available. (☎683-0200. Permit required to bike trails, but visitors report that it is rarely enforced; $20 per year.) The premier location for wildlife observation in the Philadelphia area is the **John Heinz National Wildlife Refuge,** just off I-95 near the south end of Philadelphia in Tinicum. This 205-acre freshwater tidal marsh is home to hundreds of bird species, including migrants from both tropical and northern climes.

The abandoned **Waterworks,** Greek-style ruins by the waterfall immediately behind the Museum of Art, were built between 1819 and 1822. Free 90min. tours of the Waterworks' romantic architecture and technology begin on Aquarium Dr., behind the museum. (☎685-4935; www.fairmountwaterworks.org. Open Tu-Sa 10am-5pm, Su 1-5pm.) Farther down the river, Philly's place in the rowing world is evidenced by a line of crew clubs forming the historic **Boathouse Row.** The Museum of Art hosts the Schuylkill Stroll, a $8 guided tour of Boathouse Row (F 6-7:30pm, Su 1-2:30pm), as well as trolley tours to some of the mansions in Fairmount Park (Mansion tour schedules ☎763-8100). The area near Boathouse Row is also one of Philly's most popular in-line skating spots, and joggers seeking the refreshing river breeze crowd the local paths. In the northern arm of Fairmount Park, trails follow the secluded Wissahickon Creek for 5 mi., as the concrete city fades into a distant memory. The **Japanese House and Garden,** off Montgomery Dr., near Belmont Ave., is designed in the style of a 17th-century *shoin*. (☎878-5097; www.shofuso.com. Open May-Oct. Tu-F 10am-4pm, Sa-Su 11am-5pm; call for winter hours. Ask about the tour. $5, ages 6-17, over 55, and students $3.) The park and the surrounding neighborhoods are not safe at night.

⮞ DAYTRIP FROM PHILADELPHIA

VALLEY FORGE

Valley Forge lies 40min. from Philadelphia by car. To get to the Visitors Center, take I-76 west from Philadelphia for about 12 mi. until Exit 327 (formerly Exit 25) and make a right at the bottom of the ramp. SEPTA runs buses from Philadelphia to the Visitors Center daily; catch #125 in front of the Sheraton Hotel at 16th and JFK ($3.50). Valley Forge is open daily 9am-10pm. Free.

In 1777-78 it was the frigid winter, not the British military, that almost crushed the Continental Army. When George Washington, looking for a retreat from which to monitor British-occupied Philadelphia, selected Valley Forge as the winter camp for his 12,000 troops after a defeat at Germantown in October, he could not have predicted the fate that would befall his soldiers. Three arduous months of starvation, bitter cold, and disease nearly halved his forces. It was not until Baron Friedrich von Steuben arrived with reinforcements and supplies on February 23, 1778, that recovery seemed possible. Reinvigorated, the Continental Army left Valley Forge on June 19, 1778 to win the Battle of Monmouth.

The hills that once tormented the frost-bitten soldiers now constitute the **Valley Forge National Historical Park.** The **Visitors Center,** 1400 Outer Line Dr., features a small museum and a 20min. film. (☎610-783-1099; www.nps.gov/vafo. Open daily in summer 9am-6pm; in winter 9am-5pm.) Visitors can explore the park by bicycle, bus, car, foot, or even horse, but no in-line skates or skateboards are allowed. The 10 mi. self-guided **auto tour** (tape $10, CD $12), begins at the Visitors Center. If you prefer live narration and question time, the quarter-mile **walking tour,** led by a knowledgeable park ranger and culminating in an **antique musket demonstration,** also leaves from the Visitors Center. (In summer daily 10:50am, 12:30, 1:50pm; in winter Sa-Su 10:50am and 1:50pm. Free.) The park also rents bikes for a 2hr. park cruise ($15, children $12). The 1½hr. **bus tour** allows visitors to explore sites in air-conditioned comfort. (In summer M and Th-Su. $16, ages 13-16 $11, under 12 $7.50.) All tours pass Washington's headquarters, reconstructed soldier huts and fortifications, and the Grand Parade Ground where the Continental Army drilled. The park has three picnic areas but no camping. Joggers can take a trip down a fairly flat, paved 6 mi. trail through deer-populated forests. Near the park, shoppers delight in the **King of Prussia Mall,** the nation's largest retail mall, conveniently located in a region that exempts clothing from sales tax. Follow signs from I-76 or use SEPTA bus #125.

LANCASTER COUNTY   ☎717

Lancaster County is known as the heart of Pennsylvania Dutch Country, but its residents, so-called the Pennsylvania Dutch, aren't actually Dutch. When Amish and Mennonite settlers migrated to the area in the 1700s in search of religious freedom and introduced themselves as "Deutsch," English settlers mistook the German word for "Dutch." Lancaster County is still home to the largest Old Order Amish population in the US, a group that strives to maintain its simple lifestyle in the face of modernity. Metropolitan Lancaster, however, is a thoroughly modern small town with a remarkably diverse population.

🛈 **PRACTICAL INFORMATION.** Amtrak, 53 McGovern Ave., in Lancaster City (☎291-5080; www.amtrak.com; ticket office open M-F 5:30am-9pm, Sa-Su 7am-8:45pm), runs **trains** to Philadelphia (1½hr., 8-10 per day, $14) and Pittsburgh (6½hr., 2 per day, $43). Capitol Trailways (☎397-4861; open daily 8am-10pm), in the same location, runs **buses** to Philadelphia (2hr., 3 per day, $17) and Pittsburgh (7hr., 3 per day, $58). Red Rose Transit, 45 Erick Rd., has **bus service** within Lancaster City and to Bird-in-Hand, Paradise, Park City, and other areas in the surrounding countryside. (☎397-4246. Buses run daily approx. 5am-6pm. $1.25-$2.45.)

Lancaster County covers an area almost the size of Rhode Island. Driving in from Philadelphia and other cities to the east is easiest on **Route 30 W;** from southern destinations, take **Route 83 N** to **Route 30 E.** County seat **Lancaster City,** in the heart of Dutch country, has red brick rowhouses huddled around historic **Penn Square.** The rural areas are mostly accessible by car (or horse and buggy), but it is easy to see the tourist sites with a bike or to walk the mile or two between public transit drop-offs. To sample the Amish and Mennonite traditions, stick to the towns along Rte. 340, such as **Bird-in-Hand** and the unfortunately named **Intercourse.** Because the area is heavily Mennonite, most businesses and all major attractions are closed on Sundays. The **Pennsylvania Dutch Visitors Bureau,** 501 Greenfield Rd., on the east side of Lancaster City off Rte. 30, distributes info on the region, including maps and walking tours. (☎299-8901 or 800-723-8824; www.padutchcountry.com. Open Nov.-May M-Sa 8:30am-5pm, Su 9am-5pm; late May-Oct. M-Sa 8am-6pm, Su 9am-5pm.) **Post office:** 1400 Harrisburg Pike. (☎396-6925 or 800-275-8777. Open M-F 7:30am-7pm, Sa 9am-2pm.) **Postal Code:** 17604.

TIP **DON'T SHOOT.** Tempted as you may be to point your camera at those oh-so-quaint Amish folk, please refrain out of respect for their culture. Most Amish and Mennonite orders consider photographs to be sacrilegious graven images, and take offense at rapacious tourist paparazzi.

ACCOMMODATIONS. Hundreds of hotels, campgrounds, and B&Bs cluster in this area, as do several working farms with guest houses. The lodging guide published by the Visitors Center is an essential resource for wading through all the options. If you are considering staying in a B&B, call the **Authentic Bed and Breakfasts of Lancaster County Association** (☎ 800-552-2632; www.authenticbandb.com). The amicable staff at the **Mennonite Information Center** (see **Sights**, p. 163) can put you in touch with Mennonite-run guest houses. For an affordable stay in a convenient working farm home, head to the **Verdant View Farm Bed and Breakfast** ❸, 429 Strasburg Rd., in Paradise. The farmhouse has five bedrooms, all with A/C and three with private baths, plus a visitors' cottage with a full kitchen. Guests interested in the "Mennonite experience" can milk cows, feed calves, crawl through hay tunnels, and attend church service with their hosts. (☎ 687-7353 or 888-321-8119; www.verdantview.com. Check-in 2-5pm. Doubles $65-96. AmEx/MC/V.) Six miles east of Lancaster lies the **Amish Country Motel** ❸, 3013 Old Philadelphia Pike, where the price of a room includes a 2hr. bus tour of the area. (☎ 768-8396. Closed Dec.-Mar. Double rooms $59-99; peak rates from mid-June to early Sept. AmEx/D/MC/V.) For the B&B experience on a budget, look to the **Blue Ball B&B** ❸, 1075 Main St., in Blue Ball, east of Lancaster City on Rte. 23. This cozy guesthouse provides A/C, cable TV, a full breakfast, and a private bath, all at $20 less than its competitors. (☎ 800-720-9827; www.blueballbandb.com. Singles and doubles $70-80.) The quiet wilderness of **Beacon Hill Camping** ❶, Rte. 772 W, a half-mile from Rte. 340, makes it a perfect place to spend a night in one of 50 level sites. (☎ 768-8775. Check-in 1pm. Sites $30, with full hookup $32. Cabins $50. 7th night free. D/MC/V.)

FOOD. Amish food, German in derivation and generous in portion, is characterized by a heavy emphasis on potatoes and vegetables. Palatable alternatives to high-priced "family-style" restaurants are the **farmers' markets** and produce stands that dot the roadway. The **Central Market,** in downtown Lancaster City at the northwest corner of Penn Sq., next to the Heritage Center Museum, has been doing business since the 1730s. Nowadays, simply dressed Pennsylvania Dutch pour into the city to sell affordable fresh fruit, bologna, seasonings, and homemade desserts. (☎ 291-4739. Open Tu and F 6am-4pm, Sa 6am-2pm.) To be treated like the VIP that you are, head to **The Pressroom** ❸, 26 W. King St., in Lancaster City. Deep leather booths give this lunch and dinner spot a club-like feel, while airier outdoor dining is available at the small fountain-decorated **Steinman Park** next door. Try one of the sandwiches ($7-9) or pizzas ($8-14), which remain economical choices even at dinner. Entrees ($19-35), however, are strictly for the fat cats. (☎ 399-5400; www.thepressroomrestaurant.com. W-Th live jazz 7-10pm. Lunch daily 11:30am-3pm. Dinner Tu-Th 5-9:30pm, F-Sa 5-10:30pm, Su 5-9pm.) If you have a hankering for something a little more historic, the **Revere Tavern** ❸, 3063 Lincoln Hwy., in Paradise, has a legacy of excellent service that dates back to its construction in 1740. Seven fireplaces give the dining room a cozy feel in the winter. Lunch options here include croissant sandwiches ($5-10), snapper turtle soup ($4), and a deli buffet. (☎ 687-8601. Dinner entrees $11-30. Open M 5-10pm, Tu-Sa 11am-2pm and 5-10pm, Su 4-9pm.) At **The Family Cupboard** ❸, 3029 Old Philadelphia Pike, in Bird-in-Hand, quilts for sale hang on the walls surrounding tables where patrons devour Amish specialties. Though hardly an authentic family restaurant, it's perfect for big groups; see the petting zoo at the crafts shop next door for child-friendly fun. (☎768-8886. Entrees about $10. Open June-Aug. M-Sa 7:30am-9pm; in spring and fall M-Sa 8am-8pm; call for winter hours.)

◙ SIGHTS. From April to October every year, quilt and art fanatics flock to Amish country to see the **People's Place Quilt Museum,** 3510 Old Philadelphia Pike in Intercourse. (☎800-828-8218; www.ppquiltmuseum.com. Open Apr.-Oct. M-Sa 9am-5pm. Free.) The Mennonites believe in outreach and have established the **Mennonite Information Center,** 2209 Millstream Rd., off Rte. 30 east of Lancaster, to help tourists distinguish between the Amish and Mennonite faiths. Kind hostesses guide guests through the Biblical Tabernacle. (☎299-0954; www.mennoniteinfoctr.com. 2hr. private tours available.) To explore the Amish countryside by car, try winding through the fields off U.S. 340, near Bird-in-Hand. Cyclists can capture the simple spirit on the **Lancaster County Heritage Bike Tour,** a reasonably flat 46 mi. route past covered bridges and historic sites maintained by the Visitors Center. A visit to Lancaster is not complete without using the preferred mode of local transportation, the horse and buggy. ◙**Ed's Buggy Rides,** 253 Hartman Bridge Rd., on Rte. 896, 1½ mi. south of U.S. 30 W in Strasburg, offers 3 mi. tours that bump through scenic backwoods, covered bridges, and working farms. (☎687-0360; www.edsbuggyrides.com. Open daily 9am-5pm. Rides $9, under 11 $4.) **Amish Country Tours** leads 1½hr. trips that include visits to one-room schoolhouses, Amish cottage industries, cheery farmland vistas, as well as roadside produce and craft stands. (☎768-8400. Tours Apr.-Oct. M-Sa 10:30am and 2pm, Su 11:30am; Nov. daily 11:30am; Dec.-Mar. Sa-Su 11:30am. $27, ages 4-12 $11.) Old country crafts, food, and even a mock hanging can be found from late June to early July at the **Pennsylvania Dutch Folk Life and Fun Festival,** in Kutztown, which offers an unusual combination of polka bands, pot pies, and petting zoos. (☎888-674-6463; www.kutztownfestival.com. $12 per day, seniors $11, under 12 free.)

GETTYSBURG   ☎717

In the sweltering heat of July 1-3, 1863, perhaps the most memorable period of the Civil War, Union and Confederate forces met at Gettysburg in a spectacularly destructive battle. The Union forces ultimately prevailed, though the victory cost over 50,000 casualties. President Lincoln arrived in Gettysburg four months later to dedicate the Gettysburg National Cemetery, where 979 unidentified Union soldiers still rest alongside hundreds of other marked graves. Today, the National Soldier's Monument towers where Lincoln once delivered his legendary Gettysburg Address. Sights here are heavily historical; each year thousands of visitors from north and south of the Mason-Dixon line visit to retrace the movements of Generals Meade and Lee.

⊠ PRACTICAL INFORMATION. Inaccessible by Greyhound or Amtrak, Gettysburg is in south-central Pennsylvania, about 30 mi. south of Harrisburg and a straight shot along U.S. 15. The **Gettysburg Convention and Visitors Bureau,** 102 Carlisle St., has maps and brochures. (☎800-337-5015; www.gettysburgcvb.com. Open daily 8:30am-5pm.) **Post office:** 115 Buford Ave. (☎337-3781 or 800-275-8777. Open M-F 8am-4:30pm, Sa 9am-noon.) **Postal Code:** 17325.

⌂ ACCOMMODATIONS. From downtown Gettysburg, follow Carlisle St./Rte. 34 N. (north of the traffic circle) to Rte. 233 to reach the closest hostel, ◙**Ironmasters Mansion Hostel (HI) ❶,** 1212 Pine Grove Rd., 20 mi. from Gettysburg, within Pine Grove Furnace State Park. Large and luxurious, the building holds 46 beds in a tranquil area. Spacious porches, an ornate dining room, a piano, and a decadent jacuzzi make this hostel seem more like a resort. (☎486-7575. Kitchen, laundry, ping-pong, volleyball. Internet access $3 per 15min. Linen $2. Reception 7:30-9:30am and 5-10pm. Reservations recommended year-round, required in Jan. Dorms $23, members $20.) Many motels line Steinwehr Rd. near the battlefield, but finding summer rates below $100 is difficult in downtown. For those willing to sacrifice proximity to attractions, the **Red Carpet Inn** ❸, 2450 Emmitsburg Rd., 4 mi. south of Military Park, has a pool and comfortable rooms with A/C. (☎334-1345 or 800-336-1345. Singles and doubles $70-$100. AAA discount.) The gracious hosts at **The Brickhouse Inn** ❺, 452 Baltimore St., in downtown, offer 14 mid-to-upscale B&B rooms in two Victorian houses, one of which continues to bear the scars of gunfire from the war. (☎338-9337 or 800-864-3464; www.brickhouseinn.com. Breakfast and parking included. Check-in 3:30-8pm. Check-out 11am. Rooms in summer $109-159; in winter less; check website for specials.) **Artillery Ridge** ❶, 610 Taneytown Rd., 1 mi. south of the Military Park Visitors Center, maintains over 200 campsites with access to hot showers, laundry, a pond, a pool, and stables. (☎334-1288; www.artilleryridge.com. Open Apr.-Oct. daily; Nov. Sa-Su. Sites $31, with partial hookup $39, with full hookup $42. Each additional adult $4, child $2.)

❏ FOOD. In addition to its battlefields' scenic beauty, Gettysburg features a downtown area full of small shops and lively restaurants. Hefty rations prevail in the town's square and just beyond the battlefield entrance. Vegetarians would do well to seek out the sizable salads on most tavern menus since there aren't many other options. Local nightlife takes the form of saloons that cluster around the central square. In Gettysburg's first building (c. 1776), now the ▩**Dobbin House Tavern** ❸, 89 Steinwehr Ave., patrons can create their own grilled burger ($6-7) and view an Underground Railroad shelter. For finer dining, the tavern also serves elegant entrees for $20-32. (☎334-2100; www.dobbinhouse.com. Salads $6. Sandwiches $8. Open daily 11:30am-9pm.) At **Kilwins** ❶, 37 Steinwehr Ave., guests indulge in ice cream (cones $3-4) and assorted confectionery staples. The peanut fudge ($15 per lb.; free ½ lb. with 1 lb. purchase) is as addictive as it is pricey. (☎337-2252. Open M-Th and Su 11am-10pm, F-Sa 11am-midnight.)

◧ SIGHTS. A sensible starting point is the **National Military Park Visitors Information Center**, 97 Taneytown Rd., which distributes free maps for an 18 mi. self-guided driving tour. Ranger walks are also available by reservation. (☎334-1124, ext. 431, ranger walk reservations 877-438-8929; www.nps.gov/gett. Visitors Center open daily June-Aug. 8am-6pm; Sept.-May 8am-5pm. Park open daily 6am-10pm. Free.) An electronic map inside the Visitors Center uses lights to show the course of the Battle of Gettysburg. ($4, seniors $3, under 15 $2.) Be prepared to spend some extra cash for an in-depth look at the historic grounds. The Visitors Center bookstore carries a variety of **audio driving tours** (2hr.; CD $13-18, cassette $11-12). For a personalized experience, one of the ▩**licensed battlefield guides** will squeeze into the family car to guide visitors through the monuments, narrating and answering questions. (☎334-1124, ext. 470; www.gettysburgtourguides.com. 2hr. tours 8am-close. 1-6 people $45, 7-15 people $65, 16-49 people $100. Arrive by 9am to ensure a time slot or pay a surcharge to reserve in advance. Cash or traveler's checks only.) The chilling sights and sounds of battle surround the audience at the **Cyclorama Center**, a short walk down Taneytown Rd. from the Visitors Center. The Center shows "Gettysburg 1863" (20min., begins 5min. after the hr.), "The American Civil War" (10min., 35min. after the hr.), and a 20min. light show (every 30min.) around a 9500 sq. ft. mural of the battle. The "cyclorama" itself is an 1824 oil painting of Pickett's Charge that is 26 ft. high and 356 ft. in circumference. (☎334-1124, ext. 422. Open daily 9am-5pm. Last show 4:30pm. $3, seniors $2.50, ages 6-16 $2. Cash or traveler's checks only.) Bus tours to the

Eisenhower House and Farm include a 20min. house tour and self-guided tour of the grounds. (Departures every 30min. 9am-4pm. $6, ages 13-16 $4.50, ages 6-12 $3.50.) Artillery Ridge Campgrounds (see **Accommodations,** above) conducts **horseback tours.** (1hr. horseback tour $38, 2hr. horseback and history tour $62. No one under 8 or more than 240 lb.) Adjacent to the campground office is a meticulously detailed **diorama** of the Gettysburg battle, along with other exhibits ($4.50, children and seniors $3.50). **Historic Tours** shuttles visitors around the battlefield in double-decker buses. (☎334-8000; www.gettysburg.com. 2½hr. tours $20, AAA and AARP members $19, children $13.)

The ■**Shriver House,** 309 Baltimore St., a museum dedicated to the civilian experience of the Civil War, features energetic tour guides in period costume. A house tour covers daily 19th-century life as revealed in the diary of a wartime inhabitant of the house. The tour also showcases relics discovered under the floorboards of the house's attic and takes visitors deep into the cellar, where the original owner once ran a saloon. (☎337-2800; www.schriverhouse.com. Open Apr.-Nov. M-Sa 10am-5pm, Su noon-5pm; Dec. and Feb.-Mar. Sa-Su noon-5pm. $7, seniors $6.50, ages 6-12 $4.75.) Based on the chilling tales told by author Mark Nesbitt, a former park ranger and inhabitant of a haunted Gettysburg house, candlelit **Ghosts of Gettysburg,** 271 Baltimore St., reawakens the war's dead. Three different tours, covering different parts of the town and their resident ghosts, run each night. (☎337-0445; www.ghostsofgettysburg.com. Tours Mar.-Nov. 8, 8:15, 9, 9:45pm; call for low-season times. Reservations recommended. $8-8.50, under 8 free.) Don't miss the living history programs or the disturbingly lifelike multimedia presentations on display at the **American Civil War Museum,** 297 Steinwehr Ave., across from the Military Park entrance. (☎334-6245; www.e-gettysburg.com. Open Mar.-Dec. daily 9am-8:15pm; Jan.-Feb. weekends and holidays only. $5.50, ages 13-17 $3.50, ages 6-12 $2.50, under 6 free. Cash or traveler's checks only.)

PITTSBURGH   ☎412

While other Rust Belt cities staggered and stumbled after the steel industry fell flat, Pittsburgh dusted itself off and transformed into a center for higher education, health care, and robotics. The city has not had an easy time emerging from the shadow of better-touristed Philadelphia; still, it has cultivated a heady music scene, tightly knit ethnic neighborhoods, and an affordable housing market. Streets plunge up and down steep embankments that have prompted some to dub Pittsburgh "a poor man's San Francisco," but abundant riches are in store for the traveler who veers off the beaten path to explore the city's charms.

MID-ATLANTIC

▐ TRANSPORTATION

Airport: Pittsburgh International (PIT; ☎472-3525; www.pitairport.com), 15 mi. west of downtown, encircled by I-279 and Rte. 60. The Port Authority's **28x Airport Flyer** bus serves downtown and Oakland. Runs daily every 20min. 5:45am-midnight. $2.25. **Airlines Transportation Company** (☎472-3180 or 800-991-9890) runs downtown M-F every 30min. 7am-11:40pm; reduced service Sa. $20. Taxi to downtown $35-45.

Trains: Amtrak, 1100 Liberty Ave. (☎471-6170; www.amtrak.com), at Grant St., on the northern edge of downtown, near Greyhound and the post office. Be careful in this area at night. Station open 24hr. To **Chicago** (9½hr., daily 11:59pm, $106), **New York City** (11hr., 3 per day, $60-90), and **Philadelphia** (8-10hr., 2 per day, $45-58).

Buses: Greyhound, 990 2nd Ave. (☎392-6504). Open 24hr. To **Chicago** (10-13hr., 5 per day, $51.50), **Cleveland** (2½-4hr., 6 per day, $25), and **Philadelphia** (6-8hr., 9 per day, $41).

Public Transit: Port Authority of Allegheny County (☎442-2000; www.ridegold.com). Within downtown, subway free and bus free until 7pm. Beyond downtown, bus and light rail $1.75-2.75; transfers $0.50; weekly pass $16.50. Ages 6-11 ½-price.

Taxi: Yellow Cab, ☎321-8100.

✈ 🛈 ORIENTATION AND PRACTICAL INFORMATION

Pittsburgh's downtown, the **Golden Triangle,** is shaped by two rivers (the **Allegheny** to the north and the **Monongahela** to the south) that flow together to form a third river, the **Ohio.** Streets in the Triangle that run parallel to the Monongahela are numbered one through seven. The **University of Pittsburgh** and **Carnegie Mellon University** lie east of the Triangle in Oakland. Be careful in the area north of PNC Park. The city's streets and 40-odd bridges are notoriously difficult to navigate; don't venture into one of Pittsburgh's many dense neighborhoods without getting directions first. The **Wayfinder system** helps tourists and locals alike navigate the city's often confusing streets. The 1500 color-coded signs point the way to major points of interest, business areas, and universities.

Visitor Info: Pittsburgh Convention and Visitors Bureau, 425 6th Ave., 30th fl. (☎281-7711 or 800-359-0758; www.visitpittsburgh.com). Open M-F 8:30am-5:30pm. There are 2 **Visitors Centers,** 1 downtown on Liberty Ave. (open M-F 9am-5pm, Sa 9am-3pm, Su 10am-3pm) and 1 at the airport (open M 9am-4pm, Tu-F 10am-5pm, Sa 10am-6pm, Su 2pm-6pm).

Hotlines: Hate Crime Hotline, ☎820-0111. **Rape Action Hotline,** ☎866-363-7273. Both operate 24hr. **Gay & Lesbian Community Center,** ☎422-0114. Operates M-F 6:30-9:30pm, Sa 3-6pm.

Internet Access: Carnegie Library of Pittsburgh, 4400 Forbes Ave. (☎622-3114). Free. Open M-Th 10am-8pm, F-Sa 10am-5:30pm, Su 1-5pm.

Post Office: 700 Grant St. (☎642-2984). Open M-F 7am-6pm, Sa 7am-2:30pm. **Postal Code:** 15219.

🏕 🏠 CAMPING AND ACCOMMODATIONS

Dealing a major blow to budget travelers, the sole hostel closed in 2004. Those in search of a cheap bed should try along U.S. 60 near the airport or I-79 at Exit 60A.

Motel 6, 211 Beecham Dr. (☎922-9400), off I-79 at Exit 60A. Basic rooms with TV and A/C. Singles $36; doubles $42. AmEx/MC/V. ❷

Bear Run Campground, 184 Badger Hill Rd. (☎724-368-3564 or 888-737-2605), in Portersville, 40min. north of Pittsburgh. From I-79 N, take PA-488 Exit 96, turn right, then turn left on Badger Hill Rd. Next to Morain State Park, the 60-acre Bear Run campground has fishing, hiking, and other outdoor activities. Check-in 4pm. 2-person sites $25, with water and electricity $33, with full hookup $38. 4-person cabins $69; security deposit $30. Each additional adult $10. AmEx/MC/V. ❶

🍴 FOOD

Aside from the pizza joints and bars downtown, **Oakland** is the best place to find a good, inexpensive meal. Collegiate watering holes and cafes pack **Forbes Avenue** around the University of Pittsburgh, while colorful eateries and shops line **Walnut Street** in Shadyside and **East Carson Street** in the South Side. The **Strip District** on Penn Ave. between 16th and 22nd St. (north of downtown along the Allegheny) bustles with Italian, Greek, and Asian cuisine. The Saturday morning **farmers' market** in the Strip District sells an abundance of fresh produce and fish.

MID-ATLANTIC

Pittsburgh

▲▲ ACCOMMODATIONS
Bear Run Campground, **3**
Motel 6, **2**
Outside Inn, **1**

🍴 FOOD
Beehive Coffeehouse
and Desserterie, **4**
The Church Brew Works, **12**
Primanti Brothers, **9**

The Quiet Storm, **10**
Spice Island Tea House, **8**
Zenith, **5**

🍸 NIGHTLIFE
Brillobox, **13**
Garfield Artworks, **11**
Jack's, **6**
Mr. Roboto Project, **14**
Pegasus Lounge, **7**

🍽 **Zenith,** 86 S 26th St. (☎481-4833), at Sarah St. This vegetarian cafe and antiques store rotates its menu every week with seasonal ingredients, but expect an entree to be about $10. If you like the plates or table settings, you can buy them—everything, from the silverware to the tablecloths, is for sale. The antiques store is quite large with a collection of vintage clothing to boot. Open Th-Sa 11am-9pm, Su 11am-3pm. ❸

🍽 **The Church Brew Works,** 3525 Liberty Ave. (☎688-8200). The hand-finished pews and stained-glass windows are right where the diocese left them, but copper and steel brewing equipment have replaced the altar in this church-cum-brewpub. The menu's fussier entrees run over $20, but brick-oven pizzas are a good bet at $9-15. Get the $5 sampler to try all their beers. Pints $3. Open M-Th 11:30am-midnight, F-Sa 11:30am-1am, Su noon-10pm. Kitchen closes M-Th 9:30pm, F-Sa 11pm, Su 9pm. AmEx/D/MC/V. ❹

🍽 **Beehive Coffeehouse and Desserterie,** 1327 E. Carson St. (☎488-4483), on the South Side. With a disco ball, clouds painted on the ceiling, and a lime-green study room crackling with Wi-Fi, Beehive could have been transplanted to Pittsburgh directly from Amsterdam. Art students doodle in their sketchbooks and devour sandwiches, while waifish grungeboys sip yerba mate ($2.20) and hum absentmindedly under their breath. Open M-Th 9am-1am, F-Su 9am-2am. Cash only. ❶

Spice Island Tea House, 253 Atwood St. (☎687-8821), in Oakland. Votive candles and warm earth tones set the mood for deep plates of curry ($8-12.50) and fried rice ($7). A large pot of after-dinner darjeeling ($4) can be a great way to draw out an early-evening date. Open M-Th 11:30am-9pm, F-Sa 11:30am-10pm. D/MC/V. ❷

The Quiet Storm, 5430 Penn Ave. (☎661-9355). From the mismatched armchairs to the retro pinball machine in back, this vegetarian cafe keeps East End hipsters happy with options like the maelstrom quesadilla ($6), served with chickpeas, mushrooms, spinach, and a glob of herbed *tzatziki*. Su brunch 10am-2pm. Open M-F 7:30am-10pm, Sa 9am-10pm, Su 9am-9pm. Cash only. ❷

Primanti Brothers, 46 18th St. (☎263-2142), in the Strip District. Designed for truckers with big appetites and no time for side orders, the cheesesteaks ($5) are piled high with cole slaw, tomato, and french fries. Add on a bowl of Pittsburgh-style chili ($2.75), and wash it all down with an Iron City beer for the true 'Burgh experience. Open 24hr. 4 other locations in the city. Cash only. ❶

◎ SIGHTS

GOLDEN TRIANGLE. The **Golden Triangle** is home to **Point State Park** and its famous 200 ft. fountain. Near the entrance, the **Fort Pitt Museum** is in the shape of the battlements that once guarded the rivers. (☎281-9284; www.fortpittmuseum.com. Open W-Su 9am-5pm. $5, seniors $4, ages 6-17 $2.) The **Monongahela** and **Duquesne Inclines,** in the South Side, hoist visitors up for a view of the Pittsburgh skyline. (Inclines operate M-Sa 5:30am-12:45am, Su 8:45am-midnight. $1.75, ages 6-11 $0.85.)

CARNEGIE'S LEGACY. Industrialist Andrew Carnegie's rise to wealth involved ruthless business practices on par with the other so-called robber barons of America's Gilded Age. After Carnegie sold his empire to New York financiers in 1901, however, he built a legacy for himself as a philanthropist by endowing museums, libraries, and universities. The beloved dinosaur collection at the **Carnegie Museum of Natural History** returns to its home in November 2007 after two years of restoration in New Jersey. (4400 Forbes Ave. ☎622-3131; www.carnegiemuseums.org. Open Tu-Sa 10am-5pm, Su noon-5pm; July-Aug. also M 10am-5pm. $10, seniors $7, ages 3-18 and students $6.) The **Carnegie Museum of Art's** impressive hall of sculpture includes a life-sized replica of the interior of the Parthenon. (440 Forbes Ave. ☎622-3131; www.cmoa.org. Open Tu-Sa 10am-5pm, Su noon-5pm; July-Aug. also M 10am-5pm. $10, seniors $7, children and students $6.) Up on the North Shore, the **Carnegie Science Center,** next to Heinz Field, sends visitors into the bowels of a WWII submarine and gives them aerodynamic foam wings to test a wind tunnel. The SportsWorks annex features a 25 ft. climbing wall and a chance to sprint against a digitally projected Jackie Joyner-Kersee. (1 Allegheny Ave. ☎237-3400; www.carnegiesciencecenter.org. Open M-F and Su 10am-5pm, Sa 10am-7pm. $14, ages 3-18 and seniors $10. OMNIMAX $10/8.)

FLORA AND FAUNA. Just south of the Carnegie museums, the **Phipps Conservatory and Botanical Gardens** has plants from around the world and allows visitors to walk amidst live butterflies. (1 Schenley Park. ☎622-6914; www.phipps.conservatory.org. Open daily 9:30am-5pm; May-Nov. also W-F 7-10pm. $12.50, seniors $11.50, students $11.50, ages 2-18 $7.50; evening admission for non-members $15, for members $7.50.) Northeast of downtown, the **Pittsburgh Zoo & PPG Aquarium** leads visitors through Asian forests and African savannahs, while sharks and stingrays dart around Pennsylvania's only public aquarium. (1 Wild Pl. ☎665-3640 or 800-474-4966; www.pittsburghzoo.com.

Open daily late May-Aug. 9am-6pm; Sept.-Dec. 9am-5pm; Jan.-March 9am-4pm; Apr.-May 9am-5pm. Apr.-Nov. $10, seniors $9, ages 2-13 $8; Dec.-Mar. $8, seniors and ages 2-13 $7. Parking $3.50.) Back on the North Side, the **National Aviary** is home to more than 600 exotic and endangered birds. *(Allegheny West Commons. ☎ 323-7235; www.aviary.org. Open daily 9am-5pm. $9, seniors $8, ages 2-12 $7.50.)*

OTHER SIGHTS. The ⬛**Andy Warhol Museum,** on the North Side, is the world's largest museum dedicated to a single artist. Seven floors of the Pittsburgh native's artwork include his familiar soup cans, oxidation sculptures of urine on metal, and an installation called "Silver Clouds," where visitors can play among floating metallic pillows. *(117 Sandusky St. ☎ 237-8300; www.warhol.org. Open Tu-Th and Sa-Su 10am-5pm, F 10am-10pm. $12, seniors $9, ages 3-18 and students $8; F 5-10pm ½-price)* Deeper into the North Side, ⬛**The Mattress Factory** has dedicated itself to site-specific installation art daring artists to engage with the parameters of a converted warehouse space in creating new pieces. Check the website for directions. Be careful in the surrounding area. *(500 Sampsonia Way, between Brighton and Federal St. ☎ 231-3169; www.mattress.org. Open Tu-F 10am-5pm, Sa 10am-7pm, Su 1-5pm. $9, students and seniors $6, under 12 free; Th ½-price.)* The soaring Gothic spires of the **Cathedral of Learning** have become symbols of the **University of Pittsburgh,** featuring 26 "nationality classrooms" decorated by artists from the city's many ethnic traditions. The stark arches of the Armenian room and the baroque grandeur of the Austrian room are among the most striking. Remarkably, Chancellor John Gabbett Bowman relied on 90,000 $0.10 contributions from the city's schoolchildren to finance the Cathedral's construction. *(☎ 624-6000; www.pitt.edu/~natrooms. Audio tours Sa 9:30am-2:30pm, Su 11am-2:30pm; May-Aug. also M-F 9am-2:30pm. $3, seniors $2, ages 8-18 $0.50.)* In Penn Hills, an eastern suburb of Pittsburgh sits the elegantly carved **Sri Venkateswara (S.V.) Temple,** modeled after a 7th-century temple in the Andhra Pradesh in India; it has become a major pilgrimage site for American Hindus. Non-Hindus can see the Great Hall and observe prayer services. *(1230 S. McCully Dr. ☎ 373-3380; www.svtemple.org. Open M-Th and Sa-Su 9am-8:30pm, F 9am-9:30pm.)*

🎵🎭 ENTERTAINMENT AND NIGHTLIFE

The weekly *City Paper* provides a recommended "Short List" and a comprehensive "Big List" of entertainment options. The three conductors of the acclaimed **Pittsburgh Symphony Orchestra** take their bows at **Heinz Hall,** 600 Penn Ave. (☎ 392-4900; www.pittsburghsymphony.org. Box office open M-F 9am-8pm, Sa noon-4pm. Tickets $19-73; student rush tickets 2hr. before performance $14.) The **Pittsburgh Public Theater** performs at the **O'Reilly Theater,** 621 Penn Ave. (☎ 316-1600; www.ppt.org. Box office open M 10am-5:30pm, Tu-Sa 10am-curtain, Su noon-curtain. Tickets $30-76, students and under 26 $12.) Musicals, ballets, and operas light up the stage at the **Benedum Center,** 719 Liberty Ave. (☎ 456-6666; www.pgharts.org. Box office open M-Sa 9am-9pm, Su noon-6pm. Matinees $23-64, evening shows $20-76; ½-price student tickets to select shows available 1hr. before curtain.) **Pittsburgh Filmmakers,** 477 Melwood Ave., screens indie and foreign films at three theaters around Pittsburgh, and sponsors the **Three Rivers Film Festival** each November. (☎ 681-5449; www.pghfilmmakers.org. Most films $6-10.)

On the North Shore, the **Pirates** (☎ 321-2827; tickets $9-35) round the bases at **PNC Park,** 115 Federal St. The **Steelers** (☎ 323-1200) storm the gridiron down the road at **Heinz Stadium,** but it's nearly impossible to score tickets. The NHL's **Penguins** (☎ 800-642-7367; tickets $20-107) compete at **Mellon Arena. East Carson Street,** on the South Side, is jammed with revelers throughout the week, while the galleries and performance spaces along the **Penn Corridor** echo with the city's best underground music. The **Station Square** complex, across the Smithfield St. Bridge, is another option for boisterous clubs and music venues.

▨ **Brillobox,** 4104 Penn Ave. (☎621-4900). Preserves the vibe of a neighborhood bar downstairs, while its upstairs performance space is one of Pittsburgh's best venues for hearing live indie music. The Christmas lights and mock moose head set the tone at the bar. Su at 6pm there's a homestyle vegan dinner, and trivia night is a flashy multimedia experience extremely popular with locals. Beer $2.50-4. W-Th DJ. F-Sa live music by indie rock and hip-hop acts. Cover Th-F $2-5. AmEx/MC/V.

▨ **Garfield Artworks,** 4931 Penn Ave. (☎361-2262; www.garfieldartworks.com). Displays work by local artists in one of Pittsburgh's hippest music venues for alt-country, folk, and indie rock. With no liquor license, it's the music and the sense of community that keep scenesters coming back. Cover $5-7. Most shows start at 8pm. Call for schedule.

Mr. Roboto Project, 722 Wood St. (☎247-9639; www.therobotoproject.org), in Wilkinsburg. Founded in 1999 as a cooperatively run music venue and magazine library, this unpretentious storefront has become a node of Pittsburgh's punk and hardcore scene with Sept. all-vegan Punks' Picnic and as many as 20 shows per month. Cover $5-7. Most shows start at 7pm. Call for schedule.

Jack's, 1117 E. Carson St. (☎431-3644), at S. 12th St., in the South Side. This rowdy, neon-splashed Pittsburgh institution keeps its doors open 365 days a year; an unpretentious, back-slapping climate makes Jack's an obligatory stop on South Side pub crawls. M hot dogs $0.25. W wings $0.15. Open M-Sa 7am-2am, Su 11am-2am.

Pegasus Lounge, 818 Liberty Ave. (☎281-2131), in downtown. Features a sweaty, jam-packed dance floor thronged by young gay men and their admirers. W drag shows. 21+, Tu and Th-F 18+. Open Tu-Sa 9pm-2am.

▶ DAYTRIPS FROM PITTSBURGH

FALLINGWATER AND KENTUCK KNOB. Fallingwater, 8 mi. north of Ohiopyle on Rte. 381, is a masterpiece by the king of modern architecture, Frank Lloyd Wright. Designed in 1935, the house exemplifies Wright's concept of organic architecture, incorporating original boulders into its structure and striking a perfect symbiosis with its surroundings. The house appears as though it will cascade over the waterfall it sits on, and the water's gentle roar can be heard in every room. (☎724-329-8501; www.paconserve.org. Open mid-Mar. to Nov. Tu-Su 10am-4pm; also some weekends in Dec. and the first 2 weekends in Mar. 10am-3pm. Reservations required. Grounds $6. Tours M-F $16, ages 6-12 $10. In-depth tours $55. Under 9 not allowed.) For a more intimate and quaint Frank Lloyd Wright home, head to the nearby **Kentuck Knob,** on Kentuck Rd., 6 mi. north of U.S. 40, where a guided tour examines the rustic house and the grounds. (☎724-329-1901; www.kentuckknob.com. Open Mar.-Dec. Tu-Su 10am-4pm. Call for reservations. Tours M-F $16, under 18 $10; Sa-Su $15/12. In-depth tours $55.)

OHIOPYLE STATE PARK. Two hours south of Pittsburgh, Ohiopyle's 8 mi. of Class III and IV rapids draws masses each year. Some of the best whitewater rafting in the East, the rapids take about 4-5hr. to conquer. For novices, Class I and II rapids ease rafts down the river. Four outfitters front Rte. 381 in "downtown" Ohiopyle: **White Water Adventurers** (☎800-992-7238; www.wwaraft.com), **Wilderness Voyageurs Outfitters** (☎800-272-4141; wilderness-voyageurs.com), **Laurel Highlands River Tours** (☎800-472-3846), and **Ohiopyle Trading Post** (☎888-644-6795). Trip prices on the Youghiogheny River ("The Yough," pronounced "YOCK" by locals) vary depending on the season, day of the week, length of trip, and difficulty ($20-145). Prices for rentals are more stable. (rafts $17-55 per person; canoes $40-150). In order to float anything without a guide, you need a **launch permit** from the park office. (☎724-329-8592. M-F free, Sa-Su $2.50. $3 shuttle fee. Call at least 2 weeks in advance for Sa permits. Rental companies provide free permits.) Ohiopyle also offers biking, fishing, rock climbing, and camping opportunities. The **Visitors Center,** off Rte. 381 on Sheridan St., has info on the park and surroundings. (☎ 724-329-1127, camping reservations 888-727-2757. Visitors Center open May-Oct. daily 10am-4:30pm; July-Aug. M-Th 10am-4:30pm, F-Su 10am-7pm; Nov.-Apr. M-F 8am-4pm. Primitive sites $12-17, with full hookup $14-19. Cottages $32-36.)

DELAWARE

Tiny Delaware is a sanctuary of beaches, B&Bs, and tax-free shopping in a region dominated by the sprawling cities of New York, Philadelphia, and Washington, D.C. Though Delaware was first explored by Henry Hudson in 1609, it was not until 1664 that it was officially claimed as one of England's 13 colonies in the New World. In 1787, Delaware proudly became the first state to ratify the US Constitution. The more recent history of Delaware centers around the wealthy DuPont clan, whose gunpowder mills evolved into one of the world's biggest chemical companies. Today, Delaware's laid-back mix of city and shore attracts visitors in search of a break from the Mid-Atlantic's hustle and bustle, while its favorable tax laws offer local businesses a different kind of break.

⁊ PRACTICAL INFORMATION

Capital: Dover.

Visitor Info: Delaware State Visitors Center, 406 Federal St., Dover 19901 (☎302-739-4266; www.destatemuseums.org/vc). Open M-Sa 8am-4:30pm, Su 1:30-4:30pm.

Postal Abbreviation: DE. **Sales Tax:** 8% on accommodations only.

WILMINGTON/BRANDYWINE VALLEY ☎302

In 1683, a Swedish ship, the *Kalmar Nyckel*, sailed from Europe to the banks of what was then called the "South River," leaving its passengers to successfully establish the colony of New Sweden. Originally the epicenter of the DuPont manufacturing empire, modern Wilmington has morphed into a major financial hub, though it maintains a close connection to its industrial roots. While businesspeople jet in and out of the city throughout the week, weekend visitors are drawn to the natural beauty of the Brandywine Valley and the colonial charm of the DuPont estates that surround the city.

⁊⁊ ORIENTATION AND PRACTICAL INFORMATION. Wilmington is situated in northern Delaware, across the Delaware Memorial Bridge from New Jersey. **I-95** connects Wilmington to Philadelphia 29 mi. to the north and Baltimore 76 mi. to the southwest. Downtown Wilmington is set up on a grid of one-way streets. Numbered streets run east-west starting from the south, while named streets run north-south. The two major roads leading into the downtown are **Martin Luther King, Jr. Boulevard (Route 48)** and **Delaware Avenue (Route 52),** which also runs out of town, toward the DuPont estates. Exercise caution in the area between the restored riverfront and downtown and in the non-riverfront areas south of 8th St. Parking is free at riverfront attractions and curbside on weekends and after 6pm on weekdays. Otherwise, lots charging $5-8 per day can be found through the **Wilmington Parking Authority** (☎655-4442). **Airport: Philadelphia International Airport (PHL;** ☎215-937-6937; www.phl.org) is 20 mi. north of Wilmington on I-95. **Amtrak,** 100 S. French St., runs trains to Boston (5-6½hr., 10 per day, $84) and Washington, D.C. (1½hr., $46). Use caution in this area at night. (☎800-872-7245; www.amtrak.com. Open M-F 5:45am-9:30pm, Sa 6am-8:45pm, Su 6am-9:30pm.) **Greyhound,** 101 N. French St. (☎655-6111; www.greyhound.com), in the Wilmington Transport Center, runs to Boston (9-12hr., $59), New York (4hr., $35), and Washington, D.C. (4-6hr., $22). **DART** runs buses in the Wilmington area: #7 criss-crosses downtown (M-F 8am-4pm), and #32 runs between the riverfront and downtown (M-F 7am-7pm, Sa 7:45am-7:30pm). (☎800-652-3277; www.dartfirststate.com. $1.15; all-day pass $2.40. Bus #32 $0.25 per ride.) For a **taxi,** call **Yellow Cab,** ☎658-4340. **Greater Wilmington Convention and Visitors Bureau** is at 100 W. 10th St., Ste. 20, at Orange St. (☎652-4088 or 800-489-6664; www.visitwilmingtonde.com. Open M-F 9am-5pm.) **Internet Access: Wilmington Public Library,** at 10th and Market St. (☎571-7400. Free. Open M-Th 9am-8pm, F-Sa 9am-5pm.) **Post Office:** 1101 N. King St., at 11th St. (☎800-276-8767. Open M-F 7am-5:30pm, Sa 9am-2pm.) **Postal Code:** 19801.

⌂ ACCOMMODATIONS. Wilmington's hotels cater to businesspeople, so rates tend to be far lower on weekends than during the week. Upscale chains and the city's landmark **Hotel DuPont** can be found on **King Street** downtown. Otherwise, look to **Newark, DE,** just south on I-95, for budget chain motels. **The Inn at Wilmington ❹,** 300 Rocky Run Pkwy., at the Concord Pike (Rte. 202) offers a 24hr. convenience center, continental breakfast, and an exercise room, in addition to spacious accommodations. (☎479-7900 or 800-444-2775. Doubles M-Th and Su from $101-120, F-Sa $97-114.) B&Bs in the Brandywine Valley range from pricey to very pricey. For those willing to splurge, the elegant and relaxing **Faunbrook B&B ❺,** 699 W. Rosedale Ave., in West Chester, PA, 20min. north of Wilmington on Rte. 100, is a perfect base from which to explore the Brandywine River Valley. Faunbrook's Italian-style estate, complete with a vast mahogany porch, boasts seven guest rooms with private baths and two acres of gardens. (☎610-436-5788; www.faunbrook.com. No smoking. 3-course candlelight breakfast included. Check-in 3-9pm. Check-out 11am. Rooms $125-195.) Though there is no camping in the immediate Wilmington vicinity, **Lums Pond State Park ❶,** 1068 Howell School Rd., 30 mi. south of the city, offers a retreat from the urban grind. Drive south on I-95 to Exit 1A (Middleton), onto Rte. 896 S., then follow it 6 mi. until you cross Rte. 40. Turn left onto Howell Rd. at the third light after Rte. 40. Campers have access to bicycle and horseback-riding trails, fishing, flush toilets, rowboat and canoe rentals, and showers. (Reservations ☎368-6989 or 877-987-2757; www.destateparks.com. No alcohol allowed. Rowboats $7 per hr., $35 per day; canoes $8/40. 4-person tent sites $24, with electricity $27. Each additional person $2.)

◨◧ FOOD AND NIGHTLIFE. For simple diner fare, head to the **Sterling Grill ❶,** 919 Orange St., a local breakfast and lunch favorite in the center of town that serves short stacks of pancakes ($2.45) and waffles ($3.50). Add an order of "scrapple," a regional meat medley ($3.50), to satisfy the carnivore in you. (☎652-3575. 9 in. subs $4.15. Open M-F 5:30am-3pm, Sa 7:30am-1pm.) The **Iron Hill Brewery ❹,** 710 S. Madison St., serves Asian fusion cuisine beside a relaxing view of the Brandywine River. Patrons also get a look at the brewing process through a glass display that showcases the pipes, cisterns, and hoppers involved in making beer. (☎472-2739; www.ironhillbrewery.com. Entrees $14-27. Open M-Sa 11:30am-1am, Su 11am-1am. AmEx/D/MC/V.) For mixed drinks in a calmer setting, try the restaurant-bars along the **Riverfront.** Meanwhile, a rowdier crowd gathers at college bars and clubs in the **Trolley Square** area on the northwest side of town, centered around Delaware Ave. **Baxter's,** 2006 Pennsylvania Ave., at Union St., draws a mixed, gay-friendly crowd to its upscale lounge. (☎654-9858; www.baxtersclub.com. W and Su karaoke. 21+. No cover M-Th and Su. Cover varies F-Sa; call ahead. Happy hour M-F 4-7pm; drinks $1 off. Open M-F 4pm-2am, Sa 5pm-2am, Su 6pm-2am.)

◩◪ SIGHTS AND ENTERTAINMENT. The **DuPont estates** are among the most popular attractions in the area. Closest to downtown Wilmington, the **Hagley**

Museum, 1 Brandywine Blvd., emphasizes the home and work life of the DuPonts, with tours of the original family home and black powder works. Mechanical minds flock to see the enormous stone mills, water turbines, steam engines, and powder testers, while techies of all ages may enjoy sitting inside Jeff Gordon's NASCAR racer, complete with a roll cage and steerable wheels. From downtown Wilmington, take I-95 south to Exit 5B (Newport), follow Rte. 141 north for 7 mi., and after crossing Rte. 100 look for the Hagley entrance on the left. (☎658-2400; www.hagley.lib.de.us. Open daily mid-Mar. to Dec. 9:30am-4:30pm; Jan. to mid-Mar. Sa-Su 9:30am-4:30pm, plus a tour M-F 1:30pm. $11, seniors and students $9, ages 6-14 $4.) Botany enthusiasts should not miss the **Winterthur Estate and Gardens,** on Rte. 52, 6 mi. northwest of Wilmington. Samuel DuPont used specific combinations of flowers to create harmony of both color and design. The mansion's interior and furnishings are so extensive that several differently themed guided tours are required to cover it all. (☎888-4600 or 800-448-3883; www.winterthur.org. Open Tu-Su 10am-5pm. Last entry 3:45pm. Guided tours leave frequently; call ahead for info about particular seasonal tours. Garden tram operates Mar.-Dec. Wheelchair-accessible. Garden and gallery pass $15, seniors and students $13, ages 2-11 $5.) The farthest DuPont estate from Wilmington is the **Longwood Gardens,** over 1050 acres of woodlands, meadows, and (surprise!) gardens. Nature lovers will delight in Longwood's fountains, lakes, meadows, open-air theaters, topiaries, and wild and hothouse flowers. Take Rte. 52 northwest 12 mi. from Wilmington, just over the Pennsylvania state line, then turn west onto Rte. 1 and follow it to Kennett Sq. (☎610-388-1000 or 800-737-5500; www.longwoodgardens.org. Open daily Apr.-Oct. 9am-6pm; Nov.-Mar. 9am-5pm. In summer Tu and F-Sa hours extended to 10pm. Wheelchair-accessible. $16, seniors $14, children and students $6.) On Rte. 1, just east of Longwood Gardens in Chadds Ford, PA, the ▧**Brandywine River Museum** displays an extensive collection of the works of N.C., Andrew, and Jaimie Wyeth in a restored mill house. From Wilmington, take Rte. 52 N to Rte. 1 and follow it east approximately 3½ mi. (☎610-388-2700; www.brandywinemuseum.org. Open daily 9:30am-4:30pm. $8; ages 6-12, seniors, and students $5.)

The story of the first Swedish settlers in Delaware is retold daily at **Fort Christina Park** and the **Kalmar Nyckel Shipyard,** 1124 E. 7th St. (☎429-7447 or 888-783-7245; www.kalmarnyckel.org. The *Kalmar Nyckel* still sails on tour Sa in summer; call for hours. $5, students $4, under 12 $3. Pirate-themed trips to Lewes Sa in summer; 3hr., call for departure times. $60, under 17 $40.) At the **Old Swedes Church and Hendrickson House Museum,** 606 Church St., just west of the shipyard, visitors can tour a Swedish farmhouse and church built in the 1690s, as well as the Hendrickson's collection of colonial artifacts. (☎652-5629; www.oldswedes.org. Tours W-Sa 10am-4pm. $2. Church service in summer Su 9:30 and 10am. Free.) The **Delaware History Museum,** 504 Market St. Mall, is home to the interactive exhibit "Distinctively Delaware" and covers over 400 years of history, beginning with the region's Native American inhabitants. (☎656-0637; www.hsd.org. Open Tu-F 11am-4pm, Sa 10am-4pm. $4, seniors $3, under 18 $2.)

Music, theater, and dance venues cluster in the downtown area, particularly on **Market Street.** The **Grand Opera House,** 818 N. Market St. (☎652-5577), the ornate cream-colored home of OperaDelaware, also presents Broadway-bound shows for much less than the cost of tickets in a larger city and even hosts the occasional pop-music performance.

REHOBOTH BEACH ☎302

Rehoboth Beach lies between Lewes and Ocean City both geographically and culturally. While Lewes tends to be quiet and family-oriented and Ocean City attracts rowdy high-schoolers, Rehoboth manages to balance discount-boardwalk fun with serene, historic B&Bs. The outlet mall on Rte. 1 on the way into town floods Rehoboth with bargain hunters eager to snag tax-free Delaware deals all year long. On summer weekends, the beach is a zoo, packed end to end with vacationing families and the town's burgeoning gay population.

■ ▮ **ORIENTATION AND PRACTICAL INFORMATION.** To reach Rehoboth, take **Route 1B** to **Rehoboth Avenue** and follow it to the water. Parking near the beach is a rare commodity—rather than worry constantly about the pesky meter monitors, drop your friends and family off at the beach with your gear and find a parking spot off the main drag. Most parking spots on side streets are either metered or require a permit (before 5pm). The southern end of Rehoboth Ave. is lined with shops and small restaurants; hotel accommodations tend to be farther north.

Greyhound/Trailways, 801 Rehoboth Ave. (☎227-1080 or 800-454-2487; www.greyhound.com), runs buses to Boston (11hr., $49), Philadelphia (4hr., $29), and Washington D.C. (3½ hr., $29). The 1¾hr. **ferry** to Cape May is the best option for island-hopping. (☎800-643-3779; www.capemaylewesferry.com. Office open daily 8:30am-4:30pm. 8 per day. Reservations required; call at least 24hr. in advance. Check-in 30min. prior to departure. Apr.-Oct. $29 per car, $24 per motorcyclist, $9.50 per pedestrian or bicyclist; Nov.-Mar. $23/18/7.) The **Rehoboth Beach Chamber of Commerce,** 501 Rehoboth Ave., around the traffic circle next to an imitation lighthouse, provides info on area attractions, dining, and accommodations. (☎227-2233 or 800-441-1329; www.beach-fun.com. Open M-F 9am-5pm, Sa-Su 9am-1pm.) **Internet Access: Rehoboth Beach Public Library,** 226 Rehoboth Ave. (☎227-8044. Free. Open M and F 10am-5pm, Tu and Th noon-8pm, W 10am-8pm, Sa 10am-3pm). **Post Office:** 179 Rehoboth Ave., at 2nd St. (☎227-8406. Open M-F 9am-5pm, Sa 8:30am-12:30pm.) **Postal Code:** 19971.

▮ ▯ **ACCOMMODATIONS AND FOOD.** Inexpensive lodging in Rehoboth disappears as the summer season reaches its peak. Unless you want to spend over $100 (or, more likely, over $200), forget staying on the Boardwalk. The comfortable, B&B-style **Abbey Inn ❸,** 31 Maryland Ave., is just a block from Rehoboth Ave. (☎227-7023. 2-night min. stay. Open late May-early Sept. Singles and doubles with shared bath from $58; larger rooms from $68. Weekends 15% more.) The Kandler family owns and operates the **Pirate's Cove Motel ❹,** 625 Rehoboth Ave., and prides itself on the clean rooms. (☎227-2844; www.rehobothbeach.com/piratescove. A/C and cable TV. Rooms $89-169. Peak rates in July. AmEx/D/MC/V.) Just off of Rehoboth Ave., three long blocks from the beach, the **High Seas Motel ❹,** 12 Christian St., provides cable TV, a microwave, and a mini-fridge in each simple, comfortable room. (☎227-2022. Rooms Apr.-May M-F $35-55, Sa-Su $60-85; June-early Sept. M-F $65-100, Sa-Su $100-130; Memorial, Independence, and Labor Day weekends $120-150. AmEx/D/MC/V.) **Big Oaks Family Campground ❶,** 1 mi. off Rte. 1 on Rte. 270, has a bus to the beach, a general store, laundry, and a pool. (☎645-6838. Tent sites $38, RV sites $45.)

Rehoboth is known for its high-quality beach cuisine, but a lot of it comes at resort prices. At the charming **Back Porch Cafe ❹,** 59 Rehoboth Ave., just blocks from the beach, you can enjoy a healthy gourmet lunch on the open-air patio. Go for its tasty lunch entrees ($11-14) or dinner dishes ($28-36), or revel in its live music and art shows, hosted occasionally. (☎227-3674. Su brunch 11am-3pm. Open daily 11am-3pm and 6-10pm.) At **Cafe Papillon ❷,** 42 Rehoboth Ave., in the Penny Lane Mall, French cooks serve fresh crepes, croissants, pastries, and sandwiches. (☎227-7568. Crepes $3-8. Sandwiches $5-8. Open June-Aug. M-Sa 8am-11pm; call for hours in May and Sept. Cash only.) **Royal Treat ❷,** 4 Wilmington Ave., flips pancakes and bacon for just $6.75. Omelets start at $6.25. (☎227-6277. Open June-Aug. daily 8am-11:30pm. Breakfast served until 11:30am.)

🎵 **NIGHTLIFE.** Rehoboth partygoers head out early to maximize time before 1am last calls. **The Summer House Saloon,** 228 Rehoboth Ave., across from City Hall, is by night a favorite flirtation spot for college-aged singles. (☎227-3895; www.summerhousesaloon.com. M ½-price burgers. Th live blues-rock 9:30pm-1:30am. F live DJ 9pm-1am. Su ½-price daquiris 4-8pm. Open May-Sept. M and Sa-Su 4pm-1am, Tu-F 5pm-1am. AmEx/D/MC/V.) Look for live music on weekends at **Dogfish Head Brewings & Eats,** 320 Rehoboth Ave. Try one of their 13 award-winning homemade microbrews, or get a five-beer sampler for $5. (☎226-2739; www.dog-fish.com. Happy hour M-F 3-6pm; $1 off appetizers and Dogfish's homemade beer. F-Sa live music 10pm-1am. Open May-Aug. M-Th 4-11pm, F 4pm-1am, Sa noon-1am, Su noon-11pm; Sept.-Apr. M and Th 4pm-midnight, F 4pm-1am, Sa noon-1am, Su noon-11pm.) **The Frogg Pond,** on the corner of 1st St. and Rehoboth Ave., caters to a diverse crowd of locals, tourists, twentysomethings, and seniors, and is known for serving the best Buffalo wings and quesadillas (both $8) in town. (☎227-2234. Happy hour M-F 4-7pm. Th karaoke. F-Sa live music. Open M-Sa 11am-1am.)

MARYLAND

Once upon a time, folks on Maryland's rural eastern shore trapped crabs, raised tobacco, and ruled the state. Meanwhile, across the bay in Baltimore, workers loaded ships and ran factories. Then the federal government expanded, industry shrank, and Maryland had a new focal point: the Baltimore-Washington Pkwy. As a result, suburbs grew, Baltimore was revitalized, and the Old Line State gained a new, liberal urbanity. Still, even as D.C.'s generic suburbs swell and Baltimore revels in its immensity, Annapolis—the state capital—remains a small town of sailors.

🔢 PRACTICAL INFORMATION

Capital: Annapolis.

Visitor Info: Office of Tourism, 217 E. Redwood St., 9th fl., Baltimore 21202 (☎866-639-3526; www.mdisfun.org).

Postal Abbreviation: MD. **Sales Tax:** 5%.

BALTIMORE ☎410

Nicknamed "Charm City" for its mix of small-town hospitality and big-city flair, Baltimore impresses visitors with its lively restaurant and bar scene, first-class museums, and devotion to history. The city's pulse lies beyond its star attraction, the glimmering Inner Harbor, in Baltimore's overstuffed markets, coffee shops, and diverse citizenry. The city's Southern heritage is evident in Roland Park, where friendly neighbors greet you from front porches in a "Bawlmer" accent. Though it would be unwise to head into Baltimore expecting to find only the shining tourist sights, gentrification and restoration efforts have succeeded in returning the Inner Harbor, Fells Point, Camden Yards, and Canton to their former glory, complete with attractive, walkable streets.

🚊 TRANSPORTATION

Airport: Thurgood Marshall Baltimore-Washington International (BWI; ☎859-7111; www.bwiairport.com), on I-195 off the Baltimore-Washington Pkwy. (I-295), about 10 mi. south of the city. Take MTA bus #17 to the Nursery Rd. light rail station. Airport **shuttles** to hotels (☎703-416-6661 or 800-258-3826; www.supershuttle.com) run daily every 30min. 5:45am-11:30pm. $11 to downtown. Shuttles leave for D.C. daily every hr. 5:45am-11:30pm ($26-34). **Amtrak** trains from BWI run to Baltimore ($14) and D.C. ($14). **MARC** commuter trains run M-F to Baltimore ($3.25) and D.C. ($5).

Trains: Penn Station, 1500 N. Charles St., at Mt. Royal Ave. Easily accessible by bus #3 or 11 from Charles Station downtown, or by Light Rail to the University of Baltimore/ Mount Royal stop. **Amtrak** (www.amtrak.com) trains run every 30min.-1hr. to **New York City** (2½-3hr., 10 per day, $76), **Philadelphia** (1hr., 10 per day, $47), and **Washington, D.C.** (45min., 10 per day, $17). On weekdays, **MARC commuter rail** (☎539-5000) connects to D.C.'s Union Station from Penn Station (with stops at BWI; $7) or **Camden Station,** at Howard and Camden St. Ticket office open daily 5:30am-9:30pm; self-serve ticketing kiosks available 24hr.

Buses: Greyhound (☎800-231-2222; www.greyhound.com) has 2 locations: downtown at 2110 Haines St. (☎752-7682); and 5625 O'Donnell St. (☎633-6389), 3 mi. east of downtown, at Exit 57 off I-95, just north of the toll tunnel. To **New York City** ($38), **Philadelphia** ($22), and **Washington, D.C.** ($14).

Public Transit: Mass Transit Administration (MTA), 300 W. Lexington St. (☎866-743-3682, schedule info 539-5000 M-F 6am-7pm; www.mtamaryland.com), near N. Howard St. Bus, Metro, and Light Rail service to most major sights in the city. Some buses run 24hr. Metro runs M-F 5am-midnight, Sa 6am-midnight. Light Rail runs M-F 6am-11pm, Sa 8am-11pm, Su 11am-7pm. $1.60, disabled and seniors $0.55; higher on Light Rail to outer suburbs. Day pass $3.50.

Water Taxi: Harbor Boating, 1732 Thames St. (☎563-3901 or 800-658-8947; www.thewatertaxi.com). Main stop in Inner Harbor; other stops at harbor museums and restaurants, Harborplace, Fells Point, and Little Italy. Runs Apr.-Oct. every 15min.; Nov.-Mar. every 40min. Service May-Aug. M-Th 10am-11pm, F-Sa 10am-midnight, Su 10am-9pm; Apr. and Sept.-Oct. M-Th 11am-8pm, F 11am-midnight, Sa 10am-midnight, Su 10am-8pm; Nov.-Mar. daily 11am-6pm. Day pass $8, under 10 $4.

Taxi: American Cab, ☎636-8300. **Arrow Cab,** ☎261-0000.

✦✦ 🏷 ORIENTATION AND PRACTICAL INFORMATION

Baltimore lies 35 mi. north of D.C. and about 150 mi. west of the Atlantic Ocean. From D.C., take the **Baltimore-Washington Parkway.** Exit 53 from Rte. 395 leads right into the **Inner Harbor;** without traffic, the trip takes less than 1hr. **Baltimore Street** (east-west) and **Charles Street** (north-south) divide the city. The **Inner Harbor,** at Pratt and Charles St., is home to historic ships and attractions. **Little Italy,** served by city buses #7 and 10, sits on the bay a few blocks east of the Inner Harbor, past the Jones Falls Expressway. A short walk to the southeast brings you to bar-happy **Fells Point,** also served by city bus #10. Be careful: moving north or east from Fells Point, away from the waterfront, will lead you into dangerous neighborhoods. The trendy **Mount Vernon** neighborhood, home to museums, bars and theaters, occupies **North Charles Street,** north of Baltimore St., around **Monument Street** and **Centre Street:** it is served by city buses #3 and 11 and by the Light Rail (Centre Street stop). Old-fashioned **Federal Hill,** accessed by city buses #1 and 64, contains Fort McHenry. Use caution in Federal Hill and areas to the south. The **Camden Yards** baseball stadium and M&T Bank Stadium lie across I-395 from Federal Hill. Venturing more than a few blocks north of Camden Yards will place you in the historic, but dangerous, West Side.

Visitor Info: Baltimore Area Visitors Center, 401 Light St. (☎877-225-8466; www.baltimore.org). Provides maps, brochures, and the free *Quickguide.* Open daily 9am-6pm.

Hotlines: Suicide Line, ☎531-6677. **Sexual Assault and Domestic Violence,** ☎828-6390. Both 24hr. **Gay and Lesbian Line,** ☎837-8888. Operates daily 7pm-midnight.

Downtown Baltimore

▲ ACCOMMODATIONS
Aunt Rebecca's B&B, 4
Mr. Mole B&B, 1

🍴 FOOD
Attman's Deli, 6

Babalu Grill, 7
The Helmand, 2
Rusty Scupper, 9

🎭 NIGHTLIFE
Fletcher's, 8
Grand Central, 3
Howl At The Moon, 5

Internet Access: Library, 400 Cathedral St. (☎396-5430; www.pratt.lib.md.us). Free. Open M-W 11am-7pm, Th 10am-5:30pm, F-Sa 10am-5pm; Oct.-May also Su 1-5pm.

Post Office: 900 E. Fayette St. (☎347-4202). Open M-F 7:30am-10pm, Sa 8:30am-5pm. **Postal Code:** 21233.

ACCOMMODATIONS

Expensive hotels dominate the Inner Harbor. To reserve B&Bs, contact **Bed and Breakfast Accommodations, Ltd.** (☎413-582-9888; www.bedandbreakfastdc.com. From $65 per night. Open M-F 9am-5pm.)

▨ **Aunt Rebecca's B&B,** 106 E. Preston St. (☎625-1007; www.auntrebeccasbnb.com), at N. Calvert St. in Mount Vernon. Full of gilded mirrors and chandeliers. Only 3 bedrooms, but if you book one you'll save big over downtown hotels. Free parking. Queen bedroom with full breakfast $100; each additional person $15. AmEx/D/MC/V. ❺

Mr. Mole Bed and Breakfast, 1601 Bolton St. (☎728-1179; www.mrmolebb.com), in Bolton Hill. This small B&B offers its 5 suites for the same price as standard rooms downtown. A/C, Dutch breakfast, phone, and private bath. Suites from $149. AmEx/D/MC/V. ❺

Capitol KOA, 768 Cecil Ave. (☎923-2771 or 800-562-0248), in Millersville, 20min. from Baltimore. Take I-97 south 8½ mi. to Exit 10A (Benfield Blvd. E). Turn right at the KOA sign. Mostly RVs, some cabins, and a small wooded area for tents. Pool, playground, toilets, and showers. Free shuttle to MARC train Odenton Station M-F; to New Carrollton Metro Sa-Su. Open Mar. 25-Nov. 1. 2-person sites $33-41, with water and electricity $38-54, with full hookup $43-57. 1-room cabin $58-69; each additional person $5. ❷

FOOD

For cheap eats, locals flock to **Lexington Market** (Metro: Lexington Market), a panoply of independent food stands serving everything from fried chicken and crab cakes to Polish sausage. Better-known chain restaurants are clustered in the Inner Harbor's **Harborplace.** The smaller **Cross Street Market** in Federal Hill is a charming, characteristically Baltimorean food pavilion similar to Lexington.

▨ **Babalu Grill,** 32 Market Pl. (☎234-9898), in Power Plant Live. Cuban sides like rice and beans ($4) go well with creative entrees like lobster and coconut rice ($31). Turns into a hot salsa club F-Sa nights (cover $5 10-11pm, $10 after 11pm). Open Tu-Th 5pm-10pm, F-Sa 5pm-11pm. Club open F-Sa 11pm-2am. AmEx/D/MC/V. ❹

The Helmand, 806 N. Charles St. (☎752-0311; www.helmand.com). The best Afghan restaurant in town, with dishes like *kabuli* (rice baked with chunks of lamb tenderloin, raisins, and glazed carrots; $14). Plenty of vegetarian options and enough desserts to satisfy any sweet tooth. Open M-Th and Su 5-10pm, F-Sa 5-11pm. AmEx/D/MC/V. ❷

The Rusty Scupper, 402 Key Hwy. (☎727-3678), in the Inner Harbor. A landmark, serving fresh seafood with a waterfront view. The "waterman's po' boy," with oysters or popcorn shrimp ($10) is justly famous. Su jazz brunch 11am-2pm. Open M-Th 11:30am-10pm, F-Sa 11:30am-11pm, Su 10am-10pm. AmEx/D/MC/V. ❹

Attman's Deli, 1019 E. Lombard St. (☎563-2666), on Baltimore's Corned Beef Row. Has made a name for itself serving hot pastrami ($6) and corned beef sandwiches ($6) just like you'd find in New York City. An intimate crowd and friendly staff make it feel like home. Open M-Sa 8am-6:30pm, Su 8am-5pm. MC/V. ❷

SIGHTS

Downtown Baltimore ends with a colorful bang in the **Inner Harbor,** a body of water surrounded by five blocks of eateries, museums, and boardable ships.

■**THE NATIONAL AQUARIUM.** The **National Aquarium** is one of the US's best places to ogle and learn about sealife. Though a visit to the outdoor sea pool to watch slap-happy seals play is free to the general public, it is worth the time and money to venture inside. The eerie **Wings in the Water** exhibit showcases 50 species of stingrays in an immense backlit pool. In the steamy **Tropical Rainforest,** piranhas, parrots, and a pair of two-toed sloths peer through the dense foliage in a 157 ft. glass pyramid. At the **Marine Mammal Pavilion,** dolphins perform every hour on the half-hour. Plan about 2hr. for the tour of the entire aquarium. *(Pier 3, 501 E. Pratt St., in the Inner Harbor. ☎576-3800; www.aqua.org. Open July-Aug. M-Th and Su 9am-6pm, F-Sa 9am-8pm; Mar.-June and Sept.-Oct. M-Th and Sa-Su 9am-5pm, F 9am-8pm; Nov.-Feb. M-Th and Sa-Su 10am-5pm, F 10am-8pm. Last entry 1½hr. before closing. $22, seniors $20, children $13; with admission to dolphin show $25/24/14. Tickets are sold for a particular entrance time on busy summer days and can be purchased in advance online.)*

BALTIMORE MARITIME MUSEUM. Several ships grace the harbor by the aquarium, most of which belong to the Baltimore Maritime Museum. Visitors may clamber through the **USS Torsk,** the intricately-painted submarine that sank the last WWII Japanese combat ship, or board one of the survivors of the Pearl Harbor attack, the Coast Guard cutter **Roger B. Taney,** and ascend the **octagonal lighthouse** on Pier 5. For these historic sites and more, purchase the **Seaport Day Pass,** which grants access to the **Maritime Museum,** the **Museum of Industry,** and the **USS Constellation,** the last all-sail warship built by the US Navy. The pass also includes admission to Baltimore's **World Trade Center,** the world's tallest pentagonal building, which offers an overhead view of the city from its observation deck. Water taxi service to and from attractions is included. *(Piers 3 and 5. ☎396-3453; http://baltomaritimemuseum.org. In the summer the Taney is open daily 10am-5:30pm; the Chesapeake lightboat 10am-6pm; the Torsk 10am-8:30pm. All boats open in spring and fall M-Th and Su 10am-5pm, F-Sa 10am-6pm; in winter F-Su 10am-5pm. Last entry 1hr. before closing. $7, seniors $6, ages 5-13 $4. Seaport Day Pass $24.50, seniors $22, ages 15-17 $16.75, ages 6-14 $13.75.)*

MARYLAND SCIENCE CENTER. From the prehistoric to the futuristic, the **Maryland Science Center** is a kid- and adult-friendly museum that explores the mysteries of science in everyday life. The Hubble Space Telescope Visitors Center and the Davis Planetarium are perfect for space enthusiasts, and children will dig the dinosaur dig exhibit. An impressive IMAX theatre features a rotating series of films, with frequent new additions. *(601 Light St. ☎685-5225; www.marylandsciencecenter.org. Open in summer M-W and Su 10am-6pm, Th-Sa 10am-8pm; in low season Tu-F 10am-5pm, Sa 10am-6pm, Su noon-5pm. $16.25, military and seniors $15.25, children $11.75. Traveling exhibit $5.50/5.50/4. IMAX tickets $8.)*

WALTERS ART MUSEUM. Spanning 50 centuries, the **Walters Art Museum** houses one of the world's largest private art collections. The museum's pride and joy is its ancient art, featuring sculpture, jewelry, and metalwork from Egypt, Greece, and Rome. Byzantine, Romanesque, and Gothic art are also on display. At the **Hackerman House,** a mansion attached to the Walters, rooms filled with dark furniture, patterned rugs, and velvet curtains display Asian and South Asian art. Just north of the museum is Baltimore's **Washington Monument,** which predates the more famous iteration in Washington, D.C., and is in fact the first monument to honor the life of the first president of the US. *(600 N. Charles St. Take bus #3 or 11. ☎547-9000; www.thewalters.org. Permanent collection free. Free audio tour available on request.)*

FORT MCHENRY. After watching the British troops bombard this harbor fort during the war of 1812, Francis Scott Key was inspired to compose the Star-Spangled Banner, which would become the National Anthem of the US in 1931. The first official 49- and 50-star American flags were flown here and can still be viewed by the public. Other items of note are the cannons used to defend Baltimore from attack,

LOCAL LEGEND

THE DEATH OF POE

In late September 1849, Edgar Allan Poe boarded a train in Richmond, VA, bound for New York; a week later, he was discovered on a Baltimore street in a state of delirium. He was taken to a nearby hospital, where in early morning hours of October 7, he died mysteriously.

Poe was just 40 years old, and had in the years prior enjoyed great success as a writer. In his best-known work, "The Raven" (1845), Poe writes about a man trying to forget a lost love. For him, the events of the poem would prove sadly prophetic: in 1847, two years after the poem was published, his wife (and cousin) Virginia died suddenly at the age of 24. An inconsolable Poe traveled around aimlessly writing, drinking and grieving.

To this day, no one knows the exact cause of Poe's death. Alcohol poisoning was the official explanation, but this was disputed by an attending physician. Seizures, cholera and even rabies are all common theories.

The Poe mystery is alive and well in Baltimore. Every year for the past 58 years, a shadowy figure arrives on the morning of Poe's birthday at the poet's grave on Amity St. He then drinks a shot of cognac and leaves the bottle and three roses on the grave.

For more information, call the Poe House and Museum (☎ 396-7932).

which are still fired on occasion, and the prisons in which Confederate captives were housed during the American Civil War. (☎ 962-4290; www.nps.gov/fomc. 2400 E. Fort Avenue; take the water taxi from the Inner Harbor or Bus #1. $7, under 15 free.)

EDGAR ALLAN POE HOUSE. American mystery and suspense pioneer Edgar Allan Poe made this Amity St. house his home for a time in the 1830s. In between doses of opium, Poe penned famous stories such as *The Tell-Tale Heart* and *The Pit and the Pendulum*, as well as his poems *The Raven* and *Annabel Lee*. Now a preserved historical landmark, the house shows exhibits about its former owner and is impeccably maintained by a staff eager to regale visitors with all sorts of Poe stories. Steer clear of this neighborhood at night. *(203 N. Amity St., near Saratoga St. Take bus #15 or 23. From Lexington Market, walk on N. Lexington St. away from downtown and turn right on Amity St. It is the 2nd house on the right. ☎ 396-7932. Open Aug.-Dec. W-Sa noon-3:45pm. $3, active military and under 13 free.)*

JOHNS HOPKINS UNIVERSITY. Approximately 3 mi. north of the harbor, prestigious **Johns Hopkins University (JHU)** spreads out over the Roland Park neighborhood. Hopkins was the first research university in the country and remains a world leader in developments in the research and study of medicine, public health, and engineering. The campus was originally the Homewood estate of Charles Carroll, Jr., the son of the longest-lived signer of the Declaration of Independence. Free 1hr. campus tours begin at the **Office of Admissions** in Garland Hall. *(3400 N. Charles St. Take bus #3 or 11. ☎ 516-8171; http://apply.jhu.edu/visit/ guidedtours.html. Tours Sept.-May M-F 10am and 1pm, Sa by reservation; call for summer hours.)* One mile north of the main campus, **Evergreen House** is an exercise in excess—the bathroom of this elegant mansion is plated in 23-carat gold. Purchased in 1878 by railroad tycoon John W. Garret, the ornate house, along with its collections of fine porcelain, rare artwork, and Tiffany silver, was bequeathed to JHU in 1942. *(4545 N. Charles St. ☎ 516-0341; www.jhu.edu/~evrgreen/evergreen.html. Take bus #11. Open Tu-F 11am-4pm, Sa-Su noon-4pm. Tours every hr.; last tour 1hr. before close. $6, seniors $5, children and students $3.)*

🎵 ENTERTAINMENT

Much of Baltimore's finest entertainment can be enjoyed free of charge. At Harborplace, street performers delight tourists with magic acts and juggling during the day. The **Baltimore Museum of Art** offers jazz concerts on summer Saturdays at 7pm (May-Sept.) in its sculpture garden. The museum's permanent exhibit focuses on impressionists, with the world's largest single Matisse collection. (☎396-6314; www.artbma.org. Open W-F 11am-5pm, Sa-Su 11am-6pm. Free. Jazz concerts $18.) The **Pier 6 Concert Pavilion** presents concerts from May to October, ranging from classical to R&B. (☎625-3100; www.piersixpavilion.com. Tickets $15-50. Pier Pass for 2 people to 4 concerts $100.) Never thought you were the type to go to the orchestra? The **Baltimore Symphony Orchestra** is out to change your mind. The orchestra plays at **Meyerhoff Symphony Hall**, 1212 Cathedral St., from September to May and during the month-long Summerfest. The real secret is the venue's college nights: $10 student tickets include a reception with complimentary food and $1 beers. (☎783-8000; www.baltimoresymphony.org. Box office open M-F 10am-6pm, Sa-Su noon-5pm, and 1hr. before performances. Tickets $15-52. Discounts available 1hr. before concerts.)

The **Lyric Opera House**, 140 W. Mt. Royal Ave., near Maryland Ave., hosts the **Baltimore Opera Company** from October to May. (☎727-6000; www.baltimoreopera.com. Box office, down the road, open M-F 10am-5pm. Tickets $37-130.) The **Theater Project**, 45 W. Preston St., near Maryland St., experiments with theater, poetry, music, and dance. (☎752-8558; www.theatreproject.org. Shows Th-Sa 8pm, Su 3pm. Box office open 1hr. before shows; call to reserve tickets. Tickets from $16, seniors and students from $11.) The **Arena Players,** the longest continually running African-American theater company in the country, performs comedies, drama, and musicals. (801 McCulloh St., at Martin Luther King, Jr. Blvd. ☎728-6500. Box office open M-F 11am-2pm, Sa 10am-8pm, Su noon-4pm. Tickets from $15.) From June through October, the **Showcase of Nations Ethnic Festivals** celebrate Baltimore's numerous ethnic neighborhoods with food, music, vendors, and special ceremonies. A different culture is featured each week. Call the Baltimore Area Visitors Center for info (p. 176).

The beloved **Baltimore Orioles** play baseball at **Camden Yards,** situated just a few blocks from the Inner Harbor at the corner of Russell and Camden St. (Box office ☎685-9800. Open M-Sa 9am-5pm, Su noon-5pm. Tickets $9-55.) The NFL's **Ravens** play in **M&T Bank Stadium,** which is right next to Camden Yards. (☎261-7283; www.baltimoreravens.com. Single game tickets $50-345.)

■ NIGHTLIFE

Nightlife in **Mount Vernon** is reminiscent of the TV show *Cheers*, with neighborhood bars that know their middle-aged patrons by name, while the loud music and sweaty dance floors of **Fells Point** and **Power Plant Live** cater to a college and twentysomething crowd. Be prepared for the 1:30am last call. If you make it through the dozens of bars in Fells Point, head to **Canton** and **Federal Hill** for a similar scene.

Howl At The Moon, 22 Market Pl. (☎783-5111; www.howlatthemoon.com), in Power Plant Live. An amusing dueling-piano bar where the crowd runs the show, with frequent sing- (or "howl-") alongs. Crowd ranges from barely-adults to could-be-your-parents. More relaxed than Fells Point's testosterone-fueled bars. Beer $3.50-5. Mixed drinks $4.50-8. Happy hour F 5-8pm; ½-price drinks and free buffet. Piano shows W-Th 7:45pm, F 5:45pm. Cover Th $5 after 9pm, free with college ID; F-Sa $8 after 8pm. Open W-Th 7pm-2am, F 5pm-2am, Sa 5:30pm-2am.

Grand Central, 1001-1003 N. Charles St. (☎752-7133; www.centralstationpub.com), at Eager St. Chill under chandeliers from the set of *A Few Good Men* and *Batman* or play some pool with a mixed gay-straight crowd. The disco club next door is the spot for bumping and grinding (W-Su 9pm-2am; cover $6). Happy hour daily 4-8pm; beer $1 off. F 9-11pm all drinks $1.75. Su Skyy vodka drinks $2. Open daily 4pm-2am.

Fletcher's, 701 S. Bond St. (☎558-1889; www.fletchersbar.com), brings in live bands on the weekend to entertain its barflies, most often featuring rock, rap, and blues acts.

"Noise in the Basement" on F nights brings in aspiring local rockers. Happy hour M-Th 4:30-6:30pm and all day Su. Beer from $2.50. Cover $5-13. Doors open at 7, 8, or 9pm depending on the show. Closes daily 2am.

ANNAPOLIS   ☎ 410

Annapolis became the capital of Maryland in 1694, and in 1783 enjoyed a stint as capital of the US. Since then, the city has lived a dual life of residential port town and naval garrison. The historic waterfront district retains its 18th-century appeal despite the presence of ritzy boutiques. Crew-cut "middies" ("midshipmen," a nickname for Naval Academy students) do sailors proud at the pubs while shaggier students from St. John's (the country's third oldest college) chill at the coffeeshops, all amid middle-age couples ogling the US's highest concentration of historical homes.

▲⁊ ORIENTATION AND PRACTICAL INFORMATION. Annapolis lies 30 mi. east of D.C. and 30 mi. south of Baltimore. The city extends south and east from two landmarks: **Church Circle** and **State Circle. School Street,** in a blatantly unconstitutional move, connects Church and State. **East Street** runs from the State House to the Naval Academy. **Main Street,** where food and entertainment venues abound, starts at Church Cir. and ends at the docks. Downtown is compact and easily walkable, but finding a cheap parking space can be tricky. If a convenient metered spot doesn't come your way, parking at the Visitors Center ($1 per hr., $8 max. weekdays, $4 max. weekends) is the best bet. There is also free weekend parking in State Lots A and B, at the corner of Rowe Blvd. and Calvert St. Greyhound (☎ 800-231-2222; www.greyhound.com) **buses** stop at the Mass Transit Administration bus stop, 308 Cinquapin Rd., and run to Baltimore (30min., 3 per day, $10), Philadelphia (4-5hr., 3 per day, $24), and Washington, D.C. (1-2hr., 3 per day, $14). Tickets (cash only) are available from the bus driver. The **Annapolis Department of Public Transportation** operates a web of buses connecting the historic district with the rest of town. (☎ 263-7964. Buses run M-Sa 5:30am-10am, Su 8am-7pm. $0.75, seniors and disabled $0.35.) **Taxi:** Annapolis Cab Co., ☎ 268-0022. Checker Cab, ☎ 268-3737. **Car Rental:** Budget, 2001 West St. (☎ 266-5030). **Visitor Info: Annapolis and Anne Arundel County Conference and Visitors Bureau,** 26 West St., has free maps and brochures. (☎ 280-0445; www.visit-annapolis.org. Open daily 9am-5pm.) **Post Office:** 1 Church Cir. (☎ 263-9292. Open M-F 9am-5pm.) **Postal Code:** 21401.

⋔ ACCOMMODATIONS. The heart of Annapolis favors elegant and pricey B&Bs over cheap motels. Rooms should be reserved in advance, especially for weekends, spring graduations, and the summer. The **Annapolis Bed and Breakfast Association** (www.annapolisbandb.com) is a good place to start your search. The **Historic Inns of Annapolis ❺,** 58 State Circle, three properties that ring the state capitol, sometimes offer their beautifully appointed rooms for bargain rates. (☎ 263-2641; www.annapolisinns.com. Breakfast included. Rooms $110-200. AmEx/D/DC/MC/V.) The **Scotlaur Inn ❺,** 165 Main St., sits atop Chick & Ruth's Delly. Ten guest rooms with queen, double, or twin beds, A/C, TV, and private bath grace this homey "bed & bagel." (☎ 268-5665; www.scotlaurinn.com. Check-in 2pm. Check-out 11am. Rooms $100-145. MC/V.)

◖◗ FOOD. Most restaurants cluster around **City Dock,** an area packed with people in the summer. Find cheap eats at the **Market House** food court, at the center of City Dock, where a hearty meal costs less than $6. A Swedish coffeehouse with an Idaho twist, **Potato Valley Cafe ❷,** 47 State Cir., across from the State House, specializes in giant oven-roasted potatoes stuffed with fillings ($5-7). Toppings range from standard sour cream to exotic curry dressing with pineapple. (☎ 267-0902.

Open M-F 10am-5pm, Sa 11:30am-5pm. MC/V.) Of course, Main St. wouldn't be complete without a lovable deli. The staff at **Chick and Ruth's Delly ❷,** 165 Main St., serves up over 40 specialty sandwiches ($3.50-7), along with a bewildering array of salads, desserts, and all-day breakfasts. (☎269-6737; www.chickandruths.com. Dinner platters $5-10. Open M-Th and Su 6:30am-11:30pm, F-Sa 6:30am-12:30am Cash only.) Locals flock to **Carrol's Creek Bar & Cafe ❷,** 410 Severn Ave., in the Annapolis City Marina Complex, for home-cooked food and cheap drinks along the waterfront. Texas barbecued shrimp ($10) and Maryland crab soup ($6.50) are favorites. Happy hour (M-F 5-7pm) features half-price appetizers. (☎263-8102; www.carrolscreek.com. Open M-Sa 11:30am-4pm and 5-10pm; Su $19 all-you-can-eat brunch 10am-1:30pm, dinner 3-9pm. AMEx/D/MC/V.)

◎ SIGHTS. In many senses the **US Naval Academy,** 52 King George St., is the soul of Annapolis. The legendary military school turns harried, short-haired "plebes" (first-year students) into Naval-officer "middies" (midshipmen) through rigorous drilling and physical and emotional obstacles. President Jimmy Carter and billionaire H. Ross Perot are among the Academy's celebrity alumni. Once at the Academy, the first stop should be the **Leftwich Visitors Center,** in the Halsey Field House, which doubles as a food court and hockey rink. (☎263-6933; www.navyonline.com. Open Mar.-Dec. 9am-5pm, Jan.-Feb. 9am-4pm.) Guided walking tours take visitors through historic Bancroft Hall, the chapel's crypt, a dorm room, and the athletic facilities, where the middies test their seafaring prowess on land. **King Hall,** the world's largest dining facility, is a madhouse at lunchtime, when the entire student populace assumes "Brigade Meal Formation" and is served in under 20 frenzied minutes. On Saturdays in the summer, alumni weddings take place in the Academy's chapel (open M-Sa 9am-4pm, Su 1-4pm). Underneath the chapel is the final resting place of **John Paul Jones,** father of the United States Navy, who uttered the famous words, "I have not yet begun to fight!" as he rammed his sinking ship into an attacking British vessel. (75min. campus tours July-Aug. M-Sa 9:30am-3pm, Su 12:30-3pm; Apr.-June and Sept.-Nov. M-F 10am-3pm, Sa 9:30am-3pm, Su 12:30-3pm; Dec.-Mar. M-Sa 10am-2:30pm, Su 12:30-2:30pm. $7.50, seniors $6.50, students $5.50.)

The historic **Hammond-Harwood House,** 19 Maryland Ave., an elegant 1774 building designed by colonial architect William Buckland, retains period decor right down to the candlesticks. The **William Paca House,** 186 Prince George St., was the first Georgian-style home built in Annapolis, and has two acres of lush vegetation. Paca, an early governor of Maryland, was one of the original signers of the Declaration of Independence. Both houses feature exhibits on life in the late 1700s, stocked with artifacts from archaeological digs on the grounds. (Hammond-Harwood: ☎263-5553; www.hammondharwoodhouse.org. Open Apr.-Oct. W-Su noon-5pm; Nov.-Mar. F-Sa noon-4pm. 40min. tours every hr.; last tour 1hr. before close. $6, students $5.50, under 12 $3. William Paca House: ☎990-4538 or 800-603-4020; www.annapolis.org. Open Mar.-Dec. M-Sa 10am-5pm, Su noon-5pm. Tours every 30min. Garden or house $5, seniors and AAA $4, ages 6-17 $3; garden and house $8/$7/$5. Uniformed armed service personnel and ages 5 and under free.)

Built between 1772 and 1779, the Corinthian-columned **State House,** in the center of State Circle, is the oldest functioning capitol building in the nation. It was the US capitol building from 1783 to 1784; the Treaty of Paris was signed here on January 14, 1784. Visitors can explore the historical exhibits and silver collection, or watch the state legislature bicker (politely, of course) in two exquisite marble halls. Cordial guides clad in colonial garb gladly field questions. (☎974-3400. Open M-F 9am-5pm, Sa-Su 10am-4pm; grounds 6am-11pm. Tours daily 11am and 3pm. Legislature in session mid-Jan. to mid-Apr. Free.)

🎵🎭 **ENTERTAINMENT AND NIGHTLIFE.** Locals and tourists engage in one of two activities in Annapolis: wandering along City Dock or schmoozing 'n' boozing at the city's upscale pubs. The bars and taverns that line downtown Annapolis draw crowds every night. If you want more culture than drink can provide, check out **The Colonial Players, Inc.,** 108 East St., for performances of innovative and often unknown plays. (☎268-7373; www.cplayers.com. Shows Th-Sa 8pm, Su 2:30 and 7:30pm. $15, students $10.) In the summer, the **Annapolis Summer Garden Theater,** 143 Compromise St., presents musical "theater under the stars" on a terraced lawn overlooking an open courtyard theater. (☎268-9212; www.summergarden.com. Th-Su at 8:30pm. Lawn seats $12.) The **Naval Academy Band** performs on City Dock every Tuesday night at 7:30pm. (☎293-0263; www.usna.edu/usnaband. Free.)

As close as you can get to the water without falling in, **Pusser's Landing,** 80 Compromise St., facing City Dock, is located on a working pier. (☎626-0004; www.pussers.com. Beer $2-4. Kitchen open M-Th and Su 7am-11pm, F-Sa 7am-midnight; bar open daily until 2am.) Midshipmen and tourists alike enjoy 135 different ales, lagers, and stouts at **Ram's Head Tavern,** 33 West St. Happy hour (M-F 4-7pm) includes $2 drafts and free tacos. There is free live music on the patio many evenings; for bigger-name bands, a dinner and show combination ticket gets you a 10% discount on your meal and a free drink. (☎268-4545. Happy hour with $2 drafts daily midnight-1am. Open daily 10am-2am.) Locals and officers pack in under the two-story ficus tree that grows through **Irish McGarvey's,** 8 Market Space. Two bars in the establishment serve Aviator Lager, the manliest-sounding beer in town (10 oz. draft $3.50, pint $5.50), but not much else. Summer parties on Tuesday nights invite patrons to don tropical attire and enjoy frozen Zombies ($4) with their red beans and rice ($6). Happy hour (M and W 10pm-2am) features buffalo wings for $3-10, 32 oz. drafts for $3, and 10 oz. mugs for $1. (☎263-5700. Th 6pm-1am house beer $1.50. Open M-Sa 11:30am-2am, Su 10am-2am.)

ASSATEAGUE AND CHINCOTEAGUE ☎757

Local legend has it that wild mustangs first came to Assateague Island by swimming ashore from a sinking Spanish galleon. A more likely theory is that miserly colonial farmers put their horses out to graze on Assateague to avoid mainland taxes. Whatever their origins, the famous wild ponies (so called because of their stunted growth) now roam free across the unspoiled beaches and forests of the island, and, on the last Wednesday and Thursday in July, swim from Assateague to Chincoteague during Pony Penning.

> **TIP**
> **BUG FOOD.** To avoid being seen as a tasty and vulnerable treat by the islands' mosquitoes, come prepared: bug spray and long sleeves are a must.

📍❼ **ORIENTATION AND PRACTICAL INFORMATION.** Telling the two islands apart, especially since their names are sometimes used interchangeably, can often leave visitors bewildered. **Assateague,** largely covered by wilderness, is the longer barrier island facing the ocean, while the tourist-oriented **Chincoteague Island** is nestled between Assateague and mainland Delmarva Peninsula. Maryland and Virginia share Assateague Island, and **Chincoteague Wildlife Refuge** is actually on Assateague. As Assateague remains mostly undeveloped, resources are located primarily on Chincoteague. The best way to get to Chincoteague is by car; the best way to explore it is by bike. From D.C., take Rte. 50 E to Salisbury, MD; then take Rte. 13 S and turn left onto Rte. 175 E. The **Chincoteague Chamber of Commerce** is at 6733 Maddox Blvd. (☎336-6161; www.chincoteaguechamber.com. Open M-Sa 9am-4:30pm; Memorial Day-Labor Day also Su 12:30-5pm.) **Internet Access: Vacation**

Internet Cafe, 4407 Deep Hole Rd. (☎336-3616; www.vacationinternetcafe.com. Free Wi-Fi with $3 food purchase. Internet access $3 per 15min., $10 per hr. Open M-Sa 9am-6pm.) **Post Office:** 4144 Main St. (☎336-2934. Open M-F 8am-4:30pm, Sa 8am-noon.) **Postal Code:** 23336.

🏠🏠 ACCOMMODATIONS AND FOOD. Unless you're planning to snuggle up with the ponies and graze on grass, the only accommodations and food are located on Chincoteague. The **Blue Heron Inn ❸**, 7020 Maddox Blvd., has clean, spacious rooms with A/C, phones, refrigerators, cable TV, a pool, and boat/camper parking. Be sure to check out the pony corral in the motel's gravel parking lot. (☎336-1900 or 800-615-6343; www.chincoteague.com/blueheron. Room rates peak at $139 during Pony Penning. Rooms June-early Sept. $96-125; Sept.-May $55-75. Weekend rates $10 more. AmEx/D/MC/V.) For rooms with breathtaking views and access to pools and an exercise room, head to the waterfront **Island Motor Inn Resort ❺**, 4391 Main St. (☎336-3141; www.islandmotorinn.com. Check-in 4pm. Check-out 11am. Rooms June-Sept. $110-195; Mar.-May $88-160; Dec.-Feb. $68-150. Low season senior discount 10%. AmEx/D/MC/V.) The sprawling **Maddox Family Campground ❶**, 6742 Maddox Blvd., across from the Visitors Center, has 550 campsites, hot showers, laundry, and a pool. (☎336-3111. For full hookup, reserve 3 months in advance. Sites with water and electricity $35, full hookup $40.) Another camping option is **Tom's Cove Park ❶**, which operates a large campground with available waterfront sites. Make a right on Main St. coming off the Chincoteague Rd. drawbridge and then a left on Beebe Rd. (☎336-6498. Tent sites $29, with electricity and water $35, full hookup $39, waterfront $41. Open Mar.-Nov.)

    AJ's on the Creek ❹, 6585 Maddox Blvd., specializes in steaks and grilled fish in a dining room decked out in lace and mahogany. Lunchtime brings a variety of seafood specialties, including oyster and crab cake sandwiches ($6.50-9) guaranteed to please even seasoned seafood lovers. (☎336-5888. Lunch entrees $4-10. Dinner entrees $15-25. Open in summer M-Sa 11:30am-9:30pm. Lounge open until 1am. AmEx/D/MC/V.) **Not Just Salads ❶**, 6349 Maddox Blvd., is a beachtown-chic eatery with an all-you-can-eat salad bar ($7), but, as the name suggests, also serves sandwiches, burgers, and subs. (☎336-7333. Open daily 10am-9pm. MC/V.) Treat yourself to towering ice-cream cones and inventive sundaes at **Mister Whippy ❶**, 6201 Maddox St. (☎336-5122. Cones $1.50. Open daily 11am-10:30pm. Cash only.)

◨ SIGHTS. The █Chincoteague National Wildlife Refuge stretches across the Virginia side of Assateague Island. Avid bird-watchers come to see rare species like snowy egrets and black-crowned night herons. The **Pony Penning,** held the last consecutive Wednesday and Thursday in July (after the month-long Chincoteague Volunteer Firefighter's Carnival), brings thousands of tourists to Assateague. During low tide, firemen herd the ponies together and swim them from Assateague to Chincoteague Island, where the fire department auctions off the foals the following day. The remaining horses swim back to Assateague to mate, providing next year's herd. Head to the **Visitors Center,** located just inside the refuge, to learn about biking, hiking, walking, and bird and nature tours. Guided wildlife bus tours are also available. (☎336-3696. Tours run Memorial Day-Labor Day daily 10am, 1, 4pm; Labor Day-Memorial Day 1 per day. $12, over 62 $10, ages 2-12 $5.) Trails include the 3 mi. **Wildlife Loop,** which circles a fresh-water impoundment (open 3pm-dusk for cars, all day for pedestrians and bicyclists), the forested 1½ mi. **Woodland Trail** (cars not permitted), and the quarter-mile **Lighthouse Trail,** which runs to the historic Assateague Lighthouse (pedestrians only). The ponies can be viewed from overlooks along the road leading into the park. Visitors should maintain a safe distance from the wild ponies and resist the urge to feed them: if fed by guests, the ponies could become dependent on humans for survival. (8231 Beach

MID-ATLANTIC

Rd. ☎336-6122; http://chinco.fws.gov. No pets permitted. Park open daily May-Sept. 5am-10pm; Apr. and Oct. 6am-8pm; Nov.-Mar. 6am-6pm. Visitors Center open daily Memorial Day-Labor Day 9am-5pm; Labor Day-Memorial Day 9am-4pm. 7-day pass $10 per car; allows access to a spacious beach with free parking.) The **Oyster & Maritime Museum** is a nonprofit museum that recounts island history with a focus on the oystering and seafood industry. Don't miss the 1865 First Order Fresnel lens from the Assateague Lighthouse, one of only 21 in the US. Retired in 1961, its light could be seen from 23 mi. away. (7125 Maddox Blvd. ☎336-6117. Open May-Sept. daily10am-5pm. Free.) The **Chincoteague Pony Centre** offers pony rides and showcases veterans of the pony swim. (6417 Carriage Dr. ☎336-2776; www.chincoteague.com/ponycentre. Heading north on Main St., turn right onto Church St., left onto Chicken City Rd., and right onto Carriage Dr. Open in summer M-Sa 9am-10pm. Pony rides M-Sa 9am-1pm and 3:30-6pm. Rides $5.)

OCEAN CITY   ☎410

Ocean City (OC) is a lot like a kiddie pool—it's shallow and plastic, but can be a lot of fun if you're the right age or in just the right mood. This 10 mi. strip of prime Atlantic beach packs endless bars, all-you-can-eat buffets, boardwalks, mini-golf courses, flashing neon lights, and sun-seeking tourists into a thin region between the ocean on the east and the Montego, Assawoman, Isle of Wight, and Sinepuxent bays to the west. The siren call of senior week beckons droves of recent high-school and college graduates to alcohol and hormone-driven fun, turning OC into a city-wide block party in late May and June. During July and August, the city caters more to families and professional singles looking for fun in the sun.

■■ **ORIENTATION AND PRACTICAL INFORMATION.** Driving is the least painful mode of transportation to reach the ocean resort, though beach traffic can make getting to OC a headache no matter how you plan to do it. From the north, simply follow Rte. 1, which becomes **Coastal Highway (Philadelphia Avenue).** From the west, Rte. 50 also leads directly to Ocean City. From points south, take Rte. 113 to Rte. 50. **Philadelphia Avenue** and **Baltimore Avenue** run north-south, though the latter is for northbound traffic only. **Wilmington Avenue** is a narrow two-way alley that runs parallel. Numbered streets run east-west, linking the ocean to the bay. Most hotels are in the lower-numbered streets to the south, toward the ocean; most clubs and bars are uptown toward the bay. On the southern end of the island, the orderly street grid spills into the inlet parking lot, which houses an amusement park and a series of shops, stands, bars, and clubs.

Greyhound/Trailways, (☎289-9307; www.greyhound.com; open daily 10am-1:30pm), at 2nd St. and Philadelphia Ave., sends **buses** to Baltimore (3¾hr., 2 per day, $35) and Washington, D.C. (4½-5½hr., 3 per day, $48). In town, **public buses** (☎723-1607; operate 24hr.) run the length of the strip and are the best way to get around town (unlimited rides $2 per day). The **Ocean City Visitors Bureau,** 4001 Coastal Hwy., at 40th St. in the Convention Center, gives out coupons and brochures for local establishments. (☎723-8610 or 800-626-2326; www.ococean.com. Open M-F 8am-5pm, Sa-Su 9am-5pm.) **E-Point Internet Cafe,** 1513 Philadelphia Ave., in the 15th St. Shopping Center complex, offers Internet access. (☎289-9844. $4 per 30min., $7 per hr. Open daily 10am-2am. Cash only.) **Post Office:** 7101 Coastal Hwy. (☎524-4978. Open M-F 9am-5pm, Sa 9am-noon.) **Postal Code:** 21842. **Area Codes:** 410, 443. In text, 410 unless otherwise noted.

⌐ **ACCOMMODATIONS.** Reservations are highly recommended at any time from May to early September, especially if you plan to stay more than a couple of days. Weekend prices are about $20-25 higher than weekday prices, but many guest houses and motels offer weekly rates at a discount. The **Atlantic House Bed and Breakfast ❺**, 501 N. Baltimore Ave., half a block from the ocean and the boardwalk, provides a full breakfast buffet and a wholesome change of pace from the Ocean City motel trend. (☎289-2333; www.atlantichouse.com. Complimentary beach chairs, towels, and umbrellas. A/C, cable TV, hot tub, and parking. Open Apr.-Sept. May-Aug. rooms with shared bath $85-150, with private bath $115-195. D/MC/V.)

🏛 **FOOD.** Ocean City's cuisine oscillates between linen-napkin gourmet and cheap, grease-laden buffet. Ice cream, funnel cakes, and sno-ball stands beckon from the boardwalk, but most sit-down eateries are just off the beach. ▨**Brass Balls Saloon & Bad Ass Cafe ❶**, on the Boardwalk between 11th and 12th St., is known for its $1.25 Jell-O shots (after 10pm) and its motto: "Drink Hearty, Eat Healthy." Specials like $5.25 Oreo waffles and $7 pizzas seem to defy the latter imperative, though college crowds can't get enough of the "drink hearty" part. (☎289-0069. Th karaoke. Open Mar.-Oct. M-F 8:30am-2am, Sa-Su 8am-2am. AmEx/D/MC/V.) **Dumser's ❶** maintains several locations in the city (including the south inlet parking lot and at 49th St.), and specializes in quick seaside fare, including milkshakes, floats, hot dogs and buckets of clams, chicken, and fish. In addition to a takeout booth, the 49th St. location has a sit-down restaurant. (☎524-1588. Sandwiches $3-8. Open daily 11am-1am. MC/V.) With fresh catches and a friendly atmosphere, **The Embers ❺**, 2305 Philadelphia Ave., boasts the biggest seafood buffet in town. All the clams, oysters, Alaskan crab legs, prime rib, steak, sides, and dessert you can eat come for $28. (☎289-3322 or 888-436-2377; www.embers.com. Open daily 2-9:30pm. AmEx/D/MC/V.)

🎭🎵 **ENTERTAINMENT AND NIGHTLIFE.** Ocean City's star attraction is its beautiful beach. The wide stretch of surf and sand runs the entire 10 mi. length of the town and can be accessed by taking a left onto any of the numerous side streets off Philadelphia and Baltimore Ave. The breaking waves know no time constraints, but the beach is technically only open daily 6am-10pm. When the sun goes down, professional party-goers will be impressed by **Seacrets**, on 49th St., in the bay, a virtual adult entertainment mecca and amusement park. This oasis features 17 bars, including two floating on the bay. Wander from bar to bar or listen to live bands while floating on a personal raft. A magnificent sunset view ushers in early revelers for mixed drinks in the raft pool. (☎524-4900; www.seacrets.com. 21+. Cover Th $5

ON THE MENU

CRABCAKES 101

Eating crabs is a pricey hobby for Marylanders as it is for anyone else: in local eateries, a **crabcake** sandwich is typically the most expensive thing on the menu. Still, that hasn't stopped the state's 5.6 million residents from indulging in the summertime ritual of cracking, peeling, caking, and baking.

Every red-blooded Marylander knows what a good crabcake should be—moist, savory, just a bit tart, and many will swear by a family recipe. Lump crabmeat (from the torso of the crab) is preferred to claw meat, but all uniformity ends there. A crabcake might make use of eggs, mustard, parsley, or none of these; it might be broiled or sautéed; it might be served plain, with tartar sauce, cocktail sauce, or lemon.

These days, though, a genuine Maryland crabcake can be tough to come by. Overfishing in the Chesapeake Bay has led to a decline in local crab production; hard-pressed to meet demand, the industry has in recent years imported much of its crab stock from the Gulf of Mexico and from Southeast Asia, especially Thailand. For the sake of authenticity, locals prefer home-raised crabs; in practice, however, it's virtually impossible to tell if your steamed crab or crabcake sandwich began life in Baltimore, in Bangkok, or on the Bayou.

after 9pm, F-Sa $5 at 5pm and goes up $1 each hr. until 10pm. Open daily 11am-2am.) The elder statesman of the bayside clubs, **Fager's Island,** 60th St., in the bay, has hordes walking the plank to its island location. Live jazz, R&B, reggae, and rock play nightly to accompany over 100 beers, and the *1812 Overture* booms every sunset. (☎524-5500; www.fagers.com. No jerseys, swimwear, caps, cutoffs, sleeveless shirts, or sagging, baggy, or oversized pants. 21+ after 8pm. Cover $5 after 9pm. Open daily 11am-2am.) **The Party Block,** 17th St. and Coastal Hwy., charges one cover for three different clubs: **Rush Club** plays hip-hop and techno, the **Paddock** has modern rock, and the **Big Kahuna** grooves to 80s music. (☎289-6331; www.partyblock.com. Budweiser longnecks $1.75. 21+. Cover $5-10 after 10pm. Open daily 8:30pm-2am.) If you're under 21 but want to party like you're older, check out the nightly dancing and occasional foam at **Club H2O,** at Worcester, off Philadelphia Ave. (☎289-7102; www.partyblock.com. Under 21 only. Cover $10 before 8:30pm, $20 after. Open daily 8pm-12:45am.)

WASHINGTON, D.C.

Visitors to the nation's capital think they've seen it all after a tour of the White House and the Lincoln Memorial. But locals and savvy travelers know that D.C. is a thriving international metropolis with a reputation for trendsetting and budget-friendly establishments. Pierre L'Enfant's diamond-shaped dream now encompasses a bewildering array of world-class cultural and culinary delights, including the avant-garde galleries of Dupont Circle, the glittering mosaic of Adams Morgan nightlife, and the colonial chic of Georgetown. Now far more than just the world's most powerful city, D.C. has hit the big-time, with Broadway shows at the Kennedy Center, the latest bands jamming on the "New U" St. corridor, and (finally!) major-league baseball in front of positively giddy fans at RFK Stadium. For expanded coverage of the D.C. area, check out ✐*Let's Go: Washington, D.C.*

■ INTERCITY TRANSPORTATION

Airports: Dulles International Airport (IAD) (☎703-572-2700; www.mwaa.com/dulles) is 25min. farther from the city. Taxis to downtown start at $45-50. The **Washington Flyer Coach Service** (☎888-927-4359; www.washfly.com) departs from Dulles every 30min. M-F 5:45am-10:15pm, Sa-Su 7:45am-10:15pm; from Metro: West Falls Church M-F 6:15am-10:45pm, Sa-Su 8:15am-10:45pm. ($9; discounts for groups of 3 or more, seniors, and international students.) Travel between Dulles and metro area takes about 30min. The **SuperShuttle** bus also runs from Dulles to downtown daily ($22; each additional person $10). **Ronald Reagan National Airport (DCA)** (☎703-417-8000; www.mwaa.com/national). Metro: National Airport. If you're flying to D.C. from within the US, this airport is your best bet: it's on the Metro and close to the city. Taxi from downtown $12-15. The **SuperShuttle** bus (☎800-258-3826; www.supershuttle.com) runs between National and the city ($12).

Trains: Amtrak operates from Union Station, 50 Massachusetts Ave. NE (☎484-7540; www.amtrak.com). 12 trains per day to: **Baltimore** (30-45min., $19); **Boston** (7¾hr., $96); **New York City** (3¼hr., $80); **Philadelphia** (2hr., $51). Maryland's commuter rail, **MARC** (☎866-743-3682), runs from Union Station to **Baltimore** ($7) and the suburbs.

▲ ORIENTATION

D.C. stretches in the four cardinal directions. The **Potomac River** forms the jagged southwest border, its waters flowing between the District and Arlington, VA. **North Capitol, East Capitol,** and **South Capitol Streets** slice the city into four quadrants: NW,

MID-ATLANTIC

Downtown Washington, D.C.

▲ ACCOMMODATIONS

Adam's Inn, 7
Hilltop Hostel, 6
Hostelling International-
Washington, D.C. (HI), 18
Hotel Harrington, 22
Tabard Inn, 16
Washington Court Hotel, 23
Washington International
Student Center, 1

🍴 FOOD

Burma Restaurant, 20
Cafe Luna, 13
Chinatown Garden, 19
The Diner, 2
Lauriol Plaza, 4
New Orleans Cafe, 3
Pasta Mia Trattoria, 5
La Tomate, 9

🎵 NIGHTLIFE

Apex, 15
The Big Hunt, 14
Brickskeller, 11
Cafe Saint-Ex, 8
Cobalt, 10
The Dubliner, 21
Eighteenth Street Lounge, 17
J.R.'s, 12
Pour House, 24

**SEE COLOR INSERTS FOR MORE
WASHINGTON, D.C. MAPS**

NE, SE, and SW. The **Mall** stretches west of the Capitol. The suffixes of the quadrants distinguish otherwise identical addresses in Washington's grid (e.g. 800 G St. NW and 800 G St. NE). Streets that run east-west are labeled alphabetically in relation to North Capitol St./South Capitol St., which runs through the Capitol. There is no J St. After W St., east-west streets take on two-syllable names, then three-syllable names, then the names of trees and flowers, all in roughly alphabetical order. Streets running north-south are numbered up to 52nd St. NW and 63rd St. NE. Addresses on lettered streets indicate the number of the cross street. For instance, 1100 D St. SE is on the corner of D and 11th. While navigation on foot is relatively easy, both drivers and pedestrians should be aware of possible road blocks and detour routes set up by city officials to protect the security of political buildings. Some streets alternate between one-way or two-way depending on the time of day.

Major roads include **Pennsylvania Avenue, Connecticut Avenue, Wisconsin Avenue, 16th Street NW, K Street NW, Massachusetts Avenue, New York Avenue,** and **North Capitol Street.** D.C. is ringed by the **Capital Beltway** (**I-495**—except where it's part of I-95). The Beltway is bisected by **U.S. 1** and meets **I-395** from Virginia. The **Baltimore-Washington Parkway** connects Washington, D.C. to Baltimore, MD. **I-595** trickles off the Capital Beltway toward Annapolis, MD, and **I-66** heads west into Virginia.

NEIGHBORHOODS

Postcard-perfect, **Capitol Hill** symbolizes the democratic ideal, with the Capitol, Supreme Court, and Library of Congress all facing each other. Extending west from the Capitol building is the grassy pedestrian **Mall,** punctuated by the Washington Monument and World War II Memorial before it ends at the Lincoln Memorial. The Mall is flanked by the Smithsonian museums and the National Gallery of Art. Cherry trees flank the Jefferson Memorial and the Potomac River Tidal Basin, just south and directly across the Mall from the **White House,** which is north of the Mall at 1600 Pennsylvania Ave. The State Department, Kennedy Center, and the infamous Watergate Complex make up **Foggy Bottom,** on the west side of the city. The **Federal Triangle** area is home to a growing commercial and banking district. It's a wonderful (corporate) life along the glass-walled blocks of **Farragut,** where government agencies, lobbying firms, and lawyers feather their nests.

There's more to D.C. than politics, though. **Adams Morgan,** in the northwest, is a hub of nightlife and good food; a wide variety of local restaurants cater to the adventurous budget traveler, with original menus ranging from Cajun to Ethiopian. In **Chinatown,** authentic Chinese restaurants bump up against the vast MCI Center and its ring of sports bars. Though its cobblestone back streets are home to Washington's power elite, picturesque **Georgetown** pairs its high-end shops with enough nightlife to keep any college student entertained. **Dupont Circle,** the city's cultural nexus, has developed a powerful trinity of tasty cuisine, trendy clubs, and cutting-edge art galleries. Another nighttime hot spot is the **U District,** a historically African-American area with clubs that blast trance and techno until the sun rises. **Upper Northwest,** an upper-class residential neighborhood, is home to American University and the National Zoo. At night, travelers in Washington D.C. should be mindful of their surroundings; it is important to be especially cautious in Dupont Circle and the U District when the sun sets.

▣ LOCAL TRANSPORTATION

Public Transit: Washington Metropolitan Area Transit Authority (☎637-7000; www.wmata.com). Operates the city's public transit. The subway, called the **"Metro,"** runs M-Th 5am-midnight, F 5am-3am, Sa 7am-3am, Su 7am-midnight. $1.35-4; day pass $6.50. The **Fast Pass** ($30) allows 7 days of unlimited travel. The **Metrobus** system serves Georgetown, downtown, and the suburbs. $1.25. Free bus transfers are available on the upper platforms of most subway stations. The **DC Circulator** (☎962-1423; www.dccirculator.com), is a cross-town bus that loops from Georgetown to Union Station and from the MCI Center to the SW Waterfront. Runs daily 7am-9pm. $1.

Taxi: Yellow Cab, ☎544-1212.

Car Rental: Union Station, 50 Massachusetts Ave., boasts several major rental agencies, including **Hertz Rent-a-Car** (☎842-0819; www.hertz.com) and **Budget** (☎800-527-0700; www.budget.com). Both open M-F 8am-6pm, Sa-Su 10am-6pm.

Bicycle Rental: Better Bikes (☎293-2080; www.betterbikesinc.com). 10-speed bikes $25 per day, $95 per week; mountain bikes $38/185; hybrids $48/215. Helmet, map, backpack, locks, and breakdown service included. $25 deposit. Open 24hr.

⁊ PRACTICAL INFORMATION

Visitor Info: Washington, D.C. Convention and Tourism Corporation, 1212 New York Ave. NW, Ste. 600 (☎789-7000; www.washington.org). Open M-F 9am-5pm. **D.C. Visitor Info Center,** 1300 Pennsylvania Ave. NW (☎866-324-7386; www.dcvisit.com), in the Reagan International Trade Center. Open high season M-F 8:30am-5:30pm, Sa 9am-4pm; low season M-F 9-4:30.

Tours: Tourmobile (☎554-5100, www.tourmobile.com). Operates daily 9:30am-4:30pm, with final reboarding 1hr. before close. $25, children $13. Purchase tickets from drivers or at Tourmobile booths.

Hotlines: Rape Crisis Center, ☎333-7273. 24hr. **Gay and Lesbian National Hotline,** ☎888-843-4564. Operates M-F 4pm-midnight, Sa noon-5pm. **Traveler's Aid Society** (www.travelersaid.org) at Union Station (☎371-1937; open M-Sa 9:30am-5:30pm, Su 12:30-5:30pm), National Airport (☎703-417-3972; open M-F 9am-9pm, Sa-Su 9am-6pm), and Dulles Airport (☎703-572-8296; open M-F 8am-9pm, Sa-Su 8am-7pm).

Medical Services: Georgetown University Medical Center, 3800 Reservoir Rd. NW (☎444-2000; www.gumc.georgetown.edu).

Internet Access: The Cyberstop Cafe, 1513 17th St. NW (☎234-2470), near P St. Close to Metro: Dupont Circle. Free Wi-Fi with purchase from cafe. $7 per 30min., $9 per hr. Open M-F 7am-midnight, Sa-Su 8am-midnight.

Post Office: Martin Luther King, Jr. Station, 1400 L St. (☎523-2001), in the lobby. Open M-F 8am-5:30pm, Sa 8am-2pm. **Postal Code:** 20005. **Area Code:** 202.

⌐ ACCOMMODATIONS

You might think that inexpensive lodgings would be harder to come by than straight-talking politicians, but the sheer size of the city and its massive volume of tourist traffic support a few reasonably priced hostels and several relatively inexpensive B&Bs. Like other major cities in the US, D.C. charges a hefty hotel tax (14.5%).

HOSTELS

▓ **Hostelling International-Washington D.C. (HI),** 1009 11th St. NW (☎737-2333; www.hiwashingtondc.org), 3 blocks north of Metro: Metro Center. Use caution in this area after dark. In the heart of D.C., 5 blocks from the White House. 250 beds. Internet access $1 per 5min. Reception 24hr. Check-in 2pm-1am; call ahead if arriving later. Check-out 11am. Wheelchair-accessible. Reservations recommended. Dorms $35, members $32; singles $72/62; doubles $82/79; quads $152. MC/V. ❷

Hilltop Hostel, 300 Carroll St. NW (☎291-9591), on the border of D.C. and Takoma Park, close to Metro: Takoma. Hostelers can come and go as they please, smoke and drink in certain areas, or fire up a grill in the backyard. A/C in some rooms. Free Wi-Fi. Satellite TV, kitchen, and coin-op laundry. Linen included. 18+. 7-night max. stay. Reception 8am-midnight. Reservations recommended. Co-ed dorms $22; private rooms with shared bath $60. Cash or traveler's check only. ❶

Washington International Student Center, 2451 18th St. NW (☎800-567-4150; www.washingtondchostel.com), in the middle of Adams Morgan. An incredible location, next door to some of D.C.'s best nightlife. Breakfast included. Towel service, kitchen, lockers, free Wi-Fi, cable TV. No smoking. Reception 8am-11pm. Co-ed dorms $23. Cash or traveler's check only. ❶

HOTELS AND GUEST HOUSES

⊠ **Adam's Inn,** 1744 Lanier Pl. NW (☎745-3600 or 800-578-6807; www.adamsinn.com), 2 blocks north of the center of Adams Morgan. 25 rooms with A/C, tasteful furnishings, and private sinks (some with private bath). Complimentary continental breakfast and snacks. Cable TV in common area, free Wi-Fi, and laundry facilities. Limited parking $10 per night. 2-night min. stay if staying Sa night. Reception M-Sa 8am-9pm, Su 1-9pm. Check-in 3-9pm. Check-out noon. Singles $99, with private bath $109; each additional person $10. AmEx/D/MC/V. ❹

Tabard Inn, 1739 N St. NW (☎785-1277; www.tabardinn.com), between 17th and 18th St. Splurgeworthy. 40 rooms in 3 townhouses done up with rich tapestry and hardwood floors. A/C, phone, Wi-Fi, and data port (but no TV). Patio, bar, and lounges. Continental breakfast and YMCA passes included. Reception 24hr. Singles $107-137, with private bath $152-227; each additional person $15. AmEx/D/MC/V. ❺

Hotel Harrington, 11th and E St. NW (☎628-8140). Metro: Metro Center or Federal Triangle. Simply furnished rooms with A/C and cable TV in a great location. Parking $10 per day. Double room with queen bed $95-109; two double beds $135; king bed $129. $10 off if you call ahead from the airport, train, or bus station; 10% off on stays of more than 5 days. AAA and student discount 10%. AmEx/D/MC/V. ❹

Washington Court Hotel, 525 New Jersey Ave. NW (☎628-21000 or 800-321-3010; www.washingtoncourthotel.com). Metro: Union Station. A 5min. walk from the Capitol. Caters primarily to government contractors and their expense accounts, but has reasonable rates given its superb location and amenities. Rooms come with A/C, marble bath, cable TV, and high-speed Internet. 2 double beds or king-sized bed $102; deluxe rooms $117. AAA discount 10%. AmEx/D/MC/V. ❺

◘ FOOD

How do you feast like a senator on an intern's budget? Savvy natives go grubbing at Happy hours, since bars often have free appetizer platters to bait early evening clients (see **Nightlife,** p. 202). For budget eateries, **Adams Morgan** and **Dupont Circle** are home to the *crème de la crème* of ethnic cuisine. Suburban **Bethesda, MD** (Metro: Bethesda), features over 100 restaurants within a four-block radius.

ADAMS MORGAN

⊠ **Bardia's New Orleans Cafe,** 2412 18th St. NW (☎234-0420). With Dixieland rattling the speakers, murals of jazz bands, and an owner who epitomizes Southern hospitality, this popular cafe rewards its customers with great jambalaya, Cajun linguine ($8-15), and gumbo ($4-8). Open Tu-F 11am-9:30pm, Sa-Su 10am-10pm. AmEx/MC/V. ❸

The Diner, 2453 18th St. NW (☎232-8800). The Diner's hours and quintessential American food earn it rave reviews from local college kids and other late-night revelers. The Portabello Cap sandwich ($6.75) with pickled red pepper strips is a standout. Vegetarian options available. Omelets $6-8. Pancakes $5. Burgers $6-8. Open 24hr. ❷

Pasta Mia Trattoria, 1790 Columbia Rd. NW (☎328-9114), near 18th St. When the moon's in the sky like a big pizza pie, huge bowls of steaming pasta are *amore*. Don't be fooled by its humble facade; Pasta Mia is an aging but perennial favorite, serving generous helpings of Italian classics ($10-13) with wine ($16-30). The tortellini in a tomato-cream sauce is delicious. No reservations accepted. Open M-Sa 6:30-10pm. ❸

CHINATOWN

Burma Restaurant, upstairs at 740 6th St. NW (☎638-1280), between G and H St. Burmese curries, unique spices, and a plethora of garnishes. Try the green tea salad ($8), followed by the squid sautéed in garlic, ginger, scallions, and country ham ($9). Vegetarians will enjoy the papaya and tofu salads ($7). Open M-F 11am-3pm and 6-10pm, Sa-Su 6-10pm. ❷

Chinatown Garden, 618 H St. NW (☎737-8887). Features an extensive 2-part menu— half Americanized fare, half authentic dishes. Try the lunch special ($6.50-7) if you're on a budget, or the sea cucumbers with stewed shrimp roe ($27) if you're feeling frisky. Lunch $6-8. Dinner $9-13. Open M-Th and Su 11am-11pm, F-Sa 11am-midnight. ❷

DUPONT CIRCLE

Lauriol Plaza, 1835 18th St. NW (☎387-0035), at T St., between Dupont Circle and Adams Morgan. Lauriol occupies half the block, with a rowdy roof deck and 3 magnificent floors of Mexican dining. Large entrees ($10-17), appetizers like fried plantains and guacamole ($4-7), and excellent margaritas ($5.75, pitchers $25). Free parking. No reservations accepted, and the wait grows exponentially—arrive early. Su brunch 11:30am-3pm. Open M-Th and Su 11:30am-11pm, F-Sa 11:30am-midnight. ❹

La Tomate, 1701 Connecticut Ave. NW (☎667-5505), at R St. This Dupont Circle mainstay features attentive service, a creative menu, and some of the best outdoor seating in the entire city. Pastas ($13-18) include *farfalle prosciutto e funghi* (bowtie pasta with prosciutto, mushrooms, and cream; $15). Entrees $15-27. Reservations recommended. Open M-Th 11:30am-11pm, F-Sa 11:30am-11:30pm, Su 11:30am-10pm. ❹

Cafe Luna, 1633 P St. NW (☎387-4005), near 17th St. A popular basement restaurant serving a mix of Italian, vegetarian, and low-fat fare in a thoroughly unpretentious atmosphere. Breakfast ($2-5) served all day. Huge sandwiches ($6-11) satisfy almost any appetite. W and Su half-price pizzas ($5-7). Brunch Sa-Su 10am-3pm ($7-11). Open M-Th 8am-11:30pm, F 8am-midnight, Sa 10am-midnight, Su 10am-11:30pm. ❷

GEORGETOWN

Clyde's of Georgetown, 3236 M St. NW (☎333-9180), between Potomac St. and Wisconsin Ave. Join the crowds of preppy students and professor-types at Clyde's for delicious sandwiches ($9-16), salads ($12-14), seafood ($13-17), and pasta ($13-15). Open M-Th 11:30am-2am, F 11:30am-3am, Sa 10am-3am, Su 9am-2am. ❹

Red Ginger, 1564 Wisconsin Ave. NW (☎965-7009). Serves flavorful Caribbean food, like adobo-spiced duck with quinoa pumpkin salad ($20). Complimentary champagne tops off the weekend brunch (Sa-Su 11:30am-5pm). Open Tu-Th and Su 11:30am-10pm, F-Sa 11:30am-11pm. ❹

Moby Dick House of Kabob, 1070 31st St. NW (☎333-4400). The huge, cheap portions of Greek and Middle Eastern food at this ramshackle hole-in-the-wall will leave you feeling like a whale beached and gone to heaven. Get salads ($4), gyros ($6), or combo meals ($8) to go, and enjoy them on a quiet bench by the C&O canal, just around the corner. Open M-Th 10am-11pm, F-Sa 11am-4am, Su noon-10pm. ❶

Patisserie Poupon, 1645 Wisconsin Ave. NW (☎342-3248), near Q St. Start the day with a buttery brioche, pear danish, or croissant ($1.30-2.25). Sandwiches and salads $4-7. Open Tu-Sa 8am-6:30pm, Su 8am-4pm. ❶

MID-ATLANTIC

Thomas Sweet, 3214 P St. NW (☎337-0616), off Wisconsin Ave. A classy yet relaxed confectionery and ice cream parlor in the center of preppy Georgetown. Customers order cones ($3.20), cappuccinos, fudge, and floats from a chalkboard menu. Ice cream flavors include amaretto, cake batter, and tiramisu. (Open M-Th 8am-midnight, F-Sa 8am-1am, Su 9-midnight. Cash only). ❶

UPPER NORTHWEST

📖 **2 Amys Neapolitan Pizzeria,** 3715 Macomb St. NW (☎885-5700), near Wisconsin Ave. Superb, fresh-from-the-oven pizzas ($8-13) in a pastel yellow and orange dining area. The "Norcia" pizza (tomato, salami, roasted peppers, mozzarella, and garlic; $13) is excellent. Many locals consider this Washington's best pizza—expect a wait at dinnertime. Open M 5-10pm, Tu-Th 11am-10pm, F-Sa 11am-11pm, Su noon-10pm. ❸

Yanni's, 3500 Connecticut Ave. NW (☎362-8871), near Metro: Cleveland Park. Find home-style Greek cooking in this airy restaurant, adorned with classical statues and murals of Greek gods. Try charbroiled octopus, crunchy on the outside and delicately tender within ($15). The strong Greek coffee ($2.50) goes well with the baklava ($5). Entrees $6-17. Vegetarian options $9-12. Open daily 11:30am-11pm. ❸

Mama Maria and Enzio's, 2313 Wisconsin Ave. NW (☎965-1337), near Calvert St. Amazing southern Italian cuisine with a casual, family atmosphere and exceptionally warm service. Shrimp in lemon sauce ($16) is worth the price. Pizzas $9-12. Calzones $7. Cannoli $5. Lunch $7-11. Open M-F 11:30am-10pm, Sa 5-10pm, Su 5-9pm. ❸

Max's Best Ice Cream, 2416 Wisconsin Ave. NW (☎333-3111), just south of Calvert St. Known as D.C.'s premier purveyor of homemade ice cream, Max himself dishes out old favorites and exotic flavors. The only hard part is choosing from his extensive menu. Single scoop $3. Open M-Sa noon-midnight, Su noon-10pm. Cash only. ❶

👁 🏛 SIGHTS AND MUSEUMS

CAPITOL HILL

THE CAPITOL. The ■US Capitol impresses visitors with a grandeur that sets it apart from the city's other historical buildings and memorials. From the time of 19th-century frontiersman Andrew Jackson to the present, it has been the site of the presidential inauguration. The East Front entrance, facing the Supreme Court, brings visitors into the 180 ft. high rotunda, where weary soldiers slept during the Civil War. From the lower-level crypt, visitors can climb to the second floor for a view of the House or Senate visitors chambers. Though much of the real political action takes place behind the scenes, visitors can get gallery passes to view the legislative show—just don't be disappointed if all that's going on is a roll call vote. Americans may obtain gallery passes from the office of their Representative or Senator in the House or Senate office buildings near the Capitol; foreigners can get one-day passes by presenting identification at the appointments desks in the crypt. *(Metro: Capitol South or Union Station.* ☎ *225-6827; www.aoc.gov. Generally open M-Sa*

> **⁂TIP** **CAPITOL TOURS.** For a longer, more informative tour of the Capitol, call your Representative or Senator's office at least a week in advance of your trip to reserve gallery passes and schedule a tour. You will be assigned to a Congressional intern, usually a bright-eyed, bushy-tailed college student who will happily lead you on a detailed tour (often lasting over 1hr.) and answer all your questions. Because of the way the building is set up, it's wise to book through your Representative's office; there's much more to see, including historical artifacts, murals, and the Hall of Columns, on the House side of the Capitol.

9am-4:30pm. Access by 30min. guided tour only. Free, but tickets are required. Same-day tickets available at the Garfield Circle kiosk on the West Front, across from the Botanic Gardens. Kiosk is open from 9am until all tickets are distributed; get there about 45-60min. before opening to guarantee a ticket.) Congress's real business, however, is conducted in **committee hearings.** Most are open to the public; check the *Washington Post*'s "Today in Congress" box for times and locations. If you can find a staff member to chaperone you, you can take a ride on the free **Capitol subway** (the "Capitol Choo-Choo"), which shuttles between the basement of the Capitol and the House and Senate office buildings; a buzzer and flashing light signal an imminent vote.

SUPREME COURT. In 1935, the **Supreme Court** justices decided it was time to take the nation's separation of powers literally and moved from their makeshift offices in the Capitol into a new Greek Revival courthouse across the street. Oral arguments are open to the public; show up early to get a seat. *(1 1st St. Metro: Capitol South or Union Station. ☎ 479-3221; www.supremecourtus.gov. In session Oct.-June M-W 10am-noon and open 1-3pm for 2 weeks every month; courtroom open to the public when Justices are on vacation. The "3min. line" shuffles visitors through standing gallery of the courtroom for a glimpse. Court open M-F 9am-4:30pm. Seating before 8:30am. Free.)*

LIBRARY OF CONGRESS. With over 126 million objects stored on 532 mi. of shelves (including a copy of *Old King Cole* written on a grain of rice), the ☒**Library of Congress** is the world's largest library. The collection was torched by the British in 1814 and then reincarnated using Thomas Jefferson's personal stash. These days, it's open to anyone of college age or older with a legitimate research purpose. Facility tours are also available; exhibits change frequently and range from collections of Pulitzer Prize-winning political cartoons to texts documenting the Supreme Court decisions that ended racial segregation in public schools. The **Jefferson Building's** green copper dome and gold-leafed flame top a spectacular reading room. *(1st St. SE. Metro: Capitol South. ☎ 707-8000; www.loc.gov. Great Hall open M-Sa 10am-5:30pm. Tours M-F 10:30, 11:30am, 1:30, 2:30, and 3:30pm; Sa 10:30, 11:30am, 1:30, and 2:30pm. Visitors Center and galleries open daily 10am-5pm. Free.)*

MONUMENTS

☒**WASHINGTON MEMORIAL.** With a $9.4 million restoration project completed in 1999, this shrine to America's very first president is truly impressive. Once nicknamed the "the Beef Depot monument" after the cattle that grazed in the surrounding area during the Civil War, the Washington Monument was built with rock from multiple quarries, which explains the subtle variations in the color of its stones. The beautiful Reflecting Pool mirrors Washington's obelisk. *(Metro: Smithsonian. ☎ 426-6841; www.nps.gov/wamo/homt.htm. Open daily 9am-5pm. Tours every 30min. 9am-4:30pm. Admission to the monument by timed ticket. Free if obtained on day of visit; arrive early. $1.50 if reserved in advance.)*

☒**VIETNAM VETERANS MEMORIAL.** Maya Lin, the memorial's designer, received a "B" when she submitted her concept for a grade as a Yale senior. She went on to beat her professor in the public memorial design competition. In her words, the monument is "a rift in the earth—a long, polished black stone wall, emerging from and receding into the earth." The wall contains the names of the 58,235 Americans who died in Vietnam, indexed in books at both ends. *(Constitution Ave. at 22nd St. NW. Metro: Smithsonian or Foggy Bottom-GWU. ☎ 634-1568; www.nps.gov/vive. Open 24hr. Free.)*

☒**LINCOLN MEMORIAL.** The Lincoln Memorial, at the west end of the Mall, recalls the rectangular grandeur of Athens's Parthenon, complete with 36 Doric columns. It was from these steps that Martin Luther King, Jr. gave his famous "I Have a Dream" speech during the 1963 March on Washington, D.C. Inside, a seated

MID-ATLANTIC

Lincoln presides over the admiring visitors. Though you may find Lincoln's lap inviting, climbing on the 19 ft. president is a federal offense; a camera will catch you if the rangers don't do it first. *(Metro: Smithsonian or Foggy Bottom-GWU. ☎426-6841; www.nps.gov/linc. Open 24hr. Free.)*

JEFFERSON MEMORIAL. A 19 ft. hollow bronze statue of Thomas Jefferson stands in this open-air rotunda, encircled by massive Ionic columns and overlooking the Tidal Basin. Quotes from the Declaration of Independence, the Virginia Statute of Religious Freedom, and *Notes on Virginia* adorn the walls. *(A long walk from Metro: L'Enfant Plaza or Smithsonian. ☎426-6841; www.nps.gov/thje. Open 24hr. Free.)*

KOREAN WAR MEMORIAL. The 19 colossal polished-steel statues of the Korean War Memorial trudge up a hill, rifles in hand, expressions of weariness and fear frozen upon their faces. The statues are accompanied by a black granite wall with over 2000 sandblasted photographic images from this war, in which 54,246 Americans lost their lives. *(At the west end of the Mall, near Lincoln. Metro: Smithsonian. ☎426-6841; www.nps.gov/kwvm. Open daily 8am-midnight. Free.)*

FRANKLIN DELANO ROOSEVELT MEMORIAL. Occupying a broad stretch of West Potomac Park, the FDR Memorial deviates from the presidential tributes nearby, replacing their marble statuary with serene sculpted gardens, cascading fountains, and thematic alcoves. Four "rooms" each represent a phase of FDR's lengthy presidency. Whether or not to display the disabled Roosevelt in his wheelchair was hotly debated; as a compromise, Roosevelt is shown seated, as in a famous picture of him taken at Yalta. *(A long walk from Metro: Smithsonian, but a short walk from the Jefferson or Lincoln Memorials. ☎426-6841; www.nps.gov/fdrm. Open daily 8am-midnight. Free.)*

NATIONAL WWII MEMORIAL. Its place of prominence on the Mall may have been a subject of local controversy, but this newest monument makes clear how impossible it is to understate the impact of World War II on modern American history. This immense neo-classical plaza is part tribute to the 16 million Americans who served in the armed forces during WWII, including the more than 400,000 soldiers who died, and part triumphal arch, with an archway symbolizing each of the major theaters of battle, 56 granite pillars to represent the contribution of each of the US's states and territories, and a shimmering rainbow pool. *(Metro: Smithsonian or Foggy Bottom-GWU. ☎426-6841; www.nps.gov/nwwm. Open 24hr. Free.)*

THE MALL

The Smithsonian Institution's museums on the Mall constitute the world's largest museum complex. The **Smithsonian Castle,** on the south side of the Mall, has an introduction to and info on all of the Smithsonian buildings. *(Metro: Smithsonian or Federal Triangle. ☎357-2700; www.si.edu. Open daily 8:30am-5:30pm.)*

■ **NATIONAL AIR AND SPACE MUSEUM.** This is the world's most popular museum, with 7.5 million visitors each year. Record-breaking airplanes and space vehicles hang from the ceilings. Exhibits include the Wright brothers' original biplane, which hangs in the entrance gallery, the walk-through Skylab space station, the Apollo XI command module, and a DC-7. *(On the south side of the Mall. Metro: Smithsonian or Federal Triangle. ☎357-2700; www.nasm.si.edu. Free.)*

■ **NATIONAL GALLERY OF ART.** The National Gallery is not a part of the Smithsonian, but is considered a close cousin because of its prime Mall-front location. The West Building, the gallery's original home, contains masterpieces by Leonardo da Vinci, El Greco, Rembrandt, Vermeer, and Monet. The East Building is devoted to 20th-century art, from Magritte and Matisse to Man Ray and Miró. Don't miss the whimsical sculpture garden behind the West Building. *(Metro: Smithsonian or Federal Triangle. ☎737-4215; www.nga.gov. Open M-Sa 10am-5pm, Su 11am-6pm. Free.)*

MID-ATLANTIC

HIRSHHORN MUSEUM AND SCULPTURE GARDEN.
The Hirshhorn is D.C.'s best collection of modern, postmodern, and post-postmodern works from around the world. The slide-carousel-shaped building has outraged traditionalists since 1966. Each floor consists of two concentric circles: an outer ring of paintings and an inner of sculptures. *(On the south side of the Mall, west of Air and Space. Metro: Smithsonian. ☎633-4674; www.hirshhorn.si.edu. Open daily 10am-5:30pm. Free.)*

FREER GALLERY OF ART. The Freer's collection is an intriguing jumble of American and Asian art. The permanent American collection, as dictated by Charles L. Freer himself, focuses on works by James McNeill Whistler, a close friend of the collector. The rotating Asian collections run from 2500 BC through the present. *(On the south side of the Mall, just west of the Hirshhorn. Metro: Smithsonian or Federal Triangle. ☎357-4880; www.asia.si.edu. Open daily 10am-5:30pm. Free.)*

NATIONAL MUSEUM OF AMERICAN HISTORY. The NMAH's plexiglass-encased clutter of old goods have earned it the nickname "the nation's attic." When the Smithsonian inherits quirky pop culture artifacts, like Dorothy's slippers from *The Wizard of Oz*, they end up here. The Hands On History Room contains a working telegraph and an interactive introduction to the Cherokee language. *(On the north side of the mall. Metro: Smithsonian or Federal Triangle. ☎357-2700; www.americanhistory.si.edu. Open daily 10am-5:30pm. Free.)*

NATIONAL MUSEUM OF NATURAL HISTORY. The NMNH contains three floors of rocks, animals, gift shops, and displays selected from the museum's 124 million possessions. The Hope Diamond and dinosaur skeletons are major attractions. The Behring Hall of Mammals presents stuffed and fossilized mammals in recreations of their natural habitats. The museum is rightly proud of its IMAX & Jazz Cafe, where you can enjoy a live performance and then take in the latest nature or action film. *(Metro: Smithsonian or Federal Triangle. ☎633-1000; www.mnh.si.edu. Open daily 10am-5:30pm. Free. IMAX & Jazz shows F 6-10pm; cover $10.)*

OTHER MUSEUMS. Built in 1987, the **National Museum of African Art** and the **Arthur M. Sackler Gallery** hide their treasures underground, below the four-acre **Enid A. Haupt Garden.** The Museum of African Art displays artifacts from sub-Saharan Africa, such as masks, ceremonial figures, and musical instruments. *(Metro: Smithsonian or Federal Triangle. ☎633-4600; www.nmafa.si.edu. Open daily 10am-5:30pm. Free.)* The Sackler Gallery showcases an extensive collection of illuminated manuscripts, Chinese and Japanese paintings, jade miniatures, and friezes from Egypt, Phoenicia, and Sumeria. *(Metro: Smithsonian or Federal*

THE LOCAL STORY

SECRET SYMBOLS

No need to confine your conspiracy theories to the CIA or FBI—an initiated eye can spot the influence of Freemasonry practically everywhere you look in D.C. This secret society pervaded the Revolutionary generation—52 of the original 55 signatories of the Declaration of Independence were Masons. Capitol architect Benjamin Latrobe, White House architect James Hoban, Washington Monument architect Robert Mills: all Masons. The George Washington Masonic Memorial features a large mural depicting the man himself laying the cornerstone of the Capitol in full Masonic regalia.

The very shape of the city reflects the tenets of Freemasonry, which treasures symbols like the builder's square. Look at the original plan for Washington, D.C., which used to encompass Arlington, VA, and a square is exactly what you get. Members seek to "turn to the light," so perhaps it's no mistake that the statue of Freedom atop the Capitol faces due east, towards the rising sun. Freemasons were also taken with Egyptian symbolism, traces of which can be seen in many of the city's memorials, including one tall, central monument in particular.

Interested in exploring these symbols? The George Washington National Masonic Memorial now gives free tours that explore the famous Freemason's life. Call ☎703-683-2007 for info.

Triangle. ☎*633-4880; www.asia.si.edu. Open daily 10am-5:30pm. Free.)* The Smithsonian's newest addition to the Mall is the sweeping **National Museum of the American Indian.** Created through ongoing collaboration with existing American Indian tribes, the exhibits focus on contemporary interpretation and performance to retell the stories of Native American peoples from the Inca to the Inuit. *(Metro: Smithsonian or Federal Triangle.* ☎*633-1000; www.nmai.si.edu. Open daily 10am-5:30pm. Free.)*

SOUTH OF THE MALL

▨**HOLOCAUST MEMORIAL MUSEUM.** Opened in 1993, the privately-funded Holocaust Memorial Museum examines the atrocities of the Holocaust. Special exhibitions, which can be viewed without passes, include the **Wall of Remembrance**—a touching collection of tiles painted by American schoolchildren in memory of the 1.5 million children killed during the Holocaust—the Wexner Learning Center, and an orientation film. The permanent gallery is divided into three chronologically organized floors. *(14th St. between C St. and Independence Ave. SW. Metro: Smithsonian.* ☎*488-0400; www.ushmm.org. Open daily 10am-5:30pm. Film every 30min. 10:45am-4:15pm. Not recommended for children under 11; kids can tour the exhibition "Daniel's Story," an account of Nazi occupation told from a child's perspective. Arrive early to ensure tickets. Free.)*

BUREAU OF ENGRAVING AND PRINTING. The buck starts here, at the Bureau of Engraving and Printing, the largest producer of currency, stamps, and security documents in the world. Guided tours of the presses that print $696 million in money and stamps each day are available. *(At 14th and C St. SW. Metro: Smithsonian.* ☎*874-2330 or 866-874-2330; www.moneyfactory.gov. Mar.-Aug. ticket booth opens M-F at 8am to distribute free tickets for same-day tours 9am-2pm. Arrive early to obtain tickets; most are gone by 9am. Sept.-Feb. no tickets required; tours 10am-2pm.)*

FEDERAL TRIANGLE

▨**NATIONAL ARCHIVES.** Visitors line up at the National Archives to view the original Declaration of Independence, US Constitution, and Bill of Rights as they make their daily appearance from the recesses of a nuclear-bomb-proof vault. This building houses 16 million pictures and posters, 18 million maps, and billions of pages of text—about 2-5% of the documents the government produces each year. *(8th St. and Constitution Ave. NW. Metro: Archives-Navy Memorial.* ☎*501-5000; www.nara.gov. Open daily Apr.-early Sept. 10am-9pm; early Sept.-Mar. 10am-5:30pm. Exhibit Hall open daily Mar.-early Sept 10am-7pm; daily Sept. to mid-March 10am-5:30pm. Free.)*

INTERNATIONAL SPY MUSEUM. Visitors navigating the flash-bang movie set-like backdrops may wonder whether this is an amusement park about to blow its museum cover, but the Spy Museum is legitimately overloaded with fascinating facts and artifacts from centuries of espionage, doing justice to the city with the world's highest concentration of spies. For your inner James Bond, check out tools of the trade, like necktie cameras, secret writing inks, and lipstick pistols. The museum also offers Operation Spy, an hour-long interactive role-playing program that demonstrates to visitors the rigors of espionage. *(800 F St. NW, at 9th St. Metro: Gallery Place-Chinatown.* ☎*393-7798; www.spymuseum.org. Open daily Apr.-Aug. 9am-8pm; Aug.-Oct. 10am-8pm; Oct.-Mar. 10am-6pm. Last entry 2hr. before closing. Tickets with timed admission $16, seniors and military $15, children $13, under 5 free. Operation Spy $14. Combination ticket with museum admission $24. Long lines late in the day yield entry times that may be more than 1hr. after ticket purchase.)*

OLD POST OFFICE. A refuge from D.C.'s summer heat, this classical masterpiece of arched windows, conical turrets, and a clock tower actually holds an expansive food court and shopping pavilion. If you can't make it up to the Washington Monument, the Old Post Office's soaring tower has the second-best view of the city. *(Pennsylvania Ave. and 12th St. NW. Metro: Federal Triangle. ☎ 289-4224; www.oldpostofficedc.com. Tower open mid-Apr. to mid-Sept. M-Sa 9am-7:45pm, Su 10am-5:45pm; low season M-F 9am-4:45pm, Sa-Su 10am-5:45pm. Shops open M-Sa 10am-8pm, Su noon-7pm. Free.)*

NATIONAL MUSEUM OF WOMEN IN THE ARTS. Housed in a former Masonic Temple, the National Museum of Women in the Arts showcases works by the likes of Mary Cassatt, Georgia O'Keeffe, and Frida Kahlo. This museum is the only one in the world dedicated solely to the celebration of achievements of women in the visual, performing, and literary arts, and comprises over 3000 pieces dating from the 16th century to the present. *(1250 New York Ave. NW. Metro: Metro Center. ☎ 783-5000; www.nmwa.org. Open M-Sa 10am-5pm, Su noon-5pm. $10, over 60 and students $8, under 19 free; 1st Su of each month free.)*

WHITE HOUSE AND FOGGY BOTTOM

▨ WHITE HOUSE. With its simple columns and expansive lawns, the White House seems a compromise between patrician lavishness and democratic simplicity. Thomas Jefferson proposed a design for the building, but his entry lost to that of amateur architect James Hoban. Today the President's staff works in the West Wing, while the First Lady's cohorts occupy the East Wing. Staff who cannot fit in the White House work in the nearby **Old Executive Office Building.** The President's official office is the **Oval Office,** site of many televised speeches. *(1600 Pennsylvania Ave. NW. ☎ 456-7041; www.whitehouse.gov. Tours of the White House can be arranged only by calling your congressional representative more than 1 month in advance. Phone numbers for representatives available at www.house.gov. All tours free.)*

LAFAYETTE PARK. Historic homes surround Lafayette Park north of the White House and include the Smithsonian-owned **Renwick Gallery Craft Museum,** which has some remarkable 80s sculptures. *(17th St. and Pennsylvania Ave. NW. Metro: Farragut North, Farragut West, or McPherson Sq. ☎ 633-2850; www.americanart.si.edu/renwick. Open daily 10am-5:30pm. Free.)* The nearby neo-classical **Corcoran Gallery** boasts an expansive collection ranging from colonial to contemporary American art. *(17th St. between E St. and New York Ave. NW. ☎ 639-1700; www.corcoran.org. Open M, W and Su 10am-6pm; Th 10am-9pm; F-Sa 10-5pm. $14, seniors and military $12, students $10.)* The **Octagon House,** designed by Capitol architect William Thornton, was home to President and Mrs. Madison after the White House was burned down by British soldiers during the War of 1812. Today this example of Federalist architecture allegedly houses several ghosts. *(Open Tu-Su 10am-4pm. $5, seniors and students $3.)*

KENNEDY CENTER. Completed in the late 60s, the **John F. Kennedy Center for the Performing Arts** is a monument to the assassinated president, boasting four major stages, a film theater, three breathtaking halls replete with sumptuous red carpets and crystal chandeliers, and a roof deck with stunning views of the Potomac and the D.C. skyline. *(25th St. and New Hampshire Ave. NW. Metro: Foggy Bottom-GWU. ☎ 467-4600 or 800-444-1324; www.kennedy-center.org. Open daily 10am-midnight. Free tours leave from the level A gift shop M-F 10am-5pm, Sa-Su 10am-1pm; call ☎ 416-8340 for details.)* Across the street is "Tricky Dick" Nixon's **Watergate Complex.**

GEORGETOWN

▨ DUMBARTON OAKS ESTATE. Home to several acres of some of the most beautiful gardens in Washington, Dumbarton Oaks was the site of the 1944 Dumbarton Oaks Conference, which helped form the United Nations charter. The estate is now a museum with a collection of Byzantine and pre-Columbian art. *(1703 32nd*

MID-ATLANTIC

St. NW, between R and S St. ☎339-6401, tour info 339-6409; www.doaks.org. Mansion: open Tu-Su 2-5pm. Suggested donation $1. Gardens: open daily mid-Mar. to Oct. 2-6pm; Nov. to mid-Mar. 2-5pm. High season $8, seniors and children $5; low season free.)

GEORGETOWN UNIVERSITY. Archbishop John Carroll oversaw construction in 1788, and Georgetown University opened the following year, becoming the nation's first Catholic institution for higher learning. Today the original Neo-Gothic spires overlook a bustling campus, with several stores, cafes, and sporting venues open to the public. *(37th and O St. ☎687-3600; www.georgetown.edu. Campus tours M-Sa mornings through the admissions office; call for details.)*

UPPER NORTHWEST

■**WASHINGTON NATIONAL CATHEDRAL.** Since its construction in 1909, religious leaders from Rev. Martin Luther King, Jr. to the Dalai Lama have preached from its pulpit. The solemnity of the vast Gothic nave is lightened by fanciful stained glass and sculpture, including a Darth Vader gargoyle near the ceiling. The Pilgrim Observation Gallery reveals D.C. from the city's highest vantage point. *(Massachusetts and Wisconsin Ave. NW. From Metro: Tenleytown, take a 30-series bus toward Georgetown; or, from Metro: Woodley Park-Zoo, walk up Cathedral Ave. ☎537-6200; www.nationalcathedral.org. Open mid-May to early Sept. M-F 10am-5:30pm, Sa 10am-4pm, Su 8am-6:30pm; early Sept. to mid-May M-F 10am-5:30pm. Su mass 8, 9, 11am. Organ demonstration 12:45pm. Tours M-F 10am-11:30am and 12:45-4pm, Sa 10-11:30am and 12:45-3:15pm, Su 12:45-2:30pm. Suggested donation $3, seniors $2, children $1. Behind-the-scenes tours July-Feb. M-F at 10:30am and 1:30pm, $5.)*

NATIONAL ZOO. Founded in 1889 and designed by Frederick Law Olmsted, who also designed New York City's Central Park (p. 103), the zoo is popular with both locals and tourists. Tigers, elephants, and gorillas (oh my!) await. The zoo's giant pandas are perpetual Washington celebrities; both parents and cub are now receiving visitors. The zoo features two roaming endangered golden lion tamarin monkeys who wander freely in a contained environment. *(3001 Connecticut Ave. Metro: Woodley Park-Zoo. ☎673-4800; www.si.edu/natzoo. Grounds open daily Apr.-Oct. 6am-8pm; Nov.-Mar. 6am-6pm. Zoo buildings open daily Apr.-Oct. 10am-6pm, Nov.-Mar. 10am-4:30pm. Free.)*

DUPONT CIRCLE

■**PHILLIPS COLLECTION.** Situated in a stately mansion, the Phillips was the nation's first museum of modern art and still turns heads with its variety of Impressionist and Post-Impressionist masters. Visitors gape at Renoir's masterpiece, *Luncheon of the Boating Party*, and works by Delacroix, Miró, and Turner. Rothko and Kandinsky are also featured prominently. *(1600 21st St., at Q St. NW. ☎387-2151; www.phillipscollection.org. Open Tu-W and F-Sa 10am-5pm, Th 10am-8:30pm; in summer also Su 11am-6pm. Tu-F permanent collection free; Sa $10, students and seniors $8, under 18 free. Audio tours free with admission.)*

ART GALLERY DISTRICT. A triangle of creativity, the **Art Gallery District** contains over two dozen galleries displaying everything from contemporary photographs to tribal crafts. They hold a joint open house on the first Friday of each month (6-8pm) with complimentary drinks at each venue. *(Bounded by Connecticut Ave., Florida Ave., and Q St. www.artgalleriesdc.com lists any changes to open house schedule.)*

EMBASSY ROW. The stretch of Massachusetts Ave. between Dupont Circle and Observatory Circle is also called **Embassy Row.** Before the 30s, socialites lived along the avenue in extravagant edifices; diplomats later found the mansions perfect for their purposes (and sky-high budgets). At the northern end of Embassy Row, flags line the entrance to the **Islamic Center.** Inside the brilliant white mosque, stunning designs stretch to the tips of spired ceilings. *(2551 Massachusetts Ave. NW. ☎332-8343. No shorts allowed; women must cover their heads, arms, and legs. Open daily 10am-5pm. Prayers 5 times daily.)*

🎵 ENTERTAINMENT

MUSIC

D.C.'s punk roots run deep, but performers of all kinds call the city home. Check the *Weekend* section in the Friday edition of the *Washington Post* for details on upcoming concerts, shows, and other events. The bigger, more mainstream events take place at the sports arenas: **RFK Stadium,** 2400 E. Capitol St., in the summer (box office ☎608-1119; open M-F noon-5pm), and the **Verizon Center,** 601 F St., year-round (box office ☎628-3200; open daily 10am-5:30pm). In its 73rd season, the ◢**National Symphony Orchestra** continues to delight D.C., primarily in the Kennedy Center's concert hall (☎467-4600 or 800-444-1324; www.kennedy-center.org/nso). D.C. also has a diverse and thriving jazz and blues scene, with venues perfect for any budget. The **Kennedy Center** (p. 199) and **Smithsonian Museums** (p. 196) often sponsor free shows, especially in the summer.

THEATER AND DANCE

Arena Stage, 6th St. and Maine Ave. SW, is often called the best regional theater company in America due to its innovative take on classics and frequent successes with new works. (Metro: Waterfront. ☎488-3300; www.arenastage.org. Box office open M-Sa 10am-8pm, Su noon-8pm. Tickets $47-74. Discounts for students, seniors, and the disabled. A limited number of half-price tickets usually available 1½hr. before start of show.) The ◢**Kennedy Center,** at 25th St. and New Hampshire Ave., presents various ballet, opera, and dramatic productions. (☎416-8000, for rush ticket info 467-4600; www.kennedy-center.org. Tickets $10-75.) The **Shakespeare Theatre** at the Lansburgh, 450 7th St. NW, at Pennsylvania Ave., puts on lively performances. Each summer the theater puts on the "Free for All," a no-charge production of a Shakespearean work, usually one of the comedies. (Metro: Archives-Navy Memorial. ☎547-1122 or 877-487-8849; www.shakespearetheatre.org. Tickets $23-68; during preview week $13-59. Discounts for students and seniors. $10 standing-room tickets available 1hr. before sold-out performances.) To further satisfy any Shakespearean craving, head to the stately **Folger Theater,** 201 E. Capitol St. SE. The theater is a reproduction of the Bard's Globe in London, and a small museum is adjacent to the performance space. In 2008, look for *Macbeth* (Feb. 28-Apr. 6) and *The School for Scandal* (May 7-June 15). Students receive 20-25% discounts on most regular tickets and 50% rush discounts 1hr. prior to showtime. Seniors, teachers, and military personnel receive 15-20% discounts on most regular tickets. (☎544-7077; www.folger.edu. Box office open M-F 10am-5pm in person, M-Sa noon-4pm by phone.) In the **14th Street Theater District,** tiny repertory companies explore and experiment with new shows; check *CityPaper* for listings. ◢**The Source Theatre,** 1835 14th St. NW, between S and T St., is dedicated to the local community of artists. (Metro: U St.-Cardozo. ☎462-1073; www.sourcetheatre.com.) The famous ◢**Woolly Mammoth Theater Company** offers pay-what-you-can and under-25 performances of contemporary works; a list of plays for 2008 includes *The Unmentionables* and *Measure for Pleasure.* (Metro: Gallery Place-Chinatown. ☎393-3939; www.woollymammoth.net.)

SPORTS

The 20,000-seat **Verizon Center,** 601 F St. NW, in Chinatown, is D.C.'s premiere sports arena. (Metro: Gallery Pl.-Chinatown. ☎628-3200. Open daily 10am-5:30pm.)

The **Wizards,** Washington D.C.'s official NBA team, calls the impressive Verizon Center home. (☎661-5065; www.washingtonwizards.com. Tickets $7-120.) The WNBA's **Mystics** play from May to September. (www.wnba.com/mystics. Tickets $8-60.) The **Capitals** are back with the rest of the NHL for the 2008 season, running October-April. (☎661-5065; www.washingtoncaps.com. Tickets $10-100.) Washington's most successful and least known pro sports team is soccer's **D.C. United,** with a strong local fan base and several MLS championship titles. (☎587-5000; www.dcunited.mlsnet.com. Tickets $16-$40.) Washington's current baseball heroes are the **Nationals,** who used to round the bases in **RFK Stadium** but move to **Nationals Park** in 2008. (www.washington.nationals.mlb.com. Tickets $5-65.) Will Washington, D.C. always remain a football town? Their beloved, if politically incorrect, **Redskins** still draw faithful to **Fed-Ex Field,** Raljon Dr., in Raljon, MD. (☎301-276-6050; www.redskins.com. Season runs Sept.-Dec. Tickets $40-200.)

⚑ NIGHTLIFE

BARS AND CLUBS

Talk about a double life: D.C. denizens who crawl through red tape by day paint the town red by night. If you find yourself taking Jell-O body shots off a beautiful stranger at an all-you-can-drink-fest, don't say we didn't warn you. If you ache for a pint of amber ale, swing by the Irish pub-laden **Capitol Hill.** Hit up **Georgetown** for youthful prepsters in upscale bars. **Dupont Circle** is home to glam GLBT nightlife, while **Adams Morgan** hosts an international crowd. To party with rock stars, head to the hopping **U District.** For additional tips, try www.dcnites.com.

DUPONT AND U DISTRICT

▨ **Brickskeller,** 1523 22nd St. NW (☎293-1885). The largest selection of beer in the world, with 1072 different bottled brews to choose from ($3.25-19). With so many options, expect to get laughed at if you order a Miller Lite. Try a "beer-tail," a mixed drink made with beer ($3.25-6.50). Monthly beer tastings Sept.-May. Open M-Th 11:30am-2am, F 11:30am-3am, Sa 6pm-3am, Su 6pm-2am. Kitchen closes 1hr. earlier.

Eighteenth Street Lounge, 1212 18th St. NW (☎466-3922; www.eslmusic.com/lounge). For the last decade, ESL has set the bar for the D.C. lounge scene with its top-shelf DJs, most of whom are signed to ESL's independent record label. Jazz bands often chill out the top floor while DJs work it downstairs, spinning house, hip-hop, and dance. Cover generally $10-20; Tu no cover. Women often free after midnight. Open Tu-W 9:30pm-2am, Th 5:30pm-2am, F 5:30pm-3am, Sa 9:30pm-3am.

Cafe Saint-Ex, 1847 14th St. NW (☎265-7839; www.saint-ex.com), at T St. The vintage aviation-themed bar, named after Antoine de Saint-Exupery, aviator and author of *The Little Prince,* attracts a mixed crowd of alt-hippies and legal yuppies. It anchors an increasingly lively row of funky nightspots along 14th St. Upstairs bar and patio cafe that serves lunch (M-F 11am-5pm) and brunch (Sa-Su 11am-4pm). Downstairs Gate 54 lounge. Beer $3-6, rail drinks $6. Happy hour daily 5:30-7pm; drinks $3. 21+ after 10:30pm. No cover. Open M-F 5pm-2am, Sa-Su 11am-2am.

The Big Hunt, 1345 Connecticut Ave. NW (☎785-2333). The steam isn't a prop at this jungle-themed 3-floor bar, where the casual khaki-and-flip-flops crowd hunts for "mates, food and drink." The name is a perfect fit for this notorious pickup joint for the college crowd. 24 brews on tap ($3.75-5). Solid pub fare, plus surprisingly good Guinness ice cream. Pool table. Happy hour M-F 4-7:30pm. 21+. No cover. Open M-Th 4pm-2am, F-Sa 4pm-3am, Su 11am-midnight.

ADAMS MORGAN

▓ **Madam's Organ,** 2461 18th St. NW (☎667-5370; www.madamsorgan.com), near Columbia Rd. A 3-floor blues bar with an intimate rooftop patio serving soul food. Live band plays nightly on first floor to an international crowd. Pool tables. 2-for-1 drinks during Happy hour (M-F 5-8pm), and redheads always drink Rolling Rock for ½-price. Drafts $3.75-5.75. Mixed drinks $4.75-6.75. Pitchers $14. 21+. Cover M-Th and Su $2-4, F-Sa $5-7. Open M-Th and Su 5pm-2am, F-Sa 5pm-3am.

Millie & Al's, 2440 18th St. NW (☎387-8131). This jukebox bar draws a trendy crowd operating under a down-home disguise—pitchers over martinis. Cheap pizza, fries, subs, and $1 jello shots. Nightly specials 4-7pm. DJs play rock and hip-hop F-Sa. Draft beer $2-3.50; bottles $3-4.25. 21+. No cover. Open M-Th 4pm-2am, F-Sa 4pm-3am.

Larry's Lounge, 1840 18th St. NW (☎483-1483), at the southern end of Adams Morgan. This funky bar may be a trek from the Metro, but its Singapore Slings ($6.50) make the trip worth it. Happy hour daily 4-8pm. Open daily 4pm-2am.

CAPITOL HILL

▓ **The Dubliner,** 520 N. Capitol St. NW (☎737-3773). Metro: Union Station. A subdued crowd enjoys Guinness and the house brew, Auld Dubliner Amber Ale (pints $5), in what many consider to be D.C.'s most authentic Irish pub. A large patio turns lounge-style for celebrators as the night ticks on. Live Irish music nightly around 9pm. Open M-Th and Su 7am-2am, F-Sa 7am-3am. Kitchen closes at 1am.

Pour House, 319 Pennsylvania Ave. SE (☎546-1001; www.politiki-dc.com). Metro: Capitol South. 3 levels: German biergarten atmosphere downstairs, martini bar upstairs (Tu-Sa), and a typical sports bar in between that stays packed with Hill staffers all week long. Nightly drink specials. Free buffet M-Th and Su 4pm-1:30am. Happy hour M-F 5:30-8pm. Open M-Th 4pm-1:30am, F 3pm-2:30am, Sa-Su 10am-2:30am.

GLBT NIGHTLIFE

The *Washington Blade* is the best source for gay news and club listings; published every Friday, it's available in virtually every storefront in Dupont Circle. *Metro Weekly*, a gay and lesbian Washington-area magazine, is another good reference for weekend entertainment and nightlife.

▓ **J.R.'s,** 1519 17th St. NW (☎328-0090), at Church St. D.C.'s busiest gay bar for good reasons: hot bartenders, fun events like bachelor auctions, and great drink deals. Packed every night with hordes of "guppies" (gay urban professionals). Happy hour (M-W 5-8pm) brings $3 mini-pitchers, $2 rail drinks and domestic beers, and $1 sodas; the famous Power Hour follows (8-9pm), during which everything is ½-price. Open M-Th 4pm-2am, F-Sa 12:30pm-3am, Su noon-2am.

▓ **Cobalt,** 1639 R St. NW (☎462-6569), at 17th St. No sign marks this hot spot; look for the blue light and bouncer. Shirtless bartenders serve drinks ($4.75-5.75) to a preppy gay male and straight female crowd. Tu 70s and 80s night. No cover M-W or Su. Cover Th $8, open bar; F after 11pm and Sa $5. Open Tu-Th 10pm-2am, F-Sa 10pm-3am, Su 8:30pm-2am. Downstairs, **30°** is a relaxed lounge with ½-price martinis during Happy hour (M-F 5-8pm). 21+. Open M-Th and Su 5pm-2am, F-Sa 5pm-3am.

Apex, 1415 22nd St. NW (☎296-0505), near P St. Formerly Badlands, this 2-story dance complex is one of Dupont's old standbys. DJs attract a young crowd with house, trance, and Top 40. Sa "Liquid Ladies" night, with $7 cover and $3 Long Island iced teas, draws a crowd of lesbians. Drag karaoke starts 11pm. Th college night; cover $5, free with student ID, mixed drinks $3. Cover F $9. 18+. Open Th-Sa 9pm-4am.

■ DAYTRIPS FROM D.C.

ARLINGTON, VA

Metro: Arlington Cemetery, for Drug Enforcement Administration Pentagon City.

The 612-acre **Arlington National Cemetery** holds the graves of over 260,000 service-men and women, including veterans of every American war from the Revolution-ary War to the present. A simple walking tour can begin at the **Tomb of the Unknowns,** which honors unidentified servicemen who died fighting for the US. It is guarded by soldiers from the Army's Third Infantry, who execute a perfect chang-ing of the guard with stunning precision (Apr.-Sept. every 30min. 8am-6pm; Oct.-Mar. every hr. 8am-4pm). A 10min. walk directly north of the Tomb are the **Kennedy gravesites.** Here lie the remains of President John F. Kennedy, his brother Robert F. Kennedy, and his wife Jacqueline Kennedy Onassis. It is said that shortly before that fateful day in November, JFK visited this hillside spot and was so enchanted by the view that he declared "I could stay here forever"; now the Eternal Flame flickers above the simple memorial stone commemorating his final resting place. A brief walk up the hill from the Kennedy gravesites toward the distinctive orange columns of **Arlington House** is a memorial to **Pierre L'Enfant,** whose grave overlooks the city he designed. The classical edifice, Arlington House (open daily 9:30am-4:30pm) was once the home of Confederate general Robert E. Lee, who was origi-nally offered command of the Union Army by President Lincoln. Torn between his country and his state, Lee decided he could not fight against his fellow Virginians and left for Richmond. The Union Army occupied Arlington House shortly thereaf-ter and, to ensure that Lee never returned, began burying their war dead on the property. Lee's home, now a museum of antebellum life, provides one of the best views of D.C.

Farther down the hill among the plain headstones lies General of the Armies **John J. "Black Jack" Pershing,** commander of US forces during WWI, who asked to be buried with his men. Arlington also holds the bodies of Arctic explorers **Robert E. Peary** and **Richard Byrd,** legendary politician **William Jennings Bryan,** and heavy-weight champion **Joe Louis.** Each year on Memorial Day, a small American flag is placed on each of the cemetery's gravesites; the President lays a wreath at the Tomb of the Unknowns and makes a speech commemorating the day. The **Women in Military Service for America Memorial** fits into its somber surroundings with a cir-cular stone wall and reflecting pool. A memorial for the victims of the September 11th attacks and a memorial dedicated to the crew of the space shuttle *Columbia* were recently added. (☎703-607-8000; www.arlingtoncemetery.org. Open daily Apr.-Oct. 8am-7pm; Oct.-Mar. 8am-5pm. Free. Parking $1.25 per hr. for 1st 3hr., $2 per hr. thereafter.)

Exit the cemetery through Weitzel Gate and walk north for 20min. to get to the **Iwo Jima Memorial,** based on Joe Rosenthal's Pulitzer Prize-winning photo of Marines straining to raise the US flag on Mt. Suribachi. **The Pentagon,** south of the Arlington National Cemetery, is the world's largest building, with 17½ mi. of hall-ways, 7754 windows, 131 stairways, and four postal codes of its own. The wall that took the impact of the hijacked airplane on September 11, 2001, has been com-pletely restored. Tours of the Pentagon are currently suspended due to security concerns; the Tour Office (☎703-695-3324) has information about the future of Pentagon tours. Just down S. Hayes St. from the Pentagon is the **Drug Enforcement Administration,** which operates a fascinating museum on the history of illegal drugs in America. Changing exhibits have focused on topics such as drugs' effects on their users and how the agents operate on land, in air, and on sea. (☎307-3463; www.deamuseum.org. Open Tu-F 10am-4pm. Free.)

ALEXANDRIA, VA

Metro: King Street; 10min. drive from downtown over Roosevelt Bridge and south on George Washington Parkway.

Alexandria was once the young nation's sixth-busiest port, but it didn't become a tourist attraction until the 80s, when city residents backed away from proposed high-rises and decided to revitalize Old Town. Capitalizing on original 18th-century architecture and the legacy of historical all-stars like George Washington and Robert E. Lee, the town re-cobbled the streets, re-bricked the sidewalks, installed gardens, restored over 1000 original facades, and invited tall ships and hip shops. As a result, **Old Town Alexandria** is now packed with tourists (tours offered at the Visitors Center M-Sa 10:30am and Su 2pm). **King Street,** Old Town's main thoroughfare, is a long tree-shaded street lined with shops and restaurants that runs down to the Potomac waterfront. Sights cluster along Washington and King St. Looming over western Alexandria, the lofty **George Washington Masonic National Memorial,** 101 Callahan Dr., is an imposing testament to the strength of Masonry and the legacy of Washington, the only person in history to have been a Masonic chartermaster and US president at the same time. (☎ 703-683-2007; www.gwmemorial.org.) Formerly a hotbed of political, business, and social life, the restored **Gadsby's Tavern,** 134 N. Royal St., takes you back to ye good olde days of hospitality, when as many as four hotel guests slept in one bed. Adams, Jefferson, Madison, and Lafayette all quaffed here. (☎ 703-838-4242; www.gadsbystavern.org. Open Apr.-Oct. M and Su 1-5pm, Tu-Sa 10am-5pm; Nov.-Mar. W-Sa 11am-4pm, Su 1-4pm. Last 30min. tour 15min. before closing. $4, students 11-17 $2, ages under 10 free.) The **Ramsay House Visitors Center,** 221 King St., offers free maps. The house, a 1724 building shipped upriver from Dumfries, VA, was the home of Scottish merchant and Lord Mayor William Ramsay. (☎ 703-838-4200; www.alexandriacity.com. Open daily 9am-5pm.)

MOUNT VERNON

Fairfax Connector 101 bus from Metro: Huntington, or George Washington Pkwy. S, which becomes Washington St. in Alexandria.

George Washington's fabulous **Mount Vernon** estate is easily accessible in Fairfax County, VA. Enthusiastic curators have turned the estate into a living 1760s experience. Visitors can tour Washington's bedroom and tomb and watch demonstrations on the estate's fields, where slaves once grew corn, wheat, and tobacco. The rocking chairs on the mansion's immense veranda are perfect for enjoying the breezes off the Potomac River below. Eschewing modesty, Washington once bragged, "No estate in United America is more pleasantly situated than this." The estate maintains 30-40% of Washington's original furnishings, all of which are on display. Seafaring types may want to take advantage of a 40min. cruise on the Potomac ($9, children $5); also offered are tours of Washington's grist mill and whiskey distillery, still in operation ($2). The fit and adventurous can bike the scenic, 20 mi. Mt. Vernon trail. (☎ 703-780-2000 or 800-429-1520; www.mountvernon.org. Open daily Apr.-Aug. 8am-5pm; Mar. and Sept.-Oct. 9am-5pm; Nov.-Feb. 9am-4pm. $13, seniors $12, ages 6-11 $6, under 6 free.)

VIRGINIA

Many of America's formative experiences took place in Virginia—the English settlement of North America, the boom in the slave trade, the definitive establishment of American independence, and much of the Civil War. The powerful antebellum imagery proffered by the state's many historical sites can be over-

MID-ATLANTIC

whelming, especially since today's cosmopolitan Virginia is a far cry from its colonial origins. Travel down the state's eastern shore to indulge your historical nostalgia, and if you seek solitude and rejuvenation, head west to explore towering Appalachian forests and fascinating underground caverns.

🛈 PRACTICAL INFORMATION

Capital: Richmond.

Visitor Info: Virginia Division of Tourism (motto: "Virginia is for lovers"), 901 E. Byrd St., Richmond 23219 (☎800-847-4882; www.virginia.org). Open M-F 8:30am-5pm. **Department of Conservation and Recreation,** 203 Governor St., Ste. 213, Richmond 23219 (☎804-786-1712; www.dcr.state.va.us). Open M-F 8am-5pm.

Postal Abbreviation: VA. **Sales Tax:** 5%.

RICHMOND ☎ 804

Virginia's capital city has a survivor's history of conflicts, disasters, and triumphs. Richmond was officially chartered in 1742, but William Mayo—who laid out the city of Richmond—found his handiwork burned to the ground in 1781 thanks to a British attack led by American traitor Benedict Arnold. The city was rebuilt and went on to become the capital of the ill-fated Confederate States of America during the Civil War. However, this tenacious town held on after the South's bitter loss, and by 1946 Richmond's economy and industrial strength outpaced nearly every other US city.

🚊 TRANSPORTATION

Trains: Amtrak, 1500 East Main St. (☎800-872-7245; www.amtrak.com). To: **Baltimore** (3-4hr., 3 per day, $47-55); **Virginia Beach** (3½hr., 2 per day, $30-33); **Washington, D.C.** (2¼hr., 3 per day, $26-40); **Williamsburg** (1¼hr., 2 per day, $19). Station open 24hr. Taxi to downtown $17-18.

Buses: Greyhound, 2910 N. Blvd. (☎254-5910 or 800-231-2222; www.greyhound.com), 2 blocks from downtown. To: **Baltimore** (3-5hr., 19 per day, $23-25); **Charlottesville** (1¼hr., 4 per day, $18); **New York City** (7-8hr., 22 per day, $55-59); **Norfolk** (2½hr., 6 per day, $18-20); **Philadelphia** (6-8hr., 10 per day, $42-45); **Washington, D.C.** (2½hr., 14 per day, $19-21); **Williamsburg** (1hr., 5 per day, $10).

Public Transit: Greater Richmond Transit Co., 101 S. Davis Ave. (☎358-4782). Maps available in the basement of City Hall (900 E. Broad St.), at the 6th St. Marketplace Station, and in the Yellow Pages. Most buses leave from stops on Broad St. downtown. Bus #24 goes to the Greyhound station. $1.25; seniors and disabled $0.50; transfers $0.15. Supersaver tickets 10 for $10.

Taxi: Veterans Cab, ☎275-5542.

🛩️🛈 ORIENTATION AND PRACTICAL INFORMATION

Broad Street is the city's central artery, and its cross streets are numbered from west to east. Most parallel streets to Broad St., including **Main Street** and **Cary Street,** run one way. Both **I-95,** going north to Washington, D.C., and **I-295** encircle the city's urban section—the former to the east and north, the latter to the south and west. On the southeast edge of the city, **Shockoe Slip** and **Shockoe Bottom** overflow with partiers at night. Farther east, on the edge of town, the **Court End** and **Church Hill** districts comprise the city's historic center. **Jackson Ward** to the north, bounded by Belvedere, Leigh, Broad, and 5th St., underwent major construction

Downtown Richmond

▲ ACCOMMODATIONS
Be My Guest
Bed and Breakfast, **2**
Pocahontas State Park, **7**
Travelodge, **1**

● FOOD
Bottoms Up, **6**

Strawberry St. Cafe
and Market, **3**
Zuppa, **4**

🔔 NIGHTLIFE
The Tobacco Company
Club, **5**

several years ago to revamp its City Center and revitalize the surrounding community—visitors should still use caution in this area at night. The **Fan** is bounded by the Boulevard, I-195, the walk of statues along **Monument Avenue,** and **Virginia Commonwealth University.** The Fan has a notoriously dangerous reputation, but has become more gentrified in recent years. The pleasant bistros and boutiques of **Carytown,** west of the Fan on Cary St., and the tightly knit working community of Oregon Hill add texture to the cityscape. Be careful in Oregon Hill at night.

Visitor Info: Richmond Metropolitan Visitor's Bureau, 405 N. 3rd St. (☎783-7450; www.richmondva.org), in the Richmond Convention Center. Tours, maps, and discounted lodging. Open daily Memorial Day-Labor Day 9am-6pm; low season 9am-5pm.

Hotlines: Rape Crisis; ☎643-0888. 24hr. **AIDS/HIV;** ☎800-533-4148. Operates M-F 8am-5pm.

Internet Access: Richmond Public Library, 101 E. Franklin St. (☎646-4867). Free with photo ID. Open M-W 9am-9pm, Th-F 9am-6pm, Sa 10am-5pm.

Post Office: 1801 Brook Rd. (☎775-6304). Open M-F 7am-6pm, Sa 9am-2pm. **Postal Code:** 23232.

⛺ ACCOMMODATIONS

▓ Be My Guest Bed and Breakfast, 2926 Kensington Ave. (☎358-9901). Located in the heart of Richmond, Be My Guest is truly a hidden deal: it doesn't have a sign or appear in a phone book. Pleasing decor, full breakfast, and friendly owners make this B&B worth the hunt. Reservations recommended. Rooms $70-135. Cash only. ❹

Travelodge, 5221 Brook Rd. (☎266-7603 or 800-637-3297). Take I-95 to Exit 81, bear right at the first light, and make a left on Brook Rd. This brand-new location offers continental breakfast, free parking, an outdoor pool, cable TV, and microfridges. Singles and doubles weekdays $50-64, weekends $64-69. AAA discount. AmEx/D/MC/V. ❸

Pocahontas State Park, 10301 State Park Rd. (☎796-4255 or 800-933-7275; www.dcr.state.va.us). Take I-95 south to Rte. 288 (Exit 67); after 5 mi., connect to Rte. 10, exit on Ironbridge Rd. east, and turn right on Beach Rd.; the park is 4 mi. down on the right. Showers, biking, boating, picnic areas, and the second-largest pool in Virginia. Rent a canoe, rowboat, or paddleboat (each $6 per hr.), or a kayak ($8-10 per hr.). Sites with water and electricity $24-29. MC/V. ❶

🍴 FOOD

Strawberry Street Cafe and Market, 421 and 415 Strawberry St. (cafe ☎353-6860, market 353-4100; www.strawberrystreetcafe.com). Offers an unlimited salad bar ($8), a brunch bar (Sa-Su until 3pm; $10), and an array of American classics ($7-14) in a pleasant setting. Located in an upscale, youthful Fan neighborhood. Try the French Dip sandwich ($8.75), served on a croissant with broth on the side for dipping. Open M-Th 11am-3pm and 5-10:30pm, F 11am-3pm and 5-11pm, Sa 11am-11pm, Su 10am-10:30pm. AmEx/MC/V. ❸

Bottoms Up, 1700 Dock St. (☎644-4400), at 17th and Cary St. Perfect for post-nightclub pizza cravings, with creative toppings to suit any taste. Create your own, or go with the Chesapeake (spicy crabmeat). Slices $4.25-7; pies $10-21.50. Open M-Tu and Su 11am-10pm, W-Th 11am-11pm, F-Sa 11am-2am. AmEx/D/MC/V. ❷

Zuppa, 104 N. 18th St. (☎249-8831), in Shockoe Bottom. A mostly professional crowd enjoys freshly baked bread, a daily selection of soups, and just-about-gourmet salads, sandwiches, and appetizers. Zuppa's is the place to go for a quick and tasty meal. Sandwiches $6. Soup $2-5. Open Tu-Th 11am-10pm, F 11am-2am, Sa 5pm-3am. AmEx/D/MC/V. ❶

📷 SIGHTS

ST. JOHN'S CHURCH AND ENVIRONS. St. John's Church is the site of Patrick Henry's famed "Give me liberty or give me death" speech. In the summer, orators re-create the 1775 speech on Sundays at 2pm. The church still serves as an active house of worship. *(2401 E. Broad St. ☎648-5015; www.historicstjohnschurch.org. 25min. tours M-Sa 10am-3:30pm, Su 1-3:30pm. Services Su 8:30 and 11am. Admission $5, ages over 62 $4, ages 7-18 $3.)* Nearby is the **Edgar Allan Poe Museum,** in Richmond's oldest standing house (circa 1737), where visitors try evermore to unravel the author's untimely death. Poe memorabilia fill the museum. *(1914 E. Main St. ☎648-5523; www.poemuseum.org. Open Tu-Sa 10am-5pm, Su 11am-5pm. Tours every hr.; last tour 4pm. $6; AAA, seniors, and students $5; under 9 free. Self-guided tours $5.)*

CONFEDERATE SOUTH. Explore the historical relevance of the Civil War at the **Museum of the Confederacy.** The poignant painting "Last Meeting of Lee and Jackson" and the collection of military medical artifacts are especially intriguing. Next door, friendly guides run tours through the **White House of the Confederacy.** *(1201 E. Clay St. ☎649-1861; www.moc.org. Museum open M-Sa 10am-5pm, Su noon-5pm. White House guided tours every 30min-1hr. Museum tickets $8, over 62 $7, ages 7-18 $4. Tickets to White House $8/7/4. Combination tickets $11/10/6.)*

FAN DISTRICT. Richmond's old-world section is home to the country's largest and best-preserved Victorian neighborhood. Stroll down **Monument Avenue,** a boulevard lined with graceful old houses and towering statues of Virginia heroes—Richmond's memory lane. The statue of **Robert E. Lee** faces south toward his beloved Dixie; **Stonewall Jackson** faces north so that the general can scowl at the Yankees for all eternity. The statue of African-American tennis hero **Arthur Ashe** created a storm of controversy when it was added to the end of the avenue that had previously featured only Civil War generals.

MUSEUM ROW. The ◪**Virginia Historical Society** maintains an impressive collection in an even more impressive building. Marvel at the elegant classical architecture before moving on through the extensive "Story of Virginia" exhibit, tracing the history of Virginians from pre-history to the present. The museum's showcase feature is a series of murals known as the "Four Seasons of the Confederacy," painted by the French artist Charles Hoffbauer between 1914 and 1921. *(428 N. Blvd. ☎358-4901; www.vahistorical.org. Open M-Sa 10am-5pm, Su 1-5pm. $5, seniors $4, students and children $3.)* The **Virginia Museum of Fine Arts** is the South's largest art museum, and houses a collection by some of the world's most renowned painters—Monet, Renoir, Picasso, and Warhol—as well as ancient treasures from Rome, Egypt, and Asia. *(200 N. Blvd. ☎340-1400; www.vmfa.state.va.us. Open W-Su 11am-5pm. Suggested donation $5; admission for special exhibitions varies.)*

🎵 📷 ENTERTAINMENT AND NIGHTLIFE

At the marvelous old **Byrd Theatre,** 2908 W. Cary St., movie buffs buy tickets for just-out-of-theaters movies from a tuxedoed agent. On Saturdays, guests are treated to midnight shows and a Wurlitzer organ concert. (☎353-9911; www.byrdtheatre.com. Shows $2; Sa midnight movie $3.) **Friday Cheers** presents free concerts at Brown's Island on Friday evenings during the summer. Check at the Visitors Center for schedules. *Style Weekly*, a free magazine available at the Visitors Center, and *Punchline*, found in most hangouts, list concert lineups and events. Cheer on the **Richmond Braves,** Richmond's AAA minor-league baseball team, at The Diamond, Exit 78 off I-95. (☎359-4444; www.rbraves.com. General admission $7, box seats $10.)

Student-driven nightlife enlivens **Shockoe Slip** and the **Fan.** After dark, **Shockoe Bottom** turns into college-party central, with bars pumping bass-heavy music. Be cautious in the Bottom's alleys after dark. At **The Tobacco Company Club,** 1201 E. Cary St., in the Tobacco Company Restaurant, an older crowd drinks martinis, smokes cigars, and revels in the comfort of Southern living. (☎782-9555; www.the-tobaccocompany.com. Live music in restaurant Tu-Sa 9pm. No bikini contests here—or tennis shoes, jeans, or boots. 21+. Happy hour M-F 4:30-7pm. Cover $3. Open Th-Sa 8pm-2am.)

WILLIAMSBURG   ☎757

Colonial Williamsburg is a living snapshot of American life on the eve of the Revolutionary War; every part of the reconstructed town screams 1770. The historical re-creation extends right down to the fife-and-drum corps that periodically marches down the town's streets. If Williamsburg alone doesn't satiate your colonial nostalgia, check out the nearby towns of Jamestown, the first permanent British settlement in what would become the United States of America, and Yorktown, the most decisive battle of the American Revolutionary War.

▐ TRANSPORTATION

Airport: Newport News and Williamsburg International Airport (PHF) (☎877-0221; www.nnwairport.com), 20min. away in Newport News. Take state road 199 W to I-64 S. Several shuttles serve the airport, including **Williamsburg Limousines** (☎877-0279). To Newport News $26, Norfolk $65; call ahead for reservations.

Trains: Amtrak (☎800-872-7245 or 229-8750; www.amtrak.com), 468 N. Boundary St. To: **Baltimore** (5-6hr., 2 per day, $44-59); **New York City** (7-9hr., 2 per day, $77-91); **Philadelphia** (6-7hr., 2 per day, $58-77); **Richmond** (1¼hr., 2 per day, $16-21).

Buses: Greyhound, 468 N. Boundary St. (☎800-231-2222 or 229-1460; www.greyhound.com). Ticket office open M-F 8am-noon and 1-5pm, Sa 8am-noon and 1-2pm. To: **Baltimore** (5½-7hr., 7 per day, $45-48); **Norfolk** (1-2hr., 5 per day, $12-14); **Richmond** (1hr., 6 per day, $9-10); **Virginia Beach** (2½hr., 3 per day, $16-18); **Washington, D.C.** (4-6hr., 6 per day, $30-32).

Public Transit: Williamsburg Area Transport (WAT; ☎259-4093; www.williamsburgtransport.com). Bus service along Rte. 60 and to all major Williamsburg destinations. 8 lines operate May-Sept. M-Sa 6am-10pm; Sept.-May M-Sa 6am-8pm. $1.25, seniors and disabled $0.50. All-day pass $1.50. Transfer $0.25.

Taxi: Yellow Cab, ☎722-1111.

▐ ▐ ORIENTATION AND PRACTICAL INFORMATION

Williamsburg lies 53 mi. southeast of Richmond. The beautiful **Colonial Parkway** connects the three towns in the historic triangle—Williamsburg, Jamestown, and Yorktown. Take the Colonial Pkwy. Exit off I-64 to reach Colonial Williamsburg.

Visitor Info: Williamsburg Area Convention and Visitors Bureau, 421 N. Boundary St. (☎253-0192 or 800-368-6511; www.visitwilliamsburg.com), ½ mile northwest of the Transportation Center. Provides information about area attractions. Open M-F 8:30am-5pm. **Colonial Williamsburg Visitors Center,** 100 Visitors Center Dr. (☎229-1000 or 800-447-8679; www.colonialwilliamsburg.com), 1 mi. northeast of the Transportation Center. Open daily 8:45am-5:30pm; winter hours vary.

Post Office: 425 N. Boundary St. (☎800-275-8777). Open M-F 8am-5pm, Sa 9am-2pm. **Postal Code:** 23185.

ACCOMMODATIONS

Williamsburg is teeming with upscale hotels and unique B&Bs. Budget chains cluster around the junctions of Rte. 5, 31, 60, 132, and 162. The 1 mi. walk into the colonial area might be strenuous during the scorching summers, but if you can't get a room in town, this may be your best bet. **Econolodge ❸**, 1800 Richmond Rd., has some of the lowest prices in town and a central location. (☎229-6600. Wheelchair-accessible rooms available. Outdoor pool and continental breakfast. Doubles M-F $65, Sa-Su $75. AmEx/D/MC/V.) **Days Inn ❸**, 902 Richmond Rd., located on Williamsburg's main thoroughfare, is not far from the College of William and Mary. (☎229-5060. Outdoor pool and continental breakfast. Singles $61; doubles $72. Discounts for AAA members. AmEx/D/MC/V.)

FOOD

The Old Chickahominy House, 1211 Jamestown Rd. (☎229-4689), 1½ mi. from Williamsburg's historic district. A combination antiques shop and restaurant, Chickahominy offers traditional Southern fare. The "Complete Luncheon" has Virginia ham, hot biscuits, fruit salad, homemade pie, and iced tea or coffee for $7.25. 2 pancakes $5. Open M-F 8:30-10:30am and 11:30am-2:30pm, Sa-Su 8:30-10am and 11:45am-2pm. MC/V. ❷

Chowning's Tavern, Duke of Gloucester St. (☎229-2141 or 800-828-3767). Quasi-authentic British pub grub. Costumed waiters sing 18th-century ditties and challenge guests to card games and sing-alongs over light meals ($3.50-5.50). Seating arrangements make Chowning's better for large groups. Sandwiches $5-14. Cover $3, no cover for dinner guests. Open daily 11am-9pm. AmEx/D/MC/V. ❷

Berret's, 199 S. Boundary St. (☎253-1847), located at Merchant's Sq. Combines 2 restaurants in 1. The more casual **Tap House Grill ❸** serves upscale sandwich plates like the chicken pecan apple salad sandwich ($8-12) and seafood entrees ($14-19). Open daily 5-10pm. **Berret's Restaurant and Bar ❺** features mouth-watering (albeit pricey) dishes such as the chilled shrimp in puff pastry with herbed goat cheese appetizer ($8.50). Live music in summer Su 6:30-9:30pm. Open daily 11:30am-3:30pm and 5:30-10pm. AmEx/D/MC/V.

SIGHTS

COLONIAL WILLIAMSBURG. Every day is a historical reenactment at Colonial Williamsburg. In the summer, ask the pedestrians in 18th-century apparel what's on their minds and visitors will enjoy an informed discussion of the issues of 1776. The year 1774 is reenacted in the spring, 1775 in the fall, and 1773 in the winter. Armed with enthusiastic actors and meticulously restored buildings, the site prides itself on its authenticity. Immersing yourself in the colonists' world doesn't require a ticket: visitors can walk the streets, interact with the locals, and use the restrooms without ever opening their wallets. However, to enter any building, with or without an actor inside, or to attend any of the performances, you will have to pay for a ticket. The focal point is the Palace Green in front of the reconstructed Governor's Palace, which housed Patrick Henry and Thomas Jefferson during their respective gubernatorial reigns; tours are offered throughout the day at 7-15min. intervals. **Duke of Gloucester Street** is a large pedestrian mall lined with colonial-style buildings that house a variety of shops and restaurants. The weekly *Visitor's Companion* newsletter lists free events, evening programs, and complete hours. (☎229-1000; www.colonialwilliamsburg.org. Visitors Center open daily 8:45am-5:30pm. Most sights open 9am-5pm. Day pass $36, ages 6-17 $18; 2 consecutive days and admission to Governor's Palace $49/$24.)

COLLEGE OF WILLIAM AND MARY. Spreading west from the corner of Richmond and Jamestown Rd., the College of William and Mary, founded in 1693, is the second-oldest college in the United States (after Harvard University in Massachusetts, p. 274) and has educated such luminaries as Presidents Jefferson, Monroe, and Tyler. The Christopher Wren Building is the oldest academic building in continuous use in America, still hosting classes to this day. The Office of Admissions, in Blow Hall, leads free tours throughout the year. (☎ 221-4223; www.wm.edu. Tours M-F 10am and 2:30pm, also Sa 10am.)

◤ DAYTRIPS FROM WILLIAMSBURG

JAMESTOWN AND YORKTOWN

The Historic Triangle brims with US history. Less crowded than the Colonial Williamsburg tourist empire, Jamestown and Yorktown show visitors where it all really began. The **Colonial National Park** preserves American colonial and revolutionary history with branches in both Jamestown and Yorktown. Southwest of Williamsburg on Rte. 31, at the Jamestown branch, you'll see the remains of the first permanent English settlement in America (founded in 1607) and exhibits on colonial life. The Visitors Center presents a film emphasizing the courage of America's first settlers, a 35min. walking tour (10:15am and 2:45pm; free with admission), and a 45min. audio tape tour ($2) for the Island Loop Route. Southeast of Williamsburg on the Colonial Pkwy., Yorktown recreates the last battle of the Revolutionary War with an engaging film and a map. The Visitors Center rents cassettes and players ($2) for the battlefield's 3- or 5-mi. car routes. (☎ 229-1733; www.nps.gov/colo. Open daily 9am-5pm. Visitors Centers close 30min. before park. Jamestown $8, Yorktown $5, under 17 free; both parks $10. Passes good for 7 days.)

On Rte. 31, near the Jamestown branch of Colonial National Park, the **Jamestown Settlement** has a museum with changing exhibits, a reconstruction of James Fort, a Native American village, and full-scale replicas of the three ships that brought the original settlers to Jamestown in 1607. Children will enjoy the educational riverfront "discovery area." On the Colonial Parkway near the recreated Settlement is the original **Historic Jamestowne**, the site of the first permanent English-speaking colony in North America. The site includes an archaeological dig, a statue of Pocahontas, and a 1907 church built on the foundation of the 17th-century original. (☎ 253-4838 or 888-593-4682. Open daily June 15-Aug. 15 9am-6pm; Aug. 16-June 14 9am-5pm. $12, ages 6-12 $6. Combination ticket including Yorktown Victory Center $17.75, ages 6-12 $8.75, under 6 free.)

The 1781 American and French triumph over British forces in the final battle of the Revolutionary War is celebrated daily at the Yorktown Victory Center. The Center features two re-created areas—a Continental Army camp and a traditional 1780s farm—where reenactors interpret history. Admission to the center also includes informative exhibits and a 30min. film about the battle of Yorktown. (☎ 253-4838 or 888-593-4682; www.historyisfun.org. Visitors center open daily 9am-4:30pm. $8.75, ages 6-12 $4.50, under 6 free.)

VIRGINIA BEACH ☎ 757

This boardwalk-centered town overflows with the all-you-can-eat buffets, age-old motels, and cheap discount stores that are the hallmarks of seemingly every beach town in America. Load up on saltwater taffy, homemade fudge, and tacky t-shirts; the best part of a Virginia Beach vacation is not getting wrapped up in the stuffiness that can plague more pretentious resort towns.

MID-ATLANTIC

⌐ TRANSPORTATION

Trains: Amtrak (☎800-872-7245 or 245-3589; www.amtrak.com). The nearest train station, at 9304 Warwick Blvd. in Newport News, runs 45min. bus service to and from the corner of 19th and Pacific St. Open daily 7:30am-8pm. Trains go to: **Baltimore** (6½hr., 2 per day, $50-91); **New York City** (8½hr., 1 per day, $77-138); **Philadelphia** (7½hr., 1 per day, $58-104); **Richmond** (2hr., 1 per day, $20-37); **Washington, D.C.** (4hr., 1 per day, $40-75); **Williamsburg** (30min., 1 per day, $16-31).

Buses: Greyhound, 14407 Warwick Blvd. (☎800-231-2222 or 872-4405; www.greyhound.com). Open daily 8am-9:30am, 11:30am-1pm and 3-8pm. Buses go to **Richmond** (1¾hr., 5 per day, $19.50), **Washington, D.C.** (5¼hr., 5 per day, $31.50), and **Williamsburg** (40min., 5 per day, $9.50).

Public Transit: Virginia Beach Transit/Trolley Information Center (☎222-6036; www.gohrt.com), at Atlantic Ave. and 24th St. Info on area transportation and tours, including trolleys, buses, and ferries. Trolleys transport riders to most major points in Virginia Beach. The Atlantic Ave. Trolley runs from Rudee Inlet to 42nd St. Other trolleys run along the boardwalk, the North Seashore, and to Lynnhaven Mall. Open May-Sept. daily 8am-2am. $1, seniors and disabled $0.50, under 38 in. free. All-day passes $3, 3-day pass $5, 5-day pass $8.

Taxis: Beach Yellow Cab, ☎460-0605. **Beach Taxi,** ☎486-6585.

◀◤ 🄝 ORIENTATION AND PRACTICAL INFORMATION

In Virginia Beach, east-west streets are numbered and the north-south avenues, parallel to the beach, are named. **Atlantic Avenue** is next to the beach and home to many of the town's hotels and shops. The major thoroughfare, **Pacific Avenue,** is the next street over. **Arctic, Baltic,** and **Mediterranean Avenue** are farther inland.

Tourist Office: Virginia Beach Visitors' Center, 2100 Parks Ave. (☎800-822-3224 or 491-7866; www.vbfun.com), at 22nd St. Info on budget accommodations and area sights. Open daily June-Aug. 9am-8pm; Sept.-May 9am-5pm.

Internet Access: Virginia Beach Public Library, 4100 Virginia Beach Blvd. (☎431-3001). Open June-Sept. M-Th 10am-9pm, F-Sa 10am-5pm; Oct.-May also Su 1-5pm. Free.

Post Office: 501 Viking Dr. (☎340-0981). Open M-F 7:30am-6pm, Sa 10am-2pm. **Postal Code:** 23452.

🄵 ACCOMMODATIONS

Virginia Beach has two kinds of lodging: high-rise hotels along the boardwalk and motor courts one block off the boardwalk. The ocean-view high-rises don't come cheap; in summer the cheapest rooms go for $150. Most motels run $70-100, and are still convenient to the beach and the boardwalk's social scene.

▨ **Ocean Cove Motel and HI Hostel (HI),** 302 24th St. (☎428-4690; www.angiescottage.com). The staff welcomes international guests with coveted parking passes and advice about the beach. Guests at The Cove are mostly in their 20s and share bunk beds in separate-sex dorm-like rooms. 34 beds. A/C. Kitchen, lockers, and beach mats available. Free Linen. Check-in 11am-9pm. Check-out 10am. Reservations recommended. Open Apr.-Oct. High season dorms $20, members $17; singles $38; doubles $60. Low season dorms $17, members $13; singles; $32 doubles $48. MC/V. ❶

MacThrift Motor Inn, 311 22nd St. (☎422-2639; www.macthriftvb.com). This motel with an honest name and some Scottish charm is 1 block from the beachfront and has many amenities including free cable TV. Free parking, doubles with 2 beds available. High season $74-100. Low season $55-74. Under 12 free. D/MC/V. ❸

First Landings, 2500 Shore Dr. (☎412-2300 or 800-933-7275; www.dcr.state.va.us/ parks/1stland), about 8 mi. north of town on Rte. 60. 2-bedroom cabins and campsites amidst the beauty of the Virginia coastline. Cabins are close to picnic areas, public beach area, a bathhouse, and boat launching areas. Campsites with hot showers and grills available. Reservations are recommended for campsites. June-Aug. cabins $126. Apr.-May and Sept.-Nov. $76. Campsites $24, with water and electricity $30. ❸

False Cape State Park (☎800-933-7275 or 426-7128). Exit I-64 on Indian River Rd. E, drive 13 mi. and turn left on Newbridge Rd., right on Sandbridge Rd., and right on Sandpiper Rd. to parking at Little Island City Park. The 4 primitive campsites with drinking water and pit toilets, are worth the 6-9 mi. hike to their secluded locations. Reservations required. Parking in summer M-F $3, Sa-Su $4. Campsites $9. ❶

🍴 FOOD

Cuisine and Co., 3004 Pacific Ave. (☎428-6700; www.cuisineandcompany.com). Gourmet sandwiches to go. Specialties include the California grilled chicken with avocado ($7.60) and turkey with cranberry mayonnaise ($7.20). Open early Sept. to late May M-Sa 9am-7pm, Su 9am-6pm. AmEx/D/MC/V. ❷

Guadalajara, 200 21st St. (433-0140; www.guadalajaravb.com). This authentic Mexican restaurant is a hot post-beach spot for cooling down with a margarita ($6.25, jumbo $10.25). Burritos $5.50-8. Crabmeat quesadillas $9.75. Open M-Th 5pm-1am, F-Su noon-1:30am. AmEx/D/MC/V. ❷

Tropical Smoothie Cafe, 211 25th St. (☎422-3970; www.tropicalsmoothie.com). Silky smoothies ($3.80-4.30), healthful wraps ($5.50), and fresh salads ($7.60) served in a modern beach-inspired setting near the oceanfront. Open M-Sa 9am-11pm, Su 10am-6pm. AmEx/MC/V. ❶

👁 SIGHTS

BACK BAY NATIONAL WILDLIFE REFUGE. This national refuge is a sanctuary for an array of endangered species and other wildlife. Visitors camping, hiking, or fishing in the park can gawk at nesting bald eagles, white-tailed deer, ospreys, egrets, and other wildlife on a tram tour departing daily from Little Island City Park, up the road. *(Take General Booth Blvd. to Princess Anne Dr., turn left; then turn left on Sandbridge Rd. and continue 6 mi. Turn right on Sandpiper Rd., which leads directly to the Visitors Center. ☎721-2412; http://backbay.fws.gov. Visitors Center open Apr.-Oct. M-F 8am-4pm, Sa-Su 9am-4pm. $5 per car, $2 per family on foot or bike. Tram daily Apr.-Oct. 9am-1pm. ☎426-3643; www.bbrf.org. $8, seniors and under 12 $6.)*

FALSE CAPE STATE PARK. The origin of "False Cape" comes from the 17th century, when ships trying to reach Cape Henry, the landing site of America's first English settlers, would mistakenly touch shore in the present-day state park. The Back Bay National Wildlife Refuge's tram stops at False Cape State Park, where walkers trek 1 mi. to the beach. If you miss the tram, prepare for an adventurous 4 mi. hike or canoe ride, as foot and water are the only ways to get around the park. *(☎426-7128; www.dcr.state.va.us/parks.)* **Kayak Nature Tours** offers kayak excursions to these areas. *(☎480-1999 or 888-669-8368 for 2½hr. tours. Sunset or moonlight tour $15. Prepare to get wet on the summer-time dolphin tours as kayaks may flip over. $45.)*

VIRGINIA AQUARIUM AND MARINE SCIENCE MUSEUM. One mile south of the downtown boardwalk on Pacific Ave. (which becomes General Booth Blvd.), the Virginia Marine Science Museum contains Virginia's largest aquarium and is home to hundreds of fish species, including sharks and stingrays. The aquarium and museum also houses a six-storey IMAX theater and offers excursion trips for dolphin observation in summer and whale-watching in winter. *(717 General Booth Blvd. ☎385-3474; www.vmsm.com. Open Memorial Day-Labor Day daily 9am-7pm; Labor Day-Memorial Day 9am-5pm. $12, over 61 $11, under 11 $8. IMAX tickets $7.50/6.75/6.50. Combined museum and IMAX admission $17/16/13.)*

NIGHTLIFE

Mahi Mah's, 615 Atlantic Ave. (☎437-8030; www.mahimahs.com). At 7th St. inside the Ramada Hotel. This hot spot hosts live rock performances every night. Bathing suit-wearers mingle with a well-dressed crowd to enjoy sushi or just a night of entertainment and drinks. Limited late-night menu. Music daily 7-11pm. Open daily 7am-1:30am. ❷

Chicho's, 2112 Atlantic Ave. (☎422-6011), on "The Block" of college bars clustered between 21st and 22nd St. One of the hottest spots catering to a twenty-something crowd. Cheesy pizza $2.50-$3.75. Drinks $5-7. M live rock 'n' roll. 21+ after 10pm. Open daily 6pm-1:30am. ❶

Harpoon Larry's, 216 24th St. (☎422-6000; www.harpoonlarryskillerseafood.com). Serves tasty fish in an everyone-knows-your-name atmosphere. Hot crab dip $6.95. M $0.35 oysters. W $0.25 jalapeño poppers and wings. F $10.95 prime rib and crab legs. Happy hour M-F 4-7pm. Open daily noon-2am. ❷

CHARLOTTESVILLE ☎434

Thomas Jefferson, colonial Renaissance man and the primary author of the Declaration of Independence, built his dream house, Monticello, high atop his "little mountain" just southeast of Charlottesville. Around his personal paradise, Jefferson endeavored to create the ideal community. In a last-ditch effort to breed intellect and keep himself busy, Jefferson created the University of Virginia (UVA), which blends college town vivacity with old-fashioned Southern charm.

TRANSPORTATION

Airport: Charlottesville-Albemarle Airport (CHO; ☎973-8342; www.gocho.com), 8 mi. north of Charlottesville, 1 mi. west of Rte. 29 on Airport Rd.

Trains: Amtrak, 810 W. Main St. (☎296-4559 or 800-872-7245; www.amtrak.com). Ticket office open daily 6am-9pm. To **New Orleans** (23hr., 1 per day, $205) and **Washington, D.C.** (3hr., 1 per day, $24-30).

Bus: Greyhound/Trailways, 310 W. Main St. (☎295-5131 or 800-231-2222; www.greyhound.com). To **Baltimore** (5hr., 3 per day, $40), **Richmond** (1¼hr., 3 per day, $16), and **Washington, D.C.** (3¼hr., 2 per day, from $21).

Public Transit: Charlottesville Transit Service (☎296-7433). Bus service within city limits M-Sa 6:30am-midnight. $0.75, seniors and disabled $0.35, under 6 free. All-day pass $2. Free trolley service between UVA and downtown area runs daily 6am-midnight.

Taxi: Carter's Airport Taxi, ☎981-0170. **AAA Cab Co.,** ☎975-5555.

ORIENTATION AND PRACTICAL INFORMATION

Charlottesville's streets are numbered from east to west, using compass directions; 5th St. NW is 10 blocks from (and parallel to) 5th St. NE. There are two downtowns: **The Corner,** on the west side across from the university, is home to student delis and coffee shops; **Historic downtown** is about a mile east, centered on a pedestrian mall on E. Main Street. The two are connected by the east-west **University Avenue,** which starts as Ivy Rd. and becomes Main St.

TRUCKIN' ALONG. Gas prices can differ wildly between states, and it's easy to pay too much at gas stations on unfamiliar highways. Along interstates throughout the US, truck stops like Pilot Travel Centers have consistently low prices for gasoline, plus cheap coffee to keep you alert behind the wheel.

Visitor Info: Chamber of Commerce, 415 E. Market St. (☎295-3141), at 5th St. Maps, guides, and info about lodging and local events. Open M-F 9am-5pm. **Charlottesville-Albemarle County Convention and Visitors Bureau** (☎977-1783 or 877-286-1102; www.charlottesvilletourism.org), off I-64 on Rte. 20. Open daily 8:30am-5:30pm.

Hotlines: Region 10 Community Services; ☎972-1800. **Sexual Assault Crisis Center;** ☎977-7273. Both 24hr. **Mental Health;** ☎977-4673. Operates M-F 9am-5pm.

Internet Access: Jefferson Madison Regional Library, 201 E. Market St. (☎979-7151). Free. Open M-Th 9am-9pm, F-Sa 9am-5pm; Sept.-May also Su 1-5pm.

Post Office: 513 E. Main St. (☎963-2661). Open M-F 8:30am-5pm, Sa 10am-1pm. **Postal Code:** 22902.

ACCOMMODATIONS

The Budget Inn, 140 Emmet St. (☎800-293-5144; www.budgetinn-charlottesville.com). The closest motel to the university. 36 large rooms with sunlight, cable TV, and Wi-Fi. Rooms Apr.-Sept. $45-75. Oct. $60-90. Nov.-Mar. $40-70. Each additional person $5. AAA discount. AmEx/D/MC/V. ❸

English Inn of Charlottesville, 2000 Morton Dr. (☎800-786-5400; www.englishinncharlottesville.com). Has standard rooms with A/C, airport shuttle, full breakfast, cable TV, Internet, a pool, and access to a local health club. Rooms M-Th $100-120, F-Su $110-150. AAA and AARP discount. AmEx/D/MC/V. ❺

Charlottesville KOA Kampground, 3825 Red Hill Rd./Rte. 708 (☎296-9881 or 800-562-1743; www.charlottesvillekoa.com), 9 mi. south of downtown. Take Rte. 20 S to Rte. 708. Shaded campsites with bathrooms and a pool. Sites $22, with water and electricity $26, full hookup $28. Cabins $42-60. Each additional person $5. MC/V. ❶

FOOD

Littlejohn's, 1427 University Ave. (☎977-0588). This deli is as overstuffed as its sandwiches at lunch. In the wee hours of the morning, barflies trickle in to kick back and relax with the "Easy Rider" (baked ham, mozzarella, and cole slaw; $3.75). Beer $2-3. 3-egg omelettes $3.50. Breakfast 5-11am. Open 24hr. MC/V. ❶

Jaberwocke, 1517 University Ave. (☎984-4973). Looks like a trendy bar, but make no mistake: Jaberwocke is a famed local pizza joint. The turkey and brie sandwich ($8), served on sourdough with apple slices and honey spread, is to die for. Entrees $8-10. Sandwiches $5-8. Large pizzas from $10. Open M-W and Su 11am-10pm, Th-Sa 11am-11pm. AmEx/D/MC/V. ❷

Chaps, 223 E. Main St. (☎977-4139). A favorite for homemade ice cream and cheap grub with a diner-that's-been-here-forever feel. Burgers and sandwiches $3.50-7. Open M-Th 8am-10pm, F-Sa 8am-11pm, Su 11am-9pm. Cash only. ❶

SIGHTS

UNIVERSITY OF VIRGINIA (UVA). Most activity on the grounds of the **University of Virginia** clusters around the fraternity-lined **Rugby Road** and the ✦**Lawn,** a terraced green carpet and one of the prettiest spots in American academia. Professors live in the Lawn's pavilions, each designed in a different architectural style. (☎ 924-7969. *Free tours meet at Rotunda entrance facing the Lawn. Tours mid-Jan. to mid-Dec. daily 10, 11am, 2, 3, 4pm; no tours early to mid-May. Free.*)

HISTORIC MANSIONS. Jefferson oversaw every stage of the development of his beloved homestead at ◪**Monticello,** which reflects the personality of its creator. The house is a quasi-Palladian jewel filled with fascinating 18th-century innovations, such as a fireplace dumbwaiter and a mechanical manuscript copier. Tours meet in the parking lot; a free shuttle takes visitors up the mountain to the house. (*1184 Monticello Loop. ☎ 984-9844; www.monticello.org. Open daily Mar.-Oct. 8am-5pm; Nov.-Feb. 9am-4:30pm. $15, ages 6-11 $7. 30min. tour included with admission.*) **Ash Lawn-Highland** was the 535-acre plantation of President James Monroe. Though less majestic than Monticello, the estate provides a glimpse of family life in the early 19th century. (*1000 James Monroe Pkwy. Off Rte. 792, 2½ mi. east of Monticello. ☎ 293-9539; www.ashlawnhighland.org. Open daily Apr.-Oct. 9am-6pm; Nov.-Mar. 11am-5pm. Tours $9, seniors and AAA $8, ages 6-11 $5.*) The partially reconstructed **Michie Tavern** has an operating grist mill and a general store. Lagers and ales are served alongside a Southern buffet lunch. (*Just west of Monticello on Thomas Jefferson Pkwy. ☎ 977-1234; www.michietavern.com. Open daily 9am-5pm. Last tour 4:20pm. Tours $8, seniors and AAA $7, ages 6-11 $3. Buffet lunch $14.50, ages 12-15 $10, ages 6-11 $7.25, under 5 free. $27 President's Pass Combination Ticket includes tours of Ash Lawn, Monticello, and Michie Tavern.*) Twenty-seven miles north of Charlottesville on Rte. 20, James Madison's **Montpelier** once supported his slaves and tobacco crops. (*11407 Constitution Hwy./Rte. 20. ☎ 540-672-2728; www.montpelier.org. Open Apr.-Oct. 9:30am-5:30pm, Nov.-Mar. 9:30am-4:30pm. $12, seniors and AAA $10, ages 6-14 $6. Audio tours available.*)

▧ NIGHTLIFE

Buddhist Biker Bar and Grille, 20 Elliewood Ave. (☎ 971-9181). UVA students and local twentysomethings—though few bikers or bona fide Buddhists—flock to this bar for its huge lawn and drink specials. Try the spinach dip ($4) or pork dumplings ($5). Beer $2.50-4. M beer $1. W mixed drinks $2. Tu-W live music. Open M-Sa 3:30pm-2am.

Baja Bean, 1327 W. Main St. (☎ 293-4507). Cheap burritos, tamales, and chimichangas go for $5-8 in this festively decorated Mexican bar and restaurant. Beer $2-3.50. M open mic night; occasional karaoke nights. Tu Coronas $2. Happy hour M-F 3-7pm. Open daily 11am-2am. Kitchen closes at midnight.

Orbit Billiards and Cafe, 102 14th St. NW (☎ 984-5707). A geek-chic bar and restaurant combo with a *2001: A Space Odyssey* theme downstairs. 8 pool tables and another bar upstairs. Happy hour daily 5-9pm. Th $3 draft night. Su occasional live acoustic music. Open daily 5pm-2am. Kitchen closes at 1am.

SHENANDOAH NATIONAL PARK ☎ 540

When Shenandoah National Park was purchased by the state of Virginia in 1926, it was a 280-acre tract of over-logged and over-hunted land. A 1936 decree from Franklin Roosevelt made Shenandoah America's first great nature reclamation project. The park now spans 10,600 acres and contains more plant species than all of Europe. In the same day, visitors can explore mineral-encrusted caves and pay homage to Civil War battlefields.

◪ ▣ ORIENTATION AND PRACTICAL INFORMATION

The park runs nearly 105 mi. along the famous **Skyline Drive,** which extends from Front Royal in the north to Rockfish Gap in the south before evolving into the **Blue**

AT A GLANCE

AREA: 300 sq. mi.

CLIMATE: Varied, with a long growing season and a harsh winter.

FEATURES: Peaks Stonyman and Hawksbill, both of which exceed 4000 ft.

HIGHLIGHTS: Hiking the Appalacian Trail, fishing, biking, and horseback riding.

GATEWAYS: Front Royal, Thornton Gap, Swift Run Gap, Rockfish Gap.

CAMPING: Tourists permitted to camp in any of 5 campgrounds or in the back-country.

FEES AND RESERVATIONS: Hiking permit free. Check website for entrance fee.

Ridge Parkway. Skyline Drive remains open year-round except during bad weather, and from dusk to dawn on some nights in hunting season. Mile markers are measured north to south and denote the location of trails and stops. Three major highways divide the park into sections: the **North Section** runs from Rte. 340 to Rte. 211; the **Central Section** from Rte. 211 to Rte. 33; and the **South Section** from Rte. 33 to I-64. A park pass is required to enter the park and is valid for seven days. (Entrance fee $15 per vehicle. Mar.-Feb. $8 per hiker, biker, or bus passenger; Dec.-Feb. $5. Disabled persons free.) Most facilities close in winter; call ahead.

The **Dickey Ridge Visitors Center,** at Mi. 4.6, and the **Byrd Visitors Center,** at Mi. 51, answer questions and maintain small exhibits about the park. The park rangers conduct informative presentations on local wildlife, guide short walks among the flora, and wax romantic during outdoor, lantern-lit evening discussions. Pick up a free *Shenandoah Overlook*, available at park entrances and Visitors Centers, for a complete listing of programs. (Dickey Ridge: ☎635-3566. Byrd: ☎999-3283. For both, visit www.nps.gov/shen for camp and park info and www.visitshenandoah.com for info and reservations. Both open Apr.-Oct. daily 8:30am-5pm; July-Sept. also F-Sa until 6pm.) For **emergencies,** call ☎800-732-0911.

TIP

DRIVING SKYLINE DRIVE. When planning your trip through Shenandoah National Park, give yourself plenty of extra driving time—the speed limit in the park is only 35 mph, and tourists love to pull on and off the road to admire the wildlife and scenery.

ACCOMMODATIONS

The Appalachian Trail Conference's **Bears Den Hostel ❶**, 18393 Blue Ridge Mountain Rd., 35 mi. north of Shenandoah on Rte. 601, sleeps 20 travelers in two dorms. There are also private cabins for families or groups and a third bunk room for Appalachian Trail hikers. An in-house convenience store, kitchen, sleepsacks, and laundry ($2) are available. Take Rte. I-81 to Rte. 7 E and follow it for 17 mi. to Blue Ridge Mountain Rd.; turn right and drive a half mi. until you see a gate and a sign for the Bears Den on the right. (☎554-8708; www.bearsdencenter.org. 5-day max. stay. Reception 8-9am and 5-10pm. Check-out 9:30am. Curfew and quiet hours from 10pm. Camping $6 per person. Dorms $18; doubles $50. MC/V.) The park maintains two lodges—essentially motels with rustic rooms. **Skyland Resort ❹**, Mi. 42 on Skyline Dr., offers wood-furnished cabins and more upscale motel rooms. (☎743-5108 or 800-999-4714. Dining available. Wheelchair-accessible rooms available. Open Apr.-Nov. Cabins $66-124; lodge rooms $87-131. AmEx/D/MC/V.) **Lewis Mountain Cabins ❸**, Mi. 57, also owned by the park service, operates cabins with private baths and outdoor grill areas, as well as sparsely furnished "tent cabins." (☎743-5108 or 800-999-4714. Open May-Oct. Tent cabins $25; cabins $76-123. AmEx/D/MC/V.)

CAMPING

The park service (☎800-365-2267; reservations.nps.gov; open 10am-10pm) maintains four major campgrounds. The northernmost, **Mathews Arm ❶**, Mi. 22 (179 sites; $16), is convenient to nearby **Elkwallow**, Mi. 24, which has a gas station, eatery, and gift shop. The popular **Big Meadows ❶**, Mi. 51 (sites $20), boasts secluded sites close to a Visitors Center, another gas station, major trailheads, and several waterfalls; it also features a "Story of the Forest" nature trail, a 1.8 mi. looping path and a case study of the changes that occur over time in forest vegetation. **Lewis Mountain ❶**, Mi. 58 (sites $17), is more private. Closest to the southern entrance, **Loft Mountain ❶**, Mi. 80 (sites $16), has shaded sites. The latter three have stores, showers, and laundry. All but Lewis Mountain have dump stations; none have hookups. Only Big Meadows accepts reservations. All campgrounds have a 14-day maximum stay, allow pets, and are open from spring through October.

A 101 mi. section of the **Appalachian Trail (AT)** runs the length of the park. Twelve three-sided shelters are strewn at 8-10 mi. intervals along the AT. Unwritten trail etiquette usually reserves the cabins for those hiking long stretches of the trail. **Backcountry camping ❶** is free, but you must obtain a permit. Camping without a permit or above 2800 ft. is illegal and unsafe. The **Potomac Appalachian Trail Club (PATC) ❶**, 118 Park St. SE, Vienna, VA, a volunteer organization, maintains six cabins in backcountry areas of the park that sleep 8-12 people each; these are accessible by foot only. Bring lanterns and food; the primitive cabins contain only bunk beds, blankets, and stoves. Pit toilets and spring water are nearby. (☎703-242-0693; www.patc.net. 1 group member must be over 21. Headquarters open M-W 7-9pm, Th noon-2pm and 7-9pm, F noon-2pm. M-W and Su $25 per group, Th-Sa $40. Reservations required. MC/V.) Trail maps and the PATC guide can be obtained at the Visitors Centers. The PATC also puts out topographical maps ($6).

OUTDOOR ACTIVITIES

HIKING

The trails off Skyline Dr. are heavily used and generally safe for cautious day-hikers with maps, appropriate footwear, and water. The middle section of the park, from **Thorton Gap**, Mi. 32, to **South River**, Mi. 63, bursts with photo opportunities and stellar views, although it also tends to be crowded with tourists. Rangers can recommend hikes of appropriate length and difficulty level for any visitor.

Whiteoak Canyon Trail (Mi. 42.6; 4½ mi., 4hr. round-trip) is a strenuous hike that opens up on the park's 2nd-highest waterfall (86 ft.), rewarding those who ascend the 1040 ft. elevation with views of the Limberlost hemlocks.

Limberlost Trail (Mi. 43; 1¼ mi., 1hr. round-trip) is the park's easiest and only wheelchair-accessible trail. From the trailhead (½ mi. from Skyland Lodge), Limberlost plunges into forest, weaves through orchards, and passes over a footbridge. No pets.

Corbin Cabin Cutoff Trail (Mi. 37.8; 4 mi., 2½ hr. round-trip) is popular among history buffs. The trail leads down into a hollow where an old cabin has been preserved so that hikers can see how the area's settlers lived. The ascent back up is fairly strenuous.

OTHER ACTIVITIES

There are two other ways to explore Shenandoah: by boat and by beast. **Downriver Canoe Company** in Bentonville offers canoe, kayak, raft, and tube trips. From Skyline Dr., Mi. 20, follow U.S. 211 W for 8 mi., then take U.S. 340 N 14 mi. to Bentonville; turn left on Rte. 613 and go 1 mi. The store is on the right. (☎635-5526 or 800-338-1963; www.downriver.com. Open M-F 9am-6pm, Sa-Su 7am-7pm.) Guided **horseback rides** are available at the Skyland Lodge, Mi. 42. (☎999-2210; www.visitshenandoah.com. Riders must be at least 50 in. $30. per 1hr. 1-day advance reservation required. Open Apr.-Nov.)

📷 DAYTRIPS FROM SHENANDOAH

LURAY CAVERNS. Though the billboards that appear every 10 mi. along the highway scream tourist trap, the **Luray Caverns** defy all expectations. Take Exit 264 from U.S. 81 onto U.S. 211 E; signposts lead to the caverns from there. The 1hr. guided tours feature a variety of formations; don't miss Dream Lake, an underground pool that creates such a convincing optical illusion that you can't even tell the water is there, and Pluto's Ghost, a bright white formation that seems to follow the cave's visitors around on their tour. The equally unforgettable cathedral room houses the world's largest natural musical instrument: a 37-mallet organ created from the caverns' own stalactites. It took Leland W. Sprinkle, a Virginia organist, three years and over 3000 trials of different cave formations to finish his masterpiece in 1957; since that time the room has hosted hundreds of underground weddings. Bring a sweater for the cool caverns, and your patience along with it—the caverns can get extremely busy in the summer. A ticket to the caverns will also get you into the **Car and Carriage Museum,** which has over 140 vehicles on display. Car enthusiasts of all ages will enjoy this homey vintage showroom that features many automotive milestones, including the 1913 Stanley Steamer, the 1904 Curved Dash Oldsmobile, and a variety of prewar Mercedes-Benz, Pierce-Arrow, Rolls-Royce, and Hispano-Suiza models. (☎743-6551; www.luraycaverns.com. Open mid-June to early Sept. daily 9am-7pm; Apr. to mid-June and Sept.-Oct. daily 9am-6pm; Nov. to Mar. M-F 9am-4pm, Sa-Su 9am-5pm. Wheelchair-accessible. Adults $19, seniors $16, ages 6-12 $9.)

ENDLESS CAVERNS. Discovered in 1879, the **Endless Caverns** are considered "endless" because they encompass over 5 mi. of mapped cave passages with no visible end. Take Exit 257 or 264 from US 81 and continue to the intersection of U.S. 11 and U.S. 211 in New Market; continue on US 11; follow the signs from here to 1800 Endless Caverns Rd. Bring a jacket and sturdy shoes; cave floors are slippery and the temperature hardly ever varies from its standard 55°F. (☎896-2283; www.endless-caverns.com. Open daily mid-Mar. to mid-June 9am-5pm; mid-June to early Sept. 9am-6pm; early Sept.-Oct. 9am-5pm; Nov. to mid-Mar. 9am-4pm. $16, ages 4-12 $8, under 4 free.)

SKYLINE CAVERNS. Smaller than Endless and Luray Caverns—and perhaps more kid-friendly than either—are the Skyline Caverns, on U.S. 340, 1 mi. from the entrance to the Shenandoah National Park. Skyline is famous for their collection of orchid-like anthodites. These rare crystal formations, which only grow 1 in. every 7000 years, have formed a garden of white rock spikes. Tour stops include the Capitol Dome, the Wishing Well, Cathedral Hall, and Rainbow Falls, which pours 37 ft. from one of the three cavern streams. (☎635-4545 or 800-296-4545; www.skylinecaverns.com. Open June-Aug. daily 9am-6pm; Sept.-May M-F 9am-5pm, Sa-Su 9am-6pm. $16; seniors, AAA, and military $14; ages 7-13 $8, under 6 free.)

WEST VIRGINIA

With 80% of the state cloaked in untamed forests, commercial expansion and economic prosperity once seemed a distant dream for West Virginia. When the state's coal reserves began to run out, government officials decided to capitalize on the area's raging rivers and wooded wilderness. Today, thousands of tourists forge paths into West Virginia's breathtaking landscape, and thousands more settle for good. Park officials and state planners now face the challenging task of trying to accommodate the new human residents without encroaching too much upon the animals that already call West Virginia home.

🛂 PRACTICAL INFORMATION

Capital: Charleston.

Visitor Info: Department of Tourism, 90 MacCorkle Ave. SW, South Charleston 25305; P.O. Box 30312 (☎800-225-5982; www.callwva.com). **US Forest Service,** 200 Sycamore St., Elkins 26241 (☎304-636-1800; www.fs.fed.us/r9/mnf). Open M-F 8am-4:45pm.

Postal Abbreviation: WV. **Sales Tax:** 6%.

HARPERS FERRY   ☎304

Harpers Ferry, situated at the confluence of the Shenandoah and Potomac Rivers, earned its fame when a band of abolitionists led by John Brown raided the US armory there in 1859. Although Brown was captured and executed, the raid brought the clash over slavery to a new height and is considered a precursor to the American Civil War. The town of Harpers Ferry also became a major theater of conflict, changing hands eight times during that war. Today, Harpers Ferry's guests are more mild-mannered, ranging from outdoors enthusiasts to field trippers looking for a taste of American history.

🔂🛂 **TRANSPORTATION AND PRACTICAL INFORMATION.** Harpers Ferry is on West Virginia's eastern panhandle, less than a 10min. drive south to Virginia or north to Maryland. Amtrak (☎800-535-6406; www.amtrak.com; no ticketing office), on Potomac St. on the eastern side of the historic district, runs **trains** to Washington, D.C. (1¾hr., 1 per day, $20). At the same depot you'll find the Maryland Rail Commuter (MARC; ☎866-743-3682; www.mtamaryland.com), which offers cheaper, more frequent **rail** service to Washington, D.C. (M-F 2 per day, $9). Pan Tran, also at the train station, sends **buses** to Charles Town for $1.50 per person. (☎263-0876; www.pantran.com. Buses run M-F 6am-7pm, reduced hours Sa.) The **Jefferson County Convention and Visitors Bureau,** is on Shoreline Dr. just off Rte. 340 in Harpers Ferry (☎535-2627; www.hello-wv.com). The **Cavalier Heights Visitors Center** is inside the Harpers Ferry National Historic Park entrance, off Rte. 340. (☎535-6298; www.nps.gov/hafe. Open daily 8am-5pm.) The Cavalier Heights Visitors Center is the closest **public parking** to the historic district; $6 park admission is charged at the entrance to the Visitors Center and parking lot. The **Historic Town Area Visitor Information Center,** at the end of Shenandoah St., has free tour info. (☎535-6029; www.nps.gov/hafe. Open daily 8am-5pm.) **Internet Access: Bolivar and Harpers Ferry Public Library,** 151 Polk St. (☎535-2301. Free. Open M-Tu and F-Sa 10am-5:30pm, W-Th 10am-8pm.) **Post Office:** 1010 Washington St., at the corner of Washington and Franklin St. (☎535-2479. Open M-F 8am-4pm, Sa 9am-noon.) **Postal Code:** 25425.

🏠 **ACCOMMODATIONS.** Ragged hikers are welcome at the social 🏴**Harpers Ferry Hostel (HI) ❶,** 19123 Sandy Hook Rd., at Keep Tryst Rd. off Rte. 340 in Knoxville, MD. This renovated auction house has a backyard trail to Potomac overlooks, a library, Internet access, kitchen, and shuttle pickup from the Greyhound station in Frederick, MD. (☎301-834-7652; www.harpersferryhostel.org. Laundry $2. Check-in 6-10pm. Check-out 7-9am. 5-night max. stay. Open mid-Mar. to mid-Nov. Dorms $23, members $20. Camping $9; includes use of kitchen and bathrooms. D/MC/V.)

The **Hillside Motel ❷**, 19105 Keep Tryst Rd., 3 mi. from town in Knoxville, MD, has clean rooms and a fairly convenient location. (☎301-834-8144. Summer singles $45, doubles $55; winter $35/45. AmEx/D/V.) Those who like to rough it can camp along the **C&O Canal ❶**, where free primitive sites lie 5 mi. apart all along the canal's 180 mi. length. Camping is first come, first served. **Greenbrier State Park ❶**, on Rte. 40 E off Rte. 66, has 165 campsites and a lakeside recreation area. (☎301-791-4767; http://reservations.dnr.state.md.us. Open Apr.-Oct. Sites $25, with electricity $30. Reservations recommended. MC/V.)

◨◨ **FOOD AND NIGHTLIFE.** Chain restaurants welcome fast-food fanatics along Rte. 340. Nearby Charles Town's ▨**La Mezzaluna Cafe ❸**, Somerset Village Ste. B3, off Rte. 340 S, serves delicious Italian favorites. (☎728-0700. Pasta $9-15. Open Tu-Th 11am-3pm and 4-9pm, F-Sa 11am-3pm and 4-10pm, Su 2:30-9pm. AmEx/D/MC/V.) Across the street from the Hillside Motel, the **Cindy Dee Restaurant ❶**, 19112 Keep Tryst Rd., in Knoxville, MD, is usually full of people clamoring for fried chicken (from $5.75) and delicious apple dumplings. (☎301-695-8181. Open daily 6am-11pm. AmEx/D/MC/V.) Harpers Ferry's historic area around High St. and Potomac St. caters to the lunch crowd and empties out during dinner hours when most tourists have left. One exception is the **Armory Pub ❸**, 109 Potomac St., which gives pub fare a twist with fresh fish ($12) and chargrilled burgers ($6) and has live music on weekend nights. (☎535-2469. Open daily 11am-10:30pm. MC/V.) A tiny college town, **Shepherdstown**, 11 mi. north of Harpers Ferry, is a veritable culinary oasis in these quiet parts. Take Rte. 340 S for 2 mi. to Rte. 230 N, or bike 13 mi. along the C&O towpath. Caffeine fiends flock to ▨**Lost Dog ❶**, 134 E. German St., which brews 30 different blends of coffee and over 50 kinds of tea. College kids and old-schoolers alike chill to indie rock in the bright seating area. (☎876-0871. Open M-Th and Su 6:30am-6pm, F-Sa 6:30am-7pm. AmEx/D/MC/V.) Amid the colonial architecture of E. German St., the **Mecklinburg Inn,** 128 E. German St., provides rock 'n' roll and Rolling Rock ($2.50) on open mic nights every Tuesday from 9pm to midnight. (☎876-2126. Happy hour M-F 4:30-6:30pm. 21+. Open M-Th 3pm-12:30am, F 3pm-1:30am, Sa 1pm-2am, Su 1pm-12:30am.)

◧ **SIGHTS.** The **Harpers Ferry National Historic Park** is composed of several museums. Entrance to the museums, parking, and shuttle rides from the parking lot to the historic area are all included with admission. (☎535-6298. Open daily 8am-5pm. Shuttles every 10min., last pickup 5:45pm. 3-day admission $6 per car; $4 per pedestrian, biker, or motorcyclist.) Parking in historic Lower Town is nearly nonexistent. Unless you snag one of the pricey spots in the lot at the end of Shenandoah St., it's necessary to park at the Visitors Center and board the free shuttles to town or walk about 20min. The bus stops at **Shenandoah Street,** where a barrage of replica 19th-century shops greets visitors. The **Harpers Ferry Industrial Museum,** on Shenandoah St., describes the methods used to harness the powers of the Shenandoah and Potomac rivers and details the town's status as the endpoint of the nation's first successful rail line. The unsung stories of Harpers Ferry captivate visitors at **Black Voices,** on the corner of High and Shenandoah St., where visitors can listen to audio clips from actors reading the memoirs of freed slaves expressing their opinions on John Brown and his raid. Next door on High St., the plight of Harpers Ferry's slaves is further elaborated upon in the **Civil War Museum. John Brown's Museum,** at the corner of Shenandoah and Potomac Aves., is a solid general introduction to the attack that made the town famous. A dauntingly steep staircase hewn into the hillside off High St. follows the **Appalachian Trail** to **Upper Harpers Ferry,** which has fewer sights but is laced with interesting historical tales. The staircase leads to **Harpers House,** the restored home of town founder Robert Harper, and **St. Peter's Church,** where a pastor flew the Union Jack during the Civil

War to protect the church. Just a few steps uphill from St. Peter's lie the ruins of **St. John's Episcopal Church,** used as a hospital and barracks during the Civil War.

◪ OUTDOOR ACTIVITIES. After digesting the town's historical sights, many revel in the beauty of the outdoors. The park's Visitors Center offers meticulously detailed trail maps. The moderately difficult **Maryland Heights Trail,** across the railroad bridge in the Lower Town of Harpers Ferry, wanders 4 mi. through the Blue Ridge Mountains and includes glimpses of crumbling Civil War-era forts. The strenuous 7½ mi. **Loudon Heights Trail** starts across the Shenandoah River in Virginia and leads to Civil War trenches and scenic overlooks. The moderate 2½ mi. **Camp Hill Trail** passes by the Harper Cemetery. Civil War era battlefields and infantry trenches dominate the **Bolivar Heights Trail,** which starts at the northern end of Whitman Ave. If you just need to walk off a heavy lunch, scamper along the **Virginius Island Trail,** a flat 0.9 mile walk that begins near the shuttle bus stop and runs parallel to the Shenandoah River. All park trails close after dark.

The **Chesapeake & Ohio Canal** towpath, off the end of Shenandoah St. and over the railroad bridge, serves as a lasting reminder of the town's industrial roots and is the point of departure for a 180 mi. bike ride to Washington, D.C. The determined can—and often do—ride the whole towpath in one day, but only by getting on the trail at or before daybreak. The **Appalachian Trail Conference** (see **Transportation and Practical Information**), 799 Washington St., at Jackson St., offers catalogs with deals on hiking books and trail info. (☎535-6331; www.appalachiantrail.org. Open M-F 9am-5pm; May-Oct. also Sa-Su 9am-4pm. Membership $30, seniors and students $25.) **River & Trail Outfitters,** 604 Valley Rd., 2 mi. from Harpers Ferry off Rte. 340 in Knoxville, MD, rents canoes, kayaks, inner tubes, and rafts. They also organize everything from scenic daytrips to wild overnights, all on the Shenandoah River. (☎301-695-5177 or 888-446-7529; www.rivertrail.com. Raft trips $53-67, under 16 $47-61. Canoes $60 per day. Tubing $25 per day.) At **Butt's Tubes,** on Rte. 671 off Rte. 340, adventurers and loungers can float down the river without having to dig too deep into their wallets. (☎888-434-9911 or 800-836-9911; www.buttstubes.com. Open M-F 10am-3pm, last pickup from the river at 5pm; Sa-Su 10am-4pm, last pickup 6pm. Tube $15-25; $45 per half-day, $80 per full day.) **Elk Mountain Trails,** 921 Hoffmaster Rd., off Sandy Hook Rd., leads horseback riding trips in the area. (☎301-834-8882; www.elkmountaintrails.com. Rides $25-150.)

MONONGAHELA NATIONAL FOREST ☎304

Monongahela National Forest sprawls across the eastern portion of West Virginia and is home to nine endangered species, limestone caverns, and hordes of weekend canoers, fly-fishermen, cavers, and skiers. The **Cranberry Mountain Nature Center** (☎653-4826 or 653-8564; www.fs.fed.us/r9/mnf; open Apr.-Nov. Th-Su 9am-4:30pm), near the Highland Scenic Hwy. at the junction of Rte. 150 and Rte. 39/55, proudly displays excellent wildlife exhibits, provides maps of local hiking trails and shows movies on local wildlife and scenery upon request. The Center also conducts free weekend tours of the **Cranberry Glades** (½-1hr. tours June-Aug. Sa-Su 2pm). Wrapping around the glades is the **Cow Pasture Trail** (6 mi.), which passes a WWII German prison camp. Two popular hikes are **Big Beechy Trail** (6½ mi.; the trailhead is next to a parking lot at the Highland Scenic Hwy. and Rte. 461 junction) and the awesome **Falls of Hills Creek Trail** (1½ mi.), off Rte. 39/55 south of the Nature Center, with three waterfalls ranging from 25 to 63 ft. in height. A small concrete pathway leads to a cascade of wooden steps down to the falls.

The **Highland Scenic Highway (Route 150),** accessible from the parking lot of the Nature Center, stretches 43 mi. from Richwood to U.S. 219, 7 mi. north of Marlinton, and affords gorgeous views. This is particularly true for the section of **Route**

39 from Marlinton to Goshen, VA, which passes by swimming sites on the Maury River which are signposted from the highway. Tempting as it is to gaze at the forest's splendor, driving on the winding and often foggy roads can be treacherous.

Those with several days to spend might choose to hike, bike, or ski part of the **Greenbrier River Trail** (75 mi., 1° grade), which runs from Cass to North Caldwell; the trailhead is on Rte. 38 off U.S. 60 in North Caldwell. Lined with access points and campgrounds, the trail offers easily hikeable and bikeable terrain and, in the late summer, a chance to witness monarch butterfly migration, during which millions of these distinctively patterned butterflies make a trans-continental flight to their warm winter sanctuary in Mexico.

Downhill delights abound on the 54 ski trails at the **Snowshoe Resort,** accessible from Rte. 66 between Rte. 219 and Rte. 28. (☎572-1000 or 877-441-4386; www.snowshoemtn.com. Lift tickets $50, students and seniors $45, children $36; F-Su $65/60/47. Ski rental $26-30; children $18-22. Open Dec.-Mar. daily 8:30am-10pm.) When the snow melts, mountain bikers move in for the summer. The **Mountain Adventure Center** at Snowshoe offers bike rentals, tours, and lift passes. (☎877-441-4386; ride.snowshoemtn.com. Bike rentals $40-125. Trail access passes with access to the lift and mountain bike park $37 per day.)

Travel north to ▨**Cass Scenic Railroad State Park,** off Rte. 28/92, for novel train rides on the remaining 11 mi. of the once-burgeoning 3000 mi. lumber railroad lines of West Virginia. Ascend to 4842 ft. on the oldest steam engine locomotive in continual use in the US; specialty trips and overnight stays on Cheat Mountain are offered. (☎456-4300 or 800-225-5982; www.cassrailroad.com. Trains run Memorial Day-Oct., call for schedules. $15-24, ages 5-12 $10-17, depending on day of the week and destination.) Science aficionados will appreciate the **National Radio Astronomy Observatory,** off Rte. 28/92 in Green Bank, which houses **The Robert C. Byrd Green Bank Telescope,** the largest fully steerable radio telescope in the world. Not only is this where the Search for Extra-Terrestrial Intelligence (the SETI Project) started, it is also the largest moveable structure on land. Free tours take you to the base of the looming 17 million lb. telescope. (☎456-2150; www.gb.nrao.edu. Tours late May-early Sept. every hr. daily 9am-6pm; early Sept.-Oct. W-Su 9am-6pm; Nov.-late May W-Su 11am, 1, 3pm.)

Each of Monongahela's six districts has a campground and recreation area, with ranger stations off Rte. 39 east of Marlinton and in the towns of Bartow and Potomack. Established sites are $8; backcountry camping is free, though you must register at the Cranberry Mountain Nature Center. **Cranberry Campground ❶,** in the Gauley district, 13 mi. from Ridgewood on Forest Rd. 76, has hiking trails through cranberry bogs and campsites. (☎846-2695. Sites $8.) **Watoga State Park ❶,** 14 mi. south of Marlinton, has maps of available campsites and features a stunning lake. (☎799-4087; www.watoga.com. Sites $17, with electricity $20. AmEx/D/MC/V.) If you don't feel like roughing it, travel up a wildflower-lined driveway to the ▨**Morning Glory Inn ❹,** 1½ mi. north of Slatyfork on Rte. 219. This B&B offers gargantuan rooms with cathedral-like ceilings, whirlpool tubs, and a sprawling porch. (☎572-5000 or 866-572-5700; www.morninggloryinn.com. Check-in 4-9pm. Check-out 11am. Doubles Apr.-Dec. $80-100; Jan.-Mar. $100-160. AmEx/D/MC/V.) Five miles farther from the slopes, the **Jerico B&B ❸,** on Jerico Rd., off Rte. 219 in Marlinton just south of the junction with Rte. 39, has pre-Civil War themed cabins in addition to bedrooms in the main house. (☎799-6241 or 888-499-6241; www.jericobb.com. Rooms $50-$85; cabins $85-185. AmEx/D/MC/V.)

The Restaurant at Elk River ❹, on Rte. 219 in Slatyfork, has a steak- and seafood-based menu with similar prices but a less touristy feel than the posh resort restaurants. The rainbow trout is a specialty. (☎572-3771. Open Th-Su 5-9:30pm. AmEx/D/MC/V.) The **Route 66 Sub Shop ❶,** on Rte. 66 at the base of Snowshoe, serves salads, pizzas, and wraps that will fill you up without breaking the bank. Visitors are greeted by multicolored slabs of homemade fudge ($10 per lb.); the dining room doubles as an antiques and gift shop. (☎572-1200. Breakfast served all day. Subs $4-6. Open M-F 7am-9pm, Sa-Su 7am-10pm. AmEx/D/MC/V.)

Amtrak, 315 W. Main St., across from the Greenbrier Resort, is in White Sulphur Springs at the forest's southern tip. (☎800-872-7245; www.amtrak.com. No ticket office.) Trains run W, F, and Su to Washington, D.C. ($48). **Greyhound** (☎800-231-2222; www.greyhound.com) will drop passengers with a Charleston ticket off along Rte. 60 but does not run from the forest. The forest **Supervisor's Office,** 200 Sycamore St., in Elkins, distributes a list of campsites and fees, as well as fishing and hunting info. (☎636-1800. Open M-F 8am-4:30pm.)

NEW RIVER GORGE   ☎304

The New River Gorge is a testament to the raw beauty and power of nature. New River is (ironically) one of the oldest rivers in the world, responsible for carving a narrow gorge through the Appalachian Mountains, creating precipitous valley walls that tower 1000 ft. above the churning white waters. These steep slopes remained untouched until 1873, when industrialists drained the region to uncover coal and timber. With the coal mines now defunct, the New River Gorge has become a sanctuary for outdoors enthusiasts, with rafters cruising its rapids and climbers ascending its cliffs.

◰◪ TRANSPORTATION AND PRACTICAL INFORMATION. Amtrak, on Rte. 41 N in Prince and Hinton, runs through the heart of the gorge. (☎253-6651 or 800-872-7245; www.amtrak.com. Prince open W, F, Su 9:30am-9pm. Hinton open W, F, Su 11am-1pm and 4:30-6:30pm.) Greyhound stops at 105 3rd St. in Beckley. (☎800-231-2222 or 253-8333; www.greyhound.com. Open M-Sa 7am-5pm, Su 7-10am and 2-5pm.) **Buses** go to Charleston (1hr., 3 per day, $20), Charlottesville (7hr., 2 per day, $59), and Philadelphia (6hr., 3 per day, $96). The park operates four Visitors Centers, each of which has info on hiking trails and the area's history. Off Rte. 19 just north of Fayetteville and the New River Gorge Bridge, █**Canyon Rim** provides the best view in the entire park. (☎574-2115. Open daily 9am-5pm.) If you're heading to New River Gorge from the south, **Sandstone,** on Rte. 64 east of Beckley, is a good place to start. The gorgeous building is eco-friendly and features a scale model of the New River and its tributaries in colored stone, as well as a room full of enticing hands-on exhibits. (☎466-0417. Open daily 9am-5pm.) **Grandview,** on Rte. 9 near Beckley, attracts visitors in May when the rhododendrons are in bloom. (☎763-3715. Open May-Sept. daily noon-5pm.) **Thurmond,** on Rte. 25 off I-19, has access to hiking trails down in the river valley. (☎465-8550. Open May-Sept. daily 10am-5pm.) Signs on Rte. 19 labeled "Rafting and Recreation Information" lead to the **New River Convention and Visitors Bureau,** 310 Oyler Ave., in Oak Hill, which has extensive information on rafting outfitters, area attractions, and various Bridge Day festivities. (☎465-5617; www.newrivercvb.com. Open daily 9am-5pm.)

▛ ACCOMMODATIONS. A slew of budget motels can be found off I-77 in Beckley ($45-60). The **Green Bank Motel ❷,** 505 S. Eisenhower Dr., in Beckley, is a basic motel with rooms that come with HBO, microwaves, and refrigerators. (☎253-3355. Singles $50; doubles $55. AmEx/D/MC/V.) **Babcock State Park ❶,** on Rte. 41 south of U.S. 60, 15 mi. west of Rainelle, has shaded campsites, a bath house, laundry facilities, and 28 cabins, including two deluxe cabins with kitchen and A/C. Activities include swimming, horseback riding, and tennis. (☎438-3004 or 800-225-5982. No alcohol. Campground open Apr.-Oct. Sites $17, with electricity $20; cabins $49-110. Cash only, unless booking by phone.) Many raft companies operate private campgrounds that offer both lodging and packaged rafting-lodging-dining deals. **ACE Adventure Center ❶,** at the end of Minden Rd., in Oak Hill, offers rafting, recreation, and lodging options. From Rte. 19, take the Oak Hill Main St. Exit eastbound and turn left onto Minden Rd. (☎800-787-3982; www.aceraft.com. Tent sites $11 per person; bunkhouses for groups of 6 or more $17, $15 per child under 17; RV sites $29; cabin tents $45 per 1-2 people. AmEx/D/MC/V.) **North American River Runners (NARR) ❶,** on Hwy. 60, has rafting, kayaking, bath houses, and a cafe. Lodging options include primitive camping, four-person cabin tents, and 24-person bunkhouses. (☎800-950-2585; www.narr.com. No outlets or linens. Sites $10 per person; bunk houses $15; cabin tents $80. On-base activities include paintball ($30) and a high ropes course ($25). AmEx/D/MC/V.)

🍴 **FOOD.** The **Sedona Grill ❸,** on Rte. 16, just north of the Appalachian Dr. Exit from Rte. 19, offers upscale New American cuisine. The Sedona offers lunch wraps and sandwiches ($6-8) and delicious entrees like barbecued pork ($14-18) and the more exotic shrimp and apple curry ($15). (☎574-3411. Open M-Tu and Th 4-9pm, F-Sa 11:30am-10pm, Su 11:30am-9pm. AmEx/D/MC/V.) If only barbecue can satisfy your post-rafting hunger, try **Dirty Ernie's Rib Pit ❹,** at 310 Keller St. near the northern Fayetteville Exit off Rte. 19. Racks of ribs start at $12; prime rib is $16. For the rib-averse, options include a variety of "bun-buster" sandwiches for $8. (☎574-4822. Open daily 4-10pm. AmEx/D/MC/V.) Scaling rocks and scampering over trails can really wear you out; cool down with a custard cone at **Berkshire's Frozen Custard ❶** roadside stand, on Eisenhower Dr./Rt. 19 in Beckley. Homemade, hand-rolled waffle cones ($3) are filled with creamy frozen custard. Perennial favorites include vanilla, chocolate and strawberry, but Berkshire's also features enticing flavors of the week like maple walnut. Outdoor patio seating is available. (Open daily during the summer. D/MC/V.)

🎯 **SIGHTS.** In 1973, the breathtaking ◪**New River Gorge Bridge** was completed, becoming the second-highest bridge in the US. Best seen on foot, the bridge towers 876 ft. above New River and claims the world's largest single steel arch span. The Canyon Rim Visitors Center offers a decent vista, but for an unobstructed view, take the time to descend the zig-zag wooden stairs to the lower level lookout—it's worth it. On **Bridge Day,** the third Saturday in October, thousands of extreme sports enthusiasts leap off the bridge by bungee or parachute as on-lookers enjoy the festival's food and crafts. (☎800-927-0263; www.wvbridgeday.com.) In Beckley, retired coal miners lead 35min. tours down a mine shaft at the **Beckley Exhibition Coal Mine,** on Ewart Ave., Exit 44 from I-77, at New River Park. Visitors can see how coal mines operated while riding in a coal car through 150 ft. of underground passages. The tunnels are chilly; bring a jacket. (☎256-1747. Open Apr.-Oct. daily 10am-6pm, Nov.-Mar. Tu-Sa 10am-5pm; closed until Apr. 2008 for renovations. $15, seniors $13, ages 4-12 $10. Last tour leaves 30min. before close.)

🏞 **OUTDOOR ACTIVITIES.** The **New River Gorge National River** runs north from Hinton to Fayetteville, falling over 750 ft. in 50 mi. In order to conserve its magnificent natural and historic value, the New River Gorge has been protected by the National Park Service since 1958. Rafting companies offer trips on the Upper (gentler) and Lower (wilder) New River, as well as the Gauley River, 15 mi. north of New River National Park. The **West Virginia Division of Tourism** (☎800-225-5982; www.callwva.com), will connect you to outfitters on both rivers.

Though the renowned rapids draw the most tourists, leisurely hiking allows visitors time to take in the scenery. The most rewarding trails are the strenuous **Kaymoor Trail** (2 mi.) and the easy **Thurmond-Minden Trail** (round-trip 6½ mi., main overlook round-trip 3 mi.). Kaymoor starts at the bridge on Fayette Station Rd., near Canyon Rim Visitors Center, and runs past the abandoned coal-processing ovens of Kaymoor, a coal-mining community that shut down in 1962. Thurmond-Minden is fairly flat and has vistas overlooking the New River and Dunloup Creek, but is not clearly marked in some areas. To get to the trailhead, exit Rte. 19 at Main St. in Oak Hill. Turn left onto Main St. if coming from the south—right if from the north—then make a left on Minden Rd. Continue for 2 mi. and take a right across a small bridge. The trail is distinguished from the other paths in the vicinity by the gate that blocks vehicles from entering. Hikers of all levels can take advantage of the gorge's spectacular rock-climbing opportunities with **New River Mountain Guides,** at Wiseman and Court St., in downtown Fayetteville. (☎574-3872 or 800-732-5462; www.newriverclimbing.com. Half-day trips with climbing and rapelling from $95, full-day trips $200. $50 deposits required to book any course; reserve ahead of time.) Experienced climbers can climb the challenging **Endless Wall,** which runs southeast along the New River and has impressive river views from a height of 1000 ft. The wall is accessible from a 2½ mi. trail off Lansing-Edmond Rd. (Rte. 5) north of the Canyon Rim Visitors Center along Rte. 19.

Horseback-riding trips are another way to explore the gorge. ◙**New River Trail Rides,** in Oak Hill, leads 2hr. rides, sunset trips, and overnight adventures year-round from their stables off Wonderland Rd. From E. Main St., turn on Gatewood Rd. eastbound, then right on Wonderland Rd. (☎465-4819 or 888-742-3982; www.ridewva.com. 2½hr. rides from $42. Scenic Overlook Ride departs 9:30am, 1pm, 3:30pm. Sunset rides depart June-Aug. 6:30pm, May and Sept. 5:30pm, Mar.-Apr. and Oct. 5pm; $55.) Bike tours, rentals, and repairs are available at **New River Bike and Touring,** 103 Keller Ave., off the Fayetteville Historic District Exit on Rte. 19. (☎574-2453; www.newriverbike.com. Open daily 9am-6pm. Bike rentals $35 per half-day, $60 per full day. Bike tours $70 half-day, $110 full day.) **ACE Adventure Center,** on Minden Rd. in the town of Oak Hill, also provides rentals and tours. (☎888-223-7238; www.bikewv.com. Bike rentals $36-39 per half-day, $49-59 per full day. Tours $54-65.)

MID-ATLANTIC

NEW ENGLAND

New England considered itself a mecca for intellectuals and progressive politicians long before the States were United, and still does today. Scholars from every corner of the planet inundate New England's colleges and universities each fall, and town meetings still evoke the democratic spirit that inspired the American Revolution. While the region is heavy on historical landmarks that detail its break from "Old" England, New England's history didn't stop at Lexington and Concord, evident in its diversity and ever-evolving culture. Still, some things never change: the region's unpredictable climate can be particularly disconcerting to unsuspecting tourists, but long-time locals are accustomed to the occasional May snowstorm or February heat wave. Today's visitors seek adventure in the rough edges that nearly ruined early settlers, flocking to the coastline to meander on pebbled beaches or heading to the slopes of the Green and White Mountains to ski, hike, and canoe. The perennial New England trademark is magnificent fall foliage, which fills northern roads in the gap between summer and ski season and transforms quiet towns into postcard-worthy bursts of brilliance.

HIGHLIGHTS OF NEW ENGLAND

CRACK the shell of a succulent Maine **lobster** in Bar Harbor (p. 234), which serves the freshest seafood around, and don't miss out on New England clam "chowda."

SPRAWL on the lawns of **Tanglewood** (p. 288) as classical music, performed by some of the world's most illustrious musicians, washes over you.

BUNDLE UP before you tackle the frigid and beautiful slopes that comprise the East Coast's best **skiing** and **snowboarding** (p. 238 or p. 248).

CRANE your neck to take in the stunning fall **foliage** as you drive along scenic highways in Franconia Notch (p. 243).

TRANSPLANT yourself to the days of revolutionary ferment and colonial austerity while walking the **Freedom Trail** (p. 265) or visiting **Plimoth Plantation** (p. 277).

MAINE

Ever since Leif Ericson and the Vikings set foot on the shores of Maine nearly a millennium ago, travelers have been captivated by the state's distinctive blend of sea salt and pine forest, schooners and logging trucks, and, more recently, workboots and polo shirts. Thousands pour into Maine each summer, swimming in the cool Atlantic waters and reveling in the towns and cities that line the coast. Journey inland, and you'll find a quieter side of Maine, where small towns and vast expanses of wilderness await the adventurous traveler.

◪ PRACTICAL INFORMATION

Capital: Augusta.

Visitor Info: Maine Tourism Information, 59 State House Station, Augusta 04333 (☎207-623-0363 or 888-624-6345; www.visitmaine.com). **Maine Information Center,** in Kittery, 3 mi. north of the Maine-New Hampshire bridge. (☎207-439-1319.) Open

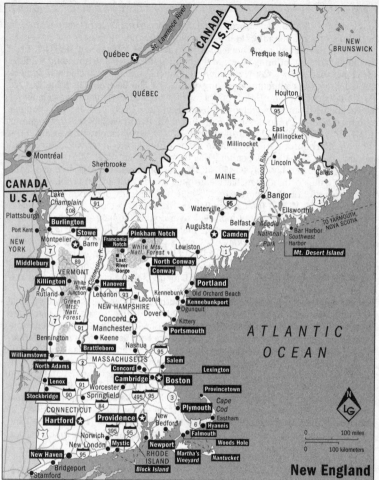

New England

daily July-early Oct. 8am-6pm; mid-Oct. to June 9am-5:30pm. **Bureau of Parks and Lands,** State House Station #22 (AMHI, Harlow Bldg.), Augusta 04333 (☎207-287-3821; www.state.me.us/doc/parks). **Maine Forest Service,** Department of Conservation, State House Station #22, Augusta 04333. (☎207-287-2791.)

Postal Abbreviation: ME. **Sales Tax:** 5%.

NORTHERN MAINE COAST

Much like the coastal region south of Portland, the north boasts eye-catching cliffs, windswept ocean panoramas, and quintessential New England towns. Here, where hiking boots give way to loafers, lodging and food isn't cheap. Still, passing through rewards even the budget traveler with the classic New England feel that sustains summer vacationers. U.S. 1 is the area's only thoroughfare, and it moves at a snail's pace for most of the summer.

CAMDEN ☎207

In the summer, khaki-clad crowds mingle with the sea captains of Camden, 100 mi. north of Portland, docking their yachts alongside the tall-masted schooners in Penobscot Bay. If you don't have a private yacht, 2hr. **cruises** sail May-Oct. from the public landing, offering views of the many lighthouses and abundant wildlife. (**Schooner Olad** ☎236-2323; www.maineschooners.com. $29. **Windjammer Surprise** ☎236-4687; www.camdenmainesailing.com. $30.) The **Camden Hills State Park ❶**, 1¼ mi. north of town on U.S. 1, offers over 80 wooded sites, usually available for arrivals before 2pm. This secluded retreat also offers 25 mi. of trails and a popular auto road leading to a lookout from the top of Mt. Battie. (☎236-3109, reservations in ME only 800-332-1501, out of state 287-3824; www.campwithme.com. Free showers. Park information available at the office at the entrance to the campground; open 7am-10pm. Open mid-May to mid-Oct. Sites $20, ME residents $15; reservations $2 per day. Day use $3. MC/V.) The **Birchwood Motel ❸**, in Lincolnville off U.S. 1, 3 mi. north of town, has clean, quiet rooms with A/C and cable TV, along with a beautiful outdoor porch. (☎236-4204; www.birchwoodmotel.com. Rooms $65-90. AmEx/D/MC/V.) **The Camden Deli ❷**, 37 Main St., stacks a variety of sandwiches at a good price. An outdoor deck overlooking the harbor and a full bar on the 2nd floor with daily drink specials make this a versatile option. (☎236-8343. Open daily 7am-9pm. AmEx/D/MC/V.) **Cappy's Chowder House ❸**, 1 Main St., serves up seafood specialties (entrees $10-14) and homemade pies in its bakery. (☎236-2254. Open daily 11am-11pm. Kitchen closes 10pm. MC/V.) Schooner crews crowd into **Gilbert's Publick House,** on Bay View Landing, for the cheap pub food, entertainment, and local brews. (☎236-4230. Open noon-12:45am.)

Maine Sports, on U.S. 1 in Rockport, just south of Camden, rents and sells a wide array of boats. (☎236-7120 or 800-722-0826. Open mid-June to Aug. daily 9am-8pm; Sept. to mid-June M-Sa 9am-6pm, Su 10am-5pm. Single kayaks $25-40 per day; doubles $30-50. Canoes $30 per day.) The **Maine State Ferry Service,** 5 mi. north of Camden in Lincolnville, floats to Islesboro Island, a quiet residential island. (☎800-491-4883. 20min.; 5-9 per day, last return trip 4:30pm; round-trip $5.25 per person, with bike $10.25, car and driver $15.) The ferry also has an agency at 517A Main St., on U.S. 1 in Rockland, that runs to Vinalhaven and North Haven. (☎596-2202. Rates and schedules change with weather; call ahead.) The **Camden-Rockport Lincolnville Chamber of Commerce,** located just ashore from the public landing, has helpful information and an informative guide to the area. (☎236-4404 or 800-223-5459; www.camdenme.org. Open M-F 9am-5pm, Sa 10am-5pm, Su 10am-4pm; mid-Oct. to mid-May closed Su.)

PORTLAND ☎207

Tucked between forested land and a wild sea, Portland is Maine's largest port town. The city thrives as an urban center in an otherwise rural area with a mixture of industry, arts, and well-preserved relics of colonial times. In summer, the streets fill with the exuberant sounds of parades and festivals. Laughter can be heard long into the night in the Old Port district, where pubs beckon the city's spirited youth to set aflame even the coldest night.

■ ▮ **ORIENTATION AND PRACTICAL INFORMATION.** Downtown is located in the middle of the peninsula along **Congress Street,** between State St. and Pearl St. A few blocks south, between Commercial and Middle St. on the waterfront, lies the **Old Port.** These two districts contain most of the city's sights and attractions. **I-295** (off I-95) forms the northwestern boundary of the city. Amtrak, 100 Thompson's Point Rd., on Connector Rd., off Congress St. (☎800-872-7245; www.thedowneaster.com; ticket office open M-F 5:30am-4:05pm, Sa-Su 5:30am-

6:35pm), runs **trains** to Boston (2¾hr., 4 per day, $23). Concord Trailways (☎828-1151; office open daily 4:30am-9:30pm), in the same building, runs **buses** to Bangor (2½hr., 3 per day, $23) and Boston (2hr., 12 per day, $19). Metro buses run to and from the station (M-Sa every 20min., Su every hr.). Greyhound/Vermont Transit, 950 Congress St., on the western outskirts of town (☎772-6587; www.greyhound.com), runs **buses** to Bangor (2½-3½hr., 5 per day, $22-28) and Boston (2hr., 6 per day, $17-27). Use caution in this area at night. Metro Bus services downtown Portland. Routes run 5:30am-11:45pm; brochures are at the Visitors Center. (☎774-0351. $1, seniors with Medicare card $0.50, under 5 free.) **The Visitors Information Bureau,** is at 245 Commercial St., between Union and Cross St. (☎800-306-4193; www.gotoportland.com. Open M-F 8am-5pm, Sa 10am-3pm.) **Internet Access: Portland Public Library,** 5 Monument Sq. (☎871-1700. Free with guest library card. Open M, W, and F 9am-6pm, Tu and Th noon-9pm, Sa 9am-5pm.) **Post Office:** 400 Congress St. (☎871-8464. Open M-F 8am-7pm, Sa 9am-1pm.) **Postal Code:** 04101.

♖ ACCOMMODATIONS. Portland has some inexpensive accommodations during the winter, but in summer prices jump steeply, especially on weekends. Lodging in the smaller towns up and down the coast can be less expensive. Three miles from downtown, the **Budget Inn Motel ❸,** 634 Main St. off U.S. 1/Main St. in South Portland, offers clean rooms at reasonable prices. (☎773-5722. Rooms $55-75. AmEx/D/MC/V.) **Wassamki Springs ❶,** 56 Saco St., in Scarborough, is the closest campground to Portland. Take I-95 S. to 22 W., Exit 46. RVs and tents cluster around a lake surrounded by sandy beaches. (☎839-4276. Free showers and flush toilets. Reserve 2 weeks in advance, especially July-Aug. Open May to mid-Oct. 2-person sites with water and electricity $41, with hookup $43; lakefront sites $3 extra. Each additional person $5. MC/V.)

▯ FOOD. Portland's harbor overflows with seafood, but non-aquatic and vegetarian fare is easy to find. The organic pizzas at the ▨**Flatbread Company ❸,** 72 Commercial St., have creative names like "Punctuated Equilibrium" (with roasted red pepper and onion) and cost $8-14. (☎772-8777. Open in summer M-Th 11:30am-10pm, F-Sa 11am-10:30pm; in winter M-Th 11:30am-9pm, F-Sa 11:30am-10pm. AmEx/MC/V.) **Federal Spice ❶,** 225 Federal St., just off Congress St., seasons all its wraps and soft tacos (all under $6) with fiery Caribbean, South American, and Asian ingredients. (☎774-6404. Open M-Sa 11am-9pm. V.) **Gilbert's Chowder House ❸,** 92 Commercial St., is the local favorite for seafood. A large bread bowl of chowder ($7-11) is a meal in itself. (☎871-5636. Entrees $10-21. Open June-Sept. M-Th and Su 11am-10pm, F-Sa 11am-11pm; Oct.-May call for hours. AmEx/D/MC/V.) The ▨**Portland Public Market,** at 477 Congress St., in Monument Sq., sells ethnic foods, seafood, and baked goods from small vendors. (☎228-2000; www.portlandmarket.com. Open M-Sa 9am-7pm, Su 10am-5pm.)

◪ SIGHTS. Offshore islands with secluded beaches are just a ferry ride from the city limits. **Casco Bay Lines,** on State Pier near the corner of Commercial and Franklin, runs daily to **Long Island** and **Peaks Island,** as well as a few other destinations. (☎774-7871; www.cascobaylines.com. Long Island: operates M-Sa 5am-9:30pm, Su 7:45am-9:30pm. Round-trip $9.50, seniors and ages 5-9 $4.75. Peaks Island: operates M-Sa 5:45am-11:30pm, Su 7:45am-11:30pm. Round-trip $7.25, seniors and ages 5-9 $3.60.) Peaks Island has great biking and kayaking and holds a reggae concert every Monday in the summer at Jones Landing. **Brad's Recycled Bike Shop,** 115 Island Ave., on Peaks Island, rents bikes. (☎766-5631. Open daily 10am-5pm. $5 per hr., $8.50 per 3hr., $12 per day.) A trip to the still-functioning **Portland Head Light** in **Fort Williams Park** is definitely worth the scenic detour. From Rte. 77 N. turn right at the flashing signal onto Shore Rd. and proceed to the park. The **Portland**

NEW ENGLAND

Observatory, 138 Congress St., the last maritime signal tower in the US, offers unrivaled views of the city and an excellent historical tour. (☎774-5561; www.portlandlandmarks.org. Open daily 10am-5pm; last tour 4:40pm. Admission and tour $6, ages 6-16 $4.) It takes about eight days to brew a batch of beer at the **Shipyard Brewing Co.,** 86 Newbury St., but it only takes 30min. to tour the brewery and try a free sample. (☎761-0807. Tours every 30min. in summer M-F 3-5pm, Sa-Su noon-5pm; in winter W-F 3-5pm, Sa noon-5pm. Free.) The **Portland Museum of Art,** 7 Congress Sq., at the intersection of Congress, High, and Free St., holds a fascinating display of 19th-century American art. The museum includes the recently restored McLellan House, originally built in 1801, as well as a stunning collection of Winslow Homer paintings. (☎775-6148 or 800-639-4067; www.portlandmuseum.org. Open M-Th and Sa-Su 10am-5pm, F 10am-9pm; mid-Oct. to May closed M. Wheelchair-accessible. $10, students and seniors $8, ages 6-12 $4; F 5-9pm free.) The **Wadsworth-Longfellow House,** 489 Congress St., has been excellently restored and serves as a window into the life of the poet. (☎774-1822, ext. 208; www.mainehistory.org. Open June-Oct. M-Sa 10am-4pm, Su noon-4pm. Tours every hr. $7, students and seniors $6, ages 5-17 $3. Price includes admission to a neighboring history museum.)

🎭🎟 **ENTERTAINMENT AND NIGHTLIFE.** Signs for theatrical productions decorate Portland, and schedules are available at the Visitors Center (p. 231). The **Portland Symphony** presents concerts renowned throughout the Northeast. (Performances at the Merrill Auditorium, 477 Congress St. ☎842-0800. Tickets through Porttix, online at www.porttix.com, or at 20 Myrtle St. Open M-Sa noon-6pm. Occasional 50% student discount.) Info on Portland's jazz, blues, and club scene is available in the *Portland Phoenix* and *FACE*, which are both free and widely distributed. During the last week of spring, the three-day **Old Port Festival** (☎772-6828) fills the blocks from Federal to Commercial St. with parades, music, and free public entertainment before the flood of summer tourists arrives. Throughout the summer, the **Weekday Music Series** (☎772-6828; www.portland-maine.com) hosts bands in Post Office Sq. between Middle and Exchange St. The Old Port area, known as "the strip"—especially **Fore Street** between Union and Exchange St.—livens up after dark, as patrons from countless bars overflow into the cobblestone streets. **BrianBorú,** the red building at 57 Center St., provides a mellow pub scene with top-notch nachos for $8. (☎780-1506. Su live Irish music and $2 pints 3-7pm. Open daily 11:30am-1am.) **Gritty MacDuff's,** 396 Fore St., brews beer (pints $2.50), serves hearty pub food ($7-13), and entertains locals with live music Saturday and Sunday nights. (☎772-2739. Open daily 11:30am-1am.)

KENNEBUNK AND KENNEBUNKPORT ☎207

Just 20 mi. south of Portland, Kennebunk and its coastal counterpart 8 mi. east, Kennebunkport, are popular hideaways for the wealthy—Kennebunkport is famous as the summer home of former President George H.W. Bush—but their true charm lies in the little art galleries and bookstores that fill each town. Surfers, swimmers, and sunbathers enjoy the five public beaches, a short trip from town. Parking is $10 per day, $20 per week, and $50 for a season pass. Narrated **scenic cruises** aboard the *Deep Water II* offer glimpses of wildlife and historic sites along the coast. (☎967-5595. Ticket booth on Ocean Ave. in front of The Landing Restaurant. 1½hr. $15, seniors $12.50, ages 3-12 $7.50.) The 55 ft. gaff-rigged *Schooner Eleanor,* leaving from Arundel Wharf on Ocean Ave., provides a relaxed 2hr. yachting experience. (☎967-8809. Call for reservations and times. $40.) **Old Salt's Pantry ❶,** 5 Ocean Ave., serves breakfast and lunch. Be sure to sample one of the gigantic muffins for $1.50. (☎967-4966. Open daily 9:30am-5:30pm. MC/V.) For a quick lunch, **Aunt Marie's ❶,** 13 Ocean Ave., serves great burgers ($3.50) and amaz-

> **TIP** **SLOW DOWN, YOU WILD CHILD.** As you drive along the southern coast, be forewarned that speed traps are as common as clambakes in this area, and an out-of-state license plate is as good as a bulls-eye. When a speed limit sign carries the clause "strictly enforced," know that going 27 mph in a 25 mph zone will get you nailed faster than you can say "Kennebunkport."

ing freshly squeezed lemonade. (☎967-0711. Hours vary. Cash only.) With river views, good brews, and live music, **Federal Jack's ❸**, 8 Western Ave., is the jack-of-all-trades for Kennebunkport dining. (☎967-4322. F-Sa live music. Th and Su karaoke. Open daily 11:30am-1am. AmEx/D/MC/V.) The **Kennebunk-Kennebunkport Chamber of Commerce**, 17 U.S. 9/Western Ave., in Kennebunkport, has a free area guide. (☎967-0857; www.visitthekennebunks.com. Open in summer M-F 11am-5pm.) The Chamber of Commerce runs a hospitality center, 2 Union Center, next to Ben & Jerry's. (☎967-0857. Open M-F 10am-9pm, Sa 9am-9pm, Su 10am-8pm.)

MT. DESERT ISLAND   ☎207

Roughly half of Mt. Desert Island is covered by Acadia National Park, which harbors some of the last protected marine, mountain, and forest environments on the New England coast. Sweetly-scented air, icy waters, stunning vistas, and an abundance of wildlife, including the peregrine falcon, await the many tourists who frequent the island each summer. Bar Harbor, on the eastern side, is by far the most crowded and glitzy part of the island. Once a summer hamlet for the affluent, the town now welcomes a motley crowd of vacation-seekers.

■ **ORIENTATION AND PRACTICAL INFORMATION.** Mt. Desert Island is shaped roughly like a 16 mi. long and 13 mi. wide lobster claw. It promises not to hurt you, but keep an eye on your wallet. Rte. 3 reaches the island from the north and runs south to Bar Harbor, becoming Mount Desert St. and then Main St. **Mount Desert Street** and **Cottage Street** are the major areas for shops, restaurants, and bars in Bar Harbor. Continuing on Rte. 3, **Seal Harbor** rests on the southeast corner of the island. **Northeast Harbor** is just south on Rte. 198, near the cleft. Across Somes Sound on Rte. 102, **Southwest Harbor** is where fishing and shipbuilding thrive. Rte. 102 cuts through the western half of the island, while Rte. 3 circles the eastern half. **Bar Harbor Chamber of Commerce**, 93 Cottage St. (☎288-5103; open June-Oct. M-F 8am-5pm, Nov.-May M-F 8am-4pm), has an **info booth** at 1 Harbor Pl., on the town pier. (Open mid-May to mid-Oct. daily 9am-5pm.) **Downeast Sexual Assault Helpline** (☎800-228-2470). Operates 24hr. **Internet Access: The Opera House**, 27 Cottage St. (☎288-3509. $2.50 for 1st 15min., $0.15 per min. thereafter.) Open daily May-June 8am-11pm.; July-Oct. 7am-11pm. **Post Office:** 55 Cottage St. (☎288-3122. Open M-F 8am-4:30pm, Sa 9am-noon.) **Postal Code:** 04609.

■ **TRANSPORTATION.** Greyhound (☎288-3211; www.greyhound.com) **buses** leaves Bar Harbor daily at 8:30am from the Villager Motel, 207 Main St., for Boston (7hr., $60) via Bangor (1½hr., $14). Beal & Bunker runs mail boat **ferries** (☎244-3575; open June to Sept. daily 8am-4:30pm; call for winter hours) from the Northeast Harbor town dock to Great Cranberry Island and Islesford, a.k.a. Little Cranberry. (15min.; 6 per day in summer; round-trip $14, under 12 $7, bicycles $5). Bay Ferries (the Cat), 121 Eden St., runs to Yarmouth, Nova Scotia. (☎888-249-7245; www.catferry.com. 3hr.; 1-2 per day; $73, children $53; cars $105, bikes $11. Reservations recommended, $5 fee.) The ticket shop and tourist information center are in Bar Harbor, at 4 Cottage St. (☎288-3395. Open daily 10am-9pm.) Free Island Explorer **buses** depart from Bar Harbor Green for the park and its campgrounds

NEW ENGLAND

and run about every 30min. from each stop. A park pass is required to go through Acadia. *Acadia Weekly*, free and widely available in Bar Harbor, has schedules. Acadia Bike & Canoe, 48 Cottage St., in Bar Harbor, rents **bikes** and **boats** and leads **kayak** tours. (☎288-9605 or 800-526-8615. Bikes $15 per half-day, $20 per day. Kayak tours per day $69, per half-day $45. Open May-Oct. daily 8am-6pm.)

ACCOMMODATIONS. Though grand hotels recall the island's exclusive resort days, budget-friendly motels dot **Route 3** north of Bar Harbor. However, expect to pay $65-85 in peak season at most places. The newly renovated and sparkling clean ☒**Bar Harbor Youth Hostel ❶**, 321 Main St., accommodates 32 people in two dorm rooms, an annex dorm, and one private room that houses four people. A state-of-the-art kitchen, movie nights, lime-green walls, and magenta sheets add to this hostel's bright and perky charm, and the kind staff will help you navigate Bar Harbor with ease. (☎288-5587. Linen included. Check-in 5-8:30pm. Lockout 10am-5pm. Curfew 11pm. Open May-Nov. Dorms $25; private room $80. MC/V.) The simple **Robbins Motel ❷**, 4 mi. north of Bar Harbor on Rte. 3, offers the best deal in town. (☎288-4659; www.acadia.net/robbins. Reservations recommended. Doubles $56. D/MC/V.) Camping spots cover the island, especially on Rtes. 102 and 198 west of town. Most campgrounds charge $20-30 for a site. **White Birches Campground ❶**, on Seal Cove Rd. 1 mi. west of Rte. 102 in Southwest Harbor, has 60 wooded sites in a remote location ideal for hiking. (☎244-3797 or 800-716-0727. Showers, toilets, and pool. Coin-op laundry. Reservations recommended. Office open daily mid-May to mid-Oct. 8am-8pm. Sites for up to 4 people $27, with hookup $30. Each additional person $4.)

FOOD. Watch some flicks and munch on a few slices at ☒**Reel Pizza ❸**, 33 Kennebec Pl., at the end of Rodick off Main St. This movie theater/pizzeria shows two films every night for $6 and serves creative pizza pies like the "Godfather," topped with artichoke, garlic, tomato, and onion. Three rows of the theater are comfy couches and chairs. (☎288-3828. Pizzas $11-21. Open daily 5pm to end of last screening. MC/V.) **Beal's ❸**, off Main St. at the end of Clark Point Rd. in Southwest Harbor, sells lobsters live or boiled at superb prices on a bustling dock. Landlubbers (a person unfamiliar with the sea or seamanship) can get turf food at a nearby stand. (☎244-3202 or 800-245-7178; www.bealslobster.com. Boiled lobster $10 per lb. Open daily May-Oct. 7am-8pm; Nov.-Apr. 7am-4pm; seafood sold daily year-round 9am-5pm. AmEx/MC/V.) **Ben and Bill's Chocolate Emporium ❶**, 66 Main St., near Cottage St., boasts 76 flavors of homemade ice cream and gelato, including—no kidding—lobster. (☎288-3281. Fudge $14 per lb. Cones $4-6. Open mid-Feb. to Jan. daily 9am-11:30pm. MC/V.) Those looking for a lighter fare should try the **Little Notch Bakery and Cafe ❶**, 11 Apple Ln., has exceptional pizzas ($10-17) and gourmet sandwiches ($7) on homemade Italian breads. (☎244-4043. Open in summer 7am-8pm; hours vary in low season.)

SIGHTS. The staff at the **Mount Desert Oceanarium**, off Rte. 3 on the northeast edge of the island, are masters of the marine. The facility's museum and hatchery teaches everything that you need to know about lobsters with a museum and hatchery. Its sister oceanarium, at the end of Clark Pt. Rd. near Beal's in Southwest Harbor, has fascinating exhibits and a museum geared toward children. (☎244-7330. Open mid-May to mid-Oct. M-Sa 9am-5pm. Main oceanarium $10-12, ages 4-12 $7; Southwest Harbor $8/6.) Just north of Bar Harbor, **Bar Island** is accessible at low tide, when receding waters reveal a gravel path accessed via Bridge St., off Rte. 3. (Tide times are published in *Acadia Weekly*.) At the end of Main St., pedestrians wander the **Shore Path** along the eastern edge of the harbor. The path offers the chance to explore the rocky coast's numerous tidal pools and boasts great views of nearby islands. For a relaxing and scenic drive, go north from Northeast Harbor on **Sargent Drive,** which runs along Somes Sound, the only fjord on the east coast. The four-masted schooner *Margaret Todd,* docked in front of the Bar Harbor Inn, dominates the harbor view and runs 2hr. tours of the islands. (☎288-4585 or 288-2373; www.downeastwindjammer.com. Ticket office at 27 Main St. Tours depart 10am, 2pm, and sunset. $30, under 12 $20.)

⚑▨ ENTERTAINMENT AND NIGHTLIFE. Most after-dinner pleasures on the island can be found in Bar Harbor's laid-back bars. **Geddy's Pub,** 19 Main St., provides a backdrop of brightly colored signs and lobster traps for the dancing frenzy that breaks out on summer nights. (☎288-5077. Pub-style entrees $10-26. Live music, mostly acoustic rock and folk, daily 7-10pm. No cover. Open Apr.-Oct. daily 11am-1am, kitchen closes 10pm; winter hours vary. MC/V.) **Improv Acadia,** 15 Cottage St., is a Chicago-based comedy outfit that induces laughing fits and serves local treats like Bar Harbor Ales ($3.50) and ice cream. (☎288-2503. Call for showtimes. Tickets $12.) Locals adore the **Lompoc Cafe & Brew Pub,** 36 Rodick St., off Cottage St., which keeps the crowd content with Bar Harbor Real Ale ($4), a bocce court, and jazz, Celtic, and folk music. (☎288-9392. Th open mic. F-Sa live music. No cover. Open May-Oct. daily 11:30am-1am.)

ACADIA NATIONAL PARK ☎207

The jagged, oceanside perimeter of Acadia National Park is lined with pine and birch forests and punctuated by dramatic rocks and secluded shores. Park preservation efforts were aided by the philanthropy of millionaire John D. Rockefeller, Jr. Fearing that the island would be overrun by cars, he funded 57 mi. of **carriage roads** accessible to hikers, mountain bikers, and skiers. For info on which trails are groomed for skiing, contact **The Friends of Acadia** (☎288-3340 or 800-625-0321). An ideal road for biking is the **Eagle Lake Loop** (6½ mi.), accessible from Rte. 233 or the park loop road, which has gentle grades and a spectacular lake view. Weekly **park passes** cost $20. Seniors can purchase a $10 lifetime pass, which entitles them to half-price camping at the park campgrounds. The *Biking and Hiking Guide to the Carriage Roads* ($6), available at the Visitors Center, offers invaluable hiking information. **Wildwood Stables,** along Park Loop Rd. in Seal Harbor, takes tourists around the island via horse and carriage. (☎276-3622. Reservations recommended. Wheelchair-accessible with advance notice. 1hr. tour $16, ages 6-12 $8, under 5 $4.50. 2hr. tour $18-22.)

GIVING BACK

TRAIL CREW

Each year thousands of hikers tackle a portion of the Appalachian Trail, a route stretching 2175 miles from Maine to Georgia. Few, however, realize that the trail was built entirely by volunteers, and that today volunteerism is what maintains its beauty. The **Appalachian Trail Conservancy,** a non-profit organization charged with maintaining the trail, sponsors 12 one-week sessions for a new generation of volunteers to do the backbreaking work required to provide for the trail's future. Spread along the length of the trail, crews make steps, move boulders, build bridges, cut underbrush, and sometimes blaze new routes. The work is tough, often leaving crews without showers and summoning them at the break of dawn. Nonetheless, volunteers come from all walks of life. Some are students, some are dedicated hikers, some are foreigners looking for a meaningful way to experience the American East, while others are professionals who seek a brief respite from the demands of modern life. Previous trail maintenance or hiking experience is not required—only a willingness to work and a love for the Appalacian Trail.

For further information, contact the Appalachian Trail Conservancy, P.O. Box 807, 799 Washington St., in Harpers Ferry, WV 25425. (☎953-3571; www.appalachiantrail.org).

Peregrine falcons, Acadia's most famous residents, nest along the **Precipice Trail** (1½ mi.), on the western side of Mt. Champlain. The hike is quite strenuous and involves the use of iron ladders to ascend the cliffs. When the trail is closed to accommodate the nesting falcons (June-late Aug.), the birds may be viewed with telescopes that are provided to visitors by the park service daily 9am-noon in the trail parking lot. On the eastern half of the island, popular hikes include the moderate blueberry-lined **Mt. Champlain/Bear Brook** (2½ mi. round-trip) and the strenuous **Beehive** (¾ mi. round-trip), both of which provide dramatic views of the Atlantic coastline. An easy half-mile amble along the **Bowl** trail from the summit of Mt. Champlain rewards hikers with a view of Sand Beach and Otter Point. To reach incredible vistas of both land and sea from the summit of Cadillac Mountain (1530 ft.), hike the **Cadillac Mountain North** (4½ mi.) or **South Ridge** (7½ mi.) trails or cruise up the paved **auto road** (accessed from the Park Loop Rd.; open 1hr. before dawn to midnight). Early birds are among the first people in the US to see the sun rise. About 4 mi. south of Bar Harbor on Rte. 3, the **Park Loop Road** traces the granite shore of the island, making a 27 mi. circuit through the forests. About 2-3hr. before high tide, strong waves crash against a rock chasm at **Thunder Hole,** along the Otter Cliffs at the southwest side of the coast. Soft sand and warm waters await at **Echo Lake,** along Rte. 102. **Sand Beach,** on the Park Loop along the island's eastern shore, is a beautiful spot sheltered by rocky cliffs, but the water is frigid, even in summer.

Acadia National Park campgrounds include **Blackwoods ❶,** 5 mi. south of Bar Harbor on Rte. 3. Nestled within Acadia's thick birch forests, Blackwoods is in the heart of the park, and its 286 sights are tightly packed in summer. (☎ 800-365-2267. Office open daily 8am-10pm. No hookups. Coin-operated showers available at private facility just outside of the campground. Reservations recommended. Park pass required for entry. Sites mid-Mar. to Oct. $20; call for low-season rates.) On Rte. 102A south of Southwest Harbor, **Seawall ❶** campground offers 214 sites available on a first come, first served basis. No reservations. (☎ 800-365-2267. Office open 8am-10pm. Coin-op showers nearby. No hookups. Sites $14.) Along the Park Loop Rd., **Jordan Pond House ❹** serves weary travelers tea and popovers ($8.25) under sweet-smelling white birch canopies. (☎ 276-3316. Lunch $10-20. Dinner $15-25. Open mid-May to late Oct. daily 11:30am-9pm; hours vary. Popovers served until 5:30pm. Reservations recommended. AmEx/MC/V.) **Acadia National Park Visitors Center,** located 3 mi. north of Bar Harbor on Rte. 3, has a topographical map, a bookstore, and helpful rangers on staff. A basic 15min. video introducing the park is shown to visitors every 30min. (☎ 288-5262. Open daily mid-June to mid-Sept. 8am-6pm; mid-Apr. to mid-June and mid-Sept. to Oct. 8am-4:30pm.) The **Park Headquarters,** 3 mi. west of Bar Harbor on Rte. 233, provides visitor info during the low season. (☎ 288-3338. Open M-F 8am-4:30pm.) **Emergency: Acadia National Park Law Enforcement** (☎ 288-3369).

NEW HAMPSHIRE

There are two sides to New Hampshire: the rugged landscape and natural beauty of the White Mountains, and the tax-free outlets, tourist traps, and state liquor stores that line most highways in and out of the state. New Hampshire's inland towns often revolve around their "three seasons" resort destinations, catering to outdoorsmen in the summer, leaf-lovers in the colorful autumn, and skiers in the long New England winter season. The first colony to declare its independence from Great Britain, New Hampshire has retained its patriotic charm along with its motto, "Live Free or Die."

🔢 PRACTICAL INFORMATION

Capital: Concord.

Visitor Info: Office of Travel and Tourism, 172 Pembroke Rd., P.O. Box 1856, Concord 03302 (☎271-2666 or 800-386-4664; www.visitnh.gov). **NH Parks and Recreation** (☎271-3556; www.nhparks.state.nh.us). The **Fish and Game Department,** 2 Hazen Dr., Concord 03301 (☎603-271-3421; www.wildlife.state.nh.us), provides info on regulations and licenses. **US Forest Service,** 719 N. Main St., Laconia 03246 (☎603-528-8721; www.fs.fed.us/r9/white). Open M-F 8am-4:30pm.

Postal Abbreviation: NH. **Sales Tax:** 8% on meals and lodgings.

PORTSMOUTH   ☎603

Though only 13 mi. of its perimeter touch the Atlantic Ocean, New Hampshire makes the most of its toehold on the water. Portsmouth, the colonial capital, boasts a rich history and a vibrant atmosphere. Colonial history is an integral part of Portsmouth (most buildings date from the 18th century) but hip restaurants and artistic productions throughout the city reveal an affinity for present-day style.

📠🔢 TRANSPORTATION AND PRACTICAL INFORMATION. Just 57 mi. north of Boston, Portsmouth is situated at the junction of U.S. 1, 1A, and I-95. Cheap parking ($0.50-1 per hr.) is available downtown, but the town is best navigated by foot. **State Street/U.S. 1** and **Congress Street** are major roads that run northeast-southwest through town. **Market Street** runs southeast-northwest and is the central intersecting road. Vermont Transit/Greyhound, 22 Ladd St. (☎436-0163; www.greyhound.com; open 7am-6pm), inside Federal Tobacconists, sends **buses** to Boston (1¼hr., 3 per day, $17). Purchase tickets on-site. Seacoast Trolley (☎431-6975) is a scenic touring company that runs every hour in the summer from 11am-3pm, with 14 stops around Portsmouth. (Partial loop $3, full loop with reboarding privileges $6.) For a **taxi** call Blue Star Taxi, ☎436-2774. The **Greater Portsmouth Chamber of Commerce** is at 500 Market St., outside downtown. (☎436-1118; www.portcity.org. Open M-F 8am-5pm, Sa-Su 10am-4pm.) The Chamber of Commerce **info kiosk** is in Market Sq. (Open May to mid-Oct. daily 10am-5pm.) **Hotlines: Violence and Rape Hotline,** ☎800-336-3795. **Medical Services: Portsmouth Regional,** 333 Borthwick Ave. (☎436-5110 or 800-991-4325). **Internet Access: Portsmouth Public Library,** 8 Islington St. (☎427-1540. Free Wi-Fi. Open M-Th 9am-9pm, F 9am-5:30pm, Sa 9am-5pm.) **Post Office:** 80 Daniel St. (☎800-275-8777. Open M-F 7:30am-5:30pm, Sa 8am-12:30pm.) **Postal Code:** 03801.

📠📶 ACCOMMODATIONS AND FOOD. Portsmouth is not exactly budget-friendly when it comes to hanging your hat; a common tactic to avoid steep prices is to take a short trip over the border to Maine, where accommodations are pleasant and more reasonably priced. **Camp Eaton ❷,** in York Harbor, ME, about 15 mi. north of Portsmouth off Rte. 1A, is mere steps from a beautiful New England beach. Immaculate bathrooms and well-kept, wooded sites make camping here a relative bargain. (☎207-363-3424. 2-person sites in summer $56; low season $38. Each additional person $6. MC/V.) The **Farmstead B&B ❹,** 999 Goodwin Rd., just east of the intersection with Rte. 236, in Eliot, ME, offers pristine rooms with views of the countryside only 10 mi. from downtown Portsmouth. (☎207-748-3145 or 207-439-5033; www.farmstead.qpg.com. Rooms $85. D/MC/V.)

Portsmouth offers a plethora of dining options, with establishments of every persuasion peppering Market St. 🔲**The Friendly Toast ❷,** 121 Congress St., a block and a half from Market Sq., is cluttered with the most ghastly artifacts the 50s could produce: mannequins, pulp novels, formica what-nots, and stroke-inducing bad art. Menu items like the "mission burrito" ($8) are nearly impossible to finish alone. (☎430-2154. Breakfast served all day. Entrees $6-8. Open M-Th and Su 7am-9pm, F-Sa 24hr. AmEx/D/MC/V.) With a giant golden stein above the entrance, **The Portsmouth Brewery ❷**, 56 Market St., offers great pub fare ($6-10) and some excellent brews. Their "Smutty Nose IPA" is ranked the #1 IPA in the US, and their "Old Brown Dog" is a local favorite. (☎431-1115. Open daily 11:30am-12:30am. AmEx/D/MC/V.) When you're sick of seafood, transport yourself down South at the **Muddy River Smokehouse ❸**, 21 Congress St. For the particularly ravenous, "The Squealer" includes a rack of pork ribs, a pound of pulled pork, half a smoked chicken, a pint of baked beans and mashed potatoes, and cornbread ($30). A downstairs club staves off the food coma with live blues. (☎430-9582. Entrees $10-22. Open M-Th and Su 11am-9pm, F-Sa 11am-10:30pm. Blues club open Th-Sa. 21+. Cover and times vary. AmEx/D/MC/V.)

◉ ♫ **SIGHTS AND ENTERTAINMENT.** Modern Portsmouth sells itself with its colonial past. The prestigious **Strawbery Banke Museum,** on the corner of Marcy and Hancock St., encompasses several blocks of buildings and beautiful gardens, each restored to recreate the region as it evolved over time. Museum employees in period garb populate the various houses and shops. To find the museum, follow the signs that lead toward the harbor through a maze of shops. (☎433-1100; www.strawberybanke.org. Open May-Oct. M-Sa 10am-5pm, Su noon-5pm. $15, ages 7-17 $10; families $40. Tickets good for 2 consecutive days.) Across the street, **Prescott Park** hugs the bank of the Piscataqua River. A great place to picnic, these small, well-tended gardens offer an amazing view. Naval enthusiasts can climb aboard through the hatches of the **U.S.S. Albacore,** 600 Market St., a research submarine built locally at the Portsmouth Naval Shipyard. (☎436-3680. Open May-Oct. daily 9:30am-5pm; winter hours vary. $5, over 62 or military with ID $3.50, ages 7-17 $2; families $10.) The **Music Hall,** 28 Chestnut St., a 125-year-old theater, hosts shows in the summer, including movies, concerts, dances, and plays. (☎436-2400; www.themusichall.org. Box office open M-Sa noon-6pm or until 30min. after the show has started. Films $8; military, students, seniors, and under 21 $6.) Head to the **Press Room,** 77 Daniel St., which hosts nightly jazz, folk, and blues in an intimate, colonial-feeling pub. (☎431-5186. Cover up to $5.)

NEW HAMPSHIRE SKI RESORTS ☎ 603

With sizeable mountains and abundant snowfall from November to April, New Hampshire is one of the East Coast's most popular skiing destinations. When the White Mountains thaw, each resort blossoms into a summer diversion. **Ski New Hampshire** (☎745-9396 or 800-937-5493; www.skinh.com), in Lincoln, provides information and reservations for five resorts in the White Mountains. **Cranmore,** in North Conway (p. 245), offers 39 trails, more than 200 skiable acres, and great shopping. Its children's summer camps offer tennis, hiking, swimming, and more. (☎800-786-6754; www.cranmore.com. Lift operates in winter M-F 9am-4pm, Sa-Su 8:30am-4pm. Lift tickets $39, ages 13-18 $29, ages 6-12 and over 65 $19.) Located on U.S. 302 by North Conway, pricey **Attitash** has two mountains, 51 trails (evenly divided among beginner, intermediate, and expert), and 25 acres of glades. Biking, horseback riding, water slides, a climbing wall, trampolines, and an alpine slide keep summer visitors busy. (☎374-2368; www.attitash.com. Lift tickets in winter M-F and Su $49, Sa and holidays $55; ages 13-18 $39/45, ages 6-12 and seniors $19/25. Water slide open in summer daily 10am-6pm. Single ride $15. Summer full-day value pack without golf and horseback riding $35, ages 2-7 $15.)

Just outside Pinkham Notch on Rte. 16, **Wildcat Mountain** features 47 trails (25% beginner, 45% intermediate, 30% expert) and mountainscape views from its 4062 ft.

peak. (☎888-754-9453; www.skiwildcat.com. Lift tickets $55, ages 13-18 $42, ages 6-12 $25. Gondola rides late May-Oct. daily. $13, over 65 $9, ages 6-12 $7.) Three miles east of Lincoln on Rte. 112, **Loon Mountain** has 43 ski trails, along with biking and horseback riding in warmer months. (☎745-8111; www.loonmtn.com. Lift tickets M-F $52, Sa-Su $59; ages 13-19 $42/49; under 13 $32/37.) Just off I-93 in Franconia Notch State Park (p. 243), **Cannon Mountain** has 42 trails (15% beginner, 50% intermediate, 35% expert) at slightly lower prices than other local resorts; on Tuesdays and Thursdays, a 2-person pass is just $40. Summer hiking, biking, canoeing, and swimming keep visitors active, while the Aerial Tramway (p. 245) whisks weary travelers up the mountain. (☎823-8800; www.cannonmt.com. Lift tickets M-F $34, Sa-Su $45; ages 13-17 $23/37; seniors and children $23/29.)

WHITE MOUNTAINS ☎ 603

The White Mountains' 780,000 forest acres create a playground for any outdoor enthusiast. While many associate the area with powdery ski slopes, its warm-weather alternatives—hiking, camping, canoeing, kayaking, and fishing—make the White Mountains an attractive destination year-round.

▐ TRANSPORTATION. However you approach the White Mountains, the scenery is breathtaking. Concord Trailways (☎228-3300 or 800-639-3317) runs **trains** from Boston to Conway (First Stop Market, on W. Main St.; 2 per day, $28), and Franconia (Kelly's Foodtown, Exit 38 off I-93; daily, $31). For hikers, the Appalachian Mountain Club (AMC) runs a **shuttle** between locations on the Appalachian Trail in the White Mountains. Consult AMC's *The Guide* for a map of routes and times or pick up a schedule at the AMC Pinkham Notch Visitors Center. (☎466-2727. June to mid-Oct. daily 8am-4pm. Reservations highly recommended for all stops; required for some. $12, AMC members $10.)

▰▱ ORIENTATION AND PRACTICAL INFORMATION. The White Mountains can be daunting to an unfamiliar traveler, but are easily navigated with a good map and guide. The immense forest, spanning both New Hampshire and Maine, is bordered by a dozen or so towns and contains several commercial ski resorts. Many of the region's highlights can be found in three areas: **Pinkham Notch** (p. 242), northeast of the forest near Mt. Washington; the **Franconia Notch** area (p. 243), northwest of the National Forest; and **North Conway** (p. 245), to the southeast.

Any unattended vehicle parked on White Mountain National Forest land must have a **parking pass,** sold by the US Forest Service, the Appalachian Mountain Club, and the White Mountain Attraction Center; vehicles parked at national forest campground sites are an exception. (☎528-8721. $5 per week, $20 per year.) Purchase daily passes at any of the forest trailheads for $3. The **US Forest Service** operates four **ranger stations,** each of which provides free information on recreational opportunities, camping, and safety precautions in the White Mountains. **Pemigewasset/Ammonoosuc,** on Rte. 175 in Plymouth near Exit 25 off I-93, covers the southwest region of the forest. (☎869-2626. Open M-F 8am-4:30pm.) **Androscoggin,** 2½ mi. south of Gorham on Rte. 16, oversees the northern region. (☎466-2713. Open in summer daily 8am-5pm; in winter M-Sa 8am-4:30pm.) **Evans Notch,** 18 Mayville Rd., in Bethel, ME, covers the Maine section of the national forest. (☎207-824-2134. Open in summer daily 8am-4:30pm; winter Tu-Sa 8am-4:30pm.) **Saco,** 100 yd. west of the Rte. 16 junction on Hwy. 112 (Kancamagus Hwy.), oversees the southeast section of the forest. (☎447-5448. Open daily 8am-4:30pm.)

The **White Mountain Gateway and Visitors Center,** P.O. Box 10, North Woodstock 03262, at Exit 32 off I-93, has info on mountain recreation. (☎745-8720. Open daily

July-Sept. 8:30am-6pm; Apr.-July and Sept. to mid-Oct. 8:30am-5:30pm; mid-Oct. to Apr. 8:30am-5pm.) The **Appalachian Mountain Club (AMC)** is a nonprofit conservation and recreation organization that maintains 1400 mi. of trails in the northeastern US. They teach outdoor skills workshops, run environmental programs, and provide lodging at backcountry shelters, camps, and lodges. Members of the AMC receive discounts at their hiking destinations. Individual ($50) or family ($75) memberships may be purchased online (www.outdoors.org) or at the AMC's **Pinkham Notch Visitors Center,** 10 mi. north of Jackson on Rte. 16. As the base camp for Mt. Washington, the Visitors Center is the best source of info on weather and trail conditions, with maps, current weather reports, and a packroom, bathrooms, and showers for hikers. They handle lodging reservations and have comprehensive information on White Mountain trails, wilderness safety, and eco-friendly "Leave No Trace" backpacking. (AMC headquarters ☎617-523-0636; www.outdoors.org. Visitors Center ☎466-2727. Open daily 6:30am-10pm.)

⌂ ACCOMMODATIONS. Outside the forest, numerous accommodations, from hostels to high-end resorts, lie within an hour's drive. For a guide to lodgings near the White Mountains, pick up the small *White Mountains Travel Guide,* free and available at any **info booth.** Other than ski resorts, most accommodations within the National Forest are operated by the AMC. The AMC operates **huts** along the White Mountains' stretch of the Appalachian Trail, used by trail hikers to break up the trail's vast distance. A free *AMC Huts and Lodges* brochure, available at the **Pinkham Notch Visitors Center,** has descriptions and locations. The huts only have co-ed bunkrooms, and some huts have no showers or electrical outlets. The **full-service huts ❸** provide a bunk, mattress, pillow, and three wool blankets, as well as breakfast and dinner. There are toilets, single-sex washrooms, and cold water. Bring sleeping gear and a flashlight. At the **self-service huts ❶,** guests must provide their own food, but have use of a kitchen stocked with cookware. Blankets are not provided—bring a warm sleeping bag. (☎466-2727; www.outdoors.org. No pets. No smoking or open flames. Huts open June to mid-Sept.; 6 huts open to mid-Oct.; 3 self-service huts open in winter. Some discounts for longer stays. Full-service huts $87-94, under 15 $26-58; AMC members $79/48. Self-service huts $27, members $25. Reservations with AmEx/MC/V.) For car-accessible lodging, the AMC runs the **Joe Dodge Lodge ❸** (p. 243). The **Highland Center at Crawford Notch ❸,** off Rte. 302, is open year-round, with private and shared rooms as well as 16 bunks in the Shapleigh Bunkhouse. (☎466-2727. Dorms with breakfast and dinner $49, AMC members $43; doubles with breakfast and dinner $131/109. Call for low-season rates. AmEx/MC/V.) The **White Mountains Hostel ❶** (p. 246) is also close by.

✂ CAMPING. The US Forest Service maintains 23 designated **National Forest campgrounds ❶,** all of which are accessible by car. Four remain open in winter, although only one has plowed access. Some sites are first come, first served, but these can fill quickly. On weekends, arrive around check-out time (usually 10-11am) to snag a site. Bathrooms and firewood are usually available. (Reservations ☎877-444-6777; www.reserveusa.com. Cars parked at a campsite do not require a parking pass. Reservations accepted after Jan. 1 and must be made at least 1 week in advance. Sites $16-18; reservation fee $9, change/cancellation fee $10.) Camping is less expensive or free of charge at the many **backcountry campsites ❶,** which are only accessible via hiking trails. Regulations prohibit camping and fires above the treeline (approximately 4000 ft.); within 200 ft. of trails, certain bodies of water, and a few specific roads; or within a quarter mile of huts, shelters, tent platforms, lakes, streams, trailheads, or roads. Rules are even stricter in the Great Gulf Wilderness around Mt. Washington—no wood or charcoal fires are allowed. Other areas have more special regulations; consult the US Forest Service's *Backcountry*

Appalachian Trail

0 20 miles
0 20 kilometers

MAINE
ATLANTIC OCEAN
Portland
Sebago Lake
Pinkham Notch
Mt. Washington
6288ft
North Conway
Conway
White Mountain National Forest
Franconia Notch State Park
Lake Winnipesaukee
Portsmouth
Newfound Lake
Concord
Hanover
Manchester
Lake Sunapee
Nashua
Lowell
NEW HAMPSHIRE
Green Mountain National Forest
Killington
VERMONT
Brattleboro
Worcester
Quabbin Reservoir
MASSACHUSETTS
North Adams
Springfield
Albany
Lenox
Stockbridge
Hartford
CONNECTICUT
Waterbury
New Haven
NEW YORK
Pine Hill
Phoenicia
Woodstock
Bridgeport
Catskill Forest Preserve
New York City
Delaware Water Gap National Recreation Area
Newark
PENNSYLVANIA
Scranton
NEW JERSEY

Mt. Katahdin
5267ft
MAINE
QUÉBEC
SEE EXPANSION LEFT
VERMONT
NEW HAMPSHIRE
MASS.
CONNECTICUT
NEW YORK
NEW JERSEY
PENNSYLVANIA
DE.
MARYLAND
VIRGINIA
Shenandoah National Park
George Washington National Forest
WEST VIRGINIA
Jefferson National Forest
KY.
Cherokee National Forest
Great Smoky Mountains National Park
Pisgah National Forest
NORTH CAROLINA
SOUTH CAROLINA
Nantahala National Forest
TENNESSEE
Springer Mtn.
3782ft
Chattahoochee National Forest
GEORGIA

0 50 miles
0 50 kilometers

NEW ENGLAND

> ❗ **BEAR CARE.** No matter where you camp, **bears** are a threat. Stop by a ranger station or the AMC Visitors Center to pick up information on how to minimize the danger. Keep food hung high or secured in bear canisters and well away from sleeping areas. Do not keep anything with the scent of food on it (clothes worn while cooking, for example) in or near your tent. If you do encounter a bear, stay calm and back away slowly, and do not make direct eye contact. When hiking, make sufficient noise to alert bears to your presence, allowing them to move away from the trail.

Camping Rules, available for reference at any of the four regional ranger stations, for more info. A plethora of **private campgrounds ❷,** the majority of which cater to RVs and families, surround the borders of the forest. A copy of *New Hampshire's Guide to Camping,* available at any highway rest stop or information booth in the state, provides a map, prices, and campgrounds' phone numbers.

🏞 **OUTDOOR ACTIVITIES.** If you are planning to do a significant amount of hiking, the invaluable *AMC White Mountain Guide* ($23; available in the AMC Visitor's Center and most bookstores) includes maps and descriptions of every mountain trail. To estimate hiking time, allow 30min. for every horizontal mile and 1hr. for every 1000 ft. of elevation gain. Weather and physical condition may affect this time. Because weather in the mountains is unpredictable, hikers should bring three layers of clothing in all seasons: one for wind, one for rain, and at least one for warmth—preferably wool or a synthetic material like polypropylene or fleece (not cotton). Black flies, ticks, and mosquitoes make insect repellent a must-have. Always bring more than enough water; dehydration can be a serious problem and hikes in the region are often more strenuous than anticipated. A high-calorie snack, like trail mix, is also a good idea.

Cycling is another popular way to tour the White Mountains. For help with planning, ask a ranger or consult *30 Bicycle Tours in New Hampshire* ($13; at local bookstores and outdoor equipment stores). **Great Glen Trails Outdoor Center,** across Rte. 16 from the Mt. Washington Auto Rd., rents bikes for use only on their trails. They also offer guided kayaking trips and, in winter, ski rentals. (☎ 466-2333. Open daily 9am-5pm. Trail fee $7; included in rental. Bikes $20 per 2hr., under 18 $14 per 2hr.; $30/20 per 4hr. Helmets $3 per day. Winter trail pass $15 per day, ages 6-12 and over 62 $10; $11/7 per afternoon half day. Kayaking $75-150.)

To see the National Forest in a less strenuous way, drive along the 📷**Kancamagus Scenic Highway (Route 12),** which connects the towns of Lincoln and Conway. The 35 mi. drive takes at least 1hr., though the many wooded outlooks are perfect for a picnic. It's a good idea to get gas at Lincoln—no gas is available in the park—then head east on "the Kanc" to enjoy the scenic splendor all the way to Conway.

PINKHAM NOTCH ☎ 603

Pinkham Notch, New Hampshire's easternmost mountain pass, lies in the shadow of the tallest mountain in the northeastern US—the 6288 ft. **Mount Washington.** Pinkham's proximity to the peak makes it more crowded than neighboring areas, but secluded areas can be found if you're willing to look. AMC's **Pinkham Notch Visitors Center** lies between Gorham and Jackson on Rte. 16.

Stretching from behind the Pinkham Notch Visitors Center all the way up to the summit of Mt. Washington, **Tuckerman's Ravine Trail,** despite the deceiving 4¼ mi. distance, demands 4-5hr. of steep hiking each way. Authorities urge caution when climbing—Mt. Washington claims at least one life every year. Mt. Washington is one of the most dangerous mountains in the world because of its highly unpredictable weather, including wind speeds that frequently reach hurricane force. It has never been recorded to be warmer than 72°F on top of Mt. Washington, and the average temperature on the peak is a bone-chilling 27°F. The summit of Mt. Washington boasts the highest winds ever recorded (231 mph) and the peak is shrouded in fog 300 days of the year. In the right conditions, however, the trek offers excellent vistas and some of the best views in New England—on a clear day hikers are rewarded with a view of five states and Canada. A less daunting option for the steepest part of the ascent is the **Lion's Head Trail,** which diverges from the Tuckerman's Ravine Trail about 2 mi. into the hike. Because Tuckerman's Ravine is closed in winter (due to frequent avalanches), the Lion's Head Trail is the only option for adventurers hiking in the snowy months.

Motorists can take the **Mt. Washington Auto Road,** a partially paved road that winds 8 mi. to the summit. For most vehicles, the ascent is a minor test, but 1000 ft. drop-offs and an absence of guard rails will tax even steel nerves. Drivers sturdy enough to reach the top receive bragging rights in the form of a free "This Car Climbed Mt. Washington" bumper sticker. The road begins 3 mi. north of the Pinkham Notch Visitors Center on Rte. 16. (☎466-3988. Road open daily June-Aug. 7:30am-6pm; May-June and Sept.-Oct. 8:30am-5pm. Road may close due to weather conditions. $20 per car and driver, free audio tour included. Each additional passenger $8, ages 5-12 $5.) To enjoy the view without the drive (and to save your brakes from the long ride down), take a **stage tour,** across Rte. 16 from the Auto Road, where well-trained drivers escort you up the mountain. (☎466-2333. Open daily 8:30am-5pm. $26, seniors $23, ages 5-12 $11.)

Many of the region's lodging options are on or near Mt. Washington. Accessible by car, the **Joe Dodge Lodge ❸,** immediately behind the Pinkham Notch Visitors Center, gives sleepy travelers over 100 comfortable bunks to choose from. Those who don't fall asleep immediately can make use of seven family rooms, a small library, and a living room. (☎466-2727. Breakfast and dinner included. Check-in 2pm. Check-out 10:30am. Reservations recommended. $56-76, under 16 $37-43; AMC members $51-63/34-39; without meals $43-54/25-30, AMC members $39-49/$23-27. Call for low-season rates. AmEx/MC/V.) About 2hr. up the Tuckerman Ravine Trail, **Hermit Lake Shelter ❶** has bathrooms but no showers, and sleeps up to 90 people on a first come, first served basis. Nightly passes are sold at the Visitors Center ($10). **Lakes of the Clouds Hut ❸,** 1½ mi. from Mt. Washington's summit, is one of AMC's most popular full-service huts. (Reservations ☎466-2727. See **Accommodations,** p. 246)

FRANCONIA NOTCH AREA   ☎603

Carved by glacial movements that began 400 million years ago, the granite peaks of Franconia Notch State Park are one of the most majestic spots in the White Mountains. Although one of the biggest attractions in the area, the famous rocky profile known as the "Old Man of the Mountain," collapsed in 2003, Franconia is still home to stunning waterfalls, woodlands, and natural rock formations.

■▸ **ORIENTATION AND PRACTICAL INFORMATION.** Most of the area highlights are accessible directly from I-93. It's important to note that the highway exit numbering system has recently changed. The old Exit 1 on the Franconia Notch Pkwy. corresponds to the new 34A; Exit 2 to 34B; and Exit 3 to 34C. The **Franconia Notch Chamber of Commerce,** on Main St. in Franconia, has maps and information on the region. (☎823-5516; www.franconianotch.org. Open mid-May to mid-Oct. Tu-Su 10am-5pm.)

▸▪ **ACCOMMODATIONS AND FOOD.** Franconia Notch is a popular place for camping, but make sure to bring insect repellent if you plan to stay in the great outdoors. Nestled in the middle of the park, **Lafayette Place Campground ❶**, off I-93 S between Exits 34A and 34B, offers spacious campsites in an ideal location. (☎823-9513, reservations 271-3628; www.nhstateparks.org. Camp store, clean facilities, and coin-op showers. Reservations strongly recommended and must be made at least 3 days in advance for a $5 fee. Open mid-May to mid-Oct. 2-person sites $19-24. Each additional adult $9.50-12, under 18 free. MC/V.) The scenic Pemi Trail passes through the campground; follow it toward the Flume (3½ mi.) and the Basin (2 mi.) to the south and toward Profile Lake and Cannon Mtn. (2½ mi.) to the north. A peaceful evening can be found at the **Fransted Family Campground ❶**, 3 mi. north of the Notch on Rte. 18. The expansive grounds contain over 100 well-tended sites, a small beach, volleyball, and an 18-hole miniature golf course. Facilities include showers, bathroom, and coin-op laundry. (☎823-5675. Open May-Oct. Tent sites $30-36, with electricity and water $36, with full hookup $38. MC/V.) Numerous cottages, private campgrounds, and motels cluster along the stretch of Rte. 3 between Woodstock and the entrance to Franconia Notch. For a quieter option, head north to the **Hillwinds Lodge ❸**, off Rte. 18 in Franconia, next to the scenic Gale River. In addition to clean rooms, guests enjoy the perks of nearby Franconia Inn, including free mountain bikes and an outdoor pool. (☎823-5551 or 800-473-5299. Rooms $55-75. AmEx/MC/V.)

🖼Polly's Pancake Parlor ❷, on Rte. 117 in Sugar Hill, just 2 mi. from Exit 38 off I-93, is a homey restaurant with a dining room overlooking Mt. Washington. A stack of Polly's superb pancakes arrives with a tray of maple syrup, maple spread, and granulated maple sugar from the restaurant's own product line. (☎823-5575; www.pollyspancakeparlor.com. 6-pancake stack $6. Unlimited pancakes $12. Open mid-May to mid-Oct. daily 7am-3pm; Apr. and Nov. Sa-Su 7am-3pm only. AmEx/D/MC/V.) The endless menu at the **Woodstock Inn Brewery ❸**, on Rte. 3 in Woodstock, is sure to fuel your engine, with everything from not-so-standard sandwiches like the "Train Wreck" (roasted chicken, beef, and a big red Anaheim chili; $8), to pasta and seafood. (☎745-3951. Open daily 11:30am-10pm. AmEx/D/MC/V.)

🔳 **SIGHTS.** Traveling north from Lincoln on I-93, 🖼The Flume, Exit 34A on I-93, is a 2 mi. walk cutting through a spectacular granite gorge. An optional shuttle bus takes you to the highlights of the gorge and cuts the walk to half a mile. Although only 12-20 ft. apart, the moss-covered canyon walls are 70-90 ft. high. Take a leisurely stroll over centuries-old covered bridges and past the 35 ft. Avalanche Falls. Tickets can be purchased from the **Flume Visitors Center**, which provides area information and shows an excellent 15min. film acquainting visitors with the landscape and geological history of the area. (☎745-8391; www.flumegorge.com. Open daily May-June and Sept.-Oct. 9am-5pm; July-Aug. daily 9am-5:30pm. $8, ages 6-12 $5.) A 9 mi. paved **bike path** begins at the Visitors Center and parallels I-93 N through the park, providing easy access to attractions and sights along the way. To rent some wheels, head to 2 mi. north to **Franconia Sports Shop**, off Main St. in Franconia. (☎823-5241. Bike rental $7 per hr., $15-19 per half-day, $19-25 per full-day. Open M-Sa 10am-6pm, Su 10am-4pm.) Between Exits 34A and 34B on I-93, visitors can find a well-marked turn-off for **The Basin.** A 10min. walk leads to a 20 ft. whirlpool that has been carved into the granite by a 15 ft. waterfall. (Wheelchair-accessible.)

For years Franconia had been known as the home of the **Old Man of the Mountain,** but in May 2003, the granite profile fell from its perch. The viewing areas at Exit 34B on I-93 and between Exit 34A and 34B on I-93 are still open and provide a diagram and explanation of the Old Man's fall. A pleasant 10min. walk down the designated path from the parking lot at Exit 34B brings viewers to the banks of **Profile Lake**, which affords the best available view of the cliff where the Old Man used to rest. Also at Exit 34B, a small display of Old Man memorabilia and the history regarding his discovery and rise to popularity can be found at the **Old Man of the Mountain Museum.** (☎823-7722, ext. 717. Open daily mid-May to mid-Oct. 9:30am-5pm. Free.) The 80-passenger **Cannon Mountain Aerial Tramway,** Exit 34B, climbs over 2000 ft. in 7min. and carries visitors to the summit of the Cannon Cliff, a 1000 ft. sheer drop into the cleft between Mt. Lafayette and Cannon Mountain. (☎823-8800. Open daily mid-May to mid-Oct. 9am-5pm; mid-Dec. to mid-Apr. 9am-3:45pm. Trams run every 15min. $8, round-trip $10, ages 6-12 $6.) In winter, the tram takes skiers up the mountain (see **New Hampshire Ski Resorts,** p. 238). Back at the base of the mountain, right next to the tramway station, sits the one-room **New England Ski Museum,** home to a variety of old ski equipment and an exhibit on Hannes Schneider, who started the first ski school in America. (☎823-7177. Open mid-May to mid-Oct. and mid-Dec. to mid-Apr. daily 10am-5pm. Free.) While skiers enjoy Cannon Mtn. during the winter, on summer days, the lifeguard-protected beach at **Echo Lake,** just off Exit 34C on I-93 at the base of Cannon Mtn., offers cool but often crowded waters. The lake is accessible until 10pm. (☎823-8800, ext. 784. Lifeguard on duty mid-June to early Sept. daily 10am-5pm. $3, ages 6-11 $1. Free when lifeguard not on duty. Canoe or paddleboat rental ☎823-8800, ext. 783. $10 per hr. Last rental 4pm. 7 RV sites with hookup $29.)

HIKING. Franconia Notch provides excellent day-hikes and views; the **Hiking Information Center,** adjacent to Lafayette Place Campground, is the best source in the area for hiking suggestions and safety tips. (Open daily 8am-4pm.) In this area be prepared for severe weather, especially above 4000 ft. On the western rim, the **Lonesome Lake Trail** (2 mi.) winds from Lafayette Place Campground to **Lonesome Lake,** where the AMC operates its western-most hut. The trails on the eastern rim boast an extensive network stretching into the wilderness of Franconia Notch. The **Greenleaf Trail** (2½ mi.), which starts at the aerial tramway parking lot, and the **Old Bridle Path** (3 mi.), beginning from Lafayette Place and known for its stellar views, are more ambitious. Both lead up to the AMC's **Greenleaf Hut,** near the summit of Mt. Lafayette overlooking Echo Lake. From Greenleaf, a 7½ mi. trek east along the **Old Bridle Path** and **Garfield Ridge** leads to the AMC's most remote hut, the **Galehead.** Mt. Garfield's summit is above the timberline, and storms intensify quickly. Ambitious hikers seek the **Falling Waters Trail,** accessed from Lafayette Place. With three waterfalls within 1½ mi. of the trailhead and a 1600 ft. elevation change, the trail is a strenuous hike. The well-maintained eastern rim trails are interconnected and can occupy trekkers for days; make sure to get adequate supplies before starting out.

LOST RIVER GORGE

Outside of Franconia Notch State Park, **Lost River Gorge,** located 6 mi. west of North Woodstock on Rte. 112, is a deep glacial gorge with a network of caves, massive boulders, complex rock formations, and beautiful waterfalls. The park also maintains a nature garden and a forestry center with information about the area. The walk through the gorge is less than 1 mi. along well-maintained suspended wooden walkways and bridges, but exploring the caves can easily take over an hour; each creatively named cavern (like the Lemon Squeezer) is open for exploration to those agile enough to wrench themselves through. (☎745-8031; www.findlostriver.com. Open daily July-Aug. 9am-6pm; mid-May to June and Sept. to mid-Oct. 9am-5pm. Last entry 1hr. before closing. Solid walking shoes and active wear recommended. $11, ages 4-12 $7. Garden and forestry center free.)

NORTH CONWAY AND CONWAY   ☎603

Proximity to the White Mountains makes North Conway one of New Hampshire's most popular vacation destinations. Rte. 16, the traffic-infested main road, houses the usual crop of outlet stores and a variety of smaller local shops. The town of

Conway, 5 mi. south, has fewer touristy shops, but several excellent options for meals and lodging. The **Mt. Washington Chamber of Commerce,** on Rte. 16 in North Conway, has info on area attractions. (☎800-367-3364; www.mtwashingtonvalley.com. Open June-Oct. M-F 9am-5pm, Sa-Su 10am-5pm. Call ahead for winter hours.) Numerous stores in the North Conway area rent outdoor equipment for the slopes, the water, and the roads. For ski equipment in winter or bike and boat rentals during other seasons, **Joe Jones,** 2709 White Mtn. Hwy. at Mechanic St. in North Conway, has it all. (☎356-9411. Alpine skis, boots, and poles $20 per day, $36 per 2 days; cross-country equipment $15/26; snowboards $25/46. Bike rental $15 per 4hr., $30 per 8hr. Canoes M-F $30 per day, Sa-Su $35 per day; kayaks $20/25 per day. Open July-Aug. daily 9am-8pm; Sept.-Nov. and Apr.-June M-Th and Su 10am-6pm, F-Sa 9am-6pm; Dec.-Mar. M-F 8:30am-6pm, Sa-Su 8:30am-8pm.) **Eastern Mountain Sports (EMS),** north on White Mtn. Hwy. in the lobby of the Eastern Slope Inn, sells camping equipment and rents tents, sleeping bags, snowshoes, packs, and skis. The knowledgeable staff provides free first-hand info on climbing and hiking; EMS also offers a summer climbing school. (☎356-5433. Tents $20 for first day, each additional day $10. Sleeping bags $15/5. Open June-Sept. M-Sa 8:30am-9pm, Su 8:30am-6pm; Oct.-May M-Th and Su 8:30am-6pm, F-Sa 8:30am-9pm.)

Located in the heart of Conway and maintained by a friendly staff, the **White Mountains Hostel (HI) ●,** 36 Washington St., off Rte. 16 at the intersection of Rte. 153, is meticulously clean and environmentally friendly. The hostel has 43 comfy bunks, a kitchen, Wi-Fi, and a common room. (☎447-1001. Locker key deposit $10. Linen included. Towels $0.50. Laundry $3. Reception 7:30-10am and 5-10pm. Check-out 10am. Lockout 10am-noon. Reservations recommended during the summer and peak foliage season. Dorms $23, members $20; private rooms $48. MC/V.) Owned by Babe Ruth's son-in-law, the hostel at the beautiful **Cranmore Mt. Lodge ●,** 859 Kearsarge Rd., in North Conway, has 22 bunks. The lodge is about 2 mi. from downtown, and has a living room, pool, jacuzzi, cable TV, refrigerator, Wi-Fi, tennis courts, and a duck pond. A delicious full breakfast ($8) makes up for the tight bunkrooms and thin mattresses. Be sure to bring a warm blanket to ward off the nightly temperature drop in the basement rooms. (☎356-2044 or 800-356-3596. Linen and towels $3. Check-in 3-9pm. Check-out 11am. Reservations recommended. Dorms $30. MC/V.)

Wooden canoes and Adirondack decor mingle with sombreros on the pink and purple walls at **Cafe Noche ❷,** 147 Main St. in Conway. On a menu filled with delicious Mexican dishes, the Montezuma Pie (Mexican lasagna; $8.50) comes highly recommended. (☎447-5050. Open daily 11:30am-9pm. AmEx/D/MC/V.) At **Delaney's ❷,** north of town along Rte. 16, hungry locals feast on sushi and excellent sandwiches like the "Cranmore Carver," with ham, turkey, and swiss smothered in peppercorn dressing and served on a honey loaf. (☎356-7776. Sandwiches $6-9. W night live music. Open daily 11:30am-late. Kitchen closes 11pm. AmEx/D/MC/V.)

HANOVER ☎603

Home to the beautiful campus of Dartmouth College, the quiet little town of Hanover comes alive when students flood the classrooms and streets, as well as the many trails, paths, and waterways that make the area ideal for those who love the outdoors. Full of muddy boots, ancient Ivy League streets, and classy bars, Hanover is an appealing blend of the wild and sophisticated.

■■ **ORIENTATION AND PRACTICAL INFORMATION.** Located along the Connecticut River near the Vermont border, and along Rte. 10 and 120, Hanover is accessible from both I-91 and I-89. Nearby towns are **Lebanon** (5 mi. south on Rte. 120), **White River Junction** (4 mi. south on Rte. 10, encompassing the confluence of the White and Connecticut Rivers), and **Norwich** (1½ mi. northwest in Vermont). Vermont Transit (☎800-552-8737) runs **buses** from Hanover that stop in front of the Hanover Inn, 35 S. Main St. Buy tickets on the bus or from Garber Travel, 57 S. Main St. (☎643-2700). **Buses** go to Boston (3-4hr., 4-5 per day, $25) and Burlington (2½hr., 4-5 per day, $21-27). Amtrak (station information ☎295-7160, schedules and reservations 800-872-7245; www.amtrak.com), on Railroad Row off N. Main St. in White River Junction, sends **trains** to Burlington (2hr., 1 per day, $19-27) and New York City (7½hr., 1 per day, $61-67). The **Hanover Chamber of Commerce,** 53. S. Main St., has area info. (☎643-3115; www.hanoverchamber.org. Open M-F 9am-4pm. Booth open daily June-Sept. 7:30am-5pm.) **Internet Access: Howe Library,** 13 E. South St. (☎643-4120. Free. Open M-Th 10am-8pm, F 10am-6pm, Sa 10am-5pm; Sept.-May also Su 1-5pm.) **Post Office:** 50 S. Main St. (☎643-4544. Open M-F 8:30am-5pm, Sa 8:30am-noon.) **Postal Code:** 03755.

▜▟ ACCOMMODATIONS AND FOOD. The **Sunset Motor Inn ❸** has simple rooms with soft beds. Just 2 mi. south of Hanover on Rte. 10, this small motel features river views and some of the area's most reasonably priced accommodations. (☎298-8721. A/C. Reservations recommended. Rooms $53-100 depending on season and room type. AmEx/D/MC/V.) Camping with wooded sites, restrooms, pool access, two lake beaches, tennis courts, hiking, and hot showers is available at **Storr's Pond ❶,** 2 mi. north of Hanover off Rte. 10. (☎643-2134. Open May 15-Oct. 15. Reservations recommended. Sites for 1-4 people $25, with electricity and water $30. Each additional person $5. Cash only.) For a quick bite, try **Lou's ❶,** 30 S. Main St., which has been humming with the conversations of Dartmouth students and locals since 1947. The $1 crullers—choose from glazed, cinnamon sugar, chocolate frosted, or jelly-filled—are especially delicious. (☎643-3321. Most meals $5-7. Open M-F 6am-3pm, Sa-Su 7am-3pm. AmEx/MC/V.) For late-night munchies, travelers should head to **Everything But Anchovies ❷,** 5 Allen St. "EBA's" has an all-day buffet ($6) big enough to make it a perennial favorite of hungry Dartmouth athletes. Pizza, sandwiches ($7-8), and free Wi-Fi add to the perks. (☎643-6135; www.ebas.com. Open M-F 9am-2am, Sa-Su 7am-2am. AmEx/MC/V.) Coffee connoisseurs are attracted to the **Dirt Cowboy ❶,** 7 S. Main St., by the individually brewed cups of coffee, selected from over 30 varieties of beans, while students come for hot drinks, light fare, and a hip atmosphere at the edge of campus. (☎649-8288. Open daily 7am-6pm.)

◉ SIGHTS. Virtually synonymous with Hanover is **Dartmouth,** the Ivy League crown's rural jewel (☎646-1110; www.dartmouth.edu). The college offers tours starting from the admissions office in McNutt Hall on N. Main St. (☎646-2875. Open M-F 8am-4pm. Tours free, times vary.) The **Hood Museum of Art,** on Wheelock St., houses collections that include African, Native American, ancient Asian, and contemporary art. (☎646-2808; www.hoodmuseum.dartmouth.edu. Open Tu and Th-Sa 10am-5pm, W 10am-9pm, Su noon-5pm. Free.) With the Appalachian Trail passing through town, Hanover is an ideal base for hiking. The **Dartmouth Outing Club,** in Robinson Hall on N. Main St., maintains hundreds of miles of trails, sells the *Dartmouth Outing Guide* ($15) as well as detailed maps ($1-3), and provides information about hiking in the area. A downstairs bulletin board provides lodging and food information for through-hikers. (M-F 8am-4pm ☎646-2428; Robinson Hall office ☎646-2429. Open M-Th and Su 2-6pm.)

▧ NIGHTLIFE. While crashing a Dartmouth party may be a option, a year-round supply of students ensure that the nightlife in Hanover is always in full swing. **Murphy's on the Green,** 11 S. Main St., is a preppy restaurant by day and a wild party by night. At 10pm, tables move aside for the throngs of students that crowd into the

NEW ENGLAND

bar to enjoy dancing, drinks (pitchers $10), and music. (☎643-4075. Entrees $10-22. Open daily 11:30am-1am.) At **5 Olde Nugget Alley,** descend into a dimly lit, cozy basement bar with different specials each night of the week. Cheers resound from the fans watching ESPN at the bar, while subdued conversation emanates from the secluded tables. (☎643-5081. W Buffalo wings $0.25. Open daily 11:30am-1am.)

VERMONT

In 1609, the explorer Samuel de Champlain dubbed the area "green mountain" in his native French, and the name Vermont stuck. Here, lush forests and crystal clear waterways share the land with roaming Holstein cattle. The Vermont of Champlain's time still exists in the Green Mountain National Forest, and rural charm can be found in the myriad villages tucked into hillsides and valleys. But the region has also taken on the world, drawing thousands to the natural beauty of its ski slopes and the trendy commercialism of its outlet stores and gift shops. A mix of these features can be seen in the state's cities, which boast a unique metropolitan atmosphere tinged with true Vermont sensibility and culture.

⚡ PRACTICAL INFORMATION

Capital: Montpelier.

Visitor Info: Vermont Information Center, 134 State St., Montpelier 05602 (☎802-828-3237; www.vermontvacation.com). Open daily 7:45am-8pm. **Department of Forests, Parks, and Recreation,** 103 S. Main St., Waterbury 05671 (☎802-241-3670). Open M-F 7:45am-4:30pm. **Vermont Snowline** (☎802-229-0531; www.skivermont.corn) gives snow conditions Nov.-May. 24hr.

Postal Abbreviation: VT. **Sales Tax:** 5%, meals and lodgings 9%.

VERMONT SKI RESORTS   ☎802

Every winter, skiers pour into Vermont and onto the Northeast's finest slopes; in the summer and fall, these inclines melt, becoming the stomping grounds of hikers and mountain bikers. Towns surrounding each of the mountains make their livelihood on this annual avalanche, offering a range of tourist attractions. For information, contact **Ski Vermont,** 26 State St., P.O. Box 368, Montpelier 05601. (☎223-2439; www.skivermont.com. Open M-F 7:45am-5:30pm.) The Vermont Information Center (see **Practical Information,** above) also provides helpful info. Cheaper lift tickets can be found during low-season—before mid-December and after mid-March.

With three mountains, 78 trails, the highest vertical drop in Vermont, and the only triple-black-diamond run in the eastern US, **Smugglers' Notch,** just north of Stowe on Rte. 108, can satisfy even the most extreme adventure seekers. The resort also offers great family programs. In summer, hiking and canoeing prevail. (☎644-8851 or 800-451-8752; www.smuggs.com. Lift tickets $56, ages 7-18 $40, over 70 free.) A beautiful but dangerous passage south through Smugglers' Notch along Rte. 108 leads to the **Stowe Mountain Resort.** Only minutes from the village of Stowe, the resort offers one-day lift tickets ($65, seniors and ages 6-12 $45) for 48 trails (16% beginner, 59% intermediate, 25% expert), and impressive summer facilities, including alpine slides (single ride $14, ages 6-12 $10), a golf course, and a country club. (☎253-3000 or 800-253-4754; www.stowe.com. 3 alpine slide rides, 1 gondola ride, bungee, trampoline, climbing wall $49; seniors and ages 6-12 $44.) West of Brattleboro on Rte. 100, in the town of West Dover, **Mount Snow** boasts 145 trails (22% beginner, 49% intermediate, 29% expert), 23 lifts, excellent snowmaking capabilities, and the first snowboard park in the Northeast. In summer, mountain bikers take advantage of the 45 mi. of trails. (☎800-245-7669; www.mounts-now.com. Open mid-Nov. to late Apr. M-F 9am-4pm, Sa-Su 8am-4pm; May-early Nov. daily 9am-4pm. Lift tickets M-F $59, Sa-Su $67; ages 13-19 $44/46; under 13 and seniors $31/33. Mountain biking $30 per day.) At the junction of U.S. 4 and Rte. 100 N, the mammoth **Killington Resort** is unrivaled as the largest of Vermont's frozen playgrounds. Maintaining a city of resort complexes at the base of its seven peaks and 200 trails, it hosts the east coast's longest ski season (mid-Oct. to early June). The summer keeps a fair pace in Killington (see below) with hiking, biking, and fishing. (☎800-621-6867; www.killington.com. Lift tickets $67, ages 13-18 $54, seniors and ages 6-12 $43.) Near the Canadian border in Vermont's Northeast Kingdom, **Jay Peak,** in Jay on Rte. 242, catches more snowfall than any other New England peak. With excellent glade skiing, Jay Peak is an appealing option for thrill-seekers. (☎988-2611 or 800-451-4449; www.jaypeakresort.com. 76 trails; 40% expert. Lift tickets $56, half-day $42; ages 7-17 $42/32.) Challenging visitors to "Ski it if you can," **Mad River Glen,** in Waitsfield, has loads of expert-level trails (only 15% with snowmaking) and the last surviving single chair lift. Snowboarding is not allowed. (☎496-3551; www.madriverglen.com. Lift tickets $50, seniors and ages 6-12 $37.) Other resorts include **Stratton** (☎297-2200 or 800-787-2886; 90 trails, 16 lifts), on Rte. 30 N in Bondville, and **Sugarbush** (☎583-6100 or 800-537-8427; www.sugarbush.com; 2 mountains, 115 trails, 17 lifts), in Warren. Cross-country resorts include the **Trapp Family Lodge** (see **Stowe,** p. 256); **Mountain Meadows,** in Killington (☎775-7077; 90 mi. of trails); and **Woodstock** (☎457-1100; 40 mi. of trails).

TIP **QUIET TIME.** Many ski towns in Vermont empty out when the snow melts, which can mean lower rates and less traffic for summer travelers. Be warned, however, that some restaurants and nightspots can close for months at a time in the low season, so it's best to call ahead to establishments on your itinerary.

KILLINGTON ☎802

With 4241 ft. Mt. Killington rising overhead, the town of Killington is a shrine for those who worship chairlifts and snow. While winter brings out Killington's best, summer travelers will find numerous opportunities for hiking, biking, and more.

TRANSPORTATION AND PRACTICAL INFORMATION. Vermont Transit (☎800-552-8737), in the Killington Deli on Rte. 4 at the intersection with Rte. 100 N, runs buses to White River Junction (1hr., depart 7am, $7.50-8.50). **The Bus** leaves from the transit station to shuttle visitors to over 15 stops around Rutland and Killington. (☎773-3244; www.thebus.com. Jan.-Mar. 12 per day 7:15am-11:15pm; Apr.-June and Sept.-Dec. 6 per day 7:15am-5:15pm; July-Aug. 10 per day 7:15am-7:15pm. $2.) If you need more flexible wheels, **Gramp's Shuttle** (☎236-6600) will come to your aid. The **Killington Chamber of Commerce,** on U.S. 4, just west of Killington Rd., is the best source of area info. (☎773-4181 or 800-337-1928; www.killingtonchamber.com. Open M-F 9am-5pm; Dec.-Mar. M-Sa 9am-5pm.) To gear up for the slopes, visit **The Basin Ski Shop,** 2886 Killington Rd., where the friendly staff will suit you up for a day on the mountains. (☎422-3234. Open late Oct.-May M-Th 8:15am-9pm, F 8:15am-midnight, Sa-Su 7:15am-9pm; May-late Oct. M and Th-Sa 10am-6pm, Tu-W and Su 10am-5pm. Ski, boot, and pole package $28 per day.) **Internet Access: Sherburne Memorial Library,** 2 mi. south of the intersection of Rte. 4 and Rte. 100, on River Rd. (☎422-9765. Free. Open M and F 10am-5:30pm, T and Th 1-5:30pm, W 10am-8pm, Sa 9am-1pm.) **Post Office:** 2046 Rte. 4, just west of the intersection with Killington Rd., attached to the Chamber of Commerce. (☎775-4247. Open M-F 8:30am-4:30pm, Sa 8:30am-noon.) **Postal Code:** 05751.

🛏🍴 ACCOMMODATIONS AND FOOD. Prices for area lodgings are highly seasonal, lowest in the summer months and highest over holiday weekends at the peak of ski season. **Trailside Lodge ❸,** on Rte. 100 N 2½ mi. from the intersection with Rte. 4, is the best bargain in town. Peak-season perks include a full breakfast buffet, four-course family-style dinner, big-screen TV in the lounge, lift ticket discounts, hot tub and heated outdoor pool, and free bus tickets to the resort. Rates are directly proportional to group size; each bunk-style room can accommodate up to 6 people. (☎422-3532 or 800-447-2209; www.trailsidelodge.com. Early and late season $96-123 per person; mid-winter and holidays up to $167 per person. AmEx/MC/V.) In summer, camping at one of 27 sites or 21 lean-tos at the **Gifford Woods State Park ❶** is an inexpensive option with well-kept campsites. (May to mid-Oct. ☎775-5354, Jan.-May 888-409-7579. Hot showers $0.25 per 5 min. 4-person sites $14-16; lean-tos $21-23; each additional person $4. MC/V.)

A plow car that formerly kept the rail track clear of snow now houses **Casey's Caboose ❸,** 2½ mi. up Killington Rd. from Rte. 4., a restaurant and bar that gives away 40,000 lb. of free chicken wings every winter. Munch away on the raised deck or snuggle into a booth for salmon or prime rib for $16-22. (☎422-3795. Free wings daily 3-6pm. Open daily 3pm-midnight. AmEx/D/MC/V.) **Johnny Boy's Pancake House ❶,** 923 Killington Rd., is a good place to begin the morning with big breakfasts ($3.50-7.50) that will keep you energized all day. (☎422-4411. Open M and Th-F 8am-1pm, Sa-Su 7am-2pm.)

🥾🎶 OUTDOOR ACTIVITIES AND NIGHTLIFE. During the green season in Vermont, the slopes and surrounding mountains turn into hiking and biking throughways. **Gifford Woods State Park,** on Rte. 100, ¾ mi. from the intersection of Rte. 4 and Rte. 100 N, offers connecting trails to Vermont's major trails, the **Appalachian Trail (AT)** and the **Long Trail.** Trail information can be obtained at the park office. (☎775-5354. Park office open May to mid-Oct. M-Th and Su 9am-8:30pm, F-Sa 9am-9pm. Day-use fee $2.50, ages 4-13 $2. Fishing licenses available at the park office; $15 per day, $41 per season.) The **Killington Resort Complex** also provides summer recreation options at Killington and Pico mountains. (☎422-3333. All-day adventure center pass $30, ages 6-12 and seniors $25; with mountain biking $40/35. Mountain bike rentals $30 per 2hr., $35 per 4hr., $45 per day; under 12 $15/17/22. Alpine slide $7, children $5.) Rent less expensive wheels at **First Stop,** south of the resort complex along Rte. 4. (☎422-9050. Open May-Sept. M and Th-Su 9am-6pm. Bikes $25 per day.)

When the temperature drops, two of Vermont's best nightlife spots open up on Killington Rd. After Halloween, the **Wobbly Barn,** halfway up the Killington Rd., has dancing, live acts, and a free nacho bar. (☎422-6171; www.wobblybarn.com. Call for schedule.) Just past the Killington Shops at the Shack, **The Pickle Barrel,** (☎422-7433) whose past performers include Blues Traveler and Ziggy Marley, warms things up with Happy hour events and late-night hubbub. (☎422-3035; www.picklebarrelnightclub.com. Info on tickets available online.) Free rides from the resort to the nightclub are provided by The Pickle Barrel.

BURLINGTON   ☎802

On the shore of Lake Champlain, Burlington's thriving downtown lures young and old to classy restaurants, independent bookstores, and excellent shopping. Along pedestrian-friendly Church St., the Birkenstocks of college students share the street with the worn sneakers of street performers and leather oxfords of office-bound businessmen; but with the Adirondacks rising over the lake and the Green Mountains beckoning just beyond the city limits, even those who don only hiking boots have an excuse to venture to Burlington.

Burlington

🏠 ▲ ACCOMMODATIONS
G.G.T. Tibet Inn, **3**
Lang House, **2**
North Beach Campsites, **1**

🍎 FOOD
Muddy Waters, **8**
Sweetwater's, **5**
Zabby and Elf's
Stone Soup, **6**

🍷 NIGHTLIFE
Nectar's, **9**
Red Square, **7**
Ri-Ra, **4**

TRANSPORTATION AND PRACTICAL INFORMATION. Two roads lead to Burlington: **Route 7** from Shelburne in the south, and **Route 2** connecting to I-89 from the east. Three miles east of Burlington, off Rte. 2, **Burlington International Airport (BTV);** (☎863-2874) flies to a handful of major cities. **Chittenden County Transit Authority (CCTA)** runs U Mall/Airport shuttles to the airport. CCTA also serves the downtown area with unbeatable access and reliable service. Connections to Shelburne and other outlying areas also run frequently; catch **buses** downtown at the intersection of Cherry and Church St. (☎864-2282; www.cctaride.org. Buses operate at least every 30min. M-Sa 6:15am-10:10pm, depending on routes. Schedules available at the Chamber of Commerce. $1.25; ages 6-18, disabled, and seniors $0.60.) Amtrak, 29 Railroad Ave., Essex Jct., (station info ☎879-7298, schedules and pricing 800-872-7245; www.amtrak.com; open 1hr. before and after departures.) 5 mi. east of Burlington on Rte. 15, runs **trains** to New York City (9hr., 1 per day, $62-68) and White River Junction (2hr., 1 per day, $19-27). Vermont Transit, 345 Pine St., (☎864-6811 or 800-552-8737; open daily 5:30am-9:30pm) runs **buses** to: Albany (4¾hr., 3 per day, $38); Boston (4¾hr., 4 per day, $45); Middlebury (1hr., 2 per day, $12); Montreal (2½hr., 5 per day, $26); White River Junction (2hr., 4 per day, $21). **Ski Rack,** 85 Main St., rents bikes and ski equipment. (☎658-3313 or 800-882-4530. Open M-F 10am-7pm, Sa 9am-6pm, Su 11am-5pm. Mountain bikes $12 per hr., $20 per 4hr., $25 per day. Credit card required.) **Lake Champlain Regional Chamber of Commerce** is at 60 Main St., Rte. 100. (☎863-3489 or 877-686-5253;

www.vermont.org. Open May to mid.-Oct. M-F 8am-5pm, Sa-Su 10am-5pm; mid-Oct. to Apr. M-F 8am-5pm.) **Internet Access: Fletcher Free Library,** 235 College St. (☎863-3403. Free. Open M-Tu and Th-F 8:30am-6pm, W 8:30am-9pm, Sa 9am-5pm, Su noon-6pm.) **Post Office:** 11 Elmwood Ave., at Pearl St. (☎863-6033. Open M-F 8am-5pm, Sa 8am-1pm.) **Postal Code:** 05401.

⌐ ACCOMMODATIONS. The Chamber of Commerce has the complete rundown on area accommodations, which tend toward upscale lodgings. B&Bs can be found in the outlying suburbs. Reasonably priced hotels and guest houses line **Shelburne Road (Route 7),** south of downtown, and **Main Street (Route 2),** east of downtown. If you're looking to drop some serious cash, look no further than the soft beds, five-star furnishings, and first-class service of the **Lang House ❺,** 360 Main St., only a 5-10min. walk from Church St. and downtown. With a view of Lake Champlain from the third floor rooms and a full gourmet breakfast, Lang House ensures a luxurious stay. (☎652-2500 or 877-919-9799; www.langhouse.com. Rooms with A/C and TV $145-235. AmEx/D/MC/V.) With low prices and sparkling clean rooms, the **G.G.T. Tibet Inn ❸,** 3 mi. south of Burlington on Rte.7, has A/C, outdoor pool, refrigerators, and a small library with books about the owner's native Tibet. (☎863-7110; www.ggttibetinn.com. Rooms $40-75. AmEx/MC/V.) The **North Beach Campsites ❶,** on Institute Rd., 1½ mi. north of town by North Ave., have 137 sites with access to a beach on Lake Champlain. Take Rte. 127 to North Ave., or the "North Ave." bus from the main terminal on Pine St. (☎862-0942 or 800-571-1198. Showers $0.25 per 5min. $5 parking fee for non-campers. Open May to mid-Oct. Sites $22, with water and electricity $28, with full hookup $30-31. AmEx/MC/V.) North Beach, is open to non-campers, and rents canoes and kayaks. (Beach open 24hr. for campers; beach parking closes at 9pm. Lifeguards on duty mid-June to Aug. 10am-5:30pm.) See **Champlain Valley** (p. 253) for more camping options.

◖ FOOD. With all the fantastic restaurants that crowd the Church Street Marketplace and its adjacent sidestreets, visitors could eat in this food lover's paradise for weeks without hitting the same place twice. A mostly vegetarian cafe, **◪Zabby and Elf's Stone Soup ❷,** 211 College St., offers a wide variety of stews, casseroles, rice, and customizable salads from the hot and cold bars ($6 per lb.), as well as sandwiches ($6-7) made with freshly baked bread. (☎862-7616. Open M 7am-7pm, Tu-F 7am-9pm, Sa 9am-7pm. Cash or check only.) The college crowd heads to **Muddy Waters ❶,** 184 Main St., where large cups of coffee ($1.50), a selection of light fare (veggie chili $3.50), and a rustic, comfortable cafe area keep the conversation going for hours. (☎658-0466. Open M 7:30am-8:30pm, Tu-Sa 7:30am-midnight, Su 8:30am-10pm. Cash or check only.) At **Sweetwater's ❸,** 120 Church St., high ceilings and vast wall paintings dwarf those who come for the delicious french onion soup ($6) and wide variety of sandwiches ($7-10). When the warm weather rolls around, dine al fresco. (☎864-9800. Entrees $10-18. F and Sa evenings live music. Open M-Sa 11:30am-midnight, Su 11:30am-11pm. AmEx/D/MC/V.)

◙ SIGHTS. The **◪Shelburne Museum,** 7 mi. south of Burlington on Rte. 7 S. in Shelburne, houses one of the most impressive collections of Americana in the country. Visitors can see the enormous paddleboat Ticonderoga, a 50s home, a 19th-century Vermont church, printing presses, a lighthouse, a covered bridge, and even a small collection of works by Degas, Monet and Cassatt. (☎985-3346; www.shelburnemuseum.org. Open mid-May to late Oct. daily 10am-5pm. $18, students $13, ages 6-18 $9; after 3pm $10/10/5; families $48.) Discover ecology, culture, and history at **ECHO,** 1 College St., a science center and lake aquarium near the water. The multitude of hands-on exhibits and interactive demos are fun, especially for kids. (☎864-1848; www.echovermont.org. Open M-W and F-Su 10am-

5pm, Th 10am-8pm. $9, students and seniors $8, ages 3-17 $6.) The **Ethan Allen Homestead** rests north of Burlington on Rte. 127 in the Winooski Valley Park. In the 1780s, Allen, his Green Mountain Boys, and Benedict Arnold forced the surrender of Fort Ticonderoga and helped establish the state of Vermont. Now, hourly tours visit the cabin and tell the famed frontiersman story. (☎865-4556; www.ethanallen-homestead.org. Open May-Oct. M-Sa 10am-4pm, Su 1-4pm; Nov.-Apr. Sa 10am-4pm. $5, seniors $4, ages 5-17 $3; families $15.) **Magic Hat,** 5 Bartlett Bay Rd., a top New England brewer, offers free samples and tours at its Gothic, industrial-themed brewery. (5 mi. south on Rte. 7. ☎658-2739. Open M-Sa 10am-7pm, Su noon-5pm. Tours offered Th-Su in the afternoon.)

Amateur historians love **South Willard Street,** where **Champlain College** occupies many of the Victorian houses that line the street. **City Hall Park,** downtown, and **Battery Street Park,** on Lake Champlain near the edge of downtown, are a wonderful escape to cool shade on hot summer days. For travelers who long to feel the wind in their sails, just north lies the **Lake Champlain Community Sailing Center,** 1 Lake St., where sailboat rentals ($25-42 per hr.) and private instruction on the water ($45 per hr.; each additional person $20 per hr.) are available. (☎864-2499; www.lccsc.org. Open M-F 9am-8pm, Sa-Su 10am-8pm. Lessons M-Th 5-8pm, Sa-Su 9am-noon.) The **Spirit of Ethan Allen III** runs a narrated, 500-passenger scenic cruise that departs from the boathouse at the bottom of College St. (☎862-8300; www.soea.com. 1½hr. cruises late May to mid-Oct. daily 10am, noon, 2, 4pm; 2½hr. sunset cruise 6:30pm. Sunset cruise mid June-Sept. $17, ages 3-11 $13; Oct-May $12/6.) At Lake Champlain rent boats that are available from **Umiak.** (☎253-2317. Open daily 10am-5pm. Canoes $18 per hr.; kayaks $12-25 per hr.)

🌺 🎵 **FESTIVALS AND NIGHTLIFE.** With so many colleges in the area, Burlington's nightlife scene is always alive and kicking. A pedestrian haven, Church St. Marketplace nurtures offbeat puppeteers and musicians who entertain the crowds at all hours. Pick up a free *Seven Days* newspaper, available all over Burlington, to get the skinny on what's happening around town.

In the summer, the **Vermont Mozart Festival** brings Bach, Beethoven, and Mozart to local barns, farms, and meadows. (☎862-7352; www.vtmozart.com. Concerts late July-early Aug.) In mid-June, the **Discover Jazz Festival** features over 1000 musicians, with past performers including Ella Fitzgerald, Dizzy Gillespie, and Betty Carter. (☎863-7992; www.discoverjazz.com. Some performances are free but others are sold through the Flynn Theater Box Office.) The **Champlain Valley Folk Festival,** located about halfway between Burlington and Middlebury, enlivens summer days in early August. (☎877-850-0206; www.cvfest.org. Tickets $25-75.) The **Flynn Theater Box Office,** 153 Main St., handles sales for the Folk Festival and the Discover Jazz Festival, as well as its own series of concerts and plays. (☎652-4500; www.flynncenter.org. Open M-F 10am-5pm, Sa 11am-4pm.)

The birthplace of the band Phish, **Nectar's,** 188 Main St., still rocks with inexpensive food, including their legendary gravy fries ($3). The large stage and dance floor cater nightly to live tunes of all genres from local and mainstream bands. (☎658-4771. Cover varies. Open M-Tu 11am-2:30am, W-F 6am-2:30am, Sa-Su 7am-2:30am.) One of Burlington's most popular night spots, **Red Square,** 136 Church St., rocks out to live music nightly. Bands play everything from funk to classic rock in the alley if the crowd gets large. (☎859-8909. Cover varies. Open daily 4pm-2am.) For a laid-back pint, try **Ri-Ra,** 123 Church St., a traditional Irish pub with deep booths and a quieter crowd. (☎860-9401. Beer $2.50-4.50. W Irish music 7pm. Sa live music 10pm. Open M-Sa 11:30am-2am, Su 11:30am-1am.)

🌄 **DAYTRIP FROM BURLINGTON: CHAMPLAIN VALLEY.** Stretching 100 mi. between Vermont's Green Mountains and New York's Adirondacks, **Lake Cham-**

plain boasts plentiful opportunities for biking, hiking, and camping in the many well-kept state parks that dot the lake's shorelines. Visitors can take a bridge or ferry across the lake to gain the best views of its silvery surface. The **Lake Champlain Ferry,** located on the dock at the bottom of King St., sails from Burlington to Port Kent, NY, and back. (☎864-9804; www.ferries.com. 1hr. each way. July-Aug. 11-13 per day 7:30am-7:30pm; mid-May to late June and Sept. to mid-Oct. 9 per day 8am-6:35pm. $14.75 per car. Each additional person $4, ages 6-12 $1.60.) Throughout the day, service from Grand Isle, VT to Plattsburg, NY and from Charlotte, VT, to Essex, NY is also offered. ($8.25 per car. Each additional person $3, ages 6-12 $1.) Campers can stock up on anything from fishing gear to local maple syrup at the **Hero's Welcome** complex, in North Hero off Rte. 2. The buildings house an eclectic array of food and goods at reasonable prices with seating overlooking Lake Champlain. (☎372-4161; www.heroswelcome.com. Open daily 6:30am-6pm.)

Fog drifts over the grasslands hiding the countless migratory birds that come to rest in the marsh of the **Missisquoi National Wildlife Refuge,** 2 mi. to the northwest of Swanton, VT on Rte. 78 at the northern end of the lake. The refuge provides extensive lands for hiking, birdwatching, kayaking, and canoeing in warm weather, and cross-country skiing and snowshoeing in the winter. (☎868-4781. Office 5 mi. northwest of Swanton off Tabor Rd. Open M-F 8am-4:30pm. Refuge open dawn-dusk. Free.) **Mount Philo State Park ❶,** 15 mi. south of Burlington, off Rte. 7, offers pleasant, easy-to-moderate hiking and picnic facilities with an expansive view of deep forests, green pastures, and winding roads leading to a mountainous horizon. Camping is offered on seven sites and three lean-tos nestled on the side of the mountain. (☎425-2390, 14-day advance reservations at any Vermont state park 888-409-7579. Open mid-May to mid-Oct. daily 10am-dusk. Entrance fee $2.50, ages 4-13 $2. 2-night min. stay. Sites $14; lean-tos $21.)

Also north of the lake, **Burton Island State Park ❶** is accessible only by private boats and a ferry which runs five times daily from Kill Kare State Park, 35 mi. north of Burlington and 3½ mi. southwest of U.S. 7 off of Town Rd., near St. Albans Bay. This secluded park provides a tranquil place to hike, swim, and picnic. (☎524-6353. Open late May to early Sept. daily 8am-8pm; call for schedule. Ferry service $3 each way. Bike rental $1. 4-night min. stay. 17 tent sites $16 each; 26 lean-tos $23 each. Each additional person $4. Day use $2.50, ages 4-13 $2. MC.) Also along the Champlain Islands are myriad **biking trips** (☎597-4646; www.champlainbikeways.org), **state parks** available for day use (**Alburg Dunes** ☎796-4170; **Knight Point** ☎343-7236; **North Hero** ☎372-8727; **Knight Island** ☎524-6353; www.vtstateparks.com), and the **Lipizzan Stallions,** horses known for their grace and strength. (Past the drawbridge between Grand Isle and North Hero on Rte. 2 W in Knight Point State Park. Champlain Islands Chamber of Commerce ☎372-8400 or 800-262-5226; www.champlainislands.com. Performances July-Aug. Th-F 6pm, Sa-Su 2:30pm; $17, seniors $14, ages 6-12 $10.) Call for more info.

MIDDLEBURY ☎802

Built on the foundations of the countryside's ample marble supply, Middlebury now thrives on the thick tourist wallets, while maintaining an atmosphere hip enough for the discriminating Middlebury College student. Middlebury's lush green hills and diverse residents create a blend of culture and history that makes this charming town stand out from the crowd.

◧ ▚ TRANSPORTATION AND PRACTICAL INFORMATION. Middlebury sits along U.S. 7, 42 mi. south of Burlington. Vermont Transit **buses** stop at the Exxon station, 16 Court St., west of Main St. (☎388-9300. Station open daily 6am-10pm.) **Buses** run to: Albany (4hr., 3 per day, $31); Boston (6hr., 3 per day, $48); Burlington

(1hr., 3 per day, $11); Rutland (1½hr., 3 per day, $8). Addison County Transit Resources provides free **shuttle** service in the immediate Middlebury vicinity, making stops every hr. at the town green, Marbleworks, Middlebury College, and along U.S. 7 S. (☎388-1946. Runs M-F 7am-8:30pm, Sa-Su 9am-5pm.) Exploring on foot is probably the easiest way around town, but for those who prefer wheels, the **Bike Center**, 74 Main St., rents bikes. (☎388-6666; www.bikecentermid.com. Open M-Th and Sa 9:30am-5:30pm, F 9:30am-8pm; June-Sept. also Su 1-4pm. Bikes from $20 per day.) The staff at the **Addison County Chamber of Commerce**, 2 Court St., provides free area maps, bus schedules, and event information. (☎388-7951 or 800-733-8376; www.midvermont.com. Open M-F 10:30am-5pm.) **Internet Access: Ilsley Public Library**, 75 Main St. (☎388-4095. Free. Open M, W, and F 10am-6pm; Tu and Th 10am-8pm; Sa 10am-4pm.) **Post Office:** 10 Main St. (☎388-2681. Open M-F 8am-5pm, Sa 8am-12:30pm.) **Postal Code:** 05753.

▐ ACCOMMODATIONS. Lodging with four walls and no mosquitoes isn't cheap in Middlebury. The **Sugar House Motel ❸**, 202 Ethan Allen Hwy., 2 mi. north on Rte. 7, has clean rooms with A/C, microwave, refrigerator, and TV; the complex has a pool. (☎388-2770 or 800-784-2746. Reservations recommended. Rooms from $49-99, depending on season. MC/V.) **Branbury State Park ❶**, 7 mi. south on U.S. 7, then 4 mi. south on Rte. 53, stretches along Lake Dunmore, offering 45 spacious sites and seven lean-tos on grassy fields shaded by a leafy canopy. (☎247-5925. Hot showers $0.25 per 5min. Canoes $7.50 per hr., $35 per day. Paddleboats $5 per 30min. Open late May to mid-Oct. Sites $16-18; lean-tos $23-25.)

▐▐ FOOD AND NIGHTLIFE. Middlebury's restaurants cater chiefly to plump wallets, but a student presence ensures the survival of less-expensive options. **Noonie's Deli ❶**, 137 Maple St., in the Marbleworks building just behind Main St., makes terrific sandwiches ($4-5) on thick slices of homemade bread in a lovely cafe. (☎388-0014. Open M-F 8am-8pm, Sa 9am-8pm, Su 11am-7pm. Cash or check only.) Turquoise and peach decor complements the larger-than-life murals on the walls of **Amigos ❸**, 4 Merchants Row, which offers creative Mexican dishes like the three-enchilada Mexican Flag for $11. (☎388-3624. Lunch $6-8. Dinner $8-18. Open M-Sa 11:30am-10:30pm, Su 4-10:30pm. Kitchen closes daily at 9pm. AmEx/D/MC/V.) **Mister Up's ❸**, a popular hangout on Bakery Ln., just off Main St., blends a friendly pub atmosphere with outdoor, airy, cafe-style dining. Ample sandwiches ($6-7) are perfect

ON THE MENU

FROM COW TO SPOON

Along Rte. 100 in Waterbury, VT. lies a little scoop of heaven for anyone with a sweet tooth: **Ben & Jerry's Ice Cream Factory.**

What began as two high school friends making ice cream in an old Burlington gas station has become an ice cream phenomenon. Today, people from across the country celebrate triumphs and nurse broken hearts with their favorite Ben & Jerry's flavor.

Closer to the company's local roots, visitors line up at the Waterbury factory for tours of the facility and a scoop of ice cream fresh off the conveyor belt. The tour starts with a short film about the company's history, then guests are taken to a viewing area to see the the making of the frozen treats below. The cherry on top is the tasting room, where the tour concludes with two delectable sample flavors.

A short walk from the factory lies the flavor graveyard, where short-lived concoctions like Miz Jelena's Sweet Potato Pie, Ethan Almond, and Holy Cannoli melt off into the sunset.

Sound good? The ambitious traveler might want to see if the factory has any openings—each employee gets three pints of ice cream to take home per day. Now that's a job with benefits!

Ben & Jerry's Ice Cream Factory, *☎882-3586. Call for tour times. $3, seniors $2, under 12 free.*

with the nightly drink specials. (☎388-6724. Entrees $9-14. Open M-Sa 11:30am-midnight, Su 11am-midnight. AmEx/MC/V.) Night owls head to **Angela's Pub,** 86 Main St., for live rock, the jukebox, or the cheers of a heated game of pool. (☎388-6936. Tu $1.50 Labatt pints. F DJ. Sa live band. 21+. No cover. Open Tu-Th and Sa 8pm-2am, F 6pm-2am.) For a more mellow drinking atmosphere, laughter and the clinking of glasses harmonize with live jazz and rock at **Two Brothers,** 88 Main St. (☎388-0002. Beer $1.75-3.50. M $1 off all pints and wine. Tu $1.50 Labatt pints. No cover. Open M-F 11:30am-2am, Sa-Su 11am-2am.)

■ **SIGHTS.** Most of the town's cultural events are hosted by **Middlebury College;** the concert hall in the college **Arts Center,** just outside of town on S. Main St., has a terrific concert series. The **box office** has details on events sponsored by the college. (☎443-4168; www.middlebury.edu/cfa. Open Sept.-May M-F noon-5pm, also 1hr. before start of shows. Many events free, most $5-12.) Inside the Arts Center, the **Middlebury College Museum of Art** offers an intimate gallery filled with ancient art, sculpture, and innovative modern exhibits. (☎443-5007. Open Tu-F 10am-5pm, Sa-Su noon-5pm. Call for exact hours. Free.) Through the summer months, Middlebury's **International Film Festival** screens movies on Saturdays at 7 and 9:30pm in the Dana Auditorium. (☎443-5510; www.middlebury.edu/ls/film. Free.) **Tours** from the admissions office, in Emma Willard Hall on S. Main St., showcase the white marble houses and manicured fields of Middlebury's picturesque campus. (☎443-3000. Tours daily 10am and 2pm; Aug-Nov. also Sa 10am. Self-guided tour brochures are also available.) If you're too cheap for a pint or just want some local flavor, trek three quarters of a mile north of town to the **Otter Creek Brewery,** 793 Exchange St., for a free tour and samples of their award-winning copper ale. (☎800-473-0727. Tours daily 1, 3, 5pm. Shop open M-Sa 10am-6pm, Su 11am-4pm.) Fifteen miles east of the Middlebury College campus, the **Middlebury College Snow Bowl** entertains skiers in winter with 14 trails and three lifts. (☎388-4356; www.middlebury.edu/~snowbowl. Lift tickets M-F $28, Sa-Su $35; seniors and students $23/28; preschoolers $7.) The **Henry Sheldon Museum of Vermont History,** 1 Park St., offers a house full of artifacts collected by Henry Sheldon, who founded the museum in 1884. Wooden canes, furniture, silverware, and textiles paint a portrait of life in Addison County during the 19th century. (☎388-2117; www.henrysheldonmuseum.org. Open M-Sa 10am-5pm; call ahead for winter hours. $5, seniors $4.50, students $4, ages 6-18 $3.)

The scenic outdoors surrounding Middlebury make for great hiking and paddling. Hiking and camping information for Green Mountain National Forest is provided by the **Middlebury Ranger Station,** 1077 Rte. 7 S. (☎388-4362. Open M-F 8am-4:30pm.) For paddling supplies, **Middlebury Mountaineer,** 5 Park St., can meet your needs and provide you with a license to hunt or fish. (☎388-1749; www.mmvt.com. Single kayak $50 per day; tandem kayak $60 per day; each additional day ½ price. Licenses $15 per day, $41 per season. Open M-Sa 10am-5:30pm, Su noon-3pm.) Exercise your mind at the **Robert Frost Interpretive Trail,** an easy 1 mi. trail starting from a parking lot 2 mi. east of Ripton on Rte. 125. Excerpts from the poet's works are mounted on plaques along the path in spots similar to ones that may have inspired the poems' creation. (☎388-4362. Free.)

STOWE ☎802

Stowe curls gracefully up the side of Mt. Mansfield, Vermont's highest peak at 4393 ft. A mecca for outdoor activities in all seasons, Stowe tries to offer the charm and character of an alpine ski village. The proliferation of Swiss chalets evokes the feeling of a charming Swiss village lost in the mountains of Vermont.

NEW ENGLAND

⚑⚐ TRANSPORTATION AND PRACTICAL INFORMATION. Stowe is 10 mi. north of I-89 off Exit 10, 27 mi. southwest of Burlington. The ski slopes lie along **Mountain Road (Route 108),** northwest of Stowe. Vermont Transit (☎244-7689 or 800-552-8737; open M-Sa 5am-9pm, Su 6am-8pm) **buses** come only as close as **Depot Beverage,** 1 River Rd., in Waterbury, 11 mi. from Stowe, and run to Boston (4hr., 1 per day, $53) and Burlington (30min., 1 per day, $8-9). Peg's Pick-up/Stowe Taxi (☎253-9490 or 800-370-9490) **cars** will take you into Stowe for about $25 plus $5 for each additional passenger; call ahead. In winter, the Stowe Trolley runs up and down Mountain Rd. every 20-30min. (☎223-7287; www.stoweshuttle.org. **Trolley** runs in winter 7:30am-10pm. $1, seniors and under 17 $0.50; weekly pass $10, season pass $20. July to mid-Oct. 1½hr. tours leave from town hall daily 11am. $2.) **The Stowe Area Association** is at 51 Main St. (☎253-7321 or 800-247-8693; www.gostowe.com. Open June to mid-Oct. and mid-Dec. to Mar. M-Sa 9am-8pm, call for Su hours; mid-Oct. to mid-Dec. and Apr.-June M-F 9am-5pm.) Pick up the free *Stowe Scene* and the *Vacation Planner* for event and recreation info. **Internet Access: Stowe Free Library,** 90 Pond St. (☎253-6145. Free. Open M, W, and F 9:30am-5:30pm; Tu and Th 2-7pm; Sa 10am-3pm.) **Post Office:** 105 Depot St., off Main St. (☎253-7521. Open M-F 8am-5pm, Sa 9am-noon.) **Postal Code:** 05672.

⚑ ACCOMMODATIONS. Foster's Place ❷, 4968 Mountain Rd., offers primarily long-term and group dorm rooms with a lounge, laundry, game room, outdoor pool, and hot tub/sauna in a recently renovated school building. (☎800-330-4880. Reservations recommended. Singles $35-39, with private bath $49-59; quads $55. Call for seasonal rates. AmEx/D/MC/V.) A converted 19th-century farm house and adjacent motel, the **Riverside Inn ❸,** 1965 Mountain Rd., 2 mi. from town, offers good rates and great perks, such as free mountain bike loans, pool table, and fireplace in the lodge. (☎253-4217 or 800-966-4217. Rooms $49-109. AmEx/MC/V.) **⛺Smugglers' Notch State Park ❶,** 6443 Mountain Rd., 8 mi. west of Stowe, just past Foster's Place, has hot showers, tent sites, and lean-tos. Secluded sites, new facilities, and beautiful views of Mt. Mansfield make this an excellent camping option. (☎253-4014. Reservations recommended. Open late May to mid-Oct. 4-person sites $14; lean-tos $21; each additional person $4.)

⚐⚑ FOOD AND NIGHTLIFE. At the **⛾Depot Street Malt Shoppe ❶,** 57 Depot St., sports pennants and vinyl records deck the walls, while rock 'n' roll favorites liven up the outdoor patio seating. The cost of a 1950s-style hot fudge sundae has been adjusted for inflation ($4), but prices remain enticing. (☎253-4269. Entrees $5-8. Open M-Th and Su 11:30am-8pm, F-Sa 11:30am-9pm. AmEx/D/MC/V.) Creative pizza and a busy lounge bring adventurous diners to **Piecasso ❷,** 1899 Mountain Rd., a large yellow house with pseudo-cubist decor. **Gracie's Restaurant ❸,** on Mountain Rd. outside Stowe, will have you howling in delight with pooch-themed delights like "doggone good" burgers ($9-10) and an on-site bakery. Don't forget to check out their "doggie bag" desserts. (☎253-8741. Open M-Th 11:30am-10pm, F-Su 11:30am-11pm. AmEx/D/MC/V.) Fans of little green men and all things not of this planet will enjoy **Pie in the Sky ❸,** 492 Mountain Rd. Their yummy pizzas include the "Blond Vermonter" with olive oil, Vermont cheddar, apples, and ham. (☎253-5100. Pizza $8-17. Open daily 11:30am-10pm. MC/V.) For sports fans, the **Sunset Grille and Tap Room,** 140 Cottage Club Rd., off Mountain Rd., allows its guests to face off at the pool tables while they watch sporting events on more than 25 TVs. The adjacent restaurant offers an award-winning BBQ platter for $14. (☎253-9281. Lunch $5-10. Dinner $10-20. Kitchen open daily 11:30am-midnight. Bar open until 2am.) Head to the **Rusty Nail,** 1 mi. from town center on Mountain Rd., to sample their full martini bar, dance to live music, or tap into one of the few sources of Wi-

Fi on the mountain. In the winter, the front patio becomes an ice bar that draws a large contingent. (☎253-6245. Th-Sa live music or DJ 9pm-2am. 21+. Cover $5-15. Open daily 11:30am-2am. Kitchen closes 10pm.)

🏂 **SKIING.** Stowe's ski offerings include the Stowe Mountain Resort (☎253-3000 or 800-253-4754) and Smugglers' Notch (☎644-8851 or 800-451-8752; see **Vermont Ski Resorts,** p. 248). Brush up on your skiing history at the **Vermont Ski Museum,** just south of the intersection of Mountain Rd. and Main St. in town. The small museum hosts a pseudo-chandelier of chairlifts and is filled with skiing memorabilia. (☎253-9404. Open M and W-Su noon-5pm. Free, suggested donation $3.) The hills are alive with cross-country skiing on 37 mi. of groomed trails and 25 mi. of back-country trails on the softly undulating mountainsides surrounding **The Trapp Family Lodge,** 2 mi. off Mountain Rd., accessed from Luce Hill Rd. Budget travelers beware: prices for lodging climb to as much as $960 in the high season. However, inexpensive rentals and lessons coupled with the unparalleled serenity of back-country skiing make this alpine winter wonderland hard to resist. (☎253-5719 or 800-826-7000; www.trappfamily.com. Trail fee $16. Ski rentals $20 per day. Lessons $15-45 per hr. Ski school package includes all 3 for $40.) **AJ's Ski and Sports,** 350 Mountain Rd., rents ski equipment. (☎253-4593 or 800-226-6257. Downhill equipment rental $26 per day, $50 per 2 days; cross-country $15/28. Snowboard and boots $22 per day. Open in winter M-Th and Su 8am-8pm, F-Sa 8am-9pm.)

🎭📷 **SIGHTS AND OUTDOOR ACTIVITIES.** In summer, Stowe's frenetic pace drops off some, but it still burns with outdoor enthusiasts' energy. **AJ's Ski and Sports** (see above) also rents bikes and kayaks in the summer. (Open in summer daily 9am-6pm. Bikes $18 per half-day, $27 per full day; children $16/24. Tandem kayak or canoe $42 per day.) Stowe's 5½ mi. asphalt **recreation path** runs parallel to Mountain Rd. (Rte.108) and begins behind the church on Main St. in Stowe, ascending toward Smugglers' Notch through peaceful meadows and thick forest glades. Perfect for biking, skating, and strolling in the summer, the path accommodates cross-country skiing and snowshoeing in the winter. A few miles past Smugglers' Notch on Mountain Rd. (Rte. 108), the road shrinks to one lane and winds past huge boulders and 1000 ft. high cliffs. Road closures through the pass are common in the winter, and strong caution should be observed if attempting any winter ascent. Several **hiking** trails begin at the Smuggler's Notch picnic area and lead to the "mouth," "nose," and "chin" of Mt. Mansfield. All are approximately 4 mi. round-trip and gain around 2000 ft. Stowe boasts several mountain streams, including the Winooski River, prime for fly-fishing. Seasoned and aspiring fly-fishers should head to the **Fly Rod Shop,** 2½ mi. south of Stowe on Rte. 100, to pick up the necessary fishing licenses ($15 per day, $30 per week, $41 per year; VT residents $20 per year), rent fly rods and reels, and enroll in the free fly-fishing classes at the shop's pond. (☎253-7346 or 800-535-9763. Open Apr.-Oct. M-Sa 9am-6pm, Su 10am-4pm; Nov.-Mar. M-Sa 9am-5pm, Su 10am-4pm. Classes W 4-6pm, Sa 9-11am. Rods and reels $15 per day.) **Umiak,** on Rte. 100, ¾ mi. south of Stowe Center, rents kayaks and canoes in the summer. (☎253-2317. Open daily 9am-6pm. 2hr. river trip $30 per person, 4hr. trip $40 per person. Kayaks $25 per half-day after 1pm, $35 per day; canoes $35/45.) Just 1¼ mi. north on Edson Rd., off Mountain Rd. north of Stowe, **Edson Hill Manor Stables** offers guided 1hr. horseback rides ($35) on the southeastern ridge of Smugglers' Notch through cool woodlands and green meadows. (☎253-8954 or 253-7371. Refreshments provided upon return. Call for tours and availability.) **Ziemke Glassblowing Studio,** 7 mi. south of Stowe along Rte. 100, allows free viewing of the entire glassblowing process—from a molten mass in the 2100°F furnace to finished vases, glasses, and candleholders. The wares being made are also for sale in the gallery. (☎244-6126. Open daily 10am-6pm.)

BRATTLEBORO   ☎802

Increasingly gentrified hippie roots run deep in Brattleboro, where bookstores, art galleries, and independent cafes compete with majestic scenery and outdoor adventure for attention. Bridging the divide between rural and urban sensibilities, Brattleboro's distinct mix of psychedelic progressivism and traditional values infuses the city with excitement. While downtown Brattleboro is always buzzing with activity, hiking and skiing in nearby parks provide a perfect environment for fun and relaxation.

■■▐ **ORIENTATION AND PRACTICAL INFORMATION.** Located along the southern part of the Vermont-New Hampshire border, Brattleboro is most easily reached by I-91 or Rt. 9. Amtrak, 10 Vernon St. (☎800-872-7245; www.amtrak.com; open 11:30am-1:30pm and 3:30-5:30pm; no ticket office), **trains** go to New York City (6hr., 12:30pm, $42), and Greyhound, Jct. Rtes. 5 and 9 (☎254-6066; www.greyhound.com; open M-F 8:15am-noon and 2-4pm, Sa-Su 8am-noon and 2-3:25pm), runs **buses** to Boston (4hr., 3:10pm, $36) and New York City (5½hr., 3 per day, $46). For visitor information, the **Brattleboro Chamber of Commerce,** 180 Main St., has hundreds of brochures about the area. (☎254-4565; www.brattleborochamber.org. Open M-F 9am-5pm, Sa 10am-2pm.) **Bike Rental: Brattleboro Bicycle Shop,** 165 Main St. (☎ 254-8644; www.bratbike.com. $20 per day. Open M-F 10am-6pm, Sa 10am-5pm, Su noon-4pm.) Access the **Internet** at **Brooks Memorial Library,** 224 Main St. (☎254-5290; www.brooks.lib.vt.us. Open in winter M-W 10am-9pm, Th-F 10am-6pm, Sa 10am-5pm; in summer also Su 10am-1pm. Wi-Fi available.) **Post Office** is at 204 Main St. (☎275-8777. Open M-F 8am-5pm, Sa 9am-noon.) **Postal Code:** 05301.

▐▐ **ACCOMMODATIONS AND FOOD.** Follow South Main St. out of downtown to reach **Fort Dummer State Park ❶,** 517 Old Guilford Rd., which has 50 well-maintained campsites and 10 lean-tos, as well as picnic areas and two hiking trails. (☎254-2610. Hot showers. Open mid-May to Labor Day. Sites $14, lean-tos $21.) Outside of town, along Rtes. 5 and 9, the **Colonial Motel and Spa ❹,** 889 Putney Road, boasts a tavern, an indoor pool and a spa, A/C, and cable TV. (☎257-7733; www.colonialmotelspa.com. Rooms $65-120. AmEx/D/MC/V.) An on-site bakery and casual seating overlooking the river make **Amy's Bakery Arts Cafe ❶,** 113 Main St., the perfect choice for a fresh sandwich ($5.25-6) or pastry. (☎251-1071. Open daily 11am-4pm.) For caffeine and conversation, locals head to ▓**Mocha Joe's ❶,** 183 Main St., where the coffee is brewed with beans from around the world. Mexican hot chocolate ($2.25) is a specialty. (☎257-5637; www.mochajoes.com. Open M-Th 7am-8pm, F 7:30am-10pm, Sa 7:30am-10pm, Su 7:30am-7pm.) Sweeping river views await at **Riverview Cafe and Bar ❹,** 36 Bridge St., where you can sample goat cheese cakes ($7.25) or "Chicken Under a Brick" ($17) while supporting local farms. (☎254-9841; www.riverviewcafe.com. Open M-Th 11am-8pm, F-Sa 11am-9pm, Su 11am-8pm. AmEx/D/MC/V.)

▣▐ **SIGHTS AND NIGHTLIFE.** The **Brattleboro Museum & Art Center,** 10 Vernon St., housed in a renovated railway station, has rotating exhibits of contemporary works by internationally renowned artists on display and an exceptionally friendly, volunteer staff. (☎257-0124; www.brattleboromuseum.org. Open M and W-Su 11am-5pm. $4, seniors and students $2, under 6 free.) A map of Vermont's famous covered bridges, which can be seen throughout the state, is available at the Brattleboro Chamber of Commerce. The 125-year-old **Creamery Covered Bridge,** 0.3 mi. west on Rte. 9 from I-91, deserves a short visit for its simple beauty and idyllic setting. Grab drinks and check out local bands at **Mole's Eye Cafe,** 4 High St., where you can enjoy simple entrees ($4-8), relax at the large bar, or indulge in the

NEW ENGLAND

heavenly chocolate truffle cake. (☎257-0771; www.moleseyecafe.net. Th open mic night. Open M-Th 4pm-midnight, F-Sa 11:30am-1pm. Kitchen open until 9pm.)

MASSACHUSETTS

Massachusetts regards itself, with some justification, as the nation's intellectual center. Since the 1636 establishment of Cambridge's Harvard College, the oldest college in America, Massachusetts has been a breeding ground for academics and literati. The undisputed highlight of the state is Boston, the "Cradle of Liberty" and birthplace of the American Revolution, where colonial landmarks and cobblestone streets coexist with hip eateries and crowded T stops. Beyond the hubbub of the Hub, Cape Cod's ample beaches and sea breezes fill the roads with sun-seeking tourists, while inland, the Berkshires draw those looking for art, inspiration, and stunning fall foliage in the area's bountiful golden hills.

⚡ PRACTICAL INFORMATION

Capital: Boston.

Visitor Info: Office of Travel and Tourism, 10 Park Plaza, Ste. 4510, Boston 02116 (☎617-973-8500 or 800-227-6277; www.massvacation.com). Free *Getaway Guide* available online or in person. Open M-F 9am-5pm.

Postal Abbreviation: MA. **Sales Tax:** 5%; no tax on clothing or pre-packaged food.

BOSTON   ☎617

Perhaps more than any other American city, Boston reveals the possibilities of the "melting pot." The Financial District's corporate sanctuaries are visible from the North End's winding streets. Aristocratic Beacon Hill is just across Boston Common from the nation's first Chinatown. The trendy South End abuts the less-gentrified neighborhoods of Roxbury and Dorchester. While Boston's famed Freedom Trail will expose you to some of the earliest history of the US, a walk through Boston's neighborhoods lends a glimpse into a still-evolving metropolis. For more comprehensive coverage of the Boston area, see 📖*Let's Go: Boston.*

✈ INTERCITY TRANSPORTATION

Airport: Logan International (BOS; ☎800-235-6426; www.massport.com/logan), 5 mi. northeast of downtown. T: Airport; a free shuttle connects all 5 terminals to the T stop. **Back Bay Coach** (☎888-222-5229; www.backbaycoach.com) runs door-to-door service to and from the airport (24hr. advanced reservation recommended). A **taxi** to downtown costs $15-20.

Trains: Amtrak (☎800-872-7245; www.amtrak.com) pulls into **South Station,** at Summer St. and Atlantic Ave. T: South Station. Open 24hr. Trains run to **New York City** (3½-4½hr., 10 per day, $66-94), **Philadelphia** (5-6hr., 10 per day, $82-163), and **Washington, D.C.** (6½-8hr., 10 per day, $91-176).

Buses: Buses depart from South Station.

Bonanza Bus (☎888-751-8800; www.bonanzabus.com) runs to **New York City** (4¾hr., 15 per day, $30) and **Providence** (1hr., 16 per day, $8-9).

Greyhound (☎800-231-2222; www.greyhound.com) runs to **New York City** (4½-6½hr., every 30min.-1hr., $35), **Philadelphia** (7-8½hr., every 1-2hr., $55), and **Washington, D.C.** (10-11hr., every 1-2hr., $66).

Peter Pan (☎800-237-8747; www.peterpanbus.com) runs to **Albany** (4-4½hr., 2-3 per day, $37).

Boston
SEE COLOR INSERTS FOR
MORE BOSTON MAPS

Plymouth and Brockton St. Railway (☎508-746-0378; www.p-b.com) goes to **Plymouth** (1hr., every 1-2hr., $11) and **Cape Cod,** including **Hyannis** (1½hr., 25 per day, $16) and **Provincetown** (3¼hr., 2 per day, $26).

Vermont Transit (☎800-552-8737; www.vermonttransit.com) goes north to **Burlington** (5hr., 4 per day, $49) and **Montréal** (8hr., 5 per day, $61).

⊞ ORIENTATION

Boston, the capital of Massachusetts and the largest city in New England, is situated on a peninsula that juts into the Massachusetts Bay (bordered to the north and west by the **Charles River** and to the east by **Boston Harbor**). The city proper centers on the grassy **Boston Common;** the popular **Freedom Trail** (p. 265) begins here and links most of the city's major sights. The Trail heads east through crowded **Downtown** (still the same compact 3 sq. mi. settled in 1630), skirting the city's growing **Waterfront** district to the southeast. The Trail then veers north to the charming **North End,** Boston's "Little Italy," bounded by the **Fitzgerald Expressway (I-93),** before crossing the river to historic **Charlestown.**

Boston Common is sandwiched between aristocratic **Beacon Hill** to the north and **Chinatown** to the south. Much of Chinatown overlaps the nightlife-heavy **Theater District** to the west. Just west of the Common, **Back Bay's** grand boulevards and brownstones surround beautiful Copley Sq., Newbury St.'s elegant shops, and Boylston St., a true bar-hopper's paradise. The **Massachusetts Turnpike (I-90)** separates Back Bay from the artsy and predominantly gay **South End,** which has a lion's share of the city's best restaurants. Farther west are **Kenmore Square** and **Fenway,** home to baseball's Red Sox, major museums, and the clubs of Lansdowne St. South of the Fenway is vibrant, gay-friendly **Jamaica Plain,** filled with green spaces and cheap restaurants.

▤ LOCAL TRANSPORTATION

Public Transit: Massachusetts Bay Transportation Authority (MBTA; ☎222-5000; www.mbta.com). Known as the T, the subway has 5 colored lines—Red, Blue, Orange, Green (Green splits into lettered lines B-E), and Silver—that radiate from Downtown. "Inbound" trains head toward T: Park St. or T: Downtown Crossing; "outbound" trains head away from those stops. All T stops have maps and schedules. Lines run daily 5:30am-12:30am. Fare $2 ($1.70 with plastic CharlieCard), seniors $0.60, under 11 free. **Visitor passes** for unlimited subway and bus use are good for 1 day ($7.50), 3 days ($18), or 7 days ($35). **MBTA Commuter Rail** trains run from T: **North Station** (Green/Orange) to **Concord** (Fitchburg line; $5), **Plymouth** (Plymouth/Kingston line; 1hr., $6), and **Salem** (Newburyport/Rockport line; 30min., $3.75).

Taxi: Boston Cab ☎262-2227. **Checker Taxi** ☎494-1500. **Town Taxi** ☎536-5000.

Car Rental: Dollar Rent-a-Car (☎634-0006 or 800-800-3665), at the airport. Open 24hr. Under-25 surcharge $30 per day. AAA discount 10%. Must be 21+ with major credit card. All other agencies have desks at the airport.

❼ PRACTICAL INFORMATION

Visitor Info: Greater Boston Convention and Visitors Bureau (☎800-733-2678; www.bostonusa.com) has a booth at Boston Common, outside T: Park St. Open M-F 8:30am-5pm. Downtown's **National Historic Park Visitor Center,** 15 State St. (☎242-5642), has Freedom Trail info and tours. T: State. Open daily 9am-5pm.

Tours: Boston Duck Tours (☎267-3825; www.bostonducktours.com). Wacky conductors drive WWII amphibious vehicles past sights before splashing down in the Charles,

offering cheesy commentary and quacking all the way. 1½hr. tours depart the Prudential Center, T: Prudential. Apr.-Nov. daily every 30-60min. 9am-1hr. before sunset. $25,
students and seniors $22, ages 3-11 $16. Tickets sold online or at the Museum of Science, Faneuil Hall, and the Prudential Center M-Sa 8:30am-8pm, Su 8:30am-6pm.

Hotlines: Rape Crisis Center: ☎492-7273. 24hr. **GBLT Help Line:** ☎267-9001. Operates M-F 6-11pm, Sa-Su 5-10pm.

Post Office: 25 Dorchester Ave. (☎800-275-8777), at T: South Station. Open M-F 6am-
midnight, Sa 8am-7pm, Su noon-7pm. **Postal Code:** 02205.

ACCOMMODATIONS

Finding cheap accommodations in Boston is hard. Rates and bookings are highest
in summer and during college-rush times in September, late May, and early June.
Reservation services promise to find discounted rooms, even during sold-out periods. Try **Boston Reservations** (☎332-4199), **Central Reservation Service** (☎569-3800 or
800-332-3026; www.bostonhotels.net), or **Citywide Reservation Services** (☎267-7424
or 800-468-3593). Listed prices do not include Boston's 12.45% room tax.

▨ **Oasis Guest House,** 22 Edgerly Rd. (☎267-2262; www.oasisgh.com), at Stoneholm St.,
in Back Bay. From T: Hynes/ICA, exit onto Massachusetts Ave. Cross Boylston St. and
turn right onto Haviland St.; the next left is Edgerly Rd. This rambling 16-room guest
house *is* an oasis, serving as a calm respite from the city's hustle and bustle. Continental breakfast daily 8-11am. Reservations recommended up to 2 months in advance.
May to mid-Nov. singles $59; doubles with shared bath $69, with private bath $89.
Mid-Nov. to Apr. all rooms $90-$250. AmEx/MC/V. ❸

▨ **Newbury Guest House,** 261 Newbury St. (☎437-7666; www.newburyguesthouse.com),
between Gloucester and Fairfield St. T: Hynes/ICA. This urban B&B offers 32 immaculate, bright, and tastefully decorated double rooms with private bath and digital cable.
Breakfast daily 7:30-10:30am. Reception 24hr. Check-in 3pm. Check-out noon. Doubles Apr.-Oct. $125-170. Nov.-Mar. $99-125. AmEx/D/MC/V. ❺

Boston International Youth Hostel (HI-AYH), 12 Hemenway St. (☎536-1027;
www.bostonhostel.org), in Back Bay. From T: Hynes/ICA, walk down Massachusetts
Ave., turn right onto Boylston St., then turn left onto Hemenway St. Central location,
spotless bathrooms, and quiet dorms. Kitchen. Continental breakfast, lockers, and
linen included. Laundry facilities. Check-in noon. Check-out 11am. Dorms $31-48,
members $28-45. AmEx/MC/V. ❷

FOOD

Once a barren gastronomical wasteland whose only claim to fame was baked
beans, Boston may not be a culinary paradise, but its cuisine has certainly become
much more palatable. Trendy bistros, fusion restaurants, and a globetrotting array
of ethnic eateries have taken their place alongside the long-standing "chowda"
shacks, greasy spoons, soul food joints, and welcoming pubs.

DOWNTOWN

Downtown is the most heavily touristed part of Boston, so expect mediocre food,
big crowds, and high prices. The best and most affordable food options are the
interchangeable sandwich shops (sandwiches $5-7) found on almost every street
corner and the more diverse food court inside **Quincy Market** (p. 266). Downtown is
also near the fresh seafood shops lining Boston's **Waterfront** district.

Durgin Park, 340 Faneuil Hall Marketplace (☎227-2038). T: Government Ctr. Boston's
most touristed restaurant, Durgin Park has been serving traditional New England dishes

like fried seafood, Yankee pot roast, and Indian pudding since 1827. Entrees $11-33. Open M-Sa 11:30am-10pm, Su 11:30am-9pm. AmEx/D/MC/V. ❹

No Name, 17 Fish Pier St. W (☎338-7539), the next pier over from the World Trade Center. Take the free shuttle to the WTC from T: South Station. This waterfront eatery is one of Boston's best and cheapest seafood spots, serving fish fresh off the boat since 1917. Entrees $8-12. Open M-Sa 11am-10pm, Su 11am-9pm. Cash or check only. ❸

NORTH END

Boston's Italian-American enclave is the place to go for authentic Italian fare, with over 100 restaurants packed into 1 sq. mi. Most establishments line **Hanover Street,** accessible from T: Haymarket. After dinner, try one of the countless *caffès*. For cannoli ($2-3) and other Italian sweets, join the lines at ◙**Mike's Pastry,** 300 Hanover St., or **Modern Pastry,** 257 Hanover St.

Trattoria Il Panino, 11 Parmenter St. (☎720-1336), at Hanover St. A romantic North End trattoria—warm lighting, exposed brick, and intimate seating—with gigantic portions of classic fare. *Antipasti* $11-13. Entrees $10-17. Open M-Th and Su 11am-11pm, F-Sa 11am-midnight. AmEx/D/MC/V. ❹ Il Panino also runs the cheaper lunch counter **Il Panino Express,** at 1001 Mass Ave. in Cambridge. Calzones, 1 ft. subs, and salads $5-8. Open daily 11am-11pm. Cash only. ❷

L'Osteria, 104 Salem St. (☎723-7847). Turn left off Hanover St. onto Parmenter St., then right onto Salem St. A simple, reliable trattoria that serves all the robust Italian favorites found on Hanover St., but at lower prices. *Antipasti* $8.50-15. Entrees $10-24. Open M-Th and Su noon-10pm, F-Sa noon-11pm. AmEx/MC/V. ❸

CHINATOWN

Chinatown (T: Chinatown) is *the* place for filling, cheap Asian food (not just Chinese) any time. Stuck between the skyscrapers of the Financial District and the chaos of the Big Dig, the neighborhood is slightly grimy and run-down, but the prices are unbeatable, and most places stay open until 3 or 4am.

Shabu-Zen, 16 Tyler St. (☎292-8828; www.shabuzen.com), off Beach St. The signature do-it-yourself Japanese dish, *shabu-shabu,* is named for the swish-swish sound of dipping thinly sliced meat or veggies in your own pot of boiling broth. Entrees $10-19. Open M-W and Su 11:30am-11pm, Th-Sa 11:30am-midnight. AmEx/MC/V. ❸

Jumbo Seafood Restaurant, 5-7-9 Hudson St. (☎542-2823). Greet your dinner swimming in the tanks by the entrance at the best of Chinatown's Hong Kong-style seafood spots, with huge portions, a light touch, and a glowing velvet mural on the wall. Lunch specials $5-6. Dinner entrees $10-20. Open daily 11am-midnight. D/MC/V. ❸

BACK BAY

The diverse eateries of Back Bay line elegant **Newbury Street,** accessible from T: Hynes/ICA or T: Back Bay. Though Newbury is known as Boston's expensive shopping district, affordable restaurants do exist.

◙ **Parish Café,** 361 Boylston St. (☎247-4777), near T: Arlington. Locals crowd tables and barstools to order sandwiches ($10-12) designed by the city's hottest chefs, who do marvelous things with chicken, portobello, lobster, brioche, and focaccia. Outdoor seating. Open M-Sa 11:30am-1am, Su noon-1am. Bar open until 2am. AmEx/MC/V. ❸

Island Hopper, 91 Massachusetts Ave. (☎266-1618), at Newbury St. Trendy yet casual, Island Hopper brings huge portions flavored with authentic Southeast Asian spices to this bright and spacious restaurant. All-day special combos $8. Entrees $10-25. Open M-Th 11:30am-11pm, F-Sa 11:30am-midnight, Su noon-11pm. AmEx/MC/V. ❸

Kashmir, 279 Newbury St. (☎536-1695), at Gloucester St. Marble floors and plush red seats create a setting as exotic as the subtle curries ($12-15) and vegetarian menu. Don't miss the *tandoori* specials. Entrees $15-25. All-you-can-eat buffet M-F 11:30am-3pm ($9), Sa-Su noon-3pm ($12). Open daily 11:30am-11pm. AmEx/D/MC/V. ❹

SOUTH END

The long waits and hefty bills here are worth it: the South End's upscale restaurants creatively meld flavors and techniques from around the world, creating amazing meals. Most eateries line **Tremont Street,** accessible from T: Back Bay.

🌄**Addis Red Sea,** 544 Tremont St. (☎426-8727). Curry- and veggie-heavy Ethiopian cuisine in an intimate setting. Entrees ($9-15) are served utensil-free, to be scooped up with spongy *injera* bread. Open M-F 5-11pm, Sa-Su noon-11pm. AmEx/D/MC/V. ❸

Flour, 1595 Washington St. (☎267-4300), at Rutland St. Near T: Prudential, Mass. Ave, or Back Bay. Chef/owner Joanne Chang bakes the most mouth-watering cakes, cookies, and pastries ($1-4) in the city. Gourmet sandwiches $6.50. Open M-F 7am-9pm, Sa 8am-6pm, Su 9am-3pm. AmEx/D/MC/V. ❷

JAMAICA PLAIN

Restaurants in "JP" are some of the best bargains in the city, with a wide variety of ethnic eateries—the Mexican offerings and vegetarian options are especially noteworthy. The action is, not surprisingly, centered on **Centre Street,** which runs parallel to the Orange Line (between T: Jackson Sq. and T: Forest Hills).

🌄 **Bella Luna,** 405 Centre St. (☎524-6060). T: Jackson Sq. Those who trek to the heart of Jamaica Plain will be rewarded with upscale food at affordable prices. The interior twinkles with red walls, candles, and lanterns that stand out against the drab concrete of the surrounding neighborhood. Choose from 13 artful pizza creations ($5-17) or carefully constructed entrees ($12-17), such as chicken marsala and spinach ravioli. The airy crème brûlée and homemade tiramisu ($6.50) are out of this world. Open M-Th 11:30am-3pm and 5-10pm, F-Sa 11:30am-3pm and 5pm-11pm, Su 11:30am-10pm. AmEx/D/MC/V. ❸

El Oriental de Cuba, 416 Centre St. (☎524-6464). Turn right out of T: Jackson Sq. A cheerful local spot with a plantain- and meat-heavy menu. Don't miss the Cuban sandwiches or Puerto Rican *mofongo* (mashed garlicky plantains). Tropical shakes $2.50. Entrees $5-12. Open M-Th 8am-9pm, F-Sa 8am-10pm, Su 8am-8pm. AmEx/MC/V. ❷

◎ SIGHTS

THE FREEDOM TRAIL

Passing the landmarks that put Boston on the map in colonial times, the 2½ mi. red-brick Freedom Trail is a great introduction to the city's history. Start at the **Visitors Center,** where the National Park Service offers free guided tours of the portion of the Trail from the Old South Meeting House to the Old North Church. *(15 State St., opposite Old State House. ☎242-5642; www.nps.gov/bost. At least 2 tours daily mid-June to Nov.; times vary, call ahead.)* You can also embark on the Freedom Trail from the **Visitors Center** on Boston Common, outside T: Park St.

BEACON HILL. The Freedom Trail first runs uphill to the **Robert Gould Shaw Memorial,** honoring the first black regiment of the Union Army in the American Civil War and their Bostonian leader. Opposite the memorial is the gold-domed **Massachusetts State House.** *(State House tours ☎720-1713. Open daily 9am-5pm. $5, students and seniors $4, ages 6-18 $1.)*

DOWNTOWN. Passing the **Park Street Church** (☎523-3383), the trail reaches the **Granary Burial Ground**, where John Hancock, Samuel Adams, Elizabeth Goose ("Mother Goose"), and Paul Revere rest. **Kings Chapel and Burying Ground** is America's oldest Anglican church; the latest inhabitants are Unitarian. The city's 1st cemetery, next door, is the final resting place of midnight rider William Dawes. *(58 Tremont St. Chapel ☎227-2155. Chapel open Tu-Su 10am-4pm. Donations accepted. Burying Ground open daily Mar.-Nov. 9am-5pm; Dec.-Feb. 9am-3pm. Wheelchair-accessible. Free.)* The Charles Bulfinch-designed **Old City Hall** (☎523-8678), on School St., was built on the original site of the country's 1st public school, the Boston Latin School, which has since relocated to the Fenway. The **Old Corner Bookstore**, 1 School St., was once the city's intellectual and literary center. The **Old South Meeting House** was the site of the preliminary meeting that set the mood for the Boston Tea Party. *(310 Washington St. ☎482-6439; www.oldsouthmeetinghouse.org. Open daily Apr.-Oct. 9:30am-5pm; Nov.-Mar. 10am-4pm. $5, students and seniors $4, ages 6-18 $1, under 6 free.)* Formerly the seat of British government, the ▧**Old State House** is now a museum chronicling the history of Boston. *(206 Washington St. ☎720-1713. Open daily 9am-5pm; extended hours in summer. $5, students and seniors $4, ages 6-18 $1.)* The Trail passes a brick circle marking the site of the **Boston Massacre** en route to **Faneuil Hall** and **Quincy Market.** A former meeting hall and current mega-mall, the complex houses a food court and carts selling kitschy items. *(Faneuil Hall ☎523-1300. Open M-Sa 10am-10pm, Su noon-6pm.)*

NORTH END. Heading into the Italian-American North End, the Trail crawls through Big Dig rubble to the **Paul Revere House,** where a self-guided tour helps visitors navigate meticulously recreated 18th-century rooms. *(19 North Sq. ☎523-2338; www.paulreverehouse.org. Open mid-Apr. to Oct. daily 9:30am-5:15pm; Nov.-Dec. and early Apr. daily 9:30am-4:15pm; Jan.-Mar. Tu-Su 9:30am-4:15pm. $3, college students with ID and seniors $2.50, ages 5-17 $1, under 5 free.)* The **Old North Church** is where Robert Newman was instructed by Revere to hang lanterns—"one if by land, two if by sea"—warning patriots in Charlestown that the British were coming. The church still houses such Revolutionary relics as George Washington's wig and tea from the Boston Tea Party. *(193 Salem St. ☎523-6676. Open daily 9am-6pm. Donations accepted. Behind the Scenes tour $8, children $5.)* **Copp's Hill Burying Ground,** up Hull St. from the church, is a final resting place for numerous colonial Bostonians and was a key vantage point in the Battle of Bunker Hill.

CHARLESTOWN. The Battle of Bunker Hill is the focus of much of the rest of the Trail, which heads across the Charles River to the **U.S.S. Constitution** (a.k.a. "Old Ironsides") and its museum. *(☎426-1812; www.ussconstitution.navy.mil. Ship open in summer Tu-Su 10am-5:50pm; in winter 10am-3:50pm. Tours every 30min. Museum open daily in summer 9am-6pm; in winter 10am-5pm. Free; donations accepted.)* The Trail winds through residential Charlestown toward the **Bunker Hill Monument,** which is actually on Breed's Hill—fitting given that the entire Battle of Bunker Hill was actually fought on Breed's Hill. A grand view awaits atop the obelisk's 294 steps. *(☎242-5641. T: Community College. Monument Sq. Open daily 9am-4:30pm. Visitors Center open daily 9am-5pm. Free.)* The Trail loops back to Boston from Monument Sq., passing **City Square,** settled in 1629 shortly after the Puritans' arrival in the Boston area.

DOWNTOWN

In 1634, Massachusetts Bay colonists designated **Boston Common** as a grazing ground for their cattle. Today, street vendors, runners, and tourists roam the green and congregate near the **Frog Pond,** a wading pool in summer and ice-skating rink in winter. *(T: Park St.)* Across Charles St. from the Common is the lavish **Public Garden,** the nation's 1st botanical garden. Bronze versions of the title characters from the children's book *Make Way for Ducklings* point the way to the **Swan Boats,** graceful paddleboats that float around a willow-lined pond. (☎ 522-1966; T: Arlington, Boylston, or Park St. www.swanboats.com. Park open daily dawn-dusk. Wheelchair-accessible. Boats open daily mid-Apr. to mid-June 10am-4pm; mid-June to Labor Day 10am-5pm; Sept. M-F noon-4pm, Sa-Su 10am-4pm, weather permitting. 15min. ride $2.75, seniors $2, ages 2-15 $1.25.) Steps from the Common is the pedestrian mall at **Downtown Crossing**, a shopping district centered around legendary **Filene's Basement**, a chaotic feeding frenzy for bargain hunters. (426 Washington St. T: Downtown Crossing. ☎ 542-2011. Open M-F 9:30am-8pm, Sa 9am-8pm, Su 11am-7pm.)

BEACON HILL

Looming over the Common is posh Beacon Hill, an exclusive residential neighborhood that was the 1st spot on the Shawmut Peninsula settled by Puritans. Antique shops, pricey cafes, and ritzy boutiques now line charming **Charles Street,** the neighborhood's main artery. For generations, the Hill was home to Boston's intellectual, political, and social elite, christened the "Boston Brahmins." For a taste of Brahmin life, visit the **Nichols House,** restored to its 19th-century state. (55 Mt. Vernon St., off Charles St. T: Charles/MGH. ☎ 227-6993; www.nicholshousemuseum.org. Open Apr.-Oct. Tu-Sa noon-4pm; Nov.-Mar. Th, F, and Sa noon-4pm. Entrance by 30min. guided tour only, every 30min. Last tour 4pm. $7, under 12 free.) Quiet **Louisburg Square,** between Mt. Vernon and Pinckney St., was the birthplace of neighborly Christmas caroling.

Boston was the 1st city in America to outlaw slavery, and many African-Americans moved to the Beacon Hill area after the Civil War. The **Black Heritage Trail** is a free 2hr. (1½ mi.) walk through Beacon Hill sights that were important during Boston's abolitionist era. The tour begins at the foot of Beacon Hill, near the Shaw Memorial (p. 265), and ends at the free **Museum of Afro-American History,** which contains a small collection of art and artifacts, a church, and an exhibit about Boston's relationship with slavery. (46 Joy St. ☎ 725-0022; www.afroammuseum.org. Museum open in winter M-Sa 10am-4pm; in summer M-W and F-Sa 10am-4pm, Th 10am-8pm. Heritage Trail tours Memorial Day-Labor Day. Both free; donations accepted.) Also at the foot of the hill is the cheesy **Bull and Finch Pub,** 84 Beacon St., the inspiration for the bar in *Cheers.*

WATERFRONT

The Waterfront district refers to the wharves along Boston Harbor that stretch from South Station to the North End. The excellent ◼**New England Aquarium** features cavorting penguins, an animal infirmary, and briny beasts in a four-story tank. (Central Wharf at T: Aquarium. ☎ 973-5200; www.neaq.org. Open M-Th 9am-6pm, F-Su 9am-7pm. $19, ages 3-11 $11. IMAX $9. Whale Watch $35, under 11 $29.) The Long Wharf, north of Central Wharf, is **Boston Harbor Cruises'** departure point. They lead history-minded sightseeing cruises and whale-watching excursions, and charter boats to the Harbor Islands. (☎ 227-4321; www.bostonharborcruises.com. Open Apr.-Oct. Sightseeing cruise 45min.-1½hr.; 3 per day; $19, seniors $17, under 12 $15. Whale-watching cruise 3hr., $35/32/29; families $100. Reservations recommended.)

BACK BAY

Back Bay was initially an uninhabitable tidal flat tucked into the "back" corner of the bay until the late 19th century. Today elegant Back Bay's stately brownstones and spacious, shady promenades are laid out in an easily navigable grid. Cross-streets are labeled alphabetically from Arlington to Hereford St. Running through Back Bay, fashionable **Newbury Street,** accessible from T: Hynes/ICA, is where Boston's trendiest strut their stuff and empty their wallets.

COPLEY SQUARE. Named for painter John Singleton Copley, Copley Sq. is popular with both lunching businessmen and busy Newbury St. tourists. The square is dominated by H.H. Richardson's Romanesque fantasy, **Trinity Church,** reflected in

NEW ENGLAND

the 14 acres of glass used in I.M. Pei's stunning **John Hancock Tower,** now closed to the public. *(T: Copley. Church ☎ 536-0944, tower 247-1977.)* Facing the church, the dramatic ▊**Boston Public Library** is a museum in disguise; don't miss John Singer Sargent's restored *Triumph of Religion* murals or the hidden courtyard. *(☎ 536-5400; www.bpl.org. Free Wi-Fi. Open M-Th 9am-9pm, F Sa 9am-5pm. Free.)* The 50th floor of the **Prudential Center** mall next door to Copley Sq. is home to the **Prudential Skywalk,** which offers a 360-degree view of Boston from a height of 700 ft. *(T: Prudential. ☎ 859-0648. Skywalk open daily 10am-9:30pm. Last entry 9:30pm. $10.50, over 65 and students with ID $8.50, under 10 $7.)*

CHRISTIAN SCIENCE PLAZA. Down Massachusetts Ave. from Newbury St., the 14-acre Christian Science Plaza is Boston's most under appreciated public space. This epic expanse of concrete, centered on a smooth reflecting pool, is home to the Byzantine-revival "Mother Church," a.k.a. **First Church of Christ, Scientist,** a Christian denomination of faith-based healing founded in Boston by Mary Baker Eddy. *(T: Symphony. ☎ 450-2000. Open to public during services W noon and 7:30pm; July-Aug. Su 10am, Sept.-June Su 10am and 7pm. Doors open 30min. before each service.)* The adjacent **Mary Baker Eddy Library,** another of Boston's library/museum hybrids, has exhibits on Mrs. Eddy's life and a surreal "Hall of Ideas," where holographic words bubble out of a fountain and crawl all over the floor and walls. Step inside the ▊**Mapparium,** a three-story stained-glass globe that depicts the world as it was in 1934 and details the changes that have occurred since then. The globe's perfect acoustics let you whisper in the ear of Pakistan and hear it in Suriname. *(☎ 888-222-3711; www.marybakereddylibrary.org. Open Tu-Su 10am-4pm. $6; ages 6-17, over 62, and students with ID $4; under 6 free.)*

JAMAICA PLAIN

Jamaica Plain offers everything quintessentially un-Bostonian: ample parking, good Mexican food, and Mother Nature. Although it's one of Boston's largest green spaces (over 265 acres), many Boston residents never make it to the lush **Arnold Arboretum,** which has flora and fauna from all over the world. A haven for bikers, joggers, and skaters, the Arboretum is the next-to-last link in Frederick Law Olmsted's Emerald Necklace, a ring of nine parks around Boston. *(T: Forest Hills. ☎ 524-1718. Open daily dawn-dusk.)* To conclude your JP junket, salute beer-guzzling patriots at the **Sam Adams Brewery.** At the end of the tour, the experts teach you how to "taste" beer. *(30 Germania St. T: Stony Brook. ☎ 368-5080. Tours every 30min. Th noon-2pm, F noon-5:30pm, Sa 11am-3pm. Tastings 21+. Free.)*

🏛 MUSEUMS

MUSEUM OF FINE ARTS. The exhaustive MFA showcases an international array of artwork from Samurai armor and contemporary American art to medieval instruments. The ancient Egyptian and Nubian galleries (lots of mummies), Impressionist collection (the largest outside France), and colonial portrait gallery (includes the painting of George Washington found on the $1 bill) are a few highlights. Swing by for MFA Fridays (first F of the month), where you can schmooze over mixed drinks and canvases with people who pretend to know what they're talking about. *(465 Huntington Ave., in Fenway. T: Museum. ☎ 267-9300; www.mfa.org. Open M-Tu 10am-4:45pm; W-F 10am-9:45pm, Th-F only West Wing open after 5pm; Sa-Su 10am-5:45pm. $17; students and seniors $15; ages 7-17 M-F $6.50, after 3pm free. W after 4pm free.)*

ISABELLA STEWART GARDNER MUSEUM. This astounding private collection remains exactly as eccentric Mrs. Gardner arranged it over a century ago—empty frames even remain where stolen paintings once hung. Solve the case and claim a $5 million reward! The Venetian-style palazzo architecture draws as much atten-

TIP

BEANTOWN MUSEUM BINGE. Consider a **CityPass** (www.citypass.com), which covers admission to the JFK Library, MFA, the Museum of Science, Harvard's Museum of Natural History (p. 274), the Aquarium (p. 267), and the Prudential Center Skywalk (p. 267). Passes, available at museums or online, are valid for 9 days. (CityPass $39.50, ages 3-11 $21.50.)

tion as the Old Masters, and the courtyard garden alone is worth the price of admission. Highlights include an original of Dante's *Divine Comedy* and Titian's *Europa*, considered the most important Italian Renaissance work in North America. *(280 Fenway, in Fenway. T: Museum. ☎ 566-1401; www.gardnermuseum.org. Open Tu-Su 11am-5pm. M-F $10, Sa-Su $11; students $5; under 18 free. Individuals named "Isabella" always free with valid ID.)*

JOHN F. KENNEDY LIBRARY AND MUSEUM. In a glass tower designed by I.M. Pei, this is a monument to Boston's favorite son, 35th US President John Francis Fitzgerald Kennedy. Exhibits trace JFK's career from the campaign trail to his assassination. *(At Columbia Point, just off I-93 in Dorchester, south of Boston. From T: JFK/UMass, take free shuttle #2 "JFK Library." ☎ 514-1600; www.jfklibrary.org. Open daily 9am-5pm. Wheelchair-accessible. $10, students and seniors $8, ages 13-17 $7, under 13 free.)*

INSTITUTE OF CONTEMPORARY ART. Boston's bastion of the avant-garde has installations from major contemporary artists beside lesser-known works. Thought-provoking exhibits rotate every three to four months. *(100 Northern Ave. T: Courthouse. ☎ 478-3100; www.icaboston.org. Open Tu-W and Sa-Su 10am-5pm, Th-F 10am-9pm. $12, students and seniors $10, under 17 free. Th 5-9pm free.)*

SPORTS MUSEUM OF NEW ENGLAND. The only way to understand Boston's fanatical sports obsession is to step inside it. Interactive exhibits each cover a different Boston sports franchise using archival footage, authentic gear, and reconstructions of lockers belonging to Boston's all-time greats. Don't miss the stuffed bruin (an animal, not a former player) or Larry Bird's size-14 shoes. *(Inside the TD Banknorth Garden, downtown. T: North Station. ☎ 624-1235. Open non-game days 11am-5pm. Hours vary on game days; call ahead. $6, seniors and ages 6-17 $4, under 6 free.)*

MUSEUM OF SCIENCE. Boston's Museum of Science educates and entertains children of all ages with its countless interactive exhibits. The must-sees are the giant *Tyrannosaurus rex;* the wacky Theater of Electricity; and the Soundstair, stairs that sing out a tune when you step on them. A five-story OMNI Theater and various trippy laser shows are at the Hayden Planetarium. *(Science Park. T: Science Park. ☎ 723-2500; www.mos.org. Open M-Th and Sa-Su 9am-5pm, F 9am-9pm. $16, seniors $14, ages 3-11 $13. IMAX, laser show, or Planetarium tickets $9/7/8; discounts after 6pm.)*

🎭 ENTERTAINMENT

The best publications for entertainment listings are the weekly *Boston Phoenix* (free from streetside boxes) and the *Boston Globe* Calendar section ($0.50, included with the Thursday *Boston Globe*). **Bostix** sells tickets to most major theater shows, and half-price, day-of-show tickets for select shows at locations in Faneuil Hall (p. 266) and Copley Sq. (p. 267). The website and booths post which shows are available for sale each day. (☎ 262-8632; www.artsboston.org. Half-price tickets go on sale daily 10am. Cash only.)

THEATER

Boston's tiny two-block Theater District, near T: Boylston, west of Chinatown, was once the nation's premier pre-Broadway tryout area. Today it's a stop for tour-

NEW ENGLAND

ing Broadway and West End productions, not to mention a lively nightlife district. The **Charles Playhouse,** 74 Warrenton St., is home to the whodunit *Shear Madness* and the dazzling performance art of Blue Man Group. (*Shear:* ☎426-5225; $34. Blue Man: ☎426-6912. $43-53. Box office open M-Tu 10am-6pm, W-Th 10am-7pm, F 10am-6pm, Sa 10am-9pm, Su 11am-4pm. Half-price student rush tickets often available from 10am on day of show. Volunteer to usher Blue Man Group and watch for free—call at least 5 days in advance.) The giant **Wang Center,** 265 Tremont St., hosts Broadway shows and other productions. (☎482-9393; www.wangcenter.org. Box office open M-Sa 10am-6pm. Tickets $20-90; student discounts available for some shows.) For more avant-garde productions, check out the **Boston Center for the Arts,** 539-551 Tremont St. (☎426-5000), near T: Back Bay.

CLASSICAL MUSIC

Modeled on the world's most acoustically perfect music hall (the Gewandhaus in Leipzig, Germany), **Symphony Hall,** 301 Massachusetts Ave., T: Symphony, is home to both the **Boston Symphony Orchestra (BSO)** and its light-hearted sister, the **Boston Pops.** Every Fourth of July, the Pops gives a free evening concert at the **Hatch Shell,** near T: Charles/MGH, with patriotic music, fireworks, and Tchaikovsky's *1812 Overture*—with real cannons. (☎266-1200. Box office open M-F 10am-7pm and Sa 10am-6pm. BSO: season runs Sept.-Apr. Tickets $27-105. Rush Tu and Th 5pm, F 9pm; $8. Pops: season runs May-June. Tickets $18-130.)

SPORTS

While the sights along the Freedom Trail testify to Boston's Revolutionary roots, the city's true heart beats at the storied **Fenway Park;** the home-team Boston Red Sox finally won baseball's World Series in 2004 for the first time since 1918. The nation's oldest, smallest, and most expensive baseball park, Fenway is also home to the Green Monster (the left field wall) and one of only two manual scoreboards left in the major leagues (the other is at Chicago's Wrigley Field; p. 526). Get tickets from the **Ticket Office,** 4 Yawkey Way, T: Kenmore. (☎482-4769. Bleachers $12-23, grandstands $27-45, field boxes $45-90.) The **TD Banknorth Garden,** 50 Causeway St.; T: North Station, formerly the FleetCenter, was built on the site of the legendary Boston Garden and hosts concerts and games for basketball's **Celtics** and hockey's **Bruins.** (☎624-1750. Box office open M-F 10am-5pm. Celtics $10-140. Bruins $19-99.) At the newly-built **Gillette Stadium** in Foxborough, the 2003 and 2004 Super Bowl champion **New England Patriots** grind it out on the gridiron from September to January (www.patriots.com).

Run every Patriot's Day (3rd M in Apr.), the **Boston Marathon** (www.bostonmarathon.org), the nation's oldest foot race and one of Boston's greatest sporting traditions, is a 26.2 mi. run that starts in Hopkinton, MA, in the west, passes over "Heartbreak Hill," and ends amid much hoopla at Copley Sq. The **Head of the Charles** (www.hocr.org), the world's largest crew regatta, has beckoned preppy throngs to the river banks every October since 1965.

◪ NIGHTLIFE

Before you set out to paint the town red, there are a few things to keep in mind. Boston bars and clubs are notoriously strict about age requirements (usually 21+), so bring back-up ID. While bars are easy to stumble upon, dance clubs are scarcer. Landsdowne St. is where the most popular clubs reside, but changes are being made. Avalon and Axis are set to merge, with construction to be completed by spring 2008. Puritanical zoning laws require that all nightlife shuts down by 2am. The T stops running at 12:30am, so bring extra cash for the taxi ride home.

BARS AND PUBS

Boston's large student population means the city is filled with countless great bars and pubs. Most tourists stick to the various faux Irish pubs around **Downtown,** while the **Theater District** is the premier after-dark destination of the city's international elite. The shamelessly yuppie meat markets on Back Bay's **Boylston Street** are also popular.

Bukowski's Tavern, 50 Dalton St. (☎437-9999), in Back Bay off Boylston St., 1 block south of T: Hynes/ICA. Named for boozer poet Charles Bukowski, the casual ambience and over 99 bottles of beer on the wall is a welcome respite from Boylston St.'s trendy chic. Pints $3-20. 21+. No cover. Open M-Sa 11:30am-2am, Su noon-2am. Cash only.

Mantra/OmBar, 52 Temple Pl. (☎542-8111), in downtown. T: Temple Pl. Seductive. Scandalous. Incomprehensible. And that's just the bathroom, which has 1-way mirrored stalls and ice cubes in the urinals. A pricey Franco-Indian fusion restaurant by day, Mantra becomes OmBar by night, with a bar in the bank vault downstairs and a plush, smoke-free "hookah den" upstairs. Mixed drinks $9. Open M-Sa 5:30pm-2am.

Emily's Nightclub Boston, 48 Winter St. (☎423-3649), in downtown. T: Park St. Top 40 dance club that was catapulted to fame as the top hangout for the cast of MTV's *Real World: Boston.* Beer $4. Cover around $5. 21+. Open Tu-Th 5pm-midnight, F-Sa 5pm-2am.

Purple Shamrock, 1 Union St. (☎227-2060), in downtown. From T: Government Ctr., walk through City Hall Plaza to Congress St. Popular with professionals winding down after work and college kids preparing for a night on the town. If you're feeling decadent, try the sinfully sweet Chocolate Cake Martini ($8). Karaoke Tu starts 9-10pm. 21+ after 9pm. Cover Th-Sa $5. Open M-Sa 11:30am-2am, Su 11am-2am.

The Kells, 161 Brighton Ave. (☎782-9082; www.thekells.com). This popular bar corners the hard-to-find Irish-pub-slash-Asian-food niche. Sample the tasty kung pow chicken ($8) with a Guinness ($4.75). Doubles as a classy dance club, where you can boogie on 2 floors and schmooze at the bar. Open daily 4pm-2am. Kitchen closes M-F and Su 1am, Sa 2am.

DANCE CLUBS

Boston is a town for pubbers, not clubbers. The city's few clubs are on or near Kenmore Sq.'s **Lansdowne Street,** near T: Kenmore. Nightclubs often card by night; different clubs have different themed nights, but if you are going to a dance club (i.e. not a concert) you're out of luck if you're under 21. Students report that this is sporadically enforced, and clubs can get written permission to extend the age limit for a special event. Check listings for more thorough information, and also check the website—themes and nights change often in the club world.

Avalon, 15 Lansdowne St. (☎262-2424; www.avalonboston.com). The flashy, trashy grand dame of the club scene, and the closest Puritanical Boston gets to Ibiza. World-class DJs, amazing light shows, gender-bending cage dancers, and throngs of hotties pack the giant dance floor. Cover $10-15. Open Tu-Sa 11pm-2am, Su 11pm-2pm.

Gypsy Bar, 116 Boylston St. (☎482-7799; http://gypsybarboston.com), in the Theater District. T: Boylston. Gypsy Bar has quickly become one of Boston's uber-trendy socialite nightspots, with top 40 and house. The opulent interior is especially popular with international students and locals yearning for that exotic foreign student hook-up. The 4 bars mean easy access to your next drink, and while the prices may make you think again, Gypsy Bar makes for a fun splurge and a classy night out. Cover W $15, F-Sa $10. Bar open W-Sa 5pm-2am. Club open W and F-Sa 10pm-2am.

Sophia's, 1270 Boylston St. (☎351-7001). From T: Kenmore, walk down Brookline Ave., turn left onto Yawkey Way, then right onto Boylston St. Far from Lansdowne St. in distance and style, Sophia's is a fiery Latin dance club with 4 floors of Latin music from a mix of live bands and DJs. Trendy, international crowd. Cover $10; no cover before 9:30pm W-Th and Sa. Open Tu-Sa 6pm-2am.

Axis, 13 Lansdowne St. (☎262-2437). Smaller and less crowded than Avalon, but with a similar college crowd. M "alternative styles" night, which is sometimes highlighted by amateur stripping contests. F feature mash-ups, classics, and top-20 hits. Cover $10-20. Open M and Th-Sa 10pm-2am. Tired of the dance floor? Chill upstairs in the chic lounge **ID.** 19+. Cover $15. Open Th-Sa 10pm-2am.

LIVE MUSIC

Boston's live music scene is impressive—no surprise for the town that gave the world rockin' acts like Aerosmith and the Dropkick Murphys. The best acts often play across the river in **Cambridge** (p. 273). **Wally's Café,** 427 Massachusetts Ave., at Columbus Ave., is in the South End. Turn right out of T: Massachusetts Ave. or T: Symphony. Established in 1947, Wally's is Boston's longest-standing jazz joint, and has only improved with age. (☎424-1408. 21+. No cover. Live music daily 9pm-2am. Cash only.) **Paradise Rock Club,** 969 Commonwealth Ave., is visible from T: Pleasant St. This smoky, spacious venue has hosted rock acts including U2 and Soul Asylum. (☎562-8800. 18+. Cover $12-25. Call for schedule and hours.)

GLBT NIGHTLIFE

For up-to-date listings of gay and lesbian nightlife, pick up a free copy of the South End-based *Bay Windows*, a gay weekly available everywhere, or check the lengthy listings in the free *Boston Phoenix* and *Improper Bostonian*. The **South End's** bars and late-night restaurants, accessible from T: Back Bay, are all gay-friendly (sorry, ladies, these are mostly spots for the boys). The sports bar **Fritz,** 26 Chandler St. (☎482-4428), and divey **The Eagle,** 520 Tremont St. (☎542-4494), are exclusively for gay men. Also check out **Jacques Cabaret,** 79 Broadway (☎426-8902). In Fenway is the all-encompassing **Ramrod,** 1254 Boylston St. (☎266-2986), a leather-and-levis spot that has spawned a non-fetish dance club known as **Machine.** Popular gay nights at straight clubs include Avalon's Sunday bash (p. 271)—preceded by the early evening "T-Dance" at **Vapor**—and sassy drag night at Axis on Monday (p. 272). Lesbians flock to **Jamaica Plain's** bookstores and cafes, many of which are queer-owned, and to lesbian-friendly **Midway Café,** 3496 Washington St. (☎524-9038), south of T: Green St. Also popular is **Tribe** at **Felt Nightclub,** 533 Washington St. (☎350-5555; www.tribenightclub.com. Women only every Th 9pm-2am.)

◪ OUTDOOR ACTIVITIES

For a major urban center, Boston has a number of outdoor opportunities, thanks largely to the **Emerald Necklace,** a string of nine parks ringing the city. Designed by Frederick Law Olmsted (1822-1903), who also created New York City's Central Park (p. 103) and San Francisco's Golden Gate Park (p. 852), the Necklace runs from Boston Common and the Public Garden along the Commonwealth Avenue Mall, the Back Bay Fens and Riverway, Jamaica Plain's Olmsted Park, Jamaica Pond, and Arnold Arboretum (p. 268), ending at far-flung Franklin Park.

The **Charles River** separates Boston from Cambridge. Though swimming in the unsettling grimy water is strongly discouraged, runners, bikers, and skaters crowd the **Charles River Esplanade** park, which runs along its banks. The Esplanade is home to the **Hatch Shell,** where Boston's renowned Fourth of July festivities take place. Rent watercraft from **Charles River Canoe and Kayak,** beyond Eliot Bridge near T: Riverside. (☎965-5110. Open Apr.-Oct. M-F 10am-sunset, Sa-Su 9am-sunset; Oct.-Mar. by appointment. Canoes $13 per hr., $52 per day; kayaks $14/56.)

Serious hikers should consider the **Harbor Islands National Park,** made up of the roughly 30 wooded islands floating in Boston Harbor. The most popular islands include Lovell's (with the islands' best beach) and Bumpkin (a wildberry paradise). **Boston Harbor Cruises** runs ferries from Long Wharf at T: Aquarium to George's Island. (☎227-4321; www.bostonislands.com. Open May-Oct. daily 9am-sunset, hours vary by island. Ferries run daily July-Aug. on the hr. 9am-5pm; May-June and Sept.-Oct. 10am, 2, 4pm. Ferry ticket $10, seniors $7, children $6; includes free water taxis to 5 other islands from George's Island.)

🔁 DAYTRIPS FROM BOSTON

CAMBRIDGE ☎ 617

Separated from Boston only by the Charles River, Cambridge (pop. 100,000), is often called Boston's "Left Bank" for its liberal politics and bohemian flair. The city has thrived as an intellectual hotbed since the colonial era, when it became the home of prestigious Harvard University, the nation's first college. The Massachusetts Institute of Technology (MIT), the country's foremost school for science and technology, moved here in the early 20th century. Cambridge counterculture has relaxed since its 60s heyday, but the city remains vibrant, with tons of bookstores and coffeeshops, a large student population, great food and lively nightlife.

🔳🔁 ORIENTATION AND PRACTICAL INFORMATION. Cambridge is easily reached by public transit—it's just a 10min. T ride from downtown Boston. Cambridge's main artery, **Massachusetts Avenue ("Mass Ave."),** runs above the T's Red Line, which makes stops along the street. The **Kendall/MIT** stop is just across the river from Boston, near MIT's campus. The Red Line continues to: **Central Square,** a bar-hopper's paradise; **Harvard Square,** the city's chaotic heart; and largely residential **Porter Square.** Harvard Sq. sits at the intersection of Mass. Ave., Brattle St., JFK St., and Dunster St. The **Cambridge Office for Tourism** runs a booth outside T: Harvard with plenty of maps and info. (☎441-2884; www.cambridge-usa.org. Open M-Sa 9am-5pm, Su 10am-5pm. Hours may vary.) **Internet Access: Adrenaline Zone,** 40 Brattle St., in Harvard Sq. (☎876-1314. $5 per hr. Open M-Th and Su 11am-11pm, F-Sa 11am-midnight.) **Post Office:** 770 Mass. Ave. (☎876-0550), in Central Sq., and 125 Mt. Auburn St. (☎876-3883), in Harvard Sq. (Both open M-F 7:30am-6pm, Sa 7:30am-3pm.) **Postal Code:** 02138.

🔲 FOOD. Cambridge is a United Nations of ethnic eateries, from Mexican to Tibetan. Most visitors stick to the spots in Harvard Sq. Indian restaurants come a dime-a-dozen in Cambridge, and most offer a budget-friendly all-you-can-eat lunch buffets ($7-9, served daily 11:30am-3pm). 🔳**Tanjore ❷,** 18 Eliot St., off JFK St., stands out from the crowd with its encyclopedic menu and range of regional specialties. (☎868-1900. Open daily 11am-3pm and 5-11pm. AmEx/D/MC/V.) 🔳**Darwin's Limited ❷,** 148 Mt. Auburn St., is a 5min. walk from Harvard Sq. proper. Exit the T onto Brattle St. and turn right at the Harvard Square Hotel onto Mt. Auburn St.; it's six blocks up on the left. The bohemian staff crafts Boston's best gourmet sandwiches ($5.75-8), named after nearby streets. (☎354-5233. Open M-Sa 6:30am-9pm, Su 7am-9pm. V.) 🔳**Felipe's Taqueria ❶,** 83 Mt. Auburn St., is quickly becoming a Harvard Sq. institution with wicked cheap Mexican grub—filling chicken burritos, decadent *carnitas* quesadillas, and tacos are served with fresh ingredients by a friendly staff. (☎354-9944. Open M-W and Su 10am-midnight, Th-Sa 11am-2am. Cash only.) **Punjabi Dhaba ❷,** 225 Hampshire St., in Inman Sq., gives it a run for its rupees, offering a cheap menu of spicy dishes. (☎547-8272. Veggie dishes $5. Combos $8. Open daily noon-midnight. MC/V.) For over 40 years, **Bartley's Burger Cottage ❸**, 1246 Mass Ave., has served some of the area's juiciest burgers, named after famous folk. Try the Ted Kennedy, a "plump liberal" burger. (☎354-6559. Burgers $5-12. Open M-Sa 11am-9pm. Cash only.) **Emma's Pizza ❷**, 40 Hampshire St., opposite the 1 Kendall Sq. complex, dishes up gourmet pizza with toppings like roasted sweet potatoes and rosemary chicken. (☎864-8534. 6-slice 12 in. pies $8; 8-slice 16 in. pies $11. Open M-W and Su 11am-10pm, Th-Sa 11am-11pm. AmEx/MC/V.)

◙ SIGHTS. Harvard Sq. is, of course, named after **Harvard University.** The free student-led tours offered by **Harvard Events and Information,** Holyoke Center Arcade (across Dunster St. from the T), are the best way to tour the university's dignified red-brick-and-ivy campus and learn about its history. (☎495-1573; www.harvard.edu. Open M-Sa 9am-5pm. Tours Sept.-mid-May M-F 10am and 2pm, Sa 2pm; June to mid-Aug. M-Sa 10, 11:15am, 2, and 3:15pm.) **Harvard Yard,** just off Mass Ave., is the heart of undergraduate life and the site of Commencement. The massive **Harry Elkins Widener Memorial Library,** in Harvard Yard, houses nearly 5 million of Harvard's 13.3 million books, making it the world's largest university library collection. Harvard's many museums are well worth a visit. The **Arthur M. Sackler Museum,** 485 Broadway, at Quincy St. just off Mass. Ave., has four floors of East Asian, pre-Columbian, Islamic, and Indian treasures. Across the street, the **Fogg Art Museum,** 32 Quincy St., offers a small survey of North American and European work from the Middle Ages to the early 20th century, with a strong Impressionist collection and several van Gogh portraits. Inside the Fogg, the excellent **Busch-Reisinger Museum** is dedicated to modern German work. (All 3 museums: ☎495-9400; www.artmuseums.harvard.edu. Open M-Sa 10am-5pm, Su 1-5pm. $5, students and seniors $4, under 18 free. W and Sa 10am-noon free.) Next door, the Le Corbusier-designed **Carpenter Center,** 24 Quincy St., displays the hottest contemporary art by both students and professionals. The **Harvard Film Archive (HFA),** in the basement of the Carpenter Center, has a great art-house film series. Schedules are posted outside the door. (Carpenter: ☎495-3251. Open M-Sa 9am-11pm, Su noon-11pm. Galleries free. HFA: ☎495-4700. $7, students and seniors $5.) The **Harvard Museum of Natural History,** 26 Oxford St., has exhibits on botany, zoology, and geology, including the famous **Glass Flowers**—over 3000 incredibly life-like, life-sized glass models of plants. (☎495-3045. Open daily 9am-5pm. $7.50, students and seniors $6, ages 3-18 $5. Su 9am-noon and Sept.-May W 3-5pm free.)

Kendall Sq. (T: Kendall/MIT) is home to the **Massachusetts Institute of Technology (MIT),** the world's leading institution dedicated to the study of science. Free campus tours begin at the **MIT Info Center,** 77 Mass. Ave., in Lobby 7/Small Dome building, and include visits to the Chapel and Kresge Auditorium, which touches the ground in only three places. (☎253-1000; www.mit.edu. Tours M-F 10am and 2pm.) The ◙**MIT Museum,** 265 Mass. Ave., features technological wonders in dazzling multimedia exhibitions. Highlights include a gallery of "hacks" (elaborate, if nerdy, pranks) and the world's largest hologram collection. (☎253-4444. Open Tu-F 10am-5pm, Sa-Su noon-5pm. $5; college students with ID, seniors, and ages 5-18 $2.)

◙◙ ENTERTAINMENT AND NIGHTLIFE. Harvard Sq.'s ◙**Club Passim,** 47 Palmer St., at Church St., off Mass. Ave., is a folk music legend: a 17-year-old Joan Baez premiered here, and Bob Dylan played between sets. Countless acoustic acts have hit this intimate venue before making it big. (☎492-5300. Shows 7-11:30pm. Tu open mic 7pm. Cover $8-25.) Some of the Boston area's best live music spots are in Central Sq., T: Central. **The Middle East,** 472-480 Mass. Ave. (☎864-3278), and **T.T. the Bear's Place,** 10 Brookline St. (☎492-2327), at Mass. Ave., feature live music every night from the nation's hottest indie rock and hip-hop acts.

On weekend nights, **Harvard Square** is equal parts gathering place, music hall, and three-ring circus, with tourists, locals, students, and pierced suburban punks enjoying the varied street performers. Harvard Sq. abounds with bars, but Cambridge's best nightlife options are in **Central Square,** a bar-hopper's heaven. Most bars are open until 1am, and some stay open until 2am on the weekends. ◪**The People's Republik,** 878 Mass. Ave., keeps the proletariat happy with cheap beer and cheeky chalkboards enticing passersby to drop in for a drink with adages like "Drink beer—it's cheaper than gasoline." (☎491-6969. Beer $2-4. Mixed drinks $4-4.50. 21+. No cover. Open M-W and Su noon-1am, Th-Sa noon-2am. Cash only.) The harem-like **Enormous Room,** 567 Mass. Ave., unmarked save an outline of a bull elephant on the window, is too seductive to resist. Amidst sultry, arabesque lighting and floor pillows for lounging, a trendier-than-thou crowd jives to music from a hidden DJ. "Enormous plates" of appetizers ($14, vegetarian $12) include hummus, grape leaves, salmon skewers, and anything else that strikes the chef's fancy. (☎491-5550. Beer $4. Mixed drinks $6-9. 21+. Cover $3 after 10pm. Open M-F 5:30pm-1am, Sa-Su 7pm-1am. Cash only.) A typical pub from the outside, **The Phoenix Landing,** 512 Mass. Ave., keeps a lively college crowd dancing with some of the area's best electric and downtempo grooves. (☎576-6260. 21+, W 19+. Cover $3-5. Open M-W and Su 11:30am-1am, Th-Sa 11:30am-2am.)

LEXINGTON AND CONCORD ☎781

"Stand your ground. Don't fire unless fired upon, but if they mean to have a war, let it begin here," said Captain John Parker to the colonial Minutemen on April 19, 1775. Although no one is certain who fired the "shot heard 'round the world," the American Revolution did indeed erupt in downtown Lexington. The site of the fracas lies in the center of town at **Battle Green,** where a Minuteman statue stands guard. Across the street, the **Buckman Tavern,** 1 Bedford St. (☎862-5598), housed the Minutemen on the eve of their decisive battle. The nearby **Hancock-Clarke House,** 36 Hancock St. (☎861-0928), and the **Munroe Tavern,** 1332 Mass. Ave. (☎862-1703), also played significant roles in the birth of the revolution. All three can be seen on a 30min. tour that runs continuously. (All open Apr.-Oct. M-Sa 10am-5pm, Su 1-5pm; hours subject to change, call ahead. $5 per site, ages 6-16 $3; combo ticket for all 3 $12/7.) The **Museum of Our National Heritage,** 33 Marrett Rd. (Rte. 2A), emphasizes a historical approach to understanding popular American life, especially at the time of the Revolution. (☎861-6559; www.monh.org. Open M-Sa 10am-5pm, Su noon-5pm. Free.) The road from Boston to Lexington is a straight shot up Mass Ave. from Boston or Cambridge; the **Minuteman Trail** is an excellent bike trail to downtown Lexington (access off Mass Ave. in Arlington, or Alewife St. in Cambridge). MBTA bus #62/76 from T: Alewife runs to Lexington (20min., $0.90). A model and description of the Battle of Lexington adorns the **Visitors Center,** 1875 Mass. Ave., opposite Battle Green. (☎862-2480. Open Apr.-Nov. daily 9am-5pm; Dec.-Mar. M-Sa 10am-4pm.)

Nearby Concord was the site of the 2nd conflict of the American Revolution, and is famous both for its military history and its status as a 19th-century intellectual center. The period rooms at the **Concord Museum,** 200 Lexington Rd., on the Cambridge Turnpike, move through Concord's three centuries of history. Highlights include the original lamp from Paul Revere's midnight ride and Henry David Thoreau's bed, desk, and chair. (☎978-369-9609. Open June-Aug. daily 9am-5pm; Sept.-Dec. M-Sa 9am-5pm, Su noon-5pm; Jan.-Mar. M-Sa 11am-4pm, Su 1-4pm; Apr.-May M-Sa 9am-5pm, Su noon-5pm. $8, students and seniors $7, ages 5-18 $3.) Down the road from the museum, the **Orchard House,** 399 Lexington Rd., was once home to the multi-talented Alcotts, whose daughter Louisa May wrote *Little Women.* (☎978-369-4118. Open Apr.-Oct. M-Sa 10am-4:30pm, Su 1-4:30pm; Nov.-Mar. M-F

NEW ENGLAND

11am-3pm, Sa 10am-4:30pm, Su 1-4:30pm. Entry by guided tour only. $8, students and seniors $7, ages 6-17 $5; families $20.) Farther down the road lies **Wayside,** 455 Lexington Rd., the former residence of the Alcotts and Hawthornes. (☎978-369-6975. Open for tours June-Aug. Tu-Th 2 and 4pm, Sa-Su 11am, 1:30, 3, and 4:30pm. $4.) Today, Alcott, Hawthorne, Emerson, and Thoreau reside on "Author's Ridge" in the **Sleepy Hollow Cemetery** on Rte. 62, three blocks from the center.

The Battle of Concord, the 2nd battle of the revolution, was fought at the **Old North Bridge.** From the parking lot, a 5min. walk brings visitors to the **North Bridge Visitors Center,** 174 Liberty St., to learn about the town's history, especially its involvement in the Revolutionary War. The **Minuteman National Historical Park,** off Rte. 2A between Concord and Lexington, best explored along the adjacent 5mi. **Battle Road Trail,** includes an impressive **Visitors Center** that organizes battle reenactments and screens a multimedia presentation on the "Road to Revolution." (☎978-369-6993. Off Rte. 2A between Concord and Lexington. Open daily Oct.-Nov. 9am-4pm; reduced hours in winter.) Concord, north of Boston, is served by the Fitchburg commuter rail train ($5) that runs from T: North Station.

WALDEN POND   ☎978

In 1845, Thoreau retreated 1½ mi. south of Concord "to live deliberately, to front only the essential facts of life" (though the harsh essence was eased somewhat by his mother's home cooking; she lived within walking distance of his cabin). In 1845, he published his thoughts on his time here in *Walden,* one of the major works of the Transcendentalist movement. The **Walden Pond State Reservation,** 915 Walden St., off Rte. 126, draws picnickers, swimmers, and boaters. No camping, pets, or flotation devices allowed. (☎369-3254. Open daily 8am-dusk. Parking $5.)

SALEM   ☎978

Although Salem has more to offer than witch kitsch, its infamous past has spawned a Halloween-based tourist trade that culminates in the month-long **Haunted Happenings** festival in October (www.hauntedhappenings.org). The **Salem Witch Museum,** 19½ Washington Sq. N, gives a multimedia presentation detailing the history of the witch trials of 1692. It also has an exhibit on scapegoating throughout history. (☎744-1692. Open daily July-Aug. 10am-7pm, Sept.-June 10am-5pm; extended hours in Oct. $6.50, seniors $6, ages 6-14 $4.50.) Engraved stones commemorate the trials' 20 victims at the **Witch Trials Memorial,** off Charter St. next to the Old Burying Point Cemetery. The **Witch House,** 310½ Essex St., was owned by witch trial judge Jonathan Corwin and is the only remaining building in Salem with direct links to the trials. (☎744-0180. Open daily Mar. to early Nov. 10am-5pm; extended hours in Oct. $7, seniors $6, ages 6-14 $4. AAA discount $1.)

Escape the witch frenzy at the recently renovated and expanded ◪**Peabody Essex Museum,** on the corner of Essex and New Liberty St., itself worth the trip to Salem. The museum presents objects and art in their cultural contexts, including excellent exhibits of maritime, Asian export, and American decorative art. The museum's prize jewel is Yin Yu Tang, a Qing Dynasty merchant's house that was relocated piece by piece from China. (☎745-9500 or 866-745-1876; www.pem.org. Open daily 10am-5pm. $13, seniors $11, students $9, ages 16 and under free. Yin Yu Tang requires timed tickets, free with admission.) The **House of the Seven Gables,** 54 Turner St., became famous after the release of Nathaniel Hawthorne's gothic romance of the same name. (☎744-0991. Open daily July-Oct. 10am-7pm; Nov.-Dec. and mid-Jan. to June 10am-5pm. Closed early Jan. Entry by 30min. guided tour only. $11, seniors and AAA members $10, ages 5-12 $7.25.)

The **Salem Maritime National Historic Site Visitors Center,** 2 New Liberty St., has free maps. (☎740-1650. Open daily 9am-5pm.) Salem, 15 mi. northeast of Boston, is accessible by the Newburyport/Rockport commuter rail train (30min., $3.75) from

T: North Station, by MBTA bus #450 or 455 (45min., $3.45) from T: Wonderland, or by car from I-95 or U.S. 1 N to Rte. 128 and Rte. 114. **Area Code:** 978.

PLYMOUTH ☎508

The Pilgrims' first step onto the New World was not actually at Plymouth—they stopped first at Provincetown (p. 280), then left because the soil was inadequate. **Plymouth Rock** is a small stone that has dubiously been identified as the rock on which the Pilgrims disembarked the second time. A symbol of liberty during the American Revolution, it has since moved three times before ending up beneath a portico on Water St., at the foot of North St. After several vandalizations and one dropping (in transit), it's cracked and under "tight" security.

Three miles south of town off Rte. 3A, the historical theme park ◙**Plymoth Plantation** recreates the Pilgrims' early settlement. Costumed actors carry out their daily tasks in the **Pilgrim Village,** while **Hobbamock's Homesite** represents a Native American village of the same period. (☎746-1622. Open Mar.-Nov. daily 9am-5pm. $21, seniors $19, ages 6-12 $12.) Docked off Water St., the **Mayflower II** is a scale replica of the Pilgrims' vessel and is staffed by actors to recapture the atmosphere of the original ship. (Open Mar.-Nov. daily 9am-5pm. $8, seniors $7, ages 6-12 $6. Both sights $24, students and seniors $21, ages 6-12 $14.)

Plymouth, 40 mi. southeast of Boston, is best explored by car; take Exit 6A from Rte. 3, off I-93. The Plymouth/Kingston commuter rail **train** goes from T: North Station to the Cordage Park Station (45min., 3-4 per day, $6). Plymouth and Brockton Bus (☎746-0378; www.p-b.com) runs **buses** from T: South Station to the Exit 5 Info Center. (45min.; $10, seniors $8.) From the info center and Cordage Park Station, catch a local GATRA bus ($1, seniors and children $0.50) to Plymouth Center. The **Plymouth Visitors Center** is at 170 Water St. (☎747-7533 or 800-872-1620; www.visit-plymouth.com. Open M-F 8am-4pm.)

CAPE COD AND ISLANDS ☎508

In his book *Cape Cod*, Henry David Thoreau wrote: "[the Cape] is wholly unknown to the fashionable world, and probably will never be agreeable to them." Needless to say, Thoreau was wrong. This thin strip of land, now one of New England's premier vacation destinations, draws droves of tourists with its charming towns and sun-drenched landscapes—everything from sandy beaches to cranberry bogs. Though parts of the Cape are famous for their frolicking blue-bloods and sky-high prices, it can be a good choice for budget travelers, thanks in large part to abundant shoreline activities and excellent hostelling and camping options.

▪ ORIENTATION

Stretching out into the Atlantic Ocean south of Boston, Cape Cod resembles a flexed arm, with **Falmouth** and **Woods Hole** at its armpit, **Hyannis** at its tricep, **Chatham** at its elbow, the **National Seashore** tattooed on its forearm, and **Provincetown** at its clenched fist. The southern islands **Martha's Vineyard** (p. 282) and **Nantucket** (p. 285) are accessible by ferries from Woods Hole or Hyannis. **Upper Cape** refers to the suburbanized area closer to the mainland. Proceeding eastward away from the mainland and curving up along the Cape, you travel "down-Cape" through **Mid-Cape** (where two hostels are located, near **Eastham** and **Truro**) to the **Lower Cape** and the National Seashore. In the summer, "Cape traffic" is hellish; most vacationers drive down on Friday and return Sunday afternoon, so avoid traveling then.

Cycling is the best way to travel the Cape's terrain. The Cape has many trails, and the excellent *Cape Cod Bike Book* ($3) is available at most Cape bookstores.

The 135 mi. **Boston-Cape Cod Bikeway** connects Boston to Provincetown, and scenic trails line either side of the **Cape Cod Canal,** in the National Seashore, and the 25 mi. **Cape Cod Rail Trail** from Dennis to Wellfleet. For discount coupons, pick up a free *Official 2007 Guide to Cape Cod* or *Cape Cod Best Read Guide* available at most Cape info centers.

FALMOUTH AND WOODS HOLE   ☎508

Coming from Boston, Falmouth and Woods Hole are the 1st true Cape towns daytrippers encounter. Unlike other places on the Cape, these towns sustain a decent-sized year-round population and have less of a touristy feel, since most people bypass them to drive farther up the Cape or catch the ferry to Nantucket or Martha's Vineyard. The beach reigns as the main attraction, but on hot days, it's hard to find the sand in the sea of umbrellas. Check out **Chapoquoit,** south of Old Silver, on the western shore of North Falmouth to avoid the crowds and relax peacefully. **Falmouth Heights** on the southern shore of Falmouth, along Grand Ave., provides soft sands and great swimming. **Old Silver** and **Stoney** beaches are also popular. At the end of Water St., the **Woods Hole Science Aquarium** has two playful harbor seals outside and lots of local sealife swimming in indoor tanks. (☎495-2001. Open Tu-Sa 11am-4pm. Free.) Lodgings are plentiful and nearly identical. For diet-busting fried seafood ($5-12), check out the lively **Clam Shack ❷,** 227 Clinton Ave., an always-busy spot right on the water. (☎540-7758. Open late May-early Sept. daily 11:30am-7:45pm. Cash only.) Enjoy an enchanted evening at the **Firefly ❸,** 271 Main St., with wood-grilled pizza, a sleek bar, and frequent live entertainment. (☎548-7953. Entrees $8-20. Opens daily at 4:30pm and closes when patrons filter out. AmEx/D/MC/V.) After hours, don't miss **Captain Kidd,** 77 Water St., just after the drawbridge in Woods Hole. A local bar adorned with the wheels and props of old ships, local fishermen and tourists flock here for strong drinks and to watch boats motor by in the harbor. (☎548-8563. Open daily 11am-1am.) Bonanza (☎888-751-8800; www.bonanzabus.com) sends **buses** from Falmouth Bus Station, on Depot St., to Boston (1½hr., 12 per day, $19). Buses also go from Logan Airport and South Station in Boston to Falmouth and on to the ferry in Woods Hole.

HYANNIS   ☎508

Mostly a transportation hub (ferries to Nantucket depart from here) and industrial center, Hyannis offers less charm than the villages farther down the Cape. However, the town does boast a long Main St. lined with trendy stores, pubs, and motels. Hyannis's fame comes from its proximity to JFK's famous summer home in nearby Hyannisport, and its excellent beaches. **Kalmus Park Beach,** on Ocean St. in Hyannisport, is popular with windsurfers, while **Orrin Keyes Beach,** on Sea St., attracts more of a local crowd. **Veteran's Park Beach,** off Ocean St., is great for families. All have parking ($10), lifeguards, bath houses, snack bars, picnic areas, and wheelchair accessibility. The pride of the Hyannis industrial complex is the **Cape Cod Potato Chip Factory,** 100 Breeds Hill Rd. Tours trace the history and process of chip-making, and visitors are rewarded with a free bag of delicious kettle-cooked chips. (☎775-3358. Tours M-F 9am-5pm. Free.) Hyannis is full of cookie-cutter motels and inns. The immense **Hyannis Inn Motel ❸,** 473 Main St., has spacious rooms with cable TV and mini-fridges, a sauna, and an indoor swimming pool. (☎775-0255 or 800-922-8993. Open mid-Mar. to mid-Oct. Doubles $40-160. AmEx/D/MC/V.) Upscale seafood restaurants line Main St., with entrees averaging $12-20. For inexpensive, delicious sandwiches ($4-6), head to **Box Lunch ❶,** 357 Main St., a Cape Cod chain that serves rolled sandwich combos in cute little boxes. (☎790-5855. Open M-F 9am-6pm, Sa 10am-10pm, Su 10am-5pm. Cash only.) Plymouth & Brockton (☎746-0378) **buses** run from Boston's South Station to the new Hyannis Transportation Center, off Main St. (1½hr.; M-F 24 per day, Sa-Su 17 per day; $17).

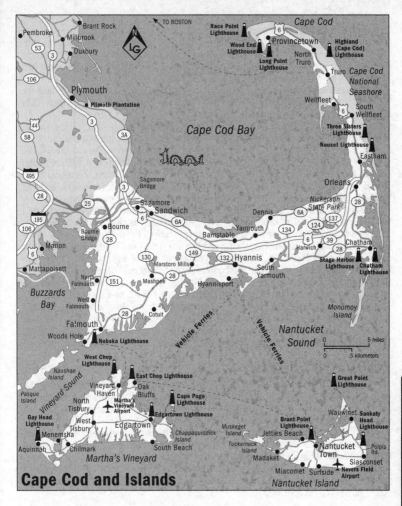

Cape Cod and Islands

CAPE COD NATIONAL SEASHORE ☎ 508

As early as 1825, the Cape had suffered so much damage at the hands of mankind
that the town of Truro required local residents to plant beach grass and keep their
cows off the dunes. These conservation efforts culminated in 1961, when the
National Park Service created the Cape Cod National Seashore. The seashore
includes much of the Lower and Outer Cape, from Provincetown south to
Chatham, and has six beaches: **Coast Guard** and **Nauset Light,** in Eastham; **Marconi,**
in Wellfleet; **Head of the Meadow,** in Truro; and **Race Point** and **Herring Cove,** in Provincetown. **Parking** at the beaches is expensive (summer Sa-Su and low-season holidays $10 per day). A $30 pass is the best deal, covering all areas in the park for an
entire season. Among the best of the seashore's 11 self-guided **nature trails** are the
Great Island Trail and the **Atlantic White Cedar Swamp Trail.** The moderately difficult

Great Island Trail, in Wellfleet, traces an 8 mi. loop through pine forests and grassy marshes, rewarding trekkers with panoramic views of the bay and Provincetown. The most popular trail, the 1¼ mi. Atlantic White Cedar Swamp Trail, starts at Marconi Station in south Wellfleet and winds past swampy waters and under towering trees. There are also three bike trails: **Nauset Trail** (1½ mi.), **Head of the Meadow Trail** (2 mi.), and **Province Lands Trail** (5 mi.). Park rangers at the National Seashore's **Salt Pond Visitors Center,** at Salt Pond off Rte. 6 in Eastham, provide maps, schedules for guided tours, and additional information about the park. (☎255-3421. Open daily July-Aug. 9am-5pm; Sept.-June 9am-4:30pm.)

Camping in the National Seashore is illegal, but numerous private campgrounds are squeezed into the narrow space between Rte. 6 and the boundaries of the park. Two hostels on the seashore provide the most affordable accommodations on the Cape. With a beautiful private beach nearby and a spacious kitchen, ■**Truro Hostel (HI) ❶,** 111 N. Pamet Rd., in Truro, is a genuine treasure for budget travelers. From Rte. 6, take the Pamet Rd. Exit, which becomes N. Pamet Rd. (☎508-349-3889 or 888-901-2086. Free linen. Check-in 10am-10pm. Check-out 10am. Open late June-early Sept. Dorms $33-38, members $30-35. MC/V.) Eastham's **Mid-Cape Hostel (HI) ❶,** 75 Goody Hallet Dr., close to the bike path known as the **Cape Cod Rail Trail,** offers communal bungalow living in a woodsy location. From Rte. 6, take the Rock Harbor Exit at the Orleans Ctr. traffic circle, turn right onto Bridge Rd., then right again onto Goody Hallet Dr. By Plymouth & Brockton bus, ask the driver to let you off as close as possible, and call the hostel for the "short-cut" directions along bike paths. (☎255-2785 or 888-901-2085. Shared baths, kitchen, and barbecue facilities. 7-day max. stay. Open late May to mid-Sept. Dorms $28-32, members $25-229. MC/V.) Plymouth & Brockton (☎746-0378) runs **buses** from Boston's South Station through the towns on the seashore (2½ to 3 hr.), including Orleans ($23), Eastham ($24), and Truro ($26). To access the seashore by car, take Rte. 3 to Rte. 6 west, cross the Sagamore Bridge, and follow the signs.

PROVINCETOWN   ☎508

The Pilgrims' first landing site in 1620, Provincetown was a key fishing and whaling center in the 1800s. In the early 20th century, the town's popularity soared with resident artists and writers like Norman Mailer, Tennessee Williams, and Edward Hopper. Today, Provincetown's tradition of open-mindedness has attracted a large gay community, making it a premier destination for gay vacationers, who fill the town to capacity in summer. Locals and visitors rock the town during the annual **Carnival Week,** which augments everything fun about P-town. Though far from inexpensive, Provincetown has better options for outdoor activities, dining, and nightlife than most of Cape Cod. It's easily accessible by public transit and just as easily navigated on foot.

■■ **ORIENTATION AND PRACTICAL INFORMATION. Commercial Street,** the town's main drag—home to countless art galleries, novelty shops, and trendy bars and eateries—runs along the harbor, centered on **MacMillian Wharf. Bradford Street,** the other main street, runs parallel to Commercial St. one block inland. Standish St. divides P-town into the **East End** and **West End.** Take the Provincetown Shuttle (CCRTA) to outlying areas, including Herring Cove Beach and North Truro. Buy tickets on the bus or at the Chamber of Commerce. (☎800-352-7155. Operates late June-Aug. daily every hr. 7-9am, every 20min. 9am-12:30am. $1, seniors and ages 6-16 $0.50, under 6 free. Day pass $3; seniors, disabled, and children $1.50.) Plymouth & Brockton (☎746-0378) runs **buses** from Boston's South Station to Provincetown (3¼hr., $27). All but officially known as the "Fairy Ferry," Boston Harbor Cruises runs **catamarans** from Long Wharf, near T: Aquarium, in Boston. (☎617-

227-4321 or 877-733-9425; www.bostonharborcruises.com. 1½hr.; $45, seniors $40.) P-town Bikes, 42 Bradford St., rents **bikes** (☎487-8735; www.ptown-bikes.com. $10 per 2hr., $20 per day. Open daily 9am-6pm.) The **Provincetown Chamber of Commerce,** 307 Commercial St., is on MacMillian Wharf. (☎487-3424; www.ptownchamber.com. Open June-Sept. daily 9am-5pm; reduced hours in low season.) Head to the **Province Lands Visitors Center,** on Race Point Rd. off Rte. 6, for park info. (☎487-1256. Open May-Oct. daily 9am-5pm.) **Internet Access: Provincetown Public Library,** 330 Commercial St., has Wi-Fi. (☎487-7094. Open M and F 10am-5pm, Tu and Th noon-8pm, W 10am-8pm, Sa 10am-2pm, Su 1-5pm.) **Post Office:** 219 Commercial St. (☎487-3580. Open M-F 8:30am-5pm, Sa 9am-noon.) **Postal Code:** 02657.

▶ ACCOMMODATIONS. Provincetown teems with expensive lodging. **Sunset Inn ❺,** 142 Bradford St., the inspiration for Edward Hopper's painting *Rooms for Tourists,* offers an excellent location, simple, well-kept rooms with shared bath, and a "clothing optional" sundeck. (☎487-9810 or 800-965-1801. Rooms June-Sept. $90-165. Apr.-May and Oct. $50-120. D/MC/V.) Though the **Truro Hostel ❷** (p. 280) is infinitely better and just a few miles down the road, the only truly budget accommodation in P-town is **Outermost Hostel ❶,** 28 Winslow St., with five cramped cottages. (☎487-4378. Tiny kitchen for guest use. Linen $3. Key deposit $10. Reception 8-9:30am and 5:30-10pm. Open May to mid-Oct. Dorms $20. Cash only.) Excellent (and expensive) campgrounds border the dunes of the park. **Dunes Edge Campground ❶,** off Rte. 6, 1 mi. from Provincetown, has 100 wooded sites near the dunes. (☎487-9815. Reservations recommended 6 weeks in advance in summer. 2-person sites $38-46. Up to 4 additional people $14 each. V/MC.)

◗ FOOD. Sit-down meals in Provincetown are quite pricey. Fast-food joints line the Commercial St. extension (next to MacMillan Wharf) and farther west by the Aquarium Mall. Groceries are available at **Grand Union,** 28 Shankpainter Rd., in the West End. (☎487-4903. Open M-Sa 7am-11pm, Su 7am-10pm.) **Karoo Kafe ❷,** 338 Commercial St., is a self-described "fast food safari," serving up South African and Mediterranean favorites from falafel to tofu with peri-peri sauce. (☎487-6630. Most entrees $5-9. Open June to mid-Sept. M-F and Su 11am-8pm, Sa 11am-9pm; Mar.-May and Sept.-Nov. lunch hours only. D/MC/V.) Stop for some quick and delicious takeout at **Mojo's ❶,** 5 Ryder St., with a long list of surf and turf options that come at amazingly low prices. (☎487-3140. Open daily in summer 11am-11pm. Cash only.) **Tofu A Go-Go ❷,** 336 Commercial St., serves fresh vegetarian options on a balcony overlooking a sea of tourists. (☎487-6237. Entrees $5-12. Open June-Aug. M-Th 11am-4pm, F-Su 11am-9pm; call for hours Apr.-May and Sept.-Oct. Cash or traveler's check only.) **Café Edwidge ❸,** 333 Commercial St., serves American cuisine in a candlelit dining room adorned with local artwork. (☎487-4020. Breakfast $6-10. Dinner $8-22. Open late June-Aug. daily 8am-1pm and 6-10pm; mid-May to late June and Sept. to mid-Oct. Sa-Su 8am-1pm and 6-10pm. MC/V.)

◖◚ SIGHTS AND OUTDOOR ACTIVITIES. The **Pilgrim Monument,** the tallest granite structure in the US at 253 ft., and the **Provincetown Museum,** on High Pole Hill just north of the center of town, commemorate the Pilgrims' 1st landing. Hike up to the top of the Italian Renaissance-style tower for stunning views of the Cape and the Atlantic. (☎487-1310. Open daily July-Aug. 9am-6:15pm; Apr.-June and Sept.-Nov. 9am-4:15pm. $7, students and seniors $5, ages 4-12 $3.50, under 4 free.) A large bas-relief **monument,** in the small park at Bradford St. and Ryder St. behind the town hall, depicts the signing of the Mayflower Compact on November 11, 1620, in Provincetown Harbor.

The **National Seashore** (2 mi. from town) stretches out from Race Point Rd. with beaches, forests, and sand dunes. At **Race Point Beach,** waves roll in from the Atlantic, while **Herring Cove Beach,** at the west end of town, shelters calmer waters. The **Visitors Center** offers free daily guided tours and activities during the summer. Directly across from Snail Rd. on Rte. 6, an unlikely path leads to a world of **sand dunes;** look for shacks where writers like Tennessee Williams, Norman Mailer, and John Dos Passos spent their days. At the west end of Commercial St., the 1¼ mi. **Breakwater Jetty** takes you to a secluded peninsula, with two working lighthouses and the remains of a Civil War fort.

Provincetown seafarers have traded harpoons for cameras, but they still enjoy whale-hunting—whale watches rank among P-town's most popular attractions. Most companies guarantee whale sightings. A 3hr. tour averages $30-35, but grab discount coupons at the Chamber of Commerce. **Boston Harbor Cruises Whale Watch** (☎617-227-4321 or 877-733-9425), **Dolphin Fleet** (☎349-1900 or 800-826-9300), and **Portuguese Princess** (☎487-2651 or 800-422-3188) all leave from MacMillian Wharf.

■ **NIGHTLIFE.** Nightlife in P-town is almost completely gay- and lesbian-oriented. **Crown & Anchor,** 247 Commercial St., has a restaurant, two cabarets, the Wave video bar, and the techno-filled **Paramount Club,** where the boys flock nightly. (☎487-1430. Beer $3.50-4.50. Mixed drinks $4-8. Sa "Summer Camp." 21+. Cover $10; no cover for Wave. Open in summer daily 11pm-1am; low season Sa-Su 11pm-1am.) Founded in 1798, the **Atlantic House,** 6 Masonic Pl., just off Commercial St., still attracts its fair share of seamen with the low-key "little bar," the Leather & Levis "macho bar," and the "big room," where you, too, can be a dancing queen. (☎487-3821. Beer $3.50. Mixed drinks $4-10. 21+. Cover for dance club $10. Open daily 10pm-1am.) The major club for women is **Vixen,** 336 Commercial St., with liquor in the front and a dance floor out back. (☎487-6424. Beer $3. Mixed drinks $5-8. 21+. Cover $5. Bar open daily noon-1am. Club open daily 10pm-1am.)

MARTHA'S VINEYARD   ☎508

Martha's Vineyard is a favorite summertime escape, with New England's characteristic beaches, charm, and exorbitant prices. Since President Bill Clinton began summering here, "the Vineyard" has become one of the most popular vacation destinations for the region's socialites; in summer, the population swells from 15,000 to over 105,000. Savvy travelers might consider a weekend visit to the Vineyard in the spring or fall, when many private beaches are open and B&B prices plunge.

 THE WHEELS ON THE BUS. The bus system on Martha's Vineyard is easily the best way to navigate the island. The VTA schedule can be complicated, though, so it's a good idea to notify the driver of your intended destination, especially if you need to make a quick transfer. The drivers can often accommodate requests, especially if the route isn't crowded.

■ ■ **ORIENTATION AND PRACTICAL INFORMATION.** Six major towns and a smattering of smaller villages make up Martha's Vineyard. The rural towns of West Tisbury, Chilmark, and Aquinnah (Gay Head) take up the western side of the island, called **up-island** because sailors tack upwind to get to it. The three major **down-island** towns are Oak Bluffs, Edgartown, and Vineyard Haven (Tisbury). Only Oak Bluffs and Edgartown sell alcohol. Vineyard Haven has the main ferry port and the **Chamber of Commerce,** on Beach Rd., which has info on lodging, transportation, and island attractions. (☎693-0085. Open June-Oct. M-F 9am-5pm, Sa 10am-4pm, Su noon-4pm; Nov.-May M-F 9am-5pm, Sa 10am-2pm.)

The island is accessible by ferry or airplane only, but the latter is prohibitively expensive (flights begin at $130 each way). Bonanza Bus (☎888-751-8800; www.bonanzabus.com) runs **buses** from Boston's South Station to Woods Hole on Cape Cod (1½hr., $19), where the Steamship Authority (on Martha's Vineyard ☎693-9130, elsewhere 477-8600; www.steamshipauthority.com) sends 12-17 **ferries** per day to Vineyard Haven (45min.; daily 7am-9:30pm; $7, ages 5-12 $3.50, cars $65, bikes $3) and Oak Bluffs (45min., May-Oct. daily 10:15am-5:45pm, same prices as Vineyard Haven). Martha's Vineyard Regional Transit Authority (MVRTA) runs summer **shuttles** between and within the six towns on the island. (☎693-9440. $1 per town; day pass $6.) Pick up a free schedule and map of all 15 routes at the ferry terminal, Chamber of Commerce, or info booths. **Bikes** may seem like a scenic option, but parts of the island are outside of biking range. Anderson's, on Circuit Ave. in Oak Bluffs, has rentals. (☎693-9346. Bikes $20 per day, includes maps and helmet. Open daily July-Aug. 8am-6pm; Apr.-June and Sept.-Oct. 9am-5pm.) For a **taxi**, call AdamCab, ☎800-281-4462; Atlantic Cab, ☎877-477-8294. **Post Office:** 1 Lagoon Pond Rd., in Vineyard Haven. (☎693-2818. Open M-F 8:30am-5pm, Sa 9:30am-1pm.) **Postal Code:** 02568.

▌ ACCOMMODATIONS. ◙**Martha's Vineyard Hostel (HI) ❶**, on Edgartown-West Tisbury Rd., has the 74 cheapest beds on the island and serves as a base camp for travelers on bikes looking to explore the less-crowded beaches and wildlife preserves up-island. From Vineyard Haven, take VTA bus #3 to West Tisbury and then bus #6 to the hostel. (☎693-2665 or 888-901-2087. Lockers $0.75. Linen included. Open Apr.-Oct. Dorms $23-27, members $20-24. MC/V.) **Attleboro House ❹**, 42 Lake Ave., in Oak Bluffs, has a no-frills atmosphere in one of Oak Bluffs' famous gingerbread houses. (☎693-4346. Open June to mid-Sept. Doubles $90-140. Each additional person $15. AmEx/D/MC/V.) Reserve months in advance for **Martha's Vineyard Family Campground ❷**, 556 Edgartown Rd., just outside of Vineyard Haven, which has sites with hot showers, laundry, playground, and access to bike paths and bus routes. Call for directions and reservations. (☎693-3772; www.campmvfc.com. 2-person tent sites $46; RV sites $52. Up to 4 additional people $15 each.)

◘ FOOD. Vineyard food is mostly overpriced, but cheap lunch places dot Vineyard Haven and Oak Bluffs. ◙**Aquinnah Shop Restaurant ❺**, 27 Aquinnah Cir., in Aquinnah, serves excellent seafood and freshly brewed sun tea ($2.50) on a balcony atop the cliffs. The food here is rivaled only by the view.

(☎ 645-3867. Entrees $18-40. Seafood $12-15. Open July-Aug. daily 8am-9pm; Apr.-June and Sept.-Oct. M-Th 8am-3pm, F-Su 8am-sunset. AmEx/D/MC/V.) The island's tourists have made several excellent (but pricey) establishments very popular, including the **Black Dog** eateries (tavern and two bakeries in Vineyard Haven; ☎ 693-9223), **Mad Martha's** ice cream parlor (locations in Vineyard Haven, Oak Bluffs, and Edgartown; ☎ 693-5883), and **Murdick's Fudge**, which markets delicious homemade sweets (locations in Vineyard Haven, Oak Bluffs, and Edgartown; ☎ 888-553-8343). Some of the Vineyard's best restaurants lie outside the main towns, often sporting great views and better deals. ◪**The Bite ❷**, on Basin Rd. near the beach in Menemsha, features phenomenal service in a low-key setting, topped only by their decadent fried seafood and famous quahog chowder. (☎ 645-9239. Entrees $12-28. Open late May-early Oct. daily 11am-sunset. Cash only.) Straight from the 1700s, **Newes From America ❷**, 23 Kelley St., in Edgartown, has a dedicated local following. (☎ 627-4397. Beer $4-5.50. Entrees $8-12. Open daily 11:30am-midnight. AmEx/MC/V.) You'll be flying high at **The Aviator ❷**, next to the Katama Airfield near South Beach, where you can enjoy dishes like the "Seatbelt Extender" (3 eggs, meat, home fries, and pancakes; $12.50) as you watch private planes fly onto the grassy landing strip. (☎ 627-9018. Breakfast $5-9. Sandwiches $7-8.50. Open daily 7am-4pm. Cash only.)

◪ **SIGHTS.** Oak Bluffs, 3 mi. west of Vineyard Haven on Beach Rd., is the most youth-oriented of the Vineyard villages. A tour of **Trinity Park,** near the harbor, includes the elaborate, Victorian **Gingerbread Houses,** while the **Flying Horses Carousel,** in the center of town, is the oldest operating carousel in the nation. Snatch the brass ring and win a free ride. (☎ 693-9481. Open mid-May to Sept. daily 10am-10pm. $1.50.) **Chicama Vineyards,** a 1 mi. walk up a dirt road from the MVRTA #3 bus stop, in West Tisbury, has free tours and wine tastings. (☎ 693-0309. Open June-Oct. M-Sa 11am-5pm, Su 1-5pm; Nov.-Dec. M-Sa 1-4pm; Jan.-May Sa 1-4pm. Tours June-Oct. M-Sa noon, 2, 4pm; Su 2 and 4pm.) Martha's Vineyard has always been known for its shopping. The best shops are in **Vineyard Haven,** but with five locations, the famous **Black Dog** boutique can satisfy your tourist-trendy needs.

◪ **OUTDOOR ACTIVITIES.** Exploring the Vineyard should involve more than pedaling around—hit the beach or trek down one of the great trails. **Felix Neck Wildlife Sanctuary,** on the Edgartown-Vineyard Haven road, offers five trails that meander through 350 acres and lead to the water. (☎ 627-4850. Office open June-Sept. M-Sa 8am-4pm, Su 10am-3pm; Oct.-May Tu-Sa 8am-4pm, Su 10am-4pm. Gate opens with office and closes around 7pm. $4, seniors and ages 3-12 $3.) **Menemsha Hills Reservation,** off North Rd. in the village of Menemsha, has 4 mi. of trails along the rocky Vineyard Sound Beach, leading to the island's 2nd-highest point. **Cedar Creek Tree Neck,** off Indian Hill Rd. on the western shore, harbors 250 acres of heathland with trails throughout, while **Long Point Park** in West Tisbury preserves 633 acres and a shore on the Tisbury Great Pond. The 20-acre ◪**Polly Hill Arboretum,** 809 State Rd., in West Tisbury, boasts a complete collection of island plant species in a peaceful and remote setting. (☎ 693-9426. Open in summer M-Tu and Th-Su 7am-7pm; in low season dawn-dusk. Visitors Center open in summer M-Tu and Th-Su 9:30am-4pm. Suggested donation $5.)

South Beach (Katama Beach), at the end of Katama Rd., 3 mi. south of Edgartown (shuttle from Edgartown $2), and **State Beach,** on Beach Rd. between Edgartown and Oak Bluffs, are free and open to the public. South Beach boasts sizeable surf but an occasionally nasty undertow. State Beach's warmer waters once set the stage for parts of *Jaws* (1975), the granddaddy of beach horror films. For the island's best sunsets, stake out a spot at **Menemsha Town Beach** or ◪**Aquinnah Beach (Moshup Beach),** New England's best clothing-optional spot. To access a private beach frequented by nude bathers, go to the beach's main entrance where signs say "no nudity," then walk down toward the cliffs. The native Wampanoag used to save sailors shipwrecked on the **Gay Head Cliffs,** near Aquinnah. The 100,000-year-old precipice shines brilliantly and supports one of the island's five lighthouses. (☎645-2211. Lighthouse open F-Su 1½hr. before sunset to 30min. after sunset. $3, under 12 free.)

NANTUCKET   ☎508

Nantucket has entered modern lore as Martha's Vineyard's conservative little sister. The spellbinding trance of the island's cobblestone streets, precious cottages, and gorgeous beaches is quickly broken when the price tag of such flavor is revealed. Nevertheless, a good hostel and a number of cheap sandwich shops make Nantucket a relatively affordable luxury.

█▐ ORIENTATION AND PRACTICAL INFORMATION. As any fan of the TV show *Wings* (set in Nantucket's Tom Nevers Field airport) knows, flights are out-of-reach pricey, so take one of the **ferries** from Hyannis, on Cape Cod (both are near the bus station). Hy-Line Cruises, on Ocean St. Wharf (☎778-2600), runs to Nantucket's Straight Wharf on slow **boats** (2hr.; in summer 3 per day, low season 1-3 per day; $18.50, ages 5-12 $10, bikes $6) and fast boats (1hr., 5-6 per day, $38/29/6). The Steamship Authority, South St. Wharf (☎477-8600), goes to Steamboat Wharf on slow **boats** (2hr.; May-Oct. 6 per day, Nov.-Dec. 3 per day; $15, ages 5-12 $8, bikes $6) and fast boats (1hr., 5 per day 6am-7:20pm, $29/22/6).

Steamship Authority ferries dock at Steamboat Wharf, which becomes **Broad Street** inland. Turn left off Broad St. onto S. Water St. to reach **Main Street.** Hy-Line ferries dock at the base of this street. Nantucket Regional Transit Authority (☎228-7025; www.shuttlenantucket.com) has **shuttles** to destinations throughout the island. **Buses** to **Siasconset** and **Surfside** leave from Washington and Main St. (near the lamppost). Buses to **Miacomet** leave from Washington and Salem St., a block up from Straight Wharf; those to **Madaket** and **Jetties Beach** leave from Broad St., in front of the Peter Foulger Museum. (Buses run daily 7am-11:30pm; surfside bus every 40min. 10am-5:20pm. Fare $1-2, seniors ½-price, under 6 free.) With most beaches close to town, **bikes** are the best way to see Nantucket. The cheapest rentals are at Cook's Cycle, 6 S. Beach St., right off Broad St. (☎228-0800. $25 per day. Open Apr.-Nov. daily 9am-5pm.) Get bus maps, island maps, brochures, and accommodation info at **Nantucket Visitor Services,** 25 Federal St., off Broad St. (☎228-0925. Open in summer daily 9am-6pm; in winter M-Sa 9am-5:30pm.)

▐ ACCOMMODATIONS. While lodging on Nantucket seems exclusively for the trust-fund set, creative visitors can stay on the island without digging too deep into their pockets. Note that camping on the island is illegal. Across the street from the beach, the **Nantucket Hostel (HI) ❶,** 31 Western Ave., a 3½ mi. bike ride from town at the end of the unlit Surfside Bike Path, is housed in a gorgeous 130-year-old life-saving station with three large, clean dorm rooms. (☎228-0433 or 888-901-2084. Shuttle to hostel available during peak season daily 10am-6pm; $2. Full kitchen. Linen included. 7-day max. stay. Check-in 3-10pm. Lockout 11am-3pm. Open Apr.-Oct. Dorms $33-38, members $30-35. MC/V.) The **Nesbitt Inn ❹,** 21 Broad St., one block from the wharf, is the oldest and cheapest inn on Nantucket. It has small rooms and shared baths, but guests are treated to a fireplace, deck, continental breakfast, and beach towels. (☎228-0156. Open Mar.-Dec. Reservations required. Singles $95; doubles $105; quads $145. Mar.-Apr. and Oct.-Dec. $10 less. MC/V.) Most other accommodations on Nantucket are more expensive; the **Nantucket Accommodations Bureau** (☎228-9559) or **Nantucket & Martha's Vineyard Reservations** (☎800-649-5671) can help find deals, especially on last-minute accommodations.

NEW ENGLAND

🗋 **FOOD.** If you want a sit-down meal on the island, be prepared to shell out $15-20 for an entree. The cheapest options are the takeout places on Steamboat Wharf. Get groceries at the **Grand Union,** off Straight Wharf. (☎228-9756. Open M-Sa 7am-10pm, Su 7am-7pm.) 🖾**Something Natural ❶,** 50 Cliff Rd., a short walk north of town, serves warm cookies and amazing sandwiches—perfect for enjoying on the picnic tables out back. (☎228-0504. Half sandwiches $4-5, full sandwiches $7-8. Open May-Oct. M-Th 8am-6pm, F-Su 8am-6:30pm. Cash only.) **The Atlantic Café ❸,** 15 S. Water St., is nautical and nice, with friendly employees and American pub fare. (☎228-0570. Sandwiches $8-15. Entrees $13-22. Open daily May-Oct. 11:30am-1am; Nov.-Apr. 11:30am-midnight. Kitchen closes at 10pm. MC/V.) For a gourmet meal that doesn't break the bank, **Even Keel Cafe ❸,** 40 Main St., serves grilled salmon salad ($15) and lobster risotto ($25) that are pure heaven. (☎228-1979. Open daily 7am-late. AmEx/D/MC/V.)

🔲 **SIGHTS.** The **Nantucket Whaling Museum,** 7 Broad St., displays the skeleton of a 40 ft. sperm whale, whaling tools, and a collection of intricate scrimshaw. A combination ticket grants access to four of Nantucket's oldest buildings, including the **Old Gaol** and a **Quaker meeting house.** (☎228-1894; www.nha.org. Open M-W and F-Sa 10am-5pm, Th 10am-9pm, Su noon-5pm. Tickets $15, ages 6-17 $8; combination ticket $18/9.) For a panoramic view of the island, climb 92 stairs to the top of the **Congregational Church Tower,** 62 Centre St., off Broad St. The north vestry is an 18th-century church attached to the modern one. (☎228-0950. Open mid-June to Oct. M-Sa 10am-4pm; Apr. to mid-June F-Sa 10am-2pm. $2.50, ages 5-12 $0.50.)

🔳🏄 **BEACHES AND OUTDOOR ACTIVITIES.** Nantucket's silky public beaches are the island's highlight. The northern beaches (Children's, Jetties, and Dionis) edge much calmer seas than the southern beaches (Cisco, Surfside, Nobadeer). **Dionis** and **Jetties,** near town, are the most popular, with full facilities for daytrippers, while **Siasconset** and **Madaket** are more isolated. On the southern shore, **Miacomet** is the most peaceful, while the biggest waves are at **Nobadeer** and **Cisco,** which is the headquarters for the **Nantucket Island Surf School.** (☎560-1020; www.surfack.com. Rentals $40 per day, $25 per half-day. 1hr. private lesson $65; 2hr. group lesson $80.) **Nantucket Community Sailing,** at Jetties Beach, rents watercraft and gives sailing lessons. (Lessons ☎228-6600. Rentals 228-5358. Kayaks $15 per hr. Open mid-June to mid-Sept. daily 9am-5pm.) **Barry Thurston's,** 5 Salem St., at Candle St., left off Straight Wharf, rents rods and reels. (☎228-9595. Pole, reel, and three lures $23 per day. Open Apr.-Dec. M-Sa 8am-6pm, Su 8am-5pm.) There are two popular **bike routes** on Nantucket. To reach them from Steamboat Wharf, turn right on N. Water St. and bear left on Cliff Rd. to head for **Madaket Beach** (6¼ mi.). Many combine this with the **Sanford Farm Hike,** a single trail made up of several loops running through the brushy flatlands and gentle slopes of the old Sanford Farm, a preserved area at the heart of the island. A longer bike route runs to Siasconset (8¼ mi. of flat terrain) from Straight Wharf. Head up Main St. and turn left onto Orange St.; there are signs to the path after the traffic circle. To see more of the island, return from Siasconset Beach on the 10 mi. Polpis Road path. Look for maps of the bike routes at the Visitors Center and rental shops.

THE BERKSHIRES ☎413

An easy drive from Boston and New York City, the Berkshires are an attractive weekend getaway destination. Small towns sprinkled throughout the mountains offer homemade ice-cream, country stores, and scenic rural drives, as well as picturesque colleges and spas. Both modern and traditional, the Berkshires offer an amazing assortment of theater, music, contemporary art, and outdoor adventure.

NEW ENGLAND

▦ 🛈 ORIENTATION AND PRACTICAL INFORMATION

The **Berkshire** region comprises the western third of Massachusetts, bordered on the north by Rte. 2 (the Mohawk Trail) and Vermont, and on the south by Connecticut. From Williamstown, Peter Pan/Bonanza Bus Lines (☎888-751-8800; www.bonanzabus.com) runs **buses** to Boston (4hr., 2 per day, $34) via Pittsfield and Springfield. The **Berkshire Visitors Bureau** is at 3 Hoosac St., in Adams. (☎743-4500 or 800-237-5747; www.berkshires.org. Open M-F 8:30am-5pm.) The **Pittsfield Visitor Center,** 121 South St., in Pittsfield, also provides information about the region. (☎395-0105. Open M-Sa 8:30am-5pm.) For info on hiking and camping at the 12 state parks in Berkshire County, stop by the **Region 5 Headquarters,** 740 South St., in Pittsfield. (☎442-8928. Open M-F 8am-5pm.)

NORTH ADAMS   ☎413

In its heyday as a large industrial center, North Adams had 100 trains passing through the Hoosac Tunnel each day. Over time, the factories changed into art studios and galleries—some of the best in New England—and today modern art stands where assembly lines and machinery once loomed. ▨**Mass MoCA,** 1040 Mass MoCA Way, has galleries in 27 old factory buildings and is the largest center for contemporary visual and performing arts in the country. Pushing the envelope of modern art, the museum houses upside-down trees and large multimedia displays, as well as fascinating rotating exhibits. (☎662-2111; www.massmoca.org. Open July-Labor Day daily 10am-6pm; early Sept.-late June M and W-Su 11am-5pm. $11, students $9, ages 6-16 $5.) The **Contemporary Artists Center,** 189 Beaver St. (Rte. 8 N.), contains an artists' studio and a stunning gallery inside an enormous brick factory. (☎663-9555; www.thecac.org. Open W-Sa 11am-5pm, Su noon-5pm. Free.) Celebrating the history of the Hoosac Tunnel, the **Western Gateway,** 115 State St., just after the Hadley Overpass off Rte. 8, is one of Massachusetts's five Heritage State Parks. The complex consists of a Visitors Center, railroad museum, and a gallery. There are also free outdoor concerts during the summer. (☎663-6312. Open daily 10am-5pm. Summer concerts Th 7pm. Donations accepted.) On Rte. 8, half a mile north of downtown, **Natural Bridge State Park** is home to a white marble bridge that spans a 60 ft. deep chasm. Navigate the labyrinth of stairs and stone leading to the bridge, or picnic on the grounds. (May-Oct. ☎663-6392, Nov.-Apr. ☎663-8469. Open late May to mid-Oct. daily 9am-5pm. Parking $2.)

   Clarksburg State Park ❶, 1199 Middle Rd., a few miles north of town on Rte. 8, has 44 wooded campsites and nearly 350 acres of woods and water. (☎664-8345. No lifeguard on duty. Free showers. Reservations recommended on weekends. Sites $14, MA residents $12. Day use $5. D/MC/V.) **Moulton's Pizzeria ❷,** 117 Main St., serves crispy pizza with festive Italian flare. Try the "Mayor," which is piled high with everything but anchovies. (☎663-3770. Medium pizzas $8-10. Delivery available. Open M-Th 11am-10pm, F-Sa 11am-midnight. MC/V.) Follow Rte. 2 east from Mass MoCa for the **North Adams Visitors Center,** on Union St. (Rte. 2/Rte. 8), where enthusiastic volunteers are happy to help travelers. (☎663-9204. Open June-Sept. daily 10am-4pm.)

WILLIAMSTOWN   ☎413

With a purple cow named "Ephs" (after college founder Ephraim Williams) as a mascot and a lively student population, **Williams College** injects youthful vitality into an otherwise quiet town. Maps of the campus are available from the admissions office, 33 Stetson Ct., in Bascom House. (☎597-2211; www.williams.edu. Open M-F 8:30am-4:30pm. Tours daily; call for times.) The **Williams College Museum of Art,** 15 Lawrence Hall Dr., #2, houses over 12,000 pieces ranging from medieval religious works to modern art. (☎597-2429; www.wcma.org. Open Tu-Sa 10am-

5pm, Su 1-5pm. Wheelchair-accessible. Free.) Half a mile down South St. from the traffic circle, the 🎨Clark Art Institute, 225 South St., features impressive 19th-century works by artists like Renoir, Degas, and Cassat, as well as unique temporary exhibits. The 140-acre grounds encourage patrons to picnic in the gardens or stroll through the hillside pastures. Construction to expand the museum began in the fall of 2005, but it remains open to the public. (☎458-2303. Open July-Aug. daily 10am-5pm; Sept.-June Tu-Su 10am-5pm. Wheelchair-accessible. Nov.-May free; June-Oct. $12.50, students with ID and under 18 free.) As the summer heats up, so do the stages at the Williamstown Theater. The Tony-award-winning 🎭Williamstown Theater Festival hosts plays and musicals on two main stages and several secondary stages around town. (☎597-3399; www.wtfestival.org. Box office at 1000 Main St. Open mid-June to late Aug. Tu-Sa 10am-8pm, Su 10am-4pm. Performances Tu-Su. Main Stage $20-52; Nikos Stage $33-35; F afternoon play readings $3.) The Hopkins Memorial Forest (☎597-2346) offers over 2500 acres of free hiking and cross-country skiing on 15 mi. of trails. Take Rte. 7 N. (North St.), turn left on Bulkley St., and turn right onto NW. Hill Rd. For bike, snowshoe, or cross-country ski rentals, check out The Mountain Goat, 130 Water St. (☎458-8445. Bike and ski rentals $25 per day, $35 per weekend, $100 per week. Open M-W and F-Sa 10am-6pm, Th 10am-7pm, Su noon-5pm.) At 3491 ft., Mt. Greylock is the tallest peak in Massachusetts and has more than 50 mi. of trails, including the Appalachian Trail. At the top stands the Veterans War Memorial Tower.

Affordable motels cluster along Rte. 2 east of town. The Maple Terrace Motel ❹, 555 Main St. (Rte. 2), is one of the nicest places in town, with beautiful gardens, bright rooms with cable TV, a heated outdoor pool, and continental breakfast. (☎458-9677; www.mapleterrace.com. Reservations strongly recommended. Rooms in summer $93-148. In low season $56-6101. AmEx/D/MC/V.) At the summit of Mt. Greylock sits 🏔Bascom Lodge ❷, which offers bunks, private rooms, and expansive mountain views. (☎743-1591; www.naturesclassroom.org. Accessible by Notch Rd., off Rt. 2, from the north and North Main St., off Rt. 7, from the south. Breakfast $8. Dinner $16. Parking $2. Bunks M-F $26, Sa-Su $36. Private rooms M-F $68-98. Reservations required for lodging and meals. Closed until 2009. AmEx/MC/V.)The comfortable Chimney Mirror Motel ❸, 295 Main St., is slightly cheaper, but rates on summer weekends jump significantly. Rooms are simple and clean, with private baths and A/C. (☎458-5202; www.chimneymirror.com. Breakfast included. Rooms in summer M-Th and Su $62-88, F-Sa $109-130. In low season $60-78. Lower rates may be available upon request. Discounts for extended stays. D/MC/V.) For a quick and easy meal, stroll to Pappa Charlie's Deli ❶, 28 Spring St., and sink your teeth into $5 celebrity-themed sandwiches, such as the meaty "Columbo." (☎458-5969. Open M-Sa 8am-8pm, Su 8am-7pm. Cash only.) Serving gourmet ice cream ($3), incredible milkshakes ($3.50), and grilled burgers and hot dogs, Lickety Split ❶, 69 Spring St., is hopping in the early afternoon. (☎458-1818. Open Feb.-Nov. daily 11am-11pm; Dec.-Jan. M-Sa 11:30am-4pm. Cash only.) Students gather to study and chat over locally roasted coffee at Tunnel City Coffee ❶, on Spring St. (☎488-8010. Daily 6:30am-6:30pm.) The Williamstown Chamber of Commerce operates a Visitors Information Booth at the intersection of Rte. 2 and 7 with info on events, lodging, and dining. (☎485-9077; www.williamstownchamber.com. Open 24hr.; staffed July-Aug. daily 10am-6pm; Sept. F-Su 10am-6pm.)

LENOX ☎413

🎵Tanglewood, an enormous and scenic music center off Rte. 7, west of Lenox Village on West St. (Rte. 183), is one of the Berkshires' greatest treasures and the summer home of the Boston Symphony Orchestra. For an enchanting evening or a relaxing Sunday afternoon, lawn tickets and picnics are the way to go. Chamber concerts, showcasing the young musicians training at Tanglewood, provide regular evening entertainment. The Boston Pops also give summer concerts. For a rare treat, hear Tchaikovsky's 1812 Overture punctuated by cannon shots and fireworks at **Tanglewood on Parade,** held each year in late July. The summer comes to a close with a **jazz festival** at the end of August. (Tickets and schedules ☎888-266-1200; www.bso.org. Orchestral concerts late June-late Aug. F 8:30pm, 6pm prelude; Sa 8:30pm; Su 2:30pm. Open rehearsals Sa 10:30am. Auditorium or "Music Shed" $19-96; lawn seats $16-23, under 12 free. Students with valid ID ½ price on F.) Over 20 historic buildings, a bevy of farm animals, and informative, scholarly displays bring Shaker history to life at the **Hancock Shaker Village,** located west of Pittsfield on Rt 20. (☎443-0188. Open daily 10am-5pm. Adults $12.50, children $5.) Though best known for her works of fiction, **Edith Wharton** also dabbled in architecture, designing her own sparkling white mansion. Shakespeare's works never go out of style at **Shakespeare & Company,** 70 Kemble St. (Rte. 7A). Enjoy plays written by Berkshire authors at the **Founders' Theater.** Free matinees are also performed *al fresco* in the Rose Footprint, modeled after the Elizabethan Rose Playhouse. (☎637-3353; www.shakespeare.org. Box office open mid-Apr. to late Oct. daily 10am-2pm, or until performance begins. Call for showtimes. Founders Theater $10-50. Rose Footprint shows free.)

At the base of Lenox Mountain, the **Pleasant Valley Wildlife Sanctuary** contains 1300 acres and 7 mi. of trails through forest, meadows, and wetlands. (☎637-0320; www.massaudubon.org. From Pittsfield, take Rte. 20 S to W. Dugway Rd. Follow W. Dugway 1½ mi. to the Nature Center. Open July-Sept. daily dawndusk. Nature Center open late Oct.-June M 9am-4pm, Tu-Sa 9am-5pm, Su 10am-4pm; July-late Oct. M and Su 10am-4pm, Tu-Sa 9am-5pm. No pets allowed. $4, ages 3-12 $3.)

The perfectly located **October Mountain State Forest ❶,** offers 46 campsites within 10min. of the Tanglewood grounds. Campsites fill early on concert weekends. (☎413-243-1778. Free showers. Sites $14.)

Serving breakfast, lunch, and the occasional psychic reading, **Carol's ❷,** 8 Franklin St., will satisfy any craving for home cooking. With breakfast all day, you can try local celebrity James Taylor's favorite omelet or sample some of Carol's delicious pancakes. (☎637-8948. Pancakes from $5. Open daily 7am-3pm. Cash only.) The **SoCo Creamery ❶,** 26 Housatonic St, serves the country's only ice cream made soley from the milk of Jersey cows for a particularly creamy treat. (☎637-9192. M-Th and Su 11am-10pm, F-Sa 11am-midnight.)

TANGLEWOOD

Each year, the Boston Symphony Orchestra draws almost 300,000 people to its 210-acre summer home in the Berkshires of western Massachusetts. For some **Tanglewood,** is a concert experience of the highest order. Whether an inventive performance of contemporary works, or the BSO's annual performance of Beethoven's 9th in the legendary acoustics of the Koussevitzky Music Shed, Tanglewood concerts are a delight. Before concerts, the lawn surrounding the Shed looks like tailgating for the upper-crust, dotted with elaborate, gourmet picnic spreads and regal couples reclined in lawn chairs. For 150 elite young musicians, a summer spent studying and performing at the Tanglewood Music Center is a capstone experience before launching a career as a professional musician. It is estimated that the Center has educated 20 percent of the members of professional American orchestras since its founding in 1936.

From early July to mid-August, the BSO gives concerts each and every weekend, while gifted members of the Tanglewood Music Center perform chamber music during the week.

For tickets or more info: Boston Symphony Orchestra, 301 Massachusetts Ave., in Boston. ☎617-266-1492; www.bso.org.

STOCKBRIDGE   ☎ 413

Stockbridge, like many other small towns in the Berkshires, glimmers with natural beauty and the afterglow of the Gilded Age. Enjoy some old-fashioned Americana at the ⬛**Norman Rockwell Museum,** 9 Glendale Rd. (Rte. 183), where you can visit the artist's studio and the largest single collection of his original works, including many *Saturday Evening Post* covers. (☎298-4100; www.nrm.org. Open May-Oct. daily 10am-5pm; Nov.-Apr. M-F 10am-4pm, Sa-Su 10am-5pm. $12, students $7, under 18 free. Audio tours available.) Just down the road lies **Chesterwood,** the home and studio of sculptor Daniel Chester French, best known for his sculpture at the Lincoln Memorial in Washington, D.C. (☎298-3579; www.chesterwood.org. Open May-Oct. daily 10am-5pm. $12, under 18 $5, under 5 free; families $25.) Enjoy fresh fragrances and stunning flower arrangements at the 15-acre **Berkshire Botanical Gardens,** at the intersection of Rte. 102 and 183. (☎298-3926; www.berkshirebotanical.org. Open May-Oct. daily 10am-5pm. $7, seniors and students $5, under 12 free.) Set in the rolling hills overlooking Stockbridge, **Naumkeag,** 5 Prospect Hill Rd., is the 44-room Choate family mansion surrounded by lavish gardens, a blue-roofed Chinese temple, and perfectly manicured trees. (☎298-3239; www.thetrustees.org. Open daily 10am-5pm. Last tour 4pm. Admission and tour $10, ages 3-12 $3. Admission to garden without tour $8/3.)

RHODE ISLAND

Founded in 1636 by religious outcast Roger Williams, Rhode Island is the smallest state in the Union, but makes good use of its territory. Its winding coastline is smattered with seaside hamlets, while its scenic interior is criss-crossed with bike trails. Still, not everything in the state is tiny—Providence's cosmopolitan flair and the Gilded Age mansions of Newport are giants in their own right.

🛈 PRACTICAL INFORMATION

Capital: Providence.

Visitor Info: Providence/Warwick Convention and Visitors Bureau: 1 W. Exchange St., (☎751-1177 or 800-233-1636; www.visitrhodeisland.com), in downtown Providence, RI 02901. Open M-Sa 9am-5pm. **Division of Parks and Recreation,** 2321 Hartford Ave., Johnston 02919. (☎401-222-2632.) Open M-F 8:30am-4pm.

Postal Abbreviation: RI. **Sales Tax:** 7%.

PROVIDENCE   ☎ 401

Located at the mouth of the Seekonk River, Providence is undergoing a renaissance from the inside out. Artistic and collegiate flavors have brought trendy shops and restaurants to this compact city. Downtown rests at the base of two hills—one home to two world-class institutes of higher education, and the other to the State Capitol—allowing Providence to seamlessly blend the hustle and bustle of a busy capital city with the laid-back feel of a college town.

▐ **TRANSPORTATION. T.F. Green Airport (PVD),** south of the city at Exit 13 off I-95, is a Southwest Airlines hub. Amtrak, 100 Gaspee St., operates from a station southeast of the state capitol. (☎800-872-7245; www.amtrak.com. Open daily 5am-10:45pm; ticket booth open 5am-9:45pm. Wheelchair-accessible.) **Trains** run to Boston (40min., 10 per day, $12) and New York City (3-4hr., 10 per day, $51-105). The Massachusetts Bay Transit Authority (MBTA) operates from the same station and sends **trains** to Boston (1hr., 15 per day, $7.75). Greyhound has an info and ticket booth in Kennedy Center. (☎454-0790 or 800-231-2222; www.greyhound.com. Ticket window open 6:30am-8pm.) **Buses** run to Boston (1hr., 7-8 per day, $8.50) and New York City (4-5hr., 9-12 per day, $24). Bonanza Bus, 1 Bonanza Way, at Exit 25 off I-95 and at the RIPTA info booth in Kennedy Center (☎888-751-8800; www.bonanzabus.com; station open daily 4:30am-11pm, Kennedy Center ticket window daily 7am-6pm), has **bus** service to Boston (1hr., 18 per day, $8) and New York City (4-5hr., 7 per day, $36). Rhode Island Public Transit Authority (RIPTA), 265 Melrose St., runs an **info booth** at Kennedy Plaza that provides free bus maps. (☎781-9400; www.ripta.com. Terminal open 6am-8pm; ticket window open M-F 7am-6pm, Sa 9am-noon and 1-5pm.) RIPTA's service includes Newport and a variety of other locations. (Schedules vary. **Buses** run daily 5am-midnight. $1.50; day pass $6.) Providence Link run by RIPTA, runs **trolleys** ($1.50) in the city with stops at sights. Yellow Cab (☎941-1122) provides **taxis** in the Providence metro area.

🔳🔂 ORIENTATION AND PRACTICAL INFORMATION. I-95 and the **Providence River** run north-south and split Providence into three sections. West of I-95 is **Federal Hill**; between I-95 and the Providence River is **Down City**. East of the river is **College Hill**, home to **Brown University** and **Rhode Island School of Design** (RISD, or Risdee). When driving to the city from the north, make sure to keep an eye out for the famous ▧**Big Blue Bug**, the 9 ft. mascot of New England Pest Control, perched to the right of the highway. Walking or taking the Providence Link are the best ways to see the city during the day. **Providence/Warwick Convention and Visitors Bureau,** 1 Sabin St., is on the first floor of the convention center downtown. (☎751-1177 or 800-233-1636; www.goprovidence.com. Open M-Sa 9am-5pm.) The **Providence Preservation Society,** 21 Meeting St., at the foot of College Hill, has info on historic Providence and the *Guide to Providence Architecture* ($25), which outlines 11 self-guided tours. (☎831-7440; www.ppsri.org. Open M-F 8:30am-5pm.) **Internet Access: Providence Public Library,** 225 Washington St. (☎455-8000. Free. Open M noon-8pm, Tu-Th 10am-6pm, F-Sa 9am-5pm.) **Post Office:** 2 Exchange Terr. (☎421-5214. Open M-F 8am-5pm.) **Postal Code:** 02903.

📍 ACCOMMODATIONS. Downtown motel rates make Providence an expensive overnight stay, and rooms fill up well in advance for graduation season in May and early June. Head 10 mi. south on I-95 to **Warwick** or **Cranston**, or northeast to **Seekonk, MA,** on Rte. 6, for cheaper motels. Catering largely to the university's international visitors, the stained-glass windows of the **International House of Rhode Island ❸,** 8 Stimson Ave., off Hope St., near the Brown campus, shine light on three comfortable and unique rooms. Reservations are required and should be made far in advance. (☎421-7181. Fridge, laundry facilities, private bath, shared kitchen, TVs. Reception June-July M-F 8:30am-4pm; Aug.-May M-F 9:30am-5pm. Singles $60, students $40; doubles $70/55. $5 per night discount for stays of 5 nights or more. Monthly rate $550/450. Cash only.) The **Knights Inn ❸,** 50 Mink St., on Rte. 6, 1 mi. after entering Seekonk, has a kind staff and cushy rooms. (☎508-336-8050. Continental breakfast included. Singles $75-79; doubles $82-90. Each additional person $6.) The nearest campgrounds lie 30min. from town. **Colwell's Campground ❶,** in Coventry, has showers and hookups for 75 sites along the Flat River Reservoir, perfect for swimming or water-skiing. From Providence, take I-95 S to Exit 10, then go west 8½ mi. on Rte. 117 and look for Peckham Lane on the right. (☎397-4614. Check-in 3-9pm. Reservations recommended. Sites $18, with hookup $20.)

◖ FOOD. Providence provides excellent culinary options. **Atwells Avenue,** on Federal Hill, just west of downtown, is Providence's "Little Italy"; **Thayer Street,** on College Hill to the east, is home to offbeat student hangouts and ethnic restaurants; and **Wickenden Street,** in the southeast corner of town, has inexpensive eateries. For cheap food downtown, the **Arcade,** the 1st indoor mall in America, has plenty of sandwich shops, as does its counterpart, the food court in the massive **Providence Place Mall. Geoff's Superlative Sandwiches ❶,** 163 Benefit St., in College Hill, attracts a diverse clientele with 85 creatively named sandwiches ($5-7), like the "Kevorkian," a sandwich that, with pastrami, bacon, and Frank's Hot Sauce, might facilitate your demise. Dive into the huge pickle barrel for a treat to complement your meal. (☎751-2248. Open M-F 8am-9pm, Sa-Su 9:30am-9pm. Cash only.) Specializing in Eggs Benedict (five varieties; $5-8), **Julian's ❸,** 318 Broadway, near Federal Hill, is a funky sit-down eatery. (☎861-1770. Wraps and sandwiches $5-8. Dinner $11-22. Open M-F 9am-1am, Sa 9am-3pm and 5pm-1am, Su 9am-3pm and 6pm-1am. AmEx/D/MC/V.) A Federal Hill institution, **Angelo's Civita Farnese ❷,** 141 Atwells St., serves up Italian favorites family-style at reasonable prices. (☎621-8171. Entrees $3-12. Sandwiches $4-6. Open daily noon-6:30pm. Cash only.) For refreshing frozen lemonade beloved by locals, be on the lookout for **Del's ❶,** which has stands and trucks. (1999 Weybosset Ave. and 1527 Mineral Spring Ave.)

🅖 **SIGHTS.** Take a jaunt down Benefit St. in College Hill, past the artsy RISD students, and stop by the 🟥**RISD Museum of Art,** 224 Benefit St. The museum's three floors of galleries have a collection of Native American, Egyptian, Indian, Impressionist, medieval, and Roman art, as well as a giant 12th-century Japanese Buddha. (☎454-6500; www.risd.edu/museum.cfm. Open Tu-Su 10am-5pm. $8, seniors $5, students $3, ages 5-18 $2. Free Su 10am-1pm, every 3rd Th 5-9pm, F noon-1:30pm, and last Sa of the month 11am-4pm.) Established in 1764, **Brown University** has a plethora of 18th-century buildings, including the **Corliss-Brackett House,** 45 Prospect St., now the Office of Admission. (☎863-2378; www.brown.edu/admission. Open M-F 8am-4pm. Free campus tours M-F 9am-4pm.) The stunning marble dome of the **Rhode Island State Capitol** is visible from nearly every vantage point in the city. (☎222-3938; www.state.ri.us. Open M-F 8:30am-4:30pm. Free guided tours every hr. M-F 9am-noon. Tour guides on duty in the library until closing. Reservations recommended for groups. Self-guide tour booklets available in the library.) The **John Brown House Museum,** 52 Power St., is steeped in tranquil elegance. The 1hr. tour includes a brief video introducing the house built by John Brown himself in the late 18th century. Guides are well-versed in the house's priceless antiques and exquisite architecture. (☎273-7507. Open Tu-Sa 10am-5pm, Su noon-4pm. $7, students and seniors $5.50, ages 7-17 $3; families $18.) The Pawtucket factory that started the American industrial revolution is preserved at the **Slater Mill Historic Site,** 67 Roosevelt Ave., along the rushing waters of the Blackstone River. (☎725-8638; www.slatermill.org. Open June-Nov. Tu-Sa 10am-5pm, Su 1-5pm; call for winter hours. 1½hr. tours available continuously. $9, seniors $8, ages 6-12 $7, under 6 free; tour included.) In addition to founding Rhode Island, Roger Williams founded the **First Baptist Church of America** in 1638. Its 1775 incarnation stands today at 75 N. Main St. (☎454-3418; www.fbcia.org. Guided tours available after the Su service. Self-guided tours during all other hours. Open M-F 10am-noon and 1-4pm, Sa 10am-noon. Free.)

🎵🅖 **ENTERTAINMENT AND NIGHTLIFE.** For film, theater, and nightlife listings, read the "Weekend" section of the *Providence Journal* or pick up a free *Providence Phoenix.* On several evenings each summer, floating and stationary bonfires span the entire length of the downtown rivers during 🟥**WaterFire,** a public art exhibition and festival. (☎272-3111; www.waterfire.org. Free.) The regionally acclaimed **Trinity Repertory Company,** 201 Washington St., usually offers $15 student rush tickets on the day of performances. (☎351-4242; www.trinity-rep.com for ticket info. Tickets $28-50.) The **Providence Performing Arts Center**

(PPAC), 220 Weybosset St., hosts a variety of high-end productions including concerts and Broadway musicals. (☎421-2787; www.ppacri.org. Box office open Sept.-May M-F 10am-6pm, Sa noon-5pm; May-Sept. M-Th 10am-3pm, or until curtain on show days. Tickets $30-68. Half-price tickets for students and seniors sometimes available 1hr. before weekday showtimes; call ahead.) The **Cable Car Cinema and Cafe,** 204 S. Main St., one block down from Benefit St., shows arthouse and foreign films in a small theater with comfy couches and refreshments. (☎272-3970. 2 shows per evening; times vary. Cafe open M-F 7:30am-11pm, Sa-Su 9am-11pm. $8, M-W students $6.)

Brownies, townies, and RISDs rock the night away at several hot spots throughout town. Something's going on every night at **AS220,** 115 Empire St., between Washington and Westminster St., a nonprofit, totally uncensored cafe/bar/gallery/performance space. (☎831-9327; performance info www.as220.org. Cover usually around $6. Open M-F 3pm-1am, Sa-Su 7pm-1am.) **Trinity Brewhouse,** 186 Fountain St., behind Trinity Repertory Theatre, serves award-winning beer and hosts live blues on Wednesday nights. Diners and drinkers enjoy themselves under a "Last Supper" painting of musical greats from Beethoven to Lennon. (☎453-2337. Open M-Th 11:30am-1am, F 11:30am-2am, Sa noon-2am, Su noon-1am.)

NEWPORT   ☎401

Money has always found its way into Newport. Once a center of transatlantic shipping, the coastal town later became the summer escape for the elite of America's elite. Today, the awe-inspiringly opulent mansions of big-business tycoons still remain, but they are only a part of this high-priced tourist town—world-famous music festivals and the beautiful landscape are now big draws as well.

⌨🔢 TRANSPORTATION AND PRACTICAL INFORMATION. Bonanza **buses** (☎846-1820; www.bonanzabus.com) depart from the Gateway Center, as do Rhode Island Public Transit Authority (RIPTA; p. 291) **buses.** Parking at the Gateway Center is a cheap option ($2 per day with RIPTA receipt, 30min. free with Visitors Center validation). Ten Speed Spokes, 18 Elm St., rents **bikes.** (☎847-5609. Bikes $5 per hr., $25 per day. Credit card and photo ID required. Open M-F 10am-6pm, Sa 10am-5pm, Su noon-5pm.) Parallel to the shore, **Thames Street** is home to the tourist strip and the wharves, while **Bellevue Avenue** contains many of Newport's mansions. The Newport/Pell bridge requires a $2 toll. A mecca of information, the **Newport County Convention and Visitors Bureau,** 23 America's Cup Ave., two blocks from Thames St., in the Newport Gateway Center, has floor-to-ceiling pictures and large maps. Be sure to ask at the information counter for visitor guides. (☎800-976-5122; www.gonewport.com. Open daily 9am-5pm.) **Internet Access: Public Library,** 300 Spring St. (☎849-8720. Free Wi-Fi. Open M 11am-8pm, Tu-Th 9am-8pm, F-Sa 9am-6pm.) **Post Office:** 320 Thames St. (☎847-2329. Open M-F 8:30am-5pm, Sa 9am-1pm.) **Postal Code:** 02840.

🏠 ACCOMMODATIONS. Small and expensive lodging crowds Newport, but a new hostel proves that Newport's vacationers have changed since the days of railroad and steel monopolies. For less-expensive lodging, Rte. 114 (W. Main Rd.) and the adjacent Coddington Hwy. have a variety of standard chain motels about 4 mi. from Newport. Many hotels and guest houses book solid two months in advance for summer weekends, especially during the popular festivals. A breakthrough for budget travelers, the newly opened ⬛**William Gyles Guesthouse ❷,** 16 Howard St., treats visitors to hostel accommodations in the heart of town, breakfast, an evening tour of Newport, and other goodies. (☎369-0243. Laundry $3. 3-night max. stay. Check-out 10am. Reservations recommended. Dorms in summer $20-29, during festivals $49, in winter $16. Inquire about student discounts. MC/V.) A few minutes from Newport's harbor front, the **Newport Gateway Hotel ❺**, 31 W. Main Rd., in Middletown, has alluring doubles with A/C, cable TV, and a mini-fridge. (☎847-2735. Breakfast included. Rooms M-Th and Su $65-99, F-Sa $159-195. AmEx/D/MC/V.) **Fort Getty Recreation Area ❶**, on Fort Getty Rd., on Conanicut Island, provides 15 small tent sites in an open field with a great view of an old lighthouse. (☎423-7211. Free hot showers and beach access. Reservations recommended. June-Oct. tent sites $20; RV sites $40. Cash only.)

⬛ FOOD. The vegetarian-friendly **Panini Grill ❶**, 186 Thames St., grills tasty sandwiches ($5-6) in a small and funky basement. (☎847-7784. Open M-Th and Su 11am-9:30pm, F-Sa 11am-2am. MC/V.) Choice mollusks are always the catch of the day at **Flo's Clam Shack ❸**, 4 Wave Ave., across from the east end of Easton Beach. This place is the perfect summer treat, but locals have already figured that out—be prepared for lines on hot evenings. (☎847-8141. Seafood platters with cole slaw and fries $8-14. Open in summer M-Th and Su 11am-9pm, F-Sa 11am-10pm; call for low-season hours. Cash only.) A Rhode Island staple, the **Newport Creamery ❷**, on Bellevue Ave., across from the Tennis Hall of Fame, serves three meals and ice cream inside or at the takeout window. (☎846-6332. Locations throughout Rhode Island. Open 6:30am-11pm. AmEx/D/MC/V.) The **Franklin Spa ❶**, 229 Spring St., prepares breakfasts like the "Portuguese Sailor," with *chorizo* and eggs. (☎847-3540. Breakfasts $7-8. Open M-W 6am-2pm, Th-Sa 6am-3pm, Su 7am-1:30pm.)

◪◩ SIGHTS AND BEACHES. George Noble Jones built the first "summer cottage" in Newport in 1839, anchoring the town's extravagant string of palatial summer estates. Most mansions lie south of downtown on Bellevue Ave. A self-guided walking tour or, in some mansions, a guided tour by the **Preservation Society of Newport**, 424 Bellevue Ave., gives you a chance to ogle the decadence. (☎847-1000; www.newportmansions.org. Open in summer daily 9am-5pm; in winter M-F 9am-5pm.) The five largest mansions are **The Elms**, 367 Bellevue Ave.; **The Breakers**, 44 Ochre Point Ave.; **Chateau-sur-Mer**, 474 Bellevue Ave.; **Rosecliff**, 548 Bellevue Ave.; and ▣**Marble House**, 596 Bellevue Ave. (☎847-1000. Mansions open M-F 10am-5pm. $15-20 per house, ages 6-17 $4. Combination tickets $27-37.)

Newport's gorgeous beaches are as crowded as its streets. The most popular sandy spot is **Easton's Beach**, or First Beach, on Memorial Blvd. (☎848-6491. Parking late May-early Sept. M-F 10am-9pm $8, before 10am $6, Sa-Su $10.) Other beaches line Little Compton, Narragansett, and the shore between Watch Hill and Point Judith. Starting at Easton's Beach or Bellevue Ave., the ▣**Cliff Walk** traverses Newport's eastern shore as a 3½ mi. walking/running trail (www.cliffwalk.com). Wildflowers and a rocky shoreline mark one side of the trail, while gorgeous mansions border the other. **Fort Adams State Park,** south of town on Ocean Dr., 2½ mi. from the Visitors Center, has showers, picnic areas, fishing piers, and a gorgeous view of downtown Newport alongside the largest coastal fort in America. (☎847-2400; www.fortadams.org. Park open daily dawn-dusk. Guided tours of fort every hr. 10am-4pm. Tours $8, ages 5-17 $5; families $20.) Near Fort Adams, **Ocean Drive** is a breathtaking car or bike ride along the coast.

Baseball has been played at **Cardine's Field**, across from the Gateway center, for almost 100 years. In the summer, the field is home to the Newport Gulls, New England's champion collegiate summer league. (☎845-6832. Tickets $4, children $2. 2-4 games per week during summer.) Built in 1763, the **Touro Synagogue,** 85 Touro St., is the oldest synagogue in the US. (☎847-4794, www.tourosynagogue.org. Tours M-W, F, and Su every 30min. 10am-5pm. Adults $5, under 12 free.) The **Tennis Hall of Fame,** 194 Bellevue Ave., is a white-and-green Victorian building that contains an in-depth look at the sport's history and a Wimbledonesque grass court. (☎849-3990; www.tennisfame.com. Open daily 9:30am-5pm. $9, students and seniors $7, under 17 $5; families $23.)

📷📷 **ENTERTAINMENT AND NIGHTLIFE.** From June through August, Newport gives lovers of classical, folk, jazz, and film each a festival to call their own. Festival tickets sell out months in advance; look early if you want to attend. The **Newport Jazz Festival,** at Fort Adams State Park, is one of the oldest and best-known jazz festivals in the world. Also at Fort Adams State Park, folk singers entertain at the **Newport Folk Festival,** where former acts include Bob Dylan and Joan Baez. (Both festivals ☎847-3700; www.festivalproductions.net. Tickets $53-100 per day, under 12 $5.) The **Newport Music Festival** brings classical musicians from around the world for more than 60 concerts during two weeks in July. (☎846-1133, box office 849-0700; www.newportmusic.org. Box office: 850 Aquidneck Ave., in Middletown. Open M-F 10am-6pm, Sa 10am-1pm. Tickets $35-45.) In June, the **Newport International Film Festival** screens films in the **Jane Pickens Theater** and the **Opera House Cinema.** (☎846-9100; www.newportfilmfestival.com).

Even if you can't get to a festival, music fills the streets every night. Pubs and clubs line Thames St., but bring proper ID, as clubs are strict. The **Rhino Bar and Grille's Mamba Room,** 337 Thames St., is the place to dance the night away. (☎846-0707. 21+. Cover $5-20. Open W-Sa 9pm-1am.) **The Newport Blues Cafe,** 286 Thames St., hosts live music ranging from blues to rock to reggae. (☎841-5510. Live music daily after 9:30pm. Business casual, no hats. Cover up to $15. Open in summer daily 6pm-1am. Kitchen closes 10pm. Call for winter hours.) With three bars, a dockside location, and live music, **Christies,** 351 Thames St., keeps crowds coming back. (☎847-5400. Open in summer daily 11:30am-1am; call for winter hours.)

📷 **DAYTRIP FROM NEWPORT: BLOCK ISLAND.** A popular daytrip 20 mi. southwest of Newport, teardrop-shaped **Block Island** possesses an untamed natural beauty. All beaches are free, but many are a hike from the ferry stops; cycling is the best way to explore the island. **Aldo's Rentals,** on Chapel St., behind the Harborside Inn, rents bikes and other contraptions. (☎466-5018. Mountain bikes $7 per hr., $25 per day; mopeds $40/85; kayaks $15 per hr., $35 per half-day; cars $90-155 per day. Coupons available at the Visitors Center. Open mid-May to mid-Oct. daily 8am-6pm.) A three-quarter mile hike along the shore to **North Light,** the granite lighthouse and maritime museum that rests on the northern tip of the island, is a pleasant excursion. (Open early July-early Sept. daily 10am-5pm. $2.) Don't miss the trail hidden behind the lighthouse that leads through the sand dunes to the northern coast. Follow the coast up to the very northern tip of the island, where a narrow pathway leads out into the Atlantic. Enjoy the most beautiful and secluded sands on the island, but do not swim here—currents are downright lethal.

The island does not permit camping; it's best to make it a daytrip unless you're willing to shell out at least $70, and probably much more, for a room in a guest house. Most moderately priced restaurants hover near the ferry dock in Old Harbor, but a few others are located in New Harbor, 1 mi. inland. **Rebecca's Seafood Restaurant ❶,** on Water St. across from the dock, serves beach favorites in a small dining room and sunny patio. (☎466-5411. Seafood sandwiches $4-6. Open M-Th 7am-8pm, F-Su 7am-2am. Cash only.) Luscious sweets like thick slices of banana bread ($2.50-5) and iced coffee ($2-3) can be found alongside Internet terminals ($1 per 5min.) at **Juice 'n' Java ❶,** on Dodge St. (☎466-5220. Open daily 7am-midnight. Cash only.) If you reach Block Island with a hankering for pancakes and bacon, look no farther than **Ernie's Old Harbor Restaurant ❷,** on Water St. at Old Harbor. (☎466-2473. Open daily 6:30am-noon. MC/V.) The popular restaurant and bar at **Ballard's Inn** has live music most summer afternoons, which can be enjoyed for free on their public beach at the end of Water St.

The Interstate Navigation Company (☎783-4613 or 866-783-7340) provides **ferry service** to Block Island from State Pier at Point Judith, in Galilee (1hr.; mid-June to early Sept. 8-9 per day; $10.60, seniors $9, ages 5-11 $5.20; car $45 by reservation only, driver and passengers must pay regular fare; bike $3); and Fort Adams State Park in Newport (2hr.; July-Aug. 1 per day; $10.35, seniors $9.85, ages 5-11 $4.25; bike $2.50). The Block Island Express (☎ 860-444-4624) runs a high-speed ferry from New London, CT (1hr.; mid-June to mid-Sept. 4-5 per day, last ferry 7pm; $21, ages 2-11 $10; bike $10). Schedules are available at any of the terminals. The **Block Island Chamber of Commerce** (☎466-2982 or 800-383-2474; www.blockislandchamber.com), located at the ferry dock in Old Harbor, provides maps and information on accommodations on the island. (Lockers and ATM in the Visitors Center next door. Open in summer daily 9am-5pm; low-season hours vary.)

CONNECTICUT

Connecticut is like a patchwork quilt; industrialized centers like Hartford and New Haven are interspersed with serene New England villages, a vast coastline, and woodland beauty. Home to Yale University and the nation's first law school, Connecticut has a rich intellectual history. The "work hard, play hard" ethic seems to work here, however: Connecticut is also the state that brought us the three-ring circus and the largest casino in the US.

🛈 PRACTICAL INFORMATION

Capital: Hartford.

Visitor Info: Connecticut Vacation Center, 505 Hudson St., Hartford 06106 (☎800-282-6863; www.ctbound.org). Open M-F 8am-4:30pm.

Postal Abbreviation: CT. **Sales Tax:** 6%.

HARTFORD   ☎860

Hartford may be the world's insurance capital, but travelers will be more interested in the cool museums, the historical sites, and the lively theater scene. As Mark Twain—a revered resident for 17 years—boasted, "of all the beautiful towns it has been my fortune to see, this is the chief."

🖿🛈 TRANSPORTATION AND PRACTICAL INFORMATION. Hartford marks the intersection of the **Connecticut River, I-91,** and **I-84.** Union Place, between Church and Asylum St., houses Amtrak (☎727-1778; www.amtrak.com; office open M-F 6am-7:30pm, Sa-Su 6:30am-7:30pm), which runs **trains** to New Haven (1hr., $11) and New York City (3hr., $34), and Greyhound (☎724-1397; www.greyhound.com; station open daily 5:45am-10pm), which sends **buses** to Boston (2hr., 12 per day, $24), New Haven (1½hr., 4-5 per day, $12), and New York City (2½-3hr., 17 per day, $25). **Connecticut Transit Information Center** is the round terminal at State and Market St. (☎525-9181; www.cttransit.com. Open M-F 7am-6pm, Sa 9am-3pm. **Buses** within the city $1.25, students $1, seniors $0.60; day pass $3.25.) For a **taxi,** call Yellow Cab, ☎666-6666. **Greater Hartford Welcome Center** is at 45 Pratt St. (☎244-0253 or 800-793-4480; www.hartford.com. Open M-F 9am-5pm.) The **Old State House,** 800 Main St., also provides tourist info. (☎522-6766. Open M-Sa 10am-4pm.) **Internet Access: Hartford Public Library,** 500 Main St. (☎695-6300. Free Wi-Fi. Open M-Th 10am-8pm, Sa 10am-5pm; Oct.-May also Su 1-5pm.) **Post Office:** 80 State House Sq. (☎240-7553. Open M-F 8am-5pm.) **Postal Code:** 06103.

█ █ ACCOMMODATIONS AND FOOD. The **Mark Twain Hostel (HI) ❶**, 131 Tremont St., has 42 bunks. It's not exactly squeaky clean, but the price is right. Head west on Farmington Ave., then turn right on Tremont St., or take the "Farmington Ave." bus west. (☎523-7255. Kitchen. Linen included. Laundry $2.50. Check-in 5-10pm. Check-out 10am. Dorms $24, members $20. Cash only.)

Eateries in downtown Hartford consist mainly of cheap lunch places and trendy restaurants. Corporate clock-punchers crow the food carts near the Old State House and fill the food court at State House Square in the middle of the day. **Black-Eyed Sally's BBQ & Blues ❷**, 350 Asylum St., serves down-home Southern cooking. Enjoy jambalaya ($16) while you decipher the thousands of signatures covering the walls. (☎278-7427; www.blackeyedsallys.com. Sandwiches $7-9. Half-rack of ribs $14. W-Sa night live blues. Cover F-Sa $5-10. Open M-Th 11:30am-10pm, F 11:30am-11pm, Sa 5-11pm. Bar open late. AmEx/MC/V.) The alternative and business crowds mingle, if not mix, at **Jojo's Coffee ❶**, 22 Pratt St., which roasts its own coffee. (☎800-524-1488. Free Wi-Fi.)

█ SIGHTS. The ◪**Wadsworth Athenaeum,** 600 Main St., has collections of contemporary and Baroque art, including one of three Caravaggio paintings in the US. Rotating exhibitions, a breathtaking collection of Hudson River School landscapes, and a display of German and French porcelain round out an exceptional gallery. (☎278-2670. Open W-F 11am-5pm, Sa-Su 10am-5pm. $10, seniors $8, ages 13-18 and students with ID $5. Call ahead for tour and lecture info.) Designed by Charles Bulfinch in 1796, the gold-domed **Old State House,** 800 Main St., housed the state government until 1878. Now, historical actors take you into the chambers where Reverend Hooker delivered his revolutionary sermon in 1638 and the Amistad Trial began in 1839. On a lighter note, the museum of curiosities inside includes a crocodile, a tiger, and a two-headed calf. (☎522-6766; www.ctosh.org. Open M-F 10am-4pm, Sa 11am-4pm. Free.) **Bushnell Park,** at Jewell St., has a 1914 **carousel,** complete with an organ. (☎585-5411. Open May-Oct. Tu-Su 11am-5pm. Rides $1.) The **Mark Twain House and Museum,** 351 Farmington Ave., presents entertaining tours of the intricately textured home where the author penned parts of *The Adventures of Huckleberry Finn* and *Tom Sawyer*. From the Old State House, take any "Farmington Ave." bus west. (☎247-0998. Open M-W and F-Su 9:30am-5:30pm, Th 9:30am-8pm; Jan.-Apr. closed Tu. Tours fill quickly. Last tour 1hr. before closing. $13, seniors $11, ages 6-12 $8.) The **Harriet Beecher Stowe House,** 77 Forest St., adjacent to Twain's home, has tours with information about the life and times of the *Uncle Tom's Cabin* author, whom Abraham Lincoln called "the little lady that started the big war." (☎522-9258; www.harrietbeecherstowe.org. Open June to mid-Oct. Tu-Sa 9:30am-4:30pm, Su noon-4:30pm; mid-Oct. to May closed M. $8, seniors $7, ages 6-16 $4.)

█ █ ENTERTAINMENT AND NIGHTLIFE. The Tony Award-winning **Hartford Stage Company,** 50 Church St., stages productions of traditional works, American classics, and contemporary works. (☎527-5151; www.hartfordstage.org. Tickets $20-60.) **TheaterWorks,** 233 Pearl St., is an off-Broadway-style theater that presents a variety of recent plays. (☎527-7838; www.theaterworkshartford.org. Tickets $35-55.) For more shows, head to **The Bushnell,** 166 Capitol Ave., home of Hartford's symphony, ballet, and opera companies, as well as a venue for Broadway hits, jazz, and family favorites. (☎987-5900; www.bushnell.org. Box office open M-Sa 10am-5pm, Su noon-4pm. Rush and student-rate tickets sometimes available.)

Downtown is pretty empty on weeknights, but on weekends Hartford's nightlife is concentrated along Asylum St. and around the train station. Take advantage of the ultimate combination of food, nightlife, and entertainment at the **City Steam Brewery and BrewHaHa Comedy Club,** 942 Main St. Pool tables fill one room while red

NEW ENGLAND

velvet couches line lounges complete with card tables and TVs. Nine brewing tanks hold home-brewed masterpieces like "Naughty Nurse" Pale Ale. Upstairs, the comedy club keeps guests in stitches. (☎525-1600. M margaritas $2, M-F 10pm-midnight martinis $3. W Irish music. Th comedy shows 8pm, F 9pm, Sa 7 and 10pm; cover $5-15. F-Sa live rock and blues. Open M-Th 11:30am-midnight, F-Sa 11:30am-1am, Su 4-10pm. Kitchen closes M-Th 10:30pm, F-Sa midnight.) With a loyal clientele, pool table, and weekday drink specials, **McKinnon's,** 114 Asylum St., is the best place to find cool brews and good times. (☎524-8174. M karaoke. 21+. Cover varies. Open M-Th 11am-1am, F-Sa 11am-2am.) If you want to ditch the raucous crowds, try **Tapas On Ann,** 126 Ann St., where great Greek food and tapas complement the full bar. (☎525-5988. Open M-Th 11am-1am, F 11am-2am, Sa 5pm-2am. Kitchen closes M 9pm, Tu-Th 10pm, F-Sa 11pm.)

NEW HAVEN   ☎203

In an effort to shake a bad reputation that continues to haunt it, New Haven is growing from the inside out. The center of the Elm City is home to the solid stone foundations of Yale University, a shining academic light that continues to expand into the darker areas of the city's troubled past. Today, the "new" New Haven, especially the area immediately around Yale's campus, sustains a healthy assortment of ethnic restaurants, art galleries, divey pizza parlors, and coffee shops supported by both students and townies alike.

■ **ORIENTATION AND PRACTICAL INFORMATION.** New Haven lies at the intersection of **I-95** and **I-91,** 40 mi. south of Hartford, and is laid out in nine squares surrounded by radial roads. Between Yale University and City Hall, the central square, called **The Green,** provides a pleasant place to sit and relax. At night, don't wander too far from the immediate downtown and campus areas; some of the surrounding sections can be very unsafe. Amtrak, at Union Station, on Union Ave., Exit 1 off I-91 (☎773-6177; www.amtrak.com; ticket office open daily 6:30am-9:30pm), runs **trains** to: Boston (2½hr., 16 per day, $55); Mystic (1hr., 3-4 per day, $21); New York City (1½hr., 10 per day, $31); Washington, D.C. (5½hr., 10 per day, $94). Also at Union Station, Greyhound (☎772-2470; www.greyhound.com; ticket office open daily 7am-8pm) runs frequent **buses** to Boston (3½-5hr., 11 per day, $30), New York City (2½hr., 11 per day, $21), and Providence (2½hr., 11 per day, $22). The **New Haven Trolley Line** services the downtown area and Yale. (☎288-6282. Runs every 15min. M-Sa 11am-6pm. Free.) For a **taxi,** call MetroTaxi, ☎777-7777. **Internet Access: New Haven Public Library,** 133 Elm St. (☎946-8130. Free with photo ID. Open mid-Sept. to May M noon-8pm, Tu-Th 10am-8pm, Sa 10am-5pm; June to mid-Sept. M-Th 10am-6pm, F 10am-5pm.) **Post Office:** 150 Court St., in the federal building. (☎752-3283. Open M-F 7:30am-5pm, Sa 8am-noon.) **Postal Code:** 06510.

■ **ACCOMMODATIONS.** Inexpensive lodgings are sparse; the hunt intensifies and prices jump around Yale Parents Weekend (mid-October) and Commencement (early June). Head 10 mi. south on I-95 to **Milford** for affordable motels. **Hotel Duncan ❸,** 1151 Chapel St., located in the heart of Yale's campus, exudes old-fashioned charm. Guests enjoy spacious rooms and the chance to ride in the state's oldest manually operated elevator. (☎787-1273. Reservations recommended on weekends. Singles $49-55; doubles $65-75. AmEx/MC/V.) **Hammonasset Beach State Park ❶,** 20min. east of New Haven off I-95 N Exit 62 in Madison, has 558 sites just a few minutes from woods and a long sandy beach. (☎245-1817. Office open mid-May to Oct. daily 8am-10:30pm. Lifeguard on duty 8am-8pm. Free hot showers. Sites $15, walk-ins $18. Day use M-F $10, Sa-Su $14. Cash only.)

🔆 **FOOD.** For great, authentic Italian cuisine, work your way along Wooster St., in Little Italy, a 10min. walk east of downtown. Try to beat the lines at ⊠**Frank Pepe's Pizzeria ❸**, 157 Wooster St., which claims to be the originator of the American pizza, originally known as "tomato pie," in the 20s. The thin-crust pizza is served dripping with sauce and cheese and comes with an essential stack of napkins. (☎865-5762. Open M-Th 4-10pm, F-Sa 11:30am-11pm, Su 2:30-10pm. Cash only.) Next door, **Libby's ❶**, 139 Wooster St., has yummy cannoli ($1.50-2.50) and gelato. (☎772-0380. Open M and W-Th 11:30am-10pm, F-Sa 11:30am-11pm, Su 11:30am-9pm. Cash only.) No condiments are allowed at **Louis' Lunch ❶**, 263 Crown St. Cooked in suspended grills, the beloved burgers ($4.50) go well with apple pie. (☎562-5507. Open Tu-W 11am-4pm, Th-Sa noon-2am. Cash only.)

📷 **SIGHTS.** The majority of the sights and museums in New Haven are located on or near the **Yale University** campus. Most of the campus buildings were designed in the English Gothic or Georgian Colonial styles, many of them with intricate moldings and a few with gargoyles. The **Yale Visitors Center,** 149 Elm St., faces the Green and is the starting point for campus tours. (☎432-2300; www.yale.edu. Open M-F 9am-4:45pm, Sa-Su 11am-4pm. Free 1hr. tours M-F 10:30am and 2pm, Sa-Su 1:30pm.) Bordered by Chapel, College, Grove, and High St., the charming Old Campus contains **Connecticut Hall,** which, raised in 1753, is the university's oldest remaining building. A block north, on the other side of Elm St., **Sterling Memorial Library,** 120 High St., is designed to resemble a monastery—even the telephone booths are shaped like confessionals. The design is not entirely without a sense of humor, though—carved stone brackets portray students sleeping, smoking, and lounging. (☎432-1852. Open Sept.-June M-Th and Su 8:30am-midnight, F 8:30am-10pm, Sa 10am-7pm; July-Aug. M-W and F 8:30am-5pm, Th 8:30am-10pm, Sa 10am-5pm. Free Internet access.) Paneled with Vermont marble cut thin enough to be translucent, **Beinecke Rare Book and Manuscript Library,** 121 Wall St., is a massive modern structure containing more than 600,000 rare books and manuscripts, including one of Gutenberg's Bibles. Rotating exhibits allow visitors to see the collection. (☎436-1254. Open M-Th 8:30am-8pm, F 8:30am-5pm. Free.) Open since 1832, the **Yale University Art Gallery,** 1111 Chapel St., at York St., holds over 100,000 pieces, including an impressive array of classical Greek sculpture and works by Monet, Van Gogh, Matisse, and Picasso. (☎432-0600. Open Tu-W and F-Sa 10am-5pm, Th 10am-8pm, Su 1-6pm. Self-guided audio tours available. Free.) Just down the road, the **Yale Center for British Art,** 1080 Chapel St., holds the largest collection of British art outside the United Kingdom. (☎432-2800. Open Tu-Sa 10am-5pm, Su noon-5pm. Free.) The **Peabody Museum of Natural History,** 170 Whitney Ave., Exit 3 off I-91, houses Rudolph F. Zallinger's Pulitzer Prize-winning mural "Age of Reptiles" in a room populated with dinosaur skeletons. The museum also has a 100-million-year-old 8 ft. turtle and a mummy. (☎432-5050. Open M-Sa 10am-5pm, Su noon-5pm. $7, seniors $6, students and ages 3-15 $5.) Outside the campus area and accessed from East Rock Rd. northeast of the city, **East Rock Park** provides an excellent sunset view of New Haven and the Long Island Sound from an overlook 325 ft. above sea level. (☎782-4314. Open dawn-dusk.)

🎭📷 **ENTERTAINMENT AND NIGHTLIFE.** New Haven was once the testing ground for Broadway-bound plays, and its theatrical tradition remains, fueled by student crowds. The **Yale Repertory Theatre,** 1120 Chapel St. (☎432-1234), performs a variety of classic and contemporary plays throughout the school year. Now more than 40 years old, the **Long Wharf Theatre,** 222 Sargant Dr. (☎787-4282), still serves as a springboard for new plays hoping to make the leap to Broadway. The **Shubert**

Performing Arts Center, 247 College St. (☎562-5666 or 800-955-5566), is New Haven's entertainment centerpiece, offering musicals, dance, and opera.

🏠**Toad's Place,** 300 York St., has hosted Bob Dylan, the Rolling Stones, and George Clinton. Also a popular spot with students, Toad's throws dance parties on Wednesday and Saturday nights during the school year. (☎562-5694, recorded info 624-8623. Box office open M-F 11am-6pm; buy tickets at the bar after 8pm. 21+. Cover $5-35 for shows; $5 for dance nights. Open M-Th and Su 8pm-1am, F-Sa 8pm-2am; closed when no show.) **Bar,** 254 Crown St., is a cool hangout with a pool table, lounge, dance floor/theater, five homemade beers brewing in tanks at the bar, and brick-oven pizza. Alternative Night every Tuesday ("Boom") attracts a large gay crowd. (☎495-8924. Live music 3-4 nights per week. Cover Tu $3, Sa $6. Open M-Tu and Su 4pm-1am, W-Th 11:30am-2:30pm and 4pm-1am, F-Sa 11:30am-2am.)

MYSTIC AND THE CONNECTICUT COAST   ☎860

When Herman Melville's white whale became a legend in *Moby Dick,* Connecticut's coastal towns were busy seaports full of dark, musty inns and tattooed sailors. Today, vacationers and sailing enthusiasts still head to the coast seeking a whale of a good time. Along the Mystic River, **Mystic Seaport,** 1 mi. south on Rte. 27 from I-95 at Exit 90, offers a look at 18th-century whaling. In the recreated village, staff demonstrate historic life-saving techniques and help visitors navigate the decks of the museum's ships. (☎888-973-2767; www.mysticseaport.org. Open daily Apr.-Oct. 9am-5pm, F-Sa until 8pm; Nov.-Mar. 10am-4pm. $17, seniors and students $15, ages 6-12 $12. Tickets good for 2 days.) A few dollars more puts you on an authentic 1908 coal-fired steamboat for **Sabino Charters'** cruise along the Mystic River. (☎572-5351. 30min. trips every 30min. mid-May to early Oct. daily 10:30am-3:30pm. $5.50, ages 6-17 $4.50. 1½hr. cruise at 4:30pm. $12/10.) The **Mystic Aquarium and Institute for Exploration,** 55 Coogan Blvd., at Exit 90 off I-95, has a menagerie of seals, penguins, sharks, and white beluga whales. (☎572-5955; www.mysticaquarium.org. Open daily July-early Sept. 9am-6pm; early Sept.-June 9am-5pm. $19.75, seniors $19.25, ages 3-12 $14.25.) The **Denison Pequotsepos Nature Center,** 109 Pequotsepos Rd., 1½ mi. east of downtown, offers 8 mi. of trails through three diverse ecosystems. The nature center also has interactive exhibits like "After Dark in the Meadow." (☎536-1216; www.dpnc.org. Nature center open M-Sa 9am-5pm, Su 10am-4pm. Park open dawn-dusk. $6, seniors and under 12 $4.)

Budget lodgings are scarce in Mystic, though there are a few hotels at the intersection of Rte. 27 and I-95. The **Stonington Motel ❸,** 901 Stonington Rd., 5 mi. from Mystic on Rte. 1 N, has tidy rooms with A/C, cable TV, a microwave, and a minifridge. (☎599-2330. Rooms $55-80. AmEx/MC/V.) Close to Mystic, **Seaport Campground ❶,** on Rte. 184, 3 mi. north of Rte. 27 from Mystic, boasts a pool, mini-golf course, fishing pond, and live music on weekends. (☎536-4044. Open mid-Apr. to late Oct. Check-in before 11pm. Mid-May to mid-Sept. tent sites with water and electricity $38; RV sites $42. Apr. to mid-May and mid-Sept. to late Oct. $31/34. Each additional adult $7, child $1.50. D/MC/V.) Though Julia Roberts is no longer serving, **Mystic Pizza ❷,** 56 W. Main St., made famous by the film of the same name, still serves heavenly slices of pizza. (☎536-3700. Pizza $6-11. Open 11am-11pm. AmEx/D/MC/V.) For takeout that's almost gourmet, head to **Mystic Market East ❶,** 63 Williams St., which has terrific sandwiches ($5-7), like the Black Forest ham with French brie. (☎572-7992. Open M-Sa 7am-7pm, Su 7am-5pm. AmEx/D/MC/V.) A throwback to the days of sea captains and grog, 🏠**Captain Daniel Packer Inne,** 32 Water St., serves the "Dark and Stormy," black rum with a splash of ginger beer. (☎536-3555. Live music begins at 10pm. Dining room open daily 11am-4pm and 5-10pm; bar open M-Th and Su until 1am, F-Sa until 2am.)

NEW ENGLAND

Amtrak (☎800-872-7245; www.amtrak.com; open daily 10am-4pm; no ticket office), half a mile east of Mystic on Rte. 1, runs **trains** to Boston (1½hr., 3 per day, $34), New Haven (1hr., 3 per day, $21), and New York City (3hr., 4 per day, $42). The **Mystic Tourist and Information Center,** Bldg. 1D in Olde Mistick Village, at the corner of Rte. 27 and Coogan St., offers maps, discounted tickets to attractions, a 24hr. digital hotel board with listings of all vacancies, and a direct phone line to accommodations in the region. (☎536-1641; www.mysticinfo.com. Open mid-June to Sept. M-Sa 9:30am-6pm, Su 10am-5pm; Oct. to early June M-Sa 9am-5:30pm, Su 10am-5pm.) **Internet Access: Mystic and Noank Library,** 40 Library St., in Mystic. (☎536-7721. $0.25 per 15min. Open M-W 10am-9pm, Th-Sa 10am-5pm; mid-June to early Sept. closes Sa 1pm.) **Post Office:** 23 E. Main St. (☎536-8143. Open M-F 8am-5pm, Sa 8:30am-12:30pm.) **Postal Code:** 06355.

THE SOUTH

The American consciousness has become much more homogeneous since the 1860s, but differences, though not as dramatic, persist between North and South. Outside the area's commercial capitals, Southerners continue to live slower-paced lives than their northern countrymen. Nevertheless, the South's legacy of racial tension is still an ugly blemish on its history; the effects of slavery have not yet been completely washed away, and the Civil Rights movement is too recent a development to be comfortably relegated to textbooks.

At the same time, the South's racial differences have inspired many aspects of American culture for which the country is known the world over, from great literature to nearly *all* music native to the country: gospel, blues, jazz, country, R&B, and rock 'n' roll all claim the South as their birthplace. The South's distinctive architecture, cuisine, and language are all products of its Spanish, French, and Native American influences throughout the years. Landscapes are equally varied—the region is filled with mountains, beaches, and of course, the bayou. The traveler here should forget facile stereotypes and discover a part of the world that is overlooked and underestimated. In the South you'll find Bible factories and booze distilleries, rural backcountry and raging cities, traditional comfort food and finger-lickin' good barbecue, and some of the best entertainment the US has to offer.

HIGHLIGHTS OF THE SOUTH

GNAW on juicy ribs at local joints like **Dreamland Barbecue** (p. 393) and wash them down with some old-fashioned Southern sweet tea.

GYRATE like Elvis at **Graceland** (p. 328), kick up your heels to zydeco in **New Orleans** (p. 412), or wallow in your sorrows in **Memphis** (p. 331), where blues is king.

FANCY yourself a Southern Belle as you tour **historic plantations** like the ones in Charleston, SC (p. 358), that capture the grandeur of the Old South.

REMEMBER the Civil Rights Movement at **The Martin Luther King Center** (p. 370) in Atlanta, GA and the **Birmingham Civil Rights Institute** (p. 391) in Birmingham, AL.

In August 2005, Category Five Hurricane Katrina struck the Gulf Coast of the United States, devastating cities and killing thousands in the states of Alabama, Louisiana, and Mississippi. While much progress has been made, parts of the South are still trying to recover from the disaster's emotional and physical impact. *Let's Go: USA's* coverage reflects the South's state as of August 2007.

KENTUCKY

Legendary for its duels, feuds, and the stubborn spirit exhibited by its early inhabitants (such as the infamous Daniel Boone), Kentucky invites travelers to kick back, take a shot of the legendary local bourbon, and relax amid rolling hills and the sound of bluegrass. The state also boasts an extensive network of caves, including the longest known cave in the world. Today, the spirit of Kentucky can be boiled down to one pastime: going fast. The state is home to the signature American sports car, the Corvette, and to the world's premier horse race, the Ken-

The South

tucky Derby. Louisville tends to ignore its vibrant cultural scene and active night-life at Derby time, and Lexington devotes much of its farmland to breeding champion racehorses.

⚡ PRACTICAL INFORMATION

Capital: Frankfort.

Visitor Info: Kentucky Dept. of Tourism, Capital Plaza Tower, 500 Mero St., Ste. 2200, Frankfort 40601 (☎502-564-4930 or 800-225-8747; www.kentuckytourism.com). **Kentucky State Parks,** Capital Plaza Tower, 500 Mero St., Ste. 1100, Frankfort 40601 (☎800-255-7275; www.parks.ky.gov).

Postal Abbreviation: KY. **Sales Tax:** 6%.

LOUISVILLE   ☎ 502

When the familiar gremlins of white flight and deindustrialization caught up with Louisville (LOO-uh-vuhl) in the 50s, Kentucky's largest city spent a few decades adrift before setting its sights on revitalization. Residents can't quite agree on what a revitalized Louisville should look like, but new development determined to "keep Louisville weird" has begun. Louisville's biggest draw is still the Kentucky Derby. The horse race that some call "the greatest two minutes in sports" will return to town on May 6, 2008.

🖿⚡ TRANSPORTATION AND PRACTICAL INFORMATION. The Louisville International Airport (SDF; ☎367-4636; www.louintlairport.com) is 15min. south of downtown on I-65; take bus #2 into the city. A **taxi** to downtown costs around $16. Greyhound, 720 W. Muhammad Ali Blvd. (☎561-2805; www.greyhound.com; open 24hr.), between 7th and 8th St., runs **buses** to: Chicago (6hr., 9 per day, $48.50); Cincinnati (2hr., 8 per day, $24); Indianapolis (2hr., 9 per day, $25); Lexington (2-4hr., 4 per day, $24). The Transit Authority River City (TARC) **bus** system serves the metro area. (☎585-1234; www.ridetarc.com. Schedules vary by route; buses run as early as 4:30am until as late as 11:30pm. $1.25, ages 6-17 and over 65 $0.50 with TARC ID; transfers free.) Two **trolley** routes service Main St./Market St. (M-F 6:45am-6:30pm, Sa 10am-6pm) and 4th St. (M-F 7am-11pm, Sa 9:30am-10pm). **Trolley** rides cost $0.50. For a **taxi,** call Cardinal Cab ☎636-5511.

Interstates through the city include **I-65** (north-south expressway), **I-71,** and **I-64.** The easily accessible **Watterson Expressway (I-264)** rings the city, while the **Gene Snyder Freeway (I-265)** spirals farther out. In central downtown, **Main Street** and **Market Street** run east-west in opposite directions (both are one-way), and **Preston Highway** and **19th Street** run north-south. The **West End,** beyond 20th St., is a rough area. **Visitor Info:** The **Louisville Visitor Information Center** is at 301 S. 4th St., in the Hyatt Regency Hotel. (☎584-2121; www.gotolouisville.com. Open M-Sa 10am-6pm, Su noon-5pm; Oct.-Mar. closed Su.) **Internet Access:** The **Louisville Free Public Library** is at 301 York St. (☎574-1611. Free with photo ID. Limit 1hr. Open M-Th 9am-9pm, F-Sa 9am-5pm, Su 1-5pm.) **Hotlines: Rape Hotline,** ☎581-7273. **Crisis Center,** ☎589-4313. Both operate 24hr. **GLBT Hotline:** ☎454-7613. Operates daily 6-10pm. **Post Office:** 835 S. 7th St. (☎587-8546. Open M-F 8am-5pm.) **Postal Code:** 40203.

🏠 ACCOMMODATIONS. Lodging options downtown are plentiful, but pricey. Budget motels are on **I-65** near the airport or across the river in **Jeffersonville, IN. Newburg Road,** 6 mi. south, is also a budget haven. Derby Week lodging is expensive; make reservations up to a year in advance. Starting around January, the Visitors Center helps travelers arrange rooms for the event. The cheapest beds are the foam mattresses in the basement of the **Emily Boone Guest House and Hostel ❶,** 102

Pope St., off Franklin Ave. The entrance to the hostel is on the side of the house at the garage door. Call ahead to make sure Ms. Boone will be home to receive you. Boone houses up to three backpackers at a time in exchange for 20min. of chores around her house and yard. Expect to get cozy with her long-haired dog, Violet, who also sleeps in the basement. (☎585-3430. No linens provided. Bed $10. Cash only.) For more in the way of comfort, **Super 8 ❸**, 101 Central Ave., near Churchill Downs and the University of Louisville, has clean rooms and a stellar location. (☎635-0799. Laundry. Breakfast and airport shuttle included. Singles $55; doubles $65. AmEx/D/MC/V.) **Louisville Metro KOA ❶**, 900 Marriott Dr., across the river in Indiana, has campsites 10min. from town. (☎812-282-4474. Reserve well in advance. 2-person sites $28-31, with hookup $31. Each additional person $4, under 18 $2.50. 2-person cabins $40-45.)

❒ FOOD. Good budget food is hard to find downtown. **Bardstown Road** is lined with cafes, budget eateries, and global cuisine, while **Frankfort Road** is rapidly catching up. Downtown, **Fourth Street Live!**, at Broadway and 4th St., has various lunch options. The mannequin legs jutting out of the day-glow walls at ◙ **Lynn's Paradise Cafe ❸**, 984 Barret Ave., give an inkling of what it would be like to live in a surrealist painting where breakfast is served all day. Try the pancakes filled with cinnamon granola ($7.25) or dinner platters, like fried catfish with mustard-shallot sauce ($14.25), available after 11am. (☎583-3447. Open M-F 7am-10pm, Sa-Su 8am-10pm. AmEx/MC/V.) **Cafe 360 ❷**, 1582 Bardstown Rd., is a cafe and hookah bar that serves vegan-friendly sandwiches and ethnic cuisine to a chatty, younger set. Salads and soups are a lunch deal—fill up on the vegetarian chili for $3. The fully stocked bar starts serving at 6am. (☎473-8694. Open 24hr. except M 4am-11am. Sandwiches $4-5. Hookah $6. AmEx/MC/V.)

◙ SIGHTS. Browsing the record stores, cafes, boutiques, and antique shops on the **Highlands** strip can easily fill an afternoon. The strip runs along Baxter Ave. and Bardstown Rd. between Broadway and Trevilian Way. (Take buses #17 or 23.) Down by the University of Louisville campus, the **Speed Art Museum**, 2035 S. 3rd St., shows off a treasure trove of European paintings. As the largest art museum in Kentucky, the Speed also draws major temporary exhibitions. The permanent collection includes Cezanne's celebrated painting *Two Apples on a Table*. (☎634-2700; www.speedmuseum.org. Open Tu-W and F 10:30am-4pm, Th 10:30am-8pm, Sa 10:30am-5pm. Free; special exhibitions $5-10.) J.F. Hillerich & Son started out manufacturing butter churns in the 1870s, but the enormous baseball bat leaning up against the **Louisville Slugger Factory and Museum**, 800 W. Main St., belongs to the company's more lucrative product line. The museum traces the history of the Slugger, while a factory tour leads visitors through sawdust and past lengths of wood that have been earmarked for specific major-leaguers. At the tour's end, visitors receive a miniature bat of their own. (☎877-775-8443; www.sluggermuseum.org. Open Jan.-June M-Sa 9am-5pm, Su noon-5pm; July to mid-Aug. M-Sa 9am-6pm, Su noon-6pm; mid-Aug. to Nov. M-Sa 9am-5pm, Su noon-5pm. $9, seniors $8, ages 6-12 $4.) The **American Printing House for the Blind**, 1839 Frankfort Ave., has a small but fascinating museum on the development of Braille and other technologies for aiding the blind. The facility is the world's largest publishing house dedicated to the visually impaired. (☎895-2405; www.aph.org. Open M-F 8:30am-4:30pm, Sa 10am-3pm. 1hr. tours M-Th 10am and 2pm. Wheelchair-accessible. Free.)

◙◙ ENTERTAINMENT AND NIGHTLIFE. Two free weeklies, *Leo* and *Velocity*, are available throughout the city and spotlight current happenings. Broadway shows, comedy acts, and big-name music performers take the stage at the lavishly decorated **Louisville Palace**, 625 S. 4th Ave. (☎361-3100. Tickets $20-100. Box office open M-F noon-5pm.) The respected **Actors Theatre,** 316 W. Main St., raises the curtain on a season of comedy, drama, and March's **Humana Festival of New American Plays.** (☎584-1205; www.actorstheatre.org. Box office open M 10am-5:30pm, Tu-W 10am-8pm, Th-Sa 10am-8:30pm, Su 1-8pm. Student and senior rush tickets 15min. before curtain; $17) On the **First Friday** of every month, more than a dozen of Louisville's downtown galleries treat visitors to special openings and refreshments until 9pm. Trolleys provide free transportation between galleries 5-11pm. The **Kentucky Shakespeare Festival,** at the amphitheater in Central Park in Old Louisville, struts upon the stage from late June to July. (☎637-4933; www.kyshakes.org. Performances 8pm. Free.) Quirky **Lebowski Fest** draws fans of the Coen brothers' comedy *The Big Lebowski* (1998) for a summer weekend of bowling, live music, and opportunities to quote obscure dialogue to like-minded "Achievers." (☎583-9290; www.lebowskifest.com. Tickets $10-40.) Clubs cluster on Baxter Ave. near Broadway. **The Pink Door,** 222 Dundee Rd., serves noodle dishes ($5) to aficionados of Asian cuisine and hipsters who like their dinner with a heavy dose of irony—menu includes dishes with ramen noodles, an infamous college staple. After dinner, dance to live music (Th-Sa) or relax and chat on the comfy sofas in the lounge. (☎413-5204. Beer $2.50-4. Open M-W 5pm-2am, Th-Sa 5pm-4am, Su 8pm-2am.) **The Connection,** 120 S. Floyd St., is the crown jewel of Kentucky's gay nightlife, with six amazing venues under one roof. Multiple bars, a showroom for drag performances, and a vast dance floor draw capacity crowds as the week wears on. (☎585-5752. 21+. Cover $3-5, includes all bars. Happy hour daily 5-10pm. Open M-Tu 7pm-2am, W-Su 7pm-4am. Dance floor open W-Sa 9pm-4am.)

◥ DAYTRIPS FROM LOUISVILLE

BARDSTOWN. Kentucky's 2nd-oldest city, 17 mi. east on Rte. 245 from I-65 Exit 112, charms visitors with its historic downtown district. The real attractions, however, are the bourbon distilleries outside of town. Bardstown, once home to 29 distilleries, is still proudly known as the "Bourbon Capital of the World." It all started in 1791, when Kentucky Baptist Reverend Elijah Craig left a fire unattended while heating oak boards to make a barrel for his aging whiskey. The boards were scorched, but Rev. Craig carried on, and bourbon was born in that charred oak barrel. Today, 90% of America's native bourbon still hails from Kentucky, and 60% of that is distilled in Nelson and Bullitt Counties.

    Jim Beam's American Outpost, 15 mi. west of Bardstown in Clermont, off Rte. 245, treats visitors to samples of the world's best-selling bourbon (M-Sa), lemonade, coffee, and bourbon candies. Peek into a warehouse with thousands of the 53-gallon barrels of aging bourbon stored at the distillery, check out an authentic moonshine still and Jeremiah Beam's historic home, or watch a video about the company's 200-year history. (☎502-543-9877. Open M-Sa 9am-4:30pm, Su 1-4pm. Free.) Visitors can take a factory tour at **Maker's Mark Distillery,** 19 mi. southeast of Bardstown on Rte. 52 E in Loretto. Any day but Sunday, buy a bottle and hand-dip it in the trademark red wax. (☎270-865-2099; www.makersmark.com. Tours every hour M-Sa 10:30am-3:30pm, Su 1:30-3:30. Gift shop open M-Sa 10am-4:30pm; Mar.-Dec. also Su 1-4:30pm.) Bardstown also hosts the **Kentucky Bourbon Festival** (☎800-638-4877; www.kybourbonfestival.com) every September, with several days of tours, events, and bourbon-drinking. **Bardstown-Nelson County Tourism Office,** 1 Court Sq., is in the courthouse. (☎502-348-9545; www.visitbardstown.com. Open in summer M-F 8am-6pm, Sa 9am-6pm, Su 11am-3:30pm; call for winter hours.)

MAMMOTH CAVE NATIONAL PARK. Plummeting sinkholes and narrow crawlspaces burrow their way through the limestone underneath **Mammoth Cave National Park,** 80 mi. south of Louisville in central Kentucky. From I-65, turn off at

Exit 48 (Park City) or Exit 53 (Cave City) and follow signs to the Visitors Center. With over 365 mi. of mapped caves, Mammoth Cave comprises the world's longest network of cavern corridors—over three times longer than any other known cave system. Tours depart from the Visitors Center. (☎758-2180 or 800-967-2283; www.nps.gov/maca. Open daily 8:30am-7pm; low season 8:45am-5pm. Call for tour schedule.) The **Frozen Niagara Tour** (¾ mi., 2hr.) provides a good introduction to the cave's geology ($10, ages 6-12 $8), while the **Violet City Lantern Tour** (3 mi., 3hr.) shuns electricity in favor of some old-fashioned spelunking ($15/11); reservations for the lantern tour should be made in advance. Bring a jacket, even in summer, as temperatures underground hover around 54°F year-round. Above ground, the 52,000-acre park has walking, biking, and horseback riding trails, plus fishing and canoeing. Camping with bathhouses, a camp store, and laundry is available at the pleasant **Headquarters Campground ❶**, near the Visitors Center. (☎758-2424. RVs allowed, but sites have no hookups. Showers $2. Open Mar.-Nov. Sites $17.) Free **backcountry camping** permits can also be obtained at the Visitors Center, and motel rooms start from $35 on the outskirts of nearby Cave City.

LEXINGTON   ☎859

Home to the first institution of higher learning west of the Alleghenies, Lexington has more than two centuries of experience as a college town. These days, the basketball wizardry of the University of Kentucky plays second fiddle only to the thoroughbred horses that are groomed for the Kentucky Derby on farms outside the city. Lexington is Kentucky's 2nd-largest city, yet the pedestrian-friendly downtown lends the place a relaxed, down-home feel.

▌ TRANSPORTATION

Airport: Blue Grass Airport (LEX), 4000 Terminal Dr. (☎425-3114; www.bluegrassairport.com), off Man O' War Blvd. about 6 mi. west of downtown. Ritzy downtown hotels run shuttles, but there is no public transit. Taxi to downtown about $15.

Buses: Greyhound, 477 W. New Circle Rd. NW. (☎299-0428). Open daily 8am-6pm, 9pm-11pm. To **Cincinnati** (1½hr. 3 per day, $22); **Knoxville** (3½hr., 5 per day, $48.50); and **Louisville** (2-5hr., 4 per day, $22).

Public Transit: LexTran (☎253-4636; www.lextran.com). Buses leave from the Transit Center, 220 E. Vine St., on a long block between Limestone and Rose St. Office open M-F 6am-6pm, Sa 8am-noon. Serves the university and city outskirts. Most routes run 5am-9pm. $1, ages 5-18 $1, seniors and disabled $0.50; transfers free.

Taxi: Lexington Yellow Cab, ☎231-8294.

✷ ⚡ ORIENTATION AND PRACTICAL INFORMATION

I-64 and **I-75** pass Lexington to the northeast. **New Circle Road (Route 4, U.S. 60 bypass, U.S. 421 bypass,** and **U.S. 25 bypass)** loops around the city, intersecting with many roads that connect the downtown district to the surrounding towns. **High, Vine** and **Main Street,** running east-west, and **Limestone** and **Broadway Street,** running north-south, are the major routes through downtown. Beware of the curving one-way streets downtown and near the **University of Kentucky (UK)** to the south.

Visitor Info: Lexington Convention and Visitors Bureau, 301 E. Vine St. (☎233-7299 or 800-845-3959; www.visitlex.com), at Rose St. Open in summer M-F 8:30am-5pm.

Hotlines: Crisis Intervention, ☎253-2737 or 800-928-8000. **Rape Crisis,** ☎253-2511 or 800-656-4673. Both 24hr.

Medical Services: Saint Joseph East Hospital, 150 N. Eagle Creek Dr. (☎967-5000).

Internet Access: Lexington Public Library, 140 E. Main St. (☎231-5500), at Limestone St. 1hr. slots. Open M-Th 9am-9pm, F-Sa 9am-5pm, Su 1-5pm.

Post Office: 210 E. High St. (☎254-6156). Open M-F 8am-5pm. **Postal Code:** 40507.

▎ ACCOMMODATIONS

Three-star hotels and antique-heavy B&Bs offer little in the way of affordable lodgings downtown. The cheapest rooms are outside the city on New Circle Rd. or near I-75 at Winchester Rd. and Newtown Pike.

Motel 6, 2260 Elkhorn Rd. (☎293-1431), off I-75 at Exit 110, 3½ mi. west of downtown. Young families and weekend revelers can make it a noisy place to stay, but you'll sleep easier knowing that you're getting the lowest rates around. A/C, cable TV, and pool. Singles M-Th and Su $40, F-Sa $50. Each additional person $6. AmEx/D/MC/V. ❷

Extended Stay America, 2750 Gribbin Dr. (☎266-4800 or 800-398-7829; www.ext-stay.com). From New Circle Rd., take Exit 15 and follow Richmond Rd.; turn right onto Patchen Dr. and left onto Gribbin Dr. Spacious rooms include cable TV with HBO, fully equipped kitchenettes, and free local calls. Pool and on-site laundry facilities. Studio with queen bed $55. Stays 1 week or longer $42 per night. AmEx/D/MC/V. ❸

Kentucky Horse Park Campground, 4089 Ironworks Pkwy. (☎259-4257 or 800-370-6416, ext. 257; www.kyhorsepark.com), 10 mi. north of downtown off I-75 at Exit 120. 260 well-manicured campsites with bath houses, Internet access, laundry, playground, basketball/volleyball/tennis courts, and swimming pool. Apr.-Oct. tent sites $15, with hookup $20. Nov.-Mar. $13/19. ❶

▎ FOOD

On the east end of downtown, cafes and sandwich shops cluster around **South Broadway** and the one-time slave market of **Cheapside.** Funkier student haunts line **High Street,** on the southern edge of the UK campus. The **Lexington Farmers' Market** sells fresh produce, breads, and cheeses in summer. The stalls at **200 South Broadway** open at 7am on Tuesdays and Thursdays, while the **300 Southland Drive** vendors start hawking their wares at 11am on Sundays.

▨ **Alfalfa Restaurant,** 141 E. Main St. (☎253-0014; www.alfalfarestaurant.com). Certainly praiseworthy for its exposed-brick dining room and live music. But it's the food that puts this downtown mainstay in a league of its own. Vegetarian entrees $12-16. F-Sa live music 8-10pm. Open M-Tu 11am-2pm, W-Th 11am-2pm and 5:30-10pm, F 11am-2pm and 5:30-11pm, Sa 9am-2pm and 5:30-11pm, Su 9am-2pm. MC/V. ❸

Third Street Stuff, 257 N. Limestone (☎255-5301). A bright purple alternative gift shop and coffeehouse with vegetarian sandwiches ($3-6). Try the olive-infused cream cheese sandwich ($4). Free Wi-Fi and cheap espresso drinks ($2-3). Open M-Th and Su 7am-11pm, F-Sa 7am-midnight. MC/V. ❷

Ramsey's, 496 E. High St. (☎259-2708). Dishes up generous portions of meatloaf and country-fried steak. Play it safe with a side of mashed potatoes or expand your horizons with fried green tomatoes. Dinner platter $10.50. 2-for-1 mixed drinks 4-7pm. Open M-Th and Su 11am-11pm, W-Sa 11am-1am. AmEx/MC/V. ❷

▎ SIGHTS

A HORSE OF COURSE. A visit to one of the private horse farms in the Lexington area is the best way to get an insider's perspective on life beyond the Derby; the Visitors Center distributes a list of farms that welcome visitors. Farms rarely charge an up-front fee, but plan to tip the groom $5-10. **Kentucky Horse Park** is a more touristy alternative to individual visits, with live horse shows, horse-drawn tours of the grounds, and two small museums that trace the role of the horse in human history. On Sunday afternoons in summer, thrifty enthusiasts can watch polo matches for only the cost of parking. *(4089 Ironworks Pkwy., off Exit 120 from I-75. ☎233-4303 or 800-678-8813; www.kyhorsepark.com. Open mid-Mar. to Oct. daily 9am-5pm; Nov. to mid-Mar. W-Su 9am-5pm. Mid-Mar. to Oct. $15, ages 7-12 $8; Nov. to mid-Mar. $9/6; horse shows, museums, and 15min. horse-drawn tours included. 45min. horseback rides additional $22; over 7 only. Pony rides $5; under 13 only. Parking $3.)*

The *Lexington-Herald-Leader* has described the **Keeneland Race Track,** west of the city off U.S. 60, as the "closest thing to a non-religious cathedral" for its ivy-covered grandstand and procession of maple trees along the main drive. Every April, the final prep race for the Kentucky Derby is run on the original dirt track. Other races take place in April and October, and a new synthetic training track means that visitors can watch morning workouts year-round. A sparkling new library houses historical photographs, while the Track Kitchen offers breakfast for $3.75 and the chance to chat up a jockey or horse owner. *(4201 Versailles Rd., across U.S. 60 from the airport. ☎254-3412 or 800-456-3412; www.keeneland.com. Races Apr. and Oct. $3. Dirt track workouts mid-Mar. to Nov. 6-10am, training track year-round 6-11am. Workouts free and open to the public. Library open M-F 8:30am-5pm. Track kitchen open daily 6-11am.)*

UNIVERSITY OF KENTUCKY. When local residents profess to "bleed blue" for the Wildcats and the entire metropolitan area changes its area code to spell out "UKY" on the keypad, it should come as no surprise that the state's largest university plays a prominent role in Lexington's cultural life. The **University of Kentucky Art Museum,** 116 Singletary Ctr., at Rose St. and Euclid Ave., has an eclectic collection that ranges from 19th-century portraits and landscapes to splashy Abstract Expressionist canvases. *(☎257-5716; www.uky.edu/artmuseum. Permanent collection free. Exhibitions $5, students free. Open Tu-Th and Sa-Su noon-5pm, F noon-8pm.)* On the other side of campus, the **University of Kentucky Arboretum and State Botanical Garden,** 500 Alumni Dr., offers a 2 mi. "Walk Across Kentucky" with plants from each of the state's seven regional landscapes. *(☎257-6955; www.uky.edu/arboretum. Open daily dawn-dusk. Visitors Center open M-F 8:30am-4:30pm. Free.)*

HISTORIC HOMES. The austere Federal-style homes in South Hill and their stately Greek Revival neighbors in Gratz Park give visitors an inkling of Lexington's rich architectural heritage. Four historic homes in and around the city are open to the public for tours, and the Visitors Center sells an invaluable combo pass for just $10. **The Hunt-Morgan House,** 201 N. Mill St., was home to infamous Confederate General John Hunt Morgan, who was said to have steered his horse up the front steps and out the back door with Union troops in hot pursuit. *(☎233-3290; www.bluegrasstrust.org/hunt-morgan. Admission by guided tours only. Tours leave 15min. past the hr. Open mid-Mar. to mid-Dec. W-F 1-5pm, Sa 10am-4pm, Su 1-5pm. $7, students $5.)* A few blocks to the south, the **Mary Todd Lincoln House,** 578 W. Main St., was the childhood home of the misunderstood presidential widow. *(☎233-9999; www.mtl-house.org. Open mid-Mar. to Nov. M-Sa 10am-4pm. $7, ages 6-12 $4.)* West of downtown, in Ashland, **The Henry Clay Estate,** 120 Sycamore Rd., is an 18-room mansion with the original furnishings of the Southern orator's family. *(☎266-8581; www.henryclay.org. Guided tours on the hr. Open Feb.-Dec. M-Sa 10am-4pm, Su 11am-4pm; Nov.-Mar. closed M. $7.)*

▣ NIGHTLIFE

The pages of *Ace Weekly* and *Nougat* are full of ideas for evening entertainment; both are free and available throughout the city. The "Weekender" section of Friday's *Herald-Leader* ($0.50) is also a valuable resource.

THE SOUTH

▧**Woodsongs Old-Time Radio Hour,** 214 E. Main St. (☎252-8888; www.wood-songs.com), at the Kentucky Theatre. This nationally syndicated radio program tapes live bluegrass and folk music on M nights. Mountain music at its best. Tapings 6:45pm. Reservations required. $5.

The Dame, 156 W. Main St. (☎226-9005; www.dameky.com). For live rock and punk shows, look no further. Pale girls in vintage sundresses and skinny boys with mod haircuts abound. 21+. Cover $3-10. Shows M-Sa; doors open 8-9pm.

The Bar, 224 E. Main St. (☎255-1551; www.thebarcomplex.com). Draws a gay and lesbian crowd with a neon-soaked dance fl., mod art in the lounge, and drag shows Th-Su nights. Th and Sa nights are best. Th-Sa DJs 11pm-2:30am. 21+. Cover F-Sa $5 after 8pm. Happy hour M-Sa 4-7pm. Open M-W 4pm-1am, Th-Sa 4pm-2:30am.

TENNESSEE

Though Tennessee's land ranges from the Great Smokies to the flat banks of the Mississippi River in the west, the Volunteer State has one unifying theme: music. From the twang of eastern bluegrass and the woes of Nashville country to the gut-wrenching blues of Memphis and the roots of rock 'n' roll at Graceland, music is the soul of the state. Other elements of the state seem to cancel each other out—Tennessee distills Jack Daniel's Tennessee whiskey while simultaneously producing the largest number of Bibles in the US—but both the boozin' and the proselytizin', and just about anything else you can think of, can be found in the music.

▨ PRACTICAL INFORMATION

Capital: Nashville.

Visitor Info: Tennessee Department of Tourist Development, Tennessee Towers, Charlotte Ave. between 7th and 8th Ave. N, Nashville 37243 (for travel advice ☎615-741-2159, for personally tailored advice or a free guide 800-462-8366; www.tnvacation.com). Open M-F 8am-4:30pm. **Tennessee State Parks Information,** 401 Church St., Nashville 37243 (☎888-867-2757; www.tnstateparks.com). Open M-F 8am-4:30pm.

Postal Abbreviation: TN. **Sales Tax:** 9.25% (13.25% for accommodations).

NASHVILLE   ☎615

Nashville is often called "nouveau dixie", for all of the money spent on gaudy, glitzy entertainment. Nashville also has a number of other unusual nicknames. Known as "the Athens of the South," the city is home to an array of Greek architecture. The area has also been called the "buckle of the Bible belt," a reference to its Southern Baptists. But Nashville's most popular moniker is "Music City USA," and for good reason: this town has long been the banjo-pickin', foot-stompin' capital of country music. Today, the city is home to a much broader music scene that attracts performers of all music genres seeking that classic Nashville inspiration (and maybe a recording contract while they're at it). Past visitors to the city will be surprised by downtown's renovated face, but the historical highlights of the Music City remain in pristine condition. No matter which Nashville you visit, you're sure to have a rollicking good time, with music and beer flowing around the clock.

▣ TRANSPORTATION

Airport: Nashville International Airport (BNA), 1 Terminal Dr. (☎275-2098, information center 275-1675; www.flynashville.com), 8 mi. south of downtown. From downtown,

Downtown Nashville

ACCOMMODATIONS
Drake Inn, **6**
Music City Hostel, **8**
Nashville Country
RV Park, **1**

FOOD
Big River Grille and
Brewing Works, **3**
Jack's Bar-B-Que, **4**
Loveless Cafe, **7**

NIGHTLIFE
Belcourt Theater, **9**
Bluebird Cafe, **10**
Play, **5**
Wildhorse Saloon, **2**

take I-40 E and turn off at Exit 216A. **Gray Line Tours** runs a **shuttle** (☎275-1180) to major hotels daily 6am-11pm. $12, round-trip $18. Taxi to downtown about $20.

Buses: Greyhound, 200 8th Ave. S (☎255-3556; www.greyhound.com), at Demonbreun St., downtown. Borders a rough area, but the station is well-lit. Open 24hr. To: **Birmingham** (4hr., 6 per day, $32); **Chattanooga** (2½hr., 6 per day, $23); **Knoxville** (3½hr., 5 per day, $30); **Louisville** (3½hr., 15 per day, $30); **Memphis** (4hr., 6 per day, $36).

Public Transit: Metropolitan Transit Authority (MTA; ☎862-5950; www.nashvillemta.org). Buses operate on limited routes. Times vary route to route, but none run M-F before 5:30am or after 11:15pm. Sa last bus from downtown 10:15pm, Su last bus from downtown 9:15pm and only hourly service. Local fare $1.25, express $1.75, under 19 $0.70, seniors and disabled $0.60, under 4 free; transfers $0.10. All-day pass $3.75; under 19, seniors, and disabled $2.25. Weekly pass $15, under 19 $9.

Taxi: Nashville/Allied Cab, ☎242-7070. **Music City Taxi,** ☎742-3030.

THE SOUTH

⊀ ⁊ ORIENTATION AND PRACTICAL INFORMATION

Nashville's roads are fickle, interrupted by parkways and one-way streets. Names change without warning, as do traffic signals—be cautious at lights. **Broadway,** the main east-west road, runs through downtown, then veers left after passing over I-40; **West End Avenue** continues ahead. Broadway joins **21st Avenue** after a few blocks, passing through **Vanderbilt University.** Downtown, numbered avenues run north-south, parallel to the Cumberland River and divided by Broadway into north and south. The curve of **James Robertson Parkway** encloses the north end, becoming **Main Street** on the other side of the river (later **Gallatin Pike**) and turning into **8th Avenue** downtown. There are worthwhile bars and restaurants south of Broadway between 2nd and 7th Ave., but it can be unsafe at night and it is best to not walk there alone. Metered street parking is free after 12:30pm on Saturdays and all day Sundays; spots are hot commodities at night, when lot parking costs $10.

Visitor Info: Nashville Visitor Information Center, 501 Broadway (☎259-4747; www.musicccity.com), in the Sommet Center, off I-65N/I-40 at Exit 209A; from the exit ramp, follow Broadway east-bound toward downtown. Open M-Sa 8:30am-5:30pm, Su 10am-5pm, and on event days until the event starts. Attraction ticket packages, coupon book, walking tour guide, and info on events distributed for free.

Hotlines: Crisis Line, ☎244-7444. 24hr.

Internet Access: Nashville Public Library, 615 Church St. (☎862-5800), between 6th and 7th Ave. Wi-Fi. Open M-Th 9am-8pm, F 9am-6pm, Sa 9am-5pm, Su 2-5pm.

Post Office: 901 Broadway (☎256-3088), in the same building as the Frist Center for the Visual Arts. Open M-F 8:30am-5pm. **Postal Code:** 37203.

▚ ACCOMMODATIONS

Rooms in downtown Nashville can be expensive, especially in summer. The Visitors Center offers several deals on motel rooms, and budget motels are plentiful around **West Trinity Lane** and **Brick Church Pike,** off I-65 at Exit 87. There are cheap hotels around **Dickerson Road** and **Murfreesboro,** and near downtown, motels huddle on **Interstate Drive** over the Woodland St. Bridge.

Nashville Country RV Park, 1200 Louisville Hwy., Goodlettsville, TN (☎859-0348), 12 mi. north of downtown off I-65 at Exit 98. Significantly cheaper than the campgrounds surrounding Opryland USA, located only a few exits from attractions outside the city. Shaded sites, showers, laundry, a pool, an exercise room, and free Wi-Fi. Occasional live music and camp dinners. Office closes at 7pm, but late-night registration available with advance reservations. Sites $16, with water and electricity $17.25. MC/V. ❶

Music City Hostel, 1809 Patterson Ave. (☎692-1277), between 18th and 19th Ave. N. A 20min. walk down Church St. to downtown, but the immediate area provides hip nightlife that's an alternative to the country-music scene. Friendly staff make traveling a communal effort. Long-term housing options available. Advance online booking recommended. Bunks $25. Private rooms $70; 2-person max., based on capacity. ❶

Drake Inn, 420 Murfreesboro Rd. (☎256-7770). Conveniently located within a 5min. drive from downtown. Features small, clean, comfortable rooms. Fridge, hair dryer, and country music-influenced murals. Laundry and a pool. Singles M-Th $40, F-Su $45; doubles M-Th $43, F-Su $49. AmEx/D/MC/V. ❸

◖ FOOD

In Nashville, the initials of the Grand Ole Opry grace even the local candy: **goo-goo clusters** (peanuts, pecans, chocolate, caramel, and marshmallow) are sold in specialty shops throughout the city. Nashville's other finger-lickin' traditions—barbecue and fried chicken—are no less sinful. Restaurants catering to collegiate tastes (and budgets) cram **21st Avenue, West End Avenue,** and **Elliston Place,** near Vanderbilt. Travelers looking to make their own food can find ingredients at Nashville's **Farmers' Market,** 900 8th Ave. (Open daily 8am-6pm.)

Loveless Cafe, 8400 Rte. 100 (☎646-9700; www.lovelesscafe.com), at the end of the Natchez Trace Pkwy. Follow West End Ave. to where it becomes Harding Pike/Rte. 100. A Nashville tradition since 1951. Expect significant wait on weekends, but tables turn quickly. Visit the Ham and Jams Country Store while you wait for a must-eat experience. Breakfast all day. Open daily 7am-9pm. AmEx/D/MC/V. ❸

Jack's Bar-B-Que, 416A Broadway (☎254-5715; www.jacksbarbque.com). A bit of a legend, both for the flashing neon-winged pigs above the door and for its succulent, tender pork. Sandwiches $3-5. Plates $8-12. Open in spring and summer M-Th 10:30am-8pm, F-Sa 10:30am-10pm, Su noon-6pm; in winter Th 10:30am-8pm, F-Sa 10:30am-10pm. Also at 334 W. Trinity Ln. (☎228-9888). AmEx/D/MC/V. ❷

♪ **EAVESDROPPING.** On some nights, patrons at Jack's Bar-B-Que's outdoor patio can hear performances from the Ryman Auditorium next door.

Big River Grille and Brewing Works, 111 Broadway (☎251-4677; www.bigrivergrille.com). A microbrewery in the heart of downtown. Their rotating choice of specialty beers and selection of salads come as a relief to vegetarians and those looking for respite from fried fare. Meals $8-14. Open M-Th 11am-midnight, F-Sa 11am-1am, Su 11am-10pm. Kitchen closes 1hr. earlier. AmEx/D/MC/V. ❸

👁 SIGHTS

COUNTRY LOVIN'. Country music drives this city. The first stop for any traveler—country fan or not—should be the state-of-the-art **Country Music Hall of Fame,** where visitors can view live performances and design their own CDs. Even travelers uninterested in country music will find themselves engaged as the museum's exhibits connect country music's history to the greater history of American popular culture. Only about 20% of the archived material is on display, but special exhibitions regularly show such stored items. Wander through the well-crafted displays on the history of country, listen to samples from music legends Johnny Cash and Patsy Cline, and watch videos of performances and interviews with modern artists. For an extra $8, country music fans can enjoy a guided tour of RCA's **Studio B,** where over 1000 American Top 10 hits have been recorded. A Grayline shuttle runs between the two venues. (222 5th Ave. S. ☎416-2001; www.countrymusichalloffame.com. Open daily 9am-5pm. $18, seniors and students $16, ages 6-17 $10, under 6 free. AAA discount $1. Audio tours and combination passes with Ryman Auditorium available.) Two-step over to the **Ryman Auditorium,** where its legendary **Grand Ole Opry** radio show was recorded for more than 30 years. The Opry eventually moved to a bigger studio to accommodate the growing crowd of fans, but the Ryman continues to host fantastic shows. View a short video outlining the history of the building, peruse display cases of costumes and photos, and even climb on stage. (116 5th Ave. N. ☎889-3060; www.ryman.com. Open daily 9am-4pm. $12.50, ages 4-11 $6.25. Guided backstage tour $16.25, ages 4-11 $10. Times and prices for shows vary.) The primary country venue in the nation is the **Grand Ole Opry House.** Though the Opry has moved from its original home at the Ryman, visitors can enjoy musical performances, tour the backstage areas, or visit the free self-guided museum detailing the Opry's history. Upcoming weekend shows are listed in *The Tennessean* and online. Tickets for tours of the stage area may only be purchased on the day of the tour, at the gift shop. *(2804 Opry Mills Dr. Exit 11 off Hwy. 155, accessible from both I-40 (Exit 215B) and I-65 (Exit 90B). ☎871-6779; www.opry.com. Museum open daily 10am-5pm. Free. Tours M and W-Th 10am, noon, 2, 3:30pm; Tu and F-Sa 10am, noon, 2pm; Su 12:30pm, 2, 3:30pm. Wheelchair-accessible. Tours $11.50, ages 4-11 $5. Shows F 8-10pm, Sa 6:30-9pm and 9:30-11:30pm; Mar.-Dec. also Tu 7pm. Tickets $34.50-47.50, available at ☎800-871-6779, online, or through Ticketmaster.)*

MUSEUMS AND MORE. Right in the heart of downtown, the **Frist Center for the Visual Arts** inspires both young and old with an array of rotating exhibits and a hands-on learning center that allows visitors to paint, draw, and make prints. *(919 Broadway. ☎244-3340; www.fristcenter.org. Open M-W and F-Sa 10am-5:30pm, Th 10am-9pm, Su 1-5:30pm. Wheelchair-accessible. $8.50, students with ID $6.50, active military and over 65 $7.50, under 18 free.)* **Fisk University's Carl Van Vechten Gallery** displays selections from Alfred Steiglitz's private collection. The gallery is tiny, but the fascinating photographs hanging among Picassos, Cézannes, and Renoirs should not be missed. Across the way on the third floor of University Library, Fisk presents its own collection in selected exhibitions at the **Aaron Douglas Gallery.** *(1000 17th Ave. N. ☎329-8720. Open during the school year Tu-F 10am-5pm, Sa-Su 1-5pm; in summer Tu-F 10am-5pm. Donations accepted.)* Across West End Ave. from Vanderbilt, the pleasant **Centennial Park** stretches between 25th and 28th Ave. A visit to the park will reveal why Nashville is known as the "Athens of the South": a full-scale replica of the Greek **Parthenon** sits on top of a low hill. Built as a temporary exhibit for the Tennessee Centennial in 1897, the Parthenon was so popular that it was maintained and finally rebuilt with permanent materials in the 1920s. The 42 ft. golden statue of Athena inside completes the illusion. In its first floor gallery, the building contains the **Cowan Collection of American Paintings,** a selection of 19th- and early 20th-century American art. *(☎862-8431; www.parthenon.org. Open Tu-Sa 9am-4:30pm; in summer also Su 12:30pm-4:30pm. Wheelchair-accessible. $5, ages 4-17 and over 62 $2.50.)* At the **Capitol,** a stately Greek Revival building on Charlotte Ave. north of downtown, visitors can tour the Governor's Reception Room, the legislative chambers, the former Tennessee Supreme Court, and the tomb of President James K. Polk. Walk around the building to see the view of the **Bicentennial Mall Park** from the south entrance and gaze out to the mountains of Tennessee. *(On Charlotte Ave. between 6th and 7th Ave. ☎741-0830. Photo ID required. Open M-F 8am-4pm. Tours every hr. M-F 9-11am and 1-3pm; self-guided tours also available. Wheelchair-accessible. Free.)* Take a trip back down Capitol Hill to see the expansive **Tennessee World War II Memorial** at the Bicentennial Mall State Park. Erected in 1997, the memorial features a series of large marble and stone installations, as well as statues honoring the fallen soldiers and the surviving war heroes. Inspirational quotes from some of the South's finest writers frame the sometimes difficult state history, and a series of fountains installed in the ground provide a humorous self-mockery of Tennessee's frequent droughts. Children and parents enjoy hot summer days running through the fountains and have picnics of fresh produce from the farmers' market just next door. *(598 James Robertson Pkwy. Contact Tennessee State Parks ☎888-TN-PARKS.)*

CHEEKWOOD MUSEUM AND BELLE MEADE MANSION. For a break from the bustle of downtown, head to the **Cheekwood Botanical Garden and Museum of Art.** The well-kept gardens, complete with a woodland sculpture trail, are a peaceful spot for a stroll or a family picnic. The museum features American and contemporary sculpture and paintings and a collection of English and American decorative arts. *(1200 Forrest Park Dr., off Page Rd., between Rte. 100 and Belle Meade Blvd. 8 mi. southwest of town. ☎356-8000; www.cheekwood.org. Open Tu-Sa 9:30am-4:30pm, Su 11am-4:30pm. $10, seniors $8, students and ages 6-17 $5; families $30.)* The nearby **Belle Meade Plantation** was once one of the nation's most famed thoroughbred nurseries. The lavish 1853 mansion has hosted seven US presidents, including the 380 lb. William Howard

Taft, who allegedly spent some time stuck in the mansion's bathtub. Today, visitors can explore the house and grounds, including a collection of antique carriages and a haunting exhibit of a restored slave cabin that details the dark side of the plantation's history. *(5025 Harding Rd. ☎ 356-0501 or 800-270-3991. Open M-Sa 9am-5pm, Su 11am-5pm. 2 guided tours per hr.; 1st tour 30min. after opening, last tour 4pm. 1st fl. and grounds wheelchair-accessible. $14, seniors $12, ages 6-12 $6. AAA discount.)*

THE HERMITAGE. The **Hermitage,** the graceful manor of the seventh President of the United States, Andrew Jackson, holds an impressive array of its original furnishings. Admission includes a 15min. film about Jackson's life, access to the house and grounds, and a visit to the nearby **Tulip Grove Mansion** and **Hermitage Church.** An extra $7 will get you a ride on a horse-drawn wagon through the plantation, and is the best way to get a sense of the farm's former grandeur. *(4580 Rachel's Ln. Exit 221 off I-40 E, continue 4 mi. on Old Hickory Blvd.; entrance is on the right. ☎ 889-2941; www.thehermitage.com. Open daily 9am-5pm. Last entry 4pm. Partial wheelchair-accessibility. Guided tour included in admission. $14, ages 13-18 and 62+ $12, ages 6-12 $6, families $38, active military free. AAA discount.)*

🎵 ENTERTAINMENT

The hordes of visitors that swoop down upon Nashville have turned the **Grand Ole Opry** (p. 313) into a grand ole American institution. However, there are many other great forms of entertainment in the capital city as well. The **Tennessee Performing Arts Center,** 505 Deaderick St. at 6th Ave. N, hosts the Nashville Symphony, opera, ballet, Broadway shows, and other theater productions. (☎ 255-2787; www.tpac.org. Wheelchair-accessible. Tickets $15-75.)

Two professional franchises dominate the Nashville sports scene. The NFL's **Tennessee Titans** play at **LP Field,** 460 Great Circle Rd., just across the river from downtown. (☎ 565-4200; www.titansonline.com. Open M-F 8:30am-5pm. Tickets $12-52.) The NHL's **Nashville Predators** face off at the **Sommet Center,** 501 Broadway. (☎ 770-2040. Open M-F 10am-5:30pm. Tickets $10-85.)

🐾 NIGHTLIFE

Nashville has a vivacious nightlife scene fueled by country music; line dancing aficionados will love the downtown bar scene. Other, smaller scenes, such as hip-hop spots and gay clubs, are located a bit farther from the city center. Downtown, country nightlife centers on Broadway and 2nd Ave. Parking can be difficult in summer, especially when something is going on at the Sommet Center. Near Vanderbilt, **Elliston Place** hops with college-oriented music venues, and **Hillsboro Village,** on 21st Ave. at Belcourt Ave., attracts a young crowd to its late-night bars and coffee shops. A new "gayborhood" has developed in the last few years on Church St. around the **Outloud Bookstore,** 1703 Church St. (☎ 340-0034), a great resource for info on GLBT night (and day) life in Nashville, with a cafe attached and a new community outreach center.

🍴 **Bluebird Cafe,** 4104 Hillsboro Pkwy. (☎ 383-1461; www.bluebirdcafe.com), near the mall at Green Hills. From 21st Ave., it's on the left after you cross Richard Jones Rd. This famous bird sings original country and acoustic every night. Line up outside the door an

TIP **THE EARLY 'BIRD.** The Bluebird Cafe hosts some of Nashville's most talented songwriters each week. Although their late show at 9:30pm has a cover charge and sells out quickly, their early show, at 6:30pm, is a good way to hear some great music in a relaxed, coffeehouse-style atmosphere with no cover.

THE SOUTH

hour before showtime; the place gets packed quickly. $7 min. per person. if sitting at a table. Cover for shows usually $8-15; Su no cover. Reservations recommended Tu-Sa. Open M-Sa 5:30pm-close, Su 6pm-close. Early show 6:30pm.

Wildhorse Saloon, 120 2nd Ave. N (☎902-8200; www.wildhorsesaloon.com). Bring your boots and hat and two-step 'til dawn in this country dance hall. It's loud and brash, but ain't that country? Dance lessons M-F 7-9pm, Sa-Su 6-9pm. Live music Tu-Sa. Cover after 7pm M-Th and Su $4, F-Sa $6. Open M-Th and Su 11am-1am, F-Sa 11am-3am.

Belcourt Theater, 2102 Belcourt Ave. (☎383-9180; www.belcourt.org), at 21st St. in Hillsboro Village. Once a silent movie theater, the Belcourt now profits from the marketing miracle of blockbusters and booze. Indie and classic films with beer and wine to make your entertainment experience that much better. Tickets $8, matinees $6. Call or check online for showtimes and events.

Play, 1519 Church St. (☎322-9627). The hottest dance bar in Nashville, Play is a trendy gay club, but everyone, straight or otherwise, is welcome and attends. Best drag show in town brings in crowds on W and F-Sa. W college night, free with valid college ID. 18+. Cover varies. Open W-Su 9pm-3am.

KNOXVILLE   ☎865

Knoxville was settled after the Revolutionary War and later named for George Washington's Secretary of War, Henry Knox. It was once the capital of the "Territory South of the River Ohio," part of which became the state of Tennessee. Shaded by the stunning Great Smoky Mountains and hemmed in by vast lakes created by the Tennessee Valley Authority, Knoxville is a friendly, easily-navigated city that is home to the 26,000 students of the University of Tennessee (UT). Though less glitzy and touristy than Nashville, Knoxville features a lively college town atmosphere and a vibrant bluegrass and country music scene.

ⅅ⨌ TRANSPORTATION AND PRACTICAL INFORMATION. Downtown Knoxville stretches north from the Tennessee River, bordered by **Henley Street** and **World's Fair Park** to the west and **Clay Street** to the east. The **McGhee Tyson Airport** (**TYS;** ☎342-3000; www.flyknoxville.com) is on Hwy. 129, 10 mi. south of downtown and just past the intersection of Hwy. 129 and I-140. Greyhound, 100 E. Magnolia Ave. (☎524-0369 or 800-231-2222; www.greyhound.com; open 24hr.), at Central St., sends **buses** to: Chattanooga (2-8hr., 5 per day, $21.25); Lexington (3½hr., 3 per day, $48); Nashville (3-3½hr., 3 per day, $33). Be cautious in this area and don't walk alone here at night. Public **KAT buses** cover the city. (☎637-3000 or 525-1525; www.katbus.com. Buses run weekdays 6:15am-7:15pm; reduced service on Sa. Call for availability. Night Rider and Sunday Rider routes run M-F 8:45pm-midnight, Sa 6:45pm-midnight, Su 10:15am-6:30pm. $1, under 18 or over 65 $0.50, under 4 free; transfers $0.20.) Four free **trolley** lines run throughout the city: Blue (M-F 6am-6pm) runs to the Coliseum, Blount Mansion, and the Women's Basketball Hall of Fame; Orange (M-F 7am-6pm) heads downtown and westward to World's Fair Park and the UT campus; Green (M-F 7am-6pm) travels between the Fort Sanders neighborhood and UT; the Late Line (Aug.-May F-Sa 8pm-3:30am) serves UT, the Cumberland Avenue Strip, Market Square, and the Old City. Trolley and bus schedules are available at the Visitors Center downtown.

The **Visitors Center** at 301 S. Gay St. downtown has a coffeehouse with musical performances weekdays at noon. (☎523-7263 or 800-727-8045; www.knoxville.org. Open M-F 7:30am-6pm, Sa 9am-5pm, Su noon-4pm.) **Hotlines: Sexual Assault Crisis Center.** (☎522-7273. 24hr.) **Internet Access: Lawson McGhee Public Library,** 500 W. Church Ave. (☎215-8700. 1hr. free Internet access with guest card. Open M-Th 9am-8:30pm, F 9am-5:30pm, Sa noon-5pm, Su 1-5pm.) **Post Office:** 501 W. Main Ave. (☎522-1070. Open M-F 7:30am-5:30pm.) **Postal Code:** 37902.

THE SOUTH

⌐ ACCOMMODATIONS. Several mid-range motels can be found off of I-75 and I-40 west of downtown and I-75 north of downtown. The **Knoxville Hostel ❶**, 404 E. 4th Ave., is just a 10min. walk from the restaurants and clubs of the Old City. The hostel has a kitchen and common room, plus free Internet access and breakfast. Be cautious around this neighborhood at night—don't walk here alone. The hostel is small but comfortable, with friendly international guests. Manager Al has plenty of advice for travelers, and he's a great source for Knoxvillian lore. Arrange reservations in advance during summer months, though management does its best to accommodate. Call ahead to arrange for pick-up from the Greyhound station. (☎546-8090. Shuttle service to Gatlinburg $7.60, students $6.45, hostel guests $6. Laundry $2. Reception usually daily 8am-noon and 1-6pm. Beds $17. Cash or check only.) **Volunteer Park Family Campground ❷**, 9514 Diggs Gap Rd., at Exit 117 off I-75, is 12 mi. from the city and has a pool, basketball court, coin-op laundry, a convenience store, and live bluegrass and country music during the summer. (☎938-6600; www.volpark.com. Tent sites $20, with water and electricity $25. Rates are for 2 adults and 2 children, each additional person $4.) The basic rooms at **Scottish Inns ❸**, 201 Callahan Rd., at Exit 110 off I-75, are farther from downtown. Odd-numbered rooms face away from I-75 and are quieter than even-numbered rooms. Wi-Fi is available in some rooms, but the front office has a computer for Internet use. (☎689-7777. Continental breakfast included. Outdoor pool. A/C. HBO. Singles M-Th and Su $30, F-Sa $37; doubles $40/50. AAA discount $2. D/MC/V.)

◖ FOOD. Market Square, a shaded plaza with restaurants and fountains east of World's Fair Park, bustles during the day. The other center for dining, browsing, and carousing, the **Old City,** spreads north up Central and Jackson St. and is usually hopping until at least 2am. Part of Cumberland Ave. along campus proper, **The Strip** is lined with student hangouts, bars, and restaurants. **The Tomato Head ❶**, 12 Market Sq., prepares gourmet pizzas (slices $1.40-5) and sandwiches ($5-7), with a variety of creative vegetarian options. The outdoor patio area becomes a hangout, as customers and passersby alike chat it up with the friendly waitstaff. (☎637-4067. Open M 11am-3pm, Tu-Th 11am-9:30pm F-Sa 11am-10:30pm, Su 10am-9pm. AmEx/MC/V.) **La Costa ❹**, 31 Market Sq., features an exciting Latin-Southern fusion menu. While dinner entrees are priced steeply ($15-23), the restaurant features an incredible weekend brunch (Sa-Su until 3pm). (☎566-0275; www.lacosta-onmarketquare.com. Mimosas and Bloody Marys $4. Sangria 1L $7. M-Th and Su 4-10pm, F-Sa 4-11pm, Sa-Su brunch 10am-3pm.)

◙ SIGHTS. The ▨**Women's Basketball Hall of Fame,** 700 Hall of Fame Dr., traces the history of amateur and professional women's basketball and inducts new members at a ceremony each June. Visitors can watch a video called "Hoop Full of Hope," sit in on simulated locker room pep-talks by famous coaches, and show off their skills on the indoor court. (☎633-9000; www.wbhof.com. Open May 1-Labor Day M-F 10am-5pm, Sa 10am-6pm, Su 1-5pm; Labor Day-April 30 Tu-F 10am-5pm, Sa 10am-6pm, Su 1-5pm. Wheelchair-accessible. $8, seniors and ages 6-15 $6. AAA discount $2.) Across the street, the **James White Fort,** 205 E. Hill Ave., preserves portions of the original stockade built in 1786 by Knoxville's founder. Guided tours describe the lives of the first white settlers in the area. (☎525-6514. Open Mar. to mid-Dec. M-Sa 9:30am-5pm; Jan.-Feb. M-F 10am-4pm. Tours by appointment or walk-in 9:30am-3:30pm. Admission by tour only. $5, AAA $4, ages 5-12 $2.) The **Museum of Appalachia,** 16 mi. north of Knoxville at Exit 122 off I-75 in Norris, showcases 300 years of Appalachia's cultural history. The museum consists of old buildings relocated from the surrounding countryside, including barns, a blacksmith's shop, a smokehouse, and the cabin where Mark Twain's family lived. Live mountain music is played daily from 9:30am to 4:30pm. Also at the museum is the

THE SOUTH

annual **Tennessee Fall Homecoming Festival,** which is held the second full weekend in October and draws musicians, writers, craftspeople, and huge crowds. (☎494-7680; www.museumofappalachia.com. Open daily May-Aug. 8am-8pm; Sept.-Apr. 8am-7pm; Oct.-Mar. 8am-6pm; Nov.-Feb. 8am-5pm. $13, seniors and AAA $10, ages 6-12 $5, families $30; higher during festival.) **World's Fair Park,** west of downtown, underwent major reconstruction that expanded the convention center and added a vast green swath stretching toward the river. (Open daily dawn-dusk.) The **Knoxville Museum of Art,** 1050 World's Fair Park Dr., has fascinating rotating exhibits on display and a small but dynamic permanent collection of modern and postmodern art. The museum hosts "Alive after Five" on Fridays, with live music, food, and drinks. (☎525-6101; www.knoxart.org. Open Tu-Th Sa 10am- 5pm, F 10am-8pm, Su 1-5pm. Wheelchair-accessible. $5, under 17 free; Tu free. "Alive after Five" typically bi-monthly F in spring and summer, 5:30-8pm. $6.)

🎵 🎭 **ENTERTAINMENT AND NIGHTLIFE.** Knoxville is a great place for sports fans; UT's **football** (in the Neyland Stadium) and **women's basketball** (in the Thompson Bowling Arena) consistently rank among the top teams in the nation. (☎656-1200; www.utsports.com. Football tickets $38-45. Basketball $8-14.) **Smokies Park,** 20 mi. east of downtown on I-40, Exit 407, is home to the Tennessee Smokies, a AA minor league baseball team that plays over 60 home games from April to September each year. Most games start at 7:15pm. (☎286-2300; www.smokiesbaseball.com. Tickets $5-9.) **Sundown in the City,** a free concert series held in Market Sq., draws big-name rock and blues bands on Thursday nights in summer. (☎523-2665; www.sundowninthecity.com. Apr.-July Th 6-10pm.) The annual **Dogwood Arts Festival** brings crafts, food, a parade, and biking competition to Market Sq. every April. (www.dogwoodarts.com. Apr. 11-13, 2008. Free.)

   The Old City is the center of Knoxville's nightlife; the Strip and Market Sq. also have popular bars. For goings-on around town, pick up a copy of the free *Metro Pulse* (www.metropulse.com). The hip **Blue Cats,** 125 E. Jackson St., is a cool venue in a gritty district that draws big rock, blues, and country acts. (☎544-4300; www.bluecatslive.com. Beer from $3. 18+. Cover varies. Doors usually open at 9pm.) The club transforms itself some evenings into **Tonic or Fiction,** Knoxville's hottest dance party. (www.fictionfx.com. Cover $5-7. 18+. Open Sa 10pm-3am.) **Preservation Pub,** 28 Market Sq., is a happening, friendly bar with great beer ($3.50) and fun quotes on the walls. (☎524-2224. Live music nightly. Happy hour daily 4-9pm, draft beers from $1-2. 21+. Open daily 3pm-2:30am.) **Kurt's,** 4928 Homburg Dr. in the Homburg Place mini-mall, is a relaxed, friendly gay bar west of the city. Take the Kingston Pike from downtown and Homburg Dr. will be on the left. Escape the crowded interior bar for the outdoor grotto area. (☎558-5720. 21+. Happy hour W-Su 6-8pm. Open M-Tu 9pm-3am, W-Su 6pm-3am.)

GREAT SMOKY MOUNTAINS   ☎865

Great Smoky Mountains National Park encompasses over 500,000 acres of gray-green Appalachian peaks bounded by the North Carolina and Tennessee valleys, making it the largest wilderness area in the eastern US. Described by the Cherokee as "shaconage," or "blue, like smoke," the mountains are populated by black bears, wild hogs, and turkeys, along with more than 1500 species of flowering plants. Spring sets the landscape ablaze with wildflowers; in June and July, rhododendrons bloom. By mid-October, the mountains are a vibrant quilt of autumnal color.

✳ 🛈 **ORIENTATION AND PRACTICAL INFORMATION**

The **Newfound Gap Road (U.S. 441)** is the only road connecting the Tennessee and the North Carolina sides of the park. On the Tennessee side, **Gatlinburg** and **Pigeon**

Forge lie just outside of the park; both are overwhelmingly touristy, especially in summer. Travelers should take the Gatlinburg Bypass Road off of U.S. 441 to avoid the midday mayhem of downtown Gatlinburg. **Townsend,** to the west near Cades Cove, is less crowded. The town of **Cherokee** lies near the park entrance on U.S. 441 in North Carolina. **Bryson City,** near the Deep Creek campground, is quieter. The free *Smokies Guide* details the park's tours, lectures, activities, and changing natural surroundings. U.S. 441 is lined with tourist info and welcome centers, but beware: these are not run by the park and they rope travelers in with deals to Dollywood and other attractions. Travelers solely interested in the park should wait for Visitor Centers located within the park that are run by park rangers.

Visitors Centers: Sugarlands (☎436-1291), on Newfound Gap Rd. 2 mi. south of Gatlinburg, next to the park's headquarters. Shows a video that introduces the Smokies. There is also an interesting and comprehensive exhibit on regional plants and animals. Visitors have access to recent weather updates, bear sightings, and campsite availability. Open daily June-Aug. 8am-7pm; Apr.-May and Sept.-Oct. 8am-6pm; Mar. and Nov. 8am-5pm; Dec.-Feb. 8am-4:30pm. On the North Carolina side of the park, **Oconaluftee** (☎828-497-1900), on U.S. 441 about 2 mi. north of Cherokee, shares its grounds with the **Mountain Farm Museum,** which is made up of historic buildings relocated from throughout the park in the 50s. Open daily 8am-dusk; low-season hours vary. Free.

Hotlines: Park Info Line (☎436-1200; www.nps.gov/grsm). Operates daily Dec.-Feb. 8am-4:30pm; Mar. and Nov. 8am-5pm; Apr.-May and Sept.-Oct. 8am-6pm; June-Aug. 8am-7pm. **Park Headquarters:** ☎436-1294.

Post Office: 130 Slope St., Bryson City, NC (☎828-488-3481). Open M-F 8:30am-5pm, Sa 10am-noon. Another office at 1216 E Parkway (☎800-275-8777), in Gatlinburg, TN. Open M-F 9am-5pm, Sa 9-11am. **Postal Code:** 28713 (Bryson City), 37738 (Gatlinburg). **Area Code:** 865; 828 in Cherokee and Bryson City, NC. In text, 865 unless otherwise noted.

ACCOMMODATIONS

The chain **motels** lining Rte. 441 and Rte. 321 decrease in price with increasing distance from the park. Small motels are clustered in Cherokee and Gatlinburg, but there are few "budget" options. Rooms are at least $40 and prices soar on weekends and during the summer and fall. The best value is to camp in the park or stay in hostel-style accommodations a little farther out. Congested traffic on U.S. 441 also makes camping the best option for travelers who expect to spend the majority of their time in the park.

Nantahala Outdoor Center (NOC), 13077 U.S. 19 W (☎888-662-2199), 13 mi. southwest of Bryson City. Beckons with cheap beds and 3 restaurants. Also arranges beginner-friendly whitewater rafting on the nearby river. Hot showers. Kitchen. Laundry facilities. Call ahead. True mountaineers can bunk in simple "basecamp" cabins with self-provided linens for $15. Private cabins and suites also available. ❶

Folkestone Inn, 101 Folkestone Rd. (☎828-488-2730 or 888-812-3385; www.folkestone.com). From Rte. 19 southbound in Bryson City, turn right onto Everett St. and follow signs for Deep Creek Campground. Hot breakfast. Children must be 10 or older. 2-night min. stay on weekends May-Oct. Check-in 3-7pm. Check-out 11am. Call ahead. Rooms $104-158; each additional person $20. AmEx/D/MC/V. ❹

Landmark Inn North, 680 Winfield Dunn Pkwy., Rte. 441/66 (☎865-429-7797 or 800-429-7798; www.landmarkinnthesmokies.com), in Sevierville off Rte. 441 in front of Kroger's. 15 mi. from the park entrance. Landmark offers standard rooms and reasonable rates. Singles M-Th $32-42, F-Sa $42-52; doubles $36.50-46.50/48.50-58.50. AmEx/D/MC/V. ❷

THE SOUTH

📷 CAMPING

Ten 📷campgrounds ❶ lie scattered throughout the park, each with tent sites, limited trailer space, water, and bathrooms with flush toilets. There are no showers or hookups. **Smokemont, Elkmont,** and **Cades Cove,** the largest and most popular campgrounds, accept reservations from mid-May to late October. Cades Cove and Smokemont are open year-round, while the other campgrounds open between March and May and close in October or November. (Sites $17-20 during reservation period; $14 rest of the year. River sites around $23.) The other campgrounds are first come, first served; Visitors Centers have info about availability. In summer, reserve spots as early as your travel plans allow. (☎800-365-2267, park code GRE; http://reservations.nps.gov. Open daily 10am-10pm. Sites $12-14.) The riversites at Elkmont are perfect for families who are looking for the idyllic camping experience, but locals and park rangers agree that the sites at **Cosby** are the go-to spot for campers looking for a more rustic, solitary experience. **Backcountry camping** ❶ permits that allow access to the park's 100 primitive backcountry sites can be obtained for free at ranger stations. (☎436-1231. Office open daily 8am-6pm.)

🍴 FOOD

Although there are many chain restaurants in and around the park, the most affordable option is to bring packed food to the park. **The Village General Store,** 9400 Hwy. 19 W, opposite Nantahala Village Lodge, is a good place to stock up on supplies and food if you're entering the park from the south. If entering the park from the north, the **Kroger's** supermarket behind the Landmark Inn on Rte. 441 in Sevierville is accessible and affordable. If coming down from the park to pick up additional supplies, try the **Food Lion** on U.S. 441 in Pigeon Forge.

> **Pizza by the River,** on Hwy. 19, 1½ mi. past Nantahala Outdoor Ctr., 14½ mi. southwest of Bryson City. This roadside stand with outdoor decks overlooking the Nantahala is a local favorite. If coming by river, look for the Italian pizza flag or the skull and crossbones on the right as you go downstream. Slices $2.50-3. 12 in. pies $10. Sandwiches $5-7. Open Apr. to mid-Oct. M-Th and Su 11am-10pm, F-Sa 7am-10pm. ❷
>
> **Pear Tree Cafe,** Rt. 441 in downtown Gatlinburg (☎430-8082), at the intersection of Rtes. 441 and 321. A taste of gourmet at reasonable prices. Off-the-beaten-path specialties include fried green tomatoes ($6.50), and chilled pear and mint soup ($5). Sandwiches $7-9. Internet access $3. Open in high season M-Th and Su noon-8pm, F-Sa noon-9pm; low-season hours vary. D/MC/V. ❷
>
> **Parton's Deli,** 332 Parkway (☎436-9625), just past the Galinburg Bypass Rd. on U.S. 441 near the beginning of the Gatlinburg main drag. Perfect place to pick up some simple sandwiches for a daytrip. A necessary stop for campers on their way up to the park to pick up basic camp food supplies. Made-to-order sandwiches $3.50-5. Homemade potato salad $0.85. ❶

🏔 OUTDOOR ACTIVITIES

HIKING

Over 900 mi. of hiking trails and 170 mi. of road meander through the park. Trail maps and a guide to area day-hikes are also available at the Visitors Centers ($1 each; the $5 "starter pack" has all the maps you need for day hiking, fishing, auto touring, and camping). The Great Smokies are known for phenomenal **waterfalls,** and many of the park's most popular hikes culminate in stunning vistas or fantastic views of the surrounding mountains. Less-crowded areas include **Cosby** and **Cat-**

aloochee, both on the park's eastern edge. Wherever you go, bring water and don't feed the bears. **Rainbow Falls** (5½ mi., 4hr. round-trip), accessible from Cherokee Orchard Rd., is the park's most popular hike, a moderate to strenuous trek that reveals the Smokies' highest single-plunge waterfall. About 4 mi. west of Sugarlands Visitors Center on Little River Rd., **Laurel Falls** (2½ mi., 2hr. round-trip) is one of the easier (and more crowded) hikes on the Tennessee side of the park, following a paved trail through a series of cascades before reaching the 60 ft. falls; it gets crowded as the day wears on, but the path is virtually empty before 9:30am. Accessible from the Maddron Bald trailhead east of Gatlinburg, **Albright Grove Loop** (6½ mi., 4hr. round-trip via Maddron Bald Trail) is less crowded and passes by some gigantic ancient maple trees. **Ramsay Cascades** (8 mi., 5hr. round-trip) is a strenuous hike leading to 100 ft. cascades. The trailhead is in the Greenbrier area—from Gatlinburg, the park entrance is 6 mi. east on Hwy. 321. **Clingman's Dome** (1 mi., 30min. round-trip), off Clingman's Dome Road, ascends a steep, paved path to a viewing tower atop the highest vantage point in the park, which offers fantastic views of sunrise and sunset. **Chimney Tops** (4 mi., 2hr. round-trip) is a steep scramble leading up to two 4755 ft. rock spires. **Newfound Gap** offers handicapped-accessible views from Newfound Gap Road.

BIKING

Biking is permitted along most roads within the park, with the exception of the Roaring Fork Motor Nature Trail. The best opportunities for cyclists are at the **Foothills Parkway, Cades Cove,** and **Cataloochee.** On Wednesday and Saturday mornings from May to September, the 11 mi. Cades Cove Loop is closed to car traffic to allow bicyclists full use of the road from dawn to 10am. While the Smokies have no mountain biking trails, a few gravel trails in the park, including the **Gatlinburg Trail,** the **Oconaluftee River Trail,** and **Deep Creek** (lower section) allow bicycles. Another option is neighboring **Tsali Recreation Area,** where there are four mountain biking loops available for a small fee. Contact the Cheoah Ranger in the **Nantahala National Forest** for more information. (☎828-479-6431. Open M-F 8am-5pm.) Bike rental is available at **Cades Cove Campground Store.** (☎448-9034. $4 per hr., $20 per day. Open June to mid-Aug. daily 9am-7pm; late Aug. M-F 9am-5pm, Sa-Su 9am-7pm; Apr.-May and Sept.-Oct. daily 9am-5pm, last rental 2:30pm. W and Sa bike rental begins 7am. Closed-toe shoes required.)

FISHING

Forty species of fish swim in the park's rivers and streams. The Smokies permit fishing in open waters year-round from 30min. before dawn to 30min. after sunset. Anglers over 12 (over 15 in North Carolina) must possess a valid Tennessee or North Carolina **fishing license.** The park does not sell licenses; check with local chambers of commerce, sports shops, and hardware stores to purchase a license, or buy one online before leaving for your trip (https://www3.wildlifelicense.com/tn/). Visitors Centers have a free leaflet and map detailing fishing regulations.

RIDING

Over 500 mi. of the park's trails are open to horses. For travelers with horses, five drive-in **horse camps** provide facilities within the park: **Cades Cove, Big Creek, Cataloochee, Round Bottom,** and **Tow String.** (☎800-362-2267; http://reservations.nps.gov for reservations. Reservations required. $20-25 per night. Open mid-Mar. to Oct.) There are also four **riding stables** offering guided rides on scenic trails. (**Cades Cove Riding Stable:** ☎448-6286; open mid-Mar. to Nov. **Smokemont Riding Stable:** ☎828-497-2373; open mid-Apr. to Thanksgiving. **Smoky Mountain Riding Stable:** ☎436-5634; open mid-Mar. to Oct. **Sugarlands Horseback Riding Stable:** ☎436-3535; open mid-Mar. to Nov. All $20 per hr. Age and weight restrictions vary.)

THE SOUTH

AUTO TOURS

The park offers a number of auto tours. The **Cades Cove Loop, Newfound Gap Road,** and **Roaring Fork** tours are favorites, and can get crowded in summer and on weekends. Pamphlets and maps are available in the Visitors Centers ($1 each). Prices for area-specific guides vary. The **Cataloochee** tour ($1) goes through the area where elk have been reintroduced.

WHITEWATER RAFTING

South of Bryson City, NC, Rte. 19 winds past whitewater rafting outfitters on the Nantahala River. The **Nantahala Outdoor Center (NOC),** 13077 U.S. 19 W (☎888-662-2199), 13 mi. southwest of Bryson City, is the largest and most comprehensive of these, offering guided and unguided rafting trips in four-, six-, and eight-person rafts as well as one- and two-person "duck-boats." (Guide-assisted rafting trips for beginners M-F $33 per person, Sa-Su $37 per person. Guide and rental rates vary depending on season, type of raft, and length of rental. Call for details.)

⊠ DAYTRIP FROM SMOKY MTNS: CHEROKEE RESERVATION

The Cherokee Indian Reservation, on the southeast border of the national park, has a number of attractions, including a 24hr. dry casino in the town of Cherokee itself. For a look at the history and traditions of the Cherokee people, visit the **Museum of the Cherokee Indian,** at Drama Rd. and Tsali Blvd./U.S. 441. (☎828-497-3481; www.cherokeemuseum.org. Open June-Aug. M-Sa 9am-7pm, Su 9am-5pm; Sept.-May daily 9am-5pm. $9, ages 6-12 $6.) The reservation offers tours of the **Oconaluftee Indian Village,** 276 Drama Rd., a recreated mid-18th-century Cherokee village. Tours educate visitors about Cherokee crafts, political organization, and village life. (☎828-497-2315; www.cherokee-nc.com. Open mid-May to late Oct. daily 9am-4:30pm. Tours 1-1½hr., every 10min. Wheelchair-accessible. $16, ages 6-13 $6.) **"Unto these Hills,"** an outdoor drama, chronicles the story of the Cherokee people from the first European arrival to the Trail of Tears. Follow signs from Rte. 441. (☎828-497-2111. Box office on U.S. 441, downtown Cherokee. Shows early June-late Aug. daily 8:30pm, pre-show singing 8pm. Reserved seating $22, ages 6-12 $10; general admission $18/8.) For lighter entertainment, roll the dice at **Harrah's Cherokee Casino,** 777 Casino Dr. off Hwy. 19 N. More than 2800 games, three restaurants, and an entertainment pavilion keep visitors entertained into the night. (☎800-427-7247 or 828-497-7777; www.harrahs.com. 21+. Open 24hr.) The **Cherokee Visitors Center,** 498 Tsali Blvd./Rte. 441, provides information; follow the signs. (☎800-438-1601 or 828-497-9195; www.cherokee-nc.com. Open mid-June to late Aug. 8:15am-7pm; low-season hours vary.)

CHATTANOOGA ☎423

Chattanooga, once famous for being home to the legendary "Chattanooga Choo-Choo," has recently made great strides towards modernization. Although its history as a transportation hub still flavors the city, Chattanooga is a bustling family destination, complete with a new "21st Century Waterfront," the result of a renovation project that has forever changed the face of the city. Now, Chattanooga's plot on the shores of the Tennessee River is adorned with fountains, greenery, and newly expanded cultural attractions that complement the city's old charm.

▧ ☑ ORIENTATION AND PRACTICAL INFORMATION. Chattanooga straddles the Tennessee-Georgia border at the junction of I-24, I-59, and I-75. **Downtown, Lookout Mountain,** and the **Bluff View Art District** comprise the city's most popular areas. The **Chattanooga Metropolitan Airport (CHA)** lies about 5 mi. east of the city. From

downtown, take I-24 E to I-75 N, Exit 4, and follow signs to the airport. (☎855-2200; www.chattairport.com.) Greyhound, 960 Airport Rd. (☎892-1277; www.greyhound.com; open daily 6:30am-10pm) sends **buses** to: Atlanta (2-2¾hr., 7 per day, $23); Knoxville (2hr., 3 per day, $20); Nashville (2½hr., 5 per day, $24). Chattanooga Area Transportation Authority (CARTA) operates a **free downtown electric shuttle** service with stops on every block between the aquarium and the Holiday Inn. (☎629-1473; www.carta-bus.org. Shuttles run every 5min. M-F 6am-9:30pm, Sa 9am-9:30pm, Su 9am-8:30pm. Wheelchair-accessible.) The **Visitors Center,** 2 Broad St., is next to the aquarium. (☎800-322-3344; www.chattanoogafun.com. Discounted attraction tickets and free city maps. Open daily 8:30am-5:30pm.) **Physician's Care,** 403 McBrien Rd. (☎894-3589; open M-F 8am-9pm, Sa-Su 10am-3pm), offers a walk-in clinic. **Internet Access: Public Library,** 1001 Broad St., at 10th St. (☎757-5310. Free. Open M-Th 9am-9pm, F-Sa 9am-6pm, Su 2-6pm.) **Post Office:** 900 Georgia Ave., between Martin Luther King Blvd. and 10th St. (☎267-1609. Open M-F 8am-4:30pm.) **Postal Code:** 37402.

ACCOMMODATIONS. Chain hotels congregate east of the city on I-24/I-75. **King's Lodge ❷,** 2400 West Side Dr., Exit 181A off I-24 E or Exit 181 off I-24 W, has inexpensive, clean rooms and a nice view of the city. (☎698-8944 or 800-251-7702. A/C, cable TV, HBO, pool, and Wi-Fi. Doubles M-Th and Su $40, F-Sa $45. AmEx/D/MC/V.) The **Stadium Inn ❸,** 100 W. 21st St., Exit 178B off I-24, has clean, standard rooms in a convenient downtown location. (☎265-3151. A/C, cable TV, HBO, pool, continental breakfast. Rooms in high season from $59; low-season from $49. AAA and AARP discount 10%. AmEx/D/MC/V.) **Best Holiday Trav-L-Park ❶,** 1709 Mack Smith Rd., occupies a Civil War battlefield. From Chattanooga, take I-24 E to I-75 S and turn off at Exit 1. Turn right at the top of the ramp, then left at the 2nd light. (☎706-891-9766 or 800-693-2877; www.chattacamp.com. Bathrooms, showers, laundry, Wi-Fi, and a pool. Tent sites with no hookups for 2 people $23; with water and electricity $27. RV sites with full hookup for 2 people $31; Big Rig sites with 50 AMP $33. Extra person over 6 $3. Weekly rates available. AARP discount 10%.)

FOOD. In the Bluff View Art District, **⬛Rembrandt's Coffee House ❶,** 204 High St., offers gourmet sandwiches and salads ($3-6) at reasonable prices. The lovely brick patio is the perfect spot to relax and sample the incredible pastries (under $4) or sip some coffee. (☎265-5033. Open M-Th 7am-10pm, F 7am-11:30pm, Sa 8am-11:30pm, Su 8am-10pm. AmEx/D/MC/V.) Within the same inlet of restaurants, cafes, and galleries as Rembrandt's is **Back Inn Cafe ❸,** 412 E 2nd St. Though pricier than its neighboring establishments, Back Inn has prime location over Bluff View, providing an exquisite location for romantic evening dinners or relaxing afternoon lunches. The lunch options (entrees $7-15) are significantly cheaper than those on the dinner menu (entrees $14-31), but the sunset on Bluff View makes this stop a worthwhile splurge. Items vary from prime-cut steaks to seafood and pasta dishes, and the menu also features creative drink options. (☎265-5033. M-Th and Su 11am-10pm, F-Sa 11am-11pm.) **Jack's Alley** is lined with places to eat.

SIGHTS. Downtown Chattanooga, a small area between 10th St. and the river, is crammed with attractions, shops, and restaurants. The **⬛Tennessee Aquarium,** 1 Broad St., on Ross's Landing, is home to the world's largest freshwater tank as well as the newly opened "Ocean Journey" exhibit featuring sharks and other ocean life. The aquarium entertains visitors with an IMAX screen, mesmerizing seahorses, and some hideously ugly fish. (☎800-262-0695; www.tnaqua.org. Open daily 10am-6pm; extended hours in summer. $20, ages 3-12 $11; IMAX screening $8/5.50; aquarium/IMAX combo pass $25/15. Behind-the-scenes-tour daily 3-4:45pm $15. Tour ages 10+ only.) Dedicated in 2005, **The Passage,** on Market St.

THE SOUTH

next to the aquarium, is a memorial to the Trail of Tears which celebrates the art, culture, and history of the Cherokee Native Americans. The memorial exits into **Riverfront Park,** which has great views of the Tennessee River. The **International Towing and Recovery Hall of Fame and Museum,** 3315 S. Broad St., chronicles the creation and life of the tow truck. Even if you're not interested in trucks, this museum is worth seeing as a testament to American ingenuity. (☎267-3132; www.internationaltowingmuseum.org. Open M-Sa 9am-5pm, Su 11am-5pm. $8, ages 6-18 and over 55 $7, under 6 free. AAA discount.) The **Bluff View Art District** (www.bluffviewartdistrict.com) is a neighborhood of upscale shops and cafes, anchored by the ⬛**Hunter Museum of American Art,** 10 Bluff View Ave. From downtown, take 4th St. to High St. and turn left. Exhibits include contemporary art and classical American paintings. (☎267-0968; www.huntermuseum.org. Th special events and classes 6-9pm. Open M-Tu and F 10am-5pm, W and Su noon-5pm, Th 10am-9pm. Wheelchair-accessible. $7, seniors $6, ages 4-17 $3.50, under 4 free. Students may purchase year-long membership with unlimited visits for $5 with current student ID. AAA discount.) Across the street, the **Houston Museum,** 201 High St., is the life work of Anna Houston, an eccentric who lived in a barn she built herself. She left her belongings, including music boxes and an amazing glass collection, to a committee that started a museum on the river banks. To see the exhibits, visitors must join a 45min. tour. (☎267-7176; www.thehoustonmuseum.com. Open M-F 9:30am-4pm, Sa 11am-5pm. $7, ages 4-12 $3.50, under 4 free.)

One of Chattanooga's most popular destinations is **Lookout Mountain.** Take S. Broad St. and follow the signs. Billed as "America's most amazing mile," the **Incline Railway** is the world's steepest passenger railway, chugging visitors up an insane 72.7% grade to an observation deck. The deck is accessible by car, allowing you to take in the incredible views for free. (☎821-4224; www.ridetheincline.com. Open summer 8:30am-9:30pm, last train around 9:10pm; Apr.-May and Sept.-Oct. 9am-6pm, last train around 5:20pm; Nov.-Mar. 10am-6pm. $12, round-trip $10; ages 3-12, seniors, and disabled $6/5.) The nature trail at **Rock City Gardens** combines scenic lookouts and narrow rock passages with singing and dancing elves and strategically placed shops. (☎706-820-2531 or 800-854-0675; www.seerockcity.com. Open daily Jan.-May 8:30am-5pm; June-Aug. 8:30am-8pm; Sept. to mid-Nov. 8:30am-6pm. Open mid-Nov. to Dec. until 4pm and 6-9pm for the "Enchanted Garden of Lights." $13, ages 3-12 $7.) One thousand feet inside the mountain lies the **Ruby Falls** cavern formations and an impressive 145 ft. waterfall—complete with colored lights and sound effects—add pizzazz to a day of sightseeing, but be prepared to endure long waits and narrow passageways crowded with tourists. (☎821-2544; www.rubyfalls.com. Open daily 8am-8pm. 1hr. tour $13, ages 3-12 $6.) **Combo passes** ($40; children, seniors, and disabled persons $21) for Incline Railway, Rock City, and Ruby Falls are available.

🔲🎭 **ENTERTAINMENT AND NIGHTLIFE.** For entertainment listings, check the "Weekend" section of the Friday *Chattanooga Times Free Press* or *The Pulse* and *Enigma,* two weekly alternative papers. Most nightlife options are downtown, especially in the area surrounding **Jack's Alley,** from Broad St. to Market St., between 4th and 5th St. There are several bars off the commercialized alley; **Taco Mac's,** 423 Market St., has the best selection of beers with over 50 on tap. (☎267-8226. Outdoor seating available. Beer from $3. Happy hour M-F 4-7pm. Open M-F 11am-3am, Sa-Su 11:30am-3am.) Nearby, the **Big River Grille and Brewing Works,** 222 Broad St., offers six original beers, plus seasonal ales and lagers. (☎267-2739. Pints $3.25. Happy hour M-F 4-7pm. Pool tables. Open M-Th and Su 11am-1am, F-Sa 11am-2am. Kitchen closes M-Th and Su 11pm, F-Sa midnight.) **Rhythm and Brews,** 221 Market St., has consistently hot bands every night. (☎267-4644; www.rhythmbrews.com. 21+. Cover $5-20. Usually open W-Sa 8pm-late; music starts around

9:45pm.) **Alan Gold's,** 1100 McCallie Ave., just over the bridge from Central on National, is a popular gay venue that boasts two bars, a dance floor, lounge areas, and balconies. (☎629-8080. Drag shows daily 12:30am. 21+. Cover F-Sa $5, Su $3. Open daily 4:30pm-3am.)

The **Chattanooga Lookouts,** a minor league baseball team for the Reds, play at the AT&T Field, 201 Power Alley. (☎267-2208; www.lookouts.com. Tickets $4-8, seniors and under 12 $2.) For nine nights in June, the riverfront shuts down for live rock, country, blues, jazz, and reggae during the **Riverbend Festival.** (☎756-2211; www.riverbendfestival.com. Tickets $35, $26 in advance.) The mountains surrounding Chattanooga also offer opportunities for whitewater rafting; ask for info at the Visitors Center.

MEMPHIS   ☎901

Music is the pulse of Memphis and what compels travelers to visit the city. All the blues, funk, soul, country, and rock is deeply entwined with the history of civil rights and social change in the United States. White farmers brought country music, black workers brought the blues, and their synthesis resulted in a melting pot of contemporary musical styles. Black and white musicians also played together, challenging the segregation laws of the time. Today, most visitors make the Memphis pilgrimage to see Graceland, the former home of Elvis Presley and one of the most deliciously tacky spots in the US. There's plenty to do after you've paid your respects to "The King"; unusual museums, fantastic ribs, and live music are just some of the reasons to stay a few more days.

▐ TRANSPORTATION

Airport: Memphis International (MEM), 2491 Winchester Rd. (☎922-8000; www.mscaa.com), south of the southern loop of I-240. Taxi to the city about $25—negotiate in advance.

Trains: Amtrak, 545 S. Main St. (☎526-0052; www.amtrak.com), at G.E. Patterson Ave., on the southern edge of downtown. This area can be unsafe. Main St. trolley runs to the station. Ticket office open daily 6:30am-11pm. To **Chicago** (10½hr., 1 per day, $155), **Jackson** (4½hr., 1 per day, $46), and **New Orleans** (8½hr., 1 per day, $68).

Buses: Greyhound, 203 Union Ave. (☎523-9253 or 800-231-2222; www.greyhound.com), at 3rd St. downtown. The area can be unsafe at night. Open 24hr. To **Chattanooga** (7-10hr., 4 per day, $41), **Jackson** (4-6hr., 6 per day, $35), and **Nashville** (4hr., 13 per day, $32).

Public Transit: Memphis Area Transit Authority, or **MATA** (☎274-6282; www.matatransit.com), at Auction Ave. and Main St. Bus routes cover most suburbs but run infrequently (every 30min. at best). Major routes run on Front, 2nd, and 3rd St. Buses run M-F beginning between 4:30 and 6am and stopping between 7 and 11pm, depending on the route. Sa-Su service less frequent. $1.50, transfers $0.10. Refurbished 19th-century **trolley cars** cruise Main St. and the Riverfront, operating M-F 6am-midnight, Sa 9:30am-1am, Su 9am-6pm. $1, seniors $0.50, under 5 free. Exact change required. 1-day pass $3.50, 3-day pass $8.

Museum Shuttles: Sun Studio and Graceland both offer free shuttle service between attractions. The **Elvis Express,** operated by Graceland, runs between Graceland and Beale St. The **Sun Studio shuttle** transports travelers between Graceland, Sun Studio, and the Rock 'n' Soul museum, departing from Graceland on the hr., from Sun Studio at 15min. past the hr., and from the Rock 'n' Soul Museum on the ½hr. daily 10am-6pm. Call attractions for further info. (☎800-441-6249; www.sunstudio.com.)

Taxi: City Wide, ☎722-8294. **Yellow Cab,** ☎577-7700.

✈ 🛈 ORIENTATION AND PRACTICAL INFORMATION

Downtown, named avenues run east-west and numbered ones run north-south. **Madison Avenue** divides north and south addresses. Two main thoroughfares, **Poplar** and **Union Avenue,** are east-west; **2nd** and **3rd Street** are the major north-south routes downtown. **I-240** and **I-55** encircle the city. **Riverside Drive** takes you to U.S. 61, which becomes **Elvis Presley Boulevard** and leads south to Graceland. **Midtown,** east of downtown, is home to a funky music scene and gay venues, and is a break from the tourist attractions (and traps) of **Beale Street. South Main Street** is becoming a hip neighborhood of coffee shops, niche restaurants, and specialty shops.

Visitor Info: Tennessee Welcome Center, 119 N. Riverside Dr. (☎543-6757; www.memphistravel.com), at Jefferson St. Open daily 7am-6pm; building closes 10pm.

Hotlines: Crisis Line, ☎274-7477. **Gay/Lesbian Switchboard, ☎**278-4297. Both 24hr.

Internet Access: Cossitt Branch Library, 33 S. Front St. (☎526-1712), downtown at Monroe. Open M-F 10am-5pm. Farther away, the **Main Library** is at 3030 Poplar Ave. (☎415-2700). Open M-Th 9am-9pm, F-Sa 9am-6pm, Su 1-5pm. Both free.

Post Offices: 1 N. Front St. (☎576-2037). Open M-F 8:30am-5pm, Sa 9am-1pm. **Postal Code:** 38103. Second location at 555 S. 3rd St. (☎521-2559). Open M-F 8:30am-5pm. **Postal Code:** 38101.

🏠 📷 ACCOMMODATIONS AND CAMPING

Few downtown motels have prices in the budget range, but more budget lodgings are available near Graceland at **Elvis Presley Boulevard** and **Brooks Road.** Coupons from the Visitors Center are good for substantial discounts at many chain hotels, particularly midweek, but call ahead to confirm room availability. For the celebrations of Elvis's historic birth (Jan. 8) and death (Aug. 16), as well as for the Memphis in May festival, book rooms six months to one year in advance.

American Inn, 3265 Elvis Presley Blvd. (☎345-8444), Exit 5B off I-55, close to Graceland. Despite its shabby exterior, the large, comfy rooms and the Elvis-themed mural in the lobby will win you over. A/C, cable TV, continental breakfast, and pool. Singles $30; doubles $46. AmEx/D/MC/V. ❷

Homestead Studio Suites Hotel, 6500 Poplar Ave. (☎767-5522, www.homesteadhotel.com). Though 16 mi. from downtown, these impeccable rooms come with Internet, a full kitchen, and access to laundry facilities--just like your own apartment. The surrounding area also offers plenty of dining options. Rooms $70-90. Weekly rates $385-455. Check website for discounts. AAA and AARP discount. AmEx/D/MC/V. ❸

Memphis-Graceland RV Park and Campground, 3691 Elvis Presley Blvd. (☎396-7125 or 866-571-9236), beside the Heartbreak Hotel, a 2min. walk from Graceland. Very little privacy, but the location is great. Pool and laundry facilities. Reservations recommended. Sites $24, with water and electricity $34, with full hookup $39. 2-person cabins $42. Each additional person $5, ages 12 and under $2. D/MC/V. ❶

🍴 FOOD

In Memphis, barbecue is as common as rhinestone-studded jumpsuits. It remains an art that Memphians practice in two forms—the local "dry rub" specialty and the more traditional "wet BBQ"; the city even hosts the **World Championship Barbecue Cooking Contest** in May. Don't fret if gnawing on ribs isn't your thing—Memphis has plenty of other Southern restaurants with down-home favorites like fried chicken, catfish, chitlins, and grits.

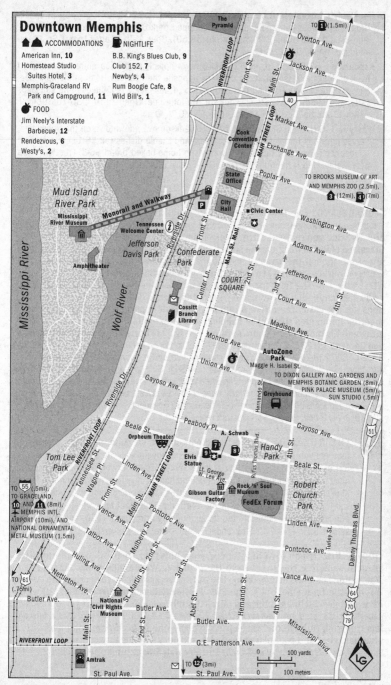

Downtown Memphis

🏠🏠 ACCOMMODATIONS   📠 NIGHTLIFE

American Inn, **10**

Homestead Studio
   Suites Hotel, **3**

Memphis-Graceland RV
   Park and Campground, **11**

🍗 FOOD

Jim Neely's Interstate
   Barbecue, **12**

Rendezvous, **6**

Westy's, **2**

B.B. King's Blues Club, **9**

Club 152, **7**

Newby's, **4**

Rum Boogie Cafe, **8**

Wild Bill's, **1**

The Pyramid

TO 🍺 (1.5mi)

Overton Ave.

Jackson Ave.

RIVERFRONT LOOP

Front St.

Main St.

MAIN STREET LOOP

Market Ave.

I-40

Cook
Convention
Center

Exchange Ave.

State
Office

Poplar Ave.

TO BROOKS MUSEUM OF ART
AND MEMPHIS ZOO (2.5mi),
🏨 (12mi), 🏨 (7mi)

Washington Ave.

Mud Island
River Park

Mississippi
River Museum

Monorail and Walkway

Tennessee
Welcome Center

Riverside Dr.

Front St.

P

Jefferson
Davis Park

Confederate
Park

City
Hall

■ Civic Center
✚

COURT
SQUARE

Main St. Mall

2nd St.

3rd St.

Adams Ave.

Jefferson Ave.

Court Ave.

4th St.

Mississippi River

Wolf River

Amphitheater

Center Ln.

Cossitt
Branch
Library

Madison Ave.

Monroe Ave.

Union Ave.

AutoZone
Park

Maggie H. Isabel St.

TO DIXON GALLERY AND GARDENS AND
MEMPHIS BOTANIC GARDEN (8mi),
PINK PALACE MUSEUM (5mi),
SUN STUDIO (.5mi)

Gayoso Ave.

Riverside Dr.

Hernando St.

Greyhound

Gayoso Ave.

51

Beale St.

Orpheum Theater

Peabody Pl.

A. Schwab

Handy
Park

Tom Lee
Park

RIVERFRONT LOOP

Tennessee St.

Wagner Pl.

Linden Ave.

Front St.

Main St.

MAIN STREET LOOP

Elvis
Statue

7

9

8

Lt. George
W. Lee Ave.

Gibson Guitar
Factory

Rock 'n' Soul
Museum

FedEx Forum

Rufus Thomas Blvd.

Beale St.

4th St.

Robert
Church
Park

Linden Ave.

Pontotoc Ave.

Vance Ave.

Tulley St.

Danny Thomas Blvd.

64

70

79

TO 55 (.5mi),
TO GRACELAND,
🏨 AND 🏕 (8mi),
MEMPHIS INTL.
AIRPORT (10mi), AND
NATIONAL ORNAMENTAL
METAL MUSEUM (1.5mi)

Vance Ave.

Pontotoc Ave.

Mulberry St.

2nd St.

3rd St.

Talbot Ave.

Huling Ave.

TO 61
(.75mi)

Butler Ave.

Nettleton Ave.

St. Martin St.

National
Civil Rights
Museum

Butler Ave.

2nd St.

Abel St.

Butler Ave.

Hernando St.

4th St.

Mississippi Blvd.

RIVERFRONT LOOP

Main St.

G.E. Patterson Ave.

0   100 yards

0   100 meters

N

LG

🚆 Amtrak

St. Paul Ave.

✉ TO 🍗 (3mi)

St. Paul Ave.

THE SOUTH

Jim Neely's Interstate Barbecue, 2265 S. 3rd St. (☎775-2304), off I-55 at Exit 7. Great barbecue, plain and simple. The chopped pork Bar-B-Q sandwich ($5) is excellent, as is the rib dinner (full rack of ribs $8.50). Open M-Th 11am-11pm, F-Sa 11am-midnight. AmEx/D/MC/V. ❷

Rendezvous, 52 S. 2nd St. (☎523-2746; www.hogsfly.com). The entrance is around back on Maggie H. Isabel St., in the alley opposite the Peabody Hotel. A Memphis legend, serving charcoal-broiled ribs (half-rack $14, full-rack $17), cheese and sausages ($8), and sandwiches ($6-7). Look for the long line. Open Tu-Th 4:30-10:30pm, F 11am-11pm, Sa 11:30am-11pm. AmEx/D/MC/V. ❸

Westy's, 346 N. Main St. (☎543-3278), at Jackson Ave., downtown on the trolley line. Serves delicious tamales, stuffed potatoes, and Creole dishes (all $6-11) in a relaxed atmosphere. Over 270 beers. Sandwiches on home-baked bread $6-8. Free Wi-Fi and pool tables. Happy hour daily 4-7pm. Open daily 10:45am-3am. AmEx/D/MC/V. ❷

◉ SIGHTS

GRACELAND. The best strategy for visiting Elvis Presley's home is to know what you want to get out of it before you go—it's easy to be overwhelmed by the crowds once you're there. Crowds are lightest in the mornings before 10am. The **Graceland Mansion** itself can be seen in about 1½-2hr.; it takes a whole morning or afternoon to visit the array of secondary shops, museums, and restaurants. The crush of tourists swarms in a delightful orgy of gaudiness around the tackiest mansion in the US. The faux-fur furnishings, mirrored ceilings, green shag-carpeted walls, ostrich-feather pillows, and yellow-and-orange decor of Elvis's 1974 renovations are not easily forgotten. A blinding sheen of hundreds of gold and platinum records illuminates the **Trophy Building,** where exhibits detail Elvis's stint in the army and his more than 30 movie roles. The King is buried in the adjacent **Meditation Gardens.** *(3763 Elvis Presley Blvd. Take I-55 S. to Exit 5B or bus #43 "Elvis Presley." ☎332-3322 or 800-238-2000; www.elvis.com contains info on Graceland as well as all peripheral attractions. Ticket office open Mar.-Nov. M-Sa 9am-5pm, Su 10am-4pm; Dec.-Feb. M and W-Su 10am-4pm. Attractions remain open 2hr. after ticket office closes. Mansion closed Tu. Trophy Building and Meditation Gardens are fully wheelchair-accessible; mansion only partially accessible. Graceland Mansion tour including audio headset $25, students and over 62 $22.50, ages 7-10 $10, under 7 free. Parking $6, oversized vehicles $10.)*

> (deal) **THE ROYAL DEAL.** Graceland now offers a **VIP Entourage Tour** package that lets you skip the lines to get in and includes a souvenir "backstage" pass. But at $68 (under 7 free), it's a lot of money spent for very little time saved: once inside, even VIPs have to wait behind hordes of visitors moving through The King's palace. Those interested in seeing The King beyond the castle while conserving cash are best off with the **Platinum Tour Package,** which discounts admission to the mansion and its surrounding attractions. ($30, students and seniors $27, ages 7-12 $15, under 7 free). —*Stephen Travierso*

MORE ELVIS. If you love him tender, love him true, visit the peripheral Elvis attractions across the street from the mansion. **Walk a Mile in My Shoes,** a free 20min. film screened every 30min., traces Elvis's career from the early (slim) years through the later (fat) ones. The **Elvis Presley Automobile Museum** has a fleet of Elvis-mobiles, including pink and purple Cadillacs and motorized toys. *(Wheelchair-accessible. $8, students and over 62 $7.20, ages 7-12 $4.)* Visitors to **Elvis's Custom Jets** can walk through the King's private plane, the *Lisa Marie,* complete with a blue suede bed and gold-plated seatbelts, and peek into the tiny *Hound Dog II* Jetstar. *($7, seniors $6.30, children $3.50.)* The **Sincerely Elvis** exhibit offers a glimpse into

Elvis's private side, displaying his wedding announcements, a collection of Lisa Marie's toys, items from his wild wardrobe, as well as memorabilia and heaps of fan letters. *(Wheelchair accessible. $6, seniors $5.40, children $3.)*

MUSIC: THE MEMPHIS HEARTBEAT. Memphis's musical roots run deep into the fertile cultural soil of the Mississippi delta region. During the early- and mid-1900s, Memphis's musical scene blended jazz, soul, and folk traditions to create a new and unique blues sound. Downtown Memphis's historic **Beale Street** saw the invention of the blues and the soul hits of the Stax label. At the must-see ⧈**Rock 'n' Soul Museum,** the numerous artifacts on display include celebrity stage costumes and B.B. King's famous guitar, Lucille. Best of all, the audio tour contains 100 complete songs. The museum, which houses exhibitions designed with help from the Smithsonian Institute, also provides an account of rock 'n' roll's origins, from the cotton fields to the union of black and white music. *(On 3rd St. across from the Gibson Guitar factory. 1 block south of Beale St. ☎ 205-2533; www.memphisrocknsoul.org. Open daily 10am-7pm. Wheelchair-accessible. $10, ages 5-17 $7; audio tour included with over 100 mp3 recordings available for listening throughout the tour.)* For rock 'n' roll fans, no visit to Memphis is complete without a visit to ⧈**Sun Studio,** where rock 'n' roll was conceived. In this legendary one-room recording studio, Elvis was discovered, Johnny Cash walked the line, and Jerry Lee Lewis was consumed by great balls of fire. Tours go through a small museum area and proceed to the studio itself, where visitors listen to the recording sessions that earned the studio its fame. *(706 Union Ave. ☎ 800-441-6249; www.sunstudio.com. Open daily 10am-6pm. 35min. tours every hr. on the half-hr. $10, under 12 free. AAA discount.)* Long before Sam Phillips and Sun Studio produced Elvis and Jerry Lee Lewis, the **Gibson Guitar Factory,** across the street from the Rock 'n' Soul Museum, was lovingly crafting guitars. Even these days, the factory only produces about 35 instruments each day. Tours detail the various stages of the guitar-making process; visit during the week to see the craftsmen at work. Coupons for the tour are available at www.memphistravel.com. *(145 Lt. George W. Lee Ave. ☎ 544-7998, ext. 4075; www.gibsonmemphis.com. 35-45min. tours run M-Sa 11am-4pm, Su noon-4pm. Must be 12 or older. $10.)*

UNIQUE MUSEUMS. On April 4, 1968, Dr. Martin Luther King, Jr. was assassinated at the **Lorraine Motel** in Memphis. Today, the powerful ⧈**National Civil Rights Museum** occupies the original building. Relive the courageous struggle of the Civil Rights move-

ALL SHOOK UP

Elvis Presley's Graceland mansion receives thousands of visitors every day of the year. During Memphis's annual celebration of "Elvis Week" in August, die-hard Elvis fans join rhinestone-clad impersonators for a week of commemoration and revelry. Elvis Week events range in tone from light-hearted to somber and include Elvis film festivals, impersonator contests, Elvis karaoke, and even Elvis bingo. The week reaches its climax with a candlelight vigil from sundown on August 15th at Graceland until the morning of August 16th, the date of Elvis's death (Aug. 2007 marked the 30th anniversary).

Fans who attend Elvis Week emphasize his significance as a successful challenger to the cultural and racial barriers of 50s America. Though Elvis's music and live performances may seem tame by today's standards, his gyrating pelvis caused such a scandal that the *Ed Sullivan Show* would only film him from the waist-up when he performed on television. As historian Michael Bertrand argues in *Race, Rock, and Elvis*, Elvis's music blended black and white musical traditions into a new sound with cross-racial appeal that helped to break down cultural segregation among American youth.

For more Elvis Week info see www.elvis.com. Elvis Week 2008 occurs August 9-17.

CONTROVERSIAL COMMEMORATION

Most visitors to Memphis's Civil Rights Museum wouldn't think twice about the educational value of its exhibits, but the debate over how best to preserve the memory of Dr. Martin Luther King, Jr. for future generations remains unresolved. Jacqueline Smith has camped out across the street from the Civil Rights Museum for over 19 years in protest of a museum that she argues has betrayed Dr. King's vision. Suggesting that the museum has turned the site of Dr. King's assassination into a sensationalized tourist trap, Smith criticizes the museum's exhibit on the assassination of Dr. King. Why spend millions commemorating King's death, Smith argues, when the poverty and racial segregation he fought against are still present in Memphis?

The Civil Rights Museum's powerful exhibits provide at least one compelling answer to Smith's criticisms—only by learning about past struggles against racial injustice can we understand how to face the problems of the present. Regardless of your opinions on the issue, don't miss the opportunity to engage with this issue yourself—Ms. Smith and the museum both plan on sticking around for a while.

For more info on Smith's protest, see www.fulfillthedream.net.

ment through photographs, videos, and interviews in this moving exhibit, which ends in Dr. King's motel room. The main exhibition's presentation of the Civil Rights movement of the 60s is comprehensive, engaging, and among the best of the South's many similar museums. Even so, the museum's annex across the street devotes an entire floor to the assassination of Dr. King and the investigation and trial of James Earl Ray, which some may find overwhelming. *(450 Mulberry St. ☎ 521-9699; www.civilrightsmuseum.org. Open June-Aug. M and W-Sa 9am-6pm, Su 1-6pm; Sept.-May M and W-Sa 9am-5pm, Su 1-5pm. $12, students and over 55 $10, ages 4-17 $8.50. Free M after 3pm. 1hr. audio tours $2; children's version available. AAA and military discounts.)* South of downtown, the ⚑**National Ornamental Metal Museum,** the only institution of its kind in the US, displays fine metalwork from international artists. Get a better idea of the artistic process at the working blacksmith shop behind the museum, and check out the front gate as you walk in. *(374 Metal Museum Dr., Exit 12C from I-55. ☎ 774-6380; www.metalmuseum.org. Open Tu-Sa 10am-5pm, Su noon-5pm. $5, over 62 $4, students and children $3, under 5 free. AAA discount $1.)* A general store, antique museum, and clothing shop rolled into one, **A. Schwab** has stood on Beale St. since 1876. Used clothing treasures abound for the bargain-hunter. *(163 Beale St. ☎ 523-9782. Open M-Sa 9am-5pm.)*

OVERTON PARK. The **Brooks Museum of Art,** in the southwest corner of Overton Park, east of downtown, showcases a diverse collection of paintings and decorative art and features visiting exhibits. On the 1st Wednesday of each month, the museum hosts a celebration (6-9pm, $5) with food, films, live music, and drinks. *(1934 Poplar Ave. ☎ 544-6200; www.brooksmuseum.org. Open Tu-F 10am-4pm, Sa 10am-5pm, Su 11:30am-5pm. Wheelchair accessible. $7, over 65 $6, students and ages 7-17 $3; special exhibitions sometimes more. W free. AAA discount 50%. Audio tour $3/2/2.)* Also in the park, the small but impressive **Memphis Zoo** is one of four places in the US where you can see giant pandas. Kids will enjoy the sea lion show (daily 10:30am and 2:30pm) and taking a spin on the carousel. *(2000 Prentis Pl. ☎ 276-9453; www.memphiszoo.org. Open daily Mar.-Oct. 9am-6pm; Nov.-Feb. daily 9am-5pm; last admission 1hr. before close. Wheelchair-accessible. $13, over 60 $12, ages 2-11 $8. Parking $3. Tram tour $1.)*

MUD ISLAND RIVER PARK. A quick walk or monorail ride over the Mississippi to **Mud Island** allows you to stroll and splash along the ⚑**River Walk,** where children slide their way down a scale model of the Mississippi River the length of five city blocks. Free tours of the River Walk run several times daily. The

Mississippi River Museum on the island charts the river's history and culture over the past 10,000 years with videos, musical recordings, and life-size replicas of steamboats and ironclads. *(Monorail leaves from 125 N. Front St. every 10min., round-trip $4; pedestrian bridge free. ☎576-7241 or 800-507-6507; www.mudisland.com. Park open in summer Tu-Sa 10am-6pm; spring and fall 10am-5pm. Last entry 1hr. before closing. 3-5 tours daily. Wheelchair-accessible. Museum $8, over 62 $6, ages 5-12 $5. Monorail free with museum admission.)* Visitors can paddle around the Mississippi or pedal through the streets of downtown. *(1-person kayak $15 per hr.; 2-person kayak or canoe $20 per hr. Bike $10 per 2hr.)* The newest feature is the **Sleep Out on the Mississippi,** held the 2nd Friday of each month in summer. It may sound like a form of political protest, but it's a camping trip under the stars with dinner, music, kayaks, and breakfast. *(Reserve in advance. Reservations ☎576-7241 or 800-507-6507. $40.)*

PARKS AND GARDENS. The 96-acre **Memphis Botanic Garden,** with 22 distinct gardens, is the perfect place for a stroll. Relish the fantastic 57-variety rose garden, the sensory garden, or the peaceful Japanese garden. *(750 Cherry Rd., in Audubon Park off Park Ave. ☎576-4100; www.memphisbotanicgarden.com. Open M-Sa 9am-6pm; Su 11am-6pm. Wheelchair-accessible. $5, over 62 $4, ages 3-12 $3, under 2 free.)* Across Park Ave., the **Dixon Gallery and Gardens** flaunts an impeccable garden, an impressive range of sculptures, and a collection of European art with work by Renoir, Degas, and Monet. *(4339 Park Ave. ☎761-2409 or 761-5250; www.dixon.org. Open Tu-F 10am-4pm, Sa 10am-5pm, Su 1-5pm. $7, seniors and students $5, ages 7-17 $3. Audio tours $3.)*

🎵 ENTERTAINMENT

The majestic **Orpheum Theatre,** 203 S. Main St., hosts Broadway shows and big-name performers. On Fridays during the summer, the grand old theater shows classic movies with an organ prelude and a cartoon. *(☎525-3000; www.orpheum-memphis.com. Box office open M-F 9am-5pm and before shows. Movies 7:15pm; $6, seniors and under 12 $5. Concerts and shows $15-55; $3 booking fee except on day of show.)* Just as things are really beginning to heat up in the South, the legendary **Memphis in May** celebration hits the city, continuing throughout the month with concerts, art exhibits, food contests, and sporting events. *(☎525-4611; www.memphisinmay.org.)* One such event is the **Beale Street Music Festival,** featuring some of the biggest names from a range of musical genres. There's also the **World Championship Barbecue Cooking Contest** and the **Sunset Symphony,** a concert near the river given by the Memphis Symphony Orchestra.

🎸 NIGHTLIFE

W.C. Handy's 1917 "Beale St. Blues" claims that "you'll find that business never closes 'til somebody gets killed." Today's visitors are more likely to encounter the Hard Rock Cafe and the mega-commercialism that comes with it than the rough-and-tumble juke joints of old. Despite all the change, the strip between 2nd and 4th St. is still the place to go for live music. On Friday and Saturday nights, a wristband lets you into any club on the strip, except Alfred's (wristband F $10, Sa $15). You must show ID to get into **Beale St.** at night; police officers card at entrances to the pedestrian area. The free *Memphis Flyer* and the "Playbook" section of the *Friday Memphis Commercial Appeal* can tell you what's goin' down in town.

BEALE STREET BLUES
Beale St. is a great place to enjoy a quiet beer on weeknights, but come on the weekend and people are cartwheeling down the street. While some bars are frequented by a spring-break crowd, older (and pricier) standbys feature the music that put Beale St. on the map.

Rum Boogie Cafe, 182 Beale St. (☎528-0150). One of the first clubs on Beale St., Rum Boogie still rocks with homegrown blues and a friendly ambience. Check out the celebrity guitars hanging from the ceiling. Live music M-Th and Su 8pm, F-Sa 9pm. 21+ M-Th and Su after 9pm, F-Sa after 8pm. Cover M-Th and Su after 8pm $3, F-Sa after 9:30pm $5. Happy hour M-F 5-7pm. Open M-Th and Su 11am-12:30am, F-Sa 11am-2am.

B.B. King's Blues Club, 143 Beale St. (☎524-5464; www.bbkingsclub.com). The live blues makes this place popular with locals, visitors, and celebrities. Drinks are expensive, even for Beale St. B.B. himself occasionally plays a show, though tickets can reach $200 and typically sell out. Entrees $11-19. Music starts at 6pm, house band at 8:30pm. Cover $5-7. Open M-Th and Su noon-1:30am, F-Sa 11am-3am.

Club 152, 152 Beale St. (☎544-7011). One of the most popular clubs on Beale, offering 3 fl. of dancing and drinks. Live music acts range from blues to techno; on weekends DJs spin upstairs. Check out the "mood elevator," a wildly painted elevator that takes you to hip hop (F 2nd fl.), techno (Sa 3rd fl.), and beyond. Beer from $3.50. 21+. Cover Th $5, F $5-8, Sa $5-10. Open M-Th and Su 11am-2am, F-Sa 11am-5am.

NIGHTLIFE OFF BEALE STREET

For a collegiate climate, try the **Highland Street** strip near **Memphis State University.** The city's gay bars are located in **Midtown;** take the Main St. trolley down Madison to the end of the line. This area can be unsafe after dark. Ask any bar to call you a cab. For info on gay clubs and happenings, *Triangle Journal News* can be found in any gay venue.

Newby's, 539 S. Highland St. (☎452-8408; www.newbysmemphis.com), is a dark, lively college bar with pool tables, comfy red booths, and a patio. Live bands play everything from rock to reggae almost every night beginning at 10pm. Beer from $3. 21+. Cover usually $3-5, check website. Happy hour daily 3-10pm. Open daily 3pm-3am.

Wild Bill's, 1580 Vollintine Ave. (☎726-5473), a neighborhood restaurant and music joint, lies off the beaten track and contrasts with touristy places downtown. Live music F-Sa 11pm, Su 10pm. Cover F-Su $5. Open M-Th 11am-7pm, F-Su 10am-3am.

NORTH CAROLINA

Fields of tobacco, pastel sunsets, and rocking chairs on porches—these generalizations about North Carolina aren't far from the truth, but visitors rarely just sit around drinking mint juleps. Outdoorsy types revel in the awesome landscapes of the western mountains, while the central Piedmont region, filled with cultural activities and historical sights, combines the sophistication of the North with the South's slower pace. There's no denying the state's marked diversity; North Carolina is home to gorgeous beaches, some of the nation's top universities, and the country's second-largest financial center. One thing can be said for the whole of the "Tarheel State": natural beauty and Southern hospitality are the rule.

⚡ PRACTICAL INFORMATION

Capital: Raleigh.

Visitor Info: Dept. of Commerce, Travel, and Tourism, 301 N. Wilmington St., Raleigh 27601 (☎919-733-8372 or 800-847-4862; www.visitnc.com). **Division of Parks and Recreation,** 512 N. Salisbury St., Archdale Building 7th fl., Room 732 (☎919-733-4181).

Postal Abbreviation: NC. **Sales Tax:** 7%.

THE RESEARCH TRIANGLE   ☎919

Clustered in the northern Piedmont region, the Research Triangle is comprised of Raleigh, Durham, and Chapel Hill. In the 1950s, the three towns were united by the creation of the spectacularly successful Research Triangle Park, a research hub responsible for such medical developments as the AIDS drug AZT. **Raleigh**, the state capital and home to North Carolina State University (NC State), is a historic town with recently revamped museums and shops. **Durham**, formerly a major tobacco producer, now supports medical research projects devoted to finding cancer cures, and is home to Duke University. The University of North Carolina (UNC), chartered in 1789 as the nation's first state university, is located down the road in **Chapel Hill**. College culture infuses all three cities with a hot music scene, popular bars, and unconventional stores.

▛ TRANSPORTATION

Flights: Raleigh-Durham International (**RDU**; ☎840-2123; www.rdu.com), 10 mi. southeast of Durham and 10 mi. northwest of Raleigh, between U.S. 70 and I-40 on Aviation Blvd. From Durham, take Exit 284B from I-40 E or Exit 292 from U.S. 70 E. From Raleigh, take Exit 285 from I-40 W or Exit 292 from U.S. 70 W. A **taxi** to downtown Raleigh or Durham costs about $30; to Chapel Hill costs about $35. Triangle Transit Authority has shuttle service from RDU to surrounding areas; see **Public Transit,** below.

Trains: Amtrak (www.amtrak.com) has stations in Raleigh and Durham. Raleigh: 320 W. Cabarrus St. (☎833-7594), 4 blocks west of the Civic Ctr. Open daily 5:30am-10:30pm. To: **Durham** (30min., 2 per day, $5-8); **New York City** (10hr., 1 per day, $77-160); **Richmond** (3½hr., 1 per day, $27-60); **Washington, D.C.** (6hr., 1 per day, $43-93). Durham: 400 W. Chapel Hill St. Open daily 7am-9pm. Trains to **Raleigh** (30min., 2 per day, $4-7).

Buses: there are several options for bus travel in this area. For information on traveling between all three cities, visit www.gotriangle.org.

  Greyhound: www.greyhound.com. Stations in both Raleigh and Durham. Raleigh: 314 W. Jones St. (☎834-8275). Open 24hr. Buses to **Charleston** (7-8hr., 2 per day, $59), and **Durham** (20-40min., 9 per day, $7). Durham: 412 W. Chapel Hill St. (☎687-4800). Open daily 6:30am-10pm. Buses to **Washington, D.C.** (6hr., 8 per day, $48).

  Public Transit: Triangle Transit Authority: ☎549-9999; www.ridetta.org. Buses run throughout the Triangle M-F 6am-10pm, Sa 7am-6:30pm. $2.

  Capital Area Transit: ☎485-7433, in Raleigh. Buses run throughout the city M-Sa 5am-10:30pm. $0.75; transfers free.

  Durham Area Transit Authority (DATA): ☎485-2755; http://data.durhamnc.gov. Most routes start downtown at 521 Morgan St. Operates daily; hours vary by route and day. $1, seniors and ages under 13 free, disabled $0.50; transfers free.

  Chapel Hill Transit: ☎968-2769; www.townofchapelhill.org/transit, in Chapel Hill. Offers a **free shuttle** between Duke's East and West campus. Buses run M-F 6am-7pm, Sa-Su 7am-6pm. Free.

Taxi: Cardinal Cab, ☎828-3228. Serves all 3 cities.

▟ PRACTICAL INFORMATION

Visitor Info: All 3 of the cities' Visitors Centers provide brochures, guides to the cities, maps, and helpful advice. **Capital Area Visitor Center,** 5 East Edenton St. in Raleigh (☎807-7950; www.nccapvisit.org). Open M-Sa 9am-5pm. **Durham Convention and Visitors Bureau,** 101 E. Morgan St. in Durham (☎687-0288 or 446-8604; www.durham-nc.com). Open M-F 8:30am-5pm, Sa 10am-2pm. **Chapel Hill Orange County Visitors Bureau,** 501 W. Franklin St., near Carrboro (☎968-2060 or 888-968-2060; www.chocvb.org). Open M-F 8:30am-5pm, Sa 10am-2pm.

THE SOUTH

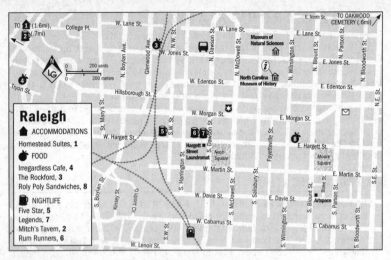

Raleigh

🔺 ACCOMMODATIONS
Homestead Suites, 1

🍴 FOOD
Irregardless Cafe, 4
The Rockford, 3
Roly Poly Sandwiches, 8

🎵 NIGHTLIFE
Five Star, 5
Legends, 7
Mitch's Tavern, 2
Rum Runners, 6

Hotlines: Mental Health and Detox Crisis Hotline, ☎683-8628. 24hr.

Internet Access: The public libraries in all 3 cities provide 1hr. free Internet access. Bring identification for a visitor's library card. **North Regional Library,** 7009 Harps Mill Rd. in Raleigh (☎870-4000). Take Exit 8 from the Rte. 440 beltline, head north on Six Forks Rd., then turn left on Horizon Dr. Open M-F 9am-9pm, Sa 10am-5pm, Su 1-5pm. **Durham County Public Library,** 300 N. Roxboro St. in Durham (☎560-0100), near the Visitors Center. Open Aug.-May M-Th 9am-9pm, F 9am-6pm, Sa 9:30am-6pm, Su 2-6pm; June-July closed Su. **Chapel Hill Public Library,** 100 Library Dr. in Chapel Hill (☎968-2777). From UNC, go down Franklin St. toward Durham. Turn left on Estes Dr. and it's on the right. Open M-Th 10am-9pm, F 10am-6pm, Sa 9am-6pm, Su 1-8pm.

Post Office: Raleigh: 311 New Bern Ave. (☎832-1604). Open M-F 8am-5:30pm, Sa 8am-noon. **Postal Code:** 27611. **Durham:** 323 E. Chapel Hill St. (☎683-1976). Open M-F 8:30am-5pm. **Postal Code:** 27701. **Chapel Hill:** 125 S. Estes St. (☎929-9892). Open M-F 7:30am-6:00pm, Sa 8:30am-3pm. **Postal Code:** 27514.

🏠 ACCOMMODATIONS

Budget lodging in Raleigh surrounds the major exits to the Rte. 440 beltline, especially at Glenwood Ave., Forest Rd., and Capital Blvd. In Durham, economy motels line I-85, especially between Exits 173 and 175, north of Duke. Mid-range motels can be found at the intersection of I-40 and U.S. 15/501 in Chapel Hill.

Homestead Suites, 4810 Bluestone Dr. (☎510-8551; www.homesteadhotels.com), off Glenwood Ave. in Raleigh. New, comfortable rooms with A/C, cable TV, full kitchens, and free local calls. Free access to local gym. Internet access $5 per day. Coin-op laundry facilities available. Single with queen bed $56; double with 2 queens or king and pull-out couch $66. Weekly rate $36; doubles $46. AmEx/D/MC/V. ❷

Best Value Carolina Duke Inn, 2517 Guess Rd. (☎286-0771 or 800-438-1158), off I-85 at Exit 175 in Durham, has friendly service, coin-op laundry facilities, pool, A/C, and cable TV. Free local calls and continental breakfast. Doubles have fridge and microwave. DATA bus access across the street. Wheelchair accessible. Singles $52; doubles $50; family rooms $60. AAA and AARP discount 10%. AmEx/D/MC/V. ❷

THE SOUTH

Falls Lake State Recreation Area, 13304 Creedmoor Rd. (☎676-1027; www.ils.unc.edu/parkproject/visit/fala/home.html), about 10 mi. north of Raleigh off Rte. 98, 1 mi. north of N.C. 50. Falls Lake has 4 campgrounds. The main campground, **Holly Point,** is adjacent to the lake and has both open lakefront sites and secluded shady sites, warm showers, boat ramps, 2 swimming beaches, and a dump station. 14-day max. stay within a 30-day period. Gates close May-Aug. 9pm; Apr. and Sept. 8pm; Mar. and Oct. 7pm; Nov.-Feb. 6pm. Reservations recommended during high season and holidays. Walk-in sites and non-electric sites $15, over 62 $10. Sites with electricity $20/$14. Day-use $5 per car, seniors $3. Cash or check only. ❶

🍴 FOOD

Local universities have given rise to a haven of affordable eateries; Raleigh's **Hillsborough Street** and **Capital Boulevard,** Durham's **9th Street,** and Chapel Hill's **Franklin Street** cater to a college (read: budget-oriented) crowd. In Raleigh, travelers can find good dining options in **City Market's** shops, cafes, and bars a few blocks from the capitol. In Durham, **Brightleaf Square,** a mile east of 9th St. on Main St., has renovated warehouses that hold galleries, shops, and quality restaurants.

RALEIGH

The Rockford, 320½ Glenwood Ave. (☎821-9020), near Hillsborough St. A trendy and kid-friendly 2nd fl. restaurant that serves delightful food. The ABC sandwich (apple, bacon, and cheddar on french toast; $6.75) is popular. Entrees $7 or less. Beer from $1.50. Open M-W 11:30am-2pm and 5:30-10pm, Th-Sa 11:30am-2pm and 6-10:30pm, Su 6-10pm. Bar open M-W and Su 5pm-midnight, Th-Sa 5pm-2am. AmEx/MC/V. ❶

Irregardless Cafe, 901 W. Morgan St. (☎833-8898; www.irregardless.com), after Morgan splits off of Hillsborough St. International gourmet food that focuses on seafood, vegetarian, and vegan dishes. The warm goat cheese salad ($7) is divine. Entrees $8-11. Lunch $6-10. Live jazz, acoustic, or bluegrass every night. Dancing Sa 9:30-11pm. Lunch Tu-F 11:30am-2:30pm. Dinner Tu-Th 5:30-9:30pm, F-Sa 5:30-10pm. Brunch Su 10am-2pm. D/MC/V. ❸

Roly Poly Sandwiches, 137 E. Hargett St. (☎834-1135; www.rolypoly.com), in downtown. Serves 53 different imaginative wraps, including the "Peachtree Melt" (baked ham, melted brie and swiss, peach and pepper relish served with dill horseradish). Vegetarians will enjoy the "Nut and Honey." Half wraps $3.25-4. Full wraps $5.25-7. Open M-F 10am-4pm, Sa 11am-3pm. AmEx/D/MC/V. ❶

DURHAM

🏆 **The Mad Hatter's Cafe and Bake Shop,** 1802 W. Main St. (☎286-1987; www.madhattersbakeshop.com), 1 block from 9th St. This bright, colorful restaurant is decorated with modern contemporary artwork and has an outdoor patio. Most food is locally grown and organic. A wide selection of delectable dishes including grilled sandwiches, Asian noodles, and wraps ($7-8). Cookies $1.50-2.25. Occasional live music. Open M-Th 7am-9pm, F-Sa 7am-11pm, Su 8am-4pm. AmEx/V. ❷

Francesca's, 706 9th St. (☎286-4177). Specializes in beverages and desserts, and their focus is worth it. Sample the homemade gelato and sorbet for just $2.50. Some vegan options available. Sandwiches $5-7. Drinks from full coffee bar $1.25-$3.25. Pastries and cake $1.75-4.50. Open M-Th 11am-11pm, F-Sa 11am-midnight, Su 11am-10pm. D/MC/V. ❶

Pao Lim Asian Bistro and Bar, 2505 Chapel Hill Blvd. (☎419-1771), just off the 15/501 Business Rte. Serves exceptional Asian cuisine, blending Chinese, Indian, and other flavors for an all-ages crowd. Dinner entrees from $9-12. Lunch specials $5.50-

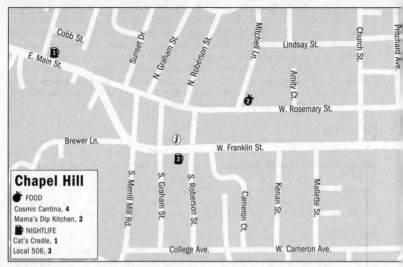

Chapel Hill

🍴 FOOD
Cosmic Cantina, **4**
Mama's Dip Kitchen, **2**

📻 NIGHTLIFE
Cat's Cradle, **1**
Local 506, **3**

7.50. Open M-Th 11:30am-9:30pm, F 11:30am-9:30pm, Sa 11am-10pm, Su noon-9:30pm. AmEx/D/MC/V. ❷

CHAPEL HILL

Jack Sprat Cafe, 161 E. Franklin St. (☎933-3575). Whips up salads, hot and cold sandwiches ($8), coffee, and desserts in a pleasant, stylish environment. Order the "Salad Sampler" ($8) to try 3 different selections, or come in during the night for drinks. Daily drink specials include Th $3 Long Island Iced Tea. Open M-Th 8am-9pm, F-Sa 8am-10pm, Su 8am-5pm. D/MC/V. ❷

Mama Dip's Kitchen, 408 W. Rosemary St. (☎942-5837). This soul food restaurant serves country cookin' for lunch, dinner, and Su brunch. From the sweet potato biscuits to the chicken and dumplings, Mama Dip's serves some of the best regional delicacies around. Most entrees $9-13. Open M-Sa 8am-10pm, Su 8am-9pm. MC/V. ❸

Cosmic Cantina, 128 E. Franklin St. (☎960-3955), in the Franklin Centre shopping complex. Delicious burritos quesadillas and speedy service. Entrees $1-6.50. Sangria $3. Open daily 11am-2am. AmEx/MC/V. Also in Durham, 1920 Perry St. (☎286-1875), at the end of the 9th St. shops. ❶

🔆 SIGHTS

RALEIGH

MUSEUMS. Downtown Raleigh offers several free attractions. Across from the capitol building in the center of downtown Raleigh are two unique museums. The **Museum of Natural Sciences** has four floors full of exhibits that both adults and children will enjoy. Highlights include a 15 ft. giant ground sloth unearthed near Wilmington, and "Willo," a rare dinosaur fossil with an iron concretion within its ribcage—possibly a fossil of the creature's heart! (11 W. Jones St. ☎733-7450 or 877-462-8724; www.naturalsciences.org. Open M-Sa 9am-5pm, Su noon-5pm. Free. Audio tours $2.) Just down the block, the **North Carolina Museum of History** displays such exhibits as "Decorative Arts," "A Call to Arms," the NC Sports Hall of Fame, and a variety of temporary attractions. **Calvert Cafe** serves up tasty pastries for $5 or less with a full coffee bar. Program

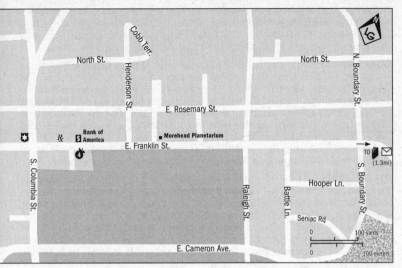

and tour info is available on the website. (5 E. Edenton St. ☎807-7900; www.ncmuseumof-history.org. Open Tu-Sa 9am-5pm, Su noon-5pm. Free.)

ARTSPACE. This collection of 30 artists' studios in three exhibition galleries features work by regional, national, and international artists. Watch masters create art of all types, from watercolor and oil paintings to 3D fabric arts. Call ahead or check online for guided tours and special events. (201 E. Davie St. ☎821-2787; www.artspacenc.org. Open Tu-Sa 10am-6pm, 1st F of each month 10am-10pm. Studio hours vary. Free.)

OAKWOOD. Stretching east from the Visitors Center, **Historic Oakwood** is a Victorian neighborhood featuring some of Raleigh's most impressive architecture, with colonial homes constructed in the late 19th and early 20th centuries. This neighborhood and the adjacent **Oakwood Cemetery** provide a pleasant escape from the bustle of the city center. (Historic Oakwood is bordered by Franklin, Watauga, Linden, Jones, and Person St. Free walking tour guides available at the Visitors Center in the lobby of the North Carolina Museum of History. Cemetery entrance at 701 Oakwood Ave. ☎832-6077. Open daily 8am-4pm. Free maps available in the cemetery office.)

DURHAM

DUKE UNIVERSITY. The Duke family's principal legacy, Duke University, is divided into East and West Campus. The majestic, neo-Gothic **Duke Chapel,** completed in the 1930s, presides over West Campus. Over a million pieces of glass were used to make the 77 stained glass windows depicting hundreds of figures from the Bible and Southern history. (☎684-2572. Open daily June-Aug. 8am-8pm; Sept.-May 8am-5pm. Free. Self-guided tour available. Chapel closed to public during weddings and other ceremonies.) Nearby on Anderson St., the gorgeous **Sarah P. Duke Gardens** have over 55 acres divided into the Bloomington garden of native plants, the Culberson Asiatic arboretum, and the Terraces. (☎684-3698. Open daily 8am-dusk. Free. 1½hr. guided tours by appointment; donations accepted. 45min. trolley rides $25.)

MUSEUM OF LIFE AND SCIENCE. At the other end of Durham, the Museum of Life and Science is a must-see for families with children. Visitors can romp through the musical playground, pet barnyard animals, ride a train through the

THE SOUTH

Nature Park, and explore hands-on exhibits about everything from bubbles to outer space. In the **Magic Wings Butterfly House,** almost 1000 butterflies flutter above lush tropical plants. *(433 Murray Ave., off N. Duke St. ☎ 220-5429; www.ncmls.org. Open M-Sa 10am-5pm, Su noon-5pm. $9.50, over 65 $8.50, ages 3-12 $7.50, under 3 free. Train $2.)*

DUKE HOMESTEAD. Visitors can explore the original farm, home, and factories where Washington Duke first planted and processed the tobacco that would become Durham's key to prosperity. Duke's sons founded the American Tobacco Company, which dominated the industry for decades, putting the city on the map and generating enough profits to found the university. The free historic tour includes an early factory, a curing barn, and a packhouse as well as the restored home. The adjoining **Tobacco Museum** explains the history of the tobacco industry and displays fascinating old cigarette advertisements. *(2828 Duke Homestead Rd., off Guess Rd. ☎ 477-5498. Open Tu-Sa 10am-4pm. Free homestead tours depart every hr.)*

OTHER SIGHTS. The 1988 movie *Bull Durham* was filmed in **Durham Athletic Park,** 409 Blackwell St., the **Durham Bulls'** ballpark. The AAA farm team for the Tampa Bay Devil Rays plays here, without Kevin Costner, who starred as a minor league baseball player in the film. *(☎ 687-6500, tickets 956-2855; www.durhambulls.com. Games Apr.-Sept. Tickets $5-8.)* Travelers visiting the area during June and July should not miss modern dance performances showcasing the likes of the Paul Taylor Dance Company at the **American Dance Festival,** hosted annually at Duke. *(☎ 684-6402; www.americandancefestival.org. Tickets $12-40.)*

CHAPEL HILL

UNIVERSITY OF NORTH CAROLINA. Chapel Hill and neighboring Carrboro are inseparable from the beautiful **University of North Carolina at Chapel Hill.** *(Tour info ☎ 962-1630 or www.unc.edu. Tours M, W, F 1:30pm. Brochures and maps available in the lobby of the Morehead Planetarium.)* The **Dean Dome** hosts a variety of sporting events and concerts. *(Tickets ☎ 834-4000; www.ticketmaster.com.)* Until 1975, NASA astronauts trained at UNC's **Morehead Planetarium;** of the 12 astronauts who have walked on the moon, 11 spent time at Morehead. Today, Morehead gives live sky shows and presentations in the 68 ft. domed Star Theater, and houses small exhibits on outer space. If you're feeling adventurous, try the astronaut ice cream ($3) sold in the gift shop. *(250 E. Franklin St. ☎ 962-1236; www.moreheadplanetarium.org. Open mid-June to mid-Aug. M and Su 12:30-5pm, Tu-W 10am-5pm, Th-Sa 10am-5pm and 6:30-9pm. Call for low-season hours and showtimes. Shows $5.25; students, seniors, and children $4.25. Exhibits free.)* For more info about campus attractions, including the **Ackland Art Museum** and the **North Carolina Botanical Garden,** visit the **Campus Visitors Center** in the Planetarium.

🎵📷 ENTERTAINMENT AND NIGHTLIFE

Pick up a free copy of the weekly *Independent* magazine, available at restaurants and bookstores, for listings of Triangle events. Info on events in Raleigh can be found at www.raleighnow.com. Chapel Hill offers the best restaurants, bars, and clubs in the Triangle. Popular bars line Franklin St. and several live music clubs are clustered where Franklin St. becomes Main St. in the neighboring town of Carrboro. **Cat's Cradle,** 300 E. Main St. in Carrboro, hosts local and national musical acts ranging from hip-hop to country. *(☎ 967-9053; www.catscradle.com. Cover $5-15. Doors open 7:30-9pm, shows usually begin 8-10pm.)* **Local 506,** 506 W. Franklin St., focuses on indie rock. *(☎ 942-5506, call after 7pm; www.local506.com. Most nights 18+. Cover from $5. Open daily 2pm-2am; shows start around 10pm.)*

Nightlife options are also plentiful in Raleigh; the area around Glenwood by Hillsborough St. is home to a number of popular bars. **Mitch's Tavern,** 2426 Hillsborough St., a second-floor bar across from NC State, is a favorite among students and locals for a late-night brew. The dark, smoky charm of the tavern's interior led the producers of *Bull Durham* to select this as the set for two scenes. (☎821-7771; www.mitchs.com. Pints $2.25-3.50. Pitchers $8-13. Open M and Su 11:30am-midnight, Tu-Sa 11:30am-2am.) **Rum Runners,** 208 E. Martin St., a boisterous bar with a tropical flair, hosts interactive "piano-offs" where two pianists compete for glory. Rum runners are $6.25. (☎755-6436; www.rumrunnersusa.com. Open W and F-Sa 6pm-2am, Th and Su 8pm-2am.) For dancing, head to **Five Star,** 511 W. Hargett St., in downtown Raleigh. This popular Chinese restaurant becomes a nightclub Th-Sa around 11pm. (☎833-3311. Th-Sa live DJs. F-Sa 21+ after 10:30pm. No cover. Open daily 5:30pm-2am. Kitchen open 5:30pm-midnight.) **Legends,** 330 W. Hargett St., is gay- and transgender-friendly. (☎831-8888; www.legends-club.com. Tu cabaret night, W women's night, Th "Dark Waves" gothic night, Su drag show 12:30am. Cover $2-8, under 21 up to $8. Open nightly 9pm-3am, F-Sa later.)

WINSTON-SALEM ☎336

As its name suggests, Winston-Salem was originally two different towns. Salem was founded in 1766 by the Moravians, a Protestant sect from the present-day Czech Republic. One of America's most successful utopian communities, Salem was bolstered by religious fervor, dedication to education, and the production of crafts. Winston, meanwhile, was home to the tobacco mogul R.J. Reynolds and rose to prominence as a center of tobacco production. When the two towns merged in 1913, a dynamic, bustling city was born. Today, the skyline of Winston-Salem testifies to the towns' continued prominence. Visitors can experience the history of the two towns when they visit Old Town Salem or the Reynolda House.

 TRANSPORTATION. The **Piedmont Triad International Airport (GSO)** (☎721-0088; www.flyfrompti.com), at Exit 210 off I-40, 9 mi. west of the intersection of I-85 and I-40, is the closest commercial airport. Amtrak Connector **buses** run from 236 East Washington St. (☎800-872-7245; www.amtrak.com. Early morning debaters. Return trips available at night.) Greyhound **bus** station, 250 Greyhound Ct., is downtown at Exit 110A off Rte. 52N. (☎724-1429; www.greyhound.com. Open daily 8am-1am.) **Winston-Salem Transit Authority** has its main depot at 100 W. 5th St. between Liberty and Trade St. (☎727-2000. Buses operate M-F 5:30am-11:30pm, Sa 6am-6:30pm. $1, transfers free.)

 PRACTICAL INFORMATION. The **Winston-Salem Visitor Center,** 200 Brookstown Ave., has brochures and maps. (☎728-4200 or 866-728-4200; www.visitwinstonsalem.com. Open daily 8:30am-5pm.) Check **email** at the **Public Library,** 660 W. 5th St., at Spring St. (☎703-2665. Open Sept.-May M-W 9am-9pm, Th-F 9am-6pm, Sa 9am-5pm, Su 1-5pm; June-Aug. closed Su. Free.) **Post Office:** 1500 Patterson Ave. (☎721-6070. Open M-F 8:30am-5pm.) **Postal Code:** 27101.

 ACCOMMODATIONS. Winston-Salem has scores of motels perfect for budget travelers on the way into town at Exit 184 off I-40. On the northern side of the city, budget motels center around Rte. 52, just past Patterson Ave. Most rooms run $39-69, and many hotels off the I-40 Business Route run $59 specials on weekend nights. The **Microtel Inn ❸,** on Hanes Mall Blvd., between I-40 and the Silas Creek Pkwy., is a great value with free local and long distance calls, cable TV, data ports, and a pool. (☎659-1994. Singles $57; doubles $67-95. AAA discount. AmEx/D/MC/V.) The **Innkeeper ❸,** 2113 Peters Creek Pkwy., is close to downtown and offers large rooms as well as a pool, A/C, cable TV, and continental breakfast. (☎721-0062. Rooms from $41. AAA and AARP discount. AmEx/D/MC/V.) **Summit Street Inns ❺,** 434 Summit St., at W. 5th St. a few blocks from downtown, is a two-house

THE SOUTH

B&B worth the splurge. The luxurious rooms are outfitted with jacuzzis, stereos, HD TVs with hundreds of DVDs to choose from, bathrobes, and refrigerators. (☎777-1887; www.bbinn.com. Exercise room and pool table. One room without jacuzzi for 1-2 people M-Th and Su $89-99, F-Sa $99-109. Doubles M-Th and Su $119-169, F-Sa $149-189. All rooms non-smoking. AmEx/D/MC/V.)

◨ **FOOD.** The **West End Cafe ❷**, 926 W. 4th St., has cozy booths and a wooden bar and makes every kind of sandwich under the sun. Patrons line up for the vegetarian reuben ($6), the honey-mustard pretzel-encrusted salmon ($11), and other creative masterpieces. (☎723-4774. Salads $5.25-9. Burgers $5.25-6.75. Dinner entrees $10-22. Open M-F 11am-10pm, Sa noon-10pm. AmEx/D/MC/V.) Winston-Salem is the birthplace of national doughnut company Krispy Kreme, and no visit to the city would be complete without stopping by the **Krispy Kreme Shop ❶**, 259 S. Stratford Rd., where you can watch the famous doughnuts being made fresh on-site. (☎724-2484. Doughnuts $0.70-0.90. Open M-Th and Su 6am-11pm, F-Sa 6am-midnight. Drive-thru open M-Sa 6am-midnight, Su 6am-11pm. AmEx/D/MC/V.) In the heart of the Old Salem Village, **Old Salem Tavern ❺**, 736 Main St., delights the eyes and tantalizes the taste buds with dishes served by waiters in traditional Moravian garb. Lunch entrees range from quiche to Southern-style catfish. Dinner includes selections such as salmon corn cakes, pork schnitzel, and duck. (☎748-8585; www.old-salemtavern.com. Lunch and dinner entrees $6.50-22.50. Open for lunch M-F 11:30am-2pm, Sa 11:30am-2:30pm, Su 11am-2pm; dinner M-Th 5-9pm, F-Sa 5-9:30pm. Closed Su in Jan. Reservations recommended. AmEx/MC/V.)

◨ **SIGHTS.** **Old Salem Village** takes visitors back in time to a restored Moravian village, outlining its fascinating history and traditions. The area stretches south from downtown and includes a Visitors Center, museums exhibiting Moravian life, and a multitude of traditional Moravian homes and buildings, including a cobbler shop and a gunsmith. Tickets include admission to all of the museums and buildings. (☎888-653-7253; www.oldsalem.org. Visitors Center open Tu-Sa 8:30am-5:30pm, Su 12:30-5:30pm. Most attractions open Tu-Sa 9am-5pm, Su 1-5pm. Tickets $21-22, ages 6-16 $10. AAA discount $3; look for other discounts on the website.) Old Salem's **Frank L. Horton Museum Center** features a number of museums, the most extensive of which is the **Museum of Early Southern Decorative Art (MESDA).** The MESDA showcases furnishings dating from 1690-1820 from the Southeast and around the world. Not only are the rooms set up entirely "ropes free," to recreate the full feel of Southern homes, but all of the furnishings are original, right down to the bricks in the fireplace. (Open M-Sa 9:30am-3:30pm, Su 1:30-3:30pm. 1hr. guided tours every 30min.; appointment required at the ticketing desk or Visitors Center. Free with admission to Old Salem Village.) The **Toy Museum,** in the same building, displays toys spanning 1700 years. Don't be fooled by its name—this museum is geared toward adults and older children. All of the toys are delicate antiques housed in glass cases.

Winston-Salem's other premier attraction is the **Reynolda House,** 2250 Reynolda Rd., one of the most famous homes in the South. The Reynolda was once home to tobacco tycoon R.J. Reynolds and his wife, Katherine, who made the household completely self-sufficient by growing vegetables and producing power to sustain it as a working "village" on the grounds. Today, the manor's primary allure is the two-acre garden that surrounds it. The Reynolda is now affiliated with Wake Forest University. (☎758-5150 or 888-663-1149; www.reynoldahouse.org. Open Tu-Sa 9:30am-4:30pm, Su 1:30-4:30pm. No admittance after 4pm. Wheelchair accessible. $10, seniors $9, with AAA $8.50, students and children free.) The **Reynolda House Museum of American Art** is a new addition to the Reynolda family compound. The museum offers exhibits of American art from 1755 to the present, all prominently displayed in this historic home and shiny new exhibition wing. The hours are the same as the Reynolda House. The **Reynolda Garden,** created for the enjoyment of the public as well as the Reynolds family, remains one of the most beautiful spots in Winston-Salem. (☎ 758-5593. Open daily dawn-dusk. Free.)

🎵 **ENTERTAINMENT.** Look for listings of local events in the free weekly newspaper *Go Triad* or in *Relish,* the Thursday entertainment supplement to the *Winston-Salem Journal.* On weekends from May to August, the city hosts three live music performance series in the downtown area: **Alive After Five** every Thursday evening (Corpening Plaza, 100 W. 2nd St.), **Fourth Street Jazz and Blues** every Friday evening (W. 4th St.), and **Summer on Trade** every Saturday evening (6th and Trade St.). Check out www.winstonsalemevents.com for more info. You'll find quality live rock, roots, and reggae music at **Ziggy's,** 433 Baity St., off University Pkwy. near the Coliseum. (☎ 748-1064; www.ziggyrock.com. Beer from $2. Cover $5-25. Open Tu-Su 8pm-2am, live music starts around 9pm.) Musicians also rock out at **The Garage,** 110 W. 7th St., at Trade St. Call ahead or check online—featured bands play new blue grass, pop punk, and everything in between. (☎ 777-1127; www.thegarage.ws. Beer from $2. Cover $5-15, under 21 $2 extra. Open Th-Sa, sometimes W. Showtimes vary.)

CHARLOTTE   ☎ 704

Named in the mid-1700s after the wife of England's King George III, Charlotte is still referred to as the "Queen City." Settlers flooded the region in the nation's first gold rush, which occurred around the turn of the 18th century, when a boy discovered a 17 lb. gold nugget near Charlotte. Shortly thereafter, the first branch of the US Mint was established here in 1837. Now the Carolina's biggest city, Charlotte has expanded both outward and upward. For visitors, the city offers top-notch museums, ritzy clubs, and a wide variety of professional sports.

🖥🎵 **TRANSPORTATION AND PRACTICAL INFORMATION. Charlotte-Douglas International Airport (CLT),** about 7 mi. west of the city at 5501 Josh Birmingham Pkwy. (☎ 359-4910; www.charlotteairport.com), accessible from the Billy Graham Pkwy. (Rte. 521), is a hub for US Airways. Amtrak, 1914 N. Tryon St. (☎ 376-4416 or 800-872-7245; www.amtrak.com; open 24hr.), sends **trains** once per day to Atlanta (5½hr., $48) and New Orleans (17hr., $106), and twice daily to New York City (12hr., $92-157), Raleigh (4hr., $24), and Washington D.C. (9hr., $94-117). Greyhound, 601 W. Trade St. (☎ 375-3332; www.greyhound.com; open 24hr.), sends **buses** to Charleston, WV (6½hr., 3 per day, $72-77), Columbia, SC (1¾hr., 34 per day, $17-18.50), and Richmond, VA (5½ -8½hr., 11 per day, $58). The Charlotte Area Transit System (CATS) operates **local buses;** the central terminal is at 310 E. Trade St. (☎ 336-7433; www.ridetransit.org. Most buses operate M-Sa 5:30am-1:30am, Su 6:30am-1:30am. $1.30, $2.60 for express service in outlying areas; most transfers free, local to express transfers.) Uptown, CATS runs Gold Rush, **free shuttles** that resemble cable cars. The nucleus of Charlotte, the busy uptown area, has numbered streets laid out perpendicular to named streets in a simple grid pattern. **Tryon Street,** running north-south, is the major crossroad. **I-77** crosses the city north-south, providing access to uptown, while **I-85** runs southwest-northeast, connecting the uptown to the UNC campus. Uptown is also accessible from **I-277,** a beltway, and is called the **John Belk Freeway** to the south of uptown and the **Brookshire Freeway** to the north. A **Visitors Center** is located at 330 S. Tryon St. (☎ 800-231-4636; www.visitcharlotte.com. Open M-F 8:30-5pm, Sa. 9am-3pm.) Local 24hr. hotlines include **Rape Crisis** (☎ 375-9900) and **suicide line** (☎ 358-2800). Both 24hr. The **Gay/Lesbian Community Center** hotline is ☎ 333-0144, and it operates M-Th and Su

6:30-9:30pm. Check **email** at the **Public Library of Charlotte and Mecklenburg County,** 310 N. Tryon St., uptown. (☎336-2572. 2hr. free Internet access per day. Open M-Th 9am-9pm, F-Sa 9am-6pm, Su 1-6pm.) **Post Office:** 201 N. McDowell St. (☎704-333-2542. Open M-F 7am-6pm, Sa 10am-1pm.) **Postal Code:** 28204.

▐▛ ▐ ACCOMMODATIONS AND FOOD. There are several clusters of budget motels in the Charlotte area: on Independence Blvd. off the John Belk Freeway; off I-85 at Exit 41, Sugar Creek Rd.; off I-85 at Exit 33 near the airport; and off I-77 at Exit 7, Clanton St. The **Continental Inn ❷,** 1100 W. Sugar Creek Rd., Exit 41 off I-85, has immaculate and inviting rooms. (☎597-8100. A/C, cable TV with free HBO, and continental breakfast. Rooms $42-45. AAA and AARP discount 10%. AmEx/D/MC/V.) **Homestead Studio Suites Hotel ❸,** 710 Yorkmont Rd., near the airport, provides clean, spacious rooms with full kitchenettes and Wi-Fi connections (activation fee $4) as well as coin-operated laundry facilities and free access to a local Bally's health club. (☎676-0083; www.extendedstayhotels.com. Reception 24hr. Rooms from $66; rates drop to $38 for stays of a week or longer. AAA and AARP discount 10%. AmEx/D/MC/V.) The **McDowell Nature Preserve ❶,** 15222 York Rd., offers RV, rent-a-tent, and primitive campsites in a shady, tranquil environment. RV and rent-a-tent sites have water and electricity; rent-a-tent sites include a 9x12 tent and two cots. (Go south on Tryon St. until it becomes York Rd. ☎583-1284; www.parkandrec.com. Open year-round. Primitive sites $9. RV sites $18. Rent-a-tent sites $38.)

Two areas outside of uptown offer attractive dining options at reasonable prices. **North Davidson ("NoDa"),** around 36th St., is home to a small artistic community inhabiting a set of historic buildings. South of the city center, the **Dilworth** neighborhood, along East and South Blvd., is lined with restaurants serving everything from authentic ethnic meals to pizza and pub fare. For eccentric, tasty cuisine, the hip **Cosmos Cafe ❸,** 300 N. College St., at E. 6th St., has a versatile menu ranging from tapas and *mezes* ($5.75-9.25) to sushi and wood-fired pizzas ($8.75-10). The restaurant becomes a popular yuppie bar around 10:30pm; swing by Wednesday nights for superb gourmet martinis at half price. (☎372-3553; www.cosmoscafe.com. 2-for-1 tapas M-Sa 5-7pm. Th Latin night with free salsa lessons. Open M-F 11am-2am, Sa 5pm-2am. AmEx/D/MC/V.) For an inexpensive tastebud pleaser try **Penguin Drive-In ❶,** 1921 Commonwealth Ave. This local favorite serves up 50s-style sandwich classics like "Fried Bologna" ($4.50) or "The Boss Hogg" ($5.25), a grilled honey ham sandwich. (☎375-6959. M-Sa 11am-2am, Su noon-2am.) Find scrumptious organic food at **Talley's Green Grocery ❶,** 1408-C E. Blvd. in Dilworth, an upscale market behind the Outback Steakhouse. Cafe Verde, in the back of the store, offers excellent sandwiches and prepared dishes. (☎334-9200; www.talleys.com. Sandwiches premade $7; made to order $8, served until 2pm. Open M-Sa 9am-9pm, Su 10am-7pm. AmEx/D/MC/V.) The friendly staff at the **Smelly Cat Coffeehouse ❶,** 514 E. 36th St., in NoDa, serve great coffee drinks ($1.50-4) as well as several pastries. Add a sugar rush to your caffeine high with the "El Guapo" ($4.25), a cinnamon chai drink made into a milkshake. (☎374-9656. Ice cream $1.75. Cinnamon rolls $2.25. Live music some weekends. Open M-W 7am-8pm, Th 7am- 8pm, F 7am-midnight, Sa 8am-midnight, Su 8:30am- 8pm. D/MC/V.)

◙ SIGHTS. Charlotte has a number of museums that give visitors an insider's perspective on the region; most are located in the uptown area. The **▧Levine Museum of the New South,** 200 E. 7th St., is a fantastic new museum that explores the history of the Charlotte and Carolina Piedmont area. From a working cotton gin to a re-creation of a soda fountain that was occupied during the civil rights sit-ins, the Levine shows how the "New South" has developed from the end of the Civil War to the present. (☎333-1887. Open Tu-Sa 10am-5pm, Su noon-5pm. $6; students, seniors, and ages 6-18 $5; under 6 free.) For a trip outdoors visit the **Carolina Raptor Center,** 6000 Sample Rd. Take I-77 to Exit 16-B. Turn right at second light onto Beatties Ford Rd. Take Beatties Ford Rd. to Sample Rd. which leads to Latta Plantation Nature Preserve. The Raptor Center is six-tenths of a mile on the left. The Raptor Center is a home for eagles, hawks, owls, vultures and falcons that have been injured. (☎875-6521; http://carolinaraptorcenter.org. Open M-Sa 10am-5pm, Su noon-5pm. Adults $6, seniors $5, students $4.) Admission to the **Mint Museum of Craft and Design,** 220 N. Tryon St., uptown, also grants you access to the **Mint Museum of Art,** 2730 Randolph Rd., about two and a half miles to the southeast. The Museum of Craft and Design features contemporary work in glass, wood, metal, and fiber. Even the chandelier in the lobby is an impressive work of craftsmanship, and previous exhibits have highlighted such topics as goldsmithing and quilting. The **Museum of Art** focuses on more traditional painting and ceramics and displays pieces from local students. The building that now houses the art museum once functioned as Charlotte's mint; visitors can peruse coins produced here. (Both museums ☎337-2000; www.mintmuseum.org. Craft and Design Museum open Tu-Sa 10am-5pm, Su noon-5pm. Museum of Art open Tu 10am-10pm, W-Sa 10am-5pm, Su noon-5pm. Adults $6, students and over 62 $5, ages 6-17 $3. Craft and Design Museum free Tu 10am-2pm. Museum of Art free Tu 5-10pm.)

🎭🎸 **ENTERTAINMENT AND NIGHTLIFE.** In addition to its arena football, NHL, NFL, NBA, WNBA, and AAA baseball teams, Charlotte is also home to the fastest-growing sport in national popularity—stock car racing. The **Lowe's Motor Speedway,** Exit 49 off I-85, hosts several major NASCAR events each year. (Tickets and schedule information ☎800-455-3267; www.gospeedway.com.) The latest expansion team to enter the NBA, the **Charlotte Bobcats,** is owned by Black Entertainment Television founder Robert Johnson. The Bobcats and Charlotte's WNBA team, the **Sting,** shoot hoops in the new **Charlotte Arena,** 333 E. Trade St. (Tickets ☎800-495-2295; www.newcharlottearena.com. Call or check website for box office hours.) Football fans can catch an NFL game when the **Carolina Panthers** play at the **Bank of America Stadium,** 800 S. Mint St. (Tickets ☎522-6500; www.carolinapanthers.com. Tickets $45-70. Stadium tours $4, over 55 $3, ages 5-15 $2.) Ten miles south, the Charlotte **Knights** play AAA minor league baseball at **Knights Castle,** off I-77 S at Exit 88. (Tickets ☎364-6637; www.charlotteknights.com. Box office open M-F 10am-5pm and 10am until game time on game days. Tickets $6-10.)

To check out nightlife, arts, and entertainment listings, grab a free copy of *Creative Loafing* in one of Charlotte's shops or restaurants, visit www.charlotte.creativeloafing.com, or look over the E&T section of the *Charlotte Observer*. Many of Charlotte's hippest clubs can be found uptown, especially on College St. from 5th to 7th St. For live rock bands, head to **Amos's Southend,** 1423 S. Tryon St. Live acts are often cover bands of rock's greats, from Led Zeppelin and Pink Floyd to Guns N' Roses and Journey. Beer $3, import $4; mixed drinks $5. (☎377-6874; www.amossouthend.com. Call for showtimes, cover, and age restrictions). **The Evening Muse,** 3227 N. Davidson St., in NoDa, is a laidback venue for a wide variety of musical acts, including acoustic, jazz, and rock. (☎376-3737; www.theeveningmuse.com. Cover from $5. Open W-Th 6pm-midnight, F-Sa 6pm-2am.)

CAROLINA MOUNTAINS

The sharp ridges and rolling slopes of the southern Appalachian range create some of the most spectacular scenery in the Southeast. Scholars, ski bums, farmers, and artists all find reasons to call this gorgeous region home. The aptly named High Country stretches from Boone in the north to Asheville in the south. The 469 mi.

THE SOUTH

Blue Ridge Parkway, cuts through the mountaintops and connects Virginia's Shenandoah National Park in the north to Tennessee's Great Smoky Mountains National Park in the south. Views from many of the Parkway's scenic overlooks are staggering, particularly on days when mist shrouds the tree-carpeted peaks.

ASHEVILLE   ☎ 828

Hazy blue mountains, deep valleys, and spectacular waterfalls form the impressive backdrop of this small, friendly city. Once a popular retreat for the well-to-do, Asheville hosted enough Carnegies, Vanderbilts, and Mellons to fill a 1920s edition of *Who's Who on the Atlantic Seaboard*. The population today leans toward dreadlocks and vegetarianism, providing funky nightlife and festivals all year. The urban feel extends to Asheville's downtown, where boutiques and polished office buildings look like they belong in Manhattan rather than Appalachia.

E TRANSPORTATION. The **Asheville Regional Airport (AVL)** is at Exit 9 off I-26, 15 mi. south of the city. (☎ 684-2226; www.flyavl.com.) Greyhound, 2 Tunnel Rd. (☎ 253-8451; www.greyhound.com), 2 mi. east of downtown near the Beaucatcher Tunnel, sends **buses** to Charlotte (3hr., 5 per day, $25.50), Knoxville (2½hr., 7 per day, $27), and Raleigh (8-11hr., 5 per day, $39-61). The Asheville Transit System handles **bus service** within city limits. Pick up a copy of bus schedules and routes from the Visitors Center or visit the **Asheville Transit Center,** 49 Coxe Ave., by the post office. (☎ 253-5691. Buses run M-Sa between 6am and 7pm; though hours vary by route. $1, short trips in downtown area free. Discounts for seniors, disabled, and multi-fare tickets; free transfers.)

7 PRACTICAL INFORMATION. The **Chamber of Commerce and Visitor Center,** 151 Haywood St., Exit 4C off I-240, situated on the northwest end of downtown, dispenses a wealth of knowledge about activities and accommodations in the area, as well as offering a free downtown-area map. (☎ 258-6101 or 800-257-1300; www.exploreasheville.com. Open M-F 8:30am-5:30pm, Sa-Su 9am-5pm.) Check **email** at the **Pack Memorial Library,** 67 Haywood St. (☎ 255-5203. $2. 55min. limit. Open M-Th 10am-8pm, F 10am-6pm, Sa 10am-5pm; Sept.-May also Su 2-5pm.) **Post Office:** 33 Coxe Ave., off Patton Ave. (☎ 271-6429. Open M-F 7:30am-5:30pm, Sa 9am-1pm.) **Postal Code:** 28802.

⌐ ACCOMMODATIONS. ✦Bon Paul and Sharky's Hostel ❶, 816 Haywood Rd., features a number of amenities, including a common room with a huge TV and a DVD collection, outdoor hot tub, foosball table, communal kitchen, free lockers, linens, and Wi-Fi, off-street parking, bicycles for biking downtown, and free bus station and airport pickup. (☎ 350-9929; www.bonpaulandsharkys.com. Reception daily 9am-noon and 5-10pm. Check-in 24hr. Dorms $20, $17 if staying for 3 nights or if 3 people are staying together; singles $50; camping on grounds $8 per person. 21 day max. stay. Cash only.) The funky, new-age **Arthaus Hostel ❶,** 16 Ravenscroft Rd., is located downtown and offers brightly painted, spotless rooms, a communal kitchen, and free Wi-Fi. (☎ 225-3278. Ages 18-40, unless supervised. Linens included. Call to arrange check-in. Restricted access noon-4pm. Private rooms for groups of 2 to 6 $50-100. MC/V.) The **Log Cabin Motor Court ❸,** 330 Weaverville Hwy., 5 mi. north of downtown, provides immaculate, inviting cabins with HBO, A/C, Wi-Fi, and laundry. The more expensive cabins also have fireplaces and kitchenettes. (☎ 645-6546. Reception 10am-8pm. Cabins with one bedroom and bath $55, with kitchenette $75; with 2 bedrooms and bath from $110. AAA and military discount 10%. AmEx/D/MC/V.) **Days Inn ❸,** 201 Tunnel Rd., has huge rooms with A/C, cable, coffeemakers, microwaves, and refrigerators, as well

as a pool and full breakfast. (☎252-4000. Singles $59-79; doubles $75-119. AAA and
AARP discount. AmEx/D/MC/V.) **Powhatan Lake Campground ❶**, 375 Wesley Branch
Rd., 12 mi. southwest of Asheville off Rte. 191, is in the **Pisgah National Forest** and
has wooded sites on a trout lake open for swimming and fishing. Sites fill fast in
summer. (☎670-5627, reservations 877-444-6777. Some hookups; hot showers and
dump station available. Open Apr.-Oct. Gates close at 10pm. Sites $17-20.)

🍴 **FOOD.** Downtown Asheville is packed with excellent places to eat. At the
🌿**Laughing Seed Cafe ❸**, 40 Wall St., the international lineup of vegetarian dishes,
including the "Havana Cuban Sandwich"($9), tastes even better when served on
the sunny patio. (☎252-3445. Entrees $9-15. Sandwiches $5-8.50. Dinner specialties
$13-$16. Open M-Th 11:30am-9pm, F-Sa 11:30am-10pm, Su 10am-9pm. AmEx/D/
MC/V.) Nearby, the **Tupelo Honey Cafe ❷**, 12 College St., prepares Southern home
cookin' with organic ingredients and an innovative twist. Try the Charleston
Chicken Sandwich ($8.50) or the Southern vegetable gnocchi ($15). (☎255-4404.
Sandwiches $7-8.50. Entrees $6-12.75. Open Tu-Th 9am-3pm and 5:30-10pm, F-Sa
9am-3pm and 5:30-midnight, Su 9am-3pm. AmEx/MC/V.) If you like Southern-style
barbecue try **Ed Boudreaux's Bayou Bar-B-que ❷**, 48 Biltmore Ave., where they prepare barbecue for the meat-eater and the vegetarian. Choose from the slow-
smoked "St. Louis" style or Creole seasoning. Try Applewood-smoked Pulled Pork
($9) or for the vegetarian, BBQ Tempeh Po' Boy ($9). (Sandwiches $7-8. BBQ plat-
ters $9-$22. Open M-Th 11am-11pm, F-Sa 11am-midnight, Su noon-10pm.)

📷 **SIGHTS.** George Vanderbilt's palatial **Biltmore Estate**, 1 Approach Rd., just
north of I-40, was constructed in the 1890s and is the largest private home in America. A self-guided tour of the house and grounds can take all day; try to arrive early.
Entrance fee includes complimentary wine tastings at the on-site winery. (☎225-
1333 or 800-543-2961; www.biltmore.com. Estate open daily Jan.-Mar. 9am-4pm;
Apr.-Dec. 8:30am-5:30pm. Winery open daily Jan.-Mar. noon-6pm; Apr.-Dec. 11am-
7pm. Most of the estate is wheelchair accessible. $38, ages 10-17 $19.50, under 5
free. Audio tour $8. Behind the Scenes tours of North and South Wings $15. Carriage rides $35. Trail rides $60.) If Biltmore is a bit more than your wallet can handle, enjoy the **Thomas Wolfe Memorial**, 52 N. Market St., between Woodfin and
Walnut St., which celebrates one of the early 20th century's most influential American authors with a museum and the "old Kentucky home" where Thomas Wolfe
grew up. (☎253-8304; www.wolfememorial.com. Open Apr.-Oct. Tu-Sa 9am-5pm,
Su 1-5pm; Nov.-Mar. Tu-Sa 10am-4pm, Su 1-4pm. 45min. tours the bottom of every
hr. $1, students $0.50., under 12 free.) The **Asheville Art Museum**, 2 S. Pack Sq., displays 20th-century American artwork. While there are over 3000 artists on exhibit,
the most prominent ongoing display is "Vantage Points: Perspectives on American
Art 1960-1980." (☎253-3227; www.ashevilleart.org. Open Tu-Th and Sa 10am-5pm,
F 10am-8pm, Su 1-5pm. Wheelchair accessible. $6; students, seniors, and ages 4-15
$5.) Twenty-five miles southeast of Asheville on U.S. 64/74A, the scenic setting for
Last of the Mohicans rises almost half a mile in **Chimney Rock Park.** After driving
to the base of the Chimney, take the 26-story elevator to the top or walk up for a 75
mi. view. Savor your time on the mountaintop with one of the five hikes that range
in length from a half-mile to 1½ mi., some leading to breathtaking waterfalls.
(☎625-9611 or 800-277-9611; www.chimneyrockpark.com. Ticket office open daily
Apr.-Oct. 8:30am-5:30pm; Nov.-Mar. 8:30am-4:30pm. Park open 1½hr. after office
closes. $14, ages 6-15 $6.) Enjoy the free **Botanical Gardens**, 151 W. T. Weaver Blvd.,
which contains plants native to the Carolina Mountains. The best time to visit is
when the wildflowers are blooming, from April to mid-May. (☎252-5190;
www.ashevillebotanicalgardens.org. Open daily dawn-dusk.)

THE SOUTH

🎵🎬 **ENTERTAINMENT AND NIGHTLIFE.** The downtown area, especially the southeast end around the intersection of Broadway and College St., is a haven for music, munchies, and movies. The free weekly paper *Mountain Xpress*, and *Community Connections*, a free gay publication, have arts, events, and dining listings. **Jack of the Wood,** 95 Patton Ave., heats up at night with live Celtic, bluegrass, and old-time mountain music. While you enjoy the soundtrack, fill up with traditional pub fare. (☎252-5445. Local beer $3.50. M trivia night 8pm. 21+ after 10pm. Cover F-Sa $5-7. Open M-F 4pm-2am, Sa noon-2am, Su 3pm-2am.) The popular **Asheville Pizza and Brewing Company,** 675 Merrimon Ave., shows second-run movies for $2 and serves pizza ($9-11.50 for 12"). Try the Funky Chicken (barbecue chicken, bacon, red onions; $11) and home-brewed beer. (☎254-1281. Th all pints $3. Open daily 11am-midnight.) Indie and arthouse flicks play at the **Fine Arts Theatre,** 36 Biltmore Ave. (☎232-1536; www.fineartstheatre.com. $8, seniors and matinees $5.75. Box office opens at 12:30pm. Ticket sales begin 30min. before showtimes.) **Shakespeare in Montford Park,** at the Hazel Robinson Amphitheater, produces three to five plays each summer. (☎254-4540; www.montfordparkplayers.org. Performances June-Oct. F-Su 7:30pm. Free.)

BOONE   ☎ 828

Nestled among the High Country's breathtaking mountains, Boone has a laid-back feel. Home to Appalachian State University, the small city is heavily populated with students but also attracts skiers, nature lovers, and everyone in between. Thrift shops and used book stores abound, and the bright colors of tie-dye and vegetarian cuisine are everywhere you turn.

🚍🛈 **TRANSPORTATION AND PRACTICAL INFORMATION. Boone AppalCart,** 274 Winklers Creek Rd., provides local bus service. (☎264-2278. Hours vary. $0.50.) **Visitor Info: Boone Area Chamber of Commerce,** 208 Howard St. (☎800-852-9506; www.visitboonenc.com. Open M-F 9am-5pm.) **The North Carolina High Country Host Visitor Center,** 1700 Blowing Rock Rd./U.S. 321. (☎800-438-7500; www.mountainsofnc.com. Open M-Sa 9am-5pm, Su 9am-3pm.) **Internet access: Watauga County Public Library,** 140 Queen St., at N. Depot St. (☎264-8784. Open M-Th 9am-7pm, F-Sa 9am-5pm.) **Post Office:** 544 Blowing Rock Rd. (☎264-3813; M-F 5:30am-9pm.) **Postal Code:** 28607.

🛏🍴 **ACCOMMODATIONS AND FOOD.** The neighboring community of Blowing Rock offers plenty of pricey inns. In Boone, the **Hidden Valley Motel ❸,** 8725 Hwy. 105 S, is located in the stunning Foscoe Valley, reasonably close to downtown, and offers large, well-decorated rooms. (☎963-4372. A/C, cable TV. Singles $50-80; doubles $55-90. D/MC/V.) Along the Parkway near Boone, the **Julian Price Campground ❶,** Mi. 297, has spectacular tent and RV sites. Sites around Loop A are on a lake. (☎963-5911. Flush toilets and water; no hookups or showers. Open May-Oct. Sites $15. Cash or check only.)

King St. offers great little restaurants, most with a healthy, earthy feel. The small, hip **Black Cat ❶,** 127 S. Depot St., off King St., makes humongous and tasty burritos; vegetarian options are cooked on a separate grill. Bluegrass, rock, and country musicians perform some weeknights during the school year. (☎263-9511. Burritos, quesadillas, and nachos from $4. Beer and wine $2.50-4.50. Open M-Th 11:30am-9pm, F-Sa 11:30am-10pm, Su 11:30am-9pm. MC/V.) Vegetarians have plenty of options, but none combine quality with low prices as well as **Angelica's ❷,** 506 W. King St., which prepares gourmet sandwiches ($6-10), smoothies ($4), and vegetarian sushi. (☎265-0809. Open M-Th 11am-9pm, F-Sa 11am-9pm, Su 11am-9pm. AmEx/MC/V.) For less healthy but equally filling fare, head to **Mel's Diner ❶,** 1286 Hwy. 105 S, which serves burgers, sandwiches, and breakfast atop a pastel pink counter. (☎265-1344. Burgers and sandwiches $6-9. Breakfast $3.50-7. Open M-Th 7am-midnight, F-Sa 7am-11pm. MC/V.)

◪ **SIGHTS.** ▨**Grandfather Mountain,** near the intersection of U.S. 221 and the Blue Ridge Parkway (Mi. 305), is a great destination for families and wildlife enthusiasts. The habitat walk features bald eagles, black bears, mountain lions, and other animals; a nature museum, suspension bridge, and a series of hikes round out the park. (☎800-468-7325; www.grandfather.com. Open daily June-Aug. 8am-7pm; Mar.-May and Sept.-Nov. 8am-6pm; Dec.-Feb. 8am-5pm. Last entry 1hr. before closing. Some areas are wheelchair accessible. $14, seniors $12, ages 4-12 $6, under 4 free.) Hiking or camping on Grandfather Mtn. requires a camping and vehicle permit ($10), available at the park entrance or at several area stores, including the historic **Mast General Store,** 630 W. King St., downtown. (☎262-0000. Open M-Sa 10am-6pm, Su noon-6pm. AmEx/V/MC.) There are two locations in the Valley and three locations in the High Country. The free *Grandfather Mountain Trail Map and Backcountry Guide,* available anywhere permits are sold, details area hikes. The carless can take the **Boone AppalCart** (p. 346) up to the mountain. Near Boone, Wilson Creek offers waterfalls, swimming holes, and trails. Linville Gorge is perfect for backcountry camping and rock climbing. For more info, call the ranger's office (☎737-0833).

Didn't think you could ski this far south? Think again. Boone is conveniently located near three ski resorts. **Sugar Mountain,** off Hwy. 184 in Banner Elk (☎898-4521 or 800-784-2768; www.skisugar.com; weekend lift tickets $59, ages 4-11 $40, under 4 and over 70 free), with hiking and biking trails open May 1 to October 1, and **Ski Beech,** 1007 Beech Mtn. Pkwy. also off Hwy. 184 (☎800-438-2093; www.skibeech.com; weekend lift tickets $50, ages 5-12 and 60-69 $37, under 5 and over 70 free), are the largest resorts. The Appalcart runs a free winter shuttle from Boone to Sugar Mountain. Call ☎800-962-2322 for info about daily ski conditions.

ASU's **Appalachian Cultural Museum,** on University Hall Dr. off Blowing Rock Rd. (U.S. 321), strives to preserve the rich cultural traditions of the region with exhibits on crafts, storytelling, moonshine, and even NASCAR. (☎262-3117. Open Tu-Sa 10am-5pm, Su 1-5pm. Wheelchair accessible. $4, seniors $3.50, ages 10-18 $2.)

◪▧ **ENTERTAINMENT AND NIGHTLIFE.** In the town of Todd, 11 mi. north of Boone at the edge of Ashe County, the **Todd General Store** hosts live mountain music concerts on Friday nights 7pm to 9:15pm and Saturday afternoons during the summer. From downtown Boone, take U.S. 421 South and turn left on Hwy. 194; continue 11 mi. and make a right onto Todd Railroad Grade Rd. It's on the left after half a mile. (☎336-877-1067. Most events free, with suggested donations. Times vary; call for schedule.) For a cold beer or a game of pool, head to **Murphy's Pub,** 747 W. King St. (☎264-5117. Beer $2.25-3. Live music ranging from hip-hop to bluegrass usually Th-Sa. 21+. Cover $3-5. Open daily 11am-2am. Kitchen closes at 11pm.) For a little culture with your drink, check out the **Boone Saloon,** 489 W. King St., which has billiards, modern art decor, and live music of all varieties during the week. (☎264-1811. Beer $1.75-5. 21+ after 10pm. Open M-Sa 11:30am-2am, Su 6pm-2am, sometimes closes earlier.) The **Boone Bowling Center,** 261 Boone Heights Dr., has a variety of special deals. Glow bowling takes place every Friday (8pm-11pm; $3.75 per game, $2.50 for shoes). The 3rd Friday of every month is Christian cosmic night (10pm-midnight; $12.50 including shoes). Saturday is cosmic night (11pm-2am; $17.75 per game including shoes). Daytime bowling on weekdays is less flashy, but cheaper. (☎264-3166; www.boonebowling.com. Open M-F 10am-11pm, Sa 10am-2am, Su 2-10pm. M-F before 5pm $2.75 per game, seniors and under 10 $2; after 5pm $3/2.50; Sa-Su $3.75. Shoe rental $2.50.)

NORTH CAROLINA COAST

Lined with islands that shield inlanders from Atlantic squalls, the Carolina Coast has a history as stormy as the hurricanes that pummel its beaches. England's first attempt to colonize North America ended in 1590 with the peculiar disappearance of the Roanoke settlement, now known as the "Lost Colony." Later, the coast earned the title "Graveyard of the Atlantic"—over 1000 ships have foundered on the Outer Banks' southern shores, leaving hundreds of wrecks for scuba exploration. The winds that sank ships lifted the world's first flight in 1903, with some assistance from the Wright brothers. Flying now forms the basis of much of the area's recreational activities such as hang-gliding, parasailing, kiteboarding, and good ol' kite-flying. Those not interested in taking to the sky can take advantage of the abundance of natural sea life by fishing, crabbing, or aquarium hopping.

OUTER BANKS   ☎ 252

Locals claim that the legendary pirate Blackbeard once roamed the waters off the Outer Banks; some think that his treasures still lie beneath the beaches. But whether or not you dig up Blackbeard's loot, there are plenty of other gems on these islands, from historic lighthouses to gorgeous sand dunes. On the northern half of Bodie Island, the three contiguous towns of **Kitty Hawk, Kill Devil Hills,** and **Nags Head** are heavily trafficked, commercial, and filled with restaurants, mini-golf courses, and souvenir super-stores. However, follow Rte. 12 south to Hatteras Island to find largely undeveloped, pristine beaches, thanks to the protection of the National Park Service. **Ocracoke Island,** the southernmost of the islands, retains a sense of community despite its growing popularity.

▐▀ TRANSPORTATION

Ferries: Free ferries run between **Hatteras** and **Ocracoke** (40min., daily 5am-midnight. No reservations accepted. Lines to board and disembark from the ferry may take 10min. Toll ferries run between **Ocracoke** and **Cedar Island,** east of New Bern on Rte. 12, which becomes U.S. 70 (2¼hr.; pedestrians $1, bicycles $3, motorcycles $10, cars $15). Toll ferries also travel between Ocracoke and **Swan Quarter,** (2½hr., same prices as Cedar Island). Call ahead for schedules and reservations: ferries from **Ocracoke** ☎800-345-1665, from Cedar Island ☎800-856-0343, from Swan Quarter ☎800-773-1094. General info and reservations at ☎800-293-3779; www.ncferry.org.

Taxis: In Nags Head **Beach Cab** (☎441-2500). In Bodie Island **Coastal Cab** (☎449-8787). In Cape Hatteras **Island Hopper Shuttle** (☎995-6771).

Bike Rental: Ocean Atlantic Rental (☎441-7823), in Nags Head. $10 per day, $40 per week. Open daily 9am-9pm.

✴ ORIENTATION

The Outer Banks consist of four narrow islands strung along the northern half of the North Carolina coast. The northernmost, **Bodie Island,** is joined to the mainland by the **Wright Memorial Bridge,** which allows U.S. 158 to run the length of the island. For most of Bodie Island, Rte. 12 (known as the Beach Road and the Virginia Dare Trail) and U.S. 158 (called the Bypass) run parallel to each other. **Roanoke Island** lies between the southern end of Bodie and the mainland. U.S. 64 runs from the mainland to **Manteo** on Roanoke over the Virginia Dare Bridge and then to Bodie Island just south of Nags Head over the Washington Baum Bridge. From the **Whalebone Junction,** where U.S. 158 ends and U.S. 64 runs into Rte. 12, the **Cape Hatteras**

National Seashore stretches south for 70 mi. Rte. 12 is the only major road running north-south through the Cape Hatteras National Seashore and connects Bodie to Hatteras Island by another bridge. Southernmost **Ocracoke Island** is linked by ferry to Hatteras Island to the north and mainland towns to the south. Ocracoke Island is almost all park land and has only one town, Ocracoke Village. Directions to locations on Bodie Island and Hatteras Island are usually given in terms of miles from the Wright Memorial Bridge. There is no public transit on the Outer Banks. During high season be prepared for hectic traffic with extra caution and travel time.

🛈 PRACTICAL INFORMATION

Tourist Offices: Outer Banks Welcome Center on Roanoke Island, 1 Visitors Center Cir. (☎877-629-4386; www.outerbanks.org), at the base of the bridge to the mainland in Manteo. Info for all the islands except Ocracoke. Open daily 8am-5:30pm. **Aycock Brown Welcome Center** (☎261-4644; www.outerbanks.com/dare/brown.htm), Mile 1.5 on U.S. 158 in Kitty Hawk, has maps and tons of brochures. Open daily 9am-5:30pm. **Cape Hatteras National Seashore Information Centers: Bodie Island** (☎441-5711), on Rte. 12 between mi. 22 and 23 at the north entrance to the National Seashore at Whalebone Junction. Open daily June-Aug. 9am-6pm; Sept.-May 9am-5pm. **Hatteras Island Visitor Center** (☎995-4474) on Rte. 12 at the Cape Hatteras Lighthouse. Open high season 9am-6pm; low season 9am-5pm. **Ocracoke Island Visitor Center** (☎928-4531), next to the ferry terminal at the south end of the island. Open daily June-Aug. 9am-6pm; Sept.-May 9am-5pm. Park info online at www.nps.gov/caha.

Internet Access: Free in the **Dare County Libraries.** On Bodie, the **Kill Devil Hills Branch,** 400 Mustian St. (☎441-4331), is 1 block west of U.S. 158, behind the post office. Open M and Th-F 9am-5:30pm, Tu-W 10am-7pm, Sa 10am-4pm. **Manteo Branch** on Rte. 64 at Burnside St. (☎473-2372), in Roanoke. Open M and Th 10am-7pm, Tu-W and F-Sa 10am-4pm. **Hatteras Branch** (☎986-2385), on Hwy. 12 in the Community Building. Open M-Tu and Th-F 9:30am-5:30pm, W 1-7pm, Sa 9:30am-12:30pm.

Post Office: 3841 N. Croatan Hwy./Rte. 158 (☎261-2211), in Kitty Hawk. Open M-F 9am-4:30pm, Sa 10am-noon. **Postal Code:** 27949.

🛏🍴 ACCOMMODATIONS AND FOOD

Most motels line **Route 12** on crowded Bodie Island. More privacy awaits farther south; Ocracoke is the most secluded. Rates everywhere are highest from June through August, especially on weekends. Although inter-season rates are good for April, May, September, and October, April can be rainy, October cold, and September hurricane-ridden. For a good deal without sacrificing pleasant weather, schedule for May. During high season make reservations at least three days in advance.

CAMPING

While sleeping on public beaches is punishable by fine and oceanview hotel rooms cost an arm and a leg, you can nod off to the sounds of the surf if you camp in one of the National Park Service's four oceanside **campgrounds ❶**. Each of the campgrounds is located on the Cape Hatteras National Seashore and has water, restrooms, picnic tables, grills, and cold-water showers. The northernmost site is **Oregon Inlet,** near the southern tip of Bodie Island and thus best-suited for town excursions. The next two sites, **Cape Point** and **Frisco,** both lie near the elbow of Hatteras Island, close to the lighthouse. Cape Point's flat terrain tends to flood in wet weather. A number of Frisco's campsites are perched atop dunes, allowing for unobstructed views of the Atlantic. Farthest south, **Ocracoke** is located on Ocracoke Island, 3.5 mi. north of Ocracoke Village. Soil in the campgrounds is sandy;

rangers recommend bringing longer-than-usual stakes for tents. There are no shade trees in the campgrounds. (Reservations may be made only for Ocracoke ☎800-365-2267; all others first come, first served. Cape Point open late May to early Sept.; all others open late Mar. to mid-Oct. All sites $23. RVs allowed; no hookups available.)

BODIE ISLAND

A cheaper (though non-oceanside) option on Beach Rd. is the **Ebb Tide Motel ❸**, mi. 10 on Beach Rd., which offers rooms with refrigerator, microwave, cable TV, and A/C, as well as a pool and restaurant. (☎441-4913. June-Aug. room with double bed $63. Sept.-May $59. Prices higher on weekends. MC/V.) One alternative to the pricier beachside options is **Cavalier Motel ❹**, 601 Beach Rd., near mi. 8.5. This motor court comes with most of the amenities of a large hotel at a fraction of the price: refrigerators, microwaves, free local calls, cable TV, A/C, pool, hot tub, children's play area, and volleyball court. (☎441-5585; www.thecavaliermotel.com. Room with twin and double bed June-Aug. $93; Apr.-May and Sept. $9; Oct.-Mar. $39-45. Year-round ocean view and 2 double beds $59-176. Multiple-bedroom cottages available. D/MC/V.). **Adventure Campground ❶**, 1004 W. Kitty Hawk Rd., is the best deal on the northern islands. Late risers, beware: peacocks live on the premises and begin screeching at sunrise. (☎261-2294. Reception 9am-9pm. $20, each additional adult $5, under 12 $2.50, under 5 free. Cash and traveler's checks only.)

 Tortuga's Lie ❸, mi. 11 on Beach Rd. in Nags Head, serves Caribbean-influenced seafood, sandwiches, pasta, and grill items in a stylish setting with license plates from all over the country covering the ceiling. The Pork Antonio ($15) is a spicy option rubbed with jerk seasoning and topped with habanero yellow currant glaze. (☎441-7299. Sandwiches and burgers $4-8. Dinner entrees $13-15. W sushi night. Open daily 11:30am-10:30pm. No reservations. AmEx/D/MC/V.) Pacific Rim fare reigns at **Mama Kwan's Tiki Bar and Grill ❷**, mi. 9.5 on U.S. 158, where Asian flair enhances local dishes in a faux thatch hut. Try the popular "Jawaiian Spiced Chicken Breasts" (a fusion of Hawaiian and Jamaican flavors drizzled with butter-rum sauce; $16), or try vegetarian pad thai for $7. (☎441-7889. Sandwiches $7-9. Open M-Sa 11:30am-2am, Su noon-2am. MC/V.) With a "no grits, no glory" motto, **Grits Grill ❶**, Mi. 14 on U.S. 158 in the Outer Banks Mall, serves the Southern specialty with breakfast items ($2.80-9), sandwiches ($3-7.50), and fresh Krispy Kreme Donuts in a 50s-style diner setting. (☎449-2888. Open daily 6am-2pm.) **Howard's Pub and Raw Bar Restaurant ❷**, Highway 12, was established in 1854. Legend has it Howard was Blackbeard's quartermaster and had served drinks here in the mid 1800s. Now young and old enjoy Howard's wooden deck, game room and over 200 selections of beer. Try their sub sandwiches (half $4.95, whole $6.95). (☎928-4441. Open daily 11am-1am.)

OCRACOKE ISLAND

Hatteras Island is almost exclusively parkland, so there are few lodging options other than at one of the area's many campgrounds. On Ocracoke, accommodations and restaurants cluster on the southern tip in Ocracoke Village. **Edwards of Ocracoke ❸**, at Old Beach and Sand Dollar Rd., offers bright rooms for reasonable prices. (☎928-4801; www.edwardsofocracoke.com. A/C, cable TV, laundry. In summer 2-person bungalow $70; in spring $48 on weekdays; $58 on weekends. MC/V.) The juniper wooden rooms at the **Sand Dollar Motel ❸**, 70 Sand Dollar Rd., in Ocracoke, have a natural allure. (☎928-5571. Open Apr. to late Nov. Breakfast included. Refrigerators, microwaves, A/C, cable TV, and pool. Low season queen bed $60, 2 double beds $65. High season $85/90. Winter rates vary. AmEx/D/MC/V.) For pleasant, wood-paneled rooms at some of Ocracoke's lowest prices, head to **Blackbeard's Lodge ❹**, 111 Back Rd. Turn right off Rte. 12 before the boat filled with seashells. The swing and rocking chairs on the front porch are perfect for relaxing and people-watching. Check out the game room and lobby designed in a pirate theme with nautical accents (☎928-3421, reservations 800-892-5314; www.blackbeardslodge.com. A/C, cable TV, game room, and heated pool. Double beds $85. D/MC/V.)

Seafood lovers will feel right at home at **Jolly Roger ❷**, on Rte. 12. Come enjoy eating outside on the waterfront: the view is great for glimpsing all the different species of birds of the island. Inhale the ocean breeze while indulging in local fresh fish specials and sandwiches. (☎928-3703. Beer from $2.50 per pint or $7.50 per pitcher. Open mid-Mar. to mid-Nov. daily 11am-10pm. AmEx/D/MC/V.)

SIGHTS

The first flight in Kitty Hawk inspired many more airborne activities. The largest hang gliding school in the world is located at **Jockey's Ridge State Park,** mi. 12 on U.S. 158. **Kitty Hawk Kites** (☎441-4124 or 877-359-8447; www.kittyhawk.com) trains aspiring hang-gliding pilots. Beginner lessons (from $89) last 3hr. and include five solo flights. Those preferring ground-level excitement can slide down Jockey Ridge's dunes, the tallest on the East Coast, which comprise some 30 million tons of sand. (Park ☎441-7132. Open daily in summer 8am-9pm; low season closes between 6pm and 8pm. Free.)

The **Wright Brothers National Memorial,** mi. 7.5 on U.S. 158, marks the spot where Orville and Wilbur Wright soared in history's first powered flight. Exhibits in the Visitors Center and First Flight Pavilion document aerospace technology from the first airplane to the first moon landing. (☎441-7430; www.nps.gov/wrbr. Open daily 9am-5pm. $4, under 15 free.)

Roanoke Island offers several historic and cultural attractions. The **Fort Raleigh National Historic Site,** 1409 National Park Rd., just off U.S. 64, marks the spot where the British first attempted to settle in the New World. Settlers occupied this area beginning in 1585, but a lack of supplies and tensions with local tribes forced their return to England. A second colony, established in 1587, disappeared without explanation around 1590. Today, visitors can see artifacts from the settlement and attend talks by park interpreters at the Lindsay Warren Visitor Center. (☎473-5772; www.nps.gov/fora. Open daily in summer 9am-6pm; low season 9am-5pm.) During the summer, actors perform **The Lost Colony,** a musical version of the settlers' story, in a theater near the Fort Raleigh site. (☎473-3414; www.thelostcolony.org. Shows June-Aug. M-Sa 8:30pm. $16, over 62 $15, under 12 $8.)

Just down U.S. 64, the child-friendly **Roanoke Island Festival Park** is home to a spectacle of museum exhibits, costumed reenactments, outdoor activities, and historical replicas reflecting 400 years of Outer Banks history. (☎475-1500; www.roanokeisland.com. Park and museum open daily June-Aug. 10am-7pm; Apr.-May and Sept.-Oct. 10am-6pm; mid-Feb. to Mar. and Nov.-Dec. 10am-5pm. Two-day tickets $8, ages 6-17 $5, under 6 free. Drama, dance, and music performances in the park's outdoor pavilion in July Tu-Sa 8pm.) Nearby, in the romantic **Elizabethan Gardens,** visitors can wander among fountains, antique statues, and beds of seasonal flowers. (☎473-3234; www.elizabethangardens.org. Open June-Aug. M-Sa 9am-8pm, Su 9am-7pm; low-season hours vary. Wheelchair accessible. $8, under 5 free.)

SCENIC DRIVE: CAPE HATTERAS NATIONAL SEASHORE

Cape Hatteras National Seashore actually offers two shores for the price of one: on **Route 12** running between Whalebone Junction and Ocracoke Village, you can see the Atlantic Ocean to the east and the Pamlico Sound to the west. During high season the traffic may force you to crawl along at 30 mph if you drive south from Hatteras to Ocracoke, but the leisurely pace is perfect for appreciating the unob-

THE SOUTH

structed bi-coastal view. Route 12 is a paved two-lane road and the main artery of the park, running from the northern entrance of the park at Nags Head on Bodie Island to the southern tail in the town of Ocracoke Village. A free 40min. ferry shuttles cars from Hatteras to the northern end of Ocracoke Island (see **Transportation**, p. 348). Total transport time from Whalebone to Ocracoke is about 2½hr.

All of the park's major attractions are accessible and clearly marked from Rte. 12. The chief of these are the Outer Banks' three lighthouses on Bodie, Hatteras, and Ocracoke Islands. The tallest brick lighthouse in North America is the 196 ft. **Cape Hatteras Lighthouse,** built in 1870. Due to beach erosion, the lighthouse was relocated in 1999. To scale the tower for an impressive view, take one of the self-guided tours. (Tickets sold 8am to 20min. before closing. Open daily Apr. 9am-5pm; June-Aug. 9am-6pm; Sept. 9am-5pm. Adults $7; under 12, disabled, and ages over 62 $3.50.) Duck into the **Visitors Center** to see a section of the original lens, an inspiring feat of early engineering. (☎995-4474. Open daily in summer 9am-6pm; low season 9am-5pm.) Another set of attractions along Rte. 12 reminds visitors that lighthouses have value apart from being picturesque—several shipwrecks can be seen from the shore. Turn off Rte. 12 at Coquina Beach to see the wreck of the *Laura A. Barnes,* which was grounded in 1921. Visibility varies. Pick up the free paper *In The Park* for a list of dates of snorkeling tours and fishing trips.

The **Pea Island National Wildlife Refuge** on the northern tip of Hatteras Island boasts over 365 species of birds, including endangered peregrine falcons. The **Charles Kuralt Nature Trail,** next to the Visitors Center, affords hikers a chance to glimpse blackbirds, pelicans, loggerhead turtles, and Carolina salt marsh snakes. The half-mile **North Pond Wildlife Trail,** also beginning at the Visitors Center, is wheelchair accessible. (Visitors Center ☎987-2394; www.peaisland.fws.gov. Open daily 9am-5pm. Beaches in the refuge are open only during daylight.) Farther south, the **Pony Pasture,** on Rte. 12 in Ocracoke, is the stomping ground for a herd of semi-wild horses, said to be the descendants of horses left by shipwrecked explorers in the 16th or 17th century.

WILMINGTON ☎910

Situated on the Carolina coast at the mouth of the Cape Fear River and only a few miles from the Atlantic beaches, Wilmington has long been an important center for shipping. Home to the largest film production facility east of Los Angeles, the city is sometimes referred to as "Wilmywood" and "Hollywood East." Over 400 feature films and TV projects have been shot along the picturesque Cape Fear coast since 1983, including the hit TV series *Dawson's Creek* and *One Tree Hill.* Even if you don't glimpse a celebrity, the historic downtown area has plenty to offer, from historic memorials and excellent restaurants to gorgeous views of the waterfront.

◧ TRANSPORTATION. Wilmington International Airport (ILM), 1740 Airport Blvd. (☎341-4333; www.flyilm.com.), off 23rd St., 2 mi. north of Market St. and the downtown area. Greyhound **buses,** 201 Harnett St. (☎762-6073, 800-231-2222; www.greyhound.com; open daily 9:30am-1:30pm, 4:15-6pm), between 3rd and Front St., about a mile north of downtown, depart to (6¾hr., 1 per day, $54) and Raleigh (3hr., $38). The **Wilmington Transit Authority** or **Wave Transit** (☎343-0106; www.wavetransit.com) runs **local buses** (M-F 6am-9:30pm, Sa 8:30am-9:30pm, Su 9:30am-6pm; $1; over 65, disabled, and students $0.50) and a **free trolley** that travels Front St. between Ann St. and Hanover St. (M-F 6:30am-9:30pm, Sa 11am-9:30pm). A **river taxi** ferries passengers across the river between downtown Market St. and the *USS North Carolina,* aboard the *J.N. Maffitt.* (☎343-1611 or 800-676-0162. Runs June-Aug. daily 10am-5pm. 15min., round-trip $4. 1½hr. sightseeing cruises also available at 11am and 3pm; $15, under 12 $5.) **Port City Taxi** (☎762-1165).

⏷ PRACTICAL INFORMATION. Visitors Center, 24 N. 3rd St., is at the corner of 3rd and Princess. (☎341-4030 or 800-222-4757; www.capefearcoast.com. Open M-F 8:30am-5pm, Sa 9am-4pm, Su 1-4pm.) The Visitors Center also runs an **information kiosk** at the foot of Market St. by the waterfront. (Open daily June-Aug. 9:30am-5pm; Apr.-May and Sept. 9am-4:30pm.) Check **email** at the **New Hanover County Library,** 201 Chestnut St., at 3rd St., one block from the Visitors Center. (☎798-6302. Open M-Th 9am-8pm, F-Sa 9am-5pm, Su 1-5pm. Must purchase $2 card. Internet access limited to 1hr.) **Post Office:** 152 N. Front St., at Chestnut St. (☎313-3293. Open M-F 9am-5pm, Sa 9am-noon.) **Postal Code:** 28401.

⏷ ACCOMMODATIONS. Wilmington's best lodging comes in the form of B&Bs; most are conveniently in the historic downtown area. Though rooms usually cost $100-200 per night, the unique decor, convenient location, and riverfront views make Wilmington's B&Bs worth the extra cash. Be sure to reserve far in advance, especially during the summer. For less expensive lodging, nearly every budget chain can be found on Market St. between College Rd. and 23rd St. Weekend rates often run $10-20 higher than weekday prices. The **Greentree Inn ❷,** 5025 Market St., has large comfy rooms with A/C and cable TV. (☎799-6001; www.greentreenc.com. Continental breakfast, pool. June-Aug. M-Th and Su from $56, F-Sa from $78-90. AmEx/D/MC/V.) **Travel Inn ❷,** 4401 Market St., a single-floor motor court, provides comfortable rooms for some of the lowest rates around. (☎763-8217. A/C, cable TV with HBO, pool. Rooms in summer M-F $50, Sa-Su $70. Lower in winter. AAA and AARP discount 10%. AmEx/D/MC/V.) The **Dragonfly Inn ❺,** 1914 Market St., differs from antiques-and-lace B&Bs with an earthy, holistic approach to hospitality, complete with a delicious full breakfast, all-natural bath products, and aromatherapy offerings. (☎762-7025; www.dragonflyinn.com. Internet access, off-street parking. Doubles from $89-$99. AmEx/D/MC/V.) The **Carolina Beach State Park ❶,** about 15 mi. south of Wilmington on U.S. 421, offers spacious, wooded campsites as well as hiking, picnic areas, and a marina. (☎458-8206. Laundry facilities, grills, spotless restrooms, hot showers. No RV hookups. Open year-round. Sites $15.)

⏷ FOOD. Quality restaurants are plentiful in historic downtown Wilmington. **⏷Rim Wang ❷,** 128 S. Front St., offers authentic Thai cuisine, with options that will please travelers with mild to wild palates. Lunch specials range from traditional pad thai ($11) to chicken massaman and include a bowl of zesty coconut soup. (☎763-5552. Lunch specials $9. Most noodle, rice, stir-fry, and curry dishes $11. Open M-Th 11am-3pm and 5-10pm, F 11:30am-3pm and 5-11pm, Sa 11:30am-11pm, Su 3-10pm. AmEx/D/MC/V.) **Nikki's ❶,** 16 S. Front St., is a downtown bistro where the atmosphere is laid-back, the waitresses friendly and efficient, and the vegetarian fare delectable; sample the "Avocado on Wheat" ($6.25) for a healthy treat. (☎772-9151. Sandwiches $4.25-7. Wraps $5.25-6.50. Sushi from $3.50 for 8 pieces. Open M-Th 11am-10pm, F-Sa 11am-11pm, Su noon-10pm. MC/V.) Head over to **Middle and McDaniel Farms Creamery and Restaurant ❶,** 614 S. College Rd., for some home cookin'. Housed in a barn complete with a silo, McDaniel Farms makes homemade ice cream, in addition to sandwiches, burgers, and other entrees for a family-oriented crowd. The banana bread pudding ice cream is a delight. (☎793-9994; www.mcdanielfarms.com. Free Wi-Fi. Entrees $5-15. Open M-Th 11am-11pm, F-Sa 11am-midnight. AmEx/MC/V.)

⏷ SIGHTS. No visit to historic Wilmington would be complete without an afternoon spent winding down at the relaxing **Wrightsville Beach.** From Market St. downtown, take Eastwood Rd. to the bridge leading over Wrightsville Sound to the beach. Fifteen miles down Rte. 421, **Carolina Beach** has a charming boardwalk and a state park where the carnivorous Venus flytrap plant flourishes. Five miles far-

THE SOUTH

ther on Rte. 421 is **Kure Beach,** a state recreation area. The **Fort Fisher Aquarium** in Kure Beach draws visitors from all over the country to see three habitat exhibits: freshwater, coastal marsh, and open ocean. Don't miss the freshwater alligators or the quarter-million gallon Cape Fear Shoals tank, full of eels, sharks, coral reefs, and varying fish species. (☎458-8257; www.ncaquariums.com. Open daily 9am-5pm. $8, over 62 and active military $7, ages 6-17 $6, under 6 free.)

For Wilmington's glamorous side, take a visit to **Screen Gems Studios,** 1223 N. 23rd St., near the airport, the largest movie and TV production facility east of Hollywood. Guided 1hr. studio tours provide a fascinating behind-the-scenes glimpse of the industry. (☎343-3500; www.screengemsstudios.com. Tours June-Aug. Sa-Su noon and 2pm; Sept.-May Sa noon. $12, under 12 $8.) Art aficionados shouldn't miss the **Louise Wells Cameron Art Museum,** 3201 S. 17th St., at its intersection with Independence Blvd., which displays the work of American masters, including Mary Cassatt, and North Carolinian artists from the 18th to 21st centuries. (☎395-5999; www.cameronartmuseum.com. Open Tu-Sa 10am-5pm, Su 10:30am-4pm. $7, ages 6-18 $2, ages under 6 and active military free, families $15.)

The military-minded might like the self-guided tour of the **Battleship North Carolina,** in the Cape Fear River across from downtown, at the junction of Hwys. 17, 74, 76, and 421. This warship, which carried 2339, participated in every major Pacific naval offensive during WWII. Highlights include the bridge, the soldiers' quarters, and the galley. (☎251-5797; www.battleshipnc.com. Open daily mid-May to mid-Sept. 8am-8pm; mid-Sept. to mid-May 8am-5pm. Ticket sales end 1hr. before closing. $12, over 65 and military $10, ages 6-11 $8, under 6 free.) Take in a jazz or folk concert at the **Airlie Gardens,** 300 Airlie Rd., just off Oleander Dr., or stroll through the **New Hanover County Arboretum,** 6206 Oleander Dr., which includes a Japanese garden and teahouse. (Airlie Gardens ☎798-7700; www.airliegardens.org. Open Tu-Su 9am-5pm. $5, children under 6-10 and over 65 $3, under 6 free. Free concerts Apr.-Oct. 1st and 3rd F 6-8pm. Arboretum open daily dawn-dusk. Free.)

📺🎭 **ENTERTAINMENT AND NIGHTLIFE.** For local entertainment info, pick up a free copy of *Encore* or *The Outrider*, weekly newspapers with event listings that are available in most hotels and cafes. Wilmington's historic **Thalian Hall,** 310 Chestnut St., offers a wide range of entertainment, including theater, dance, music, and comedy acts. Tours of the hall showcase its history, from the design created by famous architect John Trimble to the famous guests—including Buffalo Bill Cody and John Philip Sousa—hosted during its nearly 150 years of continuous use. (Box office ☎343-3664 or 800-523-2820; www.thalianhall.com. Purchase tickets 2hr. prior to show. Box office open M-F noon-6pm, Sa 2-6pm. Tour info ☎343-3660. Tours by appointment. $6.)

Downtown Wilmington is jumping on Friday and Saturday nights; most bars and clubs cluster around Front St. The **Reel Cafe,** 100 S. Front St., offers three big-screen TVs, a rooftop bar, a dance floor, and live music on the courtyard patio. (☎251-1832; www.thereelcafe.net. No backward hats or baggy pants allowed. 18+ after 11pm. Cover F men $5, women free; Sa both $5. Open daily 11am-2am. Rooftop bar open Th-Su, dance floor F-Sa.)

Are your socks dirty? Spend an evening at **Soapbox,** 255 N. Front St., a "Laundro-Lounge" where you can do your laundry as you booze. Downstairs, you'll find foosball, pool, occasional live music, a bar, and plenty of washers and dryers. Upstairs is a conventional nightclub with another bar and a stage for live music, which plays almost every night and ranges from hip-hop and reggae to jazz and good old rock 'n' roll. (☎251-8500; www.soapboxlaundrolounge.com. Cover downstairs $3, upstairs $5-15. Open daily noon-2am.) For a change of pace, head to **Lula's,** 138 Orange St., off S. Front St., a charming pub popular with Wilmingtonians of all ages. (☎763-0070. Tu $2.25-3 pint night. Open daily 7pm-2:30am.)

SOUTH CAROLINA

To some, the display of South Carolina's pride in the Palmetto State may seem extreme. Inspired by the state flag, the palmetto tree logo decorates hats, bottles, and bumper stickers across the area. This pride is justified, though, in the Grand Strand's unrivaled beaches and Charleston's stately elegance. Columbia, though less well known, offers an impressive artistic and cultural experience without the smog and traffic that plague other cities of the New South. Tamed for tourists and merchandising, the Confederate legacy of this first state to secede from the Union is groomed as a cash cow. Beyond the commercialized strips, however, South Carolina retains its old-style grace and charm—not to mention its rebellious spirit.

⑦ PRACTICAL INFORMATION

Capital: Columbia.

Visitor Info: Department of Parks, Recreation, and Tourism, 1205 Pendleton St., Rm. 110, Columbia 29201 (☎803-734-1700; www.discoversouthcarolina.com). **South Carolina Forestry Commission,** 5500 Broad River Rd., Columbia 29212 (☎803-896-8800).

Postal Abbreviation: SC. **Sales Tax:** 7.5%.

CHARLESTON ☎843

Built on rice, cotton, and indigo, Charleston's antebellum plantation system yielded vast riches that are now visible in its numerous museums, historic homes, and ornate architecture. Three hundred years' worth of cultural capital flows like the locals' long, distinctive drawl. Several of the South's most renowned plantations dot the city, while two venerable educational institutions, the **College of Charleston** and **The Citadel,** add a youthful vitality. Horse-drawn carriages, cobblestone streets, pre-Civil War homes, beautiful beaches, and some of the most delicious cuisine in the Southeast explain why Charleston often tops the list of the nation's most popular destinations.

▛ TRANSPORTATION

Trains: Amtrak, 4565 Gaynor Ave. (☎744-8264; www.amtrak.com), 8 mi. west of downtown. Open 6pm-midnight. Trains go to **Richmond** (7hr., 2 per day, $62-102), **Savannah** (1¾hr., 2 per day, $17-20), and **Washington, D.C.** (9½hr., 2 per day, $82-107).

Buses: Greyhound, 3610 Dorchester Rd. (☎744-4247; www.greyhound.com), in N. Charleston. Avoid this area at night. Open daily 7:30-10:30pm. Runs to **Charlotte** (7hr., 2 per day, $47), **Myrtle Beach** (2½hr., 1 per day, $29), and **Savannah** (2½-5½hr., 2 per day, $31). CARTA's "Upper Dorchester" bus serves this area.

Public Transit: CARTA, 36 John St. (☎724-7420). Runs area buses and the **Downtown Area Shuttle (DASH)** trolleys that circle downtown. $1.25, seniors $0.60, disabled $0.35; 1-day pass $4, 3-day $9. DASH runs daily 6am-11pm. CARTA 5:30am-1am. Visitors Center has schedules.

Taxi: Yellow Cab, ☎577-6565.

Bike Rental: The Bicycle Shoppe, 280 Meeting St. (☎722-8168), located between George and Society St. Open M-F 9am-7pm, Sa 9am-6pm, Su 1-5pm. Beach cruisers: $5 per hr., $20 per day. City bikes: $10 per hr., $40 per day. Hybrid bikes: $10 per hr., $40 per day.

ORIENTATION AND PRACTICAL INFORMATION

Old Charleston lies at the southernmost point of the mile-wide peninsula below **Calhoun Street**. The major north-south routes are **Meeting, King,** and **East Bay Streets**. **Savannah Highway (U.S. 17)** cuts across the peninsula going south to Savannah and north across two towering bridges to Mt. Pleasant and Myrtle Beach. There are plenty of metered parking spaces and plenty of police officers giving tickets.

Visitor Info: Charleston Visitors Center, 375 Meeting St. (☎853-8000; www.charleston-cvb.com), across from Charleston Museum. Open daily Apr.-Oct. 8:30am-5:30pm; Nov.-Mar. 8:30am-5pm. Parking in the Visitors Center garage $8 per day.

Hotlines: Crisis Line: ☎744-4357. **People Against Rape:** ☎745-0144 or 800-241-7273. Both 24hr.

Medical Services: Charleston Memorial Hospital, 326 Calhoun St. (☎792-2300).

Internet Access: Charleston County Public Library, 68 Calhoun St. (☎805-6801). Free. 1 hr. limit. Open M-Th 9am-9pm, F-Sa 9am-6pm, Su 2-5pm.

Post Office: 83 Broad St. (☎577-0690). Open M-F 9am-5pm. **Postal Code:** 29402.

ACCOMMODATIONS

Luckily for budget travelers, Charleston has a great hostel: motel rooms in historic downtown Charleston are quite expensive. If you want to splurge, opt for the charming B&Bs. Cheap motels are just outside the city, around Exits 209-211 on I-26 W in N. Charleston, or across the Ashley River on U.S. 17 S in Mt. Pleasant. For information on discounted rates, talk to the folks at the Visitor Center.

Charleston's Not So Hostel, 156 Spring St. (☎722-8383; www.notsohostel.com). Friendly, clean, and comfortable, with dorms, private rooms, and a camping platform. Themed rooms make for a cozy stay. Bunks may be co-ed. Internet access, make-your-own waffle breakfast, and off-street parking included. Laundry facilities available. Check-in 5-10pm. Dorms $21; private rooms $60; camping $10. AmEx/D/MC/V. ❶

1837 Bed and Breakfast, 126 Wentworth St. (☎723-7166 or 877-723-1837; www.1837bb.com), in a wealthy cotton planter's former home. Within walking distance to downtown sights, this B&B is sure to charm. Each of the 9 rooms is beautifully furnished with period antiques and maintained with modern amenities like A/C, free Wi-Fi, cable TV, and microfridges. The sit-down gourmet breakfast—with homemade sticky buns and delicious sausage pies—is definitely worth it. Reservations recommended. Rooms $79-199. AmEx/D/MC/V. ❹

Campground at James Island County Park (☎795-4386 or 800-743-7275). Take U.S. 17 S to Rte. 171 to Hwy. 700 and follow the signs. 125 spacious sites, including picnic tables, bicycle trails, and a small water park. Activity center has movies, pancake breakfast, and bingo. Schedule varies; check ahead at registration. Bike and boat rental. Hot water showers. Park gates closes 10pm. Primitive sites $22, tent sites $33 for water and electricity. Hookup $35-40. Senior discount 10%. ❶

FOOD

Most restaurants cater to big-spending tourists, but there are plenty of budget-friendly opportunities to sample the Southern cooking, barbecue, and fresh seafood that have made the Low Country famous.

Jestine's Kitchen, 251 Meeting St. (☎722-7224). Jestine died at the age of 112, leaving behind a legacy of deep-fried Southern home cookin'. Jestine's has become a local favorite with daily Southern blue plate specials (fried pecan chicken $13) and famous

Downtown Charleston

▲▲ ACCOMMODATIONS

1837 Bed and Breakfast, **6**
Campground at James Island County Park, **1**
Charleston's Not So Hostel, **2**

♥ FOOD

Dave's Carry Out, **3**
Gaulart & Maliclet, **9**
Jestine's Kitchen, **7**

🍸 NIGHTLIFE

A.C. Bar & Grill, **4**
Coast, **5**
Meritage, **8**

desserts (like fudge Coca-Cola cake) that keep even Oprah coming back for more. Open Tu-Th 11am-9:30pm, F-Sa 11am-10pm, Su 11am-9pm. MC/V. ❷

Gaulart & Maliclet, 98 Broad St. (☎577-9797). Francophiles flock to this French restaurant, known colloquially as "G & M," "Fast & French," and "Pig & Chicken." This gem of a cafe serves inexpensive, delectable, French-inspired fare, from vegetarian escargot (sauteed mushrooms; $6.50) to hot goat cheese on a croissant ($7), finished with chocolate fondue for 2 ($7.40). Open M 8am-4pm, Tu-Th 8am-10pm, F-Sa 8am-10:30pm. AmEx/D/MC/V. ❷

Dave's Carry-Out, 42 Morris St. (☎577-7943). Quick, cheap, and delicious Southern specialities. Dave's famous sandwiches ($3.50-5.50) delight locals and tourists alike. Offers a generously portioned fried fish sandwich ($3.50). F special includes BBQ ribs and Turkey Wings ($3.50-6.50). All entrees include sides from lima beans to red rice. Tu-F 11:30am-until the lunch crowd leaves and 6pm-until the bar is full. ❶

🖙 SIGHTS

Charleston's ancient homes, historical monuments, churches, galleries, and gardens can be seen by foot, car, bus, boat, horse-drawn carriage, or on one of the ten ghost tours. **City Market,** 188 Meeting St., stays abuzz in a newly restored 19th-century building. (Open daily 9am-5pm.)

GRITS GALORE

Every April, the population of St. George, SC swells to about 20 times its normal size as tens of thousands of people from all over the world descend on this small town (pop. 2100) to celebrate the annual World Grits Festival.

In 1985, the manager of a local supermarket was placing an order with the broker of a large grits company when the broker remarked that his company sure shipped a lot of grits to St. George, given its small size. Subsequent research revealed that St. George residents ate more grits per capita than anywhere else in the world. They considered themselves grits-eating champions. To celebrate, they held the first-ever grits festival.

Now, the three-day festival includes a multitude of grits-themed events, such as grits eating contests, grits grinding, and the popular Roll in Grits contest, in which contestants are weighed before and after diving into a huge pool of grits and win by amassing the most "grits weight." Roll in Grits strategies include wearing clothing with lots of pockets, and showing up to the event with unbelievably long hair. Whether you love the dish or have never even tried it, the festival is the perfect opportunity to dive in and soak up some grits.

The 2006 World Grits Festival takes place in April. For more information, visit www.worldgritsfestival.com.

PLANTATIONS AND GARDENS. The best value to be had is at **Drayton Hall,** a 265-year-old plantation that has survived both the Revolutionary and Civil Wars, as well as numerous earthquakes and hurricanes. Entrance includes a guided tour of the stately plantation house and a stroll along the scenic marsh. Bring a picnic lunch to enjoy on tables under moss-draped oak trees. *(On Rte. 61, 9 mi. northwest of downtown. ☎ 769-2600; www.draytonhall.org. Open daily Mar.-Oct. 8:30am-5:30pm, last entry 4pm; Nov.-Feb. 8:30am-4:30pm, last entry at 3pm. Tours are every hr. on the hr. Wheelchair accessible. $14, ages 12-18 $8, 6-11 $6. Grounds only $5. AAA discount.)* The 300-year-old **Magnolia Plantation and Gardens** is by far the most majestic of Charleston's plantations and the oldest major public garden in the country. Visitors can enjoy the Drayton family's staggering wealth by exploring their 50 acres of gorgeous gardens. Other attractions include a hedge maze, swamp, and bird sanctuary. *(On Rte. 61, 10 mi. out of town off U.S. 17. ☎ 571-1266 or 800-367-3517; www.magnoliaplantation.com. Open daily Mar.-Oct. 8am-dusk, last entry 5:30pm; winter hours 9am-dusk. Gardens and grounds $15, ages 6-12 $9. House tour $7 per person; swamp $7; nature train $7; nature boat tour $7; under 6 free for all attractions.)* Farther away from Charleston, **Cypress Gardens** lets visitors paddle their own boats out onto the eerie, gator-filled swamps or embark on guided tours every hour for no extra charge. *(3030 Cypress Gardens Rd. Off Rte. 52. ☎ 553-0515; www.cypressgardens.info. Open daily 9am-5pm. $10, over 65 $9, ages 6-12 $5.)*

PATRIOT'S POINT AND FORT SUMTER. Visitors can climb aboard four Naval vessels, including a submarine and a giant aircraft carrier, at **Patriot's Point Naval and Maritime Museum,** the world's largest naval museum. *(40 Patriots Point Rd. Across the Cooper River in Mt. Pleasant. ☎ 884-2727; www.patriotspoint.org. Open daily 9am-6:30pm, last entry 5pm. $14, seniors and military $12, ages 6-11 $7.)* From Patriot's Point in Mt. Pleasant, **Spirit Line Cruises** leads boat excursions to the National Historic Site where Confederate soldiers bombarded Union forces in April 1861, turning years of escalating tension into open war. Tour guides maintain that the first Confederate casualty haunts one of the American flags on display. There is a dock at Liberty Square next to the South Carolina Aquarium in Charleston. *(Fort Sumter ☎ 883-3123, Tours ☎ 881-7337; www.spiritlinecruises.com. Six 2¼hr. tours per day. $14, seniors $12.50, ages 6-11 $8.)*

CHARLESTON MUSEUM AND HISTORIC HOMES. The **Charleston Museum** and its **Historic Homes** make up the nation's oldest museum and are a great way to become acquainted with the city's historical offerings. The museum boasts outstanding exhibits on the

Revolutionary and Civil Wars and a thorough look into the Low Country's history. Across the street, the **Joseph Manigault House** reflects the lifestyle of a wealthy, rice-planting family and the African American slaves who lived there. Farther downtown, the **Heyward-Washington House** was home to Thomas Heyward, Jr., a signer of the Declaration of Independence. It was rented to George Washington during his 1791 trip through the South. *(Museum: 360 Meeting St. ☎722-2996; www.charlestonmuseum.org. Open M-Sa 9am-5pm, Su 1-5pm. Joseph Manigault House: 350 Meeting St. ☎723-2926. Heyward-Washington House: 87 Church St. ☎722-0354. Both houses open M-Sa 10am-5pm, Su 1-5pm. Museum $10, 1 house $10, 2 sights $16, 3 sights $22. Wheelchair accessible.)* To tour historic homes, try the **Nathaniel Russell House:** the gracefully restored interior demonstrates the luxurious lifestyle of its former owner. The audio tour of the **Aiken Rhett House** is heavily focused on the slave quarters. *(Nathaniel Russell House: 51 Meeting St. ☎724-8481. Aiken Rhett House: 48 Elizabeth St. ☎723-1159. Both houses open M-Sa 10am-5pm, Su 2-5pm. Each house $10, both $16.)*

BEACHES. Folly Beach is popular with Citadel, College of Charleston, and University of South Carolina students who enjoy the shops and bars that line the beach. Charleston's beaches are great surfing haunts for novices and experts. *(Over the James Bridge and U.S. 171, about 20 mi. southeast of Charleston. ☎588-2426.)* The more expansive **Isle of Palms** extends for miles toward the less-crowded **Sullivan's Island.** *(Isle of Palms: Across the Cooper Bridge; drive 10 mi. down Hwy. 17 N, turn right onto the Isle of Palms Connector. ☎886-3863.)*

LIBERTY SQUARE. Two of Charleston's finest sights are located in Liberty Square. The **Charleston Aquarium's** regional exhibits showcase aquatic life from swamps, marshes, and oceans. Stare down the fishies at the 330,000 gallon, Great Ocean Tank, which boasts one of the nation's tallest viewing windows. *(At the end of Calhoun St. on the Cooper River, overlooking the harbor. ☎720-1990; www.scaquarium.org. Open Apr. to mid-Aug. M-Sa 9am-6pm, Su noon-5pm, last entry 5pm; mid-Aug. to Mar. M-Sa 9am-6pm, Su noon-5pm, last entry 4pm. Wheelchair accessible. $16, seniors, students, and military $14, ages 2-11 $8.)* Next door, the **Fort Sumter Visitor and Education Center** has a great exhibit on the cultural, economic, and political differences between the North and South prior to the Civil War. *(340 Concord St. ☎577-0242. Open daily 8:30am-5pm. Free.)*

BULL ISLAND. To get away from civilization, take a ferry to 5000-acre Bull Island, off the coast. Boats are often greeted by dolphins swimming in some of the planet's cleanest water. On the island there are 16 mi. of hiking trails populated by 278 different species of birds, like the striking wood stork and the green egret. *(☎881-4582. Ferries depart from Moore's Landing, off Seewee Rd., 16 mi. north of Charleston off U.S. 17. Depart Mar.-Nov. Tu and Th-Sa 9am, 12:30pm; returns Tu and Th-Sa noon, 4pm. Departs Dec.-Feb. Sa 10am; returns 3pm. Round-trip $30, under 12 $15.)*

🎵 📷 ENTERTAINMENT AND NIGHTLIFE

The density of bars and clubs downtown, combined with the abundance of twentysomethings attending the city's colleges, gives Charleston a lively nightlife scene. Free copies of *City Paper*, in stores and restaurants, list concerts and other events. College kids head to **A.C's Bar & Grill,** 467 King St., creating a lively atmosphere. Domestic drafts ($2), along with the drink of the month, complement the popular late-night menu, including loaded nachos for $4.75. (☎577-6742. Kitchen closes at 1:30am.) Big-name bands take center stage at **Music Farm,** 32 Ann St. (☎853-3276. Call for schedule and ticket prices.) Charleston's trendiest flock to **Coast,** 39-D John St. With its high ceilings and tropical decor, and a few drinks, you'll swear you're on the beach. The largest crowds come on Sunday nights, when all bottles of wine are half-price until 8pm, and tacos are $3. (☎722-

8838. Th live jazz. Su DJ. Open daily 5pm-late. Kitchen open M-Th and Su 5:30-10pm, F-Sa 5:30-11pm.) **Meritage,** 235 E. Bay St., is popular for its late-night scene. Wash down the tasty tapas ($4-9), and Charleston's famous she-crab soup ($5.25) with a wide selection of brews that keep the party going strong. (☎723-8181. Live music Tu-Th. Open daily 5pm-2am. Kitchen closes 1am.) The city explodes with music, theater, dance, and opera, as well as literature and visual arts when Charleston hosts the annual **Spoleto Festival USA,** the nation's most comprehensive arts festival. Founded in 1977, it is the counterpart to the **Festival of Two Worlds** in Spoleto, Italy. (☎722-2764; www.spoletousa.org. $10-125.)

COLUMBIA   ☎803

Much is made over Columbia's Civil War heritage, and understandably so, as Old South nostalgia brings in big tourist dollars. Despite this nostalgia, more antebellum buildings have been lost to developers in the last century than were burned by Sherman and his troops. Still, the town is the heart of the nation's "rebel" child, and a defiant spirit imbues Columbia's bars, businesses, and citizens. Southern pride and passion are perpetuated at the University of South Carolina (USC), with its sprawling green spaces and fascinating museums.

⎚⎚ TRANSPORTATION AND PRACTICAL INFORMATION. The city is laid out in a square, bordered by Huger and Harden St. running north-south and Blossom and Calhoun St. east-west. **Assembly Street** is the main drag, running north-south through the city, and **Gervais Street** is its east-west equivalent. The Congaree River marks the city's western edge. The Beltline offers little for tourists and, for safety purposes, is best avoided. **Columbia Metropolitan Airport (CAE),** 3000 Aviation Way (☎822-5000; www.columbiaairport.com), is in West Columbia. A taxi to downtown costs about $15-17. Amtrak, 850 Pulaski St. (☎252-8246; www.amtrak.com; open daily 10pm-5:30am), sends one **train** per day to Miami (16½hr., $66-146), Savannah (2¾hr., $25-55), and Washington, D.C. (11hr., $70-153). Greyhound, 2015 Gervais St. (☎256-6465 or 800-231-2222; www.greyhound.com), at Harden St., sends **buses** to Atlanta (4hr., 7 per day, $52.50), Charleston (2½hr., 2 per day, $28-31.50), and Charlotte (1¾hr., 3-4 per day, $20). Central Midlands Regional Transit Authority runs **buses** and **trolleys** throughout Columbia. (☎255-7100; www.gocmrta.com. Runs M-F 6:30pm-8pm, Sa 6am-midnight, Su 7am-7:30pm; call for schedules. $1.50, seniors and disabled $0.75; transfers free.) For a **taxi,** call Capital City Cab. (☎233-8294.) The **Columbia Metropolitan Convention and Visitors Bureau,** 1501 Lincoln St., has maps and visitor info. (☎545-0000; www.columbiacvb.com. Open M-F 9am-5pm, Sa 10am-4pm.) For info on USC, visit the **University of South Carolina Visitors Center,** 816 Bull St. (☎777-0169 or 800-922-9755. Open M-F 8:30am-5pm, Sa 11am-3pm. Free parking.) The **Palmetto Richland Memorial Hospital** is at 5 Richland Medical Park. (☎434-7000.) **Internet Access: Richland County Public Library,** 1431 Assembly St. (☎799-9084. 1hr. free per day. Open M-Th 9am-9pm, F-Sa 9am-6pm, Su 2-6pm.) **Post Office:** 1601 Assembly St. (☎733-4643. Open M-F 7:30am-6pm.) **Postal Code:** 29201.

⎚ ACCOMMODATIONS. Generally, the cheapest digs lie farthest from the city center. A short drive from downtown, the **Masters Inn ❷,** 613 Knox Abbott Dr., has great rates and offers spacious, modern rooms with free local calls, microwaves, mini-fridges, cable TV, and a pool. Take Blossom St. across the Congaree River, where it becomes Knox Abbott Dr. (☎796-4300. Singles $41-49; doubles $46-63. AmEx/D/MC/V.) If the Masters Inn is full, a good alternative is the nearby **Riverside Inn ❷,** 111 Knox Abbott Dr., which provides large, well-furnished rooms with free local calls, a coffee maker, cable TV, A/C, a pool, and continental breakfast. (☎939-

4688. Singles $57; doubles $62. AAA and AARP discount 10%. AmEx/D/MC/V.) Inexpensive motels also line the three interstates (I-26, I-77, and I-20) that circle the city. Rooms at the **Knights Inn ❷**, 1987 Airport Blvd., Exit 113 off I-26, have refrigerators, microwaves, cable TV, A/C, free Wi-Fi and local calls, and pool access; some have kitchenettes. (☎794-0222. Singles and doubles M-Th and Su $39, F-Sa $47. AAA, AARP, and senior discount 10%. AmEx/D/MC/V.) The 1400 acres of **Sesquicentennial State Park ❶** include 30 acres surrounding a lake for kayaking and fishing. The park includes a nature center, hiking trails, and 85 wooded campsites with electricity and hot water hookups. Public transit does not serve the park; take I-20 to Two Notch Rd./U.S. 1, Exit 17, and head 3 mi. northeast. (☎788-2706. Boat rentals $5 per hour, $15 per day. Open daily Apr.-Oct. 8am-6pm and 9pm-8am; Nov.-Mar. 7am-9pm. Campsites M-Th and Su $16-18, F-Sa $18-21. D/MC/V.)

◘ **FOOD.** The popular, funky **Hunter Gatherer ❸**, 900 Main St., offers a variety of tasty sandwiches, pizzas, and entrees in addition to home-brewed beer. (☎748-0540. Sandwiches and pizzas $6-10. Entrees $10-16. Beer $3.50. Th jazz night. Open Tu-Sa 4-11pm. Bar open until midnight. AmEx/D/MC/V.) Customers are immediately drawn to **Sake Tumi Grill and Sushi Bar ❸** for deals as fresh as their fish. Try the Bangkok Crabcakes ($8). At happy hour (6:30-9:30pm), many of their rolls are only $2. (☎803-931-0700; http://www.sakitumigrill.com. Sushi $18-40. Open daily 4:30-10pm. Cash only.) Gamecocks past and present give highest marks to **Groucho's ❷**, 611 Harden St., where the famous "dipper" sandwiches (from $6) have been delighting patrons for over 60 years. (☎799-5708. Open M-Sa 11am-4pm. AmEx/MC/V.) At the **Flying Saucer ❷**, 931 Senate St., their logo is "friends don't let friends fly drunk." Try the vegetarian Hippie burger ($6.29) or Buffalo Chicken ($7.29). With over 200 different beers, it is easy to find a favorite to match the great pub fare. (☎933-9712; www.beerknurd.com. Open M-W 11am-1am, Th-Sa 11am-2am, Su noon-midnight.)

◙ **SIGHTS.** Bronze stars mark the impact of Sherman's cannonballs on the **Statehouse,** 1100 Gervais St., an Italian Renaissance high-rise. Home to South Carolina's state government, it also holds the state's two most prized symbols—the Senate Sword and a British mace, both of which reflect Carolinians' rebellious reputation. Survey the surrounding grounds, which have monuments and sculptures scattered throughout lush and tranquil gardens. (☎734-2430. Open M-F 9am-5pm, Sa 10am-5pm; 1st Su each month 1-5pm. Wheelchair accessible. Free tours.) Across Sumter St. from the Statehouse is the central green of the USC campus—the **Horseshoe.** Here, students play frisbee, sunbathe, study, and nap beneath a canopy of trees. At the head of the green, **McKissick Museum,** 816 Bull St., explores the folklore of South Carolina and the Southeast through history, art, and science. (☎777-7251; www.cla.sc.edu/mcks. Open M-F 8:30am-5pm, Sa 11am-3pm. Free.) One of the top 10 zoos in the country, **Riverbanks Zoo and Garden,** on I-126 at Greystone Blvd., northwest of downtown, recreates natural habitats that house over 2000 species. After ogling the adorable koalas and wallabies at the Koala Knockabout, check out the zoo's newest addition—a baboon exhibit and a new male lion. (☎779-8717; www.riverbanks.org. Open mid-Apr. to mid-Oct. M-F 9am-5pm, Sa-Su 9am-5:45pm; mid-Oct. to mid-Apr. M-F 9am-4pm, Sa-Su 9am-5pm. $9.75, over 62 $8.25, ages 3-12 $7.75). The **South Carolina Confederate Relic Room and Museum,** 301 Gervais St., traces South Carolina's military history and contains an exhaustive collection of Civil War artifacts and displays. (☎737-8095; www.state.sc.us/crr. Open Tu-Sa 10am-5pm; 1st Su of each month 1-5pm. Wheelchair accessible. $4, under 21 free.) Two 19th-century mansions, the **Robert Mills Historic House and Park** and the **Hampton-Preston Mansion,** 1616 and 1615 Blanding St., two blocks east of Bull St., compete as examples of antebellum opulence and are both survivors of Sherman's Civil War rampage. Both have been lovingly restored with period finery. For a broader experience of 19th-century life, stop by the **Manns-Simons Cottage**, 1403 Richland St., once owned by a freed slave, and the **Woodrow Wilson Boyhood Home**, 1705 Hampton St. (☎252-1770; www.historiccolumbia.org. Tours every hr. Tu-Sa 10am-4pm, Su 1-5pm. Tours $5; students, over 65, military, and AAA $4; ages 6-17 $3; under 6 free. Combo tickets with tours of all 4 houses $18/14/10. Buy all tickets at Mills House Museum Shop.)

🎵 **NIGHTLIFE.** Columbia's nightlife centers around the collegiate **Five Points District**, at Harden and Devine St., and the slightly more mature **Vista** area on Gervais St. before the Congaree River. The weekly publication *Free Times* gives details on Columbia's club and nightlife scene. *In Unison* is a weekly paper listing gay-friendly nightspots. In the Vista, the **Art Bar**, 1211 Park St., attracts a funky crowd to match its ambience. Glow paint, Christmas lights, 50s bar stools, and a troop of life-sized plastic robots complement eclectic music. (☎929-0198. Open M-F 8pm-late, Sa-Su 8pm-2am.) The oldest bar in Columbia, **Group Therapy**, 2107 Greene St., offers drinks like the Mullet (warm Jack Daniel's with a touch of Budweiser; $8.75) to help locals drown their sorrows the old-fashioned way. (☎256-1203. Open daily 4:30pm-late.) At the popular late-night spot, **Bar None**, 620 Harden St., patrons hone their shuffleboard skills. (☎254-3354. Open M-F 4pm-6am, Sa-Su 4pm-2am.)

MYRTLE BEACH AND THE GRAND STRAND ☎843

Each summer, millions of Harley-riding, RV-driving Southerners make Myrtle Beach the country's second-most-popular summer tourist destination in the country. During spring break and early June, Myrtle Beach is jammed with students looking for a good time. The rest of the year, families, golfers, and shoppers partake in the proud kitchyness of the town's themed restaurants, amusement parks, and shops. The pace slows significantly on the rest of the 60 mi. Grand Strand. South of Myrtle Beach, Murrell's Inlet is the place to go for good seafood, Pawley's Island is lined with beach cottages and beautiful private homes, and Georgetown showcases white-pillared 18th-century-style rice and indigo plantation homes.

📠 **TRANSPORTATION AND PRACTICAL INFORMATION.** Greyhound, 511 7th Ave. N (☎448-2471 or 800-231-2222; www.greyhound.com; open daily 10am-1pm and 2-7pm), runs **buses** once daily to: Atlanta (9-10hr., $7.50); Charleston (2½hr., $27.50); Columbia (4½hr., $37); New York City (17hr., $91); Washington D.C. (13hr., $70). The Waccamaw Regional Transportation Authority (WRTA), 1418 3rd Ave., provides minimal **busing;** pick up a copy of schedules and routes from the Chamber of Commerce or from area businesses. (☎488-0865. Runs daily 5am-11pm. Local fares $1.50-1.75.) WRTA also operates the **Ocean Boulevard Lymo,** which shuttles tourists up and down the main drag. (☎488-0865. Runs daily 8am-11pm. $1.75) Rent bikes at **The Bike Shoppe,** 715 Broadway, at Main St. (☎448-5335. Beach cruisers, $10 per day, mountain bikes $15 per day. Open M-F 8am-6pm, Sa 8am-5pm.) Most attractions are on **Kings Highway (Route 17),** which splits into a business route and a bypass 4 mi. south of Myrtle Beach. **Ocean Boulevard** runs along the ocean, flanked on either side by hotels and motels. Avenue numbers repeat after reaching 1st Ave. in the middle of town; note whether the Ave. is "north" or "south." Take care not to confuse north **Myrtle Beach** with the town **North Myrtle Beach,** which has an almost identical street layout. **Route 501** runs west toward Conway, **I-95,** and the factory outlet stores. Unless otherwise stated, addresses on the Grand Strand are for Myrtle Beach. **Visitor Information** at the **Myrtle Beach Chamber of Commerce,** 1200 N. Oak St., parallel to Kings Hwy., at 12th Ave. N. (☎626-7444; www.myrtlebeachinfo.com. Open M-F 8:30am-5pm, Sa-9am-5pm, Su 10am-2pm.) **Grand Strand Regional Medical Center,** 809 82nd Pkwy. (☎692-1000.) **Internet access: Chapin Memorial Library,** 400 14th Ave. N. (☎918-1275. Mandatory library card $8. 1hr. max. per day. Open M and W 9am-6pm, Tu and Th 9am-8pm, F-Sa 9am-5pm; closed Sa 1pm in summer.) **Post Office:** 505 N. Kings Hwy., at 5th Ave. N. (☎626-9533. Open M-F 8:30am-5pm, Sa 9am-1pm.) **Postal Code:** 29577.

ꜰ ACCOMMODATIONS. Hundreds of motels line Ocean Blvd.; those on the ocean side fetch higher prices than those across the street. Cheap motels also dot Rte. 17. From October to March, prices plummet as low as $20-30 per night for the luxurious hotels right on the beach. Call the **Myrtle Beach Lodging Reservation Service,** 12th Ave N. Oak Street, for free help with reservations. (☎800-626-7477. Open M-F 8:30am-5pm, Sa 9-5pm, Su 10-2pm.) Across the street from the ocean, the family-owned **Sea Banks Motor Inn ❷,** 2200 S. Ocean Blvd., has immaculate rooms with mini-fridges, cable TV, laundry, and pool and beach access. (☎448-2434 or 800-523-0603; www.seabanks.com. Mid-Mar. to mid-Sept. singles $35-45; doubles $45-78. Mid-Sept. to mid-Mar. singles $25-28; doubles $26-40. AmEx/D/MC/V.) **The Coastal Breeze Motel ❸,** 2010 S. Ocean Blvd., has big, clean rooms with access to a pool and hot tub. (☎626-3531; www.myrtlefindlodging.com. High-season singles $70-95; doubles $75-85. Low season singles $35-45. Ask about a walk-in special. D/MC/V.) **Huntington Beach State Park Campground ❶,** 3 mi. south of Murrell's Inlet on U.S. 17, is located in a diverse environment including lagoons, salt marshes, and a beach; campsites are situated around a mostly open field as well as in a more wooded area. (☎237-4440, reservations 866-345-7275. Open daily Apr.-Oct. 6am-10pm; Nov.-Mar. 6am-6pm. Tent sites Apr.-Oct. M-Th and Su $17, F-Sa $19. With water and electricity M-Th and Su $23, F-Sa $25, full hookup $28; Nov.-Mar. $17/21/25. Day-use $54.) The **Coral Sands Motel ❷,** 301 N. Ocean Blvd., is three blocks from the Family Kingdom amusement parks and has small rooms with A/C, cable TV, fridges, and microwaves. (☎448-3584 or 800-248-9779. High season singles $110; doubles $150. Low season singles $25; doubles $40. D/MC/V.)

◖ FOOD. The Grand Strand offers hungry motorists over 1800 restaurants serving every type of food in every imaginable setting. Massive family-style all-you-can-eat joints beckon from beneath the glow of each traffic light. **Route 17** offers countless steakhouses, seafood buffets, and fast-food joints. Seafood, however, is best on **Murrell's Inlet.** With license plates adorning the walls and discarded peanut shells crunching underfoot, the **River City Cafe ❶,** 404 21st Ave. N., celebrates a brand of American informality bordering on delinquency. Peruse the patrons' signatures on tables and walls as you polish off a burger ($3-6) or knock back a $3-4 beer. (☎448-1990. Open daily 11am-10pm. D/MC/V.) While most of the restaurants in the Broadway at the Beach entertainment complex (see below) seem to sacrifice quality for elaborate decor, **Amici's ❸,** in the "Caribbean Village" section, serves delightful stuffed shells ($10) and calzones ($8.50) that will make you forget the screaming children and blaring lights outside. (☎444-0006. Open daily 11am-10:30pm. D/MC/V.) Take a break from Ocean Dr. at **Dagwood's Deli ❷,** 400 11th Ave. N., where beach bums and businessmen come together to enjoy a "Shag" (ham, turkey, and swiss cheese; $8), reminiscent of the monster sandwiches from the comic strip. (☎448-0100. Sandwiches $5-9. Open M-Sa 11am-4pm.) If you're looking for country cookin' on the beach, **Caroline's Cafe ❷,** 1709 N. Ocean Blvd., has all-you-can-eat breakfast and lunch buffets with stewed apples, fried bacon, and other South Carolinian fare. (☎626-5926. Open daily 6am-1:30pm. MC/V.)

◖◖ SIGHTS AND NIGHTLIFE. The boulevard and the beach are both "the strand," where fashionable teens strut their stuff, low-riders cruise the streets, and beachgoers showcase their sunburns. Never pay full price for any attraction in Myrtle Beach; pick up a copy of the *Monster Coupon Book, Sunny Day Guide, Myrtle Beach Guide,* or *Strand Magazine* at any tourist info center or hotel.

THE SOUTH

The colossal **Broadway at the Beach,** Rte. 17 Bypass and 21st Ave. N. (☎444-3200 or 800-386-4662), is a sprawling 350-acre complex designed to entertain with shops, theaters, a waterpark, mini-golf, 26 restaurants, nightclubs, and other attractions. In Broadway's **Ripley's Aquarium,** guests roam through a 330 ft. underwater tunnel and gaze upward at the ferocious sharks and circling piranhas swimming above. (☎916-0888 or 800-734-8888; www.ripleysaquarium.com. Open daily 10am-11pm. Wheelchair accessible. $17, ages 5-11 $10, ages 2-4 $4.) The reptile capital of the world is ▨**Alligator Adventure,** 4604 Rte. 17, in North Myrtle Beach at Barefoot Landing, where fans are mesmerized by the exotic collection of snakes, lizards, and frogs as well as hourly gator feedings. Don't miss the park's 20 ft., 2000 lb. resident, Utan—the world's largest captive croc. (☎361-0789; www.alligatoradventure.com. Open daily June-Aug. 9am-11pm; call for low-season hours. Wheelchair accessible. $17, seniors $15, ages 4-12 $10.)

The **NASCAR Speedpark,** across from Broadway at the Beach at 1820 N. 21st St., has seven tracks of varying difficulty levels, all catering to those with a need for speed. (☎918-8725. Open daily high season 10am-11pm; low season 10am-8pm. Unlimited rides $30.) The 9100 acre **Brookgreen Gardens,** 1931 Brookgreen Dr., off Rte. 17 opposite Huntington Beach State Park, south of Murrell's Inlet, provides a respite from the touristy tackiness that dominates Myrtle Beach. Over 500 American sculptures are scattered beneath massive oaks. Guided tours of the gardens and wildlife trail are offered in addition to summer drama, music, and food programs. (☎235-6000; www.brookgreen.org. Open daily mid-June to mid Aug. 9:30am-5pm, daily 9:30am-9pm. Wheelchair accessible. 7-day pass $12, seniors and ages 13-18 $10, 6-12 $5, 5 and under free.)

For a night on the town, try the New Orleans-style nightclub district **Celebrity Square,** at Broadway at the Beach, which features 10 different nightclubs, ranging from classic rock to Latin. **2001,** 920 Lake Arrowhead Rd. off Rte. 17, just south of North Myrtle Beach, brings partygoers from three clubs all under one roof. (☎449-9434. In summer M and Su teen nights 8pm-midnight. 21+. Cover varies. Open daily Tu-Sa 8pm-2am.)

GEORGIA

Georgia has many faces; the rural southern region contrasts starkly with the sprawling north's commercialism. Atlanta packs the punch of a booming metropolis, while Savannah fosters a distinctively antebellum atmosphere, and collegiate Athens breeds new up-and-coming rock bands. Perhaps nowhere are the state's contrasting natures as evident as at Cumberland Island, where deserted beaches and marshes lie just hundreds of yards from the crumbling ruins of Gilded Age mansions. In this state of contradictions, only one thing remains constant: enduring Southern hospitality.

▧ PRACTICAL INFORMATION

Capital: Atlanta.

Visitor Info: Georgia Department of Economic Development, Tourism Division, 75 5th St. Ste. 1200, Technology Sq., Atlanta 30308 (☎404-962-4000 or 800-847-4842; www.georgia.org). **Department of Natural Resources,** 2 Martin Luther King, Jr. Dr. SE, Ste. 1252, East Tower, Atlanta 30334 (☎404-656-3500).

Postal Abbreviation: GA. **Sales Tax:** 4-7%, depending on the county.

ATLANTA ☎404

An increasingly popular destination for recent college grads wary of fast-paced cities, Atlanta is a cosmopolitan center with a smile. Northerners, Californians, the third-largest gay population in the US, and a host of ethnic groups have diversified the South's unofficial capital, modifying its distinctly Dixie feel. An economic powerhouse, Atlanta houses 400 of the Fortune 500 companies, including the headquarters of Coca-Cola, UPS, and CNN. Nineteen colleges, including Georgia Tech, Morehouse College, Spelman College, and Emory University, also call "Hotlanta" home. Brand new attractions include the Georgia Aquarium, the world's largest aquarium, and the colossal World of Coca-Cola (WOCC). The city is equally blessed with hidden gems; touring Atlanta's streets reveals an endless number of delightful restaurants and beautiful old houses.

◼ INTERCITY TRANSPORTATION

Airport: Hartsfield International Airport (ATL; ☎209-1700; www.atlanta-airport.com), off I-85/75 south of the city. The "airport" line of the MARTA goes downtown, with rides departing from the Airport Station (20min., daily 5am-1am, $1.75).

Atlanta Airport Shuttle (☎524-3400 or 866-545-9633; theatlantalink.com) runs vans to over 100 locations in the metropolitan area and outlying areas (every 15min. 7am-midnight, to downtown $16.50; from downtown back to airport runs every 30 min.).

Trains: Amtrak, 1688 Peachtree St. NW (☎800-872-7245; www.amtrak.com), 3 mi. north of downtown at I-85, or 1 mi. north of Ponce de Leon Ave. on Peachtree St. Take bus #23 from MARTA: Arts Center. Open daily 7am-9:30pm. Trains go to **New Orleans** (11¾hr., 1 per day, $57-110) and **New York City** (17hr., 1-3 per day, $119-232).

Buses: Greyhound, 232 Forsyth St. SW (☎584-1728 or 800-231-2222; www.greyhound.com), across from MARTA: Garnett. To **New York City** (19-21hr., 14 per day, $101), **Savannah** (5hr., 6 per day, $39-45), and **Washington, D.C.** (14-16hr., 14 per day, $82).

◼ ORIENTATION

Atlanta sprawls across 10 counties in the northwest quadrant of the state at the junctures of **I-75, I-85** (the city "thruway"), and **I-20. I-285** (the "perimeter") circumscribes the city. Maneuvering around Atlanta's main thoroughfares, which are arranged much like the spokes of a wheel, challenges even the most experienced native. **Peachtree Street** (one of over 100 streets bearing that name in Atlanta), is a major north-south road; **Spring Street,** which runs only south, and **Piedmont Avenue,** which runs only north, are parallel to Peachtree St. On the eastern edge, **Moreland Avenue** traverses the length of the city, through Virginia Highland, Little Five Points (L5P), and East Atlanta. **Ponce de Leon Avenue** is the primary east-west road and takes travelers to most major destinations (or intersects with a street that can). To the south of "Ponce" runs **North Avenue,** another major east-west thoroughfare. Navigating Atlanta requires a full arsenal of transportation strategies. Midtown and downtown attractions are best explored using MARTA. The outlying areas of Buckhead, Virginia Highlands, and L5P are easiest to get to by car; once you're there, the restaurant- and bar-lined streets encourage walking.

NEIGHBORHOODS

Sprouting out of downtown Atlanta, the **Peachtree Center** and **Five Points MARTA** stations deliver hordes of tourists to shopping and dining in and around **Peachtree Center Mall** where you can find some of Atlanta's best dining establishments. To

THE SOUTH

> ⚠ **LET'S NOT GO.** While recent efforts to increase police presence in high-risk areas of the city are having an effect, travelers—especially women—should exercise caution in the area south of Five Points, and especially the West End. Be aware that panhandlers throughout the city may be verbally aggressive.

pick up a souvenir, stop at Underground Atlanta, which shares this MARTA stop. Downtown is also home to **Centennial Olympic Park** as well as Atlanta's major sports and concert venues. Directly southwest of downtown, the **West End** is one of the city's oldest historic quarters. From Five Points, head northeast to **Midtown,** from Ponce de Leon Ave. to 17th St., for museums and **Piedmont Park.** East of Five Points at Euclid and Moreland Ave., the **Little Five Points (L5P)** district is a local haven for artists and youth subculture. North of L5P, **Virginia Highland,** a trendy neighborhood east of Midtown and Piedmont Park, attracts yuppies and college kids. The **Buckhead** area, north of Midtown on Peachtree St., greets both Atlanta's professionals and its rappers, housing designer shops and dance clubs.

▤ LOCAL TRANSPORTATION

Public Transit: Metropolitan Atlanta Rapid Transit Authority, or **MARTA** (☎848-4711; trains run daily 5am-1am, bus hours vary). Clean, uncrowded trains and buses provide hassle-free transportation to Atlanta's major attractions, making MARTA the "SMARTA" way to get around downtown. Multiday visitor passes (1-7 days) range $8-15. The new $1.75 MARTA breeze card has replaced the tokens and is good for both trains and buses, as well as free transfers between either. Exact change or a breeze card from a station machine needed. Unlimited weekly pass $13. Pick up a system map at the **MARTA Ride Store** (at Five Points Station downtown), or at the airport, Lindbergh, or Lenox stations. Most trains, rail stations, and buses are wheelchair accessible.

Taxis: Atlanta Yellow Cab, ☎521-0200.

Car Rental: Atlanta Rent-a-Car, 3185 Camp Creek Pkwy. (☎763-1110), 2½ mi. east of the airport, inside I-285. 21+ with credit card. $39 per day, $0.24 per mi. over 150 mi.

⁈ PRACTICAL INFORMATION

Visitor Info: Visitors Center, 65 Upper Alabama St., on the upper level of Underground Atlanta. MARTA: Five Points. Open M-Sa 10am-6pm, Su noon-6pm. The **Atlanta Convention and Visitors Bureau,** 233 Peachtree St. NE, Peachtree Center #100 (☎521-6600 or 800-285-2682; www.atlanta.net), is geared toward convention planning but operates an automated **information service** (☎222-6688). Available M-F 8:30am-5:30pm.

GLBT Resources: Gay Yellow Pages (☎770-216-9856; www.atlantagaypages.com).

Rape Crisis Counseling: ☎616-4861. 24hr.

Medical Services: Piedmont Hospital, 1968 Peachtree Rd. NW (☎605-5000).

Internet Access: Central Library, 1 Margaret Mitchell Sq. (☎730-1700). Open M-Th 9am-9pm, F-Sa 9am-6pm, Su 2-6pm. Online cards $2 per hr.

Post Office: Phoenix Station (☎524-2960), at the corner of Forsyth and Marietta St., 1 block from MARTA: Five Points. Open M-F 9am-5pm. **Postal Code:** 30303. **Area Code:** 404 inside the I-285 perimeter, 770 outside. In text, 404 unless otherwise noted.

▥ ACCOMMODATIONS

Atlanta International Hostel, 223 Ponce de Leon Ave. (☎875-9449 or 800-473-9449; www.hostel-atlanta.com), in Midtown. From MARTA: North Ave., exit onto Ponce de Leon and walk 3½ blocks east to Myrtle St., or take bus #2. This family-owned hostel has

Downtown Atlanta

🏠 🏠 **ACCOMMODATIONS**

Atlanta International Hostel, **13**

Masters Inn, **1**

Motel 6, **2**

Stone Mountain Family
  Campground, **3**

Travelodge, **16**

🍴 **FOOD**

The Flying Biscuit, **7**

Gladys Knight's and Ron Winans's
  Chicken and Waffles, **15**

Krispy Kreme, **11**

Mary Mac's Tea Room, **10**

Outwrite Bookstore & Coffeehouse, **9**

The Varsity, **12**

Zocalo, **6**

🍸 **NIGHTLIFE**

Blake's, **8**

Club 112, **5**

The EARL, **17**

Eastside Lounge, **18**

Flatiron, **19**

The Heretic, **4**

Masquerade, **14**

clean dorms in a home with TV, pool table, and kitchen. Internet access $5 for entire stay. Free lockers. Towels $1. Dorms $23; private rooms $49-69. AmEx/D/MC/V. ❶

Red Roof Inn, 311 Courtland St. NE (☎659-4545; www.redroof.com), off Highway I-75 at Exit 249-A. Completely renovated and situated in the heart of downtown Atlanta, this hotel is within walking distance to many restaurants and the new Georgia Aquarium. Clean rooms, A/C, cable TV, pool, free WI-FI, continental breakfast. Free parking and a friendly desk staff. Rates vary in summer; call ahead for reservations. Singles $89-99; doubles $99-109. AAA and AARP discount 10%. AmEx/D/MC/V. ❹

Masters Inn, 2682 Windy Hill Rd. (☎770-951-2005 or 800-633-3434). A standard hotel with clean rooms 15min. from Downtown, Atlanta Exit 260 off I-75 in Marietta. A/C, cable TV, and free Wi-Fi. Singles from $41; doubles $45. AmEx/D/MC/V. ❷

The Highland Inn, 644 N. Highland Ave. NE (☎874-5756; www.thehighlandinn.com). This boutique hotel was built in 1927 and renovated for the 1996 Olympics. With over 80 uniquely decorated rooms; you won't get the standard cookie-cutter feel of other hotels here. A/C, cable TV, mini-fridges, and continental breakfast. Reception 24hr. Rooms $81-105. AAA and AARP discount 10% during low season. AmEx/MC/V. ❹

Stone Mountain Family Campground (☎770-498-5710), on U.S. 78. Far from the city's commotion, this campground has stunning sites and beautiful lake sites. Wi-Fi $8 per day, $18 per week. 2-wk. max. stay. Primitive sites $23-25; sites with water and electricity $25-29. Most campsites closed during winter months. RV sites with full hookup $28. Entrance fee $8 per car. AmEx/D/MC/V. ❶

◖ FOOD

From Vietnamese to Italian, fried to fricasseed, Atlanta cooks options for any craving, but soul food—Southern cuisine consisting of fried chicken, collard greens, and even waffles—nourishes the city. Head to "Chicken and Waffles" restaurants for the uncommon and terrific combination. A depot for soul food's raw materials since 1923, the **Sweet Auburn Curb Market,** 209 Edgewood Ave., has come a long way with an eye-popping assortment of goodies, from their famous sweet potato pie (ask devoted fan Bill Clinton) to Southern favorites like pig's feet and pecans. (☎659-1665. Open M-Sa 8am-6pm.) Whether you're looking for a full meal or just a quick snack, **Cafe Aquaria** ❷, located in the new Georgia Aquarium, will satisfy your hunger after a long day of swimming with the fishes. With a wide array of baked goods (pecan chocolate tart $4) and upscale lunch (goat cheese pizza $5-7) as well as hot sandwiches ($7), the Cafe will fill your stomach without emptying your wallet. Diners must pay aquarium admission. (Open May 25-Aug.11 M-Th 8am-6pm, F-Su 8am-7pm; Aug.12-May 24 M-Th 10am-5pm, F-Su 9am-6pm.)

BUCKHEAD

Fellini's Pizza, 2809 Peachtree Rd. NE (☎266-0082). 3 watchful gargoyles and an angel welcome customers to this pizzeria, the flagship of 5 Atlanta locations, complete with a spacious deck and mouth-watering pizza. If you're craving pizza before you go out in Hotlanta, come to this brightly colored restaurant with fast service. Enjoy a slice (from $1.65) or pie ($10.50-19) inside, where classic rock is combined with a romantic atmosphere. Open M-Sa 11am-2am, Su noon-midnight. MC/V. ❶

The Shipfeifer, 1814 Peachtree Rd. (☎875-1106). The Shipfeifer serves up fresh Mediterranean and vegetarian food at reasonable prices. Peachtree patio dining with casual Mediterranean fare and lots of vegan options. Entrees $8.25-10. Wraps $5-7. Quesadillas and burritos $4.50-6.50. Open M-Th and Su 11am-10pm, F 11am-11pm, Sa 11:30am-11pm. AmEx/D/MC/V. ❷

MIDTOWN

▨ **Gladys Knight's and Ron Winans's Chicken and Waffles,** 529 Peachtree St. (☎874-9393). MARTA: North Ave. This upscale but reasonably priced joint screams "soul" with incredible dishes like the Midnight Train (4 Southern-fried chicken wings and a waffle; $8.75). Among the side dishes are collard greens, cinnamon raisin toast, and corn muffins. Don't forget to try their delicious sweet potato cheesecake. Open M-Th 11am-11pm, F-Sa 11am-4am, Su 11am-8pm. AmEx/D/MC/V. ❷

Eats, 600 Ponce de Leon Ave. (☎888-9149). Quickly whips up terrific pasta, meat, and vegetables including sweet potatoes, collard greens, and many more choices and for amazingly low prices. Meat and vegetable plates $3.50-7. Pasta $4-7. Try the special of meatloaf or chicken and two sides ($6.50). Takeout available. Open daily 11am-10pm. MC/V. ❶

The Varsity, 61 North Ave. NW (☎881-1706), at Spring St. MARTA: North Ave. Established in 1928, The Varsity claims to be the world's largest drive-in restaurant. Subject of a landmark Supreme Court ruling in the 1960s abolishing racial segregation in restaurants, The Varsity has since delighted patrons with cheap and delicious hamburgers ($1.10), classic Coke floats ($2.30), and famous onion rings ($1.50). Open M-Th and Su 10am-11:30pm, F-Sa 10am-12:30am. Cash only. ❶

10TH STREET

The Flying Biscuit, 1001 Piedmont Ave. (☎874-8887). With creamsicle-colored walls painted with flying biscuits, this restaurant serves scrumptious sandwiches and breakfast bites all day. Loyal patrons, mostly young professionals, pack this joint to enjoy the Flying Biscuit Breakfast ($7.25) with a poinsettia (cranberry and champagne mixed drink). Open M-Th and Su 7am-10pm, F-Sa 7am-10:30pm. AmEx/MC/V. ❷

Outwrite Bookstore and Coffeehouse, 991 Piedmont Ave. (☎607-0082). Rainbow disco balls grace the windows at this unique gay-friendly establishment. A relaxed and stylish air with remarkably friendly service. Large assortment of books and DVDs for sale. Try the espresso specialty drink "Shot in the Dark" ($2.15) or one of their delicious baked goods ($0.75-4). Open daily 10am-11pm. AmEx/D/MC/V. ❶

Zocalo, 187 10th St. (☎249-7576). Equipped with tequila advertisements, cool patio seating, and fresh salsa made right in front of you, Zocalo has a relaxing atmosphere great for people-watching. Their inventive margaritas are some of the best in Atlanta and they have all the Mexican favorites. Try the Atlantarito—peach and orange Schnapps with Jose Cuervo. Margaritas $9. *Chiles rellenos* $11. Taquitos $8. Open M-Th 11am-11pm, F-Sa 11am-midnight, Su 10am-10pm. AmEx/D/MC/V. ❸

VIRGINIA HIGHLAND

Doc Chey's, 1424 N. Highland Ave. (☎888-0777). Serves heaping mounds of noodles at super prices. This pan-Asian restaurant is ultra-popular among young Atlanta locals. Try the delicious Chinese lo mein ($6.50), Red Curry with veggies ($6.50), or the Marco Polo (shrimp, vegetables, and udon noodles in a zesty Thai sauce; $8.50), one of Doc's originals. Open M-Th and Su 11:30am-10pm, F-Sa 11:30am-11pm. AmEx/D/MC/V. ❷

Everybody's, 1040 N. Highland Ave. (☎873-4545). Receives high accolades for Atlanta's best pizza. It's difficult to choose from the array of personal pizzas, but if you try the Paradiso with pesto ($9-15), or opt for one of their inventive pizza salads ($14), you won't be sorry. Full bar with lots of great beer on tap. Open M-Th 11:30am-11pm, F-Sa 11:30am-1am, Su noon-10:30pm. AmEx/D/MC/V. ❸

Highland Tap, 1026 N. Highland Ave. (☎875-3673). Home of greatest steaks in the Highlands; springing for the tap steak burger ($8.50) is well worth it. Happening bar scene on weekends. Steaks $18-28. Burgers $8.50-12.50. Open M-Sa 11:30am-3am, Su 12:30am-2am. Kitchen open M-Th 5pm-midnight, F 11:30am-3pm and 5pm-1am, Sa 11am-3pm and 5pm-1am, Su 11am-3pm. AmEx/D/MC/V. ❸

◉ SIGHTS

SWEET AUBURN DISTRICT

MARTIN LUTHER KING, JR. The most moving sights in the city run along Auburn Ave. in Sweet Auburn. The Reverend Martin Luther King, Jr.'s birthplace, church, and grave are all part of the 23-acre ▤**Martin Luther King, Jr. National Historic Site.** The Visitors Center houses poignant displays of photographs, videos, and quotations oriented around King's life and the African-American struggle for civil rights. *(450 Auburn Ave. NE. MARTA: King Memorial. ☎331-5190; www.nps.gov/malu. Open daily*

Virginia Highland

🏠 ACCOMMODATIONS

The Highland Inn, **7**

🍎 FOOD

Doc Chey's, **1**
Eats, **6**
Everybody's, **3**
Highland Tap, **4**

🍸 NIGHTLIFE

Mama Q's, **2**
Blind Willie's, **5**
The Vortex, **8**

June-Aug. 9am-6pm; Sept.-May 9am-5pm. Free.) The Center also gives tours of the Birth Home of MLK. (501 Auburn Ave. Tours June-Aug. every 30min.; Sept.-May every hr. Arrive early; reservations not accepted.) Across the street from the Visitors Center stands **Ebenezer Baptist Church,** where King gave his first sermon at age 17 and co-pastored with his father from 1960 to 1968. (407 Auburn Ave. ☎688-7263. Open June-Aug. M-Sa 9am-6pm, Su 1-6pm; Sept.-May M-Sa 9am-5pm, Su 1-5pm.) Next door at the **Martin Luther King, Jr. Center for Nonviolent Social Exchange** lies a beautiful blue reflecting pool with an island on which King has been laid to rest in a white marble tomb. The center's Freedom Hall contains a collection of King's personal articles (including his Nobel Peace Prize medal), an overview of his role model, Gandhi, and an exhibit on Rosa Parks. (449 Auburn Ave. NE. ☎526-8920. Open daily June-Aug. 9am-6pm; Sept.-May 9am-5pm. Free.) In the surrounding area, plaques describing the architecture and past residents of this historic neighborhood line the streets.

DOWNTOWN VICINITY

GEORGIA AQUARIUM. The world's largest aquarium is conveniently located in the heart of Atlanta. This new aquarium has five unique and engaging exhibits: Cold Water Quest (featuring Beluga whales, California sea lions, and African Blackfooted penguins), Georgia Explorer (an interactive gallery where you can touch everything from horseshoe crabs to stingrays housed in pools), Ocean Voyager (where visitors walk through a 100 ft. long acrylic tunnel and gaze at the gigantic viewing window to watch thousands of fish swim by), River Scout (which includes electric African fish and Georgian sealife), and Tropical Diver (with curious garden eels and fish resembling Nemo). The 4D Theater for children or the young-at-heart features a 3D movie with many other special effects. If you are really hankering for more knowledge about how an aquarium operates, take the behind-the-scenes tour where you view everything from the top of the Beluga tank to the largest ocean exhibit tank in North America. *(225 Baker St., NW. ☎581-4000. Open May 25-Aug.11 M-Th 8am-6pm, F-Su 8am-7pm; Aug. 12-May 24 M-Th 10am-5pm, F-Su 9am-6pm. Peak times include spring break and summer. Wheelchair accessible. Adults $24, over 55 $20, ages 3-12 $18. 1hr. tours daily every 30min. noon-5pm.)*

WORLD OF COCA-COLA (WOCC). The World of Coca-Cola may seem like a big advertisement, but the museum impresses and educates tourists on the rise of "the real thing" from its humble beginnings in Atlanta to its position of world domination. This newly renovated and green-friendly museum is twice the size of the beverage company's former museum. While you uncap the secrets of Coke, walk through 1200 artifacts from around the world including expressions of the brand in pop culture (with Andy Warhol and Norman Rockwell designs), and learn about the science behind the refreshment. Sentimentality aside, the best part of the tour is the tasting lounge where guests can sample more than 80 international Coca-Cola products. Try all the flavors to experience a bona fide Coca Cola sugar buzz. The 4D Theater, featuring the search of the secret formula for Coca Cola, is aimed to entertain kids and those who want to experience the museum in full. Theater tickets are sold separately. *(121 Baker St. ☎800-676-2653; http://www.woccatlanta.com. Open daily Sept.-May 9am-5pm, June-Aug. 8am-6pm. Wheelchair accessible. Adults $15, seniors $13, ages 5-12 $9, under 4 free; $1 discount online.)*

CNN. Overlooking beautiful Centennial Park is the global headquarters of the **Cable News Network (CNN).** Check out the 1 hr. studio tour, which reveals "the story behind the news." Sit inside a replica control room, learn the secrets of teleprompter magic, and peer into the renowned CNN newsroom. *(At Centennial Olympic Park Dr. and Marietta St. MARTA: Omni/Dome/GWCC Station at W1. ☎827-2300; www.cnn.com/studiotour. Tours every 20min. daily 9am-5pm. Wheelchair-accessible tours 3 times per day; call for times. $10, seniors $8, ages 4-12 $7.)*

CARTER PRESIDENTIAL CENTER. Just north of L5P, a charming garden and a circle of state flags surrounding the American flag welcome visitors to this museum, which relates the works, achievements, and events of Jimmy Carter's life and presidency. Attached to the museum, the **Jimmy Carter Library** serves as a depository for historic materials from the Carter Administration. *(441 Freedom Pkwy. Take bus #16 to Cleburne Ave. ☎865-7101; www.jimmycarterlibrary.org. Museum open M-Sa 9am-4:45pm, Su noon-4:45pm. Grounds open daily 6am-9pm. Wheelchair accessible. $8; students, seniors, and military $6; under 16 free.)*

OLYMPIC PARK. Amidst the commerce and concrete of bustling downtown Atlanta, you can find serenity at the **Centennial Olympic Park,** a 21-acre state park that is both a public recreation area and a lasting monument to the 1996 Olympic Games. Eight enormous torches and an array of flags (each representing a nation that has hosted one of the modern Olympic Games) surround the park's central feature, the **Fountain of Rings,** which enthralls (and soaks) children and adults alike. Twenty-minute fountain shows feature water spouts set to symphonic melodies and dazzling lights. *(265 Park Ave. West NW. MARTA: Peachtree Center. ☎222-7275; www.centennialpark.com. Park open daily 7am-11pm. Wheelchair accessible. Fountain shows daily 12:30, 3:30, 6:30, 9pm.)*

ZOO ATLANTA. Lions, tigers and...giraffes are common for zoos, but Zoo Atlanta is one of only four in the nation to exhibit giant pandas. Coupled with the meerkats and warthogs, this is a trip worth taking. *(800 Cherokee Ave. SE. Take bus #97 from Five Points. ☎624-5600; www.zooatlanta.org. Open Apr.-Oct. M-F 9:30am-4:30pm, Sa-Su 9:30am-5:30pm; Nov.-Mar. daily 9:30am-4:30pm. Wheelchair accessible. $18, seniors $14, ages 3-11 $13.)*

STATE CAPITOL. At Washington and Mitchell St. is the **Georgia State Capitol Building,** a classical structure built in 1889 with Georgia's own natural resources: Cherokee marble, Georgian oak, and gold mined in Lumpkin County. Exhibits detail the state's tumultuous history. *(☎463-4536; www.sos.state.ga.us. Open M-F 8am-5pm. Tours 30-40min; 8am-3pm; call for availability. Free.)*

WALKING TOURS. From March to November, the **Atlanta Preservation Center** offers walking tours of seven popular areas, including Druid Hills, the setting of the film *Driving Miss Daisy.* Other tour destinations include Inman Park, Atlanta's first trolley suburb, and Historic Downtown. *(327 St. Paul Ave. NE. ☎688-3350; www.preserveatlanta.com. Call ahead for wheelchair-accessible tours. $10, over 60 and students $5.)*

GRANT PARK CYCLORAMA. The world's largest painting (42 ft. tall and 358 ft. in circumference) is in Grant Park, directly south of Oakland Cemetery and Cherokee Ave. The 121-year-old Cyclorama takes visitors back in time, revolving them on a huge platform in the middle of the "1864 Battle of Atlanta." *(800 Cherokee Ave. SE. Take bus #97 from Five Points. MARTA: King Memorial. ☎624-1071. Open daily 8:50am-4:30pm. Wheelchair accessible. $7, seniors and students $6. AAA or military ID discount $1.)*

UNDERGROUND ATLANTA. This former railroad underpass is now a subterranean mall with places to get a snack or shop for souvenirs. Once a hot spot for alternative music, the underground now resembles a carnival-like labyrinth of marketing and merchandise. *(Descend at the entrance beside the Five Points subway station. ☎523-2311. Shops open June-Sept. M-Sa 10am-9:30pm, Su 11am-7pm; Oct.-May M-Sa 10am-9pm, Su noon-6pm. Bars and restaurants close later.)*

AFRICAN-AMERICAN HISTORY. Dating from 1835, the **West End** is Atlanta's oldest neighborhood. A tour of the historic **Wren's Nest** offers a twist on the typical "historic home" tour. Home to Joel Chandler Harris, who popularized the African folktale trickster Br'er Rabbit, the Wren's Nest offers a glimpse into middle-class life at the beginning of the 20th century. *(1050 Ralph David Abernathy Blvd. SW. Take bus #71 from West End Station/S2. 5 blocks left of the MARTA: West End Station. ☎753-7735. Open Tu-Sa 10am-2:30pm. No tour reservations. Storytelling Sa 1pm. Wheelchair accessible. $8, seniors and ages 13-19 $7, ages 4-12 $5.)* The Hammonds House, the home-turned-gallery of Dr. Otis Hammonds, a renowned African-American physician and art lover, displays contemporary and historic works in Georgia's premier collection dedicated to African-American and Haitian art.*(503 Peeples St. SW. ☎752-8730; www.hammondshouse.org. Open Tu-F 10am-6pm, Sa-Su 1-5pm. Wheelchair accessible. $4; children, students, and seniors $2.)* Born a slave, Alonzo F. Herndon founded Atlanta Life Insurance Co., eventually becoming Atlanta's wealthiest African American in the 1900s. A Beaux-Arts Classical mansion, the Herndon Home was built in 1910; today it is dedicated to the legacy of Herndon's philanthropy. *(587 University Pl. NW. Take bus #3 from Five Points station to the corner of Martin Luther King, Jr. Dr. and Maple, then walk 1 block west, turn right on Walnut, and walk 1 block. ☎581-9813; www.herndonhome.org. Tours by appointment. Wheelchair accessible. $5.)*

THE SOUTH

MIDTOWN

WOODRUFF ARTS CENTER. Cultural connoisseurs, the **Woodruff Arts Center (WAC)** is your place. To the west of Piedmont Park, Richard Meier's award-winning buildings of glass, steel, and white porcelain are rivaled only by the treasures they contain. Within the WAC, the **High Museum of Art** features a rotation of incredible temporary exhibits and the permanent "Louvre in Atlanta" exhibit, displaying different objects from the Louvre on rotation. *(1280 Peachtree St. NE. MARTA: Arts Center; exit at Lombardy Way. WAC: ☎733-4200. High Museum of Art: ☎733-4400; www.high.org. Open Tu-W 10am-5pm, Th 10am-8pm, F-Sa 10am-5pm, Su noon-5pm. $15, students with ID and seniors $12, ages 6-17 $10.)*

MARGARET MITCHELL HOUSE. Margaret Mitchell wrote her Pulitzer Prize-winning novel, *Gone with the Wind*, in an apartment she called "The Dump" located in Midtown. Tour the apartment and view her typewriter and autographed copies of the book. Across the street, the **Gone with the Wind Movie Museum** has memorabilia such as the door to Tara Plantation and the portrait of Scarlett at which Clark Gable hurled a cocktail onscreen—complete with stain. *(990 Peachtree St., at 10th St., adjacent to MARTA: Midtown. ☎249-7015; www.gwtw.org. Open daily 9:30am-5pm. Tours 1hr. every hr. $12, students and seniors $9, ages 6-12 $5.)*

WILLIAM BREMAN JEWISH HERITAGE MUSEUM. The largest Jewish museum in the Southeast features a powerful Holocaust exhibit and a gallery tracing the history of Atlanta's Jewish community from 1845 to the present. *(1440 Spring St. NW. From MARTA: N5/Arts Center, walk 3 blocks north to 18th St. and Spring St. ☎873-1661; www.thebreman.org or www.shalomatlanta.org. Open M-Th 10am-5pm, F 10am-3pm, Su 1-5pm. Wheelchair accessible. $10, seniors $6, students $4, ages 3-6 $2, under 3 free.)*

FERNBANK MUSEUM OF NATURAL HISTORY. Sporting outstanding dinosaur and sealife exhibits, an IMAX theater, and interactive discovery centers, the Fernbank is one of the best science museums in the South. *(767 Clifton Rd. NE. Off Ponce de Leon Ave.; take bus #2 from North Ave. or Avondale Station. ☎929-6300; www.fernbank.edu/museum. Open M-Sa 10am-5pm, Su noon-5pm. Wheelchair accessible. Museum $13, students and seniors $12, ages 3-12 $11; with IMAX $17/15/13.)* The adjacent **R.L. Staton Rose Garden** blossoms from spring until December. *(Corner of Ponce de Leon Ave. and Clifton Rd. Free.)*

CENTER FOR PUPPETRY ARTS. The complexity and sophistication of "puppeteering" will surprise and interest even those who haven't watched "The Muppet Show" in years. As it happens, the highlight of the tour is the Jim Henson exhibit, which showcases some of the puppet master's most famous creations. Play with an animatronic puppet and learn all of the operations that go into animating, from moving its head to blinking its eyes. To see the puppets play, call for showtimes. *(1404 Spring St. NW, at 18th St. ☎873-3391; www.puppet.org. Open Tu-Sa 9am-5pm, Su 11am-5pm. Wheelchair accessible. $8, students and seniors $7, under 18 $6.)*

BUCKHEAD

A drive through **Buckhead,** north of Midtown and Piedmont Park, off Peachtree St. near W. Paces Ferry Rd., reveals Atlanta's own version of Beverly Hills. The majority of the gaudy mansions in this area were built by Coca-Cola bigwigs; as such, the architectural style of this area has been aptly dubbed "Rococo-cola." The main drag along Peachtree Dr. is slowly changing from a hip yuppie hangout to that of a younger, and often more unruly, crowd. The area remains conducive to wining and dining, however, and is strung with clubs and restaurants frequented by Atlanta's twentysomethings.

BUCKHEAD ATTRACTIONS. One of the most exquisite residences in the Southeast, the Greek Revival **Governor's Mansion** has elaborate gardens and one of the finest collections of furniture from the Federal Period. *(391 W. Paces Ferry Rd. ☎261-1776. Tours Tu-Th 10-11:30am. Free.)* In the same neighborhood, the **Atlanta History Center** traces Atlanta's development from a rural area to an international cityscape. Its Civil War Gallery spotlights the stories of both Confederate and Union soldiers, while the Folklife Gallery details Southern culture from grits to banjos. Also on the grounds are exquisite mansions from the early 20th century, including the **Swan House,** a lavish Anglo-Palladian Revival home built in 1928, and the **Tullie Smith Farm,** an 1845 Yeoman farmhouse. Abutting the homes, 33 acres of trails and gardens are perfect for an afternoon stroll. *(130 W. Paces Ferry Rd. NW. ☎814-4000; www.atlantahistorycenter.com. Open M-Sa 10am-5:30pm, Su noon-5:30pm. Wheelchair accessible. $15, students and seniors $12, ages 4-12 $10; house tours free with museum admission.)*

🎭 ENTERTAINMENT

For hassle-free fun, buy a MARTA breeze card (see **Public Transit,** p. 366) and pick up the city's free publications on music and events. *Creative Loafing*, the *Hudspeth Report*, and "Leisure" in the Friday edition of the *Atlanta Journal and Constitution* contain the latest info and are available in most coffee shops and on street corners. Check for free summer concerts in Atlanta's parks.

The **Woodruff Arts Center** (see **Midtown,** p. 369) houses the Atlanta Symphony, the Alliance Theater Company, the Atlanta College of Art, and the High Museum of Art. **Atlantix,** 65 Upper Alabama St. and 3393 Peachtree Rd. NE at Lenox Sq., MARTA: Five Points, offers same-day, half-price rush tickets to dance, theater, music, and other attractions (walk-up service only). Full price advance tickets are available online. (☎678-318-1400; www.atlantaperforms.com. Open Tu-Sa 11am-6pm, Su noon-4pm.) The **Philips Arena,** 1 Philips Dr. (☎878-3000), hosts concerts, the **Atlanta Hawks** NBA team, the **Atlanta Thrashers** NHL team and **Georgia Force.** Atlanta's pride and joy, the National League's **Atlanta Braves,** play at **Turner Field.** (755 Hank Aaron Dr., MARTA: Georgia State, or take Braves Shuttle from Five Points. ☎522-7630; Ticketmaster 800-326-4000. Tickets $1-53.) One-hour tours of Turner Field include views of the diamond from the $200,000 skyboxes. (☎614-2311. Open non-game days M-Sa 9am-3pm, Su 1-3pm; evening game days M-Sa 9am-noon; no tours on afternoon or Su game days. $10, under 14 $5.) See the **Atlanta Falcons** play football at the **Georgia Dome,** MARTA: OMNI/Dome/World or Vine City, the world's largest cable-supported dome. (☎223-8687. Open daily 10am-3pm. Tours available Tu-Sa on the hr., except during events; call ahead. $6, students and seniors $4.)

Six Flags Over Georgia, 275 Riverside Pkwy., at I-20 W, is one of the nation's largest amusement parks. Take bus #201 (Six Flags) from Hamilton Homes. Check out the 54 mph "Georgia Scorcher" roller coaster and the "Superman" roller coaster, with a pretzel-shaped inverted loop. (☎770-948-9290. Open mid-June to July M-F 10am-9pm, Sa 10am-10pm; low-season hours vary, call ahead. $50, seniors and under 4 ft. $29. Parking $15-20.)

🌙 NIGHTLIFE

Atlanta's rich nightlife lacks a clear focal point. Fortunately, however, it also lacks limits—young people can be found partying until the wee hours and beyond. Scores of bars and clubs along Peachtree Rd. and Buckhead Ave. in **Buckhead** cater to a younger crowd. Pricier **Midtown** greets the glitzy and glamorous. Alternative **L5P** plays host to bikers and goths, while **Virginia Highland** and up-and-coming **East Atlanta** feature an eclectic mix.

THE SOUTH

BARS AND PUBS

■ **Blind Willie's,** 828 N. Highland Ave. NE (☎873-2583). Blind Willie's is the quintessential blues club: the brick-lined interior is dark, and the bar serves mostly beer ($3-5) to local musicians and newcomers. Despite its hole-in-the wall appearance, Blind Willie's is an Atlanta legend. Live Chicago blues, zydeco (Southern Cajun), and folk music start around 9:30pm on weekdays and 10pm on weekends. Limited menu. Cover $3-12. Open M-Th 7pm-1:30am, F and Sa 7pm-2am.

Fado Fado, 3035 Peachtree Rd. NE (☎841-0066). The interior of this bar was imported from Ireland—right down to the wood of the bar itself. The top yuppie and sports fan hang-out in Buckhead. The boxty (rolled Irish pancake; $13-15) complements a Guinness nicely. Try the "Beef and Cabbage" ($13). Free Wi-fi. Open M-Sa 11:30am-3am, Su 11:30am-midnight.

The Vortex, 438 Moreland Ave. (☎688-1828), in L5P. An incredible restaurant that doubles as an even cooler bar, The Vortex is the spot for serious eaters and drinkers. With mammoth burgers like "Coronary Bypass" ($8) and "Italian Stallion" ($7.50), you'll need a drink to make it through the night. Open M-W and Su 11am-midnight, Th-Sa 11am-3am, Sa-Su brunch 11am-3pm. Th-Sa kitchen open late. Patio seating available.

Masquerade, 695 North Ave. NE (☎577-8178). Occupies an original turn-of-the-century mill. The bar has 3 levels: "heaven," with live music from touring bands; "purgatory," a more laid-back pub and pool house; and "hell," a dance club with everything from techno to 40s big band jazz. An outside space provides dancing under the stars, while the 4000-seat amphitheater caters to metal and punk tastes. Cover from $3. Call for showtimes. Tickets can be purchased at the box office M-F 10am-7pm; cash only.

Steamhouse, 3041 Bolling Way (☎233-7980). For those who like raw oysters (12 on the half shell $6.50-8) with their beer, Steamhouse has plenty of both. On lazy hot summer evenings, the party often spills out onto the patio. Beer $3.50. Open M-Sa 11:30am-2am, Su 11:30am-midnight. Kitchen closes at 11:30pm.

Eastside Lounge, 485 Flat Shoals Ave. SE (☎522-7841). If you're looking for a place to dance, come to the Eastside Lounge. Strobe-lit dance area located upstairs in a small room where the DJ spins. Couches near the bar and tables in the small upstairs offer rest for the weary, but be prepared to stand with the rest of the trendsetters. F-Sa DJ. Cover weekends $5. Open M-Sa 9pm-3am.

DANCE CLUBS

■ **Tongue and Groove,** 3055 Peachtree Rd. NE (☎261-2325; www.tongueandgrooveonline.com). This club has taken Atlanta by storm, featuring some inventive and delicious drinks, earning praise from both the media and locals. Kick back at one of the 2 gorgeous bars or shake it on the dance floor. Dress code strictly enforced. Cover from $10. Open W-Sa 10pm-3am.

Havana Club, 247 Buckhead Ave. (☎869-8484). Latin hot spot with a mature crowd. M night hip hop. Live music F-Sa. Cover men $10 after 11pm. Open M-Sa 8pm-3am.

GLBT NIGHTLIFE

Atlanta is the gay capital of the South, which makes **Midtown** the mecca of Southern gay culture. In Atlanta, straight and gay often party together, since some of the city's best all-around joints are rainbow-colored. For information on gay nightlife and events, check out the free *Southern Voice* newspaper, available everywhere.

Blake's, 227 10th St. (☎892-5786). Midtown males flock to this friendly bar, where see-and-be-seen is a way of life. A prime location in gay-friendly Midtown and just steps from Piedmont Park, this popular bar is also a destination for the young lesbian crowd. Open M-Sa 3pm-3am, Su 3am-midnight.

Mama Q's, 560 B. Amsterdam Ave. (☎875-625), in Amsterdam Walk. 3 pool tables and air hockey. Predominantly a lesbian bar, Mama Q's has a relaxed atmosphere. M free pool, Sa karaoke 10pm. 21+. Open M-Sa 4pm-2am, Su 3pm-midnight.

The Heretic, 2069 Cheshire Bridge Rd. NE (☎325-3061), a little outside of the center of Midtown. Many guys head here for a night of fun. If the action on the smoky dance floor gets a little too hot for you, cool off on the outdoor patio. W Dress Code Boy (shirtless and uniform only). 21+. Cover F-Sa after 10pm $4. Open M-Sa 9am-3am, Su 10am-midnight.

🏔 OUTDOOR ACTIVITIES

In the heart of Midtown, **Piedmont Park** is a hotbed of fun, free activities. Look for the **Dogwood Festival** (www.dogwood.org), a spring art festival, and the **Jazz Festival** (www.atlantafestivals.com) in May. In June, the park celebrates the **Gay Pride Festival** (www.atlantapride.org), and on July 4th, Atlanta draws 55,000 people to the world's largest 10K race, the Peachtree Road Race. Every summer Turner Broadcasting and HBO present **"Screen on the Green,"** a series of free films shown once a week in the meadow behind the Visitors Center. The **Atlanta Botanical Garden** occupies the northern end of the park and provides refuge from the hustle and bustle of everyday life. Stroll through 15 acres of landscaped gardens, a hardwood forest with trails, and an interactive children's garden focusing on health and wellness. The Garden is also home to the Storza Woods and the **Dorothy Chapman Fuqua Conservatory,** which houses some of the world's rarest plant species. (1345 Piedmont Ave. NE. Take bus #36 or MARTA: Arts Center; on Su, bus #27 from MARTA: Five Points. ☎876-5859; www.atlantabotanicalgarden.org. Open Apr.-Oct. Tu-Su 9am-7pm; Nov.-Mar. Tu-Su 9am-5pm. $12, seniors $9, students $7. Tu $2 off.)

Sixteen miles east of the city on U.S. 78, one of Georgia's top natural attractions, **Stone Mountain Park,** provides a respite from the city with beautiful scenery and the remarkable **Confederate Memorial.** Carved into the world's largest mass of granite, the 825 ft. "Mt. Rushmore of the South" profiles Jefferson Davis, Robert E. Lee, and Stonewall Jackson. On summer nights, be sure to check out the dazzling laser show that illuminates the side of the mountain. (Take bus #120 "Stone Mountain" from MARTA: Avondale. ☎770-498-5600; www.stonemountainpark.com. Park open daily 6am-midnight. Attractions open daily in summer 10am-8pm; low season 10am-5pm. Entrance $8 per car, $7 per attraction. All-day pass $24, ages 3-11 $19. Free laser show daily 9:30pm.)

ATHENS ☎706

In the grand Southern tradition of naming college towns after great classical cultural centers, Athens is perhaps the most successful at living up to its eponym. Still, the only Greeks around here live in the University of Georgia's (UGA) fraternities and sororities, and the city is better known for its production of rock stars than philosophers or mathematicians—the university and surrounding bars have spawned hundreds of popular bands, including R.E.M. and the B-52s. Strolling around the beautiful campus and downtown, it's easy to see why the nearly 34,000 students who live in Athens choose to spend their college years here.

📇 TRANSPORTATION AND PRACTICAL INFORMATION. Situated 70 mi. northeast of Atlanta, Athens can be reached from I-85 via U.S. 316, which runs into U.S. 29. Although the **Athens-Ben Epps Airport (AHN),** 1010 Ben Epps Dr.; is located in Athens (☎613-3420), it's easier to fly into Atlanta and take the AAA Airport Express **shuttle** (☎800-354-7874) to various points in and around Athens ($40).

THE SOUTH

Southeastern Stages, 220 W. Broad St., runs **buses** to Atlanta and Augusta. (☎549-2255. Call for schedules and prices. Open M-F 8:30am-8:30pm, Sa-Su 8:30am-4pm.) The Athens Transit System runs **buses** throughout Athens. (☎613-3430. Buses M-F 6:15am-10:45pm, Sa 7:30am-10:15pm; call for schedules. $1.25, ages 6-18 $1, seniors $0.60; transfers free.) UGA's **Campus Transit System** runs everywhere on campus and to some stops downtown. (☎369-6220. Buses daily 7am-12:45am. Free.) Two blocks north of the UGA campus is the **Athens Welcome Center,** 280 E. Dougherty St., in the Church-Waddel-Brumby House. (☎353-1820. Open mid-Apr. to mid-Oct. M-Sa 10am-6pm, Su noon-6pm; mid-Oct. to mid-Apr. M-Sa 10am-5pm, Su noon-5pm.) The **UGA Visitors Center,** at the intersection of College Station and River Rd. on campus, provides info on UGA attractions. (☎542-0842. Open M-F 8am-5pm, Sa 9am-5pm, Su 1-5pm.) Local hotlines include: **Sexual Assault Crisis Line** (☎353-1912); **Community Connection** (☎353-1313). The **Athens Regional Medical Center** is at 1199 Prince Ave. (☎549-9977). **Post Office:** 115 E. Hancock Ave. (☎354-8066. Open M-F 8am-5pm). **Postal Code:** 30601.

⌂ ACCOMMODATIONS. Accommodations are usually reasonably priced, but rates rise during football weekends. The **Perimeter Inn ❷,** 3791 Atlanta Hwy., 5 mi. from downtown, is a comfortable, independently owned motel with Spanish flair. (☎548-3000. Cable, A/C, continental breakfast. Rooms $56-61.) For a luxurious stay, check out **The Foundry Park Inn ❺,** 295 E. Dougherty St. at Thomas St., in one of Athens's oldest historic sites. Thoughtfully decorated rooms and suites come with A/C, down bedding, cable TV, coffeemakers, microwaves, minifridges, and free Wi-Fi. (☎549-7020; www.foundryparkinn.com. Rooms from $105. AmEx/D/MC/V.) For camping closer to the city, try **Sandy Creek Park ❶,** 400 Bob Holman Rd., 4 mi. north of Athens Hwy. 441 N, 3 mi. outside of the loop. (☎613-3631. Open in summer Tu-Su 7am-9pm; call for low-season hours. Primitive sites $10.) **Watson Mill Bridge State Park ❶,** 650 Watson Mill Rd., 21 mi. east of Athens, is the best place in the area to camp, with horse and hiking trails, canoe and boat rentals, and plenty of fishing. (☎783-5349 or 800-864-7275. Park open daily 8am-10pm; office 8am-5pm. Sites $15-17, with water and electricity $17-19; secluded primitive sites $20. AmEx/D/MC/V.)

◖ FOOD. The **Last Resort Grill ❸,** 174 and 184 W. Clayton St., at the corner of Hull St., is an eclectic restaurant with a gourmet atmosphere and reasonable prices. You may never again see a fried green tomato sandwich ($4.75) presented so elegantly. (☎549-0810; http://lastresortgrill.com. Lunch $4-8. Dinner $8-15. Open M-Th and Su 11am-3pm and 5-10pm, F-Sa 11am-3pm and 5-11pm. Bar until 2am. AmEx/D/MC/V.) **The Grit ❷,** 199 Prince Ave., advertises itself as the "greatest vegetarian restaurant in town," and it certainly comes close. This restaurant stays true to its motto—"Vegetarian Food for Carnivores"—dishing up delicious substitutes that everyone will enjoy. Serving a wide array of tempting and exclusively vegetarian food ranging from the teriyaki tofu wrap ($5.25) or chik'n on texas toast ($6), the Grit is sure to please vegetarians and their meat-loving friends. (☎543-6592. Sandwiches $5-6. Entrees $4-7. Open M-F 11am-10pm, Sa-Su 10am-3pm and 5-10pm. MC/V.) R.E.M. fans who wonder what "automatic for the people" means should ask Dexter Weaver, the owner of **Weaver D's Fine Foods ❶,** 1016 E. Broad St., to whom the phrase originally belongs. Located in a small roadside house, Weaver D's offers a true taste of Athens, with pork chop sandwiches ($4.25) and soul food lunches ($4-9). R.E.M. repaid Weaver for the use of his phrase as their 1992 album title by inviting him to the Grammy Awards. (☎353-7797. Open M-Sa 11am-6pm. AmEx/D/DC/MC/V.) **The Grill ❷,** 171 College St., is Athens's version of the all-night burger-and-malt joint. In addition to the standard hamburger platter ($6.25) and luscious malts ($3.50), the Grill has a mean vegetarian side. (☎543-4770. Open

24hr. AmEx/D/MC/V.) For the best baked goods in town, head to **Big City Bread ❶**, 393 N. Finley St., which serves biscuits and sandwiches on home-baked bread. (☎353-0029. Sandwiches $6-8. Open M-Sa 7am-6pm, Su 7am-3pm. AmEx/MC/V.)

◙ **SIGHTS.** The **University of Georgia,** chartered in 1785 as the first land-grant college in the US, is the very reason Athens exists, and it also tops Athens's list of tourist attractions. The campus **Visitors Center,** at the corner of College Station and River Rd. in south campus, has self-guided tours, maps, and helpful information. (☎542-0842. Open M-F 8am-5pm, Sa 9am-5pm, Su 1-5pm.) The campus begins downtown on Broad St., where the arch guards the official entrance to the institution. **Sanford Stadium** is the home turf of UGA's "Dawgs," the white English bulldogs that serve as the school's mascot. **Butts-Mehre Heritage Hall,** on the corner of Pinecrest Dr. and Rutherford St., houses the school's athletic offices and the Heritage Museum, which celebrates UGA athletes and, more importantly, white English bulldogs. (☎542-9036. Open M-F 8am-5pm.) The **Georgia Museum of Art,** 90 Carlton St., in the Performing and Visual Arts Complex off East Campus Dr., is an impressive state-funded collection of over 7000 works of art. (☎542-4662. Open Tu and Th-Sa 10am-5pm, W 10am-9pm, Su 1-5pm. Suggested donation $2.)

Beyond the university, Athens boasts a wealth of historic sites, homes, and artifacts chronicling the town's rich history. The many lush gardens and arboretums encourage long walks and picnics. Maps and tours of the city's historic areas and green spaces are available at the Athens Welcome Center (see **Practical Information,** p. 378), the oldest residence in town. The **US Navy Supply Corps School and Museum,** 1425 Prince Ave., was originally a teacher's college, then a Carnegie library, and is now one of only 11 official US Navy Museums. Exhibits of ship models, uniforms, and all manner of Navy flotsam are on display. (☎354-7349. Open M-F 9am-5:15pm. Visitors must call ahead. Free.) The city's most elaborate garden, the **State Botanical Garden of Georgia,** 2450 S. Milledge Ave., houses trails, a tropical conservatory, and a day chapel. (☎542-1244. Open daily Apr.-Sept. 8am-8pm; Oct.-Mar. 8am-6pm. Visitors Center open Tu-Sa 9am-4:30pm, Su 11:30am-4:30pm. Free.)

If you hesitate to bequeath your property to undeserving offspring, consider making your favorite plant an heir. Professor William H. Jackson set the legal precedent when he willed to a beloved oak tree all the land within 8 ft. of its trunk. Today, **The Tree That Owns Itself** flourishes at the intersection of Finley and Dearing St., south of Broad St. downtown. By far Athens's best Civil War relic, the nearby **Double-Barreled Cannon** was a great idea that failed spectacularly. On the grounds of City Hall, at Washington and College St., the two barrels are still ominously pointed north.

🎵🎭 **ENTERTAINMENT AND NIGHTLIFE.** Athens has cradled hundreds of fledging bands in all genres of music over the years. R.E.M. is arguably Athens's most well-known homegrown band, but those plugged into the music world will know that most musicians show up in Athens at one point or another to play in a true-blue music mecca. In late June, **Athfest** takes over the town. (☎548-1973; www.athfest.com. $10 per day, entire festival $15.) Take a look at Athens's free weekly newspaper, *Flagpole Magazine*, available everywhere downtown, to find out which bands are in town. As soon as you're within spitting distance of Athens, tune in to **WUOG 90.5,** one of the nation's last bastions of real college radio. The students who run the station play tons of local music and liven it up with unscripted, unplanned, and occasionally incoherent commentary. R.E.M. played many early shows at **The 40 Watt Club,** 285 W. Washington St. Conceived in 1979 as a raucous Halloween party lit by a single 40-watt bulb, the club has had numerous incarnations and locations, but currently kicks with live music most nights. (☎549-7871. Cover $5-15. Open daily 8pm-2am.) Downtown, bars line the streets between Lumpkin and Thomas St., where you're sure to find a bar that fits your style, though the **Flicker Theater and Bar,** 263 W. Washington St. (☎546-0039; open M-Sa 4pm-2am), **The Globe,** 199 N. Lumpkin St. (☎353-4721; open M-Sa 11am-2am, Su 11am-midnight), and the **Manhattan Cafe,** 337 N. Hull St. (☎369-9767), are current hot spots. If you're looking for something beyond music and booze, try **Jittery Joe's,** 1210 S. Milledge Ave., which offers a classy coffeeshop atmosphere. (☎208-1979. Open M-F 6:30am-midnight, Sa 6:30am-1am, Su 7:30am-midnight.) **The Morton Theatre,** 195 W. Washington St., was built in 1910 as a vaudeville theater and was entirely owned and operated by African-Americans. Today it is a fully restored, high-tech performing arts center home to all sorts of theater and music. (☎613-3771; www.mortontheatre.com. Call for schedules and ticket prices.)

ANDERSONVILLE   ☎229

Fifty-five miles south of Macon and 10 mi. northeast of Americus on Rte. 49, the **Andersonville National Historic Site** preserves the location where 45,000 Union soldiers were confined in a primitive prison pen without food, water, or shelter in 1864 near the end of the Civil War. Nearly 13,000 men died horrible deaths within the camp's wooden walls due to the barbaric conditions and severe overcrowding—at one point more than 32,000 men were confined in a space intended to hold 10,000. On the grounds, the excellent **National Prisoner of War Museum** memorializes the experiences of American POWs with artifacts, interactive video testimonials, recordings, photographs, and journals. The museum is extraordinarily sobering: visitors pass actual rations that kept men alive for days, myriad portrayals of horrible suffering and amazing strength, and a small outdoor memorial in the sunlight. Also on the grounds, the **Andersonville National Cemetery** is a fitting place to end the visit. (☎924-0343; www.nps.gov/ande. Park open daily 8am-5pm. Museum open 8:30am-5pm. Special talks daily 11am and 2pm. Audio driving tours $1.) Directly across Rte. 49 from the park exit is the tiny town of Andersonville. The **Welcome Center,** 114 Church St., doubles as a little museum stuffed with bric-a-brac.

SAVANNAH   ☎912

In February 1733, General James Oglethorpe and his band of 120 vagabonds founded the city of Savannah and the state of Georgia. General Sherman later spared the city during his Southern rampage. Some say he found Savannah too pretty to burn, presenting it instead to President Lincoln as a Christmas gift. Today, anyone who sees Savannah's stately oak trees and Federalist and English Regency houses interwoven with spring blossoms will agree with Sherman.

◨◪ TRANSPORTATION AND PRACTICAL INFORMATION. Savannah rests on the coast of Georgia at the mouth of the **Savannah River,** which runs north of the city along the border with South Carolina. The city stretches south from bluffs overlooking the river. The restored 2½ sq. mi. **downtown historic district,** bordered by East Broad St., Martin Luther King Jr. Blvd., Gwinnett St., and the river, is best explored on foot. A parking pass ($8), available at the Visitors Center, allows two-day unlimited use of all metered parking, city lots, and garages. **Savannah/Hilton Head International Airport (SAV),** 400 Airways Ave. (☎964-0514; www.savannahairport.com), at Exit 104 off I-95, serves coastal Georgia and the South Carolina Low Country. Amtrak, 2611 Seaboard Coastline Dr. (☎234-2611; www.amtrak.com; open daily 4:30pm-midnight), **trains** chug to Charleston (1¾hr., 1 per day, $21-44). Greyhound, 610 W. Oglethorpe Ave. (☎232-2135; www.greyhound.com; open 24hr.), at Fahm St., sends **buses** to Atlanta (5hr., 7 per day, $39-42), Charleston (2½hr., 2 per day, $31), and Jacksonville (2-3hr., 13 per day, $28). Chatham Area Transit (CAT), 124 Bull St. (☎233-5767), in the Chatham County Court House, runs

buses and a **free shuttle** through the historic area. (Open daily 7am-11pm. Shuttle operates M-Sa 7am-7pm, Su 9:40am-4:20pm. Bus $1, seniors $0.50; no transfers. Weekly pass available at 124 Bull St.; $12.) For a **taxi,** call Yellow Cab (☎236-1133). The **Rape Hotline** (☎233-7273) operates 24hr. The **Savannah Visitors Center,** 301 Martin Luther King Jr. Blvd., at Liberty St., is housed in a former train station. (☎944-0455; www.savannahgeorgia.com. Open M-F 8:30am-5pm, Sa-Su 9am-5pm.) The **Georgia Regional Hospital** is at 1915 Eisenhower Dr. (☎356-2045). **Internet Access: Public Library,** 2002 Bull St. (☎652-3600. Open M-Th 9am-9pm, F-Sa 9am-6pm, Su 2-6pm. Wi-Fi available.) **Post Office:** 2 N. Fahm St., at Bay St. (☎800-275-8777. Open M-F 7am-6pm, Sa 9am-3pm.) **Postal Code:** 31402.

⌐ ACCOMMODATIONS. Downtown motels cluster near the historic area, Visitors Center, and Greyhound station. Venture into the Historic District for a number of very fine B&Bs. For those with cars, **Ogeechee Road (U.S. 17)** has several budget options. **Savannah Pension ❷,** 304 E. Hall St., only minutes from some of Savannah's greatest sights, is the best budget accommodation in the historic district, featuring pastel-hued, clean rooms with A/C and free street parking. Some of the cheaper rooms are dorm-style with bunk beds and shared bathrooms. (☎236-7744. Reservations required at least 7 days in advance. May have rooms available on a first-come, first-served basis. Call for reservations 7am-10am and 5-11pm. Rooms $40-70. Cash and check only.) The **Thunderbird Inn ❸,** 611 West Oglethorpe Ave., has retro, spacious rooms with a 27-inch TV, fridge, and free high-speed Internet. It's also conveniently located near the Savannah civic center and the convention center. (☎232-2661. High season $99-149; low season $89-139. AAA and AARP discount 10%. AmEx/D/MC/V.) Beyond the 8-ft. walls of the courtyard, **The President's Quarters ❺,** 225 E. President St., offers 16 beautiful rooms with period furnishings and modern amenities, like high-speed Internet and complementary parking. (☎233-1600 or 800-233-1776; www.presidentsquarters.com. Expanded continental breakfast and daily tea. Reservations recommended. Ask for daily "walk-in" specials. Rooms $173-252. AmEx/D/MC/V.) **Skidaway Island State Park ❶** is 6 mi. southeast of downtown off Diamond Causeway; take Liberty St. east until it becomes Wheaton St., turn right on Waters Ave., and follow the signs. (☎598-2300 or 800-864-7275. Restrooms, hot showers, electricity, and water. Open daily 7am-10pm. Check-in before 10pm. Sites $24, with hookup $26.)

⌐ FOOD. Mrs. Wilkes Boarding House ❸, 107 W. Jones St., is a Southern institution where friendly strangers gather around large tables for the homestyle atmosphere and delicious soul food. Fried chicken, butter beans, and superb biscuits are favorites. Guests must clear their dishes. (☎232-5997. All-you-can-eat $13. Open M-F 11am-2pm. Cash only.) **Clary's Cafe ❶,** 404 Abercorn St., has been serving some of Savannah's best breakfasts since 1903 and was the setting for many of the scenes in *Midnight in the Garden of Good and Evil* (1997). Weekend brunch features $5 malted waffles. (☎233-0402. Open M-Th 7am-4pm, F 7am-5pm, Sa 8am-5pm, Su 8am-4pm. AmEx/D/MC/V.) **Wall's BBQ ❶,** 515 E. York Ln., in an alley running from Houston to Price St., parallel to York St. and Oglethorpe Ave., serves mouth-watering barbecue in an honest-to-goodness hole-in-the-wall location. Don't plan on devouring your delicious barbecue sandwich ($5-11) or red velvet cake ($4) here; most locals relish their incredible meal in one of the neighboring public squares. (☎232-9754. Baked deviled crabs $3.25. Open Th-Sa 11am-9pm. Cash only.) The **Crystal Beer Parlor ❷,** 301 W. Jones St., at Jefferson St., serves up some of the best burgers and seafood. Try the CBP Crab Stew ($5) or the Crystal Cornbread ($1), staple dishes of this 72-year-old restaurant. (☎443-9200. Burgers and sandwiches $7-9. Happy hour M-F 4-6pm. Live jazz F 7:30-10:30pm. Open M-Th 11am-10pm; F-Sa 11am-midnight. Kitchen closes at M-Th 9:30pm, F-Sa 11pm. AmEx/D/MC/V.)

THE SOUTH

SO SWEET. A cold drink may sound refreshing on a hot Southern afternoon, but only Yanks order "iced tea." To blend in, ask for "sweet tea" instead, but beware: the drink is pre-sweetened and can range in sweetness from barely noticeable to practically gag-inducing. If you'd rather add sugar your tea yourself, order an "unsweet tea" and stir in as much (or as little) as you'd like.

SIGHTS AND ENTERTAINMENT. Most of Savannah's 21 squares contain some distinctive centerpiece. Elegant antebellum houses and drooping vine-wound trees often cluster around the squares, adding to the classic Southern aura. Bus, van, and horse carriage **tours** leave from the Visitors Center and City Market, but walking can be more rewarding. Two of Savannah's best-known historic homes are the **Davenport House,** 324 E. State St., on Columbia Sq., and the **Owens-Thomas House,** 124 Abercom St., one block away on Oglethorpe Sq. Built in 1820, the Davenport House is nearly exactly as Isaiah Davenport left it in the mid-19th century, complete with the original furniture, cantilevered staircase, and exemplary woodwork. The Owens-Thomas House is similar, but the carriage house, which contains artifacts and stories about slave life, is free. Walk the beautiful grounds and see the nation's first indoor plumbing facility. (Davenport: ☎236-8097; www.davenportsavga.com. Open M-Sa 10am-4pm, Su 1-4pm. $10, ages 7-18 $4. Owens-Thomas: ☎233-9743. Open M noon-5pm, Tu-Sa 10am-5pm, Su 1-5pm; last tour 4:30pm. $8, seniors $7, students $4, ages 6-12 $2. Both homes $15.) The **Green Meldrim House,** 14 W. Macon St., on Madison Sq., is a Gothic Revival mansion that served as General Sherman's Savannah headquarters following his famed "march to the sea." It was from this house that Sherman wrote the famous telegram to President Lincoln, giving him the city as a gift. (☎233-3845. Open Tu and Th-F 10am-4pm, Sa 10am-1pm. Tours every hr. on the hr. $7, students $2.)

Savannah's four forts once protected the city's port from Spanish, British, and other invaders. The most intriguing, **Fort Pulaski National Monument,** 15 mi. east of Savannah on U.S. 80 E and Rte. 26, marks the Civil War battle where Union forces first used rifled cannons to decimate the Confederate opposition. (☎786-5787. Partially wheelchair accessible. Call for more ahead for more information. Open daily 9am-5pm. $3, under 16 free.) Special events in Savannah include the annual **NOGS Tour of the Hidden Gardens of Historic Savannah** (☎961-4805), where private walled gardens are opened to the public, with the chance to partake in a special Southern teatime. Green is the theme of the **St. Patrick's Day Celebration on the River,** a multi-day, beer- and fun-filled party that packs the streets and warms up celebrants for the annual **St. Patrick's Day Parade,** the second-largest in the US. (Parade: ☎233-4804. Begins 10:15am.) **First Saturday on the River** (☎234-0295) brings arts, crafts, entertainment, and food to historic River St. each month. The free paper *Connect Savannah,* found in local stores, has the latest in news and entertainment.

NIGHTLIFE. The waterfront area running along Savannah's **River Street** brims with endless oceanfront dining opportunities, street performers, and a friendly pub ambience. While you're allowed to freely walk the streets with one drink in hand in a plastic cup, better not have two or the police will peg you with a $150 ticket. At **Kevin Barry's Irish Pub,** 117 W. River St., the Guinness flows, and the entire bar jigs with live Irish folk music. The classic corned beef and cabbage ($14) keeps the Irish heritage alive, while the bourbon pecan pie ($4.75) pays homage to local flavors. (☎233-9626. Music daily 8:30pm-12:30am. Cover $2 for the entertainment room. Open M-F 2pm-3am, Sa 11:30am-3am, Su 12:30pm-2am. Kitchen closes at 2am.) The **Warehouse,** 18 E. River St., boasts the "coldest and cheapest beer in town." (☎234-6003. Drafts $2-5. Live music most nights. Happy hour M-F 2:30-7pm; domestic pitchers $6 and 2-for-$1 well drinks. Open M-Th and Su 11am-2am, F-Sa

11am-3am.) Students eat, drink, and shop at **City Market,** the largest historic district in the US. (Jefferson at W. St. Julian St.) For the best alternative scene and a gay-friendly atmosphere, check out **Club One,** 1 Jefferson St. near Bay St., where Lady Chablis, a character featured in *Midnight in the Garden of Good and Evil*, performs regularly. (☎232-0200. Cover $3-10. Open M-Sa 5pm-3am, Su 5pm-2am.)

CUMBERLAND ISLAND ☎912

The prize jewel of Georgia's National Seashore, Cumberland Island was once a playground for wealthy Gilded Age robber barons. Hundreds of wild horses now outnumber the few remaining private homes, loggerhead turtles lay their eggs on the island's beaches, playful manatees swim next to the harbor, and maritime forests are slowly reclaiming the ruins of enormous mansions. The **Ice House Museum,** at Dungeness Dock, displays historical artifacts from the island. (No phone. Restrooms. Open daily 8am-4pm.) Off the main road about half a mile south of Dungeness Dock lie the ruins of **Dungeness,** the abandoned winter home of Thomas Carnegie. **Plum Orchard,** the ruins of a Georgian-Revival home built for Carnegie's son and his wife in 1898, is accessible by a short hike from the main road about 7 mi. north of Sea Camp Dock or by bi-monthly ferry from the dock. (Ferries 2nd and 4th Su of each month. Depart Sea Camp Dock at 12:45pm, return at 4:15pm. $6. Free ranger presentation 1:30pm.) The northern and central portions of the island are covered by pine and hardwood forests, while the western side is a tidal marsh excellent for birdwatching. The ranger-led **Dungeness Trail** runs from Dungeness Dock to the beach, passing the Carnegie mansion's spooky ruins along the way. The more adventurous can catch the **Parallel Trail** at Sea Camp Beach and follow it 5½ mi. through shady oak groves and palmetto stands to the Hickory Hill campsite, where a number of other trails converge for further exploration. Since most visitors head straight for the trails, sun-lovers can have the beautiful white sand beaches practically to themselves.

If you wish to spend the night on the island, come prepared—aside from water, all provisions must be carried on and off. The only developed campground, **Sea Camp Beach ❶,** is a 15min. walk from the Sea Camp dock and has restrooms, cold showers, and drinking water. Sites are under a canopy of beautifully gnarled oaks and just steps from the beach ($4 per person). A slightly longer trek rewards hardy campers with **backcountry camping ❶,** magnificent in its isolation and scenery. Each of the four camping areas—**Stafford Beach, Hickory Hill, Yankee Paradise,** and **Brickhill Bluff**—has a well, but the water should be treated before drinking. Campfires are not permitted in the backcountry, so bring a cook stove. (☎882-4335 or 888-817-3421. All camping requires a reservation and a permit that can be obtained at the ranger station at Sea Camp Dock. $2 per person.) For those less inclined to the outdoors, St. Mary's has plenty of overnight options. The **Cumberland Kings Bay Lodges ❷,** 603 Sand Bar Dr., at Charlie Smith Sr. Hwy./U.S. 40 Spur, is 10min. from the dock and offers mini-suites with kitchenettes, a pool, and continental breakfast. (☎882-8900. Singles $39; doubles $43. AmEx/D/MC/V.) The **Riverview Hotel ❸,** 105 Osborne St., is located across the street from the ferry docks. (☎882-3242. Continental breakfast included. Singles $55-69; doubles $63-69; includes 12% tax. AmEx/D/MC/V.) As there is no food on the island, either bring your own or stuff yourself silly before you board the ferry. There are numerous restaurants near the ferry dock, though the **Riverside Cafe ❷,** 106 St. Mary's St., is one of the better choices, offering an extensive selection of tasty breakfast dishes, sandwiches, burgers, and entrees (stir-fry shrimp $11) for reasonable prices. (☎882-3466. Entrees $6-11. Open M 7:30am-2pm, Tu-Su 7:30am-9pm. D/MC/V.)

Cumberland Island, Georgia's southernmost coastal island, is 17½ mi. long and nearly 3 mi. wide. The vast majority of the land is owned and operated by the

THE SOUTH

National Park Service. **The Cumberland Queen,** a ferry operated by the National Park Service from St. Mary's, GA (Exit #3 off I-95), is the only transportation to the island and leaves from the dock at St. Mary's St. and Osborne Rd., arriving at Dungeness Dock and Sea Camp Dock, about 1 mi. north of Dungeness Dock. Reservations are strongly recommended. No pets, bicycles, kayaks, or cars allowed. (Departs St. Mary's Mar.-Nov. daily 9 and 11:45am; Dec.-Feb. M and Th-Su 9 and 11:45am. Departs Dungeness Dock and Sea Camp Dock on Cumberland Island Mar.-Nov. daily 10:15am and 4:45pm; Dec.-Feb. M and Th-Su 10:15am and 4:45pm; also Mar.-Sept. W-Sa 2:45pm.) The **Cumberland Island National Seashore Visitors Center,** 113 St. Mary's St., is located next to the dock in St. Mary's. Make reservations in advance for island accommodations. Seats on the ferry are first-come, first-served. (☎888-817-3421; www.nps.gov/cuis. State park fee $4, under 12 free. Ferry roundtrip $17, under 12 $12, ages 65+ $15. Open daily 8:15am-4:30pm.) On the island, the **Sea Camp Ranger Station,** at Sea Camp Dock, has restrooms, water, and exhibits on the island's natural history, and trail info. (Open daily 8am-4:30pm.)

ALABAMA

Forty years later, the "Heart of Dixie" is still haunted by its controversial role in the Civil Rights movement of the 60s, when Governor George Wallace fought a vicious campaign opposing integration. Today, the state has made efforts to improve its image and has constructed a series of important monuments and homages to the tumult of the Civil Rights movement. While the state's rich colonial past, Native American heritage, and legacy of immigration are on full display, Alabama "the beautiful" offers unique cuisine, nationally acclaimed gardens, and frequent festivals that constantly create an alternative image for the state.

🛈 PRACTICAL INFORMATION

Capital: Montgomery.

Visitor Info: Alabama Bureau of Tourism and Travel, 401 Adams Ave., Ste. 126, Montgomery 36104 (☎334-242-4169 or 800-252-2262; www.touralabama.org). Open M-F 8am-5pm. **Division of Parks,** 64 N. Union St., Montgomery 36104 (☎800-252-7275). Open M-F 8am-5pm.

Postal Abbreviation: AL. **Sales Tax:** usually 10%, varies by county.

MONTGOMERY   ☎334

Montgomery's numerous monuments and historical sites commemorate its turbulent past as the first capital of the Confederacy and the birthplace of America's Civil Rights movement. Montgomery's role in the movement began in 1955 with the arrest of Rosa Parks, a black seamstress and activist who refused to give up her seat to a white man on a city bus. The success of the ensuing bus boycott, organized by local minister Dr. Martin Luther King, Jr., encouraged nationwide reform. Montgomery's marketing now relies on its prominent past, proclaiming itself "courageous, visionary, rebellious."

🖎🛈 ORIENTATION AND PRACTICAL INFORMATION. Downtown follows a grid pattern. Major east-west routes are **Madison Avenue** downtown and **Vaughn Road** south of **I-65**; main north-south roads are **Perry Street** and **Decatur Street,** which becomes Norman Bridge Rd. farther south. **Dexter Avenue** is Montgomery's main street, running east-west up an imposing hill to the capitol. West of downtown, **I-65**

runs north-south and intersects **I-85**, which forms downtown's southern border. A ring road, varyingly called East, South, West, and North Blvd., encircles both downtown and the outlying neighborhoods. Greyhound, 950 W. South Blvd. (☎286-0658, for reservations 800-231-2222; www.greyhound.com; open 24hr.), at Exit 168 on I-65 and a right onto South Blvd., runs **buses** to: Atlanta (3-4hr., 10 per day, $31); Birmingham (2hr., 5 per day, $20); Mobile (3-4hr., 8 per day, $34); Selma (1hr., 5 per day, $20); Tuskegee (45min., 7 per day, $20). Montgomery Area Transit System (MATS) runs **local buses.** (Operates M-Sa 6am-6pm. "Fixed route" bus $1.) The **Lightning Route Trolley** arrives every 25min. at well-marked stops near downtown attractions. Take the Gold route for the State Capitol and Civil Rights Monument and the Green route for the Rosa Parks Museum and the Old Town Museum. (Operates M-Sa 9am-5:40pm. $0.25 per stop, disabled with MAP card and seniors $0.10. Day pass $1; seniors, children, and disabled $0.50.) For a **taxi,** call New Deal Cab (☎262-4747). A **Visitors Center,** 300 Water St., in Union Station, has a short video about the city and free maps. (☎262-0013; www.visitingmontgomery.com. Open M-Sa 8am-5pm, Su noon-4pm.) **Hotlines: Council Against Rape, ☎**286-5987 or 800-656-HOPE. Operates 24hr. **Internet Access: Montgomery City-County Public Library,** 245 High St., between McDonough and Lawrence St. (☎584-7144. Free. Open M-Th 9am-9pm, F-Sa 9am-6pm, Su 1-6pm.) Free Wi-Fi is also available in the center of downtown in the area surrounding the **Court Square fountain,** a new centrally located downtown fixture. **Post Office:** 135 Catoma St. (☎263-4974. Open M-F 9am-5pm.) **Postal Code:** 36104.

ACCOMMODATIONS. For those with a car, South Blvd., Exit 168 off I-65, overflows with inexpensive lodging options, while most exits off I-85 lead to standard, more expensive chains. Beware: the cheapest of the cheap can be fairly seedy. If you're looking to stay close to the historic downtown, the **Red Bluff Cottage ❹,** 551 Clay St., is a B&B worth the price tag. Gorgeous rooms, full baths, free Internet, TV, bathrobes, and flowers add to the cottage's allure. (☎264-0056 or 888-551-2529; www.redbluffcottage.com. Rooms $110-215. AmEx/D/MC/V.) **America's Best Inn ❸,** 977 West South Boulevard, Exit 168 off of I-65 S, has particularly spacious rooms with cable TV, a pool, and Wi-Fi access in most rooms. Good quality for bargain rates. (☎288-5740. Singles $49; doubles $53. AmEx/D/MC/V.) The site of a 1763 French stronghold, **Fort Toulouse Jackson Park ❶,** 12 mi. north of Montgomery on Ft. Toulouse Rd., off U.S. 231, has 39 sites with water and electricity under hanging Spanish moss in beautiful woods. (☎567-3002. Reception daily 8am-5pm. In spring and fall, reservations recommended 2 weeks in advance. Tent sites $11; RV sites with hookups $14, over 62 $11.)

FOOD. In a tiny pink house with lovely paintings and posters, **⧉Martha's Place ❶,** 458 Sayre St., is a family affair. Fried chicken, pork chops, collard greens, and black-eyed peas are all included in the gigantic, authentic soul food lunch. Don't miss the pound cake and sweet tea. (☎263-9135. Traditional lunch $5.50. 4-vegetable plate $4. Open M-F 11am-3pm. AmEx/MC/V.) **⧉Farmers Market Cafe ❷,** 315 N. McDonough St., is an institution, founded in 1958. Grab breakfast or lunch canteen-style; a two-course lunch is $7.60. Montgomery's politicians eat here, as do farmers and builders on their way to or from work. (☎262-1970. Open M-F 5:30am-2pm. AmEx/D/MC/V.) The oldest restaurant in town, **Chris's Hot Dogs ❶,** 138 Dexter Ave., has been making hot dogs ($1.70) like nobody else since 1917. A stone's throw from the State House, Chris's draws in the politicos for hamburgers ($1.70), grilled cheese ($1.70), and other diner fare. "Freedom Fries" are only $1.40. (☎265-6850. Open M-Th and Sa 10am-7pm, F 10am-8pm. Cash only.) **Arirang ❸,** 1633 Eastern Blvd., in the mall across from Lowe's and Best Buy, serves very good Korean specialties. Grilled meat you cook yourself runs $13-15, while other meat and vegetarian dishes range $9-13. (☎215-3251. Open daily 11am-10pm. AmEx/D/MC/V.)

THE SOUTH

"COLD CASES" REIGNITED

The **Southern Poverty Law Center (SPLC)** has a longstanding tradition of defending disenfranchised members of society who are left without a voice but remain victim to prejudice of color, creed, nationality, gender, and sexual orientation. In the courtroom and in the classroom, the Center has combated civil abuse through their leading example that dates back to landmark cases in the fallout of the heat of the civil rights movement of the 60s.

The **Civil Rights Memorial,** and its adjoining education center, were built in recognition and reminder of 40 heroes of that early civil rights movement who were fatally victimized by prejudice. As the SPLC website notes, however, only six of these murders have been met with court convictions.

In February 2007, the Federal Bureau of Investigation announced it would reopen the case files of the unsolved murder cases of over 70 victims of racial violence. The FBI's recognition of these "cold cases" reignites the flames of the civil rights movement, and the Civil Rights Memorial Center offers that reminder daily to its visitors.

For more info visit the Southern Poverty Law Center website (www.splcenter.org), or the Civil Rights Memorial Center in Montgomery, AL.

■ **SIGHTS.** The **State Capitol,** at Bainbridge St. and Dexter Ave., is an imposing Greek Revival structure sporting marble floors, cantilevered staircases, and neat echo chambers. On the front steps, a bronze star commemorates the spot where Jefferson Davis took the oath of office as president of the Confederacy. (☎242-3935. Self-guided tours available. Open M-Sa 9am-5pm. Free.) Only a few feet away is the 112-year-old **King Memorial Baptist Church,** 454 Dexter Ave., where Martin Luther King, Jr. was pastor for six years. (☎263-3970. Open Tu-Sa 10am-4pm. $3, children $2. Cash only.) The **◙Civil Rights Memorial,** designed by Maya Lin, the architect of the Vietnam Veterans Memorial in Washington D.C. (p. 195), has been a mark of beauty in the center of the city since its construction in 1989. A circular black granite table over which water continuously flows pays tribute to activists who died fighting for civil rights. (Open 24hr. Wheelchair-accessible. Free.) The **◙Civil Rights Memorial Center,** 400 Washington Ave., opened in 2005, now furthers the educational outreach and emotional response to the history of the movement. The brainchild of the Southern Poverty Law Center, an institution notable in the protection of civil rights, the Center extends the simple but evocative art of Lin's initial design and features state-of-the-art technology to revive the troubled history that occurred 40 years ago within only 1 mi. of where the museum now stands. An engaged and friendly staff encourages the continuation of discourse on civil rights in the past, present, and future, with its motto, "The March Continues." (Open M-F 9am-4:30pm, Sa 10am-4pm. $2.) The **Alabama Department of Archives and History,** 624 Washington Ave., not only houses important state documents, but also is a museum. Come here to explore Civil War and Civil Rights history or, for younger visitors, to interact with the past in the "Hands-On Gallery." Visit the second-floor exhibit of Spider Martin's "Selma to Montgomery: A March for the Right to Vote" photography exhibit. Twenty-two of Martin's images—from Bloody Sunday to the 54 mi. march from Selma to Montgomery—are housed here. (☎242-4365. Museum open M-F and 1st Sa of every month 8:30am-4:30pm. Wheelchair-accessible. Free.) The **Rosa Parks Library and Museum,** 252 Montgomery St., was dedicated 45 years after Rosa Parks refused to give up her bus seat on December 1, 1955. The museum uses video, artifacts, audio, and an actual 1955 Montgomery bus to recreate that fateful day and the subsequent events that influenced the nation. (☎241-8661. Open M-F 9am-5pm, Sa 9am-3pm. Last entry 1hr. before closing. Call ahead for scheduled tours. $5.50, under 12 $3.50.) **Old Alabama Town,** 301 Columbus St., at Hull St., reconstructs 19th-century Alabama with over 40 period buildings, including a pioneer homestead, an 1892 grocery, and an early African-American church. Allow at least 2hr. to wander around the grounds and use the audio tour at your own pace; if you only want to visit a few blocks rather than the whole museum, you can get a reduced entrance fee. (☎240-4500. Tickets sold M-Sa 9am-2:30pm. Grounds open M-Sa 9am-4pm. Last entry 1½hr. before closing. $8, seniors $7.20, ages 6-18 $4.) The **Hank Williams Museum,** 118 Commerce St., across from the Montgomery Civic Center, features the Montgomery native's outfits, memorabilia, and even the '52 Cadillac where the songwriter died at the young age of 29. (☎262-3600. Open M-Sa 9am-6pm, Su 1-4pm. $8, under 12 $3. AAA discount $1.) A modest exterior hides the quirky **F. Scott and Zelda Fitzgerald Museum,** 919 Felder Ave., off Carter Hill Rd. at Dunbar. The curator will be happy to show you photographs, Zelda's paintings, Scott's original manuscripts, and evidence of the couple's stormy marriage. (☎264-4222. Open W-F 10am-2pm, Sa-Su 1-5pm. Free.) The **Montgomery Museum of Fine Arts,** 1 Museum Dr., part of the Blount Cultural Park (see below), houses 19th- and 20th-century American paintings including works by painters Georgia O'Keeffe and Edward Hopper. (☎244-5700. Open Tu-W and F-Sa 10am-5pm, Th 10am-9pm, Su noon-5pm. Free; donations accepted.)

🎭🎬 **ENTERTAINMENT AND NIGHTLIFE.** The nationally acclaimed **Alabama Shakespeare Festival,** considered by many to be Montgomery's leading attraction, is staged at the **Carolyn Blount Theater** on the grounds of the 300-acre private estate, **Wynton M. Blount Cultural Park.** From Exit 6 off I-85, follow Eastern Blvd. south and turn left on Woodmeere Blvd.; the park will be on the right. The theater also hosts a mix of contemporary and Shakespearean plays year-round on its two stages. (☎271-5353 or 800-841-4273; www.asf.net. Box office open M-Sa 10am-6pm, Su noon-4pm; performance nights until 9pm. Tickets range $20-45; student tickets available. Senior discount 10%.) For regional music, head to Montgomery's **1048 Bar,** 1104 E. Fairview Ave., to enjoy a beer and listen to the best acts in town. It's jazz and blues night daily 10pm-2:30am, and the house jazz band plays every Sunday 5:30-9pm. (☎834-1048. Domestic beer $2.75, imported $3.75-5. Maker's Mark on the rocks $5.25. 21+. Cover most nights $3. Open M-F and Su 4pm-3am, Sa 4pm-2am.) **Gator's,** 5040 Vaughn Rd., at Vaughn Plaza, blasts delta, acoustic, blues, and rock in its cafe and nightclub. (☎274-0330. Tu-Sa live music usually 8pm-late. Kitchen open M-W 11am-2pm and 4-9pm, Th-Sa 4-10pm, Su 11am-2pm.) Montgomery's only independent movie theater, **Capri Theater,** 1045 E. Fairview, shows arthouse films nightly. (☎262-4858. Tickets $7, children $2.) The Thursday *Montgomery Advertiser* ($0.50), *The Buzz,* and *King Kudzu* (both free) list more entertainment options.

🅿 **DAYTRIP FROM MONTGOMERY: TUSKEGEE.** After Reconstruction, "emancipated" blacks in the South remained segregated and disenfranchised. **Booker T. Washington,** a former slave, believed that blacks could best improve their situation through hard work and learning a trade, and the curriculum of the college he founded reflected that philosophy. "What we need we will ourselves create," Washington asserted, a claim made concrete by the fact that virtually the entire school was built by student labor. Today, a more academically oriented **Tuskegee University** (☎727-8347 for free tours by the Park Service) fills 160 buildings on 5000 acres, while the buildings of Washington's original institute comprise a national historical site. On campus, the **George Washington Carver Museum** has exhibits and films on its namesake and Booker T. Washington, and on the history of Tuskegee University. Artist, teacher, scientist, and head of the Tuskegee Agricultural Department, Carver improved the daily lives of Macon County's poor by discovering hundreds of practical uses for common, inexpensive products like the peanut. (☎727-3200. Open daily 9am-4:30pm. Free.) Across the street from the campus lies

The Oaks, a restoration of Washington's home. (Tours daily 30min.; call for schedule.) Grab a wholesome and hearty meal in the **Kellogg Conference Center ❷** on campus. The lunch buffet is $8.75; Sunday brunch is $11. (☎727-3000. Open for lunch M-Sa 11am-2pm, Su 11am-3pm. Open for dinner M-Th 5:30-8:30pm, F-Sa 5:30-9pm. AmEx/MC/V.) To get to Tuskegee, take I-85 toward Atlanta, get off at Exit 32, and follow the signs. Greyhound, 205 E. MLK, Jr. Blvd./Hwy. 80 (☎727-1290; www.greyhound.com; open M-F 8:30am-5pm, Sa 8:30am-2pm), runs **buses** to and from Montgomery (45min., 7 per day, $11).

SELMA   ☎ 334

Selma, perhaps more than any other place in Alabama, is haunted by the past. The small Southern town was shaped by two defining events that took place 100 years apart. As a stronghold for the Confederate armies, its fall in 1865 marked a decisive victory for the North. A century later, Selma gained notoriety during the Voting Rights movement. In the Selma of 1964, state-imposed restrictions gave only 1% of eligible blacks the right to vote. In 1965, Civil Rights activists organized an ill-fated march on the state capitol that was quashed by troops using night sticks, cattle prods, and tear gas. Their spirits battered but not destroyed, the marchers kept trying. A third attempt resulted in the 54 mi. trek from Selma to Montgomery that Dr. King declared the "greatest march ever made on a state capitol in the South." Five months later, Congress passed the Voting Rights Act, prohibiting states from using prerequisites to disqualify voters on the basis of color.

Today, these events are memorialized in museums and sights around town. Selma has the largest historical district in Alabama and calls itself home to one of America's most unique festivals, the **Tale Tellin' Festival.** Storytellers and yarn-spinners from across the South converge on Selma during the second Friday and Saturday in October. (☎800-457-3562; http://taletellin.selmaalabama.com. $10, children $5.) The **National Voting Rights Museum and Institute,** 1012 Water Ave., houses memorabilia relating to the Voting Rights Act of 1965 and continues to disseminate information about voting rights and responsibilities. (☎418-0800. Open M-F 9am-5pm, Sa 10am-3pm. $8; children, seniors, and students $6.) The **Slavery and Civil War Museum,** 1410 Water Ave., is a sister museum to the Voting Rights Institute. The exhibits recreate the harrowing slave experience by casting visitors in the roles of slaves on the journey through the Middle Passage. (☎418-4889. Open T-F 11am-5pm, Sa 10am-3pm. $6; children, seniors, and students $4. Call ahead to schedule the reenactment tours. Inquire about combined ticketing with the Voting Rights Museum.) The **Brown Chapel AME Church and King Monument,** 410 Martin Luther King, Jr. St., served as the headquarters for many Civil Rights meetings during the movement and was the starting point for the march to Montgomery. (☎874-7897. Call for hours and tours.) South of Water Ave., at the end of Broad St., you can walk over the famous **Edmund Pettus Bridge,** where the march left Selma on its way to Montgomery. The **Old Depot Museum,** 4 Martin Luther King, Jr. St., explores Selma's history with artifacts of past and present, some dating back to the area's original inhabitants, the Cherokee and Creek Indians. Check out the photography collection by the 19th-century Alabama native Mary Morgan Keipp. (☎874-2197. Open M-Sa 10am-4pm, Su by appointment. $4, seniors $3, students 19-25 $2, ages 6-18 $1, children under 6 free.) The **Vaughan Smitherman Museum,** 109 Union St., is housed in a mansion that was a hospital for Confederate soldiers. The museum recounts Selma's history and is worth visiting in conjunction with the Voting Rights Museum for two starkly contrasting perspectives on Selma's history. (☎874-2174. Open Tu-Sa 9am-4pm. $3.)

For lodging options, **Budget Inn ❷,** 601 Highland Ave. (Hwy. 80 W), opposite McDonald's, is the best of the budget motels along Highland Ave., with basic, clean rooms and a pleasant staff. (☎872-3451. Cable TV, free local calls, pool, fridge, and microwave. Singles $41; doubles $49. AmEx/D/MC/V.) ▨**Strong's #2 ❷**, 118 Washington St. off Broad St., offers superb soul food prepared from scratch and is worth the wait. Really fresh chicken (boxes $4.50-5.75), fish ($4.50-6.25), and a choice of 15 vegetable side orders ($1.30) make for a wholesome and filling meal. (☎875-8800. Open M-F 10am-7pm, Sa 10am-6pm. Cash only.)

Downtown Selma is bordered by **Jeff Davis Avenue** to the north and the **Alabama River** to the south. **U.S. 80,** which becomes **Broad Street,** runs straight through town. Greyhound, 434 Broad St. (☎874-4503; www.greyhound.com; open daily 7am-10pm), runs **buses** to Atlanta (4½-6hr., 5 per day, $38), Dallas (12-13½hr., 4 per day, $102), and Montgomery (1hr., 5 per day, $15). **Internet Access: Selma/Dallas County Public Library,** 1103 Selma Ave., 2nd fl. (☎874-1727. Free with library card. Open M-Sa 9am-5pm.) **Post Office:** 1301 Alabama Ave. (☎874-4678. Open M-F 8am-4:30pm, Sa 8am-noon.) **Postal Code:** 36703.

BIRMINGHAM   ☎205

For many, Birmingham is a reminder of the struggle for black civil rights in the 60s. Leaders like Martin Luther King, Jr. and Fred Shuttlesworth faced some of their toughest fights in what was labeled "Bombingham" after dozens of bombs rocked the city in the early 60s. Alabama's largest city has made efforts in coming to terms with its past, strides that are evident in many of its excellent museums, especially the Civil Rights Museum, and its push to build a substantial medical research community in recent years. The city's past looms large, however, in today's residential segregation and the downtown sites in the old black neighborhoods where many of the worst racial crimes took place.

▉ TRANSPORTATION

Airport: Birmingham International Airport (**BHM;** ☎595-0533; www.flybirmingham.com), Exit 129 off I-20. Info Center (☎599-0500), 1st fl. by baggage claim.

Trains: Amtrak, 1819 Morris Ave. (☎324-3033 for station information or 800-872-7245 for ticket purchases; www.amtrak.com), south of 1st Ave. N at 19th St. Open daily 9am-5pm. 1 train per day to **Atlanta** (4hr., $20-49) and **New Orleans** (7hr., $23-57). Use caution in this area, especially at night.

Buses: Greyhound, 618 19th St. N. (☎252-7190; www.greyhound.com). Open 24hr. To: **Atlanta** (3hr., 7 per day, $28); **Mobile** (6hr., 5 per day, $48); **Montgomery** (2hr., 5 per day, $21.50); **Nashville** (3½-5½hr., 6 per day, $32).

Public Transit: Metropolitan Area Express (MAX) and **Downtown Area Rapid Transit** (**DART;** ☎521-0101; www.bjcta.org). MAX: most routes M-F 6am-8pm. $1, students $0.60; transfers $0.25. DART trolley runs to downtown tourist destinations. Most routes every 10min. M-Th 10am-5pm, F-Sa 10am-midnight, Su 10am-9pm. Free.

Taxi: Yellow Cab, ☎252-1131.

✴❷ ORIENTATION AND PRACTICAL INFORMATION

While most of the city is pancake-flat, the southeastern edge climbs up suddenly into the bluffs, and the streets curl, wind, and become both very beautiful and very confusing. Downtown Birmingham is organized in a grid with numbered avenues running east-west and numbered streets running north-south. **Richard Arrington, Jr. Boulevard** is the one exception, running along what should have been called 21st St. Downtown is divided by railroad tracks running east-west through the center of the city—thus avenues and streets are designated "N" or "S." Avenue numbers decrease as they near the railroad tracks (with 1st Ave. N and S running alongside them), while street numbers increase from 11th St. at the western edge of downtown to 26th St. at the east. Many streets end unexpectedly and pick up again on the other side of interstate highways or residential highways, and one-way traffic allowances are in effect on many blocks. See the Visitor Bureau for maps of the downtown area that highlight these changes. The center of downtown shuts down for most of the weekend, especially on Sunday when very few businesses or restaurants remain open. However, **Five Points South,** the center of nightlife, is lively all week, no matter what day or time. Five Points South is at the intersection of 20th St. S and 11th Ave. S. The **University of Alabama-Birmingham** is northwest of Five Points South, between 6th and 10th Ave. along University Blvd.

Visitor Info: Greater Birmingham Convention and Visitors Bureau, 2200 9th Ave. N (☎458-8000; www.birminghamal.org). Has helpful staff and useful city maps. Open M-F 8:30am-5pm. **Birmingham Fun Line** (☎458-8000) has weekly information on upcoming events.

Hotlines: Crisis Center, ☎323-7777. **Rape Response,** ☎323-7273. Both 24hr.

Internet Access: Birmingham Public Library, 2100 Park Pl. (☎226-3600), at the corner of Richard Arrington, Jr. Blvd. near the Visitor Bureau. Say you're from out of town to use their Internet computers or Wi-Fi. Open M-Tu 9am-8pm, W-Sa 9am-6pm, Su 2-6pm.

Post Office: 351 24th St. N (☎521-7990). Open M-F 7am-8pm. **Postal Code:** 35203.

ACCOMMODATIONS

Relatively cheap hotels and motels dot the greater Birmingham area along the various interstates. The closer to downtown, the more expensive the room.

The Hospitality Inn, 2127 7th Ave. S (☎322-0691), 4 blocks north of Five Points South near the university, is a good value and boasts a convenient location. Rooms with 2 twin beds $47.50; 2 double beds $52.50. Wheelchair-accessible. AmEx/D/MC/V. ❷

Delux Inn and Suites/Motel Birmingham, 7905 Crestwood Blvd. (☎956-4440). Take Exit 132B from I-20 E. Turn right at Montevallo Rd. and left on Crestwood Blvd. Comfortable rooms, A/C, cable TV, patios, continental breakfast, and a pool. One of the better deals for its price. Rooms for 1-2 people M-Th $50, F-Su $59. AmEx/D/MC/V. ❸

Oak Mountain State Park Campground (☎620-2527 or 800-252-7275), 15 mi. south of the city off I-65 in Pelham at Exit 246. 10,000 acres of horseback riding, golfing, and hiking, and an 85-acre lake with a beach and fishing. A bit of a hike from the city. Campground has bathrooms, showers, and laundry. Park open 7am-8pm. 2-night min. stay required for reservations; no min. for walk-ins, depending on availability. Sites $10.75, with water and electricity $15, with full hookup $17. ❶

FOOD

An old streetcar suburb near the University of Alabama-Birmingham, Five Points South, at the intersection of 20th St. S and 11th Ave. S, is the best place to find great restaurants with reasonable prices. On weekends, most establishments throughout the city are closed, with the exception of those in Five Points, which are open late night seven days a week.

Jim 'n Nick's B-B-Q, 1908 11th Ave. S (☎320-1060), in Five Points South. Jim 'n Nick's began as a roadside barbecue joint over 50 years ago and has grown into a casual restaurant. The ribs are excellent (half-rack $14, full-rack $20). Open M-Th and Su 10:30am-9pm, F-Sa 10:30am-10pm. AmEx/D/MC/V. ❸

Bogue's, 3028 Clairmont Ave. (☎254-9780). Follow University Ave. east until it turns into Clairmont. Established in 1936, Bogue's is a Birmingham institution known for its hearty breakfasts, but their signature sweet rolls are a must for any meal. Breakfast platters $4.75-6.75. Lunch specials with choice of two vegetables and sweet rolls $6.45. Open M-Sa 6am-2pm. AmEx/MC/V. ❷

Pyramid's, 1207 20th St. S (☎930-0078), in Five Points South. Though the city has many Mediterranean options, Pyramid's stands out for quality and price ($4.50-6). Authentic falafel bar with fresh-made falafel, as well as other sandwich options. A good choice for vegetarians and late-night eaters. Open daily noon-4am. AmEx/MC/V. ❶

🔵 SIGHTS

CIVIL RIGHTS. Birmingham's commemoration of the 50s and 60s civil rights struggles centers around the **Birmingham Civil Rights District,** nine blocks dedicated to the battles and bombings that took place there. **Kelly Ingram Park** was the site of numerous protests, and commemorative statues and sculptures now grace the green lawns. (At 5th and 6th Ave. N between 16th and 17th St. Open daily 6am-10pm. Audio tours available at Civil Rights Institute Tu-Sa 10am-3pm. Tours $5.) The **Sixteenth Street Baptist Church** served as the focal point of Birmingham's Civil Rights movement. Four young black girls were killed here on September 15, 1963, when white segregationists bombed the building, spurring protests in the nearby park. A small exhibit in the church's basement chronicles its past. (1530 6th Ave. N. ☎251-9402. Open Tu-F 10am-4pm, Sa by appointment. $3.) Across the street from the church, the fascinating ⬛Birmingham Civil Rights Institute traces the nation's Civil Rights struggle through the lens of Alabama's segregation battle. Displays and documentary footage balance imaginative exhibits and disturbing artifacts from the Jim Crow era, like the burnt-out shell of a torched Greyhound bus and the Birmingham Segregation Ordinances. (520 16th St. N. ☎328-9696 or 866-328-9696; www.bcri.org. Open Tu-Sa 10am-5pm, Su 1-5pm. $10, seniors $5, students $4, under 18 free; Su free, donations accepted. Audio walking tours of neighboring Kelly Ingram Park $5 with ID deposit.)

4TH AVENUE. In the heart of the old historic black neighborhood, now known as the **4th Avenue District,** sits the ⬛Alabama Jazz Hall of Fame. Jazz greats from Erskine Hawkins to the magnificent Ella Fitzgerald each get a small display. There are free concerts on Sundays 1-3pm and 2-4pm. (1631 4th Ave. N, in the Carver Theater 1 block south of Kelly Ingram Park. ☎254-2731. Open Tu-Sa 10am-5pm. $2. Guided tours $3. AmEx/D/MC/V.) Two blocks away, the ⬛Birmingham Museum of Art is the largest municipal art museum in the South, containing over 18,000 works and a sculpture garden. The gallery also houses the Hanson Library, which features the largest collection of Wedgewood china outside the UK. (2000 8th Ave. N. ☎254-2565. Open Tu-Sa 10am-5pm, Su noon-3pm. Self-guided audio tour available. Donations accepted.) Alabama's sports greats, from Willie "The Say Hey Kid" Mays to runner Carl Lewis, are immortalized in the **Alabama Sports Hall of Fame.** (2150 Civic Center Blvd., at the corner of 22nd St. N. ☎323-6665. www.ashof.org. Open M-Sa 9am-5pm, Su 1-5pm. $5, seniors $4, students $3, under 6 free. AAA $1 discount. Make tour reservations online. AmEx/MC/V.)

SMELTING. Birmingham remembers its days as the "Pittsburgh of the South" at the **Sloss Furnaces National Historic Landmark.** Although the blast furnaces closed 20 years ago, they are the only preserved example of 20th-century iron smelting in the world. Plays and concerts are held in a renovated furnace shed by the stacks. (20 32nd St. N, adjacent to the 1st Ave. N overpass off 32nd St. downtown. ☎324-1911; www.slossfurnaces.com. Open Tu-Sa 10am-4pm, Su noon-4pm. Call ahead to schedule tours. Free.) For more insight into the city's history, head to **Vulcan,** 1701 Valley View Dr., the largest statue ever made in the US and the largest cast-iron statue in the world. Vulcan, the Roman god of metallurgy, was sculpted by Italian artist Giuseppe Moretti to represent Alabama at the 1904 St. Louis World's Fair and rises to a height of 180 ft. on top of a hill to the south of the city. From the top you get a 360-degree view of the region, but you can also get a great view of Birmingham from the base for free. If you do go up the tower, the first thing you'll see as you emerge from the elevator is Vulcan's huge iron butt. Don't worry; the view gets better. *(Go south on 20th St. S and follow the signs. ☎ 933-1409; www.vulcanpark.org. Open M-Sa 10am-6pm, Su 1-6pm; open until 10pm some nights for great nighttime views. Wheelchair-accessible. $6, seniors $5, ages 5-12 $4, under 5 $3. Evenings $3 for all.)*

OTHER SIGHTS. For a break from the heavy-duty ironworks, revel in the marvelously manicured grounds of the **Birmingham Botanical Gardens.** Spectacular floral displays, an elegant Japanese garden, and an enormous greenhouse occupy a 67-acre site. Arrange a tour if you want expert commentary on the garden's flora and fauna. *(2612 Lane Park Rd., off U.S. 31. ☎ 414-3900. Garden Center open daily 8am-5pm; gardens open dawn-dusk. Free.)* If you prefer cogs and grease to petals and pollen, the **Mercedes-Benz U.S. International Visitors Center** is a 24,000 sq. ft. museum that spares no technological expense to celebrate the history of all things Mercedes. *(I-20/59 off Exit 89 on Mercedes Dr. at Vance St. ☎ 507-2253 or 888-286-8762; www.mbusi.com. Visitors Center and museum open M-F 8:30am-4:30pm. Factory tours Tu and Th 9 and 9:15am.)*

🎵 🎭 ENTERTAINMENT AND NIGHTLIFE

Opened in 1927, the **Historic Alabama Theater,** 1817 3rd Ave. N, is booked 300 nights of the year with films, concerts, and live performances. Their organ, the "Mighty Wurlitzer," entertains the audience before each show. *(☎ 251-0418. Open M-F 9am-4pm. Order tickets at the box office 1hr. prior to show. Showtimes generally 7pm, Su 2pm. Organ plays 15min. before the official show time. Free.)* Mid-June means everything from country to gospel to big-name rock groups at **City Stages.** The three-day festival, held on multiple stages in downtown's blocked-off streets, is the year's biggest event and includes food, crafts, and children's activities. *(☎ 251-1272 or 800-277-1700; www.citystages.org. 1-day pass $25, 3-day weekend pass $45 if purchased well in advance, $50 2 weeks before the festival.)*

Nightlife centers around **Five Points South,** at 20th St. S and 11th Ave. S. The hippest people jam at **The Nick,** 2514 10th Ave. S, at the corner of 26th St. Locals call it "the place." *(☎ 252-3831. Live rock music most nights. Cover $5-6 for local bands, $10-15 for big names; M usually free. Happy hour M-F 3-9pm. Open M-F 3pm-late, Sa-Su 8pm-6am.)* **The Garage,** 2304 10th Terrace S, is a very cool bar tucked out of sight down 23rd St. A former architecture studio turned antique store, all the materials are still there—customers just drink around the statues, tools, and artwork. Try a German Jubel beer in the weed-covered courtyard, or munch on a simple sandwich among the nymphs and Greek art. *(☎ 322-3220. Open daily 11am-3am.)*

TUSCALOOSA AND MOUNDVILLE ☎ 205

Moundville is one of the best-preserved and most important sites in Native American history. From AD 1000 to 1500, the Mississipian people's fortified city of 3000 people was the prehistoric metropolis of the South. The settlement thrived thanks to rich soil, ample water, and a long growing season. Its dirt mounds were constructed over a 300-year span, and their orderly arrangement suggests ambitious city planning that is still not fully understood. Tuscaloosa, the nearest city, is 13 mi. north of Moundville on Hwy. 69 and 60 mi. southwest of Birmingham along I-59/20. **Moundville Archaeological Park** is well worth the effort of getting there. You can drive around the earthen mounds and climb the highest one, which at 60 ft. is thought to be the original chief ceremonial mound and provides a great view of the lesser mounds. The park provides an informative video. *(For tours ☎ 371-2234. $4; children, seniors, and students $2; under 5 free.)* Inside the park, the **Jones Archae-**

ological Museum displays exhibits and mound artifacts, and a model Native American village features reenactments of the daily life of the Mississipian people. Every year during the first full week of October, the **Moundville Native American Festival** is held on the grounds and celebrates traditional dances, crafts, and storytelling. (☎371-2234. Open M-F 9am-4pm, Sa 9am-5pm.)

In Tuscaloosa, home to the University of Alabama, sail the Black Warrior River aboard the paddle ship **Bama Belle,** 1 Greensboro Ave. (☎339-1108; www.bama-belle.com). Sunset cruises with live entertainment set sail Tuesdays at 6:30pm and "Something to Do" cruises run Sundays at 3pm. (Both 1½hr. $9, seniors $8, ages 2-12 $6). It also offers dinner cruises on Fridays (1½hr. Reservations required. $40.)

The **Tuscaloosa Visitors Center** (☎391-9200; open M-F 8:30am-5pm, Sa 10am-2pm) is housed in the basement of the **Jemison-Van de Graf House,** 1305 Greensboro Ave., one of the finest examples of Italianate architecture in the South. The 1862 mansion is open to visitors; inquire at the Visitors Center. Accommodations in Tuscaloosa cluster along McFarland Blvd./Hwy 82 near the University of 'bama. **Masters' Inn ❷,** 3600 McFarland Blvd. E, has clean, standard rooms, some with continental breakfast, microwave, and refrigerator. (☎556-2010. Singles $40; doubles $45. AAA discount. AmEx/D/MC/V.) **La Quinta Inn ❸,** 4122 McFarland Blvd. E, is a comfortable motel with a pool and good breakfast. (☎349-3270. Free Wi-Fi. Room with 2 beds $50-60. AAA discount. D/MC/V.) **Camping ❶** is available in Moundville in a quiet, wooded setting among the mounds and under the stars. The 30 sites come with hot showers, electricity; some have sewage connections for RVs. (☎371-2572. Registration at the Jones Museum daily 9am-5pm. Tent and RV sites $10.) In Tuscaloosa, ▨**Dreamland Barbecue ❸,** 5535 15th Ave. E., is pure barbecue heaven. From McFarland Blvd. E, turn onto Jug Factory and look for the sign. There's no menu to complicate things here—just choose from a plate of three ribs for $6, six for $9.50, or a full slab for $18. (☎758-8135. Open M-Th 10am-9pm, F-Sa 10am-10pm, Su 11am-9pm. AmEx/MC/V.) The **Super China Buffet ❷,** 4127 McFarland Blvd. E, around the corner from Foodworld, offers a huge selection of Chinese food, made-to-order stir-fry, and sushi. (☎752-8998. Dinner buffet $8. Lunch buffet M-Sa $5.25, Su $6.50. Open M-Th and Su 11am-10pm, F-Sa 11am-11pm. AmEx/MC/V.) In Moundville, **Miss Melissa's Cafe ❶,** 384 Market St., resembles a small school cafeteria—but the cooking you get here is the real deal. There's an all-you-can-eat breakfast ($5) and a canteen-style lunch with meat and three vegetables for $5.70. (☎371-9045. Open M-Sa 6am-2pm. Cash or check only.)

In Tuscaloosa, Greyhound, at 2520 Stillman Blvd. (☎758-6651; www.greyhound.com; open M-F 7:30am-6pm, Sa 7:30am-5pm, Su 7:30-9am and 1:30-5pm), runs **buses** to: Birmingham (1hr., 7 per day, $12); Jackson (3-8hr., 6 per day, $22); Memphis (7-10hr., 5 per day, $47). **Postal Code:** 35405.

HUNTSVILLE   ☎256

Huntsville, 80 mi. north of Birmingham, was the first English-speaking settlement in Alabama and the location of the state's Constitutional Convention in 1819. Far more momentous, however, was the 1950 decision to locate the nation's rocket program here. Initially proposed by Wernher von Braun, the program has endowed the city with a museum, Visitors Center, and Space Camp, as well as one of NASA's 10 national research facilities. A 363 ft. replica of a Saturn V rocket at the **US Space and Rocket Center,** Exit 15 off I-565, is visible for miles around, and the center features space-flight simulators, an IMAX theater, and decommissioned rockets, missiles, and spacecraft, including the original Apollo 16 capsule. The Center is also home to Space Camp, which celebrated its 25th anniversary in 2007. (☎837-3400; www.ussrc.com. Open daily 9am-5pm. Last entry 4pm; allow 3hr. for museum and film. Museum $16, ages 3-12 $11. Combination ticket with IMAX screening and special exhibits $21/16. Inquire about senior discounts.) **Huntsville**

Botanical Garden, 4747 Bob Wallace Ave., provides welcome relief from dull strip malls. Designed for kids' entertainment as well as adults' appreciation, the garden has bonsai trees, inviting water features, a new butterfly house, an aquatic garden, and a 110-year-old dogwood tree. (☎830-4447; www.hsvbg.org. Open Memorial Day-Labor Day M-Sa 9am-6pm, Su noon-6pm; winter M-Sa 9am-5pm, Su 1-5pm. $10, seniors $8, ages 3-18 $5.) The **Huntsville Stars,** a AA affiliate of the Milwaukee Brewers, round the bases at **Joe Davis Stadium** from April to September. (☎882-2562; www.huntsvillestars.com. Tickets $5-8.)

Miles of budget motels and chain restaurants are located on **University Drive,** northwest of downtown, and also at the exits near the airport. Hotel lodging tends to be more expensive the closer you are to the downtown area. To peruse possible lodgings, get off I-565 at Exit 19 and head northwest to University Dr. For discount lodging vouchers, pick up a copy of *Alabama Travel Coupons* at the Visitors Center. **Knight's Inn ❷,** 4404 University Dr., has 60 rooms with refrigerator, Wi-Fi, and microwave in a two-story complex. (☎864-0388. Free local and long-distance calls. Continental breakfast included. Rooms $43-57. AmEx/D/MC/V.) The **Red Carpet Motel ❷,** 3200 University Dr., has clean rooms and a pool. From I-565, exit Jordan Ln. N and take a right on University Dr. (☎539-8448. Check-out 11am. Singles $35-37; doubles $42. AmEx/D/MC/V.) For a bite to eat, the **Wild Rose Cafe ❷,** 121 N. Side Sq., is easy to find in the main square, opposite the courthouse. A traditional lunch counter with constantly shifting daily and weekly menus, it serves quality meat-and-three (vegetables) platters for $6. There are at least 17 vegetables to choose from each day, while desserts start at $1.25. (☎539-3658. Open M-F 7-9:30am and 11am-2pm. AmEx/D/MC/V.) **Papou's ❷,** 110 South Side Ave. above Judge Crater's, features Greek cuisine, as well as daily lunch specials. (☎534-5553. Entrees $6-8. Open M-Tu 11am-2pm, W-F 11am-2pm and 5-9pm, Sa 5-9pm. AmEx/D/MC/V.)

Greyhound, 601 Monroe St. (☎534-1681; www.greyhound.com; open daily 8am-8pm), runs **buses** to: Birmingham (2½-7hr., 4 per day, $21); Memphis (6½-11¼hr., 2 per day, $68.50); Nashville (2½hr., 3 per day, $24). A **tourist shuttle** runs between downtown, museums, points on University Dr., and the Space and Rocket Center. The **trolley** can also make hotel pickup stops by reservation. (1 per hr. M-F 6:40am-6:40pm, Sa 8:40am-7:10pm. $1, all-day pass $2. Wheelchair-accessible.) **Huntsville Shuttle** runs 11 routes infrequently; the tourist loop is one. (☎532-7433 for schedule. Runs M-F 6am-6pm. $1; students, seniors, and children under 7 $0.50; transfers free.) **Visitor Info,** 500 Church St., has a very helpful and talkative staff who can provide a variety of local and state maps. (☎551-2230 or 800-772-2348; www.huntsville.org. Open M-Sa 8am-5pm, Su noon-5pm.)

MISSISSIPPI

The pervasive legacy of cotton, slavery, racial strife, and economic ruin are still visible in Mississippi. Cotton is now machine-harvested and mention of slavery is confined to museums, but racial tension persists. In spite of, or perhaps because of this complex past, Mississippi also had its share of triumphs. Mississippi produced several renowned authors, including William Faulkner, Eudora Welty, and Tennessee Williams. Notably the American home of the blues, the Crossroads State is the birthplace of Robert Johnson, Bessie Smith, W.C. Handy, Muddy Waters, and B.B. King, whose riffs spread upriver and throughout the world.

◪ PRACTICAL INFORMATION

Capital: Jackson.

Visitor Info: Division of Tourism, P.O. Box 849 Jackson 39205 (☎800-927-6378; www.visitmississippi.org). **Department of Parks,** P.O. Box 451, Jackson 39205 (☎800-467-2757).

Postal Abbreviation: MS. **Sales Tax:** 7%. **Hotel Tax:** 10%.

JACKSON   ☎601

As Mississippi's political and cultural capital, Jackson boasts impressive museums, sights, and a cultured perspective. It is one of only four cities in the world to host the International Ballet Competition, held at the Thalia Mara Center every four years. North Jackson's lush homes and country clubs epitomize wealthy Southern living, while refreshing reservoirs and forests invite outdoor exploration in nearby state parks. Just don't arrive on a Sunday—true to its deep Southern roots, Jackson is always closed for a day of rest.

🖪🔃 TRANSPORTATION AND PRACTICAL INFORMATION. Jackson-Evers International Airport (JAN), 100 International Dr. (☎939-5631; www.jmaa.com), is east of downtown off I-20. Amtrak, 300 W. Capitol St. in Union Station (☎355-6350; www.amtrak.com; open daily 10:15am-5:45pm), runs **trains** to Memphis (4½hr., 7 per week, $33) and New Orleans (4hr., 7 per week, $21). Greyhound, in Union Station (☎353-6342; www.greyhound.com; open 24hr.), sends **buses** to Memphis (5hr., 1 per day, $30-32); Montgomery (5hr., 7 per day, $50-53), and New Orleans (4½hr., 4 per day, $27-29). Jackson Transit System (JATRAN) offers limited **public transit.** Find maps at bus stops and JATRAN headquarters, 1025 Terry Rd. (☎948-3840. Open M-F 8am-6pm. Runs from Union Station M-F 5:30am-6:30pm every 30min.; Sa 7am-6pm every hr. $1, transfers free.) For a **taxi,** call City Cab ☎355-8319.

West of I-55 and north of I-20, downtown is bordered on the north by **High Street,** on the south by **South Street,** and on the west by **Lamar Street.** North-south **State Street** bisects the city. **Jackson Convention and Visitors Bureau** is at 111 E. Capitol St., in downtown. (☎960-1891 or 800-354-7695; www.visitjackson.com. Open M-F 8am-5pm.) **Internet Access:** The **Jackson Library** is at 300 State St. (☎968-5801. Free. Open M-Th 9am-5pm, F 9am-6pm, Su 1-5pm.) **Post Office:** 401 E. South St. (☎351-7096. Open M-F 7am-6pm, Sa 8am-noon.) **Postal Code:** 39205.

🛏🛏 ACCOMMODATIONS AND CAMPING. Standard mid-range chains crowd **I-20** and **I-55.** During the summer months, Jackson plays host to a number of business conferences and hotels book fast. Try to reserve ahead, or be patient in your search for a room. **Parkside Inn ❷,** 3720 I-55 N., at Exit 98B off the access road, is a cheap, clean motel with cable TV, free local calls, and a pool. (☎982-1122. Some rooms with fridge and microwave. Singles $40; doubles $50. AmEx/D/MC/V.) The more expensive but extremely comfortable **Cabot Lodge ❹,** 120 Dyess Rd., in Ridgeland, has an extensive breakfast, free Internet access, mixed drinks, and a pool. (☎957-0757 or 800-342-2268; www.cabotlodgejacksonnorth.com. Rooms $99-109, based on availability. AmEx/D/MC/V.) For camping, head to **Timberlake Campgrounds ❶.** Take I-55 N. to Lakeland East (Exit 98B), turn left after 6 mi. onto Old Fannin Rd., and go 4 mi.; it's inside the Barnett Reservoir. (☎992-9100. Office open daily 8am-11pm. Tent sites with water and electricity $15, with full hookup $20. MC/V.)

🍴 FOOD. Delicious and deliciously cheap, the 🖪**Big Apple Inn ❶,** 509 N. Farish St., serves up tasty biscuit sandwiches with your choice of sausage, hamburger, or pig's ear for $1. Six hot tamales go for $4. (☎354-9371. Open M-Sa 7:30am-9pm. MC/V.) **Two Sisters ❸,** 707 N. Congress St., around the corner from George St., offers another Southern smorgasbord in a delightful, creaky-staired home. Eat all you want for $9.50; salad bar and dessert are included. (☎353-1180. Open M-F and Su 11am-2pm. AmEx/D/MC/V.) **Mayflower Cafe ❷**, 123 W. Capitol St., has been serving diner fare and fresh seafood since 1935. A scene from the movie *Ghosts of Mississippi* was shot in the cafe. (☎355-4122. Blue-plate lunch specials $6. Seafood dinners $11-16. Open M-F 11am-10pm, Sa 4:30-10pm. AmEx/D/MC/V.)

◪ **SIGHTS.** The ▨**International Museum of Muslim Cultures (IMMC)**, 117 E. Pascagoula St., was created initially as a temporary satellite to an exhibit at the Mississippi Museum of Art, but became permanent in response to overwhelming community enthusiasm. The museum has extraordinary exhibits on world mosques and the Muslim diaspora. (☎960-0440; www.muslimmuseum.org. Open Tu-Sa 10am-5pm, Su noon-5pm. $7; seniors $5; students, children, and disabled $4. Tickets for special exhibits may have additional charges.) The **New State Capitol**, 400 High St., between West and President St., completed in 1903, was restored to preserve its Beaux Arts grandeur. Don't miss the antique elevator when you visit the galleries of the House and Senate chambers. (☎359-3114. Self-guided tours M-F 8am-5pm. Free.) The **Mississippi Museum of Art (MMA)**, 380 S. Lamar St., amazes visitors with galleries displaying over 3100 works of art, from regional and local artists to rotating national and international exhibits. (☎960-1515; www.msmuseumart.org. Open Tu-Sa 10am-6pm, Su noon-6pm. $12, seniors $10, students $6, under 5 free.) Adjacent to the MMA, the **Russell C. Davis Planetarium**, 201 E. Pascagoula St., presents movies and astronomy shows with music and lasers. (☎960-1550. Movies $6.50, seniors and under 12 $5.50. Planetarium shows $5.50/4.50)

Tour the sumptuous Pumpkin Bedroom and Gold Bedroom in the grandiose **Governor's Mansion**, 300 E. Capitol St., one of only two inhabited governor's mansions in the US. (☎359-6421. Tours every 30min. Tu-F 9:30-11am. Free.) The **Old Capitol Museum**, at Capitol and State St., houses Mississippi's old House and Senate chambers and a small collection of exhibits on the state's history. (☎359-6920. Open M-F 8am-5pm, Sa 9:30am-4:30pm, Su 12:30-4:30pm. Free.) Both are expected to re-open in fall of 2007 after renovations are completed.

▧ **NIGHTLIFE.** To get the scoop on all the goings-on in Jackson, pick up the *Clarion-Ledger* on Thursday for a list of weekend events. Two other free publications with events listings are the *Planet Weekly* and *Jackson Free Press* (www.jacksonfreepress.com), the city's alternative magazine, available around town. **930 Blues Cafe,** 930 N. Congress St., has live blues every night at 8:30pm in a restored 1901 house. National and regional bands play on Fridays and Saturdays. (☎948-3344. Cover W-Th $5, F-Sa $10. Open M-Sa 5:30pm-late.) **Hal & Mal's Restaurant and Brew Bar,** 200 S. Commerce St., near the corner of State and Pascagoula, has live music in a huge, old, relic-strewn warehouse. Acts range from bluegrass on Wednesdays to jazz on Thursdays and country on Fridays. (☎948-0888. Gumbo $6. Cover F-Sa under $5. Restaurant open M 11am-3pm, Tu-F 11am-11pm, Sa 5-11pm. Bar open Tu-Th until midnight, F-Sa until 2am.) **Dick and Jane's,** 206 W. Capital St., attracts a young twentysomething crowd with live alt-rock bands. (☎944-0123. Bar serves beer only. Cover $5 for 21+, under 21 $7. Open Th-Sa 9pm-late.)

VICKSBURG ☎601

President Lincoln said the Civil War would "never be brought to a close until that key is in our pocket." The "key" was Vicksburg, and after a 47-day siege, the Confederacy surrendered to Ulysses S. Grant's army on July 4, 1863. Memorials and combat site markers riddle the grassy 1700-acre **Vicksburg National Military Park,** giving the grounds a sacred air. The park sits on the eastern and northern edges of the city. The **Visitors Center** is on Clay St., directly across from the entrance to the park, about a half-mile west of I-20 Exit 4B. Driving along the 16 mi. path, there are three options: taking a self-guided tour with a free map available at the entrance, using an informative audio tour, or hiring a guide. (☎636-0583; www.nps.gov/vick. Park center open daily 8am-5pm. Grounds open daily in summer 7am-7pm; in winter 7am-5pm. $8 per car. Tape $6.50, CD $11, live guide $35. Driving tour 1-3hr.) In the park, the **USS Cairo Museum** contains artifacts salvaged from the sunken and saved battleship. (☎636-2199. Usually open daily Apr.-Oct. 9:30am-6pm; Nov.-Mar. 8:30am-5pm. Free with park admission.) During the 1863 siege of Vicksburg, Confederate troops used the cupola at the **Old Courthouse Museum,** 1008 Cherry St., as a signal station and held Union prisoners in the courtroom. The restored building now houses Jefferson Davis memorabilia and the gift store sells a range of civil war relics. (☎636-0741; www.oldcourthouse.org. Open Apr.-Sept. M-Sa 8:30am-5pm, Su 1:30-5pm; Oct.-Mar. M-Sa 8:30am-4:30pm, Su 1:30-5pm. $5, seniors $4.50, grades 1-12 $3, kindergarten and younger free.) Vicksburg also has attractions not related to the war; most are along the river on **Washington Street.** One half of the ⬛Corner Drug Store, 1123 Washington St., is a fully operating modern pharmacy. The other half is an elaborate 1800s drug store museum, complete with exhibits on cocaine, arsenic, opium, and hashish. Old implements adorn the walls and moonshine jugs sit in the corner. (☎363-2756. Open M-Sa 8am-6pm, Su 9-11am. Free.) Grab an ice cream at the **Biedenharn Museum of Coca-Cola Memorabilia,** 1107 Washington St. In the 1900 soda fountain you can learn all about the bottling of "the ideal brain tonic." (☎638-6514. Open M-Sa 9am-5pm, Su 1:30-4:30pm. $3, ages 6-12 $2. AAA discount $1.)

The **Battlefield Inn ❸,** 4137 I-20 N/Frontage Rd., is built on part of the actual battlefield—complete with cannons—right next to the National Military Park. (☎800-359-9363. Breakfast and evening mixed drinks included. Laundry, mini-golf, pool, and Wi-Fi. Singles $69; doubles $79. AmEx/D/MC/V.) The well-worn but adequate rooms at the **Beechwood Motel ❶,** 4449 E. Clay St., have cable TV and fridges; some have microwaves. (☎636-2271. Singles $40; doubles $50. AmEx/D/MC/V.) Close to the military park is **Battlefield Kampground ❶,** 4407 I-20/Frontage Rd., off Exit 4B. (☎636-2025. Pool and laundry. Free shuttle to casinos. Tent sites with water and electricity $12, with full hookup $22. Motel rooms $40.) At ⬛Walnut Hills ❸, 1214 Adams St., just north of Clay St., noon is "dinnertime." First-rate all-you-can-eat round-table dinners of catfish, ribs, okra, snap peas, biscuits, iced tea, and dessert cost $12. The individual "blue plate special" comes with meat, three vegetables, iced tea, and dessert for $7.40. (☎638-4910. Round-table dinners M-F and Su 11am-2pm. Open M-F 11am-8:30pm, Su 11am-2pm. D/MC/V.) At the **Tree House Cafe ❸,** 1837 Cherry St., you can play pinball or race miniature slot cars while you eat. Entrees can get quite pricey, but sandwiches and po' boys ($7-8) are reasonable. (☎638-7561. Open M-F 11am-2pm and 5-10pm, Sa 11am-11pm. AmEx/D/MC/V.)

A car is necessary in Vicksburg. The bus station, the Visitors Center, downtown, and the far end of the sprawling military park mark the city's extremes; no public transit runs between them. Greyhound, 1295 S. Frontage Rd. (☎638-8389; www.greyhound.com; open daily 7am-8:30pm), sends **buses** to Jackson (1hr., 4 per day, $12). The **Tourist Information Center,** on Clay St., across from the military park entrance west off I-20, has a helpful city map and coupons. (☎636-9421 or 800-221-3536; www.visitvicksburg.com. Open in summer daily 8am-5:30pm; in winter M-F 8am-5pm, Sa-Su 8am-4pm.) **Post Office:** 3415 Pemberton Blvd., off U.S. 61 S. (☎636-1022. Open M-F 8:30am-5pm, Sa 9am-noon.) **Postal Code:** 39180.

OXFORD   ☎662

When westward explorers first came to this site in northern Mississippi, they decided to name it "Oxford" in hopes of getting the state government to open a university here. The plan worked brilliantly, eventually landing Oxford the **Univer-**

sity of Mississippi (Ole Miss). Today, the lively college-town atmosphere is an even greater attraction than Oxford's historical architecture and rich past.

ORIENTATION AND PRACTICAL INFORMATION. Oxford is 30 mi. east of **I-55** on **Rte. 6** (Exit 243), 55 mi. south of Memphis and 140 mi. north of Jackson. The main east-west roads are **Jackson Avenue** and **University Avenue,** while **Lamar Boulevard** runs north-south. The center of town is **Courthouse Square,** at the intersection of Jackson Ave. and Lamar St., bordered by Van Buren Ave. Greyhound, 715 Hwy. 35 N. (☎563-3046; www.greyhound.com), operates **buses** out of Batesville, a 20min. drive from Oxford. The **Oxford Tourism Info Center,** 107 Courthouse Sq., in the back of the City Hall, offers free audio walking tours and info on William Faulkner. (☎232-2367 or 800-758-9177. Open M-F 8am-5pm. Skipwith Cottage, next door, replaces the info center at City Hall on weekends and is open Sa 10am-4pm, Su 1-4pm.) **Internet Access:** The **Public Library,** 401 Bramlett Blvd., is at Jackson Ave. (☎234-5751. Free. Open M-Th 10am-8pm, F-Sa 10am-5:30pm, Su 2-5pm.) **Post Office:** 401 McElroy Dr. (☎234-5615. Open M-F 9am-5pm, Sa 9:30am-12:30pm.) **Postal Codes:** 38655 (Oxford); 38677 (University of Mississippi).

ACCOMMODATIONS AND FOOD. Lodging is easy to find in Oxford—unless you're in town during the Ole Miss football season. The **Ole Miss Inn ❷,** 1517 E. University Ave., is within walking distance of downtown and has clean, basic rooms. (☎234-2424. Singles $45; doubles $49. AmEx/D/MC/V.) The **Downtown Oxford Inn & Suites ❺,** 400 N. Lamar Blvd., just past Courthouse Sq., has lovely rooms and is literally in the center of this quaint town. Easy access to downtown shops and restaurants, as well as the Ole Miss campus, make this comfortable inn a perfect choice for a weekend getaway. (☎234-3031. Breakfast, on-site dry cleaning and laundry, Internet access, 24hr. exercise facility, and pool. Rooms $99-119. AmEx/D/MC/V.)

The bustling **Courthouse Square,** at Jackson Ave. and Lamar Blvd., is bursting with quaint and quirky shops, cafes, and restaurants, all housed in pastel-painted storefronts that appear like renovated relics of the Old West. ◙**Square Books ❶,** 160 Courthouse Sq. is one of the best independent bookstores in the nation. The owner also happens to be the city's mayor. Expand your belly while opening your mind—coffee drinks and pastries cost just $1-2. Local and internationally recognized authors alike often come for book-signings and readings. (☎236-2262. Open M-Th 9am-9pm, F-Sa 9am-10pm, Su 10am-6pm. AmEx/D/MC/V.) ◙**L&M's Restaurant and Salumeria ❹,** 306 N. Lamar Blvd., is a worthwhile splurge that many Ole Miss parents swear by when visiting their kids. This traditional Italian trattoria cures its own meats for spectacular entrees and pasta dishes, and has a fine selection of cheeses and wines for tasting menus. Though some entrees can get pricey ($20-30), there are several reasonably-priced options ($12.50-$15) that make this a find for real foodies. Sunday brunch dishes range $8-10. (☎238-7780, Lunch W-Sa 11am-2:30pm; dinner Tu-Sa 5:30-10pm; brunch Sa-Su 10am-2pm.) Lunchtime at nearby ◙ **Ajax Diner ❷,** 118 Courthouse Sq., means excellent meat-and-veggie platters ($9) accompanied by jalapeño cornbread. (☎232-8880. Dinner entrees $9-11. Open M-Sa 11:30am-10pm. AmEx/D/MC/V.) The **Bottletree Bakery ❷,** 923 Van Buren Ave., serves large deli sandwiches ($7-8) and fresh pastries in a relaxed atmosphere with brightly painted walls and recycled furniture. (☎236-5000. Open Tu-F 7am-3pm, Sa 9am-3pm, Su 9am-2pm. MC/V.)

At night, live music rolls from the renovated **Proud Larry's,** 211 S. Lamar Blvd., where hand-tossed pizzas are served piping hot. Big names like Elvis Costello have played here in recent history. (☎236-0050. Pizzas $8-10. Cover $5-7. Music F-Sa 10pm-1am, also some weeknights 10pm-midnight. Kitchen open M-Sa 11am-10pm, Su 11:30am-2:30pm. AmEx/D/MC/V.) Four student-friendly bars lie on Jackson

Ave., just west of Courthouse Sq. Of these, **Jubilee,** 1002 West Jackson Ave., is the most reliably cool, with a variety of bar food (wraps and sandwiches $7-8) and live music most Tuesdays. (☎236-3757. Kitchen open daily 11am-10pm. Bar open M-Th and Su until midnight, F-Sa until 1am.) For local entertainment listings, check the free weekly *Oxford Town.*

⑤ SIGHTS. William Faulkner remains the South's favorite son, and his home, **Rowan Oak,** just south of downtown on Old Taylor Rd., off S. Lamar Blvd., is Oxford's biggest attraction. Entranced by the home's history (it once belonged to a Confederate general), Faulkner bought the place in 1930 and named the property after the Rowan tree, a symbol of peace and security. The plot outline of his 1954 novel *A Fable* is etched in pencil on the walls of the study. (☎234-3284. Mansion open for self-guided tours Tu-Sa 10am-4pm, Su 1-4pm. Grounds open sunrise to sunset. Adults $5, students free. W free.) Oxford's sights are all affiliated with another symbol of Southern intellectualism—Ole Miss. The town's covered side-walks and tall cedar trees make it a fitting home for the **Center for the Study of Southern Culture,** a university department in the old Barnard Observatory. The cen-ter hosts the ever-popular annual **Faulkner & Yoknapatawpha Conference** during the last full week of July. Other conferences and festivals sponsored by the center include the **Oxford Conference on the Book,** in April, which celebrates a different author each year, and the **Southern Foodways Symposium,** which brings people together in late October to discuss weighty academic subjects like barbecue and other Southern food traditions. (☎915-5993; www.olemiss.edu/depts/south. Center open M-F 8am-5pm. Free.) Oxford also hosts a **film festival** during the 2nd week in February (☎236-6429; www.oxfordfilmfest.com). Dedicated in 2006, the **Civil Rights Memorial,** next to the library, "commemorates equality in education" on the Ole Miss campus in the form of life-size statue of James Meredith, the 1st African-American student on the Ole Miss campus. Blues fans love the **Ole Miss Blues Archive,** on the 2nd floor of the main library on University Circle, which has one of the largest collections of blues memorabilia in the world. (☎915-7753. Open M-F 8am-5pm. Free.)

TUPELO   ☎662

This former industrial town was the birthplace of Elvis Presley and now milks that fact for all it's worth. Tupelo is 1½hr. east of Oxford along Hwy. 6; a prettier drive, however, is along Rte. 30 through the **Holly Springs National Forest** and Rte. 78 from New Albany. The **Elvis Presley Birthplace,** 306 Elvis Presley Blvd., is definitely worth a visit (something that can't be said of the peripheral sights), especially if you've never been to Graceland. There's also an **Elvis Presley Museum** and the **Memorial Chapel** for meditation, features like a fountain, a statue of 13-year-old Elvis, and a walking tour that explores his life. You can even take an Elvis driving tour and visit places he frequented as a kid. (☎841-1245; www.elvispresleybirthplace.com. Open M-Sa 9am-5pm, Su 1-5pm; May-Sept. open M-Sa until 5:30pm. Birthplace $2.50, children $1.50. Museum $6/3. Combination ticket $7/3.50.) Antique car fanatics will be in heaven at the **Tupelo Automobile Museum,** 1 Otis Blvd., off E. Main St., which includes hot rides like a gull-wing DeLorean and a customized Corvette. (☎842-4242; www.tupeloauto.com. Open Tu-Sa 10am-6pm, Su noon-5pm. $10, seniors and AAA $8, children $5.) Tupelo is also home to the headquarters of the **Natchez Trace Parkway,** a beautiful, if slow, drive from Natchez, MS, to Nashville, TN. The parkway follows old Native American routes and is free of commercial traffic and advertising. Civil War buffs may want to visit the **Tupelo National Battle-field** (☎305-7417), on W. Main St., where the last Civil War battle in Mississippi was fought, as well as **Brice's Crossroads** (☎365-3969; www.bricescrossroads.com), on Rte. 45 north of town, the site of a major Confederate victory. The Trace's **Visitors**

THE SOUTH

Center, 2680 Natchez Trace Pkwy., near the Rte. 78/45 junction, includes information on early settlers, nature, and history along the route. (☎680-4025 or 800-305-
7417; www.nps.gov/natr. Open daily 8am-5pm.)

Accommodations are concentrated around the intersection of McCullough Blvd.
and Gloster St. **Economy Inn ❷,** 708 N. Gloster St., is a great value with clean, spacious rooms close to downtown. (☎842-1213. Microwaves, fridges, free Wi-Fi. Singles $30; doubles $40. AmEx/D/MC/V.) **Commodore Motel ❷,** 1800 E. Main St., east
of downtown, is located close to Elvis's birthplace and provides basic rooms.
(☎842-9074. Rooms $30-40. Cash only.) Six miles south of the city, **Tombigbee State
Park ❶,** 264 Cabin Dr., has primitive campsites overlooking Lake Lee and slightly
less-attractive developed campsites with electricity, showers, and water. (☎842-
7669; reservations at www.reserveamerica.com. Entrance fee $2. Reception 8am-
5pm. Park gates close at 10pm. Primitive sites $11; developed sites $18. Cabins
$50-75; 3-night min. stay. MC/V.) Grab a bite at Elvis's old haunt, **Johnnie's Drive-In
❶,** 908 E. Main St., where a barbecue burger and shake will run you only $5. (☎842-
6748. Open M-Sa 6am-9pm, closed Su because they've "gone to church." Cash
only.) **Romie's ❶,** 804 W. Jackson St., is a local favorite for lunch with a $6 meat
and vegetable special. (☎842-8986. Open M-F and Su 11am-2pm. AmEx/D/MC/V.)

Greyhound, 201 Commerce St. (☎842-4557 or 800-231-2222; www.grey-
hound.com; open M-F 8am-5pm, Sa-Su 9am-noon), sends **buses** to Jackson (6-
12hr., 4 per day, $43), Memphis (2½hr., 4 per day, $28), and Nashville (6-9hr., 2 per
day, $51-55). For a **taxi,** call A-1 Taxi Cab (☎842-5262) or Tupelo Cab Company
(☎842-1133). The **Convention and Visitors Bureau** is at 399 E. Main St. and has a
guidebook with lots of useful coupons. (☎841-6521. Open M-F 8am-5pm.) **Internet
Access:** The **Lee County Library** is at 219 N. Madison St., at the corner of Jefferson
and Madison. (☎841-9027. Free. Open M-F 9am-8pm, Sa 9am-5pm.) **Post Office:** 500
W. Main St. (☎841-1286. Open M-F 8:30am-5pm.) **Postal Code:** 38804.

LOUISIANA

After exploring the Mississippi River Valley in 1682, Frenchman René-Robert Cavalier proclaimed the land "Louisiane" in honor of Louis XIV. The name has
endured three centuries, though French ownership of the region has not. The territory was tossed among France, England, and Spain before Thomas Jefferson and
the US snagged it in the Louisiana Purchase of 1803. Nine years later, a smaller,
redefined Louisiana was admitted to the Union. Each successive government
lured a new mix of settlers to the bayous: Spaniards from the Canary Islands,
French Acadians from Nova Scotia, Americans from the East, and free blacks from
the West Indies. Louisiana's multinational history, Creole culture, Catholic govern-
mental structure (under which counties are called "parishes"), and Napoleonic
legal system are unlike anything found in the other 49 states. Here the swamps
seep into the towns, French words slide into local speech, and a certain *joie de
vivre* is evident in bars and music venues that never close.

🛈 PRACTICAL INFORMATION

Capital: Baton Rouge.

Visitor Info: Office of Tourism, P.O. Box 94291, Baton Rouge 70804 (☎225-342-8100;
www.louisianatravel.com).

Postal Abbreviation: LA. **Sales Tax:** 4%.

NEW ORLEANS ☎ 504

First explored by the French, la Nouvelle Orléans was ceded secretly to the Spanish government in 1762; the citizens of the town didn't find out about the change until 1766. Spain returned the city to France just in time for the fledgling US to grab it in 1803. Centuries of cultural cross-pollination in the city have resulted in a heady cultural melange of Spanish courtyards, Victorian verandas, Cajun jambalaya, and French *beignets*, to name but a few unique hallmarks of New Orleans.

Though intended to reflect the carefree attitude characteristic of this infamous party destination, the city's nickname, "The Big Easy," has been put to the test by recent events that have challenged the physical and spiritual being of New Orleans. The devastation incurred by Hurricane Katrina upon the Gulf Coast in August 2005 has left an indelible impression on the city and its people. Though tempestuous weather had always threatened the area, no storm has ever affected New Orleans in such a way. Levees along the Mississippi River gave way, and the city that sits well-below sea level was submerged in flood waters. Two years later, the areas most affected by these breaks are still in significant need of repair, and only an estimated 255,000 of the city's pre-Katrina 455,000 residents have returned to New Orleans. The Lakefront, Lower Ninth Ward, and East New Orleans remain in dire need of reconstruction efforts, and visitors should be advised of the shocking sights one might still encounter in these damaged areas.

Two years after the tragedy, a common misconception for travelers to New Orleans remains: that the New Orleans of lore is still damaged and unwelcoming. In reality, the major tourist areas were largely unaffected by the storm. The city's main economic sector lies in tourism, and travelers who are looking to support the reconstruction effort would do well to come and enjoy the New Orleans they've always dreamed about visiting—the grand Greek revival mansions of the Garden District still stand tall, the madness of Mardi Gras continues to grow beyond the reaches of Bourbon St. each year, and the solemn comfort of blues played by the world's best jazz musicians in the French Quarter and the Marigny gives way to the healing that this city so richly deserves. A city built with tumultuous beginnings and fought over by pirates and kings for its land throughout history, New Orleans will pay heed to no storm, and the indomitable spirit of its people reflect that history in contemporary times of crisis.

■ INTERCITY TRANSPORTATION

Airport: Louis Armstrong New Orleans International Airport (MSY), 900 Airline Dr. (☎464-0831), 15 mi. west of the city. Cab fare to the Quarter is set at $28 for 1-2 people; $12 each additional person. An **airport shuttle** (☎522-3500; www.airportshuttle-neworleans.com) runs to and from downtown hotels. $13. The **Louisiana Transit Company,** 118 David Dr. (☎818-1077), travels from the airport to Loyola Ave. downtown M-F 5:20am-9:20pm, Sa and holidays 6:20am-9:20pm, Su 7:20am-9:20pm. Buses run every 23min., and every 10-15min. during peak times in the afternoon and evening. After 7pm, buses go to Tulane Ave. and Carrollton Ave. (mid-city) until 11:30pm. Station open M-F 8am-4pm. $1.60; exact change needed. Pickup on the upper level of the airport, near the exit ramp, outside Delta Airlines area.

Trains: Amtrak, 1001 Loyola Ave. (☎800-872-7245; www.amtrak.com), in the Union Passenger Terminal, a 10min. walk to Canal St. via Elk St. Station. Open daily 6am-10pm. Ticket office open M, W, and F-Sa 6:15am-8:30pm; Tu, Th, and Su 6:15am-11pm. To **Atlanta** (11½hr., 1 per day, $57) and **Memphis** (8¼hr., 1 per day, $48).

Buses: Greyhound, 1001 Loyola Ave. (☎524-7571 or 800-231-2222; www.greyhound.com), located in the Union Passenger Terminal. Station open 24hr.; tickets sold

5:15am-1:30am. To **Atlanta** (11½-16½hr., 4 per day, $79) and **Baton Rouge** (1¾hr., 8 per day, $16.50).

▣ ORIENTATION

The majority of New Orleans's attractions crowd around the city center. The city's main streets follow the curve of the **Mississippi River,** hence the nickname "the Crescent City." Directions from locals reflect watery influences—"lakeside" means north, referring to **Lake Pontchartrain,** and "riverside" means south. Uptown lies west, upriver; downtown is downriver. The city is concentrated on the Mississippi's east bank, but **"The East"** refers only to the easternmost part of the city. On-street **parking** in New Orleans is abundant. Many streets throughout the city have meters, which are free on weekdays after 6pm, on weekends, and on holidays.

NEIGHBORHOODS

Tourists flock to the **French Quarter (Vieux Carré),** bounded by the Mississippi River, **Canal Street, Rampart Street,** and **Esplanade Avenue.** Streets in the Quarter follow a grid pattern. Just northeast, or "downtown/downriver," of the Quarter across Esplanade Ave. is **Faubourg Marigny,** a residential neighborhood full of trendy nightclubs, bars, and cafes. Northwest of the Quarter across Rampart St., the little-publicized African-American neighborhood of **Tremé** has a storied history, but has been ruined somewhat by the encroaching construction of a highway overpass and the housing projects lining its Canal St. border. Uptown, the residential **Garden District,** bordered by **Saint Charles Avenue** to the north and **Magazine Street** to the south, is distinguished by its elegant homes. The scenic **Saint Charles Streetcar route** picks up passengers at Canal St. and Carondelet St., and passes through parts of the **Central Business District** ("CBD" or "downtown"), the Garden District via St. Charles Ave., and the **Uptown** and **Carrollton** neighborhoods along **South Carrollton Avenue** and past **Tulane** and **Loyola Universities.** Less populated regions of the city, like **Algiers Point,** are on the **West Bank** across the river. For a guide to the city's neighborhoods, pick up *Historic Neighborhoods of New Orleans* at the Jackson Sq. Visitors Center.

▣ LOCAL TRANSPORTATION

Public Transit: Regional Transit Authority (RTA; ☎248-3900; www.norta.com). Most buses and streetcars $1.25 in exact change; over 65 $0.40, under 3 and disabled free; transfers $0.25. Express buses $1.50. 1-day pass $5, 3-day pass $12; passes sold at major hotels in the Canal St. area and on streetcars.

Taxi: United Cabs, ☎522-9771. **Checker Yellow Cabs,** ☎943-2411.

! Travelers should be aware of New Orleans's capacity for quick change—safe and decidedly unsafe areas are often separated by a block or less, and usually safe areas can become dangerous in a heartbeat. The tenement areas directly north of the French Quarter and northwest of Lee Circle pose particular threats to personal safety; after dark, do not linger in the area of the bus station—head into the French Quarter and do not venture northwest. At night also avoid Tremé and the area immediately north of Carondelet in the Garden District. Travelers who choose to investigate areas still under reconstruction should go only during the daytime. Stick to busy, well-lit roads, never walk alone after dark, and downplay your tourist image.

St. Charles Streetcar

Lake Pontchartrain

Lakeshore Dr.

Pontchartrain Park

LAKE VISTA

University of New Orleans

West End Park

Lake Pontchartrain Causeway

Robert E. Lee Blvd.

Franklin Ave.

TO 1 (.5mi)

WEST END

Canal Blvd.

Paris Ave.

Elysian Fields Ave.

Bombabel Ave.

W. Esplanade Ave.

Oaklawn Ave.

Lake Ave.

Pontchartrain Blvd.

City Park

Bayou St. John

Wisner Blvd.

GENTILLY

Gentilly Blvd.

Harrison Ave.

Dillard University

S. Causeway Blvd.

Veterans Memorial Blvd.

10

610

St. Bernard Ave.

Almonaster Ave.

Florida Ave.

Inner Harbor Navigation Canal

Intracoastal Waterway

TO 2 (18mi)

Metairie Rd.

Metairie Cemetery

Storyland and Botanical Garden

New Orleans Museum of Art

City Park Ave.

TREME

Esplanade Ave.

Ursuline Ave.

N. Claiborne Ave.

St. Claude Ave.

FAUBOURG MARIGNY

TO AIRPORT (10mi)

OLD METAIRIE

Canal St.

Longue Vue House and Gardens

MID-CITY 3

4

N. Broad St.

N. Brolienville St.

Orleans Ave.

FRENCH QUARTER

Airline Dr.

Earhart Expwy.

61

Xavier University

Jefferson Davis Pkwy.

Tulane Ave.

Jackson Square

3139

Jefferson Hwy. River Rd.

90

Earhart Blvd.

Broadway

Carrollton Ave.

Poydras

10

SEE "DOWNTOWN NEW ORLEANS," p. 405

Lafayette Square

ALGIERS POINT

Patterson Rd.

Gen. Meyer Ave.

Gov. Huey P. Long Bridge

River Rd.

Lake Ave.

S. Clairborne Ave.

Fountainbleau

Loyola University

Napoleon Ave.

Washington Ave.

Louisana Ave.

90

Franklin

BUS 90

Crescent City Connection Toll Bridge

18 Old Spanish Trail

90

WESTWEGO

Sophie Newcomb University

UPTOWN

Tulane University

5

St. Charles Ave.

GARDEN DISTRICT

Audubon Park

Jefferson Ave.

Prytania St.

Magazine St.

Tchoupitoulas St.

Audubon Zoo

10

Mississippi River

4th St.

18

18 BUS 90

0   1 mile

0   1 kilometer

🍎 FOOD
Dunbar's, 5
Juan's Flying Burrito, 8

🍸 NIGHTLIFE
Mid City Lanes
Rock 'n' Bowl, 3
Tipitina's, 10

New Orleans

🏠 ACCOMMODATIONS
Columns, 9
India House, 4
Jude Travel Park and Guest House, 1
Marquette House New Orleans
  International Hostel (HI-AYH), 6
St. Bernard State Park, 2
St. Charles Guest House, 7

🛈 PRACTICAL INFORMATION

Visitor Info: Metropolitan Convention and Visitors Bureau, 529 St. Ann St. (☎568-5661; www.neworleanscvb.com), by Jackson Sq. in the French Quarter. Beware of private Visitors Centers in the Quarter that give less than impartial information, pushing their own services 1st—the Jackson Sq. center is the only official center in the French Quarter. Though the staff is few in number, visitors to the city quickly find that talking to these locals is the best way to get to the heart of New Orleans. Open daily 9am-5pm.

Hotlines: Cope Line, general crisis help, ☎523-2673. **Domestic Violence Hotline,** ☎486-0377. Both 24hr.

Medical Services: Charity Hospital, 1532 Tulane Ave., and **University Hospital,** 2021 Perdido St. (both hospitals ☎903-3000).

Internet Access: New Orleans Public Library, 219 Loyola Ave. (☎529-7323), 1½ blocks west of Canal St. Open M-Th 10am-6pm, F-Sa 10am-5pm. If they know you're from out of town, it's $3 per hr. Most of the city has free Wi-Fi, though you must register for 24hr. access with a street address.

Post Office: 701 Loyola Ave. (☎589-1258), near the bus station. Open M-F 7am-8pm, Sa 8am-5pm, Su noon-5pm. **Postal Code:** 70113.

⌐ ACCOMMODATIONS

Finding inexpensive yet decent rooms in the **French Quarter** can be as difficult as staying sober during Mardi Gras. Luckily, other parts of the city compensate for the absence of cheap lodging downtown. Several hostels cater to the young and almost penniless, as do guest houses near the **Garden District,** the area of town that also happens to be host to New Orleans's cheapest and most youthful bar scene. Accommodations for Mardi Gras and the Jazz Festival get booked up to a year in advance. During peak times, proprietors will rent out any extra space, so be sure you know what you're paying for. However, rates tend to sink in the low season (June-early Sept.) when business is slow, and negotiation can pay off. As for campers, there are tons of campsites to discover, but even those get pricey during Mardi Gras. The *Louisiana Official Tour Guide,* available at the Jackson Sq. Visitors Center, has the most comprehensive, unbiased campground listings available.

▨ **India House,** 124 S. Lopez St. (☎821-1904), at Canal St. between N. Broad and Jefferson Davis. What this bohemian haunt lacks in tidiness it makes up for in character. Murals and pictures of past guests fight for space on the walls. Communal eating (and, on busier nights, sleeping) and a backyard patio with pool. Canal St. streetcar provides easy access to French Quarter and downtown (15min. ride). A/C, kitchen, lounge areas, and turtle pond out back. Internet access $2 per 30min. Key deposit $5. Coin laundry $1.50. Reception 24hr. Dorms $17; long-term guests may be able to help with housekeeping duties for discounted lodging. Private rooms $45. MC/V. ❶

▨ **St. Charles Guest House,** 1748 Prytania St. (☎523-6556; www.stcharlesguesthouse.com). In the Garden District, one of New Orleans's most spectacular neighborhoods, a 5min. walk from the St. Charles streetcar. Clean rooms, a leafy courtyard, pool, and continental breakfast. Large antique signs hang haphazardly in the hallway, and the friendly staff lives out back. Small, single "backpacker" rooms $45-65, with A/C and private bath $65-75. Rooms with 1 queen-size bed or 2 twins $55-95, during Jazz Fest and Mardi Gras $100-150; summer rates lower. AmEx/MC/V. ❷

Marquette House New Orleans International Hostel, 2249 Carondelet St. (☎523-3014, www.neworleansinternationalhostel.com), in the Garden District, near the St. Charles streetcar route. A very quiet hosteling experience and a pretty safe bet due to its no-alcohol policy, cleanliness, and mandatory quiet hours (midnight-7am). Large, semi-rustic private rooms also available. 200 beds. A/C, kitchen (no stove), and study rooms. Linen $2, towel $0.50. Key deposit $5. Wheelchair-accessible. Dorms $22, weekly $126; 2-person private rooms with bath and kitchenette $53-66. Each additional person $10. MC/V. ❷

Lamothe House Hotel, 622 Esplanade Ave. (☎947-1161 or 800-367-5858). An imposing 1839 pink townhouse across the street from the French Quarter. 20 rooms featuring antique furniture, A/C, cable TV, and full bath. Continental breakfast is served in the house's decadent dining room, and the large pool is an ideal place to enjoy the complimentary afternoon sherry. Rooms May-Sept. and Dec. $74-90; Mardi Gras and holidays $165-185; call for low-season rates. AmEx/D/MC/V. ❸

CAMPING

Jude Travel Park, 7400 Chef Menteur Hwy./U.S. 90 (☎241-0632 or 800-523-2196, www.judetravelpark.com), just east of the eastern junction of I-10 and U.S. 90, Exit 240B. From downtown New Orleans, take the #55 bus to the corner of Gentilly Blvd. and Elysian Fields and transfer to the #98 bus, which drives past the front gate of the Travel Park. Pool and hot tub, laundry, showers, and 24hr. security. Tent sites $25; sites with electricity $30-50. Weekly and monthly rates available. ❶

St. Bernard State Park, 501 St. Bernard Pkwy. (☎682-2101), 18 mi. southeast of New Orleans; take I-10 Exit 246A, turn left onto Rte. 46, travel for 7 mi., then turn right on Rte. 39 S for 1 mi. 51 sites with water and electricity, as well as swimming pools and walking trails. Office open daily 7am-9pm. Sites $15. ❶

🍴 FOOD

If the eats in the Quarter prove too trendy, touristy, or tough on the wallet, there are plenty of other options, most notably on **Magazine Street** and in the Tulane area, both of which are accessible via the St. Charles Streetcar or via a short and reasonable cab ride.

FRENCH QUARTER

🍴 **Napoleon House,** 500 Chartres St. (☎504-9752), at the corner of St. Louis St. A classy joint with a courtyard and a candlelit dining room with portraits of General Bonaparte, Napoleon's is known for mixed drinks like the Pimm's Cup ($5) and a menu of New Orleans favorites. Beer $3.50-4.50. Po' boy $6.50. Open M 11:30am-5pm, Tu-W 11:30am-10pm, Th 5-10pm, F-Sa 11:30am-11pm. Cash only. ❷

🍴 **Cafe du Monde,** French Market (☎525-4544), across Decatur St. from Jackson Sq. Centrally-located in the heart of the Quarter, Cafe du Monde is the place to go for a *beignet* ($1.60 for an order of 3), the fried, puffed-up doughnut that is a French Quarter tradition. Enjoy with a *cafe au lait* ($1.60). Open 24hr. MC/V. ❶

The Court of Two Sisters, 613 Royal St. (☎522-7261; www.courtoftwosisters.com). Experiencing their live jazz brunch is a true wonder, with classic Cajun dishes sitting side by side with more traditional brunch fare. The fancy fare is enough to make the most squeamish eaters comfortable with taking a taste of the turtle soup, even if they'd prefer the made-to-order omelets or eggs benedict. The prices are steep for the evening Creole dinner, but the daily jazz brunch costs $29, and perhaps even a bit more for a mimosa. Be sure to request a table outside in the courtyard to listen to the jazz band under the canopy of trees. Reservations recommended, especially on weekends. Jazz brunch buffet M-Th 11am-3pm, F-Su 9am-3pm. Creole a la carte dinner M-Sa 5:30-9pm. AmEx/D/MC/V. ❺

Coop's Place, 1109 Decatur St. (☎525-9053), near the corner of Ursuline Ave., has some of the Quarter's best Southern cooking. The gumbo ($4.75-9.50) is thick and spicy, the beer-battered alligator bits ($9) have won awards, and the jambalaya ($4.75-8) is unbeatable. Portions are large for these local treats. Open M-Th and Su 11am-3am, F-Sa 11am-4am. AmEx/D/MC/V. ❷

Johnny's Po' Boys, 511 St. Louis St. (☎524-8129), near the corner of Decatur St. This French Quarter institution, with 40 varieties of the famous sandwich, has been the place to grab a po' boy ($4-7.50) since 1950. Creole fare is also on the menu. Lines may be long, but service is speedy. Gumbo $5. Open M-F 8am-4:30pm, Sa-Su 9am-4pm. MC/V. ❷

Clover Grill, 900 Bourbon St. (☎598-1010). Greasy and delicious burgers grilled under an American-made hubcap (makes 'em cook faster), as well as breakfast available all day. The only place in New Orleans where bacon comes with a side of sexual innuendo—"You can beat our prices, but you can't beat our meat." Burgers from $4.50. Breakfast $3-7. Sandwiches $5-8. Open 24hr. MC/V. ❶

Acme Oyster House, 724 Iberville St. (☎522-5973). At the bar, patrons slurp fresh oysters (6 for $4, 12 for $7) shucked before their eyes by Hollywood, the senior shucker. Typically crammed full of tourists, Acme is at least partly responsible for Bourbon St. debauchery—their motto is "Eat Louisiana oysters, love longer." Open M-Th and Su 11am-10pm, F-Sa 11am-11pm. AmEx/D/MC/V. ❷

OUTSIDE THE QUARTER

Adolfo's Restaurant, 611 Frenchmen St. (☎948-3800). Hardly noticeable from outside, but this true hole-in-the-wall, above the Apple Barrel Bar, is a casual but romantic hideaway, serving up Creole-Italian cuisine for reasonable prices. The fusion of flavors works marvelously, and most entree dishes range $12-16. ❷

Juan's Flying Burrito, 2018 Magazine St. (☎569-0000). Makes some of the best burritos on the planet. Get the "gutter punk" ($6.50), a meal the size of your head, and wash it down with Mexican beer ($2.50). Open M-Sa 11am-11pm, Su noon-10pm. MC/V. ❶

Dunbar's, 4927 Freret St. (☎899-0734), at Robert St. Take St. Charles Ave. west to Upperline St., turn right on Upperline, and then left onto Freret. Residents call it the best place to get mama-just-cooked-it soul food. Po' boy $5-9. Seafood and barbecue plates $11-13. Open M-Sa 7am-9pm. AmEx/D/MC/V. ❸

Hookah Cafe, 500 Frenchmen St. (☎943-1101). Indian food in a friendly and fun atmosphere. The elegant dining room has plenty of cozy nooks in which to enjoy over 20 flavored hookah tobaccos ($11-20). Live music nightly around 10pm. Open daily 5:30pm-2am. AmEx/D/MC/V. ❸

⊙ SIGHTS

FRENCH QUARTER

The 24hr. revelry of the French Quarter epitomizes New Orleans's unbeatable spirit. Unchanged by Katrina, the Quarter remains an attraction that has brought tourists in and rarely ever let them out. Allow at least a full day in the Quarter. The oldest section of the city is famous for its ornate wrought-iron balconies—French, Spanish, and uniquely New Orleans architecture—and raucous atmosphere. Known as the **Vieux Carré** (vyuh ca-RAY), the historic district encompasses dusty used bookstores, voodoo shops, museums, art galleries, bars, and tourist traps. **Bourbon Street** is packed with touristy bars, strip clubs, and pan-handlers disguised as clowns, but there's a distinct change as you leave the trashy straight end and cross the "Lavender Line" into the more sophisticated gay end, where there's less neon and you can hear yourself. **Decatur Street** has mellow cafes and bars. Though Bourbon Street is credited as the home of jazz, musicians and audiences alike now prefer to head northeast of the Quarter to **Frenchmen Street,** a block of bars preferred by locals.

ROYAL STREET. A streetcar named "Desire" once rolled down Royal St., one of the French Quarter's most pleasing avenues. With its historically preserved

NOSHING IN N'AWLINS

With a lingo all its own, dining in New Orleans can be more than a little confusing without a guide to the most popular local cuisine.

Beignet: A "French-style" donut, the beignet is a deep-fried blob of dough that is typically smothered in powdered sugar. Cafe du Monde and Cafe Beignet have them.

Gumbo: New Orleans's seafood gumbo starts with a *roux* broth with regional spices, is usually thickened with okra, and can include crab, shrimp, or crawfish. Coop's Cafe makes a good one. N'awlins natives like theirs in large quantities—note when to order a bowl or a cup.

Muffuletta: Invented in 1906 by Salvatore Lupo, the owner of the Central Grocery on Decatur St., the muffuletta has ham, salami, provolone cheese, and olive relish between slices of round muffuletta bread. These can get messy to eat, but are worth the extra napkins. Try one at Central Grocery or Mama Rosa's.

Po' boy: A New Orleansian pronunciation of "poor boy," this is basically New Orleans's version of the grinder, hoagie, submarine or hero sandwich. The name originates from the Great Depression of the 30s, when oyster po' boys were the cheapest meal you could buy in the city. Served on french bread, today's po' boy may feature oysters, catfish, shrimp, or more traditional lunch meats.

buildings and lines of antique shops and coffee bars, Royal St. remains a perfect spot for respite from the raunchier areas of the Quarter. Pick up the free *French Quarter Self-Guided Walking Tour* from the Visitors Center on St. Ann St. to begin an informed jaunt past Louisiana's oldest commercial and government buildings. Don't miss **Maison LeMonnier,** known as the "first skyscraper," which towers three stories high, or **LaLaurie House,** rumored to be haunted by the souls of the slaves abused by the LaLaurie family. *(LeMonnier: 640 Royal St. LaLaurie: 1140 Royal St.)*

JACKSON SQUARE. During the day, much of the activity in the French Quarter centers around **Jackson Sq.,** a park dedicated to Gen. Andrew Jackson, victor of the Battle of New Orleans. The square swarms with artists, mimes, musicians, psychics, magicians, and con artists. Bargain down a horse-drawn tour of the Quarter to $10; wait on the Decatur St. side. The oldest Catholic cathedral in the US, **Saint Louis Cathedral,** though inconspicuous from the outside, has gorgeous murals inside. Open since 1718, the cathedral still holds daily services. *(615 Père Antoine Alley. ☎525-9585; www.stlouiscathedral.org. Open M, W, and F-Su 7am-5pm; Tu and Th 7am-6pm. Tours every 15-20min. Free.)* Behind the cathedral lies **Cathedral Garden,** also known as Saint Anthony's Garden, bordered by Pirate's Alley and Père Antoine's Alley. Legend has it that **Pirate's Alley** was the site of covert meetings between pirate Jean Lafitte and Andrew Jackson as they conspired to plan the Battle of New Orleans. In reality, the alley wasn't even built until 16 years later. Pirate's Alley is also home to **Faulkner House Books,** where the late American author William Faulkner wrote his first novel, *Soldier's Pay*. The small bookshop is a treasure trove of Faulkner's essays and books, alongside an extensive catalogue of other Southern writers. Manager Joanne Sealy works magic in perusing the high shelves for the perfect read, tailored to the visitor's greatest interest in New Orleans, a city that has lured nearly every major American writer through its mystery and revelry. *(624 Pirate's Alley. ☎524-2940. Open daily 10am-6pm.)*

FRENCH MARKET. The historic French Market takes up several city blocks east of Jackson Sq., toward the water along N. Peters St. and Decatur St. *(☎522-2621. Shops open daily 9am-8pm.)* The market begins at the famous **Café du Monde** and for the first few blocks is a strip mall of touristy shops in a historical building. By Gov. Nicholls St., it becomes the outdoor **Farmers' Market,** which never closes and has been selling "most anything that grows" since 1791. Beyond the Farmers' Market is the **Flea Market,** where vendors sell everything from feather boas to woodcarvings. The Jackson Sq. Visitor Center has free maps. *(Flea Market open daily 8:30am-5pm.)*

OTHER SIGHTS. The **Jean Lafitte National Historical Park and Preserve Visitors Center** conducts free walking tours through the Quarter. *(419 Decatur St. ☎589-2636. 1½hr. tour daily 9:30am. Come early; tickets are given out starting at 9am; only the first 25 people are taken. Other programs on New Orleans culture and history begin at 11:30am. Office open daily 9am-5pm.)* Just south of Decatur St. along the Riverfront streetcar line, the **Moon Walk** has great views of the Mighty Mississippi. Be extremely careful in this area at night. At the southwest corner of the Quarter, the **Aquarium of the Americas** houses an amazing collection of sea life and birds. Though its populations were devastated by Katrina-related damage, the aquarium has regenerated its assemblage of rare marine life. Among the 500 species are endangered sea turtles and extremely rare white alligators. Come face to face with sharks as you walk through a 30 ft. acrylic-and-glass tunnel. The new **Energy IMAX Theater** accompanies the aquarium with documentary features that explore the depths of the oceans beyond the limits of the aquariums glass tanks. *(1 Canal St. ☎581-4629. Open Tu-Su 9am-5pm. Aquarium only $17, ages 2-12 $13, over 65 $10; IMAX $8/7/5; Combination Aquarium and IMAX showing $22/17/12. Combination tickets available with Audubon Zoo, as well as bus transportation on Audubon Express.)* From a dock near the aquarium, the steamboat **Natchez** breezes down the Mississippi on 2hr. cruises with live jazz and narration on riverside sights. (☎ 586-8777 or 800-233-2628. Departs M-Su 2pm, F-Su also at 11:00am. Morning and afternoon cruises $20, with lunch $30. Evening cruises $33.50, with live jazz band and buffet dinner $56.50. AmEx/D/MC/V.) The **John James Audubon Zoo Cruise** plies the river between the aquarium and the zoo. (Limited schedule; call for dates and times. $17.50, with zoo entry $26.50, with aquarium entry $30.25.)

OUTSIDE THE QUARTER

WATERFRONT. For an up-close view of the Mississippi River and a unique New Orleans district, take the free **Canal Street Ferry** to Algiers Point. The Algiers of old was home to many of New Orleans's African-Americans and was the birthplace of several of the city's famous jazz musicians. Once called "The Brooklyn of the South," it is now a quiet, beautiful neighborhood best explored by foot. Stop at the **Dry Dock Cafe,** just off the ferry landing, to pick up a free map of the area. At night, the ferry's outdoor observation deck affords a panoramic view of the city's sights. (Departs daily every 30min. 5:45am-midnight from the end of Canal St. Free for pedestrians. Cars $1. For further information contact the Mississippi Bridge Authority ☎ 376-8100.) The **Riverwalk,** a multimillion-dollar conglomeration of overpriced shops overlooking the port, stretches along the Mississippi. (☎ 522-1555. Open M-Sa 10am-9pm, Su 11am-7pm.) Dispose of your spare change at **Harrah's New Orleans Casino,** at Canal St. and the river, where an endless Mardi Gras of slot machines depressingly suck down endless buckets of quarters. (☎ 800-427-7247. 21+. Open 24hr.)

CEMETERIES. To counter the adverse effects to the city's high water table, New Orleans's cemeteries are crowded with above-ground tombs that range from the plain to the extravagant, keeping the resting at peace. Cemeteries are free and open most weekdays from 9am-4pm. **Lafayette Cemetery #1** is one block south of the Washington Ave. stop on the St. Charles streetcar. The most lavish tombs can be found at the sprawling **Metairie Cemetery** at the northern end of the Canal St. streetcar. Cemeteries can be dangerous; use caution and go with a group. Stay safe by shadowing the many guided tours. Do not go to the cemeteries at night.

WAREHOUSE/ARTS DISTRICT. Relatively new to the downtown area, the **Warehouse/Arts District,** centered roughly at the intersection of Julia and Camp St., contains several revitalized warehouse buildings turned contemporary art galleries and many of the city's museums, and is quickly following other urban trends in transforming into chic lofts for young professionals. The galleries feature free exhibition openings the first Saturday of every month. On **White Linen Night,** the first Saturday in August, thousands attend the galleries in their fanciest white finery. (Arts District info: www.neworleansartsdistrictassociation.com.) In an old brick building with a modern glass-and-chrome facade, the **Contemporary Arts Center** mounts exhibits ranging from puzzling to cryptic. (900 Camp St. ☎ 528-3805; www.cacno.org. Open Th-Su 11am-4pm. Galleries rotate frequently; call ahead for details. Internet access free with any purchase in the cafe. Exhibits $5, students and seniors $3, under 12 free.) In the rear studio of the **New Orleans School of Glassworks and Printmaking Studio,** observe students and instructors transform blobs of molten glass into vases and sculptures. (727 Magazine St. ☎ 529-7277. Open in summer M-F 10:30am-5pm; in winter M-Sa 10am-6pm. Glassblowing usually runs from Sept.-May. Free.) The **Jonathan Ferrara Gallery** hosts local artists and the annual "No Dead Artists: A Juried Exhibition of New Orleans Art Today" every April. Ferrara was nationally recognized for his involvement in "Guns in the Hands of Artists," a 1996 program in which people turned in guns to be made into works of art. (841 Carondelet St. ☎ 522-5471; www.jonathanferraragallery.com. Open M-Sa 11am-5pm. Free.) The **Zeitgeist Multi-Disciplinary Arts Center** is moving north of the Warehouse District, but will continue to present challenging works to viewers. The center

THE SOUTH

offers films, theatrical and musical performances, and art exhibitions. Alternative, experimental, and provocative, the center's mission is, "Something for and against everyone!" *(2940 Canal St.* ☎ *827-5858; www.zeitgeistinc.net. Open Tu-Sa 10:30am-5pm.)* A few blocks west on St. Charles Ave., in **Lee Circle,** a bronze statue of Gen. Robert E. Lee faces north, continuing to stare down the Yankees.

▣ **SAINT CHARLES STREETCAR.** Much of the Crescent City's fame derives from the **Vieux Carré,** but areas uptown have their fair share of beauty and action. The famed **Saint Charles Streetcar** was put on hold in the aftermath of Katrina, but the lines of the streetcar extend with each month and the full line is expected to be operational by late fall of 2007. The streetcar runs west of the French Quarter, passing some of the city's finest buildings, including the 19th-century homes along **Saint Charles Avenue.** *Gone With the Wind* fans will recognize the whitewashed bricks and elegant doorway of the house on the far right corner of Arabella St.—it's a replica of Tara. But frankly, my dear, it's not open to the public. For more views of fancy living, get off the streetcar in the **Garden District,** an opulent neighborhood around Jackson and Louisiana Ave. Homes that harken back to plantation days loom over lush gardens, fertilized by soil enriched by a levee break much earlier in the 20th century. For a great introduction to these neighborhoods, buy a $5 streetcar day-pass from any streetcar driver and hop on and off the St. Charles line as much as you want.

CITY PARK. Brimming with golf courses, ponds, statues, Greek Revival gazebos, softball fields, a stadium, and **Storyland** (a theme park for kids), City Park is a huge green wonderland of non-alcoholic activities. An antique carousel and fishing from paddle boats in the 11 mi. of lagoons make Storyland the kind of kids' entertainment parents love. Though the majority of the plant life at the **New Orleans Botanical Gardens** died in the aftermath of Katrina, the Gardens maintained their structures and reopened in March of 2006 with the help of generous donations. *(1 Palm Dr., at the northern end of Esplanade Ave. www.neworleanscitypark.com. Storyland open weekends 10am-5pm. $3. Gardens open Tu-Su 10am-4:30pm. Maps at Jackson Sq. Visitors Center. $5, children 5-12 $2, under 5 free.)*

HISTORIC HOMES AND PLANTATIONS

Across from downtown New Orleans, **River Road** curves along the Mississippi River and accesses several preserved 19th-century plantations. *Great River Road Plantation Parade: A River of Riches*, available at the New Orleans or Baton Rouge Visitors Centers, contains a good map and descriptions of the houses. Choose carefully, since a tour of all the privately owned plantations is expensive, and some are a 45-60min. drive from downtown New Orleans.

LAURA: A CREOLE PLANTATION. ▣**Laura,** unlike the others on the riverbank, was owned and operated by slave-owning Creoles who lived a different life from that of white antebellum planters. A 45min. drive from downtown New Orleans, Laura is also the only plantation near New Orleans that has preserved slave quarters. Br'er Rabbit hopped into his first briar patch here, the site of the first recorded "Compair Lapin" West African stories. Laura presents a valuable and unique look at Southern plantation life, and the dedicated and knowledgeable staff give engaging and animated tours that give creed to the humor and life-force of Creole culture. In celebration of Creole heritage, tours in French are available by appointment. Though the plantation was undamaged by Hurricane Katrina, the sudden decrease in tourism has forced it to offer fewer tours. Call ahead or check the website for regular updates. *(2247 Hwy. 18/River Rd., at the intersection of Rte. 20 in Vacherie. Take Exit 194 off I-10, then take Rte. 641 S and follow signs.* ☎ *225-265-7690 or 888-799-7690. 1hr. tours based on the "memories" of the old plantation home daily 9:30am-4pm. Max. 20min. wait. $10, ages 6-17 $5. AAA discount $1. Cash only.)*

LONGUE VUE HOUSE AND GARDENS. Called the "Great Showplace of New Orleans," **Longue Vue** epitomizes grand Southern estate living with lavish furnishings, opulent decor, and sculpted gardens inspired by the Spanish Alhambra. A 10min. drive from downtown New Orleans, this plantation is much closer to the city than similar estates. (*7 Bamboo Rd., off Metairie Rd. ☎ 488-5488. 35min. guided tours depart every hr. M-Sa 10am-4:30pm, Su 1-5pm. Self-guided tours available in 6 languages. $10, seniors $9, students $5, under 5 free. AAA/AARP discount $1.*)

NOTTOWAY PLANTATION. The largest plantation home in the South, **Nottoway** is often called the "White Castle of Louisiana." A 64-room mansion with 22 columns, a large ballroom, and a three-story stairway, it was the first choice for the filming of *Gone with the Wind*, but the owners wouldn't allow it. (*30970 Hwy. Rte. 405., between Bayou Goula and White Castle, 18 mi. south of Baton Rouge on the southern bank of the Mississippi. 1hr. from New Orleans. ☎ 225-545-2730 or 888-323-8314. Open daily 9am-5pm. Lunch served daily 11am-3pm. Admission and 1hr. tour $10, under 12 $4, under 5 free.*)

OAK ALLEY PLANTATION. The name **Oak Alley** refers to the magnificent lawn-alley bordered by 28 oaks that correspond to the 28 columns surrounding the bright pink Greek Revival house. Peering through the wrought-iron gates past the lines of oak trees, you get a good impression of the grandeur of the home and its estate. (*3645 Rte. 18., between St. James and Vacherie St. 5min. west of Laura plantation, 50min. from downtown New Orleans. ☎ 800-442-5539. Tours daily every 30min. Mar.-Oct. 9am-5:30pm; Nov.-Feb. 9am-5pm. $10, ages 13-18 $5, ages 6-12 $3.*)

HISTORIC HOMES DOWNTOWN. Located in the French Quarter and built in 1831, **Hermann-Grima Historic House** exemplifies urban elegance with guillotine windows, a fan-lit entrance, and parterre beds. On Thursdays from October to May, volunteers demonstrate period cooking in an 1830s Creole kitchen. (*820 St. Louis St. ☎ 525-5661. Open M-F 10am-4pm. Tours every hr. in the morning, every 30min. in the afternoon. Last tour 3pm. $6, seniors and ages 8-18 $5.*) Nearby, the **Gallier House Museum** is another example of antebellum architecture. James Gallier, Jr., the city's most famous architect, lived here in the 1860s. (*1118-1132 Royal St. ☎ 525-5661. Open M-Sa 10am-4pm. Last tour 3pm. $6; students, seniors, and ages 8-18 $5; under 8 free. Combination tickets for both houses may be purchased at either location for $10/9.*)

🏛 MUSEUMS

▨ **NATIONAL WORLD WAR II MUSEUM.** The WWII Museum, or D-Day Museum as it is also known, was founded by historian Stephen Ambrose and dedicated in 2000 by Tom Hanks and Steven Spielberg. The museum is a sobering study of heroism and horror that confronts visitors with the lesser-known, gruesome Pacific battles and issues of race and propaganda. The museum is truly remarkable for its unbiased scrutiny of the way, but the sometimes graphic exhibits fill the walls with such intensity that the museum might be a bit mature for children. Allow at least 2hr. to experience the magnitude of the exhibits, or feel free to reenter the museum throughout the day with an admission sticker. (*945 Magazine St., at Andrew Higgins Dr. in the Historic Warehouse District. ☎ 527-6012. Open daily 9am-5pm. $14; students, seniors, and military $8; under 12 $6; military in uniform and under 5 free. AAA discount $2.*)

▨ **NEW ORLEANS PHARMACY MUSEUM.** This enthralling look into medical history is housed in an apothecary shop built by America's first licensed pharmacist in 1823. Among the exhibits are 19th-century "miracle drugs" like cocaine and opium, voodoo powders, a collection of old spectacles, and live leeches. (*514 Chartres St., between St. Louis and Toulouse St. ☎ 565-8027; www.pharmacymuseum.org. Open Tu and Th 10am-2pm, W and F-Sa 10am-5pm. $5, seniors and students $4, under 6 free.*)

THE SOUTH

NEW ORLEANS MUSEUM OF ART (NOMA). This museum houses art from North and South America, a magnificent glass collection, opulent works by the jeweler Fabergé, a strong collection of French paintings, and impressive African and Japanese cultural collections. The inspiring new sculpture garden sprawls over acres of walkways. *(In City Park, at the City Park/Metairie Exit off I-10. ☎ 488-2631; www.noma.org. Open W-Su 10am-4:30pm. $8, seniors $7, ages 3-17 $4. Call for tickets to special exhibits.)*

LOUISIANA STATE MUSEUM. The "State Museum" really encompasses eight separate museums, six of which are in New Orleans. *(All museums ☎ 800-568-6968; http://lsm.crt.state.la.us.)* The **Cabildo** presents the history of Louisiana and houses Napoleon's death mask. *(701 Chartres St.)* The **Arsenal** recounts the history of the Mississippi River and New Orleans as a port city. *(615 St. Peter, enter through the Cabildo.)* The **Presbytère** features an interactive exhibit about Mardi Gras. *(751 Chartres St.)* The **1850 House** is—you guessed it—a recreated house from the 1850s. *(523 St. Ann St., on Jackson Sq.)* **Madame John's Legacy** showcases Creole architecture as well as contemporary self-taught Louisiana artists. *(632 Dumaine St.)* The **Old US Mint** focuses not only on currency, but on the history of jazz in an exhibit that includes Satchmo's first horn. *(400 Esplanade. All museums open Tu-Su 9am-5pm. Old US Mint, Cabildo, Presbytère: $5; students, seniors, and active military $4. 1850 House, Mme. John's Legacy: $3/2. Under 12 free at all museums. 20% discount on tickets to 2 or more museums.)* Note: The 1850 House, Madame John's Legacy, and the Old US mint were all closed as of July 2007 due to requisite Katrina renovations.

THE VOODOO MUSEUM. Learn why dusty shops in the Quarter sell *gris-gris* and alligator parts. A priest or a priestess will do a reading for $30, or visitors can just walk through the rooms full of artifacts for the entrance fee. *(724 Dumaine St., in the Quarter. ☎ 680-0128. Open daily 10am-6pm. $7; students, seniors, and military $5.50; high school students $4.50; ages 5-12 $3.50, under 5 free.)*

MUSÉE CONTI WAX MUSEUM. Thirty-one tableaux of wax figures make for a great mix of the historically important, sensationally infamous, and just plain kitschy history of New Orleans. *(917 Conti St., between Burgundy and Dauphine St. ☎ 525-2605 or 800-233-5405. Open M-Sa 10am-5:30pm. $7, seniors $6.25, under 17 $6.)*

🎵 ENTERTAINMENT

THEATER AND MUSIC

Le Petit Théâtre du Vieux Carré, 616 St. Peter St., is the oldest continuously operating community theater in the US. The 1789 building replicates the early 18th-century abode of Joseph de Pontalba, Louisiana's last Spanish governor. About five musicals and plays go up each year, as well as three fun productions in the "Children's Corner." *(☎ 522-9958; www.lepetittheatre.com. Box office open Tu-Sa 10:30am-5:30pm, Su noon-showtime. Plays $23; musicals $28, with student ID $25. Shows F-Su 8pm; weekly matinee Su 2pm.)* Born at the turn of the century in **Armstrong Park,** traditional New Orleans jazz still wails nightly at the tiny, historic **Preservation Hall,** 726 St. Peter St. With only two small ceiling fans trying to move the air around, the joint heats up in more ways than one. *(Daytime ☎ 522-2841 or 800-785-5772, after 8pm 523-8939; www.preservationhall.com. No food or drink allowed. Cover $5. Doors open at 8pm; music 8:15pm-midnight.)* Keep your ears open for **Cajun** and **zydeco** bands, which use accordions, washboards, triangles, and drums to perform hot dance tunes and saccharine waltzes. Anyone who thinks couple-dancing went out in the 50s should try a *fais-do-do,* a traditional dance that got its name from the custom parents had of putting their children to sleep before dancing the night away. *(Fais-do-do* is Cajun baby talk for "to make sleep.")* **Uptown** tends to play host to Cajun dance halls and popular university hangouts, while the **Marigny** is home to New Orleans's alternative/local music scene and is becoming an increasingly hip neighborhood for locals and visitors alike. Check out *Off Beat*, free in many local restaurants; *Where Y'At*, another free entertainment weekly; or the Friday *Times-Picayune* to find out who's playing where.

FESTIVALS

New Orleans's **Mardi Gras** celebration is the biggest party of the year, a world-renowned, epic bout of lascivious debauchery that fills the three weeks leading up to Ash Wednesday—the beginning of Lent and a time of penance and deprivation in the Catholic tradition. Mardi Gras, which literally means "Fat Tuesday," is an all-out hedonistic pleasure-fest before 40 days of purity—and tourists pour in by the plane-full (flights into the city and hotel rooms fill up months in advance). In 2008, Mardi Gras falls on February 5th, and though this will be the earliest Mardi Gras of the decade, the writhing crowds are sure to keep the heat on high at Bourbon St. For those looking to experience the festival as true New Orleanians do, the biggest parades and the bulk of the partying will take place the two weeks prior to that. In fact, most locals venture to the Uptown bars and the neighborhoods just outside the Quarter, such as the Marigny, for the festival and to avoid the Quarter's debauchery—though the party is inescapable wherever you might be in the Crescent City. The ever-expanding **New Orleans Jazz and Heritage Festival** attracts 7000 musicians from around the country to the city's fairgrounds. The likes of Aretha Franklin, Bob Dylan, and New Orleans native Wynton Marsalis have graced this festival. Music plays simultaneously on 12 stages in the midst of a food and crafts festival; the biggest names perform at evening riverboat concerts. (☎522-4786; www.nojazzfest.com. Last weekend in Apr.-1st weekend in May.)

SPORTS

The NFL's **Saints** play at the **Louisiana Superdome.** (Sugar Bowl Dr., off I-10. ☎587-3663. Tickets at www.ticketmaster.com.) Catch the NBA's **Hornets** shoot hoops at the **New Orleans Arena.** (1501 Girod St. ☎587-3663, tickets ☎525-4667; www.ticketmaster.com.) The **New Orleans Zephyrs,** a AAA affiliate of Major League Baseball's Washington Nationals, play home games from April to August at **Zephyr Field,** on Airline Dr., west of Transcontinental Dr. (☎734-5155; www.zephyrsbaseball.com. Tickets $6-10, children and seniors $6-9.) The state of Louisiana is big in college athletics, and many of **LSU's Tigers** teams, also known as the Bayou Bengals, have a strong following. (Team info, schedules, and tickets at www.lsusports.net.)

▧ NIGHTLIFE

BARS

FRENCH QUARTER

▧ **Funky Butt,** 714 N. Rampart St. (☎558-0872). An awesome hideout to hear live jazz and marvel at the wonder of the *derrière.* Walk in to face a languorous nude painting and hear the riffs of a live band 5 ft. from the door. New Orleans native Fats Domino's hat hangs above the bar. Stay to sip a funkybuttjuice ($6) and sit with a select group in the tiny space alongside the band. Beer $3-4. House band plays nightly 7:30-9:30pm. Sets most nights 10pm and midnight. Cover $5-10. Open daily 7pm-2am.

▧ **Lafitte's Blacksmith Shop,** 941 Bourbon St. (☎522-9377), at Phillip St. Appropriately, one of New Orleans's oldest standing structures is a bar, one of the oldest bars in the US. Named for the scheming hero of the Battle of New Orleans, it offers shaded relief from the elements of the city and a dimly lit hiding place for celebrities. Beer $4-5. Live piano 8pm-late. Open daily 10 or 11am-4 or 5am.

THE REAL DEAL. For those seeking to engage in the true Mardi Gras spirit all night long, drinks in the French Quarter, especially along Bourbon St., can quickly take their toll on your wallet. The best way to kick off a night in the Quarter is, surprisingly enough, with a trip to the bars **uptown.** Any number of hole-in-the-wall institutions offer bourbon-and-cokes for as little as $1.50, and beers just under that cost. Classics include Miss Mae's (4336 Magazine St. at the corner of Napoleon Ave.), a 24hr. joint. Places like Miss Mae's aren't typical fare for Magazine St.'s traditionally posh crowd, but this is a regular stop for uptown college students. An $8 cab ride here will be cheaper than the first round of drinks in the Quarter. —*Stephen Travierso*

Pat O'Brien's, 718 St. Peter St. (☎525-4823 or 800-597-4823). Housed in the 1st Spanish theater in the US, Pat O'Brien's is one of the most famous bars in the French Quarter, bursting with rosy-cheeked patrons who carouse in the courtyard. The piano bar is packed at night, but stalk around long enough and you're sure to grab a seat. If you're feeling sentimental, purchase your first drink in a souvenir glass ($9, without glass $6.50). Open M-Th 11am-4am, F-Su 10am-5am.

Donna's, 800 N. Rampart St. (☎596-6914), at St. Ann. As one fan says, this is "the place where you can sit and watch New Orleans roll by." On the edge of the Quarter, with good barbecue, music, and a relaxed air. Open M, W, and F-Su 8:30pm-1:30am.

Fritzel's, 733 Bourbon St. (☎561-0432), between Orleans and St. Ann. Opened over 30 years ago by a German proprietor who wanted to give musicians of all abilities the chance to play. It hosts some of the best traditional and Dixie band jazz in the Quarter every night. Although drinks are pricey (most beers $5-6), there's no cover. Entertainment begins at 8 or 9pm. Open daily 1pm-2am.

Pirate's Alley, 622 Pirate's Alley (☎524-9332), down the alley on the left when facing the St. Louis Cathedral. Its location on a side street, compounded by the plain wooden walls and awnings, make this bar feel like a safe haven in what can be a sensory-overload city. Beer $3-8. Open daily noon-close.

OUTSIDE THE QUARTER

The Spotted Cat, 623 Frenchmen St. (☎943-3887). Offers what you might have imagined most New Orleans bars would have: cheap beer ($2-4), a place to sit and chill, and passion-filled trumpets, voices, and piano solos. The wooden walls and floors make for excellent acoustics. Early band 6:30pm, late band 10pm. Domestic beers $2 during Happy hour. Live music until 2am. 1-drink min. Open M-F 2pm to 2 or 3am, Sa-Su noon-4 or 5am.

d.b.a., 618 Frenchmen St. (☎942-3731), next to Snug Harbor. Popular, wood-paneled bar with free Wi-Fi and a wide selection of beers on tap ($3-7). A twentysomething kind of place. Live music most nights at 10pm. No cover; 1-drink min. Open daily 1pm-4am.

Snug Harbor, 626 Frenchmen St. (☎949-0696), near Decatur St. Regulars include big names in jazz like Charmaine Neville and Ellis Marsalis. Cover is sometimes steep ($10-25), but the music, played in the intimate cypress "jazz room," is incredible. Shows nightly 8 and 10pm. All ages. Restaurant open M-Th and Su 5-11pm, F-Sa 5pm-midnight; bar until 1am. The kitchen closes early some nights; call ahead to find out if they are serving. Advance ticket purchase recommended, especially for weekend events.

Igor's Checkpoint Charlie, 501 Esplanade (☎281-4847), is a combination bar, laundromat, and restaurant that feels like a cozy neighborhood coffeeshop or a wild nightclub, depending on where you're standing. You can drink while you wash your clothes ($1.50 per load), listen to a poetry slam over jazz, buy a used book, or have a greasy burger while shooting a game of pool. Beer $3-4, pitchers $7.50. Burgers $5-7. Live music nightly, usually starting around 8pm. Open 24hr.

DANCE CLUBS

■ **Tipitina's,** 501 Napoleon Ave. (☎895-8477; www.tipitinas.com) in uptown. The best local bands and some big national names—like the Neville Brothers and Harry Connick, Jr.—play so close you can almost touch them. Beer $2-5. Cajun *fais-do-dos* (p. 412) Su 5-9pm. 18+. Cover $7-10, higher for national acts. Music usually W-Su 9pm-3am; buy tickets online, or call for times and prices. Box office open M-F 10am-2pm. Also at 233 N. Peters St., in the French Quarter.

House of Blues, 225 Decatur St. (☎301-49999; www.hob.com), in the French Quarter. A sprawling complex with a large music/dance hall (capacity over 1000) and a balcony and bar overlooking the action. Call ahead to inquire if the legendary Su gospel brunch has returned. Concerts nightly 9:15pm. 18+. Tickets $12-50. Restaurant open M-Th and Su 11am-10pm, F-Sa 11am-11pm.

Mid City Lanes Rock 'n' Bowl, 4133 S. Carrollton Ave. (☎482-3133, www.rockand-bowl.com), in the mini-mall at Tulane Ave. Since 1941, this place has attracted multi-tasking partiers to its rockin' lanes. The "home of Rock 'n' Bowl" is a bowling alley by day and dance club by night (you can bowl at night, too). Drinks $2-3.50. Lanes $18 per hr., shoes $1. Live music Tu-W 8:30pm, F-Sa 10pm; local zydeco Th 9:30pm. 18+ when the bar gets hopping at night. Cover $5-10. Open daily noon-1 or 2am.

◧ GLBT ACTIVITIES

New Orleans has a long history of sexual diversity, touching on all strands of society, but it never really met with public approval. In spite of the private clubs and mixed bars that have existed for hundreds of years, only today does the city have an open and vibrant gay scene. It is an anomaly to the city's regional counterparts, and still a singularity in comparison to other American urban gay communities because of its laid-back setting and free flow into the surrounding straight community. Many straight people visit gay venues because the drinks are cheaper and stronger. Someone is also keeping track of gay history in New Orleans: Robert Batson, "history laureate," leads the ◧**Gay Heritage Tour**—a walking tour through the French Quarter—leaving from Alternatives, 909 Bourbon St. It lasts 2½hr. and is perhaps the best possible introduction to New Orleans for anyone, gay or straight. (☎945-6789. W 4pm and Sa 1pm. $20 per person. Reservations required.)

You'll find the majority of gay establishments toward the northeast end of Bourbon St. ("downriver"), and along St. Ann St., known to some as the **"Lavender Line."** If the proud presence of rainbow flags and the 24hr. loop of techno music aren't strong enough signals of crossing the line, a good point of reference is where St. Ann and Bourbon St. cross—**Oz** is to the river side and **Bourbon Pub** is to the lake side. These are the city's two biggest gay dance clubs and principal gay institutions. To find the real lowdown of gay nightlife, get a copy of *The Whiz Magazine*, a local guide; there's always a copy on top of the radiator in Cafe Lafitte in Exile. *Ambush* is a mass-produced gay entertainment mag that can be found at many French Quarter businesses. **Faubourg-Marigny Art and Books,** 600 Frenchmen St., on the corner of Frenchmen St. and Chartres St. in Marigny, has books, photos, and art on GLBT New Orleans. (☎947-3700. Open daily noon-7pm.)

The gay community recongregates in the Quarter past the Lavender Line every Labor Day weekend in the summer for **Southern Decadence** (www.southerndecadence.net), perhaps the only true rival to the everlasting party that is Mardi Gras. For information, tailored entertainment and community fact sheets, go to the **Lesbian and Gay Community Center of New Orleans,** 2114 Decatur St., in Marigny. (☎945-1103; www.gayneworleans.com. Open M-F 2-8pm, Sa 11am-6pm. Report hate crimes to ☎943-4325.)

THE SOUTH

GLBT NIGHTLIFE

Cafe Lafitte in Exile, 901 Bourbon St. (☎522-8397; www.lafittes.com). Exiled from Lafitte's Blacksmith Shop in 1953 when Lafitte's came under new management, the ousted gay patrons trooped up the street, founding America's oldest gay bar. On the opening night, surrounded by patrons dressed as their favorite exile, Cafe Lafitte in Exile lit an "eternal flame" (it still burns today) that aptly represents the soul of the New Orleans gay community. Today, though Cafe Lafitte has video screens, occasional live music, pageants, and shows, it's still the same old neighborhood gathering place at heart. The weekday crowd is slightly older, but when the weekend Lavender Line is hopping, this place is packed with people of all ages. Open M-Tu 1pm-5am, W-Su 24hr.

Good Friends, 740 Dauphine St. (☎566-7191; www.goodfriendsbar.com). Could be a gay "Cheers" episode. A cozy, friendly neighborhood bar full of locals happy to welcome in a refugee from Bourbon St. Despite the occasional pool tournament, drink specials, and "hot buns" contest, things are usually pretty calm. Don't miss Su afternoon sing-alongs. Open M-Th and Su 1pm-2am, F-Sa 1pm-3am.

Cowpokes, 2240 St. Claude Ave. (☎947-0505), 1 block off Elysian Fields in Marigny. Line dancing, W lube wrestling, 10-gallon hats, and spurs can be as wholesome as you want to make them. This self-styled neighborhood bar welcomes cowgirls and pardners. Tu free line dancing lessons 8pm. Happy hour 4-9pm. Open M-Th and Su 4pm-1am, F-Sa 4pm-2am. Cowpokes also has a great **theater** that puts up 4 productions per year (for info ☎947-0505; www.dramano.org). Take a cab here; area can be unsafe at night.

◪ OUTDOOR ACTIVITIES

The St. Charles streetcar eventually makes its way to **Audubon Park,** near **Tulane University.** Audubon contains lagoons, statues, stables, and the award-winning ◪**Audubon Zoo,** 6500 Magazine St., where white alligators swim in a recreated Louisiana swamp. Elephants, rhinos, sea lions, and tigers, among others, are grouped into exhibit areas that highlight historical and natural regions of the globe, while peacocks roam the walkways freely. A free museum shuttle runs between the streetcar stop and zoo entrance every 15min. (☎581-4629. Zoo open in summer M-F 9:30am-5pm, Sa-Su 9:30am-6pm. $12, seniors $9, ages 2-12 $7. Combination zoo/aquarium/IMAX tickets $28/24/18. AAA discount.)

One of the most unique sights in the New Orleans area, the coastal wetlands along Lake Salvador make up a segment of the **Jean Lafitte National Historical Park** called the ◪**Barataria Preserve,** 7400 Barataria Blvd., south of New Orleans; take Business 90 to Rte. 45 southbound, turn left onto Lafitte Pkwy. and follow signs to the preserve. (☎589-2330. Daily park-sponsored walking tour through the swamp 11am. Ranger-led canoe trips Mar.-May Sa 9:30am. Free maps and trail guides for ¼-2 mi. walks. Open daily 9am-5pm; closed Dec. 25 and Mardi Gras, extended summer hours. **Visitors Center** in French Quarter open daily 9am-5pm. Free.) Many commercial boat tours operate in the park. Tours typically travel by airboat and involve feeding alligators. Prices vary and many have discounts in the *Sizzlin' Summer* coupon book available at the New Orleans Visitor Center next to Jackson Park. Ask how many people fit into each tour boat; boats vary from small airboats to large pontoon cruisers. **Cypress Swamp Tours** will pick you up from your hotel. (☎581-4501 or 800-633-0503. 2hr. tours 9:30, 11:30am, 1:30pm. $22, with hotel pickup $39; ages 6-12 $12/22. Call for reservations.)

BATON ROUGE ☎225

Once the site of a tall cypress tree marking the boundary between rival Native American tribes, Baton Rouge ("red stick") has grown into Louisiana's 2nd-largest city. Though the city's meat-and-potatoes flavor contrasts with the sauciness of New Orleans, fiery state politics have shaped this town—it was once home to governor, senator, and demagogue Huey "Kingfish" Long—and Louisiana State University (LSU) adds an element of youthful vigor and rabid Tigertown loyalty.

🔲🔁 TRANSPORTATION AND PRACTICAL INFORMATION. Close to downtown, Greyhound, 1253 Florida Blvd. (☎383-3811 or 800-231-2222; www.greyhound.com; open 24hr.), at 12th St., sends **buses** to Lafayette (1hr., 8 per day, $15) and New Orleans (2hr., 6 per day, $17). Use caution in this area at night. Capitol Transportation (☎389-8282) runs **buses** through downtown every 30min. 7:15am-7:30pm. ($1.25, seniors and children $0.90.) For a **taxi,** call ABC Transit, ☎355-3133.

From east to west, the three main streets in Baton Rouge are **N. Foster Drive, N. Acadian Throughway,** and **22nd Street.** Beginning in the north, Florida Blvd. and Government St. run perpendicular to these. Public transportation is useful for getting around downtown, but driving is the best way to see other areas of the city. **Visitor Info:** The **State Capitol Visitors Center,** on the 1st floor of the state capitol, has maps and brochures. (☎342-7317. Open daily 8am-4:30pm.) **Internet Access: State Library of Louisiana,** 701 N. 4th St., is a beautiful library with free Internet access. (☎342-4915. Open M-F 8am-5pm.) On weekends, access is available at **East Baton Rouge Parish Library,** 7711 Goodwood Blvd. (☎231-3740. Free. Open M-Th 8am-10pm, F-Sa 8am-6pm, Su 2-10pm.) **Post Office:** 750 Florida St., off River Rd. (☎381-0325. Open M-F 7:30am-5pm, Sa 8am-12:30pm.) **Postal Code:** 70821.

🔳 ACCOMMODATIONS. Downtown rooms are pricey, especially during midweek when state capitol business is underway. The university area is home to several motels, but you don't get what you don't pay for: some of these less expensive options are less than reliable for quality and service. A good idea for budget travelers is to drop a few extra dollars to stay at one of the many mid-priced options. The **Highland Inn ❸,** 2605 S. Range Ave., at Exit 10 off I-12 in Denham Springs, is 15min. from downtown. (☎667-7177. Cable TV, continental breakfast, free local calls, and pool. Singles $59; doubles $69. AmEx/D/MC/V.) **KOA Kampground ❶,** 7628 Vincent Rd., 1 mi. off I-12 at the Denham Springs Exit, keeps 110 great sites, clean facilities, hot showers, and a pool. (☎664-7281 or 800-562-5673. Sites with full RV hookup from $35. Cabins from $43. MC/V.)

🔳🔲 FOOD AND NIGHTLIFE. Downtown, sandwich shops and cafes line 3rd St.; the **casinos** boast some of the city's best cuisine. For simple, small-town fare, check out the **Frostop ❶,** 402 Government St., downtown, with a giant, gracefully aging root beer can out front. Burgers with "freedom fries" and a drink go for $5.50, but po' boy sandwiches ($4.50-6) and seafood platters ($8-10) are also popular. (☎344-1179. Floats and shakes $2-4. Open M-F 10am-7pm, Sa noon-7pm.) Head to LSU at the intersection of Highland Rd. and Chimes St., off I-10, for cheap chow, bars, and smoothie shops. At **The Chimes ❸,** 3357 Highland Rd., at Chimes St., you can sample a beer from almost every country; Chimes stocks 120 brews with 30 on tap. Start with Louisiana alligator (fried or blackened, with Dijon mustard sauce) for $8, then dig into some crawfish *étouffée* for $9. (☎383-1754. Entrees $10-15. Open M-Sa 11am-2am, Su 11am-11:45pm. AmEx/D/MC/V.) Next door is the **Varsity Theatre,** 5535 Highland Rd., which has hosted big names like Tori Amos and They Might Be Giants. (☎383-7018. Beer $2.50-4. Cover $10-45, depending on band. Usually open 8pm-2am; hours vary.) Thirsty LSU students flock to **Tigertown,** a collection of nearly identical bars along Bob Pettit Blvd. west of Nicholson Drive, for live music and drinks. For nightlife listings, pick up a copy of *Reveille,* LSU's free bi-weekly paper (published daily during school time), at Louie's cafe.

THE SOUTH

◙ **SIGHTS.** In a move reminiscent of Ramses II, Huey Long ordered the construction of the ◙**Louisiana State Capitol,** referred to as "the new capitol"—a somewhat startling skyscraper completed over a mere 14 months in 1931 and 1932. "The house that Huey built" was meant to raise Louisiana's prestige and pave Long's path to the presidency. Ironically, Long was assassinated inside it three years later; a display marks the spot of the shooting. The **observation deck,** on the 27th floor, provides a panoramic view of the surrounding area. (☎342-5914. Open daily 8:30am-4:00pm. Free.) The **Old State Capitol,** 100 North Blvd., resembles a cathedral with a fantastic cast-iron spiral staircase and domed stained glass. Inside, interactive political displays urge voter responsibility alongside exhibits about the "Kingfish" and Louisiana's tumultuous (and often corrupt) political history. (☎800-488-2968. Open Tu-Sa 10am-4pm, Su noon-4pm. $4, seniors $3, students $2.) The **Old Governor's Mansion,** 502 North Blvd., may look familiar—Huey Long insisted that his governor's residence resemble his dream dwelling, the White House. Inside, peruse many of Long's personal belongings, including a book he wrote, somewhat prematurely, called *My First Days in the White House.* (☎387-2464. Open M-F 10am-4pm; hours may vary. Last tour 3pm. $6, seniors $5, K-12 students $4.) The **Louisiana Art and Science Museum (LASM),** 100 S. River Rd., is a strange combination of art gallery and hands-on science museum that recently opened a state-of-the-art planetarium. (☎344-5272; www.lasm.org. Open Tu-F 10am-4pm, Sa 10am-5pm, Su 1-5pm. Planetarium open until 8pm on Sa. Galleries and planetarium $8; students, seniors, and children $7. 1st Su of every month galleries free and planetarium discounted.) At the **USS Kidd and Nautical Center,** 305 S. River Rd., at Government St., you can check out the destroyer *Kidd,* which was hit directly by a kamikaze during its career and has been restored to its WWII glory. (☎342-1942. Open daily 9am-5pm. Museum and restored *Kidd* $8, seniors $6; restored *Kidd* exhibit only $7/6; ages 6-12 $4, under 5 free.) The **LSU Rural Life Museum,** 4560 Essen Ln., just off I-10 at Exit 160, depicts the life of 19th-century Creoles and working-class Louisianans through their original furnished shops, cabins, and storage houses. Next door, explore the lakes, paths, and flowers of the **Windrush Gardens.** The semi-formal gardens contain native plants used during the time period. (☎765-2437. Both open daily 8:30am-5pm. Joint admission $7, seniors $6, ages 5-11 $4, under 5 free.)

NATCHITOCHES ☎318

Don't say it how it's spelled. Pronounced "NAK-ah-tish," the oldest city in Louisiana was founded in 1714 by the French as an outpost to guard against the Spanish. The town was named after the original Native American inhabitants of the region. With its strategic location along the banks of the Red River, Natchitoches should have become a major port city; a big logjam, however, changed the course of the city's history, redirecting the river and leaving the town high and dry, with only a 36 mi.-long lake running along historic downtown. Today, it makes for a romantic setting as you stroll along the manicured lakefront park.

◙◙ **TRANSPORTATION AND PRACTICAL INFORMATION.** Greyhound, 5123 University Pkwy. (☎357-7983; www.greyhound.com; open daily 9am-9pm), sends **buses** to Dallas (4¾-6hr., 2 per day, $62); Houston (13¾hr., 1 per day, $68.50); and New Orleans (6½hr., 2 per day, $58).

Downtown Natchitoches is tiny. **Highway 6** enters town from the west off I-49 and becomes **Jefferson Street** which, in turn, transforms into the cobbled road that is **Front Street,** the main drag, where it follows the **Cane River,** running north until it becomes Hwy. 6 again. **Second Street** runs parallel to Front St., and the town stems across the lake from those two streets. Historic homes populate downtown, while plantations lie 7 to 18 mi. south, off **Route 1 S.** The plantations and Rte. 1 follow the Cane River. Maps and accommodations info are at the **Natchitoches Convention and Visitors Bureau,** 781 Front St. (☎352-8072 or 800-259-1714; www.natchitoches.net. Open daily 9am-5pm.) **Internet Access: Natchitoches Public Library,** 450 2nd St. (☎357-3280. Free. Open M-F 9am-6pm, Sa 9am-5pm.) **Post Office:** 250 St. Denis St. (☎352-0378. Open M-F 8am-4:30pm, Sa 9-11am.) **Postal Code:** 71457.

⌂ ACCOMMODATIONS. Natchitoches isn't a cheap town. As the "B&B Capital" of Louisiana, the city abounds with cozy rooms in historic homes, but during the annual **Christmas Festival of Lights** (p. 420), held the 1st weekend in December, room rates can triple, and reservations are needed months in advance. For those seeking a quiet, romantic Southern getaway, this lakeside town provides a pleasant escape. Get an authentic taste of Natchitoches at the elegant and reasonably priced ◪**Chaplin House Bed and Breakfast ❸,** 434 2nd St. The well-traveled proprietors of this exquisitely restored and decorated 1892 home boast a wealth of local knowledge. The house has recently undergone further renovation, and is a welcoming and private accommodation for travelers seeking peace and quiet. (☎471-9505. Full continental breakfast, including fresh home-baked bread included. Singles $75; doubles $100. MC/V.) One of the best deals is the **Fleur de Lis Bed and Breakfast ❹,** 336 2nd St., near the southern end of town, an adorable, gingerbready Victorian with a whimsical pastel exterior and quirky flavor all its own. (☎352-6621 or 800-489-6621. Rooms $65-80; higher during Festival of Lights. AmEx/MC/V.) Farther out, the 600,000-acre **Kisatchie National Forest** offers basic camping with trails and scenic overlooks. The park is about 25 mi. south of the Rte. 6 Ranger Station near Natchitoches. Many of its sites, though equipped with bathhouses, are primitive. The **Kisatchie Ranger District ❶,** 106 Rte. 6 W., has maps and park conditions, and provides help finding the well-hidden, primitive sites. (☎473-7160. Office open M-F 7am-4pm. No bathrooms. Sites $2-3.)

◧◪ FOOD AND NIGHTLIFE. ◪**Lasyone's ❷,** 622 2nd St., is the place to go for down-home cooking. Their specialty is meat pie ($3), and travelers can get an eyeful of the 5 ft. meat pie model in the window before enjoying one of more manageable meals. (☎352-3353. Lunch specials $6. Open M-Sa 7am until usually after 6pm. MC/V.) **Mama's Oyster House ❷,** 606 Front St., is a downtown institution, cooking lunch gumbo for $9 a bowl and oyster po' boys for $7. For dinner, fried crawfish ($12) complements live jazz and rock on the 1st and 3rd Friday of each month. (☎356-7874. Open M-Sa 11am-10pm. MC/V.) Next door to Mama's is, of course, **Papa's Bar and Grille ❶,** 604 Front St., with Natchitoches meat pies for $7 and po' boys and burgers for $6-7. (☎356-5850. Open M-Sa 11am-10pm.) One of the few establishments in Natchitoches open late is the **Pioneer Pub,** 812 Washington St., opposite the Visitors Center. Its neon lighting and musty old-world charm work surprisingly well. Skip the mediocre food and have a beer ($2-3) instead. (☎352-4884. Sa live music 9pm. Open daily 11am-2am, or until the crowd leaves. MC/V.)

◉♫ SIGHTS AND ENTERTAINMENT. Much of Natchitoches' charm lies on the Cane River Lake along **Front Street,** where coffeeshops, casual restaurants, and antique stores fill the storefronts of historical buildings that date back to the mid-19th century. To see Natchitoches' landmarks—including many of the sites where *Steel Magnolias* was filmed—from the comfort of a large, green trolley or a horse-drawn carriage, take a 1hr. ride with the **Natchitoches Transit Company,** 100 Rue Beau Port, next to the Visitors Center. (☎356-8687. Trolley only runs with large groups, around 10 people. Carriages available for smaller groups or individuals. Call for departure times. $12.) Many of the most popular tourist destinations are in the **Cane River National Heritage Area,** the plantation-dotted countryside around

THE SOUTH

Natchitoches. The Visitors Center has information about all the plantations and a free tourist guide, *Cane River Heritage Area*, which lists points of interest. The **Fort St. Jean Baptiste State Historic Site,** 155 Rue Jefferson, provides a glimpse of daily life in Natchitoches's original French outpost, founded in 1714. The 15min. video and full-scale replica of the Fort explain the history of French and Native American settlement in the area. (☎357-3101. Open daily 9am-5pm. $2, under 13 and over 62 free.) To see a zoo's worth of bayou wildlife, drive out to **Alligator Park,** 8 mi. north of Natchitoches off Rte. 1 N (look for the school bus in the shape of a gator off Rte. 1). Originally a conservation project, the park now entertains visitors with regular feeding shows every 30min., a snake house, an aviary, and an exhibit on nutria, swamp rats the size of small dogs. (☎354-0001 or 877-354-7001. Open mid-Apr. to mid-Aug. daily 10am-6pm; mid-Aug. to early Oct. Sa-Su 10am-6pm. Alligators hibernate when it's cold, so plan accordingly. $7, children $5. Seniors and AAA discount 10%.) A string of plantation homes lines the Cane River, south of downtown along Rte. 1. The **Melrose Plantation,** 14 mi. south on Rte. 1, then left on Rte. 493, is unique in origin—its female founder was an ex-slave. The **African House,** one of the outbuildings, is the oldest example of Congo-like architecture in North America. An engaging, but long (1½-2hr.) tour leaves daily at noon. Don't miss the gorgeous 🎨**paintings** by folk artist Clementine Hunter upstairs. (☎379-0055. Open Tu-Su noon-4pm. $7, ages 13-17 $4, ages 6-12 $3.)

While Natchitoches may not see a white Christmas, she'll most definitely see a bright one. The town's residents spend months putting up some 300,000 Christmas bulbs, only to be greeted in turn by 150,000 camera-toting tourists flocking like moths to the **City of Lights** display, held during the **Christmas Festival of Lights.** After a barge parade down the river on Friday, the month-long exhibition peaks the first Saturday in December when a carnival-like atmosphere fills the town. (☎800-259-1714; www.christmasfestival.com.) From April to November, all can enjoy the **Cane River Green Market,** a wonderful farmers' market on the banks of the Cane River downtown. It's big on organic produce, locally grown fruit, and recycling initiatives. (☎352-2746. Open Apr.-Nov. Sa 9am-1pm; June-July also Tu 4-8pm.)

ACADIANA

Throughout the early 18th century, the English government in Nova Scotia became increasingly jealous of the prosperity of French settlers (Acadians) and deeply offended by their refusal to kneel before the British Crown. During the war with France in 1755, the British rounded up the Acadians and deported them by the shipload in what came to be called *le grand dérangement*, or "the Great Upheaval." The "Cajuns" (as they are known today) of St. Martin, Lafayette, New Iberia, and St. Mary parishes are descendants of these settlers. In the 20s, Louisiana passed laws forcing Acadian schools to teach in English. Later, during the oil boom of the 70s and 80s, oil executives and developers envisioned the Acadian center of Lafayette as the Houston of Louisiana and threatened to flood the area with mass culture. The proud people of southern Louisiana have resisted such homogenization and the state is officially bilingual.

LAFAYETTE ☎337

The center of Acadiana, Lafayette is ripe with soul-moving zydeco, the sweet flavor of boiled crawfish, and the splendor of the magnificent Atchafalaya Basin. Get beyond the highway's chains and into downtown on Jefferson St., and there is no question that Cajuns rule the roost. Dance floors heat up every night of the week, and many locals continue to answer their phones with a proud *bonjour*. Though

THE SOUTH

you may simply plan to pass through on your way to one of the better known party destinations, expect to extend your stay once arriving in this friendly and comfortable corner of the Bayou.

ORIENTATION AND PRACTICAL INFORMATION. Amtrak, 133 E. Grant St. (☎800-872-7245; www.amtrak.com), is where the "Sunset" **train** comes three times per week en route to Houston (5½hr., $36); New Orleans (4hr., $21); and San Antonio (11hr., $55). Next door, Greyhound (☎235-1541; www.greyhound.com; open 24hr.) runs **buses** to Baton Rouge (1hr., 6 per day, $13.50) and New Orleans (3-5hr., 5 per day, $21). The Lafayette Bus System, 100 Lee Ave., is centered at Lee and Garfield St. (☎291-8570; schedules at www.lafayettelinc.net. Operates **local buses** approximately every 30min. M-Sa 6:30am-6:30pm; some routes until 11:30pm. $0.75, ages 5-12 $0.50, seniors and disabled $0.35.) For a **taxi**, call Yellow/Checker Cab Inc., ☎234-2111.

Lafayette stands at a crossroads. **I-10** leads east to New Orleans and west to Lake Charles, **U.S. 90** heads south to New Iberia and the Atchafalaya Basin, and **I-49** heads north to Alexandria and Shreveport. Most of the city is west of the **Evangeline Throughway (I-49/U.S. 90),** which runs north-south. **Johnston Boulevard** intersects Evangeline Thwy. and is the main street through town. **Jefferson Street (I-167)** runs north-south through central downtown and is full of fun places to eat and drink. The **Lafayette Parish Convention and Visitors Commission,** is at 1400 N. Evangeline Thwy. (☎232-3808; www.lafayettetravel.com. Open M-F 8:30am-5pm, Sa-Su 9am-5pm.) **Medical Services: Lafayette General Medical Center,** 1214 Coolidge Ave. (☎289-7991). **Internet Access: Lafayette Public Library,** 301 W. Congress St. (☎261-5787. Free. Open M-Th 9am-9pm, F 9am-6pm, Sa 9am-5pm, Su 1-5pm.) **Post Office:** 1105 Moss St. (☎269-7111. Open M-F 8am-4:30pm.) **Postal Code:** 70501.

ACCOMMODATIONS. A comfortable and friendly lodging experience awaits at ◪**Blue Moon Guest House ❶,** 215 E. Convent St., a refreshing signpost of growing American hostelling. As you enter, check out the walkway paved with (fake) doubloons and the local art showcased on the surrounding walls. A large dorm with A/C and comfy private rooms with private baths are accompanied by a spacious common area, a deck, and a "saloon" where bands whoop it up Wednesday through Saturday. Guests get free concert access and a complimentary drink at the bar, as well as Internet access (Wi-Fi available) and use of the kitchen and laundry room. Though the active backyard nightlife might make this a less desirable option for families, it welcomes a variety of guests, from weekending married couples to road-tripping college kids. Exceptionally affordable prices and prime location in the center of town make this the South's best-kept secret. (☎877-766-2583; www.bluemoonhostel.com. Key deposit $5. Dorms $18; private rooms $70-90. AmEx/MC/V.) Inexpensive hotels line the Evangeline Thwy. **Travel Host Inn South ❷,** 1314 N. Evangeline Thwy., rents large, clean rooms with cable TV, continental breakfast, microwaves, an outdoor pool, and refrigerators. (☎233-2090. Singles $40; doubles $50. AmEx/D/MC/V.) The lakeside but more commercial **KOA Lafayette ❶,** 5 mi. west of town off I-10 at Exit 97, has over 200 sites, mini-golf, two pools, and a store. (☎235-2739. Reception M-Th and Su 7:30am-8pm, F-Sa 7:30am-9pm. Tent sites with water and electricity for up to 4 people $26. Each additional person $5. Reservations recommended. D/MC/V.)

FOOD. It's not hard to find reasonably priced Cajun and Creole cuisine in Lafayette, a city that prides itself on food. Of course, music is also a priority, and can be found live in most of those same restaurants at night. Since 1927, ◪**Dwyer's Cafe ❶,** 323 Jefferson St., a diner with stained-glass windows and murals on the walls, has been the best place in town to get breakfast and lunch. They serve a

THE SOUTH

bang-up breakfast (grits, eggs, ham, biscuits, juice, and coffee) for $4. At lunch, locals saunter in from the heat to eat a plate lunch (different every day; $7) of gigantic proportions. Breakfast crowds can fill up the cafe on weekends, but it is worth the wait for a table. (☎235-9364. Open M and Su 6am-2pm, Tu-Sa 6am-2pm and 5:30pm-late. AmEx/D/MC/V.) Down Jefferson St. from Dwyer's, ⬛**Borden's ❶**, 1103 Jefferson St., has great malts ($2.50-4.25), sundaes ($2.50-3.50), and huge banana splits ($4). Established in 1940, the joint gets jumping on Sundays after church as patrons indulge in the heavenly strawberry cheesecake ice cream. (☎235-9291. Open Tu-Th 1-8pm, F-Sa noon-9pm, Su noon-8pm. Cash or check only.) For great alternative cuisine on the cheap check out the **Cedar Deli ❶**, 1115 Jefferson St., across the parking lot from Blue Moon Guest House (p. 421). For 25 years, Syrian owner Nabil Loli has been serving up muffulettas, gyros, halloumi, and falafel. (☎233-5460. Open M-F 9am-5pm, Sa 9am-4pm. Cash only.) Save room for ice cream at **The Filling Station ❷**, 900 Jefferson St. Occupying the shell of an old gas station, the restaurant also serves gigantic burritos and burgers ($4.75-7.25) and, from March to May, shrimp and crawfish ($8). Their full bar will fill your tank nicely, and you can rock out to live music on Thursdays and Fridays. (☎291-9625. Beer $2.75-4. Kitchen open M-F 11am-9pm, Sa 5pm-9pm. Bar open until people empty out. AmEx/D/MC/V.)

🅖 **SIGHTS.** Driving through south-central Louisiana means driving over America's largest swamp, the **Atchafalaya Basin.** It's a unique environment consisting of hundreds of miles of shallow waterways inhabited by alligators, wildcats, and residential and migratory birds. The **Atchafalaya Freeway** (I-10 between Lafayette and Baton Rouge) crosses 32 mi. of swamp and cypress trees. For swamp tours, **McGee's Landing,** 1337 Henderson Rd., sends three 1½hr. **boat tours** into the basin each day. (☎228-2384. Tours daily 10am, 1, 3pm. Spring and fall sunset tours by reservation. $18, seniors $15, under 12 $12, under 2 free.) The ⬛**Acadian Cultural Center,** 501 Fisher Rd. (take Johnston St. to Surrey, then follow the signs), is a unit of the **Jean Lafitte National Historical Park and Preserve,** which runs throughout the delta region of Louisiana. The Acadian Center has a dramatic 40min. documentary chronicling the arrival of the Acadians in Louisiana, as well as a 16min. film on conservation efforts in the Atchafalaya swamp and terrific bilingual exhibits on Cajun history and culture. (☎232-0789. Open daily 8am-5pm. Shows every hr. 9am-4pm. Free.) Next door to the cultural center, you can take a self-guided tour of a "living museum" that recreates the Acadian settlement of **Vermilionville,** 300 Fisher Rd., with Acadian music, crafts, food, actors in costume, and dancing on the Bayou Vermilion banks. (☎233-4077 or 800-992-2968. Live bands Su 1-4pm. Cajun cooking demos daily 10:30am, 12:30, 1:30pm. Open Tu-Su 10am-4pm. Last entry 3pm. $8, seniors $6.50, ages 6-18 $5. AAA discount $1.) **Acadian Village,** 200 Greenleaf Rd., is similar and features authentic 19th-century Cajun homes with an array of artifacts and period displays. While at the village, see the collection of 19th-century medical paraphernalia at the **Doctor's House.** (☎981-2489 or 800-962-9133. Both open daily 10am-4pm. $8, seniors $7, ages 6-14 $5. AAA discount $1. Bluegrass concerts in summer; call Lafayette Visitors Commission, p. 421, for info. Tickets $10.)

Closer to downtown, the University of Louisiana's recently-opened **University Art Museum,** 710 E. St. Mary Blvd., houses temporary and permanent exhibits of sculpture, photography, and paintings in a gorgeous glass building. (☎482-2278; www.louisiana.edu/UAM. Open Tu-Sa 10am-5pm. $5, over 50 $4, ages 5-17 $3. Tu and Sa 10am-noon free.) The **Cathedral of Saint John the Evangelist,** 515 Cathedral St., is worth a peek for its stunning 19th-century ecclesiastical architecture. (☎232-1322. Open daily 6am-6pm. Free.) Skip the church museum and check out the nearby **Saint John's Cathedral Oak,** 914 St. John St., which shades an entire lawn with spidery branches reaching from a trunk 19 ft. in circumference. Astronomy buffs may want to check out the **Lafayette Natural History Museum and Planetarium,** 433 Jefferson St., which has planetarium shows and a variety of rotating exhibits, like one on Chinese astronomy. (☎291-5544. Open M-F 9am-5pm, Sa 10am-6pm, Su 1-6pm. $5, seniors $3, children $2.)

🔊🎵 **ENTERTAINMENT AND NIGHTLIFE.** While in Lafayette, be sure to take advantage of the many local festivals and music performances. The **Festival International de Louisiane** is the largest free outdoor francophone festival in the US, and transforms Lafayette into a gigantic French-speaking fairground for one wild weekend in April. The festival expands each year and is beginning to rival the greatest fetes of Louisiana's better-known city of revelry, New Orleans. Book a hotel or campground well in advance; rates will likely be twice as high as normal. (☎232-8086; www.festivalinternational.com. Apr. 23-27, 2008.) The **Festivals Acadiens** began with the idea of educating Acadiana youth about their Cajun culture. It now attracts some of the state's best Cajun and zydeco musicians and has tons of other cultural and culinary events. (☎232-3737; www.festivalsacadiens.com. Mid-Sept. to mid-Oct.) The **Breaux Bridge Crawfish Festival** in nearby Breaux Bridge, 10 mi. east on I-10 at Exit 109, stages crawfish races, live music, dance contests, cook-offs, and a crawfish-eating contest. (☎332-6655; www.bbcrawfest.com. May 2-4, 2008.) Local college students frequent the numerous bars and dance clubs along Jefferson St. downtown. Some bars have live music on Fridays or Saturdays; pick up a free copy of the *Independent* for listings. To find the best zydeco in town, check out *The Times*, free at restaurants and gas stations. Most clubs and bars have cover charges around $5-10 when they feel like it or depending on bands playing that night.

> ◤ **THE LONG RIDE HOME.** The city-provided **Tipsy Taxi** anonymously provides free taxi service from bars in an effort to cut down drunk driving. Speak to the bartender at the end of the night if you feel uncomfortable getting behind the wheel.

On Sunday afternoons, the place to be is **Angelle's Whiskey River Landing,** 1365 Henderson Levee Rd., in Breaux Bridge, where live Cajun music has people dancing on the very lip of the levee looking out over the swamp. On weekends you'll see boatmen pulling ashore right outside and coming in to join the party—it sometimes feels like the whole floor could collapse into the swamp with all the stamping. (☎228-8567. Live music F-Sa occasionally, Su 4-8pm.) **Hamilton's Zydeco Club,** 1808 Verot School Rd., is one of the best places in Louisiana to cut loose at night, since live Cajun bands make for some wild dancing. (☎991-0783. Open sporadically; call or drive by to see the marquee for upcoming events and times.) **Grant Street Dance Hall,** 113 Grant St., features bands playing everything from zydeco to metal. (☎237-8513. 18+. Cover usually $5-10, up to $50 depending on the act. Open on show days, usually F-Sa nights; call ahead.)

ARKANSAS

Encompassing the Ozark and Ouachita mountains, the clear waters of Hot Springs, and miles of lush pine forests, the "Natural State" lives up to its nickname. Arkansas can be divided into distinct regions: the mountainous northwest is home to the University of Arkansas at Fayetteville and gave birth to Wal-Mart, while the flat plains of the southeast are poorer and support cotton and rice farming. The bluesy Mississippi Delta region seeps into east Arkansas, while Hot Springs National Park is an easy daytrip from the capital.

🗓 PRACTICAL INFORMATION

Capital: Little Rock.

Visitor Info: Arkansas Department of Parks and Tourism, 1 Capitol Mall, Little Rock 72201 (Tourism Office ☎501-682-7777 or 800-628-8725, Parks Office 501-682-1191; www.arkansas.com). Open daily in summer 8am-6pm; low season 8am-5pm.

Postal Abbreviation: AR. **Sales Tax:** 6%.

LITTLE ROCK ☎ 501

Located squarely in the middle of the state along the Arkansas River, Little Rock became a major trading city in the 19th century, when a small rock served as an important landmark for boats pushing their way upstream. Though this "little rock" is still visible today, it doesn't loom as large as the historical landmark of Central High School, where, in 1957, Governor Orval Faubus and local white segregationists violently resisted nine black students who entered the school under the protection of the National Guard. Today, this and other historical events are remembered in the many museums in the downtown area. The late 90s and early 2000s saw a brilliant clean-up effort in the city, which now abounds in grassy parks, clean streets, and fine eateries. The most recent attraction is the Clinton Presidential Library, which overlooks the Arkansas River.

🖩🗓 TRANSPORTATION AND PRACTICAL INFORMATION. Amtrak, 1400 W. Markham St. (☎372-6841; www.amtrak.com; open daily 11pm-7:45am), at Victory St., runs **trains** from Union Station Sq.; take bus #1 or 8. Trains run to Dallas (6½hr., 1 per day, $60), Malvern, AR (1hr., 1 per day, $10), and St. Louis (7hr., 1 per day, $53). Greyhound, 118 E. Washington St. (☎372-3007; www.greyhound.com; open 24hr.), is in North Little Rock; take bus #7 or 18. **Buses** run to Memphis (2½hr., 8 per day, $27), New Orleans (12½hr., 4 per day, $78), and St. Louis (8½hr., 1 per day, $52). Central Arkansas Transit (CAT) operates an extensive and tourist-friendly **bus system** through downtown and the surrounding towns. Catch CAT buses and get detailed route info at the River Cities Travel Center, 310 E. Capitol St. (☎375-1163. Buses run every 30-40min. M-Sa 6am-6pm, some routes until 10pm; Su 9am-4pm. $1.25, seniors $0.60; transfers $0.05.) CAT also runs two **trolley** routes. The South trolley route runs east-west along Clinton Ave. and 2nd St., while the North trolley route runs north-south along Main St. from Clinton Ave. across the river to 7th St. in North Little Rock. (☎375-1163. M-W 11am-10pm, Th-Sa 11am-midnight, Su 11am-5pm. $0.50, seniors $0.25.)

Little Rock is at the intersection of **I-40** and **I-30,** 140 mi. west of Memphis. Downtown, numbered streets run east-west, while named streets run north-south. The four major thoroughfares are **I-630, Cantrell Road, University Avenue,** and **Rodney Parham Road.** Near the river, Markham is 1st St. and Capitol is 5th St. The east side of Markham St. is now President Clinton Ave. and moves through the lively **Riverwalk** district. **North Little Rock** is linked to downtown Little Rock by three bridges spanning the Arkansas river. Note that when crossing the bridges North Little Rock repeats a similar street pattern to Little Rock. **Little Rock Visitor Information Center** is at 615 E. Capitol Ave., in the newly renovated Curran Hall. Take the 6th or 9th St. exit off I-30 and follow the signs. (☎371-0076 or 877-220-2568; www.little-rock.com. Open M-Sa 9am-5pm, Su 1-5pm.) **Internet Access:** The **Main Library** is at 100 Rock St., near River Market. (☎918-3000. Free. Open M-Th 9am-8pm, F-Sa 9am-6pm, Su 1-5pm.) **Post Office:** 600 E. Capitol Ave. (☎375-5155. Open M-F 7am-5:30pm.) **Postal Code:** 72701.

ACCOMMODATIONS. Budget motels are dense around I-30 southwest of town and at the intersection of I-30 and I-40 in North Little Rock. Exit 130 off I-30 has a cluster of discount hotels lining the access road. The **Cimarron Inn ❷**, 10200 I-30, off Exit 130 on the westbound access road, has clean, standard rooms with fridge and microwave, and a pool. (☎565-1171. Singles $35; doubles $40. AmEx/MC/V.) **Maumell Park ❶**, 9009 Pinnacle Valley Rd., on the Arkansas River, has 129 sites near the beautiful Pinnacle Mountain State Park. From I-430, take Rte. 10 (Exit 9) west 2½ mi., turn right on Pinnacle Valley Rd., continue for 2 mi., and look for the sign. (☎868-9477 or 753-0086. Office open daily 10am-10pm. Sites with 30-amp hookup $20, 50-amp hookup $22; riverside sites $24.)

FOOD. The city has revamped the downtown area starting with **River Market**, 400 President Clinton Ave. The downtown lunch crowd heads here for a wide selection of food shops, coffee stands, delis, and an outdoor **farmers' market.** The River Market Grocery holds a variety of gourmet and ethnic treats, with a variety of food stands and grocery items. (☎375-2552. Market Hall open M-Sa 7am-6pm; many shops only open for lunch. Farmers' market open May-Oct. Tu and Sa 7am-3pm.) Near Market Hall, **The Flying Fish ❷**, 511 President Clinton Ave., has quickly become downtown's most popular hangout for its unpretentious atmosphere and walls covered with photos of fish caught by patrons. Hungry diners clamor for catfish baskets (2 fillets $6), oyster and catfish po' boy sandwiches ($7), and on-tap brews. (☎375-3474. Open daily 11am-10pm. MC/V.) Just past the Hillcrest area, **Pizza D'Action ❶**, 2919 W. Markham St., boasts some of the area's tastiest pizza and most eclectic crowds, along with live music most nights. (☎666-5403. Large pies $11-15. Burgers and sandwiches $4-6. Open M 3pm-1am, Tu-Su 11am-1am. AmEx/D/MC/V.) Chef Nate Townsend cooks up fantastic feasts at **Grampa's Catfish House ❷**, 100 Shadow Oaks, near Rt. 67/167. In addition to the popular catfish dinners ($8-10), you can try the chicken-fried steak, oysters, and scallops. (☎758-4654. Open Tu-Su 4:30-9:30pm. AmEx/D/MC/V.)

SIGHTS. Tourists can visit **"La Petite Roche,"** the actual "little rock" of Little Rock, at Riverfront Park at the north end of Rock St. From underneath the railroad bridge at the north end of Louisiana St., look straight down. Look carefully; the rock is part of the embankment (it's that small), and it's been covered in graffiti since its plaque was stolen. The **Clinton Presidential Library,** 1200 E. President Clinton Ave., is an architecturally distinctive glass building hailed by admirers as a metaphor for Clinton's "Bridge to the 21st Century." Highlights include Clinton's presidential limo, replicas of the Oval Office and Cabinet Room, and a presentation on White House humor. The library hosts a wealth of documents and memorabilia from Clinton's personal life, as well as from beyond his time in office. Visitors may take several hours to look through the well-documented exhibits. (☎370-8000; www.clintonpresidentialcenter.com. Open M-Sa 9am-5pm, Su 1-5pm. $7; students, seniors, and retired military $5; ages 6-17 $3; active military free. With audio tour $10/8/6/3.) The aftermath of Little Rock's Civil Rights struggle is manifest at the corner of Daisy L. Gatson Bates Dr. (formerly 14th St.) and Park St., where **Central High School** remains a fully functional school. It's therefore closed to visitors, but a **Visitors Center,** 2125 Daisy L. Gatson Bates Dr., in a restored gas station across the street, contains an excellent exhibit on the "Little Rock Nine." In September 2007, President Clinton returned to Little Rock for the commemoration of a new Visitors Center in honor of the 50th anniversary of the integration of Central High School. (☎374-1957; www.nps.gov/chsc. Open daily 9am-4:30pm. Free.) The **Arkansas Art Center,** 501 E. 9th St., is a huge complex with out-of-the-ordinary landscapes and still lifes; one of the most prominent sculptures, *Heavy Dog Kiss*, depicts a huge human head kissing a huge dog head. (☎372-4000; www.arkarts.com. Open Tu-Sa 10am-5pm, Su 11am-5pm. Free, suggested donation $5.) When the legislature is not in session, visitors can explore the **State Capitol,** at the west end of Capitol St. Survey the grounds to see the many statues dedicated to Arkansas's history, such as **Testament,** a marbled recreation of the Little Rock Nine surrounded by inspirational quotes from each of students. (☎682-5080. Open M-F 8am-5pm, Sa-Su and holidays 10am-3pm.) In the middle of downtown, the **Historic Arkansas Museum,** 200 E. 3rd St., recreates life in 19th-century Little Rock using period actors who show off old-time tricks of frontier living. (☎324-9351; www.arkansashistory.com. Open M-Sa 9am-5pm, Su 1-5pm. Free. Tour of historic downtown $2.50, seniors $1.50, under 18 $1.) Just a 15min. drive west of the city is **Pinnacle Mountain State Park,** 11901 Pinnacle Valley Rd., in Roland. The interpretive trails and the **Arkansas Arboretum** provide info on area flora. (☎868-5806; www.arkansasstateparks.com. Call for hours.)

🎵 **NIGHTLIFE. Vino's,** 923 W. 7th St., at Chester St., is Little Rock's original microbrewery-nightclub with a diverse range of clientele including lunchtime's corporate businessmen and midnight's younger patrons. (☎375-8466. Pizza slices $1.15. Live rock music Th-Sa. 18+ at night. Cover $5-10. Open M-W 11am-10pm, Th 11am-11pm, F 11am-midnight, Sa 11:30am-midnight, Su 1-9pm.) **Sticky Fingerz,** 107 S. Commerce St., across President Clinton Ave. from the River Market, serves signature chicken fingers ($5.50) with a side of alt-rock. (☎372-7707; www.stickyfingerz.com. Open M-F 11am-2pm and 4:30pm-late, Sa 11am-late.) **The Underground Pub,** 500 President Clinton Ave., offers British fare. Enjoy music, darts, pool, and football (British style) on big-screen TVs. (☎707-2537. Happy hour daily 4-7pm. Open M-W 11am-midnight, Th-F 11am-2am, Sa 11am-1am.) **Weekend Theater,** on W. 7th St. across from Vino's, stages Off-Broadway theater productions. (☎374-3761. Call for showtimes.)

HOT SPRINGS ☎501

Since the region was settled in 1807, visitors have flocked to Hot Springs seeking health and relaxation in its steamy waters. Today, the springs manifest themselves in fountains and water outlets around the town of Hot Springs, most of which are very hot (143°F, or 62°C): consider yourself warned. The main drag of Hot Springs, known as **Bathhouse Row,** is lined with spas and baths. A former bathhouse, **Fordyce House Visitors Center,** 369 Central Ave., is home to the Hot Springs National Park Visitor Center, which has free, self-guided tours of the restored Fordyce Bathhouse and ranger-guided tours of Bathhouse Row. (☎620-6715. Open daily 9am-5pm. Guided tours in summer 9:30, 10:30am, and 2:30pm; call ahead to confirm.) The **Buckstaff House,** 509 Central Ave., three houses up the road, is the only bathhouse continuously active since 1912. Visitors can rejuvenate with mineral baths ($22) and Swedish massages ($27). Reservations are required for manicures, pedicures, and facials. (☎623-2308; www.buckstaffbaths.com. Open M-Sa 7-11:45am and 1:30-3pm, Su 8am-1pm; Dec.-Feb. closed Sa afternoons and Su. Last entry 15min. before closing) The **hot springs** themselves are in town along Central Ave., and drinking the water is actually encouraged by the National Park. On a clear day at the **Hot Springs Mountain Tower,** 401 Hot Springs Mountain Dr., you can see 70 mi. in every direction. From the end of Bathhouse Row, turn right down Fountain St., then continue up Hot Springs Dr. (☎623-6035; www.hotsprings.org. Open daily 9am-9pm. $6, seniors $5, ages 5-11 $3.) **Walking trails** of all levels crisscross Hot Springs Mountain. Trail maps are available at Fordyce House and the Visitors Center, both on Central Ave. During the first two weeks of June, the **Hot Springs Music Festival** brings thousands to the town for classical music concerts. (☎623-4763; www.hotmusic.org. June 1-14, 2008.)

Heavy tourism has pushed lodging prices sky-high in Hot Springs, and it can be difficult to find a room on weekends. One of the best values in town is the **Happy Hollow Motel ❸**, 231 Fountain Ave., on the edge of the park. Built in the late 40s, it has a funky aluminum patio and clean rooms in a quiet location. (☎321-2230; www.happyhollowmotel.com. Fridge, microwave, VCR, and free Wi-Fi. Rooms $58-95. D/MC/V.) Just outside of town, the **Alpine Inn ❷**, 741 Park Ave., has spacious themed rooms with refrigerators and a pool. (☎624-9164; www.alpineinnhotsprings.com. Singles $49-55; doubles $55-75. AmEx/D/MC/V.) **McClard's ❸**, 505 Albert Pike Rd., an old Clinton hangout, has served fabulous Southern fare in large portions for over 75 years. The tamales (2 for $8.35) are delectable and the selection of ribs is mouth-watering. (☎623-9665; www.mcclards.com. Open Tu-Sa 11am-8pm. Cash only.) For a fast, cheap meal, **King Kone Drive-In ❶**, 1505 Malvern Ave., is an original burger joint with burgers ($2-3), ice cream, and pickle juice slushies. (☎321-9766. Open M-Sa 9am-10pm. Cash or check only.) **Vicki's Cafe ❶**, 406 Central Ave., serves sandwiches ($4-6) and provides cool relief on hot summer days with a large selection of ice cream and other frozen treats. (Internet access available. Open M-Th 8am-6pm, F-Sa 8am-7pm, Su 10am-5pm.) To occupy Hot Springs's steamy evenings, the amazing **Poet's Loft,** 514B Central Ave., is a groovy hangout with a variety of poetry readings, music recitals, and jam sessions. (☎627-4224; www.poetsloft.com. Open W and F-Sa 5-10pm.) **100 Exchange Jazz Lounge,** 100 Exchange Pl., has live jazz Wednesdays, blues on Thursday, and dance music on Saturdays. (☎624-9463 or 623-3663. 21+. Open W-F 4pm-3am, Sa noon-2am.)

One hour southwest of Little Rock, Hot Springs is easy to reach. Most of the town's noteworthy buildings, plus the National Park headquarters, are along **Central Avenue.** The downtown **Visitors Center,** 629 Central Ave. (open daily winter 9am-5pm, spring-fall 9am-7pm) has tourist info. Greyhound, 229 W. Grand St. (☎623-5574; www.greyhound.com; open daily 8am-noon and 4-7pm), runs **buses** to Atlanta (12hr., 1 per day, $120), Little Rock (1hr., 2 per day, $14), and Memphis (4hr., 2 per day, $40). Wi-Fi is available at the cyber cafe in the **Convention and Visitors Bureau,** 134 Convention Blvd. (Free. Open M-F 9am-5pm.) **Post Office:** 100 Reserve St., in the Federal Building. (☎623-8217. Open M-F 8am-4:30pm, Sa 9am-noon.) **Postal Code:** 71901.

OZARKS

The mountains that encompass the northwest region of Arkansas are accessible from the capital and provide a convenient escape with good roads, good food, and great green scenery. Up until the last few decades, the region was isolated, but a booming tourist industry and an influx of retirees has helped the Ozarks grow in recent years. Mountain View and Eureka Springs are two of the most popular towns to visit, although they can get very busy during the summer months.

EUREKA SPRINGS   ☎479

Achieving an intoxicatingly high quaintness-to-square-footage ratio, Eureka Springs, near the intersection of Hwy. 62 and Rte. 23 in northwest Arkansas, peddles its patent charm, natural scenery, and slow pace to travelers. The site of the 1st Native American and white settlements in Eureka Springs, the **Blue Spring Heritage Center,** at the end of Eureka Springs Garden Road off Hwy. 62, has 33 acres of gardens, trails, and azure spring waters. (☎253-9244; www.bluespringheritage.com. Open daily Mar. 15-Thanksgiving 9am-6pm. $7.25, ages 10-17 $4, under 10 free. AAA discount $1.) **Turpentine Creek Wildlife Refuge,** on Hwy. 23, 7 mi. south of Eureka Springs, is home to over 100 lions, tigers, and leopards rescued from around the US. The best time to see the cats is at their 6pm feeding time; otherwise

THE SOUTH

they'll probably be dozing. (☎253-5841; www.turpentinecreek.org. Open daily 9am-7pm. Tours daily every hr. 11am-5pm. $15; military, seniors, and under 12 $10.) If you're driving from Little Rock, take a detour to the ◪**Dickson Street Bookshop**, 325 W. Dickson St. in downtown Fayetteville, an hour west of Eureka Springs. Behind a humble storefront, a seemingly endless maze of shelves overflows with used books ranging from bargain paperbacks to out-of-print collector's items. (☎442-8182. Open M-Sa 10am-9pm, Su 1-6pm.) Eureka's most famous tourist attraction is **The Great Passion Play**, 935 Passion Play Rd., off Hwy. 62, and the Bible-inspired sights that surround it. Hundreds of actors depict the final days of Christ on an elaborate outdoor set. The dialogue is pre-recorded, but at least it's not in Aramaic. (☎253-9200 or 800-882-7529; www.greatpassionplay.com. Tickets $23.25, ages 6-11 $10. Shows May-Aug. M-Tu and Th-Sa 8:30pm; Sept.-Oct. M-Tu and Th-Sa 7:30pm.) The **Bible Museum** has over 6000 copies of the Good Book in 600 languages, and the **Sacred Arts Center** features works inspired by Christ. Both are located on the grounds of the Passion Play and are open from 10am-8pm on days that it is running. Admission is included in the ticket price. Nearby, visitors marvel at the seven-story **Christ of the Ozarks** statue.

Lodging prices fluctuate greatly with the ebb and flow of tourists; peak season is from late September to early October. The Visitors Center has detailed information on the numerous hotels, motels, and B&B lodgings, with price-range comparisons available. The line of hotels and motels along Hwy. 62 E. provide the best budget deals. **The Trails Inn ❷**, 2060 E. Van Buren/Hwy. 62, is one of the better motels on Hwy. 62, with clean rooms, breakfast, Wi-Fi, and a pool. (☎253-9390 or 800-962-4691; www.thetrailsinn.com. Singles $42-45; doubles $42-69. AmEx/D/MC/V.) The **Lookout Lodge ❷**, on Hwy. 62 east of downtown, is a good value with surprisingly comfortable rooms. (☎253-9335. Rooms on weekdays $49-69; weekends $59-99. AmEx/D/MC/V.) Campers head to **Kettle Campgrounds and Cabins ❶**, 4119 E. Van Buren St./Hwy. 62, which offers tent and RV sites as well as laundry, showers, Wi-Fi ($3) and a pool. (☎253-9100 or 800-899-2267. Primitive sites $13, with water and electricity $17, with full hookup $21. Cabins $40. Cash or check only.) Hwy. 62 offers plenty of all-you-can-eat dinner buffets packed with Southern food staples at reasonable prices. The subterranean **Mud St. Cafe ❷**, 22G S. Main St., serves breakfast ($3-7), sandwiches, burgers, and delicious desserts. Local artwork funkifies the classic timber and stained-glass saloon decor, and the menu provides plenty of tantalizing vegetarian options. (☎253-6732; www.mudstreetcafe.com. Open Feb.-Dec. M-Tu and Th-Su 8am-3pm. AmEx/MC/V.) For dinner, **Ermilio's ❸**, 26 White St., lets patrons mix and match a variety of pastas and homemade sauces ($10-12) in a casual dining room. Patrons enjoy friendly conversation and mixed drinks outside on the patio. (☎253-8806. Open daily 5-9pm. Closed mid-Feb. to mid-Mar. MC/V.) At **Bubba's BBQ ❷**, 166 W. Van Buren St., barbecue sandwiches ($4-7) are topped with cole slaw in the traditional Southern fashion. Heaping dinner plates run $9-12. (☎253-7706. Open M-Sa 11am-9pm. Cash or check only.) The **Pine Mountain Jamboree**, 2075 E. Van Buren St., and **Ozark Mountain Hoedown**, 3140 E. Van Buren St., have live country variety shows, with bluegrass, gospel, and country music and comedy routines. (Pine Mountain ☎253-9156. Shows Mar.-Dec. M-Sa 7:30pm. Tickets $20, seniors $19, children under 12 free. AmEx/D/MC/V. Ozark Mountain ☎253-7725. Shows nightly 8pm, pre-show bluegrass 7:30pm. Tickets $21.50, seniors $20, military $17.50, under 12 free. MC/V) Wash down that wholesome feeling with a cold one at **Chelsea's Corner**, 10 Mountain St., off Center St. (☎253-8231. Live music weekends. 21+. Cover $5. Open M-Th noon-10pm, F-Sa noon-midnight, Su 4-8pm.)

Downtown is hilly but walkable; park at free lots on Rte. 23 N south of the railroad or on Hwy. 62 W. **Trolleys** run to every destination around town. (☎253-9572;

www.eurekatrolley.org. Operates May-Oct. M-Th and Su 9am-5pm, F-Sa 9am-8pm; Mar.-Apr. and Nov. daily 9am-5pm; Dec.-Feb. limited service F-Sa 10am-4pm. Day pass $4.50, ages 7-11 $1.25; 2-day pass $7; 1-ride pass $2.) The **Eureka Springs Chamber of Commerce Visitors Center** is on Hwy. 62 W, two blocks west of Hwy. 23 N. (☎253-8737 or 800-638-7352; www.eurekaspringschamber.com. Open daily 9am-5pm.) **Post Office:** 101 Spring St. (☎253-9850. Open M-F 8:15am-4:15pm, Sa 10am-noon.) **Postal Code:** 72632.

MOUNTAIN VIEW   ☎ 870

Mountain View is located 123 mi. north of Little Rock, the closest big city. The self-proclaimed "folk music capital of the world" has plenty of music to offer, starting with the free outdoor music on central **Courthouse Square.** Locals bring along deck chairs or sit on the grass to listen and some even join in. Other venues offer music at a price. The **Jimmy Driftwood Barn,** 2 mi. north of town past the junction of Hwy. 5/9/14 N, is a performance space created by Jimmy Driftwood, known as the "Bard of the Ozarks" and most famous for his song "The Battle of New Orleans." Although Jimmy died in 1998, you can still hear folk music there year-round. (☎269-4578. Shows F and Su 7pm. Gospel concerts 2nd Sa of each month 7pm. Free, donations accepted.) **Cash's White River Hoedown,** 507 Sylamore Ave., at the junction of Hwy. 5/9/14 N just north of town, has a family-oriented comedy and music show. (☎800-759-6474. Apr.-May and Aug. F-Sa comedy warm-up 7:30pm, show 8pm; June, July, and Oct. Th-Sa warm-up 7:30pm, show 8pm; Nov.-Dec. Sa warm-up 7pm, show 7:30pm. $18, seniors $16, under 16 free.) **Brickshy's Backstreet Theater,** on Jefferson St., behind White River Furniture, rotates four bands: Harmony, The Leatherwoods, The River Rat Band, and Homemade Jam. (☎269-6200. Shows Apr.-Aug. Th-Sa at 8pm; Sept.-Nov. Th-Sa 7:30pm. Tickets available after 5pm. $15, under 17 free. Senior discount available upon request.) The **Mountain View Gospel Opry** performs on Thursdays and Saturdays at 7pm in the Folklore Society building, on Franklin St. just off the square. In the nearby **Ozark National Forest,** the spectacular **Blanchard Springs Caverns** offer fascinating underground tours. From downtown, take Hwy. 5/9/14 N to 14 W. There are three levels of caverns; two are accessible to the public. The **Dripstone Trail** tour takes visitors through the highlights. The area also has hiking trails, a mountain-bike trail, and a shooting range. (☎757-2211 or 888-757-2246. Tours run 9:30am-6pm, last tour 4:30pm. Tours $10, ages 6-15 $5, under 5 free.)

MODERN EMPIRE

Although Wal-Mart is currently the largest private employer in America with revenues rivaling the economies of small nations, it traces its humble beginnings back to Bentonville, a tiny town that once blended into the unassuming landscape of northwestern Arkansas. It was here that Sam Walton opened his first Walton's 5 and 10 over 50 years ago. Walton's business has since grown into a corporate fixture whose motto, "Always Low Prices," has seeped into popular culture and revolutionized how (and for how much) Americans shop. Though Walton died in 1992, according to Forbes Magazine his commercial visions have left his heirs with a collective fortune of over $90 billion.

Bentonville is now home to Wal-Mart global headquarters and the Wal-Mart Visitor Center. The nerve center for Wal-Mart's nationwide distribution network, the town has recently sought to expand its airport to accommodate its growing population of Wal-Mart's corporate management officers. Although Bentonville's prairie charm may not be able to match the California chic of Silicon Valley, with over 20 new Wal-Marts opening each month, Wal-Mart is unlikely to go the way of the 90s dot-com bubble anytime soon. In fact, it just might be Middle America's next and greatest corporate enterprise.

Angler's White River Inn ❸, at the junction of Hwy. 5/9/14, provides motel-style accommodations with a fabulous deck overlooking the river. (☎585-2226 or 800-794-2226; www.anglerswhiteriver.com. Boat and kayak rentals, guided fishing trips, and river floats available with the White River Resort staff. Rooms $60-65. Lofts $70-90. MC/V.) **Mountain View Motel ❷,** two blocks east of Court House Square on Main St., has small but clean rooms decorated like your grandmother's guest room. (☎269-3209. Singles $33-42; doubles $37-47. Cash or check only.) The cheapest place to stay is at one of the **Ozark National Forest Campgrounds ❶,** near the Blanchard Springs Caverns, 15 mi. northwest of Mountain View. The campsites are first come, first served, with showers, toilets, and plenty of local fishing, swimming, and hiking trails. (☎269-3228. Sites $10.) Just north of town on Rte. 14, the **Sylamore Creek Campground ❶** has cabins as well as campsites, with clean bathrooms and hot showers. (☎585-2326 or 877-475-4223; www.sylamorecreek.com. Sites $10, with electricity $15, with full hookup $17. 2-person cabins $65-90. Each additional person $5. AmEx/D/MC/V.) One block west of Court House Sq., ▨**Woods Pharmacy and Soda Fountain ❶,** 301 W. Main St., recreates an old-fashioned soda fountain with "phosphate" sodas that come with your choice of flavored syrup ($1.80). A fully functional pharmacy, Woods also serves ice cream sodas and sandwiches. (☎269-8304. Open M-Sa 8am-5pm. MC/V.) At **Jo Jo's Catfish Wharf ❷,** 6 mi. north of town on Hwy. 5 N, chow down on classic Arkansas catfish in a no-nonsense setting by the river. (☎585-2121. Open M-Th and Su 11am-8pm, F-Sa 11am-9pm. AmEx/D/MC/V.)

Getting to Mountain View is virtually impossible without a car; the town is not accessible by bus and there is no public transit within the town. Your best bet is to drive up from Little Rock. The **Chamber of Commerce and Tourist Information Center** is at 199 Peabody St. (☎269-8068; www.yourplaceinthemountains.com. Open M-F 9am-5pm, Sa 10am-2pm.) **Post Office:** 802 Sylamore Ave. (☎269-3520 or 888-679-2859. Open M-F 8:30am-4:30pm.) **Postal Code:** 72560.

FLORIDA

Ponce de León landed in Florida in 1513, looking for the elusive Fountain of Youth. Although the multitudes who flock to Florida today aren't seeking fountains, many find their youth restored in the Sunshine State, whether they're dazzled by the spectacle of Disney World or bronzed by the sun on the state's seductive beaches. Droves of senior citizens also migrate to Florida—jokingly referred to as heaven's waiting room—where the sun-warmed air is just as therapeutic as de León's fabled magical elixir. Florida's recent population boom has strained the state's natural resources; commercial strips and tremendous development have turned pristine beaches into tourist traps. Still, it is possible to find a deserted spot on the peninsula on which to plop down with a paperback and dig your toes into the sand.

HIGHLIGHTS OF FLORIDA

WALTZ around Walt's magical collection of amusements at **Disney World** (p. 435).

SOAK up the rays and the cocktails at the beaches and nightclubs of **Miami** (p. 452).

HOP aboard a cruise through the swamps and islands of the **Everglades** (p. 460).

DIG into a slice of the famous **Key Lime Pie** in the Florida Keys (p. 463).

PRACTICAL INFORMATION

Capital: Tallahassee.

Visitor Info: Florida Division of Tourism, 126 W. Van Buren St., Tallahassee 32301 (☎888-735-2872; www.flausa.com). **Division of Recreation and Parks,** 3900 Commonwealth Blvd., #536, Tallahassee 32399 (☎850-488-9872).

Postal Abbreviation: FL. **Sales Tax:** 6%. **Accommodations Tax:** 11%.

CENTRAL FLORIDA

ORLANDO   ☎407

When Walt Disney was flying over the small towns of Central Florida in search of a place to put his Florida operation, he marveled at the endless lakes and streams that dominate the Orlando area. Amidst this beautiful setting, he foresaw a world full of thrill-packed amusement rides and life-sized, cartoonish figures. While Orlando is older than Disney World, most of the city's resources are dedicated to supporting the tourism industry that is the lifeblood of its economy. Theme parks, hotels, diners, and other kitschy treats line every major street; even downtown Orlando, 20 mi. from Disney, overflows with tourist attractions.

TRANSPORTATION

Airport: Orlando International (MCO), 1 Airport Blvd. (☎825-2001; www.orlandoairports.net). From the airport take Rte. 436 N, Exit to Rte. 528 W/Bee Line Expressway., then head east on I-4 for downtown, and west on I-4 to the attractions, including Disney and Universal. LYNX buses #42 and 51 make the trip to International Drive and down-

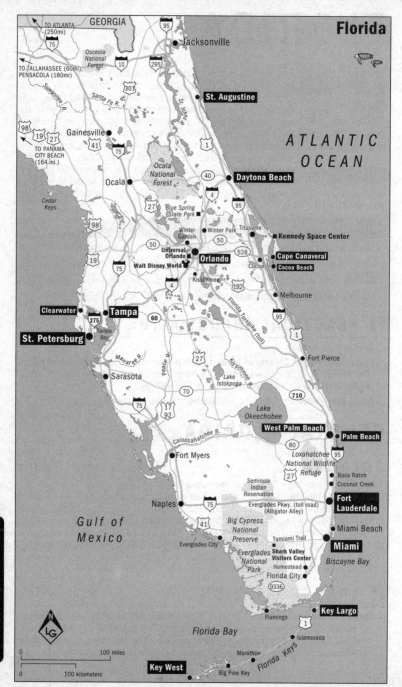

Florida

TO ATLANTA (250mi)

GEORGIA

TO TALLAHASSEE (60mi), PENSACOLA (180mi)

Osceola National Forest

Suwannee R.

TO PANAMA CITY BEACH (164 mi.)

Cedar Keys

Santa Fe R.

Jacksonville

St. Augustine

Gainesville

Ocala National Forest

Ocala

ATLANTIC OCEAN

Blue Spring State Park

Daytona Beach

Winter Garden   Winter Park   Titusville

Universal Orlando   **Orlando**

Walt Disney World

Kissimmee

Kennedy Space Center

Cape Canaveral

Cocoa

Cocoa Beach

Melbourne

Clearwater   **Tampa**

St. Petersburg

Tampa Bay

Manatee R.

Sarasota

Peace R.

Lake Istokpoga

Kissimmee R.

Florida Turnpike (toll)

Fort Pierce

Lake Okeechobee

Caloosahatchee R.

West Palm Beach

Palm Beach

Fort Myers

Loxahatchee National Wildlife Refuge

Boca Raton

Coconut Creek

Seminole Indian Reservation

Gulf of Mexico

Naples

Everglades Pkwy. (toll road) (Alligator Alley)

Fort Lauderdale

Big Cypress National Preserve

Miami Beach

Everglades City

Tamiami Trail

Miami

Everglades National Park

Shark Valley Visitors Center

Biscayne Bay

Homestead

Florida City

Flamingo

Key Largo

Islamorada

Florida Bay

0   100 miles

0   100 kilometers

Marathon

Florida Keys

Key West

Big Pine Key

FLORIDA

town for $1.50. **Mears Motor Shuttle** (☎423-5566; www.mearstransportation.com) has booths at the airport for transportation to most hotels ($17, round-trip $27-31). Walk-up service at airport. No shuttle reservations are necessary from the airport; for return, call 1 day in advance.

Trains: Amtrak, 1400 Sligh Blvd. (☎843-7611; www.amtrak.com), 3 blocks east of I-4. Take S. Orange Ave., head west on Columbia, turn right on Sligh. Station open daily 7:30am-6:30pm. To: **Jacksonville** (3hr., 2 per day, $21-47); **Kissimmee** (20min., 2 per day, $5-13); **Miami** (6hr., 1-2 per day, $34-74); **Tampa** (2hr., 2 per day, $10-21).

Buses: Greyhound, 555 N. John Young Pkwy. (☎292-3424; www.greyhound.com), just south of W. Colonial Dr. (Rte. 50). Open 24hr. To **Jacksonville** (3¾hr., 10 per day, $30-34) and **Kissimmee** (45min., 5 per day, $9.50-11).

Public Transit: LYNX, 455 N. Garland Ave. (☎841-2279; www.golynx.com). Downtown terminal 5 blocks north of Central St., 1 block west of Orange Ave., and 1 block east of I-4. Buses operate daily 4:30am-2am, hours vary with route. $1.50, seniors 0.75; transfers free. Weekly pass $12. Look for signposts with a colored paw. Serves the airport, downtown, and all major parks. The **Lynx Lymmo** is a free downtown transportation service with 11 stations and 8 stops scattered along and around Magnolia Ave.

Taxi: Yellow Cab ☎699-9999.

▟❷ ORIENTATION AND PRACTICAL INFORMATION

Orlando lies at the center of hundreds of lakes, toll highways, and amusement parks. **Orange Blossom Trail (Route 17/92 and 441)** runs north-south and **Colonial Drive (Route 50)** east-west. The **Bee Line Expressway (Route 528)** and the **East-West Expressway (Route 408)** exact several tolls for their convenience. The major artery is **I-4**, which actually runs east to west through the center of town, despite being labeled an east-west highway. The parks—**Disney World, Universal Orlando,** and **Sea World**—await 20 mi. southwest of downtown; **Winter Park** is 3-4 mi. northeast.

Visitor Info: Orlando Official Visitor Center, 8723 International Dr., Ste. 101 (☎363-5872; www.orlandoinfo.com), southwest of downtown; take bus #8. Free "Magic Card" offers discounts at sights, restaurants, and hotels. Open daily 8am-7pm. Tickets sold 8am-6pm.

Hotlines: Sexual Assault Hotline ☎497-6701. **Crisis Hotline** ☎843-4357.

Internet Access: Orlando Public Library, 101 E. Central Blvd. (☎835-7323). Open M-Th 9am-9pm, F-Sa 9am-6pm, Su 1-6pm. Internet access 7-day use $10; 2hr. per day.

Post Office: 46 E. Robinson St. (☎425-6464). Open M-F 7am-5pm. **Postal Code:** 32801.

▛ ACCOMMODATIONS

With over 120,000 hotel rooms, Orlando has options for all wallet sizes. Prices rise as you approach Disney. **Irlo Bronson Memorial Highway (U.S. 192)** runs from Disney World to downtown Kissimmee and has cheap motels. **International Drive (I-Drive),** a north-south road that parallels the interstate, is the center of Orlando's lodging world. Many accommodations have free transportation to Universal and Disney.

Palm Lakefront Resort & Hostel, 4840 W. Irlo Bronson Hwy./U.S. 192 (☎396-1759). Features simple dorm-style rooms, private rooms, and a common kitchen. Only 5 mi. from Disney with easy bus access (Bus 56), the hostel is a great crash pad for serious park hoppers. Free Wi-Fi. Dorms $19; private rooms $40. MC/V. ❶

Gator Motel, 4576 W. Irlo Bronson Hwy./U.S. 192 (☎396-0127; http://gatormotel.com); look for the large green gator. Has quiet, bright, clean, remodeled rooms, and offers A/C, cable TV, free Internet access, a pool, and close proximity to Disney. Continental breakfast included. Rooms $24-50; each additional person $6. AmEx/D/MC/V. ❷

Disney's All-Star Resorts (☎939-6000), in Disney World. Caters to vacationing families looking for full Disney immersion. From I-4, take Exit 64B and follow the signs to Animal Kingdom; the resorts are just behind it. Disney's All-Star Movie, Music, and Sports Resorts, the "value resorts," are a great deal for large groups. Each of the hotels has 3 pools, a food court, a pool bar, laundry facilities, and convenient free self parking. Get info and tickets at the Guest Services Desk to avoid long lines at park gates. Buses to Disney transportation. A/C, phone, and TV. Wi-Fi $10. Rooms $99-150; under 18 free with adult. AmEx/D/MC/V. ❹

The Courtyard at Lake Lucerne, 211 N. Lucerne Circle E (☎648-5188 or 800-444-5289), 30min. from Disney. From I-4, take Exit 82C on to Anderson St., right on Delaney Ave., and right on N. Lucerne Circle. This beautiful B&B offers lavish rooms in 4 houses (of which Norment Perry is the best deal). Complimentary wine upon arrival and nightly Happy hour 6-7pm. Free Wi-Fi, phone, and TV. Continental breakfast. Rooms $99-250. AmEx/D/MC/V Reservations recommended. ❺

◪ FOOD

Most eating in the Orlando area is either fine dining or done on-the-run. Prices are exorbitant inside theme parks; pack food if you have space. Cheap buffets line International Dr., U.S. 192, and Orange Blossom Trail.

Viet Garden, 1237 E. Colonial Dr. (☎896-4154), near Mills Ave. Nestled in a strip of international restaurants, this little gem serves delectable Vietnamese and Thai cuisine. Savor the pineapple fried rice ($10) for a familiar favorite, or mix it up with different rice platters, featuring pork, chicken, beef, and quail ($6-8). Open M-Th and Su 10am-9pm, F-Sa 10am-10pm. AmEx/D/MC/V. ❶

Tijuana Flats, 50 E. Central Blvd. (☎839-0007). Colossal burritos like the "megajuana" with beef, steak, or chicken ($7-9) will satisfy any appetite, and vegetarians will enjoy the spinach artichoke quesadilla ($6). Taquitos ($6) are a meal of more manageable portions. Open M-Th 10:30-10pm, F-Sa 11am-10:30pm, Su 11am-9pm. Am/MC/V. ❶

Beefy King, 424 N. Bumby Ave. (☎894-2241), off E. Colonial Dr. Voted "Best Beefy Experience" by Florida Magazine, this family eatery has been pleasing residents for 30 years with fantastic sandwiches served on a different-sized kaiser rolls (junior $3, regular $4, extra large $5). Sit at the old-fashioned lunch counter to enjoy their roast beef sandwich. Open M-F 10am-3pm, Sa 11am-3pm; drive-through open M-F 10am-5:30pm. MC/V. ❶

♫ ENTERTAINMENT AND NIGHTLIFE

The best options for one-stop partying are Disney's **Pleasure Island** or Universal's **CityWalk** (p. 440), but downtown is also lively. Check the listings found in the Calendar in Friday's *Orlando Sentinel* or the free *Orlando Weekly.* Cheap bars line **North Orange Avenue.** For tourist-oriented attractions, head to the bright lights of **International Drive,** where mini-golf, a Ripley's Believe It or Not museum, the world's largest McDonald's, and Wonderworks (a science funhouse in an upside-down building) await.

▨ SAK Comedy Lab, 380 W. Amelia St. (☎648-0001), at Hughey Ave., in downtown. With its trademark family-friendly humor, SAK manages to produce top-notch hilarity that all audiences can enjoy. Enjoy the funniest improvisional comedy in town with theatre-style concessions. Shows Tu-W 9pm, Th 8pm, F-Sa 8 and 10pm. Tickets $2-12 depending on the night. Discounted tickets with college ID.

Waitiki, 26 Wall St. (☎481-1199), in downtown. Polynesian antique-lovers will admire the huge tiki statue in the middle of this bar and cafe, while after-workers enjoy $3 mojitos at Happy hour, and $3 Red Stripe all day. On F-Sa 10pm, the street shuts down, outdoor stages go up, and $5 gets you into all 8 bars on the block. W-Th live reggae 10pm, F-Sa live bands 9-10pm. Open daily 11am-2am. Kitchen closes at 11pm.

Tabu, 46 N. Orange Ave. (☎648-8363; www.tabunightclub.com), in downtown. An upscale South Beach-style haven for twentysomethings with the neighborhood's largest dance floor. Tu and Th is college night, with all-you-can-drink included in the cover. Stylish dress. Usually 18+. Cover $12. Open Tu-Sa 10pm-3am.

WALT DISNEY WORLD ☎407

Disney World is lot like Rome: all roads lead to it. Its name is more apt than one might imagine, as Disney indeed creates a "world" of its own, even hosting a full marathon run entirely on its grounds. Within this Never-Neverland, theme parks, resorts, theaters, restaurants, and nightclubs all come together as the embodiment of fun. The only setback is that magical amusement comes at a price—everything in Walt Disney's world costs almost twice as much as it does in the real world. Every attraction here is a marketing machine, and all rides end in their very own gift shop. In the end, though, the Disney empire leaves no one bored.

> **THE REAL FASTPASS.** Though the FASTPASS option numbs some of the pain induced by Disney theme park crowds, it only takes the relief so far. Getting a FASTPASS for a particular ride may prevent you from being able to obtain another pass for a set amount of time (sometimes upward of an hour). If you're looking to avoid long lines, arrive in the evening, or visit Disney during the quieter (and cooler) low-season months.

🛈 PRACTICAL INFORMATION

Disney dominates **Lake Buena Vista,** 20 mi. west of Orlando via I-4 (☎824-4321 or 939-4636; www.disneyworld.com). Ticketing options are vast and complex, and the best way to acquaint yourself with them is to visit the Disney World website. The one-day basic ticket ($71, ages 3-9 $59) admits visitors to one of the four parks, allowing them to leave and return later in the day. The **Park-Hopper Pass** is a better value, allowing admission to all four parks for a flat rate of $45, plus the cost of a one- or multiple-day base ticket. The **Park-Hopper Plus** includes a set number of days at the four parks and a specified number of visits to other Disney attractions for $45 plus the cost of a one- or multiple-day Park-Hopper Pass. Hopper passes need not be used on consecutive days, but must be used within 14 days of the first use unless the **No Expiration** option ($15 or more) is added.

Disney provides free transportation between attractions. Attractions that charge separate admissions include: **Typhoon Lagoon** ($41, ages 3-9 $35), **Blizzard Beach** ($41/35), **Disney's Wide World of Sports** complex ($11.25/8.50) and **Pleasure Island** ($28; under 18 must be accompanied by an adult). For descriptions, see **Other Disney Attractions** (p. 439). Avoid paying full fare for a Disney park by purchasing Park Hopper Passes at official Visitors Centers for about $10-15 less.

Disney World opens its gates 365 days a year, but hours fluctuate by season. Expect the parks to open at 9am and close between 9 and 11pm, but call beforehand—the schedule is only set a month in advance. Prepare for crowds (and afternoon thunderstorms) in summer, but the crowded peak times are Christmas, Thanksgiving, and spring break. The parks are least crowded in January and October. The free **FASTPASS** option at all of the parks allows you to bypass long lines on popular rides. Simply insert your park entrance ticket into a FASTPASS station, and you will receive a ticket telling you when to return, usually 30min. to 2hr. later.

👁 PARKS

MAGIC KINGDOM

Seven lands comprise the Magic Kingdom: **Main Street, USA; Tomorrowland; Fantasyland; Liberty Square; Frontierland; Adventureland;** and **Mickey's Toontown Fair.** More than any of the other Disney parks, the Kingdom is geared toward children.

MAIN STREET, USA. As the entrance to the "Most Magical Place on Earth," Main Street captures the spirit and bustle of early 20th-century America, with parades and vendors peddling everything from glass-blown figurines to original Mickey animation cells. The aroma of freshly baked, overpriced cookies and cakes beckons from **Main Street Bakery,** and the **Emporium** is a one-stop shop for Magic Kingdom souvenirs. A horse-drawn trolley carries visitors up the crowded Main St. to **Cinderella's Castle,** Disney World's centerpiece, where there are frequent dancing and singing shows by favorite Disney characters.

TOMORROWLAND. In the 90s, Tomorrowland received a neon facelift that skyrocketed it out of the space-race days of the 60s and into a futuristic intergalactic nation. The indoor coaster **Space Mountain** dominates the landscape, providing thrills in the blackness of outer space. A bonus is the long corridor with A/C in which guests can beat the heat while waiting. **Buzz Lightyear's Space Ranger Spin** equips *Toy Story* fans with laser cannons to fight the Evil Emperor Zurg.

MICKEY'S TOONTOWN FAIR AND FANTASYLAND. Visitors can meet their favorite characters at the **Hall of Fame** and **Mickey's Country House.** To meet Mickey, come to the **Judge's Tent** equipped with an autograph book and a camera, but be ready to wait in lines (average wait 20min.-120min.) with dozens of eager children. **Fantasyland** brings some of Disney's all-time favorite animated films to life. Soar above London and Neverland in a pirate ship sprinkled with pixie dust at **Peter Pan's Flight,** then dance with dwarves at **Snow White's Scary Adventures.** Board a honey pot and journey into the Hundred Acre Wood at **The Many Adventures of Winnie the Pooh,** where you will withstand a blustery day, bounce with Tigger, and encounter bizarre Heffalumps. Meet mechanical children from around the world on the classic boat ride **"It's a Small World,"** which will fiendishly burn its happy, happy song into your brain.

LIBERTY SQUARE AND FRONTIERLAND. Welcome to Americana, Disney-style. Liberty Square introduces visitors to educational and political aspects of American history, while Frontierland showcases the America of cowboys and Indians. The **Hall of Presidents** is a fun exhibit on US heads of state, from George Washington to George W. Bush. Next door, the spooky **Haunted Mansion** houses 999 happy ghouls. In Frontierland, take a lazy raft ride over to **Tom Sawyer Island** and explore, or take on the two thrill rides—**Splash Mountain** and **Big Thunder Mountain Railroad.**

ADVENTURELAND. The classic **Pirates of the Caribbean** steals the show. You can expect to wait in long lines to see a Johnny Depp imposter: a new animatronic Captain Jack Sparrow has been recently added. Fly on the **Magic Carpets of Aladdin** for an aerial view of the park. One of the original rides from the park's opening, the **Jungle Cruise,** provides a tongue-in-cheek take on exploration, touring the world's amazing rivers while supplying good, wet fun and lots of bad puns.

EPCOT CENTER

For those above 12 years of age or without a Mickey fetish, EPCOT may be the most appealing of the Disney World parks. In 1966, Walt dreamed up an "Experimental Prototype Community Of Tomorrow" (EPCOT), which would evolve con-

Orlando Theme Parks

▲ ACCOMMODATIONS   ★ FOOD

The Courtyard at
Lake Luceme, **2**
Disney's All-Star Resorts, **6**
Gator Motel, **8**
Palm Lakefront Resort
& Hostel, **7**

Beefy King, **1**
Tijuana Flats, **3**
Viet Garden, **4**

TO BLUE SPRING (32mi),
STATE PARK (32mi),
DOWNTOWN ORLANDO AND
EXPERIENCE (3mi), WINTER PARK (7mi),

① (10mi) THE HOLY LAND
② (5mi), ③ (8.5mi), ④ (19mi)

Orlando Official
Visitors Center

stantly to incorporate new ideas from US technology, eventually becoming a self-sufficient, futuristic utopia. At present, EPCOT is divided into Future World and the expansive World Showcase. After a day of walking around EPCOT, you'll see why some joke that the acronym actually stands for "Every Person Comes Out Tired." The trademark 180 ft. high geosphere (or "golf ball") at the entrance of **Future World** houses the **Spaceship Earth** attraction, in which visitors board a "time machine" for a tour through the evolution of communication. **Body Wars** takes visitors on a simulated tour of the human body. At nearby **Test Track,** riders experience life in the fast lane, one of Disney's fastest and longest rides.

In the **World Showcase,** architectural styles, monuments and crafts represent 13 countries from around the world, while people in traditional dress perform various forms of cultural entertainment. **Maelstrom** is an amusing and thrilling boat ride through Norway, complete with Vikings and evil trolls. Every night at 9pm, EPCOT presents a magnificent mega-show called **IllumiNations** with music, dancing fountains, laser lights, fireballs, and fireworks. The World Showcase also specializes in regional cuisine—each "country" offers both a sit-down restaurant and a more reasonably priced cafeteria-style option. The prices at the **Restaurant Akershus ❸,** in the Norway Pavilion, make it a Disney dining bargain. The traditional *Kjottkake* ($7.75) makes for a great regional treat. Call ahead to avoid long waits. (Entrees range $7.25-11.) Those with an affinity for brew can create their own around-the-world tour, sampling a beer from each country. Though drinking a Corona in Mexico and a Casablanca in Morocco is truly magical, at $4-7 a beer, doing so will demolish both your sobriety and your budget.

DISNEY-MGM STUDIOS

Disney-MGM Studios is a living movie set, built around stunt shows and mini-theatricals. Restaurants resemble their Hollywood counterparts, and movie characters stroll the grounds signing autographs. Movie fanatics will love the **Great Movie Ride,** housed inside a replica of Grauman's Chinese Theatre. The ride represents about every genre of film, from western and romance to action and adventure, and is hosted by a cast member. The **Studios Backlot Tour** takes visitors on a 35-40min. behind-the-scenes tour into the magic of movie making. The **Twilight Zone Tower of Terror** drops guests 13 stories in a runaway elevator. The thrilling, twisting, "limo" ride **Rock 'n' Roller Coaster** will take you from 0 to 60 mph in less than three seconds with the force of a supersonic F-14 while Aerosmith blasts in your ears; it's also the only Disneyworld ride to take you upside down. Based on the hit TV game show, **Who Wants to Be a Millionaire? Play It!** replicates the real show, save affable host Regis Philbin. The **Indiana Jones Epic Stunt Spectacular** shows off some of the greatest scenes from the trilogy in live action. If screeching, synchronized cars are your thing, check out the new **"Lights, Motors, Action" Extreme Stunt Show** and learn what goes into creating complex vehicle stunts. **The Magic of Disney Animation,** a tour that introduces you to actual Disney animators, explains how Disney animated films are created and offers a sneak peak at sketches of upcoming flicks.

DISNEY'S ANIMAL KINGDOM

If plastic characters are getting to be too much, the Animal Kingdom is a dose of reality, in a carefully managed Disney presentation, of course. Animal Kingdom's walkways and wildlife are a great respite from the fast-paced park environment, but it has something for the die-hard thrill-seekers as well. Animal Kingdom's newest attraction, **Expedition Everest,** is more aggressive than Space Mountain—this high-altitude, high-speed coaster is full of surprises. **Kilimanjaro Safaris** depart for the Harambe preserve, where elephants, hippos, giraffes, and other creatures of the African savannah roam. A **Maharajah Jungle Trek** drops riders among tigers, tapirs, and bats, and the **Kali River Rapids** is a whitewater adventure exposing the threats facing our planet. Like any Disney park, shows and rides make up a large part of Animal Kingdom (the park's catchphrase is NAHTAZU: "not a zoo"). **DINO-SAUR,** the park's best ride, puts travelers in the middle of the early Cretaceous. Another 3D spectacular, **It's Tough to be a Bug!,** put on by the cast of the animated flick *A Bug's Life,* is sure to entertain all ages and species.

OTHER DISNEY ATTRACTIONS

Besides the four main parks, Disney offers several other draws with different themes and separate admissions. **Blizzard Beach** is a water park built on the premise of a melting mountain. Ride a ski lift to the fastest water-slide in the world and plummet down the 120 ft. descent. **Typhoon Lagoon,** a 50-acre water park, centers on the nation's largest wave pool and its seven-foot waves. In addition to eight water slides, the lagoon has an inner-tubing creek and a saltwater coral reef with tropical fish and harmless sharks. Water parks fill up early on hot days; late arrivals may be turned away. With venues for over 30 sports, **Disney's Wide World of Sports** complex is a hub of athletic activity. Catch the Atlanta Braves in spring training and the Tampa Bay Buccaneers during pre-season camp. The larger-than-life **Downtown Disney** is a neon conglomeration of theme restaurants, nightlife, and shopping encompassing the **Marketplace, Pleasure Island,** and the **West Side.** Pleasure Island is hedonistic Disney with an attitude. Party the night away at eight clubs, from comedy to jazz to 70s and 80s pop. **Mannequins,** with a spinning dance floor and stunning strobes, trumps any South Beach club in terms of venue, though perhaps not clientele coolness. (Under 18 with parent. Cover $21. Open daily 7pm-2am.) In the Marketplace at the **LEGO Imagination Center,** take a photo with LEGO sculptures or create your own. In the West Side, **Cirque Du Soleil** presents La Nouba, a blend of circus acrobatics and theater with a price higher than the tightropes ($63-97, ages 3-9 $50-90). Next door, the high-tech games of **Disney Quest** guarantee a "virtually" exciting time at the interactive indoor park ($29-35).

LIFE BEYOND DISNEY   ☎ 407

Believe it or not, it exists. In fact, many visitors say Universal's **Islands of Adventure** is Orlando's best park. Disney has such a domination that the other parks band together to compete with Mickey: "FlexTickets" combine admission to various parks at a discount, though prices can fluctuate. A four-park ticket ($186, ages 3-9 $153) covers **Sea World,** both **Universal Studios** parks, and **Wet 'n' Wild,** and allows 14 days with free transportation. The five-park ticket ($227/187; 14 days) adds **Tampa's Busch Gardens** (p. 443). Universal City Travel (☎800-224-3838) sells tickets.

🜨 PARKS

UNIVERSAL ORLANDO

Swap Mickey and Goofy for Spider-Man and Shrek, and you get a theme park for comic fans and animation lovers. Universal has movie-themed rides that thrill, spin, and make you squeal. With two parks **(Universal Studios Florida and Islands of Adventure),** three resort hotels, and an entertainment complex, **CityWalk,** Universal stands toe-to-toe with the "other park." *(I-4 Exit 74B or 75A. ☎363-8000. Open daily 9am, closing times vary. CityWalk open until 2am. 2-park pass $75/$65. CityWalk is ungated and free; club, dinner, and movie packages available. Parking $11, free after 6pm.)*

UNIVERSAL STUDIOS FLORIDA. The first park to "ride the movies" showcases a mix of rides and behind-the-scenes extravaganzas. Live the fairy tale courtesy of "OgreVision" at **Shrek 4D,** the park's most popular attraction. **Back to the**

Future...The Ride, a staple of any visit, utilizes seven-story OmniMax screens and spectacular special effects. **Men in Black: Alien Attack** puts you through agent training as you navigate through an alien-infested city armed with your own blaster gun, competing against other players to see who is the best alien sharp shooter.

ISLANDS OF ADVENTURE. This park encompasses 110 acres of rides and typically has short waits. Five islands portray different themes, ranging from cartoons to Jurassic Park. **The Amazing Adventures of Spider-Man** is the park's crown jewel. A fast-moving car whizzes around a 3D video system as you and Peter Parker find the stolen Statue of Liberty. The most amusing island is **Seuss Landing,** home of the **Green Eggs & Ham Cafe ❷** (green eggs and ham-wich $6). **The Cat in the Hat** turns the classic tale into a ride on a wild couch that loops its way through the story. If that's too tame, the ◪**Dueling Dragons** is the world's first inverted, dueling roller coaster.

CITYWALK. CityWalk greets the eager tourist upon entering Universal Studios. A unique mix of restaurants, bars, clubs, and a cineplex makes it an appealing alternative to Pleasure Island. **The NASCAR Cafe, Jimmy Buffet's Margaritaville,** and **Emeril's** are a few of the pricey theme restaurants that line the main street. Clubs on the walk include **Bob Marley's** and **The Groove.** Packages make it possible to enjoy a meal, a movie, and partying at an affordable price. *(All-club access $10, with a movie $14. Meal with a movie or club access $20.)* For cheap eats on the walk, head to **Pastamore ❸,** an indoor and outdoor cafe with many Italian classics at an affordable price. Try their pizza ($8-9) or their warm goat cheese dip ($7). If you're craving something sweet, try their pistachio ice cream ($3). For rock 'n' roll and good food head to the world's largest **Hard Rock Cafe.** In addition to sampling the dishes, visitors can take the Hard Rock Tour to see the VIP area of the building and to learn about some of the rock memorabilia that the restaurant holds dear.

SEA WORLD

One of the largest marine parks in the US, **Sea World Adventure Park** makes a splash with shows, rides, and exhibits. In recent years, it has worked to transform itself into a full-fledged park emphasizing the marvels and mysteries of sea creatures. Eels, barracudas, sharks, and other beasties lick their chops in **Shark Encounter,** the world's largest collection of dangerous sea creatures. **The Shamu Adventure** thrills with aquatic acrobatics smartly executed by a family of orcas and their trainers. Whale belly flops send waves of salt water into the cheering "soak zone." The park's first thrill ride, **Journey to Atlantis,** gets rave reviews, as does **Kraken,** a floorless roller coaster billed as the highest, fastest, and longest in Orlando. In summer, stick around until 10pm for **Mystify,** a fireworks spectacular. *(12 mi. southwest of Orlando off I-4 at Rte. 528/Bee Line Expressway. Take bus #8. ☎ 351-3600. Open daily 9am-7pm; extended hours in summer. $60, ages 3-9 $48. Parking $8.)* Orlando's newest destination is the adjacent **Discovery Cove.** Swim with dolphins, snorkel among tropical fish, and frolic in an aviary with more than 200 birds. *(☎877-434-7268; www.discoverycove.com. Open daily 9am-5:30pm. Reservations required. $129-409.)*

OTHER SIGHTS. Step back in time at the Holy Land Experience, a small, controversial, proselytizing park billed as a "living biblical museum." Take in the architecture and sights of ancient Jerusalem and watch costumed performers reenact biblical scenes. The Scriptorium is a one-of-a-kind museum displaying Bible-related artifacts. *(4655 Vineland Rd. I-4 Exit 78. ☎ 367-2065; www.holylandexperience.com. Open M-F 10am-5pm, Sa 10am-6pm, Su noon-6pm; extended seasonal hours. $35, seniors $30, ages 6-12 $23, under 5 free; cheaper tickets available online.)* The botanical garden at Cypress Gardens features over 8000 varieties of plants and flowers amidst winding walkways and boat rides. Despite the pretty flowers, the water-ski shows attract the biggest crowds and the loudest applause. *(Southwest of Orlando in Winter Haven.*

Take I-4 SW to Rte. 27 S, then Rte. 540 W. ☎863-324-2111. Open daily 10am-6pm; extended hours in summer. $45, ages 6-12 and seniors $40.)

TAMPA   ☎813

Even with beautiful weather and ideal beaches, Tampa has avoided the plastic pink flamingos that plague its Atlantic Coast counterparts. While Busch Gardens is Tampa's primary tourist attraction, the rest of the city provides less-commercial fun. Ybor (EE-bor) City, Tampa's Cuban district, is a hotbed of energy and activity where sun-kissed tourists can find many of Tampa's best restaurants and bars.

🖪🖬 ORIENTATION AND PRACTICAL INFORMATION. Tampa wraps around Hillsborough Bay and sprawls northward. **Nebraska Avenue** and **Dale Mabry Road** parallel **I-275** as the main north-south routes; **Kennedy Boulevard, Columbus Street,** and **Busch Boulevard** go east-west. With some exceptions, numbered streets go north-south and numbered avenues run east-west. **Ybor City** is bounded roughly by Nuccio Pkwy., 22nd St., Palm Ave., and 5th Ave. Be careful outside these boundaries; the surrounding area can be dangerous. **Tampa International Airport** (**TPA**; ☎870-8770; www.tampaairport.com) is 5 mi. west of downtown, Exit 39 off I-275. HARTline bus #30 runs between the airport and downtown. Amtrak, 601 Nebraska Ave. (☎221-7600; www.amtrak.com; open daily 9am-6pm), at the end of Zack St. two blocks north of Kennedy St., runs **trains** to Miami (5-5½ hr., 1 per day, $29-45). Greyhound, 610 Polk St. (☎229-2174; www.greyhound; open 24hr.), sends **buses** to Atlanta (12-13hr., 5 per day, $73), Miami (8-9hr., 11 per day, $38-41), and Orlando (2hr-2½ hr., 8 per day, $20-21). Hillsborough Area Regional Transit (HARTline) provides **public transit** in the Tampa area. Buses #8 and 46 run to Ybor City from downtown. (☎254-4278. $1.50, ages 5-17 and seniors $0.75; exact change required.) HARTline operates Tampa's Streetcar System (☎254-4278; www.tecolinestreet-car.org; $1.75) as well, which runs **streetcars** from Ybor City to downtown Tampa. **Visitor Info:** The **Tampa Bay Convention and Visitors Bureau** is at 401 East Jackson St. N, Ste. 2100. (☎223-1111 or 800-448-2672; www.visittampabay.com. Open M-F 8am-5pm.) **Tampa Bay Visitor Information Center** is at 615 Channelside Dr. Ste. 108A (☎223-2752 or 800-448-2672. Open M-Sa 9:30am-5:30pm, Su 11am-5pm.) **Hotlines: Crisis Hotline,** ☎234-1234. **Internet Access: John F. Germany Public Library,** 900 N. Ashley Dr., in downtown. (☎273-3652. Free. Open M-Th 9am-9pm, F 9am-6pm, Sa 9am-5pm, Su 10am-6pm.) **Post Office:** 401 S. Florida Ave. (☎223-4332. Open M-F 8:30am-4:30pm.) **Postal Code:** 33601.

🖡 ACCOMMODATIONS. The only hosteling option is **Gram's Place ❶**, 3109 N. Ola Dr., Exit 46B off I-275 N. What the "train" dorm lacks in spaciousness it makes up for in quirkiness, and you're sure to bunk alongside interesting travelers. Photos of rock 'n' roll legend Gram Parsons line the hostel between the Little Amsterdam and Little Montreal sections. Be prepared: showers and toilets are outside. (☎221-0596. Dorms M-Th and Su $22.50, F-Sa $25; private rooms from $55. AmEx/MC/V.) Chain hotels and motels hug I-275 and can be found at most exits. With spacious, comfy rooms, the classy **Baymont Inn ❷**, 9202 N. 30th St., is a great alternative to motels. (☎930-6900 or 877-229-6668. A/C, cable TV, free Internet, and continental breakfast. Rooms $69-75. AAA and AARP discount 10%. AmEx/D/MC/V.)

🖪 FOOD. Ybor City's 7th Ave. is lined with a number of fun and funky eateries, many of which stay open late to satiate post-clubbing cravings. Since 1905 **🖾Columbia ❸**, 2117 East 7th Ave., has been serving up award-winning Cuban/Spanish food. Columbia is Florida's oldest restaurant, and its delicious fare is served in a beautiful Spanish-style building. The atmosphere doesn't come cheap, but you can still

GUAVAWEEN

Every year during the last week of October, more than 100,000 people flock to Tampa to participate in one of the nation's biggest and baddest street parties. Held in the notoriously festive neighborhood of Ybor City, Guavaween is a Halloween celebration infused with Latin spice and Southern soul.

In the 19th century, Tampa residents tried to cultivate a guava industry on the Gulf Coast, and, though the effort was largely unsuccessful, guavas became synonymous with the region. Columnist Steve Otto noted that if New York City was the "Big Apple," then Tampa could be called the "Big Guava." The analogy stuck, and for the last 20 years, "Mama Guava" has kicked off the Guavaween bash by leading the legendary "Mama Guava Stumble Parade" through the streets of Ybor. The festival has tons of concerts and costume contests, and winners take home prizes of up to $2000. Guavaween has recently toned down some of its wild antics and now appeals to both partiers and families, entertaining children during the day with a scavenger hunt. Still, don't be fooled—sin and skin prevail when the sun goes down, as revelers party early into the morning in search of a trick or a treat. The countdown to the next Guavaween has already begun.

For more information on Guavaween, call ☎ 248-0721 or visit www.cc-events.org/gw.

find a reasonable meal by selecting from their many tapas, soups, and salads. Try their famous Spanish bean soup (garbanzo beans, smoked ham, chirozo sausage; cup $4, bowl $5). Tapas range from $6-9. Try the scallops "Casmiro" ($9) if you're in the mood for seafood. (☎ 248-4961; www.columbiarestaurant.com. M-Sa flamenco dancers 7 and 9:30pm. Open M-Th 11am-10pm, F-Sa 11am-11pm, Su noon-9pm.) Mostly a dinner spot, the swanky **Bernini ❹**, 1702 E. 7th Ave., whips up delicious pasta dishes ($18-23). Try Jason's Favorite (capellini with grilled chicken breast, tomatoes, and garlic; $18) or the pistachio nut encrusted grouper ($24). Hungry customers enjoy their meals under photos and replicas of the eponymous sculptor's works. (☎ 248-0099. Open M-Th 11:30am-10pm, F 11:30am-11pm, Sa 4-11pm, Su 5-10pm. AmEx/D/MC/V.) The king of buffets, **Sweet Tomatoes ❷**, 1902 N. Dale Mabry Hwy., greets diners with an extensive salad bar, delectable soups, fresh baked goods, three types of pasta, a sundae bar, and fresh fruit. A meal here won't put too much of a dent in your wallet, either; lunch (all-you-can-eat salad and soup) is a mere $8, and dinner ($9) is just as much bang for your buck. (☎ 874-6566. Open M-Th and Su 11am-9pm, F-Sa 11am-10pm. AmEx/D/MC/V.)

◗ **SIGHTS.** Tampa blossomed through Ybor City, a planned community once known as the cigar capital of the world. Early 20th-century stogie manufacturer Vincent Martínez Ybor employed a host of immigrants, and the city soon displayed the influence of intermingled Cuban, Italian, and German heritages. The **Ybor City State Museum**, 1818 9th Ave., details the rise and fall of the tobacco empire and its workers. Exhibits include a detailed look at 19th- and early 20th-century Ybor life, while a display is dedicated to the art of hand-rolled cigars, complete with a viewing of a cigar roller at work. (☎ 247-6323; www.ybormuseum.org. Open daily 9am-5pm. Neighborhood walking tours Sa 10:30am. $3, under 6 free. Tours $6.)

The **Florida Aquarium**, 701 Channelside Dr., invites you to get up close and personal with fish from Florida's lagoons. Head into the wetlands exhibit to gape at gators, turtles, and fighting river otters, and then check out the coral reef, where menacing sharks and enigmatic jellyfish haunt the waters. Wild dolphins of the Gulf stage a meet and greet on **Dolphin Quest Eco-Tours** in Tampa Bay. (☎ 273-4000; www.flaquarium.org. Open daily 9:30am-5pm. Eco-Tours M-F 2pm, Sa-Su 2 and 4pm. $18, seniors $15, ages 3-11 $12. Eco-tours $20/19/15; first-come, first-served basis. Combo tickets available.) Built in 1891, Henry B. Plant's Tampa Bay Hotel was once considered the most luxurious resort in the South. A wing of the lavish hotel is open today as the

Henry B. Plant Museum, 401 W. Kennedy Blvd. The restored Moorish architecture, opulent furnishings, and tropical gardens at this national landmark will transport you back to the Victorian age. The museum comes complete with Edison carbon-filament lighting and classical music. (☎254-1891; www.plantmuseum.com. Open Tu-Sa 10am-4pm, Su noon-4pm. Suggested donation $5.)

Anheuser-Busch's addition to Florida's theme parks, **Busch Gardens,** 3605 E. Bougainvillea Ave., is the most prized weapon in the Tampa tourism arsenal. Thrill-seekers head for roller coasters Kumba, Montu, and Gwazi, while others watch animals roam, fly, slither, and swim through the African-themed zoo areas. The "Edge of Africa" safari experience is among the park's most popular attractions. (☎987-5082 or 888-800-5447; www.buschgardens.com. Hours vary, usually open daily 9:30am-7:30pm. $62, ages 3-9 $59. Parking $11.)

🎭🎶 **ENTERTAINMENT AND NIGHTLIFE.** Brief yourself on city entertainment with the free *Tampa Weekend* or *Weekly Planet,* in local restaurants and bars and on street corners. Gay travelers should check out the free *Stonewall.* Every year during the last week of January, the **José Gasparilla,** a 165 ft., fully rigged pirate ship loaded with "buccaneers," invades Hillsborough Bay, kicking off a month of pirate-themed parades and festivals (www.gasparillapiratefest.com). Thousands pack Ybor City on the last Saturday in October for **Guavaween** (☎242-4828; www.cc-events.org), a Latin-style Halloween celebration (see box at left). With over 35 clubs and bars, Ybor City is brimming with energetic nightlife.

Most nighttime hangouts are on bustling 7th Ave., though fun can be found on 8th and 9th Ave. as well. Use caution when walking down side streets. During the week, many restaurants close at 8pm, and clubs don't open until 10pm. 7th Ave. is closed to vehicular traffic at night, making bar-hopping very easy. For those first drinks, **Green Iguana Bar & Grill,** 1708 E. 7th Ave., serves cheap, tasty food by day and turns into a multi-level clubbing extravaganza at night, with $1 drinks on Wednesdays. Try the award-winning Mambo King's Bacon and Cheeseburger Deluxe ($7) or artichoke chicken ($9) from their delicious food menu. (☎248-9555. Open daily 11am-3am. Kitchen closes at midnight.) **Coyote Ugly Saloon,** 1722 E. 7th Ave., is the hottest club on the Ybor strip. Taking its cue from the movie *Coyote Ugly,* the rowdy bar serves mostly liquor shots with complimentary bar dancing and body licking. Their motto: "You will get drunk, you will get ugly." (☎228-8459. 21+. Happy hour daily 5-7pm. Open daily 5pm-3am.)

ST. PETERSBURG
AND CLEARWATER
☎ 727

Across the bay, 22 mi. southwest of Tampa, St. Petersburg (a.k.a. St. Pete) is home to a relaxed beach community of retirees and young singles. The town basks in soft white beaches, emerald water, and about 361 days of sunshine each year. The St. Petersburg-to-Clearwater stretch caters to beach bums and city strollers alike. While the outdoor scenery draws crowds, indoor activities are equally captivating—museum exhibits on Salvador Dalí and John F. Kennedy rival even the sunset.

🧭🔢 **ORIENTATION AND PRACTICAL INFORMATION.** In St. Petersburg, **Central Avenue** parallels numbered avenues, running east-west downtown. **34th Street (U.S. 19), I-275,** and **4th Street** are major north-south thoroughfares. The beaches line a strip of barrier islands on the west side facing the Gulf of Mexico. Several causeways, including the **Clearwater Memorial Causeway (Route 60),** lead to the beaches from St. Pete. Clearwater sits at the far north of the strip. **Gulf Boulevard** runs down the coastline, through Belleair Shores, Indian Rocks Beach, Indian Shores, Redington Shores, Madeira Beach, Treasure Island, and St. Pete Beach.

Greyhound, 180 9th St. N, at 2nd Ave. N, in St. Petersburg (☎898-1496; www.greyhound.com; open daily 4:30am-11:30pm), runs **buses** to Clearwater (30min., 5 per day, $11) and Orlando (3hr., 6 per day, $21). The Clearwater station is at 2811 Gulf-to-Bay Blvd. (☎796-7315. Open M-Sa 6am-9pm, Su 6am-noon and 1:30-9pm.) Pinellas Suncoast Transit Authority (PSTA) handles **public transit;** most routes depart from Williams Park at 1st Ave. N and 3rd St. N. (☎540-1900. $1.50, students $1, seniors $0.75; day pass $3.50.) To reach Tampa, take bus #100X from the Gateway Mall ($1.75). A **beach trolley** runs up and down the shore. (Daily every 20-30min. 5am-10pm. $1.50; day pass $3.50.) Jump on the Looper Trolley ($0.50), which runs a 30min. tour of downtown St. Pete (☎821-5166). For a **taxi,** call Yellow Cab, ☎799-2222. The **St. Petersburg Area Chamber of Commerce** is at 100 2nd Ave. N. (☎821-4069; www.stpete.com. Open M-F 8am-5pm, Sa 10am-5pm, Su noon-5pm.) **The Pier Information Center,** 800 2nd Ave. NE., is also in St. Petersburg. (☎821-6443. Open M-Th 10am-9pm, F-Sa 10am-10pm, Su 11am-7pm.) **Hotlines: Rape Crisis,** ☎530-7233. **Medical Services: Bayfront Medical Center,** 701 6th St. S. (☎823-1234.) **Internet Access: St. Petersburg Main Library,** 3745 9th Ave. N. (☎893-7724. Free. Open M, W, and F 9am-6pm, Tu-Th 11-8pm, Su 10am-6pm.) **Post Office:** 3135 1st Ave. N., at 31st St. (☎322-6696. Open M-F 8am-6pm, Sa 8am-2:30pm.) **Postal Code:** 33701.

⌂ ACCOMMODATIONS. Many cheap motels line **4th Street N.** and **U.S. 19** in St. Pete. To avoid the worst neighborhoods, stay on the north end of 4th St. and the south end of U.S. 19. In Clearwater, several inexpensive motels cluster along **Gulf Boulevard.** Tucked snugly away on the sandy Clearwater shore, the **Clearwater Beach International Hostel (HI) ❶,** 606 Bay Esplanade Ave., off Mandalay Ave. at the Sands Motel in Clearwater Beach, is the ultimate beach pad, with spacious, well-furnished rooms and a friendly staff. Bikes and kayaks are available for cruising the beaches. (☎443-1211. Free Wi-Fi. Linen and key deposit $5. Laundry $3. Reception 9am-noon and 5-9pm. Dorms $17; private rooms $39-65. MC/V.) **Fort De Soto County Park ❶,** 3500 Pinellas Bayway S, composed of five islands, has perhaps the best camping in all of Florida. Though its namesake, Fort De Soto, is available for exploration, you may never want to leave your beautiful campsite. (☎582-2267; www.pinellascounty.org/park. Hot showers, electricity, and laundry. Front gate locked 9pm. Curfew 10pm. Sites $28.) In downtown St. Petersburg, the **Landmark Motel ❷,** 1930 4th St. N., has bright rooms nestled among tropical plants. (☎895-1629. A/C and cable TV. Singles from $50-60; doubles from $60. AmEx/D/MC/V.)

▯ FOOD. St. Petersburg's cheap, health-conscious restaurants cater to retirees and generally close by 8 or 9pm. After a day of relaxing under the Clearwater sun, make your way over to **Frenchy's Cafe ❸,** 41 Baymont St., and cool off with a salted margarita ($3). Have a seat at one of the benches for the boiled shrimp (half-order $8), which comes dusted with secret seasonings. The famous smoked fish spread with crackers ($7) delights all patrons. (☎446-3607. Open M-Th 11:30am-11pm, F-Sa 11:30am-midnight, Su noon-11pm. AmEx/MC/V.) The cheapest breakfast in town doesn't have to be just a bagel. At **The Beach Shanty Cafe ❶,** 397 Mandalay Ave., you can get a huge freshly cooked breakfast for a few bucks. Try the one egg, homefries, and toast special ($2.50) or the waffles with strawberries and whipped cream ($6) if you're feeling slightly more adventurous. (☎443-1616. Breakfast 7-11:30am; lunch served after 11:30am. AmEx/D/MC/V.) Also in St. Pete is the **Fourth Street Shrimp Store ❷,** 1006 4th St. N., a purveyor of all things shrimp: the chipotle shrimp salad ($7) or the popcorn shrimp poggie ($8) will fill any traveler's shrimp void. (☎822-0325. Open M and Su 11am-8:30pm, Tu-Sa 11am-9pm. MC/V.)

◐ SIGHTS. Grab *See St. Pete* or the *St. Petersburg Official Visitor's Guide* for the lowdown on area events, discounts, and useful maps. The highlight of St.

Petersburg is the ▓**Salvador Dalí Museum,** 1000 3rd St. S, the largest private collection of the surrealist's work in the world. Come see Dalí's famous "Hallucinogenic Toreador." The South's most-visited museum houses 95 of Dalí's oil paintings and provides guided tours offering fascinating glimpses into the enigmatic artist's life and works. (☎823-3767 or 800-442-3254; www.salvadordalimuseum.org. Open M-W and Sa 9:30am-5:30pm, Th 9:30am-8pm, F 9:30am-6pm, Su noon-5:30pm. Free tours daily every hour. Wheelchair-accessible. $15, seniors $13.50, students $10; Th after 5pm $5.) Downtown St. Pete is cluttered with museums and galleries, including the **Florida International Museum,** 244 2nd Ave. N. The "Cuban Missile Crisis: When the Cold War Got Hot" exhibit allows visitors to relive the Cold War era of the 1960s, recounting day-by-day the Cuban Missile Crisis. "John F. Kennedy: The Exhibition" provides a look at JFK's personal and political life. (☎822-3693 or 800-777-9882; www.floridamuseum.org. Open Tu-Sa 10am-5pm, Su noon-5pm; last entry 4pm. $10, AAA and seniors $8, students $5. Wheelchair-accessible.) The **Florida Holocaust Museum,** 55 5th St. S, in an old bank, traces Jewish life and anti-Semitism from early Europe to the present. (☎820-0100; www.flholocaustmuseum.org. Open daily M-F 10am-5pm; last entry 4pm. $8, seniors and students $7, ages 6-18 $4.)

The museum exhibits may impress you with their thorough and informative displays, but for a scene a little more characteristic of gulf coast Florida, hit the beaches. The nicest beach in the area may be **Pass-a-Grille Beach,** but its parking meters eat quarters by the bucketful. Check out **Clearwater Beach,** at the northern end of the Gulf Blvd. strand, where mainstream beach culture finds a fantastic white-sand setting. The **Sunsets at Pier 60** festival brings arts and entertainment to Clearwater Beach, but it's the sunsets that draw the crowds. (☎449-1036; www.sunsetsatpier60.com. Festival daily 2hr. before sunset until 2hr. after.)

▓ **NIGHTLIFE.** St. Petersburg caters to those who want to end the night by 9 or 10pm, fairly early in the evening; most visitors looking for nightlife head either to Tampa or the beach. If you're staying in downtown St. Pete and are in the mood for a concert, don't overlook **Jannus Landing,** 16 2nd St. N, which hosts local and big-name bands. The courtyard accommodates 1500 people and the bar keeps listeners in good spirits. (☎896-1244; www.jannuslandingconcerts.com. Most shows open to all ages. Limited bar menu. Call for tickets.) For a more consistent scene infused with youthful energy, Clearwater's hotels, restaurants, and parks often host free concerts. Free copies of *Weekly Planet* or *Tampa Tonight/Pinellas Tonight* can be found at local restaurants and bars, though an evening stroll through the blocks surrounding the rotary should turn up the night's hottest spot. The younger crowd heads for the big party at **Shepard's,** 619 South Gulfview Blvd., (☎441-6875). Sip a Shepard Margarita ($6) while you listen to the live music out on the dock at this two-level nightclub.

ATLANTIC COAST

DAYTONA BEACH   ☎ 386

When locals first started auto-racing on the hard-packed shores of Daytona Beach more than 60 years ago, they combined two aspects of life that would come to define the town's entire mentality: speed and sand. Daytona played an essential role in the 1947 founding of the **National Association of Stock Car Auto Racing (NASCAR),** and the mammoth Daytona International Speedway still hosts several big races each year. Though races no longer occur on the sand, 23 mi. of Atlantic beaches still pump the community's lifeblood.

FLORIDA

■ ORIENTATION. Daytona Beach lies 53 mi. northeast of Orlando and 90 mi. south of Jacksonville. **I-95** parallels the coast and the barrier island. **Atlantic Avenue (Route A1A)** is the main drag along the shore, and a scenic drive up A1A goes to St. Augustine and Jacksonville. **International Speedway Boulevard (U.S. 92)** runs east-west from the ocean, through downtown and to the racetrack and airport. Daytona Beach is a collection of smaller towns; many street numbers are not consecutive and navigation can be difficult. To avoid the gridlock on the beach, arrive early (8am) and leave early (around 3pm). Visitors must pay $5 to drive onto the beach, and police strictly enforce the 10 mph speed limit. Free parking is plentiful during most of the year but sparse during spring break, Speedweek, Bike Week, Biketoberfest, and the Pepsi 400. See p. 447 for festival dates.

■ TRANSPORTATION AND PRACTICAL INFORMATION. Amtrak, 100 North Atlantic Ave. (☎734-2322; www.amtrak.com. Open daily 6am-10pm.) Amtrak commuter shuttle takes passengers to their train connections at this curbside stop. Runs to Miami (8¼hr., 2 per day, $79-92). **Greyhound,** 138 S. Ridgewood Ave. (☎255-7076; www.greyhound.com; open daily 7:30am-10:30pm), 4 mi. west of the beach, runs to Jacksonville (2hr., 6 per day, $20) and Orlando (50min.-90min., 7 per day, $11-14). **Volusia County Transit Co. (VOTRAN),** 950 Big Tree Rd., operates local buses and a trolley that covers Rte. A1A between Granada Blvd. and Dunlawton Ave. All buses have bike racks. (☎761-7700. Regular service M-Sa 5:30am-midnight, Su 6:30am-6:30. Night service on select routes. Trolley M-Sa noon-midnight. $1.25, day pass $3, seniors and ages 6-17 $0.60. Free maps available at hotels.) For a **taxi,** call **Yellow Cab,** ☎255-5555. The **Daytona Beach Area Convention and Visitors Bureau** is at 126 E. Orange Ave., on City Island. (☎255-0415; www.daytonabeachcvb.org. Open M-F 9am-5pm.) **Hotline: Rape Crisis Line,** ☎258-7273. 24hr. **Medical Services: Halifax Medical Center,** 303 N. Clyde Morris Blvd. (☎254-4000). **Internet Access: Volusia County Library Center,** 105 E. Magnolia Ave. (☎257-6036. Free. 1hr. limit. Open M-Th 9am-7pm, F 9am-5pm, Sa 9am-3pm, Su 1-5pm.) **Post Office:** 220 N. Beach St. (☎258-9352. Open M-F 8:30am-5pm, Sa 10am-noon.) **Postal Code:** 32114.

■ ACCOMMODATIONS. Almost all of Daytona's lodgings front **Atlantic Avenue (Route A1A),** either on the beach or across the street; those off the beach offer the best deals. Spring break and race events drive prices upward of $150 per night even at budget places, but low-season rates are more reasonable. Many of the motels facing the beach cost $70 for a low-season single; prices range from $40-45 on the other side of the street. The **Camellia Motel ❷,** 1055 N. Atlantic Ave. (Rte. A1A), across the street from the beach, has cozy, bright rooms, free local calls, cable TV, free Wi-Fi, and A/C. (☎252-9963. Singles from $42; doubles from $47. Rates drop to $30 for stays of a week or longer. MC/V.) The gay-friendly **Streamline Hotel ❷,** 140 S. Atlantic, has some of the cheapest rooms in town. The top floor is a sky-roof bar with an expansive view of the beach. All rooms have a fridge, cable TV, and A/C. (☎258-6937. No reservations. Singles with up to 2 additional people from $33-100. 3-night special $89; week stay $200; special events $100. MC/V.) For a change in budget motel scenery, try the **Travelers Inn ❷,** 735 N. Atlantic Ave. Each of the 22 rooms has a different theme—find the force in the *Star Wars* room or rock out in the Jimi Hendrix or Beatles rooms. (☎253-3501 or 800-417-6466. Kitchen use $10. Singles $45-55; doubles $55-79; each additional person $10. AmEx/D/MC/V.) **Tomoka State Park ❶,** 2099 N. Beach St., 8 mi. north of Daytona in Ormond Beach, has 100 campsites under a tropical canopy. Enjoy salt water fishing (fishing supplies provided for a fee), nature trails, and a sculpture museum. (☎676-4050, reservations 800-326-3521. Open daily 8am-dusk. All sites $20, includes gas and electricity; additional person $4; pedestrians and bicyclists $1.)

◘ FOOD. The **Dancing Avocado Kitchen ❶**, 110 S. Beach St., is a delicious alternative to the Daytona seafood-and-grill scene, serving fantastic breakfasts. Enjoy the shrimp, avocado, and onion omelet ($8.75), or for lunch chow down on a grilled chicken quesadilla ($6.25) or the signature symphony salad ($5.50) in this endearing organic eatery. The tofu and vegetable scramble ($6.50) is just one of many vegan options. (☎947-2022. Open M-Sa 8am-4pm. AmEx/D/MC/V.) One of the most famous seafood restaurants in the area is **Aunt Catfish's ❸**, 4009 Halifax Dr., at Dunlawton Ave. on the mainland side of the Port Orange Bridge. Order any seafood, and you're in for a treat; the lobster and crab receive the most praise. (☎767-4768. Entrees $10-16. Salad buffet $10. Open M-Sa 11am to 9 or 10pm, Su 9am to 9 or 10pm. AmEx/D/MC/V.) At **Maria Bonita ❷**, 1784 S. Ridgewood Ave., the food is authentic and delicious, the servers are friendly, and the portions generous. It is heralded for its Mexican food, but the Cuban specials take the prize. The *tamales vegetarianos* (vegetarian tamales; $8.75) is a great choice for vegetarians. (☎767-9512. Th after 4pm 2-for-1 mojitos. Cuban Specialities ($8.25-12). Open M-Th 11:30am-9pm, F 11:30am-10pm, Sa noon-10pm, Su noon-9pm. AmEx/D/MC/V.) Though a little out of the way, **Boondocks ❷**, 3948 South Peninsula, in Wilbur by the Sea, an entirely outdoor casual dining option overlooking the Halifax River, serves excellent burgers, sandwiches, and a variety of seafood and meat entrees. Take Atlantic Ave. south and turn right onto Mallard Ave. (☎767-4768. Sandwiches and burgers $4-8. Entrees $9-20. Open daily 11am-10pm. MC/V.)

⚑ START YOUR ENGINES. The center of the racing world, the **Daytona International Speedway** hosts NASCAR's biggest race, the Daytona 500 (Feb. 17, 2008). **Speedweek** (Feb. 9-17, 2008) precedes the legendary race, while the **Pepsi 400** (for those who think young) heats up the track in early July 2008. (NASCAR tickets ☎866-761-7223; www.daytonainternationalspeedway.com.) Next door, **Daytona USA**, 1801 W. International Speedway Blvd., is a must-see for any NASCAR fan, though the admission price will seem ridiculous if you're not. This interactive experience includes a new simulation ride, an IMAX film on NASCAR, and a fun teaching program on NASCAR commentators. The breathtaking **Speedway Tour** is a unique chance to see the garages, grandstands, and famous 31-degree banked turns up close. (☎947-6800. Open daily 9am-7pm. Event hours 8am-7pm. Tours every 30min. daily 9:30am-5:30pm. $24, seniors $19, ages 6-12 $16.) The **Richard Petty Driving Experience** puts fans ages 14 or older in a stock car for a ride-along (which lasts a few minutes) at 150 mph, or fans ages 16 or older in their own driving experience, which can last up to four hours. Drivers must have a valid license and know how to use manual transmission. (☎800-237-3889. Ride-along $134, drive $525-2100.) When you have had your fill of race cars check out Daytona's artsy side at the grand **Seaside Music Theater**, 221 N. Beach St. (☎252-6200), located conveniently at the News Journal Center. This theater company has been home to plays, comedies, and musicals for nearly 30 years. (For more information on upcoming shows visit their website www.seasidemusictheater.com. Tickets $27-45.) **Bike Week** draws biker mamas for various motorcycle duels, and **Biketoberfest** brings them back for more. (Bikeweek: Mar. 2-11, 2008; www.bikeweek.com. Biketoberfest: Oct. 18-21, 2008; www.biketoberfest.com.)

◙ NIGHTLIFE. When spring break hits Daytona, all manner of concerts, hotel-sponsored bashes, and other events answer the call of party-hungry students. News about these events travels fastest by word of mouth, but the *Calendar of Events* and *See Daytona Beach* make good starting points. On mellow nights, head to the boardwalk to play volleyball or party at the **Oceanfront Bandshell**, an open-air amphitheater made of *coquina* (a mixture of crushed seashells and con-

FLORIDA

crete). Dance clubs line Seabreeze Blvd. just west of N. Atlantic Ave. **Zeba's,** 200 South Beach St., is one of Daytona's few gay bars. Come for the $12 all-you-can-drink special on weeknights from 10pm-2:30am. The basket of fries ($4) is just one of many late-night bar options. (☎238-6001. Open M-Th 11am-3am, Sa-Su 5-10pm.) **Ocean Deck,** 127 S. Ocean Ave., stands out among the clubs with live music on the beach, nightly drink specials, and beach-friendly motto, "No shirt, no shoes, no problem." Chow down on the "shipwreck" (shrimp, crab, oysters, and clams; $20) with some friends and boogie down to reggae, jazz, calypso, or rock. (☎253-5224; www.oceandeck.com. Music daily 9:30pm-2:30am. 21+ after 9pm. Open daily 11am-3am. Kitchen closes 2am.) **Razzle's,** 611 Seabreeze Blvd., caters to a traditionally spring break crowd with high-energy dance floors, flashy light shows, and nightly drink specials. (☎257-6236. Cover varies. Open daily 8pm-3am.)

COCOA BEACH AND CAPE CANAVERAL   ☎321

During the Cold War, Cape Canaveral and the surrounding "Space Coast" were the base of operations for major space explorations, from the Apollo moon landings to the current International Space Station effort. Even the local area code (3, 2, 1… liftoff!) reflects the space obsession. The towns of Cocoa Beach and nearby Melbourne are home to Florida's best waves; surfers head to ◙**Ron Jon Surf Shop,** 4151 N. Atlantic Ave., for two floors of boards, shirts, shorts, and sunscreen. (☎799-8888. Open 24hr.) All of **NASA's** shuttles take off from the **Kennedy Space Center (KSC),** 18 mi. north of Cocoa Beach on Rte. 3; by car via Rte. 405 E off I-95, or Rte. 528 E from the Bee Line Expressway. From Cocoa Beach, take Rte. A1A to Rte. 528, then follow Rte. 3 N. The renovated ◙**Kennedy Space Center Visitors Complex** has two 3D IMAX theaters, a Rocket Garden, exhibits on current space exploration, and a new launch simulator that produces the feeling of being launched into space. Standard admission ($38, children 3-11 $28) will let you into the Visitors Complex, including the off-site Astronaut Hall of Fame (8min. away on 405) and simulators. The G-force simulator—which recreates how Air Force pilots feel during flying and diving maneuvers—is perfect for daredevils. **NASA Up Close** tours the shuttle launch pads and gets into the International Space Station Center; the tour **Cape Canaveral: Then and Now** guides visitors through America's first launch sites from the 60s, the Air Force Space & Missile Museum, and the Cape Canaveral Lighthouse (tours $22, children $16). Check NASA's **launch schedule**—you may have a chance to watch space shuttles thunder off into the blue yonder. (☎449-4444; www.kennedyspacecenter.com. Open daily 9am-5:30pm; extended hours in summer.) Nearby, the **Merritt Island National Wildlife Refuge** teems with sea turtles, manatees, wild hogs, otters, and over 300 bird species. Take Exit 80 off I-95 and go east on Garden St. to Rte. 402. (☎861-0667. Open daily dawn-dusk. Visitors Center open Apr.-Oct. M-F 8am-4:30pm, Sa 9am-5pm; Nov.-Mar. M-F 8am-4:30pm, Sa-Su 9am-5pm. Closed 4 days before and day of NASA launches.)

Around summer launch dates, tourists pack the area and hotel prices soar into the stratosphere. **Canaveral National Seashore** is an undeveloped beach with gorgeous dunes. Take Rte. 406 E off U.S. 1 in Titusville. (☎267-1110. Open daily Apr.-Oct. 6am-8pm; Nov.-Mar 6am-6pm. Closed 3 days before and day of NASA launches. Cars $5, pedestrians and bicyclists $3.). Year after year, loyal patrons return to the lovely **Luna Sea Motel ❷,** 3185 N. Atlantic Ave., to bask in the sun by the pool and at the nearby beach. (☎783-0500 or 800-586-2732. Cable TV, A/C, microwave, fridge, and breakfast catered by a local restaurant. Rooms from $69. AAA and AARP discount 10%, military discount 15%. AmEx/D/MC/V.) You can pitch your tent at the small **Jetty Park Campgrounds ❶,** 400 E. Jetty Rd., at the northern tip of Cape Canaveral. (☎783-7111. Jan.-Apr. primitive sites $20, with water and electricity $28, with full hookup $31; May-Dec. $20/22/26.) **The Dixie Motel ❷,**

301 Forrest Ave., has clean basic rooms with huge windows, A/C, and cable TV, and a pool. (☎632-1600. Coin-op laundry. Must be 21+ to rent a room. Rooms $55-70. AmEx/MC/V.) Partying teenagers and vacationing families flock to the **Cocoa Beach Comfort Inn ❸**, 3901 N. Atlantic Ave., offers rooms with A/C, cable TV, and free Wi-Fi. (☎783-2221. Pool and whirlpool. Rooms Nov.-Apr. from $100; May-Oct. from $110. AAA and AARP discount 10%. AmEx/D/MC/V.) Bikini contests, live music, karaoke, drink specials, and tasty seafood make **Coconut's on the Beach ❸**, 2 Minutemen Cswy. at Rte. A1A, a popular local hangout. (☎784-1422. Entrees $7-22. Open daily 11am-2am. D/MC/V.) **The Omelet Station ❶**, 5590 N. Atlantic Ave., is a great Americana breakfast joint. The Snappy Omelet (ham and cheese; $7) and the Eggs Benedict a la Fisherman ($9) are sure to please. (☎783-1038; www.theomeletstation.com. Egg-based meals $6-9.50. Sandwiches $7-$8.)

The Space Coast, 50 mi. east of Orlando, consists of mainland towns Cocoa, Titusville, Rockledge, oceanfront Cocoa Beach and Cape Canaveral, and Merritt Island. Greyhound, 1220 S. Washington Ave. (☎267-8760; www.greyhound.com; open M-Sa 6am-2am, Su 7am-midnight), in Titusville, 15 mi. north of Cocoa, runs **buses** to Daytona Beach (3-5hr., 3 per day, $16) and Orlando (1hr., 3 per day, $16). Space Coast Area Transit (SCAT) has North Beach and South Beach routes and stops at every town in Brevard County. (☎633-1878. Operates M-F 8am-9:30pm, Sa-Su service on some routes. $1; disabled, seniors, and students $0.50; transfers free.) **The Cocoa Beach Chamber of Commerce** is at 400 Fortenberry Rd., on Merritt Island. (☎459-2200; www.visitcocoabeach.com. Open M-F 9am-5pm.) **Space Coast Office of Tourism** is at 2725 Judge Fran Jamieson Way, in Viera. (☎637-5483 or 877-572-3224. Open M-F 8am-5pm.) **Medical Services: Cape Canaveral Hospital,** 701 W. Cocoa Beach Cswy. (☎799-7111). **Internet Access: Cocoa Beach Public Library,** 550 N. Brevard Ave. (☎868-1104. Free. Open M-W 9am-9pm, Th 9am-6pm, F-Sa 9am-5pm, Su 1-5pm.) **Post Office:** 500 N. Brevard Ave., in Cocoa Beach. (☎783-2544. Open M-F 9am-5pm, Sa 9am-noon.) **Postal Code:** 32931.

ST. AUGUSTINE   ☎904

Spanish adventurer Pedro Menéndez de Áviles founded St. Augustine in 1565, making it the first European colony in North America and the oldest continuous settlement in the US. Thanks to preservation efforts and a desire to trap as many tourist dollars as possible, much of St. Augustine's Spanish flavor remains. This city's pride lies in its provincial cobblestone streets, *coquina* walls, and antique shops rather than in its token beaches. With a little effort the tourist traps can be avoided and the charm, history, and lively nights of St. Augustine can be yours.

▌▓ TRANSPORTATION AND PRACTICAL INFORMATION

Most sights lie within a 10-15min. walk from the hostels, motels, and bus station, which is convenient since narrow streets and frequent one-ways make driving unpleasant. The city's major east-west routes, **King Street** and **Cathedral Place,** run through downtown and become the **Bridge of Lions** that leads to the beaches. **San Marco Avenue** and **Avenida Menéndez** run north-south. **Castillo Drive** grows out of San Marco Ave. near the center. **Saint George Street,** a charming north-south pedestrian-only route, has most of the shops and sights in town. Greyhound, 1711 Unit A Dobbs Rd. (☎829-6401; www.greyhound.com; open daily 8:30am-9:30pm), about 2 mi. outside of downtown, runs **buses** to Daytona Beach (45min., 3 per day, $16-18) and Jacksonville (45min., 3 per day, $10-11.50). If the station is closed, drivers accept cash. Sightseeing Trains, 170 San Marco Ave., shuttles travelers on a 21-stop **trolley** that hits all the major attractions. (☎829-6545 or 800-226-6545. Runs every 15-20min. 8:30am-5pm. $19, ages 6-12 $6, under 5 free. Ticket good for 3 consecutive days.) For a **taxi** call Ancient City Taxi (☎824-8161). The **St. Augustine Visitor Information Center,** is at 10 Castillo Dr., at San Marco Ave. From the bus station, walk three blocks north on Riberia St., then turn right on Orange St. (☎825-1000. Open daily 8:30am-5:30pm. Parking $1.35 per hr., or $7 per day) **Post Office:** 99 King St. (☎825-0628. Open M-F 8:30am-6pm, Sa 9am-2pm.) **Postal Code:** 32084.

ACCOMMODATIONS

☑ **Pirate Haus Inn and Hostel,** 32 Treasury St. (☎808-1999), just off Saint George St. From Rte. 16 E, go south on U.S. 1, make a left on King St. and then turn left on Charlotte St.; parking is available in the metered lot behind the inn. Hands-down the best place to stay, with spacious dorms, pirate-themed private rooms, and a central location. Free lockers. Internet access $1 per 15min., $2 per 30min., $3 per hr., $5 per 2hr. A/C. Laundry $4. Key and linen deposit $5. Reception 8-10am and 5-10pm. No lockout for registered guests. Dorms $20; private rooms M-Th and Su $60-70, F-Sa $65-80. Under 13 free. Single parent discount. MC/V. ❶

Seabreeze Motel, 208 Anastasia Blvd. (☎829-8122), has retro, clean rooms with refrigerators and pool access. A/C, cable TV, and free local calls. Singles M-Th and Su $40-49, F-Sa $59; holidays and special events $69; doubles $50-59/69/79. D/MC/V. ❷

Casablanca Inn, 24 Avenida Menéndez (☎829-0928), in Historic Downtown. Stands out among St. Augustine's many B&Bs. Feast on a 2-course gourmet breakfast and unwind on the porch with rocking chairs and a spectacular view of the river. Large rooms boast cable TV, pleasant artwork, and fireplaces. Rooms $99-349. AmEx/D/MC/V. ❺

Anastasia State Recreation Area (☎461-2033, reservations ☎800-326-3521), on Rte. A1A, 4 mi. south of the historic district. From town, cross the Bridge of Lions and turn left just past the small alligator farm. Small but shady and secluded campsites. Nearby opportunities for great windsurfing, fishing, swimming, and hiking. Reception daily 8am-dusk. Sites with water and electricity $25. $3-5 per car, $1 per pedestrian. ❶

FOOD AND NIGHTLIFE

The bustle of daytime tourists and the abundance of budget eateries make lunch in St. Augustine's historic district a delight, especially in the cafes and bars of **Saint George Street.** If you're looking for late-night grub to accompany your booze, head to **A1A Ale Works ❸,** 1 King St., overlooking historic downtown, which brews its own beer and serves food late into the night. Wash down the delicious sandwiches (blackened mahi mahi $10) with their homemade brew. (☎829-2977. Happy hour M-F 4-7pm. Live music Th-Sa. Open daily 11am-1am.)Worth the short drive, the **Manatee Cafe ❶,** 525 S. Rte. 16 #106, is a delightful little eatery that serves mostly organic and vegetarian fare (Cajun-style tofu $6.50), and provides a small natural food selection at the front of the store. For something light on your stomach and your wallet, order half an entree for half the price plus $1. (☎826-0210. Open M-Sa 8am-4pm, Su 8am-3pm. AmEx/MC/V.) You'll get more barbecue than you can handle at **Scarlett O'Hara's ❷,** 70 Hypolita St., at Cordova St. Patrons will never go hungry again after discovering the burgers ($7.50-10) and full slabs of ribs ($15) dished up in this slat-board house. Enjoy your ribs al fresco on the large wooden porch outside, or salivate over the many Scarlett O'Hara paintings inside. Live music, usually rock or acoustic, entertains each night. (☎824-6535. Happy hour M-F 4-7pm. Open M-Sa 11am-1am, Su 11am-midnight. AmEx/D/MC/V.) Looking for pizza and only have a couple of minutes? Grab a slice at **Pizza Time ❷,** 124 St. George St. Make some time for a thin crust pizza pie ($14) or grab a slice ($2.50) to go. (☎819-0133. Open M-Th and Su 10:30am-10:30pm, F-Sa 10:30am-11:00pm.)

Many of St. Augustine's bars are on Rte. A1A S and Saint George St. *Folio Weekly,* free and available throughout the city, has event listings. Local string musicians play on the two stages at the **Milltop,** 19½ Saint George St., a tiny but illustrious bar above an old water mill in the restored district. (☎829-2329. Music daily 1pm-close. F-Sa cover $2. Open M-Sa 11am-1am, Su 11am-10pm.) Get dinner, a movie, and a beer all at once at **Pot Belly's,** 36 Granada St. Screening just-out-of-theaters movies, this combination pub, deli, and cinema serves a range of sandwiches ($2.50-5), snacks (from $2.25), and brews (pitchers $7.50) to in-house tables. (☎829-3101. Movie tickets $5. Call for showtimes. Cash only.) Sample your choice of 24 drafts at the **Oasis Deck and Restaurant,** 4000 Rte. A1A S at Ocean Trace Rd., a family restaurant by day and romping party by night. (☎471-3424. Gator tail $7. Seafood sandwiches $6-8. Happy hour 4-7pm. Live music nightly. Open daily 6am-11pm.) Throw back a few with Flagler College students at their campus watering hole, the **St. George Tavern,** 116 Saint George St. Come on Wednesday for $0.50 domestic beers, or get a pitcher for just $3.50. (☎824-4204. Happy hour daily 4-8pm; beer $2.25. Open daily 11am-1am.)

👁 SIGHTS

SPANISH HERITAGE. The oldest masonry fortress in the continental US, **Castillo de San Marcos National Monument** has 14ft-thick *coquina* walls. The fort, built by the Spanish in 1627, is shaped like a four-pointed star with drawbridge and moat. It has a museum, large courtyard, jail, and chapel, and the original cannon brought overseas from Spain. (*1 Castillo Dr., off San Marco Ave.* ☎829-6506. *Open daily 8:45am-5:15pm, last entry 4:45pm. $7, under 16 free.*) Thanks to Spanish settlers, **La Leche Shrine and Mission of Nombre de Dios** became the birthplace of American Catholicism, 55 years before Plymouth rock. A huge steel cross marks the city's religious roots, and the shaded lawns make for peaceful strolls. (*27 Ocean St., off San Marco Ave.* ☎824-2809. *Open M-F 8am-5pm, Sa 9am-5pm, Su 9:30am-5pm. Donation suggested.*)

ESCAPE TO THE WILD. Across the Bridge of Lions, the ▧**St. Augustine Alligator Farm** allows visitors to get personal with the gators. The park, delighting visitors since 1893, is the only place in the world where all 23 known crocodilian species live. The park is also home to wide array of wildlife from green egrets to galapagos turtles. (*On Rte. A1A S.* ☎824-3337. *Open daily 9am-6pm. Presentations every hr. Feeding daily at noon and 3pm. $20, ages 5-11 $11. AAA, military, and senior discount.*)

HISTORICAL SIGHTS. For the best view of the city and the water, climb the 219 stairs of the **St. Augustine Lighthouse and Museum,** one of only six lighthouses in the state open to the public. Tour the 19th-century tower and keeper's house to learn about marine archaeological studies in the surrounding waters. (*81 Lighthouse Ave., off Rte. A1A across from the alligator farm.* ☎829-0745. *Open daily 9am-6pm. House and grounds $6, seniors $5, ages 7-11 $4. Tower, grounds, and house $8/$7/$6.*) The **González-Álvarez House** is the oldest house listed on the National Registry of Historic Places. Built in the 17th century, the tiny house now serves as a tourist haven, with exhibits on the area's Spanish, British, and American heritage. (*14 Saint Francis St.* ☎824-2872. *Open daily 9am-5pm. Last entry 4:30pm. Partially wheelchair accessible. $8, seniors $7, students $5, families $16.*) In the **Colonial Spanish Quarter,** period craftsmen, soldiers, and housewives go about their business in a charming recreation of an 18th-century colonial Spanish town. Luckily for us, 18th-century Spanish colonists were apparently bilingual. (*53 Saint George St.* ☎825-6830. *Open daily 9am-5:30pm. $7; seniors, military, and college students $4.25; families $14.*)

RESTORATIONS. Flagler College is a small liberal arts institution in the restored Spanish Renaissance-style **Ponce de León Hotel.** Built by railroad and Standard Oil tycoon Henry Flagler in 1888, the hotel was the playground for America's social elite. Celebrity heavyweights like John Rockefeller and Will Rogers once strolled

FLORIDA

through the gorgeous interior. *(74 King St. ☎823-3378; www.flagler.edu. Tours mid-May to mid-Aug. daily on the hr. 10am-3pm. Wheelchair accessible. $6, under 12 $1.)* The **Memorial Presbyterian Church,** a beautiful model of St. Mark's Cathedral in Venice, was also built by Flagler, but these Tiffany windows are fake. The workmanship is so fine that no one would guess that the church only took 361 days to finish. *(36 Sevilla St. ☎829-6451. Open M-Sa 9am-4pm, Su 12:30-4pm. Services Su 8:30 and 11am. Free.)* In 1947, Chicago publisher and art lover Otto Lightner converted the Alcazar Hotel into the **Lightner Museum,** which now holds an impressive collection of cut, blown, and burnished glass, along with old clothing and oddities. Today, the museum's eccentricity is its strongest feature, as it houses everything from a shrunken head to nuns' and monks' beer steins. *(75 King St. ☎824-2874; www.lightnermuseum.org. Open daily 9am-5pm. Live 18th-century music daily 11am and 2pm. Wheelchair accessible. $8, military $6, students and ages 12-18 $2.)*

SOUTH FLORIDA

MIAMI   ☎305

No longer just a vacation spot for "snowbirds" (wealthy East Coasters escaping harsh winters), Miami's heart pulses to a beat all its own, fueled by the largest Cuban population this side of Havana. Appearance rules in this city, and nowhere is this clearer than on the shores of South Beach, where visual delights include Art Deco hotels and tanned beach bodies. South Beach is home to a nightclub scene that attracts some of the world's most beautiful and famous people. But it's not all bikinis—Miami is the entry point for one of America's great natural habitats, the Everglades, as well as the gateway to the Florida Keys and the Caribbean.

> **MIAMI FOR POCKET CHANGE.** With a little know-how, travelers can enjoy Miami's glamour without breaking the bank. Before holing up at the hip new **Jazz Hostel** (p. 455), savor a deliciously cheap meal at the **Flamingo Cafe** (p. 456). On Fridays from 6-9pm, the **Wolfsonian Museum** (p. 457) has free admission. If you prefer beautiful people to beautiful paintings, the price of an espresso will buy you hours of people-watching pleasure at **Ocean Drive's** trendy cafes (p. 456). Of course, die-hard sun-worshippers know that Miami's public **beaches** (p. 457) can always be enjoyed *gratis.*

▐ TRANSPORTATION

Airport: Miami International (MIA; ☎876-7000; www.miami-airport.com), at Le Jeune Rd. and NW 36th St., 7 mi. northwest of downtown. Bus #7 runs downtown. From downtown, take bus "C" or "K" to South Beach. Taxi to Miami Beach $32-35 flat rate.

Trains: Amtrak, 8303 NW 37th Ave. (☎835-1223; www.amtrak.com), near the Northside Metrorail station. Bus "L" goes to Lincoln Rd. Mall in South Beach. Open daily 5:45am-9:30pm. To: **Charleston** (13hr., 1 per day, $67-148); **Orlando** (5-7hr., 2 per day, $34-75); **Tampa** (5½hr., 1 per day, $34-75); **Washington, D.C.** (23-27hr., 2 per day, $114-248).

Buses: Greyhound, 4111 NW 27th St. (☎871-1810; www.greyhound.com). Open 24hr. To: **Atlanta** (15-17hr., 8 per day, $111); **Fort Lauderdale** (45min.-1hr., 20 per day, $6.50); **Key West** (4½hr., 3 per day, $39); **Orlando** (5hr., 13 per day, $45).

Public Transit: Metro Dade Transportation (☎770-3131; info M-F 6am-10pm, Sa-Su 9am-5pm).

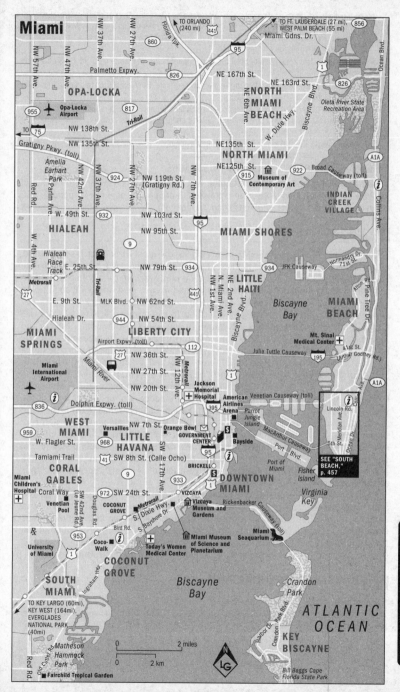

Miami

TO ORLANDO (240 mi)

TO FT. LAUDERDALE (27 mi), WEST PALM BEACH (55 mi)
Miami Gdns. Dr.

Ocean Blvd.

860
95
826

Palmetto Expwy.
NE 167th St.
NE 163rd St.

NW 37th Ave.
NW 27th Ave.
NW 47th Ave.
NW 57th Ave.

856
1

OPA-LOCKA

NE 6th Ave.
NE 8th Ave.

NORTH MIAMI BEACH

826

Oleta River State Recreation Area

955 Opa-Locka Airport
817
Tri-Rail

NW 138th St.

TO 75

Gratigny Pkwy. (toll)

NW 135th St.

NE135th St.

NORTH MIAMI

W. Dixie Hwy.
Biscayne Hwy.

A1A

Amelia Earhart Park

Parim Ave.
Red Rd.
NW 42nd Ave.
NW 37th Ave.
NW 27th Ave.

924

NW 119th St. (Gratigny Rd.)

NW 7th Ave.

NE125th St.

915 922 Museum of Contemporary Art

Broad Causeway (toll)

INDIAN CREEK VILLAGE

Collins Ave.

W. 49th St.

932

NW 103rd St.

95

MIAMI SHORES

HIALEAH

W. 4th Ave.

NW 95th St.

Hialeah Race Track
9

E. 25th St.
NW 79th St.

934

934 JFK Causeway

Normandy Dr. 71st St.

MIAMI BEACH

Pine Tree Dr.
Alton Rd.

Metrorail
27
Tri-Rail

E. 9th St.
MLK Blvd.
NW 62nd St.

441

NE 2nd Ave.
NE 1st Ave.
N. Miami Ave.

Biscayne Bay

Hialeah Dr.
944
NW 54th St.

LITTLE HAITI

Mt. Sinai Medical Center

1st St.

MIAMI SPRINGS

LIBERTY CITY

Biscayne Blvd.

Julia Tuttle Causeway
1st St. (Arthur Godfrey Rd.)

27
Airport Expwy. (toll)
112

195

NW 36th St.

Miami River

NW 12th Ave.
Metrorail

NW 27th St.

A1A

Miami International Airport

NW 20th St.

1

Venetian Causeway (toll)

Collins Ave.

836

Dolphin Expwy. (toll)

Jackson Memorial Hospital

395

American Airlines Arena

Parrot Jungle Island

Lincoln Rd.

WEST MIAMI

959

NW 7th St.
Versailles
968

Orange Bowl
GOVERNMENT CENTER
Bayside

MacArthur Causeway

5th St.

Meridian Ave.
Ocean Dr.

SEE "SOUTH BEACH," p. 457

W. Flagler St.
Tamiami Trail

LITTLE HAVANA

41
SW 8th St. (Calle Ocho)

SW 17th Ave.

95
BRICKELL

Port Blvd.
Port of Miami

CORAL GABLES

9

Miami Children's Hospital
Coral Way

972
SW 24th St.

933
1

DOWNTOWN MIAMI

Fisher Island

Virginia Key

Venetian Pool

SW 42nd Ave. (Le Jeune Rd.)
Douglas Rd.

COCONUT GROVE
Metrorail
S. Dixie Hwy.

VIZCAYA
Vizcaya Museum and Gardens

Rickenbacker Causeway (toll)

Rx

953
Coco-Walk
Bird Rd.

Miami Museum of Science and Planetarium

Miami Seaquarium

University of Miami

1

S. Bayshore Dr.

Today's Women Medical Center

Crandon Park

SOUTH MIAMI

COCONUT GROVE

Ingraham Hwy.

Biscayne Bay

ATLANTIC OCEAN

TO KEY LARGO (60mi), KEY WEST (164mi), EVERGLADES NATIONAL PARK (40mi)

Harbor Dr.
Crandon Park Blvd.

KEY BISCAYNE

Red Rd.
Cutler Rd.

Matheson Hammock Park

0   2 miles
0   2 km

Fairchild Tropical Garden

Bill Baggs Cape Florida State Park

N
LG

FLORIDA

Metrobus lines converge downtown, where most long trips transfer. Over 100 routes, but the major lettered bus routes A, C, D, G, H, J, K, L, R, S, and T serve Miami Beach. Runs M-F 24hr., most services every 30min. $1.50, disabled, seniors, and students $0.75; transfers $0.50/0.25. Call for weekend schedule. Exact change only.

Metrorail serves downtown's major business and cultural areas. M-F 5am-midnight; Sa-Su 5:20am-midnight. $1.50, rail-to-bus transfers $0.50.

Metromover loop downtown is linked to the Metrorail stations. Runs daily 6am-midnight. It glows at night and is free.

Tri-Rail (☎800-874-7245) connects Miami, Fort Lauderdale, and West Palm Beach. Trains run M-F 4am-11pm, Sa 7am-11pm, Su 7am-9pm. $2-10; children, students, seniors, and disabled with Tri-Rail ID discount varies.

Electrowave (☎843-9283) sends shuttles along Washington Ave. from S. Pointe to 17th St. Pick up a brochure or just hop on in South Beach. $0.25.

Taxi: Metro, ☎888-8888. **Central Cab,** ☎532-5555.

Bike Rental: Miami Beach Bicycle Center, 601 5th St. (☎531-4161), at the corner of Washington Ave. Open M-Sa 10am-7pm, Su 10am-5pm. $8 per hr., $40 per day, $80 per week. Credit card or $200 cash deposit required.

ORIENTATION

Three highways crisscross the Miami area. **I-95,** the most direct north-south route, merges into **U.S. 1 (South Dixie Highway)** just south of downtown. U.S. 1 runs to the Everglades entrance at Florida City and then continues as the Overseas Hwy. to Key West. **Route 836 (Dolphin Expressway),** a major east-west artery through town, connects I-95 to **Florida's Turnpike,** passing the airport in between.

When looking for addresses, pay attention to the systematic street layout; it's easy to confuse addresses in North Miami Beach, West Miami, Miami Beach, and Miami (all different places). Streets in Miami run east-west, avenues north-south; both are numbered. Miami divides into NE, NW, SE, and SW quadrants; the dividing lines downtown are **Flagler Street** (east-west) and **Miami Avenue** (north-south). Some numbered roads also have names; be sure to get a map that lists both.

Several causeways connect Miami to **Miami Beach.** The most useful is **MacArthur Causeway,** which becomes 5th St. Numbered streets run east-west across the island, increasing as you go north. In South Beach, **Collins Avenue (A1A)** is the main north-south drag, parallel to the club-filled **Washington Avenue** and the beachfront **Ocean Drive.** The commercial district sits between 6th and 23rd St. One-way streets, traffic jams, and limited parking make driving around **South Beach (SoBe)** frustrating, but there are plenty of parking places available. Tie on your most stylish sneakers and enjoy the small island at your leisure—it only takes about 20min. to walk up Collins Ave. from 6th to 16th St.

Back in Miami, the life of **Little Havana** is on **Calle Ocho**—between SW 8th Ave. and SW 27th Ave.; take bus #8, 11, 17, or 37. **Coconut Grove,** south of Little Havana, centers on the shopping and entertainment on **Grand Avenue** and **Virginia Street. Coral Gables,** an upscale residential area, rests around the intersection of **Coral Way (SW 24th Street)** and **Le Jeune Road,** also known as **SW 42nd Avenue.** Though public transit is generally reliable and safe, a car can be useful to get around the city.

PRACTICAL INFORMATION

Visitor Info: Miami Beach Visitors Center, 1920 Meridian Ave. (☎672-1270; www.miami-beachchamber.com). Open M-F 9am-6pm, Sa-Su 10am-4pm. **Coconut Grove Chamber of Commerce,** 2820 McFarlane Rd. (☎444-7270). Open M-F 9am-5pm. **Greater Miami Convention and Visitors Bureau,** 701 Brickell Ave. (☎539-3000; www.miamiandbeaches.com), 27th fl. of Bank of America Bldg., in downtown. Open M-F 8am-5pm.

Hotline: **Crisis Line,** ☎358-4357. 24hr.

Medical Services: **Mt. Sinai Medical Center,** 4300 Alton Rd. (☎674-2121), in Miami Beach. **Rape Treatment Center and Hotline,** 1611 NW 12th Ave. (☎585-7273), at Jackson Memorial Hospital. Open 24hr.

Internet Access: **Miami Public Library,** 101 W. Flagler St. (☎375-2665), across from the Museum of Art. Free; 1hr. limit. Open M-Sa 9am-6pm.

Post Office: Downtown: 500 NW 2nd Ave. (☎371-7099). Open M-F 8am-5pm, Sa 8am-1:30pm. Miami Beach: 1300 Washington Ave. (☎672-2447). Open M-F 8am-5pm, Sa 8:30am-2pm. **Postal Code:** 33101; Miami Beach 33119.

⌂ ACCOMMODATIONS

Cheap rooms abound in South Beach. Hostels in Miami Beach are the cheapest option for solo travelers. If young and bohemian isn't your thing, cruise down Collins Ave. to the funky, hot-pink Art Deco hotels. Get a discount when you stay more than two nights in one of the trendy **South Beach Group Hotels,** including Whitelaw, Mercury, Shelly, Chelsea, Chesterfield, and Lily. High season for Miami Beach runs late December through mid-March; during low season, hotel clerks are often quick to bargain. The Miami Beach Visitors Center (see **Practical Information,** above) can get you the cheapest rates. Camping is not allowed on Miami Beach.

HOSTELS

▨ **The Clay Hotel and International Hostel (HI),** 1438 Washington Ave. (☎534-2988 or 800-379-2529), at Collins Ave. and Española Way; take bus C from downtown. This Mediterranean-style building is home to the best hostel in SoBe and hosts an international crowd. A/C, kitchen, laundry facilities. Dorms come with phone and fridge; some have TV. Internet access $0.10 per min. Lockers $1 per day. Linen/key deposit $10. 4- to 8-bed dorms M-F $28, Sa-Su $30; members $26/28. Private rooms with shared bath $56-60, with private bath $68-74. MC/V. ❶

Jazz Hostel, 321 Collins Ave. (☎672-2137); from airport take the J to 41st St. and Sheridan Ave. Transfer to bus M, get off at 3rd St. and walk a block to 3rd and Collins Ave. The newest hostel to hit the block, the Jazz offers clean dorm rooms, Internet kiosks, and free Wi-Fi. Dorms come with hair dryers, fridges, and closet. The staff organizes daily party outings that are walking distance to many bars and clubs. Reception 24hr. No curfew. Laundry facilities. 8-bed dorms $20. ❶

Miami Beach International Travelers Hostel (9th St. Hostel), 236 9th St. (☎534-0268 or 800-978-6787), at Washington Ave. From the airport take bus 237 (midnight-6am) or bus "C" to "J" (6am-midnight); 1hr. In the heart of SoBe's club scene and the beach. Common room with TV and movies. Laundry $1. Free Wi-Fi. Internet access $5 per hr. Dorms with A/C and bath $25. Singles from $59; doubles from $69. MC/V. ❶

The Tropics Hotel/Hostel, 1550 Collins Ave. (☎531-0361), across from the beach. From the airport, take bus J to 41st St., transfer to bus C to Lincoln Rd., walk 1 block south on Collins, next to the parking garage. This quiet refuge from the SoBe scene offers large, comfy rooms with A/C, large pool, and an outdoor kitchen. Lockers at front desk. Linens included. Laundry $1. Internet access $1 per min. Key deposit $10. Low-season dorms $27. MC/V. ❶

HOTELS

▨ **Kent Hotel,** 1131 Collins Ave. (☎604-5068; www.thekenthotel.com), 1 block from the beach. The Kent's tagline, "savvy affordability," is right on the mark. The dramatic lobby is decorated with orange, yellow, and purple furniture. Lavender rooms with A/C, a fridge, a large plasma TV, and DVDs. Free Internet access. No parking garage. Rooms Oct.-Apr. $80-120; May-Sept. $75-100. AmEx/D/MC/V. ❹

FLORIDA

Whitelaw Hotel, 808 Collins Ave. (☎398-7000). Complimentary mixed drinks served 7-8pm in the bright white leather and chrome lobby. Rooms are pink with big closets. The clerks offer VIP passes to some of SoBe's clubs. A/C, plasma TV, free airport shuttle. Wi-Fi $15 per day. Doubles Oct.-Mar. $65-300; Apr.-Sept. $75-125. AmEx/MC/V. ❹

Chesterfield Hotel, 855 Collins Ave. (☎531-5831), a block from the beach. House music pumps through this uber-chic retreat. Within walking distance of bars. The rooms have a double bed and mirrored showers. Hotel has a helpful staff, bar, cafe, free airport shuttle, and free VIP passes to area clubs. A/C and TV. Internet access $15 per day. Free Wi-Fi. Doubles Dec.-Mar. $150-175; Apr.-Nov. from $75-110. AmEx/MC/V. ❹

Hotel Shelley, 844 Collins Ave. (☎531-3341). With marble bathrooms and bright white bedspreads, the Shelley offers luxury for less. Lobby has free Wi-Fi, TV, A/C, fridge, complimentary mixed drinks, VIP passes for clubs, and free airport shuttle. High season $195; low season $105. Book online for discounts. AmEx/MC/V. ❹

🍴 FOOD

Food in Miami is incredibly diverse. Four-star restaurants owned by celebrities and celebrity chefs are as prevalent in the city as local sandwich counters known for their affordability. The South Beach strip along Ocean Dr. has regulars like **TGI Friday's** and **Johnny Rockets,** favorites like **News Cafe,** and clubs that attract mainly tourists, like **Mango.** Head at least one block inland from the beach to find more wallet-pleasing prices.

🦪 **Opa,** 36 Ocean Dr. (☎673-6730). At 7pm every night, the music strikes up and the manager tosses hundreds of napkins in the air while Greek belly dancers gyrate on table tops. Come for the fun and enjoy their delicious baklava (walnut, honey cinnamon pastry; $4). *Souvlaki* $6. Oak-grilled pork loin $11. Vegetarian-friendly *spanakopita* (spinach and feta pastry) $5. Entrees range from $11-$14. Open daily from 4pm until the *ouzo* runs out. AmEx/D/MC/V. ❸

News Cafe, 800 Ocean Dr. (☎538-6397). Though the food is outstanding, you're really paying for one of the best people-watching locations on Ocean Dr. Try their homemade *empanadas* with choice of cheese, beef, or chicken ($7.25) or 1 of their 8 different kinds of Caesar salad ($7.75-13.75). Go in the evening for dessert (strawberries and champagne with chocolate fondue for 2; $20) and stare at stylish hardbodies strolling by. Celebrities from Paris Hilton to Hulk Hogan frequently dine here when they're in town. Full bar. Drafts served in a souvenir Pilsner glass $6.75. Open M-Th and Su 6:30am-1am, F-Sa 24hr. AmEx/D/MC/V. ❸

Big Pink Diner, 157 Collins Ave. (☎531-0888). Hard to miss—it's the only light pink building on the street. Serves excellent diner food, including oversized "pyramid" salads (flaked salmon salad; $12) and the "Churrasco Wrap" (steak and fried plantains; $10.50). Red velvet cake ($7) makes a great dessert. Open M-W 8am-midnight, Th 8am-2am, F-Su 8am-5:30am. ❷

Pizza Rustica, 863 Washington Ave. (☎674-8244). This popular eatery, along with its 2 other Miami locations, serves up some of the best pizza in South Florida. Try the spinach and blue cheese, the NY steak, or the tomato and basil. Slices $3-$4.50. Whole pizzas $12-$17. Open daily 11am-midnight. Cash only. ❶

Versailles, 3555 SW 8th St. (☎444-0240), in Little Havana. Miami-Cuban to the core. Sit in the company of power-brokers as you enjoy classic Cuban dishes like the deliciously salty *ropa vieja* (your choice of meat with tomato and dry white wine; $10) with a side of fried sweet plantains ($10). Open M-Th 8am-2am, F 8am-3:30am, Sa 8am-4:30am, Su 9am-2am. AmEx/D/MC/V. ❸

Flamingo Cafe, 1454 Washington Ave. (☎673-4302), near the Clay Hostel in Miami Beach. Overwhelming amounts of delicious food for staggeringly low prices. Exotic natural shakes ranging from guanabana to papaya ($2) will energize your afternoon. Breakfast plate with eggs, toast, and meat $2.80. Beef tacos and salad $3. *Frijoles con queso* (beans with cheese; $3). Lunch specials $5-7. Open M-Sa 6:30am-9:30pm. AmEx/D/MC/V. ●

🄖 SIGHTS

SOUTH BEACH. South Beach is the reason to come to Miami. The liberal atmosphere, hot bodies, Art Deco design, and excellent sand make the 17 blocks between 6th and 23rd St. seem like their own little world. **Ocean Drive** is where Miami's hottest come to see and be seen. Bars and cafes cram this tiny strip of land, which is part fashion show, part raging party. The **Art Deco Welcome Center** dispenses free maps and advice, features a free museum, and hosts walking tours. *(1001 Ocean Dr. ☎531-3484; www.mdpl.org. Open M-Sa 9am-7pm, Su 9am-6pm. 90min. walking tours W and F-Su 10:30am, Th 6:30pm. $20, seniors and students $15.)* In the heart of South Beach is the fantastic 🄖**Wolfsonian Museum.** 300 works range in a variety of forms from books to architectural models, paintings, postcards, and sculptures all reflecting reform movements, world's fair, advertisements, and political propaganda from all over the world. The museum's collection of modern art and design projects far outstrips its floor space, so call or check the website for current exhibition info. *(1001 Washington Ave. ☎531-1001; www.wolfsonian.org. Open Th-F 11am-9pm, Sa-Su noon-6pm; in winter also M-Tu 11am-6pm. Tours Th-F 6pm. Wheelchair-accessible. $7, seniors and students $5; F 6-9pm free.)* The **Holocaust Memorial** commemorates the six million Jews who fell victim to Nazi genocide in WWII. The 42 ft. bronze arm protruding from the ground, the

South Beach

🏠 **ACCOMMODATIONS**

Chesterfield Hotel, **15**
The Clay Hotel and
   International Hostel (HI), **6**
Hotel Shelley, **14**
Jazz Hostel, **18**
Kent Hotel, **9**
Miami Beach International
   Travelers Hostel (9th
   St. Hostel), **12**
The Tropics Hotel/Hostel, **3**
Whitelaw Hotel, **16**

🍴 **FOOD**

Big Pink, **20**
Flamingo Cafe, **4**
News Cafe, **17**
Opa, **21**
Pizza Rustica, **13**
Taystee Bakery, **5**

🍸 **NIGHTLIFE**

Cameo, **7**
Laundry Bar, **1**
Mango's Tropical Cafe, **11**
Mansion, **8**
Privé, **19**
Score, **2**
Twist, **10**

FLORIDA

ARTFUL LIVING

Walking along the streets of Miami, it's hard to ignore the sea of pastel buildings. These hot pinks, neon blues, and light greens are part of the history of Miami's **Art Deco** movement. The history of Art Deco goes back to the 1920s, when rich vacationers built these homes to reflect the style of the day with their own Miami twist. As the population changed in the 1950s, some of the colorful hotels were transformed into retirement homes. The booming real estate industry led to concern that the Art Deco buildings would soon be razed to build skyscraping hotels and condos. Preservationists brought together local businessmen, politicians, and residents to help restore the area's unique architecture. In 1976, the Miami Design Preservation Center was formed in order to restore the beach's historical buildings. In the 80s, Andy Warhol became one of many celebrity representatives to support the Center's mission. Miami's Art Deco neighborhoods were immortalized with the 1984 hit television series *Miami Vice*, which used many of these buildings for its action scenes.

For more info, see the Art Deco Welcome Center, 1001 Ocean Dr. (☎531-3484), for books and guided tour schedules.

base of which is supported by dozens of sculpted human figures struggling to escape persecution, makes an impact. *(1933-45 Meridian Ave. ☎538-1663. Open daily 9am-9pm. Wheelchair-accessible. Free.)* Since 1936, visitors to **Parrot Jungle Island** have walked among free-flying parrots, flamingos, and swinging orangutans. Also on-site are the Parrot Bowl amphitheater, the Serpentarium, the clay cliffs of Manu Encounter, and the Treetop Ballroom. Go down the Hippo, the park's newest attraction, a 168 ft. water slide. *(1111 Parrot Jungle Tr. From downtown, take MacArthur Cswy. east toward South Beach. Parrot Jungle Tr. is the first exit after the bridge. ☎258-6453; www.parrotjungle.com. Open daily 10am-6pm. $28; military, seniors, and students $26; ages 3-10 $23. Parking $7.)*

COCONUT GROVE. A stroll through lazy **Coconut Grove** uncovers an unlikely combination of haute boutiques and tourist traps. People-watching abounds at the open-air mall, **CocoWalk**, along Grand Ave. On the bayfront between the Grove and downtown stands the ◘**Vizcaya Museum and Gardens.** The 70-room Italianate villa was created by wealthy industrial realist James Deering. All the rooms are decorated in period designs, and some rooms contain Roman antiques that are over 2000 years old. Vizcaya is one of the most romantic attractions in Miami because of its lush gardens, view of the waterfront, and rooms designed in elegant decor from all over the world. *(3251 S. Miami Ave., Exit 1A off I-95. ☎250-9133; www.vizcayamuseum.com. Open daily 9:30am-5pm; last entry 4:30pm. Partially wheelchair-accessible. $12, with college ID $9, ages 6-12 $5. ISIC discount $1.)*

BAYSIDE. On the waterfront downtown, Miami's sleek **Bayside** shopping center hops nightly with street performers. Stores and restaurants cater mostly to cruise ship guests and tourists, though a tour through the center and its surrounding statues makes it a worthwhile trip. *(From Miami Beach, take bus F or C. ☎577-3344. Open M-Th 10am-10pm, F-Sa 10am-11pm, Su 11am-9pm; restaurants and bars stay open later.)*

CORAL GABLES. In addition to the **University of Miami,** scenic **Coral Gables,** 7 mi. south of downtown, boasts one of the most beautiful planned communities in the region. Nearby, the family-friendly **Venetian Pool,** built in 1923 from a coral rock quarry, is a national historic site. The pool, which resembles a lagoon, draws visitors to its 800,000 gallon oasis. Waterfalls and Spanish architecture dress up this swimming hole, which is always crowded on hot summer weekends. *(2701 De Soto Blvd. From U.S. 1, head north of Granada Blvd. ☎460-5356; www.venetianpool.com. Partially wheelchair-accessible. Open Apr. and Sept.-Oct. Tu-F*

*11am-5:30pm, Sa-Su 10am-4:30pm; May-Aug. M-F 11am-7:30pm, Sa-Su 10am-4:30pm; Nov.-
Mar. Tu-Su 10am-4:30pm. Apr.-Oct. $10, ages 3-12 $6.75; Nov.-Mar. $5.50/3.50.)*

NORTH MIAMI. The **Museum of Contemporary Art (MOCA)** is known for its often
eccentric exhibits and displays. The latest, "Make Your Own Life: Artists In and
Out of Cologne," features multimedia from artists who had a lasting impact on
contemporary art. MOCA supports uncommon means of artistic expression. The
last Friday of the month has free jazz concerts (7-10pm); donations are accepted.
*(770 NE 125th St.; Exit 10A off I-95. ☎893-6211; www.mocanomi.org. Open Tu-Sa 11am-5pm,
Su noon-5pm. Wheelchair-accessible. $5, seniors and students $3.)*

♪ 🎭 ENTERTAINMENT AND NIGHTLIFE

For news on Miami entertainment, check out the "Living Today," "Lively Arts," and
"Weekend" sections of the *Miami Herald.* Weekly *Oceandrive, New Times,
Street,* and *Sun Post* list local happenings. *TWN* and *Miamigo,* free gay papers,
are available along Ocean Dr. Music is a big part of Miami life, whether it's grinding techno in a SoBe nightclub, a street performance on **Calle Ocho** in little Havana,
or the nightly performances at **CoCoWalk.** Spring and summer are festival season,
which opens with **Carnaval Miami,** the nation's largest Hispanic festival, filling 23
blocks of Calle Ocho in early March with the world's longest conga line.

Nightlife in the South Miami Beach Art Deco district starts late (after midnight)
and continues until well after sunrise. Gawk at models, stars, and beach bunnies
while eating at one of Ocean Drive's open cafes or bars, then head down to **Washington Avenue,** between 6th and 18th St., for some serious fun. Miami Beach's club
scene is transient; what's there one week may not be there the next. Clubs themselves change character depending on the night—check beforehand or you may be
in for a surprise. Many clubs don't demand covers until after midnight, and often
the $20+ door charge includes an open bar. However, even a willingness to pay a
steep cover is no guarantee of admission. Difficult doormen can prove impossible
after 1am, so it is to your advantage to show up early. Stunningly beautiful or
scantily clad women generally have the easiest time. Most clubs have dress codes
and everyone dresses to the nines, even on so-called "casual" nights. If discos
aren't your thing, check out one of the frat-boy party bars along the beach.

Cameoobar, 1445 Washington Ave. (☎325-2667 or 531-8225). If you're searching out
a club with the "dark and the dirty side" of disco then you found it here. Under new
management, this disco-inspired club is packed most nights. 21+. Cover about $20-25.
Open M and Th-Su 10pm-5am.

Mansion, 1235 Washington Ave. (☎532-1525; www.mansionmiami.com). An assault
on the senses, the richly decorated Mansion sets the standard among SoBe clubs. The
VIP section is littered with celebrities sipping Cristal. By midnight lines are around the
corner, so arrive early. 21+. Cover around $20. Open Tu-Su 11pm-5am.

Privé, 136 Collins Ave. (☎531-5535). SoBe's best hip-hop party. If you forgot your white
linen Armani suit, you'll have a bit more luck at the door here than at some of the other
clubs. The club has an oriental theme with Buddhist statues, giant Chinese lanterns,
and a huge dance floor covered by a white canopy. The Th Betty Ford party is legendary.
Cover $20. Open 10pm-5am.

Mango's Tropical Cafe, 900 Ocean Dr. (☎673-4422). The noise you hear while walking
up Ocean Dr. is coming from here. Mango's is the place for tourists and locals to party
till the early morning. Order a "Surfer on Acid" (Jagermeister, peach schnapps, and
pineapple juice) and stay for a live music set, concluded with a bar-top dance by the
wait staff. The party atmosphere prevails, be it 2pm or 2am. No cover during the day;
$10-20 at night. Open daily 11am-5am.

FLORIDA

GLBT NIGHTLIFE

South Beach's vibrant gay scene takes to the street almost every night of the week, in a constant search for the new "it club." Gay and mixed clubs in the area have bragging rights as the most trendy, amorphous hot spots, attracting a large crowd of both gay and straight partiers.

Twist, 1057 Washington Ave. (☎538-9478). A popular club with an outdoor lounge, dance floor, and 7 bars. Although stylish Twist hosts a predominately gay male crowd, it appeals to everyone with embossed copper ceilings, wooden bars, and emerald green walls. 21+. "Never a cover, always a groove." Happy hour daily 1-9pm; 2-for-1 drinks. Open daily 1pm-5am.

Score, 727 Lincoln Rd. (☎535-1111), in Lincoln Mall, near Meridian. Men frequent this multi-bar hot spot with a packed dance floor, plenty of style, and a hip attitude. For a more sophisticated and intimate setting head upstairs to the cream lounge. Tu is the night to be here. Daily drink specials. 21+. Cover Tu and F-Sa $5-10. Happy hour 3-9pm; half-price drinks. Open daily M-Sa 3pm-5am, Su 3pm-3am.

Laundry Bar, 721 N. Lincoln Ln. (☎531-7700). Men and women alike flock to the unusual Laundry Bar, where the chic and friendly clientele sip mixed drinks to the beat of DJ-spun house music and the hum of real laundry machines. A great place for an early drink, especially with the 2-for-1 drink specials daily noon-1pm. 21+ after 10pm. No cover. Open 7am-5am.

EVERGLADES NATIONAL PARK ☎305/239

Encompassing the entire tip of Florida and spearing into Florida Bay, Everglades National Park spans 1.5 million acres, making it the second-largest national park and of one of the world's most unique and fragile ecosystems. Vast prairies of sawgrass range through broad expanses of shallow water, creating the famed "river of grass," while tangled mazes of mangrove swamps wind up the western coast. To the south, delicate coral reefs lie below the shimmering blue waters of the bay. A host of species, many of which can be found nowhere else in the world, inhabits these lands and waters: American alligators, dolphins, and sea turtles, as well as the endangered Florida panther, Florida manatee, and American crocodile.

AT A GLANCE

AREA: 1,508,508 acres.

CLIMATE: Subtropical grassland.

HIGHLIGHTS: Be terrified by the denizens of the Everglades Alligator Farm and amazed by the flora and fauna of Anhinga Trail. Sleep it off at the spectacular Everglades International Hostel.

CAMPING: Reservations can be made in person, at least 1 day in advance, at the Flamingo or Gulf Coast Visitors Centers. $14. $10 permit plus $2 per person for backcountry camping; free in summer.

FEES: $10 per car, $5 per pedestrian or cyclist, good for 7 days.

✚🗷 ORIENTATION AND PRACTICAL INFORMATION

The **Ernest Coe Visitors Center,** 40001 State Road Rte. 9366, is at the park's main entrance, just inside the eastern edge of the Everglades. (☎242-7700; www.nps.gov/ever. Open daily 9am-5pm. Hours may be reduced June-Sept.; call ahead.) Rte. 9366 cuts 40 mi. through the park to the **Flamingo Visitors Center** (☎239-695-2945; open daily mid-Nov. to Apr. 8am-5pm; hours vary in summer). At the northern end of the park off U.S. 41, the **Shark Valley Visitors Center** has access to a 15 mi. loop through a swamp by foot, bike, or tram. Shark Valley is an ideal site for those who want a taste of the freshwater ecosystem but aren't inclined to venture too deep into the park. (☎305-221-8776. Open daily in wet season 9am-5pm; in dry season 8:45pm-5:15pm.) The **Gulf Coast Visitors Center,** 815 Copeland Ave. S, in Everglades City in the northwestern end of the park, provides access to the western coastline and the vast river network throughout the park. (☎239-695-3311. Open daily Nov.-Apr. 8am-4:30pm; May-Sept. 9am-4:30pm.) The **entrance fee** is $10 per car, $5 per pedestrian or cyclist at the Ernest Coe and Shark Valley entrances. Your receipt gets you into the park for the next seven days. The Gulf Coast entrance is free. For info on lodgings, check out the **Tropical Everglades Visitors Association,** on U.S. 1 in Florida City. (☎245-9180 or 800-388-9669; www.tropicaleverglades.com. Open M-Sa 9am-5pm, Su 10am-2pm.) **Emergency: Park Headquarters,** ☎247-7272. **Area Codes:** 305 and 239; in text, 305 unless otherwise specified.

🏠 🛏 ACCOMMODATIONS AND FOOD

Outside the eastern entrance to the park, **Florida City** offers cheap motels along U.S. 1, but the ⬛**Everglades International Hostel (HI) ❶,** 20 SW 2nd Ave., off Rte. 9336 (Palm Dr.), is a far better option. After venturing into the Everglades on one of the guided tours, hang out with fellow travelers in the hostel's gazebo, gardens, or kitchen, which has a big-screen TV and free video collection. This amazing hostel is also a fantastic base for daytrips to the Keys. (☎248-1122 or 800-372-3874; www.evergladeshostel.com. Internet, A/C, and free parking. Laundry $1. Linen $2. Bike rental $15. Canoe rental $30. Dorms $22. Ask about free-spirited travelers Discounts: walk-ins pay for four nights and get the fifth night free. In the park, both **Long Pine** and **Flamingo Campgrounds ❶** offer developed camping. Flamingo is a sun-bleached campground offering beautiful vistas of the day, while Long Pine provides a bit more shade. (☎800-365-2267. Reservations required. Long Pine has hot water showers. Nov.-Apr. Long Pine sites $26, Flamingo sites $16. Both parks free in summer.) There are dozens of **backcountry camping ❶** options in the park, though many are accessible only by boat (see **Boating,** p. 462). Required **permits** are available on a first come, first served basis at the Flamingo and Gulf Coast Visitors Centers. (Applications can be made in person up to 24hr. in advance. Permits Dec.-Apr. $10 plus $2 per person, good for 14 days. Mid-Apr. to mid-Nov. free.)

Across the street from the hostel, **Rosita's ❶,** 199 Palm Dr., has fabulous Mexican food. *Huevos rancheros* ($5) can get you ready for a long day of exploring the park. Try their enchiladas (chicken or beef, $6.50) for lunch, or come back to relax at dinner with great, affordable Mexican food. (☎246-3114. Open daily 8:30am-9pm. AmEx/MC/V.) In Homestead, Florida City's neighboring town, you will find a Cuban gem: **Calindos Cafe ❷,** 30530 South Dixie Hwy, (☎242-0333.) The *cubano especial* (ham, pork, and cheese on Cuban bread; $6) backs up the promise in their logo: it really is the "Best Sandwich in Town." Open daily 10-9pm. AmEx/D/MC/V. **Farmers' Market Restaurant ❸,** 300 N. Krome Ave., urges you to enjoy hearty portions of oh-so-fresh produce. The market breakfast (2 eggs, bacon, homefries, and a muffin; $6) will fill you up for a day of travel and exploration. For dinner, feast on fried conch ($10) for a truly Floridian experience. (☎242-0008. Breakfast $4.50-9. Lunch $6-11. Dinner $9-15.50. Open daily 5:30am-9pm. MC/V.)

🏔 OUTDOOR ACTIVITIES

The park is swamped with fishing, hiking, canoeing, biking, and wildlife-watching opportunities. Forget swimming within the park—alligators, sharks, and barracuda patrol the waters. If you're hot for some water sports, the nearby Biscayne National Park is there to satisfy (see **Swimming,** p. 462). From November through April, the park sponsors amphitheater programs, canoe trips, and ranger-guided Slough Slogs (swamp tours).

HIKING. The Everglades offer hikes suited for both skilled adventurers and novices who wish to stay within sight of their cars. Even for short hikes, it is advisable to pick up a copy of the *Wilderness Trip Planner,* which provides info on trails and conditions. All trails take about 25min. to complete. The wheelchair-accessible **Anhinga Trail** yields a good time with minimal commitment. Those willing to brave the half-mile stroll down the boardwalk are guaranteed up-close encounters with alligators, birds, and turtles. Low water from December to March makes for a higher concentration of wildlife, though the walk is a must any time of year. Take the turnoff for the Royal Palms Visitors Center, 4 mi. inside the park from the main entrance. The **Pa-hay-okee Overlook,** 13 mi. from the main entrance off Rte. 9336, rewards visitors with a stunning view of the park after a quarter-mile boardwalk stroll. For a more difficult trail, try the Long Pine Key (6 mi. from the main entrance), where the **Long Pine Key Trail** ventures through 10 mi. of slash pine forests. Another arduous hike is the **Mahogany Hammock Trail** (20 mi. from the main entrance, wheelchair-accessible). The trail is made up of incredible routes through freshwater prairie and pineland, but mosquitoes have the run of the land in the summer, making it most enjoyable in the winter.

BOATING. To experience the Everglades, start paddling. The 99 mi. **Wilderness Waterway** winds its way from the northwest entrance to the Flamingo station in the south. **Camping** spots include chickees (elevated wooden platforms above swamps), beaches, and groundsites. **Everglades National Park Boat Tours,** at the **Gulf Coast Visitors Center,** rents canoes ($25) and is the best option for guided boat tours. The **Ten Thousand Island Cruise** ($21, ages 5-12 $11) is a 1½hr. tour through the Everglades' tiny islands. Expect to see bald eagles, dolphins, and manatees. The **Mangrove Wilderness Cruise** ($35/17.50) is a 1¼hr. narrated cruise through the inland swamps that brings you face-to-face with alligators. (☎239-695-2591. Tours 9am; call for schedule.) For more information about canoe rentals consult the rangers at the **Flamingo Visitor Center.**

BIKING. While the Everglades mostly cater to those with walking sticks and canoe paddles, it does boast some excellent biking opportunities for visitors. By far the best route starts at the **Shark Valley Visitors Center,** an adventurous 15 mi. loop. The trail peaks at an incredible observation tower that offers great views of the park. (Bike rental daily 8:30am-3pm. $6.25 per 1hr., includes helmet. Return bikes by 4pm.) For the less athletic, tram tours through the Shark Valley area (2hr. round-trip) are worth the time and money. (Runs daily Dec.-Apr. hourly 9am-4pm; May-Nov. 9:30, 11am, 1, 3pm. Wheelchair-accessible. Reservations recommended. $14.50, under 12 $8.75.)

SWIMMING. It can be very easy to overlook the nearby **Biscayne National Park,** as 95% of it is submerged under water. Just 15min. from the Everglades Hostel, Biscayne features amazing diving and snorkeling, and remote camping on Boca Chita and Elliott Key, accessible only by boat. (Visitors Center: 9700 SW 328th St. ☎230-7275. Snorkel cruise and Keys ferry info ☎230-1100.) For a lazy swim in a heavenly (and gator-free) lagoon, stop by the **Homestead Bayfront Park,** south of the Biscayne Visitors Center.

GARDENS AND GATORS. View gators, crocs, and snakes at the **Everglades Alligator Farm,** 40351 SW 192 Ave., 4 mi. south of Palm Dr. Though touristy, this is the place to see thousands of gators, from little hatchlings clambering for a bit of sunlight to 18 ft. monsters clambering for a bite of you. Call ahead for pricing information to take a wild airboat ride. (☎247-2628 or 800-644-9711; www.everglades.com. Open daily 9am-6pm. Feedings noon and 3pm. Wheelchair-accessible. Alligator shows free with admission; 11am, 2, 5pm. $19, ages 4-11 $12.)

KEY LARGO ☎305

Over half a century ago, Hollywood stars Humphrey Bogart and Lauren Bacall immortalized the name "Key Largo" in their hit movie of the same name. Quick-thinking locals of Rock Harbor, where some of the scenes were shot, soon changed the name to Key Largo to attract tourists. Even though Bogart and Bacall never step foot on Rock Harbor (their scenes were filmed in a Hollywood set), it worked—Key Largo is now the gateway to the enchanting Florida Keys. Though laid-back in attitude, the Keys can be hard on the budget, especially during winter high season. Key Largo can be a bit cheaper than the more westward Keys and is renowned for natural beauty, coral reefs, and great fishing. Pennekamp State Park was the country's first underwater park, and divers of all abilities flock to the isle for the chance to glimpse at the reef ecosystem and the numerous shipwrecks.

▮▨ TRANSPORTATION AND PRACTICAL INFORMATION. Greyhound, Mi. 99.6 (☎800-231-2222; www.greyhound.com), runs to Key West (3hr., 3 per day, $29) and Miami (1¾hr., 3 per day, $16.50). Most drivers will stop at mile markers along the road, though you must do all in your power to get their attention. Greyhound signs along the highway indicate **bus** stops (usually hotels), where you can buy tickets or call the **info line** on the red phones. For a **taxi,** call **Mom's Taxi,** ☎852-6000.

The **Overseas Highway (U.S. 1)** bridges the divide between the Keys and the southern tip of Florida, stitching the islands together. Mile markers section the highway and replace street addresses. **Biking** along U.S. 1 is treacherous due to fast cars and narrow shoulders; instead of riding, bring your bike on the bus. Spirits flow freely in the Keys, and drunk driving has recently become a problem—stay alert when on the roads. The **Key Largo Chamber of Commerce/Florida Keys Visitors Center,** 106000 U.S. 1, Mi. 106, has a coffee bar. (☎451-1414 or 800-822-1088; www.keylargo.org. Open daily 9am-6pm.) **Medical Services: Mariners Hospital,** Mi. 91.5 (☎434-4000). **Post Office:** 100100 U.S. 1, Mi. 100. (☎451-3155. Open M-F 8am-4:30pm, Sa 10am-1pm.) **Postal Code:** 33037.

▮ ACCOMMODATIONS. Ed and Ellen's Lodgings ❸, 103365 U.S. 1, Mi. 103.4 (on Snapper Ave.), has well-kept, 300 sq. ft. rooms with A/C, cable TV, and kitchenettes. Ed, the entertaining owner, is helpful with everything from restaurant suggestions to diving and snorkeling reservations. It's also within walking distance to Pennekamp State Park. (☎451-9949 or 888-333-5536; www.ed-ellens-lodgings.com. Doubles $59-79; low season $49-59. Each additional person $10. Rates increase on weekends, holidays, and during lobster season. MC/V.) Reservations are strongly recommended for the popular **John Pennekamp Coral Reef State Park Campground ❶** (see **Sights,** p. 464). The 47 sites have water, electricity, picnic tables, and grills, and are well-located (5min. walk Pennekamp beach), making them worth the effort required to obtain reservations. Most sites (90%) are available for reservation online; the other 10% are set aside for walk-ins on a first-come, first-served basis. (☎451-1202; www.reserveamerica.com. Bathrooms and showers. Pets allowed. 14-day max. stay. Park open 8am-sunset. Sites $32. AmEx/D/MC/V.) The waterside **Hungry Pelican ❸,** Mi. 99.5, boasts an explosion of bougainvillea vines, tropical birds in the trees, and cozy rooms with double beds, fridges, DVD players, and cable TV. You can watch dolphins and manatees from this beachfront campsite. Large outdoor hut outside for socializing and eating. (☎451-3576. Free use of paddleboats, canoes, and kayaks. Continental breakfast included. Rooms $60-170. Each additional person $10. AmEx/D/MC/V.)

◖ FOOD. Seafood restaurants of varying price, quality, and specialty litter Overseas Hwy. The neighboring Islamorada boasts one of the best seafood restaurants

FLORIDA

in the Keys. The **Islamorada Fish Company ❸**, Mi. 81.5, offers an incredible array of seafood sandwiches ($7-15) and entrees ($17-20), which patrons enjoy under the sunset. For dessert, try the legendary Key Lime Pie. (☎664-9271 or 800-258-2559. Open daily 11am-9pm, sometimes later. AmEx/D/MC/V.) The Cuban Cafe, **Calypso's ❸**, 1 Seagate Blvd., at Ocean Bay Dr. near Mi. 99.5, offers delectable buffalo shrimp and dolphin fish sandwiches ($9) and freshly cut fries. Try the butter pecan mahi mahi ($18) for dinner. (☎451-0600. Open M-W 11am-10pm, F-Sa 11:30am-11pm, Su noon-9:45pm. Cash only.) **Mrs. Mac's Kitchen ❷**, Mi. 99.4 on the bay side, cooks up overwhelming hamburgers ($5.50-$7.45) and famous steak sandwiches ($6-7) for eager patrons. While you're waiting to dine, check out the license plates from all over the country. (☎451-3722. Open M-Sa 7am-9:30pm. AmEx/D/MC/V.) For a scrumptious breakfast, head to **The Hideout Restaurant ❶**, on the ocean side of Mi. 103.5, at the end of Transylvania Ave. Plate-size pancakes (2 for $4) and unforgettable french toast ($4) make this the affordable meal you can't miss. Stop by this hidden treasure on Friday nights for an all-you-can-eat fish fest for $10. (☎451-0128. Open daily 7am-2pm; also F 5-9pm. Cash only.)

⬛ SIGHTS. Key Largo is the self-proclaimed "Dive Capital of the World," and many diving instructors offer their services via highway billboards. The best place to go is **John Pennekamp Coral Reef State Park,** Mi. 102.5. The park extends 3 mi. into the Atlantic Ocean, safeguarding a part of the coral reef that runs the length of the Keys. (☎451-1202; www.pennecamppark.com. Vehicle with 1 occupant $3.50, 2 occupants $6; each additional person $0.50. Pedestrians or bicycles $1.50.) Stop by the park's Visitors Center for free maps, boat and snorkeling tour info, and films on the park. To see the reefs, visitors must bring or rent their own boat, or hop on a charter. (☎451-9570, reservations 451-6325. Open daily 8am-5pm. Canoes $12 per hr. 18 ft. motor boat $135 per 4hr. Deposit required.) Hidden away on Hwy. 1, **The Turtle Hospital,** 2396 Overseas Hwy., Marathon, FL, rehabilitates rescued sea turtles. This charitable organization treats sea turtles for a variety of ailments, from boat collisions to viral infections. Admission gives you a 90min. guided tour of the site, where you can see the patients at different stages of rehabilitation. (☎743-2552; www.turtlehospital.org. Reservations required. Tours daily 10am, 1, 4pm. $15, ages 4-12 $7.50.) **Scuba trips** leave from the dive shop. (☎451-6322. 9:30am and 1:30pm. 2-tank dive $45 per person. Deposit required.) A **snorkeling tour** also allows you to enjoy the underwater quiet and mingle with barricuda, parrot fish, and other ocean life. (☎451-6300. 2½hr. total, 1½hr. water time. Tours 9am, noon, 3pm. $29, under 18 $24; equipment $6. Deposit required.) **Glass Bottom Boat Tours** provides a crystal clear view of the reefs without wetting your feet. (☎451-6300. 2½hr. tours 9:15am, 12:15, 3pm. $22, under 12 $15.) Head to any of the local marinas to charter a spot on a **fishing boat.** To avoid paying a commission, hang out on the docks and ask one of the friendly captains yourself. At Mi. 100 on the ocean side, the **Holiday Inn** also runs a plethora of scuba, snorkel, and boat trips. The best-known is the **Key Largo Princess,** which leads 2hr. glass bottom boat tours. (☎451-4655. $25.) Aside from its active dock, the hotel has become a tourist destination, as it houses the **African Queen** the original boat on which Humphrey Bogart and Katherine Hepburn sailed in the movie of the same title.

KEY WEST   ☎305

The small "last island" of the Florida Keys, Key West has always drawn a cast of colorful characters to its shores since its days of pirates and smugglers. Henry Flagler, Ernest Hemingway, Tennessee Williams, Truman Capote, and Jimmy Buffett have all called the quasi-independent "Conch Republic" home. Today thousands of tourists hop on the Overseas Hwy. to glimpse the past, visit hundreds of bars, and kick back under the sun. The crowd is as diverse as Key West's past: families take

Key West

🏠 ACCOMMODATIONS
Boyd's Campground, **5**
Caribbean House, **14**
Key West Youth Hostel and
Sea Shell Motel, **16**

🍴 FOOD
Blue Heaven, **13**
The Cafe, **6**
El Siboney Restaurant, **15**

🍸 NIGHTLIFE
801 Bourbon, **12**
Aqua, **10**
The Bourbon Street Pub, **11**
Captain Tony's Saloon, **3**
The Green Parrot, **7**
Kelly's Caribbean Bar, **4**
Kwest Men, **9**
Rick's, **2**
Sloppy Joe's, **1**

a week to splash in the water, twentysomethings come to party and work, and a swinging gay population finds a haven of gay-only clubs and resorts. Key West is as far south as you can get in the continental US. This is the end of the road—enjoy it.

▕▘ TRANSPORTATION

Airport: Key West International Airport (EYW), 3491 South Roosevelt Blvd. (☎296-7223), off U.S. 1A, on the eastern side of the island.

Buses: Greyhound, 3535 S. Roosevelt Blvd. (☎296-9072; www.greyhound.com), at the airport. Open daily 8am-6pm. To **Miami** (4½hr., 3 per day, $33.50; slightly higher on weekends and holidays).

Taxi: Keys Taxi, ☎296-6666.

Bike Rental: Keys Moped & Scooters, 523 Truman Ave. (☎294-0399). Open daily 9am-8pm. Bikes $10 per day. Single scooter $40 per day, double scooter $65 per day.

◢ ▞ ORIENTATION AND PRACTICAL INFORMATION

Key West lies at the end of **Overseas Highway (U.S. 1),** 155 mi. southwest of Miami (3-3½hr.). The island is divided into two sections. The eastern part, known as **New Town,** harbors tract houses, chain motels, shopping malls, and the airport. Beautiful old conch houses fill **Old Town,** west of White St. **Duval Street** is the main north-south thoroughfare in Old Town; **U.S. 1 (Truman Avenue)** is a major east-west route. A car is the easiest way to get to Key West, though driving in town is neither easy nor necessary. Do not park overnight on the bridges.

Visitor Info: Key West Welcome Center, 3840 N. Roosevelt Blvd. (☎296-4444), just north of the intersection of U.S. 1 and Roosevelt Blvd. A private reservation service. Open daily 8:30am-5:30pm. **Key West Chamber of Commerce,** 402 Wall St. (☎294-2587 or 800-527-8539; www.keywestchamber.org), in old Mallory Sq. Open M-F 8am-6:30pm, Sa-Su 9am-6pm.

GLBT Resources: The Key West Business Guild Gay and Lesbian Information Center, 513 Truman Ave. (☎294-4603; www.gaykeywestsl.com). Helps find gay guest houses. Open daily 9am-5pm.

Hotlines: Help Line, ☎296-4357. 24hr.

Internet Access: Crossroads, 500 Truman Ave. #7 (☎294-9118). $10 per 1hr. Open daily 9am-8pm.

Post Office: 400 Whitehead St. (☎294-9539), west of Duval St., at Eaton St. Open M-F 8:30am-5pm, Sa 9:30am-noon. **Postal Code:** 33040.

ACCOMMODATIONS

Key West is packed with visitors year-round, but especially from January to March; reserve rooms far in advance. **Pride Week** (www.pridefestkeywest.com), held every June, is generally a busy time of the year. In Old Town, the multicolored 19th-century houses capture the flavor of the Keys. B&Bs dominate and "reasonably priced" still means over $50. Some of the guest houses in Old Town are exclusively for gay men.

Key West Youth Hostel and Sea Shell Motel, 718 South St. (☎296-5719). The cheapest option in town, with simple rooms and a good location. No TV. Free Wi-Fi and parking. Dorms $34, 3-night stay $29 per night; motel rooms $75-175. Each additional person $20. HI and ISIC discounts. MC/V. ❶

Casablanca Hotel, 900-904 Duval St. (☎296-0815), in the center of the main drag. This stately B&B once played host to Humphrey Bogart. A/C, cable TV, Internet access, pool. Reserve early during Fantasy Fest (late Oct.). Rooms Dec.-May $155-250; June-Nov. $125. AmEx/MC/V. ❺

Caribbean House, 226 Petronia St. (☎296-0999). Has rooms with Caribbean-influenced decor. A/C, cable TV, fridge, and comfy double beds. In winter, rooms $100. In summer $85. AmEx/D/MC/V. ❹

Boyd's Campground, 6401 Maloney Ave. (☎294-1465). Heading south, take a left off U.S. 1 onto Macdonald Ave., which becomes Maloney. Sprawls over 12 oceanside acres and provides modern facilities. 2-person sites $60, with water and electricity $75, full hookup $95. In summer $50/65/75. Each additional person $10. Waterfront sites additional $10-15. MC/V. ❷

FOOD

Expensive, trendy restaurants line festive **Duval Street.** Side streets offer lower prices and fewer crowds, but many visitors seem to just skip the chow and jump straight to the bars.

Blue Heaven, 729 Thomas St. (☎296-8666). Feast upon the town's best cuisine in a lovely outdoor setting. Healthful breakfasts include fresh banana bread ($4-11), Caribbean or Mexican lunches ($7-12), and heavenly dinners ($11.50-34). The vegetarian stir-fry ($16) is a great accompaniment to the scallop appetizer ($14). Don't forget their fantastic Key Lime pie ($9) topped with a huge dollop of meringue. Open mid-Oct. to Aug. daily 8am-2pm and 6:30-10pm. AmEx/D/MC/V. ❸

The Cafe, 509 Southard St. (☎296-5515). Ideal for vegetarians and vegans. Serves up a wide variety of tempting dishes, from tofu parmesan ($9.25) and Szechuan stir-fry ($9.25) to barbecued tofu sandwich ($8), plus better prices than anywhere else in all of Old Town. The seared coconut cake with ginger ice cream ($7) is just one of many delicious homemade desserts. Open M-Sa 11am-10pm. MC/V. ❷

El Siboney, 900 Catherine St. (☎296-4184). Breaking with the Key West tradition of overpriced food, this Cuban establishment serves heaping mounds of beans, rice, and meat—all for around $10. Try the pork roast with plantains, beans, and rice ($9) for a hearty meal. Open M-Sa 11am-9:30pm. Cash only. ❷

👁 SIGHTS

ON LAND. Because of limited parking, traversing Key West by bike or moped is more convenient and comfortable than driving. For those who would rather take a tram, the **Conch Tour Train** is a fun but pricey 1½hr. narrated ride through Old Town. *(Leaves from Mallory Sq. ☎294-5161. Runs daily 9am-4:30pm. $27, ages 4-12 $13.)* **Old Town Trolley** runs a similar narrated tour, but you can get on and off throughout the day at 10 stops. *(☎296-6688. Tours daily 9am-5:30pm. Full tour 1½hr. $27, ages 4-12 $13.)* No one can leave Key West without a visit to the ◪**Ernest Hemingway Home,** where "Papa" wrote *For Whom the Bell Tolls* and *The Snows of Kilimanjaro.* Take a tour with hilarious guides who relate Hemingway and Key West history, then strut through on your own among 47 descendants of Hemingway's cat, half of which have 6 toes. *(907 Whitehead St. ☎294-1136; www.hemingwayhome.com. Open daily 9am-5pm. Partially wheelchair-accessible. $11, ages 6-12 $6.)* Tucked into the affluent Truman Annex Gated Community, the **Harry S. Truman Little White House Museum** provides insight into the life of President Truman and his idyllic getaway in Key West. *(111 Front St. ☎294-9911; www.trumanlittlewhitehouse.com. Open daily 9am-5pm. Last tour 4:30pm. Partially wheelchair-accessible. $11, children $5; includes tour.)* In addition to its serene garden, the **Audubon House** shelters fine antiques and a collection of original engravings by naturalist John James Audubon, who amassed his fortune from selling his art and engaging in piracy. *(205 Whitehead St. ☎294-2116; www.audubon-house.com. Wheelchair-accessible. Open daily 9:30am-4:30pm. $11, seniors $10, students $6.50, ages 6-12 $5.)*

MARITIME MUSEUMS. Feel the weight of an actual bar of gold at the **Mel Fisher Maritime Heritage Society Museum.** This museum brings to life the amazing discovery and salvaging of the Spanish galleon Atocha, which sank off the Keys in the 17th century with millions of dollars in gold and silver. Many different artifacts of the shipwreck can be seen here, including jewelry and cannon balls. The museum also has an entire floor dedicated to the study of the slave trade. *(200 Greene St. ☎294-2633; www.melfisher.org. Open daily 8:30am-5pm. $11, students $9.50, ages 6-12 $6.)* The **Key West Shipwreck Historeum Museum,** located in Mallory Sq., boasts the remains of the *Isaac Allerton*, the 594-ton ship that sank in 1856. Live demonstrations give a glimpse into the lives of classic adventurers by surveying artifacts and the original cargo that the Allerton was carrying. The museum's 65 ft. lookout tower offers a great view of the island. *(1 Whitehead St. ☎292-8990; www.shipwreckhistoreum.com. $11, ages 4-12 $5. Open daily 9:45am-5pm.)* On Whitehead St. is the 92 ft. **Key West Lighthouse and Museum.** Climb the 88 steps to the top to be rewarded with the best view of Key West in town. *(938 Whitehead St. ☎294-0012. Open daily 9:30am-4:30pm. Partially wheelchair-accessible. $9, AAA and seniors $8, students $5.)*

FLORIDA

ON WATER. The **glass-bottomed boat** *Pride of Key West* cruises to the reefs and back. (☎ *296-6293. 2hr. cruises daily noon, 2, 4pm; champagne cruise 6pm. $35; ages 5-12 $15.)* Down Whitehead St., past the Hemingway House, you'll come to the southernmost point in the continental US, at the fittingly named **Southernmost Beach.** A colorful, buoy-like monument marks the spot: "90 miles to Cuba." Key West has one of the most spectacular sunsets you can see in the continental United States. Beachgoers take part in the daily tradition of watching the sun go down. At the **Mallory Square Dock,** street entertainers and kitsch-hawkers work the crowd, while boats parade in revue during the daily **Sunset Celebration.**

⬛ NIGHTLIFE

The free *Island News*, found in local restaurants and bars, lists dining spots, music, and clubs. Nightlife in Key West, centered around upper **Duval Street,** revs up at 11pm and winds down in the wee daylight hours. Key West nightlife reaches its annual high in the third week of October during **Fantasy Fest** (☎ 296-1817; www.fantasyfest.net), when decadent floats filled with drag queens, pirates, and locals take over Duval St.

Capt. Tony's Saloon, 428 Greene St. (☎ 294-1838). The oldest bar in Key West and allegedly the preferred watering hole of Tennessee Williams and Truman Capote. If drinking isn't your thing, come see the huge oak tree where, according to legend, 73 pirates were hung. This wild saloon decorated with hundreds of business cards and brassieres has been serving since the 30s. Live music nightly. Open M-Sa 10am-2am, Su noon-2am.

The Green Parrot, 601 Whitehead St. (☎ 294-6133). Though a 7min. walk from the main drag, this neighborhood hangout has enough of a reputation to have warranted a nod from Playboy as Key West's best. Try the root beer barrel (root beer and Schnapps; $4). Open daily 11am-4am.

Sloppy Joe's, 201 Duval St. (☎ 294-5717). For the best party you'll most likely forget, stop by Hemingway's favorite hangout. There are no sloppy joes served here: Hemingway named the bar after suggesting to the owner it needed a more appropriate name. Try their "Bacardi Piña Colada" or the "Frozen Pain in the Ass" ($7) to get in the mood for your next stop. 21+ after 9pm. Open M-Sa 9am-4am, Su noon-4am.

GLBT NIGHTLIFE

Known for its wild, outspoken gay community, Key West hosts more than a dozen fabulous drag lounges, night clubs, and private bars for the gay man's enjoyment. Most clubs also welcome straight couples and lesbians, but check with the bouncer first before entering. Most gay clubs in town line Duval St., just south of Fleming Ave. Check out *Conch Color* or *The Gay Ray* for extensive coverage of the Key West gay and lesbian community.

Aqua, 711 Duval St. (☎ 294-0555). Has become the hottest drag club in Key West. You're likely to see many wide-eyed tourists checking out the singing beauties, the Aquanettes. Long Island iced tea $3. Happy hour daily 3-8pm. Open M-Th and Su 3pm-2am, F-Sa 3pm-4am.

The Bourbon Street Pub, 724 Duval St. (☎ 294-9354; www.bourbonstreetcomplex.com). Lacking the jock-strap-clad waiters common at many of the other bars, this is a more traditional bar, though antics can still get wild. Try the Absolut 7, a different flavor of Absolut every day ($5). Drag shows daily 9 and 11pm. Open M-Sa 11am-4am, Su noon-4am.

801 Bourbon, 801 Duval St. (☎ 294-9354). Bourbon's sister club. Also very popular. Open M-Sa 11am-4am, Su noon-4am.

FORT LAUDERDALE ☎ 954

During the past two decades, Fort Lauderdale has transformed from a beer-stained spring break mecca to the largest yachting center in North America. City streets and highways may be fine for the commoner's transportation needs, but Fort Lauderdale adds another option: canals. Intricate waterways connect ritzy homes with the intracoastal river and even mere mortals can cruise the canals via the Water Taxi, an on-the-water bus system. "The Venice of America" also boasts 23 mi. of beach where spring break mayhem still reigns supreme, making Fort "Liquordale" fun even for those who can't afford a yacht.

▐▀ TRANSPORTATION

Airport: Fort Lauderdale/Hollywood International (FLL), 320 Terminal Dr. (☎359-6100; www.broward.org/airport), 3½ mi. south of downtown on U.S. 1. Or take I-595 E from I-95 to Exit 12B. Buses to and from the airport go through Broward Country Transit Central Terminal (☎367-8400). Take bus #1 to and from the airport.

Trains: Amtrak, 200 SW 21st Terr. (☎587-6692; www.amtrak.com), just west of I-95, ¼ mi. south of Broward Blvd. Take bus #22 from downtown. Open daily 6:45am-9:00pm. To **Orlando** (4¾hr., 2 per day, $32-70). **Tri-Rail** (☎800-874-7245) connects West Palm Beach, Fort Lauderdale, and Miami. Trains run M-F 4am-10pm, Sa 7am-11pm, Su 7am-9pm. Schedules available at airport, motels, or Tri-Rail stops. $2-10; children, disabled, students, and seniors with Tri-Rail ID 50% discount.

Buses: Greyhound, 515 NE 3rd St. (☎764-6551; www.greyhound.com), at Federal Hwy., 3 blocks north of Broward Blvd., in downtown. Be careful in this area, especially at night. Open 24hr. To **Daytona Beach** (7hr., 6-7 per day, $38), **Miami** (45min., 20 per day, $6), and **Orlando** (4½-5½hr., 13 per day, $40).

Public Transit: Broward County Transit (BCT) (☎357-8400). Central Terminal at NW 1st Ave. and Broward Blvd. downtown. Buses #11 and 36 run north-south on A1A through the beaches. Operates daily 6am-11pm. $1; disabled, seniors, and under 18 $0.50. 1-day pass $2.50, 7-day pass $9, 10-ride pass $8. Schedules available at hotels, libraries, and the central terminal. **Sun Trolley** (☎761-3543) loops through downtown and between Sunrise and Las Olas Blvds. Runs every 30min. F-Sa 6pm-1am. $0.25-0.50.)

Taxi: Yellow Cab, ☎777-7777. **Public Service Taxi,** ☎587-9090.

Bike Rental: Big Wheels Cycles, 5429 N. Federal Hwy. (☎493-5277). Open M-F 10am-7pm, Sa 10am-5pm. Bicycles $20 per day, $50 per week; racing bikes $30/100. Credit card deposit.

◤ ORIENTATION

North-south **I-95** connects West Palm Beach, Fort Lauderdale, and Miami. **Rte. 84/I-75 (Alligator Alley)** slithers 100 mi. west from Fort Lauderdale across the Everglades to Florida's Gulf Coast. Florida's Turnpike runs parallel to I-95. Fort Lauderdale is bigger than it looks, extending westward from its 23 mi. of beach to encompass nearly 450 sq. mi. Streets and boulevards run east-west and avenues run north-south, and all are labeled NW, NE, SW, or SE. The two major roads in Fort Lauderdale are **Broward Boulevard,** running east-west, and **Andrews Avenue,** running north-south. The brick-and-mortar downtown centers around **U.S. 1 (Federal Highway)** and **Las Olas Boulevard,** about 2 mi. west of the oceanfront. Between downtown and the waterfront, yachts fill the ritzy inlets of the **Intracoastal Waterway. The Strip** (a.k.a. Rte. A1A, Fort Lauderdale Beach Blvd., 17th St. Causeway, Ocean Blvd., or Seabreeze Blvd.) runs 4 mi. along the beach between Oakland Park Blvd. to the north and Las Olas Blvd. to the south.

⚡ PRACTICAL INFORMATION

Visitor Info: Greater Fort Lauderdale Convention and Visitors Bureau, 100 E. Broward Blvd. Ste. 200 (☎765-4466, travel directions and hotel info 800-227-8669 9am-9pm; www.sunny.org), has the useful *Superior Small Lodgings*, a comprehensive list of low-priced hotels. Open M-F 8:30am-5pm. **Chamber of Commerce,** 512 NE 3rd Ave. (☎462-6000), 5 blocks north of Broward Blvd., just north of 5th St. Open M-F 8am-5pm.

Hotlines: First Call for Help, ☎537-0211. **Sexual Assault and Treatment Center,** ☎761-7273. Both 24hr.

Medical Services: Fort Lauderdale Hospital, 1601 E. Las Olas Blvd., at SE 16th Ave. (☎463-4321).

Internet Access: Broward County Library, 100 S. Andrews Ave. (☎357-7444). Free with ID. Open M-Th 9am-9pm, F-Sa 9am-5pm, Su noon-5:30pm.

Post Office: 1900 W. Oakland Park Blvd. (☎765-5720). Open M-F 7:30am-7pm, Sa 8:30am-2pm. **Postal Code:** 33310.

🛏 ACCOMMODATIONS

Thank decades of spring breakers for the abundance of beachfront hotels. It's easy to find a room at any time of the year, depending on how much you are willing to pay. Motels north of The Strip and a block west of Rte. A1A are the cheapest. High season runs from mid-February to early April and many hotels offer low-season deals for under $50. The **Greater Fort Lauderdale Lodging and Hospitality Association,** 1412 E. Broward Blvd. (☎462-5663), provides a free directory of area hotels. The *Fort Lauderdale News* and the *Miami Herald* occasionally print listings by local residents who rent rooms to tourists in spring.

Fort Lauderdale Beach Hostel, 2115 N. Ocean Blvd./Rte. A1A and 21 Ave. (☎567-7275), between Sunrise and Oakland Park Blvd. Take bus #11 from the central terminal. Mingle in the tropical courtyard, TV-equipped common room, and kitchen. A/C, coin-op laundry, grill, and local phone calls. Continental breakfast included. Free lockers. Linen deposit $10. Free Wi-Fi. Call ahead for free daytime pickup. Reservations suggested Dec.-June. Dorms $22; singles $45, doubles $55. MC/V. ●

Bridge II Hostel, 506 SE 16th St. (☎522-6350). From downtown take bus #1 or 40 and get off at 17th St. Across the street from Floyd's and home to backpackers and boat crews. Spacious dorms, free Wi-Fi, kitchens, cable TV, free local calls, and swimming pool. Dorms $26.50; private rooms $33-35. Weekly dorms $148; private rooms $230-250. D/MC/V. ●

Floyd's Hostel/Crew House, 445 SE 16th St. (☎462-0631). From downtown take bus #1 or 40 and get off at 17th St. Call ahead for free pickup in the Fort Lauderdale area. A homey hostel catering to international travelers and boat crews. Close to shops, restaurants, and gifts on Las Olas Blvd., 1 mi. from the beach. Free Wi-Fi, cable TV, laundry, linen, and lockers. Check-in until midnight. Passport or US driver's license required. 4-bed dorms $20; private rooms $25. Weekly dorms $125. MC/V. ●

🍴 FOOD

Though clubs along The Strip offer massive quantities of free Happy hour grub—wieners, chips, and hors d'oeuvres come on surfboard-sized platters—most bars have hefty cover charges (from $5) and drink minimums (from $3).

The Floridian, 1410 E. Las Olas Blvd. (☎463-4041). A local favorite, serving up heaping portions of delicious fare. The Red Conch Chowder ($4) and Jumbo Fried Clams ($12)

Fort Lauderdale

⌂ ACCOMMODATIONS

Bridge II Hostel, **9**
Floyd's Hostel/Crew House, **8**
Fort Lauderdale Beach
    Hostel, **2**
Tropic-Cay Beach Hotel, **11**

🍎 FOOD

Argie Grill , **6**
Lulu's Bait Shack, **12**
The Floridian, **7**
Jaxson's, **10**

▣ NIGHTLIFE

Dicey O'Riley's Irish Pub, **3**
Elbo Room, **13**
Ramrod, **1**
Tarpon Bend, **4**
The Voodoo Lounge, **5**

are great regional favorites. The milkshakes ($4) are to die for. Marilyn Monroe fans will love this restaurant; the walls are decorated with gorgeous pictures from her daily life, as well as some fantastic glam shots. Open 24hr. AmEx. ❷

Jaxson's, 128 S. Federal Hwy. (☎923-4445), in Dania Beach. This sparkling red building contains scrumptious ice cream and before-dessert fare. Try the Kitchen Sink to see just how much ice cream your stomach can handle ($10 per person). Cold sandwiches $8.75-$10.25. Gourmet platters $12-$17. Open M-Th 11:30am-11pm, F-Sa 11:30am-midnight, Su noon-11pm. AmEx/D/MC/V. ❷

Argie Grill, 300 SW 1st St., Ste. 105 (☎463-2686). Offers 19 varieties of *empanadas* like the spinach and portobello ($3.65), in addition to sandwiches, pizza, salads, and burgers. Open M-Th and Su 11am-10pm, F-Sa 11am-4:30am. MC/V. ❶

🅖 SIGHTS

Most visitors flock to Fort Lauderdale to lounge on the sunny beaches. When floating in the crystal-clear waves of the Atlantic, it's easy to forget the city's other notable attractions. Cruising down the palm-lined shore of Beachfront Ave. (Rte. A1A), biking through a nature preserve, or boating through the winding intracoastal canals reveals Fort Lauderdale's less-sandy side.

FLORIDA

ON THE BEACH. Spring break lasts 365 days a year on Fort Lauderdale Beach, with the help of a Corona or two in any of the big bars along Rte. A1A. If extreme inebriation isn't your thing, have no fear: the beach area offers plenty of booze-free activities. If you'd like to hit the water in more active style, **Water Sports Unlimited** has water sport rentals and trips. Sail the ocean or enjoy its serene blue water from above on a parasailing trip. Wave runners are also available. *(301 Seabreeze Blvd./Rte. A1A. ☎ 467-1316. Open daily 9am-5pm. Boat rental $219-599 per 2 hr. Parasailing trips $75 per 12min.; $95 per 17min.)* Get lost in an oasis of subtropical trees and animals in the middle of urban Fort Lauderdale at **Hugh Taylor Birch State Park.** Bike, jog, canoe, or drive among mangroves and royal palms, or relax in the freshwater lagoon area with herons, gophers, tortoises, marsh rabbits, and even wild iguanas. *(3109 E. Sunrise Blvd., west off Rte. A1A. ☎ 564-4521. Open daily 8am-dusk. $4 per vehicle, $1 per person. Canoes $5.30 per hr.)* For a different kind of high-seas adventure, doggy-paddle over to the **International Swimming Hall of Fame and Museum** for exhibits on the sport and its greatest athletes, including old-fashioned bathing suits. *(1 Hall of Fame Dr., 1 block south of Las Olas Blvd. on Rte. A1A. ☎ 462-6536; www.ishof.org. Open M-F 9am-7pm, Sa-Su 9am-5pm. Wheelchair-accessible. $8, military, seniors, and students $4, under 12 free.)* For a family-friendly overview of Fort Lauderdale, take a tour aboard the **Jungle Queen.** The captain's commentary acquaints you with the changing scenery as you cruise up the New River. *(801 Seabreeze Blvd. At the Bahía Mar Yacht Center, on Rte. A1A, 3 blocks south of Las Olas Blvd. ☎ 462-5596; www.junglequeen.com. 3½-4hr. tours daily 9:30am, 1:30, 6pm. $14, ages 2-12 $11; 7pm tour $35/17.50; dinner included.)*

IN TOWN. The **Riverwalk** provides a shaded stroll along the banks of the New River, which cuts through downtown. Beginning at U.S. 1, the brick-lined, oak-shaded path meanders along the river, passing numerous sights and enormous mega-yachts. *(☎ 468-1541; www.goriverwalk.com.)* First along the route is Fort Lauderdale's **Museum of Art,** 1 E. Las Olas Blvd., home to an extensive collection of American painters and remarkable temporary exhibits, which have included everything from Surrealism to photojournalism. The museum is kicking off its 50th anniversary with two new exhibits: The Great Age of American Automobiles (from exotic cars to antique classics), and an exhibit on the life and work of the late Dorothy Draper. *(☎ 525-5500; www.moafl.org. Open M-W and F-Su 11am-7pm, Th 11am-9pm. Wheelchair-accessible. $10, seniors $7, students 6-17 $7.)* The next stop is the **Las Olas Waterfront,** 2 SW 2nd St., the latest on-the-beach mall, boasting a bevy of clubs, restaurants, and bars. Two hundred yards farther, the Riverwalk cuts through **Old Town** (known locally as **Himmarshee Village**) which is loaded with bars and cheap eateries. The **Water Taxi** offers a relaxing way to beat the rush-hour traffic. The friendly captains will drop you off anywhere along the Intracoastal Waterway of New River. Alternatively, ride through the entire route for an intimate viewing of the colossal houses along the canal. *(651 Seabreeze Blvd./Rte. A1A. ☎ 467-6677; www.watertaxi.com. Open 10am-11:30pm. 1-day unlimited pass $11, seniors and under 18 $9.)*

A bit farther from downtown are a number of attractions. Anointed by Guinness as the "fastest game in the world," *jai alai* still remains mostly unknown to Americans outside the state of Florida. Take a break from the beach heat and watch a match at **Dania Jai-Alai** with a diverse crowd, which sports one of the largest *frontons* (courts) in the state. *(301 E. Dania Beach Blvd. Off U.S. 1, 10min. south of Fort Lauderdale. ☎ 927-2841. Games Tu and Sa noon and 7pm, W-F 7pm, Su 1pm. General admission $1.50.)* Cast your line at the **International Game Fishing Association's Fishing Hall of Fame and Museum,** where a gallery of odd fish, the inside scoop on fishing spots, and an interactive reel exercise amaze even the most determined non-fisherman. Check out the wooden replicas of world-record catches adorning the museum's ceiling and the film *Journeys* in the big-screen theater. *(300 Gulf Stream*

Way. Off I-95 at Griffin Rd., Exit 23. ☎922-4212; www.igfa.org. Open daily 10am-6pm. Wheel-chair-accessible. $6, seniors and ages 3-16 $5. IGFA members free.)

▓ NIGHTLIFE

Locals will tell you that the real nightlife action is in **Himmarshee Village.** On 2nd St. near the **Riverwalk** district, the 100 yds. of Himmarshee Village are packed with raucous bars, steamy clubs, cheap eats, and a stylish crowd. Geared toward spring break spending money, the **Strip** houses popular nightspots across from the beach.

▓ **Tarpon Bend,** 200 SW 2nd St. (☎523-3233). Always the busiest place on the block. Starched shirts from the office converge with flirty black tube tops around the icy beer tubs of "the Bends." Pair the crab cake burger ($11) with the Mamacita Martini ($8) for a happy meal. Happy hour daily 4-7pm, F until 9pm. M-Sa live music. M reggae night, ladies drink free from 7pm until close. Beer $3-4.50. Open daily 11:30am-2:30am.

Dicey O'Riley's Irish Pub, 217 SW 2nd St. (☎522-1908). This establishment has undergone beautiful renovations to its interior, which is packed on F nights. Happy hour pints (domestic $2, imported $3), a free buffet on F afternoons, live music W-Sa 10pm-2am, and cheap, delicious fare (shepherd's pie $8) keep this place hopping. Open M-F 5pm-4am, Sa-Su 4pm-4am.

Ramrod, 1508 NE 4th Ave. (☎763-8219; www.ramrodbar.com). Gay club with daily Happy hour 3-9pm. Open M-Th and Su 3pm-2am, F-Sa 3pm-3am.

PALM BEACH/WEST PALM BEACH ☎561

Nowhere else in Florida is the line between the "haves" and the "have-nots" as visible as at the intracoastal waterway dividing the aristocratic vacationers of Palm Beach Island from the blue-collar residents of West Palm Beach and surrounding areas. Five-star resorts and guarded mansions reign over the "Gold Coast" island, while auto repair shops and fast-food restaurants characterize the mainland. Budget travel may be difficult here, but the region still offers some unique museums, beautiful beaches, and stunning houses.

▓▓ **ORIENTATION AND PRACTICAL INFORMATION.** Palm Beach is approximately 60 mi. north of Miami and 150 mi. southeast of Orlando. **I-95** runs north-south through West Palm Beach, continuing south to Fort Lauderdale and Miami. The more scenic coastal highway, **A1A,** also travels north-south, crossing Lake Worth at the Flagler Memorial Bridge to Palm Beach. Large highways cut through urban areas and residential neighborhoods; finding your way around can be a bit confusing. Stick to the major roads like north-south **Highway 1** (which turns into S. Dixie Hwy.), A1A, east-west **Palm Beach Lakes Boulevard,** and **Belvedere Road.** The heart of downtown West Palm Beach is **Clematis Street,** across from the Flagler Memorial Bridge, which offers both affordable restaurants and wild nightclubs.

Palm Beach International Airport (PBI) (☎471-7420; www.pbia.org), 1000 Turnage Blvd., at Belvedere and Australian Ave., between Exits 68 and 69 on I-95 N, is 2½ mi. east of downtown West Palm Beach. The Tri-Rail (see below) stops at the airport, as does **bus** #44 from the downtown West Palm Beach Quadrille station. Amtrak, 201 S. Tamarind Ave. (☎832-6169; www.amtrak.com; open daily 10:15am-6:15pm), east of I-95 in the downtown West Palm Beach Quadrille runs **trains** to Charleston (11½hr., 1 per day, $64-120) and Orlando (3½-5½hr., 2 per day, $26-57). Greyhound sends **buses** from the same station (☎833-8534; www.greyhound.com. Open daily 7am-11:30pm) for Miami (2hr., 14 per day, $10.50) and Orlando (3¾hr., 12 per day, $36). Palm Tran, 3201 Electronics Way, has 32 routes from North Palm Beach Gardens to Boca Raton, with #1 traveling through the Palm Beach area. The major hub is at the intersection of Quadrille Blvd. and Clematis St. in downtown West Palm Beach. Schedules are available on all buses, at the main office, or at any public library. (☎841-4200. $1.25; seniors, under 21, and disabled $0.60; 1-day pass $3/2.) **Tri-Rail** connects West Palm Beach to Fort Lauderdale and Miami and leaves from the train station on Tamarind. (☎800-874-7245. Hours vary by route; runs M-F 4am-10pm, Sa 7am-11pm, Su 7am-9pm. $2-10; students, seniors, and disabled half-price; under 4 free.) For a **taxi**, call Yellow Cab, ☎689-2222. The **Palm Beach County Convention and Visitors Bureau** is at 1555 Palm Beach Lakes Blvd. (☎233-3000 or 800-833-8733; www.palmbeachfl.com. Open M-F 8:30am-5:30pm.) **Medical Services: Columbia Hospital,** 2201 45th St. (☎842-6141). **Hotlines: Center for Information and Crisis Services,** ☎383-1111. **Internet Access: Clematis St. News Stand,** 206 Clematis St. (☎832-2302. $4 per 30min. Open M-W and Su 7:30am-10pm, Th-Sa 7:30am-midnight.) **Post Office:** 640 Clematis St., in West Palm Beach. (☎833-0929. Open M-F 8:30am-5pm.) **Postal Code:** 33401.

█ ACCOMMODATIONS. Extravagant resorts and skyscraper hotels are arguably the most notable attractions lining the Gold Coast. While the idea of mingling with royalty might sound like a fairy tale come true, the words "budget" and "hostel" will only receive blank stares from receptionists. Many reasonably priced B&Bs are booked far in advance; reserve a room early. West Palm Beach is the best bet for an affordable room near the action, but the absolute cheapest options are the chain hotels near I-95. **Hotel Biba ❹,** 320 Belvedere Rd., is accessible by bus #44. This historic building is located in beautiful West Palm Beach, and has been revamped with a funky, art deco ambience. Rooms are painted in pastel and bold tones, and beautiful people lounge on the pool deck. Wednesday nights feature house music with a live DJ, creating a cool scene that burns until 2am. (☎832-0094; www.hotelbiba.com. Continental breakfast included. Free Wi-Fi. Rooms mid-Nov. to mid-Apr. $140-200; mid-Apr. to mid-Nov. $109. AmEx/MC/V.) Built in 1922 by a former Palm Beach mayor and elegantly restored in 1990, **Hibiscus House Bed & Breakfast ❹,** 501 30th St., in West Palm Beach at the corner of Spruce St. west of Flagler Dr., is affordable without sacrificing luxury. Sleep in one of five antique-decorated bedrooms and wake up to a two-course gourmet breakfast. Rooms have A/C, phones, TVs, and terraces. (☎863-5633 or 800-203-4927; www.hibiscushouse.com. Rooms Dec.-Apr. $100-250; May-Nov. $95-150. AmEx/D/MC/V.)

▐▌ FOOD AND NIGHTLIFE. Clematis St. in downtown West Palm Beach offers a lively option for travelers on the cheap, and a Wednesday to Saturday nightlife scene that rivals any college town. Voted "Best Burger" and "People's Choice" in a recent cook-off, **Sushi Jo ❷,** 319 Belvedere Rd. #12, stays open on Wednesday until 2am when parties wind down. The Resort Roll (spicy white tuna, scallion, sesame seeds; $10) is sure to satisfy. (☎868-7893. Open M-Tu and Th-Sa 11:30am-2pm and 5-11pm, W 11:30am-2pm and 5pm-2am, Su 5-11pm. AmEx/MC/V.) **O'Shea's Irish Pub and Restaurant ❷,** 531½ Clematis St., at Rosemary St., will modify any dish to fit vegetarian needs. For a special treat, try their fish and chips ($8). Locals and those nostalgic for Dublin flock here for the live music W-Sa, usually Irish rock or folk, and for Mrs. O'Shea's $10 savory chicken pie. (☎833-3865. Open M-Tu and Su 11am-10pm, W-Th 11am-midnight, F-Sa 11am-1am. Bar open M-Th and Su until 3am, F-Sa until 4am. AmEx/D/MC/V.) **Paradise Bar and Grill ❷,** 300 Clematis St., serves Caribbean-influenced dishes like pulled pork ($7) and coconut shrimp ($9). Paradise also boasts over 70 different beers and live music Thursday through Saturday. (☎296-2337. Happy hour M-F 4-7pm. Open M-W and Su 11:30am-11pm, Th-Sa 11:30am-3am. AmEx/D/MC/V.)

Known for exclusive dinner parties and black-tie galas, nightlife on Palm Beach is an invitation-only affair. You won't find a "local bar" anywhere in the ritzy downtown area. You will, however, find **Sprinkles Ice Cream & Sandwich Shop ❶**, 279 Royal Poinciana Way, the best bargain for a hungry stomach. For a sweet treat, try their triple chocolate fudge. Flo's curried chicken salad wrap ($7) will feed a hungrier stomach. (☎659-1140. All wraps $7. Salad bar $8. Homemade ice cream $4. Open M-Th and Su 10am-10pm, F-Sa 10am-11pm. AmEx/D/MC/V.)

◙ SIGHTS. The prize of blue-collar West Palm Beach is **▧Ragtops,** 2119 S. Dixie Hwy., as fine a collection of automotive Americana as you'll find. It just so happens that all the items have four wheels and some muscle under the hood. Once a Cadillac dealership, the five show floors are now home to over 70 beautiful classic cars, and should you fall in love with one, you need not leave broken-hearted—most of the cars are for sale. (☎655-2836; www.ragtopsmotorcars.com. Open M-Sa 10am-5pm. Wheelchair-accessible. $5, seniors $4, ages 8-12 $3, under 8 free.) The **Norton Museum of Art,** 1451 S. Olive Ave., is well known for its well-chosen collection of European, American, Chinese, and contemporary art. Stop by the central garden, which features its own fountain of youth. (☎832-5196; www.norton.org. Open May-Sept. Tu-Sa 10am-5pm, Su 1-5pm; Nov.-Apr. M-Sa 10am-5pm, Su 1-5pm. Tours daily 2-3pm; lectures Nov.-Apr. M-F 12:30-1pm. Wheelchair-accessible. $8, ages 13-21 $3, under 13 free. Tours free.)

In early spring, catch the training seasons of the **Florida Marlins** and **St. Louis Cardinals** at **Roger Dean Stadium,** 4751 Main St. in Jupiter, 14 mi. north of West Palm Beach. (☎775-1818. Call for schedules.) In Palm Beach, walking around can be one of the most enjoyable (and affordable) activities. Known as the "Rodeo Drive of the South," **Worth Avenue,** between S. Ocean Blvd. and Cocoanut Row, outfits Palm Beach's rich and famous in the threads of fashion heavyweights. Walk or drive along **Ocean Boulevard** to gawk at the spectacular, enormous mansions owned by celebrities and millionaires. One particularly remarkable complex is **The Breakers,** 1 S. County Rd., a sizable Italian Renaissance resort. Even if you can't afford the bare-minimum $285 price tag for a night of luxury, you can still live vicariously and stroll the resort grounds or take a guided tour. (☎655-6611 or 888-273-2537. Tour W 2pm. $15 for all non-guests.) Of course, a trip to Palm Beach County would be incomplete without relaxing on one of its picturesque beaches. Although you'll see few residents swimming, the sand is beautiful and the water is serene. Good options on Palm Beach include the popular **Mid-town Beach,** 400 S. Ocean Blvd., and **Phipps Ocean Park,** 2145 S. Ocean Blvd. (☎585-9203).

GREAT LAKES

Though the region's alternative name—the Midwest—evokes a bland image of cornfields and small-town, white-picket-fence America, the states that hug the five Great Lakes encompass a variety of personalities. The world's largest freshwater lake, Lake Superior, and its unpopulated, scenic coast cradle some of the most stunning natural features in the region—from the dense forests in northern Wisconsin to the waterfalls of the Upper Peninsula in Michigan. Meanwhile, the Lake Michigan coast hosts sand dunes, swimming, sailing, and deep-water fishing. Minneapolis and St. Paul form a bona fide coastal metropolis, while Chicago dazzles with a stunning skyline, incredible culinary offerings, and world-class museums.

HIGHLIGHTS OF THE GREAT LAKES

DEVOUR deep-dish **pizza** in Chicago (p. 520), traditional **pasties** in Michigan's Upper Peninsula (p. 510), and the feast-like results of a Door County **fish boil** (p. 545).

SIMPLIFY your life among the Amish in Ohio's **Hardin County** (p. 484).

GROOVE to the music at the **Motown Historical Museum** (p. 498) and the **Rock and Roll Hall of Fame** (p. 480).

DON your stovepipe hat and iconic facial hair for the brand-new **Abraham Lincoln Presidential Library and Museum** (p. 532).

PRESS your nose against the glass of the fish tanks and watch penguins pummel each other at the **Shedd Aquarium** (p. 527).

OHIO

America's eyes were trained on Ohio on Nov. 2, 2004, as George W. Bush squeaked past John Kerry to pick up the state's 20 electoral votes and a second term in the White House. Ohio's inscrutable political climate reflects the diversity of the state's population; unionized machinists in Cleveland, farmers in the western plains, and coal miners on the Allegheny Plateau will not always see eye to eye. Even so, Midwestern friendliness and a practical view of the world make natives of Ohio the perfect candidates to welcome visitors into the Great Lakes region.

🛈 PRACTICAL INFORMATION

Capital: Columbus.

Visitor Info: State Office of Travel and Tourism, 77 S. High St., 29th fl., Columbus 43215 (☎614-466-8844; www.discoverohio.com). Open M-F 8am-5pm. **Ohio Tourism Line** ☎800-282-5393.

Postal Abbreviation: OH. **Sales Tax:** 6%.

CLEVELAND   ☎216

Ohio Congressman Louis Stokes once observed that "the Cuyahoga will live in infamy as the only river that was ever declared a fire hazard." The industrial ooze that once lapped up on the shores of Cleveland is now gone, and Cleveland has

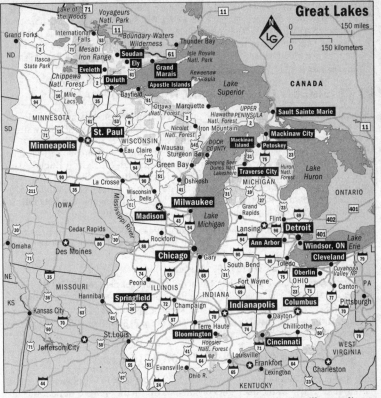

Great Lakes

0 — 150 miles
0 — 150 kilometers

CANADA

Lake Superior

Lake Huron

Lake Michigan

Lake Erie

ONTARIO

made valiant efforts to spruce up its civic center. Yet, the city is still struggling to reinvent itself. Hip coffee shops and music venues abound on the eastern and western edges of Cleveland, and residents are hopeful that these enclaves will become increasingly integrated with the museums and playhouses downtown.

TRANSPORTATION

Airport: Cleveland Hopkins International (CLE; ☎265-6000; www.clevelandairport.com), 13 mi. southwest of downtown. RTA line #66X "Red Line" to Terminal Tower downtown. Trains depart every 15min. during the day. The trip takes 30min. Taking a taxi downtown takes roughly 22min. and costs $20.

Trains: Amtrak, 200 Cleveland Memorial Shoreway (☎696 5115; www.amtrak.com), across from the Browns Stadium. Open daily midnight-1pm and 9:30pm-midnight. To **Chicago** (7hr., 2 per day, $41-64) and **Pittsburgh** (3½hr., 1 per day, $19-30).

Buses: Greyhound, 1465 Chester Ave. (☎781-0520; www.greyhound.com), at E. 14th St., 7 blocks from Terminal Tower. Open 24hr. To: **Chicago** (7-8hr., 5 per day, $45.50); **Cincinnati** (5hr., 6 per day, $37); **Columbus** (2½hr., 6 per day, $20.50); **New York City** (9-14hr., 7 per day, $67); **Pittsburgh** (2½-4hr., 6 per day, $25.50).

Public Transit: Regional Transit Authority (RTA), 1240 W. 6th St. (☎621-9500; www.rid-eRTA.com). Open M-F 7am-6pm. Bus lines, connecting with Rapid Transit trains, travel from downtown to most of the metropolitan area. Service daily 5am-midnight; call for info on "owl" service after midnight. Train $1.50. Bus $1.25, express $1.50, downtown loop $0.75. Day pass $3, children and seniors $1. Park for free at one of the park-and-rides and take the train to Terminal Square for $1.50. The **Waterfront Line** runs along the Lake Erie waterfront and serves the Science Center and Rock 'n' Roll Hall of Fame.

Taxi: Ace Taxi, ☎ 361-4700. **Americab,** ☎ 881-1111.

ORIENTATION AND PRACTICAL INFORMATION

Terminal Tower, in **Public Square,** at the intersection of Detroit Ave. and Ontario St., forms the center of downtown and splits the city into east and west. Many street numbers correspond to the distance of the street from Terminal Tower; e.g., E. 18th St. is 18 blocks east of the Tower. To reach Public Sq. from **I-90** or **I-71,** take the Ontario St./Broadway Exit. From **I-77,** take the 9th St. Exit to Euclid Ave., which runs into Public Sq. The residential stretch of the East Side between 30th and 80th should be avoided, even during the daytime, and travelers should be cautious in downtown at night. **Coventry Road,** in Cleveland Heights, and **Ohio City,** to the southwest, are the happening spots for food and nightlife.

Visitor Info: Cleveland Convention and Visitors Bureau, 100 Public Sq. (☎ 875-6600; www.travelcleveland.com), on the ground floor of Terminal Tower. Open M-F 8am-5:30pm, Sa 9am-2pm.

Hotline: Rape Crisis Line, ☎ 619-6192. Operates 24hr.

Internet Access: Cleveland Public Library, 325 Superior Ave. (☎ 623-2800). Allows free 1hr. slots at its terminals. Open M-Sa 9am-6pm, Su 1-5pm; in summer closed Su.

Post Office: 2400 Orange Ave. (☎ 443-4494, after 5pm 443-4046). Open M-F 7am-8pm, Sa 8am-4pm. **Postal Code:** 44101. **Area Code:** 216; 440 or 330 in suburbs. In text, 216 unless otherwise noted.

ACCOMMODATIONS AND CAMPING

With hotel taxes (not included in prices below) as high as 14.5%, cheap lodging is hard to find. Those with cars might consider staying in the suburbs or near the airport, where prices tend to be lower. Most places will not rent to those under 21.

Cuyahoga Valley Stanford Hostel (HI), 6093 Stanford Rd. (☎ 330-467-8711), in Peninsula, 22 mi. south of Cleveland in the Cuyahoga Valley National Park. Set in a 19th-century farmhouse, this idyllic hostel offers cozy dorms and nightly cricket serenades. Lockout 9am-5pm. Curfew 10pm, but arrangements can be made for later arrivals. Reservations recommended. Dorms $19. Under 18 with guardian ½-price. MC/V. ❶

Danes Guest House, 2189 West Blvd. (☎ 961-9444). Follow I-90 west of downtown to the West Blvd. Exit. 2 rooms in a 20s colonial revival house are a particularly good deal for travelers in groups. There is no sign; drivers should keep eyes peeled for the address. Homemade breakfast included. Room with double bed $60-70, with queen bed $70-80, two rooms $110. $10 off stays of more than 2 nights. Cash only. ❸

Punderson State Park, 11755 Kinsman Rd. (☎ 440-564-1195), off Exit 29 on I-271, 45min. east of downtown. Once a vacation spot for wealthy Clevelanders, the park now has 196 campsites and 26 2-bedroom cottages, plus trails and a golf course. Sites $23-24. Cottages from $99. AmEx/D/MC/V. ❶

FOOD

Colorful cafes grace **Coventry Road,** in **Cleveland Heights** between Mayfield Rd. and Euclid Heights Blvd. The sounds of Italian crooners fill the sidewalks of **Little Italy,**

Downtown Cleveland

■■ ACCOMMODATIONS ■ 🍴 FOOD

Cuyahoga Valley Stanford Hostel (HI), **8**
Dane's Guest House, **7**
Punderson State Park, **4**

Lelolai Bakery and Cafe, **5**
Talkies, **6**
Tommy's, **2**

📌 NIGHTLIFE

The Grid, **1**
Grog Shop and B-Side Liquor Lounge, **3**

around **Mayfield Road.** Over 100 vendors hawk fresh produce, meat, and cheese at the old-world-style **West Side Market,** 1979 W. 25th St., at Lorain Ave. (☎781-3663; www.westsidemarket.com. Open M and W 7am-4pm, F-Sa 7am-6pm.)

Talkies, 2521 Market Ave. (☎696-3456). Converts its cafe-restaurant space into a screening room for classic movies at night. Model projectors even decorate the bathrooms. During the day free Wi-Fi, creative sandwiches named after movies (try the West Side Story, an artichoke heart melt; $5), and vintage paraphenalia from cinema's golden age attract quiet, reflective regulars who leisurely read the paper or furiously type away at their next great American novel. Cash only. ❶

Tommy's, 1824 Coventry Rd. (☎321-7757; www.tommyscoventry.com), in Cleveland Heights. This bright, spacious cafe stays busy throughout the day serving 11 types of grilled cheese sandwiches ($5-6), vegetarian fare ($4.50-7), and a tempeh reuben

($7). Meat-eaters get in on the action with juicy burgers ($3.50-6). Open M-Th 7:30am-10pm, F-Sa 7:30am-11pm, Su 9am-10pm. MC/V. ❶

Lelolai Bakery and Cafe, 1889 W. 25th St. (☎771-9956), in Ohio City. Revered for its velvety flan ($2) and sandwiches slathered with garlic mayonnaise ($5.50), this Hispanic bakery also offers buttery breakfast pastries ($1.50) that are perfect with a steaming cup of *café con leche*. Open M-W 8am-5pm, Th-Sa 8am-6pm. D/MC/V. ❶

◎ SIGHTS

DOWNTOWN. A spit of land jutting out into Lake Erie became the focal point of downtown revitalization with I.M. Pei's ▨**Rock and Roll Hall of Fame.** The permanent collection traces a chronology of rock music, narrated through artifacts ranging from a Jimi Hendrix guitar to a Madonna bustier. *(1 Key Plaza. ☎781-7625; www.rockhall.com. Open M-Tu and Th-Su 10am-5:30pm, W 10am-9pm; June-Aug. Sa until 9pm. $20, students $18, seniors $14, ages 9-11 $11, under 9 free.)* Next door, the **Great Lakes Science Center** trots out high-tech toys, like a solar car, to create interactive exhibits that are fun for all ages. *(601 Erieside Ave. ☎694-2000; www.greatscience.com. Open daily 9:30am-5:30pm. Science Center or OMNIMAX $9.50, seniors $8.50, ages 3-17 $7.50; combined ticket $13/11/9. Parking for Hall of Fame and Science Center $7.50.)*

THE WILD SIDE. Nearly 20,000 acres of undeveloped land comprise the **Cleveland Metroparks,** perfect for biking, horseback riding, and hiking; the trail along the northern edge of Big Creek Reservation's Lake Isaac is a great place to listen for songbirds. The **Cleveland Metroparks Zoo,** 5 mi. south of Cleveland on I-71 at the Fulton Rd. Exit, offers a more manicured look at Mother Nature, from the nation's largest primate collection to the "Australian Adventure" walk. *(☎661-6500; www.clemetzoo.com. Open daily 10am-5pm. $10, children 2-11 $7, under 2 free.)*

UNIVERSITY CIRCLE. A compound of museums, parks, and academic buildings forms a kind of second downtown on the eastern edge of Cleveland. The **Cleveland Museum of Art** will be displaying a limited selection from its holdings as it undergoes a massive renovation expected to be completed in 2011. *(11150 East Blvd. ☎421-7340; www.clevelandart.org.)* In the meantime, the **Cleveland Museum of Natural History** showcases a menagerie of animals preserved by taxidermists, while live river otters and great horned owls populate the Wildlife Center outside. *(1 Wade Oval Dr. ☎231-4600 or 800-317-9155; www.cmnh.org. Open M-Tu and Th-Sa 10am-5pm, W 10am-10pm, Su noon-5pm. $9; ages 7-18, seniors, and students $7; ages 3-6 $6.)* The **Cleveland Botanical Garden's** Eleanor Armstrong Smith Glasshouse recreates a Costa Rican cloud forest and the spiny desert of Madagascar, while outdoor herb and rose gardens offer an ideal place to stroll. *(11030 East Blvd. ☎721-1600; www.cbgarden.org. Open Apr.-Oct. M-Sa 10am-5pm, Su noon-5pm; Nov.-Mar. closed M. $7.50, ages 3-12 $3.)* On the far side of the Botanical Garden, Frank Gehry's **Peter B. Lewis Building** houses the Weatherhead School of Management at Case Western Reserve. The building's undulating, metallic armature echoes Gehry's iconic Guggenheim Museum in Bilbao. *(10900 Euclid Ave. Reservations ☎368 2030; www.weatherhead.cwru.edu/tour. 30min. tours offered Sa-Su 1-3:30pm. Free.)*

🎭 🎟 ENTERTAINMENT AND NIGHTLIFE

Football reigns supreme in Cleveland, where the **Browns** grind it out on the gridiron at the **Cleveland Browns Stadium,** north of Lakeside Ave. between W. 3rd St. and E. 9th St. (☎891-5050. Tickets from $25.) Baseball's **Indians** round the bases at **Jacobs Field,** 2401 Ontario St. (☎420-4487. Tickets from $10.) The NBA's **Cavaliers** take the court at **Gund Arena,** 1 Center Ct. (☎420-2000. Tickets from $10.) The **Cleve-**

land Orchestra can be heard at **Severance Hall,** 11001 Euclid Ave. (☎231-1111; www.clevelandorch.com. Box office open June-Aug. M-F 9am-6pm; Sept.-May M-F 9am-6pm, Sa 10am-6pm. Tickets from $30; $10-15 student tickets available for select performances; call for info.) The **State Theater,** 1519 Euclid Ave., hosts the **Cleveland Opera** (☎575-0903; www.clevelandopera.org. Box office open daily 11am-6pm.) The **Cleveland Institute of Art Cinematheque,** 11141 East Blvd., screens classic and foreign films. (☎421-7450; www.cia.edu/cinematheque. Shows W-Su. $8.)

A few pubs and music venues stay open at major hotels downtown. The **Warehouse District** features upscale clubs, while edgier crowds favor nightspots along **Coventry Road** in Cleveland Heights or along **W. 25th Street** in Ohio City. For more info on clubs and concerts, pick up a free copy of *Scene* or the *Free Times*. For info on Cleveland's GLBT scene, the *Gay People's Chronicle* and *OUTlines* can be found at libraries and bookstores.

🎵 **Grog Shop,** 2785 Euclid Heights Blvd. (☎321-5588; www.grogshop.gs), at Coventry Rd., in Cleveland Heights. A mainstay of Cleveland's punk, indie rock, and hip-hop scenes. Cover $6-12, under 21 $2 extra. Open daily 8pm-2am. Downstairs, the **B-Side Liquor Lounge** mixes martinis (from $7) for an eclectic crowd splayed on sleek leather couches. Open M-Th and Su 8pm-2:30am, F-Sa 8pm-2:30am.

◄**Wish,** 621 Johnson Ct. (☎902-9474), just off W. 6th St. in the Warehouse District. While this shadowy, 3-floor complex has lost some of its gothic edge, it's still a funky dance club that isn't afraid to work The Smiths into the evening's playlist. No cover. Open Th and Su 10pm-2:30am, F-Sa 9pm-2:30am.

The Grid, 1437 St. Clair Ave. (☎623-0113). Attracts a predominantly gay crowd with 3 bars and strategic views of the dance floor. W lesbian night. Th male strippers. Sa cover $7, under 21 $10. Open daily 5pm-2:30am; dance floor open F-Sa until 3:30am.

🔲 DAYTRIPS FROM CLEVELAND

OBERLIN
From Cleveland, drive 30mi. west on I-90 to Exit 140, then follow Rte. 53 into Oberlin's downtown area.

Two young missionaries from the East Coast founded the Oberlin Collegiate Institute in 1833. Their commitment to coeducation and racial integration left its imprint on the small town of Oberlin; three years before the Civil War broke out, local abolitionists swarmed the nearby village of Wellington to rescue a fugitive slave who was being returned to captivity. Progressive politics are still alive and well in Oberlin, as Birkenstocked students from **Oberlin College** pad around South Main St. and dream of a free Tibet. The college's **Conservatory of Music** is one of the nation's best, and free recitals are open to the public year-round. (☎440-775-8044; www.oberlin.edu/con.) The **Allen Memorial Art Museum,** 87 N. Main St., features a strong collection of 17th-century Dutch and Flemish canvases, although its modern holdings, including wall drawings by minimalist pioneer Sol LeWitt, are also vast. (☎440-775-8665; www.oberlin.edu/allenart. Open Tu-Sa 10am-5pm, Su 1-5pm. Free.) Town-gown relations are at their rosiest during the **Big Parade,** held on the first Saturday in May, while mid-June's **Juneteenth** celebration commemorates the signing of the Emancipation Proclamation in 1865. Grilled sandwiches ($5.50-7) and salads ($5-7) are daytime staples at **The Feve ❶,** 30 S. Main St., and the upstairs bar gets lively during the school year with $3 drafts. (☎440-774-1978. F night live jazz. Restaurant open June-Aug. M-F 11am-10pm, Sa 10am-10pm, Su 10am-2:30pm; Sept.-May M-F 11am-midnight, Sa-Su 9:30am-midnight. Bar open June-Aug. M-Sa 5pm-1am, Su 9pm-1am; Sept.-May daily 5pm-2:30am. AmEx/MC/V.) **MindFair Books,** 13 W. College St., delights bookworms, and the upstairs annex hosts live jazz and

GREAT LAKES

spoken-word on Friday nights during the school year. (☎440-774-6463. Open M-W and Sa 9am-6pm, Th-F 9am-8pm, Su noon-5pm.)

OTHER DAYTRIPS

CUYAHOGA VALLEY NATIONAL PARK. Just 10 mi. south of Cleveland lies the northern edge of the scenic **Cuyahoga Valley National Park.** The park's lifeline is the **Cuyahoga River,** which winds 30 mi. through dense forests and open farmland, passing stables, aqueducts, and mills along the way. The best way to see the park is to hike or bike its long trails. The **Ohio & Erie Canal Towpath Trail** runs through shaded forests and past the many locks used during the canal's heyday, when it served as a vital link between Cleveland and the Ohio River. One of the park's several **Visitors Centers,** 7104 Canal Rd., has maps and info on the canal. (☎524-1497 or 800-445-9667; www.nps.gov/cuva. From Cleveland, take I-77 south to Rockside Rd., take a left after the Exit, continue to Canal Rd., and make a right into the park. Open daily 10am-4pm.)

■ CEDAR POINT AMUSEMENT PARK. Consistently ranked the "best amusement park in the world" by *Amusement Today*, **Cedar Point Amusement Park,** off U.S. 6, 65 mi. west of Cleveland in Sandusky, earns its superlatives. Many of the world's highest and fastest roller coasters reside here. The towering **Top Thrill Dragster** takes the cake in both categories, launching thrill-seekers 420 ft. before plummeting down at 120 mph, while the brand new **maXair** spins riders until their inner ears beg for mercy. (☎419-627-2350 or 800-237-8386; www.cedarpoint.com. Off U.S. 6 in Sandusky, 65 mi. west of Cleveland. Open daily June to mid-Aug. 10am-10pm; May 10am-8pm; Sept.-Oct. hours vary. Laser light shows in summer nightly at 10pm. $42, over 3 and less than 4 ft. $12. Parking $10.)

COLUMBUS   ☎ 614

Less a single, coherent metropolis than a collection of freeway exits, Columbus pulled past Cleveland in 1990 to take its place as Ohio's most populous city. White-collar workers hit the freeways at 5pm and make for the suburbs, while immigrants and young artists keep parts of downtown aglow after dark. Though no one would call mild-mannered Columbus "edgy" and keep a straight face, the capital's museums and galleries are well worth a day or two of exploration.

⊟ ⁊ TRANSPORTATION AND PRACTICAL INFORMATION. Port Columbus International Airport (CMH), 4600 International Gateway (☎239-4000; www.port-columbus.com), is 8 mi. east of downtown. A taxi to downtown is about $23. Greyhound, 111 E. Town St. (☎228-2266; www.greyhound.com); offers **bus** service to Chicago (7-12hr., 5-7 per day, $53.50); Cincinnati (2-3½hr., 9-11 per day, $18.50), and Cleveland (2-4½hr., 6 per day, $20.50). The Central Ohio Transit Authority (COTA), 60 E. Broad St., runs **local buses** until 11pm or midnight, depending on the route. (☎228-1776; www.cota.com. $1.50, express $2; transfers $0.75.)

Columbus is laid out in a simple grid. **High Street,** running north-south, and **Broad Street,** running east-west, are the main thoroughfares, dividing the city into quadrants. Most of the city's activity is centered around **High Street,** which heads north from downtown to the galleries and coffee shops of the **Short North.** It continues up through the campus of **Ohio State University (OSU).** South of downtown, the **German Village** and **Brewery District** recall the Old World with narrow streets and traditional crafts. **Visitor Info: Experience Columbus** maintains an administrative office downtown at 90 N. High St., and a **Visitors Center** on the first floor of the Easton Town Mall, north of the airport on I-270. (☎221-6623 or 800-345-2657; www.experience-columbus.com. Visitors Center open M-Sa 10am-9pm, Su noon-6pm. Administrative office open M-F 8am-5pm.) For a **taxi,** call Yellow Cab ☎444-4444. **Internet**

Access: Columbus Metropolitan Library, 96 S. Grant St. (☎645-2275. Photo ID required. Free. Limit 1hr. per day. Open M-Th 9am-9pm, F-Sa 9am-6pm, Su 1-5pm.) **Post Office:** 850 Twin Rivers Dr. (☎469-4226. Open M-F 8am-7pm, Sa 8am-2pm.) **Postal Code:** 43216.

▟◖ ACCOMMODATIONS AND FOOD. A city ordinance prevents hotels from renting to visitors under age 21. Budget options can be found at almost any exit off I-270. In the summer, **OSU ❷,** 85 Curl Dr., in the Royer Activity Centers, offers clean dorm rooms near High St.'s bars and restaurants. (☎292-9725. Open mid-June to mid-Aug. Rooms $36, with linen $38; with A/C $38, with A/C and linen $46. MC/V.) Northwest of downtown, the **Westerville Inn Bed and Breakfast ❸,** 5 S. West St., maintains three homey rooms in an 1854 cottage. Take I-270 to Exit 27; take Cleveland Ave. north, turn right on W. Main St., then right on West St. (☎882-3910. Complimentary 3-course breakfast. Rooms $95-115. D/MC/V.) The **German Village Inn ❸,** 920 S. High St., has large rooms with A/C and cable TV. (☎443-6506. Singles M-Th and Su $48, F-Sa $54; doubles $54/59. Each additional person $5. AmEx/D/MC/V.) For great budget eats, don't miss the **North Market ❶,** 59 Spruce St., in the Short North Arts District, which is packed with food vendors selling everything from falafel to chocolate. (☎463-9664. Meals about $5. Open Tu-F 9am-7pm, Sa 8am-5pm, Su noon-5pm.) ▧**Katzinger's Delicatessen ❸,** 475 S. 3rd St., charges a whopping $11.25 for its incredible half-pound reuben. But with Black Angus corned beef shipped down from Detroit and Bill Clinton's personal approval, Katzinger's can't be beat for sandwiches ($9-12) or Sunday morning bagels and lox. (☎228-3354. Open M-F 8:30am-8:30pm, Sa-Su 9am-8:30pm. AmEx/MC/V.) If you're less of a meat-lover and more of a cow-hugger, head over to **Northside ❸,** 951 N. High St., where vegan and vegetarian burgers ($9.60) and pizzas ($7.70) are served to trendy twentysomethings and the environmentally conscious in a large room with high ceilings. (☎298-9999. Open daily 7:30am-10pm. AmEx/MC/V.) **Nancy's Home Cooking ❶,** 3133 N. High St., offers diner-style counter service to regulars who swear by the $1 pancakes. (☎265-9012. Open M-Th 6am-2pm and 4-7pm, F 6am-2pm, Sa-Su 6am-noon. Cash only.)

◗ SIGHTS. OSU's newly renovated **Wexner Center for the Arts,** 1871 N. High St., now sports a five-story "permanent scaffold," an aesthetic of unfinished construction that matches its commitment to avant-garde visual art and performance. (☎292-0330; www.wexarts.org. Call for hours. Galleries free. Films $7, students and seniors $5, under 12 $3.) The **Columbus Museum of Art,** 480 E. Broad St., has an unusually strong permanent collection of early modern canvases, from European luminaries like Matisse and Klee to lesser-known Americans like George Bellows. (☎221-6801; www.columbusmuseum.org. Open Tu-W and F-Su 10am-5:30pm, Th 10am-8:30pm. Wheelchair-accessible. $6; students, seniors, and ages 6-18 $4. Su Free. Parking $3.) Down the street in Franklinton, the superb **Center of Science and Industry (COSI),** 333 W. Broad St., is part museum and part theme park, ruffling feathers with giant propellers in the Gadgets exhibit and sending kids out on a high-wire unicycle. (☎228-2674; www.cosi.org. Open M-Sa 10am-5pm, Su noon-6pm. Wheelchair-accessible. $12.50, seniors $10.50, ages 2-12 $7.50. "Extreme Screen" movie $7.50. Combo tickets $18.50/16.50/13.50.) Back by the Museum of Art, James Thurber's childhood home, the **Thurber House,** 77 Jefferson Ave., off E. Broad St., is a shrine to the beloved writer-illustrator and a literary center with monthly readings. Watch out: the house is supposedly haunted—listen closely for a ghost running up and down the back stairs. (☎464-1032. Open daily 1-4pm. Guided tours Su. Free. Tours $2.50, students and seniors $2.)

South of downtown, the **German Village** neighborhood appeals to pedestrians with brick streets, slate roofs, and ivy-covered mansions. Rescued from the wreck-ing-ball version of urban renewal in the 60s, German Village combines young professionals and families into a community-minded clan of neighbors. The **German Village Society Meeting Haus,** 588 S. 3rd St., provides visitors with info and arranges late June's annual *Haus und Garten* tour. (☎221-8888; www.germanvillage.com. Open M-F 9am-4pm, Sa 10am-2pm; shorter hours in winter. Tour $20.)

🎵🎭 **ENTERTAINMENT AND NIGHTLIFE.** Alternative weeklies *Columbus Alive* and *The Other Paper* run a list of entertainment options and are available throughout the city. The **Ohio State Buckeyes** play football in historic **Ohio Stadium.** It's not easy to score tickets, but call the Athletic Ticket Office, 411 Woody Hayes Dr. (☎292-2624; open M-F 8am-5pm), for more info. Major League Soccer's **Columbus Crew** (☎447-2739; tickets $20-40) hit the field at **Crew Stadium,** while the NHL's **Blue Jackets** (☎246-3350; tickets $15-150) play at **Nationwide Arena.** In early August, the **Ohio State Fair** continues its 150-year tradition, with livestock competitions, rides, and concerts. (☎888-646-3976; www.ohioexpocenter.com. Take Exit 111 off I-71 to 17th Ave. $8, seniors and ages 5-12 $7. Ride wristbands $20. Parking $5.)

Columbus's nightlife scene is driven by rock 'n' roll, and it's hard to find a bar that doesn't have live music on the weekend. Big national acts stop at the **Newport,** 1722 N. High St. (☎294-1659; www.newportmusichall.com. Tickets $5-40.) To see alternative bands before they hit the big time, head to **Surly Girl's,** 1126 N. High St., which looks like a dark saloon from the Wild West with a playful, feminine twist— pictures of cow girls and Shirley Temple line the walls. (☎294-4900. 24 draught beers $3-4. Pizza $10. Tu punk rock aerobics. W open mic comedy. Th live music, no cover. Su jazz DJ. Open daily 11:30am-2:30am.) The **Varsity Club,** 278 W. Lane Ave., at the upper edge of North Campus near the intersection of High St., is the favorite haunt of students and alums. (☎299-6269. Draft beer $2, pitchers $6.75. Open daily 11am-2am; opens at 9am for home football games.) Gay and lesbian partygoers spend their weekends at **Axis,** 775 N. High St., where the third Friday of every month brings a "steam" party with showers dropping down from the ceiling. (☎291-4008. 18+. Cover $3-6. Open F-Sa 10pm-2:30am, sometimes Su for drag shows or other special performances.)

🔷 DAYTRIPS FROM COLUMBUS

HARDIN COUNTY

Most visits start in the county seat of Kenton. From Columbus, take I-270 N to Exit 17B, and then Rte. 33 W. to Marysville. Pick up Rte. 31 N., and follow the scenic 2-lane road 30 mi. north into Kenton.

The winding country roads and serene fields of undiscovered Hardin County offer budget travelers a chance to see small-town Ohio at its best. The **Hardin County Historical Museum,** 223 N. Main St., showcases local history in a lovely Victorian mansion. Keep an eye out for the ghost at the top of the staircase. (☎419-673-7147; www.hardinmuseums.org. Open M-F 1-4pm. Free.) Just down the street, the **Hardin County Convention and Visitors Bureau,** 128 N. Main St., arranges outdoor excursions and directs visitors to the Amish farms southeast of Kenton. (☎888-642-7346; www.tourhardin.com. M-F 8:30am-4:30pm) Roughly 130 Amish families live in the area east of Rte. 31 and south of Rte. 309; look for the simple white signs along the road to see what products a family has to offer. The Hardin County Amish have managed to avoid the commercialism that has overtaken other Amish communities in Ohio. Leave your camera in the car—it's considered sacrilegious to take pictures—and be sure to respect the families' privacy, especially on Sundays. The front porch of **Pfeiffer Station General Store ❶,** at the intersection of Rtes. 144 and 265, is a great place for a dish of homemade ice cream ($2) and watch horse-drawn buggies on their way back from the fields. (☎419-674-4103. Open M-F 8am-7pm, Sa 9am-6pm, Su noon-5pm. Cash only.)

HOPEWELL CULTURE PARK
The park, at 16062 Rte. 104, is open daily dawn-dusk. Entrance costs $5 per car.

One hour south of Columbus, the area around Chillicothe (CHILL-ih-CAW-thee) features several Native American cultural sights. The **Hopewell Culture National Historical Park** swells with 23 Hopewell burial mounds spread over 13 acres. A small museum offers theories on the mounds and background on the 2000-year-old Hopewell culture. (☎740-774-1126; www.nps.gov/hocu. Visitors Center open daily 8:30am-5pm; June-Aug. until 6pm.) Between mid-June and late August, the **Tecumseh Sugarloaf Mountain Amphitheater,** in Chillicothe, off Rte. 23, presents a reenactment of Shawnee leader Tecumseh's life. (☎775-0700; www.tecumsehdrama.com. Shows M-Sa 8pm. Tickets M-Th $17, under 10 $10; F-Sa $19, under 10 $12.)

CINCINNATI ☎513

Founded in 1788 as a frontier outpost, Cincinnati soon emerged as a vital gateway between the South and the West. Industry thrived as trade routes passed through the city, and a profusion of meat-packing plants earned Cincinnati the nickname "Porkopolis"—slightly less flattering than the title coined by Longfellow, "Queen City of the West." Recently, an aggressive downtown development plan and a burgeoning art scene have put Cincinnati on the map as a fun-loving hub of activity.

▐ TRANSPORTATION

Airport: Cincinnati/Northern Kentucky International (CVG; ☎859-767-3151; www.cvgairport.com), in Kentucky, 13 mi. south of Cincinnati and accessible by I-71, I-74, and I-75. **Airport Executive Shuttle** whisks new arrivals into downtown Cincinnati. (☎859-261-8601. Reserve 24hr. in advance. $15.) The **Transit Authority of Northern Kentucky (TANK;** ☎859-331-8265; www.tankbus.org) sends the #2X Airport Express to and from downtown daily 5am-midnight ($1.50).

Trains: Amtrak, 1301 Western Ave. (☎651-3337; www.amtrak.com), in Union Terminal. Open Tu-Su 11pm-6:30am. To **Chicago** (10½hr., 1 per day, $76) and **Indianapolis** (3½hr., 1 per day, $40). Be cautious in the area to the north of the train station, especially along Liberty St.

Buses: Greyhound, 1005 Gilbert Ave. (☎352-6012; www.greyhound.com), 1 block east of the intersection of E. Court and Broadway. Open 24hr. To **Cleveland** (5hr., 6 per day, $37); **Columbus** (2hr., 6 per day, $18.50); and **Louisville** (2hr., 6 per day, $22).

Public Transit: Cincinnati Metro and **TANK,** 121 E. 5th St. (☎621-4455; www.sorta.com), both in the bus stop in the Mercantile Center. Open daily 4am-1:30am. Most buses run down 5th and Main St. $1; zone 2 $1.50; transfers $0.25; $1 extra to suburbs.

Taxi: Yellow Cab, ☎241-2100. From airport to downtown $25.

▐ ORIENTATION AND PRACTICAL INFORMATION

The downtown business district is an easy grid centered around **Fountain Square,** at **5th** and **Vine Street.** Numbered cross streets are designated E. or W. by their relation to Vine St. **Downtown** is bounded by E. Central Pkwy. on the north, Broadway on the east, 3rd on the south, and Central Ave. on the west. The **University of Cincinnati** spreads out from the Clifton area north of the city. To the south, the **Great American Ballpark,** the **Serpentine Wall,** and the **Riverwalk** border the Ohio River. Be careful outside of the downtown area at night, especially north of E. Central Pkwy.

Downtown Cincinnati

🏠🏠 ACCOMMODATIONS
Ross Bed and Breakfast, **6**
Stonelick State Park, **8**
Xavier University, **3**

🍴 FOOD
Graeter's, **4**
Myra's Dionysus, **2**
Skyline Chili, **7**

🍸 NIGHTLIFE
Blind Lemon, **5**
Northside Tavern, **1**

Visitor Info: Cincinnati Visitor's Bureau, 50 E. Rivercenter, Covington, KY (☎ 859-581-2260 or 800-344-3445; www.cincinnatiusa.com), is 8min. south of the city by car. Open M-F 8:30am-5pm.

Hotlines: Rape Crisis Center, ☎ 872-9259. **Gay/Lesbian Community Switchboard,** ☎ 591-0200. Both operate 24hr.

Internet Access: Cincinnati Public Library, 800 Vine St. (☎ 369-6900). Free. Limit 90min. slots. Open M-W 9am-9pm, Th-Sa 9am-6pm, Su 1-5pm.

Post Office: 525 Vine St. (☎ 684-5659). Open M-F 8am-5pm. **Postal Code:** 45202. **Area Codes:** 513; Kentucky suburbs 859. In text, 513 unless otherwise noted.

🏕 ACCOMMODATIONS

Cheap hotels are scarce in downtown Cincinnati. About 30 mi. north, in **Sharonville,** budget motels lie along **Chester Road.** Twelve miles south of the city, inexpensive accommodations line I-75 in **Florence, KY.** Closer to downtown, the motels at **Central Parkway** and **Hopple Street** offer good, mid-priced lodging.

Xavier University, 17 University Dr., Brockman Hall (☎ 745-3203; www.xavier.edu/reslife). Take I-71 N. to Exit 5, turn right on Dana St. and then right again on Ledgewood

Ave. Rock-bottom weekly rates for dorm rooms are affordable even for 2 or 3 nights. Common bathrooms, kitchen, and laundry. Reserve 1 week in advance. Open mid-May to early Aug. Shared double $70 per week; private single $95 per week. D/MC/V. ❸

Ross Bed and Breakfast, 88 Silverwood Cir. (☎671-2645). Take I-75 N. to I-275 W., and take Exit 42B to Kemper Ave. An affable couple rents out 2 rooms with a private bath in their home. Rooms $59. Reservations recommended. Cash only. ❸

Stonelick State Park, 2895 Lake Dr. (☎625-6593, reservations 866-644-6727), 35 mi. east of the city, outside the I-275 loop. 114 campsites at the edge of a lake with boating, fishing, and swimming. Sites $19, with electricity $23, lakeside $25. ❶

🟦 FOOD

Cincinnati's greatest culinary innovation is its chili, which consists of noodles, meat, cheese, onions, kidney beans, and a distinctive secret ingredient (some say chocolate). The city has also given rise to a number of noteworthy fast-food chains. Fine restaurants can be found in the **Mount Adams** area, while more moderately priced chains are common at **Newport on the Levee** and **Covington Landing** just across the river.

Skyline Chili, 643 Vine St. (☎241-2020; www.skylinechili.com), at 7th St. With locations all over Cincinnati, it dishes up the best beans in town. Skyline's curiously sweet, meaty sauce is one of the first things transplanted Cincy natives say they miss. 5-way chili from $4. Open M-F 10:30am-8pm, Sa noon-4pm. AmEx/D/MC/V. ❶

Graeter's, 332 Ludlow Ave. (☎281-4749), between Walnut and Vine St., in downtown, with 14 other stores. An institution since 1870, Graeter's uses a time-intensive "French pot" process to make ice cream 2 gal. at a time. Oprah is a devoted fan. Single-dip cone $2.35. Open M-Sa 7am-10:45pm, Su 9am-10:45pm. AmEx/D/MC/V. ❶

Myra's Dionysus, 121 Calhoun Ave. (☎961-1578), on the edge of the University of Cincinnati. This tiny vegetarian cafe has 25 soups on rotation. The *gado gado* ($6.50) packs a punch. Open M-Th 11am-10pm, F-Sa 11am-11pm, Su 5-10pm. MC/V. ❶

🟦 SIGHTS

DOWNTOWN. Downtown Cincinnati centers around the **Tyler Davidson Fountain,** at 5th and Vine St., a towering 19th-century bronze masterpiece. Around **Fountain Square,** business complexes and shops are connected by a series of skywalks. The 49th-floor observation deck atop **Carew Tower,** Cincinnati's tallest building, provides a ranging view of the riverfront. *(441 Vine St. ☎579-9735. Open M-Th 9:30am-5:30pm, F-Sa 9:30am-9pm, Su 11am-5pm. $2, ages 5-11 $1.)* Just to the east, the **🔲Contemporary Arts Center** has been called "the most important American building to be completed since the end of the Cold War." Baghdad-born architect Zaha Hadid is the first woman ever to win the prestigious Pritzker Prize, and her airy, angular design houses six floors of avant-garde art. *(44 E. 6th St. ☎345-8400; www.contemporaryartscenter.org. Open M 10am-9pm, W-F 10am-6pm, Sa-Su 11am-6pm. $7.50, seniors $6.50, students $5.50, ages 3-13 $4.50. M 5pm-9pm free.)* At the eastern edge of downtown, the **Taft Museum of Art** contains a modest collection of Old Masters and Chinese ceramics in an 1820 mansion. *(316 Pike St. ☎241-0343; www.taftmuseum.org. Open Tu-Su 11am-5pm. $8, seniors and students $6, under 18 free. W free.)*

EDEN PARK. Flowering trees and a sea of daffodils mark the arrival of spring in Eden Park, although skating on Mirror Lake ensures that Cincinnati's own Garden of Eden remains charming even in winter. Just be sure to steer clear of the Tree of Knowledge. *(Northeast of downtown and Mt. Adams. Take bus #49 to Eden Park Dr. Open daily 6am-10pm. Free)* The impressive **Cincinnati Art Museum,** inside the park, greets visitors with a serpentine chandelier designed by glassblower Dale Chihuly. Highlights of the collection include Impressionist landscapes from both sides of the Atlantic, and the Cincinnati Wing with period furniture and portraits of native son Frank Duveneck. *(953 Eden Park Dr. ☎ 639-2984; www.cincinnatiartmuseum.org. Open Tu and Th-Su 11am-5pm, W 11am-9pm. Tours Tu-F 1pm, Sa 2pm, Su 1 and 2pm. Free. Some temporary exhibitions $6.)* The nearby **Krohn Conservatory** teems with tropical plants, while May and early June bring a cloud of butterflies to the conservatory's Show Room. *(950 Eden Park Dr. ☎ 421-5707; www.cinci-parks.org. Open daily 10am-5pm. Suggested donation $5, under 17 $2. Butterfly show $6/4.)* To encounter some more sizable wildlife, head to the **Cincinnati Zoo,** where you can rub elbows with rare Sumatran rhinos and duck into the domed Vanishing Giants building for a glimpse of an Asian elephant. *(3400 Vine St. ☎ 281-4700; www.cincyzoo.org. Open June-Aug. daily 9am-6pm; check website for low-season schedule. $13, seniors $11 ages 2-12 $8. Parking $6.50.)*

MUSEUM CENTER. Built in 1933 as part of a West End renaissance, the enormous Art Deco **Union Terminal** fell into disrepair in the 70s, and then reopened in 1990 with three major museums. The **Cincinnati History Museum** takes visitors back to Cincy's past as a garrison town of the Early Republic and the cultural mecca of the Civil War era. A giant mastodon skeleton welcomes visitors into the **Museum of Natural History and Science,** where explorers can uncover the secrets of the Ice Age and descend into a cave's damp depths to see bats. Kids are in control at the **Cinergy Children's Museum,** where they can clamber through a giant playscape or try to generate hydropower in the WaterWorks area. *(1301 Western Ave. ☎ 287-7000; www.cincymuseum.org. Open M-Sa 10am-5pm, Su 11am-6pm. 1 museum $7.25, ages 3-12 $5.25; 2 museums $10.25/7.25; 3 museums $13.25/9.25. Parking $5.)*

OTHER SIGHTS. Across the river in Kentucky, the spectacular ◪**Newport Aquarium** routes visitors through glass tunnels where tiger sharks swim 6 in. from their heads. Tiny American alligators are about as cute as carnivorous reptiles get, while the aquarium's beautiful Jellyfish Gallery features chandeliers and gilded frames. *(At Newport on the Levee. ☎ 859-261-7444; www.newportaquarium.com. Open in summer M-F and Su 9am-7pm, Sa 9am-9pm; in winter daily 10am-6pm. $18, children 3-12 $11.)* A mile from downtown, the **William Howard Taft National Historic Site** was the childhood home of the portly US President and Supreme Court Justice. *(2038 Auburn Ave. ☎ 684-3262; www.nps.gov/wiho. 30min. tours leave on the hour daily 8am-4pm. Free.)*

♫ ENTERTAINMENT

The free newspapers *City Beat, CinWeekly,* and *Downtowner* list happenings around town. Cincinnati's **Playhouse in the Park,** 962 Mt. Adams Cir., won a 2004 Tony award for best regional theater in the US with dramas, comedies, and musicals inside Eden Park. *(☎ 421-3888; www.cincyplay.com. Performances mid-Sept. to June Tu-Su. $34-48. Senior and student rush tickets 2hr. before show $18.)* The **Music Hall,** 1241 Elm St. *(☎ 744-3344),* hosts the **Cincinnati Symphony Orchestra** and the **Cincinnati Pops Orchestra** from September through May. *(☎ 381-3300. $17-77. Student tickets sold the week of the concert $10.)* The **Cincinnati Opera** sings in the Hall's Springer Auditorium. *(☎ 241-2742; www.cincinnatiopera.org. $27-136.)* A summer series of classical concerts and operas takes place at the **Riverbend Music Center,** 6295 Kellogg Ave., on the banks of the Ohio River. The **Cincinnati Ballet** *(☎ 621-5219; www.wguc.org/cincinnatiballet)* performs at the **Aronoff Center for the Arts,** 650 Walnut St., which also hosts the **Broadway in Cincinnati** series. *(☎ 241-7469. Ballet performances late Sept. to mid-May $18-47. Broadway Sept.-June $25-65.)* Early June kicks off the edgy, mixed-media productions of the ◪**Cincinnati Fringe Festival** *(☎ 300-5669; www.cincyfringe.com),* while September brings almost 300 bands to town for the **MidPoint Music Festival** *(☎ 877-572-8690; www.mpmf.com).*

GREAT LAKES

Northeast of the city, off I-71 at Exit 24, **Paramount's King Island** cages **The Beast,** the world's longest wooden roller coaster, while the new **Italian Job** puts thrillseekers behind the wheel for a car chase full of special effects. (☎573-5800 or 800-288-0808; www.pki.com. Open late May to late Aug. daily 10am-10pm; call for low-season hours. $45, seniors and ages 3-6 $30. Parking $10.) Major League baseball's **Reds** (☎381-7337; tickets $5-45) take the field at the **Great American Ball Park,** 100 Main St., and football's long-suffering **Bengals** (☎621-8383; tickets $49-60) play at **Paul Brown Stadium** five blocks west.

🎵 NIGHTLIFE

Overlooking downtown from the east, the winding streets of **Mount Adams** have spawned some offbeat bars and music venues, creating a relaxed environment removed from the bustling city below. On the Kentucky side of the river, a more commercialized nightlife scene has emerged in **Newport.**

Northside Tavern, 416 Hamilton Ave. (☎542-3603), in the Northside. Pool tables and a jukebox set the tone inside this favorite twentysomethings hangout. Drafts $3-4. Live music daily 10pm. 21+. Open M-F 5pm-2:30am, Sa-Su 8pm-2:30am.

Blind Lemon, 936 Hatch St. (☎241-3885), at St. Gregory St. Live blues and rock fill the cavernous tavern where Jimmy Buffett got started. During the colder months, bonfires light up the outdoor courtyard Th-Sa. Drafts $2. Live music daily 8:30pm. 21+. Open M-F 5pm-2am, Sa-Su 3pm-2:30am.

INDIANA

The cornfields of southern Indiana's Appalachian foothills give way to expansive plains in the industrialized north, where Gary's smokestacks spew black clouds over the waters of Lake Michigan and urban travel hubs string along the interstates. Despite its official motto—"The Crossroads of America"—Indiana is a modest, slow-paced state, where farms roll on and on, big cities are a rarity, and countless Hoosier school kids dream of becoming the next Larry Bird.

🚩 PRACTICAL INFORMATION

Capital: Indianapolis.

Visitor Info: Indiana Division of Tourism, 1 N. Capitol Ave., #700, Indianapolis 46204 (☎317-232-8860 or 800-677-9800; www.in.gov/visitindiana). **Division of State Parks,** 402 W. Washington St., #W-298, Indianapolis 46204 (☎317-232-4124; www.in.gov/dnr/parklake).

State Bird: Larry. **Postal Abbreviation:** IN. **Sales Tax:** 6%.

Time Zone: Indiana adopted Daylight Savings Time in the summer of 2006; this marked the first time that the entire state had ever turned its clocks forward. 17 counties in the north and southwestern parts of Indiana are on central time. The remaining 75 counties are on Eastern Standard Time.

INDIANAPOLIS   ☎317

After years of being known by such epithets as "Napville" and "India No Place," Indiana's sprawling state capital resolved to build a cultural infrastructure that would outlast the seasonal boom of the Indianapolis 500. Superb museums and a diverse music scene promptly rose to the occasion. Bands of poverty still separate the sparkling downtown from outlying neighborhoods, but on the whole, Indianapolis pulses with the energy of a city on the move.

TRANSPORTATION AND PRACTICAL INFORMATION. The **Indianapolis International Airport** (**IND**; ☎487-7243; www.indianapolisairport.com) is located 7 mi. southwest of downtown off I-465, Exit 11B; take bus #8 "Washington St." Taxi to downtown costs around $17. Amtrak, 350 S. Illinois St. (☎263-0550; www.amtrak.com; open daily midnight-2:30pm and 11pm-midnight), runs **trains** to Chicago (5hr., 3 per day, $29-64) and Cincinnati (3hr., 1 per day, $32). Greyhound, inside the same terminal (☎267-3076; www.greyhound.com; open 24hr.), sends **buses** to Chicago (3-4hr., 8 per day, $34); Cincinnati (2-5hr., 7 per day, $22.50); and Detroit (7-11hr., 4 per day, $47.25). Indygo, 209 N. Delaware St., runs routes throughout the city, as well as **shuttles** to special events. (☎635-3344; www.indygo.net. $1.50, under 6 free.) For a **taxi,** call Yellow Cab, ☎487-7777.

The city is laid out in concentric circles, with a dense central cluster of skyscrapers and low-lying outskirts. The very center of Indianapolis is just south of **Monument Circle,** at the intersection of **Washington Street (U.S. 40)** and **Meridian Street.** Washington St. divides the city north-south; Meridian St. divides it east-west. **I-465** circles the city and provides access to downtown. **I-70** cuts through the city east-west. Metered parking is abundant along the edge of the downtown area. The **Artsgarden Cultural Concierge,** on the 1st floor of Circle Centre Mall, gives out info on arts events and the Cultural Districts Guide. (☎624-2563; www.indyarts.org. Open M-Sa 10am-9pm, Su noon-6pm.) **Post Office:** 125 W. South St., across from Amtrak. (☎464-6852. Open M-F 7am-5:30pm.) **Postal Code:** 46206.

ACCOMMODATIONS. Budget motels line the I-465 beltway, 5 mi. from downtown. Make reservations a year in advance for the Indy 500, which drives rates up drastically in May. The friendly **Indy Hostel ❶,** 4903 Winthrop Ave., three blocks from N. College Ave., has quickly carved out a niche for itself with summer interns in the city. Short-term guests also find the convivial common spaces, well-stocked kitchen, and open-door atmosphere refreshing. (☎727-1696; www.indyhostel.us. Free Internet access. Laundry $1. Dorms M-Th and Su $22, F-Sa $25; private room $45/49. MC/V.) **Motel 6 ❷,** 6330 Debonair Ln., at Exit 16A off I-465, may be the middle ground between hostel prices and hotel comfort; expect pleasant rooms with A/C and cable TV. (☎293-3220. Singles M-Th and Su $34, F-Sa $37; doubles $40/43. AmEx/D/MC/V.) The **Indiana State Fairgrounds Campgrounds ❶,** 1202 E. 38th St., bus #4 or 39 from downtown, has 170 sod-and-gravel sites packed with RVs. (☎927-7523. Sites $16, with hookup $25.)

FOOD. Ethnic food stands, vegetable markets, and knick-knack vendors fill the spacious **City Market,** 222 E. Market St. Meals start around $5. (☎634-9266. Open M-F 6am-6pm, Sa 8am-4pm.) Massachusetts Ave. houses some of the city's liveliest restaurants and bars; in the summer, diners crowd outdoor patios. **Bazbeaux Pizza ❸,** 334 Massachusetts Ave. (☎636-7662) and 832 E. Westfield Blvd. (☎255-5711), is the go-to spot for a casual date and a legendary slice of thin crust. Stay basic with the margherita pizza ($10), or try the intoxicating Tchoupitoulas ($11.50) and brave the one-two punch of Cajun shrimp and andouille sausage. (Both locations open M-Th and Su 11am-10pm, F-Sa 11am-11pm. AmEx/D/MC/V.) **The Abbey ❷,** 825 Pennsylvania Ave., cultivates a celestial vibe with cloud-painted ceilings, church-style lanterns, and an array of vegetarian sandwiches ($7-8) that puts most other coffeeshops to shame. (☎269-8426. Free Wi-Fi. Open M-Sa 9am-midnight, Su 8am-11pm. MC/V.)

◉ **SIGHTS.** The attractions in and around White River State Park, bordered by West St. and W. Washington St., form an axis of activity that has anchored the city's downtown revitalization efforts. At the eastern edge of the park, the **Eiteljorg Museum of American Indians and Western Art,** 500 W. Washington St., includes a gallery of provocative pieces by contemporary Native American artists, rounding out the museum's collection of tribal crafts and paintings of frontier life. (☎636-9378; www.eiteljorg.org. Open M and W-Sa 10am-5pm, Tu 10am-8pm, Su noon-5pm; Oct.-Apr. closed M. Tours daily 1pm. Wheelchair-accessible. $8, seniors $7, students and ages 5-17 $5.) The **Indiana State Museum,** 650 W. Washington St., has a fascinating collection of artifacts that create evocative portraits of life in the 19th and 20th centuries; look for the bottles of patent medicine and the 1887 barber's chair. (☎232-1637; www.in.gov/ism. Open M-Sa 9am-5pm, Su 11am-5pm. Wheelchair-accessible. $7, over 60 $6.50, ages 3-12 $4. IMAX $9/7.50/6. Combo $12.50/11/8.) No sports fan should miss the **NCAA Hall of Champions,** 700 W. Washington St., which pays homage to the best in American college sports. Experience the passion of the Final Four in the March Madness Theater and try your hand at hitting a clutch shot in the 30s-style gymnasium. (☎916-4255; www.ncaahallofchampions.org. Open Tu-Sa 10am-5pm, Su noon-5pm. $3, students $2, under 5 free.) A majestic stained-glass dome graces the marbled interior of the **State House,** 200 W. Washington St. (☎233-5293. Open M-F 8am-5pm. Tours Sa 10:15am, 11am, noon, 1pm; tours Su 11:15am, noon, 1, and 2. $8. 3-5 1hr. guided tours per day. Call ahead. Free.) Animal-lovers should check out the seemingly cageless **Indianapolis Zoo,** 1200 W. Washington St. Adjacent to the zoo, frolic with butterflies amidst exotic flora at **White River Gardens.** (☎630-2001; www.indyzoo.com. Open June-Aug. M-Th 9am-5pm, F-Su 9am-6pm; Sept.-Oct. M-Th 9am-4pm, F-Su 9am-5pm. Zoo and gardens Mar.-Oct. $13.50, ages 2-12 and over 62 $8.50; Jan.-Feb. and Nov.-Dec. $8.50/6.50. Parking $5.) Although it is almost 4 mi. north of downtown, the ◨**Indianapolis Museum of Art,** 4000 Michigan Rd., rewards those who make the trek with its galleries and stunning formal gardens. The African art collection reopened in 2006. The StarStudio gives kids a crack at edgy, interactive installation work. (☎923-1331; www.ima-art.org. Open Tu-W and Sa 11am-5pm, Th-F 11am-9pm, Su noon-5pm. Free.) Young people are foremost on the agenda of the **Indianapolis Children's Museum,** 3000 N. Meridian St., where the mood-lit fossils of the museum's signature Dinosphere exhibit open up on an art studio and a simulated archaeological dig. (☎334-3322; www.childrensmuseum.org. Open Mar.-Aug. daily 10am-5pm; Sept.-Feb. Tu-Su 10am-5pm. $12.50, over 60 $11.50, ages 2-17 $7.50.)

🏎 **DAYS OF THUNDER.** America's passion for fast cars reaches fever pitch during the **500 Festival** (☎927-3378; www.500festival.com), an entire month of parades and hoopla leading up to race day at the **Indianapolis Motor Speedway,** 4790 W. 16th St., off I-465 at the Speedway Exit. (Take bus #25.) The festivities begin with time trials in mid-May and culminate with the "Gentlemen, start your engines" of the **Indianapolis 500** the Sunday before Memorial Day. During quieter times, buses full of tourists drive around the 2½ mi. track at slightly tamer speeds. (☎492-6784; www.indy500.com. Track tours daily 9:30, 11:15am, 1:15, 3pm. $3, ages 6-15 $1.) The **Speedway Museum,** at the south end of the infield, houses the Indy **Hall of Fame** and a collection of cars that have tested their strength on the storied track over the years. (Open daily 9am-5pm. $3, ages 6-15 $1.) Tickets for the race usually sell out within a week after the previous year's race. After the smoke clears from the racetrack, more than 400 bands pull into town for August's **Midwest Music Summit.** (☎459-8634; www.midwestmusicsummit.com. 3-day pass $25.) The recently opened **Indianapolis Fringe Theatre Festival** features experimental plays in four venues around the city. (☎822-4386; www.indyfringe.com. Tickets $10 per show.)

October brings the feel-good flicks of the **Heartland Film Festival.** (☎464-9405; www.heartlandfilmfestival.org. Tickets $7 per film; $50 for 10 tickets.)

🎭🎬 ENTERTAINMENT AND NIGHTLIFE. The **Madame Walker Theatre Centre,** 617 Indiana Ave., used to be the headquarters of African-American entrepreneur Madame C.J. Walker's beauty enterprise. Today, the national historic landmark hosts arts programs, including the bi-weekly **Jazz on the Avenue.** (☎236-2099; www.walkertheatre.com. Tours M-F 9am-3:30pm. $5, children $3. Jazz every other F 6-10pm. $10.) The **Indianapolis Symphony Orchestra** performs in the **Hilbert Circle Theater** on Monument Cir. (☎639-4300; www.indyorch.org. Box office open M-F 10am-6pm, Sa 10am-2pm.) The shining star of the city's theater scene is the **Indiana Repertory Theatre,** 140 W. Washington St. (☎635-5252; www.indianarep.com. Box office open M-F 10am to 30min. before showtime. Tickets from $25.) Basketball fans watch the **Pacers** from November to April at **Conseco Fieldhouse,** 125 S. Pennsylvania St. (☎917-2500. Tickets $10-96.) The WNBA's **Indiana Fever** take over in the summer months. (☎239-5151. Tickets $10-75.) The NFL's **Colts** toss the pigskin at the **RCA Dome,** 100 S. Capital Ave. (☎239-5151. Tickets $15-65.) Adjacent to the campus of Butler University, the **Broad Ripple** area, 6 mi. north of downtown at College Ave. and 62nd St., is the best area for nightlife. **The Jazz Kitchen,** 5377 N. College Ave., draws intimate trios and swinging big bands alike. (☎253-4900; www.thejazzkitchen.com. M no cover. Th Latin dance party 9pm. 21+. Sets usually begin at 9pm and 11pm. Cover $7-10; $15-20 for national acts. Open M-Sa 5pm-midnight.) **The Vogue,** 6259 N. College Ave., hosts national acts in a restored movie house and transforms itself into the city's favorite megaclub after hours. Expect to wait in a line that stretches half-way down the block. (☎259-7029; www.thevogue.ws. Shows 8pm. 21+. Cover $3-5; F ladies free. Open W and F-Sa 10pm-3am.) Back downtown, the **Slippery Noodle,** 372 S. Meridian St., is the oldest bar in Indiana, as well as one of the country's best venues for live blues. (☎631-6974. Beer $3-5. 21+. Cover Th-Sa $5. Open M-Sa 11am-3am, Su 4pm-12:30am.)

BLOOMINGTON   ☎812

While the rolling hills of Monroe County are home to tiny communities, they also open up on the cosmopolitan college town of Bloomington. **Indiana University** (IU) drums up a rowdy fan base for Big Ten basketball games, while scruffy kids skateboard by ethnic restaurants and students chalk "not my government" on the sidewalk. With the shores of Monroe Lake just 10 mi. to the south, Bloomington is within striking distance of natural resources that rival its heady cultural life. At the eastern end of Kirkwood Ave., the **Sample Gates** mark the entrance to the IU campus. Veer to the left past the red-roofed Student Building and cut across **Dunn Meadow,** where students have been known to stage protests and erect shantytowns. Several blocks further east, I.M. Pei's angular, sunlit **Art Museum,** 1133 E. 7th St., counts Stuart Davis' bold *Swing Landscape* as a cornerstone of its collection. (☎855-5445; www.indiana.edu/~iuam. Open Tu-Sa 10am-5pm, Su noon-5pm. Free.) Nearby, the **Mathers Museum of World Cultures,** 416 N. Indiana Ave., near E. 8th St., has just unveiled a new permanent exhibit comparing and contrasting the Bloomington of the 60s to the Hausa tribe of central Africa. (☎855-6873; www.indiana.edu/~mathers. Open Tu-F 9am-4:30pm, Sa-Su 1-4:30pm. Free.) South of town, the **Tibetan Cultural Center,** 3655 Snoddy Rd., recently came within days of foreclosure, but a new board of directors promises to keep the compound's sacred *stupas* and interfaith temple open for years to come. (☎336-6807; www.tibetancc.com. Grounds and center open daily during daylight hours.) Inexpensive rooms crowd the intersection of Rte. 46 and N. Walnut St. Usually, rooms at the **Scholars Inn Bed & Breakfast ❹,** 801 N. College Ave., go for over $100, but on weekdays the comfortable beds drop in price. (☎332-1892. Gourmet breakfast included. Check-in 4-6pm. Rooms from $99. AmEx/MC/V.) **Paynetown "Peyton" State Recreation Area ❶**, 10 mi. southeast of downtown on Rte. 446, has open campsites on Lake Monroe with access to trails, a beach, boat rentals, and a fishing dock. (☎837-9546. Primitive sites M-W and Su $10, Th-Sa $13; with electricity $17/25. Vehicle registration $7, IN residents $4.) Rent boats from **Lake Monroe Boat Rental.** (☎837-9909; www.lake-monroeboatrental. Kayaks and canoes $9 per hr., $25 per 8hr.; Fishing boats $75 per 8hr., deposit $50; $85 per day, deposit $100.) The **Snow Lion ❸**, 113 S. Grant St., serves authentic Tibetan cuisine on the cheap (entrees $8-9). It has been blessed by the Dalai Lama and is owned and run by his holiness' nephew. (☎336-0835. Open M-Sa 11am-3pm and 5pm-10am. AmEx/MC/V.) The brightly colored picnic tables out on the deck of the Kenwood Manor Building point the way into **Laughing Planet Cafe ❶**, 322 E. Kirkwood Ave. Burritos bulging with beans and brown rice ($5.25) can get messy, but a tabletop guide recalls that it is "a violation of Natural Law" to eat a burrito with a fork. (☎323-2233. Open daily 11am-9pm. MC/V.) Downstairs, **The Cinemat,** 123 S. Walnut St., screens foreign and independent films at bargain-basement prices. (☎333-4700; www.thecinemat.com. $4, matinees $3.) **Nick's English Hut,** 423 E. Kirkwood Ave., looks just like a quaint Yorkshire cottage on the outside, with crowds of IU students squeezing into its myriad booths during termtime. (☎332-4040. Pints from $2.25. 21+ after 8pm. Open M-Sa 11am-2:30am, Su noon-midnight.)

The city of Bloomington is south of Indianapolis on Rte. 37. **North Walnut Street** and **College Avenue** are the main north-south thoroughfares. The town centers on **Courthouse Square.** Bloomington Transit sends **buses** through town and IU's campus. Service is infrequent. (☎336-7433; www.bloomingtontransit.com. $0.75, seniors and ages 5-17 $0.35.) The campus also has a **shuttle bus** ($0.75). The **Visitors Center,** 2855 N. Walnut St., offers free local calls and a helpful staff. (☎334-8900 or 800-800-0037; www.visitbloomington.com. Open Apr.-Oct. M-F 8:30am-5pm, Sa 9am-4pm; Nov.-Mar. M-F 8:30am-5pm, Sa 10am-3pm. Brochure area open 24hr.)

MICHIGAN

While pressing up against four of the Great Lakes, the state's two peninsulas present visitors with two distinct Michigans. The sparsely populated Upper Peninsula hangs over Lake Michigan, containing moose, wolves, and the stunning waterfalls of the scenic Hiawatha National Forest. Campers and hikers have recently discovered the UP, and the resplendent forests entertain both backpackers and families. In the Lower Peninsula, beach bums hang out in quaint communities along the state's western coast, sunning and boating along some of Michigan's 3000 mi. of coastline. Those craving an urban environment head to Ann Arbor, the state's intellectual center, or to industrial Detroit for world-class museums.

▨ PRACTICAL INFORMATION

Capital: Lansing.

Visitor Info: Travel Michigan, 300 N. Washington Sq., Lansing 48913 (☎800-644-2489; www.michigan.org).

Department of Parks and Recreation, Mason Building, 3rd floor, P.O. Box 30031, Lansing 48909 (☎517-373-9900). State parks require a motor vehicle permit ($8 per day, $29 per day; MI residents $6/24 per year). Call ☎800-447-2757 for reservations.

Postal Abbreviation: MI. **Sales Tax:** 6%.

GREAT·LAKES

DETROIT ☎ 313

Heavyweight boxing champ Joe Louis is one of Detroit's best-known native sons and a fitting icon for the city; Detroit resembles an aging contender, caught up on the ropes in the seventh round but determined to stay standing until the final bell. Violent race riots in the 60s spawned a massive exodus to the suburbs, while the decline of the auto industry in the late 70s chiseled away the city's industrial base and left behind the weary, crumbling shell of Motown's glory days. Detroit continues to shrink with each succeeding census, and yet the stalwarts who have stayed behind love their city with an almost cultish ferocity.

▐ TRANSPORTATION

Airport: Detroit Metropolitan (DTW; ☎734-247-7678; www.metroairport.com), 20 mi. southwest of downtown, off I-94 at Merriman Rd., in Romulus. **Metro Airport Taxi** (☎800-745-5191) offers taxi service to downtown for $41.

Trains: Amtrak, 11 W. Baltimore St. (☎873-6938; www.amtrak.com). Open daily 6:45am-1am and 3:45-11pm. To **Chicago** (5½hr., 3 per day, $27-67) and **New York** (16hr., 1-3 per day, $93-146). **VIA Rail,** 298 Walker Rd. (☎888-842-7245; www.viarail.ca), in Windsor, ON runs to **Toronto** (4hr., 4 per day, CDN$91) and other Canadian spots.

Buses: Greyhound, 1001 Howard St. (☎961-8011; www.greyhound.com). Station open 24hr.; ticket office open daily 5:30am-11:30pm. Be cautious in this area at night. To **Ann Arbor** (1½hr., 3 per day, $8), **Chicago** (5½-7½hr., 5 per day, $34), and **Cleveland** (3½-4½hr., 6 per day, $30.50).

Public Transit: Detroit Department of Transportation (DOT), 1301 E. Warren Ave. (☎933-1300; www.ci.detroit.mi.us/ddot). Serves downtown, with limited service to the suburbs. Many buses stop service at midnight. $1.50; transfers $0.25. An elevated tramway, **People Mover,** 1420 Washington Blvd. (☎962-7245; www.thepeoplemover.com), circles the Central Business District on a 2¾ mi. loop; worth a ride just for the view of the riverfront and downtown. Runs M-Th 7am-midnight, F 7am-2am, Sa 9am-2am, Su noon-midnight. $0.50. **Suburban Mobility Authority for Regional Transportation (SMART),** 660 Woodward Ave. (☎866-962-5515; www.smartbus.org). Runs bus service to the suburbs daily 4am-midnight. $1.50; transfers $0.25.

▐▐ ORIENTATION AND PRACTICAL INFORMATION

Detroit lies on the Detroit River, which connects Lake Erie and Lake St. Clair. Across the river to the south, the town of **Windsor, ON,** can be reached by a tunnel just west of the Renaissance Center (toll $3.50), or by the Ambassador Bridge (toll $3.25). Those planning to make the crossing should expect delays due to heightened security. American citizens need to have a passport or copy of their birth certificate, not just a driver's license. Detroit can be a dangerous town, but it is generally safe during the day; expect to be approached by panhandlers, and **avoid walking alone at night.** Office buildings and sports venues dominate the downtown, while up-and-coming neighborhoods like **Corktown** open out to the west. Driving is the best way to get around town.

Detroit's streets form a grid. The numbered Mile Roads run east-west and measure the distance away from downtown. **Eight Mile Road** is the city's northern boundary and the beginning of the suburbs. **Woodward Avenue/Route 1** is the city's main north-south artery and divides Detroit into "East Side" and "West Side." **Gratiot Avenue** flares out northeast from downtown, while **Grand River Avenue** shoots west. Both I-94 and I-75 pass through downtown. Streets tend to end suddenly and reappear several blocks later; for a particularly helpful map, check *Visit Detroit*, available at the Visitors Bureau.

GREAT LAKES

TO 🏛 MOTOWN
HISTORICAL
MUSEUM (1mi)

TO 🎭 DETROIT
REPERTORY
THEATRE (2.5mi)

TO 🚗 (0.5mi),
DETROIT ZOO (9mi),
CRANBROOK (18mi)

94

TO HAMTRAMCK (5mi),
PALACE AT AUBURN HILLS (20mi)
(19 mi.)

TO ✈ (2mi),
🏛 HENRY FORD MUSEUM (10mi).

Palmer St.

Ferry St.

Downtown Detroit

🏠 🏔 ACCOMMODATIONS

Pontiac Lake Recreation Area, 1
Shorecrest Motor Inn, 10
University of Windsor, 12

🍎 FOOD

American Coney Island, 7
Cass Cafe, 2
Slows, 5
Xochimilco, 6

🍺 NIGHTLIFE

Garden Bowl, 3
Papa Cheney's Whiskey Well, 11
Phog, 13
Saint Andrews Hall, 9
The Old Shillelagh, 8
Town Pump Tavern, 4

WAYNE STATE
UNIVERSITY

Detroit
Historical
Museum

Kirby St.

Kirby St.

Kirby St.

David Adamany
Undergraduate
Library

Detroit
Public
Library

Detroit
Institute
of Arts

Frederick Douglass Ave.

Farnsworth St.

Frederick Douglass Ave.

Rivard St.

Russell St.

Putnam St.

CULTURAL
CENTER

Warren Ave.

The New Detroit
Science Center

Museum of
African-American
History

Warren Ave.

Hancock St.

Forest Ave.

Forest Ave.

Garfield St.

Prentis St.

Garfield St.

Canfield St.

75

Willis St.

Cass Ave.

Willis St.

John R St.

Superior St.

Alexandrine St.

W. Service Dr.

Alexandrine St.

Selden St.

Brush St.

Leland St.

Illinois St.

Orchestra Hall

Parsons St.

St. Antoine

St. Joseph St.

Chrysler Dr.

Rivard St.

Russell St.

Brainard St.

Davenport St.

Mack St.

Myrtle St.

Stimson St.

Eliot St.

Pierce St.

Peterboro St.

Erskine St.

Watson St.

Beaubien St.

Wilkins St.

Erskine St.

Watson St.

EASTERN MARKET

Charlotte St.

Edmund St.

Brewster St.

Brewster St.

Cass
Park

Temple St.

Alfred St.

Alfred St.

Alfred St.

Ledyard St.

Sproat St.

Division St.

Divison St.

Sibley St.

Adelaide St.

Farmers ■
Market

Henry St.

Park Ave.

75

Old Tiger
Stadium

Kaline St.

Plum St.

Fox Theatre

Columbia St.

Montcalm St.

Comerica
Park

Ford
Field

TO HEIDELBERG
PROJECT
(1.5mi)

CORKTOWN

TO 5 (.3mi)

Plum St.

Elizabeth St.

Elizabeth St.

State Theatre

Adams St.

TO MEXICAN
TOWN, 6 (2mi)

Bagley St.

Grand Circus
Park

Madison St.

Harmonie
Park

Mullet St.

375

Bagley St.

Bagley St.

Clinton St.

Labrosse St.

Michigan Ave.

Downtown People Mover

Macomb St.

Porter St.

6th St.

Woodward Ave.

GREEK-
TOWN

Abbott St.

Abbott St.

2nd St.

1st St.

State St.

Griswold St.

Library St.

Monroe St.

Lafayette St.

Howard St.

5th St.

3rd St.

Campus
Martius
Park

Cadillac Sq.

9

Beaubien St.

Chrysler Dr.

TO BELLE ISLE
(3mi)

TO AMBASSADOR
BRIDGE (3 mi.)

W. St.

3

John K. King Used
and Rare Books

Washington Blvd.

Shelby St.

Congress St.

Randolph St.

10

E. Jefferson Ave.

Jefferson Ave.

Larned St.

Woodbridge St.

Franklin St.

TO DETROIT

Dieppe
Gardens

Riverside Dr.

Detroit–
Windsor
Tunnel (Toll)

Casino ■
Windsor

11

Goyeau Ave.

Joe Louis
Arena

Cobo
Hall

HART
PLAZA

Renaissance
Center

Atwater St.

TO 12
(3mi),
13 (400ft)

University Ave.

Ouellette Ave.

Park St.

McDougall Ave.

City
Hall

Detroit River

MICHIGAN (U.S.A.)
ONTARIO (CANADA)

TO WINDSOR, ON (.25mi)
(SEE INSET)

Detroit–Windsor
Tunnel (toll)

500 yards

0
500 meters

Visitor Info: Convention and Visitors Bureau, 211 W. Fort St., 10th fl. (☎202-1800 or 800-338-7648; www.visitdetroit.com). Open M-F 9am-5pm.

GLBT Resources: Triangle Foundation of Detroit, 19641 W 7 Mile Rd. (☎537-3323). **Affirmations,** 195 W. 9 Mile Rd. (☎248-398-7105; www.goaffirmations.org), in Ferndale, has a large library.

Hotlines: Crisis Hotline, ☎224-7000. **Rape Counseling Center,** ☎833-1660. 24hr.

Internet Access: Detroit Public Library, 5201 Woodward Ave. (☎833-1490). Offers free Internet access in 1hr slots. Open Tu-W noon-8pm, Th-Sa 10am-6pm. The **David Adamany Undergraduate Library** 5155 Gullen Mall, at Wayne State University, offers free Internet access in 1hr. slots. Photo ID required. Open May-Aug. M-Th 8am-11pm, F 8am-6pm, Sa 9am-5pm, Su 11am-7pm; Sept.-Apr. M-Th 8am-11pm, F 8am-9pm, Sa 9am-9pm, Su 11am-11pm.

Post Office: 1401 W. Fort St. (☎226-8075). Open 24hr. **Postal Code:** 48233. **Area Codes:** 313 (Detroit); 810, 248, and 734 (suburbs). In text, 313 unless noted.

■ ACCOMMODATIONS

Staying in downtown Detroit often leaves travelers with the choice of high-end hotels or questionable dives. There are a few options along **East Jefferson Avenue,** but it may be easier to find chain motels in the northern suburbs or across the border in **Windsor.** *Visit Detroit* lists accommodations and prices by area.

■ **University of Windsor,** 750 Sunset Ave. (☎519-973-7041 or 1-888-561-5552), in Windsor. In the summer rents several townhouses at hostel rates. Communal kitchen and living room included. Also rents palatial, hotel-style dorm rooms. A/C, free Internet access, and refrigerators. Open early May-late Aug. Linen CDN$7.50. Parking CDN$5 per day. Hostel bed CDN$32. 2-bedroom suite with continental breakfast CDN$79. AmEx/MC/V. ❷

Shorecrest Motor Inn, 1316 E. Jefferson Ave. (☎568-3000 or 800-992-9616), located 3 blocks east of the Renaissance Center. Rooms have A/C and fridge. Key deposit $20. Reservations recommended. 21+. Singles $71; doubles $91. AmEx/D/MC/V. ❸

Pontiac Lake Recreation Area, 7800 Gale Rd. (☎248-666-1020; reservations 800-447-2757), in Waterford, 45min. northwest of downtown. Take I-75 to Rte. 59 W, turn right on Williams Lake north and left onto Gale Rd. 176 wooded sites with electricity and showers. Vehicle permit $8 per day, $29 per year; MI residents $6/24. Sites $16. ❶

■ FOOD

Gourmet restaurants may have cast their lot in the northern suburbs, but city-dwellers continue to dine in the city's ethnic neighborhoods. At the **Greektown** People Mover stop, Greek restaurants line one block of Monroe St., east of Beaubien St. Joseph Campau Ave., in **Hamtramck** (Ham-TRAM-eck), is the center for Polish fare, while **Mexican Town,** 3 mi. west of downtown, brims with affordable restaurants and markets. The **Eastern Market,** at Gratiot Ave. and Russell St., is a 43-acre bonanza of open-air produce and farm-fresh meat; almost 50,000 people turn up on Saturdays to gather ingredients. (☎833-9300. Open Sa 7am-5pm.)

■ **Slows,** 2138 Michigan Ave. (☎962-9828). Neighboring Detroit's old abandoned train station in Corktown, Slows specializes in BBQ, supplying four of its original sauces with every meal. Served on thick slices of texas toast, the pulled pork sandwich ($7) is stuffed with so much meat that it spills out of the sandwich at the first bite. There are also vegetarian options; locals praise the macaroni and cheese ($9). Open M-F 11am-2am, Sa-Su noon-2am. MC/V. ❷

Cass Cafe, 4620 Cass Ave. (☎831-4100). Displaying local artists' work on the walls ($250-3000), Cass has understated white walls, skylights, and a lentil-walnut burger ($6) that will satisfy the appetite of any carnivore. Entrees $8-12.50. Su live DJ. Open M-Sa 11am-2am, Su 5pm-midnight. AmEx/D/MC/V. ❷

Xochimilco, 3409 Bagley St. (☎843-0179). Draws huge crowds with delicious enchiladas and burritos ($5-8). Among the entrees the standout dish is the *nopalitos (*pieces of cactus mixed with onions, peppers and eggs; $7.75). The dim lighting may force you to squint a bit, but the mural, great service, and warm chips with salsa make Xochimilco (so-she-MEEL-ko) exceptional. Open daily 11am-2am. AmEx/DC/MC/V. ❷

◉ SIGHTS

The freeways and housing projects that divide downtown Detroit mean that public space can be hard to come by. Both civic leaders and local artists have worked to carve out new areas for people to congregate, even as they respect the institutions that have anchored the community for decades. **John K. King Used and Rare Books,** 901 W. Lafayette St., is one of these institutions, a resolutely uncomputerized warehouse for books ranging from $0.75 paperbacks to a $6500 Hemingway first edition. Friendly staff use walkie-talkies to help guide customers through the cavernous building. (☎961-0622. Open M-Sa 9:30am-5:30pm.)

CAMPUS MARTIUS PARK. The same firm that gave the Bellagio casino in Las Vegas its famous fountains designed the centerpiece of Detroit's newest public space. The park borrows its name from an 18th-century military drill ground that occupied this site and has already emerged as a center for activity with its shaded gardens and outdoor skating rink that opens during the winter months. From June through September, there are free outdoor screenings of family-friendly films on Saturdays at 8pm. (*800 Woodward Ave., between Fort and Michigan Ave. Open M-Th 7am-10pm, F 7am-midnight, Sa 9am-midnight, Su 9am-8pm.)*

DETROIT ZOO. Exotic animals, like tigers and red pandas, roam the grounds of the **Detroit Zoological Park.** The National Amphibian Conservation Center allows visitors to get up close and personal with enormous salamanders, while the Arctic Ring of Life exhibit showcases polar bears and a trek through the tundra. *(8450 W. Ten Mile Rd., just off the Woodward Exit of Rte. 696 in Royal Oak. ☎248-541-5717; www.detroit-zoo.org. Open daily 10am-5pm. $11, seniors $9, ages 2-12 $7. Parking $5.)*

CRANBROOK SCHOOLS. Founded by Detroit philanthropists in 1922, the **Cranbrook Schools** give more than 1600 students a world-class education in the posh suburb of Bloomfield Hills, 15 mi. north of Detroit. Public gardens and a house designed by noted architect Eliel Saarinen are well worth a look, and the **Cranbrook Institute of Science,** 39221 N. Woodward Ave., will be sure to please the entire family. The new Bat Zone area houses bats, sloths, and other creatures that creep around at night. (*☎248-645-3209 or 877-462-7262; www.cranbrook.edu. Open daily 10am-5pm. $8, seniors and ages 2-12 $6. Planetarium shows $4, under 2 $1. Bat Zone free. Hourly shows cost an extra $4/1.)*

THE HEIDELBERG PROJECT. Drawing on the imagery of painters like Dubuffet and Basquiat, Tyree Guyton has spent the better part of two decades transforming a row of run-down crack houses and abandoned lots on Detroit's Near East Side into installation art. Neatly aligned rows of vacuum cleaners line up in waist-high weeds like a formation of soldiers, while hundreds of stuffed animals hang from the sides of a nearby building. (*Heidelberg St., between Ellery and Mt. Elliott; take Gratiot Ave. downtown and follow it north for 1 mi. Heidelberg St. will be on the right. ☎267-1622; www.heidelberg.org. Free.)*

🏛 MUSEUMS

🎵**MOTOWN HISTORICAL MUSEUM.** Entrepreneur and producer Berry Gordy founded Motown Records with an $800 loan from his family and built it into a recording empire that would leave a permanent impression on American music. Knowledgeable tour guides lead visitors past the hat and gloves donned by Michael Jackson in his "Thriller" video, before descending to the legendary Studio A where Stevie Wonder and Diana Ross laid down their first soulful tracks. *(2648 W. Grand Blvd. ☎ 875-2264; www.motownmuseum.org. Open Tu-Sa 10am-6pm. $10, under 13 $8.)*

HENRY FORD MUSEUM. The astonishing eight acres of exhibit space in the Henry Ford Museum includes iconic artifacts, like the bus where Rosa Parks stood her ground and the convertible in which JFK breathed his last breath. In addition to chronicling the history of transportation in America, the museum offers snapshots of popular culture through the 20th century; sit for a few minutes to play with a vintage Mr. Potato Head. Next door, the Greenfield Village outdoor museum is an overly precious tribute to Americana, while the new and impressive Ford Rouge Factory Tour brings visitors out on a catwalk over the F-150 assembly line. *(20900 Oakwood Blvd., off I-94 in Dearborn. Take SMART bus #200 or 250. ☎ 313-982-6001. Museum open daily 9:30am-5pm. Factory open daily 9:30am-2:30pm, tours every 30min. Museum and factory tour $14 each, seniors $13, ages 5-12 $10. Greenfield Village $20/19/14. Combination pass including museum, village, and factory tour $30/28/22.)*

DETROIT INSTITUTE OF ARTS. The most recent reports indicate that major renovations to Detroit's Museum of Fine Art are slated to drag on until late 2007. For the moment, handpicked selections from the permanent collection hold down the fort, along with the signature Diego Rivera mural depicting scenes from Detroit's industrial history. *(5200 Woodward Ave. ☎ 833-7900; www.dia.org. Open W-Th 10am-4pm, F 10am-9pm, Sa-Su 10am-5pm; first F of each month 11am-9pm. Suggested donation $4.)*

MUSEUM OF AFRICAN AMERICAN HISTORY. The MAAH features a core exhibit entitled "And Still We Rise" that follows the African Diaspora from a marketplace in Benin to a reconstructed 60s lounge from Detroit's East Side. *(315 E. Warren Ave. ☎ 494-5800; www.maah-detroit.org. Open Tu-Sa 9:30am-5pm, Su 1-5pm. Reception with free hors d'oeuvres F 6pm. $8, seniors and ages 3-12 $5.)*

THE NEW DETROIT SCIENCE CENTER. Interactive exhibits that manage to be both educational and fun abound at the Science Center. Write a concerto on the stringless laser harp, or take a trip through the human body at the IMAX Dome theater, where the three-story-tall screen covers the whole dome. *(5020 John R St. ☎ 577-8400; www.detroitsciencecenter.org. Open M-Th 9am-5pm, F 9am-9pm, Sa 10am-10pm, Su 10am-6pm. $8, seniors and ages 2-12 $7; IMAX $4.)*

DETROIT HISTORICAL MUSEUM. The Detroit Historical Museum explores the region's transformation from "frontiers to factories"—visitors can tour a streetscape of old town Detroit and gawk at a working piece of the Cadillac assembly line. *(5401 Woodward Ave. ☎ 833-7935; www.detroithistorical.org. Open W-F 9:30am-3pm, Sa 10am-5pm, Su noon-5pm. $6, seniors and children 5-18 $4. Parking $3.)*

🎭 ENTERTAINMENT

The brassy anthems of The Supremes and the surly guitar riffs of The White Stripes may define Detroit's sonic palette in the popular imagination, but the **Detroit Symphony Orchestra** sticks to a more traditional repertoire with concerts at **Orchestra Hall,** 3711 Woodward Ave., at Parsons St. (☎ 576-5100, box office 576-

5111; www.detroitsymphony.com. Open M-F 10am-6pm. Tickets $36-170. Student and senior rush tickets 1½hr. prior to show $20-15.) The **Theater District**, on either side of Woodward Ave. at Grand Circus Park, is anchored by the historic **Fox Theatre**, 2211 Woodward Ave., which draws nationally recognized musicians and entertainers. (☎248-433-1515. Box office open M-Sa 10am-6pm. Tickets $25-100.) The **Fillmore Detroit**, 2115 Woodward Ave. (☎961-5451; www.statetheatredetroit.com), hosts smaller concerts, and the **Detroit Repertory Theatre**, 13103 Woodrow Wilson Ave., shakes things up with a deep-seated commitment to race-transcendent casting. (☎868-1347; www.detroitreptheatre.com. Shows Th-F 8:30pm, Sa 3 and 8:30pm, Su 2 and 7:30pm. $20, advance tickets $17.)

Detroit is a big sports town. During the summer, baseball's **Tigers** play in the newly built **Comerica Park**, 2100 Woodward Ave. (☎866-668-4437. $5-60.) Football's **Lions** hit the gridiron next door at **Ford Field**, 2000 Brush St. (☎262-2003. $40-70.) Inside the **Joe Louis Arena**, 600 Civic Center Dr., the **Red Wings** play hockey. (☎396-7444. $20-40.) Thirty minutes north of Detroit in Auburn Hills, basketball's **Pistons** play at **The Palace at Auburn Hills**, 4 Championship Dr. (☎248-377-0100. $10-110.)

✿ FESTIVALS

Hart Plaza, a sprawling green space on the banks of the Detroit River, is the epicenter of Detroit's open-air festivals. **Movement** draws electronic music enthusiasts from around the country for a futuristic Memorial Day weekend full of skittering jungle beats. (www.demf.com. Day pass $21, 3-day pass $41.) In late August, two million square feet of Downtown Detroit from Hart Plaza to the Campus Martius Park is transformed by the four-day **Ford Detroit International Jazz Festival** (☎447-1248; www.detroitjazzfest.com). Late June's **International Freedom Festival** (☎923-7400) celebrates the friendship between the US and Canada, and the continent's largest fireworks display erupts over the Detroit River with 10,000 colorful explosions. Steer clear of the crowds at Hart Plaza and head out to Belle Isle for an equally spectacular view. More than a million visitors arrive for the **African World Festival** (☎494-5800; third weekend in August), and the **Michigan State Fair** (☎369-8250), at Eight Mile Rd. and Woodward Ave., celebrates over 100 years of bake-offs and 500 lb. pumpkins for two weeks during the heart of August.

◪ NIGHTLIFE

Metro Detroit's trendiest lounges and nightclubs tend to be in the northern suburbs, and Ferndale has cultivated a lasting reputation for GLBT nightlife. Still, the downtown area has its own hot spots; check the *7daysindetroit* section of the free weekly *Real Detroit* for listings. **Garden Bowl**, 4120 Woodward Ave., is a bar combined with a live music venue and a bowling alley. The mishmash of entertainment options attracts a decidedly hip crowd which doesn't take its bowling too seriously. After 9pm, black lights illuminate the bowling alley. The bar itself features 40 types of bottled beers and shares space with a pizzeria. (☎833-9700. Pizza $1.50 per slice. Beer $3-7. Bowling lanes $8 per hr. during the day, $16 per hr. at night. Rental shoes $2, socks $3. Live music Th-Sa. Buy tickets for the live music at the door $8-20. Open daily 11am-2pm. AmEx/MC/V.) Things get rowdy weekend nights at **The Old Shillelagh**, 349 Monroe St., where the upstairs audience loudly sings along to traditional Irish songs, often drowning out the band. Don't clap if you want to look like a local—regulars slam their beers on the table to cheer on the house band, the Black Mist, who have performed here every weekend for over 20 years. Downstairs, a DJ spins trademark Detroit techno to a less raucus set of revelers. (☎964-0007. Beer $4-5. Pitcher $8. F-Sa DJ and live music. Cover F-Sa $5.

Open M-Sa 11am-2:30am, Su noon-2:30am.) If all you want is a good pint, try the **Town Pump Tavern**, 100 W. Montcalm St., behind the State Theater. Good beer abounds at this watering hole, which is cloaked in ivy and features a mock study with comfy leather chairs. (☎961-1929. Th and Sa-Su live music. Drafts $4-5. Open daily M-Sa 11am-2am, Su noon-2am. Kitchen closes 11pm.)

▶ DAYTRIP FROM DETROIT

WINDSOR, ONTARIO   ☎519

Though Windsor may not quite live up to its utopian portrayal in Michael Moore's documentary *Bowling for Columbine*, Canada's southernmost city does offer a respite from the gritty streets of Detroit. Riverfront parks and sidewalk cafes give the City of Roses a leisurely European feel, while a string of auto plants employs workers outside the tourist economy. Though Windsor made a name for itself in the 1800s as a terminus of the Underground Railroad, today it is underage refugees from Detroit's 21+ bar scene.

Cupped between Riverside Dr. and the Detroit River, the **Odette Sculpture Garden** stretches east from the Ambassador Bridge and includes standout pieces like Edwina Sandys' *Eve's Apple* and Ted Bieler's *Tower Song*. (☎253-2300; www.windsorsculpturepark.com. Open daily dawn-dusk. Free. Parking available.) At the eastern edge of the park, the **Art Gallery of Windsor**, 401 Riverside Dr. W, boasts a strong permanent collection of Canadian painters, including works by Lauren Harris and F.H. Valery, two of the founding members of the Group of 7, a turn-of-the-century Canadian art collective. The collection also highlights work by contemporary artists in the Detroit-Windsor area. (☎977-0013; www.artgalleryof-windsor.com. Open W 11am-8pm, Th-F 11am-9pm, Sa-Su 11am-5pm. CDN$3.) **Point Pelee National Park of Canada ❶**, 407 Monarch Ln., Leamington, ON, 45 mi. southeast of Windsor, houses more endangered species of plants and animals than any other Canadian national park. Birdwatchers flock to the park in May, and monarch butterfly enthusiasts make the trip in September. (☎322-2365 or 888-773-8888. Open daily Apr. and June-Oct. 6am-10pm; May 5am-10pm; Nov.-Mar. 7am-7pm. CDN$7, seniors CDN$6, children 6-16 CDN$3.45; families CDN$17.30. Self-guided park activity pack CDN$5. Campsites with showers CDN$13.)

Inexpensive Chinese and Vietnamese restaurants are plentiful along Wyandotte Ave. as it approaches the University of Windsor. Just across from the tunnel Exit, **Tunnel Bar-B-Q ❸**, 58 Park St. E, has been serving up finger-lickin' barbecue ribs for more than 40 years. You can't go wrong with an order of the half-strip rib dinner (CDN$14)—unless you forget to ask for extra napkins. (☎258-3663. Open M-W and Su 8am-midnight, Th 8am-2am, F-Sa 8am-4am. AmEx/D/MC/V.) Sidewalk dining is the name of the game along Ouellette (OH-let) Ave., downtown, where flush-faced American minors stumble in and out of sweaty pubs doling out $2 shots. Those looking to dance the night away also flock to Ouellette where several clubs line both sides of the street north of Park St. Indie rock shows and local microbrews (CDN$5.50) cultivate a very different vibe at **◼phog,** 157 University Ave. W, where hipsters recline on a battered-chic leather couch rescued from the curb. (☎253-1605; www.phoglounge.com. Th-Sa live music; check website for other shows in summer. Cover CDN$3-5. Open daily 4pm-2am.) **Papa Cheney's Whiskey Well,** 63 E. Riverside Dr. is a two floor pub/restaurant on the waterfront. Its 2nd story lounge has leather couches and bay windows for enjoying the sunset on the water (lounge opens 4:30pm). Known locally for its perogies (Cajun-style "Voodoo" perogies, $9), the bar's best feature is its CDN$2 locally produced Candian Club Rye Whiskey. (☎258-1334. Beer CND$4.75. Open daily 11am-2am.

AmEx/MC/V.) **Casino Windsor,** 377 Riverside Dr., offers three floors of gambling and draws gamers from across the river who have told themselves that they are losing less money because of the exchange rate. (☎800-991-7777; www.casinowindsor.com. 19+. Open 24hr.)

Canada's national **rail** service, VIA Rail, 298 Walker Rd. (☎888-842-7245; www.viarail.ca; ticket window open daily 5:15am-7:30pm), provides service to Toronto (4hr., 4 per day, CDN$109). Transit Windsor, 3700 N. Service Rd. E, sends **buses** throughout the city. (☎944-4111. CDN$2.35, seniors CDN$1.60.) For a **taxi,** call Veteran's Cab, ☎256-2621. The **Convention and Visitors Bureau of Windsor, Essex County, and Pelee Island** is at 333 Riverside Dr. W, #103. (☎255-6530 or 800-265-3633; www.visitwindsor.com. Open M-F 8:30am-4:30pm.) The **Ontario Travel Center,** 110 Park St., offers maps, currency exchange, and a knowledgeable staff. (☎973-1338 or 800-668-2746; www.ontariotravel.net. Open daily June-Aug. 8am-8pm; Sept.-May 8:30am-5pm.) **Post Office:** City Centre, at Park St. and Ouellette Ave. (☎253-1252. Open M-F 8am-5pm.) **Postal Code:** N9A 4K0.

ANN ARBOR   ☎734

Ann Arbor's namesakes, Ann Rumsey and Ann Allen—the wives of two of the area's early pioneers—supposedly enjoyed sitting under grape arbors. Now known to locals as "A2," the town has managed to prosper without losing its relaxed charm, despite being tucked between several major industrial hubs. Meanwhile, the huge and well-respected University of Michigan adds a hip collage of young, liberal, middle-Americans. Ann Arbor is the prototype for a great college town, and is well worth a visit for anyone traveling in the area.

▐▀▌ **TRANSPORTATION AND PRACTICAL INFORMATION.** Amtrak, 325 Depot St. (☎994-4906; www.amtrak.com; ticket window open daily 7:15am-11:30pm), runs **trains** to Chicago (4½hr., 3 per day, $25-67) and Detroit (1hr., 3 per day, $11). Greyhound, 116 W. Huron St. (☎662-5511; www.greyhound.com; open M-F 9am-6pm, Sa-Su 9am-4pm), sends **buses** to Chicago (6½hr., 2 per day, $34), Detroit (1½hr., 3 per day, $8), and Grand Rapids (6hr., 2 per day, $22.50). Ann Arbor Transportation Authority (AATA), 331 S. 4th Ave., provides **public transit** in Ann Arbor and neighboring Ypsilanti. (☎996-0400; www.theride.org. Station open M-F 7:30am-9:30pm, Sa noon-6:15pm. **Buses** run M-F 6:45am-10:30pm, Sa-Su 8:30am-7pm. $1, ages 6-18 $0.50; seniors can obtain card for $0.25-0.50 fares.) AATA's Nightride provides door-to-door transportation within city limits. (Reservations ☎528-5432 at least 1hr. in advance. Runs M-F 11pm-6am, Sa-Su 7pm-7:30am. $5.) Checker Sedan runs between Ann Arbor and the Detroit Metro Airport. (☎963-1000. $56. Reserve in advance.)

Ann Arbor's streets lie in a grid, but watch out for the slant of Packard St. and Detroit St. **Main Street** divides the town east-west, and **Huron Street** cuts it north-south. The central campus of the **University of Michigan (U of M)** lies east of Main St. and south of E. Huron, a 5min. walk from downtown. In spite of plentiful meter parking, authorities ticket ruthlessly, and one-way streets and frequent dead-ends can make driving stressful. Luckily, downtown Ann Arbor is walkable, and a car is generally unnecessary. Yuppies and business professionals congregate along the many bars and restaurants that line Main St. Students don't venture far from the central campus; most student hangouts and affordable venues can be found within an area bound by S. State St. to the west and S. University St. to the north. The **Ann Arbor Area Convention and Visitors Bureau** is at 120 W. Huron St., at Ashley. (☎995-7281 or 800-888-9487; www.annarbor.org. Open M-F 8:30am-5pm.) The **University of Michigan,** 530 S. State St., provides maps of Ann Arbor. and has a free Internet terminal. (☎764-4636. Open M-Th 7am-midnight, F-Sa 7am-2am, Su 9am-midnight.) **Hotlines: Sexual Assault Crisis Line,** ☎483-7273. **Psychiatric Emergency Services,** ☎936-5900. (Both 24hr.) **Internet Access: Ann Arbor District Library,** 343 S. 5th Ave. (☎327-4200. Free with ID. Open M 10am-9pm, Tu-F 9am-9pm, Sa 9am-6pm, Su noon-6pm.) **Post Office:** 2075 W. Stadium Blvd. (☎665-1105. Open M-F 8am-7pm, Sa 10am-4pm.) **Postal Code:** 48103.

🏠 ACCOMMODATIONS. Rooms in Ann Arbor don't come cheap; keep an eye out for discount chains on the southern edge of town or in Ypsilanti, 5 mi. southeast along I-94. Frederika the Hungarian watch-cat keeps an eye on guests at 🛏**The Eighth Street Trekkers Lodge ❸,** 120 8th St., where innkeeper Heather O'Neal sells Nepalese crafts out of her garage and plans excursions into the Himalayas. (☎369-3107. Breakfast included. Reserve in advance. Doubles $75. Cash only.) Should you have a falling out with Frederika, seven **campgrounds ❶** lie within a 20 mi. radius of Ann Arbor, including the **Pinckney Recreation Area,** 8555 Silver Hill, in Pinckney, and the **Waterloo Recreation Area,** 16345 McClure Rd., in Chelsea. (Pinckney ☎426-4913. Waterloo ☎475-8307. Primitive sites $10, with water and electricity $22. Vehicle permit $8 per day, $29 per year. MI residents $6/24.)

🍴 FOOD. Where there are students, there are cheap eats. The cheapest cram the sidewalks of **State** and **South University Street,** while more upscale establishments line **Main Street.** 🍽**Zingerman's Deli ❸,** 422 Detroit St., is an Ann Arbor institution deservedly famous for its gourmet breads, cheeses, and deli sandwiches ($8-12). Expect a line out the door during the lunchtime rush. Try **Zingerman's Next Door ❶** for baked goods and gelato made with imported Italian machines and flavor syrups served from an Italian freezer. (☎663-3354. Gelato $4 per cone. Open daily 7am-10pm. AmEx/D/MC/V.) **Krazy Jim's Blimpy Burger ❶,** 551 S. Division St., near campus, caters to the college crowd with gorgeously greasy "cheaper than food" burgers, from a single patty all the way up to the monstrous half-pound "Quint." (☎663-4590. Burgers $3-6. Open M-Sa 11am-10pm, Su noon-8pm. Cash only.) For something less likely to induce cardiac arrest, hit up **Seva ❸,** 314 E. Liberty St., for vegetarian entrees like spinach lasagna and North African couscous. (☎662-1111. Entrees $10-14. Lunch specials M-F 11am-3pm. Open M-Th 11am-9pm, F-Sa 11am-10pm, Su 10am-9pm. AmEx/D/MC/V.)

📷🎭 SIGHTS AND ENTERTAINMENT. Not surprisingly, the University of Michigan is the driving force behind Ann Arbor's rich cultural life. The **University of Michigan Museum of Art (UMMA),** 525 S. State St., houses one of the country's foremost university art collections, although the exhibition hall closed its doors in July 2006 for a major renovation that will continue into 2008. (☎764-0395; www.umma.mich.edu. Open Tu-W and F-Sa 10am-5pm, Th 10am-9pm, Su noon-5pm. Free.) A pair of enormous mastodon skeletons, flanked by a saber-tooth tiger and a T-Rex skull, guards the second floor of the **University of Michigan Exhibit Museum of Natural History,** 1109 Geddes Ave. The anthropology exhibits on the 4th floor are a bit spotty, but weekend shows at the planetarium bring the stars that much closer. (☎764-0478; www.exhibits.lsa.umich/edu. Open M-Sa 9am-5pm, Su noon-5pm. Museum free. Planetarium $3.75.) Security won't escort you to the door for touching displays at the **Ann Arbor Hands-On Museum,** 220 E. Ann St., which has four floors of exhibits designed to be tugged, twisted, and turned. (☎995-5439; www.aahom.org. Open M-Sa 10am-5pm, Su noon-5pm. $7. Students, seniors, and ages 2-17 $6.) The stalls in front of the historic **Kerrytown Shops** play host to a vibrant **farmers' market,** 315 Detroit St. (☎994-3276. Open May-Dec. W and Sa 7am-3pm; Jan.-Apr. Sa 8am-3pm.) Paintings and pottery take over the market space on Sundays, when local artists display their creations at the **Artisans' Market.** (☎734-

Downtown Ann Arbor

🏠 **ACCOMMODATIONS**

The Eighth Street
Trekkers Lodge, **3**

🍴 **FOOD**

Fleetwood Diner, **4**
Krazy Jim's Blimpy Burger, **10**
Seva, **7**
Zingerman's Deli, **1**

🌙 **NIGHTLIFE**

\áut\bar, **2**
Ashley's, **9**
Blind Pig, **5**
Conor O'Neill's, **8**
Firefly Club, **6**

913-9622. Open May-Dec. Su 11am-4pm.) It's nearly impossible to get tickets for a **Wolverine football game** at U of M's 115,000 capacity stadium, but fans can give it a shot by calling the athletics office (☎764-0247). After the students depart for the summer, the **Ann Arbor Summer Festival** (☎994-5999; www.annarborsummerfestival.org) draws local crowds from mid-June to early July for dance and musical performances at the **Power Center.** Thrifty festiva-lgoers tend to prefer **Top of the Park,** a nightly series of free movies and concerts held on top of a Fletcher St. parking garage. Check the summer festival website for the 2008 location. Late July draws thousands for the **Ann Arbor Street Art Fair** (☎994-5260; www.artfair.org), while the **University Musical Society** sponsors classical concerts from September to April. (☎764-2538 or 800-221-1229; www.ums.org. Balcony seats from $10.)

🎵 **NIGHTLIFE.** Free in restaurants and music stores, the monthly *Current* has detailed nightlife listings, although Detroit's *Metro Times* and the monthly *Ann Arbor Paper* are also good resources. For GLBT info, pick up a copy of the Detroit-based *Between the Lines.* For gritty rock 'n roll shows and a cool indie vibe, nobody upstages the **Blind Pig,** 208 S. 1st St. (☎996-8555; www.blindpigmusic.com. Tu-Sa shows 9:30pm. 18+. Cover $4-8, varies depending on the act; check the website. Under 21 $3 extra. Open daily 3pm-2am.) The **Firefly Club,** 637 S. Main St., offers an intimate setting for jazz, ranging from traditional big band to modern avant-garde. It was voted one of the 100 best jazz clubs in the world by *Downbeat*

Magazine, the "Bible" of contemporary jazz. (☎665-9090; www.fireflyclub.com. Th Latin jazz. 21+. Cover $5-10. Open daily 4pm-2am.) There are Irish bars, and then there are bars that like to think that they're Irish bars. **Conor O'Neill's**, 318 S. Main St., is solidly in the first camp; a mixed crowd of locals and students gather under retro Guiness advertisements to take in local sports on TV. (☎665-2968. Open daily 11:30am-2am. Beer $2.50-4. Breakfast served Sa-Su 8am-2pm. Kitchen closes M-Th and Su 11pm, F-Sa midnight. AmEx/D/MC/V). **\áut\ bar,** 315 Braun Ct., near the intersection of Catherine St. and 4th Ave., is a straight-friendly gay bar which caters to college boys and a laid-back older crowd. (☎994-3677. Su brunch 10am-3pm. Open M-Sa 4pm-2am, Su noon-2am.)

LAKE MICHIGAN SHORE

The freighters that once powered the rise of Chicago still steam along the coast of Lake Michigan, but these days they are greatly outnumbered by pleasure boats cruising along the coast. Valleys of sand beckon sunbathers, while hikers trek through the untouched forests of Michigan's state parks. When autumn comes, the weather forbids swimming, but inland, festivals celebrate local fruits and blossoms, from cherries in July to apples in September. Snow covers much of the coast in winter, drawing snowmobiling, skiing, and ice-skating enthusiasts. The coastline stretches 350 mi. north from the Indiana border to the Mackinac Bridge; its southern end is a scant 2hr. from downtown Chicago.

◼ PRACTICAL INFORMATION

Many of the region's attractions lie in the small coastal towns that cluster around **Grand Traverse Bay** in the north. **Traverse City,** at the southern tip of the bay, is the famous "Cherry Capital of the World." The main north-south route along the coast is **U.S. 31.** Numerous green "Lake Michigan Circle Tour" signs lead closer to the shoreline, providing an excellent view. Coastal accommodations can be expensive; head inland for cheaper lodging. Determined travelers can occasionally find a good deal lakeside, and numerous camping options exist in the summer months. Based in Grand Rapids, the **West Michigan Tourist Association,** 3665 28th St. SE, Ste. B, hands out info on the area. (☎616-245-2217 or 800-442-2084; www.wmta.org. Open M-F 8:30am-5pm.) **Area Codes:** 616 and 231.

CENTRAL MICHIGAN SHORE

SLEEPING BEAR DUNES   ☎231

The Sleeping Bear Dunes lie along the western shores of the Leelanau Peninsula, 20 mi. west of Traverse City on Rte. 72. **Sleeping Bear Dunes National Lakeshore** encompasses 25 mi. of shoreline in Leelenau and Benzie Counties, as well as both the Manitou Islands, located a few miles off the mainland coast. Access to both mainland and offshore areas of the Lakeshore is administered by the National Park Service, and visitors hoping to do anything more than drive along the county roads must pay an entrance fee at the **National Parks Service Visitors Center,** 9922 Front St., in Empire. (☎326-5134. $10 per car, $5 per pedestrian or cyclist; fee includes 7-day admission. Open daily June-Aug. 8am-6pm; Sept.-May 8am-4pm.)

Near the historic Fishtown shops at the end of River St., **Manitou Island Transit,** in Leland, makes daily trips to slightly less rugged South Manitou from June to August. The ferry schedule makes South Manitou an ideal destination for day hikers, dropping visitors off at 11:30am and whisking them back to Leland at 4:30pm. Visitors who set foot on North Manitou should take note—the ferry returns to

Leland immediately after dropping off passengers at 11am, and hikers are cut off from the modern world until the next morning. The ferries will not run during bad weather—campers on either island should bring at least two extra days of supplies. (☎256-9061. Check-in 9:15am. Trips to North Manitou 3-5 times per week in June, daily July-Aug. Call ahead for May and Sept.-Nov. schedule. Reservations recommended. Round-trip $29, under 13 $15.) Hardcore backpackers looking for an adventure can **camp** on both islands by purchasing a **camping permit** ($5) from the Manitou Island Transit office, though there is an entrance fee ($10 per week; available at the Visitors Center). The Manitou Islands do not allow wheeled vehicles, including cars and bikes.

Back on the mainland, hikers can make an exhausting 3 mi. trip up the side of a sand dune and down to the waters of Lake Michigan. The **Dune Climb** starts 5 mi. north of Empire on Rte. 109; the full route takes roughly 3hr. to complete, and hikers should bring plenty of drinking water. Visitors in search of a more leisurely day at the beach should turn off Rte. 22 just before it crosses the Platte River, and follow Lake Michigan Rd. all the way to the end. The waters of Lake Michigan are often quite cold until August, but the Platte River flows into the lake at **Platte River Point** and creates warmer conditions in early summer. After toweling off, drivers can inch their way along the 7 mi. **Pierce Stocking Scenic Drive**, off Rte. 109 just north of Empire. The best-known outlook presents a sweeping view from the top of a sand cliff 450 ft. above the surface of Lake Michigan. The drive stays open from late April to early November, weather permitting. As night falls on the dunes, the silver screen lights up at **Cherry Bowl Drive-in Theatre**, 9812 Honor Hwy., in Honor. Heading south on Rte. 22, take a left onto Rte. 708 and drive 5 mi. until you see the signs. (☎325-3413; www.cherrybowldrivein.com. Open daily June-Aug. Movies start at dusk. $8, under 12 free.) **Riverside Canoes**, on Rte. 22 at Platte River Bridge, organizes 2½hr. canoe and kayak excursions, as well as relaxed tubing trips. (☎325-5622; www.canoemichigan.com. Open May-early Oct. daily 8am-10pm. Inner tubes $15 per 2hr. Kayak trips from $26. Canoe trips from $36.)

The Sleeping Bear Dunes are home to four different **campgrounds. Platte River ❶**, just off of Rte. 22, 10 mi. south of Empire, is the most luxurious, with 179 sites, showers, and electrical hookups. (☎325-5881 or 800-365-2267. Sites $16, with electricity $21. Showers $1.) **D.H. Day ❶**, 1 mi. west of Glen Arbor on Rte. 109, offers drinking water and flush toilets. (☎334-4634. Sites $12.) Two backcountry campsites, **Whitepine ❶** and **Valley View ❶**, have fire rings and vault toilets; reservations are not accepted, but permits can be purchased for $5 at Platte River or D.H. Day. Whitepine is popular for its proximity to the water.

TRAVERSE CITY   ☎231

Bearing a certain resemblance to the Ann Arbor of 20 years ago, Traverse City is quickly emerging as a hip town and a magnet for young people from around the state. Bikes are a popular way to explore the surrounding area, and abandoned railroad beds have been reclaimed as the **Traverse Area Recreation and Transportation (TART)** trail that extends 19 mi. northwest of Traverse City to Suttons Bay. The demanding **Vasa Pathway** draws mountain bikers to the hills of Pere Marquette State Forest, while the **Cherry Capital Cycling Club** leads Monday evening excursions up into scenic Old Mission Peninsula, northeast of town. **McLain Cycle and Fitness**, 750 E. 8th St., rents road bikes and mountain bikes. (☎941-7161. Open in summer M-F 9am-6pm, Sa 9am-5pm; low season closed Su. All bikes $10 per 2hr. Road bikes and mountain bikes $25 per day.)

With half of America's cherries produced in the region around Traverse City, the **National Cherry Festival** (☎947-4230 or 800-968-3380; www.cherryfestival.org), held during the first full week of July, celebrates arguably nature's sexiest fruit. Eight nights of live music and daily events ranging from a pit-spitting tournament to a fireworks display ensure that festivalgoers will get a chance to see Traverse City with all of its flags flying. In early to mid-July, many orchards near Traverse City let visitors pick their own cherries. Try **Elzer Farms,** 1214 Center Rd., 9 mi. north of Traverse City on Rte. 37 (☎223-713. Cherries $1.75 per lb. Cherry pie filling $6. Open May-Sept. daily 10am-6pm.) Sophisticated fruit connoisseurs can also indulge their taste buds at one of the area's many well-respected wineries.

East Front St. (U.S. 31) is lined with motels, and during the summer rates generally start at $50. **Northwestern Michigan College ❷,** 1701 E. Front St., West and East Halls, offers simple dorm rooms with unyielding mattresses, and is most cost-effective for travelers in bigger groups. Guests have access to coin-op laundry, a common room, and outdoor athletic facilities. (☎995-1400; www.nmc.edu/housing/summer. Reserve several weeks in advance. Open June-Aug. Single beds $40; 2-bed suites $70; 4-bed suites $140. D/MC/V.) For those who prefer to commune with nature, **Traverse City State Park ❶,** 1132 U.S. 31 N, 2 mi. east of town, has 343 wooded sites crowded along U.S. 31, adjacent to the beach. (☎922-5270 or 800-447-2757. Toilet and shower facilities. Sites with hookup $27; cabins $45. Cars $8 per week, $29 per year; MI residents $6/24.) Sit down at **Green House Cafe ❷,** 115 E Front St (☎929-7687) to sample the famous french onion soup covered with a thick coat of melted cheese ($3; with soup and salad $6.60) or go for a burger ($6). The owner uses the walls as gallery space for his striking underwater photography, which mesmerizes the children of families having brunch. Walk west on Front St., take a left on to Division St., and take a right onto 11th St. and walk two blocks, bearing right, to get to **Another Cuppa Joe ❶,** 11th St. west of Division St., inside building 50 (☎947-7730). Free Wi-Fi comes with your vegetarian wrap ($6-7) and espresso drink ($2.75-3.50) as you sit inside this abandoned psychiatric ward. Polish off a mid-afternoon snack at **Grand Traverse Pie Company ❶,** 525 W. Front St., where Old Mission cherry pie sells by the slice ($3) and by the pan. (☎922-7437; www.gtpie.com. Open M-F 7am-8pm, Sa 8am-7pm, Su 10am-4pm. AmEx/D/MC/V.) If you're looking for a spot to bring a date for dinner, **Poppycock's ❸,** 128 E. Front St., offers pasta ($12-15) and multi-ethnic vegetarian entrees ($13-14) in a bistro setting that manages to be both convivial and elegant. From Thursday to Saturday, the restaurant dims the lights and brings in live jazz. (☎941-7632. Open in summer M-W 11am-10pm, Th-Sa 11am-midnight, Su noon-9pm; low season M-W 11am-9pm, Th-Sa 11am-midnight. MC/V.)

After hours, head down to **Union Street Station,** 117 S. Union St., where an artsy twentysomething crowd grooves to live music and $3 drafts. (☎941-1930. Live music Tu and Th-Sa 10pm. No cover Tu or Th; F-Sa $5. Open M-Sa 11am-2am, Su noon-2am. AmEx/MC/V.) For an alternative to the bar scene, stop by the recently opened **InsideOut Gallery,** 229 Garland St., behind the Visitors Center, where TC's alternative set congregates for live music and rotating exhibitions of pop art. (☎929-3254; www.insideoutgallery.com. Open Tu-Th 11am-5pm, F-Sa 11am-6pm. Free.) For more entertainment info, pick up the excellent weekly *Northern Express* at corner kiosks in the city, or seek out the sporadically published *Thirdeye* for a more radical take on life in Traverse City.

Indian Trails, 115 Hall St. (☎946-5180 or 800-231-2222), runs **buses** to Grand Rapids (3½hr., 1 per day, $23) and destinations on the Upper Peninsula via St. Ignace (3hr., 1 per day, $19). The Bay Area Transportation Authority (BATA) runs five **regular bus routes** around Traverse City with a service called the **Cherriot.** They also pick up passengers if given 24hr. notice. (☎941-2324. Open daily 6am-6:40pm. Cherriot routes $1, seniors and under 12 $0.50; pickup service $2/1.) **The Traverse City Convention and Visitors Bureau,** at Union St. and Grandview Pkwy., maintains a binder with info on weekly events. (☎947-1120 or 800-872-8377; www.mytraversecity.com. Open M-F 9am-6pm, Sa 9am-5pm, Su 11am-3pm.) **Internet** access: **Traverse City District Library,** 610 Woodmere Ave. (☎932-8558. Free. 1hr. limit. Open

M-Th 9am-9pm, F-Sa 9am-6pm, Su noon-5pm). **Post Office:** 202 S. Union St. (☎946-9616. Open M-F 8am-5pm.) **Postal Code:** 49684.

NORTHERN MICHIGAN SHORE

STRAITS OF MACKINAC   ☎231

First things first: Mackinac is pronounced "MACK-i-naw," so curb the urge to rhyme your syllables by saying "MACK-i-nack." The **Mackinac Bridge** ("Mighty Mac") soars over the intersection of Lake Michigan and Lake Huron, connecting **Mackinaw City** to St. Ignace in the Upper Peninsula. Measuring 950 ft. longer than the Golden Gate Bridge, the 5 mi. span is the world's third-longest suspension bridge. A local tradition that is not to be missed is the annual **Labor Day Bridge Walk,** where Michigan's governor leads thousands north across the bridge to St. Ignace. Chain motels and tacky gift shops dominate the town, although the **Mackinac State Historic Parks** are well worth a look. Just west of the Mackinac Bridge's southern landfall, **Colonial Michilimackinac** reconstructs a fort built in 1715 by French fur traders and recently unearthed by a tireless team of archaeologists. (☎436-4100; www.mackinacparks.com. Open daily May-June 9am-4pm; June-Oct. 25th 9am-6pm. 7th. $10, ages 6-17 $6, under 6 free.) A 5min. walk away, the **Old Mackinac Point Lighthouse** opened in 2005 as a restoration project in progress. Warped wood and cracked plaster walls give a sense of the work that remains to be done, although the four-story climb to the tower already offers a sweeping view of the surrounding straits. (Open daily mid-May to early June and late Aug.-early Oct. 9am-4pm; early June-late Aug. 9am-5pm. $6, ages 6-17 $3.50, under 6 free.) **Fort Mackinac** (on Mackinac Island, see below) and **Historic Mill Creek,** a complex with a water-powered sawmill and nature trails 3 mi. south of Mackinaw City, round out the list of Mackinac State Historic Parks. (Mill Creek open daily early May-early June and late Aug.-early Oct. 9am-4pm; early June-late Aug. 9am-5pm. $7.50, ages 6-17 $4.50, under 6 free.) A Mackinac "triple choice" ticket gives you one daily admission to any three of the four ticketed parks. ($22, ages 6-17 $13.25. Available at all 4 sights.)

   Lakeshore accommodation options abound on Rte. 23, south of the city. The best lodging deals in the area lie across the Mackinac Bridge on the **I-75 Business Loop** in St. Ignace.For an outdoor escape, campers can crash at one of the 600 sites of **Mackinac Mill Creek Campground ❶,** 3 mi. south of town on Rte. 23. The grounds provide beach access and biking trails. (☎436-5584; www.campmackinaw.com. Internet access, public showers, heated pool. Free shuttle to island ferry. Sites from $24, with full hookup $36. Cabins in summer from $55; low season from $30. AmEx/D/MC/V.) Their recipe for the Upper Peninsula's favorite meat pie may trace its way back to Cornwall, but **Mackinaw Pastie & Cookie Co. ❶,** 117 W. Jamet St., two blocks south of Colonial Michilimackinac, recruits summer workers from overseas in the spirit of cultural exchange. Ask the workers at the counter which country they call home. (☎231-436-8202; www.mackinawpastie.com. Pasties $5-8. Open daily 9am-11pm. Additional location at 516 S. Huron. AmEx/D/MC/V.) The **Michigan Welcome Center,** on Nicolet St. off I-75 at Exit 338, has maps and brochures about area attractions. (☎436-5566. Open daily mid-June to Aug. 8am-6pm; Sept. to mid-June 9am-5pm. Free reservation service.)

MACKINAC ISLAND   ☎231

Mackinac Island, a 16min. ferry ride from the mainland, has been a destination for summer vacationers since the 1870s. Railroad barons lined the south-facing bluffs with elegant Victorian homes and, by banning automobiles from the island in 1896, tried to guarantee that Mackinac would retain its genteel, unhurried atmosphere for years to come. The slew of shops pressing **Mackinac fudge** (half-lb. $7) on day-trippers proves that the early inhabitants weren't entirely successful, although there are still quiet corners of the island to explore. Walk off the ferry landing, cross the garish strip that is Main St., and never look back.

Commanding a lofty view of the island's southern harbor, **Fort Mackinac** was a hotly contested piece of military architecture during the War of 1812. Today cannon firings, carefully restored buildings, and the sounds of fife and drum lure a steady stream of visitors up to the bluffs. (☎436-4100; www.mackinacparks.com. Open daily May to early June 9am-4:30pm; June 9-June 21 9:30am-6pm; June 22-Aug. 25 9:30am-8pm; Aug 26-Oct. 7 9:30am-4:30pm. $10, ages 6-17 $6, under 6 free.) June through August, tickets to the fort also include access to a number of historic buildings on Market St. (open daily 11am-6pm) as well as Mission Church, near the southeastern corner of the island (open daily noon-4pm). Travelers willing to don a three-cornered hat should inquire into weeklong fort **volunteer opportunities,** which include free housing on the island. Call for details. **Mackinac Island Carriage Tours,** on Main St., sends horse-drawn buggies on a 2hr. trot around the southern half of the island veering as far east as the Arch Rock formation before circling back to showcase the sumptuous grounds of the Grand Hotel. Keep an eye out for weepy devotees of the 1980 Christopher Reeve film *Somewhere in Time,* which was set at the hotel. (☎906-847-3307; www.mict.com. Tours daily early May to mid-Oct. 9am-3pm; July-Aug. until 5pm. $23, ages 5-12 $9.) For those who would rather take the reins themselves, **Jack's Livery Stable,** 331 Mahoney Ave., off of Cadotte Ave., rents saddle horses and buggies. (☎847-3391. Open daily May-Oct. 8am-5pm; June-Aug. until 6pm. Saddle horses $35 per hr. Horse and 2-person buggy $54 per hr.; 4-person buggy $60 per hr.) Bicycles are the best way to see the island's beaches and forests. Rental shops line Main St. by the ferry docks and generally offer identical rates ($4 per hr., $25 per day). Encompassing 80% of the island, **Mackinac Island State Park** features a circular 8¼ mi. shoreline road that takes about 1hr. by bike and 2hr. by foot.

Hotel rates on the island generally reach into the stratosphere, but ◧**McNally Cottage** ❹, on Main St., offers a haven for thrifty travelers. Situated in the heart of downtown, this B&B has been owned and operated by the same family every summer since its construction in the 1880s. (☎847-3565; www.mcnallycottage.net. Shared baths. Call well in advance for reservations. Single room with twin bed $50; double beds $65-70. Cash only.) Take your cue from the locals and "shop across" in Mackinaw City for food; everything is more expensive on the island, whether you buy it in a restaurant or a convenience store. **Marquette Park,** just below Fort Mackinac, is a good spot for a picnic; otherwise, carry your food up shady, flower-lined Cupid's Pathway behind the fort and grab a cold can of beer ($2) at **Harrison-ville General Store,** on Hoban Ave. This outpost is the spot where year-round residents stop for groceries and gossip during the low season. (Open daily May-Sept. 10am-8pm; Nov.-Apr. noon-5:30pm. Cash only.) If you're just not the picnicking type, stop by **3 Brothers Sarducci Pizzeria** ❶, on Main St., for an oversized slice of Sicilian-style pizza ($4.25) and a song on the jukebox. (☎847-3880. Open daily in summer 11am-8pm; low-season 11am-5pm. Cash only.)

Transportation to the island via ferry is quick and pleasant, if egregiously over-priced. Three ferry lines, **Shepler's** (☎800-828-6157), **Arnold Transit Co.** (☎800-542-8528), and **Star** (☎800-638-9892), leave Mackinaw City (in summer every 30min. M-Th and Su 8am-10pm, F-Sa 8am-11pm) and St. Ignace, though service from St. Ignace is slightly less frequent. (16min. round-trip $19, ages 5-12 $9.50, bikes and strollers $7.50. All lines charge identical rates.) The **Mackinac Island Tourism Bureau,** on Main St., has a free visitors guide. (☎800-454-5227; www.mackinacis-land.org. Open daily 9am-5pm.)

SCENIC DRIVE: NORTHERN MICHIGAN SHORE

Heading north from Traverse City, the northern shore of Lake Michigan skirts cherry orchards, moneyed resort towns, and broadleaf forests before meeting up with Lake Huron at the Straits of Mackinac. U.S. 31 follows the shoreline for some 65 mi. north of Traverse City, while Rte. 119 picks up the route at Petoskey and terminates in Cross Village. Drivers should expect to be both careful and patient on the 27 mi. stretch of Rte. 119 between Harbor Springs and Cross Village. Known as the **Tunnel of Trees,** this stretch of road is very narrow and twists through many sharp curves, keeping speeds down around 30 mph and giving drivers plenty of time to enjoy glimpses of the lake through the branches.

From Traverse City, U.S. 31 winds its way east along the southern shore of Grand Traverse Bay, and then passes through miles of cherry orchards just south of tiny **Acme.** For a more leisurely look at the orchards, turn right on Elk Lake Rd. as you pull into the town of **Elk Rapids,** 10 mi. north of Acme. Follow the road over the county line as far as Williamsburg and then double back to the main road. Just north of Elk Rapids, U.S. 31 threads its way across a narrow spit of land between Grand Traverse Bay to the west and Elk and Torch Lakes to the east; in Eastport, at the tip of Torch Lake. **Barnes County Park** beckons to swimmers and sunbathers with a quiet, sandy beach. The town of **Charlevoix** (SHAR-le-voy) is the next major stop along U.S. 31, and while the community once inspired Ernest Hemingway to pen his series of Nick Adams stories, today it is a yachting hub filled with upscale shopping. However, affordable accommodations can be found south of town. The west-facing rooms at **Courtside Motel ❷,** 1528 Bridge St., get warm in the afternoon, but A/C and in-room fridges manage to cool things down. (☎547-0505. In summer singles $50-65, doubles $65-99; low season $35/48. AmEx/D/MC/V.) Campers who don't mind going without showers and electricity can take one of 81 rustic sites on the shores of Lake Michigan at **Fisherman's Island State Park ❶,** on Bells Bay Rd., 5 mi. south of Charlevoix on U.S. 31. The park offers 5 mi. of virgin shoreline, and the bell-like whistle of the endangered piping plover can be heard near the water. (☎547-6641 or 800-447-2757. Sites $10. $8 per car, MI residents $6. MC/V.)

Charlevoix also serves as the gateway to **Beaver Island,** the most remote inhabited island in the Great Lakes and a paradise of loon-dotted shores and apple groves. **Ferries** depart from the dock located at 103 Bridge St. in Charlevoix. (☎547-2311 or 888-446-4095; www.bibco.com. 2hr., 1-4 per day. Round-trip $42, ages 5-12 $22; bikes $18.) The **Beaver Island Chamber of Commerce** is just north of the ferry dock and has info about campgrounds. (☎448-2505; www.beaverisland.org. Open M-F 9am-1pm; in summer open until 3pm.)

You can circle back to Charlevoix for a good night's rest, but in the meantime continue north for 16 mi. as far as **Petoskey,** a resort town that has developed into a hub for galleries and traditional crafts. **Crooked Tree Arts Center,** 461 E. Mitchell St., has led the way with rotating collections of visual art and music classes, as well as theater and dance performances. (☎347-4337; www.crookedtree.org. Galleries open M-F 9am-5pm, Sa 10am-4pm; in summer also Su noon-4pm. Art collections free. Call for student discounts on select performances.) In the heart of Petoskey's quaint **Gaslight District,** an arch-shaped mosaic of colorful coffee cups marks the entrance to the **Roast & Toast Cafe ❶,** 309 E. Lake St. A young, funky staff serves fresh sandwiches ($6-7) and coffee that's roasted on-site; bring your grub out to the patio on a sunny day. (☎347-7767. Free Wi-Fi. Open in summer daily 7am-9pm; low season M-Th 7am-7pm, F-Su 7am-8pm. AmEx/D/MC/V.) On Friday and Saturday nights, young people head out on the town to **The Upstairs Club,** 434 E. Mitchell St. (☎347-2739. Cover $5. 21+. Open F-Sa 10:30pm-1:30am.) Sunday nights during summertime mean taking in a set by the Jelly Roll Blues Band at the **Legs Inn,** on the left as Rte. 119 pulls into Cross Village. (☎526-2281;

www.legsinn.com. Check website for live music on other nights. Cover $5. Open mid-May to mid-Oct. M-Sa noon-9:30pm, Su noon-1am.) Early July also brings the earthy-crunchy ◪**Blissfest Music Festival** to the northern Michigan shore, as three days of folk music unfolds just east of Cross Village on an old farmstead. (☎348-7047; www.blissfest.org. 1-day ticket $30-40, weekend pass $80. Rustic camping $18 per night.) If these plans fall through, then there's no better way to finish a day on the Lake Michigan shore than watching the sunset from the gazebo at **Sunset Park Scenic Overlook,** just off Rte. 31 in Petoskey.

UPPER PENINSULA

Overlooked by natives and first-time visitors alike, Michigan's Upper Peninsula (UP) has vast stretches of unspoiled land and a low cost of living that makes it a must-see region for budget travelers. With only 20,000 people in **Marquette,** the peninsula's largest town, locals joke that they can always spot tourists because they're the only ones who tuck their purses under their arms when they go up to the salad bar. Sophistication may not be the UP's strong suit, but the opportunities for world-class hiking, kayaking, and snowshoeing more than make up for its spotty cell phone reception.

The UP's state parks give beginners plenty of opportunities for day hikes, while seasoned trailblazers make their way across Michigan's section of the **North Country Trail,** a scenic trail extending from New York to North Dakota. The **North Country Trail Association,** 229 E. Main St., Lowell MI 49331 (☎866-445-3628; www.north-countrytrail.org), provides details on the path. At its best, Michigan's fall foliage can rival New England's vivid colors, making autumn an appealing time to hike the UP. In the winter, cross-country skiers and snowmobilers replace hikers as layers of snow blanket the trails. After the ice thaws, dozens of pristine rivers beckon canoers. Those who heed the call of the water should contact the **Michigan Association of Paddlesport Providers,** 801 S. Garfield Ave., Traverse City MI 49686 (☎231-947-3345; www.michigancanoe.com), for canoeing tips.

Lodging is fairly inexpensive throughout the UP, and outside the major tourist spots motel rooms start at around $30. The peninsula is littered with **campgrounds.** (Reservations at National Forest sites: ☎877-444-6777; www.reserveusa.com. Reservations at state parks: ☎800-447-2757; www.michigan.gov/dnr.) Bring extra blankets, as temperatures here can drop to 50°F or lower, even in July. Keep in mind that the counties of the UP that border Wisconsin are on Central Time, while the northern counties are on Eastern Time. And be sure to save room for a **pastie** (PASS-tee) during your stay; the meat pie was imported by Cornish miners during the 19th century. Tourists tend to drown the concoction in brown gravy, but ask for a bottle of ketchup if you want to pass for a local.

▓ PRACTICAL INFORMATION

Michigan Travel Centers surround the Upper Peninsula at its six main entry points: **Ironwood,** 801 W. Cloverland Dr. (☎932-3330; open daily June-Aug. 8am-6pm, Sept.-May 8am-4pm); **Iron Mountain,** 618 S. Stephenson Ave. (☎774-4201; open daily June-Aug. 7am-5pm, Sept.-May 9am-5pm); **Marquette,** 2201 U.S. 41 S (☎249-9066; open daily June-Aug. 9am-5pm, Sept.-May 9am-5pm); **Menominee,** 1343 10th Ave. (☎863-6496; open daily 8am-6pm); **Saint Ignace,** on I-75 N north of the Mackinac Bridge (☎643-6979; open daily June-Aug. 8am-6pm, Sept.-May 9am-5pm); and **Sault Sainte Marie,** 843 Portage Ave. (☎632-8242; open daily 9am-7pm). The **Upper Peninsula Travel and Recreation Association** (☎774-5190 or 800-562-7134; www.uptravel.com; info line staffed M-F 8am-4:30pm) publishes the invaluable *Upper Peninsula*

Travel Planner. For additional help planning a trip in the area, write or call the **USDA Forest Service** in the Hiawatha National Forest, 2727 N. Lincoln Rd., Escanaba 49829 (☎786-4062).

SAULT SAINTE MARIE   ☎906

The shipping industry has long been the hallmark of gritty Sault ("Soo") Ste. Marie, although an emerging tourist industry is gussying up the pedestrian-friendly downtown. St. Mary's River, the only waterway linking Lake Superior to the other Great Lakes, drops 21 vertical ft. over 1 mi. here, and Ojibwe traders were once forced to carry their canoes and skirt the rocky rapids on land. In 1853, entrepreneurs built the first modern canal between the lakes, and today more than 11,000 vessels make their way through the three locks each year. This volume of commercial traffic has also brought Sault Ste. Marie under the scrutiny of the Department of Homeland Security; don't mistake a certain wariness to answer questions about the locks as unfriendliness on the part of locals.

There are a number of ways to watch ships passing through the locks. **Soo Locks Park,** which faces E. Portage Ave., gives visitors a good view of the 1000 ft. freighters that make their way through the southernmost MacArthur lock. As many as 15 ships pass through within a 24hr. period. (☎253-9101. Park open 8am-midnight. Visitors Center open May-Nov. daily 8am-8pm.) On **Engineers' Day,** the last Friday in June, the public can venture behind the fence that normally cordons off the locks and see the passing ships up close. For travelers with other plans in late June, a 2hr. **Soo Locks Boat Tour** leaves from both 515 and 1157 E. Portage Ave., and explains the mechanics of the locks' operation even as it gets lifted up to the level of the lake. (☎632-6301 or 800-432-6301; www.soolocks.com. Tours leave every hr. July-Aug. 9am-5pm, at least 3 per day mid-May to June and Sept. to mid-Oct. $19.50, ages 4-12 $9.50, under 4 free. Call ahead for specific dock.) Diehard history buffs might take time to ascend the **Tower of History,** 326 E. Portage Ave., but even stubborn landlubbers should be sure to visit the ☒**Museum Ship Valley Camp,** on the waterfront, at the end of Johnston St. Wander the decks of a 1917 steam-powered freighter, peering into the tiny quarters of the ship's crew and surveying the mangled lifeboats that washed ashore after the sinking of the *Edmund Fitzgerald.* (☎632-3658. Open daily mid-May to June 10am-5pm; July-late Aug. 10am-7pm; late Aug.-Sept. 10am-6pm; early Oct. 10am-5pm. $9, ages 6-16 $4.50, under 6 free.)

Chain motels line the I-75 Business Spur, and the most reasonable rates can be found closer to the downtown. Locals head to **Penny's Kitchen ❶,** 112 W. Spruce St., for fresh sandwiches ($6-7) and thick slices of warm raspberry pie ($3.25). Three computers against the back wall provide free Internet access for customers. (☎632-1232. Open M-F 7am-6pm, Sa 8am-5pm. AmEx/D/MC/V.) A string of bars on E. Portage Ave. gets lively during the school year, when students from Lake Superior State University trot downhill for dance and drink.

MIDDLE OF THE PENINSULA   ☎906

The West Unit of the **Hiawatha National Forest** runs like a thick green stripe down the middle of the peninsula, offering hiking and cross-country skiing opportunities all the way from the Superior to the Michigan lakeshores. The **Visitors Center,** at the junction of Rte. 28 and County Rte. H-58 in **Munising,** serves as the primary gateway to the forest and helps administer over a dozen rustic **campsites ❶,** south of town on County Rte. 13. (☎387-3700, reservations at all National Forest Service sites ☎877-444-6777. Open mid-May to mid-Oct. daily 8am-6pm; mid-Oct. to mid-May M-Sa 9am-5pm. Pit toilets, fire rings, well water. Campsites open mid-May to Sept. Sites $10-40.) The Munising Visitors Center also administers the remarkable **Pictured Rocks National Lakeshore,** where Lake Superior's waters—saturated with copper, manganese, and iron oxide—paint the sandstone cliffs with multicolored bands. Prices are steep, but the **Pictured Rocks Boat Cruise,** at the city dock in Munising, gives the best view of the cliffs. (☎387-2379; www.picturedrocks.com. Tours leave daily July to mid-Aug. every hr. 9am-5pm; June and mid-Aug. to mid-Oct. 10am, 1 and 4pm. 3hr. tour $31, ages 6-12 $13, under 6 free.)

Four miles east of Munising on County Rte. 58, Miner's Castle Rd. leads up to the **Miner's Castle Overlook,** affording the best view of the cliffs accessible from the road. Miner's Castle Rd. also has the trailhead to **Miner's Falls,** a 60 ft. cascade accessible by a 10min. hike down a gravel trail lined with sugar maples and yellow birch. More intrepid hikers can ogle the colorful cliffs along Lake Superior via the 9 mi. **Chapel Basin loop.** The route takes approximately 5hr. to complete, and the trailhead can be found at the end of unpaved Chapel Rd., off of County Rte. 58 in Melstrand. Rte. 58 is paved as far east as Melstrand, but then reverts to primitive conditions until the **Log Slide Overlook,** west of Grand Marais. The unpaved sections of bumpy gravel road can be an adventure, but they can also be a precursor to a front-end alignment; conditions are best after the road is graded in the spring. For a quicker and less jarring route from Munising to Grand Marais, go east on Rte. 28, then north on Rte. 77. The white sands of **Twelvemile Beach** are most easily accessed from the Grand Marais end of Rte. 58, and self-registered rustic **campsites** ❶ go for $12. (Pit toilets, well water. Open May-Oct. Cash only.)

For those campers looking to venture farther off the beaten path, **backcountry camping permits** ❶ are available from the Munising Visitors Center (p. 511) or the **Grand Sable Visitors Center,** 3 mi. west of Grand Marais on Rte. 58. (☎494-2660. Open mid-May to early Oct. daily 9am-5pm. Reservations must be made 2 weeks in advance. Permits $4 per person; group reservation fee $15.) Inexpensive motels are plentiful in Newberry, 1hr. east of Munising on Rte. 28 and 30min. south of **Tahquamenon Falls State Park** (say "phenomenon", and then substitute in the right consonants). The ruddy waters of the Upper Falls take their color from tannin leached out of tree roots. The waterfall is one of the largest east of the Mississippi River. Hike 4 mi. down to the burbling Lower Falls, where the observation deck at the boardwalk gets you close enough to feel the spray on your face. (☎492-3415. Open daily May-Oct. 8am-10pm; Nov.-Apr. 8am-4:30pm. Cars $8 per day, $29 per year; MI residents $6/24.)

KEWEENAW PENINSULA   ☎906

Arching its way north into Lake Superior, the Keweenaw (KEE-wa-naw) Peninsula is possibly the wildest quadrant of the UP. The copper mine and mill industries once put a chicken in every family's pot, but when labor unrest and new technologies started to erode the bottom line, Big Copper up and left. A tourist economy has started to emerge, but thus far, the peninsula's geographical isolation has conspired to leave it largely undeveloped.

The **Porcupine Mountain Wilderness State Park** ❶, affectionately known as "The Porkies," hugs Lake Superior at the base of the peninsula, 18 mi. west of **Ontonagon** on Rte. 107. (☎800-447-2757; www.michigan.gov/dnr. Backcountry sites and outpost sites with outhouses $14; sites with toilets, showers, and electricity at Union Bay $21. Call the park directly at ☎885-5275 for 2- to 8-person cabins, $60. Lakeside cabins come with rowboats for use within the park; reserve well in advance.) The **Visitors Center** on S. Boundary Rd. near the junction of Rte. 107, provides required vehicle permits good for all Michigan state parks. (☎885-5208. Open mid-May to mid-Oct. daily 10am-8pm. Permits $8 per week, MI residents $6; $29/24 per year.) Eight miles inside the park on Rte. 107, the **Lake of the Clouds** scenic overlook opens up on a stunning mountain lake nestled in the Big Carp River valley. **Summit Peak,** off S. Boundary Rd., is the highest point in the park, and the observation tower affords an expansive view of Michigan's largest continuous expanse of undisturbed forest. 13 mi. farther to the end of S. Boundary Rd. are the three roaring waterfalls at **Presque Isle.** Casual hikers can pick up the 4 mi. **Union Spring Trail** just south of the Visitors Center, while more experienced hikers can make a 12 mi. loop through the old growth forest found on the **Big Carp River, Correction Line,** and **North Mirror Lake Trails.**

The college towns of **Houghton** and **Hancock** link the Porkies to the rest of the peninsula. During January, Houghton's Michigan Technological University campus is taken over by the construction of 40 ft. **snow sculptures,** which are judged during the festivities of early February's Winter Carnival. To the east in Lake Linden, the **Houghton County Historical Museum** pieces together artifacts from the copper boom and gives visitors a ride on a restored steam locomotive. (☎296-4121; www.houghtonhistory.com. Open June-Sept. daily 10am-4pm. $8, seniors and students $5, under 12 free.) One of the river dredges used by the Quincy Mining Company is still visible from Rte. 26 as it passes through Hubble. Today **Quincy Mine Hoist and Underground Mine,** just north of Hancock on Rte. 41, offers 2hr. tours that descend deep into the old mine shafts. (☎482-3101; www.quincymine.com. Open daily 9:30am-5pm. Tours depart less frequently in low season. Tours $15, seniors $14, ages 6-12 $8, under 6 free.) Houghton and Hancock are also home to an enclave of fiercely proud Finns, and locals head to **Suomi ❶,** 54 Huron St. in downtown Houghton, for pannukakku ($3.65), a thick breakfast custard served with raspberry jam and sweet toast. (☎482-3220. Entrees $4-8. Open M-Sa 6am-3pm, Su 7am-2pm. Cash only.) Farther north, in Calumet, a yellowing 1906 mural overlooks the antique wooden bar at **Michigan House Cafe & Brewpub ❸,** 300 6th St., five blocks off of Rte. 41. Sink your teeth into a charbroiled Black Angus burger ($8) and wash it down with a mug of in-house Oatmeal Espresso stout ($3.50), the most northerly brew in Michigan. (☎337-1910. Entrees $7-12. Occasional live music F-Sa; call for schedule. Open M-Tu and Th-Sa 11:30am-10pm, Su noon-9pm. D/MC/V.) There's strong coffee and free Internet (three computer terminals and Wi-Fi) at **Cyberia Cafe ❶,** 524 Sheldon Ave. (☎482-2233. Espresso drinks $1.25-3.25.) Eight miles south of Calumet on Rte. 203, **McLain State Park ❶** offers campsites in close proximity to a 2 mi. agate beach and a small lighthouse at the end of a pebbly sandbar. (Reservations ☎482-0278 or 800-447-2757. 10 walk-in sites available. 103 sites with electricity $26; cabins $45-60. $8 per car, MI residents $6.)

Rte. 41 is the most direct route to the northern tip of the peninsula, although drivers and bikers can take Rte. 26, off Rte. 41, to wind their way through lakeside villages and desolate ghost towns where copper miners once toiled. Rising over 1300 ft. above sea level, the breathtaking **Brockway Mountain Drive** (6 mi.), between Eagle Harbor and Copper Harbor, presents a panoramic view of the pine-covered peaks and sloping valleys of the Upper Peninsula. In **Copper Harbor,** the northernmost town in the entire state of Michigan, the **Keweenaw Adventure Company,** 155 Gratiot St., provides kayaks and mountain bikes to those who wish to explore Keweenaw's wild side. (☎289-4303. 2½hr. guided kayak tours depart daily 9:30am, 1, 7:30pm. Register 30min. before departure. $33. Full day kayak rental $45. Bike rentals $38 per half-day, $50 per full day.)

ILLINOIS

At first glance, Illinois seems like a state with dual personalities. In the northern part of the state, Chicago gleams as a Midwestern metropolis with top-notch museums, stunning architecture, and suburban sprawl stretching all the way into two neighboring states. Once removed from suburbia, a second Illinois—the

"Land of Lincoln"—reaches outward with endless miles of corn fields and small towns. In its politics and its culture, Illinois is a compromise between these contrasting landscapes and can claim a mix of urban chic and rural values as perhaps no other state can.

⁊ PRACTICAL INFORMATION

Capital: Springfield.

Visitor Info: Chicago Cultural Center, 77 E. Randolph St., Chicago 60607. (☎800-226-6632; www.enjoyillinois.com). Springfield Convention and Visitors Bureau, 109 N. 7th St. (☎800-545-7300; www.visit-springfieldillinois.com). Open M-F 8:30am-5pm.

Postal Abbreviation: IL. **Sales Tax:** 6.25-9.25%, depending on the city.

CHICAGO   ☎312

Chicagoans take pride in their city's mix of cosmopolitan sophistication and Midwestern accessibility. Known in the 20s as a center for railroads, gangsters and blue-collar labor, Chicago had cleaned up municipal corruption and lost more than half of its blue collar jobs by 1980. Contrasting neighborhoods converge on one another with Swedish delis next to Turkish bakeries and public housing projects near upscale apartments. Now an intellectual and financial hub, Chicago still fancies itself a haven for the working man and woman.

⌐ INTERCITY TRANSPORTATION

Airports: O'Hare International (**ORD;** ☎773-686-2200; www.ohare.com), off I-90. Although O'Hare is only 18 mi. away, the drive from downtown can take up to 2hr., depending on traffic. The cheapest and most convenient route to the city center is on the Blue Line of Chicago's rapid transit system, called "the El." It runs between the Airport El station and downtown (40-60min., 24hr., $1.75). **Midway Airport** (**MDW;** ☎773-838-0600), on the western edge of the South Side, often offers cheaper flights. To get downtown, take the El's Orange Line from the Midway stop.

Continental Airport Express (☎888-284-3826; www.airportexpress.com). Connects to downtown hotels from O'Hare (45-60min., daily every 10-15min. 4am-11:30pm, $25) and Midway (30-45min., daily every 15min. 4am-10:30pm, $20).

Trains: Amtrak, Union Station, 225 S. Canal St. (☎655-2101; www.amtrak.com), at Adams St. just west of the Loop. Amtrak's nationwide hub. From O'Hare, take the Blue Line El to Clinton (1hr.) and then walk 2 blocks north on Clinton. A number of CTA buses also make stops at the station, including buses #1, 60, 125, 126, 151, and 156. Station open daily 5:30am-10:30pm; tickets sold daily 6am-10pm. To: **Detroit** (6½hr., 3 per day, $27-38); (1½hr., 7 per day, $21); **New York City** (21-28hr., 4-5 per day, $101-126); **St. Louis** (5½hr., 3-5 per day, $22-62).

Buses: Greyhound, 630 W. Harrison St. (☎408-5800; www.greyhound.com), at Jefferson and Desplaines Ave. Take the El to Linton, or buses #60, 125, 156, or 157 to the terminal. Station open 24hr.; tickets sold 24hr. To **Detroit** (7hr., 5 per day, $34), **Indianapolis** (3½-4½hr., 8 per day, $31.50), and **Milwaukee** (2hr., 9 per day, $14). **Van Galder** in Union Station (☎608-752-5407 or 800-747-0994; www.vangalderbus.com) runs to **Madison** (3-4hr., 4 per day, $26).

Chicago

🏠 ACCOMMODATIONS
International House, **9**
Chicago International
Hostel, **1**

🍎 FOOD
Ann Sather, **4**
Dixie Kitchen &
Bait Shop, **8**
Harold's Chicken
Shack, **6**
Kopi, A Traveler's Cafe, **2**
Reza's, **3**
Veggies to Go, **7**

🍸 NIGHTLIFE
The Green Mill, **5**

MORTON GROVE

SKOKIE

NILES

■ Northwestern
University

EVANSTON

N. Harlem Ave.

94

N. Skokie Blvd.

N. Crawford Ave.

N. McCormick Blvd.

N. Shore Channel

Chicago Ave.

Sheridan Rd.

Rogers
Park

LINCOLNWOOD

N. Lincoln Ave.

Loyola University
of Chicago

TO ✈ O'HARE
INT'L. AIRPORT
(4mi)

90

Forest
Preserve

N. Nelson Ave.

W. Devon Ave.

W. Peterson Ave.

W. Foster Ave.

N. Western Ave.

N. Ashland Ave.

Andersonville

❸ ❷

❹ 🍎 ❺

N. Lake Shore Dr.

HARWOOD
HEIGHTS

W. Lawrence Ave.

W. Montrose Ave.

W. Irving Park Rd.

W. Addison St.

W. Belmont Ave.

W. Fullerton St.

N. Milwaukee Ave.

Irving Park

Uptown

Wrigleyville

Lakeview

Central Ave.

S. Laramie Ave.

S. Cicero Ave.

W. Armitage Ave.

N. Br. Chicago River

90
94

SEE "NORTHSIDE,"
p. 521

Lincoln
Park

0   2 miles

0   2 kilometers

Frank Lloyd Wright
House and Studio

W. North Ave.

W. Division Ave.

W. Chicago Ave.

W. Lake St.

Bucktown
Wicker Park

Humboldt
Park

W. Grand Ave.

SEE "BUCKTOWN/
WICKER PARK,"
p. 519

Gold Coast

SEE "DOWNTOWN
CHICAGO," p. 517

Near North

N

LG

Austin

ⓘ

Ernest Hemingway
Birthplace and Museum

River
North

Chicago River

Lake Michigan

OAK PARK

W. Washington St.

Garfield
Park

Greektown

290

Congress Pkwy.

United Center ■

Little Italy

Hull
House

Grant
Park

W. Roosevelt Rd.

Cook County
Hospital ✚

University of Illinois
at Chicago

Soldier Field ■

CICERO

Douglas
Park

Chicago River

BERWYN

W. Cermak Rd.

S. Archer Ave.

Pilsen

South Side

Chinatown

Lake Shore Dr.

Des Plaines River

W. 31st St.

W. Pershing Rd.

Chicago Sanitary and Ship Canal

55

Bridgeport

Comiskey Park ■

Burnham
Park

Back of
the Yards

W. 43rd St.

W. 47th St.

W. 51st St.

S. Michigan Ave.

90
94

DuSable Museum of
African-American History

❻ ❼ ❽

Roble
House

Museum of Science
and Industry

W. 55th St.

University of
Chicago ■

❾

Jackson
Park

BEDFORD PARK

Midway
Airport ✈

Englewood

Hyde Park

E. 67th St.

W. 63rd St.

BURBANK

Marquette
Park

S. Damen Ave.

S. Ashland Ave.

S. Halsted St.

Oriental
Institute 🏛

E. 71st St.

E. 75th St.

S. Shore Dr.

W. 79th St.

S. Cicero Ave.

S. Western Ave.

S. Kedzie Ave.

S. Pulaski Rd.

90

S. Cottage Grove Ave.

S. Martin L. King Jr. Dr.

S. Chicago Ave.

S. Stony Island Ave.

OAK LAWN

W. 87th St.

W. 95th St.

294

S. Harlem Ave.

S. Central Ave.

S. Ridgeland Dr.

Dan
Ryan
Woods

TO INDIANA DUNES
STATE PARK (38mi)

Calumet River

WORTH

EVERGREEN
PARK

W. 103rd St.

W. 111th St.

Morgan
Park

57

Pullman

94

Lake
Calumet

William W. Powers
State Conservation Area

Calumet Sag Channel

ALSIP

S. Crawford Ave.

⚒ ORIENTATION

Chicago dominates the entire northeastern corner of Illinois, running along 29 mi. of the southwest Lake Michigan shorefront. Almost all roads lead to Chicago; the city sits at the center of a web of interstates, rail lines, and airplane routes; most cross-country traffic swings through the city. Chicago's streets are laid out in straight lines forming a grid. The grid makes navigating the city straightforward whether by car or on foot. The grid system's blocks are large, with eight blocks to a mile. A good map is essential for navigating Chicago's extensive mass transit system; pick up a free one at the tourist office or any CTA (Chicago Transit Authority) station. At the city's center is the **Loop** (p. 524), Chicago's downtown business district and the public transit system's hub. Directions in *Let's Go* are from downtown, unless otherwise noted. The Loop is bounded loosely by the Chicago River to the north and west, Wabash Ave. to the east, and Congress Pkwy. to the south. South of the Loop, east-west street numbers increase toward the south. Many ethnic neighborhoods lie in this area (see **Neighborhoods,** p. 516), but travelers should avoid the struggling **South Side.** Most of the city's best spots for food and nightlife jam into the first few miles north of the Loop. Beware the 45 mph speed limit on **Lake Shore Drive,** a scenic freeway hugging Lake Michigan that offers express north-south connections.

To avoid driving and parking in the city, daytrippers can leave their cars in one of the suburban park-and-ride lots ($2 per day); call CTA (p. 518) for info. Parking downtown costs around $8-15 per day. Check out the lots west of the South Loop and across the canal from the **Sears Tower** (p. 524) for the best deals.

NEIGHBORHOODS

Diverse, distinctive, and ethnically and economically homogenous neighborhoods make up the Windy City. North of the Loop, LaSalle Dr. loosely defines the west edge of the posh **Near North** area; here, most activity is centered along the Magnificent Mile of Michigan Ave. between the Chicago River and Oak St. A trendy restaurant and nightlife district, **River North** lines N. Clark St., just north of the Loop and west of Michigan Ave. The primarily residential Gold Coast shimmers on N. Lake Shore Dr. between Oak St. and North Ave. The **Bucktown/Wicker Park** area, at the intersection of North, Damen, and Milwaukee Ave., is the place to be for artsy, cutting-edge cafes and nightlife. **Lincoln Park** revolves around the junction of N. Clark St., Lincoln Ave., and Halsted St. To the north, near the 3000 block of N. Clark St. and N. Halsted St., sits **Lakeview,** a gay-friendly area teeming with food and nightlife that becomes **Wrigleyville** in the 4000 block. **Andersonville,** 5 mi. farther up N. Clark St. north of Foster Ave., is the center of the Swedish community, though immigrants from Asia and the Middle East have recently settled here.

> **LET'S NOT GO.** It is a good idea to stay within the boundaries of tourist maps. Aside from small pockets such as Hyde Park and the University of Chicago, areas south of the loop and west of the little ethnic enclaves are mostly industrial or residential and pose a safety threat to the unwary tourist. **Cabrini Green** (bounded by W. Armitage Ave. on the north, W. Chicago Ave. on the south, Sedgwick St. on the east, and Halsted St. on the west) was once the site of an infamously dangerous public housing development and sits within tourist map borders. The neighborhood is now part of a city experiment in mixed-income housing and is surrounded by redeveloped areas, but travelers should still be cautious.

Downtown Chicago

🏠 ACCOMMODATIONS

Hostelling International–
Chicago (HI), **10**

🍴 FOOD

Al's Italian Beef, **1**
Artopolis, **8**
Billy Goat's Tavern, **4**
Frontera Grill, **3**

Orange, **11**
Pegasus, **7**
Gold Coast Dogs, **5**
Lou Mitchell's, **9**
The Parthenon, **6**

🍸 NIGHTLIFE

Funky Buddha
Lounge, **2**

The near south and west sides are filled with other vibrant ethnic districts. While much of the German community has scattered, the beer halls and restaurants in the 3000 and 4000 blocks of N. Lincoln Ave. keep local German culture alive. The former residents of **Greektown** have also moved, but S. Halsted St. still houses authentic Greek restaurants. This area is bustling and generally safe until the restaurants close, at which point tourists wisely clear out. Although nearby **Little Italy** has fallen prey to the encroachments of the **University of Illinois at Chicago (UIC),** good dining options remain. Jewish and Indian enclaves center on Devon Ave., from Western Ave. to the Chicago River. The **Pilsen** neighborhood, around 18th St., offers a glimpse of Mexico and a developing art community. Chicago's Polish population is the largest of any city outside of Warsaw; those seeking Polish cuisine should go to N. Milwaukee Ave. between blocks 2800 and 3100.

☐ LOCAL TRANSPORTATION

Public Transit: The **Chicago Transit Authority (CTA),** 567 W. Lake (☎888-968-7282; www.transitchicago.com), runs efficient trains, subways, and buses. The **elevated rapid transit train system,** called the **El,** encircles the Loop. The El operates 24hr., but check ahead for schedules, as late-night service is infrequent. Some buses do not run all night; call the CTA for schedules and routes. Many routes are "express," and different routes may run along the same track. Helpful CTA maps are available at many stations and at the Chicago Visitor Information Center. Train and bus fare $1.75; express routes $2. Transfers ($0.25) allow for up to 2 more rides on different routes during the 2hr. after purchase. Buy **transit cards** (min. $1.75) for fares and transfers at all CTA stations, on the Internet, and at some museums. CTA also offers a variety of consecutive-day passes for tourists, available at airports and Amtrak stations ($5-18, depending on length of pass). On Sa from early May to late Oct., a **Loop Tour Train** departs on a free 40min. elevated tour of the downtown area (pick up tickets at the **Chicago Cultural Center;** see p. 518. Tours start at 10am and 10:40am).

Commuter Rail: METRA, 547 W. Jackson St. (M-F 8am-5pm ☎322-6777, Sa-Su ☎836-7000; www.metrarail.com). Distributes free maps and schedules for its extensive rail network of 12 rail lines and 4 downtown stations. Suburban stations open M-F 5am-1pm; downtown stations M-Su 6am-1pm. Fare $2-10.35, depending on distance.

Suburban Bus: PACE (☎847-364-7223; www.pacebus.com). Runs the suburban bus system. Many free or cheap shuttle services run throughout the Loop.

Taxi: Yellow Cab, ☎829-4222; www.yellowcabchicago.com. **Flash Cab,** ☎773-561-4444.

Car Rental: Dollar Rent-a-Car (☎800-800-3665; www.dollar.com), at O'Hare and Midway. 21+ with major credit card. Under 25 surcharge $25 per day.

Bike Rental: McDonald's Cylce Center (☎888-245-3929; www.bikechicago.com), 239 E. Randolph St. On the NE corner of Millenium Park. Offers bike tours of the lakefront and historic Chicago neighborhoods. Bikes $10 per day for 4 days; lock included. Tours M-F $30; Sa-Su $40. Open in summer M-F 6:30am-8pm, Sa-Su 8am-8pm; spring and fall open M-F 6:30am-7pm, Sa-Su 10am-6pm; winter M-F 6:30am-6:30pm.

☐ PRACTICAL INFORMATION

Visitor Info: Chicago Cultural Center , 77 E. Randolph St. (☎744 6630; www.chicagoculturalcenter.org), at Michigan Ave. Houses a Visitor Information Center with maps and brochures. Take a peek at the building's free art galleries before heading out into the city. Open M-F 10am-6pm, Sa 10am-5pm, Su 11am-6pm. **Water Works Visitors Center,** 163 E. Pearson St. at Michigan Ave., in the Water Tower Pumping Station. Open daily 7:30am-7pm. **Visitor hotline,** ☎877-244-2246. 24hr.

Bucktown and Wicker Park

🍎 FOOD
Alliance Bakery & Cafe, **5**
Pontiac Cafe, **3**
The Smoke Daddy, **4**

🎵 NIGHTLIFE
Hideout, **1**
Subterranean, **2**

GLBT Resources: Gay and Lesbian Hotline, ☎773-929-4357. Operates daily 8am-10pm. For current info on events and nightlife, pick up the Windy City Times or Gay Chicago at Lakeview's **Unabridged Books,** 3251 N. Broadway (☎773-883-9119). Open M-F 10am-9pm Sa-Su 10am-7pm. For the most comprehensive listings of GLBT events online go to www.chicagopride.com.

Medical Services: Northwestern Memorial Hospital, 251 E. Huron St. (☎926-2000), near Michigan Ave. **Emergency division,** 250 E. Erie St. (☎926-5188). Open 24hr.

Internet Access: Free at the **Chicago Public Library.** Main branch at 400 S. State St. (☎747-4999), at Congress. Check for other locations at www.chipublib.org. Open M-Th 9am-7pm, F-Sa 9am-5pm, Su 1-5pm.

Post Office: 433 W. Harrison St. (☎800-275-8777), at the Chicago River. Open M-Sa 8am-5pm. **Postal Code:** 60607. **Area Code:** 312 (downtown) or 773 (elsewhere in Chicago); 708, 630, or 847 (outside the city limits). In text, 312 unless otherwise noted.

🏠 ACCOMMODATIONS

Find cheap beds at one of Chicago's three hostels or in the moderately priced motels on **Lincoln Avenue** in Lincoln Park. **At Home Inn Chicago** (☎800-375-7084) offers a reservation and referral service for many downtown B&Bs. Most have a two-night minimum stay, and rooms average $120. Travelers should be aware of Chicago's 15% tax on most accommodation rates.

Arlington House, 616 W. Arlington Pl. (☎ 773-929-5380; www.arlingtonhouse.com). Take the El Red or Blue to Fullerton, walk 3 blocks east on Fullerton, then turn left on Orchard and right on Arlington. Located on a quiet residential street in trendy Lincoln Park, this tidy and inexpensive hostel is a 10min. walk from the dance clubs and bars that line nearby N. Halstead St. Free Internet. Kitchen, TV room, coin-operated laundry. Check-out 11am. Dorms $29; doubles with shared bath $64, with private bath $78. MC/V. ❶

Hostelling International—Chicago (HI), 24 E. Congress Pkwy. (☎ 360-0300; www.hichicago.org), off Wabash Ave. in the South Loop. Large hostel with tidy, sparsely decorated rooms. Vibrant and friendly staff make up for the lack of cool decor. Frequent and varied excursions into Chicago's many neighborhoods and the nearby Loop. Internet $2 per 20min. Kitchen and coin-op laundry. Check-out 11am. Reservations recommended. 10-bed dorms $35, 6-bed dorms $39. HI members $3 discount. MC/V. ❷

Chicago International Hostel, 6318 North Winthrop Ave. (☎ 773-262-1011; www.chicagointernationalhostel.com), just south of the Loyola University campus. Take the El Red to Granville, turn right out of the station, and then left on Winthrop. Travelers willing to make the 40min. train ride from the loop to reach this hostel enjoy its easy-going staff and low prices. Internet $4 per hr. Laundry and kitchen. Lockout 11am-2pm. Check-out 9:30am. Reservations for private rooms should be made in advance online. Dorms $25.50; doubles $40-86. MC/V. ❶

International House, 1414 E. 59th St. (☎ 773-753-2270), in Hyde Park, off Lake Shore Dr. Take the METRA South Shore Line to 59th St. and walk 1 block west. On the grounds of the University of Chicago; avoid walking off-campus at night. All dorm rooms are singles and come with a desk, bureau, and linens. Guest rooms are larger with TVs. Communal bathrooms. Wi-Fi $7 per day. Must have valid student ID. Dorms $57; guest suites $62. Call for details. ❸

🞂 FOOD

Chicago is best known as the home of the deep dish pizza, but this reputation does little justice to the city's independent cafes, ethnic eateries, and upscale restaurants. From old-fashioned diners downtown to trendy Thai tapas bars in Lakeview, Chicago boasts a dizzyingly diverse array of dining options other than pizza. One of the best guides to city dining is the monthly *Chicago* magazine, which includes an extensive restaurant section indexed by price, cuisine, and quality. It can be found at tourist offices and newsstands everywhere.

THE LOOP

As Chicago's historic business district, the Loop once teemed with elegant steakhouses and all-American diners. Today, dime-a-dozen fast-food chains dominate the culinary landscape, although there are a handful of notable exceptions. The best bet for cheap eats in the pricey city center is to buy groceries at **Jewel-Osco,** 1224 S. Wabash (☎ 663-4646).

🞖 **Lou Mitchell's,** 565 W. Jackson Blvd. (☎ 939-3111), 2 blocks west of the Sears Tower. Situated at the jumping-off point of historic Route 66, this old-school diner has been stuffing faithful customers for more than 80 years. Start the day with "meltaway pancakes" that take up the whole plate ($6) or hearty omelets served simmering in the skillet ($8-9). Open M-Sa 5:30am-3pm, Su 7am-3pm. Cash only. ❷

Orange, 75 W. Harrison St. (☎ 773-549-4400), between S. Clarke St. and S. Federal St. Bright and airy with high ceilings and packed tables, Orange specializes in playfully inventive brunch and breakfast dishes such as green eggs and ham ($9) and eggs

Northside

▲ ACCOMMODATIONS
Arlington House, **8**

☕ FOOD
Bourgeois Pig, **9**
Cozy Noodles
  & Rice, **1**
Mia Francesca, **3**
Penny's Noodle Shop, **6**
Sura, **5**

🍸 NIGHTLIFE
Hydrate, **2**
Kingston Mines, **7**
Smart Bar, **4**

benedict caprese (with basil-infused hollandaise sauce, $9). Signature dish is Frushi (sushi with fruit instead of fish; 2 for $3.50). Open M-F 8am-2pm, Sa-Su 8am-3pm. ❷

Gold Coast Dogs, 159 N. Wabash Ave. (☎917-1677), located between Randolph and Lake St. This Chicago-based chain is favored by locals for serving up hot dogs Second City style: on a poppy-seed bun, topped with hot peppers, tomato, celery salt, and a long pickle spear. Magnificent Dog $2.50. Open M-F 9:30am-8pm, Sa 10am-6pm, Su 11am-5pm. Cash only. ❶

RIVER NORTH

River North houses some of the trendiest eateries in town, as well as Chicago's famous pizzerias.

▨ Billy Goat's Tavern, 430 N. Michigan Ave. (☎222-1525), on the lower level of Michigan Ave. Don't let the curt service make you angry. This no-frills Chicago institution is famous for its gruff waitstaff. Grab a "cheezeborger" ($3) from the grill and watch some sports with the regulars at the bar. Beer $3.50. Open M-F and Su 6am-2am, Sa 10am-3am. Cash only. ❶

Frontera Grill, 445 N. Clark St. (☎661-1434), between Illinois and Hubbard St. Take the El Red Line to Grand. When locals are willing to wait 1½hr. for a table, you know that something good must be cooking. Frontera is widely acclaimed for its delicate, sophisticated approach to Mexican cuisine, which uses fresh seasonal ingredients in superb entrees (lunch $11-23; dinner $17-27). Make your own tacos ($15) at lunch. Open Tu 11:30am-2:30pm and 5:20-10pm, W-Th 11:30am-2:30pm and 5-10pm, F 11:30am-2:30pm and 5-11pm, Sa 10:30am-2:30pm and 5-11pm. AmEx/D/MC/V. ❹

Al's Italian Beef, 169 W. Ontario (☎943-3222), at Wells. Featuring layers of beef on top of a huge sausage, an Italian beef sandwich ($5) is a Chicago institution set to expand your waistline. Open M-Th 10am-midnight, F-Sa 10am-3am, Su 11am-10pm. AmEx/D/MC/V. ❶

SOUTH SIDE

The **South Side** is home to the city's best and cheapest soul food with healthy portions of greasy ribs, fried chicken, and collard greens. Eateries around the University of Chicago cluster on 53rd street east of Ellis Ave. Be very careful south of the Loop, though, especially after dark. **Wicker Park,** to the north, is another safer option for soul food.

Dixie Kitchen & Bait Shop, 5225A S. Harper St. (☎773-363-4943). Take bus #6 to 51st and Lake Park, walk 2 blocks south, and cut through the parking lot on the right. You'll see this local hot spot at the back. Feast on an oyster po' boy sandwich smeared with New Orleans remoulade ($9.25), and wash it down with a Purple Haze beer ($3.75). Open M-Th and Su 11am-10pm, F-Sa 11am-11pm. AmEx/D/MC/V. ❷

Veggies To Go, 1375 E. 53rd St. (☎773-667-8344), on the South Side. Take bus #6. For vegetarians who have a hankering for soul food, try the vegetarian riblet ($5) at this vegan-friendly sandwich and smoothie shop. 6-inch subs $5. Smoothies $4.50. Open daily 11am-9pm. MC/V. ❶

Harold's Chicken Shack, 1208 E. 53rd St. (☎773-752-9260), in Hyde Park on the South Side near University of Chicago campus. Ordering at the bulletproof glass window in this cheap soul food restaurant is a quintessential South Side experience. All meals come with 2 slices of wonderbread to sop up the grease. 9 nuggets and fries $3. 2 wings and fries $2.50. Large gizzard and fries $3.50. Open M-Th 11am-11pm, F-Sa 11am-12pm, Su 11am-10pm. Cash only. ❶

GREEKTOWN

Pegasus, 930 S. Halstead St. (☎226-3377;www.pegasuschicago.com). Enjoy views of downtown Chicago from Pegasus's roof deck while sampling traditional saganaki (flaming cheese; $5.75) or sipping traditional Greek wine ($6). The dessert menu notes that the delicious "Galaktoboureko" (custard wrapped in philo pastry and garnished with honey; $4) is also the longest word in Greek. AmEx/MC/V. ❷

The Parthenon, 314 S. Halsted St. (☎726-2407). The jewel of Chicago's Greek restaurants continues to impress. Waiters prepare flaming, brandy-soaked cheese ($5.25) at tableside, while the combination plate ($13) gives guests a taste of grape leaves, moussaka, and roast lamb. Open daily 11am-midnight. AmEx/MC/V. ❷

Artopolis, 306 S. Halsted St. (☎559-9000). After dinner, loosen your belt a notch and then duck into this "bakery, and cafe, and agora" for dessert. Play it safe with baklava ($3.25), or branch out with the mango yogurt mousse ($2.50). Open M-Th and Su 9am-11pm, F-Sa 9am-midnight. AmEx/MC/V. ❷

LINCOLN PARK

Bourgeois Pig, 748 W. Fullerton Ave. (☎773-883-5282; www.bpigcafe.com). A neighborhood institution, complete with creaky hardwood floors and well-worn Oriental rugs. Sink your teeth into a Great Gatsby sandwich on herbed focaccia (grilled with pesto, mayonnaise, avocado, swiss cheese, bacon, tomatos, and spinach; $7.75), or settle down with a cup of coffee ($1.75) or iced chai ($3.50) brewed on-site. Open M-Sa 7am-11pm, Sa-Su 8am-11pm. AmEx/MC/V. ❶

Sura, 3124 N. Broadway St. (☎773-248-7872; www.surachicago.com), at Barry Pl. Newly-opened Sura serves inventive gourmet Thai tapas in style. Order duck crepes ($6) and shrimp pad thai ($5) to share. Sit back to see the white walls slowly change colors in the soft lights. You can also wait for your meal while swinging in the bar's bubble chairs, suspended from the ceiling by white chains. Dinner entrees $10-16. Open M-Th 5-11:30pm, F-Sa 5pm-2am, Su 5pm-midnight. AmEx/V/MC. ❷

Penny's Noodle Shop, 950 W. Diversey Ave. (☎773-281-8448), at Sheffield Ave. One of the best budget options in town, Penny's presents generous portions of Asian noodles (under $7) in a bright, inviting setting. Pad thai $6.40. Red curry $6.40. Open M-Th and Su 11am-10pm, F-Sa 11am-10:30pm. Call for additional locations. MC/V. ❷

BUCKTOWN AND WICKER PARK

Pontiac Cafe, 1531 N. Damen Ave. (☎773-252-7767). Housed in an old garage, this restaurant and bar serves up healthy portions of traditional American sandwiches (burger $7), grilled sandwiches (the Pontiac; prosciutto, tomato, basil; $8), and appetizers (gazpacho $4) to a decidedly untraditional local set of bike messengers and artists. F live band karaoke. Su honky-tonk bingo. Open daily 11am-2am. MC/V. ❶

The Smoke Daddy, 1804 W. Division St. (☎773-772-6656; www.thesmokedaddy.com), north of the Loop in Wicker Park. Pulled pork sandwiches ($8.50) and finger-lickin' rib platters ($12.25-22). Live blues and jazz M-W and Su 8:30pm, Th-Sa 9:30pm. Open M-W and Su 11:30am-midnight, Th-Sa 11:30am-1am. AmEx/MC/V. ❷

Alliance Bakery & Cafe, 1736 W. Division St. (☎773-278-0366). Cheap pastries, strong coffee, and free Wi-Fi attract students and young professionals to this neighborhood coffeeshop. Giant cinnamon roll $1.65. Coffee $1.60. Espresso drinks $2.50-4. Open M-Sa 6am-9pm, Su 7am-9pm. AmEx/MC/V. ❶

WRIGLEYVILLE

Cozy Noodles & Rice, 3456 N. Sheffield Ave. (☎773-327-0100). The curries ($6.50) and rice noodles ($6.25) are tasty and inexpensive, but it's the playful ambience and attentive waitstaff that lift Cozy head and shoulders above other Thai spots in the area. Open M-Th 11am-10pm, F-Su 11am-10:30pm. AmEx/D/MC/V. ❷

Mia Francesca, 3311 N. Clark St. (☎773-281-3310). A stylish urban trattoria decorated with black-and-white photographs of rural Italy. An ideal spot for a date. Entrees $14-25. Pizzas $8. Reservations recommended. Open M-Th 5-10pm, F-Su 5-11pm. AmEx/D/MC/V. ❹

ANDERSONVILLE

🖾 **Kopi, A Traveler's Cafe,** 5317 N. Clark St. (☎773-989-5674). Take the El Red to Berwyn and walk 10min. down Berwyn Ave. to Clark. Named after the Indonesian word for coffee, Kopi caters to locals and visitors alike with an extensive travel library. Nestle into the pillows by the window, where nose-ringed moms sip hearty miso soup ($3.35) and soothing barley grass smoothies ($3.75). Open M-Th 8am-11pm, F-Sa 8am-midnight, Su 10am-11pm. AmEx/D/MC/V. ❶

Ann Sather, 5207 N. Clark St. (☎773-271-6677). Rustic murals adorn the walls of this popular Swedish-American eatery, known for the gooey cinnamon rolls ($3) that accompany its dishes. Swedish pancakes with lingonberries ($6.50) are available all day. Try pairing a burger ($8-10) with a side of pickled herring ($2). Open M-F 7am-2pm, Sa-Su 7am-4pm. AmEx/D/MC/V. ❷

GREAT LAKES

◉ SIGHTS

Only a fraction of Chicago's eclectic sights are revealed by tourist brochures, bus tours, and strolls through the downtown area. Sights range from well-publicized museums to undiscovered back streets, from beaches and parks to towering skyscrapers. To see it all requires some off-the-beaten-path exploration.

THE LOOP

When the **Great Fire of 1871** razed Chicago's downtown, the burgeoning metropolis had an opportunity to start anew. Bounded by the river on one side and **Lake Michigan** on the other, the city was forced to build up rather than out. Drawing on new technologies including steel-frame construction and the elevator brake, the Windy City assembled a daring skyline regarded today as one of America's most elegant.

TOURS. Visitors can take a crash course on columns and cornices through **walking tours** organized by the **Chicago Architecture Foundation.** Two-hour tours of skyscrapers and architecture start at the foundation's gift shop. Highlights include the stained glass windows of the Marquette Building, the Art Deco flourishes of the Board of Trade, and the revolutionary aesthetics of Mies van der Rohe. *(224 S. Michigan Ave. ☎ 922-3432, ext. 240; www.architecture.org. Historic Skyscrapers May-Oct. M-Tu and Th-Su 10am and 3pm, W 10am; Nov.-Apr. daily 10am. Modern Skyscrapers daily 1pm. $15, students and seniors $12. Call for tours in French, German, or Italian.)*

SEARS TOWER. A few blocks west on Jackson, the 1454 ft. tall Sears Tower is undoubtedly Chicago's most recognizable landmark. Early in 1997, the Petronas Towers in Malaysia edged out the Sears Tower as the tallest buildings in the world; however, the Tower can still claim the highest occupied floor. The ear-popping elevator ride to the 103rd floor Skydeck earns visitors a view of four states on a clear day. *(233 S. Wacker Dr.; enter on Jackson. ☎ 875-9449; www.theskydeck.com. Open daily May-Sept. 10am-10pm, last entrance 9:30pm, top closes at 10pm; Oct.-Apr. 10am-8pm. Last entry 30min. before closing. $13, children $9.50. Expect waits of at least 1hr., or try visiting after 5pm for shorter lines, especially on the weekends.)*

STATE STREET. State and Madison St., the most famous intersection of "State Street, that great street," forms the focal point of the Chicago street grid. Louis Sullivan's signature **Carson Pirie Scott** store is adorned with exquisite ironwork and wide Chicago windows. Sullivan's other masterpiece, the **Auditorium Building,** sits several blocks south at the corner of Congress St. and Michigan Ave. Once Chicago's tallest building, it typifies Sullivan's obsession with form and function, housing a hotel and an opera house with some of the world's finest acoustics.

OTHER ARCHITECTURAL WONDERS. Burnham and Root's **Monadnock Building** deserves a glance for its alternating bays of purple and brown rock. *(53 W. Jackson Blvd.)* Just to the southeast lies the grandeur of the **Fine Arts Building** *(410 S. Michigan Ave. ☎ 427-7602).* The $144 million **Harold Washington Library Center** is a researcher's dream, as well as a postmodern architectural delight. *(400 S. State St. ☎ 747-4300. Open M-Th 9am-7pm, F-Sa 9am-5pm, Su 1-5pm.)* On the north side of the Loop, at Clark and Randolph, the glass **State of Illinois Building** offers an elevator ride to the top that gives a thrilling (and free) view of a sloping atrium, circular floors, and hundreds of employees.

SCULPTURE. In addition to its architectural masterpieces, Chicago is decorated with a fantastic collection of outdoor sculpture. The Chicago Cultural Center (p. 518) sells the *Loop Sculpture Guide* for $4. The piece known simply as "The Picasso," at the foot of the **Daley Center Plaza,** was the first monumental modern statue to be placed in the Loop, eventually becoming an unofficial symbol of the city.

(Intersection of Washington and Dearborn St.) Across Washington St. rests Surrealist Joan Miró's *Chicago*, the artist's gift to the city. (69 W. Washington St.) Two blocks north on Clark St., Jean Dubuffet's *Monument with Standing Beast* stands guard at the State of Illinois Building (see above). Three blocks south on Dearborn at Adams, Alexander Calder's *Flamingo*, a stark red structure, stands in front of the **Federal Center Plaza,** which was designed by Mies van der Rohe. Calder's other Chicago masterpiece, *The Universe*, swirls in the lobby of the Sears Tower.

NEAR NORTH

MAGNIFICENT MILE. Chicago counts Paris as one of its sister cities, and the Magnificent Mile must be the Windy City's answer to the Champs-Elysées. Expensive shopping on the order of Tiffany's and Cartier lines the stretch of N. Michigan Ave. between the Chicago River and Oak St. Up as far as Pearson Ave., the squat **Chicago Water Tower** and **Pumping Station** stand out among the surrounding glass office buildings. Built in 1869, these two limestone buildings were the only ones in the area to survive the Great Chicago Fire. The Pumping Station houses a Visitors Center (p. 518), and the Water Tower has a free gallery dedicated to photography exhibits. (Gallery open M-Sa 10am-6:30pm, Su 10am-5pm.) One block north, the **John Hancock Building's** exoskeleton of black steel girders and glass casts a stunning figure on the skyline. (☎ 654-2892. Observation deck open daily 9am-11pm. Last entry 10:45pm. $11.30, seniors $8.80, ages 5-12 $7-15.)

TRIBUNE TOWER. Critics of the Tribune Tower, a 1925 skyscraper, dubbed it the "Cathedral of Commerce" for its marriage of Gothic religious architecture and the spirit of corporate America. *The Chicago Tribune* still publishes the city's largest newspaper from the tower's upper floors. At street level, the **Freedom Museum** (☎ 222-4860; www.freedommuseum.us) displays rotating exhibits and hosts events promoting freedom and the first amendment. (435 N. Michigan Ave. For museum info, check www.mccormickmuseum.org. Open M and W-Su 10am-6p. $5, children free.)

NAVY PIER. With a concert pavilion, dining options, nightspots, sightseeing boats, a spectacular Ferris wheel, a crystal garden with palm trees, a Shakespearean theater, and an IMAX theater, the mile-long pier is like Las Vegas, Mardi Gras, and the State Fair rolled into one. From here, explorers can rent bicycles to navigate the Windy City's streets or book a seat on a boat tour to take in Chicago's skyline. (600 E. Grand Ave. ☎ 595-7437; www.navypier.com. Take the El Red Line to Grand/State and transfer to a free pier trolley bus. Open April-Oct. M-Th and Su 10am-8pm, F-Sa 10am-10pm; Nov.-Mar. M-Th 10am-8pm, F-Sa 10am-10pm, Su 10am-7pm. Pier admission free. Rides $5-6. **Shoreline Sightseeing** (☎ 222-9328; www.shorelinesightseeing.com) offers architecture and boat tours on the Chicago River departing from the west end of Navy Pier June-Aug. M-F 10, 11:30am, 12:15, 1, 1:45, 2:30, 3:15, 4:00, 4:45, 5:30pm; Sa-Su every 30min. from 10am-5:30pm. 1hr. cruises $24, seniors $21, under 12 $13.)

OLD TOWN. The bells of the pre-fire **Saint Michael's Church** ring 1 mi. north of the Magnificent Mile in **Old Town,** settled by German immigrants and later transformed into a hub for the Chicago counterculture. Long since gentrified, Old Town still maintains ties to its past through the annual **Old Town Art Fair** and through performances at the **Old Town School of Folk Music,** 4544 N. Lincoln Ave. (Take the El Purple or Brown to Armitage or Sedgwick. The Old Town Art Fair takes place in early June. Call ☎ 773-728-6000 or check www.oldtownschool.org for info about performances at the School of Music.)

NORTH SIDE

LINCOLN PARK. Bounded by Armitage Ave. to the south and Diversey Ave. to the north, swanky Lincoln Park caters to young professionals and (increasingly) to families. Proximity to greenspace keeps property values high, while cafes and nightspots draw in visitors from other parts of the city.

LAKEVIEW. North of Diversey Pkwy. on N. Clark St., the streets of Lincoln Park become increasingly diverse as they melt into Lakeview around the 3000 block. Shopping plazas alternate with markets and vintage stores in this one-time summer getaway for Chicago's upper crust, while apartment towers and hotels spring up between aging two-story houses. North of Belmont St., N. Halsted also serves as the center of "Boystown," one of the city's most visible gay communities, but nightlife in Boystown increasingly caters to gay and straight partygoers alike.

WRIGLEYVILLE

Around the 4000 block of N. Clark, Lakeview shifts into **Wrigleyville.** Even though the **Cubs** (p. 530) haven't won a World Series since 1908, Wrigleyville residents remain fiercely loyal to their hometown team. Tiny, ivy-covered **Wrigley Field** is the North Side's most famous institution, and tours of the historic park are available during summer weekends when the Cubs are away. *(1060 W. Addison St., just east of the junction of Waveland Ave. and N. Clark St. Take bus #22 "Clark" or #152 "Addison."* ☎ *773-404-2827. Tours $15.)*

NEAR WEST SIDE

Old St. Patrick's Church remains a symbol of the area's Irish roots, although waves of immigrants from southern and eastern Europe, as well as African-Americans from the American South, arrived into the 1950s. The area is still negotiating tensions between new development and affordable housing for longtime residents.

JANE ADDAMS HULL-HOUSE MUSEUM. The Corinthian mansion of real estate magnate Charles Hull became the epicenter of the American settlement house movement, under the stewardship of activists Jane Addams and Ellen Gates Starr. Today, the museum commemorates Addams's and Starr's work in immigrant communities of the early 20th century and occasionally sponsors public lectures on issues in present-day immigration. *(800 S. Halsted St. Take the El Blue Line to UIC-Halsted.* ☎ *413-5353; www.hullhousemuseum.org. Open Tu-F 10am-4pm, Su noon-4pm. Free.)*

SOUTH OF THE LOOP

HYDE PARK AND THE UNIVERSITY OF CHICAGO. Seven miles south of the Loop along the lake, the scenic campus of the ivy-clad **University of Chicago** dominates the **Hyde Park** neighborhood. The university's efforts at revitalizing the area have resulted in a community of scholars and a lively campus life amidst the poorer and more dangerous neighborhoods surrounding it. University police patrol the area bounded by 51st St. to the north, Lakeshore Dr. to the east, 61st St. to the south, and Cottage Grove to the west—but don't test these boundaries, even during the day. Lakeside Burnham Park, east of campus, is fairly safe during the day, but not at night. The impressive **Oriental Institute** *(1155 E. 58th St.;* ☎ *773-702-9514; free, suggested donation $5),* **Museum of Science and Industry** (see **Museums,** p. 527), and **DuSable Museum of African-American History** are all in or near Hyde Park. On the first weekend in May, the **Festival of the Arts** *(http://fota.uchicago.edu)* showcases the area's diverse cultural offerings. *(From the Loop, take bus #6 "Jefferson Express" or the METRA Electric Line from the Randolph St. Station south to 59th St.)*

ROBIE HOUSE. On campus, Frank Lloyd Wright's famous **Robie House,** designed to resemble a hanging flower basket, is the seminal example of his Prairie-style house. Now in the midst of a 10-year restoration project to return to its original 1910 state, the house will remain open to visitors during the renovation. *(5757 S.*

Woodlawn, at the corner of 58th St. ☎ 773-834-1847. Tours M-F 11am, 1, 3pm; Sa-Su every 20min. 11am-3:30pm. Not wheelchair-accessible. $12, seniors and ages 7-18 $10.)

WEST OF THE LOOP

OAK PARK. Gunning for the title of the most fantastic suburb in the US, Oak Park sprouts off Harlem St. *(10 mi. west of downtown, I-290 W to Harlem St.)* Frank Lloyd Wright endowed the downtown area with 25 of his spectacular homes and buildings, all of which dot the Oak Park Historic District. His one-time home and workplace, the **Frank Lloyd Wright House and Studio,** offers an unbeatable look at his interior and exterior stylings. *(951 Chicago Ave. ☎ 708-848-1976; www.wrightplus.org. Bookshop open daily 10am-5pm. 45min. house tours M-F 11am, 1, 3pm; Sa-Su every 20min. 11am-3:30pm. 1hr. self-guided Oak Park tours, with a map and audio cassette, available daily 10am-3:30pm. Guided tours Mar.-Nov. Sa-Su every hr. 11am-4pm; Dec.-Feb. Sa-Su every hr. noon-2pm. Limited wheelchair access. $12, seniors and under 18 $10; combination interior/exterior tour tickets $20/16.)* Throughout the year, fans flock to the **Ernest Hemingway Birthplace and Museum** to take part in the many events honoring an architect of the modern American novel. The museum features rare photos of Hemingway, his letters, and other memorabilia. *(Birthplace: 339 N. Oak Ave. Museum: 200 N. Oak Park Ave. ☎ 708-848-2222; www.ehfop.org. House and museum open Th-F and Su 1-5pm, Sa 10am-5pm. $7, seniors and under 18 $5.50.)* Swing by the **Visitors Center** for maps, guidebooks, tours, and local history. *(1118 Westgate. ☎ 708-524-7800; www.visitoakpark.com.)*

🏛 MUSEUMS

Chicago's museums range from some of the largest collections in the world to one-room galleries. The first five listings (known as the **Big Five**) provide a diverse array of exhibits, while a handful of smaller collections target specific interests. Lake Shore Dr. has been diverted around Grant Park, linking the Field Museum, Adler, and Shedd. This compound, known as **Museum Campus,** offers a free shuttle between museums. Visitors who plan on seeing the Big Five, plus the Hancock Observatory, can save money by purchasing a **CityPass** that grants admission to the sights and provides discount coupons for food and shopping. ($50, ages 3-11 $39; available at each attraction and good for 9 days.) All museums are wheelchair-accessible unless otherwise noted.

🖼 ART INSTITUTE OF CHICAGO. It's easy to feel overwhelmed in this expansive museum, with a collection of art from around the world spanning 4 millennia. Make sure to see Chagall's stunning *America Windows*—the artist's blue-stained glass tribute to the country's bicentennial—between visits to Wood's *American Gothic,* Hopper's *Nighthawks,* and Monet's *Haystacks.* If you have time, check out the basement's Touch Gallery where you can touch the sculptures on display, including a 2000-year-old bust of a Chinese imperial guard. *(111 S. Michigan Ave., at Adams St. in Grant Park. Take the El Green, Brown, Purple, or Orange Line to Adams. ☎ 443-3600; www.artic.edu/aic. Open M-W and F-Su 10:30am-5pm, Th 10:30am-8pm. $12, students and children $7, under 12 free. Th 5-8pm free; summer Th-F 5-9pm free.)*

🖼 SHEDD AQUARIUM. The Shedd, the world's largest indoor aquarium, has 650 species of fish and marine life. The Oceanarium features Beluga whales, dolphins, and penguins in a giant pool that appears to flow into Lake Michigan. Explore Wild Reef coral formations, or greet piranhas in the steamy Amazon Rising exhibit. *(1200 S. Lake Shore Dr., in Grant Park. Take the El Red to Roosevelt, then bus #12 or the museum trolley away from the Loop. ☎ 939-2438; www.sheddaquarium.org. Open June-Aug. daily 9am-6pm; Sept.-May M-F 9am-5pm, Sa-Su 9am-6pm. $23, seniors and ages 3-11 $16.)*

■ FIELD MUSEUM OF NATURAL HISTORY. Home to the largest tyrannosaurus rex skeleton ever unearthed and the body of the largest man-eating lion on record, the Field Museum of Natural History displays many of the most fearsome animals in earth's history. Tribal masks, mummies, and a life-sized reconstruction of a Native American dwelling shed light on ancient and foreign cultures. Summer 2008 will feature 100 of the greatest (and oldest) maps ever made in an exhibit on maps and map making. *(1400 S. Lake Shore Dr., on the Museum Campus in Grant Park. ☎922-9410; www.fieldmuseum.org. Open daily 9am-5pm. Last entry 4pm. Free tours M-F 11am and 2pm, Sa-Su 11am and 1pm. $12, students and seniors $7, ages 4-11 $7, under 4 free.)*

MUSEUM OF CONTEMPORARY ART. The cutting-edge white and chrome building provides an ideal backdrop for the ambitious rotating exhibitions within. The impressive permanent collection includes sculpture by Joseph Beuys (a suit made of felt) and Sol LeWitt's minimalist painting. Check the website for info on First Fridays, a hip cocktail hour held monthly at the museum. *(220 E. Chicago Ave., 1 block east of Michigan Ave. Take the El Red to Chicago, and then walk 4 blocks east on E. Chicago. ☎280-2660; www.mcachicago.org. Open Tu 10am-8pm, W-Su 10am-5pm. $10, students and seniors $6, under 12 free. Tu 5-8pm free.)*

MUSEUM OF SCIENCE AND INDUSTRY. Earmark the better part of a day for reaching and then exploring the largest museum of science in the western hemisphere. The crown jewel of its collection is the German U-boat captured by the U.S. Navy in 1944; tours of the interior are $5, but the exhibit is free. Other highlights include the Apollo 8 command module and a full-sized replica of an Illinois coal mine. *(5700 S. Lake Shore Dr., at 57th St. in Hyde Park. Take buses #2, 6, or 10 south from the Loop; #10 runs in summer daily, rest of the year Sa-Su and holidays. ☎773-684-1414; www.msichicago.org. Open June-Aug. M-Sa 9:30am-5:30pm, Su 11am-5:30pm; Sept.-May M-Sa 9:30am-4pm, Su 11am-4pm. $11, seniors $9.50, ages 3-11 $7.50. Parking $12.)*

ADLER PLANETARIUM. Traditional and digital sky shows bring you face to face with the awesome glory of the cosmos. Colorful, hands-on exhibits illustrate the complex science behind black holes and quasars. Also home to the giant, metallic Atwood Sphere, which was the only walk-in planetarium in North America when it was built in 1913. *(1300 S. Lake Shore Dr., on the Museum Campus in Grant Park. ☎322-0336; www.adlerplanetarium.org. Open daily 9:30am-4:30pm. Admission and choice of sky show $19, seniors $17, ages 4-17 $15. Digital sky shows $4 extra.)*

CHICAGO HISTORY MUSEUM. Renovated in 2006, this Neo-georgian colonial building atop a hill in the centre of Lincoln Park houses Chicago's oldest cultural institution. The extensive collection of Lincoln memorabilia includes a replica of the president's deathbed. On the second floor are dioramas illustrating Chicago's history from settlement by a fur trader of African descent in 1785 to its rebirth as host of the 1893 Columbian Exposition, which the museum also commemorates with a large collection of souvenirs from the event. A life-sized replica of a Chicago trolley from 1895 and other colorful interactive exhibits dominate the rest of the renovated space. *(1601 N. Clark St., in Lincoln Park. ☎642-4600; www.chicagohistory.org. Open M-W and F-Sa 9:30am-4:30pm, Th 9:30am-8:00pm, Su noon-5pm. $12, students and seniors $10, children free. M free.)*

♫ ENTERTAINMENT

The free weeklies *Chicago Reader* and *New City*, available in many bars, record stores, and restaurants, list the latest events. The *Reader* reviews all major shows with times and ticket prices. *Chicago* magazine includes theater reviews alongside exhaustive club, music, dance, and opera listings. *The Chicago Tribune* includes an entertainment section every Friday. *Gay Chicago* provides info on social activities as well as other news for the area's gay community.

THEATER

One of North America's foremost theater centers, Chicago's more than 150 theaters feature everything from blockbuster musicals to off-color parodies. Downtown, the recently formed Theater District centers around State St. and Randolph, and includes the larger venues in the city. Smaller theaters are scattered throughout Chicago. Most tickets are expensive. Half-price tickets sold on the day of performance at **Hot Tix Booths**, 78 W. Randolph (open Tu-F 8:30am-6pm, Sa 10am-6pm, Su noon-5pm), and 163 E. Pearson in the Water Works Visitors Center (☎977-1755; open Tu-Sa 10am-6pm, Su noon-5pm). Purchases must be made in person. **Ticketmaster** (☎559-1212) supplies tickets for many theaters; ask about discounts at all Chicago shows. The "Off-Loop" theaters on the North Side put on original productions, with tickets usually under $18.

Steppenwolf Theater, 1650 N. Halsted St. (☎335-1650; www.steppenwolf.org). Where Gary Sinise and John Malkovich, who are still known to stop by occasionally, got their start. Tickets $30-60, rush tickets available. Student tickets can be purchased at the box office 1hr. before showtime; $15 dollars with student ID. Box office open M-Sa 11am-5pm, Su 11am-7:30pm.

Goodman Theatre, 170 N. Dearborn (☎443-3800; www.goodman-theatre.org). Presents consistently solid original works. Tickets around $10-68; half-price after 6pm or after noon for matinees. Box office open M 10am-5pm, Tu-Th 10am-7:30pm, F 10am-8pm, Sa noon-8pm, Su noon-7:30pm.

Bailiwick Repertory, 1229 W. Belmont Ave. (☎773-883-1090; www.bailiwick.org), in the Theatre Bldg. Mainstage and experimental studio space. Tickets from $20. Box office open M-W 10am-6pm, Th-Sa 10am-8pm, Su noon-6pm.

COMEDY

Chicago boasts a plethora of comedy clubs. The most famous is the legendary **Second City,** 1616 N. Wells St. (☎664-4032; www.secondcity.com), at North Ave., which spoofs Chicago life and politics. Alums of the club include Bill Murray, Chris Farley, and John Belushi. Most nights a free improv session follows the main show. At next-door **Second City Etc.,** 1608 N. Wells St., up-and-coming comics offer even more laughs for interested patrons. (☎664-4032. Tickets M $14, Tu-Th and Su $19, F-Sa $24. Shows for Second City M-Th 8pm, F-Sa 8 and 11pm, Su 7pm; free improv sessions M-Th 10pm, Sa 1am, Su 9pm. Box office opens M-Sa 10am-9pm, Su noon. Reservations recommended for weekend shows.) Watch improv actors compete against each other at **Comedy Sportz,** 777 N. Green St. Two teams of comedians create sketches based on audience suggestions. (☎733-6000. Tickets $19. Shows Th-F 8pm, Sa 8 and 10pm.)

DANCE, CLASSICAL MUSIC, AND OPERA

Ballet, comedy, live theater, and musicals are performed at **Auditorium Theatre,** 50 E. Congress Pkwy. (☎922-2110; www.auditoriumtheatre.org; box office open M-noon-6pm). From September through June, the **Chicago Symphony Orchestra** performs at **Symphony Center,** 220 S. Michigan Ave. (☎294-3000; www.cso.org). **Ballet Chicago,** 218 S. Waba-sh Ave., 3rd fl., holds its performances at the **Athenaeum Theatre,** 2936 N. Southport. (☎251-8840; www.balletchicago.org. Tickets $18-30.) The **Lyric Opera of Chicago** performs from September through March at the **Civic Opera House,** 20 N. Wacker Dr. (☎332-2244; www.lyricopera.org). The **Grant Park Music Festival** (☎742-7638; www.grantparkmusicfestival.com) provides classical music for free. From mid-June through late August, the acclaimed **Grant Park Symphony Orchestra** plays a few free evening concerts per week at the new **Jay Pritzker Pavilion** in **Millennium Park.**

FESTIVALS

The city celebrates summer on a grand scale. The **Taste of Chicago** festival cooks for eight days in late June and early July. Seventy restaurants set up booths with endless samples in Grant Park, where crowds chomp to the blast of big-name bands. The Taste's fireworks are the city's biggest (free entry; 11 food tickets for $7). In mid-June, the **Blues Festival** and the **Chicago Gospel Festival** celebrate Chi-town's soul, and locals gets a taste of Nashville during the **Country Music Festival** at the end of the month. The **¡Viva Chicago!** Latin music festival steams up in late August, while the **Chicago Jazz Festival** scats over Labor Day weekend. All festivals center at the Grant Park Petrillo Music Shell. For more information on these events, contact the Mayor's Office's **Special Events Hotline** (☎744-3370; www.city-ofchicago.org/specialevents). The **Ravinia Festival,** in the northern suburb of High-land Park, runs from late June to early September. During the festival's 14-week season, the Chicago Symphony Orchestra, ballet troupes, folk and jazz musicians, and comedians perform. On certain nights, the orchestra allows students free lawn admission with student ID. (☎847-266-5100; www.ravinia.org. Shows 8pm, occasion-ally 11am, 4:30, and 7pm—call ahead. The festival runs 2hr. every night. Round-trip on the METRA costs about $5. Charter buses $12. Lawn seats $10-20, other seats $20-100.)

SPORTS

The National League's **Cubs** step up to bat at **Wrigley Field,** 1060 W. Addison St., at N. Clark St., one of the few ballparks in America to retain the game's early grace and intimate feel. (☎773-404-2827; www.cubs.com. Tickets $30-60.) The **White Sox,** Chicago's American League team, swing on the South Side at new **US Cellular Field,** 333 W. 35th St. (☎866-769-4263. Tickets $30-60.) The NFL **Bears** play at the newly renovated **Soldier Field,** 425 E. McFetridge Dr. (☎866-788-2482; www.chicago-bears.com. Tickets $45-1000.) The **Bulls** have won three NBA championships at the **United Center,** 1901 W. Madison, west of the Loop. (☎455-4000; www.nba.com/bulls. Tickets $35-850.) Hockey's **Blackhawks** skate onto United Center ice when the Bulls aren't hooping it up. (☎455-7000; www.chicagblackhawks.com. Tickets $25-100.)

⊠ NIGHTLIFE

The birthplace of blues, Chicago has hosted innumerable blues performers over the years. Jazz, folk, reggae, and punk clubs throb all over the **North Side.** The **Buck-town/Wicker Park** area stays open late with various bars and clubs. Aspiring pickup artists swing over to **Rush Street** and **Division Street.** Full of bars, cafes, and bistros, **Lincoln Park** is frequented by singles and young couples, both gay and straight. The bustling center of gay culture is between 3000 and 4500 **North Halsted Street.** Many of the more colorful clubs and bars line this area. For more upscale raving and dis-coing, there are plenty of clubs near **River North,** in Riverwest, and on Fulton St.

LIVE MUSIC

⊠ **Hideout,** 1354 W. Wabansia Ave. (☎773-227-4433; www.hideoutchicago.com). Take the El Red to North and Clybourn, then take bus #72 to Elston. Walk 2 blocks up Elston, in a group if possible, and then turn right on Wabansia. Tucked away in a municipal truck parking lot, this bar and performance space lures hipsters with indie rock shows and families with a late Sept. block party. Beer $2-5. Cover Tu-F $5-10. Open M 7:30pm-2am, Tu-F 4pm-2am, Sa 7:30pm-3am. Cash only.

The Green Mill, 4802 N. Broadway Ave. (☎773-878-5552; www.greenmilljazz.com). Take the El Red to Lawrence. Once a Prohibition-era speakeasy favored by Al Capone, the Green Mill has phased out gangsters and gun-runners in favor of elegant live jazz.

Home to the nation's first and longest running weekly poetry slam (Su 6-9pm). Patrons keep their voices low during sets, but things get lively again late in the evening, especially during the cover-free jam sessions after weekend headliners wrap up. Beer $4-5. Cover $6-12. Open M-F 9pm-4am, Sa 8pm-5am, Su 7pm-4am. AmEx.

Kingston Mines, 2548 N. Halsted St. (☎ 773-477-4646; www.kingstonmines.com). Mick Jagger and Led Zeppelin have been known to drop in for a jam session at this venerable club, which has dueling blues acts alternating on 2 stages. Live blues M-F and Su 9:30pm, Sa 8pm. M-W and Su college students with ID free. 21+. Cover M-Th and Su $12-15, F-Sa from $15. Open M-Th and Su 8pm-4am, F-Sa 8pm-5am.

Subterranean, 2011 W. North Ave. (☎ 773-278-6600; www.subt.net), in Wicker Park. Take the El Blue to Damen. Sink into a green leather couch in the downstairs lounge of this funky hangout, or else clamber upstairs to take in live music in the opulent, recently renovated ballroom. Tu hip-hop open mic. Beer $3-5. Cover for shows $5-20. Open M 7pm-2am, Tu-F 6pm-2am, Sa 7pm-3am, Su 8pm-2pm. AmEx/DC/MC/V.

BARS AND CLUBS

Funky Buddha Lounge, 728 W. Grand Ave. (☎ 666-1695; www.funkybuddha.com). Take the El Blue to Chicago. Trendy, eclectic dance club where hip-hop and funk blend with leopard and velvet decor. Caters to the ecologically minded partier with organic juices, energy drinks, and liquor. W and Su soul. Cover $10; free before 10pm. Open M-W 10pm-2am, Th-F 9pm-2am, Sa 9pm-3am, Su 6pm-2am.

Smart Bar, 3730 N. Clark St. (☎ 773-549-4140; www.smartbarchicago.com). Resident DJ spins punk, techno, hip-hop, and house. Swing by after 2am to rub elbows with music industry types. Beer $4-6. Mixed drinks $5-8. 21+. Cover $10-15. Open M-F and Su 10pm-4am, Sa 10pm-5am.

Hydrate, 3458 N. Halsted St. (☎ 773-575-5244), in Lakeview. Cool off with a frozen martini ($9) after grooving on this trendy gay bar's hot dance floor. Beer $4-5. Cover M and Th $5, F-Sa $5-10. Open M-F 8pm-4am, Sa 6pm-4am, Su 6pm-4am. MC/V

⚠ OUTDOOR ACTIVITIES

A string of lakefront parks fill the area between Chicago proper and Lake Michigan. On sunny afternoons, dog walkers, in-line skaters, and skateboarders storm the shore. Close to downtown, the two major parks are Lincoln and Grant. ◪**Lincoln Park** extends across 5 mi. of lakefront on the north side with winding paths, groves of trees, and asymmetrical open spaces. The Lincoln Park Zoo features some of humankind's distant cousins in its acclaimed Great Apes exhibit. (☎ 742-2000; www.lpzoo.com. Zoo grounds open in summer daily 9am-6pm, buildings daily 10am-5pm; low season daily 10am-4:30pm. Free.) Next door, the Lincoln Park Conservatory provides a glass palace of plants from varied ecosystems. (☎ 742-7736. Open daily 9am-5pm. Free.) Grant Park, covering 14 lakefront blocks east of Michigan Ave., follows the 19th-century French park style: symmetrical and ordered with corners, a fountain, and wide promenades. The Grant Park Concert Society hosts free summer concerts in the Petrillo Music Shell, 520 S. Michigan Ave. Colored lights illuminate Buckingham Fountain from 9-11pm. On the north side, Lake Michigan lures swimmers and sunbathers to Lincoln Park Beach and Oak Street Beach. Beware, though: the rock ledges are restricted areas, and swimming from them is illegal. Although the beaches are patrolled 9am-9:30pm, they can be unsafe after dark. The Chicago Parks District (☎ 742-7529) has more info. The ◪Indiana Dunes State Park and National Lakeshore lie 45min. southeast of Chicago on I-90, but a world away. The State Park's gorgeous dune beaches on Lake Michigan harbor trail through dunes, woods, and marshes. Info about the

State Park is available at the park's office, 1600 N. 25 E in Chesterton, IN (☎219-926-1952). Obtain Lakeshore details at their Visitors Center, 1100 N. Mineral Springs Rd., in Porter, IN (☎219-926-7561).

SPRINGFIELD   ☎217

"The town that Lincoln loved" was a hotbed of political activity during the years leading up to the Civil War, and half a century later, the capital of Illinois became the birthplace of the NAACP. Today, Springfield pays tribute to the legacy of the Great Emancipator, even as fiercely political lo-fi radio stations remind listeners that America is still in the process of desegregating.

The crown jewel of Springfield's Lincoln sights is the new ◙Abraham Lincoln Presidential Library and Museum, 112 N. 6th St., which welcomed more than 200,000 visitors in its first three months of operation. The library is geared toward scholarly research, but the superb museum tells the story of Lincoln's life through realistic recreations and iconic artifacts like the president's stovepipe hat. (☎558-8844; www.alplm.org. Open daily 9am-5pm. $7.50, seniors and students $5.50, ages 5-15 $3.50, under 5 free.) On the other side of Springfield's sleepy downtown, the Lincoln Home Visitors Center, 426 S. 7th St., distributes free tickets for tours of the Lincoln Home, at 8th and Jackson St., where Abraham and Mary Todd Lincoln raised their sons during the 1840s and 50s. (☎492-4241. Open daily 8:30am-5pm. 20min. tours every 5-10min., starting at the front of the house. Arrive early in summer. Free.) Lincoln served as a legislator in the Old State Capitol, where he gave his prophetic "House Divided" speech in 1858. (☎785-9363. Open Tu-Sa Mar.-Oct. 9am-5pm; Nov.-Feb. 9am-4pm. 30min. tours every 10-20min. Last tour 1hr. before closing. Suggested donation $2.) The fallen president's final resting place is marked by the imposing Lincoln Tomb, 1500 Monument Ave., inside Oak Ridge Cemetery. (☎782-2717. Open daily Mar.-Oct. 9am-5pm; Nov.-Feb. 9am-4pm.) Should you start to overdose on Honest Abe, the Dana-Thomas House, 301 E. Lawrence Ave., was one of Frank Lloyd Wright's early experiments in the Prairie style and still features the original fixtures. (☎782-6776. Open W-Su 9am-4pm. 1hr. tours every 15-20min. Last tour 3:45pm. Suggested donation $3, under 18 $1.)

Chain motels line I-55 south of downtown, and the cheapest rooms are at Motel 6 ❷, 6011 S. 6th St. (☎529-1633. A/C, cable TV, and pool. Singles M-Th and Su $40, F-Sa $49; doubles $50/59. AmEx/D/MC/V.) Trout Lily Cafe ❶, 218 S. 6th St., offers sandwiches ($4.50-5.50), quiche ($4.50), and espresso drinks ($2-4). Stop by on weekdays between noon and 1pm for an hour of acoustic music. (☎391-0101. Open M-F 7am-4:30pm, Sa 9am-3pm. MC/V.) Cozy Drive-In ❶, 2935 S. 6th St., is a landmark on historic Rte. 66 and the birthplace of the "Cozy Dog," or corndog ($1.75). Today, it's a family-owned diner devoted to roadside memorabilia and deep-fried food. (☎525-1992. Burger $2. Open M-Sa 8am-8pm. Cash only.) For live music, look no farther than the Underground City Tavern, 700 E. Adams St., beneath the Hilton Springfield. Americana and country-rock bands take the stage during the week, while early July's Rooftop Roots Fest draws big names like blues guitarist Corey Harris. (☎789-1530. Shows 10pm. Beer $3. 21+. Cover $5-10. Open M-Th 3pm-1am, F 3pm-3am, Sa noon-3pm.)

Amtrak (☎753-2013; www.amtrak.com; station open daily 5am-11pm), at 3rd and Washington St., near downtown, runs trains to Chicago (3½hr., 4 per day, $18-50) and St. Louis (2hr., 5 per day, $13-36). Greyhound, 2351 S. Dirksen Pkwy., (☎544-8466; www.greyhound.com; depot open M-F 8am-noon and 2-7pm, Sa-Su 8am-noon and 2-4pm), sends buses to Chicago (4-6hr., 6 per day, $38.50); Indianapolis (4-9hr., 2 per day, $48); and St. Louis (2hr., 4 per day, $20.75). For a taxi, call Lincoln Yellow Cab, ☎522-7766. Springfield Convention and Visitors Bureau, 109 N. 7th St., provides parking passes. (☎789-2360 or 800-545-7300; www.visit-springfieldillinois.com. Open M-F 8:30am-5pm.) Internet Access: Lincoln Library, 326 S. 7th St.

(☎753-4900. Free. 30min. slots, limit 2hr. per day. Open June-Aug. M-Th 9am-9pm, F 9am-6pm, Sa 9am-5pm; Sept.-May also Su noon-5pm.) **Post Office:** 411 E. Monroe St. (☎753-3432. Open M-F 7:30am-5pm.) **Postal Code:** 62701.

WISCONSIN

Hospitality is served up with every beer and every piece of Wisconsin cheddar sold in the Great Lakes's most wholesome party state. A wide variety of wily creatures make themselves at home in the thick woods of Wisconsin's extensive park system, while the state's favorite animal—the cow—grazes near highways. Along the shoreline, fishermen haul in fresh perch, and on rolling hills, farmers grow barley for beer. Visitors to "America's Dairyland" encounter cheese-filled country stores en route to the ocean-like vistas of Door County and the ethnic *fêtes* (not to mention other, less-refined beer bashes) of Madison and Milwaukee.

🛈 PRACTICAL INFORMATION

Capital: Madison.

Visitor Info: Department of Tourism, 201 W. Washington Ave., P.O. Box 8690, Madison 53708 (☎608-266-2161 or 800-432-8747; www.tourism.state.wi.us).

Postal Abbreviation: WI. **Sales Tax:** 5%.

MILWAUKEE   ☎414

Home to beer and countless festivals, Milwaukee is a city with a reputation for *Gemütlichkeit* (hospitality). Ethnic communities throw rollicking, city-wide parties each summer weekend, from the traditional Oktoberfest to the Asian Moon festival. When the weather turns cold, the city celebrates with the International Arts Festival Milwaukee, during which galleries and museums extend their hours. Milwaukee's countless bars and taverns fuel the revelry with boatloads of beer. In addition to merrymaking, the city boasts top-notch museums, German-inspired architecture, and scenic lakeshores.

⌐ TRANSPORTATION

Airport: General Mitchell International Airport (MKE), 5300 S. Howell Ave. (☎747-5300; www.mitchellairport.com). Take bus #80 from 6th St. downtown (30min.; $1.75), or try out Amtrak's new Hiawatha service from the downtown train station (11min., 6-7 per day, $7).

Airport Connection, ☎769-2444 or 800-236-5450. 24hr. pickup from most downtown hotels. $12, round-trip $22. Reservations required.

Trains: Amtrak, 433 W. St. Paul Ave. (☎271-0840; www.amtrak.com), in downtown. Use caution in the area at night. To **Chicago** (1½hr., 6-7 per day, $21) and **St. Paul** (6½hr., 1 per day, $82-107). Station open daily 5:30am-10pm; tickets sold 5:30am-9pm.

Buses: Greyhound, 606 N. James Lovell St. (☎272-2156; www.greyhound.com), off W. Michigan St., 3 blocks from the train station. To **Chicago** (2-3hr., 11 per day, $13) and **Minneapolis** (7hr., 6 per day, $56). Station open 24hr.; tickets sold daily 6am-7:15pm. **Coach USA Milwaukee** (☎262-542-8861 or 800-236-2028), in the same terminal, covers southeastern Wisconsin. **Badger Bus,** 635 N. James Lovell St. (☎276-7490; www.badgerbus.com), is across the street. To **Madison** (1½hr., 7 per day, $15). Open M-Sa 6:30am-8pm, Su 9:30am-8pm. Be cautious near these stations at night.

Public Transit: Milwaukee County Transit System, 1942 N. 17th St. (☎344-6711; www.ridemcts.com). Efficient metro area service. Most lines run daily 5am-12:30am. $1.75, seniors and children $0.85, weekly pass $16. Fare includes transfer that can be used for 1hr. after 1st ride. Free maps at the library or at Grand Avenue Mall. Call for schedules. The **Trolley** (☎344-6711) runs in a loop through downtown. Free.

Taxi: Veteran, ☎220-5000. **Yellow Cab Co-op,** ☎271-1800.

ORIENTATION AND PRACTICAL INFORMATION

Most of Milwaukee's action is downtown, which lies between **Lake Michigan** and **10th Street.** Address numbers increase north and south from **Wisconsin Avenue,** the center of east-west travel. North-south streets west of the Milwaukee River are numbered, increasing toward the west. The **interstate system** forms a loop around Milwaukee: **I-43 S** runs to Beloit; **I-43 N** runs to Green Bay; **I-94 E** is a straight shot to Chicago; **I-94 W** goes to Madison and then Minneapolis/St. Paul; **I-794** cuts through the heart of downtown Milwaukee; and **I-894** connects with the airport.

Visitor Info: VISIT Milwaukee Information Center, 500 N. Harbor Dr. (☎273 7222; www.visit-milwaukee), inside Discovery World, 1st fl. Open daily 9am-5pm. **Greater Milwaukee Convention and Visitors Bureau,** 400 W. Wisconsin Ave. (☎287-6252 or 800-554-1448), in the Midwest Airlines Center lobby. Hours depend on conventions being held at the Midwest Airlines Center.

Hotlines: Crisis Intervention, ☎257-7222. **Women's Center Hotline,** ☎933-2722. Both operate 24hr.

Internet Access:

Node Coffee Shop, 1504 E. North Ave (☎431-9278). Wi-Fi $2 per hr. Internet access $4 per hr. Open 24hr.

Rochambo Coffehouse, 1317 E. Brady St. (☎291-0095; www.rochambo.com). Free Wi-Fi. Coffee $1.25. Specially brewed iced coffee $3.30. Open M-F 7am-midnight, Sa 8am-midnight, Su 9am-midnight.

Milwaukee Public Library, 814 W. Wisconsin Ave. (☎286-3000). $2 per week; 2hr. per day limit. Open M-W 9am-8:30pm, Th-Sa 9am-5:30pm; Oct.-Apr. also Su 1-5pm.

Post Office: 345 W. St. Paul Ave. (☎270-2308), east of the Amtrak station at 4th Ave. Open M-F 7:30am-8pm. **Postal Code:** 53201.

ACCOMMODATIONS

The rates at the hotels located along Wisconsin Ave. downtown are almost all expensive, but thankfully motels with more reasonable rates are just a short ride away in the northern and western suburbs, as well as down by the main airport.

Wellspring Hostel (HI), 4382 Hickory Rd. (☎262-675-6755), in Newburg. Take I-43 N to Exit 96, and then follow Rte. 33 W 10 mi. into Newburg. Bear right onto Main St. and take a sharp right onto Hickory Rd. This homey 10-bed hostel shares the grounds of a rambling organic farm and garden school. It's only 35min. to downtown Milwaukee, but the city feels like it's a world away. Linens included. Reception daily 8am-9pm. Dorms $25, members $20. MC/V. ❶

University of Wisconsin at Milwaukee (UWM), Sandburg Hall, 3400 N. Maryland Ave. (☎229-4065 or 299-6123). Take bus #30 north one stop past Hartford Ave. Spotless dorm-style suites close to East Side restaurants and bars. Linens provided. Laundry facilities and free local calls. Parking M-Sa $8.50 per day, Su free. 48hr. advance reservations required. Open June to early Aug. Singles with shared bath $40, with A/C $51; doubles $47/73. Cash only. ❷

Downtown Milwaukee

⌂ ACCOMMODATIONS

Golden Key Motel, **9**
University of Wisconsin at
   Milwaukee (UWM), **2**
Wellspring Hostel (HI), **1**

🍴 FOOD
Alterra at the Lake, **5**
Comet, **4**
La Fuente, **10**
La Perla, **11**
Mader's German Restaurant, **6**

🍸 NIGHTLIFE
Art Bar, **3**
Cage, **12**
Old German Beer Hall, **7**
Safehouse, **8**

Golden Key Motel, 3600 S. 108th St. (☎543-5300), in Greenfield. Take I-894 to Exit 3, then turn right on W. Beloit Rd. Proceed for ½ mi. and turn right on S. 108th. With a pool and high-speed Internet, this basic motel packs in more than its fair share of amenities. Singles $45-85; doubles $60-65. 10% AAA discount. AmEx/D/MC/V. ❸

🍴 FOOD

From *bratwurst* to *bier*, Milwaukee is best known for its German traditions. Downtown restaurants tend to favor traditional menus heavy on meat and potatoes, although the **Friday Night Fish Fry** cuts through the formal veneer with a table-bending feast (polka band optional). Inexpensive Polish and Mexican fare crop up on the **South Side,** while **Bradley Street** and the **Water Street Entertainment District** are each a nexus for trendy, upscale dining.

La Perla, 734 S. 5th St. (☎645-988), in the South Side. In a neighborhood of good Latin-American restaurants, La Perla stands out by virtue of its large mechanical pepper (rides $0.25). Its menu features Tex-Mex staples like chimichangas ($8.50). The best deal are the lunch combos (available 11am-2pm) with an enchilada and a chimichanga for $7.25. Roof seating provides a good neighborhood view and an excellent people-watching spot. Open daily 11am-10pm. AmEx/MC/V. ❷

Comet, 1947 N. Farwell St. (☎273-7677). Hip diner by day and cocktail lounge by night, Comet serves distinctive lunch dishes in healthy portions (meatloaf with beer gravy; $9.25) and quirky breakfast plates (pancakes with bacon in them; $7.50. Extensive beer list includes everything from cheap "working man" beer ($1.50) to fruit-flavored imports ($10). Open M-Sa 10:30am-2am, Su 9:30am-9pm. MC/V. ❷

La Fuente, 625 S. 5th St. (☎271-8595), in the South Side. Locals flock here for traditional Mexican food and Milwaukee's best margaritas ($5). Murals, mariachi music, and an expansive patio add to the laid-back atmosphere. 3 tacos $7.15. 3 enchiladas $9.50. Open M-Th and Su 10am-10pm, F-Sa 10am-11:30pm. AmEx/D/MC/V. ❷

Mader's German Restaurant, 1037 N. Old World Third St. (☎271-3377). Founded in 1902, and known for serving the likes of Cary Grant and Ronald Reagan. Traditional German fare against a backdrop of dark wood, stained glass, and armor. Entrees $8.50-14. Reservations recommended. Open M-Th 11:30am-9pm, F-Sa 11:30am-10pm, Su 11am-9pm. AmEx/D/MC/V. ❸

The Old German Beer Hall, 1009 N. Old World Third St. (☎226-2728), next door to Mader's. Recreates a traditional Munich beer hall complete with a seemingly mile-long bar and a wide selection of imported German beer. Beer $3.50-11. Basic bar food includes classic German dishes like wiener (hot dog; $4) and *bratwurst* ($5). Th-Sa live music. Open daily 11am-2am. AmEx/MC/V. ❶

◉ SIGHTS

BREWERIES. Although many of Milwaukee's breweries have relocated, beer is still a tried-and-true staple. The **Miller Brewery,** a corporate giant well-known to American college students for low-end brands like *Milwaukee's Best,* aka "the Beast," offers a free 1hr. tour with a three-screen video presentation and a complementary sample at the end. *(4000 W. State St. ☎931-2337; www.millerbrewing.com. Under 18 must be accompanied by an adult. ID required. Open M-Sa 10am-7pm. 2 tours per hr., last tour 4:30pm.)* Of course, breweries needn't be huge to be successful; workers at the **Lakefront Brewery** joke that the volume of beer they sell each year is roughly the same amount Anheuser-Busch spills on the floor in one shift. Tours are informal, even raucous, and the souvenir pint glasses given to visitors don't stay empty for long. *(1872 N. Commerce St. ☎372-8800; www.lakefrontbrewery.com. Tours year-round F 2, 3, 5:30, 6 and 7pm; Sa 1, 2 and 3pm; in summer also M-Th 2, 3pm. $5, non-beer drinkers $3. 21+ unless accompanied by legal guardian.)* For a taste of a few other microbreweries, take a 3hr. **Riverwalk Boat Tour.** Their boat, the aptly named "The Brew City Queen," travels to the Lakefront Brewery, the Milwaukee Ale House, and the Rock Bottom Brewery for guided tours and samples. *(☎283-9999; www.cafevecchio.com/riverwalkboat. Tours in summer Sa-Su. 3 per day, each starting from one of the 3 breweries. Must be 21+. $20.)* One of the state's most renowned microbreweries, **Sprecher Brewing** is the champion of traditional Old World brewing techniques. The 1hr. tour, which includes a visit to an old lager cellar and the **Rathskeller Museum of Beer Memorabilia,** is followed by four beer samples. *(701 W. Glendale, 5 mi. north on I-43, then east on Port Washington St. ☎964-2739; www.sprecherbrewery.com. Tours F 4pm; Sa 1, 2, and 3pm; Su 1:30 and 2:30pm; June-Aug. additional tours M-Th 4pm. $3, under 21 $1. Reservations required; call ahead to confirm tour times.)*

MUSEUMS. Without question, the pride and joy of Milwaukee's public art space is the lakeside ◪**Milwaukee Art Museum,** with its dramatic white pavilion and enormous sunscreen designed by Santiago Calatrava. The art on the walls is just as impressive, ranging from paintings from the Renaissance to the largest collection of Haitian art outside of Haiti. The permanent collection also include paintings by Georgia O'Keeffe, Picasso, and Kandinsky. *(700 N. Art Museum Dr., on the lakefront*

GREAT LAKES

downtown. ☎ 224-3200; www.mam.org. Open M-W and F-Su. 10am-8pm. $8, seniors $6, students $4, under 12 free. Feature exhibitions $2-4 extra. Free audio tour available.) Newly opened **Discovery World**, 500 N. Harbor Dr. (☎ 765-9966 or 708-6544) is a strange marriage between an aquarium and a science-technology museum. Observers can walk through glass tubes running through the aquarium's tanks to get a 360-degree view of the fish. There are also "touch tanks" for petting various fresh and salt water species. Live out your spy film fantasies by scanning your retinas at the technology museum, or make a spy film yourself at the museum's TV studios, complete with a green screen. Most notable among the interactive exhibits is the bed of nails, which allows museum visitors, with some assistance, to lie down on thousands of nails. *(Open Tu-Su 9am-5pm. $16, senior $14, child $12. MC/V.)* Beleaguered by a budgetary crisis over the last several years, the **Milwaukee Public Museum** is doing what it can to preserve the luster of signature exhibits like the Rainforest and the Streets of Old Milwaukee. *(800 W. Wells St., at N. 8th St. ☎ 278-2702; www.mpm.edu. Open M-Sa 9am-5pm, Su noon-5pm. Parking available. Wheelchair-accessible. $11, seniors $8, children $6, under 2 free.)* The **Charles Allis Art Museum,** an almost perfectly preserved 1911 mansion, combines period art and furnishings with rotating exhibitions of contemporary Wisconsin artists. *(1801 N. Prospect Ave. at E. Royal Pl., 1 block north of Brady. Take bus #15 or 30. ☎ 278-8295; www.cavtmuseums.org. Open W-Su 1-5pm. $5, students and seniors $3, children free.)* The 1892 **Pabst Mansion** came within weeks of being turned into a Holiday Inn parking lot, but it was scooped up by a group of civic-minded benefactors and today stands as a monument to the extravagance of Milwaukee's beer barons. *(2000 W. Wisconsin Ave. ☎ 931-0808; www.pabstmansion.com. Open M-Sa 10am-4pm, Su noon-4pm. $8, students and seniors $7, ages 6-17 $4. Prices increase at Christmas. Self-guided tours available. Tours leave on the hr.; last tour at 3pm.)*

PARKS. With almost 15,000 acres of parks in Milwaukee County, you won't need to go far out of town to get some grass under your feet while in Milwaukee. Lake, Back Bay, and Veterans Parks are all popular spots by Lake Michigan. Farther afield, the **Boerner Botanical Gardens** cultivate gorgeous blossoms and host open-air concerts on Thursday nights. *(9400 Boerner Dr. in Hales Corner, Exit I-894 at S. 92nd St. ☎ 525-5601. Open April-Oct. daily 8am-7pm. $4.50, seniors $3.50, ages 6-17 $2.50.)* The **Mitchell Park Horticultural Conservatory,** otherwise known as "The Domes," has recently fallen on hard times, although the seven-story conical glass greenhouses are still in place, waiting to be restored to their former splendor. *(524 S. Layton Ave., at 27th St. Take bus #10 west to 27th St., then #27 south to Layton. ☎ 649-9800. Open daily 9am-5pm. $5, ages 5-17 $3.50, under 5 free.)*

OTHER SIGHTS. A road warrior's nirvana, locally-headquartered **Harley-Davidson** gives free 1hr. tours of its engine plant that will enthrall any aficionado. *(11700 W. Capitol Dr. in Wauwatosa. ☎ 343-7850. Tours at regular intervals M-F 9:30am-1pm; call ahead for details and plan to arrive early. Reservations required for groups larger than 10. Closed-toe shoes must be worn. No children under 12. Photo ID required for over 18.)* Olympic hopefuls in figure skating and speed skating train at the **Pettit National Ice Center,** but daily open skates ensure that even beginners get ice time. *(500 S. 84th St., at I-94, 10min. west of downtown. ☎ 266-0100; www.thepettit.com. Open skate M 11:30am-9pm, Tu 11am-1pm, W 11:30am-1pm, Th 7:15am-9pm, F 11am-9pm Sa 1:15pm-4pm, Su 1-4pm. $7, seniors and children $5. Skate rental $3.)*

♪ ENTERTAINMENT

Summer brings free entertainment to Milwaukee, like the popular **Cathedral Park Jazz** series (☎ 271-1416), Thursdays at 6:30pm in Cathedral Square Park, at N. Jackson St. between Wells and Kilbourn St. In Père Marquette Park, at 3rd and Kilbourn St., **River Flicks** (☎ 276-6696) screens free family-oriented movies at dusk on

HAVIN' A BALL

With tickets to see the Milwaukee Brewers starting at just $10, there's no need to travel any farther than Miller Park for a dose of America's pastime. Yet minor-league baseball has an allure all its own. It has a laid-back charm that comes hand-in-hand with hokey promotions between innings, kids wandering around while parents socialize, and speculation that one of the players snagging fly balls might be called up to the majors for a date with destiny. Budget-friendly ticket prices are just icing on the cake.

The Beloit Snappers play in the Class A Midwest League, and they square off against rivals like their in-state nemesis, the Wisconsin Timber Rattlers. Their home turf, Pohlman Field, holds 3500 fans, and the shaded bleacher seats in the center sections are always coveted. Sunburnt dads bring radar guns to the game to clock the speed of pitches as they streak toward home plate, and a large snapping turtle mascot (call him Snappy) appears at regular intervals to rev up the crowd. Whether or not the Beloit players are teetering on the brink of big-league glory, they play a snappy game of small-town ball.

*The **Beloit Snappers** (☎362-2272; www.snappersbaseball.com) at Pohlman Field. From Milwaukee, take I-43 south into Beloit, and turn right on Cranston Rd; the field is 1½ mi. farther on the right. $5.50, ages 5-14 $4.50.*

Fridays in August. The **Marcus Center for the Performing Arts,** 929 N. Water St., (☎273-7121; www.marcuscenter.org; concerts Tu noon and 7:30pm) is the seat of Milwaukee's high culture as home to the **Milwaukee Symphony,** the **Orchestra,** and the **Milwaukee Ballet Florentine Opera Company.** (Box office ☎273-7206. Symphony tickets from $20, ballet tickets from $22, and opera tickets from $10. Ballet and symphony offer ½-price student rush tickets; opera student rush tickets $15. Box office open M-F 11:30am-9pm, Sa-Su noon-9pm.) From September through May the **Milwaukee Repertory Theater,** 108 E. Wells St., opens its three stages, presenting a mix of innovative shows and classics. (☎224-9490; www.milwaukeerep.com. $12.50-55; students and seniors $2 discount. ½-price rush tickets 30min. before shows. Box office open M-F noon-6pm) Baseball's **Brewers** step up to bat at **Miller Park,** at the interchange of I-94 and Rte. 41. (☎902-4000 or 800-933-7890; www.milwaukeebrewers.com. Seats from $5. Tours daily Apr.-Sept. 10:30am, noon, 1:30, 3pm; no tours on gamedays. $6, seniors and under 14 $3.) The NBA's **Bucks** shoot hoops at the **Bradley Center,** 1001 N. 4th St. (☎227-0500. Tickets from $10.)

※ FESTIVALS

With street fairs lined up for every single weekend during the summer months, it's not hard to see why Milwaukee is known to call itself "the city of festivals." ▓**Summerfest** is the mother of them all, drawing more than a million visitors to the city during 11 days of big-name music, roasted corn, and overpriced beer. (☎273-2680 or 800-273-3378; www.summerfest.com. Late June-early July. Tickets from $15, seniors and ages 3-10 $3; 2-day pass $23.) In early August, the **Wisconsin State Fair** rolls into the fairgrounds, next to the Pettit National Ice Center, with live music, rides, cream puffs, fireworks, and an aquatic pig race. (☎266-7000 or 800-884-3247; www.wistatefair.com. $8, seniors $6, ages 7-11 $3.) Smaller, but still popular, ethnic festivals are held in the **Henry W. Maier Festival Park,** on the lakefront of the Historic Third Ward. Among the most popular are: **Asian Moon** (☎483-8530; www.asianmoon.org) and **Polish Fest** (☎529-2140; www.polishfest.org), both in mid-July; **Festa Italiana** (☎223-2808; www.festaitaliana.com) in mid-July; **Bastille Days** (☎271-1416; http://bastille.easttown.com) around July 14; and **German Fest** (☎464-9444; www.germanfest.com) in late July. (The Milwaukee County Transit System runs shuttles directly to the festivals. For more info, call ☎344-6711. Most festivals $8-10, under 12 free. Some free plus cost of food.)

■ NIGHTLIFE

Milwaukee never lacks activity after sundown. The downtown business district becomes desolate at night, but the area along **Water Street** between Juneau and Highland Ave. hosts breweries and Irish pubs frequented by a staunchly local clientele. The college crowd heads toward the intersection of **North Avenue** and **North Farwell Street,** near the UWM campus. Running east-west between Farwell St. and the Milwaukee River, **Brady Street** tends to have more upscale lounges, while **South 2nd Street** hosts Latin dancing and most of the city's gay nightlife.

Safehouse, 779 N. Front St. (☎271-2007; www.safe-house.com), across from the Pabst Theater downtown. An enigmatic sign that reads "International Exports, Ltd." welcomes guests to this bizarre world of spy hideouts and secret passwords. Teeming with atmosphere and intrigue, Safehouse prides itself on an "Ultimate Martini" that's propelled 665 ft. through a maze of pneumatic tubes before being served without so much as a hint of vermouth. Mixed drinks $5-6. Cover $3-5. Open M 11:30am-1:30am, Tu-Th 11:30am-2am, F-Sa 11:30am-2:30am, Su 4pm-midnight. AmEx/MC/V.

Art Bar, 722 E. Burleigh St. (☎372-7880). This bright and laid-back back coffee house and bar lets local artists display work on the walls. If you feel like the art's over your head, there's always the solace of drinking one of the 15 beers ($2.50-6.50) or knocking back exotic shots—the house special is the pineapple upside down cake shot ($3). Th-F night DJ. Su canvas night, when a local artist paints on a canvas in the bar. Beer $2.50-$6.50. Open daily 6am-2am. DC/MC/V.

Cage, 801 S. 2nd Ave. (☎383-8330; www.cagenightclub.com). A two-decade veteran of Milwaukee's nightlife, Cage draws a primarily gay crowd with 5 bars, a massive dance floor, and a cage suspended from the ceiling. Weekday nights can be quiet, but Saturdays always crackle with energy. Tu male dancers. F Drag show. Cover F-Sa $6. Open M-Th and Su 9pm-2am, F-Sa 9pm-2:30am.

MADISON   ☎608

Locals in Madison refer to their downtown as "the Isthmus." For the geography-averse, an isthmus is a narrow strip of land that connects two larger landmasses. It is a dramatic place to build a city and places the Capitol and the University of Wisconsin-Madison in very close quarters. The coupling results in an active, lively community with a strong sense of history seen in its museums, outdoor activities, restaurants, and arts. Madison's distinct flavor is a fine blend of mature stateliness and youthful vigor.

▐ TRANSPORTATION

Airport: Dane County Regional Airport (MSN), 4000 International Ln. (☎246-3380; www.co.dane.wi.us/airport), 5 mi. northeast of downtown. Take U.S. 151 (E. Washington Ave.) to U.S. 51N (Stoughton St.). Taxis to downtown run $12-16. Bus to downtown: Metro #24 to North Transfer Point, then #2 or 4 to Capital Square.

Buses: Greyhound, 2 S. Bedford St. (☎257-3050; www.greyhound.com), at W. Washington Ave. Goes to **Chicago** (3-4hr., 6 per day, $30) and **Minneapolis** (5-6hr., 4 per day, $30-42). **Badger Bus** (☎255-6771; www.badgerbus.com), at the same address, or from Memorial Union on the UW campus, runs to **Milwaukee** (1½hr., 6-8 per day, $15). Open daily 6:30am-9pm.

Public Transit: Madison Metro Transit System, 1101 E. Washington Ave. (☎266-4466; www.ci.madison.wi.us/metro). Serves downtown and campus. $1.50, 1-day pass $3.40, 10-ride card $12. Open M-F 6:15am-6pm, Sa 6am-4:30pm, Su 12:30pm-4:30pm.

Taxi: Union Cab (☎242-2000; www.unioncab.com). Wheelchair-accessible cabs available. $3 base fare. **Badger Cab** (☎256-5566; www.badgercab.com). Fares by zone.

ORIENTATION AND PRACTICAL INFORMATION

Madison's main attractions are centered on the Capitol and the University of Wisconsin-Madison. **State Street,** which is reserved for pedestrians, bikers, and buses, connects the two and is the city's hub for eclectic food, shops, and nightlife. **Williamson (Willy) Street,** northeast of the university, is the comfortable home of Madison's yuppie-hippies; shops, cafes, restaurants, and even the Willy Street Co-op, a community-oriented supermarket, attest to this funky atmosphere. **Lake Monona** to the southeast and **Lake Mendota** to the northwest lap at Madison's shores. The northeastern and southwestern ends of the isthmus are joined by **Washington Avenue (U.S. 151),** the city's main thoroughfare, which, along with **Regent Street,** divides streets into north and south. **Wisconsin Avenue** and **Martin Luther King, Jr. Boulevard** split streets into east and west. **I-90** and **I-94** skirt the city to the west. I-94 E goes to Milwaukee, then Chicago; I-94 W goes to Minneapolis/St. Paul; I-90 E goes directly to Chicago through Rockford, IL; I-90 W goes to Albert Lea, MN.

Visitor Info: Greater Madison Convention and Visitors Bureau, 615 E. Washington Ave. (☎255-2537 or 800-373-6376; www.visitmadison.com). Open M-F 8am-5pm.

Internet Access: Madison Public Library, 201 W. Mifflin St. (☎266-6300; www.madisonpubliclibrary.org). Free. Ask at information desk for code for Wi-Fi. Open M-Th 9am-9pm, F 9am-6pm, Sa 9am-5pm; Oct.-Apr. also open Su 1-5pm.

Post Office: 215 Martin Luther King, Jr. Blvd., Ste. 101 (☎250-6487). Open M-F 8am-5pm, Sa 9am-noon. **Postal Code:** 53703.

ACCOMMODATIONS

Motels stretch along E. Washington Ave. (U.S. 151) just west of its intersection with I-90, with rooms from $40-60. From the Capitol, bus route #6 drives the 5 mi. between the Washington Ave. motels and downtown. Prices get steeper downtown, starting around $60-80.

Hostelling International–Madison (HI), 141 S. Butler St. (☎441-0144; www.madisonhostel.org), at King St. A good bet for budget travelers. No-shoe policy helps keep rooms clean and comfortable. Directions to most of Madison's sights are printed on colored slips of paper and hung on a wall. Free Internet access, kitchen, and coin-op laundry. Reception in summer M-Th and Su 8am-9pm, F-Sa 8am-10pm; in winter daily 8-11am and 5-9pm. Call ahead for after-hours arrival. Parking $5 per night; reserve ahead. Dorms $21, members $17; private rooms $44/41. MC/V. ❶

Memorial Union, 800 Langdon St. (☎262-1583), on the UW campus. Spacious rooms with excellent lake and city views. A/C, cable TV, and free parking. Call ahead; the 6 rooms fill—especially on football weekends—up to a year in advance. College cafeterias dole out quick and cheap meals. Check-in 2pm. Check-out 11am at the UW Visitors Center. Singles $68; doubles $78-85; 1 suite $95. MC/V. ❸

Select Inn, 4845 Hayes Rd. (☎249-1815; www.selectinn.com), west of the junction of I-94 and U.S. 151. Large rooms with A/C, cable TV, hot tub, laundry, and refrigerators. Free Wi-Fi. Singles from $54; doubles from $59; suites from $86. AmEx/D/MC/V. ❸

Lake Kegonsa State Park, 2405 Door Creek Rd. (☎873-9695, reservations 888-947-2757; www.wiparks.net), south on I-90 to Stoughton (Exit 147). Pleasant single, family, and group sites near beaches. Showers, flush toilets. Parking $10 per day. Office open 8am-11pm; park open 6am-11pm. Reservations highly recommended. Campground open May-Oct. Sites M-F $10, WI residents $8; Sa-Su $12/$10. Electricity $5. ❶

Downtown Madison

TO PICNIC POINT (2.25mi)

TO OLBRICH BOTANICAL GARDENS, BOLZ CONSERVATORY AND MSN AIRPORT (5mi), James Madison Park (6.5mi), (75mi), (3mi)

Lake Mendota

Lake Monona

ACCOMMODATIONS
Hostelling International-Madison (HI), 9
Lake Kegonsa State Park, 16
Memorial Union, 4
Select Inn, 1

FOOD
Cleveland's, 6
The Great Dane, 13
Himal Chuli, 12
Jin's, 11
The Nitty Gritty, 14
Mediterranean Cafe, 7
Michael's Frozen Custard, 3

NIGHTLIFE
Essen Haus, 6
Paul's Club, 8
State Street Brats, 10
Greenbush Bar, 15
The Weary Traveler, 2

FOOD

German-inspired pub fare, myriad coffee shops, and an impressive array of ethnic restaurants line **State Street,** which tends to be more expensive and refined toward the Capitol and more student-oriented near the campus. The numerous Madison originals attract travelers and locals alike and serve up reasonable, tasty food. At the Library Mall on State St.'s west end, vendors peddle juices, candy, and international delicacies, including Thai, Indonesian, and East African treats.

Greenbush Bar, 914 Regent St. (☎257-2874), at N. Park St. In the former Italian Workers' Club of Madison, this underground pizza sensation dazzles. The perpetual darkness, alleviated only by colored strands of Christmas lights, makes the arrival of the thin-crust pizzas all the more brightening. Patrons add toppings like homemade sausage to pizzas, which come in 3 sizes and 2 crust thicknesses ($10-14; toppings $1-4). Antipasti ($3.50-10), creative salads, pasta ($7-14), and sandwiches ($7) round out the menu. Open M-Th 4-11pm, F-Sa 4pm-midnight. ❷

The Great Dane, 123 E. Doty St. (☎284-0000; www.greatdanepub.com), at King St., near the Capitol. This brew pub serves hearty sandwiches, burgers, and other pub favorites along with a range of hand-crafted beers. Outdoor garden patio in summer. Entrees $8-19. Open M-Th and Su 11am-2am, F-Sa 11am-2:30am. AmEx/D/MC/V. ❸

Mediterranean Cafe, 625 State St. (☎251-8510). Some students affectionately deem this lunch eatery "Med-Caf" in appreciation of its cheap, nutritious provisions perfect for both sit-down and take-out meals. There's table service in the back, or you can order your falafel sandwich ($4); chicken, beef, or falafel and hummus plate ($6.50); or seriously budget soup ($1.50) to go. Open M-Sa 10am-4:30pm. ❶

Cleveland's, 410 E. Wilson St. (☎251-4455), near S. Hancock St. Cheap, warm, and open early, Cleveland's has a menu that reads like a standard diner's, but its food exceeds all expectation. Potato pancakes served with sour cream and applesauce ($3.50) give a German twist to a menu featuring the otherwise standard but decent array of egg sandwiches, french toast, and omelets ($3.50-5). A lunch menu exists, but breakfast is served until 1:30pm, so why bother? Open Tu-Sa 6am-1:30pm, Su 8am-1:30pm. Cash only. ❶

Himal Chuli, 318 State St. (☎251-9225). This family-owned Newar eatery welcomes patrons with the aromas of exotic spices. With Nepalese specialties such as *daal* (bean soup) and *momo* (steamed dumplings), the menu is vegetarian- and carnivore-friendly. Entrees $6-15. Open M-Sa 11am-9pm, Su noon-9pm. Cash only. ❸

The Nitty Gritty, 223 N. Frances St. (☎251-2521; www.nittygrittybirthdayplace.com), at W. Johnston St. For your fill of beer and burgers, head to the Nitty Gritty, which celebrates a gazillion birthdays each day with free beer (for the of-age birthday person only). Pub fare $5-10. Open M-Sa 11am-late, Su noon-midnight. AmEx/D/MC/V. ❷

Jin's Chicken and Fish, N. Frances St., away from State St., past Brat's. There are 2 choices and 1 long line at the cart Jin sets up. He fries chicken or fish, sandwiches them in a big white roll, and adds mayo or spicy sauce to satiate students' late-night hunger. Sandwiches $5. Open most days midnight-3:30am. ❶

Michael's Custard, 3826 Atwood Ave. (☎222-4110). A Madison institution, Michael's delicious frozen custard resembles neither hard nor soft ice cream. It can be topped with assorted indulgences. There are 4 locations, but this one is not far from the Botanical Gardens. Also at 2531 Monroe St. Small cone $3, shake $4. Open M-Th and Su 10:30am-11pm, F-Sa 10:30am-midnight. ❶

◉ SIGHTS

INSIDE MADISON

As the seat of local government and home to a thriving college scene, the Isthmus has an eclectic mix of sights—many of them free. The **State Capitol,** at the center of downtown, boasts beautiful ceiling frescoes, mosaics, and an observation deck. Stunning views unfold below the observation deck of the capitol building, by law the city's tallest building. (☎266-0382. Open M-F 8am-6pm, Sa-Su 8am-4pm. Observation desk open M-Sa 10am-4pm, Su noon-4pm. Free tours every hr. from the ground floor info desk M-F 9am-noon and 1-4pm, Sa 9-11am and 1-3pm, Su 1-3pm.) The **Madison Museum of Contemporary Art,** 227 State St., opened its Cesar Pelli-designed doors in 2006. Large galleries host visiting exhibits and small one displays works from the permanent collection. A sculpture garden on the roof overlooks State St. (☎257-0158; www.mmoca.org. Open Tu-W 11am-5pm, Th-F 11am-8pm, Sa 10am-8pm, Su noon-5pm. Free.) Between the Capitol and Lake Monona lies the **Monona Terrace Community and Convention Center,** 1 John Nolen Dr., at Martin Luther King, Jr. Blvd., an adaptation of a design by Frank Lloyd Wright. The rooftop gardens offer beautiful views and often host performances. (☎261-4000; www.mononaterrace.com. Open daily 8am-5pm. Free. 1hr. guided tours available daily 1pm. Tours $3.)

Every Wednesday and Saturday morning from late April to early November, visitors swarm the capitol grounds for the **Dane County Farmers' Market,** where farmers, food vendors, and artisans sell fresh-picked crops and other local treats. The uninitiated should try fresh cheese curds. (☎455-1999; www.dcfm.org. Open Apr.-Nov. W 8:30am-2pm, Sa 6am-2pm.) One of the state's most acclaimed art museums, the **Chazen Museum of Art,** 800 University Ave., on the UW campus, devotes one floor to a collection of ancient Greek vases, one to American and European sculpture and painting, and one to contemporary art. (☎263-2246; www.chazen.wisc.edu. Open Tu-F 9am-5pm, Sa-Su 11am-5pm. Tours Th 12:30pm, and Su 2pm. Free. Audio tours $1.) In the mornings before 10:30am, visitors can watch their favorite ice-cream flavors being made at UW's own **Babcock Hall Dairy Store,** 1605 Linden Dr., at Babcock Dr. (☎262-3045; www.wisc.edu/foodsci/store. Open M-F 9:30am-5:30pm, Sa 10am-1:30pm.) Visitors and locals alike seek refuge from bustling metropolitan Madison in two green spaces present in the heart of the city. **Olbrich Botanical Gardens** and indoor **Bolz Conservatory,** 3330 Atwood Ave., showcase changing plant exhibits, from butterfly-attracting flora to the exquisite Thai Pavilion, constructed out of teak, adorned in gold leaf, and imported from Thailand. (Take E. Washington Ave., turn right on Fair Oaks Ave., then left on Atwood Ave. ☎246-4550; www.olbrich.org. Gardens open daily Apr.-Sept. 8am-8pm; Oct.-Mar. 9am-4pm. Free. Conservatory open M-Sa 10am-4pm, Su 10am-5pm. $1, under 5 free; W and Sa 10am-noon free.)

Hikers and botanists alike enjoy trekking the 20 mi. of trails among the 1260 acres of the **University Arboretum,** with entrances at the intersection of North Wingra Dr. and S. Mills St. and also at McCaffrey Dr. and Seminole Hwy. (☎263-7888. Grounds open daily 7am-10pm.) For more info, visit the **UW Visitors Center,** 716 Langdon St., inside the Memorial Union. (☎263-2400. Open M-F 9:30am-4pm, Sa-Su 12:30-4pm.) Next door to the Arboretum, the **Henry Vilas Park Zoo,** 702 S. Randall Ave., is small but has plans to add polar bears to its already comprehensive collection. (☎266-4732; www.vilaszoo.org. Grounds open daily 9:30am-5pm. Buildings open daily 10am-4pm. Free.) For children under 8, the **Madison Children's Museum,** 100 State St., will provide educational entertainment for the entire family with interactive displays, many of them Wisconsin-oriented. (☎256-644; www.madison-childrensmuseum.org. Open Tu-F 9am-4pm, Sa 9am-5pm, Su noon-5pm; Memorial Day-Labor Day also M 9am-4pm. $5, seniors $4; 1st Su of each month free.)

OUTSIDE MADISON

It's worth taking a jaunt outside the city to see what smaller surrounding towns have to offer. Forty miles from Madison in Spring Green, Frank Lloyd Wright's famed **Taliesin** home, farm, and architecture school hug the hills that inspired his organic designs. One of five well-led tours ($16-80) must be purchased to enter the estate. (Take U.S. 14 W to Rte. 23 and County C. ☎877-588-7900; www.taliesin-preservation.org. Open April-Oct. daily 9am-6pm. Call for tour schedules.) Next door, the **American Players Theatre** puts on satires, Shakespeare, and other plays in an outdoor theater. (☎588-2361; www.playinthewoods.org. Shows June-early Oct. Tickets $35-48.) Nine miles south of Taliesin, the **House on the Rock,** 5754 Rte. 23, is an unparalleled multilevel house built into a chimney of rock and stocked with a kitschy collection of bizarre trinkets and artifacts. Home to the world's largest carousel—of its 269 animals, not one is a horse—the house is interesting but may not be worth the steep admission price. (☎935-3639; www.thehouseontherock.com. Open daily mid-June-Aug. 9am-7pm; late April to mid-June and late Aug.-early Sept. 9am-6pm; Sept. to early Nov. 9am-5pm. One of 3 self-guided tours $11.50, all $26.50; ages 4-17 $7.50/15.50, under 3 free. MC/V.) Those in the know pull off U.S. 12 at **Delaney's Surplus,** 35 mi. north of Madison. Tom Every, a.k.a. Dr. Evertron, has made it his life's work to transform scrap metal into sculpture. His ⊠**Forever-ton,** the world's largest scrap metal sculpture, depicts a space-bound voyage in a unique and exciting way. Surrounding it are birds, monsters, and musicians, created by both Every and his family members. (☎219-7830. Free.)

In Baraboo, 40 mi. northwest of Madison on U.S. 12, the **Circus World Museum,** 550 Water St., once the winter home of the world-famous Ringling Brothers Circus, pays homage to circus history with a full lineup of big-top shows and other events. (☎866-693-1500; www.circusworldmuseum.com. Open with performances mid-May to early Sept. daily 9am-6pm; mid-April to mid-May and Sept.-Nov. daily 10am-4pm; Jan. to mid-April and Nov.-Dec. M-F 10am-4pm. $15, seniors $13, ages 5-11 $8. AmEx/D/MC/V.) Seven miles north of Baraboo, the **International Crane Foundation,** on Shady Lane Rd., displays the birds it's trying to save—plus miles of winding prairie trails. (☎356-9462; www.savingcranes.org. Open Apr. 15-Oct. 31 daily 9am-5pm. Tours Memorial Day-Labor Day at 10am, 1, and 3pm. Adults $8.50, seniors $7, children $4. MC/V.)

♪ ENTERTAINMENT

One-hundred thousand music-lovers flood Capitol Sq. for six Wednesday nights in late June and July when the **Wisconsin Chamber Orchestra** performs free **Concerts on the Square.** (☎257-0638; www.wcoconcerts.com. Concerts at 7pm.) Leading out from the Capitol, State St. exudes a lively college atmosphere, sporting many offbeat clothing stores and record shops, as well as a host of bars and restaurants. Next door to the Museum of Contemporary Art, the **Overture Center for the Arts,** 201 State St., is a catch-all for theater, music, visual art, and dance venues. (Tickets and info ☎258-4141; www.overturecenter.com. Ticket office open M-F 11am-5:30pm, Sa 11am-2pm. Tours June-Aug. M, W, F 2pm; Sa 11am and noon. Tours $4. Call for info on student discounts.) The **Madison Symphony Orchestra,** the **Madison Repertory Theatre,** and a huge concert organ, installed in 2004, all make their homes here. (Symphony Orchestra ☎257-3734; www.madisonsymphony.org. Season runs late Aug.-May. Tickets $15-85. Reporatory Theatre ☎256-0029; www.madison-rep.org. Showtimes vary. Tickets from $15.) Across from the Overture Center, the **Orpheum,** 216 State St., brings indie and rock bands to its intimate auditorium. (☎255-6005; www.orpheumtheatre.net.) Students and locals pass their days and nights on the signature chairs of UW's gorgeous **Memorial Union Terrace,** 800 Langdon St., on Lake Mendota (☎265-3000). The terrace is home to free concerts which take place on the lakeshore in the summer and move indoors for winter.

◈ NIGHTLIFE

Fueled by the 40,000-plus students who pack an aptly labeled party school, Madison's nightlife scene is active, with crowded bars scattered throughout the isthmus, particularly along **State Street.** On game days, revelry kicks off at about 9am. Look out for great Happy hour specials and lots of live music.

State Street Brats, 603 State St. (☎255-5544; www.statestreetbrats.com). Head to "Brats" (as in German sausages—not spoiled kids) for a healthy dose of collegiate debauchery and some serious sports, especially on Tu nights. Long list of Wisconsin microbrews (pints $3.25-4, pitchers $8.50-11). Brats and burgers $3-8. Open M-F 11am-2am, Sa 9am-2am.

Essen Haus, 514 E. Wilson St. (☎255-4674; www.essen-haus.com), at S. Blair St. A lively German bar known for its "beer boot" (from $15) and traditionally dressed waitstaff. On the menu, German fare rubs shoulders with American cuisine. Incredible beer selection from $1.50. Open Tu-Sa 3pm-late, Su 3-10pm. Kitchen closes at 10pm.

Paul's Club, 212 State St. (☎257-5250). Mingle under the branches of the real, preserved tree that adorns the bar at Paul's Club, a laid-back lounge that offers a quieter alternative to the many bars with louder, younger crowds, though it still gets packed. Enticing leather couches provide a great place to chat. Open M-Th 4pm-2am, F 4pm-2:30am, Sa noon-2:30am, Su 5pm-2am.

The Weary Traveler, 1201 Williamson St. (442-6207). A laid-back, local crowd from the neighborhood eats and drinks at this watering hole. A closet full of games, including an oversized chess board, enliven the place, as do varied mixed drinks ($4.50-8), regional draft beers (pints $3-5, pitchers $11-14), and an eclectic menu cooked from local ingredients. Burgers $6. Chili (vegan and meat) $3.25-7. Open M 4pm-2am, Tu-Su 11:30-2am. Kitchen open M 4pm-1am, Tu-Su 11am-1am.

⚞ OUTDOOR ACTIVITIES

Madison's many parks and lakeshores offer ample recreational activities. There are 10 gorgeous public **beaches** along the two lakes for swimming or strolling; closest is the one at James Madison Park, 614 E. Gorham St. Back on dry land, **bicycling** is possibly the best way to explore the city and surrounding parklands. Madison is, in fact, the bike capital of the Midwest, with more bikes than cars traversing the landscape. **Budget Bicycle Center,** 1230 Regent St., rents all types of two-wheeled transportation. (☎251-8413. Bikes $10-20 per day, $30 per week; tandems $15-30 per day. Open in summer M-F 9am-9pm, Sa 9am-7pm and Su 11am-7pm; in winter M-F 11am-6:30pm, Sa 10am-5pm, Su noon-4pm.) Its large rental selection, informed staff, and two city locations make **Willy Bikes,** 640 W. Washington St., near the bus station, and 3729 E. Washington St., near U.S. 51, the best bet for bike rentals. (W. Washington ☎255-5292, E. Washington ☎244-2453; www.willy-bikes.com. Hybrid bikes $15 per day; tandems and road bikes $30 per day. Open in summer M-F 10am-8pm, Sa 9am-6pm, Su 11am-6pm.) Hikers and picnickers can enjoy great views of the college at **Picnic Point** on Lake Mendota, a bit of a hike off University Bay Dr. For other city parks, the **Parks Department,** 215 Martin Luther King, Jr. Blvd., Ste. 120, in the Madison Municipal Building, can help with specific park info. (☎266-4711; www.ci.madison.wi/us/parks. Park admission free.) At nearby Lake Wingra, southwest of downtown, the **Wingra Canoe and Sailing Center,** 824 Knickerbocker Pl., rents canoes, kayaks, and other boats. (☎233-5332; www.wingraboats.com. $35-40 per day. Open May-Oct. daily 9am-dusk.)

DOOR COUNTY   ☎920

Jutting out like a thumb from the Wisconsin mainland, the Door Peninsula is not quite the undiscovered coastal getaway that it once was. Sleepy fishing villages now hawk trinkets and fudge to tourists, while "the boat people" plan chamber music festivals in their picturesque tumbledown cottages. The world may have gotten wise to Door County, but the eastern shore's undeveloped beauty and the grassy stillness of the peninsula's county roads still testify to an earlier time.

■■◪ **ORIENTATION AND PRACTICAL INFORMATION.** Door County begins in earnest at **Sturgeon Bay,** where Rte. 42 and 57 converge and then split again. Rte. 57 hugs the eastern coast; Rte. 42 runs up the west. The peninsula's east coast contains sleepy villages and lakeside parks, while the western side tends to be more expensive and touristy. From south to north along Rte. 42, **Egg Harbor, Fish Creek, Ephraim, Sister Bay,** and **Ellison Bay** are the largest towns. Public transit only comes as close as **Green Bay,** 50 mi. southwest of Sturgeon Bay, where **Greyhound** has a station at 800 Cedar St. (☎432-4883; www.greyhound.com. Tickets sold M-F 7:30am-5pm, Sa-Su 10:30am-4:30pm.) Buses run to Madison (5-8hr., 4 per day, $25.50) and Milwaukee (2-3hr., 4 per day, $26). Reserve tickets at least a day in advance. All of the major settlements have their own Visitors Centers, but the **Door County Chamber of Commerce,** on Rte. 42/57 entering Sturgeon Bay, serves as a kind of clearinghouse for information about the county. (☎743-4456 or 800-527-3529; www.doorcounty.com. Open Apr.-Oct. M-F 8:30am-5pm, Sa-Su 10am-4pm; Nov.-Mar. M-F 8:30am-4:30pm.) **Internet Access: Door County Library,** 104 S. 4th Ave., in Sturgeon Bay. (Free. Open M-Th 9am-9pm, F 9am-6pm, Sa 9am-5pm.) **Post Office:** 359 Louisiana St., at 4th St. in Sturgeon Bay. (☎800-275-8777. Open M-F 8:30am-5pm, Sa 9:30am-noon.) **Postal Code:** 54235.

▐ **ACCOMMODATIONS.** Rooms in Door County during July and August are uniformly expensive; plan a visit for May or September to take advantage of low-season rates. Two of the best options for budget travelers are in the north-central part of the peninsula. ▨**Century Farm Motel ❸,** 10068 Rte. 57, 3 mi. south of Sister Bay on Rte. 57, rents cozy two-room cottages hand-built in the 20s. The motel, situated on a chicken farm and family homestead, is rare for its refusal to hike prices as the

ON THE MENU

BOIL, FISH BOIL, TOIL, AND TROUBLE

Bring 5 gal. fresh water to a boil in a large metal cauldron over a hot fire. Throw in 25 lb. of small red potatoes, sliced but not peeled; 9min. later, add an equal quantity of small white onions, peeled. After 3min., lower freshly caught whitefish steaks into the cauldron using a heavy-duty colander, and add a generous shovelful of evaporated salt for seasoning. The fish oil will separate and condense on the surface of the water before starting to boil over and dribble into the fire. At this point, pour a coffee can's worth of fuel oil onto the fire and get out of the way! (Leave this step to a master boiler.) The fish oil will ignite and a fireball will kick up 8ft. into the air.

After the flames die down, lift the colander with heavy gloves and serve. The **Viking Grill,** on Rte. 42 in Ellison Bay, is the granddaddy of the Door County fish boil. Though the tablecloths are plasticky, the fish sure isn't: you can drag a fork through the tender, flaky meat and pull it away easily from the bones. Owner Dan Petersen still swears by the Wickman family's original recipe, and summer after summer the fish boil continues to raise eyebrows and fill bellies.

Viking Grill, on Rte. 42 (☎854-2998; www.thevikinggrill.com). Fish boils daily May-Oct. 4:30-7pm. $14, ages 12 and under $11. Cash only.

summer progresses. (☎854-4069. A/C, fridge, and TV. Open mid-May to mid-Oct. One-bedroom cabin $50; two-bedroom cabin $60. Cash only.) Two miles to the north, **Patio Motel ❸,** 200 Orchard Dr., just off of Rte. 57, offers a more traditional motel experience, although its rates are some of the lowest in the upper half of the peninsula. (☎854-1978. Open May-late Oct. Rooms $72. D/MC/V.) North of Sturgeon Bay, budget travelers should check out **Chal-A-Motel ❷,** 3910 Rte. 42/57. It's a 30min. drive north to the other villages on the peninsula, but year-round accommodations at reasonable prices may make the commute worthwhile. (☎743-6788; www.chal-amotel.com. Doubles July-Oct. $69; Nov.-April $44. MC/V.)

▓ CAMPING. Without question, the most economical way to spend a summer night in Door County is under the stars. The area's **state parks ❶** are an appealing choice for backpackers with tents. (Reservations for all parks ☎888-947-2757; www.wiparks.net. M-Th and Su $12, WI residents $10; F-Sa $15/13.) All state parks require a motor vehicle permit, which can be purchased at the entrance of the park ($5 per hr.; $10, WI residents $7). **Peninsula State Park,** just past Fish Creek on Rte. 42, is far and away the most popular, and reservations can be made up to 11 months in advance. (☎868-3258. 469 sites with showers and toilets; 25 reserved for walk-ins. June-Aug. $3 more than state rate; sites by the shore $3 more than others.) The relatively uncrowded **Potawatomi State Park,** 3740 Park Dr., is flanked by limestone cliffs just south of Sturgeon Bay off Rte. 42/57. (☎746-2890. 123 campsites; 19 open to walk-ins. 25 with electricity.) **Newport State Park,** 7 mi. from Ellison Bay off Rte. 42, is a wilderness preserve at the tip of the peninsula. Sites are accessible by hiking only. (☎854-2500. Hike 1-2mi. to sites. 16 sites, 3 open to walk-ins. No showers.) The untamed **Rock Island State Park** offers 40 remote sites off Washington Island's northern shore. (☎847-2235. Open late May to mid-Oct. Round-trip ferry ride 15min. Departs Washington Island daily 10am, 1 and 4pm. $9, children $5; with camping gear $1.)

◖ FOOD. Restaurants that stay open for dinner tend to be expensive, so savvy travelers might want to eat out early in the day and then stock up on groceries for an evening meal. Restaurants and pubs line Madison Ave., the main thoroughfare in Sturgeon Bay. Grab groceries at **Econo Foods,** 1250 N. 14th Ave., in Sturgeon Bay (open 24 hr.). The **Piggly Wiggly Super Market,** Country Walk Dr. in Sister Bay, is a good bet up north, (open M-Sa 9am-8pm, Su 9am-5pm). Start off the day with lingonberry pancakes at **Al Johnson's**

Swedish Restaurant ❹, 700-710 N. Bayshore Dr., in the middle of Sister Bay on Rte. 42. The restaurant is hard to miss; just look for the goats grazing atop the sod-covered roof. (☎854-2626. Dinner entrees $12-19. Open daily 6am-9pm; low-season 7am-8pm. AmEx/D/MC/V.) Farther south, at **Good Eggs ❶**, 9820 Brookside Ln., just off of Rte. 42 in Ephraim, you can gorge yourself on made-to-order omelets wrapped in flour tortillas at a table improvised from surfboards. (☎854-6621. Breakfast wraps from $4.45. Open mid-May to mid-Oct. daily 7am-2pm. Cash only.) Grab an afternoon snack on the east side of the peninsula at **Town Hall Bakery ❷**, 6225 Rte. 57, in Jacksonport. Watch the lace curtains wave in the breeze as you sip a cup of soup ($3.25), or sample a dish of the famous granola ($7) that is shipped nationwide. (☎823-2116. July F live music 7:30pm. Cover $8. Open June-Aug. daily 7am-4pm; Sept. Th-Su 7am-3pm. Cash only.)

◉ ◪ SIGHTS AND ENTERTAINMENT. At the base of the peninsula, Sturgeon Bay's historic shipbuilding center houses the intriguing **Door County Maritime Museum,** 120 N. Madison St., in downtown. The museum commemorates Sturgeon Bay's local hero Captain John Roen, who recovered a sunken freighter. It showcases artifacts from steamship gauges to old outboard motors and gives visitors a glimpse into a working periscope. (☎743-5958; www.dcmm.org. Open daily May-Oct. 9am-6pm; Nov.-Apr. 10am-5pm. $7, ages 5-17 $4. MC/V.) The museum also operates an exhibit in the northern village of **Gill's Rock,** where visitors can explore a 1930s fishing boat. (☎854-1844. Open June to mid-Oct. daily 10am-5pm. $4.50, ages 5-17 $1.50.) Across the bridge from the Maritime Museum, the **Fairfield Center for Contemporary Art,** 242 Michigan St., has a permanent collection of sketches and sculptures by Henry Moore and a painting by Kandinsky. Furniture by master crafstman Michael Dorr will be featured during summer 2008. (☎746-0001; www.fairfieldcenter.org. Open M-Sa 10am-5pm, Su 10am-3pm. Free.) Trade in the hurlyburly of Sturgeon Bay for the serene grounds of **Stone's Throw Winery,** at the intersection of Rte. A and E east of Egg Harbor. Stone's Throw grows its grapes in California and then ships them overnight to Wisconsin, yielding a strong crop of wines that visitors can sample to their heart's content. (☎839-9660. Tasting $3. Bottles from $10. Open daily 10am-5pm.) A laid-back crowd of college students and locals takes in live music every summer at ▧**Fishstock,** an excellent series of acoustic concerts entering its seventh season in a renovated dairy barn. (3127 Rte. F, east of Fish Creek. ☎839-2981; www.fishstockmusic.com. Su live music 7pm July-Aug. $10. Check website for a schedule of barn dances.) The **Skyway Drive-In,** on Rte. 42 between Fish Creek and Ephraim, screens double features the old-fashioned way. (☎854-9938. $6.75, ages 6-11 $3.75, under 5 free. Films start after sunset; call for schedule.) Just south of the Skyway, Peninsula State Park plays host to the outdoor **American Folklore Theatre,** where an increasingly high-profile troupe of actors performs original Wisconsin-themed shows. (☎854-6117; www.folkloretheatre.com. $16, ages 13-19 $7.50, ages 3-12 $4.50.)

▧ OUTDOOR ACTIVITIES. Biking is the best way to take in the lighthouses, rocks, and white-sand beaches of Door's rugged eastern coastline. Village tourist offices have free bike maps. **Whitefish Dunes State Park,** off Rte. 57 south of Jacksonport, glimmers with extensive sand dunes; hiking, biking, skiing trails, and a well-kept wildlife preserve. (Open daily 8am-8pm. Vehicle permit required.) Just north of the Dunes off Rte. 57 on Cave Point Rd., **Cave Point County Park** offers unusual rock formations formed by freshwater erosion, as well as a beautiful view of the lake. (Open daily 6am-9pm. Free.) **Ridges Sanctuary,** north of Baileys Harbor off Rte. Q, is home to more than 25 species of orchids and other endangered plants, like the oddly named dwarf lake iris. Nature trails wind their way along crescent-shaped ridges formed by Lake Michigan, and travel across adjoining wet-

GREAT LAKES

lands with wooden bridges. (☎839-2802. Nature center open late May to mid-Oct. daily 9am-4pm, although trails stay open after hours. Trail fee $3. Guided tours June-Aug. daily 9:30am and 1:30pm. $5, includes trail fee.) **Baileys Harbor Ridges Beach,** an uncrowded stretch of sand that allows for secluded swimming, is attached to the sanctuary on Ridges Rd. Water temperatures are chilly, even in the summer. Accessed via Cana Island Rd. off Rte. Q, **Cana Island Lighthouse** extends into the lake, compelling visitors to cross the rocky path (at low tide) or wade through the frigid waters (at high tide) to reach the lighthouse grounds. The lighthouse is not normally open to visitors, although the Coast Guard decides on a year-by-year basis whether to offer tours on the third weekend in May. Call the Maritime Museum in Sturgeon Bay for more information. The keeper's house has a gift shop that is open throughout high season, and the island provides an expansive view of the bay. (Open May-Oct. daily 10am-5pm. $4, ages 5-17 $2.) On the opposite coast, **Peninsula State Park** draws kayakers, anglers, and families on bicycles. More crowded than the beaches around Baileys Harbor, **Nicolet Beach** attracts sunbathers from all over the peninsula. (Open daily 6am-11pm. No lifeguards. Vehicle permit required.) One mile and 110 steps up from the beach, **Eagle Tower** offers the highest view of the shore and a chance to see beyond the waters of Green Bay on a clear day. At the Fish Creek entrance to Peninsula State Park, **Edge of Park Bike & Moped Rental,** 4007 Rte. 42, rents bikes and winter equipment. (☎868-3344; www.edgeofpark.com. Bikes $6 per hr., $20 per day. Mountain bikes $7.50 per hr., $30 per day. Mopeds $45 1st hr., $22 thereafter. Open June-Oct. M-Sa 8:30am-6pm, Su 8:30am-4pm; Nov.-May M and F-Sa 10am-5pm, Su 10am-4pm.) Six miles off the northern tip of the peninsula, **Washington Island** is separated from the mainland by **Death's Door,** a treacherous channel that brought about the demise of hundreds of seafaring vessels in the 19th century. Today, Coast Guard range lights and modern ferries have made the journey much safer, allowing daytrippers to pedal over 75 mi. of quiet country roads and grill supper on **Gislason Public Beach,** across Detroit Harbor. (Washington Island Ferry,www.wisferry.com, and Island Clipper, www.islandclipper.com, departs from Gill's Rock 2-3 times per hr. in summer between 8am-7pm, less frequently in the low season. Round-trip fare $10, ages 6-11 $5. Washington Island Ferry shuttles automobiles $24, bikes $4. One-speed bikes can be rented at the island dock for $3.50 per hr.)

APOSTLE ISLANDS   ☎715

The National Lakeshore protects 22 breathtaking islands off the coast of northern Wisconsin, as well as a 12 mi. stretch of mainland shore. Bayfield, a tiny mainland town, serves as the access point to the islands. Tourism is primarily focused on the mainland and Madeline Island, where inns draw families looking for a back-to-nature weekend. Local adventure companies allow summer tourists of all levels of experience to enjoy kayaking, hiking, and camping among the sandstone bluffs.

🛈 **PRACTICAL INFORMATION.** Most excursions begin in the sleepy mainland town of **Bayfield** (pop. 611), in northwest Wisconsin on the Lake Superior coast. The **Bay Area Rural Transit (BART),** 300 Industrial Park Rd., 21 mi. south on Rte. 13 in Ashland, offers a shuttle to Bayfield. (☎682-9664. 4 per day M-F 7am-5pm. $2.25, students $1.25, seniors $1.) The **Bayfield Chamber of Commerce** is at 42 S. Broad St. (☎779-3335 or 800-447-4094; www.bayfield.org. Open M-F 8:30am-5pm, Sa-Su 9am-3pm. Lobby with free local phone open 24hr.) **National Lakeshore Headquarters Visitors Center,** 415 Washington Ave., distributes hiking info and **camping permits,** and screens a short film about the islands. (☎779-3397. Open mid-May to mid-Sept. daily 8am-6pm; mid-Sept. to mid-May M-F 8am-4:30pm. Permits $10 per night.) The **Bayfield Carnegie Library,** 37 N. Broad St., provides free **Internet** access in 30min.

slots. (☎779-3953. Open M-Tu and Th 1-7:30pm, W and F 9:30am-5pm, Sa 9:30am-3pm.) For **short-term work** picking apples or raspberries, contact the **Bayfield Apple Company**, on County Rte. J, near Betzold Rd. (☎779-5700 or 800-363-4526. Raspberries in season mid- to late July; apples late Sept. to mid-Oct. Open daily 9am-6pm.) **Post Office:** 22 S. Broad St., in Bayfield. (☎779-5636. Open M-F 9am-4:30pm, Sa 9am-11am.) **Postal Code:** 54814.

█ ACCOMMODATIONS. In summer months, the budget pickings are slim in Bayfield; rooms should be booked weeks in advance for trips during July and August. For cheaper lodgings, check the motels along Lake Shore Dr. in Ashland, an easy 30min. drive south of Bayfield. Rooms start at $40, even in high season. **The Seagull Bay Motel ❸**, off Rte. 13 at S. 7th St., offers spacious, smoke-free rooms with cable TV, free Wi-Fi and a clear lake view. (☎779-5558; www.seagullbay.com. Rooms mid-May to mid-Oct. $70-100; mid-Oct. to mid-May $40-70. MC/V.) **Greunke's Inn ❹**, 17 Rittenhouse Ave., has been accommodating guests for 140 years. Quaint country rooms and a homey atmosphere make this a great place to experience Bayfield hospitality. (☎779-5480 or 800-245-3072. Open May-Oct. Shared baths. No A/C. Rooms $55-130. AmEx/D/MC/V.) **Dalrymple Park ❶**, ¼ mi. north of town on Rte. 13, has 30 campsites and a sweeping view of Madeline Island. (Open mid-May to mid-Oct. No showers or electricity. Self-regulated. No reservations. Sites $15.) **Apostle Islands Area Campground ❶**, ½ mi. south of Bayfield on Rte. J off Rte. 13, has 60 campsites buried deep in the woods of Bayfield. (☎779-5524. Open early May to early Oct. Reservations recommended 1 month in advance for July-Aug. Tent sites $20, with hookup $24, with full sewer and electricity $28. Primitive cabins $40. Cash only.) Campers in the Bayfield area should come prepared to battle fierce mosquitoes in summer.

█ FOOD. The bright pink exterior is just the beginning at **Maggie's ❷**, 257 Manypenny Ave., where charbroiled burgers ($6.50-7.75) and zesty fajitas ($10) complement the kitschy flamingo-themed decor. (☎779-5641; www.maggies-bayfield.com. Open M-F 11:30am-9pm, Sa-Su 11:30am-10pm. AmEx/D/MC/V.) One of the oldest establishments in Bayfield, **Greunke's Restaurant ❸**, 17 Rittenhouse Ave., at 1st St., has been feeding hungry fishermen for over a century. These days, Greunke's cooks up huge breakfasts by day ($7-10) and batter-dipped whitefish livers ($16) by night. Check out the shrine to the late John F. Kennedy, Jr., located next to the 1946 Wurlitzer jukebox. (☎779-5480. Fish boils Th-Su 6:30-8pm; $13.50, children $6. Open M-Sa 6am-10pm, F-Su 7am-9:30pm. AmEx/D/MC/V.) **Egg Toss Cafe ❷**, 41 Manypenny Ave., specializes in breakfast, serving up eggs benedict with crab cakes ($10), and staple breakfast dishes such as *huevos rancheros* ($8.25) and whole wheat pancakes with eggs and sausage ($6.75) that are sure to please. (☎779-5181; www.eggtoss-bayfield.com. Open daily 6am-2pm. AmEx/D/MC/V.)

█ SIGHTS AND OUTDOOR ACTIVITIES. The recently completed **Bayfield Heritage Center**, 30 N. Broad St., offers glimpses into the settlement's past as a lumber boomtown and fishing village. (☎779-5958; www.bayfieldheritage.org. Open mid-June to mid-Sept. T-Su 1-4pm. Free) Spend an hour or two picking famously sweet strawberries up at the **James Erickson Orchard & Country Store**, 86600 Betzold Rd. (☎779-5438. U-pick strawberries $1.25 per lb. Open late May to mid-Oct. M-Sa 10am-5pm, Su noon-4pm; during late June berry season, open daily 9am-5pm). The best beach on the mainland is **Bayview Beach**, 6 mi. south of Bayfield along Rte. 13. Look for the green signs marking Bayview Park Rd., then turn down the dirt road to access Bayview's soft, red sands. Even after the summer hikers and beach bums head home for the season, Bayfield manages to attract ample tourism with its annual **Apple Festival.** An incredible 50-80 thousand visitors pour into town during the first full weekend of October. The slopeside **Big Top Chautauqua**, 3 mi. south of Bayfield off Hwy. 13 on Ski Hill Rd., draws folk and bluegrass headliners like Arlo Guthrie, in addition to staging ever-popular "house shows," original musicals about life in northern Wisconsin. (☎373-5552 or 888-244-8386; www.bigtop.org. Open June-Sept. Call for showtimes. Tickets can be purchased at the Bayfield Branch Box Office at Rittenhouse Ave. and 1st St., next to Greunke's. Reserved seating for house shows $18, under 17 $8; general admission $15/4.)

While Madeline Island (see below) is the only one of the Apostle Islands with a year-round settlement, hikers and outdoors enthusiasts use Bayfield as their gateway to a number of the other islands. Nearby **Stockton Island** and **Oak Island** are among the most popular for campers, although private sailboats dock out as far as **Rocky Island** and **York Island**. The lighthouses on **Raspberry** and **Michigan Islands** are open for tours in summer, while experienced kayakers can explore the breathtaking sea caves on **Devil's Island**. The **Apostle Islands Cruise Service** runs a narrated 3hr. tour that provides newcomers with a scenic overview of the islands. For travelers hoping to do more than look out the window, the Cruise Service also drops campers off at Stockton and Oak Islands during July and August. (☎779-3925 or 800-323-7619; www.apostleisland.com. Tours depart the Bayfield City Dock mid-May to mid-Oct. daily 10am. $38, children $23. Reservations recommended. Round-trip shuttle to Stockton or Oak Island $40, children $24. Reservations required.) **Trek and Trail**, at 1st and Washington St., in Bayfield, rents bikes and kayaks. They also lead sea kayaking tours, ranging from a 2hr. intro to a 6-day odyssey through the outer islands' caves and quarries. (☎800-354-8735. Bikes $5 per hr., $20 per day. 4hr. kayak rental from $20. All renters must complete a 3hr. kayaking safety course, offered daily 8:30am and 1pm. Safety course $50; reserve at least 1 day in advance. Tours from $30-99. Open June-Oct.)

MADELINE ISLAND   ☎715

Funkier and more free-spirited than buttoned-up Bayfield, Madeline Island brings together a provocative combination of cigar-chomping millionaires and rakish artists with dreadlocks dangling in the wind. The year-round population assembles in February for an island-wide talent show and nine holes of golf on the ice. Housed in an interconnected compound of 19th-century log buildings, the **Madeline Island Historical Museum** keeps the island's rich history alive with artifacts ranging from ice chisels and weasel traps to a Chippewa translation of the Protestant Bible. (☎747-2415. Open June to early Oct. daily 10am-5pm. $6, seniors $5, ages 5-12 $3.) Rooms in the area fill during the summer; call ahead for reservations. The **Madeline Island Motel ❹**, on Col. Woods Ave. across from the ferry landing, has private patios with hanging plants attached to each of its rooms. (☎747-3000. A/C, fridge, microwave and TV. Continental breakfast included. Open Apr.-Nov. July-early Sept. doubles $95; Apr.-June and early Sept.-Nov. $70-80. D/MC/V.) Rooms in the area fill during the summer; call well ahead for reservations. The **Island Inn ❹**, on Main St. to the left of the ferry landing, rents five small rooms near downtown Madeline Island's museums and bars. (☎747-2000. A/C and fridge. Complementary juice and coffee. Doubles $98. MC/V.) The **Inn on Madeline Island ❺**, a 10min. walk south of the ferry landing, rents out lake houses and condos that are surprisingly affordable for travelers in groups. With over 70 rental properties to offer parties of four or more, the Inn can find lodgings with a variety of configurations and amenities. (☎747-6315 or 800-822-6315; www.madisland.com. 2-3 night min. Reserve well in advance for weekends in the high season. 50% of total payment due with reservation. Rates from $100. MC/V.) Madeline Island has two campgrounds. **Big Bay Town Park ❶**, 6½ mi. from La Pointe off Big Bay Rd., rents 36 sites next to tranquil Big Bay Lagoon. (☎747-6913. Open mid-May to mid-Oct. Sites $15, with electricity $20.) Across the lagoon, **Big Bay State Park ❶** rents 60 rustic sites without electricity. (☎747-6425, reservations 888-947-2757; www.wiparks.net. Reservations $10. Sites $15-17; WI resident discount $2. Daily vehicle permit $10, WI residents $5.) On weekend mornings, crowds pack **Ella's Island Cafe ❷**, to the left of the ferry landing, to enjoy eggs benedict ($12) on the patio. (☎747-2400. Breakfast $8-11. Open F-Su 7:30am-noon. Cash only.) Take in the sunset on **Grandpa Tony's ❷** rooftop deck. The restaurant is to the right of the ferry landing. (Burgers 2 for $7.25. Caesar salad $7.25.) ◪**Tom's Burned Down Cafe,** 1 Middle Rd., is Madeline Island's nexus for all things hip, weird, and countercultural. Burned to the ground in 1992, the bar and performance space rebuilt itself with scrap metal, a huge tent, and a stubborn commitment to having a good time. (☎747-6100. Th open mic, F-Sa live music. Cover $4-15. Open daily M-Th and Su 10am-2am, F-Sa 10am-2:30am.)

With roughly five streets, downtown Madeline Island is easy to navigate. The **Madeline Island Chamber of Commerce** is on Main St. to the right of the ferry landing. (☎747-2801 or 888-475-3386; www.madeleineisland.com. Open May-Oct. M-F 9am-5pm, Sa 9am-3pm; Nov.-Apr. M-F 10am-3pm.) For pamphlets about the island, visit the chamber's booth near the ferry landing in Bayfield. **Madeline Island Ferry Line** shuttles between Bayfield and La Pointe on Madeline Island. (☎747-2051; www.madferry.com. June-Aug. daily every 30min. 9:30am-6pm, every hr. 6:30-9:30am and 6-11pm. Round-trip $10, ages 6-11 $5; bikes $5; cars $22. Apr-May and Sept.-Dec. ferries are cheaper, but run less frequently.) In winter, the state highway department builds an ice road if possible. During transition periods, the ferry service runs **windsleds** between the island and the mainland. **Motion to Go,** 102 Lake View Pl., on Middle Rd. about one block from the ferry, rents scooters and bikes. (☎747-6585. Mountain bikes $8 per hr., $30 per day. Mopeds $25 per hr. Open daily May to mid-June 9am-6pm; mid-June to July 8:30am-7pm; July-Aug. 8am-8pm; Sept. to mid-Oct. 9am-7pm.) **Apostle Island Kayaks,** 5min. to the right of the ferry landing on Main Street, rents kayaks (single $37 per 8 hr.) without requiring a water safety course. (☎715-747-3636. Open daily 9am-6pm.)The **Madeline Island Public Library,** on Library St. just off of Big Bay Rd., offers free **Internet** access. (☎747-3662. Open M and W 2-8pm, T and Th-F 10am-5pm; Sa 10am-noon.) The **Post Office** is just off the dock on Madeline Island in La Pointe. (☎747-3712. Open M-F 9am-noon and 12:30-4:20pm, Sa 9:30am-12:50pm.) **Postal Code:** 54850.

MINNESOTA

In the 19th century, floods of German and Scandinavian settlers edged native tribes out of the rich lands now known as Minnesota, a name derived from a Dakota word meaning "sky-tinted waters." Known as the Land of 10,000 Lakes, Minnesota's beauty stretches from the northern wilderness and Boundary Waters to the Twin Cities and the more settled south. From farmers to city-dwellers, Minnesotans persevere through harsh winters and cultivate warm, close-knit communities. Attempts to preserve the state's rugged northern frontier have helped raise awareness about Minnesota's natural resources and the culture of the Chippewa, the area's first inhabitants.

◪ PRACTICAL INFORMATION

Capital: St. Paul.

Visitor Info: Minnesota Office of Tourism, 100 Metro Sq., 121 7th Pl. E, St. Paul 55101 (☎651-296-5029 or 800-657-3700; www.exploreminnesota.com). Open M-F 8am-4:30pm.

Postal Abbreviation: MN. **Sales Tax:** 6.5%.

MINNEAPOLIS AND ST. PAUL ☎ 612

Native writer Garrison Keillor wrote that "the difference between St. Paul and Minneapolis is the difference between pumpernickel and Wonder bread." For years, St. Paul, viewed as a conservative, Irish-Catholic town, contrasted sharply with its young and metropolitan neighbor. Today, remnants of this distinction are evident in Minneapolis's big venues and bigger skyscrapers and St. Paul's traditional capitol and cathedrals, but it remains impossible to typecast the cities' diverse and cosmopolitan residents.

⊏ TRANSPORTATION

Airport: Minneapolis-St. Paul International (MSP; ☎ 726-5555; www.mspairport.com), 30min. south of the cities on Rte. 5, off I-494 in Bloomington. From the airport, take the Hiawatha light rail line to Minneapolis or bus #54 to St. Paul. Super Shuttle (☎ 827-7777; www.supershuttle.com) goes to some hotels and both downtowns about every 20min. Desk open 24hr. To Minneapolis ($15) and St. Paul ($13).

Trains: Amtrak, Midway Center, 730 Transfer Rd. (☎ 651-644-6012 or 800-872-7245; www.amtrak.com), off University Ave. SE and off I-94, between the Twin Cities. Open daily 6:30am-11:30pm. Bus #16 connects to both downtowns. The Empire Builder line runs once a day to **Chicago** (8hr., $50-120) and **Milwaukee** (6½hr., $48-110).

Buses: Greyhound, 950 Hawthorne Ave. (☎ 371-3325; www.greyhound.com), between 9th and 10th St. in downtown Minneapolis. In St. Paul, 166 University Ave. at Rice St. (☎ 651-222-0507), 2 blocks west of the capitol. To **Chicago** (9-15hr., 5-6 per day, $61-72) and **Milwaukee** (6-9hr., 4 per day, $50-55). $20 discount with 7-day advance purchase. Both routes depart from Minneapolis and St. Paul stations. Minneapolis station open daily 6am-12:30am. St. Paul station open daily 6am-9:30pm.

Public Transit: MetroTransit, 560 6th Ave. N (☎ 373-3333; www.metrotransit.org). Serves both cities. Most major lines have no service 1-4am. Of routes that connect the downtowns, bus #16 takes 55min., bus #94 (B, C, or D) takes 30min., and bus #50 takes 36min. Bus #50 offers limited rush hour service. Bus #16 operates 24hr. **Hiawatha Light Rail** line runs 4am-1am from the Warehouse District through downtown to the airport and Mall of America. $1.50; seniors, ages 6-12, and disabled $0.50. Downtown zone $0.50. Rush hour (M-F 6-9am and 3-6:30pm) fare $2 . Express lines $2; ages 6-12, disabled, and seniors $0.50. Student discount 5-10%. Transfers free.

Taxi: Yellow Taxi, in Minneapolis ☎ 824-4444, in St. Paul ☎ 651-222-4433.

⬛❓ ORIENTATION AND PRACTICAL INFORMATION

Public transit in the Twin Cities has improved with the Hiawatha Light Rail, but most people still rely on cars. Despite one-way streets and skewed numbered grids, the streets are not congested and driving in the cities is manageable. In addition to metered street parking, garages and parking ramps are nearly everywhere and are often free. Downtown Minneapolis lies about 10 mi. west of downtown St. Paul via **I-94. I-35** splits in the Twin Cities, with **I-35 W** serving Minneapolis and **I-35 E** serving St. Paul. **I-494** links I-35 W and E to the airport and the Mall of America, while **I-394** connects downtown Minneapolis to the western suburbs. **Hennepin Avenue** and the pedestrian **Nicollet Mall** are main roads in Minneapolis, dividing streets north-south and east-west, respectively. **Kellogg Avenue** and **7th Street** are main roads in St. Paul. For pedestrians, skyways are the main mode of movement in both downtowns, providing relief from the heat in the summer and protection from the elements during long winters.

Downtown St. Paul

FOOD
Café Latte, **4**
Cossetta, **3**
Day by Day Cafe, **5**
Mickey's Diner, **1**
Tanpopo, **2**

Downtown Minneapolis

▲ **ACCOMMODATIONS**
Evelo's Bed and Breakfast, **12**
Minneapolis International Hostel, **14**
Nan's Bed & Breakfast, **7**
Saloon Hotel, **5**

● **FOOD**
Bryant-Lake Bowl, **15**
Chino Latino, **9**
Figlio, **10**
French Meadow Bakery, **17**
Loring Pasta Bar, **11**
Midtown Global Market, **13**
Tacos Morelos, **16**
The Tin Fish, **11**

■ **NIGHTLIFE**
Brit's Pub, **8**
Escape Ultra Lounge, **4**
First Avenue and 7th St. Entry, **3**
The Gay 90s, **2**
The Local, **6**

Visitor Info: Minneapolis Convention and Visitors Association, 250 Marquette Ave. (☎767-8000; www.minneapolis.org), in Convention Center. Desk open M-F 8am-5pm. **St. Paul Convention and Visitors Bureau,** 175 W. Kellogg Blvd., #502 (☎800-627-6101 or 265-4900; www.visitstpaul.com), in River Centre. Open M-F 8am-4:30pm.

Hotlines: Crime Victim Center Crisis Line, ☎340-5400. **Rape/Sexual Assault Line,** ☎825-4357. Both 24hr. **Gay-Lesbian Helpline,** ☎822-8661. Operates M-F noon-midnight, Sa 4pm-midnight.

Internet Access: Minneapolis Public Library, 300 Nicollet Mall (☎630-6200; www.mplib.org). Wi-Fi available. Open Tu-Sa 10am-8pm. **St. Paul Public Library,** 90 W. 4th St. (☎651-266-7000; www.sppl.org), between Washington and Market St. Wi-Fi available. Open M 11:30am-8pm, Tu-F 9am-5:30pm, Sa 11am-4pm, Su 1-5pm.

Post Office: In Minneapolis, 100 S. 1st St. at Marquette Ave. Open M-F 7am-8pm, Sa 9am-1pm. In St. Paul, 180 E. Kellogg Blvd. Open M-F 8:30am-5:30pm, Sa 9am-noon. (☎800-275-8777.) **Postal Codes:** Minneapolis 55401, St. Paul 55101. **Area Codes:** Minneapolis 612, St. Paul and eastern suburbs 651, southwestern suburbs 952, northwestern suburbs 763. In text, 612 unless otherwise noted.

▌ ACCOMMODATIONS

Budget hotels in urban areas tend to be scarce, though univeristy housing and bed and breakfasts are solid options. Minneapolis caters to a younger crowd and consequently has cheaper hotels; St. Paul offers classier establishments for those with fatter wallets. The **University of Minnesota Housing Office** (☎624-2994; www.umn.edu/housing/offcampus) keeps a list of local rooms ($15-60 per night) for rent on a daily or weekly basis. The section of I-494 at Rte. 77, near the Mall of America, is lined with chain motels with rooms from $40. The nearest private campgrounds are about 15 mi. outside the city; the closest state park campgrounds include **Lake Elmo Park** (1 mi. north of I-94, 2.5 mi. from I-694, at the intersection of County Rd. 10 and 19; ☎651-430-8370), the **Three Rivers Park District** (Baker Park Reserve in Maple Plain, 21 mi. west), **Afton State Park** (20 mi. southeast; backpacker sites only), and the **William O'Brian State Park** (30 mi. east). Call **Minnesota State Parks** (☎651-296-6157 or 888-646-6367; www.stayatmnparks.com) or the **Minnesota Lodging, Restaurant, and Resort & Campgrounds Associations** (☎651-778-2400; www.hospitalitymn.com for more info).

Evelo's Bed and Breakfast, 2301 Bryant Ave. (☎374-9656), 2 blocks from Hennepin Ave. in Minneapolis. Take bus #17 to Bryant Ave. 4 lovingly tended, comfortable rooms in an exquisite 1897 Victorian home. Fresh flowers, continental breakfast, shared bathroom. Reservations and deposit required. Singles $65; doubles $85. MC/V. ❸

Saloon Hotel (Hotel Amsterdam), 828 Hennepin Ave. (☎288-0459; www.gaympls.com), in downtown Minneapolis, between 8th and 9th St. Above the Saloon nightclub, this hotel has lodging and entertainment geared toward the GBLT community, but all are welcome. Lounge with TV and Wi-Fi. Private rooms with shared bathrooms. Reservations recommended. Singles $44; doubles $50-65. MC/V. ❷

Nan's Bed & Breakfast, 2304 Fremont Ave S. (☎377-5118), 2 blocks west of Hennepin Ave. in Minneapolis. The friendly proprietors keep 3 cozy rooms and make breakfast each morning. Reservations recommended. Singles $64-69; doubles $69-75. ❷

Minneapolis International Hostel (HI), 2400 Stevens Ave. S (☎522-5000; www.minneapolishostel.com), at 24th St. W, south of downtown Minneapolis by the Institute of Arts. Take bus #17 to 24th St. and walk 2 blocks east to Stevens. One of the only budget options in town. Kitchen and Wi-Fi. Linen included. Reception daily 8am-midnight. Check-in 1pm. Check-out 11am. Reservations recommended. Dorms $28; singles $49. AmEx/MC/V. ❶

◨ FOOD

The Twin Cities' cosmopolitan vibe is reflected in its many culinary choices. **Uptown** Minneapolis, near the intersection of Lake St. and Hennepin Ave., offers funky restaurants, which abound with hip and fresh vegetarian options, and bars, which attract a mixed crowd of locals and tourists alike. In downtown Minneapolis, the **Warehouse District,** on 1st Ave. N between 8th St. and Washington Ave. is home to many of the cities' upscale options; **Nicollet Mall,** a 12-block pedestrian stretch of Nicollet Ave., attracts locals and tourists with shops and simple food options ranging from burgers to Tex-Mex. South of downtown, from 25th St. to 30th St. Nicollet turns into **Eat Street,** a stretch of serious ethnic eateries.

In St. Paul, the upscale **Grand Avenue,** between Lexington and Dale, is lined with laid-back restaurants and bars, while **Lowertown,** along Sibley St. near 6th St. downtown, is a popular nighttime hangout. Near the University of Minnesota (U of M) campus, **Dinkytown,** on the East Bank of the river, and the **Seven Corners** area of the West Bank, on Cedar Ave., cater to late-night student cravings. In the Twin Cities, locals skip restaurants and head to area **cafes** (p. 556), and many restaurants morph into bars after dinner.

The **Minneapolis Farmers' Market,** off I-94W at E. Lyndale Ave. and 3rd Ave. N, offers fruits, vegetables, and crafts. (☎333-1718; www.mplsfarmersmarket.com. Free parking under I-94 bridge. Open late Apr.-Dec. daily 6am-1pm. Also located on Nicollet Mall May-Oct. Th and Sa 6am-6pm.) The **Midtown Global Market,** 920 E Lake St., at Chicago Ave. S, is a covered market with cheap food ranging from West Indian and South American to diner fare. (☎872-4041. Open daily 7am-8pm.)

MINNEAPOLIS

French Meadow Bakery, 2610 Lyndale Ave. S (☎870-7855, www.organicbread.com), between 26th and 27th St., is the perfect place for a casual breakfast or lunch. Organic menu has vegan, vegetarian, and meat dishes served with fresh bread. Oversized cakes, scones, and muffins sit enticingly under the counter. Breakfast and lunch $4-10. Dinner $8-24. Open M-Th and Su 6:30am-10pm, F-Sa 6:30am-11pm. AmEx/D/MC/V. ❷

Chino Latino, 2916 Hennepin Ave. (☎824-7878; www.chinolatino.com), at Lake St., in Uptown. Trendy Latin-Asian cuisine that redefines "fusion." Indulge at the chic satay bar, sample the sushi, or rejuvenate after an evening out at the Late Night Borracho Breakfast (served 10:30pm-close). Settle in with drinks on the patio, beneath the glittery storefront, or in the cavernous, dimly lit interior. Happy hour daily 4:30-7pm and Su-Th 10:30pm-midnight. Open M-Th and Su 4:30pm-1am, F-Sa 4:30pm-2am. Reservations recommended. AmEx/D/MC/V. ❹

The Tin Fish, 3000 Calhoun Pkwy. E (☎832-5840; www.thetinfish.com). A lakeside stand with the best fish in the area, the Tin Fish dishes up tasty fried and grilled tacos ($3-10) and platters ($12-20). Open early spring to late fall daily 11am-9pm. MC/V. ❷

Bryant-Lake Bowl, 810 W. Lake St. (☎825-3737, show tickets ☎825-8949; www.bryantlakebowl.com), at Bryant St. near Uptown. This funky bowling alley/bar/cabaret serves food at friendly prices—ravioli and soups ensure that stylish bowlers throw strikes with full stomachs. Bowling $3. Shoes $1.50. Entrees $8-15. Open daily 8am-2am. Kitchen closes 12:30am. AmEx/D/MC/V. ❷

Loring Pasta Bar, 327 14th Ave. SE (☎378-4849; www.loringpastabar.com), in Dinkytown near the U of M campus. The large dining room draws hungry Minnesotans with regal but whimsical flair. Pastas are sauced in ingredients from Mediterranean veggies to lamb shank. Live music or performances most nights; Su salsa. Cover up to $8. Open M-Sa 11:30am-1am, Su 11am-2pm and 5:30pm-1am. Kitchen open until 11pm. AmEx/MC/V. ❸

Figlio, 3001 Hennepin Ave. (☎822-1688; www.figlio.com), at W. Lake St. in the Calhoun Square complex, in Uptown. Boasts the "Best Late Night Dining" award for its scrumptious sandwiches (from $9) and delicious pastas and pizzas (from $11). Open M-Th and Su 11:30am-1am, F-Sa 11:30am-2am. AmEx/D/MC/V. ❸

Tacos Morelos, 14 26th St. W (☎870-5053), at Nicollet Ave. More combinations of tortilla, beans, meat, and cheese than you've seen in your entire life, and probably ever will see again. Try the "Enchiladas 3 Amigos" (3 enchiladas with different sauces; $12.50), or fill up on their famous tacos ($2.50 each). Entrees $9-16. Open daily 10am-10pm. AmEx/D/MC/V. ❸

ST. PAUL

▨ **Mickey's Diner,** 36 W. 7th St. (☎651-222-5633), at St. Peter St. A 1937 diner decked-out in classic art-deco decor, Mickey's was transported from New Jersey and hasn't closed its doors since arriving in the Twin Cities. Still, it has not let fame affect the amazing quality and quantity of its food. Short stack of pancakes $4, full stack $4.50. Omelets $4.50-6. Burgers $6.50-7. Open 24hr. MC/V. ❶

▨ **Tanpopo,** 308 Prince St., #104. (☎651-209-6527), near the intersection of 4th and Broadway, in Lowertown. Among lofts and warehouses, this Japanese gem lades out filling bowls of soba or udon soups, with add-ins like tofu, tempura, and beef ($6-9). *Teishoku* are full meals that come with salad, soup, rice, and pickles ($9-10). Open M 5:30-9pm, Tu-Th 11am-2pm and 5:30-9pm, F 11am-2pm and 5:30-10pm, Sa noon-2:30pm and 5:30-10pm. MC/V. ❷

Cossetta, 211 W. 7th St. (☎651-222-3476). What began as an Italian market in 1911 now serves quality eat-in specialties. Try the veal parmigiana ($7.50), or Cossetta's famous pizza ($3-4 per slice). Open M-Th and Su 11am-9pm, F-Sa 11am-10pm; in winter M-Th 11am-9pm, F-Sa 11am-10pm, Su 11am-11pm. MC/V. ❷

Day by Day Cafe, 477 W. 7th St. (☎227-0654; www.daybyday.com). Started in 1975 by an alcoholism treatment center, Day By Day now serves the community at large, with breakfast all day ($4.50-8), as well as salads and sandwiches ($7.50-9), in its tall wooden booths and outdoor patio. Open M-F 6am-8pm, Sa 6am-3pm, Su 7am-3pm. Cash only. ❷

Café Latte, 850 Grand Ave. (☎651-224-5687), at Victoria St. More substantial than a cafe and more gourmet than its prices would suggest, this food-and-wine bar is also famous for its heavenly desserts. Changing specials, salads, and design-your-own sandwiches ($5-9) delight hungry locals. Open M-W and Su 9am-10pm, Th 9am-11pm, F-Sa 9am-midnight. MC/V. ❷

▰ CAFES

Cafes are an integral part of the Twin Cities during the day and at night. Particularly in Uptown Minneapolis, quirky coffeehouses caffeinate the masses and draw big crowds. Most complement their java with some of the cheapest food in town.

Uncommon Grounds, 2809 Hennepin Ave. S (☎872-4811), at 28th St., Uptown. The "BMW of coffeeshops" uses secret ingredients to make the tastiest coffees ($2-5) and chai teas around. Lounge in velour booths in the refurbished Victorian house. 1 drink per hr. min. Open M-F 5pm-1am, Sa-Su noon-1am. Cash or check only.

Vera's Cafe, 2901 Lyndale Ave. (☎822-3871; www.verascafe.com), between 29th and Lake St., in Uptown, welcomes both gay and straight customers with its signature, jolting "White Zombie" ($4.40), Wi-Fi, and a small bookstore nook. Regulars return daily for the great java and strong community feel. Happy hour 5-7pm. Occasional live music. Open daily 7am-11pm. MC/V.

Plan B Coffeehouse, 2717 Hennepin Ave. (☎872-1419), between 27th and 28th St., in Uptown. More subdued and intellectual, with serious readers and artwork. Try the "Tripper's Revenge" ($3.75) or frozen cheesecake on a stick ($3.25). Wi-Fi. Open M-Th and Su 9am-midnight, F-Sa 9am-1am. D/MC/V.

The Tea Garden, 2601 Hennepin Ave. S (☎377-1700) at 26th St. and 1692 Grand Ave. (☎651-690-3495). Modern and unconventional in comparison to its coffeehouse neighbors, this cafe offers all manner of tea, including trendy bubble tea ($3-5) and free Wi-Fi to customers who buy a drink. Jazz, open mic, and other events M and F-Sa. Open M-Th and Su 9am-10pm, F-Sa 9am-1am. MC/V.

◉ SIGHTS

MINNEAPOLIS

LAKES AND RIVERS. In the land of 10,000 lakes, Minneapolis claims many as its own: the city contains 22 lakes, along with 150 parks and 100 golf courses. **Lake Calhoun,** on the west end of Lake St., Uptown, is the largest of the bunch and is a recreational paradise. Scores of inline skaters, bicyclists, and runners loop the lake on all but the coldest days. Encircled by large homes, the serene **Lake of the Isles** has lovely views but no public access to the water. Just southeast of Lake Calhoun on Sheridan St., **Lake Harriet** lures locals with tiny paddleboats and a bandshell with free concerts on summer nights. The city maintains 13 mi. of lakeside trails around the three lakes for strolling and biking. The **Twin Cities Biking Club** (www.biketcbc.org) offers rides led by experienced and trained volunteers ($2). For auto touring, the city has created the "Grand Rounds National Scenic Byway" (☎230-6446; www.byways.org), a 51 mi. ribbon of road connecting the lakes with the Minnesota River. **Calhoun Cycle Center,** one block east of Lake Calhoun, rents bikes for exploring the paths. *(1622 W. Lake St. Entrance on S. James St. ☎827-8231. $7.50-10 per hour, $25-35 per 5hr. or more. Driver's license and credit card required. Open M-F 10am-8pm, Sa-Su 9am-9pm.)* At the northeast corner of Lake Calhoun, **The Tin Fish** offers canoe and kayak rentals on the side of the restaurant pavilion. *(3000 E. Calhoun Pkwy. ☎823-5840; www.thetinfish.com. Kayaks $11-15 per hr.; canoes $15 per hr.; paddle boats $16-21 per hr. Driver's license or credit card required. Open early spring-late fall daily 10am-7pm, weather permitting. Last boat out 6pm.)* **Minnehaha Park** offers striking views of the impressive **Minnehaha Falls,** immortalized in Longfellow's *Song of Hiawatha. (Park is near the airport; take the Light Rail from 5th St. downtown. Falls are off Hiawatha Ave. at Minnehaha Pkwy.)*

MUSEUMS. Lakes are only the beginning of Minneapolis's appeal—locals and visitors have plenty to do during the (at least) six months of frigid winter. The **Minneapolis Institute of Arts,** south of downtown, showcases more than 100,000 art objects spanning 5000 years, including Rembrandt's *Lucretia*, the world-famous *Doryphoros* (Polykleitos's perfectly proportioned man), and plenty of more modern work. *(2400 3rd Ave. S. ☎870-3131 or 888-642-2787; www.artsmia.org. Open Tu-Sa 10am-5pm, Th 10am-9pm, Su 11am-5pm. Free. Special exhibits $8.)* Southwest of downtown across from Loring Park, the Frank Gehry-designed ◪**Walker Art Center** fills its airy white galleries with temporary installations and works from its permanent collections, like the magnificent Minimalist "Elemental" (through Feb. 2008). *(1750 Hennepin Ave. and 725 Vineland Pl. ☎375-7600; www.walkerart.org. Open Tu-W and Sa-Su 11am-5pm, Th-F 11am-9pm. $10, seniors $8, students $6, under 13 free; Th 5-9pm and first Sa of each month free.)* Next to the Walker lies the ◪**Minneapolis Sculpture Garden,** the largest urban sculpture garden in the US. Rotating exhibits join the iconic **Spoonbridge and Cherry** sculpture. The adjacent **Cowles Conservatory** houses an array of plants and a Frank Gehry fish sculpture. *(Gardens open daily 6am-midnight; conservatory open Tu-Sa 10am-8pm, Su 10am-5pm. Both free.)* Perhaps the Twin Cities' most famous Gehry is the U of M's **Weisman Art Museum,** on the East Bank of campus. The undulating building was the rough draft for his famous Guggenheim Museum in Bilbao. Inside, visiting exhibits are not always as dramatic as the architecture. *(333 E. River Rd. ☎ 625-9494; www.weisman.umn.edu. Open Tu-W and F 10am-5pm, Th 10am-8pm, Sa-Su 11am-5pm. Free; suggested donation $3.)*

ST. PAUL

ARCHITECTURE. History and stately architecture define St. Paul. Mark Twain once said that the city "is put together in solid blocks of honest bricks and stone and has the air of intending to stay." Nowhere is this more evident than along ▨**Summit Avenue,** the nation's longest continuous stretch of Victorian houses, including the childhood home of novelist **F. Scott Fitzgerald** and the Minnesota **Governor's Mansion.** *(Fitzgerald: 593 Summit Ave. Currently a private residence. Governor's Mansion: 1006 Summit Ave. ☎ 651-297-8177. Tours May-Oct. once a week 1-3pm. Call for more information. Reservations required. Free.)* Also on Summit, the magnificent home of railroad magnate **James J. Hill**—the largest and most expensive home in the state when it was completed in 1891—offers 1¼hr. tours. *(240 Summit Ave., 1 block from the Cathedral of St. Paul. ☎ 651-297-2555; mnhs.org. Tours W-Sa 10am-3:30pm, Su 1-3:30pm. Reservations recommended. Wheelchair-accessible. $8, seniors and students $6, ages 6-17 $4.)* The 1½hr. **Walking Tours of Summit Avenue** depart from the Hill House and explore the area's architectural and social history. *(☎ 651-297-2555. Sa 11am and 2pm, Su 2pm. $4-6. Reservations recommended.)* Golden horses top the ornate ▨**State Capitol;** climb up to the roof and greet them on hourly tours. *(75 Rev. Dr. Martin Luther King, Jr. Blvd. ☎ 651-296-2881; www.mnhs.org/statecapitol. Open M-F 9am-4pm, Sa 10am-3pm, Su 1-4pm. Tours every hr. M-F 9am-4pm, Sa 10am-3pm, Su 1-4pm. Free.)* The **Cathedral of St. Paul,** on a hill at the start of Summit Ave., faces the capitol. *(239 Selby Ave. ☎ 651-228-1766; www.cathedralsaintpaul.org. Mass M-Th 7:30am and 5:15pm; F 7:30am; Sa 8am and 7pm; Su 8, 10am, noon, 5pm. Open M-Th 7am-5:30pm, F 7am-4pm, Sa 7am-7pm, Su 7am-5pm. Tours M, W, and F 1pm.)*

HISTORY AND SCIENCE. The innovative ▨**Minnesota History Center** houses interactive, hands-on exhibits that entertain young and old alike. Learn how Minnesotans cope with their extreme seasons in "Weather Permitting," where you can experience the terror of a tornado in a darkened "shelter." *(345 Kellogg Blvd. W. at John Ireland Blvd. ☎ 651-296-6126 or 888-727-8386; www.mnhs.org. Open Memorial Day-Labor Day M and W-Sa 10am-5pm, Tu 10am-8pm, Su noon-5pm; Sept.-May closed M. Wheelchair-accessible. $8, seniors and students $6, ages 6-17 $4.)* Downtown's **Landmark Center** is a grandly restored 1894 Federal Court building replete with towers and turrets, a collection of pianos, a concert hall, and four courtrooms. *(75 W. 5th St. ☎ 651-292-3225; www.landmarkcenter.org. Open M-W and F 8am-5pm, Th 8am-8pm, Sa 10am-5pm, Su noon-5pm. Free tours Th 11am, Su 1pm.)* Out front, **Rice Park,** the oldest park in Minnesota, is an ideal place for a stroll or a picnic—just ask two members of Charles M. Schulz's Peanuts gang, immortalized in bronze in the middle of the park. The **Science Museum of Minnesota** includes a beautiful atrium, an exhibit on the human body, and an expanded paleontology hall. The "Virtual River Pilot" allows visitors to take a ride on the Mississippi River. *(120 W. Kellogg Blvd. ☎ 651-221-9444; www.smm.org. Open mid-June to early Sept. M-Sa 9:30am-9pm, Su noon-5pm; low season M-W 9:30am-5pm, Th-Sa 9:30am-9pm, Su noon-5pm. $8.50, seniors and ages 4-12 $6.50; combo with Omnitheater and 3D cinema $16/12.50.)* For those with children, the **Children's Museum** is a big, interactive playground. In the summer, the roof becomes the Rooftop Artpark. *(10 W. 7th St. ☎ 651-225-6000; www.mcm.org. Open Tu-Th and Sa-Su 9am-5pm, F 9am-8pm; in summer also M 9am-5pm. $8.)*

AMUSEMENTS. Located on 500 wooded acres out in Apple Valley, the **Minnesota Zoo** houses local and exotic animals in their natural habitats, including 50 endangered species, a Tiger Lair exhibit, and native beavers, lynx, and wolverines. *(13000 Zoo Blvd. Take Rte. 77 S to Zoo exit and follow signs. ☎952-431-9500 or 800-366-7811; www.mnzoo.org. Open June-Aug. daily 9am-6pm; Sept. and May M-F 9am-4pm, Sa-Su 9am-6pm; Oct.-Apr. daily 9am-4pm. $12, seniors $8.25, ages 3-12 $7. Parking $5.)* From St. Paul, escape to **Como Park,** off Lexington Pkwy., where you can visit the zoo and an impressive conservatory with an award-winning collection of Bonsai trees and orchids. *(☎651-487-8200; www.comozooconservatory.org. Open daily Apr.-Sept. 10am-6pm; Oct.-Mar. 10am-4pm. Free; suggested donation $2.)* In Shakopee, even the most daring thrill-seekers will be satisfied at **Valleyfair,** an amusement park with five coasters and the heart-stopping Power Tower, which drops approximately 20 stories. *(1 Valleyfair Dr. Take I-35W south to Hwy. 13 W, then 13 W to Cty. Rd. 101. ☎800-386-7433; www.valleyfair.com. Open daily June-Aug. 10am, call for closing times.; May and Sept. select days. $36, under 48 in. tall $12, under 2 free. Parking $9.)*

🎭 ENTERTAINMENT

Second only to New York City in number of theater seats per capita, the Twin Cities are alive with drama and music. Most parks offer free concerts and shows on summer weekends, while theaters present classical and contemporary plays in winter. Music is also big here—the thriving alternative, pop, and classical music scenes fill out the wide range of options. For more info, read the free *City Pages* (www.citypages.com) and the *Pulse of the Twin Cities* (www.pulsetc.com).

THEATER

The renowned repertory 🏛**Guthrie Theater,** 818 S. 2nd St., on the river's west bank, draws praise for its mix of daring and classical productions. Its new building has three stages, upscale dining options, and open public lobbies with Wi-Fi. (☎377-2224; www.guthrietheater.org. Box office open M-F 11am-8pm, Sa 10am-8pm, Su hours vary. Tickets $20-90. Rush tickets no later than 10min. before show $15-25; line starts 1-1½hr. before show. Cash or check only for rush tickets.) The historic **State Theatre,** 805 Hennepin Ave.; the **Orpheum Theatre,** 910 Hennepin Ave. N; and the **Pantages Theatre,** 710 Hennepin Ave., comprise the Hennepin Theater District in downtown Minneapolis, with touring Broadway shows and musical events. (Box office ☎339-7007; www.hennepintheaterdistrict.org. Located at the

INSIDE AMERICA

The Mall of America is part shopping center, part amusement park, and part chain dining extravaganza all under one roof. One could get lost in the parking lot alone for days.

Just inside the mall, there's an info center for orientation (you'll need it). The whole place is centered around an amusement park, featuring a monstrous Ferris wheel, roller coaster, and log flume. Then it branches off into four wings, each bounded by a nationally known department store. These are anywhere from two to four stories, depending on the section of the mall in which you find yourself.

Despite the fact that very few items sold in the Mall of America are in fact unique or one-of-a-kind, the very experience of wandering its labyrinthine corridors and marveling at its impressive structure is irreplaceable. People come from hours away to spend days here, eating Nathan's, sipping Orange Julius, shopping for trinkets, and hurtling through the air on a high-speed rollercoaster. It's sheltered and mundane—but somehow, the whole is greater than its run-of-the-mill parts. Welcome to America.

The Mall of America is located at the intersection of U.S. 494 and Hwy. 77, 15min. from downtown Minneapolis/St. Paul. ☎952-883-8800; www.mallofamerica.com.

State Theatre. Open M-F 10am-6pm, Sa noon-3pm. Box offices at Orpheum and Pantages open at 5pm or 2hr. before matinees. Tickets from $22.) For family-oriented productions, the **Children's Theatre Company,** 2400 3rd Ave. S, next to the Minneapolis Institute of Arts, has first-rate plays. (☎ 874-0400; www.childrenstheatre.org. Season runs late Aug.-early June. Box office open in season M-F 10am-5pm, Sa 9am-2pm, Su noon-5pm; in summer M-F 10am-4pm. $15-50; children, seniors, and students $9-40. Rush tickets 15min. before show.) The ingenious **Théâtre de la Jeune Lune,** 105 1st St. N, stages critically acclaimed, off-the-beaten-path productions in an old warehouse. (☎ 332-0048, box office 333-6200; www.jeunelune.org. Box office open M-F 10am-6pm. Tickets $20-26.) **Brave New Workshop,** 2605 Hennepin Ave. at 26th St., in Uptown, stages comedy shows and improv in an intimate club. (☎ 332-6620; www.bravenewworkshop.com. Box office open W-Th noon-5pm, F 9:30am-8pm, Sa 10am-8pm. Tickets $23-27.)

MUSIC

The Twin Cities' vibrant music scene jams with everything from polka to hip-hop. **Sommerfest,** a month-long celebration of Viennese music put on in July by the **Minnesota Orchestra,** is the best of the cities' classical offerings. **Orchestra Hall,** 1111 Nicollet Mall, in downtown Minneapolis, hosts the event. (☎ 371-5656 or 800-292-4141; www.minnesotaorchestra.org. Box office open M-F 10am-5pm, Sa 10am-3pm, and 2hr. prior to performances. $15-65. Student rush tickets 30min. before show $10. Free pre-performances in Peavy Plaza.) Nearby, **Peavey Plaza,** on Nicollet Mall, holds free nightly concerts and occasional film screenings. The **Saint Paul Chamber Orchestra,** the **Schubert Club,** and the **Minnesota Opera Company** all perform at St. Paul's glass-and-brick **Ordway Center for the Performing Arts,** 345 Washington St., which also hosts Broadway productions. (☎ 651-224-4222; www.ordway.org. Box office open M-F 10am-5pm, Sa 11am-3pm. Tickets $15-85. Student rush tickets 10min. before performances.) Bands gravitate to the artist Prince's studio complex, formerly and currently known as **Paisley Park,** in nearby Chanhassen.

SPORTS

The puffy **Hubert H. Humphrey Metrodome,** 900 S. 5th St., in downtown Minneapolis, houses the Twin Cities' most popular team, the NFL's **Minnesota Vikings** (☎ 338-4537; www.vikings.com), whose few single tickets sell out fast. Baseball's **Minnesota Twins** (☎ 375-7454; www.twinsbaseball.com) also play in the Metrodome, although a new venue may be in the works. The NBA's **Timberwolves** (☎ 673-1600; www.timberwolves.com) and the WNBA's **Lynx** (☎ 673-1600; www.wnba.com/lynx) howl at the **Target Center,** 601 1st Ave. (☎ 673-0900), between 6th and 7th St. in downtown Minneapolis. The NHL team the **Wild** (☎ 651-602-6000; www.wild.com) takes to the ice at St. Paul's **Xcel Energy Center,** 175 W. Kellogg Blvd. (☎ 651-265-4800; www.rivercentre.com). The soccer craze hits the Great Plains with the minor-league **Thunder** (www.mnthunder.com) at the **National Sports Center** (☎ 763-785-5600; www.nscsports.com) in suburban Blaine.

FESTIVALS

The Twin Cities celebrate countless festivals, both to liven up the dreary winter days and to celebrate the coming of summer. In late January and early February, the **St. Paul Winter Carnival** (☎ 651-223-4700; www.winter-carnival.com), centered on Harriet Island, cures cabin fever with ice fishing, skating, and an ice palace. Leading up to the 4th of July, St. Paul celebrates the **Taste of Minnesota** (☎ 651-772-9980; www.tasteofmn.org) with fireworks, concerts, and regional and ethnic cuisine from hordes of local vendors. The **Minneapolis Riverfront Fourth of July Celebration and Fireworks** is a family affair with trolley rides, concerts, food, and fireworks. On its coattails rides the 10-day **Minneapolis Aquatennial** (☎ 376-7669;

www.aquatennial.org), with concerts and art exhibits glorifying the lakes and their city. During the two weeks prior to Labor Day, everyone heads to the **Minnesota State Fair,** at Snelling and Como St. between Minneapolis and St. Paul. With cheese curds and walleye-on-a-stick, horse contests, and a variety of music, the fair provides a sampling of the area's flavor. (☎651-288-4400 or 651-642-2372; www.mnstatefair.org. $11, seniors $9, ages 5-12 $8, under 5 free. Advance tickets $8. Parking $9.)

🎵 NIGHTLIFE

Minneapolis's vibrant youth culture feeds the Twin Cities' nightlife. Anchored by strong post-punk influences, the area's music scene remained localized until bands such as Soul Asylum, Hüsker Dü, and The Replacements made it big. A cross-section of the diverse nightlife options can be found in the downtown **Warehouse District** on Hennepin Ave., in **Dinkytown** by U of M, and across the river on the **West Bank** (bounded on the west by I-35 W and to the south by I-94), especially on **Cedar Avenue.** All bars and clubs in both Minneapolis and St. Paul are smoke-free.

Brit's Pub, 1110 Nicollet Mall (☎332-3908; www.britspub.com), between 11th and 12th St. in Minneapolis. Allows patrons to go "lawn bowling" (Sa-Su noon-11pm; Sa $5 per hr., Su $2.50 per hr.) on the rooftop garden. 18 beers ($5.50), the Stilton burger ($10), and fish and chips ($10-15) add to the British flavor. Open daily 11am-2am.

The Local, 931 Nicollet Mall (☎904-1005; www.the-local.com), at 10th St. in downtown Minneapolis. Irish pub that doubles as a restaurant (weekday lunch specials $10) and bar. Outdoor patio and dark interior make for a mellow, intimate night out. Open M-F 11am-2am, Sa-Su 9am-2am.

First Avenue and 7th St. Entry, 701 1st Ave. N (☎332-1775, box office ☎338-8388; www.first-avenue.com), in downtown Minneapolis. Rocks with some of the area's best live music. Tickets are a must for concerts, which feature the nation's hottest bands. A second stage offers smaller acts at lower ticket prices. 21+ most nights, 18+ Sa. Sa night dance parties $3, free with student ID. Cover $3-10, for concerts $15-40. Open M-Th 8pm-2am, F-Sa 9pm-3am, Su 7pm-2am.

Triple Rock Social Club, 629 Cedar Ave. S (☎333-7499; www.triplerocksocial-club.com), between 6th and 7th St. S in Minneapolis. Triple Rock attracts punk bands and their fans and a variety of other music groups. Come for the live music and grungy-chic atmosphere. Stay for the often vegan-friendly bar food; an extensive menu goes well with the 12 beers on tap. Shows all ages, 18+ and 21+; check website. Tickets $5-20. Kitchen open M-F 4pm-1am, Sa-Su 10am-1am.

Escape Ultra Lounge, 600 Hennepin Ave. (☎333-8855; www.escapeultralounge.com), above the Hard Rock Cafe in the Warehouse District of Minneapolis. Has a DJ every night. Huge plasma screens and occasional live music draw new crowds each night. 21+, sometimes 18+; call ahead. Cover $5. Open daily 5pm-2am.

The Gay 90s, 408 Hennepin Ave. (☎333-7755; www.gay90s.com), at 4th St. in Minneapolis. Serves dinner and then lets loose for the night. Gigantic complex hosts thousands of gay and lesbian partiers in 6 bars and 3 dance floors, though the straight crowd is sizeable. Drag shows upstairs Tu-Su 9:30pm. M-Tu and F-Sa 21+, W-Th and Su 18+. Cover after 9pm $3-5. Open M-Sa 8am-2am, Su 10am-2am.

DULUTH ☎218

Originally an industrial town built upon timber and mining, Duluth today has tremendous appeal outside its role as a freshwater port harboring ships from over 60 different countries. The popularity of Canal Park and the Aerial Lift Bridge have

SPAM SPAM
THANK YOU MA'AM

"Welcome to America," says the "butcher" sitting next to plastic sausages and pork tenderloins. He is actually a guard at the SPAM museum in Austin, MN. He points at pictures showing Mr. Hormel, the SPAM man, when he was first opening his butcher shop in the late 19th century.

After that, the museum's displays vary; historical artifacts and interactive exhibits (like can-your-own SPAM) make the museum a popular destination. It's a testament to the power of propaganda—if you learn anything here, it is how SPAM's marketing schemes made people crave salted pig parts stuffed in cans.

"Processed" is a buzz word here, and it appears on posterboards and TV screens alike as you walk through the palace of pork. Hormel pigs get "processed" into SPAM, visitors learn, at an extremely rapid rate; there is of course no elaboration of the transition from living thing to edible mass.

Still, since admission is waived by friends at Hormel foods, which still operates a big factory in Austin, those driving through Northern Iowa or Southern Minnesota can't deny themselves a detour off I-90 to Austin and the friendly blue-and-yellow museum of SPAM.

1937 SPAM Blvd., Austin, MN. ☎*437-5100; www.spam.com. Open M-Sa 10am-5pm, Su noon-4pm. Free.*

enticed microbreweries, theaters, and museums to occupy the old factories down on the wharf, creating a sparkling haven on beautiful Lake Superior.

◨ TRANSPORTATION AND PRACTICAL INFORMATION. Greyhound, 4426 Grand Ave. (☎722-5591; www.greyhound.com; ticket office open M-F 7am-4pm, Sa-Su 7-8am, 2-4pm), stops 4 mi. south of downtown; take bus #1, 2, or 3. Buses run to Minneapolis (3hr., 2 per day, $27.50). Buy discounted tickets **two weeks in advance.** The **Duluth Transit Authority,** 2402 W. Michigan St., runs buses within the city. (☎722-7283; www.duluthtransit.com. Peak fare M-F 7-9am and 2:30-6pm $1.25, students $0.75; off-peak $0.60.) The **Port Town Trolley** takes tourists through downtown, Canal Park, and the Waterfront. (☎722-7283. Runs every 30min. June-Labor Day daily 11:30am-7pm. $0.50.) The **Convention and Visitors Bureau** is at 21 W. Superior St. at N. Lake Ave. (☎722-4011; www.visitduluth.com. Open M-F 8:30am-5pm.) **Hotlines: Crisis Line,** ☎723-0099. 24hr. **Internet Access: Duluth Public Library,** 520 W. Superior St. (☎730-4200; www.duluth.lib.mn.us. 1hr. free per day. Open M-Tu 10am-8:30pm, W-F 10am-5:30pm.) **Post Office:** 2800 W. Michigan St. (☎723-2557. Open M-F 8am-5pm, Sa 9am-1pm.) **Postal Code:** 55806.

⌂ ACCOMMODATIONS. Rates rise and rooms fill quickly during the summer months in Duluth. **Voyageur Lakewalk Inn ❸,** 333 E. Superior St., off the Lakewalk, has comfortable rooms and free morning coffee. (☎722-3911. Office open daily 7am-11pm. Rooms in summer M-Th and Su from $54, F-Sa $70-74; prices lower in winter. AmEx/D/MC/V.) The **Chalet Motel ❸,** 1801 London Rd., 2 mi. north of downtown, offers well-decorated rooms with A/C near scenic Leif Erickson Park, which overlooks Lake Superior. (☎728-4238 or 800-235-2957. Singles M-Th and Su $46, F-Sa $57; doubles $59/70. Prices lower in winter. D/MC/V.) A few miles south of town, the **Duluth Motel ❷,** 4415 Grand Ave., houses visitors in affordable, well-kept rooms across from the Greyhound station. (☎628-1008. In summer singles $40; doubles $45. Prices lower in winter. AmEx/D/MC/V.) For a less urban feel, the rocky **Jay Cooke State Park ❶,** 780 Hwy. 210, southwest of Duluth, draws in travelers with hiking, snowmobiling, cross-country skiing, and 83 campsites among the trees of the St. Louis River Valley. (☎384-4610 or 800-246-2267; www.stayatmnparks.com. Turn left at Exit 242 off I-35 and look for signs. Office open daily 9am-9pm. Reservations recommended; reservation fee $8.50. Backpacking sites $11, with showers $18, with electricity $19. Vehicles $5 per day. MC/V.)

▓▓ **FOOD AND NIGHTLIFE. Fitger's Brewery Complex,** 600 E. Superior St., and the **Canal Park** region, south of downtown along Lake Ave., feature plenty of pleasant eateries. **The Brewhouse ❷,** located in Fitger's, has home-brewed beer like Big Boat Oatmeal Stout ($4), root beer on tap, and specialty burgers and sandwiches. (☎279-2739; www.brewhouse.net. Live entertainment or music most nights. Open M-W and Su 11am-1am, Th-Sa 11am-2am. Kitchen closes M-Sa 11pm, Su 10pm. AmEx/D/MC/V.) Italian cafe **Va Bene ❸,** 734 E. Superior St, has a refined dining room and seating on the terrace. Follow appetizers like mixed antipasti ($6) and spinach salad ($6) with design-your-own pastas ($9-12): choose your pasta shape, then add sauces, veggies, and meat. (☎722-1502. Open M-Th and Su 8am-9pm, F-Sa 8am-10pm. Pasta bar open 11am-2pm and 5pm to close. AmEx/MC/V.) Located in an old pipe-fitting factory in Canal Park, **Grandma's Sports Garden ❷,** 425 S. Lake Ave., is a popular place, especially among the young and boisterous college crowd. Casual dining, original bonottas (rolled and stuffed pizzas), and a thriving after-hours scene keep hordes of people coming over the river and through the woods to Grandma's. (☎722-4724. Entrees $8-14. DJs W and F-Sa. Happy hour M-F 3-6pm, Th all day. Restaurant open June-Aug. daily 11am-10pm; Sept.-May W-Th 5-10pm, F-Su 11:30am-10pm. Bar open daily 11am-2am. AmEx/D/MC/V.) Located in the basement of the DeWitt-Seitz Marketplace, **Amazing Grace Bakery & Cafe ❶,** 394 Lake Ave. S, serves fresh sandwiches ($6; half $4) in a funky atmosphere. (☎723-0075; www.amazinggracebakery.com. Live entertainment and music most nights; usually no cover. M open mic. Open daily 7am-11pm. AmEx/D/MC/V.) **Sara's Table ❸,** 1902 E. 8th St. at 19th Ave. E, cooks up a great veggie burger with sweet potato fries ($8) as well as other delicious, healthy dishes. (☎723-8569; www.taransmarketplace.com. Wi-Fi. Open in summer M-Sa 7am-9pm, Su 8am-4pm. Kitchen closed 3:30-5pm. MC/V.)

▓▓ **SIGHTS AND ENTERTAINMENT.** Duluth's proximity to majestic **Lake Superior** is its biggest draw. Nearly 400 mi. across, it is the world's largest body of fresh water—indeed, it is so massive that when frozen, each person in the world could lay out his own 6 ft. by 6 ft. picnic blanket on its surface. Many visitors head down to **Canal Park** to watch the big ships go by at the ▓**Aerial Lift Bridge.** Accompanied by deafening horn blasts, this unique bridge climbs 138 ft. in 1min. to allow vessels to pass. Traffic is generally heavier in the late afternoon, but check the **Boatwatcher's Hotline** (☎722-6489) and the **Duluth Shipping News** (☎722-3119; www.duluthshippingnews.com), published daily at the **Lake Superior Maritime Visitors Center,** by the Aerial Lift Bridge at Canal Park. The Visitors Center has displays on the history of commercial shipping on Lake Superior and makes announcements as ships come in. (☎727-2497; www.lsmma.org. Open in summer daily 10am-9pm; call for low season hours.) Canal Park is also the beginning and end of the **Duluth Lakewalk,** a beautiful 3 mi. promenade.

Waterfront tours aboard the docked giant steamer **William A. Irvin** and the US Coast Guard Cutter *Sundew* reveal more of Duluth's shipping past. The *Irvin*, docked at Duluth's Downtown Waterfront, is longer than two football fields and was the "Queen of the Lakes" in her prime. (☎722-7876. Open Memorial Day-Labor Day M-Th and Su 9am-6pm, F-Sa 9am-8pm; May and Sept. to mid-Oct. M-Th and Su 10am-4pm, F-Sa 10am-6pm. 1hr. tours every 20min. $11, seniors and students $10, children $8.50.) ▓**Great Lakes Aquarium,** 353 Harbor Dr., is America's first and only all-freshwater aquarium. Stop by to see spotted stingrays and bioluminescent fish. (☎740-3474; www.glaquarium.org. Open daily 10am-6pm. $13, seniors $10, ages 3-11 $7. Parking $3.) Across the Aerial Lift Bridge, **Park Point** stretches on for seven miles and has excellent but cold swimming areas (Lake Superior's water averages 40°F), parks, and sandy beaches.

The scenic **Willard Munger State Trail** links West Duluth to Jay Cooke State Park and continues on to Hinckley, providing 80 mi. of paved path perfect for bikes; the **Willard Munger Inn**, 7408 Grand Ave., takes care of rentals. (☎624-4814; www.mungerinn.com. $15 per 2hr., $20 per 4hr. AmEx/MC/V.) In an old train station in Canal Park, the **Midnight Sun Adventure Company,** 100 Lake Pl., rents bikes and kayaks, and leads guided adventure tours. (☎727-1330; www.midnightsunsports.com. Bike rentals $16 per half-day, $30 per full day. Kayak rentals $50/95. Open M-Sa 10am-8pm, Su 10am-5pm.)

The Depot, 506 W. Michigan St., a former railroad station, contains a performance space for music and ballet as well as four museums, including the **Lake Superior Railroad Museum** (www.lsrm.org), which allows visitors to enjoy the North Shore Scenic Railroad trip. (☎727-8025; www.duluthdepot.org. Open June-Aug. daily 9:30am-6pm; Sept.-May M-Sa 10am-5pm, Su 1-5pm. Museum $10, ages 3-13 $5.50. Railroad trip $12/5.50.) A 39-room Neo-Jacobian mansion built on mining wealth, the **Historic Congden Estate,** 3300 London Rd./Hwy. 61, lies on the northeastern outskirts of town and provides visitors with a glimpse of Duluth's most prosperous period. (☎726-8910 or 888-454-4536; www.glensheen.org. Open May-Oct. daily 9:30am-4pm; Nov.-Apr. Sa-Su 11am-2pm. Mandatory tours every hr. $12, seniors $11, ages 6-12 $7, families $35. Grounds $5.) Opera, musicals, and jazz all come to Duluth in July and August thanks to the **Sieur du Luth** festival, run by the University of Minneota Duluth. Events take place at the Marshall Performing Art Center and Weber Music Hall, on campus, which is northwest of downtown. (☎726-8561; www.d.umn.edu/sfa/sumarts. Box office open M-F 10am-4pm. Tickets $7-20.) Across the road from the *Irvin* is the **Duluth OMNIMAX Theatre,** 301 Harbor Dr. (☎727-0022; www.duluthomnimax.com. $7.50, seniors and students $6.50, 12 and under $5.50. Check website for schedule.)

CHIPPEWA NATIONAL FOREST   ☎218

The Lost Forty of Chippewa National Forest are a small group of virgin red and white pines, untouched by logging due to a mapper's error that plotted them underwater. Each tree is more than 300 years old and forms part of the habitat that makes the forest home to one of the highest densities of breeding bald eagles in the continental US. The national forest shares territory with the **Leech Lake Indian Reservation,** home to 3725 Chippewa tribespeople. The Chippewa, called Ojibwe in their native language, migrated from the Atlantic coast in the 18th century and, in the mid-19th century, were forced westward by the US government onto reservations such as Leech Lake.

The National Forest has plenty of affordable **camping ❶** options. **Forest Offices** (☎547-1044; www.fs.fed.us/r9/chippewa; open M-F 8am-4:30pm), just east of Walker on Rte. 200/371, and in Deer River, off Rte. 46 (☎246-2313), have info on 23 campgrounds and more than 400 free primitive sites, as well as a heap of detailed pamphlets on hiking, canoeing, biking, bald eagle watching, and must-see sights. If you'd rather rough it, national forests allow you to camp wherever you want—provided you camp at least 50 ft. from the nearest road and adhere strictly to the "Leave no Trace" ethic (p. 44).

For the northbound traveler, the town of **Walker,** in the southwest corner of the park, serves as an ideal gateway to the forest. Known as the "Fishing Capitol of Minnesota," Walker draws thousands of tourists each summer. The **Leech Lake Area Chamber of Commerce,** 205 Minnesota Ave., on Rte. 200/371 at the south end of Walker, is a good resource for the baffled traveler. (☎547-1313 or 800-833-1118; www.leech-lake.com. Open M-F 8:30am-4:30pm; May-Sept. also Sa 9am-1pm.) **Mike's Reel Repair and Video Rental,** in Hackensack, 10 mi. south of Walker on Rte. 371, has bike rentals for the Paul Bunyan Trail, or for the Pike Lake bike loop in

Chippewa. (☎675-6976. Bikes $4 per hr., $20 per day. Open M-Th 9am-8pm, F-Sa 9am-9pm.) Many of the lodges in Chippewa National Forest rent canoes and kayaks for use on its many lakes. The personalized service at Northern Adventures, in Cass Lake, 20 mi. north of Walker, facilitates Mississippi River canoe trips of varying length, with or without a guide. Scenic routes often include eagle and osprey sightings. (☎335-2078 or 766-7543. 4-6hr. trip $50 per canoe, plus $30 for transportation.) **Post Office:** 515 Michigan Ave. at 6th St. (☎547-1123. Open M-F 9am-4pm, Sa 9-11:30am.) **Postal Code:** 56484.

ITASCA STATE PARK   ☎218

One of Itasca State Park's claims to fame is the **Headwaters of the Mississippi,** which Henry Rowe Schoolcraft and his Native American guide Ozawinib discovered in 1832. Here people gather to cross over the Mississippi on the rock bridge where water flows both to the north and south. Thirty miles west of Chippewa National Forest on Rte. 200, Minnesota's popular state park is home to the oldest and largest tree in the state, representative of the large pine forests through which visitors can walk, bike, or drive. Seventeen incredible miles of paved trail and the 10 mi. Wilderness Road around the four park lakes keep visitors active and busy. A vacation spot in itself, the impeccable ▣**Mississippi Headwaters Hostel (HI),** located in the park off Main Dr., stays open for weekends in the winter to facilitate public access to the park's excellent cross-country skiing trails. (☎266-3415; www.himinnesota.org. Kitchen and laundry. Linen $4. 2- to 3-night min. stay some weekends. Reservations recommended. Check-in M-Th and Su 5-10:30pm, F-Sa 5-11pm. Vehicle permit $5 per day, $25 per year. Dorms $19-23, members $16-20; private rooms July-Aug. and Jan.-Feb. $45-64, low season $27-38. Cash or check only.) Across the street, **Itasca Sports Rental** rents bikes ($3.50 per hr.), motorized and non-motorized boats (from $5.50 per hr.), and fishing supplies. (☎266-2150, low season 657-2420; www.itascasports.com. Open daily in summer 7am-9pm; spring and fall 8am-6pm, but may vary.) The **Jacob V. Brower Visitor Center,** near the park's east entrance, has information on camping, hiking, and scenic drives (☎266-2100).

IRON RANGE   ☎218

Lured initially by rumors of gold, the miners who rushed to the **Vermillion** and **Mesabi** mountain ranges set their sights on iron instead. Today, the 120 mi. of wilderness and over 500 majestic lakes along the Iron Range serve as a corridor to the Boundary Waters, the Mississippi Headwaters, and the north shores of Lake Superior. (Info ☎800-777-8497; www.irontrail.org.) These days, the closest you can get to the mining techniques of old is a tour of the Soudan Underground Mine, but dynamite blasts still go off weekly at Hull Rust Mahoning Mine, in North Hibbing, as less concentrated iron ore continues to be excavated from the land. In **Hibbing,** on Hwy. 73, 75 mi. from Duluth, townspeople like to claim their fame as "the town that moved": during a mining rush, surveyors realized there was iron beneath where the town stood and moved most of the buildings several miles to the south. The **Hull Rust Mahoning Mine,** in North Hibbing at the northern end of Third Ave., is America's largest open pit iron mine. The Visitors Center has a panoramic view of the place; gaze at the broad black landscape to see why locals call it a manmade Grand Canyon. (☎262-4900, tickets 254-7959. Visitors Center open daily 9am-6pm. Mine tours late June to mid-Aug. W-Th noon. Tickets at Iron World Discovery Center in Chisolm. $5.) Some outsiders, however, would attribute Hibbing's fame to its rearing of folk-rock legend Bob Dylan (born Zimmerman), who moved here when he was seven. **Zimmy's,** 531 E. Howard St., is the hub of Dylan activities, which include **Dylan Days,** a two-day festival and singer-songwriter contest in May, and an underwhelming exhibit in the basement of the **Public Library,** 2020 E. 5th Ave. at

21st St. (☎262-1038. Open M-Th 9am-8pm, F-Sa 9am-5pm; closed Sa in summer.) The Zimmerman family lived at 2425 7th Ave.; it's now a private residence, but the garage door is embellished with the album cover of Dylan's "Blood on the Tracks." The **Mitchell-Tappan House ❹**, 2125 4th Ave. E., at 22nd St., was the 1897 home of a mine official and is now a yellow-and-blue wallpapered B&B. (262-3862; www.mitchell-tapanhouse.com. Cable TV and common area. Breakfast included. Check-in 4-6pm, or by arrangement. Check-out 11am. Rooms $70-90. MC/V.)

The town of **Eveleth,** 60 mi. north of Duluth on Rte. 53, has produced more elite hockey players than any other city of its size in the country. Not surprisingly, it is the home of the **US Hockey Hall of Fame,** 801 Hat Trick Ave., which honors American-born pucksters. (☎744-5167 or 800-443-7825; www.ushockeyhall.com. Open M-Sa 9am-5pm, Su 10am-3pm. $8, seniors and ages 13-17 $7, ages 6-12 $6, under 6 free.) Further proof that Eveleth takes hockey seriously is the new 110 ft., 10,000 lb. **World's Largest Hockey Stick** (built to scale), which—though it holds the world title—is technically not as big as one the Canadians built (shh!). Just follow the signs marked "Big Stick" off Rte. 53 to Monroe St. and Grant St.

A deeper experience awaits in **Soudan,** 40 mi. northeast of Eveleth, which features an unforgettable journey a half-mile underground. The ☒**Soudan Underground Mine State Park,** off Rte. 1, is the state's oldest, deepest, and purest iron ore mine. In a fascinating 1½hr. tour, visitors experience the complete dark of the mine, while learning the history of ore workers in the Iron Range. The mine's more modern guise is as a physics laboratory in search of neutrinos. Wear a jacket and sturdy shoes. (☎753-2245. Park open daily June-Sept. 9:30am-6pm. June-July tours every hr., Sept. every 2hr. 10am-4pm; physics tours twice daily. $10, ages 5-12 $6, 4 and under free; $5 state park vehicle permit required.) Two miles down the road, **McKinley Park Campground ❶**, on the shore of Lake Vermilion, has campsites with bait and tackle, bathrooms, laundry, showers, and a swimming beach. (☎753-5921, after hours 780-6860; www.mckinleypark.net. Open May-Sept. Office open M-Th and Su 8am-6pm, F-Sa 7am-9pm. 2-night min. stay on weekends, 3-night min. stay on holiday weekends. Sites $20, with electricity $35.) **Bear Head Lake State Park ❶** lies between Soudan and Ely, 7 mi. south of Hwy. 169, on Cty. Hwy. 128. Its wooded sites are popular with area families and their RVs most summer weekends. (☎365-7229. Flush toilets, showers, and fish-cleaning cabin. Sites $18. Vehicles $5 per week, $25 per year.)

The charming town of **Ely** serves as a launching pad into the **Boundary Waters Canoe Area Wilderness** (**BWCAW;** see **Boundary Waters,** p. 570), and thus supports an extensive range of wilderness outfitters who provide gear and guidance. Wildlife comes to you at the **International Wolf Center,** just east of downtown at 1396 Rte. 169, which houses eight gray and arctic wolves and blasts a recording of howls into the forest to howl back and forth with wild wolves. (☎365-4695 or 800-359-9653; www.wolf.org. Open mid-May to mid-June daily 10am-4pm; mid-June to Aug. daily 10am-6pm; Sept. to mid-Oct. W-Su 10am-4pm; mid-Oct. to mid-May Sa-Su 10am-4pm. Call for wolf communication and presentation times. $7.50, seniors $6.50, ages 6-12 $4.) Rangers issue BWCAW permits; they are moving across the street at the end of the year. (☎365-7561. Open daily May-Sept. 6am-6pm.) If wolves aren't enough, a new **North American Bear Center,** 1926 Hwy. 169, west of Ely, has its own wildlife: two bears who eat, sleep, and jump in the pond in front of a viewing window. Exhibits range from whimsical to practical and involve both teddy bears and Smokey Bear. (☎365-7879; www.bear.org. Open mid-June to Aug. M-Th 9am-6pm, F-Su 9am-8pm; May to mid-June M-F and Su 9am-6pm, Sa 9am-8pm; Sept. to mid-Oct. W-Su 9am-6pm; mid-Oct. to Apr. Sa-Su 10am-4pm. Free.) **Vince Shute Wildlife Sanctuary,** 70 mi. from Ely, on County Rd. 23 near Orr, offers a practically guaranteed opportunity to see wild black bears, who return every evening for feeding, a tradition started by a logger who used to put garbage out for the bears. (☎757-0172; www.americanbear.org. Open June-Sept. Tu-Su 5pm-dusk, except during heavy rain. $7, ages 6-17 $3.) **The Brandenburg Gallery**, 11 E. Sheridan St., has a collection of works by Jim Brandenburg, a famous National Geographic photographer. (www.jimbrandenburg.com. Open M-Sa 10am-6pm, Su 10am-5pm; in winter M-Sa 10am-5pm, Su 10am-4pm.) ◪**Stony Ridge Resort ❶**, 60 W. Lakeview Pl., off W. Shagawa Rd., has four cabins with cable, fridge, and a motor boat, as well as a few RV and tent sites. The owners also run a small cafe. (☎365-6757; www.stoneyridgeresort.com. Complimentary canoe use. Check-in 3pm. Check-out 11am. Tent sites $20; RV sites $20-$30; 1-bedroom cabins $100; 2-bedroom $120.) **Fall Lake Park ❶**, on County Road 182, offers 64 quiet RV and camping sites only 6 mi. from Ely with a beach, boat launch, canoe rentals, and direct access to BWCAW. (☎877-444-6777; www.reserveusa.com. Sites $15.) The **Front Porch Coffee & Tea Co. ❶**, 343 E. Sheridan St., has pastries, wraps, and Internet access. (☎365-2326. Open M-Sa 7am-9pm, Su 8am-5pm. AmEx/D/MC/V.)

VOYAGEURS NATIONAL PARK ☎218

Named for the French-Canadian fur traders who once traversed the area, Voyageurs is one of Minnesota's best-kept secrets, providing an undeniably unique experience as a water-based park with fewer than 10 mi. of roads. The waterways that connect Minnesota's boundary with Ontario provide ample opportunities for birdwatching, camping, canoeing, fishing, hiking, and kayaking—all of which are accessible almost solely by boat. Today's voyagers are invited to leave the auto-dominated world and push off into the serene waters of the longest inland lake waterway on the continent. Summer visitors explore the hiking trails and camp on the islands, while winter visitors bundle up to cross-country ski and snowmobile. The dangers of undeveloped wilderness, however, still remain. Water should be boiled for at least 10min. and then treated; some fish contain mercury. Ticks carrying Lyme disease have been found as well.

Hikers can get a glimpse of the park on some of its byways. A wheelchair-accessible trail at Ash River yields a great view of Kabetogama Lake and serves as the starting point for the **Blind Ash Bay Trail**. The new 24 mi. **Kab-Ash Trail** has multiple entrances for extensive hiking and skiing but users should be cautious and bring a compass because markers are not always clear, and maintenance is spotty. The 9½ mi. **Cruiser Lake Trail system,** accessible by boat only from either Rainy Lake or Kabetogama Lake, offers hiking and canoeing and is known for its ample wildlife. Many of the lodges around County Rd. 123 and 122 near Lake Kabetogama offer boat rentals to visitors not staying with them. The folks at **Sandy Point Lodge ❷**, 10606 Gamma Rd., near Lake Kabetogama, will set you up with a kayak rental or even a fully outfitted week-long Voyageurs vacation based out of their cabins. (☎875-2615 or 800-777-8595; www.sandypointlodge.com. Kayaks $25 per day, free for guests. Motor boats $50-65 per day. Wi-Fi in lodge rooms. Tent and RV sites $35. Mid-May to mid-Aug. lodge singles $65, doubles $95. Dec. to mid-May and mid-Aug. to Sept. $55/80. 3-night min. for cabins. Mid-May to mid-Aug. cabins from $655 per week. Low season from $475. Closed Oct.-Nov.)

The least intimidating way for the intrepid boatless to get their feet wet is via ranger-led boat tours. Canoe trips meander for 2hr. around the lakes on the outskirts, while daytrips on the pontoon boat venture deeper into the heart of darkness. (Reservations ☎888-381-2873. Rainy Lake and Kabetogama are departure points; for info, see the Visitors Centers, below. Canoe trips $4, children $2; pontoon boat $15-35/10-20.) **Woody's Fairly Reliable Guide Service ❹**, at Rainy Lake, off Rte. 11, features guided fishing, hunting, and snowmobiling daytrips from $295 per two people. Woody, the personable owner, also operates nine spacious suites. (☎286-5001 or 866-410-5001; www.fairlyreliable.com. 2-person suites $750 per week; 4-person $995 per week. Each additional person $25 per night. 35% discount mid-Sept. to mid-May. D/MC/V.) The cheapest way to sleep in the area is to camp inside the park. The park maintains over 200 free campsites accessible only by water. Private water taxis are available from several outfitters. The **Kettle Falls Hotel ❸**, at the Kettle Falls dam in the northeastern part of the park, is a fully operating hotel that was first a logging center, then a brothel for lonely loggers. (☎240-1724, winter 240-2070; www.kettlefallshotel.com. Water taxi service $45. Rooms from $50.) There are several car-accessible sites as well, including the 61 beautiful, primitive sites at **Woodenfrog ❶**, about 4 mi. from Kabetogama Lake Visitors Center on Rte. 122, and the nine primitive sites at **Ash River ❶**, 3 mi. from the Ash River Visitors Center on Rte. 129. (Sites $10.) Most of the area lodges have space for tent and RV camping. Just south of International Falls, which inspired the fictional Frostbite Falls of *Rocky and Bullwinkle* fame, Rte. 53 is loaded with motels, including the darling **Hilltop Motel and Cabins ❸**, 2002 2nd Ave. W at Rte. 53, which offers immaculate rooms and friendly service. (☎283-2505 or 800-322-6671. Open mid-Apr. to mid-Oct. Reservations recommended. Singles M-F $42, Sa-Su $59; doubles M-F $49, Sa-Su $69. AmEx/D/MC/V.) **International Voyageurs RV Campground ❶**, 5min. south of town on Rte. 53 at City Rd. 24, has RV and tent sites with laundry and showers. (☎283-4679. Tent sites for 1-2 people $14, with hookup $18. Each additional person $2.) For home cooking at wallet-friendly prices, try **Grandma's Pantry ❶**, 2079 Spruce St. in Ranier off Rte. 11. (☎286-5484. Open M-F 6am-7pm, Sa 6am-10:30am. D/MC/V.)

On the way into Voyageurs from the south, visitors can stop at the **Voyageurs National Park and Orr Area Info Center**, 4429 Hwy. 53 in Orr, which has information on navigating Voyageurs. (☎757-3932 or 800-357-9255. Open June-Sept. daily 9am-5pm; Oct.-May Th-Sa 9am-4pm.) Visitors can access the park through International Falls at the northern tip of Rte. 53, just below Ft. Frances, ON, or through **Crane Lake, Rainy Lake, Ash River,** or **Kabetogama Lake** (all east of Rte. 53). There are three **Visitors Centers** in the park: **Rainy Lake,** at the end of Rte. 11, 12 mi. east of International Falls (☎286-5258; www.nps.gov/voya; open mid-May to Sept. daily 9am-5pm; Oct.-Dec. W-Su 10am-4pm; Jan. to mid-May W-Su 10am-5pm), which has a large museum; **Ash River,** 8 mi. east of Rte. 53 on Rte. 129, then 3 mi. north (☎374-3221; open mid-May to Sept. daily 9am-5pm); and **Kabetogama Lake,** 5 mi. east of Rte. 53 (☎875-2111; open mid-May to Sept. 30 daily 9am-5pm). *Rendezvous,* the visitors guide to the park, is available at Visitors Centers and provides information on outdoor recreation, outfitting, and lodging.

SCENIC DRIVE: NORTH SHORE DRIVE   ☎ 218

The Lake Superior North Shore extends 646 mi. from Duluth to Sault Ste. Marie, ON, but Minnesota's **Route 61** glides through the trees from Duluth to Grand Portage and the Canadian border, offering a condensed 150 mi. version packed with beautiful shoreline and mesmerizing views of the vast lake. With jagged, glacier-carved edges and a seemingly limitless surface, the lake is a sharp contrast to the **Sawtooth Mountains,** which hover over the lake with stunning rock formations and tall, sweeping birch trees.

Though thriving fishing and logging industries once defined this area, tourism now plays a key role in the North Shore's vitality. Whether enjoying the serenity of the lake or hiking and camping on the **Superior Hiking Trail** (www.shta.org), visitors flock to the area year-round to enjoy its outdoor opportunities. Most of the small fishing towns along the shore maintain Visitors Centers; in picturesque **Two Harbors,** the knowledgeable staff at the **Lake County R.J. Houle Visitor Information Center,** 1330 Hwy. 61, 25 mi. from Duluth, offers stellar advice and personal anecdotes about each town on the Minnesota stretch of the North Shore. (☎834-4005 or 800-554-2116; www.twoharborschamber.com. Open in summer M-F 9am-5pm, Sa 9am-

6pm, Su 10am-5pm; in winter hours vary.) On summer weekends, Rte. 61 is often congested with boat-towing pickup trucks and family-filled campers. Accommodations flanking the roadside fill up fast in summer; make reservations early. Bring warm clothes—temperatures can drop as low as 40°F, even during the summer.

While state parks along Rte. 61 boast striking views of the mirror-like lake, they also provide their own attractions. With 26 gorgeous stone structures created by the Civilian Conservation Corps, **Gooseberry Falls State Park ❶** is a lovely lodging option. (☎834-3855; www.dnr.state.mn.us. Park open daily 8am-10pm. Visitors Center open daily June-Sept. 9am-7pm; Oct.-May 9am-4pm. Sites with shower $18. Vehicle permit $5 per day, $25 per year.) Gooseberry Falls offers 18 mi. of trails and five waterfalls, as well as a beautiful half-mile walk to the rocky shore. Three of the falls are located near the Visitors Center and are wheelchair-accessible.

Eight miles down the road, the **Split Rock Lighthouse** hints to the lake's industrial heyday and has a spectacular view atop a 130 ft. cliff. Visitors can enter the lighthouse and light keeper's home, restored to look as they did during operation in the 1920s. (☎226-6372; www.mnhs.org/places/sites/srl. Open mid-May to mid-Oct. daily 10am-6pm. 45min. tours every hr. $8, seniors and students $6, ages 6-17 $4.) Since Canada technically holds the upper half of a larger waterfall farther north, **Tettegouche State Park** can call itself home to Minnesota's tallest waterfall. An easy three-quarter-mile hike leads to the 60 ft. High Falls. (☎226-6365. Park open daily 9am-8pm. Visitors Center open daily 9am-3pm.) Rte. 61 then winds its way through **Superior National Forest,** passing over countless winding rivers and creeks toward Tofte, where the 1526 ft. **Carlton Peak** dominates the landscape at Temperance State Park. In Tofte, outdoors enthusiasts can rent canoes ($26-42), kayaks ($28-50), and bikes ($16-45), or join guided water trips at **Sawtooth Outfitters,** 7213 Hwy. 61. (☎663-7643; www.sawtoothoutfitters.com. Open mid-May to Aug. daily 7am-7pm; May and Sept. daily 8am-6pm; in winter M and Th-F 9am-6pm, Sa-Su 8am-6pm.) The **Coho Cafe ❷,** in Tofte on Rte. 61, serves delicious pastries, pastas ($11-18), and pizzas (from $5), as well as strong coffee. (☎663-8032. Open May-Oct. daily 7am-9pm. MC/V.) The pine-paneled **Cobblestone Cabins ❸,** off Rte. 61, 2 mi. north of Tofte, has eight guest cabins and access to a cobblestone beach, canoes, a sauna on the beach, and kitchens. (☎633-7957; www.cobblestonecabins.biz. Open year-round; no running water in winter. Cabins $60-140; weekly rates available. Cash or check only.)

GIVING BACK

EARN AND LEARN

It might surprise travelers that students at the North House Folk School in Minnesota are signing up to learn how to build so-called yurts (traditional nomadic shelters from Central Asia) in a five-day class. They can follow up with home-brewing lessons, knitting seminars, sailing overnights, and a course on orienteering in order that they might sail from place to place, yurt in tow, and settle in for the night with a cold mug of beer and a warm knit hat.

The non-profit Folk School, which was founded in 1997 and recruits teachers from across Minnesota, specializes in crafts, ecology, and skills applicable to this northern region. Some classes meet for only one afternoon; others last three weeks at a time.

Since the longer, more involved classes get pretty pricey, the Folk School has implemented an "Earn and Learn" program. Eager students can apply to work up to five days at the school, doing light manual and desk labor, and then trade in their work days for courses. This one-to-one trade-off is the kind of simple logic that characterizes both the town of Grand Marais and the useful, traditional knowledge that the Folk School's courses impart.

For more info, contact the Folk School at P.O. Box 759, in Grand Marais. ☎387-9762; www.northhousefolkschool.com.

GREAT LAKES

GRAND MARAIS AND BOUNDARY WATERS ☎ 218

Near the north end of the 150 mi. scenic drive lies the fishing village and former artists' colony Grand Marais (Ma-RAY), overlooking a large harbor with a lighthouse and marina. This popular tourist spot is a great place to sleep, eat, and enjoy the scenery. Grand Marais serves as a gateway to the **Boundary Waters Canoe Area Wilderness (BWCAW)**, and the **Gunflint Trail.** The BWCAW is a designated wilderness area of the Superior National Forest comprising 1.2 million acres of lakes, streams, and forests. It is strict about when, where, and how many people it will allow to enter in order to preserve the pristine environment; phoning ahead is essential. Make reservations with the National Recreation Reservation Service. (Camping ☎ 877-444-6777, BWCAW permits 877-550-6777; www.reserveusa.com. Reservation fee $12. Self-issue permits at trailheads for day-use free. Camping permits $10, children $5. Season pass $40/20.) More info is available at the Superior National Forest (☎ 626-4300) and the Gunflint Ranger Station (see below). The **Gunflint Trail (County Road 12)** runs 57 mi. northwest from Grand Marais to Lake Saganaga, on the border of Canada. The road offers access to amazing trails, including Eagle Mountain, Minnesota's highest point, and lakes. **The Gunflint Trail Association** lists lodges, restaurants, and private and U.S. Forest Service campgrounds spread throughout the trail. **The Two Islands Lake Campground** is close to town and has some lakeside sites. (☎ 800-338-6932; www.gunflint-trail.com.) One mile south of Grand Marais, the **Gunflint Ranger Station** distributes permits and has tourist information. (☎ 387-1750. Open May-Sept. daily 7am-5pm; Oct.-Apr. M-F 8am-4:30pm.) At Rte. 61 and Wisconsin St. is the **Gunflint Trail Information Center,** which provides information about the trail and the BWCAW, and helps to find available sites in the private and Superior National Forest **campgrounds** (sites $12-17) on the trail. (☎ 387-3191. Open daily 9am-5pm.) A variety of outfitters are stationed along the Gunflint Trail. One of the best is the family-run **Bear Track Outfitting Company,** 2011 W. Hwy. 61, right across from the Ranger Station, whose knowledgeable staff supplies rentals, fully outfits canoers and kaykers, and sends out extended guided trips (Complete outfitting for 3 days $260-318 per person; 1-2 day canoe renal $35-58 per day.) Backpacking, fly-fishing, skiing, and snowshoeing gear is also available. (☎ 387-1162 or 800-795-8068; www.bear-track.com. Open in summer M-Sa 8am-6pm, Su 9am-5pm; call for winter hours.)

   Nelson's Traveler's Rest ❷, on Rte. 61, half a mile south of town, has fully equipped cabins with fireplaces, as well as a cabin split into two cheaper motel rooms. (☎ 387-1464 or 800-249-1285; www.travelersrest.com. Open mid-May to mid-Oct. Call far in advance for reservations. 10% discounts on stays longer than 5 days. Singles $39; cabins from $55. D/MC/V.) **Grand Marais RV Park-Campground & Recreational Area ❶,** off Rte. 61 right before town on 8th Ave. W, has 300 sites by the lake. (☎ 387-1712 or 800-998-0959. Office open daily 8am-8pm. Reservations recommended. Open May to mid-Oct. Sites $22; with water and electricity $28. July-Aug. $26/33. Each additional adult $3. D/MC/V.) The consensus among locals is that the ☒**Angry Trout Cafe ❸,** has the best food in town. At this organic and environmentally conscious eatery, you can top off your meal of salad and locally caught grilled fish ($11) with a shot of pure maple syrup ($2.75). (☎ 387-1265; www.angrytroutcafe.com. Lunch $9-11. Dinner $18-22. Open May-Oct. M-Th and Su 11am-8:30pm, F-Sa 11am-9pm. MC/V.) Cheap and popular with locals and fishermen, **South of the Border Cafe ❶,** 4 W. Rte. 61, specializes in huge breakfasts and satisfying diner food. The bluefin herring sandwich is only $4. (☎ 387-1505. Breakfast under $7. Open daily 5am-2pm. Cash only.) Another favorite is the Friday fish fry ($10-15) at the **Blue Water Cafe ❷,** at Wisconsin St. and 1st Ave. W. Every other night of the week, try their burgers, salads, and sandwiches. (☎ 387-1597; www.bluewatercafe.com. Open daily 6:30am-8pm. D/MC/V.)

GREAT LAKES

The Grand Marais Visitor Information Center, 13 N. Broadway, is one block from Hwy. 61; make a right at the town's one stoplight. (☎387-2524 or 888-922-5000; www.grandmarais.com. Usually open M-Th 9am-5pm, F-Sa 9am-6pm, Su 10am-2pm; hours vary by season.)

GREAT PLAINS

In 1803, the Louisiana Purchase doubled America's size, adding French territory west of the Mississippi at the bargain price of $0.03 per acre. Over time, the plains spawned legends of pioneers, cowboys, and Native Americans as they fought over land and struggled to learn the way of life that came to define the American West. The arrival of railroads and liberal land policies in the 19th century spurred an economic boom, until a drought during the Great Depression transformed the region into a dust bowl.

Modern agriculture has reclaimed the soil, and the heartland of the US now thrives on farm products. The Plains are a truly vast swathe of land, where open sky and endless prairies stretch from horizon to horizon as far as the eye can see. While signs of humanity in the region are unmistakable—checkerboard farms, outlying Army posts, and railroad corridors—the region's most staggering sights are its works of nature, from the Badlands and the Black Hills to the mighty Missouri and Mississippi Rivers.

HIGHLIGHTS OF THE GREAT PLAINS

VENTURE into the depths of **Jewel Cave** and **Wind Cave** (p. 585) and the rugged wilderness of **Theodore Roosevelt National Park** (p. 576) and the **Badlands** (p. 580).

SLIDE down the famous "shoe chutes" at the **City Museum** in St. Louis (p. 611).

GAZE at the formidable **Mt. Rushmore** (p. 583) and **Crazy Horse Memorial** (p. 584).

UNBUCKLE your belt after feasting on the nation's best **beef** in Omaha, NE (p. 598).

MISBEHAVE like cowboys did when the West was wild in **Deadwood, SD** (p. 588).

NORTH DAKOTA

Vast open spaces usher visitors to North Dakota. An early visitor declared, "It's a beautiful land, but I doubt that human beings will ever live here." Posterity begs to differ. The stark, haunting lands that intimidated settlers eventually found willing tenants, and the territory became a state along with South Dakota on Nov. 2, 1889. One detail still muddles the event—President Benjamin Harrison concealed the order in which he signed the two bills, so both Dakotas claim to be the 39th state.

◨ PRACTICAL INFORMATION

Capital: Bismarck.

Visitor Info: Tourism Department, 1600 E. Century Ave., Bismarck 58501 (☎800-435-5663; www.ndtourism.com). **Parks and Recreation Department,** 1600 E. Century Ave., Bismarck 58501 (☎328-5357; www.ndparks.com). **Game and Fish Department,** 100 N. Bismarck Expwy., Bismarck 58501 (☎328-6300). State offices open M-F 8am-5pm.

Postal Abbreviation: ND. **Sales Tax:** 5%.

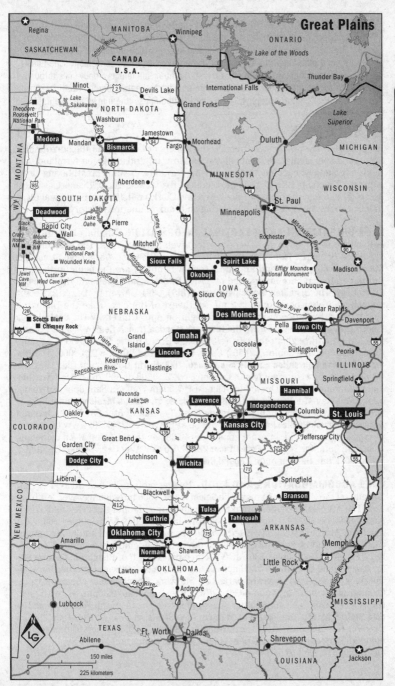

Great Plains

GREAT PLAINS

TIP

BUS' A MOVE. Greyhound has made significant schedule and route changes recently, decreasing the number of stops in the Great Plains area from 260 to 99. Many smaller bus lines have begun to pick up the slack, but travelers should plan ahead to account for higher prices and less convenient schedules. To get you from point A to point B faster, Amtrak still runs two daily lines through the region: the "Empire Builder," from Chicago to Seattle through North Dakota, and the "California Zephyr," from Chicago through southern Iowa and Nebraska.

BISMARCK

☎ 701

In Bismarck, the people are friendly, the streets are clean, and the surrounding scenery is spectacular. Seas of yellow wildflowers, grids of green farmland, and fields of golden wheat blend with surprising harmony, creating breathtaking views along the Riverside Pkwy., a scenic stretch of road that is one of Bismarck's finest assets. Located at the center of the Lewis and Clark Trail, the city is an ideal place to learn about the state's rich pioneering and Native American history.

ORIENTATION AND PRACTICAL INFORMATION. Bismarck is on I-94, halfway between Fargo and Theodore Roosevelt National Park. The **Missouri River** separates Bismarck from Mandan, its neighbor to the west. **Washington Street, 7th Street** (one-way south) and **9th Street** (one-way north) are the main north-south thoroughfares and are intersected by **Divide Street, Main Street,** and the **Bismarck Expressway.** The **Bismarck Municipal Airport (BIS),** 2301 University Dr. (☎222-6502; www.bismarckairport.com), is 2 mi. southeast of the city. Take the Bismarck Expwy. east from downtown and turn right on onto University Dr. **Capital Area Transit (CAT)** buses depart from the **Bismarck-Mandan Transit Center,** 3750 E. Rosser Ave., and run throughout the city. (☎323-9228. Buses run 6:30am-6:30pm. $1; children, disabled, and seniors $0.50.) For a **taxi,** call **Taxi 9000,** ☎223-9000. The **Bismarck-Mandan Convention and Visitors Bureau,** 1600 Burnt Boat Dr., at Exit 157 off I-94, distributes a visitor guide and coupons. (☎222-4308 or 800-767-3555; www.bismarkmandancvb.com. Open June-Oct. M-F 7:30am-7pm, Sa 8am-6pm, Su 10am-5pm; Nov.-May M-F 8am-5pm.) **Medical Services: St. Alexius Medical Center,** 900 E. Broadway Ave. (☎530-7000, Emergency and Trauma Center 530-7001). **Internet Access: Bismarck Public Library,** 515 N. 5th St. at B Ave. (☎222-6410; www.bismarcklibrary.org. Free Wi-Fi. Internet computers $0.25 per 15min. Open M-Th 9am-9pm, F-Sa 9am-6pm, Su 1-6pm.) **Post Office:** 220 E. Rosser Ave. (☎255-6963. Open M-F 7:45am-5:30pm, Sa 9am-noon.) **Postal Code:** 58501.

ACCOMMODATIONS AND FOOD. Budget motels abound off I-94 at Exit 159 and on the Bismarck Expwy. The **Select Inn ❷,** 1505 Interchange Ave., left from Exit 159 off I-94, provides breakfast, clean rooms, laundry access, and Wi-Fi. (☎223-8060 or 800-641-1000; www.selectinn.com. Singles $53; doubles $63. AAA discount. AmEx/D/MC/V.) Located two blocks from the Capitol and much homier than a chain motel, **Kay's B&B ❹,** 807 N. 6th St., is meticulously decorated. (☎258-6877. Singles $75; doubles $85. MC/V.) Three miles south of Bismarck, **General Sibley Campground ❶,** 5001 S. Washington St., has sites dotted with trees not far from the river. (☎222-1844; www.bisparks.org. Showers. Check-in and check-out 2pm. Campground open May to mid-Oct. Office open daily 8am-9:30pm. $7, with electricity $17. D/MC/V.) On the other side of the river, the beautiful **Fort Abraham Lincoln State Park ❶,** 7 mi. south of Mandan (see **Sights,** p. 575) on Rte. 1806, has 95 sites on the Missouri River. (☎667-6340 or 800-807-4723. Reservations recommended. Park entrance fee $5 per vehicle. Primitive sites mid-May to Sept. $8, with electricity $14. Oct. to mid-May $5/12.)

With an enormous Italian-inspired menu to complement its intimate atmosphere, **Walrus ❸**, 1136 N. 3rd St., in Arrowhead Plaza, is a local favorite. (☎250-0020. Pasta $10-15. Pizza $8-10. Sandwiches $5-10. Open M-Sa 10:30am-1am. D/MC/V.) Housed in the old Northern Pacific train depot, **Fiesta Villa ❸**, 411 E. Main Ave., serves quesadillas with fresh guacamole ($8-12) and other Mexican and Tex-Mex fare. Freshly blended margaritas shake up the atmosphere while rumbling trains shake the foundation below. (☎222-8075. Patio and bar 21+. Open M-Th 11am-10:30pm, F-Sa 11am-11pm. Bar open until 1am on busy evenings. D/MC/V.)

◉ **SIGHTS.** In the Capitol complex, the **North Dakota Heritage Center,** 612 E. Boulevard Ave., the official state history museum, has its own mastodon skeleton as well as colorful exhibits charting the state's goings-on since prehistory. (☎328-2666. Open M-F 8am-5pm, Sa-Su 10am-5pm. Free.) Visible from almost anywhere in the city, the **North Dakota State Capitol,** 600 E. Boulevard Ave, is a 19-story Art Deco building constructed between 1932 and 1934. The observation deck on the 18th floor is a perfect place to gaze at the prairie and the capitol's 130 acres of manicured grounds. (☎328-2480. Open M-F 7am-5:30pm. 30min. tours leave every hr. June-Aug. M-F 8-11am and 1-4pm, Sa 9-11am and 1-4pm, Su 1-4pm; Sept.-May M-F 8-11am and 1-4pm. Free.) North Dakota's oldest state park, **Fort Abraham Lincoln State Park,** lies on Rte. 1806 in Mandan, along the Missouri River, in an area once occupied by the Mandan Indians, until they succumbed to smallpox. Lewis and Clark came through this area in 1804, and General George Armstrong Custer, commanding the 7th Cavalry, took up residence here several decades later. Now, Fort Lincoln houses the **"On-a-Slant" Mandan Indian Village,** with several recon-structed earth lodges, as well as replicas of the cavalry post and Custer's well-kept Victorian home. (☎663-9571, in low-season 663-4758. Buildings open May-Oct. daily 9am-7pm. Park open daily 9am-9:30pm. Call for low-season hours. Tours every 30min. daily 9am-7pm. $6, students $4; vehicle fee $5.) The city has miles of trails for biking and walking, including the **Legacy Trail,** which connects Bismarck to Mandan and passes by historical and recreational sites. The trail has one end-point in Fort Abraham Lincoln State Park; perhaps its most scenic stretch is along Riverside Park Rd., next to the river in Bismark. The city publishes a trails bro-chure and maintains signage (a lifesaver) along the trails.

📹🎭 **ENTERTAINMENT AND NIGHTLIFE.** The **Bismarck-Mandan Symphony Orchestra** plays in the magnificent **Belle Mehus Auditorium,** 201 N. 6th St. The sym-phony celebrates holidays in style—an estimated 8000 people turn up for their 4th of July concert on the steps of the Capitol building. (☎258-8345; www.bismarck-mandansymphony.org. Concert series Sept.-Apr.) **Borrowed Buck's Roadhouse,** 118 S. 3rd St. at Front Ave., has a DJ and dancing every night. Live bands take the stage once or twice a month. (☎224-1545. 21+. Open M-Sa 4pm-1am, Su noon-1am.) In good weather, the waterfront patio at **Broken Oar,** 4724 Pintail Loop, is abuzz with

---

👁 **I-94, ROAD OF CONCRETE WONDERS.** Two gargantuan concrete monuments separated by 131 mi. of interstate symbolize North Dakota's past and present. Looming on the horizon in Jamestown, ND, at Exit 258, is the **world's largest buffalo**—a towering 24 ft. monument to the animals that once freely roamed the plains. Across the highway, a herd of real buffalo regards its concrete brother apathetically from behind a fence. In New Salem, ND, 33 mi. west of Bismarck, at Exit 127, Salem Sue, the **world's largest Holstein cow** (38 ft. tall and 50 ft. long), keeps an eye on the interstate and the spectacular patchwork fields of the plains. (Suggested donation $1.)

revelers. Take the Bismark Expwy. across the river to Mandan, then make a left at McKenzie, a left at 46th Ave., a left on 29th St., and follow it all the way to the Marina. (☎667-2159. Open daily noon-1am.) For a true country experience, try **Lonesome Dove,** 3929 Memorial Hwy. in Mandan, with live, toe-tappin' music Wednesday through Sunday. (☎663-2793. 21+. Open daily noon-1am.)

THEODORE ROOSEVELT
NATIONAL PARK ☎701

After first visiting the Badlands to hunt buffalo, pre-White House Theodore ("Teddy") Roosevelt returned for spiritual renewal after the deaths of his mother and wife. He was so influenced by its buttes and gorges, horseback riding, big-game hunting, and cattle ranching, that he later claimed, "I never would have been President if it weren't for my experiences in North Dakota." Roosevelt National Park was created in 1947 as a monument to his conservation efforts, and its vast open spaces and rugged outdoors opportunities preserve the spirit of the land that inspired the 26th President of the United States.

⬛🯄 ORIENTATION AND PRACTICAL INFORMATION. The park is split into the **North Unit** and **South Unit,** with the Little Missouri Grasslands in between. On the radio, **AM 1610** offers information about both parts of the park. The North Unit is located 52 mi. north of Exit 42 off I-94, on U.S. 85. The entrance to the more developed South Unit is at Exit 24 or 27 off I-94. The town of Medora serves as the gateway to the South Unit. Despite a year-round population of less than 100, this revamped tourist haven retains a local feel with old-fashioned ice-cream parlors and gift shops. The park **entrance fee** ($10 per vehicle; $5 per pedestrian; under 17 free) covers 7-day admission to both the North and South units. The **South Unit Visitors Center,** in Medora, maintains a mini-museum displaying Roosevelt's guns, spurs, and old letters. (☎623-4466; www.nps.gov/thro. Open daily late June-Sept. 8am-6pm; Sept. to mid-June 8am-4:30pm.) The **North Unit Visitors Center** is located next to the park entrance. (☎842-2333; www.nps.gov/thro. Open daily 9am-5:30pm. Call ahead in winter.) **Dakota Cyclery,** 275 3rd Ave., rents bikes and leads bike tours of the Badlands by reservation. (☎623-4808 or 888-321-1218; www.dakotacyclery.com. Bikes $25-35 per half-day, $30-45 per day. Tours for two people $50-80, each additional person $15-25. Open mid-May to early Oct. daily 8:30am-6pm.) Off-road biking is not allowed in either unit of the park. Medora lacks a real pharmacy and grocery store. However, both the **camp store** at Red Trail Campground, off E. River Rd. (☎623-4317; open in summer daily 7am-11pm), and **Medora Convenience and Liquor,** on Pacific Ave. at Main St. (☎623-4479; open daily 7am-10pm), sell basic pharmaceutical goods, food, and cooking items. Medora Convenience and Liquor is also the town's only gas station. There is a 24hr. **Wal-Mart** (☎225-8504; open daily 8am-10pm) in Dickinson, 30 mi. east on I-94. **Internet Access:** Ferris General Store, 251 Main St. (☎623-4447; open daily 8:30am-10pm), which has computers and free Wi-Fi. **South Unit Time Zone:** Mountain (2hr. behind EST). **North Unit Time Zone:** Central (1hr. behind EST). **Post Office:** 355 3rd Ave., in Medora. (☎623-4385. Open M-Sa 8am-7pm. Window service M-F 8am-11:45am and 12:30-4:30pm, Sa 8:15-9:45am.) **Postal Code:** 58645.

🯄🯄 ACCOMMODATIONS AND FOOD. Free **backcountry camping permits** are available from the Visitors Centers. Both units have self-registration for campgrounds 5 mi. past the river entrances. **Cottonwood Campground ❶** lies 5 mi. past the South Unit Visitors Center on Scenic Loop Dr., while the less-crowded **Juniper Campground ❶** is 5 mi. west of the North Unit Visitors Center. Be cautious: the campgrounds are frequented by buffalo. Both campgrounds have toilets and running water in the summer, but only pit toilets in the winter. (Check-out noon. No hookups or showers. Sites $10; in winter $5.) Camping outside the park usually yields more amenities and better food options. It's difficult to find cheap indoor or low-season lodging in Medora, but Dickinson, 30 mi. east on I-94, contains several affordable options year-round. Seventeen miles east of Medora, Belfield's **Cowboy Inn ❸**, 406 Hwy. 10 E., is family-run and has standard, carefully maintained rooms. Take Exit 42 off the interstate, follow Hwy. 85 over the bridge, then make a right onto 6th Ave. (☎575-8140. Wi-Fi. Singles M-Th $57, F-Sa $67; doubles $67/77. Low season M-Th $52, F-Sa $57.) The **Bunkhouse ❹**, 400 E. River Rd. S, has A/C, cable TV, and a pool. (☎800-633-6721. Register at the Badlands Motel at 500 Pacific Ave. Open late May-early Sept. Doubles M-Th and Su $75, F-Sa $85; family units $109/ 118. AmEx/D/MC/V.) For a bit more luxury, the historic **Rough Riders Hotel ❹**, 301 3rd Ave., has rooms with original furniture and an upscale restaurant. (☎623-6444. Check in at the Badlands Motel. Rooms $130-150. Restaurant open daily 7am-2pm and 5-9pm. AmEx/D/MC/V.) **Cowboy Cafe ❷**, 215 4th St., is a popular spot for inexpensive specialties like french toast and ham ($6) and the mighty caramel roll ($3), both of which offer plenty of bang for their buck. (☎623-4343. Entrees $5-9. Breakfast 6am-11am. Open daily 6am-8pm. Cash only.) Medora's **Fudge & Ice Cream Depot ❶**, on Pacific Ave., and **Marquis de Mores French Ice Cream ❶**, 330 3rd Ave., offer sweet treats. (☎800-633-6721. 1 scoop $2.50. Both open June-Aug. daily 11am-7:30pm. Cash only.) The **Iron Horse Saloon ❸**, 160 Pacific Ave., offers tons of burgers and greasy favorites, all served at the bar or on the patio. (☎623-9894. Breakfast, sandwiches, and burgers $4-9. Dinner entrees $10-20. Open daily June-Sept. 6am-1am; Oct.-May 10:30am-1am. AmEx/D/MC/V.)

> Theodore Roosevelt National Park's seclusion provides ample opportunity for wildlife contact, but be careful not to surprise the bison; you may wish to sing so they can hear you coming. Do not approach any animal, and beware of rattlesnakes and black widow spiders in prairie dog burrows. Even if you avoid the creepy-crawlies, watch out; prairie dogs' bites are worse than their barks.

◎ ♫ SIGHTS AND ENTERTAINMENT. The **Cowboy Hall of Fame**, 250 Main St., tells the story of the Plains' horse culture, from Native Americans and ranchers to rodeo stars. Upstairs, photos and stories honor the Hall of Fame's cowboy inductees. (☎623-2000; www.northdakotacowboy.com. Open daily May-Oct. 10am-7:30pm; low season by appointment. $6.50, seniors $5, students $4; families $18. AmEx/D/MC/V.) Room-by-room guides at the state historic site **Chateau de Mores,** 3448 Chateau Rd., on the west side of town, tell of the three-year stint Medora's namesake Frenchmen, the Marquis de Mores and his wife, Medora, spent here. (☎623-4355. Open May 16-Sept. 15 8:30am-6:30pm, last entry 5:50pm; in winter by appointment. $6, ages 6-15 $3, under 6 free.) The popular **Medora Musical** is a song-and-dance extravaganza celebrating the glory of Teddy Roosevelt, North Dakota, and America. The patriotic show, held in the open-air **Burning Hills Amphitheater** west of town, incorporates pyrotechnics, horses, and visiting comedians and performers. (Show runs early June-early Sept. daily 8:30-10:30pm. Tickets $30, students $16.) Before the show, at the nearby Tjaden Terrace, cast members serenade the audience as they feast at a rowdy Western **Pitchfork Steak Fondue,** where cooks put steaks on a pitchfork and dunk them into a vat of boiling oil. (Daily at 6pm. Half-steak $18, steak $23. Reservations recommended.) Tickets for both the musical and the fondue are available in town at the **Harold Schafer Heritage Center,** 335 4th St. (☎800-633-6721; www.medora.com. Open daily 10am-6pm.)

OUTDOOR ACTIVITIES. The South Unit is busier than the North Unit and includes the 36 mi. **Scenic Loop Drive,** from which all sights and trails are accessible. **Painted Canyon Overlook,** 7 mi. east of Medora off I-94, has its own Visitors Center with picnic tables, public phones, restrooms, and a breathtaking panoramic view of the Badlands. (☎575-4020. Open daily June-Aug. 8am-6pm; Apr.-May and Sept.-Oct. 8:30am-4:30pm.) The **Painted Canyon Trail** is a steep 1 mi. hiking loop that winds into the valley through shady wooded areas and scorching buttes. **Peaceful Valley Ranch,** 7 mi. into the South Unit, offers horseback excursions. (☎623-4568. Open May-Sept. Some age and height requirements. 1½hr. trail rides July-Sept. 7 daily 8:30am-4pm; May-June 5 daily 10am-3pm. Reservations by mail only. $30.) Both the **Ridgeline** and **Coal Vein Trails** are self-guided interpretive nature walks. Numbers along the trails refer to a handout with ecological and geographic insights. The three-quarter-mile Coal Vein Trail traces a seam of lignite coal that ignited and burned from 1951 to 1977; the searing heat of the blaze served as a natural kiln, baking the nearby clay and sand. Constant winds morph the soft sands of **Wind Canyon,** while a short dirt path leading along the bluffs gives a closer look at the canyon walls and the river below. There are two ways of getting to the third-largest **petrified forest** in the US: either a day's hike into the park or a drive to the park's western border. Take I-94 west to Exit 23, then take a right onto W. River Rd., a red dirt road. Drive 5½ mi., following signs with Teddy Roosevelt's face. From there, hikers must crawl beneath a gate and walk about a half-mile to the first stumps. Free tours leave every hour in the summer from 8:45am-4:15pm from the South Unit Visitors Center for **Teddy's Maltese Cross Cabin,** built circa 1883. For more info on hiking, pick up *Frontier Fragments* and the *Backcountry Guide* (both free) at one of the Visitors Centers. The 96 mi. **Maah Daah Hey Trail** connects the North and South Units through the scenic Little Missouri Grasslands. The popular trail was once a principal trade route for Native Americans in the area.

The ■**North Unit** is known for its more dramatic and varied scenery. The desert-like buttes and high grasses make for unlimited **backcountry hiking** possibilities. The North Unit's 14 mi. **Scenic Drive** is perfect for auto-touring and connects the entrance to Oxbow Overlook. The 1 mi. **Little Mo Trail** weaves through woodlands and badlands near the Juniper Campground; the first half of the 1 mi. loop is paved and wheelchair-accessible. The 4½ mi. loop **Caprock Coulee Trail** winds its way through a variety of habitats, climbing to an outlook over the Little Missouri River. The 12 mi. **Buckhorn Trail** is moderately strenuous and provides the only access to two prairie dog towns. Seasoned hikers delight in the challenging 18 mi. **Achenbach Trail,** which features vertical drops, uphill climbs, and two river crossings. Be sure to check trail conditions before attempting this hike.

SOUTH DAKOTA

With fewer than 10 people per square mile, South Dakota has the highest ratio of sights to people in all of the Great Plains. Colossal carvings such as Mt. Rushmore and the Crazy Horse Memorial, historical remnants like Deadwood, and stunning natural spectacles like the Black Hills and the Badlands draw summer crowds seeking scenic pictures and a taste of the West.

▨ PRACTICAL INFORMATION

Capital: Pierre.

Visitor Info: Department of Tourism, 711 E. Wells Ave., Pierre 57501 (☎605-773-3301 or 800-952-3625; www.travelsd.com). Open M-F 8am-5pm. **US Forest Service,** 330 Mt.

Rushmore Rd., Custer 57730 (☎605-673-4853). Open M-F 7:30am-4:30pm. **Game, Fish, and Parks Department,** 523 E. Capitol Ave., Foss Bldg., Pierre 57501 (☎605-773-3485, campground reservations 800-710-2267; www.campsd.com), has info on state parks and campgrounds. Open M-F 8am-5pm.

Postal Abbreviation: SD. **Sales Tax:** 4% (1-2% extra in some towns).

SIOUX FALLS   ☎605

As South Dakota's eastern gateway and largest city, Sioux Falls boasts a long history as a pioneer town. The city's center is **Falls Park,** the waterfall where roving settlers first claimed land. Life moves at a quicker pace on charming **Phillips Avenue,** which leads out from the park, and in the surrounding commercial boulevards, which have more character than first meets the eye. The **Washington Pavilion,** 301 S. Main Ave., at 11th St., contains the well-curated Visual Arts Center, the kid-friendly Kirby Science Discovery Center, a movie theater, and a performance space. (☎877-927-4728; www.washingtonpavilion.org. Open M-Th and Sa 10am-5pm, F 10am-8pm, Su noon-5pm. Building and Visual Arts Center free. Science Center $7, seniors $6, under 12 $5.) The **Pettigrew Home & Museum,** 131 N. Duluth Ave. at 8th St., is the former home of South Dakota's first senator, who in addition to politicking was an avid art collector. (☎367-7097; www.siouxlandmuseaums.com. Open May-Sept. M-W and F-Sa 9am-5pm, Th 9am-9pm, Su noon-5pm; Oct.-Apr. daily noon-5pm. Tours every 30min. Free.) The offbeat **Battleship South Dakota Memorial,** at the corner of Kiwanis Ave. and 12th St., honors the most decorated battleship of World War II, the *USS South Dakota.* While some parts of the enormous ship made it intact to South Dakota, other parts had to be constructed right there in the park. (☎367-7141. Museum open Memorial Day-Labor Day daily 10am-6pm. Free.) The **Sertoma Butterfly House,** 4320 S. Oxbow Ave., in Sertoma Park, is home to hundreds of butterflies from around the world. (☎334-9466; www.sertomabutterflyhouse.org. Open in summer M-Sa 10am-6pm, Su 1-5pm; in winter M-Sa 10am-4pm, Su 1-4pm. $6, over 60 $4.50, ages 4-18 $4, under 3 free.) Five miles west of Sioux Falls at Exit 390 off I-90, the recreated ghost town of **Buffalo Ridge** has over 50 quirky exhibits portraying life in the Old West. (☎528-3931. Open early Apr. to Oct. sunrise-sunset. $5, ages 5-12 $4.) The **Corn Palace,** 604 N. Main St. in Mitchell, 70 mi. west of Sioux Falls on I-90, was specifically designed to put the town on the map and now poses as a regal testament to the "a-maize-ing" power of corn. Dating back to 1892, the concrete structure is re-decorated each year using thousands of bushels of corn and grain. Come fall, it is the world's largest bird feeder. (☎866-273-2676; www.cornpalace.com. Open Memorial Day-Labor Day daily 8am-9pm; Apr.-May and Sept.-Oct. daily 8am-5pm; Nov.-Mar. M-F 8am-5pm. Festival in late Aug. Free.)

Budget motels flank 41st St. at Exit 77 off I-29. The **Red Roof Inn ❷,** 3500 Gateway Blvd., off 41st St., is a good value with continental breakfast, laundry facilities, TV, and Wi-Fi. (☎361-1864 or 800-733-7663. Singles M-F $52, Sa-Su $57; doubles $65/70. AAA discount. AmEx/D/MC/V.) Camping near Sioux Falls is available in the beautiful quartzite landscape at **Palisades State Park ❶,** 20 mi. from the city. Take I-90 E to Rte. 11 N. (☎594-3824; www.campSD.com. Water and showers. Sites $10, vehicles $5 per day. Electricity $4. Non-residence fee $5.) While in the area, visit **Devil's Gulch. Phillips Avenue,** downtown between 9th and 12th Sts., is lined with coffeehouses and restaurants. **Sanaa's Gourmet ❸,** 401 E. 8th St., is a good bet for tasty fare at reasonable prices. The Mediterranean spread in the glass cases at Sanaa's is colored by fresh salads ($3.50), dips ($3-4), and *fatayers* (pitas stuffed with spinach, eggplant, or meat; $2.50-5). Dinners ($12) include an appetizer, olives, pita, choice of main dish, salad, and coffee. (☎275-2516; www.sanaasgourmet.com. Open M 10:30am-4pm, Tu-Sa 10:30am-8pm.) **Nitwits Comedy Club,** 3224 E. 10th St., showcases local talent and Hollywood imports. (☎274-9656 or 888-798-0277; www.nitwitscomedy.com. 21+. Cover W-Th $10, F-Sa $12. Shows W-Th 7:30pm, F 8pm, Sa 7:30 and 10pm. Reservations required.) Fourteen miles of bike path make a circle around Sioux Falls, beginning in Falls Park. Also in the park, catch a historical light show shown nightly around 9:30pm from Memorial Day to Labor Day.

Jefferson Lines, 301 N. Dakota Ave., at W. 7th St., runs **buses** to Minneapolis (6hr., 3 per day, $55), Omaha (3½hr., 3 per day, $42), and Rapid City (4hr., 1 per day, $79). (☎336-0885 or 800-767-5333. Open M-Sa 8am-9pm, Su 8-11:30am and 2-9pm.) Sioux Falls Transit **buses** run throughout the city. (☎367-7183; www.siouxfalls.org/transit. Buses run M-F 5:40am-6:50pm, Sa 8am-6:50pm. $1, transfers free.) The Sioux Falls Trolley provides free **trolley** rides between Falls Park, where parking is easy, and downtown. (☎367-7183. Runs M-Sa 8am-10pm.) For a **taxi,** call Yellow Cab (☎336-1616). The **Sioux Falls Convention and Visitors Bureau** is at 200 N. Phillips St., in Falls Park. (☎336-1620; www.siouxfallscvb.com. Open Apr. to mid-Oct. daily 9am-9pm; mid-Oct. to Mar. M-F 9am-9pm, Sa-Su 9am-5pm.) **Medical Services: Sanford USD Medical Center,** 1305 W. 18th St. (☎333-1000; www.siouxvalley.org). **Internet Access: Sioux Falls Public Library,** 201 N. Main Ave., at 8th St. (☎367-8740; www.siouxlandlib.org. Wi-Fi available. Free. Open M-Th 9am-9pm, F 9am-6pm, Sa 9am-5pm; Sept.-May also Su 1-5pm.) **Post Office:** 320 S. 2nd Ave. (☎357-5021 or 357-5022. Open M-F 8am-5:30pm.) **Postal Code:** 57104.

BADLANDS NATIONAL PARK   ☎605

When faced with a mountainous wall of craggy rock formations looming over the prairie, early explorers were less than enthusiastic. The French called the hills *les mauvaises terres,* or "bad lands," and the name stuck. Still, not everyone feared the land—there is evidence that the Oglala Lakota named the lands *Paha ska,* or "white hills," and viewed them as sacred as the neighboring Black Hills. Spring and fall in the Badlands offer pleasant weather that is a relief from the extreme temperatures of summer and winter, but even at their worst, the Badlands are worth a visit. Mineral deposits lend layers of red, brown, and green to the rock formations, and the colorful moods of the Badlands change with the time and weather.

■▶ **ORIENTATION AND PRACTICAL INFORMATION.** Badlands National Park consists of the **North Unit, Western Wilderness Area,** and **South Unit.** The most accessible, the North Unit, lies 50 mi. east of Rapid City on I-90. The **entrance fee** ($15 per car, $7 per pedestrian or cyclist) comes with an extensive brochure and map. The **Ben Reifel Visitors Center,** 5 mi. inside the northeastern entrance, serves as the park headquarters. Watch their 20min. film, "Land of Stone and Light," for an overview. (☎433-5361. Open daily June to mid-Aug. 8am-6pm; mid-Apr. to June and mid-Aug. to mid-Oct. 8am-5pm; mid-Oct. to Apr. 9am-4pm.) A drive along **U.S. 240/ Badlands Loop Road,** accessible from I-90, is an excellent introduction to the northern portion of the park. This scenic byway curves through rainbow-colored bluffs and has numerous turnoffs for views of the Badlands. The gravel **Sage Creek Rim Road,** west of U.S. 240, sees very few people and lots of animals. Highlights of the area include the Roberts Prairie Dog Town and the park's herds of bison and antelope. The more remote **White River Visitor Center** is located some 55 mi. to the southwest, off B.I.A. 27 in the park's less-traversed southern section. (☎455-2878. Open June-Aug. daily 9am-5pm.) Both Visitors Centers have potable water and restrooms. The **National Grasslands Visitors Center (Buffalo Gap),** 708 Main St., in Wall, has films and exhibits on the complex ecosystem of the surrounding area. (☎279-2125. Open June-Aug. daily 8am-5pm; Sept.-May M-F 8am-4:30pm.) For more **info,** visit www.nps.gov/badl. The **First Western Bank,** 418 Main St. in Wall, has one computer with **Internet** access (Open M-F 9am-4pm). **Time Zone:** Mountain.

> While visitors are allowed to roam to their hearts' content in the Badlands back-country, it's a bit dangerous. The south unit was used as a practice bombing range during WWII, and there are still unexploded bombs around. Rangers are often spotted on the terrain collecting bombs that may or may not still be active.

FOOD AND ACCOMMODATIONS. In addition to the standard lodging and camping options, **backcountry camping ❶** (must be a half-mile from the road and out of sight) offers close contact with this austere landscape; be sure to pack plenty of water if pursuing this option. Contact one of the rangers at the Ben Reifel Visitor Center before heading out, and keep an eye out for bison, which can be extremely dangerous. Within the park, the **Cedar Pass Lodge ❸**, next to the Ben Reifel Visitor Center, rents cabins with A/C and showers. (☎433-5460; www.cedar-passlodge.com. Check-in 2pm. Check-out 11am. Reservations recommended. Open mid-Apr. to mid-Oct. 1-bed room $70; 2-bed room $85; cottage $100. 10% AAA discount. AmEx/D/MC/V.) The **Badlands Budget Host Inn ❷**, right down the road, offers clean rooms, cabins with A/C, a campground, and an on-site restaurant. (☎433-5335 or 800-283-4678. Campsites $14-21. Rooms $60-68. Cabins $30. No linens. D/MC/V.) The **Badlands Inn ❸**, half a mile outside the park on U.S. 377, has rooms with A/C and decent views of the Badlands. (☎433-5401; www.bad-landsinn.com. Check-in 2pm. Check-out 11am. Open mid-May to mid-Sept. Singles $75. AAA discount. AmEx/D/MC/V.) If you'd rather sleep under the stars, the **Cedar Pass Campground ❶**, just south of the Ben Reifel Visitors Center, is set against the dramatic Badland cliffs. (Water and flush toilets. Sites $10.) In the middle of the prairie, **Sage Creek Campground ❶**, 13 mi. from the Pinnacles entrance due south of Wall, is on a field with pit toilets and no water. (Take Sage Creek Rim Rd. off U.S. 240. Free.) Despite its tourist-friendly location at a motel and campground, **Badlands Circle 10 Cafe ❷**, half a mile west of I-90 on Rte. 240, attracts locals with its homemade fare. The salad with blue cheese, cherries, and walnuts is tempting, but platters and sandwiches, like the BLT on an English muffin, ($8-10), get you more grub for your buck. (☎800-231-3617. Breakfast $3-8. Dinner specials $11. Open M-Tu and Th-Su 8am-7:30pm. MC/V.) In the park, near the Ben Reifel Visitor Center, the **Cedar Pass Lodge Restaurant ❷** has hearty breakfasts, buffalo burgers ($7), and pricier entrees after 5pm. (☎433-5460. Open daily mid-May to Aug. 7am-8:30pm; Apr.-May and Sept.-Oct. 8am-4pm. AmEx/D/MC/V.)

SIGHTS. Since the park was originally created to preserve its fossils, check some out at the awesome **Pig Dig**, a functioning archaeological dig a quarter-mile south on Conata Road. (Open daily 10am-4pm.) From the 60s to the 90s, the Great Plains stored thousands of Minuteman intercontinental ballistic missiles (ICBM) aimed at the U.S.S.R. The National Parks system has preserved this recent history by opening up a deactivated missile site for tours. The **Minuteman Missile** office is located off the Interstate at Exit 131; the **Delta-09 launch missile silo** is at Exit 116, and the **launch control facility** is at Exit 127. (☎433-5552; www.nps.gov/mimi. Office open 8am-4:30pm. Tours of control facility in summer daily 9:30am and 1:30pm; in winter 9am. Reservations required. Free.)

OUTDOOR ACTIVITIES. The 244,000-acre park protects large tracts of prairie and stark rock formations, and the Ben Reifel Visitors Center has plenty of info on camping and hiking. The handy park brochure has schedules of guided walks and talks, delivered by park rangers from June to August. **Hiking** is permitted throughout the park, but climbing on the formations and drifting from established trails can be dangerous. Backcountry adventures come easily in the western wilderness

Don't let the intense summer heat ruin your visit! To experience the Badlands in the summer without suffering the oppressive midday heat, finish your outdoor activities by 8:30am or venture out after 7pm.

area, though well-marked trails are scarce. Hiking is discouraged in the wild and largely uncharted southern unit, which has no paved roads or trails. For backcountry hiking, bring a compass, a map, and lots of water. Despite the burning heat in summer, long pants will help ward off poison ivy, cacti, ticks, and the venomous prairie rattlesnake. Four short hiking trails begin off Loop Rd. near the Ben Reifel Visitor Center, including the **Notch Trail** (1½ mi., 1-1½hr.), which demands surefootedness through a canyon and a willingness to climb a shaky ladder at a 45-degree angle. Not for the faint of heart, the trail blazes around narrow ledges before making its way to the grand finale: a drop-off with an unbelievable view of the Cliff Shelf and White River Valley. The same parking lot gives access to the wheelchair-accessible **Door Trail** (¾ mi., 20min.), which ends at a big expanse of Badlands excellent for exploring, and the **Window Trail** (¼ mi., 10min.), which is more of a scenic overlook than an actual hike. A few miles west of Ben Reifel on Rte. 240, the **Saddle Pass** is steep and short. It scales the **Badlands Wall** and leads to both the **Castle Trail** (10 mi.) and **Medicine Root Trail** (4 mi.), the park's two longer trails, which wind through prairie and less-traversed Badlands. For horseback riding, check out **Badlands Trail Rides,** 1½ mi. south of the Ben Reifel Visitors Center on Rte. 377. (☎391-2028. Rides leave daily in summer 8am-7:30pm. Rides $15 per 30min., $20 per hr.)

BLACK HILLS REGION

The Lakota called this region *Paha Sapa*, meaning "black hills," for the dark hue that the Ponderosa pines take on when seen from a distance. They considered the region so sacred that they would not settle there. The Treaty of 1868 gave the Black Hills and the rest of South Dakota west of the Missouri River to the tribe, but when gold was discovered in the 1870s, the US government snatched back 6000 sq. mi. Today, the area attracts millions of visitors annually with its collection of natural treasures, including Custer State Park, Wind Cave National Park, and Jewel Cave National Monument. Meanwhile, Mt. Rushmore and Crazy Horse Memorial are larger-than-life symbols of the cultural clash that defines the region's history. Though Rapid City is travelers' best bet for necessities such as supermarkets, camping gear, medical attention, and movie theaters, it might not merit a long stay. Custer, more compact, touristy, and centrally located, makes a better jumping off point for Black Hills sight-seeing.

BLACK HILLS NATIONAL FOREST   ☎605

The Black Hills region contains over 100 attractions, including a reptile farm and a Flintstones theme park, but the greatest sights are the natural ones. Most of the land in the Black Hills is part of the Black Hills National Forest and exercises the "multiple use" principle—mining, logging, ranching, and recreation all take place in close proximity. The forest itself provides opportunities for backcountry hiking, horseback riding, swimming, biking, and camping. The **Centennial Trail,** 111 mi. long, runs from **Wind Cave National Park** to **Bear Butte State Park.** It is accessible by many trailheads and passes through 13 campgrounds. Bikes and horses are permitted on most portions of the trail. The 109 mi. **Mickelson Trail** is the pride of South Dakotans who hike, bike, ski, snowshoe, and ride horses on its gravel paths and wooden bridges from Deadwood down to Edgemont. Completed in 1998, it

TIP **HOG HEAVEN.** Unless you've got a Harley underneath you, the Black Hills are best avoided during the first two weeks in August, when the **Sturgis Rally** takes over the area. Nearly 500,000 motorcyclists roar through the Hills, filling up campsites and motels and bringing traffic to a standstill.

GREAT PLAINS

runs alongside the old railroads, stopping at seven towns along the way. (☎584-3896; www.mickelsontrail.com. Open 30min. before sunrise to 30min. after sunset.) Motorists stick to **Spearfish Canyon Road** (Rte. 14A), which winds through its namesake canyon, past waterfalls, creeks, and wooded cliffs. A hike along Iron Creek lets you take in the awesome landscape. U.S. 85 in Deadwood leads right to 14A. In the national forest, the **Visitors Center,** on U.S. 385 at Pactola Lake, offers a great view of the lake, wildlife exhibits, maps of the area, and details on backcountry camping. (☎343-8755. Open late May-early Sept. daily 9am-5pm.) In Rapid City, there is also the **Black Hills Visitor Information Center** at Exit 61 off I-90. (☎355-3700. Free Wi-Fi. Open daily June-Aug. 8am-8pm; Sept.-May 8am-5pm.) **Backcountry camping** in the national forest is free and allowed anywhere except around Harney Peak, Harney Trail #9, or within 200 ft. of roads, trails, or streams. Open fires are prohibited, but controlled fires in provided grates are allowed. Of the 31 **National Forest campgrounds ❶,** good ones include: **Pactola,** on the Pactola Reservoir just south of the junction of Rte. 44 and U.S. 385,; **Sheridan Lake,** 5 mi. northeast of Hill City on U.S. 385 (north entrance for group sites, south entrance for individuals); and **Roubaix Lake,** 14 mi. south of Lead on U.S. 385. Sheridan and Roubaix have some sites open in the winter. Forest campgrounds are quiet and wooded with toilets and some swimming. (Reservations ☎877-444-6777; www.reserveusa.com. No hookups. Sites at all 3 campgrounds $17-19.) The National Forest extends into Wyoming, and the **Bearlodge Ranger Station** in Sundance directs visitors to the west. (☎307-283-1361. Open M-F 8am-4:30pm.) The Wyoming side of the forest draws fewer visitors and allows campfires. **I-90** skirts the northern border of the Black Hills from Spearfish in the west to Rapid City in the east. **U.S. 385** twists from Hot Springs in the south to Deadwood in the north. Speed-demons beware: beautiful winding routes hold drivers to half the speed of the interstate. Winter in the northern area of the Black Hills offers stellar skiing and snowmobiling. However, many attractions close or have limited hours, and most resorts and campgrounds are closed in winter.

MOUNT RUSHMORE   ☎605

Mount Rushmore National Memorial boasts the faces that launched a thousand minivans. Though it's the most visited sight in the area, a pre-noon arrival should beat most of the crowds. Historian Doane Robinson originally conceived of this "shrine of democracy" in 1923 as a memorial for frontier heroes, carved among the spectacular Needles; sculptor Gutzon Borglum chose four presidents and a mountaintop instead. Borglum encountered all kinds of opposition to his work, but he defended the scale of his masterpiece, finally completing the busts of Washington, Jefferson, Theodore Roosevelt, and Lincoln in 1941. The 465 ft. tall bodies were never completed—work ceased when US funds were diverted to WWII, shortly after Borglum's death. From the observation deck above the museum, the half-mile **Presidential Trail** loops closer to the Monument with various viewing spots. The trail also leads to Borglum's studio, where visitors can view Borglum's plaster model of the carving, as well as tools and designs for Mt. Rushmore. (☎666-4448; www.rushmoreborglum.com. Ranger talks every hr. on the half-hour. Open daily mid-May to mid-Oct. 8am-7pm.) During the summer, the **Mount Rushmore Memorial Amphitheater** hosts a nightly program with a patriotic speech and film. (☎574-2523;

www.nps.gov/moru. May-Sept. 9pm. All year long, light floods the monument for 2hr. starting at dusk. Trail lights extinguished 11pm.) With presidential figures and historical scenes rendered in minute detail, the **National Presidential Wax Museum,** Hwy. 16A on the outskirts of Keystone, offers a glimpse of American history in a different medium. (☎666-4455; www.presidentialwaxmuseum.com. Open July-Aug. 9am-9pm; June 9am-8pm; Apr. and Sept.-Oct. 9am-5pm. Last entry 1hr. before closing. $10, seniors $8, ages 6-12 $7.) **Horsethief Lake Campground ❶** lies 2 mi. west of Mt. Rushmore on Rte. 244 and is operated by the Black Hills National Forest. Former President George Bush fished here in 1993; rumor has it the lake was stocked with fish to guarantee his success. (☎877-444-6777; www.reserveusa.com. Water and flush toilets. Check-out 1pm. Reservations recommended on weekends. Wheelchair-accessible sites available. Sites $23.) The commercial **Mt. Rushmore KOA/Palmer Gulch Lodge ❷,** 7 mi. west of Mt. Rushmore on Palmer Gulch Rd. off Rte. 244, has shuttle service to Mt. Rushmore ($3) and Crazy Horse ($6), bike and car rentals, cabins with showers, campsites, free Wi-Fi, horseback riding, laundry, a small strip mall, and two pools. (☎574-2525 or 800-562-8503; www.palmer-gulch.com. Make reservations up to 2 months in advance for cabins. Open May-Sept. Sites June-Aug. $30, with water and electricity $40; cabins $60-70. May and Sept. $25/34/46-55. D/MC/V.)

Mount Rushmore National Monument is 2 mi. from downtown Keystone. From Rapid City, take U.S. 16 and 16A to Keystone, and Rte. 244 up to the mountain. There is an $8 "annual parking permit" for the lot next to the entrance. The **Info Center** has maps, daily event schedules, and Ranger tours, which leave daily at 10:30, 11:30am and every 30min. 1:30pm-4:30pm. Closer to the Monument, the **Visitor Center** has a museum chronicling the Rushmore's history in addition to showing a film that explains how the carving was accomplished—about 90% of the "sculpting" was done with dynamite. (Info center ☎574-3198, museum ☎574-3165. Both open daily in summer 8am-10pm; low-season 8am-5pm. Wheelchair-accessible.) Borglum intended Mt. Rushmore to be a free attraction, and for those anxious to avoid the $8 parking fee and keep it that way, there two options. The profile-viewing parking lot is a quarter-mile west of the monument on Rte. 244 and has 15-20 spots where you can leave your car without dropping a dime. Keystone, 2½ mi. to the east of Rushmore, also has free parking. Those who walk along the highway should remember that shoulders are not sidewalks; look out for cars and roadkill. Also, be warned: "no parking" means no parking—just because a spot looks like a pull-off does not mean it is.

CRAZY HORSE MEMORIAL ☎605

In 1947, Lakota Chief Henry Standing Bear commissioned sculptor Korczak Ziolkowski to create a memorial to Crazy Horse, a famed warrior who gained respect by refusing to sign treaties or live on government reservations. Crazy Horse was stabbed in the back by a treacherous white soldier in 1877. The Crazy Horse Memorial, which at its future completion will be the world's largest sculpture, sits among the Black Hills, the Lakota tribe's sacred land, as a monumental tribute to the revered Native American leader. Construction of the monument began with a ground-breaking blast on June 3, 1948, and the completed face (all four of the Rushmore heads could fit inside it) was unveiled 50 years later. Believing that Crazy Horse should be a project funded by those who truly cared about the memorial, Ziolkowski twice refused offers of $10 million in federal funding. With admission prices covering most of the construction costs, Ziolkowski's wife Ruth and seven of their 10 children carry on his work, currently concentrating on the horse's head, which will be 219 ft. high. Eventually, Crazy Horse's entire torso and head, as well as part of his horse, will be carved into the mountain. The memorial, 4 mi. north of Custer on U.S. 385/U.S. 16, includes the **Indian Museum of North America,** the **Sculptor's Studio-Home,** and the **Native American Educational and Cultural Center,** which displays native crafts. Buses run every 15-20min. to the base of the mountain ($4). Admission includes access to a laser show detailing the history and future of the monument; ask for a re-admit pass at the info desk. (☎673-4681; www.crazyhorse.org. Open daily May-Sept. 7am-dark; Oct.-Apr. 8am-5pm. Laser show May-Sept. at dusk. Monument lit nightly about 10min. after sunset for 1hr. $24 per car. $10 per person, under 6 free.)

WIND CAVE AND JEWEL CAVE   ☎ 605

In the cavern-riddled Black Hills, the subterranean scenery often rivals the above-ground sights. After shifting plates of granite formed the Black Hills, water filled the cracked layers of limestone, creating the intricate and unusual structures that make up the area's prime underground real estate. **Wind Cave National Park** (☎745-4600; www.nps.gov/wica), adjacent to Custer State Park (p. 584) on Rte. 87 and U.S. 385, and **Jewel Cave National Monument** (☎673-2288; www.nps.gov/jeca), 13 mi. west of Custer off Rte. 16, are the area's treasured natural phenomena. Be sure to bring a sweater—Wind Cave hovers at 53°F, Jewel Cave around 49°F.

WIND CAVE. Wind Cave was discovered by Tom Bingham in 1881 when he heard the sound of air rushing out of the cave's only natural entrance. The wind was so strong that it knocked Bingham's hat off, but when he returned to show his friends, his hat got sucked in. This "breathing" of air forcefully moving in and out of the cave results from changes in outside pressure. Though Bingham found the entrance more than a century ago, scientists estimate that only 5% of the volume of the cave has been unearthed. Within the 124 mi. of the cave's depths that have been explored, geologists have found a lake over 200 ft. long. Instead of the typical crystal formations of stalagmites and stalactites, Wind Cave is known for housing over 95% of the world's "boxwork"—a honeycomb-like lattice of calcite covering its walls. Five **tours** cover a spectrum of caving abilities. For detailed information, see the park's newsletter, *Passages.* (☎745-4600. Tours June-Aug. daily 8:40am-6pm; in low season less frequently. A wheelchair-accessible tour is available by request.) The **Garden of Eden Tour** is the least strenuous. (1hr., ¼ mi., 4 per day, 150 stairs. $7, ages 6-16 $3.50, under 6 free.) The **Natural Entrance Tour** (1¼hr.; ½ mi.; 12-15 per day; 300 stairs) and the **Fairgrounds Tour** (1½hr.; ½ mi.; 8 per day; 450 stairs) are both moderately strenu-

TOUR DE FORT

At times, the Great Plains seem like the most peaceful region of the world. But, wars were once waged here, mainly against the Native Americans who inhabited the land white settlers coveted. Vestiges of military outposts remain, and many forts have been restored to resemble their original stature.

Fort Robinson, near present-day Crawford, NE, was founded in 1874. This was the starting point for many anti-Native American marches and the place where Crazy Horse and the Sioux finally surrendered. Now, the park is almost a resort; visitors can stay in many of the historic buildings where officers once lived.

Fort Laramie, in Fort Laramie, WY, features officers' houses and parade grounds, which were once said to be rowdy with partying soldiers. Fort Laramie is now a National Historic Site, and park rangers give demonstrations on remaining artillery.

Fort Atkinson, just north of Omaha, NE, has been restored to its early-19th-century glory. This fort, on the Missouri River, was a gateway to the west and was used mainly as a starting point for fur trade expeditions and western exploration. Today, the partly restored fort gives a feeling of lost grandeur.

Fort admission around $4-5.

ous, and one of the two leaves about every 30min. ($9, ages 6-16 $4.50, under 6 free.) Light your own way on the more rigorous **Candlelight Tour.** (Limited to 10 people. Min. age 8. Reservations recommended. "Non-slip" soles on shoes required. 2hr. June-Aug. 10:30am and 1:30pm. $9, ages 8-16 $4.50.) The difficult **Wild Cave Tour,** an intro to basic caving, is limited to 10 people over 16 who can fit through a 10 in. high passageway. (Parental consent required for under 18. Reservations required. 3-4hr. tour daily 1pm. $23.) Tours usually fill up an hour beforehand, so it's a good idea to buy tickets in advance. Stop by the **Visitor Center** for more info. (Open daily June to mid-Aug. 8am-7pm; mid-Aug. to Oct. and May 8am-6pm; Apr. and late Sept. to mid-Oct. 8am-5pm; mid-Oct. to early Apr. 8am-4:30pm.) The **Elk Mountain Campground ❶,** 1 mi. north of the Visitors Center, is an excellent spot in the woods that rarely fills up. (Potable water, firewood, restrooms. Self-registration. Sites mid-May to mid-Sept. $12. Mid-Sept. to mid-May $6.) **Backcountry camping** is allowed in the northwestern sector of the park. Campers must have a permit (free at the Visitors Center).

JEWEL CAVE. Distinguishing itself from nearby Wind Cave, Jewel Cave is covered with many different calcite crystal formations. These walls enticed the cave's discoverers to file a mining claim for the "jewels," but they soon realized that giving tours would be more profitable. Today the Park Service continues this tradition. The **Scenic Tour** (1¼hr.; ½ mi.; 15 per day; 723 stairs) is a moderately strenuous walk that highlights the chambers with the most interesting calcite wet formations—more commonly known as stalactites and stalagmites. (In summer every 20min. 8:20am-6pm; in winter call ahead. Reservations recommended; up to 7 days in advance. $8, ages 6-16 $4, under 6 free.) On the **Lantern Tour** (1¾hr.), you'll see roosting bats while you walk, duck, and stoop by the light of your lantern. (In summer 6 per day M-Sa 9:30am-3:45pm; Su 10:30am, 1:15pm, 3:45pm; in winter call ahead. $8, ages 6-16 $4.) Pants, long sleeves, knee and elbow pads, gloves, hiking boots, and a willingness to get down and dirty are required for the 3-4hr. The **Spelunking Tour** is limited to five people over 16. Don't wear your favorite clothes—manganese deposits will permanently stain them. (June-Aug. M-Th and Su 12:30pm. Reservations required; to book, call ☎673-2288 ext. 0. Must be able to fit through an 8½ in. by 2 ft. opening. $27.) The **Visitors Center** has more info. (☎673-2288. Open daily June to mid-Aug. 9am-5:30pm; Oct. to mid-May 8am-4:30pm.) The **Mammoth Site,** 1800 W. U.S. 18, in Hot Springs, is a working archaeological site with fossils of mammoths and other creatures. (☎745-6017; www.mammothsite.com. Open mid-May to mid-Aug. daily 8am-8pm; early May and late Aug. daily 8am-6pm; Sept.-Oct. and Mar.-Apr. daily 8am-5pm; Nov.-Feb. M-Sa 9am-3:30pm, Su 11am-3:30pm. $6.75, seniors $6.25, ages 5-12 $4.75.)

CUSTER STATE PARK   ☎605

Peter Norbeck, governor of South Dakota in the late 1910s, loved to hike among the thin, towering rock formations that punctuate the prairie south of Sylvan Lake and Mt. Rushmore. In order to preserve the land, he created Custer State Park. The spectacular **Needles Highway (Route 87)** follows his favorite hiking route—Norbeck designed this road to be especially narrow and winding so that newcomers could experience the pleasures of discovery. (Road closed Nov.-Apr.) Norbeck's scenic drive continues outside the park on **Iron Mountain Road** (U.S. 16A), which runs from Mt. Rushmore to the east entrance. It takes drivers through a series of tunnels, "pigtail" curves, and switchbacks that yield stunning views of the national monument. Inside the park, the **Wildlife Loop Road** twists past a prairie dog town and through wilderness areas near prime hiking and camping territory. The park requires an **entrance fee,** except for non-stop travel on U.S. 16A. (May-Oct. $5 per person, up to $12 per car; Nov.-Apr. $2.50/6. Good for 7 days.) The **Peter Norbeck**

Visitor Center, on U.S. 16A, half a mile west of the State Game Lodge, serves as the park's main info and program center. (☎255-4464; www.custerstatepark.info. Open daily June-Aug. 8am-8pm; Sept. 8am-6pm; Apr.-May and Oct.-Nov. 9am-5pm.) Aside from the Visitors Center, the best source for all the information on the park is found in *Tatanka,* the park's magazine guide, available at all entrances and most Visitors Centers in the area.

Both Trail 9 and Trail 4 will take you from Sylvan Lake to **Harney Peak,** (7242 ft.), the highest point east of the Rockies and west of the Pyrenees. Waiting at the top are amazing views of the Black Hills. The hike is a relatively strenuous 7 mi. round-trip, so bring water and wear good shoes. The challenging 3 mi. **Sunday Gulch Trail** offers fun hiking, rock-scrambling, and some of the park's most amazing scenery. Visitors adore ◾**Sylvan Lake,** on Needles Hwy., where you can swim, hike, fish, or boat. (☎575-2561. Boat rental $5 per person per 30min. Open daily 9am-7pm.) **Fishing** is allowed anywhere in the park, but a South Dakota fishing license is required. (Sylvan Lake store open 7am-9pm. $16 per day, SD residents $9.) One-hour horse rides are available at **Blue Bell Lodge,** on Rte. 87 about a mile from the south entrance. (☎255-4531. Reservations recommended. 1hr.; 6 per day; $28, under 12 $22.) You can rent mountain bikes at the **Legion Lake Resort,** on U.S. 16A, 6 mi. west of the Norbeck Visitors Center. (☎255-4521. $10 per hr., $25 per half-day, $40 per day.) The majestic granite of the Needles makes for great rock climbing; scramble along the 1 mi. Cathedral Spires Trail off Needles Hwy. For more professional climbing, contact **Sylvan Rocks,** 208 Main St., in Hill City, 20 mi. north of Custer, which leads guided expeditions. (☎484-7585; www.sylvanrocks.com.)

Primitive camping is available for $2 per person per night in the **French Creek Natural Area ❶.** Self-register at each end of the area, accessible from the Blue Bell Lodge or near the Norbeck Center. With the exception of Center Lake, all eight of the park's **campgrounds ❶** have sites with showers and restrooms. **Sylvan Lake** is wooded and near the best hiking trails. Sylvan Lake, **Grace Coolidge,** and **Center Lake** all have tent sites separated from RVs. Most first-come first-served sites are at **Stockade Lake** and Center Lake. No hookups are provided; only the **Game Lodge Campground** offers an RV dump station and two sites with electricity. The park's four lodges have restaurants and general stores; some have laundromats. (☎800-710-2267; www.campsd.com. Office open daily Jan.-Sept. 7am-7pm, Oct.-Dec. 9am-5pm. Reserve ahead; the entire park often fills in summer by 3pm. Sites $13-15; horse camping $18. Non-resident reservation fee $5.)

Outside the park, nearby Custer's **Mt. Rushmore Rd.** provides travelers with necessities, souvenirs, and motels. The charming **Shady Rest Motel ❸,** 238 Gordon Rd., sits on the hill overlooking Custer. It has homey cabins with kitchens, a hot tub, and friendly owners. (☎673-4478 or 800-567-8259. Closed in winter. Cabins from $60. D/MC/V.) Bold green trim distinguishes the cabins at **Chalet Motel ❷,** 933 Mt. Rushmore Rd., from the majority of Custer's run-of-the-mill motels. (☎673-2393. Wi-Fi. Singles $47; doubles $63; suites $80. D/MC/V.) The **Songbird Cafe ❶,** 440 Mt. Rushmore St., provides welcome relief from buffalo burgers with tasty wraps and sandwiches. (☎673-5125. Free Wi-Fi. W-Sa live music. Cover for shows $7-12. Open M-Th 7am-3pm and 5-8pm, F-Sa 7am-3pm and 5-10pm. MC/V.) **Baker's Bakery and Cafe ❷,** 541 Mt. Rushmore St., is a coffeeshop with a twist, offering super-fresh donuts, pies, and bread. Creatively topped burgers and sandwiches ($5-7) arrive on homemade buns. (☎673-2253. Open Tu-F 6:30am-4pm, Sa-Su 7am-4pm. MC/V.)

The **Custer Visitors Center,** 615 Washington St., helps visitors get situated in the area. (☎673-2244 or 800-992-9819; www.custersd.com. Open mid-May to Aug. M-F 8am-5pm, Sa-Su 9am-4pm; in winter M-F 10am-4pm.) **Custer County Public Library,** 447 Crook St. off U.S. 385, has Wi-Fi and computers. (☎673-8178. Free. Open M-Tu and Th-F 11am-5:30pm, W 3-7pm, Sa 10am-3pm.)

DEADWOOD ☎605

Gunslingers Wild Bill Hickok and Calamity Jane sauntered into Deadwood during the height of the Gold Rush in the summer of 1876. Bill stayed just long enough—three weeks—to spend eternity here. Jane and Bill now lie side-by-side in the **Mount Moriah Cemetery,** on a hill south of downtown. (Office open May-Sept. daily 8am-8pm. $1, ages 5-12 $0.50, under 5 free.) If these names mean nothing to you, stop at the **Adams Museum,** 54 Sherman St., to brush up on your Wild West history. (☎578-1714. Open May-Sept. daily 9am-5pm, Oct.-Apr. Tu-Sa 10am-4pm. Free.) **Saloon #10,** 657 Main St., was immortalized by Wild Bill's murder. Hickok was shot holding black aces and eights, known to poker players as a "dead man's hand." The shooting is reenacted daily in summer. (☎578-3346; www.saloon10.com. Saloon open daily 9am-2am. Reenactments daily in summer at 1, 3, 5, 7pm. Live music on weekends.) Onlookers follow the scene as assassin Jack McCall is apprehended by authorities outside of Saloon #10 (daily in summer 7:30pm) and tried at the **Masonic Temple,** 809 Main St. (daily in summer 8pm). **Trolleys** ($1) circle downtown and provide a good overview of the sights Deadwood has to offer. Tour **buses** depart from three points on Main St. and give more extensive commentary on Deadwood's sights; they also climb the hill to the cemetery. (1hr., about $7). Right outside Deadwood is Kevin Costner's interpretive center, **Tatanka: Story of the Bison,** 1 mi. north on U.S. 85, whose highlight is a dramatic outdoor sculpture of three Native American riders pursuing bison over a cliff. (☎584-5678; www.story-ofthebison.com. Open May-Sept. daily 9am-6pm. $7.50, over 65 $6.50, ages 6-12 $5.50.) Gambling takes center stage in this authentic western town—casinos line Main St., and many innocent-looking establishments have slot machines and poker tables waiting in the wings. There's live music on weekends and nightly dancing at the **Buffalo-Bodega Complex,** 658 Main St., half of which is packed with throngs of gambling spots. For the thrill of gambling without the high stakes, try your luck at the nickel slot machines. (☎578-1300. Open M-F and Su 8am-2am, Sa 7am-2am.)

Deadwood offers a few affordable accommodations, including the **Penny Motel** ❷, 818 Upper Main St., with standard rooms with A/C. (☎578-1842 or 877-565-8140; www.pennymotel.com. Reservations recommended. Rooms $59-72; suites more; call for details. AmEx/D/MC/V.) In Lead, 3 mi. from Deadwood on U.S. 85, the new **Main Street Manor Hostel** ❶, 515 W. Main St., has some of the area's lowest prices. The ten rooms occupy a charming home, in which there is a common room, kitchen facilities, and shared bathrooms. (☎717-2044; www.mainstreetmanorhostel.com. Free Wi-Fi next door at Hearst Library. Closed Dec.-Jan. Summer $25; low season $20.) The **Whistler Gulch Campground** ❶, just out of town off U.S. 85, has laundry facilities, a pool, and showers. (☎578-2092 or 800-704-7139; www.deadwood.com/whistler. Open May-Sept. Office open daily 9am-8pm. Check-out 11am. Sites $22, with full hookup $36.) Fresh food can be found in Spearfish, just west on I-90, at **Bay Leaf Cafe** ❸, 126 W. Hudson St., at Main St., where filling salads ($7-10) and appetizers like spinach pie with tabouleh ($7) provide sufficient bang for your buck. (☎642-5462. Entrees $12-20. Open M-Sa 11am-9pm, Su 4pm-9pm.) A world away from saloon food yet only two blocks away from Deadwood's main drag, **Deadwood Thymes Cafe** ❷, 87 Sherman St., serves creative sandwiches like dill havarti and pesto on multi-grain bread ($6.50). From behind the information center, take Sherman St. towards the cemetery. (☎578-7566; www.deadwoodthymes.com. Open Tu-W 10:30am-2pm, Th-F 10:30am-2pm and 5-9pm, Sa 9am-2pm and 5-9pm, Su 9am-1pm and 5-9pm.)

The **Deadwood History and Information Center,** 3 Siever St., is behind Main Street's Silverado. (☎578-2507 or 800-999-1876; www.deadwood.org. Open daily in summer 8am-7pm; in winter 9am-5pm.) **Post Office:** 68 Sherman St., in the Federal Building. (☎578-1505. Open M-F 8am-4pm, Sa 10am-noon.) **Postal Code:** 57732.

IOWA

Named for the Ioway Native Americans who lived along the state's riverbanks, Iowa contains one-fourth of all US Grade A farmland and prides itself on being the "heartland of the heartland." In this prototypical Midwestern state, agriculture and industry hold an elevated status. The land ripples with gentle hills between the two great rivers that sculpt its boundaries: the "Great Muddy" to the west and the "Mighty Miss" to the east. Despite its distinctly American landscape, Iowa's small towns and villages have managed to preserve their European cultural heritage.

GREAT PLAINS

🔁 PRACTICAL INFORMATION

Capital: Des Moines.

Visitor Info: Iowa Tourism Office, 200 E. Grand Ave., Des Moines 50309 (☎ 515-242-4705 or 888-472-6035; www.traveliowa.com). Open M-F 8am-4:30pm.

Postal Abbreviation: IA. **Sales Tax:** 5%; most towns add an additional 1-2%.

DES MOINES   ☎ 515

Des Moines hums with the activity of its affable residents. The Skywalk, a maze of passageways connecting buildings downtown, is unparalleled in the Midwest. Beautiful parks trace the area's rivers and present a welcome contrast to the now-bustling downtown area. From the "BarbeQlossal" at the World Pork Expo to world-class art, Des Moines's offerings run the gamut from kitsch to cosmopolitan.

🔲 TRANSPORTATION

Airport: Des Moines International (DSM), 5800 Fleur Dr. (☎ 256-5100; www.dsmairport.com), 5 mi. southwest of downtown. M-F take bus #90, Airport Business Express, to downtown. Taxi $7-11.

Buses: Greyhound and Burlington Trailways, 1107 Keosauqua Way (☎ 243-1773; www.greyhound.com; www.burlingtontrailways.com), at 12th St., just northwest of downtown. To: **Chicago** (7-8hr., 2-4 per day, $36-50); **Iowa City** (2hr., 2-3 per day, $21-23); **Omaha** (2hr., 3 per day, $29); **St. Louis** (9-11hr., 3 per day, $46-80). Station open 4:45am-midnight.

Public Transit: Metropolitan Transit Authority (MTA), 1100 MTA Ln. (☎ 283-8100; www.dmmta.com), south of the 9th St. viaduct. Call for info M-F 6am-7pm, Sa 7am-5pm. Routes serve Clive, Des Moines, Urbandale, West Des Moines, and Windsor Heights. Maps are at the MTA office and website. Buses run M-F usually 6:15am-9:45pm, Sa 6:45am-5:45pm. $1.25, ages 6-10 $0.75, seniors (except M-F 3-6pm) and disabled $0.50 with MTA ID card; transfers $0.10.

Taxi: Yellow Cab, ☎ 243-1111.

Car Rental: Enterprise, 5601 Fleur Dr. (☎ 285-2525), just outside the airport, with airport pickup. Open M-F 7:30am-6pm, Sa 9am-1pm.

✴🔁 ORIENTATION AND PRACTICAL INFORMATION

I-80, I-35, Rte. 5 (the "Beltway"), and **U.S. 65** encircle Des Moines; **I-235** bisects the circle from east to west. Numbered streets run east-west, named streets north-south. Addresses begin with zero downtown at the **Des Moines River** and increase as you move east or west; **Grand Avenue** divides addresses north-south. Other east-

Des Moines

🏠 ACCOMMODATIONS
The Cottage, **1**
Iowa State Fair
  Campgrounds, **2**

🍎 FOOD
Bauder's Pharmacy
  and Fountain, **3**
Cafe Su, **9**
Palmer's Deli, **4**

Raccoon River
Brewing Co., **7**

🍸 NIGHTLIFE
The Garden, **5**
Java Joe's, **8**
The Lift, **6**

west thoroughfares are **Locust Street, University Avenue** (home to Drake University), and **Hickman Road.** Note that numbered streets in Des Moines and West Des Moines are not the same; the renumbering starts at 63rd St. North-south streets change as they pass through different neighborhoods, so a map is helpful.

Visitor Info: Greater Des Moines Convention and Visitors Bureau, 400 Locust St., Ste. 265 (☎286-4960 or 800-451-2625; www.seedesmoines.com), in the Skywalk. Open M-F 8:30am-5pm. The websites www.desmoinesmetro.com and www.downtowndes-moines.com are useful for navigating the city.

Medical Services: Mercy Medical Center, 1111 6th Ave. (☎247-3185), in downtown.

Internet Access: Des Moines Public Library, 1000 Grand Ave. (☎283-4152; www.des-moineslibrary.com), at 10th St. Free. Open M-Th 9am-8pm, F 9am-6pm, Sa 9am-5pm, Su 1-5pm.

Post Office: 1165 2nd Ave. (☎283-7575), downtown just north of I-235. Open M-F 7:30am-6pm. **Postal Code:** 50318.

▐ ACCOMMODATIONS

Downtown Des Moines is cluttered with pricey hotels. Cheap accommodations lie along Fleur Dr. by the airport, off I-80, and on Merle Hay Rd., 5 mi. northwest of downtown. Remember the 7% hotel tax, and be sure to make reservations a few months in advance for visits during the **Iowa State Fair** in August and at least one month in advance during the high school sports tournament season in March.

The Cottage, 1094 28th St. (☎277-7559; www.thecottagedsm.com), at Cottage Grove Ave. near Drake University. An elegant B&B in a 20s-era home. 4 rooms with queen bed, private bath, and use of hot tub. Reservations required. Rooms $99; suites $140. AmEx/D/MC/V. ❹

Iowa State Fair Campgrounds (☎262-3111, ext. 284 or 800-545-3247; www.iowastate-fair.org). Enter the main entrance of the fairgrounds at E. 30th St. and E. Grand Ave., follow E. Grand Ave., make a right on Hoover, then a left into the campground; or take bus #1 "Fairgrounds" to the main gate and walk. More than 1800 campsites on 160 acres. No fires. Reservations accepted only during the State Fair in Aug. Open mid-Apr. to mid-Oct. Tent sites $15, with water and electricity $18, with full hookup $20; more during State Fair. ❶

◘ FOOD

Restaurants flank **Court Avenue** downtown. West Des Moines hosts budget eateries along Grand Ave. and in the antique-filled **Historic Valley Junction** at 5th St. and Railroad Ave. The **Downtown Farmers' Market** (☎243-6625) sells fresh fruit and vegetables, baked goods, and ethnic food on Saturday mornings (mid-May to Oct. 7am-noon); Court Ave. is blocked off between 2nd Ave. and 5th St. for the extravaganza. Surrounding neighborhoods hold evening (4-7pm) farmers' markets of their own throughout the week. The **Skywalk** houses many places with cafeteria-style cuisine. Many menus proudly feature local **Graziano Brothers** sausages in pastas, on pizzas, and wedged into hoagie rolls.

⊠ Bauder's Pharmacy and Fountain, 3802 Ingersoll Ave. (☎255-1124), at 38th St. A throwback to the good old days. Wax nostalgic while munching simple sandwiches ($2-4) at the lunch counter or slurping shakes, floats, and malts from the soda fountain. Open M-F 8:30am-7pm, Sa 9am-4pm, Su 10am-2pm. D/MC/V. ❶

Raccoon River Brewing Co., 200 10th St. (☎362-5222), at Mulberry St. Enjoy a freshly brewed beer with barbecue chicken pizza ($11). Music on weekends. Open M-Th 11am-midnight, F-Sa 11am-2am. Kitchen closes M-Th 10pm, F-Sa 11pm. AmEx/D/MC/V. ❸

Palmer's Deli & Market, 2843 Ingersoll Ave. (274-4004; www.palmersdeliandmarket.com), at 28th St. A fresh and healthy cafeteria-style eatery frequented by crowds of locals. Soups, lunch specials, and delicious baked goods help ease the frustration of fighting businessmen for a table. Make your own salad for $4-8 or sandwich for $4-7. Open M-F 7am-7pm, Sa 7am-3:30pm. AmEx/D/MC/V. ❷

◉ SIGHTS

The **State Capitol,** E. 9th St. and Grand Ave., is regarded as one of the most beautiful capitol buildings in the US. Its impressive interior includes grand staircases and colorful glass mosaics. The gold-domed building also offers a clear view of the Des Moines skyline. (☎281-5591. Free tours every hr. M-Sa 9:30am-3pm, except noon. Open M-F 8am-4:30pm, Sa 9am-4pm.) Nearby, the **State of Iowa Historical Building,** 600 E. Locust St., addresses the history of Iowa and Native American culture. In addition to exhibits on Iowa's past, which focus on anything from the army to lunchboxes, "Witness To Change" traces the history of a mammoth skeleton. The building also houses the state historical library, archives, and a cafe. (☎281-5111; www.iowahistory.org. Open M-Sa 9am-4:30pm, Su noon-4:30pm. Free.)

The phenomenal ◈**Des Moines Art Center,** 4700 Grand Ave., at 47th St., is composed of three contemporary buildings designed by world-renowned architects Eliel Saarinen, I.M. Pei, and Richard Meier. In addition to a collection of African tribal art, the museum contains modern masterpieces by Monet, Matisse, and Picasso, along with an expansive collection of pop, minimalist, and contemporary works by Sol LeWitt, Jasper Johns, and Robert Rauschenberg. (☎277-4405; www.desmoinesartcenter.org. Open Tu-W and F-Sa 11am-4pm, Th 11am-9pm, Su noon-4pm. Free.) Behind the Art Center lie the immaculately groomed **Rose Garden** and **Greenwood Pond,** a small lagoon accented by an Andy Goldsworthy sculpture. A branch of the center is open downtown at 800 Walnut St. (☎557-6109. Open M-F 11am-4pm. Free.) **Salisbury House,** 4025 Tonawanda Dr., lets visitors explore an early 20th-century mansion in its original condition. With an incredible collection of art and rare books, this impressive 42-room home holds an eclectic assortment of both oddball items and masterpieces. (Enter from 42nd St., off of Grand Ave. ☎274-1777; www.salisburyhouse.org. Open for tours daily 1 and 2:30pm. $7, seniors $6, ages 6-12 $3.) East of the Des Moines River, the crystagon dome of the **Botanical Center,** 909 E. Robert D. Ray Dr. (E. 1st St.), is made of 665 triangular panels and fosters exotic flora and fauna. (☎323-6290. Open daily 10am-5pm. $4, ages 6-17 and seniors $2.)

🎵 🎭 ENTERTAINMENT AND NIGHTLIFE

On Wednesday, check out *Juice* (www.dmjuice.com), published by the Des Moines Register, for dining and entertainment reviews. On Thursdays, the Register's *Datebook* has listings of concerts, sporting events, and movies. Both are distributed throughout town. *Cityview,* a free local weekly, lists free events and is available at the Civic Center box office and most supermarkets.

The **Iowa State Fair,** one of the nation's largest, takes over Des Moines for 11 days in mid-August with prize cows, crafts, cakes, and corn. (☎800-545-3247; www.iowastatefair.org. Runs Aug. 7-17, 2008 and Aug. 13-23, 2009. Call for prices and to purchase tickets in advance.) Less celebrated but equally entertaining (for carnivores) is the **World Pork Expo,** held each June. (☎847-838-6772; www.worldpork.org. June 5-7, 2008. $10.) Tickets to watch minor league baseball's **Iowa Cubs,** Chicago's farm team, are a steal. They play at **Principal Park,** 1 Line Dr. Call for game schedules. (☎243-6111 or 800-464-2827; www.iowacubs.com. Tickets $6-11.) The **Civic Center,** 221 Walnut St. (☎246-2300; www.civiccenter.org), at 2nd Ave., sponsors concerts and theater; call for info. **Jazz in July** (☎280-3222; www.metroarts.org) presents free concerts throughout the city every day of the month; grab a schedule at restaurants, the Civic Center, or Wells Fargo banks. On Fridays in June through August, East Village (between the Capitol and river) hosts **Blues Before Sunset** on the southwest outdoor terrace of the State Historical Building. (☎281-4011. 5:30-7:30pm.) **Music Under the Stars** has free concerts on the steps of the Capitol. (☎367-4845; www.dmmusicians.com/stars.htm. June-July Su 6:30-8:30pm.) On Thursdays from June through August, **Nitefall on the River** brings music to the Simon Estes Riverfront Amphitheater at E. 1st and Locust St. (☎237-1386. Concerts begin at 7pm. $8, under 12 free.)

Court Avenue and 4th Street, in the southeast corner of downtown, serves as the focal point for much of Des Moines's nightlife scene. ◈**Java Joe's,** 214 4th St., is the place to hear Des Moines's best up-and-coming bands. This hip, mellow coffeehouse with Internet ($1 per 10min., free Wi-Fi) sells exotic coffee blends and beer ($3). Vegetarians will delight in a creative array of sandwiches, all for $5-8. (☎288-5282; www.javajoescoffeehouse.com. Open M-Th 7am-11pm, F-Sa 7am-midnight, Su 9am-10pm.) Sporting some fancy art-covered walls, **The Lift,** 222 4th St., serves so many kinds of inspired martinis ($5-6), that you'll think you're at an ice cream parlor instead of a bar. (☎288-3777. Open M-Th and Su 5pm-2am, F-Sa 7pm-2am.) **The Garden,** 112 SE. 4th St., is a gay bar and nightclub with a video bar, dance floor, and performances every weekend. (☎243-3965; www.grdn.com. Happy hour daily 4-8pm. Open W-Su 4pm-2am.)

IOWA CITY   ☎319

Home to the University of Iowa's beloved Hawkeyes and aspiring poets, Iowa City is full of collegiate flavor and youthful vitality. The downtown area has tons of cheap restaurants, trendy shops, and coffeehouses, while an active nightlife scene and college football fanaticism keep students happy. In summer, cultural activities keep the city lively while students are away.

◨◪ TRANSPORTATION AND PRACTICAL INFORMATION. Greyhound and Burlington Trailways, both located at 170 E. Court St. (☎337-2127; www.grey-hound.com, www.burlingtontrailways.com; station open M-F 9am-6pm, Sa-Su 9:30am-6pm) send **buses** to: Chicago (4-6hr., 2 per day, $27-42); Des Moines (2hr., 2-3 per day, $21-23); Minneapolis (8-12hr., 2 per day, $36-61); St. Louis (12-15hr., 2-3 per day, $36-72). Iowa City Transit runs a free **downtown shuttle** (M-F 7:30am-6:30pm) when school is in session, in addition to its normal routes. (☎356-5151. Operates M-F 6am-10:30pm, Sa 6am-7pm. $0.75, ages 5-17 $0.50, seniors with pass $0.35.) The free Cambus runs **local buses** daily on campus and downtown. (☎335-8633. Usually operates M-F 6:30am-midnight; in winter also Sa-Su noon-6:30pm.) For a **taxi,** call Old Capitol Cab, ☎354-7662. Iowa City lies south of I-80, 114 mi. east of Des Moines. North-south **Madison** and **Johnson Street** and east-west **Market** and **Burlington Street** mark the boundaries of downtown. The **Convention and Visitors Bureau,** 900 1st Ave., sits across the river in Coralville between U.S. 6 and I-80. (☎337-6592 or 800-283-6592; www.iowacitycoralville.org; open M-F 8am-5pm) and also runs an **information kiosk** at the Coral Ridge Mall (open M-Sa 10am-9pm, Su 11am-6pm). More info is available at the University of Iowa's **Campus Information Center,** in the Iowa Memorial Union at Madison and Jefferson St. (☎335-3055. Open M-F 8am-6pm.) **Medical Services: Mercy Iowa City,** on Market St. at Van Buren St. (☎358-2767 or 800-358-2767; www.mercyiowacity.org) is staffed daily 7am-midnight with registered nurses. **Internet Access: Iowa City Public Library,** 123 S. Linn St., has free Wi-Fi and Internet access. (☎356-5200; www.icpl.org. Limit 30min. on library computers. Open M-Th 10am-9pm, F 10am-8pm, Sa 10am-6pm, Su noon-5pm.) **Post Office:** 400 S. Clinton St. (☎354-1560. Open M-F 8:30am-7pm, Sa 9am-3pm.) **Postal Code:** 52240.

◪◧ ACCOMMODATIONS AND FOOD. One mile from Exit 244 off I-80 and eight blocks from downtown is the **Smiths' Bed and Breakfast ❸,** 314 Brown St., an 1890s home that has been modernized with three tastefully decorated guest rooms and A/C. (☎338-1316; www.bbonline.com. Rooms $45-75. Cash or check only.) Cheap motels line U.S. 6 in **Coralville,** 2 mi. west of downtown, and **1st Avenue** at Exit 242 off I-80. One of the cheapest is the **Big Ten Inn ❷,** 707 1st Ave., which provides worn but comfortable rooms, A/C, and HBO. (☎351-6131. Singles $40; doubles $48; prices increase significantly on football weekends. D/MC/V.) **Kent Park Campgrounds ❶,** 15 mi. west on U.S. 6, has 86 secluded sites near a lake with fishing, boating, and swimming. (☎645-2315. Free showers. Check-in before 10:30pm. Sites $10, with electricity $15.) The lively downtown centers around the open-air **Pedestrian Mall** on College and Dubuque St., where musicians serenade passersby and vendors man their food carts, sometimes until 3am. The **farmers' market,** on the Chauncey Swan parking ramp between Washington and College St., has fresh produce, plants, cut flowers, and baked goods. (☎356-5110. Open May-Oct. W 5:30-

PEACE MARCH

By the time I got to Iowa City, I had driven 7000 mi. in six weeks. But on my second day there, I met Mike and Ashley, college students who had walked 2000 mi. from San Francisco, in the name of peace. My trek no longer felt so impressive.

Mike and Ashley are challenging the way people think about war and anti-war activism by walking from the west coast to the east coast. They left California in May and are planning on arriving in Washington D.C. in September. I heard about them in Omaha—they had passed through a couple of days before I had. I dawdled on my route, so we got to Iowa City at the same time. I went to a peace rally held in their honor. Both tan, very thin, and tired, they spoke for a few minutes about their goals, then made the rounds of attendees while an older Iowan strummed peace songs on his acoustic guitar.

Talking to them, I found the pair pretty nonchalant about their undertaking. I realized there was a crucial difference between their trip and my own; though I sometimes felt baseless, I could always retreat into my navy Honda and feel more or less at home. Mike and Ashley had only backpacks. While I sat in that basement, I had a strong urge to ditch the car and walk home, for peace—or for exercise—but in the end I got back in and kept on traveling.

—*Cara Eisenpress*

7:30pm, Sa 7:30-11:30am.) The city's oldest family-owned restaurant, **Hamburg Inn #2 Inc. ❷**, 214 N. Linn St., affectionately called "The Burg," serves breakfast all day along with decadent pie shakes (milkshakes with a slice of pie blended in; $5) and chicken-fried steaks. (☎337-5512; www.hamburginn.com. Open daily 6am-11pm. D/MC/V.) **Masala ❷**, 9 S. Dubuque St., Iowa City's award-winning vegetarian Indian restaurant, may offer the best deals in town with its $6.65 lunch buffet and $6 Monday dinner special. (☎338-6199. Open daily 11am-2:30pm and 5-9:30pm. AmEx/D/MC/V.)

◨ **SIGHTS.** The University of Iowa's **Museum of Art**, 150 North Riverside Dr., has an impressive collection of European, African, and American art, and two recliners set in front of a Jackson Pollack mural, perfect for contemplation. (☎335-1727; www.uiowa.edu/uima. Open W and Sa-Su noon-5pm, Th-F noon-9pm. Free.) Also on campus, the **Museum of Natural History**, at Jefferson and Clinton St., illustrates Iowa's ecology, geology, and Native American culture, with a giant Ice Age Sloth, among other mammals and birds. Downstairs, a to-scale model of the gigantopithecus, the largest known primate, has been created under the direction of a university professor. (☎335-0480; www.uiowa.edu/~nathist. Open July-Aug. Tu-Sa 10am-3pm, Su 1-5pm; school year Tu-F 10am-3pm, Sa 10am-5pm, Su 1-5pm. Free.) A short drive from downtown is **Plum Grove Historic Home**, 1030 Carroll St., off Kirkwood Ave., the 1844 home and garden of Robert Lucas, the 1st governor of the Iowa Territory. (☎351-5738; www.iowahistory.org. Open June-Oct. W-Su 1-5pm. Free.) In historic West Branch, 15min. northeast of the city (Exit 254 on I-80; follow signs), lies the **Herbert Hoover National Historic Site**. Take a walking tour of the cottage where the 31st President was born, a replica of his father's blacksmith shop, and the schoolhouse and Quaker meetinghouse he attended while growing up. The fascinating **Herbert Hoover Presidential Library-Museum** chronicles his entire life and presidency. (☎643-5301 or 643-2541; www.nps.gov/heho or www.hoover.nara.gov. Open daily 9am-5pm. 45min. tours depending on availability; call in advance. Wheelchair-accessible. $6, over 62 $3, under 17 free.)

♫▊ **ENTERTAINMENT AND NIGHTLIFE.** Each summer brings with it two exciting (and free!) festivals to Iowa City. The **Iowa Arts Festival** is held in early June and gathers local artisans, music, and food. The **Iowa City Jazz Festival** has drawn several big-name and national acts in recent years. (Both festivals ☎337-7944; www.summerofthearts.org.) n summer, the **Fri-**

day Night Concert Series offers everything from blues to salsa on the Ped Mall, in front of the Sheraton Hotel. (☎337-7944. Mid-May to mid-Sept. 6:30-9:30pm. Free.) The **Riverside Theatre,** 213 N. Gilbert St., puts on professional productions and holds a Shakespeare festival during the summer. (☎338-7672; www.riversidetheatre.org. Box office open M-F noon-4pm and 1hr. before performances. Tickets $19-22, under 18 $12.) With hordes of college students bar-hopping on the Pedestrian Mall ("Ped Mall") and loud music escaping from bars that double as dance clubs, Iowa City's weekends take up the better part of each week. ☑**Prairie Lights Bookstore,** 15 S. Dubuque St., is the intellectual hub of this writers' town, hosting popular readings and authors several times a week. (☎387-2681; www.prairielightsbooks.com. Check website for readings schedule. Open M-Sa 9am-9pm, Su 9am-6pm.) **Deadwood,** 6 S. Dubuque St., has a loyal following of students who drink coffee and work in the morning, then drink beer and socialize at night. (☎351-9417. Free Wi-Fi. Open M-F 9:30am-2am, Sa 10am-2am, Su 11am-2am.) Though the **Yacht Club,** 13 S. Linn St., is renowned for its Sunday night reggae party, the basement live music venue has an eclectic week-long schedule of live music and DJs. (☎337-6464; www.iowacityyachtclub.com. Tu DJ dance party. W jam session. Th-Sa live music. Cover $5-10. Open M-Sa 4pm-2am, Su 6pm-2am.)

EFFIGY MOUNDS

Native Americans built the mysterious and striking Effigy Mounds nearly 1400 years ago. The enigmatic mounds are low-lying piles of earth formed into distinct geometric and animal shapes for spiritual purposes. Though they once covered much of the Midwest, only a few mounds remain, thanks to farmers' plows in western Wisconsin and eastern Iowa. One of the largest concentrations of intact mounds is the **Effigy Mounds National Monument,** 151 Hwy. 76, in Marquette, IA, 106 mi. west of Madison, WI along the Mississippi River. With striking views of the Mississippi river from high, rocky bluffs, 14 mi. of winding trails provide access to the monument. North Unit features the popular Fire Point, 1hr. round-trip from the Visitors Center, and South Unit includes the best-preserved collection of mounds, the Marching Bears. Take Rte. 18 W from Madison. (☎563-873-3491; www.nps.gov/efmo. Visitors Center open June-early Sept. daily 8am-6pm; closes earlier in fall and winter. Guided tours to Fire Point 11am and 2pm. Call ahead for other events. $3, max. per car $5, under 16 free.) Seven miles south on Rte. 76 in McGregor is **Pike's Peak State Park ❶.** Follow Hwy. X56 from the southern end of Main St. in McGregor up the twisty road 3 mi. The park boasts amazing views, 24 mi. of trails, and 77 campsites. (☎563-873-2341. Park open daily 4am-10:30pm. Check-out 4pm. Reserve 2 days in advance; few sites are reserved for walk-ins. July-Aug. sites $11, with electricity $16; Sept.-June $8/13.) **Wyalusing State Park ❶,** just across the Mississippi and 10 mi. south of Prairie du Chien in Wisconsin, offers 110 campsites overlooking the Wisconsin and Mississippi Rivers. Take U.S. 18 to County Rd. P, County Rd. X, then follow signs. (☎608-996-2261 or 888-947-2757; www.wyalusing.org. Campsites $12, non-residents $14; vehicles $10. Electricity $5.)

SPIRIT LAKE AND OKOBOJI   ☎712

In a dubious attempt to rival its neighbors, Iowa boasts its own "Great Lakes." **Spirit Lake, West Okoboji** (o-ka-BO-ja) **Lake,** and **East Okoboji Lake** form a popular resort destination. The 10,000-year-old, glacier-carved West Okoboji Lake ranks with Switzerland's Lake Geneva and Canada's Lake Louise as one of the most beautiful blue-water lakes in the world. It's hard to miss the amusement park in **Arnolds Park,** off Rte. 71, with its 1927 wooden roller coaster, kiddie rides, and ice-cream shops. (☎332-2183 or 800-599-6995; www.arnoldspark.com. Open late May to mid-Sept. Usually opens at 11am, closing time 7-10pm. $20, children 3-4 ft. tall

BLOWIN' IN THE WIND

The pre-corn season Iowa landscape is remarkably flat. Neither the silos nor the budding corn stalks represent its most striking feature; rather, stark wind turbines characterize the landscape.

Iowa is the third-largest producer of wind-energy in the United States. Though not perfected, wind turbines can generate electricity from gusts of wind with zero emissions. Energy generated from wind promises cleaner air, a way to combat global warming, and even, some argue, more jobs for Iowans.

Iowa has long relied on coal brought in from neighboring states to fill its energy needs. These days, both citizens and lawmakers are intent on finding alternative, local ways of fueling the state. People are sick of the emissions from fossil fuels, and they say so—on signs mounted around Iowa's back roads. Because of the state's geographical layout, wind energy, is a very viable alternative source of power. As with all bureaucratic measures, the transfer to greener power sources will require time and raise many questions. We only have to look to Minnesota's Bob Dylan to know, however, that the answer (to fuel emissions) is blowin' in the wind.

To learn more about Iowa's commitment to clean and renewable wind energy, visit the Iowa Energy Center's website at www.energy.iastate.edu/renewable/wind.

and seniors $16, under 3 ft. free. Individual ride tickets $1. AmEx/D/MC/V.) During summer, the park hosts concerts in the **Roof Garden** at 6pm on Thursdays and in the **Preservation Plaza** at 7:30pm on Saturdays (call the park for info). The **Higgins Museum of Money,** 1507 Sanborne Ave., in Okoboji, has one of the most extensive collections of National Bank notes. Check out the invaluable error note, with $20 printed on one side and $10 on the other. (☎332-5859. Open mid-May to mid-Sept. Tu-Su 11am-5pm. Free.) **Lakes Art Center,** 2201 Hwy. 71, is a fun and funky space with an art gallery, tours, and a cool interactive "smart art" exhibit that experiments with drawing, color, and perspective. (☎332-7013; www.lakesart.org. Open Tu-W and F-Sa 10am-4pm, Th 10am-9pm; June-Aug. also Su noon-3pm.) Theater buffs can catch productions next door at the **Stephens College Okoboji Summer Theater.** (☎332-7773. Box office open M 10am-6pm, Tu-Sa 10am-9pm, Su 1-7pm. 9 shows June-Aug. Performances Tu-Sa at 8pm, Sa also 4:30pm, Su 6pm. $13, musicals $15; groups, students and seniors $11/13; under 12 $6.50/7.50.) If you'd like a quick dose of the outdoors, signs all over the area point to trailheads for the network of **Dickinson County Recreational Trails** on which visitors hike, bike, or run. Rent bikes at **Okoboji Expedition Co.,** 1021 Rte. 71 in Okoboji before the bridge. (☎332-9001; www.expeditionco.com. Open M, W, and F-Sa 9am-6pm; Tu and Th 9am-5:30pm; Su 10am-4pm. Bike rental $20 per 3hr., $25 per day.) Beaches line the coasts of Spirit and Okoboji Lakes. The beach at Gull's Point Campground is more tranquil; Sunset Beach by the "boardwalk" in Arnolds Park has more going on. Rent kayaks, boats, and jet skis at **Funtime Rentals** in Arnold's Park, south of the bridge on U.S. 71. (☎332-2540. Kayaks $25 for 1st hr., $5 each hr. thereafter. Boats $40-105 per hr. Jet skis $95 per hr. Open daily 9am-9pm. Credit card required.)

Indoor budget accommodations in the immediate lake area are scarce. Cheap motels cluster around U.S. 71 in Spencer, 15 mi. south of Okoboji. **The Northland Inn ❸,** 2051 Hwy. 9, at the junction of Rtes. 9 and 86, north of West Okoboji Lake, has a family atmosphere and rooms with fridges and microwaves. (☎336-1450; www.northlandinnspiritlake.com. May-Sept. singles M-Th and Su $50, F-Sa $71; doubles $60/81. Oct.-Apr. singles $44; doubles $54. AmEx/D/MC/V.) The area has numerous state parks and private campgrounds, for camping both on and near the lakes. Pitch your tent year-round at tranquil **Marble Beach Campground ❶** (☎336-4437), on the shores of Spirit Lake. **Gull's Point ❶** (☎337-3870), off Rte. 86 on beautiful West Okoboji Lake, is a gorgeous spot with a beach and a playground. (☎337-3211. Sites $11.

Electricity $16.) The **Koffee Kup Kafe ❶**, 43 U.S. 71, just before Broadway St., serves breakfast all day, with tasty pancakes for $1-3. (☎332-7657. Lunch $5-8. Open daily 6am-1pm. Cash only.) Down by the water, at Parks Marina, beach bums while away summer evenings with drinks and simple food at **Barefoot Bar ❶**, 2447 178th St., in Okoboji. Ribs ($10), burgers ($9), and mojitos ($6, pitcher $20) accompany slightly tacky tiki decor. (☎332 7303. Th Karaoke. Call for other events and performances. Open May-Sept. daily 11am-10pm.) At night, vacationers linger in Arnolds Park. Broadway St., between U.S. 71 and the park, is lined with bars.

Okoboji Spirit Center, 243 W. Broadway Ave., houses a brochure-packed welcome center and a maritime museum that traces the history of the local lake industry. (☎800-270-2574; www.vacationokoboji.com. Open M-Sa 9am-7pm, Su 10am-5pm.) **Internet Access: Spirit Lake Public Library,** 702 16th St. off Hill Ave. (☎336-2667; www.spiritlakepubliclibrary.org. Free. 30min. max. Wi-Fi available. Open M-Th 11am-8pm, F-Sa 10am-5pm. Computer lab closes 30min. before closing time.) **Post Office:** 1513 Hill Ave., in Spirit Lake. (☎336-1683. Open M-F 8:30am-4:30pm, Sa 8:30-11:30am.) **Postal Code:** 51360.

NEBRASKA

Nebraska suffers from accusations of being boring, flat, and empty, but in reality, the landscape is the state's greatest attraction. Central Nebraska features the Sandhills, a region full of windblown, grassy dunes, and tiny rural towns. The Panhandle has Western-style mountains and canyons, historical trails, and national monuments. For the more urbane traveler, Omaha and Lincoln feature quality sports, fine music, and some of America's best meat. While many might have the urge to speed through the Cornhusker State, patient travelers are rewarded with a surprisingly pleasant Great Plains experience.

⁊ PRACTICAL INFORMATION

Capital: Lincoln.

Visitor Info: Nebraska Tourism Office, 301 Centennial Mall S, Lincoln 68509 (☎402-471-3796 or 877-632-7275; www.visitnebraska.org). Open M-F 8am-5pm. **Nebraska Game and Parks Commission,** 2200 N. 33rd St., Lincoln 68503 (☎402-471-0641 or 800-826-7275; www.outdoornebraska.org). Open M-F 8am-5pm. **State Soft Drink:** Kool-Aid.

Postal Abbreviation: NE. **Sales Tax:** 5.5%.

OMAHA   ☎402

A city of seemingly endless sprawl, Omaha stretches over miles and miles of Nebraska's prairie. The heart of the city, however, is refreshingly compact, and Omaha's museums, world-renowned zoo, and sports complex are the envy of other cities. Downtown, the Old Market lures visitors with breweries, cafes, and nightclubs, while the Gene Leahy Mall boasts a popular and beautiful green path down to the banks of the Missouri River. The town has settled comfortably into its role as a gateway to the West, but is still constantly embracing new trends.

▦⁊ ORIENTATION AND PRACTICAL INFORMATION. Omaha is framed to the east by the **Missouri River,** to the west and north by **I-680,** and to the south by **I-80.** The city has numbered streets that run north-south and increase from the river; you can divide building numbers in addresses on named streets (east-west) by 100 to get the nearby numbered street. Inside the city, **Dodge Street** (Hwy. 6) is the main east-west thoroughfare, while **I-480/Route 75** (Kennedy Expwy.) is the main north-south road. Downtown lies between the river and 24th St. and between Cuming and Leavenworth St. At night, avoid the north and south ends of 24th St., Ames Ave., and the area north of I-480. **Eppley Airfield (OMA),** 4501 Abbott Dr., 4 mi. northeast of downtown, has domestic flights and is accessible from I-480/Rte. 75, Pershing Dr., or Cuming Dr. (☎661-8017; www.eppleyairfield.com.) Amtrak, 1003 S. 9th St. (☎342-1501; www.amtrak.com), at Pacific St., sends **trains** to Chicago (10hr., 1 per day, $62-109) and Denver (10hr., 1 per day, $65-113). Greyhound, 1601 Jackson St. (☎341-1906; www.greyhound.com; open daily 5am-10pm), runs **buses** to Des Moines (2-3hr., 3 per day, $26-29) and St. Louis (9-10hr., 2 per day, $36-80). Metro Area Transit (MAT), 2222 Cumming St., handles **local transportaion.** Check website for schedules. (☎341-0800; www.metroareatransit.com. Open M-F 8am-4:30pm. Buses run M-F 6am-7pm, Sa 7am-7pm, Su 8am-5:30pm. $1.25, ages 10-18 $1, ages 5-9 $0.50; transfers $0.05.) For a **taxi,** call Happy Cab, ☎339-8294. The **Greater Omaha Convention and Visitors Bureau** is at 1001 Farnam St., in downtown. (☎444-4187 or 866-937-6624; www.visitomaha.com. Open M-Sa 9am-4:30pm.) The **Nebraska Travel Information Center,** 1212 Bob Gibson Blvd., is at Exit 454 off I-80 by the zoo. (☎595-3990. Open Apr.-Oct. daily 9am-5pm; Nov.-Mar. M-F 9am-5pm.) **Hotlines: Rape Crisis,** ☎345-7273 (24hr.), **First Call for Help,** ☎444-6666 (operates daily 7am-7pm). **Internet Access: Omaha Library,** 215 S. 15th St., between Douglas and Farnham. (☎444-4800; www.omahapubliclibrary.org. Free. Open M-Th 10am-8pm, F-Sa 10am-6pm, Su 1-6pm; Su hours vary in summer.) **Post Office:** 1124 Pacific St. (☎348-2696. Open M-F 7:30am-6pm, Sa 7:30am-noon.) **Postal Code:** 68108.

⋔ ACCOMMODATIONS. Most budget-friendly lodgings are on the outskirts of downtown and midtown. The usual chains are located at I-80 Exits 445 and 449 (L St.) and near the airport. **Relax Inn Motel & Suites ❸,** 4578 S. 60th St., just south of I-80 at Exit 450, has standard rooms with laundry and Wi-Fi. (☎731-7300. Continental breakfast included. Singles M-Th and Su $51, F-Sa $61; doubles $56/66. D/MC/V.) You won't miss the **Satellite Motel ❷,** 6006 L St., south of I-80 at Exit 450 (60th St.), with its round building and wedge-shaped rooms equipped with cable TV, fridge, and microwave. (☎733-7373. Singles $51; doubles $55. MC/V.) **Glen Cunningham Campground ❶,** on Rainwood Rd. north of I-680 Exit 9 (72nd St.), has lovely, shaded sites next to Cunningham Lake. (☎444-4628. Showers. Open Apr. 15-Oct. 15. Sites $9, with electricity $11, with full hookup $15.)

🞐 FOOD. It's no fun being a chicken, cow, or vegetarian in Omaha, where there is a fried chicken joint on every block and a steakhouse in every district. Mexican food abounds in South Omaha, along S. 24th St. where the vibrant immigrant community cooks up a storm. Once a warehouse area, the brick streets of the **Old Market,** on Jackson, Howard, and Harney St., between 10th and 13th, now feature popular bars, shops, and restaurants. The **farmers' market** (☎345-5401; www.omahafarmersmarket.org) is located at 11th and Jackson St. (Open May-Oct. Sa 8am-12:30pm.) **La Buvette ❷,** pulls off the sophisticated atmosphere of an upscale wine bar as effortlessly as any good Italian or French bistro. Fresh bread, platters of feta, hummus, or carpaccio ($6-8), and salads topped with olives and your choice of cheese ($7.50), complement an excellent selection of wine by the glass. (☎344-8627. Open M-Th 11:30am-10pm, F-Sa 11:30am-midnight, Su noon-8pm. AmEx/D/MC/V.) Omaha's starving vegetarians and vegans flock to **McFoster's Natural Kind Cafe ❸,** 302 S. 38th St. in midtown, which fries vegetable tempura ($6), stews tofu in Indian curry ($7-10), and mixes fruit, nuts, and yogurt into unique salads ($8). Fish and free-range chicken also grace the menu. (☎345-7477; www.mcfosters.com. Open M-Th 11am-10pm, F-Sa 11am-11pm, Su 10am-3pm. MC/V.) For the acclaimed Omaha steakhouse experience, it's worth bopping over to old-fashioned **Johnny's Cafe ❹**, 4702 S. 27th St., which has fed Omaha's hungry carnivores since 1922. The dark, wood-paneled dining room is the perfect environment for savoring a juicy steak. Take Rte. 75 to the L St. Exit in South Omaha. (☎731-4774. Steaks $20-46. Open M-Th 11am-2pm and 5pm-9:30pm, F-Sa 11am-2pm and 5pm-10pm. AmEx/D/MC/V.) When you get sick of the classic American food available everywhere in the city, head to Ahmed's **Persian Cuisine ❸**, 1006 Howard St. in the Old Market, which attracts worldly patrons with the smells of Mediterranean spices. (☎341-9616. Lunch entrees $6-8. Dinner $7-17. Open daily 11:30am-2pm and 5:30-10pm. AmEx/D/MC/V.)

◪ SIGHTS. With the world's largest desert dome, indoor rainforest, and nocturnal exhibit, the ever-evolving **◪Henry Doorly Zoo**, 3701 S. 10th St., has recently added the Orangutan Forest, whose residents swing wildly among the tree-tops, and the Hubbard Gorilla Valley, where great apes roam (sort of) free and gawk at visitors. (☎733-8400; www.omahazoo.com. Take Exit 454 from I-80 and follow signs. Open daily 8:30am-5pm. $10.75, over 62 $9.25, ages 3-11 $7.) About 30min. west on I-80, the **Wildlife Safari Park** lets visitors drive 4½ mi. through a nature preserve inhabited by bison, elk, sandhill cranes, wolves, and other beasts. (☎944-9453. Open Apr.-Oct. daily 9:30am-5pm. $5, seniors $4, ages 3-11 $3.)

The **Durham Western Heritage Museum**, 801 S. 10th St., occupies the former **Union Train Station**, an impressive Art Deco structure. Visitors can eavesdrop on the conversations of talking statues based of 40s train station employees before indulging in a malted milkshake at an authentic 1931 soda fountain. (☎444-5071; www.dwhm.org. Open Tu 10am-8pm, W-Sa 10am-5pm, Su 1-5pm. $7, seniors $6, ages 3-12 $5.) Across the river in Council Bluffs, the **Union Pacific Railroad Museum**, 200 Pearl St., off Rte. 6, includes furniture from a train car intended for President Lincoln before his assassination, a locomotive simulator, and exhibits on the evolving technology of the railroad. (☎712-329-8307. Open Tu-Sa 10am-4pm. Free.) The **Joslyn Art Museum**, 2200 Dodge St., displays American and European art, including the original plaster cast of Degas's famous "Little Dancer" sculpture and colorful glasswork by Dale Chihuly. (☎342-3300; www.joslyn.org. Open Tu-Sa 10am-4pm, Su noon-4pm. "Jazz on the Green" July-Aug. Th 7-9pm; free. $7, seniors and with college ID $5, ages 5-17 $4. Sa 10am-noon free.) Temporary contemporary art exhibits grace the converted warehouse walls of the **Bemis Center for Contemporary Arts**, 724 S. 12th St. Interactive installations often take over the galleries, where visitors become more than passive observers. (☎341-7130; www.bemiscenter.org. Open Tu-Su 11am-5pm. Free.) See the gargantuan remnants of US airpower from the past half-century, including the most recent wars, in the enormous **Strategic Air and Space Museum**, at Exit 426 off I-80, in Ashland. The museum displays military aircraft, including a B-52 bomber and an SR-71—still one of the world's fastest planes. (☎827-3100 or 800-358-5029; www.strategicairand-space.com. Open daily 9am-5pm. $7, military and seniors $6, ages 5-12 $3.)

◪◪ ENTERTAINMENT AND NIGHTLIFE. The spanking new **Qwest Center Omaha**, 455 N. 10th St., hosts concerts and sporting events. (☎341-1500; www.omahameca.com.) At **Rosenblatt Stadium**, across from the zoo on 13th St., you can watch the **Omaha Royals** round the bases from April to September. (☎738-5100; www.oroyals.com. Wheelchair-accessible. Tickets $6-10.) The stadium also hosts the NCAA College Baseball World Series every June. From late June to early July, **Shakespeare on the Green** stages free performances in Elmwood Park, on 60th and Dodge St. (☎280-2391. Shows Th-Su 8pm.)

Punk and progressive music fans have found their niche near several area universities; check the windows of **Homers**, 114 Howard St., in the Old Market, for the scoop on shows. The **13th Street Coffee Company,** 519 S. 13th St., brews three different varieties daily and provides a comfortable atmosphere for chatting, reading, and working. (☎345-2883. Free Wi-Fi. Open M-Th 6:30am-11pm, F 6:30am-midnight, Sa 8am-midnight, Su 9am-11pm.) Saddle Creek Records, the name behind such indie acts as Bright Eyes, owns the **Slowdown,** 729 N. 14th St., between Cuming St. and Webster St., near the Qwest center. It's a champion of a bar, with board games, a free jukebox, a photobooth, and a moveable wall that connects the main bar to the live music venue in back. (☎345-7575; www.theslowdown.com. Music tickets $5-20. Happy hour daily 4pm-7pm. Open daily 4pm-1am.) **The Max,** 1417 Jackson St., is one of the state's most popular gay bars. With a dance floor, DJs, five bars, fountains, and a patio, The Max also attracts a sizeable straight crowd on Saturday nights. (☎346-4110; www.themaxomaha.com. 21+. Cover F $3, Sa $5, Su varies. Happy hour daily 4-9pm. Open daily 4pm-1am.)

LINCOLN   ☎402

The spirit of Lincoln rises and falls with the success of its renowned college football team, the Nebraska Cornhuskers, though a recent drought of Top-25 finishes has mellowed the city's famous football fervor. Off the field, Lincoln mixes stateliness with a distinctly collegiate atmosphere, hosting both the Nebraska state legislature and rows of bars heaving with frat-style hijinks.

■🛈 **ORIENTATION AND PRACTICAL INFORMATION.** Lincoln's grid makes sense—numbered streets increase as you go east, and lettered streets progress through the alphabet as you go north. **O Street** is the main east-west drag, becoming Hwy. 6 west of the city and Rte. 34 to the east. **R Street** runs along the south side of the **University of Nebraska-Lincoln (UNL).** Downtown lies between 7th and 16th St. and M and R St. There is plenty of metered, on-street, and garage parking available. **Lincoln Municipal Airport (LNK),** 2400 W. Adams St., (☎458-2480; www.lincolnairport.com), at W. 12th St., is located 5 mi. northwest of downtown off Cornhusker Hwy.; take Exit 399 off I-80. Amtrak, 201 N. 7th St. (☎476-1295; www.amtrak.com), runs **trains** once daily to Denver (8hr., $63-125), Chicago (11hr., $67-131), and Omaha (1hr., $11-20). Greyhound, 2500 NW. 12th St., (☎474-1071; www.greyhound.com; ticket window open M-F 9am-3pm and 5:30-10:30pm, Sa-Su 9am-2pm and 6pm-10:30pm), near the airport, sends **buses** to Chicago (12-13hr.; 1 per day; $55-98) and Minneapolis (11hr., 1 per day, $36-73). StarTran, 710 J St., handles **public transit.** Schedules are available on buses, at the office on J St., and at many locations downtown. (☎476-1234. Buses run M-F 5:15am-7:10pm, Sa 6am-7:10pm. $1.25, seniors $0.60.) For a **taxi,** call Yellow Cab, ☎477-4111. The **Lincoln Visitors Center** is at 201 N. 7th St., at P St., in Lincoln Station. (☎434-5348 or 800-423-8212; www.lincoln.org. Open May-Sept. M-F 9am-8pm, Sa 8am-5pm, Su noon-4pm.) **Medical Services: Bryan LGH Medical Center East,** 2300 SW. 16th St., at South St. (☎475-1011; www.bryanlgh.org.) **Internet Access: Lincoln Bennett Martin Public Library,** 136 S. 14th St., at N St. (☎441-8500. Free. Open M-Th 10am-9pm, F-Sa 10am-6pm, Su 1:30-5:30pm.) **Post Office:** 700 R St. (☎473-1738. Open M-F 7:30am-6pm, Sa 9am-2pm.) **Postal Code:** 68501.

🛏 **ACCOMMODATIONS.** There are few inexpensive lodging options downtown. Cheaper places are on W. O St., near the airport or east around the 5600 block of Cornhusker Hwy. (U.S. 6). Lincoln's **Microtel Inn and Suites ❸,** 2505 Fairfield St., is new and clean, and its simple rooms have pleasant window seats. Follow 27th St. north of O St. and take a left onto Fairfield. (☎476-2591 or 888-771-7171. Singles M-Th and Su $49, F-Sa $59; doubles $59/69. D/MC/V.) **The Great Plains Budget Host Inn ❷,** 2732 O St., at 27th St., has large rooms with A/C and fridge. Take bus #9, the "O St. Shuttle." (☎476-3253 or 866-556-4315. Free parking and kitchenettes available.

Singles $40; doubles $44. AAA discount 10%. AmEx/D/MC/V.) The elegant **Atwood House Bed and Breakfast ❺**, 740 S. 17th St., at G St., two blocks from the Capitol, is a gorgeous 1894 mansion that dazzles guests with antiques nestled in every corner and whirlpool baths in most suites. (☎438-4567 or 800-884-6554; www.atwoodhouse.com. Reservations required. Rooms $85-199. AmEx/D/MC/V.) To reach the convenient **Camp-A-Way ❶**, 200 Campers Cir., at 1st and Superior St., take Exit 401a from I-80, then Exit 1 from I-180/Rte. 34. Though next to a highway, the sites are peaceful and shaded. (☎476-2282 or 866-719-2267; www.camp-a-way.com. Heated pool, laundry, showers, and Wi-Fi. Office open daily 8am-9pm. Reservations recommended in summer. Sites $18, with water and electricity $29, with full hookup $36. AAA discount. D/MC/V.)

◪◫ FOOD AND NIGHTLIFE. Historic Haymarket, between 7th to 9th St. and O to R St., is a renovated warehouse district near the train tracks with restaurants, shops, and a **farmers' market.** (☎435-7496. Open mid-May to mid-Oct. Sa 8am-noon.) **◪Maggie's Vegetarian Wraps ❶**, 311 N. 8th St., at Q St., sustains Lincoln's vegetarians and vegans with $1-2 pastries, huge $6-7 wraps, and the $7 free-range breakfast burrito, all served in an intimate rainbow interior. (☎477-3959; www.maggiesvegetarian.com. Open M-F 8am-8pm, Sa 11am-3pm. Cash only.) If you thought Nebraska was all meat-and-potatoes, stop by **La Mexicana ❸**, 1637 P St., in the back of a Mexican grocery, for huge dishes of meat, rice, and beans. (☎477-4845. Lunch specials $5-7. Entrees $13-14. Open daily 9am-9pm. D/MC/V.) **Lazlo's Brewery and Grill ❹**, 710 P St., prides itself on locally brewed beer ($4), fresh fish ($12-18), and steak ($16-24) served in a mellow, casual setting. (☎434-5636. Burgers, salads, and sandwiches $6-9. Open M-Th and Su 11am-10pm, F-Sa 11am-11pm. AmEx/D/MC/V.) The ivy-covered **Green Gateau Cafe ❹**, 330 10th St., at M St., draws people in for delicious and reasonably priced breakfast, brunch, and lunch dishes, like strawberry-stuffed french toast. (☎477-0330. Breakfast and brunch $5-10. Open M-F 11am-2pm and 5pm-9pm, Sa 8am-10pm, Su 8am-3pm. MC/V.) Coffee-shops in and around the Haymarket attract readers, conversationalists, and drinkers at all times of day.

With as many as 10 bars per block, Lincoln is obviously a college town. The greatest concentration of nightlife is on and around O St., between 13th and 15th streets, and in the Haymarket. For Lincoln's live blues scene, try the suitably dark **Zoo Bar**, 136 N. 14th St., where Lincoln's sophisticated crowd congregates. (☎435-8754; www.zoobar.com. Tu-Sa live music. Cover $4-15. Open Tu-F 3pm-1am, Sa 2pm-1am, Su 5-10pm.) **The Bricktop**, 1427 O St., caters to bumping, grinding, and all manner of shaking it with live music, DJ nights, and a hip, young crowd. (☎202-8780. 21+. Open M-Sa 7pm-1am, Su 8pm-1am.) **Duffy's Tavern**, 1412 O St., takes the college atmosphere to new and glorious heights with communal "fishbowls" in myriad flavors ($11-22), making drinking a team sport. (☎474-3543. Nightly drink specials. Open M-Sa 4pm-1am, Su 6pm-1am.)

◪ SIGHTS. Intricate mosaics and murals cover the walls, floor, and ceiling of the sophisticated "Tower on the Plains," the 400 ft. ◪**Nebraska State Capitol**, at Centennial Mall, a renamed portion of 15th St. and K St. Since much of the art inside was not completed until relatively recently, it makes for a colorful surprise

---

(deal) **EL VERDADERO ACUERDO.** Nebraskan and Iowan meatpacking cities boast large Hispanic immigrant populations. As they've settled, some have opened restaurants serving delicious homemade cuisine. Taco joints in these Midwestern towns and cities are often surprisingly good and delightfully inexpensive—perfect for the budget traveler looking for "the real deal."

in this official building. "The Sower" sits atop the building as a reminder of Nebraska's agricultural roots. (☎471-0448; www.capitol.org. Open M-F 8am-5pm, Sa 10am-5pm, Su 1-5pm. Free 45min. tours every hr. except 8am and noon.) Also on Centennial Mall, the **Museum of Nebraska History,** at P St., has a phenomenal collection of headdresses, moccasins, jewelry, and other artifacts from the Plains Native Americans, as well as a display on Nebraska's agricultural contributions to World War II. (☎471-4754. Open Tu-F 9am-4:30pm, Sa-Su 1-4:30pm. Suggested donation $2.) The **University of Nebraska State Museum,** at 14th and U St., in Morrill Hall, boasts a fossil collection that includes Archie, the largest mounted mammoth in any American museum. (☎472-2642; www.museum.unl.edu. Open M-Sa 9:30am-4:30pm, Su 1:30-4:30pm. $5, ages 5-18 $3, under 5 free; families $10.) Also on campus is the **Sheldon Memorial Art Gallery and Sculpture Garden,** at 12th and R St. With a focus on modern art, this is Lincoln's only (and therefore best) art museum. (☎472-2461. Open Tu-Th and Sa 10am-5pm, F 10am-8pm, Su noon-5pm. Free.) For a wheel-y good time, roll to the **National Museum of Roller Skating,** 4730 South St., at 48th St., located at the USA Roller Sports headquarters. (☎483-7551, after office hours ext. 16; www.rollerskatingmuseum.com. Open M-F 9am-5pm. Free.) At the end of August, the **Nebraska State Fair** entertains with live music, car races, tractor pulls, and more fried food than you'll ever want to eat. (☎474-5371; www.statefair.org. M-F $6, Sa-Su $8; ages 6-12 $2.) **Pioneers Park,** 3201 S. Coddington Ave., a quarter-mile south of W. Van Dorn, is a perfect spot for a prairie picnic. In winter there is a lighted sled run open until 11pm.

SCOTTS BLUFF AND CHIMNEY ROCK   ☎308

Known to the Plains Indians as *Meapate* ("hill that is hard to go around"), the imposing clay and sandstone highlands of **Scotts Bluff National Monument** were landmarks for people traveling the Oregon Trail in the 1800s. For some time the bluff was too dangerous to cross, but in the 1850s a single-file wagon trail was opened just south of the bluff through narrow **Mitchell's Pass,** where wagon wheels wore deep marks in the sandstone. Today, visitors can walk along a half-mile stretch of the original **Oregon Trail** at the pass, complete with a pair of covered wagons. The **Oregon Trail Museum,** at the **Visitors Center** and entrance on Rte. 92, relates the contradictory accounts of the mysterious death of Hiram Scott, the fur trader who gave the bluffs their name. (☎436-4340; www.nps.gov/scbl. Open daily in summer 8am-7pm; in winter 8am-5pm. $5 per car, $3 per motorcycle.) To get to the top of the bluffs, hike the moderate **Saddle Rock Trail** (3 mi. round-trip) or motor up **Summit Drive.** (Shuttle available for hikers. Summit Dr. closes at 6:30pm.) At the top, you'll find two short **nature trails.** Guidebooks ($0.50) are available at the trailheads and the Visitors Center. The **North Overlook** is a half-mile paved walk with a view of the North Platte River Valley. The short and easy **South Overlook** (¼ mi.) provides a spectacular view of Scotts Bluff and the Oregon Trail route.

From I-80, take Rte. 71 45 mi. north to Rte. 92; the monument is on Rte. 92 about 2 mi. west of **Gering** (not in the town of Scottsbluff). A 1¼ mi. bike trail links Gering with the **Visitors Center** at the base of the bluffs. Festive folk pack the towns near Gering each year for the carnival, concerts, and chili cook-off of the annual **Oregon Trail Days** festival. (☎436-4457; www.oregontraildays.com. Mid-July.) Twenty miles east on Rte. 92, south of Bayard, the 475 ft. spire of **Chimney Rock,** visible from miles away, served as another landmark for travelers on the Oregon Trail. There is no path up to the base of the rock due to the rough terrain and rattlesnakes. The **Nebraska State Historical Society** operates a Visitors Center on Chimney Rock Rd. off Rte. 92. (☎586-2581; www.nps.gov/chro. Open daily 9am-5pm.) If you have time, continue down the road past the Visitors Center, take a right onto the gravel road, and follow it half a mile to the end. Here you will find a graveyard of Oregon Trail settlers and a closer view of the rock itself.

In **Scotts Bluff,** national motel chains dominate the intersection of 20th St. and 21st Ave., while charming, locally owned places grace Rte. 71. Just north of the city on Rte. 71, **Lake Minatare Recreational Area ❶,** has modern and primitive campsites and permits travelers to set up tents right on the beach, with nice views of the landscape. (☎783-2911; www.ngpc.state.ne.us. Entrance fee $4 per vehicle per week, $20 per year. Sites $6, with hookup $15. Cash or check only for self-service sites.) The **Emporium Coffeehouse and Cafe ❸,** 1818 1st Ave, at 18th St., has appetizing, fresh food. The lunch menu abounds with filling salads ($7-8), sandwiches, and paninis ($6-8). Though dinner entrees are more expensive, portions are enormous and can be shared. (☎632-6222; www.emporiumcoffeehouseandcafe.com. Open M-Sa 7am-10pm, Su 7am-3pm. D/MC/V.) **Time Zone:** Mountain.

SCENIC DRIVE: SANDHILLS SCENIC BYWAY

The **Sandhills Journey Scenic Byway** (Rte. 2) is 272 mi. in length from Grand Island to Alliance, 50 mi. from the South Dakota border. The two-lane route parallels I-80 and is about the same length (allow 5hr.) but much more rural, passing through endless rolling sand dunes covered in short prairie grass, interrupted only by bright blue lakes and the largest hand-planted forest in the US, the **Nebraska National Forest,** at the intersection with Rte. 86b. (☎432-0300; www.fs.fed.us/r2/nebraska. Day-use $3. Camping $8, with hookup $15.) **Visitors Centers** in many towns are at local restaurants and hotels; look for the Sandhills Journey emblem. Brochures and maps contain historic information and point to sights off the main road. Check the website for a trip planner and info about the Byway's towns (www.sandhillsjourney.com). **Time Zone:** Mountain time (2hr. behind EST) west of Seneca, Central time (1hr. behind EST) east of Seneca.

Broken Bow is the most charming of the dozen or so towns along the Byway; it has a grassy town square and some places to stop along the route. A good base for exploring central Nebraska, **Grand Island,** at the junction of Rte. 2, Hwy. 281, and U.S. 30, 10 mi. north of I-80, has several budget accommodations and a few attractions of its own. The beautiful, immaculate **Hall County Park Campground ❶,** off Rte. 34, is perfect for a stop-over and offers shady, grassy sites with showers. (Heading south from the city, make a left on Rte. 34. ☎385-5087; www.hcgi.org. Open Apr. 15.-Oct. 15. 3-night max. stay. Sites $7, with hookup $13.) For coffee and simple meals in Grand Island, try the **Blue Moon ❶,** 313 W. 3rd St., which serves lunch, coffee, and delicious baked goods. (☎398-5214. Open M-Th 7:30am-5pm, F-Sa 7:30am-10pm. Cash or check only.) For an escape from the summer heat of the Great Plains, **Island Oasis Water Park** is a sure bet for fun in the sun at amazingly cheap prices. (☎385-5381; www.grand-island.com/oasis. Open June-Aug. usually noon-9pm. $6, ages 5-15 and seniors $5; families $20.) The **Visitors Center,** 2424 S. Locust St., Ste. C, south of the intersection with Stolley Park Rd., is not far from the water park. (☎382-4400; www.visitgrandisland.com. Open M-F 8-5:30pm.)

A short detour 3 mi. north of Alliance on Hwy. 87 will bring you to **Carhenge,** a rough replica of Stonehenge made entirely out of stacked American cars from the 50s and 60s. Jim Reinders created the structure in 1987 with Stonehenge in mind and continues to maintain the site. (www.carhenge.com. Open dawn-10pm. Free.)

KANSAS

Kansas may be the most landlocked state (it contains the geographic center of the United States) but Kansans look on the bright side: they are equidistant from California and New York. Almost any non-interstate highway in this most rural of states makes for an ideal scenic drive, past undulating hills and fields of tallgrass prairie dotted with cows and picture-perfect towns. As the starting point of the Civil War, "Bleeding Kansas" provides myriad opportunities for the history buff. As highway signs remind travelers, this heartland has plenty of heart to go around.

⚑ PRACTICAL INFORMATION

Capital: Topeka.

Visitor Info: Division of Travel and Tourism: 350 Speedway Blvd., Kansas City 66111 (☎800-252-6727; www.travelks.com). Open daily 9am-5pm.

Kansas Department of Wildlife and Parks, 512 SE 25th Ave., Pratt 67124 (☎620-672-5911; www.kdwp.state.ks.us). Open M-F 8am-5pm.

Postal Abbreviation: KS. **Sales Tax:** 5.3% or higher, depending on city.

WICHITA   ☎316

It may be the largest city in Kansas, but self-contained Wichita maintains a slow Midwestern pace. Since the early 20th century its economy has been shaped by aviation giants Boeing, Cessna, Learjet, and Beechcraft, all founded here. With a brick-and-gas-lantern Old Town District, and parks and museums along the grassy banks of the Arkansas River, Wichita is Kansas's cultural and economic center.

⚑ **ORIENTATION AND PRACTICAL INFORMATION.** Wichita lies on I-35, 170 mi. north of Oklahoma City and 200 mi. southwest of Kansas City. A small, quiet downtown makes for easy walking and parking. **Broadway Street** is the major north-south artery; **Douglas Avenue** is the major thoroughfare going east-west. Together, Broadway St. and Douglas Ave. divide the city into quadrants. **Kellogg Avenue (U.S. 54)** serves as an expressway through downtown and a main commercial strip. The closest Amtrak station, 414 N. Main St. (☎283-7533; www.amtrak.com; open M-F midnight-8am), 30 mi. north of Wichita in Newton, sends **trains** to Dodge City (2½hr., 1 per day, $29) and Kansas City (4½hr., 1 per day, $38). Greyhound, 308 S. Broadway St., at English St. (☎265-7711; www.greyhound.com; open daily 3am-6pm), runs **buses** to Kansas City and Oklahoma City (both 2¾hr., 2 per day, $35). Wichita Transit runs 18 bus routes in town, most of which begin at the Downtown Transit Center, 214 S. Topeka St., at William St. (☎265-7221. Transit center open M-F 6am-6:30pm, Sa 7:30am-5:30pm. Buses run M-F 5:45am-6:45pm, Sa 6:45am-5:45pm. $1, ages 6-17 $0.75, disabled and seniors $0.50; transfers $0.25.) The **Convention and Visitors Bureau** is at 100 S. Main St., at Douglas Ave. (☎265-2800 or 800-288-9424; www.visitwichita.com. Open M-F 7:45am-5:15pm.) **Internet Access: Public Library,** 223 S. Main St. (☎261-8500. 1hr. use with ID. Open M-Th 10am-9pm, F-Sa 10am-5:30pm, Su 1-5pm.) **Post Office:** 330 W. 2nd St. N, at N. Waco St. (☎267-7710. Open M-F 7:30am-5pm, Sa 9am-noon.) **Postal Code:** 67202.

⚑⚐ **ACCOMMODATIONS AND FOOD.** Wichita offers a bounty of cheap, independently run hotels about a mile north of downtown on N. Broadway St. Chains line **Kellogg Avenue,** 5-8 mi. west of downtown. **Regency Inn ❶,** 6125 W. Kellogg Dr., located 1 mile from the airport and 5 miles from downtown, has clean rooms with A/C, cable TV, fridge, microwave, and free Wi-Fi. (☎942-1341. Singles $29; doubles $35.) Only 10 blocks from downtown, the **Mark 8 Inn ❷,** 1130 N. Broadway St., has small, comfortable rooms with A/C, cable TV, fridge, laundry facilities, and free local calls. (☎265-4679 or 888-830-7268. Singles $34; doubles $38. $10 key deposit.) **All Seasons Campground ❶,** 15520 W. Maple, 9 mi. west of town, just past 151st St., has RV sites, and a grassy tree-lined area for tents, bathrooms, and hot showers. (☎722-1154. Office open M-Sa 8am-noon and 3-8pm, Su 3-8pm. Tent sites $16. RV sites $21.50-23.50. AAA discount 10%. MC/V.) In the heart of Old Town in an old brick warehouse, the **River City Brewing Co. ❷**, 150 N. Moseley St., has delicious home-brewed pints ($3.25) that complement sandwiches, burgers ($7-8), and pizza ($7-10). Try the homemade root beer with sassafras, licorice, and cinnamon. (☎263-2739. Open M-Th 11am-midnight, F-Sa 11am-2am, Su 11am-10pm. AmEx/D/MC/V.) The light Vietnamese cuisine at **Saigon ❷**, 1103 N. Broadway St., is a great alternative to barbecue. (☎262-8134. Soups $4.50-7. Noodle dishes $5.50-7. Open Su-Th 10am-8:30pm and F-Sa 10am-9:30pm. AmEx/D/MC/V.) **Hog Wild Pit Bar-B-Q ❶**, 1200 S. Rock Rd. (also at 233 S. West St. and 662 E. 47th St.), is a Wichita institution. The dinner platter (meat and two sides; $7) is lip-smackingly good. (☎618-7227. Open daily 11am-8pm. AmEx/MC/V.)

🄲 **SIGHTS.** Most of Wichita's museums are situated along the Arkansas River for handy access and scenic vistas. Take the trolley or bus #12 to "Riverside." **Old Cowtown,** 1871 Sim Park Dr., is one of the best and largest re-created Western towns in the country, with dozens of living history interpreters. (☎264-6398; www.old-cowtown.org. Generally open Apr.-Oct. M-Sa 10am-5pm, Su noon-5pm, but call ahead for hours. $7.75, seniors $6.50, AAA and ages 12-17 $6, ages 4-11 $5.50. MC/V.) The **Wichita Art Museum,** 1400 W. Museum Blvd., housed in an elegant, diamond-shaped building, has a handsome collection of 19th- and 20th-century works by the American masters, a strong focus on modernism, and several rotating exhibits of different media, with unusually progressive themes. (☎268-4921. Open Tu-Sa 10am-5pm, Su noon-5pm; $5, seniors and students with ID $4, ages 5-17 $2. Sa free.) **Botanica,** 701 N. Amindon St., is a complex containing 10 acres of lovely gardens, with themes including the aquatic world, roses, Shakespeare, and butterflies. On Tuesday evenings, complimentary hors d'oeuvres and wine are served. (☎264-0448; www.botanica.org. Open M-Sa 9am-5pm, Su 1-5pm, Tu until 8pm. $6, AAA and seniors $5, ages 6-21 $3. MC/V.) The **Kansas Aviation Museum,** 3350 George Washington Blvd., next to the McConnell Air Force Base, south of town, includes several antique aircraft, from 20s prop planes to 80s private jets, both out on the tarmac and in the 1934 Art Deco terminal building. (☎683-9243. Open Tu-F 9am-4pm, Sa 1-5pm. $6, seniors $4, ages 6-12 $2.)

MANHATTAN   ☎785

Manhattan, Kansas, nicknamed "The Little Apple" by its residents, was originally named "Boston" when it was first settled by abolitionists in 1855. While not quite as large as either of the two cities it has taken its names from, Manhattan has a quaint downtown area which runs east to west along Poyntz Street. Kansas State University, located off Manhattan Ave., is the center of activity in the town—it even has its own mini-town of Aggieville, with tons of unique restaurants and bars packed along several blocks. If you happen to be in town on New Year's Eve, you can even watch the "Little Apple" ball drop here. **The Marianna Kistler Beach Museum of Art,** located on campus at 701 Beach Lane, is host to both permanent and traveling collections of art, many focusing on the unique geography and lifestyles of Kansas. (☎532-7718. Open T-F 10am-5pm and Sa-Su 1-5pm. Free.) The **Oz Museum,** located 15 mi. outside of Manhattan in Wamego, Kansas, is an entire museum devoted to the beloved *Wizard of Oz* films and books. Filled with over 2000 artifacts dating back to 1900 and life-size statues of many of the film's characters, this museum proves that the *Wizard of Oz* is more than just a Kansas cliche. (☎866-458-8686. Open M-Sa 10am-5pm, Su 12pm-5pm. $7, ages 4-12 $4.)

Several chain motels run in and around Tuttle Creek Blvd. Two blocks away from downtown Manhattan on the corner of Pierre St. and 6th St., the **Shortridge House ❹**, built in 1871, offers cable TV, a full breakfast, and Wi-Fi. (☎565-0086,

ROADMAP TO HELL

Rumors abound about tiny **Stull, KS,** near Lake Clinton about 10 mi. outside of Lawrence. Reportedly one of the seven gateways to Hell, which are said to be especially active right around Halloween, the Stull Cemetery tends to attract a lot of attention from those with a penchant for the dark and mysterious.

The cemetery itself surrounds the ruins of a small, run-of-the-mill church built in 1859. Its setting—a small, snail-paced Midwestern town—looks too innocent to be the Devil's doorstep, but people still whisper about the Stull Cemetery.

No one is sure how this 30-year-old legend originated, but college freshmen seem determined to find out: locals often complain of teenagers and college students drunkenly parading into the cemetery late at night, ransacking the grounds in hopes of gaining entrance to Hell.

None of these rumors have been confirmed, despite many attempts to attain proof. On Halloween night in 1988, nearly $25,000 in damage was done to the headstones (which date as far back as the mid-19th century). Since then, the church has been torn down and a fence constructed to keep would-be trespassers at bay. At least for now, slurring frat boys will have to gain admission to Hell the honest way.

www.shortridgehouse.com. Reservations recommended. Rooms $95-$120.) Camping opportunities are available at **Tuttle Creek State Park ❶**, 5 mi. from downtown off Tuttle Creek Blvd. with the main park office located at 5800A River Pond Rd. The park rents kayaks and canoes and also has a full frisbee golf course. (☎538-7941. Primitive camping Apr.-Sept. $8.50, with full hook-up $14.50. Oct.-Mar. $7.50/13.50. Cabins from $55.) **Bluestem Bistro ❶**, located in the center of Aggieville at 1219 Moro St., serves a variety of coffees and has salads, sandwiches, and quiches for $5-7. Try the Grasshopper Latte ($3.50) with creme de menthe. (☎587-8888. Free Wi-Fi. Open daily May-Sept. 7am-10pm, Oct.-Apr. 7am-11pm.) **Tubby's ❶**, 1127 Moro St., is a burger joint by day and popular dance club by night. Try a half-pound burger topped with anything from peanut butter to pineapple ($7.50). The "club" part of Tubby's opens up next door at 9pm W-Sa. (☎587-8707. Open M-Tu 4pm-2am, W-Su 11:30am-2am.)

Transportation is hard to come by in Manhattan if you don't have a car. The closest Greyhound and Amtrak stations are in Topeka, KS, 60 miles away, and there is no public transit system. The **Manhattan Visitor's Bureau,** 501 Poyntz Ave., is eager to answer questions. (☎776-8829. Open M-F 8am-5pm.) **Internet Access: Public library,** 629 Poyntz Ave. (☎776-4741. Free Wi-Fi. Open M-Th 9am-9pm, F 9am-8pm, Sa 9am-6pm, Su 1pm-6pm.) **Post Office:** 500 Leavenworth St. (☎776-8851. Open M-F 8:30am-4:30pm, Sa 9:30am-noon.) **Postal code:** 66502.

LAWRENCE   ☎785

Founded by Massachusetts abolitionists who were adamant that Kansas enter the union a free state, Lawrence was fiercely progressive from the get-go. Lawrence today seems to combine the best of New England and the Midwest, managing to be chic, cultural, and cosmopolitan while remaining at heart an old-fashioned walkable town. The economy revolves around the ▨**University of Kansas's** campus (affectionately called KU to avoid confusion with the United Kingdom), situated atop Mt. Oread with commanding prairie views. The university, one of the oldest west of the Mississippi (founded 1866), is also one of the most beautiful in the country, with hilly streets and 150 years of architecture. The **KU Visitor's Center,** 1502 Iowa St., offers guidance. (☎864-3911. Open M-F 8am-5pm.) Off campus, Lawrence has numerous first-rate artistic, architectural, and historical activities. The **Watkins Community Museum of History,** 1047 Massachusetts St., has exhibits on Lawrence history, from the important (the Civil War) to the very important (KU's world-famous basketball team), all in a former bank built in 1888. (☎841-4109; www.watkinsmuseum.org. Open Tu-W 10am-6pm, Th 10am-9pm, F 10am-5pm, Sa 10am-4pm. Suggested donation $3, children $2.) **Quantrill's Raid: The Lawrence Massacre,** a driving tour, traces the events leading to the murder of 200 men by pro-slavery vigilantes on August 21, 1863. **House Styles of Old West Lawrence,** a guide to Lawrence's Victorian homes, plots a route accessible on foot (45min.) or car.

Inexpensive motels are hard to find in Lawrence; your best bet is around Iowa and 6th St., just west of campus. Three blocks west of Massachusetts St. on 10th St., the **Halcyon House Bed and Breakfast ❸,** 1000 Ohio St., has comfy, affordable rooms in a convenient location. (☎841-0314; www.thehalcyonhouse.com. Reservations recommended. Rooms $49-149.) The **Westminster Inn and Suites ❸,** 2525 W. 6th St., is the least expensive motel in town, and provides standard rooms, a pool, and a full breakfast. (☎841-8410. Singles $45-50; doubles $55-60.) Campers can take their pick of the 400 grassy, shaded sites at **Clinton Lake State Park ❶,** 798 N. 1415 Rd., 6 mi. west of town on one of largest reservoirs in Kansas. (☎842-8562. Park entry in summer $6.50; in winter $5.50. In summer sites $8.50, with water and electricity $16. In winter $7.50/15. MC/V.) Massachusetts St. abounds with culinary delights of all persuasions, and most of them are affordable. **Wheatfields Bakery and Cafe ❷,** 904 Vermont St., is a New Age cafe with tasty sandwiches that range from Cuban roasted pork to a tempeh reuben. Check out the huge cylindrical brick oven, used to bake their fresh artisan breads. (☎841-5553. Sandwiches $5-7. Coffee drinks $1-2.75. Open M-F 6:30am-8pm, Sa 6:30am-6:30pm, Su 7:30am-4pm.) For live music and a neighborhood bar feel, head to **Jazzhaus,** 926½ Massachusetts St., where local bands play five nights a week. (☎749-3320. Cover after 9pm $2-8; Tu drinks $1.50. Open M-Sa 8pm-2am; music begins at 10pm.) Cuisine at the popular **La Parilla ❷,** 814 Massachusetts St., is accented with Salvadoran, Costa Rican, Brazilian, and Mayan flavors. Try the Brazilian lemonade ($1.50), made with coconut milk and ginger. (☎841-1100. Open M and Su 11am-9pm, T-Th 11am-10pm, and F-Sa 11am-11pm.)

Lawrence, just south of **I-70,** is considered part of greater Kansas City but is separated from the suburbs of Kansas City, KS by about 10mi. of farmland. There is an unstaffed Amtrak station at 413 E. 7th St.; **trains** chug to Chicago (9½hr., 1 per day, $63-123) and Kansas City, MO (1½hr., 1 per day, $11-20). Greyhound, 2447 W. 6th St. (☎843-5622; www.greyhound.com; ticket window open M-F 7:30am-4pm, Sa 7:30am-noon) runs **buses** to Dallas (13-15hr., 5 per day, $91), Denver (12-13hr., 3 per day, $85), and Kansas City, MO (1hr., 2 per day, $15). The Lawrence Transit System (the "T"), 930 E. 30th St., has schedules in local businesses, the library, and on every bus. (☎832-3465. Open M-Sa 6am-8pm. $0.75, disabled and seniors $0.35.) The **Visitor Center,** 402 N. 2nd St., in the restored Union Pacific depot, has maps, brochures, and a 30min. film. (☎865-4499 or 888-529-5267. Open Apr.-Sept. M-Sa 8:30am-5:30pm, Su 1-5pm; Oct.-Mar. M-Sa 9am-5pm, Su 1-5pm.) **Internet Access: Public Library,** 707 Vermont Ave. (☎843-3833. Free. Open M-F 9am-9pm, Sa 9am-6pm, Su 2-6pm.) **Post Office:** 645 Vermont St. (☎843-1681. Open M-F 8am-5:30pm, Sa 9am-noon.) **Postal Code:** 66044.

MISSOURI

Nestled in the middle of the country, Missouri serves as the gateway to the West while hugging the Midwest and South, blending the three identities into a state that defies regional stereotyping. Its large cities are defined by wide avenues, lazy rivers, humid summers, and blues and jazz wailing into the night. In the countryside, Bible factory outlets stand amid fireworks shacks and barbecue pits. Missouri's patchwork geography further complicates its characterization. In the north, near Iowa, amber waves of grain undulate. Along the Mississippi, towering bluffs inscribed with Native American pictographs evoke western canyonlands, while in Hannibal, cavers enjoy the limestone caverns that inspired Mark Twain.

⑦ PRACTICAL INFORMATION

Capital: Jefferson City.

Visitor Info: Missouri Tourism Center, P.O. Box 1055, Jefferson City 65102 (☎573-751-4133 or 800-519-2100; www.missouritourism.org). Open M-F 8am-5pm; toll-free number 24hr. **Dept. of Natural Resources,** Division of State Parks, P.O. Box 176, Jefferson City 65102 (☎573-751-3443 or 800-361-4827). Open M-F 8am-5pm.

Postal Abbreviation: MO. **Sales Tax:** 5-7.5%, depending on county.

ST. LOUIS   ☎314

Directly south of the junction of the Mississippi, Missouri, and Illinois rivers, St. Louis gained prominence in the 18th and 19th centuries as the US expanded west. The silvery Gateway Arch rises above the sprawling and diverse city, framing it against the mighty river that nurtured its growth. Combining Southern hospitality, Midwestern pragmatism, and Western optimism, St. Louis offers visitors both fast-paced urban life and lazy days spent floating on the Mississippi.

▐ TRANSPORTATION

Airport: Lambert-St. Louis International (STL; ☎426-8000; www.lambert-stlouis.com), 12 mi. northwest of the city on I-70. MetroLink and Bi-State bus #66 "Clayton Airport" provides easy access to downtown ($3.50). Taxi to downtown $30.

Trains: Amtrak, 550 S. 16th St. (☎231-0061; www.amtrak.com). Open daily 3:30am-1am. To **Chicago** (5½hr., 5 per day, $23-65); **Kansas City** (5½hr., 2 per day, $25-32); and **Little Rock** (7½hr., 2 per day, $46-72).

Buses: Greyhound, 1450 N. 13th St. (☎231-4485; www.greyhound.com), at Cass Ave. From downtown, take Bi-State bus #30; the ride is less than 10min. Use caution in this area at night. Open 24hr. To **Chicago** (6-8hr., 7 per day, $40.50), **Kansas City** (4½-5hr., 5 per day, $38.25); and **Memphis** (4½-5½hr., 3 per day, $47).

Public Transit: Bi-State (☎231-2345; www.metrostlouis.org), also known as MetroBus, runs local buses. Info and schedules available at the **Metroride Service Center** (☎982-1495), in the St. Louis Center. Open M-F 6am-8pm, Sa-Su 8am-5pm. **MetroLink,** the light-rail system, runs from Lambert Airport through downtown and on to Shiloh, IL. Operates M-F 4:30am-12:15am, Sa-Su 5am-midnight. Travel for free in the "Ride Free Zone" (from Laclede's Landing to Union Station) M-F 11:30am-1:30pm. Bi-State or MetroLink $1.75, seniors and ages 5-12 $0.85; transfers $0.25/0.10. Day pass $4.50, available at MetroLink stations.

Taxi: Yellow Cab, ☎361-2345.

✈ ⑦ ORIENTATION AND PRACTICAL INFORMATION

I-64 (U.S. 40) and **I-44** run east-west through the metropolitan area. Downtown is the area east of Tucker Blvd. between **Martin Luther King** and **Market Street,** which run north-south and divide the city. Numbered streets run parallel to the Mississippi, increasing to the west. The historic **Soulard** district borders the river south of downtown. **Forest Park** and the **University City Loop,** home to **Wash-**

Downtown St. Louis

▲ ACCOMMODATIONS
Congress Airport Inn, 5
Huckleberry Finn Youth Hostel, 6
The Roberts Mayfair, 11

🍴 FOOD
Blueberry Hill, 3
Cha Yoon Elixir Bar, 2
Mangia Italiano, 9
Ted Drewes Frozen Custard, 10

🌙 NIGHTLIFE
Absolutli Goosed, 8
The Complex, 1
Pin-Up Bowl , 4
Way Out Club, 7

ington University and old, stately homes, lie west of downtown; the Italian neighborhood called **The Hill** rests south of these neighborhoods. St. Louis is a driving town: metered street parking is plentiful, and private lots are often cheap (from $2 per day). While the safety situation in St. Louis has shown improvement of late, visitors are still well advised to be alert; areas in North County can be dangerous at night, and East St. Louis—across the river in Illinois—should be avoided.

Visitor Info: St. Louis Visitors Center, 701 Convention Plaza, on the corner 7th and Washington St. (☎342-5160 or 800-888-3861). Open M-Sa 9am-5pm, Su 11am-4pm. *The Official St. Louis Visitors Guide* and the monthly *Where: St. Louis* contain helpful info and good maps.

Hotlines: Rape Hotline: ☎531-2003. **Suicide Hotline:** ☎469-6644. Both operate 24hr. **Gay and Lesbian Hotline:** ☎367-0084. Operates M-Sa 6-10pm.

Medical Services: Barnes-Jewish Hospital, in the Central West End (☎747-3000).

Post Office: 1720 Market St. (☎436-6853). Open M-F 8am-8pm, Sa 8am-1pm. **Postal Code:** 63155. **Area Code:** 314 (in St. Louis), 636 (in St. Charles), 618 (in IL); in text, 314 unless otherwise noted.

ACCOMMODATIONS

Most budget lodging is far from downtown. For chain motels, try Lindbergh Blvd. (Rte. 67) near the airport, or the area north of the I-70/I-270 junction in Bridgeton, 5 mi. beyond the airport.

Huckleberry Finn Youth Hostel, 1908 S. 12th St. (☎241-0076), at Tucker Blvd. in the Soulard District. Take bus #73 "Carondelet." Weathered dorms could use a fresh coat of paint and shower sandals are a must, but great for meeting backpackers. Reception daily 8-10am and 6-10pm. Check-out 10am. Dorms $20. Cash only. ❶

The Roberts Mayfair, 806 St. Charles St. (☎421-2500). The custom of placing choco-lates on a guest's pillow originated at this elegant Jazz Age hotel, which has played host to Cary Grant and Harry Truman. Standard rooms are spacious with marble-topped sinks and soft queen-sized beds. Rooms $90-180. AmEx/D/MC/V. ❹

Congress Airport Inn, 3433 N. Lindbergh Blvd. (☎739-5100), 1 mi. south of I-70, west of the airport. Clean accommodations just a 20min. drive from the Loop and close to the airport. Singles $45; doubles $50. AmEx/D/MC/V. ❸

Dr. Edmund A. Babler Memorial State Park, 800 Guy Park (☎636-458-3813; www.mostateparks.com), in Wildwood. 10 mi. north of I-44 off Hwy. 109. Well-main-tained facilities and hot showers nestled in a verdant setting. Tent sites Apr.-Oct. $9, Nov.-Mar. $8. RV sites with electric hookup $16. ❶

FOOD

It's worth venturing well outside the downtown area to sample St. Louis cuisine at its best. The **Central West End** offers trendy cafes and upscale bars centered on **Euclid Avenue,** just north of Lindell Blvd.; take the MetroLink to "Central West End" and walk north, or catch the Shuttle Bug. St. Louis's historic Italian neighborhood, **The Hill,** southwest of downtown and just northwest of Tower Grove Park, pro-duces plenty of inexpensive pasta; take bus #99 "Shaw-Russell." Ethnic restau-rants, ranging from Vietnamese to Middle Eastern cuisine, spice up the **South Grand** area, at Grand Blvd. just south of Tower Grove Park; board bus #70 "Grand." Coffee shops and unique restaurants cluster on **University City Loop,** on Delmar Blvd. between Des Peres and Big Bend Blvd.

Blueberry Hill, 6504 Delmar Blvd. (☎727-4444). Diners share the 9 rooms of this wacky St. Louis institution with Howdy Doody collectibles and giant baseball cards. Sand-wiches ($5-7) and burgers (from $5.50) rule the roost at street level, while musical sets in the "Duck Room" have only added to the place's reputation. Music sets 21+. Cover $10-25. Open M-Sa 11am-1:30am, Su 11am-midnight. AmEx/D/MC/V. ❷

Mangia Italiano, 3145 S. Grand Blvd. (☎664-8585). Has earned its reputation with homemade pastas like *porcini tagliatelle* ($9). After hours, the place transforms into a smoky lair for lounge lizards. Lunch buffet M-F 11am-2:30pm ($6). Open M-Sa 11am-10pm, Su 5pm-10pm. Bar open until 3am. AmEx/D/MC/V. ❸

Ted Drewes Frozen Custard, 4224 S. Grand Blvd. (☎352-7376), and 6726 Chippewa St. (☎481-2652), at Rte. 66. This roadside stand's signature blend of rich custard and candy is thick enough to be called a "concrete" ($3-4); each one undergoes a test for drips before serving. Grand Blvd. location open daily May-Aug. 11am-11pm; Chippewa St. location open daily year-round 11am-11pm. Cash only. ❶

Cha Yoon Elixir Bar, 4 N. Euclid Ave. (☎367-2209). A chic sushi joint (6-piece roll $4-8) with an encyclopedic tea menu. Lounge on leather couches and sip tieguanyin oolong ($6 per pot), said to be hand-picked by monkeys who are trained to reach the most inaccessible tea trees. Open M-Th 11am-10pm, F-Sa 11am-11pm, Su 5-9pm. Sushi bar closes 1hr. earlier. AmEx/D/MC/V. ❷

☉ SIGHTS

JEFFERSON EXPANSION MEMORIAL. At 630 ft., the **Gateway Arch**—the nation's tallest monument—towers gracefully over all of St. Louis and southern Illinois, serving as a testament to the city's historical role as the "Gateway to the West." Eero Saarinen's iconic design is impressive when viewed from the ground, and the ear-popping tram ride to the top allows visitors to see as far as 30 mi. on a clear day. Back on terra firma, the **Museum of Westward Expansion** recounts the settlement of the West through a series of photographs and artifacts that tell the white settlers' side of the story. (☎982-1410; www.nps.gov/jeff/expansion_museum. Museum and arch open daily in summer 8am-10pm; in winter 9am-6pm. Tram $10, ages 13-16 $7, ages 3-12 $3. Museum free.) Scope out the city from the water with **Gateway Riverboat Cruises;** tours leave from the docks in front of the arch. (☎877-982-1410. 1hr. riverboat tours daily; call for departure times. Limited wheelchair-accessibility. $12, ages 3-12 $6.) Across the street but still part of the Memorial, the magnificently ornate **Old Courthouse,** where the Dred Scott trial began, has been restored as a museum telling the story of the famous court case that pushed slave and free states closer to civil war. (11 N. 4th St. ☎655-1600. Open daily 8am-4:30pm. Call ahead for tour schedules. Free.)

DOWNTOWN AND WEST TOWN. Part eco-savvy installation art and part playground to end all playgrounds, the ◪**City Museum** is constructed from salvaged pieces of area buildings that were due to be demolished or discarded. The loading chutes of a former shoe factory get re-imagined as a twisting network of slides, while coils from an Anheuser-Busch cooling tank become a climbing ladder that wraps around itself like a cocoon. The recently opened World Aquarium is not worth the extra $5, but the five-story MonstroCity beckons with dizzying skywalks and lookout points like the cockpit of a passenger plane; there is no better spot for a creative date on weekend nights. (701 N. 15th St. ☎231-2489; www.citymuseum.org. Open M-Th 9am-5pm, F 9am-1am, Sa 10am-1am, Su 11am-5pm. $12, with the World Aquarium $18.) Several blocks north, the **Scott Joplin House** is a turn-of-the-century flat where the ragtime legend tickled the ivories until commercial success took him to New York in 1907. The 45min. tour delves into Joplin's long-lasting influence on American music. (2658 Delmar Blvd. ☎340-5790. Open Mar.-Oct. daily 10am-4pm; Nov.-Feb. Tu-Sa 10am-4pm. Tours leave on the hr. Last tour 3pm. Wheelchair-accessible. $2.50, ages 6-12 $1.50.)

Back downtown, the **St. Louis Cardinals Hall of Fame Museum** traces the history of the franchise from the glory days of Branch Rickey and Rogers Hornsby to the present day; the exhibit about the history of Busch Stadium has become particularly poignant since the old stadium shut its doors in 2005. An attached museum dedicated to the history of bowling should be skipped on any but the rainiest of days. (111 Stadium Plaza. ☎231-6340. Open Apr.-Sept. daily 9am-5pm, game days until 6:30pm; Oct.-Mar. Tu-Su 11am-4pm. Wheelchair-accessible. $7.50, over 66 $7, under 16 $6.)

GRANT CENTER AND THE CENTRAL WEST END. In the early 60s, the legendary nightspots and beatnik coffeehouses of **Gaslight Square** drew cultural icons like Lenny Bruce and Woody Allen to the corner of Olive St. and N. Boyle Ave. The Haight-Ashbury vibe lasted only a few years before the moneyed classes hit the suburbs; today, however, city leaders are working hard to incubate a new cultural district along N. Grand Blvd. One anchor of the new **Grant Center** area is the **Con-**

temporary Art Museum St. Louis, which has been tearing down and reassembling its galleries for new installations since it opened in 2003. *(3750 Washington Blvd. ☎535-4660; www.contemporarystl.org. Open Tu-W and F-Sa 10am-5pm, Th 10am-8pm, Su 11am-4pm. $5, senior $3, children and student free. Free W and Sa and after 5pm Th. Museum closes for up to a month between shows; call ahead to confirm opening hours.)* Just to the south, on the campus of St. Louis University, a former Jesuit chapel houses the ◙**Museum of Contemporary Religious Art (MOCRA),** which made waves in the mid-90s with a major exhibition on art and spirituality in the time of AIDS. *(221 N. Grand Blvd. ☎977-7170; http://mocra.slu.edu. Open Tu-Su 11am-4pm. Museum closes for up to a month between shows; call ahead to confirm opening hours. Free.)* Deeper into the Central West End, the **Cathedral Basilica of St. Louis** traces the history of the Catholic faith through glittering mosaics that took more than half a century to complete. *(4431 Lindell Blvd. MetroLink stop "Central West End" or bus #93 "Lindell" from downtown. ☎373-8241. Open daily 7am-5pm; tours M-F 10am-noon and 1-3pm, Su 1pm. Free.)*

FOREST PARK. Almost 500 acres larger than New York's Central Park, Forest Park attracted more than 19 million visitors to its statues and palaces in the 1904 World's Fair. Today, Forest Park upholds the City Beautiful vow to make high culture available for the masses; all of the major sights are free. *(Take MetroLink to Forest Park and catch bus #90 or bus #3. All Forest Park sites are wheelchair-accessible.)* It's easy to spend the better part of a day exploring the grounds of the **St. Louis Zoo,** from the field stations of the River's Edge exhibit to the chilly blast of the Penguin and Puffin Coast. *(☎781-0900; www.stlzoo.com. Open daily late May to early Sept. 8am-7pm; Sept.-May 9am-5pm. Free.)* The ground floor of the **St. Louis Art Museum** resembles a Who's Who of Renaissance and Impressionist art, although no visit is complete without a look at the Melanesian masks and carvings on the lower level. *(☎721-0072; www.slam.org. Open Tu-Th and Sa-Su 10am-5pm, F 10am-9pm. Free tours Tu-Su 1:30pm. Museum free. Special exhibits usually $10, seniors and students $8, ages 6-12 $6. F free.)* The "Seeking St. Louis" exhibit at the **Missouri History Museum** presents vignettes from the city's past. Galleries extending off the main atrium are reserved for temporary exhibitions. *(At Lindell and DeBaliviere. ☎454-3150; www.mohistory.org. Open M and W-Su 10am-6pm, Tu 10am-8pm. Museum free. Special exhibits usually $5, seniors and students $4.)*

SOUTH OF DOWNTOWN. The historic neighborhood of **Soulard** is bounded by I-55 and 7th St. Its 19th-century brick townhouses made it one of the first districts to draw suburbanites back downtown in the 70s. Today, the ethnically and economically diverse area is known as one of the city's most tight-knit. February brings one of the most raucous **Mardi Gras** celebrations outside New Orleans, while the **Soulard Farmers' Market** sells fresh, inexpensive produce year-round. *(730 Carroll St. From downtown, travel south on Broadway or 7th St. to Lafayette. Take bus #40 "Soulard." ☎622-4180. Open W-F 8am-5pm, Sa 6am-5pm.)* At the end of 12th St., the **Anheuser-Busch Brewery,** the largest brewery in the world, pumps out 16.5 million 12 oz. servings of beer each day. The 1½hr. tour includes a glimpse of the famous Clydesdales and two beer samples. *(1127 Pestalozzi St. at 12th and Lynch St. Take bus #40 "Broadway" south from downtown. ☎557-2333; www.budweisertours.com. Tours June-Aug. M-Sa 9am-5pm, Su 11:30am-5pm; Mar.-May and Sept.-Oct. M-Sa 9am-4pm, Su 11:30am-4pm; Nov.-Feb. 10am-4pm, Su 11:30am-4pm. Wheelchair-accessible. Free.)* North of Tower Grove Park, the stunning ◙**Missouri Botanical Garden** is the oldest in the country, with the residential compound of founder Henry Shaw dating back to 1852. The 14-acre Japanese garden at the southwest corner of the garden dazzles with wooden footbridges and cascading cherry blossoms, although the shady English woodland garden and the rose gardens to the north have subtle charms of their own. *(4344 Shaw Blvd. From downtown, take I-44 west, or ride MetroLink to "Central West End" and take bus #13 "Union-Garden." ☎577-9400; www.mobot.org. Open daily 9am-5pm; June-Aug. also W until 8pm. Guided tours daily 1pm. $8, seniors $5, under 12 free.)*

ENTERTAINMENT

Grand Center's **Powell Hall,** 718 N. Grand Blvd., is the acoustically distinguished and visually striking home of the renowned **St. Louis Symphony Orchestra.** (☎534-1700; www.slso.org. Performances late Sept. to early May F-Sa 8pm, Su 3pm. Box office open late May to mid-Aug. M-F 9am-5pm; late Sept. to late May M-Sa 9am-5pm. Tickets $15-105, students half-price for most shows.) St. Louis offers theatergoers many choices. The outdoor **Municipal Opera,** known as the "Muny," presents hit musicals on summer nights in Forest Park. (☎361-1900; www.muny.com. Box office open June to mid-Aug. daily 9am-9pm. Tickets $8-58.) Other companies include the **St. Louis Black Repertory,** 634 N. Grand Blvd., Ste. 10F (☎534-3807; tickets $35) and the **Repertory Theatre of St. Louis,** 130 Edgar Rd. (☎968-4925), on the campus of Webster University. The **Fox Theatre,** 527 N. Grand Blvd., was an opulent "Temple to the Motion Picture" during the 1930s and is now at the heart of the Grand Center renaissance with its rock concerts and Broadway musicals. (☎534-1111; www.fabulousfox.com. Box office open M-Sa 10am-6pm, Su noon-4pm. Tours Tu, Th, Sa 10:30am. Tu $5, Th and Sa $8; under 12 $3.) St. Louis ordinances permit gambling on the river for those over 21. The **President Casino on the Admiral** floats below the Arch on the Missouri side. (☎622-1111 or 800-772-3647; www.presidentcasino.com/stlouis. Open M-Th 8am-4am, F-Su 24hr. Entry tax $2.) On the Illinois side, the **Casino Queen** claims "the loosest slots in the Midwest." (☎800-777-0777; www.casinoqueen.com. Open daily 9am-7am.) Parking for both is free, and both are wheelchair-accessible. **Six Flags St. Louis,** 30min. southwest of St. Louis on I-44 at Exit 261, rattles teeth with the mighty "Boss" wooden coaster and spins swimmers around a 60 ft. funnel at Hurricane Harbor Water Park. (☎636-938-4800; www.sixflags.com/stlouis. Open June-early Aug. M-F and Sa 10am-11pm, Su 10:30am-9pm; reduced hours Apr.-May and Sept.-Oct. $45, seniors and children under 48 in. $30.) The beloved **Cardinals** play baseball at **Busch Stadium.** (☎421-2400. Tickets $16-55.) Football's **Rams** hit the gridiron at the **Edward Jones Dome.** (☎425-8830. Tickets $44-85.) The **Blues** can cheer up as hockey returns to the **Savvis Center** at 14th St. and Clark Ave. (☎622-2500. Tickets $15-125.)

NIGHTLIFE

The *Riverfront Times* (free at many bars and clubs) and the "Get Out" section of the *Post-Dispatch* list weekly entertainment. On the riverfront, north of the Arch, **Laclede's Landing** gathers a string of bars and music venues into a pedestrian-friendly complex of historic buildings. Across the river, the wild and woolly dance clubs of **East St. Louis** stay open as late as 6am, while gay nightlife back on the Missouri side tends to cluster around **Manchester Road,** southeast of Forest Park.

Pin-Up Bowl, 6191 Delmar Blvd. (☎727-5555; www.pinupbowl.com). Knock down pins while knocking back a mixed drink ($7-8). 8 lanes available by the game ($3.50-5) or by the hour ($30-50). Shoes $3. Draught beer $3.75. 21+ after 9pm. Open M-Th 3pm-3am, F-Su noon-3am.

Way Out Club, 2525 S. Jefferson Ave. (☎664-7638; www.wayoutclub-stl.com). Combines a laid-back bar for the hipster set and a performance space where local rock bands take the stage under the watchful eye of an imposing Jolly Green Giant statue. 21+. Cover for shows $3-6. Open M-Sa 8pm-1:30am.

The Complex, 3515 Chouteau Ave. (☎772-2645). Don't be put off by the dark, deserted area facing the street; circle around back to get into this popular gay club, featuring drag shows, a weekend martini lounge, and a Sa turnout that includes many straight partygoers. W drag shows 11pm and 1am. Cover F-Su $5. 21+. Open W-Su 9pm-3am.

Absolutli Goosed, 3196 S. Grand Blvd. (☎772-0400). The city's premier martini bar serves over 120 double-shot variations on the classic mixed drink. Open W-Th and Su 4pm-midnight, F 4pm-1:30am, Sa 5pm-1:30am.

HANNIBAL ☎573

Mark Twain's boyhood home sits on the Mississippi River, 100 mi. west of Spring-field, Illinois, and 100 mi. northwest of St. Louis. Hannibal slept in obscurity until Twain (born Samuel Clemens) used it as the setting of *The Adventures of Tom Sawyer*. Tourists now flock to this small town to imagine Tom, Huck, and Becky romping around its old-fashioned streets. While this outpouring of interest has left many locals scratching their heads at the fuss, the friendly spirit of small-town Missouri still lingers in Hannibal amid the chain motels and souvenir shops. The properties of the **Mark Twain Boyhood Home and Museum** line the northern half of Hannibal's Main St., with an interpretive center, 208 Hill St., selling tickets and pre-senting an illustrated timeline of the witty wordsmith's life. Glass dividers prevent visitors from getting close to the period furnishings in the cozy Clemens home, though the patent medicine bottles and draconian tooth hooks in **Grant's Drug Store** recall some of Tom Sawyer's most infamous run-ins with well-meaning adults. Farther down Main St., the **New Mark Twain Museum** features 15 illustrations done by Norman Rockwell for a reissue of Twain's classic novels. (☎221-9010; www.marktwainmuseum.org. Open June-Aug. daily 8am-6pm; Apr. and Sept.-Oct. daily 9am-5pm; May daily 8am-5pm; Nov.-Feb. M-Sa 10am-4pm, Su noon-4pm; Mar. M-Sa 9am-4pm, Su noon-4pm. Single ticket covers all sights; $8, seniors $6.50, ages 6-12 $3, under 5 free.) On the riverfront landing, the **Mark Twain Riverboat** steams down the Mississippi for a 1hr. sightseeing cruise that is part history, part folklore, and part advertisement for the land attractions. (☎221-3222; www.marktwainriverboat.com. Late May to early Sept. 3 per day; early May and late Sept. to Oct. 1 per day. $13, ages 5-12 $10.) The **Mark Twain Cave,** 1 mi. south of Hannibal on Rte. 79, winds through the complex series of caverns Twain explored as a boy. A 1hr. tour guides visitors to the author's favorite spots and details the myths and leg-ends associated with the cave. Graffiti from as early as the 1830s, including Jesse James's signature, marks the walls. The cave tour includes the only section of the cave christened by Twain: **Aladdin's Castle,** the spot where Tom and Becky were "married." (☎221-1656; www.marktwaincave.com. Open daily June-Aug. 9am-8pm; Apr.-May and Sept.-Oct. 9am-6pm; Nov.-Mar. 9am-4pm. $15, ages 5-12 $8.) Every 4th of July weekend, 100,000 fans converge on Hannibal for the fence-painting, frog-jumping fun of the **Tom Sawyer Days** festival.

Away from the river, Hannibal's historic district is dotted with beautiful 19th-century homes. The **Robard Mansion ❸,** 215 N. 6th St., is an 1871 mansion built by one of Twain's close friends and the site of an exorcism. A restored cupola offers riverfront views, but the home isn't haunted—at least not anymore. (☎248-1218; www.thegildedage.net. All rooms with A/C and private bath. Call ahead for reser-vations. Rooms $60-98. MC/V.) Wander down to the waterfront for a barbeque pork steak sandwich ($10.50) at **Bubba's ❷,** 101 Church St., or stick around for din-ner and devour a whole catfish ($10) rubbed with spicy seasonings. (☎221-5552. M 5pm-9pm, Tu-F 11am-2pm and 5-9pm Sa 11am-9pm. D/MC/V.) The old-fashioned phosphates ($1.50) at **Main Street Soda Fountain ❶,** 207 S. Main St., are as tart and refreshing as they were back when the fountain was installed in 1906; hand-dipped ice cream cones ($1.50) are another good way to cool down on a summer after-noon. (☎248-1295. Open Tu-Su 11am-5pm. Cash only.)

The **Hannibal Convention and Visitors Bureau,** 505 N. 3rd St., offers free local calls and information. (☎221-2477; www.visithannibal.com. Open M-F 8am-6pm, Sa 9am-6pm, Su 9am-5pm.) **Post Office:** 801 Broadway. (☎221-0957. Open M-F 8:45am-4:45pm, Sa 9am-noon.) **Postal Code:** 63401.

KANSAS CITY ☎816

With more miles of broad boulevard than the city of Paris and more working fountains than the city of Rome, Kansas City looks and acts more European than one might expect from the "Barbecue Capital of the World." Nonetheless, it maintains a big bad blues-and-jazz reputation in a city spanning two states: the highly suburbanized town in Kansas (KCKS) and the quicker-paced commercial metropolis in Missouri (KCMO).

▛ TRANSPORTATION

Airport: Kansas City International (KCI; ☎243-5237; www.flykci.com), 18 mi. northwest of KC off I-29. Take bus #129. **KCI Shuttle** (☎243-5000 or 800-243-6383) connects to downtown ($17), and Westport, Crown Center, and the Plaza ($20) in KCMO every 30min., and to Overland Park, Mission, and Lenexa in KCKS (up to $45) on demand. Operates daily 5:30am-midnight. Taxi to downtown $35.

Trains: Amtrak, 30 W. Pershing Rd. (☎421-3622; www.amtrak.com), in the newly renovated Union Station. Take bus #27. Open daily 6:30am-midnight. To **Chicago** (7-12hr., 2 per day, $42-112) and **St. Louis** (5-6hr., 2 per day, $25-58).

Buses: Greyhound, 1101 N. Troost St. (☎221-2835; www.greyhound.com). Open in summer 24hr.; in winter daily 5:30am-midnight. To **Chicago** (10-12hr., 7-8 per day, $60.50) and **St. Louis** (5hr., 6-7 per day, $37).

Public Transit: Kansas City Area Transportation Authority (Metro), 1200 E. 18th St. (☎221-0660; www.kcata.org), near Troost St. Most buses run 4:30am-midnight, though some routes have more limited schedules. $1.25, ages 6-11, disabled, and seniors $0.60; free transfers.

Taxi: Yellow Cab, ☎471-5000.

✦❷ ORIENTATION AND PRACTICAL INFORMATION

The Kansas City metropolitan area is split between two states, Kansas and Missouri, sprawling interminably, which makes travel difficult without a car. The Kansas side is almost entirely suburban; most sights worth visiting lie south or west of downtown on the Missouri side. All listings are for KCMO, unless otherwise indicated. **I-70** cuts east-west through the city, and **I-435** circles the two-state metro area. KCMO is laid out on a grid with numbered streets running east-west from the Missouri River well out into suburbs, and named streets running north-south. **Main Street** divides the city east-west. Metered parking is limited downtown.

Visitor Info: Convention and Visitors Association of Greater Kansas City, 1100 Main St., at 11th St. (☎221-5242 or 800-767-7700; www.visitkc.com), 22nd fl. of City Center Sq. Bldg. Open M-F 8:30am-5pm. Other locations can be found at Country Club Plaza (☎691-3866; open M-Sa 10am-6pm, Su 12pm-5pm) and Union Station (☎460-2048; open daily 9am-6pm).

Hotlines: Rape Crisis Line, ☎531-0233. **Synergy House Crisis Hotline,** ☎741-8700. Both 24hr.

Medical Services: Truman Medical Center, 2301 Holmes St. (☎404-1000).

Internet Access: Kansas City Public Library, 14 W. 10th St. (☎701-3400). 4hr. max. per day. Free Wi-Fi. Open M-W 9am-9pm, Th-F 9am-6pm, Sa 10am-5pm, Su 1-5pm.

Post Office: 30 W. Pershing Rd. (☎374-9101), inside Union Station. Open M-F 7am-7pm, Sa 8:30am-3:30pm. **Postal Code:** 64108. **Area Code:** 816 in Missouri, 913 in Kansas; in text 816 unless noted otherwise.

GREAT PLAINS

ACCOMMODATIONS

Accommodations in and around downtown KCMO tend to be overpriced—even the most meager motel room costs upward of $60. To sleep for cheap, head 10-20 mi. east on I-70. The further you go, the cheaper lodgings will be.

■ **Serendipity Bed and Breakfast,** 116 S. Pleasant St. (☎833-4719 or 800-203-4299), 10 mi. west of KCMO in Independence, MO. A 3-story 1887 brick home and carriage house within walking distance from downtown Independence. Music, bowls of candy, and Victorian-era novelties such as 19th-century Sears catalogues and stereoscopes fill each room. Rooms $45-95. D/MC/V. ❸

Interstate Inn (☎229-6311), off I-70 at Exit 18. Far from downtown, but the cheapest decent motel around. Singles from $36; doubles from $40. AmEx/D/MC/V. ❷

American Inn, 4141 S. Noland Rd. (☎373-8300), in Independence at Exit 12 off I-70, is definitely a step up in the budget hotel food chain. The American's buildings in patriotic hues feature pleasant rooms with A/C and cable TV. Several pools. Singles from $40. AmEx/D/MC/V. ❷

Lake Jacomo Campground (☎795-8200), 22 mi. southeast of KCMO. Take I-470 south to Colbern, then head east for 2 mi. Lots of water activities, 33 forested campsites, and a marina. Open year-round. Sites $10, with electricity $14, with water and electricity $18, with full hookup $20. Cash only. ❶

FOOD

Although Kansas City is best known for its ubiquitous barbecue and unusually tangy ribs, there are a variety of dining options. The **Westport** area is home to eclectic restaurants and hip coffeehouses. Expensive chains have sprung up in **Country Club Plaza,** while ethnic fare can be found on **39th Street,** just east of the state line.

■ **Succotash,** 15 E. 3rd St. (☎421-2807), in the City Market building. Easter-egg-colored walls and highly creative food, with dishes like pear pecan pancakes with bacon ($6.50) and a cheddar, tart apple, and caramelized onion sandwich ($6). Open T and Th-F 9am-3pm, W 9am-3pm and 6-9pm, Sa 8am-3pm, Su 9am-3pm. AmEx/MC/V. ❷

Blue Nile Cafe, 20 E. 5th St. (☎283-0990), in the City Market building. Delicious Ethiopian food. Intensely flavorful meat and vegetarian curries and stews ($8-13) eaten with spongy *injera* bread instead of utensils. Lunch special $7.50. Open Tu-F 11am-9pm, Sa 10am-9pm, Su 10am-2pm. AmEx/MC/V. ❸

Rheinland Restaurant, 208 N. Main St. (☎461-5383), in Independence. Authentic-tasting German goodies served by authentic-sounding waitresses. While dinner can be pricey, lunch prices are more reasonable. Sandwiches and wurst $7-9. Hefty pints $3.25. Open M and Su 11am-2:30pm, Tu-Sa 11am-9pm. ❷

Arthur Bryant's, 1727 Brooklyn Ave. (☎231-1123), 6 blocks east of 18th and Vine. Take the Brooklyn Exit off I-70 or bus #110 from downtown. The grand-daddy of KC barbecue and a perennial candidate for America's best barbecue. Bryant's "sandwiches" wimpy triangles of bread drowning in meaty perfection ($8) are a carnivore's delight. Open M-Th 10am-9:30pm, F-Sa 10am-10pm, Su 11am-8pm. AmEx/D/MC/V. ❷

d'Bronx, 3904 Bell St. (☎531-0550), on the 39th St. restaurant row. A New York deli transplanted to Middle America, d'Bronx has over 35 kinds of subs (6 in. sub $4-6). Open M-Th 10:30am-9pm, F-Sa 10:30am-11pm. AmEx/D/MC/V. ❷

Jerusalem Cafe, 431 Westport Rd. (☎756-2770). This casual, brick-walled Middle Eastern hangout is a popular stop for hungry vegetarians. Sandwiches $6-7. Kebabs $8-11. Open M-Sa 11am-10pm, Su noon-8pm. AmEx/D/MC/V. ❷

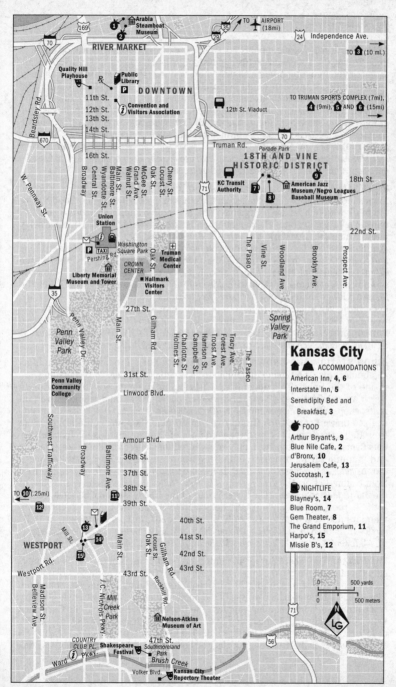

Kansas City

🏠🏠 ACCOMMODATIONS
American Inn, **4, 6**
Interstate Inn, **5**
Serendipity Bed and
    Breakfast, **3**

🍎 FOOD
Arthur Bryant's, **9**
Blue Nile Cafe, **2**
d'Bronx, **10**
Jerusalem Cafe, **13**
Succotash, **1**

🎵 NIGHTLIFE
Blayney's, **14**
Blue Room, **7**
Gem Theater, **8**
The Grand Emporium, **11**
Harpo's, **15**
Missie B's, **12**

GREAT PLAINS

◎ SIGHTS

18TH AND VINE. Jazz and blues once emanated from this neighborhood all night long. Today, the **18th and Vine Historic District,** still in the heart of KCMO's African-American community, offers a slightly more refined take on yesteryear with gussied-up buildings, museums, and performance venues (see **Nightlife,** p. 619). The ◪**Negro Leagues Baseball Museum** uses photographs, interactive exhibits, and thoughtful nostalgia to commemorate the players from before baseball was integrated. In the same building, the **American Jazz Museum** brings back the era with tributes to jazz greats and tons of memorabilia, like Louis Armstrong's lip salve. *(1616 E. 18th St. Take bus #108, "Indiana." Baseball Museum: ☎221-1920; www.nlbm.com. Jazz Museum: ☎474-8463; www.americanjazzmuseum.com. Both open Tu-Sa 9am-6pm, Su noon-6pm. One museum $6, ages 6-12 $2.50; both museums $8/4.)*

RIVER MARKET. Just south of the Missouri River, the Freeway separates downtown's monuments to capitalism from the city's hippest new neighborhood, where old brick warehouses are being converted into coffee shops, art studios, and loft units at an alarming rate. The neighborhood takes its name from the thrice-weekly farmers' market, City Market, at 5th and Walnut St. *(☎842-1271. W 8am-2pm, Sa 6am-4pm, Su 8am-4pm.)* The area also offers plenty of opportunities for pleasant strolling and jogging via the paths along the Missouri River. Just next to City Market, the ◪**Arabia Steamboat Museum** is as unique as the treasures it houses. When the steamboat *Arabia* sank in 1856, its holds were full of commercial goods. When the Missouri River shifted a century later, excavations revealed that those goods had been perfectly preserved by layers of cold mud. Today, visitors can peek at a wealth of 19th-century treasures, and can take a behind-the-scenes look at the restoration process in working labs. *(400 Grand Blvd. ☎417-4030; www.1856.com. Open M-Sa 10am-5:30pm, Su noon-5pm. $12.50, seniors $11.50, ages 4-12 $4.75.)*

UNION STATION AND CROWN CENTER. The city likes to boast of its fountains and boulevards. The Bloch Fountain in front of ◪**Union Station,** 30 W. Pershing Rd., is one of the finest. This magnificent 1914 building, the largest train station in North America outside of New York, was renovated in 1999 and is home to restaurants, shops, and a science museum. *(Open daily 6am-midnight.)* It is linked by a skywalk to **Crown Center,** 2405 Grand Ave., an upscale shopping center. Accessible from Hall's Department Store on the 3rd floor of Crown Center is the **Hallmark Visitors Center,** where extensive family-friendly exhibits chronicle the history, design, and manufacturing process behind the famous greeting cards. *(☎274-3613; www.hallmarkvisitorscenter.com. Open Tu-F 9am-5pm, Sa 9:30am-4:30pm. Free.)* Across from Union Station, the grassy slopes of **Penn Valley Park** rise to meet the base of the 217 ft. **Memorial Tower.** The tower is part of the **Liberty Memorial Museum,** 100 W. 26th St., the nation's only museum dedicated to World War I. All five allied commanders met together for the only time at the memorial's dedication in 1921. *(☎784-1918. Open Tu-Sa 10am-5pm. Tower closes at 4:15pm. Museum $8, seniors $7, ages 6-11 $4. Tower $4, ages 6-11 and seniors $3. Both $10, seniors $8, ages 6-11 $5.)*

THE PLAZA. The most "European-influenced" section of Kansas City is undoubtedly **Country Club Plaza,** known as "the Plaza," the oldest and perhaps most picturesque shopping center in the US. Modeled after buildings in Sevilla, Spain, the Plaza boasts fountains, sculptures, hand-painted tiles, grinning gargoyles, luxury chain stores, and latte-sipping yuppies. The Plaza is also famous for its Christmas lights, lit annually on Thanksgiving Eve. *(4745 Central St. Take bus #39, 51, 56, 57, or 155. Plaza Customer Service Center: ☎753-0100. Free outdoor concerts May-Aug. Th 5-8pm, Sa-Su 2-5pm.)* Three long blocks northeast of the Plaza, the world-class **Nel-**

son-Atkins Museum of Art, 4525 Oak St., contains one of the best East Asian art collections in the world, as well as European and American art from the medieval to the postmodern periods. The handsome grounds include a sculpture garden with 13 pieces by Henry Moore. *(Take bus #147, 155, 156, or 157. ☎561-4000; www.nelson-atkins.org. Open Tu-W and Su 10am-5pm, Th-Sa 10am-9pm. Live jazz in the museum's Rozzelle Court Restaurant F 5:30-8:30pm. Free, suggested donation $5, seniors and students $4, under 18 $3.)*

🎵 ENTERTAINMENT

From September to June, the **Kansas City Repertory Theatre,** 4949 Cherry St., southeast of the Plaza, stages classics ranging from Gilbert & Sullivan to Tennessee Williams. (☎235-2700; www.kcrep.org. Box office open M-F 10am-5pm. Tickets $22-50, with student ID $14-18, seniors $3 off.) **Quality Hill Playhouse,** 303 W. 10th St. downtown, produces off-Broadway plays and revues from September to June. (☎421-1700. Tickets available by phone or at the theater 1hr. before showtime. $24, seniors and students $22.) From late June to early July, the **Heart of America Shakespeare Festival** puts on free outdoor productions in Southmoreland Park at 47th and Oak St. (☎531-7728; www.kcshakes.org. Opens most nights 8pm.) Sports fans stampede to I-70 and Blue Ridge Cutoff (Exits 8-9), where the **Harry S Truman Sports Complex** houses every professional team in the city. Inside the complex, **Arrowhead Stadium** is home to football's **Chiefs** (☎920-9400 or 800-676-5488; tickets $54-103) and soccer's **Wizards** (☎920-9300; tickets $14-23). Next door, the water-fountained **Kauffman Stadium** houses baseball's **Royals.** (A stadium express bus runs from downtown and Country Club Plaza on game days for $5. Call ☎346-0348 for details. ☎921-8000 or 800-676-9257. Tickets $8-32.)

🎷 NIGHTLIFE

In the 20s, jazz musician Count Basie and his "Kansas City Sound" reigned at the River City bars. Twenty years later, saxophonist Charlie "Bird" Parker took jazz in a new direction as he cultivated the sound of "bop," the forerunner to modern jazz. Today, the **Blue Room,** 1600 E. 18th St., connected to the American Jazz Museum (p. 618), continues KC's jazz tradition four nights a week with some of the smoothest acts in the country. (☎474-2929. Cover F-Sa from $5. Bar open M 5pm-midnight, Th-F 5pm-1am, Sa 7pm-1am.) Across the street, the restored Art Deco **Gem Theater,** 1615 E. 18th St., stages top-tier regional and national blues and jazz acts. (☎474-6262. Tickets and info in the American Jazz Museum.)

Harpo's, 4109 Pennsylvania Ave. (☎753-3434). Harpo's is decidedly the cornerstone of Westport's young nightlife. $0.25 beer on Tu attracts collegiates and other budget-conscious revelers to this woodwork-laden bar. Live music Sa. Cover Tu and Sa $3. Open daily 11am-3am.

The Grand Emporium, 3832 Main St. (☎531-1504), hosts live music from reggae to blues several nights a week. Order an obscure liquor so the bartender has to climb the ladder up the 20 ft. shelves. Cover and hours vary depending on act; call for details.

Blayney's, 415 Westport Rd. (☎561-3747). The Irish tavern upstairs is decent, but the earthy "blues cavern" downstairs is where the real action is. Try to make your own sense out of the bar's primary decoration: bras. Live music M-Sa: M Americana (folk/country/rockabilly), Tu-Sa blues. Cover $2-6. 21+. Open M-Sa 5pm-3am.

Missie B's, 805 W. 39th St. (☎561-0625). This 2-story gay bar features DJs, dance floors and popular karaoke. M, W, F-Sa drag shows 11pm-2am. Cover F $3, Sa $5. 21+. Open M-Sa noon-3am.

GREAT PLAINS

◢ DAYTRIP FROM KANSAS CITY

INDEPENDENCE, MO

Independence is 10 mi. east of Kansas City, off of U.S. 24. The Park Service runs a Visitors Center at Main and Truman St. (☎816-254-9929. Open daily 8:30am-5pm.)

The small town of Independence was once the last outpost of civilization for western-bound pioneers and (much later) the home of US President Harry S Truman. Now enveloped by the sprawl of greater Kansas City, Independence still maintains a historic, small-town feel. The painstakingly preserved interior of the **Harry S Truman Home**, 219 N. Delaware St., is furnished with artifacts from the family's elegant but unpretentious lifestyle. (☎254-9929. Purchase tickets at the Visitors Center, 5 blocks west in the square on Truman Rd. Tours M 9am-4:45pm, Tu-Su 8:30am-5pm; Sept.-May closed M. $4, under 16 free.) The Visitors Center also has free maps of the **Truman Historic Walking Trail.** Among the 43 stops are the **Jackson County Courthouse**, 112 W. Lexington St., where Truman began his political life as a county judge, and **Clinton's Soda Fountain & Coffee Shop**, 100 W. Maple St., where he earned pocket change by sweeping floors. The candid ◪**Truman Presidential Museum and Library**, 500 W. Hwy. 24, recounts the life and administration of the man who became President just 82 days after taking the Vice-Presidential oath of office. Exhibits focus on the Truman administration's often-controversial decisions, such as the nuclear bombing of Japan, and invite visitors to add their own opinions in interactive displays. (☎800-833-1225. Open M-Sa 9am-5pm, Su noon-5pm. $7, seniors $5, ages 6-18 $3.) Anyone who ever tried to get their oxen to ford the river in the computer game "The Oregon Trail" will appreciate the **National Frontier Trails Center**, 318 W. Pacific St., which lets visitors "follow" each of the three routes taken by wagon trains embarking from Independence: the Santa Fe Trail, the California Trail, and of course, the Oregon Trail. Interactive exhibits simulate the critical decisions facing pioneers along the way. (☎325-7575; www.frontiertrailscenter.org. Open M-Sa 9am-4:30pm, Su 12:30-4:30pm. $5, seniors $4.50, students 6-17 $3, under 5 free.)

BRANSON   ☎ 417

Back in 1967, the Presley family had no idea of the impact the tiny theater they opened on **West Route 76** would have. Now, over 30 years later, millions of tourists clog Branson's strip to visit the "live music show capital of the world." Billboards, motels, and giant showplaces call the masses to embrace all things plastic, franchised, and "wholesome." Branson boasts over 30 indoor theaters and a few outdoor ones as well, housing family variety shows, magic acts, comedians, plays, and music. Box office prices for most shows run $20-50, depending on who's playing. Never pay full price for a show or attraction in Branson—coupon books, including the *Sunny Day Guide* and the *Best Read Guide*, offer dozens of discounts.

To see a live battle between the North and the South, head to Dolly Parton's **Dixie Stampede**, 1525 W. Hwy. 76, where a friendly competition between Yankees and Rebs is staged on the backs of ostriches, horses, and other animals that lend themselves to trick riding. Ticket prices include a four-course "feast." (☎800-520-5101. Shows Aug. daily 3, 5:30, and 8pm. $40, ages 4-11 $20. AAA discounts available.) Big-name country acts, such as Loretta Lynn and Billy Ray Cyrus, play the **Grand Palace**, 2700 W. Rte. 76. (☎334-7263 or 800-572-5223. Tickets vary by performance; call ahead for more info.) One of Branson's more unique shows is **The Shepherd of the Hills**, 5586 Rte. 76 W, an outdoor drama/dinner that tells the story of a preacher stranded in the Ozark mountains and his growing relationship with the people of the area. (☎334-4191 or 800-653-6288. Shows May Tu-W and F-Sa; June-Aug. M-Sa. Tickets $39, seniors $36, ages 4-16 $19.)

Motels along Rte. 76 generally start around $25, but prices often increase from July to September. Less tacky motels line Rte. 265, 4 mi. west of the strip, and Gretna Rd. at the west end of the strip. **Budget Inn ❶**, 325 N. Gretna Rd., has slightly dim but spacious rooms close to the action. (☎334-0292. A/C, cable TV, free local calls, pool access. Rooms $29-48.) For a more colorful option, **JR's Motor Inn ❷**, 1944 W. 76 Country Blvd., has an on-site coffeeshop, free continental breakfast, pool, and Wi-Fi. (☎800-837-8531. Rooms from $48-65.) For affordable eats, head downtown to the **Branson Cafe ❶**, 120 Main St. (☎334-3021. Burger and fries $5.25. Breakfast and lunch $6. Open M-Sa 6am-8pm. **Cakes-N-Cream ❶**, 2805 W. Rte. 76, is a 50s throwback diner, complete with jukeboxes, shiny red booths, and waitresses in poodle skirts serving American classics like pizza ($3), chicken pot pie ($5.50), and sandwiches. As its name suggests, it also serves pies, cakes, and 50 flavors of ice cream (from $2), with many sugar-free options. (☎334-4929. Open daily 11am-midnight.)

Branson is impossible without a car, but infuriating with one. On weekends, endless traffic jams clog **Hwy. 76,** the two-lane road that runs by all the town's attractions. Avoid Branson at peak tourist times. Gray Line Shuttle **bus** picks up from Springfield airport and drops off in Branson. (☎339-2550. Call to reserve. $36; 2-person minimum.) Branson's low-season runs from Jan.-Mar., when many attractions close. Beware of fake "tourist information centers". The real info center is the **Branson Chamber of Commerce and Convention and Visitors Bureau Welcome Center,** 269 Rte. 248, west of the Rte. 248/65 junction. (☎800-961-1221; www.explorebranson.com. Open M-Sa 8am-5pm, Su 10am-4pm; in summer M-Sa 8am-6pm.)

OKLAHOMA

An anomaly on the national map, the area that would become the state of Oklahoma was set aside well into the 19th century as "Indian Territory," a mixing pot where captured and subdued tribes from all over America were sent. But by the 1880s the frontier was considered closed and eager white settlers, known as "Sooners," saw Oklahoma as their last shot at free land. Today, Oklahoma is still home to the highest concentration of Native Americans in the country, though tribal names are more often associated with casinos and turnpikes than with anything else. Still, the state has plenty of culture and history, both cowboy and Native American, to go around.

🅱 PRACTICAL INFORMATION

Capital: Oklahoma City.

Visitor Info: Oklahoma Tourism and Recreation Department, 120 N. Robinson Ave., 6th fl., Oklahoma City 73152 (☎230-8400 or 800-652-6552; www.travelok.com). Open M-F 8am-5pm.

Postal Abbreviation: OK. **Sales Tax:** 4.5%. **Tolls:** Oklahoma is fond of toll booths, so keep a wad of bills (and a roll of coins for unattended booths) handy.

TULSA   ☎918

First settled by Creek Native Americans arriving on the Trail of Tears, Tulsa's location on the Arkansas River made it a logical trading outpost. Contemporary Tulsa's

HOME ON THE RANGE

It isn't just the deer and antelope that play here in America's heartland, their home on the range.

In drives across the Midwest—many of them through official wilderness areas—I've encountered cows and cranes; trout and walleye; bunny rabbits and vultures. They have been in farms, zoos, and sanctuaries; on dinner plates with exposed skin; by the side of the road, fleeing cars.

The closest I've gotten to the fauna, with the exception of the ferocious mosquitoes, has been to the eager chipmunks who dart towards my picnic table while I'm eating. More exciting still was my encounter with a moose one evening on the Gunflint Trail near the Boundary Waters; the feisty creature ran alongside my car for a quarter of a mile. My staunchest confrontation, though, was with a turtle. I had turned off the main road to check out a trailhead and was driving on dirt tire grooves with grass growing in between them. I saw a black lump in one of the grooves that looked strange enough to make me stop. I put the car into park, got out, and found a six-by-six inch turtle sitting languidly in the dirt.

Try as I might, I couldn't make it move, so I walked the rest of the way to the trailhead. Later, I had to drive all the way back up this narrow road in reverse. Like the hare before me, I had been defeated by a turtle.

—Cara Eisenpress

Art Deco skyscrapers, French villas, Georgian mansions, and a fairly substantial Native American population all reflect the varied heritage of the city that locals call "T-Town."

ORIENTATION AND PRACTICAL INFORMATION.

Tulsa is divided into 1 sq. mi. quadrants. **Main Street** (north-south) and **Admiral Boulevard** (east-west) intersect downtown. Numbered streets run parallel to Admiral Blvd. Named streets run north-south in alphabetical order; those named after western cities are west of Main St., while eastern cities are east. **Tulsa International Airport (TUL; ☎838-5000; www.tulsaairports.com)**, northeast of downtown, is accessible by I-244 or U.S. 169. A **taxi** to downtown costs $22. Greyhound, 317 S. Detroit Ave. (☎584-4428; www.greyhound.com; open 24hr.), sends **buses** to Dallas (6-7hr., 6 per day, $54), Oklahoma City (2hr., 6 per day, $21), and St. Louis (7-9hr., 5 per day, $77.50). Metropolitan Tulsa Transit Authority, 510 S. Rockford Ave., runs **local buses**. (☎582-2100. Buses start 5am-7am and finish 5:30pm-7:30pm; infrequent night service until 12:30am. $1.25, disabled and seniors $0.60, under 5 and over 74 free.) For a **taxi,** call Yellow Checker Cab, ☎582-6161.

The **Tulsa Convention and Visitors Bureau** is at Williams Center Tower Two, 2 W. 2nd St., #150. (☎585-1201 or 800-558-3311; www.visittulsa.com. Open M-F 8am-5pm.) **Medical Services: Hillcrest Medical Center,** 1120 S. Utica Ave. (☎579-1000). **Hotlines: Rape Crisis Hotline, ☎744-7273.** Check **e-mail** at the **Tulsa Public Library,** at 400 Civic Center, at 4th and Denver. (☎596-7977. Open June-Aug. M-Th 9am-9pm, F-Sa 9am-5pm; Sept.-May. also Su 1-5pm. Free Wi-Fi; 90min. limit.) **Post Office:** 333 W. 4th St. (☎732-6651. Open M-F 7:30am-5pm.) **Postal Code:** 74103.

ACCOMMODATIONS AND FOOD.

The budget accommodations in Tulsa consist of freeway-side motels, with several near Exits 222C and 232 off I-44. **Georgetown Plaza Motel ❶**, 8502 E. 27th St., on the north side of I-44 right off Exit 232, has clean rooms, reasonable rates, and Georgian architecture. (☎622-6616. Rooms $26-35. AmEx/MC/V.) The **Gateway Motor Hotel ❷**, 5600 W. Skelly Dr., at Exit 222C, has standard rooms, DVD players and free Wi-Fi. (☎446-6611. Singles $29-37. Each additional person $4. AmEx/D/MC/V.)

The Oklahoma institution **Cici's Pizza ❶**, 4949 S. Peoria St., just north of I-44, is an amazing deal: all-you-can-eat pizza, salad, and pasta for only $4.50. (☎744-8338. Open M-Th and Su 10am-10pm, F-Sa 10am-11pm. MC/V.)

◙ **SIGHTS.** In 1964, televangelist Oral Roberts dreamt that God commanded him to build a university. Today, **Oral Roberts University,** 7777 S. Lewis Ave., 6 mi. south of downtown, boasts one of the country's most whimsical, modern campuses, abounding with unusual colors and forms, as well as the world's largest bronze statue—a pair of 60 ft. high praying hands. The **Visitors Center,** in the Prayer Tower, has superb views, an orientation video, and self-guided tours. (☎495-6807; www.oru.edu. Open Tu-Sa 10am-3:30pm, Su 12:30-3:30pm.) From its vantage point in the Osage foothills, 2 mi. northwest of downtown, the **Thomas Gilcrease Museum,** 1400 Gilcrease Museum Rd., contains the world's largest collection of Western American art, focusing on landscapes and life on the frontier. The museum also displays thousands of Native American artifacts, from jewelry to pipes to weapons. Take the "Gilcrease" Exit off Rte. 412 or bus #114. (☎596-2700 or 888-655-2278; www.gilcrease.org. Open daily 10am-5pm. Suggested donation $3.) The **Philbrook Museum of Art,** 2727 S. Rockford Rd., has a little of everything, from Greek pottery to Indian basket weaving and French Impressionism, all housed in the Italian Renaissance-style villa of a 20s oil tycoon. The 23 acres of exquisitely manicured gardens are perhaps the biggest draw. (☎749-7941 or 800-324-7941; www.philbrook.org. Take bus #105. Open Tu-W and F-Sa, Th 10am-8pm. $7.50, seniors and students $5.50, under 13 free; 2nd Sa of every month free.)

◪◪ **ENTERTAINMENT AND NIGHTLIFE.** Tulsa thrives during the **International Mayfest** (☎582-6435; www.tulsamayfest.com), held May 15-18, 2008, which features live dance, music, and visual art exhibits. The **Greenwood Heritage Festival,** in the historic heart of Tulsa's African-American community, the 100 block of Greenwood Ave. just south of I-244, is held in mid-August, with jazz concerts and food. Call the Greenwood Chamber of Commerce (☎585-2084) for details. The *Tulsa Pulse,* free at local restaurants, and "The Spot," in the Friday *Tulsa World,* both have entertainment info. The area known as **Brookside,** along the 3000 block of S. Peoria Ave. and 15th St. east of Peoria, is home to the city's hippest nightlife. North of downtown in an old industrial building, the **Gypsy Coffee House,** 303 N. Cincinnati Ave., is a comfy hangout with free Wi-Fi and standard gourmet coffee drinks and sandwiches. (☎295-2181. Coffee drinks $2-4. Sandwiches $4.50-6.25. Open M-Th and Su noon-12am, F-Sa noon-3am.)

Sharing a corner with some of the city's swankies clubs and chicest wine bars, **Boston's,** 1738 Boston Ave., is more concerned with good music than the resumes of its varied clientele. Live music of every genre is played every single night, with Oklahoman "Red Dirt" music on Wednesday nights. Bar and grill food is served until 10pm. (☎583-9520. Cover F-Sa $5, under 21 $7. Open M-F 4pm-2am, Sa 6pm-2am, Su 7pm-2am.)

◪ **DAYTRIP FROM TULSA: TAHLEQUAH.** The Cherokee tribe lost nearly one-quarter of their entire population along the Trail of Tears, but they began anew by placing their capital in Tahlequah, located 66 mi. southeast of Tulsa on Rte. 51. In Cherokee Sq. stands the old **capitol building** of the Cherokee Nation, 101 S. Muskogee Ave. Built in 1870, it was the highest authority in Oklahoma until the advent of statehood. The town's **Visitors Center,** 123 E. Delaware St., has maps and information for travelers. (☎456-3742 or 800-456-4860. Open M-F 9am-5pm.) The **Cherokee Heritage Center,** 4 mi. south of town on Willis Rd., off Rte. 82, traces Cherokee history, from the Trail of Tears to self-government to the today. Included in admission is a tour of **Ancient Village,** where Cherokee interpreters reenact 19th-century life. (☎456-6007 or 888-999-6007; www.cherokeeheritage.org. Center open M-Th 10am-5pm, F-Sa 10-7pm, Su 1-5pm. Closed Jan. $8.50, seniors and students $7.50, ages 5-18 $5. AAA discount 10%.)

OKLAHOMA CITY ☎405

For years, Oklahoma City was just a dusty stop for cattle drives and railroad trains. That all changed during the land run of 1889 when the city's population exploded from a few dozen people to 15,000 virtually overnight. But the city remained relatively quiet until the tragic bombing of the Federal Building in 1995 suddenly thrust this self-proclaimed "cowtown" into the modern age. As the site of the worst terrorist attack on US soil (until 9/11), Oklahoma City became a symbol of American patriotism and solidarity around the world.

⬛🔁 ORIENTATION AND PRACTICAL INFORMATION. Oklahoma City is laid out in a nearly perfect grid. **Santa Fe Avenue** divides the city from east to west, and **Reno Avenue** slices it north to south. Street parking is cheap and plentiful. Most sights lie downtown or a few miles north. **Will Rogers World Airport (OKC;** ☎680-3200; www.flyokc.com) off Exit 116B on I-44, is southwest of downtown. Amtrak (www.amtrak.com) has an unattended station at 100 S. E.K. Gaylord Blvd., and runs **trains** to Fort Worth (4hr., daily, $24-29). Greyhound, 427 W. Sheridan Ave. (☎235-4083; www.greyhound.com; open 24hr.), at Walker St., runs **buses** to Dallas (6hr., 4 per day, $42.50), Kansas City (6-10hr., 5 per day, $74.50), and Tulsa (2hr., 6 per day, $21). Metro Transit **bus** routes leave from the main terminal, 420 NW. 5th St., which has maps and info. (☎235-7433; www.gometro.org. Buses run M-F 5:30am-7:30pm, Sa 6:30am-5:30pm. $1.25, ages 6-17 and seniors $0.60.) Look for the Oklahoma Spirit **trolley** ($0.25, disabled and over 60 $0.10) downtown and in Bricktown. For a **taxi** call: Yellow Cab, ☎232-6161. The **Oklahoma City Convention and Visitors Bureau,** 189 W. Sheridan Ave., at Robinson St., has city info. (☎297-8912 or 800-225-5652; www.okccvb.org. Open M-F 8:30am-5pm.) **Internet Access: Oklahoma City Public Library,** 300 Park Ave. at Harvey. (☎231-8650. Free Internet; 30min. limit per day. Open M-Th 9am-9pm, F 9am-6pm, Sa 9am-5pm, Su 1-6pm.) **Post office:** 305 NW. 5th St. (☎232-2198. Open M-F 7am-9pm, Sa 8am-5pm.) **Postal Code:** 73102.

📍 ACCOMMODATIONS. Motels are along I-35 near downtown in both directions. **Royal Inn ❷,** 2800 S. I-35, treats you to free local calls, HBO, and standard rooms. (☎672-0899. Singles $37; doubles $45. AmEx/D/MC/V.) **Courtesy Inn ❷,** 1307 SE. 44th St., right off I-35, is 3 mi. from downtown and offers spacious rooms (some even have sofas) with HBO, free doughnuts and coffee, a 24hr. restaurant, and free local calls. (☎672-4533 or 877-578-4836. $5 key deposit. 21+. Singles and doubles from $40.) Farther away but more scenic, **Lake Thunderbird State Park ❶** has campsites on swimmer-friendly Lake Thunderbird. Take I-40 16 mi. east to Exit 166, then go 10 mi. south on Choctaw Rd. until the road ends. The park is 1 mi. to the east. (☎360-3572. Showers. Reception M-F 8am-5pm. Sites $8, with water and electricity $16-25; fully-equipped huts $45. Day-use free.)

🔲🔳 FOOD AND NIGHTLIFE. Look for restaurants and bars in the **Paseo Arts District** (Dewey and 30th St.) and along **Western Avenue** (between 36th St. and Wilshire Blvd.). Several Asian restaurants cluster near **Classen Boulevard** and **28th Street.** In the Paseo Arts District, **Galileo Bar & Grill ❸,** 3009 Paseo St., draws a crowd of teens, college kids, yuppies, and families. (☎415-7827. Specialty martinis $5.50-7. Gourmet pizzas $8. Entrees $7-20. Open Tu-Sa 11am-2am, Su 11am-midnight. AmEx/D/MC/V.) Drawing the barbecue faithful, **Leo's Original BBQ ❶,** 3631 N. Kelley St., is a hickory-smoking outfit in the northwest reaches of town. The strawberry banana cake ($3 per slice), served warm, is heavenly. (☎424-5367. Beef brisket sandwich and baked potato $5. Open M-Sa 11am-8pm. AmEx/D/MC/V.)

Bricktown, just east of downtown, is an old warehouse district turned yuppie entertainment district. It has a 1 mi. canal system inspired by San Antonio's Riverwalk. The **Bricktown Brewery,** 1 N. Oklahoma St., at Sheridan Ave., brews five beers daily ($3.25) in an appropriately brick building. (☎232-2739. Sandwiches and burgers $7-8. Upstairs 21+. Live music F-Sa; cover $5-15. Open M-Th 11am-midnight, F-Sa 11am-2am.) **City Walk,** 70 N. Oklahoma, houses seven clubs under one roof. Judge a bikini contest at Tequila Park, line dance inside City Limits, or sing along at Stooge's piano bar. (☎232-9255. 21+. Cover $5-8. Open F-Sa 8pm-2am.)

SIGHTS AND ENTERTAINMENT. The **Oklahoma City National Memorial,** at 5th and Harvey St., downtown, is a haunting testimonial to the victims of the 1995 bombing of the Murrah Federal Building. Outside lies the Field of Empty Chairs (one for each of the 169 victims), a stone gate, and a reflecting pool. The memorial is especially powerful at night, when each chair is illuminated. Indoors, the excellent museum traces the story of the bombing from the first few minutes to the immediate and long-term relief efforts and investigation using photographs, salvaged wreckage, teddy bears that miraculously survived the bombing, and media coverage from around the world. (☎235-3313; www.nps.gov/okci. Memorial: Open 24hr. Free. Museum: Open M-Sa 9am-6pm, Su 1-6pm. $8, seniors $7, students $6, under 6 free.) **Old Cowtown** is a shopping district designed for tourists, but at its heart is a real deal: the **Oklahoma City Stockyards,** 2500 Exchange Ave. (☎235-8675), the busiest in the world. Cattle auctions (M-W) begin at 8am and may last into the night. Visitors enter for free via a catwalk that soars over cattle herds from the parking lot northeast of the auction house. The **National Cowboy and Western Heritage Museum,** 1700 NE 63rd St., houses an extensive collection of Western art as well as exhibits on rodeos and Native Americans. In the entrance hall, James Earle Fraser's poignant sculpture *The End of the Trail* symbolizes the fate of Native Americans in the West. (☎478-2250; www.nationalcowboymuseum.org. Open daily 9am-5pm. $8.50, seniors $7, ages 6-12 $4. AAA discount $1.) An oasis in the city, the downtown **Myriad Gardens,** 301 W. Reno Ave., is a 17-acre botanical garden with flora ranging from desert to rainforest. Seventy feet in diameter, the cylindrical **Crystal Bridge** provides a unique setting for a tropical conservatory. (☎297-3995. Gardens: Open daily 7am-11pm. Free. Crystal Bridge: Open M-Sa 9am-6pm, Su noon-6pm. $6, students and seniors $5, ages 4-12 $3.) The **Oklahoma City Museum of Art,** 415 Couch Dr., has a standard collection of modern and classical art, but the dazzling and wildly inventive **Dale Chihuly glass pieces** are alone worth the price of admission. (☎236-3100. Open Tu-W and F-Sa 10am-5pm, Th 10am-9pm, Su noon-5pm. $9; children, seniors, and students $7; under 5 free.) The **45th Infantry Division Museum,** 2145 NE 36th St., stocks artifacts from the Oklahoma-based 45th infantry division, covering the period from the Civil War to the Persian Gulf War. (☎424-5313. Open Tu-F 9am-4:15pm, Sa 10am-4:15pm, Su 1-4:15pm. Free.)

Oklahoma City hosts the **Red Earth Festival** (☎427-5228; in late June) is one of America's most unique celebrations of American Indian cultures and traditions. The **World Championship Quarter Horse Show** (www.aqha.com) is held in the convention center each year in mid-November.

DAYTRIPS FROM OKLAHOMA CITY. A college town with a charming Main Street, located 20 mi. south of Oklahoma City on I-35, **Norman** is home to the **University of Oklahoma (OU).** The **Fred Jones, Jr. Museum of Art** is a work of art in itself; nine hut-like galleries are connected by glass hallways. *(555 Elm Ave. ☎325-3272; www.ou.edu/fjjma. Open Tu-W and F-Sa 10am-5pm, Th 10am-9pm, Su 1-5pm. $5, seniors $4, ages 6-17 $3; Tu free.)* The **Sam Noble Oklahoma Museum of Natural History,** at the southwest corner of the OU campus, has standard exhibits on prehistoric creatures and civilizations. Ride the "dinovator" 26 ft. up to stare down the world's largest apatosaurus skeleton. *(2401 Chautauqua Ave. ☎325-4712; www.snomnh.ou.edu. Open Tu-Sa 10am-5pm, Su 1-5pm. $5, seniors $4, ages 6-17 $3.)*

GREAT PLAINS

As the location of the land grant office, **Guthrie** rose to prominence during the 1889 Land Run. The most cultured and elegant city in Oklahoma at the turn of the century, Guthrie even served as the state's first capital, though its reign only lasted three years. Nowadays, Guthrie boasts the world's largest contiguous national historic district in the country, with 400 blocks of outstanding Victorian architecture. Pick up maps and guides at the **Visitors Center.** *(212 W. Oklahoma Ave. ☎800-299-1889. Open M-F 9am-5pm.)* Guthrie is also home to the largest Masonic Temple in the world, the ◨**Scottish Rite Masonic Temple.** Guided 1¾hr. tours cover the exquisite architecture and furnishings of 12 period rooms and two auditoriums in this 6½ acre masterpiece of a building. *(900 E. Oklahoma Ave. ☎282-1281. Tours M-F 10am and 2pm. $5, children and students free.)* The **Oklahoma Territorial Museum** tells the history surrounding the stampede-like land runs that were unique to this state. *(402 E. Oklahoma Ave. ☎282-1889. Open M-Sa 8am-5pm. Suggested donation $2.)*

TEXAS

The way Texans talk about their state, you'd think Texas was its own country—actually, it *was* its own country from 1836 to 1845. The fervently proud, independent citizens of the "Lone Star State" seem to prefer it that way, with their official road signs that proclaim "Don't Mess With Texas." After revolting against the Spanish in 1821 and splitting from Mexico in 1836, the Republic of Texas stood alone until 1845, when it entered the Union as the 28th state. The state's unofficial motto proclaims that "everything is bigger in Texas." This truth is evident in prolific wide-rimmed hats, boat-sized American autos, giant ranch spreads, countless steel skyscrapers, and oil refineries the size of small towns.

HIGHLIGHTS OF TEXAS

LICK your fingers after digging into some of the US's best barbecue at **Clark's Outpost,** near Dallas (p. 639).

REMEMBER the Alamo and wander the Riverwalk in **San Antonio** (below).

PULL on your cowboy boots and place your bid at the largest **livestock auction** in the country (p. 656).

▶ PRACTICAL INFORMATION

Capital: Austin.

Visitor Info: Texas Transportation Information Centers, ☎800-452-9292. For a free guidebook, call **Texas Tourism**, ☎800-888-8839; www.traveltex.com. **Texas Parks and Wildlife Department**, Austin Headquarters Complex, 4200 Smith School Rd., Austin, TX 78744 (☎800-792-1112).

Postal Abbreviation: TX. **Sales Tax:** 6-8.25%.

SAN ANTONIO   ☎210

Though best known as the home of the Alamo, the symbol of Texas's break from Mexico, San Antonio is better defined by its integration of Anglo and Hispanic cultures. The city proudly revels in its Mexican heritage, with missions, mariachis, and margaritas around every corner. San Antonio is definitely the biggest tourist destination in Texas, attracting eight million tourists each year to its easily walkable downtown, one-of-a-kind Riverwalk, and laidback atmosphere.

▆ TRANSPORTATION

Airport: San Antonio International Airport (SAT), 9800 Airport Blvd. (☎207-3411; www.sanantonio.gov/airport), 10 mi. north of town at I-410 and U.S. 281. Bus #2 runs downtown to Market and Alamo ($1). Taxi to downtown $18-20.

Trains: Amtrak, 350 Hoefgen St. (☎223-3226; www.amtrak.com), just north of the Alamodome and south of Commerce St. To: **Austin** (2½hr., 1 per day, $10-31); **Dallas** (5-7hr., 1 per day, $26-52); **El Paso** (12½hr., 1 per day, $52-82); **Houston** (5hr., 1 per day, $67-105). Open daily midnight-8:15am and 9:30am-midnight.

Texas

Buses: Greyhound, 500 N. Saint Mary's St. (☎270-5834; www.greyhound.com). To **Dallas** (5-6hr., 11 per day, $35) and **Houston** (3½hr., 8 per day, $26). Open 24hr.

Public Transit: VIA Metropolitan Transit. Downtown info center at 260 E. Houston St. (☎475-9008. Open M-F 7am-6pm, Sa 9am-2pm.) Buses operate daily 5am-midnight; many routes stop at 6pm. Infrequent service to outlying areas. $1; transfers $0.15. Day pass $3.75. Also runs historic **streetcars** every 10min. on 4 color-coded routes to most attractions downtown. All 4 routes converge at the **Riverwalk Streetcar Station** on Alamo St. between Commerce St. and Market St.

Taxi: Yellow Checker Cab, ☎222-2222.

ORIENTATION AND PRACTICAL INFORMATION

The Alamo is the historic heart of San Antonio. The **Central Business District,** under which the Riverwalk runs, is just west of the Alamo. Major sights such as Market Square and HemisFair Park are within walking distance of the Alamo and are inside the inner loop formed by **I-35, I-37,** and **I-10.** Everything else worth seeing will be within the I-410 loop, which circles San Antonio with a 6 mi. radius.

Visitor Info: San Antonio Visitor Information Center, 317 Alamo Pl. (☎800-447-3372; www.sanantoniovisit.com), across from the Alamo. Open daily 9am-5pm.

Hotlines: Rape Crisis, ☎349-7273. Operates 24hr. **Supportive Services for the Elderly and Disabled,** ☎337-3550. Operates M-F 8am-noon and 1-5pm.

Medical Services: Metropolitan Methodist Hospital, 1310 McCullough Ave. (☎208-2200).

Internet Access: San Antonio Public Library, 600 Soledad St. (☎207-2500). Free. Open M-Th 9am-9pm, F-Sa 9am-5pm, Su 11am-5pm.

Post Office: 615 E. Houston St. (☎800-275-8777), 1 block from the Alamo. Open M-F 9am-5pm. **Postal Code:** 78205.

▐▗ ACCOMMODATIONS

For cheap motels, try **Roosevelt Avenue, Fredericksburg Road,** or **Broadway,** between downtown and Brackenridge Park. Frontage roads along **I-35** north of downtown and the **Austin Highway (Rte. 368)** are also dotted with cheaper and often safer lodgings several miles from downtown.

▓ **Bullis House Inn San Antonio International Hostel,** 621 Pierce St. (☎223-9426). From Broadway, turn right on Grayson and go ¾ mi. The #20 bus runs on Carson St. 2 blocks south. 42 beds and a pool. The main house is a B&B where the rooms have cable and queen beds. Breakfast $5. Key deposit $10. Reception daily 8am-10pm. Dorms $25. Rooms $50-$99. AmEx/MC/V. ❶/❸

▓ **Alamo KOA,** 602 Gembler Rd. (☎224-9296 or 800-562-7783), 6 mi. from downtown. Bus #24. From I-35 N, take SBC Center Pkwy. and turn left on Gembler Rd. This huge RV campground has an area with lots of grass and shade for tent campers. Amenities include a free movies, grill, laundry facilities, pool, and showers. Reception daily 8am-8:30pm. Sites $25, each additional person $3. D/MC/V. ❶

Delux Inn, 3370 I-35 N (☎271-3100), off Exit 160, 4 mi. from downtown. Reasonably priced, clean rooms with fridge, HBO, microwave, and safe. Singles M-Th and Su $38, F-Sa $58; doubles $45/68. AAA discount. AmEx/D/MC/V. ❷

▐▌ FOOD

Be prepared to pay dearly for dining along the **Riverwalk.** On weekends, hundreds of food booths crowd **Market Square.** Late in the day, prices drop and vendors are willing to negotiate. For quirky, eclectic food, head to the artsy neighborhood of **King William** on Alamo St. south of town or St. Mary's Street north of town. The Texas original diner **Pig Stand** has several locations around town, some of them even open 24hr.

▓ **Madhatters,** 320 Beauregard St. (☎212-4832; www.madhatterstea.com), at S. Alamo St., on the Blue streetcar line. Madhatters brews the best tea this side of the rabbit hole. Free Wi-Fi. Full-out tea parties available ($18 for 2 people). Quality breakfasts $4. Lunch $5. Open M-F 7am-9pm, Sa 9am-9pm, Su 9am-6pm. AmEx/D/MC/V. ❶

▓ **Liberty Bar,** 328 E. Josephine St. (☎227-1187; www.liberty-bar.com), at Ave. A. Bus #7 or 8. Only the freshest produce and cuts of meat are used in Liberty Bar's Napa Valley-inspired cuisine, and almost nothing is above $13. Try the Karkade, an iced hibiscus and mint tea mixed with fresh ginger and white grape juice ($2.50). Sandwiches run $6-9. Open M-Sa 11:30am-10:30pm, Su 10:30am-10pm. Bar open until midnight or 1am. AmEx/D/MC/V. ❷

Josephine St. Steaks/Whiskey, 400 Josephine St. (☎224-6169), just west of Hwy. 281. Rough-hewn home cookin' is the daily special here. Take your arteries for a ride with the chicken-fried steak sandwich ($9) or the bacon-wrapped filet steak ($12). Lunch specials $6.50-8.50. Open M-Th 11am-10pm, F-Sa 11am-11pm. AmEx/D/MC/V. ❸

◎ SIGHTS

COLONIAL SAN ANTONIO

THE ALAMO. Built as a Spanish mission during the colonization of the New World, **The Alamo** has come to represent those who fought for Texas's independence and serves as a touchstone of Lone Star pride. For 12 days in 1836, a motley crew of Americans, Europeans, and Hispanic *tejanos* defended the Alamo against the army of Mexican general Santa Ana, who was determined to reclaim the land for Mexico. On the 13th day, all 189 men were killed. The massacre united Texans behind the independence movement, and "Remember the Alamo!" became the rallying cry for Sam Houston's ultimately victorious forces. The site is presently under the stewardship of the Daughters of the Republic of Texas, who maintain museum exhibits, historic weapons including Jim Bowie's famous knife, and shrines to the fallen heroes. Historical talks are given every 30min. *(At the center of Alamo Pl. ☎ 225-1391; www.thealamo.org. Open M-Sa 9am-5:30pm, Su 10am-5:30pm. Free.)*

MISSIONS. Four missions built in the 1720s and 30s converted Native Americans to Catholicism and supplied San Antonio with agricultural products. Today they make up the **San Antonio Missions National Historical Park.** Stretching 23 mi. south of the city along the San Antonio River, they are connected by the brown-signed Mission Trail road, which begins at the Alamo. Stopping at each mission takes a good half-day; some may wish to see only the first two. The missions are connected by biking and hiking trails, and the first two are served by Bus #42. The first is **Mission Concepción,** the oldest unrestored stone church in North America, where visitors can watch skilled craftsmen uncovering colorful frescoes on the walls. *(807 Mission Rd. ☎ 534-1540.)* **Mission San José,** the "Queen of the Missions," is the largest of the four and home to the park's Visitors Center. Most of the compound has been rebuilt and restored to its original grandeur. Catholic masses are held each Sunday at 7:30 (in Spanish), 9, and 10:30am—the noon "Mariachi Mass" is always packed. *(6701 San José Dr. ☎ 932-1001; www.nps.gov/saan.)*

SPANISH GOVERNOR'S PALACE. When San Antonio was the capital of Texas, the seat of the government was the **Spanish Governor's Palace,** just east of Market Sq. This museum is restored with period furniture, and the staff is happy to recount history. *(105 Plaza de Armas. ☎ 224-0601. Open M-Sa 9am-5pm, Su 10am-5pm. $1.50, ages 7-13 $0.75.)* Across the plaza is **San Fernando Cathedral,** the oldest cathedral in the United States. *(115 Main Plaza. ☎ 227-1297; www.sfcathedral.org. Free.)*

DOWNTOWN SAN ANTONIO

RIVERWALK. After the Alamo, the most famous symbol of San Antonio is its 2½ mi. long **Riverwalk (Paseo del Rio),** built in the 1930s by the WPA as a combination flood control and real estate project. Following the original course of the San Antonio River, it is a 3 ft. deep river lined on both sides with shaded pathways, picturesque gardens, shops, and cafes, all of which are below street level. The Riverwalk is touristy, but it is free and immensely pleasurable to simply walk along the riverbanks. Along the southern arm of Riverwalk is **La Villita,** a Spanish-style artisan village where the public can watch artists work and purchase their creations. *(418 Villita. ☎ 207-8610. Shops open daily 10am-6pm.)* **Market Square** is a part-open-air, part-enclosed market where customers can barter with vendors. Weekends feature the upbeat tunes of *tejano* bands with a backbeat of buzzing frozen margarita machines. *(Between San Saba and Santa Rosa St. ☎ 207-8600. Shops open daily June to mid-Sept. 10am-8pm; mid-Sept. to May 10am-6pm.)* The **King William District** is a charming residential neighborhood along S. St. Mary's St., just south of downtown. Origi-

TEXAS

Downtown San Antonio

ACCOMMODATIONS

Alamo KOA, **7**
Bullis House Inn San Antonio International Hostel, **4**
Delux Inn, **5**

FOOD

Josephine St. Steaks/ Whiskey, **2**
Liberty Bar, **1**
Madhatters, **9**

NIGHTLIFE

Cowboys Dance Hall, **6**
Jim Cullum's Landing, **8**
Sam's Burger Joint, **3**

nally settled by German immigrants, the community's architecture makes for fine strolling and gallery-hopping.

HEMISFAIR PARK. Created for the 1968 World's Fair, **HemisFair Park,** on S. Alamo, contains an array of 60s era architecture, as well as the new convention center. The 750 ft. observation deck of the **Tower of the Americas** allows visitors to get a different view of the city *(600 Hemisfair Plaza Way.* ☎ *223-3101; www.toweroftheamericas.com. Open M-Th and Su 10am-10pm, F-Sa 10am-11pm. $11, seniors $10, children $9.)* At the southeast corner of the park, the **Institute of Texan Cultures** documents the histories and contributions of 20 different ethnic groups in Texas, from Czech to Chinese to Swedish. *(801 S Bowie St.* ☎ *458-2300; www.the-museum.org. Open Tu-Sa 10am-6pm, Su noon-5pm. $7, seniors $4, ages 3-12 $4.)*

ST. PAUL SQUARE. South of Commerce St. and east of I-37, **St. Paul Square** is San Antonio's former red-light district. These alleys and cobblestone streets were the center of San Antonio's speakeasy scene during Prohibition and hosted some of the biggest names in jazz. In the 60s, the largely black surrounding neighborhoods were razed to make room for HemisFair Park and, later, for the $187 million **Alamodome.** Amtrak still stops in St. Paul Square, but the old Southern Pacific Depot now belongs to **Sunset Station,** a concert venue. Pick up a free self-guided tour of the beautifully restored 1902 depot as well as the surrounding neighborhood.

OUTSIDE THE CITY CENTER

MUSEUMS. The **San Antonio Museum of Art** is housed in the former Lone Star Brewery. In addition to Egyptian, Oceanic, and Asian art, in 1998 the museum established the **Nelson A. Rockefeller Center for Latin American Art,** the first of its kind in the US. Highlights include works by Diego Rivera. *(200 W. Jones Ave. Bus #7.* ☎ *978-8100; www.samuseum.org. Open Tu 10am-8pm, W-Sa 10am-5pm, Su noon-6pm. $8, seniors $7, students $5, ages 4-11 $3; Tu 4-8pm free.)* Housed in the Spanish Mission-style McNay mansion in swanky Alamo Heights, the **McNay Art Museum** displays the collection of Impressionist, Post-Impressionist, and Expressionist masterpieces accumulated by Mrs. McNay, who stirred up controversy in the early 20th century as the first promoter of modern art in otherwise conservative Texas. The museum and 23-acre grounds are free to the public. *(6000 N. New Braunfels Ave., 3 mi. north off Broadway.* ☎ *805-1756; www.mcnayart.org. Open Tu-F 10am-4pm, Th 10am-9pm, Sa 10am-5pm, Su noon-5pm. Grounds open daily 7am-7pm.)*

BRACKENRIDGE PARK. For diversion and greenery, head north to Brackenridge Park, whose 343 acres contain bike trails, a driving range, and a miniature train. *(Train runs daily 9:30am-6:30pm. $2.50, children $2.)* The Japanese-in-name-only Japanese tea garden is a startlingly peaceful place in the middle of the city. *(3910 N. Saint Mary's St. Open 5am-11pm.)*

🎵 🎭 ENTERTAINMENT AND NIGHTLIFE

The **Fiesta San Antonio** (☎ 227-5191; www.fiesta-sa.org; April 18-27, 2008 ushers in spring with concerts, carnivals, and hoopla in honor of Texas's many heroes and cultures. The Battle of Flowers Parade is a long-standing San Antonio tradition that began as a reenactment of the Battle of San Jacinto, using floral ammunition. In an event known as **First Fridays,** the art galleries in the King William District open their doors to the public on the first Friday of each month, also providing free food and drink. The **Theatre District,** just north of the Riverwalk, puts on concerts, operas, and plays in three restored 50s movie houses. At night, the northern half of the Riverwalk transforms into a nightlife hub, albeit an expensive one. Clusters of funky independent bars and clubs can be found in the artsy residential areas of King William, N. St. Mary's St. (around Woodlawn Ave.), and Josephine St. The *Friday Express* or weekly *Current* (available at the tourist office and many businesses in town) are guides to concerts and entertainment. The Alamodome is home to the 2007 NBA Champion **San Antonio Spurs** (☎444-5000; www.spurs.com) played here for just 10 years before moving to the SBC Center in 2002. The Alamodome now hosts soccer, gymnastics, and the circus. *(100 Montana St., at Hoefgen St. Yellow streetcar stop. ☎207-3663.)*

Sam's Burger Joint, 330 E. Grayson St. (☎223-2830). Singer-songwriter open mic night W (no cover). Local rock bands play Th-Sa ($5-20 cover). While enjoying the show, try the "Big Monster Burger," a pound of beef for $7. M 7pm free swing dance lessons. Tu 10pm **Puro Poetry Slam** ($3 cover). Call for hours.

Jim Cullum's Landing, 123 Losoya St. (☎223-7266), on the Riverwalk. Old-time jazz by some old-timer musicians. Dixieland, bluegrass, jazz, swing, and standards. Cover M-Sa $6-8. Open M-F 4pm-midnight, Sa-Su noon-1am; band plays at 8pm.

Cowboys Dance Hall, 3030 Rte. 410 NE (☎646-9378). Plays 2 types of music—country and western. With a mechanical bull and 2 dance floors, you best bring your cowboy hat. Can't two-step? Don't worry: Th-Sa evenings begin with free dance lessons at 7pm. Th women free. 18+. Cover $3-20. Open W-Sa 8pm-3am.

AUSTIN   ☎512

Blending the trendiness of New York City's Soho and the mellowness of the West Coast, Austin is unlike any other place in Texas, making it an odd state capital. Refusing to turn into just another big city, Austin has maintained its soul, thanks in part to the "Keep Austin Weird" bumper sticker campaign. As the "Live Music Capital of the World" and home to 50,000 University of Texas (UT) students, liberal, alternative Austin is a lone star in the Lone Star State.

▐ TRANSPORTATION

Airport: Austin Bergstrom International (AUS), 3600 Presidential Blvd. (☎530-2242; www.ci.austin.tx.us/austinairport). Take Hwy. 71 4½ mi. east from I-35 or take bus #100 (Airport Flyer) or 350. Taxi to downtown $25.

Trains: Amtrak, 250 N. Lamar Blvd. (☎476-5684 or 800-872-7245; www.amtrak.com); take bus #38. Runs to **Dallas** (6hr., 2 per day, $30), **El Paso** (9hr., 3 per week, $131), and **San Antonio** (3½hr., 1 per day, $15).

Buses: Greyhound, 916 E. Koenig Ln. (☎458-4463 or 800-231-2222; www.greyhound.com), 3 mi. north of downtown at Exit 238A off I-35. Station open 24hr. Runs to **Dallas** (3hr., 8 per day, $30), **Houston** (3½hr., 7 per day, $34), and **San Antonio** (2hr., 9 per day, $16). Buses #7 and 15 stop across the street.

Public Transit: Capitol Metro, 323 Congress Ave. (☎474-1200 or 800-474-1201; www.capmetro.org). The office has plenty of maps and schedules. Buses run 4am-midnight, but most start later and end earlier. Office open M-F 7:30am-5:30pm. $0.50; students $0.25; seniors, children, and disabled free. Day pass $1. The **'Dillo Bus Service** runs downtown on Congress, Lavaca, San Jacinto, and 6th St. Most buses operate M-F every 10-15min.; off-peak service varies. Moonlight and Starlight 'Dillos F and Sa 6pm-3am. The 'Dillos, which look like trolleys, are always free. Free park 'n' ride lots at most 'Dillo terminals.

Taxi: American Yellow Checker Cab, ☎452-9999.

Bike Rental: Yellow bicycles are "free to ride but not to keep" as part of an effort to refurbish donated bikes for public use. Make sure to leave the bike in a conspicuous spot for the next person. **Waterloo Cycles,** 2815 Fruth St. (☎472-9253) rents bikes. Daily bike rental M-F $10-15 per day, Sa-Su $15-20 per day; includes helmet. Lock rental $5 for first day, $1.50 per day thereafter. Open M-W and F-Sa 10am-7pm, Th 10am-8pm, Su noon-5pm.

◆❷ ORIENTATION AND PRACTICAL INFORMATION

Downtown Austin sits on the north bank of the Colorado River, between **Mopac Expressway/Route 1** and **I-35,** two freeways that run north-south and parallel to one another. There are no cross-town freeways until **U.S. 290,** 3 mi. south of downtown. UT students converge on **Guadalupe Street ("The Drag"),** where music stores and cheap restaurants thrive. All downtown streets are oriented around the commanding **State Capitol,** with **Congress Avenue's** upscale eateries and classy shops leading directly toward the capitol. Funkier **South Congress (SoCo)** offers a mix of antique and thrift stores across the river, while downtown teems with nightlife, centered on **6th Street** and the **Warehouse District.** Austinites enjoy one of the country's largest greenbelt systems in the country with numerous trails and pools.

Visitor Info: Austin Convention and Visitors Bureau/Visitors Information Center, 209 E. 6th St. (☎478-0098 or 866-462-8784; www.austintexas.org). Open M-F 9am-5pm, Sa-Su 9am-6pm. Sponsors free walking tours of the capitol, downtown, UT, and historic neighborhoods Mar.-Nov. Call 454-1545 for more info.

Medical Services: St. David's Medical Center, 919 E. 32nd St. (☎476-7111). Exit 136 off I-35, north of UT. Open 24hr.

Hotlines: Crisis Intervention Hotline, ☎472-4357. **SafePlace (Austin Rape Crisis Center Hotline),** ☎267-7233. Both operate 24hr. **Outyouth Gay/Lesbian Helpline,** ☎800-969-6884. Operates M-Sa 6:30am-9pm.

Internet Access: Austin Public Library, 800 Guadalupe St. (☎974-7400). Free. 2hr. max; ID required. Open M-Th 10am-9pm, F-Sa 10am-6pm, Su noon-6pm.

Post Office: 510 Guadalupe St. (☎494-2210), at 6th St. Open M-F 8:30am-6pm. **Postal Code:** 78701.

⌂ ACCOMMODATIONS

Like its off-beat personality, Austin offers some funky, alternative budget options in addition to the standard hostels and campgrounds. ■**Co-ops** at UT peddle rooms with free meals to hostelers during the summer when school is out. (Call ☎476-5678, or check www.collegehouses.coop to find contact info for individual houses.) The **Austin Area Bed & Breakfast Association** (☎800-972-2333; www.austinareabandb.com.) coordinates several historic B&Bs, most of which start at $100 per night. Chain motels line I-35 running north and south of downtown.

21st St. Co-op, 707 W. 21st St. (☎476-5678). Take the red 'Dillo or bus #3. The spirit of the 60s lives on in this treehouse-style co-op. Colorful suites have private bedrooms. Kitchens and common rooms on each fl. Linen included. A/C. Free Wi-Fi. When you arrive, ask for the membership coordinator to set you up with a room. Single room and 3 meals per day $20. Cash only. ❶

Pearl St. Co-op, 2000 Pearl St., one block west of 21st St. Co-op (☎476-5678). Pearl St. offers similar single rooms and the same amenities, meals, and prices as 21st St. but is slightly more orderly and less colorful. Pool and sundeck. Free Wi-Fi. Cash only. ❶

McKinney Falls State Park, 5808 McKinney Falls Pkwy. (☎243-1643, reservations 389-8900), southeast of the city. Turn right on Burleson off Rte. 71 E, then right on McKinney Falls Pkwy. Campsites with ample shade and privacy near excellent swim-

Downtown Austin

🏠🏕 ACCOMMODATIONS
21st St. Co-op, **5**
McKinney Falls State Park, **11**
Pearl St. Co-op, **4**

🍎 FOOD
Bouldin Creek, **9**
The Kerbey Lane Cafe, **2**
Magnolia Cafe, **10**
Whole Foods Market, **6**

🌙 NIGHTLIFE
Alamo Drafthouse Cinema, **7**
Hole in the Wall, **3**
Oilcan Harry's, **8**
Spiderhouse, **1**

TEXAS

ming and 6 mi. of hiking trails. Gates open daily 8am-10pm. Primitive sites (accessible only by foot) $12, with water and electricity $16. Screen shelters sleep up to 8 for $37 (no cots or bedding provided). Day use $4 per person, under 13 free. ❶

🍴 FOOD

Cheap fast food and takeout are abundant near the UT campus on **Guadalupe Street.** Patrons can often enjoy free or cheap appetizers with their drinks during happy hour in the **6th Street** clubs. South of the river, **Barton Springs Road** and **S. Congress Street** are home to a range of cuisines, including Mexican and barbecue joints. The **Warehouse District** has swankier options. **Wheatsville Food Co-op,** 3101 Guadalupe St., is the place to go for groceries. (☎478-2667. Open daily 9am-11pm.)

📷 **Magnolia Cafe,** 1920 S. Congress Ave. (☎445-0000); also at 2304 Lake Austin Blvd. (☎478-8645). Blending Tex-Mex, California cuisine, and diner fare, Magnolia serves exotic dishes at not-so-exotic prices. Try the tropical turkey tacos, with turkey, cheese, pico de gallo, and pineapple (2 for $6.75). Open 24hr. AmEx/D/MC/V. ❷

📷 **Bouldin Creek,** 1501 S. 1st St. (☎416-1601), at Elizabeth St. Cheap and delicious vegetarian and vegan food. Full coffee bar and bakery with salads, sandwiches, tacos, and omelets all day. The portobello tacos ($5) are heavenly. Free Wi-Fi, books, and board games. Beer and wine. Open M-F 7am-midnight, Sa-Su 9am-midnight. MC/V. ❶

📷 **Whole Foods Market,** 525 N. Lamar Blvd. (☎476-1206), at 6th St. The organic, all-natural chain was started in Austin, and this flagship store opened in 2005 with 80,000 sq. ft., a walk-in beer cooler, and in-house nut roasteries and fish smokeries. One third of the store is set aside for takeout and prepared foods. Outdoor patio, stream, and roof terrace. Free beer and wine tastings. Free Wi-Fi. Open daily 8am-10pm; coffee bar opens 6am. AmEx/D/MC/V. ❷

👁 SIGHTS

GOVERNMENT. Proving that everything is bigger in Texas, Texans built their **State Capitol** seven feet taller than its federal counterpart. It gets its pink hue from the Texas red granite that was used instead of more traditional limestone. The capitol, its dome, the legislative chambers, and the underground extension are all open to the public. *(At Congress Ave. and 11th St. ☎463-0063. Open M-F 7am-10pm, Sa-Su 9am-8pm. Short tours M-F every 15-30min. 8:30am-4:30pm, Sa 9:30am-3:30pm, Su noon-3:30pm. Free.)* The **Capitol Visitors Center** has exhibits on the capitol's history and construction. *(112 E. 11th St. ☎305-8400. Open M-Sa 9am-5pm, Su noon-5pm. Free 2hr. parking at 12th and San Jacinto St. garage.)* Don't miss the chance to look at Dubya's old stomping grounds at the **Texas Governor's Mansion.** *(1010 Colorado St. ☎463-5516. Free tours M-Th every 20min. 10-11:40am.)*

MUSEUMS. Before the Bushes, there was another cowboy President from Texas. The 📷**Lyndon B. Johnson Library and Museum** sets the public and personal life of the Texas native—who is known for the "Great Society" and his public policy during the Vietnam War—against the backdrop of a broader history of the American Presidency. A life-sized animatronic LBJ tells jokes and anecdotes on the second floor, while the 10th floor features a model of the Oval Office and an exhibit on Lady Bird Johnson, a great leader in her own right. *(2313 Red River St. Take bus #20. ☎721-0200; www.lbjlib.utexas.edu. Open daily 9am-5pm. Free.)* Texas has a history befitting its size, and it takes a three-story museum to tell it. The **Bob Bullock Texas State History Museum** traces Texas's nearly 500 years of Western settlement, with the usual hero-worship of Travis, Houston, and Austin tempered by balanced looks at the lives of minorities and Texas's economy and culture over the years. *(1800 N. Congress Ave. ☎936-8746; www.thestoryoftexas.com. Open M-Sa 9am-6pm, Su noon-6pm. $5.50,* *seniors $4.50, ages 5-18 $3.)* The downtown **Austin Museum of Art** displays traveling exhibits of contemporary art, from photography to painting to mixed media. *(823 Congress Ave., at 9th St. ☎495-9224; www.amoa.org. Open Tu-W and F-Sa 10am-6pm, Th 10am-8pm, Su noon-5pm. M and W-Su $5, seniors and students $4, under 12 free; Tu $1.)* A second branch, at 3809 W. 35th St., is housed in a Mediterranean-style villa in a beautiful country setting with an exquisite sculpture garden. *(Open daily 11am-4pm. Free.)* The **Mexic-Arte Museum** features traveling exhibits by Mexican, Mexican-American, and Latino artists and seeks to promote cross-cultural learning and understanding. *(419 Congress Ave. ☎480-9373; www.mexic-artemuseum.org. Open M-Th 10am-6pm, F-Sa 10am-5pm, Su noon-5pm. $5, students and seniors $4, under 12 $1; Su free.)*

PARKS. Covert Park at Mount Bonnell offers a sweeping view of Lake Austin and Westlake Hills from the highest point in the city. *(3800 Mt. Bonnell Rd., off W. 35th St., 4 mi. northwest of town. Free.)* **Zilker Park**, just south of the Colorado River, has the standard recreational facilities plus several Austin-specific diversions. *(M-F free. Sa-Su parking $3.)* The **Botanical Gardens** contain a peaceful Japanese garden, a prehistoric garden that recreates the Cretaceous Period, and a garden that features plants native and well-adapted to Austin's climate. *(2100 Barton Springs Rd. Take bus #30. ☎477-8672. Open daily in summer 7am-7pm; low season 7am-5pm. Free.)* The **Umlauf Sculpture Garden** showcases the work of the late Charles Umlauf, longtime UT professor and prolific sculptor of wood, terra cotta, marble, and bronze. *(605 Robert E. Lee Rd., off Barton Springs Rd. ☎445-5582. Open W-F 10am-4:30pm, Sa-Su 1pm-4:30pm. $3.50, seniors $2.50, students $1.)* On hot days, Austinites flock to ◼**Barton Springs Pool,** a 1000 ft. long spring-fed swimming hole in Zilker Park. Flanked by walnut and pecan trees and with temperatures hovering around 68°F year-round, Barton Springs is a favorite destination of families by day and young people by night. *(☎974-6700. Open daily 5am-10pm; closed for cleaning Th 9am-7pm. $3, ages 12-17 $2, under 12 $1. Free daily 5-9am and 9-10pm.)*

The **Barton Springs Greenbelt** and several other creek trails around town offer good terrain for hiking and biking. Free spirits go *au naturel* in **Lake Travis** at **Hippie Hollow,** Texas's only public nude swimming and sunbathing haven, 15 mi. northeast of downtown. Take Mopac (Rte. 1) north to the F.M. 2222 Exit. Follow 2222 west and turn left at I-620; Comanche Tr. will be on the right. *(7000 Comanche Tr. ☎854-7275. 18+. Open daily May-Sept. 8am-9pm; Sept. 10-Oct. and Mar.-Apr. 9am-7:30pm; Nov.-Feb. 9am-6pm. No entry after 8:30pm. Cars $10, pedestrians $5.)* In a longstanding Austin tradition, folks congregate at sunset at **The Oasis,** just up the road from Hippie Hollow. With its 45 decks recently repaired from a 2006 fire, every one of the 2000 guests at this restaurant has an excellent view of the sunset over Lake Travis.

OTHER SIGHTS. In addition to its thriving nightlife, downtown Austin boasts some notable modern architecture. The new **City Hall** at 301 W. 2nd St., opened in 2004, is one of the most striking examples. The **University of Texas at Austin (UT)** is the wealthiest public university in the country, with an annual budget of over a bil-

 AUSTIN FOR POCKET CHANGE. Take advantage of the outdoors for free in Austin. Visit **Barton Springs Pool** (p. 637) before 9am or after 9pm, and swim as many laps as you can for free. Hike on up to **Covert Park** (p. 637) at Mount Bonnell for a beautiful view of the whole city, or visit the **Botanical Gardens** (p. 637) in Zilker Park. If you take one of the city's free yellow bicycles and skip the $3 parking fees, it's free. Before sunset, head over to the **Congress Avenue Bridge** to see the thousands of bats coming out of their perches. After dark, hit up a free concert at **Zilker Park** (p. 637), where the city hosts its bi-weekly Blues on the Green on alternating Wednesdays.

lion dollars, and, with over 50,000 students, is the backbone of the city's cultural life. The UT Tower, a landmark in the center of campus, was the site of the infamous Charles Whitman sniper shootings in 1966.

Just before dusk, head to the **Congress Avenue Bridge** and join thousands of others to watch the massive swarm of ▨**Mexican free-tail bats** emerge from their roosts to feed on the night's mosquitoes. When the bridge was reconstructed in 1980, the engineers unintentionally created crevices that formed ideal homes for the migrating bat colony. The city exterminated the night-flying creatures until **Bat Conservation International** moved to Austin to educate people about the benefits of their presence—the bats eat up to 3000 lb. of insects each night. Stand on the bridge itself to see the bats fly out from underneath, or on the southern riverbank under the bridge for a more panoramic view. *(www.batcon.org. For flight times, call the bat hotline at ☎ 416-5700, ext. 3636. Bats fly Mar.-Nov.)*

🎵🎭 ENTERTAINMENT AND NIGHTLIFE

Beverly Sheffield Zilker Hillside Theater (☎479-9491; www.zilker.org), across from Barton Springs pool, hosts free outdoor ballets, plays, musicals, and concerts most weekends from May to October. Entertainment industry giants and eager fans descend upon Austin for the 10-day **South by Southwest Music, Media, and Film Festival.** Nearly 1300 musical acts fill 50 stages, while movie screens show 180 films, making this festival the Southwest's premier entertainment event. (☎467-7979; www.sxsw.com. March 7-16, 2008.) The Austin Fine Arts Guild sponsors the **Fine Arts Festival,** April 12-13, 2008—featuring 200 national artists, local eateries, live music, and art activities. Austin's smaller events calendar is a mixed bag. Each spring, **Spamarama** (www.spamarama.com) gathers SPAM fans from all walks of life to pay homage to the often misunderstood meat. A cookoff, samplings, sports, and live music at the SPAM Jam are all in store.

Austin's title, "Live Music Capital of the World," is no exaggeration; on any given night, one can find literally any kind of music, from didgeridoo to jazz-rap fusion. Downtown, **6th St.** is lined with warehouse nightclubs and theme bars. Mellow night owls gather at the cocktail lounges in the **4th St. Warehouse District.** Along **Red River St.,** bars and hard-rocking clubs have less of the glamour but all of the grit of 6th St. The long-running PBS series **Austin City Limits** (www.austincitylimits.com) tapes shows with big music stars monthly at UT. Tickets are free but shows aren't announced until the morning of, and people wait in line all day. If you aren't in the mood to face club crowds, try Austin's regionally unparalleled coffeehouse scene, which is concentrated both near UT and south of the river. The weekly *Austin Chronicle* (www.austinchronicle.com) and *XL-ent* provide details on current music performances, shows, and movies.

▨ **Spiderhouse,** 2968 Fruth St. (☎480-9562), off Guadalupe St. near the UT campus. Serves a wide variety of beer (pints $2.50-3.50), wine, and liquor. Large, shaded cobblestone patio with nightly movie screenings. Free Wi-Fi. Live music W-Su runs the gamut from techno to jazz. No cover. Open daily 8am-2am.

Hole in the Wall, 2538 Guadalupe St. (☎477-4747), at 26th St. Its self-effacing name belies the popularity of this renowned music spot. Daily live music spanning all genres, usually 9-10pm. Happy hour all day M, Tu-F 1-10pm, Sa and Su noon-7pm. 21+. No cover. Open M-F 1pm-2am, Sa-Su noon-2am.

Oilcan Harry's, 211 W. 4th St. (☎320-8823). One of the biggest and best gay bars in all of Austin. Features 3 bars, a pool table, and an outdoor patio. Strippers perform Th and Sa-Su 10:30pm and midnight. Happy hour 2-10pm. 21+. No cover. Open daily 2pm-2am.

DALLAS   ☎214

Denim and diamonds define the Dallas decor, skyline, and attitude. Rugged western virility coupled with cosmopolitan offerings create the city's truly Texan aura. Big Tex, an enormous cowboy float in Fair Park, welcomes visitors to one of the country's finest collections of Asian art and a slew of restaurants. While the intrigue surrounding the assassination of President John F. Kennedy haunts the city to this day, Dallas views itself as a city imbued with a maverick's spirit where, even though an urban landscape has replaced the sprawling plains, "the people still swagger and the frontier still calls."

▐ TRANSPORTATION

Airport: Dallas-Fort Worth International (DFW; ☎972-574-8888; www.dfwairport.com) is halfway between Dallas and Fort Worth, accessible by Hwy. 183, Hwy. 114, and I-685. Catch the **Trinity Rail Express** (see below) to **Dallas** ($2.25) or **Fort Worth** ($1.25). For door-to-gate service, take the **Super Shuttle** (☎800-258-3826). 24hr. service. $27, each additional person $8.

Trains: Amtrak, 400 S. Houston St. (☎653-1101; www.amtrak.com), in Union Station. Open daily 10am-5:30pm. 1 train per day to **Austin** (6½hr., $30) and **Little Rock** (7½hr., $65).

Buses: Greyhound, 205 S. Lamar St. (☎655-7727; www.greyhound.com), 3 blocks east of Union Station. Open 24hr. To **Austin** (3hr., 11 per day, $32) and **Houston** (4hr., 9 per day, $35).

Public Transit: Dallas Area Rapid Transit (DART), 1401 Pacific Ave. (☎979-1111; www.dart.org.) Open M-F 6am-8pm, Sa-Su 8am-5pm. Buses depart from 2 downtown transfer centers, East (Pacific and Pearl St.) and West (Pacific and Griffin St.). Most buses run downtown daily 5:30am-9:30pm, to suburbs until 10pm. Get a map at any tourist office or transit station. Local fare $1.25, all-day pass $2.50; express and longer trips $2.25/4.50. **DART Light Rail** has 2 lines, Red and Blue, which converge downtown and branch out several miles north and south into the suburbs. Operates M-Sa 4am-midnight, Su 5am-midnight. Bus fares. The **M-Line Streetcar** is a free historic trolley that runs from the Downtown Arts District to Uptown along McKinney Ave. Runs M-F 7am-10pm, Sa 10am-10pm, Su 12:30-10pm. The **Trinity Rail Express (TRE)** is a commuter train service operating between Union Station and downtown Fort Worth (1hr.; M-F 22 per day, Sa 10 per day; $1.25-2.25).

Taxi: Yellow Cab Co. ☎426-6262.

▐▐ ORIENTATION AND PRACTICAL INFORMATION

Downtown Dallas is bounded by **The Mixer,** a highway loop formed by the intersections of **I-30, I-35E, I-45, U.S. 175,** and **U.S. 75.** North of downtown are the ritzy residential and shopping districts of **Turtle Creek, Oaklawn, Highland Park,** and **University Park,** as well as the **Lower Greenville** entertainment district. East of downtown are **Deep Ellum, Fair Park,** and **White Rock Lake.** The **I-635** loop surrounds Dallas. The lateral highways **I-20, I-30,** and **Hwy. 183** run east to **Fort Worth.** Beware of ravenous parking meters, which demand feeding until 10pm.

Visitor Info: Dallas Convention and Visitors Bureau, 100 S. Houston St. (☎571-1300 or 800-232-5527, 24hr. events hotline 571-1301; www.visitdallas.com), in the Old Red Courthouse. Free Internet access. Open M-F 8am-5pm, Sa-Su 9am-5pm.

GLBT Resources: Dallas Gay and Lesbian Community Center, 2701 Reagan St. (☎528-0144). Open M-F 9am-9pm, Sa-Su 9am-6pm.

Hotlines: Contact Counseling Crisis Line, ☎972-233-2233. 24hr.

Medical Services: Baylor University Medical Center, 3500 Gaston Ave. (☎820-0111).

Internet Access: Dallas Public Library, 1515 Young St. (☎670-1400), at Ervay St. Free. Limit 2 55min. sessions per day. Open M-Th 9am-9pm, F-Sa 9am-5pm, Su 1-5pm. Be careful around this area at night.

Post Office: 401 Dallas-Ft. Worth Tpk. (☎760-4545). Take Sylvan Exit. Open 24hr. **General Delivery** mail should be addressed to the downtown branch, located at 400 N. Ervay St. Open M-F 8:30am-5pm. **Postal Code:** 75201; for General Delivery 75221. **Area Codes:** 214, 972, and 817. In text, 214 unless otherwise noted.

⌂ ACCOMMODATIONS

Cheap hotel lodgings in Dallas are nearly impossible to come by; big events like college football's **Cotton Bowl** (Jan. 1, 2008) and the state fair held every October exacerbate the lodging problem. Look within 10 mi. of downtown along three of the major roads for inexpensive motels: north of downtown on **U.S. 75,** north along **I-35,** and east of **I-30.**

■ **The Hotel Lawrence,** 302 S. Houston St. (☎761-9090), conveniently located in the heart of downtown. A terrific value with stylish rooms, elegant ambience, and quality service in a historic hotel. Computer room, free fitness center, and a dining area. Free Wi-Fi. Breakfast included. Singles and doubles from $89-249. AmEx/D/MC/V. ❹

Dallas-Irving Backpacker's Stop, 214 W. 6th St., in Irving, TX, (☎972-255-9636) is located 10min. from Dallas and 20min. from Forth Worth, with local train access just 4 blocks away. With a home-away-from-home atmosphere, cable TV, free laundry facilities, full kitchen and common area, free Wi-Fi. 4 single sex dorm rooms with 4-12 beds. Dorms $20. ❶

Cedar Hill State Park (☎972-291-3900), 20min. from the city on Rte. 1382 off either U.S. 67 or I-20. 30 primitive walk-in sites and 320 sites with water and electricity nestled in a dense pine forest on a lake. Reserve at least 2 weeks in advance. Office open M-W and Su 7am-5pm, Th 8am-8pm, F-Sa 7am-10pm. 24hr. gate access with reservations. Primitive sites $7, with water and electricity $20. Park entry $5 per person. ❶

◖ FOOD

Dallas boasts that it has more restaurants per capita than New York City. The city offers eclectic dining options, coupling urban delights with tried-and-true Texan fare. For the lowdown on dining options, pick up "Startime," in the Friday *Star-Telegram.* Stock up on produce at the **farmers' market,** which takes place three blocks below Taylor St. downtown. (☎939-2808. Open daily 7am-6pm.)

■ **EatZi's,** 3403 Oaklawn Ave. (☎526-1515), at Lemmon Ave., located 1 mi. east of Oaklawn Exit from I-35 E. This grocery store, cafe, kitchen, and bakery is truly a culinary delight. Fabulous focaccia, sandwiches, and other delicacies. Fresh chef-prepared dinners ($5-10) 2-for-1 after 9pm. Sandwiches and salads $6-9. Open daily 7am-10pm. AmEx/D/MC/V. ❷

Urban Market, 1500 Jackson St. (☎741-3663). A market, cafe, and bar. Sandwiches $6. Entrees $8-11. Open M-F 7am-midnight, Sa 8am-midnight, Su 8am-3pm. ❷

Sol's Taco Lounge and Tango Bar, 2626 Commerce St. (☎651-7657). Heaping Tex-Mex combo plates ($7-10) alongside 8 different kinds of fajitas ($11-20). M selected food half-price. Happy hour M-F 3-9pm; $3 margaritas. Open M-Tu and Su 8am-11pm, W-Th 8am-12am, F-Sa 8am-3pm. AmEx/D/MC/V. ❷

TEXAS

Dallas Overview

▲ ACCOMMODATIONS
Dallas-Irving
Backpacker's Stop, **3**

■ NIGHTLIFE
Al Amir, **1**

FOOD
EatZi's, **2**

TO FORT WORTH
(32mi), **3** (12mi)

TO CEDAR HILLS
STATE PARK (20mi)

Dallas Love Field

MARKET
CENTER

UNIVERSITY
PARK

HIGHLAND
PARK

LOWER
GREENVILLE

DEEP
ELLUM

SEE DOWNTOWN
DALLAS MAP

TO
BLUE LINE (1.5mi)

Fair Park

Trinity River
Greenbelt

1 mile
1 kilometer

Downtown Dallas

▲ ACCOMMODATIONS
The Hotel Lawrence, **5**

FOOD
Sol's Taco Lounge and
Tango Bar, **3**
Urban Market, **4**

■ NIGHTLIFE
Club Dada, **2**
Trees, **1**

Baylor University
Medical Center

TO FAIR PARK
(1.5mi)

DEEP ELLUM

Exall Park

Central Expwy.

N. Good Latimer Expwy.

S. Good Latimer Expwy.

International
Marketplace and
Farmers Market

Old City Park

Pearl Expwy.

Meyerson
Symphony Center

Trammell Crow
Center

Dallas Museum
of Art

Nasher
Sculpture
Center

Fountain
Place

MCKINNEY AVE. TROLLEY

Cedar Springs Rd.

PEARL

ST. PAUL

AKARD

Public
Library

City Hall

Dallas Convention Center

DOWNTOWN

WEST END

Dallas World
Aquarium

Greyhound

Kennedy
Memorial

Dealey
Plaza

6th Floor
Museum

UNION
STATION

DOWNTOWN
CENTER

400 yards
400 meters

ON THE MENU

DAMN, THAT'S SMOKIN'

While good barbecue is plentiful in Texas, truly great barbecue is harder to find. **Clark's Outpost,** in Tioga, TX, about 1½hr. north of Dallas, is one of the best, most authentic barbecue joints around.

The restaurant has catapulted Tioga, a town that used to be marked only as the birthplace of country-music legend Gene Autry, into the barbecue spotlight. Clark's food is ecstasy-inducing, with brisket treated with a delectably spicy rub and slow-cooked for 3½ days, giving it the smoky-sweet tang and tender, succulent texture that define great barbecue. The unique "French fried corn-on-the-cob" has been fried just long enough to make each kernel crispy and buttery. Barbecue sauce is served warm in old beer bottles, and black-and-white photos of Wild West heroes, wagons, cow skulls, and boots adorn the walls. Longing for a brewski to top off that meal? Well, Tioga is in a dry county, but it's possible to get around the law by becoming a "member." Pay a one-time $3 membership fee and drink to your heart's content (by law, no more than three drinks in an hour and one drink per subsequent hour).

Clark's Outpost, 101 Hwy. 277 at Gene Autry Dr., Tioga, TX. ☎904-437-2414 or 800-932-5051. Beef sandwich $4.50. Dinner with brisket, vegetables, and Texas toast $9. Open M-Th 11am-9pm, F-Sa 11am-9:30pm, Su 11am-8:30pm.

👁 SIGHTS

Attractions in Dallas tend to be overpriced; admission-weary travelers may wish to take to the streets. Downtown's monuments to capitalism span a century of architecture, from Art Deco to I.M. Pei. Thanks to fountains, plenty of shade, and the Light Rail, these sights are surprisingly pedestrian-friendly.

JFK SIGHTS. John F. Kennedy's motorcade was passing through **Dealey Plaza** on Nov. 22, 1963 when bullets, most likely from the 6th floor of the Texas School Book Depository Building, mortally wounded the president. Today, in that same building, the **6th Floor Museum** traces the events of the assassination and the subsequent investigations, theories, and conspiracies. *(411 Elm St. on Dealey Plaza. ☎747-6660; www.jfk.org. Open M and Su noon-6pm, Tu-F 10am-6pm, Sa 10am-8pm. $10, ages 6-18, seniors, and students $9. Audio tour $3.50.)* The **Kennedy Memorial,** a sculpture by Philip Johnson, looms nearby at Market and Main St. Conspiracy hounds have expounded upon the missing pieces of the puzzle for decades.

ART AND ARCHITECTURE. The architecture of the **Dallas Museum of Art** is as graceful and beautiful as its impressive collections of Egyptian, African, early American, Impressionist, Modern, and decorative art. *(1717 N. Harwood St. ☎922-1200; www.dm-art.org. Open Tu-Su 11am-5pm, Th until 9pm. $10, ages 12-17 and seniors $7, students with ID $5. Admission includes audio tour. Free Th 5-9pm and 1st Tu of each month. Jazz concerts Th 9pm in summer.)* The **Nasher Sculpture Center** displays modern works both indoors and in the garden. Life-sized human sculptures reach heights of 100 ft. in *Walking to the Sky. (2001 Flora St. ☎242-5100. Open Tu-Su 11am-5pm, Th until 9pm. $10, seniors $7, students $5, under 12 free. Joint passes to the Museum of Art and Nasher Sculpture Center $16, seniors $12, students $8.)* Just across Harwood St., the **Crow Collection of Asian Art** has Japanese prints, Chinese jade, and Indian ivory carvings, among other pieces. *(2010 Flora St., at Hardwood and Olive St. ☎979-6430. Open Tu-Su 10am-5pm, Th until 9pm. Sculpture garden open 24hr. Free.)* Architect **I.M. Pei** lists several Dallas landmarks among his many achievements. The **Wells Fargo Building,** at Ross Ave. and Field St., makes an indelible mark on the city's skyline. **Fountain Place,** in the building's plaza, consists of cascading pools, fountains, and water gardens. Pei also designed downtown's **Energy Plaza,** at Bryan and Ervay St., and **One Dallas Center,** at Bryan St. between St. Paul and Harwood St., but it is the striking **City Hall,** at Ervay St. and Young St., that marked his career breakthrough.

FISH, FLORA, AND FLIGHT. The **Dallas World Aquarium** fits an awful lot into one urban city block, including leopards, manatees, and a multi-tiered rainforest. *(1801 N. Griffin St. ☎720-2224; www.dwazoo.com. Open daily 10am-5pm. $17, seniors $14, ages 3-12 $10).* At the **Dallas Arboretum,** 20 themed gardens occupy 66 tranquil acres near the shore of White Rock Lake. Try parking on a nearby residential street to avoid the parking fee. *(8617 Garland Rd. Bus #60. ☎515-6500. Open daily 9am-5pm. $8, seniors $7, ages 3-12 $5. Parking $5.)* The **American Airlines C. R. Smith Museum** traces the history of the world's largest airline. Exhibits give a behind-the-scenes look at airline operations using flight simulators and historic aircraft. For those who want a taste of the good life, the auditorium has first-class airplane seats. *(4601 Hwy. 360, at the FAA Rd. Exit just south of the airport. ☎967-1560. Open Tu-Sa 10am-6pm. $4; children, seniors, and students $2.)*

FAIR PARK. Home to the **State Fair** since 1886, **Fair Park** has earned national landmark status for its collection of 30s Art Deco architecture, the largest such collection in the country. The **Texas Star** ferris wheel dominates the park's skyline. *(Visit www.bigtex.com for info on the State Fair, held each Oct.)* The 277-acre park also hosts college football's **Cotton Bowl.** *(Jan. 1, 2008.)* **The Women's Museum: An Institute for the Future** has exhibits covering everything from Lucille Ball to birth control. Built in conjunction with the Smithsonian Institute, this new museum has a dramatic atrium as its centerpiece. *(3800 Parry Ave. ☎915-0860; www.thewomensmuseum.org. Open Tu-Su noon-5pm. $5, seniors and students $4, ages 5-12 $3.)*

HISTORIC DALLAS. Old City Park contains 35 restored 19th-century structures. There's a fee to tour the buildings, but the pleasant grounds are free. *(1717 Gano St., across I-30 from downtown. ☎421-5141; www.oldcitypark.org. Grounds open daily 5am-5pm. Exhibit buildings open Sept.-July Tu-Sa 10am-4pm, Su noon-4pm; Aug. Tu-Sa 10am-2pm, Su noon-2pm. Mar.-June 14 and Oct.-Dec. $7, seniors $5, children $4; June 15-Sept. and Jan.-Feb. $5, seniors $4, ages 4-12 $3.)* The **West End Historic District** is a brick-lined neighborhood of shops and restaurants a few blocks north of Dealey Plaza. Dallas's mansions are in the **Swiss Avenue Historic District** and along the ritzy streets of **Highland Park,** between Preston and Hillcrest Rd.

🎵 ENTERTAINMENT

The Observer is a free alternative weekly with unrivaled entertainment coverage. For the scoop on Dallas's gay scene, pick up copies of the *Dallas Voice* and *Texas Triangle* in Oaklawn shops and eateries.

The **Shakespeare in the Park** festival is held in Samuel-Grand Park, just northeast of Fair Park, from mid-June through July with other performances during the spring and fall. *(☎559-2778. Performances Tu-Su 8:15pm. Gates open 6:45pm; arrive early. Free tickets Tu-Th and Su.)* At Fair Park, **Music Hall** hosts Broadway tours in the **Dallas Summer Musicals** series. *(☎691-7200 for tickets; www.dallassummermusicals.org. Shows June-Oct. $11-134.)* The **Dallas Symphony Orchestra** plays in the downtown **Meyerson Symphony Center,** 2301 Flora St. *(☎692-0203, tours 670-3600; www.dallassymphony.com. Box office open M-Th 9am-6pm, F 10am-6pm. Tickets $12-100. Free tours F-Sa 1pm.)*

The **Mesquite Championship Rodeo,** 1818 Rodeo Dr., is one of the most competitive in the country. Take Exit 4 from I-635 S. and stay on the service road. *(☎972-285-8777; www.mesquiterodeo.com. Shows Apr.-late Sept. F-Sa 8pm. Gates open 6:30pm. $12, ages 3-12 and seniors $7. Pony rides and petting zoo $3. Barbecue dinner $11, children $7. Parking $5.)*

In Dallas, the moral order is God, Texas, country, and the **Cowboys.** See "The Boys" play football from September to January at **Texas Stadium,** at the junction of Rte. 12 and 183, west of Dallas in Irving. *(☎972-785-5000. Ticket office open M-F*

9am-5pm. Tickets $60-139.) **Ameriquest Field,** 1000 Ballpark Way, hosts the **Texas Rangers** from April to September. (☎817-273-5100. Ticket office open M-F 9am-6pm, Sa 10am-4pm, Su noon-4pm and 9am-9pm on game days. Tickets $6-105.) Experience the mystique of the game with a 1hr. tour of the locker room, dugout, and the press box on the **ballpark tour,** which also includes admission to **Legends of the Game Museum.** (☎817-273-5600. In-season non-game days tours every hr. M-Sa 9am-4pm, Su 11am-4pm; night-game days M-Sa 9am-2pm, Su 11am-2pm. Low season Tu-Sa 10am-4pm. $12, students with ID and seniors $10, ages 4-18 $7.)

⬛ NIGHTLIFE

Head east of downtown to **Deep Ellum,** a haven for blues legends in the 20s, and for musicians of every type since the area was revived in the 80s. The 1st Friday of every month is Deep Friday (www.deepfriday.com), when an $8 wrist band gets you into eight Deep Ellum clubs featuring local rock acts. Other nightlife centers include **Lower Greenville Avenue** and **Yale Boulevard,** near SMU's fraternity row. Gay nightlife centers on **Cedar Springs Road,** a bit north of downtown in **Oaklawn.**

> **Al Amir,** 7402 Greenville Ave. (☎ 739-2647), at Pineland. Lebanese restaurant and multi-level club with hookah (W-Th $5 per table, F-Sa $15) and belly dancers (9:30, 11:30pm). Middle Eastern, Latin, and other international dance music. F-Sa business casual dress; cover $5. F women no cover. Sa no cover for parties with dinner reservation. Bar and club 21+; restaurant all ages. Open W-Su 6pm-2am.
>
> **Club Dada,** 2720 Elm St. (☎ 744-3232). A diverse clientele, eclectic decor, and spacious outdoor patio make Club Dada a popular choice. Live acts nightly at 8pm range from rock to classical to the occasional stand-up comic. Open mic Su. 21+. Cover W-Sa $5. Open W-Su 6pm-2am.
>
> **Trees,** 2709 Elm St. (☎248-5902). A popular live music venue where grunge and swank coexist in a converted warehouse with a loft full of pool tables and tree trunks in the middle of the club. Bands play alternative rock music and everything else. 17+. Cover $2-25. Open Th-Su 7pm-2am, sometimes M-W 7pm-2am.

FORT WORTH   ☎817

If Dallas is the last Eastern city, Fort Worth is undoubtedly the 1st Western one. A mere 33 mi. west of Dallas on I-30, Fort Worth mixes raw Texan flair with cultural refinement. The city has three districts: the **Stockyards Historic District, Sundance Square,** and the **Cultural District.** Fort Worth's old stockyards, which were once the busiest in the country, have been turned into the city's largest tourist attraction. **Exchange Avenue** is the dusty main drag. Once lined with casinos and brothels catering to cowfolk with jingling pockets, its bars, restaurants, and shops now cater to the jingling pockets of tourists seeking what Fort Worth bills as a taste of the "authentic West." Catch the **cattle drive,** (www.fortworthstockyards.org.) when cowboys and cowgirls rustle a team of longhorns down Exchange Ave. The **White Elephant Saloon,** 106 Exchange Ave., a filming location in "Walker, Texas Ranger," has a ceiling plastered with celebrity cowboy hats. (☎624-8273. Cover M $2, F-Su $5-10. Open M-Th 2pm-midnight, F 2pm-2am, Sa noon-2am, Su noon-midnight.) The **Cowtown Coliseum,** 121 Exchange Ave., hosts national-level **rodeos** and **Pawnee Bill's Wild West Show.** (☎625-1025 or 888-269-8696; www.cowtowncoliseum.com. Box office open F-Sa 6-8pm. Rodeos F-Sa 8pm. $15, seniors $12, ages 3-12 $10. Pawnee Bill's June-Aug. Sa-Su 2:30 and 4:30pm. $9, seniors $7.50, ages 3-12 $5.) The world's largest honky-tonk, **Billy Bob's Texas,** 2520 Rodeo Pl., draws crowds with country music's big names. The club has a restaurant, games, and 25 bar stations. (☎624-7117. Free dance lessons Th 7pm. Bull-riding F-Sa 9 and 10pm. Families welcome; under 18 must be with parent. Cover $1 M-Th and Su before 8pm and F-Sa before 6pm. W women no cover. Open M-Sa 11am-2am, Su noon-2am.)

Sundance Square is the name given by promoters to what is essentially downtown Fort Worth. The 40-block brick-lined downtown is chock-full of trendy shops, museums, and restaurants. Parking lots are free after 5pm Monday through Friday and all day on weekends. The **Sid Richardson Collection of Western Art,** 309 Main St., is a shockingly enormous collection of western art, all donated by a wealthy oilman, Sid Richardson. Highlights include paintings by Remington. (☎332-6554; www.sidrmuseum.org. Open M-Th 9am-5pm, F-Sa 9am-8pm, Su noon-5pm. Free.) West of downtown along 7th St., Fort Worth boasts an astonishing array of high-caliber museums in the **Cultural District.** The █**Modern Art Museum,** 3200 Darnell, contains an excellent collection of art from the last half-century, including sculpture, abstract art, and photography, all housed in a stunning structure surrounded by a reflecting pool. (☎866-824-5566; www.themodern.org. Open Tu-Sa 10am-5pm, Su 11am-5pm. $10, seniors and students $4, under 12 free. W and 1st Su of month free.) The **Amon Carter Museum,** 3501 Camp Bowie Blvd., has a large collection of Western art and is renowned for its photographs of Western landscapes. (☎738-1933; www.cartermuseum.org. Open Tu-Sa 10am-5pm, Th until 8pm, Su noon-5pm. Free.)

Trinity Railway Express (p. 639), Amtrak, and **city buses** share the Intermodal Transportation Center, at the corner of 9th and Jones St. (☎215-8600. Open M-F 5am-10pm, Sa 8am-10pm, Su 10:15am-5:30pm.) The **Fort Worth Convention and Visitors Bureau** is at 415 Throckmorton St., in Sundance Sq. (☎800-433-5747; www.fortworth.com. Open M-F 8:30am-5pm, Sa 10am-4pm.) There are other branches in Stockyards, 130 E. Exchange Ave., and the Cultural District, 3401 W. Lancaster Ave. (All open M-F 9am-5pm, Sa 9am-6pm, Su 10am-6pm.) **Post Office:** 251 W. Lancaster Ave. (☎870-8104. Open M-F 8:30am-6pm.) **Postal Code:** 76102.

HOUSTON ☎713

With the fourth largest population of any US city, Houston can't hide its miles of seemingly endless strip malls and gridlocked traffic. Though known for sprawl and lack of planning, Houston has a revitalized downtown with a new light rail line, glorious modern architecture, stadiums, and several state-of-the-art performance centers. Houston's prosperity, built on the wealth of its oil and maritime industries, shows in its immaculate streetscapes, parks, and public buildings. Yet beyond the skyscrapers, culture abounds in an impressive array of world-class restaurants, museums, and cultural organizations.

▛ TRANSPORTATION

Airport: George Bush Intercontinental Airport (IAH); 25 mi. north of downtown. (☎281-230-3000; http://iah.houstonairportsystem.org.) **Express Shuttle** (☎523-8888) runs vans to downtown (1hr.; every 30min. 6:15am-11:15pm; $24, ages 5-12 $10, under 5 free) and locations in the suburbs (up to $35). **Metro bus 102** from Terminal C is cheaper (80min. to downtown; M-F every 10min., Sa-Su every 50min.; $1). **William P. Hobby Airport (KHOU/HOU),** 7800 Airport Blvd., (☎640-3000; http://hou.houstonairportsystem.org), about 10 mi. south of downtown, services Southwest and other domestic airlines.

Trains: Amtrak, 902 Washington Ave. (☎800-872-7245; www.amtrak.com). Walk toward the ferris wheel to the well-lit theater district; at night, call a cab. To **New Orleans** (10hr., 1 per day, $46-80) and **San Antonio** (5hr., 1 per day, $30-52). Open M 3pm-midnight, Tu-W and F 4am-1:45pm and 3pm-midnight, Th and Su 4am-1:45pm.

Buses: Greyhound, 2121 Main St. (☎759-6565; www.greyhound.com), 1 block south of Downtown Transit Center **METRORail** station. Be careful at night in this area. To **Dallas** (4-6hr., 8 per day, $35), **San Antonio** (3½hr., 7 per day, $26), and **Santa Fe** (24hr., 3 per day, $121). Open 24hr.

Public Transit: Metropolitan Transit Authority (☎635-4000; www.ridemetro.org). Over 130 bus lines operate within a 25-30 mi. radius of downtown. Typically operates M-Th 4:30am-1am; later on weekends. The new **METRORail** light rail, or Red Line, has 16 stops running north-south through Hermann Park, the Museum District, and downtown to University of Houston. Runs M-Th and Su until 12:45am, F-Sa until 2:15am. $1, seniors $0.40, ages 5-11 $0.25; all-day pass $2. Free maps available at the **Houston Public Library** (see **Internet Access,** p. 646), most hotels, or at METRO stores (720 Main or 1001 Travis St.; open M-F 7:30am-5:30pm).

Taxi: United Cab, ☎699-0000; www.houstondowntowncab.com. $6 flat-rate cab rides anywhere downtown.

Car Rental: Enterprise Rent-A-Car, 2101 Travis St. (☎651-7866). From $40 per day. $0.20 per mi. over 150 mi. 21+. Under-25 surcharge $10. Open M-F 7:30am-6pm, Sa 9am-3pm.

ORIENTATION AND PRACTICAL INFORMATION

Houston covers 600 sq. mi.—and that's just within the city limits. The **Houston Metroplex** is a vast agglomeration of suburbs, shopping malls, freeways, and mini-downtowns sprawling over thousands of square miles on the Gulf Plains. **Downtown Houston,** with its compact street grid, is the geographic and historic heart of the city. Much of downtown's foot traffic goes subterranean in a network of underground **tunnels** that connect most major buildings. Freeways are the prime geographic indicators, and everything is either inside or outside **The Loop (I-610).** Houston's ritzy shopping is in the **Uptown District,** which runs along Westheimer Rd. from downtown to **The Galleria,** a complex of high-end chain stores. The **Museum District** lies south of downtown and is bordered on the south by Hermann Park, Rice University, and the Texas Medical Center. The **Katy Freeway,** or **I-10,** runs west and is the axis of much of Houston's new development. Houston's vibrant gay community is concentrated in the trendy **Montrose District.** There is a small **Chinatown** just east of downtown, and a more suburban, sprawling Chinatown and **Little Vietnam,** or DiHo, along Bellaire Blvd. east of U.S. 59.

Visitor Info: Greater Houston Convention and Visitors Bureau, 901 Bagby St. (☎437-5200 or 800-446-8786; www.visithoustontexas.com), at the corner of Walker St. in City Hall. Open M-Sa 9am-4pm.

Hotlines: Crisis Center; ☎468-5463. **Rape Crisis;** ☎528-7273. **Women's Center;** ☎528-2121. **Gay and Lesbian Switchboard of Houston;** ☎529-3211. All 24hr.

Medical Services: St. Joseph Hospital Downtown, 1401 St. Joseph Pkwy. (☎757-1000). **Woman's Hospital of Texas,** 7600 Fannin St. (☎790-1234).

Internet Access: Houston Public Library, 500 McKinney St. (☎832-236-1313), at Bagby St. Open M-Sa 9am-6pm. Free Wi-Fi.

Post Office: 701 San Jacinto St. (☎800-275-8777). Open M-F 8am-5pm. **Postal Code:** 77052. **Area Codes:** 713, 281, and 832; in text, 713 unless indicated.

ACCOMMODATIONS

Cheap motels dot the city's major approaches, such as the Katy Freeway (I-10W) and the Southwest Freeway (U.S. 59). Some have rates in the $30 range, but they are often unsafe, dirty, and noisy. Motels along South Main Street (on bus route

TEXAS

HISTORICAL DISTRICT

Market Square Park

Washington St.

TO 10 (350yd)

Bagby St.

Downtown Aquarium

Wortham Center

Alley Theater

Bayou Place

Jones Hall

J.P. Morgan Chase Tower

TO BAYOU BEND (3mi)

Memorial Dr.

Hobby Center for the Performing Arts

Capitol St.

Rusk St.

Houston Heritage Society

City Hall

Houston Public Library

Dancing Fountains

Sam Houston Park

SKYSCRAPER DISTRICT

Buffalo Bayou

TO RIENZI (2.5mi)

Bagby St.

Franklin St.

Congress St.

Preston St.

Prairie St.

Texas Ave.

Old Union Station

Minute Maid Park (Houston Astros)

Capitol St.

Rusk St.

Caroline St.

Austin St.

La Branch St.

Crawford St.

Walker St.

McKinney St.

Lamar St.

Houston Center Gardens

George R. Brown Convention Center

Dallas St.

Discovery Green

Polk St.

Clay St.

Bell St.

Leeland St.

Toyota Center (Houston Rockets)

Pease St.

Jefferson St.

St. Joseph Pkwy.

Pierce St.

Gray St.

Smith St.

Louisiana St.

Milam St.

Travis St.

Main St.

Fannin St.

San Jacinto St.

Chenevert St.

Hamilton St.

St. Emanuel St.

Avenida de las America

Houston Center Gardens

0   250 yards

0   250 meters

Downtown Houston

🏠 ACCOMMODATIONS
YMCA, 2

🍸 NIGHTLIFE
Sambuca Jazz Cafe, 1

Museum District

🏠 ACCOMMODATIONS
Houston International Hostel, 12
Sara's Bed & Breakfast Inn, 16

🍎 FOOD
Brasil, 5
Tan Hzi Restaurant, 17
Ragin Cajun, 10

🍸 NIGHTLIFE
J.R.'s, 2
Montrose Mining Co., 4
South Beach, 3

🏛 MUSEUMS
Buffalo Soldiers National Museum, 9
Contemporary Arts Museum, 13
Holocaust Museum, 11
Houston Museum of Natural Science, 15
Menil Collection, 7
Museum of Fine Arts, 14
Museum of Print History, 1
Richmond Hall, 8
Rothko Chapel, 6

TO 1 (1mi)

TO 2, 3 AND 4 (300 yd)

TO BAYOU BEND 5 (.75mi)

Alabama St.

Cleburne St.

Wheeler St.

Blodgett St.

288

Mt. Vernon St.

Yoakum Blvd.

Graustark St.

Yupon St.

Alabama St.

Montrose Blvd.

Stanford St.

Branard St.

Sul Ross St.

San Jacinto St.

Fannin St.

Main St.

Crawford St.

La Branch St.

Austin St.

Caroline St.

Alameda

Washateria

6

7

Richmond Ave.

Southwest Fwy.

MUSEUM DISTRICT

Southmore Blvd.

Oakdale St.

16

11

12

Binz St.

TO 10 (3.5mi)

Dunlavy St.

13   14

15

Hermann Dr.

Mandell St.

Bissonnet St.

Rice Blvd.

Miller Outdoor Theatre

Sunset Blvd.

Japanese Gardens

Houston Zoological Gardens

Hermann Park

Outer Belt

Texas Medical Center

MacGregor Dr.

2.5 miles

0   2.5 kilometers

TO BUSH AIRPORT (10mi)

610

45

75

US 90

610

90

Katy Frwy.

10

90

16

10

90

10

90

SEE DOWNTOWN MAP

SEE MUSEUM DISTRICT MAP

904

59

Southwest Frwy.

45

TO SAN JACINTO BATTLEGROUND (11mi)

TO MANDIR (10mi), 17 (4.5mi)

TO HOBBY AIRPORT (18mi), JOHNSON SPACE CENTER (4mi)

207

288

South LOOP

610

Reliant Park

RICE UNIVERSITY

Laboratory Dr.

Stockton Dr.

Main St.

Fannin St.

University Blvd.

Moursund St.

Holcombe Blvd.

Brays Bayou

TO RELIANT PARK, ASTROWORLD, LOOP

810

0   500 yards

0   500 meters

#8) are more convenient. Most **campgrounds** in the Houston area lie a considerable distance from the city center: **Lake Houston State Park,** 30 mi. to the northeast, and **Brazos Bend,** 35 mi. to the southwest, are the nearest.

Houston International Hostel, 5302 Crawford St. (☎523-1009; www.houstonhostel.com), at Oakdale St., 3 blocks east and 5 blocks north of METRORail Museum District Station. 32 beds. Kitchen and common area. Unlimited Wi-Fi or Internet access $10. Reception 8-10am and 5-11pm. No dorm access 10am-5pm. Common area open 24 hr. Single-sex dorms $15; singles $23. Cash only. ❶

YMCA, 1600 Louisiana St. (☎758-9250; www.ymcahouston.org), between Pease and Bell St. Downtown location features singles with TVs and daily maid service. Women must stay in rooms with private baths or female-only floors. Laundry and kitchen on each floor. Towel deposit $2.50. Key deposit $10. Reception 24hr. Check-in 8am. Check-out noon. Singles $30, with private bath $35. Lower weekly and monthly rates. Additional locations at 7903 South Loop E (☎643-2804), off the Broadway Exit from I-610, near I-45. Take bus #50 to Broadway. AmEx/D/MC/V. ❶

🍴 FOOD

Houston's cuisine takes its cues from its immigrant cultures, seamlessly blending Louisiana's Cajun influence with soul food, Texas barbecue, and Mexican food. With the downtown areas newfound success has come pricier restaurants. Affordable, diverse options can be found throughout the city and on suburban commercial strips. If you're looking for the best tacos or a refreshing bubble tea, head to ethnic enclaves like the East End, Chinatown, or Little Vietnam.

🦞 **Ragin' Cajun,** 4302 Richmond Ave. (☎623-6321), just past the railroad tracks. Scarf down buckets of crawfish on checkered picnic tables amidst walls chock-full of postcards and memorabilia while zydeco plays cheerfully in the background. The Frozen Hurricane, New Orleans's favorite drink, packs quite a punch. Takeout and delivery available. Oyster bar and restaurant with table service in back. Entrees $4-17. Open M-Th 11am-10pm, F-Sa 11am-11pm, Su 11am-9pm. AmEx/D/MC/V. ❷

🦞 **Brasil,** 2604 Dunlavy St. (☎528-1993). Take bus #82 down Westheimer. This hip coffeehouse also has a bar, a restaurant, and a bakery. Snack on California-style salads and pizzas between walls lined with local artwork, or head to the foliage-enclosed patio. Plenty of vegetarian options. Breakfast served. Pizza, salads, and sandwiches $6-8. Draft beer $4-7.Live music many nights. Open M-Sa 8am-2am, Su 8am-midnight. AmEx/D/MC/V. ❷

Tan Hai Restaurant, 10780 Bellaire Blvd. (☎281-933-1666), in the shopping center parking lots between Hwy. 8 and Hillcrest Dr. Take bus #2 down Bellaire. In the heart of Little Vietnam. Menu ranges from tamer rice and vermicelli plates, to more exotic dishes, like coconut curry frog legs. The avocado smoothie ($3) is divine. Entrees $5-9. Open M-Su 9am-11pm. MC/V. ❷

👁 SIGHTS

JOHNSON SPACE CENTER. The city's most popular attraction, **Space Center Houston,** is outside Houston city limits in Clear Lake, TX. Admission includes a tour of the center's historic mission control, an abandoned prototype hangar, and the astronaut training facility, as well as educational film screenings in the Giant Screen, Texas' largest movie theater. The complex also houses models of the Gemini, Apollo, and Mercury crafts. No visit is complete without taking a moment to touch the moon rock on public display. (*1601 NASA Pkwy. 1. Take I-45 south to NASA Rd.*

(Exit 25) then head east 3 mi.; or take bus #246. ☎ 281-244-2100; www.spacecenter.org. Opens between 9-10am and closes between 5-7pm; call ahead. $19, seniors $18, ages 4-11 $15.) The **Level 9 Tour** takes visitors to areas of the Space Center not usually open to tourists, including the New Mission Control Center, the Robotics Lab, the Space Environment Simulation Lab, and the Neutral Buoyancy Lab. For the wannabe rocketman (or woman), it's the only way to see the sights. *(☎ 244-2115. 4hr., 1 per day M-F 11:45am, $70. 12-person max., over 14 only. Reservations recommended.)*

THE SAN JACINTO BATTLEGROUND STATE HISTORICAL SITE. This park commemorates Sam Houston's victory over Santa Ana's Mexican troops with a 570 ft. monument that, in true Texas fashion, is taller than the Washington Monument in the nation's capital. A small museum of Texas history (told from a Texans point of view) sits at the monument's base. The Battleship Texas, on the other side of the park, is the last remaining ship of the Dreadnought era and the only surviving battleship to have served in both World Wars. Visitors can explore the ship at will, even descending into the bowels of the engine room. *(Take Hwy. 225 E. to the Battleground Rd./Hwy. 134 Exit and head north. Park open daily 9am-6pm. Free. Museum: ☎ 281-479-2421. Open daily 9am-6pm. Free. 35min. multimedia slide show daily every hr. 10am-5pm. $4.50, seniors $4, under 11 $3.50. Battleship: ☎ 281-479-2431. Open daily 10am-5pm. $7, seniors $4, under 11 free.)*

HERMANN PARK. This 445-acre park provides respite from urban life as well as numerous opportunities for recreation. **McGovern Lake,** the reflecting pool, the Southern Pacific steam locomotive, and the **Miller Outdoor Theater** are free and open all day long. The **Japanese Tea Garden** was designed by renowned landscape architect Ken Nakajima. Pleasure-seekers can rent a paddleboat on McGovern Lake ($8) or ride the Kiddie Train ($2.25). Near the northern entrance of the park, the **Houston Museum of Natural Science** includes a planetarium, IMAX theater, and 60 ft. high butterfly center, in addition to various traveling exhibits. **Weiss Energy Hall** covers oil, and the science associated with its production. The **Houston Zoological Gardens,** at the park's southern end, features over 700 species, including a special section for animals native to Texas including the Texas Tan Tarantula, Barred Tiger Salamander, and Ornate Box Turtle. *(Museum of Natural Science: 1 Hermann Circle Dr. ☎ 639-4629; www.hmns.org. Exhibits open M-Sa 9am-5pm, Su 11am-5pm. Free Tu. Museum $9, seniors and under 12 $7; IMAX $7/$4.50; planetarium $6/$5; butterfly center $6/$5. Museum exhibits free 30min. before closing. Japanese tea garden: www.japanesegarden.org. Open daily 10am-6pm. Free. Zoo: 1513 N. MacGregor. ☎ 533-6500; www.houstonzoo.org. Open Mar.-Sept. 9am-7pm; Oct.-Feb. 9am-6pm. $8, seniors $5, ages 2-12 $4.)*

DOWNTOWN. Downtown Houston reads like a Who's Who of famous modern architects. Those who brave the heat at street level will be rewarded by over a century of the richest samplings of business architecture in the United States. At 70 floors, the **JP Morgan Chase Tower,** designed by I.M. Pei in 1981, is Houston's tallest building. The public is welcome to take the elevator to the observation deck on the 60th floor to take in the 20 mi. vista to the west. Outside the tower in the courtyard stands Juan Miró's largest freestanding sculpture in the United States. *(600 Travis St. M-F 9am-5pm. Free.)* One block north on Travis St., the public can peek through giant windows to see the *Houston Chronicle*'s **printing presses** in action. Two blocks farther up Travis St., **Market Square Park** is the historic center of the city of Houston. Having declined into a parking lot in the mid-20th century, it has been restored as a handsome park square with tiles that vividly recount the history of Houston in black-and-white photos. Six miles of **tunnels** connect Houston's downtown buildings to parking, and are a site in and of themselves, creating a veritable underground city that protects residents from the (sometimes) deadly heatwaves.

TEXAS

THURSDAYS FOR POCKET CHANGE. Almost every museum in Houston is free on Thursdays—that is, if it's not already free. On a Thursday, hop on the ultra-cheap METRORail, which runs straight into Houston's Museum District, and save yourself parking costs as well as $7 at the Fine Arts Museum. The Holocaust Museum and the hip Contemporary Arts Museum are free every day and conveniently located in the neighborhood. The McGovern Museum of Health and Medical Sciences will run you $6 unless you visit it from 2-5pm on Thursdays. After you're done expending all of that intellectual energy, take that extra $13 in your pocket, hop back on the METRORail to get to Main St. and hit up Happy hour at any of the bars lining the street.

The **Buffalo Bayou,** recently re-engineered and re-landscaped, forms the northwestern border of the downtown area.

ART ATTRACTIONS. At Houston's **Museum of Fine Arts,** the Caroline Weiss Law building showcases contemporary and modern collections, while the Audrey Jones Beck building displays everything from ancient European art to Impressionist pieces. Be sure to see Bouguereau's famous painting, "The Elder Sister," and the Glassell Collection of African gold, considered one of the best of its kind in the world. *(Museum: 1001 Bissonet. ☎ 639-7300; www.mfah.org. Open Tu-W 10am-5pm, Th 10am-9pm, F-Sa 10am-7pm, Su 12:15-7pm. $7; students, seniors, and ages 6-18 $3.50. Audio tour $10/5; Th free. Garden: 5101 Montrose Blvd. Open daily 9am-10pm. Free.)* Across the street, the **Contemporary Arts Museum** forgoes a traditional permanent collection and instead rotates the works of well-known international artists in its large, dramatic rooms. *(5216 Montrose Blvd. ☎ 284-8258; www.camh.org. Open Tu-W and F-Sa 10am-5pm, Th 10am-9pm, Su noon-5pm. Free.)* Founded in 1987 by the Menil Family, the **Menil Collection** spans five buildings in a residential neighborhood west of Montrose. Showcasing Surrealist paintings and sculptures, Byzantine and medieval artifacts, and other European, American, and African art, the Menil Collection also features touring installments. *(1515 Sul Ross. ☎ 525-9400; www.menil.org. Open W-Su 11am-7pm. Free.)* **Richmond Hall** contains nothing but the neon light sculptures of Dan Flavin. *(1500 Richmond Ave. Same hours as the Menil.)*

BAYOU BEND. Ima Hogg was once one of the city of Houston's wealthiest women, and when she left her mansion and collections as the **Bayou Bend Collection and Gardens,** Houston gained one of the finest collections of American decorative art in the US. Hidden among the collection are portraits by John Singleton Copley and silver pieces by Paul Revere. *(1 Wescott St. ☎ 639-7750; www.mfah.org/bayoubend. Enter from Memorial Dr. and walk across the suspension bridge over the bayou. 1½hr. tours leave every 15min. Tu-Sa 10-11:30am and 1-2:45pm. On Sa afternoon, Su, and all month in Aug. visitors receive audio tours in lieu of guides. $10, seniors and students $8.50, ages 10-18 $5, under 10 not permitted on tours. Gardens open Tu-Sa 10am-5pm, Su 1-5pm. 1hr. garden tours by reservation. $3, under 10 free.)* For the European counterpart to Bayou Bend, visit the **Rienzi Mansion,** located along the same ravine. Rienzi exhibits Georgian English decorative art including gilded footstools. *(1406 Kirby Dr. ☎ 639-7800. Open M and Th-Sa 10am-4pm, Su 1-5pm. $6, seniors $4. Viewing of the house is only available via tour; call ahead.)*

OTHER MUSEUMS. In the late 1800s, members of the all-black units in the American army were nicknamed "Buffalo Soldiers," both because of their naturally curly hair and as a sign of respect for their fighting spirit. The ▨**Buffalo Soldiers National Museum** contains artifacts, memorabilia, uniforms, and weapons illustrating the history of African Americans in the armed forces. Though the artifacts rival the Smithsonian's collection, the museum's limited funds means that some of these objects aren't even protected by glass. *(1834 South-more Blvd. ☎942-8920; www.buffalosoldiermuseum.com. Open M-F 10am-5pm, Sa 10am-4pm. $2)* The ▨**Museum of Print History** is in a less convenient location than its counterparts in the Museum District, but its unique subject matter sets it apart. The collections contain hundreds of documents, maps, and facsimiles produced by antique printing presses, as well as dozens of the presses themselves. Visitors can watch artists-in-residence use a model of the Gutenburg press. *(1324 West Clay. ☎522-4652; www.printingmuseum.org. Open Tu-Sa 10am-5pm. Free.)* The cylindrical architecture of the **Holocaust Museum** is meant to evoke a concentration camp's smokestack. The museum has a rotating art gallery and two films about the Holocaust. *(5401 Caroline St. ☎942-8000; www.hmh.org. Open M-F 9am-5pm, Sa-Su noon-5pm. Free.)* It looks like it belongs in 18th-century India, but **Mandir** is neither old nor a museum. Mandir is a brand-new temple of Swaminarayan Hinduism, made by thousands of pieces of marble that were carved in India. The Swaminarayans welcome the public, provided you remove your shoes and cover your shoulders and legs. The temperature inside the temple is 20° cooler because of the marble, allowing the mind and body to relax. *(1150 Brand Ln. Take U.S. 59 S to Kirkwood Exit. ☎281-499-7974; www.swaminarayan.org. Open daily 9am-8:45pm.)*

♫ ENTERTAINMENT

From March to October, symphony, opera, ballet companies, and various professional theaters stage free performances at the **Miller Outdoor Theatre** (☎284-8352; www.milleroutdoortheatre.com), in Hermann Park. Pick up a schedule at the on-site concession stand or online. The annual **Shakespeare Festival** struts and frets upon the stage in August. The downtown **Alley Theatre,** 615 Texas Ave., puts on Broadway-caliber productions at moderate prices. (☎220-5700; www.alleytheatre.org. Tickets $19-63; M-Th and Su student rush tickets 1hr. before show $13; F-Sa matinee $21.) **Bayou Place,** 500 Texas Ave., contains the **Angelika Film Center,** which plays foreign as well as mainstream domestic films. (☎333-3456. $8, students $6.) Bayou Place also holds the **Hard Rock Cafe** and the **Verizon Wireless Theater** (☎230-1666), where big-name music tours often perform. The **Hobby Center for the Performing Arts,** 800 Bagby St. (☎315-2400; www.thehobbycenter.org), features a dome ceiling with a fiber optic display of the Texas night sky and hosts **Theatre Under the Stars,** America's largest nonprofit producer of musicals, as well as traveling Broadway productions in the Broadway in Houston Series. **Jones Hall,** 614 Louisiana St. (☎227-3974), stages more of Houston's highbrow entertainment. The **Houston Symphony Orchestra** performs there from September to May. (☎224-7575. Tickets $25-106.) Between October and May, the **Houston Grand Opera** produces seven operas in the nearby Wortham Center, 501 Texas Ave. (☎546-0200; www.houstongrandopera.org. Tickets $30-275; student rush tickets available day of show $15-30; call ahead to reserve.) Major League Baseball's **Houston Astros** (www.astros.com) play at Minute Maid Park (☎295-8000), located at the intersections of Texas, Crawford, and Congress St. near Union Station downtown. From February to mid-March, both the Reliant Center and Reliant Arena house the **Houston Livestock Show and Rodeo** (☎832-667-1000; www.hlsr.com). It's nothin' but net in the new downtown Toyota Center at Polk and Crawford St., home of the NBA's **Houston Rockets** (www.rockets.com), while the NFL's **Houston Texans** (www.houstontexans.com) pass the pigskin at Reliant Stadium, 8400 Kirby Dr.

◓ NIGHTLIFE

Since the 2004 Super Bowl, downtown Houston has been reclaiming its stake in the city's nightlife. Most nightlife is concentrated along Main St., which is closed to

traffic between Capitol and Congress St. from 4pm-2am on weekends to make way
for partiers. **METRORail** heads right down Main St. and runs until 2am on weekends.
Montrose is the center of the gay nightlife scene, but while its bars tend to be
mostly gay, dance clubs in Montrose have a mixed crowd.

> **Sambuca Jazz Cafe,** 909 Texas Ave. (☎ 224-5299; www.sambucarestaurant.com). This
> wood-laden bar and restaurant hosts live jazz every night of the week. Performers range
> from blues and soft rock to free-form jazz and straight-ahead swing. Weekends tend to
> have more upbeat music for dancing. Cigar bar upstairs. Happy hour 4-7pm. Appetizers
> $3 Domestic beer $2. Martinis $4. No cover. Open M-Th and Su 11am-midnight, F
> 11am-2am, Sa 5pm-2am.

> **J.R.'s,** 808 Pacific St. (☎521-2519; www.jrsbarandgrill.com), **Montrose Mining Co.,**
> 807 Pacific St. (☎529-7488), and **South Beach,** 810 Pacific Ave. (☎529-7623;
> www.southbeachthenightclub.com). Take bus #82 down Westheimer to Crocker St.,
> and walk 2 blocks north. 3 gay bars with 3 distinct atmospheres make for ideal bar-hop-
> ping. **J.R's** is the most laid-back and traditional bar. No cover. Open daily noon-2am.
> **Montrose Mining Co.** has more of a western feel, and patrons are more likely to be
> sporting leather. Open daily 4pm-2am. Swankier **South Beach,** with an iced martini bar
> and pulsing dance floor, attracts a mixed crowd, including plenty of hip, young straight
> people. Every hr. liquid nitrogen pours down from the ceiling, instantly chilling the bar
> by 20° and plunging dancers into a sea of fog. Drink specials until 10pm. Cover up to
> $10. Open W-Su 9pm-5am.

GALVESTON ISLAND   ☎409

Although only an hour from Houston (51 mi. south), Galveston is a destination in
its own right. Over 6000 historic buildings stand testament to the fact that it was
once the largest and most powerful city in Texas. Things changed in 1900, when a
devastating hurricane ripped through the city and claimed 6000 lives. By 1915
Houston had built its ship channel and Galveston lost its key role in the maritime
industry. Today, the 32 mi. island is powered mainly by tourism, offering much-
needed respite from the Houston heat.

On the north side of the city, the historic commercial district, known as **The
Strand,** boasts one of the largest collections of commercial Victorian buildings in
the US. Trolleys clang along historic tracks that follow two routes, one to the
University of Texas Medical School and one to Seawall Beach ($1.25). Free Wi-Fi
hotspots are available at 23rd and Strand, 37th and Seawall, and 6th and Seawall.
Of the numerous museums along the Strand, two of the best explore the industries that made this region great. The **Galveston Railway Museum,** 123 Rosenburg
St., at the Strand's west end, housed in the restored Art Deco Union Station, pays
homage to that history with displays, model trains, and, best of all, dozens of
actual trains spanning an entire century. There has been no restoration; everything is in its original state, for better or for worse. With no off-limits areas, visitors are free to explore every corner of the trains, from the luxurious Pullman
car parlors to the kitchen galleys to the locomotive cabs. (☎765-5700. Open daily
10am-4pm. $6, seniors $5, ages 4-12 $3. AAA discount $1.) The one-of-a-kind **Ocean
Star Offshore Energy Center,** Pier 19, Harborside Dr. at 20th St., demystifies the
oil drilling rigs that dot the Gulf of Mexico horizon. The museum is located on
a retired oil rig anchored just offshore and can only be reached by a causeway.
Explore the history, science, politics, and ecology of off-shore drilling, then
head out to the deck of the rig to see the equipment up close. (☎766-7827. Open
daily June-Aug. 10am-6pm; Sept.-May 10am-5pm. $6, seniors $5, ages 7-18 $4.)

In addition to The Strand, there are three other national historic districts in
Galveston. Primarily residential, these are best explored on foot. Pick up a map

at the Visitors Center to see the districts' exact boundaries of the districts. Although most of the historic buildings are private homes, a few are open to public tours, including the elegant **Moody Mansion,** 2618 Broadway, at 26th St., former home of Galveston's leading family, which contains original furnishings and stunning stained glass. (☎762-7668. Open M-Sa 10am-4pm, Su noon-4pm. $6, seniors $5, ages 6-18, $3.) Three glass pyramids house a tropical rainforest, aquarium, science museum, and IMAX theater at **Moody Gardens,** 1 Hope Blvd., a tourist-oriented theme park. The grounds themselves are well-manicured and free to the public. (From Seawall Blvd., take a right on 81st St. ☎683-4200 or 800-582-4673; www.moodygardens.com. Open daily in summer 10am-9pm; winter 9am-6pm.)

The real reason most people come to Galveston is for the beaches. Taking its name from the seawall that protects Galveston from hurricanes, **Seawall Boulevard** runs along the Gulf Coast and is full of cheap eats. The beach along Seawall Blvd. is free, and so is the street parking. For more amenities, head to one of the parks farther down the island, such as **#3 Beach Pocket Park,** which has restrooms, showers, playgrounds, and a concession stand. (Open M-F 9am-5pm, Sa-Su 9am-6pm. $8 per car.) The only beach in Galveston that permits alcoholic beverages is **East Beach,** on the eastern edge of the island. Because of the booze, live music, and weekend bikini contests, it's more commonly known as "Party Beach." (www.eastbeachparty.com. $7; M-F after 5pm and Sa-Su after 7:30pm free.) For an even more raucous time, teenagers and college students take the free ferry to **Port Bolivar** and then drive to **Crystal Beach,** fondly dubbed "The Zoo" because of the abundance of booze, firecrackers, and bonfires. (Ferry operates 24hr., but the line is often over 1hr. long.) One of only four hostels in the state of Texas, **HI-Galveston ❶,** 201 Seawall Blvd., at the northern tip of town, is located inside the Sandpiper Motel and offers direct beach access, coffee, laundry, kitchen, a computer with Internet access, and a pool. The doors lock at 11pm but the 24hr. staff will let you in late. (☎765-9431; www.sandpipermotel.com. Dorms $18.50. HI members only). The oldest restaurant on the island, **The Original ❷,** 1401 Market St. dishes up tasty Tex-Mex, with enchilada plates starting at $5.50. (☎762-6001. Open M-Th 11am-9pm, F-Sa 8am-10pm, Su 8am-9:30pm.)

CORPUS CHRISTI ☎361

Corpus Christi's shoreside location makes it a tourism cash cow. The warm waters from the Gulf of Mexico produce Corpus Christi's copious amounts of tourists and crude oil. Summer vacationers are replaced in the cooler months by "winter Texans," a breed of northern mobile-home owners who head south to enjoy coastal warmth. Defined by its pricey knick-knacks, natural stretches of sand, and offshore oil derricks on the horizon, Corpus Christi is a uniquely Texan stopover.

🚍 **TRANSPORTATION. Greyhound,** 702 N. Chaparral (☎882-9206; www.greyhound.com; open daily 7:30am-12:45am), runs to Austin , (5 ½ hr., 4 per day, $40). Dallas (9-10hr., 9 per day, $47.50) and Houston (4hr., 7 per day, $30). **Regional Transit Authority** (☎289-2600), also known as the "B," operates a dozen bus routes within Corpus Christi. Get maps and schedules at the Visitors Center or at **The B Headquarters,** 1806 S. Alameda. (☎883-2287. Open M-F 8am-5pm.) City Hall, Port Ayers, Six Points, Padre Staples Mall, and the Staples St. stations are central transfer points. (M-Sa 5:30am-9:30pm, Su 10am-7:30pm. $0.75, students $0.35, seniors $0.25; transfers free.) The **Harbor Ferry** runs between the Art Museum, Aquarium, and downtown at People St. (Summer daily 10:30am-6:30pm. All-day pass $3.) On the north side of Harbor Bridge, the free **beach shuttle** travels to the beach, aquarium, and other attractions. (Summer daily 10:30am-6:30pm.) For a **Taxi,** call **Yellow Cab,** ☎884-3211.

654 ■ TEXAS

⏹ PRACTICAL INFORMATION. Greater Corpus Christi lines the shores of Corpus Christi Bay. Downtown Corpus Christi is at the eastern edge of the bay, with residential districts stretching southward and the Padre Island beaches rounding out the eastern shore of the bay. Most attractions, restaurants, and nightlife are in a walkable area either in downtown or on the island-like peninsula just north of Harbor Bridge. **Convention and Visitors Bureau,** 1823 N. Chaparral, six blocks north of I-37, has maps, brochures, and information. (☎561-2000 or 800-766-2322; www.corpuschristivb.org. Open daily 9am-5pm.) **The Spohn Hospital Shoreline** is at 600 Elizabeth St. (☎881-3000). **Hotlines include: Battered Women and Rape Victims Shelter** (☎881-8888; operates 24hr.). **Internet Access: Corpus Christi Public Library,** 805 Comanche St., just west of the Central Business District. (☎880-7000. Open M-Th 9am-9pm, F-Sa 9am-6pm, Su 2-6pm. 30min. limit.) **Post Office:** 809 Nueces Bay Blvd., just south of I-37 Exit 1E. (☎800-275-8777. Open M-F 8am-5:30pm, Sa 8am-1pm.) **Postal Code:** 78469.

⏹ ACCOMMODATIONS. Posh hotels line the shoreline in downtown. North of Harbor Bridge are several waterfront motels, but they are pricey as well. Cheap motels can be found along Leopard St. south of town or off of Exits 3-5 on I-37, a few miles north of town, with some even in the $25-35 range (though not all of those are clean or safe). **Railway Inn Suites ❸,** 4343 Ocean Dr., are located on the fashionable Ocean Dr., 4 mi. south of town on bus route #6. They take the railroad motif very seriously: there is memorabilia, artwork, and a kiddie train that follows a ¼ mi. track around the hotel. The price and free continental breakfast make it a good choice for families. (☎729-7245; www.railwayinnsuites.com. 2+ person suites M-F from $60, Sa-Su from $80.) **Camping ❶** at Padre Island beaches starts at $12 (p. 655). **Labonte Park ❶,** right off I-37 at Exit 16, 18 mi. from downtown, allows free camping in a grassy area along the river. (☎241-1464. Toilets. No showers.) Pick up a permit from the **Visitors Center** next door. (Open daily 9am-5pm.)

⏹ FOOD AND NIGHTLIFE. With the Gulf in its backyard, seafood dominates Corpus Christi's cuisine. **Pier 99 ❷,** 2822 N. Shoreline Dr., right next to the *U.S.S. Lexington,* serves it up fried, boiled, grilled, or blackened. (☎887-0764. Lunch specials $6-7. Po' boys $7. Live music F-Su. Open daily 11am-10pm.) Several bars and dance clubs line Chaparral in downtown, which is closed off for pedestrians Friday and Saturday nights. Groove to Southern rhythm 'n' blues seven nights a week at **⏹Dr. Rockits Blues Bar,** 709 Chaparral, a classic bar with high ceilings, neon lights, and Jaegermeister on tap. (☎884-7634; www.drrockitsbluesbar.com. Cover $4-8. Open M-Th 4:30pm-2am, F-Sa 7pm-2am.)

⏹ SIGHTS. Despite the ravenous gulls, Corpus Christi's **beaches** are without a doubt the city's top attraction. However, if it's beaches you're looking for, the best ones are actually located outside of the city on Padre Island, at least a 30min. drive away (p. 655). In-town swimming beaches are located next to the *U.S.S. Lexington* (metered parking) and at Magee Beach, just south of downtown (free parking). On the north side of Harbor Bridge, the **Texas State Aquarium,** 2710 N. Shoreline Blvd., focuses on animals native to the Gulf of Mexico. The state-of-the-art Dolphin Bay has above- and below-water viewing areas, with four shows per day. One exhibit features sharks and rays roaming, in true Texas fashion, beneath an oil platform. (☎881-1200 or 800-477-4853; www.texasstateaquarium.org. Open June-Aug. daily 9am-6pm; Sept.-May M-Sa 9am-5pm. $14, seniors $12, ages 4-12 $9. Parking $3.50.) Just next door floats the aircraft carrier **U.S.S. Lexington,** a WWII relic that made a cameo in the Hollywood blockbuster *Pearl Harbor.* The "Lex," as it is affectionately known, has completed secret missions in Formosa, Cuba, and Laos. The retired training vessel now welcomes tourists both below and above her decks, where 19 WWII planes sit on display. (☎ 888-4873 or 800-523-9539. Open daily June-Aug. 9am-6pm; Sept.-May 9am-5pm. $12, seniors $10, ages 4-12 $7.) **Heritage Park,** 1581 Chaparral, near the Visitors Center, is a collection of historic homes representing different immigrant groups, laid out in an attractive park. (☎ 883-0639. Free.) The **Texas Surf Museum,** 309 N. Water St., right in downtown, will remind you why you came to Corpus Christi: for the beaches. Several hundred pieces of surfing history—including more than 100 photographs and more than 50 boards dating back to the 30s—line the walls while a mock surfing garage plays a continuous loop of retro surfing videos.

NORTH PADRE ISLAND   ☎ 361

At over 100 mi., Padre Island is the longest stretch of undeveloped barrier island in the entire world. North Padre Island, east of Corpus Christi, is the more mellow cousin to rambunctious South Padre Island and its hordes of drunken spring breakers, yet it offers ample opportunities for adventure in windsurfing, swimming, and surf fishing. After reaching Padre Island by the JFK causeway from Corpus Christi, turn left for **Port Aransas** and **Mustang Island State Park,** or right for **Padre Balli County Park** and **Padre Island National Seashore (PINS).** There are also numbered beach access points that are not affiliated with any parks, but you'll need a sticker to park your car (year-long pass $12, available at Padre Balli and local convenience stores). **Mustang Island State Park ❶** charges $4 for day use and an additional $8 for tent camping on the beach, which includes free hot showers at the RV sites. **Padre Balli County Park ❶** offers less serenity but more activities. Campers choose from a narrow grass strip surrounded by asphalt or the beach itself for $10 a night. (No entrance fee; parking sticker required. Hot showers available. Full water and electric hook-up $18 per night for up to 6 people.) **Bob Hall Pier,** the main fishing pier, is located right on the beach. (Open 24hr. Entrance fee $1, seniors $0.50. Pole rentals $10.)

Part of the National Park System, PINS has the cleanest and best-protected beaches, dunes, and grassland on the island. (Entrance for 1 week $10, for 1 year $20.) **Malaquite Visitors Center** is 5 mi. south of the Causeway and bridge to the island. (☎ 949-8068; www.nps.gov/pais. Open daily in summer 8:30am-6pm; winter 9am-4pm. The **PINS Campground ❶,** 1 mi. north of the Visitors Center, has restrooms, free cold showers, and an asphalt RV area. (Sites $8.) Camping in unmarked sites farther down the beach is free, and campers still have 24hr. access to showers and bathrooms. A lucky few may spot an endangered Kemp's Ridley sea turtle and should report it to a ranger. Boat launching is possible from the **Grasslands Nature Trail,** a three-quarters of a mile paved loop through sand dunes and grasslands. Guide pamphlets are available at the trailhead. Entrance to **Bird Island Basin,** located on the far lagoon side of the island, is $10 for a yearly pass or $5 per day; entrance permits may be purchased at the entrance station or at the Malaquite Visitors Center. Also on the lagoon side, **Worldwinds Windsurfing** rents a large range of windsurfing equipment as well as various types of sea kayaks at one of the best windsurfing sites in the nation. (☎ 949-7472 or 800-793-7471. Beginner's rig and lesson $50. Singles 2 hr. $25, 3 hrs $35. Full day $45. Two-wheel drive vehicles can drive on the first 5 mi. of beach below Malaquite. Visitors with 4WD and a taste for solitude should make the 60 mi. trek to the **Mansfield Channel,** the seashore's most remote and untraveled area where shipwrecks still lie on the beach. Call the **PINS Headquarters** (☎ 949-8173), 3½ mi. south of the park entrance, for emergency assistance.

TEXAS

WEST TEXAS

AMARILLO   ☎806

Named for the yellow clay of nearby Lake Meredith (*amarillo* is Spanish for "yellow"), Amarillo began as a railroad construction camp in 1887 and ultimately evolved into a Texas-size truck stop. After years of cattle and oil, Amarillo is now the prime overnight stop for motorists en route from Dallas, Houston, or Oklahoma City to Denver and other Western destinations. For travelers, it's little more than a one-day city, but what a grand, shiny stop it is.

▄️⚄ ORIENTATION AND PRACTICAL INFORMATION. Amarillo sits at the intersection of I-27, I-40, and U.S. 287/87. Chances are, you're arriving by car, and good thing, as the city is definitely best explored behind the wheel. Rte. 335 (the Loop) encircles the city. The city's main street, **6th Avenue (Route 66),** runs east-west through downtown. **Greyhound,** 700 S. Tyler (☎374-5371; www.greyhound.com; open 24hr.), runs to Dallas (8hr., 5 per day, $67.50) and Santa Fe (11hr., 3 per day, $60). **Amarillo City Transit,** 801 SE 23rd, operates eight bus routes departing from 3rd and Fillmore St. Maps are at the office. (☎378-3095. Buses run every 15-30min. M-Sa 6:30am-6:30pm. $0.75, children 6-12 $0.60.) The **Amarillo Convention and Visitors Bureau,** 401 S. Buchanan St., has free maps and info. (☎374-8474 or 800-692-1338; www.amarillo-cvb.org. Open Apr.-Sept. M-F 9am-6pm, Sa-Su 10am-4pm; Oct.-Mar. M-F 8:30am-5:30pm, Sa noon-4pm.) **Internet Access: Public Library,** 413 E. 4th Ave., at Buchanan. (☎378-3054. Free. Open M-Th 9am-9pm, Sa 9am-6pm, Su 2-6pm.) **Post Office:** 505 E. 9th Ave., at Buchanan St. (☎373-3192. Open M-F 8am-5pm.) **Postal Code:** 79105.

▛▟ ACCOMMODATIONS AND FOOD. Budget and chain motels crowd around on all sides of I-40, I-27, and U.S. 287/87 right near Amarillo, with room rates generally running in the $25-35 range. Try the **Big Texan Motel ❸,** 7701 I-40 E (Exit 74), where each room is painted in its own color and style. There's a horse hotel out back in case you rode in on a noble steed. (☎372-5000. Restaurant and swimming pool. Singles or doubles M-W and Su $55; Th-Sa $65. AAA and AARP discount $5.) **Palo Duro Canyon** (p. 657), 23 mi. from town, has tent and RV sites for $12 and $20 respectively. **KOA Kampground ❶,** 1100 Folsom Rd., 10 mi. east of town, has friendly service and grassy, shaded tent sites. Take I-40 to Exit 75, go north to Rte. 60, then east 1 mi. (☎335-1792, reservations 800-562-3431. Pool in summer. Wi-Fi. Reception daily June-Aug. 8am-10pm; Sept.-May 8am-7pm. Tent sites for 1-2 people $27, with water and electricity $37, with full hookup $38. Each additional person $4; ages 5-13 $3.)

At I-40 and Georgia, north of the interstate, heaping portions and a friendly vibe make **Dyer's BBQ ❷** a favorite. The ribs plate includes three finger-lickin'-good ribs, apricots, baked beans, cole slaw, onion rings, and potato salad for $8.75. (☎358-7104. Open M-Sa 11am-10pm, Su 11am-9pm.) The bright yellow **Big Texan Steak Ranch ❸,** 7701 I-40 E, next to the Big Texan Motel, is a longtime Route 66 institution. Diners who can manage to eat a 72 oz. steak in under 1 hr. will receive their entire meal for free. Note, though, that an unfinished steak will set you back a whopping $50. If that's not your idea of fun, maybe the fried rattlesnake ($6.50) or Rocky Mountain "oysters" ($11) are. Their personal limo service will also pick you up from any hotel in Amarillo for free if you call. (☎372-6000, for limo pick-up ☎342-5644. Wi-Fi available. Open daily 7am-10:30pm. AmEx/D/MC/V.)

◙ **SIGHTS.** The ▨**Amarillo Livestock Auction,** 100 Manhattan St., 1½ mi. east of town off 3rd Ave., is the largest livestock auction in the country. Visitors are welcome to sit alongside real-life cowboys as they bid on cows or to scale the catwalks and get a birds-eye view of the cattle pins who rustle the cattle up for auction. (☎373-7464. Auctions held Tu 10am until all the cows have been sold, usually around 4-5pm. Free.) The largest history museum in Texas, the **Panhandle-Plains Historical Museum,** 2401 4th Ave., 10 mi. south of Amarillo in nearby Canyon, covers the gamut of human history in the Panhandle, focusing on the commercial, agricultural, and industrial innovations that made life in this harsh environment possible. The museum features life-sized recreations of agricultural homesteads, oil derricks, and farm equipment in their natural settings. (On the West Texas A&M campus. ☎651-5235. Open Memorial Day-Labor Day M-Sa 9am-6pm, Su 1-6pm; low season M-Sa 9am-5pm, Su 1-6pm. $7, seniors $6, ages 4-13 $3.) The **American Quarter Horse Heritage Center and Museum,** 2601 I-40 E, at Exit 72A, tells the history and achievements of the Quarter Horse, the first horse bred in the US and still the most popular horse in America. (☎376-5181; www.aqha.com. Open M-Sa 9am-5pm, Su noon-5pm. $4, seniors $3.50, ages 7-18 $2.50.) At the ▨**Cadillac Ranch,** eccentric millionaire Stanley Marsh III planted 10 Cadillacs—model years 1948 to 1963—at the same angle as the Great Pyramids, and, as one local noted, "they didn't take root, neither." Take Hope Rd. (Exit 62) off I-40, 9 mi. west of Amarillo, and head half mile west on S. Frontage Road.

🌠 **DAYTRIP FROM AMARILLO: PALO DURO CANYON STATE PARK.** Twenty-three miles south of Amarillo, Palo Duro Canyon, known as the "Grand Canyon of Texas," covers 20,000 acres. Take I-27 to Exit 106 and head east on Rte. 217. The breathtaking 16 mi. **scenic drive** begins at the park headquarters, then drops down to the canyon floor and criss-crosses the Red River for 8 mi. Along this road are numerous trailheads and **campgrounds ❶**. There are 146 designated campsites. (Primitive sites $12, with water and electricity $20; backcountry camping $12.) **The Cow Camp Cabin** houses up to two people for $55 and includes A/C, microwave, refrigerator and an outdoor grill, but it does not offer indoor bathrooms. (☎488-2227. $50 cash or check deposit. No linen. Cabins with indoor bathrooms available start at $100. MC/V.) Hiking opportunities range from short, shady hikes along the river, such as the **Paseo del Rio Trail** (2 mi.), to more challenging hikes involving elevation change, such as the **Lighthouse Trail** (5 mi.), which leads to a rock that was named "the lighthouse" for its uncanny resemblance. **Backcountry hiking** is permitted, but most visitors stick to the marked trails. Canyon temperatures often climb to 100°F; bring plenty of water. The **headquarters,** just inside the park, has trail maps and info on park activities. (☎488-2227. Open daily in summer 7am-10pm; winter 8am-5pm. Park open daily in summer 7am-10pm; winter 8am-10pm. $3, under 12 free.) A half-mile past the headquarters, the **Visitors Center** has exhibits on the canyon's history. (Open M-Sa 9am-5pm, Su 1-5pm.) **Old West Stables,** located inside the canyon, offers 1hr. and 4hr. guided horse tours through the canyon. (☎488-2180. Mar.-Nov. 10am, noon, 2, 4, 6pm. Rides $35 per 1hr., $140 per 4hr. Reservations required for 4hr. rides. Wagon rides for groups of 10 or more $5 per person, children $3 per person.) The entertaining musical ▨**Texas Legacies** is performed in the canyon's sprawling Pioneer Amphitheater. The play follows a Texas ranch family through joyous and turbulent times, but it is the production and natural setting that are truly spectacular. The canyon walls serve as the backdrop, and the sights and sounds of live horses and the plethora of pyrotechnics reverberate throughout the 1700-seat outdoor amphitheater. (☎655-2181. Shows June-Aug. Tu-Sa 8:30pm. Tickets $15-30, under 12 $10-25. Pre-show barbecue 6:30pm; $14, children $10.)

GUADALUPE MOUNTAINS NATIONAL PARK   ☎915

Rising austerely above the parched West Texas desert, these peaks are the highest, most remote of the West Texas ranges. Mescalero Apaches hunted and camped on these lands until they were driven out by the US army. Today, Guadalupe Mountains National Park encompasses 86,000 acres of desert, caves, canyons, and highlands. From U.S. 62/180, drivers can see the park's most dramatic sights: **El Capitán**, a 2000 ft. limestone cliff, and **Guadalupe Peak,** which at 8749 ft. is the highest point in Texas. The mountains provide over 80 mi. of challenging desert trails. The major trailhead is at Pine Springs Campground. It's a strenuous full-day hike to the summit of the imposing Guadalupe Peak (8½ mi., 5-8hr.). A shorter trek (4¼ mi., 3-4hr.) traces the sheltered streambed of **Devil's Hall.** In **McKittrick Canyon,** sometimes called the most beautiful place in Texas, the landscape transitions from desert to woodland before your eyes. To get to the trail (4½-6¾ mi., 2-4hr.), take U.S. 62/180 6 mi. north from Pine Springs to the McKittrick turnoff, which goes another 4 mi. north to the trailhead (open daily in summer 8am-6pm; winter 8am-4:30pm). The **El Capitán Trail** (11½ mi.) hugs the base of the cliff of the same name and offers a terrific view of the desert below.

The park's two campgrounds, **Pine Springs ❶,** just past park headquarters, and **Dog Canyon ❶,** south of the New Mexico border at the north end of the park, have water and restrooms but no hookups or showers. Pine Springs has 20 tent sites and 20 RV sites away from the road. (☎828-3251. No wood or charcoal fires. Reservations for groups only. Sites $8.) Dog Canyon is accessible by car via Rte. 137, 72 mi. from Carlsbad, NM and 110 mi. from Pine Springs, or by a full-day hike from Pine Springs. (☎828-3251. Office open daily June-Aug. 8am-6pm; Sept.-May 8am-4:30pm. After hours, info is posted on the outside bulletin board. $8 per night.) Free **backcountry camping ❶** is permitted in 10 designated areas; permits are available at the Visitors Center. The nearest food is at **Salt Flat Cafe ❶,** 23 mi. west of Pine Springs. Open since 1921, owner Shirley Richardson and her granddaughter serve cheap burgers, grilled cheese sandwiches, and burritos to hikers. (☎964-2838. Breakfast and lunch $3-7. Open M-Sa 6:30am-2pm. AmEx/MC/V.) Travelers should be aware that the nearest gas station west of Pine Springs is 30 mi. away.

Carlsbad, NM (p. 847), 55 mi. northeast, is a good base for visiting both Guadalupe Mountains and Carlsbad Caverns National Parks. The park's lack of development is attractive to backpackers, but it creates some inconveniences for motorists: the nearest gas station is 35 mi. north in White's City, NM. **TNM&O Coaches** runs buses along U.S. 62/180 twice per day between Carlsbad and El Paso and will stop at the Visitors Center if you call ahead. (☎532-3404 in El Paso, 806-765-6644 in Carlsbad. From Carlsbad 2½hr., $26; from El Paso 3hr., $22.) **Park Headquarters** are at Pine Springs, just off U.S. 62/180. Here, the main **Visitors Center** has maps, pamphlets, exhibits, and a theater. Park entrance is free. Hiking and backcountry access is $5 per person, payable at trailheads. (☎828-3251; www.nps.gov/gumo. Open daily June-Aug. 8am-6pm; Sept.-May 8am-4:30pm.)

EL PASO   ☎915

El Paso, the largest US border town, boomed in the 17th century as a stopover on the east-west wagon route that followed the Rio Grande through *"el paso"* (the pass) between the Rocky Mountains and the Sierra Madre. Today, the El Paso-Ciudad Juárez metropolitan area has nearly three million inhabitants. Nearly everyone speaks Spanish, and the majority are of Mexican descent. Downtown bustles during the day, but the action moves across the border after dark. Stay on El Paso St. if walking between San Antonio Ave. and the border late at night.

Historic **San Jacinto Plaza** has shaded benches and a fiberglass alligator sculpture honoring the three reptiles the city once kept there. For a view of El Paso,

> **BORDER CROSSING.** Traveling between the US and Mexico is generally an easy process, but security is still taken very seriously. Crossing can be as simple as a wave of the passport or as time-consuming as a full search of your car. To keep things moving along, make sure to have all necessary documents handy—for U.S. citizens, a driver's license is sometimes accepted. It is illegal to cross the border anywhere except an open crossing station. See **Essentials** (p. 11) for more details on documents and procedures.

Ciudad Juárez, and three states (Texas, New Mexico, and Arizona) take the **Wyler Aerial Tramway,** at the end of McKinley Ave. on the east side of the Franklin Mountains, up to the 5632 ft. peak. (☎566-6622. Open in summer M and Th noon-6pm, F-Su noon-9pm; winter M, Th, and Su noon-6pm, F-Sa and holidays noon-8pm. $7, under 12 $4.) For slightly less impressive vistas at a lower elevation, but for free, take Rim Rd./Scenic Dr. to **Murchison Park.** The **El Paso Museum of Art,** 1 Arts Festival Plaza, is one of the largest art museums in the Southwest, with over 5000 works. The collections of 19th- to 20th-century Southwestern art and 18th- to 19th-century Latin American colonial art are particularly extensive. (☎532-1707. Open Tu-Sa 9am-5pm, Su noon-5pm. Free.) In the late 1800s, a drought altered the course of the Rio Grande in such a way that a tiny piece of the US remained across the new river channel. This set off a border dispute that wasn't resolved until the 60s, when the river was re-routed a second time. **Chamizal National Memorial,** 800 S. San Marcial Dr., is located on the formerly contested site and tells the history of this geopolitical oddity. (☎532-7273. Open Tu-Sa 10am-5pm. Free.) **Hueco Tanks State Historic Site,** 32 mi. east of town off U.S. 62, has bouldering, rock climbing, and hiking in cliffs adorned with ancient pictographs. Call ahead: only 70 people are allowed on the cliffs at once. (☎849-6684. Open Oct.-Apr. daily 8am-6pm; May-Sept. M-Th 8am-6pm, F-Su 7am-7pm. $4, under 13 free.)

The **Gardner Hotel ❶,** 311 E. Franklin, conveniently located downtown, is El Paso's oldest operating hotel. Everything about the hotel is old-fashioned: ceiling fans, elevators, light switches, and the prices. (☎532-3661; www.gardnerhotel.com. A/C and cable TV. Singles with shared bath $32; doubles with shared bath $40; larger rooms with private bath $52. MC/V.) The **El Paso International Hostel ❶** is part of the same hotel and has two bunk beds per room, Internet access, kitchen, and laundry. (☎532-3661; www.elpasohostel.com. Internet $1 per 15min. Dorms $20. MC/V.) The nearest campsites are at **Hueco Tanks State Historic Site ❶,** 32 mi. east of town. (☎849-6684. Showers and water. Entrance $4. Sites $12, with electricity and water $17.) Downtown activity dies down around 5pm. Most of El Paso's restaurants are in strip malls throughout the suburbs. Along **Mesa Street,** near the University of Texas at El Paso (UTEP), are some particularly good options. Eat to your heart's delight at **Veggie Good ❶,** 3800 N. Mesa St., in University Hills Plaza, which offers a buffet with a salad bar, fajitas, sandwiches, soups, and five kinds of *aguas frescas*—all for only $7. (☎494-3068. Open M-F 11am-8pm, Sa 11:30am-7pm. AmEx/D/MC/V.)

El Paso International Airport (ELP) (☎780-4749; take Sun Metro bus #33 to the city center) has major airline service. **Amtrak** runs from **Union Train Depot,** 700 San Francisco St. (☎800-872-7245 or 545-2247; www.amtrak.com; open M 7:15am-2:30pm, Tu-Sa 7:15am-9:30pm) to San Antonio (13hr., 3 per week, $76-147) and Tucson (6hr., 3 per week, $50-98). **Greyhound,** 200 W. San Antonio (☎532-2365; www.greyhound.com), near the Civic Center, runs to Albuquerque (5½hr., 2 per day, $21-29), Dallas (12-14hr., 8 per day, $45-60), and Tucson (6hr., 5 per day, $43). **El Paso-LA Bus Lines,** 720 Oregon St. (☎532-4061), at 6th Ave., offers cheap long-distance buses to Albuquerque (3 per day, $22), Denver (3 per day, $50), and Los Angeles (3 per day, $55). **Sun Metro** (☎533-3333) operates local buses ($1, students and under

18 $0.50) and downtown trolleys ($0.25). **The Visitors Center** is at 1 Civic Center Plaza, at Santa Fe and San Francisco. (☎534-0601 or 800-351-6024; www.visitelpaso.com. Open M-F 8am-5pm.) **Post Office:** 219 Mills Ave. (☎532-8824. Open M-F 8am-5pm, Sa 8:30am-noon.) **Postal Code:** 79901.

DEL RIO   ☎830

Situated near the Chihuahuan Desert and alongside the Rio Grande is a geological and cultural oasis called Del Rio. A fine little American town in its own right, Del Rio is also a model for internationalism. Del Rio and its sister city in Mexico, Ciudad Acuña, might just be the friendliest pair of towns on the entire US border. Del Rio's **Main Street** bustles with new life and restored storefronts without falling into the cutesy clichés that plague so many Main Streets. The **San Felipe Springs** are responsible for Del Rio's lush tropical environment. Forty percent of the water in the Rio Grande south of Del Rio comes from these springs, by way of **San Felipe Creek.** A series of parks along the creek provide ideal swimming holes and excellent bird-watching. Kayaking is the most relaxing and practical way to access ▓**Parida Cave** and **Panther Cave,** where four 12,000-year-old Native American pictographs cover the cave walls in brilliant colors. (From the Pecos River ramp. 50 mi. east of Del Rio, Parida Cave is 3 mi. round-trip. Panther Cave takes all day.) Founded in 1883, long before Texas wine became the latest trend, **Val Verde Winery,** 100 Qualia Dr., off Hudson Ave., is Texas' oldest continuously-operated winery—it stayed in business during prohibition by making grape juice. (☎775-9714; www.valverdewinery.com. Free tours and tastings. Open M-Sa 10am-5pm.) **Alamo Village,** 38 mi. east of Del Rio off U.S. 90, is the largest outdoor movie set in the US. John Wayne built it for $12 million for his film *The Alamo* (1960), and it has been used for everything from *Lonesome Dove* (1989) to *The West* (1996), a documentary by Ken Burns. (☎563-2580; www.alamovillage.com. Amateur gunfight contests most Sa-Su. Open daily in summer 9am-6pm; in winter 9am-5pm. $10.75, ages 6-11 $5.)

In town, cheap motels line Veterans Blvd. **Amistad National Recreation Area ❶** has primitive lakeside campsites for $4. The **Governor's Landing ❶** sites have water hookups and cost $8. **Villa Del Rio ❹,** 123 Hudson Dr., south of town, is a small, family-run B&B in an 1887 Spanish-style home. The innkeepers serve border-influenced breakfasts every morning to guests. (☎768-1100. Rooms from $95. AmEx/MC/V.) The best food is across the border in visitor-friendly Ciudad Acuña. **La Cabañita 99 ❶,** 267 C. Galeana, in the heart of Acuña, lets you make your own tacos. The huge specialty platter, which features three meats, cilantro, sauces, onions, and corn tortillas (100 pesos; $10), is enough to feed four people. (☎877-772-1467. Cash only.) Back in the states, **Flamingo 50s Hamburgers ❶,** 1750 Veterans Blvd., has large $1.40 burgers and Hawaiian shaved ice. (☎775-4001. Open daily 9am-11pm. D/MC/V.)

Del Rio International Airport (DRT), 1104 W. 10th St. (☎774-8538), serves Houston. **Amtrak,** 100 N. Main St. (☎800-872-7245; www.amtrak.com), runs to El Paso (8½hr., 3 per week, $44-99) and San Antonio (4hr., 3 per week, $25-48). **Kerrville Bus Lines,** at the Amtrak station, has daily service to San Antonio (3¼hr., 3 per day, $25). For a **taxi** call **Del Rio Taxi Service,** (☎775-4448.) The border is 2 mi. south of Del Rio. Park and walk across the three quarter mile bridge ($2 per car, $0.75 per pedestrian; $0.30 to re-enter Texas). The **Visitors Center,** 4121 Veterans Blvd., has information on swimming, water sports, and fishing. (☎775-7491. Open daily 8am-5pm.) The **Del Rio Chamber of Commerce,** 1915 Veterans Blvd., has local info. (☎800-889-8149; www.drchamber.com. Open daily 8:30am-5pm.) **Amistad Family Violence and Rape Crisis Center** (☎775-9612) operates 24hr. **The Val Verde Regional Medical Center** is at 801 Bedell Ave. (☎703-1701). Check **email** at the **Del Rio Public Library,** 300 Spring St. (☎774-7595. Open M-Th 10am-7pm, F 10am-6pm, Sa-Su 1pm-5pm.) **Post Office:** 114 W. Broadway. (☎775-3388. Open M-F 9:30am-4:30pm.) **Postal Code:** 78840.

BIG BEND NATIONAL PARK ☎ 432

The arid Chihuahuan Desert, lofty Chisos Mountains, and muddy Rio Grande unite in a marriage of land, air, and water to form Big Bend National Park, one of Texas's most remote and wild natural areas. Roadrunners, coyotes, pig-like *javelinas*, mountain lions, and even a few black bears roam this 800,000-acre tract of land, where visitors can gaze over breathtaking desert vistas for miles on end and sleep under a clear, star-filled sky.

■ ◪ ORIENTATION AND PRACTICAL INFORMATION.

There is no public transportation into or around the park. **Amtrak** stops in Alpine, 103 mi. north of the park entrance where car rentals are also available. Three roads lead south from U.S. 90 into the park: from Marfa, U.S. 67 to Rte. 170; from Alpine, Rte. 118; from Marathon, U.S. 385 (the quickest route). There are two **gas stations** within the park, one at **Panther Junction** (☎477-2294; open daily Sept.-Mar. 7am-7pm; Apr.-Aug. 8am-6pm; credit card service 24hr.), next to the park headquarters, and one at **Rio Grande Village** (☎477-2293; open daily Mar.-May 9am-8pm; June-Feb. 9am-6pm). On Rte. 118, near the western park entrance, the **Study Butte Chevron** also sells gas (credit card access 24hr.). Park Headquarters are at **Panther Junction**, 26 mi. south of the northern park boundary. (☎477-2251, Visitors Center 477-1158; www.nps.gov/bibe. Open daily 8am-6pm. Vehicles $20 per week, pedestrians and cyclists $10 per week.) **Visitors Centers** are located at **Persimmon Gap** (☎477-2393; open daily 8am-5pm), and **Chisos Basin** (☎477-2264; open daily 9am-4:30pm). The Visitors Centers at **Rio Grande Village** (☎477-2271) and **Castalon** (☎477-2666) are only open from late May to August (both daily 9am-4:30pm). **Post Office:** The main **post office** is in Panther Junction, next to Park Headquarters. (☎477-2238. Open M-F 8am-2:30pm.) Chisos Basin's **post office** is inside the grocery store. (Open M-Sa 9am-5pm.) **Postal Code:** 79834.

▮ ▯ ACCOMMODATIONS AND FOOD.

The expensive **Chisos Mountains Lodge ❹**, in Chisos Basin, has both modern motel rooms and cottages built in the 30s. Reservations are a must in winter—the lodge is often booked a year in advance. (☎477-2291. Singles $94-115; doubles $104-125. Additional person $10. AmEx/D/MC/V.) The closest budget motel to the park, the **Chisos Mining Company Motel ❷**, on Rte. 170, ¾ mi. west of Rte. 118 in Terlingua, has clean rooms with A/C. (☎371-2254; www.cmcm.cc. Singles $49, doubles $72-98; 2- to 6-person cabins with kitchenettes from $125. AmEx/D/MC/V.) The three developed campgrounds in the park are generally first come, first served, although from November to April some sites are open for reservations up to one year in advance. During Thanksgiving, Christmas, March, and April the campgrounds fill early; call park headquarters to inquire about availability. (☎477-2251. All tent sites $14. No campfires.) **Chisos Basin Campground ❶**, at 5400 ft., has 65 sites, some with shade and privacy, all with running water and flush toilets. No hook-ups. $14 per night. In the summer it is by far the best choice for tent campers. **Castalon Campground ❶**, at 2170 ft., and **Rio Grande Vil-**

❗ DON'T FORGET TO CALL MOM. You won't have mobile phone access throughout Big Bend National Park, Terlingua, or anywhere nearby. If you're driving a car, remember there are long stretches between rest stops and gas stations, which means that half a tank of gas is sometimes the same as an empty tank of gas. When you see a sign that says you won't see a service station for 74 mi., that means you probably won't see a single living soul for those 74 mi., maybe more. If you decide to travel alone, let people know where you are, check your tires, and watch out for deer on the road.

lage Campground ❶, at 1850 ft., both feature grassy sites along the Rio Grande with lots of shade. (Castalon: 35 sites; Rio Grande; 100 sites. Sites $14 at both.) Rio Grande Village has showers ($1 per 5min.) at the **RV park ❶**, which has 25 full hookups. (Sites $21, 2 person max.; $3 per additional person.) **Backcountry camping** ❶ at any of dozens of sites is $10 and requires a permit from a Visitors Center.

  Chisos Mountains Lodge contains the park's only **restaurant ❷**, serving three meals a day. (Extensive breakfast buffet $8. Soup and salad bar $7.50. Dinner entrees $6-20. Open daily 7-10:30am, 11:30am-4pm, and 5-8pm; in winter also 8-9pm.) A small **grocery store** next to the lodge covers all food groups as well as beer at only $1.25 per can. (Open daily 9am-7pm.) Those willing to make the 25 mi. trip outside the park to **Terlingua**, or 5 mi. further west down Rte. 170 to **Terlingua Ghost Town**, will find a few additional dining and drinking establishments. At **Ghost Town Cafe ❷**, 1001 Ghost Town Rd., you probably won't find air conditioning, but you will find the best homemade cooking for 100 mi. in every direction. Try the Ghost Rider, with two slices of french toast, two eggs, and bacon for $3.75. (☎371-3000. Entrees $3-8. Breakfast served all day. Opens daily at 6am; call for hours.)

🛶 OUTDOOR ACTIVITIES. Big Bend spans over 200 mi. of hiking trails, ranging from 30min. nature walks to multi-day backpacking trips. Always carry at least one gallon of water per person per day in the desert. For those short on time, the best sightseeing is along the 🏞**Ross Maxwell Scenic Drive,** a 30 mi. paved route from the western edge of the Chisos Mountains leading down to the Rio Grande and Santa Eleña Canyon. Call ahead for road conditions.

  Pick up hiking guides and maps at any of the Visitors Centers ($1-2). Some trails have free maps at the trailheads. The **Window Trail** (5¼ mi. round-trip, 2-3hr.) slopes downhill from the Chisos Basin parking lot or campground along the basin's drainage path to "The Window," where the mountains open up to the vast desert below in an impressive panorama. Departing from the same parking lot, the **Window View Trail** offers a view of The Window, as well as sunsets, from a distance. The **Lost Mine Trail** (4¾ mi. round-trip, 3-4hr.) starts at 5600 ft. and climbs an additional 1200 ft. for breathtaking views of the Chisos and the Sierra de Carmen in Mexico. Also in the Chisos, the **Emory Peak Trail** (9 mi. round-trip, 5-8hr.) is an intense climb to the highest peak in the park (7825 ft.). If the line is too long for the showers, relax in the 104°F **hot springs** on the shores of the Rio Grande.

  Though damming has significantly decreased the river's flow, rafting on the Rio Grande is still popular. Free permits and info are available at the Visitors Center. Several companies rent kayaks and offer river trips down the 118 mi. stretch of designated **Rio Grande Wild and Scenic River.** In Terlingua on Hwy. 170, just west of Rte. 118, **Big Bend River Tours** rents canoes and rafts. Guided trips through canyons and rapids are available. (☎371-3033 or 800-545-4240; www.bigbendrivertours.com. Rafts $25 per day. Canoes $45 per day. Guided trips $65 per half-day, $100 per full day, 21-day trip $3125.)

ROCKY MOUNTAINS

Created by immense tectonic forces some 65 million years ago, the Rockies mark a vast wrinkle in the North American continent. Sculpted by eons of wind, water, and glaciers, their weathered peaks extend some 3000 mi. from northern Alberta (in Canada) down to New Mexico, soaring to altitudes exceeding two miles at some points. The highest peaks of the Rockies are accessible only to veteran mountain climbers and wildlife adapted for scant air and deep snow. Although the Rocky Mountain area supports less than 5% of the US population, each year millions flock to its spectacular parks, forests, and ski resorts, while extreme hikers follow the length of the Continental Divide. Nestled in valleys or springing from the surrounding plains, the region's mountain villages and cowboy towns welcome travelers year-round.

HIGHLIGHTS OF THE ROCKY MOUNTAINS

HIKE along the **Gunnison Route** through the Black Canyon (p. 691) or geyser-side paths in **Yellowstone National Park** (p. 700).

CRAWL through ancient Puebloan dwellings at **Mesa Verde National Park** (p. 698).

PEEK at marmots and majestic elk in **Rocky Mountain National Park** (p. 673).

CAREEN down the ski slopes in **Sawtooth** (p. 744), **Vail** (p. 681), or **Jackson** (p. 717).

CRUISE the unforgettable **Going-to-the-Sun Road** in Glacier National Park (p. 734).

COLORADO

In the high, thin air of Colorado, golf balls fly farther, eggs take longer to cook, and visitors get winded just getting out of bed. Hikers, skiers, and climbers worship Colorado's peaks and mountain enclaves. Denver, the country's highest capital, has long since shed its cow-town image and matured into the cultural center of the region. Colorado's extraordinary heights are matched only by its equally spectacular depths, like the Black Canyon of the Gunnison, etched over millions of years by the Gunnison River. Silver and gold attracted early settlers to Colorado, but it is Mother Nature's more rugged elements that appeal to modern-day adventurers.

🛈 PRACTICAL INFORMATION

Capital: Denver.

Visitor Info: Colorado Travel and Tourism Authority (CTTA), 1620 Broadway, Ste. 1700, Denver 80202 (☎303-893-3885, vacation guide 800-265-6723; www.colorado.com). **US Forest Service,** Rocky Mountain Region, 740 Sims St., Golden 80401, or P.O. Box 25127, Lakewood 80225 (☎303-275-5350). Open M-F 7:30am-4:30pm. **Ski Country USA,** 1507 Blake St., Denver 80202 (☎303-837-0793) provides info on all -area ski resorts. Open M-F 9am-5pm. **Colorado State Parks,** 1313 Sherman St., #618, Denver 80203

ROCKY MOUNTAINS

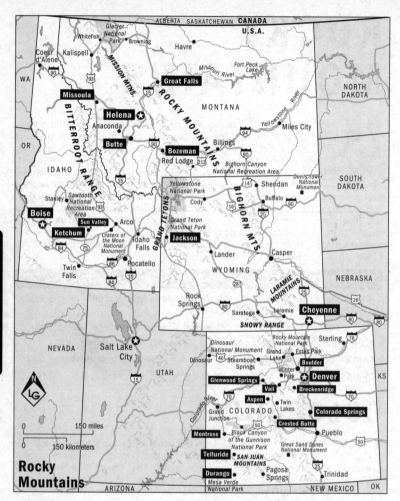

Rocky Mountains

(☎303-866-3437, state park reservations 800-678-2267). Open M-F 7am-4:45pm. $8 reservation fee for campsites; reserve at least 3 days in advance.

Postal Abbreviation: CO. **Sales Tax:** 7.4%.

DENVER
☎303

In 1858, the discovery of gold in the Rocky Mountains brought a rush of eager miners to northern Colorado. After an excruciating trek through the plains, the prospectors set up camp there before heading west into the "hills," and the frontier town of Denver was born. Modern-day Denver combines that true Western grit with urban sophistication. Boasting both the nation's largest park system and the largest amount of beer brewed in any US metropolitan area, Denver always offers something fun to do.

▣ TRANSPORTATION

Airport: Denver International (DEN; ☎342-2000; www.flydenver.com), 23 mi. northeast of downtown off I-70. Shuttles run from the airport to downtown and ski resorts. The **RTD Sky Ride** (☎299-6000) runs buses every hr. from the Market St. station to the airport. Office open M-F 6am-8pm, Sa-Su 9am-6pm. Buses operate daily 5am-1:30am. $8; seniors, disabled, and students ages 6-19 $4; under 15 free. From the main terminal, **Supershuttle** (☎370-1300 or 800-525-3177; www.supershuttle.com) runs to downtown hotels (1hr., $19). Taxi downtown $50.

Trains: Amtrak, Union Station, 1701 Wynkoop St. (☎825-2583 or 800-872-7245; www.amtrak.com), at 17th St. Office open daily 5:30am-9pm. To **Chicago** (19hr., 1 per day, $92-181), **Salt Lake City** (15hr., 1 per day, $63-124), and **San Francisco** (37½hr., 1 per day, $93-183). **Winter Park Ski Train** (☎296-4754; www.skitrain.com), leaves from the same building for **Winter Park.** Runs Jan. Sa-Su, Feb. F-Su, Mar. Th-Su, Aug. Sa only. Reservations required. Round-trip in winter $49, ages 3-13 and over 61 $44; in summer $44/39.

Buses: Greyhound, 1055 19th St. (☎293-6555; www.greyhound.com). Office open daily 5:30am-11:45pm. To: **Chicago** (21-24hr., 6 per day, $117-125); **Colorado Springs** (1½hr., 7 per day, $15-21.50); **Salt Lake City** (9½-12hr., 4 per day, $67-72); **Santa Fe** (7½-9hr., 3 per day, $57-77). **Estes Park Shuttle** (☎970-586-5151; www.estesparkshuttle.com) provides access to Rocky Mountain National Park from the airport and downtown ($45).

Public Transit: Regional Transportation District (RTD), 1600 Blake St. (☎299-6000 or 800-366-7433; www.rtd-denver.com). Serves Denver, Longmont, Evergreen, Golden, and suburbs. Hours vary; some lines shut down by 9pm, many lines shut down by midnight. $1.50, seniors and disabled $0.75. Exact change required. Regional routes go to Boulder, Nederland, and the national forests to the west for $3.75. Main terminals are at Market and 16th St., and Colfax and Broadway. A free 16th St. **mall shuttle** covers much of downtown. Runs daily 5am-1:30am.

Taxi: Yellow Cab, ☎777-7777.

Car Rental: Enterprise, 7720 Calawaba Ct. (☎342-7350 or 800-720-7222; www.enterprise.com), at the airport.

◼◼ ⊮ ORIENTATION AND PRACTICAL INFORMATION

Running north-south, **Broadway** slices downtown Denver in half. East of Broadway, **Colorado Boulevard** is another major north-south thoroughfare. Immediately west of downtown, **I-25** winds its way north-south along the South Platte River, intersects with east-west **I-70** just north of downtown, and provides the quickest access to the city center. **Colfax Avenue,** running east-west, is the main north-south dividing line. Gridded Denver is generally easy to navigate by car or bike. Travel complications most often result from confusing the numbered streets and the numbered avenues; both named and numbered streets run diagonally in the downtown area, at a 45-degree angle to the city's grid. In the rest of the city, numbered avenues run east-west and increase as you head north. Named streets run north-south. Many of the avenues on the eastern side of the city become numbered streets downtown. The pedestrian-only **16th Street Mall,** from Broadway in the southeast to Wewatta St. in the northwest, is the hub of Denver's downtown— the social, dining, and entertainment center of the city. At night, avoid traveling south of W. Colfax and west of Speer Blvd. Extra care should be taken after dark in **Lower Downtown (LoDo),** starting at Larimer St. and ending at Wewatta St., bounded by 14th and 20th St., and on the Colfax Ave. corridor.

Colorado

Visitor Info: Denver Visitors Bureau, 1600 California St. (☎892-1505; www.denver.org), in the 16th St. Mall. Open May-Oct. M-F 9am-6pm, Sa 9am-5pm, Su 11am-3pm; Nov.-Apr. M-F 9am-5pm.

GLBT Resources: The Gay, Lesbian, and Bisexual Community Services Center of Colorado (☎733-7743; www.glbtcolorado.org). Open M-F 9am-6pm.

Rape Crisis Hotline: ☎322-7273. 24hr.

Internet Access: Public Library, 10 W. 14th Ave. (☎720-865-1111; www.denverlibrary.org). Free. Open M-Tu 10am-8pm, W-F 10am-6pm, Sa 9am-5pm, Su 1-5pm.

Post Office: 951 20th St. (☎296-4692). Open M-F 7am-7pm, Sa 8:30am-7pm. **Postal Code:** 80202.

🏠 ACCOMMODATIONS

Inexpensive hotels line E. Colfax Ave., Broadway, and Colorado Blvd. Denver hotels tend to be business traveler-oriented and have better rates on weekends.

Hostel of the Rocky Mountains (HI), 1717 Race St. (☎861-7777). A family atmosphere in a pleasant residential area just east of downtown. Coin-op laundry, basement lounge with comfy couches, kitchen, library. Linen $2.50. Free Internet. Key deposit $5. Reception 8am-5pm and 8-10pm. Reservations recommended. Dorms $20; private rooms $35; refurbished guest house $40. MC/V. ❶

Melbourne International Hotel & Hostel, 607 22nd St. (☎292-6386; www.denverhostel.com), at Welton. Wooden bunks, clean bathrooms, and large kitchen. Linens and towels $3. Free Internet. Key deposit $10. Reception 6am-9pm; call ahead for late arrivals. Dorms $20, students $16; private rooms $34/29. Cash only. ❶

Broadway Plaza Motel, 1111 Broadway (☎893-0303), 3 blocks south of the Capitol. A well-preserved example of 50s architecture. Spacious rooms in a prime downtown location. Singles $50-75; doubles $60-100. AmEx/D/MC/V. ❸

Cherry Creek State Park, 4201 S. Parker Rd. (☎690-1166, reservations 470-1144 or 800-678-2267; www.parks.state.co.us), in Aurora. Take I-25 to Exit 200, go north about 3 mi. on I-225 to the Parker Rd. Exit, then continue 1 mi. south on Park Rd. to

Lehigh. Trees provide limited shade. Boating, fishing, swimming, hiking, and horseback riding available. Arrive early. Open year-round. Sites $14, with electricity $22. Additional day-use fee $7. ❶

FOOD

Downtown Denver offers a full range of cuisines, from reasonably priced Greek and Ethiopian food on **East Colfax Avenue** to trendy new American in historic **LoDo.** You may wonder what sort of delicacies **"Rocky Mountain oysters"** are, especially given the city of Denver's distance from the ocean. Be warned: these salty-sweet bison testicles, sold at the **Buckhorn Exchange,** 1000 Osage St. (☎534-9505), do not hail from the sea.

Wazee Lounge & Supper Club, 1600 15th St. (☎623-9518; www.wazeesupperclub.com), at Wazee St. in LoDo. The black-and-white tiled floor, Depression-era wood paneling, and gas lights give this diner a bohemian feel. Pizza $7-9. Stromboli $9. Happy hour M-F 4-6pm. Open M-Sa 11am-2am, Su noon-midnight. Kitchen closes M-Sa 1am, Su 11pm. AmEx/MC/V. ❷

Mercury Cafe, 2199 California St. (☎294-9258; www.mercurycafe.com), at 22nd St. Decorated with a new-age flair, "the Merc" proclaims "organic food is your birthright" and specializes in homemade wheat bread, soups ($2-3), salads ($8-16), and enchiladas ($7-10). Live bands jam in the dining room, while the upstairs dance floor hosts evening swing (Tu, Th, Su) and tango (F) lessons. Open Tu-F 5:30-11pm, Sa-Su 9am-3pm and 5:30-11pm. Cash only. ❸

Wynkoop Brewing Co., 1634 18th St. (☎297-2700; www.wynkoop.com), across from Union Station in LoDo. Colorado's first brewpub serves its own beer (pints $4), plus a menu including buffalo burgers and catfish tacos ($8-9). Th-Sa improv comedy downstairs. Happy hour M-F 3-6pm. Open M-Sa 11am-2am, Su 11am-midnight. Kitchen closes M-Th 11pm, F-Sa midnight, Su 10pm. AmEx/D/MC/V. ❷

WaterCourse Foods, 837 E. 17th Ave. (☎832-7313; www.watercoursefoods.com), at Emerson St. This innovative restaurant serves delicious vegetarian dishes, from country-fried seitan steaks ($11) to seitan fajitas ($13). For breakfast, try the banana bread french toast ($8.50). Open M-F 6:30am-10pm, Sa-Su 8am-10pm. MC/V. ❸

SIGHTS

DOWNTOWN. Denver's **Civic Center Plaza** is the heart of downtown. At the east end, at E. Colfax Ave. and Grant St., the gold-domed **Capitol Building,** built of Colorado-mined granite, marble, and limestone, is a sensible place to begin your visit to the Mile High City. A small engraving on the 15th step up to the building's entrance marks 1 mi. above sea level; according to recent satellite measurements, the mile-high point is actually on the 13th step. Oops! *(☎866-2604. Open M-F 7am-5pm. 45min. tours every 30min. June-Aug. M-F 9am-3:30pm; Sept.-May M-F 9:15am-2:30pm. Wheelchair-accessible. Free.)* Near the Capitol is the **Denver Art Museum (DAM),** a "vertical" museum housing a world-class collection of Native American art and pre-Columbian artifacts, modern and contemporary art, and works by local artists. *(100 W. 14th Ave. ☎720-865-5000; www.denverartmuseum.org. Open Tu-Th and Sa 10am-5pm, F 10am-10pm, Su noon-5pm. Tours of special exhibits daily; call for times. Wheelchair-accessible. $13, students and over 65 $10, ages 6-18 $5.)* **Grayline Tours** runs a 3hr. whirlwind introduction to Denver's major attractions with knowledgeable guides. *(☎289-2841; www.grayline.com. Departs daily at 8:30am and 1:30pm from the Cherry Creek Shopping Center. $35, ages 3-11 $17.50.)* Just north of the Pepsi Center, the **Denver Aquarium** offers spectacular exhibits on river systems and rainforests. The aquarium also houses over 15,000 marine creatures, including several species of sharks, otters, and the magnificent Napoleon wrasse. *(700 Water St., Exit 211 off I-25. RTD bus #10.* ☎ *561-4450 or 888-561-4450; www.downtownaquarium.com. Open M-Th and Su 10am-10pm, F-Sa 10am-11pm. $13.75, over 65 $13, ages 4-12 $8.25.)*

CITY PARK AREA. The gigantic **Denver Museum of Nature and Science** hosts a multitude of captivating exhibits, including the "Hall of Life," the "Prehistoric Journey," the "Edge of the Wild," and a superb exhibit on gems and minerals, including the largest gold nugget ever found in the state of Colorado. Explore the skies in the museum's digital **Gates Planetarium.** *(2001 Colorado Blvd., at Montview Blvd.* ☎ *322-7009 or 800-925-2250; www.dmns.org. Open daily 9am-5pm. Wheelchair-accessible. Call for show times. $10, students and ages 3-18 and over 60 $6; IMAX and museum $15/10; planetarium and museum $15/10.)*

COORS BREWERY. Located in nearby Golden, Coors is the largest one-site brewery in the world. It also has one of the nicest fitness centers in the corporate world, perhaps because its 3500 employees need somewhere to work off the two free beers they receive after each shift. Free tours take visitors through the Coors brewing process and finish with free samples for those over 21. *(Take I-70 W to Exit 264; turn left on 32nd Ave., head west for 4½ mi., then turn left on East St. and follow the signs. A shuttle bus runs from the parking lot to the brewery after a very short historical tour of Golden.* ☎ *277-2337. 40min. tours continuously M-Sa 10am-4pm.)*

BUTTERFLY PAVILION AND INSECT CENTER. Let exotic butterflies land on your shoulders at this unusual tropical conservatory, shielded from the Front Range's aridity by glass walls and misted water. In addition to the pavilion, a hands-on aquatic and insect center will bewitch young and old alike. *(6252 W. 104th Ave., at Westminster Blvd., in Westminster, just off U.S. 36 on the way to Boulder.* ☎ *469-5441; www.butterfly.org. Open daily in summer 9am-6pm; in winter 9am-5pm. Wheelchair-accessible. $8, seniors $6, children 4-12 $5.)*

🎵 🎭 ENTERTAINMENT AND OUTDOOR ACTIVITIES

Life in Denver is never boring for sports fans. Major League Baseball's **Colorado Rockies** play at **Coors Field,** 2001 Blake St. (☎ 762-5437 or 800-388-7625; www.colorado.rockies.mlb.com. 1¼hr. tours M-Sa on non-game days at 10am, noon, and 2pm; on evening game days 10am and noon; on afternoon game days no tours. Tickets $4-47. $4 "Rockpile" bleacher tickets available 2hr. before gametime. Tours $7, seniors $6, under 12 $5.) As a reward for their back-to-back Super Bowl victories in the late 90s, the NFL's **Denver Broncos** got a new and larger **Mile High Stadium** (officially renamed Invesco Field at Mile High), 1701 Bryant St. (☎ 720-258-3888; www.denverbroncos.com. 1¼hr. tours every hr. June-Aug. Tu-Sa 10am-2pm; Sept.-May Th-Sa 10am-2pm. $9, ages 5-12 and over 65 $7.) The stadium is also used by soccer's **Colorado Rapids** (☎ 825-4625; www.coloradorapids.com). The NBA's **Denver Nuggets** and the NHL's **Colorado Avalanche** share the state-of-the-art **Pepsi Center,** 1000 Chopper Cir. (Teams info ☎ 405-1100; www.pepsicenter.com. 1¼hr. tours M and W 10am, noon, 2pm; F 10am and noon. $6, children and seniors $5.)

Denver has more public parks per square mile than any other city in the United States, providing visitors and locals alike plenty of prime space for bicycling, walking, or sun-bathing. **Cheesman Park,** at 8th St. and Franklin St., has picnic areas, manicured flower gardens, and a view of snow-capped peaks from endless green lawns. **Confluence Park,** at Cherry Creek and the South Platte River, lures bikers and runners with paved riverside paths and kayakers with rapids. One of the best parks for sporting events, **Washington Park,** at E. Louisiana Ave. and S. Downing

Denver

▲ ACCOMMODATIONS
Broadway Plaza Motel, **11**
Cherry Creek State Park, **12**
Hostel of the Rocky
Mountains (HI), **7**
Melbourne International
Hotel & Hostel, **6**

♦ FOOD
Mercury Cafe, **5**
Wazee Lounge & Supper
Club, **4**
WaterCourse Foods, **8**
Wynkoop Brewery, **1**

♣ NIGHTLIFE
El Chapultepec, **2**
Charlie's, **9**
The Church, **10**
Fadó Irish Pub, **3**

TO ↗ (5mi)

TO BLUEBIRD THEATER (1.3mi),
COLORADO BLVD. (1.75mi),
CITY PARK AND DENVER MUSEUM OF
NATURE AND SCIENCE (2mi)

TO CHEESMAN PARK (600yd)

TO AIRPORT (20mi),
COORS BREWERY (18mi),
RED ROCKS (15mi)

TO 70

TO COORS FIELD (150yd),
DENVER AQUARIUM
(450yd)

TO BUTTERFLY PAVILION AND INSECT CENTER (11mi),
CONFLUENCE PARK (150yd), DENVER AQUARIUM
(600yd) INVESCO FIELD AT MILE HIGH (1.3mi)

TO ROXBOROUGH
STATE PARK (25mi)

0   300 yards
0   300 meters

Benedict
Fountain
Park

Molly Brown
House

State
Capitol

RTD Civic
Center
Station

Civic
Center
Park

Brown
Palace
Hotel

Museum of
Western Art

Federal
Building

Greyhound

RTD Market St.
Bus Terminal

WRITER
SQUARE

LARIMER
SQUARE

Union
Station

Skyline Park

16th St. Mall

Denver Performing
Arts Complex

Colorado
Convention
Center

Fire House
Museum

US
Mint

Greek Amphitheater

Byers/Evans
House-Denver
History Museum

Denver Art Museum

Library and
Media Center

Metropolitan
State College
Community
College of
Denver

UNIVERSITY
OF COLORADO-
DENVER

Student
Union

St. Elizabeth's

St. Francis Way

Pepsi
Center

Cherry Creek

Speer Blvd.

Santa Fe Dr.

Speer Blvd.

W. Colfax Ave.

E. Colfax Ave.

ROCKY MOUNTAINS

St., hosts impromptu volleyball and soccer games almost every summer weekend. Paths for biking, jogging, and in-line skating encircle the park, and the two lakes in the middle are popular fishing spots. **Colorado State Parks** (see **Practical Information**, p. 663) has the lowdown on nearby state parks. At **Roxborough State Park** (☎973-3959), visitors can hike among rock formations in the **Dakota Hogback** ridge. Take U.S. 85 S, turn right on Titan Rd., and follow it 3½ mi. (Open dawn-dusk.) The mammoth ◪**Red Rocks Amphitheater and Park** (☎697-4939; www.redrocksonline.com), 12 mi. southwest of Denver, on I-70 at the Morrison Exit (Exit 259), is carved into sandstone, and performers like the Dave Matthews Band and the Arcade Fire compete with the lovely view for audience attention. The park itself contains over 800 acres. (Park open daily 5am-11pm. Visitors Center open daily mid-May to Sept. 8am-7pm; in winter 10am-4pm.) Forty miles west of Denver, the road to the top of **Mount Evans** (14,264 ft.) is the highest discontinuous paved road in North America. Take I-70 W to Rte. 103 in Idaho Springs. (Info ☎567-3000. Open late May-early Sept., conditions permitting. Vehicles $10 per day.)

The **Denver Performing Arts Complex (DPAC),** at Speer Blvd. and Arapahoe St., is the largest arts complex in the nation and home to the Denver Center for the Performing Arts, the Colorado Symphony, the Colorado Ballet, and Opera Colorado. (☎893-4100 or 800-641-1222. Box office open M-Sa 10am-6pm.) The **Denver Center Theater Company** performs new shows for free the Wednesday before the show opens. (☎893-4000; www.denvercenter.org. Tickets distributed beginning at 4pm the day of performance; call for schedule.) At the intimate **Germinal Stage Denver,** 2450 W. 44th Ave., every seat is a good one. Plays range from traditional to experimental. (☎455-7108. Shows F-Su. Tickets $15-20.) **The Bluebird Theater,** 3317 E. Colfax Ave., hosts a variety of national and local musical acts. (☎322-2308; www.bluebirdtheater.net. Live music W-Sa. Tickets free-$25.)

▩ FESTIVALS

Every January, Denver hosts the **National Western Stock Show and Rodeo,** 4655 Humboldt St., the nation's largest livestock show and one of the biggest rodeos. Goodlooking cowboys compete for prize money while over 10,000 head of cattle, horses, sheep, and rabbits compete for "Best of Breed." Between big events, all sorts of oddball fun takes place, including Western battle recreations, monkey sheep herders, and rodeo clowns. (☎295-6124; www.nationalwestern.com. Jan. 12-27, 2008. Call for ticket prices.) The whole area vibrates with ancient rhythms during the **Denver March Pow-Wow,** at the Denver Coliseum, 4600 Humboldt St., when over 1000 Native Americans from tribes all over North America dance together in full costume. (☎934-8045; www.denvermarchpowwow.org. Mid-Mar. 1-day pass $6, 3-day pass $15; under 6 and over 60 free. Cash only.) The nation's most prestigious beer competition takes place every year at the end of September during the **Great American Beer Festival,** a celebration of over 1600 beers from hundreds of breweries. Admission includes a tasting cup to capitalize on the free 1 oz. samples. (☎447-0816 or 888-822-6273; www.beertown.org/events/gabf/index.htm. Tickets $45-50.)

▣ NIGHTLIFE

Downtown Denver, especially the 16th St. Mall, is an attraction in itself, with ample shopping, dining, and people-watching opportunities. A copy of the free weekly *Westword* gives the lowdown on LoDo, where the action heads after dark.

The Church, 1160 Lincoln St. (☎832-3528; www.the-church.com), at 12th St. In a remodeled chapel complete with stained-glass windows, the Church boasts 4 full bars,

3 floors of dancing, a cigar lounge, and a weekend sushi bar. Sa Latin night. Th-F and Su 18+, Sa 21+. Cover $10-15. Open Th-Su 9pm-2am.

Fadó Irish Pub, 1735 19th St. (☎297-0066; www.fadoirishpub.com/denver), on Wynkoop St., between Coors Field and the Chophouse. Built in Ireland and brought to Denver piece by piece, Fadó is authentic, from its perfect pints of Guinness to its intricate wrought-iron bar. The place to be before and after Rockies games. W and Sa live Irish music. Open M-F 11:30am-2am, Sa-Su 11am-2am. Kitchen closes 10pm.

El Chapultepec, 1962 Market St. (☎295-9126), at 20th St. A be-boppin' jazz holdover from Denver's 1950s Beat Era. Drafts from $3.75, well $4.50. Live music daily from 9pm. No cover; 1-drink min. per set. Open daily 8am-2am. Cash only.

Charlie's, 900 E. Colfax Ave. (☎839-8890), at Emerson. A popular gay-friendly bar with 2 dance floors: 1 country-western, 1 top 40. No cover. Open daily 11am-2am.

BOULDER   ☎303

The 60s have been slow to fade in Boulder; the city is known to leftists as a little liberal haven in a vast conservative wasteland and to right-wingers as "The People's Republic of Boulder." Brimming with coffee shops, teahouses, and juice bars, Boulder is also home to both the University of Colorado (CU) and Naropa University, the only accredited Buddhist university in the US. Seek spiritual enlightenment through meditation and healing workshops at Naropa, or pursue a physical awakening through Boulder's incredible outdoor activities, including biking, hiking, and rafting along Boulder Creek.

TRANSPORTATION AND PRACTICAL INFORMATION. Though Greyhound no longer serves Boulder, RTD runs **buses** from its station in Boulder, at 14th and Walnut St., to the Amtrak station in Denver. RTD also operates Boulder's extensive **public transit** system. (☎299-6000 or 800-366-7433; www.rtd-denver.com. Station open M-F 6am-8pm, Sa-Su 9am-6pm. Local fare $1.50, regional $3.75. Call for schedules.) For a **taxi,** call Yellow Cab, ☎777-7777. University Bicycles, 839 Pearl St., downtown, rents **mountain bikes.** (☎444-4196 or 800-451-3950; www.ubikes.com. Bikes with helmet and lock $15 per 4hr., $25 per day. Open in summer M-F 10am-7pm, Sa 10am-6pm, Su 10am-5pm; in winter M-Sa 10am-6pm, Su 10am-5pm.) Boulder is a small city, easily accessible from Estes Park and Denver by **Highway 36.** The commercial area lies between **Broadway (Highway 7/93)** and **28th Street (Highway 36),** two busy north-south streets. Broadway, 28th St., **Arapahoe Avenue,** and **Baseline Road** border the **University of Colorado (CU)** campus. The area west of the school, across Broadway, is known as the **Hill** and features a number of restaurants, bars, and student-oriented shopping and entertainment. The pedestrian-only **Pearl Street Mall,** between 11th and 15th St., is lined with cafes, restaurants, and posh boutiques. The **Boulder Chamber of Commerce/Visitors Service** is at 2440 Pearl St. and has info and free **Internet** access. (☎442-2911; www.bouldercoloradousa.com. Open M-Th 8:30am-5pm, F 8:30am-4pm.) A **summer visitors kiosk,** on the Pearl Street Mall at 13th, has literature and is staffed M-Tu and Su 11am-8pm, W-Sa 11am-9pm. **University of Colorado Information,** on the 2nd floor of the University Memorial Center (UMC) student union, on the corner of Broadway and Euclid St., has free Internet access and local calls. (☎492-6161. Open in summer M-Th 7am-10pm, F 7am-11pm, Sa 9am-11pm, Su noon-10pm; Sept.-May M-Th 7am-midnight, F-Sa 7am-1am, Su 11am-midnight.) **Post office:** 1905 15th St., at Walnut St. (☎938-3704. Open M-F 7:30am-5:30pm, Sa 10am-2pm.) **Postal Code:** 80302.

ACCOMMODATIONS. Nestled among CU's fraternity and sorority houses, **Boulder International Hostel ❶,** 1107 12th St., at College Ave., provides young travelers a home on the Hill with a spacious downstairs lobby, Internet access ($2 per 30min.), and cable TV. The front door is locked after 11pm, but guests are given a code to enter after hours. (☎442-0522. Kitchen, laundry. Linen $5. Key deposit $10. 3-night max. stay in dorms. Reception 8am-11pm. Lockout 10am-5pm. In summer dorms $23; singles $44; doubles $50. Call for winter rates. AmEx/D/MC/V.) Located 2 mi. west of Boulder off Canyon Blvd./Hwy. 119, **Boulder Mountain Lodge ❸**, 91 Four Mile Canyon Rd., treats guests to clean rooms, great rates, and a hot tub by Four Mile Creek. Campsites are also available on a first-come, first-served basis. (☎444-0882 or 800-458-0882; www.bouldermountainlodge. In summer singles $87, with full kitchen $97; in winter $67/77. Sites $21.) **Chautauqua Association ❸**, off Baseline Rd. at the foot of the Flatirons, has lodge rooms and private cottages. Turn at the Chautauqua Park sign and take Kinnikinic to Morning Glory Dr., or take RTD bus #203. (☎442-3282, ext. 11. Reception June-early Sept. M-F 8:30am-7pm, Sa-Su 9am-5pm; Sept.-May M-F 8:30am-5pm, Sa-Su 9am-3pm. Additional charge for stays fewer than 4 nights. Reserve months in advance. In summer lodge rooms $71-86; 1-bedroom cottages $99-139; 2-bedroom cottages $144-242; 3-bedroom cottages $179-194. In winter, cottages $94-139. AmEx/MC/V.) Camping info for **Arapahoe/Roosevelt National Forest ❶** is available from the **Boulder Ranger District,** 2140 Yarmouth Ave., north of town off Rte. 36. (☎541-2500, reservations 877-444-6777; www.recreation.gov. Open mid-May to early Sept. M-F 8am-4:30pm, Sa 7am-3:30pm; Sept. to mid-May M-F 8am-4:30pm. Campsites open mid-May to Oct. Most sites have water; none have electricity. Sites $16.) **Kelly Dahl ❶**, 21 mi. southwest of Boulder on Hwy. 119, via Nederland, is the nearest National Forest campground. Though all of the campgrounds in this district fill quickly, Kelly Dahl's 46 sites ($16), surrounded by pine trees and picnic tables, are usually available until much later in the day. For a quieter camping experience, **Rainbow Lakes ❶** lies 6½ mi. north of Nederland off Hwy. 72; turn at the Mountain Research Station (CR 116) and follow the gravel road for 5 mi. Drive slowly and carefully on the access road. The 16 primitive sites are first come, first served. (No water. Sites $10.)

❑ FOOD. The streets on the Hill, along the **Pearl Street Mall,** burst with eateries, natural food markets, and colorful bars. **◧Half Fast Subs ❶**, 1215 13th St., makes over 90 oven-baked subs, all listed in colored chalk on the walls. Seven-inch subs of every imaginable variety are deliciously inexpensive—$5.50 or less. (☎449-0404. F or Sa live music. Happy hour M-F 5-7pm; subs $4, pitchers $4.75. Open M 10:30am-10pm, Tu-W 10:30am-11pm, Th-F 10:30am-midnight, Sa 11am-midnight, Su 11am-10pm. AmEx/D/MC/V.) Everything is "daily" at the **Walnut Cafe ❶**, 3073 Walnut Ave., where there's a new variety of quiche (with 2 sides $6.75) every day, in addition to a waffle, soup, grind (of coffee), and slab (of cake) du jour. Check out "pie day" on Tuesdays, when a slice of pie is just $2.25. (☎447-2315. Open daily 7am-4pm. AmEx/D/MC/V.) **Illegal Pete's ❶**, 1320 College Ave., on the Hill, and at 1447 Pearl St., on the Mall, constructs the burritos ($5-6) that sustain CU students. (Hill location: ☎444-3055. Open daily Sept.-May 11am-8pm; June-Aug. 11am-3:30pm. Pearl St. location: ☎440-3955. Open M-W and Su 7:30am-10:30pm, Th 7:30am-midnight, Sa 7:30am-2:30am. AmEx/D/MC/V.) At the chic **Moongate Asian Bistro ❷**, 1628 Pearl St., fill up on tasty noodle or rice bowls or Thai curries all for under $10. (☎720-406-8888; www.moongateasianbistro.com. Open M-Th and Su 11am-10pm, F-Sa 11am-11pm. AmEx/D/MC/V.)

❑ ◪ SIGHTS AND OUTDOOR ACTIVITIES. The **◨Dushanbe Teahouse,** 1770 13th St., between Arapahoe and Canyon St., the only one of its kind in the Western hemisphere, was built by artists in Tajikistan, then piece-mailed from Boulder's sister city of Dushanbe. Today, a restaurant leases the building and serves exotic dishes inside or on the patio. (☎442-4993. Breakfast $6-9. Lunch $7-13. High Tea

$15. Dinner $11-16. Open M-Th and Su 8am-9pm, F-Sa 8am-9pm. Tea time 3-5pm. Reservations required for tea.) The **Celestial Seasonings Tea Company,** 4600 Sleepy- time Dr., lures visitors with tea samples and free factory tours, including the sinus- busting Mint Room, featuring the "mind-clearing power" of peppermint and spear- mint. (☎581-1202. Open M-Sa 9am-6pm, Su 11am-5pm. Tours every hr. M-Sa 10am- 3pm, Su 11am-3pm.)

Boulder is bursting with opportunities to get outdoors. Starting at **Scott Car- penter Park,** trails for biking, hiking, and in-line skating follow the sometimes congested **Boulder Creek Path** to the foot of the mountains. **Chautauqua Park** has trails varying in difficulty that climb up and around the **Flatirons.** Starting at the auditorium, the **Enchanted Mesa/McClintock Trail** is an easy 2 mi. loop through meadows and ponderosa pine forests. The challenging **Greg Canyon Trail** starts at the Baird Park parking lot and rises through pines above Saddle Rock, winding back down past Amphitheater Rocks. Before heading into the wilderness, grab a trail map at the entrance to Chautauqua Park. Road and mountain biking are both very popular; **University Bicycles** (see **Practical Information,** p. 671) rents both types of bike. One great area for smooth, shaded riding is the **Betasso Reserve** (closed W and Sa). A more technical area is **Walker Ranch,** an 8 mi. loop of mostly single-track with a few challenging climbs and exciting descents thrown in. To get there, drive 8 mi. west on Baseline; trailhead will be on the left. To meet some new cycling friends, join the casual, weekly **cruiser ride** (starts Th 7-7:30pm at Scott Carpenter Park, at Araphoe Ave. and 30th St.).

🎭🎵 **ENTERTAINMENT AND NIGHTLIFE.** An exciting street scene pounds through the Mall and the Hill; the university's kiosks have the lowdown on down- town happenings. The **University Memorial Center,** 1609 Euclid St. (16th St. becomes Euclid St. on campus; ☎492-6161), has info on events. From late June to mid- August, the **Colorado Shakespeare Festival** draws over 50,000 people to a red sand- stone amphitheater on the CU campus. (☎492-0554; www.coloradoshakes.org. Tickets $14-54, previews $7-27. Senior and student discount $5.) The **Colorado Music Festival** hosts performances July through August in Chautauqua Park. (☎449- 1397; www.coloradomusicfest.org. Tickets $12-45; lawn seats $5.) The local indie music scene is on display at the popular and retro-styled **Fox Theater and Cafe,** 1135 13th St. (☎443-3399; www.foxtheater.com).

The city of Boulder overflows with countless unique bars. For bluegrass, funk, and the best brews in Boulder (try the "Annapurna Amber"), head to the ⬛**Moun- tain Sun Pub and Brewery,** 1535 Pearl St. (☎546-0886; www.mountainsunpub.com. Su acoustic performances 10pm. Happy hour M-F 4-6pm, Sa 10pm-closing; pints $2.25. Open M-Sa 11:30am-1am, Su noon-midnight. Kitchen closes at 10pm.) Famous for serving the largest amount of Pabst Blue Ribbon within a four-state radius, the **Sundown Saloon,** 1136 Pearl St., is a large basement bar with pool tables, foosball, and a jukebox. (☎449-4987. Pitchers from $8. Free pool until 10:30pm. Open daily noon-2am.) Completely transported from Ireland piece by piece, the bar at **Conor O'Neill's,** 1922 13th St., is a great place to have a Guinness. (☎449-1922; www.conoroneills.com. Th and Su Irish car bombs $3. Live music most nights. Cover $1. Open M-F 11:30am-2am, Sa-Su 11am-2am. Kitchen closes 1am.)

ROCKY MOUNTAIN NATIONAL PARK ☎970

Of all the national parks in the United States, Rocky Mountain National Park is the closest to heaven, with over 60 peaks surpassing 12,000 ft. Here among the clouds, the alpine tundra ecosystem supports bighorn sheep, dwarf wildflowers, and arc- tic shrubs in a landscape dotted with granite boulders and crystal lakes. The city of

Estes Park, immediately east of the park, hosts the vast majority of would-be mountaineers. West of the park, the town of **Grand Lake,** on the edges of two glacial lakes, is a more tranquil base from which to explore the park's less touristed but equally stunning western side.

ORIENTATION AND PRACTICAL INFORMATION

The park is accessible from Boulder via **U.S. 36** or scenic **Route 7.** From the northeast, the park can be accessed from the Big Thompson Canyon via **U.S. 34;** beware of flash floods. **Trail Ridge Road (Highway 34)** runs 48 mi. through the park.

Visitor Info: Park Headquarters and Beaver Meadows Visitor Center (☎586-1206; www.nps.gov/romo), located 2½ mi. west of Estes Park on Rte. 36, at the Beaver Meadows entrance to the park. Open daily mid-June to Aug. 8am-8pm; Sept. to mid-June 8am-4:30pm.

Within the park, there are 3 smaller Visitors Centers:

Kawuneeche Visitor Center (☎627-3471), just outside the park's western entrance, 1¼ mi. north of Grand Lake. Open daily mid-May to Aug. 8am-6pm; Sept. 8am-5pm; Oct. to mid-May 8am-4:30pm. Evening programs in summer Sa 7pm; call for winter programs.

Alpine Visitor Center, at the crest of Trail Ridge Rd., has a great view of the tundra. Open daily mid-June to late Aug. 9am-5pm; late May to mid-June and late Aug. to mid-Oct. 10am-4:30pm.

Fall River Visitor Center, 5 mi. west of downtown Estes Park on Rte. 34 at the northern entrance to the park, is the newest center. Open May-Oct. daily 9am-5pm; in winter Sa-Su 9am-4pm only.

Entrance Fee: $20 per car, $10 per bicyclist, motorcyclist, or pedestrian; valid for 7 days.

Public Transit: A free **hiker's shuttle** runs 2 loops on the east side of the park in summer. See the park newspaper for a map of shuttle stops. From Bear Lake daily every 15min. 7am-7pm. From Moraine Park daily every 30min. 7am-7pm.

Park Weather and Road Conditions: ☎586-1333.

Medical Services: Estes Park Medical Center, 555 Prospect Ave. (☎586-2317.) **Park Emergency,** ☎586-1203.

Internet Access: Estes Park Public Library, 335 E. Elkhorn (☎586-8116; www.estes.lib.co.us). Open in summer M-Th 9am-9pm, F-Sa 9am-5pm, Su 1-5pm; in winter M-Th 10am-9pm, F-Sa 10am-5pm, Su 1-5pm.

Post Office: Grand Lake, 520 Center Dr. (☎627-3340). Open M-F 8:30am-5pm. **Postal Code:** 80447. **Estes Park,** 215 W. Riverside Dr. (☎586-0170). Open M-F 9am-5pm, Sa 10am-1pm. **Postal Code:** 80517.

ACCOMMODATIONS

ESTES PARK
Estes Park has an abundance of expensive lodges. Travelers can find better deals on beds in the winter, when temperatures drop and crowds diminish.

YMCA of the Rockies, 2515 Tunnel Rd. (☎586-3341, ext. 1010 or 800-777-9622; www.ymcarockies.org), 2 mi. from the park entrance. Follow Rte. 36 to Rte. 66. Bright rooms with great views. Mini-golf, pool, horseback rides, fly-fishing. Call ahead; reservations for summer accepted starting Apr. 21. Lodge-style rooms from $89. 4-person cabins $109, with kitchen and bath from $139; 5-person cabins $164; 7-person cabins $219. YMCA member discount $10. ❹

The Colorado Mountain School, 341 Moraine Ave. (☎586-5758 or 800-836-4008, ext. 3). Tidy, dorm-style accommodations are open to travelers unless booked by mountain-climbing students. 16 bunks with linen. Showers, kitchen. Reservations recommended. Dorms $35. AmEx/D/MC/V. ❶

The Quilt House Bed & Breakfast, 310 Riverside Dr. (☎586-0427). 4 rooms with plenty of personality and beds bedecked in homemade quilts. Least expensive B&B in town. Full breakfast included. Reservations recommended. Single $40; doubles $60; guest house with kitchenette $70. Cash only. ❷

Estes Park Hostel, 211 Cleave St. (☎586-3149 or 877-213-0549; www.estesparkhostel.com). Funky building holds basic dorms with sturdy bunks and communal atmosphere. Kitchen, no curfew. Dorms $25; singles $30; doubles $52. ❶

GRAND LAKE

Grand Lake is the snowmobile capital of Colorado and offers spectacular cross-country skiing routes. Boating and fishing are popular summertime activities on the largest natural lake in Colorado.

▨ Shadowcliff Hostel (HI), 405 Summerland Park Rd. (☎627-9220; www.shadowcliff.org). From the western entrance, go left to Grand Lake, then turn left on W. Portal Rd. With excellent views of the lake and surrounding mountains, this hand-built pine lodge has more than comfortable beds: it also views itself as a spiritual retreat. Kitchen and showers. Internet $3 per 30min. Linen $2. 7-day min. stay for cabins. Open June-Sept. Dorms $20; singles or doubles with shared bath $55, each additional person $11; 6- to 8-person cabins $125-175. AmEx/D/MC/V. ❶

Sunset Motel, 505 Grand Ave. (☎627-3318). Cozy rooms with gas fireplaces, cable TV, large bathrooms, plus friendly owners and the only heated indoor pool in Grand Lake. In summer singles $65-85, doubles $70-85. In winter $45-55/50-60. MC/V. ❸

Bluebird Motel, 30 River Dr. (☎627-9314), on Rte. 34 west of Grand Lake. Overlooks Shadow Mountain Lake and the mountains. No phones. Swimming pool access at the Sunset Motel. Singles $65-75; doubles $75-85. MC/V. ❷

▨ CAMPING

Visitors can camp for a total of seven consecutive days within Rocky Mountain National Park. In the backcountry, the maximum stay increases to 14 days, but only from October to May. Campgrounds are open during the winter, though campers are responsible for clearing their own snow. All five **national park campgrounds ❶** cost $20 in the summer; winter sites are $14 unless otherwise noted. A **backcountry camping permit** ($20) is required in summer for stays in the park's 120 backcountry areas. Backcountry sites become less crowded the farther one hikes from the trailhead. **Sprague Lake** has a wheelchair-accessible backcountry site. On eastern slopes, permits ($20 in summer, free in winter) are available from the **Beaver Meadows Backcountry Office,** next to the park headquarters. (☎586-1242. Open daily mid-May to Oct. 7am-7pm; Nov. to mid-May 8am-4:30pm.) In the west, visit **Kawuneeche Visitors Center** (p. 674).

GRAND LAKE

The only national park campground on the western side of the park is the shaded and lovely **Timber Creek,** 10 mi. north of Grand Lake. Open year-round, it offers 98 sites on a first-come, first-served basis and is usually the last to fill. Campsites can also be found in the surrounding **Arapaho National Recreation Area** and the **Arapaho National Forest. Stillwater Campground ❶,** west of Grand Lake on the shores of Lake Granby, has 129 tranquil sites, a boat ramp, flush toilets, showers, and wheelchair-accessible sites. (Open year-round; only the 11 sites in front of the gate are open in winter. Sites $19, with full hookup $24.) **Green Ridge Campground ❶,** on the south end of Shadow Mountain Lake, has 78 sites in close proximity to good fishing and hiking. (Open mid-May to mid-Nov. Sites $14.) Reservations are recommended for both campgrounds (☎877-444-6777; www.recreation.gov).

EAST SIDE OF THE PARK

Moraine Park, 3 mi. west of Beaver Meadows Park Headquarters on Bear Lake Rd., is open year-round, though only some of its 245 sites are open in winter. In summer, **Glacier Basin,** 9 mi. from Estes Park, south of Moraine Park, provides 150 secluded sites near popular hiking trails; the Bear Lake shuttle buses also stop here. Both Moraine and Glacier Basin accept summer reservations. (☎877-444-6777; www.recreation.gov.) **Aspenglen,** just west of the Fall River Visitor Center, usually fills quickly as well, with 54 first-come, first-served spots. **Longs Peak,** 8 mi. south on Hwy. 7, has 26 year-round tent sites.

◖ FOOD

ESTES PARK

Sweet Basilico Cafe, 430 Prospect Village. (☎586-3899). The always crowded restaurant overflows with patrons enjoying Italian cuisine. Sandwiches $6.75. Freshly made pastas $8-11. Reservations recommended. Open June-Sept. daily 11am-10pm; Oct.-May M-F 11am-2:30pm and 4:30-9:30pm, Sa-Su 11am-9pm. AmEx/D/MC/V. ❷

The Notchtop Bakery & Cafe, 459 E. Wonderview, #44 (☎586-0272), in the upper Stanley Village Shopping Plaza, east of downtown off Rte. 34. Breads, pastries, and pies baked fresh every morning. Wi-Fi. Soups $4-5. Salads $6.50-8.50. Sandwiches and wraps $6-9. Open M-Sa 7am-9pm, Su 7am-3:30pm. MC/V. ❷

Nepal's Cafe, 184 E. Elkhorn Ave. (☎577-7035). Serves authentic Nepalese and Indian food. Daily buffet 11am-2pm, $9. Open daily 11am-9pm. D/MC/V. ❷

GRAND LAKE

Pancho and Lefty's, 1120 Grand Ave. (☎627-8773). With a patio overlooking Grand Lake and a bar large enough to fit most of the town's residents, Pancho and Lefty's is understandably cool. Try the *rellenos fritos* ($12) or crispy chimichangas ($11.50), and wash it down with a margarita ($5-8). Th and Sa live music 8pm. Open daily June-Sept. 11am-11pm; Sept.-June 11am-9pm. Kitchen closes 9:30pm. D/MC/V. ❷

The Bear's Den, 612 Grand Ave. (☎627-3385). The best dinner deals in town. Mouthwatering chicken-fried steak $15. Open M-Sa 6am-10pm, Su 7am-9pm. D/MC/V. ❸

Grand Lake Brewing Company, 915 Grand Ave. (☎627-1711). A friendly microbrewery with a strong menu of sandwiches ($5-7), 8 delicious homemade brews ($3-4), and fresh root beer. Open in summer M-Th 2-9pm, F-Sa 11am-11pm, Su 11am-6pm; winter hours vary. AmEx/D/MC/V. ❷

⚊ OUTDOOR ACTIVITIES

SCENIC DRIVES

The star of the park is **Trail Ridge Road** (U.S. 34), a 48 mi. stretch that rises 12,183 ft. above sea level into frigid tundra, where snow patches can be found through much of the summer. The round-trip drive takes roughly 3hr. by car in perfect conditions, but slow-moving tour buses and people stopping to ogle wildlife often slow traffic. The road is sometimes closed or inaccessible (especially from October to May) due to bad weather. Many sights within the park are accessible from Trail Ridge Rd. Heading west, steal an open view of the park from the boardwalk along the highway at **Many Parks Curve** (9260 ft.). **Rainbow Curve** (10,829 ft.) and the **Forest Canyon Overlook** (11,716 ft.) offer impressive views of the vast tree-carpeted landscape, formed by glacial action. At the **Rock Cut** pullout, the 30min. **Tundra Communities Trail** is a rare opportunity to see fragile alpine tundra. Signposts along the paved trail explain local geology and wildlife. The **Lava Cliffs** attract crowds but are worth the hassle. After peaking just before **Gore Range,** Trail Ridge Rd. runs north to the **Alpine Visitors Center.** Entering the west side of the park past the Alpine Visitors Center, congestion lessens noticeably. **Wildlife viewing** along Trail Ridge Rd. is best in the early morning and evening. Elk usually congregate at higher elevations during the summer and in open meadows off the main road in fall. Natural mineral licks draw bighorn sheep to **Sheep Lakes.** Marmots and pica hang out at higher elevations, and winter visitors are treated to glimpses of ermine and snowshoe hares.

A wilder alternative is **Old Fall River Road.** Entering Rocky Mountain National Park from the east side on Rte. 34, you'll pass Sheep Lakes. Veer right toward the **Alluvial Fan** and Old Fall River Rd. Open only in the summer, Old Fall River Rd. starts at **Endovalley** picnic area and is a 9 mi., gravel, one-way, uphill road that features spectacular mountain views. (Sharp switchbacks. No trailers; max. vehicle length 25 ft.) The road intersects Trail Ridge Rd. behind the Alpine Visitors Center. **Bear Lake Road,** south of Trail Ridge Rd., leads to the most popular hiking trails within the park. **Moraine Park Museum,** off Bear Lake Rd. 1½ mi. from the Beaver Meadows entrance, has exhibits on the park's geology and ecosystem. (☎586-8842. Open in summer daily 9am-5pm.)

SCENIC HIKES

Numerous trailheads lie in the western half of the park, including the Continental Divide and its accompanying hiking trail. Trail Ridge Rd. ends in **Grand Lake,** a small town with ample outdoor opportunities. An overnight trek from Grand Lake into the scenic and remote **North** or **East Inlets** leaves the crowds behind. *Hiking Adventures in Rocky Mountain National Park* (available at Visitors Centers; $1) gives great details on the trails in the park.

Lake Nanita (11 mi., 7½hr. one-way), rewards hikers who make the effort with a Kodak-moment view. Starts at North Inlet trailhead just north of Grand Lake. Don't let the easy and well-shaded 1st 6½ mi. fool you. After reaching **Cascade Falls** (3½ mi. from the trailhead), the trail ascends 2240 ft. through pristine wilderness to a view of the lake.

Lake Verna (7 mi., 5hr. one-way), starts at East Inlet trailhead at the far east end of Grand Lake. This strenuous hike gains a total of 1800 ft. in elevation as it passes **Adams Falls,** an easy ¼ mi. from the trailhead, and **Lone Pine Lake** (5½ mi.), and rewards hikers with open views of **Mount Craig** before re-entering the forest. The culmination is a lake overlook edged by mountains and ponderosa pines.

INSECT INVASION

Driving through the mature lodgepole pine forests of the Colorado Rockies has become quite disorienting in the last few years. Slopes that should be covered in dark green are instead splotched with reddish-orange. Instead of the beloved mountain pines of the Rockies, today's pine groves resemble a deciduous forest on the cusp of autumn.

By summer, 2007, the mountain pine beetle had infested nearly half of Colorado's lodgepole pine forests, quickly turning healthy trees into dry, brown tinderboxes. Experts from the US Forest Service acknowledge that nothing can be done to contain the beetles, according to the *Rocky Mountain News.* Some foresters even see the current devastation brought to the lodgepole pines as part of the forest's natural cycle, intensified by recent warm winters, which allow the larvae to survive, and hot, dry summers that put even further stress on the trees.

Whether or not the overwhelming resurgence of pine beetles can be taken as a sign of imminent global climate change, one thing is clear: the forests of Colorado—and all of the mountainous West, for that matter—will look and feel quite different in years to come. At the very least, the changes wrought by the beetle serve to remind us that our forests are ever-changing.

MUD SEASON. During mud season (typically May and Oct.-Nov.) many places close or shorten their hours, and lodging prices are generally lower. If you're traveling in the mountains during these months, be sure to call ahead.

Mill Creek (1½ mi., 40min. one-way), beginning at Hollowell Park off Bear Lake Rd. This easy and pleasant trail (elevation gain 600 ft.) crosses an open meadow and then empties out into a serene field of aspen, providing a glimpse of beavers and soaring hawks.

Bear Lake Hikes. The park's most popular trails are all accessible from the Bear Lake Trailhead at the south end of Bear Lake Rd. The free hiker's shuttle (see **Practical Information,** p. 674) makes loop hiking possible.

    Flattop Mountain (4½ mi., 5hr. one-way), the most challenging and breathtaking of the Bear Lake hikes, climbs 2850 ft. to a vantage point along the Continental Divide. At the top, you cross the tundra at the head of the Tyndall Glacier and follow the cairns 1 mi. to Hallet Peak (12,173 ft.).

    Nymph (½ mi., 15min.); **Dream** (1 mi., 30min.); and **Emerald** (1¾ mi., 1hr.) lakes are a series of 3 glacial pools offering glimpses of the surrounding peaks. The first 2 legs of the hike are relatively easy, but the Emerald Lake portion is steep and rocky at points.

    Lake Haiyaha (2¼ mi., 1¼hr.), forking left from the trail to Emerald Lake, has switchbacks through dense sub-alpine forests and superb views of the mountains. A scramble over the rocks at the end of the trail earns you a peek at the hidden (and sometimes difficult to find) Lake Haiyaha.

WINTER ACTIVITIES

Many people find that their favorite time to visit the park is in the winter, for **snow-shoeing** and **cross-country skiing** in the Bear Lake Area, **sledding** and **tubing** in the Hidden Valley area (rentals all outside the park), and backcountry skiing throughout the park. Rocky Mountain continues to have ranger-led activities in the winter, including **snowshoe tours** (☎586-1223) and **guided cross-country skiing.** One exclusively winter activity is the popular **full moon walk,** available by reservation only Dec.-Mar. Call ahead for details (☎586-1206) as dates and locations change with the seasons. During the winter, Trail Ridge Rd. is closed from Many Parks Curve on the east side to the Colorado River trailhead on the west side, which makes the drive through the park much longer (about 3½hr. one-way via I-70).

MOUNTAIN RESORTS ON I-70   ☎970

WINTER PARK AND THE FRASER VALLEY

Hwy. 40 connects Winter Park with Fraser just 2 mi. north, and together the towns thrive as a unique mountain community with genuine small-town charm. Nestled among mountain pines in the upper Fraser River Valley, the popular **Winter Park Resort** is the closest ski and summer resort to Denver, a mere 67 mi. from downtown. Named after a local lady of pleasure, the **Winter Park Mary Jane Ski Area** (☎726-5514 or 800-979-0332; www.skiwinterpark.com) is home to the 1st man-made ski trail in the western US; the trail was laid on land Mary Jane received for providing "favors" to local railroad workers and miners. The ski area is among those boasting the most snow in Colorado, a 2610 ft. vertical drop, 25 lifts, and two mountains: Winter Park caters to families and beginners, and Mary Jane challenges experts with mogul-laden trails. The resort also hosts a variety of summer activities, including a scenic chairlift, climbing walls, bungee jumps, and the longest alpine slide in Colorado. (Open mid-June to early Sept. daily 10am-5:30pm. Park pass $44 per half-day, $49 per day.) **Fraser Tubing Hill,** half a mile off Hwy. 40 in Fraser, is another popular winter escape. (☎726-5954. Open daily, call ahead for hours. Tube and lift $17 per hr., ages 7-15 $15. Cash only.) Over 600 mi. of biking and hiking trails climb the mountains of the Continental Divide, and the **Zephyr**

ROCKY MOUNTAINS

Express chairlift blows to the summit of Winter Park Mountain, allowing bikers and hikers to start at the top and then make their way down. (☎726-1564. Open mid-June to early Sept. daily 10am-5pm. Chair pass single ride $18, includes bike haul; $25 per day. Mountain bike rentals from $55 per day.) **Viking Ski Shop,** on Hwy. 40, under the Viking Lodge, rents ski packages in winter and bikes in summer. (☎800-421-4013. Open daily June-Sept. 9am-8pm; Oct.-May 8am-8pm. Ski packages $14 per day for basic skis, $21 per day for performance skis; multi-day discounts available. Children rent skis free with adult rental. Road bikes $10 per day; mountain bikes $15. Helmets included.) **Mad Adventures** is a popular whitewater rafting company that offers guided treks on wild Clear Creek and the Colorado River. Trips leave from Kremmling, about 45min. west of Winter Park on Hwy. 40, and from Downieville, between Idaho Springs and Empire on I-70. (☎726-5290 or 800-451-4844; www.madadventures.com. Open in summer daily 8am-5pm. Trips $45 per half-day, $65 per day; ages 4-11 $38/55.) The **High Country Stampede Rodeo** bucks at the John Work Arena, west of Fraser on County Rd. 73, with competitions in calf roping, ladies' barrel racing, and bareback bronco and bull riding. (☎406-1335 or 800-903-7275; www.highcountrystampede.com. Open July-Aug. Sa nights. Western barbecue 4pm; entrees $6-12. Rodeo 7:30pm; $10, over 62 $8, ages 6-13 $8.)

The glorious ▧**Rocky Mountain Inn and Hostel ❶,** on Hwy. 40, 2 mi. north of Winter Park in Fraser, on the southern edge of town across Hwy. 40 from Safeway, has immaculate, newly renovated rooms with a Julia Child-caliber kitchen, as well as discounts on lift tickets, and ski and mountain bike rentals. (☎726-8256 or 866-467-8351; www.therockymountaininn.com. Linens $3. Free Wi-Fi. Reception 8am-10pm. Reservations recommended. Dorms $19-30; private rooms $89-119 in winter, $69-89 in summer. AmEx/D/MC/V.) The **Viking Lodge ❷,** on Hwy. 40 in Winter Park, next to the shuttle stop for the lifts, provides compact rooms with TV and access to a hot tub, sauna, and game room. (☎726-8885 or 800-421-4013; www.skiwp.com. 10% discount on rentals at the adjacent store. Reception 8am-9pm. In winter singles $50-75, doubles $55-80. In summer $40/45. AmEx/D/MC/V.) The Fraser River Valley Lions Club maintains campgrounds in the **Arapaho National Forest** from mid-May to early September. The closest campground to town, **Idlewild ❶,** just 1½ mi. south of Winter Park on Hwy. 40, contains 24 forested sites along the Fraser River. (No hookups. 14-day max. stay. Sites with water $14.) Located on Hwy. 40 in downtown Fraser, **Crooked Creek Saloon and Eatery ❷,** 401 Zerex Ave. (Hwy. 40), is a local landmark that dispenses wise advice: "Enjoy a few laughs, eat 'til it hurts, and drink 'til it feels better." Locals elbow up to the bar alongside mountain bikers and skiers year-round. (☎726-9250. Breakfast from $3.50. Burgers, pasta, and Mexican fare $7-10. Happy hour M-F 4-7pm; domestic bottles $2, hot wings $0.33. Open daily 7am-2am. Kitchen closes 10pm. AmEx/D/MC/V.) Delicious, healthy breakfasts ($6-9), lunches ($4-11), and dinners are served on the patio at **Carver's Bakery Cafe ❷,** behind Cooper Creek Sq. off U.S. 40, in downtown Winter Park. The homemade bagels are amazing. (☎726-8202; www.carversbakery.com. Massive cinnamon rolls $2.25. Open M-Tu and Su 7am-2pm, W-Sa 7am-2pm and 5-9pm. AmEx/MC/V.) After a hard day on the slopes, locals and visitors flock to the **Winter Park Pub,** at Main St. and Kings Crossing in the north end of downtown Winter Park, for live music and cheap microbrew drafts ($2.50) during Happy hour. (☎726-4929; www.winterparkpub.com. Burgers $5.50. Live music most weekends. Open M-Th and Su 11am-midnight, F-Sa 11am-2am.)

To reach Winter Park from Denver, take I-70 W to Hwy. 40. The Lift Resort Shuttle provides **free bus service** between Winter Park and Fraser. (☎726-4163. Runs July-Sept. Sa-Su and late Nov. to mid-Apr. daily 8am-5pm.) Home James Transportation Services runs **door-to-door shuttles** to and from Fraser, Winter Park, and the Denver airport. (☎726-5060 or 800-359-7503; www.ridejh.com. Office open in winter daily 8am-6pm; call for summer hours. Reservations required. $48 to airport.)

The Ski Train runs a **train** from Denver's Union Station to Winter Park. (☎303-296-4754; www.skitrain.com. Round-trip in winter $49, over 62 and 3-13 $44; in summer $44/39.) The **Winter Park-Fraser Valley Chamber of Commerce** is at 78841 Hwy. 40. (☎726-4118 or 800-903-7275; www.playwinterpark.com. Open daily 9am-5pm.) For **snow conditions,** call ☎303-572-7669 or 800-729-5813. **Internet Access: Fraser Valley Library,** 421 Norgren Rd., (☎726-5689. Free. Open M-W 10am-6pm, Th noon-8pm, F 10am-6pm, Sa 10am-4pm.) **Post Office:** 520 Hwy. 40, in Fraser. (☎726-5578. Open M-F 8am-5pm, Sa 10am-noon.) **Postal Code:** 80442.

BRECKENRIDGE

Fashionable Breckenridge lies east of Vail on I-70, 9 mi. south of Frisco on Rte 9. One of the most popular ski resorts in the country, **Breckenridge** has a 3400 ft. vertical drop, 155 trails, 29 lifts, 2358 acres of skiable terrain, and the best half-pipe in North America. (☎453-5000 or 800-789-7669, snow conditions 453-6118.; www.breckenridge.com.) Most of the summer action takes place at the **Breckenridge Peak 8 Fun Park** on Peak 8, 3 mi. west of town on Ski Hill Rd., including a scenic chairlift ride (single ride $5), a superslide ($12), Colorado's largest human maze ($7, ages 5-12 $6), and a climbing wall ($8 per climb). The **Breckenridge Mountain Bike Park** at the same location offers a variety of biking trails. (Chairlift with bike haul $15, ages 7-12 $12. Full-suspension rentals $29 per 2hr., $39 per half-day, $49 per full day.) "Super-passes" for unlimited use of the Fun Park and Mountain Bike Park are also available ($50 per half-day, $65 per day). In the summer, the **Breckenridge Music Festival** provides a wide selection of musical acts from classical and jazz to Broadway and blues. (☎453-9142; www.breckenridgemusicfestival.com. Early June-Aug. Box office open Tu-Su 10am-5pm. Some shows free. Classical concerts $22-32, under 18 $7.)

Despite the many expensive restaurants and stores in town, you can still find reasonably priced accommodations at the charming █**Fireside Inn (HI) ❷**, 114 N. French St., two blocks east of Main St. on the corner of Wellington Rd. The indoor hot tub is great for *après*-ski, and the "Afternoon Tea" presents a taste of British hospitality after a cold day on the slopes. (☎453-6456; www.firesideinn.com. Breakfast $4-8. Check-in 4-8:30pm. In winter dorms $38; private rooms $130. In summer $27/63. HI member discount $3. MC/V.) A few miles north of town on Hwy. 9, next to the Breckenridge Golf Course, **Wayside Inn ❸**, 165 Tiger Rd., offers tidy rooms with a hot tub, a fireplace in the lounge, and an attractive price. (☎453-5540 or 800-927-7669; www.breckenridgewaysideinn.com. Jan. to mid-Apr. singles $88, doubles $98; mid-Apr. to late Nov. $45/55; Dec. $69/79. AmEx/D/MC/V.) Taste the difference of high-altitude, slow-roasted coffee beans at **Clint's Bakery and Coffeehouse ❶**, 131 S. Main St., where you'll also find croissant breakfast sandwiches ($3.75), homemade quiche ($2.75), and soups made daily. The hot portobello mushroom and turkey pepperjack sandwiches ($5.25-6) are lunch favorites, as are the blackberry smoothies. (☎453-2990. Sandwiches until 3pm. Open daily 7am-10pm. MC/V.) You know the burgers are going to be big at a place called **Fatty's ❷**, 106 S. Ridge St. With 20 TVs and $2 drafts during Happy hour (daily 4-7pm), Fatty's knows how to keep the locals satisfied. (☎453-9802. Burgers $7-9. Open daily 11am-12:30am. Kitchen closes at 10pm. AmEx/MC/V.) One of two young dance clubs in town, smoke-free **Cecilia's**, 500 S. Main St., also hosts open after-parties for ski events. (☎453-2243. Nightly drink specials. W half-off all drinks. Th ladies night. Open daily 5pm-2am.)

Free Ride Breckenridge **shuttles** skiers and bikers around town and to the mountains for free. (☎547-3141. Operates daily 6:30am-midnight.) Summit Stage provides free shuttle service from Breckenridge to surrounding areas in Summit County. (☎668-0999; www.summitstage.com. Operates daily 6:30am-1:30am.) The

Breckenridge Welcome Center is at 203 S. Main St., at Washington St. (☎453-5579 or 877-864-0868; www.gobreck.com. Open daily 9am-5pm.) **Ski Conditions and Weather:** ☎453-6118. **Breckenridge Medical Center:** 555 S. Park Ave. (☎453-1010.) **Internet Access: Summit County Library,** 504 Airport Rd. (☎453-6098. Free. Open M-Th 9am-7pm, F 9am-5pm, Sa 1-5pm.) **Post Office:** 305 S. Ridge Rd. (☎547-0347. Open M-F 8am-5pm, Sa 10am-1pm.) **Postal Code:** 80424.

VAIL ☎970

The largest one-mountain ski resort in all of North America, Vail has its fair share of ritzy hotels and boutiques, but it's the mountain that wows skiers with prime powder and famed back bowls. With skiers and employees from around the world, the resort has an international feel unlike other Colorado ski towns, except for Aspen. Discovered by Lord Gore in 1854, the Vail area was swarmed by prospectors during the 1870s gold rush. According to legend, the Ute tribe adored the area's rich supply of game, but became so upset with the white settlers that they set fire to the forest, creating the open terrain beloved by so many visitors today.

■ ⊠ ORIENTATION AND PRACTICAL INFORMATION. The communities of Vail consist of **East Vail, Vail Village, Lionshead Village, Cascade Village,** and **West Vail.** Vail Village and Lionshead Village, the centers of the action, are pedestrian-only and about a 15min. walk apart; visitors must park in garages off **South Frontage Road.** Parking is free in summer, but will cost you $17 per day in winter. Free Vail Buses (☎479-2178) run a loop within and around each of the villages year-round. ECOTransit runs **buses** between Vail and the surrounding area, including Eagle, Edwards, and Beaver Creek. (☎328-3520. Office open daily in summer 7:30am-5:30pm; in winter 6am-10pm. $3.) Greyhound, in the Transportation Building next to the main Visitors Center (☎476-5137; ticket office open daily 7:30-11am and 2-6pm), buses eager skiers to Denver (2hr., 3 per day, $24-27); Glenwood Springs (1½hr., 2-3 per day, $18-20); and Grand Junction (2½-3hr., 2-3 per day, $19-21). Vail's two **Visitors Centers** are both on S. Frontage Rd. The larger one is in Vail Village, at the **Vail Transportation Center** (☎476-4940 or 800-653-4523; open summer and winter daily 9am-8pm, call for low-season hours); the smaller is at the parking lot in Lionshead Village (☎476-4941 or 800-653-4523; open summer and winter daily 9am-8pm, call for low-season hours). **Medical Services: Vail Valley Medical,** 181 W. Meadow Dr., (☎476-2451). **Weather Conditions: Road report:** ☎479-2226. **Snow report:** ☎476-4888. **Internet Access: Vail Public Library,** 292 W. Meadow Dr. (☎479-2185; www.vaillibrary.com. Free. Open M-Th 10am-8pm, F-Su 11am-6pm.) **Post Office:** 1300 N. Frontage Rd. (☎476-1494. Open M-F 8:30am-5pm, Sa 8:30am-noon.) **Postal Code:** 81657.

⌂ ACCOMMODATIONS. The phrase "cheap lodging" is not part of Vail's vocabulary. Rooms in the resort town rarely dip below $175 per night in high season, but hotels and lodges offer big discounts during the slower seasons. During the winter, beds are usually cheapest at the end of January and early February. The larger Visitors Center has a 24hr. kiosk for reading **www.vailonsale.com,** which lists last-minute lodging deals. The Visitors Centers also have sole access to a private database of last-minute deals, and the staff can make reservations. The closest thing to budget accommodations in Vail, the **Park Meadows Lodge ❺,** 1472 Matterhorn Cir., between Cascade Village and West Vail, offers clean, comfy condos with kitchenettes and outdoor hot tub. (☎476-5598 or 888-245-8086; www.parkmeadowslodge.com. In winter studio and 1-bedroom condos $99-150; 2-bedroom condos $175-270. In summer $79-89/140-189.) With cheaper rooms and easy access to the slopes, the small town of **Frisco,** located 2¼ mi. east of Vail and 9 mi. north of

Breckenridge (p. 680), is a budget skier's delight. The rates at the **Snowshoe Motel ❹**, 521 Main St., provide some relief, as do the recently refurnished rooms. (☎668-3444 or 800-445-8658; www.snowshoemotel.com. Rooms in winter $99-140. In summer $59-79. AmEx/D/MC/V.) The **Holy Cross Ranger District,** off I-70 at Exit 171, has info on the six summer campgrounds nearby. (☎827-5715. Open M-Sa 8am-5pm.) With 25 sites within hiking distance of the free East Vail Express bus, **Gore Creek ❶** is the closest campground to Vail. The 25 first-come, first-served sites fill quickly on weekends. (Drinking water, vault toilets. 10-day max. stay. Sites $16.)

🔼🔼 FOOD AND NIGHTLIFE. You'll never need to cook breakfast in Vail as long as the griddle is hot at 🟦**DJ's Classic Diner ❶**, 616 W. Lionshead Plaza, on the west end of Lionshead Village. In winter, locals ski in around the clock to warm up with crepes ($5.50-7), omelets ($5.25-9), and pasta frittatas from $7.50. (☎476-2336. Open in winter M and Su 7am-2pm, Tu-Sa 24hr.; in summer daily 7am-1pm. Cash only.) Right in the heart of Vail Village, **The Red Lion ❹**, 304 Bridge St. at Hanson Ranch Rd., is renowned for succulent barbecue brisket ($13) and ribs. (☎476-7676; www.theredlion.com. W-Sa live music. Open daily 11am-late. AmEx/D/MC/V.) **Moe's Original BBQ ❷**, 616 W. Lionshead Plaza, offers heavenly Alabama-style barbecue with soul food specialties. The box lunches (meat and two sides; $9-10) might be the best deal in town. (☎479-7888. Open in summer M-Sa 11am-sellout, usually about 3pm; in winter M-Sa 11am-9pm. Call ahead to have your food saved. MC/V.)

Both a sports bar and an upscale watering hole, **The Tap Room,** 333 Bridge St. in Vail Village, is consistently voted by locals as Vail's best place to see and be seen. (☎479-0500, ext. 3; www.taproomvail.com. M all-you-can-eat wings $5. Tu burger and beer $6. Open daily 10am-2am.) **Garfinkel's,** 536 E. Lionshead Cir., a hidden hangout accessible by foot in Vail's Lionshead Village (directly across from the gondola) calls out "Ski hard, party harder." (☎476-3789. Lunch $8-12. Dinner $15-22. Sa karaoke. Open daily 11am-2am. Kitchen closes at 10pm.)

🟦 SIGHTS. The history of Vail and the sports it loves best are extolled in the **Ski Hall of Fame,** in the **Colorado Ski and Snowboard Museum,** on the 3rd level of the Vail Transportation Center. A fascinating exhibit focuses on the 10th Mountain Division and its training in the Rockies for the rigors of fighting in the mountains of Italy during WWII. (☎476-1876; www.skimuseum.net. Open June-Sept. 10am-6pm and Nov.-Apr. Tu-Su 10am-8pm. Free, donations accepted.) In the summer, the **Gerald R. Ford Amphitheater,** at the east edge of Vail Village, presents a number of outdoor concerts, dance festivals, and theater productions. (☎845-8497; www.vvf.org. Box office open M-Sa 11am-5pm. Lawn seats $17-25. Tu free.) Next door in the lovely **Betty Ford Alpine Gardens,** stroll through the peaceful meditation and rock gardens. (☎476-0103. Guided tours M, Th, Sa 10:30am. Open May-Sept. dawn-dusk. Suggested donation $5.)

🟥 OUTDOOR ACTIVITIES. Before hitting the slopes in Vail, the unequipped visit **Ski Base,** 610 W. Lionshead Cir., west of the gondola. The store transforms into the **Wheel Base Bike Shop** in the summer months. (☎476-5799 or 888-217-9121; www.vailskibase.com. Skis, poles, and boots from $17 per day. Demo package $33 per day. Snowboard and boots from $22 per day. Path bikes $15 per 8hr.; mountain bikes from $31 per 8hr. Open daily in winter 8am-7pm; in summer 9am-6pm.) Vail caters to sun worshippers in the summer, when the ski runs turn into hiking and biking trails. The **Eagle Bahn Gondola** in Lionshead and the **Vista Bahn Chairlift,** part of the Vail Resort, whisk hikers, bikers, and sightseers to the top of the mountains for breathtaking views. (☎476-9090. Ticket office open daily 9:30am-4pm. Eagle Bahn open in summer M-W and Su 10am-4pm, Th-Sa 10am-9pm; in winter daily

8:30am-4pm. Vista Bahn open mid-July to early Sept. daily 10am-4pm. All-day pass on either Bahn $18, ages 5-12 and over 65 $11; with bike haul $23/16.) During the summer, visitors can bike the **Eagle Bahn Gondola Twilight Ride.** (Th-Sa 4-9pm. Free.) The Holy Cross Ranger District (p. 681) provides maps and information on the many snowmobile, cross-country skiing, and hiking routes clustered near Vail Pass. The **Gore Creek Fly Fisherman,** 193 Gore Creek Promenade, has free casting lessons daily at 10:30am. (☎476-3296. Rod rentals $15 per day, with boots and waders $30.) Nature trails and fascinating interpretive programs await the curious at the **Vail Nature Center,** located across Gore Creek from the Betty Ford Alpine Gardens. Call ahead for the popular beaver pond evening program, which sometimes fills weeks in advance. (☎476-2291; www.gorerange.org/vail_center. Open daily 9am-5pm. Check website or call for program schedule.)

ASPEN   ☎970

Aspen was founded in 1879 as a silver mining camp, but the silver ran out quickly, and by 1940 the town was almost gone. Wealthy visionaries took one look at the location of the foundering village and transformed it into a lavish winter playground. Today, Aspen makes a point of keeping busy, and its skiing, scenery, and festivals are matched only by the pricetags in the exclusive boutiques scattered around downtown. To catch Aspen on the semi-cheap, stay in Glenwood Springs, 40 mi. north (p. 685).

◪ **PRACTICAL INFORMATION.** Aspen Shuttles and the RFTA provide year-round **free transportation service** around town, charging a small fare in the Roaring Fork Valley. Pick up route maps on the buses or at the **Rubey Park Transit Center,** on the corner of Mill and Durant St. (☎925-8484; www.rfta.com. Open daily 6:15am-2:15am; in low season closes earlier on Su. Fare $1-9.) **Visitors Centers:** 320 E. Hyman Ave., in the Wheeler Opera House (☎920-7148; open daily 10am-6pm); 425 Río Grand Pl. (☎925-1940 or 888-290-1324; www.aspenchamber.org; open M-F 8:30am-5pm). The **Aspen Ranger District,** 806 W. Hallam, provides information on various hikes and camping within 15 mi. of Aspen. (☎925-3445. Open June-Aug. M-F 8am-4:30pm. Topographic maps $3-12.) **Roads and Weather:** ☎877-315-7623. **Snow Report:** ☎925-1221 or 888-277-3676. **Internet Access: Pitkin County Library,** 120 N. Mill St. (☎429-1900; www.pitcolib.org. Free. Open M-Th 10am-9pm, F-Sa 10am-6pm, Su noon-6pm.) **Post Office:** 235 Puppy Smith Rd. (☎925-5274. Open M-F 8:30am-5pm, Sa 9am-noon.) **Postal Code:** 81611.

▛ **ACCOMMODATIONS.** Staying in Aspen means biting the bullet and reaching deep into your pockets. Nearby Glenwood Springs has more options and is easily accessible by car or RFTA. In downtown Aspen, the friendly and conveniently-located **Tyrolean Lodge ❸,** 200 W. Main St., prices rooms by floor: darker low-floor rooms are cheaper, while airy top-floor rooms are a bit more expensive. Whichever floor you choose, you'll get 3 beds, a full kitchenette, and free shuttle rides to the ski areas. (☎925-4595 or 888-220-3809; www.tyroleanlodge.com. Office open 8:30am-7pm.) Able to charm even the hardiest ski bum with continental breakfast, a pool, a steam room, and a hot tub, the **St. Moritz Lodge ❷,** 344 W. Hyman Ave., has a European ski-lodge atmosphere. (☎925-3220 or 800-817-2069; www.stmoritzlodge.com. Wi-Fi. Reception 7am-8pm. Dorms $33-57; hotel rooms $79-248; rates depend on season.) Wake up to a full breakfast prepared by professional chefs in the adorable **Little Red Ski Haus ❸,** 118 E. Cooper Ave., which has spacious rooms and sparkling bathrooms. (☎925-3333 or 866-630-6119; www.littleredskihaus.com. Dorms $65.) Unless more than 6 ft. of snow covers the ground, **camping ❶** is available in one of the nine national forest campgrounds that lie

ROCKY MOUNTAINS

within 10 mi. of Aspen. **Silver Bar, Silver Bell,** and **Silver Queen** campgrounds sit 5 mi. southwest of town on Maroon Creek Rd. and fill quickly. Four miles southeast on Rte. 82, **Difficult** campground usually has more openings. (☎877-444-6777; www.recreation.gov. Water. No hookups. 14-day max. stay throughout the district. Open June to mid-Sept. Sites $15-18. Reservations required at the Silver grounds, recommended at Difficult.)

◖ FOOD. Always packed, the nationally-renowned **Hickory House ❸**, 730 W. Main St., smokes up award-winning barbecue favorites. (☎925-2313. Lunch specials $8-11.50. Dinner $10-20. Open daily 8am-2:30pm and 5-9pm. AmEx/D/MC/V.) Try the famed beef stew at **Little Annie's Eating House ❸**, 517 E. Hyman Ave., a longtime Aspen staple. Every day, all day long, throw back a beer and a shot for just $3. (☎925-1098. Burgers $10. Veggie lasagna $13. Open daily 11:30am-2am. Kitchen closes 10pm. AmEx/D/MC/V.) With jukeboxes and TVs blaring, **Cooper Street ❷**, 508 E. Cooper Ave., is the local hot spot. Feast on the hamburger special (burger with fries and a soda or Coors; $7.50) and gulp down Coors pitchers ($7.75) during happy hour. (☎925-7758. Happy hour 3-6pm. Open daily 11am-2am. Kitchen closes 10pm. Cash only.) The **Main Street Bakery ❷**, 201 E. Main St., serves gourmet soups ($6), vegetarian sandwiches ($8-10), and fresh-squeezed juice ($2). Their patio offers al fresco dining and a prime people-watching spot. (☎925-6446. Open M-Sa 7am-9:30pm, Su 7am-4pm. AmEx/D/MC/V.) Fast, cheap, and easy, **The Big Wrap ❶**, 520 E. Durant Ave., Ste. 101, rolls up gourmet wraps ($6.70), like the tasty (and clever) "To Thai For." (☎544-1700. Fresh salads $5.50. Smoothies $4. Open M-Sa 10am-6pm. Cash only.)

◭ SKIING. Skiing is the main attraction in Aspen. The surrounding hills contain four ski areas: Aspen Mountain, Aspen Highlands, Buttermilk Mountain, and Snowmass, known collectively as **Aspen/Snowmass.** A free **Skier Shuttle Service** runs between the four mountains 8am-4:30pm. Interchangeable lift tickets enable the four areas to operate as a single extended resort; for the best deal, buy multi-day passes at least two weeks in advance. (☎923-1227 or 877-282-7736. Day passes from $82; ages 13-17, ages 65-69, and college students under 24 $74; ages 7-12 $52; over 70 and under 7 free. Prices vary by season.) **Incline Ski Shop,** 555 E. Durant (☎800-992-2979 or 920-2760; www.inclineski.com), one of the oldest and most experienced retailers around, rents boots and skis. Each of the mountains offers unique skiing opportunities of varying difficulty. **Buttermilk's** gentle slopes are perfect for beginners interested in lessons (and snowplowing down the mountain). The largest terrain park in North America, Buttermilk has won international acclaim and will host the **Winter X Games** until 2010. The **Highlands** now includes the steep cliffs of Highland Bowl and offers a diverse selection of runs for advanced and expert skiers. **Aspen Mountain,** though smaller than the Highlands, also caters to experts; there are no easy trails. The granddaddy of the Aspen ski areas, **Snowmass,** remains the most family-friendly. Its half-pipes and terrain parks are highly popular among snowboarders.

◪ OUTDOOR ACTIVITIES. The **Silver Queen Gondola** heads to Aspen Mountain's 11,212 ft. summit, providing an unparalleled panorama. (☎923-1227 or 800-525-6200. Open mid-June to early Sept. M-F and Su 10am-4pm, Sa 8am-4pm. Day pass $22-24, ages 13-17 $16-18, ages 4-12 $11-13; week pass $40/32/21.) At Snowmass Mt., you can take a chairlift to the top and mountain bike down. (Open in summer daily 9:30am-4pm. $6, children $4.) **Aspen Bike Rentals,** 555 E. Durant, at Hunter St., has great deals on mountain bike rentals. (☎925-8200. Front-suspension bike rental $30 per half-day, $38 per full day; full-suspension bike $34/44. Open daily mid-June to Labor Day 8:30am-5:30pm.) Hikers can explore the magical **Maroon**

Bells, two of Colorado's 54 14,000 ft. peaks, on the unforgettable 1½ mi. trek to Crater Lake, a high-altitude glacial lake. Maroon Creek Rd. is closed to traffic daily 9am-5pm in an effort to preserve the wilderness. RFTA tour buses to the Bells operate during these times and leave from Aspen Highlands Village every 20min. (☎925-8484. $6 per person.) If you're planning a hike outside these times, there is a $10 fee per car to drive into the area. The steep but short **Ute Trail** (2½ mi.) departs from Ute Ave. and weaves its way to the top of Aspen Mountain, a spectacular sunset-watching spot. The gentler **Rio Grande Trail** wanders through town along the Roaring Fork and is popular for jogging and biking. Multi-day backpacking or mountain-biking treks throughout the White River Forest between Aspen, Vail, and Leadville can be complemented by night stays at the **10th Mountain Division Huts ❷,** built during WWII and carefully maintained ever since. The huts sleep 3-20 people and have heating stoves, propane burners, lighting, and mattresses. (☎925-5775; www.huts.org. Call for reservations. Open year-round. $25-41 per person.) For an adrenaline rush and a bird's-eye view of the region, **Aspen Paragliding,** 426 S. Spring St. (☎925-7625), does tandem flights ($215), as well as ski and snowboard takeoffs in the winter. Though a fly-fishing trip requires pretty deep pockets, you can learn to cast for free with the experts from the Taylor Creek Flyshop in **Wagner Park** daily at noon during the summer (for info ☎925-6331). The 25-acre Hallam Lake Nature Preserve sits peacefully on the northern edge of downtown. It is home to the **Aspen Center for Environmental Studies (ACES),** 100 Puppy Smith St., where kids and adults alike can learn about the ecosystems in and around Aspen. A self-guided nature walk (half mile round-trip) follows the beautiful Hallam Lake, and guided hikes and workshops are available on a daily basis; call or check website for details. (☎925-5756; www.aspennature.org. Open M-Sa 9am-5pm.)

GLENWOOD SPRINGS   ☎970

Next door to Aspen, Glenwood Springs allows budget travelers to stay near the famed slopes at refreshingly affordable prices. But Glenwood Springs is more than just Aspen's little brother. The hot springs are a popular year-round destination, and the spectacular Fairy Caves are considered one of the region's wonders. **Glenwood Hot Springs Lodge and Pool,** 401 N. River Rd., is a huge resort complex containing the world's largest outdoor mineral hot springs pool, a waterslide, and spas. (☎947-2955 or 800-537-7946; www.hotspringspool.com. Open daily in summer 7:30am-10pm; in winter 9am-10pm. Day pass $16.25, after 6pm $13, after 9pm $10.25; ages 3-12 $10.25/9/8.50; check website for low season and weekend prices.) Sweat out the stress of travel in 112-117°F natural steam caves at **Yampah Spa and Vapor Caves,** 709 E. 6th St. (☎945-0667; www.yampahspa.com. Open daily 9am-9pm. $12, $6.75 with pass from Glenwood Springs Hostel.) While most skiers head to Aspen, Glenwood Spring's **Sunlight,** 10901 County Rd. 117, 10 mi. west of town., has affordable, family-style skiing. (☎945-7491 or 800-445-7931. $48 per day, ages 6-13 $38; hosteler discount.) Dubbed the 8th wonder of the world in 1896, the **Fairy Caves** were reopened to the public in 1999. **Glenwood Caverns,** 51000 Two Rivers Plaza Rd., explores the caves with both family-oriented and advanced tours. There are also amusement rides at the top of the tram. (☎945-4228 or 800-530-1635; www.glenwoodcaverns.com. Tram runs 9am-8pm; call for winter hours. Tours 9am-7pm. Reservations required for 2hr. "adventure" and 3hr. "wild" tours.)

Within walking distance of the springs and downtown, the pleasantly funky ▨**Glenwood Springs Hostel (HI-AYH) ❶,** 1021 Grand Ave., has a spacious Victorian house and a newer building next door. The hostel offers a wide variety of trips and tours in the area, as well as discounts on skiing at Aspen. Amenities include two kitchens, the owner's amazing vinyl collection, a backyard patio, and a lounge with murals covering the walls. (☎945-8545 or 800-946-7835. Wi-Fi. Linen $2. Lockout 10am-4pm. 4-night max. stay. Dorms $16, 4 nights $48; private singles $25; private doubles $33. AmEx/MC/V.) One of the least expensive motels in town, the **Frontier Lodge ❸**, 2834 Glen Ave. (Rte. 82), provides clean, spacious rooms with A/C, cable TV, continental breakfast, and access to a hot tub. (☎945-5496 or 866-945-5496; www.frontierlodge.com. June-Aug. singles $90-100; doubles $100-110. Sept.-May singles $80; doubles $90. AAA discount.) Most other motels in the area are on the west side of the river on Rte. 82 or off Exit 116 from I-70. The **Daily Bread Cafe and Bakery ❷**, 729 Grand Ave., attracts locals with fresh, wholesome breakfasts and lunches. The quiche of the day (with salad or soup; $7.25) is a favorite and usually sells out by early afternoon. (☎945-6253. Open M-F 7am-2pm, Sa 8am-2pm, Su 8am-noon. D/MC/V.) Shoot some pool as you digest a delicious burger ($7-9.25) at **Doc Holliday's Saloon ❷**, 724 Grand Ave. (☎384-2379. Tu karaoke. Open daily 11am-2am. Kitchen closes 10pm. D/MC/V.)

The **Roaring Fork Transit Agency (RFTA)** (☎925-8484; www.rfta.com; open M-F 9am-5pm) runs to Aspen (1½hr.; generally every 30min.; $6, ages 6-16 $5). Visitor The **Glenwood Springs Chamber Resort Association** is at 1102 Grand Ave. (☎945-6589. Open June-Aug. M-F 9am-5pm, Sa-Su 10am-5pm; Sept.-May M-F 9am-5pm, Sa-Su 10am-3pm. Brochure area open 24hr.) **Post Office:** 113 9th St. (☎945-2701. Open M-F 8am-6pm, Sa 9am-1pm.) **Postal Code:** 81601.

COLORADO SPRINGS ☎719

Once a resort town frequented only by America's elite, Colorado Springs has grown to encompass neighboring Manitou Springs and Garden of the Gods; the metropolitan area is now the second-most visited in the state. Manitou Springs hosts the majority of the area's natural attractions, while the nearby Garden of the Gods region takes its name from a Ute legend that its stunning red rocks were petrified bodies of enemies hurled down by the gods. Today, the formations remain a popular attraction, along with the United States Olympic Complex and the United States Air Force Academy.

🖼🔁 ORIENTATION AND PRACTICAL INFORMATION. Colorado Springs is laid out in a grid of broad thoroughfares. **Tejon Street** is the main north-south strip through downtown, just east of **I-25**, though **Nevada Avenue** is generally faster. **I-25** bisects downtown, separating historic Old Colorado City from the eastern, largely residential part of town. **Colorado Avenue** and **Pikes Peak Avenue** run east-west across the city. Just west of Old Colorado City lie Manitou Springs and the Pikes Peak Area. Colorado Ave. becomes **Manitou Avenue** as it extends into Manitou Springs. **Highway 24,** which comes from Limon to the east and heads into the Pike National Forest to the west, is the main thoroughfare to move from town to town. **Greyhound,** 120 S. Weber St. (☎635-1505; www.greyhound.com; ticket office open M-Sa 7am-9:30pm), runs buses to Albuquerque (8hr., 3 per day, $73), Denver (1½-2hr., 7 per day, $20), and Pueblo (1hr., 7 per day, $14). **Metro,** 127 E. Kiowa St., at Nevada Ave., serves the local area, as well as Garden of the Gods, Manitou Springs, and Widefield. Pick up a schedule at the Kiowa bus terminal or download one from their website. (☎385-7433; www.mmtransit.com; $1.25, seniors and ages 6-11 $0.60, under 6 free. To Fountain $0.85 extra.) **Gray Line Tours,** 132 E. Animas St. (☎633-1181 or 800-345-8197; www.coloradograyline.com; open M-F 8am-5pm), offers whitewater rafting trips on the Arkansas River (7hr.; $80, under 12 $45; includes lunch), as well as a combo tour of the US Air Force Academy and the Garden of the Gods (4hr.; $35, under 12 $17.50). For a **taxi,** call **Yellow Cab,** ☎550-9300. The **Visitors Bureau** is at 515 S. Cascade Ave., at Cimarron. (☎635-7506 or 800-888-4748; www.experiencecoloradosprings.com. Open Sept.-May M-F 8:30am-5pm; June-Aug. daily 8am-6pm.) **Internet Access: Penrose Public Library,** 20 N. Cascade

Ave. (☎531-6333. Free. Open M-Th 10am-9pm, F-Sa 10am-6pm, Su 1-5pm.) **Post Office:** 201 E. Pikes Peak Ave., at Nevada Ave. (☎570-5336. Open M-F 7:30am-5:30pm, Sa 8am-1pm.) **Postal Code:** 80903.

⌂ ACCOMMODATIONS. Motels can be found all along Nevada Ave. near downtown, although the best options are farther west in and around Manitou Springs. Though many motels on the strip of Colorado Ave. between Old Colorado City and Manitou Springs are on the seedier side, two stand out. The **Mountainscape Inn ❷**, 3445 W. Colorado Ave, offers unbeatable prices accompanied by tidy rooms in well-maintained stucco. (☎578-1773. In summer rooms from $35; in winter from $28. Call ahead for reservation details. AmEx/D/MC/V.) The newly renovated **Hotel San Ayre ❸**, 3320 West Colorado Ave, provides beautiful, modern rooms but maintains charming old-world style. (☎632-4355 or 877-726-2973; www.hotelsanayre.com. Rooms from $65. AmEx/D/MC/V.) At the south entrance of the Garden of the Gods, **Red Wing Motel ❸**, 56 El Paso Blvd., is more down-to-earth—and its practicality pays off. Clean, air-conditioned rooms and a heated outdoor pool make Red Wing worth the modest price. (☎685-9547 or 800-733-9547; www.pikespeak.com/redwing. High season singles $55, with kitchen $79; doubles $69. Low season singles $42; doubles $45. AmEx/D/MC/V.) Several **Pike National Forest Campgrounds ❶** lie in the mountains flanking Pikes Peak, about 30min. from Colorado Springs. The **Pikes Peak Ranger District Office,** 601 S. Weber St. (☎636-1602; open M-F 8am-4:30pm), has maps and rangers. **Colorado, Painted Rocks,** and **South Meadows** campgrounds are near Woodland Park; others border U.S. 24 near the town of Lake George, 1hr. west of the Springs. (Generally open late May-Sept. Sites $13-15.) Farther afield is the **Eleven Mile State Recreation Area ❶**, off County Rd. 90 from U.S. 24, about 1½hr. from the Springs. (☎748-3401; reservations http://parks.state.co.us/Parks/ElevenMile. Showers, laundry. Reception 24hr. Sites $14, with electricity $18; $5 per car per day.)

▯▮ FOOD AND NIGHTLIFE. Students and locals perch at outdoor tables in front of the cafes and restaurants lining **Tejon Street.** Family establishments and fine eateries are in **Old Colorado City.** During the summer months, there are several **farmers' markets** throughout the city each week; the Visitors Center has a complete list. In Manitou Springs, the **Heart of Jerusalem Cafe ❶**, 906 Manitou Ave, Ste. 100, warmly serves fantastic falafel made from scratch ($5), delicious Shawarma ($5), espresso drinks, and ice cream from a store-front window. (☎685-9554. Open daily 9am-10pm. MC/V.) Councilman Richard Skorman sells used books next door to his **Poor Richard's Restaurant ❷**, 324½ N. Tejon St., which attracts a diverse crowd seeking healthful New York-style pizza. (☎632-7721. Cheese slices $3.50. Cheese pies $13. Sandwiches $7. Salads $5-7. Occasional live music in adjoining Rico's Cafe. Open M-W and Su 11am-9pm, Th-F 11am-10pm. AmEx/D/MC/V.) Famous for its omelets ($7-8) and country-style skillets ($7.50-8.50), **The Olive Branch ❷**, 23 S. Tejon St., serves unbeatable breakfasts. (☎475-1199. Open M-Sa 6:30am-9pm, Su 7:30am-9pm. AmEx/D/MC/V.)

Rum Bay Bourbon Street, 20 N. Tejon St., is a multilevel complex with eight clubs included under one cover charge (8pm-11pm $5, after 11pm $10). Besides the main Rum Bay club, the crowds swell into **Masquerade** (a disco club), **Wild Cats** (a rock-n-roll saloon), **Copy Cats** (a karaoke bar), **Fat City** (a blues club), **Red Martini Lounch** (a martini bar), and **Sam's**—the world's smallest bar. (☎634-3522. Mixed drinks $6-7. Shots $4.75-5.50. Th ladies night. 21+ after 8pm. Open daily 4pm-2am.) For nightlife without N. Tejon's clubbing vibe, tourists and locals alike flock to biker-friendly **Southside Johnny's,** 528 S. Tejon St., which has cover-free music, a martini bar, and plenty of beers on tap. (☎444-8487; www.southsidejohnnys.biz. Beer $3-4. W-Sa live music. 21+ F-Sa after 5pm. Open daily 11am-2am.) The two-story **Thirsty**

ROCKY MOUNTAINS

Parrot, 32 S. Tejon St., offers a taste of the Caribbean to a mixed crowd of revelers, who come seeking its famed tropical drinks ($5.75-7) and carefree atmosphere, including a multitude of grass skirts hanging from the ceiling. (☎884-1094; www.thirstyparrot.net. Beer $2-5.50. F-Sa live music. No cover. Happy hour 4-7pm. Open Tu-F 4pm-2am, Sa-Su 10am-2am.)

⑥🗻 SIGHTS. Olympic hopefuls train with some of the world's most high-tech sports equipment at the **US Olympic Complex,** 1750 E. Boulder St., on the corner of Union St. The complex has free 1hr. tours. The best times to get a glimpse of athletes in training are typically 9:30am-noon and 3-5pm, though sightings can never be guaranteed. (☎866-4618; www.usolympicteam.com. Tours depart every 30min. M-Sa beginning at 9am. Hours may vary—call for most current hours and tour times.) Tales of earlier quests for gold and land are recorded at the **Pioneers' Museum,** 215 S. Tejon Ave., which recounts the settling of Colorado Springs. Ride the birdcage elevator, walk through an old-time pharmacy, and sit in a restored courtroom. (☎385-5990; www.cspm.org. Open in summer Tu-Sa 10am-5pm. Free.) The **World Figure Skating Museum and Hall of Fame,** 20 1st St., just north of Lake St., traces the history, art, and science of skating and boasts an extensive collection of rare medals and skating outfits. (☎635-5200; www.worldskatingmuseum.org. $3, ages 6-12 and over 60 $2. Open M-Sa 10am-4pm.) Chronicling the exploits of the rough-riding American cowboy, the **Pro Rodeo Hall of Fame and Museum,** Exit 148 immediately off I-25, is a monument to the rigors and triumphs of the quintessential Western lifestyle and its two centuries of history. (☎528-4764. Open daily 9am-5pm. $6, ages 6-12 $3.) Witness the spinning, casting, and etching process that has produced museum-quality pottery for decades at **Van Briggle Pottery,** Hwy. 24 and 21st St. (☎633-7729 or 800-847-6341. Open M-Sa 8:30am-5pm, Su 1-5pm. Tours M-Sa 9am-4pm. Free.)

𝄫 OUTDOOR ACTIVITIES. Between Rte. 24 (Colorado Ave.) and 30th St. in northwest Colorado Springs, the erosion-sculpted red rock towers and spires of the **Garden of the Gods Visitor and Nature Center** rise strikingly against a mountainous backdrop. (Open daily dawn-dusk. Free.) **Climbers** are lured by the large red rock faces and the nearly 100 permanent routes (climbing guides to the area are sold at the Visitors Center). Climbers must register at the Visitors Center; $500 fines await those who climb without the free permit or proper gear. A number of exciting **mountain biking** trails cross the eastern part of the Garden as well. The park's hiking trails, including 2 mi. that are paved and wheelchair-accessible, have great views of the rock formations and can easily be completed in one day. A map is available from the park's **Visitors Center,** 1805 N. 30th St., at Gateway Rd., which has a stellar 12min. movie, shown every 20min. in summer. (☎634-6666; www.gardenofgods.com. Open daily June-Aug. 8am-8pm; Sept.-May 9am-5pm. Free guided nature walks daily 10am and 2pm; call for details on additional summer tours. Movie $2, children $1.)

The 14,110 ft. **Pikes Peak** is visible from almost any part of town. Ambitious hikers can ascend the peak along the strenuous, well-maintained **Barr Trail** (round-trip 23.4 mi., 16hr., 7400 ft. altitude gain). Overnight shelter is available at **Barr Camp** (6.8 mi. from the trailhead; also accessible by the Cog Railway) and the **Timberline Shelter** (8½ mi.). The trailhead is in Manitou Springs, just past the Cog Railway on Ruxton Ave. Down the street from the trailhead, visitors can hop on the **Pikes Peak Cog Railway,** 515 Ruxton Ave., which makes the trip to the summit every 80min. From the summit, visitors can see the Sangre de Cristo Mountains, the Continental Divide, and even the state of Kansas. (☎685-5401; www.cograilway.com. Open year-round, check website for hours. 6-8 trips per day. Round-trip $30, ages 3-12 $16. Reservations recommended.) You can also drive on your own up the gorgeous

19 mi. of the **Pikes Peak Highway,** off Rte. 24 west of Manitou Springs—it's worth every penny. (☎385-7325 or 800-318-9505. Open daily Memorial Day to Labor Day 7am-7pm; after Labor Day-late Sept. 7am-5pm; Oct.-Memorial Day 9am-3pm. $10, ages 6-15 $5; $35 max. per vehicle.)

For an underground adventure, head to the contorted caverns of the **Cave of the Winds,** on Rte. 24, 6 mi. west of Exit 141 off I-25. Discovery and lantern tours go into the more untamed areas of the cave. (☎685-5444; www.caveofthewinds.com. Guided tours daily every 15min. late May-Aug. 9am-9pm; Sept.-late May 10am-5pm. 45min. guided tour $18, ages 6-15 $9. 1-1½hr. guided lantern tour $22/12.) Just above Manitou Springs on Rte. 24, the **Cliff Dwellings Museum** contains replicas of ancestral Puebloan dwellings dating from AD 1100-1300 and actual ruins that serve as a backdrop for Santa Clara Puebloan dancers in colorful traditional dress performing from June to August. (☎685-5242 or 800-354-9971; www.cliffdwellingsmuseum.com. Open daily May-Sept. 9am-6pm; Oct., Mar.-Apr. 9am-5pm; Nov.-Feb. 10am-4pm. $8.50, seniors $7.50, ages 7-11 $6.50.) The only waterfall in Colorado to make it onto *National Geographic*'s list of the world's major waterfalls, **Seven Falls,** 10min. west of downtown on Cheyenne Blvd., cascades 181 ft. in seven distinct steps and is lit up on summer nights. The Mountain Elevator takes visitors who wish to skip the 185-step climb to a prime viewpoint. (☎632-0765; www.sevenfalls.com. Open daily in summer 8:30am-10:30pm; in winter 9am-4:15pm. Before 5pm $8.75, ages 6-15 $5.50; after 5pm $9.75/6.25.)

GREAT SAND DUNES   ☎719

In Great Sand Dunes National Park, billions of grains of sand make up dunes that have stood for between 40,000 and one million years as landmarks for travelers, from ancient North American nomads to modern outdoors enthusiasts. Thousands of years of wind and water have made these 750 ft. dunes the tallest in North America. Within the park, the most popular hiking is on the sand dunes themselves. Since wind obliterates the footprints of yesterday's explorers, no designated trails exist on the dunes, and hiking up through the soft sand can be exhausting. The best times to hike the dunes are in the morning, when the sand is coolest and the risk of thunderstorms lowest, and in the evening, especially on full-moon nights. The seasonal **Medano Creek** lies at the base of the dunes and provides a beach-like atmosphere in the middle of the high desert. A phenomenon called "surge flow," where pulses of water drive through

AMERICA'S SECOND ANTHEM

Upon reaching the summit of Pikes Peak, motorists, railroad passengers, and intrepid hikers find themselves with some unexpected history. The giant plaque atop the easternmost fourteener of Colorado commemorates the birth of "America the Beautiful" at perhaps that very spot.

The author of the poem-turned-hymn was an English professor from Wellesley College named Katharine Lee Bates, then acting as a visiting lecturer at Colorado College. One day in 1893, she stood 14,110 ft. above the sea with the expansive prairie before her and the awesome peaks of Colorado behind her, and words began to flow. She did not finalize the poem until 1913, though in 1910 it was set to the tune of a hymn written by Samuel Ward in 1882. The tune varied over the years before 1910 and was challenged thereafter, but Ward's music sticks even now.

When you listen to the words of "America the Beautiful," remember that the "amber waves of grain" mean the plains before Colorado's Front Range, "purple mountain majesties" refer to the magnificent views to the west and north of Pikes Peak, and the "pilgrim feet" belong not to the original Pilgrims, but to those who crossed the Great Plains to search for gold and silver among the Colorado Rockies.

THE GREAT VANISHING ACT

Two cowpokes sat around their fire late one night, speculating about the origin of the majestic sand dunes in southern Colorado, when a lone shepherd sauntered onto their campsite out of the pitch black. The shepherd chuckled and interrupted: "Gentlemen, you're both wrong."

"My grandfather herded sheep in the San Luis Valley, and he built a giant sheep ranch here with four of his friends. He set off to retrieve a herd of sheep that was located over the treacherous Mosca Pass. As he climbed toward the pass, the wind picked up, becoming so fierce and dangerous that he clung for dear life to a nearby tree.

"The next morning he returned to the valley, finding giant mounds of glistening white sand where the four shepherds, the 3500 sheep, and his ranch had once stood. He concluded that the windstorm had buried everyone alive."

The two cowpokes slept that night in the eerie silence that followed the strange man's harrowing tale. In the morning, the two men woke up to an empty campsite: the shepherd had vanished, as if under the sand.

For more on Local Legends of the Great Sand Dunes, check out the park's Visitors Center and ranger-led evening programs. Visit www.nps.gov/grsa for schedules.

built-up underwater sand, causes small waves perfect for splashing. The designated hiking trails elsewhere in the park often cross through multiple ecosystems in the Sangre de Cristo mountains. The half-mile **Montville Nature Trail** starts just north of the Visitors Center and meanders over rolling terrain. Off this trail, the more challenging **Mosca Pass Trail** (7 mi. round-trip) takes hikers into the high country through three different ecosystems. The worthwhile trek up **Zapata Falls**, just outside of the park (turn off at the Zapata Falls Recreation Area between Mi. 10 and 11 on Hwy. 150, follow the gravel road for 3½ mi. to the trailhead), leads hikers through a creek and narrow gorge all the way to the base of a 30 ft. hidden waterfall.

Camping is the only option for lodging within the park. People often arrive at **Pinyon Flats Campground ❶** early in the day to secure one of the 88 campsites; the most coveted have views of the dunes. (☎378-6399; www.nps.gov/grsa. No showers or hookups. Open year-round. No reservations. Sites $14. D/MC/V.) Intrepid campers can pitch their tents on the dunes themselves or in one of the seven designated **backcountry camping ❶** sites, though both of these options require hikes of at least an hour and a free backcountry permit, which can be picked up at the **Visitors Center.** (☎378-6399. Open Memorial Day-Labor Day 9am-6pm; call for off-season hours.) Maps are also available at the Visitors Center. Just outside the park, the private **Great Sand Dunes Oasis Campground and RV Park ❶**, 5400 Hwy 150 N., has showers, laundry, hookups, and panoramic views. (☎378-2222. Open May-Oct. Tent sites $18. Full hookups $28. AmEx/D/MC/V.) The cheapest and nicest indoor option in the area is the **Lodge Motel ❷**, 825 Hwy. 160 in Ft. Garland, which has clean, spacious rooms and new bathrooms. (☎379-2880; www.thelodgemotelcolorado.com. Rooms $45-55. MC/V.) The only indoor option close to the park is the **Great Sand Dunes Lodge ❹**, 7900 Hwy. 150 N., which has excellent views of the dunes from individual patios and a heated indoor pool. (☎378-2900; www.gsdlodge.com. Rooms $89. AmEx/D/MC/V.)

For those camping in the park, Oasis Campground has a small **grocery** with limited sundries, as well as a **restaurant ❶** that serves breakfast, lunch, and dinner. (☎378-2222. Breakfast $5-8. Lunch $5-8. Dinner $9-16. Open Memorial Day-Labor Day 8am-8pm.) Beyond the park, Alamosa offers a wide variety of restaurants. Tucked in the back of an antiques shop, the **Back in Thyme Eatery ❷**, 420 Main St., serves tasty gourmet soups, salads ($7.50), and sandwiches ($7). (☎587-3388. Open daily 9:30am-4pm; lunch 11am-3:30pm. AmEx/D/MC/V.)

SAN JUAN MOUNTAINS

Ask Coloradans for their favorite mountain retreats, and they're likely to name a peak, lake, stream, or town located somewhere in the San Juan Range of southwestern Colorado. Four national forests—the **Uncompahgre** (un-cum-PAH-gray), the **Gunnison,** the **San Juan,** and the **Rio Grande**—encircle this sprawling range. **Durango** is an ideal base camp for forays into these mountains. Northeast of Durango, the **Weminuche Wilderness** tempts the hardy backpacker with a vast, seemingly endless expanse of rugged terrain. You can get plenty of maps and hiking information from the **USFS headquarters** at 15 Burnett Ct., Durango. (☎247-4874. Open Apr. to mid-Dec. M-F 8am-5pm; mid-Dec. to Mar. M-F 8am-4:30pm.) The San Juan Mountains are easily accessible via U.S. 50, which is traveled by hundreds of thousands of tourists each and every summer. Greyhound serves the area, but very infrequently; traveling by car is definitely the best option. The San Juans are loaded with campgrounds, making them one of the most economical places in Colorado to visit.

BLACK CANYON OF THE GUNNISON NATIONAL PARK ☎970

Native American parents used to tell their children that the light-colored strands of rock streaking through the walls of the Black Canyon were the hair of a blonde woman—and that if they got too close to the edge they would get tangled in it and fall. The edge of **Black Canyon of the Gunnison National Park** is a staggering place, literally—watch for those trembling knees. The Gunnison River slowly gouged out the 53 mi. long canyon, crafting a steep 2500 ft. gorge that is, in some places, deeper than it is wide. The Empire State Building, if placed at the bottom of the river, would reach barely halfway up the canyon walls.

Black Canyon lies 15 mi. east of the town of **Montrose.** The **South Rim** is easily accessible via a 6 mi. drive off U.S. 50 ($15 per car, $7 per pedestrian or motorcyclist); the wilder **North Rim** can only be reached by an 80 mi., 1-3hr. detour around the canyon followed by a gravel road from Crawford off Rte. 92. The road is closed to cars in winter but open for cross-country skiing. Less than a mile past the South Rim entrance is the **Visitors Center** (see below), where the spectacular 6 mi. South Rim Drive begins. The route traces the edge of the canyon and boasts jaw-dropping vistas, including the spectacular **Chasm View.** At the **Painted Wall** overlook, visitors can stop and marvel at Colorado's highest cliff, clocking in at a whopping 2300 ft. Don't throw stones; you might kill a defenseless hiker in the canyon. On the South Rim, the moderate 2 mi. round-trip **Oak Flat Loop Trail** gives a good sense of the terrain below, while the North Rim's 7 mi. round-trip **North Vista Trail** provides a spectacular view. Those looking for backcountry adventure can scramble down the **Gunnison Route** from the South Rim, which drops 1800 ft. over a 1 mi. span, or tackle the incredibly difficult **Tomichi** or **Warner Routes,** which make good overnight hikes. Not surprisingly, the sheer walls of the Black Canyon are a rock climber's paradise; registration is required at the South Rim Visitors Center. Between the **Painted Wall** and **Cedar Point Overlooks,** a well-worn path leads to **Marmot Rocks,** which offer great bouldering for those not ready for the big walls. All inner-canyon use requires a free permit. On the South Rim, Chasm View, Sunset View, and Tomichi overlooks are all wheelchair-accessible. Balanced Rock overlook, on the North Rim, is also wheelchair-accessible.

At the canyon, the **South Rim Campground ❶** has 88 sites with pit toilets, charcoal grills, and limited water. Some sites are wheelchair-accessible. (Sites $12, RV hookup $18.) The 13 sites at the **North Rim Campground ❶** are popular with climbers. (Sites with water and toilets $12.) The automobile route into the canyon leads to the pleasant **East Portal Campground ❶.** The steep 16% grade road, although paved, prohibits large vehicles, so the campground is free of RVs. (Sites with water and toilet $12.) In Montrose, inexpensive motels line Main St./U.S. 50 east of downtown, including **Canyon Trails Inn ❷**, 1225 E. Main St. (☎249-3426 or 800-858-5911; www.canyontrailsinn.com. Hot tub, continental breakfast. Singles $40-57; doubles $48-70. Call ahead for prices. AmEx/D/MC/V.) **Starvin' Arvin's ❸**, 1320 S. Townsend, is popular with locals and visitors alike; it's been serving up cowboy-sized portions for as long as most can remember. Don't miss the 10 oz. steak and eggs breakfast for $12. (☎249-7787. All-you-can-eat pancakes $4.50. Entrees $4-12. Open daily 6am-2pm. D/MC/V.) For tasty sandwiches ($6) and breakfasts ($5.50-7), head for the **Daily Bread Bakery and Cafe ❶**, 346 Main St. (☎249-8444. Open M-Sa 6am-3pm. Cash only.) In the summer, the **farmers' market,** 1st St. between Cascade and Uncompahgre, offers fresh produce and meat. (Sa and some W 8:30am-1pm.)

Greyhound, 1360 N. Townsend, just south of the Sun Valley truck stop, travels daily to Denver (6½hr., 1 per day, $65-77), Durango (3½hr., 1 per day, $29-34), and Salt Lake City (6½hr., 1 per day, $67-78), and less frequently to other destinations, such as Las Vegas and Dallas. (☎249-6673; www.greyhound.com. Open M-F 10am-3:30pm, Sa-Su 1-3:30pm.) The bus also shuttles once a day between Montrose and the Gunnison station, 312 W. Hwy. 50 (☎641-0060), several blocks from the **Gunnison County Airport,** 711 Rio Grande, and sometimes will make an extra stop upon request on U.S. 50, 6 mi. from the canyon ($17-18). A helpful **Visitors Center** sits on the canyon's South Rim. (☎249-1914, ext. 423; www.nps.gov/blca. Open daily May-Oct. 8am-6pm; Nov.-Apr. 8am-4pm.) **Post Office:** 321 S. 1st St., in Montrose. (☎249-6654. Open M-F 8am-5pm, Sa 10am-noon.) **Postal Code:** 81401.

CRESTED BUTTE   ☎970

The compact town of Crested Butte, 27 mi. north of Gunnison on Rte. 135, was first settled by miners in the 1870s. The coal was exhausted in the 1950s, but a few years later the powder fields on the Butte began to attract skiers. Thanks to strict zoning rules, the downtown is a throwback to the early mining days. Just north of town, **Crested Butte Mountain Resort,** 12 Snowmass Rd., takes skiers to "the extreme limits," offering over 1075 acres of bowl skiing. With 15 lifts, a longest run of 2½ mi., and a drop of 3000 ft., the mountain aims to impress, and the views aren't bad either. (☎800-810-7669; www.skicb.com. Open mid-Nov. to mid-Apr. Prices vary. Generally $79 per full day, ages 13-17 $59, ages 7-12 $40; over 65 25% discount.) Crested Butte has several noteworthy summer festivals. Among these is the fun-loving **Fat Tire Bike Week** (www.ftbw.com), six days of mountain biking, racing, and fraternizing at the end of June. Visitors and locals in hilarious costumes try to coast down the mountain as fast as possible without pedaling in the famous chainless race. In 1976, a group of cyclists rode from Crested Butte to Aspen, starting the world's oldest mountain biking event. Every September, bikers repeat the trek over the 12,705 ft. pass to Aspen and back during the **Pearl Pass Tour,** organized by the **Mountain Biking Hall of Fame,** 331 Elk Ave. (☎349-1880; www.crestedbuttemuseum.com. Open Memorial Day-Labor Day daily 10am-8pm; open winter daily noon-6pm. $3, children free. MC/V.) Once on wheels, all trails are accessible right from town or via a free shuttle (see below). Be sure to check snow conditions before heading out; some trails are closed due to inclement weather well into early July. Trails begin at the base of Mt. Crested Butte and extend into the Gothic area. The famous **Trail 401** is a demanding 24 mi. round-trip loop with great views of the valley and its wildflowers along the downhill. For the same fun on a shorter ride, cut through on **Rustler's Gulch** trail. The short but beautiful **Strand Hill Trail** is an intermediate option. The **Lower Loop** leaves right from town and offers great views for beginners. For those without wheels, the hike to **Green Lake** (3 mi.) is unbeatable.

Finding budget accommodations in the winter is about as easy as striking a vein of gold. Nonetheless, the ⊠Crested Butte International Lodge and Hostel (HI) ❶, 615 Teocalli Ave., two blocks north of the four-way stop, treats travelers to gorgeous, modern facilities. Its huge kitchen and bright common area make it an ideal base for exploring the region. (☎349-0588 or 888-389-0588; www.crestedbuttehostel.com. Reception hours 8am-8pm. Showers for non-guests $5. Laundry. Rates vary depending on season; call in advance for prices and reservations. 4- to 6-bed dorms $25-38; doubles $65-95. Spacious 3rd fl. apartment $175-250 for up to 6 people. Group discounts available. D/MC/V.) The US Forest Service operates a number of campgrounds in the area. Cement Creek Campground ❶, 10 mi. south of town off Hwy. 135, is near several hiking and motorbike trails, and its namesake creek, where the adventurous can find several hot springs. Contact Gunnison National Forest Office, 216 N. Colorado, 30 mi. south in Gunnison., for more info on area camping. (☎641-0471. Open M-F 7:30am-4:30pm.) Pitas in Paradise ❷, 212 Elk Ave., a self-proclaimed "Mediterranean Cafe with Soul," wows diners with its delicious *gyros* (YEE-rohs), salads, and smoothies. Enjoy your meal on the two patios or take it with you on your next adventure. (☎349-0897. Gyros $8.50. Salads $5.50-8.50. Open daily in summer 11am-10pm; in winter 11am-9pm. D/MC/V.) Locals flock to the tiny storefront and creek-side patio at Izzy's ❷, 218 Maroon Ave., behind the post office, for scrumptious breakfast latkes ($5), homemade bagels ($1-3), and specialty "Izzwiches", ($6-8) without breaking the bank. (☎349-5630. Open M and W-Su 7am-2pm. MC/V.) The Secret Stash ❷, 21 Elk Ave., at the west end of town, specializes in mouthwatering, eclectic pizzas ($16-22). While waiting for your pizza, enjoy grilled wings (10 for $10) or a salad ($6-9) in the garden or upstairs, where the cushy couches recall a hippie's living room. (☎349-6245; www.thesecretstash.com. Open daily 5-10pm; additional lunch hours in summer and winter. D/MC/V.)

The Crested Butte Chamber of Commerce is located at 601 Elk Ave. (☎800-545-4505; www.cbchamber.com. Open daily 9am-5pm.) A free shuttle to the mountain leaves from the chamber. (☎349-7318; www.townofcrestedbutte.com. Every 20min. 7:20am-11:45pm.) Internet Access: The Old Rock Community Library, 507 Maroon Ave. (☎349-6535. Open M, W, F 10am-6pm, Tu and Th 10am-7pm, Sa 10am-2pm.) Post Office: 217 Elk Ave. (☎349-6741. Open M-F 7:30am-4:30pm, Sa 10am-1pm.) Postal Code: 81224.

TELLURIDE   ☎970

Site of the first bank Butch Cassidy ever robbed (the San Miguel), Telluride is very much a town of the Old West. Legend has it that the city's name derives from a contraction of "to hell you ride," likely a warning given to travelers headed for the notoriously rough and rowdy mining town. In the last few decades, outlaws have been replaced with film stars, and six-shooters with cinnamon buns. Skiers, hikers, and vacationers come to Telluride to pump gold and silver into the mountains, and the town also claims the most festivals per capita of any postal code in the US. In spite of its newfound fame, a small-town feeling prevails—rocking chairs sit outside brightly painted houses and dogs lounge on storefront porches.

■▪ ORIENTATION AND PRACTICAL INFORMATION. Telluride sits on Rte. 145, 120 mi. northwest of Durango in the San Juan Mountains. Most of the action lies on Colorado Ave./Rte. 145. The public bus line, Galloping Goose, runs through town on a regular basis. (☎728-5700. Every 20min. May-Oct. 7am-8pm, Nov. to mid-April 7am-midnight; call for extended festival hours. Town loop free, outlying towns $1.) A free gondola runs continuously between downtown and Mountain Village, with spectacular views of the surrounding mountains. The station is at the

ROCKY MOUNTAINS

corner of Oak St. and San Juan Ave. (☎728-0588. 15min. each way. Runs late May to mid-Oct. daily 7am-midnight; call for extended festival hours.) **Taxi** service from **Mountain Limo** serves the western slope. (☎728-9606 or 888-546-6894. Airport fare $10.) The **Visitors Center,** 630 W. Colorado Ave., at Davis St. and W. Colorado Ave. near the entrance to town, has information on trails and festivals. (☎800-525-3455; www.visittelluride.com. Open daily summer 9am-8pm; winter 9am-6pm.) **Police:** ☎728-3818. **Hotlines: Rape Crisis,** ☎728-5660. **Medical Services: Telluride Medical Center,** 500 W. Pacific St. (☎728-3848). **Internet Access: Wilkinson Public Library,** 100 W. Pacific St. (☎728-6613. Free. Open M-Th 10am-8pm, F-Sa 10am-6pm, Su noon-5pm.) **Post Office:** 150 S. Willow St. (☎728-5532. Open M-F 9am-5pm, Sa 10am-noon.) **Postal Code:** 81435.

█ ACCOMMODATIONS. If you're visiting Telluride during a festival, bring a sleeping bag; the cost of a bed is outrageous. █**Sunshine Campground ❶,** 8 mi. south on Rte. 145, is peacefully situated among the aspens on a hillside with stunning 360-degree views of all the surrounding peaks. (☎327-4261. No electricity or showers. Open May-Sept. No reservations. Sites $16.) The **Telluride Town Park Campground ❶,** east of downtown, offers 29 nice, if closely spaced, sites along the San Miguel River. (☎728-2173; www.telluride-co.gov. Full bathrooms, water, no hookups. 7-night max. stay. Office open mid-May to mid-Oct. M-W 8am-5pm, Th-F 8am-8pm, Sa-Su 8am-noon and 1-5pm. Sites $12. $16 per vehicle.) During the Bluegrass Festival, ticket holders can lottery for spots in the campground. Hot showers ($3) are available at the high school.

█ FOOD. La Cocina de Luz ❷, 123 E. Colorado Ave., serves authentic and affordable taqueria-style Mexican cuisine. Featuring fresh handmade tortillas and a daunting salsa bar, La Cocina uses organic, local ingredients in their flavorful quesadillas, tamales ($7.25-13.50), and large selection of vegetarian options. (☎728-9355. Open M-Sa 8:30am-9pm. MC/V.) The wooden benches and long tables at **Fat Alley ❸,** 122 S. Oak St., may be reminiscent of the sawdust saloons of yore, but Telluride's miners never ate barbecue like this. Specialties include the Carolina pork shoulder sandwich ($8.50) and the surprisingly ample and delicious vegetarian menu. (☎728-3985. Barbecue $8-20. Open daily 11am-10pm. AmEx/MC/V.) **Baked in Telluride ❷,** 127 S. Fir St., has enough rich coffee, pastries, pizza, and sandwiches to get you through a festival weekend, plus free Wi-Fi. The apple fritters ($2.50) and enormous calzones ($8-11) are justifiably popular. (☎728-4705. Open daily 5:30am-10pm). Telluride also has a **farmers' market,** 123 S. Oak St. (☎728-8701. Open F 11:30am-4pm.)

█ █ ENTERTAINMENT AND NIGHTLIFE. Given that only 2000 people live in Telluride, the sheer number of festivals in the town seems staggering. One weekend in July is actually designated the "Nothing Festival" to give locals a break from the onslaught of visitors and special events. For general festival info, contact the Visitors Center. Gala events occur throughout the summer and fall, from the quirky **Mushroom Festival** (☎708-0289; www.tellurideinstitute.org; late Aug.) to the renowned **Bluegrass Festival.** (☎800-624-2422; www.bluegrass.com. 3rd weekend in June. $60 per day, 4-day pass $175.) The **Telluride International Film Festival** premiers some of the hippest independent flicks; *The Crying Game* (1992) and *The Piano* (1993) were both unveiled here. (☎728-4640; www.telluridefilmfestival.com. 1st weekend in Sept.) For most festivals (including the more expensive Bluegrass Festival and Jazz Celebration, volunteering to usher or perform other tasks can result in free admission. For more info, call the contact number of the specific event a few months in advance. The beautiful **Sheridan Opera House,** 110 N. Oak St., often described as the "living room of Telluride," hosts musical performances, films, and even children's theater throughout the year. (☎728-6363; www.sheridanoperahouse.com.) Advance tickets for these events can be purchased at **Telluride Ticket** (☎728-8199; www.tellurideticket.com).

Telluride may have a New Age air by day, but its bars still burst with old-fashioned fun by night. The lively **Last Dollar Saloon**, 100 E. Colorado Ave., affectionately referred to as "the Buck," is a local favorite. Visitors owe it to themselves to try the killer margaritas. (☎728-4800. Beer $3-4.75. Open daily 3pm-2am. Cash only.) Telluride's freshest musical talent jives at **Fly Me to the Moon Saloon**, 136 E. Colorado Ave., which thrills groovers with its spring-loaded dance floor. (☎728-6666. Cover $3-25. Open daily 9pm-2am.) The historic **New Sheridan Bar**, 231 W. Colorado Ave., inspires hubbub around town with Tuesday pool tournaments in the winter and weekly open poker nights. (☎728-3911. Draft beer and well drinks $4.50. 21+ after 8pm. Open daily noon-2am.) For partiers out late, Telluride's free **"home safe" shuttle** will take you from the courthouse, 305 W. Colorado, to your front door. (Shuttle departs May 25-late Sept. F-Sa 12:45 and 2:15am. Free.)

⚡ OUTDOOR ACTIVITIES. Biking, hiking, and backpacking opportunities are endless; ghost towns and lakes are tucked behind almost every mountain crag. The tourist office has a list of suggestions for hikes in the area. The most popular trek (about 2hr.) is up the 4WD road to **Bridal Veil Falls**, the waterfall visible from almost anywhere in Telluride. The trailhead is at the end of Rte. 145. Continuing another 2½ mi. from the top of the falls will lead to **Silver Lake**, a steep but rewarding climb. Another popular hike is the **Bear Creek** trail, a gradual, easy 2½ mi. hike to the Bear Creek waterfalls that starts on S. Pine St. From from the north end of Aspen St., the **Jud Wiebe Trail** takes you on a 2¾ mi. loop with panoramas of the entire valley. For more Rocky Mountain highs, ride the free gondola to St. Sophia station at the top of the mountain, where a number of hiking trails run. At the top of the gondola, the **St. Sophia Nature Center** offers trail info and environmental programs during the summer. (☎728-7360. Open daily in summer 9am-4pm. Free.)

In winter, even avowed atheists can be spied praying before hitting the "Spiral Stairs" and the "Plunge," two of the Rockies' most gut-wrenching ski runs. For more info, contact the **Telluride Ski Resort**, 565 Mountain Village Blvd. (☎728-6900 or 800-778-8581; www.tellurideskiresort.com. Regular season lift tickets $68 per half-day, children $35; full day $79/47.) **Paragon Ski and Sport**, 213 W. Colorado Ave., rents bikes in summer and skis in winter. (☎728-4525.

THE HIDDEN DEAL

BLUEGRASS FOR LITTLE GREEN

The Telluride Bluegrass Festival is about to enter its 35th year. As the festival's notoriety increases, so does the difficulty of finding tickets. Once you do score a ticket, you'll have to worry about accommodations; hotel rates skyrocket as tourists swarm to the area. What's a bluegrass-lover on a budget supposed to do?

Volunteer. Working four 4hr. shifts garners a coveted four-day pass. These go quickly—it's good to apply at least a few months in advance.

Be creative. Some gain access to the festival by hopping on the free transportation provided between town and the free overnight festival parking areas.

Listen. If you don't mind not being in the thick of things, the mainstage bands sound almost as good on the outside of the festival perimeter, especially along the river.

Wander. Bands perform daily on the free stage in Elks Park on Main Ave., and Festivarians themselves are more than likely to strike up jam sessions on street corners.

The Telluride Bluegrass Festival is scheduled for June 19-22, 2008; June 18-21, 2009; and June 17-20, 2010. For more information about the festival, check out www.bluegrass.com. For transportation, call ☎800-525-3455.

Bikes from $22 per half-day, $33 per day. Beginner ski package $19 per day. Open daily in ski season 8:30am-7pm; in summer 9am-7pm.)

DURANGO ☎ 970

In its heyday, Durango was one of the main railroad junctions in the Southwest. Walking down the town's main thoroughfare, it's easy to see that Durango remains a crossroads. Today, this informal town attracts visitors with its mountain biking, river running, skiing, and snowboarding. Dreadlocked, hemp-clad youths share the sidewalks with weathered ranchers in ten-gallon hats and stiff Wranglers; brazen mountain bikers rub shoulders with camera-toting tourists in the bars.

🌐🚌 TRANSPORTATION AND PRACTICAL INFORMATION. Durango is at the intersection of U.S. 160 and 550. Streets run east-west and avenues run north-south, and everyone calls Main Ave., the principal road through town, **"Main St."** Greyhound, 275 E. 8th Ave. (☎259-2755; www.greyhound.com; open M-F 10:30am-1:30pm, 4:30-6:30pm; Sa-Su 11:30am-noon, 4:30-6pm), runs **buses** once per day to Albuquerque (5hr., $51), Denver (11½hr., $66), and Grand Junction (4hr., $35). **Durango Transit** provides trolley service in town. (☎259-5438; www.durangogov.org/resident/services/transit.html. Runs Memorial Day-Labor Day M-Sa 7am-10:40pm. $1, seniors $0.50.) For a **taxi:** Durango Transportation, ☎259-4818. The **Durango Area Tourism Office,** 111 S. Camino del Río, on the southeast side of town, has info on sights and local outdoor outfitters. (☎800-525-8855; www.durango.org. Open in summer M-F 8am-6pm, Sa 9am-5pm, Su 10am-4pm; in winter M-F 8am-5pm.) **Road Conditions:** ☎264-5555 or 877-315-7623. **Internet Access: Durango Public Library,** 1188 E. 2nd Ave. (☎375-3380. Free. Open M-W 9am-9pm, Th-Su 9am-5:30pm; closed Su in summer.) **Post Office:** 222 W. 8th St. (☎247-3434. Open M-F 8am-5:30pm, Sa 9am-1pm.) **Postal Code:** 81301.

🏠🍴 ACCOMMODATIONS AND FOOD. If you don't mind staying 25 mi. north of Durango, you'll be pampered at **Silverpick Lodge ❸,** 48475 U.S. 550, with luxurious rooms, goose-down comforters, hot tubs, a game room, laundry, and a library. Wooden skis adorn the walls of the lobby, completing the warm ski-lodge atmosphere. Call within 48hr. of check-in for their year-round "Last Second Special" and get any available room for only $48, about half the usual price. (☎259-6600 or 800-295-4820; www.silverpicklodge.com. Rooms May-Sept. $69-120; call for low-season rates.) The reasonably priced **Budget Inn ❷,** 3077 Main Ave., offers clean rooms, a hot tub, an outdoor pool, and laundry facilities. (☎247-5222 or 800-257-5222; www.budgetinndurango.com. Cable TV, telephone; some rooms have microwave and fridge. Rooms June-Aug. $51-82; call for low season rates.) Eighteen miles north of Durango, the **Haviland Lake Campground ❶,** off Hwy. 550, tempts campers with 45 pleasant sites and clean, well maintained facilities. (☎247-4874. No reservations. Sites $16; with water and electricity $19; lakefront $21.)

On Saturdays, locals in search of cheap, fresh produce flock to the **Durango Farmer's Market,** on 8th St. across from the post office. (☎375-6401; www.durangofarmersmarket.org. Open mid-May to late Oct. Sa 8am-noon.) Decked out with Texan and local paraphernalia, **Serious Texas BBQ ❶,** 3535 N. Main Ave. and 650 S. Camino del Rio, doles out generous half-pound portions of smoked meat ($6.50), Texas tacos ($4), and "cheezy potatoes" for $1.50. (☎247-2240 and 259-9507. Open daily in summer 11am-9pm; in winter 11am-8pm. MC/V.) Durango has a disproportionate ratio of microbreweries to people. At **Carver's Restaurant and Brewpub ❸,** 1022 Main Ave., locals enjoy pitchers of home-brewed beer ($13) and bison bratwurst ($13.50) in hammocks on the outdoor patio. (☎259-2545; www.carverbrewing.com. Breakfast $4-7.50. Open M-F 6:30am-10pm, Su 6:30am-

ROCKY MOUNTAINS

10pm. AmEx/D/MC/V.) **Steamworks Brewing Co. ❷,** 801 E. 2nd Ave., is a casual spot for a Cajun Boil (crab, shrimp, sausage, potatoes, and corn, all boiled in hot spices; $19) or a beer crafted on the premises. (☎259-9200; www.steamworksbrewing.com. Pints $4. Sa Ladies Night. Open M-W and Su 11am-2pm, F-Sa 11am-2am. Kitchen closes M-W and Su 11pm, F-Sa midnight. AmEx/D/MC/V.)

🎫🎭 **SIGHTS AND NIGHTLIFE.** More a tourist attraction than a means of transportation, the **Durango and Silverton Narrow Gauge Train,** 479 Main St., runs up the Animas River Valley to the historic mining town of Silverton. In continuous operation since 1881, the old-fashioned, 100% coal-fed locomotives wheeze through the San Juans, making a 2hr. stop in Silverton before returning to Durango. The train also offers access to the **Weminuche Wilderness,** dropping off and picking up backpackers at various scenic points; call for more info. To shorten the trip, some people take a bus one way ($9, reservations required) or drive 20min. north to Rockwood to pick up the train there. While waiting for the train, step into some of the very first iron horses at the **Railroad Museum** across the tracks. (☎247-2733 or 888-872-4607; www.durangotrain.com. Office open daily May to mid-Aug. 7am-7:30pm; mid-Aug. to Oct. 7am-7pm; Nov.-Apr. 8am-5pm. Museum open daily 7am-7pm. Morning trains from Durango and afternoon trains from Silverton 9hr.; includes stop, layover day optional. Summer $65, ages 5-11 $35. Trains to Cascade Canyon late Nov. to early May $49/29. Museum free with train fare. Reservations recommended.) The **Durango Pro Rodeo Series,** at the La Plata County Fairgrounds at 25th St. and Main Ave., moseys into town in summer. Saddling up on Friday, Saturday, and sometimes Wednesday nights, the action starts at 7pm after a barbecue at 6pm. (Call the Visitors Center for ticket info; check www.durango.org for schedule.) On U.S. 550, 7 mi. north of Durango, **Trimble Hot Springs** treats visitors to a community pool experience with better water; its mineral water fills two hot pools and an Olympic-size swimming pool. (☎247-0111; www.trimblehotsprings.com. Open in summer daily 8am-11pm; in winter M-Th and Su 9am-10pm, F-Sa 9am-11pm. $13, ages 5-11 $8.50.)

The ski-lodge atmosphere and frequent live music at **The Summit,** 600 Main Ave., a block north of the train station, attract a laid-back college crowd as the main music venue in town, with pool ($0.75) and live acts Th-Sa. (☎247-2324; www.durangosummit.com. Nightly beer and liquor specials. 21+. Cover varies. Open M-Sa 7pm-2am.) **The Lost Dog,** 1150-B Main Ave., boasts a slightly swankier atmosphere and refined decor, complete with lounge, dance floor, and outdoor tiki bar. (☎259-0430. Beer $3-5.50. Martinis $6.50. F-Sa top 40. No cover. Open M and W-Su 11:30am-2am. Kitchen closes midnight.) The family owned and operated **El Patio,** 600 Main Ave., upstairs next to The Summit, is an open-air bar. Nightly live music and $12 pitchers create a fun atmosphere. (☎382-0799. Beer $3.25. Margaritas $7. No cover. Open daily May-October 11am-11pm, weather permitting).

🚵 **OUTDOOR ACTIVITIES.** In winter, **Durango Mountain Resort,** 28 mi. north on U.S. 550, hosts skiers and snowboarders of all levels. Unlike most Colorado towns, however, Durango's busiest season is summer, when **mountain bikers** revel in the many desert and mountain trails, some of which connect to Moab, UT (p. 768) through the **San Juan Hut** system (☎626-3033; www.sanjuanhuts.com. 7-day tour $620, includes food and maps.) Durango's trails are challenging, often involving very steep climbs and technical terrain for more expert cyclists. For easier day rides, head to **Horse Gulch,** which offers mellow and smooth single-track riding after a steep half-mile climb. The extensive trail system here is well marked, with maps at every junction and both flat and mountainous trails. Watch out: the desert environment means very little shade. (Trailhead on 8th Ave., across from the bus station.) Many people head to the popular and more challenging **Hermosa Creek**

Trail; the best way to travel this 21 mi. trail is to get dropped off near the top and ride south into Durango. Numerous other marked and unmarked trails exist in the Durango area; checking in bike shops for weather conditions and difficulty levels is highly recommended. One such shop is **Hassle Free Sports,** 2615 Main St. (☎259-3874 or 800-259-3800; www.hasslefreesports.com. Full suspension $30 per half-day, $40 per full day. Ski rental packages $25-32 per day. Open in summer M-Sa 9am-6pm, Su 10am-5pm; in winter daily 7am-6pm.) **Southwest Adventure Guides,** 1205 Camino del Río, offers climbing and backpacking gear and guided tours—including mountain bike tours. (☎259-0370 or 800-642-5389; www.mtnguide.net. Bike tours $60-125. Open M-F 8am-6pm.) The Durango area is engulfed by the **San Juan National Forest.** Call the Forest Headquarters, 15 Burnett Ct., on Hwy. 160, half a mile west of Durango, for info, especially if you're planning a trip into the massive **Weminuche Wilderness,** northeast of Durango. (☎247-4874; www.fs.fed.us/r2/sanjuan. Open M-F 8am-4:30pm.)

The **Animas River** offers rapids from placid Class II splashes to intense Class V struggles. Keep in mind that the river is wilder earlier in the summer, when runoff is strongest. **Durango Rivertrippers,** 720 Main Ave., leads whitewater rafting jaunts and rents inflatable kayaks. (☎259-0289 or 800-292-2885; www.durangorivertrippers.com. Rafting trip $25 per 2 hr., children $17; half-day trip with lunch $38/28. Kayaks $30 per 2hr. Open late May to mid-Aug. daily 8:30am-9pm.) The largest area outfitter is **Mild to Wild Rafting,** 701 Main Ave. (☎247-4789 or 800-567-6745; www.mild2wildrafting.com. Mild trips $43 per half-day, children $33; full day $72/62. Intense trips $215 per full day, including narrow gauge train ticket to the jump-off point at Upper Animas River. Open Apr.-Sept. daily 9am-9pm.)

MESA VERDE NATIONAL PARK ☎970

Native American tribes began to cultivate the valleys of southern Colorado about 1400 years ago. In the centuries that followed, the Ancestral Pueblo constructed a series of cliff dwellings beneath the overhanging sandstone shelves surrounding the mesa. Around AD 1275, the Pueblo people abruptly left their eerily desolate and starkly beautiful dwellings, which weren't rediscovered until local ranchers stumbled upon the magnificent ruins of Cliff Palace in 1888. Established in 1906, Mesa Verde National Park is the only national park set aside exclusively to protect archaeological remains. Mesa Verde is not for the snap-a-shot-and-go tourist; the best sites require a bit of physical effort to reach. In honor of the park's centennial in 2006, the Mesa Verde Institute was established. It continues to provide visitors with deeper insight into the park. Check out www.mesa.verde.national-park.com for more information.

ORIENTATION AND PRACTICAL INFORMATION. The sole entrance to the park lies at its north end, half a mile from a well-marked exit for the park off U.S. 160, 10 mi. east of **Cortez** and 8 mi. west of Mancos. The park's main road runs 21 mi. from the entrance station to Chapin Mesa and the park headquarters. 15 mi. into the park on the main road, a branch road heads out 12 mi. to Wetherill Mesa. An automobile is the best way to travel through the park, but no vehicles over 25 ft. in length are allowed on the road to Wetherill Mesa. There are two other options for intra-park transport. **Aramark Mesa Verde** runs daily guided bus tours. (☎800-

WHEN TO GO. Snowy and icy conditions often make Mesa Verde an undesirable winter destination. Summer highs can hit the 90s, and afternoon thunderstorms are likely in July and August. The best times to visit are the late spring and early fall, when the weather tends to be fairly reliable and not too hot.

449-2288; www.visitmesaverde.com. Open mid-May to mid-Oct. Half-day tours $49, under 12 $38; full day $53/41.) A **tram** runs to Wetherill Mesa from the ranger kiosk in the parking lot (May-Sept., 30min. ride every 30min. 9:30am-4pm, free). Trailers and towed vehicles are prohibited past Morefield Campground; they can be parked in the lot before the entrance station. Much of the park is wheelchair-accessible, though none of the tours are.

The **Far View Visitors Center,** 15 mi. in on the main road, is the only place to buy tickets ($3) for guided tours. (☎529-5036. Open Apr. to mid-Oct. daily 8am-5pm.) When the Visitors Center is closed during the winter, head to the **Chapin Mesa Archaeological Museum.** (☎529-4631. Open daily June-Sept. 8am-6:30pm; Oct.-May 8am-5pm.) On summer evenings, the **Morefield Ranger Station** at Morefield Village offers advice and tour tickets for the following day. (☎564-6005. Open daily 5-8:30pm.) Information about the region is available at the **Colorado Welcome Center/ Cortez Chamber of Commerce,** 928 E. Main St., in Cortez. (☎565-4048. Open late May-early Sept. daily 8am-6pm; mid-Sept. to mid-May 8am-5pm.) Other services in the park include: public **showers, laundry,** and **gas** at Morefield Village (☎565-2133; open May to mid-Oct. 7am-9pm; showers and laundry 24hr.); **road and weather conditions** (☎385-1324); **general park information,** from park headquarters (☎529-4465); and **post office,** Chapin Mesa by the park headquarters and museum (☎529-4554; open M-F 8:30am-4:30pm, Sa 10am-2pm). **Postal code:** 81330.

⌐⌐ ACCOMMODATIONS AND FOOD. Lodging in the park is pricey. Budget options in neighboring Cortez are more plentiful. Spacious, affordable rooms make the **Sand Canyon Inn ❷,** 301 W. Main St., a popular choice for visitors. (☎565-8562; www.sandcanyon.com. Reception 24hr. Check-out 11am. Singles $49; doubles $63.) At the southwest corner of town, the **Ute Mountain Motel ❷,** 531 S. Broadway, has newly renovated basic rooms at attractive prices. (☎565-5392. Reception 8am-11pm. Check-out 11am. Rooms $49-69.) Mesa Verde's **Morefield Campground ❶,** 4 mi. into the park, is beautiful, and its 390 sites never fill up, though you'll have to get there early to grab one of the 15 sites with full hookup. (☎565-2133 or 800-449-2288. Open May-Oct. Reception Memorial Day-Labor Day 7am-9pm; low-season 8am-8pm. Check-out 11am. Tent sites $24; RV sites with hookup $34.) Basic camping supplies and groceries are available at the **Morefield Village General Store.** (☎565-2133. Open daily Memorial Day-Labor Day 7am-9pm; low-season 8am-8pm.) Within the park's boundaries, two cafeterias present standard buffet fare at slightly inflated prices. The **Far View Terrace Restaurant ❷,** near the main Visitors Center, offers a gourmet-style buffet ($9-11), while the **Spruce Tree Terrace Restaurant ❷,** right near the museum, serves Navajo tacos ($8), burgers ($5.45), and pizza ($6) in a thoroughly unpretentious style. (Far View Terrace open in summer daily 7am-8pm. Spruce Tree Terrace open in summer daily 9am-6pm.)

◙⌐ SIGHTS AND OUTDOOR ACTIVITIES. A good starting point, the **Far View Visitors Center** is a long 15 mi. drive from the entrance gate along Rte. 160. (☎529-4631. Open daily 8am-5pm.) After the Visitors Center, the park divides into **Chapin Mesa,** with the largest number of visible cliff dwellings, and the smaller and less-touristed **Wetherill Mesa.** The **Chapin Mesa Archaeological Museum,** along the first loop of the Chapin branch (before the dwellings), can give you an overview of the Ancestral Pueblo lifestyle and is a good place to start before exploring the mesa. Tours of the spectacular **Cliff Palace** explore the largest cliff dwelling in North America, with nearly 200 preserved rooms. (Open Apr.-Oct. daily 8:30am-6pm. 1hr. ranger-led tours depart every 30min.; $3.) The impressive **Balcony House** is a 40-room dwelling 600 ft. above the floor of Soda Canyon; entrance requires climbing several ladders and squeezing through a tunnel. (Open late Apr. to mid-Oct. daily 9am-5:30pm. 1hr. ranger-led tours depart every 30min.; $3.) A few sites are acces-

ROCKY MOUNTAINS

sible via self-guided tour from Chapin Mesa. **Spruce Tree House** is Mesa Verde's third-largest cliff dwelling and features a reconstructed *kiva* (ceremonial room) that you can explore. This is the only dwelling open in winter. (Trail ½ mi. Open daily 9am-6:30pm. Free.) A more low-key approach to Chapin Mesa is the self-guided **Mesa Top Loop Road,** which runs visitors through a 600-year history of the ruins. (6 mi. Open daily 8am-sunset. Free.)

The long drive out to Wetherill Mesa illustrates the various stages of regeneration occurring in the forest, which has suffered many significant wildfires over the past century. From the ranger kiosk, 1½hr. tours of sprawling **Long House,** composed of 150 rooms and 21 *kivas*, include a tram ride that passes many such sites. (Open late May-early Sept. daily 10am-5pm. Tickets required for tour but not for tram; ticket holders seated first when space is tight. Free.) **Step House,** also located on Wetherill Mesa, features a well-preserved set of prehistoric stairs as well as pictographs. (Open late May-early Sept. daily 10am-5pm. Free.) On both mesas, early morning visits tend to be less crowded and cooler.

Mesa Verde also offers **hiking,** though none of the pleasant day hikes around the park would challenge an experienced hiker. Staying on established trails is critical to the preservation of Mesa Verde's archaeological remains. The Visitors Center has more information on the hikes, including $0.50 interpretive trail guides. The **Petroglyph Point Trail** offers good views of the Spruce and Navajo Canyons and a few petroglyphs, and is the only trail to pass actual archeological sites along the way. (2¾ mi. Begins at the Spruce Tree House Trail.)

WYOMING

The ninth-largest state in the Union, Wyoming is also the least populated. This is a place where men don cowboy hats and boots, and livestock outnumbers citizens. It is also a land of unique firsts: it was the first state to grant women the right to vote without later repealing it, and was the first to have a national monument (Devils Tower) and national park (Yellowstone) within its borders. Those expecting true cowboy culture will not be disappointed; Cheyenne's Frontier Days festival, held every July, is a celebration of all things Western.

⁊ PRACTICAL INFORMATION

Capital: Cheyenne.

Visitor Info: Wyoming Business Council Tourism Office, I-25 at College Dr., Cheyenne 82002 (☎307-777-7777 or 800-225-5996; www.wyomingtourism.org). Open daily 8am-5pm. **Dept. of Commerce, State Parks, and Historic Sites Division,** 122 W. 25th St., Herschler Bldg., 1st fl. E, Cheyenne 82002 (☎307-777-6323; http://wyoparks.state.wy.us). Open M-F 8am-5pm. **Game and Fish Dept.,** 5400 Bishop Blvd., Cheyenne 82006 (☎307-777-4600; http://gf.state.wy.us). Open M-F 8am-5pm. **Wyoming Road Conditions:** 888-WYO-ROAD/996-7623.

Postal Abbreviation: WY. **Sales Tax:** 4%.

YELLOWSTONE NATIONAL PARK ☎307

Yellowstone National Park holds the dual distinction of being both the largest park in the contiguous United States as well as the first national park in the entire world. Though the roads are clogged with tourists eagerly snapping photos of geysers and wildlife, the park's incredible backcountry is so vast that you can go without seeing other people for days. Yellowstone also happens to be one of the largest active volcanoes in the world, with over 300 geysers and 10,000 geothermal features spewing steam and boiling water from beneath the earth's crust. Today, Yellowstone is still recovering from fires that burned over a third of the park in 1988. The destruction is especially evident in the western half of the park, where charred tree stumps line the roads. Despite the fires, Yellowstone retains its rugged beauty and sustains an incredible ecosystem. Following the reintroduction of wolves in 1995, the park once again became home to all of the animals, with the exception of the black-footed ferret, that lived in the Yellowstone area before the arrival of Europeans.

YELLOWSTONE AT A GLANCE

AREA: 2,219,791 acres.

VISITORS: Almost 3 million annually.

HIGHLIGHTS: Wait for Old Faithful to erupt, faithfully, to an astonishing 140 ft.; walk the rim of the Yellowstone Grand Canyon; gaze at the morning wildlife in the Lamar Valley.

CLIMATE: Extremely varied.

"ROUGHING" IT: Embrace corporate behemoth Xanterra's camping options ($18), or arrive early for the Park Service's first come, first served sites.

FEES: Entrance fee $25 per car, $20 per motorcycle, $12 per pedestrian. Backcountry permit free; reserve at backcountry office 48hr. in advance.

ROCKY MOUNTAINS

▐ TRANSPORTATION

The bulk of Yellowstone National Park lies in the northwest corner of Wyoming, with slivers in Montana and Idaho. There are five entrances to the park. **West Yellowstone, MT** and **Gardiner, MT** are the most developed entrance points. **Cooke City, MT,** the northeast entrance to the park, is a rustic town nestled in the mountains. East of Cooke City, the **Beartooth Highway (U.S. 212),** open only in summer, ascends the surrounding slopes for a breathtaking view of eastern Yellowstone. **Cody** lies 53 mi. east of the East Entrance to the park along U.S. 14/16/20. The southern entrance to the park is bordered by **Grand Teton National Park** (see p. 712). The only road in the park open year-round is the northern strip between the North Entrance and Cooke City. All other roads are open May-October. The park's **entrance fee** is good for seven days at both Yellowstone and Grand Teton. Roll into **Yellowstone Bicycle and Video,** 132 Madison Ave., in West Yellowstone, for mountain bike rentals. (☎406-646-7815. Mountain bikes $4 per hr., $12.50 per 5hr., $19.50 per day. Open May-Oct. daily 9am-8pm; Nov.-Apr. 11am-7pm.)

✦ ORIENTATION

Yellowstone is huge; both Rhode Island and Delaware could fit within the park's boundaries. The roadways within the park are designed in a figure-eight configura-

> Yellowstone can be a dangerous place. While roadside wildlife may appear tame, these creatures are unpredictable. Stay at least 75 ft. away from any animal, at least 300 ft. from bears. Both black bears and grizzly bears inhabit Yellowstone; consult a ranger about proper precautions before entering the backcountry. If you should see a bear, inform a ranger. Bison can travel at speeds of up to 30 mph; they gore visitors every year. Also, watch out for "widow makers"—dead trees that can fall over at any time, especially during high winds.

tion, with side roads leading to the various park entrances and some of the lesser-known attractions. The most famous natural wonders (e.g., Old Faithful) are scattered along the Upper and Lower Loops. Construction and renovation of roads is always ongoing; call ahead (☎344-2117; www.nps.gov/yell) or consult the extremely helpful *Yellowstone Today*, available at the entrance, to find out which sections will be closed during your visit. Travel through the park can be slow regardless of construction. The speed limit is 45 mph and is closely patrolled; steep grades, tight curves, and frequent animal crossings can also cause delays.

◪ PRACTICAL INFORMATION

The park's high season extends roughly from mid-June to mid-September. If you visit during this period, expect large crowds, clogged roads, and filled-to-capacity motels and campsites. Most of the park shuts down from November to mid-April, then gradually reopens as the snow melts. Even in high season, Yellowstone's busiest time is mid-week—Tuesdays often draw larger crowds than weekends.

Over 95% of Yellowstone—almost 2 million acres—is backcountry. To venture overnight into the wilds of Yellowstone requires a **backcountry permit.** The permit is free if you reserve in person at any backcountry office (check *Yellowstone Today* for locations) no earlier than 48hr. in advance of the trip. With over 300 designated campsites, there is almost always space available in the backcountry, but the more popular areas fill up in July and August. In general, the deeper into the park you hike, the less likely it is that sites will be taken. For a $20 fee, you can reserve a permit ahead of time by writing to the **Central Backcountry Office,** P.O. Box 168, Yellowstone National Park, WY 82190, and receive a **trip planning worksheet.** (☎344-2160. Open daily 8am-5pm.) Before heading into the backcountry, visitors must watch a short film outlining safety regulations. No firearms, pets, or mountain bikes are permitted in the backcountry. In many backcountry areas campfires are not permitted; bring a stove and related cooking gear. Food, cooking utensils, and any items that might attract bears or wildlife should be stored 10 ft. off the ground and 4 ft. from the nearest tree. Camps are equipped with food poles between trees at this height: use them. Consult a ranger before embarking on a trail for tips on how to avoid bears, ice, and other natural hindrances, or check out the free *Backcountry Trip Planner.*

Fishing and **boating** are both allowed within the park, provided visitors follow a number of regulations. Yellowstone-specific permits, available at the Yellowstone General Stores or any ranger station or Visitors Center, are required for fishing. Some areas may be closed due to native species conservation or feeding patterns of bears. The park's three native fish species are catch-and-release only, but if you catch the non-native lake trout, you are required to kill any specimens you do not wish to keep. (Fishing permits $15 per 3 days, $20 per 7 days, $35 per year; ages 12-15 require a free permit. State licenses not valid in Yellowstone.) In addition to Yellowstone Lake, popular fishing spots include the Madison and Firehole rivers, which are available for fly-fishing only. To go boating or even floating on the lake, you'll need a **boating permit,** available at backcountry offices (check *Yellowstone Today*), Bridge Bay Marina, and the South, West, and Northeast entrances to the park. (Motor-free vessels $5 per 7-day pass, $10 per season pass; motorized boats $10/20.) **Xanterra** rents rowboats, outboards, and dockslips at Bridge Bay Marina. (☎344-7311. Open mid-June to early Sept. Rowboats $9.50 per hr., $43 per 8hr.; outboards $46 per hr.; dockslips $15.50-21 per night.) Parts of Yellowstone Lake and some other lakes are limited to non-motorized boating; inquire at the Lake Village or Grant Village ranger stations for more advice.

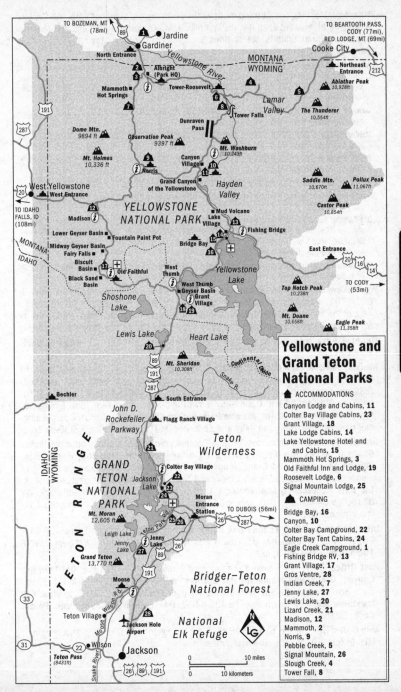

ROCKY MOUNTAINS

Yellowstone and Grand Teton National Parks

▲ ACCOMMODATIONS

Canyon Lodge and Cabins, 11
Colter Bay Village Cabins, 23
Grant Village, 18
Lake Lodge Cabins, 14
Lake Yellowstone Hotel and and Cabins, 15
Mammoth Hot Springs, 3
Old Faithful Inn and Lodge, 19
Roosevelt Lodge, 6
Signal Mountain Lodge, 25

▲ CAMPING

Bridge Bay, 16
Canyon, 10
Colter Bay Campground, 22
Colter Bay Tent Cabins, 24
Eagle Creek Campground, 1
Fishing Bridge RV, 13
Grant Village, 17
Gros Ventre, 28
Indian Creek, 7
Jenny Lake, 27
Lewis Lake, 20
Lizard Creek, 21
Madison, 12
Mammoth, 2
Norris, 9
Pebble Creek, 5
Signal Mountain, 26
Slough Creek, 4
Tower Fall, 8

Visitor Info: Most regions of the park have their own central Visitors Center. All Centers offer general info, but each has distinct hiking and camping regulations and features special regional exhibits. All stations are usually open late May-early Sept. daily 8am-7pm. Albright is open year-round, and Old Faithful is nearly so.

Albright Visitors Center (☎344-2263), at Mammoth Hot Springs. Features exhibits on the history of Yellowstone Park along with stuffed examples of natural wildlife and a gallery of Thomas Moran's artwork. Open daily late May-early Sept. 8am-7pm; Sept. 8am-5pm; Oct.-late May 9am-5pm.

Canyon (☎242-2550). Features a new exhibit on Yellowstone's supervolcano. Open late May-early Oct. daily 8am-7pm.

Fishing Bridge (☎242-2450). Exhibits describe local wildlife and Yellowstone Lake. Open daily late May-Aug. 8am-7pm; Sept. 9am-6pm.

Grant Village (☎242-2650). Has details on the 1988 fire and park wildlife. Open daily late May-Aug. 8am-7pm, Sept. 9am-6pm.

Madison (☎344-2821). Has a bookstore. Open early June-Sept. daily 9am-5pm.

Norris (☎344-2812). Major exhibit depicts "Geothermic Features of the Park." Open late May-late Sept. daily 9am-5pm.

Old Faithful (☎545-2750). Learn about geysers and eruption predictions. In temporary quarters until new Center is completed in 2010. Open daily late May-early Sept. 8am-7pm; Sept. 8am-6pm; Oct. and late Apr.-late May 9am-5pm; closed Nov. to mid-Dec. Call for winter hours. Info window open in summer until 8pm.

West Thumb, on the southern edge of the lake. Has a bookstore. Open late May-late Sept. daily 9am-5pm.

West Yellowstone Chamber of Commerce and Visitor Center, 30 Yellowstone Ave. (☎406-646-7701; www.westyellowstonechamber.com), West Yellowstone, MT, 2 blocks west of the entrance. Offers information on all area public lands. Open late May-early Sept. daily 8am-8pm; early Sept.-early Nov. and mid-Apr. to late May M-F 8am-5pm.

General Park Information: ☎344-7381. **Weather:** ☎344-2113. **Road Report:** ☎344-2117.

Medical Services: Lake Clinic, Pharmacy, and Hospital (☎242-7241), across the road from the Lake Yellowstone Hotel. Clinic open late May-late Sept. daily 8:30am-8:30pm. Emergency room open May-Sept. 24hr. **Old Faithful Clinic** (☎545-7325), near the Old Faithful Inn. Open early May to mid-Sept. daily 7am-7pm. Emergency room open May-Sept. 24hr. **Mammoth Hot Springs Clinic** (☎344-7965). Open in summer daily 8:30am-5pm, Jan.-May and Sept.-Dec. M-Th 8:30am-5pm, F 8:30am-1pm.

Disabled Services: All entrances, Visitors Centers, and ranger stations offer the *Visitor Guide to Accessible Features.* Fishing Bridge RV Park, Madison, Bridge Bay, Canyon, Mammoth, and Grant campgrounds have wheelchair-accessible sites and restrooms; Lewis Lake, Slough Creek, and Norris have wheelchair-accessible sites. The **Park Accessibility Coordinator,** P.O. Box 168, Yellowstone National Park, WY 82190 (☎344-2017, TDD only ☎344-2386; www.nps.gov/yell), is available for more information.

Internet Access: West Yellowstone Public Library, 23 N. Dunraven St. (☎406-646-9017), West Yellowstone, MT. Free. Open Tu and Th 10am-6pm, W 10am-8pm, F 10am-5pm, Sa 10am-3pm.

Post Office: There are 5 post offices located within the park: at **Lake, Old Faithful, Canyon, Grant,** and **Mammoth Hot Springs** (☎344-7764). All open M-F 8:30am-5pm. Specify which station when addressing mail. **Postal Code:** 82190. In **West Yellowstone, MT:** 209 Grizzly Ave. (☎406-646-7704). Open M-F 8:30am-5pm. **Postal Code:** 59758.

Area Codes: 307 (in the park), 406 (in West Yellowstone, Cooke City, and Gardiner, MT). In text, 307 unless otherwise noted.

ACCOMMODATIONS

Camping is cheap, and affordable indoor lodging can be found with some preparation. Lodging within the park can be hard to come by on short notice but can be a better deal than the motels situated on the parks's outskirts. During peak tourist months, motel room rates can skyrocket up to $100, but in-park lodging remains relatively inexpensive.

IN THE PARK

Xanterra (☎ 344-7311; www.travelyellowstone.com) controls all accommodations within the park, and employs a code to distinguish between cabins: "Roughrider" means no bath, no facilities; "Budget" includes a sink; "Pioneer" has a shower, toilet, and sink; "Frontier" is bigger and more plush; and "Western" is the biggest. Even the swankiest cabins, however, aren't free-standing: most share a wall or two with a neighbor. Cabins without private bath have facilities nearby. All prices are based on two adults; Xanterra charges $11 for each additional adult. Reserve cabins well in advance of the June-to-September tourist season. Unless otherwise noted, all Xanterra accommodations accept all major credit cards.

Old Faithful Inn and Lodge, 30 mi. southeast of the West Yellowstone entrance, between Madison and Grant on the lower loop. Not only conveniently located in the heart of key attractions, it is also a masterpiece unto itself. The exterior of the lodge will be undergoing renovations until 2008, but you can still admire the cavernous 6-story central lobby and massive stone fireplace from numerous balconies and stairways, all built from solid tree trunks. Open mid-May to mid-Sept. Budget cabins $64; Frontier cabins $99. Well-appointed hotel rooms from $87, with private bath $111-189. ❸

Roosevelt Lodge, in the northeast portion of the upper loop, 19 mi. north of Canyon Village. Cheap, scenic accommodations in a relatively isolated section of the park. Open June-early Sept. Roughrider cabins with wood-burning stoves $61; Frontier cabins $99. ❸

Canyon Lodge and Cabins, in Canyon Village at the middle of the figure-eight, overlooking the Yellowstone "Grand Canyon". Less rustic than Roosevelt Lodge, but centrally located and more popular among tourists. Open early June to mid-Sept. Pioneer cabins $63; Frontier cabins $87; Western cabins $126. ❸

Mammoth Hot Springs, on the northwest portion of the upper loop near the north entrance. A good base for early-morning excursions in the Lamar Valley to the east, though it sits in a busy (albeit convenient) section of the park. Open early May-early Oct. Lattice-sided Budget cabins $69; Frontier cabins (some with porches) from $99; Western cabins $169. Hotel rooms $78, with bath $105. ❸

Lake Lodge Cabins, 4 mi. south of Fishing Bridge, at the southeast corner of the lower loop. A cluster of cabins from the 20s and 50s, all just a stone's throw from Yellowstone Lake. Open mid-June to late Sept. Pioneer cabins $62; larger Western cabins $126. ❸ Next door, **Lake Yellowstone Hotel and Cabins** has yellow Frontier cabins without a lake view for $106. ❹

WEST YELLOWSTONE, MT

Guarding the west entrance of the park, West Yellowstone (pop. 1020) capitalizes on the hordes of tourists who pass through en route to the park. The closest of the border towns to popular park attractions, West Yellowstone has numerous budget motels. Housed in a historic hotel, **West Yellowstone International Hostel ❶**, 139 Yellowstone Ave., provides the best indoor budget lodging around. (☎ 406-646-7745 or 800-838-7745. Internet access $5 per hr. Open late May to mid-Oct. Dorms $26. Singles $41; doubles $50. AmEx/D/MC/V.) Comfortable, newly-appointed rooms with refrigerators and cable TV greet guests at the family-owned **Alpine Motel ❸**, 120 Madison Ave. (☎ 406-646-7544; www.alpinemotelwestyellowstone.com. Singles $69;

doubles $79; 6-person suite with full kitchen $140.) **Lazy G Motel ❸,** 123 Hayden St., has 15 spacious 1970s-style rooms with cable TV, queen beds, refrigerators, and Wi-Fi. (☎ 406-646-7586. Reservations recommended. Open May-Mar. Singles $56-63; doubles $69. D/MC/V.)

GARDINER, MT

Near the park's north entrance, Gardiner presents a more limited and somewhat more expensive selection of accommodations options. **Hillcrest Cottages ❸,** on U.S. 89, across the Cenex station, rents out tidy cabins with kitchenettes on a hillside overlooking town. (☎ 406-848-7353 or 800-970-7353; www.hillcrestcottages.com. Open May-early Sept. Singles $70; doubles $80; quints $98; 8-person duplex $150. Each additional adult $6, each additional child $2. D/MC/V.) The compact rooms at **The Town Cafe and Motel ❷,** on Park St., across from the park's northern entrance, are among the best deals around. (☎ 406-848-7322. Cable TV. No phones. June-Sept. singles $54, doubles $59; Oct.-May $32/38. MC/V.) **Eagle Creek Campground ❶,** on Jardine Rd., 2.2 mi. northeast of Gardiner, offers sites on the edge of the Gallatin National Forest with spectacular views of Mammoth's terraces, inside Yellowstone, and the surrounding country. (Pit toilets, no water. $7.)

COOKE CITY, MT

Lewis and Clark once deemed the area around Cooke City (pop. 90) impassable, and even now few people visit this rugged little town. Nonetheless, Cooke City is a great base for exploring Yellowstone's backcountry: it's conveniently situated between the park's northeast entrance and the junction of the **Chief Joseph Scenic Highway (Route 296)** and the **Beartooth Highway (Route 212).** The Beartooth Hwy. may experience delays near the park entrance due to construction (☎ 888-285-4636 for updates). Built in 1936, the cabins at **Antler's Lodge ❸,** 311 Main St. E, have plenty of personality and a great mountain view. Hemingway spent several nights editing *For Whom the Bell Tolls* here. (☎ 406-838-2432; www.cookecityantlerslodge.com. Reservations recommended. Open year-round. 2-person cabins $75, some with kitchenettes.) **Silver Gate and Pine Edge Cabins ❹,** on Hwy. 212 in Silver Gate, rents comfortable historic cabins, many with fully stocked kitchens, and five very basic motel rooms with private bath. (☎ 406-838-2371; www.pineedgecabins.com. Open year-round. Motel rooms $72; 2-person cabins $65-85; 4-person $105; 6-person $102. MC/V.)

⛺ CAMPING

Campsites fill quickly during the summer months; be prepared to make alternative arrangements. Call **Park Headquarters** (☎ 344-7381) for info on campsite vacancies or check at any of the Visitors Centers. The seven **National Park Service campgrounds ❶** are first come, first served. During the summer, these smaller campgrounds generally fill by 10am, and finding a site can be frustrating. Their popularity arises from their often stunning locations; most are well worth the effort to secure a spot. Check-out time is 10am, and the best window for claiming a campsite is 8-10am. Two of the most beautiful campgrounds are **Slough Creek Campground,** 10 mi. northeast of Tower Jct. (29 sites; vault toilets; open late May-Oct.; $12) and **Pebble Creek Campground** (32 sites; vault toilets; no RVs; open early June-late Sept.; $12). Both are located in the northeast corner of the park, between Tower Fall and the Northeast Entrance in the Lamar Valley (generally the least congested area), and offer relatively isolated sites and good fishing. Travelers in the southern end of the park might try **Lewis Lake** (85 sites; vault toilets; open mid-June to early Nov.; $12), halfway between West Thumb and the South Entrance, a rugged campground with several walk-in tent sites that tend to fill up late in the day, if at all. **Tower Fall** (32 sites; vault toilets; open mid-May to late Sept.; $12) between the Northeast Entrance and Mammoth Hot Springs, has sites situated atop a hill, with fine views over mountain meadows. **Norris** (116 sites; water and flush toilets; wheelchair-accessible sites available; open late May-late Sept.; $14); **Indian Creek,** between the Norris Geyser Basin and Mammoth Hot Springs (75 sites; vault toilets; open mid-June to mid-Sept.; $12); and **Mammoth** (85 sites; water and flush toilets; wheelchair-accessible sites available; open year-round; $14) are less scenic but still great places to camp. The lodges at Mammoth and Old Faithful have showers ($3.25), but no laundry.

   Xanterra ❶, P.O. Box 165, Yellowstone National Park, WY 82190, runs five of the 12 developed campgrounds (all $17, except Fishing Bridge RV) within the park: **Canyon,** with 272 spacious sites on forested hillsides, is the most pleasant, while **Madison,** with 277 sites on the banks of the Firehole River, has the advantage of being in the heart of the park's western attractions. **Grant Village** (425 sites) and **Bridge Bay** (432 sites), both near the shores of Yellowstone Lake, have little vegetation to provide privacy. Finally, **Fishing Bridge RV ❷** (RVs only; $35) provides closely-packed parking spots for larger motor homes and those desiring full hookups. All five sites have dump stations, flush toilets, and water. Canyon, Grant Village, and Fishing Bridge RV also have showers ($3, towel rental $0.75) and coin-op laundry facilities (open 7am-9pm). Campgrounds are usually open mid-May to early October, though Canyon has the shortest season: mid-June to mid-September. Xanterra accepts advance and same-day reservations (☎344-7311). The two largest Xanterra campgrounds, Grant Village and Bridge Bay, are the best bet for last-minute reservations.

▢ FOOD

Buying food at the restaurants, snack bars, and cafeterias in the park can get to be expensive; stick to the **general stores** at each lodging location. The stores at Fishing Bridge, Lake, Grant Village, and Canyon sell lunch-counter-style food. (Open daily 7:30am-9pm, but times may vary.) Stock up at the **Food Round-Up Grocery Store,** 107 Dunraven St., in West Yellowstone. (☎406-646-7501. Open daily in summer 7am-10pm; in winter 7am-9pm.) At the original entrance to the park, Gardiner is less touristy than West Yellowstone; it is also moderately pricier. **Food Farm,** on U.S. 89 in Gardiner, has cheap food. (☎406-848-7524. Open M-Sa 7am-9pm, Su 8am-8pm.)

   Running Bear Pancake House, 538 Madison Ave. (☎406-646-7703), in West Yellowstone. Has inexpensive breakfasts and sandwiches in a friendly down-home atmosphere. Breakfast served all day; don't miss the dinner plate-sized special walnut or peach pancakes ($3.35-6.15). Burgers, salads, and sandwiches $6-8.65. Open daily 7am-2pm. D/MC/V. ❶

   Helen's Corral Drive-In (☎406-848-7627), on U.S. 89, in Gardiner. Rounds up ½-lb. buffalo burgers and pork sandwiches ($5.50-9.50) in a lively street-side setting. Open daily June-Aug. 11am-11pm; fall 11am-8pm; winter hours vary. Cash only. ❷

   Beartooth Cafe, 114 Main St. (☎406-838-2475; www.beartoothcafe.com), in Cooke City. Serves gourmet food very unlike the usual park offerings, though its deck does have park-quality views. Sandwiches $6-9. Dinner entrees $16-25. Open daily late May-Sept. 11am-10pm. MC/V. ❹

   Beartooth Barbeque, 118 Madison Ave. (☎406-646-0227), in West Yellowstone. Offers good, cheap barbeque out of a kiosk window. Take your meal to go, or enjoy it at one of 2 picnic tables with great people-watching potential. Barbeque sandwich $6. Sides $1. Open daily 11am-9pm. Cash only. ❶

Grizzly Pad Grill and Cabins, 315 Main St. E (☎406-838-2161), on Rte. 212 on the eastern side of Cooke City. Serves the Grizzly Pad Special: a milkshake, fries, and large burger ($10). Alternatively, pick up a sack lunch ($8.50) or fried chicken (4 pc. $9.25) to go. Open daily late May to mid-Oct. 7am-9pm; Jan. to mid-Apr. hours vary. MC/V. ❷

Timberline Cafe, 135 Yellowstone Ave. (☎406-646-9349), in West Yellowstone. Prepares travelers for a day in the park with a salad bar and homemade pies. Burgers, sandwiches, and omelettes $6.50-9. Open daily 6:30am-10pm. AmEx/D/MC/V. ❷

🔵 SIGHTS

Xanterra (☎344-7311) organizes tours, horseback rides, and chuckwagon dinners. These outdoor activities are expensive, however. A cheaper option is to explore the park's trails on your own. Visitors Centers give out informative self-guided tour pamphlets with maps for each of the park's main attractions ($0.50). Trails to these sights are accessible from the road via walkways, usually extending a quarter to 1½ mi. into the various natural environments. Before you depart on a wilderness adventure, the **Yellowstone Historic Center,** on the corner of Canyon St. and Yellowstone Ave., in West Yellowstone, has extensive exhibits on the railroad, park flora and fauna, earthquakes, fires, and historical development. (☎406-646-1100. Open mid-May to mid-Oct. daily 9am-9pm. $5, over 62 $4, ages 4-12 and students $3.)

Yellowstone is set apart from other national parks and forests in the Rockies by its **geothermal features**—the park protects the largest geothermal area in the world. The bulk of these geothermal wonders can be found on the western side of the park between Mammoth Hot Springs in the north and Old Faithful in the south. The most dramatic thermal fissures are the **geysers.** Hot liquid magma close to the surface of the earth superheats water from snow and rain until it boils and bubbles, eventually building up enough pressure to burst through the cracks with steamy force. The extremely volatile nature of this area means that attractions may change, appear, or disappear without warning.

While bison-jams and bear-gridlock may make wildlife seem more of a nuisance than an attraction (park rangers joke that they can tell by the number of cars parked roadside whether tourists have spotted bison, moose, or a rarer grizzly), they afford a unique opportunity to see a number of native species co-existing in their natural environment. It is important wildlife-watching etiquette to pull off the road completely and kill the engine. The best times for viewing are early morning and just before dark, as most animals nap in the shade during the hot midday. The road between Tower-Roosevelt and the Northeast Entrance, in the untamed **Lamar Valley,** often called the "Serengeti of Yellowstone," is one of the best places to see wolves, grizzlies, and herds of bison (among other species). Some species take to higher elevations in the heat of summer, so travel earlier or later in the season (or hike to higher regions) to find the best viewing opportunities. Consult a ranger for more specific advice.

OLD FAITHFUL AREA

Yellowstone's trademark attraction, ◼**Old Faithful,** is the most predictable of the large geysers and has consistently pleased audiences since its discovery in 1870. Eruptions usually shoot 100-190 ft. in the air, typically occur every 45min.-2hr. (average 90min.), and last about 1½-5min. Predictions for the next eruption, accurate to within 10min., are posted at the Old Faithful Visitors Center. Old Faithful lies in the **Upper Geyser Basin,** 16 mi. south of the Madison area and 20 mi. west of Grant Village. This area has the world's largest concentration of geysers and boardwalks connect them all. The spectacular rainbow spectrum of **Morning Glory Pool** is an easy 1½ mi. from Old Faithful, and provides up-close-and-personal views

> ! **ON THIN EARTH.** Beware: the crust around many of Yellowstone's thermal basins, geysers, and hot springs is thin, and boiling, acidic water lies just beneath the surface. Stay on the marked paths and boardwalks at all times. In the backcountry, keep a good distance from hot springs and fumaroles.

of hundreds of hydrothermal features along the way, including the tallest predictable geyser in the world, **Grand Geyser,** and the graceful **Riverside Geyser,** which spews at a 60-degree angle across the Firehole River. Between Old Faithful and Madison, along the Firehole River, lie the **Midway Geyser Basin** and the **Lower Geyser Basin.** Many of these geysers are visible from the side of the road, and stopping for a closer look is highly recommended. The **Excelsior Geyser Crater,** a large, steaming lake created by a powerful geyser blast, and the **Grand Prismatic Spring,** the largest hot spring in the park, located in the Midway Geyser Basin, sit about 5 mi. north of Old Faithful and are well worth the trip. Two miles north is the less developed but still thrilling **Firehole Lake Drive,** a 2 mi. side loop through hot lakes, springs, and dome geysers. Eight miles north of Old Faithful gurgles the **Fountain Paint Pot,** a bubbling pool of hot, milky white, brown, and grey mud. Four types of geothermal activity present in Yellowstone (geysers, mudpots, hot springs, and fumaroles) are found along the Firehole River trails. There is a strong temptation to wash off the grime of camping in the hot water, but swimming in the hot springs is prohibited. You can swim in the **Firehole River,** near Firehole Canyon Dr., just south of Madison Jct. Prepare for a chill; the name of the river is quite deceiving. Call park info (☎ 344-7381) to make sure the river is open.

NORRIS GEYSER BASIN

Fourteen miles north of Madison and 21 mi. south of Mammoth, the colorful **Norris Geyser Basin** is the park's oldest and hottest active thermal zone. The geyser has been erupting at temperatures of up to 459°F for over 115,000 years. The area has a half-mile northern **Porcelain Basin** loop and a 1½ mi. southern **Back Basin** loop. **Echinus,** in the Back Basin, is the largest known acid-water geyser, erupting 40-60 ft. every 1-4hr. Its neighbor, **Steamboat,** is the tallest active geyser in the world, erupting over 300 ft. for 3-40min. Steamboat's eruptions, however, are unpredictable; major eruptions often occur months or even years apart.

MAMMOTH HOT SPRINGS

Shifting water sources, malleable travertine limestone deposits, and temperature-sensitive, multicolored bacterial growth create the park's most rapidly changing natural structure. The hot spring terraces resemble huge wedding cakes at **Mammoth Hot Springs,** 21 mi. north of the Norris Basin and 19 mi. west of Tower in the northwest corner of the upper loop. The Mammoth area is home to the historic **Yellowstone Fort,** where the army units in charge of managing the park headquartered before the days of the ranger began. The **Upper Terrace Drive,** 2 mi. south of Mammoth Visitors Center, winds for 1½ mi. through colorful springs and rugged travertine limestone ridges and terraces. When visiting, ask a local ranger where to find the most active springs, as they vary in intensity from year to year. In recent years, **Canary Spring,** on the south side of the main terrace, has been extremely active as it expands into virgin forest, killing trees and bushes. Also ask about area trails that provide some of the park's best wildlife viewing. Xanterra offers **horseback rides** just south of the hot springs. (☎ 344-7311; call at least 1 day ahead. Open late May to mid-Aug. 5-6 trail rides per day 8:45am-6:15pm. $35 per hr., $54 per 2hr.) Swimming is permitted in the **Boiling River,** 2½ mi. north. Park in the lot at the 49th parallel sign and take the trail along the river back toward the park to the swimming area. Check with a ranger to make sure that this area is open.

ROCKY MOUNTAINS

GRAND CANYON

The east side's featured attraction, the ⬛Grand Canyon of the Yellowstone, wears rusty red and orange hues created by hot water acting on the rock. The canyon is 800-1200 ft. deep and 1500-4000 ft. wide. For a close-up view of the mighty **Lower Falls** (308 ft.), hike down the short, steep **Uncle Tom's Trail** (over 300 steps). **Artist Point,** on the southern rim, and **Lookout Point,** on the northern rim, offer broader canyon vistas and are accessible from the road between Canyon and Fishing Bridge. Keep an eye out for osprey along the canyon's rim. Xanterra also runs **horseback rides** at Canyon and in the Tower-Roosevelt area 19 mi. north. (☎344-7311. Open June-Aug. 5-12 rides per day 7:15am-6:15pm. Reservations required. $35 per hr., $54 per 2hr.) **Stagecoach rides** ($9.35, ages 2-11 $7.50) along the canyon in yellow wagons are available early June to early September at Roosevelt Lodge.

YELLOWSTONE LAKE AREA

In the southeast corner of the park, **Yellowstone Lake** is the largest high-altitude lake in North America and serves as a protective area for the cutthroat trout. While the lake's surface may appear calm, geologists have found evidence of geothermal features at the bottom. **Xanterra** offers **lake cruises** that leave from the marina at Bridge Bay. (☎344-7311. 5-7 per day early June to mid-Sept. $11.50, ages 2-11 $7.25.) Geysers and hot springs in **West Thumb** dump an average of 3100 gal. of water into the lake per day. Notwithstanding this thermal boost, the temperature of the lake remains quite cold, averaging 45°F during the summer. Visitors to the park once cooked freshly caught trout in the boiling water of the **Fishing Cone** in the West Thumb central basin, but this is no longer permitted. Along this same loop on the west side of the lake, check out the **Thumb Paint Pots,** a field of puffing miniature mud volcanoes and chimneys. On the northern edge of the lake is **Fishing Bridge,** where fishing is now prohibited due to efforts to help the endangered trout population. The sulfurous odors of **Mud Volcano,** 6 mi. north of Fishing Bridge, can be distinguished from miles away, but the turbulent mudpots are worth the assault on your nose, caused by the creation of hydrogen sulfide gas by bacteria working on the naturally-occurring sulfur in the spring water. The unusual mudpots—with their rhythmic belching, acidic waters, and cavernous openings—have appropriate names such as **Dragon's Mouth, Sour Lake,** and **Black Dragon's Cauldron.**

OFF THE (EXTREMELY WELL) BEATEN PATH

Most visitors to Yellowstone never get out of their cars, and therefore miss out on over 1200 mi. of trails in the park. Options for exploring Yellowstone's more pristine areas range from short day-hikes to long backcountry trips. When planning a hike, pick up a topographical trail map ($9-10 at any Visitors Center) and ask a ranger to describe the network of trails. Some trails are poorly marked, so be sure of your skill with a map and compass before setting off on more obscure paths. Hikers should consult rangers to learn which areas were burned in the 1988 forest fires; burned areas have less shade, so hats, extra water, and sunscreen are musts. If planning a hike to higher elevations, be sure to bring extra layers, including a rain jacket, as weather conditions can change without warning.

In addition to the self-guided trails at major attractions, many worthwhile sights are only a few miles off the main road. The easy **Fairy Falls Trail** (5¼ mi. round-trip, 2½hr.), 3 mi. north of Old Faithful, provides a unique perspective on the Midway Geyser Basin and up-close views of 200 ft. high Fairy Falls. This easy round-trip trail begins in the parking lot marked "Fairy Falls" just south of Midway Geyser Basin. A more strenuous option is to follow the trail beyond the falls up Twin Buttes, a 650 ft. elevation gain that turns this trail into a moderate 4hr. round-trip hike. The trail to the top of **Mount Washburn** (5½ mi. round-trip, 4hr., 1380 ft. elevation gain) is enhanced by an enclosed observation area with sweeping views of the park's central environs, including the rim of the Grand Canyon and the patchwork of old and new forests caused by the 1988 fires. This trail begins at the Chittenden Rd. parking area, 10 mi. north of Canyon Village Jct., or Dunraven Pass, 5 mi. north of Canyon Village Jct. A more challenging climb to the top of **Avalanche Peak** (4 mi., 4hr., final elevation 10,568 ft.) starts 8 mi. west of the East Entrance on East Entrance Rd. A steep ascent up several switchbacks opens to stunning panoramas out over Yellowstone Lake and the southern regions of the park, west to the Continental Divide and east to Shoshone National Forest. The trail along **Pebble Creek** (12 mi. one-way) makes a great trip though some of Yellowstone's most pristine backcountry. Beginning 1½ mi. west of the Northeast Entrance, the trail climbs steeply up a 1000 ft. ridge the first 1½ mi. before descending to the Pebble Creek Valley, following it mostly downhill for the remaining 10½ mi., exiting below Pebble Creek campground. Wildlife-viewing opportunities in this area are superb.

Nearly all of Yellowstone shuts down in winter. For those intrepid souls who wish to see the geothermal features at their most spectacular, in cold and snow, **Jackson Hole Snowmobile Tours,** 515 N. Cache St. in Jackson, WY leads the way, with guided treks to Old Faithful and the Grand Canyon. (☎733-6850 or 800-633-1733; www.jacksonholesnowmobile.com. Snowmobile driver $200-250, each adult $100.)

SCENIC DRIVE: NORTH FORK DRIVE

Linking Yellowstone National Park with Cody, WY, the **Buffalo Bill Cody Scenic Byway (U.S. 14/16/20)** bridges the majestic peaks of the Absaroka Mountains (ab-SOR-ka) with the sagebrush lands of the Wyoming plains. This 53 mi. drive winds through the canyon created by the North Fork of the Shoshone River; the high granite walls and sedimentary formations of the **Shoshone Canyon** are noticeable from the road, as is the smell of sulfur from the DeMaris springs in the Shoshone River. Once the world's tallest dam, the **Buffalo Bill Dam Visitors Center and Reservoir,** 6 mi. west of Cody, was built between 1904 and 1910, and measures 353 ft. in height. (☎527-6076. Visitors Center open May-Sept. M-F 8am-8pm, Sa 8am-6pm, Su 10am-6pm.) West of the dam, strange rock formations, created millions of years ago by volcanic eruptions in the Absarokas, dot the dusty hillsides. Continuing west to Yellowstone, sagebrush and small juniper trees gradually lead into the thick pine cover of the **Shoshone National Forest,** the country's first national forest. This area, known as the **Wapiti Valley,** is home to over 20 dude ranches. The **East**

WOLFISH PATIENCE

"I thought it was just an unusually long bear," said the man to my right. I stood gazing through binoculars with fifty other people. We peered intently down the hillside to where an indistinct brownish-blackish blob moved. Much closer, three larger brown shapes were foraging in the grass, distinctly recognizable as a grizzly bear and her two cubs. But they were old news.

I raised my binoculars to my eyes and scanned the edge of the trees. The man to my right said the wolf had entered the stand not so long ago. It was my fourth time in Yellowstone, and still I had not seen one. Most of my attempts so far had been pretty lame—mostly I just drove along and kept my eyes peeled.

But tonight was different. I started stopping where other cars had parked and spending a solid amount of time in one place, just looking over of the landscape. It was then that I saw it—my first wolf. At the same time immediately familiar and like nothing I could imagine, the wolf was long, lean, and black. Though it moved like a dog, the wolf's ability to strut in front of the fifty-plus gawkers clustered above seemed to say, "I'm not going anywhere. All you need to do is look."

—Rachel Garwin

Entrance to Yellowstone National Park guards the west end of the scenic byway and is closed in winter. The **Chief Joseph Scenic Highway (Route 296)** connects Cooke City, MT, to Cody, WY, and passes through rugged mountains across **Dead Indian Summit.** The byway traces the route traveled by the Nez Percé as they evaded the US army in the summer of 1877. From Cody, follow the Buffalo Bill Cody Scenic Byway back into Yellowstone.

GRAND TETON NATIONAL PARK ☎307

The Teton Range is the youngest in the entire Rocky Mountain system. Glaciers more than 2000 ft. thick sculpted the jagged peaks, carved U-shaped valleys, and gouged out Jenny, Leigh, and Phelps lakes. Though the Shoshone Indians called the range the "hoary-headed fathers," French trappers dubbed the three most prominent peaks—South Teton, Grand Teton, and Middle Teton—"Les trois tetons," meaning "the three breasts." Grand Teton National Park delights hikers with miles of both easy and strenuous trails as well as steep rock cliffs along the range's eastern face.

🔧🛈 ORIENTATION AND PRACTICAL INFORMATION

Grand Teton's roads consist of a scenic loop through the park with approach roads coming from Jackson in the south, Dubois in the east, and Yellowstone in the north. There are three entrances to the park: Moose, Moran Jct., and near Teton Village. The east side of the main loop, **U.S. 89,** from Jackson to the Moran Jct. entrance, offers excellent free views of the Tetons. U.S. 89 in the park is open year-round. Those who enter the park must pay an **entrance fee.** ($25 per car, $20 per motorcycle, $12 per pedestrian or cyclist; annual pass $50. Passes good for 7 days in Grand Teton and Yellowstone.) Permits are required for all **backcountry camping** and are free if reserved in person within 24hr. of the trip. Reservations made more than 24hr. in advance require a $25 non-refundable fee. Requests are accepted by mail or online from January 1 to May 15; write to Grand Teton National Park, Backcountry Permits, P.O. Box 170, Moose, WY 83012, or visit www.nps.gov/grte. (For more info, contact the **Moose Visitor Center, ☎**739-3309.) Advance reservations are recommended for sites in the popular mountain canyons or near lakes. After May 15, two-thirds of all backcountry spots are available on a first-come, first-served basis; the park staff can help plan routes and find campsites. At high elevations, snow often remains into July, and the weather can become severe any time of the year, so severe weather gear is strongly advised. Bears are active in the park, so be sure to follow all food storage guidelines and other precautions.

Public Transit: Grand Teton Lodge Co. (☎800-628-9988) runs shuttles in summer from Colter Bay to Jackson Lake Lodge (7 per day, free). Shuttles also run to **Jackson** (3 per day, free) and the **Jackson Hole** airport (by reservation only, $30).

Visitor Info: Visitors Centers and campgrounds have free copies of the *Teewinot*, the park's newspaper, containing news and info on special programs, hiking, and camping. For general info and a visitor's packet, or to make backcountry camping reservations,

 CHEAP PARK-ING. Somewhere between the Grand Canyon and Grand Teton, the National Park Service's $15 and $25 entrance fees begin to add up. If you're going to be visiting four or more parks in a year, it's worth investing in an Interagency Annual Pass ($80), which gets you into most federally managed lands in the US. The passes are available at park entrances or at www.nps.gov.

contact **Park Headquarters** (☎ 739-3300; www.nps.gov/grte) or write Grand Teton National Park, P.O. Drawer 170, Moose, WY 83012.

Grand Teton Discovery and Visitors Center (☎ 739-3300), on Teton Park Rd., at the southern part of the park, ½ mi. west of Moose Jct. Open daily early June-early Sept. 8am-7pm; early Sept.-late May 8am-5pm.

Jenny Lake Visitors Center (☎ 739-3392), next to the Jenny Lake Campground at South Jenny Lake. Open daily early June-early Sept. 8am-7pm; mid-May to early June and Sept. 8am-4:30pm.

Colter Bay Visitors Center (☎ 739-3594), on Jackson Lake in the northern part of the park. Houses the Indian Arts Museum. Open daily June-early Sept. 8am-7pm; May and Sept. 8am-5pm.

Info Lines: Weather, ☎ 739-3611. **Wyoming Highway Info Center,** ☎ 733-1731. **Wyoming Department of Transportation,** ☎ 888-996-7623. **Road Conditions,** ☎ 739-3682.

Emergency: ☎ 911, **Sheriff's Office,** ☎ 733-2331. **Park Dispatch,** ☎ 739-3300.

Medical Services: Grand Teton Medical Clinic, Jackson Lake Lodge (☎ 543-2514, after hours 733-8002). Open daily late May-early Oct. 10am-6pm. **St. John's Medical Center,** 625 E. Broadway (☎ 733-3636), in Jackson.

Internet Access: Jackson Lake Lodge (☎ 543-3100).

Post Office: In Moose (☎ 733-3336), next to the Park Headquarters. Open M-F 9am-1pm and 1:30-5pm, Sa 10:30-11:30am. **Postal Code:** 83012.

🏠🍴 ACCOMMODATIONS AND FOOD

The Grand Teton Lodge Company runs several accommodations in the park. (Reservations ☎ 800-628-9988; www.gltc.com; or write to the **Reservations Manager,** Grand Teton Lodge Co., P.O. Box 250, Moran, WY 83013. Deposit required.) Lodges are pricey, but there are two options for relatively affordable cabins at Colter Bay. **Signal Mountain Lodge ❹** (☎ 543-2831 or 800-672-6012; www.signalmountain-lodge.com) has scenic lodging on the shores of Jackson Lake. Options include rustic log cabins with private bath (doubles $127), lodge-style rooms (quads $151), and lakefront retreats with living areas and kitchenettes (6 people $222). **Colter Bay Village Cabins ❷** maintains 166 log cabins near Jackson Lake. A cabin with shared bath is one of the best deals in the area; book early. (☎ 800-628-9988. Open late May-late Sept. Reception 24hr. 2-person cabins with shared bath from $45. 1 room with private bath $85-129; 2 rooms with private bath $139-165.) **Colter Bay Tent Cabins ❷** offers primitive log and canvas shelters with cement floors, wood-burning stoves, and bunks. Sleeping bags, cots, and blankets are available for rent. (☎ 800-628-9988. 66 cabins. Open early June-early Sept. Restrooms. 2-person tents $41. Each additional person $5.)

The best way to eat on a budget in the Tetons is to bring your own food. Nonperishables are available at the **Trading Post Grocery,** in the Dornan's complex near the Moose Visitors Center, and the deli makes hefty subs for $6-7. (☎ 733-2415, ext. 201. Open daily May-Sept. 8am-8pm; Oct.-Apr. 8am-6pm. Deli closes 1hr. earlier.) Jackson has an **Albertson's** supermarket, 105 Buffalo Way, at the intersection of W. Broadway and Rte. 22. (☎ 733-5950. Open daily 6am-midnight.) Gather 'round pots of ribs, stew, and mashed potatoes at **Dornan's Chuckwagon ❷,** across from the Trading Post Grocery in Moose, for an authentic Old West dinner. (☎ 733-2415, ext. 203. Breakfast $8.50. Lunch $5.50-10. Chuckwagon dinner $14, ages 6-11 $7.) The **Trapper Grill ❸,** inside Signal Mountain Lodge, tops off a day of hiking with a heaping mound of nachos ($8.25-13.75), a meal unto itself. If you've still got room, the elk chili burgers ($10.25) are unbeatable. (☎ 543-2831. Breakfasts $6.70-8.75. Open daily early May to mid-Oct. 7am-10pm.) **John Colter Cafe Court ❷,** in Colter Bay, serves burgers, burritos, and other cross-cultural fare. (☎ 543-2811. Entrees $5-8.25. Open daily 11am-10pm.) If you want a peek at wild moose and elk while nursing a mojito, the **Blue Heron Lounge,** inside the Jackson Lake Lodge, offers the perfect place to relax while the sun sets over Willow Flats. (☎543-3100. Wi-Fi. Live music most nights. Huckleberry margarita $6.50. Drafts $4.75.)

⛺ CAMPING

To stay in the Tetons without emptying your wallet, find a tent and pitch it. There are seven campgrounds in the park, five of which are operated on a first-come, first-served basis. (Info ☎739-3603. Sites generally open early May-late Sept.) All sites have cold water, fire rings, picnic tables, and restrooms; Signal Mountain, Gros Ventre, and Colter Bay have dump stations. The maximum stay is 14 days, except for Jenny Lake sites, where it is seven days. There is a maximum of six people and one vehicle per site; Colter Bay and Gros Ventre accept larger groups for $3 per person plus a $15 reservation fee. (☎543-3100 or 800-628-9988; reservations required).

Jenny Lake. Offers 50 closely-spaced sites in the shadow of towering Mt. Teewinot, within walking distance of Jenny Lake. Sites usually fill by 10am, so get there early. No RVs. Open mid-May to late Sept. Vehicle sites $19, bicycle sites $5 per person. ❶

Signal Mountain, along the southeastern shore of Jackson Lake. The 81 sites, situated on a hillside overlooking the water, are a little more secluded than at Colter Bay and have the best views and lake access of any of the campgrounds. Usually full by noon. Open early May to mid-Oct. Sites $17. ❶

Lizard Creek, closer to Yellowstone. Has 60 spacious, secluded sites along the northern shore of Jackson Lake. Fills by 2pm. Open June-early Sept. Vehicle sites $17. ❶

Colter Bay. With 350 crowded sites, a grocery store, laundromat, showers, and two restaurants, Colter is more suburb than wilderness. Sites rarely fill. Showers open 7:30am-9pm; $3.50. Open late May-late Sept. Vehicle sites $17, with full hookup $49. ❶

Gros Ventre, along the bank of the Gros Ventre River, close to Jackson. The biggest campground, with 350 sites and 5 group sites. The Tetons, however, are hidden from view by Blacktail Butte. The campground rarely fills and is the best bet for late arrivals. Open early May-late Sept. Sites $17. ❶

⛰ OUTDOOR ACTIVITIES

While Yellowstone captivates visitors with geysers and mudpots, the Tetons boast some of the most scenic mountains in the US, if not the world. Only 13 million years old, the Teton Range rises between 10,000 and 13,770 ft. in elevation. The absence of foothills creates spectacular mountain vistas that accentuate the range's steep rock faces. These dramatic rocks draw scores of climbers; hundreds of seasoned hikers flock here to experience the beauty of the Teton backcountry.

HIKING

All Visitors Centers provide pamphlets about day hikes and sell guides and maps ($3-10). Rangers also lead informative hikes; check the *Teewinot* or the Visitors Centers for details. Before hitting the trail or planning extended hikes, be sure to check in either at a Visitors Center or at the ranger station; trails at higher elevations may still be snow-covered and thus require ice axes and experience with icy conditions. During years with heavy snowfall, prime hiking season does not begin until well into July. Getting a very early start in the day helps to avoid crowds. In the past few years, bears have become more active in the park; be sure to educate yourself on bear safety and to carry bear spray (around $45) on all hikes.

The Cascade Canyon Trail to Lake Solitude (round-trip with boat ride 14½ mi., 8hr.; without boat ride 18½ mi., 10hr.; 2252 ft. elevation gain; very challenging) begins on the far side of tranquil Jenny Lake and follows Cascade Creek through a U-shaped valley carved by glaciers. The **Hidden Falls Waterfall** is located ½ mi. up; views of Teewinot, Mt. Owen, and Grand Teton are to the south. Hikers with more stamina can continue another ½ mi. upward toward **Inspiration Point** (elevation 7200 ft.), with stunning views eastward across Jackson Hole and the Gros Ventre Range. For some of the most spectacular hiking, trek 6¾ mi. farther to **Lake Solitude** (elevation 9024 ft.). Ranger-led trips to Inspiration Point depart from Jenny Lake Visitors Center every morning June-Aug. 8:30am. Hikers can reach the Cascade Canyon Trail by way of the 2 mi. trail around the south side of Jenny Lake or by taking one of the boat shuttles offered by **Jenny Lake Boating.** (☎734-9227. Boats leave Jenny Lake boat dock every 20min. daily 8am-6pm. $5, ages 4-12 $4; round-trip $9/5.) Most hikers, including many families, choose one of these options. An alternative route begins at String Lake trailhead and traverses the isolated north side of Jenny Lake for 1¾ mi. Beware: trail begins easy to moderate, but becomes more difficult.

Taggart Lake (3¼ mi. round-trip, 2hr., 277 ft. elevation gain) passes through the 1000-acre remains of the 1985 Beaver Creek fire, which conveniently removed most of the tree cover to allow an open view of the Tetons and Taggart lakeshore. This moderate trail also winds through a broad spectrum of plant and wildlife that has regrown since the fire; look out for marmots sunning themselves.

Bradley Lake (4 mi. round-trip, 3hr., 397 ft. elevation gain, moderate difficulty), beginning at Taggart Lake trailhead, proceeds up a glacial moraine to the more secluded Bradley Lake. For a longer trek, follow the trail another 1½ mi. along the eastern shore, over another moraine, and along a meadow for an elevation gain of 397 ft. before joining Amphitheater Lake Trail 1¼ mi. above the Lupine Meadows trailhead.

Surprise and Amphitheater Lakes (9¾ mi. round-trip, 8hr., 2958 ft. elevation gain, very challenging), originating just south of Jenny Lake at the Lupine Meadows parking lot, is a strenuous trek with a significant elevation change along several switchbacks. 3 mi. into the trail, a fork directs hikers either to **Garnet Canyon** to the left or **Surprise Lake** and **Amphitheater Lake** to the right. Garnet Canyon is 1¼ mi. from the fork and provides access to several mountain-climbing routes up South, Middle, and Grand Teton. Camping at the trail's end requires a permit. Climbers should consult with park rangers for info on routes. The lakes are another 1¾ mi. from the fork; both are stunning examples of high alpine tarns gouged out by glaciers long since melted. Lupines, the purple flowers visible all along the roads in the park, bloom June-July along the trail.

Hermitage Point (8¾ mi. round-trip, 4hr., 100 ft. elevation gain, easy), beginning at Colter Bay, is a gentle hike along gently rolling meadows and streams and past Swan Lake and Heron Pond. The trail provides a unique perspective on Jackson Lake, which it approaches at several points, and is a prime spot for observing wildlife.

Cunningham Cabin Trail (¾ mi. round-trip, 1hr., 20 ft. elevation gain, easy) relives the history of early homesteading in the valley. Trailhead lies 6 mi. south of Moran Jct.

CLIMBING

Two companies offer more extreme backcountry adventures, including four-day packages that let beginners work their way up the famed Grand Teton. **Jackson Hole Mountain Guides and Climbing School,** 165 N. Glenwood St., in Jackson, has a one-day beginner course for $130 and a one-day guided climbing course for $225. More advanced programs are also available: one-day guided climbs that do not require training start at $215 and four-day Grand Teton ascents at $1145. (☎733-4979 or 800-239-7642; www.jhmg.com. Open daily 8:30am-5:30pm. Reservations required.) **Exum Mountain Guides,** located near the Jenny Lake Visitors Center, has similar classes and rates. (☎733-2297; www.exumguides.com. 1-day beginner rock-climbing course $130. Guided 1- to 2-day climbs $250-375. Two-day Grand Teton ascents $645-935. Reservations required.)

ROCKY MOUNTAINS

BOATING, FISHING, AND BIKING

Getting out onto the water provides an entirely different perspective on the surrounding landscape. Non-motorized **boating** and hand-powered crafts are permitted on a number of lakes; motorboats are allowed only on Jackson, Jenny, and Phelps Lakes. Boating permits can be obtained at any Visitors Center and are good in Yellowstone National Park as well. (Motorized boat pass $20 per week, $40 per year; non-motorized craft $10/20. Jet skis prohibited on all park waterways.) **Grand Teton Lodge Company** rents boats at Colter Bay and has scenic cruises of Jackson Lake leaving from Colter Bay Marina. (☎543-1097. 1½hr. cruises $21, ages 3-11 $10. Canoes $13 per hr. Motorboats $27 per hr.; 2hr. min. Rentals available daily May-Aug. 8am-3pm, depending on water levels; call to check.) Those looking for a peaceful experience should consider renting a canoe or kayak at the **Jenny Lake Marina,** which offers a peaceful experience on the smaller, quieter lake. (☎739-9227. Canoes and kayaks $12 per hr. Scenic cruise $14.) **Signal Mountain Lodge** rents boats and kayaks at Signal Mountain Marina on Jackson Lake. (☎543-2831. Large pontoon boats $65 per hr. Motorboats $29 per hr. Canoes $13.50 per hr. Kayaks $12 per hr. Rentals available May-Aug.)

Fishing is permitted within the park with a Wyoming license, available at Moose Village Store, Signal Mountain Lodge, and Colter Bay Marina. ($10.50 Wyoming Conservation stamp required with all annual fishing licenses. $11 per day; $76 per season, ages 14-18 $15. WY residents $4/19/3.) Women interested in learning how to fly-fish can learn with **Reel Women Fly Fishing Adventures,** an Idaho-based company developed to introduce women to this traditionally male-dominated sport. (☎208-351-6410; www.reel-women.com. Full-day float trips $450, 2-day basic fly-fishing school $595. Reservations required.) **Jack Dennis Fishing Trips** also has float fishing trips on the Snake River in Grand Teton. (☎733-3270 or 800-570-3270; www.jackdennis.com. $425 for 2 people.) **Solitude Float Trips** sends raft floats down scenic Snake River. (☎733-2871 or 888-704-2800; www.solitudefloattrips.com. 10 mi. trip $50, ages 13 and under $30.)

Mountain biking is a particularly popular activity on roads in the park, but is strictly forbidden on hiking trails. Outdoor equipment rentals are in the Dornan's complex in Moose. **Adventure Sports** rents bikes and provides advice on the best trails. (☎733-3307. Open May-Oct. daily 9am-6pm. Front suspension $10 per hr., $32 per day; kayaks and canoes $46 per day. Credit card or deposit required.) **Snake River Angler** has advice and rents rods. (☎733-3699; www.snakeriverangler.com. Open May-Oct. daily 8am-6pm. Rods $15-25 per day.) **Moosely Seconds** rents mountaineering and camping equipment. (☎739-1801. Open in summer daily 8am-7pm. Climbing shoes $5 per day, $25 per week; crampons $8/40; ice axes $6/30; trekking poles $4/20.)

WINTER ACTIVITIES

In the winter, all hiking trails and the unplowed sections of Teton Park Rd. are open to **cross-country skiers** and **snowshoers.** Sign up for a free, ranger-led **snowshoe hike** at the Grand Teton Discovery and Visitors Center. (☎739-3300. 2hr. hikes depart Jan.-Mar. 2-4pm. Days and times vary; call for details.) **Snowmobiling** is only allowed on the Continental Divide Snowmobile Trail and Grassy Lake Road; pick up a $15 permit at the Moose Visitors Center and a map and guide at the Jackson Chamber of Commerce. **Grand Teton Park Snowmobile Rental,** in Moran at G.T.P. RV Resort, rents snowmobiles. (☎733-1980 or 800-563-6469. $99 per half-day, $139 per day; includes clothing, helmet, boots, and snowmobile instruction.) The Colter Bay and Moose parking lots are available for parking in the winter. All **campgrounds** close in winter, but **backcountry snow camping** (only for those with experience) is allowed with a permit obtained from the Moose Visitors Center. Before making plans, consider that temperatures regularly drop below -30°F. Be sure to carry extreme weather clothing and check with a ranger station for current weather and avalanche updates.

SCENIC DRIVE: CENTENNIAL SCENIC DRIVE

Weaving through some of the most breathtaking expanses of uninhabited wilderness on earth, this all-day drive is a vacation unto itself. For 162 mi., the Centennial Scenic Byway passes by the high peaks, roaring whitewater rapids, and broad windswept plains of western Wyoming. The drive is open year-round but occasionally closes due to snow. It begins in the small frontier town of **Dubois,** home of the **National Bighorn Sheep Interpretive Center,** 907 W. Ramshorn St., a fascinating museum that educates visitors about the majestic creatures as they exist (many in endangered states) around the globe, from Alaska to Afghanistan. (☎ 455-3429 or 888-209-2795; www.bighorn.org. Open daily late May-early Sept. 8am-7pm; in winter 9am-5pm. $2, under 12 $0.75; families $5. Wildlife tours Nov.-Mar. 9am; $25.) Leaving town on Rte. 26, the crumbly breccia of the volcanic Absaroka Mountains becomes visible to the north; the 11,920 ft. jagged pinnacles are those of **Ramshorn Peak.** Gently ascending through a conifer forest, the road eventually reaches **Togwotee Pass,** 30 mi. west of Dubois. Before the pass, 24 mi. west of Dubois, **Falls Camp ❶** is one of the region's best campgrounds, situated next to a massive waterfall concealed in the forest to the south of the highway. Even if you don't intend to stay overnight, stop to be awed by the canyon. (Toilets, no water. Sites $10.)

As the road begins to descend, the famed Teton mountain panorama becomes visible. The highest peak is Grand Teton (13,770 ft.); the exhibit at the **Teton Range Overlook** labels each visible peak in the skyline. After entering **Grand Teton National Park** (p. 712), the road winds through the flat plain of the **Buffalo Fork River.** This floodplain is the beginning of the wide, long valley known as Jackson Hole (early trappers referred to any high mountain valley as a hole). The road follows the **Snake River,** renowned for its whitewater rafting, kayaking, and fishing. Nearing Jackson (p. 717), the 24,000-acre **National Elk Refuge,** winter home to thousands of elk, is visible to the east. To bypass Jackson, take the truck route, U.S. 189/191 south. As the route turns east at Hoback Jct., one of the West's most popular whitewater rafting segments, the **Grand Canyon of the Snake,** is just downstream. The road winds through the deep and narrow Hoback Canyon. As the Tetons fade out of sight, the Wind River Range, home to several active glaciers, appears on the horizon, and soon the highest peak in Wyoming, **Gannet Peak** (13,804 ft.), rises majestically in the distance. The drive ends in the tiny, authentically Western town of Pinedale, where the **Museum of the Mountain Man,** 70 E. Hennick, chronicles the history of the Plains Indians, the fur trade, and the white settlement of western Wyoming. (☎ 367-4101 or 877-686-6266; www.museumofthemountainman.com. Open daily early May-late Sept. 9am-5pm; Oct. M-F 9am-4pm; reservations required for other months. $5, over 60 $4, ages 6-12 $3.)

JACKSON   ☎ 307

The southern gateway to both Grand Teton and Yellowstone National Parks, the town of Jackson (pop. 8000) teems with hordes of tourists in summer. However, the area is equally renowned for its skiing—when in Jackson, you are also in Jackson Hole, the valley that separates the Teton and Gros Ventre mountain ranges. A glamorous playground for the rich and famous, Jackson walks a fine line between staying chic enough for the *nouveau riche* who come to ski and Western enough for the old-time cowboys who have always been around. Regardless of how it presents itself, however, the town can't be beat as a base for hiking, biking, rafting, fishing, and exploring the Tetons and Snake River.

ROCKY MOUNTAINS

⚑ 🛈 ORIENTATION AND PRACTICAL INFORMATION. Downtown Jackson is centered around the intersection of **Broadway** (east-west) and **Cache Street** (north-south) and marked by **Town Square Park.** Most shops and restaurants are within a four-block radius of this intersection. South of town, at the intersection with Rte. 22, W. Broadway becomes U.S. 191/89/26. To get to **Teton Village,** take Rte. 22 to Rte. 390 (Teton Village Rd.) just before the town of Wilson. Winding backroads, unpaved at times, with close underbrush and frequent wildlife spottings, connect Teton Village to Moose and the southern entrance of the national park. North of Jackson, Cache St. turns into Rte. 89, leading directly into the park. **Jackson Hole Airport (JAC)** is located between Moose and Jackson (☎733-7682; www.jackson-holeairport.com). **Jackson Hole Express** (☎733-1719 or 800-652-9510) provides bus service to the **Salt Lake City Airport (SLC;** 5½hr., $75) and the **Idaho Falls Airport (IDA;** 2hr., $40). One bus to each location leaves daily at 6:30am. Reservations are required. **Jackson START** runs buses all around town and between Jackson and Teton Village. (☎733-4521; www.startbus.com. Runs daily mid-May to late Sept. 6am-10:30pm; early Dec.-early Apr. 6am-11pm; call for low-season schedule. Free in town, $1 on village roads, $3 to Teton Village; under 8 free.)

Visitor Info: The grass-covered roof of the **Jackson Hole and Greater Yellowstone Information Center,** 532 N. Cache St., hides a busy interior full of taxidermied elk, hands-on exhibits, and a wealth of information and reservations services for the area parks. It also lists the times at which park campgrounds filled the previous day. (☎733-3316. Open early June-Sept. daily 8am-7pm; Oct.-early June M-F 9am-5pm.) **Internet Access: Teton County Library,** 125 Virginian Ln. (☎733-2164. Free. Open M-Th 10am-9pm, F 10am-5:30pm, Sa 10am-5pm, Su 1-5pm.) **Post Office:** 1070 Maple Way, at Powderhorn Ln. (☎733-3650. Open M-F 8:30am-5pm, Sa 10am-1pm.) **Postal Code:** 83002.

🛏 ACCOMMODATIONS. Jackson draws hordes of visitors year-round, making rooms outrageously expensive and hard to find without reservations. **⬛The Hostel X ❸,** 3315 McCollister Dr., 12 mi. northwest of Jackson in Teton Village, lets skiers and others stay close to the slopes for cheap. The hostel has free Internet access, a lounge with TVs, ping-pong and pool tables, and shelves of puzzles and games. Perks include laundry facilities, a ski-waxing room, and a convenient location just a close stumble from The Mangy Moose (p. 719). All rooms are private with either four twin beds or one king-size bed. (☎733-3415. Open in summer and winter. Singles and doubles $60; triples and quads $74. MC/V.) Though the bunks at Jackson's own hostel, **The Bunkhouse ❶,** 215 N. Cache St., in the basement of the Anvil Motel, might not be the most appealing beds in town, they certainly are the cheapest. (☎733-3668; www.anvilmotel.com. Showers, coin-op laundry, ski storage. Showers for non-guests $6, includes towel. Bunks $25. D/MC/V.) One of the few lodgings in Jackson with rooms under $100 during peak season, **Alpine Motel ❸,** 70 S. Jean, two blocks from the town square, provides basic rooms with cable TV, free local calls, and an outdoor pool. (☎739-3200. June-Sept. singles $68; doubles $80. Oct.-May all rooms from $56.) The more expensive **Kudar Motel ❹,** 260 N. Cache, offers snug log cabins and motel-style rooms with cable TV, fridge, and microwave. (☎733-2823. Open Apr.-late Sept. Singles $90; cabin with king bed $110; family cabins $130.) The primitive campgrounds in **Grand Teton National Park** and the 4.4 million acre **Bridger-Teton National Forest** offer the area's absolutely cheapest accommodations. The park's **Gros Ventre** campground (p. 714) is only a 15min. drive north of the town of Jackson, on Rte. 89. There are exactly 37 **developed campgrounds ❶** in the Bridger-Teton National Forest, including several along U.S. 26 east of Jackson. **Backcountry camping ❶** is free in the Forest; campers must stay at least 200 ft. from water and 100 ft. from trails. Ask ranger beforehand; some areas may be restricted.

◘ FOOD. Jackson has dozens of restaurants, but few are suited to the budget traveler. Locals splurge at the **Rendezvous Bistro ❹**, 380 S. Broadway, savoring duck confit ($19) and escargot provencal ($8) in a bustling bistro setting. (☎739-1100. Open M-Th and Su 5:30-10pm, F-Sa 5:30-11pm; closed in winter Su. AmEx/D/MC/V.) **Bubba's Bar-B-Que ❸**, 515 W. Broadway, is a family restaurant that serves generous portions of ribs and sides. Most meals come with Bubba's famous barbecued beans. (☎733-2288. Lunch specials $7-10. 11 oz. New York strip $19. Open daily June-Aug. 6:30am-10pm; in winter 6:30am-8:30pm. AmEx/D/MC/V.) **The Bunnery ❷**, 130 N. Cache St., makes delicious breakfasts and baked goods, including omelets and the special OSM (oats, sunflower, and millet) bread. (☎734-0075 or 800-349-0492; www.bunnery.com. Breakfast $4-10. Omelets $8-9. Sandwiches $7-8. Pie slices $4. Open daily in summer 7am-9pm; in winter 7am-3pm. D/MC/V.) The low-key patio at **Pica's ❷**, 1160 Alpine Ln., is a great place to relax during Happy hour (3:30-6:30pm daily) or while gorging yourself on an inexpensive, taqueria-style Mexican meal. (☎734-4457. Entrees $6-12. Open M-Sa 11am-10pm. AmEx/MC/V.)

▧▣ FESTIVALS AND NIGHTLIFE. When the sun goes down on a long day of skiing, hiking, or rafting, Jackson has bars, concerts, and festivals to suit all tastes. Frontier justice is served at the **Town Square Shootout.** Live reenactments take place Monday through Saturday at 6pm during the summer in Jackson's town square. (☎733-3316. Free.) Catch cowboy fever at the **JH Rodeo**, held at the fairgrounds at Snow King Ave. and Flat Creek Dr. (☎733-2805; www.jhrodeo.com. June-early Sept. W and Sa 8pm. $12, ages 4-12 $8; reserved tickets $15; families $40.) Over Memorial Day, tourists, locals, and nearby Native American tribes pour in for the dances and parades of **Old West Days**; for info, call the Chamber of Commerce (☎733-3316; www.jacksonholechamber.com). World-class musicians roll into Teton Village each summer during the **Grand Teton Music Festival** for shows like "Moosely Mozart and a Little Wolf." (☎733-3050, ticket office 733-1128; www.gtmf.org. Early July-late Aug. Festival orchestra concerts F-Sa 8pm; $50. Spotlight concerts Th 8pm; $40. Chamber music concerts W-Sa 8pm; $25, ages 6-18 and students $10, Th-F and Su half-price seats.) In mid-September, the **Jackson Hole Fall Arts Festival** (☎733-3316; www.jacksonholechamber.com) showcases artists, musicians, and dancers in a week-long party that features everything from "Cowboy Jubilee Music" to the jubilant "Taste of the Tetons."

For nighttime fun, head to **The Mangy Moose,** in Teton Village at the base of Jackson Hole Ski Resort, a quintessential *après*-ski bar, featuring an enormous stuffed moose hanging from the ceiling. (☎733-4913, entertainment hotline 733-9779; www.mangymoose.net. Cover $5-15. Shows 10pm. Open daily 11:30am-2am. Kitchen open daily 5:30-10pm.) Slither on down to the **Snake River Brewery**, 265 S. Millward St., for the award-winning "Zonkers Stout." Pub favorite bratwursts are $9. (☎739-2337; www.snakeriverbrewing.com. Pints $3.50, pitchers $11. Happy hour 4-6pm. Open daily 11:30-midnight. Kitchen closes at 11pm.) Live music and good beer (drafts $3) make the **Stagecoach Bar,** on Rte. 22, in Wilson, popular among locals, especially on Thursday disco night. (☎733-4407. M and Su live music. W Reggae. Open M-Sa 11am-2am, Su 11am-1am.)

⚐ OUTDOOR ACTIVITIES. World-class skiing and climbing lie within minutes of Jackson, and **whitewater rafting** on the legendary Snake River is an adrenaline rush. Rafting is best in June, before the Jackson Dam flow is cut down in order to improve the fishing, which peaks in late July and August. **Barker-Ewing**, 45 W. Broadway, provides tours of varying lengths and difficulty levels, led by a highly experienced staff. (☎733-1000 or 800-448-4202; www.barker-ewing.com. 8 mi. tour on a 14-person raft $48, ages 6-12 $34; on a more agile 8-person raft $55/45. Gentle 13 mi. scenic trip $45/30. Overnight 16 mi. adventure $150/120. 16 mi. tour with breakfast: 14-person $80/60, 8-person $86/66.) **Leisure Sports,** 1075 Rte. 89, has boating and fishing equipment and the best deals on camping and backpacking rentals. (☎733-3040; www.leisuresportsadventure.com. Open daily in summer and winter 8am-6pm; in fall and spring 8am-5pm. 2-person tents $5 per day, 6-person tents $15 per day; sleeping bags $4 per day; backpacks $4 per day. Canoes and kayaks $35-65 per day; rafts $65-125 per day.) **Jackson Hole Mountain Resort,** located 12 mi. north of Jackson in the even smaller town of Teton Village, has some of the best runs in the entire United States, including the famous and jaw-droppingly steep **Corbet's Couloir.** (☎733-2292 or 888-333-7766; www.jacksonhole.com. Open early Dec.-Apr. Lift tickets $77 per day, ages 15-21 $63, seniors and under 14 $39. Half-day $58/48/29.) Even after the snow melts, the **aerial tram** whisks eager tourists to the top of **Rendezvous Mountain** (elevation 10,450 ft.) for a view of the valley. (☎739-2753. Jackson Hole is a prime locale for **cross-country skiing. Skinny Skis,** 65 W. Delorney, in downtown Jackson, rents gear. (☎733-6094. Open daily June-Aug. and Dec.-Feb. 9am-8pm; low-season 9am-6pm. Equipment rental $18 per day, $12 per half-day.)

CHEYENNE ☎307

"Cheyenne," the name of the Native American tribe that originally inhabited the region, was considered a prime candidate for the name of the whole Wyoming Territory. The moniker was struck down by notoriously priggish Senator Sherman, who pointed out that the pronunciation of Cheyenne closely resembled that of the French word *chienne*, meaning "bitch." Once one of the fastest-growing frontier towns, Cheyenne may have slowed down a bit, but its historical downtown area still exhibits rugged, traditional Western charm.

TRANSPORTATION AND PRACTICAL INFORMATION. Greyhound buses no longer serve the city, but Powder River Transportation (☎635-1327; www.coachamerica.com), 222 Deming Dr., at Warren Rd. off I-80, honors Greyhound passes and sends **buses** to Billings (10hr., 2 per day, $83-93), Denver (3½hr., 3 per day, $19-29), and Laramie (1hr., 1 per day, $13-23). For local travel, flag down one of the **shuttle buses** along the routes run by the Cheyenne Transit Program. (☎637-6253. Buses run M-F 6am-7pm, Sa 10am-5pm. $1, students $0.75. Daily 4-6pm all rides $0.50.) The Cheyenne Street Railway Trolley operates a convenient **trolley** service that loops around major sights in the town, complete with informative narration. (☎778-3133. Runs every 1½hr. M-F 10am-5:30pm. Maps and schedules available at the Visitors Center. $10, ages 2-12 $5.) Located in the southeastern corner of Wyoming, Cheyenne is much closer to Colorado than it is to many of Wyoming's top tourist destinations—the city is an entire day's drive from Yellowstone. Two major interstates border Cheyenne: **I-25** runs north-south along the western edge of the city, while **I-80** runs east-west along the southern edge. The heart of downtown is the area just north of the historic train depot, at **Carey Avenue** and **W. Lincolnway,** also known as W. 16th St.

The **Cheyenne Area Convention and Visitors Bureau** is at 15th and Capitol Ave., in the Cheyenne Depot. (☎778-3133 or 800-426-5009; www.cheyenne.org. Open May-Sept. M-F 8am-7pm, Sa-Su 9am-3pm; Oct.-Apr. M-F 8am-5pm.) **Medical Services: United Medical Center,** 214 E. 23rd St. (☎634-2273). **Hotlines: Domestic Violence and Sexual Assault Line,** ☎637-7233. Operates 24hr. **Internet Access: Laramie County Public Library,** 2800 Central Ave., has 30min. slots available. (☎634-3561; www.lclsonline.org. Free. Open mid-May to mid-Sept. M-Th 10am-9pm, F-Sa 10am-6pm; mid-Sept. to mid-May also Su 1-5pm.) **Post office:** 4800 Converse Ave. (☎772-7080. Open M-F 7:30am-5:30pm, Sa 7am-1pm.) **Postal Code:** 82009.

ACCOMMODATIONS. As long as your visit doesn't coincide with Frontier Days (the last full week of July), it's easy to land a cheap room in Cheyenne. Budget motels line Lincolnway (16th St./U.S. 30) east and west of downtown. In addition to its prime downtown location, beautiful lobby, and posh bar, the historic **Plains Hotel ❺,** 1600 Central Ave., has comfy beds and airy rooms well worth the price. (☎638-3311. Singles and doubles from $129. AmEx/D/MC/V.) Among the less expensive motels, the renovated **Guest Ranch Motel ❷,** 1100 W. Lincolnway, stands out with clean rooms and new mattresses, plus cable TV, fridge, and microwave in every room. (☎634-2137. Economy units $39; singles $44; doubles $51. AmEx/D/MC/V.) Sleep among the bison, horses, and singing cowboys in the original bunkhouses at the **Terry Bison Ranch ❷,** 51 I-25 Service Rd. E., I-25 Exit 2, 5 mi. south of Cheyenne. The ranch offers a fishing lake, bison tours, horseback riding, and even stables to board your own horse. (☎634-4171. Private rooms with shared bath $59; cabins $79. Tent sites $17.) **Curt Gowdy State Park ❶,** 1319 Hynds Lodge Rd., 24 mi. west of Cheyenne on Happy Jack Rd. (Rte. 210), provides 150 campsites centered around two lakes. The park also allows horseback riding (bring your own horse) and archery. (☎632-7946, reservations 877-996-7275; www.wyo-park.com. Boat dock, drinking water, dump station. Federal Bay and Sherman Hills areas are wheelchair-accessible. Sites $12. Day use $4.)

FOOD. Cheyenne has only a smattering of reasonably-priced, non-chain restaurants. The walls at the popular **Sanford's Grub and Pub ❷,** 115 E. 17th St., are blanketed with every type of kitsch imaginable, including hub caps and coyote skulls. The extensive menu includes everything from Cajun burgers topped with popcorn shrimp ($7-9) to crawfish jambalaya ($14). Check out the game room downstairs. (☎634-3381. 55 beers on tap, 99 bottles of beer on the wall, and 132 different liquors. Open daily 11am-10pm. AmEx/D/MC/V.) For a dirt-cheap breakfast or lunch, the **Driftwood Cafe ❶,** 200 E. 18th St., at Warren St., complements its homestyle cooking with the feel of a quintessential mom-and-pop diner. (☎634-5304. Cinnamon rolls $1.70. Burgers $3.75-7. Open M-F 7am-3pm. Cash only.)

SIGHTS. Take a free **S&V Carriage Ride** through historic downtown Cheyenne. (☎634-0167. Boards in front of the Depot at W. 15th St. and Capitol Ave. Rides M and Th-Su noon-6pm.) The downtown area has a number of well-maintained historic buildings; pick up a free walking tour guide at the Visitors Center. The **Wyoming State Capitol,** at the base of Capitol Ave. on 24th St., has beautiful stained-glass windows and a gorgeous rotunda under the gold-leaf dome; self-guided tours are available. A giant stuffed bison on the 1st level is often all alone in the building: the Wyoming legislature meets only 30 days each year. (☎777-7220. Open M-F 8am-5pm. Free.) Across from the Capitol, the newly redone **Wyoming State Museum,** 2301 Central Ave., has 10 galleries that tackle all aspects of Wyoming, from public lands and wildlife to settlement and current issues. (☎777-7022; www.wyomuseum.org. Open May-Oct. Tu-Sa 9am-4:30pm; Nov.-Apr. M-F 9am-4:30pm, Sa 10am-2pm. Free.) The **Old West Museum,** 4610 N. Carey Ave., in Frontier Park, houses a collection of Western memorabilia, including the 3rd-largest carriage collection in the nation. (☎778-7290; www.oldwestmuseum.org. Open M-F 9am-5pm, Sa-Su 10am-5pm. $6, under 12 free.) To get to **Vedauwoo Recreation Area** (☎745-2300), 28 mi. west of Cheyenne, take Happy Jack Rd. (Rte. 210), then turn south on Vedauwoo Rd., or take Exit 329 north off I-80. Vedauwoo consists of a collection of oddly jumbled rocks eroded into seemingly impossible shapes by wind and weather. Vedauwoo was once considered a sacred place for vision quests; today, rock climbers worship the area's towering formations, which also provide an excellent backdrop for hiking, picnics, and biking.

ROCKY MOUNTAINS

SADDLE UP!

Some brave few find their calling in hanging on for dear life to frantic animals—and plenty of people love to watch them try.

Gasp over thrown riders and cheer those who manage to stay on at the biggest rodeo in the world, **Cheyenne Frontier Days,** the "Daddy of 'em All." Born in 1897 as a single day festival, Cheyenne's Frontier Days has exploded into a 10-day celebration of the American West in all of its glory. Daily rodeos feature nine different events, from the ever-popular bull riding to the insane wild horse race, where teams of three attempt to catch, saddle, and ride horses fresh from the range. The steer wrestlers grab life by the horns; after racing on horseback after a steer, the cowboy leaps from his saddle onto the smaller animal, catching the steer by the horns, and tries to flip it.

Besides the roping, wrangling, and riding, Frontier Days has a good deal of singing. Country and rock legends such as Reba McEntire, Big & Rich, and Bon Jovi have graced the stage in years past. Together, the cowboys and singers make for a spectacular way to revel in the traditions of the Old West.

Frontier Days occurs during the last full week of July, in Cheyenne, WY. Info ☎ *800-227-6336; www.cfdrodeo.com. Rodeo tickets $11-23. Concert tickets $18-67.*

🎵🎭 **ENTERTAINMENT AND NIGHTLIFE.** During the last week of July, make every effort to attend the one-of-a-kind 🎵**Cheyenne Frontier Days,** a 10-day festival of non-stop Western hoopla appropriately dubbed the "Daddy of 'Em All." The town's population triples in size to see the world's largest outdoor rodeo competition and partake of the free pancake breakfasts, parades, big-name country music performances, square dancing, steer wrestling, and chuckwagon racing. (☎ 778-7222 or 800-227-6336; www.cfdrodeo.com. July 18-27, 2008. Rodeo $11-23. Concerts $18-67.) During June and July, the **Cheyenne Gunslingers,** W. 16th and Carey, reenact Wild West gunfights. (☎ 778-3133. M-F 6pm, Sa high noon.) The only brewery in town, the **Shadows Pub & Grill,** 115 W. 15th St. in the Depot, attracts a young professional crowd with its microbrews. (☎ 634-7625. Nightly drink specials $2-3. Open M-Th 11am-11pm, F-Sa 11am-1am, Su 11am-8pm. Kitchen closes M-Sa 11pm, Su 8pm.) Shoot pool upstairs at the **Crown Bar,** or descend below for hip hop, Top 40, and alternative dance at the **Crown Underground,** 222 W. 16th St., at the corner of Carey St. (☎ 778-9202. Th ladies night and $2 drinks. Th-Sa dancing 9pm-2am. Sa live music 9:30pm-1:30am. Nightly drink specials from $2. Open M-Sa 11am-2am, Su 11am-10pm. Underground open W-Sa 9pm-2am. Kitchen closes 12:30am.) Hoof it with the locals at the only bar open past 10pm on Sundays, the **Cowboy Rockin' Rodeo/Outlaw Saloon,** 312 S. Greeley Hwy. The live music and large dance floor always draw a crowd. (☎ 635-7552. Live music daily 8:30pm-1:30am. Open M-Sa 11am-2am, Su noon-2am.)

THE SNOWY RANGE   ☎ 307

Local residents call the forested granite mountains to the east of the Platte Valley the Snowy Mountain Range. Snow falls nearly year-round on the higher peaks, and when the snow melts, quartzite outcroppings reflect the sun, creating the illusion of a snowy peak. The Snowy Range, 40 mi. west of Laramie, is part of **Medicine Bow National Forest.** Cross-country skiing is popular in the winter; campsites and trails usually don't open until May or June due to heavy snowfall. On the west side of the Snowy Range along Rte. 130, chase the cold away with the geothermal stylings of **hot springs** on Walnut St., in **Saratoga,** running between 104° and 120°F, at the end of E. Walnut St. behind the **public pool.** (Open 24hr. Free.) Nearby, the **North Platte River** offers fishing and a chance to enjoy snowmelt mixed with the runoff of the hot springs. Fishing permits ($10) are available at **Hack's Tackle Outfitters,** 407 N. 1st St., in Saratoga, which also sells hunting licenses and offers both fishing advice and guided trips. (☎326-9823; www.hackstackle.com. Scenic tours $40 per half-day, $90 per day. Canoes $35 per day; $100 deposit required for guided trips. Two-person fishing trips $235 per half-day, $350 per day. Shuttles to any location on the river can be hired for a $25 flat fee, regardless of number of canoes or rafts onboard.) At **Snowy Range Ski and Recreation Area,** enjoy 27 moderately challenging downhill trails, cross-country trails, and a snowboard halfpipe. Take Exit 311 off I-80 to Rte. 130 W. (☎745-5750 or 800-462-7669; www.snowyrange.com. Open mid-Dec. to Easter. Lift ticket $41 per day, ages 6-12 $26, over 60 $33; half-day $33.)

From late May to November, cars can drive 27 mi. through seas of pine and aspen trees, around treeless mountains and picture-perfect lakes at high elevations on the **Snowy Range Scenic Byway (Route 130).** To get there from the east, exit I-80 in Laramie; approaching from the west, exit at Walcott Jct., 22 mi. east of Rawlins. Early along the Byway from the east, Barber Lake Rd. branches off along noisy Libby Creek, bypassing the entrance to the Snowy Range Ski Area before returning to Rte. 130. At the summit, the **Libby Flats Observation Point,** at the top of Snowy Range Pass (elevation 10,847 ft.), has a wildflower nature walk and an inspiring view of the surrounding alpine landscape. On bright days, delicate alpine sunflowers turn their faces to the sun. Before the road descends, don't miss the Silver Lake outlook, which features a gorgeous view of the waters and surrounding area. Keep an eye out for local fauna like bighorn sheep, pine martens, and yellow-bellied marmots. The challenging **Medicine Bow Trail** (5¼ mi., 1600 ft. elevation change) has trailheads at both **Lake Marie** and **Lewis Lake** and climbs through rocky alpine terrain to **Medicine Bow Peak** (12,013 ft.), the highest point in the forest. All 16 of the park's developed **campgrounds ❶** are only open in summer and have toilets and water, but no hookups or showers. **Sugarloaf ❶** (16 sites) and **Brooklyn Lake ❶** (19 sites) are open from July to September and are reservable through the National Recreation Reservation Service. (☎877-444-6777; www.recreation.gov. Pit toilets, water provided. 14-night max. stay. Sites $10. Reservation fee $9.) A drive up **Kennaday Peak** (10,810 ft.), Rte. 130 to Rte. 100 and 215, at the end of Rte. 215, grants an impressive view.

Biking and driving are permitted only on designated trails in the high country and on trails below 10,000 ft. The 7 mi. **Corner Mountain Loop,** just west of Centennial Visitors Center, is a roller coaster ride through forests and meadows. In winter, the trails are used for cross-country skiing and snowmobiling. **Brush Creek Visitors Center,** at the west entrance, provides hiking, biking, camping, and bear safety info. (☎326-5562. Open daily mid-May to Oct.) Get cross-country skiing equipment and trail info at the **Cross Country Connection,** 222 S. 2nd St., in Laramie. (☎721-2851; www.crosscountryconnections.com. Open M-F 10am-6pm, Sa 9am-5pm, Su noon-4pm. Ski rental $10 per day.) Downhill ski and snowboard rentals are available at **The Fine Edge,** 1660E N. 4th St. (☎745-4499; www.fineedge.net. Open in winter M-Th 9am-6pm, F-Sa 7am-6pm, Su 7am-4pm; in summer M-Sa 11am-6pm, Su 11am-4pm. Ski rental $16 per day, children $14. Snowboard rental $25/19; boots $10. $300 credit card or check deposit required for snowboards.)

MONTANA

If anything dominates Montana's landscape more than the towering mountain peaks and shimmering glacial lakes, it's the sky—welcome to Big Sky country. With 25 million acres of national forest and public lands, Montana's grizzly bears, mountain lions, and pronghorn antelope outnumber the people. Nonetheless, small towns set against unadulterated mountain vistas have attracted new populations of artists and writers and support galleries and culture disproportionate to

ROCKY MOUNTAINS

their populations. World-famous fishing rivers, 500 species of wildlife, thousands of ski trails, and endless miles of open road make Montana an American paradise.

⚡ PRACTICAL INFORMATION

Capital: Helena.

Visitor Info: Travel Montana, 301 S. Park, P.O. Box 200533, Helena 59620 (☎800-847-4868; www.visitmt.com). **National Forest Information,** Northern Region, Federal Bldg., 200 E. Broadway, Box 7669, Missoula 59807 (☎406-329-3511. Open M-F 8am-4:30pm). **Road Conditions:** ☎800-226-7623. Statewide.

Postal Abbreviation: MT. **Sales Tax:** None.

HELENA   ☎406

The outdoors appeal of Montana lures visitors to its capital city, where state politics and great hiking, biking, and fishing happily coexist. A product of the 1864 gold rush at Last Chance Gulch, Helena has transformed itself from a humble mining camp into a sophisticated city with an active art scene.

⬛⚡ TRANSPORTATION AND PRACTICAL INFORMATION. There is no Greyhound service to Helena, but Rimrock Stages, 3100 E. Hwy. 12 (☎442-5860; www.rimrocktrailways.com) runs two **buses** per day: one heads north to Great Falls (1½hr., 1 per day, $18), and one heads south, connecting to Billings (7hr., 1 per day, $52), Missoula (4hr., 1 per day, $35.50), and Salt Lake City (12½hr., 1 per day, $88). Helena Area Transportation Service (HATS) operates several **bus** routes around town. (☎447-1580. Every hr. M-F 7am-6pm. $1.50, disabled and seniors $0.85, under 5 free.) The HATS **trolley** runs in a loop to 10 downtown attractions. (☎447-1580. Every 30min. 11am-6pm. $0.50, day pass $1.50.) For a **taxi,** call Capitol Taxi, ☎449-5525. Helena sits west of I-15 on Hwy. 12. The main street has three names, starting off from the I-15 Exit as **Cedar Street,** turning into **North Main Street** at Montana Ave., and becoming **Last Chance Gulch** downtown after crossing Lyndale Ave. These streets, along with **11th Avenue** and **Euclid Avenue (Highway 12),** are the major cross-town thoroughfares. The **Helena Chamber of Commerce** is at 225 Cruse Ave. (☎447-1530 or 800-743-5362; www.helenachamber.com. Open M-F 8am-5pm.) **Medical Services: Helena Urgent Care,** 33 Neill Ave. (☎443-5354. Open M-F 8am-8pm, Sa 8am-7pm, Su 10am-5pm.) The **Helena Chamber of Commerce** is at 225 Cruse Ave. (☎447-1530 or 800-743-5362; www.helenachamber.com. Open M-F 8am-5pm.) **Internet Access: Lewis & Clark Library,** 120 S. Last Chance Gulch (☎446-1690; www.lewisandclarklibrary.org. Free. Open in summer M-Th 10am-8pm, F 10am-6pm, Sa 10am-5pm; in winter M-Th 10am-9pm, F 10am-6pm, Sa 10am-5pm, Su 1-5pm.) **Post office:** 2300 N. Harris St. (☎443-3304. Open M-F 8am-6pm, Sa 9am-noon.) **Postal Code:** 59601.

⬛ ACCOMMODATIONS. The nicest way to experience Helena is to camp in the surrounding recreation areas. If you'd rather stay in town, **Budget Inn Express ❷,** 524 N. Last Chance Gulch, has an attractive downtown location and large, tidy rooms. (☎442-0600 or 800-862-1334. Cable TV, hot tub, laundry. Singles $40, doubles $50. AmEx/D/MC/V.) The best deal in town for women, **Helena YWCA ❶,** 501 N. Park Ave., rents private singles with shared bath and use of a full kitchen and laundry facilities. (☎442-8774. Women only. Free Wi-Fi. Singles $25.) Escape the heat at **Moose Creek Campground ❶,** 10 mi. west of Helena on U.S. 12, then 4 mi. southwest on Rimini Rd., which has pleasantly cool, forested camping alongside a stream. (Vault toilets, water. Open mid-May to mid-Sept. Sites $5.) Fifteen miles east of Helena, 13 public campgrounds line **Canyon Ferry Reservoir ❶**, popular for both fishing and boating; take either Canyon Ferry Rd. or Rte. 284 from U.S. 12. The campgrounds are open year-round, but can be prohibitively hot in summer. (7 campgrounds $8 per site. 6 campgrounds free.) The free **Fish Hawk Campground ❶**, on W. Shore Dr., has tent sites and toilets, but no drinking water. The **BOR Canyon Ferry Office,** 7700 Canyon Ferry Rd. (☎475-3921), has more info.

🖪🖬 **FOOD AND NIGHTLIFE.** Local paintings and a forest of records dangle from a graffitied ceiling at the 🖪**Staggering Ox ❷,** 400 Euclid Ave., in the Lundy Center. Their patented, award-winning bread is baked in a soup can and constructed into sandwiches with names like "Yo' Momma Osama" ($7.50) and "Headbanger's Hoagie" ($5.50). The very popular "bread guts" are sold with sauces such as "Camel Spit." (☎443-1729. F live music 6-9pm. Open M-Th 11am-8pm, F-Sa 11am-9pm, Su 11am-7pm. MC/V.) Enjoy an authentic taste of southern Europe at 🖪**Mediterranean Grill ❹,** 42 S. Park Ave., enhanced by the friendly conversation of the Turkish-born chef and owner. Follow stuffed grape leaves ($6.75) with an eggplant dish ($16) or the salmon *amaretti* ($18). (☎495-1212. Open M-Sa 11am-9:30pm, Su 10am-2pm. AmEx/D/MC/V.) **Toi's Thai ❸,** 423 N. Last Chance Gulch, serves authentic Thai food with fixed-price menus, a la carte, and family-style options in a cozy setting. (☎443-6656. Reservations recommended. Open Tu-Sa 5-8:30pm. MC/V.) All the meats, grains, and produce are organic and locally-grown at **No Sweat Cafe ❶,** 427 N. Last Chance Gulch, a popular hangout where whole-wheat pancakes ($4.50) and delightful egg dishes ($5-6) reign supreme. (☎442-6954. Open Tu-F 7am-2pm, Sa-Su 8am-2pm. Cash only.) Helena's weekly **farmers' market** brings produce and crafts to Fuller Ave., in downtown. (☎439-5576. May-Oct. Sa 9am-1pm.)

    Miller's Crossing, 52 S. Park Ave., has pool tables, a large dance floor, and live blues, folk, and rock some nights. A special $2.50 microbrew is always on tap. (☎442-3290; www.millerscrossing.biz. Cover $2-5. Open daily 11am-2am.) Dancing, gambling, and occasional body shots make **Hap's,** 1550 Railroad Ave., the place to join locals for cheap drinks. Before it gets too wild, folks play horseshoes in the backyard, shoot a game of pool, and try to "cut in line" on the Internet jukebox. (☎443-2804. Drafts $1.25-1.75. Mixed drinks from $2.50. Open daily 10am-2am.) Moving from location to location, **Alive at Five** tours the city on summer Wednesdays with live music and local food vendors. (☎447-1535. Festival runs mid-May to mid-Sept. W 5pm-9pm.)

🖪🖬 **SIGHTS AND OUTDOOR ACTIVITIES.** A strategic point from which to begin an exploration of Helena, the **Montana Historical Society Museum,** 225 N. Roberts St., has chronological displays recounting the region's development through artifacts, maps, and clothing. Don't miss the stuffed rare white buffalo or the displays of military gear, including Nazi uniforms and medals brought back from WWII by American GIs. (☎444-2694 or 800-243-9900; www.montanahistoricalsociety.org. Open M-W and F-Sa 9am-5pm, Th 9am-8pm. $5, ages 5-18 $1.) The Historical Society's popular 1hr. **Last Chance Tour Train** departs in front of the museum and features commentary on the city's historical buildings and sights. (☎442-1023 or 888-423-1023; www.lctours.com. Tours May and Sept. by appointment; June 3 per day; July-Aug. 4 per day; early Sept. 2 per day. $7, seniors $6.50, ages 4-12 $6.) The **State Capitol** building, 1301 6th Ave., at Montana Ave., has several pieces of notable artwork, including a giant Charles M. Russell mural depicting the Salish Indians welcoming Lewis and Clark in 1804. At the top of the stairs is a statue of Jeannette Rankin, the first woman elected to Congress. (☎444-4789. Open 8am-5pm for self-guided tours. Tours every hr. May-Sept. M-Sa 9am-3pm, Su noon-4pm; Oct.-Apr. M-Sa in even years 10am-2pm, in odd years 9am-3pm. Free.) The towering spires of

ROCKY MOUNTAINS

the **Cathedral of Saint Helena,** at Lawrence and Warren St., are visible throughout downtown. The marble, oak, and bronze furnishings and stained glass windows of this neo-Gothic structure emulate Vienna's Votive Church of the Sacred Heart. (☎442-5825. Open June-Aug. M-Sa 7am-9pm; Sept.-May M-Sa 7am-7pm. Guided tours available Tu-Th 1-3pm. Free.) The small but lovely **Holter Museum,** 12 E. Lawrence Ave., displays paintings, photographs, and crafts. (☎442-6400; www.holtermuseum.org. Open Tu and Th-F 10am-5:30pm, W noon-8pm, Sa 10am-4:30pm, Su 11:30am-4:30pm. Suggested donation $2, seniors and students $1; families $5.) The gold vanished from **Last Chance Gulch** long ago, but today this pedestrian mall offers restaurants, shops, and public artwork. The **Myrna Loy Center,** 15 N. Ewing St. (☎443-0287; www.myrnaloycenter.com), presents foreign films, dance, music, and performance art in the historic former county jail. Artists-in-residence say there's really nowhere like "the Bray," speaking fondly of the **Archie Bray Foundation for the Ceramic Arts,** 2915 Country Club Ave. Take Euclid Ave./Hwy. 12 west, and make a right on Joslyn St. Visitors can view the incredible work in the gallery, tour the artists' studios, and take a self-guided walking tour of the grounds. (☎443-3502; www.archiebray.org. Grounds open dawn-dusk. Gallery open M-Sa 10am-5pm, Su 1-5pm. Free.)

Hikers can take in views of the entire city from the top of **Mount Helena** (5468 ft.); the trail to the summit begins at the Adams St. Trailhead, just west of Reeders Alley. Visitors can observe the Missouri River as Lewis and Clark did on a 2hr. boat tour of the ◪**Gates of the Mountains,** 18 mi. north of Helena, off I-15 at Exit 209 (even though it says "no services"). Extensive commentary on local plants and birds makes for an educating journey. The boat stops near **Mann Gulch,** where a 1949 forest fire killed 13 smokejumpers. (☎458-5241; www.gatesofthemountains.com. June-Sept. 2-7 tours per day; call or check website for times. $11, seniors $10, ages 4-17 $7.)

▶ DAYTRIPS FROM HELENA

BUTTE   ☎406

The slow-moving town of Butte was once the largest city in the entire Rockies; it was both wealthy, sitting atop an enormously rich mine, and progressive, with the first electric railroad in the region. With such a rich past, it comes as no surprise that Butte (the 2nd-largest historical district west of the Mississippi) has hidden delights for any history buff. Buildings untouched for years are now open to visitors. **Old Butte Historical Adventures,** 117 N. Main St., runs entertaining and informative tours through abandoned speakeasies, business offices, and brothels, all replete with artifacts left behind by the original inhabitants. (☎498-3424. Open in summer daily 10am-4pm; in winter by appointment only. 1½ tours depart every hr. $10, seniors $8, under 12 $5.) The wealth that supported more than 250 bars in 1917 had its roots in Butte's mineral deposits. Discover the workings of open-pit mining at the **Museum of Mining,** 155 Museum Way, located on an actual mine yard with much of the equipment and town left intact. (☎723-7211. Open daily Apr.-Oct. 9am-5:30pm. $7, over 65 $6, ages 13-18 $5, ages 5-12 $2.) Though it's not much to look at from the outside, the interior of the **Copper King Mansion ❸,** 219 W. Granite St., reflects the opulence supported by the mine. Guided tours of this magnificently ornate house are available, but even better is staying in the beautiful rooms and waking up to a full breakfast. (☎782-7580. Tours May-Sept. daily 9am-4pm; Apr. Sa-Su 9am-4pm; Oct.-Mar. by appointment only. Rooms $65-95.) Maps, brochures, and advice can be found at the **Butte Chamber of Commerce,** 1000 George St. (☎723-3177. Open M-Sa 8:30am-6:30pm, Su 9am-4pm.)

GREAT FALLS ☎406

A city planned for the railroad rather than a boom-and-bust town like so many of its neighbors, easygoing Great Falls is also known as the "Electric City" for its early development of dams and hydroelectric power. The easy-to-navigate street system and ample city parks of today were not developed until the late 1880s; when Lewis and Clark arrived in June 1805, they had to spend quite some time on the 18 mi. portage around Great Falls's series of five waterfalls. Though the falls for which the city is named are less impressive nowadays due to the dam, two museums make a stop here worthwhile. The new ▧**Lewis & Clark National Historic Trail Interpretive Center,** 4201 Giant Springs Rd., at Exit 280 off I-15, sits on the Missouri River and takes visitors through the expedition with detailed, interactive exhibits on the native peoples the explorers encountered and the flora and fauna they researched. Pelts, preserved flowers, and taxidermied birds from the expedition accompany interactive exhibits. The Center also hosts special events daily; call for details. (☎727-8733. Open June-Sept. daily 9am-6pm; Oct.-May Tu-Sa 9am-5pm. $5, under 15 free. "America the Beautiful" national parks passes accepted.) Celebrated for capturing the spirit of the West in his paintings, sculptures, and letters, Charlie Russell fell in love with Montana after moving from Missouri. His vast array of work is housed in the **C.M. Russell Museum,** 400 13th St. N., next to his home and log cabin studio. (☎727-8787. Open in summer daily 9am-6pm; in winter Tu-Su 10am-5pm. Tours in summer M-F 10am and 2pm, Sa-Su 2pm. $9, seniors $7, students and ages 6-18 $4.)

BOZEMAN ☎406

Busy Bozeman continues to grow as outdoor enthusiasts scramble to get in on the world-class fishing, skiing, and hiking. After the sun sets, this boisterous town doesn't head to bed as quickly as many other places in Montana. Montana State University (MSU) students still don cowboy hats and drive pickup trucks, but the increasing diversity of the student body reflects the cultural vigor of this thriving community. The university is also home to the wonderful Museum of the Rockies, a base for paleontologists exploring the entire region.

◧▐ **ORIENTATION AND PRACTICAL INFORMATION.** I-90 forms the northeast boundary of the city center. **Main Street** is the primary east-west road, intersecting I-90 at Exit 309. **Willson Avenue** and **19th Avenue** are the primary north-south routes, with the latter intersecting I-90 at Exit 305. Named streets run east-west; north-south avenues east of Grand Ave. are also named. North-south avenues west of Grand Ave. are numbered. Greyhound and Rimrock Stages, 1205 E. Main St. (☎587-3110; www.greyhound.com; open M-F 8am-5pm and 7-9pm, Sa 9am-5pm and 7-9pm, Su 3-5pm and 8-9pm), both send **buses** to: Billings (2½hr., 2 per day, $30); Butte (2hr., 2 per day, $22); Helena (4½hr., 1 per day, $22); Missoula (5hr., 2 per day, $33). The **Bozeman Area Chamber of Commerce** is at 2000 Commerce Way, at the corner of 19th Ave. and Baxter Ln. (☎586-5421 or 800-228-4224; www.bozemanchamber.com. Open M-F 8am-5pm.) **Internet Access: Bozeman Public Library,** 626 E. Main St. (☎582-2400; www.bozemanlibrary.org. Free. Open M-Th 10am-8pm, F-Sa 10am-5pm, Su 1-5pm; in summer closed Su.) **Post office:** 2201 Baxter Ln. (☎586-1508. Open M-F 8:30am-5pm, Sa 9am-1pm.) **Postal Code:** 59718.

▐ **ACCOMMODATIONS.** Budget motels line Main St. and 7th Ave. north of Main. Only a 5min. walk from downtown, **Bozeman Backpacker's Hostel ❶,** 405 W. Olive St., has co-ed rooms, a kitchen, a welcoming porch, and the cheapest beds in town. (☎586-4659. Linens included. Laundry facilities, Wi-Fi. Showers for non-guests $4. Dorms $20. Private rooms with shared bath $42. Cash only.) **The Imperial Inn ❸**, 122 W. Main, has clean rooms and particularly spacious singles in a prime downtown location. (☎586-3354; www.innbozeman.com. Singles $59; doubles $69. In winter $10 less. AmEx/D/MC/V.) **Langohr Campground ❶**, 11 mi. south of Bozeman, on Hyalite Canyon Rd., has mostly sunny sites along Hyalite Creek. **Hood Creek ❶** and **Chisholm ❶** campgrounds, located 4½ and 5½ mi. farther up the canyon, respectively, are situated on the shores of the Hyalite Reservoir, beneath the forested peaks of the **Gallatin National Forest.** (Reservations ☎877-444-6777; www.recreation.gov. Open mid-May to mid-Sept. Sites at all 3 campgrounds $11.) The private **Bear Canyon Campground ❶**, 4000 Bozeman Trail Rd., 4 mi. east of Bozeman at Exit 313 off I-90, has great views of the countryside from the heated outdoor pool. (☎587-1575 or 800-438-1575. Showers, laundry. Open May to mid-Oct. Sites $15, with water and electricity $23, with full hookup $28. Each additional person $4.) The **Bozeman Ranger District,** 3710 Fallon St., Ste. C (☎522-2520), has more information on camping in the Gallatin National Forest.

◻◼ FOOD AND NIGHTLIFE. Inexpensive and chain eateries aimed at the college crowd line W. College Ave. near MSU. **The Cateye Cafe ❷**, 23 N. Tracy Ave., is a downtown diner with a colorful paint job and a humorous menu, delighting in cats and all who love them. Banana bread french toast ($6.75), sandwiches on "fogatcha" bread ($7.50-7.75), and meatloaf and egg breakfasts ($7.75) satisfy any craving. (☎587-8844. Open M and W-F 7am-2:30pm, Sa-Su 7am-2pm.) **La Parrilla ❷**, 1424 W. Babcock Ave., wraps up just about everything in their giant 12 in. tortillas, including homemade barbecue, fiery jambalaya, bison meat, and fresh seafood. (☎582-9511. Wraps $5.35-9.40. Open daily 11am-9pm. AmEx/D/MC/V.) Local favorite **Main Street Overeasy ❷**, 9 E. Main St., in the indoor mall, serves stuffed french toast ($6.75) and Lewis and Clark breakfast burritos ($8.75) to young and old alike. (☎587-3205. Breakfasts $5.25-9. Sandwiches $6-8.25. Open Tu-Su 7am-2pm.) **Over the Tapas/Sweet Pea Bakery ❸**, 19 S. Willson Ave., proclaims "it's all about sharing" at this chic tapas restaurant. Treats include gazpacho, mussels, and duck skewers. (☎556-8282. Vegetarian tapas $2-9, with meat $4-11. Open daily 11am-3pm and 5pm-10pm. AmEx/D/MC/V.) The original in the popular Montana pizza chain, Bozeman's **MacKenzie River Pizza Co. ❸**, 232 E. Main St., is pure Montana, with rough-hewn tree-trunk pillars and murals of cattle herds. The selection of gourmet pizzas includes the "Sequoia," topped with basil pesto, sun-dried tomatoes, artichokes, and almonds. (☎587-0055. 12 in. pizzas $10-17.50. Open M-Sa 11am-10pm, Su noon-10pm. AmEx/D/MC/V.)

Get the lowdown on music and nightlife from the weekly *Tributary* or *The BoZone*, found at cafes, bars, and bookstores around town. Bozeman's summer concert series, **Music on Main** (Th 7-8:30pm), is a popular way to kick off an evening downtown. The rooftop patio is always packed at **Crystal,** 123 E. Main St., where buckets of beer on ice await as partiers vie for a perch amidst the crowd. (☎587-2888. 5 Coronas $10. Open M-Sa 11am-11pm, Su 2-10pm. Cash only.) Locals and travelers thirsty for good beer and great music head over to the **Zebra Cocktail Lounge,** in the basement at Rouse Ave. and Main St. The large selection of beers and hipster atmosphere draw a young, cool crowd. (☎585-8851. W-Sa DJ or bands. Open daily 8pm-2am.) One of only two non-smoking bars in all of Bozeman, the **Rocking R Bar,** 211 E. Main St., lives up to its name with hot drink specials every night, all served in a classy setting. (☎587-9355. W-Th free food 5-9pm. W and Sa live music, Th karaoke. Open daily 10am-2am.) Sample some of Montana's best brews from the selection of more than 40 beers on tap at the **Montana Ale Works,** 611 E. Main St. This former train depot for the now-defunct Northern Pacific Railway Co. now houses six pool tables for serious sharks. (☎587-7700. Beer $3.50-5.50. Open daily 4pm-midnight. Kitchen closes 11pm.)

◉▲ **SIGHTS AND OUTDOOR ACTIVITIES.** Get up close and personal with dinosaurs at the ▓**Museum of the Rockies,** 600 West Kagy Blvd., near the university. Dr. Jack Horner (the inspiration for *Jurassic Park's* Alan Grant) and other pale-ontologists make this their base for excavating prehistoric remains throughout the West. Thoughtful curation, an outdoor challenge course featuring Lewis and Clark, and an incredible amount of fossils make this museum a must-see. (☎994-3466; www.museumoftherockies.org. Open in summer daily 8am-8pm; low season M-Sa 9am-5pm, Su 12:30-5pm. $9.50, ages 5-18 $6.50. AAA discount $1/0.50.) In an old county jail, the **Gallatin Pioneer Museum,** 317 W. Main St., offers a look at gal-lows, jail cells, and a reconstructed pioneer cabin. (☎522-8122; www.pioneermu-seum.org. Open May-Sept. M-Sa 10am-5pm; mid-Sept. to mid-May Tu-Sa 11am-4pm. $3, under 12 free.)

   The Bozeman Angler, 23 E. Main St., leads trips with expert instruction in fly-fish-ing on the Yellowstone, Gallatin, Madison, and Missouri Rivers. (☎800-886-9111; www.bozemanangler.com. 2-3hr. group lesson $40 per person; full-day class $125 per person. 2-person float trip $395.) Surrounded by three renowned trout-fishing rivers—Yellowstone, Madison, and Gardiner—the small town of **Livingston,** about 25 mi. east of Bozeman off I-90, is an angler's heaven. The fly-fishing film *A River Runs Through It* was shot here. Livingston's Main St. features early 20th-century buildings, including bars, restaurants, fishing outfitters, small art galleries, and a few modern businesses. **Dan Bailey's,** 209 W. Park St., sells fishing licenses and rents gear. (☎800-356-4052. Fishing license $24.25 per 2 days, $69.25 per season. Rod and reel $20; waders and boots $15. Open in summer M-Sa 7am-7pm, Su 7am-noon; in winter M-Sa 8am-6pm.)

   The world-class ski area **Big Sky,** 45 mi. south of town on U.S. 191, has over 150 trails and short lift lines. The Lone Peak trams reach an altitude of 11,166 ft. (☎995-5000 or 800-548-4486; www.bigskyresort.com. Open mid-Nov. to mid-Apr. Lift ticket $75 per day, ages 11-17 and students $55, seniors $65. Ski rental $31-47, jun-iors $22. Snowboard rental $40.) In summer, scenic **lift rides** soar up Big Sky. (Open June-early Oct. daily 9:45am-4:30pm. $18, seniors $12, under 10 free.) Full suspension mountain bike rentals are also available at the top ($41 per hr., $83 per 8hr.). Less crowded and less expensive than Big Sky, **Bridger Bowl Ski Area,** 15795 Bridger Canyon Rd., 16 mi. northeast of town on Hwy. 86, has trails for a variety of abilities. (☎587-2111 or 800-223-9609; www.bridgerbowl.com. Open early Dec.-early Apr. Lift ticket $43 per day, ages 65-71 $35, ages 6-12 $15, over 71 free. Ski rental $25, juniors $15. Snowboard rental $25.)

   Floating in the warm and shallow **Madison River** is a cheap and relaxing way to pass a long summer afternoon in Bozeman. You ca rent inner tubes ($6-15 per day) at **Big Boys Toys,** 28670 Norris Rd., west on Main St., 7 mi. from downtown. (☎587-4747; www.bigboystoysrentals.com. Open daily in summer 7:30am-6pm; in winter 8am-6pm. Canoes $25 per day. Cash or check deposit required.) **Montana Whitewa-ter** shoots the rapids of the Gallatin River, just 7 mi. north of the Big Sky area on U.S. 191. Trips meet at the outfit's office located at Mi. 64 on U.S. 191. (☎763-4465 or 800-799-4465; www.montanawhitewater.com. Trips $47 per half-day, children $37; $79/64 per day.)

MISSOULA   ☎406

A liberal haven in a largely conservative state, Missoula attracts new residents every day with its revitalized downtown and bountiful outdoors opportunities. Missoula represents the cultural hub of the state to most native Montanans, and the students at the University of Montana (U of M) would surely not disagree. Downtown Missoula is lined with bars and coffeehouses spawned by the large stu-dent population. Twelve thousand years ago, the town was located at the very bot-

ROCKY MOUNTAINS

tom of a glacial lake; today, four different mountain ranges and five major rivers surround Missoula, supporting skiing during the winter and fly-fishing, hiking, and biking during the summer.

🛂 PRACTICAL INFORMATION. Flights stream into the **Missoula International Airport (MSO)**, 5225 Hwy. 10 W. (☎728-4381; www.flymissoula.com), 5½ mi. west of town. Follow Broadway, which turns into Hwy. 10. Greyhound, 1660 W. Broadway (☎549-2339; www.greyhound.com; ticket office open M-F 7am-noon, 1:30-5pm, and 7:45-8:30pm; Sa-Su 7:15-8am, 2:30-3:30pm, and 7:45-8:30pm), sends **buses** to Bozeman (4½hr., 2 per day, $33) and Spokane (4½hr., 2 per day, $42). From the same terminal, Rimrock Trailways (☎800-255-7655; www.rimrocktrailways.com) serves Whitefish via St. Ignatius and Kalispell (3½hr., 1 per day, $28-30) and Billings (8hr., 1 per day, $23-25). Catch a ride on Mountain Line City Buses from the Transfer Center, at Ryman and Pine St., or around town. (☎721-3333; www.mountainline.com. Buses run M-F 6:45am-7:15pm, Sa 9:45am-5:15pm. $0.85, seniors $0.35, under 18 $0.25.) For a taxi, call Yellow Cab (☎543-6644). Rent **cars** at Rent-A-Wreck, 1905 W. Broadway. (☎721-3838 or 800-552-1138; www.rentawreck.com. 21+. $35-45 per day; $0.25 per mi. after 150 mi.) The **Convention and Visitors Bureau** is at 1121 E. Broadway, Ste. 103. (☎532-3250; www.missoulacvb.org. Open in summer M-F 8am-7pm, Sa-Su 10am-2pm; in winter M-F 8am-5pm.) **Medical Services:** St. Patrick Hospital, 500 W. Broadway (☎543-7271). **Internet Access: Missoula Public Library,** 301 E. Main St. (☎721-2665; www.missoulapubliclibrary.org. Free. Open M-Th 10am-9pm, F-Sa 10am-6pm, Su 1-5pm.) **Post Office:** 1100 W. Kent St. (☎329-2200. Open M-F 8am-6pm, Sa 9am-1pm.) **Postal Code:** 59801.

🛏 ACCOMMODATIONS. There are no hostels in Missoula, but there are plenty of inexpensive alternatives along **Broadway,** both east and west of downtown. Rooms at the **City Center Motel ❸,** 338 E. Broadway, have cable TV, fridges, and microwaves. (☎543-3183 or 800-543-3184. Singles $50; doubles $55. MC/V.) West of downtown, the **Brownies Plus Motel ❷,** 1540 W. Broadway, offers large, clean rooms with A/C and cable TV, some with fridges and microwaves. (☎543-6614 or 800-543-6614; www.browniesplusmotel.com. Singles $49-64; doubles $55-67. AmEx/D/MC/V.) The **Missoula/El-Mar KOA Kampground ❶,** 3450 Tina Ave., south of Broadway, off Reserve St., has everything: all-you-can-eat pancake breakfasts, ice-cream socials, laundry facilities, mini-golf, a pool, and two hot tubs. Shaded tent sites are set apart from RVs. (☎549-0881 or 800-562-5366. 2-person sites $28, with water and electricity $32, with full hookup $40. Each additional person $3. Cabins $47-52. AmEx/D/MC/V.) Though farther afield, many **National Forest campgrounds** line the highways spreading outward from Missoula. The closest is **Lolo Creek ❶,** 15 mi. west of Lolo and 22 mi. west of Missoula on Hwy. 12, which parallels the historic Lolo Trail used by the Nez Perce, Salish, and Kootenai tribes and also explored by Lewis and Clark. (☎329-3814. 18 sites with vault toilets and water. $10.)

🍴 FOOD. The culinary capital of Montana boasts a number of innovative, delicious, and thrifty eateries. Restaurants and coffeehouses line Higgins Ave., north of the Clark Fork River, in downtown. Boasting fine espresso and billiards, the hip **Dauphine's Bakery and Cafe ❷,** 130 E. Broadway, handles heavenly slices of quiche ($4) and falafel sandwiches ($8), as well as delicious breakfasts and decadent desserts. Free Wi-Fi and funky lighting make for a great coffee-sipping atmosphere. (☎829-8188. Open M-F 7am-6pm, Sa-Su 8am-3pm. MC/V.) The busy **Hob Nob Cafe ❷,** 531 S. Higgins Ave., tempts patrons with gourmet, made-from-scratch sandwiches ($6-9), homemade breakfasts ($4-7), and salads ($6-7) as fresh as can be. (☎541-4622; www.justinshobnobcafe.com. Open M-F 7am-4pm, Sa-Su 8am-4pm. MC/V.) **Tipu's ❷,** 115½ S. 4th St. W., in the alley, was the first all-vegetarian Indian restaurant in Montana, serving samosas, its own "curritos," and delicious chai tea. (☎542-0622. Lunch buffet $8. Open M-F 11am-9pm, F-Sa 11am-9:30pm.) **Taco del Sol ❶**, 422 N. Higgins Ave., is the place for cheap eats; get $2.45 fish tacos or a hefty 14 in. Mission Burrito for $4.50. (☎327-8929. Wi-Fi. Open M-Sa 11am-9pm, Su noon-9pm. Cash only.) With wild salmon burritos ($6) and eclectic pizzas, **The Bridge Pizza ❶**, 600 S. Higgins Ave., is more than just a pizza joint. (☎542-0002; www.bridgepizza.com. Cheese slice $2.50. 12 in. pie $9-14, 16 in. $14-20. Open M-Th and Su 11am-10:30pm, F-Sa 11am-11pm. AmEx/MC/V.)

🎭📷 **SIGHTS AND ENTERTAINMENT.** Missoula's hottest sight is the **Aerial Fire Depot and Smokejumper Center,** 5756 W. Broadway, just past the airport, 7 mi. west of town. It's the nation's largest training base for smokejumpers—aerial firefighters who parachute into remote forests and serve as an initial attack against wildfires. Displays and videos recount their heroism and prodigious skill. (☎329-4934. Open May-Sept. daily 8:30am-5pm. 45min.-1hr. tours daily 10, 11am, 2, 3, 4pm. Free; donations accepted.) The **Carousel,** 101 Carousel Dr., in Caras Riverfront Park, was hand carved by local volunteer craftsmen. (☎549-8382. Open daily June-Aug. 11am-7pm; Sept.-May 11am-5:30pm. $1.50, seniors and under 16 $0.50, disabled free.) Wondering what comes out at night in Montana? Learn about nocturnal animals and astronomy, as well as how naturalists do their job, at the **Montana Natural History Center,** 120 Hickory St. Call ahead for their Saturday discovery day events. (☎327-0405; www.montananaturalist.org. Open Tu-F noon-5pm, Sa hours vary. $1, ages 4-12 $0.50.)

Out to Lunch, also in Caras Riverfront Park, offers free performances in the summer months, along with plenty of food vendors; call the Missoula Downtown Association for more information on the annual event. (☎543-4238; www.missouladowntown.com. June-Aug. W 11am-1:30pm.) If you miss "Out to Lunch," the food vendors return on Thursday nights for **Downtown Tonight,** which features live music, food, and a beer garden. (☎543-4238. June-Sept. Th 5:30-8:30pm.) Free concerts are also available on Wednesday nights courtesy of **Bonner Park Concerts,** in Bonner Park. (☎728-2400, ext. 7041. Late June-early Aug. W 8pm.) Stock up on fresh local produce, flowers, and breads at the **farmers' market** in Circle Sq. (☎543-4238. Open mid-May to mid-Oct. Sa 8:30am-noon.) The **Clark Fork River Market** adds local meat and dairy products to the Saturday morning mix near the Millennium building by Caras Park. (☎396-2954. Open mid-May to mid-Oct. Sa 8am-1pm and June-Aug. Th 5:30-7:30pm.) The **Western Montana Fair and Rodeo,** held in August, has live music by big country-western names like Brad Paisley and Chris LeDoux, plus a carnival, concession booths, a demolition derby, and a rodeo. (☎258-3280; www.westernmontanafair.com. Open 10am-10pm.)

🍸 **NIGHTLIFE.** College students swarm Missoula's downtown bar area (namely around Front St. and Higgins Ave.) throughout the school year. **The Iron Horse Brew Pub,** 501 N. Higgins Ave., always packs in a crowd on its large patios and is popular with fraternity types. (☎728-8866. Drafts $3.50. Open daily 11am-2am.) Follow the advice of the "beer coaches" at **The Kettle House Brewing Co.,** 602 Myrtle, one block west of Higgins between 4th and 5th, and "support your local brewery." The Kettle House serves a delectable assortment of beers, including unusual hemp beer called Bongwater Stout. (☎728-1660. Open M-Sa noon-9pm; no beer served after 8pm. 2 free samples; $3.50 per additional pint.) **Charlie B's,** 420 N. Higgins Ave., draws bikers, farmers, students, and hippies alike. Framed photos of longtime regulars cover the walls. (☎549-3589. Drafts $2.25. Well drinks $2.75. Open daily 8am-2am.) Something's always going on at the beautiful **Badlander,** just south of Broadway on Ryman, from free fried chicken on Mondays to live music Friday and Saturday nights. (Drafts $2.50. Mixed drinks $3. Open M-Tu 3pm-2am, W-Su 6pm-

GO NUTS!

Have you ever spied "Rocky Mountain oysters" on your menu? Hopefully, your waiter explained that the tender morsels you were about to order were not the mollusks you may have expected.

"Rocky Mountain oysters," "prairie oysters," "Montana tendergroin," and "cowboy caviar" are all names given to testicles, usually from a bull, but sometimes harvested from buffalo, boar, sheep, or calves. These western delicacies are most often served sliced and deep fried and are sometimes eaten dipped in hot sauce. Truly an acquired taste, trying some Montana tendergroin makes for a memorable Wild West experience.

Some go much further than trying once. Clinton, MT, has hosted the famous "Testicle Festival" for 25 years running. Each year, the festival draws more than 15,000 enthusiasts, who eat over 2.5 tons of the special oysters.

Fancy a taste, but prefer your genitals home-cooked? Visit www.funlinked.com/testicle, a comprehensive edible testicle website that offers over 100 recipes to help the adventurous chef serve Rocky Mountain oysters at home. Your next dinner party could give a whole new meaning to the phrase "have a ball."

Clinton, MT, is located 22 miles east of Missoula, and the Testicle Festival takes place in early August. Mosey on over to www.testyfesty.com for more information.

2am.) The *Independent* and *Lively Times*, free at newsstands and cafes, have the lowdown on Missoula's music scene. The "Entertainer" section in the Friday *Missoulian* has event schedules.

◪ OUTDOOR ACTIVITIES. Soak your weary feet at the **Lolo Hot Springs**, 35 mi. southwest of Missoula on Hwy 12. The 103-105°F springs were an ancient meeting place for local Native Americans and were visited by Lewis and Clark in 1805. (☎273-2290 or 800-273-2290; www.lolohotsprings.com. Open daily June-Sept. 10am-10pm; Oct.-May 10am-8pm. $7, ages 4-12 $5.) Farther along Rte. 12 into Idaho over the difficult Lolo Pass are two free, clothing-optional natural hot springs, **Warm Springs,** known locally as **Jerry Johnson** (35 mi. from Lolo Hot Springs at the Warm Springs Trailhead, 1½ mi. hike in), and **Weir** (45 mi. from Lolo, just pat Mocus Point Trailhead, ½mi. hike in). Indulge your sense of history at **Garnet Ghost Town,** Montana's most intact ghost town. The town is well-preserved, but not commercialized. During mining's heyday at the turn of the century, the population reached several thousand. Today it is an eerie reminder of the transience of civilization. (Info ☎329-3914. Take I-90 to Exit 109; follow Hwy. 200 to Mile 22, and turn right on Garnet Range Rd., mostly dirt and 25 mph, for 11 mi. Open to most vehicular traffic mid-May to Sept.; Jan.-Apr. snowmobiles and cross-country skis only. $3, under 16 free.)

Parks, recreation areas, and nearby wilderness areas make Missoula an outdoor enthusiast's dream gateway city. The bicycle-friendly city is located along both the Trans-America and Great Parks bicycle routes, and all major streets in town have designated bike lanes. **Open Road Bicycles and Nordic Equipment,** 517 S. Orange St., has bike rentals. (☎549-2453. Front suspension $4 per hr., $20 per day; full suspension $10/40. Open M-F 9am-6pm, Sa 10am-5pm, Su 11am-3pm.) **Adventure Cycling,** 150 E. Pine St., is the place to go for information about the Trans-America and Great Parks routes. (☎721-1776 or 800-755-2453; www.adventurecycling.org. Open M-F 8am-5pm.) The **Rattlesnake Wilderness National Recreation Area,** named after the shape of the river (there are no rattlers for miles), 11 mi. northeast of town off Exit 104 on I-90, and the **Pattee Canyon Recreation Area,** 3½ mi. east of Higgins on Pattee Canyon Dr., have excellent biking trails. Contact the **Missoula Ranger District,** Building 24 at Fort Missoula, for trail info. Take Ft. Missoula Rd. from Reserve St. and make a left at the stop sign. (☎329-3750. Open M-F 7:30am-4pm.) **Missoulians on Bicycle** (www.missoulabike.org) hosts rides and events for cyclists in a fun collegiate atmosphere.

Alpine and Nordic skiing keep Missoulians busy during winter. To indulge the Nordic craving, **Pattee Canyon Recreation Area** has groomed trails close to town. Experienced skiers should check out the **Montana Snowbowl**, 12 mi. northwest of Missoula, with a vertical drop of 2600 ft., powdered bowls, and over 35 trails. Take the Reserve St. Exit off I-90 and follow Grant Creek Rd.; turn left onto Snowbowl Rd. (☎ 549-9777 or 800-728-2695; www.montanasnowbowl.com. Open late Nov.-early Apr. daily 9:30am-4pm. $35 per day, seniors and students $32, ages 6-12 $15.)

Floating on rafts or inner tubes is a favorite local activity. The **Blackfoot River,** along Rte. 200 east of Bonner, makes a good afternoon float; take I-90 to Exit 109. Call the **Montana State Regional Parks and Wildlife Office,** 3201 Spurgin Rd., for more information about rafting locations. (☎ 542-5500. Open M-F 8am-5pm.) You can rent tubes or rafts from the **Army and Navy Economy Store,** 322 N. Higgins. (☎ 721-1315. Tubes $4 per day, $20 deposit required. Rafts $50 per day, credit card deposit required. Open M-F 9am-7:30pm, Sa 9am-5:30pm, Su 10am-5:30pm.)

Hiking opportunities abound in the Missoula area. The relatively easy 30min. hike to the "M" (for the U of M, not Missoula) on Mount Sentinel has a tremendous view of Missoula and the surrounding peaks; continue another mile to the top of the mountain (elevation gain 620 ft.). The **Rattlesnake Wilderness National Recreation Area** makes for a great day of hiking; follow Van Buren St. and then Rattlesnake Dr. 4 mi. north from Missoula to the area entrance. Other popular areas include **Pattee Canyon** and **Blue Mountain,** south of town; for Blue Mountain, travel 2 mi. southwest on U.S. 93 and turn right on Blue Mountain Rd. For maps ($6) and hiking info, try the Missoula Ranger District (see above). For equipment, stop by **The Trail Head,** 221 E. Front St. (☎ 543-6966. Open M-F 9:30am-8pm, Sa 9am-6pm, Su 11am-6pm. Tents $10-14 per day. Backpacks $9 per day. Sleeping bags $7 per day.)

Missoula is at the heart of Western Montana's **fly-fishing** country. The Bitterroot River is the place to catch brown trout, while the Blackfoot River is known for its bull trout. **Fishing licenses** are required and can be purchased from the **Department of Fish, Wildlife, and Parks,** 3201 Spurgin Rd., or from local sporting goods stores. (☎ 542-5500. One-time conservation fee $10. 2-day non-resident license $15, 10-day non-resident license $44.) **Kingfisher,** 926 E. Broadway, offers licenses and guided fishing trips. They also publish free fishing reports daily mid-Mar. to mid-Oct. on their website. (☎ 721-6141 or 888-542-4911; www.kingfisherflyshop.com. Open daily June-Aug. 7am-6pm; Sept.-May 9am-5pm. Reservations recommended. 2-person full-day guided trip with flies, reels, and rods $395.)

FROM MISSOULA TO GLACIER

Beneath the towering peaks of Mission Mountain Range, **St. Ignatius Mission,** in St. Ignatius, is home to the first Jesuit mission in the Northwest, built in 1854 by missionaries and Native Americans. The original log dormitories are still intact, as is the church built in 1891. Inside, 58 bold murals by Joseph Carignano depict St. Ignatius Loyola, the mission's namesake. (☎ 745-2768. Open daily in summer 9am-8pm; in winter 9am-5pm. Free.) **RimRock Stages** (☎ 745-3501) buses stop half a mile away in St. Ignatius, on Blaine St. The **National Bison Range** was established in 1908 in an effort to save the dwindling bison population from extinction. At one time 30-70 million of the creatures roamed the plains, but the population dropped to less than 1000 due to over-hunting. The 19,000-acre range is home to 350-500 bison as well as bighorn sheep, deer, elk, and mountain goats. (☎ 644-2211; www.fws.gov/bisonrange.com.) The 2hr. **Red Sleep Mountain** self-guided tour is a 19 mi. drive on steep gravel roads and offers a spectacular view of the Flathead Valley and glimpses of wildlife, though binoculars are helpful. The annual October roundup is not to be missed. To access the range from Missoula, take U.S. 93 north for 40 mi., then drive 5 mi. west on Rte. 200, and 5 mi. north on Rte. 212. (☎ 644-2211. Visitors

Center open M-F 8am-4:30pm. Red Sleep Mountain drive open mid-May to mid-Oct. daily 7am-7pm. $4 per vehicle.) With displays of old posters, uniforms, vintage cars, and motorcycles, the ▧**Miracle of America Museum,** on Memory Ln., the frontage road to U.S. 93 (follow the signs), at the southern end of Polson, houses one of the country's greatest collections of Americana. A general store, saddlery, barber shop, soda fountain, and gas station sit among the memorabilia. (☎883-6804. Open June-Sept. daily 8am-8pm; Oct.-May M-Sa 8am-5pm, Su 2-6pm. $4, ages 3-12 $1.) Fresh fruit and fish stands line **Flathead Lake,** on U.S. 93, between Polson and Kalispell, the largest natural lake west of the Mississippi.

WATERTON-GLACIER PEACE PARK

Waterton-Glacier transcends international boundaries to encompass one of the most strikingly beautiful portions of the Rockies. The massive Rocky Mountain peaks span both parks, providing sanctuary for many threatened bears, bighorn sheep, moose, mountain goats, and gray wolves. Perched high in the northern Rockies, Glacier is sometimes called the "Crown of the Continent," and the high alpine lakes and glaciers shine like jewels.

▨ PRACTICAL INFORMATION

Technically one park, Waterton-Glacier is actually two distinct areas: the small **Waterton Lakes National Park** in Alberta, and the enormous **Glacier National Park** in Montana. There are several **border crossings** nearby: **Piegan/Carway,** at U.S. 89 (open daily 7am-11pm); **Roosville,** on U.S. 93 (open 24hr.); and **Chief Mountain,** at Rte. 17 (open daily June-Aug. 7am-10pm; mid- to late May and Sept. 9am-6pm). The fastest way to Waterton is to head north along the east side of Glacier, entering Canada through Chief Mountain. Since snow can be unpredictable, the parks are usually in full operation only from late May to early September—check conditions in advance. The *Waterton-Glacier Visitor Guide,* provided at any park entrance, has dates and times of trail, campground, and border crossing openings. To find out which park areas, hotels, and campsites will be open when you visit, contact the **Park Headquarters,** Waterton Lakes National Park, Box 200, Waterton Park, AB T0K 2M0 (☎403-859-5133), or **Glacier National Park,** West Glacier, MT 59936 (☎406-888-7800). Mace and firewood are not allowed into Canada, and bear spray must carry an EPA certification number, which you must declare at customs.

GLACIER NATIONAL PARK ☎406

▤ TRANSPORTATION

Amtrak (☎226-4452; www.amtrak.com) **trains** trace a route along the southern edge of the park. The station in West Glacier is staffed mid-May to September, but the train still stops there in the winter. Trains chug daily to: East Glacier (1½hr., $13-17); Seattle (15hr., $82-107); Spokane (6hr., $42-54); Whitefish, MT (30min., $5-7). Amtrak also runs from East Glacier to Chicago (30hr., $182-307). A car is the most convenient mode of transport, particularly within the park. Glacier Park, Inc.'s (☎892-2525; www.glacierparkinc.com) historic red jammer **buses** run tours on Going-to-the-Sun Rd. (3hr. tours $35, 6½hr. tours $45; children $17.50/22.50.) Sun Tours offers tours from West Glacier, East Glacier, and St. Mary. (☎226-9220 or 800-786-9220; www.glaciersuntours.com. All-day tour from East Glacier $55, from St. Mary $40.) A new, **free shuttle system** whisks hikers and sightseers alike along Going-to-the-Sun Rd. to reduce traffic delays; schedules are available at Visitors Centers and in the *Waterton-Glacier Visitor Guide*.

▟ ORIENTATION

There are few roads in Glacier, and the locals like it that way. Glacier's main thoroughfare is the stunning **Going-to-the-Sun Road,** which connects the two primary points of entry, West Glacier and St. Mary. In July, 2007, the Park Service embarked on an eight-ten year project to rehabilitate Going-to-the-Sun Rd.; Visitor Centers have up-to-date information on delays. **U.S. 2** skirts the southern border of the park and is the fastest route from Browning and East Glacier to West Glacier. At the "Goat Lick," about halfway between East and West Glacier, mountain goats traverse steep cliffs to lap up the natural salt deposits. **Route 89** heads north along the eastern edge of the park past St. Mary. Those interested in visiting the northwestern section of the park can either take the unpaved **Outside North Fork Road** and enter through Polebridge or brave the rough, pothole-ridden **Inside North Fork Road,** which takes an hour longer. While most of Glacier is primitive backcountry, a number of villages provide lodging, gas, and food: St. Mary, Many Glacier, and Two Medicine in the east; West Glacier, Apgar, and Polebridge in the west.

▟ PRACTICAL INFORMATION

The park's **entrance fee** is $25 per car per week, $12 per pedestrian or cyclist, and $35 for yearly passes. Each of the three **Visitors Centers** gives good advice on campsites, day-hikes, weather, flora, and fauna. The largest, **Saint Mary,** guards the east entrance of the park. (☎ 732-7751. Open daily late June-early Sept. 7am-9pm; late May to mid-June and early Sept. 7am-5pm; mid-to-late May and late Sept. 8am-5pm.) **Apgar** is located at the west entrance. (☎ 888-7940. Open daily late June-Aug. 8am-7pm; May-June 9am-5pm; Sept. 8am-5pm.) The third graces **Logan Pass,** on the Going-to-the-Sun Rd. (Open daily July-Aug. 9am-7pm; Sept. 9am-4:30pm; June 9:30am-4:30pm, weather permitting.) The **Many Glacier** ranger station can also answer questions. (☎ 732-7740. Open daily late May to mid-Sept. 7am-4:30pm.)

Visitors planning overnight trips must obtain the necessary **backcountry permit.** With the exception of the **Nyack/Coal Creek** camping zone, all backcountry camping must be at designated campsites equipped with pit toilets, tent sites, food preparation areas, and food hanging devices. (June-Oct. camping $5 per person per night, ages 8-15 $3; Nov.-May free. For an additional $30, reservations are accepted beginning in mid-Apr. for trips between June 15 and Oct. 31.) Reservations can be made in person at the Backcountry Permit Center at Apgar, St. Mary Visitors Center, Many Glacier Ranger Station, and Polebridge Ranger Station, or by writing to Backcountry Reservation Office, Glacier National Park, West Glacier, MT 59936. Pick up a free *Backcountry Guide* from Visitors Centers or the **Backcountry Permit Center,** next to the Visitors Center in Apgar, which also has valuable info for those seeking to explore Glacier's less-traveled areas. (☎ 888-7859; www.nps.gov/glac/planyourvisit/backcountry.htm. Open daily July 7am-5pm; May-June and Sept. 8am-4pm.) **Medical Services: Kalispell Regional Medical Center,** 310 Sunny View Ln. (☎ 752-5111), north of Kalispell off Rte. 93. **North Valley Hospital,** 6575 Hwy. 93, (☎ 863-3500), in Whitefish. **Post Office:** 110 Going-to-the-Sun Rd., in West Glacier. (☎ 888-5591. Open M-F 8:30am-12:30pm and 1:30-4:45pm.) **Postal Code:** 59936.

▛ ACCOMMODATIONS

Staying indoors within Glacier National Park is expensive, but several affordable options lie just outside the park boundaries. On the west side of the park, the

> **TIP**
>
> **FANCY A FORAY OVER THE BORDER?** Canada's **Waterton Lakes National Park,** Glacier's baby cousin in Alberta, is a outdoorsman's dream come true. Waterton features spectacular scenery and activities—without the crowds that plague Glacier during summer months. Remember: traveling between the US and Canada is generally an easy process, but security is still taken very seriously. To keep things moving, make sure to have all necessary documents handy (p. 12). It is illegal to cross the border anywhere except an open crossing station. The **Waterton Lakes Visitors Center,** 5 mi. inside the park on Rte. 5, has a schedule of events and info about Waterton and the surrounding region. (☎859-5133. Open daily mid-May to Oct. 8am-7pm.)

small, electricity-less town of ■**Polebridge** provides access to Glacier's remote and pristine northwest corner. It is by far the best place in the area to see the park's two resident wolf camps. To get there from Apgar, take Camas Rd. north, then take a right onto the poorly-marked gravel Outside North Fork Rd., just past a bridge over the North Fork of the Flathead River. (Avoid Inside North Fork Rd.— your car's shocks will thank you.) From Columbia Falls, take Rte. 486 N. To the east, inexpensive lodging is found just across the park border in **East Glacier. Glacier Park, Inc.** (☎892-2525; www.glacierparkinc.com) handles reservations for most in-park lodging.

■ **North Fork Hostel,** 80 Beaver Dr. (☎888-5241; www.nfhostel.com), in Polebridge; follow the signs through town. Wooden walls and kerosene lamps are reminiscent of a hunting retreat. During the winter, wood-burning stoves warm frozen fingers after skiing or snowshoeing, and thick quilts keep guests warm at night. Hot showers and fully-equipped kitchen, but no flush toilets. Call ahead for pickup from the West Glacier Amtrak station ($40 in summer). Canoes $20 per day. Mountain bikes $10 per day. Snowshoes $5 per day. Nordic skis $5 per day. Showers $5 for non-guests. Linen $5. Check-in before 10pm. Check-out noon. Call ahead, especially in winter. Dorms $15, after 2 nights $12; tipis $30; cabins $35; log homes $75. MC/V. ❶

Brownies Grocery (HI), 1020 Rte. 49 (☎226-4426), in East Glacier Park. Reception is in the grocery store; the hostel is on the 2nd fl. Kitchen, laundry, linen, showers, and a stunning view. Internet access $1.75 per 15min. Key deposit $5. Check-in by 9pm; late arrivals call ahead. Check-out 10am. Reservations recommended; credit card required. Open mid-May to Sept., weather permitting. Tent sites $10. Dorms $16, members $13; singles $23/20; doubles $31/28; room for 4-6 $43/40. Extra bed $5. MC/V. ❶

Backpacker's Inn Hostel, 29 Dawson Ave. (☎226-9392), just east of the East Glacier Amtrak station and behind Serrano's Mexican Restaurant. 8 clean but narrow beds. Hot showers. Sleeping bags $1. Check-in by 10pm at Serrano's. Open May-Sept. Dorms $12; single with queen-sized bed and full linen $25; double $35. ❶

Swiftcurrent Motor Inn (☎732-5531, reservations 892-2525), 6 mi. from the entrance station in Many Glacier Valley. One of a few budget motels in the area. Open early June-early Sept. 1-bedroom cabins $50; 2-bedroom cabins $60, with private bath $75. ❸

⚑ CAMPING

The Park Service runs 14 **campgrounds** ❶ in the park. All three Visitors Centers have updates on availability, though Logan Pass lags in accuracy due to a lack of electricity. The most popular campground on the east side is **Many Glacier,** whose amazing views cause it to fill by early afternoon; the 25 intimate sites at **Sprague Creek** are favorites on the west side. (Sites in both $20.) **Avalanche Creek,** conveniently located on the Going-to-the-Sun Rd., and **Two Medicine,** a more secluded campground in the eastern section of the park, have very pleasant sites and prime hiking access. (Sites in both $20.) The only reservable sites are at **Fish Creek** and **St. Mary,** two of Glacier's largest campgrounds. (Reservations ☎800-365-2267; www.recreation.org. Sites $23.)

FOOD

Polebridge Mercantile Store (☎888-5105), on Polebridge Loop Rd., ¼ mi. east of N. Fork Rd. Has homemade pastries ($1-3) as splendid as the surrounding peaks. The huckleberry bearclaws are local favorites and often sell out. Gas, gifts, and groceries. Open daily June-Sept. 8am-9pm; Oct.-May 8am-6pm. MC/V. ❶

Northern Lights Saloon (☎888-5669), next to Polebridge. On Friday nights, locals and visitors flock to this friendly saloon for pizza ($11) and volleyball. On other nights, it goes gourmet with a menu that changes daily. The Montana-brewed pints ($4) are tastier sipped out of mason jars atop a tree-trunk bar stool. Entrees $8-15. F-Su live music. Open daily June-Sept. noon-3pm and 4-9pm. Bar open until midnight. Cash only. ❷

Two Sisters Cafe (☎732-5535; www.twosistersrestaurant.com), 4 mi. north of St. Mary on Hwy. 89, near Babb. Locals rave about the sandwiches served with homemade potato chips ($7-10) at this personality-laden cafe. Try the St. Mary Lake whitefish ($22), caught and processed locally. Open in summer daily 7:30am-10pm. MC/V. ❸

Whistle Stop Restaurant (☎226-9292), in East Glacier next to Brownies Grocery. Sample homemade delicacies at this restaurant best known for unbelievable deep-fried, huckleberry-injected french toast ($6.25) and tart huckleberry pie ($3.50). Breakfast served until 11:30am. Open daily mid-May to mid-Sept. 7am-9pm. ❷

HIKING

Most of Glacier's spectacular scenery lies off the main roads and is accessible only by foot, though horses are also allowed on some trails. An extensive trail system has something for everyone, from short, easy day-hikes to rigorous backcountry expeditions. Stop by one of the Visitors Centers for maps with day-hikes. Beware of bears and mountain lions; ask the rangers about wildlife activity and specific safety precautions in the area in which you plan to hike.

Avalanche Lake (4 mi. round-trip, 3hr.) is a breathtaking trail and by far the most popular day-hike in the park. Starting north of Lake McDonald on Going-to-the-Sun Rd., this moderate hike climbs 500 ft. to picture-perfect panoramas.

Trail of the Cedars (¾ mi. loop, 20min.) begins at the same trailhead as Avalanche Lake and is an easy nature walk through the easternmost edge of the Pacific Rainforest. It also has a shorter, wheelchair-accessible section.

Numa Ridge Lookout (12 mi. round-trip, 9hr.) starts from the Bowman Lake Campground, northeast of Polebridge. After climbing 2930 ft., this challenging hike ends with sweeping vistas of Glacier's rugged northwest corner.

Grinnell Glacier Trail (11 mi. round-trip, 7hr.) passes within close proximity of several glaciers and follows along Grinnell Point and Mt. Grinnell, gaining a steady and moderate 1600 ft. Trailhead at the Many Glacier Picnic Area.

OUTDOOR ACTIVITIES

BIKING AND HORSEBACK RIDING

Opportunities for bicycling are limited and confined to designated bike paths; cycling on trails is prohibited. Although Going-to-the-Sun Rd. is a popular bike

ROCKY MOUNTAINS

route, only experienced cyclists with titanium legs should attempt this grueling ride; the sometimes nonexistent shoulder of the road can create hazardous situations. From mid-June to Labor Day, bike traffic is prohibited 11am-4pm from the Apgar campground to Sprague Creek and eastbound (uphill) from Logan Creek to Logan Pass. The Inside North Fork Rd., which runs from Kintla Lake to Fish Creek on the west side of the park, is good for mountain biking, as are the old logging roads in the Flathead National Forest. Ask at a Visitors Center for info. **Glacier Cyclery** (☎ 862-6446; www.glaciercyclery.com), based in Whitefish, leads exciting "full moon" rides. Equestrians should check to make sure trails are open. Trail rides from **Swan Mountain Outfitters** (open May-early Sept.; $54 per 2hr., $80 per ½-day) are available at Many Glacier (☎ 732-4203) and Lake McDonald (☎ 888-5121).

BOATING AND FISHING

The **Glacier Park Boat Co.** (www.glacierparkboats.com) provides **boat tours** that explore all of Glacier's large lakes and peaks. Tours leave from: **Lake McDonald** (☎ 888-5727; 1hr., 5 per day, $20); **Many Glacier** (☎ 732-4480; 1¼hr., 7 per day, $20); **Rising Sun**, at St. Mary Lake (☎ 732-4430; 1-1½hr., 5 per day, $20); **Two Medicine** (☎ 226-4467; 45min., 5 per day, $20). Children ages 4-12 ride for ½-price. The tours from Two Medicine, Rising Sun, and Many Glacier provide access to Glacier's backcountry. You can rent rowboats ($12.50 per hr.) at Lake McDonald, Many Glacier, Two Medicine, and Apgar; canoes ($12.50 per hr.) at Many Glacier, Two Medicine, and Apgar; kayaks ($12.50 per hr.) at Apgar, Two Medicine, and Many Glacier; and outboards ($17 per hr.) at Lake McDonald and Two Medicine. **Glacier Raft Co.**, in West Glacier, leads trips down the middle fork of the Flathead River. (☎ 888-5454 or 800-235-6781; www.glacierraft.co.com. ½-day $44, under 13 $34; full-day trip with lunch $76/53.) The only permit required to fish in the park is the Montana state permit. Limits are generally high, but some areas are restricted, and certain species may be catch-and-release. Pick up *Fishing Regulations*, available at Visitors Centers. Lake Ellen Wilson, Gunsight Lake, and Elizabeth Lake are good places to sink a line. On Blackfeet tribal land, a special permit is needed.

IDAHO

The Rocky Mountains divide the state of Idaho into three distinct regions, each with its own natural aesthetic. Northern Idaho possesses the greatest concentration of lakes in the western US, interspersed with lush, green valleys and rugged mountain peaks. In central Idaho, ski slopes, hiking trails, and hot springs span across the semi-arid landscape. To the southeast, world-famous potatoes are cultivated in valleys rich with volcanic sediment. Averaging just over 15 people per sq. mi., much of the state is virtually untouched wilderness and national forest, making Idaho a mecca for outdoors enthusiasts. Idaho's towns and cities are also worth exploring and the mountain outposts have an appeal all their own.

▓ PRACTICAL INFORMATION

Capital: Boise.

Visitor Info: Idaho Department of Commerce, 700 W. State St., P.O. Box 83720, Boise 83720 (☎ 208-334-2470 or 800-842-5858; http://cl.idaho.gov or www.visitid.org). **State Parks and Recreation Dept.,** 5657 Warm Springs Ave., Boise 83720 (☎ 208-334-4199; www.idahoparks.org). Open M-F 8am-5pm. **Idaho Outfitters and Guide Association,** P.O. Box 95, Boise 83702 (☎ 800-494-3246; www.ioga.org).

Postal Abbreviation: ID. **Sales Tax:** 6%.

BOISE ☎208

Built along the banks of the Boise River, Idaho's remarkably cosmopolitan capital straddles the boundary between desert and mountains. A network of parks protects the natural landscape of the river banks, creating a greenbelt perfect for walking, biking, or in-line skating. Most of the city's sights cluster in the 10-block grid between the capitol and the river, making it easy to get around downtown.

ORIENTATION AND PRACTICAL INFORMATION. The **Grove** is Boise's pedestrian-friendly town plaza, and its brick walkway extends along 8th St. between Main and Front St., the two main downtown thoroughfares. Front St. becomes I-184, sometimes called the Downtown Connector, at its west end. People refer to the shopping, restaurant, and theater district bounded by **8th, Capitol, Front, 9th,** and **Myrtle Streets** as **BoDo.** One-way streets and limited street-side parking can make driving in the downtown area a chore, but public garages are abundant and affordable, and most of the city's hot spots are in walking distance from one another. Greyhound, 1212 W. Bannock St., a few blocks west of downtown, runs **buses** to Portland (11hr., 2 per day, $55), Salt Lake City (7hr., 2 per day, $57), and Seattle (14hr., 3 per day, $53) daily. (☎343-3681; www.greyhound.com. Open M-F 6am-11:30pm, Sa-Su 6am-1pm and 5-11pm.) Valley Ride has several routes through the city. (☎345-7433; www.valleyride.org. Buses operate M-F 5:15am-7:40pm, Sa 7:45am-6:45pm. $1, children $0.65, disabled and seniors $0.50. Maps available at the Visitors Center.) **McU Sports,** 822 W. Jefferson St., rents outdoor gear and offers hiking tips. (☎342-7734. Mountain bikes $15 per half-day, $25 per day. Open M-Sa 9:30am-6pm, Su 11am-5pm.) McU also has a ski shop, 2314 Bogus Basin Rd., at Bogus Basin, Boise's local ski area. (☎336-2300. Ski rental $17, children $15.) The **Visitors Center on the Grove** is at 850 W. Front. (☎344-5338; www.boise.org. Open M-F 10am-4pm.) **Internet Access: Boise Public Library,** 715 S. Capitol Blvd., across the main entrance to the Julia Davis Park. (☎384-4076. Open M-Th 10am-9pm, F 10am-6pm, Sa 10am-5pm; Sept.-May also Su noon-5pm.) **Post Office:** 750 W. Bannock St. (☎331-0037. Open M-F 8:30am-5pm.) **Postal Code:** 83702.

ACCOMMODATIONS. Budget chain motels are concentrated around Exit 53 off I-84, near the airport. For those willing to drive 20min. to the nearby town of Nampa, ◪**Hostel Boise ❶,** 17322 Can-Ada Rd., is a spectacular, inexpensive, well-kept option with mountain views, evening campfires, and a friendly staff. Take Exit 38 off I-84 W and turn right onto Garrity Blvd., which turns into Can-Ada Rd. (☎467-6858. Airport pickup or drop-off $10. Computer access and Wi-Fi included. 3-night max. stay. Check-in 5-10:30pm. Dorms $19; private room $31-35, $5 per additional person. Campsites $10. MC/V.) ◪**Bond Street Motel Apartments ❷,** 1680 N. Phillippi St., right off Fairview Ave. between Curtis and Orchard and a few minutes from the center of Boise, rents beautiful, furnished studios and one-bedroom apartments with full kitchens and Wi-Fi. From I-184 take the Curtis St. Exit, then turn right on Fairview Ave. (☎322-4407 or 800-545-5345; www.bendmotel.com. Office open M-F 8am-5pm. Studio $59; 1-bed room $55. Call for lower weekly rates. Reservations recommended. AmEx/D/MC/V.) The **Boise National Forest/Bureau of Land Management Office,** 1387 S. Vinnell Way, near Exit 50a from I-84, provides info on RV-oriented **campgrounds ❶** and the campgrounds in the National Forest land surrounding Boise, which usually cost $10-12 per night. **Schaffer Butte,** on S. Harrison Blvd. near Bogus Basin, is a short drive from town with nearby hiking trailhead access. (☎373-4007. Open M-F 7:45am-4:15pm.)

⚡📶 FOOD AND NIGHTLIFE. Boise offers much more than spuds for hungry travelers. **BoDo,** Boise's downtown district, centered around 8th and Main St., bustles with lunchtime delis, coffeeshops, ethnic cuisine, and several stylish bistros. ◼**Moon's Kitchen ❶,** 815 W. Bannock St., a vintage diner open since 1955, has blended malts ($4.50) and heaping chili burgers. (☎385-0472. Breakfast $4.50-7. Burgers $6.75-8.50. Open M-F 7:30am-7:30pm, Sa 8am-7:30pm, Su 9am-2pm. AmEx/MC/V.) Locals throng to ◼**Zeppole Baking Company ❶,** 217 N. 8th St., to enjoy gourmet sandwiches and fresh-baked bread at a steal. (☎345-2149. Lunch combos $4-5. Wi-Fi available. Open M-Sa 7am-5pm, Su 8am-4pm. Cash only.) For dinner and a movie, and for the health-minded traveler, **Satchel's Grill ❷,** 705 W. Bannock St., offers creative sandwiches, salads, and breakfast options adaptable to the gamut of dietary demands. Offers a side of movies projected from the patio at sundown (W-Sa around 9:30pm), or live music (W 6pm, Sa-Su brunch). Check online for movie and music schedule. (☎344-3742; www.satchelsgrill.com. Sa-Su breakfast sandwiches and egg scrambles $4-7. Daily lunch and dinner menu $4-$7. Open M-Tu 11am-3pm, W-F 11am-midnight, Sa 9am-midnight, Su 9am-3pm. AmEx/D/MC/V.) **Gernika Basque Pub & Eatery ❷,** 202 S. Capitol Blvd., is the place to experience a taste of Basque, a region in the Pyrenees of Spain. Order *croquetas* with a lamb or chorizo sandwich, and finish off with rice pudding. (☎344-2175. Sandwiches $6-8. Open M 11am-11pm, Tu-Th 11am-midnight, F-Sa 11am-1am. AmEx/D/MC/V.)

The heart of Boise's vibrant nightlife pulses at 6th and Main St., where a wide assortment of bars and clubs offers an atmosphere and a drink special for all crowds. For a more relaxed atmosphere and a stiff pour at a classic local hangout, visit the historic ◼**Pengilly's Saloon,** 513 W. Main St., recently named one of best bars in the US by *Esquire* magazine. (☎345-6344. M open mic night, W-Sa live music. No cover. Happy hour M-F 4-7pm; 2-for-1 drafts and well drinks. Open daily 3pm-2am.) Upstairs at **The Balcony Club,** 150 N. 8th St., #226, one block from the Grove, DJs spin nightly at the club consistently voted "Boise's best place to dance" for nearly a decade. All kinds of people gather at this gay-friendly bar to dance, relax on the outdoor terrace, and play pool. (☎336-1313. Cover F-Sa $3. Open M-F 4pm-2am, Sa-Su 2pm-2am.) Hoards of college students flock to the **Main Street Bistro,** 609 Main St., for weekly flip-cup tournaments on Tuesdays and Thursdays. "Lake Bum" Wednesdays (when men wear boardshorts and women wear bikini tops) appeal to a yupster crowd. (☎345-9515. No cover. Happy hour W and F-Sa 8-10pm; "you call it" well drinks and drafts $2, pitchers $5. Open daily 8pm-2am.) On the corner of 6th and Main St., the dance club **China Blue** throbs with hip-hop and Latin beats on weekends. Rub elbows with the hip Boise twentysomethings and big-names who happen to be in town. (☎338-6604. Club dress required. Happy hour 9-11pm; drafts $2, "you call it" well drinks $3. Open F-Sa 8pm-2am.)

◼ SIGHTS. A great starting point for exploring Boise is **Julia Davis Park** (☎384-4240; open daily sunrise to sunset), which spans between Boise State University and BoDo, Myrtle St. and Capitol Blvd. Along the paved bike paths that line the perimeter of the park and its stunning central rose garden, find paddleboating, a bandshell featuring free summer entertainment, a zoo, and several of Boise's most popular museums. The **Boise Tour Train and River Float,** which covers about 75 city sights in 1¼hr., starts and ends in the park. Train tours can be followed by relaxing raft floats down the Boise River, with guides focusing on wildlife and plant lore. (☎342-4796. Tours May and Oct. Sa-Su 1, 2:30pm; late May-early Sept. M-Sa 10, 11:15am, 12:30, 1:45, 3pm; Su noon, 1:15, 2:30, 3:45pm; Sept. W-Su noon, 1:30, 3pm. $9, over 65 $8.50, ages 3-12 $6; floats extra.) Learn about Idaho and the Old West at the **Idaho Historical Museum,** 610 Julia Davis Dr., in the park, which showcases replicas of a 19th-century bar, high-class Idahoan parlors, and working-class homesteads, as well as Native American artifacts and displays on Idaho's Basque and

Chinese populations. (☎334-2120; www.idahohistory.net/museum.html. Open May-Sept. Tu-Sa 9am-5pm, Su 1-5pm; Oct.-Apr. Tu-F 9am-5pm, Sa 11am-5pm. $2, ages 6-18 $1, under 6 free.) Next door, the **Boise Art Museum,** 670 Julia Davis Dr., displays contemporary Northwest art and a summer blockbuster traveling exhibit. (☎345-8330; www.boiseartmuseum.org. Open M-Sa 10am-5pm, Su noon-5pm; closed on M in winter; 1st Th of the month open until 9pm. In summer $8, college students and seniors $6, grades 1-12 $4; in winter $5/3/1. In summer Th half-price admission; in winter free.) One of Boise's must-see attractions is the ◪**Old Idaho State Penitentiary,** 2445 Old Penitentiary Rd. The penitentiary, in operation from 1870 until prisoner-led riots forced its closure in 1973, allows visitors to explore the 19th-century cells, death row, gallows, and solitary confinement areas. The penitentiary also houses $2 million in arms from J. Curtis Earl's private collection, which spans from the Bronze Age through both World Wars and modern artillery. All guns are kept in working order. (☎334-2844; www.idahohistory.net/oldpen.html. Open daily Memorial Day-Labor Day 10am-5pm; low season daily noon-5pm. Guided tours 2-3 times daily. Adults $5, ages 6-18 $3. MC/V.) On the grounds next to the penitentiary, the **Idaho Botanical Garden,** 2355 N. Penitentiary Rd., has extensive horticultural displays, including rose, herb, alpine, English, meditation, and water gardens. (☎343-8649 or 877-527-8233; www.idahobotanicalgardens.com. Open M-F 9am-5pm, Sa-Su 10am-6pm. $4, over 65 $3, ages 6-18 $2.) A few miles south of Boise, the **World Center for Birds of Prey,** 566 W. Flying Hawk Ln., offers an up-close look at 10 rare and striking birds of prey, including California condors, harpy eagles, and bald eagles. From I-84, take Exit 50 and go south 6 mi. on S. Cole. (☎362-8687; www.peregrinefund.org. Open Mar.-Oct. daily 9am-5pm; Nov.-Feb. Tu-Su 10am-4pm. $5, over 61 $4, ages 4-16 $3.) The fascinating **Basque Museum and Cultural Center,** 611 Grove St. at the corner of Grove St. and Capitol Blvd. on the "Basque Block," offers an interpretive exhibit about Idaho's Basque population and its old-world heritage. (☎343-2671; www.basquemuseum.com. Open Tu-F 10am-4pm, Sa 11am-3pm. Free.)

🎭 **ENTERTAINMENT.** In the **Alive After Five** series, live music infuses the Grove from June to September, every Wednesday 5-8pm. On **First Thursday,** the first Thursday of each month from 5 to 9pm, stores throughout Boise keep later hours, offer discounts, and host creative entertainment, ranging from free samples and giveaways to DJs and live music. (For both: ☎472-5200; www.visitidaho.org.) The **Capital City Public Market** takes over N. 8th St. between Main and Bannock St. from mid-April to October, every Saturday 9:30am-1:30pm, vending local produce and crafts. The **Boise River Greenbelt** provides nearly 25 mi. of paved paths that extend along the Boise River. Fishing and tubing along the Greenbelt are popular summer pursuits. The ever-growing **Idaho Shakespeare Festival** hits town from June to September. (Amphitheater located at 5657 Warm Springs Ave., behind the Idaho Department of Parks and Recreation Office. Box office ☎336-9221; www.idahoshakespeare.org. Tickets $20-38.) A little further from town, the **Ste. Chapelle Winery** hosts a summer concert series with acts ranging from classic rock to jazz and blues from 1-5pm on Sunday afternoons. Bring a picnic lunch and enjoy a bottle of one of Ste. Chapelle's signature vintages under the sun. Renowned for its summery Rieslings, Ste. Chapelle is king of the Idaho wine country. (On Lowell Road, 11 mi. from I-84 Exit 33a Nampa/Marsing on Hwy 55. ☎877-783-2427; www.stechapelle.com. See website for concert listings. $10, includes concert and wine tasting. Bottles $7.50-10.50 Winery open for tours and tastings M-Sa 10am-5pm, Su 12-5pm. Tours 11am and 2pm.) In late June, the **Spirit of Boise Balloon Classic** features hot-air balloons, a carnival, live music, and a scuba tank. (In Ann Morrison Park. ☎338-8887. June 25-28, 2008. Free.) Upcoming events are listed in Wednesday's *Boise Weekly*.

KETCHUM AND SUN VALLEY ☎ 208

In 1935, Union Pacific chairman Averill Harriman sent Austrian Count Felix Schaffgotsch to scour the western US for a site to develop into a ski resort that would rival Europe's best. After traveling for months, the Count stumbled onto the small mining and sheep-herding town of Ketchum in Idaho's Wood River Valley and was awestruck. Harriman purchased the land and built the world's first chairlift, basing his design on a pulley system he'd seen in Panama that was used for transporting bananas. Sun Valley was quickly recognized as a world-class ski resort, fulfilling Harriman's dream. Once frequented by Ernest Hemingway and Lucille Ball, Sun Valley is now a frequent destination for Arnold Schwarzenegger and Clint Eastwood. The permanent population is only 5600, but traffic extends for miles in each direction in peak months. Skiing reigns supreme in winter, while biking, hiking, and fishing draw thrill-seekers in summer.

█ ▼ TRANSPORTATION AND PRACTICAL INFORMATION. The best times to visit Sun Valley are winter and summer. The town slows down in the low season (Oct.-Nov. and May-early June), but accommodations offer lower rates and the scenery remains unchanged. Most of the food and nightlife centers around Main St. (Rte. 75) in Ketchum. Sun Valley Express **shuttles** pick up door-to-door in the Sun Valley/Ketchum area and run daily to the Boise airport. (☎ 877-622-8267; www.sunvalleyexpress.com. 3hr. From Sun Valley 8:30am; Dec.-Mar. also 6:30am and 12:30pm. From Boise 2:45pm; Dec.-Mar. also 12:45 and 5:45pm. Closed late Oct. to late Nov. $69, under 12 $59. Dec.-Mar. and Aug. $74/64. All vans TV/VCR equipped. Reservations required.) KART, Ketchum's **bus** service, runs in the city and the surrounding area. (☎ 726-7576 or 726-4628; www.kart-sunvalley.com. Runs daily 7:30am-midnight. Door-to-door service for disabled and elderly with next day advance reservations. Free within Ketchum and Sun Valley, $2.25 fare, for travel on Kart PEAK bus to outlying towns of Hailey and Bellevue.) For **visitor info,** go to **Sun Valley/Ketchum Chamber & Visitors Bureau,** 271 Washington Ave. in Ketchum; follow signs from Main St. (☎ 726-3423 or 800-634-3347; www.visitsunvalley.com or www.visitketchum.com. Open Nov.-Apr. and July-Sept. daily 9am-5:30pm; May-June and Oct. M-Sa 9am-5:30pm.) **Medical Services: St. Lukes Wood River Medical Center,** 100 Hospital Dr. (☎ 727-8800; www.stlukesonline.org). **Internet Access: Community Library,** 415 Spruce Ave. (☎ 726-3493. Free. Open M and Sa 9am-6pm, Tu and Th noon-9pm, W 9am-9pm, F 1-6pm.) **Post Office:** 151 W. 4th St. (☎ 726-5161. Open M-F 8am-5:30pm, Sa 11am-2pm. Self-service open 24hr.) **Postal Code:** 83340.

▐ ACCOMMODATIONS. From early June to mid-October, camping is by far the best option for cheap sleep in the Sun Valley area. Check with the **Ketchum Ranger Station,** 206 Sun Valley Rd., just outside of Ketchum on the way to Sun Valley. (☎ 622-5371. Open M-F 8:30am-5pm.) **Boundary Campground ❶,** 3 mi. northeast of town on Trail Creek Rd. past the Sun Valley resort, is closest to town and has eight wooded sites near a creek, as well as restrooms, water, and a picnic area. (7-night max. stay. Sites $10.) **Federal Gulch ❶** and **Sawmill Campground ❶,** both 5 mi. down E. Fork Rd., 8 mi. south of Ketchum off Hwy. 75, have three free sites amid groves of aspen trees with restrooms, grills, picnic areas, and a 3-day max. stay. Up Rte. 75 in the Sawtooth National Recreation Area (SNRA; p. 744) lie several scenic camping spots; **Murdock ❶** (11 sites with water; $10) and **Caribou ❶** (7 sites, no water; $8) are cheapest. They are, respectively, 2 and 3 mi. up the unpaved, but 2WD-suitable N. Fork Rd., which begins as a paved road to the right of the Visitors Center. **North Fork ❶** (29 sites; $11) and **Wood River ❶** (30 sites; $11) are 8 and 10 mi. north of Ketchum, respectively, along Rte. 75, and are popular fishing spots along Big Wood River. Take the first campground road north of the SNRA headquarters.

Bald Mountain Lodge ❹, 100 Picabo St., in the village at the base of the Warm Springs lift area, offers several expansive studios (as well as more expensive one-bedroom suites), complete with kitchenette. (☎726-4776. High-season studios $99, low-season $75. AmEx/D/MC/V.) For comfortable rooms, refrigerators, cable TV, an outdoor jacuzzi, and continental breakfast, try the **Lift Tower Lodge ❸,** 703 S. Main St. (☎726-5163 or 800-462-8646. Free Wi-Fi. Singles $85, each additional adult $10. AmEx/D/MC/V.)

🍴🎭 **FOOD AND NIGHTLIFE.** Ketchum's small confines bulge with over 90 restaurants, mostly catering to resort-goers' gourmet tastes, but relatively cheap food is available. Locals rave about the fish tacos and quesadillas ($4.25-$7) at **KB's Ketchum Burritos ❷,** on the corner of 6th and Washington St. Choose from their selection of "favorite" burritos ($8, vegetarian $6.25), or build your own. (☎726-2232. Open daily 11:30am-9pm. AmEx/D/MC/V.) Beer cans of all shapes and sizes grace the walls of local haven **Grumpy's ❶,** 860 Warm Springs Rd., a flavorful hangout with a porch and views of the nearby resort. (Burgers $5-6. 32 oz. beer "Schooner" $3.75. Open daily 11am-10pm.) For a quick, lighter bite, visit **Wrapcity Cafe ❶,** 180 S. Main St., with daily specials like the Caribbean Ahi and Tofu Satay wraps and the signature Chicken Ranch Club. (☎727-6766. Wraps, salads, and burritos $3.50-$6.50. Vegetarian options available. Open M-Sa 7:30am-3pm, Su 9am-3pm.) With surfboards, tiki masks, native art, and straw awnings, **No Ho's Hawaiian Cafe ❷,** 380 N. Washington Ave. at 4th St., is an island oasis in the heart of ski country, offering heaping portions of authentic Hawaiian cuisine. Phil's Ono Chicken is a notorious favorite. (☎726-8100. Lunch and dinner plate prices vary depending on size. Lighter "Menehune"-sized portions $6.50-8. Extra-large "Blahah" portions $8.50-13. Open M-F 11am-9pm, Sa noon-9pm.) Knock back stiff drinks at **Whiskey Jacques,** 251 N. Main St., which has nine televisions for sports junkies and $1 drink specials on Sunday and Tuesday. (☎726-5297. Burgers and sandwiches $7. Pizzas from $12. Live music W-Sa 9:30pm-2am. 21+ after 9pm. Cover $5. Happy hour daily 4-7pm. Open daily 4pm-2am. Kitchen open 5-9pm.) Head to the **Cellar Pub,** downstairs at 400 Sun Valley Rd., near Leadville Ave., for a young crowd, excellent burgers ($8-9), and inventive pints. (☎622-3832. 21+ after 10pm. Bar open daily 5pm-2am. Kitchen open M-Th 5-10pm, F-Su 11:30am-10pm.)

🏔 **OUTDOOR ACTIVITIES.** The **Wood River and Sun Valley trail system** consists of over 20 mi. of paved trails for bikers, skiers, skaters, joggers, and horse-

GHOST IN THE MACHINE

Deep within the mountains down a winding dirt road off of Rte. 75, the ghosts of **Custer** reside amidst the ruins of what was once a hot spot for Gold Rush miners. Custer and its twin town, Bonanza, boomed in the late 1870s when gold was discovered in the Yankee Fork of the Salmon River. The towns produced over $8 million in gold before General Custer's mine was abandoned in 1911. In 1939, the Snake River Mining Company discovered more gold in the area and constructed the formidable **Yankee Fork Gold Dredge,** extracting another $2 million in gold before it was deserted in 1952.

Today, the Dredge and remnants of the ghost town still stand. The **Art McGowns Museum,** housed inside what was once Custer's one-room schoolhouse, contains artifacts of mining life and stories about Custer's most infamous residents, including the Red Light District's Split Nose Bess and TK, a bear hunter who lost a jaw in a maul during a less successful hunt.

Yankee Fork Gold Dredge and Custer are 9 and 10 mi. respectively beyond Sunbeam Village, 13 mi. northeast of Stanley on Rte. 75, and 1 mi. north of Sunbeam Hot Springs, left down (the largely dirt) Yankee Fork Road. Museum open daily 10am-5pm. Free. Dredge self-guided tours run daily 10am-4:30pm. $4, ages 6-12 $1.

back riders. The trail starts in Bellevue and parallels Hwy. 75 north through Ketchum and east around Dollar Mountain to Sun Valley, passing ski slopes and historic sites. The *Wood River Trails* pamphlet, available at the Visitors Center, has more info. Visible for miles, **Bald Mountain** is a beacon for serious skiers. Two plazas serve "Baldy"—River Run on the north side of town and Warm Springs on the south. Need some practice? The gentle slopes of **Dollar Mountain** are perfect for beginners. (☎622-6136; www.sunvalley.com Bald Mountain: full-day lift ticket $79, under 13 $45. Dollar Mountain: full-day lift ticket $35, under 13 $30.) The **Nordic & Snowshoe Center,** behind Sun Valley Lodge, has 25 mi. of marked trails for cross-country skiing and snowshoe trekking. (☎800-786-8259. Full-day pass $16, ages 6-12 $11. Ski rental $17.) **The Elephant's Perch,** 280 East Ave., at Sun Valley Rd., has a complete stock of outdoor gear. (☎726-3497 or 866-Da Perch/327-3724; www.elephantsperch.com. Cruiser bikes $15 per 4hr., $20 per day. Backpacks $15 per day. Tents $20 per day. Nordic ski packages $20-25 per day. Open M-Sa 9am-6pm, Su 10am-5pm.) For mountain bike rentals and tips, visit **Sun Summit Ski and Cycle,** 791 Warm Springs Rd., across the street from Grumpy's. (☎726-0707. Front suspension mountain bikes $15 per ½ day, $25 per full day. Open daily.) Inquire about biking trails at bike rental shops, the Visitors Center, or the SNRA Headquarters. The **Adam's Gulch Loop, Fox Creek,** and **Corral Creek** are popular trails for both beginners as well as for seasoned riders.

The **Sun Valley Summer Symphony,** located behind the Sun Valley Lodge on the Esplanade, offers free open-air chamber and orchestral concerts from late July to mid-August. (☎622-5607. Visit www.svsummersymphony.org for exact dates. Concerts 6:30-7:30pm.) The **Ketch'em Alive Outdoor Concert Series** features rock, Latin, and bluegrass bands at Forest Service Park on 1st St. and Washington Ave. in free shows every Tuesday (7-9pm) in summer. Call the Chamber of Commerce or check www.visitsunvalley.com for band listings. After a day on the trails, locals soak their weary legs in **hot springs** hidden in Ketchum's hills and canyons. Melting snow and rain can render the springs inaccessible in spring and early summer, but they are safe for swimming once the current subsides in July. The Visitors Center has suggestions on which pools are safe and accessible. One of the more accessible, non-commercial springs is **Frenchman's Bend Hot Springs/Warfield Hot Springs,** on largely unpaved Warm Springs Rd., 11 mi. west of Ketchum, which lingers right around 100°F. (Use prohibited 10pm-4am. Nudity prohibited.) For info on fishing, including equipment rentals, stop by **Silver Creek Outfitters,** 500 N. Main St. (☎726-5282 or 800-732-5687. Open M-Sa 9am-6pm, Su 9am-5pm; longer in high season.)

SAWTOOTH RECREATION AREA   ☎208

Established by Congress in 1972, the Sawtooth National Recreation Area (SNRA) sprawls over 756,000 acres—nearly the size of Rhode Island—including 217,000 acres of untouched wilderness. The park is home to four mountain ranges with more than 40 peaks over 10,000 ft.; the glacier-scoured Sawtooth and White Cloud Mountains tower above the surrounding landscape in the north, while the Smoky and Boulder Mountains dominate the southern horizon. Over 300 alpine lakes and the headwaters of four of Idaho's major rivers are situated in the park's dense forest. Needless to say, there is ample opportunity for world-class outdoor adventure.

⬛🗗 ORIENTATION AND PRACTICAL INFORMATION. The tiny, frontier-style town of **Stanley** (pop. 100), 60 mi. north of Ketchum on Hwy. 21, near the intersection with Hwy. 75, serves as a northern base for exploring Sawtooth. The main drag is located one block south of Rte. 21, along Ace of Diamonds St. **Lower Stanley** is a continuation of the business region and lies 1 mi. north of Stanley on Hwy. 75. The **Stanley Ranger Station,** 3 mi. south of Stanley on Rte. 75, has maps and SNRA passes. (☎774-3000. Open M-F 8:30am-4:30pm.) The **Redfish Lake Visitors Center** provides additional info, including free educational programs about wildlife and geology. The Center also has a small museum about the Redfish Lake area. (☎774-3376. Open mid-June to early Sept. F-Su. 9am-5pm.) **Sawtooth National Recreation Area Headquarters,** 9 mi. north of Ketchum off Rte. 75, stocks detailed info on area forests, trails, and hot springs. (☎727-5000. Open M-F in summer 8:30am-5pm; winter hours vary.) The **Chamber of Commerce** is on Hwy. 21. (☎774-3411 or 800-878-7950; www.stanleycc.org. Open in summer daily 9am-5pm; closed in off season.) **Medical Services:** Salmon River Clinic (☎774-3565). **Internet Access: Stanley Community Library,** 33 Ace of Diamonds St. (☎774-2470. Unlimited use $3. Open M noon-8pm, Tu-W and Sa noon-4pm, Th noon-6pm, F 8am-4pm.) **Post Office:** 36 Ace of Diamonds St. (☎774-2230. Open M-F 8:30-11am and noon-5pm.) **Postal Code:** 83278.

⚲ ACCOMMODATIONS. For a real bed after a day in the wilderness, Stanley provides a few reasonably-priced options. Establishments recommend that you reserve rooms several weeks in advance for lodging in high season (late June-early Sept.). Stay in motel rooms with a kitchenette or actual log cabins at **Jerry's Country Store: Salmon River Cabins and Motel ❸,** 19055 Hwy. 75 in Lower Stanley. (☎774-3566 or 800-972-4627. Rooms $75; cabins $60-70. AmEx/D/MC/V.) **Redfish Lake Lodge ❸,** about 5 mi. south of Stanley on the shores of Redfish Lake, has comfy, historic lodge rooms with Wi-Fi; cabins come with refrigerators and kitchen areas. (☎774-3536; www.redfishlake.com. Rooms $68; in high season cabins from $130; cheaper in low season. AmEx/D/MC/V; credit cards only accepted in summer.) The remote but charming **Smiley Creek Lodge ❷,** located 37 mi. north of Ketchum and 23 mi. south of Stanley on Rte. 75, offers affordable cabins and tipis, equipped with power and electric blankets. General store and restaurant are located on the premises. (☎774-3547; www.smileycreek.com. Tipis $40; cabins $50. Restaurant open daily high season 8am-9pm, low season 9am-5pm.) The SNRA also boasts 33 campgrounds throughout the park. (Reservations ☎877-444-6777; www.recreation.gov.) **Alturas Lake ❶,** 21 mi. south of Stanley on Rte. 75 (the Alturas Lake Rd. turnoff is marked about 10 mi. north of Galena Pass), has three campgrounds with fishing and swimming nearby. These 55 sites offer greater privacy and are more scenic than some other area campgrounds. Twelve sites at **Alturas Lake Inlet** can be reserved. The other sites are first-come first-serve. (Vault toilets and water. Sites $10.) The **Redfish Lake Campgrounds ❶,** 5 mi. south of Stanley off Rte. 75, are sometimes overcrowded but are close to Stanley and a number of trailheads. (6- to 10-day max. stay. Sites $15.) East on Rte. 75, past Lower Stanley, the **Salmon River Corridor Campgrounds ❶** offer several camping options a little further from town noise and action, but close to the river for whitewater rafting. Several campground favorites include **Salmon River, Casino Creek, Mormon Bend, and Upper and Lower O'Brian.** (Water available; no hookup. First come, first served. 10-day max. stay. Sites $11.) Showers are $3 at **Papa Brunee's Laundromat** on Ace of Diamonds St.

🍴🎵 FOOD AND NIGHTLIFE. Dining options are somewhat limited in Stanley, but much of what's there is quite good. **Papa Brunee's Restaurant ❷,** on Ace of Diamonds St. downtown, serves deli sandwiches, meat-laden calzones, and pizzas with names like "The Bullfighter." (☎774-2536. 12 in. pizzas $8-10. Large calzone $6-8. Sandwiches $5.15. Open high season daily 11am-11pm; hours vary in winter. AmEx/D/MC/V.) The cozy **Stanley Baking Co. ❷,** 14 Wall St., offers wraps and sandwiches prepared on fresh bread. (☎774-6573. Breakfast $7.50-10.50. Lunch $8-10. Open daily 7am-2pm. MC/V.) Bring your appetite for a hearty, home-cooked meal at the **Elk Mountain Pot Belly Cafe ❷,** part of the Elk Mountain RV Resort located 3 mi. west of Stanley on Rte. 21. (☎774-2202; www.elkmtnrv.com. BBQ sandwiches and burgers $6. Free coffee. Open daily May-Oct. 8am-9pm.) Stock up on food, gas,

ROCKY MOUNTAINS

and fishing and hunting licenses at **Jerry's Country Store and Motel,** on Rte. 75 in Lower Stanley. (☎774-3566 or 800-972-4627. Open May-Sept. M-Sa 9am-9pm, Su 9am-5pm; winter hours vary.)

OUTDOOR ACTIVITIES. The **Sawtooth Scenic Byway** (Rte. 75) spans 60 mi. of National Forest land between Ketchum and Stanley, following the Big Wood River and crossing Galena Pass at 8701 ft. Pause at ■**Galena Overlook,** 31 mi. north of Ketchum, which rises 2000 ft. above the plain below and provides one of the finest views in the Rockies. The SNRA's backcountry is perfect for hiking, boating, fishing, and mountain biking. Pick up a free map and inquire about trail conditions at the **Stanley Ranger Station,** 3 mi. south of Stanley on Rte. 75, or the **Redfish Lake Visitors Center,** 5 mi. south of Stanley on Rte. 75, before heading into the park, particularly in early summer, when trails may be flooded. The **SNRA headquarters,** 3 mi. north of Ketchum also has info. Much of the backcountry stays buried in snow well into the warm weather. Also watch out for black bears—ranger stations have info about necessary precautions. **Redfish Lake** is the source of many trails. Some popular, leisurely hikes include those to **Fishhook Creek** (4½ mi. round-trip, elevation gain 250 ft., excellent for children). **Bench Lakes** (8 mi. round-trip, elevation gain 1225 ft.) and the **Marshall Lake trail** (10 mi. round-trip, elevation gain 1500 ft.) are more moderate hikes. Compare elevation gains on trail maps to access difficulties. Keep an eye out for native ospreys, Lincoln's sparrows, and ruby-crowned kinglets. The long, scenic loop around **Pettit, Toxaway,** and **Alice Lakes** (18½ mi. round-trip, elevation gain 2300 ft.) is a moderate overnight trip suitable for novice hikers. Starting at the **Inlet Trailhead** on the southern end of Redfish Lake, the challenging 10½ mi. round-trip trail to **Alpine Lake** (elevation gain 1800 ft.) rewards hikers with stunning views. Redfish Lake Marina (below) operates ferries to and from the south end of the lake to access the trailhead (one-way $7).

The Sawtooth Mountains have miles of mountain biking, but check a map: biking is prohibited in the Sawtooth Wilderness. **Riverwear,** on Rte. 21 in Stanley, rents bikes and offers info about trails. (☎774-3592; www.riverwear.com. Front suspension $25 per day, full suspension $32. Open daily Apr.-Oct. 7am-10pm. MC/V.) The 18 mi. **Fisher/Williams Creek Loop,** starting at the Williams Creek trailhead 10 mi. south of Stanley, is the most popular trail, ascending from 6800 ft. to an elevation of 8280 ft. Beginners will enjoy the dirt road that accesses the North Fork campgrounds from SNRA Headquarters. This passage parallels the North Fork of the Wood River for 5 mi. before branching off into narrow, steep trails for more experienced riders. The trails can be combined into loops; consult a trail map or a ranger. Another immensely popular trail is the 12 mi. **Elk Mountain Loop Trail,** designed specifically for mountain bikers and accessible from the Stanley Lake Road. The trail is relatively beginner-friendly, but has something for everyone.

Topographical maps ($6) and detailed trail books ($15-20) are available at **McCoy's Tackle and Gift Shop,** on Ace of Diamonds St., in addition to sporting goods, fishing tackle, and licenses. (☎774-3377. Licenses $11.50 for 1st day, $5 each additional day. Open June-Sept. daily 8am-8pm; low-season hours vary.) **Sawtooth Adventure Company,** on Rte. 75 in Lower Stanley, rents kayaks and rafts and leads guided kayak, Class IV whitewater rafting, and fly-fishing trips along the Salmon

! **BEARS! BEWARE!** Eastern Idaho is home to the North American Black Bear. Black Bears are a lot smaller and much more predictable than Grizzly Bears. If you come across one on a trail, stop what you're doing, avoid actions that could be interpreted as a threat, and leave the area as calmly as possible. To avoid unwanted bear encounters in the backcountry, don't leave food out around your campsite. For more info visit www.bebearaware.com.

River. They also arrange guided mountain bike tours, horseback riding, and scenic flights above Sawtooth in chartered propeller jet planes. (☎866-774-4644. Kayaks $25-50 per day. Rafts for 8 people $75 per day. Half-day kayak trips $30-65. Full-day fly-fishing trips $250. Open daily May-Sept. 7am-9pm.) For boat tours of the lake, head for **Redfish Lake Lodge Marina.** (☎774-3536. Open in summer daily 7am-8:30pm. 1hr. tours $12, ages 6-12 $5; 4-person min. Paddleboats $5 per 30min. Canoes $10 per hr., $32 per half-day, $50 per day. Single-person kayaks $7/20/35, doubles $10/32/50. Outboard motorboats $17/60/90. Aquacycles $15 per hr.) The least expensive way to enjoy the SNRA waters is to visit the hot springs just east of Stanley (info available at Chamber of Commerce; see **Practical Information** above). **Sunbeam Hot Springs,** 12 mi. northeast of Stanley on Rte. 75, triumphs over the rest at a scalding 150°F, though the springs mix with river water creating an invigorating experience for swimmers (river may be too high in late spring/early summer). Sunbeam is free and open 24hr., but proximity to drivers on Rte. 75 makes for a safer and more enjoyable visit during daylight hours.

CRATERS OF THE MOON NATIONAL MONUMENT ☎208

A visitor to the landscape of **Craters of the Moon National Monument** in the 20s claimed it was "the strangest 75 square miles on the North American continent." The same geological hot spot responsible for the thermal activity in Yellowstone National Park created the monument's 750,000 acres of twisted lava formations; eruptions ended only 2000 years ago, and are expected to resume within the next 1000. Located 70 mi. southeast of Sun Valley at the junction of Rte. 20 and 26/93, the "well-kept secret" known as Craters of the Moon promises visitors a fascinating mix of lava tube caves, ancient tree molds, and long-hardened lava flows. (Entrance $8 per car, $4 per biker or pedestrian. Accepts Interagency Annual Pass. Park entrance open 24hr.) The **Visitors Center,** right before the entrance to the monument, has videos, displays, and inexpensive printed guides outlining the area's geological past. The center hosts information sessions in the evenings in the campground and guided tours along certain trails twice daily during summer season. (☎527-3273; www.nps.gov/crmo. Open daily in summer 8am-6pm; low season 8am-4:30pm.) A 7 mi. **loop drive** winds through the major sights around the monument's northern end. In the winter, the loop drive becomes a cross-country ski and snowshoe trail. Several shorter hiking trails lead to intriguing rock formations and a variety of caves. The 2 mi. **Broken Top Loop,** starting at Tree Molds parking lot, goes through Buffalo Caves and is a quick but comprehensive survey of the surrounding land; the short ■**Caves Trail,** further along the loop, leads to three large caves, each with a distinctive character. Desert summers and arctic winters best characterize the monument's harsh climate, as black rocks absorb heat and there are no trees for miles. Don't forget sturdy shoes, plenty of water, sunscreen, and a hat. If you plan to explore the caves, bring a flashlight.

There are 51 campsites scattered throughout the monument and a single **campground ❶** located just past the entrance station. (Open year-round. Water available in summer only. In summer sites $10; in winter $6.) Wood fires are prohibited, but charcoal fires are permitted in the grills provided. Camping at unmarked sites in the dry lava wilderness of the park is possible with a free backcountry permit, available at the Visitors Center (p. 747). The inside of Echo Crater, reachable via an easy 4 mi. hike from the Tree Molds parking lot, is a popular backcountry camping destination. The town of Arco, 18 mi. east of Craters of the Moon on Rte. 20, is the closest source of services and lodging. Arco claims to have been the first city in the world powered by nuclear energy; on July 17, 1955, a local reactor fed energy to the town for two hours. Comfy, quiet, modern rooms with telephones, cable TV, and free Wi-Fi are available at the **D-K Motel ❷**, 316 S. Front St. (☎527-

ROCKY MOUNTAINS

8282 or 800-231-0134; www.dkmotel.com. Laundry facilities. Singles $35; doubles and triples $41-$53.) With a big green rocking chair in front, **Pickle's Place ❶**, 440 S. Front St., is an easy diner to identify. Home of the atomic burger ($6-8) and the Black Russian sandwich ($6), Pickle's also dishes out breakfasts ($5-8) in plentiful portions. (☎527-9944. Dinner entrees $9-12. Open daily June-Aug. 6am-11pm; Sept.-May 6am-10pm.)

The **Business Development Center/Chamber of Commerce,** 159 N. Idaho St., has local attractions info. (☎527-8977; www.cityarco.com. Open M-Th 9am-4pm.) **Police:** 256 W. Grand Ave. (☎527-8553). **Medical Services:** 551 Highland Dr. (☎527-8206). **Post Office:** 147 Lost River Dr. (☎527-3355. Open M-F 8:30am-5pm.) **Postal Code:** 83213.

THE SOUTHWEST

The Ancestral Puebloans of the 10th and 11th centuries were the first to discover that the Southwest's arid lands could support an agrarian civilization. Years later, in 1803, the US bought parts of the Southwest in the Louisiana Purchase, and claimed the rest of it in 1848 with the treaty that ended the US-Mexican War. The hope for a Western "empire of liberty," where Americans could live a virtuous farm life, motivated further expansion and inspired the region's individualist mentality. Today, the Southwest's vastness—from the dramatically colored canvas of Arizona's red rock and striking blue sky, to the breathtaking vistas of Utah's mountains—invites contemplation and awe, and the area's potential for outdoor adventures is as unparalleled as its kaleidoscopic mix of cultures. For more on the region, check out ▧*Let's Go: Southwest USA.*

HIGHLIGHTS OF THE SOUTHWEST

ACHIEVE nirvana (or at least a sense of vertigo) at the **Grand Canyon** (p. 784) and Utah's **"Fab Five"** National Parks (p. 770).

SOAK your cares away in the bubbling hot springs of **Truth or Consequences** (p. 841).

JINGLE the coins in your pocket one last time before offering them up to the shimmering slot machines of **Las Vegas** (p. 751).

SCRAMBLE past lush waterfalls to the mystical **Havasupai Reservation** (p. 793).

TITILLATE your taste buds with the chili-laden cuisine of **Albuquerque** (p. 834), **Santa Fe** (p. 824), and **Tucson** (p. 814).

NEVADA

Nevada's Great Basin stretches for hundreds of miles across land that rejects all but the hardiest life forms. Three massive lakes—man-made Lake Mead, the crystalline-blue Pyramid Lake, and mountain-ringed Lake Tahoe—provide a refreshing retreat from brutal desert heat. At the few outposts of human habitation, prostitution and gambling mark the state as a purveyor of loose, Wild West morality. Beyond patches of glaring lights, sin, and showtunes, Nevada is barren and dusty, but this hasn't kept it from becoming the fastest-growing state in the US. Nevada exemplifies America at its most excessive and contradictory.

◪ PRACTICAL INFORMATION

Capital: Carson City.

Visitor Info: Nevada Commission on Tourism, 401 N. Carson St., Carson City 89701 (☎800-638-2328). Open 24hr. **Nevada Division of State Parks,** 1300 S. Curry St., Carson City 89703 (☎775-684-2770). Open M-F 8am-5pm.

Postal Abbreviation: NV. **Sales Tax:** 6.5-7.5%; 13.5% room tax in some counties.

THE SOUTHWEST

The Southwest

LAS VEGAS ☎702

Rising out of the Nevada desert, Las Vegas is a shimmering tribute to excess. Those who embrace it find vice, greed, and one very, very good time. Those not immediately enthralled by its frenetic pace may still find sleeping (and decision-making) nearly impossible with sparkling casinos, cheap gourmet food, free drinks, and spectacular attractions at every turn. Nowhere else do so many shed inhibitions and indulge with abandon. A word of caution: know thy tax bracket; walk in knowing what you want to spend and get out when you've spent it. In Las Vegas, there's a busted wallet and a broken heart for every garish neon light.

▐ TRANSPORTATION

Airport: McCarran International (LAS); (☎261-5743**)**, at the southwest end of the Strip. **Bell Trans** (☎739-7990) runs **shuttles** to the Strip ($5.50) and downtown ($7). Operates 24 hr. Taxi to downtown $10-15; to the Strip $16-20.

Buses: Greyhound, 200 S. Main St. (☎384-9561 or 800-231-2222; www.grey-hound.com), downtown at Carson Ave., near the Plaza Hotel/Casino. Runs to **Los Angeles** (5-7hr., 16 per day, $41.50) and **San Francisco** (14-16hr., 6 per day, $74).

Public Transportation: Citizens Area Transit (CAT; ☎228-7433; www.catride.com). The "deuce" bus serves downtown and the Strip; #302 offers express service on the same route. Buses #108 and 109 serve the airport. Buses run daily 5:30am-1:30am (24hr. on the Strip). Strip routes $2, residential routes $1.25; seniors and ages 6-17 $1/0.60. Day pass $5. Wheelchair-accessible. **Downtown Transportation Center,** 300 N. Casino Center Blvd. (☎229-6025), at Stewart Ave. near the Fremont Street Experience, has schedules and maps. **Las Vegas Strip Trolleys** (☎382-1404) cruise the Strip every 20min. daily 9:30am-1:30am. $2.50; day pass $6.50. Exact fare required. The **Monorail** (☎699-8299; www.lvmonorail.com) runs along the Strip, connecting major casinos daily M-Th 7am-2am, F-Su 7am-3am. $5; day pass $8.

Taxi: Yellow, Checker, and **Star,** ☎873-2000. **Ace,** ☎736-8383.

Car Rental: Sav-Mor Rent-A-Car, 5101 Rent-A-Car Rd. (☎736-1234 or 800-634-6779). **Dollar Rent-A-Car,** 3790 S. Las Vegas Blvd. (☎400-5836).

Limousine Rental: For those livin' large. **Presidential Limousine** (☎731-5577; www.pllv.com). $35-80 per hr.

▞ ▟ ORIENTATION AND PRACTICAL INFORMATION

Driving to Vegas from L.A. is a straight, 300 mi. shot on I-15 N (4½hr.). From Arizona, take I-40 W to Kingman and then U.S. 93 N. Las Vegas has two major casino areas. The **downtown** area, around 2nd and Fremont St., has been converted into a pedestrian promenade. The **Strip,** a collection of mammoth hotel-casinos, lies along **Las Vegas Boulevard.** In its shadow is **Paradise Road,** which is also strewn with casinos. Some areas of Las Vegas should be avoided, especially downtown areas far from the casino district. Despite its debauchery, Las Vegas has a **curfew.** Those under 18 aren't allowed in most public places late at night (M-Th and Su 10pm-5am, F-Sa midnight-5am), unless accompanied by an adult. Laws are even harsher on the Strip, where no one under 18 is allowed unaccompanied 9pm-5am—ever. **The drinking and gambling age is 21.**

Visitor Info: Las Vegas Convention and Visitors Authority, 3150 Paradise Rd. (☎892-0711 or 877-847-4858; www.visitlasvegas.com), at the corner of Paradise and Convention Center Dr., 4 blocks from the Strip in the big pink convention center by the Hilton. Helpful staff with up-to-date info on headliners, shows, hotel bargains, and buffets. Open M-F 8am-5pm.

Marriage: Marriage License Bureau, 201 Clark Ave. (☎671-0600), in the courthouse. 18+; under 18 with parental consent. Licenses $55. Witness required. Open daily 8am-midnight. Cash only. **Little White Wedding Chapel,** 1301 Las Vegas Blvd. (☎382-5943 or 800-545-8111; www.littlewhitechapel.com). Frank Sinatra, Michael Jordan, and Britney Spears all got hitched here. Basic packages from $55. Available necessities include photographer, tux and gown, flowers, and, for honeymooners, a pink Caddy. Grab your marriage license 1st. Open 24hr.

Hotlines: Compulsive Gamblers Hotline, ☎800-522-4700. **Gamblers Anonymous,** ☎385-7732. **Rape Crisis Center Hotline,** ☎366-1640. **Suicide Prevention,** ☎731-2990 or 800-885-4673. All operate 24hr.

Post Office: 4975 Swenson St. (☎736-7649), near the Strip. Open M-F 8:30am-5pm. **Postal Code:** 89119.

ACCOMMODATIONS

Rates in Las Vegas fluctuate greatly; a room that normally costs $30 can cost hundreds during a convention weekend. **Vegas.com** (www.vegas.com) or **casino websites** often have the best prices. Free publications like *What's On in Las Vegas*, *Today in Las Vegas*, *24/7*, and *Vegas Visitor* list coupons, discounts, and event schedules. Hotels along the Strip are the center of the action and within walking distance of each other, but they sell out quickly and are much more expensive than comparable, off-Strip hotels. A number of motels concentrate around **Sahara Road** and **South Las Vegas Boulevard.** If you stay downtown, it is best to stay at one of the casinos near the **Fremont Street Experience** (p. 756). Budget motels also stretch along the southern end of the **Strip,** across from Mandalay Bay. In the rooms listed below, the **hotel taxes of 9%** (11% for downtown Fremont St.) are not included.

▧ **Excalibur,** 3850 S. Las Vegas Blvd. (☎597-7777 or 800-937-7777; www.excalibur.com), at Tropicana Ave. Best deal of all the major resort casinos. Features a moat and drawbridge, 2 pools, a modern spa, and a monorail station with service to Luxor and Mandalay Bay. Rooms M-Th and Su $49-109, F-Sa $109-309. AmEx/D/MC/V. ❸

USAHostels Las Vegas, 1322 Fremont St. (☎385-1150 or 800-550-8958; www.usahostels.com). Though far from the Strip's action, this hostel's staff keeps guests entertained. Nightly events include champagne limo tours of the Strip. Laundry facilities. Breakfast included. Free Wi-Fi. Passport, proof of international travel, or out-of-state college ID required. Dorms M-Th and Su $17-22, F-Sa $22-28; suites $50-52/60-62. About $3 higher in summer and peak times. ISIC discount. MC/V. ❷

Sin City Hostel, 1208 S. Las Vegas Blvd. (☎868-0222; www.sincityhostel.com). North of the heart of the Strip but south of Fremont St., this new hostel balances the pace of the city with a restful atmosphere. International passport or student ID required. Breakfast included. Dorms M-Th and Su $20; private rooms with shared bath $40, F-Sa $44. AmEx/D/MC/V. ❷

FOOD

From swanky eateries run by celebrity chefs to gourmet buffets, culinary surprises abound in Las Vegas, usually at a great price.

Dishes, 3300 S. Las Vegas Blvd. (☎894-7111), in Treasure Island. A classy buffet with offerings ranging from sushi to made-to-order salads and filling pastas. The carving stations and scrumptious desserts are hard to beat. Breakfast $12. Lunch $15. Weekday dinner $20, weekend dinner with steak and lobster $26. Champagne brunch Sa-Su $18. Open daily 7am-10:30pm. AmEx/D/MC/V. ❸

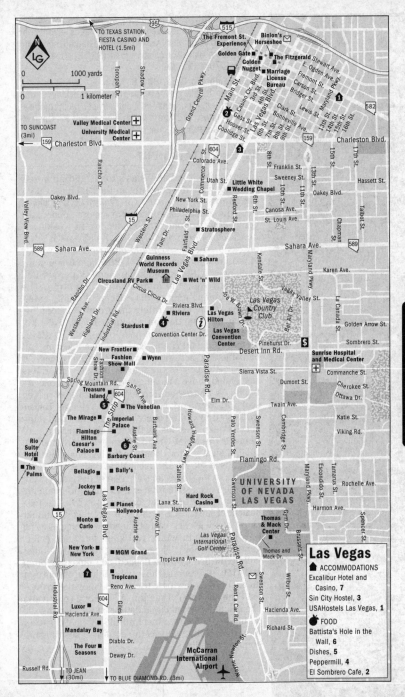

Las Vegas

🏠 ACCOMMODATIONS
Excalibur Hotel and
  Casino, **7**
Sin City Hostel, **3**
USAHostels Las Vegas, **1**

🍴 FOOD
Battista's Hole in the
  Wall, **6**
Dishes, **5**
Peppermill, **4**
El Sombrero Cafe, **2**

THE HIDDEN DEAL

DODGING DOLLARS IN LAS VEGAS

Las Vegas is a town where poker faces get you far, so it's easy to get lots of bang for your buck. Luckily, there are just as many ways to dodge Vegas's high prices as there are to bob and weave through the tourists on the Strip. How can you make sure your precious pennies stay on the tables, where they belong?

Everybody's heard of Sigfried and Roy's famous white tigers, and most visitors to Vegas want to see them in action at the Mirage's Secret Garden—but not everyone wants to shell out the dough. Why not check out the lion habitat at the MGM Grand for free? They even have a resident lion cub visitors can pet.

Don't have the bank account to furnish a wardrobe by Prada or Dolce and Gabbana? Not to worry: window shopping in the museum-like malls of the Bellagio and Caesar's Palace will make you feel just as luxurious. If you feel like coming away with a designer label and a shopping bag to make other tourists think you're a chic someone, grab one of four limited-edition silk-screened Marc Jacobs t-shirts ($20).

Beneath the Strip's garishness is a cove of fine art. To avoid big-city admission fees, wander into the Bellagio's lobby and look up: an overwhelming garden of Dale Chihuly's glass flowers bloom eagerly on the ceiling.

Peppermill, 2985 S. Las Vegas Blvd. (☎735-4177; www.peppermilllasvegas.com). A Vegas favorite for over 30 years, this Day-Glo purple restaurant serves up heaping plates of comfort food ($8-28). Open 24hr. AmEx/D/MC/V. ❷

El Sombrero Cafe, 807 S. Main St. (☎382-9234). Where locals go for authentic Mexican food. Small room, huge portions, efficient service. Their combination plates ($12) are a good value. Lunch $7. Open M-Sa 11am-9:30pm. AmEx/D/MC/V. ❷

🎵 ENTERTAINMENT

Entertainment is Las Vegas's forte, and all hotels have city-wide ticket booths in their lobbies. Check out *What's On, Showbiz,* or *Today in Las Vegas* for shows, times, and prices. For a more opinionated perspective, try one of the independent weeklies—*Las Vegas Mercury, City Life, Las Vegas Weekly,* or "Neon," the *Las Vegas Review-Journal's* weekly entertainment supplement. ◪**Blue Man Group** stuns audiences with a stimulating blend of percussion, visual effects, and audience participation. The show's unique multimedia concept is wildly entertaining and popular, filling the group's custom theater at the Venetian on a regular basis ($76-126). **Cirque du Soleil's** artistic shows—*O, Mystère, Zumanity, LOVE* and *KÀ*—are awe-inspiring but bank-busting ($60-150). Performed at the Bellagio, **O** is easily the best of the four, with agile performers suspended above a moving pool. **Mystère,** at Treasure Island, is almost as impressive, with less pricey seats. At New York-New York, cabaret-style **Zumanity,** hosted by a drag queen, caters to an adult audience. **KÀ** explores duality through the experiences of twins at the MGM Grand. The newest production, **LOVE,** is an acrobatic tribute to the legendary Beatles, and runs at the Mirage. **Jubilee!,** at Bally's, and **Folies Bergere,** at the Tropicana, are two of the last remaining true Vegas-style revues with showgirls dancing about in rhinestones and feathers ($65-88). The **Tournament of Kings,** at Excalibur, is a (k)nightly dinner show where guests feast at a medieval banquet using only their hands, while rival kings joust and evil is vanquished ($50). Those looking for an illusionist will be thrilled by **David Copperfield** (appearing often at MGM; $97), while those who think the genre of magic needs a few new tricks will enjoy the irreverent **Penn and Teller** at the Río ($75). For a (relatively) cheap laugh, **Second City Scriptless,** at the Flamingo, is an improv show that inspired the TV hit *Saturday Night Live* and features the country's best up-and-coming comedians ($45).

! **IT'S THE LAW.** The legal drinking and gambling age in Nevada is 21.

 ## CASINOS AND NIGHTLIFE

Casinos spend millions attracting big spenders to Las Vegas. Efforts to bring families to Sin City are evident everywhere, with arcades and thrill rides at every turn. Still, Vegas is no Disneyland. With steamy nightclubs, topless revues, and scantily clad waitresses serving free liquor, it's clear that casinos' priorities center on the mature, money-toting crowd. Casinos are open 24hr. Almost every casino resort has a full casino, several restaurants, a club, a buffet, and a feature show. There is valuable art and architecture at every corner. Look for casino "funbooks" that feature deals on chips and entertainment. **Gambling is illegal for those under 21.**

TIP **CASINO TIPPING.** To keep the luck flowing (and because it's nice), many players reward a good table dealer with a $1 tip next to their main bet. Casino etiquette also calls for a $1 tip per person for drink servers and buffet busers.

THE STRIP

The undisputed locus of Vegas's surging regeneration, the Strip is a neon fantasyland teeming with people, casinos, restaurants, and sadly, inflated prices. The nation's 10 largest hotels line the legendary 3½ mi. stretch of Las Vegas Blvd.

Mandalay Bay, 3950 S. Las Vegas Blvd. (☎632-7777; www.mandalaybay.com). Undoubtedly Vegas's hippest casino, Mandalay Bay tries to convince New York and L.A. fashionistas they haven't left home. With swank restaurants and clubs, gambling seems an afterthought. Shark Reef has all kinds of aquatic beasts, including 15 shark species ($16, children $11). House of Blues hosts some of Vegas's best music. Also check out the **Foundation Room.** Non-locals $30, locals $10. Open M only 11pm-5am.

Bellagio, 3600 S. Las Vegas Blvd. (☎693-7444 or 888-987-3456; www.bellagio.com). The world's largest 5-star hotel, made famous in the 2001 remake of *Ocean's Eleven.* Houses a gallery of fine art, the world's tallest chocolate fountain, and a floral conservatory. Check out the dancing fountains in front of the casino and see the water leap several stories set to music (free; every 30min. in the afternoon, every 15min. 7pm-midnight). For nightlife, enjoy **Light.** Cover $30. Open Th-su 10:30pm-4am.

Wynn, 3131 S. Las Vegas Blvd. (☎770-7000 or 877-321-9966; www.wynnlasvegas.com). This latest addition to the Strip more than competes with the Bellagio for classiest casino. The gambling floor is tastefully decorated—flashing slot machine lights are noticeably absent. Don't be put off by the subdued appearance; even if table limits are high, the dealers are friendly and the grounds are beautiful. To find late-night excitement, check out **Tryst.** Cover men $30, women $20.

New York-New York, 3790 S. Las Vegas Blvd. (☎740-6969 or 866-815-4365; www.nynyhotelcasino.com.) An eye-catching, fun-filled casino brings the Big Apple to Sin City. Towers mimic the Manhattan skyline, the streets of a miniature Greenwich Village lead to an **ESPNZone,** and a walk under the Brooklyn Bridge brings you to the Manhattan Express (open M-Th and Su 11am-11pm, F-Sa 10:30am-midnight; $12.50), a wild, loopy rollercoaster from the top of the casino to the bottom. For nightlife, check-out **Coyote Ugly.** Cover $10. Casino open daily 6pm-4am. Nightclub open daily 9pm-4am.

Luxor, 3900 S. Las Vegas Blvd. (☎262-4000 or 888-777-0188; www.luxor.com). This architectural marvel recreates ancient Egypt's majestic pyramids in steel and opaque glass. Popular with young adults, but still family-friendly, Luxor has an IMAX theater, a full-scale replica of King Tut's Tomb, and numerous clubs.

Treasure Island (TI), 3300 S. Las Vegas Blvd. (☎894-7111 or 800-288-7206; www.treasureisland.com). Caters to a younger crowd with clubs and chic lounges. See the *Sirens of TI,* one of Vegas's most scantily-clad shows (daily 7, 8:30, 10, 11:30pm). For drinks and dancing, **Tangerine** is the place to be. Cover $20. Th-Sa 10pm-4am.

Paris, 3655 S. Las Vegas Blvd. (☎946-7000 or 877-603-4386; www.parislasvegas.com). From faux French cafes to replicas of the Arc de Triomphe, the Opera House, and the Eiffel Tower, this resort adds a Parisian *je ne sais quoi* to Vegas. For an American version of Parisian nightlife, try **Risque.** Cover $20. Open F-Sa 10:30pm-early morning.

Venetian, 3355 S. Las Vegas Blvd. (☎414-1000 or 877-883-6423; www.venetian.com). Singing gondoliers serenade passengers on the chlorinated "canal" that runs through this palatial casino. Elaborate ceilings, the Guggenheim Hermitage Museum, and Madame Tussaud's wax museum evoke a little bit of old Europe, while the Blue Man Group adds some edge. For loud music and willing dance partners go to **Tao.** Cover men $30, women $20. Open Th-Sa 10:30pm-5:30am.

Caesar's Palace, 3570 S. Las Vegas Blvd. (☎731-7110 or 866-227-5938; www.caesars.com). At Caesar's, busts abound; some are plaster and others are barely covered by low-cut cocktail waitresses' outfits. The expensive Forum Shops and the Italian wishing fountain replicas provide numerous opportunities to leave your winnings in Vegas. The party never stops at **OPM.** Cover W-Th and Su $20, F-Sa men $30, women $20.

The Mirage, 3400 S. Las Vegas Blvd. (☎791-7111 or 800-374-9000; www.mirage.com). This tropical oasis is home to a 20,000 gal. aquarium, a dolphin habitat and "secret garden," and several rare white tigers and lions. A volcano that puts science fair projects to shame erupts every hr. 8pm-12am. Don't forget to check out Mirage's club **Jet.** Cover $30. Open F-Sa and M 10:30pm-4am.

MGM Grand, 3799 S. Las Vegas Blvd. (☎891-1111 or 877-880-0880; www.mgmgrand.com). A huge bronze lion guards Las Vegas's largest hotel (5000 rooms) as it glows like the Emerald City from *The Wizard of Oz.* Watch big cats frolic at the Lion Habitat. The MGM often hosts world-class sporting events and concerts. Check out club **Tabu.** Cover W-Th and Su $20, F-Sa $25. Open W-M 10pm-early morning.

Circus Circus, 2880 S. Las Vegas Blvd. (☎734-0410 or 800-634-3450; www.circuscircus.com). Though far less glamorous than its younger neighbors, the free circus acts are reminiscent of the Strip's early, outlandish days. While parents run to card tables and slot machines, children flock to one of the world's largest indoor theme parks.

DOWNTOWN AND OFF-STRIP

Many of the Strip's theme park elements are absent in "old" downtown. **Glitter Gulch** (www.glittergulchlv.com) has smaller hotels, cheaper alcohol and food, and table limits as low as $1. Years of decline were reversed with Vegas's rebound and the 1995 opening of the **Fremont Street Experience** (www.vegasexperience.com). Now, a protective canopy of neon and a pedestrian promenade have aided the area's renaissance, making it almost as entertaining as the Strip and much more welcoming to the budget traveler.

Golden Gate, 1 Fremont St. (☎385-1906 or 800-426-1906; www.goldengatecasino.com). Opened in 1906, Las Vegas's oldest hotel-casino now anchors the Fremont Street Experience and offers a thoroughly modern good time. Grab a famous $0.99 shrimp cocktail and sharpen your gambling skills in the laid-back atmosphere.

Golden Nugget, 129 Fremont St. (☎385-7111 or 800-846-5336; www.goldennugget.com). An outpost of Strip-like class downtown, this 4-star hotel charms gamblers with marble floors, elegant chandeliers, and high-end gambling.

Palms, 4321 W. Flamingo Rd. (☎942-7777 or 866-942-7777; www.palms.com). The spot to see celebrities and party with the young and beautiful. The Skin Pool Lounge has swings and cabanas to enjoy before you hit the bars and clubs on the property.

THE SOUTHWEST

⚡ DAYTRIPS FROM LAS VEGAS

HOOVER DAM

From Las Vegas, take U.S. 93/95 26 mi. to Boulder City. From Boulder City, head east 5 mi. on U.S. 93. Parking on the Nevada side costs $5; parking on the Arizona side is free.

Built to subdue the flood-prone Colorado River and give vital water and energy to the Southwest, this ivory monolith took 5000 men five years to construct. By the time the dam was finished in 1935, 96 men had died. Their labor rendered a 726 ft. colossus that pumps more than four billion kilowatt-hours of power to Las Vegas and L.A. A lasting tribute to America's "think big" era, the dam is a spectacular engineering feat, weighing 6.6 million tons and measuring 660 ft. thick at its base and 1244 ft. across the canyon at its crest. Tours and an **interpretive center** explore the dam's history and future. (☎494-2517. Open daily 9am-6pm. Last entry 5:15pm. Self-guided tours with short presentations $11, seniors $9, ages 7-16 $6.)

LAKE MEAD

From Las Vegas, take Lake Mead Blvd./Hwy. 147 off I-15 east 16 mi. to North Shore Rd.

The largest reservoir in the US, Lake Mead was created when Hoover Dam was constructed across the Colorado River in the 30s. First-time visitors will benefit from a trip to the **Alan Bible Visitors Center,** 4 mi. east of Boulder City on Hwy. 93, where the helpful staff has brochures and maps. (☎293-8990; www.nps.gov/lame. Open daily 8:30am-4:30pm. 5-day pass $5 per vehicle, $3 per pedestrian.) Falling water levels have left Lake Mead roughly half its usual depth, forcing boat ramps to close and exposing previously submerged hazards. Despite these conditions, Lake Mead is still a water recreation haven. Park service-approved outfitters rent boats and more on the shores; www.funonthelake.com has more info. Popular **Boulder Beach,** the departure point for many water-based activities, is accessible from Lakeshore Dr. at the south end of the lake. (Restrooms, water. Sites $10.) Because of the oppressively hot summer temperatures, it may be a better idea to head for the higher (and cooler) elevations west of Las Vegas in July and August.

> ❗ **IT'S THE LAW.** The legal drinking and gambling age in Nevada is 21.

RENO ☎775

Reno, with its decadent casinos cradled by snowcapped mountains, captures both the natural splendor and exciting prospects of the West. Acting as the hub of northern Nevada's tourist cluster, including nearby Lake Tahoe and Pyramid Lake, Reno is defined by a gritty glamour that falls short of the thrills of Las Vegas but still manages to supply gambling, entertainment, and dining in a few city blocks.

⚡ ORIENTATION AND PRACTICAL INFORMATION.
Fifteen miles from the California border and 445 mi. north of Las Vegas, Reno sits at the intersection of **I-80,** which stretches between Chicago and San Francisco, and **Highway 395,** which traces the eastern slope of the Sierra Nevadas from Southern California to Washington. Many of the major casinos are in the **downtown** area between West and Center St. and between 2nd and 6th St. The neon-lit streets of downtown Reno are heavily patrolled, but avoid straying too far east of the city center at night. Relatively cheap accommodations can be found south of the Truckee River along **Virginia Street,** Reno's main drag. The #1 bus services Virginia St. from downtown Reno to Meadowood Mall. The *Reno/Tahoe Visitor Planner,* available at kiosks

THE SOUTHWEST

throughout the city, contains a local map and is a helpful city guide. Amtrak sends **trains** from 280 N. Center St. (☎800-872-7245; www.amtrak.com. Open daily 7:30am-5pm.) Greyhound, 155 Stevenson St., sends **buses** to Las Vegas (15-22hr., 5 per day, $71); Salt Lake City (9½hr., 2 per day, $59); and San Francisco (5-7hr., 7 per day, $30). (☎322-2970; www.greyhound.com. Open 24hr.) The **Reno-Sparks Convention and Visitors Authority** is at 4001 S. Virginia St. (☎800-367-7366; www.visitrenotahoe.com. Call ahead for hours.) **Post Office:** 50 S. Virginia St., at Mill St. (Open M-F 7:30am-5:15pm.) **Postal Code:** 89501.

⌂ ACCOMMODATIONS. Casino resort prices fluctuate daily, so be sure to call ahead. Inexpensive independent hotels also dot the casino area. Many offer clean, simple rooms perfect for the budget traveler, but watch out: in some cases, low rates may reflect a lack of wholesomeness; inspecting your room beforehand is a wise move. Most hotels rent only to those 21 and older. The rates below don't include Reno's 13.5% hotel tax. With its huge neon heart-shaped sign, it's difficult to miss the beacon of the **Heart O' Town Motel ❷**, 520 N. Virginia St., an affordable joint in the midst of the huge hotel glitter. (☎322-4066. Rooms $62-75. AmEx/D/MC/V.) For a casino experience without handing over your entire budget, try the **Sands Regency Casino Hotel ❸**, 345 N. Arlington Ave., a bustling destination with comfortable rooms, several restaurants, and a comedy club. (☎348-2200. Rooms $43-125. AmEx/D/MC/V.) The **Bonanza Inn ❷**, 215 W. 4th St. in downtown, is a solid option for those who want to spend money on activities, not lodging. (☎322-8632 or 800-808-3303. King beds M-Th $35, F $55, Sa $65. AmEx/D/MC/V.)

◖ FOOD. Casinos offer a range of all-you-can-eat buffets, but you can escape the clutches of these giants to find inexpensive eateries with a local feel. ◪**The Pneumatic Diner ❷**, 501 W. 1st St., in Truckee River Terr., is a funky, vegetarian diner that creates unique and tasty Italian, Mexican, French, and Middle Eastern concoctions. The delightfully irreverent menu provides a glossary of terms. (☎786-8888, ext. 106. Open M-F 11am-11pm, Sa 9am-11pm, Su 8am-11pm. MC/V.) In a town filled with taquerias, **Miguel's ❷**, 1415 S. Virginia St., is the best. (☎322-2722. Open Tu-Th 11am-9pm, F-Sa 11am-10pm, Su noon-8pm. D/MC/V.) For hearty rooftop dining with in-the-know locals and a friendly, knowledgable staff, leave the casino district and head to **Silver Peak Restaurant and Brewery ❸**, 124 Wonder St. (☎324-1864. Open M-Th and Su 11am-midnight, F-Sa 11am-2am) where there is an ever-changing menu of creative, home-brewed beers.

▣ ENTERTAINMENT. Almost all casinos offer live nighttime entertainment, but most shows are not worth the steep admission prices. At **Circus Circus**, 500 N. Sierra St., a small circus on the midway above the casino floor performs a variety of "big-top" shows approximately every 30min. (☎329-0711. Shows M-Th noon-11:45pm, F-Su 11:15am-11:45pm.) For entertainment listings and info on casino events, check out the free *This Week* or *Best Bets* magazines. *The Reno News & Review* also provides an alternative look at weekly events every Thursday. The **National Automobile Museum**, 10 S. Lake St. at Mill St., houses over 200 antique and unique vehicles, including Elvis's 1973 Cadillac and a gold-plated Delorean. (☎333-9300. Open M-Sa 9:30am-5:30pm, Su 10am-4pm. $9, seniors $7, ages 6-18 $3.) Jumpstart your adrenaline at the **Ultimate Rush Speed and Thrill Park,** 2500 E. 2nd St. by the Grand Sierra Resort. The park offers the "Ultimate Rush," a combination skydiving, bungee-jumping, and hang gliding ride ($25), as well as go-karts ($6) and mini-golf ($5) for the less daring. (☎786-7005. Open daily noon-9pm.)

▣ DAYTRIP FROM RENO: PYRAMID LAKE. Located 30 mi. north of Reno on Rte. 445, on the Paiute Indian Reservation, the deep turquoise Pyramid Lake is one of the most beautiful bodies of water in the US. The lake's pristine shores are a soothing respite from Reno's clanging slot machines and a fantastic spot for world-class trout fishing and boating. **Camping ❶** is allowed anywhere on the lakeshore, but only designated areas have toilet facilities. Permits are required for day use ($6), camping ($9), and fishing ($7), and are available at the **Ranger Station** and **Marina,** which is housed in the same building, at 2500 Lakeview Dr. (☎476-1156), in Sutcliffe. The **Pyramid Lake Museum and Visitors Center,** has displays on the Paiute Tribe for curious visitors. (☎574-1088. Open M-F 8am-4:30pm; summer also Sa 10am-4:30pm. Free.)

UTAH

In 1848, persecuted members of the Church of Jesus Christ of Latter-Day Saints (colloquially called Mormons) settled on the land that is now Utah, intending to establish their own theocratic state. Mormons eventually gave up their dreams of theocracy, and statehood was granted on January 4, 1896. Today the state's population is 70% Mormon—a religious presence that creates a haven for family values. Utah's citizens dwell primarily in the 100 mi. corridor along I-15, from Ogden to Provo. Outside this area, Utah's natural beauty dominates, intoxicating visitors in a way that Utah's watered-down 3.2% beer cannot.

▇ PRACTICAL INFORMATION

Capital: Salt Lake City.

Visitor Info: Utah Travel Council, 300 N. State St., Salt Lake City 84114 (☎801-538-1030 or 800-200-1160; www.utah.com), located directly across from the capitol building. The Council office has the *Utah Vacation Planner's* lists of motels, national parks, and campgrounds, and brochures on biking, rafting, and skiing. Open M-F 8am-5pm, Sa-Su 10am-5pm. **Utah Parks and Recreation,** 1594 W. North Temple, Ste. 116, Salt Lake City 84114 (☎801-538-7220). Information on camping, boating, and highways. Open M-F 8am-5pm.

Controlled Substances: Mormons abstain from alcohol (as well as from coffee and tea). State liquor stores are sparse, and grocery stores and convenience stores only sell beer. Restaurants serve wine, but licensing laws can split a room—you may have to move to the bar if you want a mixed drink. Places that sell hard alcohol must be "members only;" tourists can find a "sponsor"—an entering patron—or get a short-term membership, usually $5 for 2 weeks.

Postal Abbreviation: UT. **Sales Tax:** 5.75-7.75%.

SALT LAKE CITY   ☎801

Tired from five months of travel across the plains, Brigham Young looked out across the Great Salt Lake and said: "This is the place." He believed that in this desolate valley his band of Mormon pioneers had finally found a haven where they could practice their religion freely. Though Mormons make up less than half of Salt Lake City's population today, Temple Square is still the focal point of downtown, and the Church of Jesus Christ of Latter-Day Saints (LDS) continues to hold tremendous sway over the city. The cultural mix engenders a city vibrant enough to have welcomed the world during the 2002 Winter Olympics. As the only American city with world-class skiing within 30min. of downtown, Salt Lake City also serves as home base for visitors to the seven surrounding ski meccas.

THE SOUTHWEST

⌐ TRANSPORTATION

Airport: Salt Lake City International (SLC), 776 N. Terminal Dr. (☎575-2400), 7 mi. west of Temple Sq. UTA bus #50 runs between the terminal and downtown ($1.50). Buses leave every 30min. M-F 6:15am-11:30pm; every hr. Sa 7am-11pm, Su 6am-6pm. Taxi to Temple Sq. about $25.

Trains: Amtrak, 340 S. 600 W. (☎322-3510 or 800-872-7245; www.amtrak.com). Open daily 10:30pm-5:30am. Use caution in this area at night. To **Denver** (15hr., 1 per day, $99) and **San Francisco** (22hr., 1 per day, $66-73).

Buses: Greyhound Intermodal Hub, 600 W. 300 S. (☎355-9579; www.greyhound.com), next to the Amtrak station. Open daily 5am-midnight; ticket window open 6:30am-11:45pm. To **Denver** (10hr., 3 per day, $70) and **Las Vegas** (8hr., 2 per day, $55).

Public Transit: Utah Transit Authority (UTA; ☎743-3882; www.rideuta.com). Frequent service to University of Utah campus, and buses to suburbs, airport, and mountain canyons. The #802 express runs to Provo ($3). TRAX light rail follows Main St. from downtown to Sandy and to the University of Utah. Buses every 20-60min. M-Sa 6am-11pm. Fare $1-2, under 5 free. Maps available at libraries and the Visitors Center. UTA buses and TRAX trains traveling downtown near the major sites are free.

Taxi: Ute Cab, ☎359-7788. **Yellow Cab,** ☎521-2100. **City Cab,** ☎363-5550.

✳❓ ORIENTATION AND PRACTICAL INFORMATION

Temple Square is the heart of downtown. Street names increase in increments of 100, indicating how many blocks east, west, north, or south they lie from Temple Sq.; the "0" points are **Main Street** (north-south) and **South Temple** (east-west). State St., West Temple, and North Temple are 100-level streets. Occasionally, streets are called 13th S. or 17th N., which are the same as 1300 S. or 1700 N. Local addresses often include cross streets. For example, a building on 13th S. (1300 S.) might be listed as 825 E. 1300 S., meaning the cross street is 800 E. (8th E.). Smaller streets and those that do not fit the grid pattern sometimes have non-numeric names.

Visitor Info: Salt Palace Convention Center and Salt Lake City Visitors Bureau, 90 S. West Temple (☎534-4902). Located in Salt Palace Convention Center. Open in summer M-F 9am-6pm, Sa-Su 9am-5pm; in winter daily 9am-5pm.

GLBT Resources: The **Little Lavender Book** (☎323-0727; www.lavenderbook.com). A directory of gay-friendly Salt Lake City services, distributed twice yearly. **Q Salt Lake** (☎649-6663; www.qsaltlake.com). A free newspaper with articles on GLBT issues and events, published bi-weekly.

Hotlines: Rape Crisis, ☎467-7273. **Suicide Prevention,** ☎261-1442. Both 24hr.

Internet Access: Salt Lake City Public Library, 210 E 400 S. (☎524-8200). A beautiful high-tech facility. Open M-Th 9am-9pm, F-Sa 9am-6pm, Su 1-5pm.

Post Office: 230 W. 200 S. (☎532-2906), 1 block south and 1 block west of Visitors Center. Open M-F 8am-5:30pm, Sa 9am-2pm. **Postal Code:** 84101.

⌐ ACCOMMODATIONS

Affordable motels cluster at the southern end of downtown, around 200 W. and 600 S., and on North Temple. Prices rise during the Sundance Film Festival.

City Creek Inn, 230 W. North Temple (☎533-9100 or 866-533-4898; www.citycreekinn.com), conveniently located by Temple Sq. Clean, ranch-style rooms. Free local calls and HBO. Singles $54; doubles $64. In winter singles $46; doubles 56. AAA discount. AmEx/D/MC/V. ❸

Salt Lake City

▲▲ ACCOMMODATIONS
The Avenues Hostel, 4
City Creek Inn, 3
Salt Lake City KOA, 5
Ute Hostel, 14

🍎 FOOD
Hires Big H, 13
Oasis Cafe, 9
One World Cafe, 6
Red Iguana, 2
Ruth's Diner, 1
Sage's Cafe, 10

NIGHTLIFE
Club Sound, 8
Burt's Tiki Lounge, 1
Port O'Call Social Club, 12
Trapp Door, 7
Squatter's Pub Brewery, 11

International Ute Hostel, 21 E. Kelsey Ave. (☎595-1645; www.internationalutehostel.com), near the intersection of 1300 S. and Main St. Offers a homey atmosphere with cozy rooms. Free pickup from the airport, bus, and train stations with advance reservations. Wi-Fi. Check-in 24hr. No curfew. Reservations recommended July-Sept. and Jan.-Mar. Dorms $20; private rooms $45. Cash only. ❶

Salt Lake City KOA, 1400 W. North Temple (☎328-0224), 14 blocks from Temple Square. Camping here is a cheap way to stay near the city and on the bus line in summer. Hot tub, pool, Wi-Fi. Expect more RVs than tents. Summer tent sites $30; RV sites with hookup $40. MC/V. ❷

🍴 FOOD

Good, cheap, and surprisingly varied restaurants pepper the city. For a quick bite, **ZCMI Mall,** across from Temple Sq., has a food court. The downtown **farmers' market** in Pioneer Park, 400 W 300 S, has fresh food. (☎333-1103; www.slcfarmersmarket.org. Open June-Oct. Sa 8am-1pm.)

🍽 **Ruth's Diner,** 2100 Emigration Canyon Rd. (☎582-5807; www.ruthsdiner.com). Take Foothill Rd. to 8th/Sunnyside and follow into the canyon. A Salt Lake City landmark known for its huge portions. A full bar with live music at night. For lunch, try the pan-seared salmon ($11). Omelets $6-8. Open daily 8am-10pm. AmEx/D/MC/V. ❷

FOOD FOR THOUGHT

World hunger got you down? The folks at One World Everybody Eats are combating hunger one Salt Lake City resident at a time. The non-profit runs the **One World Café** (at right), a "community kitchen" based on a commitment to providing fresh, organic foods every day, eliminating food waste, and ensuring that every member of the community is able to enter the kitchen with dignity and eat a healthy meal.

At One World Café, there is neither a set menu nor any fixed prices. Instead, the compassionate servers and staff ask only that community members pay what they feel is fair for their meal. Although the menu changes daily, there are always a number of vegetarian and vegan options. For those without the means to pay, One World offers two options: 1hr. of volunteer work earns you one meal voucher; alternatively, One World offers rice and dal every day for free.

One World Café opened its doors in 2003, and since then has become a sustainable non-profit. It also welcomes volunteers who may not need to work for their meal.

The community kitchen is located at 41 S. 300 E. Open daily 11am-9pm. For more info about volunteering options, call ☎801-519-2002, or visit www.oneworldeverybodyeats.org.

◙ **One World Cafe,** 41 S. 300 E. (☎519-2002; www.oneworldeverybodyeats.org). This self-styled community kitchen offers fresh, organic food with no set menu and no set prices. Management asks only that patrons contribute a fair donation to the restaurant for their delicious food. Meat, vegetarian, and vegan options. Open daily 11am-9pm. MC/V. ❶

Red Iguana, 736 W. North Temple (☎322-1489; www.rediguana.com). Famous for its *moles* ($12.30-13), this busy family-owned restaurant serves authentic Mexican food in a festive atmosphere. Veggie nachos $6.45. Daily entree combo $11. Open M-Th 11am-10pm, F 11am-11pm, Sa 10am-11pm, Su 10am-9pm. AmEx/D/MC/V. ❷

⬡ SIGHTS

LATTER-DAY SIGHTS. The center of the Mormon religion, **Temple Square** encloses the seat of the highest Mormon authority and the central temple. The square has two **Visitors Centers.** *(Both open daily 9am-9pm.)* Visitors can wander around the 35-acre square, but the temple is not open to the public. A visitor info line *(☎800-537-9703)* provides up-to-date hours and tour info. Guided 45min. tours leave from the flagpole every 10min. The beautiful **Joseph Smith Memorial Building** houses two restaurants with views of the city. *(For tours ☎240-1266. Open M-Sa 9am-9pm. Free.)* Temple Sq. is also home to the **Mormon Tabernacle** and its famed choir. Rehearsals and performances are free. *(Organ recitals M-Sa noon-12:30pm, Su 2-2:30pm; in summer also M-Sa 2-2:30pm. Choir rehearsals Th 8-9:30pm; choir performs Su 9:30-10am, doors open at 8:15am, must be seated by 9:15am.)* In summer, free concerts are held in **Brigham Young Historic Park,** at the corner of State and N. Temple. *(☎800-537-9703.)*

The **Church of Jesus Christ of Latter Day Saints Office Building** is the tallest building in town, and the elevator to the 26th floor grants a view of the Great Salt Lake. *(50 E. North Temple. ☎800-537-9703. Observation deck open M-Sa 9am-4:30pm; accessible only by guided tour.)* Access the LDS church's collection of genealogical materials at the **Family Search Center,** 15 E. South Temple St., in the Joseph Smith Memorial Building. The actual collection is located in the **Family History Library.** *(35 N. West Temple. ☎240-2331. Search Center open M-Sa 9am-9pm. Library open M 7:30am-6pm, Tu-Sa 7:30am-10pm. Free.)* Early Mormon history is recounted at the **Museum of Church History and Art,** 45 N. West Temple St., with an original 1830 Book of Mormon and Brigham Young's famous prayer bell. *(☎240-4615. Open M-F 9am-9pm, Sa-Su 10am-7pm. Free.)*

MUSEUMS. Visiting exhibits and a permanent collection of international art wow visitors to the guava-colored **Utah Museum of Fine Arts,** on the University of Utah campus, just off S. Campus Dr. (☎581-7332; www.umfa.utah.edu. Open Tu and Th-F 10am-5pm, W 10am-8pm, Sa-Su 11am-5pm. $5, students and ages 6-18 and over 65 $3.) Also on campus, the **Museum of Natural History** has interactive displays on the history of the Wasatch Front, with an emphasis on anthropology, biology, and paleontology. (☎581-6927; www.umnh.utah.edu. Open M-Sa 9:30am-5:30pm, Su noon-5pm. $6; ages 3-12, students, and over 62 $3.50; under 3 free.) The **Salt Lake Art Center** shows an impressive array of contemporary art and rotates exhibits every two to three months. (20 S. West Temple. ☎328-4201; www.slartcenter.org. Open Tu-Th and Sa 11am-6pm, F 11am-9pm. Suggested donation $2.) Twenty-five miles southwest of downtown, the museum at the ▓Kennecott Utah Copper Bingham Canyon Mine, 8362 W 10200 S, introduces visitors to the "Richest Hole on Earth." The mine itself, still fully functional, is the only manmade object besides the Great Wall of China that is visible from space. It's well worth the trip to see trucks hauling ore out of this massive copper mine. (From downtown, take I-15 S to 7200 S. Exit west and proceed to 7800 S., which merges into the Bingham Hwy. Turn left (south) on Rte. 111 toward the entrance gate. ☎252-3234. Open daily Apr.-Oct. 8am-8pm, weather permitting. Cars $5; no motorcycles.)

THE GREAT SALT LAKE. The Great Salt Lake, administered by Great Salt Lake State Marina, is a remnant of prehistoric Lake Bonneville and is so salty that only blue-green algae and brine shrimp can survive in it. The salt content varies from 5-27%, providing the buoyancy credited with keeping the lake free of drownings. Decaying organic material on the shore gives the lake its pungent odor. **Antelope Island State Park,** in the middle of the lake, separated from the city by Farmington Bay, is a great place to see wildlife or go for a briny dip. (For the lake's south shore, take I-80 17 mi. west of Salt Lake City to Exit 104. To the island, take I-15 to Exit 332 (Hwy. 108/1700 S) and go 7 mi. west. ☎773-2941; www.utah.com/stateparks/antelope_island.htm. Open daily 7am-dusk. Day use $9 per vehicle, $6 per bicycle or pedestrian.)

♫ ▓ ENTERTAINMENT AND NIGHTLIFE

Salt Lake City's summer months are jammed with evening concerts. The **Temple Square Concert Series** presents free outdoor concerts in **Brigham Young Historic Park,** at the corner of State and North Temple, with music ranging from string quartets to acoustic guitar. (☎800-537-9703. Concerts Tu and F June-July 8pm, Aug. 7:30pm. Call for schedule.) The **Utah Symphony Orchestra** performs in gold-leafed **Abravanel Hall,** 123 W. South Temple. (☎533-6683; www.utahsymphony.org. Office open M-Sa 10am-6pm. Limited summer season with outdoor venues; call 1 week in advance. Tickets Sept.-May $12-48, students $8.) The University of Utah's **Red Butte Garden,** 300 Wakara Way (☎581-4747; www.redbuttegarden.org), has a summer concert series featuring national acts in an immaculate garden with stunning views of the entire Salt Lake basin.

The free *City Weekly* and *Q Salt Lake* list events and are available at bars, clubs, and restaurants. Laws passed by early Mormon legislators make it illegal to serve alcohol in a public place. Hence, all liquor-serving institutions are "private clubs," serving only members and their "sponsored" guests. In order to get around this barrier, most bars and clubs charge a "temporary membership fee"—a cover. Despite all this, Salt Lake City has an active nightlife scene, centering on S. West Temple and the blocks near the railroad tracks.

Port O'Call Social Club, 400 S. West Temple. (☎521-0589; www.portocall.com). An unassuming sports bar by day and dance club by night where it's not surprising to see fraternity brothers partying next to middle-aged couples. Beer $3.50. W live music. Th live band karaoke. Temporary membership $4. Cover F-Sa $5. Open daily 11am-2am; during football season 10am-2am.

Burt's Tiki Lounge, 726 S. State St. (☎521-0572). A well-worn watering hole with all the typical services of a good dive bar: live music and cheap drinks in a comfortable environment. Draft beers $2. Su karaoke. Cover $5. Open daily 5pm-2am.

Trapp Door, 615 W. 100 S. (☎533-0173; www.trappdoor.com). A gay-friendly spot with clubby dance floor for all ages. Call for details on drag shows. Th indie "Dance Evolution." F "Tongue 'n' Groove." Su Latin. Drinks $3-8. Cover $5-10. Open W-Su 9pm-2am.

◤ SKIING

Utah sells itself with pictures of daring skiers on fresh powder, hailed by many (and by many Utah license plates) as the greatest snow on earth. Seven major ski areas lie within 45min. of downtown Salt Lake, making Utah's capital a good base camp for the winter vacation paradise of the Wasatch Mountains. Call or check ski area websites for deals before purchasing lift tickets. Besides being fun, the Utah ski hills are also an excellent source of employment. If you are interested in working while you ski, check the employment section on each mountain's website or call Snowbird's **job hotline** (☎947-8240). Most slopes are open in the summer for hiking, mountain biking, and horseback riding. The area code for some resorts is ☎435. Unless noted, all other numbers share SLC's ☎801 area code.

Alta (☎359-1078; www.alta.com), 25 mi. southeast of Salt Lake City in Little Cotton-wood Canyon. Cheap tickets and magnificent skiing. No-frills resort eschews opulence and rejects snowboarders. 500 in. of champagne powder annually. Open mid-Nov. to mid-Apr. daily 9:15am-4:30pm. Lift tickets: full-day $52, half-day $42-47. Day pass for beginner lifts $28; full-day joint ticket with neighboring Snowbird $71.

Brighton (☎800-873-5512; www.skibrighton.com), in Big Cottonwood Canyon. Family-friendly bargain skiing and snowboarding. Open mid-Nov. to mid-Apr. M-Sa 9am-9pm, Su 9am-4pm. Lift tickets: full-day $47, half-day $40, night $30; ages 7-10 $10; under 6 free. Rentals: ski or snowboard packages $28-35 per day, children $18.

Deer Valley (☎435-649-1000 or 800-424-3337; www.deervalley.com), in Park City. Host of several 2002 Winter Olympics events. A world-class, if expensive, ski area. No snowboards. Open Dec.-Apr. daily 9am-4:15pm. Lift tickets: full-day $79, half-day $55; seniors $56/39; children $47/38. Ski rentals: $47-58 per day, children $35.

Solitude (☎800-748-4754; www.skisolitude.com), in Big Cottonwood Canyon, 30min. south of Salt Lake. Uncrowded slopes and 6 mi. of nordic trails at Silver Lake. Open Nov. to mid-Apr. daily 9am-4pm. Lift tickets: full-day $53, half-day $45; seniors $25; children $32. Full-day joint ticket with neighboring Brighton $62. Nordic Center: full day $15, half-day $10. Rentals: skis $25-30 per day, demo skis $40, snowboards $30.

▧ DAYTRIPS FROM SALT LAKE CITY

PARK CITY

Park City is about 30 mi. east of Salt Lake City. From Salt Lake City, take I-80 east, then follow Hwy. 224 south to Park City.

Host to many of the 2002 Olympic events, nearby **Park City** is the quintessential ski town. In the winter, Park City serves as the gateway to three ski areas; in warmer months, the mountains offer great hiking and mountain biking. Watch world-class athletes train at the **Utah Olympic Park,** 3000 Bear Hollow Dr. In summer, ski-jump-ers practice on special plastic and freestylers do multiple flips into a pool. Indoors is an interactive museum where you can simulate skiing like an Olympian. (☎435-

658-4200 or 800-659-72757; www.olyparks.com. Open in summer daily 9am-6pm. Free. Guided tour $7, ages 3-17 and over 65 $5; Sa freestyle aerial shows at noon $10/7.) Park City is also teeming with festivals and major athletic events, including the **NORBA (mountain-biking) nationals** in June and **free concerts** on Wednesdays at Deer Valley. The **Visitors Center,** 1826 W. Olympic Pkwy., has more info. (☎658-4541. Open M-Sa 9am-7pm, Su 11am-4pm.)

Though prices soar during the high season, a few budget dining options still exist. A destination in its own right, the **Morning Ray ❷/La Luna Cafe ❹,** 255 Main St., inside the Treasure Mountain Inn, is a local staple for breakfast and lunch, serving omelets like the "Powderhound" and "Backcountry" ($8.25). Though its alias changes to "La Luna" at night, the cafe's fun hippie atmosphere remains the same. (☎435-649-5686. Breakfast and lunch entrees $6-10. Dinner entrees $12-18. Open daily 7am-3:30pm; W-Su also 5:30-9:30pm. AmEx/D/MC/V.) Cans line almost every inch of the walls at **Davanza's ❶,** 690 Park Ave., a pizzeria which also serves sandwiches and burgers. (☎649-2222. Slices $2.50. Burgers $5-6. Open daily 11am-11pm. AmEx/D/MC/V.) For a cold beer or a glimpse of famous skiers, **Cisero's,** 306 Main St., is a good bet on any night. (☎649-5044. Tu karaoke. W, F, Su live music . Th and Sa DJ. W mixed drinks $2. Su drafts $1, pizzas $2. Cover $5. Open daily 5pm-1am.) Locals flock to the **No-Name Saloon,** 447 Main St., home to stuffed elk heads, antler chandeliers, and a down-home fireplace. (☎649-6667; www.noname-saloon.net. Buffalo burgers $7.50-8.75. Drafts $2.50. Open daily 10am-1am.)

TIMPANOGOS CAVE NATIONAL MONUMENT

Timpanogos Cave has just one entrance, via Rte. 92 (20 mi. south of Salt Lake City off I-15, Exit 287; Rte. 92 also connects with Rte. 189 northeast of Provo). The Visitors Center (☎801-756-5238; open mid-May to late Oct. daily 7am-5:30pm) has info on the cave.

Legend has it that a set of mountain lion tracks first led Martin Hansen to the cave that bears his name. **Hansen's Cave** is only one-third of the cave system of American Fork Canyon, collectively called **Timpanogos Cave.** In a rich alpine environment, Timpanogos lures speleologists (cave nuts) and tourists alike. Though early miners shipped boxcars of stalactites and other mineral wonders back east to sell to universities and museums, plenty remain to bedazzle guests along the 1hr. walk through the depths. The cave is open to visitors only through ranger-led tours; tickets are sold at the Visitors Center. Reservations for summer weekends should be made far in advance. Bring water and warm layers: the rigorous hike to the cave climbs 1092 ft. over 1½ mi., but the temperature inside stays at 45°F. (☎801-756-5238. Open mid-May to late Oct. daily 7am-5:30pm. 3hr. hikes depart daily every 15min. 7am-4:30pm. $7, ages 6-15 $5, ages 3-5 and with Senior National Parks Pass $3, under 3 free.) An "Introduction to Caving" tour from the Visitors Center is a chance to get dirty and try spelunking for yourself. (Reservations required; call ahead for times. $15.) The National Monument is dwarfed by the **Uinta National Forest,** which blankets the mountains of the Wasatch Range. The **Alpine Scenic Drive (Route 92)** provides great views of Mt. Timpanogos and other snowcapped peaks. The 20 mi. trip takes almost 1hr. one-way. (Open late May-late Oct.; not recommended for vehicles over 30 ft. long. 3-day Forest Service pass $3 per vehicle, 14-day pass $10, annual pass $25.) Two trails lead to the peak of **Mt. Timpanogos** (11,749 ft.), the second tallest mountain in the Wasatch range. The **Timpooneke Trail** leaves from the Timpooneke Campground (15 mi. round-trip). The **Aspen Grove Trail,** which begins at the Aspen Grove Trailhead (6860 ft.), is a little shorter (14 mi. round-trip) but significantly steeper. Both trails meet before continuing to the summit. The **Pleasant Grove Ranger District** has info on area **campgrounds ❶.** (General info ☎801-785-3563, reservations 800-280-2267; www.recreation.gov. Sites $13.) **Backcountry camping ❶** in the forest requires no permit or fee as long as you respect minimum-impact guidelines. While the National Park Service forbids

THE SOUTHWEST

camping within the national monument, **Little Mill Campground ❶,** on Rte. 92 just east of the Monument, is a good starting point. (Water, vault toilets. Open early May to late Sept. Sites $13.) **Timpanooke Campground ❶,** 4 mi. farther east along the Alpine Loop, has secluded private sites. (Water, vault toilets. Open mid-June to late Sept. Reservations recommended during busy summer weekends. Sites $13.)

DINOSAUR NATIONAL MONUMENT AND VERNAL ☎ 435

In 1909, lucky paleontologist Earl Douglass came upon a river bank in eastern Utah brimming with fossilized dinosaur bones. Since then, some 350 million tons of dinosaur remains have been carted away from this Jurassic cemetery. Spectacular hiking and stark desert scenery surround the Monument and its remnants of prehistoric life. In July 2006, the Dinosaur Quarry Visitors Center was closed indefinitely due to structural instability caused by the shifting ground underneath its foundation. Though dinosaur quarry is no longer accessible to visitors, there remains plenty to do in the park. The **Temporary Visitors Center,** for instance, at the park's western entrance, offers fossil exhibits, ranger-led hikes, and shuttles to the quarry area, where visitors can still hike the easy-to-moderate **Geology Trail** (½ mi.). (☎ 781-7717. Open June-Aug. daily 8:30am-5:30pm; call for winter hours. Entrance $10 per car; $5 per cyclist, pedestrian, or tour-bus passenger.) The 4hr. **Journey Through Time** auto tour, available at Monument Headquarters (see below) is the only way to reach **Harper's Corner.** At the end of the road is an easy 2 mi. round-trip hike (1½-2hr.) leading to views of Echo Park and Whirlpool Canyon. Several hikes leave from the **Tour of the Tilted Rocks** auto tour (22 mi. round-trip), including the easy **Box Canyon** and **Hog Canyon** trails (each 1 mi. round-trip). Visitors can also explore the breathtaking Split Mountain Gorge by floating down Class III rapids on the Green River. Only two outfitters have daily permits to raft the river: **Adrift Adventures,** 9500 E. 6000 S. in Jenson, at the junction of Rte. 149 and U.S. 40; and **Don Hatch River Expeditions,** 221 N. 400 E. in Vernal. (Adrift: ☎ 789-3600 or 800-824-0150; www.adrift.com. Open May-Sept. Trips depart daily 9am. 1-day trip $75, ages 6-12 $65. Hatch: ☎ 789-4316 or 800-342-8243; www.donhatchrivertrips.com. Open M-F 8:30am-5pm, Sa-Su 8am-3pm. 1-day trip $78, ages 6-12 $68; seniors 10% off.)

The most accessible camping spot, **Green River ❶,** along Cub Creek Rd. about 5 mi. from the entrance fee station, has 88 sites. (Flush toilets and water. Closed in winter. Sites $12.) Tall cottonwoods and sheer canyon walls make **Echo Park ❶,** 13 mi. along Echo Park Rd. from Harper's Corner Dr. (4WD road; impassable when wet), the perfect location for an evening under the stars away from civilization. (21 sites. Vault toilets and water in summer. Tents only. Sites $8; free in winter when accessible.) Free **backcountry camping ❶** permits are available from Monument Headquarters or the Quarry Visitors Center. Indoor lodging is available at the **Sage Motel ❸,** 54 W. Main St., in Vernal, where each room has a different motif, ranging from "Cowboy bunkhouse" to "Golfing." (☎ 789-1442 or 800-760-1442. A/C, satellite TV, free local calls, fridge, and microwave. In summer singles $75; doubles $80. Call for winter rates. AmEx/D/MC/V.) **Stockman's ❸,** 1684 W. U.S. 40, in the Weston Plaza Hotel, 2 mi. west of town on U.S. 40, has burgers ($6-8), all-you-can-eat sirloin steak ($14), and huge desserts. (☎ 781-3030. Open M-Th 11am-9pm, F 11am-10pm, Sa 11:30am-10pm. MC/V.) For homemade chili ($3.50) or a hefty rib-eye ($18), head to the **7-11 Ranch Restaurant ❷,** 77 E. Main St. (☎ 789-1170. Sa all-you-can-eat dinner buffet. Open M-Sa 6am-10pm. MC/V.)

The monument's western entrance lies 20 mi. east of Vernal on Rte. 149, which splits from U.S. 40 southwest of the park in Jensen, UT. **Monument Headquarters,** 2 mi. east of Dinosaur, CO, on U.S. 40, is the best point to begin exploring the striking Colorado side of the park. (☎ 970-374-3000. Open June-Aug. daily 8am-4:30pm; Sept.-Oct. and Apr.-May W-Su 8:30am-4:30pm; closed Nov.-Mar.) **Gas** is available in Vernal, Jensen, and Dinosaur, CO, but provisions and resources around the park are slim. The town of **Vernal,** 20 mi. west of Dinosaur Quarry on U.S. 40, is a popular base for exploring the monument. The **Northeast Utah Visitors Center,** 496 E. Main St., inside the Utah Field House of Natural History, has interactive exhibits, fossils, and an outdoor "dinosaur garden" with 14 full-size replicas of prehistoric animals. (☎789-3799. Open daily in summer 8am-7pm; in winter 9am-5pm. $6, children and seniors $3.) The **Ashley National Forest Service Office,** 355 N. Vernal Ave., has info about outdoors activities in the Ashley and Uinta National Forests. (☎789-1181. Open M-F 8am-5pm.) **Post Office:** 67 N. 800 W. (☎789-8594; www.fs.fed.us/r4/ashley. Open M-F 9am-5pm, Sa 10am-2pm.) **Postal Code:** 84078.

FLAMING GORGE NATIONAL RECREATION AREA ☎435

At sunset, the contrast between the red canyons and the Green River's aquamarine water makes the landscape glow. The centerpiece of the Flaming Gorge National Recreation Area, however, is the 91 mi. reservoir formed in 1963 by a dam in the Green River. Boats and fishermen descend into the gorge every summer to take advantage of its 42,000 acres of shimmering water and 375 mi. of scenic shoreline.

The Green River below the dam teems with trout, providing top-notch **fishing.** To fish, get a **permit,** available at the Cedar Springs Marina (see below) and Flaming Gorge Recreation Services, at the Conoco in Dutch John. (☎885-3191; www.fishthegreen.com. Open Mar.-Oct. M-F 7am-9pm, Sa-Su 7am-10pm; Nov.-Feb. daily 9am-5pm.) For more info, call the **Utah Division of Wildlife Resources,** 1594 W. North Temple, in Salt Lake City. (☎801-538-4700; www.wildlife.utah.gov. Open M-F 7:30am-6pm.) **Cedar Springs Marina,** 2 mi. south of the dam, rents boats and offers guided fishing trips. (☎889-3795. Open Apr. 15-Oct. 15 daily 8am-6pm. 10-person pontoon boats from $140 per 3hr., $220 per day. 6-person fishing boats $70/110.) **Spinner Fall Guide Service,** 483 W 500 N in Heber City, UT, leads float trips through the gorge. (☎801-971-9553 or 877-811-3474; www.spinnerfall.com. 2-person float trip $350, includes lunch and shuttle service.) Hikers and bikers will love the area's trails, some of which snake along dangerous cliff edges. All trails allow bikes. The flat **Canyon Rim Trail** (7 mi.) has access points at Red Canyon Visitors Center and several campgrounds, and features spectacular views of Flaming Gorge. From the base of the dam, you can walk the **Little Hole** trail along the river, a scenic trail with

A TALE OF TWO CANYONS

Standing in Echo Park today, it is hard to imagine that it could have been submerged under 400 ft. of water. But for the decades-old efforts of a number of conservationists, such would be reality.

In the early 50s, a debate raged in the US Congress over a dam that was to be built at the confluence of the Green and Yampa Rivers in Dinosaur National Monument. This dam would flood the idyllic Echo Park, where John Wesley Powell and his men once found refuge after the tumultuous rapids of "Hells Half-Mile," upriver on the Green. Incensed environmental leaders at once broadcasted a message of staunch disapproval. Somewhat miraculously, their voices were heard: the dam at Echo Park would not be built.

This victory came at a cost. The Glen Canyon Dam, another concrete plug proposed as part of the same storage project, was built instead. Conservationists were powerless to stop America from forever losing one of her most majestic canyons.

Echo Park, however, remains pristine to this day. By reveling in its unique majesty, visitors can give some meaning to the loss of Glen Canyon.

Echo Park can be accessed via the 13 mi. Echo Park Road (4WD, impassable when wet), which turns east from Harpers Corner Drive some 25 mi. north of Monument Headquarters.

plenty of chances to glimpse wildlife (7 mi. one-way; the trailhead is at the Spillway Boat Ramp, just to the east of the dam). The strenuous **Elk Park Loop** (20 mi. round-trip) is perfect for mountain biking (departs from Rte. 44 at Deep Creek Rd., follows it to Forest Rd. 221 and Forest Rd. 105, skirts Browne Lake, and runs along **Old Carter and South Elk Park Trails**).

The more than 30 campgrounds around the lake make camping an easy option. The campgrounds keep 50% of their sites open for a first-come, first-served basis, so sites are generally easy to come by. (☎877-444-6777; www.recreation.gov.) The **Flaming Gorge Ranger District** (☎784-3445) also has advice on sites. **Canyon Rim ❶**, on the road to Red Canyon Visitors Center, offers views of the red-walled gorge. (Vault toilets. May to mid-Oct. sites $15; late Oct.-late Apr. free.) The 22 sunny sites at **Dripping Springs ❶**, just past Dutch John on Rte. 191, are located near prime fishing locations along the river. (Vault toilets. Reservations accepted. Sites $15.) The self-titled "civilized way to enjoy the great outdoors," the **Red Canyon Lodge ❸**, 790 Red Canyon Rd., off of Rte. 44, 24 mi. south of Manila, 2 mi. south of the Visitors Center, is the nicest indoor lodging around, complete with luxury-resort activities, a private lake, and a restaurant. (☎889-3759. 2-person cabins with bath $99; 4-person $109. Each additional adult $6, under 12 $2.)

From Vernal, follow U.S. 191 north to the recreation area on the **Flaming Gorge Scenic Byway,** which has 10 switchbacks and steep grades. The reservoir extends as far north as Green River, WY, and is also accessible from I-80 by way of Rte. 414 and Rte. 530 on the west side of the reservoir, as well as from U.S. 191, which continues along the eastern side. A recreation pass ($2 per day, $5 per 16 days, $20 per season) can be obtained at the **Flaming Gorge Visitors Center,** on U.S. 191 on the **Flaming Gorge Dam.** The Visitors Center also offers free tours of the dam. (☎885-3135. Open daily high season 8am-6pm; low season 10am-4pm.) Three miles down Red Canyon Rd., which splits from Rte. 44 to Manila 3½ mi. west of the junction with U.S. 191, the **Red Canyon Visitors Center** hangs 1360 ft. above the reservoir, offering staggering views into the canyon. (☎889-3713. Open late May-Aug. daily 8am-6pm.) **Post Office:** 690 South Blvd., in Dutch John. (☎885-3351. Open M-F 7:30am-noon and 12:30-3:30pm, Sa 8:30am-12:30pm.) **Postal Code:** 84023.

MOAB   ☎ 435

The town of Moab first got its name when the local postmaster noticed the landscape's similarity to that of the Middle East: the stones surrounding him reminded him of the red rock formations he read existed in South Jordan. When miners discovered uranium in Moab in 1952, the population grew to nearly 10,000 people in just three years, transforming the town from a quiet hamlet into a gritty yet popular desert mining outpost. Today, tourism rather than mining dominates the town. Travelers flock to Moab eager to bike the red slickrock, raft the rapids, and explore the surrounding Arches and Canyonlands National Parks. The town has adapted to its onslaught of visitors and adventure-seekers; guide companies, car repair shops, microbreweries, t-shirt shops, and organic cafes now fill the rooms of the old uranium mine headquarters on Main St.

▐▜ TRANSPORTATION AND PRACTICAL INFORMATION. Moab is 30 mi. south of I-70 on U.S. 191, just south of the junction with Rte. 128. The town center is 5 mi. south of the entrance to Arches National Park and 35 mi. north of the turnoff to the Needles section of Canyonlands National Park. U.S. 191 becomes Main St. for 5 mi. through downtown. The closest Amtrak **train** (☎800-872-7245; www.amtrak.com) and Greyhound **bus** (☎800-454-2487; www.greyhound.com) stations are in Green River, 52 mi. northwest of town. Some hotels and hostels will pick up guests from the train or bus station for a fee. Bighorn Express (☎888-655-

7433) runs **shuttles** daily to and from the Salt Lake City airport, stopping in Green River and Price. **Shuttles** leave from the Ramada Inn, 182 S. Main St. (4hr.; departs Salt Lake City airport at 2pm, departs Moab at 7:30am; $65. Reservations recommended.) Roadrunner Shuttle (☎259-9402) and Coyote Shuttle (☎259-8656) take you where you want to go in Moab. For a faster, more expensive option, Salmon Air offers **flights** between Salt Lake City airport and Moab. (Schedules and prices ☎800-448-3413 or see www.salmonair.com.) The **Moab Information Center,** 3 Center St., at the intersection of Center and Main, has free city brochures and info on area parks. (☎259-8825 or 800-635-6622. Open May-Sept. 8am-9pm; Oct. 8am-8pm; Nov.-Apr. 8am-5pm.) **Internet** access: **Grand County Library,** 257 East Center Street. (☎259-1111. Open M-W 9am-9pm, Th-F 9am-7pm, Sa 9am-5pm.) **Post Office:** 50 E. 100 N. (☎259-7427. Open M-F 8am-5pm, Sa 9am-1pm.) **Postal Code:** 84532.

ᖴ ACCOMMODATIONS. Chain motels line Main St. (U.S. 191), but rooms fill up fast from April to October. **The Kokopelli Lodge ❶,** 72 S. 100 E., a few blocks off of Main St., provides one and two person rooms along with friendly service and a convenient location. (☎259-7615. Check-in after 3pm. Check-out 11am. Reservations strongly recommended for spring, summer, and fall. Singles $65; doubles $69. AmEx/D/MC/V). **◙Lazy Lizard International Hostel ❶,** 1213 S. U.S. 191, is 1 mi. south of Moab on U.S. 191. The hostel's amenities, including access to the kitchen, lounge, outdoor patio, and hot tub draw a mix of students, backpackers, and young families. (☎259-6057. Reception 8am-11pm; late arrivals can be arranged. Check-out 11am. Reservations recommended for weekends in spring and fall. Tent sites $6; dorms $9; private rooms $22-36; cabins $27-47. AmEx/D/MC/V.)

Hundreds of campsites blanket the greater Moab area, and camping is Moab's most affordable lodging option. Goose Island, Negro Bill, Drinks Canyon, Hal Canyon, Oak Grove, Big Bend, Upper Big Bend, Fisher Towers, Onion Creek, Hittle Bottom, and Dewey Bridge **Campgrounds ❶,** all on Rte. 128 (intersection at U.S. 191 and Rte. 128), are maintained by the U.S. Bureau of Land Management (BLM) and sit right on the banks of the Colorado River. Signs for Negro Bill and Drinks Canyon are well hidden near the entrance to the other campgrounds. (☎259-2100. Fire pits. No drinking water, but toilets at all sites. Campsites are available on a first-come, first-served basis. $5 at **Negro Bill, Drinks Canyon, Upper Big Bend,** and **Onion Creek.** $10 at all other campgrounds, which also have picnic tables.) **Red Rock Lodge ❷** and Suites, 51 Route 100 W., draws guests with hot tub access, in-room TVs and refrigerators, and a downtown location. (☎269-5431. Reception 8am-noon. Check-out 11am. Reservations strongly recommended in season. Rooms with one queen bed or two double beds $60; one king bed $65. Rooms with two queen beds $70. Call for winter rates. AmEx/D/MC/V.)

◖ FOOD. Moab is filled with bookstore cafes and quirky breakfast spots that open early for adventurers looking to get a head start on their day. **◙EklectiCafé ❶,** 352 N. Main St., dishes delicious pastries and coffee in addition to specials like banana-nut pancakes ($8.75) and vegetarian dishes. You'll recognize it easily thanks to the giant mosaic of a coffee cup out front. (☎259-6896. Breakfast $4-8.75. Lunch $4.50-8.50. Open M-Sa 7:30am-2:30pm, Su 7:30am-1pm.) **◙Mondo Café ❶,** 59 S. Main St., in McStiff's Plaza, offers a variety of cool and hot beverages, in addition to breakfast and lunch options. To beat Moab's heat, try the iced latte ($3.50) or the frozen chai ($4.50). Laptop-toting customers can take advantage of Mondo's free Wi-Fi or use the cafe's computer for $0.75 per 5min. (☎259-5551. Open M-Th and Su 6:30am-7pm, F-Sa 6:30am-9:30pm. MC/V.)

▨ OUTDOOR ACTIVITIES. Mountain biking is the big draw in Moab and attracts thousands each year. **The Slickrock Trail** (10-12 mi.), beginning on Sand Flats Rd., is one of the most popular choices. Originally designed for motorcycle use, the trail is technically difficult with lots of climbing. Novices may enjoy the **Bar M Loop** (7.8 mi.) or the **Lower Monitor Loop** (7.4 mi), while those looking for a moderate challenge can check out the Sovereign Trail. **Rim Cyclery,** 94 W. 100 N, rents road and mountain bikes, does repairs, and provides friendly service and information on the trails. (☎259-5333 or 888-304-8219. Open daily 9am-6pm. Standard bikes $43 per day, $33 per half-day.) Countless rafting companies help outdoor enthusiasts explore the nearby Colorado and Green Rivers. ◪**Canyon Voyages Adventure Co.,** 211 N. Main St., has friendly, knowledgeable guides for both hiking and rafting tours who will personalize their services to meet your specific skill level. (☎259-6007 or 800-7336-6007. Rafting: half-day $42-45; full day $55. Hiking: half-day $50; full day $80. Call at least a week in advance for hiking tours. Some tours include lunch with vegetarian options.) Numerous outfitters can arrange horseback, motorboat, canoe, jeep, and helicopter rides for you. **Adrift Adventures,** 378 N. Main St., leads various rafting trips on the Colorado River and other adventure combinations, from half-day to five-day trips. (☎259-8594 or 800-874-4483. March-Oct. daily 7am-9pm. Rafting: half-day $39-42, ages 5-17 $29-31; full day $53/$40.)

UTAH'S NATURAL WONDERS

Arches, Canyonlands, Capitol Reef, Bryce Canyon, and Zion National Parks comprise Utah's Grand Circle of national parks, all connected by a series of scenic highways. In their midst lies the mammoth Grand Staircase-Escalante National Monument, sprawling south and east of Bryce Canyon and west of Capitol Reef. The spectacular arches, canyons, amphitheaters, plateaus, slickrock, and redrock of these public lands provide adventures for the experienced hiker and the cautious tourist alike, and the park's panoramic brilliance is not to be missed.

From Moab, take U.S. 191 north 5 mi. to **Arches.** Continue 60 mi. north on U.S. 191 and then take Rte. 313 west for 25 mi. to the Island in the Sky area of **Canyonlands.** To reach the Needles area of Canyonlands (87 mi.), take U.S. 191 south from Moab to Rte. 211 W. To get to **Capitol Reef,** continue south on U.S. 191, then take Rte. 95 northwest to Rte. 24. Continue west on Rte. 24, then move south onto Rte. 12 to reach **Grand Staircase-Escalante National Monument.** Scenic Rte. 12 runs south

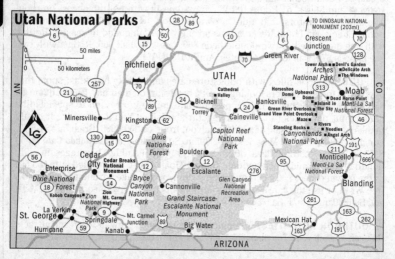

Utah National Parks

through Dixie National Forest and into **Bryce Canyon.** For **Zion,** follow Rte. 12 W to U.S. 89 S through Mt. Carmel Jct., and take Rte. 9 W. For those with less time, a trip along Rts. 12 and 95 gives a great sense of the surrounding parks.

Southern Utah's two national forests are divided into districts, some of which lie near the national parks and serve as excellent places to stay on a cross-country jaunt. **Manti-La Sal National Forest** has two sections near Arches and the Needles area of Canyonlands. **Dixie National Forest** stretches from Capitol Reef through Bryce all the way to the western side of Zion. It may be 90°F in southern Utah in June, but you'll still see snow on the ground in these forests.

> **TIP** **EXPERIENCED OR NOVICE?** When exploring the trails of Utah's national parks, park rangers and guides warn travelers to stick to their limits. Trails marked for "experienced" hikers are often long and steep, with lots of rock scrambling, while those marked for "novice" are generally flatter and shorter, and are more clearly marked. When journeying to the desert for the first time, it is important to give yourself time to adjust to the climate.

ARCHES ☎435

In the words of John Wayne, Arches National Park is where "God put the West." From its enormous balanced rocks to red sandstone walls, Arches National Park draws travelers from around the world to explore its prehistoric grandeur. Winding spires and hidden arches tower above the desert with a majesty that has emblazoned its image on Utah license plates and served as the backdrop for many movies. Though the heat may be extreme, the Arches' dramatic beauty, from "Parade of Elephants" to the "Fiery Furnace," is well worth it.

ORIENTATION AND PRACTICAL INFORMATION. The park entrance is on U.S. 191, 5 mi. north of Moab. Although no public transit serves the park, shuttle bus companies go to both Arches and Moab from surrounding towns. Many visitors come in the summer, but 100°F temperatures make hiking difficult—be sure to bring plenty of water. The weather is best in the spring and fall, when temperate days and nights make long hikes more enjoyable. An entrance pass ($10 per car, $5 for pedestrians, bicycles, and motorcycles) covers admission for seven days and comes with a map of the park and the locations of the largest, best-known arches. If you are going to several national parks, it makes sense to buy an Interagency Annual Pass ($80), good for entrance into all US National Parks as well as Fish and Wildlife Service Refuges up to a year from purchase. More detailed maps are available for purchase at the **Visitors Center** just inside the park entrance. (☎719-2299; www.nps.gov/arch. Open daily Oct.-Feb. 8am-4:30pm; extended hours Mar.-Sept. 7:30am-6:30pm.) Check out the free ranger-led programs, nature walks (daily 10am and 4:30pm) and evening "campfire talks," offered at the Devils Garden campground amphitheater (daily 9pm). For more info, ask at the Visitors Center. Sign up at least a day in advance for guided walks into the Fiery Furnace; tours fill up fast and only experienced hikers can secure a permit. (Tours daily June-Sept. 9am; Oct-June 10am, 4pm. $10. Permit $2.)

> **TIP** **WATCH WHERE YOU STEP.** Though the lumpy soil bordering the trails at Arches may look inviting, park rangers urge hikers to stay on the trails and off of the cryptobiotic (biological) soil. Hidden within the cryptobiotic soil lies a community of fungi, algae, cyanobacteria, and other simple plants. When travelers step, bike, or drive over the soil, they can damage the desert and its life forms.

✗ CAMPING. The park's only campground, **Devil's Garden ❶**, has 52 well-maintained campsites amid piñon trees and giant sandstone formations. The campground is within walking distance of the Devil's Garden and Broken Arch trailheads, but is a winding 18 mi. drive (about 30min.) from the Visitors Center. Reservations (www.reserveusa.com) are available for 28 of the sites between March 1 and October 31 for an additional $9. Reservations must be made at least four days in advance. The remaining 24 sites are available on a first-come, first-serve basis at the Visitors Center beginning at 7:30am; they can fill up very quickly in the high season. (☎719-2299. Bathrooms, water, picnic tables and fire pits. No showers or wood-gathering. 1-week max. stay. Sites $15.) If the heat is too much at Arches, the **Manti-La Sal National Forest** offers other camping options. Take Rte. 128 along the Colorado River and turn right at Castle Valley, or go south 6 mi. from Moab on U.S. 191 and turn left onto Loop Rd. Though a bit out of the way, the forest has many campgrounds, including the beautiful **Warner Lake ❶**, where sites sit 4000 ft. above Arches. (For reservations www.reserveusa.com. $10.) Contact the Manti-La Sal National Forest (☎259-7155) for more info.

◪ HIKING. While the roads that snake through Arches offer exceptional scenery for car passengers, the real points of interest are only accessible by foot. Those hiking in the summer will want to load up on water and sunscreen and start early to avoid the midday heat. Pets are not allowed on trails. The most popular hike in the park leads to the oft-photographed Delicate Arch. The trail (3 mi., round-trip 2-3hr.) begins at the Wolfe Ranch parking area and climbs 480 ft. To view the spectacular arch without the arduous hike, take the wheelchair-accessible **Delicate Arch Viewpoint Trail** which begins in the Viewpoint parking area and takes around 15min. to get to the lower viewpoint location and 30min. to the upper viewpoint. **Devil's Garden** (7 mi., 3-5hr. round-trip) is the longest of the park's trails and requires some scrambling over rocks, but hardy travelers will be rewarded by the eight arches visible along the trail. The trek is not recommended in wet or snowy conditions. **Park Avenue** (1 mi., 30min.-1hr.) is a moderate hike that is gorgeous at sunset and the closest to the park entrance. **Fiery Furnace** (3hr. guided hike) runs through a labyrinth of narrow sandstone canyons, but there is no trail; guides are strongly recommended for those who wish to explore this area (see the Visitors Center for more info on guided hikes, or to secure a hiking permit). For an easier hike suitable for small children, try **Balanced Rock** (round-trip 0.3 mi., 15-30min.), accessible from the Balanced Rock parking area, or **The Windows** (round-trip 1 mi., ½-1hr.), which offers spectacular views of two huge arches. The Windows is accessible from the Windows parking area.

CANYONLANDS   ☎435

At 527 square miles, Canyonlands is awe-inspiring in its size as well as its terrain. Divided by the Green and Colorado Rivers, each of Canyonlands' three sections has a personality all its own. The best views of the expansive red-rock canyons and the surrounding mountains are at the opposite ends of the park, in the Needles region and Island in the Sky. For the more adventurous, backpacking through the Maze's 30 mi. labyrinth can prove a technical challenge, but one that is rewarded by sights of sheer red sandstone walls and towering fins. With its diversity in hiking and camping options, as well as breathtaking views, Canyonlands truly is, as its founders intended, an "inspiration to the public."

▣◪ TRANSPORTATION AND PRACTICAL INFORMATION. The three districts of Canyonlands are **Island in the Sky**, the **Needles**, and the **Maze**, separated by the Green and Colorado Rivers. The park also includes the detached **Horseshoe Canyon** district. Island in the Sky is the most popular region, with plenty of easy trails as well as many lookout points viewable by car. Take U.S. 191 to Rte. 313, 10 mi. north of Moab and 22 mi. south of I-70. Follow Rte. 313 22 mi. southwest. The Needles, geared toward backcountry adventure, is on Rte. 211. From Moab, take U.S. 191 S for 40 mi., then Rte. 211 W for 34 mi. To reach the Maze from I-70, take Rte. 24 south for 29 mi. to a turnoff just past the entrance to Goblin Valley State Park. From there, a dirt road leads 46 mi. southeast to the ranger station. To ride the rapids of the Green or Colorado Rivers, contact one of the rafting companies based in Moab. Horseshoe Canyon is home to the art of prehistoric cultures viewable in the Great Gallery, 32 mi. east of Rte. 24 on a dirt road. None of the park districts are accessible by public transit, but the closest Amtrak **train** (☎800-872-7245; www.amtrak.com) and Greyhound **bus** (☎800-454-2487; www.greyhound.com) stations are in Green River, 52 mi. northwest of Moab on I-70. Coyote Shuttle (☎259-8656) and Roadrunner Shuttle (☎259-9402), both based out of Moab, **bus** visitors to and from Canyonlands. Entrance fees vary according to district: Island in the Sky and Needles are $10 per car, $5 per pedestrian or biker; the pass is good for one week at either entrance. The Maze is free. Island in the Sky and Needles both have a **Visitors Center,** and the Maze has a **rangers station.** (Island in the Sky Visitors Center: ☎259-4712. Needles Visitors Center: ☎259-4711. Maze Hans Flat Ranger Station: ☎259-2652. Horseshoe Canyon operates out of the Hans Flat Ranger Station. All open daily 8am-4:30pm; extended hours during high season.) Moab is the closest town to Island in the Sky (37 mi.), while Monticello (49 mi.) is the closest town to the Needles. Green River, on Rte. 70 and Hanksville, west of the park on Rte. 24, are closest to the Maze and each has several budget motels, restaurants, and cafes. Green River is 93 mi. from the Maze. Hanksville is 99 mi. away. All park areas can be contacted at www.nps.gov/cany. **Post Office:** 50 E. 100 N., in Moab. (☎259-7427. Open M-F 8am-5pm, Sa 9am-1pm.) **Postal Code:** 84532.

▟▛ ACCOMMODATIONS AND FOOD. Canyonlands does not have any indoor accommodations, so travelers who want rooms should stay in Moab, Monticello, Green River, or Hanksville, though Moab has the most options. Those who wish to camp are treated to well-maintained campgrounds. In the northern area of the park, Island in the Sky and Dead Horse Point State Park each have a campground. **Willow Flat ❶,** 7 mi. southeast of the Island in the Sky Visitors Center, has 12 first-come, first-served sites. (Pit toilets, picnic tables. No water, no hookups. Pay at campground. $10.) There are also 20 **backcountry campsites ❶** along the White Rim Road, which circles Island in the Sky (4WD vehicles only), that require a $30 backcountry permit, available at the Visitors Center or from any park ranger; reservations for permits are accepted and recommended in spring and fall. Backcountry permits go quickly, but a few walk-up permits are often available in the summer and winter. (Pit toilets. No water. ☎259-4351.) There are 21 campsites at the

---

! WATCH YOUR STEP! Much of the park is composed of slickrock. Trails on or near slickrock are extremely treacherous in wet or icy conditions. Consult the Visitors Center for daily trail conditions.

---

nearby **Dead Horse Point State Park ❶,** on Rte. 313. Seven sites are first-come, first-served and are usually filled by early afternoon. (☎800-322-3770. Reservations recommended. Limited water, hookups, picnic tables, dishwashing, sewage disposal stations, and grills. No showers. One campsite is wheelchair accessible. $15, admission to the park $7.) Additionally, camping is available in a few designated areas of the Bureau of Land Management (BLM) lands situated along Rte. 313 just east of Island in the Sky. (Sites first-come, first-served. Pay at campgrounds. $10.) Camping in the Needles area of the park is available at **Squaw Flat Campground ❶,** 3 mi. east of the Visitors Center with 27 first-come, first-served sites, drinking water, and flush toilets ($15). To camp in the Needles backcountry, make a reservation at least two weeks in advance through the Moab Needles office (☎259-4351), or one day in advance at the Needles Visitor Center (4WD vehicles only; backcountry permit $30). The Maze has no developed campsites but **primitive campgrounds ❶** (pit toilets, no water) dot the terrain and are first-come, first-served.

There is no food available in the park. In the Needles, stock up at the **Needles Outpost ❷,** just outside the park entrance, which has gas, a café with sandwiches ($7), excellent teriyaki marinated burgers ($8), and groceries. (☎979-4007. Also has a campground and showers. Sites $15. Open daily 8:30am-6pm. Cafe open daily 9am-5pm.) For Island in the Sky, check out restaurants in nearby Moab. In the Maze, Green River and Hanksville provide the closest dining options.

◙ 🛍 SIGHTS AND OUTDOOR ACTIVITIES. Each part of Canyonlands presents a unique view. Island in the Sky, a peninsula surrounded by deep canyons, is the best option for car touring. The **Grand View Point Overlook** and the **Green River Overlook,** both clearly marked, have stunning views of the mighty rivers that carved the canyons. Those wishing to stretch their legs can enjoy the beautiful and short **Mesa Arch Trail** (½ mi., 30min. round-trip), hike around the rim of the canyon on the **Grand View Point Trail** (2 mi., 1½hr. round-trip) or try the **Syncline Loop,** a steep and strenuous 8.3 mi. loop around the Upheaval Dome area with great viewpoints. For a moderate hike, try the staff favorite **Lathrop Trail** (5 mi., 4hr. round trip). For the best views of the Colorado River in Utah, (according to the park rangers) head to ◙**Dead Horse Point State Park,** a few miles north of the Island entrance on Rte. 313. (☎259-2614 or 800-322-3770. Park open daily 6am-10pm; Visitors Center open daily 8am-5pm. Entrance $7.) On the way to the Needles district, the Canyon Rims Recreation Area is the gateway to the ◙**Needles Overlook** (22 mi. past the entrance), a stunning, panoramic view of Canyonlands, perfect for sunset picnics. The eerie spires of the wilder Needles district are best explored on foot, though drivers can check out Wooden Show Arch Overlook and Big Spring Canyon Overlook for views of the canyons. **Roadside Ruin** (0.3 mi.), an easy trail to a Puebloan granary, is a quick introduction to the area's history. The **Slickrock Trail** (2.4 mi. loop, 2hr.) is an intermediate hike with good views down into the canyons, accessible at four viewpoints off of the trail's main loop. For longer, more challenging backcountry trails, secure a permit at the Visitors Center ($15). The Maze contains only very challenging and technical backcountry hiking and climbing, and it is best to consult a park ranger before starting out. Horseshoe Canyon's **Great Gallery** (6½ mi., 6hr. round-trip hike) displays looming rock art of 10 ft. human figures, estimated to have been drawn onto the cliffs sometime between 1000 and 2000 BC.

CAPITOL REEF   ☎ 435

Named for its similarity in color to the Capitol Building in Washington, D.C., as well as for its impassable nature, Capitol Reef is the middle link in Utah's famous chain of five. With its feature attraction, the 100 mi. Waterpocket Fold (where plate tectonics literally forced the land to buckle or "fold" over upon itself), in addition to red rock cliffs and miles of twisting canyons, Capitol Reef is a playground for travelers and geologists alike. Yet the cliffs and domes of the "Sleeping Rainbow," as the Navajos called it, are not the park's only attractions. Ancient Native American petroglyphs and the orchards and buildings of early Mormon settlers make Capitol Reef a fascinating blend of both natural and cultural history.

🔀🔀 ORIENTATION AND PRACTICAL INFORMATION. Capitol Reef can be found on the scenic Rte. 24, flanked by the small towns of Hanksville to the east (37 mi. from the Visitors Center) and Torrey to the west (11 mi. from the Visitors Center). The park is unreachable by major bus lines; the closest Greyhound **bus** (☎800-231-2222; www.greyhound.com) and Amtrak **train** (☎800-872-7245; www.amtrak.com) stops are in Green River. Entrance to the park is free, though the scenic drive is $5 per vehicle. The **Visitors Center,** on Rte. 24, supplies travelers with free maps, trail brochures, and info on daily activities such as campfire talks and geology lectures. Check the Center for daily program times. (☎425-3791; www.nps.gov/care. Open daily June-Aug. 8am-6pm; Sept.-May 8am-4:30pm.) **Post Office:** 75 W. Main St., in Torrey. (☎425-3716. Open M-F 7:30am-1:30pm, Sa 7:30-11:30am.) **Postal Code:** 84775.

🔀🔀 ACCOMMODATIONS AND FOOD. The park's campgrounds offer sites on a first-come, first-served basis. The main campground, **Fruita ❶,** 1.5 mi. south of the Visitors Center off Rte. 24, sits among orchard fruit trees and has 71 sites with drinking water, flush toilets, and a dump station. (Sites $10, 8-person max. Register and pay at the campsite.) All backcountry camping require a free **backcountry permit,** available at the Visitors Center. (No reservations necessary for backcountry permit.) **Torrey,** a quaint, friendly town 11 mi. west of the Visitors Center on Rte. 24, has lodging and restaurants. The **Sandcreek RV Park and Campground ❶,** 540 W Main St., has a local jewelry store, a lounge area with TV, and well-maintained lodgings, plus a spacious bathhouse and laundry room. There are 12 tent sites, two rustic cabins that sleep up to four people, and RV stations. (☎425-3577 or 877-425-3578. Showers for non-guests $4. Linens $2. Laundry $5. Reception 7:30am-7pm. Check-out 11am. Open Apr. to mid-Oct. Tent sites $12, hookups $16-20; cabins $28-34. MC/V.) The **Capitol Reef Inn ❷,** 360 W Main St., is simple and comfortable, with an adjoining gift shop that sells Southwestern memorabilia. (☎425-3271. Mini-fridge, TV, and A/C in each room. Reception 7am-10pm. Open Apr.-Oct. Rooms $44, each additional person $4. AmEx/D/MC/V.)

Though pricey, **Cafe Diablo ❺,** 599 W Main St., is definitely worth the splurge for its unique culinary approach to Southwestern cuisine. For a great meal, start with the grilled vegetables included with every entrée, move on to the beef flank steak carbon ($23), and finish with a choice from the delicious dessert platter ($8 for one dessert and one scoop of ice cream). (☎425-3070. Open Apr. 15-Oct. 15 daily 5-10pm. MC/V.) For a quick bite of Mexican food on the run, stop at **El Gringo's ❷,** located inside the Chuckwagon General Store, 12 W. Main St. El Gringo's Border Salad ($6.29) is a refreshing and delicious vegetarian option. (☎425-3290. Open daily 11:30am-8pm. AmEx/MC/V.) More affordable food awaits at **Brink's Burgers ❶,** 163 E. Main St. Their basic burger costs only $3.59, and a small ice cream cone costs $1.29. (☎425-3710. Free Wi-Fi. Takeout available. Open M-Th and Su 11am-8pm, F-Sa 11am-9pm. MC/V.) For a combined restaurant and lodging experience, the **Rim Rock Inn and Restaurant ❹,** 2523 E Highway 24., has clean and comfortable rooms in addition to an excellent restaurant. Try the BBQ pork ribs ($18) as you enjoy a stunning view of Capitol Reef. (☎1-888-447-4676 for reservations. Rooms $49-52. A/C, TV. Check-out 11am. ☎425-3388 for restaurant. Restaurant open daily 5-9pm. AmEx/MC/V.)

🔀🔀 SIGHTS AND OUTDOOR ACTIVITIES. You can see the Reef's towering, colorful rocks and canyons from your car on the 25 mi. **scenic drive,** a 1hr. round-trip route that winds around the cliffs, washes, and canyon floors on paved and improved dirt roads. Along Rte. 24, you can view the one-room **Fruita Schoolhouse** built by Mormon settlers in the late 1800s (check Visitors Center for daily operating hours), 1000-year-old **petroglyphs** etched on stone walls by the Fremont Native Americans, and **Panorama Point,** where you can see for 145 mi. on a clear day. **Chimney Rock** and the **Castle** are two striking sandstone formations also on Rte. 24, west of the Visitors Center. The ⬛**Fruita orchards,** cultivated by the Mormons, line the roads throughout the park. You're welcome to eat as much free fruit (usually cherries and apricots) as you want while in the park, but there is a fee to take fruit out of the orchards, depending on the weight of the fruit. Also be sure to check out the **Gifford Farmhouse,** built in 1908 by Calvin Pendleton, for a sense of the lifestyle of the early settlers. For adventure activities within the park **Capitol Reef Backcounty Outfitters,** 677 644 E. Rte. 24, is the umbrella organization for all area guides. (☎425-2010; www.ridethereef.com. Guided hiking tours: full day $100, half-day $75; fishing trips: $225/$135; horse rides: $35 per hr., $110 per half-day; lunch included. Open daily 8am-7pm.) If you want to strike out on your own, most trailheads lie along Rte. 24 or the scenic drive. The easy **Capitol Gorge Trail** (2 mi. round-trip, 2-3hr.) runs off the scenic drive, as does the Grand Wash Trail (4½ mi. round-trip). The **Rim Overlook and Navajo Knobs Trail** (9 mi. round-trip, 4-8hr.), one of the park's more challenging routes, departs from the Hickman Bridge parking area and climbs to the canyon rim above the river to breathtaking vistas. **Cassidy Arch** (3.5 mi. round-trip), starting on Grand Wash Rd., is a steep, challenging climb that will take you above Butch Cassidy's famous arch, but it is a shorter alternative to other hikes. In the northern and southern sections of the park, all hikes are considered backcountry travel, and overnight trips require a **free backcountry permit,** available without reservation at the Visitors Center.

BRYCE CANYON   ☎435

An unknown word to many people, "hoodoo" means both an "oddly shaped rock carved by the processes of erosion" and "to cast a spell." These famous spires are formed when ice and rainwater wear away the weak limestone that makes up the Claron Formation. Truly a "fairyland" (as one of its trails is named) with its unbeatable views and excellent trails, Bryce is a national park that is a must-see.

⬛⬛ **ORIENTATION AND PRACTICAL INFORMATION.** Approaching from the west, Bryce lies 1hr. east of Cedar City; take Rte. 14 or Rte. 20 to U.S. 89. From the east, take I-70 to U.S. 89, turn east on Rte. 12 at Bryce Jct. (7 mi. south of Panguitch), and drive 14 mi. to the Rte. 63 junction; head south 4 mi. to the park entrance. To limit traffic and preserve the air inside the park, the Park Service has a free shuttle system that takes visitors to the Visitors Center, lodge, scenic overlooks, and trailheads in air-conditioned comfort. (Shuttle runs daily every 12min. 9am-6pm, starting at Ruby's Inn, just north of the park entrance. After 6pm, use your own car.) Private vehicles can travel park roads, but the Park Service urges visitors to leave their cars outside the park and use the shuttle service. The entrance fee is $25 per car and $12 per pedestrian, and is good for seven days from date of purchase (if you elect to use the shuttle service, you can buy your ticket at Ruby's Inn). The **Visitors Center** is just inside the park, and provides maps and info on daily ranger programs, as well as guided hikes. (☎834-5322; www.nps.gov/brca. Open daily June-Aug. 8am-8pm; Apr.-May and Sept.-Oct. 8am-6pm; Nov.-Mar. 8am-4:30pm.) **Post Office:** Ruby's Inn Store, north of the park entrance. (☎834-8088. Open M-F 8:30am-noon and 12:30-4:30pm, Sa 8:30am-12:30pm.) **Postal Code:** 84764.

⬛⬛ **ACCOMMODATIONS AND FOOD. North** and **Sunset Campgrounds** ❶, both within 3 mi. of the Visitors Center, have 208 campsites, flush toilets, picnic tables, and drinking water. (North is open year-round. Reserve sites May 15-Sept. 30 for an additional $9 at ☎877-444-6777. Sunset is open late spring to early fall and is

> **TIP**
>
> **ON THE ROAD AGAIN.** Driving through southern Utah, roads near and through national parks can change from pavement to gravel or dirt without notice. Some roads may even become four-wheel drive (4WD) or all-terrain vehicle (ATV) only. Be sure to check with a local Visitors Center for road conditions before zooming down non-highway roads in a vehicle that may not be up to the task, or consider hiring a guide for extensive off-road driving.

first-come, first-served. No hookups. Sites $10. Both campgrounds are accessible via the park's shuttle service.) For overnight, backcountry hiking trips within the park, obtain **backcountry camping permits** ($5) the same day from a ranger at the Visitors Center. An additional two campgrounds lie west of Bryce on scenic Rte. 12, in Dixie National Forest. At 7400 ft., **Red Canyon Campground ❶** (15 mi. from Bryce) has 36 sites set against a backdrop of red mountains and pine trees. (☎676-9300. First-come, first-served. Bathrooms, water, picnic tables, and a dump station. Showers $2 per 8 min. No hookups. Sites $11.) **King Creek Campground ❶**, on Forest Service Rd. 087 off Rte. 12 (look for signs to Tropic Reservoir), features sites with easy access to the Tropic Reservoir (☎800-280-2267 or 676-9300. Take Rte. 12 W. for 4 mi. past Bryce, then turn left on Forest Service Rd. 087 for 7 mi. Sites first-come, first-served. Bathrooms, picnic tables, water. No hookups. Sites $10.) Indoor accommodations inside the park require a swollen wallet (rooms at the park's only hotel, the **Bryce Canyon Lodge ❺**, start at $141), but good deals line Rte. 12 in Tropic or on Rte. 89 in Panguitch, which has over 15 inexpensive, independent motels. Winter rates are much lower; during slow summers also be on the look out for bargain walk-in rates. **Bryce Pioneer Village Motel and RV Park ❷**, 80 S. Main St., has RV and tent sites as well as cabins and motel rooms. (☎800-222-0381; www.bpvillage.com. Check-out 11am. Tent sites $12; RV sites $18; motel rooms and cabins $55. AmEx/D/MC/V.) In Panguitch, the **Purple Sage Motel ❸**, 132 E. Center St., offers clean, well-outfitted rooms (☎676-2659; www.purplesagemotel.com. A/C, TV, coffeepot. Check-out 11am. Rooms with king bed $55; two queens $65. AmEx/D/MC/V.)

Inside and immediately surrounding the park, food options are scarce and require some driving. Inside the park, **Bryce Canyon General Store ❶** has pizza slices and prepackaged sandwiches. (Pizza and sandwiches $3-4. Open daily 8am-8pm. Also has showers, laundry facilities, and firewood.) For a sit-down lunch in the park, try the burgers and sandwiches ($6-8) at **Bryce Canyon Lodge Dining Room ❸**. Dinner is more expensive and reservations are recommended. (☎834-5361. Dinner $15-22. No dress code. Open Apr.-Oct. daily 6:30-10:30am, 11am-3pm, and 5:30-9:30pm. AmEx/D/MC/V.) In Tropic, **The Pizza Place ❷**, 21 N. Main St., is the only option for cheap eats. (☎679-8888. Sandwiches $5-7. Salads $4-7. Open daily 7-11am and 11:30am-9:30pm. AmEx/D/MC/V.) A few miles west of the park on Rte. 12, the **Bryce Canyon Pines Restaurant ❸** serves hearty meals. You can also pick up a pre-made picnic lunch to go for $7. (☎834-5441. Sandwiches $5-8. Open daily in summer 6:30am-9:30pm. AmEx/D/MC/V.) In Panguitch, the **C-Stop Pizza and Deli ❶**, 561 E. Center St., practically gives away 8 in. personal pizzas with up to seven toppings for $4.39. (☎676-8366. Open M-Sa 11am-10pm. MC/V.)

◆◢ SIGHTS AND OUTDOOR ACTIVITIES. Traveling along Bryce's 18 mi. main road via shuttle or car, stop at spectacular lookouts such as Bryce, Inspiration, Sunset, and Sunrise Points, which all provide quintessential postcard-worthy views of the canyon. For the best sunset pictures, guides recommend **Inspiration Point** for its western exposure. For those who wish to hike, the **Rim Trail** is an easy option with very little elevation change and can be accessed anywhere along the

THE SOUTHWEST

rim (up to 11 mi., 4-6hr.). The moderate **Navajo/Queen's Garden Loop** (3 mi., 3-4 hr. round-trip) is an excellent way to experience the canyon and see some of the park's most famous vistas. To escape from the crowds along the rim, the **Fairyland Loop,** beginning at Fairyland Point, has great views of hoodoos (8 mi., 4-5hr. round-trip). A challenging, steep trail is the **Peek-A-Boo Loop** (3 mi., 3-4hr.), which winds through Bryce Amphitheater. A word to the wise: the air is thin—if you start to feel short of breath, take a rest. Very sturdy shoes or hiking boots are a must for hiking into the canyon. **Canyon Trail Rides** arranges guided horseback rides. (☎679-8665. $40 per 2 hr., $65 per half-day. Inquire at the Bryce Canyon Lodge for info.)

GRAND STAIRCASE ESCALANTE
NATIONAL MONUMENT   ☎435

Composed of three regions—the Grand Staircase, Kaiparowits Plateau, and the Canyons of the Escalante—the Grand Staircase-Escalante National Monument is a dramatic park filled with canyons, waterfalls, and, of course, the grand staircase, a geological landform studied by geologists and archaeologists alike. One of the most unexplored and mysterious regions of the Southwest, Grand Staircase-Escalante is a relatively new monument, dedicated by President Bill Clinton in 1996. With hidden slot canyons, dinosaur tracks, and reminders of ancient Native American civilizations, the 1.9 million acre area is perfect for hiking and canyoneering.

The Staircase is big and wild, best suited to backcountry adventure. For those not interested in overnight backpacking excursions, try the moderate **Calf Creek Falls Trail,** which leads to a gorgeous 126 ft. waterfall. (6 mi. round-trip, 3-5hr. Accessible from Calf Creek Recreation Area 15 mi. east of Escalante on Rte. 12.) For a quick exploration of sandstone "hoodoos" (tall, thin spires of rock), check out **Devils Garden** (1 mi., 15 mi. down Hole-in-the-Rock Road). **Hole-in-the-Rock Road,** heading south from Rte. 12 east of Escalante, a trail originally used by early Mormon settlers, is a primary access road and gives travelers a chance to explore canyons and dinosaur tracks. (Hole-in-the-Rock Road is accessible by passenger vehicles until the last 7 mi., when it becomes 4WD high-clearance only. Allow 7-8 hr. for a round-trip drive of the road. Check with the Visitors Center for road conditions.) The beautifully narrow slot canyons, **Spooky** and **Peek-A-Boo,** are well-traveled and geared toward experienced hikers, as they require travelers to hike sideways at many points. (3-4 mi., 3-5hr. 26 mi. down Hole-in-the-Rock Road, turn at sign for Dry Fork. Guides recommended.) Dinosaur tracks, including a tail-drag, can be seen along the same road.

Death Hollow Wilderness, a 30 mi. trek of technical climbing and stretches of swimming along Pine Creek, is one of the most challenging routes. ▨**Excursions of Escalante,** 125 E. Main in Escalante, will personalize backcountry outings, backpacking trips, and canyoneering expeditions through Escalante's slot canyons to your needs. (☎800-839-7567; www.excursionsofescalante.com. Hiking trips $115 per day. Canyoneering $135 per day. Backpacking $225 per night. Prices include meals and equipment. Office hours Th-Su 11:30am-4pm.) **Utahcanyons,** 325 W. Main St., also provides knowledgeable information on the trails and area hiking opportunities, as well as gear (☎826-4976; www.utahcanyons.com). A free **backcountry permit** is required for all overnight stays in the monument and can be obtained without reservation at any Visitors Center. Most routes require technical climbing or canyoneering skills, and the slot canyons and terrain are susceptible to extremely dangerous flash floods. Unless you are a seasoned backpacker and well-prepared for your adventure, it is a wise idea to hire a guide to show you these particular areas, in addition to consulting maps and a compass. It's always best to check in at the Visitors Center before heading out on a trip.

The town of Escalante, located on Rte. 12, offers several motels, campgrounds, and cabin rentals for those wishing to explore the monument. ▣**Escalante Outfitters ❷**, 320 W Main, is a gear store, espresso bar, and restaurant, with private cabins, tent sites, and clean bathroom facilities. (☎826-4266; www.escalanteoutfitters.com. Free Wi-Fi. Tent sites $14; private cabins $45. AmEx/D/MC/V.) The 13 shaded sites at **Calf Creek Campground ❶**, 15 mi. east of Escalante, offer easy access to the Calf Creek Trail but fill up fast. (Flush toilets and drinking water. No trash, no hookups. Sites $7.) Two miles west of Escalante on Rte. 12, the **Escalante Petrified Forest State Park ❶** has 22 family-friendly sites along the banks of the reservoir; swimming is allowed and canoes can be rented ($20 per day). (☎826-4466. Showers, restrooms, hookups 8am-8pm. Sites $15, 8-person max.) The **Circle D Motel ❷**, 475 W. Main St. has clean, standard rooms. (☎435-826-4297. Reception 8am-10pm. Singles $35; doubles $40. AmEx/D/MC/V.) For breakfast or lunch with a terrific view of the monument, **Kiva Koffeehouse ❶** on Rte. 12, 12 mi. east of Escalante, is the place to go. (☎826-4550. Open M and W-Su 8:30am-4:30pm. MC/V.) To sample tasty tacos or veggie sandwiches (both $8), eat at **Georgie's Corner Deli and Café ❷**, 190 W. Main St. (☎836-4784. Open Tu-Sa 11:30am-8pm. Cash only). **Escalante Frosty Shop ❶**, 40 E. Main, has great cheap burgers and ice cream. (☎826-4488. Ice cream $2. Burgers $3. Open M-Sa 11am-9pm. Cash only.)

Stretching along Rte. 12 between Capitol Reef and Bryce Canyon, the monument's enormity necessitates a Visitors Center in each of the gateway towns— Kanab, Big Water, Cannonville, and Escalante—each specializing in a different aspect of life in the Monument. The **Escalante Interagency Visitors Center** has excellent information on the ecological resources of the region, Kanab focuses on geology and archaeology, Cannonville traces the impact of the monument on human life, and Big Water concentrates on paleontology. (Escalante Interagency Visitors Center: 755 W. Main St. in Escalante. ☎826-5499. Open daily Mar.-Oct. 7:30am-5:30pm; Nov.-Feb. 8am-4:30pm. Visitor Center in Kanab: 745 E. Hwy 89. ☎644-4680. Open in high-season daily 8am-5pm. Visitor Center in Cannonville: 10 Center St. ☎826-5640. Open in high-season daily 8am-4:30pm. Visitor Center in Big Water: 100 Upper Revolution Way. ☎675-3200. Open in high-season daily 9am-6pm. For more information and off-season hours, check out www.ut.blm.gov/monument.)

ZION NATIONAL PARK ☎435

Zion is Utah's most developed and popular national park. Each year, 2.7 million visitors come to enjoy the park's beautiful waterfalls, backcountry trails, and canyon views. In the 1860s, Mormon settlers came to the area and enthusiastically proclaimed that they had found Zion, the promised land representing freedom from persecution. Brigham Young disagreed, however, and declared that the place was awfully nice, but "not Zion." The name "not Zion" stuck for years until a new wave of explorers dropped the "not," giving the park its present name. Zion may not be the promised land, but it will humble and redeem the most adventurous cliff-climbers, narrows-seekers, and hikers. With the world's largest russet sandstone cliffs and the Virgin River, one of the last free-flowing river systems on the Colorado Plateau, Zion is its own natural wonder.

■❉❼ **ORIENTATION AND PRACTICAL INFORMATION.** Zion actually has two entrances, both on Rte. 9, which winds through the park for 24 mi. From the west, take I-15 to Hurricane, then follow Rte. 9 through the town of **Springdale** to the southern entrance. From the east, take U.S. 89 and pick up Rte. 9 to the eastern entrance. The park entrance fee is $25 per vehicle, $12 per pedestrian or per biker; both are good for one week. Inside the park, find the **Zion Canyon Visitors Center** at the southern entrance, just north of Springdale. Organic architecture and an energy-efficient design make the Visitors Center a sight in itself, while the information desk, wildlife and plant exhibits, bookstore, and permit desk make the Center a necessary stop before beginning a trip into the canyon. (☎772-3256; www.nps.gov/zion. Open daily Mar. 3-Apr. 28 8am-5pm; Apr. 29-May 26 and Sept. 2-Oct. 13 8am-6pm; May 27-Sept. 1 8am-7pm; Oct. 14-Oct. 28 8am-5pm.) Though you can access the Visitors Center by car, to travel into the park's canyons you have to hop on board the park's **free shuttle service.** The shuttle runs every 7-10min. 5:45am-11pm, and stops at the Visitors Center as well as the park's major trailheads and sites. A round-trip ride on the shuttle takes about 1½hr. and provides a great overview of the park. Shuttle maps are available at the Visitors Center and at park entrances. The park also operates a free shuttle service connecting the town of Springdale to the southern entrance (Shuttle runs every 7-10 min., 5:45am-11pm). Visitors are encouraged to leave their cars at their hotels and use the Springdale shuttle to enter the park. If you enter the park through its northwest entrance, the **Kolob Canyon Visitors Center** has maps and info on the Kolob Canyon Scenic Drive and the surrounding trails. (☎586-0895. Open daily Mar. 3-Sept. 1 8am-5pm, Sept. 2-Oct. 13 8am-4:30pm; Oct. 14-Oct. 28 8am-4:30pm.) **Emergency:** ☎911 or 772-3322. **Post Office:** For stamps and mail drop in the Visitors Center; full service is available in Springdale at 624 Zion Park Blvd, about a mile south of the park entrance. (☎772-3950. Open M-F 7:30-11:30am and noon-4:00pm., Sa 9am-noon.) **Postal Code:** 84767.

⌐ ACCOMMODATIONS. The Park Service maintains two campgrounds within the park. The **Watchman Campground ❶,** open year-round, takes reservations (☎877-444-6777; www.recreation.gov) Apr. 3-Oct 28 and has electricity hookups and river sites. (Flush toilets, drinking water, picnic tables, fire grates, dump stations. Hookup sites $18; non-hookup $16; river sites $20.) **South Campground ❶** is open on a first-come, first-served basis Mar. 9-Oct. 28, and usually fills by noon. (Flush toilets, drinking water, picnic tables, fire grates, dump stations. Sites $16.) Outside of the park, the town of Springdale offers the closest lodging options, though you'll be hard pressed to find a room for less than $50 in the summer. The **El Río Lodge ❸,** 995 Zion Park Blvd., provides clean rooms, friendly service, and dazzling views. (☎772-3205 or 888-772-3205. A/C, TV. Room with a queen bed $52; with two double beds $62; slightly lower in winter. AmEx/D/MC/V.) Across the street, the **Terrace Brook Lodge ❸,** 990 Zion Park Blvd., offers rooms with cable TV, refrigerators, microwaves, Wi-Fi, and continental breakfast. (☎800-342-6779. Singles $69, doubles $79; in winter rates are lower. AAA discount. AmEx/D/MC/V.) The **Zion Canyon Campground ❶/RV Park ❶/Quality Inn ❸,** 479 Zion Park Blvd., all in the same complex, provide some cheaper, more crowded options with access to the Virgin River, a swimming pool, coin laundry, showers, and playground. (☎772-3237; www.zioncamp.com. Tent sites $24. RV hookups $27. Hotel rooms $65. AmEx/D/MC/V.) If the prices in Springdale are too extreme, travel 30 mi. outside the park to Hurricane, where budget motels line I-15 and rooms run $40-55.

❒ FOOD. To eat inside the park, head to The Zion Canyon Lodge, which houses the only in-park concessions. The **⬛Springdale Fruit Company ❶,** 2491 Zion Park Blvd., 3 mi. south of Zion on Highway 9, sits in the midst of a breezy organic orchard. Try one of the build-your-own sandwiches or the organic fruit smoothies. The "original" smoothie, with strawberries and banana, is excellent. (☎772-3222; www.springdalefruit.com. Smoothies $3. Sandwiches $5. Open mid-Mar. to late Nov. daily 9am-7pm. AmEx/D/MC/V.) The **Castle Dome Cafe ❶,** Zion Lodge., Zion National Park, feeds hungry families and hikers. Soft-serve ice cream cones ($2-3) offer a refreshing treat. (☎772-3213. Burgers, salads, and subs $3-7. Open Apr.-Oct. daily 10am-7pm. AmEx/D/MC/V.) Located in a former Mormon church with a beer garden out back, **Zion Pizza & Noodle Co. ❸**, 868 Zion Park Blvd., lets you create your own pizza or choose from a variety of themed pizza options. (☎772-3815; www.zionpizzanoodle.com. Pizza $10-15. Pasta $10-14. Open daily 4-10pm. Cash only.) The **Mean Bean Coffeehouse ❷**, 932 Zion Park Blvd., can help get your day started with a variety of hot beverages ($2-4) and pastry ($2-5) options. For lunch, they serve yummy pressed panini sandwiches ($7). (☎435-772-0654. Open daily 6:30am-1:30pm. MC/V.) Just outside the park entrance, Springdale has a variety of hearty options. At **Oscar's Cafe ❸**, 948 Zion Park Blvd., find excellent guacamole, salads, and burgers. (☎772-3232. Burgers $8-13. Sandwiches, burritos, and salads $8-10. Open daily 8am-10pm. AmEx/D/MC/V.)

⚠ OUTDOOR ACTIVITIES. Zion accommodates both those seeking an easy stroll as well as those in search of an arduous, adventurous hike. The trails are serviced by a shuttle bus that delivers hikers to and from various trailheads and the Visitors Center (runs daily 5:45am-11pm). Shuttle maps are available at the Visitors Center. The **Riverside Walk** (2 mi., 1-2hr.), paved and wheelchair accessible, is Zion's easiest and most popular trail. It begins at the Temple of Sinawava at the north end of the shuttle route and runs along the Virgin River, leading to the Narrows. The **Emerald Pools Trail** (1-3 mi., 1-3hr.), the best way to see the park's waterfalls, is paved and easy along the lower loop; however, the middle and upper loops are rather steep and fairly narrow. Although it may seem inviting, in order to protect the water, swimming is not allowed in the pools. The **Canyon Overlook Trail** is a moderate, rocky trail that ends with a stunning view of Pine Creek Canyon. The tough, longer **Observation Point Trail** (8 mi., 5hr.) leads through Echo Canyon to Observation Point. **The Narrows,** ranger-recommended as the best hike in the park, is accessible by continuing up the Riverside Walk (1-5hr.). Alternatively, you can obtain a backcountry permit (1-2 people $10, 3-7 people $15, 8-12 people $20, available by reservation at www.nps.gov/zion, or the day before at the Visitors Center) and make the trip an overnight hike (requires a shuttle to the trailhead). The route, up to 16 mi. one-way, follows the riverbed through the neck of Zion Canyon above the end of the Riverwalk Trail. Before starting out on a backcountry hike, always check in first at the Visitors Center—the canyon's high walls make flash floods here deadly. **Kolob Canyons,** the northwest region of the park, has its own impressive vistas and hiking trails. Be sure to drive along the 🚗**Zion-Mt. Carmel Highway,** connecting the park's south and east entrances, which winds through the canyon and at

VITAL VOLUNTEERS IN NATIONAL PARKS

It may sound cheesy, but the over 360 national parks contained within the 50 United States really are national treasures. In the Southwest especially, the national parks provide endless hours of hiking, swimming, and camping joy to their visitors. While tourists can experience the beauty of America's national parks during vacations and weekend visits, many have come to know the parks in a more meaningful way, through the National Park Service's (NPS) Volunteer in Parks program. Volunteers in Parks (VIPs) are unpaid workers who assist National Parks staff by helping out with tasks ranging from working at a park Visitors Center to giving guided nature walks to serving as campground hosts. The benefits of volunteering in the parks are tremendous, and include meeting people from around the world, as well as learning specific in-depth secrets of an individual park that cannot be discovered in a single trip.

VIPs can arrange their volunteer hours to fit their schedules, and can work as frequently as every day or as little as a few hours a week; the choice is up to the volunteer. Volunteers are unpaid, and housing is not usually included.

For more information and an application, go to http:// www.nps.gov.volunteer.

one point traverses a 1 mi. long tunnel built in the 20s. Zion and the surrounding area also have a loyal mountain-biking following. **Gooseberry Mesa,** about 15 mi. from Springdale, has a variety of trails for both novice and advanced riders, while the **J.E.M. Hurricane Trail** provides a challenge with steep slickrock and large jumps. For tours and excellent advice on both mountain biking and hiking, head to **Zion Rock and Mountain Guides,** 1458 Zion Park Blvd. (☎ 772-3303; www.zionrockguides.com. Open daily 8am-8pm. Gooseberry tour $115; JEM tour $100.)

🎭 **ENTERTAINMENT.** From May to August, visitors can enjoy weekend music concerts under the stars at the 2000-seat outdoor **Tanner Amphitheater,** 1 mi. from the park entrance, at the intersection of Lion Blvd. and Zion Park Blvd.; follow Lion Blvd. for 2 mi. to the theater. Concerts range from classical orchestral pieces to jazz to country, all surrounded by Zion's stunning cliffs. (☎ 652-7994; www.dixie.edu/tanner. Concerts begin at 8pm. Tickets $9, under 18 $5.) Numerous art galleries also dot Zion Park Blvd. For funky art, sculptures, and pottery, the **Worthington Gallery,** 789 Zion Park Blvd., is the place to go. (☎ 800-626-9973; www.worthingtongallery.com. Open daily 7am-7pm.)

CEDAR BREAKS   ☎ 435

Though originally buried under a lake, movements within the Earth's crust over 20 million years ago raised Cedar Breaks National Monument to the 10,000 ft. elevation at which it stands today. Shaped like a gigantic amphitheater, the semicircle of canyons that compose Cedar Breaks measures more than 3 mi. in diameter and 2500 ft. in depth (the same depth as sixteen Statues of Liberty stacked on top of each other). Natural minerals in the earth's crust created the red, yellow, and even purple layers of sediment that are emphasized by a gallery of spires, columns, and arches viewable from the monument's famous Point Superior. To reach this geological marvel, take Rte. 14 east from Cedar City, then go north on Rte. 148 4 mi. to the entrance. From the east, take Rte. 89 to Rte. 14, then go north on Rte. 148 4 mi. to the entrance. (☎ 586-9451; www.nps.gov/cebr. $4 per person per week, ages 16 and under free.) A 28-site **campground** ❶ on the edge of an alpine meadow gives campers a place to rest. (½ mi. past Visitors Center; first-come, first-served; water, flush toilets, no hookups; open mid-June to Sept.; sites $14; 7-night max. stay. In June, call for the campground's opening date; it's dependent on snow.) The **Visitors Center** (☎ 435-586-9451; open daily June-Sept. 8am-6pm) awaits near **Point Supreme,** off of Rte. 148. Tourists travel to the Monument almost exclusively for the view, most conveniently seen by parking at the Visitors Center and walking 100 yd. to Point Supreme or by stopping at one of several vistas along the 5 mi. stretch of scenic Hwys. 148 and 143 within the monument. For those who want to hike, Cedar Breaks also maintains two trails. Starting at the **Chessman Ridge Overlook** (10,467 ft., about 2 mi. from the Visitors Center), the 2 mi. round-trip **Alpine Pond Trail** follows the rim to a spring-fed alpine lake whose waters trickle into the breaks, incrementally eroding the landscape as they descend toward the Great Basin. The hike takes 1-2hr. and can be accompanied by a trail guide available at the Visitors Center or trailhead ($1). The 4 mi. round-trip **Ramparts Trail** departs from the Visitors Center at 10,300 ft. and traces the amphitheater's edge, Spectra Point, where hikers can see some of the longest living trees, the bristlecone. With pets, the short (½ mi.) walk from the Visitor's Center to the campground is the only trail option. Though reaching the monument in the winter is difficult on snowy roads, winter recreationalists, such as snowmobilers, cross-country skiers, and snowshoers, utilize the rolling meadows and enjoy serene winter scenery. (Note: the Visitors Center is closed during the winter due to heavy snow.) There are no services inside the monument; the nearest gas, food, and lodging are in Cedar City and Brian Head.

LAKE POWELL AND GLEN CANYON ☎928

The decision to curb the Colorado River's steady flow to the Pacific to take advantage of the river's water supply, power, and recreational capacity was made in 1956, and 10 years and 10 million tons of concrete later, Glen Canyon Dam, the second-largest dam in the country, was completed. Backed into the once-remote Glen Canyon, the mighty river created the expansive Lake Powell and spawned a vacation destination that draws more than two million visitors annually to the 1.2 million acres of the Glen Canyon National Recreation Area. At the park's section near Page, Arizona, the **Rainbow Bridge National Monument,** the world's largest natural bridge, and **Antelope Canyon** serve as two of the main tourist attractions. Because the Rainbow Bridge remains sacred to area native cultures, visitors are asked not to approach, climb on, or pass through this breathtaking lesson in erosional art. Hiking to Rainbow Bridge on Navajo land is a 34 mi. round-trip, multiday hike, and requires a **hiking permit** (☎698-2808 for more information on permits). Antelope Canyon is divided by Rte. 98 into two parts: upper and lower. **Upper Antelope,** wider and flatter than **Lower Antelope,** is the more accessible; Lower Antelope involves large elevation jumps and slipping through extremely narrow gaps. To tour Antelope Canyon, Rainbow Bridge, or Lake Powell's other 96 beautiful side canyons, water transport or guide services are necessary. **Lake Powell Resorts and Marinas,** 100 Lake Shore Rd., in Page, rents houseboats, powerboats, and water toys. (☎800-528-6154; www.lakepowell.com. Houseboat rentals $54-158 per person per day; powerboat rental $375-585 per day. More info online.) **Twin Finn Diving,** 811 Vista Ave., in Page, AZ, rents kayaks for 24hr. (☎645-3114. Kayaks $35-45 per half-day; $55 per day. Life vest, paddles, and hatch covers included.)

To stay within the National Recreation Area, the **Wahweap Campground,** 6 mi. north of Page, AZ, off of Hwy. 89, is maintained by the park service and has 90 RV sites and 112 tent sites. (Reservations ☎800-528-6154. Tent site $19; RV site $34.) Cost does not include park entrance fee ($15 per vehicle per week or $16 per boat per week). Water, bathrooms, showers ($2 per 15 min.), coin laundry, picnic tables, grills, and dump stations are available. Visitors can also camp nearly anywhere on the endless Lake Powell shoreline, as long as they have a portable toilet (camping free with park entrance). Outside of the park, most indoor accommodations and restaurants are in Page, AZ, just southeast of the dam. Motels and restaurants line Lake Powell Blvd., a U-shaped road connecting with U.S. 89 both north and south of town. The **Lake Powell International Hostel ❷,** 141 S. 8th Ave., has both four-person dorms and private rooms as well as a lounge area and kitchen access. (☎645-3898. Check-in 2pm. Check-out 11am. Dorms $15; singles $30. MC/V.) To camp outside of the park, try the Page-Lake Powell Campground, 849 S. Coppermine Rd. (Rte. 98), which has tent and RV sites with an indoor pool, laundry, showers, and Internet access (☎645-3374. Reception 7am-7pm. Tent site $18; RV sites from $27. MC/V). Though dining options in Page are limited, **Stromboli's ❷,** 711 N. Navajo Dr., has excellent calzones ($6.25) big enough to share, in addition to pizzas and pasta (☎645-2605. Lunches $5-8. Open M-Sa 11am-10pm, Su noon-10pm. MC/V.) If these options don't entice you, head to **Safeway,** 650 Elm St. (☎645-8155.)

Five marinas operate along the perimeter of Lake Powell offering gas, boat rentals, and groceries, and are the only paved roads. Entrance into any marina costs $15 per vehicle, $16 per boat. The main access point from Arizona is **Wahweap Marina,** 6 mi. north of Page on Hwy. 89. The main access point from Utah is **Bullfrog Marina,** on Hwy. 267. The **Bullfrog Visitor Center** has exhibits on the area's paleontology, as well as a developed campground. (☎435-684-7423. Open Apr.-Oct. 8am-5pm.) The **Carl Hayden Visitor Center,** in Page, has info on the construction of the dam, as well as short movies, ranger programs, and a guided 1hr. tour of the dam. (☎608-6404. Open daily 8am-4pm; extended hours in the summer.) To get to Bull-

THE SOUTHWEST

frog, take Hwy. 24 S from I-70 to Hanksville, then Hwy. 95 to Hwy. 276 to Bullfrog Basin. To get to Page, follow Hwy. 89 S through Utah, or take Hwy. 89 N from Arizona. **Postal Code:** 86040.

ARIZONA

The romantic backdrop for old Westerns and wandering cowboy spirits, Arizona is typified by gun-slinging rumbles and towering red rocks, but this vibrant state defies any simple stereotype. Its borders contain the Grand Canyon, most of the Navajo Reservation, three bustling cities, and seven national forests, one of which is the world's largest ponderosa pine forest. The desolate, dusty beauty of the desert covering much of the state may send city-slickers clambering back to Phoenix or Tucson, but the perfect blue of the mid-morning sky stretching across the horizon tends to inspire visitors more often than not. Filled with hundreds of miles of hiking and mountain biking trails, as well as scenic drives, Arizona's backcountry provides enough variety for weeks of exploration, though most spend only a few days. Populated primarily by Native Americans until the end of the 19th century, the state has since been hit by waves of settlers: speculators and miners of the late 1800s, soldiers who returned after training here during World War II, and more recently, Mexican immigrants. Traces of lost Native American civilizations remain prevalent, and the tribes' descendants occupy half of Arizona.

ⓘ PRACTICAL INFORMATION

Capital: Phoenix.

Visitor Info: Arizona Tourism, 1110 W. Washington St., Ste. 155, Phoenix 85007 (☎602-364-3700 or 866-275-5816; www.arizonaguide.com). Open M-F 8am-5pm. **Arizona State Parks,** 1300 W. Washington St., Phoenix 85007 (☎602-542-4174; www.pr.state.az.us). Open M-F 8am-5pm.

Postal Abbreviation: AZ. **Sales Tax:** variable, around 5%.

Time Zone: Mountain Standard Time. With the exception of the Navajo Reservation, Arizona does not observe Daylight Saving Time.

GRAND CANYON

With brilliant sunsets, awe-inspiring size, and wealth of hiking trails, it is easy to see why over five million people come every year to visit the Grand Canyon, the pinnacle of the Southwest's national parks. At 277 mi. long and 1 mi. deep, encompassing more than 1900 sq. mi., the park offers something for all its visitors, from those who come for a short afternoon visit to those who camp for days in the canyon's backcountry. Though it may seem that Hollywood and novelists have romanticized the park's grandeur, the magnificent colors of the towering canyon walls cannot fail to amaze even the most skeptical traveler.

Grand Canyon National Park is divided into three sections: the popular **South Rim,** the more secluded **North Rim,** and the canyon gorge itself, which begins at Lake Powell, AZ, and feeds into Lake Mead, NV. Between the National Park area and Lake Mead are the **Hualapai** and **Havasupai Reservations,** which offer separate entrances into the Canyon. Traveling between rims takes approximately 5½hr. by car and even longer via a grueling 23 mi. hike, descending 5200 ft. from the South Rim and rising 6200 ft. to the North Rim.

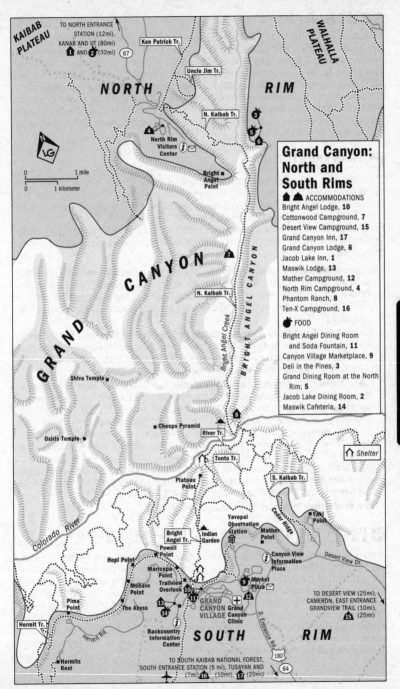

KAIBAB PLATEAU

TO NORTH ENTRANCE STATION (12mi), KANAB AND UT (80mi)
1 AND 2 (32mi)
67

WALHALLA PLATEAU

Ken Patrick Tr.

Uncle Jim Tr.

NORTH RIM

N. Kalbab Tr.

3

North Rim Visitors Center

4

5

6

Bright Angel Point

0   1 mile
0   1 kilometer

GRAND

CANYON

7

N. Kalbab Tr.

Bright Angel Creek

BRIGHT ANGEL CANYON

Shiva Temple ■

Cheops Pyramid ■

Osiris Temple ■

8

River Tr.

Tonto Tr.

Colorado River

Plateau Point

S. Kalbab Tr.

Shelter

Yaki Point ■

Yavapai Observation Station

Mather Point

Cedar Ridge

Canyon View Information Plaza

Desert View Dr.

Bright Angel Tr.

Indian Garden

Powell Point

Hopi Point

Maricopa Point

Mohave Point

Trailview Overlook

10

11

GRAND CANYON VILLAGE

Grand Canyon Clinic

Market Plaza

9

12

TO DESERT VIEW (25mi), CAMERON, EAST ENTRANCE GRANDVIEW TRAIL (10mi)
15   (25mi)

Pima Point

The Abyss

13

14

i

Backcountry Information Center

S. Entrance Rd.

SOUTH

RIM

Hermit Tr.

Hermit Rd.

Hermits Rest

TO SOUTH KAIBAB NATIONAL FOREST, SOUTH ENTRANCE STATION (5 mi), TUSAYAN AND
(7mi) 16 (10mi) 17 (20mi)

180

64

Grand Canyon: North and South Rims

ACCOMMODATIONS
Bright Angel Lodge, **10**
Cottonwood Campground, **7**
Desert View Campground, **15**
Grand Canyon Inn, **17**
Grand Canyon Lodge, **6**
Jacob Lake Inn, **1**
Maswik Lodge, **13**
Mather Campground, **12**
North Rim Campground, **4**
Phantom Ranch, **8**
Ten-X Campground, **16**

FOOD
Bright Angel Dining Room and Soda Fountain, **11**
Canyon Village Marketplace, **9**
Deli in the Pines, **3**
Grand Dining Room at the North Rim, **5**
Jacob Lake Dining Room, **2**
Maswik Cafeteria, **14**

SOUTH RIM
☎ 928

Visitors come in droves to the canyon's popular South Rim in the summer, primarily for the fantastic and easily accessible views from the lodges, restaurants, and simple day hikes. If you plan to visit at this time, be sure to make reservations for everything far in advance and prepare to battle crowds. A friendly Park Service staff, well-run facilities, and beautiful scenery generally make for enjoyable visits even despite the high volume of people that make their way to the park every year. Fewer tourists brave the canyon in the winter, so many hotels and facilities close during the low season; it's a good idea to call the Visitors Center before coming to check on service availability.

▐ TRANSPORTATION

There are two entrances to the park: the main south entrance is about 6 mi. from the Visitors Center, and the Desert View entrance is another 27 mi. away. Both are accessible via Rte. 64. From Las Vegas, the fastest route to the South Rim is U.S. 93 S to I-40 E, and then Rte. 64 N. From Flagstaff, head north on U.S. 180 to Rte. 64. From the North Rim, take Rte. 67 to Alt 89 S. to U.S. 89 S. Take Rte. 64 east to Desert View. Park entrance fees run $25 per vehicle per week, and $12 per pedestrian or biker per week.

Trains: Grand Canyon Railway (☎ 800-843-8724). Runs a restored train, the same that serviced the park in 1901, from Williams, AZ, to the Grand Canyon (2¼hr.; leaves Williams 9 and 10:30am, return trips leave Grand Canyon 3 and 4:30pm; $58, children $27). Guided train tours of the rim $28-38. Also arranges 3- and 4-day train tours of the Canyon $279-459.

Buses: Open Road Tours & Transportation (☎ 226-8060 or 800-766-7117). Departs from Flagstaff Amtrak Station (1 E. Rte. 66) daily at 8am and 3pm for the Grand Canyon. Return trips depart from Maswick Lodge at 9:45am and 4:45pm (2hr.; $27, under 11 $19, reservations recommended a week in advance).

Public Transit: The park operates 3 **free shuttle bus** routes. The Hermits Rest Route runs from the Village Route Transfer station to Hermits Rest, with stops at 8 canyon overlooks. (1¼hr. round-trip. June-Aug. every 15min. 7:30am-sunset.) The Village Route provides transportation between the Canyon View Info Plaza, Yavapai Point, hotels, restaurants, parking lots, and the backcountry permit office. (1hr. round-trip. In summer, every 15min. 6:30am-9pm.) The Kaibab Trail Route stops at the Canyon View Info Plaza, the South Kaibab Trailhead, Yaki Point, and Pipe Creek Vista. (30min. round-trip. In summer, runs every 15min. from 6:30am to 1hr. after sunset.) For early morning hikers, a **free express shuttle** runs from the Bright Angel Lodge and Backcountry Office to the South Kaibab Trailhead (in summer runs at 4, 5, and 6am).

Taxi: Fred Harvey Transportation Company ☎ 638-2822.

✷ ❷ ORIENTATION AND PRACTICAL INFORMATION

Posted maps and signs in the park make orientation easy. The Visitors Center, campground, lodges, general store, and restaurants all lie to the west of the southern entrance of the park on Rte 64. The Visitors Center, campground, and general store are farthest east, and closer to Rte. 64 than the lodges. The South Kaibab Trail is off Desert View Dr. east of the southern entrance, and is serviced by a free shuttle bus. Free shuttle buses also run to eight rim overlooks along Hermit Road in the west (closed to private vehicles in summer). Avoid walking on the main roads within the park; the rim trails are safer and more scenic. For most services in the park, call the main switchboard (☎ 638-2631).

Visitor Info: Canyon View Information Plaza, directly across from Mather Point by the entrance to the park. The one-stop center for information, as it stocks the free must-have *The Guide*, the information source for all of the parks services and trails, pamphlets, and informational kiosks on hiking in the park. To get there, either park at Mather Pt. and walk the 300 yd. to the information plaza, or park in parking lots A, B, C, D, or E and take a free Village Route shuttle bus. (☎800-858-2808; www.grandcanyon.com or www.nps.gov/grca.) The **transportation info desks** in the **Bright Angel Lodge, Yavapai Lodge,** and the **Maswik Lodge** (☎638-2631) take reservations for mule rides, bus tours, plane tours, Phantom Ranch, taxis, and more. Maswik Lodge desk open daily 6am-6:30pm. Bright Angel Lodge open daily 6am-8pm. Yavapia Lodge open daily 8am-5pm.

Equipment Rental: At the gear counter in **Canyon Village Marketplace** in Market Plaza. Hiking boots $8. Sleeping bags $7. 2-person tent $8, 4-person tent $8. Small day pack $6, large $8. Stoves $4. Deposit required. Open daily 7am-9pm.

Weather and Road Conditions: ☎638-7888, updated daily 7am.

Medical Services: Grand Canyon Clinic (☎638-2551). To get there, turn left at the 1st light after you pass through the South Rim entrance. Open M-F 7am-7pm, Sa 10am-4pm. 24hr. emergency aid.

Post Office: Grand Canyon Market Pl. (☎638-2512), next to the Marketplace. Open M-F 9am-4:30pm, Sa 11am-1pm. **Postal Code:** 86023.

▌ ACCOMMODATIONS

Indoor lodging within the park requires months of advance planning, but a few chain motels exist just outside the park's southern entrance in Tusayan and even more within an hour's drive in neighboring Williams and Flagstaff. Summer rooms in the park should be reserved 13 months in advance (☎888-297-2757 or write Xanterra, 14001 E. Iliff, Ste. 600, Aurora, CO 80014). That said, there are occasional cancellations; if you arrive unprepared, check for vacancies.

If you do somehow manage to make arrangements to stay inside in the park, be prepared for high prices; though the Maswik and Bright Angel Lodge are more reasonably priced than the neighboring El Tovar Hotel and Yavapai, Thunderbird and Kachina Lodges, the convenience that Maswik and Bright Angel offer is built into the price of their rooms.

Bright Angel Lodge (☎638-2631), in Grand Canyon Village. Designed by the famed architect Mary Colter, the Bright Angel Lodge sits right on the rim. Very close to Bright Angel Trail and shuttle buses. Single with sink $52, with toilet $58, with private bathroom $70. Rim cabins with fireplace, fridge, and TV $118-143; each additional adult $9. AmEx/D/MC/V. ❸

Phantom Ranch (☎638-2631), on the canyon floor. A day's hike or mule ride down the Kaibab Trail or Bright Angel Trail. Breakfast $17; box lunch $10; stew dinner $21; steak dinner $34; vegetarian option $21. Reservations are necessary and can be made up to 23 months in advance. If you're dying to sleep on the canyon floor but have no reservation, go to the Backcountry Office at 8am on the day prior to your planned stay and take a chance on the waiting list. Single-sex dorms $32; hard-to-get cabins for 1 or 2 people $87, each additional person $12. AmEx/D/MC/V. ❷

Grand Canyon Inn (☎635-9203 or 800-635-9203; www.grand-canyon-inn.com). Located in Valle at the junction of Hwy. 180, a 25min. drive from the entrance to the park. Clean, simply furnished rooms and a pool. 1-month advance reservations are recommended in summer. Single bed with TV and shower $49; double bed $69-79. AmEX/D/MC/V. ❸

🏕 CAMPING

While lodgings in the park are usually filled before you've even decided to visit the Grand Canyon, camping is always a good 2nd option. Reservations for the park's Mather campground can be made through **SPHERICS** (☎800-365-2267). If you do run out of options, you can camp for free in the **Kaibab National Forest,** along the park's southern border. No camping is allowed within a quarter mile of U.S. 64 or within a half mile of a developed campground. **Dispersed camping** sits conveniently along the oft-traveled N. Long Jim Loop Rd.—turn right about one mile south of the south entrance station. Forest rangers also recommend camping off Forest Roads 302, 688, and 306, off Rte. 64. Fires are heavily restricted or banned in some areas; make sure you know the rules. Sleeping in cars is not permitted in the park, but it is allowed in the Kaibab Forest. For more info, contact the **Tusayan Ranger Station** (☎638-2443), Kaibab National Forest, P.O. Box 3088, Tusayan 86023.

Mather Campground (call SPHERICS ☎800-365-2267 or 877-444-6777, or reserve online at www.recreation.gov), in Grand Canyon Village, 1 mi. south of the Canyon Village Marketplace; follow signs from Yavapai Lodge. With 327 shady sites, Mather can get crowded during peak summer months. Reservations highly recommended, but check for open spots, as cancellations are frequent. Water, flush toilets, picnic tables, fire rings. No hookups. 7-night max. stay. For Apr. to Dec., reserve up to 5 months in advance; Jan. to Mar. first-come, first-served. Individual sites $18. ●

Desert View Campground (☎638-7888), 25 mi. east of Grand Canyon Village, just west of the eastern Desert View entrance. Far from Grand Canyon Village and the Visitors Center, perfect for avoiding crowds. Flush toilets, picnic tables, fire rings, water. No hookups, campfires, or reservations. Open mid-May to Oct. Sites $12. ●

Trailer Village (☎888-297-2757). For those with RVs, Trailer Village is the only in-park camping option with hookups. On the Village Route shuttle bus line. Reservations recommended 5 months in advance. Sites $28 for 2 people, each additional adult $2. ❷

🍴 FOOD

Fast food has yet to spawn in the South Rim (the closest McDonald's is 7 mi. south in Tusayan), but you can find slightly better-quality meals at fast-food prices. The **Canyon Village Marketplace ●,** at Market Plaza, 1 mi. west of Mather Point on the main road, has a deli counter with the cheapest eats in the park, groceries, camping supplies, and enough Grand Canyon apparel to clothe your entire extended family. Try the bakery's giant muffins ($2) for a pre-hike snack. (☎638-2262. Sandwiches $5. Salads $2-5. Open daily 7am-8pm. AmEx/D/MC/V.) **Maswik Cafeteria ●,** in Maswik Lodge, also serves sandwiches and salads, and has a pasta station (pick your favorite sauce and pasta combo), tacos, burritos, and tostadas, all for $7. (☎638-2631. Sandwiches $4-5. Hot entrees $6-10. Open daily 6am-10pm. AmEx/D/MC/V.) If you want to stay close to Market Plaza, the **Yavapai Cafeteria ❷** has pizza ($5) and hot lunch entrees ($6-9). (Fried chicken $2. Open daily 6:30am-9pm. AmEx/D/DC/MC/V.) **Bright Angel Dining Room ❷,** in Bright Angel Lodge, is popular with families and serves breakfast, hot sandwiches and wraps for lunch, and Southwestern-style dinner entrees (fajitas and fish tacos are popular choices). For lunch, the Indian Garden Spinach Wrap is a good veggie option with spinach, avocado, and black beans (☎638-2631. Breakfast $6-8. Hot sandwiches $7-9. Dinner entrees $10-15. Open daily 6:30am-10pm. AmEx/D/MC/V.) Enjoy an ice cream cone from the **The Soda Fountain ●** just outside the dining room of the Bright Angel Lodge, as you look over the rim into the canyon. There you can find the basics, including eight flavors of ice cream, snack-bar sandwiches, soda, and candy. (Sandwiches and hot dogs $2. Ice cream $2. Open seasonally daily 10am-8pm.)

HIKING

Hikes in and around the Grand Canyon can be broken down into day hikes and overnight hikes. Confusing an overnight hike for a day-hike can be a dangerous mistake, so heed the warnings of rangers and don't attempt to get down to and back from the Colorado River in one day. All overnight trips (except those to Phantom Ranch) require permits obtained from the Backcountry Office, located on the west side of Parking Lot E near Maswik Lodge (permit fee $10; $5 per additional person per night). Permits often take up to four months to obtain, so request one as early as possible via the Internet (www.nps.gov/grca), mail (P.O. Box 129, Grand Canyon, AZ 86023), or walk-up (office open daily 8am-noon and 1-5pm). Those who do not have a permit but wish to hike overnight in the canyon can try to get on the permit waiting list the day before their planned departure date. For day-hikes into the canyon, remember that each hour hiked downhill into the canyon will take 2hr. on the way back to the rim. An enjoyable hike usually means beginning before 7am or after 4pm; it's best to consult a ranger at the Canyon View Information Plaza before leaving for one of the more difficult hikes. Park Service rangers also present a variety of guided hikes; daily times and details are listed in *The Guide*, as well as at the Visitors Center.

The **Rim, Bright Angel, South Kaibab,** and **River** trails are the only South Rim trails regularly maintained and patrolled by the Park Service. While other trails do exist, they are only for experienced hikers and may contain steep climbs and technical terrain, requiring sturdy hiking boots or other gear. Consult a ranger and *The Guide* before heading out.

Rim Trail (up to 12 mi. one-way, 4-6hr.). With only a mild elevation change (about 200 ft.) and the security of the nearby shuttle, the Rim Trail is an excellent way to see the canyon from all different angles and vantage points. The trail is handicap-accessible along the Village Rim in the west and has 8 viewpoints along Hermit Rd. and 3 east of it. Convenience and easy access to viewpoints also mean this trail is the most crowded in the Grand Canyon, but toward the eastern and western ends, hikers have a bit more room. Hopi, Mohave, and Pima Points all have great views of the Colorado River. To watch the sunset or sunrise, rangers recommend all overlook points along the trail. *The Guide* lists sunset and sunrise times.

Bright Angel Trail (up to 18 mi. round-trip, 1-2 days). Bright Angel's many switchbacks and water stations make it moderate hikers' into-the-canyon choice. Depending on distance, the trail can be either a day or overnight hike. Departing from the Rim Trail near the western edge of the Grand Canyon Village, the first 1-2 mi. attract droves of day hikers looking for a taste of canyon descent. Rest houses are strategically stationed 1½

! HYDRATION EXPECTATIONS. Seeing the canyon from the inside is harder than it looks. Even the young of body and heart should recall that there are no easy trails, and what starts as a downhill stroll can become a nightmarish 50° incline on the way back. Also, note that the lower you go, the hotter it gets; when it's 85°F on the rim, it's around 100°F at Indian Gardens and around 110°F at Phantom Ranch. Heat stroke, the greatest threat to a hiker, is marked by a monstrous headache and red, sweatless skin. **For a day-hike, take at least a gallon of water per person; drink at least a quart per hour hiking uphill under the hot sun.** Try not to hike during the hours of 10am and 4pm. Footwear with excellent tread is also necessary; the trails are steep, and every year careless hikers take what locals morbidly call "the 12-second tour." Parents should think twice about bringing children more than 1 mi. down any trail.

and 3 mi. from the rim, each with water May-Sept. and restrooms. **Indian Gardens,** 4½ mi. down, offers restrooms, picnic tables, 15 backcountry campsites open year-round, and blessed shade. From rim to river, the trail drops a dramatic 5200 ft. The round-trip is definitely too strenuous for a day-hike—do not under any circumstances attempt to make it one. With a permit, overnighters can camp at Indian Gardens or on the canyon floor at Bright Angel Campground. Day-hikers are advised to go no farther than Indian Gardens (9¼ mi., 6-9hr. round-trip) or Plateau Point (12¼ mi., 8-12hr. round-trip), which ends at a stunning river view. The River Trail (1¾ mi.) links the Bright Angel with South Kaibab at the base of the Canyon.

South Kaibab Trail (7 mi. to Phantom Ranch, 4-5hr.) is for those seeking a more challenging descent. Beginning at Yaki Pt. (7260 ft.), Kaibab follows the ridge into the canyon, and is trickier, steeper, and lacks shade or water, but it rewards the intrepid with a better view of the canyon. Day-hikes to Ooh-Aah Point (1.8 mi. round-trip) and Cedar Ridge (3 mi. round-trip) are reasonable only for experienced hikers due to the trail's steep grade. Kaibab meets up with Bright Angel at the Colorado River. Fewer switchbacks and a more rapid descent make the South Kaibab Trail 1½ mi. shorter than the Bright Angel to this point—guests staying at the Phantom Ranch or Bright Angel Campground can use either trail to reach the ranch. Semi-maintained trails are also available for those experienced in desert hiking. The Hermit Trail begins 500 ft. from Hermit's Rest and descends to the Waldron Basin (3 mi., 2-4hr. round-trip), Santa Maria Spring (5 mi., 5-8hr. round-trip), and Dripping Springs (7 mi., 6-9hr. round-trip).

⚠ OUTDOOR ACTIVITIES

Beyond hiking to the river or strolling along the rim, there are other ways to explore the Canyon. **Mule trips** from the South Rim are an option, but they're expensive and often booked up to 13 months in advance in advance. Call to check availability if you do not have a reservation; cancellations do occur. (☎888-297-2757. Daytrip to Plateau Point 6 mi. down the Bright Angel Trail $148, lunch included; overnight trip including lodging at Phantom Ranch and all meals $400.) Looking up at the Grand Canyon from a **whitewater raft** is another popular option but usually costs between $1500-3500 depending on trip length. Trips into the Grand Canyon span from seven to 18 days and generally require booking one year in advance. The **Trip Planner** (available by request at the info center or on linc) lists several guides licensed to offer trips in the canyon. Most guides run out of Flagstaff, AZ. **Calmwater rafting** trips are also available for those not quite ready for a wet and wild time in the heart of the canyon. Drifting from Glen Canyon Dam to Lee's Ferry generally takes a half-day. **Colorado River Discovery** leads calmwater expeditions (☎888-522-6644; www.raftthecanyon.com). Full and half-day trips can be arranged through the Bright Angel, Maswik, or Yavapai Lodge transportation desks. You can also try the higher vantages provided by one of the park's many **flightseeing** companies, located at the Grand Canyon Airport outside of Tuyasan. **Grand Canyon Airlines** flies 50min. tours hourly in the summer from 8am-5pm. (☎866-235-9422; www.grandcanyonairlines.com. $99, children $69. Reservations recommended a week in advance.) For a list of flight companies, visit the Grand Canyon Chamber of Commerce's website (www.grandcanyonchamber.org).

If you happen to visit the park on a cloudy or rainy day, fret not. The park has many options for those who want to explore the indoors. The Kolb Studio was home to pioneering photographers and is worth a visit, as is the Tusayan Museum and Ruin, where you can see exhibits on the past and present of the Grand Canyon's Native American cultures. From the **Desert View Watchtower,** climb 70 stairs to have the highest view on the South Rim. Visit the Canyon View Information Plaza for more information on other park museums and historic buildings.

NORTH RIM
☎928

If you're coming from Utah or Nevada or are looking to avoid the South Rim's crowds, the park's North Rim is rugged and serene, with a view almost as spectacular as that from the South Rim. Unfortunately, it's remote; hard to reach by public transit and a long drive by car (80 mi. from Kanab and 99 mi. from Page, AZ). The North Rim and its facilities are usually open from May 15 to October 15. The official closing date depends on snow. In summer, sunsets from the Grand Canyon Lodge, on the edge of the rim, are spectacular and worth the long trip.

✦🛈 ORIENTATION AND PRACTICAL INFORMATION

To reach the North Rim from the South Rim, take Rte. 64 E to U.S. 89 N, which runs into Alt. 89; from Alt. 89, follow Rte. 67 S through the Kaibab National Forest 43 mi. to the edge. The drive is over 220 mi. From Utah, take Alt. 89S from Fredonia. From Page, take U.S. 89 S to Alt. 89 to Rte. 67 S. Snow closes Rte. 67 from early December to mid-May, and park facilities (including the lodge) close October 15 through May 15. The park entrance fee is $25 per vehicle or $12 per pedestrian or biker. The visitor parking lot, 12 mi. south of the park entrance, is near the end of Rte. 67, close to both the Visitors Center and North Rim Lodge. Trailhead parking is also available at the North Kaibab and Widforss trails and at scenic points along the road to Cape Royal.

Buses: Transcanyon, P.O. Box 348, Grand Canyon 86023 (☎638-2820). Buses run to and from the South Rim. (4½-5hr.; late May to Oct. departs 7am from North Rim Lodge, arrives 11:30am at South Rim, departs 1:30pm from Bright Angel Lodge at the South Rim, arrives 6:30pm at North Rim; $70, round-trip $130). Reservations required at least a week in advance.

Public Transit: A **hikers' shuttle** runs on request in the morning from the North Rim Lodge to the North Kaibab Trailhead. 1st person $7, each additional person $4. Make reservations at the Grand Canyon Lodge front desk at least 24hr. in advance.

Visitor Info: North Rim Visitors Center (☎638-2611), on Rte. 67 just before the Lodge. Open May 15-Oct. 15 daily 8am-6pm. Provides info on trails and schedules of daily ranger programs. **Kaibab Plateau Visitors Center** (☎643-7298), at Jacob Lake, next to the Jacob Lake Inn. Has displays on the creation of the canyon and the ecosystem of the Kaibab National Forest. High season open daily 8am-5pm.

Weather Conditions: ☎638-7888. Updated daily 7am.

Post Office: Grand Canyon Lodge (☎638-2611). Open M-F 8am-5pm. **Postal Code:** 86052.

🏠 ACCOMMODATIONS

Staying inside on the North Rim is pricey and requires months of advance planning. If you can't get in-park lodging, many less expensive accommodations can be found 80 mi. north in Kanab, UT or 99 mi. northeast in Page, AZ.

Grand Canyon Lodge (☎638-2611, reservations 888-297-2757). The only indoor accommodation within the park's North Rim area, this wooden lodge situated on the edge of the rim offers sweeping views of the canyon. If you can't book a room in the lodge, watch the sunset from a leather sofa in the overlook near the lobby—the view and the atmosphere can't be beat. Reception 24hr. Reserve at least 13 months in advance. Open May 15-Oct. 15. Cabins $105-148; motel rooms $103. AmEx/D/MC/V. ❺

North Rim Campground (call SPHERICS ☎800-365-2267), on Rte. 67 near the Rim Visitors Center and lodge. The only in-park campground on this side of the chasm, with 93

THE SOUTHWEST

spacious sites among ponderosa trees. Groceries, showers ($1.50 per 5min.), and coin-operated laundry facilities ($2.50) can be found on the campground access road. Reservations strongly recommended in summer. Water, flush toilets, picnic tables, fire rings. No hookups. 7-night max. stay. Open May 15-Oct. 15. Sites $18. ❶

Jacob Lake Inn (☎643-7232; www.jacoblake.com), 44 mi. north of the North Rim entrance at Jacob Lake. A family-friendly hotel with lodge, gift shop, and cafe (see below). Reception daily 6am-9pm. Doubles $72-79; triples $119; motel rooms $91-99. AmEx/D/MC/V. ❸

Demotte Campground (☎643-7298), 16 mi. north of Jacob Lake on Rte. 67. Within the Kaibab National Forest, Demotte's campsites are shaded by pine trees. All sites available on a first-come, first-served basis. Drinking water, pit toilets, picnic tables, and fire rings. No hookups or showers. Sites $16; 8-person max. Pay at campsite. ❶

🄵 FOOD

Grand Canyon Lodge Dining Room (☎638-2612, ext. 160). On the edge of the canyon, the North Rim Lodge's dining room treats guests to a beautiful canyon outlook. The breakfast buffet ($10) and lunch options (salads and burgers, $6-12) are classic and tasty, providing much-needed energy for hikers. Picnic lunches, including a sandwich, chips, fruit, and water, are also available ($9). Dinners (from $15) are an expensive way to finish off the day. Reservations required a week in advance for dinner. Open daily 6:30-10am, 11:30am-2:30pm, 5-9:30pm. AmEx/D/MC/V. ❸

Deli in the Pines, at the North Rim Lodge. Specializes in to-go deli sandwiches. Salads, sandwiches, and burgers $4-6. Pizza $3-5 per slice. Open daily 7am-9pm. ❶

Jacob Lake Dining Room (☎643-7232; www.jacoblake.com), 30 mi. north of the park entrance. A good alternative to North Rim establishments. The old-fashioned diner counter, full restaurant, and tempting bakery offers gooey grilled cheese sandwiches ($6) and scrumptious peanut butter chocolate chip cookies ($1), in addition to other delectable options. Pick up a frothy milkshake ($4) for an enjoyable drive to the rim. Breakfast $5-6. Lunch $6-8. Dinner $12-15. Open daily 7am-8pm. AmEx/D/MC/V. ❷

🄰 OUTDOORS

Hiking in the leafy North Rim seems like a trip to the mountains, but the mountain just happens to be upside-down (the word "Kaibab" actually means "upside-down mountain"). The North Rim is at a surprisingly high elevation, so the air is very thin, and there are no easy trails. Rangers advise that you should never attempt to hike to the river and back in a single day. Info on trails can be found in the North Rim's version of The Guide. The **Bright Angel Point Trail** (½ mi. round-trip, 30min.) departs from the lodge area, and the **Cape Royal Trail** (¾ mi. round-trip, 30min., wheelchair-accessible), departs from the Cape Royal parking area. Both offer impressive views of the canyon with little effort. Stargazing from the Bright Angel Point Trail is highly recommended. The **Widforss Trail** (up to 10 mi. round-trip, 6hr.) is a more challenging day-hike but offers views of both canyon and forests and can be tailored into a shorter hike. Rangers often suggest only completing the 1st half of the hike; the last 2½ mi. are mostly forest. The **North Kaibab Trail** (28 mi. round-trip) is the only maintained trail into the canyon on the North Rim and is for only the most prepared and experienced hikers. Consult rangers before beginning this hike. Pick up the invaluable *Official Guide to Hiking the Grand Canyon* ($12), available in all Visitors Centers and gift shops. Overnight hikers must get **permits** from the Backcountry Office in the ranger station just north of the campground entrance, 11½ mi. from the park entrance, off of Rte. 67. (Permit $10, $5 per person per night. Open daily 8am-noon and 1-5pm.) Park rangers run **nature walks,** lectures, and evening programs at the North Rim Campground and Lodge. The info desk at the Visitors Center or campground bulletin boards have schedules. One-hour ($30), half-day ($65), and full-day ($125) **mule trips** through Canyon Trail Rides circle the rim or descend into the canyon. (☎435-679-8665. In the Grand Canyon Lodge lobby. Open May-Oct. daily 7am-5pm. MC/V.) Reservations are recommended at least 24hr. in advance, but walk-ins can be accommodated

HAVASUPAI RESERVATION   ☎928

West of the South Rim's bustle lies the beautiful Havasupai Reservation. Meaning "people of the blue-green water," the Havasupai live in a protected enclave at the base of the canyon bordered by the national park. Ringed by dramatic sandstone faces, their village, Supai, rests on the shores of the Havasu River and is only accessible by a 10 mi. trail starting at the Hualapai Hilltop. Just beyond town, rushing crystal-clear water cascades over a series of spectacular falls. Camping permits are required for overnight hiking, so reservations should be made far in advance. Those traveling to Supai should make plans to stay in Seligman, Peach Springs, or Flagstaff.

To reach the trailhead leading to Supai, take I-40 E to Rte. 66 at Seligman; follow Rte. 66 for 30 mi. until it meets Indian Rd. 18, which ends at the Hilltop after 60 mi. No roads lead to Supai, but mules and helicopters can be hired to carry bags or people. For **mule reservations,** contact Havasupai Tourist Enterprise. (☎448-2237. $75, half of which is required as a deposit. Includes 4 pieces of luggage not exceeding 130 lb. total. Groups leave at 10am.) Another option is to take the **helicopter service,** AirWest. (☎623-516-2790. $85 one way, plus baggage charge by weight; first come, first served.) The hike, a grueling, exposed 8 mi. to Supai and then an additional 2 mi. to the campground, is not to be underestimated. Do not hike down without a reservation—you may have to go right back to the trailhead. Reservations for the campground, lodge, and mules can be made by calling the Havasupai Tourist Enterprise. Visitors must check in at the **tourist office** in Supai before heading on to the campground. The village has a **post office, general store,** and **cafe.** Prices are high because everything must be brought in by mule or helicopter; bringing your own food is advised. All trash must be packed out. No gas or water is available past Rte. 66, so stock up beforehand.

The Havasupai tribe operates the ■**Havasupai Campground** and the **Havasupai Lodge,** both on the canyon floor. The campground, 2 mi. past Supai, lies between Havasu and Mooney Falls, bordering the Havasu River's blue-green water and swimmer-friendly lagoons. The tribe charges a one-time entry fee ($20 per visitor, $10 per night) at the campground. There are no showers or flush toilets. A spring provides fresh water, and the falls are close by. The Havasupai Lodge 4, in Supai, offers basic accommodations. (☎448-2111. $125 for up to 4 people, plus the entrance fee.) The trail from Supai to the campground extends to Mooney Falls (1 mi. from campground), Beaver Falls (3 mi.), and the Colorado (8 mi.). The hike down to Mooney Falls is steep; extreme caution should be exercised—shoes with good tread are a must. Swimming and frolicking are both permitted and encouraged in the lush lagoons at the bottom of the falls.

FLAGSTAFF   ☎928

Born on the 4th of July, 1876, the city of Flagstaff was founded by Mormon travelers who, on the nation's centennial, stripped a young tree of its bark and hung a flag from its top. The "Flagstaff" erected by these travelers came to symbolize the town as a safe haven, a place where those passing through could find water and grass for their cattle. Today, tourists still use Flagstaff as a rest stop on their way to the Grand Canyon, Sedona, and the Petrified Forest, all within day-tripping distance from town by car or shuttle. Those who choose to visit Flagstaff itself will find a city that is much more than a rest stop en route to someplace else; this is a bustling college town with local arts and entertainment that offers something for families, for people who love the outdoors, and for those who simply want an excellent meal. The city's citizens welcome all to their unusual rock formations during the day and their hopping breweries at night.

TRANSPORTATION

Flagstaff sits 138 mi. north of Phoenix (take I-17), 26 mi. north of Sedona on U.S. 89A, and 81 mi. south of the Grand Canyon's south rim on U.S. 180.

Trains: Amtrak, 1 E. Rte. 66 (☎774-8679; www.amtrak.com), runs once per day to: **Albuquerque** (5½hr., $54-105); **Chicago** (32hr., $129-253); **Kansas City** (24hr., $127-249); **Los Angeles** (10hr., $58-112). Station open daily 1am-9am, 4:15pm-11:30pm.

Buses: Two bus lines provide service to regional destinations. Check at the DuBeau and Grand Canyon International Hostels for their Grand Canyon and Sedona shuttles. (Grand Canyon $60; Sedona $45. Entrance fee and sack lunch included.)

Greyhound: 399 S. Malpais Ln. (☎774-4573), at intersection of Malpais and Milton Rd., behind Barnes and Noble. To: Albuquerque (6½hr., 3 per day, $50); Las Vegas (5-6hr., 3 per day, $54); Los Angeles (10-13hr., 6 per day, $60); Phoenix (3hr., 6 per day, $27.50). Terminal open 24hr.

Open Road Tours & Transportation (☎226-8060 or 800-766-7177). Offers daily trips to and from the Phoenix airport (3hr.). Departs Flagstaff at 4:30, 7:30, 9:45am, 12:30, 3:30pm; $42. Departs Phoenix Sky Harbor Airport at 9:30, 11:30am, 2:30, 4:30, 7:30pm; $42.

Public Transit: Mountain Line (☎779-6624. www.mountainline.az.gov). Routes cover most of town. Buses run every 30-60min. M-Sa. Route map and schedule available at Visitors Center in the Amtrak station. $1, seniors and children $0.50; day pass $3/1.50; book of 20 passes $18/9.

Taxi: Friendly Cab, ☎774-4444.

Car Rental: Enterprise Rent-A-Car, 100 N. Humphreys (☎774-9407).

ORIENTATION AND PRACTICAL INFORMATION

Historic downtown Flagstaff is between Beaver St. (in the west), Elm Ave. (in the north), Agassiz St. (in the east) and Butler Ave. (in the south). The Visitors Center, bus station, hostels, and inexpensive restaurants and bars are all within the confines of these streets. Split by Rte. 66, the more visited northern area is also the center of downtown. The area south of the tracks is less developed, but does have hostels and eateries.

Visitor Info: Flagstaff Visitors Center, 1 E. Rte. 66 (☎774-9541 or 800-842-7293), in the Amtrak station. Has brochures and maps. Open M-Sa 8am-5pm, Su 9am-4pm.

Police: 911 E. Sawmill Rd. (☎556-3316).

Medical Services: Flagstaff Medical Center, 1200 N. Beaver St. (☎779-3366). 24hr.

Internet Access: Macy's European Coffeehouse and Bakery (p. 795). Macy's Coffeehouse has free Wi-Fi access. **Flagstaff Public Library,** 300 W. Aspen Ave. (☎774-4000), at the corner of Aspen and Kendrick. Free. Open M-Th 10ma-9pm, F 10am-7pm, Sa 10am-6pm.

Post Office: 2400 N. Postal Blvd. (☎714-9302), on Rte. 66. Open M-F 9am-6pm, Sa 9am-4pm. **Postal Code:** 86004.

ACCOMMODATIONS

DuBeau International Hostel, 19 W. Phoenix Ave. (☎774-6731 or 800-398-7112; www.grandcanyonhostel.com). A block south of the train station, the DuBeau is clean and friendly, with 8-bed dorm rooms and private doubles. The common room with leather futons, game room with foosball table and bar stools, and 2 sunny kitchens create a lively atmosphere. Breakfast and linen included. Internet $2 per 30min. Laundry $2. Grand Canyon and Sedona tours $45-60. No A/C. Reception 7am-midnight. Checkout 11am. Dorms June-Sept. $19, Oct.-May $17; private double $41/37. MC/V. ❶

The Grand Canyon International Hostel, 19 S. San Francisco St. (☎779-9421; www.grandcanyonhostel.com). Dubeau's sister hostel, just east of the DuBeau. Same great value and friendly atmosphere. Spacious hallways, hardwood floors, and cozy 4-bed dorm rooms. Breakfast and linen included. Internet $2 per 30min. Laundry $2. Grand Canyon and Sedona tours $45-60. No A/C. Reception 7am-midnight. Dorms June-Sept. $19, Oct.-May $17; doubles $41/37. MC/V. ❶

The Weatherford Hotel, 23 N. Leroux St. (☎779-1919; www.weatherfordhotel.com), at Aspen and Leroux in downtown. Flagstaff's oldest hotel, dating to 1898, once housed William Randolph Hearst, Zane Grey, and Teddy Roosevelt. 8 spacious rooms with elegant furnishings. Reservations recommended at least 1 month in advance. Room with double bed $70, with queen bed $79, A/C, phone, and TV $125. AmEx/D/MC/V. ❸

CAMPING

Free **backcountry camping** is available in designated wilderness areas. Maps are available from the **Peaks Ranger Station,** 5075 N. 89A (☎526-0866), as well as the Mormon Lake Ranger Station, 4373 S. Lake Mary Rd (☎774-1147). All backcountry sites must be at least 200 ft. from trails, waterways, and lakes. There is a 14-night max. stay in the **Coconino National Forest;** fire restrictions apply. For info on camping, call the **Coconino National Forest Line** (☎527-3600; operates M-F 7:30am-4:30pm). Lake Mary, a popular recreation site 8 mi. southeast of Flagstaff, is surrounded by campgrounds and backcountry spots. Campers should check with the **Mormon Lake Ranger District Station,** 4373 S. Lake Mary Rd., for information on specific trails and campsites. (☎774-1147. Open M-F 7:30am-4:30pm.) The following campgrounds are all just southeast of Flagstaff on Lake Mary Rd., which is accessible off of I-17 N, but must be reached by following Milton Rd. to Beulah Dr. when coming from the north.

Canyon Vista Campground, 6 mi. south on Mary Lake Rd. 11 spacious, shady sites infused with the scent of surrounding pine trees. Has access to hiking trails. Drinking water, pit toilets, no hookups. First come, first served. $14 per vehicle per night. ❶

Lakeview Campground, on the east side of Upper Lake Mary, 11 mi. south on Lake Mary Rd. Has 30 sites on a mountainside. Drinking water, pit toilets. First come, first served. Open May-Oct. $14 per vehicle per night. ❶

Pinegrove Campground (reservations ☎877-444-6777; www.reserveamerica.com), sits 3 mi. south of Lakeview at the other end of Upper Lake Mary. Close to the lake under shady pine trees, Pinegrove is picturesque. Drinking water, flush toilets, barbecues, fire pits, dump station. No hookups. Showers $3 per 5 min. $16 per vehicle per night. ❶

FOOD

Macy's European Coffee House and Bakery, 14 S. Beaver St. (☎774-2243), behind DuBeau hostel. Has a sunny interior with wooden tables (some with chessboards) and paisley-printed chairs. Gourmet hot chocolate, organic vegan pastries, and large sand-wiches and salads beckon travelers. The Tofu Salad ($6) is a big hit with vegetarians, and the honey-sweetened lemonade ($1) is guaranteed to quench even the most parched throat. Free Wi-Fi. Open daily 6am-10pm. Kitchen closes 4pm. MC/V.) ❶

Cafe Espress, 16 N. San Francisco St. (☎774-0541). Local favorite with creative, scrumptious breakfast options. Try Over the Rainbow (citrus-infused french toast with kiwi, strawberries, and banana; $6) with the Snowstorm (espresso, steamed milk, and white chocolate; $3.50) for a filling breakfast. Open daily 7am-2pm. MC/V. ❶

Mountain Oasis Global Cuisine and Juice Bar, 11 E. Aspen St. (☎214-9270). Special-izes in international cuisine with an emphasis on Mediterranean. For lunch, try the lamb gyros ($6). Wide selection of fresh-squeezed juices and smoothies. Lunch $5-7. Dinner $8-16. Open daily 11am-9pm; may close early. AmEx/MC/V. ❸

◔ SIGHTS

Established in 1894 by Percival Lowell (who argued voraciously that intelligent life existed on Mars), the **Lowell Observatory,** 1400 W. Mars Hill Rd., 1 mi. west of downtown, uphill off Rte. 66, is home to many powerful telescopes, including the one that helped the observatory's astronomers discover the former planet Pluto in 1930. Today, visitors can tour the observatory's telescopes, as well as check out the Visitors Center for astronomy exhibits and videos. Daily tours of the observa-tory begin every hr. on the hr. from 10am-4pm and last 45min. Visitors can also come to nightly viewings of the sky, and observe the planets for themselves through the magnificent Alvan Clark refracting telescope. (☎774-3358; www.low-ell.edu. Open daily Mar.-Oct. 9am-5pm; Nov.-Feb. noon-5pm. $6, students and seniors $5, ages 5-17 $3. Alvan Clark viewings Mar.-Oct. M-Sa 5:30-10pm, Nov.-Feb. W and F-Sa 5:30-9:30pm; weather permitting.) The **Museum of Northern Arizona,** 3 mi. north of downtown on U.S. 180, details anything and everything about the land and peoples of the Colorado Plateau. If you don't have time to check out the neigh-boring Hopi and Navajo Reservations, the museum is the perfect place to get all the information you want on Northern Arizona's diverse cultures, traditions, and artistic works. The museum also has exhibits on the region's biology, paleontol-ogy, and geology. The heritage division hosts the annual Hopi (first weekend in July), Navajo (first weekend in Aug.), and Day of the Dead (last weekend in Oct.) festivals. (☎774-5213; www.musnaz.org. Open daily 9am-5pm. $6, seniors $6, stu-dents $5, ages 7-17 $4.) **Riordan Mansion State Historic Park,** 409 W. Riordan Rd., off Milton Rd. across from Northern Arizona University, is the historic home of the Riordan family, the primary developers of the Arizona Lumber and Timber Co. and major contributors to Flagstaff's initial development. The mansion, designed by Charles Whittlesey, the architect of the Grand Canyon's famous **El Tovar hotel,** has 40 furnished rooms, 20 for touring, and is a wonderful example of arts-and-crafts style architecture which emphasizes simplicity, craftsmanship, the beauty of nature, and a rustic appearance. (☎779-4395. Open daily May-Oct. 8:30am-5pm; Nov.-Apr. 10:30am-5pm. 45min. tours every hr. on the hr., beginning at 9am. Reser-vations recommended for busy summer weekends at least 24hr. in advance. Tours $6, ages 7-13 $2.50)

♫ ▣ ENTERTAINMENT AND NIGHTLIFE

North of town, across the street from by the Museum of Northern Arizona, the **Coconino Center for the Arts,** 2300 Fort Valley Rd., contains exhibits, performances, and annual festivals featuring regional artists and performers in its 4000 sq. ft. gal-lery and 170-seat theater. In June, the **Flagstaff Folk Festival** is a fun time for families. Call ahead for event details and weekend activities. (☎779-2300; www.culturalpartners.org. Tu-Sa 11am-5pm. Free.) The second weekend in June, the annual **Pine Country Pro Rodeo,** the largest pro rodeo in the county, boasts barn dances, a carnival, and a cocktail waitress race. Events are held Friday and Saturday 7-9:30pm, Sunday 2-6:30pm at the Fort Tuthill Marshall Knowles Memorial Arena, at I-17 Exit 337. (☎888-681-3556; www.pinecountryprorodeo.com. Tickets $12.) On Labor Day weekend, the **Coconino County Fair** arrives with carnival rides, games, and animal competitions. **Theatrikos,** 11 W. Cherry Ave., a local theater company, performs new shows each month at the Flagstaff Playhouse. Also features children's performances through Theatrikids. (☎774-1662; www.theatrikos.com. Mainstage tickets $14. Opening night $17.50. Box office open Tu-Th 1:30-6pm, F 11am-6pm.) **The Orpheum Theatre,** 15 W. Aspen St., is the place to get your concert kicks with nightly performances by well-known musicians playing blues, rock, and country. (☎774-5535; www.orpheumpresents.com. Ticket prices vary. Most events are 21+, under 21 with parent.) Free concerts are also offered every Wednesday evening in June and July in **Wheeler Park,** 212 W. Aspen Ave. Concerts feature local country, rock, blues, and bluegrass artists. (☎779-7690. Concerts 5:30-7:30pm. Free activities for children also available.)

Two popular nightspots reside in the Hotel Weatherford, 23 N. Leroux St. **Charly's,** on the main floor, has live music Tuesday and Thursday through Sunday nights; Tuesday is open mic night (Th-Sa gets quite packed). **Zane Grey,** upstairs, has cheap drinks in a classy setting (Crystal Palace Bar imported from Tombstone) with comfy chairs. (Both ☎779-1919. Happy hour F 5-7pm, with free taco bar at Charly's. Charly's open 11am-2am. Zane Grey open 5pm-2am.) If you feel the urge to two-step, the **Museum Club,** 3404 E. Rte. 66, a roadhouse dating back to Prohibition, was voted "Best Place to Dance" in 2006 by the *Arizona Daily Sun.* Dime beers (W 8pm-midnight) bring in waves of college students. Also hosts official rodeo dances every year. (☎526-9434. Cover $5. Open daily 11am-2am. MC/V.)

🏔 OUTDOOR ACTIVITIES

With the northern **San Francisco Peaks** and the surrounding **Coconino National Forest,** Flagstaff has abundant skiing, hiking, and biking trails for all levels. Remember, altitudes of over 7000 ft. and summer temperatures from 90° make water a necessity for outdoor activity here, regardless of the season. In late spring and summer, national and state park rangers may close trails if the potential for fire is too high. **Backcountry camping ❶** in the National Forest is free. No permit is required, but it's wise to check in and alert a ranger station of your location.

SKIING AND HIKING
For both skiing and hiking, **The Arizona Snowbowl** is one of Arizona's best sites. In winter, it features a vertical drop of 2300 ft. and maintains four chairlifts, a tow rope, and 32 trails; skiing takes place on **Agassiz Peak** (11,500 ft.). To reach the Snowbowl from Flagstaff, take U.S. 180 about 7 mi. north to Snowbowl Rd., then follow Snowball Rd. 7 mi. to the parking area. (☎779-1951; www.arizonasnowbowl.com. Open daily 9am-4pm. Lift tickets M-F noon-4pm $31, 9am-4pm $46; Sa-Su $38/46; ages 8-12 $20/25; under 7 and over 70 free.) **Equipment rental** is available on the mountain. (Adult ski package $16 per half-day, $22 per full day; under 13 ski package $10/15; snowboards $21/29.)

Though snow might still be frosting the mountain top, summer hikers hit the trails. The most popular trail in the area is the strenuous hike to the majestic **Humphrey's Peak** (12,633 ft.), Arizona's highest point (4½ mi., 6hr. round-trip). The trail begins in the first parking lot at the Snowbowl ski area (For directions, see above) and climbs nearly 3300 ft. Though difficult, the trail ends with stunning views of

EXERCISE FOR A CAUSE

There are ways for visitors to utilize Flagstaff's outdoor resources and contribute to the community at the same time. Every July, Absolute Bikes, a Flagstaff mountain biking company, hosts the **Taylor House Benefit Century Ride,** a 95-mile race through downtown Flagstaff, Wupatki and Sunset Crater National Monuments, ending with a celebratory barbecue. All proceeds benefit Taylor House, a temporary home for friends and family of patients at Flagstaff Medical Center. Raising just $50 can fund one night at Taylor House for a friend or family member of a patient at Flagstaff Medical Center. $135 funds a three-night stay.

Those who like to hike can also participate in the American Cancer Society's Climb to Conquer Flagstaff, held every August at the Arizona Snowbowl Ski and Summer Resort, off Hwy. 180. Participants can join with others to form a team to raise money for cancer research. The hike is 7 mi., though there is a bus to take participants to the top.

For more information on the Taylor House Benefit Century Ride, contact Absolute Bikes, 200 E. Rte. 66, 928-779-5969. For more information on the Climb to Conquer Flagstaff, contact the American Cancer Society at www.acsevents.org/faf, or call 928-526-3800.

the Grand Canyon, the Painted Desert, and Oak Creek Canyon. A more moderate hiking option is the **Kachina Trail** (5 mi., 5hr. round-trip). Also leaving from the first Snowbowl parking lot, it runs through aspen and conifer groves. Several other trails twist through the Coconino Forest. Detailed maps and trail advice are available at **Peaks Ranger Station**, 5075 N. 89A (☎526-0866) or the **Mormon Lake Ranger Station,** 4373 S. Lake Mary Rd. (☎774-1147). For the energetic hiker, the demanding **Elden Lookout Trail** (6 mi. round-trip, 5-8hr., 2400 ft.) offers jaw-dropping mountaintop views, as well as a look at the destruction incurred by the human-caused forest fire of 1977. The trailhead is at the Peaks Ranger Station.

Those who don't want to get a workout in order to see the view can take the **Scenic Skyride,** located at the base of the Snowbowl. This 50min. ride glides visitors up 11,500 ft. to see for over 70 miles; views include the Grand Canyon, downtown Flagstaff, and the surrounding mountains. (☎779-1951. Runs Memorial Day-Labor Day daily 10am-4pm; after Labor Day F-Su only. $10, seniors $8, ages 8-12 $6, under 7 and over 70 free.)

MOUNTAIN BIKING
Schultz Creek Trailhead, on Schultz Pass Rd. off U.S. 180 N, is the starting point for many interconnected trails in the San Francisco Mountains, including the popular **Schultz Creek Trail.** The trail begins by climbing north along the bottom of a ravine. After 3½ mi., the Schultz Loop leads onward to the right, while the main Schultz Trail continues straight ahead; both will take you to the same place, the trail's 4-mile marker, where the trail splits again into the difficult and steep **Sunset Trail,** which heads south, and the eastbound **Little Elden Trail.** Sunset Trail climbs almost straight up the side of a mountain for 3 mi. before cresting and descending along **Brookbank Trail,** a fast trail filled with roots and rocks. This 2 mi. stretch spits out riders onto **Elden Lookout Road** (Forest Service Road 557), which can be used to ride back to the trailhead or to access the rocky, rolling **Rocky Ridge Trail.** For those not looking for such a bumpy ride, **Little Elden Trail** is a fun, rolling ride along the creek. Also recommended is a 4 mi. climb on Elden Lookout Rd., followed by a ride down Catwalk Trail through the Hobbit Forest, which returns to Sunset Trail and the Schultz Creek Trailhead.

Bike rentals and excellent advice are available at **Absolute Bikes,** 200 E. Rte. 66. (☎779-5969. Bike rentals $30 per half-day, $40 per full-day. Apr.-Dec. M-F 9am-7pm, Sa 10am-6pm, Su 10am-4pm; Jan.-Mar. M-Sa 10am-6pm, Su 10am-4pm.)

▶ DAYTRIPS FROM FLAGSTAFF

SUNSET CRATER VOLCANO NATIONAL MONUMENT

Sunset Crater is 12 mi. north of Flagstaff on U.S. 89. $5, under 16 free; includes admission to Wupatki National Monument.

The 1000 ft. cinder cone of Sunset Crater Volcano National Monument is the result of one to 10 years of periodic volcanic eruptions beginning around AD 1040 (archaeologists are unsure of the exact date and length of eruptions, though different theories abound). The crater is no longer active; today, the land is used by hikers and, in the 60s, by astronauts in preparation for the first lunar missions. The easy **Lava Flow Nature Trail,** 1½ mi. east of the Visitors Center, meanders 1.3 mi. through the Bonito Lava Flow. Hiking up Sunset Crater itself is not allowed, but the **Lenox Crater Trail** is a tough quarter-mile scramble up the loose cinders of a neighboring cone (20-30 min.), followed by a quick walk back down (5min.). The Visitors Center explores the area's geology and provides an introduction to volcanoes. (☎526-0502. Open daily in summer 8am-5pm; in winter 9am-5pm.)

WUPATKI NATIONAL MONUMENT

Wupatki is 30 mi. northeast of Flagstaff (18 mi. northeast of Sunset Crater), off U.S. 89. You can reach the monument off of U.S. 89, or take the scenic Wupatki Loop Rd. for 35 mi. past Sunset Crater.

Wupatki has gorgeous views of the Painted Desert and fascinating Puebloan sights. The Sinagua people moved here after a Sunset Crater eruption forced them to evacuate in the 11th century. However, archaeologists speculate that droughts, disease, and over-farming led the Sinagua to abandon these stone houses after only 150 years. The remnants of five pueblos form a loop off U.S. 89. The largest and most accessible, Wupatki, on a half-mile round-trip loop trail from the Visitors Center, is three stories high and features a plaza, a ballroom, and a tower. Wupatki's architecture is a blend of Kayenta and Singagua styles, and more than 100 different types of pottery have been discovered in the ruins, leading experts to believe that the area was a trading center for Native American cultures from Mexico to the Great Lakes. The Doney Mountain Trail rises half a mile from the picnic area to the summit. Get info and trail guide brochures at the Visitors Center. Backcountry hiking is not permitted. (☎679-2365. Monument open daily 9am-5pm.)

SEDONA ☎928

Driving into Sedona from the north, visitors may feel like they have descended into Middle Earth; with red rock cliffs rising hundreds of feet on either side and towering pine trees shading the winding highway, it's easy to see why. Sedona's dramatic copper-toned rock formations rise from the earth so starkly that they seem like manufactured tourist attractions. Downtown may be overrun with pricey boutiques, but Sedona's sheer beauty makes the town impossible to skip.

▶ PRACTICAL INFORMATION. Sedona is 120 mi. north of Phoenix (take I-17 north to Rte. 179) and 30 mi. south of Flagstaff (take I-17 south to Rte. 179 or 89A south). The **Sedona-Phoenix Shuttle** (☎282-2066) runs eight trips daily between Phoenix and Sedona (one-way $45, round-trip $85). The **Sedona Chamber of Commerce,** at Forest Rd. and U.S. 89A, has info on accommodations and local attractions. (☎282-7722. Open M-Sa 8:30am-5pm, Su 9am-3pm.) The **South Gateway Visitors Center,** Hwy. 179 at Tequa Plaza, in Oak Creek, has similar services (☎284-5323. Open daily 8:30am-5pm.) For information on the surrounding Coconino

THE SOUTHWEST

National Forest, the Red Rock Ranger Station, located off of Fire Rd. 618 at Beaver Creek, has brochures and maps (☎282-4119. Open M-F 8am-4:30pm.) **Post Office:** 190 W. U.S. 89A. (☎282-3511. Open M-F 8:45am-5pm.) **Postal Code:** 86336.

⌂ ACCOMMODATIONS. Lodging in town is pricey, especially on weekends, so it's not a bad idea to make Sedona a daytrip from Flagstaff or Cottonwood, 15 mi. south. The **White House Inn** ❸, 2986 W. U.S. 89A (☎282-6680), is one of the cheaper options, with rooms with A/C, cable TV, and private baths from $55. Right in downtown Sedona, **La Vista Motel** ❸, 500 N. U.S. 89A, has clean rooms, friendly service, and great views of Sedona's red rocks. (☎282-7301; www.lavistamotel.com. A/C, cable TV, microwave, and refrigerator. Rooms with queen bed $55; with king bed $59. AmEx/D/MC/V.) Most campsites in the area cluster around U.S. 89A as it heads north to Flagstaff. There are plenty of private campgrounds, but most cater to the RV crowd rather than backpackers. The **US Forest Service campsites** ❶ along U.S. 89A are the best and cheapest option for tent-toters. North of Sedona, 9 to 20 mi. from town, four separate campgrounds—**Manzanita, Bootlegger, Cave Springs, and Pine Flat (East and West)** ❶—maintain over 150 campsites along the canyon floor. The shady, creek-side locations with unbeatable canyon views make these sites popular in summer, so arrive early. They all have similar facilities, with picnic tables and toilets, and all but Bootlegger have drinking water. Cave Springs also has showers. Cave Springs, Manzanita and Pine Flat West have a few reservable sites, but the rest are first-come, first-served. (☎527-3600, reservations 877-444-6777. 7-night max. stay. Tent sites $18. Manzanita open year round; all others open mid-April to mid-October.) **Dead Horse Ranch State Park** ❶, just off U.S. 89 in Cottonwood and near Tuzigoot National Monument, has 149 sites, many of which are surrounded by mesquite trees and lookouts over surrounding mountains. (☎634-5283. Toilets, showers. First-come, first-served. Tent sites $12, with hookup $19.)

◘ FOOD. The **Coffee Pot Restaurant** ❷, 2050 W. U.S. 89A, a local favorite, serves 101 varieties of omelets ($4-9) all day and a Mexican diner-style lunch. The Belgian waffles with ice cream and fruit ($6) are a special midday treat sure to beat the heat. (☎282-6626. Lunch $5-9. Open daily 6am-2:15pm. D/MC/V.) **Mesquite Grille & BBQ** ❷, 250 Jordan Rd., has an Old West atmosphere and the lowest dinner prices in town. (☎282-6533. Platters $8-12. Ribs $13. Open daily 11am-8pm. MC/V.) **Casa Rincón** ❷, 2620 W. U.S. 89A, attracts patrons with daily Happy hour (3-6pm; $3 margaritas), mouth-watering combos ($10-13), and live entertainment. (☎282-4849. Open daily 11:30am-1am. Kitchen closes 9pm. AmEx/MC/V.) For creamy, rich homemade ice cream, head over to **The Black Cow Café** ❶, 229 N. U.S. 89. Their homemade pastries are guaranteed to hit the spot. (☎203-9868. Waffle cones $3. Mix-in candies $0.50. Pastries $1-3. Open daily 8am-9pm. MC/V.)

◖ SIGHTS. One of the best ways to experience the area is to go to **Red Rock State Park,** 4050 Red Rock Loop Rd. (U.S. 89A west to Lower Red Rock Loop Rd.), which has beautiful hiking trails and an interactive Visitors Center with exhibits of the area's wildlife. Volunteer naturalists lead nature hikes (10am) into the formations, and rangers arrange daily presentations (2pm) on a variety of topics. From June to August, visitors can also join volunteer naturalists for easy sunset walks around the park (M, W, F-Sa 6pm-7:15pm). Northern flickers, kingfishers, swallows, and hummingbirds frequent the area, and bird walks (times vary seasonally; call the Visitors Center) are offered. (☎520-282-6907. $6 per vehicle, $2 per pedestrian or cyclist. Park open daily May-Aug. 8am-8pm; Apr. and Sept. 8am-6pm; Oct.-Mar. 8am-5pm. Visitors Center open daily May-Aug. 9am-6pm; Sept.-Apr. 9am-5pm.) The **Chapel of the Holy Cross,** on Chapel Rd., built on a twin-pinnacled spur, lies at the base of a 1000 ft. rock wall and is wedged into the red sandstone. Visitors of all faiths are welcome to light a candle in the chapel's antechamber, with its gorgeous panoramic views, or to take a walk around the outside. (☎282-4069. Open M-Sa 9am-5pm, Su 10am-5pm. Free.) A stretch of slippery creek bottom makes for a great natural waterpark at █Slide Rock State Park, a popular summer spot for families. Visitors can wade across colorful, smooth rocks or go down several natural water slides in the midst of Sedona's beautiful cliffs. The park also has a trail that leads through its apple orchards. (☎282-3034. Open daily in summer 8am-7pm; in winter 8am-5pm; in fall and spring 8am-6pm. $10 per vehicle, $2 per pedestrian.)

Tlaquepaque (Tlah-kee-PAH-kee), off U.S. 179, just southeast of the intersection with U.S. 89, is a resort village inside Sedona that functions as an upscale artisan market and shopping plaza with restaurants and galleries. Prices at Tlaquepaque's many art galleries may be exorbitant, but you can stroll the gardens and admire the profusion of Spanish tile, artwork, and fountains scattered around the plaza. Tlaquepaque is also home to Shakespeare Sedona, a theater troupe that presents two productions during June and July. (Info ☎800-768-9286. Tickets $25.)

Montezuma Castle National Monument, 10 mi. south of Sedona on I-17 (take Exit 293), is a remarkable 45-room cliff dwelling built by the Sinagua in the 12th century, and is one of the best-preserved cliff dwellings in North America. You can't get very close to the ruins, but the view from the 0.3 mi. loop below is excellent. (☎567-3322. Open daily Memorial Day-Labor Day 8am-6pm; Labor Day-Memorial Day 8am-5pm. $5, under 16 free.) A self-replenishing lake formed by the collapse of an underground cavern, Montezuma Well, off I-17, 11 mi. north of the castle (take Exit 289), was once a source of water for the Sinagua, and is believed to have been a sacred site. (Open daily 8am-6pm. Free.) Take U.S. 89A to Rte. 279 and continue through Cottonwood to reach Tuzigoot National Monument, 20 mi. from Sedona, which contains the remains of a Sinaguan village inhabited until 1425. (☎634-5564. Open daily Memorial Day-Labor Day 8am-6pm; Labor Day-Memorial Day 8am-5pm. $5, under 16 free.)

█ OUTDOOR ACTIVITIES. It's hard to go wrong with any of the well-maintained hiking trails in and around Sedona; most bring you to stunning views of the surrounding forests and red rock mesas. Most trailheads are on the forest service roads that snake into hills and canyons. The US Forest Service publishes a free guide to recreation (available at any Visitors Center) that lists options for hiking, biking, and driving in "Red Rock Country." In Sedona, however, even the views and hikes aren't free. In order to park at trailheads, your car has to sport a **Red Rock Pass,** a parking permit available from vending machines at most Visitors Centers and some trailheads ($5 per day, $15 per week). Hiking highlights include the difficult **Hot Loop Trail** (10 mi. one-way), with views of Bell Rock and Courthouse Butte, and the more moderate **Huckaby Trail** (6 mi.), which gives hot hikers a chance to swim in Oak Creek Canyon. For experimenting with the area's acclaimed vortex energy areas, **Boynton Canyon Trail** (5 mi.) is a moderate trail along the floor of Boynton Canyon where a combination of masculine and feminine energies can be found. To channel feminine energy, try **Cathedral Rock,** 4 mi. up Upper Red Rock Rd., and for its masculine counterpart, try **Bell Rock,** 5 mi. on Hwy. 179. Biking offers similar wonders. Considered a rival to Moab by those in the mountain biking know-how, Sedona has over 100 mi. of interconnected trails. **Broken Arrow** (4-8hr. round-trip) offers experienced bikers a challenge with its tough climbs. Tamer trails can be found along the wide and easy **Bell Rock Pathway** south of town. Bike rentals (from $25 per 2hr., $40 per day), trail information, and knowledgeable advice can be found at **Mountain Bike Heaven,** 1695 W. U.S. 89A. (☎282-1312. Open daily 8am-6pm.) Scenic drives are almost as plentiful as the rocks. The **Red Rock Loop** (20 mi., 1hr., off U.S. 89A west of town) is mostly paved, but provides some dirt road adventure and mind-blowing views of rock formations. The **Airport Mesa,** 1 mi. west on U.S. 89A, offers one of the best panoramic sunset views. For those hoping to see Sedona's wild side, many companies offer **4WD** tours. **Adventure Company,** 336 Hwy. 179 at Tlaquepaque, has guide services for some of Sedona's most famous 4WD trails. (☎204-1973. Tours daily 8:30am-5:30pm. Make reservations at least 24hr. in advance. From $45, children from $35.)

NAVAJO RESERVATION

Today, the Navajo Nation is the largest reservation in the US, covering over 27,000 sq. mi. of northeastern Arizona, southeastern Utah, and northwestern New Mexico, and is home to 250,000 people. Four sacred mountains, believed to be created in mythical times, watch over Navajo land; Mt. Blanca to the east, Mt. Taylor to the south, San Francisco Peak to the west, and Mt. Hesperus to the north. The Navajo believe that all that is good comes from the lands contained by these holy mountains, and that those who dwell within their protection will have eternal health and harmony. Anthropologists think the Diné people, more commonly known as Navajo, are descended from groups of Athapascan people who migrated to the Southwest from Canada in the 14th and 15th centuries, but the Navajo see their existence as the culmination of a journey through three other worlds into this world, the Glittering World. In the second half of the 19th century, reservations evolved out of the US government's ad hoc attempts to end fighting between Native Americans and Anglos while facilitating white settlement on native lands. The reservation system imposed a kind of wardship over Native Americans, which lasted for over a century, until Supreme Court decisions starting in the 1960s reasserted the tribes' standing as semi-sovereign nations. Today, most Navajo youth are fluent in both Navajo and English, and the importance of the native language continues to be emphasized throughout the Reservation during prayers, ceremonies, and hymns. Often highlighted as cultural heroes are the Navajo Code Talkers, marines who disguised military transmissions using the Navajo language during World War II, and helped to win the war in the Pacific. The remaining Navajo Code Talkers continue to be honored in the reservation's ceremonies.

Remember to advance your watch one hour during the summer; the Navajo Nation runs on **Mountain Daylight Time,** while the rest of Arizona, including the Hopi Reservation, does not observe daylight savings, operating on Pacific Standard Time in the summer and Mountain Standard Time in the winter. The reservation's **area code** is ☎928 in Arizona, 505 in New Mexico, 435 in Utah.

Monument Valley, Canyon de Chelly, Navajo National Monument, Rainbow Bridge, Antelope Canyon, and all their roads and trails are on Navajo land. Those planning to hike through Navajo territory need a backcountry permit, obtained by mail from one of the parks and recreation departments. Mail a **permit request** to Monument Valley Navajo Tribal Park, P.O. Box 360280, Monument Valley, UT

REMINDER. Cultural sensitivity is very important on the reservation; despite the many state and interstate roads that traverse it, the land is both legally and culturally distinct. Driving or hiking off designated trails and established routes is considered trespassing on private property unless you are with a guide. Possession and consumption of alcohol is prohibited on the reservation. The Navajo people have their own language and social norms. While many cultures find eye contact, firm handshakes, and cheerful conversation with strangers desirable, among the Navajo these behaviors are generally impolite. General photography is allowed unless otherwise stated, but photographing the Navajo people requires their permission (a gratuity is usually expected). As always, the best remedy for cultural friction is simple respect.

84536 or Navajo Parks and Recreation Department, P.O. Box 2520, Window Rock, AZ 86515. Permits can also be requested by phone at ☎978-871-6647. Flagstaff, AZ (p. 37) is a good gateway to the reservation, with car rental agencies, inexpensive accommodations, and Greyhound service on I-40. Budget travelers can camp at the National Monuments or Navajo campgrounds.

MONUMENT VALLEY   ☎435

In contrast to the arid desert landscape surrounding them, the red sandstone mesas, buttes, and spires of Monument Valley Navajo Tribal Park shock and awe the visitors who daily crowd the monument. In addition to its tourist appeal, the landscape of the monument has also provided the rocky skyline for many Hollywood westerns, but long before John Wayne, the ancient Anasazi (Navajo for "Ancient People") sustained small communities here. While you can see most of the iconic formations from Hwy. 163, you can get closer by taking the park's 17 mi. scenic **Valley Drive,** which winds around 11 of the most spectacular formations, including the famous pair of **Mittens** and the slender **Totem Pole.** The gaping ditches, large rocks, and mudholes on this dirt road, however, can be jarring to both you and your car—observe the 15 mph speed limit and allow at least 1½hr. The valley can be viewed by foot as well by hiking the park's only self-guided trail, the moderate **Wildcat Trail** (3 mi., 2hr.). To reach other parts of the valley, visitors should obtain the help of a 4WD vehicle, horse, or guide. The Visitors Center parking lot is crowded with booths selling jeep, horseback, and hiking tours. (1½hr. guided tour $50, 2½hr. $55; 1½hr. jeep tour about $35 per person, full day $100; horseback tours $65-95. For more information, call **Dineh Trailrides of Monument Valley** for horseback rides (☎419-0136), or **Totem Pole Tours** for jeep rides (☎727-3313). In winter, snow laces the rocky towers. Call the Visitors Center for road conditions. The park entrance is on U.S. 163 just south of the Utah border, 24 mi. north of **Kayenta,** at the intersection of US 163 and US 160. The **Visitors Center** has info on the park as well as the Navajo Code Breakers and a gift shop. (☎727-5870. Park and Visitors Center open daily May-Sept. 7am-8pm; Oct.-Apr. 8am-5pm. $5, under 9 free; National Passes not accepted.) **Mitten View Campground ❶,** a quarter mile from the Visitors Center and next to the parking lot, has 99 sites with views and showers, but no hookups, little shade, and a lot of exposure to visitors and park staff. (Register at the Visitors Center; first come, first served. Sites $10; in winter $5.) Cheap motels can easily be found in **Mexican Hat, UT,** and **Bluff, UT.** The only in-park dining option is **The View Restaurant ❷,** located within the Visitors Center Complex. The View serves a wide selection of burgers and sandwiches ($7-8), as well as a homemade bowl of mutton stew ($9), a "Navajo favorite." (☎727-3468. Open daily 9am-7pm. AmEx/D/MC/V.)

CANYON DE CHELLY   ☎928

The picturesque canyons of Canyon de Chelly (d'SHAY), just north of Chinle on Navajo Rte. 7 off of U.S. 191, contains evidence of nearly 5000 years of human history. From the rim overlooking two of the main canyons, Canyon del Muerto and Canyon de Chelly, you can gaze at the remains of the homes of the Anasazi, (Navajo for "ancient ones") still nestled into alcoves and perched precariously on ledges. Among these 13th century cliff dwellings, Navajo farmers can still be seen working the land of the canyon floor using traditional agricultural practices. The canyon is best viewed from one of two scenic drives. The **North Rim Drive** (37 mi., 2hr. round-trip) is a tour through four vistas of Canyon del Muerto, highlighted by petroglyphs, ancient Pueblo villages, and Massacre Cave, the site of an 1805 massacre by Spanish soldiers. The North Rim drive is especially good for morning photographs. To best capture the afternoon sun, the **South Rim Drive** (34 mi., 2hr. round-trip) is the route to take. The drive has seven viewpoints of the Canyon de Chelly, including the 800 ft. Spider Rock sandstone spire, named for the Holy Spider Woman, the Navajo deity who taught weaving. The **White House Trail,** 6 mi. from the Visitors Center along South Rim Dr., is a moderate hike (2½ mi. round-trip, 2hr.) that leads down to the canyon floor and the White House ruin; observe the whitewashed walls of the dwelling's central room that gives the ruin its name. At its peak, the White House accommodated 100 men, women, and children, and is a marvel to behold. Jewelry is frequently sold at canyon overlooks and along the White House trail; the delicate craftsmanship of the Navajo attracts browsing tourists. The drives and White House Trail are the only self-guided activities in the park; everything else must be under the supervision of an authorized **Navajo guide.** Guide services exist to lead visitors into the canyon by 4WD vehicle, horse, and foot. Totsonii Ranch offers **horseback tours** (☎245-6209); Canyon Jeep Tours provides 4WD excursions (☎245-3192). **Hiking tours** require both a permit (free from the Visitors Center) and a guide ($15 per group per hr., 3 hr. min.) If you wish to use your own 4WD vehicle to enter the canyon, you must also obtain a permit (free from the Visitors Center) and a guide ($15 per vehicle per hr., with a 3 hr. min.). For more information on guide services and prices, contact the Visitors Center.

The **Visitors Center** has archaeological and cultural displays detailing the lives of the canyon's many inhabitants and has helpful advice, as well as information on ranger programs, which range from morning coffee discussions to full-day guided hikes (Find a full list of ranger programs at ☎674-5500. Open daily 8am-5pm. Free.) Signs posted in the Visitors Center urge tourists to lock their car doors and close windows at all overlooks, as thefts can occur.

Thunderbird Lodge ❹ is the park's only indoor accommodation. Three quarters of a mile behind the Visitors Center in a historic trading post built at the end of the 19th century, the Lodge provides well-equipped, comfortable rooms. (☎674-5841. A/C, showers, cable TV, telephones. Reservations recommended in summer. Rooms from $80. AmEx/D/MC/V.) The same complex also contains a gift shop (open daily 8am-7pm); and an unremarkable cafeteria (sandwiches $5, steaks $12-18; open daily 6:30am-8:30pm). Free camping is available in the 93 tree-lined sites at **Cottonwood Campgrounds ❶,** just southwest of the Visitors Center. (Flush toilets, water, picnic tables, grills, no showers, no hookups. First come, first served. Free.) **Spider Rock Campground ❶,** 10 mi. from the Visitors Center, offers tent and RV sites and Internet access ($2) for guests. (☎877-910-CAMP. Firepits, pit toilets, potable water. Tent sites $10; RV sites $15. Hogan rentals $29-39.) For those who need an extra jolt before hitting the scenic drives, **Changing Woman Coffeehouse ❶,** right before the turn for the South Rim Drive, is a small cafe with gourmet coffee and espresso ($2-3), an outdoor patio, and mellow jazz wafting from a portable stereo.

NAVAJO NATIONAL MONUMENT ☎520

Archaeologists have determined that ancestors of today's Hopi occupied the cliffs of Tsegi Canyon from the 1250s until 1300, when a 20-year drought forced the people to move on and "continue their migration to the spiritual center of the earth." Today, the site where they lived contains the remains of three of their remarkable cliff dwellings. **Inscription House** has been closed to visitors since 1968 due to its fragile condition, and the other two admit a very limited number of visitors on a daily basis. Keet Seel, the ancestral home to Fire or Owl Burrowing Clan, Big Horn Sheep Clan, and the Coyote Clan, is one of the best-preserved ancestral Puebloan villages. Unfortunately, it can be reached only by a challenging 17 mi. round-trip hike (open Memorial Day to Labor Day). Hikers can stay overnight in a **free camp-**

ground ❶ nearby (pit toilet, no drinking water), or complete the hike in one day. Reservations for free permits to visit Keet Seel can be made through the Visitors Center up to five months in advance. Only 20 people are allowed each day, so if you don't have a reservation, show up at the Visitors Center early to secure a spot. Orientation times for Keet Seel hike 8:15am, 4pm. Call the Visitors Center for more information. Ranger-led tours to **Betatakin** (literally "House on a Ledge"), a 135-room Puebloan complex, are limited to 25 people per tour. (5 mi. round-trip, 3-5hr. May to late Sept. 8:30am, 11am; first-come, first-served.) The paved (but not wheelchair-accessible) one mile round-trip **Sandal Trail** lets you gaze down on Betatakin from the top of the canyon, and is a great option for those unable to secure a spot on the Betatakin ranger tour. The Aspen Forest Overlook Trail, another one mile hike, overlooks aspens and firs that are the remnants of an ancient forest. To get to the monument, take Rte. 564 from U.S. 160, 20 mi. southwest of Kayenta. The Visitors Center is 9 mi. down Rte. 564 and has local artisans demonstrating traditional crafts, in addition to a life-size replica of a Tsegi Canyon family home. (☎672-2700. Open daily in summer 8am-7pm; in winter 9am-5pm. Free; donations accepted.) The park also operates two free campgrounds, both located within a mile of the Visitors Center. **Sunset View ❶** has 31 sites with drinking water, picnic tables, grills, and flush toilets spread among the red sandy hills of the monument. (No hookups. First-come, first-served.) The **Canyon View campground ❶** offers 13 primitive sites with great views of the canyon. (Picnic tables, grills, pit toilets. No water or hookups. First-come, first-served).

HOPI RESERVATION   ☎928

The Hopi people reside in 12 traditional villages throughout three regions in the desolate beauty of Black Mesa's arid valleys. Landlocked by the Navajo Reservation since a US district court decision in the 80s, the Hopi Reservation is divided into three regions known, from east to west, as First, Second, and Third Mesas. Roadside stands brimming with Hopi pottery, baskets, and jewelry line the only paved highway connecting the three regions, Hwy. 264, and though prices vary from stand to stand, visitors should feel free to browse or buy. Once off the reservation, however, shoppers should be careful of imitation Hopi art and jewelry, prominent in central Arizona. **First Mesa** is the only region intended to accommodate visitors. To reach First Mesa, drive to Polacca and follow the signs to First Mesa Villages, Walpi, and the **Ponsi Hall Community Center,** a general info center and starting point for guided tours of the mesa villages, including Walpi, the most spectacular of the villages. Guided tours also include a short presentation of Hopi culture and history (☎737-2262. Open daily June-Aug. 9:30am-5pm, Sept.-May 10am-3pm. Tours last 45min. and begin at opening time; the last tour departs 1hr. prior to closing. $8, children $5. Call 3-5 days in advance to ensure tour availability.) There are no tours available on the **Second** or **Third Mesas,** and at all three, photography and recording are strictly forbidden. Though there are no tours on Second Mesa, it is home to the **Hopi Cultural Center,** 5 mi. west of the intersection of Rts. 264 and 87 and 15 mi. west of First Mesa. The Center serves as a Visitors Center and has the reservation's only museum, which focuses on the tribe's history and arts and crafts, featuring exhibits on basket-making, pottery, jewelry, and clothing. (☎734-6650. Open in summer, M-F 8am-5pm, Sa-Su 9am-3pm; in winter M-F 8am-5pm. $3, under 14 $1.) The **Hopi Cultural Center Restaurant ❷** and the **Hopi Cultural Center Motel ❹,** the only accommodations on the reservation, are in the same complex. The restaurant offers some Hopi dishes on traditional blue fry bread ($8-9), in addition to burgers and sandwiches. (☎734-2401. Restaurant open daily Apr.-Sept. 6am-9pm; Oct.-Mar. 7am-8pm. Reservations recommended for motel rooms a few weeks in advance. Rooms Apr.-Sept. $95, Oct.-Mar. $65; each additional person $5.) **Free camping ❶** is allowed at 10 dusty, sunny sites next to the Cultural Center (no toilets, water, or hookups).

One of the most spectacular parts of Hopi culture is the **sacred dances,** which take place from the winter solstice in December to July. During the dances, male members of the Kachina societies impersonate the Kachina spirits, supernatural beings who bring both balance to the universe and rain to the Hopi crops. The dances are not entertainment, but rather about "attainment of good life." For this reason, visitors are forbidden from almost all Kachina dances. As many of the dances are announced only a few days in advance and occur on weekends, it is a good idea to call the Cultural Center before making a visit to the reservation; villages close down to tourists during the ceremonies. There are a few dances that tourists are able to observe. The **Butterfly Dances,** held in August and September, are open to visitors, although shorts, tank tops, and casual wear are forbidden, as is photography. If you do choose to visit the reservation during the celebrations, remember that these dances are sacred to the Hopi people and deserve the utmost respect. For more information on the ceremonies, call the **Cultural Center** or the **Ponsi Hall Community Center.**

PETRIFIED FOREST NATIONAL PARK   ☎520

Spreading over 60,000 acres, the Petrified Forest National Park is the colorful result of geological forces millions of years in the making. Some 225 million years ago, when Arizona's desert was swampland, volcanic ash covered the logs, slowing their decay and cutting off their oxygen supply. Silica-infused water seeped through the wood, replacing the wood's cellulose. Over time, silica crystallized into quartz, combining with iron and manganese to produce rainbow hues. The same minerals stained the sediment of the park, creating the stunning colors that stripe the rock formations of the park's badlands. While these gem-like logs and the beauty of the colorful badlands are sure to fascinate, the park itself lacks the grandeur and hiking trails of neighboring national parks; it's best as a daytrip or a stop on a trip through the Native American reservations that surround the park.

Most travelers to the park opt to take the scenic 28 mi. road from north to south; all of the park's trails and viewpoints (with the exception of the Painted Desert Wilderness Area) lie off of this main road. The park can be split into two parts separated by I-40: the northern Painted Desert and the southern Petrified Forest. From the north, the **Painted Desert Rim Trail** (1 mi. round-trip) begins at Tawa Point, skirts the mesa edge above the Lithodendron Wash and the Black Forest, and ends at Kachina Point, one of the most popular views. The point provides access for travel into the **Painted Desert Wilderness Area,** the park's region for backcountry hiking and camping. The nearby Painted Desert Inn, 2 mi. from the north entrance is certainly worth a stop. A former trading post built of petrified wood, the Inn was converted into an adobe structure in the 30s by workers in the Civilian Conservation Corps, a New Deal program (p. 58). Today, the Inn houses Native American cultural history exhibits. (☎928-524-6228. Open daily 8am-4:30pm.) The Petrified Forest section of the park begins after the road crosses I-40. Native American **petroglyphs** dating thousands of years can be viewed by taking a short trail (0.3 mi. loop) through the ruins of the 100-room Puerco Pueblo, believed to have housed nearly 200 people at once. At the ruins, visitors can also observe a solar calendar marking the winter solstice. An additional 650 petroglyphs can be seen at Newspaper Rock, but only from a distance. At the fourth loop of the 3 mi. Blue Mesa drive, you can hike the **Blue Mesa Trail** (1 mi. round-trip, 45min.), a steep descent into the heart of the park's desolate and beautiful clay badlands. The **Giant Logs Trail** (0.3 mi. loop) starts at the south Visitors Center and winds past the largest logs in the park; a trail guide is available at the Visitors Center for $0.50. The **Long Logs Trail** (1.6 mi. loop) travels through the park's largest concentration of petrified wood. The **Agate House Trail** (2 mi. round-trip) leads to a partially restored pueblo of petrified wood. Both the Long Logs and the Agate House Trails depart from the south Visitors Center parking lot. While exploring the park's short trails, don't pick up the petrified wood—it's already scared enough. Also, taking fragments is illegal and considered unlucky. Unfortunately, one ton of petrified wood is taken from the park each month, depleting the park's supply.

Each end of the park's scenic 28 mi. road has an entrance station and a Visitors Center; the park can be entered from either the north or the south. (The park is open daily June-Aug. 7am-7pm; Sept.-May 8am-5pm. Entrance $10 per vehicle, $5 per pedestrian or motorcyclist.) There is no public transit to the park. To reach the northern entrance and the Painted Desert, take I-40 to Exit 311, 107 mi. east of Flagstaff and 65 mi. west of Gallup, NM. The **Painted Desert Visitors Center,** directly west of the north entrance station, shows a 20min. orientation video and has informational kiosks on the origins of the both the petrified forest and the colorful desert, as well as a schedule of daily ranger programs. (☎524-6228. Open in summer daily 7am-7pm; call for low-season hours. Free.) To reach the park' south entrance, take U.S. 180 west 36 mi. from St. Johns, AZ, or east 19 mi. from Holbrook. Inside the south entrance, the **Rainbow Forest Museum** has petrified logs and info on the park's paleontology; the forest was home to some of the earliest dinosaurs during the late Triassic period. The museum also shows the same 20min. video available at the north entrance. (☎524-6822. Open June-Aug. daily 7am-7pm, call for low-season hours. Free.) Water and restrooms are located at both Visitors Center areas. At the north entrance, the **Fred Harvey cafeteria ❶** offers burgers ($3-6), as well as other hot entrees ($5-6) for visitors. (Open daily 7am-3pm.) Visitors can also find gas and a convenience store behind the cafeteria. Next to the Rainbow Forest Museum, the **Fred Harvey Fountain ❶** serves bottomless root beer floats ($3) and huge scoops of ice cream ($2). (Open daily 7am-7pm. In case of emergency, call the ranger dispatch (☎524-9726). There are no campgrounds in the park, but **backcountry camping ❶** is allowed in the Painted Desert Wilderness with a free permit, available same day at either Visitors Center. Backpackers must park at Kachina Point and enter the Wilderness via the 1 mi. access trail. No fires are allowed. Budget motels and diners line Rte. 66, but there are none right around the park. Gallup and Holbrook offer more lodging and eating options. If you choose to stay in Holbrook, the **El Ranchero Lodge ❷**, 867 N. Navajo Blvd., has beige-themed rooms with cable TV. (☎524-3332. A/C, showers. Doubles $35. MC/V.)

PHOENIX   ☎ 602

Originally inhabited by members of the Hohokam culture, Phoenix is Arizona's— and the Southwest's—largest city. Situated in the middle of the Sonoran Desert, Phoenix has become an increasingly popular winter destination for the sun-starved traveler, and the city's many arts and sports facilities have added dimension to what could otherwise be urban sprawl. Though an adolescent city (founded in 1881), Phoenix has a wealth of restaurants, theaters, museums, and resorts that multiply by the year, ensuring the region's future expansion.

◼ TRANSPORTATION

Airport: Sky Harbor International Airport (PHX; ☎273-3300; www.phxskyharbor.com), just southeast of downtown. Take the Valley Metro red line bus into the city (3:15am-11:45pm, $1.25). **SuperShuttle** (☎244-9000 or 800-258-3826) offers transportation to and from the airport; about $7 to downtown Phoenix.

Buses: Greyhound, 2115 E. Buckeye Rd. (☎389-4200; www.greyhound.com). Station open 24hr. To: **El Paso** (9hr., 5 per day, $43); **Los Angeles** (6-10hr., 10 per day, $44); **San Diego** (7-12hr., 7 per day, $57); **Tucson** (2hr., 10 per day, $18.50). There is no direct service to Phoenix, but **Amtrak** (☎800-872-7245; www.amtrak.com) operates connector buses to and from rail stations in Tucson and Flagstaff.

Public Transit: In downtown **Valley Metro** (☎253-5000; www.valleymetro.org). Most bus lines run out of Central Station, at Central Ave. and Van Buren St. Most routes operate M-F 5am-8pm with reduced service Sa. $1.25; disabled, seniors, and children $0.60. All-day pass $3.60/2, 10-ride pass $12/6. Bus passes and system maps at the terminal or downtown Visitors Center. In Tempe, the **City of Tempe Transit Store,** 502 S. College Ave., Ste. 101 (☎480-858-2350), is the public transit headquarters. The red line runs to Tempe from Phoenix and services Mesa. Bus passes and system maps at the terminal. Loloma Station, 7084 E. 2nd St. (☎480-312-2333), just south of Indian School and Scottsdale Rd., is Scottsdale's main hub for local traffic. The green line runs from Old Town Scottsdale along Thomas Rd. to Phoenix.

Taxi: Yellow Cab, ☎252-5252.

Car Rental: Enterprise Rent-A-Car, 1702 E. Rental Car Way (☎602-225-0588; www.enterprise.com) near the airport, and at other offices throughout the city. Compact cars around $35 per day; lower weekly and monthly rates. Valid credit card and driver's license required. Airport office open daily 5am-midnight; other offices' hours vary.

✴ 🔁 ORIENTATION AND PRACTICAL INFORMATION

> **CAN I HAVE YOUR DIGITS?** Because of its explosive growth, the city has three area codes. 602 is limited to Phoenix proper, 623 is western greater Phoenix, and 480 is the East Valley (including Scottsdale, Tempe, and Mesa). Unless otherwise noted, all listings in the text are within the 602 area code.

The intersection of **Central Avenue** and **Washington Street** marks the heart of downtown. Central Ave. runs north-south, Washington St. east-west. Numbered avenues and streets both run north-south; avenues are numbered sequentially west from Central, while streets are numbered east. **Tempe,** east of Phoenix, is dominated by students from Arizona State University (ASU). **Mesa,** east of Tempe, is bigger, with a large Mormon community and many suburban neighborhoods. **Scottsdale,** north of Tempe, is an upscale district with adobe-style mansions and shopping centers. These areas combine to form what is referred to as "The Valley."

Visitor Info: Phoenix and Valley of the Sun Convention and Visitors Center (☎254-6500 or 877-225-5749, info and calendar 252-5588; www.phoenixcvb.com). Downtown at 125 N. 2nd St., Ste. 120. Open M-F 8am-5pm. Free Wi-Fi. Camping and outdoors info at the **Bureau of Land Management Office,** 1 N. Central Ave., Ste. 800 (☎417-9200), in the Phelps Dodge Building.

Hotlines: Crisis Hotline: ☎800-631-1314. **Sexual Assault Hotline:** ☎254-9000. **Suicide Prevention,** ☎480-784-1500. All open 24hr. **Gay Hotline:** ☎234-2752. Daily 10am-10pm.

Internet Access: Burton Barr Central Library, 1221 N. Central Ave. (☎262-4636). Free. Open M-Th 10am-9pm, F-Sa 9am-6pm, Su noon-6pm.

Post Office: 522 N. Central Ave. (☎800-275-8777). Open M-F 8:30am-5pm. General delivery: 1441 E. Buckeye Rd. Open M-F 8:30am-6pm. **Postal Code:** 85004.

Downtown Phoenix

🏠 ACCOMMODATIONS
Budget Lodge Motel, **8**
Metcalf Hostel (HI), **4**
YMCA Downtown
  Phoenix, **7**

🍎 FOOD
Los Dos Molinos, **9**
Welcome Diner, **5**
Dos Gringos Trailer Park, **2**

🎭 NIGHTLIFE
Amsterdam, **6**
Graham Central Station, **3**
The Willow House, **1**

W. Cypress St.
W. Monte Vista Rd.
Heard Museum
TO ARIZONA BILTMORE HOTEL (4mi)
E. Monte Vista Rd.
E. Palm Ln.
1st St.
3rd St.
7th St.
E. Coronado Rd.
Phoenix Art Museum
TO COSANTI (13mi), SCOTTSDALE (15mi), TALIESIN WEST (22mi)
E. McDowell Rd.
Townsend Park
W. Lynwood St.
Central Ave.
E. Brill St.
W. Willetta St.
E. Willetta St.
Burton Barr Central Library
W. Culver St.
10
Papago Fwy.
10
Margaret T. Hance Park
E. Moreland St.
TO (9mi) (12mi), TEMPE (5mi), PAPAGO PARK AND PHOENIX ZOO (5mi), MESA (12mi), SALT RIVER (7mi)
Portland Park
1st St.
2nd St.
E. Portland St.
W. Portland St.
W. Roosevelt St.
E. Roosevelt St.
7th Ave.
5th Ave.
3rd Ave.
1st Ave.
Central Ave.
3rd St.
4th St.
5th St.
6th St.
7th St.
9th St.
E. Garfield St.
McKinley St.
E. McKinley St.
E. Pierce St.
W. Fillmore St.
E. Fillmore St.
✉
W. Taylor St.
E. Taylor St.
E. Polk St.
Arizona Center
U. of Arizona College of Medicine-Phoenix
Central Station Transit Center
W. Van Buren St.
E. Van Buren St.
TO ✚ (1.5mi)
W. Monroe St.
Herberger Theater Center
W. Adams St.
Orpheum Theater
Renaissance Square
Phoenix Convention Center
Museum of History
HERITAGE SQUARE
W. Washington St.
CÉSAR CHÁVEZ PLAZA
PATRIOT'S SQUARE
i
Symphony Hall
Arizona Science Center
E. Washington St.
W. Jefferson St.
6th Ave.
5th Ave.
4th Ave.
3rd Ave.
2nd Ave.
1st Ave.
Central Ave.
1st St.
E. Jefferson St.
TO ✚ SKY HARBOR INTERNATIONAL AIRPORT (3mi)
7th Ave.
Madison St.
US Airways Center
E. Jefferson St.
Chase Field
E. Jackson St.
TO 🚌 GREYHOUND (3mi)
0   600 yards
0   600 meters
TO 9 (5mi)
E. Buchanan St.
N
LG
TO GAMMAGE MEMORIAL AUDITORIUM (9mi)

THE SOUTHWEST

ACCOMMODATIONS

Budget travelers should consider visiting Phoenix during July and August, when motels slash their prices by as much as 60%. In the winter, temperatures drop, the number of vacationers rises, and prices go up; make reservations early. Although several miles from the center of downtown, the areas around Papago Fwy. and Black Canyon Hwy. are loaded with motels. **Mi Casa Su Casa/Old Pueblo Homestays Bed and Breakfast,** P.O. Box 950, Tempe 85280, arranges stays at B&Bs throughout Arizona, New Mexico, southern Utah, southern Nevada, and southern California. (☎800-456-0682; www.azres.com. Open M-F 9am-5pm, Sa 9am-noon. Rooms from $65.) The reservation-less should cruise the rows of motels on **Van Buren Street** both west and east of downtown, but beware: parts of this area can be unsafe and guests should examine a motel thoroughly before checking in.

Metcalf Hostel (HI), 1026 N. 9th St. (☎254-9803), between Roosevelt and Portland northeast of downtown. This slightly worn-out hostel has a kitchen, lounge area with Wi-Fi, a dusty patio, and comfy 6-bed dorm rooms. Dorm rooms stay unlocked, so keep valuables in one of the hostel's lockers. Check-in 7am-10pm. Dorms $19, members $17; private room $30-35. Cash or traveler's check only. ❶

YMCA Downtown Phoenix, 350 N. 1st Ave. (☎253-6181). Small, clean singles with A/C and shared bathrooms for both women and men. Athletic facilities available. 18+. Reception 9am-10pm. $25 per day; $115 per week. AmEx/MC/V. ❶

Budget Lodge Motel, 402 W. Van Buren St. (☎254-7247). Has nice rooms with a lobby entrance, making it one of the safer options close to downtown. A/C, HBO, microwave, pool, and refrigerator. Reception 24hr. Rooms from $45. AmEx/D/MC/V. ❷

FOOD

Downtown businesspeople typically eat at small cafes on the ground floors of corporate buildings, most of which close on weekends. **McDowell** and **Camelback Road** have plenty of Asian restaurants, while the **Arizona Center,** an open-air shopping gallery at 3rd St. and Van Buren, has food, fountains, and palm trees. East of town, Mill Ave. in Tempe is also brimming with cheap eateries.

 Los Dos Molinos, 8646 S. Central Ave. (☎243-9113). From downtown, go 8 mi. south on Central Ave. Chile-shaped piñatas and Corona chandeliers complement fresh, authentic food filled with green and red chiles. Their motto is "some like it hot," so be ready to swallow fire. Enchiladas $4.50. Burritos $6-9. Combo platters $10. No reservations. Open Tu-F 11am-2:30pm and 5-9pm, Sa 11am-9pm. AmEx/D/MC/V. Also at 260 S. Alma School Dr. in Mesa (☎602-243-9113). ❷

Dos Gringos Trailer Park, 216 E. University Dr. (☎480-968-7879). Dos skirts the line between restaurant and nightspot with daily Happy hour (M-F 4-7pm), $0.50 Coronas (Th 9pm-midnight), and cheap, tasty Mexican dishes ($5-8). Open daily 11am-2am. AmEx/D/MC/V. ❷

Welcome Diner, 924 E. Roosevelt St. (☎495-1111). This cute little diner, with an emphasis on both "cute" and "little," is bright and has some of the best grill food around. Eat in at the red-trimmed counter, or take out. The hot dog with fried egg and cheddar cheese is a specialty ($6). Burgers $6. Open M-Sa 9am-3pm. Cash only. ❶

SIGHTS

DOWNTOWN. The center of Phoenix, Copper Park, is divided into downtown (south of I-10), with cultural and sports attractions, and uptown (north of I-10), an artistic quarter with many museums. One of the best regional museums in the country, the ⬛**Heard Museum**, 2301 N. Central Ave., has Native American ancient and contemporary art, poetry, and sculpture. The *We Are! Arizona's First People* exhibit, which details all of Arizona's Native American tribes, is particularly moving. The museum itself is a graceful adobe building with Spanish tiles, fountains, and beautifully landscaped gardens. *(☎252-8840. Open daily 9:30am-5pm. Free 45min. tours 11am, noon, 1:30, 3pm. $10, seniors $9, ages 6-12 $3, students $5. Native Americans with status cards free.)* Three blocks south, at Central and McDowell, the **Phoenix Art Museum** displays art of the American West, 19th-century European and American works, and a large collection of modern and contemporary art. A museum highlight is the **Center for Creative Photography,** featuring work by prominent schools of American photography. *(1625 N. Central Ave., at McDowell Rd. ☎257-1880. Open Tu 10am-9pm, W-Su 10am-5pm. Guided tours daily noon, 1, and 2pm. $10, students and seniors $8, ages 6-17 $4; free Tu 3-9pm. Tours free.)*

PAPAGO PARK AND FARTHER EAST. Take bus #3 east to **Papago Park,** on the eastern outskirts of the city, for spectacular views of the desert and hiking, biking, and driving trails. In the park, the **Phoenix Zoo** has a formidable collection of tropical, African, and Southwestern critters. The "Arizona Trail" walk highlights animals native to the area; all of Arizona's 11 breeds of rattlesnakes can be found in the reptile cages. *(455 N. Galvin Pkwy. ☎273-1341. Open daily Jan.-May 8am-5pm; June-Sept. M-F 7am-2pm, Sa-Su 7am-4pm; Oct. 9am-5pm; Nov.-Dec. 9am-4pm $14, seniors $9, children $6.)* The ⬛**Desert Botanical Garden** showcases colorful cacti, plants native to the Sonoran Desert, and rare breeds of succulents (plants that are able to store water in their thickened leaves, stems, and roots). Be sure to check out the Cactus House for close-up views of some of the desert's most interesting and beautiful plants. *(1201 N. Galvin Pkwy. ☎941-1225. Open daily May-Sept. 7am-8pm; Oct.-Apr. 8am-8pm. Guided tours daily Oct.-Apr. 10, 11am, and 1pm. Flashlight tours June-July Th and Sa at 7:30pm. $10, seniors $9, children ages 3-12 $4.)* Farther east of the city, in Mesa, flows the **Salt River,** one of the last remaining desert rivers in the US. **Salt River Tubing & Recreation,** in northeast Mesa, 15 mi. north of U.S. 160 on Power Rd., arranges 2-5hr. tubing trips. *(☎480-984-3305; www.saltrivertubing.com. Open May-Sept. daily 9am-4pm. Tube rental $14 per day, includes shuttle service.)*

WRIGHT SIGHTS. Taliesin West was originally built as Frank Lloyd Wright's winter home; far from the

SPACE RAISING SPIRIT

Frank Lloyd Wright, the patriarch of modern American architecture, believed that "spaces should raise spirits." At **Taliesen West**, his Scottsdale home, Wright and 27 apprentices were able to bring these principles to life, over four long winters (for only $10,000). The 45,000 sq. ft. building blends effortlessly into the surrounding desert.

Taliesen West features many key trademarks of Wright's architecture. Because Wright believed that glass was un-desertlike, the windows were originally covered ,with canvas. All of the building's fireplaces extend into the room, rather than into the wall. Wright hated the sight of electricity poles on the horizon, so he arranged for all electricity to the house to run underground. The metal furniture found throughout the house is all designed by Wright. Furthermore, the theater attached to the home is 96.5% acoustically perfect; Wright was trained by the architects who designed Carnegie Hall. Today, this stunning home is open to the public.

Taliesen West, 12621 Frank Lloyd Wright Blvd., east off the Cactus St. exit from Rte. 101. ☎480-860-2700; www.franklloydwright.org. See website for specific tour info. Tour fee $18-20, students and seniors $16-18, ages 4-12 $10-12.

center of Scottsdale, there were no building codes and the architect could be as bold and daring as he wished. Part of the building is now open to the public. Taliesin West also serves as a campus for the fellowship program he established, which educates 27 architectural "apprentices" each year. *(12621 Frank Lloyd Wright Blvd. Head east off the Cactus St. Exit from Rte. 101, follow signs for Taliesen. ☎480-860-2700; www.franklloydwright.org. Open Sept.-June daily 9am-4pm; July-Aug. M and Th-Su 9am-4pm. 1-1½hr. guided tours required; tours offered every hr. on the hr. in summer, every 30min. in winter. See website for tour info. Tours $18-20, students and seniors $16-18, ages 4-12 $10-12.)* Wright also consulted on the design for the impressive **Arizona Biltmore,** a palatial hotel with the largest gold-leaf interior in the US. Despite the hotel's posh atmosphere (guests have included every president since Herbert Hoover), viewing is free; the Aztec Room is especially magnificent. *(24th St. and Missouri. ☎955-6600.)* A design taken from Wright's archives after his death, the **Gammage Memorial Auditorium,** at ASU, is a stand-out with a unique rotunda shape, pink-and-beige earth tones, and curved accents. *(Mill Ave. and Apache Blvd., on the ASU campus in Tempe. Take bus #60 or #22 on weekends. ☎480-965-3434. 20min. tours daily in winter.)* **Cosanti** is a working studio and bell foundry designed by Paolo Soleri, one of Wright's apprentices who specializes in arcology, a combination of architecture and ecology. Visitors can watch artists sculpt and sketch from the decorative terraces. *(6433 E. Doubletree Ranch Rd., in Scottsdale. ☎480-948-6145. Open M-Sa 9am-5pm, Su 11am-5pm. Suggested donation $8.)*

🎵 🎭 ENTERTAINMENT AND NIGHTLIFE

Phoenix has many stadiums, and the large facilities make it easy to get last-minute tickets. NBA basketball action heats up with the **Phoenix Suns** (☎379-7867) at the US Airways Arena, while the **Arizona Cardinals** (☎379-0102) will play NFL football at the University of Phoenix stadium. The **Arizona Diamondbacks** (☎514-8400) use the fabulous Chase Ballpark with a retractable roof, the only swimming pool in the major leagues, and beer gardens. (☎462-6799. Tickets from $15. Tours of the stadium M-F 9:30, 11am, 12:30pm. $6, seniors, children ages 7-12 $4.)

The free *Nightlife! Magazine,* available on magazine racks, lists schedules for Phoenix's after-hours scene. The Cultural Calendar of Events covers area entertainment in three-month intervals. *'N Touch* and *Echo,* both found in bars and clubs, cover GLBT nightlife. 🏳️‍🌈**Amsterdam,** 718 N. Central Ave., is a straight-friendly gay bar with plush leather sofas, antique mirrors, over 190 types of martinis, and an outdoor patio bar. This club has a good crowd of all ages and can get crowded on Thursday through Saturday. (☎258-6122. M manicures and martinis $5 each. Open M-Th and Su 4pm-2am, F-Sa 4pm-4am.) A large, predominantly lesbian and gay bar, **Club Vibe,** 3031 E. Indian School Rd. #7, has more space devoted to pool tables than to the dance floor, but dance and hip-hop music get people moving. (☎224-9977. Th $2 pitchers. Occasional cover. Open Th-Sa 6pm-2am.) In downtown Tempe, bars and clubs line Mill Ave., catering to the college crowd and yuppies. For themed drinks and great sushi, check out **Ra,** 411 S. Mill Ave. (☎480-303-9800. Happy hour M-F 4-7pm; reverse Happy hour daily 10pm-12pm. Tu night Godzilla movies, origami, specialty sushi, and Skyy mixed drinks 8pm-midnight. Open daily 11am-1. Kitchen closes 11pm.) **The Willow House,** 149 W. McDowell Rd., is a self-proclaimed "artists' cove"; musicians and actors fill the four rooms branching off of the coffee-deli bar. (☎252-0272. Wi-Fi. No alcohol. Happy hour M-F 4-7pm; coffee half-price. M open mic night. W DJ. F-Sa live music 9pm. Open daily 6:30am-midnight.) **Graham Central Station,** 7850 S. Priest Dr., in Tempe, has four venues under one roof. The smaller top 40, retro, and karaoke venues supplement the good times of the Rockin' Rodeo, a western-themed club complete with mechanical bull. The retro club serves an older crowd; top 40 is dominated by college students and twentysomethings. (☎480-496-0799. W Ladies Night. Cover up to $7. Open W-Sa 6pm-2am.)

SCENIC DRIVE: APACHE TRAIL

A great daytrip from Phoenix, the **Apache Trail** winds from **Apache Junction,** a small mining town 40 mi. east of Phoenix (take Hwy. 60 east to the Iron Road Exit), through the rugged, haunting **Superstition Mountains.** The trail, also known less creatively as **Route 88,** takes gazers through old ghost towns, along tranquil lakes, and finally to the Roosevelt Dam. When the road was created in the early 20th century by construction workers seeking to move supplies from Phoenix to the Hoover Dam, it was hailed as "the most scenic highway in America." The road, originally named the Mesa-Roosevelt Trail, became known as the Apache Trail to the early motorists who raced around the road's harrowing turns and along its backbreaking 10% grades in their primitive cars, hoping for new records. Today, the precarious dirt road and its infamous "Horseshoe Curve" still entice motorists, though most exercise more caution than previous travelers. The trail's fantastic views, including three beautiful man-made lakes along the Salt River and the Superstition Mountain Wilderness' crags and canyons, make the steep, bumpy road and sharp switchbacks worthwhile. Although the road is only about 55 mi. one-way, trips require at least 3hr. because of the partially unpaved, narrow roadbed. Info, brochures, maps, and travel advice is available at the **Apache Junction Chamber of Commerce,** 567 W. Apache Trail. (☎480-982-3141. Open M-F 8am-5pm; Nov. 15-Apr. 15. also Sa 9am-2pm.) The car-less can drive with **Apache Trail Tours,** which offers on- and off-road Jeep tours. (☎480-982-7661. Reserve at least 48hr. in advance. 2-8hr. tours from $70-165 per person; includes lunch.)

Sights along the drive (starting from Apache Junction) include the **Superstition Mountain Museum,** 3½ mi. northeast of Apache Junction along the Apache Trail (Rte. 88), where visitors can learn about the mountain range's legends, including the stories of Geronimo's Gold Cave, Delshay's Goldmine, the Pygmy Indians, and the Circlestone Mystery. The museum also has exhibits on the American cowboy and the mining of the West. (☎480-983-4888. Open daily 9am-4pm. $5, students 6-17 $2, seniors $4.) **Goldfield Ghost Town,** along the Apache Trail, 5 mi. north of the U.S. 60 junction, is a historically preserved 1890s mining town that functions as a touristy Old West caricature complete with fudge shop, saloons, and a replica jail and train station. In the town, **Goldfield Ghost Town Mining Tours** provides humorous and informative 20min. tours of the nearby mines. (☎480-983-0333. Open daily 10am-5pm. Mine tours offered every 15min.; $6, ages 6-12 $3, seniors $5.) **Lost Dutchman State Park ❶,** 1 mi. farther north along the trails, commemorates the legend of Jacob Waltz (the Dutchman), a prospector who allegedly found a gold mine in the Superstition Mountains; his map to the mine has led many to venture into the mountains and try their luck at a search for buried treasure. The park has nature trails, picnic sites, and campsites with flush toilets and showers. (☎480-982-4485. Entrance $3-5 per vehicle. Sites $12, with electricity $20.)

The 1st body of water on the trail, **Canyon Lake,** has no shortage of recreational activities for boaters and swimmers, though a Tonto Pass is required for cars (available from the Canyon Lake Marina or from the restaurant at Tortilla Flat; $6). If you lack water transport, take the **Dolly Steamboat,** a 1½hr. narrated cruise on a vintage sternwheeler paddleboat. (☎480-827-9144; www.dollysteamboat.com. Ticket booth opens 30min. before scheduled departure. In summer departs Tu-Su noon; in winter departs noon and 2pm, as well as twilight cruises. Call for exact times. $18, children 5-12 $10.50. Cash only.) Grab a saddle for a bar stool at **Tortilla Flat,** a refurbished ghost town 18 mi. farther north on the trail. The town, once a stagecoach stop, keeps tourists fed with a restaurant (which claims to be the Lost

Dutchman's eatery), ice cream shop, and saloon. Be sure to check out the walls, which are completely covered in money. According to legend, a waitress tipped in foreign currency taped her gratuity onto the wall, and others have followed suit. Although the building burned in 1987, destroying thousands of dollars, it's estimated that $90,000 still line the walls of the restaurant. There are no phone lines to Tortilla Flat. (Restaurant open M-F 9am-6pm, Sa-Su 8am-7pm.) **Tonto National Monument,** on the trail, 5 mi. east of Lake Roosevelt, preserves the ruins of the Salado Native Americans who inhabited the Tonto Basin and upper Gila Valley in the 13th and 14th centuries. A short (½ mi.) but steep (350 ft.) trail leads from the Visitors Center up to the ruins. (☎928-467-2241. Open daily 8am-5pm. Last entry 4pm. $3 per person.) Along the trail, the rangers of **Tonto National Forest** maintain several campsites. For specific locations and facilities, call ☎602-225-5200. Sites up to $20. The trail ends at the **Theodore Roosevelt Dam** (finished in 1911), the last dam in the US built by hand, and the largest stone dam in the world at the time of its creation.

TUCSON   ☎520

A little bit country, a little bit south of the border, Tucson is a melting pot of often contradictory influences. Mexican property until 1853, the city retains much of its Mexican influence while also championing the rugged individualism of the American West. Home to the students of the University of Arizona, the soldiers of the Davis-Monthan Air Force Base, ranching cowboys, downtown artists, and suburban retirees, Tucson is the colorful fusion of a seemingly disparate variety of folk. Somehow though, amid the war machines and creative photography, honky tonk and Latin techno, the city's gradually fades away into desert sunsets.

▐ TRANSPORTATION

Airport: Tucson International Airport (TUS; ☎573-8100; www.tucsonairport.org), on Valencia Rd., south of downtown. Bus #6 goes downtown from the terminal. **Arizona Stagecoach** (☎881-4111; www.azstagecoach.com) goes downtown for $20-24.

Trains: Amtrak, 400 E. Toole Ave. (☎800-872-7245; www.amtrak.com), at 5th Ave. Open daily 10am-5:30pm and 10:15pm-5:30am. 3 trains per week run to **Albuquerque** ($99) via **Los Angeles** (10hr., $37-72), and **San Francisco** (18hr., $97) via Los Angeles. Book 2 weeks ahead for substantially lower rates.

Buses: Greyhound, 471 W. Congress St. (☎792-3475; www.greyhound.com), between Congress St. and Broadway. Station open daily 7am-midnight. To: **Albuquerque** (13-18hr., 5 per day, $90); **El Paso** (6hr., 4 per day, $43); **Los Angeles** (10-13hr., 10 per day, $52); **Phoenix** (2hr., 8 per day, $18.50).

Public Transit: Sun-Tran (☎792-9222; www.suntran.com). Buses run from the Ronstadt terminal downtown at Congress and 6th Ave. Customer service center open M-F 6am-7pm, Sa-Su 8am-5pm. Most routes M-F 5:30am-10pm, Sa-Su 8am-7pm; times vary by route. $1, seniors and disabled $0.40; day pass $2.

Taxi: Yellow Cab, ☎624-6611.

Bike Rental: Fair Wheel Bikes, 1110 E. 6th St. (☎884-9018), at Fremont. $30-40 per day with $500 credit card deposit. Open M-F 9am-6pm, Sa 9am-5:30pm, Su noon-4pm.

✳ ▐ ORIENTATION AND PRACTICAL INFORMATION

Just east of I-10, Tucson's downtown area surrounds the intersection of Broadway Boulevard and Stone Avenue, two blocks from the train and bus terminals. The

historic downtown area, known as the **Presidio District,** runs from 6th Ave. in the north to Alameda St. in the south, and is bordered by Main Ave. in the east and Church Ave. in the west. The **University of Arizona** is 1 mi. northeast of downtown at the intersection of North Park Ave. and Speedway Blvd. Avenues run north-south, streets east-west; because some of each are numbered, intersections like "6th and 6th" actually exist. Speedway Blvd., Broadway, and Grant Rd. are the quickest east-west routes through town. To go north-south, follow Oracle Rd. through the heart of the city, Campbell Ave. east of downtown, or Swan Rd. farther east.

Visitor Info: Tucson Convention and Visitors Bureau, 110 S. Church Ave. (☎624-1817 or 800-638-8350), near Broadway. Provides friendly advice, maps, and brochures on local accommodations and area attractions. Open M-F 8am-5pm, Sa-Su 9am-4pm. **The Palisade Visitors Center,** 19 mi. along General Hitchcock Highway, has maps. (☎749-7730. Open daily 8:30am-4:30pm.)

GLBT Resources: Wingspan Gay, Lesbian, and Bisexual Community Center, 425 E. 7th St. (☎624-1779). Open M-Th 11am-7pm, F 11am-6pm, Sa-Su 10am-4:30pm. **Tucson GLBT Chamber of Commerce,** P.O. Box 14312 (☎615-6436).

Hotlines: Rape Crisis, ☎624-7273. **Suicide Prevention,** ☎323-9373. Both 24hr.

Medical Services: University Medical Center, 1501 N. Campbell Ave. (☎694-0111).

Internet Access: University of Arizona Main Library, 1510 E. University Blvd. (☎520-621-6441). Free. Open Sept.-May M-F and Su 11am-9pm; June-Aug. M-Th 7:30am-11pm, F 7:30am-6pm, Sa 9am-6pm, Su 11am-11pm.

Post Office: 141 S. 6th Ave. (☎800-275-8777). Open M-F 8:30am-5pm, Sa 9am-1pm. **Postal Code:** 85701.

ACCOMMODATIONS AND CAMPING

There's a direct correlation between the temperature in Tucson and the warmth of its lodging industry to budget travelers: expect the best deals in the scorching heat of summer. The **Tucson Gem and Mineral Show** is an added hazard for budget travelers, driving prices up during its two-week run at the end of January. In addition to the **backcountry camping ❶** available in the eastern Rincon Mt. district of **Saguaro National Park** (campsites $6), there are a number of developed camping options. **Gilbert Ray Campground ❶** (☎883-4200), 3 mi. south of Saguaro West, has 150 first-come, first-served campsites with flush toilets, hookups, and drinking water, but no showers. (Tent sites $10, RV sites $20.) A variety of camping areas flank **Sky Island Scenic Byway** (General Hitchcock Highway) at Mt. Lemmon. All campgrounds charge an additional $5 road access fee. Call the Santa Catalina Ranger District for more info (☎749-7730).

Roadrunner Hostel, 346 E. 12th St. (☎628-4709). A cozy adobe home with artsy decor, filled with backpackers. The living room has a big-screen TV and comfy sectional. The owner and staff are friendly and fond of dishing out local info. Free Internet access (30min. limit), linens, and lockers. Laundry $1.75. Belgian waffle breakfast included (7-10am daily). Dorms $18; private rooms with shared bath $38. Cash only. ❶

Hotel Congress, 311 E. Congress St. (☎622-8848 or 800-722-8848). Across from the bus and train stations. Private rooms have a bath, phone, and vintage radio; no TV. Private rooms in summer $69-90; in winter $79-100. Local artists, military, and students 5% discount. AmEx/D/MC/V. ❸

The Flamingo Hotel, 1300 N. Stone Ave. (☎770-1910 or 800-300-3533). Houses guests and Arizona's largest collection of Western movie posters. Watch out, though—many are copies, because the hotel had a theft problem. All rooms have A/C, cable TV, and phone. Coin-op laundry, breakfast, and pool. Rooms June-Sept. $49; Oct.-Jan. $54; Feb.-March $59; Apr.-May $51. AAA and AARP discounts. AmEx/D/MC/V. ❸

THE SOUTHWEST

◑ FOOD

Tucson brims with inexpensive and tasty eateries; wander along 4th Ave. and University Blvd., or walk around downtown and see what strikes your fancy. Cheap Mexican definitely dominates the scene, but you can find pretty much every style of cooking imaginable.

La Indita, 622 N. 4th Ave. (☎792-0523). A family-run gem with hand-painted murals, great service, and spicy Mexican fare. Try the spinach and mushroom enchilada combo ($10). The food is still prepared by La Indita herself using unique recipes. Burritos $6-8. Open M-Th 11am-9pm, F 11am-6pm, Sa 6am-9pm, Su 9am-9pm. MC/V/D. ❶

El Charro Cafe, 311 N. Court Ave. (☎ 620-1922). The oldest family-operated Mexican restaurant in the US with several popular branches throughout Tucson. El Charro's wide selection of rice bowls, taco combos, and delicious entrees makes it worth a stop. Lunch $6-10. Dinner $10-12. Happy hour daily 3-7pm; margaritas ½-price. Open M-Th and Su 11am-9pm, F-Sa 11am-10pm. AmEx/D/MC/V. ❸

Bentley's House of Coffee and Tea, 1730 E. Speedway Blvd. (☎795-0338). A warm, colorful cafe filled with University of Arizona students and professors as well as locals looking for an afternoon pick-me-up. Linger for the Wi-Fi, a big slice of homemade chocolate cake ($3) or irresistible peanut-butter-chocolate-graham-cracker bars ($2). Beverage selection includes shakes, freezes, smoothies, and floats, as well as coffee ($1-4). Open M-Sa 7am-11pm, Su 8am-10pm. MC/V. ❶

◉ SIGHTS

UNIVERSITY OF ARIZONA. The campus is expansive and filled with parks, museums, and surrounding shops. The **Visitors Center** has details. *(Euclid Ave. and University Blvd. ☎520-621-5130. Open M-F 9am-5pm.)* Lined with restaurants, trendy shops, and galleries, **4th Avenue** between Speedway and Broadway Blvd., is a great place to stroll. **University Boulevard** leads into the university grounds from the west and is edged with breweries and cafes that appeal to the student population. The **Center for Creative Photography** acquires, preserves, and displays entire careers of photographers; the Center houses more work by 20th-century North American photographers than any other US museum. Exhibits change frequently, and range from Ralph Gibson to Ansel Adams. By appointment, visitors can view prints not currently on display. *(1030 N. Olive St. ☎621-7968. Open M-F 9am-5pm, Sa-Su noon-5pm. Call for print-viewing appointments. Free.)* The **Flandrau Science Center,** 1601 E. University Blvd., is popular with the family crowd with daily shows exploring topics from Saturn and its rings to the Arizona night sky. It also houses a mineral museum. *(☎621-7827; www.flandrau.org. Open W-F 9am-3pm and 6pm-9pm, Sa noon-9pm, Su noon-5pm. $5 includes exhibits and one show; W-F 9am-3pm $3. Call for showtimes.)* The **University of Arizona Museum of Art** has a wide collection ranging from 12th-century religious art to modern sculpture. The museum's rotating Goya exhibits are especially impressive. *(1031 N. Olive St. ☎621-7567. Open Tu-F 9am-5pm, Sa-Su noon-4pm. Free.)*

EL PRESIDIO HISTORIC DISTRICT. Bounded by 6th Ave., Alameda St., Main Ave., and Church Ave., in downtown, this adobe neighborhood was first built by the Spanish in 1775 to stake out the northern border of New Spain. Now the area is the artisan district of Tucson. Galleries, art studios, stores, and cafes line the surrounding streets, but the most interesting area can be explored by entering the **Tucson Museum of Art.** The museum encompasses an entire city block, and includes courtyards, historic homes (check out the Corbett House, a fine example of Arts and Crafts architecture), and sculpture gardens, in addition to the main galleries, which feature a diverse collection from Japanese woodblock prints to art of the

American West. *(140 N. Main Ave. ☎624-2333. Open Tu-Sa 10am-4pm, Su noon-4pm. $8, seniors $6, students $3, under 12 free; free 1st Su of the month.)*

OLD TUCSON STUDIOS. A taste of Hollywood in the desert, **Old Tucson Studios** has been the backdrop for numerous Western movies, including four John Wayne films, *The Quick and the Dead* (1995), *Arizona* (1938), and Will Smith's *Wild Wild West* (1999). Now also a studio theme park popular with families, visitors can view gunfight reenactments, have barbecue at saloons, watch daily can-can dances, and ride the carousel. Saturdays in June and July are honky-tonk nights with a rodeo. *(201 S. Kinney Rd. ☎883-0100. Open daily Feb.-Apr. 10am-6pm; May-Jan. 10am-4pm. $17, ages 4-11 $11.)*

▧**ARIZONA-SONORA DESERT MUSEUM.** The **Arizona-Sonora Desert Museum,** a fantastic combination zoo, botanical garden, and gallery, houses flora and fauna from riparian, mountain woodland, grassland, and desert habitats. With exhibits ranging from a man-made cave to a hummingbird house and more than 300 animal species, the museum is a perfect introduction to Arizona wildlife and geology. Be sure to check out the venomous reptile presentation (daily 12:15pm). Visits should be made in the morning before the animals take their afternoon siestas. *(2021 N. Kinney Rd. Follow Speedway Blvd. west as it becomes Gates Pass Rd., then Kinney Rd. ☎883-2720. Open Mar.-Sept. daily 7:30am-5pm, June-Aug. 25 M-F and Su 7:30am-5pm, Sa 7:30am-10pm; Oct.-Feb. 8:30am-5pm. June-Sept. $9, ages 6-12 $4; Oct.-May. $12/2.)*

PIMA AIR AND SPACE MUSEUM. Aerospace meets military history in an impressive museum with over 250 of the most significant aircrafts in history. Visitors can stroll through four different hangars and an outdoor display featuring planes ranging from President Kennedy's Air Force One and the SR-71 Blackbird Spyplane to the Bumblebee, the smallest piloted airplane. The **Spirit of Freedom Hangar,** home to the Arizona Aviation Hall of Fame, also has exhibits on female and African-American aviators. Visitors can amble among the exhibits themselves, go on a guided walking tour, or take a narrated, 1hr. tram ride through the museum. *(6000 E. Valencia Rd. ☎574-0462. Open daily 9am-5pm. Last entry 4pm. $11.75, seniors $9.75, under 6 free. 45min. walking tours included; call for times. Tram tours daily 10, 11:30am, 1:30, 3pm; $5.)* Bus tours of the nearby **Davis-Monthan Air Force Base** are also offered through the ticket office of the Pima Museum, but be prepared for rigorous security checks and possible cancellations. *(Tours offered M-F; call for times. $6.)*

BIOSPHERE 2. Ninety-one feet high, with an area of more than three acres, **Biosphere 2** is sealed off from Earth—"Biosphere 1"—by 500 tons of stainless steel. Opened to the public in 1990, the biosphere houses five man-made ecosystems: rainforest, savanna, marsh, ocean, and coniferous forest. The biomes help scientists understand nature's processes without atmospheric interference, and are accessible by 45min. guided tours which run every hour on the hour from 10am-3pm. *(30min. north of Tucson, follow Oracle Rd. north until it becomes Rte. 77 N, then proceed to mile 96.5. From Phoenix, take I-10 to Exit 185, follow Rte. 387 to Rte. 79/Florence Hwy., and proceed to Oracle Jct. and Rte. 77. ☎838-6200. Open daily 9am-4pm. Last entry 5pm. $20, ages 6-12 $13, AAA and seniors discount 10%.)*

🎭 🎵 ENTERTAINMENT AND NIGHTLIFE

Tucson is home to multiple theaters and performing arts centers featuring local and out-of-town acts. The **Tucson Symphony Orchestra,** 2175 N. 6th Ave., performs both classical and pops music. *(☎882-8585.* Student rush tickets available 1hr. before showtime, $7.) At the University of Arizona, **UApresents,** 888 N. Euclid Ave. *(☎621-3364)*, features a wide range of musical performances, as well as dance and theater. In downtown Tucson, the **Fox-Tucson Theater,** 17 W Congress St., has weekly showings of classic films, such as *Breakfast at Tiffany's* (1961) and *The Sound of Music* (1965), in a restored historic theater. (☎624-1515. Tickets \$10.) The free *Tucson Weekly*, published on Thursdays and available throughout the city, is the local authority on nightlife, though the weekend sections of the *Arizona Star* or *Tucson Citizen* also provide coverage. Bars and dance clubs line **University Boulevard, Speedway Boulevard,** and **North Oracle.** Downtown, **4th Avenue** supports a bustling scene where most bars have live music and a chill atmosphere.

Club Congress, 311 E. Congress St. (☎622-8848). This club alternates DJs with live indie and rock concerts. The club is in the same building as other venues within Hotel Congress, and guests tend to mingle and move from room to room, creating a diverse crowd. M 80s night with \$0.80 vodkas. Tu and W nights feature bands. Sa Bang-Bang Night, when the DJ spins only vinyl records. Cover \$2-5. Open daily 9pm-2am.

Che's Lounge, 350 4th Ave. (☎623-2088). A funky bar with enormous, modern murals caters to an eclectic crowd of local artists, yuppies, and construction workers. Show up early; there are lines early in the night on weekends and crowds during the week. Weekly \$1-3 drafts. Sa live music. Happy hour daily 4-7pm. Open daily noon-1am.

Ain't Nobody's Biz, 2900 E. Broadway Blvd. (☎318-4838), located in a strip mall. The big mama of the Tucson gay and lesbian scene (60% female, 40% male) with a large bar, themed events, and karaoke. Biz has some of the best dancing in Tucson, though no country is allowed. Open M 3-10pm, Tu 3pm-midnight, W-Su 3pm-2am.

⚡ OUTDOOR ACTIVITIES

The best hiking nearby can be found at **Saguaro National Park,** which is split into two districts flanking Tucson to the west and east. The western half **(Tucson Mountain District)** is accessed by following Speedway Blvd. out of town and taking Kinney Rd. past the Arizona-Sonora Desert Museum and Old Tucson. The **Red Hills Visitors Center** (☎733-5158) has exhibits on desert flora and fauna. The **Bajada Loop Drive** runs only 6 mi. on a graded dirt road but passes through some of the park's most striking desert scenery; the drive is especially remarkable later in the day, when the sun is beginning to set over the tall cacti. Trails in the west include the flat, wheelchair-accessible **Desert Discovery Nature Trail** (½ mi., 20min.) and the challenging **Hugh Norris Trail** (10 mi., 5-6hr.). The eastern portion of the park **(Rincón Mountain District),** accessed by going east on Speedway to Freeman Rd., is larger and has more trails, including access to the park's backcountry wilderness area. The **Rincón Visitors Center** (☎733-5153) offers natural history exhibits and guides to the park's activities. Both Visitors Centers show a 15min. introductory video throughout the day and have free copies of *The Saguaro Sentinel*, the park's free newspaper with all trail information. In the east, the **Cactus Forest Loop Drive** winds 8 mi. through impressive stands of saguaros, many of them well over 100 years old. Easier trails include the **Desert Discovery Trail,** ¼ mi., which is wheelchair-accessible and explains some of the park's plants, as well as the **Freeman Homestead Trail,** 1 mi. round-trip, which offers great views of horned owls at the trail's southern wash. Mountain biking is permitted only around the Cactus Forest Loop Drive and on the portion of the **Cactus Forest Trail** enclosed by the Drive. (Both Visitors Centers open daily 9am-5pm. Park and auto loop open 7am-sunset. \$10 per vehicle, \$5 per bike or pedestrian. \$6 backcountry camping permits for the Rincon Mt. District must be obtained by noon on day of departure; 48hr. advance reservation recommended.)

The Tucson area offers a range of opportunities for spelunking. The caves of **Colossal Cave Mountain Park,** 16721 E. Old Spanish Trail, have been known to humans for over a thousand years, first by the Hohokam Indians as a shrine from AD 900-1450, and later by train robbers who used them for hideouts from the sheriff and other local law enforcement. In addition to 45min. walking tours through-out the day (photography is allowed), a special ladder tour with helmets and flashlights through otherwise sealed-off tunnels, crawlspaces, and corridors can be arranged. The park also has a campground, a ranch, a library, and a museum. (Exit 279 on I-10. ☎647-7275. Park open mid-Mar. to mid-Sept. M-Sa 8am-6pm, Su 8am-7pm; mid-Sept. to mid-Mar. M-Sa 9am-5pm, Su 9am-6pm. Ladder tours M-F 11am or 2:30pm $15; Sa 6:30-9pm $35. Reservations required at least 24hr. in advance. Walking tours $8.50, ages 6-12 $5. Entrance fee $5 per vehicle, $2 per cyclist or pedestrian.) **Kartchner Caverns State Park,** 1300 W. Washington, required engineering feats to make it accessible to visitors without disturbing its delicate environment after it was discovered by college students in 1974. The result is a winding, dimly-lit walkway with views of wet limestone spires, helictitites (small, twisted formations), ancient "soda-straws" (long, thin, hollow stalactites), draper-ies (sheets of limestone), and the largest cave column in Arizona. Two separate 1½hr. tours are offered in the cave: one exploring the Rotunda Room (year-round) and another through the Big Room (Oct.15-Apr. 15 or once the bats have finished breeding). The Rotunda tour ends with an awe-inspiring music and light show. Taking a tour is the only way to enter the cave, and only 500 people are allowed in the cave each day (750 when the Big Room is open). Most tickets are reserved far in advance in winter, but approximately 100 tickets are held for walk-ups and dis-pensed at 7:30am. (Exit 302, 50 mi. from Tucson. ☎586-4100. Open daily 7:30am-6pm. Tours run every 20min., 8:20am-4:20pm. Entrance fee $5 per vehicle. Oct.-July tours $19, ages 7-13 $10; Aug.-Sept. $17/9. Reservations strongly recom-mended at least 24hr. in advance.) The park also has a campground with 60 sites with hookups, water, flush toilets, showers, and a dump station. (Sites $22.)

▶ DAYTRIP FROM TUCSON

CHIRICAHUA NATIONAL MONUMENT   ☎520

Locally known as the "Wonderland of Rocks," the maze of enormous balanced rock formations at **Chiricahua National Monument** (pronounced Cheer-ee-CAH-wah) is the result of a local volcanic eruption over 27 million years ago. After the erup-tion occurred, ash blew to the site of the monument, and over millions of years, ice and water sculpted the rhyolite into the formations that now include the enormous **Kissing Rocks, Duck on a Rock,** and **Big Balanced Rock.** Home to the Apache Chokonen Native Americans in the 18th and 19th centuries, today the monument is home to a diverse group of animals, including black bear, coati, quail, javelina, and over 200 species of birds, as well as 18 mi. of trails.

Winding from the Visitors Center to Masai Pt., the monument's scenic drive (6 mi.) is a great introduction to the balanced rock formations that make the park unique, though the formations are best observed by foot. Trails include the very easy **Masai Pt. Nature Trail** (½ mi. round-trip), which offers photo-friendly over-looks of the surrounding valleys and mountain ranges. The trail can be accessed from the Masai Pt. parking area. The **Bonita Creek Trail** (½ mi. round-trip), leaving from the Bonita Creek parking area, is a perfect short walk for those who want to observe the monument's wildlife; birds, deer, and javelina are often spotted from the trail. For those who want a longer, moderate challenge, the **Echo Canyon Loop Trail** (3½ mi., 2hr. round-trip) includes the **Echo Canyon, Hailstone,** and **Ed Riggs Trails.** It also passes through the **Echo Canyon Grottoes,** where hikers can walk underneath giant rock formations. For those who want to see all of the stone tow-ers that make this monument famous, the **Big Loop** (9¾ mi., 7-8hr.) encompasses Echo Canyon, Upper Rhyolite Canyon, Sarah Deming, Inspiration Point, Heart of

Rocks, Big Balanced Rock, and Mushroom Rock. You can see the massive "Duck on a Rock" and "Punch and Judy" formations from this trail. The park operates a **free hiker's shuttle** to the Echo Canyon and Masai Pt. trailheads. The shuttle runs daily at 8:30am—register the day before or the morning of at the Visitors Center.

There are no indoor accommodations, food, or gas stations inside the monument. **Bonita Creek Campground ❶,** the park's only campground, has 24 beautiful, shady sites that frame the monument's striking cliffs and formations. Sites have water, picnic tables, grills, and pit toilets. (No hookups or showers. First-come, first-served. $12.) The closest indoor accommodations and restaurants are 40 mi. northwest of the monument in Wilcox, AZ, though options in the town are slim and tend to be infested with flies, making the monument best as a daytrip from Tucson (about 2hr. away).

Chiricahua can be reached by taking I-10 to Ariz. 186 (Wilcox Exit). Follow 186 to Ariz. 181N, which leads directly to the monument. The **Visitors Center** is approximately 2 mi. past the entrance station ($5, 15 and under free) and has exhibits on the plants and wildlife of the park, as well as an 8min. video on the park's history. (☎824-3560. Open daily 8am-4:30pm.)

TOMBSTONE   ☎520

Nicknamed "the town too tough to die," Tombstone has seen two major fires, an earthquake, and enough duels to fill an entire cemetery—all in its short 120-year history. Tales of cowboys and gunfights fill backlogs of the town's newspaper, *The Epitaph*, and have steeped Tombstone in legend, folklore, and unanswerable questions. Today, the town flaunts its lawless Western, gun-slinging roots as a tourist attraction. Cowboys swagger down Allen St., stagecoaches lead tours of downtown, and dolled-up dames keep glasses full in saloons. The popular **Shootout at the O.K. Corral** reenacts a gunfight daily at 2pm at the notorious fight site between the Clantons and the Earps. Next door, in the **Tombstone Historama,** the voice of Vincent Price narrates the town's history. (☎457-3456. Shootout and historical exhibits open daily 9am-5pm; arrive before the 2pm reenactment. Historama shows daily every 30min. 9:30am-4:30pm. Both attractions $7.50.) The only original building left in Tombstone, the **Bird Cage Theater** was open 24hr. for nine years beginning in 1881, and was home to a saloon and 14 "cribs" (small wooden structures where prostitutes conducted their business). Now a museum, it was the site of the longest poker game in Western history (8 years, 5 months, and 3 days), as well as the "handkerchief" duel between Doc Holliday and the outlaw "King of the Cowboys," Johnny Ringo. Visitors can still see the bullet holes on the floor. (☎457-3421. Open daily 8am-6pm. Self-guided tour available. $10, seniors and military $9, ages 8-18 $8.) The tombstones of the town stand in **Boothill Cemetery,** on Rte. 80 just north of town. (☎457-3421 or 800-457-3423. Open daily 7:30am-6pm. Free.) Check out old copies of *The Epitaph*, as well as exhibits on the town's printing presses at the **Tombstone Epitaph Museum,** behind the Crystal Palace at South 5th St. The museum is free, but for $1 you can buy a copy of the October 1881 paper, with the original tale of the O.K. Corall shootout. (☎457-2211. Open daily 9:30am-5pm. Free.)

If you want to stay in Tombstone, inexpensive motels line Fremont St. through the middle of town. One of the cheapest options is the **Trail Riders Inn ❷,** on the corner of 7th and Fremont, which has clean, well-equipped rooms with a homey feel. (☎457-3573. A/C, cable TV, phone, pool and morning coffee. Singles from $45; doubles from $50. MC/V.) Food options revolve around thick, meaty sandwiches. **Six Gun City Crazy Horse Saloon ❷,** at 5th and Toughnut, serves burgers as well as margaritas ($3) to visitors watching theatrical Wild West shows and staged gunfights. (☎457-3827. Shows at 11:30am, 1, 3pm. Open W-Su 11am-10pm. MC/V.) **Nel-**

LOCAL LEGEND

THE WILD, WILD WEST

When in Arizona, do as the Arizonians do: in short, know your Western references. For those who have never told a "pardner" to "saddle up" or ever heard of a "handkerchief duel," here is a cheat sheet for the "Shootout at the OK Corral," reenacted daily in Tombstone, AZ.

In 1881, the town of Tombstone was the scene of constant struggle. The desire to control Tombstone's land and resources ran high among several townsmen, among them the Police Chief Virgil Earp, his brothers Wyatt and Morgan, Doc Holliday, and local cowboys Frank and Tom McLaury as well as Billy and Ike Clanton. A series of robberies, threats, and fights lead to a fateful showdown between these colorful characters.

On October 26, 1881, those eight men, some supposedly standing for the law, the others representing the wild spirit of the West, met in a dusty lot behind the OK Corral. The cowboys were hoping to confront Doc Holliday; but they weren't expecting to see the three Earp brothers. Though the men only opened fire for 30 seconds, the fight claimed three lives (all of them cowboys). Only Wyatt Earp emerged from the fight unharmed.

For more info, contact the Tombstone Visitors Center, at 4th St. and Allen. ☎520-457-3929. Open daily 9am-5pm.

lie **Cashman's Restaurant ❶,** named after the "angel of the mining camps" who was always willing to help out miners who were down on their luck, is less Old West and a bit more down-home. Delicious half-pound burgers start at $6. (☎457-2212. Open daily 11am-9pm. AmEx/D/MC/V.) For a taste of the "reuben that won the west," country music, and the remnants of dishonest underground activity, head to **Big Nose Kate's Saloon ❷** (so named for Doc Holliday's girlfriend), on Allen St. (☎457-3107. Reubens $8. "Tombstone's best pizza" $7. Open daily 11am-midnight. MC/V.)

Located some 80 mi. south of Tucson and roughly 20 mi. south of Benson, Tombstone makes a great daytrip. To get to Tombstone, take the Benson Exit off I-10 E, then go south on Rte. 80. The nearest Greyhound **bus** station is in Benson. The **Tombstone Visitors Center,** on 4th St. and Allen, provides brochures and maps, although Tombstone is so small that nothing is hard to find. (☎457-3929. Open daily 9am-5pm.) **Internet** access: Gitt Wired, at 5th and Fremont. (☎457-3250. $0.15 per min. Open 7am-4pm.) **Post Office:** Safford St. off of Hwy. 80. **Postal Code:** 85638.

BISBEE   ☎520

Located 100 mi. southeast of Tucson and 20 mi. south of Tombstone, Bisbee, a former copper-mining town, is now a small cliffside town that attracts visitors with charming B&Bs and mile-high elevation that makes it 20°F cooler than Tucson. The small galleries and tiny cafes that line the streets give Bisbee a European air, but the open pit mine on the edge of town is a reminder of its Old West roots. **Queen Mines,** 4178 Dart Rd., on the Rte. 80 interchange entering Old Bisbee, stopped operating in 1943 but now gives 1hr. subterranean tours; the mine is 47°F year-round, so bring a sweater. (☎432-2071. Tours at 9, 10:30am, noon, 2, 3:30pm. $12, ages 4-15 $5.) The Smithsonian-affiliated **Mining and Historical Museum,** 5 Copper Queen Plaza, highlights the discovery of Bisbee's copper surplus and houses the fabulous "Digging In" exhibit, which has great displays on the area's minerals as well as details on life in the mines. (☎432-7071. Open daily 10am-4pm. $7.50, seniors $6.50.) About 18 mi. west of Bisbee on Rte. 92, along Mexico's border, **Coronado National Memorial** commemorates Francisco Coronado's epic journey to find the seven Cities of Cibola in the 16th century. **Coronado Cave,** a small dry cave, is three-quarters of a mile from the **Visitors Center** along a short, steep path (elevation 500 ft.). A free permit is required to explore the cave, and can be picked up same-day at the Visitors Center; each caver must have two flashlights, in case one burns out. (☎366-5515. Park open daily dawn-dusk. Visitors Center open daily 9am-5pm.) **Ramsey Canyon Preserve,** 5 mi. farther down Rte. 92 (turn on Ramsey Canyon Rd.), attracts nearly as many bird-watchers as birds. The preserve, maintained by the Nature Conservancy, is in the middle of a key migratory flyway, and 14 species of hummingbirds throng here in summer. (Open Nov.-Jan. 9am-4pm, Feb.-Oct. 8am-5pm. Guided walks Feb.-Oct. Tu, Th, and Sa 9am. $5, under 16 free; 1st Sa of every month free.)

The **Shady Dell RV and Vintage Trailerpark ❷,** 1 Old Douglas Rd., rents vintage aluminum trailers with original decor and is a fun place to spend the night. (☎432-3567. Laundry, phones, and showers on-site. RV sites available. Trailers from $45, some with private bath.) Just outside of town off of Rte. 80 E, the **Double Adobe Campground and Recreational Ranch ❶,** 5057 W. Double Adobe Rd., has tent and RV sites in a peaceful setting. (☎364-4000. Tent sites $12, RV hookups $18.) Though a bit kitschy, the **Calumet and Guest House ❷,** 608 Powell St., has comfortable rooms brimming with old-fashioned charm. Lounge area with books and board games is open to guests. Includes a full breakfast with options from homemade granola to french toast. (☎432-4815. Rooms with A/C but no TV from $45.) For a brighten-your-day breakfast in a sunny brick building, head to the ◪**Bisbee Breakfast Club (B.B.C.) ❷,** 75 Erie St., just outside historic Bisbee. The cozy diner has a selection of sandwiches and wraps ($5-6), as well as all-day breakfast ($4-6) options. (☎432-5885. Open M and Th-Su 7am-3pm. MC/V.) **Prickly Pear Cafe ❶,** 105 Tombstone Canyon, prepares panini and salads, as well as wraps. (☎432-7337. All dishes $5-7. Open M-Th 11am-8pm, F-Sa 11am-9pm, Su 11am-4pm. MC/V.)

The **Bisbee Visitor Center,** 2 Copper Queen Plaza, has an eager-to-please staff and plenty of maps and info on accommodations. (☎432-3554. Open M-F 9am-5pm, Sa-Su 10am-4pm.) **Post office:** 6 Main St., one block south of Exit 80. (☎432-2052. Open M-F 8:30am-4:30pm.) **Postal Code:** 85603.

NEW MEXICO

In the state of New Mexico, nature's eccentricities provide outdoor enthusiasts with the landscape they need to explore the limits of both their abilities and their interests. Still, even the wildest outdoor adventurers get distracted by the many galleries of Santa Fe, the nightclubs of Albuquerque, and the pueblos of northern New Mexico. With a rich cultural mosaic of Mexican, Native American, and European influences, historical and archaeological discovery is a never-ending process in New Mexico, and travelers would be remiss not to tap into the state's rich past. After all is said and done, save some time to wander across white sand dunes or relax in the bubbly warmth of natural hot springs. They don't call it the "Land of Enchantment" for nothing.

🛈 PRACTICAL INFORMATION

Capital: Santa Fe.

Visitor Info: New Mexico Dept. of Tourism, 491 Old Santa Fe Trail, Santa Fe 87501 (☎800-545-2040; www.newmexico.org). Open M-F 8am-5pm. **Park and Recreation Division,** 2040 S. Pacheco, Santa Fe 87505 (☎505-827-7173). Open M-F 8am-5pm. **US Forest Service,** 517 Gold Ave. SW., Albuquerque 87102 (☎505-842-3292). Open M-F 8am-4:30pm.

Postal Abbreviation: NM. **Sales Tax:** 7%.

SANTA FE
☎ 505

Originally a military outpost for the Spanish Empire, Santa Fe began to develop
into the cultural haven it is today in 1821, when Mexico declared its independence
and Santa Fe was named the last stop on a major trading line. From then on, the
city became a mecca for those wishing to sell their wares to eager travelers passing through the Southwest. This 19th-century trading spirit still exists in Santa Fe,
as locals display their beautiful arts and jewelry on the streets surrounding the
Plaza. The product of Native American, Hispanic, and Anglo influences, the city
brims with a unique culture that permeates its flavorful restaurants, restful adobe
buildings, and colorful galleries. If the old-world style of downtown can't charm
you, the surrounding natural environment, including a ski mountain, a national
forest, and a wilderness area, certainly will.

▉ TRANSPORTATION

Trains: Amtrak's nearest station is in Lamy (☎466-4511; www.amtrak.com), 18 mi.
south on U.S. 285. 1 train per day to: **Albuquerque** (2hr., $20); **Flagstaff** (7½hr.,
$71); **Kansas City** (17hr., $149); **Los Angeles** (19hr., $80). Call ☎982-8829 for a
shuttle to Santa Fe ($18). Open daily 9am-4:45pm.

Buses: Greyhound, 858 St. Michael's Dr. (☎471-0008; www.greyhound.com), goes to
Albuquerque (1hr., 3 per day, $15), **Denver** (8-9hr., 3 per day, $57-75), and **Taos**
(2hr., 1 per day, $17). Open daily 11am-3pm and 6:30-10pm. **Sandía Shuttle Express**
(☎474-5696 or 888-775-5696) runs from downtown hotels to the Albuquerque airport
(the main airport that services Santa Fe) hourly 5am-6pm. From Albuquerque to Santa
Fe hourly 8:45am-10:45pm ($25, round-trip $45). Reserve at least 4 days in advance.
Office opens M-F 6am-6pm, Sa-Su 6am-5pm.

Public Transit: Santa Fe Trails, 2931 Rufina St. (☎955-2001 or 866-551-7433).
Schedules at the Visitors Center or the transit office. Runs 9 downtown buses M-F 6am-
11pm, Sa 8am-8pm, Su 10am-7pm (routes 1, 2, 4, and M only). Most routes start at
the Sheridan Transit Center, 1 block from the plaza between Marcy St. and Palace Ave.
Bus #2 goes down Cerrillos Rd., the M goes to the museums on Camino Lejo; #3/5
goes across town and passes the Greyhound station between St. Vincent Hospital and
the W. Alameda Commons. $1; seniors, students, and under 17 $0.50; day pass $2.

Car Rental: Enterprise Rent-a-Car, 2641 Cerrillos Rd. (☎473-3600). Must be 21+ with
driver's license and major credit card. Open M-F 8am-6pm, Sa 9am-noon.

▉ ORIENTATION

Abutting the **Sangre de Cristo Mountains,** Sante Fe stands at an elevation of 7000 ft.,
58 mi. northeast of Albuquerque on I-25. The streets of downtown Santa Fe seem
to wind without rhyme or reason; when the city was designed in 1610, the grid system was not yet in vogue. It may be helpful to think of the city as a wagon wheel,
with the **Plaza** in the center and roads leading outward like spokes. **Paseo de Peralta, Guadalupe,** and **Cerrillos Rd.** form a loop around the downtown area, and the
main roads leading out toward I-25 are Cerrillos Road, St. Francis Drive, and **Old
Santa Fe Trail.** Except for the museums southeast of the city center, most upscale
restaurants and sights in Santa Fe cluster within a few blocks of the downtown
Plaza. Narrow streets make driving troublesome. Several public **parking lots** are
within walking distance of the plaza; most charge $9 per day. The Visitors Centers
have maps of downtown parking areas. If you're lucky, you may be able to find a
metered parking space on the street; spaces charge $1 per hr. 2hr. max. Though
you'll be a slave to the bus schedule, look into the free parking at Museum Hill.

THE SOUTHWEST

Santa Fe

▲▲ ACCOMMODATIONS
Black Canyon
  Campground, **2**
Hyde State Park
  Campground, **1**
Santa Fe International
  Hostel, **5**
Silver Saddle Motel, **6**

🍴 FOOD
Cafe Pasqual's, **16**
French Pastry Shop and
  Crêperie, **17**
Tía Sophia's, **14**
Upper Crust Pizza, **4**

🍸 NIGHTLIFE
Cowgirl Hall of Fame, **3**
La Casa Sena Cantina, **13**

🏛 MUSEUMS
Georgia O'Keeffe Museum, **10**
Institute of American
  Indian Arts, **7**
Museum of Fine Arts, **11**
Museum of Indian Arts and
  Culture Laboratory of
  Anthropology, **8**
Museum of International
  Folk Art, **15**
Museum of Spanish
  Colonial Art, **9**
Palace of the Governors, **12**

🛈 PRACTICAL INFORMATION

Visitor Info: Visitors Information Center, 491 Old Santa Fe Trail (☎875-7336 or 800-545-2040). Open daily 8am-5:30pm; low season 8am-5pm. **Santa Fe Convention and Visitors Bureau,** 60 E. San Francisco St. (☎955-6200). Open M-F 8am-5pm. Info booth at the northwest corner of the plaza, next to the First National Bank. Open mid-May to Aug. daily 9:30am-4:30pm.

Hotlines: Rape Crisis: ☎986-9111. **Gay and Lesbian Information Line:** ☎891-3647. Both operate 24hr.

Medical Services: St. Vincent Hospital, 455 St. Michael's Dr. (☎983-3361).

Internet Access: Santa Fe Public Library, 145 Washington Ave. (☎955-6781), 1 block northeast of the Plaza. Free. Open M-Th 10am-9pm, F-Sa 10am-6pm, Su 1-5pm.

Post Office: 120 S. Federal Pl. (☎988-6351), next to the courthouse. Open M-F 8am-5:30pm, Sa 9am-4pm. **Postal Code:** 87505.

■ ACCOMMODATIONS

Home to cozy and restful inns and B&Bs, Santa Fe does not have many cheap accommodations. As early as May, start booking ahead for the **Indian Market** (3rd week in Aug.) and **Fiesta de Santa Fe** (mid-Sept.). In general, the motels along **Cerrillos Road** have the best prices, but even these places run $50-70 per night. For budget travelers, nearby **camping** is pleasant during the summer (night-time temperatures hover around 55°F), not to mention easier on the wallet. Since most campgrounds do not have showers, head to the **Fort Marcy Sports Complex,** 490 Washington Ave., at the base of Rte. 475, for hot showers and restrooms. (☎955-2500. Showers $1.85; use of sports facilities $4.)

Santa Fe International Hostel, 1412 Cerrillos Rd. (☎988-1153). Conveniently located and the only cheap option for indoor accommodations in Santa Fe, this hostel provides clean showers, free linens, a large kitchen, parking, breakfast food, and Wi-Fi Internet access ($2 per day). Chores required. Laundry $2.25. Dorms $15; private rooms $25-35. Cash or check only. ❶

Silver Saddle Motel, 2810 Cerrillos Rd. (☎471-7663). The best of the Cerillos Rd. budget motels, the Silver Saddle has comfortable adobe rooms decorated with cowboy paraphernalia and Spanish tiles. All rooms have A/C, cable TV, and phone. Some doubles have kitchenettes. Reception 7am-11:30pm. In summer singles $59; doubles $65. In winter $40/45. AmEx/D/MC/V. ❸

Black Canyon Campground (☎753-7331), 7½ mi. from Santa Fe on Rte. 475, just before the entrance to Hyde State Park in the Santa Fe National Forest. Opened in May 2007, this pine-filled, shady campground has over 30 beautifully maintained sites with picnic tables and grills. Drinking water and pit toilets. Sites $10. ❶

■ FOOD

The **Santa Fe Farmers' Market,** near the intersection of Guadalupe St. and Paseo de Peralta, has delicious fresh fruits and vegetables. (☎983-4098. Open late Apr.-early Nov. Tu and Sa 7am-noon.)

Upper Crust Pizza, 329 Old Santa Fe Trail (☎982-0000). Voted "Best Pizza" in Santa Fe in 2007, Upper Crust Pizza's fresh and wholesome ingredients, freshly baked calzones, outdoor patio, and delicious pizza make this spot the place to go for a quick slice ($2 at lunchtime). Lunch specials M-F 11am-1pm. Pizza $11-17. Calzones $7.25. Open daily 11am-11pm. AmEx/D/MC/V. ❷

The French Pastry Shop and Crêperie, 100 E. San Francisco St. (☎983-6697). Without a doubt, the best crepes, croissants, and napoleons in the entire state of New Mexico. Order one of the "crepes as meals," or get one of the fresh fruit dessert crepes ($6-7). Sandwiches on freshly baked French bread $4-6. Pastries under $5. Open daily 6:30am-5pm. Cash only. ❷

Tia Sophia's, 210 W. San Francisco St. (☎983-9880). This charming eatery with large wooden booths and colorful Spanish dresses hanging from the walls serves regional dishes loaded with green and red chiles. Anything with one of their warm, puffy sopapillas is bound to be great; try one of the daily lunch specials ($7-8) or the enormous Santa Fe plate ($8). Open M-Sa 7am-2pm. MC/V. ❷

THE SOUTHWEST

👁 🎵 SIGHTS AND ENTERTAINMENT

The grassy Plaza de Santa Fe is a good starting point for exploring the city's museums, sanctuaries, and galleries. Since 1610, the plaza has been the site of religious ceremonies, military gatherings, markets, cockfights, and public punishments. Today, it shelters galleries, Native American artisan stalls, and ornate green benches. Historic 2hr. walking tours leave from the blue doors of the Palace of the Governors on Lincoln Ave. (Apr.-Oct. M-Sa 10:15am. $10, under 17 free with adult.)

MNM MUSEUMS. Sante Fe is home to world-class museums. Five are run by the Museum of New Mexico; the Visitors Center on Museum Hill, 706 Camino Lejo, has info. (☎476-1249. Open Tu-Su 10am-4pm.) A four-day pass includes admission to all five museums and can be bought at any of them. (www.museumofnewmexico.org. All museums open daily 10am-5pm Memorial Day-Labor Day; Labor Day-Memorial Day Tu-Su 10am-5pm. $8, under 16 free; with student ID $1 discount. The 2 downtown museums—Museum of Fine Arts and Palace of the Governors—are both free F 5-8pm. 4-day pass $18.) In a large adobe building on the northwest corner of the plaza, the **Museum of Fine Arts** dazzles visitors with exhibits on the evolution of New Mexican art, as well as the works of major Southwestern artists such as Gustave Bauman and Georgia O'Keeffe. (107 W. Palace Ave. ☎476-5059.) The **Palace of the Governors,** on the north side of the plaza, housed government offices for 300 years, from 1609 until 1909, when it became the home of the Museum of New Mexico. The hacienda-style palace now houses exhibits on the history of Santa Fe. Outside, sellers of Native American art line the **Palace Portal,** an active marketplace since the 19th century. (107 W. Palace Ave. ☎476-5100.) Some of the most distinctive museums in town are 2 mi. south of the Plaza on Old Santa Fe Trail at Museum Hill. The ▧**Museum of International Folk Art** explores the beauty of everyday objects through its vibrant collection of small handmade toys, furniture, clothing, textiles, and jewelry from around the world. Be sure to check out the Girard Wing, which houses an array of miniature villages ranging from bull fights to silver palaces. (706 Camino Lejo. ☎476-1200.) Next door, the **Museum of Indian Arts and Culture Laboratory of Anthropology** displays Native American artwork, photos, and artifacts. The best exhibit, "Here, Now, and Always," is ongoing and explores how various tribes connect to the landscapes of the Southwest. (710 Camino Lejo. ☎476-1250.) The **Museum of Spanish Colonial Art** houses an extensive collection of artifacts from the Spanish settlement of New Mexico, dating from 1598. (750 Camino Lejo. ☎982-2226.)

OTHER PLAZA MUSEUMS. The popular ▧**Georgia O'Keeffe Museum** pays tribute to the famous New Mexican artist with up-close views of her vibrant flower paintings and as well as her more abstract works. Especially captivating is the museum's collection of photographs of the artist, displayed in an ongoing exhibit. (217 Johnson St. ☎946-1036. Open daily in summer 10am-5pm; closed W in winter. $8, students over 18 $4, under 17 free. F 5-8pm free. Audio tour $5.) Downtown's **Institute of American Indian Arts Museum** specializes in contemporary Native American fine art; the museum's beautiful exhibits change frequently. (108 Cathedral Pl. ☎983-8900. Open M-Sa 10am-5-pm, Su noon-5pm. $5, seniors and students $2.50, under 16 free.) The **New Mexico State Capitol** was built in 1966 in the form of the Zia sun symbol. The House and Senate galleries (accessible from the 2nd floor) are open to the public, and the building also contains an impressive art collection. The 4th floor Governor's Gallery is especially remarkable. (☎986-4589. 5 blocks south of the Plaza on Old Santa Fe Trail. Open M-F 8am-6pm. Free tours M-F 10am and 2pm.)

CHURCHES. Santa Fe's Catholic roots are evident in the Romanesque **St. Francis Cathedral,** built from 1869 to 1886 under the direction of Archbishop Lamy, the famous priest immortalized in Willa Cather's *Death Comes for the Archbishop*.

THE SOUTHWEST

(213 Cathedral Pl. 1 block east of the Plaza on San Francisco St. ☎ 982-5619. Open daily 9am-6pm. Mass M-F 7am, 5:15pm; Sa 5:15pm; Su 10am, noon, 5:15pm; in Spanish Su 8am.) The Loretto Chapel was the 1st Gothic building west of the Mississippi River, built in the style of La Sainte Chapelle in Paris. The church is famous for its spiral staircase—both its builder and the details of its construction are a mystery. *(207 Old Santa Fe Trail. 2 blocks south of the cathedral. ☎ 982-0092. Open M-Sa 9am-6pm, Su 10:30am-5pm. $2.50, children and seniors $2, under 7 free.)* About five blocks southeast of the plaza is the **San Miguel Mission,** the oldest church in the US. The Mission was built in the early 1600s by the Tlaxcalan Indians. *(401 Old Santa Fe Trail, at DeVargas St. ☎ 988-9504. Open M-Sa 9am-5pm, Su 9am-4pm; may close earlier in winter. Mass Su 5pm. $1.)*

GALLERIES. Galleries in Santa Fe line every street, alternating only with hotels and restaurants. The most successful local artists live and sell their work along Canyon Rd. To reach the galleries, leave the Plaza on San Francisco Dr., take a right on Cathedral Pl., a left on W. Alameda St., a right on Paseo de Peralta, and a left on Canyon Rd. Most galleries are open from 10am until 5pm and contain interesting and often fantastically expensive collections, from western landscapes to mammoth bronze statues. **Cruz Gallery** has beautiful silver jewelry and some more inexpensive prints, as well as a small cafe and patio. *(616 Canyon Rd. ☎ 505-995-9872. Open daily 10am-5pm.)* **Houshang's Gallery** is filled with brilliantly colorful local paintings while eclectic steel sculptures line the exterior. Though expensive, it's well worth a look. *(713 Canyon Rd. ☎ 800-756-3322. Open daily 10am-5pm.)*

🌸 🎵 FESTIVALS AND ENTERTAINMENT

The Santa Fe Plaza is home to three of the US's largest festivals. The **Spanish Market** (☎ 988-7575; www.santafefiesta.org), a combination celebration and sale of Hispanic-influenced artwork that pays tribute to the area's rich Spanish heritage, comes to town on the last weekend in July (☎ 505-982-2226. www.spanishmarket.com). On the 3rd weekend of August, the most gifted Native American artists in the US come to town for **Indian Market.** The festival is the nation's largest and most impressive showcase of Native American culture and art. The Southwestern Association for Indian Arts (☎ 983-5220; www.saia.org) has more info. Though held at Museum Hill, not the Plaza, the **International Folk Art Market** (☎ 505-476-1189; www.folkartmarket.com), held in mid-July, brings craftspeople from around the world to display their colorful collections. Don Diego de Vargas' reconquest of New Mexico in 1693 marked the end of the 13-year Pueblo Rebellion, now celebrated during the three-day **Fiesta de Santa Fe.** Held in mid-September, the festival dates back to 1712, begins with the burning of the Zozobra (a 50 ft. marionette), and includes street dancing, processions, and political satires. *The New Mexican* publishes a guide and a schedule of the fiesta's events.

Poetic verse and distinguished acting invade the city each summer when **Shakespeare in Santa Fe** raises its curtain. The shows play in an open-air theater on the St. John's College campus, just outside of downtown, from July through August. (Tickets ☎ 982-2910; call to check schedule. Shows F-Su 7:30pm. Reserved seating tickets $15-32; lawn seating free, suggested donation $5.) The **Santa Fe Opera,** on Opera Dr., draws opera fans from around the world to its outdoor theater. Nights can be cool; bring a blanket. The 2008 season includes *Falstaff, The Marriage of Figaro, Billy Budd, Radamisto,* and the American premier of *Adriana Mater.* (7 mi. north of Santa Fe on Rte. 84/285. ☎ 800-280-4654 or 986-5900; www.santafeopera.org. July W and F-Sa at 9pm; Aug. M-Sa at 8 or 8:30pm. Call the box office for a seat on the shuttle to and from Santa Fe. Box office is at opera house; call or drop by the day of the show for prices and availability. Tickets $25-170, standing room $10; with student ID 50% discount.) The **Santa Fe Chamber Music Festival** draws international artists in its celebration of the works of Baroque, Classical, Romantic, and 20th-century composers in the St. Francis Auditorium of the Museum of Fine Arts and the Lensic Theater. (☎888-221-9836 or 505-982-1890; www.sfcmf.org. Mid-July to mid-Aug. Tickets $17-57, students $10.)

NIGHTLIFE

The diverse citizens of Santa Fe—from retired Wall Street investment bankers to world-famous (or starving) artists—ensure varied, amusing nightlife. The talented waitstaff at **La Casa Sena Cantina,** 125 E. Palace Ave., perform two shows nightly for its crowd of all ages. Sit back and enjoy a margarita and the award-winning red chile chocolate soup ($10) as you listen to the mellow sounds of jazz and Broadway showtunes. (☎988-9232. Shows nightly in summer 5:30 and 8pm; in winter, shows Su-Th at 6:30pm, F-Sa at 5:30 and 8pm. Reservations recommended.) The **Cowgirl Hall of Fame,** 319 S. Guadalupe St., has nightly live rock and roll hoe-downs 9pm-1am, in addition to lively DJs spinning hip-hop. Barbecue, Mexican food, and burgers ($8) are served until midnight with 13 microbrews on tap, not including nightly beer specials. (☎982-2565. Cowgirl margaritas $5. Sa-Su ranch breakfast. Happy hour daily 4-6pm. 21+ after midnight. Cover $3-4. Open M-F 11am-2am, Sa 8:30am-2am, Su 8:30am-midnight.)

OUTDOOR ACTIVITIES

The pine-filled **Sangre de Cristo Mountains,** on Santa Fe's northern edge, reach heights of over 12,000 ft. and offer countless opportunities for hikers, bikers, and skiers. The Pecos and Río Grande rivers make great playgrounds for kayakers and rafters. Before heading into the wilderness, stop by the **Public Lands Information Center,** 1474 Rodeo Rd., near the intersection of St. Francis Rd. and I-25, to pick up maps and advice. (☎438-7542 or 877-276-9404; www.publiclands.org. Open M-F 8:30am-4:30pm.)

The closest **hiking** trails to Santa Fe are along Rte. 475 on the way to the Santa Fe Ski Area. On this road, 13 mi. northeast of town, the moderate **Tesuque Peak Road Trail** (12 mi. round-trip), winds through large stands of aspen and spruce and ends with excellent views of Santa Fe. Near the end of Rte. 475 and the Santa Fe Ski Area, trailheads venture into the 223,000 acre **Pecos Wilderness,** making them cool summer options for escaping the heat of the day. Trails departing from the Winsor Trailhead are the most popular and accessible. Call the Pecos Ranger Station (☎505-757-6121) for more info. Closer to town, the **Atayla Trail** (6 mi., 3-5hr. round-trip) offers spectacular views of Santa Fe and the surrounding mountains from its 9121 foot. summit. To reach the trail, park in the 1st parking area at St. John's College and begin at the signs for Trail 174. Forty miles southwest of Santa Fe, **Kasha-Katuwe Tent Rocks National Monument** is famous for its white, cone-shaped rocks. The national monument has two beautiful hiking trails but is largely undeveloped. (☎761-8704. Take I-25 S from Santa Fe to Exit 264 onto NM 16. From 16, turn right onto NM 22, follow signs to monument. No Visitors Center, pit toilets only. Open daily Apr.-Oct. 7am-7pm; Nov.-Mar. 8am-5pm; day use only. $5 per vehicle.)

The best **skiing** is 16 mi. northeast of downtown, at **Ski Santa Fe.** Located in the Sangre de Cristo Mountains on Rte. 475, the ski area has seven lifts (4 chairs and 2 surface lifts) servicing 67 trails (20% beginner, 40% intermediate, 40% advanced) on 660 acres with a 1725 ft. vertical drop from the summit at 12,075 ft. (☎982-4429; www.skisantafe.com. Open late Nov. to early Apr. daily 9am-4pm. Lift tickets $39 per half-day; $54 per day, teens $44, children and seniors $39. Rental packages start at $20, children $16.)

DAYTRIPS FROM SANTA FE

BANDELIER NATIONAL MONUMENT

Bandelier is 48 mi. northwest of Santa Fe. Take U.S. 285 N. to 502 W. From 502, go south on NM Rte. 4 to the monument. The park entrance fee is $12 per vehicle and $6 per pedestrian; National Park passes are accepted.

Popular Bandelier National Monument features the remnants of over 2400 cliff dwellings and pueblos amid 50 sq. mi. of mesas and tree-lined canyons. The park centers around Frijoles Canyon, the site of many natural caves and settlements along the canyon floor that were occupied for roughly 500 years. The **Visitors Center,** 3 mi. into the park at the bottom of Frijoles Canyon, has a free museum with exhibits on local prehistoric art and info on the workers of the CCC who helped create the park's roads and trails. The Center also shows a short video. There are few placards along the park's pathways, but trail guides for the most popular hikes are available at the Visitors Center for $1. (☎672-3861, ext. 517. Open daily June-Aug. 8am-6pm; Sept.-late Oct. 9am-5:30pm; late Oct. to late Mar. 8am-4:30pm; late Mar. to May 9am-5:30pm.) The 1¼ mi. **Main Loop Trail** begins at the back porch of the Visitors Center and passes the ruins of the two-storied, 400-room **Tyuonyi Pueblo** and the aptly named **Long House,** an 800 ft. section of adjoining, multi-storied homes that extend outward from the base of a cliff. Parts of the trail are wheelchair-accessible along a paved path, but caves can only be viewed up close by climbing reconstructed wooden ladders. Rangers lead guided walks of the Main Loop Trail; check the Visitors Center for daily times. Those with more time should go half a mile farther to **Alcove House,** a *kiva* carved into an enormous natural cave 140 ft. above the canyon floor and accessible only by climbing four ladders. For a longer hike, the **Falls Trail** (5 mi.) heads to the Río Grande River, passing two waterfalls along the way. Free permits are required for backcountry hiking and camping and must be obtained one day in advance at the Visitors Center. Just past the main entrance, **Juniper Campground ❶** offers the only developed camping in the park, with drinking water, grills, picnic tables, and pit toilets (sites $12).

LOS ALAMOS

Los Alamos is located 35 mi. northwest of Santa Fe. Take U.S. 285 to 502 W.

Known only as the mysterious P.O. Box 1663 during the heyday of the **Manhattan Project,** Los Alamos is no longer the nation's biggest secret. Overlooking the Río Grande Valley, scenic Los Alamos is surrounded by the Santa Fe National Forest and overlooks several nearby canyons, 35 mi. northwest of Santa Fe. The birthplace of the atomic bomb (known as "Project Y" to the select group of physicists and engineers who developed the weapon), Los Alamos attracts visitors with natural beauty, outdoor activities, and the allure of its secret past. In town, the **Bradbury Science Museum,** at 15th St. and Central, details the history of the Los Alamos National Laboratory, beginning with Project Y, as well as the lab's current projects, which range from brain mapping to the search for alternative energy sources. The museum features short documentaries and excellent hands-on exhibits. (☎667-4444. Open M-Su 1pm-5pm, Tu-Sa 10am-5pm.) The **Los Alamos Historical Museum,** at 20th St. and Central, also houses similar displays on the Manhattan Project, in addition to interesting exhibits on the town's geological history and the **Los Alamos Ranch School,** which later became the Project's base of operations during the war. (☎662-4493. Open in summer M-Sa 9:30am-4:30pm, Su 11am-5pm; in winter M-F 10am-4pm, Sa-Su 1-4pm. Free.) The **⬛Black Hole,** 4015 Arkansas Ave., is a quirky atomic junkyard that sells all the junk the laboratory doesn't want anymore, including 50-year-old calculators, fiber-optic cables, time-mark generators, and other technological flotsam. The owner's motto is "never throw anything away"; spend 5min. in the Black Hole and you'll see he's true to his word. Leave with your very own $2 atomic bomb detonator cable. (☎ 662-5053. Open M-Sa 10am-5pm.) Surrounding Los Alamos, the **Santa Fe National Forest** has countless trails for hiking and biking in and along the town's canyons. Fifteen miles west on Rte. 4, the 89,000 acres of the **Valles Caldera,** an extinct volcanic crater, was designated a National Preserve in 2000. It contains hiking trails and incredible canyon views. Certain trails only accommodate a limited number of visitors each day for hiking, fishing, and horse-drawn wagon or van tours, so make reservations in advance. If you come into town without a reservation, you can still meander along some of the Preserve's shorter hikes, including the **Coyote Call Trail** (3 mi. round-trip) and **Valle Grande Trail** (2 mi. round-trip), both of which provide views of the caldera and are accessible from Rte. 4. (☎ 866-382-5537; www.vallescaldera.gov. Permits $10, under 15 $5; other fees apply for fishing licenses and touring.)

For a terrific post-hike lunch, **Ruby K's Bagel Café ❷,** 1789 Central Ave. Ste. #2, has fresh sandwiches, salads, and homemade bagels ranging from chocolate chip to green chile. (Open M-W and Sa 6am-3pm, Th-F 6am-5:30pm, Su 7am-3pm. AmEx/D/MC/V.) Accommodations in the area tend towards chain hotels or pricey B&Bs, so it's best to spend the night in nearby Santa Fe. The **Los Alamos Visitors Center** is at 109 Central Park Sq., at Central Ave. just west of 15th St., and has area information and brochures. (☎ 661-4815. Open M-Sa 9am-5pm, Su 10am-3pm.)

TAOS   ☎ 505

Before the turn of the 20th century, Taos was a small farming community in the Sangre de Cristo Mountains. A broken wheel on the wagon of artists Bert Greer Phillips and Ernest Blumenschein changed all that. While the two painters waited for repairs 20 mi. north of town in September of 1898, they became entranced with the natural beauty and light of Northern New Mexico, decided to relocate, and convinced many of their friends to do the same. By 1915, the Taos Society of Artists was born, and soon, tourists flocked to the bohemian haven in the mountains to purchase the beautiful artwork. Now also home to multiple ski resorts, Taos has become a destination for those wishing to explore the outdoors first-hand, rather than simply through the landscapes of local artists.

■■ **ORIENTATION AND PRACTICAL INFORMATION.** Taos is 79 mi. north of Santa Fe (p. 824), between the dramatic Rio Grande Gorge and Wheeler Peak. Those coming from Santa Fe can either travel to Taos via the High Road through the mountains (take 84/285 N. to 76 to 518 to 68), or the Low Road, which winds along the river basin (take Rte. 68 N). **Paseo del Pueblo** (Rte. 68) is the town's main north-south thoroughfare, called **Paseo del Pueblo Norte** north of Kit Carson Rd. and **Paseo del Pueblo Sur** to the south. Traffic on Paseo del Pueblo can move slowly during the summer and ski season—use Rte. 240 and Upper Ranchitos Rd. as a bypass if possible. Drivers should park at the metered **Camino de la Placita,** a block west of the plaza, or at meters on side streets. The **Taos Chamber of Commerce and Visitors Bureau,** 1139 Paseo del Pueblo Sur, 2 mi. south of town at the junction of Rte. 68 and Paseo del Cañón, has maps and info on accommodations, area attractions, and restaurants, as well as free Wi-Fi. (☎ 758-3873. Open in summer daily 9am-5pm, in winter closed Su.) The **Carson National Forest Office,** 208 Cruz Alta Rd., has info on camping and hiking. (☎ 758-6200. Open M-F 8am-4:30pm.) **Internet Access: Public Library,** 402 Camino de la Placita. (☎ 758-3063. $1 per 30min. Open M noon-6pm, Tu-F 10am-6pm, Sa 10am-5pm.) **Post Office:** 318 Paseo del Pueblo Norte. (☎ 758-2081. Open M-F 8:30am-5pm.) **Postal Code:** 87571.

ACCOMMODATIONS. The **Abominable Snowmansion Hostel (HI) ❶**, located 9 mi. north of Taos in the small village of Arroyo Seco, has a friendly spirit, a large kitchen, and a comfy living room with a pool table. A hostel in summer and ski lodge in winter, the Snowmansion is also only 9 mi. west of the ski valley. Camping is also available on-site, in the warmer months. (☎776-8298. Reception 8am-noon and 4-10pm. Reservations recommended. Dec. to mid-Apr. dorms $22, private rooms $40-54. Mid-Apr. to Nov. dorms $18, tent sites $12; private rooms $32-44. MC/V.) The **Budget Host Motel ❷**, 1798 Paseo del Pueblo Sur, 3 mi. south of the plaza, has clean rooms with A/C, continental breakfast, fridge, microwave, and Wi-Fi. (☎758-2524 or 800-323-6009. Singles $64; doubles $70. AAA discount 10%. AmEx/D/MC/V.) **El Pueblo Lodge ❸**, 412 Paseo del Pueblo Norte, is one of the best deals in town with spacious rooms, continental breakfast, a hot tub, pool, and comfortable outdoor patio. Its only a 5min. walk from the plaza. (☎758-8700. Rooms from $74. AmEx/D/MC/V.)

Camping close to Taos is easy with a car, and considering the area's natural beauty and temperate climate, sleeping under the stars is an appealing option. The **Orilla Verde Recreation Area ❶**, administered by the Bureau of Land Management through the Taos Field Office, 15 mi. south of Taos on Rte. 68, has six camp-grounds on the scenic **Rio Grande Gorge.** Pilar and Rio Bravo Campgrounds have hookups; Rio Bravo has showers. (☎751-4899 or 758-8851. Water and toilets. Sites $7, with hookup $15.) The **Carson National Forest** has four campgrounds to the east of Taos along Rte. 585 and U.S. 64. Tent sites sit along a stream and are surrounded by *piñon* forest. The closest, **Las Petacas ❶**, is 4 mi. east of Taos, and has pit toilets, picnic tables, and fire pits, but no drinking water. For more information, contact the Carson National Forest Office in Taos. (☎758-6200. Sites $5.) **Backcountry camping ❶** in the forest doesn't require a permit. Dispersed camping is popular along Rte. 518 south of Taos and Forest Rd. 437; park on the side of the road and pitch your tent a few hundred feet inside.

FOOD. Restaurants cluster around Taos Plaza and Bent St., but some of the best budget eating options can actually be found in the area north of town, along Paseo del Pueblo. **◪Taos Pizza Out Back ❷**, 712 Paseo del Pueblo Norte, serves gourmet pizzas, pastas, and calzones made with locally grown organic vegetables, meats, and cheeses. The warm, thick pizza crust is spiced with rosemary and is perfect to dip into the freshly made pesto sauce served with every meal. (☎758-3112. Slice $2-7. Pizzas $15-25. Open daily 11am-10pm. MC/V.) **Michael's Kitchen ❷**, 304 Paseo del Pueblo Norte, specializes in hearty meals, with traditional Mexican and American dishes, fresh baked goods, and the best breakfast in town available all day long. Test out one of the four different cinnamon rolls, the largest the size of a dinner plate. (☎758-4178. Open daily 7am-8:30pm. AmEx/D/MC/V.) **Abe's Cantina y Cocina ❶**, 6 mi. north of Taos on the road to Taos Ski Valley in the village of Arroyo Seco, has cheap, homestyle New Mexican food (the $4 chicken, bean, and cheese burrito is a can't-beat deal) and some basic grocery items. (☎776-8516. Open M-F 7am-5:30pm, Sa 7am-1:30pm. Bar closes around 10pm. AmEx/D/MC/V.) **Taos Wrappers ❶**, 616 Paseo del Pueblo Sur, serves such inventive dishes as chicken waldorf wraps and chilled avocado soup. (☎751-9727. Wraps $5-7. Open in summer M-F 11am-4pm, Sa-Su 8am-4pm; in winter M-F 11am-1pm, Sa 11am-2pm. Cash or check only.) **Orlando's ❷**, 1114 Don Juan Valdez Ln., 1 mi. north of the plaza off of Rte. 68, is beloved by locals and tourists. The pressed tin ceilings, brightly painted walls, and smattering of Spanish tiles make this a great spot to sip a margarita ($5) and enjoy the area's best Mexican food. The deep-fried chimichangas and blue corn chicken enchiladas ($8) are delicious. (☎751-1450. Open daily 10:30am-3pm and 5-9pm. MC/V.)

THE SOUTHWEST

◙ **SIGHTS.** The ▨**Taos Art Museum at Fechin House,** 227 Paseo del Pueblo Norte, exhibits the oil paintings, watercolors, and sketches of 12 artists in the Taos Society of Artists, originally formed in 1915. While the paintings are excellent, one of the museum's real draws is the building itself: the beautiful Spanish Mission-style home of Russian immigrant, Taos resident, and painter Nicolai Fechin. (☎758-2690. Open June-Sept. Tu-Su 10am-5pm; Oct.-May W-Su 10am-4pm. $8, seniors $7, students $5, children $4.) **The Millicent Rogers Museum,** 1504 Millicent Rogers Rd., 4 mi. north of the plaza off of Rte. 64, has an extravagant collection of Indian jewelry, Navajo textiles, Pueblo pottery, and Apache baskets, the bulk of which belonged to Millicent Rogers, a fashion maven and New York socialite. The museum's showpiece is the enormous Tab Necklace, featuring 294 pieces of turquoise. There is also a gallery dedicated to the ceramic works of María Martínez, known for her innovative black-on-black pottery. (☎758-2462. Open Apr.-Oct. daily 10am-5pm; Nov.-Mar. Tu-Su 10am-5pm. $7, seniors and students $6, under 16 $2.) The **Harwood Museum,** 238 Ledoux St., associated with the University of New Mexico, houses a collection of Spanish colonial art, works by 20th-century local artists, and a gallery of Agnes Martin, a minimalist painter. (☎758-9826. Parking on Ranchitos Rd. Open Tu-Sa 10am-5pm, Su noon-5pm. $8, seniors $7, children under 11 free.) The **Martínez Hacienda,** 2 mi. southwest of the plaza on Ranchitos Rd., is one of the few surviving Spanish Colonial mansions in the US. Built in 1804, this 21-room structure housed the prosperous Martínez family, who were very active in the political community. (☎758-1000. Open daily May.-Oct. 9am-5pm; call for winter hours. $7, ages 6-15 $3.)

The five-story adobe homes of the ▨**Taos Pueblo** are between 700 and 1000 years old, making the pueblo the oldest continuously inhabited settlement in the US. Taos Pueblo was named a UNESCO World Heritage Site in 1992, and is the only pueblo in Northern New Mexico where the inhabitants still live traditionally. The pueblo includes the national historic monument **St. Jerome Church,** built in 1850, as well as ruins of the old church, destroyed in the Pueblo Revolt of 1680. Visitors can also view the pueblo's cemetery, large adobe houses, and the outside of ceremonial *kivas.* (☎758-1028. Open daily May-Sept. 8am-4:30pm; Oct.-Apr. 8am-4pm. Guided tours daily May-Sept.; self-guided tours available. $10, students $5, under 12 free. Camera permit $5.)

🏂 **OUTDOOR ACTIVITIES.** Known by most winter enthusiasts as one of the best ski resorts in the country, **Taos Ski Valley,** about 15 mi. northeast of town on Rte. 150, has 110 trails (24% beginner, 25% intermediate, 51% advanced) and 12 lifts. Ski Valley boasts over 2500 ft. vertical drop and over 300 in. annual snowfall. (☎776-2291 or 866-250-7619, lodging info 866-250-7313. Lift tickets $36-59 during the regular season.) Reserve a room in advance if you plan to come in the winter holiday season. There are also two smaller, family-oriented ski areas near Taos: **Angel Fire** (☎377-6401 or 800-633-7463; lift tickets $52, ages 7-12 $40) and **Red River** (☎800-331-7669; lift tickets $53, ages 4-12 and seniors $38, teens $47). Multi-day passes are available for use at all three resorts (from $48 per person per day). In summer, the nearly deserted ski valley and the nearby **Wheeler Peak Wilderness** become a hiker's paradise (most trails begin off Rte. 150). The ascent of **Wheeler Peak,** the highest point in New Mexico at 13,161 ft., is a strenuous 16 mi. round-trip trek that begins at the Twining Campground in Taos Ski Valley. Due to the town's location near New Mexico's wild Rio Grande, **river rafting** is very popular; the Taos Box and the Race Course are the best routes. **Los Rios River Runners** (☎776-8854 or 800-544-1181), **Far Flung Adventures** (☎758-2628 or 800-359-2627), and **Native Sons Adventures** (☎758-9342 or 800-753-7559) all offer a range of guided half-day ($49-55) and full day ($89-130) rafting trips. The best trail for mountain biking in the area is the

South Boundary Trail. Most riders take a shuttle to the trailhead near Angel Fire and then ride the rolling 27 mi., single-track trail back into town. For bike rentals, visit **Gearing Up Bicycle Shop,** 129 Paseo del Pueblo Sur. (☎751-0365. Open daily 9:30am-6pm; in winter closed Su. Mountain bikes $25 per half-day, $35 per day. Basic tune-up $40. Ride to the trailhead $80.)

ALBUQUERQUE   ☎505

Located at the crossroads of the Southwest, Albuquerque buzzes with history and culture, nurturing ethnic restaurants, offbeat galleries, first-class museums, and raging nightclubs. Legendary Rte. 66 (now Central Ave.) may no longer appear on maps, but its spirit is alive and kicking. The mythic highway radiates a palpable energy that gives shops, restaurants, and bars on the city's thoroughfare a distinctive spirit found nowhere else in the state. With its unique set of neighborhoods ranging from tranquil Old Town to trendy Nob Hill, Albuquerque has a cosmopolitan feel all its own.

▛ TRANSPORTATION

Airport: Albuquerque International (ABQ), 2200 Sunport Blvd. SE. (☎244-7700), south of downtown. Take bus #50 from 5th St. and Central Ave., or pick it up along Yale Blvd. Airport Shuttle (☎765-1234) runs to the city ($12 to Nob Hill, $7 to Old Town).

Trains: Amtrak, 214 1st St. SW. (☎842-9650; www.amtrak.com). Station open daily 10am-5pm. 1 train per day to: **Flagstaff** (5hr., $67); **Kansas City** (18hr., $102); **Los Angeles** (16hr., $76); **Santa Fe** (1hr. to Lamy and 20min. shuttle; $34). Reservations required.

Buses: Greyhound (☎243-4435; www.greyhound.com) and **TNM&O Coaches** (☎806-763-5389), at 300 2nd St. Station open 24hr. Both run buses from 3 blocks south of Central Ave. To **Denver** (10hr., 3 per day, $90), **Los Angeles** (18hr., 5 per day, $86), and **Santa Fe** (1hr., 3 per day, $15).

Public Transit: ABQ Ride, 601 Yale Blvd. SE. (☎843-9200). Open M-F 6am-8pm, Sa-Su 8am-5pm. Maps at the transit office and the main library. Most buses run M-Sa 6:30am-8:30pm and leave from Central Ave. and 5th St. Bus #66 runs down Central Ave. $1, ages 5-18 and seniors $0.35. Request free transfers from driver.

Taxi: Albuquerque Cab, ☎883-4888.

✦ ⁊ ORIENTATION AND PRACTICAL INFORMATION

Central Avenue (Route 66) is still Albuquerque's main thoroughfare, running through all the city's major neighborhoods. Central Ave. (east-west) and **I-25** (north-south) divide Albuquerque into four quadrants. All downtown addresses come with a quadrant designation: NE., NW., SE., or SW. The adobe campus of the **University of New Mexico (UNM)** spreads along Central Ave. from University Ave. to Gerard St. **Nob Hill,** the area of Central Ave. from Gerard to Carlisle St., features bookstores, coffee shops, boutiques, bars, and art galleries. **Downtown** lies on Central Ave. between 10th St. and Broadway. The historic **Old Town Plaza** sits between San Felipe, North Plaza, South Plaza, and Romero, a block north of Central Ave.

Visitor Info: Old Town Visitors Center, 303 Romero St. NW. (☎800-733-9918), in the shopping plaza west of the church. Open daily 10am-6pm.

Hotlines: Rape Crisis Center, ☎266-7711. **Gay and Lesbian Information Line,** ☎891-3647. Both operate 24hr.

Albuquerque

Old Town Albuquerque

Downtown Albuquerque

♠ ACCOMMODATIONS
Coronado Campground, **1**
Monterey Motel, **2**
Route 66 Youth Hostel, **8**
Sandía Mountain Hostel, **6**

♥ FOOD
66 Diner, **3**
Annapurna Ayuvedic Cuisine
and Chai House, **5**
Barelas, **13**

Julia's New Mexican
and Vegetarian
Café, **7**
La Montanita Co-op
Supermarket, **4**

■ NIGHTLIFE
Burt's Tiki Lounge, **11**
Maloney's, **10**
Sauce/Raw Liquid Lounge, **9**
Sunshine Theater, **12**

Medical Services: Presbyterian Hospital, 1100 Central Ave. SE. (☎841-1234).

Internet Access: Albuquerque Main Public Library, 501 Copper Ave. NW. (☎768-5141). Free Wi-Fi. Open M and Th-Sa 10am-6pm, Tu-W 10am-7pm.

Post Office: 1135 Broadway Blvd. NE. (☎346-8484). Open M-F 8am-5:30pm. **Postal Code:** 87101.

▐ ACCOMMODATIONS

Cheap motels line Albuquerque's Central Ave.; most offer similar amenities, but be sure to evaluate the quality of your room before paying. Most chain motels and hotels drop their prices in summer. During the balloon festival in October (p. 4), rooms are scarce; call ahead for reservations.

Sandía Mountain Hostel, 12234 Rte. 14 N. (☎281-4117), in nearby Cedar Crest. Take I-40 E to Exit 175 and go 4 mi. north on Rte. 14. Only 10 mi. from the Sandía Ski Area, this ski chateau has vaulted wooden ceilings and hand-crafted furniture. Well worth the 15min. drive from Albuquerque, it has a fireplace, kitchen, and spacious dorm rooms. Ask about taking a ride on one of the donkeys out back. No A/C. Reception 4:30-10pm. Dorms $14; private rooms $22-32. Cash only. ❶

Route 66 Youth Hostel, 1012 Central Ave. SW. (☎247-1813), between downtown and Old Town. An unbeatable location and simple dorm rooms. One chore per guest per day required. Key deposit $5. Reception daily 7:30am-1pm and 4-11pm. Check-out 10:30am. Dorms $18; private rooms with shared bath $24-35. Cash or check only. ❶

Monterey Motel, 2402 Central Ave. SW. (☎243-3554). By far the best of the motels along Central Ave. Pristine, nicely decorated rooms come with A/C, cable TV, a fridge, laundry access, a lovely pool, and Wi-Fi. Look for the flower-lined parking area. No smoking or pets. Singles $50; doubles $58. AAA discount. AmEx/D/MC/V. ❹

Coronado Campground (☎980-8256). About 15 mi. north of Albuquerque. Take I-25 to Exit 242, and follow signs to Coronado State Monument; the campground is just outside the park entrance. On the banks of the Río Grande. Adobe shelters at some sites offer a cool respite. Showers ($4), toilets, and water. Park open M and W-Su 8:30am-5pm. Tent sites $10, with shelters and picnic tables $14, with full hookup $18-22. ❶

▐ FOOD

A diverse ethnic community, hordes of hungry interstate travelers, and a lot of green and red chiles make Albuquerque a tasty destination. The area around the University of New Mexico is the best bet for visitors seeking inexpensive eateries. Farther east, **Nob Hill** caters to yuppies and artists. Groceries are available at **La Montanita Co-op Supermarket,** 3500 Central Ave. SE. (☎265-4631. Open M-Sa 7am-10pm, Su 8am-10pm.)

🞋 **Barelas,** 1502 4th St. (☎843-7577). This local favorite (expect a struggle to find a parking space) has the best *huevos rancheros* around ($5) and small, medium, and large New Mexican plates. The *carne adovado* ($7) is fantastic. Open M-F 7:30am-3pm, Sa 7:30am-2:30pm. D/MC/V. ❶

🞋 **Annapurna Ayurvedic Cuisine & Chai House** (☎262-2424), on the corner of Silver and Yale St. near UNM. Vegetarian Indian cuisine that is designed to leave you feeling happier, healthier, and infinitely more relaxed. The steamed mung beans and rice ($4) is recommended. Many gluten- and egg-free pastries available. Free Wi-Fi. 50% off after 5pm. Open M-Sa 7am-8pm, Su 10am-2pm. MC/V over $5. ❶

66 Diner, 1405 Central Ave. NE. (☎247-1421). Head here for great diner fare, though the real draws are the smooth, creamy, thick milkshakes and malts ($3). Cozy up inside one of the green leather booths for grilled cheese ($4), their trademark "Pile Up" ($7), or the daily blue-plate special ($6-9). Open M-Th 11am-11pm, F 11am-midnight, Sa 8am-midnight, Su 8am-10pm. AmEx/D/MC/V. ❶

Julia's New Mexican and Vegetarian Café, 303 Romero St. NW. (☎246-1854). Still family-run, Julia's has been dishing out excellent, spicy New Mexican cuisine for 5 generations. The taco salad ($8), served in a warm, fried tortilla bowl, is outstanding. Entrees $10. Open daily 8am-2pm. Cash only. ❷

◉ SIGHTS

OLD TOWN. When the railroad cut through Albuquerque in 1880, it missed Old Town by a mere 1½ mi. Though the hub of downtown grew around the railroad,

Old Town remained a vital local center. Just north of Central Ave. and east of Río Grande Blvd., the adobe plaza still looks much like it did over 100 years ago, except for the ever-present restaurants, gift shops, and jewelry vendors. Several wonderful museums and attractions are within walking distance of the plaza, the center of Old Town. To the northeast, the ◩**Albuquerque Museum of Art and History** displays the art of the American Southwest, with standing exhibits on the history of Albuquerque and art in New Mexico. The museum also houses a wonderful modern sculpture garden. (*2000 Mountain Rd. NW.* ☎*243-7255. Open Tu-Su 9am-5pm. Free guided museum tour daily at 2 pm; tour of sculpture garden Apr.-Nov. daily at 10am. $4, seniors $2, ages 4-12 $1; 1st W of each month free.*) **Walking tours** of Old Town meet at the museum. (*1hr. tours depart mid-Mar. to mid-Dec. Tu-Su 11am. Free with museum admission.*) On the north side of the plaza, the white-steepled **San Felipe de Neri Church** is a Spanish-style adobe church dating to 1706. The church is by far Old Town's most beautiful building. (☎*243-7255. Open daily 9am-5pm; museum open M-Sa 10am-4pm. Su mass in English 7 and 10:15am; in Spanish 8:30am.*) Nearby, the **National Atomic Museum** has fascinating interactive exhibits on the development of nuclear energy, with a focus on the social history of the Cold War and the Manhattan Project. It also features displays on Marie Curie and other prominent women in scientific research. (*1905 Mountain Rd. NW. Moving mid-2008 to Eubank and Southern Ave. SE., near Kirtland Air Force Base.* ☎*245-2137. Open daily 9am-5pm. $6, ages 6-17 $4, seniors $5.*) No visit to Old Town is complete without seeing the ◩**Rattlesnake Museum,** just south of the plaza. Earn a "Certificate of Bravery" by visiting the largest collection of live venomous and non-venomous rattlesnakes in the world, with over 30 species, including a family of rare albino snakes. The museum also includes several species of tarantulas. (*202 San Felipe NW.* ☎*242-6569. Open M-F 11:30am-5:30pm, Sa 10am-6pm, Su 1-5pm. $3.50, seniors and students $3, under 18 $2.50.*) Just one block off the plaza is the **Turquoise Museum,** a family-run institute that highlights the mineralogy, geology, and mining history of "America's gemstone." The museum also provides tips for those interested in purchasing turquoise, common in the area. (*2107 Central Ave. NW.* ☎*247-8650. Open M-Sa 9:30am-4pm. $4, ages 10-17 and seniors $3.*) The enormous "T-Rex Attack!" exhibit greets visitors in the lobby at the **New Mexico Museum of Natural History and Science,** where interactive exhibits allow tourists to journey through time from the Big Bang to the present. The dinosaur exhibits on the 2nd floor, particularly the "Age of Super Giants," are the museum's main attraction. The museum also features a dyna-theater and a planetarium. (*1801 Mountain Rd. NW.* ☎*841-2802. Open daily 9am-5pm; closed M in Sept. and Jan. $7, over 60 $6, ages 3-12 $4; admission and 1 attraction $13/11/7; admission and 2 attractions $19/16/10.*)

ALBUQUERQUE BIOLOGICAL PARK. A top-notch zoo, aquarium, and botanical garden in one complex make for a wild afternoon in the city. The **Albuquerque Aquarium** has a 285,000 gal. mini-ocean, complete with sharks, giant sting-rays, and a coral reef. Connected to the aquarium is the **Río Grande Botanic Garden,** which features Mediterranean and desert conservatories, as well as a Fantasy Garden sure to inspire the imagination. A couple of blocks away, the **Río Grande Zoological Park** is one of the nation's top zoos. Visitors can walk 3 mi. of trails to see exhibits such as "The Catwalk" and "The Elephant Yard." Also watch caretakers feed seals and sea lions. (*Aquarium and garden: 2601 Central Ave. NW. Zoo: 903 10th St. SW.* ☎*248-8500. Open daily 9am-5pm; June-Aug. also Sa-Su 9am-6pm. Feedings daily 10:30am and 3:30pm. Admission to zoo or aquarium and botanic gardens $7, ages 3-12 and seniors $3; 3-park pass before noon $12/5.*)

CULTURAL ATTRACTIONS. Spreading across 50 acres on the banks of the Rio Grande, **The National Hispanic Cultural Center** houses multiple performing arts centers, a technology complex, a research library, and an art museum. Center perfor-

THE SOUTHWEST

mances change frequently, but the excellent art museum's permanent collection explores Hispanic history and heritage through various media. (*1701 4th St. SW., on the corner of Bridge St.* ☎246-2261; *www.hispanicculture.org. Museum open Tu-Su 10am-5pm. $3, seniors $2, under 16 free; Su free. See website for performance info.*) The **Indian Pueblo Cultural Center** provides an introduction to the history, culture, and art of the 19 American Indian pueblos of New Mexico. The center contains two galleries of contemporary Pueblo art, a gift shop with authentic artwork and jewelry, a restaurant with traditional cuisine, and a museum on the history of the Pueblo people entitled "Emergence." (*2401 12th St. NW. Take bus #36 from downtown.* ☎843-7270. *Museum open daily 9am-5pm. Art demonstrations Sa-Su noon-3pm. Native American dances Sa-Su 11am and 2pm. $6, seniors $5.50, students and over 5 $1.*)

🎎🎭 FESTIVALS AND NIGHTLIFE

If you're looking for a departure from honky-tonk, Albuquerque will provide you with an oasis of interesting bars, jamming nightclubs, and art film houses. Check flyers posted around the university area for live music shows, or pick up a copy of *Alibi*, the free local weekly, which has extensive coverage of the local music scene. During the 1st week of October, hundreds of aeronauts take flight in the **Albuquerque International Balloon Fiesta.** Even the most grounded of souls will enjoy the week's races, musical events, and the sky full of colorful hot air balloons. The **Balloon Glow** and **Night Magic Glow,** during which lighted balloons soar through the night sky, are two of the most highly anticipated events. (☎888-422-7277; www.balloonfiesta.com. *Admission $6.*) Concert junkies should check out **Sunshine Theater,** 120 Central Ave. NW., for its frequent hip-hop performances. (☎764-0249; www.sunshinetheaterlive.com. *Tickets $8-30.*) More family-oriented concerts take place at **The Albuquerque Biological Park** on summer nights. (*Concerts Th 7pm at the Botanic Garden, F 7pm at the Rio Grande Zoo. $8, ages 3-12 $2.*) Most nightlife huddles on Central Ave., downtown, and near the university. Nob Hill establishments tend to be the most gay-friendly.

Sauce/Raw Liquid Lounge, 405 Central Ave. NW. (☎242-5839). The place to see and be seen downtown. Filled with trendy twentysomethings, Raw focuses on hip hop and R&B, while Sauce pumps top 40. 3 VIP rooms. F ladies night. W Latin-salsa. In summer Happy hour M-Sa 7-9pm. No flip-flops, t-shirts, hats. Open M-Sa 9pm-2am.

Maloney's, 325 Central Ave. NW. (☎242-7422). Packs college kids and yuppies into its comfortable brew pub interior and popular outdoor patio. Patrons watch sports from one of several TVs as they enjoy ham sliders and BLTs ($8-9). The pub also keeps 15 beers on tap ($4). Open M-Sa 11am-2am, Su 11am-midnight.

Burt's Tiki Lounge, 313 Gold Ave. SW. (☎247-2878). Situated a block south of Central Ave., Burt's is the center of Albuquerque's local music scene. Surf and tiki paraphernalia line the walls and ceiling, while anything from punk to funk takes the stage. Tropical mixed drinks $6-7. Live music M-Th and F-Su nights. No cover. Open M-Sa 8pm-2am.

🏔 OUTDOOR ACTIVITIES

The name of the **Sandía Mountains,** from the Spanish word for "watermelon," is a nod to the sunset-pink hue of their crest, which rises a mile above Albuquerque and has countless hiking trails and picnic areas. One of the most popular, though strenuous, trails, the **La Luz Trail** (7½ mi., elevation gain 3200 ft.), begins at Juan Tabo Picnic Area and climbs from a hot desert climate to the cool forest at the top of the Sandía Crest. In summer, it's best to get an early start to avoid afternoon storms. From Exit 167 on I-40, drive north on Tramway Blvd. 10 mi. to Forest Rd. 333. The **Sandía Ranger Station,** 11776 Hwy. 337, in Tijeras, has more information on hiking trails in the Sandía Mountains. (Take I-40 to Exit 175. ☎ 281-3304. Open M-F 8am-5pm, Sa-Su 8:30am-4:30pm.) To get to the top without a lot of effort, visitors can ride the world's longest tramway, the **Sandía Peak Tramway,** 10 Tramway Loop NE. From the top of the tram, see views encompassing 11,000 sq. mi. (☎ 856-7325. Runs every 20min. daily 9am-9pm. $17.50, over 62 and 13-20 $15, ages 5-12 $10.) The Sandía Mountains also have excellent biking trails. Try the moderate **Foothills Trail** (7 mi.), which starts at the Elena Gallegos Picnic Area, off Tramway Blvd. The trail winds through the desert, skirting the bottom of the mountains. The most popular place for biking is the **Sandía Peak Ski Area,** 6 mi. up Rte. 536 on the way to Sandía Crest. Bikers can take their bikes up the chairlift and then ride down on 24 mi. of mountain trails and rollers. (☎ 242-9025. Chairlifts run June Sa-Su 10am-4pm; Jul.-Aug. F-Su 10am-4pm. Bike rental at the summit $40 per day. Helmets required. Lift $9; full-day with bike $16.)

Sandía Peak Ski Area, only 30min. from downtown, is a convenient ski area for those who can't escape to Taos or Ruidoso. Four lifts service 30 short trails (35% beginner, 55% intermediate, 10% advanced) on 200 skiable acres. The summit (10,378 ft.) tops a vertical drop of 1700 ft. (☎ 242-9052. Open mid-Dec. to mid-Mar. 9am-4pm. Lift tickets $32 per half-day, $43 per day; ages 13-20 $27/35, seniors and under 13 $24/32.) There are also excellent cross-country skiing trails in the **Cibola National Forest,** particularly the North Crest and 10-K trails.

▶ DAYTRIP FROM ALBUQUERQUE

PETROGLYPH NATIONAL MONUMENT. Located on Albuquerque's west side, this national monument features more than 20,000 images etched into lava rocks between AD 1300 and 1650, mostly by Pueblo Indians. The petroglyphs, which choose when and to whom to reveal themselves (according to local Pueblo people), range from mysterious images to more recognizable animals, people, and crosses. The park encompasses over 7000 acres of Albuquerque's West Mesa, a flat "table-top" ringed with black basalt boulders that formed as a result of volcanic activity 150,000 years ago. The most accessible petroglyphs can be found via three short, easy trails (5-30min., allow 45min. to walk all three trails) at **Boca Negra Canyon,** 2 mi. north of the Visitors Center. For those interested in extended hiking, the **Rinconada Canyon Trail** (2½ mi.), 1 mi. south of the Visitors Center, is an easy desert hike with 3500 rock art images along the way. Due to recent thefts, park rangers advise all hikers not to leave any valuables in their cars at the Rinconada Canyon trailhead. To see the nearby volcanoes, take Exit 149 off I-40 and follow Paseo del Volcán to a dirt road. The volcanoes are 4 mi. north of the Exit. *(To reach the Petroglyph National Monument, take I-40 to Unser Blvd. N, Exit 154, and follow signs to the park.* ☎ *899-0205. Park open daily 8am-5pm. Boca Negra Canyon M-F $1, Sa-Su $2; National Parks Passport accepted. Rinconada Canyon and volcanoes free.)*

CHACO CULTURE NATIONAL HISTORICAL PARK ☎ 505

Sun-scorched Chaco Canyon served as the first great settlement of the Ancestral Puebloans, known as the Chacoans, and the center of a complex trading civilization that began around AD 800 and lasted nearly 300 years. The nine Great Houses found at Chaco Culture National Historical Park (NHP), massive and intricate multi-story dwellings, date from the 9th century and show the Chacoans' true genius; the carefully planned and constructed buildings feature irrigation systems, storage rooms, and enormous plazas. The most celebrated of the Great Houses is the magnificent **Pueblo Bonito,** a 4-5 story D-shaped structure with over 600 rooms, dozens of interior *kivas,* and two plazas. Though the ruins were designated a

National Monument in 1907, the significance of the Chacoans in the history of mankind's development was officially recognized in 1987, when UNESCO designated the monument a World Heritage site. Today, Chaco is admired by all visitors who venture into the desert, as well as revered by the Hopi, Navajo, and Puebloan people who consider the mystical canyon part of their sacred homeland.

The **Chaco Visitors Center,** at the east end of the park, has a free museum with Ancestral Puebloan art and two films (25min. and 1hr.) that detail the archaeology of the ruins. The free Chaco Night Sky Program—an astronomy program and solar observation—is held from April to October on Tuesday, Friday, and Saturday at 9pm. All the ruins have explanatory brochures (free to borrow, $0.50-0.75 to purchase), and from April to October, rangers lead guided tours of Pueblo Bonito (daily 10am and 2pm), beginning at the Pueblo Bonito parking lot. (☎786-7014. Open daily 8am-5pm. $8 per vehicle, pay entrance fee at Visitors Center.) The largest sites, including **Pueblo Bonito, Chetro Ketl, Pueblo del Arroyo, Hungo Pavi, Casa Rinconada,** and **Una Vida,** are accessible by short paths from the main **Canyon Loop Drive** (8 mi.). **Backcountry hiking trails** lead to the other Great Houses; get a free backcountry permit from the Visitors Center or at any trailhead. One of the best backcountry hikes is the moderate **Pueblo Alto Trail** (5½ mi. round-trip, 3-4hr.). After a steep, rocky climb to the mesa top, the trail becomes easier and loops around the mesa and canyon rims, providing access to Pueblo Alto and New Alto, as well as impressive views of Pueblo Bonito, Chetro Ketl, and the San Juan Basin. Those wanting to cut the hike shorter can stop at the **Pueblo Bonito Overlook** (2 mi. round-trip) or at **Pueblo Alto** (3¼ mi. round-trip). All trails and Canyon Loop Dr. are open daily from sunrise to sunset.

An inexpensive lodging option nearby is the ⊠**Circle A Ranch ❶,** an adobe hacienda on a sprawling mountain ranch just northwest of Cuba. The spacious living room, cheery kitchen, and two-story shady porch makes it a peaceful place to relax, aided by massages from the on-site therapists ($35 per 30min.). Hiking trails can also be found nearby. The ranch is 5 mi. east of U.S. 550 on Los Piños Rd. Turn at the cattle guard and follow the signs along Los Piños. (☎289-3350. Open May-Oct. Reservations recommended. Dorms $20; private rooms $45, with bath $55; tent sites $20. Cash or check only.) **The Gallo Campground ❶,** 1 mi. from the Visitors Center, offers serene desert camping with little shade for $10 per site; register at the campground. The 49 tent and RV sites are near a small ruin and have grills, tables, and flush toilets; the only water is at the Visitors Center. Since there is no food in the park, visitors should head to Cuba to silence their growling stomachs. **El Bruno's ❷,** 6453 Hwy. 550, in Cuba, has incredible Mexican food—their fresh ingredients and delectable marinades are an oasis in the midst of the diner food and refried beans so prevalent in western New Mexico. The chicken and beef fajitas ($15), packed with bell peppers and onions, sizzle. (☎289-9429. Entrees $8-16. Open daily 11am-10pm. AmEx/D/MC/V.) **Presciliano's Cafe ❷,** 6478 Hwy. 550, in Cuba, is great for breakfast: the giant cinnamon rolls ($2) are incredible. For lunch or dinner, the 8 oz. ranchero cheeseburger ($6) with red chile and beans is delicious. (☎289-3177. Mexican entrees $5-8. Open daily 8am-9pm. AmEx/D/MC/V.)

Chaco Canyon is 92 mi. northeast of Gallup. From the north, take U.S. 550 (formerly Rte. 44) to County Rd. 7900 (3 mi. east of Nageezi and 50 mi. west of Cuba), follow the road south for 5 mi., then turn right onto the 16 mi. unpaved County Rd. 7950 into the park. From the south, take I-40 to Hwy. 371. Follow Hwy. 371 through Crownpoint to Rte. 9. Take Rte. 9 east for 36 mi., then turn north onto the rough, unpaved Rte. 57 for 20 mi. to the park entrance. There are no services in the park, and gas stations en route are few and far between; the closest one is at the intersection of Rte. 550 and County Road 7900, about 45min. from the park. All routes leading to the park include dirt roads that are infrequently maintained. Be sure to call the park (☎988-6727) to ask about road conditions, which can deteriorate in bad weather, necessitating 4WD or leading to road closures.

EL MORRO NATIONAL MONUMENT   ☎505

Though relatively small in comparison to other Southwestern national parks and monuments, El Morro National Monument and its centerpiece, **Inscription Rock,** are still fascinating pieces of geological history. The park is best known for the names and poems carved into the 200 ft. tall Inscription Rock by Spanish and English explorers and settlers. The natural rainwater pool found at the base of the massive rock made the site a popular stop for weary desert travelers, who, beginning in 1605 with the first governor of New Mexico, signed their names into the rock to record their long journeys. The monument has two hiking options that bring visitors face-to-face with the signatures. The half-mile, wheelchair-accessible **Inscription Rock Trail** winds around the base of the rock, providing excellent views of the signatures, petroglyphs dating to the 13th century, and the rainwater pool. The **Mesa Top Trail** (2 mi., 1hr. round-trip) continues from the Inscription Rock Trail, climbing 200 ft. to the top of the rock. Before descending back to the Visitors Center, the trail circles an 875-room Pueblo built by the Anasazi in 1275. This trail is well-marked and has impressive panoramas of the region. A trail guide that details the most famous engravings and provides translations of those in foreign script is available to borrow from the Visitors Center. The trails close 1hr. before the Visitors Center. The monument is located west of the Continental Divide on Rte. 53, 125 mi. west of Albuquerque, 42 mi. west of the I-40 Exit at Grants, and 56 mi. southeast of Gallup. The **Visitors Center** includes a small museum, a 15min. video on the history of the area, and warnings against adding your own signature. (☎783-4226. Open daily Memorial Day-Labor Day 8am-7pm; Labor Day-Memorial Day 9am-6pm. $3, under 16 free.) The small, peaceful, and shady **El Morro Campground ❶** rarely fills up and has running water, picnic tables, fire pits, and pit toilets. (9 first-come, first-served sites. $5.)

TRUTH OR CONSEQUENCES   ☎505

In 1950, the popular radio game show *Truth or Consequences* (later a TV show by the same name) celebrated its 10th anniversary by seeking a town to rename in its honor. Cities from all over the US volunteered, and Hot Springs, NM was selected. Renamed Truth or Consequences on national television, this dusty town became the center of public attention. Despite two subsequent referendums to change the town's name, the residents have chosen to retain "Truth or Consequences." Today, the odd name still draws inquisitive tourists, but the majority of visitors come for the natural hot springs that lie underneath the town along the Rio Grande. The baths in "T or C" (tee-er-see) take the meaning of relaxation to a whole new level.

■■ **ORIENTATION AND PRACTICAL INFORMATION.** T or C sits about 150 mi. south of Albuquerque on I-25. Greyhound, 8 Date St., inside C.W.'s Premium Water and Ice (☎894-3649), runs **buses** to Albuquerque (3hr., 1 per day, $35.75). The **Visitors Center,** 205 Main St., has free maps and excellent area brochures. (☎894-1968. Open M-F 9am-4pm, Sa 9am-3pm, Su 11am-4pm.) **Internet Access: Public Library,** 325 Library Ln., off Third St. (☎894-3027. Free. Open M-F 9am-7pm, Sa 11am-4pm.) For Wi-Fi, head to the 4th St. **Computer Lab,** 360 W. 4th St. (☎894-4633. Open M, W, and F 10am-5pm; Tu and Th noon-5pm.) **Post Office:** 300 Main St. Open M-F 9am-3pm. **Postal Code:** 87901.

■ **ACCOMMODATIONS AND FOOD. Riverbend Hot Springs ❶,** 100 Austin St., has the nicest outdoor mineral baths in the area and is conveniently located along the Rio Grande. Friendly service and complimentary soaks make up for the small beds and dorms' worn-out appearance. (☎894-7625; www.riverbend-hotsprings.com. Kitchen and lounge area. Reception 10am-10pm; call ahead for late-night arrivals. Linen included. Dorms $25; private rooms $40-85. Tent sites $20. Discount for AAA members and college students. AmEx/D/MC/V.) Budget hotels line N. Date St., just off I-25 at Exit 70. Most offer standard lodging for around $30, but you'll have to go elsewhere for hot springs. In the center of downtown T or C, the **Charles Motel and Hot Mineral Bath Spa ❷,** 601 Broadway, has large rooms with A/C, cable TV, and kitchenettes. The motel maintains indoor mineral baths (one complimentary soak for guests) and roof-top jacuzzis. (☎894-7154 or 800-317-4518; www.charlesspa.com. Singles $35; doubles $50. AmEx/D/MC/V.) Campers at the nearby **Elephant Butte Lake State Park ❶,** which maintains over 150 sandy sites close to the water, have access to restrooms and cold showers. (Reservations ☎877-664-7787. Primitive sites $8; developed sites with showers $10, with electricity $14.)

Nearly all of the restaurants in Truth or Consequences are as easy on the wallet as the area's baths are on the body. For delicious gourmet food at budget prices, try the **Pacific Grille ❷,** 800 N. Date St. With its eclectic menu of various Asian and seafood specialties, ranging from chicken chow mein in garlic with black bean sauce ($6) to linguini with clams and blue cheese pesto ($10). Most entrees include a salad. (☎894-7687. Entrees $6-10. Open Tu-Sa 11am-2pm, 5-9pm. AmEx/D/MC/V.) **Bar-B-Que on Broadway ❷,** 308 Broadway, dishes up numerous breakfast specials that start at $2.50 and hearty barbecue lunches running $5-8. For those not in the mood for ribs, the Bar-B-Que also serves a selection of burgers and sandwiches ($4-7). For breakfast, the two egg, two pancake, two bacon special for $3.25 is an unbeatable deal. (☎894-7047. Open M-Sa 7am-4pm. AmEx/D/MC/V.) The **Happy Belly Deli ❶,** 313 Broadway, lives up to its name with satisfying food, a beautiful garden patio, and low prices, though service can be slow. Choose from their list of sandwiches (the "Green Chile Philly" is great) or build your own for $5. (☎894-3354. Open Tu-F 7am-4pm, Sa 8am-4pm. MC/V.)

■ **SIGHTS AND OUTDOOR ACTIVITIES.** The town's main attractions are its mineral baths. Apache legend and local testament claim the baths will heal virtually any ailment—doctors have been sending patients with rheumatism and arthritis here since the 30s. All mineral baths are odor-free, have a neutral pH, and are composed chiefly of sodium chloride and bicarbonate. Outdoor tubs are located at **Riverbend Hot Springs** (see above), where there are four alongside the Río Grande. You can even head for the chilly river if you want some refreshment after cleansing your pores in the hot water. Access to the baths is $10 per hr. for public baths, $15 per hr. for private bath, and complimentary for guests. (Open daily 7am-10pm.) **Hay-O-Kay Hot Springs,** 300 Austin St., also has two outdoor mineral pools with gravel bottoms and free-flowing water, in addition to five indoor tubs. (☎894-2228. Open W-Su 10am-7pm.)

Five miles north of T or C, **Elephant Butte Lake State Park** features New Mexico's largest lake (take Date St. north to a sign for Elephant Butte; turn right onto Hwy. 181 and follow the signs to the park's main entrance). Once the site of the Battle of Valverde during the Civil War, a public works project dammed up the Río Grande in 1916. The resulting lake is named after the elephantine rock formation at its southern end. The park, constructed by members of the Civilian Conservation Corps in the 30s, has miles of sandy beaches and a marina (day use $5). **Marina del Sur,** just inside the park, rents all kinds of boats for those who do not bring their own water toys. (☎744-5567. Paddleboats and kayaks $30 per hr.; waterski boats

$225 per 3hr. Must be 21+.) **Sports Adventure,** on the lake at 100 Long Point Rd. 11 mi. north of the park's main entrance, rents jet skis. (☎744-5557 or 888-736-8420. Rentals from $65 per hr.; deposit $100.) There is a **Visitors Center** at the entrance to the park with a small, free museum on the area's natural and social history. (☎877-664-7787. Open M-F 7:30am-4pm, Sa-Su 7:30am-10pm.) The **Luchini Trail,** an easy 1½ mi. hike, begins in the parking lot just past the Visitors Center.

GILA CLIFF DWELLINGS NATIONAL MONUMENT ☎505

The mysterious **Gila Cliff Dwellings National Monument** is set distantly into the Gila National Forest amid acres of mountains and pine forest. The secluded but spectacular monument contains 40 stone and timber rooms carved into a cliff's natural caves by the Mogollon tribe in 1280 AD. About a dozen families lived here for 20 years, farming beans, corn, and squash on the mesa top and along the river. During the early 14th century, however, the Mogollon abandoned their homes; archaeologists are still unsure of the exact reason for their abrupt departure. Today, visitors are not limited to photography, as is the case at many of the cliff dwellings throughout the Southwest; at Gila, tourists have the unique opportunity to explore inside the ruins, ascending to the homes via ladders and stairs.

The 1 mi. round-trip hike to the dwellings begins with a steep ascent up the canyon walls (those with bad knees should not attempt the hike), but the rest of the hike is fairly easy. A **free trail guide** is available at the trailhead, approximately 2 mi. from the Visitors Center along a paved road. Those who want more info about the ruins can go on one of the free, 1hr. ranger-guided tours (noon in winter; 11am and 2pm in summer) that meet at the first overhang—allow 20min. to hike there. (Dwellings open daily late May-early Sept. 8am-6pm; late Sept.-early May 9am-4pm. $3, under 16 free.) Visitors can also check out several **natural hot springs** in the forest. Ask at the Visitors Center for specific trail information. **Jordan Hot Spring,** at a comfortable 90°F, can be reached via **Little Bear Canyon Trail,** departing from the **TJ Corral trailhead** (6½ mi. one-way) or **Middle Fork Trail** (8 mi. one-way). **Lightfeather Hot Spring** is closer (only ½ mi. behind the Visitors Center departing from the Middle Fork Trailhead), but at 140°F, it will burn skin unless mixed with river water. 3½ mi. south of the Visitors Center, **Gila Hot Springs Campground,** on Access Rd., also maintains several sandy-bottomed hot springs. (☎536-3600. $3 to soak, $4 to camp.) A series of trails into the surrounding Gila Wilderness also depart from trailheads near the Visitors Center; ask at the Visitors Center for more information for day-long and overnight hikes.

The park has four **free campgrounds:** Forks, Grapevine, Upper Scorpion, and Lower Scorpion ❶. **Forks** and **Grapevine** are located 4 mi. south of the Visitors Center on Rte. 15, and have pit toilets but no water. **Upper** and **Lower Scorpion** are located along the road from the Visitors Center to the cliff dwellings trailhead. Water, picnic tables, grills, and pit toilets are available; there are no hookups, but the park does have a dump station. The nearest indoor accommodations can be found at **The Breathe Inn** ❸, 20 mi. south at the intersection of Forest Rd. 15 and Rte. 35. This remote lodge draws as many as 4000 hummingbirds on summer weekends, making it a tranquil place to relax and birdwatch. (☎536-3206. Singles $40-45; doubles $45-50; suites $65-75. AmEx/D/MC/V.) The adjoining **cafe** ❶ offers sandwiches, great homemade cookies, and ice cream, as well as some dinner options. (Sandwiches $3-7. Ice cream $1.25 per scoop. Open M and W-Su 8am-4pm. AmEx/D/MC/V.) In Silver City, **The Palace Hotel** ❸, 106 W. Broadway, has soft, comfortable beds and a homey atmosphere. Cable TV, continental breakfast, and gym access are included, though there is no A/C. (☎388-1811. Rooms from $44. AmEx/D/MC/V.) Nearby, **Javalina Café** ❷, 201 N. Bullard St., has the best coffee and iced tea around, chocolate-covered cinnamon rolls ($3), and free Wi-Fi. (☎388-1350.

THE SOUTHWEST

Open daily 6:30am-10pm. MC/V.) If you're looking for something more substantial, head to the locally adored **Jalisco Cafe** ❷, 103 S. Bullard St., for spicy Mexican dishes ($6-10) and hibiscus iced tea. Watch out, as its popularity makes for long lines. (☎388-2060. Open M-Sa 11am-8:30pm. MC/V.)

Gila Cliff Dwellings National Monument is 44 mi. north of Silver City on Rte. 15. The road is narrow, winding, and requires about 2hr. Road conditions can be impassable in winter, and the road is not plowed on nights and weekends, so pay attention to the weather and road conditions. The **Visitors Center,** at the end of Rte. 15, shows a film and sells maps of the Gila National Forest and Gila Wilderness Area. (☎536-9461. Open daily in summer 8am-5pm; in winter 8am-4:30pm.)

WHITE SANDS NATIONAL MONUMENT ☎505

Putting the red rocks and cacti of other monuments to shame, White Sands National Monument, the world's largest gypsum dune field, is a stark contrast to typical Southwestern terrain. The rolling dune field formed as rainwater flushed the minerals from the nearby peaks into Lake Lucero. As the lake evaporated in the desert heat, the gypsum crystals were left behind to form the 275 sq. mi. of blindingly white sand dunes. These drifts of fine sand create the appearance of the snow-covered arctic tundra, but don't be fooled: the midday sun assaults the shadeless dunes with practically unbearable light and heat—be prepared with protective clothing and eyewear, heavy-duty sunscreen, and plenty of water to prevent dehydration and sunstroke. Trekking, rolling through, or sliding down the dunes via sleds can provide hours of mindless fun or mindful soul-searching, especially at sunset or under the brilliance of a full moon.

■◪ **ORIENTATION AND PRACTICAL INFORMATION.** White Sands is on Rte. 70, 15 mi. southwest of Alamogordo and 52 mi. northeast of Las Cruces. The **Visitors Center** itself has a small museum on the dunes' formation with a 17min. introductory video and a gift shop. (☎479-6124. Park open daily June-Aug. 7am-10pm, last entrance 9pm; Sept.-May 7am-sunset. Visitors Center open daily June-Aug. 8am-6pm; Sept.-May 8am-5pm. The entrance booth distributes a park map with trail information. Park admission $3, under 16 free.) Rte. 70 from Las Cruces to just past the monument is prone to closures because of the nearby military base, and delays can run up to 1hr.; call the Visitors Center to check the road status. The park's Visitors Center has vending machines, but the nearest **ATM, restaurants, grocery store, hospital, Internet access,** and **post office** are in Alamogordo. No public transit serves the park. For more info, visit www.nps.gov/whsa.

◪ **ACCOMMODATIONS.** The only way to sleep in the park is to camp at one of the park's **backcountry campsites** ❶. Ten daily permits for the sites ($3 per person plus the park entry fee, 6-person max. per site) are first come, first served. The sites have no water or toilets (there is a restroom at the trailhead), and are not accessible by road, requiring up to a 2 mi. hike through the dunes. Campers must register in person at the Visitors Center and be at their sites before sunset. Campfires are prohibited. Sleeping amid the white dunes is extraordinary, but plan ahead because sites can fill up early on full-moon nights. Occasionally, the sites are closed due to missile range launches; call the Visitors Center for closings. For indoor lodging, the closest options are in Alamogordo. **Classic Inn** ❷, 710 N. White Sands Blvd., has comfortable and clean rooms with A/C, HBO, microwave, refrigerator, and Wi-Fi. (☎437-0210. Singles $31; doubles $35. AmEx/MC/V.) If you want to camp but can't wrangle a permit, the **Alamogordo Roadrunner Campground** ❷, 412

THE REAL DEAL. The 275 sq. mi. of snow white dunes at White Sands National Monument are spectacular, but summer temperatures over 100°F can turn a quick stroll along the sand into an exhausting, sweaty experience. To best appreciate the Monument's beauty, come to the park at dusk; the temperature drops, the stars and the moon come out, and the dunes become the perfect place for a romantic picnic or a sledding party. The park stays open until 10pm during the summer (last entry 9pm). —*Caroline Pierce*

E. 24th St., has well-maintained tent and RV sites with a pool, hot showers, and coin-op laundry. (☎437-3003; www.roadrunnercampground.com. Reception 8am-8pm. Tent sites $20, RV sites $22. MC/V.)

SIGHTS AND OUTDOOR ACTIVITIES. The 8 mi. **Dunes Drive,** beginning just past the Visitors Center, is a good way see White Sands. However, really experiencing the monument means getting out and walking or sliding down the dunes. Off-trail hiking is allowed anywhere in the park, and there are several points along Dunes Drive to park your car. Anyone considering a backcountry hike should bring a compass and map or a GPS—it's easy to get lost, though the two mountain ranges that border the dune fields can serve as valuable reference points. Rangers recommend that all backcountry hikers check in with trail registers, located at the Alaki Flat Trailhead and at the Nature Center. The park's only wheelchair-accessible trail is the **Interdune Boardwalk,** an easy half-mile walk above the sand with exhibits on area plants and wildlife. The longest hike maintained by the park is the **Alkali Flat Trail** (4½ mi., 3hr. round-trip), a moderately strenuous loop through the heart of the dunes to the prehistoric lakebed of Lake Otero, but it isn't necessary to hike the whole thing in order to see spectacular vistas. The trail is marked by white posts with orange reflective tape, but do not attempt this hike in strong winds, when blowing sand makes it easy to lose the trail. Bring lots of water and protect yourself from the sun; there is no water or shade on the trail. The **Dune Life Nature Trail,** 1 mi. round-trip, is an easier hike along the edge of the dunes.

There is a free, guided sunset stroll most evenings at 7pm (call ahead to the Visitors Center or check the website for possible cancellations), and on Friday and Saturday nights June-Aug., park rangers give evening talks on various topics (8:30pm). On full-moon nights in the summer, the park stays open late (until 11pm, last entry 10pm), and a guest speaker presents a program at the park's amphitheater on a topic relating to the Southwest at 8:30pm. A star talk takes place some Fridays during the summer at 8:30pm. Once a month, a ranger-guided expedition heads for the dry crystal bed of **Lake Lucero.** (Tours 3hr., 1½ mi. round-trip. Reservations required. Call a week in advance to secure a spot. $3.) For all ranger programs, call the Visitors Center or check the website for exact times and possible cancellations. The monument is surrounded by the **White Sands Missile Range.** Thirty miles north of the monument off U.S. 70, the White Sands Missile Range Museum, the birthplace of U.S. space and missile activity and the site of the first atomic bomb test in 1945, has an extensive collection of missiles both inside the museum and in the outdoor missile park, not to mention the original Darth Vader mask used in Star Wars. Be prepared for rigorous security checks if you want to check out the museum—driver's license, registration, and proof of insurance are required of all visitors. (☎678-8824; www.wsmr-history.org. Open M-F 8am-4pm, Sa-Su 10am-3pm. Free.) In Alamogordo, the **New Mexico Museum of Space History,** on Scenic Drive off of Hwy. 70, has four floors of interesting exhibits ranging from rocket science to satellites to the future of space exploration. The "Golden Cube," as the museum is called, also houses the **International Space Hall of Fame** and an

THE SOUTHWEST

IMAX Theater. (☎437-2840. Open daily 9am-5pm. Museum $3, military and seniors $2.75, ages 4-12 $2.50. IMAX tickets $6/5.50/4.50; call for times.)

ROSWELL ☎505

Roswell was an otherwise small town known only for its dairy industry when life was unexpectedly shaken up by extraterrestials. The fascination began in July 1947, when an alien spacecraft reportedly crashed on a ranch. The official press release reported that the military had recovered pieces of a "flying saucer," but a retraction followed the next day—the wreckage, the government claimed, was actually a weather balloon. The incident was the birth of alien-curiosity in Roswell, the beginning of multiple government conspiracy theories, and a jumping-off point for other alien and UFO sightings around the country. Today, traveling skeptics and science fiction aficionados have made tourism a far more lucrative industry than dairy cows, and most leave Roswell entertained, if not enlightened. During the first week of July, the town's **UFO Festival** celebrates the anniversary of the encounter, attracting thousands with out-of-town lecturers, music performances, an alien-infested haunted house, and the 10K/5K "Alien Chase" race. With a plastic flying saucer above its storefront, the popular **International UFO Museum and Research Center**, 114 N. Main St., recounts the events near Roswell in 1947. Exhibits contain numerous testimonials and newspaper clippings about the incident as well as the history of UFO sightings throughout time. The museum also houses an extraterrestrial themed art gallery. The research library, full of government reports, UFO documentation, magazines, and books, is the only one of its kind in the US. Peruse the shelves for such fantastic titles as "Contact Has Begun" and "Angels and Aliens." (☎625-9495. Open daily 9am-5pm. Adults $5, ages 5-15 $2, seniors and military $3. Audio tour $1.)

Roswell caters to the tourists who patronize it, and it's difficult to find restaurants and accommodations that are not part of popular chains. Such chain motels line Main St., but the **Frontier Motel ❷**, 3010 N. Main St., offers a respite with clean, large rooms, a pool, friendly service, and Wi-Fi. (☎622-1400. Continental breakfast included. Rooms from $42. D/MC/V.) Fast-food restaurants are also prevalent in Roswell, though there are a few alternatives. For sit-down meals just like Mom used to make, **Nuthin' Fancy Cafe ❶**, 2103 N. Main St., promises guests "home cooking without the mess." For breakfast, their "2-fer" deal (½ waffle, 2 eggs, 2 sausage), is filling and tasty, if a bit greasy. (☎624-5399. Steaks $9.

Burgers and sandwiches $6-7. Slice of homemade pie $2. M-Sa 6am-8:30pm, Su 6am-2pm. MC/V.) **Tía Juana's ❹**, 3601 N. Main St., beckons all travelers with its cheery outdoor patio and excellent Tex-Mex cuisine. Refresh yourself with something from the huge margarita menu. (☎624-6113. Margaritas $5-8. Entrees $10-15. F live music. Open M-Th 11am-9:30pm, F-Sa 11am-10pm, Su 11am-9pm. AmEx/D/MC/V.)

Aside from its extraterrestrial peculiarities, Roswell is a relatively normal town. The intersection of **2nd Street** (Rte. 70/380) and **Main Street** (Rte. 285) is the center of downtown, where alien-themed shops and restaurants can be found. To reach Roswell from Albuquerque, head 60 mi. west on I-40, then 138 mi. south on U.S. Hwy. 285. Greyhound, 1100 N. Virginia Ave. (☎622-2510; www.greyhound.com), in conjunction with TNM&O Coaches, runs **buses** to Albuquerque (4hr., 1 per day, $41) and El Paso (5hr., 2 per day, $44-47). Pecos Trails Transit, 515 N. Main St., runs **buses** all over town. (☎624-6766. Open M-F 6am-10:30pm, Sa 7:10am-10pm, Su 10:30am-7pm. $0.75, students $0.50, seniors $0.35.) The **Visitors Center** is at 926 N. Main St. (☎624-0889 or 623-5695. Open M-F 8:30am-5:30pm, Sa-Su 10am-3pm.) **Internet** access: **Roswell Public Library**, 301 N. Pennsylvania Ave. (☎622-7101. Open M-Tu 9am-9pm, W-Sa 9am-6pm, Su 2-6pm.) **Post Office:** 415 N. Pennsylvania Ave. (☎623-7232. Open M-F 7:30am-5:30pm, Sa 8am-noon.) **Postal Code:** 88202.

CARLSBAD CAVERNS NATIONAL PARK ☎505

Filled with enormous, haunting cave chambers, the world's deepest limestone cave, and six-story speleothems, Carlsbad Caverns can prompt even the most jaded caver to do a double-take. The caverns' jaw-dropping formations were formed over hundreds of thousands of years as water droplets trickled down limestone rock and slowly calcified in the cave's cool, moist environment. The aptly-named **Big Room** is the park's central and most accessible attraction. To call this cave spectacular would be an understatement; this is the park's must-see. An easy 1¼ mi. self-guided tour circumscribes the 14-acre chamber, highlighting subterranean wonders like the **Hall of Giants,** where the cave's three largest formations stand, the Rock of Ages, and the Bottomless Pit (not actually bottomless, the pit descends 140 ft.). The Big Room can be reached either by a steep hike down the natural entrance (800 ft. drop; 1¼ mi., 1 hr.) or via elevator. (Natural entrance open daily June to mid-Aug. 8:30am-3:30pm; mid-Aug. to May 8:30am-2pm. Elevators open daily June to mid-Aug. 8:30am-5pm; mid-Aug. to May 8:30am-3:30pm. Segments of trail wheelchair-accessible. $6, under 15 free. Audio tour $3.) To explore other areas of the park's main cave, visitors must join a ranger-led tour; reservations for all tours are recommended up to six weeks in advance. The **King's Palace Tour,** guided by a ranger, goes through four of the cave's lowest rooms at a depth of 829 ft. (May-Aug. 1½hr. tours 10, 11am, 1, 3pm; Sept.-Apr. 10am and 2pm only. Reservations recommended. $8, ages 6-15 $4.) Other guided tours in the park's main cave include a slippery tour though the **Left Hand Tunnel** lit only by lanterns (departs from Visitors Center; 2hr.; daily 9am; $7) and a moderately strenuous tour of the **Lower Cave** that descends 10 ft. via knotted rope and 50 ft. on ladders. (3hr. M-F 1pm. Helmets, kneepads, and headlamps provided. $20. Bring gloves and 4 AA batteries.) Plan your visit for late afternoon to catch the **bat flight.** The ritual, during which thousands of hungry bats storm out of the cave, is preceded by a ranger talk 30min.-1hr. before sunset. (May-Oct. daily just before sunset. Call ahead for specific times.) Be aware that while photography inside most of the cave is permitted, pictures of the bat flight are strictly forbidden. The park's **wild caves** can be explored with a backcountry cave permit, but eager spelunkers should have extensive experience with reading topographic maps, technical climbing, and hiking in a desert climate. (☎785-2232, ext. 3104. Send application to Visitors Center 1

SPELUNKING IS FOR LOVERS. If you're visiting Carlsbad Caverns National Park, be sure to bring a sweater or a light jacket (the caves are a cool 55°F in the summer). Also, a flashlight can help you to get a better look at particularly fascinating formations. Though you may want to take pictures, beware that many will not come out—the cave is simply too dark.

month in advance. Must be over 16 for most caves. Free.) **Backcountry hiking** and camping are permitted above ground (though the park's feature attractions all lie underground), but a **free permit** (available at the Visitors Center) is required and a map and at least a gallon of water per person per day are recommended. The **Caverns Visitors Center** has trail maps and tour info. (☎785-2232. Open daily June-late Aug. 8am-7pm; late Aug.-May 8am-5pm.) Make reservations through the Guided Tour Reservation Hotline (☎877-444-6777) or at www.recreation.gov.

Tours of the park's undeveloped **Slaughter Canyon Cave** can be a dirty and challenging (though exhilarating) caving experience. A car is required to get to the cave; there's no public transit, and the parking lot is a 35-40min. drive down the mostly paved Rte. 418, several miles south of the main entrance to the park on U.S. 62/180. The cave entrance is a steep, strenuous half-mile hike from the lot. Ranger-led tours, which meet at the cave's entrance (bring a flashlight), traverse difficult, slippery, and muddy terrain; there are no paved trails or handrails. (2hr. tours June-Aug. daily 10am and 1pm, Sept.-May Sa-Su 10am only. $15, ages 6-15 $7.50.) Tours of the **Hall of the White Giant** and **Spider Cave** require crawling and climbing through tight passages. (☎800-967-2283. Tours 4hr. 1 per week. $20.) Again, for all ranger-led tours, make reservations early; six weeks in advance is recommended.

The park has no indoor accommodations or campgrounds, though it does have a **restaurant ❶** with sandwiches ($4-5), pizza ($6), and burgers ($5) for pre-hike nourishment. (Open daily 8:30am-6:30pm.) A slew of budget motels line U.S. 62/180 south of downtown Carlsbad, about 15 mi. north of the park entrance. The **Stage Coach Inn ❷**, 1819 S. Canal St., offers a good value with an outdoor pool, indoor jacuzzi, and laundry. Large rooms have A/C, cable TV, microwaves, and refrigerators. (☎887-1148. Singles $42; doubles $50. AAA and AARP discount 15%. AmEx/D/MC/V.) The **Carlsbad RV Park and Campground ❶**, 4301 National Parks Hwy., 4 mi. south of town, is a campground that has it all with tent and RV sites, a playground, and two wooden cabins with a full-size bed, two bunk beds, A/C, cable, DVD player, microwave, and refrigerator. All guests have access to showers ($3) and an indoor pool. (☎885-6333. Breakfast included Sa-Su. Tent sites $16.50, RV sites $27-31. Cabin $40; linen not provided. MC/V.) Twelve miles north of downtown Carlsbad off of U.S. Hwy. 285, **Brantley Lake State Park ❶** has 51 campsites close to the lake's edge with water, hookups, picnic tables, grills, restrooms, and hot showers. (☎457-2384. 25 sites available by reservation; ☎877-644-7787; some first-come, first-served. Primitive sites $8, with full hook-up $14.) Fuel up for the trip to the caverns with fresh-baked pastries and coffee at the ▨**Blue House Bakery and Cafe ❶**, 609 N. Canyon. This converted blue house, which is very popular with locals, has sandwiches, smoothies, and a relaxing garden patio. The warm, moist buttermilk cinnamon muffin is a delicious way to start the day ($2). (☎628-0555. Open M-F 6am-2pm, Sa 7am-noon. MC/V.) For lunch or dinner, everyone in town loves **Lucy's Mexicali Restaurant and Entertainment Club ❷**, 701 S. Canal St. Lucy's serves the best tamales ($2) around, and the cheap combo plates ($5-9) are bang for your buck. (☎887-7714. Sa live music and karaoke. Open M-Th 11am-9pm, F-Sa 11am-9:30pm. AmEx/D/MC/V.)

Carlsbad Caverns National Park is located 20 mi. southwest of the town of Carlsbad on U.S. Hwy 62/180. The closest town to the park, though a bit of a tourist pit stop, is White's City, on U.S. 62/180, 20 mi. southwest of downtown Carlsbad and 6 mi. from the Visitors Center. Flash floods occasionally close the roads; call the park for road conditions. **El Paso, TX** (p. 680) is the nearest big city, 136 mi. west past **Guadalupe Mountains National Park** (p. 680). Greyhound, with TNM&O Coaches, runs three **buses** per day between El Paso and Carlsbad (3hr., $38.50) and will stop at White's City. **Post Office:** 23 Carlsbad Caverns Hwy. (☎785-2220. Open M-F 8am-noon and 1-3pm, Sa 8am-noon.) **Postal Code:** 88268.

CALIFORNIA

California and its iconic Hwy. 1 offer a wild ride—exhilaration doesn't begin to describe the feeling of being poised upon the very western edge of the country, with better times and wilder sights in the cliff-hugging turns ahead, and the past receding in your rearview mirror. Glaring movie spotlights, clanging San Francisco cable cars, vanilla-scented Jeffrey pines, alpine lakes, and ghostly desert landscapes all thrive in California. Indeed, there's so much going on you'd need a whole book (like *Let's Go: California*) to describe it.

HIGHLIGHTS OF CALIFORNIA

GAWK at the hard bodies on Venice Beach, stroll down the Walk of Fame, or (window) shop along Rodeo Drive, all while eating an In-N-Out burger, in **Los Angeles** (p. 886).

MARVEL at the tallest waterfall in North America at **Yosemite National Park** (p. 926).

GULP glass after glass of free wine at the countless vineyards of **Napa Valley** (p. 873).

PEER past the towers of San Francisco's **Golden Gate Bridge** and watch the sun fade into the Pacific Ocean (p. 850).

⚡ PRACTICAL INFORMATION

Capital: Sacramento.

Visitor Info: California Office of Tourism, P.O. Box 1499, Sacramento 95812 (☎800-862-2543; www.visitcalifornia.com). **California State Parks Department,** 1416 9th St., Sacramento 94296 (☎800-777-0369; www.parks.ca.gov).

Postal Abbreviation: CA. **Sales Tax:** 7.25-8.75%, depending on county.

SAN FRANCISCO   ☎415

If California is a state of mind, San Francisco is surely euphoria. This city will take you to new highs, leaving your mind spinning, your taste buds tingling, and your calves aching. Though it's smaller than most "big" cities, the City by the Bay more than compensates for its size with personality that simply won't quit. The city packs an incredible amount of vitality into its 47 sq. mi. of thriving art communities, bustling shops, and diverse nightlife. For more coverage of San Francisco, see *Let's Go: San Francisco.*

✈ INTERCITY TRANSPORTATION

San Francisco (SF) is 403 mi. north of Los Angeles and 390 mi. south of Oregon. The city lies at the northern tip of the peninsula that separates the San Francisco Bay from the Pacific Ocean. San Francisco is 6hr. from L.A. via I-5, 8hr. via U.S. 101, or 9½hr. via Hwy. 1. From inland California, **I-5** approaches the city from the north and south via **I-580** and **I-80,** which runs across the **Bay Bridge.** From the north, U.S. 101 and Hwy. 1 come over the **Golden Gate Bridge.**

Airport: San Francisco International (SFO; ☎650-821-8211, ground transportation info 650-821-2732; www.flysfo.com), 15 mi. south of downtown via U.S. 101. **Bay**

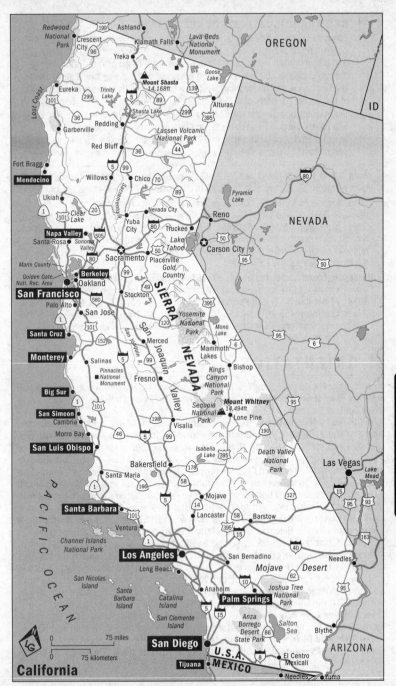

California

SAN FRANCISCO FOR POCKET CHANGE. Life in the City by the Bay isn't cheap by any means, but you don't have to leave penniless. Drop your bag at one of the city's many hostels, or camp at **Marin Headlands** (p. 872) and hike into town across the Golden Gate Bridge. To get oriented, stroll through the city's diverse neighborhoods and attractions with a free **City Guides Walking Tour** (www.sfcityguides.org). Test your bartering skills at the **produce stands** in Chinatown (p. 859) or along 24th St. in the **Mission** (p. 860), and pick up the makings of a fine meal for next to nothing. Got a spare dollar? Stop at **Dick Lee Pastry Shop,** 777 Jackson St., in Chinatown, for six delicious steamed pork buns for $1.10, or **La Victoria,** 2937 24th St., in the Mission, for the city's best *pan dulce* ($1). Remember, the **Legion of Honor** (p. 863) is free on Tuesdays.

Area Rapid Transit (BART; ☎989-2278; www.bart.gov) runs M-F 4am-midnight, Sa 6am-midnight, Su 8am-midnight. $5.15 to downtown, $1.40 within the city.

Trains: Amtrak (☎800-872-7245; www.amtrak.com). Connects from both the East Bay towns of Oakland and Emeryville to downtown SF ($4.50-7.50). To **Los Angeles** (8-12hr., 5 per day, $53-62). **Caltrain** (☎800-660-4287; www.caltrain.org), at 4th and King St. in SoMa (operates M-F 5am-midnight, Sa 7am-midnight, Su 8am-11pm), is a regional commuter train that runs south to Palo Alto ($5.75, seniors and under 12 $2.75) and San Jose ($7.50/3.75).

Buses: Greyhound runs buses from the **Transbay Terminal,** 425 Mission St. (☎495-1569; www.greyhound.com), between Fremont and 1st St., in downtown. To **Los Angeles** (8-13hr., 17 per day, $44) and **Portland** (15-17hr., 5 per day, $72). **Golden Gate Transit** (Marin County: ☎455-2000; www.goldengate.org), **AC Transit** (East Bay: ☎510-817-1717), and **SamTrans** (San Mateo County: 800-660-4287, www.samtrans.org) also stop at the terminal.

■ ORIENTATION

San Francisco's diverse neighborhoods are loosely organized along a few central arteries. **Market Street** runs on a diagonal from the Ferry Building, through downtown, and all the way to the Castro.

Retail-heavy **Union Square,** the center of downtown, is just north of Market St. North of Union Square. **North Beach,** a historically Italian area, overflows with restaurants and cafes, while **Chinatown** is the largest Chinese community outside of Asia. The skyscrapers of the **Financial District** crowd east toward the **Embarcadero** and west to the high-culture **Civic Center,** which lines Market St. and is bounded on the west by Van Ness Ave. Between Union Sq. and Civic Center is the **Tenderloin,** where drugs, crime, and homelessness prevail despite attempts at urban renewal. Northwest of Union Sq., old money presides over ritzy **Nob Hill,** newer money walks its dogs on **Russian Hill** and **Cow Hollow,** and Fillmore St. leads south to the Victorians of **Pacific Heights,** as well as the few *udon*-filled blocks of **Japantown.**

South of Market St. to the east, the **South of Market Area (SoMa)** plays host to museums near 3rd St. and thumping clubs scattered among industrial buildings down to 14th St. To the southwest of SoMa, the trendy **Mission,** largely populated by Latino residents during the day and hip barhoppers by night, takes over south of 14th St., merging into the diners and cafes of the **Castro,** a legendary gay neighborhood. To the south, **Bernal Heights** and **Noe Valley** are largely residential.

Vast **Golden Gate Park** dominates the western half of the peninsula, surrounded by the former hippie haven of the **Haight** to the east and the residential and largely Asian **Richmond District** to the north. **Lincoln Park** reaches westward to the ocean, connecting to Ocean Beach at the foot of Golden Gate Park. The majestic **Golden**

Gate Bridge stretches over the bay from the **Presidio** in San Francisco's northwest corner. Heading east from the bridge, the posh stucco of the **Marina,** cultural **Fort Mason,** and touristy **Fisherman's Wharf** line the north shore of the peninsula. **Alcatraz** sits isolated in the bay.

◨ LOCAL TRANSPORTATION

San Francisco Municipal Railway (MUNI), 1 S. Van Ness Ave. (☎673-6864; www.sfmuni.com), is a system of buses, cable cars, subways, and streetcars and is the most efficient way to get around the city. Runs daily 6am-1am. $1.50, ages 5-17 and seniors $0.50. **MUNI passports** are valid on all MUNI vehicles (1-day $11, 3-day $18, 7-day $24). A weekly pass ($15) is valid for a single work week but requires an additional $1 to ride the cable cars. Wheelchair access varies among routes; all below-ground stations, but not all above-ground sites, are accessible.

Cable cars: Operated by MUNI (see above). Noisy, slow, and usually crammed full, but charming relics. To avoid mobs, ride in the early morning. The **Powell-Mason (PM)** line, which runs to the wharf, is the most popular. The **California (C)** line, from the Financial District up through Nob Hill, is usually the least crowded, but the **Powell-Hyde (PH)** line, with the steepest hills and the sharpest turns, may be the most fun. $5, under 5 free. No transfers.

Bay Area Rapid Transit (BART; ☎989-2278; www.bart.org) operates trains along 5 lines connecting San Francisco with **East Bay** cities, including Berkeley and Oakland, and the Oakland International Airport (OAK). All stations provide maps and schedules. There are 8 BART stops in San Francisco proper. Wheelchair-accessible. Runs M-F 4am-midnight, Sa 6am-midnight, Su 8am-midnight. $1.40-5.15.

Taxi: National Cab, ☎648-4444. **Yellow Cab,** ☎333-3333.

Car Rental: City, 1748 Folsom St. (☎877-861-1312; www.cityrentacar.com), between Duboce and 14th St. $40-50 per day, $180-190 per week. 21+. Under-25 surcharge $8 per day. Open M-F 7:30am-6pm, Sa 9am-4pm. Also at 1433 Bush St. (☎866-359-1331) and 41 San Bruno Ave., near SFO (☎866-359-1331).

TIP **PREVENT RUNAWAYS.** San Francisco's hilly terrain makes parking a challenge. When parking facing uphill, turn the front wheels away from the curb, and, if driving a standard transmission, leave the car in first gear. If your car starts to roll, it will stop (hopefully) when the tires hit the curb. When facing downhill, turn the wheels toward the curb and, if driving a standard transmission, leave the car in reverse. Always set the emergency brake.

◨ PRACTICAL INFORMATION

Visitor Info: Visitor Information Center, 900 Market St. (☎391-2000, 24hr. info 391-2000; www.onlyinsanfrancisco.com), in Hallidie Plaza. Open M-F 9am-5pm, Sa-Su 9am-3pm; Nov.-June closed Su.

Hotlines: AIDS Hotline: ☎863-2437. **Crisis Line for the Handicapped:** ☎800-426-4263. **Drug Crisis Line:** ☎362-3400. **Rape Crisis Center:** ☎647-7273.

Internet Access: San Francisco Public Library Main Branch, 100 Larkin St. (☎557-4400; http://sfpl.lib.ca.us), at Grove St. Free. Open M and Sa 10am-6pm, Tu-Th 9am-8pm, F noon-6pm, Su noon-5pm. Check www.cheesebikini.com for area Wi-Fi locations.

Post Office: Pine Station, 1400 Pine St. (☎351-2435), at Larkin. Open M-F 8am-5:30pm, Sa 8am-3pm. Also at **Macy's Station,** 170 O'Farrell St., in Macy's, near Union Sq. Open M-Sa 10am-5:30pm, Su 11am-5pm. **Postal Code:** 94109.

Downtown San Francisco

🏠 ACCOMMODATIONS

Adelaide Hostel and Hotel,	1	B5
Fisherman's Wharf (HI),	2	A2
Green Tortoise Hostel,	3	C3
Hayes Valley Inn,	4	A6
The Parker Guest House,	5	B7
Phoenix Hotel,	6	A5
Red Victorian Bed, Breakfast, and Art	7	A6
San Francisco International Guesthouse,	8	B7
San Francisco Zen Center,	9	A6
San Remo Hotel,	10	B2

🍴 FOOD

Bissap Baobab,	11	A7
The Butler and the Chef Cafe,	12	D6
Café Bean,	13	B4
Cafe Mason,	14	B5
The California Culinary Academy,	15	A5
The Golden Flower,	16	C3
Home Plate,	17	A2
House of Nanking,	18	C3
King of Thai Noodle House,	19	C5
Lalita Thai Restaurant and Bar,	20	B6
La Boulangerie,	21	A4
La Méditerranée,	22	A4
L'Osteria del Forno,	23	B3

Pork Store Cafe,	24	A6
Q,	25	A4
Rigolo,	26	A4
Steps of Rome Caffe,	27	C3
Taquería Cancún,	28	A7

👁 SIGHTS

California Academy of Sciences,	29	C6
City Hall,	30	A6
City Lights Bookstore,	31	C3
Coit Tower,	32	C2
"Crookedest Street in the World,"	33	B2
Ghiradelli Square,	34	A1
Golden Gate Cookie Factory,	35	C3
Grace Cathedral,	36	B4
Maiden Lane,	37	C5
Ross Alley,	38	C3
San Francisco Art Institute,	39	B2
San Francisco Museum of Modern Art,	40	C5
War Memorial Opera House,	41	A6

Washington Square,	42	C2
Waverly Place,	43	C4
Xanadu Gallery,	44	C5
Yerba Buena Center for the Art,	45	C5

⭐ ENTERTAINMENT/NIGHTLIFE

111 Minna St.,	46	C5
Alonzo King's Lines Contemporary Ballet,	47	B6
The Bar on Castro,	48	A6
Biscuits & Blues,	49	B5
Boom Boom Room,	50	A5
Bottom of the Hill,	51	C7
Curran Theatre,	52	B5
Divas,	53	A5
El Rio,	54	A7
The EndUp,	55	C6
Geary Theater,	56	B5
Golden Gate Theatre,	57	B5
The Independent,	58	A6
Louise M. Davies Symphony Hall,	59	A6
Magic Theatre,	60	A2
The Orpheum,	61	A6
Pink,	62	A7
Swig,	63	B5
Theatre Rhinoceros	64	A7

SEE COLOR INSERTS FOR MORE SAN FRANCISCO MAPS

🏨 ACCOMMODATIONS

For those who don't mind sharing a room with strangers, many San Francisco hostels are homier and cheaper than most budget hotels. B&Bs are often the most comfortable and friendly, albeit expensive, option. A wide selection of budget and more luxurious accommodations can be found throughout the city.

HOSTELS

🏨 **San Francisco International Guest House,** 2976 23rd St. (☎641-6173), in the Mission. No sign; look for the blue Victorian with yellow trim near the corner of Harrison and 23rd St. Hardwood floors and relaxing common areas make this an excellent lodging option in the city. Passport required. Coffee, free linens, Internet, kitchens, phones, and TV area. 5-night min. stay. No reservations. Dorms $20. Cash only. ❶

🏨 **Adelaide Hostel and Hotel,** 5 Isadora Duncan Ln. (☎359-1915 or 877-359-1915; www.adelaidehostel.com), at the end of an alley off Taylor St. between Geary and Post St. in Union Sq. Classy decor and chic furniture entice an international crowd. TV and wash basin in each room. Breakfast included. Free linen, Internet, and safe deposit. Towels $1. Laundry $2, dry $2. Key deposit $10. Parking behind the building $15 per day. 4-night max. stay. Dorms from $23; private rooms from $60. AmEx/D/MC/V. ❶

Green Tortoise Hostel, 494 Broadway (☎834-1000; www.greentortoise.com), off Columbus Ave. in North Beach. Fun-seeking travelers love the spacious common room and helpful staff. Continental breakfast (daily) and dinner (M, W, F) included. Free sauna, linen, towels, Internet, and storage. Laundry wash $2, dry $1. Key deposit $20.

Downtown San Francisco

TO ALCATRAZ AND ANGEL ISLAND

U.S.S. Pampanito

Pier 39 Sea Lions

California Welcome Center

San Francisco Bay

FISHERMAN'S WHARF

The Cannery

Balcutha
Eureka
C.A. Thayer
Hyde St. Pier
Aquatic Park
Maritime Museum

Beach St.
N. Point St.
Bay St.
Jefferson St.

Ferry Terminal

The Embarcadero

Jones St.
Leavenworth St.
Hyde St.

TO FORT MASON AND (275yd)
TO (1.8mi)
Lombard St.

RUSSIAN HILL

POWELL-HYDE LINE
POWELL-MASON LINE

Van Ness Ave.
Polk St.
Larkin St.
Green St.
Vallejo St.
Broadway
Pacific Ave.
Jackson St.
Washington St.
Clay St.
Sacramento St.

Broadway Tunnel

Taylor St.
Mason St.
Powell St.
Stockton St.

Francisco St.
Chestnut St.
Lombard St.
Greenwich St.
Filbert St.
Union St.
Green St.
Vallejo St.
Broadway
Pacific Ave.

TELEGRAPH HILL

Greenwich Steps
Filbert Steps

NORTH BEACH

Columbus Ave.

Montgomery St.
Sansome St.
Battery St.
Front St.
Davis St.

Public Fishing Pier

Transamerica Pyramid

CHINATOWN

EMBARCADERO PL.
MARITIME PL.
Clay St.
Embarcadero Center

Ferry Building

NOB HILL

California St.

CALIFORNIA ST. LINE

EMBARCADERO

TO (.7mi) (1.2mi)
TO (.7mi) (2.2mi)

Pine St.
Bush St.
Sutter St.
Post St.

POWELL-HYDE LINE

Grant Ave.
Kearny St.

FINANCIAL DISTRICT

Pine St.

Market St.

Transbay Terminal

Main St.
Beale St.
Fremont St.
1st St.

MONTGOMERY

UNION SQUARE

Museum of African Diaspora

TO (1.6mi)

Geary St.
O'Farrell St.
Ellis St.
Eddy St.
Turk St.

TENDERLOIN

POWELL

Museum of Craft and Folk Art

Sony Metreon

Moscone Center

2nd St.

Golden Gate Ave.

SF Shopping Centre

Old Mint

Asian Art Museum

U.N. PLAZA

CIVIC CENTER

McAllister St.
Grove St.
Hayes St.
Fell St.

CIVIC CENTER

SOUTH OF MARKET

Mission St.
Minna St.
Howard St.
Folsom St.
Harrison St.

3rd St.
4th St.
5th St.

South Park

TO (.4mi)
TO (1.7mi) (1.3mi)
TO HAIGHT, (1mi)
(1.3mi)

Van Ness Ave.
S. Van Ness Ave.
Polk St.
Larkin St.
Hyde St.
Leavenworth St.
Jones St.
Taylor St.
Mason St.

6th St.
7th St.
8th St.
9th St.
10th St.
11th St.
12th St.

Bryant St.
Brannan St.

SBC Park

TO AND (1mi)
TO AND (.3mi),
(1.7mi)

CalTrain Depot

Townsend St.
King St.
Berry St.

Marina

TO (.7mi)

Mission Creek
Channel St.

TO MONSTER PARK (5.5mi)

TO SAN FRANCISCO INTERNATIONAL AIRPORT (12mi)

CALIFORNIA

10-night max. stay. Check-in noon. Check-out 11am. Reserve 1 week in advance in summer. Dorms $24-27; private rooms $58-81. MC/V. ❶

Fisherman's Wharf (HI), Bldg. #240, (☎771-7277), in Fort Mason. Once you enter the complex at the corner of Bay and Franklin St., the hostel is at the corner of Funston and Pope St. past the administrative buildings. Looks and feels like summer camp. Huge kitchen and cafe with vegetarian dinner. No smoking or alcohol. Bike storage, lockers, and parking. Breakfast included. Laundry $1, dry $1. Free Wi-Fi. Check-in 2:30pm. Quiet hours 11pm-7am. Reserve well in advance. Dorms $26-30; private rooms $75-100. HI hostels also near Union Square at 685 Ellis St. (☎474-5721) and 312 Mason St. (☎788-5604). AmEx/D/MC/V. ❶

HOTELS

San Remo Hotel, 2237 Mason St. (☎776-8688; www.sanremohotel.com), between Chestnut and Francisco St. in North Beach. Rooms furnished with elegant antiques. The penthouse offers a private garden and an amazing view of the city. Laundry $1.50, dry $1. Check-in 2pm. Check-out 11am. Reservations recommended. Singles and doubles $70-90. Penthouse $175-185; reserve 2-3 months ahead. AmEx/MC/V. ❸

San Francisco Zen Center, 300 Page St. (☎863-3136; www.sfzc.org), near Laguna St. in the Lower Haight. The Zen Center offers 6 breezy, unadorned rooms with courtyard views that instill a meditative peace of mind, at least until the 5am wake-up alarm. Breakfast included; all meals (vegetarian) included in the discounted weekly (10% off) or monthly (25% off) rates. Singles and doubles $72-132. AmEx/D/MC/V. ❸

BED & BREAKFASTS

Hayes Valley Inn, 417 Gough St. (☎431-9131, reservations 800-930-7999; www.hayesvalleyinn.com), just north of Hayes St. in Hayes Valley. European-style B&B with tastefully furnished rooms, shared baths, and Victorian parlor. Rooms have cable TV, phone, and private sink. Some smoking rooms. Check-in 3pm. Check-out 11am. Reservations recommended. Singles $73; doubles $84-105. MC/V. ❸

Red Victorian Bed, Breakfast, and Art, 1665 Haight St. (☎864-1978; www.red-vic.com), west of Belvedere St. Themed rooms, including the "Peacock Suit" and the "Summer of Love" room, and a mini meditation room. Reception 9am-9pm. Check-in 3-6pm or by appointment. Reservations recommended. Rooms $89-229. Discounts for stays longer than 3 days. AmEx/D/MC/V. ❹

◖ FOOD

UNION SQUARE

Cafe Mason, 320 Mason St. (☎544-0320), between Elwood St. and O'Farrell St. The sparkly vinyl booths and curving red-and-yellow ceiling are clear indications that this diner is more than just a greasy spoon. Cafe Mason functions as a diner, cafe, bistro, or watering hole, depending on the time of day, and draws a diverse clientele to match. Burgers $8. Veggie omelets $10. Pumpkin crepes $12. Open 24hr. AmEx/MC/V. ❷

King of Thai Noodle House, 184 O'Farrell St. (☎677-9991), at Powell St. Other locations around SF. Considered one of the city's best Thai restaurants, the King quickly serves up more-than-generous portions of authentic noodle dishes, soups, and curries for next to nothing. The flavorful roast duck noodle soup ($6) and vegetarian egg rolls ($4.50) are outstanding. Open daily 11:30am-1:30am. Cash only. ❶

Café Bean, 800 Sutter St. (☎346-9527). A crazy cosmopolitan atmosphere and the restorative powers of Dutch pancakes ($5-8) offer jet-setting diners much-needed respite. Parisian posters, maps of Amsterdam, and German road signs hang above makeshift couches. Creative sandwiches $5-8. Internet $3 per 20min., $7 per hr. Open M-Sa 6:30am-7pm, Su 6:30am-5pm. Kitchen closes usually 4-5pm. MC/V. ❷

NORTH BEACH AND CHINATOWN

🍴 **Chef Jia,** 925 Kearny St. (☎398-1626), at Pacific St. Chef Jia's insanely cheap and delicious food consistently draws a local crowd. Known for lunch and dinner specials ($5) served from 11:30am-4pm and celebrated signature dishes, such as rolling lettuce chicken with pine nuts ($9). Entrees $6-10. Open M-Th 11:30am-10pm, F 11:30am-11pm, Sa-Su 5-10:30pm. Cash only. ❷

L'Osteria del Forno, 519 Columbus Ave. (☎982-1124), between Green and Union St. in North Beach. The lively staff at this casual (and tiny!) Italian eatery serves terrific thin-crust pizzas (slice $3-5, whole pizza $10-19) and filling focaccia sandwiches ($5-7). Salads and antipasti $5-9. Entrees $5-15. Open M, W-Th, and Su 11:30am-10pm, F-Sa 11:30am-10:30pm. Cash only. ❸

Steps of Rome Caffe, 348 Columbus Ave. (☎397-0435), between Broadway and Vallejo St. Known for its lively and largely male waitstaff, this North Beach spot caters to young patrons in the mood for a classic Italian dinner with some entertainment on the side. Entrees $8-16. Open M-Th and Su 10am-2am, F-Sa 10am-3am. Cash only. ❷

CIVIC CENTER AND THE TENDERLOIN

The California Culinary Academy, 625 Polk St. (☎216-4329; reservations www.bay-chef.com), between Turk and Eddy St. Academy students cook behind a viewing window. The Tu-W *prix-fixe* 3-course meal indulges patrons with ambitious culinary combinations (lunch $16, dinner $24). Wine pairings with each course are a steal at $5. F grand buffet lunch ($22) and dinner ($38); reserve online 1 week ahead. Open Tu-F 11:30am-1pm and 6-8pm. AmEx/D/MC/V. ❺

Lalita Thai Restaurant and Bar, 96 McAllister St. (☎552-5744), at Leavenworth St. Mood lighting, an elaborate mural, and a touch of plastic foliage set the scene. The $20 4-course *prix-fixe* dinner special (available before 9pm) is a favorite. Intricately seasoned lunch specials $8. Dinner entrees about $11. Open M-F 11am-10pm, Sa 4:30-10pm. Dinner reservations recommended, especially on weekends. AmEx/MC/V. ❸

SOMA, THE MISSION, AND THE CASTRO

🍴 **The Butler and the Chef Bistro,** 155A S. Park St. (☎896-2075; www.thebutlerandthechef.com), between Bryant, Brannan, 2nd, and 3rd St. This stellar reproduction of a Parisian street cafe overlooks a historic park. Whether you choose the amazing *Croque Mademoiselle* ($10) or the quiche-of-the-day ($12), you get a complimentary home-made chocolate truffle. Open Tu-Sa 8am-4pm, Su 10am-5pm. AmEx/D/MC/V. ❷

Taquería Cancún, 2288 Mission St. (☎252-9560), at 19th St. Also at 3211 Mission St. (☎550-1414), at Cesar Chavez Ave., and 1003 Market St. (☎864-6773), at 6th St. Delicious burritos with veggies or meat ($4.50) and egg dishes served with chips and salsa, tortillas, and choice of sausage, ham, or salsa ($5.50). Open M-Th and Su 9am-1:45am, F-Sa 9am-2:45am. Cash only. ❶

Bissap Baobab, 2323 Mission St. (☎826-9287), at 19th St. Dine on the unique, well-seasoned cuisine of West Africa. The *dibi* chicken ($8.25) is marinated and served with a deliciously tangy onion sauce and plantains, while the *mafe* vegetables ($8) come covered in a spicy peanut sauce. Open Tu-Su 6-10:30pm. MC/V. ❷

THE HAIGHT AND THE RICHMOND DISTRICT

🍴 **Rigolo,** 3940 California St. (☎923-4470), at Laurel St. in Laurel Heights. Outstanding French-inspired pastas, sandwiches (pulled pork on olive bread $8), and thin-crust piz-

CALIFORNIA

zas. The real draws are the incredible breads and baked goods. Lasagna $10. Pizzas $8-13. Brioche $2.25. Open M-Sa 8am-9pm, Su 8am-8pm. MC/V. ❷

Pork Store Cafe, 1451 Haight St. (☎864-6981), between Masonic Ave. and Ashbury St. in the Upper Haight. 2 delicious healthy breakfast options ("Tim's Healthy Thursdays" and "Mike's Low Carb Special"; each $7.50) pack in enough spinach, avocado, and salsa to hold their own against the Piggy Special ($8). The biscuits and gravy deserve especially high praise. Open M-F 7am-3:30pm, Sa-Su 8am-4pm. AmEx/D/MC/V. ❷

Q Restaurant, 225 Clement St. (☎752-2298), at 3rd Ave. in Inner Richmond. The funky decor doesn't quite match up with the amazing comfort food, but with macaroni and cheese with tater tots on top, who's complaining? Draws a local crowd so you may have to wait in the bar and sample the marvelous beer selection. Entrees $9-16. Open M-F 11am-3pm and 5-11pm, Sa 10am-11pm, Su 10am-10pm. MC/V. ❷

PACIFIC HEIGHTS AND THE MARINA

La Boulangerie, 2325 Pine St. (☎440-0356; www.baybread.com), at Fillmore St. Homesick, friendly management serves Parisian-style *macarons*, richly textured *cannelés,* and the most delicious almond croissants this side of the Seine. Breads $2-7. Pastries $1-3. Mouth-watering selection of savory tarts and sandwiches $4.50-8.50. Check the website for additional SF locations. Open daily 6am-7pm. MC/V. ❶

Home Plate, 2274 Lombard St. (☎922-4663), off Pierce St. in the Marina. This inventive breakfast and lunch joint serves apple buckwheat pancakes ($5.50) and homemade apricot-pistachio granola ($5). Complimentary scones with homemade mango or mixed fruit jam. Open daily 7am-4:30pm. MC/V. ❶

La Méditerranée, 2210 Fillmore St. (☎921-2956; www.lamediterranee.net), between Sacramento and Clay St. Also at 288 Noe St. (☎431-7210), at 16th and Market St. in the Castro and 2936 College Ave. (☎510-540-7773), in Berkeley. Harkens back to modest Greek and Lebanese traditions but adds a chic twist. Lunch specials (served until 5pm; $7.25) and entrees are light and Mediterranean-inspired. Entrees $8-10. Open M-W and Su 11am-10pm, F-Sa 11am-11pm. AmEx/MC/V. ❶

◉ SIGHTS

UNION SQUARE

Union Square, a recently redesigned public plaza with grassy terraces perfect for street performers and people-watching, anchors this commercial and cultural district. Clothing stores, hotels, restaurants, galleries, and theaters jam the surrounding streets, but the area hasn't always been so tourist-friendly. Around 1900, murders on Union Square's Morton Alley averaged one per week and prostitutes waved to their favorite customers from 2nd-story windows. After the 1906 earthquake and fires destroyed most of the brothels, merchants moved in and renamed the alley **Maiden Lane** in hopes of changing the street's image. Today, the pedestrian-only street that extends two blocks from Union Square's eastern side is lined with the understated facades of big-name designer shops. Architecture enthusiasts will love the artful swirling brick and spiral interior of **Xanadu Gallery,** 140 Maiden Ln., the only Frank Lloyd Wright building in SF. (☎392-9999; www.xanadugallery.us. Open M-Sa 10am-6pm.)

NORTH BEACH

▦**CITY LIGHTS BOOKSTORE.** Beat writers came to national attention when Lawrence Ferlinghetti's City Lights Bookstore (est. 1953) published Allen Ginsberg's *Howl,* which was banned in 1956 and then subjected to an extended trial at the end of which a judge found the poem "not obscene." A glance around the store confirms the obvious radical leanings of a bookstore rooted in the subversive potential of intellectual countermovements. City Lights has expanded since its Beat days and now stocks a selection of fiction, poetry, and non-fiction, but remains committed to publishing young writers and providing readers with differing viewpoints. *(2261 Columbus Ave. ☎ 362-8193; www.citylights.com. Open daily 10am-midnight.)*

WASHINGTON SQUARE. North Beach's piazza, a pretty, tree-lined lawn, fills every morning with *tai chi* practitioners. By noon, sunbathers and picnickers take over. This was the site of Joe DiMaggio's wedding to his first wife, Dorothy Arnold (and not, as you may hear, to his 2nd wife, Marilyn Monroe). The **St. Peter and St. Paul Catholic Church** invites tired sightseers to take refuge in its dark wooden nave or to get a crick in the neck as they stare up at its double spires. *(666 Filbert St.)* Turn-of-the-century San Francisco philanthropist Lillie Hitchcock Coit was inspired by her rescue from a fire as a young girl to donate the **Volunteer Firemen Memorial**. *(Washington Sq. is bordered by Union, Filbert, Stockton, and Powell St.)*

COIT TOWER. Coit Tower (est. 1933) stands 210 ft. high and commands a spectacular view of the city and the bay on a clear day. During the Depression, the Works Progress Administration employed artists to decorate the interior with murals that depict laborers at work. The murals are open to the public and are all located in the tower lobby. The top of the tower can only be accessed via elevator. *(MUNI bus #39. By car, follow Telegraph Hill to the top, where there is free 30min. parking daily 10am-6:30pm. Tower: ☎ 362-0808. Open daily 10am-7pm. Free guided tour of the murals Sa 11am. Elevator $4.50, seniors $ 3.50, ages 6-12 $2, under 6 free.)*

CHINATOWN

WAVERLY PLACE. This little alley offers offbeat architecture without the garishness of Grant Ave. Near the intersection with Sacramento St., the fire escapes are painted in pinks and greens and held together by railings made of intricate Chinese patterns. Closer to Washington St., the alley is also home to **Tien Hou Temple,** the oldest Chinese temple in the US. *(Between Sacramento and Washington St. and between Stockton St. and Grant Ave. Tien Hou Temple at 125 Waverly Pl.)*

ROSS ALLEY. Ross Alley was once lined with brothels and gambling houses; today, it epitomizes the cramped look of old Chinatown. The alley has starred in such films as *Big Trouble in Little China, Karate Kid II*, and *Indiana Jones and the Temple of Doom*. *(Ross Alley is located off Washington St., between Stockton and Grant St.)* Squeeze into a tiny doorway to watch fortune cookies being shaped by hand at the **Golden Gate Cookie Factory.** All cookies that don't meet the baker's high standards are put in big tins for free taste-testing. *(56 Ross Alley. ☎ 781-3956. Open daily 9am-8pm. Bag of cookies $1-3, with "funny," "sexy," or "lucky" fortunes $5.)*

CIVIC CENTER

The palatial **San Francisco City Hall,** modeled after Rome's St. Peter's Basilica, is the centerpiece of the largest gathering of Beaux Arts architecture in the US. *(1 Dr. Carlton B. Goodlett Pl., at Van Ness Ave. ☎ 554-4000. Open M-F 8am-8pm.)* **United Nations Plaza** hosts the city's **farmers' market.** *(Just off Market St. Open in summer W 7am-5:30pm and Su 7am-5pm.)* The seating in the glass-and-brass **Louise M. Davies Symphony Hall** was designed to give most audience members a close-up view of performers. Visually, the building is a smashing success, as is the **San Francisco Symphony.** *(201 Van Ness Ave. ☎ 552-8000.)* The **San Francisco Opera Company** and **San Francisco Ballet** perform at the **War Memorial Opera House.** *(301 Van Ness Ave., between Grove and McAllister St., ☎ 864-3330. Visitors should exercise caution in this area, especially after dark.)*

NOB HILL AND RUSSIAN HILL

THE CROOKEDEST STREET IN THE WORLD. The famous curves of **Lombard Street** were installed in the 20s so that horse-drawn carriages could negotiate the extremely steep hill. From the top, both pedestrians and passengers enjoy the view of the city and harbor. *(Between Hyde and Leavenworth St., running down Russian Hill.)*

GRACE CATHEDRAL AND HUNTINGTON PARK. The largest Gothic edifice west of the Mississippi, **Grace Cathedral** is Nob Hill's stained-glass crown. The castings of its portals are such exact imitations of the Baptistry in Florence that they were used to restore the originals. Inside, murals mix San Franciscan and national history with saintly scenes. The altar of the AIDS Interfaith Memorial Chapel celebrates the church's "inclusive community." *(1100 California St., between Jones and Taylor St. ☎ 749-6300; www.gracecathedral.org. Open M-F and Su 7am-6pm, Sa 8am-6pm. Services: M-F 7:30, 9am, 12:10pm; Sa 9am and 3pm; Su 7:30, 8:15, 11am, 6pm. Additional services Th 5:15 and mid-Sept. to mid-June Su 3pm. Tours M-F 1-3pm, Sa 11:30am-1:30pm, Su 12:30-2pm. Self-guided tours available anytime. Suggested donation $5.)* Outside, the turf and trees of **Huntington Park** are equipped with a playground and sunbathers.

PACIFIC HEIGHTS AND JAPANTOWN

Between Union and Sacramento St., Pacific Heights has the greatest number of Victorian buildings in the city. The streets surrounding Alta Plaza Park and Lafayette Park have an abundance of grand homes. The public library offers free tours of Pacific Heights mansions. *(www.sfcityguides.com. Tours meet in Alta Plaza atop the stairs at Pierce and Clay St. every Sa and 3rd Tu at 11am.)* **St. Dominic's Cathedral** wows visitors with its towering altar—featuring an elaborate sculpture of Jesus and the 12 apostles—and its imposing gray stone and Gothic-style facade. *(2390 Bush St., at Steiner St. ☎ 567-7824; www.stdominics.org. Open M-Sa 6:30am-5:30pm, Su 7:30am-9pm. Mass M-F 6:30, 8am, 5:30pm; Sa 8am and 5:30pm; Su quiet mass 7:30am, family mass 9:30am, solemn choral 11:30am, Spanish 1:30pm, contemporary music 5:30pm, candlelight service 9pm.)*

THE MISSION

The Mission is slowly outgrowing its reputation as one of the most under appreciated neighborhoods in the city. The intersection of **Mission** and **16th Street** and the length of **24th St.** are perhaps the most pulsing, personality-filled areas in all of San Francisco, where shops cater to vegetarian diets, political radicals, and literary dissenters, and produce is sold on the sidewalks. It is home to some of the best nightlife in the city, and the abundance of small taquerias makes late-night eaters happy and full. Founded in 1776 in the old heart of San Francisco, the **Mission Dolores** is thought to be the city's oldest building. Due to its proximity to the Laguna de Nuestra Señora de los Dolores (Lagoon of Our Lady of Sorrows), the Mission became universally known as *Misión de los Dolores*. Bougainvillea, poppies, and birds of paradise bloom in its cemetery, featured in Alfred Hitchcock's 1958 film *Vertigo*. *(3321 16th St., at Dolores St. ☎ 621-8203. Open daily 9am-5pm. $5, ages 5-12, seniors, and students $3. Mass in English M-F 7:30 and 9am, Sa 5pm, Su 8 and 10am; in Spanish Su noon.)* The magnificent **murals** scattered throughout the mission certainly warrant straying from the main thoroughfare. Standouts include the political murals of **Balmy Alley** off 24th St. between Harrison and Folsom St., the face of **St. Peter's Church** at 24th and Florida St., and **Mona Caron's mural** at 300 Church St., at the corner of 15th St. one block south of Market St.

THE CASTRO

The concept, as well as the reality, of an all-queer neighborhood draws GLBT tourists and their friends to the Castro. Beyond the glitz of shimmering bodies and the gyms where they are sculpted, the Castro harbors a more playful side. A slew of kitschy stores and a contingent of rebellious youth add flair to the picture-perfect streets, where couples make a full-time job out of seeing and being seen. For architecture without the walk, head to the **Castro Theatre,** an Art Deco appropriation of a Mexican cathedral with a lavishly refurbished interior. *(429 Castro St.)*

TWIN PEAKS

Tourist hub by day, lovebird locale by night—the lookout-turned-make-out point atop Twin Peaks offers the best views of the city. From Alcatraz to the Transamerica Pyramid to a big rainbow flag at the foot of Market St. in the Castro, all major landmarks are on display. Scramble up the other peak for a view to the west. *(The peaks are located between Portola Dr., Clarendon Ave., and Upper Market St. From Noe Valley, take MUNI bus #48 to Diamond Heights. From elsewhere in the city, take MUNI bus K, L, or M to Forest Hills, then MUNI bus #36.)* For a scenic route by car, bike, or foot, take 17th St. to Clayton St. to Clarendon Ave. and head up Twin Peaks Blvd. to the top.

THE HAIGHT

All around Haight and Ashbury St., vestiges of the 60s remain in inexpensive bars and ethnic restaurants. Action-packed street life, anarchist literature, and shops selling pipes for, um, tobacco carry on the legacy of the free-love era. The former homes of several countercultural legends continue to attract visitors. From the corner of Haight and Ashbury St., walk up Ashbury St. to #710, just south of Waller St., to see the house occupied by the **Grateful Dead.** Look across the street for the **Hell's Angels'** house. If you walk back to Haight St., go right three blocks and make a left on Lyon St. to check out **Janis Joplin's** old abode. *(122 Lyon St., between Page and Oak St.)* Cross the Panhandle, continue three blocks to Fulton St., turn right, and wander seven blocks toward the park to see where the Manson "family" planned murder and mayhem at the **Charles Manson** mansion. *(2400 Fulton St., at Willard St.)* **Buena Vista Park,** which runs along Haight St. between Central and Baker St. and continues south, resembles a jungle complete with a dense canopy but should be avoided at night. Across **Alamo Square's** grassy slope, a string of brightly colored Victorian homes known as the **Painted Ladies** glow against the skyline.

GOLDEN GATE PARK

In-line skaters, neo-flower children, and sunbathers converge in this lush city oasis. The park has a municipal golf course, an equestrian center, sports fields, tennis courts, and a stadium. On Sundays, traffic is banned from park roads, and bicycles and in-line skates come out in full force. The **Visitors Center** is located in the Beach Chalet on the western edge of the park. *(☎ 751-2766. Open daily 9am-5pm.)*

GARDENS. The soil of Golden Gate Park is rich enough to support a wealth of flowers. The **Strybing Arboretum and Botanical Gardens** are home to over 7000 varieties of plants, including collections from Chile, New Zealand, and the tropical, high-altitude New World Cloud Forests. Within its grounds, the **Garden of Fragrance** is designed for the visually impaired; all labels are in Braille and the plants are chosen for their textures and scents. Near the Music Concourse off South Dr., the **Shakespeare Garden** contains almost every flower and plant ever mentioned by the Bard. Plaques with the relevant quotations are displayed, and maps help you find your favorite hyacinths and rue. *(Open M-F 8am-4:30pm, Sa-Su 10am-5pm. Free guided walking tours daily 1:30pm.)* The **Japanese Cherry Orchard,** at Lincoln Way and South Dr., blooms the 1st week in April. Created for the 1894 Mid-Winter Exposition, the elegant **Japanese Tea Garden** is a serene collection of wooden buildings, small pools, graceful footbridges, and carefully pruned trees. *(☎ 752-4227; www.sfbotanical-garden.org. Open daily in summer 8:30am-6pm; in winter 8:30am-5pm. $3.50, ages 6-12 and seniors $1.25. Free in summer 8:30-9:30am and 5-6pm; in winter 8:30-9:30am and 4-5pm.)*

LINCOLN PARK AND OCEAN BEACH

At the northwest end of San Francisco, **Lincoln Park** has spectacular views of the Pacific and the Golden Gate Bridge. The meandering paths and historical sights are ideal for an afternoon hike or summertime picnic. **Ocean Beach,** the largest and most popular of San Francisco's beaches, begins south of Point Lobos and extends down the northwestern edge of the city's coastline. The strong undertow along the point is very dangerous, but die-hard surfers still brave the treacherous currents, gnarly waves, and ice-cold water.

GOLDEN GATE BRIDGE AND THE PRESIDIO

When John Fremont coined the term "Golden Gate" in 1846, he meant to name the harbor entrance to the San Francisco Bay. In 1937, however, the colorful name became permanently associated with Joseph Strauss's engineering masterpiece—the **Golden Gate Bridge.** Built for a cool $35 million, the bridge stretches across 1¼ mi. of ocean, its towers looming 65 stories above the bay. It can sway up to 27 ft. in each direction during high winds. The views from the bridge are amazing, especially from the Vista Point at the Marin end. To see the bridge in its entirety, it's best to get a bit farther away. Fort Point and Fort Baker in the Presidio, Land's End in Lincoln Park, Mt. Livermore on Angel Island, and Hawk Hill off Conzelman Rd. in the Marin Headlands all offer spectacular views on clear days. *(MUNI #28 and 29 buses take passengers to the bridge. By car, take Lincoln Blvd.)*

When Spanish settlers forged up the San Francisco peninsula from Baja California in 1769, they established *presidios*, or military outposts, as they went. San Francisco's **Presidio,** the northernmost point of Spanish territory in North America, was dedicated in 1776. It was passed to the US as part of the 1848 Treaty of Guadalupe Hidalgo. It is now part of the **Golden Gate National Recreation Area (GGNRA),** run by the National Park Service, but don't go expecting to see any major sights.

MARINA AND FORT MASON

PALACE OF FINE ARTS. With its massive open-air rotunda and curving colonnades, the **Palace of Fine Arts** is one of the most impressive structures in the city, and its surrounding parklands are a popular picnic spot. It was originally built to commemorate the opening of the Panama Canal and testify to San Francisco's recovery from the 1906 earthquake. Shakespeare's plays are often performed here during the summer. *(On Baker St., between Jefferson and Bay St. next to the Exploratorium. Open daily 6am-9pm. Free.)* The **Palace of Fine Arts Theater,** located behind the rotunda, also hosts various dance and theater performances and film festivals. *(☎563-6504; www.palaceoffinearts.org. Call for showtimes and ticket prices.)*

FORT MASON. A decommissioned military post, Fort Mason is now home to many nonprofit and arts-promoting organizations. Most have very little to offer the casual visitor, and consequently the area remains unknown to most travelers, making it a quiet waterfront counterpart to the tourist blitz of Fisherman's Wharf. A seashore pathway connects Fort Mason to the Wharf area. The grounds are also the headquarters of the Golden Gate National Recreation Area and are perfect for mid-day, breezy runs. *(The park is at the eastern portion of Fort Mason, near Gashouse Cove. ☎441-3400, ext. 3; www.fortmason.org.)*

FISHERMAN'S WHARF AND THE BAY

Piers 39 through 45 on the waterfront provide access to San Francisco's most famous and touristy attractions, including Alcatraz Island.

ALCATRAZ. In its 29 years as a maximum-security federal penitentiary, **Alcatraz** harbored a menacing cast of characters, including Al "Scarface" Capone, George

"Machine Gun" Kelly, and Robert "The Birdman" Stroud. There were 14 separate escape attempts—some desperate, defiant bolts for freedom, others carefully calculated and innovative. Only one man is known to have survived crossing the bay—he was later recaptured. On "the Rock," the cell-block audio tour takes you back to Alcatraz's more infamous days. Ranger-guided tours leave throughout the day and explore the island's 200 years of occupation, from a hunting and fishing ground for Native Americans to a Civil War outpost to a military prison, a federal prison, and finally a birthplace of the Native American civil rights movement. Now part of the Golden Gate National Recreation Area, Alcatraz is home to diverse plants and tons of tourists. *(The Blue and Gold Fleet runs to Alcatraz. ☎ 705-8200, tickets 705-5555; www.blueandgoldfleet.com. 14 per day. Often sells out in summer. Reserve in advance. Round-trip with audio tour $25, ages 12-18 and seniors $21, ages 5-11 $17.)*

GHIRARDELLI SQUARE. A true chocolate-lovers' heaven, Ghirardelli Sq. houses a mall in what was once a traditional chocolate factory. Here, everyone's got a golden ticket to the **Ghirardelli Chocolate Manufactory,** with its vast selection of chocolatey goodies, as well as the **Ghirardelli Chocolate Shop and Caffe,** which sells a smaller selection of chocolates and an amazing selection of ice cream sundaes. Both hand out **free samples** of chocolate, but the Caffe is less crowded. *(Mall: 900 N. Point St. ☎ 775-5500; www.ghirardellisq.com. Stores open in summer M-Sa 10am-9pm, Su 10am-6pm. Manufactory: open M-Th and Su 10am-11pm, F-Sa 10am-midnight. Chocolate Shop and Caffe: ☎ 474-1414. Open M-Th and Su 9am-9pm, F-Sa 9am-10pm.)*

🏛 MUSEUMS

■ SAN FRANCISCO MUSEUM OF MODERN ART (SFMOMA). This black-and-white cylindrical museum houses 5 spacious floors of photography, painting, media, and sculpture, with an emphasis on architecture and design. It houses the largest selection of 20th-century American and European art this side of New York City. *(151 3rd St., between Mission and Howard St. ☎ 357-4000; www.sfmoma.org. 4 free gallery tours per day. Open Memorial Day-Labor Day M-Tu and F-Su 10am–5:45pm, Th 10am-8:45pm; Labor Day-Memorial Day M-Tu and F-Su 11am-5:45pm, Th 11am-8:45pm. $12.50, seniors $8, students $7, under 13 free. Th 6-9pm ½ price. 1st Tu of each month free.)*

EXPLORATORIUM. This museum features over 650 interactive displays—including mini-tornadoes and giant bubble-makers—that explain the world's wonders. The **Tactile Dome,** a dark maze of tunnels, slides, and crevices, refines your sense of touch. *(3601 Lyon St., in the Marina. ☎ 563-7337 or 561-0360; www.exploratorium.edu. Open Tu-Su 10am-5pm. $14; disabled, seniors, students, and ages 13-17 $11; ages 4-12 $9. Tactile Dome $17, includes museum admission; reservations recommended.)*

CALIFORNIA PALACE OF THE LEGION OF HONOR. Outside the museum, a copy of Rodin's *Thinker* beckons visitors into the courtyard, where a glass pyramid recalls the Louvre. A thorough catalogue of great masters, from the medieval to the modern, hangs inside, and extensive statuary and decorative art collections are spread throughout. Other draws include a 4500-pipe organ, played in free recitals. Outside the Palace lies the **Holocaust memorial.** *(In Lincoln Park. ☎ 750-3600; www.legionofhonor.org. Open Tu-Su 9:30am-5:15pm. Organ recitals Sa-Su 4pm. $10, seniors $7, under 17 $6, under 12 free. $2 discount with MUNI transfer. 1st Tu of each month free.)*

CALIFORNIA ACADEMY OF SCIENCES. This is the temporary location (until 2008) of the Golden Gate Park museums. The Steinhart Aquarium, home to over 600 aquatic species, is livelier than the Natural History Museum. *(875 Howard St., between 4th and 5th St. in SoMa. ☎ 750-7145; www.calacademy.org. Open daily 10am-5pm. $10; ages 12-17, seniors, and students $6.50; ages 4-11 $2. 1st W of each month free. 3rd Th of each month 5-9pm $5.)*

YERBA BUENA CENTER FOR THE ARTS. The Yerba Buena Center includes both theater and gallery space, with programs emphasizing the creative process, performance, film, viewer involvement, and local multicultural work. It is surrounded by the Yerba Buena Rooftop Gardens, a vast, popular expanse of granite terraces, waterfalls, fountains, and foliage. Also on the grounds is a restored 1906 carousel. *(701 Mission St. ☎978-2700; www.ybca.org. Open Tu-W and F-Su noon-5pm, Th noon-8pm. Free tours 1st Th of each month 6pm. $7, seniors and students $5. 1st Tu of each month free. Gardens open daily 6am-10pm. Free. Carousel runs daily 11am-6pm; 2 rides $2.)*

MUSEUM OF CRAFT AND FOLK ART. The MOCFA brings together a fascinating collection of crafts and functional art (clothing, furniture, and jewelry) from past and present, near and far, showcasing anything that makes daily life beautiful. *(51 Yerba Buena Ln., between 2nd and 3rd St. in SoMa. ☎227-4888; www.mocfa.org. Open Tu-F 11am-6pm, Sa-Su 11am-5pm. $5, ages 12-17 and seniors $4, under 18 free.)*

SAN FRANCISCO ART INSTITUTE. The oldest art school west of the Mississippi, the Institute is lodged in a converted mission and has produced several American greats, including Mark Rothko, Ansel Adams, Imogen Cunningham, Dorothea Lange, and James Weeks. To the left as you enter is the Diego Rivera Gallery, one wall of which is covered by a huge 1931 Rivera mural. *(800 Chestnut St., in North Beach. ☎771-7020 or 800-345-7324; www.sfai.edu. Open daily June-Aug. 9am-8pm; Sept.-May 9am-9pm. Weekly student exhibits with receptions Tu 5-7pm. Professional exhibits are housed in the Walter and McBean Galleries. Open Tu-Sa 11am-6pm. Free.)*

🎵 ENTERTAINMENT

MUSIC

Look for the latest live music listings in *S.F. Weekly* and *The Guardian*. Hardcore audiophiles should snag a copy of *Bay Area Music (BAM)*.

🎵 **Bottom of the Hill,** 1233 17th St. (☎626-4455, 24hr. info 621-4455; www.bottomofthehill.com), between Missouri and Texas St., in Potrero Hill. This intimate club is the best place to see up-and-comers playing everything from alternative to pop, with a focus on rock. The White Stripes, Incubus, and Kid Rock all passed through here. Most Su afternoons in summer feature local bands and all-you-can-eat barbecue for $5 (from 4pm). Usually 21+, with occasional all-ages shows. Cover $5-20. Happy hour W-F 4-7pm, otherwise doors open at 8:30pm. Reservations recommended.

The Independent, 628 Divisadero St. (☎771-1421; www.theindependentsf.com), at Hayes St., in the Lower Haight. Voted SF's best small live music venue with diverse listings of hip hop and everything from indie rock and punk to funk, jazz, and reggae. 21+. Cover $10-30. Box office open M-F 11am-6pm and 1hr. before shows. Shows 8pm.

Boom Boom Room, 1601 Fillmore St. (☎673-8000, bar 673-8040; www.boomboomblues.com), at Geary St., near Japantown. Boom Boom is known as the city's home of "blues, boogie, soul, groove, and funk." The dim interior features live music, often bigname acts, nightly at 9:20pm. Beer $2.50. Mixed drinks $4. Cover $5-15, usually free on Su. Happy hour 4-7:30pm. Open M-F 4pm-2am, Sa-Su 3pm-2am.

Biscuits & Blues, 401 Mason St. (☎292-2583; www.biscuitsandbluessf.com), at Geary St., in Union Sq. Serves Southern fare like spicy jambalaya ($14-15), but nightly live blues really makes things simmer. Entrees $12-17. Drinks $5-12. All ages. Tickets $5-20; call ahead. Open Tu-Sa 6pm-midnight. Kitchen closes at 11.

THEATER

Downtown, **Mason Street** and **Geary Street** constitute **"Theater Row,"** the city's prime place for theatrical entertainment. **TIX Bay Area,** located in a kiosk in Union Sq. on the corner of Geary and Powell St., is a Ticketmaster outlet with tickets for almost all shows and concerts in the city. Buy a seat in advance, or try for cash-only, half-price tickets on the day of the show. (☎ 433-7827. Open Tu-Th 11am-6pm, F-Sa 11am-7pm, Su 10am-3pm.)

Geary Theater, 405 Geary St. (for tickets ☎ 749-2228; www.act-sfbay.org), at Mason St., in Union Sq. Home to the renowned American Conservatory Theater, the jewel in SF's theatrical crown. The elegant theater is a show-stealer in its own right. Tickets $15-80, depending on the show (cheaper for previews and on weekdays). ½ price student, teacher, and senior tickets available 2hr. before showtime. Box office open M and Su noon-6pm, Tu-Sa noon-8pm; or purchase tickets online.

The Orpheum, 1192 Market St. (for tickets ☎ 512-7770; www.bestofbroadway-sf.com), at Hyde St., near the Civic Center. Hosts the big Broadway shows. The Orpheum box office also serves 2 sister theaters in the area: **Golden Gate Theatre,** 1 Taylor St., at Market St.; and **Curran Theatre,** 445 Geary St. Box office open M 10am-6pm, Tu-Sa 10am-8:30pm; during the run of shows also Su 11am-7pm.

Magic Theatre, Bldg. D, 3rd fl. (☎ 441-8822; www.magictheatre.org), in Fort Mason. Stages both international and American premieres. Tickets $20-75; previews $20-25; seniors, students, and teachers $5 discount. Senior and student rush tickets available 30min. before the show; $10. Shows at 8 or 8:30pm. Box office open Tu-Sa noon-5pm.

DANCE

Alonzo King's Lines Contemporary Ballet, 26 7th St. (☎ 863-3040; www.linesballet.org), at Market St., in Civic Center. One of San Francisco's premier dance companies, specializing in modern and contemporary ballet. Dancers combine elegant classical moves with athletic flair to the music of great living jazz and world music composers. Tours extensively but 2-week fall season and 1-week spring season are performed at the Yerba Buena Center for the Arts. Tickets $25-65.

San Francisco Ballet (☎ 865-2000; www.sfballet.org), in the Opera House in Civic Center. One of the largest US ballet companies. Season runs late Jan.-early May. Tickets from $30; available online or by phone M-F noon-4pm. Box office opens at noon on performance days. Military, senior, and student tickets for same-day performance $10-20.

SPORTS

The **San Francisco Giants** (tickets ☎ 800-734-4268; www.sfgiants.com) play at "the best address in baseball," **AT&T Park** (formerly Pac Bell Park and SBC Park) in SoMa, on the water off Townsend St. Barry Bonds, the single-season record holder for home runs, has hit several famous bombs into McCovey Cove, a portion of San Francisco Bay just beyond right field where ball-hungry boaters congregate. Most games sell out before the season starts, except for 500 seats reserved for day-of-game sale. Those not wanting to pay or unable to get tickets can watch the action for free through a fence below the right field bleachers. (☎ 972-2400. Tickets $10-54. Tours of the park at 10:30am and 12:30pm daily, except game days. $10.) The NFL's **49ers** (☎ 562-4949; www.49ers.com) still play at the windy **Candlestick Park** (☎ 467-1994). Now officially called **Monster Park,** the stadium is 8 mi. south of the city with its own exit off U.S. 101. MUNI (transit info ☎ 511; www.sfmuni.com) offers express round-trip service to the park via the 9x, 28x, and 47x buses.

FESTIVALS

Musical, cultural, ethnic, and queer festivals take place year-round in San Francisco. The High Holy Day of the queer calendar, **Pride Day** celebrates with a parade and events downtown starting at 10:30am. (☎ 864-3733; www.sfpride.org.

ALL IS FAIR

The word "fair," as it stands alone, hearkens images of hot air balloons, ferris wheels, prize pigs, and the 1800s. No wonder: county fairs have begun a tradition where locals bring their best goods to show off and compete in the vein of American individuality and homegrown merit-winning. Everyone wants to make a name for themselves, and a local fair is a perfect place to start.

Nowadays we have "fairs" for everything: craft fairs, farmers' markets, carnivals, music festivals, historical fairs—all venues for self-starters and enthusiasts to show the general public what they can do, make or grow, and why they deserve the gold medal.

Check local literature for fair and festival listings, or seek out the following:

Stern Grove Music Festival in San Francisco. A free, summer-long music set in among the tall majetic trees of Stern Grove park. Check www.sterngrove.org for schedules and artists.

San Diego Arts Festival in the San Diego Convention Center over Thanksgiving weekend. Live artist demonstrations and clothes from local designers.

Monterey Bay Strawberry Festival in Monterey, CA. A mid-summer strawberry extravaganza. Local farmers come out with their best in this cheerful, berry-laden fest. Don't forget the pie-eating contest. www.watsonvillestrawberryfestival.com for details.

Last week of June.) The leather-and-chains gang lets it all hang out at the **Folsom Street Fair,** Pride Day's ruder, raunchier little brother. (On Folsom St. between 7th and 11th St. ☎777-3247; www.folsomstreetfair.com. Last week of Sept.) In fall, the **SF Fringe Festival** (☎931-1094; www.sffringe.org), beginning the 1st Thursday after Labor Day, is experimental theater at its finest, with over 60 international companies presenting, all for less than $8. **Ghirardelli Square Chocolate Festival** (☎775-5500; www.ghirardellisq.com), in Ghirardelli Sq., makes the beginning of September a chocolate paradise. Six tastings will cost you $10; 12 go for $20. Follow the drummers and dancing skeletons to **Día de los Muertos** ("Day of the Dead"; ☎821-1155, www.dayofthedeadsf.org), the festive Mexican celebration in honor of the dead. The party starts on the evening of November 2 at the Mission Cultural Center, 2868 Mission St., at 25th St.

◪ NIGHTLIFE

Everyone from the shy first-timer to the bearded strap daddy can find places to go on a Saturday (or Tuesday) night. The spots listed below are divided into bars and clubs, but the lines get pretty blurred in SF after dark, and even cafes hop at night. For additional information, check out the nightlife listings in the *S.F. Weekly, S.F. Bay Guardian,* and *Metropolitan.* For online listings go to www.sfstation.com. **All clubs listed are 21+.**

BARS AND LOUNGES

◪ **Noc Noc,** 557 Haight St. (☎861-5811), between Steiner and Fillmore St., in the Lower Haight. The only place in the Haight that gets happening before 10pm. Neo-hippies and other inheritors of the Haight-Ashbury aesthetic mingle on high-backed bar stools, relax cross-legged on the padded floor cushions. Happy hour daily 5-7pm; pints $3. Open daily 5pm-2am.

111 Minna St. 111 Minna St. (☎974-1719; www.111minnagallery.com), at 2nd St., in SoMa. A funky gallery by day and hipster groove-spot by night. The bar turns club W 5-10pm for a crowded night of progressive house music. Check for openings and receptions. Mixed drinks and beer $4. Cover usually $5-10. Gallery open Tu-F noon-5pm. Bar hours vary widely; call or check website for calendar and hours.

Swig, 561 Geary St. (☎931-7292; www.swig-bar.com), between Taylor and Jones St., in Union Sq. With an intimate back room and an upstairs smoking lounge, this chic morning cafe, trendy power lunch site, and hopping nightclub has entertained Eminem and the Wallflowers. Open daily 6am-2am.

CLUBS

El Río, 3158 Mission St. (☎282-3325, www.elriosf.com), between César Chavez and Valencia St., in the Mission. El Río sprawls in all directions with a chill lounge and expansive dance floor. The patio is center stage for young, stylin' urbanites who while away the hours playing cards and smoking cigars. Diverse international crowd. M $1 drinks all day. Tu $2.50 margaritas, free pool. Th "BraziLive". F world music. Su live salsa. Check website for events calendar. Cover M $2, Th after 10pm $5, Su $7. Happy hour Tu-F 5-9pm. Open Mar.-Nov. M-Th 5pm-2am, F 4pm-2am, Su 3pm-2am; Dec.-Feb. M-Th and Sa-Su 5pm-2am, F 4pm-2am.

Pink, 2925 16th St. (☎431-8889, www.pinksf.com), at S. Van Ness Ave., in the Mission. Pink satin and gossamer draperies lend a chic lounge feel during the week, but expect clubbers F-Sa. A mix of world music, soulful house, Cuban jazz, and Afro beats blasts on the speakers. Cover Tu-Th and Su $5, F-Sa $10. Open Tu-Th and Su 9:30pm-2am, F-Sa 9:30pm-3am; hours vary based on events.

The EndUp, 401 6th St. (☎646-0999; www.theendup.com), at Harrison St. in SoMa. A wide range of people, many of them beautiful, inevitably end up here for after-hours fun. DJs spin progressive house for a very energetic crowd. Sa "Ascension" party 6am-1pm. Su infamous "T" Dance (29 years strong) 5:30am-2am; cover $7. Cover $10-15. Open Th 10:30pm-4am, F 10pm-6am, Sa 6am-1pm and 10pm-4am, Su 6am-8pm.

GLBT NIGHTLIFE

▧ Divas, 1081 Post St. (☎474-3482; www.divassf.com), at Polk St., in the Tenderloin. This full-time transgender nightclub is simply fabulous and gets even better after 11:30pm. 1st level bar, 2nd level dance floor, 3rd level TV lounge. Drinks $4-8. Tu Talent (singing, comedy, lip synching); $50 prize. W-Th pole dancers. F-Sa midnight drag show. Ladies free before 11pm. Cover W-Sa $10. Happy hour M-F 5-7pm; well drinks, wine, and domestic beer $3. Open daily 6am-2am.

The Bar on Castro, 456 Castro St. (☎626-7220), between Market and 18th St. Padded walls and plush couches for eyeing the stylish young crowd and scoping the dance floor. 80s-themed "Manic Mondays" feature $0.80 mixed drinks 8-10pm. Su beer $1.75. Happy hour M-F 3-8pm; beer $2.25. Open M-F 4pm-2am, Sa-Su noon-2am.

Wild Side West, 424 Cortland Ave. (☎647-3099), at Wool St., in Bernal Heights. The oldest lesbian bar in SF is a friendly neighborhood favorite for women and men alike. The hidden highlight is a backyard jungle with benches, fountains, and scrap-art statues contributed by patrons. Open daily 1pm-2am.

THE BAY AREA

BERKELEY   ☎510

Berkeley emerged as a haven for progressive iconoclasts in 1964, when activist Mario Savio led the University of California at Berkeley student body in a series of highly visible protests. While the town remains staunchly liberal, true radicals may chuckle at the irony of today's yuppified Berkeley, where polished storefronts sell organic goods to a niche market of Marxists with bourgeois incomes. Catering to its stylish students and hippies, Berkeley's restaurants range from high-end California cuisine to family-run cheap Asian takeout, and its bookstores provide the perfect material for an afternoon spent sunning in the park, making the city an ideal trip from San Francisco.

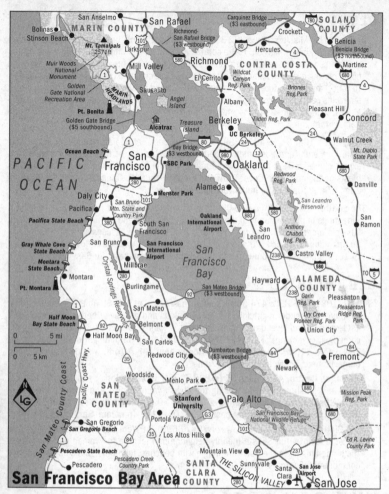

San Francisco Bay Area

TRANSPORTATION AND PRACTICAL INFORMATION. Bay Area Rapid Transit (BART) has **trains** to three Berkeley stops. The Downtown Berkeley station, 2160 Shattuck Ave., at Center St., is near the western edge of campus, while the North Berkeley station, at Delaware and Sacramento St., lies four blocks north of University Ave. The Ashby stop, at Ashby and Adeline St., provides access to South Berkeley. (☎465-2278; www.bart.gov. 20-30min. to downtown SF, $3.25.) City **buses** #15, 40, 43, and 51 run from the Berkeley BART station to downtown Oakland on Martin Luther King, Jr. Way, Telegraph Ave., Shattuck Ave., and Broadway, respectively ($1.75; seniors, disabled, and ages 5-12 $0.85; under 5 free; transfers $0.25). Berkeley lies across the Bay Bridge northeast of San Francisco, just north of Oakland. If you're driving from SF, cross the Bay Bridge on **I-80** and take one of the four Berkeley exits. The **University Avenue Exit** leads most directly to UC Berkeley and downtown. **Shattuck Avenue** is west of campus and is

Berkeley's main north-south route. The heart of town, **Telegraph Avenue**, runs south from the UC Berkeley Student Union. **Berkeley Convention and Visitor Bureau**, 2015 Center St., at Milvia St., has area maps and brochures. (☎549-7040. www.visitberkeley.com. Open M-F 9am-5pm.) **UC Berkeley Visitors Center**, 101 University Hall, at the corner of University Ave. and Oxford St., offers maps, campus info, and tours. (☎642-5215; www.berkeley.edu/visitors/. Open M-F 8:30am-4:30pm.) **Internet Access: Berkeley Public Library**, 2090 Kittredge St. (☎981-6100. Free. Open M-Tu 10am-8pm, W-Sa 10am-6pm, Su 1-5pm.) **Post Office:** 2000 Allston Way, at Milvia St. (☎649-3155. Open M-F 9am-5pm, Sa 9am-3pm.) **Postal Code:** 94704.

🛏🍴 ACCOMMODATIONS AND FOOD. Though the naive visitor might expect to find Berkeley overrun with communes and hostels, it has surprisingly few cheap accommodations. The **Berkeley-Oakland Bed and Breakfast Network** (☎547-6380; www.bbonline.com/ca/berkeley-oakland) coordinates some great East Bay B&Bs with a range of rates (singles $90-190). No-frills motels line University Ave. between Shattuck and Sacramento St.; ritzier places are downtown, especially on Durant Ave. **UC Berkeley Summer Visitor Housing ❸** has simple college dorms, a great location, shared baths, and free linens, towels, and Internet access. (☎642-4108. Open June to mid-Aug. Check-in 3-6pm or call ahead. Singles and doubles $57, $342 per week. D/MC/V.) The **YMCA ❷**, 2001 Allston Way, features a communal kitchen, computer room, shared bath, and TV lounge. Use of the pool and fitness facilities is included. (☎848-6800. 10-night max. stay. Reception 7am-9:30pm. 18+. Singles $39-46; doubles $50-60.)

Berkeley's **Gourmet Ghetto**, at Shattuck Ave. and Cedar St., is where "California cuisine" (p. 885) began. The north end of **Telegraph Avenue** caters to student appetites and wallets, with late-night offerings of all varieties along **Durant Avenue.** If you'd rather talk to a cow than eat one, you're in luck; Berkeley does greens like nowhere else. A growing number of international eateries are helping to diversify the area. **Solano Avenue** to the north is great for Asian cuisine and budget grub, while **4th Street** to the west is home to trendy upscale eats. **◪Chez Panisse ❺**, 1517 Shattuck Ave., epitomizes California cuisine, and was opened by chef Alice Waters in 1971. Alice still prepares the nightly fixed menu (4 courses; $50-85) in the cozy downstairs restaurant. Upstairs, the more casual cafe serves similar, but less expensive, fare. (☎548-5525, cafe 548-5049; www.chezpanisse.com. Appetizers $7.50-14. Entrees $18-27. Reservations for restaurant or cafe strongly recommended; available up to 1 month in advance. Restaurant open M-Th 5-10:30pm, F-Sa 5-11:30pm. 2 dinner seatings nightly. Cafe open M-Th 11:30am-3pm and 5-10:30pm, F-Sa 11:30am-3:30pm and 5-11:30pm.) Voted the best pizza in the Bay Area by the *San Francisco Chronicle*, **◪Zachary's Pizza ❸**, 1853 Solano Ave., at Colusa Ave., attracts a cult-like following for its Chicago-style stuffed pies. The spinach and mushroom is Zachary's "Pride and Joy," and if you're not hungry, but will be, you can take home one of their "half-baked" pizzas to heat up in your B&B's kitchen. (☎525-5950. Large pies $20.25-28.25. Open M-Th and Su 11am-9:30pm, F-Sa 11am-10:30pm. Cash only.) **Café Intermezzo ❶**, 2442 Telegraph Ave., at Haste St., serves heaping salads ($4-7), huge sandwiches on freshly baked bread, and hot soups. (☎849-4592. Sandwiches $5.30. Open daily 10am-10pm. Cash only.)

◪ SIGHTS. In 1868, the private College of California and the public Agricultural, Mining, and Mechanical Arts College united as the **University of California.** The 178-acre university in Berkeley was the first of nine University of California campuses, so by seniority it has sole right to the nickname "Cal." The campus is bounded on the south by Bancroft Way, on the west by Oxford St., on the north by Hearst Ave., and on the east by Tilden Park. From Telegraph Ave., enter through **Sather Gate** into **Sproul Plaza,** both sites of celebrated student sit-ins and bloody confrontations

CALIFORNIA

MUSIC TO MY EARS

From its 1990 founding on Telegraph Ave., Amoeba Music has been called a "shoppers' paradise" and the "world's greatest record store." The store was created by music lovers (all staff are either musicians, music junkies, or both) to cater to smaller, niche markets and to allow their customers to create the best music collections possible.

As the world's largest independent record store, they stock thousands of titles criss-crossing all genres and media. You'll find Gwen Stefani and Coldplay next to Ella Fitzgerald on vinyl and New Kids on the Block on cassette. On top of that, there is a selection of imported music and a massive video and DVD collection.

Most appealing to the budget traveler, the racks of used music and movies are dirt-cheap, with CDs you'd actually want to listen to going for as little as $2. The only thing Amoeba lacks is the all-too-common record store music snobbery. As an added bonus, the friendly staff members may transform into in-house DJs in the San Francisco or Hollywood stores during the evening. At Amoeba, it's all about the music.

Amoeba Music, 2455 Telegraph Ave. (☎510-549-1125). Open M-Sa 10am-10:30pm, Su 11am-9pm. Other locations in San Francisco and Hollywood.

with police. Free 1½hr. tours explore the campus each day. (Tours M-Sa 10am, Su 1pm. Weekday tours depart from 101 University Hall; weekend tours depart from the Campanile.) **Sather Tower** is the official name of the Campanile, the tallest building on campus; you can ride to its observation level for a great view of the San Francisco Bay. (Open M-F 10am-4pm, tip-top is not wheelchair-accessible; $2.) The ⬛**Berkeley Art Museum (BAM),** 2626 Bancroft Way, is most respected for its collection of 20th-century American and Asian art. The **Pacific Film Archive** is a branch of BAM and has over 500 public screenings each year; check online for details. (☎642-0808; www.bampfa.berkeley.edu. Open W and F-Su 11am-5pm, Th 11am-7pm. $8; students, seniors, disabled, and ages 12-17 $5. First Th of each month free.) You haven't really visited Berkeley until you've been on **Telegraph Avenue,** lined with a motley assortment of cafes, bookstores, and used clothing and record stores—plus a few sidewalk stands where the mutterings of ex-hippies provide a soundtrack for window shopping. A visit to legendary **Amoeba Records** is a Berkeley must. In the forested hills in the eastern part of the city lies beautiful **Tilden Regional Park.** By car or bike, take Spruce St. to Grizzly Peak Blvd. then to Canon Ave. Hiking, biking, running, and riding trails criss-cross the park and provide impressive views of the Bay Area. (☎562-7275. Open daily 8am-10pm. Free.) Inside the park, the small beach at **Lake Anza** is a popular swimming spot on the hottest summer days. (☎843-2137. Open May-Oct. daily 11am-10pm; lifeguards on duty until 6pm. $3.50, seniors and children $2.50.)

🖫 NIGHTLIFE. ⬛**Jupiter,** 2181 Shattuck Ave., near the BART station, houses a huge beer garden and offers live music and terrific wood-fired pizza for $8-13. (☎843-8277. Open M-Th 11:30am-1am, F 11:30am-1:30am, Sa noon-1:30am, Su 1pm-midnight.) **Blakes,** 2367 Telegraph Ave., near Durant Ave., is a jam-packed and unabashed meat market. (☎848-0886. M acoustic open mic. W-Sa local bands. Drink specials 9pm-midnight; W $1 beer and fries, Th college night, $2 well drinks and $1 pints. Cover $2-12. Open M-F 11:30am-2am, Sa-Su noon-2am.) The boisterous and friendly **Triple Rock Brewery,** 1920 Shattuck Ave., north of Berkeley Way, was the first of Berkeley's many brewpubs. Come Thursday nights for delicious and highly alcoholic Monkey Head ale. (☎843-2739. Award-winning Red Rock Ale $3.75. Open M-W and Su 11:30am-midnight, Th-Sa 11:30am-1am. Rooftop garden closes 10pm. Kitchen closes M-W and Su 10pm, Th-Sa 11:30pm.)

MARIN COUNTY
☎415

Just across the Golden Gate Bridge, Marin (muh-RIN) County is strikingly beautiful, politically liberal, and visibly wealthy. Suburbia rules in the east part of the county, but on the west side, the cathedral-like stillness of ancient redwoods, sharp scent of eucalyptus (though not a native species), brilliant wildflowers, windy bluffs, and crashing surf converge along Hwy. 1.

▐ TRANSPORTATION

Buses: Golden Gate Transit (☎455-2000, in SF 923-2000; www.goldengate.org). Provides bus service between San Francisco and Marin County via the Golden Gate Bridge, as well as local service in Marin ($3.60-5.30). **West Marin Stagecoach** (☎499-6099; www.marintransit.org) provides weekday service connecting West Marin communities to the rest of the county. Stops include: Muir Beach, Pt. Reyes Station, Samuel P. Taylor Park, San Anselmo, and Stinson Beach. Call for schedules and routes. $2.

Ferries: Golden Gate Ferry (☎455-2000). Runs from San Francisco to the Sausalito terminal at the end of Market St. and to the Larkspur terminal ($7.10; seniors, disabled and under 18 $3.55). **Blue and Gold Fleet** (☎705-8200; www.blueandgoldfleet.com) runs ferries from Pier 41 at Fisherman's Wharf to Sausalito and Tiburon ($9, ages 5-11 $5, under 5 free). Offices open M-F 6am-8pm, Sa-Su 7am-8pm.

Taxi: Belaire Cab Co. ☎388-1234.

Bike Rental: Cycle Analysis (☎663-9164; www.cyclepointreyes.com), a trailer in the empty, grassy lot at 4th and Main St. off Hwy. 1 in Point Reyes Station. Rents unsuspended bikes ($10 per hr., $32 per day), front-suspension mountain bikes ($15/40), and child trailers ($30 per day). Emergency repairs and advice for self-guided tours. Open M-Th by appointment, F-Su 10am-5pm.

▐ ORIENTATION AND PRACTICAL INFORMATION

The Marin peninsula lies at the northern end of the San Francisco Bay and is connected to the city by **U.S. 101** via the **Golden Gate Bridge.** U.S. 101 extends north inland to Santa Rosa and Sonoma County, while **Route 1** winds north along the Pacific coast. The **Richmond-San Rafael Bridge** connects Marin to the East Bay via I-580. Gas is scarce and expensive in West Marin, so fill up in town before you head out for the coast. Drivers should exercise caution in West Marin, where roads are narrow, sinuous, and perched on the edges of cliffs.

Visitor Information: There are several Visitors Centers throughout the county; one for Marin County itself and several for its parks and outdoors attractions.

Marin County Visitors Bureau, 1 Mitchell Blvd., Suite B (☎925-2060; www.visit-marin.org). In San Rafael near the Freitas Pkwy. Exit off U.S. 101. Open M-F 9am-5pm.

Point Reyes National Seashore Headquarters (also referred to as Bear Valley Visitor Center; ☎464-5100; www.nps.gov/pore), on Bear Valley Rd., ½ mi. west of Olema. Open M-F 9am-5pm, Sa-Su and holidays 8am-5pm.

Pan Toll Ranger's Station, 801 Panoramic Hwy. (☎388-2070), in Mt. Tamalpais State Park, about 2½ mi. inland from Stinson Beach. Bus #63 stops on weekends (about 5 per day). Open daily June-Aug. 9am-6pm; Sept.-May intermittently.

Muir Woods National Monument Visitors Center (☎388-2596; www.nps.gov/muwo), near the entrance to Muir Woods. Muir Woods trail map $1 (free download on website). Open daily Sept.-May 9am-6pm; June-Aug. 8am-8pm.

Marin Headlands Visitors Center, Bldg. 948, Fort Barry (☎331-1540), located at Bunker and Field Rd. The center is also a museum. Wheelchair-accessible. Open daily 9:30am-4:30pm.

Post Office: 15 Calle del Mar (☎868-1504), at Shoreline Hwy. in Stinson Beach. Open M-F 8:30am-5pm. **Postal Code:** 94970.

ACCOMMODATIONS

🏠 **West Point Inn** (☎388-9955, reservations 646-0702), on Mt. Tamalpais, 2 mi. up Old Stage Rd. Park at the Pan Toll Ranger Station ($6, seniors $5) and hike or bike up. Not luxurious, but one hell of an experience. Propane-generated heat, light, and refrigeration; no electricity. Bring sleeping bag, food, and flashlight. 7 private rooms, 5 private cabins, and a well-equipped kitchen. Self clean-up required. Reservations required. Sa vacancies are rare. Closed M and Su nights. $35, under 18 $18, under 5 free. ❷

Marin Headlands Hostel (HI) (☎331-2777; www.norcalhostels.org) at Fort Berry . Take the Alexander Ave. Exit and follow the signs at Fort Berry. A converted century-old house with an international collection of backpackers. Linen $1. Towels $0.50. Alcohol prohibited. Reception open 7:30am-11:30pm. Dorms $18-22. ❶

Point Reyes Hostel (HI) (☎663-8811; norcalhostels.org/reyes), just off Limoatour Rd., 2 mi. from Limatour beach in the Point Reyes National Seashore. Miles from civilization, this unique hostel provides shelter and solace in the wilderness. Linen $1; sleeping bags encouraged. Towels $1. Chore required. Check-in 4:30-9:30pm. Check-out 10am. Lockout 10am-4:30pm. Dorms $20, under 17 $10. ❶

FOOD

Marinites take their fruit juices, tofu, and double-shot cappuccinos very seriously; restaurateurs know this, and raise their alfalfa sprouts and prices accordingly.

Venice Gourmet Delicatessen, 625 Bridgeway (☎332-3544), in Sausalito. Serves a wide variety of sandwiches ($5.50-8) and side dishes ($1.50-5) in a Mediterranean-style marketplace. A few outdoor tables have a stunning view of the San Francisco skyline, but the sandwiches are perfect for a picnic at the beach. Open daily 9am-6pm; in summer till 7pm. ❷

Avatar's Punjabi Burrito, 15 Madrona St. (☎381-8293), in Mill Valley. Take chickpeas, rice, chutney, yogurt, and spice; add tofu and meats; and wrap in yummy Indian flatbread for an inspired and filling meal. Burritos $5.50-8.50. Open M-Sa 11am-8pm. ❷

Bubba's Diner, 566 San Anselmo Ave. (☎459-6862), in San Anselmo. A local favorite with all the essentials. All-day breakfast, including "chocoholic" pancakes ($9), prepared next to the old-fashioned counter. Open W-F 9am-9pm, Sa-Su 8am-9pm. ❸

SIGHTS

Marin's proximity to San Francisco makes it a popular daytrip destination. Almost everything worth seeing or doing in Marin is outdoors. An efficient visitor can hop between parks and enjoy several short hikes along the coast and through the redwood forests in the same day, topping it off with dinner in one of the small cities, but the roads are winding and the RVs ahead of you will probably slow you down.

MARIN HEADLANDS. Fog-shrouded hills just west of the Golden Gate Bridge constitute the Marin Headlands. These windswept ridges, precipitous cliffs, and hidden sandy beaches offer superb hiking and biking within minutes of downtown SF. For instant gratification, drive up to any of the several look-out spots and pose for your own postcard-perfect shot of the Golden Gate Bridge and the city skyline.

POINT REYES NATIONAL SEASHORE. Surrounded by nearly 100 mi. of isolated coastline, Point Reyes National Seashore is a wilderness of pine forests, chaparral ridges, and grassy foothills. *(Hwy. 1 provides direct access to the park from the north or south; Sir Francis Drake Blvd. comes west from U.S. 101 at San Rafael.)* The **Point Reyes Lighthouse** is at the very tip of the dramatic, windswept point. From December to February, migrating gray whales can be spotted from the overlook. *(Follow Sir Francis Drake Blvd. to its end, 20 mi. from the Visitors Center. Lighthouse Visitors Center ☎ 669-1534. Access to lighthouse via 300 stairs. Open M and Th-Su 10am-4:30pm. Free.)*

MOUNT TAMALPAIS AND MUIR WOODS. Between the towns of eastern Marin and the rocky bluffs of western Marin rests beautiful **Mount Tamalpais State Park** (Mt. Tam; 2571 ft.). The park has miles of challenging trails on and around Mt. Tam. The bubbling waterfall on Cataract Trail *(off Hwy. 1, follow signs)* and the Gardner Lookout on the east peak are worthy destinations. *(☎ 388-2070. 7am-sunset; road access opens at 9am. Free. Parking $6, seniors $5.)* Visit the Pan Toll Ranger Station, on Panoramic Hwy., for trail suggestions and biking restrictions. On weekends and holidays, bus #63 stops at the ranger station between the Golden Gate Bridge and Stinson Beach. At the center of the state park is **Muir Woods National Monument,** a 560-acre grove of ancient redwoods. Spared from logging by the steep sides of Redwood Canyon, these massive redwoods tower over the rest of the silent forest. Go in the evening to avoid crowds. *(5 mi. west of U.S. 101 on Hwy. 1. ☎ 388-2596. Open 8am-dusk. $3, under 15 free.)*

BEACHES. Sheltered **Muir Beach** is scenic and popular with families. The crowds thin out significantly after a 5min. climb on the shore rocks to the left. *(Open dawn-9pm.)* Six miles to the north, ▓**Stinson Beach** attracts a younger, rowdier surfer crowd, although cold and windy conditions often leave them languishing on dry land. *(Bus #63 runs from Sausalito to Stinson Beach on weekends and holidays. Open 9am-1hr. after sunset.)* From July to October, the Bard visits Stinson Beach for **Shakespeare at Stinson.** *(☎ 868-1115; http://www.marinwebpro.com/stinson/tiks.html.)* Between Muir and Stinson Beaches lies **Red Rocks Beach,** where many beachgoers do without their swimsuits. The beach is a secluded spot reached by a steep hike from a parking area 1 mi. south of Stinson Beach.

WINE COUNTRY

NAPA VALLEY ☎707

Napa catapulted American wine into the big leagues in 1976, when a bottle of red from the area's Stag's Leap Vineyards beat a bottle of critically acclaimed (and unfailingly French) Château Lafitte-Rothschild in a blind taste test in Paris. Napa Valley is certainly the best-known of America's wine-growing regions. Its grape-dotted hills, natural hot springs, and consistently gorgeous weather attract everyone from the well-to-do urbanite staying in a high-priced B&B to the group of tourists cruising in a rental limousine. Expect insufferable traffic congestion, especially at the south end of Napa where all the major highways meet. Napa's dense collection of vineyards promises winery after winery of intoxicating pleasure and vistas that are equally disarming.

▐ TRANSPORTATION

Buses: Valley Intercity Neighborhood Express (VINE), 1151 Pearl St. (☎ 800-696-6443, TDD 226-9722; www.napavalleyvine.net), has a few bus services that cover the

CALIFORNIA

entire stretch of Napa Valley from Vallejo to Calistoga. Schedules vary, generally M-Sa 6:30am-7pm. $1.25-2.75, ages 6-18 $1-2, seniors $0.60-1.35. Ask for free transfers. The nearest Greyhound station is in Vallejo at 1500 Lemon St. (☎643-7661 or 800-231-2222; www.greyhound.com).

Bike Rental: ■**St. Helena Cyclery,** 1156 Main St. (☎963-7736; www.sthelenacyclery.com). Hybrid bikes $10 per hr., $30 per day; road bikes $60 per day; tandem bikes $70 per day. All bikes come with maps, helmet, and a lock. Reservations recommended, although no reservations necessary for hybrid bikes. Open Tu-Sa 9:30am-5:30pm, Su 10am-5pm.

▦▮ ORIENTATION AND PRACTICAL INFORMATION

Scenic **Route 29 (Saint Helena Highway)** runs north from **Napa** through Napa Valley and the well-groomed villages of **Yountville** and **Saint Helena** (where it's called Main St.) to **Calistoga's** soothing spas. The relatively short distances between wineries may seem unpleasantly long on weekends when the roads crawl with visitors. The **Silverado Trail,** parallel to Rte. 29, is much less crowded and accesses many wineries, but watch out for cyclists. Napa is 14 mi. east of Sonoma on **Route 12.** From San Francisco, take U.S. 101 over the Golden Gate Bridge, then follow Rte. 37 east to catch Rte. 29, which runs north to Napa.

Visitor Info: Napa Valley Conference & Visitors Bureau, 1310 Napa Town Ctr. (☎226-7459; www.napavalley.com). Provides free maps, helpful info, and the useful *Napa Valley Guidebook* ($6). Ask about any specials from local businesses. Open daily 9am-5pm. **St. Helena Chamber of Commerce,** 1010A Main St. (☎963-4456; www.sthelena.com). Eager to help. Open M-F 10am-5pm, Sa 11am-3pm. **Calistoga Chamber of Commerce,** 1506 Lincoln Ave. (☎942-6333; www.calistogachamber.com). Open M-F 10am-5pm, Sa 10am-4pm, Su 11am-3pm.

Winery Tours: Napa Valley Wine Train, 1275 McKinstry St. (☎253-2111 or 800-427-4124; www.winetrain.com), offers dining and drinking on board, traveling from Napa to St. Helena and back. Train ride 3hr. M-F 11am and 6pm; Sa-Su 8:30am, 12:10, 5:30pm. Ticket and meal plans $40-90. Advance reservations and payments required.

Police: 1539 1st St. (☎257-9223), in Napa; 1234 Washington St. (☎942-2810), in Calistoga.

Medical Services: Queen of the Valley Hospital, 1000 Trancas St. (☎252-4411), in Napa.

Post Office: 1625 Trancas St. (☎255-0190), in Napa. Open M-F 9am-5pm. **Postal Code:** 94558.

▮ ACCOMMODATIONS

Rooms in Napa Valley go quickly despite high prices; reserve ahead. Though Napa is close to the Bay Area, smaller towns prove more wallet-friendly. Although certainly not cheap, Calistoga is a good first choice; the quaint town is a short drive from many wineries and is close to Bothe-Napa State Park. It is also home to natural hot-spring spas. Campers will save, but should be prepared for summer heat.

Golden Haven Hot Springs Spa and Resort, 1713 Lake St. (☎942-6793; www.goldenhaven.com), a few blocks from Lincoln Ave., in Calistoga. Large and tastefully decorated rooms. TV, fridge, and private bath but no phones. Mineral swimming pool and hot tub access. No children under 16 F-Sa. 2-night min. stay on weekends. Room with queen-sized bed $79-95, with private sauna $145-175; king-sized bed $85-99, with kitchenette $135-169, with jacuzzi $165-219. Check online for internet specials and spa packages. ❹

Calistoga Inn and Brewery, 1250 Lincoln Ave. (☎942-4101; www.calistogainn.com), at the corner of Rte. 29, in Calistoga. 18 simple, country rooms that barely fit a queen-sized bed. Shared bathrooms. Microbrewery and restaurant downstairs. Rooms Apr.-Oct. M-Th and Su $89, F-Sa $139. Low season M-Th and Su $75, F-Sa $125. ❹

Bothe-Napa Valley State Park, 3801 Rte. 29 (☎942-4575, reservations 800-444-7275; www.napanet.net/~bothe), 5 mi. north of St. Helena. 50 rustic sites near Ritchey Creek Canyon. Toilets, fire pits, and picnic tables at each site. Firewood $5. Pool $3, under 17 $1. Hot showers $0.25 per 3min. Check-in 2pm. Park open daily 8am-dusk. Sites for up to 8 and 1 vehicle $25. Picnic area day use $6. ❶

🍴 FOOD

Extremely cheap eats aren't an option in Wine Country. Picnics are a potentially inexpensive alternative—many wineries have picnic grounds but most require patronage. The **Napa Farmer's Market,** 500 1st St., at Soscol Ave., offers a sampling of local produce. (☎252-7142. Open Tu and Sa 7:30am-noon.) **Cal Mart,** 1491 Lincoln Ave. (☎942-6271), in Calistoga, provides groceries. **Taylor's Automatic Refresher ❷,** 933 Main St., on Rte. 29, in St. Helena, is a roadside stand with burgers, sandwiches, fries, and the obligatory wine selection. The "Texas Burger" (pepper jack cheese, guacamole, salsa, and jalapenos; $8.50) pairs well with a thick milkshake. (☎963-3486; www.taylorsrefresher.com. Outdoor seating. Open daily 10:30am-8:30pm.) **First Squeeze Cafe and Juice Bar ❷,** 1126 1st St., in Napa, has a friendly staff that serves healthful favorites like the "Vanessa" (grilled tofu with avocado on nut bread), *huevos rancheros* ($8), and fruit smoothies. (☎224-6762. Beer and wine $2.50-3.50. Breakfast served until 3pm. Open daily M-F 7am-3pm, Sa-Su 8am-3pm. AmEx/D/MC/V.)

Napa Valley

⚡ WINERIES

There are over 250 wineries in Napa County, nearly two-thirds of which line Rte. 29 and the Silverado Trail in Napa Valley. Some wineries have free tastings, some have free tours, and some charge for both; all have large selections of bottled wine available for purchase at prices cheaper than in stores. A good way to begin your Napa Valley experience is with a tour such as the ones offered at **Domaine Carneros,** 1240 Duhig Rd. in Napa (☎716-2788), or a tasting class, like the one on Saturday mornings at **Goosecross Cellars,** 1119 State Ln. in Yountville. (☎944-1986. Open daily 10am-4:30pm; classes Sa 10:30am-noon. $10.) ⬛**V. Sattui,** 1111 White Ln., at Rte. 29, in St. Helena was named "Best Winery in California" at the 2007 California State Fair, is one of the few wineries in the valley that only sells at its winery, which means great prices. The family-owned operation also has a gourmet cheese counter, meat shop, and bakery. (☎963-7774 or 800-799-2337; www.vsattui.com. Open daily Mar.-Oct. 9am-6pm; Nov.-Feb. 9am-5pm. Picnic area for customers. Very popular and crowded free tastings.) ⬛**Mumm Napa,** 8445 Silverado Trail in Rutherford, produces only sparkling wines, but has a variety designed to fit any palette. A free tour illuminates the sparkling wine-making process and tastings are done in a seated, restaurant-like atmosphere. The winery also houses a magnificent photography gallery. (☎686-6272; www.mummnapa.com. Open daily 10am-5pm. Tours every hr. 10am-3pm. Free. No reservation needed. $5-20 depending on selections.) ⬛**Kirkland Ranch,** 1 Kirkland Ranch Rd., south of Napa off Rte. 29., is a family-operated winery with windows overlooking the production facilities. True to its country-western style, the winery's log walls are adorned with family pictures of cattle-herding cowboys, and the very drinkable wines are surprisingly affordable. (☎254-9100; www.kirklandranch-winery.com. Open daily 10am-4pm. Tours by appointment. Tastings $5 for 4 selections.) **Robert Mondavi Winery,** 7801 Rte. 29, 8 mi. north of Napa, is massive and touristy, with a beautiful mission-style visitors complex, three tasting rooms selling by taste and by the glass ($3-20), and the atmosphere of a luxury resort. (☎963-9611 or 888-766-6328; www.robert-mondaviwinery.com. Open daily 10am-5pm. Vineyard and winery tour daily every hr. 10am-4pm; includes 3 tastes. Reservations at least 1hr. in advance are recommended.) **Rubicon Estate Winery** (formerly **Niebaum-Coppola**) at 1991 St. Helena Hwy., was purchased by famed director Francis Ford Coppola and his wife in 1975. Restoring the historic 1880 Inglenook Chateau and Niebaum vineyards to production capacity, Coppola also added a free Coppola family history museum upstairs that contains film memorabilia, including the desk from *The Godfather* and his Oscar and Golden Globe statues. Newest additions to the vineyard include the upstairs "magic lantern" exhibit and a series of caves that house barrels and barrels of wine. (☎968-1100; www.niebaum-coppola.com. Open daily 10am-5pm. $25, includes 5 tastes and a historical tour. Free valet parking and baguettes. Vineyard tours daily 11am, $15; historical tours on the half hr.)

OUTDOOR (AND INDOOR) ACTIVITIES

Napa's gentle terrain makes for an excellent bike tour. The area is fairly flat, although small bike lanes, speeding cars, and blistering heat can make routes more challenging, especially after a few samples of wine. The 26 mi. Silverado Trail has a wider bike path than Rte. 29. To soothe your weary quads and hamstrings, visit Calistoga, which is known as the "Hot Springs of the West." Its odoriferous mud baths, luxuriant massages, and refreshing mineral showers will feel even more welcome after a hard day of wine-tasting. Be sure to hydrate beforehand; alcohol-thinned blood and heat don't mix. A basic package with a mud bath, mineral bath, eucalyptus steam, and blanket wrap costs about $60. Salt scrubs and facials cost each about $50. The Calistoga Village Inn and Spa boasts friendly service and heavenly treatments. (☎942-0991. Mud bath $60. 50min. massage $80. Body wrap $95.) Golden Haven also offers full spa services. (☎942-6793; www.goldenhaven.com. 30min. facial $49. Mud bath $75. 30min. massage $49-60. Prices lower in winter.)

SONOMA VALLEY ☎707

A carefully crafted charm prevails in the sprawling Sonoma Valley, providing a quieter alternative to Napa. Many wineries are on winding side roads rather than a freeway strip, dispersing traffic and creating a more intimate wine-tasting experience. Sonoma Plaza is surrounded by art galleries, novelty shops, clothing stores, and restaurants. Petaluma, west of the Sonoma Valley, has more budget-friendly lodgings than the expensive wine country.

TRANSPORTATION

From San Francisco, take **U.S. 101 N.** over the Golden Gate Bridge; then follow Rte. 37 E to Rte. 116 N., which turns into Rte. 121 N. and crosses Rte. 12 N. to Sonoma. Alternatively, follow U.S. 101 N. to Petaluma and cross over to Sonoma by Rte. 116. Driving time from San Francisco is about 1-1½hr. **Route 12** traverses the length of Sonoma Valley, from **Sonoma** through **Glen Ellen** to **Kenwood** in the north. The center of downtown Sonoma is **Sonoma Plaza,** which contains City Hall and the Visitors Center. **Broadway** dead-ends at Napa St. in front of City Hall. Numbered streets run north-south. **Petaluma** lies to the west and is connected to Sonoma by **Route 116,** which becomes **Lakeville Street** in Petaluma.

Buses: Sonoma County Transit (☎576-7433 or 800-345-7433; www.sctransit.com) serves the entire county. Bus #30 runs from **Sonoma** to **Santa Rosa** (daily every 1-1½hr. M-F 6am-9:30pm, Sa-Su 7am-7pm; $2.50, students $2.15, seniors and disabled $1.25, under 6 free); #44 and 48 go from **Santa Rosa** to **Petaluma** (daily; $2.10, students $1.80, seniors and disabled $1.05). Within Sonoma, county buses must be flagged down at bus stops (daily 8am-4:25pm; $1.10/0.90/0.55). **Golden Gate Transit** (from Sonoma County ☎541-2000, from SF 415-923-2000) runs buses frequently between **San Francisco** and **Santa Rosa.**

CALIFORNIA

Bike Rental: Sonoma Valley Cyclery, 20093 Broadway (☎935-3377). $6 per hr., $20-25 per day; includes helmet, lock, and bags. Open M-Sa 10am-6pm, Su 10am-4pm.

🛈 PRACTICAL INFORMATION

Visitor Info: Sonoma Valley Visitors Bureau, 453 1st St. E (☎996-1090; www.sonomavalley.com), in Sonoma Plaza. Maps available. Open daily 9am-5pm. **Petaluma Visitors Program,** 800 Baywood Dr. (☎762-2785), at Lakeville St. The free visitor's guide has listings of restaurants and activities. Open daily 9am-5pm.

Police: In Sonoma ☎838-1234. In Petaluma ☎778-4451.

Medical Services: Petaluma Valley Hospital, 400 N. McDowell Blvd. (☎778-1111).

Post Office: Sonoma, 617 Broadway (☎996-9311), at Patten St. Open M-F 8:30am-5pm. **Postal Code:** 95476. Petaluma, 120 4th St. (☎800-275-8777). Open M-F 8:30am-5pm, Sa 10am-2pm. **Postal Code:** 94952.

🛏 ACCOMMODATIONS

Pickings are pretty slim for lodging; rooms are scarce even on weekdays and generally start at $90. Less-expensive motels cluster along **U.S. 101** in Santa Rosa and Petaluma. Campers with cars should try the **Russian River Valley** to the west.

🏨 **Sonoma Creek Inn,** 239 Boyes Blvd. (☎939-9463 or 888-712-1289), west off Hwy. 12, in Sonoma. Just 10min. from the Sonoma Plaza. Cheaper than most places in the area, but just as nice. Colorful rooms with cable TV, fridge, full bath, and phone; most with adobe patio. Rooms Nov.-Mar. $79-119; Apr.-June $109-169; July-Oct. $129-179. ❹

Redwood Inn, 1670 Santa Rosa Ave. (☎645-0474), in Santa Rosa. At least a 30min. drive from Sonoma. Comfortable, motel-style rooms with bath, cable TV, phone; some with kitchenette. Rooms with 1 bed $60-75, with 2 beds $70-85; $5 less in winter. ❸

Sugarloaf Ridge State Park, 2605 Adobe Canyon Rd. (☎833-5712, reservations 800-444-7275; www.reserveamerica.com), off Rte. 12, north of Kenwood in the Mayacamas mountains. 49 sites with tables and fire rings. Arranged around a central meadow with flush toilets and running water (but no showers). In summer and fall, take advantage of Ferguson Observatory inside the park; see www.rfo.org for details. Sites $15-20. Parking $6. ❶

🍴 FOOD

Seasonal produce is available directly from area farms or at roadside stands and farmers' markets. Those in the area toward the end of the summer should ask about the ambrosial **crane melon,** a tasty hybrid of fruits grown only on the Crane Farm north of Petaluma. The **Sonoma Market,** 500 W. Napa St., in the Sonoma Valley Center, is an old-fashioned grocery store with deli sandwiches ($4.25-7) and produce. (☎996-3411. Open daily 6am-9pm.) The **Fruit Basket,** 18474 Sonoma Hwy., sells inexpensive fruit. (☎996-7433. Open daily 7am-7pm.) A deli-style boulangerie, the **Basque Cafe ❷,** 460 1st St. E, specializes in fresh breads, pastries, and delicious sandwiches. Their breakfast ($1.35-5) is a great way to start the day, and the prosciutto and brie sandwich ($8.35) will keep energy levels high. (☎935-7687. Open daily 7am-6:30pm.) In Sonoma, even the pubs are classy, as is evident at **Murphy's Irish Pub ❸,** 464 1st St. E, with a warm wood interior and a good-natured staff that welcomes newcomers with a perfectly pulled pint. Favorites include the fish and chips ($13), and any of the beers, ales, or whiskeys. (☎935-0660; www.sonomapub.com. Live music Th 7:30pm, F-Sa 8pm, Su 6pm. Open M-Th and Su 11am-11pm, F-Sa 11am-midnight.)

🎗 WINERIES

Sonoma Valley's wineries, near Sonoma and Kenwood, are less touristy but just as elegant as Napa's. As an added bonus, there are more complimentary tastings of current vintages. ◼**Benziger,** at 1883 London Ranch Rd., is certified as biodynamic and is a family-owned and operated winery that brings a great deal of care to the winemaking process in order to preserve the natural character of its grapes. (☎888-490-2739 or 935-4014; www.benziger.com. Open daily 10am-5pm. Self-guided tours lead from the parking lot through the vineyards and peacock aviary. Comprehensive 45min. tractor-tram tour through the vineyards runs in summer daily every 30min. 11am-3:30pm, includes reserve tasting and 20% off purchases. $10, under 21 $5. Tastings of current vintage $5, estate and reserves $10.) ◼**Gundlach-Bundschu,** at 2000 Denmark St., off 8th St. E., established in 1858, is the 2nd-oldest winery in Sonoma and the oldest family-owned and run winery in the country. A quiet, refined tasting room and high-quality wines draw people from across the country. (☎939-3015; www.gunbun.com. Open daily 11am-4:30pm. Free wine storage cave tours Sa-Su 1:30 and 3pm. Tastings $5 for 4-6 samples.) **Buena Vista,** 18000 Old Winery Rd. Take E. Napa St. from Sonoma Plaza and turn left on Old Winery Rd., is the oldest premium winery in the valley. Famous stone buildings are preserved just as Mr. Haraszthy built them in 1857 when he founded the California wine industry. Its park-like grounds are a great stop for learning a little bit about the history of American winemaking. (☎938-1266; www.buenavistawinery.com. Tours $10. Reservations for group tours for 8 or more can be made in advance by calling the winery. Tastings $5-20; includes glass. Open daily 10am-5pm.) Be greeted by a chorus of adorable bleating sheep as you enter the driveway of the **Larson Family Winery,** 23355 Millerick Rd., just off Hwy. 121, is a cozy farmhouse vineyard that also boasts a llama named Dolly. Enjoy award-winning wine and a casual chat with the pourers, and help yourself to bread and local olive oil as you taste. If you have enough energy, stay for a game of bocce in their lawn court. (☎938-3031. Open daily 10am-5pm. $5 for 6 tastes.) **Ledson Winery and Vineyards,** 7335 Sonoma Hwy., is a relatively new Merlot estate, does not market its wines. The stunning French-Normandy "castle" houses a lavish parlor and an equally impressive gourmet marketplace featuring fine cheeses, sauces, and exclusive fruit spreads. (☎537-3810; www.ledson.com. Monthly events themed around holidays. Open daily 10am-5pm. Tastings $5-15.)

🌀 SIGHTS

SONOMA STATE HISTORIC PARK. A series of structures surround the town plaza and are known collectively as the historic park. At the northeast corner of the square, an adobe church stands on the site of the **Mission San Francisco-Solano,** the northernmost and last of the 21 Franciscan missions. Built in 1826 by Padre Jose Altimira, the mission contains a fragment of the original California Republic flag, the rest of which was burned in the 1906 San Francisco earthquake fires. Other attractions include Gold Rush era hotels, army barracks, and the Victorian home of General Vallejo. *(E. Spain and 1st St. ☎938-9560. Open daily 10am-5pm. $2, children under 17 free. Includes access to all sites.)*

JACK LONDON STATE PARK. Around the turn of the 20th century, hard-drinking and hard-living Jack London, author of *The Call of the Wild* and *White Fang*, bought 1400 acres here, determined to create his dream home. London's hopes were frustrated when the estate's main building, **Wolf House,** was destroyed by arsonists in 1913. London died three years after the fire and is buried in the park, his grave marked by a volcanic boulder intended for the construction of his house. The remains of Wolf House are accessed by a half-mile trail. The nearby **House of Happy Walls,** built by London's widow in his honor, is now a two-story museum devoted to the writer. Scenic trails cross the property, allowing access to what London called "Beauty Ranch." *(Take Hwy. 12 4 mi. north from Sonoma to Arnold Ln. and follow signs.* ☎ *938-5216. Park open daily 10am-dusk. Museum open daily 10am-5pm. Free.)*

THE CENTRAL COAST

The 400 mi. stretch of coastline between Los Angeles. and San Francisco embodies all things Californian—rolling surf, a seaside highway built for cruising, dramatic bluffs topped by weathered pines, self-actualizing New-Age adherents, and always a hint of the offbeat. This is the solitary magnificence that inspired John Steinbeck's novels and Jack Kerouac's musings. The landmarks along the way—Hearst Castle, the Monterey Bay Aquarium, the historic missions—are well worth visiting, but the real highlight of the Central Coast is the journey itself.

SANTA CRUZ ☎ 831

Negotiating the liminal space between NorCal and SoCal, Santa Cruz (pop. 56,000) embraces sculpted surfers, aging hippies, free-thinking students, and same-sex couples. The atmosphere here is fun-loving but far from hedonistic, intellectual but nowhere near stuffy. This small city exudes fun, whether you find it gobbling cotton candy on the Boardwalk or downing wheatgrass at poetry readings.

◪◲ TRANSPORTATION AND PRACTICAL INFORMATION. Greyhound, 425 Front St. (☎ 423-1800; www.greyhound.com; open daily 6-6:30am, 8:30am-12:30pm, 2:30-7:15pm, 9:30-10pm), runs **buses** to Los Angeles (8-10hr., 8 per day, $44), San Francisco (2½-3hr., 5 per day, $13), and San Jose (1hr., 4 per day, $7.50). Santa Cruz Metropolitan Transit District (SCMTD), 920 Pacific Ave., handles **local transportation.** (☎ 425-8600; www.scmtd.com. Open M-F 8am-4pm. Buses run daily 6am-11pm. $1.50, disabled and seniors $0.75, under 46 in. free; day pass $4.50/2.25/free.) Santa Cruz is on the northern tip of Monterey Bay, 65 mi. south of San Francisco. Through west Santa Cruz, Hwy. 1 becomes **Mission Street.** The **University of California at Santa Cruz (UCSC)** blankets the hills inland from Mission St. Southeast of Mission St. lies the waterfront, where **Beach Street** and **West Cliff Drive** run roughly east-west along the coastline. The many shops, restaurants, and clubs of downtown straddle **Pacific Avenue.** Many lots around downtown offer 3hr. free **parking,** and day-long free parking can be found west of town along W. Cliff Dr., about a 10min. walk from the beach. Pick up the *Santa Cruz County Traveler's Guide* at **Santa Cruz County Conference and Visitor Council,** 1211 Ocean St. (☎ 425-1234 or 800-833-3494; www.santacruzca.org. Open M-Sa 9am-5pm, Su 10am-4pm.) **Post Office:** 850 Front St. (☎ 426-8184. Open M-F 9am-5pm.) **Postal Code:** 95060.

◪◲ ACCOMMODATIONS AND FOOD. Santa Cruz gets jam-packed in summer, especially on weekends; room rates skyrocket and vacancies plummet. Always make reservations. **Carmelita Cottage Santa Cruz Hostel (HI) ❶,** 321 Main St., is a collection of small Victorian cottages that functions as a 40-bed hostel. (☎ 423-8304. Chores requested. Towels $0.50. Day-parking permit $1.25. July-Aug. 3-night max. stay. Reception 8-11am and 5-10pm. Lockout 11am-5pm. Strict curfew 11pm. No alcohol. Dorms $23, members $21, ages 12-17 $15, ages 3-11 $10, under 3 free. MC/V.) The **Harbor Inn ❸,** 645 7th Ave., is a beautiful, historic 19-room hotel east of the harbor and well off the main drag. In late June, pick plums from the trees out back. (☎479-9731. Free parking. Cable TV, fridges, microwaves. Office open M-Sa 10am-7pm, Su noon-5pm. Rooms in summer $65-95, with bath $85-175.) Camping may be the best budget option. Twenty-five miles northwest of Santa Cruz, ☒**Big Basin Redwoods State Park ❶,** California's oldest state park and home to 18,000 acres of old growth and recovering redwood forest, has great sites and breezy trails. (☎338-8860; www.bigbasin.org. Sites $25.)

A few eateries can be found along the beachfront, but downtown is home to the most reasonably priced restaurants, pizza joints, and coffee shops. Fresh produce and ready-to-eat goodies are sold at the **farmers' market** (W 2:30-6:30pm) at Lincoln and Cedar St. downtown. **Zoccoli's ❷,** 1534 Pacific Ave., downtown, is a tasty Italian deli that uses only the freshest ingredients and has all of the makings for a semi-gourmet beachside picnic. (☎423-1711. Sandwiches $5-6. Open M-Sa 9am-6pm, Su 10am-6pm.) After a day at the beach, grab a generously-sized burrito ($2) with the locals at **Las Palmas Taco Bar ❶,** 55 Front St., by the wharf. Tasty tacos cost $1.50 and combo plates with rice, beans, and excellent tortillas run $4.50-7. (☎429-1220. Open M-Th and Su 10am-9pm, F-Sa 10am-10pm.)

■ **SIGHTS.** Santa Cruz has a great beach, but the water is frigid—it requires courage (and sometimes a wetsuit) to take full advantage of the waves. Many casual beachgoers catch their thrills on the **Santa Cruz Beach Boardwalk.** First opened in 1907, the boardwalk is now a three-block strip of rides, guess-your-weight booths, shooting galleries, arcade games, and corn-dog vendors. It's a gloriously tacky throwback to 50s-era beach culture. The traditional favorite is the **Giant Dipper,** the 1924 wooden roller coaster where Dirty Harry met his enemy in 1983's *Sudden Impact.* (Boardwalk open daily Memorial Day-Labor Day, plus many low-season weekends and holidays; arcade open year-round. Rides require 4-6 tickets each. All-day pass $29. 60 tickets $38. Mini-golf $5. Look for flyers with special deals.) The **Santa Cruz Wharf,** off Beach St., is the longest car-accessible pier on the West Coast. Seafood restaurants and souvenir shops will try to distract you from expansive views of the ocean. Snack on a caramel apple from local favorite **Marini's,** at the wharf's end, and watch the sea lions on the rocks below. (☎423-7258. Open M-Th and Su 10am-9:30pm, F-Sa 10am-11pm.)

■▲ **BEACHES AND OUTDOOR ACTIVITIES.** The **Santa Cruz Beach (Cowell Beach)** is broad, reasonably clean, and packed with volleyball players. Novice surfers and families may prefer semi-sheltered **Cowell Cove,** just west of the wharf, and the more secluded beaches that line Hwy. 1. The best vantage points for watching surfers are along W. Cliff Dr. To learn more about surfing, stop in at the small **surfing museum** in the lighthouse overlooking **Steamer Lane** at Lighthouse Point, the deep water where Hawaiian "Duke" Kahanamoku kick-started California's surf culture a century ago. For surfing lessons, contact the **Richard Schmidt Surf School** or ask around for him at the beach. (☎423-0928; www.richardschmidt.com. 1hr. private lesson $80, 2hr. group lesson $80 per person. Lessons include equipment.)

Around the point at the end of W. Cliff Dr. is **Natural Bridges State Beach.** Only one natural bridge remains standing, but the unblemished beach still has fascinating tidepools and tours during **monarch butterfly** season (Oct.-Mar.). In November and December, thousands of the stunning *lepidoptera* swarm the beach and cover the nearby eucalyptus groves with their orange wings. (☎423-4609. Open daily 8am-dusk. Parking $6, disabled $3, seniors $5.) **Kayak Connection,** 413 Lake Ave., offers tours of Elkhorn Slough and Santa Cruz Harbor ($50), and rents **sea kayaks** at decent rates. (☎479-1121. Open M-F 10am-5pm, Sa-Su 9am-6pm. Closed-deck singles $35 per 4hr., $40 per day; plastic doubles $50-60 per day. Paddle, life jacket, brief instruction, and wetsuit included.)

⚐ NIGHTLIFE. There are comprehensive events listings in the free *Metro Santa Cruz*, and in "Spotlight" in Friday's *Sentinel*. The Boardwalk bandstand offers free summertime Friday concerts around 6:30 and 8:30pm. Make it onto the Wall of Fame at ⚑**99 Bottles of Beer on the Wall Restaurant and Pub**, 110 Walnut Ave., in the heart of downtown, by making it through all 99 beers they have on tap—though hopefully not in one sitting. (☎459-9999. Beer $3-6, pitchers $12-15. W trivia night. Th "Local Night." 21+ after 10pm. Happy hour M and F 4-6pm, Tu-W 10pm-close, and Th all day. Open M-Th 11:30am-1:30am, F-Sa 11:30am-2am, Su 11:30am-midnight. Kitchen closes daily 10pm.) The mega-popular club **Blue Lagoon**, 923 Pacific Ave., has won many awards, including "best place you can't take your parents." (☎423-7117. Stronger-than-the-bouncer drinks $4-6. Cover $1-3 after 10pm. Happy hour daily 4-9pm; $3 drinks. Open daily 4pm-2am.)

MONTEREY ☎831

Monterey (pop. 33,000) is rightfully proud to be considered the cradle of Californian history. The bay was claimed by the Spanish in the 16th century and briefly served as the first capital of California. After lapsing into obscurity in the mid-19th century, Monterey was revived as a resort town by vacationers eager to experience its natural beauty. Luxury hotels and tourist shops are plentiful nowadays, and though the Cannery Row of Steinbeck fame has all but vanished, red-tiled roofs and a bustling waterfront stand as testimony to the city's colorful past.

⚐⚐ TRANSPORTATION AND PRACTICAL INFORMATION. Monterey-Salinas Transit (MST; ☎888-678-2871; www.mst.org) is the convenient public transit system. A free MST trolley serves major tourist sights during the summer. The free *Rider's Guide*, available on buses, at motels, and at the Visitors Center, has complete route info. ($2; exact change only. Day pass $4.50, with service to Big Sur $9.) The **Monterey Peninsula Visitor and Convention Bureau** is at 150 Olivier St. (☎657-6400 or 888-221-1010; www.montereyinfo.org. Open M-Sa 9am-5pm, Su 10am-4pm.) **Post Office:** 565 Hartnell St. (☎372-3021. Open M-F 8:30am-5pm, Sa 10am-2pm.) **Postal Code:** 93940.

⚐⚐ ACCOMMODATIONS AND FOOD. Inexpensive hotels line the 2000 block of **Fremont Street** in Monterey (bus #9 or 10). Others cluster along **Munras Avenue** between downtown Monterey and Hwy. 1. The **Monterey Hostel (HI) ❷**, 778 Hawthorne St., one block west of Lighthouse Ave., is a modern 45-bed hostel with a big common room. (☎649-0375. Free linen and parking. Towels $0.50. Check-in 5-8pm. Curfew 1am. Reservations essential June-Sept. In summer dorms $28, members $25. In winter $26/23. Ages 7-17 $17 year-round. Private rooms for 2-5 people $60-74. MC/V.) **Del Monte Beach Inn ❹**, 1110 Del Monte Ave., near downtown and across from the beach, is a Victorian-style inn with pleasant rooms. (☎649-4410. Check-in 2-6pm. Reservations recommended. Rooms $66, with private bath $77-88.) Call the **Monterey Parks** line (☎755-4895 or 888-588-2267) for camping info.

Once a hub for the canned sardine industry, Monterey Bay now yields crab, red snapper, and salmon. Seafood is bountiful but expensive—early-bird specials (usually 4-6:30pm) are easiest on the wallet. **Fisherman's Wharf** has stalls with smoked salmon sandwiches ($7) and free chowder samples. Get free samples of fruit, cheese, and seafood at the **Old Monterey Market Place**, on Alvarado St. (☎655-2607. Open daily 9am-5pm.) ⚑**First Awakenings ❷**, 125 Oceanview Blvd., in the outlet mall near the Aquarium, specializes in big portions of healthy, homemade brunch favorites. A single plate-sized signature pancake is a meal ($4), and a full stack ($7) is food for a day. Try them with wheat germ for a satisfying crunch, or order up an overstuffed omelet ($7-9) or towering reuben ($8.30) to enjoy by the firepit. (☎372-1125. Open M-F 7am-2pm, Sa-Su 7am-2:30pm.) **Turtle Bay Taquería ❶**, 431 Tyler St., at Bonifacio in downtown, combines fresh local produce and sea-food to create flavorful and filling Mexican-inspired dishes. Top a calimari Cozumel taco ($2.75) or tilapia Cancun burrito ($6.50) with the zesty mango salsa. (☎333-1500. Open M-Th 11am-9pm, F-Sa 11am-9:30pm, Su 11:30am-9pm.)

◙ SIGHTS. The extraordinary ▨**Monterey Bay Aquarium**, 886 Cannery Row, with nearly 200 outstanding exhibits and galleries, has been voted the nation's best. Gaze through the world's largest window at an enormous marine habitat with sea turtles, giant sunfish, large sharks, and yellow- and blue-fin tuna, or marvel at the three-story kelp forest. Special exhibits relate jellyfish to various art forms and explore the myths and mysteries of sharks. The thrice-daily sea-otter feeding is a crowd-pleaser; for a literal feeding frenzy, check out **Outer Bay** (Tu, Th, and Sa-Su 11am). The lines are always long, so pick up tickets the day before and save 20-40min. (☎648-4888 or 800-756-3737; www.montereybayaquarium.org. Open daily June-early Sept. and holidays 9:30am-6pm; early Sept.-May 10am-6pm. $25, over 65 and students $23, ages 3-12 $16.) **Cannery Row** was once a dilapidated street of lan-guishing sardine-packing plants, but restaurants and T-shirt shops have begun to take over. The **Great Cannery Row Mural** covers 400 ft. of a construction-site barrier on the 700 block with depictions of 30s and 40s Monterey. The best time to go **whale-watching** is during gray whale migration season (Nov.-Apr.), but humpbacks and blue whales can be spotted on a hit-or-miss basis year-round. **Chris' Whale Watching**, 48 Fisherman's Wharf, offers tours and charters. (☎375-5951. 3hr. tours May-Nov. $30, under 13 $20. 2hr. gray whale migration tours Dec.-Apr. $22/15.) In nearby Carmel, the amazing 550-acre, state-run wildlife sanctuary of ▨**Point Lobos Reserve** is popular with skindivers and day-hikers. From the cliffs, watch otters, sea lions, seals, brown pelicans, and gulls. There are also tidepools, scuba access, and marvelous vantage points for watching the winter whale migration. (☎624-4909. Open daily Apr.-Oct. 9am-7pm; Nov.-Mar. 9am-5pm. $8 per car, or park on the highway and walk or bike in for free. Diving reservations required; ☎624-8413. Dive fee $7.)

SANTA BARBARA   ☎805

Santa Barbara (pop. 92,500) epitomizes worry-free living, and with mountains on one side and the ocean on the other, there's no reason to complain. Spanish Revival architecture dominates State St., a pedestrian-friendly, palm-lined prome-nade of cafes, thrift stores, boutiques, and galleries. The city's golden beaches, scenic drives, and leisurely pace make it a frequent weekend escape for the wealthy and an attractive destination for surfers, artists, and backpackers.

▐ TRANSPORTATION

Many downtown parking lots and streets offer 1¼hr. of **free parking;** try the under-ground lots at Paseo Nuevo, accessible on the 700 block of Chapala St. All parking is free on Sundays. **Biking** is a nice alternative to driving. The **Cabrillo Bikeway** runs east-west along the beach from the Bird Refuge to the City College campus.

> **Trains: Amtrak,** 209 State St. (☎963-1015 or 800-872-7245; www.amtrak.com). Be careful around the station after dark. Open daily 5:45am-10pm. To **Los Angeles** (3hr., 6 per day, $25) and **San Francisco** (10hr., 3 per day, $76).

> **Buses: Greyhound,** 34 W. Carrillo St. (☎965-7551; www.greyhound.com), at Chapala St. Open daily 5am-8:15pm and 11pm-midnight. To **Los Angeles** (2-3hr., 6 per day, $12) and **San Francisco** (8-10hr., 5 per day, $39). **Santa Barbara Metropolitan Tran-**

CALIFORNIA

sit District (MTD), 1020 Chapala St. (☎683-3702), at Cabrillo Blvd. behind the Greyhound station, provides bus schedules and serves as a transfer point. Open M-F 6am-7pm, Sa 8am-6pm, Su 9am-6pm. The MTD runs a purple **crosstown shuttle** from Franklin Center on Montecito St. to Mountain and Valerio. $1.25, disabled and seniors $0.60, under 45 in. free; 10-ride pass $10; transfers free. Runs M-F 7am-6pm. The **downtown-waterfront shuttle** along State St. and Cabrillo Blvd. runs every 15min. M-Th and Su 10am-6pm, F-Sa 10am-10pm. Stops marked by circular blue signs. $0.25.

ORIENTATION AND PRACTICAL INFORMATION

Santa Barbara is 92 mi. northwest of Los Angeles and 27 mi. from Ventura on **U.S. 101.** Since the town is built along an irregular stretch of shoreline, its street grid is slightly skewed. The beach lies at the south end of the city, and **State Street,** the main drag, runs northwest from the waterfront. All streets are designated east and west from State St. The major east-west artery is **U.S. 101,** and **Cabrillo Boulevard** runs along the coastline.

Visitor Info: Tourist Office, 1 Garden St. (☎965-3021 or 800-676-1266), at Cabrillo Blvd., across from the beach. Open July-Aug. M-Sa 9am-6pm, Su 10am-5pm; Sept.-Nov. and Feb.-June M-Sa 9am-5pm, Su 10am-5pm; Dec.-Jan. M-Sa 9am-4pm, Su 10am-4pm. 24hr. computer with info on dining, shopping, hotels, and entertainment.

Medical Services: Cottage Hospital, (☎682-7111), on Pueblo St. at Bath St.

Internet Access: Santa Barbara Public Library, 40 E. Anapamu St. (☎962-7653). Free Wi-Fi. Open M-Th 10am-9pm, F-Sa 10am-5:30pm, Su 1-5pm.

Post Office: 836 Anacapa St. (☎564-2226), 1 block east of State St. Open M-F 8am-6pm, Sa 9am-5pm. **Postal Code:** 93102.

ACCOMMODATIONS

A 10min. drive north or south on U.S. 101 will lead you to cheaper lodgings than that in Santa Barbara proper. Welcoming and meticulously clean, the European-style **Hotel State Street ❹,** 121 State St., is two blocks from the beach and near the train station. (☎966-6586. Cable TV. Reservations recommended. July-Aug. $89-149. Sept.-June $59-109.) It may have cramped dorms, but the **Santa Barbara Tourist Hostel ❶,** 134 Chapala St., is also a block west of bustling State St., mere blocks from the beach and next to the train station, making it a convenient place to stay. (☎963-0154; sbhostel.com. Laundry, free linens, parking, towels, Wi-Fi. Discounted bike and boogie-board rentals. Key deposit $10. Dorms $20-29. July-Aug. private rooms $79-95. May-June and Sept. $69-89. Oct.-Apr. $55-75.) **Carpinteria State Park ❶,** 12 mi. south of Santa Barbara, has beachfront camping. (☎800-444-7275. Reservations recommended. Sites $25.)

FOOD

Hip State St. is lined with fashionable cafes while cheap taquerias lie four blocks west, along Milpas St. The reproduction of the Sistine Chapel ceiling at **Palazzio ❹,** 1026 State St., is nearly as impressive as the enormous pasta dishes ($17-23, half-portion $14-17), amazing garlic rolls, and self-serve wine. (☎564-1985. Lunch $8-11. Open M-Th and Su 11:30am-3pm and 5:30-11pm, F-Sa 11:30am-3pm and 5:30pm-midnight.) Bourbon St. spice meets Santa Barbara class at **The Palace Grill ❺,** 8 E. Cota St., a Cajun-Creole-Caribbean restaurant worth the splurge. (☎963-5000. Fish and grill selections $15-25. Boozey bread pudding souffle $7. Open M-Th and Su 11:30am-3pm and 5:30-10pm, F-Sa 11:30am-3pm and 5:30-11pm.) Hungry Santa

Barbarans rave about the authentic French cuisine at **Pacific Crepes ❷**, 705 Anacapa St. (☎882-1123. Open Tu-Sa 10am-3pm and 5:30-9pm, Su-M 10am-3pm.)

👁 SIGHTS

ZOOLOGICAL GARDENS. This delightfully leafy habitat has such an open feel that the animals seem kept in captivity only by sheer lethargy. A mini-train provides a tour of the exhibits, including a miniaturized African plain where giraffes stroll lazily, silhouetted against the Pacific. Make sure to see the zoo's magnificent pair of endangered snow leopards. *(500 Niños Dr., off Cabrillo Blvd. from U.S. 101. Take bus #14 or the downtown-waterfront shuttle. ☎962-5339. Open daily 10am-5pm. $10, ages 2-12 and seniors $8, under 2 free. Train $2, children $1.50. Parking $3.)*

BEACHES AND ACTIVITIES. The city's beaches are breathtaking, lined on one side by flourishing palm trees and on the other by sailboats around the harbor. The powdery sand and happy sunbathers at **East** and **Leadbetter Beaches** flank the wharf on either side. **Wheel Fun Rentals** will rent beachgoers a 🌀**retro surrey**—a covered wagon (often with fringe on top), or a Flintstone-esque bicycle seating up to nine. *(22 State St. ☎966-2282. Surreys $24-44 per 2hr., depending on number of riders. Regular bikes $7 per hr. Open daily 8am-8:30pm.)* **Beach House** rents surfboards and bodyboards. *(10 State St. ☎963-1281. Surfboards $7 per hr., $10 per ½-day. Bodyboards $4/10. Wetsuits $4/10. Credit card required. Open M-Th and Su 9am-7pm, F-Sa 9am-8pm.)*

STATE STREET. State St., Santa Barbara's red-tiled tribute to its Hispanic roots, runs a straight, tree-lined 2 mi. through the center. Among the shops, restaurants, and clubs are cultural and historical landmarks, not to mention countless opportunities for people-watching. The **Red Tile Tour**, a free walking-tour guide and map available at the Visitors Center, leads pedestrians to some of Santa Barbara's finest Spanish-style architecture. Farther down State St., the **Santa Barbara Museum of Art** owns an impressive collection of classical Greek, Asian, and European works, mostly donated by wealthy local residents. *(1130 State St. ☎963-4364. Open Tu-Su 11am-5pm. $9, seniors $6, students ages 6-17 $6, under 6 free. Su free.)*

HIKING. The very popular **Inspiration Point** is a 3½ mi. round-trip hike that climbs 800 ft. Half of the hike is an easy walk on a paved road; the other half consists of a series of mountainside switchbacks. The reward on a clear day is an extensive view of the city, the ocean, and the Channel Islands. Following the creek upstream will lead to **Seven Falls.** *(From Mission*

ON THE MENU

MAKE MINE A CALIFORNIAN

Not all US states can boast golden beaches, pines and snow-capped mountains, hipper-than-hip cities, and peaceful deserts. The lucky California even has a cuisine all its own. Upon entering the Golden State, visitors will immediately begin to notice the term "Californian" on menus.

Anything "Californian" has the ubiquitous **avocado** in it and usually features a combination of robust Mexican flavors, like lime and cilantro, and the best seafood the Pacific has to offer. The flavors are clean, positively unfried, and fresh. A popular breakfast item in California is the "Californian Benedict," which replaces the fatty meats of this American classic with avocado and tomato but doesn't forget the necessary Hollandaise sauce.

One restaurant, popular with in-the-know locals, is making a name for itself amongst dining gurus everywhere because of decidedly Californian cuisine. **Fresco!**, in downtown Santa Barbara, deserves its built-in punctuation and its Italian name, meaning "fresh." Tortilla soup, fresh seafood, leafy salads, and sandwiches dominate this restaurant's menu. Check it out for a dining experience that will only set you back about $10-20.

Fresco!, 3987 State St., in downtown Santa Barbara. ☎967-6037. Open M-Sa 8am-9pm.

Santa Barbara, drive toward the mountains and turn right onto Foothill Rd. Turn left onto Mission Canyon Rd. and continue 1 mi. Bear left onto Tunnel Rd. and drive 1¼ mi. to its end.) **Rattlesnake Canyon Trail** (3½ mi. round-trip, 1000 ft. elevation gain) is a moderate hike up-canyon to the Tunnel Trail junction. It starts along a shady, secluded creek, then climbs through chaparral to a high desert meadow. *(From Mission Santa Barbara, drive toward the mountains and turn right onto Foothill Rd. Turn left onto Mission Canyon Rd. and continue for ½ mi. Make a sharp right onto Las Conas Rd. and travel 1 mi. Look for a large sign on the left side of the road.)*

UNIVERSITY OF CALIFORNIA AT SANTA BARBARA (UCSB). This beautiful outpost of the UC system is actually in Goleta, an unremarkable suburb of Santa Barbara, but the beachside dorms and gorgeous student body more than make up for its peripheral location. UCSB's excellent **art museum** houses the Sedgwick Collection of 15th- to 17th-century European paintings. *(From Santa Barbara, take U.S. 101 7 mi. north to the UCSB Exit, or take bus #11. ☎893-2951. Open W-Su noon-5pm. Free.)* From November to February, hordes of **monarch butterflies** cling to the eucalyptus trees in Ellwood Grove, just west of UCSB, and at the end of Coronado St. off Hollister Ave.; take the Glen Annie/Storke Rd. Exit off U.S. 101.

☕ NIGHTLIFE

Every night, the clubs on **State Street,** particularly the stretch of street between Haley and Cañon Perdido St., are packed. Consult the *Independent* to see who's playing on any given night. ☕**Sharkeez,** 416 State St., is a wild college hangout, with tons of drink specials and events nightly to ensure an early-morning bedtime and late-afternoon wakeup. *(☎963-9680; www.sharkeez.net. Tu 2-for-1 margaritas. Th college night; domestic draft beers, shots, and mixed drinks $1.50. Su 2-for-1 beers 10pm-2am. Happy hour M-F 3-6:30pm; 2-for-1 beers, shots, cocktails, pitchers, and yes, buckets. Open M-F 11am-2am, Sa-Su 9am-2am. Kitchen closes 10pm.)* **Q's Billiards Club,** 409 State St., is classy but fun, boasting four full bars on three levels and eight pool tables. *(☎966-9177. Sushi $3-14. Sake $3-5. Happy hour M-F 4-7pm; 20% off sushi rolls, 50% off drinks and selected appetizers. M international night. Tu 80s night. W karaoke. Th college night. No jeans, tanks, or sandals. Cover Sa $5 after 9pm. Open M-Sa 4pm-2am.)*

LOS ANGELES

There's a reason 17 million people choose to live in the sprawling collection of neighborhoods and freeways known as the City of Angels. Yes, the traffic is terrible, the smog is worse, the socio-economic divisions are tense, and the plastic surgery rate is high. However, many find L.A.'s ever-changing scene enthralling, and battle to seek out the trendiest beaches, freshest clubs, hottest artists, and best ethnic food as the sun shines through their car windows. In this movie-obsessed town, everyone either works in the industry, knows someone who works in the industry, or dreams of working in the industry.

✈ INTERCITY TRANSPORTATION

Three major freeways connect Los Angeles to the rest of the state of California. **I-5,** which travels the length of California, bisects L.A. on a north-south axis; it continues north to Sacramento and south to San Diego. **U.S. 101** links L.A. to other coastal cities, heading west from Pasadena before turning north toward San Francisco and running parallel to I-5. **I-10** stretches west from L.A., providing access to Las Vegas and Arizona.

Los Angeles and Vicinity
SEE COLOR INSERTS FOR MORE LOS ANGELES AREA MAPS

Airport: Los Angeles International Airport (LAX) is in Westchester, about 15 mi. south-west of downtown. LAX information (☎310-646-5252) aids English and Spanish speakers. Airport police (☎310-646-7911) patrol 24hr. Traveler's Aid, a service for airport info, transportation, accommodations, and major transit emergencies, is in all terminals. (☎310-646-2270.) Open M-F 9am-5pm.

Trains: Amtrak, Union Station, 800 N. Alameda St. (☎213-683-6897 or 800-872-7245; www.amtrak.com), at the northeastern edge of downtown. Open 24hr.

Buses: Greyhound (☎800-231-2222 or 213-629-8401; www.greyhound.com). The most convenient service is at the **Hollywood Terminal,** 1715 N. Cahuenga Blvd. (☎323-466-6384. Open daily 6:30am-9:30pm.) From there, buses run to: **Las Vegas** (5-8hr., 15 per day, $41.50); **San Diego** (2½-4hr., 17 per day, $16); **San Francisco** (7-12hr., 14 per day, $44); **Santa Barbara** (2½hr., 6 per day, $12); **Downtown**

Tijuana, Baja California (3½-5hr., 5 per day, $25). The downtown station, 1716 E. 7th St. (☎213-629-8401), at Alameda St., is in an extremely rough neighborhood. If you must get off in downtown, be very careful near 7th and Alameda St., one block south-west of the station, where you can catch MTA bus #60 traveling north to Union Station.

■ ORIENTATION

I-5 (Golden State Freeway), I-405 (San Diego Freeway), I-110 (Harbor Freeway), U.S. 101 (Hollywood Freeway), and the **Pacific Coast Highway (PCH or Highway 1)** all run north-south. **I-10 (Santa Monica Freeway)** runs east-west, connecting Santa Monica to downtown and beyond. I-5 intersects I-10 east of downtown and is one of the two major north-south thruways. I-405, which stretches from Orange County in the south all the way through L.A., parallels I-5 closer to the coast, separating Santa Monica and Malibu from the inland Westside, and is often gridlocked. The best way to orient yourself is by learning a couple of important freeways and remaining aware of L.A.'s natural landmarks; the ocean is west and the mountains are east.

THE COAST. Santa Monica reigns over the coast with high-end shopping and lavish houses. **Malibu,** its wealthier neighbor to the north, is purely focused on the beach, and its seaside cliffs are home to many incognito celebrities. **Venice** and **Marina del Rey** extend south along Santa Monica's ocean beach path. Drum circles and in-line skaters populate Venice, while Marina del Rey caters to the yachting set. The beaches of South Bay are relaxed and fun.

THE WESTSIDE. East of I-405, the Westside sits comfortably along Santa Monica Blvd. This is the cleanest, most happening part of the city. UCLA brings students to **Westwood** and **West L.A.,** while the neighboring hills of **Bel Air, Brentwood,** and **Pacific Palisades** accommodate stellar homes and the impressive Getty Center. **Beverly Hills** is, as always, the land of luxury shopping and gaudy mansions. Still on the Westside, but inching toward eastern messiness, predominantly gay **West Holly-wood** is the center of much of the city's best nightlife and shopping.

HOLLYWOOD. Hollywood, in its faded glamour and neon excitement, lies just up Sunset Blvd. from West Hollywood. It's ideal for late-night eats and celebrity stalking, and it holds many of the city's most famous landmarks. Lodging here is among the cheapest available. South of Hollywood, the **Wilshire District** houses Miracle Mile, home to many prestigious museums.

EAST OF HOLLYWOOD. East of Hollywood are the bohemian neighborhoods **Los Feliz** and **Silver Lake,** and the greenery of Griffith Park. Southeast, **downtown L.A.** does exist and is undergoing a rejuvenation, with the recent construction of Frank Gehry's **Walt Disney Concert Hall** and future additions of housing complexes. Farther east, at the foot of the San Gabriel Mountains, **Pasadena** has old-time charm and hosts the Rose Bowl. Movies are made and recreation parks reign in the **San Fernando Valley,** north of downtown on I-5.

■ LOCAL TRANSPORTATION

Whether they're driving pimped-out low-riders, road-hugging sports cars, or sparkling luxury sedans, Angelenos love their cars with a fervor that comes from constant contact with the road. L.A.'s roadways are often jammed; heavy traffic moves toward downtown from 7 to 10am on weekdays and streams outbound from 4 to 7pm. However, since L.A. has a huge population that doesn't work 9 to 5, traffic can be as bad at 1pm as it is at 6pm. No matter how crowded the freeway is, it's almost always quicker and safer than taking surface streets to your destination.

AREA CODES. L.A. is big. Really big. **213** covers Downtown L.A. **323** covers Hollywood, Huntington Park, Montebello, and West Hollywood. **310** covers Beverly Hills, Santa Monica, and the Westside. **562** covers Long Beach and the South Bay. **626** covers Pasadena. **818** covers Burbank, Glendale, and the San Fernando Valley. **909** covers San Bernardino and Riverside.

The **Automobile Club of Southern California**, 2601 S. Figueroa St., at Adams Blvd., has additional driving info and maps. Club privileges are free for AAA members and cost $2-3 for non-members. (☎213-741-3686, emergency assistance 800-400-4222. Open M-F 9am-5pm.) Anyone needing non-emergency roadside assistance can dial #399 on their cellphone to be connected with the appropriate aid.

As a result of this obsession with driving, public transportation systems are limited and inconvenient. Though renting a car is expensive, your own set of wheels is the best way to navigate the sprawling city. If you must forgo the rental, use the subway and the bus to get around. Walking or biking around the city is simply not feasible—distances are just too great. However, some colorful areas such as Melrose, the Third St. Promenade in Santa Monica, Venice Beach, Hollywood, and Old Town Pasadena, are best explored by foot. At night, those on foot, especially outside the Westside, should exercise caution. *Let's Go* **does not recommend hitchhiking.** It is exceptionally dangerous, not to mention illegal. Don't even consider it.

Local Buses: Metropolitan Transit Authority (MTA) Metro Customer Center, Gateway Transit Center, Union Station E. Portal (open M-F 6am-6:30pm) in downtown. Bus fare $1.25, seniors and disabled $0.55; transfer $0.30/0.10; exact change required. The Metro Day Pass ($5) allows for unlimited rail and bus rides and can be purchased on any metro bus or rail station. Transfers can be made between MTA lines or to other transit authorities. Unless otherwise noted, all route numbers are MTA; BBBus stands for **Big Blue Bus** and indicates Santa Monica buses. (☎800-266-6883; www.mta.net.) Open M-F 6am-8:30pm, Sa-Su 8am-6pm. The local **DASH shuttle** (☎213-808-2273; www.ladottransit.com), designed for short neighborhood hops, serves many major tourist destinations. Fare $0.25.

Subway: The **Blue Line** runs north-south between Long Beach and Los Angeles. The **Green Line** goes east-west from Norwalk to Redondo Beach, with shuttle service to LAX at Aviation/I-105. The **Red Line** runs from Union Station and downtown through Hollywood to the San Fernando Valley. The **Purple Line** follows the Red Line for six stops, then extends out to the mid-Wilshire area. The new **Gold Line** (Pasadena line) connects to the Red Line at Union Station and then runs northeast to Pasadena. $1.25, bus and rail transfers $0.30; seniors and disabled $0.55/0.10. All lines run daily 5am-12:30am.

Taxi: Independent, ☎323-666-0050 or 800-521-8294. **L.A. Taxi/Yellow Cab Co.,** ☎310-808-1000 or 800-333-3305. **Bell Cab,** ☎888-235-5222.

Car Rental: Universal Rent-A-Car, 920 S. La Brea Ave. (☎323-954-1186). Cars from $20 per day with 150 mi. free, $140 per week with 1050 mi. free. No under-25 surcharge. Open M-F 8am-6pm, Sa-Su 9am-5pm.

⌷ PRACTICAL INFORMATION

Visitor Info: L.A. Convention and Visitor Bureau, 685 S. Figueroa St. (☎213-689-8822; www.visitlanow.com), between Wilshire Blvd. and 7th St. in the Financial District. Staff speaks English, French, German, and Japanese. Detailed bus map of L.A. available, along with tourist and entertainment info. Open M-F 8:30am-5pm.

Hotline: Rape Crisis, ☎310-392-8381.

Medical Services: Cedars-Sinai Medical Center, 8700 Beverly Blvd. (☎310-423-3277, emergency 423-8605). **Good Samaritan Hospital,** 1225 Wilshire Blvd. (☎213-977-2121, emergency 977-2420). **UCLA Medical Center,** 10833 Le Conte Ave. (☎310-825-9111, emergency 825-2111).

Post Office: Central branch at 7001 S. Central Ave. (☎800-275-8777). Open M-F 7am-7pm, Sa 7am-3pm. Hollywood branch at 6457 Santa Monica Blvd. Open M-F 8:30am-7pm, Sa 8:30am-5pm. **Postal Code:** 90052.

ACCOMMODATIONS

When choosing where to stay, the first consideration should be location. Those visiting for beach culture should choose lodgings in Venice or Santa Monica. Avid sightseers will be better off in Hollywood or the more expensive (but cleaner and nicer) Westside. One campground fairly close to Los Angeles is **Leo Carrillo State Beach ❶** (☎805-488-5223), on Hwy. 1 about 20 mi. north of Malibu. It has 135 sites equipped with flush toilets and showers (sites $9-25). Listed prices do not include L.A.'s 14% hotel tax.

THE COAST

Los Angeles Surf City Hostel, 26 Pier Ave. (☎798-2323), in Pier Plaza in Hermosa Beach, the center of the local scene. A young, mostly international clientele enjoys the beach by day and the clubs by night. Helpful staff dispenses advice and maps, and coordinates tours. Free breakfast, linens, and towels. Passport or driver's license required. Key deposit $10. 28-night max. stay; US citizens 3 night max. Reservations recommended. Dorms $21-23; private rooms $50. MC/V. ❶

Seaview Motel, 1760 Ocean Ave. (☎310-393-6711), in Santa Monica. Tastefully decorated rooms, a patio ideal for sunbathing, and a path straight to the beach. Prime location at a reasonable price. Singles to quads $90-125. MC/V. ❹

Venice Beach Cotel, 25 Windward Ave. (☎310-399-7649; www.venicebeachcotel.com). Situated right off the Venice Boardwalk and easily identifiable by its row of international flags on display. International staff and guests. Tennis rackets, table tennis, and boogie boards ($20 deposit). Passport required. Key deposit $5. Reservations recommended. Dorms with ocean view and bath $22-26. Doubles $52; triples with bath $70. MC/V. ❶

THE WESTSIDE

Orbit Hotel and Hostel, 7950 Melrose Ave. (☎323-655-1510 or 877-672-4887; www.orbithotel.com), a block west of Fairfax Ave., in West Hollywood. Self-titled the "sexiest hostel in the world," it has a central location and retro-chic decor. TV and game room, courtyard, and late-night party room with bright furniture. Small cafe with breakfast and dinner for around $5. Dorms only accept international students with passport. Free linens, towels, and parking. Internet access and free coffee and tea all day. Dorms $20-24; private rooms for up to 4 $59-99. MC/V. ❶

Hotel Claremont, 1044 Tiverton Ave. (☎310-208-5957 or 800-266-5957), near UCLA in Westwood Village. The Claremont is a house-like hotel in a beautiful area, still owned by the same family that built it over 60 years ago. All rooms are equipped with ceiling fans and small private baths. Fridge and microwave next to a Victorian-style TV lounge. Free newspapers and Wi-Fi. Reservations recommended. Singles $60; doubles $70-79. AmEx/D/MC/V. ❸

HOLLYWOOD

USA Hostels Hollywood, 1624 Schrader Blvd. (☎323-462-3777 or 800-524-6783; www.usahostels.com), south of Hollywood Blvd., west of Cahuenga Blvd. Buzzing with young travelers and filled with energy. Nice kitchen and big-screen TV lounge. Special events nightly. Free beach shuttles run Tu, Th, Sa. Pancake breakfast included. Linens and Wi-Fi free. International passport or out-of-state student ID required. Parking usually about $6 per day. Dorms $23-29; private rooms for 2-4 $58-72. MC/V. ●

Orange Drive Manor, 1764 N. Orange Dr. (☎323-850-0350). A converted 20s mini-mansion in a residential neighborhood just a block off Hollywood Blvd. Grandeur (and lack of sign) disguise this rambling hostel. Cable TV lounge. Lockers $0.75. Internet $1 per 10min. Key deposit $20. Parking $5 per day. Reservations recommended. Dorms $25-29; private rooms $55-69. ISIC discount $2. Cash or traveler's check only. ❷

Hollywood International Hostel, 6820 Hollywood Blvd. (☎800-750-6561), across the street from Hollywood and Highland. Lounge, kitchen, shared baths. Breakfast included. Linens free. International passport required. Roomy dorms from $17, private rooms from $40. Cash only. ●

🖸 FOOD

From celebrity eateries to taco wagons, there's no shortage of great food in L.A. The city's diversity is reflected in its exotic cuisine. If you like to cook, **Trader Joe's** specializes in cheap gourmet food. There are 74 locations in SoCal; call ☎800-746-7857 to find one. (Most open daily 9am-9pm.) L.A.'s 🖻**farmers' market,** 6333 W. 3rd St., at Fairfax Ave., draws 3 million people every year with produce stalls, international food booths, handicraft shops, and a phenomenal juice bar. A cheaper and less touristy source of produce is the **Grand Central Public Market,** 317 S. Broadway, between 3rd and 4th St. downtown. Entrances are on both Broadway and Hill St. between 3rd and 4th St. (☎213-624-2378. Open daily 9am-6pm.)

THE COAST

🖻 **Rose Cafe and Market,** 220 Rose Ave. (☎310-399-0711), at Main St., in Venice. Cafe features local art, industrial architecture, and healthy deli specials, including sandwiches ($9) and a wide variety of salads ($10) available from 11:30am. Open M-F 7am-5:30pm, Sa 8am-6pm, Su 8am-5pm. Limited menu after 3pm. AmEx/MC/V. ❷

Fritto Misto, 601 Colorado Ave. (☎310-458-2829), at 6th St., in Santa Monica. Create your own pasta (from $6) at this "Neighborhood Italian Cafe." Weekend lunch special ($12) includes all-you-can-eat calamari and salad. Vegetarian entrees $8-12. Open M-Th 11:30am-10pm, F-Sa 11:30am-10:30pm, Su 11:30am-9:30pm. AmEx/D/MC/V. ❸

The Spot, 110 2nd St. (☎310-376-2355; www.worldfamousspot.com), in Hermosa Beach. L.A.'s oldest vegetarian restaurant, and a favorite with local hippies. "Inflation Buster" combos like the "Dear George" include veggies on pasta or rice with tofu ($6-8). Homemade bread and desserts $4. Open daily 11am-10pm. Cash only. ❷

THE WESTSIDE

🖻 **The Apple Pan,** 10801 W. Pico Blvd. (☎310-475-3585), 1 block east of Westwood Blvd., across from the Westside Pavilion, in West L.A. Not much has changed since the diner opened in 1947. No tables, no frills, just a white linoleum counter where you can enjoy juicy hickory burgers ($7), crispy fries ($2), and humongous slices of fresh-baked apple pie ($5.25). Open Tu-Th and Su 11am-midnight, F-Sa 11am-1am. Cash only. ❷

Sak's Teriyaki, 1121 Glendon Ave. (☎310-208-2002), in Westwood. UCLA students pack this teriyaki joint, ordering the not-so-authentic but oh-so-tender skewers of meat and veggies (with rice, gyoza, and salad; $4-9). Open daily 11am-10pm. Cash only. ●

Barney's Beanery, 8447 Santa Monica Blvd. (☎310-656-5777). Brings back L.A.'s good ol' days with nostalgic furnishings and a menu that lists the famous celebrities that have enjoyed the house specialty chili ($5). Barney's proudly boasts "if we don't have it, you don't need it" and with over 1000 menu items and 125 bottled beers, they're probably right. Specialty pizzas $6-24. Potato skins with any toppings you can think of $7-10. Open daily 11am-1am. AmEx/MC/V. ❸

HOLLYWOOD

🏆 **Canter's,** 419 N. Fairfax Ave. (☎323-651-2030), north of Beverly Blvd. An L.A. institution and the heart and soul of historically Jewish Fairfax since 1931. Baseball-sized matzah balls in chicken broth ($7), and giant pastrami or corned beef sandwiches ($11.25) are wildly popular. Beer $3. Lounge with nightly free rock, blues, jazz, and cabaret-pop (from 10pm). Observant eaters beware: Canter's is Kosher-style, not Kosher. Open 24hr. AmEx/D/MC/V. ❷

Roscoe's House of Chicken and Waffles, 1514 Gower St. (☎323-466-7453), at Sunset Blvd. Also at 5006 W. Pico Blvd, in West L.A. The down-home feel and comfort food menu make this place popular. "1 succulent chicken breast and 1 delicious waffle" $8. Open M-Th 8:30am-midnight, F-Sa 8:30am-4am, Su 8am-midnight. AmEx/MC/V. ❷

Pink's Hot Dog Stand, 709 N. La Brea Ave. (☎323-931-4223; www.pinkshollywood.com), at Melrose Ave. Pink's serves up chili-slathered goodness in a bun, attracting droves of tourists and Angelenos alike. Try the special "Ozzy Osbourne Spicy Dog" for $5.40. Standard chili dogs run $3. Open M-Th and Su 9:30am-2am, F-Sa 9:30am-3am. Cash only. ❶

EAST OF HOLLYWOOD

🏆 **Philippe, The Original,** 1001 N. Alameda St. (☎213-628-3781; www.philippes.com), 2 blocks north of Union Station, downtown. Philippe invented the French Dip sandwich here back in 1918, when he dropped a roll into a pan filled with sizzling hot oil. Choose from pork, beef, ham, turkey, or lamb filling ($5). Free parking. Open daily 6am-10pm. Cash only. ❶

Fair Oaks Pharmacy and Soda Fountain, 1526 Mission St. (☎626-799-1414), at Fair Oaks Ave., in South Pasadena. From Colorado Blvd., go south 1 mi. on Fair Oaks Ave. to Mission St. Open since 1915, this old-fashioned soda fountain serves huge triple-decker club sandwiches ($8.50) and their famous phosphates made with soda water and flavored syrup ($2.25). Shakes and malts $5. Lunch served until 6pm daily. Soda fountain open M-Th 9am-9pm, F-Sa 9am-10pm, Su 10am-7pm. AmEx/D/MC/V. ❶

The Pantry, 877 S. Figueroa St. (☎213-972-9279), in downtown. Since 1924, it hasn't closed once—not for

ON THE MENU

THE INS-N-OUTS OF IN-N-OUT

From its simple beginning in 1948 as a burger stand in Baldwin Park, just east of Los Angeles, **IN-N-OUT Burger** has come a long way. Its distinctive yellow-and-red sign is now ubiquitous across California, Nevada, and Arizona. Many first-time visitors are surprised to see a menu with just five choices (hamburger, cheeseburger, double-double, fries, and shake), but IN-N-OUT offers far more. The restaurant also has a "secret menu" from which many more items can be ordered simply by knowing what to ask for. Next time you place your order, keep these other options in mind. They aren't on the menu, but they're available at all locations.

Animal Style: Burger of your choice grilled in mustard with lettuce, tomato, pickles, grilled onions, and IN-N-OUT's special sandwich spread.

Protein Style: Burger of your choice wrapped in lettuce instead of a bun.

Double Meat: Two beef patties, no cheese.

Flying Dutchman: Two beef patties, two slices of cheese, and nothing else.

Wish Burger: No meat.

3x3: Three beef patties, three slices of cheese, lettuce, tomato, and spread on a bun. (Also available in 4x4.)

Fries Animal Style: Fries with cheese, special spread, onions.

the earthquakes, not for the 1992 riots (when it served as a National Guard outpost), and not even when a taxicab drove through the front wall. This diner is known for its large portions, free cole slaw, and fresh sourdough bread. Giant breakfast specials $4-8. Lunch sandwiches $8. Open 24hr. Cash only. ❷

◎ SIGHTS

SANTA MONICA

Santa Monica is known more for its lively shoreside scene than for its surf, and the area on and around the carnival pier is filled with hawkers and local tourist activity. The fun spills over onto the pedestrian-only Third St. Promenade, where street performers and a farmers' market add a bit of spice to the outdoor mall-ish ambience. Farther inland, along Main St. and beyond, a smattering of galleries, design shops, and museums testify to the city's love for art and culture.

SANTA MONICA PIER, PACIFIC PARK, AND THE BEACH. The famed pier is the heart of Santa Monica Beach and home to the roller coasters, arcades, and Ferris wheels of Pacific Park. Look for the small aquarium and free TV show tickets near the north entrance to the pier. *(Off Hwy. 1 on the way to Venice Beach from Santa Monica Beach.* ☎ *310-458-8900; www.santamonicapier.org. Pier open 24hr. Park open in summer M-Th and Su 11am-11pm, F-Sa 11am-12:30am; winter hours vary. Last entry 30min. before closing. Pier free. Tickets $2 each; most rides 2-3 tickets. Day pass $20, children under 42 in. $11.)* The paved **Ocean Front Walk** is a palm-lined mini-freeway of cyclists, skaters, and runners, stretching 20¼ mi. along the beach between Santa Monica and Torrance. Immediately south of the pier on Ocean Front Walk, skilled players match wits at the public chess tables at the **International Chess Park.** Opposite the chess masters is the original location of **Muscle Beach** (now in Venice Beach), where bodybuilders and athletes lifted impossibly heavy weights and posed in briefs from the 30s to the 50s.

THIRD STREET PROMENADE. Angelenos claim that nobody walks in L.A., but if shopping is involved, all rules go out the car window. The Third Street Promenade, three ultra-popular pedestrian blocks of mosaic art tiles, fountains, and patio restaurants, is home to trendy shopping ranging from overpriced bikini shops to some of L.A.'s best specialty bookstores. On Wednesday and Saturday mornings, the area transforms into a popular **farmers' market** selling fresh California flowers and produce. The market features exclusively organic products on Saturdays. *(Between Broadway and Wilshire in downtown Santa Monica. 4th St. Exit from I-10. Open W 8:30am-1:30pm, Sa 8:30am-1pm.)*

MALIBU, VENICE, AND SOUTH BAY

North of Santa Monica along the Pacific Coast Highway (PCH), the cityscape gives way to appealing stretches of sandy, sewage-free shoreline. **Malibu's** beaches are clean, relatively uncrowded, and easily the best in L.A. County for surfers, sunbathers, and swimmers alike. Along the 30,000 block of PCH, 30min. west of Santa Monica, stretches ◪**Zuma Beach,** L.A. County's northernmost, largest, and most popular sandbox. **Zuma Westward,** located at Point Dume State Beach, just south of Zuma Beach, is less crowded and more relaxing. You can jet through the wave tubes at **Surfrider Beach,** a section of Malibu Lagoon State Beach north of the pier at 23000 PCH. Walk there via the Zonker Harris Access Way at 22700 PCH. Free parking along PCH. On your way back from the beach, turn into any uphill street along PCH for a self-guided tour of the area's hippest, most beautiful homes.

Venice is a carnivalesque beach town where guitar-toting, wild-eyed, tie-dyed residents sculpt masterpieces in sand, compose them in graffiti, or just talk gibberish. Grab a corn dog and head to **Ocean Front Walk,** where street people converge on clusters of benches, evangelists drown out off-color comedians, and panhandlers solicit donations. Bodybuilders of both sexes pump iron in skimpy spandex outfits at **Muscle Beach,** 1800 Ocean Front Walk, closest to 18th St. and Pacific Ave. For some exercise to punctuate all your L.A. driving, take a scenic walk around the **Venice Canals,** or venture on a run along the Venice beach pedestrian walkway. About 20 mi. southwest of downtown L.A. are the South Bay beaches of **Manhattan Beach, Hermosa Beach,** and **Redondo Beach.** Manhattan Beach is favored for surfing; Hermosa Beach, L.A. County's most popular urban beach, is also one of the cleanest. Both host elite beach volleyball and surf competitions (☎ 426-8000; www.avp.com or www.surffestival.org). Most visit Redondo Beach for its harbor, pier, and seafood-rich boardwalk. **The Strand** is a concrete bike path that runs from Santa Monica (where it's called Ocean Front Walk) to Hermosa Beach.

WESTWOOD

Westwood, an area east of I-405 and north of Wilshire Blvd., is home to the **University of California at Los Angeles (UCLA),** a prototypical California university, with grassy open spaces, dazzling sunshine, massive brick buildings, and deeply tanned bodies on 400 acres in the foothills of the Santa Monica Mountains. Once voted the #1 jock school in the country by *Sports Illustrated,* UCLA also boasts an illustrious film school whose graduates include James Dean, Jim Morrison, Oliver Stone, Francis Ford Coppola, and Tim Robbins. Just south of campus, the **Hammer Art Museum,** 10899 Wilshire Blvd., houses the world's largest collection of works by 19th-century French satirist Honoré Daumier, as well as Van Gogh's *Hospital at Saint-Rémy.* (☎310-443-7000; www.hammer.ucla.edu. Open Tu-W and F-Sa 11am-7pm, Th 11am-9pm, Su 11am-5pm. $5, seniors $3, students and under 17 free; Th and summer months free. Museum validates parking for garage on Westwood Blvd.) UCLA's art collection continues outdoors with the **Murphy Sculpture Garden,** in the northeast corner of campus, which contains over 70 pieces by major artists, like Auguste Rodin and Henri Matisse, scattered under the trees. Over 5000 plant species flourish in the **UCLA Botanical Gardens,** in the eastern part of campus, at the intersection of Le Conte and Hilgard Ave. Stop at an information booth inside each entrance to get a parking day pass ($7). Just south of UCLA, **Westwood Village** is a walkable area with trendy stores and affordable restaurants.

BEVERLY HILLS

Beverly Hills glows in the mystique of expensive hotels, ritzy boutiques, and movie stars galore. You can live it up here simply by throwing on your trendiest jeans, slipping on some shades, and making clerks work for the money they think you have. Pick up a star map, available all over town for around $5, to drive by celebrities' houses (and don't be too disappointed when all you can see are their nicely manicured hedges). The heart of designer shopping pulses along **Rodeo Drive** and throughout the **Golden Triangle,** a wedge formed by Beverly Dr., Wilshire Blvd., and Santa Monica Blvd. Stroll past the stone storefronts, breathe in the sweet smell of money, and check out your hot self in the smoked glass windows of **Armani,** 436 N. Rodeo Dr. The divine triple-whammy of **Cartier** (370 N. Rodeo Dr.), **Gucci** (347 N. Rodeo Dr.), and **Chanel** (400 N. Rodeo Dr.) sits on prime real estate, where rents approach $40,000 per month. At the south end of Rodeo Dr. (the end closest to Wilshire Blvd.) is pedestrian-only **2 Rodeo Drive,** a.k.a. **Via Rodeo,** which houses **Dior, Tiffany,** and numerous salons frequented by the stars. Across the way is the venerable **Regent Beverly Wilshire Hotel,** 9500 Wilshire Blvd., where Julia Roberts went from Hollywood hooker to Richard Gere's queen in *Pretty Woman.* A ludicrously extravagant retreat as famous as the starlets who romanced here, the salmon-colored **Beverly Hills Hotel,** 9641 Sunset Blvd. (☎276-2251), sits among 12 acres of tropical gardens and pools. Marilyn Monroe reportedly had trysts with both JFK and RFK in one of the 22 "bungalows." In case you were wondering, rooms run $395-455, bungalows $450-3400, and suites $835-5200.

WEST HOLLYWOOD

Bring your walking shoes and spend a day on the 3 mi. strip of **Melrose Avenue** from Highland Ave. west to the intersection of Doheny Dr. and Santa Monica Blvd. This strip began to develop its funky flair in the late 80s when art galleries, designer stores, lounge-like coffee shops, used clothing and music stores, and restaurants began to take over. Now the hippest stretch lies between La Brea and Fairfax Ave. North of the mammoth **Beverly Center Mall,** 8500 Beverly Blvd. (☎310-854-0071; open M-F 10am-9pm, Sa 10am-8pm, Su 11am-6pm), is the **Pacific Design Center,** 8687 Melrose Ave. (☎310-657-0800; www.pacificdesigncenter.com), a sea-green glass complex nicknamed the Blue Whale and constructed in the shape of a wave.

HOLLYWOOD

Exploring the Hollywood area takes a pair of sunglasses, a camera, some cash, and a high tolerance for crowds. **Hollywood Boulevard** is the center of tourist madness, home to the Walk of Fame, famous theaters, and ubiquitous souvenir shops.

HOLLYWOOD SIGN. Those 50 ft. high, 30 ft. wide, slightly crooked letters perched on Mt. Lee in Griffith Park stand as the city's universal symbol. The original 1923 sign read "HOLLYWOODLAND" as an advertisement for a new subdivision in the Hollywood Hills. The sign has been a target of many college pranks, which have made it read everything from "Hollyweird" to "Ollywood" (after the infamous Lt. Col. Oliver North). A fence keeps you 40 ft. away and views are sometimes obscured by smog. *(Getting close requires a strenuous 2½ mi. hike. Take plenty of water. From Franklin Ave., go north on Canyon Dr. to its end, where parking is free. Walk up beyond the gates; Brush Canyon Trail starts where Canyon Dr. becomes unpaved. At the top of the hill, follow the road to the left; the sign looms just below. For those satisfied with driving, go east on Franklin Ave. and then north on Beachwood, and drive up until you are forced to drive down.)*

GRAUMAN'S CHINESE THEATRE. Loosely modeled on an ancient Chinese temple, this monumental, eye-catching theater is a Hollywood icon and frequently rolls out the red carpet for movie premieres. The exterior columns were imported from China, where they once supported a Ming Dynasty temple. The theatre houses a collection of celebrity footprints as well as other star trademarks— Whoopi Goldberg's dreadlocks, R2D2's wheels, and George Burns's cigar. *(6925 Hollywood Blvd., between Highland and Orange St. ☎323-463-9576. 4-5 tours per day; call ahead. $12, children and seniors $8.)*

WALK OF FAME. Pedestrian traffic along Hollywood Blvd. mimics L.A.'s congested freeways, as tourists stop mid-stride to gawk at the sidewalk's over 2000 bronze-inlaid stars, which are inscribed with the names of the famous, the infamous, and the downright obscure. Stars are awarded for achievements in movies, radio, television, recording, or live performance; only Gene Autry has a star in all five categories. The stars have no particular order, so don't try to find a method to the madness. Scheduled inductees for 2008 include Cate Blanchett, Vince McMahon, and Ricky Martin. To catch today's (or yesterday's) stars in person, call the Chamber of Commerce for info on star-unveiling ceremonies. *(☎323-469-8311; www.hollywoodchamber.net. Free.)*

HOLLYWOOD AND HIGHLAND. The sprawling **Hollywood and Highland Center** contains brand-name stores, high-profile restaurants, nightlife, a 640-room hotel, and the $94 million **Kodak Theater,** built specifically for the Academy Awards, and now also home to American Idol finales. *(☎323-467-6412. Center open M-Sa 10am-10pm, Su 10am-7pm; various restaurants, theaters, and clubs open later. Parking $2 per 4hr. with validation. Kodak box office ☎323-308-6363. Open daily 10am-6pm; on performance days until 9pm. Tours in summer every 30min. 10:30am-4pm; in winter 10:30am-2:30pm. $15, seniors and under 12 $10.)*

CAPITOL RECORDS TOWER. The **Capitol Records Tower** was designed to look like a stack of records with a needle on top blinking H-O-L-L-Y-W-O-O-D in Morse code. A faded, yet still impressive mural of jazz legends occupies the building's southern face, and the tower becomes Hollywood's tallest Christmas tree in December. *(1750 Vine St., at the famous Hollywood and Vine address.)*

GRIFFITH PARK AREA

GRIFFITH PARK. For a breath of fresh air and a respite from city life, take to the rugged slopes of Griffith Park, the nation's largest municipal park, nestled in the hills between U.S. 101, I-5, and Rte. 134. A stark contrast to the concrete heights of downtown and the star-studded streets of Hollywood, the park's dry grass foothills and scrub-forested valleys are the site of many outdoor diversions. Some 52 mi. of hiking trails, three golf courses, a planetarium, a zoo, museums, and the 6000-seat Greek Theatre are all found within its rolling 4107 acres. The grounds are perfect for biking, and rentals are available at the Griffith **Park Bicycle Rental** at the Visitors Center. *(Visitors Center and ranger headquarters: 4730 Crystal Spring Dr. ☎323-913-4688, emergency 913-7390. Open daily 5am-10:30pm.)* The park has numerous equestrian trails and places to saddle up, such as **J.P. Stables.** *(914 S. Mariposa St., in Burbank. ☎818-843-9890. Open daily 7:30am-6pm. $25 for 1st hr., $15 per hr. thereafter. Cash only.)*

AUTRY MUSEUM OF THE AMERICAN WEST. City slickers and lone rangers may discover that the American West is not what they thought—this museum insists that the real is not the reel, drawing the line between Old West fact and fiction. The main level focuses on myth and imagination in the creation of the American West, and visitors can gawk at items like Annie Oakley's pistols and Hopalong Cassidy's costume alongside the sketches and paintings of 19th-century American artists. The lower level explores the West with Indian artifacts, a trading post replica, and a tribute to cowboys of the past and present. *(4700 Western Heritage Way. ☎323-667-*

PULLING THE GRAVEYARD SHIFT

Every summer thousands of Los Angelenos emerge from their swank apartments or beach bungalows and head out for the evening—to the graveyard! For Los Angeles residents, the coming of June means the coming of a long-standing annual tradition called **Cinespia,** a film.festival that screens cult favorite films for an audience seated among the memorials at the **Hollywood Forever Cemetery** on Santa Monica Blvd. Film lovers young and old indulge with picnic fare and wine as they watch flicks like *Fast Times at Ridgemont High* (1982) and *One Flew Over the Cuckoo's Nest* (1975). The films are projected against a large building, and can be seen from virtually any seat in the yard. Some lucky graveyard-goers will even witness a celebrity introduction to the films (Drew Barrymore took the stage before the Summer 2007 screening of *Fast Times.)* The presence of impossibly thin hipsters and celebutantes complete the experience, making it quintessentially L.A. Admission is a suggested $10 (but pay it so they can keep showing films in a cemetery). Parking is limited and it gets incredibly crowded, so try to get there early or prepare to hike.

All screenings at the Hollywood Forever Cemetery on 6000 Santa Monica Blvd. at Gower. For more information, visit www.cinespia.org.

2000. Open Tu-W and F-Su 10am-5pm, Th 10am-8pm. $9, students and seniors $5, ages 2-12 $3; free Th after 4pm and 2nd Tu of each month.)

PLANETARIUM AND OBSERVATORY. The world-famous white stucco and copper domes of the mountaintop observatory would be visible from nearly any point in L.A. were it not for the smog. The observatory parking lot lends a terrific view of the Hollywood sign. You may remember the planetarium from the James Dean film *Rebel Without A Cause* (1955). Visitors can also check out the modest displays and mini-planetarium at the **Griffith Observatory Satellite** in the northern corner of Griffith Park. *(Drive to the top of Mt. Hollywood on Vermont Ave. or Hillhurst St. from Los Feliz Blvd., or take MTA #180 or 181 from Hollywood Blvd. ☎323-473-0800; www.griffithobs.org. Open Tu-F noon-10pm, Sa-Su 10am-10pm. Free.)*

L.A. ZOO. Much of the zoo is undergoing renovations due to a large fire in Griffith park that destroyed much of the landscape, but rare animals from around the world are still on display throughout the 113 well-kept acres. The zoo's five sea lions are a big hit, as are the red apes and chimps. *(5333 Zoo Dr. From Los Feliz Blvd., take Crystal Springs Dr. into the park; the zoo will be on the left. ☎644-4200; www.lazoo.org. Open daily July-Aug. 10am-6pm; Sept.-June 10am-5pm. Animals are put away starting 1hr. before closing. $10, seniors $7, ages 2-12 $5.)*

DOWNTOWN

The **DASH Shuttle** runs six lines downtown that cover most of the major tourist destinations ($0.25; ask for a free transfer). Due to expensive short-term lot parking ($3 per 20min.) and exorbitant meter prices ($0.25 per 10min.), it's best to park in a public lot ($5-10 per day) and hit the pavement on foot. The **L.A. Visitors Center,** 685 S. Figueroa St., between Wilshire and 7th St., has pamphlets and answers to your travel queries. (☎213-689-8822. Open M-F 8am-4pm, Sa 8:30am-5pm.)

EL PUEBLO HISTORIC PARK. The historic birthplace of L.A. is now known as **El Pueblo de Los Angeles Historical Monument,** bordered by Cesar Chávez Ave., Alameda St., Hollywood Fwy., and Spring St. (DASH B). Established in 1825, the Plaza is the center of El Pueblo, and hosts several festivals including **Cinco de Mayo** (May 5), the Mexican Independence celebration (Sept. 16), and **Día de los Muertos** celebrations (Nov. 1-2). As you wander through the area, check out the plaques found on the walls and sidewalks for all sorts of fun historical facts about the area and its former inhabitants. **Olvera Street** resembles a colorful Mexican marketplace, selling all sorts of things you don't really need. Feel free to bargain at *puestos* (vendor stalls) for everything from Mexican handicrafts and food to personalized t-shirts. The **Avila Adobe** (circa 1818), 10 E. Olvera St., is the oldest house in the city, and the **Sepulveda House,** 12 Olvera St., contains a small museum and Visitors Center, providing information and a short film on the history of Los Angeles. *(Avila Adobe open daily 9am-3pm. Sepulveda House open M-Sa 10am-3pm. Free.)*

MUSIC CENTER. The Music Center is an enormous, beautiful complex most easily identified by the sweeping silver curves of the Frank Gehry-designed ◨**Walt Disney Concert Hall.** This gleaming 2265-seat structure is the brand-new home of the L.A. Philharmonic and the L.A. Master Chorale. *(151 S. Grand Ave. ☎213-972-7211; www.disneyhall.org. Audio tours available 10am-3pm daily. Free.)* The musical fun continues next door with the **Dorothy Chandler Pavilion,** home of the L.A. Opera *(☎213-972-8001; www.laopera.org)* and former site of the Academy Awards. Also part of the Music Center are the **Mark Taper Forum** and the **Ahmanson Theatre,** known for their world-class shows. *(☎213-628-2772; www.taperahmanson.com. Tours of the center M-F 11:30am, 12:30, 1:30pm as performances permit. Go to the information booth in the large outdoor courtyard between the theaters. Free.)*

MUSEUM OF CONTEMPORARY ART (MOCA). MOCA features an extensive and varied collection of American and European art dating from 1940, including abstract expressionism, pop art, and photography. Check out the permanent Richard Tuttle collection of drawings and sculpture in the Grand Ave. building. The Frank Gehry-renovated **MOCA at the Geffen Contemporary** was once the garage for the LAPD fleet. The "Temporary Contemporary" and its highly-acclaimed art exhibitions eventually became permanent, to the delight of its adoring public. *(250 S. Grand Ave. ☎ 213-626-6222; www.moca.org.)* Additional visual arts displays can be found at the **Pacific Design Center** complex. *(8687 Melrose Ave. All locations open M and F 11am-5pm, Th 11am-8pm, Sa-Su 11am-6pm; PDC closed M. All 3 locations $8 each, students and seniors $5, under 12 free. Free Th 5-8pm. Admission good for both MOCA locations. Shuttle between the 2 locations available.)*

OTHER SIGHTS. One of the best-known buildings in SoCal, **City Hall** "has starred in more movies than most actors." *(200 N. Spring St.)* Bargain hounds can haggle to their hearts' delight in the **Fashion District,** which is bordered by 6th and 9th St. along Los Angeles St. At 1017 ft., the tallest building between Chicago and Hong Kong, the **US Bank Tower,** punctuates the L.A. skyline with its glass crown and is brilliantly lit at night. *(633 W. 5th St.)* The **Westin Bonaventure Hotel** is composed of five sleek cylinders sheathed in black glass, and has appeared in the films *Rain Man*, *In the Line of Fire*, and *Heat*. *(404 S. Figueroa St.)* Slightly southeast of the Bonaventure is the historic **Millenium Biltmore Hotel,** designed by Schultze and Weaver, the design team best known for New York's Waldorf-Astoria. *(506 S. Grand Ave.)* After trekking around downtown, visit the soothing **James Irvine Garden,** better known as Seiryu-en or "Garden of the Pure Stream." *(244 S. San Pedro St., by the Japanese American Cultural and Community Center in Little Tokyo. ☎ 213-628-2725; www.jaccc.org. Garden open daily 9am-5pm. Closed for renovations until Jan. 2008.)* North of **Exposition Park**—an enticing location in and of itself, thanks to a host of fascinating museums—the **University of Southern California (USC)** brings a youthful character to the streets of downtown. *(☎ 213-740-2311; www.usc.edu. Campus tours offered M-F every hr. 10am-3pm; call ☎ 213-740-6605 to confirm availability.)*

PASADENA

Though just 15min. northeast of downtown L.A., Pasadena cultivates a very different atmosphere, affording visitors the feel of a small town while still offering the shopping, entertainment, and attractions of the big city. **Old Town,** the area surrounding the intersection of Fair Oaks Blvd. and Colorado Blvd., and **Paseo Colorado,** just east along Colorado Blvd., are vibrant shopping and dining districts located at the heart of the reinvigorated historical city.

▓ NORTON SIMON MUSEUM OF ART. West of Old Town, the **Simon Museum** houses a world-class, well-curated collection of Western and Southeast Asian art spanning seven centuries. Paintings by Van Gogh, Monet, and Picasso are featured. The bronzes by Degas and the 79,000 sq. ft. sculpture garden surrounding a Monet-inspired lily pool are particularly impressive. *(411 W. Colorado Blvd. ☎ 626-449-6840. Open M, W-Th, and Sa-Su noon-6pm, F noon-9pm. $8, seniors $4, students and under 18 free. Audio guide $3. Free parking.)*

▓ HUNTINGTON LIBRARY, ART GALLERY, AND BOTANICAL GARDENS. South of Pasadena in San Marino, the Huntington's 150 stunning acres of gardens are broken into 15 thematic areas including the Rose Garden, the Desert Garden, and the Japanese Garden. As tempting as the grounds may be, picnicking and sunbathing among the greens are strictly forbidden. The library holds one of the most important collections of rare books and British and American manuscripts in the world, including a Gutenberg Bible, Benjamin Franklin's handwritten autobiography, a 1410 manuscript of Chaucer's *Canterbury Tales*, and a number of Shakespeare's first folios. The art gallery is known for its 18th- and 19th-century British and French paintings. No visit here is complete without taking tea in the Rose Garden Tea Room. *(1151 Oxford Rd., between Huntington Dr. and California Blvd. ☎405-2100; www.huntington.org. Open Memorial Day-Labor Day Tu-Su 10:30am-4:30pm; Labor Day-Memorial Day Tu-F noon-4:30pm, Sa-Su 10:30am-4:30pm. $15, seniors $12, students $10, ages 5-11 $6, under 5 free; free 1st Th of each month. Rose Garden set tea Tu-Su $20; reservations required, call ☎683-8131.)*

ROSE BOWL. Pasadena's most famous landmark, the Rose Bowl is a sand-colored, 90,000-seat stadium that is home to the college football showdown between the champions of the Big Ten and Pac 10 conferences each New Year's Day. *(1001 Rose Bowl Dr., west of town. ☎577-3100; www.rosebowlstadium.com.)* The Bowl also hosts a huge flea market with upward of 2000 vendors. *(☎323-560-7469. 2nd Su of each month 9am-4:30pm.)*

CALTECH. Some of the world's greatest scientific minds do their work at the sunny, stone-and-tile campus of the California Institute of Technology (Caltech), southeast of Old Town between Del Mar Blvd. and California Blvd. Founded in 1891, Caltech has amassed a faculty that includes several Nobel laureates and a student body that prides itself both on its staggering collective intellect and its loony practical jokes, which range from unscrewing all the chairs in a lecture hall and bolting them in backwards to reworking the Hollywood sign to read "Caltech." *(1201 E. California Blvd., about 2½ mi. southeast of Old Town. ☎626-395-6327. Self-guided tour brochures available at the Visitors Center, 315 S. Hill Ave., between Colorado Blvd. and Del Mar Blvd. Tours M-F 2pm.)* NASA's **Jet Propulsion Laboratory,** about 5 mi. north of Old Town, executed the journey of the Mars Pathfinder. Ask to see pictures of the face of Mars. *(4800 Oak Grove Dr. ☎818-354-9314. Free tours by appointment.)*

SAN FERNANDO VALLEY

The Valley can't seem to shake the infamy it gained for breeding the Valley Girl, who started a worldwide trend in the 80s with her huge hair, and, ohmigod, like, totally far-out mall adventures. But the Valley deserves some respect; all of the major movie studios (and many pornographers) make their blockbusters here. Passing Burbank on Rte. 134, you may catch glimpses of the Valley's most lucrative studios: Universal, Warner Bros., NBC, and Disney. To best experience the industry, attend a free TV show taping or take a studio tour.

■ **UNIVERSAL STUDIOS.** A movie and TV studio that happens to have the world's first and largest movie-themed amusement park attached, Universal Studios Hollywood is the most popular tourist spot in Tinseltown. The signature Studio Tour tram brings riders face-to-face with King Kong and Jaws, rattles through a massive earthquake, and wanders past blockbuster sets including *War of the Worlds*, *Apollo 13*, *Jurassic Park*, *Psycho*, and many more. But for some, the 45min. tour plays second fiddle to the park's interactive attractions. While the movie may have bombed, the live stunts and pyrotechnics at *Waterworld* are impressive, and you can test your mettle by participating in *Fear Factor Live*, an extreme audience participation show. *(Take U.S. 101 to the Universal Center Dr. Exit. By MTA rail: Exit North Hollywood Red Line at Universal Station. ☎800-864-8377; www.universalstudioshollywood.com. Hours vary, check online; generally open July-Aug. M-Th 9am-8pm, F-Su 9am-9pm; Sept.-June M-F 10am-6pm, Sa-Su 10am-7pm. $61, under 48 in. $51, under 3 free. Parking $10.)*

■ **J. PAUL GETTY CENTER & MUSEUM.** Wedding classical materials with modernist form, renowned architect Richard Meier designed the stunning $1 billion complex known as "The Getty." The museum consists of five pavilions containing the Getty's manuscripts, drawings, photographs, decorative arts, sculptures, and paintings spanning seven centuries. The pavilions surround the Robert Irwin-designed Central Garden, a living work of art that changes with the seasons. Park at the base and take the free tram up to the galleries, performance-oriented exhibits, and outdoor cafes. *(1200 Getty Center Dr. Take the Getty Center Dr. Exit off I-405 or Sepulveda Blvd. ☎310-440-7300; www.getty.edu. Open Tu-Th and Su 10am-6pm, F-Sa 10am-9pm. Free. Audio guides $5. Parking $8.)*

UNIVERSAL CITY WALK. This neon strip of shopping, dining, movie theaters, and nightlife is the Valley's more colorful, less charming answer to Santa Monica's Third St. Promenade. You can find everything from a mammoth green guitar outside the Hard Rock Cafe to trendy clothing or mechanical bulls at Saddle Ranch restaurant-nightclub. *(At Universal Studios. ☎818-622-4455; www.citywalkhollywood.com. M-Th and Su 11am-9pm, F-Sa 11am-11pm. Free. City Walk parking $10; rebate with purchase of 2 or more movie tickets.)*

MAGIC MOUNTAIN. At the opposite end of the Valley, 40min. north of L.A. in Valencia, is thrill-ride heaven **Six Flags Magic Mountain,** boasting the most roller coasters in the world. Its newest addition, **Scream!,** is Southern California's first floorless mega-coaster where your feet dangle in the air as you scream through 4000 ft. of twists, plunges, and loops. **X** boasts of being the world's only 4D roller coaster with front and back flips. It also happens to have mammoth lines, so go early in the day. Next door, Six Flags's waterpark **Hurricane Harbor** features the world's tallest enclosed speed slide. *(Take U.S. 101 N to U.S. 170 N to I-5 N to Magic Mountain Pkwy. Magic Mountain: ☎661-255-4100; www.sixflags.com/magicmountain. Open Apr.-Aug. daily; Sept.-Mar. weekends and holidays. Hours vary; check the website. $60, seniors and under 48 in. $30, under 2 free. Check for online specials and discounts. Parking $15. Hurricane Harbor: ☎661-255-4527. Open May-Sept.; hours vary. $25, seniors and under 48 in. $21, under 2 free. Both parks $70.)*

MIRACLE MILE

Museums are found all over the greater Los Angeles area, but a district known as the **Miracle Mile,** on Wilshire Blvd. between La Brea and Fairfax, is home to many of the most impressive.

LOS ANGELES COUNTY MUSEUM OF ART (LACMA). Opened in 1965, LACMA is the largest museum on the West Coast. The Steve Martin Gallery, in the Anderson Building, holds the famed comedian's collection of Dadaist and Surrealist works. *(5905 Wilshire Blvd. in the Wilshire District. ☎323-857-6000; www.lacma.org. Open M-Tu and Th noon-8pm, F noon-9pm, Sa-Su 11am-8pm. $9, seniors and students $5, under 18 free; free 2nd Tu of each month and daily after 5pm. Free jazz F 6-9pm, chamber music Su 6-7pm. Film tickets $8, seniors and students $6. Parking $5-8.)*

PETERSEN AUTOMOTIVE MUSEUM (PAM). The PAM showcases one of L.A.'s enduring symbols—the automobile. PAM is the world's largest car museum, with over 150 classic cars, hot rods, motorcycles, and celebrity cars on display at any given time. A joint exhibition with Fender Guitars pairs rock stars with their cars and guitars. Special exhibits on alternative power cars, microcars, and Ferarris are slated to appear throughout 2008. *(6060 Wilshire Blvd. at Fairfax Ave., in the Wilshire District. ☎323-930-2277; www.petersen.org. Open Tu-Su 10am-6pm; Discovery Center closes 4pm. $10, seniors and students $5, ages 5-12 and military $3, under 5 free. Parking $6.)*

GEORGE C. PAGE MUSEUM OF LA BREA DISCOVERIES. The smelly La Brea Tar Pits fill the area with an acrid petroleum stench and provide bones for this natural history museum. The skeletons of thirsty prehistoric animals who became stuck and perished in these oozing tar pools are on display. You can feel what it's

CALIFORNIA

like to be trapped in tar and play with the sabertooth cat skull. A viewing station, where archaeologists work in the summer, is at Pit 91. *(5801 Wilshire Blvd. ☎ 323-934-7243; www.tarpits.org. Museum open M-F 9:30am-5pm, Sa-Su 10am-5pm. $7, seniors and students $4.50, ages 5-12 $2; free 1st Tu of each month. Parking $6 with validation.)*

🎬 ENTERTAINMENT

FILM AND TELEVISION STUDIOS

A visit to the world's entertainment capital isn't complete without some exposure to the business of making a movie or TV show. Fortunately, most production companies oblige. **Paramount** (☎323-956-5000), **NBC** (☎818-840-3537), and **Warner Bros.** (☎818-954-1008) offer 2hr. guided tours that take you onto sets and through backlots. The best way to get a feel for the industry is to land yourself tickets to a taping. Tickets are free, but studios tend to overbook, so holding a ticket does not always guarantee you'll get in; show up early. **NBC**, 3000 W. Alameda Ave., at W. Olive Ave. in Burbank, is your best bet. Arrive at the ticket office on a weekday before 8am for passes to Jay Leno's **Tonight Show,** filmed at 4:30pm the same day (2 tickets per person, must be 16+). Studio tours run on the hour. (☎818-840-3537. Tours M-F 9am-3pm. $7.50, ages 5-12 $4.) Many of NBC's "Must-See TV" shows are taped at **Warner Bros.,** 4000 Warner Blvd. (☎818-954-6000), in Burbank—call the studio at least five business days in advance to secure tickets.

A **CBS box office,** 7800 Beverly Blvd., next to the farmers' market (p. 894) in West Hollywood, hands out free tickets to various tapings, such as the Late Late Show with Craig Ferguson. Tickets can be difficult to obtain. (☎323-575-2458. 18+. Open M-F 9am-5pm.) If all else fails, **Audiences Unlimited, Inc.,** 100 Universal City Plaza, Building 4250, Universal City, CA 91608 (☎818-506-0067; www.tvtickets.com), is a great resource. Most sitcoms do not film in the late spring to early summer months, but resume in late July or early August.

MOVIES

L.A.'s movie palaces show films the way they were meant to be seen—on a big screen, in plush seats, and with top-quality sound. The huge theaters at **Universal City,** as well as those in **Westwood Village** near UCLA, are incredibly popular, especially on weekends; expect long lines. **Santa Monica** has 22 screens within the three blocks between Santa Monica Pl. and Wilshire Blvd. along Third St. Promenade.

To ogle the stars as they walk the red carpet into the theater for a premiere, check the four main premiere venues: **Grauman's Chinese** (about 2 per month), **El Capitán** (Disney films only), and **Mann's Village** and **Bruin,** in Westwood. For info on what's playing, call ☎323-777-3456 or read the daily Calendar section of the *L.A. Times.* Devotees of second-run, foreign-language, and experimental films are rewarded by the Santa Monica theaters away from the Promenade. Foreign films play consistently at the eight **Laemmle Theaters** in Beverly Hills (☎310-274-6869), West Hollywood (☎323-848-3500), Santa Monica (☎310-394-9741), Pasadena (☎626-844-6500), and downtown L.A. (☎213-617-0268).

LIVE THEATER AND MUSIC

L.A.'s live theater scene does not hold the weight of New York's Broadway, but its 115 "equity waiver theaters" (under 100 seats) offer dizzying, eclectic choices for theatergoers, who can also view small productions in art galleries, universities, parks, and even garages. Browse listings in the *L.A. Weekly* to find out what's hot.

L.A.'s music venues range from small clubs to massive amphitheaters. The **Wiltern** (☎213-380-5005) shows alternative-rock/folk acts. Midsized acts head for the **Gibson Amphitheater** (☎818-622-4440). Huge indoor sports arenas, such as **The**

Forum (☎310-330-7300) and the **Staples Center** (☎213-742-7100), double as concert halls for big acts. Few dare to play at the 100,000-seat **Los Angeles Memorial Coliseum and Sports Arena;** only U2, Depeche Mode, Guns 'n' Roses, and the Warped Tour have filled the stands in recent years. Call Ticketmaster (☎213-480-3232) to purchase tickets for any of these venues.

▧ **Hollywood Bowl,** 2301 N. Highland Ave. (☎323-850-2000, www.hollywoodbowl.com), in Hollywood. L.A.'s premier outdoor music venue hosts a music festival from early July to mid-Sept. Free rehearsals by the Philharmonic and visiting performers usually Tu and Th 10:30am. Call Ticketmaster (☎213-480-3232) to purchase tickets or order them at the Hollywood Bowl website. Parking ($11-12) at the Bowl is limited. Other lots at 10601 and 10801 Ventura Blvd., near Universal City; at the Kodak Theatre at 6801 Hollywood Blvd.; and at the L.A. Zoo, 5333 Zoo Dr. (parking $5, shuttle $2.50 each way; departs every 10-20min. starting 1½hr. before showtime).

Geffen Playhouse, 11301 Wilshire Blvd. (☎310-208-5454), at Brentwood Theater, in Westwood. Fresh from renovation, it's home to Off-Broadway and Tony Award-winning shows. Tickets $34-46; student rush tickets $10, available 1hr. before the show, or ahead of time through Ticketmaster (☎213-480-3232).

Pasadena Playhouse, 39 S. El Molino Ave. (☎626-356-7529; www.pasadenaplayhouse.org), in Pasadena. California's premier theater and historical landmark has spawned Broadway careers and productions. Tickets $35-60. Call for rush tickets. Shows Tu-F 8pm, Sa 5 and 9pm, Su 2 and 7pm.

SPORTS

Exposition Park and the often dangerous city of **Inglewood,** directly southwest of the park, are home to many sports teams. The **USC Trojans** play football at the **L.A. Memorial Coliseum,** 3911 S. Figueroa St. (☎213-765-6388). The NBA's **L.A. Clippers** (☎213-742-7500) share playing space with the post-dynasty **L.A. Lakers** (☎310-426-6000) at the new **Staples Center,** 1111 S. Figueroa St. (☎213-742-7100, box office 213-742-7340), along with the **L.A. Kings** hockey team (☎213-742-7100) and the WNBA's **L.A. Sparks** (☎310-330-3939). Call Ticketmaster (☎213-480-3232) for tickets. About 3 mi. northeast of downtown, **Elysian Park** curves around the northern portion of Chávez Ravine, home of **Dodger Stadium** and the popular **L.A. Dodgers** baseball team. Single-game tickets ($10-30) are a hot commodity during the April to October season, especially if the Dodgers are playing well. (Call ☎323-224-1448 for info and advance tickets.)

▧ NIGHTLIFE

L.A.'s nightlife scene is constantly shifting. Pick up a copy of *L.A. Weekly* or the *L.A. Times*'s Calendar section for the latest news on goings on about town. Given the extremely short shelf life and unpredictability of the L.A. club scene, late-night restaurants have become the reliable fallback option, popular with underage club kids and of course celebs in rehab. Many coffeehouses stay open late and have open-mic nights or live music. Though it's hard to barhop when the best places are a 30min. drive from each other (don't forget your designated driver), L.A.'s **bars** run the gamut from casual beach hangouts to swanky hotel lounges. With the highest number of bands per capita in the world, L.A. is also justly famous for its club scene, much of which focuses around the Sunset Strip and comes with a hefty price tag. To enter the club scene, it's best to be at least 21 years of age (it also helps to be a beautiful woman). If you're over 18, you can still find a space to dance, though it may mean a hefty cover charge in a less desirable venue than those options open to patrons over the age of 21. **All bars and clubs are 21+ unless otherwise noted.**

CALIFORNIA

THE COAST

The waterfront areas are packed with brewpubs, dance clubs, and surfer hangouts. ▨**The Kettle,** 1138 Highland Ave., at the corner of Manhattan Beach Blvd. in Manhattan Beach, is filled with surfers feasting on heaping platefuls of homestyle cooking. After sipping beer or wine (served until midnight), prepare for the morning with the "Mardi Gras" omelet ($10), containing turkey, avocado and jack cheese. (☎310-545-8511. Salads and sandwiches $8-12. Open 24hr.) The dark red glow of "eastern" decor and the cool live music give **Temple Bar,** 1026 Wilshire Blvd., in Santa Monica, its smooth vibe. The food and drink, like house favorites Caribbean jerk blackened red snapper quesadillas ($10) and mojitos ($12), complete the bar's eclectic mix. (☎310-393-6611; www.templebarlive.com. Live music nightly. Open daily 8pm-2am.)

THE WESTSIDE

The Sunset Strip and West Hollywood contain the city's densest concentration of nightlife. Chic lounges, grungy clubs, and happy group hangouts can all be found.

▨ **Standard Lounge,** 8300 Sunset Blvd. (☎323-822-3111), in the Standard Hotel. No cover, no guest list, but you'd never know it. No dress code for the lounge, but make sure to leave your flip-flops at home if you want to gain entry to the dance club connected to the 24hr. restaurant. Insanely chic—Carrie Bradshaw drank in the mirrored, jewel-toned interior in the "Sex and Another City" episode of *Sex and the City*. Look for the scantily clad girl lounging in the glass case behind the hotel registration desk. Drinks $9. DJ nightly. Open daily 10pm-2am.

Jerry's Famous Deli, 8701 Beverly Blvd. (☎310-289-1811), at San Vicente Ave., West Hollywood. Also at 10925 Weyburn Ave. (☎310-208-3354), in Westwood, and 12655 Ventura Blvd. (☎818-980-4245), in Studio City in the Valley; www.jerrysfamousdeli.com. The valet should be your 1st indication that this is no regular deli. The sleek red leather and sky-high prices should be your 2nd. That said, the atmosphere is inviting, and the food is perfect for your 4am snack. Jumbo triple-deckers $15. Salads served in a pizza crust $10-13. Open 24hr.

Miyagi's, 8225 Sunset Blvd. (☎323-650-3524). With 3 levels, 7 sushi bars (rolls $6-14), 6 liquor bars, and indoor waterfalls, this Japanese-themed restaurant, bar, lounge, and hip-hop dance club is a Strip hot spot. Sake bomb $5. Open daily 5:30pm-2am.

HOLLYWOOD AND POINTS EAST

Hollywood and its immediate neighboring areas are up-and-comers in the Los Angeles nightlife world. Known for being more laidback than the uber-ritzy clubs of the Sunset Strip, these distinctive nightspots have managed to gather a strong following and can be just as fashionable as any on the Strip.

3 of Clubs, 1123 N. Vine St. (☎323-462-6441), at Santa Monica Blvd., in Hollywood, in a strip mall. Look for the small "cocktails" sign. Simple, classy, and spacious bar famous for its starring role in the movie *Swingers*. A local watering hole early in the week, a happening club on the weekend. Th live bands. F-Sa DJ. Open daily 6pm-2am.

Lucky Strike Lanes, 6801 Hollywood Blvd. (☎323-467-7776; www.bowlluckystrike.com), in the Hollywood & Highland Complex. You're more likely to be bowling next to a celebrity than your Uncle Joe and his buddies. With 12 lanes, plush seating, state-of-the-art video screens, a pumping audio system, DJs, and a full bar, Lucky Strike is an upscale, hip version of any bowling alley you've ever been to. Call for lane reservations. Bowling $5-8; shoes $4. 21+ after 7pm. Open M-F noon-2am, Sa-Su 11am-2am.

The Derby, 4500 Los Feliz Blvd. (☎323-663-8979; www.clubderby.com), at Hillhurst Ave., in Los Feliz. Ladies, grab your pearls and Marilyn Monroe-tribute dress; many dress and dance the 40s part. Full bar. $10 swing lessons Su 7-9pm. Cover F-Sa $5-12. Open M-F 5pm-2am, Sa 9pm-2am, Su 6pm-2am. Bar open daily 5pm-2am.

Beauty Bar, 1638 Cahuenga Blvd. (☎323-464-7676; www.beautybar.com), in Hollywood. Get a manicure while sipping a mixed drink in a time warp of a 60s beauty parlor. Martinis are so much headier when sitting under an old-school hair dryer. Beautify while boozing on drinks like the "Perm" or the "Platinum Blonde" ($8, with manicure $10). DJ nightly 10pm. Open M-W and Su 9pm-2am, Th-Sa 6pm-2am. Manicures available Th-Sa 6-11pm.

Bourgeois Pig, 5931 Franklin Ave. (☎323-464-6008), between Tamarind and N. Bronson. The dim interior of this late night coffeehouse and hangout is not nearly as darkly intriguing as its mysterious and brooding Hollywood clientele, most of whom appear to be artist types and eccentric night owls. Come during the day for local brew and free Wi-Fi, and return at night for some of the most interesting people-watching in town. Open daily 8am-2am. Cash only.

COMEDY CLUBS

L.A.'s comedy clubs are among the world's best. You can catch new comedians or watch skilled veterans hone new material. The **Comedy Store,** 8433 Sunset Blvd., in West Hollywood, has three rooms, each featuring a different type of comedy. The Main Room and Original Room host headliner comedians, while the Belly Room provides a testing ground for up-and-comers. (☎323-650-6268. Drinks $5-9. 21+. Main Room and Original Room cover M-F $15, Sa-Su $20. Belly Room no cover. 2-drink min. Showtimes vary; call a week ahead to reserve tickets. Open daily until 2am; Main Room only open Sa.) The **Groundling Theater,** 7307 Melrose Ave., in Hollywood, is one of the most popular improv and comedy clubs in town. Illustrious alums of the club include Pee Wee Herman and many current and former *Saturday Night Live* regulars, including Will Ferrell and Chris Kattan. (☎323-934-4747; www.groundlings.com. Shows W-Th 8pm, F-Sa 8 and 10pm, Su 7:30pm. Tickets $15-22.)

GLBT NIGHTLIFE

The slice of Santa Monica Blvd. in West Hollywood is the Sunset Strip of GLBT nightlife. All of the clubs listed below are in West Hollywood. In addition to clubs in that area, many "straight" clubs have gay nights; check *L.A. Weekly* or contact the Gay and Lesbian Community Services Center for more information. The free weekly magazine *fab!* lists happenings in the GLBT community. **All clubs are 21+ unless otherwise noted.**

🖼 **The Abbey,** 692 N. Robertson Blvd. (☎310-289-8410), at Santa Monica Blvd. 6 candlelit rooms, 2 huge bars, a large outdoor patio, and a hall of private booths make this beautiful lounge and dance club the best gay nightspot in town. The comfy couches cry out for some lovin', but get there early or wait outside. Open daily 8am-2am.

Micky's, 8857 Santa Monica Blvd. (☎310-657-1176; www.mickys.com). On Sa night when bars close, head to Micky's for another 2hr. of grooving. Music is mostly electronica and techno, although hip-hop is sometimes sprinkled into the mix. Tu college night; 18+. Cover $3-10 after 10pm. Happy hour M-F 4-9pm. Open Tu-F 4pm-2am, Sa 11pm-4am, Su 11pm-2am. Expected to reopen after a fire in late summer 2007; call ahead.

Here, 696 N. Robertson St. (☎310-360-8455), at the corner of Santa Monica Blvd. Known for Su nights when the bartenders dress up in scandalous surfer shorts, this sleek gay bar and dance club caters to the well-dressed and trendy. DJs spin a mix of house and hip-hop. Don't miss the frozen cosmopolitans ($8). Th lesbian night. Happy hour daily 4-8pm; drinks $2-3 off. Open W-Su 6pm-2am.

BEYOND LOS ANGELES

ORANGE COUNTY ☎714/949

Directly south of L.A. County lies Orange County. Composed of 34 cities, it is a microcosm of SoCal: dazzling sandy shoreline, bronzed beach bums, oversized shopping malls, homogenous suburban neighborhoods, and frustrating traffic snarls. As one of California's staunchest wealthy enclaves, Orange County (and no, they don't actually call it "The O.C.") has the multimillion-dollar hillside mansions oozing luxury cars and disaffected teens to prove it. Disneyland, the stronghold of the Walt Disney Company's ever-expanding empire, is the premier inland attraction. The coast runs the gamut from the budget- and party-friendly surf burg of Huntington Beach to the opulent excess of Newport Beach and the artistic vibe of Laguna. Farther south lies the quiet mission of San Juan Capistrano, set amid rolling hills that spill onto the laid-back beaches of Dana Point and San Clemente.

▆ TRANSPORTATION

Airport: John Wayne Airport (SNA), 18601 Airport Way; (☎949-252-5200), in Santa Ana. 20min. from Anaheim. Domestic flights only.

Trains: Amtrak (☎800-872-7245; www.amtrak.com) stations, from north to south: **Fullerton,** 120 E. Santa Fe Ave. (☎714-992-0530); **Santa Ana,** 1000 E. Santa Ana Blvd. (☎714-547-8389); **Irvine,** 15215 Barranca Pkwy. (☎949-753-9713); **San Juan Capistrano,** 26701 Verdugo St. (☎949-240-2972). Call for hours.

Buses: Greyhound (☎800-231-2222; www.greyhound.com) has 3 stations in the area. **Anaheim,** 100 W. Winston Rd. (☎714-999-1256), 3 blocks south of Disneyland. Open daily 6:30am-12:45pm and 2:40-9:15pm. **Santa Ana,** 1000 E. Santa Ana Blvd. (☎714-542-2215). Open daily 6:30am-8:30pm. **San Clemente,** 2421 S. El Camino Real (☎949-366-2646). Open daily 7am-9pm.

Public Transit: Orange County Transportation Authority (OCTA; ☎714-636-7433; www.octa.net), 550 S. Main St., in Orange. Useful for getting from Santa Ana and Fullerton Amtrak stations to Disneyland and for beach-hopping along the coast. Long Beach, in L.A. County, serves as the destination for several OCTA lines. Bus #1 travels the coast from Long Beach to San Clemente (every hr. until 8pm); #25, 33, and 35 travel from Fullerton to Huntington Beach; #91 goes from Laguna Hills to San Clemente. ($1.25, day pass $3.) **Info center** open M-F 7:30am-5:30pm. **MTA Info** (☎213-626-4455 or 800-266-6883) available by phone daily 5am-10:45pm. MTA buses run from L.A. to Disneyland and Knott's Berry Farm.

▟ PRACTICAL INFORMATION

Visitor Info: Anaheim Area Visitors and Convention Bureau, 800 W. Katella Ave. (☎714-765-8888; www.anaheimoc.org), in Anaheim Convention Ctr. Open M-F 8am-5pm. **Newport Visitors Bureau,** 110 Newport Center Dr., #120 (☎949-719-6100 or 800-942-6278), in Newport Beach. Eager-to-help staff, maps of area attractions, and events brochures. Open M-F 8am-5pm. **Laguna Beach Visitors Bureau,** 252 Broadway (☎949-497-9229). Open M-F 10am-4pm, Sa-Su 10am-2pm.

Police: Anaheim, 425 S. Harbor Blvd. (☎714-765-1875). **Huntington Beach,** 2000 Main St. (☎714-960-8811).

Hotlines: Sexual Assault Hotline, ☎714-957-2737. **Orange County Referral Hotline,** ☎714-894-4242. **Surf and Weather Conditions,** ☎213-554-1212.

Medical Services: St. Jude Medical Center, 101 E. Valencia Mesa Dr. (☎714-446-5050), in Fullerton. **Lestonnac Free Clinic,** 1215 E. Chapman Ave. (☎714-633-4600). Open Tu-F 9am-5pm; sometimes Sa. Hours can vary; call for an appointment.

Post Office: 701 N. Loara St. (☎714-520-2639 or 800-275-8777), 1 block north of Anaheim Plaza, in Anaheim. Open M-F 8:30am-5pm, Sa 9am-3pm. **Postal Code:** 92803. **Area Codes:** 714 (Anaheim, Santa Ana, Orange, Garden Grove), 949 (Newport, Laguna, Irvine, Mission Viejo, San Juan Capistrano).

ACCOMMODATIONS

Countless budget chain motels and garden-variety rooms flank Disneyland on all sides, but travelers with cars might want to consider staying in one of L.A.'s many hostels instead. Keep watch for family or group rates posted on marquees; seek out establishments offering the **3-for-2 passport** (3 days of Disney for the price of 2).

Fullerton Hostel (HI), 1700 N. Harbor Blvd. (☎714-738-3721), in Fullerton, 10min. north of Disneyland. Shuttle from LAX $21. OCTA bus #43 runs along Harbor Blvd. to Disneyland. In the woods (and away from nearby Anaheim's themed craziness) this hostel has a homey, suburban feel and a diverse crowd. The enthusiastic staff invites questions but forbids drinking. Kitchen, relaxed living room, communal bathrooms. Laundry $1.50. 7-night max. stay. Check-in 10:30am-11:30pm. Reservations recommended; does not accept residents of L.A. or Orange County. Open June-Sept. Single gender and co-ed dorms $25, members $22. MC/V. ❶

Hotel Laguna, 425 S. Coast Hwy. (949-494-1151), on the sand in Laguna Beach. This posh place was Laguna's first hotel. The modern interior has handsomely furnished rooms, many with outstanding ocean and garden views. Continental breakfast included. May-Sept. rooms from $150. Sept.-May from $120. AmEx/D/MC/V. ❺

FOOD

With wealthy residents and a location on the coast, Orange County thrives on light California cuisine and exquisitely fresh seafood.

Rutabegorz, 211 N. Pomona Blvd. (☎714-738-9339; www.rutabegorz.com), 1 block east of Harbor Blvd., in Fullerton. Also at 264 N. Glassell St. (☎714-633-3260), in Orange, and 158 W. Main St. (☎731-9807), in Tustin. This hippie-cum-hipster joint has a 20-page recycled newsprint menu. Crepes, curries, quesadillas, and club sandwiches are all fresh and veggie-heavy (all $8-11). Check for the delicious and constantly changing $1 specials. Smoothies, veggie juices, and coffee drinks $2.25-5. Open M-Th 11am- 9pm, F-Sa 11am-11pm, Su 4-9pm. AmEx/D/MC/V. ❷

Michele's Sugar Shack Cafe, 213½ Main St. (☎714-536-0355), in Huntington Beach. Big omelets, crispy hashbrowns, and blue plate lunch specials (each $5-6). Open M-Tu and Th 5am-4pm, W 5am-8:30pm, F-Su 5am-5pm. AmEx/D/MC/V. ❷

C'est la Vie Restaurant and Bar, 373 S. Coast Hwy. (☎949-497-5100), just south of Broadway, in Laguna Beach. Enjoy rich quiches, light salads, lunch specials, and designer martinis on the patio. Most dishes $8-16. Martinis $9. Open M-Th 9:30am-10:30pm, F-Sa 8:30am-11:30pm, Su 8:30am-10:30pm. AmEx/D/MC/V. ❸

SIGHTS AND BEACHES

DISNEYLAND. Disneyland calls itself the "Happiest Place on Earth," and the child in everyone agrees. After a full day there, your feet and your precious wallet may not. Weekday and low-season visitors will undoubtedly be the happiest. Clever vis-

CALIFORNIA

itors can wait for parades and gigantic Disney characters to distract shrieking children, utilize the line-busting FastPass program, or come at night to avoid the worst of the crowds. Recently, Disneyland introduced its kid brother, **California Adventure,** to the theme park family. Current fun-filled Disney projects include a submarine ride based upon the blockbuster animated film, *Finding Nemo:* stay tuned! The park features ambitious attractions divided into four districts. **Sunshine Plaza,** the gateway to the park, is anchored by a 50 ft. tall sun enlivened by a flood of red, orange, and yellow lights at night. **Golden State** offers an eight-acre mini-wilderness, a citrus grove, a winery, and even a replica of San Francisco. **Paradise Pier** is dedicated to the so-called "Golden Age" of amusement parks, with rollercoasters like California Screamin' and the stomach-dropping Tower of Terror. Finally, the **Hollywood Pictures Backlot** fulfills your aspirations of stardom without any embarrassing before-you-were-famous photos. *(Main entrance on Harbor Blvd., a smaller one on Katella Ave. ☎ 714-781-4565; www.disneyland.com. Disneyland open daily in summer 8am-midnight; hours vary by season. California Adventure open daily in summer 8am-10pm; hours vary by season. Disneyland passport or California Adventure passport $63, ages 3-9 $53, under 3 free; allows repeated single-day entrance. Combination Park Hopper ticket $83, ages 3-9 $73. 2- and 3-day passes also available. Parking $11.)*

(K)NOT(T) DISNEYLAND. Knott's Berry Farm has more intense rides and is slightly easier on the wallet than Disney, although this means a smaller size and more common rides. The park's highlights include **Camp Snoopy** for the kids, roller coasters like **Boomerang** and **Ghostrider,** the largest wooden roller coaster in the West, for the brave. The latest addition, **Xcelerator,** goes from 0 to 80 mph in 2.3 seconds. *(8039 Beach Blvd., at La Palma Ave., 5 mi. northeast of Disneyland. Recorded info ☎ 714-220-5200. Open M-Th and Su 10am-10pm, F-Sa 10am-11pm; hours may vary. $49, ages 3-11 $19, under 3 free; after 4pm all tickets half-price. Parking $10.)* **Soak City USA,** a 50s beach-theme town, is Knott's effort to make a splash in the already-drenched water park scene. *(Next to Knott's. ☎ 714-220-5200. Open M-Th and Su 10am-6pm, F-Sa 10am-7pm; hours may vary. $28, ages 3-11 $17, under 3 free.)*

SPORTS. For more evidence of Disney's world domination, catch a game by one of the teams they own. The major league Los Angeles **Angels** of Anaheim play baseball from early April to October at **Angel Stadium** in Anaheim. *(☎ 714-940-2000 or 800-626-4357; http://losangeles.angels.mlb.com. General tickets $9-60.)* The NHL's 2007 Stanley Cup champions, the **Anaheim Ducks,** play at **Honda Center** *(☎ 714-704-2400; http://ducks.nhl.com).*

ORANGE COUNTY BEACH COMMUNITIES. Orange County's beach communities have cleaner sand, better surf, and less madness than their L.A. counterparts; L.A. residents seek refuge here. Huntington Beach is a perfect beach bum playground with a large beach, volleyball nets, and waves. This town has surf lore galore: the proof is on the **Surfing Walk of Fame** and in the **International Surfing Museum.** *(Walk of Fame: the sidewalk along PCH at Main St. Museum: 411 Olive St. ☎ 714-960-3483. Open daily noon-5pm; in spring and summer Sa-Su open 11am-5pm. $2, students $1.)* Multimillion-dollar homes, the world's largest leisure-craft harbor, and Balboa Peninsula are all packed closely enough on the **Newport Beach** oceanfront to make even New Yorkers feel claustrophobic. Surfing, beach volleyball, shopping, and looking hot are all popular activities. Punctuated by rocky cliffs, shady coves, and lush hillside vegetation, lovely, artsy **Laguna Beach's** character is decidedly Mediterranean. **Ocean Avenue,** at the Pacific Coast Hwy., and **Main Beach** are the prime parading areas. The **Laguna Art Museum** showcases local and state art, including some excellent early 20th-century Impressionist works. *(307 Cliff Dr. ☎ 949-494-8971; www.lagunaart-museum.com. Open M-W and F 11am-5pm, Th 11am-9pm, Sa-Su 10am-6pm. Tours daily 2pm. $10, seniors and students $8, under 12 free.)* The evocative **Mission San Juan Capistrano,**

30min. south of Anaheim on I-5, was established by Father Junípero Serra and is considered the jewel of the California missions. *(On the corner of Ortega Hwy. and Camino Capistrano. ☎949-234-1300; www.missionsjc.com. Open daily 8:30am-5pm. $7, over 60 $6, ages 4-11 $5, under 3 free.)*

BIG BEAR
☎909

Big Bear is easily Southern California's most popular mountain and lake resort. Los Angelenos hit the slopes in the winter, and in the summer, the central lake provides ample opportunities for fishing, sailing, and watersports, while the nearby mountains and forest offer enjoyable hikes and well-preserved campgrounds.

Hiking the trails in the surrounding mountains is a superb way to explore the San Bernardino wilderness. Head to the **Big Bear Discovery Center (BBDC),** on Hwy. 38, for maps, trail descriptions, and the *Visitor's Guide to the San Bernardino National Forest.* (☎382-2790. Open daily 8:30am-4:30pm.) The 3½ mi. **Alpine Pedal Path** follows a paved course from the Stanfield Cutoff to the BBDC along the lake's north shore. The moderately difficult 2½ mi. **Castle Rock Trail,** starting 1 mi. east of the dam on Hwy. 18, is a steep haul to stupendous views of Big Bear Lake. In summer, **mountain biking** takes over the Big Bear area. Grab a *Ride and Trail Guide* at the BBDC or at **Snow Summit,** 1 mi. west of Big Bear Lake, which runs lifts in summer, providing access to the surrounding Forest Service lands. If you aren't ready to grind down the mountain, a scenic round-trip ride can be picked up for the same price. (☎866-5766. Open M-F and Su 9am-4pm, Sa 8am-5pm. One-way with bicycle $10, ages 7-12 $5. Helmet required.) **Bear Valley Bikes,** 40298 Big Bear Blvd., rents bikes for use on the mountain. (☎866-8000. $9 per hr., $25 per 4hr., $35 per day; helmet included.) Big Bear Lake is well-stocked with rainbow trout and catfish. State **fishing** licenses are available at sporting goods stores ($12.50 per day, $48 per season). Boats can be rented at **Holloway's Marina,** 398 Edgemor Rd., on the south shore. (☎866-5706 or 800-448-5335; www.bigbearboating.com. $80-230 per day.)

When snow conditions are favorable, ski areas quickly run out of lift tickets, which may be purchased through Ticketmaster (☎714-740-2000). **Big Bear Mountain Resorts** (www.bigbearmountainresorts.com) splits 55 runs between two ski resorts. The huge vertical drops and adventure skiing terrain at **Bear Mountain,** 43101 Goldmine Dr., are geared toward freestyle skiing and snowboarding. (☎585-2519; www.bearmtn.com.) **Snow Summit,** 880 Summit Blvd., is a more family-oriented resort with snowmaking, night skiing, and a well-rounded assortment of beginner runs. (☎866-5766; www.snowsummit.com. Lift tickets are interchangeable, and a shuttle runs between the 2 parks. Lift tickets $49, ages 13-21 $39, ages 7-12 $19; holidays $59/49/25. Skis $27 per day; snowboards $30 per day. Deposit required for rentals.) **Snow Valley,** 35100 Hwy. 18, near Running Springs, is the most family-oriented resort in Big Bear and even has a "snow play" area if you want to frolic in the fluffy white stuff without strapping skis on. (☎867-2751; www.snow-valley.com. Lift tickets $49, ages 7-12 $19. Ski and boot rental $26; snowboard $30.) **Renting** ski equipment from the ski stores along Big Bear Blvd. can save you up to half the price of renting at the mountains. **Cross-country skiing** is very popular in Big Bear. The **Rim Nordic Ski Area,** across from Snow Valley, is a network of cross-country ski trails. An Adventure Passport (free at the Visitors Center) is required.

As Big Bear is a year-round destination, rooms below $50 a night are often only found down the mountain in San Bernardino. **Big Bear Boulevard** is lined with lodging possibilities. **Robinhood Inn ❹,** 40797 Lakeview Dr., has a courtyard complete with spa and barbecue, and many rooms have fireplaces and kitchenettes. (☎866-4643. Singles and doubles in summer from $64; suites for up to 6 people under $100. Winter rates much higher; call for details. AmEx/D/MC/V.) **Serrano ❶,** 40650

N. Shore Ln., off Hwy. 38, in Fawnskin, is the most popular campground in Big Bear, with flat, roomy sites, many of which are located right along the highway. (☎866-8021, reservations 877-444-6777. Flush toilets and showers. Sites $26, with hookup $36.) Food can get pricey, so those with kitchens should buy groceries at **Stater Bros.**, 42171 Big Bear Blvd. (☎866-5211. Open M-Sa 7am-11pm, Su 7am-10pm.) Cutesy cafes and roadside burger stands circle the lake, providing ample opportunity to satisfy your stomach. For a more relaxing meal, the **Peppercorn Grille ❷**, 553 Pine Knot Ave., in the Village, has $9 lunch specials of mainly American and Californian cuisine. (☎866-5405. Open daily 11am-3pm and 5-9pm.)

To reach Big Bear, take **I-10** to **Route 30** in San Bernardino and follow Rte. 30 north to **Route 330** (Mountain Rd.), which turns into **Route 18,** a winding 30-45min. ascent. Rte. 18 hits the west end of Big Bear Lake and forks—Rte. 18 goes along the south shore to Big Bear Lake City and **Route 38** goes along the north shore to the BBDC. Driving time from L.A. is about 2½hr., barring serious weekend traffic or road closures. Driving to Big Bear should not be attempted during the winter without checking road conditions with **CalTrans** (☎427-7623; www.dot.ca.gov). **Mountain Area Regional Transit Authority (MARTA)** runs two **buses** per day (M-Sa) from the Greyhound station in San Bernardino to Big Bear. (☎878-5200. Round-trip $5.) The **Big Bear Visitors Center,** 630 Bartlett Rd., in Big Bear Village, has a treasure trove of maps and brochures. (☎866-4608; www.bigbearchamber.com. Open daily 9am-5pm.) **Post Office:** 472 Pine Knot Blvd. (☎866-7481. Open M-F 8:30am-5pm, Sa 10am-noon). **Postal Code:** 92315.

SAN DIEGO ☎619

The locals call it "America's Finest City," and visitors pulling into this picturesque port will soon understand why. In a state where every town stakes a claim on paradise, San Diego may be Southern California's best return on the promises of a golden state, offering perfectly sunny weather almost every day of the year and a vibrant, varied city that is simultaneously cosmopolitan and relaxed.

▐ TRANSPORTATION

San Diego is in the southwest corner of California, 127 mi. south of L.A. and 15 mi. north of the Mexican border. **I-5** runs south from L.A. through the cities of Oceanside and Carlsbad, skirting the eastern edge of downtown on its way to the Mexican border; **I-15** runs northeast through the desert to Las Vegas; and **I-8** runs east-west along downtown's northern boundary, connecting the desert with Ocean Beach.

Airport: San Diego International (SAN) (Lindbergh Field), at the northwest edge of downtown. Call **Airport Ambassadors** (☎231-7361 or 231-5230) for info. Open daily 8am-11pm. Bus #992 goes downtown ($2.25), as do cabs ($8-10). **Cloud 9 Shuttle** (☎800-974-8885) offers affordable shared van transportation throughout the region.

Trains: Amtrak, 1050 Kettner Blvd. (☎800-872-7245; www.amtrak.com), north of Broadway in the Santa Fe Depot. Station has bus, trolley, car, and boat transportation info. Ticket office open daily 5:15am-10:15pm. To **Los Angeles** (10 per day, 3 hr., $34).

Buses: Greyhound, 120 W. Broadway (☎239-8082 or 800-231-2222; www.greyhound.com), at 1st St. Ticket office open 24hr. To **Los Angeles** (18 per day, $16) and **Tijuana, Mexico** (4 per day, $12).

Public Transit: San Diego Metropolitan Transit System (MTS). 24hr. info line, **Info Express** (☎238-0100), has info on San Diego transit (Fares $1.25-3 depending on distance). The **Transit Store,** at 1st Ave. and Broadway, also has info. Open M-F 9am-5pm, closed weekends and holidays. Get a 1- to 4-day **Day Tripper Pass** if you plan to use public transit more than once. 1-day pass $5, 2-day $9, 3-day $12, 4-day $15.

Downtown San Diego

▲ ACCOMMODATIONS
Old Town Inn, 1
San Diego Downtown Hostel (HI), 20
USA Hostels San Diego, 18

🍎 FOOD
Casa Guadalajara, 2
The Corvette Diner, 4
Kansas City Barbecue, 19
Kono's Surf Club, 3

🍸 NIGHTLIFE
The Bitter End, 17
Bourbon Street, 6
The Casbah, 7
Croce's, 16
The Flame, 5

🏛 MUSEUM
Aerospace Museum, 13
Automotive Museum, 12
Maritime Museum, 14
Museum of Art, 9
Museum of
  Contemporary Art, 15
Museum of Man, 8
Museum of Natural History, 10
Museum of
  Photographic Arts, 11

CALIFORNIA

Car Rental: Atwest Rent A Car, 3045 Rosecrans St., #215 (☎877-928-9378; www.atwestrentacar.com), near the airport. Cars from $35 per day. Under-25 surcharge $5-15 per day. Insurance $17 per day if driving to Mexico. Open daily 8am-8pm; office hours extended to 11pm with reservation only.

◢ 🇿 ORIENTATION AND PRACTICAL INFORMATION

The epicenter of inland San Diego tourism is historic **Balboa Park.** Northwest of the park is the stylish **Hillcrest** neighborhood, the city's gay enclave and home to plenty of great shopping and restaurants. **Downtown** attractions are centered in the corridor that includes the area's business and **waterfront** districts. The downtown core is laid out in a grid, with many one-way streets. The **Gaslamp Quarter,** the nexus of San Diego nightlife, sits in the southern section of downtown between 4th and 6th

St. and contains many of San Diego's signature theaters, clubs, and restaurants. Farther north and near the water, **Little Italy** is its own tiny international epicenter of food and entertainment. Just north of downtown in the southeast corner of the I-5 and I-8 junction lies a little slice of old Mexico known as **Old Town.** Along the **coast,** San Diego Bay opens up south of downtown, bounded by classy **Coronado Island.** Northwest of town sits the collection of shiny beaches and man-made inlets known as **Mission Bay,** home to several laidback, sun-soaked communities including **Ocean, Mission,** and **Pacific Beaches.** A jaunt up the coast leads to the tourist haven **La Jolla.**

Visitor Info: San Diego Visitors Center, 2688 Mission Bay Dr. (☎276-8200; www.sandiego.org). Offers maps, activity guides, and discounts. (Open M-Sa 9am-5pm, Su 9:30am-4:30pm.

Library: San Diego Public Library, 820 E St. (☎236-5800). Provides free **Internet** access and Wi-Fi. Open M and W noon-8pm, Tu and Th-Sa 9:30am-5:30pm, Su 1-5pm.

Police: ☎531-2000.

Hotlines: GLBT Crisis Line, ☎800-479-3339. **Rape Hotline,** ☎800-385-4657.

Post Office: Hillcrest Station, 3911 Cleveland Ave. (☎295-5091). Open M-F 7:30am-6pm, Sa 8:30am-4pm. **Postal Code:** 92103.

Area Code: Most of San Diego, including downtown, Coronado, and Ocean Beach: 619. Northern San Diego area codes (including Del Mar, La Jolla, parts of North County, and Pacific Beach): 858 and 760. In text, 619 unless otherwise noted.

ACCOMMODATIONS

Beyond the hostel and residential hotel scene, San Diego is littered with generic chain motels, which are generally clean and safe. There is a popular cluster known as **Hotel Circle** (2-3 mi. east of I-5 along I-8), where summer prices begin at $65 for a single and $75 for a double during the week ($75 and $85, respectively, on weekends). If you're willing to drive a bit to save on hotel bills, better deals can often be found in the surrounding area of Chula Vista, to the south. Several beaches in North County, as well as one on Coronado, are state parks and allow camping, but you'll want to reserve early, especially on weekends.

USA Hostels San Diego, 726 5th Ave. (☎232-3100 or 800-438-8622; www.usahostels.com), between F and G St. in the Gaslamp Quarter. Right in the middle of a popular clubbing street. Hosts parties and organizes Tijuana tours and Gaslamp pub crawls. Free breakfast, linen, and lockers. Coin-op laundry. Internet $20 per day. Reserve private rooms in advance. International passport or out-of-state student ID required. June-Sept. dorms $27; private rooms $61. October-May dorms $22; private rooms $46. BUNAC, ISIC, and VIP discount $2. MC/V. ●

San Diego Downtown Hostel (HI), 521 Market St. (☎525-1531 or 800-909-4776, ext. 156; www.sandiegohostels.org), at 5th Ave., in the heart of the Gaslamp Quarter. Same amenities as the hostel above, with a slightly calmer atmosphere. Its clean and colorful interior and many common areas draw an international crowd. No alcohol. Breakfast, linen, and towels included. Discounted bike rentals and tours. Lockers (bring a lock) and laundry available. Internet $4 per hr. Reception 6:30am-12:30am. 4- to 10-bed dorms $22-27, members $19-24; private rooms $47-57. MC/V. ●

Old Town Inn, 4444 Pacific Hwy. (☎800-643-3025), near I-5 and I-8, a 10min. walk from Old Town. Features several clean rooms with standard array of amenities. Across the street from the trolley station; perfect for those without cars. Some rooms have kitchenettes. Pool access. Large continental breakfast included. Standard rooms from $60. AmEx/D/MC/V. ●

◨ FOOD

With its large Hispanic population and proximity to Mexico, San Diego is renowned for exemplary Mexican cuisine. The culinary scene is truly dominated, however, by the opposing forces of trendy, upscale restaurants in the Gaslamp Quarter and Hillcrest, and the cheap, deliciously filling beachfront eateries.

Casa Guadalajara, 4105 Taylor St. (☎299-5111), in Old Town, just north of Plaza del Pasado. With its brightly painted tiles, heavy wooden furniture, and lush, shady patio you'll feel the freshness of Mexican beaches at Guadalajara. Big combination platters ($10-17) and heaping plates of delectable *carnitas* with guacamole and fresh tortillas ($12) are overshadowed only by the intoxicating selection of margaritas ($5-12). Open M-Th and Su 7am-10pm, F-Sa 7am-midnight. AmEx/D/MC/V. ❸

The Corvette Diner, 3946 5th Ave. (☎542-1436), in Hillcrest. This 50s-style diner has more chrome than Detroit and more neon than Las Vegas. Greasy-spoon classics and a number of unique creations like the Rory Burger (peanut butter and bacon burger; $8). Open M-Th and Su 11am-10pm, F-Sa 11am-midnight. AmEx/D/MC/V. ❷

Kono's Surf Club, 704 Garnet Ave. (☎483-1669), across from the Crystal Pier in Pacific Beach, serves up legendary burritos. Expect long lines. M-F 7am-3pm. ❶

◉ SIGHTS

San Diego's world-famous attractions are varied enough to keep any traveler engaged. Pick up the free weekly *Reader* for local event listings. The **San Diego 3-for-1 Pass** ($107, ages 3-9 $77) offers unlimited admission for five consecutive days at a discounted price to three of the city's premier sights: Sea World, the San Diego Zoo, and the San Diego Wild Animal Park. Visit www.sandiegozoo.org or the websites of the other two parks for information and online ticketing.

SAN DIEGO ZOO. With over 100 acres of exquisite habitats, this zoo well deserves its reputation as one of the world's finest. At the legendary **panda exhibit** you can get close enough to see the bamboo stuck between the animals' teeth, but go before noon to avoid long lines. The educational 40min. **double-decker bus tour** covers about 75% of the zoo. The express bus will take you to any of five stops throughout the park anytime during the day. The **Skyfari Aerial Tramway** rises 170 ft. above the park and can save on walking time. Don't expect to see anything but the tops of trees and the skyline. *(One-way $3.)* Purchase bus and train tickets with zoo admission. *(2920 Zoo Dr., Balboa Park. ☎234-3153; www.sandiegozoo.org. Open daily late June-early Sept. 9am-10pm; early Sept.-late June 9am-dusk. $33, ages 3-11 $22. Includes unlimited use of narrated bus tour, express bus, and aerial train. Military in uniform free. Free on Founder's Day, the 1st M in Oct.)*

DOWNTOWN. Petco Park, the new home of the **San Diego Padres,** offers excellent views from almost every seat. *(Games Mar.-Oct. Check www.padres.com for schedule and tickets.)* The **Gaslamp Quarter** contains antique shops, Victorian buildings, trendy restaurants, and nightclubs (see **Entertainment and Nightlife,** p. 916). The steel-and-glass structure of the **San Diego Museum of Contemporary Art** is a small gallery whose two floors display frequently changing exhibits. *(1001 Kettner Blvd. ☎858-454-3541; www.mcasd.org. Open M-T and Sa-Su 11am-6pm, Th-F 11am-pm, closed Wednesday. $10, MCASD members free.)* Housed within some of San Diego's oldest ships, the **San Diego Maritime Museum** showcases San Diego's rich maritime history and maintains three ships. *(1492 N. Harbor Dr. ☎234-9153; www.sdmaritime.org. Open daily 9am-8pm. $12, military and seniors $9, ages 6-17 $8; with 30min. boat excursion $15/12/11.)* The **Embarcadero** has boardwalk shops and museums that face moored windjammers,

CALIFORNIA

cruise ships, and the occasional naval destroyer. *(Most afternoon tours of naval craft free.)* The jewel of San Diego's redevelopment efforts is **Horton Plaza,** at Broadway and 4th, a pastel, open-air, multi-level shopping center.

BALBOA PARK AND THE EL PRADO MUSEUMS. Constructed and painstakingly landscaped for the 1915 Panama-California and the 1935 California Pacific International Expositions, Balboa is America's largest urban cultural park. It is a central feature of San Diego, containing 15 museums, several performing arts venues, and eight gardens within its 1200 beautiful acres. Most of the museums reside within the Spanish-Renaissance buildings that line El Prado St., which runs east-west through the park's central Plaza de Panama. The Passport to Balboa Park provides admission to (and is available for purchase at) all park museums. It's a great way for adults to see all of the museums, but those eligible for student and senior discounts should make sure the passport benefits them. The Best of Balboa Park passport also includes admission to all ticketed options at the zoo. The Balboa Visitors Center, in the Plaza de Panama, sells park maps and the Passport to Balboa Park. *(1549 El Prado St. ☎ 239-0512; www.balboapark.org. Open daily late June-early Sept. 9:30am-5pm. Passport to Balboa Park $35. Best of Balboa Park $59. Park maps $0.50.)* Creationists beware: the **Museum of Man** dedicates an entire floor to the 98.4% of DNA we share with chimpanzees. Another hall displays mummies from around the world. *(On the west end of the park. ☎ 239-2001; www.museumofman.org. Open daily 10am-4:30pm. $8, seniors $6, ages 6-17 $4; free 3rd Tu of each month.)* The small, ultra-modern **Museum of Photographic Arts (MOPA)** features classic and contemporary photography. Its film program ranges from cult classic film festivals to technical examination of more serious cinematic works. *(☎ 238-7559; www.mopa.org. Open Th-Su 10am-5pm. $6; military, seniors, and students $4; free 2nd Tu of each month. Films $6-10.)* The **Reuben H. Fleet Space Theater and Science Center** has interactive exhibits sure to delight your inner nerd, plus the world's first hemispheric Omnimax theater. *(1875 El Prado Way. ☎ 238-1233; www.rhfleet.org. Open daily at 9:30am, closing times vary. $8, with Omnimax show $12.50; seniors $6.75/9.75; ages 3-12 $6.75/9.75. Free 1st Tu of each month.)* The **San Diego Museum of Art** has a collection ranging from ancient Asian and European masterpieces to contemporary Californian works. At the adjoining outdoor Sculpture Garden Court, a sensuous Henry Moore piece presides over other large abstract blocks. *(☎ 232-7931; www.sdmart.org. Open Tu-W and F-Su 10am-6pm, Th 10am-9pm. $10, seniors and military $8, students with ID $7, ages 6-17 $4. Special exhibits $2-20.)* The **Air and Space Museum** displays 24 full-scale replicas and 44 original planes, as well as exhibits on aviation history and the International Space Station project. *(2001 Pan American Plaza. ☎ 234-8291; www.aerospacemuseum.org. Open daily 10am-4:30pm; in summer hours extended. $12, seniors and students $10, ages 6-17 $6, military and under 6 free. Free 4th Tu of each month.)* The fragrant **Botanical Building** may look like a giant wooden cage, but it's filled with plants, not birds. The orchid collection, set among murmuring fountains, is particularly striking. *(2200 Park Blvd. ☎ 235-1100. Open M-W and F-Su 10am-4pm. Free.)* At the east side of the park, the **Desert Garden** and **Rose Garden** prove a salient floral contrast. The surprisingly lush Desert Garden is in full bloom from January to March, while the roses are best admired between April and December.

OLD TOWN. In 1769, Father Serra, supported by a brigade of Spanish infantry, established the first of 21 missions that would eventually line the California coast in the area now known as **Old Town.** The remnants of this early settlement have become one of San Diego's tourist mainstays. The most popular of the area's attractions is **Plaza del Pasado,** containing museums, shops, and restaurants in the State Park's early 19th-century buildings. Visitors are free to wander the grounds and explore the many museums and living history displays as they learn about California's early days. Guided tours are also available M-F 11am,

Sa-Su 11am and 2pm, leaving from the Robinson-Rose House, which functions as a **Visitors Center.** *(Open daily 10am-5pm.)* Daytime tours of the **Whaley House,** which stands on the site of San Diego's first gallows, are little more than a walk through an old house. Nighttime tours are said to be much more interesting, as it is one of two official haunted houses recognized by the State of California. *(2482 San Diego Ave. ☎ 298-2482, tours 293-0117. Open daily 10am-10pm. $6, seniors $5, ages 3-12 $4; after 7pm $10/8/5.)* The stout adobe walls of the **Serra Museum** were raised at the site of the original fort and mission in 1929 and now present displays on the history of California. *(2727 Presidio Dr., in Presidio Park. ☎ 297-3258. Open F-Su 10am-4:30pm. $5; military, seniors, and students $4; ages 6-17 $2.)*

CORONADO ISLAND. A slender 7 mi. strip of hauled sand known as the "Silver Strand" tethers lovely Coronado "Island" to the mainland near Imperial Beach. Coronado's most famed sight is its Victorian-style **Hotel Del Coronado,** one of America's largest wooden buildings. *(1500 Orange Ave. ☎ 435-6611.)* Coronado also has a huge military presence, and its entire northern chunk comprises the **North Island Naval Air Station,** the birthplace of American naval aviation. In fact, it was Navy men who carted sand to connect the island to the rest of Coronado in 1947. Park and have a bite at one of Orange St.'s many chic, casual outdoor cafes, and then make your way to Imperial Beach for a seaside stroll.

OCEAN, MISSION, AND PACIFIC BEACHES. Much of San Diego's younger population flocks to these communities for the surf and hopping nightlife; not surprisingly, noisy bars and grills crowd these shores. The three beaches line up consecutively, but each has its own flavor. **Ocean Beach (OB)** cultivates a home-grown, earthy atmosphere. With local hippies lounging in the gentle surf, OB is the most laid-back of the beaches and the best place to learn the art of wave-riding. Farther north, **Mission Beach,** at the corner of W. Mission Bay Dr. and Mission Blvd., is a people-watcher's paradise. **Belmont Park,** a combination amusement park and shopping center, draws a large, family-friendly crowd. **Pacific Beach**, with its coveted alcohol permit, caters to the good-looking, beer-drinking college crowds, and its boisterous **Garnet Avenue** is home to the best nightlife. **Ocean Front Walk** is packed with joggers, cyclists, and beachfront shops.

SEA WORLD. With its occasionally oppressive crowds and often long lines, you may forget why you're there, but Seaworld remains a staple San Diego attraction. Each year millions flock to the park to see Shamu, the park's famous killer whale, soak his audience with his signature bellyflop splash. There are many other goofy and surprisingly charming animal shows. The dolphin show, featuring highly trained and intelligent Atlantic bottlenose dolphins, including the high-jumping Dolly the Dolphin, is a crowd favorite. Those looking to cool down without a face full of saltwater should head to the free **Budweiser's Beer School and brewery.** The 30min. class, ☒**free beer,** and general merriment come courtesy of Anheuser-Busch, the proud owners of Sea World. *(☎ 800-257-4268; www.seaworld.com. Open in summer daily 9am-11pm; opens at 10am in winter, but closing hours vary. $57, ages 3-9 $47; special deals sometimes available online. Parking $10, RVs $15.)*

LA JOLLA. This affluent seaside neighborhood has few budget options, but offers some of the finest public beaches in the San Diego area. **La Jolla Cove,** a small beach lined with sandstone cliffs near the commercial district, is popular with photographers, picnickers, snorkelers, and brilliantly colored Garibaldi goldfish. Wander south along the cliffs to a striking semi-circular inlet known as **The Children's Pool** or **Casa,** home to a thriving sea lion community. Some of the best breakers in the county are in La Jolla at **Tourmaline Beach** and **Wind 'n' Sea Beach.** However, these are notoriously territorial spots, so outsiders may be advised to surf elsewhere. **La Jolla Shores** has gentle swells ideal for new surfers and boogie boarders. ■**Black's Beach** is not officially a nude beach, but that doesn't seem to stop sunbathers from going *au naturel*. The beach is accessible only via a precarious 1 mi. path from Torrey Pines State Beach, so use caution getting there, but then catch some rays and look out for hangliders on the cliffs above.

Overlooking La Jolla Shores, the ■**Birch Aquarium at the Scripps Institute of Oceanography** has great educational exhibits including a tank of oozing jellyfish, a large collection of seahorses, and a 70,000-gallon kelp and shark tank. *(2300 Expedition Way, off Torrey Pines. ☎858-534-3474; www.aquarium.ucsd.edu. Open daily 9am-5pm. $11, seniors $9, students $8, ages 3-17 $7.50.)* The **San Diego Museum of Contemporary Art**, bigger and better than the downtown branch, houses parts of the permanent collection of pop, minimalist, and conceptualist art from the 1950s onward, as well as rotating exhibitions. The museum is as visually stunning as the art it contains, with gorgeous ocean views, high ceilings, and light-filled spaces. *(700 Prospect St. ☎858-454-3541; www.mcasd.org. Open M-Tu and F-Su 11am-5pm, Th 11am-7pm. $10, military and seniors $5, under 25 free; free 3rd Tu of every month.)* Be sure to check out the glass terraces and buttresses of **Geisel Library** at the **University of California, San Diego (UCSD)**, a space-age structure endowed by La Jolla resident Theodore Geisel, better known as Dr. Seuss, the late children's author. *(☎858-534-2208.)*

🎵🍸 ENTERTAINMENT AND NIGHTLIFE

Nightlife is concentrated in several distinct pockets. Posh locals and party-seeking tourists flock to the Gaslamp Quarter, where numerous restaurants and bars feature live music. The Hillcrest area, next to Balboa Park, draws a young, large, loud, and flamboyant crowd to its clubs and dining spots. Away from downtown, the beach areas (especially Garnet Ave. in Pacific Beach) are loaded with clubs, bars, and cheap eateries that attract college-age revelers. The city's definitive source of entertainment info is the free *Reader*, available in coffeehouses and Visitors Centers. Listings can also be found in the Thursday *San Diego Union-Tribune*. If boozin' isn't your idea of nightlife, you can spend a more sedate evening at one of San Diego's excellent theaters, such as the Lyceum Theatre, 225 Broadway Ave. (☎544-1000), or the Horton Grand Theatre, 444 4th Ave. (☎234-9583), both downtown. The La Jolla Playhouse, 2910 La Jolla Village Dr., presents shows on the UCSD campus. (☎858-550-1010; www.lajollaplayhouse.com.)

■ **Croce's Jazz Bar** and **Croce's Top Hat Bar and Grille,** 802 5th Ave. (☎233-4355; www.croces.com), at F St. in the Gaslamp Quarter. A warm, classy rock/blues bar and jazz bar opened by Ingrid Croce, widow of Jim Croce. Live music nightly from 8:30pm. Cover $5-$10. Jazz Bar open daily 5:30pm-12:30am. Top Hat open F-Sa 7pm-1:30am.

The Bitter End, 770 5th Ave. (☎338-9300; www.thebitterend.com), in the Gaslamp Quarter. This 3-level dance club is always packed with those dressed to impress, so leave the torn Levi's and sandals at home. The main floor is a popular watering hole, while upstairs is a swanky lounge. DJs spin everything from hip-hop and top 40 to trance downstairs. Happy hour Th-F 3-7pm. 21+. Cover $10 after 9pm. Restaurant open daily 3pm-2am; dance club opens at 10pm.

Bourbon Street, 4612 Park Blvd. (☎291-0173), in University Heights. A perennially popular gay bar with nightly entertainment. Watch the game in the front pub area, then move to the covered patio and dance floor for some more serious mixing and mingling. Tu karokee 9pm. Martinis $3 4-7pm. 21+. No cover. Open daily 4pm-2am.

The Casbah, 2501 Kettner Blvd. (☎232-4355), at Laurel St., near the airport. Eddie Vedder of Pearl Jam owns this intimate spot, one of the city's best live music venues. Cover varies. 21+. Hours vary; usually 8:30pm-2am.

The Flame, 3780 Park Blvd. (☎295-4163), in Hillcrest. One of the most popular lesbian dance clubs in the nation. Come early to find parking. 21+. Open daily 5pm-2am.

DAYTRIP FROM SAN DIEGO: TIJUANA, MEXICO

> **BORDER CROSSING.** At the world's largest border crossing, northbound lanes often have backups of more than 150 cars. The best time to cross is during weekday mornings. The southbound ride is almost always smoother, but weekends can be rough in both directions. If you're crossing into Tijuana for a day or so, it's easier to leave your car in a lot on the US side and walk across the border. Remember that a tourist card (roughly US$20) is needed if you plan to stay longer than seven days. Regardless of which way you are crossing, bring proper ID (p. 12) and leave your bushels of fruit, truckloads of livestock, stashes of drugs, and armory of weapons behind.

TIJUANA, BAJA CALIFORNIA ☎664

Just minutes from San Diego lies the most notorious specimen of border subculture: Tijuana. Often referred to as "TJ," the city's cheap booze, haggling vendors, and kitschy, unapologetic hedonism attract 30 million US visitors each year. Most travelers stick to Revolución, the city's main strip, which reverberates with mariachi bands, thumping dance beats from the packed nightclubs, and the sounds of eager tourists unloading wads of cash on everything from colorful trinkets to slimy strip shows. To the vast majority of visitors, Tijuana is simply **Avenida Revolución. La Revo,** as it is commonly known, forms the heart of the **Zona Centro.** While the most entertaining sights in town belong to "La Revo," Tijuana's parks and museums offer another side of local culture that is often overlooked. The ▓**Centro Cultural Tijuana (CECUT),** Av. Paseo de los Héroes 9350, Tijuana's most visually striking feature. The main attraction is the **Museo de las Californias,** where a collection of artifacts and models with bilingual descriptions and interactive terminals traces the history of the peninsula. (CECUT ☎687-9641; www.cecut.gob.mx. Museum open Tu-Su 10am-7pm. 20 pesos, students and children 12 pesos. Cine Omnimax tickets 44 pesos, students and children 25 pesos.) If you want to visit a museum in Tijuana without losing sight of La Revo's tackiness, make a beeline for the **Museo de Cera,** Calle 1 and Madero, the city's wax museum, where 86 life-size figures welcome you, organized into Mexican History, International Politics, Stage and Screen, and Horror. Memorable combinations (of which there are several) include President Vicente Fox and Fidel Castro towering over Mother Teresa and Mahatma Gandhi. (☎688-2478. Open daily 10am-6pm. 15 pesos.) The flow of Americans thirsty for booze remains unencumbered, and many take advantage of the low drinking age (18) to circumvent US prohibitions. Stroll down Revolución after dusk and you'll be bombarded by lights, music, and club promoters hawking overpriced two-for-one margaritas. Tijuana's young, artsy crowd hangs out at the ▓**Revolver Cine Cafe,** Madero between Calles 5 and 6, next to Hotel Catalina. (☎685-1233; www.myspace.com/revolvercinecafe. Open M and Th-Su 10am-10pm, Tu-W 10am-midnight. Cash only.) **Iguanas-Ranas**, on Revolución at Calle 3, is a sublimely wacky world of life-size plaster clowns, balloons, and kitschy US pop-culture paraphernalia. (☎688-3885. Open M-Th 10am-2am, F-Su 10am-5am. Cash only.) **Animale**, on Revolución at Calle 4, is the biggest, glitziest, and loudest hedonistic haven of them all. Watch out—the similarly named Animale Continental next door is an altogether more "adult" experience. (www.clubanimale.com. Open daily 10am-4am. Cash only.)

As a general rule, hotels in Tijuana become less reputable the farther north you go. Avoid any in the Zona Norte. Though crowded during the day, even the Zona Centro can be unsettling at night, especially between Revolución and Constitución close to the Zona Norte. Take a cab if you need to cross this area at night. Reserve ahead for weekends. **Hotel Catalina ❶**, Madero 2039, on the corner of Calle 5, has a friendly staff. The singles are miniature, but other rooms are spacious. (☎685-9748 or 688-1005. Singles 220 pesos; doubles 260 pesos, with TV 320 pesos. Cash only.) Like most things in Tijuana, restaurants are often loud and in-your-face; promoters try to drag tourists into the pricey joints lining Revolución. Sometimes, however, paying a couple of extra pesos can reap delicious benefits. For cheap fast food, try the taco stands in the *centro*. The Spanish-style **Restaurant Chiki Jai ❸**, on Revolución and Calle 7, has provided dishes from across the Atlantic since 1947. (☎685-4955. Large portions of seafood paella 100 pesos. Tapas 30-60 pesos. Open daily 11am-9pm. Cash only.) **Los Panchos Taco Shop ❶**, on Revolución at Calle 3, is a handy pit stop for hungry clubbers. Juicy burritos are filled generously with *carne asada* and cost 13-17 pesos. (☎685-7277. Open M-Th and Su 8am-midnight, F-Sa 8am-4am. Cash only.)

From San Diego, grab a **trolley** on the blue line and ride to the border. (25min. from downtown.) From there, follow the instructions for San Ysidro. By car, take US I-5 South or US 805 South (25min.). Both lead to the San Ysidro border crossing. "Centro" signs lead to Calle 2a. The **Tourist Office** is a small, freestanding booth at Revolución and Calle 3 (☎685-2210. English-speaking staff with good maps. Open daily 10am-4pm. Branch at the border crossing.) The **Customs Office**, at the border on the Mexican side after crossing the San Ysidro bridge, sells tourist permits. (☎624-2280, www.aduanos.gob.mx. Open 24hr.) **Banks** along Revolución exchange money. **Emergency:** ☎066. **Police:** Constitución 1616, at Calle 8 (☎685-6557, 24hr. tourist help line ☎078). **Red Cross**, on Gamboa at Silvestre, across from Price Club. (☎621-7787.) **Hospital General,** Centenario 10851, in the Zona Río. (☎684-0237 or 684-0922.) **Internet Access: Matrix Internet Place**, at Revolución and Calle 5. (☎688-2273. 16 pesos per hr. Open daily 10am-midnight.) **Cafe Internet**, on Calle 5 between Madero and Revolución. (☎290-0508; www.cybertijuana.com. 15 pesos per hr., or free with a drink order. Open daily 8am-10pm.) **Post Office:** on Negrete at Calle 11/Elías Calles. (☎684-7950. Open M-F 8am-5pm, Sa 9am-1pm.) **Postal Code:** 22000. **Country Code:** 52.

THE CALIFORNIA DESERT

California's desert is one of the most beautiful places in the world; it's also one of the loneliest. Deserted roads cut through endless expanses of barren earth and landscapes that seem completely untouched by civilization. Exploration turns up elusive treasures: diverse flora and fauna, staggering topographical variation, and scattered relics of the American frontier. Throughout the year, the desert switches from a pleasantly warm refuge to an unbearable wasteland and back again.

PALM SPRINGS   ☎760

From its first known inhabitants, the Cahuilla, to today's fun-loving geriatrics, the restorative oasis of Palm Springs has attracted an odd menagerie of old and young. With warm winter temperatures, celebrity residents, funky art galleries, and a casino, this city is a sunny break from everyday life.

Mt. San Jacinto State Park, Palm Springs's primary landmark, offers outdoor recreation like hiking and cross-country skiing. If the 10,804 ft. peak seems too strenuous, the world-famous **Palm Springs Aerial Tramway** can whisk you to the top in

10min. and even rotates to ensure you get a full view of the valley floor. After 3pm, the Ride & Dine option includes dinner at the cafeteria-style Top of the Tram restaurant. (☎325-1449 or 888-515-8726. Trams run at least every 30min. M-F 10am-10:30pm, Sa-Su 8am-10:30pm. Round-trip $22, over 60 $20, ages 3-12 $15. Ride & Dine $35.50, children $23.) Experience Palm Springs's heralded golf scene by hitting the links at **Tahquitz Creek Golf Resort,** 1885 Golf Club Dr., a club managed by Arnold Palmer. (☎328-1005 or 800-743-2211. Green fees $110 in high season; sharp discounts in summer.)

Despite Palm Springs's reputation as a luxury getaway, affordable lodgings do exist; check out the north and south edges of the downtown area just off Palm Canyon Dr. or look online for deals before you go. The **Royal Sun Inn ❸**, 1700 S. Palm Canyon Dr., has large, well-furnished rooms for more-than-reasonable rates. Many have views of the nearby San Jacinto Mountains. (☎327-1504. Breakfast included. King bed $79 in winter; $39 in summer. AmEx/D/MC/V.) Palm Springs offers an array of culinary treats, from standard burger joints to ultra-trendy fusion cuisine. Satisfying and inexpensive Thai cuisine is served at ▨**Thai Smile ❷**, 651 N. Palm Canyon Dr. Don't miss the $8 lunch specials. (☎320-5503. Open daily 11:30am-10pm. AmEx/D/MC/V.) The shaded patio of the **Rock Garden Cafe ❷**, 777 S. Palm Canyon Dr., is the perfect place to enjoy one of their many burgers, mixed drinks, or omelets. (☎327-8840. Burgers $8. Omelets $8. Cocktails $5-7. Open daily 7am-midnight. AmEx/D/MC/V.) To experience Palm Springs's heralded nightlife, head to **Village Pub,** 266 S. Palm Canyon Dr., and relive your college days by swilling beer and grooving to folksy rock with a diverse international crowd. (☎323-3265. Open daily 11am-2am. AmEx/D/MC/V.)

Greyhound, 311 N. Indian Canyon Dr. (☎325-2053; www.greyhound.com), runs buses to Los Angeles (3-4hr., 5 per day, $29), Las Vegas (6-9hr., 4 per day, $65), and San Diego (4-11hr., 5 per day, $32). **SunBus** covers Coachella Valley cities. (☎343-3451 or 800-347-8628. $1.) With plenty of brochures and info, the **Visitor Center,** 2901 N. Palm Canyon Dr. (☎778-8415 or 800-347-7746; www.palm-springs.org), is a good stop for first-time visitors. **Post Office:** 333 E. Amado Rd. (☎322-4111. Open M-F 8am-5pm, Sa 9am-3pm.) **Postal Code:** 92262.

JOSHUA TREE NATIONAL PARK ☎760

When devout Mormon pioneers crossed this faith-testing desert in the 19th century, they named the enigmatic tree they encountered after the Biblical prophet Joshua. The tree's crooked limbs resembled the Hebrew general, and, with arms upraised, seemed to beckon these Latter-Day pioneers to the Promised Land. The Joshua tree forests still inspire reverent awe, but the park, centered around the intersection of the Colorado and Mojave deserts, is also home to some of the most popular climbing rocks in the US.

■■ 🔏 **ORIENTATION AND PRACTICAL INFORMATION.** The park is bordered by three highways: **I-10** to the south, **Route 62 (Twentynine Palms Highway)** to the west and north, and **Route 177** to the east. The north entrances are off Rte. 62 at the towns of **Joshua Tree** and **Twentynine Palms.** The south entrance is at **Cottonwood Spring,** off I-10 at Rte. 195, southeast of Palm Springs. The park entrance fee ($10 per car, $5 per person.) is valid for one week. **The Headquarters and Oasis Visitor Center** is at 74485 National Park Dr. (☎367-5500; www.nps.gov/jotr. Open daily 8am-5pm.) **Post Office:** 73839 Gorgonio Dr., in Twentynine Palms. (☎800-275-8777. Open M-F 8:30am-5pm, Sa 9am-noon.) **Postal Code:** 92277.

▌🖸 **ACCOMMODATIONS AND FOOD.** Most park campgrounds don't accept reservations, but reservations can be made at Black Rock, Indian Cove, and all

THE DRAW OF THE DESERT

Joshua Tree National Park is near and dear to a lot of famous visitors' hearts: beyond being the inspiration for U2's famed 1987 album *The Joshua Tree*, it was a favorite haunt of ground-breaking musician Gram Parsons, a pioneer in the country/rock fusion genre now represented by bands like Wilco. A UFO and drug enthusiast, Parsons sought solace and inspiration during his frequent visits to the spiny-treed park, where he would play music and watch for flying saucers with such notable friends as The Rolling Stones' Keith Richards.

During a 1973 visit, Parsons died from a mysterious heroin overdose in a room at the Joshua Tree Inn (the Inn, which still remains, has dedicated this fateful room to the musician). His devastated family felt the best thing to do would be to ship his body back to the Parson homestead in Louisiana for a ceremony and burial—but his friends and bandmates had different plans for their wayward pal, who had expressed to them his desire to have his ashes spread over Joshua Tree. Using false identification and drug-induced tales told to airport officials, these rocker bandits managed to steal Parson's body and bring it back to the California desert, where they burned it, coffin and all, and scattered their friend about the landscape he so loved.

group sites (☎800-365-2267). **◗Jumbo Rocks ➊,** 4400 ft., near Skull Rock Trail on the eastern edge of Queen Valley, is the highest campground in the park, with sites amongst granite formations. (Pit toilets, no water. Free.) **Indian Cove ➊,** 3200 ft., on the north edge of Wonderland of Rocks, is popular among climbers. (Sites $10; group sites $20-35.) **Cottonwood ➊,** in the south, and **Black Rock➊,** near Yucca Valley, offer water and flush toilets ($10 and $12, respectively). Experienced campers can register for a **back-country permit** at the Visitors Center or at self-service boards throughout the park. Those who can't stomach desert campgrounds will find inexpensive motels in Twentynine Palms or Joshua Tree proper, like the **Safari Motor Inn ➌,** 61959 Twentynine Palms Hwy., which offers friendly service, consecutive night deals, and a swimming pool. (☎366-1113. In winter from $49; summer from $39. AmEx/D/MC/V.) The **29 Palms Inn ➍,** 73950 Inn Dr., is an attraction in its own right: in addition to 33 bungalows and rooms facing the Mora Oasis, Robert Plant composed "29 Palms" here. (☎367-3505; www.29palmsinn.com. Continental breakfast, pool. Reservations required Feb.-Apr. Doubles Oct.-May M-Th and Su $85-115, F-Sa $120-165; June-Sept. $70-95/85-125. AmEx/D/MC/V.)

For casual, filling and healthy fare, head to local favorite **Crossroads Cafe and Tavern ➋,** 61715 Twentynine Palms Hwy., and snag an omelet ($6-8) for breakfast, or opt for cheap nostalgia at lunchtime with a peanut butter, honey, and banana sandwich ($5.25). (☎366-5414. M-T, Th, and Su 7am-8pm; F-Sa 7am-9pm. AmEx/D/MC/V.) Add some jazz to dinner at **The Beatnik Cafe ➊,** 61597 Twentynine Palms Hwy., where you can munch on a yummy build-your-own salad ($4.25-6) while you listen to local live music. (☎366-2090. M-T, Th-F, Su 11am-11pm; W and Sa 11am-midnight. AmEx/D/MC/V.)

▟ OUTDOOR ACTIVITIES. Over 80% of Joshua Tree is designated wilderness, safeguarding it against development and paved roads. Even so, many of the densest stands of Joshua Trees and more curious rock formations are to be found along the roadways in the western portion of the park, making a **driving tour** an easy way to explore. All roads are well marked, and signs labeled "Exhibit Ahead" lead to unique floral and geological formations. One of these tours, a 34 mi. stretch winding through the park on **Park Boulevard,** provides access to the park's most outstanding sights and hikes. An especially spectacular detour is **Keys View** (5185 ft.), 6 mi. off Park Blvd. and just west of Ryan Campground. On a clear day, you can see Palm Springs and Mexico, and the sunrise from here is always spectacular. Toward Cottonwood, on Pinto Basin Rd., the **Cholla Cactus Garden** is home to many "teddy bear" cacti but is mostly known as a transition zone between the ecosystems of the Colorado Desert and the higher, slightly cooler Mojave Desert. Those with **4WD** vehicles have even more options for exploration, including the 18 mi. **Geology Tour Road,** west of Jumbo Rocks off Park Blvd., which climbs through striking rock formations and ends in the Little San Bernardino Mountains.

Hiking is the best way to see Joshua Tree, but those eager to explore should pack plenty of water and be alert to changing weather and possible flash flood conditions. Anticipate slow progress even on short walks; the oppressive heat and the scarcity of shade can strain even the hardiest hikers. The easy **Hidden Valley Trail** leads you between boulders and into a tucked-away hollow that was once the secret hideaway of cattle rustlers (1 mi. loop with interpretive signs). The summit of **Ryan Mountain** provides a 360 degree panorama of the surrounding country, but those with less time will want to forgo the sunbaked, 3 mi. round-trip climb in favor of scrambling up the bluff at Keys View. Visitors Centers have info on the park's other hikes, from a 15min. wheelchair-accessible stroll leading to the **Oasis of Mara** to a three-day trek along the 35 mi. **California Riding and Hiking Trail.**

The crack-split granite of Joshua Tree provides some of the best rock climbing and bouldering in the world for experts and novices alike. The renowned boulders at **Wonderland of Rocks** and **Hidden Valley** are always swarming with hard-bodied climbers, making Joshua Tree the most climbed area in America. Adventurous beginners will find thrills at the **Skull Rock Interpretive Walk,** which runs between Jumbo Rocks and Skull Rock. The walk offers info on local plants and animals and exciting yet non-technical scrambles to the tops of monstrous boulders.

DEATH VALLEY NATIONAL PARK   ☎ 760

The devil owns a lot of real estate in Death Valley's 3.3 million acres: he grows crops at Devil's Cornfield and hits the links at Devil's Golf Course. In fact, the park is home to Hell's Gate itself. Indeed, the area's extreme heat and surreal landscape make it inhospitable enough to belong to the dark side. Winter temperatures dip well below freezing in the mountains, and summer readings in the valley average 115°F. The second-highest temperature ever recorded in the world (134°F in the shade) was measured at the valley's Furnace Creek Ranch on July 10, 1913.

▐ **TRANSPORTATION.** Cars are the only way to get to and around Death Valley, but conditions are notoriously hard on vehicles. **Radiator water** (not for drinking) is available at critical points on Rte. 178 and 190 and Nevada Rte. 374. There are only four **gas stations** in the park (Furnace Creek, Scotty's Castle, Stovepipe Wells, Panamint Springs), and though prices are hefty, keep the tank at least half full at all times. Travel with two gallons of water per person per day. In case of breakdown, stay in the shade of your vehicle. Of the seven **park entrances,** most visitors choose Rte. 190 from the east. The road is well maintained, and the Visitors Center is relatively close. Since most of the major sights adjoin **Badwater Road,** the north-south road, daytrippers can see more by entering from the southeast (Rte. 178 W from Rte. 127 at Shoshone) or the north (direct to Scotty's Castle via Nevada Rte. 267). Unskilled mountain drivers in passenger cars should not attempt to enter on the smaller Titus Canyon or Emigrant Canyon Dr. While it may look convenient to enter the park's north end near Big Pine, the road is not maintained and its use is not advisable at most times of year. No regular public transportation runs in the Valley. Attempting to hitchhike through Death Valley is akin to suicide.

▐ **PRACTICAL INFORMATION. Visitor Info: Furnace Creek Visitors Center,** on Rte. 190 in the Valley's east-central section. (☎786-3244; www.nps.gov/deva. Open daily Mar.-Nov. 8am-6pm, Dec.-Feb. 8am-5pm.) Contact stations are at **Grapevine** (☎786-2313), at Rte. 190 and 267 near Scotty's Castle; **Shoshone** (☎832-4308), at Rte. 127 and 178 outside the Valley's southeast border; and **Beatty, NV** (☎702-553-2200), on Nevada Rte. 374. Pick up a copy of the *Death Valley Visitor's Guide* newspaper at any ranger station. Fill up on gas outside Death Valley at Lone Pine, Olancha, Shoshone, or Beatty, NV. **Post Office: Furnace Creek Ranch** (☎800-275-8777). Open M-F 8:30am-5pm. **Postal Code:** 92328.

ACCOMMODATIONS. Motel rooms in surrounding towns are cheaper than those in Death Valley but can be over an hour away from top sights. Never assume that rooms will be available, but your chances (and the prices) will be better in the summer. In winter, camping with a stock of groceries saves money and driving time. In summer, camping can get quite uncomfortable. **Furnace Creek Ranch ❹**, in Furnace Creek, has a supremely convenient location next to the Visitors Center. You can also tee up on the world's lowest golf course. (☎786-2345; www.furnacecreekresort.com. Singles and doubles in summer from $116; in winter from $120. AmEx/D/MC/V.) The National Park Service maintains nine **campgrounds ❶** in Death Valley. All have toilets but no showers, and stays are limited to 30 days, except Furnace Creek, with a 14 day limit. (Sites free-$18.) **Backcountry camping ❶** is free and legal. You must check in at the Visitors Center and pitch tents at least 2 mi. from your car and any road and a quarter mile from any backcountry water source.

SIGHTS. With the blooming of desert plants, springtime brings special beauty to Death Valley. Year-round, the area's slanted mountains melt into canyons colored by trace minerals, making for surprisingly pretty hiking. **Golden Canyon Trail** is an easy trail winding through one such colorful draw (2 mi. round-trip from Golden Canyon trailhead, 2 mi. south of Hwy. 190 on Badwater Rd.). There are countless other trails to occupy the gentlest wanderer and hardiest adventurer. Visitors should keep in mind that Death Valley can be a very dangerous place to hike. Not only is it hot and shadeless, but distances can be very deceiving; mountains that appear to be close to the road can actually be several miles away. No matter what your plans are, carry at least a gallon of water per person and start drinking before you are thirsty to prevent dehydration. Ironically, flash floods are a real danger, so be aware of the weather at all times. Camera-toters should keep in mind that the best photo opportunities are at sunrise and sunset. Rangers often set up telescopes at **Zabriskie Point** to capitalize on the Valley's clear skies. Many of the park's most spectacular sights are accessible from the air-conditioned comfort of your car. One of the best views is at **Dante's View,** reached by a 13 mi. paved road from Rte. 190. **Badwater,** a briny pool four times saltier than the ocean, is at the lowest point (282 ft. below sea level) in the Western Hemisphere. **Artist's Drive,** 10 mi. south of the Visitors Center, is a one-way loop that contorts its way through brightly colored rock formations. The loop's early ochres and burnt siennas give way at **Artist's Palette** to vivid green, yellow, periwinkle, and pink mineral deposits in the hillside. About 5 mi. south is **Devil's Golf Course,** a vast expanse of gnarled salt pillars formed by flooding and evaporation; jagged crystalline deposits, some quite delicate and beautiful, stretch as far as the eye can see.

THE SIERRA NEVADA

The Sierra Nevada Mountain Range is known as California's backbone, stretching 450 mi. from stifling Death Valley in the south to near the Oregon border in the north. Its magnificent, jagged peaks—including Mt. Whitney, the tallest mountain in the continental US—are a tribute to the area's active geological past. Breathtaking U-shaped valleys testify to the more recent tempering influence of granite-smoothing glaciation. The Sierra Nevada, whose name fittingly translates as "snowy range," also contains Lake Tahoe's crystalline waters, Sequoia National Park's towering redwoods, and Yosemite's incredible waterfalls.

LAKE TAHOE   ☎ 530

Shimmering blue water, pristine beaches, immense mountains, and an unobtrusive but ubiquitous commercial presence make Tahoe an ideal destination for boating, fishing, skiing, hiking, and spending money. Each season brings wonders of its own to Tahoe; accordingly, tourist season is year-round.

⌐ TRANSPORTATION

Trains: Amtrak, 10000 E. River St. (☎800-872-7245; www.amtrak.com), in Truckee, CA. 1 train daily to **Oakland/San Francisco** (6½hr., $37-48), **Reno** (1hr., $13), and **Sacramento** (4½hr., $25-38). Open daily 9am-5pm.

Buses: There are a few options available to those seeking bus transport in Tahoe.

Greyhound, 10065 Donner Pass Rd. (☎800-231-2222; www.greyhound.com), in Truckee. The closest station to Tahoe. Buses roll to **Reno** (1hr., 2 per day, $12), **Sacramento** (3hr., 3 per day, $26), and **San Francisco** (5½hr., 3 per day, $31).

Tahoe Area Regional Transport (**TART**; ☎550-1212 or 800-736-6365; www.laketahoe-transit.com). Connects the western and northern shores from Incline Village to Meeks Bay, where it joins with South Lake Tahoe (BlueGO) buses in the summer at a transfer station. Stops daily every 30-60min., depending on the route. Buses also run from Tahoe City to Truckee and Squaw Valley and back (5 per day 7:30am-4:45pm). $1.50, day pass $3.50; exact fare required.

BlueGO (☎541-7149; www.bluego.org). Operates routes along the South Shore, including from Stateline, NV to the Hwy. 89/50 transit center. Runs approximately 6:40am-12:40am. $1.75, day pass $3, 10-ride pass $15. Also offers seasonal service to Heavenly Ski Resort.

BlueGO Door to Door (☎541-7149). Runs door-to-door service within city limits (24hr., $3) and within El Dorado County (7am-7pm, $5).

◢▐ ORIENTATION AND PRACTICAL INFORMATION

Located in the northern Sierra Nevada Mountain Range right on the California-Nevada border, Lake Tahoe is about a 3hr. drive from San Francisco. The lake sits 100 mi. northeast of Sacramento (via **Highway 50**) and 35 mi. southwest of Reno (via **Highway 395** and **431**). Lake Tahoe is divided into two main regions, **North Shore** and **South Shore.** The North Shore includes **Tahoe City** in California and **Incline Village** in Nevada; the South Shore includes **South Lake Tahoe** in California and **Stateline** in Nevada.

Visitor Info: N. Lake Tahoe Visitors Bureau, 380 N. Lake Blvd. (☎581-6900; www.gotahoenorth.com). A helpful office with tons of info on the area. Open M-F 8:30am-5pm, Sa-Su 8:30am-5pm. **Taylor Creek Visitors Center** (USFS; ☎543-2600; www.fs.fed.us/r5/ltbmu), 3 mi. north of S. Lake Tahoe on Hwy. 89. Permits for Desolation Wilderness. Camping fee $5 per person per night, $10 per person for 2 or more nights, yearly pass $20; under 12 free. Reservations (☎644-6048; $5) are available for overnight permits mid-June to mid-Sept. Open daily mid-June to Sept. 8am-5:30pm; May 31 to mid-June and Oct. 8am-4pm.

CALIFORNIA

Medical Services: Incline Village Community Hospital, 880 Alder Ave. (☎775-833-4100), off Hwy. 28 in Incline Village. **Barton Memorial Hospital,** 2170 South Ave. (☎541-3420), at 3rd St. and South Ave. off Lake Tahoe Blvd. in South Lake.

Post Office: Tahoe City, 950 N. Lake Blvd. (☎800-275-8777). Open M-F 8:30am-5pm. **Postal Code:** 96145. **South Lake Tahoe,** 1046 Al Tahoe Blvd. (☎800-275-8777). Open M-F 8:30am-5pm, Sa noon-2pm. **Postal Code:** 96150. **Area Code:** 530 in CA, 775 in NV; in text, 530 unless otherwise noted.

ACCOMMODATIONS

The South Shore has many of the cheapest motels, with basic amenities. Accommodations on the North Shore, while pricier and fewer in number, are generally more refined. In Tahoe City and Incline Village, the priciest lodgings are booked solid for weekends and holidays. Fall and spring are the cheapest times to visit. Whatever your budget, campgrounds are great options in warmer months.

Tahoe Valley Lodge, 2214 Lake Tahoe Blvd. (☎800-669-7544 or 541-0353; www.tahoevalleylodge.com), in South Lake. Enjoy exquisite comfort in rooms decorated with a log-cabin theme. All rooms come equipped with a queen-size bed, cable TV, coffee-maker, and gas fireplace; many have jacuzzi, microwave, and refrigerator. Queen beds M-Th and Su $95, F-Sa $125. AmEx/MC/V. ❹

Elizabeth Lodge, 3918 Pioneer Trail (☎544-2417), in South Lake, 1 block off Lake Tahoe Blvd. Simple rooms with perhaps the lowest prices in town. Queen bed with TV and phone M-Th and Su $28, F $39, Sa $49. AmEx/D/MC/V. ❷

Tahoe State Recreation Area (☎583-3074 or 800-444-7275 for reservations), on the eastern edge of Tahoe City off Hwy. 28. In these 39 compact sites within walking distance of downtown Tahoe City (and adjacent to a shopping center), you may not feel like you're camping. Water and flush toilets. Showers ($0.50). Open May-Nov. Sites $15; each additional vehicle $4. ❶

FOOD

On the South Shore, casinos offer low-priced buffets while posh dining clubs line the lakefront, but grills and burger joints promise food at reasonable prices.

Sprouts Natural Foods Cafe, 3123 Harrison Ave. (☎541-6969), at the intersection of Lake Tahoe Blvd. and Alameda Ave., in South Lake. Creative natural foods for a health-conscious crowd. Try a breakfast burrito with avocados ($6.50) or a fresh smoothie ($3.75-4). Open daily 8am-9pm. Cash or local check only. ❶

The Red Hut Cafe, 2749 Lake Tahoe Blvd. (☎541-9024), in South Lake. Also at 227 Kingsbury Grade (☎775-588-7488), in Stateline. A Tahoe original since 1959. Friendly staff serves homestyle cooking and outstanding daily specials. Whipped cream and strawberries atop a waffle $7. Avocado burgers $8. Open daily 6am-2pm. Cash only. ❶

Bridgetender Tavern and Grill, 65 W. Lake Blvd. (☎583-3342), in Tahoe City. A local favorite known for juicy ½ lb. burgers ($8). Both the rustic interior or the scenic outdoor patio overlooking the Truckee River are great for recovering from a busy day on the lake. Open M-Th and Su 11am-11pm, F-Sa 11am-midnight. MC/V. ❸

OUTDOOR ACTIVITIES

BEACHES
Many beaches surround Lake Tahoe, providing the perfect setting for sun-bathing and people-watching. Parking costs $3-8; bargain hunters should park in turn-outs

on the main road and walk. On the North Shore, **Sand Harbor Beach,** 2 mi. south of Incline Village on Hwy. 28, has granite boulders and clear waters that attract swimmers, snorkelers, and boaters. **Baldwin Beach,** on the South Shore, and neighboring **Pope Beach,** near the southernmost point of the lake off Hwy. 89, are popular, shaded expanses of shoreline. Quiet spots on both can be found on the edges. **Nevada Beach,** on the east shore, 3 mi. north of South Lake Tahoe off Hwy. 50, is close to casinos but offers sanctuary from slot machines. Recently renovated **Zephyr Cove Beach,** 5 mi. north of S. Lake Tahoe, hosts a youthful party crowd keen on beer and bikinis. The West Shore offers **Meeks Bay,** 12 mi. south of Tahoe City, a family-oriented beach with picnic tables and volleyball courts. **D.L. Bliss State Park,** 17 mi. south of Tahoe City on Hwy. 89, is home to **Lester** and **Calawee Cove Beaches** on striking **Rubicon Bay** and is a trailhead for the **Rubicon Trail.**

HIKING

The 165 mi. **Tahoe Rim Trail** was decades in the making and now encircles the lake, following the ridge tops of the basin, and welcomes hikers, equestrians, and, in most areas, mountain bikers. On the western shore, the route is part of the Pacific Crest Trail. In the north, **Mount Rose,** at 10,778 ft., is one of the tallest mountains in the region as well as one of the best climbs. The panoramic view from the summit includes views of the lake, Reno, and the surrounding Sierra Nevada. Take Hwy. 431 north from Incline Village to the trailhead (over 6 mi., strenuous 2200 ft. climb). The rugged trails and mountain streams of **Granite Chief Wilderness,** west of Squaw Valley, wind through forests in 5000 ft. valleys up to the summits of 9000 ft. peaks. The **Alpine Meadows Trailhead,** at the end of Alpine Meadows Rd. off Hwy. 89 between Truckee and Tahoe City, and the **Pacific Crest Trailhead,** at the end of Barker Pass Rd. (Blackwood Canyon Rd.), provide convenient access into the wilderness. The picturesque ⚑**Emerald Bay,** on Hwy. 89 between S. Lake Tahoe and Tahoe City, is breathtaking from the road but is best explored on foot. Waterfalls cascade down the mountains above this partially enclosed bay, which contains Lake Tahoe's only island, Fannette. The Rubicon Trail, accessible from **Emerald Bay State Park, D.L. Bliss State Park,** or **Vikingsholm,** winds along the beach and granite cliffs (6 mi.). The various trailheads allow you to customize the length and difficulty of your hike, but stunning vistas are found all along the way.

ROCK CLIMBING

Alpenglow Sports, 415 N. Lake Blvd., in Tahoe City, provides climbing literature and know-how. (☎583-6917. Climbing shoe rental $10 per day. Open M-F and Su 10am-6pm, Sa 9am-6pm.) Pleasant climbs abound in Lake Tahoe, but safety precautions are a must. The inexperienced can try bouldering in **D.L. Bliss State Park.** The South Shore has many popular climbing spots, including the celebrated **Ninety-Foot Wall** at Emerald Bay, **Twin Crags** at Tahoe City, and **Big Chief** near Squaw Valley. **Lover's Leap,** in S. Lake Tahoe, is an incredible, albeit crowded, route spanning two cliffs.

SKIING

With world-class slopes, 15 ski resorts, knee-deep powder, and California sun, Tahoe is the stuff of skiers' dreams. Conditions range from winter storms to t-shirt weather; snow covers the slopes into early summer. Rates listed are for peak season. ⚑**Squaw Valley,** 5 mi. north of Tahoe City off Hwy. 89, site of the 1960 Winter Olympics, has 4000 acres of terrain across six Sierra peaks. The 33 ski lifts, including the 110-passenger cable car and high-speed gondola, access runs for all levels. (☎583-5585 or 888-766-9321; www.squaw.com. Open late Nov.-May. full day lift ticket $55-73. Half-day $39, ages 13-18 $39, ages 65-75 $32, under 12 $5, ages over 76 free. Night skiing mid-Dec. to mid-Apr. daily 4-9pm; $20.) The largest and most popular resort is **Heavenly,** on Ski Run Blvd. off S. Lake Tahoe Blvd., with over

4800 acres and 91 runs. Its vertical drop is 3500 ft., Tahoe's biggest. (☎775-586-7000; www.skiheavenly.com. Full day lift ticket $61, ages 13-18 $45, ages 6-12 $29.)

A great way to enjoy Tahoe's snow-covered forests is to **cross-country ski** along the thick braid of trails around the lake. **Spooner Lake,** at the junction of Hwy. 50 and 28, offers 57 mi. of machine-groomed trails and incredible views. (☎775-749-5349; www.spoonerlake.com. Morning half-day $16; ages 13-18 $10. Full day M and W-Su $21, Tu $12.) **Tahoe X-C,** 2 mi. northeast of Tahoe City on Dollar Hill off Hwy. 28, maintains 40 mi. of trails for all abilities. (☎583-5475, www.tahoexc.org. Dayfarmers' marketfarmers' market $21, after 12:30pm $16, after 3pm $11; ages 10-17 and over 60 $5 discount.) Skiing is a blast, but snowshoeing is often easier to pick up. Follow hiking or cross-country trails and look for fresh powder to walk through. Equipment rentals are readily available at local sporting goods stores for about $15 per day.

YOSEMITE NATIONAL PARK ☎209

Yosemite became a national park over 100 years ago, but the park's geological history of the park began eons before that. About 50 million years ago, the flat floor and granite walls of Yosemite Valley, the park's most spectacular and popular area, were no more than a slow-moving river and rolling hills. Then the Sierra Nevada rose, the Merced River slowly etched deeper into the valley floor, and glaciers carved out the valley's trademark "U" shape. Today, Yosemite is the most famous of the national parks and for good reason; world-class sightseeing, outdoor activities, an unimaginable geologic history, and incredible biodiversity are just a few of its offerings. Yosemite Valley, the bustling, awe-inspiring heart of the park, still lives up to its old name, "The Incomparable Valley."

AT A GLANCE

AREA: 1189 sq. mi.

CLIMATE: Temperate forest.

FEATURES: Tuolumne (tuh-WALL-um-ee) Meadows, Mariposa Grove, Hetch Hetchy Reservoir, Yosemite Valley.

HIGHLIGHTS: Swimming in Tenaya Lake, climbing El Capitán, getting sprayed at Vernal Falls.

GATEWAYS: Fresno, Merced, Manteca, and Lee Vining.

CAMPING: Reservations are necessary. 7-night max. stay in the valley and Wawona; 14-night max. stay elsewhere. Free wilderness permit is required for backcountry camping in the high country; backcountry camping is not permitted in Yosemite Valley.

FEES AND RESERVATIONS: Entrance fee $20 per car; $10 per pedestrian, cyclist, or bus passenger. Valid for 7 days. Annual pass $40.

▪ **TRANSPORTATION. Yosemite VIA** runs buses from the Merced bus station at 16th and N St. (☎888-727-5287. 4 trips per day, $10.) VIA also meets Amtrak trains and Greyhound buses at the Merced train station. Tickets can be purchased from the driver. (☎800-842-5463. Operates M-F 8am-5pm. Fares include park entry.) **Yosemite Area Regional Transportation System (YARTS)** provides four daily trips to Yosemite from Merced, making convenient stops along the way, and sends one bus a day along Rte. 120 and 395, hitting Mammoth and June Lakes, Lee Vining, and Tuolumne Meadows. (☎388-9589 or 877-989-2787. Buses depart Merced 7, 8:45, 10:30am, 5:25pm. Round-trip $20. Fares include park entry.) **Amtrak** (☎800-872-7245; www.amtrak.com) runs **trains** from Los Angeles (6hr., 5 per day, $38-42) and San Francisco (3hr., 4 per day, $34-38) to Merced and then a bus from Merced to Yosemite (4 per day, $24). Despite traffic, the best way to see Yosemite is by **car.** Be sure to fill the tank before heading out, as there is no gas in Yosemite Valley

Yosemite National Park

Lake Eleanor

Lake Vernon

Benson Lake

Rodgers Lake

TO 395, LEE VINING, MONO LAKE (11mi)

Pettit Peak 10,788ft

Pacific Crest Trail

GRAND CANYON OF THE TUOLUMNE RIVER

Tuolumne R.

Tioga Pass 9945ft

120

Hetch Hetchy Reservoir

Hetch Hetchy Rd.

Hetch Hetchy Entrance

Harden Lake

Lukens Lake

White Wolf

Yosemite Cr.

May Lake

Tioga Rd.

Tuolumne Meadows Visitor. Ctr.

Tuolumne Meadows Lodge

Tioga Entrance

Eleanor Rd.

Bald Mountain 7261ft

Tioga Rd. (closed in winter)

Yosemite Creek

Porcupine Flat

Cathedral Lakes

Tuolumne Meadows

Mammoth Peak 12,117ft

120

Big Oak Flat Entrance

120

Olmsted Point

Tenaya Lake

Cathedral Peak 10,940 ft

Evelyn Lake

CATHEDRAL RANGE

Hodgdon Meadow

El Capitan 7569ft

Yosemite Falls

Ireland Lake

Tuolumne Grove

Tamarack Flat

Ribbon Meadow

YOSEMITE VILLAGE

TENAYA CANYON

Half Dome 8836ft

John Muir Trail

Merced Lake Ranger Station

Mt. Ansel Adams 11,760ft

Merced Grove

Crane Flat

Big Oak Flat Rd.

Valley View

SEE INSET

Little Yosemite Valley

Merced Lake

Washburn Lake

TO YOSEMITE BUG RUSTIC MOUNTAIN RESORT (25mi), MERCED (78mi)

Merced R.

140

Arch Rock Entrance

El Portal

Tunnel View

Bridalveil Fall

Cathedral Rocks

Vernal Fall

Nevada Fall

Glacier Point Rd.

Glacier Point

CLARK RANGE

Merced R.

Foerster Peak 12,057ft

S. Fork of the Merced R.

Bridalveil Creek

Badger Pass Ski Area

Wawona Rd.

TURNER RIDGE

BUENA VISTA CREST

Buena Vista Peak 9709ft

Merced Peak 11,728ft

Inyo National Forest

Sierra National Forest

Wawona

Pioneer Yosemite History Center

Wawona

South Entrance

Mariposa Grove

41

TO FRESNO (85mi)

0   5 miles

0   5 kilometers

▲ Ranger Station
△ Summer Only

N

YOSEMITE VILLAGE

Ahwahnee Hotel

North Pines

Stables

Northside Dr.

Housekeeping Camp

Lower Pines

TO CAMP 4 (.6mi)
YOSEMITE LODGE (.5mi)

Southside Dr.

Curry Village

Upper Pines

Shuttlebus Only

.5 miles

.5 kilometers

Nature Center at Happy Isles

Yosemite Valley

---

except for emergency gas at the Village Garage ($15 per 5 gallons). There are pricey 24hr. gas stations at Crane Flat, Tuolumne Meadows, and Wawona. (☎372-8320. Open daily 8am-noon and 1-5pm. 24hr. towing service. Emergency gasoline available. AAA and National Auto Club accepted.) Rent **bikes** from **Yosemite Lodge** (☎372-1208) or **Curry Village.** (☎372-8319. Bikes $7.50 per hr., $24.50 per day. Driver's license or credit card required as deposit. Both open in summer daily 8:30am-7pm, weather permitting; open on a limited basis after first week in Sept.)

ORIENTATION AND PRACTICAL INFORMATION. Yosemite covers 1170 sq. mi. of terrain, 95% of which is designated as wilderness. The park has four main entrances: Hwy. 120 in the west (Big Oak Flat), Hwy. 120 in the east (Tioga Pass), Hwy. 140 in the west (Arch Rock), and Hwy. 41 in the south (Wawona). Hwys. 120 and 140 lead to the center of activity, **Yosemite Valley,** which contains the area's most enduring monuments, including **El Capitán, Half Dome,** and **Yosemite Falls. Yosemite Village,** the Valley's service and info center, is the least natural and most crowded part of the park, with most of the park's dining and accommodations. **Tuolumne Meadows,** a rock-strewn alpine meadow in the northeast, is the heart of Yosemite's high country and the park's backpacking base camp. **Wawona,** in the south, is a historic, upscale development that features museums and a golf course. **Mariposa Grove,** near Wawona, is the park's largest stand of giant sequoia trees. In the northwest corner, **Hetch Hetchy Reservoir,** created by the damming of the Tuolumne River to provide water for San Francisco, is the park's quietest area, yet still offers much of the same natural beauty. Yosemite has a phone number and website for **General Park Information** (☎379-2486; www.yosemite.org). For other park info, visit the **Yosemite Valley Visitors Center** in Yosemite Village. (☎372-0299. Open daily in summer 8am-6pm; in winter 9am-5pm.) The **Wilderness Center** in Yosemite Village takes wilderness permit reservations up to 24 weeks in advance. (☎372-0740; www.nps.gov/yose/wilderness. $5 per person per reservation. Open M-F 8:30am-4:30pm.) **Tuolumne Meadows Visitors Center,** near the campground of the same name, is the high-country headquarters. (☎372-0263. Open in summer daily 9am-7pm.) **Yosemite Mt. Mountaineering School,** in Tuolumne Meadows and Curry Village, teaches rock climbing classes and rents sleeping bags ($10.50 per day) and backpacks ($8.50 per day; 3rd day half-price), with a driver's license or credit card as deposit. (☎372-8344. Open daily 8:30am-noon and 1-5pm.) Yosemite operates a 24hr. number for **Weather and Road Conditions.** (☎372-0200.) For medical services, head to the **Yosemite Medical Clinic,** in Yosemite Valley. (☎372-4637. 24hr. emergency room. Open M-Sa 8am-5pm.) **Post Office: Yosemite Village,** next to the Visitors Center. (Open M-F 8:30am-5pm, Sa 10am-noon.) **Postal Code:** 95389.

ⵏ ACCOMMODATIONS. When American Transcendentalist Ralph Waldo Emerson visited Yosemite in 1884, the park's accommodations were so simple that he was awakened in the morning by the clucking of a hen climbing over his bed. These days, Yosemite's lodgings have become much more comfortable. Reservations are necessary and can be made up to one year in advance (☎559-252-4848; www.yosemitepark.com). All park lodgings provide access to dining, laundry, showers, and supplies. **Curry Village ❹,** 2 mi. southeast of Yosemite Village, has a wide range of dining options, a comfortable lounge, a pool, an outdoor amphitheater, a store, and an ice rink from November to February. It is the park's most convenient lodging in the park, but the area is always crowded. (☎252-4848. Canvas tent cabins $74; cabins $90, with bath $108; standard motel rooms $123. AmEx/D/MC/V.) The army barracks-style **Housekeeping Camp ❸** is a less developed and more adventurous option. "Camping shelters" for up to four include two bunk beds, a double bed, a picnic table, and a fire pit. (☎372-8338. Camping equipment rental. Shelters for 1-4 people $70. AmEx/D/MC/V.) Outside the park, the **🛏Yosemite Bug Rustic Mountain Resort (HI) ❷,** on Rte. 140 in Midpines, 25 mi. west of the park, is a woodsy, spirited hostel where backpackers lounge on the porches and in the affordable cafe, which serves hearty, healthful fare. (☎966-6666; www.yosemitebug.com. Swimming hole. Free Wi-Fi. Dorms $18, members $15; tent cabins $30-50; private rooms $40-70, with bath $55-115. D/MC/V.)

ⵏⵎ CAMPING AND FOOD. One of visitor's first views of Yosemite during the summer may be of the endless "tent cities" in the valley. Make reservations as far in advance as possible, especially in summer. (☎800-436-7275; http://reservations.nps.gov. Reserve by phone or online daily 7am-7pm.) All Valley campgrounds fill completely every summer night. No matter how pretty it looks, all natural stream water must be boiled, filtered, or treated. **Backcountry camping ❶** is prohibited in the Valley but encouraged outside it. Information and permits can be obtained at the Wilderness Centers at Yosemite Village, Wawona, or Big Oak Flat. Catering to seasoned climbers, **Camp 4 ❶,** 4000 ft., at the western end of the valley, past Yosemite Lodge, has 35 walk-in sites that fill up before 9am. Meet new friends; every site is filled with six random people. (Water, flush toilets, and tables. First come, first served. Limited parking. Sites $5 per person.) Escape the RVs in the 25 sites kept for walk-in hikers at **Tuolumne Meadows ❶,** 8600 ft., on Rte. 120, 55 mi. east of the Valley. (152 sites require advance reservations, 152 saved for same-day reservations. Open July-Sept., depending on snow. Drive-in sites $18 per car; backpacker sites $3 per person.) Crowded but convenient, the **Pines Camp-grounds** ❶ (Upper, Lower, and North) are located in the Valley and provide 379 sites for tents or RVs. (☎877-962-7690. Reservations required. All sites $18.)

Even with its inflated prices, the wide selection at the **Village Store** is your best bet for groceries. (Open daily June-Sept. 8am-10pm; Oct.-May 8am-10pm.) With views of Yosemite Falls from nearly every seat, **Mountain Room Restaurant** ❻, in Yosemite Lodge, is ideal for a post-hike dinner. (☎372-1274. Hearty fare $17-29. Casual dress. Open daily 5:30-9:30pm. AmEx/D/MC/V.) **Degnan's Delicatessen** ❷, in Yosemite Village, has great sandwiches and an inexpensive convenience store. (☎372-8454. Sandwiches $6. Open daily 7am-5pm. AmEx/D/MC/V.)

🏔 OUTDOOR ACTIVITIES. Although the view is better outside of the car, you can see a lot of Yosemite from the bucket seat, and if you only have one day in the park, **scenic drives** are the way to see the sights. **Highway 120 (Tioga Road)** is the highest highway strip in America. The road is only open during the summer, and travelers are treated to spectacular panoramas and beautiful glades from Crane Flat in the west to Tuolumne Meadows in the east. Tioga Rd. then crests Tioga Pass (9945 ft.) before descending to the lunar landscape of Mono Lake outside the park's eastern boundary. No less incredible are the views afforded by the southern approach to Yosemite, **Route 41.** Most recognizable is the **Wawona Tunnel Turn-out** (also known as Inspiration Point), which gives outstanding panoramic views that many visitors will recognize from Ansel Adams photographs. From here, Yosemite Valley unfurls its humbling beauty. **El Capitán,** the largest granite monolith in the world (3593 ft. base to summit), looms over awestruck crowds. Opposite El Capitán, **Bridalveil Falls** drops 620 ft. (the equivalent of a 62-story building). A drive into the valley's heart leads to the staggering Upper and Lower **Yosemite Falls** (combined, the highest waterfall in North America at 2425 ft.). Incredible views of the falls are available at many parking lots and turn-outs, but completely avoiding the traffic jams and shoulder-to-shoulder tourists photographing the sight may be difficult. In the valley's eastern end stands **Half Dome** (8842 ft.), a distinctive rounded rock formation that can be seen from virtually everywhere in the valley.

Glacier Point Road, off Hwy. 41 in the southern part of the park, meanders past lush meadows and rounded domes. At its end, **Glacier Point** gives a bird's-eye view of the Valley floor, considered one of the most spectacular views on earth. If you can maneuver around the other awestruck tourists, you'll be treated to a view of Half Dome presiding over the Valley's east side and the riotous Nevada Falls seemingly reduced to a tranquil silver ribbon. Arrive at sunset and watch the fiery colors fade over the valley as the stars and moon appear. When the moon is full, this is an extraordinary (and even more popular) place to visit.

With two or more days in Yosemite, it's worthwhile to explore some of its trails. World-class hiking abounds for anyone willing to lace up a pair of boots, though sneakers will suffice for a few trails. Day-hike trails are well populated—at nearly any point in the day, you may find yourself stuck behind groups of other tourists. Set your alarm clock, because hiking just after sunrise is the best and sometimes only way to beat the crowds; even then, trails like Half Dome are busy. The Visitors Center has leaflets listing day-hikes for all hiking levels and maps of all regions of the park. The exceptional **Mist Trail** (6 mi.) starts at Happy Isles trailhead (shuttle bus stop #16) at the valley's eastern end. The trail runs parallel to the Merced River to the base of Vernal Falls. From there, steep and slippery steps carved out of the granite put you next to the falls, which sprinkles, sprays, or drenches hikers with its mist, depending on the time of year. The trail ends at the top of the falls, but those with buns of steel can continue to the top of Nevada Falls and then circle back down to the trailhead along the John Muir Trail. The strenuous hike to the top of **Half Dome** is another popular option. This hike, also starting

CALIFORNIA

at the Happy Isles trailhead, yields the thrill of conquering Yosemite's most recognizable monument. The 16 mi. hike is only recommended for those in good shape and comfortable with heights. Half Dome attracts lightning and mid-summer thunderstorms; early-morning departures are best. Expect your hike to take 10-12hr.

The **Mirror Lake Loop** is a flat 3 mi. walk past Mirror Lake (½ mi.), up Tenaya Creek, and back. This is also a popular biking trail. The **Lower Yosemite Falls Trail** is a favorite, starting across from Yosemite Lodge. On moonlit nights, mysterious moonbows (nighttime rainbows) can often be spotted above the water. **Upper Yosemite Falls Trail,** a backbreaking 3½ mi. trek to the summit, climbs 2700 ft. but rewards the intrepid hiker with an overview of the dizzying 2425 ft. drop. Those with energy to spare can trudge on to **Yosemite Point** or **Eagle Peak,** where views of the Valley below rival those from Glacier Point. The trail begins with an extremely steep, unshaded ascent. Leaving the marked trail is not wise—a sign warns, "If you go over the waterfall, you will die." The steep **Four Mile Trail** (actually 4½ mi. long) is a switchbacked climb from the Valley to Glacier Point. The strenuous hike through white fir and sugar pine forests has sporadic Valley views, giving a sense of the Valley's soaring heights.

WINTER ACTIVITIES. In Yosemite's quietest season, the landscape undergoes a facelift as the waterfalls freeze and the meadows frost over. Unlike much of the park, Yosemite Valley remains accessible year-round. **Route 140** from Merced, an all-weather entrance, is usually open and clear. Although Tioga Pass and Glacier Point Rd. close at the first sign of snow, **Route 41** and **Route 120** typically remain traversable. Always be sure to verify road conditions before traveling (☎372-0200) and carry tire chains.

Well-marked trails for **cross-country skiing** and **snowshoeing** cut into the backcountry of the Valley's South Rim at Badger Pass and Crane Flat. Rangers host snowshoe walks from mid-December to March, but the serene forests are perhaps best explored without guidance. Guided cross-country skiing trips to Glacier Point (☎327-8444) with meals and hut lodgings are available. The state's oldest ski resort, **Badger Pass Ski Area,** on Glacier Point Rd. south of Yosemite Valley, is the park's only downhill ski area, and has a family atmosphere. **Ice skating** at Curry Village is beautiful, with Half Dome towering above a groomed outdoor rink encircled by snow-covered pines. (☎372-8341. Open in winter daily 3:30-6pm and 7-9:30pm; also Sa-Su 8:30-11am and noon-2:30pm. $6.50, children $5. Skate rental $3.25.)

MAMMOTH LAKES ☎760

Home to one of the most popular ski resorts in the entire United States, the small town of Mammoth Lakes (pop. 7156) is a giant year-round playground. The snowfall averages over 350 in. per year, creating an impressive 3500 acres of skiable terrain. When the snow melts, mountain bikers invade to take on Mammoth Mountain, skateboarders come to test their skills in competitions, and fisherfolk come to the magma-warmed creeks. A **free shuttle bus (MAS)** transports skiers between lifts and the ski lodge.

Devil's Postpile National Monument is a stunning 60 ft. wall that, although formed naturally, appears made up of eerily uniform hexagonal rock columns. Pristine wilderness surrounds the Postpile, with brilliant **Rainbow Falls** accessible via a moderate 2½ mi. one-way hike. (Open in summer daily 7am-7:30pm.) The **Inyo Craters** are curious open pits 600 ft. across with blue-green water at the bottom formed by volcanic activity within the last 2000 years. The quarter mile path to the craters can be reached from Mammoth Scenic Loop Rd. The climbing walls and 80 mi. of twisted bike trails at **Mammoth Mountain Adventure Center,** home of the **Mammoth Mountain Bike Park** at Mammoth Mountain base camp, is a fun diversion for novices and experienced climbers and bikers. (☎934-0706. Open daily 8am-6pm. $7 per climb, $19 per hr. Bike rentals $37 per day, $95 per 3 days. Helmets required.) The **Mammoth Mountain Gondola** affords mile-high views. (☎934-2571. Open daily 9am-4:30pm. Round-trip $18, children $14; day pass $37.) Once you reach the top of the gondola, visit the new **Top of the Sierra Interpretive Center and Cafe.** From 11,053 ft. up, this center offers information on the area's volcanic and cultural history, as well hot sandwiches and soups. (Cafe open daily in summer 9:30am-3:30pm; in winter 10:30am-2:30pm. Free.) The high altitude and piles of snow often allow **Mammoth Mountain,** a favorite for southern California's Tahoe-less skiers, to stay open into June. (☎800-626-6684 or 934-0745; www.mammothmountain.com. Open in winter daily 8:30am-4pm. $79, ages 13-18 $60).

As in most ski resort towns, lodging is much more expensive in the winter months than in the summer. Condo rentals are good for groups of three or more and start at $100 per night. **Mammoth Reservation Bureau** (☎800-462-5571; www.mammothvacations.com) can make arrangements. For lone travelers, dorm-style motels are cheapest. Reservations are highly recommended. **Davison St. Guest House ❶,** 19 Davison Rd., at Lake Mary Rd., is the best value in town, offering guests small yet comfortable rooms and an inviting common room with views of the surrounding mountains. (☎924-2188, reservations 858-755-8608; www.mammoth-guest.com. Dorms $25; singles $55, with bath $75. Check or money order only.) There are nearly 20 Inyo Forest public **campgrounds ❶** in the area. All sites have piped water and most are near fishing and hiking. (Sites $14-16.) Contact the **Mammoth Lakes Welcome Center,** 2500 Main St., for free camping, wildlife and fire permits, and for information on free campsites. (☎924-5500 . Open daily 8am-5pm). **Paul Schat's Bakery and Cafe ❶,** 3305 Main St. has the best sandwiches in town. (☎934-6055. Cafe open M-Th and Su 5:30am-6pm, F-Sa 5:30am-8pm. Deli open daily 10am-3pm. MC/V.) **Angel's ❶,** 3516 Main St., serves homestyle cooking, excellent barbecue, and a variety of beers that will hit the spot after a long day on the mountain. (☎934-7427. Open daily 11:30am-9pm. AmEx/D/MC/V.) For a hearty breakfast, try **The Stove Restaurant ❷,** 644 Old Mammoth Rd. This cozy town favorite offers fast, friendly service, and they make a mean country biscuit. (☎934-2821. Open daily 6:30am-2pm and 5-9pm. MC/V.)

THE NORTH COAST

Windswept and larger than life, the North Coast winds from the San Francisco Bay Area to the Oregon border. Redwoods tower over black-sand beaches deserted save for the sea lions, otters frolic next to jutting rock formations, and U.S. 101 snakes along cliffs between pounding surf and humbling redwoods. The North Coast's untouched wilderness is simply stunning.

MENDOCINO ☎707

Teetering on bluffs over the ocean, isolated Mendocino (pop. 1008) is a coastal community of art galleries, craft shops, bakeries, and B&Bs. Just west of the village, the earth falls into the Pacific at the impressive ■**Mendocino Headlands.** A meadow of tall grass and wildflowers separates the town from the rocky shore. Poor drainage and thin, acidic soil have created stunted vegetation at the **Pygmy Forest** in **Van Damme State Park.** To get to the forest, drive 3 mi. south of town, past the main park entrance, then turn left on Little River Airport Rd. and drive 3 mi.

Jughandle Creek Farm ❶, about 3 mi. north of Mendocino off Hwy. 1, across the street from the Jug Handle State Reserve, is a beautiful 39-acre complex of gardens, forest, campsites, small rustic cabins, and a century-old Victorian home with private and dorm rooms. Trails from the property lead directly onward to the coast. (☎964-4630. Reservations recommended in summer. Rooms $30, students $23; cabins $38/30 per person. Sites $12. $5 off with1hr. of chores.) Inside the main entrance of Van Damme State Park, three **campgrounds ❶**—one traditional, one hike and bike, and one environmental—provide a wide range of options for travelers. (☎937-5804. Traditional has running water and toilets; others are primitive. Sites $15-20.) The four campgrounds at **MacKerricher State Park ❶**, 2½ mi. north of Fort Bragg, total 184 campsites scattered between 9 mi. of beaches and the shores of Lake Cleon. The sites have excellent views of tide-pool life, passing seals, sea lions, and migratory whales. (☎964-9112. Showers, flush toilets, bathrooms, and drinkable water. Sites $20.) For picnic supplies, head to **Harvest Market at Mendosa's**, 10501 Lansing St., which stocks all the basics you might need, plus some organic produce and breads. (☎937-5879. Open daily 7:30am-10pm.) Mendocino restaurants are often pricey, but the food is excellent. The **Bay View Cafe ❸**, 45040 Main St., lives up to its name with big picture windows overlooking the headlands, making it a great place to enjoy the decadent hot crab sandwich ($15) or peppery clam chowder. Look for the wooden water tower and walk up the steps. (☎937-4197. Open daily 8am-9pm. Cash only.)

Tiny Mendocino sits on **Highway 1,** right on the Pacific coast, 30 mi. west of U.S. 101 and 12 mi. south of Fort Bragg. Like all northern coast areas of California, Mendocino can be very chilly, even in the summer months. Travelers should expect 40-70°F temperatures and dress accordingly. The nearest Greyhound **bus** station (☎800-231-2222; www.greyhound.com) is approximately 2hr. away in Ukiah. Mendocino Transit Authority, 241 Plant Rd. (☎800-696-4682), in Ukiah, makes one round-trip daily between Mendocino and Santa Rosa ($20), stopping at Willits ($3.25) and Ukiah ($4.75) on the way. The **bus** leaves from the Cookie Company, at Lansing and Ukiah St. **Fort Bragg-Mendocino Coast Chamber of Commerce** is at 332 N. Main St., in Fort Bragg. (☎961-6300 or 800-726-2780: www.mendocino-coast.com. Open M-F 9am-noon and 12:30-5pm, Sa 9am-3pm.) For **Park Info,** call ☎937-5804, or go to the **Ford House Mendocino Headlands Visitors Center** on Main St. in Mendocino. Historical museum and free hot cider are inside. (☎937-5804. Open M-F 11am-4pm.) **Internet Access:** The **Fort Bragg Library,** is at 499 Laurel St., in Fort Bragg. (☎964-2020. Free. Open Tu and Th 10am-6pm, W noon-8pm, F-Sa 10am-5pm.) **Medical Services: Mendocino Coast District Hospital,** 700 River Dr. (☎961-1234), in Fort Bragg. **Post Office:** 10500 Ford St., in Mendocino. (☎937-5282. Open M-F 7:30am-4:30pm.) **Postal Code:** 95460.

AVENUE OF THE GIANTS   ☎707

About 10 mi. north of Garberville on U.S. 101 in Humboldt Redwoods State Park, the Avenue of the Giants splits off the highway and winds its way through 32 mi. of redwoods, the world's largest living organisms above ground level. The roads can be narrow enough for you to worry about the fate of your side mirrors, but that's part of the fun. The staff at **Humboldt Redwoods State Park Visitors Center** can highlight the avenue's groves, facilities, trails, and bike routes. (☎946-2409. Open daily Apr.-Oct. 9am-5pm; Nov.-Mar. 10am-4pm.) Sleep under the massive trees at the park's many **campsites ❶,** which have coin showers, flush toilets, and fire rings. (☎946-2409. Sites $20.) For some up-close giant viewing, try the half-mile loop at **Founder's Grove,** featuring the 1300- to 1500-year-old **Founder's Tree** and the former tallest tree in Humboldt Redwoods State Park, the fallen 362 ft. **Dyerville Giant,** whose massive, three-story root-ball looks like a mythic entanglement of evil. Uncrowded trails wind through **Rockefeller Forest** in the park's northern section, which contains the largest grove of continuous old-growth redwoods in the world.

REDWOOD NATIONAL AND STATE PARKS
☎ 707

The redwoods are the last remaining stretch of the old-growth forest that used to blanket two million acres of northern California and Oregon. Within the parks, the world's tallest trees continue to grow in quiet splendor while black bears and mountain lions roam the backwoods and elk graze the meadows.

🛈 **PRACTICAL INFORMATION. Redwood National and State Parks** is an umbrella term for four contiguous parks. From south to north, they are: **Redwood National Park, Prairie Creek Redwoods State Park, Del Norte Coast Redwoods State Park,** and **Jedediah Smith Redwoods State Park. Fees** vary by park and are different for camping, parking, and hiking. There is usually no entrance fee. Day-use fees ($5 per car) for parking and picnic areas are typical. **AAA Emergency Road Service** is available 24hr. at ☎ 800-222-4357; www.aaa.com. **Redwood National Park Headquarters and Information Center,** 1111 2nd St., in Crescent City, is the headquarters of the entire park, but 3 other Visitors Centers are also well informed. (☎ 464-6101, ext. 5826. Open daily 9am-5pm.) **Sutter Coast Hospital,** 800 E. Washington Blvd. (☎ 464-8511; www.suttercoast.org), in Crescent City, offers medical services. **Del Norte County Library,** 190 Price Mall, at 2nd St. and I St., in Crescent City, has **Internet acces.** (☎ 464-9793. $1 per 30min. Open M and W-Th 10am-6pm, Tu noon-8pm.) **Post Office:** 751 2nd St., at H St., in Crescent City. (☎ 464-2151. Open M-F 8:30am-5pm, Sa noon-2pm.) **Postal Code:** 95531.

🛏🍴 **ACCOMMODATIONS AND FOOD.** ✉**Redwood Hostel (HI) ❶,** 14480 U.S. 101, at Wilson Creek Rd., 7 mi. north of Klamath, is a beach location with great sunset views. (☎ 482-8265 or 800-295-1905; www.redwoodhostel.com. Free Internet. Check-in 5-10pm. Check-out 10am. Summer reservations recommended. Dorms $20, under 17 $10; private rooms for 1-3 people $49. MC/V.) **Jedediah Smith Redwoods State Park ❶,** 9 mi. east of Crescent City off U.S. 199, has 106 RV and tent sites in old-growth redwood forest. Campfire programs and nature walks are offered during the summer. (☎ 458-3018. Picnic tables, restrooms, showers, and water. Sites $20; day-use $5.) **Mill Creek Campground ❶,** 6 mi. south of Crescent City off U.S. 101, in Del Norte Coast Redwoods SP, has 145 RV and tent sites in second-growth redwood forest. (☎ 800-444-7275. Restrooms, showers, and bear-proof lockers. Open June-Aug. Sites $20; day-use $5.)

There are more picnic tables than restaurants in the area, so the best option for food is probably the supermarket. In Crescent City, head to the 24hr. **Safeway,** 475 M St. (☎ 465-3663), on U.S. 101 between 2nd and 5th St. The **Klamath Market,** 166 Klamath Blvd., has an ATM. (☎ 482-0211. Open M-Sa 8am-9pm, Su 9am-5pm.) The mom-and-pop **Palm Cafe ❷,** on U.S. 101, is one of the few places to eat in Orick; the homemade pies are wonderful. (☎ 488-3381. Pie slices a la mode $3.75. Open daily 6am-8pm. MC/V.) **Glen's Bakery and Restaurant ❶,** 722 3rd at G St., in Crescent City, opened in 1947 and has always been a family affair. Dedicated regulars love the plate-sized pancakes. (☎ 464-2914. Breakfast served all day. Sandwiches $5.50-8. Pancakes $4. Open Tu-F 5am-6:30pm, Sa 5am-2pm. MC/V.)

🏔 **OUTDOOR ACTIVITIES.** All plants and animals in the park are protected—even feathers dropped by birds of prey are off-limits to visitors. California **fishing licenses** ($12 per day) are required for fresh and saltwater fishing off any natural formation, but fishing is free from any man-made structure in the parks. There are minimum-weight and maximum-catch requirements specific to both fresh and

CALIFORNIA

saltwater fishing. Contact the **Fish and Game Department** (☎916-445-0411; www.dfg.ca.gov) for more information.

The **Orick Area** covers the southernmost section of Redwood National and State Parks. The **Kuchel Visitors Center** lies on U.S. 101, 1 mi. south of Orick (☎465-7765). A popular sight is the **Tall Trees Grove,** a 3 mi. trail down to a grove of some of the world's tallest trees. The grove is accessible by car to those with permits (free from the Visitors Center in Crescent City) when the road is open. Allow at least 3-4hr. for the trip. The 70 mi. of criss-crossing trails in the **Prairie Creek Area** can be confusing. Be sure to pick up a trail map ($1) at the **Prairie Creek Visitor Center,** off U.S. 101 in Prairie Creek Redwoods State Park. (☎465-7354. Open daily Memorial Day-Labor Day 9am-5pm.) The **James Irvine Trail** (4mi.) snakes through a prehistoric garden of towering old-growth redwoods. The less ambitious can cruise part of the **Foothill Trail** (¾ mi.) to a 1500-year-old behemoth, the 306 ft. **Big Tree.** The northern **Klamath Area** connects Prairie Creek with Del Norte State Park; the main attraction is the spectacular coastline. The **Klamath Overlook,** where Requa Rd. meets the steep **Coastal Trail** (42 mi.), is an excellent whale-watching site. Crescent City is the nearest substantial city and an outstanding base for exploring the parks. The **Battery Point Lighthouse** is on a causeway jutting out from Front St. and houses a museum open only during low tide. (☎464-3089. Open Apr.-Sept. W-Su 10am-4pm, tide permitting; Nov.-Mar. F-Sa at low tide. $3, children $1.) From June to August, **tidepool walks** leave from Enderts Beach. (At the turnoff 4 mi. south of Crescent City; call ☎458-3209 for schedules.)

PACIFIC NORTHWEST

The Pacific Northwest became the center of national attention when gold rushes and the Oregon Trail ushered hordes of settlers into the region. In the 1840s, Senator Stephen Douglas argued that the Cascade Range would make a good natural border between Oregon and Washington, but the Columbia River, perpendicular to the Cascades, became the border instead. Yet even today, the range and not the river is the region's most important cultural divide: in the wet, lush land west of the Cascades lie the two microchip, mocha, and music meccas of Portland and Seattle; to the east sprawls farmland and an arid plateau. For more info on the region, see ▇*Let's Go: Pacific Northwest Adventure Guide.*

HIGHLIGHTS OF THE PACIFIC NORTHWEST

SIP java while strolling through the offbeat neighborhoods, spectacular museums, and quirky cafes of **Seattle** (p. 959).

EXPLORE the remains of a volcano at **Crater Lake National Park** (p. 956) or the icy peaks of the dormant **Mt. Rainier** (p. 977).

MEDITATE upon the mossy grandeur of **Olympic National Park** (p. 972).

SKIM through hundreds of dusty volumes at **Powell's City of Books** (p. 941).

REVEL in the low prices and natural beauty of **Vancouver, British Columbia** (p. 984).

OREGON

Lured by plentiful forests and promises of gold and riches, entire families liquidated their possessions, sank their life savings into covered wagons, corn meal, and oxen, and high-tailed it to Oregon (OR-uh-gun) in search of prosperity and a new way of life. The resulting population of outdoors-enthusiasts and fledgling townspeople joined the Union in 1859, and has since become an eclectic mix of treehuggers and suave big-city types. Today, Oregon remains as popular a destination as ever for backpackers, cyclists, anglers, beach crawlers, and families alike. With everything from excellent microbrews to untouched wilderness, Oregon is still a great reason to cross the Continental Divide.

▇ PRACTICAL INFORMATION

Capital: Salem.

Visitor Info: Oregon Tourism Commission, 670 Hawthorne Ave., Ste. 240, Salem 97310 (☎503-378-8850 or 800-547-7842; www.traveloregon.com). **Oregon State Parks and Recreation Dept.,** 725 Summer St. NE, Ste. C, Salem 97301 (☎503-986-0707 or 800-551-6949; www.prd.state.or.us).

Postal Abbreviation: OR. **Sales Tax:** None.

PORTLAND   ☎ 503

An award-winning transit system and pedestrian-friendly streets make Portland
feel more like a pleasantly overgrown town than a crowded metropolis. With over
250 parks, the pristine Willamette River, and snow-capped Mt. Hood on the horizon, the City of Roses basks in the natural beauty surrounding it. In the rainy season, Portlanders flood pubs and clubs to sip java while musicians strum and sing.
In the summer, music from outdoor performances fills the air from Pioneer Courthouse Square to the lawn of the Oregon Zoo in Washington Park. And throughout
it all, the best beer pours from the taps in the microbrewery capital of the US.

▐ TRANSPORTATION

Airport: Portland International Airport (PDX; ☎460-4232 or 877–739-4636; www.fly-
pdx.com) is well-served by almost every major airline. The airport is connected to the
city center of Portland by **MAX Red Line,** an efficient Light Rail system (38min., every
15min. 5am-11:30pm, $1.70).

Trains: Amtrak, 800 NW. 6th Ave. (☎273-4864 or 800-872-7245; www.amtrakcas-
cades.com), in Union Station, at Hoyt St. Open daily 7:30am-9pm. To **Eugene** (2½hr.,
5 per day, $13-22) and **Seattle** (4hr., 4 per day, $28-44). Also has daily service to **Chicago** and **San Francisco.**

Buses: Greyhound, 550 NW. 6th Ave. (☎243-2361 or 800-231-2222; www.grey-
hound.com), at NW. Glisan St. by Union Station. Ticket counter open daily 5:45am-
11:30pm. To **Eugene** (2½-4hr., 5 per day, $18.50-20), **Seattle** (3-4½hr., 8 per day,
$25-27), and **Spokane** (7½-11hr., 4 per day, $41-44).

Public Transit: Tri-Met, 701 SW. 6th Ave. (☎238-7433; www.trimet.org), in Pioneer
Courthouse Sq. Open M-F 8:30am-5:30pm. Self-service lobby open Sa 10am-4pm.
Buses generally start as early as 5am and run as late as 1:30am on weekdays,
12:30am on weekends. $1.70-2, ages 7-18 $1.35, disabled and over 65 $0.85; day
pass $4.25. All of the city's public transit is free in the **No-Fare Zone ("Fareless
Square"):** north and east of I-405, west of the river and south of NW. Irving St.; see
www.trimet.org/fares/fareless.htm for specific info. **MAX** (☎228-7246), based at the
Customer Service Center, is Tri-Met's Light Rail train running between downtown, Hillsboro in the west, and Gresham in the east. Blue Line runs in the west side; Yellow Line
spans 5 mi. of Interstate Ave.; Red Line runs to the airport. M-F around 4am-1:30am,
Sa 5am-12:30am, Su 5am-11:30pm.

Taxi: Radio Cab, ☎227-1212. **Broadway Cab,** ☎227-1234.

Car Rental: Crown Auto Rental, 1315 NE. Sandy Blvd. (☎230-1103).

✦❷ ORIENTATION AND PRACTICAL INFORMATION

Portland lies in the northwest corner of Oregon, where the Willamette River joins
the Columbia River. **I-5** connects Portland with San Francisco and Seattle, while **I-
84** follows the path of the Oregon Trail through the Columbia River Gorge, heading along the Oregon-Washington border toward Boise, ID. West of Portland, **U.S.
30** follows the Columbia downstream (northwest) to Astoria, but **U.S. 26,** heading
west to Mt. Hood, is the most direct path to the coast. **I-405** runs in a loop west
from I-5, encircling downtown and linking I-5 with U.S. 26 and 30.

Every street name in Portland carries one of five prefixes: **N., NE., NW., SE.,** or
SW., indicating where in the city the address is found. **Burnside Street** divides the
city into north and south, while east and west are separated by the **Willamette River.**
Southwest Portland, home to Jefferson Park and the University, is known as **downtown** but also includes the southern end of Old Town and a slice of the wealthier

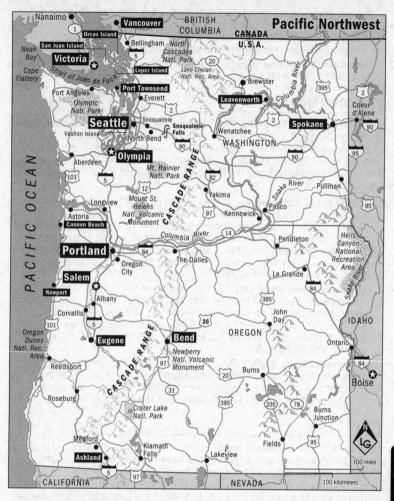

West Hills. Old Town, mostly in **Northwest** Portland, encompasses the city's historic sector. Be cautious at night in the areas around W. Burnside St. To the north, **Nob Hill** and **Pearl District** hold revitalized homes and snazzy shops, and are hip and trendy. Casual **Southeast** Portland contains parks, factories, and residential areas of all income brackets; a rich array of restaurants and theaters lines **Hawthorne Boulevard. Williams Avenue** frames "the North." **North** and **Northeast** Portland are largely residential, but punctuated by vibrant stretches of entertainment, food, shopping, and nightlife on **Alberta Street, Mississippi Avenue,** and **Fremont Street.**

Visitor Info: Portland Oregon Information Center (Portland Oregon Visitors Association; POVA), 701 SW. 6th Ave. (☎275-8355 or 275-9750; www.travelportland.com), at SW. Morrison St. in Pioneer Courthouse Sq. Has maps and other handouts. Open M-F 8:30am-5:30pm, Sa 10am-4pm.

Internet Access: Found at the elegant **Central Library,** 801 SW. 10th Ave. (☎988-5123; www.multcolib.org), between Yamhill and Taylor. 1hr. free with a guest pass from customer service. Open M and Th-Sa 10am-8pm, Tu-W 10am-6pm, Su noon-5pm. Much of the downtown area has free Wi-Fi through the expanding Portland MetroFi Network.

Post Office: 715 NW. Hoyt St. (☎800-275-8777). Open M-F 7am-6:30pm, Sa 8:30am-5pm. **Postal Code:** 97208.

ACCOMMODATIONS

Although chain hotels dominate downtown and smaller motels steadily raise prices, Portland still welcomes the budget traveler. Prices drop as you leave the city center, and inexpensive motels can be found on SE. Powell Blvd. and the southern end of SW. 4th Ave. Accommodations in Portland fill up during the summer months, especially during the Rose Festival and Blues Festival, so make your reservations early.

Portland Hostel Northwest (HI), 425 NW. 18th Ave. (☎241-2783 or 888-777-0067; www.2oregonhostels.com), at Glisan St., between Nob Hill and the Pearl District. This Victorian building has a kitchen, Internet access ($1 per 16min.), lockers, laundry, and a manageable walk to many of Portland's most popular attractions. 3 blocks from "fare-less square." Reception 8am-11pm. Dorms June-Sept. $25, members $22; private doubles from $49. Oct.-May dorms $20, members $17; private doubles from $36. Reservations recommended. MC/V. ●

Portland Hawthorne Hostel (HI), 3031 SE. Hawthorne Blvd. (☎236-3380; www.portlandhostel.org). Take bus #14 to SE. 30th Ave. A laid-back, bohemian hostel with a lively common space and a huge porch. Pancakes $1. Linen included. Internet access $1 per 16min. Reception 8am-10pm. Check-out 11am. Dorms June-Sept. $25, members $22; private rooms $51/48. Oct.-May dorms $20, members $17; private rooms $43/40. AmEx/D/MC/V. ●

McMenamins White Eagle Rock'n'Roll Hotel, 836 N. Russell St. (☎335-8900; www.mcmenamins.com), at N. Mississippi, near the northern I-5/I-405 interchange, in North Portland. 11 simple but welcoming rooms. Cafe, beer garden, and saloon. Bunk room $30; room with full bed $40, with queen bed $50-60. AmEx/D/MC/V. ●

FOOD

Downtown can be expensive, but the quirky restaurants and cafes outside of the Pearl District have reasonable prices. The **lunch trucks** dispersed throughout the city generally have tasty authentic food for cheap. Most restaurants in the city have a firm respect for **Happy hour,** making lighter fare in even the fanciest of Portland's restaurants accessible to the budget traveler before peak hours. Although Happy hour is usually held from 4:30 to 6:30pm, many bars and restaurants offer a late-night special as well.

▩ **Montage,** 301 SE. Morrison St. (☎234-1324; www.montageportland.com). Take bus #15 to the east end of the Morrison Bridge and walk under it. Straight-laced, mainstream Portlanders enter a surreal land of Cajun dining while seated Last-Supper-style underneath a macaroni-framed mural. Tricky to find, but well worth the effort. No reservations, but La Merde lounge is a cozy place to hang and wait for a table. Oyster shooters $1.75. Frog legs $9.50. Gator jambalaya $10.25. Open M and Su 6pm-2am, Tu-Th 11:30am-2pm and 6pm-2am, F 11:30am-2pm and 6pm-4am, Sa 6pm-4am. MC/V. ❷

▩ **Le Happy,** 1011 NW. 16th Ave. (☎226-1256; www.lehappy.com), between Lovejoy and Marshall St. Classy, chic, and perhaps the best date spot in all of Oregon. Wine and mixed drink bar attracts a fun and vibrant crowd of artists and inspired types at peak

Downtown Portland

▲ **ACCOMMODATIONS**
McMenamins White Eagle
Rock'n'Roll Hotel, **2**
Portland Hawthorne
Hostel (HI), **12**
Portland Hostel
Northwest (HI), **5**

◆ **FOOD**
Garbonzos, **1**
Montage, **10**
Muu-Muu's Big World Diner, **3**
Nicholas Restaurant, **9**
Palio Dessert and
Espresso House, **14**

♥ **THEATERS**
Bagdad Theater and Pub, **13**
Oregon Symphony
Orchestra, **8**
Portland Center Stage, **11**

🏛 **NIGHTLIFE**
Laurelthirst Public House, **4**
Ohm, **6**
Red Cap Garage
and Boxxes, **7**

ALSO SEE COLOR INSERT MAP

Bus Route
Streetcar
MAX
Fareless Square

PACIFIC
NORTHWEST

times, while couples fill up on fantastic, affordable crepes in a cozy atmosphere during dinner and late-night hours. Dinner and dessert crepes $4-8. Open M-Th 5pm-1am, F 5pm-2:30am, Sa 6pm-2:30am.

Nicholas Restaurant, 318 SE. Grand Ave. (☎235-5123; www.nicholasrestaurant.com), between Oak and Pine. Phenomenal Lebanese and Middle Eastern food in a relaxed atmosphere. The *mezzas* ($8.75) are fantastic. Sandwiches $6-8. Open M-Sa 10am-9pm, Su noon-9pm. Cash or check only. ❷

🅖 SIGHTS

PARKS AND GARDENS. Less than 2 mi. west of downtown, in the middle of the posh neighborhoods of **West Hills,** mammoth 🅜**Washington Park** has miles of beautiful trails and serene gardens. If possible, schedule in a day to enjoy the park to its fullest. *(Take MAX lightrail to Washington Park Station.)* The pride of the City of Roses, the **Portland International Rose Test Garden** is the most spectacular of Washington Park's attractions, boasting over 550 varieties of roses. The 4½ acres of crimson, pink, and yellow blooms are more than just a beautiful garden for people to gawk at; they're a testing ground for new breeds of roses. *(400 SW. Kingston St. ☎823-3636; www.rosegardenstore.org. Open daily 7:30am-9pm. Free.)* Just across from the Rose Garden, the peaceful and pristine **Japanese Garden** completes the park's one-two punch. *(611 SW. Kingston Ave. ☎223-1321; www.japanesegarden.com. Open Apr.-Sept. M noon-7pm, Tu-Su 10am-7pm; Oct.-Mar. M noon-4pm, Tu-Su 10am-4pm. Tours daily Apr.-Oct. 10:45am, 1, 2:30pm. $8, seniors and college students with ID $6.25, under 6 free.)* Forming the wooded backdrop for the rest of Washington Park's sights, the **Hoyt Arboretum** features 183 acres of trees and 21 mi. of trails. *(4000 SW. Fairview Blvd. ☎865-8733; www.hoytarboretum.org. Open daily 10am-6pm. Visitors Center open M-F 9am-4pm, Sa 9am-3pm. Free guided tours leave from the Visitors Center 1st Sa of each month at 10am.)* **Forest Park,** 5400 acres of wilderness stretching north from Washington Park, provides an idea of what the area was like before the arrival of Lewis and Clark. A web of trails and over 30 mi. of bike paths lead into abundant forests, past scenic overviews of Mt. Hood and Mt. St. Helens, and through idyllic picnic areas. The largest Ming-style garden outside of China, the **Classical Chinese Garden,** occupies an entire city block. *(NW. 3rd and Everett. ☎228-8131; www.portlandchinesegarden.org. Open daily Apr.-Oct. 9am-6pm; Nov.-Mar. 10am-5pm. Last entry 30min. before closing. Free guided tours at noon and 1pm daily. $7, seniors $6, students $5.50, under 6 free.)*

MUSEUMS. The **Portland Art Museum (PAM)** sets itself apart from the rest of Portland's arts scene on the strength of its spectacularly diverse collections, especially in Asian and Native American art. Special exhibitions for 2008 include "The Dancer: Degas, Ferain, and Toulouse-Lautrec in fin-de-siècle Paris" and "The Columbia River Gorge." *(1219 SW. Park, at Jefferson St. on the west side of S. Block Park. Bus #6, 58, 63. ☎226-2811; www.portlandartmuseum.org. Open Tu-W and Sa 10am-5pm, Th-F 10am-8pm, Su noon-5pm. In winter Th-F closes at 5pm. $10, students and seniors $9, ages 5-18 $6, under 5 free. Special exhibitions $2-5 more.)* The 🅜**Oregon Museum of Science and Industry (OMSI)** keeps visitors mesmerized with exhibits like an earthquake simulator chamber, an Omnimax theater, and the Kendall Planetarium. *(1945 SE. Water Ave., 2 blocks south of Hawthorne Blvd., next to the river. Bus #63. ☎797-4000; www.omsi.edu. Open early June-early Sept. daily 9:30am-7pm; early Sept.-early June Tu-Su 9:30am-5:30pm. Omnimax ☎797-4640. Shows on the hr. M-Tu and Su 10am-7pm, F-Sa 11am-9pm. Planetarium*

THE "BIG DEAL." Portland "Big Deal" Attractions pass offers entrance to 10 of Portland's top attractions at huge discounts. It's available at the Visitors Center (☎877-678-5263; www.portlandbigdeal.com) for $35, ages 5-18 $29.

☎ 797-4646. Shows daily every 30min. 11am-4:30pm. Museum $9, seniors and ages 3-13 $7. Omnimax $8.50/6.50, under 3 free. Planetarium $5.50. Combo ticket for museum, Omnimax, and either the planetarium or the submarine $19, seniors and ages 3-13 $15.)

OTHER SIGHTS. The still-operational **Pioneer Courthouse,** at 5th Ave. and Morrison St., is the centerpiece of the **Pioneer Courthouse Square.** Tourists and urbanites of every ilk hang out in the brick quadrangle known as "Portland's Living Room." (701 SW. 6th Ave. ☎ 223-1613.) On the southern edge of the NW. district, ⬛**Powell's City of Books** is a must-see for anyone who gets excited about the written word. Nine color-coded rooms and 77,000 sq. ft. of floor space that spans four floors on an entire city block contain more than four million new and used books. If you like to dawdle in bookstores, be sure to bring a sleeping bag and rations. (1005 W. Burnside St. Bus #20. ☎ 228-4651 or 800-878-7323; www.powells.com. Open daily 9am-11pm.) Across the street from Powell's, **Everyday Music** sells new and used CDs and **Buffalo Exchange** sells trendy "Portland approved" new and used clothing for a steal. Boutiques in the SE. district brim with affordable, hip clothes from creative and edgy independent designers.

The Grotto, a 62-acre Catholic sanctuary, has magnificent religious sculptures and shrines. (Sandy Blvd. at NE. 85th. ☎ 254-7371; www.thegrotto.org. Open daily late May-early Sept. 9am-7:30pm; early Sept.-late Nov. and Feb.-late May 9am-5:30pm; late Nov.-Jan. 9am-4pm.) The **Oregon Zoo** has gained fame for its successful efforts at ⬛**elephant breeding.** Exhibits include a goat habitat and a marine pool. (4001 SW. Canyon Rd. ☎ 226-1561; www.oregonzoo.com. Open daily Apr.-Sept. 8am-6pm; Oct.-Mar. 9am-4pm. $9.75, over $8.25, ages 3-11 $6.75, under 3 free; 2nd Tu of each month $2.) You can find a **farmers' market** in Portland every day of the week, but the **Portland Saturday Market,** under the Burnside Bridge between SW. 1st Ave. and SW. Naito Pkwy., is far and away the biggest and best, hosting all types of artisans selling their crafts and an international food court. (☎ 222-6072; www.saturdaymarket.org. Open Mar.-Dec. Sa 10am-5pm and Su 11am-4:30pm.)

🎵 🎆 ENTERTAINMENT AND FESTIVALS

Portland's daily newspaper, the *Oregonian*, lists upcoming events in its Friday edition (www.oregonlive.com/oregonian). The free cultural reader, the Wednesday *Willamette Week*, is a reliable guide to local music, plays, and art (www.wweek.com). For a more irreverent take on entertainment, check out the weekly **Portland Mercury** (www.portlandmercury.com), the go-to guide for Portland's twentysomethings. Founded in 1896, the **Oregon Symphony Orchestra,** 923 SW. Washington St., at the **Arlene Schnitzer Concert Hall,** plays classical and pop concerts from September to June. On Mondays and Sundays, students can buy $5 tickets one week before showtime. (☎ 228-1353 or 800-228-7343; www.orsymphony.org. Box office open M-F 9am-5pm, in **Symphony Season** also Sa 9am-5pm. $17-76; "Symphony Sunday" afternoon concerts $10-15.) **High Noon Tunes,** at Pioneer Courthouse Sq., hosts rock, jazz, folk, and world music. (☎ 223-1613. July-Aug. Tu and Th noon-1pm.)

Portland Center Stage, in the Gerding Theater at the Armory, will perform *Twelfth Night, Sometimes a Great Notion,* and *Doubt, a Parable* in its 2008 season. (☎ 274-6588; www.pcs.org. Open late Sept.-Apr. $27-55, under 30 $15 except F and Sa night and Su matinees.) The **Bagdad Theater and Pub,** 3702 SE. Hawthorne Blvd., is housed in a former vaudeville theater, with a separate pub in front. The theater plays third-run films, while the pub offers over 200 ales. (☎ 236-9234; www.mcmenamins.com. Some shows 21+. Open M-Sa 11am-1am, Su noon-midnight.) The **Portland Trail Blazers** play at the **Rose Garden Arena,** 1 Center Ct. (☎ 321-321; www.nba.com/blazers).

PACIFIC NORTHWEST

The **Northwest Film Center,** 934 SW. Salmon Ave., shows classics, documentaries, and off-beat flicks almost everyday. The Center also hosts the **Portland International Film Festival** in the last three weeks of February, with a constantly growing number of films from around the world. Screenings are at the **Whitsell Theatre** across the street, next to the Portland Art Gallery. (☎221-1156; www.nwfilm.org. Box office opens 30min. before each show; tickets also available online. $7, students and seniors $6.)

Portland's premier summer event is the **Rose Festival** (☎227-2681; www.rosefestival.org), during the first three weeks of June. In early July, the outrageously fun multi-day ▨**Waterfront Blues Festival** draws some of the world's finest blues artists. (☎973-3378 or 800-973-3378; www.waterfrontbluesfest.com. Admission $58 and 2 cans of food to benefit the Oregon Food Bank.) The **Oregon Brewers Festival,** on the last full weekend in July, is the continent's largest gathering of independent brewers at an incredible party at Tom McCall Waterfront Park, with food vendors and exhibits, live music, and over 70 hand-crafted beers from 14 states. (☎778-5917; www.oregonbrewfest.com. Tasting mug $4; tastings $1 each, $4 to fill. Under 21 must be accompanied by parent.) On **First Thursday** (www.firstthursdayportland.com) in the Pearl District, art galleries open their doors to visitors, and street performers line the bustling streets. ▨**Last Thursday** (www.artonalberta.org) on Alberta St. in the NE. district, is the NE. district's version, with a little less pomp and lot more funk.

◩ NIGHTLIFE

Once a rowdy frontier town, always a rowdy frontier town. Portland's clubs cater to everyone from the college athlete to the neo-goth aesthete. There are dozens of brewpubs throughout the city. Each neighborhood has a few happening blocks. In SE., **Belmont** is the place to be after dark; **21st Avenue** between Irving and Everett Streets in the NW.; five blocks of Historic **Mississippi Avenue** above N. Fremont St.; and **Alberta Street** between 15th and 33rd Ave. in the NE. district. **Old Town** and **Chinatown** in the W. district around Burnside are perhaps the best known hot spots, but keep within the 1st four streets of Burnside in the NW. after dark.

Doug Fir Lounge, 830 E. Burnside (☎231-9663; www.dougfirlounge.com). This restaurant-bar-lounge is the place to be according to locals. Hosts a plethora of local acts (see website for details) and draws a mostly twentysomething crowd. The late-night munchies (F-Sa midnight-2:15am; $5-6) will keep you going after most other bars have shut down. Domestic bottles $3. House wine $4. Well drinks $3. Happy hour daily 3-6pm. Bar open all day. Open daily 7am-2:30am.

Laurelwood NW Public House, 2327 NW. Kearney St. (☎228-5553; www.laurelwoodbrewpub.com). Victorian-era residence refurbished as a relaxed, welcoming pub, ideal for Happy hour or a low-key evening. A satellite of the Laurelwood Public House & Brewery downtown, the NW Public House serves hand-crafted organic microbrews and a full menu. Open daily 11am-11pm.

Red Cap Garage and Boxxes, 341 SW. 10th Ave. (☎221-7262; www.boxxes.com). 2 gay bars that become 1 around 10pm. Magic happens at the 23-screen video and karaoke bar in Boxxes, while Red Cap fills an upscale niche. Cover Th, F, and Sa $2-5 after 10pm. Open Tu-Su 3pm-2:30am.

CANNON BEACH   ☎503

Cannon Beach is home to an impressive array of boutiques, bakeries, and galleries, making it a more refined alternative to the commercialism and miles of strip-malls that have developed in many Oregon coastal towns. **Ecola State Park** ($3), at the north end of town, attracts picnickers, hikers, and surfers alike with its view of the dramatic volcanic coastline (☎368-5943. Open sunrise-sunset.) Ecola Point's view of hulking **Haystack Rock,** covered with seagulls, barnacles, puffins, and the occasional sea lion, is stunning. **Indian Beach,** accessible off U.S. 101 north of Cannon Beach, is a gorgeous surfing destination where surfers can catch waves between volcanic rock walls and then rinse off the salt in the nearby freshwater stream. **Sandcastle Day** transforms Cannon Beach's shores into a fantastic architectural menagerie on one Saturday in the middle of June.

Pleasant but pricey motels line Hemlock St. In the slightly less ritzy neighboring town of Seaside, ⬛**Seaside International Hostel (HI) ❶,** 930 N Holladay Dr., is immaculate, warm, and inviting, with nightly movies, a full kitchen, and an espresso bar. (☎738-7911; www.seasideinternational.net. Reception 8am-11pm. Free Wi-Fi. Internet access $1 per 15min. Canoe rental $10 per 2hr. Single kayak $12 per 2hr. Dorms $25, members $26; private rooms $64/57. Touring cyclists $2 off. MC/V.) **Oswald West State Park ❶,** 10 mi. south of Cannon Beach, is a tiny headland rainforest with 30 campsites accessible by a quarter-mile trail off U.S. 101. The park provides wheelbarrows for transporting gear from the parking lot. Beach and trailhead access and stunning scenery make the site so desirable that it can be difficult to find a spot on busy summer weekends. (☎800-551-6949. Open Mar.-Oct. First come, first served. Sites May-Sept. $14; Oct.-Apr. $10.) Most of the dining deals in Cannon Beach are down Hemlock St. in mid-town. With funky, fun decor and amazing homemade crab cakes ($9), ⬛**Cranky Sue's ❷,** 308 Fir St., "furiously good food" is a sure fix to even the foulest of moods. (☎436-0301; www.crankysues.com. Chowder $4. Sandwiches $6. Open M-Tu and Th-Su 11am-7pm.) **Bill's Tavern ❷,** 188 N. Hemlock St., is a local spot for down-to-earth eatin' and drinkin'. (☎436-2202. Pints $3.25. Burgers $6-8. Open M-Tu and Th-Su 11:30am-midnight, W 4:30pm-midnight. Kitchen closes around 9:30pm. D/MC/V.)

Cannon Beach lies 8 mi. south of Seaside, 42 mi. north of Tillamook on U.S. 101 and 79 mi. from Portland via U.S. 26. The four exits into town from U.S. 101 all lead to Hemlock St., which is lined with galleries and restaurants. Cannon Beach Shuttle-traverses the downtown area daily. Rides around downtown are free in a 6½ mi. loop from Les Shirley Park on the north end to Tolovana Park at the south end. (☎862-7433. Buses to Seaside $1.25.) Look for visitor info at the **Cannon Beach Chamber of Commerce Visitor Center,** 207 Spruce St. (☎436-2623; www.cannon-beach.org. Open M-Sa 10am-5pm, Su 11am-4pm.) **Mike's Bike Shop,** 248 N. Spruce St., rents mountain bikes. (☎436-1266 or 800-492-1266; www.mikesbike.com. Open daily 10am-6pm. $9 per hr., $30 per day. Beach tricycles $10 per 1½hr.) **Cannon Beach Police** (☎436-2811). **Post Office:** 163 N. Hemlock St. (☎436-2822. Open M-F 9am-5pm.) **Postal Code:** 97110.

NEWPORT   ☎541

After the miles of malls along U.S. 101, Newport's renovated waterfront area of pleasantly kitschy restaurants and shops is a delight. Newport's claim to fame, however, is the ⬛**Oregon Coast Aquarium,** 2820 SE. Ferry Slip Rd., at the south end of the bridge. This world-class aquarium housed Keiko, the much-loved orca star of the movie *Free Willy,* before he returned to his childhood waters near Iceland. (☎867-3474; www.aquarium.org. Open daily Memorial Day-Labor Day 9am-6pm; Labor Day to Memorial Day 10am-5pm. $13.25, seniors $11.25, ages 3-12 $7.75.) The **Mark O. Hatfield Marine Science Center** is the hub of Oregon State University's coastal research. The live octopus is off-limits, but sea anemones, slippery slugs, and bottom-dwelling fish await your curiosity in the touch tanks. Daily presentations and guided walks are available in the summer months. (2030 Marine Science Dr., at the south end of the bridge. ☎867-0100; www.hmsc.oregonstate.edu/visitor.

Open daily Memorial Day-Labor Day 10am-5pm; Labor Day-Memorial Day M and Th-Su 10am-4pm. Suggested donation $4, families $10.) Three miles to the north of Newport, you can explore the tide pools or ascend the lighthouse and see grey whales, harbor seals, bald eagles, and countless species of sea birds from the **Yaquina Head Outstanding Natural Area.** (☎574-3100. Open daily sunrise-sunset. Lighthouse open in summer 9am-4pm; in winter noon-4pm. $5 per vehicle.) In town, the wide, sandy ◙**Nye Beach** is perfect for relaxing along the coast. Bordered on either side by the **Newport Centers for Visual and Performing Arts,** Nye Beach is well-known as Newport's edgy artist enclave. Weekly entertainment, festivals, and outdoor events in Newport and neighboring towns are published in Friday's *Oregon Coast Today* and at www.oregoncoasttoday.com.

The serene ◙**Sylvia Beach Hotel ❸,** 267 NW Cliff St., at Nye Beach, has a hostel-style dorm and a variety of rooms uniquely decorated for the writers who inspired them. Try the Edgar Allen Poe room if you dare, but be sure to make reservations early. (☎265-5428 or 888-795-8422; www.sylviabeachhotel.com. Breakfast included. Dorms $30; private rooms $68-178. AmEx/MC/V.) Campgrounds teem with families seeking a weekend getaway in summer months; don't show up without a reservation. The stunning and heavily-wooded ◙**Beverly Beach State Park ❶,** 7 mi. north of Newport on Hwy. 101, has trails extending to Yaquina Head and Otter Rock, serene shoreline, and points for whale-watching. (☎265-9278 or 800-551-6949, for reservations 800-452-5687; www.oregonstateparks.org. 128 tent sites $17; 75 sites with water and electricity $21; 53 RV sites with full hookup $21. Oct.-Apr. $4 less.) One mile south of the Bay Bridge, **South Beach State Park ❶** has camping near the quiet beach. (☎867-4715, reservations 800-452-5687. Sites $4; RV sites $22.) Decorated entirely by local artists and boasting quirky entertainment ranging from acoustic gigs and local theater to gypsy music, punk hillbilly, and fire dancers, ◙**Cafe Mundo ❶,** at the corner of NW 2nd Court and Coast St., epitomizes Nye Beach's creative alternative spirit. The menu is as eclectic as the patrons who offer fish tacos ($6.50), sushi, seasonal specials (from $10) made with local products, plus a full range of vegetarian options. Cafe Mundo also plans on creating camp space; call in fall of 2007 to check. (☎574-8134. Open Tu-Th 2pm-10pm, F-Sa 2pm-midnight, Su 8am-2pm; in winter closed Tu.) The granddaddy of all Newport establishments, ◙**Mo's Restaurant ❷,** 622 Bay Blvd., is famous for its clam chowder ($4.25). If "Old Mo's" is packed, head across the street to **Mo's Annex ❷,** at 657 Bay Blvd., which dishes up the same food in a less historic atmosphere. (Mo's Restaurant: ☎265-2979; www.moschowder.com. Open daily 11am-10pm. Annex: ☎265-7512. Open M-W and F-Su 11am-9pm, Th 11am-10pm. AmEx/D/MC/V.) **Rogues Ales,** 2320 OSU Dr. (☎867-3600), is a commercial brewery and an icon in Newport, offering brewery tours, a tasting room, and a pub house.

Newport is bordered on the west by the foggy Pacific Ocean and on the south by Yaquina Bay. U.S. 101, known as the **Coast Highway,** divides east and west Newport. U.S. 20, known as **Olive Street,** bisects the north and south sides of town. Greyhound, 956 10th St. SW (☎265-2253 or 800-231-2222; www.greyhound.com), at Bailey St., runs **buses** to Portland (3½-5hr., 3 per day, $21), San Francisco (17-23hr., 3 per day, $95), and Seattle (7-9hr., 3 per day, $51). The **Greater Newport Chamber of Commerce,** 555 Coast Hwy. SW, provides tourist info. (☎265-8801 or 800-262-7844; www.newportchamber.org.) **Samaritan Pacific Communities Hospital** offers medical care. (☎265-2244. Open M-F 8:30am-5pm.) **Post Office:** 310 2nd St. SW. (☎800-275-8777. Open M-F 8:30am-5pm, Sa 10am-noon.) **Postal Code:** 97365.

EUGENE ☎541

Epicenter of the organic foods movement and a hippie haven, Eugene has a well-deserved liberal reputation. Home to the University of Oregon, Oregon's third-largest city is packed with college students during the school year but mellows out considerably in summer. Eugene's Saturday market, nearby outdoor activities, and overall sunny disposition charm every one of its visitors.

⬛🔢 ORIENTATION AND PRACTICAL INFORMATION. Eugene lies 111 mi. south of Portland on I-5. The main north-south arteries are, from west to east, **Willamette Street, Oak Street,** and **Pearl Street. High Street Highway 99** also runs east-west and splits in town—**6th Avenue** goes west, and **7th Avenue** goes east. The numbered avenues run east-west and increase toward the south. Eugene's main student drag, **13th Avenue,** leads to the **University of Oregon (U of O)** in the southeast of town. The Whiteaker area, around Blair Blvd. near 6th Ave., can be unsafe at night. Amtrak, 433 Willamette St. (☎687-1383; www.amtrak.com; open daily 5:15am-9pm), at 4th Ave., runs **trains** to Portland (2½-3hr., 5 per day, $19-32) and Seattle (6-8hr., 3 per day, $38-65). Greyhound 987 Pearl St. (☎344-6265; www.greyhound.com; open M-F 6am-9:30pm, Sa-Su 9:30am-9:30pm), at 10th Ave., runs **buses** to Portland (2-4hr., 8 per day, $20) and Seattle (6-9hr., 6 per day, $38). Lane Transit District (LTD) handles **public transit** in and around Eugene and Springfield. Buses also periodically run east to the MacKenzie Ranger Station, west to Veneta, and to several other rural destinations. Map and timetables are at the **LTD Service Center,** in Eugene Station at 11th Ave. and Willamette St. (☎687-5555; www.ltd.org. Major routes run M-F 6am-10:45pm, Sa 7:30am-10:45pm, Su 8:30am-7:30pm. $1.25, seniors and under 18 $0.60. Day pass $2.50/1.20.) The **Lane County Convention and Visitors Association** is at 754 Olive St., just off 8th St. (☎484-5307 or 800-547-5445; www.visitlanecounty.org. Courtesy phone. Free maps and **Internet** access. Open late May-early Sept. M-F 8am-5pm, Sa-Su 10am-4pm; early Sept.-late May closed Su.) The **Ranger Station,** about 60 mi. east of Eugene on Rte. 126, sells maps and Northwest Forest Passes ($5) for use at trailheads. (☎822-3381; www.fs.fed.us\r6\willamette. Open late May to mid-Oct. daily 8am-4:30pm; mid-Oct. to late May closed Sa-Su.) **Internet Access: Eugene Public Library,** 100 W. 10th Ave. (☎682-5450. Day pass $1. Open M-Th 10am-8pm, F-Su 10am-6pm.) **Post Office:** 520 Willamette St., at 5th Ave. (☎800-275-8777. Open M-F 8:30am-5:30pm, Sa 10am-2pm. Self-service open M-Sa 5am-7:30pm, Su 6am-7:30pm.) **Postal Code:** 97401.

🔢🔳 ACCOMMODATIONS AND FOOD. The cheapest motels are on E. Broadway and W. 7th Ave. Make reservations early; motels are packed on big football weekends. The newly renovated ⬛**Eugene Whiteaker Hostel ❶,** 970 W. 3rd Ave., offers clean and comfy dorm lodging and private rooms to guests, along with continental breakfast, Wi-Fi, pretty porches, and a big back yard. Unmatched hospitality makes the hostel a delightful place to stay and a difficult one to leave. (☎343-3335 or 206-5205; www.eugenewhiteakerhostel.com. Bike rental $10 per day. Laundry $2.50. Dorms $22; private rooms $30-45. Backyard camping $12, 2 people $20.) The **Eugene International Hostel ❶,** 2352 Willamette St., is a quaint neighborhood home just outside of the city, with a book-lined living room, full kitchen, Wi-Fi, and a mellow atmosphere. (☎349-0589. Check-in 5-10pm. Lockout 1-4pm. Dorms $20; private rooms from $30.) East on Rte. 58 and 126, the immense **Willamette National Forest ❶** is full of campsites. The Ranger Station (see above) has info and maps. (Most sites first-come, first-served, though some are reservable; for reservations call ☎877-444-6777, or book online at www.recreation.gov. Sites free-$18.) Eugene's downtown area specializes in gourmet food. The University hangout zone at 13th Ave. and Kincaid St. has grab-and-go joints, and natural food stores are everywhere. ⬛**Keystone Cafe ❶,** 395 W. 5th St., serves creative breakfast and lunch concoctions to vegans, vegetarians, and omnivores alike. (☎342-2075; www.keystonecafe.com. Pancakes $4.25. Breakfast burritos $6. Vegan burgers $7. Open M-Th 7am-2pm, F-Sa 7am-3pm, Su 8am-3pm. Cash or check only.) **Cafe**

A "PRE"MIER RUNNER

With one leg shorter than the other, the gangly young **Steve "Pre" Prefontaine** seemed an unlikely candidate for international acclaim in track and field. But the sleeper pick from the small town of Coos Bay took the world by storm as a college athlete at the University of Oregon in the early 70s, and in his short-lived career changed the face of distance running forever. He broke almost every American distance record, fanning hysteria for the sport that established Eugene as Track Town, USA.

Pre was on the rise and favored to win a gold in the 1976 Olympics in Montreal before a tragic car collision ended his career. He died at the age of 24 in Eugene on the way home from a party but has gone down in history as arguably the best American distance runner to have ever lived. Today, "Pre's Rock," the spot where he died, has become a mecca of sorts for runners around the world.

In 2008, for the first time in nearly 30 years, the Olympic Trials for Track and Field will return to Hayward Field, Pre's former training grounds, at the University of Oregon.

Yumm! ❶, 130 Oakway Ctr., offers funky fresh "Yumm bowls" ($4-7), staples for Eugene veg-heads. (☎225-0121; www.cafeyumm.com. Open M-F 8am-8pm, Sa 10am-8pm, Su 10am-5pm). Additional location at 1801 Willamette St. (☎431-0204. Open M-F 8am-9pm, Sa 10am-9pm, Su 10am-5pm.)

◪ SIGHTS. Every Saturday the area around 8th Ave. and Willamette St. fills up for the popular ◪**Saturday Market,** with over 300 artisans hawking everything from hemp shopping bags to tarot readings. Next to the shopping stalls is the **farmers' market,** where you can buy organic produce among lots of food booths and live music all day. (☎686-8885; www.eugenesaturdaymarket.org. Open Apr. to mid-Nov. Sa 10am-5pm; May-Oct. also Tu 10am-3pm. Free parking and admission.) Take time to see the ivy-covered halls that set the scene for National Lampoon's Animal House at the **University of Oregon,** E. 13th Ave. and Agate St. (☎346-3014; www.uoregon.edu. Tours M-F 10am and 2pm, Sa 10am.) Since the 70s, Eugene, or "Track Town, USA," has been a production powerhouse and mecca for world-renowned track & field athletes, including the late distance running legend Steve Prefontaine (see **A "Pre"mier Runner,** at left). The only city to host three consecutive Olympic trials (in 1972, 76, and 80), Eugene is ecstatic to have the trials return to **Hayward Field,** 15th and Agate St., in the heart of U of O's campus. Tickets to the trial held June 30 through July 6, 2008, sold out in early 2007, but all are welcome to the celebration. Festivals with beer gardens, live music entertainment, and large-screen televised coverage of the trials will commence next-door to Hayward Field on June 26 and continue through the last day of the trials on July 6, 2008. Visit www.eugene08.com or call Lane County Convention and Visitor's Association (see above) for details. Monday's *Eugene Weekly* (www.eugeneweekly.com) lists concerts and local events. During the University of Oregon's Grammy award-winning **Oregon Bach Festival,** which runs for 17 days in late June and early July every year, Baroque authority Helmut Rilling conducts performances of Bach and great composers he influenced. (☎346-5666 or 800-457-1486; www.oregonbachfestival.com. Range of lectures, concerts, and events free-$60.) The vast ◪**Oregon Country Fair,** the most exciting event of the summer, takes place in **Veneta,** 12 mi. west of town on Rte. 126. Started in 1969 as a fundraiser for a local school, the fair has become a magical annual gathering of hippies, musicians, misfits, and activists. (☎343-4298; www.oregoncountryfair.org. Every year on the weekend after the 4th of July; in 2008 July 11-13.)

🏃 OUTDOOR ACTIVITIES. The **Ridgeline Park** system consists of over 1000 acres of ridgeline and 12 mi. of trails for bikers and hikers centered around Spencer's Butte (2054 ft. high) and the marker of the southern tip of the Willamette Valley, from which you can see all of Eugene and surrounding areas. The trails are great for wildlife viewing and are an invigorating break from the hustle and bustle of downtown Eugene. **Alton Baker Park,** Eugene's largest park (over 400 acres), is not far from the downtown action. In addition to providing miles of trails for outdoor enthusiasts, Alton Baker Park hosts festivals and events and is close to some of Eugene's bigger tourist attractions. The large, popular Cougar Lake features the Terwilliger Hot Springs, known by all as **Cougar Hot Springs.** Drive through the town of Blue River, 60 mi. east of Eugene on Rte. 126, and then turn right onto Aufderheide Dr. (Forest Service Rd. 19), and follow the road 7¼ mi. as it winds on the right side of Cougar Reservoir. (Open dawn-dusk. Clothing optional. No glass permitted. $5 parking fee.)

East of Eugene, Rte. 126 runs adjacent to the beautiful McKenzie River, and on a clear day, the **Three Sisters of the Cascades** are visible. Just east of the town of McKenzie Bridge, about 70 mi. east of Eugene, the road splits into a scenic byway loop; Rte. 242 climbs east to the lava fields of McKenzie Pass, while Rte. 126 turns north over Santiam Pass and meets back with Rte. 242 in Sisters. Often blocked by snow until July, Rte. 242 tunnels between **Mount Washington** and the **Three Sisters Wilderness** before rising to McKenzie Pass. The 26 mi. **McKenzie River Trail** starts 1½ mi. west of the ranger station and leads through mossy forests to two of Oregon's most spectacular waterfalls—**Koosah Falls** and **Sahalie Falls.** Ambitious hikers can sign up for overnight permits at the ranger station and head for the high country, where hiking opportunities are endless.

📻 NIGHTLIFE. Come nightfall, bearded hippies mingle with pierced anarchists and muscle-bound frat boys in Eugene's eclectic nightlife scene. **☒Sam Bond's Garage,** 407 Blair Blvd., is a laid-back hangout in the Whitaker neighborhood. There is live music Tuesday to Sunday night, complemented by an always-evolving selection of local microbrews pints for $3.50. (☎431-6603; www.sambonds.com. Microbrew glasses $2.75, pints $3.50. Pizza $3.50 per slice. M night bingo. Tu bluegrass. Su Irish music. 21+ after 8:30pm. Cover varies. Happy hour daily 4-7pm; pints $2.50. Open daily 4pm-2:30am.) **John Henry's,** 77 W. Broadway, is Eugene's prime site for punk, reggae, and virtually any other kind of live music. Call or check the website for schedule and covers. John Henry's also hosts a Broadway Review Burlesque show on Sundays at 10pm. (☎342-3358; www.johnhenrysclub.com. Open daily 9pm-2:30am.) **Diablo's Downtown Lounge,** 959 Pearl St., is a casual scene with pool tables upstairs and a hip crowd shaking their thangs downstairs. (☎343-2346; www.diablosdowntown.com. W-Sa live music. Cover at least $3. 21+ after 9pm. Open M-F 11am-2:30am, Sa-Su 1pm-2:30am.)

WILLAMETTE VALLEY

Draw a straight line across the globe from the heart of French Burgundian wine country and eventually you'll plow into Oregon's Willamette Valley, a vibrant and burgeoning center of New World wine production and the home of over 250 of Oregon's 300 wineries and more vineyards than you could count. Situated along the 45th parallel, Willamette's cool climate is ideal for growing the mighty Pinot grape, and some of the world's leading Pinot Noirs and Pinot Gris come from the region. Oregon's generally laid-back and friendly demeanor affords wine tasting in the Willamette an accessibility you won't find in the Old World or in the more commercialized Napa region. With endless wineries to visit and routes to choose from,

STAY CLASSY, EAGER OENOPHILE. Too much freeloading can be upsetting and hurtful to winery owners. Although most wineries welcome visitors to sample their wines, refrain from excessive "free tasting" if you have no intention of buying a bottle. At the same time, visitors should not feel coerced into purchasing wine after a free sample.

there's no wrong way to take on the expansive American Viticultureal Area (AVA) of the Willamette Valley. The best way to visit the following wineries while on a budget is to use nearby towns (Eugene for Lane County Wineries, and Salem for Eola-Amity Hills) as the foundation for exploration.

LANE COUNTY WINERIES   ☎541

The best way to explore Lane Country wineries is by using the town of Eugene as a home base. From Eugene, take Hwy. 126 east to Veneta, then head south on Territorial Hwy. Each winery has clearly-marked turn-offs from the highway. The following wineries are listed in geographical order from Eugene. Named not for the honey taste of its award-winning Rieslings, but for the voluptuous curves of the vineyard's hillsides, the sophisticated and relaxed **Sweet Cheeks Winery and Vineyards,** 27007 Briggs Hill Rd., has a tasting room with a chic outdoor terrace overlooking rose-lined fields. "Twilight Tastings" (in summer F 6-9pm) offer live music, barbecue facilities, and spectacular sunset views. (☎349-9463 or 877-309-9463; www.sweetcheekswinery.com. Open daily noon-6pm. Free tasting. Tours upon request.) Across the street, Lane County's oldest winery, **Silvan Ridge at Himman Vineyards,** 27012 Briggs Hill Rd., has views of Sweet Cheeks' "sweet cheeks" and a variety of great wines beyond the Willamette's signature Pinots. Their semi-sparkling Muscat makes waves among seasoned wine enthusiasts and those who've never had a sip. (☎345-1945; www.silvanridge.com. Free tasting. Open daily noon-5pm.) Just beyond the beaten path, **Iris Hill Winery,** 82110 Territorial Rd., at Iris Hill Ln., is named for the cascades of blues and purples that wash the hillsides in early spring. The wine, along with the enthusiastic staff, is well-worth the brief dirt road trek if the tasting room is open. (☎895-9877; www.iris-hill.com. Open Th-Su noon-5pm and by appointment. Tasting $5 for 7 wines, refunded upon purchase.) The largest winery in Oregon, the titan **King Estate,** 80854 Territorial Rd., reigns over its competitors as lord of Lane County. While tastings are on the pricier side (starting at $6 for 4 wines), the sprawling campus is a sight to behold. In summer, tours run daily noon-5pm on the hour. (☎942-9874; www.kingestate.com. Tasting room and restaurant open daily 11am-9pm.) The outdoor **Market Place at King Estate** promises a more casual and relaxed atmosphere with home-grown organic produce, fresh-cut flowers, special events with local artisans, and barbecue lunches. (Open seasonally Th-Su 11am-6pm.) Tucked away in evergreen groves and overlooking a private lake, the cozy **Chateau Lorane,** 27415 Siuslaw Rd., is known for originality, using rare grapes like Huxelrebe, Baco Noir, and Marachel Foch to produce stellar and creative wines. Honey Mead wines, made with huckleberries, raspberries, and apricots, are a treat on a hot summer's day. (☎942-8028; www.chateaulorane.com. Free tasting. Open daily June to mid-Oct. noon-5pm. MC/V.) Near Exit 176 off I-5 just south of Eugene, the family-owned and operated **Saginaw Vineyard,** 80247 Delight Valley Rd., exudes country charm, with tastings in a cozy red barn surrounded by sheep pastures and sunflowers. Specializing in fruity blackberry and blueberry wines, in addition to the staple Pinots, Saginaw is a quaint repose from some of its larger-scale neighbors (☎942-1364; www.saginawwineyard.com. Free tasting. Tasting room open daily 11am-5pm.)

EOLA-AMITY HILLS   ☎503

Easily explored as a Salem-based region, Eola-Amity hills is part of the Willamette Valley AVA and lies in the northern area of the valley. From Salem, head north on Rte. 221. Wineries below are listed in geographical order. ◪**Redhawk Winery, Inc.,** 2995 Michigan City Ave., 3 mi. north of Salem on Hwy 221, prides itself on being "not stiffy and stuffy," with creative, unpretentious wines like its signature Pinot Noir "Grateful Red"—a steal at $12 a bottle. Picnic tables and stunning views make Redhawk the perfect place to spend a weekend afternoon. (☎362-1596; www.redhawkwine.com. Free tasting. Open daily 11am-5pm. AmEx/MC/V.) **Cristom Vineyards** brings a smooth "New World" style to their Pinots, and festive flowers and friendly staff make the tasting room a fun stop. (☎375-3068; www.cristomwines.com. Tasting $5, refunded upon purchase. Open in summer M and W-Su 11am-5pm; low season Sa-Su 11am-5pm.) **Witness Tree,** 711 Spring Valley Rd. NW, next door to Cristom, is named for the 200-year-old tree that rests in the middle of the vineyards, a former plot marker for settlers fresh off the Oregon Trail. Their most delightful wines bear the names of the winemakers' grandchildren. (☎585-7874. Free tasting. Tasting room open daily 11am-5pm.) **Bethel Heights Vineyard,** 6060 Bethel Heights Rd. NW, teems with sophistication and staff as sunny as its glass-paned tasting rooms, eager for seasoned wine enthusiasts. Those new to tasting can experience the award-winning Pinot Noirs of one of the oldest and most highly acclaimed wineries in central Willamette. (☎581-0943; www.bethelheights.com. Free tasting. Tasting room open in summer Tu-Sa 11am-5pm; lowseason Sa-Su 11am-5pm.) The big red barn atop the hillside differentiates ◪**Amity Vineyards,** 18150 SE Amity Vineyards Rd., off 99W, left from Rice Rd., from the patchwork green acres of grape fields on rolling hills that surround it, and its reputation for being "not too fancy and just a little funky" sets Amity apart from some of the slightly stuffy big-name producers of northern Willamette. (☎835-2362; www.amityvineyards.com. Tasting room open daily June-Sept. 11am-5pm; Oct.-May noon-5pm.) If the world of wine is a mystery to you, visit the **Oregon Wine Tasting Room at Bellevue Market,** 19690 SW Hwy. 8, in McMinnville, where friendly and endlessly knowledgeable staff will answer all of your burning questions, letting you taste wines from their collection of over 300 wines from 100 different Oregon wineries. They also provide information and directions for the other wineries in the area. (☎843-3787. Tasting daily 11am-5:45pm.)

SALEM   ☎503

The home of Willamette University and the second largest urban center in Oregon, Salem gives off the vibe of a much smaller city. As the center of state government, Salem isn't best-known for tourism, but the history and fine museums, renowned wineries, and attractions like the Oregon State Fair draw throngs of visitors.

✦ ▐ ORIENTATION AND TRANSPORTATION

Salem is 47 mi. south of **Portland** and 64 mi. north of **Eugene** on **I-5.** While I-5 runs north and south through the city, **Highway 22** runs east and west. **Willamette University** and the **capitol building** dominate the center of the city, and the nearby shops make up the heart of downtown. To reach downtown, take Exit 253 off I-5, or take Hwy. 22W. Street addresses are divided into quadrants: the **Willamette River** divides east from west, while **State Street** divides southeast from northeast.

> **Trains: Amtrak,** 500 13th St. SE (☎371-7130 or 800-872-7245), across from the Visitors Center. Open daily 6:15am-7:45pm. To: **Portland** (1½hr., 4 per day, $11-19); **Seattle** (5-7hr., 2 per day, $34-57); **San Francisco** (17hr., 1 per day, $67-137).

Buses: Greyhound, 450 Church St. NE (☎362-2428). Open M-F 5:30am-8:30pm, Sa 5:30am-8:30pm. To: **Portland** (1½hr., 9 per day, $10); **Eugene** (1½-2hr., 10 per day, $14); **Seattle** (6hr., 7 per day, $31).

Local Transportation: Cherriots Customer Service Office, 220 High St. NE (☎588-2877; www.cherriots.org), provides monthly passes ($25) and free bus maps. Routes leave from High St. from the courthouse every hr. M-F 6:15am-9:30pm, Sa 7:45am-9:30pm. All buses have bike racks. $1, over 60 or disabled $0.50, under 19 $0.75.

Taxis: Salem Yellow Cab Co. (☎362-2411). $2.50 base, $1.90 per mi. 24hr.

ⓩ PRACTICAL INFORMATION

Tourist Information: 1313 Mill St. SE (☎581-4325 or 800-874-7012; www.scva.org), in the Mission Mill Museum complex; take I-5 Exit 253 and follow signs. Open M-F 8:30am-5pm, Sa 10am-5pm.

Police: 555 Liberty St. SE (☎588-6123), in City Hall room 130.

Hospital: Salem Hospital, 665 Winter St. SE (☎561-5200).

Internet Access: Salem Public Library, 585 Liberty St. SE (☎588-6315; www.salemlibrary.org). Free Internet access on 25 computers. Limit 1hr. Metered parking in the adjacent garage. Open June-Aug. Tu-Th 10am-9pm, F-Sa 10am-6pm; Sept.-May also open Su 1-5pm.

Post Office: 1050 25th St. SE (☎800-275-8777). Open M-F 8:30am-5pm. **Postal Code:** 97301.

⚑ ⚑ ACCOMMODATIONS AND CAMPING

The Visitors Center has a list of **B&Bs,** which provide comfortable and often classy lodgings on the pricier side. A number of cheaper hotels line Lancaster Dr. along the length of I-5, and camping options are also available, including **Silver Falls State Park ❷**(see Sights, below).

Salem Campground and RV, 3700 Hagers Grove Rd., SE (☎581-6736 or 800-826-9605; www.salemrv.com). Take Exit 253 off I5. Has tent and full-hookup RV sites a short drive from downtown. Plenty of amenities and the only camping available within city limits. Tent sites $18; RV sites $24. MC/V. ❶

Crossland Economy Studios, 3535 Fisher Ln. (☎363-7557; www.crosslandstudios.com). Provides clean and cozy furnished studios with kitchenettes. Laundry, cable, Wi-Fi. Office open daily 7am-11pm. Singles from $46. Reduced weekly rates. AmEx/D/MC/V. ❷

McMenamins Hotel Oregon, 310 N.E. Evans St. (☎472-8427 or 888-472-8427; www.mcmenamins.com). In downtown McMinnville: take a left onto 3rd St. off of 99W, which becomes Adams St. A fun and edgy place to rest your head after a day in the Willamette wine country. Enjoy a microbrew or local wine at the legendary rooftop bar, which overlooks the countryside and is the highest point in Yamhill County. Singles from $50. ❸

🍴 🍷 FOOD AND NIGHTLIFE

Salem is no city for the budget gourmet, but restaurants pride themselves on using organic and sustainable goods from local producers. Groceries await at **Roth's,** 702 Lancaster Dr. NE. (☎585-5770. Open daily 6am-10:30pm.) Hit the **farmers' market,** at the corner of Marion and Summer St., for local produce and crafts. (☎585-8264; www.salemsaturdaymarket.com. Open May-Oct. Sa 9am-3pm.)

Off-Center Cafe, 1741 Center St. NE (☎363-9245). Mismatched furniture and local banter fill this quirky diner tucked away just off Center St. Offers a good selection of reasonably-priced burgers, soups, and scrambles ($3-8). Open Tu-F 7am-2:30pm, W-Sa 6-9pm, Sa-Su 8am-2pm. ❷

Fuji Rice Time, 159 High St. SE (☎364-5512; www.fujiricetime.com). Serves traditional Japanese food in a calm atmosphere to a local crowd. Grab a seat at the counter to watch the chef at work while you nibble on sushi ($4-7). Lunch bowls $5-7. Dinner entrees $12-18. Open M-F 11am-2:30pm and 5-9pm, Sa 5-9pm. MC/V. ❷

Boon's Treasury, 88 Liberty St. NE (☎399-9063; www.meminamins.com), in the restored Oregon State Treasury and General Store from the 1860s. Great beer, great music, and great company. Microbrews $3.15 per pint. Burgers $3.45. W-Sa live music ranging from alternative and rock to bluegrass. No cover. 21+ after 9pm. Happy hour 4-6pm and 10pm-midnight. Open M-Th 11am-midnight, F-Sa 11am-1am, Su noon-11pm.

◉ ♫ SIGHTS AND ENTERTAINMENT

STATE CAPITOL. This gigantic marble building, topped by a 23 ft. gilt-gold statue of the "Oregon Pioneer," is located in the heart of Salem. *(900 Court St. NE. Bounded by Court St. to the north, Waverly St. to the east, State St. to the south, and Cottage St. to the west. ☎986-1388. Open M-F 10am-6pm. In summer, a free tour to the top of the rotunda and a tour of the various chambers leave every hr.; call for low-season tours.)*

SILVER FALLS STATE PARK. A 7 mi. loop trail has spectacular views and passes by 10 waterfalls. Those with less time on their hands can check out **South Falls,** at the head of the Canyon Trail and only an eighth of a mile from the main day-use parking lot. *(Take Rte. 22 east for 5 mi., then take the exit for Rte. 214N and follow it for about 18 mi. ☎873-8681, camping reservations 800-452-5687; www.oregonstateparks.org $3.)*

FESTIVALS AND FETES. Salem celebrates the end of summer in the 12 days leading up to Labor Day with the annual **Oregon State Fair.** With a whirl of rides, baking contests and performances, Salem is invaded and transformed from a picture of complacent suburbia to a barnyard celebration. *(2330 17th St. NE, at the Expo Center. ☎947-3247 or 800-833-0011; www.oregonstatefair.org. Open M-Th and Su 10am-10pm, F-Sa 10am-11pm. Tickets available in advance online. $7, over 65 $3, ages 6-12 $2, slightly higher at gate.)* During the 3rd weekend of July, the Salem Art Association hosts the free **Salem Art Fair and Festival** in Bush's Pasture Park. While the food booths do brisk business and the local wineries pour from their most recent vintage, the artsy and crafty display their wares as bands strum away the afternoon. The Visitors Center has info on the fair and on local wineries. *(600 Mission St. SE. ☎581-2228; www.sale-mart.org/fair.)* February 14, 2009 marks the **150th anniversary** of Oregon statehood and the beginning of a six-month-long birthday party for the Beaver state from Valentine's Day through the Oregon State Fair, with a special pre-statehood exhibit at the **Mission Mill Museum,** 1313 Mill St. SE, and raucous festivities throughout the summer. *(Call the Visitors Center or visit www.oregon150.org for details.)* Apart from the birthday party, the Museum is a sight to behold in and of itself, bringing visitors inside a 19th century woolen mill and three restored Mission houses from the 1840s. *(☎585-7012; www.missionmill.org. Open M-Sa 10am-5pm. Tours daily. Adults $8, seniors $7, youth $4. MC/V.)*

BEND   ☎541

Surrounded by a dramatic landscape, with volcanic remnants to the south, the Cascades to the west, and the Deschutes River running through its heart, Bend attracts outdoors enthusiasts from all over the Pacific Northwest. Its proximity to wilderness areas makes Bend an unbeatable base for hiking, rafting, and skiing, while the charming downtown is packed with restaurants, pubs, and shops. Set-

PACIFIC NORTHWEST

tled in the early 1800s as "Farewell Bend," a pioneer trail waystation along the Deschutes, Bend is no longer a well-kept secret. SUVs toting bikes, boards, or boats (or all three) on top have replaced covered wagons, and the Three Sisters to the west are viewed as insurance against boredom, not a daunting obstacle.

✦ ⌘ ORIENTATION AND TRANSPORTATION

Bend is 160 mi. southeast of Portland and 144 mi. north of Klamath Falls on **US 97,** and 100 mi. southeast of Mt. Hood via **US 26.** US 97 (Bend Parkway) bisects the town. West along the Deschutes River is downtown; **Wall Street** and **Bond Street** are the two main arteries. Avenues run east-west and are labeled alphabetically starting in the south. Streets run north-south and are numbered increasing toward the west. From east to west, Franklin Ave. becomes Riverside Blvd.; at the edge of Drake Park, Tumalo Ave. becomes Galveston Ave.; Greenwood Ave. becomes Newport Ave.; 14th St. becomes Century Dr. and is the first leg of the **Cascade Lakes Highway.** Grab free useful maps of the city and surrounding scenic byways at the Visitors Center.

Buses: Bend Oregon Bus Station, 1555 NE Forbes Rd., in the Lava Lanes Bowling Center lobby. (☎382-2151). Tickets may also be purchased online at www.greyhound.com. Station open daily 10am-3pm. To **Portland** (6¼hr., 1 per day, $48). **Central Oregon BREEZE** (☎389-7469 or 800-847-0157; www.cobreeze.com) shuttles people to and from Portland daily, with stops at the Portland airport. Shuttles from Bend depart at 7:30 and 11am. Shuttles from Portland depart at 1:30 and 6pm. Call or visit website for schedule and pickup locations. 4-4½hr. One way $45, round-trip 81; seniors and students $40/72; ages 2-10 half price with adult. BREEZE available for chartered trips.

Bend Area Transit (BAT), 575 NE 15th Street, Ste. B (☎322-5870; www.bendareatransit.com). Bend's new bus system. Single ride $1, unlimited day pass $2. Discounts for seniors and disabled.

Taxi: Owl Taxi, 1919 NE 2nd St. (☎382-3311). $2 base, $2.50 per mi. 24hr.

🛈 PRACTICAL INFORMATION

Visitor Info: Bend Visitors and Convention Bureau, 917 NW Harriman St. (☎382-8048 or 800-949-6086; www.visitbend.com). Offers a mother lode of brochures in addition to an "Attractions and Activities Guide" and a map of the area. Open M-Sa 9am-5pm, Sa 10am-4pm.

Outdoor Information: Bend/Fort Rock District Ranger Station, 1230 NE 3rd St. #A262 (☎383-4000; www.fs.fed.us/r6/deschutes), has additional info on Deschutes National Forest. Open M-F 7:45am-4:30pm. **Oregon Department of Fish and Wildlife,** 61374 Parrell Rd. (☎388-6363; www.dfw.state.or.us), sells fishing licenses for $12 per day; inquire about hunting permits. Open M-F 8am-5pm.

Equipment Rental:

Redpoint Climbers Supply, just off US 97 in **Terrebonne** at 975 Smith Rock Way (☎923-6207; www.redpointclimbing.com or www.goclimbing.com). They'll have what you need to replace the #2 cam that you just couldn't get out of the crack. Also has clothing and info on local routes. Open M 9am-8pm, Tu-Th and Sa 8am-8pm, F 8am-9pm, Su 8am-6pm. **First Ascent Climbing Services** (☎800-325-5462; www.goclimbing.com) has lessons for first-timers. Private lessons $230 per ½ day; groups $90-130 per person per ½ day. Equipment included.

Sunnyside Sports, 930 NW Newport Ave. (☎382-8018; www.sunnysidesports.com). Front suspension bikes ($15 per ½ day, $20 per full day, each additional day $10), full suspension bikes ($25 per ½ day, $40 per full day; each additional day $20), road bikes (first day $40, each additional day $20), cross-country skis (first day $15-20, each additional day $5), and snow shoes ($10 per day). Trail maps $9-11. Open daily mid-May to Oct. 9am-7pm; winter hours vary.

PURCHASE YOUR PASSES. Visitors need parking permits to park at trailheads, and they must be obtained at a Visitors Center or a sporting outfitter. **Tumalo State Park** and **Deschutes National Forest** require different passes. (Generally $5 per day, $30 per year.) At Smith Rock State Park, passes can be purchased for $3 from a park ranger or an automatic machine with exact change. Without a permit, you'll have to leave the park. ●

Pine Mountain Sports, 255 SW Century Dr. (☎385-8080; www.pinemountainsports.com). Rents cross-country skis, mountain bikes, and backcountry hiking and camping gear. Tents $10, sleeping bag $10, backpacks $10 per day. Cross-country ski package $10 per ½ day, $15 per full day. Snowshoes $10 per ½ day, $15 per full day. Splitboards $20 per ½ day, $30 per full day. Hard tail mountain bikes $20 per ½ day, $25 per full day. Front suspension bikes $35 per ½ day $35, $45 per full day. Road bikes $35 per ½ day, $45 per full day. Open Apr.-Oct. M-Sa 10am-7pm, Su 10am-6pm; winter daily 8am-6pm.

Skjersaas, 130 SW Century Dr. (☎382-2154; www.skibend.com). Impossible to pronounce, but well-known for the lowest rates in town, Skjersaas (SHEER-shaws) is the go-to place for downhill ski rentals. Ski and snowboard rental packages (skis, poles, boots, and bindings) are $25 per day, with every 4th day free. Junior rentals $15 per day. Performance demo rentals $40 per day. Open M-Th 8am-6pm, F 8am-7pm, Sa-Su 7:30am-7pm.

Police: 555 NE 15th St. (☎388-0170).

Medical Services: St. Charles Medical Center, 2500 NE Neff Rd. (☎382-4321).

Internet Access: Bend Public Library, 601 NW Wall Ave. (☎617-7040; www.dpls.lib.or.us). Free. Open M-Th 10am-8pm, F 10am-6pm, Sa 10am-5pm, Su 1-5pm.

Post Office: 2300 NE 4th St. (☎318-5068). Open M-F 8:30am-5:30pm, Sa 10am-1pm. **Postal Code:** 97701.

ACCOMMODATIONS AND CAMPING

Most of the cheapest motels line 3rd St. on the fringe of downtown, and rates are generally affordable. Camping in the national forest is cheap and pleasant.

Deschutes National Forest, 1645 NE. Hwy. 20, west of town. Maintains a huge number of lakeside campgrounds. Backcountry camping in the national forest area is free, though Northwest Forest Pass required to park at trailheads. Contact the Bend/Ft. Rock Ranger District Office (above) for more info. $10-14 per tent. ❶

Tumalo State Park, 62976 O.B. Riley Rd. (general info ☎388-6055, reservations 800-452-5687), 4 mi. north of Bend off US 20W. Popular riverside campsites in loop. Though the campground can at times be crowded with people, curious chipmunks generally vastly outnumber humans. Lots of tubing nearby. Tumalo day-use pass ($3) required to park at trailheads and boat ramps. Solar showers $2. 65 sites, each $17; 22 full RV sites, each $22; 7 yurts, each $29; hiker and biker sites $4. MC/V. ❶

Rainbow Motel, 154 NE Franklin Ave, 2 blocks from Hwy. 97. (☎382-1821 or 877-529-2877). Large, clean rooms with fridge, microwave, and TV. Continental breakfast included. Singles $45; doubles $59. Lower weekly and winter rates. ❸

FOOD AND NIGHTLIFE

Bend has many affordable restaurants and one of the highest per capita ratios of breweries to people of any city in the world. Four mega-markets line S. 3rd St.

🗗 **Mother's Juice Cafe,** 1255 NW Galveston Ave. (☎318-0989). Friendly staff blends exquisite organic smoothies for $4.25, with ginkgo biloba or ginseng for another $0.50.

Food menu standouts include the Mt. Everest sandwich ($7, half $5.25). Open in summer M-F 7am-7pm, Sa 8am-7pm, Su 8am-6pm; closes daily at 5pm in winter. ❷

Pizza Mondo, 811 NW Wall St. (☎330-9093). Once the sun sets, you'll have to fight through the crowds to get a slice of New York-style pizza ($3) or a 15 in. creative pie ($14), but it's worth it. Daily lunch special (slice, salad, and soda) for $5. Open M-Th and Su 11:30am-9:30pm, F-Sa 11am-10pm; in winter M-Th and Su closes at 9pm. ❷

D&D Bar & Grill, 927 NW Bond St. (☎382-4592). A Bend institution since 1943 with bullet holes still in the ceiling from a historic bar brawl. Grill serves full breakfast, lunch, and dinner menus all day. Try a Bloody Mary with D&D's secret spicy veggie-infused vodka, but be forewarned of the bar's signature double pour. Happy hour daily 4:30-6:30pm; drafts $2, well drinks $3. 21+ after 9pm. Open daily 7am-2am.

👁 ❋ SIGHTS AND FESTIVALS

▨HIGH DESERT MUSEUM. The museum is one of the premier natural and cultural history museums in the Pacific Northwest. Life-size dioramas recreate rickety cabins, cramped immigrant workshops, and Paiute tipis. The desertarium provides a peek at shy desert creatures. Don't miss the 7000 sq. ft. wing featuring birds of prey in their natural habitats, like the endangered spotted owl. *(59800 Hwy. 97 S, 3½ mi. south of Bend on U.S. 97. ☎382-4754; www.highdesertmuseum.org. Open daily 9am-5pm. $15, over 66 $12, ages 5-12 $9. Entry good for 2+ days.)*

BREWERIES. Bend's youngest brewery, ▨**Silver Moon Brewing Company,** 24 NW Greenwood Ave., is the least institutionalized, and its popularity is on the rise. The staff is generally happy to give brewery tours upon request during off-peak hours. Silver Moon has the best deal in town—64 oz. "Growler" microbrews are $6.50. Try the Hop Knob I.P.A. or Badlands Bitter. (Light pub menu served all day. Live music acts ranging from bluegrass and folk to hip hop Wednesday and Saturday nights. ☎388-8331; www.silvermoonbrewing.com. Free Wi-Fi. 21+ after 8pm. Open M-Sa 11am-10pm, Su 11am-3pm.) Beer enthusiasts far and wide come to Bend to see the mecca of breweries, **Deschutes Brewery,** 901 SW Simpson St., and check out how the flagstaff Black Butte Porter and Mirror Pond Pale Ale are made. *(☎385-8606; www.deschutesbrewery.com. Tasting room open Tu-Sa 12-5pm. Tours Tu-F at 1, 2:30, and 4pm, Sa upon request.)* Visit the **Deschutes Brewery Pub House** brewpub and restaurant location for exclusive brews that don't make it to stores. *(1044 NW Bond St. ☎382-9242. 20 oz. drafts $4. Open M-Th 11am-11pm, F-Sa 11am-midnight, Su 11am-10pm.)*

DRAKE PARK AND THE CASCADE FESTIVAL OF MUSIC. Picnic by the river or float down on a raft at beautiful Drake Park. The park hosts many events and festivals, most notably the Cascade Festival of Music, a week-long series of classical and pop concerts during the week before Labor Day. *(Between Mirror Pond and Franklin St., 1 block from downtown. ☎382-8381; www.cascademusic.org. Tickets $15-38; rush tickets, students, and under 12 half price.)* Bend's **Old Mill District** *(☎312-0131; www.theoldmill.com; open M-Sa 10am-8pm, Su 11am-6pm)* is the town's main shopping district, and the place to find great restaurants, the cinema, and the **Les Schwab Amphitheatre,** 520 SW Powerhouse Dr., which draws in crowds for blockbuster music acts and a free **Summer Sunday Concert Series** that runs weekly June through Labor Day. Call or visit website for listings. *(Take Exit 138 or 139 from Hwy 97 for Old Mill District and Amphitheatre. ☎322-9383; www.bendconcerts.com. Gates open at 1pm, shows begin at 2:30pm.)*

🏔 OUTDOOR ACTIVITIES

The outdoors opportunities near Bend are limitless and without peer in Oregon. From skiing, snowboarding, and snowshoeing in the winter to hiking, biking, climbing, and whitewater rafting in the summer, Bend is an inexpensive outdoor adventure waiting to happen. The **Three Sisters Wilderness Area,** north and west of the Cascade Lakes Hwy., is one of Oregon's largest and most popular wilderness areas. Pick up a parking permit at a ranger station or the Visitors Center ($5). Within the wilderness, the ⬛**South Sister** makes for the best trek as well as the most accessible peak, offering a simple, if long (11 mi., 5000 ft. vertical), hike in late summer that threads between glaciers. The other Sisters provide more difficult technical climbs, with opportunities for multi-pitch ice or rock climbs.

⬛ **SKIING.** Those who ski the 9065 ft. **Mount Bachelor,** with its 3365 ft. vertical drop, are in good company—the mountain has been home to the US Ski Team and the US Cross-Country Ski Team, and hosts many of the largest snowboarding competitions in the country. Just 22 mi. southwest of Bend on the Cascade Lakes Hwy., it's considered by many to be the best ski resort in Oregon. (☎800-829-2442, snow report 382-7888; www.mtbachelor.com. Call for 2008 lift ticket prices.) Many nearby lodges offer **ski packages** (contact the Bend Visitors and Convention Bureau at ☎ 382-8048 or 800-949-6086 for info). **Chairlifts** run for sightseers in summer. (Open daily 11am-8pm. 11am-4pm $15, over 65 $12, ages 6-12 $9, under 6 free; 5-8pm $12/10/7/free.) A parking permit from the ranger is necessary on the mountain. See **Orientation and Practical Information,** p. 952, for equipment rental info. For cross-country skiers, **South Sister** and **Todd Lake** have stunning scenery, with easily accessible trailheads across from Mt. Bachelor.

⬛ **MOUNTAIN BIKING.** Mountain biking is forbidden in the well-signed wilderness area, but Benders have plenty of other places to spin their wheels. Be forewarned: the loose "pummy dust"—ground-up pumice—makes riding slow and corners sketchy until you reach higher elevations. The most renowned area for biking is **Phil's Trail Area** (9 mi.) which fills the space between Skyliners Rd. and the Cascade Lakes Hwy. west of Bend and has trails for all levels. A map is necessary (available at Sunnyside Sports, $8-14). Lower elevation climbs indicate beginner-friendly terrain. Go west on Skyliners Road out of Bend 2½ mi., then make a left (south) on Forest Rd. 220. Try **Deschutes River Trail** (6 mi.) for a fairly flat, forested trail ending at **Deschutes River.** To reach the trailhead, go 7½ mi. west of Bend on S. Century Dr. (Cascade Lakes Hwy.) until Forest Rd. 41, then turn left and follow the signs to Lava Island Falls. For a technical ride, hit **Waldo Lake Loop,** a grueling 22 mi. around the lake (4-4½hr.). Bring insect repellent—the summertime mosquitoes are brutal. Take Cascade Lakes Hwy. to Forest Rd. 4290. For rental information, consult **Orientation and Practical Information,** p. 952. While Bend's bike lanes skirt closely to traffic congestion, nearby resort towns of Sun River and Black Butte have separated paths for road bikers.

⬛ **RAFTING AND KAYAKING.** Bend has a large kayaking and rafting community. The powerful **Deschutes River** has year-round flows thanks to dam releases for irrigation, and its rapids—formed by lava flows—are unusual and range from Class II to unrunnable gnar-gnar. **Big Eddy** is the other big play spot, although the recovery pools are brief at summertime high flows, necessitating either a quick roll or a facemask. The class III-IV or IV stretch, depending on flow, is accessed by

> **!** Many of Bend's kayaking and rafting trips should not be done alone unless you are very experienced. Sun Country's most popular tour is the "Big Eddy Thriller," which does the trail safely. However, if you stay on too long—but are unguided and miss the stop—you're in Benham Falls with Class V waterfalls. Seek the guidance of a reputable tour company for a safer trip.

taking 14th St. south 6½ mi. from Bend, and then making the next left after passing the Inn of the Seventh Mountain. Take the road marked by "Big Eddy/Aspen." A common run is to put in at Aspen and take out above Lava Island Falls. Along the same road, several of the Deschutes' falls (really huge rapids, not waterfalls), including Lava Island Falls, have extreme descents.

Rafting companies take 3hr. trips on the Upper Deschutes' tame waters from Aspen to above Lava Island Falls. Full-day trips require a 1hr. drive to Maupin to run the Class III+ rapids of the Lower Deschutes. Family-friendly **Sun Country Tours** runs half-day and full-day trips out of the Sun River Resort, 17 mi. south of Bend off U.S. 97, and at 531 SW 13th St. in Bend. The 1¼hr. Big Eddy Thriller tour is a favorite ($44). Longer half-day ($73) and full-day tours ($98+) to McKenzie or Lower Deschutes run several days a week. (☎382-6277 or 800-770-2161; www.sun-countrytours.com.)

☒ ROCK CLIMBING. Smith Rock State Park (☎541-548-7501 or 800-551-6949; www.smithrock.com), 4 mi. east of Hwy. 97 at Terrebonne, is home to the best rock climbing north of Yosemite. Sheer, jagged rock formations rise abruptly for hundreds of feet, towering over the Crooked River and the several miles of trail that wind their way through the park. A popular loop starts at the bridge below the main parking area and tours the most spectacular areas of the park in 3½ mi. before returning to the bridge. (If you're feeling adventurous, cut some distance off this trail by going left at the bridge and then scrambling over Asterisk Pass half a mile into the hike). Even those with a fear of heights can enjoy watching the climbers make their way up the impossibly minute holds on the walls. From the loop trail you can call across a 300 ft. deep void to climbers just 20 ft. away on the Monkey Face formation (you'll see immediately how it got its name). The park is also home to several birds of prey, most notably bald eagles.

CRATER LAKE NATIONAL PARK   ☎541

The deepest lake in the US, the seventh deepest in the world, and one of the most beautiful anywhere, Crater Lake is one of Oregon's signature attractions. Formed about 7700 years ago in a cataclysmic eruption of Mt. Mazama, the lake began as a deep caldera and gradually filled with centuries worth of snowmelt. The circular lake plunges from its shores to a depth of 1943 ft., enchanting tourists with its impossibly blue waters. It is only a 300 ft. walk from the **Rim Village Visitors Center** (☎594-3090, www.nps.gov/crla; open June-Sept. daily 9:30am-5pm) to the **Sinnott Memorial Overlook,** the park's most panoramic and accessible view. Above the lake, **Rim Drive,** which does not open entirely until mid-July, is a 33 mi. loop around the rim of the caldera. **Steel Information Center,** located 4 mi. north of the South entrance and 3 mi. below the Rim Village, is open all year and provides maps, information about hiking trails and camping, historical exhibits, backcountry permits, and postal services (information center open daily 9am-5pm; **post office** open M-Sa 9am-noon and 1-3pm). ▨**Garfield Peak** (3.4 mi., 2-3hr. round-trip), adjacent to the Crater Lake Lodge, is a moderate to difficult trail that skirts the caldera rim and offers hikers arresting lake views. Trails to **Watchman Peak** (¾ mi., 1hr.), on the lake's west side, are the most spectacular. The strenuous 2½ mi. hike up **Mount Scott,** the park's highest peak (almost 9000 ft.), starts at the lake's eastern edge. The steep **Cleetwood Cove Trail** (2¼ mi., 2hr.) leaves from the north edge of the lake and is the only route down to the lake's edge, from which **Volcanic Boat Cruises** depart for **Wizard Island,** a cinder cone rising 760 ft. above the western portion of the lake. Cruises run from late June to mid-September. (☎830-8744. $25.50, ages 3-11 $15.) All trails provide breathtaking views of Wizard Island and **Phantom Ship Rock,** a spooky rock formation in the southeast edge. In addition to trails around the lake, the park has over 140 mi. of wilderness trails. Picnics, fishing (with artificial lures only), and swimming are allowed, but water temperatures only reach about 50°F. Permits are required to scuba dive in the caldera. Park rangers lead free tours periodically in the summer and winter. (Tour info ☎594-3000.)

The closest town to Crater Lake is Fort Klamath (pop. 89), 7 mi. south of the South entrance to Crater Lake on Rte. 62. **The Aspen Inn ❸,** 52250 Hwy 62, has understated but peaceful and pristine motel rooms and cabins, with microwaves and outdoor grill access. Dogs welcome. (☎381-2321; www.theaspeninn.com. Office open daily 8am-9pm. Open Apr.-Nov. Rooms $65.) The **Klamath General Store,** 52608 Hwy 62, has gasoline, basic groceries, toiletries, a grill and deli, and the latest scoop on small-town gossip. (☎381-2263. Open daily in summer 7am-9pm, in winter 7am-6pm.) The distant, but more urban **Klamath Falls** has several affordable hotels and restaurants. The **Townhouse Motel ❶,** 5323 6th St., 3 mi. south of Main St., has very tidy rooms. (☎882-0924. Cable TV, A/C. Singles $34; rooms with full kitchens $48. Lower weekly rate. MC/V.) There are two campgrounds within the Crater Lake National Park area and ample opportunity for backcountry camping (permits available at the Visitors Center or Ranger Station). Near the park's south entrance off Hwy. 62, the mammoth **Mazama Village Campground ❶** provides 212 tent and RV sites (half reservable and half first come, first served). A gas station, restaurant, and general store are located in Mazama Village nearby. (☎888-774-2728; www.xanterra.com or www.craterlakelodges.com. Showers $0.75 per 4 min. Laundry $1.75. Open early June to mid-Oct. Tent sites $18; RV sites $20, full hookup $23.) The idyllic and secluded **Lost Creek Campground ❶,** in the southeast corner of the park on Spur Rd., has 16 first come, first served sites with water and vault toilets exclusively for tent camping. Call National Park Service for info. (☎594-3100. Open mid-July to mid-Sept. Sites $10.) While eating cheap isn't easy in Crater Lake, Klamath Falls has some affordable dining and a **Safeway,** 2740 S. 6th St. (☎273-3510). Where's **Waldo's Mongolian Grill and Tavern ❷?** It's at 610 Main St. and grills your choice of veggies and meat. (☎884-6863. Bowls $7-11. Open daily 11:30am-9pm. MC/V.)

Crater Lake averages over 44 ft. of snow per year, and snowbound roads can keep the northern entrance and parts of the Rim Drive closed until July (call ☎594-3000 for road closures). The park's southern entrance is open year-round. The **entrance fee** is $10 per car and $5 per hiker or cyclist. Amtrak, 1600 Oak St. (☎884-2822; www.amtrak.com; open daily 7:30-11am and 8:30-10:15pm), and Greyhound, 435 S. Spring St. (☎883-2609; www.greyhound.com; open M-F 9am-5pm, Sa-Su 9-11am), are both in Klamath Falls. One **train** per day runs to Redding, CA (4½hr., $32), and one **bus** per day rolls to Eugene (6½hr., $39) and then on to Portland ($46-50). The **Chamber of Commerce** is at 706 Main St. (☎884-5193 or 877-552-6284; www.klamath.org. Open M-F 8am-5pm.) The **William G. Steel Center** issues free backcountry camping permits. (☎594-3000; www.nps.gov/crla. Open daily 9am-4pm.) **Post Office:** 317 S. 7th St. in Klamath Falls. (☎800-275-8777. Open M-F 7:30am-5:30pm, Sa 9am-noon.) **Postal Code:** 97604.

ASHLAND ☎541

Situated near the California border, Ashland mixes hip youth culture with a certain dead British man, setting an unlikely but intriguing stage for the world-famous ▧**Oregon Shakespeare Festival** (☎482-4331 or 800-219-8161; www.osfashland.org). From mid-February to October, drama devotees can choose from 11 Shakespearean and contemporary works performed in Ashland's three elegant theaters: the outdoor Globe Theatre replica **Elizabethan Stage,** the **Angus Bowmer Theater,** and the **New Theater.** The 2008 schedule includes "A Midsummer Night's Dream," "Othello," "The Comedy of Errors," and Thornton Wilder's "Our Town." During summer months, buy tickets in advance. (Children under 6 not admitted. In summer $30-75; in spring and fall $27-56. Discounts for under 18.) At 9:30am, the **box office,** 15 S. Pioneer St., releases any unsold tickets for the day's performances and sells 20 standing-room tickets ($12) for sold-out shows on the Elizabethan Stage. Half-price rush tickets are sometimes available 1hr. before performances. **Backstage tours** provide a wonderful glimpse of the festival from behind the curtain. (Tours Tu-Su 10am. In summer $11, ages 6-17 $8.25; low season $8.25/5.25.)

In winter, Ashland is a budget paradise; in summer, hotel and B&B rates double and the hostels bulge. Only rogues and peasant slaves arrive without reservations. Medford, 12 mi. north of town on I-5, has affordable chain motels if Ashland's budget beds are filled. **◪Ashland Hostel ❶,** 150 N. Main St., is well-kept, immaculate, charming, and cheery, making it an ideal place to sleep. (☎482-9217. Free Internet access. Kitchen access. Check-in 5-9pm. Lockout 10am-5pm. Dorms $25; singles $59. Cash only.) A short walk from the heart of downtown, the friendly and bustling **Ashland Commons ❶,** 437 Williamson Way, has hostel-style dorm accommodations and private rooms available to large groups or lone travelers. (☎482-6753. Dorms $25.) The incredible food selection on N. and E. Main St. has earned the plaza a strong culinary reputation. **The Ashland Food Cooperative,** 237 1st St., stocks organic groceries. (☎482-2237; www.ashlandfood.coop. Open daily 7am-9pm.) If you're sick of the Man keeping you down, fight back at **Evo's Java House and Revolutionary Cafe ❶,** 376 E. Main St., where the politics are as radical as the coconut yerba mates, and the veggie burritos are delicious. (☎482-2261. Free Wi-Fi. Open daily 6:30am-6pm. AmEx/D/MC/V.) Nobody doth protest too much about the food at **Morning Glory ❸,** 1149 Siskiyou Blvd. (☎488-8636; www.morninggloryrestaurant.com. Half-orders available upon request. Open daily 8am-2pm. AmEx/D/MC/V.) Ashland's nightlife concentrates around N. and E. Main St. Try the excellent microbrews and legendary fish and chips at **Jefferson State Pub,** 31 Water St., just off N. Main St. (☎482-7718; www.thejeffersonstatepub.com. Live music daily 9pm. 21+ after 9pm. Cover $3-5. Happy hour daily 11am-9pm. Open daily in summer 11am-2am; in winter hours vary.)

Ashland proper is located in the foothills of the Siskiyou and Cascade Ranges, 285 mi. south of Portland and 15 mi. north of the California border, near the junction of **I-5** and **Route 66. Route 99** cuts directly through the middle of town on a northwest-southeast axis and becomes **North Main Street** as it enters town from the west; it then splits briefly into **East Main Street** and **Lithia Way.** The **Chamber of Commerce** is at 110 N. 1st St. (☎482-3486; www.ashlandchamber.com. Open M-F 9am-5pm.) The **post office** is at 120 N. 1st St. (☎800-275-8777. Open M-F 9am-5pm.) **Postal Code:** 97520.

WASHINGTON

On Washington's western shores, Pacific storms feed one of the world's only temperate rainforests in Olympic National Park. Just east, clouds linger over Seattle through much of the year, hiding the Emerald City. Visitors to the Puget Sound area can experience everything from isolation in the San Juan Islands to cosmopolitan entertainment on the mainland. Past the Cascades, the state's eastern half spreads out into fertile farmlands and grassy plains.

◪ PRACTICAL INFORMATION

Capital: Olympia.

Visitor Info: Washington State Tourism, Dept. of Community, Trade, and Economic Development, P.O. Box 42500, Olympia 98504 (☎800-544-1800; www.experiencewashington.com). **Washington State Parks and Recreation Commission,** P.O. Box 42650, Olympia 98504 (☎360-902-8844 or 888-226-7688; www.parks.wa.gov).

Postal Abbreviation: WA. **Sales Tax:** 7-9%, depending on the county.

SEATTLE   ☎206

Seattle's mix of mountain views, clean streets, espresso stands, and rainy weather was the magic formula of the 90s, attracting transplants from across the US. The droves of newcomers provide an interesting contrast to the older residents who remember Seattle as a city-town, not a metropolis swarming with young millionaires. Money from local successes like Microsoft and Amazon has helped drive rent sky-high in some areas, but the grungy, punk-loving street culture still prevails. The city is under cloud cover 200 days a year, but when the skies clear, Seattleites rejoice that "the mountain is out," heading outside to soak up the sun.

▐ TRANSPORTATION

Airport: Seattle-Tacoma (Sea-Tac) International (SEA; ☎433-5388; www.portseattle.org), 15 mi. south of Seattle, exit right off I-5 to Rte. 518 (follow signs).

Trains: Amtrak, King St. Station, 303 S. Jackson St. (☎382-4125, reservations 800-872-7245; www.amtrak.com), 1 block east of Pioneer Sq., enter from 3rd Ave. S and King St. Ticket office open daily 6:15am-8pm. To: **Portland** (3½hr., 4 per day, $25-40); **Spokane** (8hr., 1 per day, $37-81); **Tacoma** (45min., 4 per day, $6-16); **Vancouver** (3½hr., 1 per day, $25-39). Amtrak also offers 4 buses per day to Vancouver for $25 from King St. Station.

Buses: Greyhound (☎628-5526 or 800-231-2222; www.greyhound.com), at 8th Ave. and Stewart St. Ticket office and station open daily 6:30am-1am. To: **Portland** (4hr., 5 per day, $25); **Spokane** (6-7hr., 3 per day, $33); **Tacoma** (1hr., 5 per day, $5); **Vancouver** (4hr., 5 per day, $25).

Ferries: Washington State Ferries (☎464-6400 or 888-808-7977; www.wsdot.wa.gov/ferries) has 2 terminals in Seattle. The main one is downtown, at Colman Dock, Pier 52. Service to **Bainbridge Island** (35min.; $6.10, with car $13.30) and **Bremerton** on the Kitsap Peninsula (1hr.; $6.10, with car $13.30). Ferries for Bremerton and Bainbridge depart frequently 6am-1am, arrive 1hr. early in high season. The **Victoria Clipper** (☎800-888-2535, reservations 448-5000; www.victoriaclipper.com) goes to **Victoria, B.C.** from Pier 69. (3hr.; 3 per day mid-May to early Sept., 1 per day mid-Sept. to Apr.; $71-86, under 12 half-price; bikes $10, discounts for advance booking, no cars.)

Public Transit: Metro Transit, Customer Service Offices, King St. Center, 201 S. Jackson St., at 2nd Ave. S, and the Transit Tunnel in Westlake Station, downtown. (☎553-3000, or 800-542-7876; http://transit.metrokc.gov.) King St. Center open M-F 8am-5pm; Westlake Station open M-F 9am-5pm. Fares are based on a 2-zone system. **Zone 1** is everything within the city limits (peak hours $1.50, off-peak $1.25). **Zone 2** is everything else (peak $2, off-peak $1.25). Ages 5-17 always $0.50. **Peak hours** in both zones are M-F 6-9am and 3-6pm. Weekend day passes $2.50. Ride free daily 6am-7pm in the downtown **ride free area,** bordered by S. Jackson St. to the south, 6th Ave. and I-5 to the east, Battery St. on the north, and the waterfront to the west. Outside ride free area, pay-as-you-board buses head toward downtown and pay-as-you-leave buses head away from downtown. Transfers free.

Taxi: Farwest Taxi, ☎622-1717. **Orange Cab Co.,** ☎522-8800.

■ ORIENTATION

Seattle stretches from north to south on an isthmus between **Puget Sound** and **Elliott Bay** to the west and **Lake Washington** to the east. The city is easily accessible by car via **I-5**, which runs north-south through the city, and by **I-90** from the east, which ends at I-5 southeast of downtown. Get to **downtown** (including **Pioneer Square, Pike Place Market, Belltown,** and the **waterfront**) from I-5 by taking any of the exits between James and Stewart St. Take the Mercer St./Fairview Ave. Exit to the **Seattle Center;** follow signs from there. The Denny Way and Olive Way Exits lead to **Capitol Hill,** and, farther north, the NE 45th St. Exit heads toward the **University District.** During rush hour, Seattle's main arteries can slow to a crawl, making the less crowded **Route 99,** also called Aurora Ave., a convenient alternative; it runs parallel to I-5 along the waterfront and skirts the western side of downtown.

■ PRACTICAL INFORMATION

Tourist Information: Seattle's **Citywide Concierge Center** is housed inside the **Convention and Visitors Bureau** (☎461-5840; www.seeseattle.org), at 7th and Pike St., on the 1st fl. of the convention center. Helpful staff doles out maps, brochures, newspapers, and Metro schedules, and can help visitors find lodging. Open late May-early Sept. M-F 9am-6pm, Sa-Su 10am-4pm; early Sept.-late May M-F 9am-5pm.

Outdoor Information: Seattle Parks and Recreation Department, 100 Dexter Ave. N (☎684-4075; www.ci.seattle.wa.us/parks). Open M-F 8am-5pm. **Outdoor Recreation Information Center,** 222 Yale Ave. (☎470-4060; www.nps.gov/ccso/oric.htm), in REI. Does not sell permits. Free brochures on hiking trails. Open daily 10am-6pm; late Sept.-late spring closed M.

Medical Services: International District Emergency Center, 720 8th Ave. S, Ste. 100 (☎461-3235). Medics with multilingual assistance available. Clinic open M-F 9am-6pm, Sa 9am-4:30pm; phone 24hr. **Swedish Medical Center, Providence Campus,** 500 16th Ave. (☎320-2111), for urgent care and cardiac. 24hr.

Internet Access: Seattle Central Library, 1000 4th Ave. (☎386-4636; www.spl.org), at Madison. 15min. free Internet with photo ID.; free unlimited Wi-Fi. Open M-Th 10am-8pm, F-Sa 10am-6pm, Su noon-6pm. Free Wi-Fi also available with purchase at all **Tully's Coffee** locations around the city.

Post Office: 301 Union St. (☎748-5417 or 800-275-8777), at 3rd Ave. downtown. Open M-F 7:30am-5:30pm. **Postal Code:** 98101.

■ ACCOMMODATIONS

Pacific Reservation Service (☎439-7677 or 800-684-2932) can arrange B&B singles for $50-65. For motels away from downtown, drive north on Aurora Ave. or take bus #26 to Fremont.

Green Tortoise Hostel, 105 Pike St. (☎340-1222; www.greentortoise.net), across the street from Pike Place Market, at Pike St. on the #174 or 194 bus. Known for throwing parties from time to time. W open mic. Breakfast included. Free Internet access. Key deposit $20, cash only. Reception 24hr. Dorms $25-29; private rooms $77. Small additional charge for credit cards. MC/V. ❶

Moore Hotel, 1926 2nd Ave. (☎448-4851 or 800-421-5508; www.moorehotel.com), 2 blocks east of Pike Place Market. Built in 1907, the Moore Hotel has a swanky lobby and cavernous hallways. "European-style" (with smaller beds and shared bathrooms) singles $54; doubles $66. Singles $70; doubles $82-92. Suites $104-175. MC/V. ❷

Downtown Seattle

🏠 **ACCOMMODATIONS**
The College Inn, **1**
Green Tortoise Backpacker's
   Hostel, **17**
Moore Hotel, **12**

🍎 **FOOD**
Araya's Vegetarian Place, **2**
Ayutthaya, **11**
Bimbo's Bitchin' Burrito Kitchen, **10**

Beecher's Homemade Cheese, **14**
Emmett Watson's Oyster Bar, **13**
Flowers Bar & Restaurant, **3**
Ho Ho Seafood Restaurant, **25**
House of Hong, **23**
Ivar's Fish Bar, **19**
Mae Phim Thai Restaurant, **21**
Piroshky, Piroshky, **15**
Ristorante Machiavelli, **6**
Uwajimaya, **24**
Victrola Coffee & Art, **4**

ALSO SEE COLOR INSERT MAP

✉ **NIGHTLIFE**
The Alibi Room, **18**
Club Noc Noc, **16**
Contour, **20**
J & M Cafe and Cardroom, **22**
Havana, **9**
Linda's Tavern, **7**
Neighbours, **8**
Viceroy Cocktail Lounge, **5**

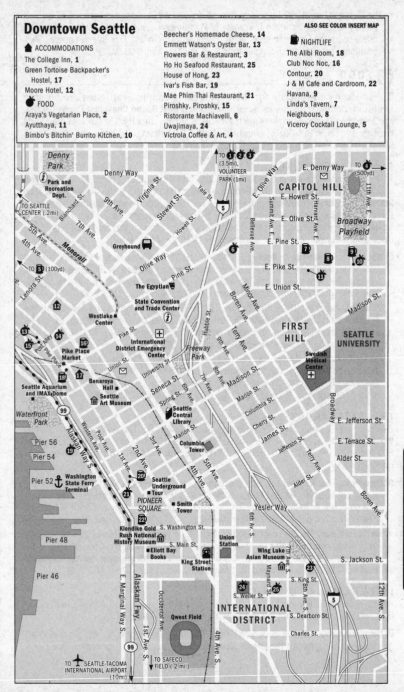

The College Inn, 4000 University Way NE (☎633-4441; www.collegeinnseattle.com), across the street from the University of Washington campus. This historic landmark offers charming European-style rooms. Continental breakfast. Free Internet access. Reservations recommended. Singles from $50; doubles from $60. MC/V/D. ❸

🍴 FOOD

Though known primarily for their espresso-worship, Seattleites are big into healthful, organic cuisine, especially seafood. **Puget Sound Consumer Coops (PCCs),** are local health-food markets with locations across the city. (In Green Lake: 7504 Aurora Ave. N, ☎525-3586.) Capitol Hill, the U District, and Fremont close main streets on summer Saturdays for **farmers' markets.**

PIKE PLACE MARKET
In 1907, angry citizens got fed up with the middle-man, and local farmers began selling produce directly to locals by the waterfront, creating the ◪**Pike Place Market**. Today tourists mob the marketplace for fresh produce, artisan food vendors, the original Starbucks location, and the flying fish that are hurled from shelves to scales in the Main Arcade. (Most stalls open M-Sa 9am-6pm, Su 11am-5pm. Produce and fish open earlier; restaurants and lounges close later.)

◪ **Beecher's Handmade Cheese,** 1600 Pike Pl. (☎956-1964), between Pine and Stewart St. Pull up a milk-jug stool and enjoy this fromagerie's signature "World's Best" mac and cheese ($6), while you watch the artisan cheesemakers create the sinfully tasty Flagship Reserve cheese from scratch. Open daily 9am-6pm. AmEx/MC/V. ❶

Piroshky, Piroshky, 1908 Pike Pl. (☎441-6068), between Virginia and Stewart St. The Russian piroshky is a croissant-like dough baked and stuffed with sausages, mushrooms, cheeses, salmon, or apples doused in cinnamon ($3-4). The $6 soup and piroshky combo is a steal. Open daily 8am-6pm. MC/V. ❶

Emmett Watson's Oyster Bar, 1916 Pike Pl.(☎448-7721), inside the main market building between Virginia and Stewart St. Serves seafood in blue-checkered booths. Try the Oyster Bar Special—2 oysters, 3 shrimp, and a heaping bowl of chowder ($8). Open M-Th 11:30am-7pm, F-Sa 11:30am-8pm, Su 11:30am-6pm. MC/V. ❷

THE WATERFRONT
Budget eaters, steer clear of Belltown and Pioneer Sq. Instead, take a picnic to **Waterfall Gardens,** on the corner of S. Main St. and 2nd Ave. S. The garden sports tables and chairs and a man-made waterfall that masks traffic outside. (Open daily dawn-dusk.)

◪ **Mae Phim Thai Restaurant,** 94 Columbia St. (☎624-2979), a few blocks north of the waterfront between 1st and Post Ave. Delicious, inexpensive Thai cuisine served quickly in a no-frills hole-in-the-wall location. For lovers of pad thai, this spot is hard to beat. All dishes $5.50. Open M-F 11am-7pm, Sa-Su 11:30-6:30pm. Cash only. ❷

Ivar's Fish Bar, Pier 54 (☎467-8063). A fast-food window that serves all kinds of seafood—from clam chowder ($2.50) to clams and chips ($5.30). Open M-Th and Su 11am-midnight, F-Sa 11am-2am. MC/V. ❶ For a more upscale meal, try **Ivar's Restaurant** next door. Open M-Th and Su 11am-10pm, F-Sa 11am-11pm. MC/V. ❸

INTERNATIONAL DISTRICT
Along King and Jackson St., between 5th and 8th Ave. east of Qwest Field, Seattle's International District is packed with great Asian eateries.

◪ **Uwajimaya,** 600 5th Ave. S (☎624-6248). The Uwajimaya Village is a city block of Asian groceries and gifts; it's the largest Japanese department store in the region. Don't miss the food court's panorama of delicacies. Open M-Sa 9am-10pm, Su 9am-9pm. Food court closes daily 9pm. ❷

House of Hong, 409 8th Ave. S (☎622-7997), at S. Jackson St. An upscale restaurant. Standard Chinese cuisine $8-13. Dim sum daily 10am-5pm. Open M-F 10am-midnight, Sa 9:30am-midnight, Su 9:30am-10pm. AmEx/MC/V. ❸

Ho Ho Seafood Restaurant, 653 S. Weller St. (☎382-9671). Generous portions of Cantonese-prepared seafood, including steamed rock cod ($8.25). Lunch until 4pm $5-7. Dinner $7-12. Open M-Th and Su 11am-1am, F-Sa 11am-3am. MC/V. ❷

CAPITOL HILL

With bronze dance-steps on the sidewalks and neon storefronts, Broadway Ave. is home to numerous espresso houses, imaginative cafes, and funky nightclubs.

Bimbo's Bitchin' Burrito Kitchen, 1013 E. Pike St. (☎329-9978). The name explains it, and the decorations prove it. Walk right through the door to the bar, **Cha Cha,** for $3.50 tequila shots (open until 2am). Spicy Bimbo's burrito $4.25. Tacos $2.50. Happy hour daily 4-7pm. Open M-Th noon-11pm, F-Sa noon-2am, Su 2-10pm. MC/V. ❶

Ristorante Machiavelli, 1215 Pine St. (☎621-7941). A small, bustling Italian place with simple decor and hearty food. The gnocchi is widely considered the best in town. Pasta $8-10. Open M-Sa 5pm-2am. Kitchen closes 11pm. MC/V. ❸

Ayutthaya, 727 E. Pike St. (☎324-8833). Thai food infused with Caribbean spices in a quiet mint-green nook. Generous lunch entrees $6-6.50; go for those with spice if you can handle the kick, but be sure to save room for the deep-fried banana dessert ($2.50). Open M-Sa 11am-2:30pm and 5-9:30pm. AmEx/D/MC/V. ❷

UNIVERSITY DISTRICT

The neighborhood around the immense **University of Washington** ("U-Dub"), north of downtown between Union and Portage Bay, supports funky shops, international restaurants, and coffeehouses. The best of each lies within a few blocks of University Way, known as "the Ave."

🎖 **Araya Vegetarian Place,** 1121 NE. 45th St. (☎524-4332). One of the top vegan restaurants in Seattle, Araya's lunch buffet has all the Thai classics—curries and pad thai—plus some unconventional offerings ($7). Buffet 11:30am-3:30pm. Open M-Th 11:30am-9pm, F-Sa 11:30am-9:30pm, Su 5-9pm. AmEx/D/MC/V. ❷

Flowers Bar & Restaurant, 4247 University Way NE (☎633-1903). This 20s landmark was a flower shop; now, the mirrored ceiling reflects an all-you-can-eat vegan Mediterranean buffet ($8). Drink specials daily. Open M-Sa 11am-2am, Su 11am-midnight. Bar open Th-Sa 6pm-2am. AmEx/D/MC/V. ❷

█ CAFES

The coffee bean is Seattle's 1st love; you can't walk a single block without passing an institution of caffeination. The city's obsession with Italian-style espresso drinks even has gas stations pumping out thick, dark, soupy java.

🎖 **Victrola Coffee & Art,** 411 15th Ave. E (☎325-6520; www.victrolacoffee.com). On mellow 15th Ave., this cafe possesses atmosphere in abundance, balancing private sitting space with inviting sofas. Signature espresso roasts (double shot $2), sandwiches ($5-6), and top-notch pastries ($2). Open daily 5:30am-11pm. ❶

Cafe Besalu, 5909 24th Ave. NW (☎789-1463). The coffee is good, but the real draw is Cafe Besalu's delectable pastries—from artisan bread to croissants and brioches ($1-3.25)—baked fresh in the open kitchen. Open W-Su 7am-3pm. ❶

⊙ SIGHTS

Most of the city's major sights are within walking distance or in the Metro's "ride free" zone. Seattle has unparalleled public art installations downtown (self-guided tours begin at the Visitors Center) and plentiful galleries. While dot-com success drove Seattle's collective worth up and some of the local artists out, the money has begun to pay off; the investments of Seattle-based millionaires have brought about an architectural renaissance, with the Gehry-designed Experience Music Project (EMP), the edgy postmodern Seattle Central Library, the expanded Seattle Art Museum (SAM), and the new waterfront Olympic Sculpture Park.

DOWNTOWN AND PIKE PLACE MARKET

Designed by noted Prada architect Rem Koolhaas, the transparent, ultra-modern **⧉Seattle Central Library,** 1000 4th Ave., at Madison St., hovers above the downtown streets with jagged angles and floating floors. (☎386-4636; www.spl.org. Open M-Th 10am-8pm, F-Sa 10am-6pm, Su noon-6pm. Free 1hr. general tours M-W 12:30, 2:30, 4:30pm; Th-Sa 10:30am, 12:30, 2:30, 4:30pm; Su 2 and 4pm. Free 1hr. architectural tours M-W 5:30 and 6:45pm, Sa-Su 1:30 and 3:30pm.) The heart of Seattle, **⧉Pike Place Market,** 1531 Western Ave., is definitely worth a visit, even if food is not on your mind. Join the crowds gawking at the famed fish throwers, enjoy a latte at the original Starbucks, and peruse the arts and crafts from hundreds of local vendors. Tours start at the **Market Heritage Center.** (☎682-7453; www.pike-placemarket.com. $7, under 18 and over 60 $5. Open W-Su 11am and 2pm.) The **Pike Place Hillclimb** descends from the south end of Pike Place Market to Alaskan Way and the waterfront. The **Seattle Art Museum (SAM),** 100 University St., at 1st Ave., boasts the region's largest collection of African, Native American, and Asian art. In 2007, SAM moved to a sleek new building, with a contemporary new look to complement its rapidly growing Modern art collection. Be sure to check out the installation in the lobby, with a series of mid-90s Ford Tauruses suspended from the ceiling. (☎654-3100; www.seattleartmuseum.org. Open Tu-W and Sa-Su 10am-5pm, Th-F 10am-9pm. $13; over 62 $10, students and ages 13-17 $7; under 12 free; 1st Th of the month free. Special exhibits $5-15.)

WATERFRONT

Showcasing provocative artwork in a spectacular outdoor location overlooking Elliott Bay, the **⧉Olympic Sculpture Park,** 2901 Western Ave., at Broad St., was an immediate success when it opened in 2007. (☎654-3100; www.seattleartmuseum.org/visit/OSP/. Open daily May-Sept. 6am-9pm, Oct.-Apr. 7am-6pm. Free.) Explore over 400,000 gallons of Pacific Northwest sea life at the recently renovated **Seattle Aquarium,** 1483 Alaskan Way, at Pier 59. Check out the Life on the Edge exhibit, where a wave tank simulates the rough conditions of Washington's tidal zones. (☎654-3100; www.seattleaquarium.org. Open daily 9:30am-5pm. $15, ages 4-12 $10, under 4 free.)

THE SEATTLE CENTER

The 1962 World's Fair demanded a Seattle Center to herald the city of the future. Now the Center houses everything from carnival rides to ballet performances. It is bordered by Denny Way, W. Mercer St., 1st Ave., and 5th Ave., and has eight gates, each with a map of its facilities. It is also accessible by a short **monorail** which runs from downtown's **Westlake Center.** (400 Pine St. ☎625-0280; www.seattlemono-rail.com. Monorail every 10min. M-F 7:30am-11pm, Sa-Su 9am-11pm. $1.50, seniors $0.75, ages 5-12 $0.50.) The Center's anchor point is the **Center House,** which holds a food court and info desk. (For info about special events, call ☎684-7200; www.seat-tlecenter.com. Info desk open daily 11am-6pm.) The **Experience Music Project (EMP),** 325 5th Ave., at the Seattle Center, the brainchild of Seattle billionaire and Microsoft co-founder Paul Allen, was initially intended as a shrine to Allen's music idol, Jimi Hendrix. The project eventually ballooned to include a $350 million budget, a collection of over 80,000 musical artifacts, and the world-renowned architect Frank Gehry. The result? The rock 'n' roll museum of the future. Inside, rock fanatics will appreciate the guitar Hendrix smashed on a London stage, computer teaching devices that let you try your own hand at music making, a collection of guitars covering the past two centuries, and On Stage, a first-class karaoke stage gone haywire. (☎367-5483 or 877-367-5483; www.emplive.org. Open late May to early Sept. daily 10am-8pm; early Sept. to late May M-Th and Su 10am-6pm, F-Sa 10am-8pm. Free live entertainment Tu-Su in the lounge. $15; military with ID, seniors, and ages 5-17 $12.) The **Space Needle** was built in 1962 for the World's Fair. When this 607 ft. rotating building was constructed, it was hailed as futuristic and daring. Today, the Space Needle is the symbol of Seattle. It has a great view and is an invaluable landmark for the disoriented. The needle houses an observation tower and a revolving restaurant with appropriately sky-high prices. (400 Broad St. ☎905-2100; www.spaceneedle.com. Open daily 9am-midnight. $13, seniors $11, ages 4-13 $6.)

THE INTERNATIONAL DISTRICT/PIONEER SQUARE

The ⬛**Wing Luke Asian Museum,** 407 7th Ave. S, gives a description of life in an Asian-American community, showing work by local Asian artists. One permanent exhibit is Camp Harmony, a replica of barracks from a Japanese internment camp during WWII. (☎623-5124; www.wingluke.org. Open Tu-F 11am-4:30pm, Sa-Su noon-4pm. $4, students and seniors $3, ages 5-12 $2. 1st Th of each month free.) The **Seattle Underground Tour,** 608 1st Ave., in Pioneer Sq., offers an entertaining glimpse into Seattle's clumsy beginnings, including exploring subterranean Pioneer Sq. buildings that were ground level a century ago. Tours are guided by a knowledgeable, funny staff. (☎682-4646; www.undergroundtour.com. 3-9 1½hr. tours daily 10am-6pm, but call ahead. $14, seniors and ages 13-17 $12, ages 7-12 $7.)

CAPITOL HILL

What do you do when you have too much good art to exhibit all at once? Open a second museum, which is what SAM did, creating the **Seattle Asian Art Museum (SAAM),** 1400 E. Prospect St., in Volunteer Park, just past the water tower. The collection is particularly strong in Chinese art, but the museum also has exhibits on Buddhist art and daily life in Japan. (☎654-3100; www.seattleartmuseum.org/visit/visitSAAM.asp. Open Tu-W and F-Su 10am-5pm, Th 10am-9pm. Suggested donation $5, seniors and ages 13-17 $3, under 12 free; free with SAM ticket from the previous 7 days; SAAM ticket good for $3 discount at SAM. 1st Th and Sa of every month free.) The **University of Washington Arboretum,** 10 blocks east of Volunteer Park, has excellent trails packed amongst over 4000 species of trees and flowers. Take bus #11, 43, or 48 from downtown. Explore the carefully crafted gardens, including a serene Japanese Garden, Rhododendron Glen, and Azalea Way. Tours depart the Graham Visitor Center, at the southern end of the arboretum on Lake Washington Blvd. (☎543-8800; http://depts.washington.edu/wpa. Open daily dawn-dusk. Visitors Center open daily 10am-4pm. Free tours 1pm on the 1st Su of each month or by appointment. Japanese Garden open Apr.-Nov. 10am-dusk. $2.50, students and over 60 $1.50.)

🎵 ENTERTAINMENT

Seattle has a world-renowned underground music scene and a bustling theater community. For concerts and other listings, check out Seattle's free weekly publication, the *Seattle Weekly* (www.seattleweekly.com). One regular occurrence in the city is the free **Out to Lunch** series (☎623-0340; schedules at www.downtownseattle.com), which brings everything from reggae to folk dancing to parks, squares, and buildings. (June-Sept. M-F noon-1:30pm.)

PACIFIC NORTHWEST

MUSIC

The **Seattle Opera** performs from October to August in **McCaw Hall.** The culmination of a 10-year renovation project, the Opera House reopened in 2003, with a glass facade, decked-out lobbies, and a modernized auditorium. Opera buffs should reserve in advance, but rush tickets are sometimes available. (☎389-7676 or 800-426-1619; www.seattleopera.com. Ticket office at 1020 John St., below the 13 Coins Restaurant parking lot. Students and seniors can get half-price tickets 1½hr. before performances at the ticket office. Open M-F 9am-5pm. Tickets from $35.) The **Seattle Symphony** performs in the beautiful **Benaroya Hall,** 200 University St., at 3rd Ave., from September to June. Free organ concerts attract crowds on the first Monday of every month at 12:30pm. (☎212-4700, tickets 215-4747; www.seattlesymphony.org. Ticket office open M-F 10am-6pm, Sa 1-6pm. Ticket prices vary by concert, but most nights have a limited amount of $15 seats; most tickets $25-39; seniors and students $10 day of show when available.)

THEATER AND CINEMA

Seattle has many plays and alternative pieces, often by talented amateurs. Rush tickets are often available at half-price on the day of the show from **Ticket/Ticket.** (☎324-2744. Locations in Capitol Hill, Downtown, and Pike Place. Cash only.) **The Empty Space Theatre,** 3509 Fremont Ave. N, 1½ blocks north of the Fremont Bridge, presents comedies from October to early July. (☎547-7500. Tickets $20-40; half-price tickets 30min. before curtain.) **Seattle Repertory Theater,** 155 Mercer St., at the Bagley Wright Theater in the Seattle Center, has productions from September to May. (☎443-2222; www.seattlerep.org. Ticket office open M-F 10am-6pm. Tickets $15-45, over 65 $32, under 25 $10; rush tickets 30min. before curtain.)

Seattle is a cinephile's paradise. Most of the theaters screening non-Hollywood films are on Capitol Hill and in the University District. On summer Saturdays (mid-June to late Aug.), **Fremont Outdoor Movies** begins at dusk at the corner of 35th Ave. and Finney Ave. N in Fremont, in the U-Park lot. (☎781-4230. Entrance 7pm; live music 8pm. $5.) **The Egyptian,** 801 E. Pine St., at Harvard Ave. on Capitol Hill, hosts the **Seattle International Film Festival** (☎324-9997; www.seattlefilm.com) at the end of May and the 1st week of June. (☎781-5755. $9, seniors $6.)

SPORTS

The Mariners, or "M's," play baseball in the $500 million, hangar-like Safeco Field, at 1st Ave. S and Royal Brougham Way S near Pioneer Sq., under a giant retractable roof. (☎622-4487; www.mariners.org. Tickets from $7.) Across the street, the NFL **Seahawks** play in **Qwest Field,** one of the world's most modern football fields. (☎628-0888; www.seahawks.com. Tickets from $33.) On the other side of town, **Key Arena,** in the Seattle Center, hosts Seattle's NBA basketball team, the **Supersonics.** (☎628-0888; www.supersonics.com. Tickets from $9.)

▒ FESTIVALS

Pick up the Visitors Center's *Calendar of Events* (www.seeseattle.org/events) for coupons and listings. On the first Thursday of each month, the art community sponsors **First Thursday,** a free gallery walk where galleries and art cafes open to the city. The **Fremont Fair** (☎694-6706; www.fremontfair.com), in honor of the summer solstice, is in mid-June, with the **Fremont Solstice Parade,** led by hundreds of bicyclists wearing only body paint. The **International District** holds an annual two-day bash in mid-July, with arts and crafts, East Asian and Pacific food booths, and presentations by groups ranging from the Radical Women/Freedom Socialist Party to cultural dancers. Call **Chinatown Discovery** for info (☎382-1197; www.seattlechinatowntour.com). **Seafair,** in early August, is a weekend festival on Lake Washington with hydroplane races and airshows by the Blue Angels (☎ 728-0123; www.seafair.com). **Bumbershoot,** a giant three-day festival, caps off Labor Day weekend with major rock bands, street musicians, and a young, exuberant crowd. (☎ 281-7788; www.bumbershoot.org. Individual day $30 in advance, $35 same day; 3 day pass $75 in advance, up to $95 same day. Some events require additional tickets.)

Puget Sound's yachting season starts in May. **Maritime Week,** in the 3rd week of May, and the **Shilshole Boats Afloat Show** (☎ 634-0911; www.boatsafloatshow.com), in mid-September, let boaters show off their craft. Over the 4th of July weekend, the Center for Wooden Boats sponsors the free **Wooden Boat Festival and Classic Speedboat Show** (☎ 382-2628; www.cwb.org) on Lake Union, which includes a demonstration of boat-building skills. The finale is the **Quick and Daring Boatbuilding Contest,** in which competitors sail wooden boats of their own design that they built in the previous 24hr. using limited tools and materials.

🅦 NIGHTLIFE

DOWNTOWN AND BELLTOWN

Home to many of Seattle's most popular bars, 1st and 2nd Ave. in Belltown are packed with trendy hot spots.

🅦 **Viceroy Cocktail Lounge,** 2332 2nd Ave. (☎ 956-8423; www.viceroyseattle.com). Oozes so much vintage cool you'll think you've picked up a 70s issue of GQ. Enjoy a drink under the boar's head, or join the live DJ on the intimate dance fl. Open daily 5pm-2am.

The Alibi Room, 85 Pike St. (☎ 623-3180; www.alibiroom.com), across from Market Theater, in Post Alley in Pike Place. A friendly indie director-type hangout, with a bookshelf of scripts at the entrance. Bar with music. Downstairs dance floor open F-Sa. Mediterranean-style cuisine; brunch Sa-Su. Open daily 11am-2am.

Club Noc Noc, 1516 2nd Ave. (☎ 223-1333; www.clubnocnoc.com), between Pike and Pine. Casual and spacious, with exposed brick walls, lots of red lighting, and a dance floor, Club Noc Noc embraces everyone from goths to frat boys. Drink specials feature Pabst Blue Ribbon (M $0.50, Su $0.25) and an outstanding Happy hour 5-9pm (drinks $2). Cover $5 after 9pm. Open daily 5pm-2am.

PIONEER SQUARE

Artfully quirky by day, Pioneer Sq. transforms into a loud mix of bars and clubs at night, hopping with twentysomethings and cover bands.

J & M Cafe and Cardroom, 201 1st Ave. (☎ 292-0663), in the center of Pioneer Sq. A member of the "Club Stamp," which gives patrons access to a total of 9 participating Pioneer Sq. bars for 1 charge (M-Th and Su $5, F-Sa $10-12). Open daily 11am-2am.

Contour, 807 1st Ave. (☎ 447-7704; www.clubcontour.com). Intimate and elegant, the paintings, windows, and swanky statues make for a decadent dance spot. Happy hour M-F 3-8pm, Sa-Su 2-8pm; food $2, beer $2, mixed drinks $3.75. Cover up to $12. Open M 3pm-2am, Tu-Th 11:30am-2am, F 11:30am-5am, Sa 2pm-5am, Su 2pm-2am.

CAPITOL HILL

Centered around Broadway, Pike St., and Pine St., Capitol Hill is a lively, funky low-rise neighborhood with numerous clubs and bars. It is also the main hub of Seattle's GLBT scene.

🅦 **Linda's Tavern,** 707 E. Pine St. (☎ 325-1220). A quirky post-gig local scene with pool tables and comfort food ($4-10). On Tu DJ spins jazz, alternative, and rock. Happy hour 7-9pm. Open daily 4pm-2am.

■ **Havana,** 1010 E Pike St. (☎323-2822). So cool that even the entrance is a secret (look for the unmarked black awning in the parking lot off Pike), Havana's Cuban decor and world-famous mojitos keeps Seattle hedonists dancing all night. Open daily 4pm-2am.

Neighbours, 1509 Broadway (☎324-5358). Enter from the alley off Pike. A fixture in Seattle's gay scene, Neighbours is a techno-slick dance club. Frequent drag nights. Open Tu-W and Su 4pm-2am, Th 4pm-3am, F-Sa 4pm-4am.

◤ OUTDOOR ACTIVITIES

Biking is very popular in Seattle: the city prides itself on 30 mi. of bike-pedestrian trails, 90 mi. of signed bike routes, and 16 mi. of bike lanes on city streets. Each year up to 8000 cyclists participate in the 190 mi. **Seattle to Portland Classic (STP)** in mid-July. Call the **Cascade Bicycle Club** (☎522-3222; www.cascade.org) for info. On **Bicycle Saturdays/Sundays** from May to September (usually on the 2nd Sa and 3rd Su of each month), Lake Washington Blvd. is open only to cyclists 10am-6pm. Contact the **Seattle Parks and Recreation Activities Office** (☎684-4075; www.cityofseattle.net/parks) for info.

OLYMPIA   ☎ 360

From musicians and artists to politicians and lobbyists, an undeniably diverse crowd occupies Washington's capital city. Evergreen State College lies a few miles from the city center, throwing a liberal, tree-hugging student body into the mix. Located at the southern end of Puget Sound, Olympia is a gateway to the Olympic Peninsula and only a short hop from Mt. Rainier and the rest of the Cascade range. With a population just over 40,000, the city has a pleasant daytime town feel that transforms into a remarkably active bar scene at night.

◨ PRACTICAL INFORMATION. Settled at the junction of **I-5** and **U.S. 101** between **Tumwater** (to the south, I-5 Exit 102) and **Lacey** (to the east, I-5 Exit 108), Olympia makes a convenient stop on any north-south journey. Amtrak, 6600 Yelm Hwy. (☎923-4602; www.amtrak.com; open daily 8:15am-noon, 1:45-3:30pm, and 5:30-8:30pm), runs **trains** to Portland (2-2½hr., 45 per day, $23-32) and Seattle (1¾hr., 4 per day, $18-22). Greyhound, 107 7th Ave. SE (☎357-5541; www.greyhound.com), at Capitol Way, sends **buses** to Portland (2-2¾hr., 5 per day, $25) and Seattle (1¾hr., 5-6 per day, $12). Intercity Transit (IT) runs almost everywhere in Thurston County. (☎786-1881 or 800-287-6348; www.intercitytransit.com. $0.75; day pass $1.50.) To get to the **Washington State Capitol Visitors Center,** 103 14th Ave. SW, follow the signs from I-5. (☎586-3460; www.ga.wa.gov/visitor. Open Oct.-Apr. M-F 8am-5pm; May-Sept. also Sa-Su 9am-4pm.) The **Olympic National Forest Headquarters,** 1835 Black Lake Blvd. SW, has info on trails and camping on the nearby Olympic Peninsula. (☎956-2400; www.fs.fed.us/r6/olympic. Open M-F 8am-4:30pm.) **Post Office:** 900 Jefferson St. SE (☎357-2289. Open M-F 7:30am-6pm, Sa 9am-4pm.) **Postal Code:** 98501.

◨◧ ACCOMMODATIONS AND FOOD. Motels in Olympia and their $60-80 rooms generally cater to policy-makers; chains in nearby Tumwater are more affordable. Try **Motel 6 ❷,** 400 W. Lee St. (☎754-7320. Singles from $42; doubles from $48.) **Millersylvania State Park ❶,** 12245 Tilly Rd. S, 10 mi. south of Olympia, has 168 sites. Take Exit 95 off I-5, turn onto Rte. 121 N, and follow signs. (☎753-1519, reservations 888-226-7688. Showers $0.25 per 3min. Hiker or biker sites $14; drive-in sites $19, with hookup $26.) Diners, coffee shops, veggie cafes, and Asian quickstops line 4th Ave. east of Columbia. The ■**Olympia Farmers' Market,** 700 N.

Capitol Way, sells baked goods and other fantastic fare. (☎352-9096; www.olympi-afarmersmarket.com. Open Apr.-Oct. Th-Su 10am-3pm; Nov.-Dec. Sa-Su 10am-3pm.) Looking like the set of an old film noir, **The Spar Cafe & Bar ❸**, 114 E. 4th Ave., has been an icon for beer, burgers, and cigars for decades. (☎357-6444. Sa live jazz. Cafe open M-Th 6am-9pm, F-Sa 6am-10pm, Su 6am-8pm. Bar open M-Th 11am-midnight, F-Sa 11am-2am. AmEx/D/MC/V.)

◙ SIGHTS. Olympia's crowning glory is the **State Capitol**, 416 14th Ave. SW, a complex of government buildings, fountains, manicured gardens, veterans' monuments, and the recently remodeled Legislative Building, styled after St. Peter's Basilica in Rome. Tours depart from just inside the front steps, at 4th and Capitol. (☎902-8880. Tours every hr. daily. 10am-3pm. Building open M-F 8am-5pm, Sa-Su 10am-4pm.) **Wolf Haven International**, 3111 Offut Lake Rd., 10 mi. south of the capital, is a permanent home for captive-born gray wolves reclaimed from zoos and illegal owners. Tours offer an up-close look at this beautiful, oft-vilified species. (☎264-4695 or 800-448-9653; www.wolfhaven.org. Open Apr.-Sept. M and W-Sa 10am-4pm, Su noon-4pm; Oct.-Mar. only Sa-Su. 45min. tours every hr. Last tour 3pm. $8, seniors $7, ages 3-12 $6.) The **Nisqually National Wildlife Refuge** shelters 500 species of plants and animals by protecting the Nisqually River's estuary and its diverse mix of tidal mudflats, marshes, grasslands, and forest ecosystems, all laced with miles of trails. Visitors come to walk and to birdwatch, as both bald eagles and Northern spotted owls nest in the area. The Visitors Center loans out free binoculars and info packets—just leave behind some form of ID. Take Exit 114 off I-5 between Olympia and Tacoma. (☎753-9467; www.fws.gov/nisqually. Visitors Center office open W-Su 9am-4pm. Park office open M-F 7:30am-4pm. Park open dawn-dusk. Trails closed to cyclists, joggers, and pets. $3 per car.)

◖ NIGHTLIFE. Olympia's thriving nightlife seems to have outgrown its daylife. The *Olympian* (www.theolympian.com) lists live music events. ◙**Fish Tale Brewpub**, 515 Jefferson St. SE, reflects Olympia's love for the sea and beer; the locally-brewed British ales served here are named after fish. (☎943-3650; www.fish-brewing.com. Ales $3.50. Happy hour M-Th 9-11pm. Open M-Sa 11am-midnight, Su noon-10pm.) At **Eastside Club and Tavern**, 410 4th Ave. E, patrons come to dance, play pool, and sip microbrews. (☎357-9985; www.theeastsideclub.com. Pints $2.75; M $1.75, Th $2. Happy hour daily 4-7pm; pints $2.50. Open M-F noon-2am, Sa-Su 3pm-2am.) Locals gather for "slabs" of pizza, seafood baskets, live music, and 26 regional microbrews at **4th Avenue Alehouse & Eatery**, 210 4th Ave. E. (☎786-1444; www.the4thave.com. Pizza $5.25. Pints $3. Free Wi-Fi. Th-Sa live music 9pm. Happy hour daily 5-7pm. Cover $3-10. Open M-F 11:30am-2am, F-Sa noon-2am.)

SAN JUAN ISLANDS ☎360

Made up of hundreds of tiny islands and forested parks, the San Juan Islands are an explorer's dream, enjoying nearly perfect weather. From May to September, the sun shines almost every day, and only a few inches of rain fall each summer month in this "rain shadow" of the Olympic Mountains. Tourists storm the islands in July and August; early June and September tend to be slightly less packed.

◪ INTER-ISLAND TRANSPORTATION

Washington State Ferries has frequent daily service to Lopez (50min.), Orcas (1½hr.), San Juan Island (1½hr.), and Shaw (1¼hr.) from Anacortes. Travel time to the islands depends on the number of stops. To save on fares, travel directly to the westernmost island on your itinerary, then return: eastbound traffic travels for

PACIFIC NORTHWEST

free. The ferries are packed in the summer, so arrive at least 1hr. (2hr. on weekends) before departure. (☎206-464-6400 or 800-843-3779; www.wsdot.wa.gov/ferries. May to mid-Oct. $12, vehicles $44-49, bikes $4; mid-Oct. to May $10/33-37/2. Cash only outside Anacortes. Eastbound traffic free. Westbound inter-island: passengers free, vehicles $19.35.)

The **Bellingham Airporter** (☎380-8800 or 866-235-5247; www.airporter.com) **buses** go between Sea-Tac and Anacortes (12 per day to Anacortes, 10 continue to ferries; $31). Island Commuter (☎738-8099 or 800-443-4552; www.islandcommuter.com) **ferry** departs Bellingham for Friday Harbor (2½hr., 1 per day) and islands on the way ($39, round-trip $49; ages 6-12 $25/20; under 6 free). Victoria Clipper (☎800-888-2535; www.victoriaclipper.com) departs Seattle's Pier 69 daily for San Juan Island, arriving at Spring St., landing in Friday Harbor (2½hr.; June to mid-Sept. 1 per day, late Sept. Sa-Su 1 per day; round-trip $60-75, ages 11 and under $30-35).

SAN JUAN ISLAND

The biggest and most popular of the islands, San Juan is easy to explore because the ferry docks right in town, the roads are good for cyclists, and a shuttle bus services the island. The **West Side Road** traverses gorgeous scenery and provides the best chance for seeing orcas. Mullis Rd. merges with Cattle Point Rd. and goes straight into **American Camp,** on the south side of the island, one of two parts of the **San Juan National Historical Park. English Camp,** the other half of the park, lies on West Valley Rd. in **Garrison Bay.** (Buildings open June-Aug. daily 9am-5pm.) On Saturday afternoons in June and July, the two camps alternate performing reenactments of daily life from the time of the Pig War, a mid-19th-century squabble between the US and Britain over control of the islands. (☎378-2240. Open June-Aug. daily dawn-11pm; Sept.-May Th-Su dawn-11pm. Visitors Centers open June-Aug. daily 9am-5pm; Sept.-May Th-Su 8:30am-4:30pm. Guided walks June-Sept. Sa 11:30am. reenactments Sa 12:30-3:30pm.) **Lime Kiln Point State Park,** along West Side Rd., is the best whale-watching spot in the area.

🔲**Wayfarer's Rest ❶,** 35 Malcolm St., is a 10min. walk from the ferry onto Argyle St.; turn left at the church. This house-turned-hostel has driftwood bunks, a patio, a full kitchen, and laundry. (☎378-6428; www.rockisland.com/~wayfarersrest. Bike rental $15 per day. Linen included. Check-in 2-9pm. May-Sept. dorms $25; private rooms and cabins from $60. Oct.-April $22/55. MC/V.) **San Juan County Park ❶,** 50 San Juan Park Rd., 10 mi. west of Friday Harbor, has 20 sites perched on a bluff with a fantastic sunset view. (☎378-1842; www.co.san-juan.wa.us/parks. Reservations strongly recommended in summer; in winter, all sites are first come, first served. Reservation fee $7. Sites $6; vehicle sites $25.) **Hungry Clam Fish and Chips ❷,** 205 A St., serves fresh beer-battered seafood. (☎378-3474. Open daily late May-early Sept. 11am-9pm; early Sept.-late May 11am-7pm. MC/V.)

San Juan Transit (☎378-8887 or 800-887-8387; www.sanjuantransit.com) **buses** travel from Friday Harbor to Roche Harbor on the hour. ($5; day pass $15. Tours depart Friday Harbor at 11am and 1:30pm. $17.) Island Bicycles, 380 Argyle Ave., rents **bikes.** (☎378-4941; www.islandbicycles.com. $7 per hr., $35 per day. Open daily 9am-6pm.) The **Chamber of Commerce,** 1 Front St. 2A, is at Front and Spring St. (☎378-5240 or 888-468-3701; www.sanjuanisland.org or www.guidetosanjuans.com. Open Apr.-Nov. M-F 10am-4pm. Call for low-season hours.)

ORCAS ISLAND

A small population of retirees, artists, and farmers dwells here in understated homes surrounded by red madrona trees. **Moran State Park** is unquestionably Orcas's star attraction. Over 30 mi. of hiking trails range from a 1hr. jaunt around **Mountain Lake** to a day-long trek up the south face of **Mount Constitution** (2407 ft.), the highest peak on the islands. The peak, also accessible by car, features a stone ⬛**observation tower** at the top, offering one of the best 360-degree marine viewpoints in North America. Partway down, **Cascade Falls** is spectacular in the spring and early summer. South of Moran, the trail to **Obstruction Pass Beach** is the best way to clamber down to the rocky shores. **Shearwater Adventures** runs sea kayak tours exploring various parts of the island. (☎376-4699; shearwaterkayaks.com. 3hr. tour with 30min. of dry-land training $49 per person.) **Crescent Beach Kayak,** on the highway 1 mi. east of Eastsound, rents kayaks for use around Crescent Beach. (☎376-2464. Open daily 9am-7pm. $18 per hr., $50 per half-day.)

Doe Bay Resort ❶, on Pt. Lawrence Rd., off Olga Rd., is a relaxing former commune complete with a hot tub, volleyball, horseshoes, and yoga classes. (☎376-2291; www.doebay.com. Sauna $10 per day. 1½hr. yoga classes $10. Reception 11am-9pm. Dorms $25-30; campsites $30/35; private rooms from $65-75; yurts $75-85. MC/V.) The resort also houses a **cafe ❷** which serves organic dishes. (☎376-8059. Open daily 8am-2pm; W-Su also 5-9pm. MC/V.) The **farmers' market** in Eastsound on North Beach Rd. is another good place for grub. (Open May-Oct. Sa 10am-3pm.) **Moran State Park ❶,** on Horseshoe Hwy. (Olga Rd.), is 15 mi. from the ferry landing. Follow Horseshoe Hwy. into the park, 14 mi. from the ferry on the east side. The 151 campgrounds spread out along **Cascade Lake ❶** are the islands' most popular camping. (☎902-8844, reservations 888-226-7688. 12 primitive sites open year-round. Showers $0.50 per 3min. Standard sites $16; primitive sites $10.)

The ferry lands on the southwest tip of Orcas; the main town of Eastsound is 9 mi. northeast. Olga and Doe Bay are an additional 8 and 11 mi., respectively, down the island's eastern side. Orcas Island Shuttle (☎376-7433; www.orcasislandshuttle.com) runs **public buses** through most of the island ($5; day pass $10; bikes $1 extra per ride). Dolphin Bay Bicycles, at the ferry landing, rents **bikes** for $30 per day. (☎376-4157; www.rockisland.com/~dolphin. Reservations recommended.)

LOPEZ ISLAND

Smaller than either Orcas or San Juan, Lopez lacks some of the tourist facilities of the larger islands. Still, the island is a blessing for those looking for solitary beaches, bicycling without car traffic, and a small-town atmosphere. On the southwest end of the island, the small **Shark Reef County Park** has well-maintained hiking trails leading to a rocky beach. The even smaller **Agate Beach Country Park** is home to a calm, deserted beach. **Lopez Village** is a tiny town 4½ mi. from the ferry dock off Fisherman Bay Rd. Roads on the island are ideal for biking.

Spencer Spit State Park ❶, on the northeast corner of the island about 3½ mi. from the ferry terminal, has seven beach sites and 30 wooded sites. (☎468-2251, reservations 888-226-7688. Park open Apr.-Oct. dawn-10pm. Reservations required. Sites $16.) Find delicious breads ($3-5) and pastries ($3) at ⬛**Holly B's Bakery ❶,** Lopez Plaza in Lopez Village. The ham and Gruyère croissant ($3) is a favorite. (☎468-2133. Open early Apr. to late Nov. M and W-Sa 7am-5pm, Su 7am-4pm; winter hours vary. Cash only.) To rent a **bike,** go to Lopez Bicycle Works. (☎468-2847; www.lopezbicycleworks.com. Open June-Aug. daily 10am-6pm, May and Sept. daily 10am-5pm. Bikes $5 per hr., $25 per day.)

OLYMPIC PENINSULA

Due west of Seattle and its busy Puget Sound neighbors, the Olympic Peninsula is a backpacking paradise. Olympic National Park dominates much of the peninsula, preserving its glacier-capped mountains and temperate rainforests. To the west, the Pacific Ocean stretches from rugged beaches to a distant horizon; to the north, the Strait of Juan de Fuca separates the Olympic Peninsula from Canada's Vancouver Island; and to the east, Hood Canal and the Kitsap Peninsula isolate this sparsely inhabited wilderness from Seattle's urban intensity.

PORT TOWNSEND ☎360

When rumors circulated in the late 1800s that the railroad would connect Port Townsend to the east, wealthy families flocked to the overlooking bluffs, constructing elaborate Victorian homes and stately public buildings. The railroad actually bypassed Port Townsend, but the neglected town was rediscovered in the 70s and turned into a vibrant and creative community. Now, in addition to cafes, galleries, and bookstores, Port Townsend takes advantage of its 19th-century flavor to entice those heading to the park onto Rte. 20 into town. **Point Hudson,** where Admiralty Inlet and Port Townsend Bay meet, is the hub of a small shipbuilding area. Check out boatbuilders crafting sea kayaks and sailboats. North of Point Hudson are several miles of beach and the beautiful **Chetzemoka Park,** at Garfield and Jackson St., with an ocean view and endless manicured flowerbeds.

The ◧**Olympic Hostel (HI) ❶,** 272 Battery Way, in Fort Worden State Park, 1½ mi. from town, is a converted WWII barracks and one of the best hostels in the Pacific Northwest with immaculate rooms and beautiful setting. (☎385-0655; olympichostel@olympus.net, www.olympichostel.org. Make-your-own pancake breakfast $2-3. Check-in 5-10pm. Check-out 9:30am. Reservations recommended. Dorms $20, members $17. MC/V.) To reach the small, homey **Marrowstone Island Hostel (HI) ❶,** 10621 Flagler Rd., in Fort Flagler State Park, on Marrowstone Island 20 mi. from Port Townsend, go south on Rte. 19, which connects to Rte. 116 E and leads into the park. (☎385-1288. Check-in 5-10pm. Lockout 10am-5pm. Reservations recommended. Open June-Sept. Dorms $17, members $14. MC/V.) Camp close to the beach or in the nearby forest at the 116-site **Fort Flagler State Park ❶.** (☎385-1259 or ☎888-226-7688. Check-in 2:30pm. Check-out 1pm. Quiet hours 10pm-6:30am. Open for camping Mar.-Oct. Reservations recommended. Hiker or biker sites $12; car sites $17; RV sites $24.) Indulge in organic sandwiches and sweets at the cheery **Sweet Laurette & Cyndee's Cafe and Patisserie ❷,** 1029 Lawrence St., in uptown. The lemon ricotta pancakes are divine. (☎385-4880. Breakfast $5-9. Lunch $7-12. Open M-Sa 8am-2:30pm, Su 8am-2pm. MC/V.) **El Sarape ❷,** 628 Water St., serves a variety of Mexican dishes with a full bar to boot. (☎379-9343. Burritos $5-7. Dinner $7-11. Open in summer M-Th and Su 11am-9pm, F-Sa 11am-10pm; in winter M-Th and Su 11am-8pm, F-Sa 11am-9pm. AmEx/D/MC/V.)

Port Townsend sits at the terminus of **Route 20** on the northeastern corner of the Olympic Peninsula. It can be reached by **U.S. 101,** or from the Kitsap Peninsula across the Hood Canal Bridge. **Washington State Ferries** (☎206-464-6400; www.wsdot.wa.gov/ferries) go between Port Townsend and Keystone on Whidbey Island (30min.; 16 per day; $2.50, car and driver $9-11). **P.T. Cyclery,** 2352 Tyler St., rents mountain bikes. (☎385-6470; www.ptcyclery.com. $7 per hr., $25 per day. Open M-Sa 9am-6pm.) **Visitor Info:** The **Port Townsend Chamber of Commerce,** 2437 E. Sims Way, is west of town on Rte. 20. (☎385-2722 or 888-365-6978; www.ptchamber.org. Open M-F 9am-5pm, Sa 10am-4pm, Su 11am-4pm.) **Post Office:** 1322 Washington St. (☎385-1600. Open M-F 9am-5pm, Sa 10am-2pm.) **Postal Code:** 98368.

OLYMPIC NATIONAL PARK ☎360

Olympic National Park (ONP) is certainly the centerpiece of the Olympic Peninsula, sheltering one of the most diverse landscapes of any region in the world. The towering peaks, covered in snow from the water-laden winds and drastically carved by ancient glaciers, form the most dramatic feature of the park. Roads lead to many corners of Olympic National Park, but with over 90% of the park roadless, they only hint at the depths of its wilderness. A foray into the backcountry leaves summer tourists behind and reveals the park's richness and diversity.

ORIENTATION AND PRACTICAL INFORMATION

Each side of the park has one major settlement—**Port Townsend** to the east, **Port Angeles** to the north, and **Forks** to the west. U.S. 101 forms an upside-down "U," passing through almost every small town. The park's eastern rim runs up to Port Townsend, from which the heavily touristed northern rim extends westward. Along a winding detour on Rte. 112, off U.S. 101 going west, the tiny town of **Neah Bay** and stunning **Cape Flattery** perch at the tip of the peninsula. Temperate rainforests lie on the west side of ONP and in the **Hoh, Queets,** and **Quinault River valleys,** where low valleys claim the ocean moisture before it slides up the mountains' sides. July, August, and September are the best months for visiting Olympic National Park, as roads and trails become saturated in early fall, though visitors can enjoy beach walks throughout spring and fall. **Entrance passes** are available at ranger stations and park entrances ($15 per car, $5 per hiker or biker; good for 1 week). **Olympic National Park Visitors Center,** 3002 Mt. Angeles Rd., is off Race St. in Port Angeles. (☎565-3130; www.nps.gov/olym. Open daily May-early Sept. 9am-4:30pm; late Sept. to Apr. M and Th-Su 10am-4pm.) The staff at the **Olympic National Park Wilderness Information Center** (☎565-3100; www.nps.gov/olym), just behind the Visitors Center, helps design trips within the park.

ACCOMMODATIONS AND CAMPING

The closest budget accommodations are at the ⬛**Rainforest Hostel ❶,** 169312 U.S. 101, 20 mi. south of Forks. Follow the signs from U.S. 101. The hostel boasts a large co-ed dorm, two rooms for couples, and a family room. (☎374-2270; www.rainforesthostel.com. Chore required. Reservations required. Internet $0.10 per min. for 1st 15min., $0.05 each additional min. Laundry $2. Sites $4.25. Dorms $8.50; couples' rooms $18. Cash or traveler's checks only.) Olympic National Park maintains 16 **campgrounds ❶.** Sites at Kalaloch campground ($14 per night) can be reserved (www.recreation.gov), but the other campgrounds are first-come, first-served. **Backcountry camping ❶** in the park costs $2 per person, and there is a $5 registration fee per group. The Washington Department of Natural Resources allows free backcountry camping 300 ft. from any state road on DNR land, mostly accessible via the western shore along the Hoh and Clearwater Rivers. From July to September, most spaces are taken by 2pm, but very popular sites fill by noon.

OUTDOOR ACTIVITIES

EASTERN RIM
The eastern rim stuns visitors with its canals and grandiose views of the peninsula and Puget Sound. Steep trails lead up **Mt. Ellinor,** 5 mi. past Staircase on Rte. 119. Hikers can choose the 3 mi. path or an equally steep but shorter journey to the summit; look for signs to the Upper Trailhead along Forest Rd. #2419-04. Adventurers who hit the mountain before late July should bring snow clothes to "mach" (as in Mach 1) down a quarter-mile snow chute. In the nearby National Forest, a 3¼ mi. hike goes to **Lena Lake,** 14 mi. north of Hoodsport off U.S. 101; follow Forest Service Rd. 25 off U.S. 101 for 8 mi. to the trailhead. The Forest Service charges $3 per trailhead pass. The **West Forks/Dosewallips River Trail,** a 10½ mi. trek to **Mount Anderson Glacier,** was the shortest route to any glacier in the park—however, a washout has recently closed part of the access road, adding an extra 5½ mi. of hik-

ing to reach the trailhead. The US Forest Service has yet to release a statement about when the access road will re-open. The road to **Mount Walker Viewpoint,** 5 mi. south of Quilcene on U.S. 101, has sheer dropoffs and shouldn't be attempted in bad weather or in a temperamental car. A view of Hood Canal, Puget Sound, Mt. Rainier, and Seattle awaits travelers at the top.

NORTHERN RIM
The most developed section of Olympic National Park lies along its northern rim, near the Port Angeles settlement, where glaciers, rainforests, and sunsets over the Pacific are only a short drive away. Farthest east off U.S. 101, accessible by an 18mi. narrow, winding road, lies **Deer Park,** where trails tend to be uncrowded. Also on the northern rim, the **Royal Basin Trail** meanders 6¼ mi. to the **Royal Basin Waterfall.** The road up **Hurricane Ridge** is a curvy drive, so be cautious. Before July, walking on the ridge usually involves some snow-stepping. Clear days provide splendid views of Mt. Olympus and Vancouver Island set against a foreground of snow and indigo lupine. A number of trails of varying levels of difficulty are available on and around Hurricane Ridge (check at the Hurricane Ridge Visitor Center for suggestions and a map). On weekends from late December to late March, the Park Service organizes snowshoe walks on the ridge. Farther west, the **Sol Duc trailhead** is a starting point for those heading up, but crowds thin dramatically above **Sol Duc Falls.** The **Eagle Ranger Station** has information. (☎327-3534. Open in summer daily 8am-4:30pm.)

NEAH BAY AND CAPE FLATTERY
At the westernmost point on the Juan de Fuca Strait and north of the park's western rim is **Neah Bay,** known as the "Pompeii of the Pacific." The only town in the **Makah Reservation,** Neah Bay is a 500-year-old village that was buried in a landslide at Cape Alava. The Makah Nation, whose recorded history goes back 2000 years, still lives here. Just inside the reservation, the **Makah Cultural and Research Center,** in Neah Bay on Rte. 112, has archaeological artifacts. (☎645-2711; www.makah.com/mcrchome.htm. Open June to mid-Sept. daily 10am-5pm; mid-Sept. to May W-Su 10am-5pm. Free tours W-Su noon-4pm. $5, students and seniors $4.) For over 80 years, local Native Americans have come for canoe races, dances, and bone games during **Makah Days,** a festival held on the last weekend of August. (☎645-2711; www.makah.com/makahdays.htm. $7 permit required per car.) **☒Cape Flattery,** the northwesternmost point in the contiguous US, lies just outside Neah Bay. Take the road through town until it becomes dirt, then past the "Marine Viewing Area," where a half-mile trail leads to the cape's breathtaking cliffs well worth the long drive. **Clallam Transit System** runs bus #14 from Oak St. in Port Angeles to Sappho, then #16 to Neah Bay. (☎452-4511; www.clallamtransit.com. $0.75, ages 6-19 $0.50, seniors $0.25; day pass $2.) You can also reach Neah Bay and Cape Flattery by detour from U.S. 101. From Port Angeles, Rte. 112 leads west to Neah Bay; Rte. 113 runs north from Sappho to Rte. 112.

COASTAL ZONE
Pristine coastline traces the park's far western region for over 70 mi., separated from the rest of ONP by U.S. 101 and non-park timberland. Eerie fields of driftwood, sculptured arches, and dripping caves frame flaming sunsets, while the waves are punctuated by rugged sea stacks. Between the Quinault and Hoh Reservations, U.S. 101 hugs the coast for 15 mi., with parking lots a short walk from the sand. North of Kalaloch, **Beach #4** has abundant tide pools plastered with sea stars. **Beach #6,** 3 mi. north at Mi. 160, is a favorite whale-watching spot. Near Mi. 165, sea otters and eagles hang amid tide pools and sea stacks at **Ruby Beach.** Beach camping (wilderness permit required) is permitted north of the Hoh Reser-

vation between **Oil City** and **Third Beach** and north of the Quileute Reservation between **Hole-in-the-Wall** and **Shi-Shi Beach.** Day hikers and backpackers adore the 9 mi. loop that begins at **Ozette Lake.** The trail has two 3 mi. legs leading along boardwalks through the rainforest. One heads toward sea stacks at **Cape Alava,** and the other goes to a beach at **Sand Point.** A 3 mi. hike down the coast links the two legs, passing ancient petroglyphs. The **Wilderness Information Center** has more info (☎565-3100). Campers should be sure to reserve permits in advance.

WESTERN RIM
In the rainforests of ONP's western rim, ferns, mosses, and giant old-growth trees blanket the earth. The drive along the **Hoh River Valley,** actively logged land outside the park's boundaries, is alternately overgrown and barren. **Hoh Rainforest Visitors Center** is a 45min. drive from U.S. 101 on the western rim. (☎374-6925; www.nps.gov/olym. Open mid-June to early Sept. daily 9am-4pm; in winter F-Su only.) From the Visitors Center, take the three-quarter-mile. **Hall of Mosses Trail** for a tour of the rainforest. With educational panels scattered throughout providing information about the rainforest plants and animals, the **Spruce Nature Trail** leads 1¼ mi. through the forest and along the Hoh River. The **Hoh Rainforest Trail** starts at the Visitors Center and edges the Hoh River for 18 mi. before reaching **Blue Glacier** on the shoulder of Mt. Olympus. The 4 mi. **Quinault Lake Loop** and half-mile **Maple Glade Trail** begin at the **Quinault Rain Forest Ranger Station,** on the Quinault North Shore Rd. (☎288-2525. Open May-Sept. M-F 8am-4:30pm, Sa-Su 9am-4pm; Oct.-Apr. M-F 9am-4:30pm.) **Quinault Lake** lures anglers, rowers, and canoers. The **Lake Quinault Lodge,** on the south shore, rents boats. (☎288-2900 or 800-562-6672; www.visitlakequinault.com. Rentals from $13 per hr.)

CASCADE RANGE

Intercepting the moist Pacific air, the Cascades divide Washington into the lush, wet green of the west and the dry plains of the east. The Cascades are most accessible from July to September; many of the mountain passes are snowed in during the rest of the year, making access extremely difficult. Mt. Baker, Vernon, Glacier, Adams, and the stunning Mt. Rainier and Mt. St. Helens are accessible by four major roads. The North Cascades Hwy. (Rte. 20) is the most breathtaking and runs to North Cascades National Park. Scenic U.S. 2 leaves Everett for Stevens Pass and descends along the Wenatchee River. U.S. 12 approaches Mt. Rainier through White Pass and reaches Mt. St. Helens from the north. I-90 sends four lanes from Seattle past the ski resorts of Snoqualmie Pass and eastward towards Spokane.

MOUNT SAINT HELENS ☎360
In one cataclysmic blast on May 18, 1980, Mt. St. Helens erupted, transforming what had been a perfect cone into a crater. The force of the ash-filled blast reduced the mountain's height by 1300 ft. and razed forests, strewing trees like matchsticks. Ash from the crater rocketed 17 mi. upward, blackening the sky. The explosion with 27,000 times the force of the atomic bomb dropped on Hiroshima. Today, Mt. St. Helens is comprised of part of the **Gifford Pinchot National Forest,** as well as **Mount Saint Helens National Volcanic Monument.** Mt. St. Helens is still an active volcano and began to belch smoke and ash once more in September 2004.

■■ ❼ ORIENTATION AND PRACTICAL INFORMATION. To take the most popular and worthwhile approach into town, take Exit 49 off **I-5** and use **Route 504,** otherwise known as the **Spirit Lake Memorial Highway.** The 52 mi. road has astounding views of the crater and includes the Mt. St. Helens Visitor Center, the Coldwater Ridge Visitor Center, and the Johnston Ridge Observatory. **Route 503** skirts the south side of the volcano until it becomes **Forest Service Road 90.** From there, **Forest Service Road 83** leads to lava caves and the Climber's Bivouac, a launching pad for treks up the mountain. Views from this side don't highlight the destruction from the 1980 eruption, but the green glens and remnants of age-old lava and mud flows make up for it with great camping and hiking. For a northern approach, take **U.S. 12** east from I-5 (Exit 68). The towns of **Mossyrock, Morton,** and **Randle** along U.S. 12 offer the closest major services. Vigorous winter rains often spoil access roads; check at a ranger station for road closures before heading out.

The monument charges entrance fees at almost every Visitors Center, viewpoint, and cave. (1-day all-access $8, under 16 free. Individual monument fees $3/1.) With interactive exhibits, **Mount Saint Helens Visitors Center,** across from Seaquest State Park at milepost 5 on Rte. 504, is most visitors' first stop. A detailed exhibit looks at the events leading up to the 1980 eruption in increments of years, months, days, and finally, seconds. (☎274-0962. Open daily May-late Oct. 9am-5pm; late Oct.-Apr. 9am-4pm.) Coldwater Ridge Visitors Center, 38 mi. farther at milepost 43 on Rte. 504, has a superb view of the crater along with trails leading to Coldwater Lake and exhibits about the eruptions impact on plants and wildlife in the area. (☎274-2114. Open in summer daily 10am-6pm; call for winter hours.) Overlooking the crater, **Johnston Ridge Observatory,** at the end of Rte. 504 at milepost 52, focuses on geological exhibits and offers the best roadside view of the crater. A fantastic 16min. film features a digital recreation of the blast that fills in the space between the famous stills depicting the eruption. (☎274-2143. Open May-Oct. daily 10am-6pm.) **Pine Creek Information Station,** 17 mi. east of Cougar on Rd. 90, shows a film of the eruption. This station is the only place in the south of the park with free water. (☎449-7800. Open mid-June to Sept. daily 9am-6pm.) **Apes Headquarters,** at Ape Cave on Rd. 8303 on the south side of the volcano, is 3 mi. north of the Rd. 83/Rd. 90 junction. Rangers guide lantern walks into a 1900-year-old lava tube. (Open late May-Sept. daily 10am-5:30pm. Guided walks on the half-hour daily 10:30am-4:30pm.)

🏕🍴 **CAMPING AND FOOD.** Although the monument itself has no campgrounds, a number are scattered throughout the surrounding national forest. Free dispersed camping is allowed within the monument, but finding a site takes luck. **Iron Creek Campground ❶** is the closest campsite to Mt. St. Helens, situated in a moss- and fern-filled forest with good hiking nearby. All 97 sites can fill up on busy weekends. (☎877-444-6777; www.recreation.gov. Reservations strongly recommended in summer. Sites $16-18.) **Swift Campground ❶,** 30min. east of Cougar on Rd. 90, just west of the Pine Creek Information Station, has spacious sites on Swift Reservoir and is one of the most popular campgrounds in the area. 93 Sites ($14) go on a first come, first served basis. (Open late Apr.-Nov.) Along Yale Lake are **Cougar Campground ❶** and **Beaver Bay ❶,** 2 and 4 mi. east of Cougar, respectively. Cougar Park (open Memorial Day-Labor Day) has 60 sites that are more spread out and private than Beaver Bay's 78 sites. Reservations required at Cougar Campground, while Beaver Bay is first come, first served. (☎503-813-6666. Sites $14-26). **Jack's Restaurant and Country Store ❷,** 13411 Louis River Rd., 5 mi. west of Cougar (I-5 Exit 21) on Rte. 503, serves standard American fare. (☎231-4276. Breakfast $4-8. Lunch $6-9. Dinner $6-10. Open M-Th and Su 6am-9pm, F-Sa 6am-10pm. AmEx/D/MC/V.)

🥾 **OUTDOOR ACTIVITIES.** Along each approach, short trails loop into the landscape. The 1hr. drive from the Mt. St. Helens Visitors Center to Johnston Ridge offers spectacular views of the crater and its resurgence of life. Another 10 mi.

east, the hike along **Johnston Ridge,** where geologist David Johnston died studying the eruption, offers unbeatable views of the crater. On the way west along Rd. 99, **Bear Meadow** provides the first stop, an excellent view of Mt. St. Helens, then continues until Rd. 99 ends at **Windy Ridge.** The monument begins just west of Bear Meadow, where Rd. 26 and 99 meet. Rangers lead half-mile walks around emerald **Meta Lake;** meet at Miner's Car at the junction of Rd. 26 and 99. (Tours late June-Sept.) Farther west on Rd. 99, **Independence Pass Trail #227** is a difficult 3½ mi. hike overlooking Spirit Lake, with views of the crater and dome. For a serious hike, continue along this trail to its intersection with the spectacular **Norway Pass Trail,** which runs 8 mi. through the blast zone to **Mt. Margaret** peak. Farther west, the 2 mi. **Harmony Trail #224** provides the shore access to Spirit Lake. From Windy Ridge, a steep ash hill called the "sand ladder" grants a magnificent view of the crater from 3½ mi. away. As of June 2007, those who wish to climb the actual mountain (5 mi., elevation 4500 ft.) must obtain **climbing permits** online (www.fs.fed.us/gpnf/mshnvm/; $22). Be sure to do so early, since permits are capped at 100 per day. Although climbing is allowed, entry in the actual volcanic crater is prohibited. Before your climb, you must register outside of Jack's Restaurant and Country Store (see above). Cavers should head to **Ape Cave,** 5 mi. east of Cougar just off Rd. 83. The cave is a broken 2½ mi. lava tube formed by an ancient eruption. When exploring the cave, wear a jacket and sturdy shoes, and take at least two flashlights. Rangers lead 10 free guided cave explorations per day (p. 976).

MOUNT RAINIER NATIONAL PARK ☎ 360

At 14,411 ft., Mt. Rainier (ray-NEER) presides regally over the Cascade Range as the giant among giants. The Klickitat native people called it Tahoma, or "Mountain of God," but Rainier is simply "the Mountain" to most Washington residents. Perpetually snowcapped, this dormant volcano draws thousands of visitors from around the globe. Clouds mask the mountain at least 200 days each year, frustrating visitors who come solely to see its distinctive summit. Its sharp ridges, steep gullies, and glaciers make Rainier inhospitable to the thousands of climbers who attempt its summit each year. Non-alpinists can explore over 305 mi. of trails that weave through old-growth forests, alpine meadows, and bubbling hot springs.

■ ☷ **ORIENTATION AND PRACTICAL INFORMATION.** To reach Mt. Rainier from the northwest, take **I-5** to Tacoma, then go east on **Route 512,** south on **Route 7,** and east on **Route 706.** Rte. 706, open year-round, runs through the town of Ashford and into the park by the **Nisqually** entrance, leading to the Visitors Centers of **Longmire** and **Paradise.** Snow usually closes all other park roads from November to May. **Stevens Canyon Road** connects the southeast corner of the national park with Paradise, Longmire, and the Nisqually entrance, unfolding superb vistas of Rainier and the Tatoosh Range along the way. Mt. Rainier is 65 mi. from Tacoma and 90 mi. from Seattle; call a ranger station for road updates.

The best place to plan a backcountry trip is at the **Longmire Wilderness Information Center** (☎569-4453; open late May to early Oct. daily 7:30am-5pm), east of the Nisqually entrance; or the **White River Wilderness Information Center** (☎569-6030; open late May to Sept. M-F and Su 7am-8pm, Sa 7am-5pm), off Rte. 410 on the park's east side. Both distribute free **backcountry permits,** good for seven days. **Jackson Visitor Center** (☎569-6036; www.nps.gov/mora; open daily June-Sept. M-F and Su 7am-7pm, Sa 6am-6pm; open mid-Oct. to Apr. weekends only.), at Paradise, is also available. An **entrance fee** is required. ($15 per car, $5 per hiker. Gates open 24hr.) **Rainier Mountaineering, Inc. (RMI),** 20027 S.R. 706 E, in the Rainier Base Camp complex, in Ashford, leads summit climbs. (☎569-2227 or 888-892-5462; www.rmiguides.com. Open May-Sept. daily 7am-8pm; Oct.-Apr. M-F 9am-5pm.) All kinds of equipment are available to rent or buy at **Whittaker Mountaineering,** 30027 S.R. 706 E, in Ashford. (☎800-238-5756; www.whittakermountaineering.com. Sleeping bag $30 per day, $50 per 5 days. Ice axe $17 per day, $32 per 5 days. Open in summer M-F 9am-5pm, Sa-Su 8am-6pm; call for low-season hours.) **Post Office:** Inside National Park Inn, in Longmire. (Open M-F 8:30am-5pm, Sa 8:30am-noon.) **Postal Code:** 98397.

⬛⬛ ACCOMMODATIONS AND FOOD. ⬛ Hotel Packwood ❷, 104 Main St., in Packwood, was established as a Historic Landmark in 1912. (☎494-5431; www.packwoodwa.com. Singles $29; doubles from $35. D/MC/V.) Originally a logger and mill workers bunkhouse, **Whittaker's Bunkhouse ❶,** 30205 Rte. 706 E, in Ashford, 6 mi. west of the Nisqually entrance, offers homey rooms loosely reminiscent of an alpine lodge, with a hot tub and espresso bar, but no kitchen or linens. **Camping ❶** in the park is largely first come, first served from mid-June to late September, with some reservable sites. (Low-season reservations ☎877-444-6777; www.recreation.gov. Prices range from free to $15.) National park campgrounds all have wheelchair-accessible facilities, but no hookups or showers. Coin-operated showers are available at Jackson Memorial Visitors Center, in Paradise. **Cougar Rock ❶** (173 sites, $12-15), 2¼ mi. north of Longmire, is in the southwest. The serene high canopy of **Ohanapecosh ❶** (188 sites, $15) is 11 mi. north of Packwood on Rte. 123, in the southeast. **White River ❶** (112 sites, $12) is 5 mi. west of White River Entrance on the way to Sunrise, in the northeast. **Backcountry camping ❶** requires a **permit,** free from ranger stations and Visitors Centers. Fires are prohibited in the backcountry. Hikers with a valid permit can camp at trailside, alpine, and snowfield sites (most with toilets and water). **Blanton's Market,** 13040 U.S. 12, in Packwood, is the closest decent supermarket and has an ATM. (☎494-6101. Open M-F 7am-9pm, Sa-Su 7am-10pm.) **Wild Berry Restaurant ❷,** 37718 S.R. 706 E, 1 mi. outside the Nisqually entrance, serves home-style meals with several vegetarian options and fresh pies. Sack lunches are also available. (☎569-2042. Sandwiches $7. Dinner $8-9. Open daily 7am-9pm. D/MC/V.)

⬛ OUTDOOR ACTIVITIES. There are far too many hiking trails to list—Mt. Rainier National Park is Washington's most versatile area, with room for summer tourists, rugged winter explorers, and all those in between. One option is a **ranger-led interpretive hike,** which can cover anything from area history to local wildflowers. Each Visitors Center conducts its own hikes, and most campgrounds have evening talks. The most interesting and inevitably full are those at Paradise.

Mt. Adams and Mt. St. Helens can be seen from mountain trails like **Paradise** (1½ mi.), **Pinnacle Peak** (2½ mi.), **Eagle Peak** (7 mi.), and **Van Trump Park** (5½ mi.). One of the oldest stands of trees in Washington, the **Grove of Patriarchs** grows near the Ohanapecosh Visitors Center. An easy 1½ mi. walk leads to these 500- to 1000-year-old Douglas firs, cedars, and hemlocks. The **Summerland** and **Indian Bar Trails** are excellent for serious backpacking—this is where rangers go on their days off. **Carbon River Valley,** in the park's northwest corner, is one of the only inland rainforests in the US and provides access to the Wonderland Trail. Winter storms keep the road beyond the Carbon River entrance in constant disrepair. The hike to **⬛Camp Muir** (9 mi. round-trip), the most popular staging ground for summit attempts, is also a challenging day hike, beginning on **Skyline Trail,** a scenic 6 mi. loop reaching its peak at the 7000 ft. Panorama Point. The latter half of the hike to Muir is covered in snow throughout the year; only those skilled in snow travel with the proper equipment should attempt it. A segment of the **Pacific Crest Trail,** which runs from Mexico to the Canadian border, dodges in and out of the park's southeast corner. The undeniable behemoth of all the park's routes is the infamous **Wonderland Trail,** 94 mi. of challenging terrain that circumnavigates the whole mountain. Arguably more difficult than the mountain ascent, the route passes through every type of scenery imaginable: dark forest, bright snowfields, rushing rivers, and rocky moraines. A full hike requires experience and careful planning; be sure to spend plenty of time at a ranger station before setting out. **A trip to the summit requires substantial preparation and expense.** The ascent involves a vertical rise of more than 9000 ft. over a distance of 9 mi., usually taking two days and an overnight stay at Camp Muir on the south side (10,000 ft.) or Camp Schurman on the east side (9500 ft.). Permits for summit climbs cost $30. Guided trips are available through Rainier Mountaineering, Inc. in Ashford near the Nisually entrance.

NORTH CASCADES NATIONAL PARK ☎ 360

Over half a million acres of vertical rock peaks with tenacious glaciers clinging to their sides and cascades of water pouring through their valleys make the North Cascades National Park one of the wildest places left in the country. These dramatic pinnacles rise abruptly from the neighboring deep glacial valleys, creating some of the most complex and challenging mountaineering in the continental US. Over 93 percent of the park is designated part of the Stephen Mather Wilderness: the area protects alpine meadows, over 300 of the about 600 US glaciers outside of Alaska, and abundant wildlife, including the grizzly bear and northern grey wolf.

⌐ TRANSPORTATION. To reach North Cascades National Park from the west, take I-5 to Burlington and take the Rte. 20 Exit. Coming from the east, take Rte. 20 west from Twisp. The park and its surrounding recreation areas are always open, but access is limited by snow, ice, and avalanche danger in winter. Rte. 20 is partially closed from mid-November to mid-April due to winter conditions. Many people tend to view the North Cascades as a scenic drive along **Route 20,** also known as the **North Cascades Scenic Highway.**

◢◤ ORIENTATION AND PRACTICAL INFORMATION. The park itself consists of four sections: **North Unit, South Unit, Ross Lake National Recreation Area,** and **Lake Chelan National Recreation Area.** The North Unit reaches up to the Canadian border and is the most remote area of the park. The South Unit, pocked by glaciers, is accessible from trails leaving Rte. 20 along both its north and east sides. Ross Lake National Recreation Area, running along Rte. 20 and north along Ross Lake, contains the park's main throughway and sees most of the park's recreation. The Lake Chelan National Recreation Area at the park's southernmost tip protects the beautiful wilderness around Stehekin and the northern tip of Lake Chelan.

North Cascades National Park and the Ross Lake and Lake Chelan National Recreation Areas are all managed as one entity—the North Cascades National Park Service Complex. The **North Cascades National Park Headquarters Information Station** is located in Sedro-Woolley, a logging hamlet nestled in the rich farmland of the lower Skagit Valley and the westernmost town of note on Rte. 20. It is also home to the **Mt. Baker-Snoqualmie National Forest Headquarters,** which borders the western side of the park. Northwest Forest Passes, required for parking, are sold here. (810 Rte. 20, near the intersection with Rte. 9. ☎854-7200; www.nps.gov/noca. Open daily 8am-4:30pm; mid-Oct. to May closed Sa-Su.) The **Chelan Ranger Station** in Chelan near the lake is an office of the Wenatchee National Forest and offers information on the Lake Chelan National Recreation Area. (☎509-682-2549. Open daily 7:45am-4:30pm; Sept. to mid-June closed Sa-Su.) The **◪North Cascades National Park Visitors Center,** mi. 120 near Newhalem, has an extensive display on the area's ecosystems found at each elevation, featuring films, photos, and preserved animals, a visually stunning 25min. film on the park's history and legacy, interactive maps and models, and numerous trails. (☎206-386-4495, ext. 11. Open summer daily 9am-6pm; winter Sa-Su 9am-4:30pm.) The **North Cascades Chamber of Commerce/Visitors Center,** 59831 Rte. 20, is the best resource for backcountry trip-planning in the North Cascades. The Center has updates on trails and weather and is the place to pick up free but required backcountry permits (see **Camping,** below). They also sell the Northwest Forest Pass required for parking at trail-heads. (☎873-4500, ext. 39; www.marblemount.com. Open July-Aug. M-Th and Su 7am-6pm, F-Sa 7am-8pm; in winter call ahead.) There are **no major service stations** for 69 mi. east of Marblemount. **Post Office:** 60096 Rte. 20, in **Marblemount. (**Open M-F 8am-noon and 12:45-4:30pm.) **Postal Code:** 98267.

⚑ CAMPING. Backcountry camping requires a **permit,** free from ranger stations and Visitor Centers (☎873-4500, ext. 39). Permits must be picked up in person no earlier than the day before trip date and are on a first-come, first-served basis. There are campsites available at two parks along Hwy. 20 in the Marblemount area: **Rockport State Park** and **Howard Miller Steelhead Park ❶.** Geared towards RVs, Rockport is embedded within old-growth Douglas-firs, providing a sublime spot to rest for the night. (☎853-8461 or 800-233-0321. 62 sites with hookups, $22.) Howard Miller Steelhead, a county campground with numerous amenities, includes a playground, Adirondack shelters (3-sided wooden buildings), and free showers. (☎853-8808. 15 primitive sites, $20; 44 sites with hookups, $26.) More remote options are on Cascade Road, including at **Cascade Island ❶.** (☎902-1000. 15 tent sites, free.) The National Park Service-run **⛺Colonial Creek Campground ❶** lies nestled along the shore of Diablo Lake, with turquoise waters lapping at the foot of some sites; all spots are shaded by a lush and verdant canopy. Take a frigid dip in the lake waters, or explore for an afternoon of fishing or boating. Easy access to numerous trails. Nightly naturalist talks are hosted in the site's impressive amphitheater. (☎206-386-4495. Open mid-Apr. to mid-Oct. 140 sites, $12.)

⚞ OUTDOOR ACTIVITIES. While most people encounter the park via the North Cascades Hwy., there are ample opportunities for on-foot exploration as well. Those determined to penetrate the park should bring a stout pair of boots and allot plenty of time. A park this daunting demands multi-day hiking, and the Marblem-ount Info Center is the authority on backcountry trekking (see **Practical Information,** p. 979). There's no shortage of day hikes, either; ask at Marblemount for a trail suggestion to fit your specific need.

The best short hiking in the Marblemount area is the moderate 4 mi. climb though wildflower meadows in spring to a viewpoint on **Sauk Mountain.** (On Forest Rd. 1030 off Hwy. 20, about 3hr.) In Newhalem, take the brief but breath-taking **Sterling Munro Trail** for 300 yd. to a view of the rugged southern Pickett Range. The trail leads directly from the North Cascades Visitors Center (p. 979) and should not be missed.

While the mountains of the park are surely its main attraction, the lakes created by dams earlier in the century along the stretch of road past Newhalem come in a close second. The **Gorge Overlook Trail** is an easy half mile to an impressive view of Gorge Lake, while both **Diablo** and **Ross Lakes** have designated **overlooks** just off the side of Rte. 20 that include multiple explanatory plaques and signs. For a more private overlook of Ross Lake, there is a 1½ mi. round-trip hike from the highway to the dam. From Colonial Creek Campground, the **Thunder Knob Trail** takes hikers to the over 7000 ft. lookout over Diablo Lake in a short but steep 3½ mi. round-trip. These lakes beg to be seen from the water, and that's an urge you shouldn't resist. Boat rentals are available at **Ross Lake Resort** or in towns to the east (Mazama, Winthrop, and Twisp) and west (Sedro-Woolley).

The stretch of road from **Ross Lake,** near the Eastern border of North Cascades National Park, to **Winthrop,** in the Okanogan National Forest, is the most beautiful section of Rte. 20. Leaving the basin of Ross Lake, the road begins to climb, revealing the craggy peaks of the North Cascades. The **Pacific Crest Trail** (p. 978) crosses Rte. 20 at **Rainy Pass** (mi. 157) on one of the most scenic and difficult legs of its 2500 mi. course from Mexico to Canada. From the Rainy Pass parking lot there are numerous well-maintained day hikes into the picturesque surroundings; many can be hiked in sneakers, provided the snow has melted (about mid-July). The most heavily trodden path is the **Rainy Lake Nature Trail,** an easy 1¾ mi. round-trip hike that takes visitors to a lakeside picnic area facing a waterfall and the impressive Lyall Glacier. Another easy longer daytrip is the hike to **Lake Ann** and **Maple Pass,** bringing you first to trout-stocked the lake, then after another 2 mi. to outstanding views from the pass at 6800 ft. (6¼ mi. round-trip).

Only slightly farther east is the overlook at **Washington Pass** (mi. 162), rewarding visitors with one of the state's most dramatic panoramas, an astonishing view of the red rocks exposed by **Early Winters Creek** in **Copper Basin,** and one of the few spots that really reveals the contrast of the wet western and drier eastern climates.

LEAVENWORTH ☎509

After Leavenworth's logging industry collapsed in the 60s, desperate officials undertook a daring experiment in tourism and transformed the town into a German village. Now Leavenworth is thriving, complete with Bavarian-style buildings, free-flowing beer, and polka music. Visitors to "Washington's Little Bavaria" can almost always be guaranteed a celebration of some sort, though there are some that stand out. **Icefest,** in mid-January, is a winter festival with sleigh rides, dogsled rides, and a dogsled competition, while mid-May brings **Maifest,** with a parade and live music. (☎548-5807; www.leavenworth.org.) Summers host a new set of festivals and events almost every week, but the **Leavenworth Summer Theater** at the Ski Hill Amphitheater is a favorite town tradition. Productions vary each year, but *The Sound of Music* has a permanent place on the playbill. Theater performances run frequently throughout July and August. (☎548-2000; www.leavenworthsummertheater.com. Tickets from $14.) Still, no Bavarian town—contrived or otherwise—would be complete without its own **Oktoberfest,** held during the first three weekends in October. (☎548-7021; www.oktoberfestleavenworth.com.) Most famous of all is the **Christmas Lighting Festival** in the first three weekends of December, when Santa Claus roams the streets and Leavenworth's proverbial stocking runneth over with holiday cheer. Visitors book lodgings as early as a year in advance. (☎548-5807; www.leavenworth.org). Accommodations for both Oktoberfest and Christmas Lighting Festival should be made at least a year in advance. Leavenworth's main outdoor attraction is the **Alpine Lakes Wilderness,** also home to Icicle Valley. Icicle Creek Canyon, with **Icicle Ridge** to the north and **Mount Stuart** to the south, stretches into the eastern core of the Wilderness and contains some of the best-loved trails in Washington backcountry. The moderate **Icicle Ridge Trail** (26 mi. one-way), off Icicle Rd. on the south end of U.S. 2, follows the ridge all the way to Steven Pass and connects the trails on the northern side. East of Mt. Stuart, the mystical **Enchantment Basin,** a chain of backcountry lakes framed by rock peaks, attracts backpackers willing to trudge up to the 7000 ft. basin and climbers anxious to try their hand at its jagged spires, called the Cashmere Crags.

Leavenworth's booming tourist industry has generated a niche for dozens of expensive faux-Bavarian lodgings. **Mrs. Anderson's Lodging House ❸,** 917 Commercial St., is the oldest building in Leavenworth and a quaint, affordable option in the heart of the downtown district. Each room is named after a quilt and decorated with antiques and vintage clothing. (☎548-6173 or 800-253-8990. Rooms from $58.) Camping is available at several different sites on Icicle Creek Rd., which heads southwest out of town on Hwy. 2. The closest sites, **Eightmile ❶,** are—surprise—8

PACIFIC
NORTHWEST

mi. out, at a National Forest campground (45 sites, $13). For more info, contact the Leavenworth Ranger District (see below). Off Hwy. 2, Turnwater has 84 sites 11 mi. from town ($14). Predictably, Leavenworth's food mimics German cuisine; surprisingly, it often succeeds. There are more pubs serving up goulash and wieners than you can imagine; one worth trying is **Andreas Keller Restaurant ➋**, 829 Front St., if only for its $10 bratwurst reuben. (☎548-6000; www.andreaskellerrestaurant.com. Open M-Th and Su 11am-9pm, F 11am-10pm, Sa 11am-10:30pm. Live Bavarian music Jan.-June M and F-Su from 6pm; June-Jan. nightly 6pm-closing. AmEx/MC/V.) **Renaissance Cafe ➊**, 217 8th St., is one of the few places in town with plenty of vegetarian options, in addition to terrific sandwiches, a few Bavarian classics, and a full breakfast menu. (☎548-6725. Omelets $5. Wi-Fi.)

Leavenworth is near Washington's geographic center, on the eastern slope of the Cascades. From Seattle, follow I-5 north to Exit 194, then U.S. 2 east for 126 mi. From Spokane, take U.S. 2 west, or take I90 to Hwy. 97. The **Chamber of Commerce,** 940 Hwy. 2, has brochures. (☎548-5807; www.leavenworth.org. Open M-Th 8am-5pm, F-Sa 8am-8pm, Su 8am-4pm.) The **Wenatchee River Ranger District Ranger District,** 600 Sherborne St., has extensive information on trails and permits. (☎548-6977.) **Internet Access: Leavenworth Community Library,** 700 Hwy. 2. (☎548-7923.) **Post Office**: 960 Hwy. 2 (☎548-4354. Open M-F 9am-5pm, Sa 9-11am.) **Postal Code**: 98826.

SPOKANE   ☎509

Spokane (spoe-KAN) may have peaked when the 1974 World's Fair came to town; parks, department stores, and skyways sprang up in preparation for a promising future that never quite arrived. Today, cafes catering to the college crowd from Gonzaga and nearby Eastern Washington Universities along with 50s-style burger joints make for a suburban atmosphere, but the surrounding wilderness provides plenty of opportunities to enjoy the dry climate and diverse terrain.

◪◪ TRANSPORTATION AND PRACTICAL INFORMATION. Spokane is 280 mi. east of Seattle on I-90, between Exits 279 and 282. **Spokane International Airport (GEG),** 900 W. Airport Dr. (☎455-6455; www.spokaneairports.net) is off I-90, 8 mi. southwest of town. Amtrak, 221 W. 1st Ave. (☎624-5144 or 800-872-7245; www.amtrak.com; station open 24hr.; ticket office open daily 10am-5:30am), at Bernard St., runs **trains** to Portland (7hr., 2 per day, $43-95) and Seattle (8hr., 1 per day, $43-95). Greyhound, 221 W. 1st Ave. (☎624-5251 or 800-231-2222; www.greyhound.com.), is in the same building as Amtrak. Station is open 24hr. **Buses** go to Portland (7-10hr., 3 per day, $40) and Seattle (6hr., 5 per day, $30). Spokane Transit Authority, 1230 W. Boone Ave., serves the greater Spokane area. (☎325-6000; www.spokanetransit.com. STA plaza bus shop open M-F 6:30am-6pm, Sa noon-5pm. $1, seniors $0.50.) The **Spokane Regional Convention and Visitors Bureau** is at 201 W. Main Ave; take Exit 281 off I-90. (☎624-1341, tourist info 747-3230 or 888-776-5263; www.visitspokane.com. Open M-F 8:30am-5pm, Sa 9am-5pm.) **Internet Access: Spokane City Public Library,** 906 W. Main Ave. (☎444-5300; www.spokanelibrary.org.) Free Internet access in 15min. slots. Open Tu-W 10am-8pm, Th-Sa 10am-6pm. **Post Office:** 904 W. Riverside Ave. (☎800-275-8777). Open M-F 8am-5pm. **Postal Code:** 99210.

◪◪ ACCOMMODATIONS AND FOOD. Numerous motels are sprinkled in the outskirts of downtown, especially along I-90, Rte. 2, and Division Ave. Clean and affordable chains can be found close to the airport, Exit 277 from Rte. 2. The **Ramada Limited City Center ➌**, 123 S. Post St., has basic rooms in a convenient location. (☎838-8504 or 800-210-8465. Breakfast included. Shuttle to the airport $5. Singles from $60; doubles from $70. AmEx/D/MC/V.) **Riverside State Park ➊** is 6 mi.

from downtown on Rifle Club Rd., off Rte. 291 (Nine Mile Rd.), and has 16 standard sites and 15 utility hookup sites near the beautiful Spokane River. (☎465-5064; www.riversidestatepark.org. Standard sites $15; utility hookup sites $18-21.) ☑**High Nooner Gourmet Sandwiches ❷,** 237 W. Riverside Ave., offers sandwiches loaded with fresh ingredients. The "Unforgettable Nooner," with turkey, bacon, avocado, tomato, and cream cheese ($6.20), is definitely unforgettable. (☎838-5288; www.highnooner.com. Open M-F 10am-3pm. AmEx/MC/V.) (☎747-8798. Breakfast $4-8. Open daily 6am-9pm. D/MC/V.) At **Dick's Hamburgers ❶,** 10 E. 3rd Ave., at Division St., customers eat in parked cars and pay 50s-era prices. (☎747-2481. Burgers $0.83. Shakes $1.23. Fish and chips $2.75. Open daily 8am-1am. Cash only.) **Jack and Dan's Bar and Grill,** 1226 N. Hamilton Street, transforms from a favorite lunchspot for three generations of locals during the day to a lively spot for college students at night. (☎487-6546; www.jackanddans.com. Pints $2.35. Open M-Sa 10am-2am, Su noon-midnight.)

◼️🗺️ **SIGHTS AND OUTDOOR ACTIVITIES.** One of the most beautiful spots in Spokane, the 90 acres of ☑**Manito Park** boasts six distinct areas of lovingly-maintained flowerbeds, with 150 varieties of blooming roses and Japanese and Lilac gardens. *(4 W. 21st Ave. From downtown, go south on Bernard St. or Grand St. and turn left on 21st Ave. Park open summer 4am-11pm; winter 5am-10pm. Buildings open 8am-dusk. Free.)* Developed for the 1974 World's Fair, the **Riverfront Park** is Spokane's civic center and the perfect place for a pleasant stroll. Riverfront's **IMAX Theater** houses a five-story movie screen, ice-skating rink, and a small amusement park. On the park's edge lies the historic **Carousel,** hand carved by Charles Loof of Coney Island carousel fame. *(507 N. Howard St. ☎456-4386 or 800-336-7275; www.spokaneriverfrontpark.com. IMAX: ☎626-6686. Open daily 10:30am-10pm. $7.75, ages 13-17 $6.75, ages 3-12 $5.75; higher for special engagements. Carousel: Open M-Th and Su 10am-8pm, F-Sa 10am-10pm. $2, children $1. Day pass to several attractions $15.)* The **Northwest Museum of Arts and Culture,** or the MAC, as it is known, is the crown jewel of Spokane's attractions, with five galleries focusing on local artists. *(2316 W. 1st Ave. ☎456-3931; www.northwestmuseum.org. Open Tu-Su 11am-5pm. $7, students and over 62 $5, under 6 free. 1st F of the month admission by donation.)* Friday's **Spokane 7** (www.spokane7.com) lists upcoming entertainment in town.

Only 30 mi. northeast of the city, **Mount Spokane State Park** provides 14,000 acres of outdoor options, including 100 mi. of hiking trails and the massive **Ski and Snowboard Park** with a 2065 ft. vertical drop. *(29500 N. Mt.*

HOOP DREAMS

Between the extra police force on duty and the chalk scrawled across 40 blocks of city streets closed to traffic, an outsider who stumbles into Spokane on the last weekend in June might think disaster has struck. But those in the know realize that **Hoopfest** fever has taken over again. The event that began as a mere fundraiser for the Special Olympics in 1990 has since grown into the world's largest three-on-three basketball tournament, drawing 25,000 players on over 6000 different teams.

Amateurs and seasoned players of all ages take to the city streets to play on the 400 courts that volunteers have chalked across downtown Spokane. Brackets run the gamut of backgrounds, with specific divisions for 3rd and 4th graders, family teams, college players, men over six feet tall, and players in wheelchairs. In just two days, Hoopfest facilitates 13,000 basketball games amidst concerts, street vendors, and city-wide festivities for athletes and enthusiasts. While the 1974 World Fair put Spokane on the map, Hoopfest is now the city's claim to fame and the slam-dunk event of the year.

The next Hoopfest is scheduled for June 28-29, 2008; registration opens March 15, 2008. For more info see www.spokanehoopfest.net.

Spokane Park Dr. ☎238-2220; www.mtspokane.com. Scheduled to open Dec. 1, 2007 for the new season.) Try the 1½ mi. **Entrance Loop Trail** for a brief stroll, the easy 5 mi. **Day Mountain Loop** to see rocky meadows, or the 4½ mi. **Hay Ridge Loop** for scenic stream-crossings. *(At the end of State Rd. 206, 15 mi. east of Rte. 2. ☎238-4258. Camping available in summer at the Bald Knob Campground. Sites $17, with full hookup $24. Parking $5 per day. Park open summer 6:30am-dusk, winter 8am-10pm.)* In **Riverside State Park**, the scenic **Centennial Trail** runs 37 mi. from Nine Mile Dam all the way to the Idaho border and is paved for the benefit of hikers, bikers, skiers, and sledders alike. *(9711 W. Charles Rd. ☎465-5054; www.riversidestatepark.org.)*

VANCOUVER (BC, CANADA) ☎604

Even more so than most cities in North America, Vancouver, British Columbia (BC) boasts a thriving multicultural populace; the Cantonese influence is so strong that it is commonly joked that Chinese will soon become Canada's 3rd national language. You'll find Asian flavor in everything from peaceful manicured gardens and raucous annual festivals, to the cuisine in one of the largest Chinatowns in North America. It may sound like an overwhelming metropolis but, surrounded on three sides by water and closely hemmed in by the Coast Mountain Range, Vancouver can never stray too far from its humble logging-town roots.

> **BORDER CROSSING.** Traveling between the US and Canada is generally an easy process, but security is still taken very seriously. Crossing can be as simple as a wave of the passport or as time-consuming as a full search of your car. To keep things moving along, make sure to have all necessary documents handy. It is illegal to cross the border anywhere except at an open crossing station. See **Essentials,** p. 11, for more details on documents and procedures.

⬛🔢 TRANSPORTATION AND PRACTICAL INFORMATION. Vancouver is in the southwestern corner of mainland British Columbia. Amtrak, 1150 Station St. (☎604-640-3798 or 800-872-7245; www.amtrak.com), sends **trains** to Seattle, WA (4hr., 5 per day, US$28-43). Greyhound USA, 1150 Station St. (☎800-229-9424; www.greyhound.com), runs **buses** to Seattle, WA (5hr., 6 per day, CDN$26-28). Quick Shuttle (☎940-4428 or 800-665-2122; www.quickcoach.com) makes 8 trips per day from the Holiday Inn on 1110 Howe St. to Seattle, WA (4hr.; CDN$33, students CDN$22) and Sea-Tac Airport (4½hr.; CDN$41, students CDN$29). For a **taxi,** try Vancouver Taxi (☎871-1111) or Black Top Cabs (☎731-1111; 24hr.). For **Visitor Info,** go to 200 Burrard St. at plaza level. (☎683-2000; www.tourismvancouver.com. Open daily 8:30am-6pm.) **GLBT Resources: The Centre,** 1170 Bute St. (☎684-5307; www.lgtbcentrevancouver.com. Open M-F 9am-7pm.) **Hotlines: Crisis Center** (☎872-3311; operates 24hr.). **Medical Services: Vancouver General Hospital,** 855 W. 12th Ave. (☎875-4111). **UBC Hospital,** 2211 Westbrook Mall (☎822-7121), on the UBC campus. **Internet Access: Vancouver Public Library,** 350 W. Georgia St. (☎331-3600; www.vpl.vancouver.bc.ca. Free. Open M-Th 10am-9pm, F-Sa 10am-6pm, Su 1-5pm.) **Post Office:** 349 W. Georgia St. (☎662-5725). Open M-F 8am-5:30pm. **Postal Code:** V6B 3P7. **Country Code:** 1.

🔳🔲 ACCOMMODATIONS AND FOOD. Vancouver has plenty of options for the budget traveler, from huge hostels in the center of Vancouver's booming nightlife districts to smaller, serene respites from the fast pace of city life. The best hostels book quickly in summer months. ◣**Vancouver Jericho Beach (HI) ❶,** 1515 Discovery St., is in serene Jericho Beach Park: follow 4th Ave. west past Alma, go right at the fork, and follow signs; or take bus #4 from Granville St. The former army barracks

are now a pleasant and inviting getaway, serving breakfast and dinner. (☎224-3208 or 888-203-4303. Kitchen. Linen included. Laundry facilities. Check-in 24hr. Check-out 11am. Open May-Sept. CDN$24, members CDN$20. MC/V.) **Vancouver Hostel Central (HI) ❶**, 1025 Granville St., is in a former hotel located in the heart of the entertainment and nightlife district. (☎685-5335 or 888-203-8333. Breakfast and linen included. Free Wi-Fi. Reception 24hr. Check-in noon. Check-out 11am. Dorms June-Sept. CDN$32, members CDN$28; private rooms CDN$66/58. Oct.-May dorms CDN$24, members CDN$20; private rooms CDN$76/68. MC/V.) The city is best known among young crowds for shockingly cheap fresh sushi joints (CDN$5 specials) and CDN$1-per-slice pizza parlors. ⛱**The Naam ❷**, 2724 W. 4th Ave., half a block east of MacDonald St., off of bus #4, 7 or 27 from Granville Mall, offers a diverse vegetarian menu in a welcoming, homey atmosphere. (☎738-7151; www.thenaam.com. Naam Dragon Bowl CDN$10. Buddha's Feast CDN$11.50. Gravy fries CDN$5. Live music nightly 7-10pm. Open 24hr. AmEx/MC/V.) **Subeez Cafe ❸**, 891 Homer St., at Smithe St., in downtown, is a cavernous cafe populated with hipster youth. (☎687-6107; www.subeez.com. Entrees CDN$10-20. Th-Su DJs 10pm-1am. Open M-F 11:30am-1am, Sa 11am-1am, Su 11am-midnight. MC/V.)

🄶 **SIGHTS.** The ⛱**Vancouver Art Gallery,** 750 Hornby St., in Robson Sq. hosts fantastic temporary exhibitions and a varied collection of contemporary art and design from the West Coast. (☎662-4700, 24hr. info line 662-4719; www.vanartgallery.bc.ca. Open Apr.-Oct. M, W, and F-Su 10am-5:30pm, Tu and Th 10am-9pm; call for hours Nov.-Mar. CDN$19.50, seniors CDN$15, students CDN$14, children 6-12 $6.50. Tu 5-9pm pay by donation. 3rd Su of each month under 12 free.) Some 55 acres of former golf course have been converted into the immense **VanDusen Botanical Garden,** 5251 Oak St., at W. 37th, which showcases 7500 kinds of plants from six continents, an international sculpture collection, an Elizabethan maze, and over 60 species of birds interspersed in the Fragrance Garden and Bonsai House. (☎878-9274. Open daily June-Aug. 10am-9pm; Sept. and Apr. 10am-6pm; Oct.-Mar. 10am-4pm; Apr. 10am-6pm. Free parking. Wheelchair-accessible. Apr.-Sept. CDN$7.75, over 65 CDN$5.50, ages 13-18 CDN$5.75, ages 6-12 CDN$4; families CDN$12. Sept.-Mar. rates about CDN$2 less.) Journey to the tropics inside the **Bloedel Floral Conservatory,** a triodetic dome made of plexiglass and aluminum tubing. (Center of Queen Elizabeth Park on Cambie and 33rd Ave., a few blocks east of VanDusen. ☎257-8570 or ☎257-8584. Open Apr.-Sept. M-F 9am-8pm, Sa-Su 10am-9pm; Feb.-Mar. daily 10am-5:30pm; Nov.-Jan. daily 10am-5pm; Feb.-Mar. daily 10am-5:30pm. CDN$4.50, seniors CDN$3.15, ages 13-18 CDN$3.40, ages 6-12 CDN$2.25, under 6 free.)

One of the best places to visit at the **University of British Columbia (UBC)** is the fascinating ⛱**Museum of Anthropology,** 6393 NW. Marine Dr. The high-ceilinged building contains indigenous totems, African tribal masks, and European ceramics that span several centuries of civilization's development. (☎822-5087; www.moa.ubc.ca. Open June-Sept. M and W-Su 10am-5pm, Tu 10am-9pm; Oct.-May Tu 11am-9pm, W-Su 11am-5pm. CDN$9, students and over 65 CDN$7, under 6 free. Tu after 5pm pay by donation.) Just down the road, a single gardener tends the **Nitobe Memorial Garden,** the finest classical Shinto garden outside of Japan. During a visit the garden, the current Emperor of Japan allegedly said, "I am in Japan." (☎822-6038; www.nitobe.org. Open daily mid-Mar. to mid.-Oct. 10am-6pm; mid-Oct. to mid-Mar. 10am-2:30pm. Mid-Mar. to mid-Oct. CDN$5, over 65 CDN$4, students CDN$3; mid-Oct. to mid-Mar. admission by donation.)

Established in 1889 at the tip of the downtown peninsula of Vancouver, the sprawling 1000-acre **Stanley Park** is a testament to the foresight of Vancouver's urban planners. The thickly wooded park is laced with numerous cycling and hiking trails and surrounded by a popular 10km **seawall promenade.** (Take the #19 bus.

☎257-8400; www.vancouverparks.ca. A free shuttle runs throughout the park late June-Sept. on the ½hr. 10am-6:30pm.) The ▨**Vancouver Aquarium** features exotic aquatic animals, a shark tank with weekly feedings, and, in the summer months, up to 8000 Costa Rican butterflies. Dolphins, beluga whales, sea otters, and sea lions perform in shows daily. (☎659-3474; www.vanaqua.org. Open daily July-Aug. 9:30am-7pm; Sept.-June 9:30am-5pm. CDN$20; students, seniors, and ages 13-18 CDN$15; ages 4-12 CDN$12; under 3 free.) Nature walks start from the **Nature House,** underneath the Lost Lagoon bus loop, on the SE corner of Lost Lagoon at the foot of Alberni St. (☎257-8544; www.stanleyparkecology.ca. 1¾hr. nature walks Su noon and F 1pm. Cultural and birding walks offered as well. CDN$10, under 12 free. Nature House open June-Aug. F-Su 11am-7pm. Free, donations accepted.) The park's edges boast a few restaurants, tennis courts, a cinder running track, beaches, and an outdoor theater, featuring the summer "Theatre Under the Stars" series, the **Malkin Bowl** (☎687-0174).

▨▨ **ENTERTAINMENT AND NIGHTLIFE.** The **Vancouver Symphony Orchestra** (☎876-3434; www.vancouversymphony.ca) plays from October to early June in the **Orpheum Theatre,** at the corner of Smithe and Seymour St. The **Vancouver Playhouse Theatre Co.** (☎873-3311), on Dunsmuir and Georgia St., and the **Arts Club Theatre** (☎687-1644), on Granville Island, stage various low-key shows throughout the year. The **Ridge Theatre,** 3131 Arbutus, shows foreign and vintage double-features. (☎738-6311; www.ridgetheatre.com. CDN$6, W matinee CDN$5.) The **Vancouver International Jazz Festival,** centered on Granville Island, is held during the last week in June. It features over 400 performances, many of which are free, with artists from 18 countries. (☎872-5200; www.coastaljazz.ca. Free events in clubs around towns. Shows at concert venues begin at $15. Festival 3-pack $33. AmEx/MC/V.)

The biggest nightlife draw in Vancouver for younger people is Canada's drinking age (19). ▨**The Irish Heather,** 217 Carrall St., is the second-highest seller of Guinness in BC, serving 20 oz. drafts (CDN$6.20), as well as bangers and mash (CDN$14). (☎688-9779; www.irishheather.com. Th live music. Open daily noon-midnight.) In the back find its sister establishment, the **Shebeen Whiskey House,** which boasts innumerable varieties of whiskey from CDN$5 and up… way up. (Open Th-Sa 5pm-midnight.) **The King's Head,** 1618 Yew St., just downhill from 1st St., in Kitsilano, has cheap drinks and food in a fun location near the beach. Bands play acoustic sets Wednesday through Saturday. (☎738-6966. Daily specials. Pints CDN$3.75. Open M-Sa 8am-1am, Su 8am-midnight.)

APPENDIX

CLIMATE

Avg. Temp. Precipitation	January			April			July			October		
	°C	°F	mm	°C	°F	mm	°C	°F	mm	°C	°F	mm
Atlanta	2/11	36/52	125	11/22	52/72	94	21/31	70/88	119	12/22	54/72	66
Boston	-7/2	19/36	91	3/12	37/53	89	17/27	63/81	84	8/17	46/63	84
Chicago	-8/0	18/32	51	4/13	39/55	71	19/27	66/81	84	8/16	46/31	66
Dallas	2/13	36/55	64	13/24	55/75	107	24/34	75/93	71	14/26	57/79	71
Detroit	-7/1	19/34	53	3/13	37/55	64	17/28	63/82	84	7/16	45/61	61
Kansas City	-6/3	21/37	33	8/18	46/64	81	21/32	70/90	104	9/20	48/68	71
Little Rock	1/10	34/50	122	12/22	53/72	130	22/32	72/90	86	12/32	53/90	71
Los Angeles	8/18	46/64	79	10/21	50/70	25	16/27	61/81	0	12/24	53/75	15
Miami	16/23	61/73	71	19/27	66/81	81	24/31	75/88	155	22/28	72/82	234
Minneapolis	-14/-6	7/21	25	2/13	36/55	58	17/28	63/82	86	5/15	41/59	53
Nashville	-1/8	30/46	117	9/21	48/70	109	20/31	68/88	91	10/22	50/72	66
New Orleans	8/17	46/63	117	16/25	61/77	122	24/32	75/90	168	18/26	64/79	89
New York City	-4/3	25/37	94	6/14	42/57	81	19/28	66/82	107	13/20	55/68	10
Phoenix	4/18	39/64	20	12/28	53/82	10	25/40	77/104	25	4/19	39/66	38
Salt Lake City	-8/2	18/36	33	3/17	37/63	51	16/33	61/91	15	12/20	53/68	25
San Francisco	7/13	45/55	119	9/17	48/63	38	12/18	53/64	0	8/15	46/59	74
Seattle	2/7	36/45	122	6/14	42/57	58	12/22	53/72	15			
Washington DC	-3/6	27/42	86	7/18	45/64	84	20/31	68/86	112	9/19	48/64	74

MEASUREMENT CONVERSIONS

The US uses Imperial (English) units of measure as well as the metric system. For Imperial units, the basic unit of measure is the **yard (yd.)**, which is divided into three **feet (foot; ft.)**, or 36 **inches (in.)**. There are 1760 yards in a **mile (mi.)**. Fluids are measured by the **pint (pt.)**, which is composed of 20 fluid **ounces (oz.)**. There are two pints in a **quart (qt.)**, and eight pints in a **gallon (gal.)**. For the metric system, the basic unit of length is the **meter (m)**, which is divided into 100 **centimeters (cm)**, or 1000 **millimeters (mm)**. One thousand meters make up one **kilometer (km)**. Fluids are measured in **liters (L)**, each divided into 1000 **milliliters (ml)**. A liter of pure water weighs one **kilogram (kg)**, divided into 1000 **grams (g)**, while 1000kg make up one metric **ton**.

1 in. = 25.4mm	1mm = 0.039 in.
1 ft.= 0.30m	1m = 3.28 ft.
1 yd. = 0.914m	1m = 1.09 yd.
1 mi. = 1.609km	1km = 0.62 mi.
1 oz. = 28.35g	1g = 0.035 oz.
1 lb. = 0.454kg	1kg = 2.205 lbs.
1 fl. oz. = 29.57ml	1ml = 0.034 fl. oz.
1 gal. = 3.785L	1L = 0.264 gal.

DISTANCES (MI.) AND TRAVEL TIMES (BY BUS)

	Atlanta	Boston	Chic.	Dallas	D.C.	Denver	L.A.	Miami	New Or.	NYC	Phila.	Phnx.	St. Lou.	Sa. Fran.	Seattle	Trnto.	Vanc.	Mont.
Atlanta		1108	717	783	632	1406	2366	653	474	886	778	1863	560	2492	2699	959	2825	1240
Boston	22hr.		996	1794	442	1990	3017	1533	1542	194	333	2697	1190	3111	3105	555	3242	326
Chicago	14hr.	20hr.		937	715	1023	2047	1237	928	807	767	1791	302	2145	2108	537	2245	537
Dallas	15hr.	35hr.	18hr.		1326	794	1450	1322	507	1576	1459	906	629	1740	2112	1457	2255	1763
D.C.	12hr.	8hr.	14hr.	24hr.		1700	2689	1043	1085	2375	139	2350	845	2840	2788	526	3292	665
Denver	27hr.	38hr.	20hr.	15hr.	29hr.		1026	2046	1341	1785	1759	790	860	1267	1313	2404	1458	1864
L.A.	45hr.	57hr.	39hr.	28hr.	55hr.	20hr.		2780	2005	2787	2723	371	1837	384	1141	1564	1285	2888
Miami	13hr.	30hr.	24hr.	26hr.	20hr.	39hr.	53hr.		856	1346	1214	2368	1197	3086	3368	1320	3505	1676
New Or.	9hr.	31hr.	18hr.	10hr.	21hr.	26hr.	38hr.	17hr.		1332	1247	1535	677	2331	2639	496	3085	1654
NYC	18hr.	4hr.	16hr.	31hr.	5hr.	35hr.	53hr.	26hr.	27hr.		104	2592	999	2923	2912	503	3009	386
Phila.	18hr.	6hr.	16hr.	19hr.	3hr.	33hr.	50hr.	23hr.	23hr.	2hr.		2511	904	2883	2872	2069	1654	465
Phoenix	40hr.	49hr.	39hr.	19hr.	43hr.	17hr.	8hr.	47hr.	30hr.	45hr.	44hr.		1503	753	1510	810	2276	2638
St. Louis	11hr.	23hr.	6hr.	13hr.	15hr.	17hr.	35hr.	23hr.	13hr.	19hr.	16hr.	32hr.		2113	2139	2630	951	1128
San Fran.	47hr.	60hr.	41hr.	47hr.	60hr.	33hr.	7hr.	59hr.	43hr.	56hr.	54hr.	15hr.	45hr.		807	2623	146	2985
Seattle	52hr.	59hr.	40hr.	40hr.	54hr.	25hr.	22hr.	65hr.	50hr.	55hr.	54hr.	28hr.	36hr.	16hr.			4563	2964
Toronto	21hr.	11hr.	10hr.	26hr.	11hr.	26hr.	48hr.	29hr.	13hr.	11hr.	13hr.	48hr.	14hr.	49hr.	48hr.			655
Vancvr.	54hr.	61hr.	42hr.	43hr.	60hr.	27hr.	24hr.	67hr.	54hr.	57hr.	56hr.	30hr.	38hr.	18hr.	2hr.	53hr.		4861
Montreal	23hr.	6hr.	17hr.	28hr.	12hr.	39hr.	53hr.	32hr.	31hr.	7hr.	9hr.	53hr.	23hr.	56hr.	55hr.	7hr.	55hr.	

INDEX

INDEX (side tab)

GET CONNECTED & SAVE
WHEN YOU STAY WITH HI-USA

Stay with HI-USA and be close to all the sites, clubs, attractions and more. So you can really experience fantastic citites like New York, Boston, Chicago, Washington, San Francisco and Los Angeles, or explore the open road.

Enjoy great rates and a warm HI welcome!

 Hostelling International USA

Book your next stay online today at HIUSA.ORG

MAP INDEX

MAP LEGEND

- Site/Point of Interest
- Hotel/Hostel
- Camping
- Food
- Nightlife
- Entertainment
- (i) Tourist Information
- Hospital
- Police
- Pharmacy
- Library
- Post Office

- Internet
- Bank
- Museum
- Theater
- Golf Course
- Skiing
- Beach
- Ship/Submarine
- Aquarium
- Observatory
- Church/Cathedral
- Synagogue
- Mission

- Lighthouse
- Waterfall
- Forest
- Park Ranger Station
- Shelter
- Mountain Peak
- Mountain Range
- Mountain Pass
- Bus Station
- Train Station
- Ferry Landing
- Airport
- Parking

- Ferry
- Railroad
- Pedestrian Area
- Steps
- Trail
- Subway
- Tunnel
- Cemetery
- Beach
- Park

The Let's Go compass always points NORTH.